Baseball Prospectus

2013

Baseball Prospectus 2013

THE ESSENTIAL GUIDE TO THE 2013 SEASON

EDITED BY KING KAUFMAN AND CECILIA M. TAN

R.J. Anderson • Michael Bates • Craig Brown • Russell A. Carleton

Derek Carty • Jason Cole • Jason Collette • Bradford Doolittle • Ken Funck • Jay Jaffe

King Kaufman • Matthew Kory • Ben Lindbergh • Ian Miller • Sam Miller

Rob McQuown • Bill Parker • Jason Parks • Daniel Rathman • Josh Shepardson

Adam Sobsey • Paul Sporer • Cecilia M. Tan • Doug Thorburn • Jason Wojciechowski

Colin Wyers • Geoff Young

WILEY

Published by John Wiley & Sons, Inc., Hoboken, New Jersey
Published simultaneously in Canada

For general information about our other products and services, please contact our Customer Care Department within the United States at (800) 762-2974, outside the United States at (317) 572-3993 or fax (317) 572-4002.

Wiley also publishes its books in a variety of electronic formats and by print-on-demand. Some content that appears in standard print versions of this book may not be available in other formats. For more information about Wiley products, visit us at www.wiley.com.

Library of Congress Cataloging-in-Publication Data:

ISBN 978-1-118-45919-5 (pbk); 978-1-118-45920-1 (ebk);
978-1-118-45921-8 (ebk); 978-1-118-45918-8 (ebk)

Printed in the United States of America

10 9 8 7 6 5 4 3 2 1

CONTENTS

Foreword

Jeff Luhnow, General Manager, Houston Astros

After hiring Mike Fast and Kevin Goldstein away from Baseball Prospectus and into the front office of the Houston Astros, I assumed I would be *persona non grata* among the BP editors for having stripped them of two incredibly talented individuals. I was wrong. Instead, I was asked to write the foreword for this year's annual! I immediately accepted. I feel honored, as it is a publication that not only sits on my shelf, but is used frequently as a reference throughout the year. It is a good sign that BP is proud of its alumni and supports these individuals as they seek to accomplish career goals. This is sound human-resource management, and something one should expect from a progressive, forward-looking operation.

So what can I say that can possibly add to the robust analysis and insights consistently provided by this book? I think what most analytically oriented baseball fans want to know is how major-league teams develop and use information to make decisions, and how that is changing over time.

Much has been made about the divide between those people driven by statistics and those people driven by first-hand experience. This type of controversy provides as much fodder for bloggers and sportswriters as a good old-fashioned bench-clearing brawl. Of course, there are people who lean more heavily on their intuition and experience in making recommendations and decisions, and there are those who rely on the comfort of analysis and past performance. In general, though, the gulf between the two sides is exaggerated. All teams have experienced scouts and coaches who use their best judgment to evaluate players and situations. All teams have at least one person—and in most cases several people—dedicated to crunching numbers and providing analysis. Therefore, all teams use a variety of information gathered from a variety of sources and methods to make baseball decisions. That is a fact.

Each team finds itself in a unique position and oftentimes the right decision for one team is not the right decision for another. What makes sense for the Houston Astros in 2013 is not the same as what makes sense for the Texas Rangers. Each team operates in a distinct market with its own portfolio of player contracts and prospects in the system. Even two teams that have similar resources and are in similar markets will see things differently because of the relative strengths and weaknesses of their farm systems and the state of their big-league rosters.

One thing that I think many fans underestimate is how difficult it is to make many baseball decisions. Why? It's because we are trying to predict the future—and very few things are more uncertain than what is to happen. It's hard enough to agree on what already happened (hence the vigorous debates about MVP, Cy Young, and Hall of Fame qualifications). It's an order of magnitude more difficult to predict what will happen—especially in a game with so many variables, that takes place over the course of a 162-game season. It's so hard, in fact, that it's easy to get discouraged and give up trying because of how often one will be wrong. People have always said baseball is a humbling game—a successful batter will fail 70 percent or more of the time, and everyone eventually goes through slumps. The same can be said of front offices. Most of us get it wrong—often—and it can be not only humbling, but discouraging.

The first time I saw the BP PECOTA projections, I realized that someone out there understood the inherent variability in attempting to predict the future, but they also understood the value of attempting to do it in a systematic and thoughtful way. What made the PECOTA projections so interesting to me and others was how clearly the system described the different types of outcomes. Clearly the people behind it had a good sense of variability and value and used both to make the predictions. Why? I've never spoken to Nate Silver about it, but I'm sure it's because he looked closely at the past and tried as best as he could to explain what happened and how that affects what might happen in the future. Nate, as we all know, took his show to the political arena and is now widely recognized as the most reliable forecaster of national elections—having run the table last November by predicting all 50 states correctly in the presidential election. If only it were that easy in baseball!

So, as you read this book and watch the upcoming baseball season, keep in mind that what each player will do is essentially a roll of the dice: Some (few) will roll a double six while some (few) will roll the snake eyes. Most will be somewhere in between. The difference between baseball players and dice is that every player is unique and changing all the time. In order to best understand the possible outcomes, you need to have a good sense of what outcomes have occurred in the past, as well as how each player may be changing as he ages and becomes more or less skilled at various parts of the game of baseball. This book is a good place to start, so enjoy it, and we hope to see you at the ballpark!

Preface

Two decades ago, a movie came out called *1991: The Year Punk Broke*. The title was amusing to those of us who thought punk broke in 1977 and had been tickled in 1991 when it came back around for our nephews and nieces. *Nostalgia cycles are so quick these days,* we thought.

If 1991 was the year punk broke, 2012 was the year analytics broke: A huge crowd came on board a ship that had been sailing for a long time. Welcome aboard, world.

Nate Silver, longtime Baseball Prospectus writer and the inventor of the PECOTA forecasting system that's at the heart of this book, was the breakout media star of 2012, correctly predicting the outcome of the presidential election in all 50 states on his *New York Times* blog—one state better than his 2008 performance. Silver became the nation's foremost expert on political polling by applying sabermetrics to politics. He did the math, and it made his analysis much sharper than that of a thousand pundits extrapolating from their assumptions.

Sound familiar, baseball fans?

In baseball, we may have all agreed long ago that the old scouts vs. stats war had been overstated, even as talk of it flared in the mainstream media with the release of the *Moneyball* movie late in 2011, but the end of the 2012 baseball season was dominated by a donnybrook worthy of the one you might have had with your Uncle Casey at Thanksgiving, 2001, a pitched battle between the traditional and the sabermetrically inclined over the American League Most Valuable Player award.

Miguel Cabrera of the Detroit Tigers was on his way to the Triple Crown. *Case closed!* the old-schoolers cried. A Triple Crown is a nice bauble, retorted the new-agers (as the old-schoolers like to call them) and Cabrera is an astonishingly great hitter, but Mike Trout of the Los Angeles Angels has been better at baseball this year. His baserunning and defense, combined with some pretty great hitting of his own, make him a far more valuable player than Cabrera. One need only look at his 9-plus WARP, half again better than Cabrera's total.

And the traditional crowd complained about WARP and WAR and VORP and BABIP and FRA and here's where they inevitably make up a funny acronym, like SHINDIG or BIEBER. *It's like we're not even talking the same language,* the Cabrera-for-MVPers said.

And they were right. We're not.

The traditional folks won this round. Cabrera is the 2012 AL MVP and always will be. But, more and more every year, the language of baseball is sabermetrics, advanced statistical analysis that, along with scouting, is part of the foundation of any successful franchise in the twenty-first century. No team is without experts in analytics—a trend that has cost Baseball Prospectus many fine writers over the last decade, as MLB teams have harvested the expertise of BP's staff. We're always sad to see them go, but also thrilled for them, and by the increasing influence of sabermetric thinking in big-league baseball, an influence in which we like to think Baseball Prospectus has played no small part.

This year we said goodbye to one of BP's stars, Kevin Goldstein, who led our coverage of prospects before new Astros general manager Jeff Luhnow hired him away to head up Houston's pro scouting department. We thought the least Luhnow could do in return was to write the foreword to this book, and he said he was thrilled to do it. We're thrilled too, but we're not going to let him know that. Jason Parks, already well known to Prospectus readers, has taken the lead on prospects coverage both online and for this book, and he coordinated the team of writers that created this year's Top 101 Prospects list. Just like a big-league team, BP replenishes its roster with fresh talent, and we're very happy to welcome some sharp new minds (and tongues) to the lineup this year.

That's one of a few changes we hope you'll enjoy. We've also redesigned the team essays this year. They are shorter and more direct than they have been in the past. Each team's essay is divided into sections on the 2012 season, the 2013 season, and the overall state of the organization, and each of those sections begins with a brief overview. The idea is to make it easier for you to get a handle on the information you're looking for quickly, which after all is the goal of a reference book. The new format also gives us space to include comments about more players—the nearly 2200 players profiled in this annual is a new Baseball Prospectus record—and to bring something back that had been squeezed out in recent years: essays on topics broader than any one team. Colin Wyers takes a look at the year in sabermetrics itself, while Russell Carleton takes a more philosophical tack on the subject of analytical research as it is conducted these days.

One thing to remember as you read about your favorite teams and players and how they're likely to fare is that the 2013 season will be the third one preceded by a World Baseball Classic—and you know what that means. Don't you? Neither do we. There was some concern following the last WBC in 2009 that a large number of pitchers who had participated ended up on the disabled list over the course of that season. But a lot of pitchers end up on the DL every season. It's impossible to sort out cause and effect after only two tournaments have been played, in 2006 and '09. But the WBC does have big-league pitchers cranking it up in more-meaningful-than-usual competition in March. It's probably wise to have a little extra concern about the health of any hurlers who take part.

A change we made last year continues in the 2013 edition: Whenever possible, players are listed in the chapter of the team they'll be with on Opening Day, not the team they finished last year with. It's not a perfect system because this book went to press around Christmas, and plenty of moves were made between Christmas Day and when you read this. Unsigned free agents and later-traded players will still be listed with their old teams, but we believe it's better to make our best effort to get as many onto the right teams as possible than to have, say, Jose Reyes sitting in the chapter on the Marlins, a team he left three and a half months before spring training began.

Even minor changes to the familiar are often met with boos, but we hope you'll enjoy the 2013 annual as much as ever. One thing that hasn't changed is that Baseball Prospectus is at the center of the sabermetrics movement in baseball, and we plan to stay there even as that movement becomes the mainstream.

And we'll be watching as the same impulses that drove the baseball world to a new and better way of thinking drive people in other areas. At a journalism conference late in the year, Harper Reed, the punk-styled engineer who had been the chief technology officer of the successful Obama campaign, was asked what advice he would give to journalists.

"F---ing do math," he said.

At Baseball Prospectus, we've been doing it for decades.

King Kaufman, San Francisco
Cecilia M. Tan, Boston
December 24, 2012

Statistical Introduction

Colin Wyers

It's the eternal refrain—why don't you get your nose out of those numbers and watch a game?

It's a false dilemma, of course. I would wager that Baseball Prospectus readers watch more games than the typical fan. They also probably pay better attention when they do. The numbers do not replace observation, they supplement it. Having the numbers allows you to learn things not readily seen by mere watching, and to keep up on many more players than any one person could on their own.

So this book doesn't ask you to choose between the two—instead we combine numerical analysis with the observations of a lot of very bright people. They won't always agree—just as the eyes don't always see what the numbers do, the reverse can be true. In order to get the most out of this book, however, it helps to understand the numbers we're presenting and why.

Offense

At the core of everything we do to measure offense is True Average, which attempts to measure everything a player does at the plate—hitting for power, taking walks, striking out and even "productive" outs—on the familiar scale of batting average. A player with a TAv of .260 is average, .300 is exceptional, .200 is awful.

True Average also accounts for the context a player performs in—the baseline for average is not what the typical player has done, but what we expect the typical player would have done given similar opportunities. That means we adjust based on the mix of parks a player plays in. For example, rather than use a blanket park adjustment for every player on a team, a player who plays a disproportionate amount of his games at home will see that reflected in his numbers. We also adjust based upon league quality: The average player in the AL is better than the average player in the NL, and True Average accounts for this.

Because batting runs isn't the entirety of scoring runs, we also look at a player's Baserunning Runs. BRR accounts for the value of a player's ability to steal bases, of course, but also for his ability to go first to third on a single, or advance on a fly ball.

Defense

Defense is a much thornier issue. The general move in the sabermetric community has been toward stats based on zone data, where human stringers record the type of batted ball (grounder, liner, fly ball) and its presumed landing location. That data is used to compile expected outs to compare a fielder's performance to.

The trouble with zone data is two-fold. First, unlike the sorts of data that we use in the calculation of the statistics you see in this book, the data used in purportedly advanced fielding stats wasn't made publicly available. It was recorded by commercial entities that kept it private, only disclosing it to a select few who paid large sums for it. Second, as we've seen the field of zone-based defensive analysis open up—more data and more metrics based upon that data coming to light—we see that the conclusions of zone-based defensive metrics don't hold up to outside scrutiny. Different data providers can come to very different conclusions about the same events. And even two metrics based upon the same data set can come to radically different conclusions based upon their starting assumptions—assumptions that haven't been tested, using methods that can't be duplicated or verified by outside analysts.

The quality of the fielder can bias the data: Zone-based fielding metrics will tend to attribute more expected outs to good fielders than bad fielders, irrespective of the distribution of batted balls. Scorers who work in parks with high press boxes will tend to score more line drives than scorers who work in parks with low press boxes. Simply put, there is no evidence to show that the inclusion of zone-based data improves defensive metrics over the short run, and much evidence that incorporating the data causes severe distortions over the long run.

Our Fielding Runs Above Average incorporates play-by-play data, allowing us to study the issue of defense at a granular level without resorting to the sorts of subjective data used in some other fielding metrics. We count how many plays a player made, as well as expected plays for the average player at that position based upon a pitcher's estimated groundball tendencies and the handedness of the batter. There are also adjustments for park and the base-out situations.

Pitching

Of course, how we measure fielding influences how we measure pitching.

Most sabermetric analysis of pitching has been inspired by Voros McCracken, who wrote, "There is little if any difference among major-league pitchers in their ability to prevent hits on balls hit in the field of play." When first published, this statement was extremely controversial, but later research has by-and-large validated it. McCracken (and others) went forth from that finding to come up with a variety of defense-independent pitching measures.

The trouble is that many efforts to separate pitching from fielding have ended up separating pitching from pitching—looking at only a handful of variables (typically walks, strikeouts, and home runs—the "three true outcomes") in isolation from the situation in which they occurred. What we've done instead is take a pitcher's actual results—not just what happened, but when it happened—and adjust it for the quality of a pitcher's defensive support, as measured by FRAA.

Applying FRAA to pitchers in this sense is easier than applying it to fielders. We don't have to worry about figuring out which fielder is responsible for making an out, only identifying the likelihood of an out being made. So there is far less uncertainty here than there is in fielding analysis.

Note that Fair Runs Allowed means exactly that, a number scaled to a pitcher's runs allowed per game, not his earned runs allowed per game. Looking only at earned runs tends over time to overrate three kinds of pitchers:

1. Pitchers who play in parks where scorers hand out more errors. Looking at error rates between parks tells us scorers differ significantly in how likely they are to score any given play as an error, as opposed to an infield hit;
2. Groundball pitchers, because a substantial proportion of errors occur on groundballs; and
3. Pitchers who aren't very good. Good pitchers tend to allow fewer unearned runs than bad ones because they have more ways to get out of jams. They're more likely to get a strikeout to end the inning, and less likely to give up a home run.

For a metric that provides a more forward-looking perspective, we have Fielding Independent Pitching, a metric developed independently by Tom Tango and Clay Dreslough that says what a pitcher's expected ERA would be given his walks, strikeouts, and home runs allowed. FIP is attempting to answer a different question than Fair RA; instead of saying how well a pitcher performed, it tells us how much of a pitcher's performance we think is due to things the pitcher has direct control over. Over time, we see pitchers who consistently over- or underperform their FIPs through some skill that isn't picked up by the rather limited components; FIP may be useful in identifying pitchers who were "lucky" or "unlucky," but some caution must be exercised, lest we throw the baby out with the bathwater.

Projection

Of course, many of you aren't turning to this book just to see what a player has done. You want to know what a player is going to do. That's what the PECOTA projections touted on the cover of the book are all about.

PECOTA, initially developed by Nate Silver (who has moved on to greater fame as a political analyst), consists of three parts:

1. Major-league equivalencies, which allow us to use minor-league stats to project how a player is expected to perform in the majors;
2. Baseline forecasts, which use weighted averages and regression to the mean to produce an estimate of a player's true talent level,
3. A career-path adjustment, which incorporates information on how comparable players' stats changed over time.

Now that we've gone over our stats, let's go over what's inside the book.

The Team Prospectus

The bulk of this book is comprised of team chapters, with one for each of the 30 major-league franchises. On the first page of each chapter, you will be greeted by a box laying out some key statistics for each team.

DIAMONDBACKS PROSPECTUS

2012 W-L: 81-81, 3rd in NL West

Pythag	.530	13th	DER	.699	25th
RS/G	4.53	8th	B-Age	28.2	16th
RA/G	4.25	15th	P-Age	26.7	1st
TAv	.264	12th	Salary	$75.9	23rd
BRR	-11.1	29th	M$/MW	$1.93	9th
TAv-P	.257	11th	DL Days	650	25th
FIP	3.85	11th	DL WARP	3.2	16th

Three-Year Park Factors

Overall	103
HR/RH	109
HR/LH	105
AVG/RH	104
AVG/LH	109

Chase Field (1998)
Att. % of Capacity: 55.3% (26th)
Dim. 330, 376, 407, 376, 335

Only Coors Field and Fenway Park yielded more doubles than the park we still want to call the Bob.

2012 W-L is exactly as it sounds—the straight and unadjusted tally of wins and losses. Pythag tallies wins and losses on an adjusted basis by taking the runs scored per game (RS/G) and allowed (RA/G) by a team in a season and running them through a version of Bill James's Pythagorean formula refined and developed by David Smyth and Brandon Heipp called "Pythagenpat."

A team's runs scored is accompanied by True Average and Baserunning Runs to give a picture of how a team scores its runs. In terms of run-prevention ability, we present a team's TAv against, FIP, and Defensive Efficiency Rating, which is its rate of balls in play turned into outs.

Then we have several measures not directly related to on-field performance. B-Age and P-Age tell us the average age of a team's batters and pitchers, respectively. Salary tells us how much the team cost to put on the field, and Doug Pappas's Marginal Dollars per Marginal Win (abbreviated M$/MW) tells us how much bang for the buck a team got out of its payroll.

This year we're expanding the annual's coverage of injuries. We count up the number of disabled-list days a team has, as well as the estimated WARP that a team lost in those DL days, to quantify the impact of the specific players who were out of commission.

We also have a summary of a team's run environment, based upon its home park. We have a team's overall park factor as well (considering its home park and the road parks it's slated to play in), plus park factors broken down for left- and right-handed hitters and home-run park factors for left- and right-handed hitters.

Position Players

After an opening essay that gives overviews of how a team fared in 2012, expectations for 2013, and the shape the organization's in, each chapter moves on to the player comments. Position players are listed first, in alphabetical order, and each player is listed with the major-league team with which he was employed as of December 25, 2013, meaning that free agents who changed teams after that date will be listed under their previous employer. As an example, take a gander at the 2012 AL Rookie of the Year, Mike Trout

The player-specific sections begin with biographical information, such as a player's age, height, and weight. Stats from the past three years are listed, though if a hitter got fewer than five plate appearances at a minor-league level, we left it out. The column headers begin with more standard information such as year, team, level (majors or minors, and which level of the minors), and the raw, untranslated tallies found on the back of a baseball card: PA (Plate Appearances), R (Runs), 2B (doubles), 3B (triples), HR (home runs), RBI (runs batted in), BB (walks), SO (strikeouts), SB (stolen bases), and CS (caught stealing).

Following those are the untranslated triple-slash-rate statistics: batting average (AVG), on-base percentage (OBP), and slugging percentage (SLG). Their "slash" nickname is derived from the way they're often presented: Joey Votto hit .309/.416/.531. Put together, they describe the "shape" of a hitter's production—whether he's a slap-hitting "punch and judy" type, an all-or-nothing slugger, or simply an all-around amazing hitter. The slash line is followed by True Average, which rolls all those things and more into one easy-to-digest number, as described above.

Batting Average on Balls in Play is meant to show how well a player did when he hit the ball and it didn't leave the park. An especially low or high BABIP may mean a hitter was especially lucky or unlucky—but it may not. Line-drive hitters tend to have high BABIPs from season to season; so do speedy hitters who are able to beat out more grounders for base hits.

Next is Baserunning Runs (BRR), which, as mentioned earlier, covers all sorts of baserunning accomplishments, not just stolen bases. It's followed by a player's fielding performance. This year we've added the number of games a player has played in parenthesis after the position, followed by the player's FRAA.

The last column is Wins Above Replacement Player. WARP combines a player's Batting Runs Above Average (derived from a player's True Average), BRR, FRAA, an adjustment based upon position played, and a credit for plate appearances based upon the difference between the "replacement level" (derived from looking at the quality of players added to a team's roster after the start of the season) and the league average.

Why the replacement level adjustment? Why not leave everything relative to average? The answer is playing time:

Mike Trout **CF**

Born: **8/7/1991** Age: **21**
Bats: **R** Throws: **R** Height: **6' 2"**
Weight: **200** Breakout: **6%**
Improve: **63%** Collapse: **6%**
Attrition: **16%** MLB: **99%**

Comparables:
Ken Griffey,Jason Heyward,Justin Upton

YEAR	TEAM	LVL	AGE	PA	R	2B	3B	HR	RBI	BB	SO	SB	CS	AVG_OBP_SLG	TAv	BABIP	BRR	FRAA	WARP
2010	CDR	A	18	368	76	19	7	6	39	46	52	45	9	.362/.452/.526	.347	.418	7.2	CF(78): -2.2, LF(2): 0.1	5.3
2010	RCU	A+	18	232	30	9	2	4	19	27	33	11	6	.306/.384/.434	.319	.341	2.3	CF(58): -3.7, LF(3): 0.2	2.3
2011	ARK	AA	19	412	82	18	13	11	38	45	76	33	10	.326/.414/.544	.329	.390	4.1	CF(51): -1.0, LF(1): -0.0	2.6
2011	ANA	MLB	19	135	20	6	0	5	16	9	30	4	0	.220/.281/.390	.264	.247	0.8	CF(13): 0.9, RF(13): -0.3	0.4
2012	SLC	AAA	20	93	21	4	5	1	13	11	16	6	1	.403/.467/.623	.383	.476	-0.3	CF(8): -1.1, LF(3): 0.4	0.9
2012	ANA	MLB	20	639	129	27	8	30	83	67	139	49	5	.326/.399/.564	.357	.383	8.7	CF(110): 6.1, LF(67): 2.7	9.1
2013	*ANA*	*MLB*	*21*	*542*	*85*	*22*	*6*	*18*	*62*	*48*	*117*	*35*	*7*	*.289/.357/.473*	*.302*	*.342*	*4.4*	*CF -3, LF 0*	*4.1*

If you have two players who are totally average (in terms of hitting, fielding, position, and baserunning) but one plays in a dozen games and one plays in 120 games, the latter of the two is clearly more valuable to his team. At the same time, it's easy to envision a player who plays so poorly he is less valuable the more he plays—a first baseman who bats .200 with a lack of walks and power to match is hurting his team more the more he plays. Replacement level gives us a way to see how a player's playing time is helping—or hurting—his team.

Pitchers

Now let's look at how pitchers are presented, looking at a certain knuckleballing phenom (on the next page):

The first line and the YEAR, TM, LVL, and AGE columns are the same as in the hitter's example above. The next set of columns—W (Wins), L (Losses), SV (Saves), G (Games pitched), GS (Games Started), IP (Innings Pitched), H (Hits), HR, BB, and SO—are the actual, unadjusted cumulative stats compiled by the pitcher during each season.

Next is GB%, which is the percentage of all batted balls that were hit on the ground. That includes both outs and hits. The average GB% for a major-league pitcher in 2012 was about 46.6; a pitcher with a GB% anywhere north of 50 can be considered a good groundball pitcher. As mentioned above, this is based upon the observation of human stringers and can be skewed based upon a number of factors. We've included the number as a guide, but please approach it skeptically.

BABIP is the same statistic as for batters, but often tells you more in the case of pitchers, since most pitchers have very little control over their batting average on balls in play. A high BABIP is most likely due to a poor defense, or bad luck, rather than a pitcher's own abilities, and may be a good indicator of a potential rebound. A typical league-average BABIP is around .295–.300.

WHIP and ERA are known to most fans, with the former measuring the number of walks and hits allowed on a per-inning basis while the latter shows earned runs allowed per nine innings pitched. Neither is translated or adjusted in any way.

We went into Fair RA in some depth above. It's the basis of WARP for pitchers. Incorporating play-by-play data allows us to set different replacement levels for starting pitchers and relievers. Relief pitchers have several advantages over starters: They can exert maximum effort on every pitch, and hitters have fewer chances to pick up on what they're doing. That means it's significantly easier to find decent replacements for relief pitchers than it is for starting pitchers, and that's reflected in the replacement level for each.

We also credit starters if they pitch deeper into games and "save the pen." A starting pitcher who's able to pitch effectively deep into a game allows a manager to keep his worst relievers in the bullpen and bring his best relievers out to preserve a lead.

All of this means that WARP values for relief pitchers (especially closers) will seem lower than what we've seen in the past—and may conflict with how we feel about relief aces coming in and "saving" the game. But the save stat, while a model of how we feel about a pitcher's performance—a successful save means a win, while a failed save typically means a loss—does not describe how teams win games. In other words, saves give extra credit to the closer for what his teammates did to put him in a save spot to begin with; WARP is incapable of feeling excitement over a successful save, and judges it dispassionately.

PECOTA

Pitchers and hitters both have PECOTA projections for this season, as well as a set of biographical details that describe the performance of that player's comparable players according to PECOTA.

The 2013 line is the PECOTA projection for the player in the upcoming season. Note that the player is projected into the league and park context as indicated by his team abbreviation. All PECOTAs represent a player's projected major-league performance. The numbers beneath the player's name—Breakout, Improve, Collapse, and Attrition—are also a part of PECOTA. These estimate the likelihood of changes in performance relative to a player's previously established level of production, based upon the performance of comparable players:

- Breakout Rate is the percent chance that a player's production will improve by at least 20 percent relative to the weighted average of his performance over his most recent seasons.
- Improve Rate is the percent chance that a player's production will improve at all relative to his baseline performance. A player who is expected to perform just the

R.A. Dickey
Born: **10/29/1974** Age: **38**
Bats: **R** Throws: **R** Height: **6' 3"** Weight: **220**
Breakout: **10%** Improve: **29%** Collapse: **26%**
Attrition: **10%** MLB: **77%**
Comparables:
Dennis Martinez,Derek Lowe,Early Wynn

YEAR	TEAM	LVL	AGE	W	L	SV	G	GS	IP	H	HR	BB	SO	EqBB9	EqSO9	GB%	BABIP	WHIP	ERA	FIP	FRA	WARP
2010	BUF	AAA	35	4	2	0	8	8	60^2	55	3	8	37	1.2	5.5	56%	.272	1.04	2.22	3.26	4.04	2.2
2010	NYN	MLB	35	11	9	0	27	26	174^1	165	13	42	104	2.2	5.4	56%	.276	1.19	2.84	3.67	4.39	2.8
2011	NYN	MLB	36	8	13	0	33	32	208^2	202	18	54	134	2.3	5.8	53%	.278	1.23	3.28	3.74	4.38	14.8
2012	NYN	MLB	37	20	6	0	34	33	233^2	192	24	54	230	2.1	8.9	48%	.275	1.05	2.73	3.31	3.74	47.3
2013	*TOR*	*MLB*	*38*	*12*	*8*	*0*	*26*	*26*	*175^1*	*176*	*22*	*54*	*126*	*2.7*	*6.5*	*50%*	*.291*	*1.31*	*4.22*	*0.00*	*4.59*	*1.5*

same as he has in the recent past will have an Improve Rate of 50 percent.

- Collapse Rate is the percent chance that a position player's equivalent runs produced per PA will decline by at least 25 percent relative to his baseline performance over his past three seasons.
- Attrition Rate operates on playing time rather than performance. Specifically, it measures the likelihood that a player's playing time will decrease by at least 50 percent relative to his established level.

Breakout Rate and Collapse Rate can sometimes be counterintuitive for players who have already experienced a radical change in their performance levels. It's also worth noting that the projected decline in a given player's rate performances might not be indicative of an expected decline in underlying ability or skill, but rather something of an anticipated correction following a breakout season.

The final piece of information, listed just to the right of the player's Attrition Rate, are his three highest-scoring comparable players, as determined by PECOTA, and a similarity score from 0–100 describing how similar a player's comps are to him. Occasionally, a player's top comparables will not be representative of the larger sample that PECOTA uses. It's also important to note that established major leaguers are compared to other major leaguers only, while minor-league players may be compared to major- or minor-league players, with PECOTA strongly preferring the latter. All comparables represent a snapshot of how the listed player was performing at the same age as the current player, so if a 23-year-old hitter is compared to Sammy Sosa, he's actually being compared to a 23-year-old Sammy Sosa, not the decrepit version of Sosa who played for the Orioles, nor to Sosa's career as a whole.

Managers

Each team chapter ends with a manager's comment and data breaking down his tactical tendencies. Though it's often difficult to isolate a manager's contributions to a team, comparing specific data modeled after well-documented plays and styles to the league average helps determine what a manager likes to do, even if we are still unable to translate that information into actual wins and losses.

Following the year, team, and the actual record, Pythag +/- lets us know by how many games the team under- or overperformed its Pythagenpat record. That isn't necessarily a reflection of the manager, but it does tell us how well a team performed compared to a somewhat less noisy assessment of the underlying talent.

Pitching staff usage follows, first with Avg PC reporting the average pitch count of his starting pitchers; 100+P and 120+P track the number of games in which the starters exceeded certain pitch thresholds. QS is the total number of quality starts—a start of at least six innings and with no more than three runs allowed—a manager received from his starting pitchers. BQS is Blown Quality Starts, a Baseball Prospectus stat that measures games in which the starter delivered a quality start through six innings before losing it in the seventh inning or later by allowing runs to give him four or more. That said, a Blown Quality Start is not necessarily an indictment of the manager's ability or tactics—a number of factors, ranging from excellent offensive support to extremely poor bullpen support, can lead a manager to leave his starter in a game after he's thrown six quality innings. Conversely, the decision by a manager to "bank" quality starts by restricting his starters to only six innings can have downsides as well, as it increases the bullpen's workload and gives it more opportunities to blow games in which a starter was cruising.

The next stats in the manager table tally how many pitching changes a manager made over the course of the season (REL) and how many times the reliever called upon didn't allow any runners, his own or inherited, to score (REL w Zero R). Bequeathed runners also count against REL w Zero R, meaning that relievers who exit with runners on that subsequently score prevent a manager from "padding" his tally here. Concluding the pitching section, IBB is simply the number of intentional walks the manager ordered during the given season, which can be a mark of managerial strategy so long as outlying intentional-walk recipients such as Albert Pujols are accounted for.

Managers do more than manage pitchers, however; their usage of a bench can lead to added or lost performance. Subs lets us know the number of defensive replacements

MANAGER: DAVEY JOHNSON

YEAR	TEAM	W-L	Pythag +/-	Avg PC	100+ P	120+ P	QS	BQS	REL	REL w Zero R	IBB	PH	PH Avg	PH HR	SB2	CS2	SB3	CS3	SAC Att	SAC %	POS SAC	Squeeze	Swing	In Play
2012	WAS	98-64	1	93.6	48	1	97	2	482	378	32	244	.288	4	18	4	1	1	80	72.5%	27	1	303	78

the manager employed throughout the regular season, while PH, PH Avg, and PH HR report the offensive statistics of pinch-hitters called upon. We then turn to the so-called small-ball tactics, starting with the running game. The manager's aggressiveness on the bases is broken down by successful steals of second and third base (SB2, SB3) and times caught (CS2, CS3). We also provide the number of sacrifices a team attempted (SAC Att) and their success rate (SAC %). Be sure to keep in mind the differences between leagues as National League sacrifice attempts are greatly inflated by the fact that the pitchers bat. To correct for this, we list the number of times a manager got a successful sacrifice from a position player (POS SAC), which allows for comparisons between the two leagues. We finish up with Squeeze, which counts the number of successful squeeze plays the team executed over the season. Finally, we have a couple of statistics that attempt to measure the manager's hit-and-run tactics. Swing is the number of times a hitter swung at a pitch while the runners were in motion, while In Play reflects how many times hitters swung and made contact while those runners were off to the races. Granted, swings on steal attempts do not always translate to hit-and-run attempts, but managers who greatly deviate from the average can be assumed to be staunch proponents or opponents of the strategy.

2012: The Year in Sabermetrics

Colin Wyers

I'm sure if you talked to 10 different sabermetricians and asked what the fundamental insight of sabermetrics is, you'd get a dozen different answers. Here's mine:

Nobody is ever going to know everything there is to know about baseball. More generally speaking, not even all of us together will ever know everything there is to know about baseball.

Why should you listen to this one?

- It is right.
- It is universally useful—it can be applied to hitting, pitching, fielding, managing, economics, your day job, raising your children, questions of eschatology and more.
- It is the fundamental thing that makes being a sabermetrician distinct from someone who uses numbers to talk about baseball, because anyone can do that, and quite a few people whom nobody would mistake for a sabermetrician do.

Now, the period where Bill James and Pete Palmer and a handful of other diligent researchers were basically founding the field of sabermetrics as we know it will never be rivaled in terms of the sheer quantity (or quality) of discoveries by a person or even the whole field, despite the fact that the field has grown much larger and has much better tools to work with. There were decades of ossification being overcome in the space of a few years, an incredible accomplishment that we won't see the likes of again.

But there are still things left undiscovered, as well as old discoveries that are waiting to be overturned or walked back a little. The most important thing a sabermetrician can learn isn't the findings of James and his contemporaries and followers but their spirit of inquiry, their sense of always having more questions than answers. (That said, learn about their actual findings, too.)

So in that spirit, let's talk about what we learned in 2012 about baseball that we may not have known before. I say "we" to refer to the nebulous concept of the general sabermetric community; I talked to several others to help curate this list, but in the end what it really reflects is my judgment of findings that are new and interesting. I am reasonably well-read in the field, but obviously (see the fundamental insight) I cannot know everything and do not claim to. In other words, I can't guarantee that these findings are new. They're just new to me.

Let's start off with something of my own. Many considered 2012 the year of the shift, and early on I decided to investigate the shift in general and the shifting of Brett Lawrie in particular. Lawrie, third baseman for the Toronto Blue Jays, played in a rather peculiar version of the Ted Williams Shift, where Lawrie moved to the spot normally occupied by the second baseman in the shift, short right field. By May, Lawrie had a very high rating in Defensive Runs Saved, a fielding metric published by Baseball Info Solutions. Baseball Info Solutions had also published research showing that the shift was becoming more prevalent and causing teams to improve defensively overall. I went to investigate two questions:

1. Was Brett Lawrie's defensive rating being unduly influenced by the shift, and
2. Was there any evidence that the shift was having a significant impact on league-wide fielding?

To try to answer the first question, I watched video of Lawrie and counted the number of shifts he made. I counted 12–16 shift plays, depending on how one defines the term. Then I estimated how many runs he saved using two different methods.[1] One was an attempt to follow BIS's methods as outlined in *The Fielding Bible III*. BIS uses batted-ball location data to estimate how likely an average fielder would be to make a play on a ball hit at a given speed to a certain area, then subtracts likely plays from actual plays made to determine Defensive Runs Saved. The other method I used instead looked at the likelihood of *any* fielder, regardless of position, making a play given the same inputs. I thought that by ignoring this metric, BIS was not accounting for areas of shared responsibility and thus overstating individual fielding performances.

Lawrie provided such an obvious example of this overstatement that it was impossible to overlook; because third basemen never play in short right field, the expected play value was essentially zero, even though we can presume there was some chance of a play being made if no such shift was employed. BIS discovered its error in July and altered its fielding system to exclude shift plays from individual fielder ratings, which solves the Lawrie issue but doesn't address

1. Colin Wyers, "Who Gives A Shift?," Baseball Prospectus, *http://www.baseballprospectus.com/article.php?articleid=17183.*

the more general issue of shared areas of responsibility.[2] At the team level, if X is plays made and Y expected plays made, then X minus Y is team fielding performance. Things should break down the same way at the player level, but BIS is throwing away parts of Y, so individual fielding performance won't add up to what team fielding performance should be.

With the differences between the two methods, as many as 10 runs of Lawrie's May DRS rating could have been due to overstating the impact of the shift. Baseball Info Solutions lowered Lawrie's Defensive Runs Saved from 30 to 16 in July. Lawrie was still the best defensive third baseman in the league, but he wasn't *that* good.

For the second question, I had to use somewhat more indirect methods to examine the shift[3]. The work I did on counting shift plays by Lawrie simply wouldn't scale up to tracking a whole league, at least not working by myself. (There are also questions about how well you can track less extreme shift alignments using video.) Instead, I looked at hitters who were likely shift candidates (slow, left-handed power hitters) over time, to see if their BABIP relative to the league was dropping, which is what we would expect if the shift were becoming more prevalent and/or more effective. Instead I saw no significant change, and I also found no increase in bunts that would have indicated that lefty sluggers were attempting to "beat" the shift more often. In other words, if teams really are shifting more, it seems there's no evidence that it's helping them field more batted balls.

My Baseball Prospectus colleague Russell Carleton took on a different question: Is there a point at which players tend to stop developing? In other words, at some point, is a player too old to be expected to show significant improvement?

Russell took a battery of stats—OBP, HR/PA, and so on—and looked at the year-to-year correlation for those stats depending on the age of the player.[4] What he found was that the correlation increased significantly around age 26. That is, if your favorite player hasn't seemed to reach his potential by age 26, he isn't likely to do so, because across the population of players development slows significantly at that age. Talent is far more stable year-to-year for players in their late 20s, Russell found, and then there is a corresponding decrease in correlation around age 29, when players' talent typically becomes less stable again. This is a generalization, not an absolute law.

These ages seem to line up with our traditional model of player age, but, as Russell notes, it's not a validation of the standard peak model. "These numbers tell me that we need to view 24–26 as more of a chaotic, malleable period," Russell wrote in a comment on his own piece. "Some will take bigger jumps than others. Some will fall. At 26 though, the chaos stabilizes. At 29, some start to decline, while others hold." Russell's findings hint at several new and interesting questions about how players develop: Are there ways to identify players who learn better than others? Are there better ways to teach skills to players who have reached the age where players typically stop developing?

And, as noted above, if sabermetrics should be about having more questions than answers, answers that raise additional questions are the best sorts of answers.

Glenn DuPaul of the Hardball Times looked at whether a hitter's approach at the plate is a useful predictor of his future batting average.[5] Specifically, he wanted to see if a hitter's ability to be patient at the plate could be used to predict how well he would hit for average. What Glenn found was that while a hitter's strikeout rate is useful in predicting his future batting average, his walk rate isn't. Glenn went on to discuss some potential areas for improvement in the study (such as selective sampling issues).

It's admirable to discuss shortcomings and reservations with one's own studies. It demonstrates an awareness and puts the findings in the appropriate context. It's also a good thing to publish nonfindings as well as findings: Glenn went looking for an effect and instead found no evidence for it. Such results may be discouraging for researchers, but our community is better off when these things are discussed openly.

Max Marchi of Baseball Prospectus examined pitch velocities, looking to see what factors influenced how fast a pitch was thrown.[6] Thanks to the PITCHf/x systems MLB Advanced Media has installed in every major-league stadium, we now have very accurate data on almost every pitch thrown in the highest level of baseball, and Max has been one of the best in interrogating that data to learn new things about it.

Very accurate data is not perfect, however, and Max wanted to examine how well the PITCHf/x systems in different parks were measuring speed relative to each other. To that end, he examined how different factors affect pitch speed. Month is important, as is temperature (the two are correlated across MLB, but different stadiums will be affected differently by temperature, even controlling for month). Pitch speeds tend to increase as the season goes on and temperatures rise, though pitchers also throw harder, on

2. John Dewan, "Brett Lawrie—Best Defensive Third Baseman in Baseball?," Bill James Online, *http://www.billjamesonline.com/brett_lawrie—best_defensive_third_baseman_in_baseball_/*.
3. Colin Wyers, "What We Really Know About the Shift," Baseball Prospectus, *http://www.baseballprospectus.com/article.php?articleid=17265*.
4. Russell Carleton, "When Do Players Stop Developing?,", Baseball Prospectus, *http://www.baseballprospectus.com/article.php?articleid=18501*.
5. Glenn DuPaul, "Controlling the strike zone and batting average," The Hardball Times, *http://www.hardballtimes.com/main/article/controlling-the-strike-zone-and-batting-average/*.
6. Max Marchi, "All About Velocity," Baseball Prospectus, *http://www.baseballprospectus.com/article.php?articleid=16888*.

average, at night, when it's cooler. And, unsurprisingly, pitch speeds drop the more pitches a hurler has thrown in a game.

Even when controlling for those factors, though, Max still found significant differences in how speed is measured in different parks. It's a caution to be careful with raw data, even data as good as what the PITCHf/x system delivers.

Not all findings are directly about baseball itself. Some are about how we interpret the models we use to analyze baseball. The blogger Kincaid at 3-D Baseball did a rather thorough examination of how various metrics treat home runs.[7] He looked at three different metrics:

1. Run Expectancy, which is how many additional runs an event typically creates, given the base-out situation when it occurs.
2. Win Probability Added, which is similar to run expectancy, but looks at the home team's win percentage instead of runs scored, and considers the inning and score differential in addition to the bases and outs.
3. Win Probability Added/Leverage Index, which is WPA divided by the average change in win probability given the base-out situation at the start of the play (in other words, its "leverage index").

What Kincaid discovered was that while RE and WPA provided similar event values, WPA/LI had a significantly larger value for the home run than the other two methods. Kincaid found that the value of the home run was negatively correlated with the leverage index of the play, and that home runs were more likely in negative leverage-index situations. What that means is that home runs are less likely to be hit when the game is on the line and more likely to be hit when they mean less to the outcome of the game. This means that WPA/LI (and stats based on it, like some popular measures of "clutch" hitting) will overstate the value of players who hit a lot of home runs.

This points out a general warning for sabermetric researchers: While models are often useful, they are not the same as what we are studying, and care ought to be taken to examine our conclusions to ensure that they apply to baseball itself, not just our models of it.

Dave Studeman of the Hardball Times decided to take a look at a much older tool, one developed by Bill James himself: the Pythagorean win estimate, which estimates a team's winning percentage from its runs scored and allowed. Sabermetricians favor the Pythagorean estimate, or Pythagorean winning percentage, because it does a better job predicting future performance than actual winning percentage, but Studeman wanted to see if Pythagorean was simply a proxy for regression to the mean (what Bill James called the Plexiglass principle: Extreme observations tend to be less extreme in larger sample sizes).

What Dave did was to look at the predictive value of Pythagorean winning percentage compared to regressed winning percentages, not raw records.[8] To avoid the problem of roster turnover, he looked at how well a team's performance correlated from month to month, not season to season, and to get a large enough set of observations to work with, he looked at all teams and months from 1970 through 2012. And what he found was that if you know a team's Pythagorean winning-percentage estimate, knowing its regressed actual wins adds nothing to your predictive value.

Now, this finding corroborates something that sabermetrics has long held to be true, that a team's run differential is a better predictor of future results than its won-loss record, and that teams that outperform their run differential tend not to do so in the future. But it's an interesting way of framing the question, and it helps clarify what exactly is being measured.

Not all conclusions are about what happens on the field. Sabermetricians are increasingly turning their attention to the way teams are constructed, the purview of general managers and owners. One important tool in those evaluations is Marginal Dollars per Marginal Wins, developed by Doug Pappas in 2004. What Pappas designed is a tool for looking at how efficiently teams spend their payroll. A problem with the metric is that teams that scrimp on payroll and manage not to have historically bad seasons come out looking very good.

Matt Swartz, also at Hardball Times, decided to dig deeper, dividing players into two pools: young, cost-controlled players, and those who were acquired as free agents.[9] That way, he could measure how efficient teams were at free-agent spending, without the confounding factor of how reliant a team was on players not yet eligible for free agency. In 2011, for example, the Marlins spent hardly anything on free agents and posted a decent 79–83 record. Thus, they led the majors in Marginal Dollars per Marginal Wins. The Yankees, on the other hand, got more wins above replacement from their free agents than any other team. What Matt found, though, was that the two clubs were about even in terms of free-agent efficiency, both in the middle of the MLB pack. That is, the free agents the Yankees bought weren't any better or worse, on average, than the free agents the Marlins bought. The Yankees just bought a whole lot more of them.

Like Russell's findings about player development, what's exciting about this isn't so much the questions it answers as

7. Kincaid, "Clutch, WPA/LI, and the Home Run Bias," 3-D Baseball, *http://www.3-dbaseball.net/2012/06/clutch-wpali-and-home-run-bias.html.*

8. Dave Studeman, "Of Runs And Wins," The Hardball Times, *http://www.hardballtimes.com/main/article/of-runs-and-wins/*

9. Matt Swartz, "Free agent value and building teams from within," The Hardball Times, *http://www.hardballtimes.com/main/article/free-agent-value-and-building-teams-from-within1/*

the questions it raises. Is it better to spend free-agent dollars efficiently, or to avoid free agency altogether? Can a team effectively do both?

As we come to the end of this list, the elephant in the room is how little PITCHf/x figures on it, relative to analysis that can be done with data that was around when James was doing much of his work or shortly thereafter. Part of this is because teams have been snatching up the most prominent PITCHf/x analysts to work for them, taking much of the best work out of the community. (Mike Fast's work on catcher framing for Baseball Prospectus was one of the most important advances of 2011; Mike now works for the Houston Astros.) But there are still analysts out there working, and there's still room for a lot of exciting new PITCHf/x analysis, if one goes looking for it.

Besides PITCHf/x, what sorts of things might we see on this list next year? Fielding is quite possibly the most exciting frontier remaining in sabermetrics. It's certainly the most controversial. And, of course, fielding and pitching cannot be so easily separated from each other.

That's both the joy and the curse of sabermetrics: There's always something new to learn, new discoveries to make. I hope you'll join me in asking more questions than we have answers for.

Arizona Diamondbacks

2012: SNAKES ON A PLAIN

The Diamondbacks' .500 record didn't do justice to their performance. They outscored opponents by 46 runs, but any playoff hopes were hamstrung by a 15–27 mark in one-run ballgames. Arizona's third-order winning percentage fell within a rounding error of both the Dodgers and the Giants, and the cost-conscious D-Backs fielded a competitive club without a single player earning as much as $8 million.

They stayed in contention until the dog days before fading to third place down the stretch, but the organization continued to develop a foundation of talent at the big-league level in what amounted to a building year in Phoenix. The Diamondbacks experienced first-hand the growing pains that come with raising pitchers, suffering the loss of starter Daniel Hudson to Tommy John surgery, while 2011 revelation Ian Kennedy fought a losing battle with statistical regression on balls in play.

One of the league's youngest pitching staffs demonstrated veteran-level control of the strike zone in 2012, finishing with the second-fewest walks allowed in the circuit, though a contact-oriented approach placed them 12th in the NL in strikeouts on the mound. The batters worked deeper counts, resulting in the offense posting the league's second-highest walk total, though a summer-long power outage by former wunderkind Justin Upton effectively muted the Arizona attack. One of the least efficient base-stealing teams in the NL, the D-Backs' 64.6 percent success rate only surpassed that of the Pirates, and the top thief on the club was 230-pound first baseman Paul Goldschmidt.

DIAMONDBACKS PROSPECTUS

2012 W-L: 81-81, 3rd in NL West

Pythag	.530	13th	DER	.699	25th
RS/G	4.53	8th	B-Age	28.2	16th
RA/G	4.25	15th	P-Age	26.7	1st
TAv	.264	12th	Salary	$75.9	23rd
BRR	-11.1	29th	M$/MW	$1.93	9th
TAv-P	.257	11th	DL Days	650	25th
FIP	3.85	11th	DL WARP	3.2	16th

Three-Year Park Factors	
Overall	103
HR/RH	109
HR/LH	105
AVG/RH	104
AVG/LH	109

Chase Field (1998)
Att. % of Capacity: 55.3% (26th)
Dim. 330, 376, 407, 376, 335

Only Coors Field and Fenway Park yielded more doubles than the park we still want to call the Bob.

2013: RATTLING THE CAGE

The Diamondbacks have an organizational nucleus of nascent talent around which to build this season, with a syllabus that includes the expansion of workloads for their prime-age pitchers and an injection of new blood into the rotation. They will mix in a healthy blend of seasoned position players who are within the range of their physical peak, which should help to stabilize the offense. If Upton can manage to jump back onto a Hall-worthy career-track, that would cover for the potential regression of a couple of veterans who are coming off big 2012 campaigns.

Arizona prioritized the organizational need for a shortstop over the offseason, emphasizing glove-savvy fielders at the expense of offense, a nod to the team's recent emphasis toward groundball-friendly pitchers. GM Kevin Towers made quite a statement when he traded starting center fielder Chris Young and enigmatic pitching phenom Trevor Bauer. Those trades returned veteran glove man Cliff Pennington to hold things down at short until fellow offseason acquisition Didi Gregorius is ready to take over full-time, plus Heath Bell, in the hope that Towers can use his Midas touch for relievers to re-kindle Bell's career.

The trade of Young to the Athletics cleared the path for rookie Adam Eaton to stake his claim to the center-field pasture at Chase Field, a positional swap of familiar names that will no doubt register some moments of déjà vu for Towers from his time spent shuffling pitchers for his old Padres teams. Eaton's on-base skills could turn him into a spark plug at the top of the order, though his defensive limitations might be a liability to the pitchers on staff, further weakening a unit that ranked 13th in the NL in defensive efficiency last season. There is considerable potential for growth on Kirk Gibson's ballclub, with a nucleus that was strong enough to contend in 2012 and is now poised for improvement.

STATE OF THE ORGANIZATION: PHOENIX RISING

The Snakes are a shining example of financial flexibility in the modern age. They are tied to just a handful of long-term contracts, as the only players from the 2012 roster with guaranteed commitments beyond 2013 are Upton, Miguel Montero, and Trevor Cahill. The front office can also bask in the security of knowing that the roster is covered for future seasons, with minimal turnover required, as most of Arizona's core players are under team control for the foreseeable future and several key players are not yet eligible for arbitration.

The management team is set for the next several years, with the club holding options that could keep both Towers and Gibson in Arizona through the 2016 season, while team president and CEO Derrick Hall is in the middle of an eight-year extension that runs through 2015. The team's local broadcasting deal expires in 2015, and at the going rate of inflation for television contracts, the time for the Diamondbacks to renegotiate with Fox might just align with designs to maintain a roster that will become increasingly expensive. Upton is the priciest player on the books, with compensation that peaks at $14.5 million in 2015, in the last year of a contract that conveniently overlaps with the final year of the television deal.

The Diamondbacks have played conservatively with free agency in recent years, signing middle-tier players to short-term deals and showing a willingness to acquire bats yet avoiding the treacherous arms race. Towers is a shrewd negotiator who prefers to improve his ballclub through trade rather than test the shark-infested waters of free agency. The risk of a negative R.O.I. escalates when dealing with free-agent pitchers, and the D-Backs are well-positioned to leverage their organizational wealth of pitching talent to exploit this particular market inefficiency.

The attrition rate that is inherent to mound work provides further incentive for Arizona to stockpile pitchers in the minor leagues. The Snakes have a cadre of arms coming through the organizational pipeline, as the system is oozing with pitching depth at the major-league level as well as the minors. On the other side of the ledger, the minor-league coffers are nearly barren of offensive support, so the D-Backs may need to lure free-agent bats with promises of big flies and swimming-pool splashdowns at Chase Field.

HITTERS

Lars Anderson **1B**

Born: **9/25/1987** Age: **25**
Bats: **L** Throws: **L** Height: **6' 5"**
Weight: **215** Breakout: **2%**
Improve: **68%** Collapse: **1%**
Attrition: **8%** MLB: **95%**

Comparables:
Keith Hernandez, Orlando Merced, Andre Thornton

YEAR	TEAM	LVL	AGE	PA	R	2B	3B	HR	RBI	BB	SO	SB	CS	AVG_OBP_SLG	TAv	BABIP	BRR	FRAA	WARP
2010	PME	AA	22	71	13	5	0	5	16	7	16	1	1	.355/.420/.677	.378	.415	-0.7	1B(17): -1.9	0.7
2010	PAW	AAA	22	462	49	32	3	10	53	44	109	2	2	.262/.342/.428	.262	.334	-6.5	1B(105): -3.6	-0.7
2010	BOS	MLB	22	43	4	1	0	0	4	7	8	0	0	.200/.326/.229	.220	.250	0.5	1B(18): -0.2	0.0
2011	PAW	AAA	23	577	65	31	2	14	78	80	120	5	0	.265/.369/.422	.274	.322	-2.5	1B(94): 2.8	0.6
2011	BOS	MLB	23	5	2	0	0	0	0	0	3	0	0	.000/.000/.000	.012	.000	0.1	1B(6): 0.1	-0.1
2012	COH	AAA	24	69	4	5	0	0	7	9	18	0	0	.196/.319/.286	.250	.275	0.3	1B(5): 0.2	0.0
2012	PAW	AAA	24	401	49	22	2	9	52	56	89	1	0	.259/.359/.415	.252	.320	0.3	1B(59): 0.2, LF(14): -0.9	-0.2
2012	BOS	MLB	24	8	1	0	0	0	0	0	3	0	0	.125/.125/.125	.104	.200	0.3	LF(4): -0.1, 1B(2): 0.0	-0.1
2013	*ARI*	*MLB*	*25*	*250*	*25*	*12*	*1*	*5*	*27*	*26*	*61*	*0*	*0*	*.240/.324/.376*	*.254*	*.306*	*-0.3*	*1B -6, LF -0*	*-0.6*

Once viewed as an elite prospect, Anderson checked in at a high of 17 on both the Baseball Prospectus and *Baseball America* lists in 2009. He then suffered through a terrible season at Double-A as a 21-year-old, with a 673 OPS, easily his worst as a pro, and despite a 2010 rebound, his stock has been tumbling since. Entering his age-25 season, the year when prospects meet the fork in the road and become either major leaguers or former prospects, Anderson is desperately hoping to regain the third and most important of the true outcomes that he used to possess: power. It showed up as a force in his game just once, though, and that was way back in 2008.

Josh Bell **3B**

Born: **11/13/1986** Age: **26**
Bats: **B** Throws: **R** Height: **6' 4"**
Weight: **220** Breakout: **4%**
Improve: **57%** Collapse: **2%**
Attrition: **11%** MLB: **93%**

Comparables:
Doug Decinces, Mike Lowell, Roy Howell

YEAR	TEAM	LVL	AGE	PA	R	2B	3B	HR	RBI	BB	SO	SB	CS	AVG_OBP_SLG	TAv	BABIP	BRR	FRAA	WARP
2010	NOR	AAA	23	344	43	25	0	13	50	23	78	2	4	.278/.331/.481	.276	.333	-1.4	3B(73): -1.4	1.3
2010	BAL	MLB	23	161	15	5	0	3	12	2	53	0	1	.214/.224/.302	.204	.301	-0.6	3B(49): 1.5	-0.4
2011	NOR	AAA	24	438	62	12	2	19	57	40	118	4	0	.253/.320/.438	.236	.310	1	3B(47): 1.4	0.0
2011	BAL	MLB	24	65	6	0	0	0	6	4	25	0	0	.164/.215/.164	.157	.278	1.2	3B(21): -1.4, LF(1): -0.0	-0.7
2012	RNO	AAA	25	371	60	25	2	12	75	33	70	3	4	.311/.372/.509	.258	.356	-1.3	3B(26): -1.9, 1B(4): 0.1	-0.5
2012	ARI	MLB	25	56	3	2	0	1	4	4	14	0	0	.173/.232/.269	.166	.216	-0.2	3B(12): -0.5	-0.4
2013	*ARI*	*MLB*	*26*	*250*	*24*	*11*	*1*	*7*	*28*	*14*	*70*	*1*	*1*	*.230/.276/.368*	*.232*	*.296*	*-0.4*	*3B -2, 1B 0*	*-0.4*

An example of the rapport between Kevin Towers and Orioles GM Dan Duquette, Bell was acquired from the Orioles in May for pitcher Michael Belfiore. Bell is a bat-first player whose defensive struggles could confine him to DH for an American League club, but as long as he remains property of the Diamondbacks, the team will have to hold out hope his glove comes around. The offensive skills that were on display in the minors have yet to translate to the majors. Bell's first 100 games in the bigs have exposed the holes in his swing, leading to a strikeout-to-walk ratio of 92-to-10.

Willie Bloomquist UT

Born: **11/27/1977** Age: **35**
Bats: **R** Throws: **R** Height: **6' 0"**
Weight: **185** Breakout: **1%**
Improve: **40%** Collapse: **9%**
Attrition: **24%** MLB: **77%**

Comparables:
Jerry Hairston,Edgar Renteria,Alvin Dark

YEAR	TEAM	LVL	AGE	PA	R	2B	3B	HR	RBI	BB	SO	SB	CS	AVG_OBP_SLG	TAv	BABIP	BRR	FRAA	WARP
2010	CIN	MLB	32	18	0	0	0	0	0	1	3	0	0	.294/.333/.294	.220	.357	-0.2	RF(5): 0.0, LF(3): -0.0	-0.1
2010	KCA	MLB	32	181	31	10	1	3	17	8	25	8	5	.265/.296/.388	.239	.294	-0.3	RF(21): -1.1, 3B(11): 0.6	0.2
2011	ARI	MLB	33	381	44	10	2	4	26	23	51	20	10	.266/.317/.340	.233	.300	0.3	SS(59): -2.8, LF(25): -0.3	-0.4
2012	ARI	MLB	34	338	47	21	5	0	23	12	55	7	10	.302/.325/.398	.262	.362	0.7	SS(64): -9.4, 3B(11): 0.2	0.2
2013	*ARI*	*MLB*	*35*	*328*	*38*	*12*	*3*	*3*	*23*	*18*	*54*	*13*	*7*	*.261/.305/.346*	*.236*	*.306*	*0*	*SS -2, LF 0*	*0.2*

Bloomquist is the type of player you don't mind using in a pinch, but repeatedly seeing his name in the starting lineup brings the risk of night terrors. He cracked a 700 OPS for the first time in his 10-year career last year, though his secondary skills were sorely lacking. He posted a career-worst walk rate, failed to hit a home run, and had a horrific track record on the basepaths. An empty .300 batting average was enough to establish a new career-high in VORP, though he gave a large chunk of that value back with his tepid defense. Willie's stay in Paradise City might be on the verge of expiration, but nobody can take away his multimillion-dollar memories.

Keon Broxton CF

Born: **5/7/1990** Age: **23**
Bats: **R** Throws: **R** Height: **6' 4"**
Weight: **195** Breakout: **11%**
Improve: **51%** Collapse: **6%**
Attrition: **19%** MLB: **82%**

Comparables:
Nelson Mathews,Sil Campusano,Billy Murphy

YEAR	TEAM	LVL	AGE	PA	R	2B	3B	HR	RBI	BB	SO	SB	CS	AVG_OBP_SLG	TAv	BABIP	BRR	FRAA	WARP
2010	SBN	A	20	603	74	17	19	5	32	65	172	21	13	.228/.313/.360	.245	.324	-1.7	CF(131): -0.3	0.4
2011	SBN	A	21	85	8	0	2	0	1	7	30	6	4	.231/.294/.282	.212	.375	0	--	0.0
2011	VIS	A+	21	483	69	14	5	7	44	62	142	27	8	.251/.349/.362	.267	.360	2.1	CF(49): -3.5, LF(5): 0.8	0.5
2012	VIS	A+	22	536	84	24	1	19	62	40	136	21	8	.267/.326/.437	.275	.332	3	CF(87): -1.5, LF(12): -0.9	1.8
2013	*ARI*	*MLB*	*23*	*250*	*27*	*8*	*2*	*4*	*18*	*15*	*80*	*7*	*3*	*.202/.253/.306*	*.203*	*.284*	*0.6*	*CF -5, LF -0*	*-1.2*

The best tools in the system began to materialize at the plate in 2012 as Broxton's bat took a step forward in his second trip through the California League. He nearly doubled his career total for homers and broke the .260 batting-average barrier for the first time. A deterioration of his walk rate and an associated drop in strikeouts suggest that Broxton was swinging earlier in the count, identifying pitches that he could drive, though the net result was a shrunken on-base percentage. "Neon Keon" might lose his nickname if the speed indicators keep trending in the wrong direction, but Broxton could have a bright future if his various talents coalesce into a well-rounded blend of speed, power, and patience.

Eric Chavez 3B

Born: **12/7/1977** Age: **35**
Bats: **L** Throws: **R** Height: **6' 2"**
Weight: **210** Breakout: **0%**
Improve: **29%** Collapse: **9%**
Attrition: **16%** MLB: **89%**

Comparables:
Don Money,Joe Torre,Al Smith

YEAR	TEAM	LVL	AGE	PA	R	2B	3B	HR	RBI	BB	SO	SB	CS	AVG_OBP_SLG	TAv	BABIP	BRR	FRAA	WARP
2010	OAK	MLB	32	123	10	8	0	1	10	8	31	0	0	.234/.276/.333	.243	.301	0.3	1B(1): -0.0	0.0
2011	NYA	MLB	33	175	16	7	1	2	26	14	34	0	0	.262/.320/.356	.240	.320	0.3	3B(42): 0.1, 1B(3): -0.0	0.1
2012	NYA	MLB	34	313	36	12	0	16	37	30	59	0	0	.281/.348/.496	.293	.300	-1.2	3B(64): 0.6, 1B(10): 0.2	1.6
2013	*ARI*	*MLB*	*35*	*267*	*28*	*13*	*1*	*7*	*29*	*20*	*57*	*0*	*0*	*.251/.308/.395*	*.252*	*.298*	*-0.4*	*3B -0, 1B -0*	*0.3*

After five straight seasons with a 60-day DL stint, Chavez avoided the disabled list completely in 2012, and with his back feeling better than it had in years, he was able to generate enough torque to drive the ball, posting his best TAv since 2004. It didn't hurt that Yankees manager Joe Girardi hid him from lefties, sending him to the plate with the platoon advantage in nearly 90 percent of his PA, but Chavez's unlikely renaissance probably owed more to the team's doctors and trainers than it did to any managerial moves. After contemplating retirement during each of the last two winters, Chavez warmed up this time around with a one-year, $3 million deal with the Diamondbacks.

Brent Clevlen OF

Born: **10/27/1983** Age: **29**
Bats: **R** Throws: **R** Height: **6' 2"**
Weight: **205** Breakout: **4%**
Improve: **54%** Collapse: **5%**
Attrition: **13%** MLB: **87%**

Comparables:
Rick Monday,Ray Lankford,Mack Jones

YEAR	TEAM	LVL	AGE	PA	R	2B	3B	HR	RBI	BB	SO	SB	CS	AVG_OBP_SLG	TAv	BABIP	BRR	FRAA	WARP
2010	GWN	AAA	26	214	19	8	0	3	29	22	62	3	0	.257/.333/.346	.238	.365	-1.4	RF(51): 0.9	-0.2
2010	ATL	MLB	26	4	2	1	0	0	0	0	1	0	0	.250/.250/.500	.182	.333	0.1	LF(2): 0.2	0.0
2011	REA	AA	27	134	26	12	0	6	20	21	34	5	2	.336/.440/.602	.338	.438	2	RF(21): 1.0, CF(2): -0.0	1.0
2011	LOU	AAA	27	96	9	2	1	3	10	7	28	0	1	.247/.302/.393	.203	.328	-0.7	CF(17): 0.5	-0.4
2012	MOB	AA	28	259	45	15	3	10	39	30	64	3	1	.260/.345/.489	.312	.314	0.3	LF(22): -0.0, CF(17): 0.1	1.6
2012	RNO	AAA	28	86	17	5	2	3	17	8	24	3	0	.377/.430/.610	.262	.510	1.1	RF(9): 0.9, LF(2): 0.0	0.4
2013	*ARI*	*MLB*	*29*	*250*	*27*	*10*	*2*	*7*	*30*	*23*	*76*	*2*	*1*	*.240/.312/.400*	*.253*	*.324*	*0.1*	*RF 0, CF -0*	*0.4*

A minor-league veteran of nine years, Clevlen last winced at the bright lights in a four-game cameo with Atlanta back in 2010. In the past three years he's treated NL organizations like a game of Q-Bert, hopping across teams in pursuit of fame and fortune. Clevlen has only played six complete big-league games, start to finish, in his career, but his age-27 and 28 seasons were loaded with peak performances for various minor-league clubs. Clevlen still has a window of opportunity to contribute at the major-league level, but Arizona's outfield depth might convince the mercenary to hop to the next cube.

Matt Davidson 3B
Born: **3/26/1991** Age: **22**
Bats: **R** Throws: **R** Height: **6' 4"**
Weight: **225** Breakout: **3%**
Improve: **55%** Collapse: **2%**
Attrition: **10%** MLB: **98%**
Comparables:
Roy Howell,Scott Rolen,Brett Lawrie

YEAR	TEAM	LVL	AGE	PA	R	2B	3B	HR	RBI	BB	SO	SB	CS	AVG_OBP_SLG	TAv	BABIP	BRR	FRAA	WARP
2010	SBN	A	19	475	58	35	3	16	79	43	109	0	2	.289/.374/.504	.302	.359	-2.4	3B(52): 0.5	2.7
2010	VIS	A+	19	84	6	1	0	2	11	12	25	0	0	.169/.298/.268	.204	.227	-1.2	3B(20): 0.7, 1B(1): -0.0	-0.4
2011	VIS	A+	20	606	93	39	1	20	106	52	147	0	1	.277/.348/.465	.289	.340	0.2	1B(33): 0.5, 3B(30): -2.1	1.4
2012	MOB	AA	21	576	81	28	2	23	76	69	126	3	4	.261/.367/.469	.297	.304	-4.4	3B(91): -0.2	2.0
2013	*ARI*	*MLB*	*22*	*250*	*26*	*11*	*1*	*9*	*31*	*17*	*70*	*0*	*0*	*.225/.290/.395*	*.244*	*.281*	*-0.4*	*3B 1, 1B -0*	*0.2*

After splitting time at first and third base in 2011, Davidson was stationed at the hot corner for all of 2012 as the Diamondbacks assess whether the former supplemental first-rounder has a future on the left side of the infield. His offensive game took a step forward, improving in the power and patience departments, but he doesn't have a first baseman's bat. Davidson's career path will largely be dictated by his glove work at third, where a clear path to playing time exists.

Adam Eaton CF
Born: **12/6/1988** Age: **24**
Bats: **L** Throws: **L** Height: **5' 10"**
Weight: **180** Breakout: **1%**
Improve: **58%** Collapse: **3%**
Attrition: **5%** MLB: **97%**
Comparables:
Lee Mazzilli,Andrew McCutchen,Jacoby Ellsbury

YEAR	TEAM	LVL	AGE	PA	R	2B	3B	HR	RBI	BB	SO	SB	CS	AVG_OBP_SLG	TAv	BABIP	BRR	FRAA	WARP
2010	MSO	Rk	21	282	48	14	4	7	37	35	44	20	8	.385/.504/.575	.388	.457	0.7	CF(39): 3.1, LF(28): 2.1	4.5
2011	VIS	A+	22	301	54	15	3	6	39	42	41	24	8	.332/.455/.492	.335	.379	2	CF(22): 1.3, RF(8): -0.4	2.0
2011	MOB	AA	22	255	31	7	4	4	28	30	35	10	6	.302/.409/.429	.293	.345	-2.4	RF(23): 2.5, CF(1): -0.1	0.4
2012	MOB	AA	23	51	11	1	0	0	3	6	8	6	1	.300/.451/.325	.234	.375	0.9	CF(4): 0.2	0.3
2012	RNO	AAA	23	562	119	46	5	7	45	53	68	38	10	.381/.456/.539	.306	.432	5.4	CF(36): -3.6, RF(10): 1.7	1.9
2012	ARI	MLB	23	103	19	3	2	2	5	14	15	2	3	.259/.382/.412	.296	.294	1.9	CF(21): -3.2, LF(1): -0.0	0.5
2013	*ARI*	*MLB*	*24*	*250*	*34*	*12*	*2*	*3*	*21*	*21*	*46*	*13*	*4*	*.278/.356/.392*	*.272*	*.331*	*0.7*	*CF -1, RF 0*	*1.0*

The trade of Chris Young opened the door for Eaton to establish himself as Arizona's center fielder of the future, though the presence of Gerardo Parra will push the rookie to perform if he wants to earn playing time. Eaton is more than a figment of Reno's imagination. He cracked his way to a .355 batting average across four minor-league levels spanning almost 1,500 plate appearances, and his penchant for the walk and efficient base-thievery add to his intriguing profile atop a major-league lineup. The jury is still out on Eaton's defense. He needs to work on his routes in order take full advantage of his speed, but the lasting memory of his catch-and-throw double-play on September 9 will buy some benefit of the doubt with the local fan base.

Paul Goldschmidt 1B
Born: **9/10/1987** Age: **25**
Bats: **R** Throws: **R** Height: **6' 4"**
Weight: **245** Breakout: **1%**
Improve: **56%** Collapse: **3%**
Attrition: **6%** MLB: **99%**
Comparables:
Boog Powell,Will Clark,Frank Robinson

YEAR	TEAM	LVL	AGE	PA	R	2B	3B	HR	RBI	BB	SO	SB	CS	AVG_OBP_SLG	TAv	BABIP	BRR	FRAA	WARP
2010	VIS	A+	22	599	102	42	3	35	108	57	161	5	1	.314/.390/.606	.337	.395	-2.4	1B(128): -5.8	5.0
2011	MOB	AA	23	457	84	21	3	30	94	82	92	9	3	.306/.435/.626	.387	.331	2.3	1B(43): 0.1	2.8
2011	ARI	MLB	23	177	28	9	1	8	26	20	53	4	0	.250/.333/.474	.284	.323	1.4	1B(43): -2.3	0.5
2012	ARI	MLB	24	587	82	43	1	20	82	60	130	18	3	.286/.359/.490	.308	.340	2.6	1B(139): -3.3	2.9
2013	*ARI*	*MLB*	*25*	*493*	*65*	*28*	*1*	*21*	*70*	*49*	*123*	*9*	*2*	*.265/.341/.478*	*.290*	*.320*	*0.4*	*1B -7*	*1.3*

Tim Lincecum probably gets holiday cards from Goldschmidt, having given up five of the first baseman's 28 lifetime homers in the majors. Goldy started slowly in 2012, hitting just two homers before May 27, but a sudden power surge at the beginning of the summer saw him club five bombs in a seven-game span. After that he settled into a comfortable 20-homer pace. He led all of baseball in line-drive percentage and is overflowing with secondary skills. Goldschmidt's a star-in-the-making who could make a leap forward if a handful of doubles find their way into the pool, and who could have every kid in Phoenix clamoring for Paulie-boy to "stay Gold."

Didi Gregorius SS

Born: **2/18/1990** Age: **23**
Bats: **L** Throws: **R** Height: **6' 2"**
Weight: **175** Breakout: **5%**
Improve: **40%** Collapse: **11%**
Attrition: **24%** MLB: **95%**

Comparables:
Robin Yount,Alfredo Griffin,Dickie Thon

YEAR	TEAM	LVL	AGE	PA	R	2B	3B	HR	RBI	BB	SO	SB	CS	AVG_OBP_SLG	TAv	BABIP	BRR	FRAA	WARP
2010	DYT	A	20	548	65	16	11	5	41	33	62	16	7	.273/.324/.379	.258	.300	3.1	SS(119): -2.4	2.3
2011	BAK	A+	21	203	30	12	1	5	28	10	25	8	8	.303/.333/.457	.281	.323	1	SS(26): 0.8	0.8
2011	CAR	AA	21	160	18	6	3	2	16	9	25	3	2	.270/.312/.392	.245	.314	0	--	0.0
2012	PEN	AA	22	359	45	11	8	1	31	29	49	3	4	.278/.344/.373	.240	.323	-2.7	SS(21): -5.2	-0.7
2012	LOU	AAA	22	202	25	10	3	6	23	12	31	0	2	.243/.288/.427	.243	.262	1.8	SS(34): -3.6, 2B(3): 0.1	0.1
2012	CIN	MLB	22	21	1	0	0	0	2	0	5	0	0	.300/.300/.300	.218	.400	0.2	SS(6): -0.4	0.0
2013	*ARI*	*MLB*	*23*	*250*	*24*	*9*	*3*	*3*	*19*	*9*	*44*	*2*	*2*	*.240/.270/.340*	*.219*	*.279*	*-0.1*	*SS -1, 2B -0*	*-0.1*

Aggression, thy name is Gregorius. Actually, his name is Mariekson but he goes by Didi and is a flashy defensive shortstop who sometimes gets too excited at the plate, on the bases, and in the field. He hasn't shown much with the bat yet but impressed in the Arizona Fall League, with one veteran observer calling him the circuit's best athlete. If Gregorius can play under more control and avoid silly mistakes, he could have a career as a shortstop who bats toward the bottom of a lineup. Think Alfredo Griffin.

Jonathan Griffin 1B

Born: **4/29/1989** Age: **24**
Bats: **R** Throws: **R** Height: **6' 8"**
Weight: **250** Breakout: **7%**
Improve: **56%** Collapse: **5%**
Attrition: **19%** MLB: **98%**

Comparables:
Brandon Snyder,Nick Evans,Brett Wallace

YEAR	TEAM	LVL	AGE	PA	R	2B	3B	HR	RBI	BB	SO	SB	CS	AVG_OBP_SLG	TAv	BABIP	BRR	FRAA	WARP
2011	MSO	Rk	22	313	47	12	0	18	59	29	77	4	0	.295/.355/.532	.297	.339	0	--	0.0
2012	VIS	A+	23	548	87	19	3	26	98	49	107	0	0	.300/.363/.511	.290	.331	-1.2	1B(85): -2.0	1.2
2013	*ARI*	*MLB*	*24*	*250*	*26*	*9*	*1*	*9*	*32*	*15*	*58*	*0*	*0*	*.241/.289/.411*	*.248*	*.279*	*-0.2*	*1B -1*	*-0.2*

It is rare to see a 21st-round pick make an immediate impact, and despite Griffin's advanced age and the premier offensive tools that are required for a first baseman, he has provided every reason to be optimistic about his future. Griffin will need considerable plate coverage to avoid exploitation at the highest level: He's a massive presence at the plate and his big strike zone could open up holes in his swing. He brought his power to a five-game cup of coffee at Double-A, hitting the home run that proved to be the difference in a 1-0 victory for the Southern League championship. Griffin will be challenged to prove himself at every stop. He's already exceeded expectations.

Aaron Hill 2B

Born: **3/21/1982** Age: **31**
Bats: **R** Throws: **R** Height: **6' 0"**
Weight: **200** Breakout: **1%**
Improve: **33%** Collapse: **4%**
Attrition: **8%** MLB: **97%**

Comparables:
Mark Ellis,Orlando Hudson,Brandon Phillips

YEAR	TEAM	LVL	AGE	PA	R	2B	3B	HR	RBI	BB	SO	SB	CS	AVG_OBP_SLG	TAv	BABIP	BRR	FRAA	WARP
2010	TOR	MLB	28	580	70	22	0	26	68	41	85	2	2	.205/.271/.394	.239	.196	-0.2	2B(137): 4.0	0.9
2011	ARI	MLB	29	142	23	12	2	2	16	12	19	5	4	.315/.386/.492	.299	.356	1.5	2B(33): 2.2	1.2
2011	TOR	MLB	29	429	38	15	1	6	45	23	53	16	3	.225/.270/.313	.215	.242	-1.4	2B(104): -5.1	-2.0
2012	ARI	MLB	30	668	93	44	6	26	85	52	86	14	5	.302/.360/.522	.295	.317	0.3	2B(153): 20.5	5.9
2013	*ARI*	*MLB*	*31*	*609*	*79*	*30*	*2*	*20*	*67*	*39*	*86*	*12*	*4*	*.258/.313/.425*	*.263*	*.272*	*0.1*	*2B -0*	*2.4*

Hill was a key cog in in the Diamondbacks machine last season, rounding out the right side of the infield and enjoying the best season of his career on both sides of the ball. He eclipsed his offensive explosion of 2009 with career-high marks in each of the slash categories, and the man has raised his career batting average by eight points in a little over a full season in the desert. Hill has been the most valuable player taken on the first day of the 2003 draft, based on major-league performance to date, yet classmates such as Nick Markakis and Rickie Weeks have received far more attention. In compliance with Arizona Law, Hill carries his signed contract in his bat bag in order to avoid deportation back to the Blue Jays.

Eric Hinske 4C

Born: **8/5/1977** Age: **35**
Bats: **L** Throws: **R** Height: **6' 3"**
Weight: **235** Breakout: **3%**
Improve: **29%** Collapse: **11%**
Attrition: **22%** MLB: **90%**

Comparables:
Dale Long,Chili Davis,David Dellucci

YEAR	TEAM	LVL	AGE	PA	R	2B	3B	HR	RBI	BB	SO	SB	CS	AVG_OBP_SLG	TAv	BABIP	BRR	FRAA	WARP
2010	ATL	MLB	32	320	38	21	1	11	51	33	75	0	0	.256/.338/.456	.277	.308	-0.6	LF(50): -0.1, 1B(32): -0.3	0.8
2011	ATL	MLB	33	264	24	10	0	10	28	26	71	0	1	.233/.311/.403	.249	.288	0.2	LF(31): -0.1, RF(16): -0.4	0.0
2012	ATL	MLB	34	147	9	7	1	2	13	14	41	0	0	.197/.272/.311	.204	.267	-0.1	1B(15): 0.5, LF(6): -0.3	-0.8
2013	*ARI*	*MLB*	*35*	*250*	*27*	*12*	*1*	*8*	*31*	*25*	*63*	*1*	*0*	*.230/.311/.403*	*.255*	*.280*	*-0.4*	*LF -0, 1B 0*	*0.4*

After years of providing unsung value off the bench, the dependable Hinske finally threw a rod. He made contact and damaged mistakes less often en route to a horrendous season. Hinske is an aging hitter with old-player skills, so you have to wonder if he's nearing the end. His tremendous clubhouse reputation should open the door for a post-playing career in baseball, one that may be almost ready to begin.

Mike Jacobs **1B**
Born: **10/30/1980** Age: **32**
Bats: **L** Throws: **R** Height: **6' 4"**
Weight: **215** Breakout: **1%**
Improve: **40%** Collapse: **6%**
Attrition: **14%** MLB: **88%**
Comparables:
Paul Sorrento,Adam LaRoche,Richie Zisk

YEAR	TEAM	LVL	AGE	PA	R	2B	3B	HR	RBI	BB	SO	SB	CS	AVG_OBP_SLG	TAv	BABIP	BRR	FRAA	WARP
2010	BUF	AAA	29	371	53	23	3	15	57	28	65	1	0	.260/.316/.478	.260	.282	1.1	1B(63): 2.4	0.6
2010	LVG	AAA	29	157	26	6	0	6	34	21	21	0	0	.308/.404/.492	.318	.330	0.7	1B(31): -2.3	0.9
2010	NYN	MLB	29	28	1	1	0	1	2	3	7	0	0	.208/.296/.375	.243	.250	0	1B(7): 0.1	0.0
2011	CSP	AAA	30	495	70	30	1	23	97	58	105	3	3	.298/.376/.534	.277	.340	-0.8	1B(66): -4.3	-0.1
2012	RNO	AAA	31	378	59	15	0	18	60	44	83	2	2	.279/.362/.486	.254	.322	-0.6	1B(37): -2.3	-0.8
2012	ARI	MLB	31	23	4	1	0	0	2	4	6	0	0	.211/.348/.263	.228	.308	0.1	1B(4): -0.1	-0.1
2013	*ARI*	*MLB*	*32*	*250*	*28*	*10*	*1*	*10*	*34*	*20*	*64*	*0*	*0*	*.232/.293/.420*	*.251*	*.272*	*-0.4*	*1B -2*	*-0.2*

The minor-league veteran spent his summer in Reno, gambling that the Snakes would need some replacement pop in the event of an injury to Goldschmidt and raking his way through yet another high-octane environment. After a string of stops in launching-pad ballparks such as Las Vegas and Colorado Springs, Jacobs might be expected to further expand his enormous strike zone as he ups the aggression to pad his counting stats. But the 30-something slugger has posted the best walk rates of his minor-league career while playing the majority of his games in the hitter havens of the Pacific Coast League.

Chris Johnson **3B**
Born: **10/1/1984** Age: **28**
Bats: **R** Throws: **R** Height: **6' 4"**
Weight: **220** Breakout: **2%**
Improve: **40%** Collapse: **4%**
Attrition: **4%** MLB: **94%**
Comparables:
Doug Decinces,Larry Parrish,Tony Perez

YEAR	TEAM	LVL	AGE	PA	R	2B	3B	HR	RBI	BB	SO	SB	CS	AVG_OBP_SLG	TAv	BABIP	BRR	FRAA	WARP
2010	ROU	AAA	25	163	26	10	1	8	33	9	23	0	0	.329/.371/.570	.324	.347	-0.1	3B(37): -1.7	1.2
2010	HOU	MLB	25	362	40	22	2	11	52	15	91	3	0	.308/.337/.481	.285	.387	-0.7	3B(90): -10.9	1.0
2011	OKL	AAA	26	94	18	7	0	4	15	10	25	1	1	.272/.372/.506	.301	.346	0	--	0.0
2011	HOU	MLB	26	405	32	21	3	7	42	16	97	2	2	.251/.291/.378	.244	.317	-1.1	3B(101): -10.2	-1.0
2012	ARI	MLB	27	160	12	7	2	7	35	8	40	1	0	.286/.321/.503	.281	.340	-2.7	3B(39): -2.3	0.0
2012	HOU	MLB	27	368	36	21	3	8	41	23	92	4	1	.279/.329/.428	.256	.360	-1.1	3B(88): -8.3, 1B(6): 0.6	-0.4
2013	*ARI*	*MLB*	*28*	*472*	*49*	*25*	*4*	*13*	*57*	*21*	*116*	*3*	*1*	*.265/.304/.427*	*.257*	*.328*	*-0.2*	*3B -1, 1B -0*	*0.8*

The D-Backs' acquisition of Johnson was curious on multiple levels. First, the Snakes parted ways with a couple of prospects who have the upside to handle an infield corner in Bobby Borchering and Marc Krauss. Then there was the statistical profile: A front office that had blatantly shunned the strikeout-saturated ways of Mark Reynolds decided to make a play for Johnson, whose 25 percent K rate was among the highest in the National League and whose strikeout-to-walk ratio was the worst in the circuit. Johnson's value stems from his ability to hit line drives. He ranked just behind Goldschmidt with the second-highest mark in the NL, 24 percent. That was consistent with his career norms.

Kila Ka'aihue **1B**
Born: **3/29/1984** Age: **29**
Bats: **L** Throws: **R** Height: **6' 5"**
Weight: **235** Breakout: **7%**
Improve: **52%** Collapse: **7%**
Attrition: **10%** MLB: **92%**
Comparables:
Andre Thornton,Todd Helton,Jeff Bagwell

YEAR	TEAM	LVL	AGE	PA	R	2B	3B	HR	RBI	BB	SO	SB	CS	AVG_OBP_SLG	TAv	BABIP	BRR	FRAA	WARP
2010	OMA	AAA	26	416	67	16	1	24	78	88	69	2	0	.319/.465/.598	.365	.342	0.4	1B(75): 0.6	5.1
2010	KCA	MLB	26	206	22	6	1	8	25	24	39	0	1	.217/.307/.394	.243	.231	0.3	1B(34): 0.1	-0.2
2011	OMA	AAA	27	388	43	19	0	11	65	57	81	1	1	.272/.379/.433	.266	.325	-1	1B(18): -1.0	-0.1
2011	KCA	MLB	27	96	6	4	0	2	6	12	26	0	0	.195/.295/.317	.234	.255	0.7	1B(19): -0.7	-0.2
2012	SAC	AAA	28	305	44	16	0	15	52	44	60	1	1	.256/.367/.496	.298	.273	2.2	1B(9): 0.5, LF(4): -0.6	0.6
2012	OAK	MLB	28	139	13	9	0	4	14	10	28	1	0	.234/.295/.398	.249	.271	-0.1	1B(22): -0.7	-0.3
2013	*ARI*	*MLB*	*29*	*250*	*32*	*10*	*1*	*11*	*35*	*35*	*53*	*0*	*0*	*.244/.352/.449*	*.285*	*.271*	*-0.4*	*1B -2, LF -0*	*0.8*

The quintessential minor-league thumper who wears a Quadruple-A label on his back, the elder of the Hawaiian Ka'aihue brothers was seemingly a perfect fit for Oakland, following in the footsteps of fellow under-appreciated take-and-rake batsmen. But then Ka'aihue reminded us that scouts can often see through the numbers, as his power failed to show up at the highest level, where mistake pitches seem to evaporate into thin air, and those hitters who fail to adjust end up hooked on Dramamine to keep from getting sick of the bus leagues. At 29 years old, Ka'aihue is running out of prime-age at bats, with a dwindling opportunity to shed the label of 5 o'clock slugger.

Jason Kubel **LF**
Born: **5/25/1982** Age: **31**
Bats: **L** Throws: **R** Height: **6' 1"**
Weight: **220** Breakout: **0%**
Improve: **52%** Collapse: **6%**
Attrition: **9%** MLB: **94%**
Comparables:
Cliff Floyd,Luke Scott,Roy Sievers

YEAR	TEAM	LVL	AGE	PA	R	2B	3B	HR	RBI	BB	SO	SB	CS	AVG_OBP_SLG	TAv	BABIP	BRR	FRAA	WARP
2010	MIN	MLB	28	582	68	23	3	21	92	56	116	0	1	.249/.323/.427	.264	.280	-2.9	RF(83): -2.0, LF(16): 0.2	0.6
2011	MIN	MLB	29	401	37	21	1	12	58	32	86	1	1	.273/.332/.434	.274	.326	-2	RF(50): -1.8, LF(9): -0.3	0.5
2012	ARI	MLB	30	571	75	30	4	30	90	57	151	1	1	.253/.327/.506	.286	.296	-5.7	LF(124): -14.1, RF(2): -0.0	0.3
2013	*ARI*	*MLB*	*31*	*503*	*60*	*24*	*3*	*21*	*71*	*46*	*111*	*1*	*1*	*.258/.328/.461*	*.277*	*.297*	*-0.7*	*LF -1, RF 0*	*1.9*

Kubel provided some of the power that was missing from Justin Upton's bat, taking advantage of his cozy new home with an exaggerated fly-ball rate that far exceeded his career norms. Kubel hit half of his balls in play in the air, leading the majors, and his frequency of fly balls that went out placed him in the top 10 in the NL. After two years spent trying to master the cold dimensions of Minnesota's Target Field, Kubel's free-agency move to the desert was a breath of thin air, and his all-or-nothing approach resulted in half of his hits going for extra bases, with an isolated power of .253 that represented a career high.

Alfredo Marte RF

Born: **3/31/1989** Age: **24**
Bats: **R** Throws: **R** Height: **6' 1"**
Weight: **190** Breakout: **8%**
Improve: **55%** Collapse: **1%**
Attrition: **15%** MLB: **92%**

Comparables:
Tony Tarasco,Ruben Mateo,Candy Maldonado

YEAR	TEAM	LVL	AGE	PA	R	2B	3B	HR	RBI	BB	SO	SB	CS	AVG_OBP_SLG	TAv	BABIP	BRR	FRAA	WARP
2010	VIS	A+	21	565	76	26	3	9	61	34	107	9	5	.260/.313/.374	.250	.309	-1.3	CF(129): 8.9	2.0
2011	VIS	A+	22	250	35	15	3	7	33	14	43	5	0	.299/.344/.479	.273	.342	0.6	RF(25): -0.9, LF(3): 0.0	0.0
2012	MOB	AA	23	446	68	25	3	20	75	34	72	6	6	.294/.363/.523	.307	.314	2.6	RF(76): 2.9, LF(4): 1.1	2.8
2013	*ARI*	*MLB*	*24*	*250*	*23*	*11*	*1*	*6*	*27*	*10*	*54*	*2*	*1*	*.236/.275/.374*	*.230*	*.277*	*-0.2*	*RF 0, CF -1*	*-0.2*

Marte exploded in his first real taste of Double-A, enjoying a tremendous power spike in conjunction with an emerging affinity for taking a walk. The combination added up to an OPS that was the highest of his professional career. Marte built upon the improvements that he had made in 2011, and the performance earned him a trip to the Futures Game. The ability to make adjustments is a critical skill at the highest level, where a batter's weaknesses are quickly identified and exploited. Marte's pattern of statistical improvement as he faces tougher competition is a ringing endorsement of his potential.

John McDonald SS

Born: **9/24/1974** Age: **38**
Bats: **R** Throws: **R** Height: **5' 10"**
Weight: **180** Breakout: **2%**
Improve: **18%** Collapse: **18%**
Attrition: **18%** MLB: **77%**

Comparables:
Alan Trammell,Juan Castro,Jose Vizcaino

YEAR	TEAM	LVL	AGE	PA	R	2B	3B	HR	RBI	BB	SO	SB	CS	AVG_OBP_SLG	TAv	BABIP	BRR	FRAA	WARP
2010	TOR	MLB	35	163	27	9	2	6	23	6	26	2	1	.250/.273/.454	.253	.260	1.9	2B(23): -0.7, SS(19): -0.0	0.6
2011	ARI	MLB	36	63	2	2	0	0	2	4	9	0	0	.169/.222/.203	.194	.200	-0.2	SS(17): 1.2	0.0
2011	TOR	MLB	36	182	19	8	1	2	20	8	18	2	4	.250/.285/.345	.234	.267	0.8	3B(26): 2.3, 2B(21): 1.3	0.6
2012	ARI	MLB	37	213	16	9	0	6	22	12	33	0	1	.249/.295/.386	.232	.272	1.2	SS(54): -0.8, 3B(5): -0.0	0.0
2013	*ARI*	*MLB*	*38*	*250*	*22*	*11*	*1*	*4*	*23*	*10*	*36*	*2*	*2*	*.236/.272/.342*	*.221*	*.258*	*-0.5*	*SS 0, 2B 0*	*0.0*

McDonald has carved out a 14-year career in the major leagues as a backup infielder. The 38-year-old's ability to play up the middle is the only thing keeping him in the bigs. He has little to offer on offense, lacking power, patience, or even speed on the basepaths, and his career VORP lies in the red. Yet McDonald has more than $10 million in lifetime earnings, and he'll collect another $1.5 million from Arizona this season. With the Diamondbacks' questionable layout on the left side of the infield, he could be in line for another 150-200 plate appearances.

Miguel Montero C

Born: **7/9/1983** Age: **29**
Bats: **L** Throws: **R** Height: **6' 0"**
Weight: **215** Breakout: **2%**
Improve: **31%** Collapse: **10%**
Attrition: **20%** MLB: **97%**

Comparables:
Ryan Doumit,Gary Carter,Johnny Romano

YEAR	TEAM	LVL	AGE	PA	R	2B	3B	HR	RBI	BB	SO	SB	CS	AVG_OBP_SLG	TAv	BABIP	BRR	FRAA	WARP
2010	ARI	MLB	26	331	36	20	2	9	43	29	71	0	1	.266/.332/.438	.256	.318	-2.8	C(79): 0.5	1.2
2011	ARI	MLB	27	553	65	36	1	18	86	47	97	1	1	.282/.351/.469	.279	.317	-2	C(134): 1.8	3.3
2012	ARI	MLB	28	573	65	25	2	15	88	73	130	0	0	.286/.391/.438	.295	.362	-6.8	C(139): 2.1	3.8
2013	*ARI*	*MLB*	*29*	*534*	*60*	*29*	*1*	*16*	*67*	*50*	*108*	*1*	*1*	*.270/.347/.439*	*.280*	*.318*	*-1*	*C 1*	*3.6*

Montero will be the Diamondbacks' highest-paid player this year after signing a five-year contract extension in May worth $60 million that will keep him behind the plate through 2017. It was the largest contract in team history, and Montero responded with his lowest ISO since his rookie year, though his plate discipline soared to new heights as he finished with the fourth-highest walk rate among National League qualifiers. His competence at the plate overshadows some of his struggles behind it: Montero's sub-par pitch-framing cost Arizona pitchers approximately 15 runs, according to our metrics. If those struggles persist, Diamondbacks pitchers could be in for a frustrating summer of uncalled strikes.

Wil Nieves C

Born: **9/25/1977** Age: **35**
Bats: **R** Throws: **R** Height: **6' 0"**
Weight: **190** Breakout: **3%**
Improve: **24%** Collapse: **12%**
Attrition: **28%** MLB: **89%**

Comparables:
Brook Fordyce,Tony Pena,Bo Diaz

YEAR	TEAM	LVL	AGE	PA	R	2B	3B	HR	RBI	BB	SO	SB	CS	AVG_OBP_SLG	TAv	BABIP	BRR	FRAA	WARP
2010	WAS	MLB	32	172	10	8	0	3	16	8	29	0	0	.203/.244/.310	.194	.228	-0.7	C(51): 0.9	-0.6
2011	GWN	AAA	33	79	8	2	0	1	6	6	11	1	0	.282/.333/.352	.247	.317	0	--	0.0
2011	NAS	AAA	33	95	3	2	0	1	6	4	11	0	0	.170/.213/.227	.044	.182	-0.7	C(8): -0.0	-0.7
2011	MIL	MLB	33	54	2	2	0	0	0	3	12	0	0	.140/.189/.180	.120	.184	0.3	C(17): 0.7	-0.4
2012	CSP	AAA	34	123	15	4	0	3	16	6	20	1	1	.306/.336/.423	.243	.344	0.1	C(23): 0.3	0.3
2012	ARI	MLB	34	38	4	1	0	1	3	1	8	0	1	.306/.324/.417	.246	.370	0.2	C(12): 0.0	0.1
2012	COL	MLB	34	51	3	2	0	1	5	3	9	0	0	.298/.333/.404	.229	.342	-2.9	C(12): 0.1, 1B(2): -0.0	-0.4
2013	*ARI*	*MLB*	*35*	*250*	*21*	*10*	*1*	*3*	*21*	*14*	*49*	*1*	*1*	*.233/.278/.318*	*.214*	*.277*	*-0.4*	*C 1, 1B -0*	*0.0*

The journeyman receiver has played for four different organizations in the past three years, but his 2012 route through Colorado and Arizona was the most offensively pleasant detour of his career. Aging backstops can carry a reserve gig for years, playing once or twice a week while collecting a big-league paycheck, joining NFL long-snappers among the ranks of gainfully employed athletes who rarely sniff the field of play. Nieves has played just 391 games over the past six years in the majors and minors combined, with the vast majority of his time spent spitting sunflower seeds on a big-league bench.

Chris Owings SS

Born: **8/12/1991** Age: **21**
Bats: **R** Throws: **R** Height: **5' 10"**
Weight: **175** Breakout: **3%**
Improve: **57%** Collapse: **8%**
Attrition: **16%** MLB: **97%**

Comparables:
Jack Heidemann,Jose Lopez,Garry Templeton

YEAR	TEAM	LVL	AGE	PA	R	2B	3B	HR	RBI	BB	SO	SB	CS	AVG_OBP_SLG	TAv	BABIP	BRR	FRAA	WARP
2010	SBN	A	18	271	39	19	2	5	28	9	50	1	3	.298/.325/.447	.271	.351	-0.2	SS(62): 2.8	1.7
2011	VIS	A+	19	555	67	29	6	11	50	15	130	10	4	.246/.274/.388	.245	.305	1.6	SS(64): 7.9	1.3
2012	VIS	A+	20	257	51	16	2	11	24	13	63	8	3	.324/.362/.544	.288	.399	1.3	SS(44): -0.4	1.4
2012	MOB	AA	20	310	35	10	3	6	28	11	69	4	3	.263/.291/.377	.229	.324	-0.2	SS(53): 4.2	0.5
2013	*ARI*	*MLB*	*21*	*250*	*24*	*11*	*2*	*5*	*22*	*4*	*66*	*2*	*1*	*.232/.247/.353*	*.212*	*.294*	*0*	*SS 3*	*0.2*

Owings conquered the California League on his second go-round, but his hacktastic approach was exposed against the advanced pitchers in Double-A. Owings has been young for his levels, and the Diamondbacks can afford to be patient with his timetable as long as he continues to make adjustments, but his atrocious strikeout-to-walk ratios are a harbinger of doom. Pitch recognition will only get tougher as he climbs the minor-league ladder, with increasing diets of off-speed pitches as he reaches the upper levels. By the end of 2013 the Diamondbacks should have a much better idea whether Owings will be a meaningful part of their long-term plans.

Gerardo Parra OF

Born: **5/6/1987** Age: **26**
Bats: **L** Throws: **L** Height: **6' 0"**
Weight: **200** Breakout: **3%**
Improve: **59%** Collapse: **6%**
Attrition: **10%** MLB: **96%**

Comparables:
David Murphy,Shane Victorino,David DeJesus

YEAR	TEAM	LVL	AGE	PA	R	2B	3B	HR	RBI	BB	SO	SB	CS	AVG_OBP_SLG	TAv	BABIP	BRR	FRAA	WARP
2010	ARI	MLB	23	393	31	19	6	3	30	23	76	1	0	.261/.308/.371	.234	.322	1.1	LF(76): 6.7, RF(36): 1.0	0.9
2011	ARI	MLB	24	493	55	20	8	8	46	43	82	15	1	.292/.357/.427	.275	.342	0.8	LF(125): 14.7, RF(14): 0.3	3.0
2012	ARI	MLB	25	430	58	21	2	7	36	33	77	15	9	.273/.335/.392	.259	.323	2.8	CF(48): -3.6, LF(47): -0.3	0.8
2013	*ARI*	*MLB*	*26*	*417*	*46*	*19*	*4*	*7*	*41*	*29*	*75*	*10*	*4*	*.276/.329/.400*	*.258*	*.323*	*0.4*	*LF 3, CF -0*	*1.3*

There was a minor outcry when Arizona signed Kubel to a lucrative deal to patrol left field, a move that relegated the up-and-coming Parra to a reserve role, but the combination of Kubel's power surge and Young's injuries quickly silenced the critics. Parra is the type of well-rounded ballplayer whose lack of a single elite tool can cause him to drift under the radar, but all of his skills took a step backward in 2012, and a glove that was elite in left suffered when spread around the outfield. Parra will have a shot to claim the center-field job out of spring training, but his failure to build his résumé last season has opened the door for Eaton to fly past him on the organizational depth chart.

Cliff Pennington SS

Born: **6/15/1984** Age: **29**
Bats: **B** Throws: **R** Height: **5' 11"**
Weight: **215** Breakout: **6%**
Improve: **44%** Collapse: **5%**
Attrition: **15%** MLB: **93%**

Comparables:
Alan Trammell,Rafael Furcal,Edgar Renteria

YEAR	TEAM	LVL	AGE	PA	R	2B	3B	HR	RBI	BB	SO	SB	CS	AVG_OBP_SLG	TAv	BABIP	BRR	FRAA	WARP
2010	OAK	MLB	26	576	64	26	8	6	46	50	96	29	5	.250/.319/.368	.268	.296	4.2	SS(155): 13.0	5.4
2011	OAK	MLB	27	570	57	26	2	8	58	42	104	14	9	.264/.319/.369	.257	.314	-1.3	SS(147): -11.9	0.4
2012	OAK	MLB	28	462	50	18	2	6	28	35	90	15	6	.215/.278/.311	.234	.259	3	SS(93): 7.0, 2B(32): 3.1	1.5
2013	*ARI*	*MLB*	*29*	*458*	*51*	*21*	*4*	*6*	*40*	*40*	*85*	*17*	*5*	*.251/.320/.363*	*.247*	*.296*	*1.2*	*SS 0, 2B -0*	*1.5*

Pennington's bat was a poor fit for Oakland, where his inclination toward hitting the ball in the air caused his value to be sucked dry by the Coliseum's super-sized foul territory. The change of scenery should do well to highlight his strengths. The Diamondbacks will look to Pennington to buffer the infield defense, and any offensive production will just be icing on the cake for a team that endured a carousel of light-hitting shortstops last season. There is an outside chance Pennington fulfills his first-round promise in the desert.

A.J. Pollock OF

Born: **12/5/1987** Age: **25**
Bats: **R** Throws: **R** Height: **6' 2"**
Weight: **205** Breakout: **14%**
Improve: **58%** Collapse: **2%**
Attrition: **21%** MLB: **97%**

Comparables:
Mickey Stanley,Gil Flores,Johnny Damon

YEAR	TEAM	LVL	AGE	PA	R	2B	3B	HR	RBI	BB	SO	SB	CS	AVG_OBP_SLG	TAv	BABIP	BRR	FRAA	WARP
2011	MOB	AA	23	608	103	41	5	8	73	44	86	36	7	.307/.357/.444	.252	.346	-0.7	CF(56): -6.1, RF(5): 0.2	-0.6
2012	RNO	AAA	24	471	65	25	3	3	52	32	52	21	8	.318/.369/.411	.253	.353	4.5	CF(25): 0.1, LF(13): -1.3	0.2
2012	ARI	MLB	24	93	8	4	1	2	8	9	11	1	2	.247/.315/.395	.251	.257	-1.5	CF(14): 0.7, LF(7): 0.4	0.1
2013	*ARI*	*MLB*	*25*	*250*	*30*	*12*	*1*	*3*	*19*	*15*	*44*	*12*	*3*	*.250/.297/.353*	*.235*	*.293*	*1*	*CF -1, RF -0*	*0.1*

Arizona's second of two consecutive first-round picks in the 2009 draft, Pollock has the talent to be a future cog in a major-league outfield, though the presence of Parra and Pollock's similar skill set clouds his future in Phoenix. Pollock's offensive potential is heavily reliant on bat control to hit 'em where they ain't, and a lack of secondary skills puts tremendous pressure on the bat to continue spraying liners from gap to gap. The Notre Dame product can play all three outfield positions, while his makeup and baseball instincts receive high grades that should allow his performance to outplay his raw tools.

Cody Ransom 3B
Born: **2/17/1976** Age: **37**
Bats: **R** Throws: **R** Height: **6' 3"**
Weight: **190** Breakout: **2%**
Improve: **22%** Collapse: **9%**
Attrition: **22%** MLB: **72%**
Comparables:
Ron Cey,Jose Valentin,Eddie Joost

YEAR	TEAM	LVL	AGE	PA	R	2B	3B	HR	RBI	BB	SO	SB	CS	AVG_OBP_SLG	TAv	BABIP	BRR	FRAA	WARP
2010	LEH	AAA	34	443	58	25	1	18	63	40	108	5	2	.261/.335/.467	.274	.316	1.6	3B(81): -11.7, SS(10): 0.2	0.9
2010	PHI	MLB	34	46	6	0	0	2	5	3	11	1	0	.190/.244/.333	.210	.207	0.7	3B(9): -0.5, 2B(6): 0.0	0.0
2011	RNO	AAA	35	432	86	29	3	27	92	55	94	10	3	.317/.405/.629	.344	.358	0	--	0.0
2011	ARI	MLB	35	37	3	2	0	1	4	3	9	1	0	.152/.243/.303	.187	.174	0.5	SS(8): 0.3, 3B(6): 0.3	-0.1
2012	ARI	MLB	36	88	11	7	0	5	16	7	30	0	0	.269/.352/.551	.305	.372	-0.3	3B(18): -0.8, SS(7): -0.4	0.3
2012	MIL	MLB	36	194	18	7	0	6	26	23	79	0	1	.196/.293/.345	.225	.325	0.5	SS(40): 0.4, 3B(17): 1.0	0.1
2013	*ARI*	*MLB*	*37*	*250*	*27*	*11*	*1*	*8*	*30*	*23*	*75*	*2*	*1*	*.218/.295/.387*	*.245*	*.283*	*-0.3*	*3B -1, SS -1*	*0.3*

A minor-league lifer, Ransom has played ball in the bush leagues for 15 years, including the past 12 seasons spent dodging hot-dog cannons in Triple-A. He started 2012 in the D-Backs system and finished the season in Arizona, but over the summer Ransom pursued a brewing internship that earned him close to 200 plate appearances in Milwaukee. His 30s have brought maturity as well as power to his game, but Father Time has Ransom in his sights and is closing fast.

Cody Ross RF
Born: **12/23/1980** Age: **32**
Bats: **R** Throws: **L** Height: **5' 11"**
Weight: **195** Breakout: **1%**
Improve: **36%** Collapse: **3%**
Attrition: **10%** MLB: **90%**
Comparables:
Jose Guillen,George Hendrick,Scott Hairston

YEAR	TEAM	LVL	AGE	PA	R	2B	3B	HR	RBI	BB	SO	SB	CS	AVG_OBP_SLG	TAv	BABIP	BRR	FRAA	WARP
2010	FLO	MLB	29	487	60	24	3	11	58	30	100	9	1	.265/.316/.405	.260	.319	1.9	CF(77): -4.9, RF(46): 2.8	1.1
2010	SFN	MLB	29	82	11	4	0	3	7	7	21	0	1	.288/.354/.466	.275	.360	-0.8	LF(21): -0.7, CF(12): -0.9	0.2
2011	SFN	MLB	30	461	54	25	0	14	52	49	96	5	2	.240/.325/.405	.272	.279	-0.3	LF(83): 2.6, RF(35): -0.5	1.0
2012	BOS	MLB	31	528	70	34	1	22	81	42	129	2	3	.267/.326/.481	.289	.317	0.1	RF(96): 1.4, LF(22): -2.4	2.1
2013	*ARI*	*MLB*	*32*	*485*	*55*	*26*	*2*	*17*	*63*	*33*	*108*	*4*	*2*	*.254/.312/.438*	*.267*	*.298*	*-0.5*	*RF -0, LF -0*	*1.4*

Ross loved Fenway Park and it loved him. His pull swing was built for its short left-field porch (921 home OPS vs a 684 road OPS), and he started out with a bat-flipping party (.282/.352/.576 through June) that put him in the faithful's good graces. That production and an uncanny ability to avoid serious injury (he was the only Boston outfielder to play more than 100 games) carried the good feelings forward even as his production fell off. Signed by the Diamondbacks in the offseason, Ross will miss exploiting the Green Monster on a regular basis, though his transition should be eased by the homer-friendly confines of Chase Field. Kirk Gibson will have plenty of options when coordinating the crowded Arizona outfield, and his deployment of Ross might be influenced by a career OPS 200 points higher against southpaws.

Stryker Trahan C
Born: **4/25/1994** Age: **19**
Bats: **L** Throws: **R** Height: **6' 2"**
Weight: **215** Breakout: **0%**
Improve: **61%** Collapse: **39%**
Attrition: **39%** MLB: **100%**
Comparables:
Robin Yount,Ed Kranepool,Wayne Causey

YEAR	TEAM	LVL	AGE	PA	R	2B	3B	HR	RBI	BB	SO	SB	CS	AVG_OBP_SLG	TAv	BABIP	BRR	FRAA	WARP
2012	DIA	Rk	18	211	29	11	3	5	25	40	48	8	1	.281/.422/.473	.319	.362	0.3	C(10): 0.1	0.0
2013	*ARI*	*MLB*	*19*	*250*	*28*	*8*	*1*	*5*	*19*	*13*	*76*	*13*	*3*	*.189/.234/.296*	*.191*	*.251*	*1.7*	*C 0*	*-0.2*

The path to the majors for a high-school catcher is arduous, given the amount of training necessary to handle the game's most demanding position. Trahan's main priorities will be to learn how to handle a pitching staff, to scout opposing hitters, and to optimize his receiving skills. His need for defensive homework was evident from the 18 passed balls in just 40 games last year, and though he has a strong arm, Trahan threw out just 24 percent of opposing baserunners. The left-handed hitter is built like a linebacker, with uncommon athleticism for a backstop, and his advanced pitch-recognition skills are useful at the plate as well as behind it.

Justin Upton RF
Born: **8/25/1987** Age: **25**
Bats: **R** Throws: **R** Height: **6' 3"**
Weight: **205** Breakout: **5%**
Improve: **51%** Collapse: **2%**
Attrition: **8%** MLB: **97%**
Comparables:
Jay Bruce,Ben Johnson,Jack Clark

YEAR	TEAM	LVL	AGE	PA	R	2B	3B	HR	RBI	BB	SO	SB	CS	AVG_OBP_SLG	TAv	BABIP	BRR	FRAA	WARP
2010	ARI	MLB	22	571	73	27	3	17	69	64	152	18	8	.273/.356/.442	.275	.354	-0.8	RF(128): 2.9	1.9
2011	ARI	MLB	23	674	105	39	5	31	88	59	126	21	9	.289/.369/.529	.310	.319	2.3	RF(159): 4.1	4.5
2012	ARI	MLB	24	628	107	24	4	17	67	63	121	18	8	.280/.355/.430	.279	.327	0.3	RF(149): 8.2	2.6
2013	*ARI*	*MLB*	*25*	*599*	*80*	*28*	*4*	*23*	*81*	*58*	*138*	*17*	*7*	*.274/.351/.471*	*.290*	*.328*	*0.4*	*RF 5*	*3.8*

It has been almost eight years since the Diamondbacks chose Upton with the top selection of the 2005 draft, and each passing season of uneven skill development serves as an eerie reminder of the trail that was blazed by Justin's big brother, B.J. Justin is just entering his theoretical prime, leaving plenty of room for optimism about his long-term outlook, but it's an ominous sign that we're also still waiting for Bossman Junior to realize his ceiling. The precipitous drop in power was likely related to the thumb injury Upton sustained in April, an ailment he attempted to play through. The hindrance on his bat-grip likely contributed to the lowest isolated power in his six years in the bigs. Despite industry-wide speculation that the Diamondbacks will actively look to unload him, Upton enters 2013 with his trade value at an all-time low.

PITCHERS

Heath Bell

Born: **9/29/1977** Age: **35**
Bats: **R** Throws: **R** Height: **6' 4"** Weight: **260**
Breakout: **24%** Improve: **55%** Collapse: **26%**
Attrition: **13%** MLB: **80%**

Comparables:
Eddie Guardado,Akinori Otsuka,Rich Gossage

YEAR	TEAM	LVL	AGE	W	L	SV	G	GS	IP	H	HR	BB	SO	BB9	SO9	GB%	BABIP	WHIP	ERA	FIP	FRA	WARP
2010	SDN	MLB	32	6	1	47	67	0	70	56	1	28	86	3.6	11.1	45%	.322	1.20	1.93	2.08	2.43	1.6
2011	SDN	MLB	33	3	4	43	64	0	62^{2}	51	4	21	51	3.0	7.3	45%	.261	1.15	2.44	3.20	3.06	0.7
2012	MIA	MLB	34	4	5	19	73	0	63^{2}	70	5	29	59	4.1	8.3	48%	.342	1.55	5.09	3.76	4.33	0.4
2013	*ARI*	*MLB*	*35*	*3*	*1*	*28*	*65*	*0*	62^{1}	*53*	*5*	*19*	*62*	*2.8*	*9.0*	*49%*	*.305*	*1.17*	*3.26*	*3.17*	*3.54*	*1.0*

Bell crossed the threshold from undervalued asset to overpaid money-sink in the blink of an eye, and Kevin Towers hopes that a return to the National League and a reunion with the old boss will be the antidote that Bell needs to re-harness his stuff. The familiarity with upper management will have to compensate for the difficult transition to Chase Field, which does not bode well for a guy who was last successful when he had the San Diego marine layer to knock down big flies. After Bell's $27 million contract expires, one can envision him following the Sam Malone path to retirement, buying a bar in downtown Phoenix and telling old stories to the baseball junkies who flock to spring training every year.

Archie Bradley

Born: **8/10/1992** Age: **20**
Bats: **R** Throws: **R** Height: **6' 5"** Weight: **225**
Breakout: **44%** Improve: **68%** Collapse: **14%**
Attrition: **4%** MLB: **88%**

Comparables:
Gary Nolan,Madison Bumgarner,Sandy Koufax

YEAR	TEAM	LVL	AGE	W	L	SV	G	GS	IP	H	HR	BB	SO	BB9	SO9	GB%	BABIP	WHIP	ERA	FIP	FRA	WARP
2011	MSO	Rk	18	0	0	0	2	1	2	1	0	0	4	0.0	18.0	—	.333	0.50	0.00	0.28	0.31	0.0
2012	SBN	A	19	12	6	0	27	27	136	87	6	84	152	5.6	10.1	56%	.246	1.26	3.84	3.87	4.10	0.5
2013	*ARI*	*MLB*	*20*	*2*	*2*	*0*	*7*	*7*	35^{2}	*32*	*4*	*22*	*34*	*5.4*	*8.5*	*50%*	*.300*	*1.50*	*4.94*	*4.60*	*5.37*	*-0.1*

The seventh pick of the 2011 draft, Bradley burst out of the gate in his first full season of pro ball, though issues with pitch command foreshadowed a horrific summer swoon when his mechanical timing fell off the wagon. Bradley retained his velocity, but he plunked 15 batters and uncorked 17 wild pitches on the season. Bradley will need to iron out the inconsistencies in order to maximize effectiveness, and he must learn to trust that he can locate his mid-90s fastball in any situation. He has the prototypical build for a workhorse, but the development of a changeup might determine whether his future will be spent starting big-league games or finishing them.

Trevor Cahill

Born: **3/1/1988** Age: **25**
Bats: **R** Throws: **R** Height: **6' 5"** Weight: **225**
Breakout: **18%** Improve: **48%** Collapse: **19%**
Attrition: **17%** MLB: **94%**

Comparables:
Joe Blanton,Mike Pelfrey,Enrique Gonzalez

YEAR	TEAM	LVL	AGE	W	L	SV	G	GS	IP	H	HR	BB	SO	BB9	SO9	GB%	BABIP	WHIP	ERA	FIP	FRA	WARP
2010	SAC	AAA	22	1	0	0	2	2	8^{2}	7	0	5	8	5.2	8.3	48%	.304	1.38	1.03	3.47	3.41	0.3
2010	OAK	MLB	22	18	8	0	30	30	196^{2}	155	19	63	118	2.9	5.4	57%	.236	1.11	2.97	4.16	5.44	0.1
2011	OAK	MLB	23	12	14	0	34	34	207^{2}	214	19	82	147	3.6	6.4	57%	.302	1.43	4.16	4.14	5.15	-0.7
2012	ARI	MLB	24	13	12	0	32	32	200	184	16	74	156	3.3	7.0	63%	.289	1.29	3.78	3.89	4.22	1.8
2013	*ARI*	*MLB*	*25*	*12*	*8*	*0*	*28*	*28*	*175*	*157*	*18*	*58*	*129*	*3.0*	*6.6*	*56%*	*.284*	*1.23*	*3.87*	*4.06*	*4.21*	*1.4*

The acquisition of Cahill last offseason underscored a growing organizational emphasis toward groundball pitchers inspired by the home park. Cahill's 2012 grounder rate was baseball's highest among starting pitchers, and the 25-year-old with a frame built for pitching and a clean medical record is well-tailored for his new home. By some measures, last season was the finest of his brief career. Cahill's core ratios improved across the board. A sustained growth trend in critical categories teases the possibility that Cahill has yet to reach his ceiling.

Andrew Chafin

Born: **6/17/1990** Age: **23**
Bats: **R** Throws: **L** Height: **6' 3"** Weight: **205**
Breakout: **26%** Improve: **52%** Collapse: **24%**
Attrition: **17%** MLB: **91%**

Comparables:
Juan Morillo,Gio Gonzalez,Ken Cloude

YEAR	TEAM	LVL	AGE	W	L	SV	G	GS	IP	H	HR	BB	SO	BB9	SO9	GB%	BABIP	WHIP	ERA	FIP	FRA	WARP
2011	DIA	Rk	21	0	0	0	1	1	1	1	0	0	2	0.0	18.0	%	.500	1.00	0.00	3.37	0.79	0.1
2012	VIS	A+	22	6	6	0	30	22	122^1	112	12	69	150	5.1	11.0	53%	.324	1.48	4.93	4.38	5.10	1.8
2013	*ARI*	*MLB*	*23*	*2*	*2*	*0*	*7*	*7*	*36^1*	*33*	*4*	*19*	*34*	*4.6*	*8.5*	*48%*	*.307*	*1.43*	*4.62*	*4.33*	*5.02*	*0.0*

Chafin has been known to fall in love with his slider, particularly in strikeout situations, and the southpaw generally stays away from opposing hitters to avoid their strengths. His fastball command needs refinement—he can find the inner half against right-handed batters, but his issues with mechanical timing lead to an inconsistent release point, leaving him vulnerable to the vagaries of missed targets. He stumbled over the summer, and a particularly bad stretch during the first half of July precipitated a temporary move to the bullpen. But Chafin was able to make the necessary adjustments and make a triumphant return to the rotation. His capacity to deal with adversity bodes well for his development.

Josh Collmenter

Born: **2/7/1986** Age: **27**
Bats: **R** Throws: **R** Height: **6' 3"** Weight: **235**
Breakout: **21%** Improve: **56%** Collapse: **17%**
Attrition: **5%** MLB: **94%**

Comparables:
Joe Blanton,Shawn Hill,Joel Pineiro

YEAR	TEAM	LVL	AGE	W	L	SV	G	GS	IP	H	HR	BB	SO	BB9	SO9	GB%	BABIP	WHIP	ERA	FIP	FRA	WARP
2011	RNO	AAA	25	1	0	0	1	1	6	2	1	2	7	3.0	10.5	—	.091	0.67	1.50	4.62	5.02	0.0
2011	ARI	MLB	25	10	10	0	31	24	154^1	137	17	28	100	1.6	5.8	35%	.255	1.07	3.38	3.77	4.00	1.8
2012	DIA	Rk	26	0	0	0	3	3	8	5	0	0	11	0.0	12.4	67%	.267	0.62	0.00	1.63	-1.44	0.3
2012	ARI	MLB	26	5	3	0	28	11	90^1	92	13	22	80	2.2	8.0	40%	.304	1.26	3.69	3.97	4.64	0.8
2013	*ARI*	*MLB*	*27*	*5*	*4*	*0*	*19*	*13*	*86*	*83*	*10*	*25*	*66*	*2.6*	*6.9*	*40%*	*.295*	*1.25*	*3.92*	*4.05*	*4.26*	*0.7*

The deception that buoyed Collmenter's rookie season was less convincing the second time around. After a handful of ugly April starts the right-hander with the extreme over-the-top delivery was jettisoned to the bullpen. Batters have teed off on Collmenter the second time through the order, a factor that plagued him during his breakout rookie campaign. An arsenal that is predicated on changing speeds was more effective in short stints last season, when batters lacked the opportunity to make adjustments. Collmenter's modest fastball comes tumbling down from a high arm slot, with a trajectory that minimizes the number of throws that miss wide of the zone, though his additional downhill plane fails to produce the desired groundball effect.

Patrick Corbin

Born: **7/19/1989** Age: **23**
Bats: **L** Throws: **L** Height: **6' 4"** Weight: **165**
Breakout: **27%** Improve: **63%** Collapse: **18%**
Attrition: **11%** MLB: **96%**

Comparables:
Brian Matusz,Jon Niese,Mike Mussina

YEAR	TEAM	LVL	AGE	W	L	SV	G	GS	IP	H	HR	BB	SO	BB9	SO9	GB%	BABIP	WHIP	ERA	FIP	FRA	WARP
2010	CDR	A	20	8	0	0	9	9	58^1	52	2	10	42	1.5	6.5	50%	.289	1.06	3.86	3.28	4.84	0.4
2010	RCU	A+	20	5	3	0	11	11	60^1	57	7	18	64	2.7	9.6	52%	.307	1.24	3.88	4.06	5.01	0.6
2010	VIS	A+	20	0	1	0	8	8	26	17	1	9	30	3.1	10.4	52%	.271	1.00	1.38	2.96	3.58	0.7
2011	MOB	AA	21	9	8	0	26	26	160^1	172	15	40	142	2.2	8.0	48%	.311	1.32	4.21	3.72	4.98	0.8
2012	MOB	AA	22	2	0	0	4	4	27	22	0	8	25	2.7	8.3	49%	.300	1.11	1.67	2.29	1.52	0.4
2012	RNO	AAA	22	3	2	0	9	9	52^1	57	4	15	55	2.6	9.5	51%	.349	1.38	3.44	3.47	3.91	0.9
2012	ARI	MLB	22	6	8	1	22	17	107	117	14	25	86	2.1	7.2	46%	.317	1.33	4.54	4.04	4.49	1.3
2013	*ARI*	*MLB*	*23*	*7*	*5*	*0*	*18*	*18*	*101^2*	*101*	*13*	*28*	*81*	*2.5*	*7.2*	*46%*	*.304*	*1.27*	*4.23*	*4.10*	*4.59*	*0.5*

Corbin exemplifies the benefits of pitching depth at the minor-league level. The control artist filled in admirably when Daniel Hudson went down, first in late April and then for good over the summer, and though his contact-oriented approach might leave him susceptible to the whims of his defense, Corbin's pinpoint accuracy offer a refreshing contrast from the inefficient strikeout-pursuing tactics of his fellow young rotation-mates. Strike-throwing lefties are a rare commodity, as the insistence of pitching coaches on advocating steep angles and other batter-disruption strategies for their southpaws often gets in the way of the basics. But Corbin may have been able to circumvent such approaches due to a funky stride that supports his lefty persona.

David Hernandez

Born: **5/13/1985** Age: **28**
Bats: **R** Throws: **R** Height: **6' 3"** Weight: **250**
Breakout: **19%** Improve: **46%** Collapse: **33%**
Attrition: **13%** MLB: **88%**

Comparables:
Luis Tiant,Angel Guzman,Joel Hanrahan

YEAR	TEAM	LVL	AGE	W	L	SV	G	GS	IP	H	HR	BB	SO	BB9	SO9	GB%	BABIP	WHIP	ERA	FIP	FRA	WARP
2010	BAL	MLB	25	8	8	2	41	8	79^1	72	9	42	72	4.8	8.2	29%	.285	1.44	4.31	4.45	4.84	0.3
2011	ARI	MLB	26	5	3	11	74	0	69^1	49	4	30	77	3.9	10.0	34%	.253	1.14	3.38	2.91	3.73	0.9
2012	ARI	MLB	27	2	3	4	72	0	68^1	48	4	22	98	2.9	12.9	30%	.291	1.02	2.50	2.13	2.64	1.7
2013	*ARI*	*MLB*	*28*	*3*	*2*	*3*	*53*	*2*	*61*	*50*	*7*	*24*	*65*	*3.6*	*9.5*	*34%*	*.289*	*1.22*	*3.62*	*3.74*	*3.93*	*0.7*

When Hernandez was acquired from Baltimore in the winter of 2010-11, much of the focus was on the player who went the other direction. The exile of Mark Reynolds spoke volumes about the D-Backs' commitment to shedding strikeouts from the lineup. But when the smoke cleared, it became apparent that

Arizona had acquired a helluva relief pitcher. Hernandez has improved in each of the past three seasons, beginning with his transition to the bullpen in May 2010, and last year he took his game to the level of baseball's burgeoning class of elite relievers. His pitch velocity has increased since his Oriole days, and Hernandez has both the numbers and the stuff to challenge J.J. Putz for the closer throne. Hernandez may have to wait for Putz's contract to expire before he can begin compiling his own salary-inflating save totals.

David Holmberg
Born: **7/19/1991** Age: **21**
Bats: **R** Throws: **L** Height: **6' 5"** Weight: **219**
Breakout: **28%** Improve: **60%** Collapse: **17%**
Attrition: **4%** MLB: **89%**
Comparables:
Jordan Lyles,Alex Fernandez,Hayden Penn

YEAR	TEAM	LVL	AGE	W	L	SV	G	GS	IP	H	HR	BB	SO	BB9	SO9	GB%	BABIP	WHIP	ERA	FIP	FRA	WARP
2010	GRF	Rk	18	1	1	0	8	8	40^1	52	2	9	29	2.0	6.5	63%	.378	1.51	4.47	4.01	5.45	0.2
2010	MSO	Rk	18	1	4	0	7	7	37^1	47	2	7	47	1.7	11.3	56%	.398	1.45	3.86	3.05	4.13	0.8
2011	SBN	A	19	8	3	0	14	14	83	65	3	13	81	1.4	8.8	—	.278	0.94	2.39	2.60	2.83	0.0
2011	VIS	A+	19	4	6	0	13	13	71^1	73	5	35	76	4.4	9.6	48%	.361	1.51	4.67	4.33	3.73	1.1
2012	VIS	A+	20	6	3	0	12	12	78^1	62	6	14	86	1.6	9.9	44%	.281	0.97	2.99	3.15	3.73	1.9
2012	MOB	AA	20	5	5	0	15	15	95	104	8	23	67	2.2	6.3	47%	.319	1.34	3.60	3.62	4.17	0.9
2013	*ARI*	*MLB*	*21*	*3*	*3*	*0*	*7*	*7*	45^2	*48*	*6*	*17*	*32*	*3.4*	*6.3*	*46%*	*.312*	*1.44*	*5.06*	*4.62*	*5.50*	*-0.3*

Holmberg keeps hitters off-balance with a plus changeup, offsetting a fastball that has matured since he was chosen by the White Sox in the second round of the 2009 draft. Holmberg, who came to the Diamondbacks in the Edwin Jackson trade, has added a couple ticks to his fastball over the last couple of years to reach the low 90s. His advanced command is reflected in his walk rates as well as his ability to discourage hard contact, as a well-placed change can devastate the fastball-feasting batters of the lower minors. Holmberg has scuffled when transitioning to new levels, but organizational pitching depth will allow the Diamondbacks to be patient with him as he makes the necessary adjustments.

Daniel Hudson
Born: **3/9/1987** Age: **26**
Bats: **R** Throws: **R** Height: **6' 4"** Weight: **230**
Breakout: **28%** Improve: **62%** Collapse: **14%**
Attrition: **12%** MLB: **98%**
Comparables:
Matt Garza,Jered Weaver,Matt Cain

YEAR	TEAM	LVL	AGE	W	L	SV	G	GS	IP	H	HR	BB	SO	BB9	SO9	GB%	BABIP	WHIP	ERA	FIP	FRA	WARP
2010	CHR	AAA	23	11	4	0	17	17	93^1	81	13	31	108	3.0	10.4	43%	.286	1.20	3.47	3.91	4.00	1.6
2010	ARI	MLB	23	7	1	0	11	11	79^2	51	7	16	70	1.8	7.9	40%	.216	0.84	1.69	3.24	3.60	1.4
2010	CHA	MLB	23	1	1	0	3	3	15^2	17	1	11	14	6.3	8.0	30%	.356	1.79	6.32	4.20	4.99	0.0
2011	ARI	MLB	24	16	12	0	33	33	222	217	17	50	169	2.0	6.9	42%	.295	1.20	3.49	3.25	3.99	3.2
2012	RNO	AAA	25	1	0	0	1	1	5	5	0	1	2	1.8	3.6	47%	.294	1.20	3.60	3.47	1.06	0.0
2012	ARI	MLB	25	3	2	0	9	9	45^1	62	9	12	37	2.4	7.3	39%	.368	1.63	7.35	4.88	6.00	-0.1
2013	*ARI*	*MLB*	*26*	*5*	*3*	*0*	*12*	*12*	*71*	*62*	*7*	*19*	*62*	*2.4*	*7.9*	*42%*	*.292*	*1.14*	*3.48*	*3.54*	*3.78*	*1.0*

After a season spent torturing White Sox fans with what might have been, Hudson traveled a rocky road in 2012 that began when a shoulder impingement shelved him after just three April starts. His summer return was short-lived, and he was claimed by the operating table after 45 unmerciful innings when his ulnar collateral ligament gave way and Tommy John called for a surgical consult. In the aftermath of the injury, Hudson was quoted as saying, "With my arm action, I just kind of figured it came with the territory," a frightening admission for a player who carries the weight of a future rotation anchor on his right arm. The D-Backs must hope that Hudson can make the adjustments necessary to avoid a return trip under the knife.

Ian Kennedy
Born: **12/19/1984** Age: **28**
Bats: **R** Throws: **R** Height: **6' 1"** Weight: **190**
Breakout: **28%** Improve: **68%** Collapse: **14%**
Attrition: **6%** MLB: **92%**
Comparables:
Ervin Santana,Chris Young,Jered Weaver

YEAR	TEAM	LVL	AGE	W	L	SV	G	GS	IP	H	HR	BB	SO	BB9	SO9	GB%	BABIP	WHIP	ERA	FIP	FRA	WARP
2010	ARI	MLB	25	9	10	0	32	32	194	163	26	70	168	3.2	7.8	39%	.256	1.20	3.80	4.35	4.77	2.2
2011	ARI	MLB	26	21	4	0	33	33	222	186	19	55	198	2.2	8.0	40%	.270	1.09	2.88	3.19	3.68	3.5
2012	ARI	MLB	27	15	12	0	33	33	208^1	216	28	55	187	2.4	8.1	40%	.306	1.30	4.02	4.08	4.43	2.4
2013	*ARI*	*MLB*	*28*	*13*	*8*	*0*	*29*	*29*	*186*	*163*	*21*	*51*	*168*	*2.5*	*8.1*	*39%*	*.289*	*1.15*	*3.62*	*3.68*	*3.93*	*2.2*

After two consecutive seasons spent riding the coattails of an ultra-low BABIP, Kennedy was knocked around the ballpark for the first half of the 2012 season. His true-outcome rates were nearly identical between 2011 and 2012, but his results suffered when the gloves came into play. Kennedy's fly-ball tendencies are a risk at Chase Field, so his ability to repeat his delivery is necessary to minimize his mistakes by keeping the free passes off the bases. Kennedy did everything in his power to contribute on offense. He lacks the stick-handling skills to make solid contact, but he exhibited the patience to run up opposing pitch counts to the tune of 11 walks, easily the highest total among NL hurlers, and his 10 sacrifice bunts led the team.

Matt Lindstrom

Born: **2/11/1980** Age: **33**
Bats: **R** Throws: **R** Height: **6' 4"** Weight: **220**
Breakout: **17%** Improve: **42%** Collapse: **27%**
Attrition: **22%** MLB: **91%**

Comparables:
Ramon Hernandez,Matt Guerrier,Mike Timlin

YEAR	TEAM	LVL	AGE	W	L	SV	G	GS	IP	H	HR	BB	SO	BB9	SO9	GB%	BABIP	WHIP	ERA	FIP	FRA	WARP
2010	HOU	MLB	30	2	5	23	58	0	53^1	68	5	20	43	3.4	7.3	50%	.358	1.65	4.39	3.84	4.68	0.2
2011	CSP	AAA	31	0	0	0	2	0	2	4	1	0	4	0.0	18.0	33%	.600	2.00	13.50	6.28	5.01	0.1
2011	COL	MLB	31	2	2	2	63	0	54	52	3	14	36	2.3	6.0	50%	.288	1.22	3.00	3.27	4.25	0.5
2012	ORI	Rk	32	0	0	0	2	2	2	2	0	0	2	0.0	9.0	83%	.333	1.00	4.50	1.43	2.58	0.1
2012	BOW	AA	32	0	0	0	2	1	2^1	4	0	1	1	3.9	3.9	70%	.400	2.14	3.86	3.63	5.79	0.0
2012	ARI	MLB	32	0	0	0	12	0	10^2	10	0	2	10	1.7	8.4	53%	.312	1.12	2.53	2.10	2.92	0.1
2012	BAL	MLB	32	1	0	0	34	0	36^1	35	2	12	30	3.0	7.4	51%	.308	1.29	2.72	3.43	4.19	0.4
2013	*ARI*	*MLB*	*33*	*3*	*1*	*1*	*49*	*0*	45^2	*44*	*4*	*14*	*37*	*2.8*	*7.3*	*47%*	*.309*	*1.27*	*3.87*	*3.64*	*4.21*	*0.3*

Lindstrom has played for five teams in the past four years, and one can understand any club's interest in a hard-throwing reliever with groundball tendencies. Once disguised as a closer, Lindstrom has parlayed two poor seasons that happened to generate saves into $9.2 million in major-league earnings, though the Diamondbacks wised up and declined his $4 million option for 2013. Perhaps Lindstrom lacks the intestinal fortitude to earn the "proven closer" label, as his performance has been much stronger outside of the role. But sheer velocity will put him in the conversation of ninth-inning options if the best-laid plans of his new employers go awry.

Brandon McCarthy

Born: **7/7/1983** Age: **29**
Bats: **R** Throws: **R** Height: **6' 8"** Weight: **200**
Breakout: **14%** Improve: **39%** Collapse: **23%**
Attrition: **4%** MLB: **96%**

Comparables:
Dave Bush,Joe Blanton,Roy Oswalt

YEAR	TEAM	LVL	AGE	W	L	SV	G	GS	IP	H	HR	BB	SO	BB9	SO9	GB%	BABIP	WHIP	ERA	FIP	FRA	WARP
2010	OKL	AAA	26	4	2	0	11	9	56^1	51	8	11	44	1.8	7.0	52%	.271	1.10	3.36	4.61	4.50	1.1
2011	STO	A+	27	1	0	0	2	2	10	7	0	0	8	0.0	7.2	59%	.235	0.70	0.00	2.35	2.79	0.2
2011	OAK	MLB	27	9	9	0	25	25	170^2	168	11	25	123	1.3	6.5	48%	.296	1.13	3.32	2.90	3.60	2.4
2012	SAC	AAA	28	0	1	0	2	2	9^2	9	1	3	11	2.8	10.2	56%	.333	1.24	5.59	3.67	4.98	0.0
2012	OAK	MLB	28	8	6	0	18	18	111	115	10	24	73	1.9	5.9	43%	.295	1.25	3.24	3.71	4.07	1.0
2013	*ARI*	*MLB*	*29*	*8*	*5*	*0*	*19*	*19*	117^1	*110*	*11*	*24*	*89*	*1.9*	*6.8*	*43%*	*.294*	*1.14*	*3.54*	*3.52*	*3.85*	*1.5*

McCarthy has a reputation for being as brittle on the field as he is likable off of it. One of baseball's best tweeters has eight trips to the DL on his résumé, including six, in four different years, for stress fractures to his scapula. He's revamped his delivery over the last couple of years, resulting in marked improvement across the board, and his ability to repeat his motion underlies a walk rate that was cut in half in his Oakland tenure during which he finally lived up to his promise. Alas, McCarthy's season was once again ravaged by injury. He missed half of the summer with right-shoulder soreness, and then disaster struck on September 5, when he was hit on the side of the head by a line drive, fracturing his skull, ending his season, and necessitating life-saving brain surgery. Miraculously, he's expected to make a full recovery, and the Diamondbacks are banking on a return to form with a two-year, $15.5 million pact that effectively triples McCarthy's career earnings.

Anthony Meo

Born: **2/19/1990** Age: **23**
Bats: **R** Throws: **R** Height: **6' 3"** Weight: **185**
Breakout: **27%** Improve: **56%** Collapse: **25%**
Attrition: **21%** MLB: **93%**

Comparables:
Edinson Volquez,Tyler Clippard,Juan Morillo

YEAR	TEAM	LVL	AGE	W	L	SV	G	GS	IP	H	HR	BB	SO	BB9	SO9	GB%	BABIP	WHIP	ERA	FIP	FRA	WARP
2011	DIA	Rk	21	0	0	0	1	1	1	0	0	0	2	0.0	18.0	1.%	.000	0.00	0.00	0.37	0.74	0.1
2011	MSO	Rk	21	0	0	0	1	0	2	0	0	0	1	0.0	4.5	—	.000	0.00	0.00	3.28	3.57	0.0
2012	VIS	A+	22	9	8	0	26	25	140	134	15	71	153	4.6	9.8	50%	.320	1.46	4.11	4.78	4.56	1.9
2013	*ARI*	*MLB*	*23*	*2*	*2*	*0*	*7*	*7*	38^2	*37*	*5*	*19*	*33*	*4.5*	*7.8*	*47%*	*.307*	*1.45*	*4.85*	*4.65*	*5.27*	*-0.1*

BP Hall of Famer Kevin Goldstein recognized Meo as an arm to watch out of the 2011 draft, and the right-hander began 2012 in a prospect-laden rotation at High-A Visalia. He was expected to move quickly, but his progression was stunted by the control problems that plague so many young arms. Meo walked a batter for every two innings pitched, uncorked 17 wild pitches, and plunked 11 batters. His ERA, though, was suspiciously lowered by 14 runs that were deemed unearned. With a fastball that hits the mid-90s and a plus breaking ball, Meo has the raw tools to succeed at the highest level, but his mastery of a suitable changeup could decide whether that future is in the bullpen or as a starter.

Wade Miley

Born: **11/13/1986** Age: **26**
Bats: **L** Throws: **L** Height: **6' 2"** Weight: **220**
Breakout: **34%** Improve: **61%** Collapse: **12%**
Attrition: **19%** MLB: **86%**

Comparables:
Clayton Richard,Zach Duke,Matt Harrison

YEAR	TEAM	LVL	AGE	W	L	SV	G	GS	IP	H	HR	BB	SO	BB9	SO9	GB%	BABIP	WHIP	ERA	FIP	FRA	WARP
2010	VIS	A+	23	4	5	0	14	14	80^{1}	81	1	37	50	4.1	5.6	66%	.312	1.47	3.25	4.07	5.80	-0.1
2010	MOB	AA	23	5	2	0	13	13	72^{2}	60	5	28	63	3.5	7.8	61%	.276	1.21	1.98	3.74	4.49	0.6
2011	MOB	AA	24	4	2	0	14	14	75^{1}	74	6	28	46	3.3	5.5	54%	.296	1.35	4.78	4.36	6.52	-0.4
2011	RNO	AAA	24	4	1	0	8	8	54^{1}	53	4	16	56	2.7	9.3	—	.327	1.27	3.64	3.56	3.87	0.0
2011	ARI	MLB	24	4	2	0	8	7	40	48	6	18	25	4.1	5.6	48%	.321	1.65	4.50	5.04	5.75	-0.2
2012	ARI	MLB	25	16	11	0	32	29	194^{2}	193	14	37	144	1.7	6.7	45%	.293	1.18	3.33	3.19	3.84	3.2
2013	*ARI*	*MLB*	*26*	*9*	*8*	*0*	*24*	*24*	*140^{2}*	*146*	*15*	*43*	*94*	*2.7*	*6.0*	*51%*	*.307*	*1.34*	*4.51*	*4.17*	*4.90*	*0.1*

The control artist personified the general pitching approach in Arizona this year, limiting walks and keeping the ball in the park. His walk rate was the fifth-lowest mark in the National League among qualifying starters, and his 4.6 percent rate of fly balls clearing the fence trailed only Gio Gonzalez among NL frontmen. Miley carries a couple of mechanical advantages in his signature delivery, with a naturally elevated arm slot that allows him to create a tall release point without sacrificing balance and a closed stride that supports a deceptive angle without tarnishing his release point. Miley may have reached a new level of pitch efficiency, but the lack of similar command indicators in his minor-league stat line provides reason for caution.

Joe Paterson

Born: **5/19/1986** Age: **27**
Bats: **R** Throws: **L** Height: **6' 2"** Weight: **210**
Breakout: **26%** Improve: **52%** Collapse: **28%**
Attrition: **15%** MLB: **80%**

Comparables:
Tim Crabtree,Ryan Braun,Ronald Belisario

YEAR	TEAM	LVL	AGE	W	L	SV	G	GS	IP	H	HR	BB	SO	BB9	SO9	GB%	BABIP	WHIP	ERA	FIP	FRA	WARP
2010	SJO	A+	24	1	0	1	7	0	11	9	0	2	15	1.6	12.3	70%	.333	1.00	0.82	1.55	2.08	0.4
2010	FRE	AAA	24	4	3	2	46	0	54^{1}	55	2	24	49	4.0	8.1	52%	.323	1.45	3.48	3.75	4.28	0.9
2011	ARI	MLB	25	0	3	1	62	0	34	28	1	15	28	4.0	7.4	55%	.265	1.26	2.91	3.41	4.49	0.0
2012	RNO	AAA	26	2	2	2	48	0	43^{1}	41	7	16	40	3.3	8.3	50%	.279	1.32	4.15	5.30	8.06	-0.3
2012	ARI	MLB	26	0	0	0	6	0	2^{2}	15	2	3	0	10.1	0.0	52%	.619	6.75	37.12	16.26	11.21	-0.3
2013	*ARI*	*MLB*	*27*	*2*	*1*	*0*	*43*	*0*	*37*	*34*	*4*	*15*	*32*	*3.5*	*7.8*	*50%*	*.299*	*1.31*	*4.18*	*4.09*	*4.54*	*0.1*

A Rule 5 selection from the Giants, Paterson was used very carefully in 2011 as the D-Backs limited his exposure, but a solid performance in the LOOGY role opened the door for an extended look. He broke camp with the team in 2012, but he got lit up like a Disney parade during the first month of the season and would not resurface in Phoenix. A pitcher who had excelled at keeping the ball in the park became homer-prone last year, giving up as many bombs in his 46 innings split between the majors and minors as he had surrendered in his entire career coming into the season, spanning 218 innings in the pros.

J.J. Putz

Born: **2/22/1977** Age: **36**
Bats: **R** Throws: **R** Height: **6' 6"** Weight: **250**
Breakout: **29%** Improve: **46%** Collapse: **36%**
Attrition: **9%** MLB: **79%**

Comparables:
Kazuhiro Sasaki,Brendan Donnelly,Rich Gossage

YEAR	TEAM	LVL	AGE	W	L	SV	G	GS	IP	H	HR	BB	SO	BB9	SO9	GB%	BABIP	WHIP	ERA	FIP	FRA	WARP
2010	CHA	MLB	33	7	5	3	60	0	54	41	4	15	65	2.5	10.8	49%	.276	1.04	2.83	2.49	3.58	1.0
2011	DIA	Rk	34	0	0	0	2	2	2	1	0	0	0	0.0	0.0	75%	.250	0.50	0.00	4.37	5.33	0.0
2011	RNO	AAA	34	0	0	0	2	0	2	1	0	0	3	0.0	13.5	—	.250	0.50	0.00	0.78	0.85	0.0
2011	ARI	MLB	34	2	2	45	60	0	58	41	4	12	61	1.9	9.5	44%	.247	0.91	2.17	2.51	3.31	0.9
2012	ARI	MLB	35	1	5	32	57	0	54^{1}	45	4	11	65	1.8	10.8	46%	.301	1.03	2.82	2.42	3.03	1.1
2013	*ARI*	*MLB*	*36*	*3*	*1*	*37*	*52*	*0*	*49^{1}*	*40*	*4*	*15*	*54*	*2.8*	*9.9*	*45%*	*.298*	*1.11*	*3.03*	*2.98*	*3.30*	*0.9*

His old 97-mph fastball may not have survived the trip, but Putz has put together consecutive seasons of solid performance at the closing end of Arizona's bullpen. Putz's most devastating weapon is a split-finger fastball that he'll keep in his back pocket until he gets ahead in the count. His control of the strike zone stands out among the league's firemen: The only NL stopper with a better walk rate was the Giants' Sergio Romo. Putz's track record suggests that the plus command could be fleeting, and a checkered injury history has caused the Diamondbacks to be careful with his workloads. The right-hander has not pitched more than 60 innings in a season since 2008, his last in Seattle.

Matt Reynolds

Born: **10/2/1984** Age: **28**
Bats: **L** Throws: **L** Height: **6' 6"** Weight: **240**
Breakout: **27%** Improve: **42%** Collapse: **30%**
Attrition: **6%** MLB: **88%**

Comparables:
Jerry Blevins,Aaron Fultz,Damaso Marte

YEAR	TEAM	LVL	AGE	W	L	SV	G	GS	IP	H	HR	BB	SO	BB9	SO9	GB%	BABIP	WHIP	ERA	FIP	FRA	WARP
2010	CSP	AAA	25	1	3	7	50	0	55	49	2	16	67	2.6	11.0	48%	.333	1.18	2.62	2.55	3.63	1.5
2010	COL	MLB	25	1	0	0	21	0	18	10	2	5	17	2.5	8.5	43%	.182	0.83	2.00	3.83	4.77	0.2
2011	COL	MLB	26	1	2	0	73	0	50^{2}	48	10	18	50	3.2	8.9	39%	.286	1.30	4.09	4.65	4.53	0.3
2012	COL	MLB	27	3	1	0	71	0	57^{1}	65	11	17	51	2.7	8.0	44%	.318	1.43	4.40	4.74	5.20	0.1
2013	*ARI*	*MLB*	*28*	*3*	*1*	*1*	*62*	*0*	*52^{1}*	*46*	*6*	*15*	*51*	*2.6*	*8.8*	*45%*	*.295*	*1.16*	*3.63*	*3.60*	*3.95*	*0.6*

Selected by the Rockies in the 20th round of the 2007 draft, Reynolds has done more than the other 29 players taken that round combined. He is a LOOGY whose slow curve is tough on lefties but who gives up too many hits and homers. Last year he struggled against right-handed batters, who hit him like the 1994 version of Andres Galarraga. Reynolds hadn't shown such vulnerability to righties in the past, but for the second straight season his performance plummeted in the second half. There are six or seven guys in most modern bullpens. Reynolds is one of them.

Takashi Saito

Born: **2/14/1970** Age: **43**
Bats: **L** Throws: **R** Height: **6' 3"** Weight: **200**
Breakout: **18%** Improve: **24%** Collapse: **39%**
Attrition: **39%** MLB: **64%**

Comparables:
Jeff Fassero, John Franco, Doug Brocail

YEAR	TEAM	LVL	AGE	W	L	SV	G	GS	IP	H	HR	BB	SO	BB9	SO9	GB%	BABIP	WHIP	ERA	FIP	FRA	WARP
2010	GWN	AAA	40	0	0	0	1	1	1	1	0	0	1	0.0	9.0	%	.500	1.00	0.00	1.29	0.59	0.1
2010	ATL	MLB	40	2	3	1	56	0	54	41	4	17	69	2.8	11.5	44%	.282	1.07	2.83	2.46	2.73	1.2
2011	NAS	AAA	41	0	0	0	6	0	5^{2}	3	0	0	7	0.0	11.1	50%	.000	0.53	0.00	1.31	1.77	0.0
2011	MIL	MLB	41	4	2	0	30	0	26^{2}	21	2	9	23	3.0	7.8	45%	.260	1.12	2.03	3.37	3.70	0.3
2012	DIA	Rk	42	0	0	0	4	4	4	2	0	0	4	0.0	9.0	%	.500	0.50	0.00	2.38	-0.23	0.1
2012	VIS	A+	42	0	0	0	1	1	1	1	0	1	0	9.0	0.0	%	.333	2.00	0.00	6.81	566.15	0.0
2012	RNO	AAA	42	0	1	0	4	0	2^{2}	7	1	1	2	3.4	6.8	%	.500	3.00	10.12	8.17	8.41	0.0
2012	ARI	MLB	42	0	0	0	16	0	12	17	4	5	11	3.8	8.2	44%	.333	1.83	6.75	7.14	7.54	-0.3
2013	*ARI*	*MLB*	*43*	*2*	*1*	*1*	*43*	*0*	38^{1}	*32*	*4*	*13*	*40*	*2.9*	*9.5*	*43%*	*.300*	*1.17*	*3.36*	*3.49*	*3.66*	*0.5*

The peak velocity has held relatively firm as Saito advances through his 40s, but his body has failed to withstand the kinetic toll of his pitching motion. Continued leg problems kept him on the shelf for most of the 2012 season. The run of calf and hamstring strains is not entirely surprising for an aging pitcher whose delivery requires considerable leg strength, as Saito employs the distinct pause in his pitching motion that is common among hurlers with Japanese roots, then bursts forward from a stork-like position after the lift leg reaches its apex. The injury sequence suggests that Saito may have to augment his approach to physical preparation to try to combat the aging process.

Tony Sipp

Born: **7/12/1983** Age: **29**
Bats: **L** Throws: **L** Height: **6' 1"** Weight: **190**
Breakout: **27%** Improve: **42%** Collapse: **37%**
Attrition: **16%** MLB: **92%**

Comparables:
Frank Dipino, Damaso Marte, Brian Fuentes

YEAR	TEAM	LVL	AGE	W	L	SV	G	GS	IP	H	HR	BB	SO	BB9	SO9	GB%	BABIP	WHIP	ERA	FIP	FRA	WARP
2010	CLE	MLB	26	2	2	1	70	0	63	48	12	39	69	5.6	9.9	33%	.250	1.38	4.14	5.29	5.18	-0.3
2011	CLE	MLB	27	6	3	0	69	0	62^{1}	45	10	24	57	3.5	8.2	28%	.219	1.11	3.03	4.47	5.30	-0.1
2012	CLE	MLB	28	1	2	1	63	0	55	47	9	23	51	3.8	8.3	37%	.255	1.27	4.42	4.63	5.20	-0.2
2013	*ARI*	*MLB*	*29*	*3*	*1*	*1*	*58*	*0*	51^{2}	*41*	*7*	*22*	*56*	*3.9*	*9.7*	*36%*	*.283*	*1.23*	*3.76*	*4.07*	*4.09*	*0.5*

Joe Smith passed Sipp for the third spot in Cleveland's bullpen pecking order last season, due in part to Sipp's career-worst ERA, which surprisingly was a result of some bad luck with runners on and not regression from the ridiculous BABIPs he has a habit of posting. He has enough stuff—a rising 92-mph fastball, changeup, and curve—to generate strikeouts, but that arsenal creates an extreme fly-ball profile, and his control is below average. It wouldn't be surprising to find him working low-leverage innings before long.

Tyler Skaggs

Born: **7/13/1991** Age: **21**
Bats: **L** Throws: **L** Height: **6' 5"** Weight: **195**
Breakout: **33%** Improve: **55%** Collapse: **9%**
Attrition: **6%** MLB: **93%**

Comparables:
Scott Kazmir, Frank Tanana, Clayton Kershaw

YEAR	TEAM	LVL	AGE	W	L	SV	G	GS	IP	H	HR	BB	SO	BB9	SO9	GB%	BABIP	WHIP	ERA	FIP	FRA	WARP
2010	CDR	A	18	8	4	0	19	14	82^{1}	78	6	21	82	2.3	9.0	53%	.316	1.20	3.61	3.48	4.98	0.6
2010	SBN	A	18	1	1	0	4	4	16	13	1	4	20	2.2	11.2	58%	.324	1.06	1.69	2.67	3.28	0.4
2011	VIS	A+	19	5	5	0	17	17	100^{2}	81	6	34	125	3.0	11.2	54%	.304	1.14	3.22	3.40	3.78	1.6
2011	MOB	AA	19	4	1	0	10	10	57^{2}	45	4	15	73	2.3	11.4	45%	.370	1.04	2.50	2.56	2.27	1.1
2012	MOB	AA	20	5	4	0	13	13	69^{2}	63	8	21	71	2.7	9.2	45%	.294	1.21	2.84	3.55	4.17	0.9
2012	RNO	AAA	20	4	2	0	9	9	52^{2}	49	4	16	45	2.7	7.7	47%	.308	1.23	2.91	3.91	4.51	0.4
2012	ARI	MLB	20	1	3	0	6	6	29^{1}	30	6	13	21	4.0	6.4	36%	.264	1.47	5.83	5.90	6.90	-0.6
2013	*ARI*	*MLB*	*21*	*4*	*3*	*0*	*11*	*11*	*59*	*55*	*7*	*20*	*52*	*3.1*	*8.0*	*46%*	*.303*	*1.28*	*4.06*	*4.00*	*4.41*	*0.4*

Skaggs was the key figure in the trade that sent Dan Haren to the Angels, and his tall arm slot could invoke mirror-image memories from the south side of the rubber. Skaggs has a long way to go before he can reach Haren-level efficiency. He struggles to repeat a delivery that depends on sharp angles for deception. The velocity spread between his heat and off-speed stuff is an exceptional 10-12 miles per hour, and his mid-70s breaking ball provides myriad options for Skaggs to exploit a batter's timing. However, it could take time for him to overcome the issues with command, and if his batted-ball rates were to regress, he'd be headed for difficult times in his first full trial in the bigs.

Brad Ziegler

Born: **10/10/1979** Age: **33**
Bats: **R** Throws: **R** Height: **6' 5"** Weight: **205**
Breakout: **19%** Improve: **43%** Collapse: **32%**
Attrition: **18%** MLB: **89%**

Comparables:
Jose Mesa, Dave Smith, Matt Guerrier

YEAR	TEAM	LVL	AGE	W	L	SV	G	GS	IP	H	HR	BB	SO	BB9	SO9	GB%	BABIP	WHIP	ERA	FIP	FRA	WARP
2010	OAK	MLB	30	3	7	0	64	0	60^{2}	54	4	28	41	4.2	6.1	56%	.276	1.35	3.26	4.09	5.07	-0.2
2011	ARI	MLB	31	0	0	0	23	0	20^{2}	15	0	6	15	2.6	6.5	66%	.259	1.02	1.74	2.41	3.39	0.2
2011	OAK	MLB	31	3	2	1	43	0	37^{2}	38	0	13	29	3.1	6.9	73%	.325	1.35	2.39	2.64	3.13	0.6
2012	ARI	MLB	32	6	1	0	77	0	68^{2}	54	2	21	42	2.8	5.5	76%	.264	1.09	2.49	3.25	4.85	0.6
2013	*ARI*	*MLB*	*33*	*3*	*1*	*1*	*64*	*0*	57^{2}	*52*	*4*	*19*	*42*	*2.9*	*6.6*	*62%*	*.297*	*1.22*	*3.59*	*3.63*	*3.90*	*0.6*

Ziegler's bizarre delivery is reminiscent of submarine folk hero Chad Bradford. Not surprisingly, Ziegler has inherited the same extreme grounder-inducing tendencies. His groundball rate was the best in baseball for any pitcher who spent more than a week on a big-league roster, contributing to one of the lowest rates of homers allowed in the National League. Not bad for a guy whose fastball tops out in the upper 80s. The right-hander is essentially a one-trick pony, but it's a good trick. His loopy pitches trace a path that, more often than not, lead to harmless contact.

LINEOUTS

HITTERS

PLAYER	TEAM	LVL	AGE	PA	R	2B	3B	HR	RBI	BB	SO	SB-CS	AVG/OBP/SLG	TAv	BABIP	BRR	FRAA	WARP
C H. Blanco	ARI	MLB	40	67	6	3	0	1	7	3	18	1-0	.188/.224/.281	.192	.244	0.1	C(21): 0.5	-0.1
2B T. Bortnick	MNT	AA	24	404	46	18	8	4	48	46	61	23-3	.253/.352/.385	.294	.297	0.1	2B(26): -0.6	0.5
	RNO	AAA	24	151	11	7	0	2	12	14	26	5-2	.212/.293/.311	.217	.250	-0.5	2B(9): 2.7, 3B(3): -0.2	-0.1
OF T. Graham	RNO	AAA	28	72	7	0	2	1	6	8	12	1-1	.115/.239/.230	.091	.125	1	LF(5): 0.4	-0.5
MI T. Harbin	RNO	AAA	26	513	73	43	3	5	70	21	52	18-1	.308/.341/.441	.263	.333	12.7	2B(25): 2.6, SS(23): 0.8	2.1
SS J. Munoz	DIA	Rk	18	193	25	4	2	2	20	16	53	4-4	.260/.326/.341	.307	.364	0.2	SS(11): -1.0	-0.1
2B D. Nick	MOB	AA	22	497	49	23	2	5	43	28	85	13-5	.249/.296/.341	.242	.294	0.2	2B(84): -12.3	-1.4
C M. Perez	MSO	Rk	19	254	43	16	5	10	60	20	72	0-1	.293/.358/.542	.282	.381	-1.6	C(18): -0.0	0.8
4C M. Teahen	SYR	AAA	30	500	60	28	4	3	63	45	102	9-3	.260/.328/.360	.239	.328	0.5	1B(71): 1.3, LF(17): 1.8	-0.5

Henry Blanco followed up the best hitting ratios of his career with an empty performance that exposed his age, a harsh reminder that his days as a hard-throwing catcher-caddy are numbered. **Tyler Bortnick** was acquired from the Rays for Ryan Roberts in a deal at the 2012 deadline, and his blend of patience and speed could start delivering positive equity on the D-Backs' investment by 2013. A fractured shoulder knocked **Tyler Graham** out for all but the last month of the minor-league season, and despite a forgettable experience in Reno upon his return, the speed demon got his first taste of the majors when rosters expanded in September. **Taylor Harbin** enjoyed a PCL-fueled breakout, delighting Triple-A fantasy players with a power-speed combo that's rare in the middle of the diamond and a versatility that even included the occasional trip to the mound. **Jose Munoz** committed 25 errors in just 45 games at shortstop and his bat failed to show up for his first taste of professional ball, but the second-rounder's value lies in his long-term projection. **David Nick**'s bat is supposed to carry him, but his first exposure to Double-A was a disaster at the plate that ultimately clouds his future **Michael Perez** enjoyed a fantastic small-sample introduction, raking through the Pioneer League and establishing his cannon as a registered firearm: He gunned down 52 percent of would-be base thieves. **Mark Teahen** hasn't cracked a 750 OPS in the majors since his age-25 season, and he failed to breech the 700 mark in 2012 at Triple-A. This is the way the Teahen ends, not with a bang but a whimper.

PITCHERS

PLAYER	TEAM	LVL	AGE	W	L	SV	IP	H	HR	BB	SO	BB9	SO9	GB%	BABIP	WHIP	ERA	FIP	FRA	WARP
C. Anderson	MOB	AA	24	5	4	0	104	91	9	25	97	2.2	8.4	46%	.292	1.12	2.86	3.36	4.17	0.8
B. Bergesen	NOR	AAA	26	4	3	1	80^{1}	90	10	23	41	2.6	4.6	44%	.297	1.41	4.03	4.69	6.30	-0.6
	ARI	MLB	26	2	1	0	29^{2}	29	2	7	18	2.1	5.5	45%	.290	1.21	3.64	3.61	4.44	0.2
C. Brewer	RNO	AAA	24	11	7	0	133^{2}	177	26	34	104	2.3	7.0	44%	.346	1.58	5.99	5.47	7.57	0.5
E. De La Rosa	MOB	AA	22	4	4	8	63^{1}	47	3	17	68	2.4	9.7	36%	.277	1.01	2.84	2.51	3.37	1.1
M. Gorgen	MOB	AA	25	1	2	7	35	27	0	18	49	4.6	12.6	41%	.329	1.29	2.83	1.97	2.75	0.8
	RNO	AAA	25	1	2	0	27	27	4	7	22	2.3	7.3	42%	.280	1.26	3.00	4.74	5.60	0.1
E. Marshall	MOB	AA	22	6	3	16	48^{2}	55	2	16	27	3.0	5.0	60%	.311	1.46	3.51	3.68	4.82	0.0
K. Munson	MOB	AA	23	3	5	3	53	55	3	27	64	4.6	10.9	43%	.364	1.55	6.28	3.39	4.01	0.6
K. Winkler	VIS	A+	22	3	1	0	43	51	2	24	38	5.0	8.0	44%	.355	1.74	5.44	4.40	5.22	0.5

Chase Anderson has been throwing strikes for years (enough to get him drafted by the Twins multiple times), and though injuries have slowed his progression, he can contribute to a major-league rotation if he can keep the ball in the yard. One of a slew of arms that have exchanged Orioles uniforms for Arizona Red in recent years, **Brad Bergesen** flew the coop for Japan this winter. **Charles Brewer** suffered the fate of so many strike-throwers who have attempted to conquer Reno, sitting center stage in the Aces Stadium pinball machine while relentless rounds of multi-ball put him on tilt. **Eury De La Rosa** was unfazed by an aggressive promotion to Double-A, and the 5'9" dynamo flourished after claiming the closer role for the Bay Bears in the final month of the season. **Matt Gorgen** stands just an inch taller than De La Rosa but with more than 40 additional pounds on his frame, and yet the pair shares a penchant for run prevention that supersedes their physical dimensions. **Evan Marshall** was on the fast track to the majors and tearing through Mobile, but he hit a speed bump in August that threw him from the closer role in favor of De La Rosa. **Kevin Munson** has struggled with keeping the baseball in the strike zone throughout his minor-league career, to the extent that his 2012 walk rate was actually a big improvement, though it leads one to wonder whether all seven of his hit batsmen were entirely accidental. **Kyle Winkler**'s minor-league debut was delayed until mid-May as he recovered from Tommy John surgery. When he regained the mound, the 22-year-old from TCU was greeted by a plethora of baserunners.

MANAGER: KIRK GIBSON

YEAR	TEAM	W-L	Pythag +/-	Avg PC	100+ P	120+ P	QS	BQS	REL	REL w Zero R	IBB	PH	PH Avg	PH HR	SB2	CS2	SB3	CS3	SAC Att	SAC %	POS SAC	Squeeze	Swing	In Play
2010	ARI	34-49	0	188.7	83	83	56	3	247	181	38	302	.235	0	3	1	0	1	64	84.4%	24	0	153	31
2011	ARI	94-68	1	96.9	80	0	90	6	463	375	16	248	.206	5	16	2	0	0	96	61.5%	26	3	306	79
2012	ARI	81-81	1	95.2	63	3	85	5	461	382	18	225	.234	3	14	4	0	0	96	72.9%	24	2	281	72

Kirk Gibson is the Ron Swanson of baseball managers, down to the mustache-wearing skills and the cabin in the woods, so it figures that Gibby prefers the libertarian view that lets athletes play with little interference from a governing body. He rarely calls for a pinch-hitter, is frugal with incurring short-distance charges on the bullpen phone, and takes a conservative approach to positional shifting on defense. His non-pitchers executed only 15 successful sacrifice bunts all season, while the 18 intentional walks that Gibson ordered were the fewest in the National League. The general's men were lulled into relative complacency on the basepaths due to his reluctance to put runners in motion: A tarnished stolen-base rate crippled his confidence in the hit-and-run, a factor that may have been associated with the 19 outs that were registered via pick-offs.

In-game tactics are just part of the managerial equation, and it is easy to underestimate the difficulty in managing the personalities of 25 rich men for six months at a time. Gibson admitted after the season that his players lacked the drive of 2011's squad, and he had to manage both a superstar's slump and a phenom's ego through a tumultuous season under a new postseason format. After a 22-28 start that dropped the team's playoff odds to 11 percent on May 29, Gibson orchestrated a summer surge that brought his team within two games of the division lead in early August, but they failed to keep pace with the torrid Giants down the stretch and finished third.

Atlanta Braves

2012: HUMBLE PIE

The Braves made the postseason for the second time in general manager Frank Wren's five years, earning a spot in the first-ever wild-card game against the Cardinals. The playoff run would end there, however, thanks to sloppy defensive play—a Chipper Jones throwing error loomed large—and a controversial infield-fly-rule call. The Braves had a successful season despite the quick exit, one marked by strong performances from Michael Bourn, Jason Heyward, Kris Medlen, and Craig Kimbrel.

Wren kept most of the 2011 roster in place, and his patience paid off. Fueled by the ultra-talented Heyward's recovery from a deep sophomore slump, the offense scored 59 more runs than in 2011, while the pitching staff remained one of the National League's stingiest. Those extra runs led to a five-game improvement in the standings, not enough to catch the ascendant Nationals for the division title, but more than enough to leave the faltering Phillies eating their dust.

Refusing to hit the panic button wasn't the only wise choice made by the front office. Another was the decision to start the year with Medlen in the bullpen. Doing so allowed Atlanta to limit his innings without shutting him down late in the season. The parallels to—and differences from—the Stephen Strasburg situation in Washington were hard to ignore. Medlen was available to start in the postseason while Strasburg sat.

Other highlights included a historic campaign by Kimbrel, as the Braves closer again earned Cy Young and MVP votes while becoming the first pitcher in history to strike out more than half the batters he faced while pitching at least six innings. That's not a typo. Nobody had done it even in a tiny seven-inning sample size. The club's long-term solution to its game of musical chairs at shortstop may have arrived in the person of Andrelton Simmons, as the young Curacao native displayed a slick glove and potential at the plate. Heyward is once again on the path to superstardom, while on the other side of the career arc, 2012 marked the end for Jones, who at 40 put up a solid 832 OPS in 112 games. He should keep the summer of 2018 free. He'll be wanted in Cooperstown.

BRAVES PROSPECTUS

2012 W-L: 94-68, 2nd in NL East

Pythag	.570	5th	DER	.716	7th
RS/G	4.32	17th	B-Age	28.4	18th
RA/G	3.70	5th	P-Age	27.8	13th
TAv	.257	19th	Salary	$93.5	17th
BRR	12.4	3rd	M$/MW	$1.76	8th
TAv-P	.244	2nd	DL Days	764	18th
FIP	3.78	8th	DL WARP	2.1	25th

Three-Year Park Factors	
Overall	100
HR/RH	96
HR/LH	105
AVG/RH	99
AVG/LH	101

Turner Field (1997)
Att. % of Capacity: 60.4% (20th)
Dim. 335, 380, 400, 385, 330

More neutral than people realize, Turner Field is actually a pretty comfy park for lefty power hitters.

2013: PIE IN THE SKY

Although this will be the first Braves team in more than two decades to enter the season without Jones or Bobby Cox in uniform, the real question around Atlanta is not just whether the team will make the postseason, but whether this is the year it makes a serious run at the World Series.

The Braves hit the offseason running. Before teams convened in early December for the Winter Meetings, Atlanta had already signed B.J. Upton to a five-year deal worth $75 million—the largest in franchise history—to replace Bourn in center field. They also added Gerald Laird as the new backup catcher. Martin Prado will be trotting in from left field to take over at the hot corner, but someone else will need to step up to fill Chipper's shoes if the offense is to avoid taking a step backward this year.

The rotation will look a lot like the one that ended last season, and should remain an asset. Tommy Hanson and Jair Jurrjens are gone, but Tim Hudson, Medlen, Mike Minor, and Paul Maholm, along with one of their young arms, should be a solid group. The club hopes promising Brandon Beachy, whose breakout 2012 was cut short by Tommy John surgery in June, can return in time to contribute down the stretch. Meanwhile, a high-octane bullpen that features Kimbrel, Jonny Venters, Jordan Walden, and Eric O'Flaherty should again rank among the best in the league.

THE STATE OF THE ORGANIZATION: PIE WITH EXTRA CHEESE

Wren and crew have positioned the Braves to be relevant for years to come, thanks in no small part to a deep supply of arms. The front office will have to continue its good work to fight off a constantly improving NL East and to cancel out the suppressive effects of one of the worst television deals in the league.

The Braves spent the offseason adding talent to the lineup—a sensible approach given the departures and the club's ability to reinforce the pitching staff from within. As is seemingly always the case, the strength of Atlanta's farm system is in its pitchers. Julio Teheran and J.R. Graham are the top two talents on the farm, but others—like Zeke Spruill, Lucas Sims, Mauricio Cabrera, Alex Wood, and Sean Gilmartin—give the Braves an enviable variety of upside and safeness, polish and projection.

Those arms will come in handy, not only when the Braves have to deal with injury or bad performance, but potentially as trade chips as well. The Nationals have matured into a formidable division foe, and while the Phillies, Mets, and Marlins all have their struggles, none of them, with the possible exception of Miami, figures to be down for long. In order to keep up, the Braves will have to be creative, because they won't be able to outspend their rivals.

The Braves signed a 25-year pact for their television rights prior to the start of the 2007 season. While teams like the Dodgers are reportedly nearing new deals with total values in the billions, the Braves are reportedly collecting one of the smallest per-year amounts in the league. The 2031 season is a long way off, and one wonders if the Braves made a miscalculation or just suffered from bad timing. Either way, Wren will have to work around the revenue restraints.

He should be up for that challenge. Wren has shown an aptitude for building bullpens and benches on the cheap. Likewise, his ability to find veteran fits at the deadline has given the Braves that extra late-season boost. Make no mistake: Atlanta's margin for error is wider than the Tampa Bays and Oaklands of the world. But the Braves will have to continue exhibiting their own brand of genius in order to validate Wren's efforts to date.

HITTERS

Nick Ahmed **SS**

Born: **3/15/1990** Age: **23**
Bats: **R** Throws: **R** Height: **6' 4"**
Weight: **205** Breakout: **9%**
Improve: **40%** Collapse: **12%**
Attrition: **20%** MLB: **89%**

Comparables:
Oswaldo Navarro,Roy Smalley,Eddie Leon

YEAR	TEAM	LVL	AGE	PA	R	2B	3B	HR	RBI	BB	SO	SB	CS	AVG_OBP_SLG	TAv	BABIP	BRR	FRAA	WARP
2011	DNV	Rk	21	284	46	13	2	4	24	30	46	18	6	.262/.346/.379	.251	.305	2.3	SS(34): 7.3	1.1
2012	LYN	A+	22	571	84	36	4	6	49	49	102	40	10	.269/.337/.391	.249	.325	6	SS(101): 18.0	3.3
2013	*ATL*	*MLB*	*23*	*250*	*29*	*11*	*1*	*3*	*17*	*16*	*58*	*12*	*3*	*.217/.269/.313*	*.213*	*.270*	*1.1*	*SS 7*	*0.8*

No one questioned Ahmed's passion for the game coming out of the University of Connecticut. What people did question was his long-term viability at shortstop and the potential potency of his bat. Ahmed's first full professional season was a step in the right direction, and scouts are now convinced he has the defensive ability to stick at shortstop. He didn't hit a ton, but he still has gap power and good speed. A baseball rat, Ahmed is expected to max out his tools. His upside is starting shortstop. His downside is solid utility infielder.

Jeff Baker **UT**

Born: **6/21/1981** Age: **32**
Bats: **R** Throws: **R** Height: **6' 3"**
Weight: **210** Breakout: **2%**
Improve: **32%** Collapse: **9%**
Attrition: **22%** MLB: **86%**

Comparables:
Geronimo Berroa,Craig Monroe,Jeff Conine

YEAR	TEAM	LVL	AGE	PA	R	2B	3B	HR	RBI	BB	SO	SB	CS	AVG_OBP_SLG	TAv	BABIP	BRR	FRAA	WARP
2010	CHN	MLB	29	224	29	13	2	4	21	16	50	1	0	.272/.326/.413	.249	.340	-0.6	3B(33): 2.0, 2B(26): -0.3	0.5
2011	CHN	MLB	30	212	20	12	1	3	23	10	46	0	0	.269/.302/.383	.246	.333	2.5	1B(19): -0.7, 2B(18): -0.2	-0.2
2012	ATL	MLB	31	20	1	0	0	0	1	1	10	0	0	.105/.150/.105	.098	.222	0	LF(3): -0.1, RF(1): -0.0	-0.4
2012	CHN	MLB	31	144	16	10	1	4	20	8	28	4	1	.269/.306/.448	.260	.308	-0.3	1B(20): -2.3, RF(14): 0.1	-0.2
2012	DET	MLB	31	37	1	2	0	0	4	2	10	0	0	.200/.243/.257	.209	.280	0	RF(11): -0.2, 3B(4): 0.0	-0.2
2013	*ATL*	*MLB*	*32*	*250*	*24*	*13*	*1*	*5*	*27*	*17*	*61*	*2*	*1*	*.248/.299/.383*	*.249*	*.313*	*-0.1*	*1B -0, 2B -0*	*0.2*

After a strong first half, Baker changed hands twice in a matter of weeks: once from the Cubs to the Tigers, then again from the Tigers to the Braves. Baker's value lies in his ability to hit left-handed pitching and play multiple defensive positions. He makes for a decent utility infielder, though his inability to play shortstop makes him a flawed one. Unfortunately for him, he didn't do much hitting with either Detroit or Atlanta, lowering his stock as he heads into free agency.

Christian Bethancourt C

Born: **9/2/1991** Age: **21**
Bats: **R** Throws: **R** Height: **6' 3"**
Weight: **190** Breakout: **3%**
Improve: **52%** Collapse: **14%**
Attrition: **18%** MLB: **93%**

Comparables:
Del Crandall,Ivan Rodriguez,Buck Martinez

YEAR	TEAM	LVL	AGE	PA	R	2B	3B	HR	RBI	BB	SO	SB	CS	AVG_OBP_SLG	TAv	BABIP	BRR	FRAA	WARP
2010	ROM	A	18	420	31	19	2	3	34	14	62	11	3	.251/.280/.331	.237	.290	-1.4	C(80): -0.1	0.3
2011	ROM	A	19	235	25	10	3	4	33	8	27	6	3	.303/.323/.430	.277	.323	2.3	C(36): 1.1	1.2
2011	LYN	A+	19	175	11	6	0	1	20	3	35	3	2	.271/.277/.325	.213	.328	1.6	C(24): -0.3	-0.1
2012	MIS	AA	20	288	30	5	1	2	26	11	45	8	6	.243/.275/.291	.235	.281	-2	C(18): 1.0	-0.2
2013	*ATL*	*MLB*	*21*	*250*	*20*	*9*	*1*	*3*	*22*	*4*	*53*	*3*	*2*	*.229/.241/.315*	*.200*	*.275*	*-0.1*	*C 0*	*-0.5*

Bethancourt is blessed with all the right tools to become a special defender. The only thing holding him back from claiming a big-league gig is his bat. There's some potential to be found in his raw power and bat speed, but his approach is tedious. Bethancourt looks fastball and swings fastball, regardless of the location of the pitch or situation. Age is still on his side, and he could become a backup without much offensive improvement. Bethancourt remains a candidate to post the worst walk-to-strikeout ratio on his team.

Michael Bourn CF

Born: **12/27/1982** Age: **30**
Bats: **L** Throws: **R** Height: **6' 0"**
Weight: **180** Breakout: **0%**
Improve: **38%** Collapse: **2%**
Attrition: **10%** MLB: **92%**

Comparables:
Rajai Davis,Manny Mota,Kenny Lofton

YEAR	TEAM	LVL	AGE	PA	R	2B	3B	HR	RBI	BB	SO	SB	CS	AVG_OBP_SLG	TAv	BABIP	BRR	FRAA	WARP
2010	HOU	MLB	27	605	84	25	6	2	38	59	109	52	12	.265/.341/.346	.251	.329	10.4	CF(138): 6.6	3.4
2011	ATL	MLB	28	249	30	8	3	1	18	15	50	22	7	.278/.321/.352	.252	.346	2.2	CF(53): -5.2	0.1
2011	HOU	MLB	28	473	64	26	7	1	32	38	90	39	7	.303/.363/.403	.271	.381	4.4	CF(103): -1.8	1.7
2012	ATL	MLB	29	703	96	26	10	9	57	70	155	42	13	.274/.348/.391	.272	.349	11.7	CF(153): 0.4	3.7
2013	*ATL*	*MLB*	*30*	*664*	*87*	*26*	*7*	*5*	*46*	*58*	*140*	*48*	*12*	*.263/.329/.357*	*.249*	*.330*	*5.3*	*CF 2*	*2.1*

Bourn hit free agency as an intriguing option: a capable leadoff hitter, good center fielder, and good basestealer. There were some concerns about him, however. He's faded in the second half in back-to-back seasons, and his strikeout-heavy approach to hitting is unusual for a speed-and-defense center fielder. With a relatively weak free-agent class, Bourn stood out as one of the best players on the market.

Jose Constanza OF

Born: **9/1/1983** Age: **29**
Bats: **L** Throws: **L** Height: **5' 10"**
Weight: **150** Breakout: **0%**
Improve: **34%** Collapse: **3%**
Attrition: **11%** MLB: **83%**

Comparables:
Brock Davis,Luis Polonia,Rudy Law

YEAR	TEAM	LVL	AGE	PA	R	2B	3B	HR	RBI	BB	SO	SB	CS	AVG_OBP_SLG	TAv	BABIP	BRR	FRAA	WARP
2010	COH	AAA	26	448	69	11	8	1	32	35	54	34	6	.319/.367/.394	.252	.359	2.7	RF(63): -2.8, CF(55): -3.2	0.3
2011	GWN	AAA	27	363	47	2	4	1	25	25	41	23	8	.312/.361/.351	.262	.353	0	--	0.0
2011	ATL	MLB	27	119	21	1	1	2	10	6	14	7	4	.303/.339/.385	.288	.333	1.8	LF(17): 1.8, RF(16): 0.6	0.7
2012	GWN	AAA	28	392	54	10	4	1	27	36	43	14	6	.314/.380/.375	.253	.354	5.1	LF(26): 2.9, CF(7): 1.5	1.0
2012	ATL	MLB	28	86	8	2	0	0	4	8	21	5	2	.250/.321/.276	.226	.345	0.5	LF(21): 1.5, CF(5): -0.4	0.0
2013	*ATL*	*MLB*	*29*	*250*	*29*	*8*	*2*	*2*	*18*	*18*	*41*	*10*	*3*	*.274/.327/.354*	*.247*	*.318*	*0.8*	*LF 1, CF -0*	*0.4*

At one point in 2011, Constanza overtook Jason Heyward as master of the Braves' right-field domain. Constanza's success proved fleeting—as is often the case for 28-year-old slap hitters with minimal big-league experience. Nonetheless, he can help a club as a fifth outfielder. His speed plays up on defense and on the basepaths and his contact-heavy tendencies can help in certain pinch-hitting situations. Asking anything more of him is asking too much.

Todd Cunningham CF

Born: **3/20/1989** Age: **24**
Bats: **B** Throws: **R** Height: **6' 1"**
Weight: **200** Breakout: **1%**
Improve: **36%** Collapse: **8%**
Attrition: **11%** MLB: **94%**

Comparables:
Mike Hershberger,Mickey Stanley,Tom Umphlett

YEAR	TEAM	LVL	AGE	PA	R	2B	3B	HR	RBI	BB	SO	SB	CS	AVG_OBP_SLG	TAv	BABIP	BRR	FRAA	WARP
2010	ROM	A	21	263	32	9	3	1	20	14	30	7	4	.260/.340/.338	.244	.292	0.8	CF(45): 1.7, RF(19): 0.0	0.3
2011	LYN	A+	22	386	59	12	4	4	20	33	47	14	6	.257/.348/.353	.262	.289	3.9	CF(51): -0.6, LF(9): -0.4	0.8
2012	MIS	AA	23	519	77	23	6	3	51	38	51	24	8	.309/.364/.403	.280	.340	4.3	CF(34): -3.1, RF(6): -0.7	1.2
2013	*ATL*	*MLB*	*24*	*250*	*27*	*10*	*2*	*3*	*19*	*12*	*41*	*6*	*2*	*.246/.294/.345*	*.232*	*.281*	*0.4*	*CF -2, RF -0*	*-0.2*

Cunningham, the Braves' second-round pick in 2010, took steps forward in 2012. The Jacksonville State product is a tweener, lacking the speed to play in center field every day, the arm for right field, or the power for either corner. Cunningham's deficiencies put a lot of pressure on his hit tool and on-base abilities. There's some reason to think he can develop into a second-division starter, but a future as a fourth outfielder seems more likely.

Brandon Drury 3B

Born: **8/21/1992** Age: **20**
Bats: **R** Throws: **R** Height: **6' 3"**
Weight: **190** Breakout: **21%**
Improve: **54%** Collapse: **7%**
Attrition: **20%** MLB: **86%**

Comparables:
Claudell Washington, Ed Kranepool, Al Kaline

YEAR	TEAM	LVL	AGE	PA	R	2B	3B	HR	RBI	BB	SO	SB	CS	AVG_OBP_SLG	TAv	BABIP	BRR	FRAA	WARP
2010	BRA	Rk	17	207	20	7	1	3	17	9	50	2	2	.198/.248/.292	.188	.250	0.4	3B(37): -2.5, SS(9): 0.3	-1.2
2011	DNV	Rk	18	278	40	23	0	8	54	6	35	3	0	.347/.367/.525	.285	.373	0.2	3B(25): -1.0, 2B(5): 0.0	0.7
2012	ROM	A	19	480	47	22	3	6	51	20	73	3	4	.229/.270/.333	.217	.259	-3.4	1B(44): -2.6, 3B(37): -2.4	-2.6
2013	*ATL*	*MLB*	*20*	*250*	*16*	*9*	*1*	*3*	*21*	*5*	*65*	*0*	*0*	*.191/.209/.279*	*.177*	*.242*	*-0.4*	*3B 1, 1B -1*	*-1.8*

After nearly leading the Appalachian League in hitting in 2011, Drury took a step back in the Sally. He's a big-framed third baseman with a quick swing and above-average raw power potential. His flaw is an overly aggressive approach at the plate. Advanced pitchers are able to pick him apart, as they did last season. There's still plenty of time for Drury to get back on the horse, but he'll need to become more selective to live up to his potential.

Juan Francisco 3B

Born: **6/24/1987** Age: **26**
Bats: **L** Throws: **R** Height: **6' 3"**
Weight: **240** Breakout: **4%**
Improve: **51%** Collapse: **4%**
Attrition: **13%** MLB: **95%**

Comparables:
Bill Melton, Matt Williams, Chris Davis

YEAR	TEAM	LVL	AGE	PA	R	2B	3B	HR	RBI	BB	SO	SB	CS	AVG_OBP_SLG	TAv	BABIP	BRR	FRAA	WARP
2010	LOU	AAA	23	329	46	24	4	18	59	16	81	1	0	.286/.327/.565	.294	.335	-1.1	3B(61): -5.9, LF(5): 0.3	1.7
2010	CIN	MLB	23	59	3	3	0	1	7	4	20	0	1	.273/.322/.382	.233	.412	-0.4	3B(12): -0.9	-0.1
2011	LOU	AAA	24	314	46	23	1	15	50	10	65	0	0	.307/.334/.540	.278	.348	-0.9	3B(40): 0.2, RF(1): -0.1	0.8
2011	CIN	MLB	24	97	10	7	1	3	15	4	24	1	0	.258/.289/.452	.249	.318	0.8	3B(24): -1.8	0.1
2012	ATL	MLB	25	205	17	11	0	9	32	11	70	1	1	.234/.278/.432	.240	.316	-1.9	3B(49): -1.4	-0.3
2013	*ATL*	*MLB*	*26*	*250*	*28*	*13*	*1*	*11*	*35*	*11*	*69*	*1*	*0*	*.256/.291/.455*	*.261*	*.315*	*-0.3*	*3B -1, LF -0*	*0.5*

In need of Chipper Jones insurance, the Braves added Francisco from the Reds just before Opening Day 2012. Francisco's skill set is all about strength. He has impressive raw power and a strong throwing arm. His game lacks nuance and his troubles with left-handed pitching limit him to a platoon role. Nonetheless, what he brings to the table should be enough to keep him around through his cost-controlled years.

Freddie Freeman 1B

Born: **9/12/1989** Age: **23**
Bats: **L** Throws: **R** Height: **6' 6"**
Weight: **225** Breakout: **4%**
Improve: **63%** Collapse: **3%**
Attrition: **8%** MLB: **94%**

Comparables:
Kent Hrbek, Prince Fielder, Jason Thompson

YEAR	TEAM	LVL	AGE	PA	R	2B	3B	HR	RBI	BB	SO	SB	CS	AVG_OBP_SLG	TAv	BABIP	BRR	FRAA	WARP
2010	GWN	AAA	20	519	73	35	2	18	87	43	84	6	2	.319/.384/.521	.296	.359	-0.5	1B(110): -0.9	2.3
2010	ATL	MLB	20	24	3	1	0	1	1	0	8	0	0	.167/.167/.333	.195	.200	-0.1	1B(11): 0.1	-0.1
2011	ATL	MLB	21	635	67	32	0	21	76	53	142	4	4	.282/.346/.448	.282	.339	-2.1	1B(156): -5.1	0.2
2012	ATL	MLB	22	620	91	33	2	23	94	64	129	2	0	.259/.340/.456	.285	.295	1.7	1B(146): -6.9	0.9
2013	*ATL*	*MLB*	*23*	*585*	*69*	*31*	*1*	*21*	*78*	*50*	*125*	*3*	*1*	*.267/.335/.451*	*.281*	*.311*	*-0.9*	*1B -4*	*1.3*

Freeman spent the previous winter lifting weights. A typical offseason pursuit for a professional ballplayer—except, apparently, for Freeman, who claimed it was the first time he had done so. The hard work with the dumbbells paid off as he increased his power production while also improving his walk and strikeout rates in 2012. Freeman is becoming one of the top first basemen in the National League based on his age, defensive reputation, and offensive production to date. He's also on his way to earning the Captain Marvel Jr. nickname.

Evan Gattis LF

Born: **8/18/1986** Age: **26**
Bats: **R** Throws: **R** Height: **6' 5"**
Weight: **230** Breakout: **6%**
Improve: **55%** Collapse: **7%**
Attrition: **14%** MLB: **96%**

Comparables:
Matt Holliday, Mel Hall, Allen Craig

YEAR	TEAM	LVL	AGE	PA	R	2B	3B	HR	RBI	BB	SO	SB	CS	AVG_OBP_SLG	TAv	BABIP	BRR	FRAA	WARP
2010	DNV	Rk	23	242	33	10	0	4	29	6	44	0	0	.288/.342/.387	.266	.345	0.6	C(35): 0.7	0.9
2011	ROM	A	24	377	58	24	2	22	71	25	53	2	4	.322/.386/.601	.348	.328	0.3	C(38): -0.4, 1B(5): 0.0	3.0
2012	LYN	A+	25	94	14	7	0	9	29	10	12	1	1	.385/.468/.821	.453	.356	-0.3	C(7): 0.1, LF(1): 0.0	1.4
2012	MIS	AA	25	207	24	13	4	9	37	20	29	1	1	.258/.343/.522	.396	.262	0.1	C(8): -0.1, LF(5): -0.3	0.8
2013	*ATL*	*MLB*	*26*	*250*	*28*	*11*	*1*	*11*	*35*	*13*	*54*	*0*	*0*	*.247/.294/.447*	*.261*	*.273*	*-0.4*	*C -0, LF -0*	*0.8*

There are long shots and then there is Gattis. He gave up the game as an amateur only to return and play at a Division III school. The Braves drafted Gattis just before he turned 24, and they tried to make up for lost time by pushing him through the system and, last year, moving him from catcher to the outfield. Gattis has a large frame, plus-plus raw power, and a surprising knack for contact. All he's done since turning pro is hit, hit, and hit some more. If that continues, he could see the majors by the end of the season.

Jason Heyward **RF**

Born: **8/9/1989** Age: **23**
Bats: **L** Throws: **L** Height: **6' 6"**
Weight: **240** Breakout: **6%**
Improve: **60%** Collapse: **5%**
Attrition: **4%** MLB: **97%**

Comparables:
Tom Brunansky,Justin Upton,Wladimir Balentien

YEAR	TEAM	LVL	AGE	PA	R	2B	3B	HR	RBI	BB	SO	SB	CS	AVG_OBP_SLG	TAv	BABIP	BRR	FRAA	WARP
2010	ATL	MLB	20	623	83	29	5	18	72	91	128	11	6	.277/.393/.456	.306	.335	-0.1	RF(140): 1.2	4.1
2011	ATL	MLB	21	454	50	18	2	14	42	51	93	9	2	.227/.319/.389	.257	.260	-0.6	RF(122): 3.0	0.2
2012	ATL	MLB	22	651	93	30	6	27	82	58	152	21	8	.269/.335/.479	.294	.319	7.7	RF(153): 14.7, CF(2): -0.1	5.4
2013	*ATL*	*MLB*	*23*	*572*	*74*	*26*	*3*	*20*	*74*	*64*	*125*	*14*	*5*	*.258/.346/.446*	*.287*	*.304*	*0.4*	*RF 3, CF -0*	*3.3*

The problem with a big rookie season is living up to it in the years thereafter. Fortunately for Heyward, while last season might not have been his best by True Average, he did set career-highs in home runs and stolen bases, among other traditional stats. One of those stats, games played, is an encouraging step forward for a player who'd had his toughness questioned the year before. Add in fantastic defense in right field, and Heyward, still just 23, is living up to the hype as a potential impact talent.

Paul Janish **SS**

Born: **10/12/1982** Age: **30**
Bats: **R** Throws: **R** Height: **6' 3"**
Weight: **200** Breakout: **0%**
Improve: **30%** Collapse: **9%**
Attrition: **15%** MLB: **92%**

Comparables:
Larry Brown,Bucky Dent,Don Kessinger

YEAR	TEAM	LVL	AGE	PA	R	2B	3B	HR	RBI	BB	SO	SB	CS	AVG_OBP_SLG	TAv	BABIP	BRR	FRAA	WARP
2010	CIN	MLB	27	228	23	10	0	5	25	22	30	1	3	.260/.338/.385	.257	.283	-1.3	SS(61): -2.4, 3B(11): 0.1	0.5
2011	LOU	AAA	28	53	9	2	0	1	3	7	4	1	0	.256/.377/.372	.199	.256	0.4	SS(9): -0.7	-0.2
2011	CIN	MLB	28	366	27	14	1	0	23	18	46	3	2	.214/.259/.262	.203	.244	-0.2	SS(103): 6.0, 3B(8): -0.6	-0.5
2012	LOU	AAA	29	194	27	12	1	4	11	20	26	0	1	.237/.332/.391	.246	.259	1.7	SS(38): -5.3, 2B(3): -0.4	-0.1
2012	ATL	MLB	29	186	18	6	1	0	9	17	30	1	0	.186/.269/.234	.198	.226	1	SS(55): 5.8	0.2
2013	*ATL*	*MLB*	*30*	*250*	*22*	*12*	*1*	*2*	*20*	*19*	*40*	*1*	*1*	*.221/.291/.312*	*.224*	*.254*	*-0.4*	*SS 1, 3B 0*	*0.2*

Atlanta needed another shortstop after Andrelton Simmons and Jack Wilson went down with injuries, so Frank Wren called up Walt Jocketty and made a deal for Janish. Janish is a crazy-good defensive shortstop and a crazy-bad hitter. The profile is enough to merit comparison to Rey Ordonez. Except here's the thing: Ordonez's career True Average is higher by one point. Yikes. The fewer plate appearances Janish gets, the happier his employers should be.

Reed Johnson **OF**

Born: **12/8/1976** Age: **36**
Bats: **R** Throws: **R** Height: **5' 11"**
Weight: **180** Breakout: **1%**
Improve: **27%** Collapse: **7%**
Attrition: **20%** MLB: **77%**

Comparables:
Trenidad Hubbard,Dom Dimaggio,Steve Finley

YEAR	TEAM	LVL	AGE	PA	R	2B	3B	HR	RBI	BB	SO	SB	CS	AVG_OBP_SLG	TAv	BABIP	BRR	FRAA	WARP
2010	LAN	MLB	33	215	24	11	2	2	15	5	50	2	2	.262/.291/.366	.243	.336	1.5	LF(61): 3.8, RF(22): -0.0	0.6
2011	CHN	MLB	34	266	33	22	1	5	28	5	63	2	1	.309/.348/.467	.286	.394	0.4	RF(43): 1.4, LF(27): -0.5	0.9
2012	ATL	MLB	35	105	7	5	0	0	4	3	18	0	1	.270/.305/.320	.241	.329	-1.4	LF(19): -0.7, CF(8): -1.0	-0.3
2012	CHN	MLB	35	183	23	9	3	3	16	10	43	2	1	.302/.355/.444	.277	.390	0.1	RF(24): 0.1, CF(22): -0.1	0.6
2013	*ATL*	*MLB*	*36*	*266*	*29*	*14*	*1*	*4*	*23*	*11*	*58*	*2*	*2*	*.264/.311/.378*	*.250*	*.327*	*-0.4*	*RF 0, CF -0*	*0.4*

Acquired to replace Matt Diaz, Johnson stumbled, though the Braves still re-signed him to a one-year deal with a club option for 2014. There are plenty of aspects of Johnson's game to dislike—for example, that he strikes out too much given his walk rate and power production—but teams love having him around. He can play each outfield spot, though he's a bit stretched in center, and he has a superb clubhouse reputation.

Kyle Kubitza **3B**

Born: **7/15/1990** Age: **22**
Bats: **L** Throws: **R** Height: **6' 4"**
Weight: **190** Breakout: **9%**
Improve: **61%** Collapse: **4%**
Attrition: **14%** MLB: **94%**

Comparables:
Denny Gonzalez,Hank Blalock,Denis Menke

YEAR	TEAM	LVL	AGE	PA	R	2B	3B	HR	RBI	BB	SO	SB	CS	AVG_OBP_SLG	TAv	BABIP	BRR	FRAA	WARP
2011	DNV	Rk	20	190	36	16	3	1	34	24	38	9	3	.321/.407/.475	.311	.408	0.6	3B(18): -1.3, LF(1): -0.1	0.8
2012	ROM	A	21	531	68	24	9	9	59	73	127	18	11	.239/.349/.393	.278	.310	1.3	3B(73): 0.6	1.7
2013	*ATL*	*MLB*	*22*	*250*	*23*	*9*	*2*	*4*	*22*	*24*	*79*	*5*	*2*	*.192/.271/.296*	*.212*	*.273*	*0*	*3B 1, LF -0*	*-0.6*

Kubitza is an athletic third baseman with the tools to stick, a powerful left-handed hitter with the approach to succeed, and a total wild card. His strikeout rate is worrisome. It's one thing to fan a quarter of the time in the majors, doing so in the low minors is a red flag—especially when the player has collegiate experience, as Kubitza does. Keep an eye on Kubitza because he could be a nice player if he gets the strikeout woes in check.

Gerald Laird **C**

Born: **11/13/1979** Age: **33**
Bats: **R** Throws: **R** Height: **6' 2"**
Weight: **225** Breakout: **5%**
Improve: **37%** Collapse: **10%**
Attrition: **21%** MLB: **88%**

Comparables:
Jim Sundberg,Jerry Grote,John Wathan

YEAR	TEAM	LVL	AGE	PA	R	2B	3B	HR	RBI	BB	SO	SB	CS	AVG_OBP_SLG	TAv	BABIP	BRR	FRAA	WARP
2010	DET	MLB	30	299	22	11	0	5	25	18	57	3	1	.207/.263/.304	.201	.243	-0.3	C(87): 1.9	-0.1
2011	SLN	MLB	31	108	11	7	1	1	12	9	19	1	1	.232/.302/.358	.229	.276	-2	C(31): 0.4, 1B(1): -0.0	-0.4
2012	DET	MLB	32	191	24	8	1	2	11	14	21	0	0	.282/.337/.374	.251	.309	0.5	C(56): 0.1	0.5
2013	*ATL*	*MLB*	*33*	*250*	*23*	*12*	*1*	*3*	*21*	*18*	*44*	*2*	*1*	*.233/.296/.331*	*.228*	*.271*	*-0.3*	*C -0*	*0.2*

Don't quite believe in the idea of small sample sizes and how they aren't necessarily indicative of a player's skill? Take a look at Laird's career as a backup catcher. He has been all over the map, but his actual skill hasn't been spiking in concert. What you see is what you get: a capable backup who can survive with the bat, but sometimes in 200ish plate appearances, things aren't going to go his way and the returns will be soft.

Matt Lipka CF

Born: 4/15/1992 Age: 21
Bats: R Throws: R Height: 6' 2"
Weight: 195 Breakout: 4%
Improve: 55% Collapse: 9%
Attrition: 14% MLB: 95%

Comparables:
Oscar Gamble,Curt Flood,Thad Bosley

YEAR	TEAM	LVL	AGE	PA	R	2B	3B	HR	RBI	BB	SO	SB	CS	AVG_OBP_SLG	TAv	BABIP	BRR	FRAA	WARP
2010	BRA	Rk	18	210	33	8	4	1	24	14	22	20	3	.302/.359/.401	.309	.337	3.9	SS(41): -1.0	2.0
2011	ROM	A	19	585	78	21	3	1	37	42	83	28	14	.247/.305/.304	.230	.288	0.9	SS(61): -0.1, 2B(31): 2.4	-0.2
2012	LYN	A+	20	229	32	5	1	2	13	20	32	12	6	.271/.335/.337	.274	.308	-0.8	CF(42): -0.1	0.9
2013	*ATL*	*MLB*	*21*	*250*	*25*	*8*	*1*	*2*	*15*	*12*	*52*	*9*	*4*	*.217/.253/.285*	*.200*	*.266*	*0.3*	*SS 1, CF -1*	*-0.6*

One of the early positives of Lipka's career is his status as a hard-working diamond rat. The Braves tested him in 2012 by moving him from the infield to center and pushing him to a new level despite his struggles in 2011. He responded well, hitting better and showing enough in center field to have people buy into him sticking there for the long haul. Lipka's best attributes are his quick bat and quicker feet. If he continues to progress, he should find himself batting near the top of the order in the near future.

Brian McCann C

Born: 2/20/1984 Age: 29
Bats: L Throws: R Height: 6' 4"
Weight: 230 Breakout: 5%
Improve: 40% Collapse: 7%
Attrition: 15% MLB: 97%

Comparables:
Yogi Berra,Victor Martinez,Ted Simmons

YEAR	TEAM	LVL	AGE	PA	R	2B	3B	HR	RBI	BB	SO	SB	CS	AVG_OBP_SLG	TAv	BABIP	BRR	FRAA	WARP
2010	ATL	MLB	26	566	63	25	0	21	77	74	98	5	2	.269/.375/.453	.294	.297	-3.4	C(136): 1.3	4.5
2011	ATL	MLB	27	527	51	19	0	24	71	57	89	3	2	.270/.351/.466	.287	.287	-2.6	C(126): 3.3	3.1
2012	ATL	MLB	28	487	44	14	0	20	67	44	76	3	0	.230/.300/.399	.245	.234	-0.9	C(114): 2.8	0.8
2013	*ATL*	*MLB*	*29*	*465*	*58*	*23*	*0*	*19*	*65*	*47*	*75*	*3*	*1*	*.265/.343/.461*	*.286*	*.281*	*-0.7*	*C 2*	*3.5*

For the first time in a long time, McCann did not look special, posting career lows across the board and riding pine while David Ross caught the first pitch in wild-card playoff game history. To what extent a torn labrum impacted McCann is unquantifiable. We do know he's likely to miss the first two weeks of the new season, and perhaps more. With McCann hitting free agency after the season, it's in his and the team's best interest to let him heal properly before returning—even if that means relying on Laird for longer than any team would like to.

Ernesto Mejia 1B

Born: 12/2/1985 Age: 27
Bats: R Throws: R Height: 6' 6"
Weight: 245 Breakout: 3%
Improve: 41% Collapse: 5%
Attrition: 10% MLB: 91%

Comparables:
Josh Phelps,Tony Clark,Lee May

YEAR	TEAM	LVL	AGE	PA	R	2B	3B	HR	RBI	BB	SO	SB	CS	AVG_OBP_SLG	TAv	BABIP	BRR	FRAA	WARP
2010	WIL	A+	24	188	25	13	2	5	21	14	41	0	0	.288/.346/.476	.298	.355	-0.6	1B(42): 0.3	0.8
2010	NWA	AA	24	293	36	18	0	11	48	22	86	1	0	.268/.339/.464	.271	.360	-2.1	1B(9): -0.3	0.4
2011	MIS	AA	25	573	82	37	1	26	99	58	156	4	3	.297/.375/.531	.307	.377	0	--	0.0
2012	GWN	AAA	26	559	73	32	1	24	92	34	132	10	4	.296/.347/.502	.295	.355	-1.8	1B(33): 1.1	0.7
2013	*ATL*	*MLB*	*27*	*250*	*27*	*12*	*1*	*9*	*32*	*13*	*73*	*2*	*1*	*.242/.286/.418*	*.250*	*.308*	*-0.2*	*1B -3*	*-0.2*

Mejia looked like a non-prospect as recently as two seasons ago due to injuries and poor performance. He left the Braves organization after the 2009 season, signing with the Royals as a minor-league free agent, but returned to Atlanta's system in 2011. Since then, Mejia has hit 50 home runs. He's a big guy, and those types tend to have issues with long swings and strikeouts. Mejia is no different. His immobility leaves him at first base, where he's nothing special defensively. He has not shown a knack for drawing walks, either. If Mejia gets to the show it'll be as a bench bat, and it'll be because of his pop.

Lyle Overbay 1B

Born: 1/28/1977 Age: 36
Bats: L Throws: L Height: 6' 3"
Weight: 220 Breakout: 1%
Improve: 24% Collapse: 20%
Attrition: 21% MLB: 85%

Comparables:
Keith Hernandez,Harold Baines,Andre Thornton

YEAR	TEAM	LVL	AGE	PA	R	2B	3B	HR	RBI	BB	SO	SB	CS	AVG_OBP_SLG	TAv	BABIP	BRR	FRAA	WARP
2010	TOR	MLB	33	607	75	37	2	20	67	67	131	1	0	.243/.329/.433	.270	.285	-2.1	1B(153): -0.7	0.9
2011	ARI	MLB	34	49	3	4	0	1	10	6	11	1	0	.286/.388/.452	.289	.367	0.1	1B(11): 0.8	0.2
2011	PIT	MLB	34	391	40	17	1	8	37	36	77	1	1	.227/.300/.349	.232	.269	-1.5	1B(98): -2.9	-1.3
2012	ARI	MLB	35	110	11	9	0	2	10	12	26	0	0	.292/.367/.448	.273	.377	-3.5	1B(21): 0.1	-0.2
2012	ATL	MLB	35	21	1	1	0	0	0	1	8	0	0	.100/.143/.150	.104	.167	0.2	1B(2): -0.0	-0.3
2013	*ATL*	*MLB*	*36*	*250*	*26*	*13*	*1*	*6*	*27*	*28*	*54*	*1*	*0*	*.242/.329/.384*	*.259*	*.294*	*-0.4*	*1B 1*	*0.3*

Arizona's decision to cut bait with Overbay despite a sparkling line raised some eyebrows. His inability to make consistent contact with Atlanta lowered those eyebrows back into place. Further complicating matters is that Overbay's defense can no longer overcome his mediocre offensive production. Now 36, with back-to-back disappointing seasons under his belt, his days as a starter could be over.

Tyler Pastornicky SS
Born: 12/13/1989 Age: 23
Bats: R Throws: R Height: 6' 0"
Weight: 170 Breakout: 3%
Improve: 38% Collapse: 13%
Attrition: 21% MLB: 93%
Comparables:
Toby Harrah,Rudy Meoli,Alan Trammell

YEAR	TEAM	LVL	AGE	PA	R	2B	3B	HR	RBI	BB	SO	SB	CS	AVG_OBP_SLG	TAv	BABIP	BRR	FRAA	WARP
2010	DUN	A+	20	331	50	16	0	6	35	39	49	24	7	.258/.345/.376	.264	.289	4.3	SS(46): 2.6, 2B(30): -4.8	1.6
2010	MIS	AA	20	160	22	5	2	2	15	16	22	11	2	.254/.323/.366	.276	.274	-0.1	SS(37): -4.1	0.7
2011	MIS	AA	21	395	50	13	5	6	36	24	34	20	8	.299/.345/.414	.267	.315	0	--	0.0
2011	GWN	AAA	21	117	15	2	0	1	9	8	11	7	3	.365/.407/.413	.299	.398	0	--	0.0
2012	GWN	AAA	22	167	15	15	1	1	20	11	21	3	3	.268/.317/.399	.247	.301	0.5	SS(10): -0.2, 2B(6): -0.9	0.0
2012	ATL	MLB	22	188	21	6	1	2	13	10	32	2	0	.243/.287/.325	.227	.287	1.4	SS(46): -4.6, 2B(3): 0.1	-0.4
2013	*ATL*	*MLB*	*23*	*250*	*29*	*11*	*1*	*4*	*20*	*17*	*45*	*7*	*2*	*.243/.297/.354*	*.235*	*.280*	*0.4*	*SS -1, 2B -0*	*0.4*

Pastornicky started the season as the Braves' every-day shortstop. Between an early-season slump and Andrelton Simmons' potential, Pastornicky found himself back in the minors. He's an instinctual player with big-league bloodlines, but his arm limits his ability to make the tough throws from the hole, and that limits a team's willingness to play him at shortstop as well as his upside. If nothing else, Pastornicky brings enough to the table to become a solid utility infielder.

Martin Prado LF
Born: 10/27/1983 Age: 29
Bats: R Throws: R Height: 6' 2"
Weight: 190 Breakout: 1%
Improve: 31% Collapse: 6%
Attrition: 16% MLB: 91%
Comparables:
Mike Greenwell,Bill Sample,Conor Jackson

YEAR	TEAM	LVL	AGE	PA	R	2B	3B	HR	RBI	BB	SO	SB	CS	AVG_OBP_SLG	TAv	BABIP	BRR	FRAA	WARP
2010	ATL	MLB	26	651	100	40	3	15	66	40	86	5	3	.307/.350/.459	.285	.335	5.6	2B(98): -1.7, 3B(43): 1.4	4.3
2011	ATL	MLB	27	590	66	26	2	13	57	34	52	4	8	.260/.302/.385	.247	.266	-1	LF(100): -2.7, 3B(41): 4.9	0.3
2012	ATL	MLB	28	690	81	42	6	10	70	58	69	17	4	.301/.359/.438	.285	.322	0.8	LF(118): -9.6, 3B(25): -1.1	2.3
2013	*ATL*	*MLB*	*29*	*628*	*77*	*38*	*3*	*13*	*64*	*44*	*74*	*8*	*4*	*.286/.337/.429*	*.275*	*.305*	*-0.8*	*LF 1, 3B 1*	*2.7*

A rough 2011 season proved to be nothing but a hiccup for Prado. The one constant between his '11 and '12 seasons is the complaint about his profile not fitting left field. Prado depends on contact and average, not power, and that's a skill set that often fits better in the middle of the diamond. With Chipper Jones retiring, Prado is expected to move a few rungs back up the defensive spectrum to third base. Not quite the middle of the diamond, but it works. A free agent at season's end, Prado can ill afford a repeat of 2011.

Edward Salcedo 3B
Born: 7/30/1991 Age: 21
Bats: R Throws: R Height: 6' 4"
Weight: 195 Breakout: 3%
Improve: 46% Collapse: 8%
Attrition: 30% MLB: 97%
Comparables:
Brooks Robinson,Kevin Bell,Aramis Ramirez

YEAR	TEAM	LVL	AGE	PA	R	2B	3B	HR	RBI	BB	SO	SB	CS	AVG_OBP_SLG	TAv	BABIP	BRR	FRAA	WARP
2010	ROM	A	18	209	23	5	4	2	16	11	56	6	5	.197/.236/.295	.206	.259	0.9	SS(52): 7.5	0.4
2011	ROM	A	19	566	83	27	6	12	68	41	105	23	10	.248/.315/.396	.262	.289	4.5	3B(65): 1.5, SS(19): 3.8	1.6
2012	LYN	A+	20	511	65	26	2	17	61	33	130	23	14	.240/.295/.412	.233	.295	-1.9	3B(94): 4.8	0.1
2013	*ATL*	*MLB*	*21*	*250*	*25*	*9*	*1*	*6*	*24*	*10*	*74*	*7*	*4*	*.205/.239/.328*	*.206*	*.265*	*0.2*	*3B 4, SS 0*	*-0.3*

The waiting is the hardest part. Salcedo has the raw tools to become a special player down the road. He can hit for average and power alike, and his strong arm and reactions should play at third base. Add in the credit he receives for good makeup and you get the feeling he's going to push himself as hard as he can to reach his upside. But no amount of pushing can speed up the developmental process. He's still young, raw, and at least two years away.

Jordan Schafer CF
Born: 9/4/1986 Age: 26
Bats: L Throws: L Height: 6' 2"
Weight: 200 Breakout: 5%
Improve: 64% Collapse: 6%
Attrition: 25% MLB: 95%
Comparables:
Dave Collins,Donell Nixon,Jeff Salazar

YEAR	TEAM	LVL	AGE	PA	R	2B	3B	HR	RBI	BB	SO	SB	CS	AVG_OBP_SLG	TAv	BABIP	BRR	FRAA	WARP
2010	MIS	AA	23	72	7	3	0	0	5	8	12	1	1	.175/.268/.222	.224	.216	0.2	LF(13): 0.2, CF(4): -0.3	0.1
2010	GWN	AAA	23	209	16	5	1	1	8	14	47	9	8	.201/.250/.254	.192	.253	-2.3	CF(48): 4.1, RF(4): 0.5	-0.8
2011	GWN	AAA	24	186	21	8	0	1	21	14	28	6	3	.256/.309/.323	.229	.297	0	--	0.0
2011	ATL	MLB	24	219	32	6	3	1	7	18	42	15	4	.240/.307/.316	.237	.301	1.4	CF(51): 0.2	0.0
2011	HOU	MLB	24	118	14	4	0	1	6	10	28	7	0	.245/.314/.311	.232	.321	2.2	CF(27): 0.5	0.1
2012	HOU	MLB	25	360	40	10	2	4	23	36	106	27	9	.211/.297/.294	.224	.304	4.2	CF(86): -4.2	-0.7
2013	*ATL*	*MLB*	*26*	*335*	*41*	*12*	*2*	*4*	*22*	*31*	*88*	*18*	*6*	*.218/.293/.308*	*.223*	*.288*	*1.3*	*CF -1, LF -0*	*-0.2*

Nearly 900 plate appearances into his big-league career, it's time to admit that Schafer is unlikely to become a tolerable hitter. His defensive reputation is solid, and his ability to swipe bases at a fair clip gives him value. He could be useful as a fifth outfielder. Atlanta reacquired Schafer off waivers a little more than a year after sending him to Houston in the Michael Bourn trade.

Andrelton Simmons SS
Born: **9/4/1989** Age: **23**
Bats: **R** Throws: **R** Height: **6' 3"**
Weight: **170** Breakout: **2%**
Improve: **39%** Collapse: **11%**
Attrition: **19%** MLB: **91%**

Comparables:
Osvaldo Martinez,Bucky Dent,Harvey Kuenn

YEAR	TEAM	LVL	AGE	PA	R	2B	3B	HR	RBI	BB	SO	SB	CS	AVG_OBP_SLG	TAv	BABIP	BRR	FRAA	WARP
2010	DNV	Rk	20	269	36	11	1	2	26	16	14	18	4	.276/.343/.356	.295	.286	0.7	SS(62): 11.9	3.7
2011	LYN	A+	21	570	69	35	6	1	52	29	43	26	18	.311/.351/.408	.271	.334	-0.5	SS(88): 14.1	3.6
2012	MIS	AA	22	203	29	9	2	3	21	20	20	10	2	.293/.372/.420	.272	.314	-0.6	SS(14): 3.4	0.7
2012	ATL	MLB	22	182	17	8	2	3	19	12	21	1	0	.289/.335/.416	.264	.310	1.8	SS(49): 7.5	1.5
2013	*ATL*	*MLB*	*23*	*250*	*28*	*11*	*2*	*3*	*20*	*13*	*33*	*8*	*3*	*.258/.299/.361*	*.239*	*.284*	*0.2*	*SS 6*	*1.2*

The wackiest rumor of spring 2012 had Simmons opening the season as the Braves' every-day shortstop. Right, we all said, as if the Braves would rush a 22-year-old without experience above A-ball to the majors. Sure enough, Simmons started the season in Double-A. But while Simmons started off like a house on fire, Pastornicky started off like that house after its flames were extinguished: cold, wet, and stinky. The Braves made the switch and didn't regret it. Simmons is a special defender and will become one of the top shortstops in the league if his bat doesn't hold him back.

Joe Terdoslavich 3B
Born: **9/9/1988** Age: **24**
Bats: **B** Throws: **R** Height: **6' 2"**
Weight: **200** Breakout: **15%**
Improve: **56%** Collapse: **3%**
Attrition: **18%** MLB: **95%**

Comparables:
Brandon Snyder,Mike Ivie,Adrian Gonzalez

YEAR	TEAM	LVL	AGE	PA	R	2B	3B	HR	RBI	BB	SO	SB	CS	AVG_OBP_SLG	TAv	BABIP	BRR	FRAA	WARP
2010	DNV	Rk	21	205	27	10	2	2	24	15	27	3	3	.296/.351/.402	.293	.338	-0.2	1B(30): -2.4, 3B(18): 0.4	0.9
2010	ROM	A	21	85	7	9	0	0	10	5	18	0	0	.316/.365/.430	.289	.410	-1.6	3B(18): -2.5, 1B(3): 0.1	0.0
2011	LYN	A+	22	536	72	52	2	20	82	41	107	2	0	.286/.341/.526	.283	.324	-0.3	1B(71): 0.5, 3B(2): -0.2	1.2
2012	MIS	AA	23	333	43	24	5	5	51	27	62	4	0	.315/.372/.480	.339	.377	-1.4	1B(19): -0.1, 3B(4): -0.6	0.5
2012	GWN	AAA	23	215	19	4	0	4	20	19	50	3	0	.180/.252/.263	.223	.220	2.4	3B(16): -1.5	-0.1
2013	*ATL*	*MLB*	*24*	*250*	*22*	*12*	*1*	*5*	*26*	*15*	*61*	*0*	*0*	*.232/.278/.362*	*.230*	*.288*	*-0.3*	*1B -3, 3B -0*	*-0.8*

Terdoslavich followed up a breakout season by changing positions. He moved back across the diamond to third base after reaching Triple-A. The book on Terdoslavich has been that he can hit well but lacks the raw power to merit consideration as a first-base prospect. At third, the expectations for power are lower. With some passable defense, Terdoslavich may develop into a second-division starter. Provided, that is, his bat bounces back from an ugly stint at Gwinnett.

Dan Uggla 2B
Born: **3/11/1980** Age: **33**
Bats: **R** Throws: **R** Height: **6' 0"**
Weight: **205** Breakout: **1%**
Improve: **30%** Collapse: **3%**
Attrition: **9%** MLB: **92%**

Comparables:
Woodie Held,Bobby Grich,Ryne Sandberg

YEAR	TEAM	LVL	AGE	PA	R	2B	3B	HR	RBI	BB	SO	SB	CS	AVG_OBP_SLG	TAv	BABIP	BRR	FRAA	WARP
2010	FLO	MLB	30	674	100	31	0	33	105	78	149	4	1	.287/.369/.508	.309	.330	0.6	2B(158): -5.0	5.2
2011	ATL	MLB	31	672	88	22	1	36	82	62	156	1	3	.233/.311/.453	.272	.253	1.9	2B(159): -3.6	1.9
2012	ATL	MLB	32	630	86	29	0	19	78	94	168	4	3	.220/.348/.384	.271	.283	0	2B(152): 13.8	3.3
2013	*ATL*	*MLB*	*33*	*600*	*76*	*25*	*1*	*27*	*85*	*71*	*150*	*3*	*2*	*.239/.335/.444*	*.280*	*.282*	*-1.3*	*2B -3*	*3.0*

Here's a thought sure to keep Braves fans up all night: Uggla has three years remaining on his contract. The closest thing baseball has to a Popeye lookalike made contact at a career-worst rate in 2012. When he did hit the ball, he didn't do as much damage as in the past, as evidenced by a career-low ISO. Uggla did walk a ton, but he's at the uncomfortable point where a complete offensive collapse would surprise no one. This could be a long three years because Uggla's bat is his one positive attribute.

B.J. Upton CF
Born: **8/21/1984** Age: **28**
Bats: **R** Throws: **R** Height: **6' 4"**
Weight: **185** Breakout: **1%**
Improve: **38%** Collapse: **2%**
Attrition: **7%** MLB: **95%**

Comparables:
Merv Rettenmund,Carlos Beltran,Chris Young

YEAR	TEAM	LVL	AGE	PA	R	2B	3B	HR	RBI	BB	SO	SB	CS	AVG_OBP_SLG	TAv	BABIP	BRR	FRAA	WARP
2010	TBA	MLB	25	610	89	38	4	18	62	67	164	42	9	.237/.322/.424	.268	.304	4.6	CF(154): 4.5	3.7
2011	TBA	MLB	26	640	82	27	4	23	81	71	161	36	12	.243/.331/.429	.278	.298	2.3	CF(151): 1.5	3.0
2012	TBA	MLB	27	633	79	29	3	28	78	45	169	31	6	.246/.298/.454	.277	.294	3.5	CF(142): -6.5	2.1
2013	*ATL*	*MLB*	*28*	*598*	*79*	*31*	*3*	*17*	*66*	*63*	*150*	*37*	*10*	*.246/.327/.409*	*.265*	*.309*	*3.3*	*CF 6*	*3.2*

For the third straight year, Upton waited until late to get hot, this time after also waiting to get started at all after a spring training back injury cost him the first three weeks of the season. After July 31, he exploded, hitting 19 of his 28 homers to help bring his final numbers remarkably close to 2011's, albeit with fewer walks and an FRAA plunge. But was his wow September (941 OPS, 12 homers) traceable not only to a career trend but also to contract-year urgency? Upton's inconsistent productivity, focus, and (perceived) effort have vexed his adherents, because he's clearly a gifted five-tool player who can carry a team when it matters. He has just entered his prime. Whose prime will it be, though? Curtis Granderson's? Alfonso Soriano's? Or will Upton mature into a more taciturn Torii Hunter? One parting question: How will natural grass affect his game?

PITCHERS

Luis Avilan

Born: **7/19/1989** Age: **23**
Bats: **L** Throws: **L** Height: **6' 3"** Weight: **165**
Breakout: **29%** Improve: **50%** Collapse: **26%**
Attrition: **24%** MLB: **87%**

Comparables:
Julian Tavarez,Seth Morehead,Fabio Castro

YEAR	TEAM	LVL	AGE	W	L	SV	G	GS	IP	H	HR	BB	SO	BB9	SO9	GB%	BABIP	WHIP	ERA	FIP	FRA	WARP
2010	ROM	A	20	2	1	0	10	0	20^{2}	15	1	9	21	3.9	9.1	54%	.255	1.16	2.61	3.58	4.07	0.2
2010	MYR	A+	20	4	3	9	31	0	48	42	5	18	37	3.4	6.9	48%	.264	1.25	3.94	4.53	5.59	-0.4
2011	MIS	AA	21	4	8	1	36	13	106^{1}	113	10	36	78	3.0	6.6	—	.300	1.40	4.57	4.30	4.68	0.0
2012	MIS	AA	22	3	6	1	16	12	61^{1}	50	7	31	55	4.5	8.1	54%	.268	1.32	3.23	4.40	5.24	0.2
2012	ATL	MLB	22	1	0	0	31	0	36	27	1	10	33	2.5	8.2	48%	.268	1.03	2.00	2.58	2.87	0.6
2013	*ATL*	*MLB*	*23*	*2*	*1*	*0*	*20*	*2*	*37^{2}*	*35*	*4*	*17*	*32*	*4.0*	*7.6*	*46%*	*.299*	*1.38*	*4.40*	*4.24*	*4.78*	*0.0*

Avilan showed effectiveness against lefties and righties alike in his first big-league season. His sinker showed added pep coming out of the bullpen, sitting at around 93 miles per hour. Meanwhile, he kept batters off balance with his curveball and changeup. There were some questions about how Avilan's stuff would translate, not just to the majors but the upper minors, too. The last two seasons have gone a long way to confirm Avilan as big-league quality.

Miguel Batista

Born: **2/19/1971** Age: **42**
Bats: **R** Throws: **R** Height: **6' 2"** Weight: **210**
Breakout: **16%** Improve: **33%** Collapse: **23%**
Attrition: **8%** MLB: **65%**

Comparables:
Murry Dickson,Virgil Trucks,Woodie Fryman

YEAR	TEAM	LVL	AGE	W	L	SV	G	GS	IP	H	HR	BB	SO	BB9	SO9	GB%	BABIP	WHIP	ERA	FIP	FRA	WARP
2010	WAS	MLB	39	1	2	2	58	1	82^{2}	71	9	39	55	4.2	6.0	51%	.256	1.33	3.70	4.79	5.58	-0.4
2011	BUF	AAA	40	3	0	0	10	8	46^{2}	46	4	25	36	4.8	6.9	52%	.260	1.52	4.24	4.54	4.93	0.1
2011	NYN	MLB	40	2	0	0	9	4	30^{2}	22	0	14	15	4.1	4.4	53%	.234	1.17	2.64	3.58	4.06	0.2
2011	SLN	MLB	40	3	2	0	26	1	29^{1}	27	2	19	16	5.8	4.9	39%	.260	1.57	4.60	5.14	5.74	-0.4
2012	BIN	AA	41	0	1	0	1	1	7	4	1	4	3	5.1	3.9	52%	.150	1.14	5.14	5.92	6.30	-0.1
2012	GWN	AAA	41	1	1	0	6	4	24	19	2	10	21	3.8	7.9	57%	.262	1.21	3.38	3.87	4.54	-0.1
2012	ATL	MLB	41	0	0	0	5	0	6	5	1	2	2	3.0	3.0	40%	.211	1.17	3.00	5.64	5.81	-0.1
2012	NYN	MLB	41	1	3	0	30	5	46^{2}	53	5	31	34	6.0	6.6	49%	.322	1.80	4.82	5.13	5.50	-0.4
2013	*ATL*	*MLB*	*42*	*3*	*2*	*0*	*32*	*5*	*58^{2}*	*58*	*7*	*31*	*40*	*4.7*	*6.1*	*47%*	*.292*	*1.51*	*5.07*	*4.97*	*5.51*	*-0.5*

Batista opened the season with the Mets and made 35 appearances in New York, including five starts, before his July release. The Braves signed him for depth purposes and later gave him five appearances of little consequence. He turned 42 in February and there's reason to think this could be the end of the line. If so, Batista spent time with 11 teams over 18 seasons and set himself up for a second career as an author.

Brandon Beachy

Born: **9/3/1986** Age: **26**
Bats: **R** Throws: **R** Height: **6' 4"** Weight: **215**
Breakout: **28%** Improve: **59%** Collapse: **12%**
Attrition: **10%** MLB: **99%**

Comparables:
Adam Wainwright,Pedro Martinez,Vida Blue

YEAR	TEAM	LVL	AGE	W	L	SV	G	GS	IP	H	HR	BB	SO	BB9	SO9	GB%	BABIP	WHIP	ERA	FIP	FRA	WARP
2010	MIS	AA	23	3	1	1	27	6	73^{2}	53	3	22	100	2.7	12.2	43%	.298	1.02	1.47	2.18	2.50	2.3
2010	GWN	AAA	23	2	0	1	8	7	45^{2}	40	2	6	48	1.2	9.5	45%	.295	1.01	2.17	2.28	3.39	1.0
2010	ATL	MLB	23	0	2	0	3	3	15	16	0	7	15	4.2	9.0	33%	.356	1.53	3.00	2.51	2.52	0.5
2011	GWN	AAA	24	1	0	0	1	1	5	4	1	2	8	3.6	14.4	—	.300	1.20	1.80	3.84	4.17	0.0
2011	ATL	MLB	24	7	3	0	25	25	141^{2}	125	16	46	169	2.9	10.7	36%	.307	1.21	3.68	3.16	3.60	2.1
2012	ATL	MLB	25	5	5	0	13	13	81	49	6	29	68	3.2	7.6	42%	.200	0.96	2.00	3.53	4.14	1.0
2013	*ATL*	*MLB*	*26*	*5*	*3*	*0*	*16*	*12*	*76^{1}*	*63*	*7*	*24*	*76*	*2.8*	*9.0*	*40%*	*.292*	*1.14*	*3.25*	*3.34*	*3.53*	*1.2*

We may look back one day and wonder what could have been. A case of elbow soreness led to a case of Tommy John surgery in June. The operation ended Beachy's season and his Cy Young candidacy with a thud. While all the projections that labeled Beachy a back-end starter in the making appear silly now, it's worth noting that Justin Verlander threw more innings last season than Beachy has in his big-league career. There's no question Beachy has pitched like a frontline starter over the past two seasons. You'd just like to see him cement himself by making a full slate of starts.

Billy Bullock

Born: **2/27/1988** Age: **25**
Bats: **R** Throws: **R** Height: **6' 7"** Weight: **225**
Breakout: **30%** Improve: **53%** Collapse: **26%**
Attrition: **8%** MLB: **84%**

Comparables:
Wesley Wright,Frank Francisco,Stan Belinda

YEAR	TEAM	LVL	AGE	W	L	SV	G	GS	IP	H	HR	BB	SO	BB9	SO9	GB%	BABIP	WHIP	ERA	FIP	FRA	WARP
2010	FTM	A+	22	0	4	14	28	0	37^{1}	39	2	19	45	4.6	10.9	46%	.398	1.55	3.62	3.49	3.79	0.5
2010	NBR	AA	22	2	4	13	30	0	36^{2}	34	3	24	60	5.9	14.7	40%	.380	1.58	3.43	3.36	3.21	0.9
2011	MIS	AA	23	3	1	11	50	0	49^{2}	35	2	34	65	6.2	11.8	—	.284	1.39	4.53	3.81	4.14	0.0
2011	GWN	AAA	23	1	0	0	1	0	1	2	0	0	1	0.0	9.0	—	.500	2.00	0.00	1.24	1.34	0.0
2012	MIS	AA	24	1	2	1	26	0	39^{1}	30	3	33	41	7.6	9.4	46%	.273	1.60	3.89	4.80	6.16	-0.2
2012	GWN	AAA	24	0	0	0	14	0	20^{1}	33	4	23	26	10.2	11.5	44%	.453	2.75	11.07	6.70	8.61	-0.6
2013	*ATL*	*MLB*	*25*	*1*	*0*	*1*	*26*	*0*	*35^{2}*	*32*	*4*	*21*	*38*	*5.4*	*9.7*	*42%*	*.316*	*1.49*	*4.72*	*4.29*	*5.13*	*-0.2*

The jokes wrote themselves when the Twins traded Bullock to the Braves for Scott Diamond—trading a hard-thrower for a soft-thrower is such a Twins thing to do. But while Diamond had a successful season for the Twins in 2012, Bullock spent the year walking nearly a batter per inning in the upper minors. Bullock has the stuff to become a late-inning force—a mid-90s fastball and occasionally plus slider—but his command and control issues may sabotage his efforts. He'll give the upper minors another go in 2013. Hopefully this time his pitches can find the plate.

David Carpenter
Born: **7/15/1985** Age: **27**
Bats: **R** Throws: **R** Height: **6' 3"** Weight: **210**
Breakout: **26%** Improve: **52%** Collapse: **32%**
Attrition: **29%** MLB: **66%**
Comparables:
Chad Orvella, Luis Perdomo, Jorge Julio

YEAR	TEAM	LVL	AGE	W	L	SV	G	GS	IP	H	HR	BB	SO	BB9	SO9	GB%	BABIP	WHIP	ERA	FIP	FRA	WARP
2011	CCH	AA	25	0	1	5	14	0	14	14	4	3	17	1.9	10.9	—	.303	1.21	4.50	5.73	6.23	0.0
2011	OKL	AAA	25	0	0	9	19	0	19	15	0	6	21	2.8	9.9	—	.306	1.11	0.00	2.52	2.74	0.0
2011	HOU	MLB	25	1	3	1	34	0	27^{2}	28	3	13	29	4.2	9.4	44%	.329	1.48	2.93	4.15	4.51	0.1
2012	LVG	AAA	26	0	1	1	16	0	17^{2}	15	1	7	19	3.6	9.7	42%	.298	1.25	3.57	3.61	4.38	0.3
2012	OKL	AAA	26	1	0	3	7	0	8^{2}	7	1	0	6	0.0	6.2	52%	.231	0.81	2.08	3.78	5.94	0.0
2012	HOU	MLB	26	0	2	0	30	0	29^{2}	43	4	14	27	4.2	8.2	43%	.402	1.92	6.07	4.59	4.61	0.2
2012	TOR	MLB	26	0	0	0	3	0	2^{2}	8	1	2	4	6.8	13.5	54%	.583	3.75	30.38	8.30	6.84	-0.1
2013	*ATL*	*MLB*	*27*	*2*	*1*	*1*	*38*	*0*	*38^{2}*	*37*	*4*	*17*	*35*	*3.9*	*8.1*	*41%*	*.314*	*1.40*	*4.55*	*4.05*	*4.94*	*-0.1*

Since last July, Carpenter has been employed by four organizations, finally landing with Atlanta after the Braves claimed him off of waivers from Boston at the end of November. Such is the life of a replacement-level relief pitcher. Carpenter shined for the Astros in the second half of 2011, but a propensity for putting runners on base soured his sophomore effort, a year in which he was one of only five pitchers to throw at least 30 innings with an earned-run average north of eight.

Randall Delgado
Born: **2/9/1990** Age: **23**
Bats: **R** Throws: **R** Height: **6' 4"** Weight: **200**
Breakout: **35%** Improve: **63%** Collapse: **18%**
Attrition: **21%** MLB: **93%**
Comparables:
Juan Morillo, Homer Bailey, Tyler Clippard

YEAR	TEAM	LVL	AGE	W	L	SV	G	GS	IP	H	HR	BB	SO	BB9	SO9	GB%	BABIP	WHIP	ERA	FIP	FRA	WARP
2010	MYR	A+	20	4	7	0	20	20	117^{1}	89	7	32	120	2.5	9.2	54%	.271	1.03	2.76	3.13	4.02	1.3
2010	MIS	AA	20	3	5	0	8	8	43^{2}	36	2	20	42	4.1	8.6	44%	.274	1.28	4.74	3.57	4.55	0.4
2011	MIS	AA	21	5	5	0	21	21	117^{1}	116	11	46	110	3.5	8.4	—	.312	1.38	3.84	3.93	4.27	0.0
2011	GWN	AAA	21	2	2	0	4	4	21^{2}	19	4	11	25	4.6	10.4	—	.288	1.38	4.15	4.85	5.27	0.0
2011	ATL	MLB	21	1	1	0	7	7	35	29	5	14	18	3.6	4.6	40%	.220	1.23	2.83	5.11	5.80	-0.3
2012	GWN	AAA	22	4	3	0	8	8	44^{1}	47	6	21	51	4.3	10.4	44%	.353	1.53	4.06	4.11	5.83	0.0
2012	ATL	MLB	22	4	9	0	18	17	92^{2}	89	8	42	76	4.1	7.4	52%	.299	1.41	4.37	4.11	4.70	0.9
2013	*ATL*	*MLB*	*23*	*5*	*5*	*0*	*15*	*15*	*80^{2}*	*77*	*10*	*37*	*68*	*4.1*	*7.6*	*46%*	*.301*	*1.41*	*4.65*	*4.50*	*5.06*	*-0.2*

There were murmurs early in the season that Delgado was tipping his pitches, with batters able to see more white on the ball during his delivery on curveballs. If the observation is true, and there's no reason to believe it isn't, then you'd be hard-pressed to find proof of it in the numbers, which remained constant throughout the year. Pitch-tipping or not, Delgado projects to become a third starter behind his fastball-changeup combination. Should he live up to the billing, the comparisons to Jair Jurrjens of yesteryear will look silly.

Chad Durbin
Born: **12/3/1977** Age: **35**
Bats: **R** Throws: **R** Height: **6' 3"** Weight: **225**
Breakout: **17%** Improve: **65%** Collapse: **25%**
Attrition: **8%** MLB: **82%**
Comparables:
Jim Gott, Kerry Ligtenberg, Dave Veres

YEAR	TEAM	LVL	AGE	W	L	SV	G	GS	IP	H	HR	BB	SO	BB9	SO9	GB%	BABIP	WHIP	ERA	FIP	FRA	WARP
2010	CLR	A+	32	1	0	0	2	0	3	0	0	0	3	0.0	9.0	50%	.000	0.00	0.00	1.44	2.76	0.1
2010	PHI	MLB	32	4	1	0	64	0	68^{2}	63	7	27	63	3.5	8.3	45%	.296	1.31	3.80	3.99	4.24	0.6
2011	CLE	MLB	33	2	2	0	56	0	68^{1}	86	12	26	59	3.4	7.8	41%	.339	1.64	5.53	4.89	4.59	0.4
2012	ATL	MLB	34	4	1	1	76	0	61	52	9	28	49	4.1	7.2	48%	.251	1.31	3.10	4.82	5.30	-0.3
2013	*ATL*	*MLB*	*35*	*3*	*1*	*0*	*56*	*0*	*56^{2}*	*51*	*6*	*23*	*50*	*3.7*	*7.9*	*45%*	*.296*	*1.32*	*4.13*	*4.03*	*4.49*	*0.1*

There was reason to expect little from Durbin when the Braves signed him. Not only was he coming off a poor season with Cleveland but the Nationals then released him before the season started. Nonetheless, Durbin provided value. He held right-handers in check while ducking left-handers as often as he could. The bounce-back should give Durbin enough credibility to land another middle-relief job on a big-league deal.

Cory Gearrin
Born: **4/14/1986** Age: **27**
Bats: **R** Throws: **R** Height: **6' 4"** Weight: **200**
Breakout: **39%** Improve: **49%** Collapse: **40%**
Attrition: **16%** MLB: **87%**
Comparables:
Andrew Brown, Sergio Santos, Josh Roenicke

YEAR	TEAM	LVL	AGE	W	L	SV	G	GS	IP	H	HR	BB	SO	BB9	SO9	GB%	BABIP	WHIP	ERA	FIP	FRA	WARP
2010	GWN	AAA	24	3	5	0	52	0	80^{1}	72	6	32	66	3.6	7.4	62%	.284	1.30	3.36	4.15	5.10	0.4
2011	GWN	AAA	25	4	1	4	35	0	50	42	0	20	60	3.6	10.8	—	.328	1.24	1.80	2.22	2.41	0.0
2011	ATL	MLB	25	1	1	0	18	0	18^{1}	17	0	12	25	5.9	12.3	61%	.370	1.58	7.85	2.56	3.26	0.3
2012	GWN	AAA	26	3	3	9	39	0	54^{2}	43	0	22	66	3.6	10.9	68%	.317	1.19	2.30	2.06	2.56	0.8
2012	ATL	MLB	26	0	1	0	22	0	20	17	1	5	20	2.2	9.0	58%	.308	1.10	1.80	2.84	4.04	0.2
2013	*ATL*	*MLB*	*27*	*1*	*1*	*0*	*29*	*0*	*37^{2}*	*31*	*3*	*16*	*39*	*3.8*	*9.3*	*54%*	*.300*	*1.25*	*3.68*	*3.44*	*4.00*	*0.3*

If Atlanta has a Peter Moylan succession plan, you better believe Gearrin is the fulcrum. He shares a lot of qualities with Moylan: arm slot, stuff, and relative strengths and weaknesses. There isn't much left for Gearrin to do at Triple-A since he's spent the past three seasons there. Gearrin will become a fixture in Atlanta's bullpen at some point soon, likely as a right-handed specialist.

Sean Gilmartin

Born: **5/8/1990** Age: **23**
Bats: **L** Throws: **L** Height: **6' 3"** Weight: **195**
Breakout: **28%** Improve: **61%** Collapse: **17%**
Attrition: **12%** MLB: **92%**

Comparables:
Mike Mussina, Dontrelle Willis, Ryan Feierabend

YEAR	TEAM	LVL	AGE	W	L	SV	G	GS	IP	H	HR	BB	SO	BB9	SO9	GB%	BABIP	WHIP	ERA	FIP	FRA	WARP
2011	BRA	Rk	21	0	1	0	1	1	2	3	0	0	1	0.0	4.5	38%	.375	1.50	9.00	2.42	6.12	0.0
2011	ROM	A	21	2	1	0	5	5	21^{1}	18	3	2	30	0.8	12.7	29%	.341	0.94	2.53	2.82	3.54	0.5
2012	MIS	AA	22	5	8	0	20	20	119^{1}	111	9	26	86	2.0	6.5	47%	.283	1.15	3.54	3.44	4.64	0.3
2012	GWN	AAA	22	1	2	0	7	7	37^{2}	41	6	13	25	3.1	6.0	34%	.285	1.43	4.78	4.94	6.40	-0.1
2013	*ATL*	*MLB*	*23*	*2*	*3*	*0*	*8*	*8*	*41^{1}*	*43*	*6*	*12*	*29*	*2.6*	*6.3*	*42%*	*.304*	*1.32*	*4.57*	*4.55*	*4.97*	*-0.0*

The Braves' first-round pick in 2011, Gilmartin reached Triple-A in his first full professional season. There's reason to believe he could reach Atlanta in his second. Gilmartin throws strikes and attacks batters with a three-pitch mix. His changeup is the best offering of the bunch, and grades out as an above-average offering. The fastball is nothing special from a velocity standpoint—often sitting in the high-80s—but Gilmartin can put it where he wants and cut it when he wants. His outlook varies from mid- to back-end starter, depending on how sold you are on his ability to overcome his so-so stuff.

J.R. Graham

Born: **1/14/1990** Age: **23**
Bats: **R** Throws: **R** Height: **6' 1"** Weight: **185**
Breakout: **26%** Improve: **57%** Collapse: **21%**
Attrition: **14%** MLB: **83%**

Comparables:
Vance Worley, Alex Sanabia, Sean O'Sullivan

YEAR	TEAM	LVL	AGE	W	L	SV	G	GS	IP	H	HR	BB	SO	BB9	SO9	GB%	BABIP	WHIP	ERA	FIP	FRA	WARP
2011	DNV	Rk	21	5	2	0	13	8	57^{2}	52	0	13	52	2.0	8.1	60%	.266	1.13	1.72	2.71	4.07	0.7
2012	LYN	A+	22	9	1	0	17	17	102^{2}	88	6	17	68	1.5	6.0	59%	.269	1.02	2.63	3.38	4.86	0.8
2012	MIS	AA	22	3	1	0	9	9	45^{1}	35	2	17	42	3.4	8.3	56%	.266	1.15	3.18	3.12	3.45	0.1
2013	*ATL*	*MLB*	*23*	*2*	*3*	*0*	*7*	*7*	*39^{1}*	*40*	*5*	*14*	*25*	*3.3*	*5.8*	*53%*	*.301*	*1.40*	*4.77*	*4.65*	*5.19*	*-0.1*

Graham may have entered the season as a sleeper arm in the system, but his performance in the Southern League served as an alarm clock. Nobody's sleeping anymore. Although Graham is a small right-hander, his fantastic athleticism and sinker—one of the best in the league—give him a shot at starting, as does the development of his secondary offerings. He'll need to keep working, but the odds of him sticking in the rotation are higher now than they were a year ago.

Tim Hudson

Born: **7/14/1975** Age: **37**
Bats: **R** Throws: **R** Height: **6' 2"** Weight: **175**
Breakout: **13%** Improve: **44%** Collapse: **29%**
Attrition: **21%** MLB: **83%**

Comparables:
Chris Carpenter, R.A. Dickey, Derek Lowe

YEAR	TEAM	LVL	AGE	W	L	SV	G	GS	IP	H	HR	BB	SO	BB9	SO9	GB%	BABIP	WHIP	ERA	FIP	FRA	WARP
2010	ATL	MLB	34	17	9	0	34	34	228^{2}	189	20	74	139	2.9	5.5	65%	.249	1.15	2.83	4.12	5.14	1.6
2011	ATL	MLB	35	16	10	0	33	33	215	189	14	56	158	2.3	6.6	58%	.273	1.14	3.22	3.36	4.41	1.7
2012	ROM	A	36	0	2	0	2	2	7	13	0	1	1	1.3	1.3	67%	.433	2.00	7.71	4.15	6.25	0.0
2012	GWN	AAA	36	2	0	0	2	2	10^{2}	8	0	5	8	4.2	6.8	62%	.235	1.22	0.84	3.06	2.63	0.0
2012	ATL	MLB	36	16	7	0	28	28	179	168	12	48	102	2.4	5.1	56%	.270	1.21	3.62	3.82	5.13	0.1
2013	*ATL*	*MLB*	*37*	*11*	*8*	*0*	*26*	*26*	*166^{2}*	*151*	*15*	*46*	*110*	*2.5*	*6.0*	*59%*	*.282*	*1.18*	*3.53*	*3.88*	*3.84*	*1.9*

Hudson failed to record 200 innings for the first time since 2009. He missed most of April while recovering from offseason back surgery to correct a herniated disc. When Hudson returned, he proved his five-pitch mix remains effective. He fills up the bottom of the zone on both sides of the plate, putting on a clinic in how to sequence and keep batters guessing. Hudson turns 38 in July and is under contract for one more season. There's no telling how long he wants to pitch, but it would be a surprise if he finishes his career outside of Atlanta.

Juan Jaime

Born: **8/2/1987** Age: **25**
Bats: **R** Throws: **R** Height: **6' 2"** Weight: **230**
Breakout: **35%** Improve: **61%** Collapse: **11%**
Attrition: **6%** MLB: **89%**

Comparables:
Bobby Bolin, Daniel Bard, Tom Gordon

YEAR	TEAM	LVL	AGE	W	L	SV	G	GS	IP	H	HR	BB	SO	BB9	SO9	GB%	BABIP	WHIP	ERA	FIP	FRA	WARP
2012	LYN	A+	24	1	3	18	42	0	51^{1}	31	4	33	73	5.8	12.8	36%	.257	1.25	3.16	3.72	3.95	0.9
2013	*ATL*	*MLB*	*25*	*1*	*1*	*1*	*29*	*0*	*36*	*30*	*4*	*22*	*40*	*5.5*	*9.9*	*40%*	*.307*	*1.45*	*4.45*	*4.26*	*4.84*	*-0.1*

Jaime is a 25-year-old reliever without so much as a cup of Double-A coffee, and he missed the 2010 and 2011 seasons after undergoing Tommy John surgery. Yet teams cannot help themselves from claiming him on waivers. Such is the allure of an arm with plus-plus velocity. Whether Jaime will ever use that velocity effectively is the big question. His command profile is poor thanks to his delivery, and his secondary offerings are lacking. Expect Jaime to receive plenty of opportunities to develop into a big-league caliber arm.

Jair Jurrjens

Born: **1/29/1986** Age: **27**
Bats: **R** Throws: **R** Height: **6' 2"** Weight: **200**
Breakout: **17%** Improve: **45%** Collapse: **27%**
Attrition: **9%** MLB: **94%**

Comparables:
Jon Garland, Brian Bannister, Shawn Hill

YEAR	TEAM	LVL	AGE	W	L	SV	G	GS	IP	H	HR	BB	SO	BB9	SO9	GB%	BABIP	WHIP	ERA	FIP	FRA	WARP
2010	GWN	AAA	24	1	1	0	3	3	13	20	2	6	9	4.2	6.2	58%	.391	2.00	5.54	5.29	6.76	-0.1
2010	ATL	MLB	24	7	6	0	20	20	116^1	120	13	42	86	3.2	6.7	43%	.300	1.39	4.64	4.22	4.62	1.1
2011	GWN	AAA	25	1	0	0	1	1	6	4	1	2	3	3.0	4.5	—	.176	1.00	3.00	5.40	5.87	0.0
2011	ATL	MLB	25	13	6	0	23	23	152	142	14	44	90	2.6	5.3	44%	.269	1.22	2.96	3.95	4.77	0.2
2012	GWN	AAA	26	4	6	0	14	14	72^1	79	10	16	39	2.0	4.9	42%	.284	1.31	4.98	4.58	7.90	-0.3
2012	ATL	MLB	26	3	4	0	11	10	48^1	72	8	18	19	3.4	3.5	40%	.354	1.86	6.89	5.68	5.92	-0.3
2013	*ATL*	*MLB*	*27*	*5*	*5*	*0*	*14*	*14*	*80^2*	*77*	*8*	*25*	*58*	*2.8*	*6.4*	*45%*	*.294*	*1.26*	*3.96*	*3.98*	*4.31*	*0.5*

My, my, my, what a mess. A season removed from an All-Star appearance, Jurrjens fell to pieces. Four disastrous starts were enough to merit a trip down to the minors. Jurrjens pitched poorly against Triple-A batters yet still had the nerve to complain that he didn't feel wanted. When he returned to the majors, he made seven appearances and allowed 23 runs in 32 innings. The Braves shut him down in early August due to a strained groin, ending his season two months early. Atlanta had two choices with Jurrjens: Trade him for a song or non-tender him. Given Jurrjens' arbitration eligibility and price tag ($5.5 million), cutting him loose was an easy call.

Craig Kimbrel

Born: **5/28/1988** Age: **25**
Bats: **R** Throws: **R** Height: **6' 0"** Weight: **205**
Breakout: **20%** Improve: **43%** Collapse: **23%**
Attrition: **12%** MLB: **93%**

Comparables:
Jonathan Broxton, David Robertson, Francisco Rodriguez

YEAR	TEAM	LVL	AGE	W	L	SV	G	GS	IP	H	HR	BB	SO	BB9	SO9	GB%	BABIP	WHIP	ERA	FIP	FRA	WARP
2010	GWN	AAA	22	3	2	23	48	0	55^2	28	3	35	83	5.7	13.4	59%	.238	1.13	1.62	3.11	3.74	0.8
2010	ATL	MLB	22	4	0	1	21	0	20^2	9	0	16	40	7.0	17.4	28%	.281	1.21	0.44	1.56	0.51	0.9
2011	ATL	MLB	23	4	3	46	79	0	77	48	3	32	127	3.7	14.8	45%	.315	1.04	2.10	1.49	2.18	2.1
2012	ATL	MLB	24	3	1	42	63	0	62^2	27	3	14	116	2.0	16.7	49%	.250	0.65	1.01	0.82	1.44	2.2
2013	*ATL*	*MLB*	*25*	*3*	*2*	*38*	*56*	*0*	*57*	*31*	*3*	*25*	*91*	*3.9*	*14.4*	*48%*	*.292*	*0.99*	*1.82*	*2.01*	*1.98*	*1.9*

If not for Fernando Rodney's record-breaking ERA, Kimbrel might have received the attention he deserved as arguably the best relief pitcher in the league. Choosing a ridiculous factoid to print here among ample options proved harder than you might anticipate. In the end, the winner was this: Kimbrel had more multi-strikeout appearances (41) than appearances in which he allowed a baserunner (33). Injury might be the only thing preventing Kimbrel from dominating over the next decade, as his fastball-slider combination makes the best hitters in the world look like they're swinging at a Wiffle ball.

Paul Maholm

Born: **6/25/1982** Age: **31**
Bats: **L** Throws: **L** Height: **6' 3"** Weight: **220**
Breakout: **14%** Improve: **57%** Collapse: **16%**
Attrition: **12%** MLB: **81%**

Comparables:
Jarrod Washburn, Chris Oxspring, Joe Saunders

YEAR	TEAM	LVL	AGE	W	L	SV	G	GS	IP	H	HR	BB	SO	BB9	SO9	GB%	BABIP	WHIP	ERA	FIP	FRA	WARP
2010	PIT	MLB	28	9	15	0	32	32	185^1	228	15	62	102	3.0	5.0	53%	.327	1.56	5.10	4.21	4.64	1.7
2011	PIT	MLB	29	6	14	0	26	26	162^1	160	11	50	97	2.8	5.4	52%	.286	1.29	3.66	3.75	4.43	1.2
2012	ATL	MLB	30	4	5	0	11	11	68^2	63	8	19	59	2.5	7.7	54%	.281	1.19	3.54	3.81	4.52	0.3
2012	CHN	MLB	30	9	6	0	21	20	120^1	115	12	34	81	2.5	6.1	51%	.281	1.24	3.74	4.18	4.93	0.1
2013	*ATL*	*MLB*	*31*	*10*	*9*	*0*	*26*	*26*	*154^2*	*153*	*14*	*44*	*108*	*2.6*	*6.3*	*52%*	*.306*	*1.27*	*4.14*	*3.83*	*4.50*	*0.6*

After chasing Ryan Dempster for weeks, including reportedly acquiring him in a deal contingent on his approval, the Braves turned their attention to another Chicago starter. Maholm lacked Dempster's sizzle but gave Atlanta a boost down the stretch, recording seven quality starts in 11 tries. The veteran southpaw pounds the bottom of the zone in order to generate a high rate of groundballs. It's not a sexy package, but the Braves were pleased enough to exercise Maholm's club option, worth $6.5 million.

Cristhian Martinez

Born: **3/6/1982** Age: **31**
Bats: **R** Throws: **R** Height: **6' 2"** Weight: **185**
Breakout: **19%** Improve: **45%** Collapse: **33%**
Attrition: **8%** MLB: **82%**

Comparables:
Wilbur Wood, Dave Borkowski, Steve Gromek

YEAR	TEAM	LVL	AGE	W	L	SV	G	GS	IP	H	HR	BB	SO	BB9	SO9	GB%	BABIP	WHIP	ERA	FIP	FRA	WARP
2010	GWN	AAA	28	5	1	0	23	2	52^2	45	3	8	49	1.4	8.4	49%	.282	1.01	3.07	2.63	4.40	0.6
2010	ATL	MLB	28	0	0	0	18	0	26	28	3	6	22	2.1	7.6	60%	.316	1.31	4.85	3.61	4.55	0.1
2011	GWN	AAA	29	2	1	0	4	4	22	26	2	2	18	0.8	7.4	—	.329	1.27	2.86	3.05	3.32	0.0
2011	ATL	MLB	29	1	3	0	46	0	77^2	56	8	19	58	2.2	6.7	49%	.218	0.97	3.36	3.69	5.43	-0.5
2012	ATL	MLB	30	5	4	1	54	0	73^2	80	6	19	65	2.3	7.9	48%	.332	1.34	3.91	3.20	3.63	1.0
2013	*ATL*	*MLB*	*31*	*2*	*1*	*0*	*42*	*0*	*66^1*	*65*	*7*	*17*	*47*	*2.3*	*6.3*	*48%*	*.296*	*1.24*	*4.04*	*3.92*	*4.39*	*0.2*

Last year we warned the Braves not to fall victim to the Peter Principle by promoting Martinez to a role above his talent level. Atlanta listened. Martinez returned to his designated long-reliever slash rubber-arm role that works so well for him. He went multiple innings in 22 of his outings, and threw without a day of rest on a career-high 15 occasions. Martinez might be the best long reliever in the game, and that isn't a backhanded compliment.

Kris Medlen
Born: **10/7/1985** Age: **27**
Bats: **B** Throws: **R** Height: **5' 11"** Weight: **190**
Breakout: **16%** Improve: **52%** Collapse: **21%**
Attrition: **8%** MLB: **94%**
Comparables:
Roy Oswalt,Tim Belcher,Taylor Buchholz

YEAR	TEAM	LVL	AGE	W	L	SV	G	GS	IP	H	HR	BB	SO	BB9	SO9	GB%	BABIP	WHIP	ERA	FIP	FRA	WARP
2010	ATL	MLB	24	6	2	0	31	14	107^{2}	108	13	21	83	1.8	6.9	44%	.299	1.20	3.68	3.80	4.59	1.0
2011	ATL	MLB	25	0	0	0	2	0	2^{1}	1	0	0	2	0.0	7.7	33%	.167	0.43	0.00	1.28	2.65	0.0
2012	GWN	AAA	26	0	2	0	3	3	13^{1}	15	2	6	12	4.1	8.1	35%	.342	1.58	4.72	4.88	6.57	-0.2
2012	ATL	MLB	26	10	1	1	50	12	138	103	6	23	120	1.5	7.8	54%	.261	0.91	1.57	2.46	3.37	3.1
2013	*ATL*	*MLB*	*27*	*6*	*4*	*0*	*32*	*11*	*97^{2}*	*84*	*9*	*22*	*90*	*2.0*	*8.2*	*46%*	*.296*	*1.09*	*3.01*	*3.23*	*3.28*	*1.8*

Atlanta's handling of Medlen was genius. By keeping the small right-hander in the bullpen for most of the season, the Braves were able to limit his outings without shutting him down. Medlen pitched well no matter the role. Watch him slice and dice hitters using a three-pitch mix through location and deception, and you'll begin to understand the Greg Maddux comparisons. Medlen should start the season in the rotation, giving him the opportunity to put to rest any concerns about his small frame enduring a starter's workload.

Mike Minor
Born: **12/26/1987** Age: **25**
Bats: **R** Throws: **L** Height: **6' 5"** Weight: **205**
Breakout: **24%** Improve: **58%** Collapse: **22%**
Attrition: **10%** MLB: **97%**
Comparables:
Micah Owings,Anthony Reyes,Ervin Santana

YEAR	TEAM	LVL	AGE	W	L	SV	G	GS	IP	H	HR	BB	SO	BB9	SO9	GB%	BABIP	WHIP	ERA	FIP	FRA	WARP
2010	MIS	AA	22	2	6	0	15	15	87	74	8	34	109	3.5	11.3	48%	.317	1.24	4.03	3.28	3.92	1.2
2010	GWN	AAA	22	4	1	0	6	6	33^{1}	19	1	12	37	3.2	10.0	47%	.234	0.93	1.89	2.54	3.70	0.7
2010	ATL	MLB	22	3	2	0	9	8	40^{2}	53	6	11	43	2.4	9.5	38%	.379	1.57	5.98	3.79	5.36	-0.1
2011	GWN	AAA	23	4	5	0	16	16	100^{2}	93	12	27	99	2.4	8.9	—	.295	1.19	3.13	3.68	4.00	0.0
2011	ATL	MLB	23	5	3	0	15	15	82^{2}	93	7	30	77	3.3	8.4	39%	.350	1.49	4.14	3.36	3.80	1.5
2012	ATL	MLB	24	11	10	0	30	30	179^{1}	151	26	56	145	2.8	7.3	37%	.252	1.15	4.12	4.42	5.09	0.4
2013	*ATL*	*MLB*	*25*	*9*	*7*	*0*	*24*	*24*	*134^{2}*	*122*	*16*	*42*	*125*	*2.8*	*8.3*	*40%*	*.299*	*1.21*	*3.77*	*3.82*	*4.10*	*1.2*

After struggling in the first half, Minor finished the season strong. His peripherals improved across the board in the second half, including his home run rate—he went from allowing more than one long ball per start to allowing one every other start. Whether Minor's second half represents an epiphany is unclear. If not, Minor might be what he seems to be: a slightly better-than-average starter who always leaves you wanting more.

Navery Moore
Born: **8/10/1990** Age: **22**
Bats: **R** Throws: **R** Height: **6' 3"** Weight: **212**
Breakout: **13%** Improve: **59%** Collapse: **24%**
Attrition: **13%** MLB: **85%**
Comparables:
Mike Fornieles,Bruce Kison,Jack Fisher

YEAR	TEAM	LVL	AGE	W	L	SV	G	GS	IP	H	HR	BB	SO	BB9	SO9	GB%	BABIP	WHIP	ERA	FIP	FRA	WARP
2012	ROM	A	21	8	3	0	26	13	102^{2}	83	3	45	84	3.9	7.4	51%	.269	1.25	3.86	3.75	5.04	0.7
2013	*ATL*	*MLB*	*22*	*1*	*2*	*0*	*9*	*5*	*35^{2}*	*36*	*4*	*18*	*25*	*4.5*	*6.3*	*46%*	*.303*	*1.52*	*5.23*	*4.77*	*5.68*	*-0.3*

Atlanta surprised everyone by taking Moore in the 14th round of the 2011 draft and signing him to an overslot deal. Formerly Vanderbilt's closer, Moore spent part of his first professional season in the rotation in order to hasten his development. Armed with the right makeup, a plus fastball, and a potentially plus slider, Moore has the potential to become a late-inning force.

Peter Moylan
Born: **12/2/1978** Age: **34**
Bats: **R** Throws: **R** Height: **6' 3"** Weight: **225**
Breakout: **12%** Improve: **28%** Collapse: **43%**
Attrition: **14%** MLB: **81%**
Comparables:
Dennys Reyes,Hoyt Wilhelm,Bob Wickman

YEAR	TEAM	LVL	AGE	W	L	SV	G	GS	IP	H	HR	BB	SO	BB9	SO9	GB%	BABIP	WHIP	ERA	FIP	FRA	WARP
2010	ATL	MLB	31	6	2	1	85	0	63^{2}	53	5	37	52	5.2	7.4	69%	.274	1.41	2.97	4.33	5.30	-0.4
2011	GWN	AAA	32	0	1	0	6	1	6	5	0	4	10	6.0	15.0	—	.333	1.50	0.00	1.90	2.07	0.0
2011	ATL	MLB	32	2	1	0	13	0	8^{1}	12	0	3	10	3.2	10.8	84%	.480	1.80	3.24	1.67	2.11	0.2
2012	BRA	Rk	33	0	0	0	4	3	4^{2}	4	1	1	4	1.9	7.7	67%	.273	1.07	7.71	5.79	10.28	-0.2
2012	ROM	A	33	0	1	0	4	0	4	5	0	2	3	4.5	6.8	61%	.385	1.75	9.00	4.33	5.56	0.0
2012	MIS	AA	33	1	0	0	1	0	1^{1}	0	0	0	1	0.0	6.8	75%	.000	0.00	0.00	1.64	2.11	0.0
2012	GWN	AAA	33	0	0	0	12	0	12^{2}	18	0	5	13	3.6	9.2	67%	.429	1.82	5.68	2.29	1.69	0.2
2012	ATL	MLB	33	1	0	1	8	0	5	3	1	2	2	3.6	3.6	59%	.125	1.00	1.80	6.14	7.17	-0.1
2013	*ATL*	*MLB*	*34*	*2*	*1*	*1*	*48*	*0*	*37^{2}*	*33*	*3*	*16*	*33*	*3.7*	*7.8*	*61%*	*.300*	*1.29*	*3.83*	*3.76*	*4.16*	*0.3*

Shoulder and back surgeries have limited Moylan to 13 innings over the past two seasons. When he pitches, he generates a high rate of groundballs in the midst of dominating right-handed hitters. The Braves have an in-house alternative in Gearrin, so Moylan's pending free signals his end in Atlanta. Of course, we wrote the same thing last year and Moylan returned.

Eric O'Flaherty

Born: **2/5/1985** Age: **28**
Bats: **L** Throws: **L** Height: **6' 3"** Weight: **220**
Breakout: **23%** Improve: **45%** Collapse: **31%**
Attrition: **5%** MLB: **82%**

Comparables:
Doug Slaten,Craig Breslow,Luke Gregerson

YEAR	TEAM	LVL	AGE	W	L	SV	G	GS	IP	H	HR	BB	SO	BB9	SO9	GB%	BABIP	WHIP	ERA	FIP	FRA	WARP
2010	GWN	AAA	25	0	0	0	3	0	4	1	0	1	5	2.2	11.2	88%	.125	0.50	0.00	1.54	3.17	0.1
2010	ATL	MLB	25	3	2	0	56	0	44	37	2	18	36	3.7	7.4	58%	.282	1.25	2.45	3.36	3.92	0.4
2011	ATL	MLB	26	2	4	0	78	0	73^{2}	59	2	21	67	2.6	8.2	57%	.275	1.09	0.98	2.51	3.00	1.2
2012	ATL	MLB	27	3	0	0	64	0	57^{1}	47	3	19	46	3.0	7.2	66%	.275	1.15	1.73	3.31	4.13	0.3
2013	*ATL*	*MLB*	*28*	*3*	*1*	*1*	*61*	*0*	*54*	*46*	*4*	*16*	*48*	*2.7*	*8.0*	*54%*	*.295*	*1.16*	*3.20*	*3.27*	*3.48*	*0.8*

O'Flaherty was one of the better waiver-wire claims in recent history. Since joining Atlanta in 2009, he has averaged 69 appearances per season with a 1.95 ERA. His work against left-handers reached its apex in 2012, and his pending free agency after the 2013 season creates a conundrum for the Braves. Do they re-sign O'Flaherty, who has become a reliable workhorse, or look for the next O'Flaherty?

Carlos Perez

Born: **11/20/1991** Age: **21**
Bats: **L** Throws: **L** Height: **6' 3"** Weight: **195**
Breakout: **21%** Improve: **65%** Collapse: **7%**
Attrition: **5%** MLB: **71%**

Comparables:
Mark Littell,Wade Blasingame,Ken Brett

YEAR	TEAM	LVL	AGE	W	L	SV	G	GS	IP	H	HR	BB	SO	BB9	SO9	GB%	BABIP	WHIP	ERA	FIP	FRA	WARP
2010	DNV	Rk	18	2	0	0	6	6	32	20	0	14	27	3.9	7.6	61%	.255	1.06	1.12	3.54	5.26	0.0
2010	ROM	A	18	0	1	0	2	2	7	8	1	3	4	3.9	5.1	69%	.280	1.57	3.86	5.96	7.54	-0.2
2011	ROM	A	19	4	10	1	28	23	125	138	7	66	109	4.8	7.8	47%	.309	1.63	4.82	4.19	5.03	0.8
2012	DNV	Rk	20	3	2	0	16	0	30^{2}	20	0	15	50	4.4	14.7	42%	.323	1.14	2.05	2.30	2.39	0.9
2012	ROM	A	20	0	3	0	7	4	19	33	3	19	12	9.0	5.7	43%	.417	2.74	12.79	7.53	7.97	-0.3
2013	*ATL*	*MLB*	*21*	*1*	*2*	*0*	*9*	*5*	*33^{2}*	*37*	*4*	*21*	*22*	*5.7*	*5.8*	*46%*	*.313*	*1.73*	*6.23*	*5.31*	*6.77*	*-0.6*

Lefties with low-90s fastballs and the feel for two secondary offerings always get a fair share of attention. As intriguing as Perez's upside is, his inconsistency is at least that irritating. Perez has been bedeviled by a complicated delivery that proves difficult to repeat. His secondary offerings do flash potential, but the quality fluctuates on a pitch-by-pitch basis. Perez has a middle-of-the-rotation ceiling that can feel off on his bad nights. He turned 21 in November, so the ride will last for a few more years. Expect some highs and some lows.

Lucas Sims

Born: **5/10/1994** Age: **19**
Bats: **R** Throws: **R** Height: **6' 3"** Weight: **195**
Breakout: **19%** Improve: **54%** Collapse: **46%**
Attrition: **46%** MLB: **64%**

Comparables:
Rick Wise,Lew Krausse,Von McDaniel

YEAR	TEAM	LVL	AGE	W	L	SV	G	GS	IP	H	HR	BB	SO	BB9	SO9	GB%	BABIP	WHIP	ERA	FIP	FRA	WARP
2012	BRA	Rk	18	0	0	0	3	3	7	2	1	1	10	1.3	12.9	50%	.091	0.43	1.29	3.29	4.10	0.1
2012	DNV	Rk	18	2	4	0	8	8	27	26	2	12	29	4.0	9.7	44%	.316	1.41	4.33	4.18	4.55	0.3
2013	*ATL*	*MLB*	*19*	*2*	*3*	*0*	*9*	*9*	*34*	*37*	*5*	*21*	*24*	*5.7*	*6.3*	*43%*	*.315*	*1.71*	*6.08*	*5.55*	*6.61*	*-0.5*

Sims's intriguing combination of athleticism and polish caused the Braves to pick him in the first round. Depending on the day, he can flash three plus offerings. His fastball is one of them, and can touch the upper-90s. His two breaking pitches—a low-80s slider and low-70s curve—are the other two. Sims will need to refine his changeup and his fastball command as he matures, but there's more than enough to like here already.

Zeke Spruill

Born: **9/11/1989** Age: **23**
Bats: **B** Throws: **R** Height: **6' 5"** Weight: **184**
Breakout: **23%** Improve: **60%** Collapse: **13%**
Attrition: **9%** MLB: **84%**

Comparables:
Kyle Kendrick,Dan Haren,Greg Reynolds

YEAR	TEAM	LVL	AGE	W	L	SV	G	GS	IP	H	HR	BB	SO	BB9	SO9	GB%	BABIP	WHIP	ERA	FIP	FRA	WARP
2010	BRA	Rk	20	0	0	0	2	2	3	4	0	1	1	3.0	3.0	83%	.333	1.67	3.00	3.84	5.14	0.0
2010	MYR	A+	20	3	5	0	14	13	65	83	4	13	41	1.8	5.7	53%	.339	1.48	5.54	3.73	5.47	-0.3
2011	LYN	A+	21	7	9	0	20	20	129^{2}	108	7	23	92	1.6	6.4	57%	.243	1.01	3.19	3.23	4.94	0.3
2011	MIS	AA	21	3	2	0	7	7	45	45	3	17	16	3.4	3.2	–	.273	1.38	3.20	4.93	5.36	0.0
2012	MIS	AA	22	9	11	0	27	27	161^{2}	158	8	46	106	2.6	5.9	52%	.294	1.26	3.67	3.44	4.47	1.0
2013	*ATL*	*MLB*	*23*	*3*	*3*	*0*	*8*	*8*	*47*	*52*	*6*	*16*	*26*	*3.1*	*5.1*	*51%*	*.307*	*1.45*	*5.24*	*4.77*	*5.69*	*-0.4*

Spruill is a tall, gangly right-hander who draws comparisons to Derek Lowe. A second-round pick in 2008, Spruill's slow development is close to paying off. His best offering is his sinker, which has good arm-side run and flirts with the mid-90s on occasion. Spruill has two decent secondary offerings in his slider and changeup. After making 34 starts in Double-A over the past two seasons, Spruill can expect to spend some time in Triple-A in 2013.

Julio Teheran

Born: **1/27/1991** Age: **22**
Bats: **R** Throws: **R** Height: **6' 3"** Weight: **175**
Breakout: **28%** Improve: **63%** Collapse: **16%**
Attrition: **7%** MLB: **90%**
Comparables:
Jair Jurrjens,Shairon Martis,Steve Karsay

YEAR	TEAM	LVL	AGE	W	L	SV	G	GS	IP	H	HR	BB	SO	BB9	SO9	GB%	BABIP	WHIP	ERA	FIP	FRA	WARP
2010	ROM	A	19	2	2	0	7	7	39^1	23	1	10	45	2.3	10.3	46%	.237	0.84	1.15	2.71	2.79	1.1
2010	MYR	A+	19	4	4	0	10	10	63^1	56	6	13	76	1.8	10.8	42%	.312	1.09	2.99	3.09	3.65	1.2
2010	MIS	AA	19	3	2	0	7	7	40	29	2	17	38	3.8	8.6	38%	.260	1.15	3.38	3.49	4.47	0.4
2011	GWN	AAA	20	15	3	0	25	24	144^2	123	5	48	122	3.0	7.6	—	.288	1.18	2.55	3.10	3.37	0.0
2011	ATL	MLB	20	1	1	0	5	3	19^2	21	4	8	10	3.7	4.6	30%	.262	1.47	5.03	5.84	6.10	-0.3
2012	GWN	AAA	21	7	9	0	26	26	131	146	18	43	97	3.0	6.7	38%	.318	1.44	5.08	4.79	6.45	0.0
2012	ATL	MLB	21	0	0	0	2	1	6^1	5	0	1	5	1.4	7.1	22%	.278	0.95	5.68	2.03	2.65	0.1
2013	*ATL*	*MLB*	*22*	*2*	*3*	*0*	*8*	*8*	42^1	*42*	*6*	*16*	*33*	*3.4*	*6.9*	*41%*	*.301*	*1.37*	*4.78*	*4.62*	*5.19*	*-0.1*

Teheran started the season as one of the top pitching prospects and ended it as a giant question mark. The Braves sent organizational pitching guru Dom Chiti to Gwinnett to work with him and were reportedly pleased with the results. There's still reason for optimism. Teheran's feel for the game is superb, as is his fastball-changeup combination. The key for him to live up to the front-of-the-rotation billing is sharpening his breaking ball and fine-tuning his command. Without that, Teheran might struggle even to find a home in the middle of a rotation.

Anthony Varvaro

Born: **10/31/1984** Age: **28**
Bats: **R** Throws: **R** Height: **6' 1"** Weight: **195**
Breakout: **29%** Improve: **60%** Collapse: **16%**
Attrition: **16%** MLB: **85%**
Comparables:
Steve Bedrosian,Jack Meyer,John Wyatt

YEAR	TEAM	LVL	AGE	W	L	SV	G	GS	IP	H	HR	BB	SO	BB9	SO9	GB%	BABIP	WHIP	ERA	FIP	FRA	WARP
2010	WTN	AA	25	1	3	9	31	0	39^1	27	2	21	46	4.8	10.5	42%	.260	1.22	3.21	3.31	3.83	0.7
2010	TAC	AAA	25	0	0	0	19	0	25^2	24	1	14	26	4.9	9.1	47%	.326	1.48	5.25	4.17	4.33	0.5
2010	SEA	MLB	25	0	1	0	4	0	4	6	2	6	5	13.5	11.2	46%	.364	3.00	11.25	11.55	12.46	-0.4
2011	GWN	AAA	26	2	8	1	38	0	59	37	3	35	69	5.3	10.5	—	.250	1.22	2.90	3.44	3.74	0.0
2011	ATL	MLB	26	0	2	0	18	0	24	15	3	11	23	4.1	8.6	35%	.203	1.08	2.62	4.08	4.62	0.1
2012	GWN	AAA	27	0	2	6	33	1	44^1	39	1	24	47	4.9	9.5	41%	.311	1.42	2.23	3.02	2.07	1.1
2012	ATL	MLB	27	1	1	0	12	0	16^2	16	2	9	21	4.9	11.3	43%	.333	1.50	5.40	4.16	4.03	0.2
2013	*ATL*	*MLB*	*28*	*1*	*0*	*0*	*27*	*0*	35^2	*32*	*4*	*21*	*34*	*5.3*	*8.6*	*42%*	*.299*	*1.48*	*4.74*	*4.52*	*5.15*	*-0.2*

A strained pectoral muscle sabotaged Varvaro's shot at making the Opening Day bullpen. He spent most of the season at Gwinnett, where he pitched well enough to merit a promotion. Varvaro's cameo in the majors was more of the same old, same old. He misses bats and the zone consistently, but has not missed barrels enough to become a full-fledged big-league reliever. Varvaro is without options, so he should start the season in the majors—with Atlanta or some other team.

Jonny Venters

Born: **3/20/1985** Age: **28**
Bats: **L** Throws: **L** Height: **6' 4"** Weight: **195**
Breakout: **32%** Improve: **56%** Collapse: **31%**
Attrition: **9%** MLB: **86%**
Comparables:
Phil Coke,Renyel Pinto,Dave Righetti

YEAR	TEAM	LVL	AGE	W	L	SV	G	GS	IP	H	HR	BB	SO	BB9	SO9	GB%	BABIP	WHIP	ERA	FIP	FRA	WARP
2010	GWN	AAA	25	1	0	0	2	1	6^2	4	0	1	6	1.3	8.1	72%	.222	0.75	1.34	1.95	2.30	0.2
2010	ATL	MLB	25	4	4	1	79	0	83	61	1	39	93	4.2	10.1	69%	.288	1.20	1.95	2.72	3.41	1.4
2011	ATL	MLB	26	6	2	5	85	0	88	53	2	43	96	4.4	9.8	74%	.242	1.09	1.84	2.74	3.17	1.1
2012	GWN	AAA	27	0	0	0	1	1	1	0	0	0	0	0.0	0.0	33%	.000	0.00	0.00	3.16	3.43	0.0
2012	ATL	MLB	27	5	4	0	66	0	58^2	61	6	28	69	4.3	10.6	64%	.357	1.52	3.22	3.80	3.37	0.8
2013	*ATL*	*MLB*	*28*	*3*	*1*	*1*	*60*	*0*	60^1	*51*	*5*	*26*	*59*	*3.9*	*8.8*	*59%*	*.301*	*1.28*	*3.69*	*3.61*	*4.01*	*0.5*

Venters was not his usual dominant self in 2012. He allowed more hits and runs than we're accustomed to seeing, and pitched fewer innings. Granted, the decrease in workload seemed like an organizational emphasis to reduce the burden placed on the pillars of the bullpen. Given Venters's walk- and strikeout-heavy approach, it's not a bad idea as he's always liable to run a high pitch count. An increase in home runs allowed would be alarming, except the bout of gopheritis was contained to the first half. Venters may not return to excellence, but he should still provide value as a set-up man.

Jordan Walden

Born: **11/16/1987** Age: **25**
Bats: **R** Throws: **R** Height: **6' 6"** Weight: **235**
Breakout: **34%** Improve: **55%** Collapse: **9%**
Attrition: **10%** MLB: **90%**
Comparables:
Bill Slayback,Len Barker,Jonathan Papelbon

YEAR	TEAM	LVL	AGE	W	L	SV	G	GS	IP	H	HR	BB	SO	BB9	SO9	GB%	BABIP	WHIP	ERA	FIP	FRA	WARP
2010	ARK	AA	22	1	1	8	38	0	43	44	2	22	38	4.6	8.0	56%	.339	1.53	3.35	3.54	4.91	-0.1
2010	SLC	AAA	22	0	0	0	6	0	6^2	8	0	2	3	2.7	4.0	38%	.333	1.49	4.03	3.58	3.76	0.1
2010	ANA	MLB	22	0	1	1	16	0	15^1	13	1	7	23	4.1	13.5	63%	.353	1.30	2.35	2.26	1.77	0.5
2011	ANA	MLB	23	5	5	32	62	0	60^1	49	3	26	67	3.9	10.0	47%	.295	1.24	2.98	2.83	3.14	0.9
2012	SLC	AAA	24	0	1	0	3	0	2^2	3	0	0	3	0.0	10.1	38%	.375	1.12	6.75	2.54	2.38	0.1
2012	ANA	MLB	24	3	2	1	45	0	39	35	3	18	48	4.2	11.1	40%	.311	1.36	3.46	2.97	3.63	0.5
2013	*ATL*	*MLB*	*25*	*2*	*1*	*10*	*41*	*0*	40^1	*37*	*4*	*18*	*40*	*4.0*	*8.9*	*50%*	*.310*	*1.35*	*4.04*	*3.84*	*4.40*	*0.2*

That Walden lost his ninth-inning job with the Angels wasn't a shock; half the league's closers lose theirs most seasons. But he lost it early, after just one blown save and four total innings. The quick hook came after a Brandon Allen walk-off home run in Tampa Bay April 26, but there's a backstory: As a rookie closer in 2011, despite a good ERA and excellent peripherals, Walden blew the most saves in the AL. He hits 98 mph and stares down batters, but between the blown saves, short record of success, secondary pitches he can't control, and a tendency toward walks and wild pitches, he's not a quiet ninth. As a result, the Braves will try him in the seventh.

Alex Wood

Born: **1/12/1991** Age: **22**
Bats: **L** Throws: **L** Height: **6' 5"** Weight: **215**
Breakout: **29%** Improve: **47%** Collapse: **19%**
Attrition: **18%** MLB: **87%**

Comparables:
Brad Hand,Ryan Feierabend,Jon Niese

YEAR	TEAM	LVL	AGE	W	L	SV	G	GS	IP	H	HR	BB	SO	BB9	SO9	GB%	BABIP	WHIP	ERA	FIP	FRA	WARP
2012	ROM	A	21	4	3	0	13	13	52^2	39	1	14	52	2.4	8.9	66%	.368	1.01	2.22	2.76	3.24	0.4
2013	*ATL*	*MLB*	*22*	*2*	*3*	*0*	*7*	*7*	35^2	*37*	*5*	*17*	*27*	*4.3*	*6.7*	*47%*	*.310*	*1.51*	*5.21*	*4.94*	*5.66*	*-0.3*

Wood, Atlanta's second-round pick, comes by way of the University of Georgia. An unorthodox delivery, with Wood propelling backward after landing, overshadows an intriguing package of size and velocity. He's a well-built southpaw with an above-average fastball. His changeup is solid and represents his go-to secondary offering. Ultimately, Wood will need to develop a better breaking ball or a cutter in order to avoid the bullpen.

LINEOUTS

HITTERS

PLAYER	TEAM	LVL	AGE	PA	R	2B	3B	HR	RBI	BB	SO	SB-CS	AVG/OBP/SLG	TAv	BABIP	BRR	FRAA	WARP
C B. De La Rosa	BRA	Rk	18	73	5	1	0	1	3	2	30	0-1	.162/.194/.221	.139	.263	0	C(3): -0.1	-0.2
UT B. DeWitt	IOW	AAA	26	118	5	3	0	0	5	14	23	0-0	.127/.246/.157	.145	.165	-0.4	LF(11): -0.0, 1B(6): 0.1	-1.2
	CHN	MLB	26	30	1	1	0	0	1	0	2	0-0	.138/.133/.172	.157	.143	0.8	2B(4): 0.1, LF(1): 0.0	-0.1
2B P. Gosselin	MIS	AA	23	547	55	23	3	3	46	46	90	12-4	.242/.317/.320	.290	.289	3.3	2B(36): -2.9	1.1
CF M. Jones	LYN	A+	25	437	45	27	3	3	30	34	64	22-8	.253/.327/.363	.229	.296	2.1	CF(68): -4.7, LF(17): -0.5	-0.4
	MIS	AA	25	98	11	0	0	0	0	9	25	7-5	.141/.232/.141	.204	.200	-0.4	CF(6): 0.2, RF(1): -0.1	0.0
2B T. La Stella	LYN	A+	23	358	43	22	5	5	56	36	24	13-2	.302/.386/.460	.283	.305	0.1	2B(59): -2.6	1.1
OF A. Milligan	LYN	A+	24	367	45	21	2	15	49	20	134	3-0	.255/.306/.463	.252	.372	-1.5	LF(24): 0.5, RF(9): 0.6	-0.2
	MIS	AA	24	114	4	5	0	1	9	8	38	0-0	.176/.248/.255	.109	.266	-2.4	LF(6): -0.5, RF(1): -0.0	-1.0
OF J. Parraz	GWN	AAA	27	133	14	6	1	2	9	11	26	5-1	.288/.364/.407	.273	.356	-0.3	RF(8): 0.5, LF(2): 0.3	0.1
INF R. Pena	SWB	AAA	26	404	40	13	3	2	29	34	74	1-3	.258/.325/.328	.253	.317	-0.4	SS(56): 8.5, 2B(14): -1.8	1.1

Catcher **Bryan De La Rosa** has a plus-plus arm and all the tools to become a special defender, but his bat is too raw to project as more than a backup. **Blake DeWitt** looked like a solid if unspectacular third-base option once upon a time. His stock has fallen to organizational depth. **Philip Gosselin** has the reputation for being an instinctual player, but he struggled upon his introduction to Double-A. **Mycal Jones** is now at the age where potential is less important than production, though he doesn't seem to realize it. **Tommy La Stella** is a smallish second baseman who must continue to hit to make it. Outfielder **Adam Milligan** showed off impressive raw power before a promotion to Double-A. Injuries have often been his undoing, but last season it was advanced pitchers. With another year passed, **Jordan Parraz**'s chances of becoming someone's fourth outfielder are slipping away. Remember how we used to joke about **Ramiro Pena** being Derek Jeter's glove? Now he's Tyler Pastornicky's glove.

PITCHERS

PLAYER	TEAM	LVL	AGE	W	L	SV	IP	H	HR	BB	SO	BB9	SO9	GB%	BABIP	WHIP	ERA	FIP	FRA	WARP
M. Cabrera	DNV	Rk	18	2	2	0	57^{2}	45	2	23	48	3.6	7.5	44%	.256	1.18	2.97	4.05	5.09	0.0
D. Carrasco	NYN	MLB	35	0	0	0	3^{2}	6	2	0	3	0.0	7.4	36%	.333	1.64	7.36	9.41	9.60	-0.2
D. Delgado	LYN	A+	23	7	7	0	128^{2}	144	7	39	80	2.7	5.6	43%	.328	1.42	3.92	3.94	4.53	1.4
R. Fish	ARK	ARK	AA	23	1	0	30^{1}	21	1	18	41	5.3	12.2	56%	.250	1.29	3.26	2.98	4.44	0.2
D. Hale	MIS	AA	24	8	4	0	145^{2}	121	11	67	124	4.1	7.7	48%	.272	1.29	3.77	4.01	5.90	0.3
C. Jones	MIS	AA	23	2	5	2	60	69	1	19	61	2.8	9.1	58%	.366	1.47	3.90	2.33	1.83	1.3
C. Martin	LYN	A+	22	12	7	0	107^{1}	93	7	34	123	2.9	10.3	40%	.314	1.18	2.93	3.09	3.78	1.0
L. Merejo	BRA	Rk	17	0	5	0	41	38	1	9	53	2.0	11.6	—	.349	1.15	4.61	2.04	2.22	0.0
A. Northcraft	LYN	A+	22	10	11	0	151^{2}	143	4	53	160	3.1	9.5	62%	.329	1.29	3.98	2.82	4.39	1.2
C. Rasmus	MIS	AA	24	3	5	7	58^{2}	45	3	32	62	4.9	9.5	38%	.291	1.31	3.68	3.43	3.56	0.6

Mauricio Cabrera is a projectable right-hander with velocity to burn. He can hit the upper-90s, and the early returns on his secondary pitches are encouraging. Veteran **D.J. Carrasco** made five minor-league appearances before Atlanta released him. **Dimasther Delgado** missed the 2010 season following a horrific car crash. He has not regained his pre-crash prospect status yet, but as a once-promising southpaw, he figures to get plenty of chances. A Rule 5 pick, **Robert Fish** is a lefty with a mid-90s fastball and power breaking ball. He missed the 2012 season with elbow trouble. Righty **David Hale** attended Princeton, where he majored in operations research and financial engineering and minored in arm strength. Acquired for Derek Lowe, **Chris Jones** is a deceptive southpaw with better numbers and deception than stuff—code for left-handed specialist. **Cody Martin** has bloodlines and a good feel for the game, but his stuff limits him to a fifth-starter projection. Scouts love **Luis Merejo**'s advanced feel for pitching. His fastball can touch the mid-90s and both his curveball and changeup have the potential to become solid offerings. **Aaron Northcraft** doesn't throw hard, but a good sinker and altered mechanics helped him earn a spot on the 40-man roster. Former first-round pick **Cory Rasmus**, the younger brother of Colby, still has a chance to reach the majors as a reliever.

MANAGER: FREDI GONZALEZ

YEAR	TEAM	W-L	Pythag +/-	Avg PC	100+ P	120+ P	QS	BQS	REL	REL w Zero R	IBB	PH	PH Avg	PH HR	SB2	CS2	SB3	CS3	SAC Att	SAC %	POS SAC	Squeeze	Swing	In Play
2010	FLO	34-36	1	191.5	70	69	52	1	193	141	36	202	.211	2	3	1	1	1	68	76.5%	14	2	148	45
2011	ATL	89-73	1	95.9	56	0	86	3	510	435	73	257	.175	8	6	1	0	3	115	70.4%	39	2	289	86
2012	ATL	94-68	1	93.3	53	1	79	3	460	404	40	249	.158	4	17	5	1	2	85	69.4%	23	3	288	93

Gonzalez's second season at the helm in Atlanta went better than the first. For starters, he didn't overtax his top relievers. Instead he used his bullpen's depth and distributed the innings in a manner that didn't harm the Braves' chances of winning games. Gonzalez did not bench potential franchise cornerstone Jason Heyward in favor of Jose Constanza, or anything similar. He also shied away from having his positional players bunt. He did, on the other hand, issue a bunch of intentional walks. Gonzalez seems to have a solid relationship with the players and an understanding of the Braves Way of doing things. The entire package adds up to a decent manager, which is a big step forward from where things stood with Gonzalez a year ago.

Baltimore Orioles

2012: BUDGET GOURMET

We suggested in this space last year that the Orioles trying to compete in the AL East was akin to storming Mount Olympus with a butter knife. Perhaps that's not as bad a strategy as it sounds; the Orioles surprised everyone this year as that butter knife sliced and diced Zeus and company to the tune of a .574 winning percentage, losing the division title on the last day of the season but making the playoffs for the first time in 15 years. Baltimore may also have captured Circe, the Greek goddess of luck, as the team's .496 third-order win percentage betokens either some good fortune, some good managing, or a combination of both.

While Buck Showalter's managerial tally was surely on the plus side of the ledger this year, a lot of that Pythagorean-beating came as a result of Baltimore's stellar (read: mostly lucky) performance in one-run (29–9) and extra-innings games (16–2).

ORIOLES PROSPECTUS

2012 W-L: 93-69, 2nd in AL East

Pythag	.505	16th	DER	.715	9th
RS/G	4.40	14th	B-Age	28.0	14th
RA/G	4.35	17th	P-Age	27.4	7th
TAv	.259	15th	Salary	$84.9	19th
BRR	-4.8	22nd	M$/MW	$1.61	6th
TAv-P	.261	16th	DL Days	1264	7th
FIP	4.15	20th	DL WARP	2.9	18th

Three-Year Park Factors	
Overall	**100**
HR/RH	**111**
HR/LH	**115**
AVG/RH	**109**
AVG/LH	**107**

Oriole Park at Camden Yards (1992)
Att. % of Capacity: 57.9% (23rd)
Dim. 333, 364, 400, 373, 318

Better for power than average, Camden featured the fourth-most homers, but was 14th in BABIP.

Though the Orioles might have been some lucky ducks (or birds, but that doesn't rhyme), had they merely performed to their third-order win percentage and won 80 games last year, they would have finished 11 wins ahead of their 2011 record—and 14 wins ahead of their 2011 third-order record. That's no easy leap to make. Much credit goes to new GM Dan Duquette, who took what most viewed as a lemon of a job and made lemonade. And damn good lemonade at that. None of that watered-down nonsense kids these days serve. The book *Mind Game* highlighted Duquette's skills at assembling cost-effective talent to supplement core pieces, and he did that with nine players in particular, for whom he paid just $1.5 million per win—less than a third of the going rate. Duquette's acquisitions helped turn a rotation that had the worst ERA in baseball in 2011 (worse even than a staff of replacement-level pitchers would be expected to post) into a 13th-ranked one in 2012, thanks to the additions of four mid-rotation starters and three quality bullpen arms, all for near pennies.

Dan Duquette's Cost-Effective Acquisitions

Starters	*WARP/200 IP*
Jason Hammel	4.6
Miguel Gonzalez	2.8
Joe Saunders	2.2
Wei-Yin Chen	2.0
Relievers	*WARP/70 IP*
Darren O'Day	1.5
Luis Ayala	1.0
Matt Lindstrom	0.8
Hitters	*WARP/650 PA*
Nate McLouth	2.5
Wilson Betemit	0.5
Total WARP	10.7
Total Salary	$15.9 million
$/WARP	$1.5 million/WARP

2013: A SEAT AT THE TABLE

As will be the case until owner Peter Angelos succeeds in bribing Bud Selig to realign Baltimore into the NL West, the Orioles must continue to elbow their way into relevance in baseball's toughest division. The Yankees are still the Yankees. The Rays are still the Rays. The Red Sox and Jays made big splashes this offseason. Baltimore has a strong offensive core and a solid bullpen, but it lacks the star power of New York and the front-line starting pitching of Tampa Bay.

The team has one true star now in Adam Jones, and Chris Davis's breakout adds him to a core that also includes Matt Wieters, J.J. Hardy, and Nick Markakis—though none (save Jones) are stars on the level of Robinson Cano, Curtis Granderson, or Mark Teixeira. On the offensive side, Baltimore's ability to be competitive may hinge on how well Nolan Reimold and mega-prospect Manny Machado play and how effectively Duquette can plug second base.

Duquette has assembled more than enough mid-level pitching, but until top prospect Dylan Bundy is ready, the team lacks a true ace or even a formidable second starter. Jake Arrieta is the Orioles' best in-house bet to front the rotation until Bundy arrives, and if Chris Tillman can squeeze a few more whiffs out of his quality stuff, he could be the number two. Baltimore's chances of punching a return ticket to the playoff dance may well hinge on Arrieta and Tillman's success. Improved control would help young flamethrower Pedro Strop establish himself as a viable eighth-inning man, improving an already stellar bullpen and making Baltimore a very well-rounded club, capable of earning a playoff spot for the second consecutive year—something the O's have accomplished just once since the mid-1970s.

STATE OF THE ORGANIZATION: FARM-TO-TABLE

The Orioles lack the resources of the Yankees and Red Sox, but if 2012 is any indication, their brainpower is at least competitive with the great minds of the AL East (something we weren't so sure about at this time last year). While Hardy and Markakis are no longer spring chickens, most of Baltimore's core is either in their prime or has yet to reach it. Better still is that their primary weaknesses—front-line pitching, second base, and third base—stand to be filled by high-quality prospects within a few years.

Machado has already reached the bigs, and Jonathan Schoop could join him in the infield within a year or two. Bundy is fast approaching MLB-readiness and could give the team a much-needed ace, and he could be followed soon after by Kevin Gausman.

While the Orioles are in a solid position for the next few years, their long-term success will ultimately be determined by their ability to draft and develop quality talent. Prior to Duquette, the O's track record was one of the worst in baseball. Despite seven picks in the top 10, 12 in the top 20, and 26 in the top 50 from 1998 to 2008, the O's developed only seven prospects who played in the majors for more than a year, and a mere two All-Stars. Duquette acknowledge the need to do better shortly after being hired: He overhauled the scouting department, most notably turning over personnel while increasing the club's amateur scouting ranks (at the expense of in-person pro scouting). The jury is still out on his 2012 draft, but its success (and the success of subsequent drafts) will have a large impact on Baltimore's overall success in the AL East . . . assuming that realignment doesn't come through.

HITTERS

Xavier Avery **CF**

Born: **1/1/1990** Age: **23**
Bats: **L** Throws: **L** Height: **6' 0"**
Weight: **180** Breakout: **5%**
Improve: **44%** Collapse: **6%**
Attrition: **12%** MLB: **91%**

Comparables:
Curt Flood,Gary Thomasson,Dave Martinez

YEAR	TEAM	LVL	AGE	PA	R	2B	3B	HR	RBI	BB	SO	SB	CS	AVG_OBP_SLG	TAv	BABIP	BRR	FRAA	WARP
2010	FRD	A+	20	498	73	25	6	4	48	42	96	28	14	.280/.348/.389	.261	.347	4.5	CF(70): -6.7, LF(42): -3.6	0.8
2010	BOW	AA	20	120	10	6	0	3	18	7	34	10	0	.234/.288/.374	.248	.306	1.1	CF(27): 1.5	0.4
2011	BOW	AA	21	626	72	31	2	4	26	49	156	36	14	.259/.324/.343	.241	.352	-0.2	CF(99): -14.8	-1.7
2012	NOR	AAA	22	458	57	13	5	8	34	51	106	22	7	.236/.330/.356	.238	.301	3.7	CF(58): -4.9, LF(22): -0.0	-0.7
2012	BAL	MLB	22	107	14	6	1	1	6	11	23	6	3	.223/.305/.340	.235	.286	0.7	LF(27): -0.0, CF(1): -0.0	-0.1
2013	*BAL*	*MLB*	*23*	*250*	*31*	*10*	*1*	*4*	*19*	*17*	*63*	*11*	*4*	*.229/.288/.336*	*.219*	*.293*	*0.9*	*CF -3, LF -0*	*-0.6*

Avery, one of the most athletic players in Baltimore's organization, made his debut as an injury replacement for the big boys last season. While he has good speed and defensive skills, his approach at the plate is suspect and reviews of his bat are mixed. The hit tool is what will ultimately determine whether he becomes a starter or a fourth outfielder, and signs point to the latter. He doesn't make hard contact, and there are doubts about his ability to handle breaking pitches. And while he's been improving of late, he's had a sketchy work ethic in the past.

Wilson Betemit **INF**

Born: **11/2/1981** Age: **31**
Bats: **B** Throws: **R** Height: **6' 3"**
Weight: **220** Breakout: **1%**
Improve: **37%** Collapse: **13%**
Attrition: **21%** MLB: **94%**

Comparables:
Jim Dyck,Phil Nevin,Brooks Conrad

YEAR	TEAM	LVL	AGE	PA	R	2B	3B	HR	RBI	BB	SO	SB	CS	AVG_OBP_SLG	TAv	BABIP	BRR	FRAA	WARP
2010	OMA	AAA	28	135	9	6	2	2	17	17	23	1	1	.265/.364/.407	.266	.315	-0.7	SS(12): -0.9, 1B(8): 0.6	0.4
2010	KCA	MLB	28	315	36	20	0	13	43	36	74	0	0	.297/.378/.511	.312	.361	-2.1	3B(53): -3.9, 1B(5): -0.2	1.8
2011	DET	MLB	29	133	11	7	3	5	19	11	47	1	0	.292/.346/.525	.315	.429	-0.9	3B(40): -0.2	0.9
2011	KCA	MLB	29	226	29	15	1	3	27	20	58	3	1	.281/.341/.409	.260	.372	-0.3	3B(47): 0.9, 1B(3): 0.2	0.5
2012	BAL	MLB	30	376	41	19	0	12	40	31	103	0	1	.261/.322/.422	.267	.336	-0.2	3B(74): -4.5, 1B(15): -0.8	0.3
2013	*BAL*	*MLB*	*31*	*351*	*38*	*19*	*1*	*11*	*44*	*30*	*98*	*1*	*1*	*.252/.317/.421*	*.259*	*.327*	*-0.6*	*3B -2, 1B 0*	*0.5*

See the "B" up there next to "Bats:"? That's kind of misleading, since Betemit is a switch-hitter in name only. Not once has he been allowed to bat from the right side even 90 times during a season, and it's easy to see why: his career TAv is .204 vs. lefties and .301 against righties. Betemit has spent a long career treating southpaws like *Resident Evil* zombies genetically engineered to throw 500 mph. That seems out of line with Umbrella's M.O. to us, but we're not the ones with the delusion . . . or the 100-point platoon split. He'd be more valuable if he could feign playing defense, but as a part-time player or the strong-half of a DH platoon, he can definitely help a ballclub.

Alexi Casilla INF

Born: **7/20/1984** Age: **28**
Bats: **B** Throws: **R** Height: **5' 10"**
Weight: **185** Breakout: **0%**
Improve: **30%** Collapse: **10%**
Attrition: **11%** MLB: **94%**

Comparables:
Steve Sax, Dave Cash, Chris Getz

YEAR	TEAM	LVL	AGE	PA	R	2B	3B	HR	RBI	BB	SO	SB	CS	AVG_OBP_SLG	TAv	BABIP	BRR	FRAA	WARP
2010	MIN	MLB	25	170	26	7	4	1	20	13	17	6	1	.276/.331/.395	.255	.304	1.5	SS(30): 1.5, 2B(23): 0.3	0.8
2011	MIN	MLB	26	365	52	21	4	2	21	28	45	15	4	.260/.322/.368	.256	.294	2.1	2B(56): 4.7, SS(36): 1.4	1.8
2012	MIN	MLB	27	326	33	17	2	1	30	16	52	21	1	.241/.282/.321	.223	.283	0.7	2B(96): -1.1, 3B(4): 0.1	-0.3
2013	*BAL*	*MLB*	*28*	*314*	*36*	*13*	*2*	*5*	*28*	*24*	*44*	*14*	*3*	*.256/.318/.367*	*.242*	*.282*	*1.6*	*2B -3, SS -0*	*0.5*

The Twins waited for Casilla to develop into the every-day second baseman they were expecting for almost seven seasons. And at times, 2008 in particular, Casilla actually looked like he was going to blossom. But he never developed plate discipline and alternated good seasons with embarrassingly poor ones, and the Twins grew understandably frustrated. He is a capable defender at second, but a move to short didn't pan out in 2011. He is a very good basestealer, with an 89 percent career success rate. He was waived in November and claimed by the Orioles, where he will serve as a utility infielder and insurance for Brian Roberts.

Endy Chavez OF

Born: **2/7/1978** Age: **35**
Bats: **L** Throws: **L** Height: **6' 1"**
Weight: **170** Breakout: **1%**
Improve: **28%** Collapse: **14%**
Attrition: **25%** MLB: **81%**

Comparables:
Scott Podsednik, Mickey Hatcher, Jim Piersall

YEAR	TEAM	LVL	AGE	PA	R	2B	3B	HR	RBI	BB	SO	SB	CS	AVG_OBP_SLG	TAv	BABIP	BRR	FRAA	WARP
2011	ROU	AAA	33	142	16	8	2	2	17	10	6	6	0	.305/.353/.445	.277	.306	0	--	0.0
2011	TEX	MLB	33	274	37	11	3	5	27	10	30	10	5	.301/.323/.426	.271	.321	1.6	CF(66): -3.0, LF(12): -0.4	0.6
2012	NOR	AAA	34	53	2	3	0	0	4	2	6	0	0	.149/.192/.213	.082	.163	-0.7	RF(5): 0.2, LF(4): -0.2	-0.7
2012	BAL	MLB	34	169	15	6	0	2	12	6	24	3	2	.203/.236/.278	.198	.227	-1.2	LF(35): -1.3, RF(21): 0.4	-1.1
2013	*BAL*	*MLB*	*35*	*250*	*26*	*10*	*1*	*3*	*22*	*13*	*32*	*7*	*3*	*.258/.297/.355*	*.227*	*.278*	*0.4*	*CF -0, LF 1*	*-0.1*

Despite advancing age, Chavez is still a capable fourth outfielder. Best known for his spectacular defensive plays in his younger days, he has held onto enough of those skills to continue to be an asset with the glove. His offense—never a particularly strong part of his game—has begun to decline of late; Chavez has chased more pitches over the past couple of years, leading to more strikeouts and fewer walks, and he'll need to reverse that or risk his bat being too much of a liability to justify his defensive contributions. His wheels have defended well enough against rust so that he can still beat out some groundballs, which he hits a lot of, and that gives him a small buffer to work with.

Chris Davis 4C

Born: **3/17/1986** Age: **27**
Bats: **L** Throws: **R** Height: **6' 4"**
Weight: **230** Breakout: **3%**
Improve: **39%** Collapse: **5%**
Attrition: **7%** MLB: **88%**

Comparables:
Carlos Delgado, Victor Diaz, Nate Colbert

YEAR	TEAM	LVL	AGE	PA	R	2B	3B	HR	RBI	BB	SO	SB	CS	AVG_OBP_SLG	TAv	BABIP	BRR	FRAA	WARP
2010	OKL	AAA	24	444	67	31	2	14	80	37	105	3	2	.327/.388/.520	.304	.416	-1.5	3B(59): -6.2, 1B(37): 0.8	2.4
2010	TEX	MLB	24	136	7	9	0	1	4	15	40	3	0	.192/.279/.292	.203	.275	-0.3	1B(41): 1.0, 3B(1): 0.0	-0.6
2011	ROU	AAA	25	210	39	14	1	24	66	11	58	1	0	.368/.405/.824	.386	.412	0	--	0.0
2011	BAL	MLB	25	129	16	9	0	2	13	6	39	1	0	.276/.310/.398	.270	.390	-0.9	3B(17): -2.2, 1B(16): 0.6	0.0
2011	TEX	MLB	25	81	9	3	0	3	6	5	24	0	0	.250/.296/.408	.252	.327	-1.4	1B(15): -0.6, 3B(9): -0.1	-0.3
2012	BAL	MLB	26	562	75	20	0	33	85	37	169	2	3	.270/.326/.501	.289	.335	0.6	1B(38): 1.5, RF(30): 0.8	2.1
2013	*BAL*	*MLB*	*27*	*457*	*55*	*22*	*1*	*21*	*66*	*31*	*138*	*2*	*1*	*.259/.313/.463*	*.270*	*.333*	*-0.8*	*1B -2, 3B -1*	*1.0*

For the first time in his career, a starting job was Davis's to lose, and he made the most of the opportunity. Davis may as well be followed to the plate by a blue ox given the raw power he uses to handle the lumber. That's where he's going to make his money, because his pitch recognition can be atrocious. Davis is a mistake hitter capable of being dominated by a pitcher with a good plan. His swing has definite holes, and a savvy pitcher will get him off-balance on his front foot to sap his power. Those strikeouts will never go away, but he did do a better job of staying inside the ball and using the whole field last season. As long as he capitalizes on the opportunities pitchers dangle, he's a valuable hitter capable of playing all four corner positions better than any tree stump could.

Luis Exposito **C**
Born: **1/20/1987** Age: **26**
Bats: **R** Throws: **R** Height: **6' 4"**
Weight: **210** Breakout: **6%**
Improve: **38%** Collapse: **7%**
Attrition: **17%** MLB: **89%**
Comparables:
Kyle Phillips,Bill Nahorodny,Marc Hill

YEAR	TEAM	LVL	AGE	PA	R	2B	3B	HR	RBI	BB	SO	SB	CS	AVG_OBP_SLG	TAv	BABIP	BRR	FRAA	WARP
2010	PME	AA	23	542	65	39	1	11	94	55	92	1	2	.260/.345/.416	.258	.303	-1	C(85): 0.1	1.8
2011	PAW	AAA	24	359	33	17	0	8	36	26	79	0	2	.242/.298/.367	.214	.294	0.5	C(50): -0.2	-0.6
2012	NOR	AAA	25	224	26	11	1	6	23	18	35	0	2	.268/.326/.420	.250	.297	-0.5	C(38): -0.5	0.2
2012	BAL	MLB	25	22	2	0	0	0	0	3	5	0	0	.056/.190/.056	.117	.077	-0.2	C(9): 0.0	-0.3
2013	*BAL*	*MLB*	*26*	*250*	*23*	*12*	*1*	*6*	*27*	*18*	*53*	*0*	*0*	*.232/.290/.367*	*.233*	*.273*	*-0.5*	*C -0*	*0.2*

Exposito spent the month of May backing up Matt Wieters behind the plate, and the biggest takeaway from that might just be that he looks like the love child of Dustin Pedroia and Jorge Velandia. To wit, Exposito is a solid defender (nothing more, nothing less), and he offers with the bat exactly what you'd expect from a backup catcher: very little. He has a tiny bit of pop, and catchers do generally lag behind their non-backstop counterparts offensively at Exposito's age, so he figures to have a job riding the bus between Triple-A and the majors for several more years.

Ryan Flaherty **UT**
Born: **7/27/1986** Age: **26**
Bats: **L** Throws: **R** Height: **6' 4"**
Weight: **220** Breakout: **6%**
Improve: **47%** Collapse: **4%**
Attrition: **24%** MLB: **92%**
Comparables:
Jayson Nix,Davey Johnson,Jose Castillo

YEAR	TEAM	LVL	AGE	PA	R	2B	3B	HR	RBI	BB	SO	SB	CS	AVG_OBP_SLG	TAv	BABIP	BRR	FRAA	WARP
2010	DAY	A+	23	475	65	34	3	9	63	41	74	6	3	.286/.354/.445	.291	.328	0.9	3B(51): 0.6, 2B(39): 3.4	3.3
2010	TEN	AA	23	84	10	2	0	1	9	10	12	1	0	.183/.293/.254	.204	.207	-0.6	2B(18): -2.2, 3B(3): -0.2	-0.6
2011	TEN	AA	24	344	52	20	2	14	66	40	55	4	6	.305/.384/.523	.310	.332	0	2B(11): -0.8, LF(8): -0.1	1.0
2011	IOW	AAA	24	186	22	11	1	5	22	10	44	1	0	.237/.277/.399	.232	.288	-0.5	2B(12): -1.0, 3B(10): 0.5	-0.1
2012	BAL	MLB	25	167	15	2	1	6	19	6	43	1	0	.216/.258/.359	.224	.257	-0.8	2B(28): 0.1, 3B(17): -0.3	-0.6
2013	*BAL*	*MLB*	*26*	*250*	*25*	*11*	*1*	*7*	*29*	*15*	*57*	*2*	*1*	*.236/.287/.381*	*.235*	*.279*	*-0.3*	*2B 0, 3B 0*	*0.1*

Flaherty looked overmatched last year, but that's expected for Rule 5 picks. The O's stuck with him all year, though, and even began using him as a starter against righties by the end of September. While he displays the potential for power production, he'll never get the chance to fulfill that potential unless he can improve his plate discipline. His approach was sound at times in the minors, but he appeared easily fooled last year while his patience eroded. A little seasoning at Triple-A would serve him well, and he could eventually become a useful utility player capable of playing five or six positions.

Lew Ford **OF**
Born: **8/12/1976** Age: **36**
Bats: **R** Throws: **R** Height: **6' 1"**
Weight: **200** Breakout: **0%**
Improve: **19%** Collapse: **19%**
Attrition: **20%** MLB: **77%**
Comparables:
Javy Lopez,Fernando Tatis,Bob Watson

YEAR	TEAM	LVL	AGE	PA	R	2B	3B	HR	RBI	BB	SO	SB	CS	AVG_OBP_SLG	TAv	BABIP	BRR	FRAA	WARP
2012	NOR	AAA	35	267	35	14	3	11	40	23	43	8	2	.331/.390/.550	.319	.365	-1.2	CF(11): -0.8, RF(4): 0.2	1.4
2012	BAL	MLB	35	79	7	3	0	3	4	7	13	1	0	.183/.256/.352	.209	.182	-0.4	LF(13): -0.1, RF(6): 0.4	-0.4
2013	*BAL*	*MLB*	*36*	*250*	*30*	*11*	*1*	*9*	*32*	*18*	*50*	*4*	*1*	*.257/.312/.435*	*.260*	*.288*	*0.2*	*LF 0, CF -0*	*0.6*

Five years removed from his last big-league stint and having played everywhere from Japan to Mexico to the independent leagues, Ford unexpectedly returned to the majors last season after the Orioles found themselves lacking organizational outfield depth. That's the high note of the story, though, as Ford was abysmal in his time with Baltimore. He showed some power at Triple-A, but there was a reason he was gone so long. Ford still plays hard and can run a bit, but the most that can be expected of him is to hold down a roster spot as a not-terrible fifth outfielder. The worst is that he's back in the bushes by this time next year.

Bill Hall **UT**
Born: **12/28/1979** Age: **33**
Bats: **R** Throws: **R** Height: **6' 1"**
Weight: **210** Breakout: **4%**
Improve: **24%** Collapse: **8%**
Attrition: **28%** MLB: **86%**
Comparables:
Deron Johnson,Paul Sorrento,Brian Daubach

YEAR	TEAM	LVL	AGE	PA	R	2B	3B	HR	RBI	BB	SO	SB	CS	AVG_OBP_SLG	TAv	BABIP	BRR	FRAA	WARP
2010	BOS	MLB	30	382	44	16	1	18	46	34	104	9	1	.247/.316/.456	.271	.300	-0.7	LF(55): 1.6, 2B(51): -1.7	1.4
2011	FRE	AAA	31	125	17	9	0	7	20	9	36	0	0	.274/.328/.540	.269	.333	-0.1	2B(7): -0.8, LF(3): 0.0	0.1
2011	HOU	MLB	31	158	18	7	2	2	13	8	55	1	1	.224/.272/.340	.210	.341	-0.8	2B(41): -6.2	-1.3
2011	SFN	MLB	31	41	6	2	0	0	1	3	8	2	1	.158/.220/.211	.143	.200	0.2	2B(10): -0.9, LF(1): 0.1	-0.5
2012	NOR	AAA	32	370	38	18	0	15	45	26	141	2	1	.246/.300/.430	.247	.369	-3.3	3B(23): -0.8, 2B(22): 0.9	0.0
2012	BAL	MLB	32	14	2	0	0	1	1	5	7	0	0	.222/.500/.556	.377	.000	-1.1	LF(1): -0.0, RF(1): -0.1	0.1
2013	*BAL*	*MLB*	*33*	*250*	*27*	*11*	*1*	*8*	*28*	*18*	*81*	*2*	*1*	*.219/.278/.379*	*.232*	*.294*	*-0.2*	*2B -2, LF 0*	*-0.2*

Hall, once a credible starter, has been diminished to a mere afterthought. He barely received a sip of coffee with Baltimore last season as his skills continued to decline. He at least showed some power at Triple-A, but that's a far cry from terrorizing big-league pitching, especially as his plate discipline continues to erode; even in the minors, Hall's strikeout rate was 38 percent last year. Still, he will continue to receive minor-league deals and spring-training invites for at least a couple of years given his past potency and current ability to provide organizational depth.

J.J. Hardy SS

Born: **8/19/1982** Age: **30**
Bats: **R** Throws: **R** Height: **6' 2"**
Weight: **200** Breakout: **2%**
Improve: **55%** Collapse: **2%**
Attrition: **3%** MLB: **92%**

Comparables:
Rich Aurilia, Miguel Tejada, Michael Young

YEAR	TEAM	LVL	AGE	PA	R	2B	3B	HR	RBI	BB	SO	SB	CS	AVG_OBP_SLG	TAv	BABIP	BRR	FRAA	WARP
2010	MIN	MLB	27	375	44	19	3	6	38	28	54	1	1	.268/.320/.394	.261	.299	-0.3	SS(100): 1.7	1.9
2011	BAL	MLB	28	567	76	27	0	30	80	31	92	0	0	.269/.310/.491	.278	.273	1.5	SS(129): 8.1	3.8
2012	BAL	MLB	29	713	85	30	2	22	68	38	106	0	0	.238/.282/.389	.234	.253	1.1	SS(158): 19.6	2.6
2013	*BAL*	*MLB*	*30*	*642*	*79*	*28*	*2*	*23*	*75*	*44*	*108*	*1*	*0*	*.254/.307/.423*	*.255*	*.273*	*-1*	*SS 2*	*2.7*

Hardy picked up in 2012 where he left off in 2011, proving that his power resurgence was for real while playing great defense. As we noted last year, the combination of health, revamped mechanics, and a favorable home ballpark did wonders for his home-run total. Some fall-off was expected, as he hit more than his fair share of fence-scrapers in 2011, but his power remains well above average by shortstop standards. He should settle in offensively somewhere between his 2011 and 2012 seasons, as PECOTA suggests. Winning the Gold Glove was fitting for Hardy, confirming that he has truly joined the ranks of the game's elite shortstops.

LJ Hoes OF

Born: **3/5/1990** Age: **23**
Bats: **R** Throws: **R** Height: **6' 2"**
Weight: **181** Breakout: **1%**
Improve: **42%** Collapse: **4%**
Attrition: **6%** MLB: **96%**

Comparables:
Melky Cabrera, Lee Mazzilli, Gerald Young

YEAR	TEAM	LVL	AGE	PA	R	2B	3B	HR	RBI	BB	SO	SB	CS	AVG_OBP_SLG	TAv	BABIP	BRR	FRAA	WARP
2010	FRD	A+	20	413	52	19	2	3	44	53	70	10	8	.278/.375/.368	.274	.337	-0.4	2B(83): -1.4	1.7
2011	FRD	A+	21	173	23	7	0	3	17	10	25	4	2	.241/.297/.342	.216	.267	0.2	2B(16): -1.1, LF(13): -0.9	-0.6
2011	BOW	AA	21	393	47	17	1	6	54	43	56	16	7	.305/.379/.413	.287	.347	-0.2	LF(48): -0.1, RF(8): -1.5	1.3
2012	BOW	AA	22	229	25	9	3	2	16	31	33	12	5	.265/.368/.372	.292	.311	-0.5	CF(43): -1.9, LF(1): -0.0	0.7
2012	NOR	AAA	22	357	54	14	4	3	38	34	43	8	7	.300/.374/.397	.260	.338	3.4	LF(34): 6.6, RF(22): 0.6	1.3
2012	BAL	MLB	22	1	0	0	0	0	0	0	0	0	0	.000/.000/.000	.002	.000	0	LF(1): -0.0	0.0
2013	*BAL*	*MLB*	*23*	*250*	*26*	*10*	*1*	*4*	*24*	*21*	*44*	*6*	*3*	*.259/.325/.367*	*.249*	*.303*	*-0.2*	*LF -0, CF -0*	*0.3*

Defensive inadequacy forced Hoes to move from second base to the outfield for good last season, which caused his stock to take a big hit. Hoes lacks the kind of power outfielders are expected to have, especially if they aren't elite speedsters or defenders. Hoes does, however, have great raw hitting tools, a good approach at the plate, and above-average baserunning skills. That combination would have played perfectly well at second base, but in the corner outfield leaves a lot to be desired. If he can find the gaps frequently enough to generate extra bases, he stands an outside chance of being a second-division starter one day.

Travis Ishikawa 1B

Born: **9/24/1983** Age: **29**
Bats: **L** Throws: **L** Height: **6' 4"**
Weight: **225** Breakout: **3%**
Improve: **43%** Collapse: **11%**
Attrition: **14%** MLB: **86%**

Comparables:
Willie Upshaw, Ken Harrelson, Ty Wigginton

YEAR	TEAM	LVL	AGE	PA	R	2B	3B	HR	RBI	BB	SO	SB	CS	AVG_OBP_SLG	TAv	BABIP	BRR	FRAA	WARP
2010	SFN	MLB	26	173	18	11	0	3	22	13	29	0	0	.266/.320/.392	.245	.307	-4.1	1B(73): 0.1	-0.4
2011	FRE	AAA	27	211	21	14	0	3	18	29	54	3	1	.251/.368/.383	.262	.345	1.5	1B(20): 1.5, RF(14): 0.9	0.4
2012	MIL	MLB	28	174	19	12	1	4	30	13	42	0	0	.257/.329/.428	.252	.327	-0.4	1B(43): -1.1, RF(3): -0.0	-0.2
2013	*BAL*	*MLB*	*29*	*250*	*28*	*13*	*1*	*8*	*31*	*21*	*58*	*2*	*1*	*.252/.320/.416*	*.258*	*.302*	*-0.4*	*1B -2, RF -0*	*0.2*

Ishikawa was once a well-regarded first-base prospect in the Giants system, but it became clear his chances of becoming an every-day player had reached approximately nil the moment his Baseball-Reference page appended "Pinch Hitter" to his list of positions. The Brewers penciled him into the starting lineup after Mat Gamel's injury in May, but soon realized his nifty glove can't overcome his middling patience and lack of power. Ishikawa's curse is that he's proven he can hit a little, especially against righties—just not enough for an offense-first position like first base. His ceiling remains that of a vagabond defensive replacement and Professional Hitter, toting his Doug Mientkiewicz impression from bench to bench.

Conor Jackson OF

Born: **5/7/1982** Age: **31**
Bats: **R** Throws: **R** Height: **6' 3"**
Weight: **215** Breakout: **0%**
Improve: **40%** Collapse: **9%**
Attrition: **19%** MLB: **92%**

Comparables:
Elmer Valo, Tony Gwynn, Willard Marshall

YEAR	TEAM	LVL	AGE	PA	R	2B	3B	HR	RBI	BB	SO	SB	CS	AVG_OBP_SLG	TAv	BABIP	BRR	FRAA	WARP
2010	ARI	MLB	28	172	19	11	0	1	11	20	18	4	1	.238/.326/.331	.251	.263	1.9	LF(36): 0.5, 1B(3): -0.1	0.4
2010	OAK	MLB	28	69	6	2	0	1	5	11	9	2	0	.228/.362/.316	.247	.255	-0.1	LF(16): 0.1	0.0
2011	BOS	MLB	29	22	2	0	0	1	5	2	3	0	0	.158/.227/.316	.194	.125	0.2	LF(3): -0.3, RF(3): 0.0	-0.1
2011	OAK	MLB	29	368	30	17	1	4	38	30	50	3	1	.249/.315/.342	.254	.281	-3	1B(50): -2.1, RF(28): 1.3	-0.7
2012	CHR	AAA	30	366	44	23	0	9	41	41	43	5	1	.277/.363/.434	.278	.294	0.4	RF(50): -2.5, LF(11): 1.5	1.0
2013	*BAL*	*MLB*	*31*	*250*	*27*	*12*	*1*	*6*	*27*	*24*	*33*	*3*	*1*	*.258/.333/.391*	*.261*	*.280*	*0*	*RF -0, LF 0*	*0.5*

In an utterly baffling move, Oakland picked up a $3.2 million option on Jackson prior to the 2011 season. Let this serve as a cautionary tale against over-emphasizing certain stats, even if they are as important as a hitter's walk and strikeout rates, both of which remain at above-average levels for Jackson. The power is gone, and he doesn't sting the ball enough to generate much batting average despite all those balls in play. He can play first base and outfield, but looks like a designated hitter while doing so.

Nick Johnson 1B
Born: **9/19/1978** Age: **34**
Bats: **L** Throws: **L** Height: **6' 4"**
Weight: **235** Breakout: **0%**
Improve: **38%** Collapse: **9%**
Attrition: **16%** MLB: **91%**
Comparables:
Ferris Fain,Carl Yastrzemski,John Olerud

YEAR	TEAM	LVL	AGE	PA	R	2B	3B	HR	RBI	BB	SO	SB	CS	AVG_OBP_SLG	TAv	BABIP	BRR	FRAA	WARP
2010	NYA	MLB	31	98	12	4	0	2	8	24	23	0	1	.167/.388/.306	.257	.213	0	1B(2): -0.1	0.1
2011	COH	AAA	32	216	20	6	0	6	13	26	52	0	1	.201/.316/.332	.234	.246	0	--	0.0
2012	BAL	MLB	33	102	9	4	0	4	11	11	26	2	0	.207/.324/.391	.254	.246	0.3	1B(5): 0.1	0.0
2013	*BAL*	*MLB*	*34*	*250*	*31*	*10*	*0*	*6*	*26*	*42*	*48*	*2*	*1*	*.247/.387/.388*	*.282*	*.295*	*-0.5*	*1B -0*	*1.1*

For the third season in a row, Johnson missed a significant chunk of time with a right wrist injury. He didn't need surgery on it this time around, as he did in 2008, 2010, and 2011. Aside from not getting to compete . . . and not getting to have fun playing the game he loves . . . and probably the frustration of it all . . . oh, and the pain of it, Johnson has a pretty sweet deal, given the kind of salaries ballplayers command. In all seriousness, Johnson is a quality player with top-notch patience and solid power when he's healthy. That just happens to be more rare than a good M. Night Shyamalan movie.

Adam Jones CF
Born: **8/1/1985** Age: **27**
Bats: **R** Throws: **R** Height: **6' 4"**
Weight: **220** Breakout: **2%**
Improve: **48%** Collapse: **6%**
Attrition: **4%** MLB: **98%**
Comparables:
Franklin Gutierrez,Will Venable,Ellis Burks

YEAR	TEAM	LVL	AGE	PA	R	2B	3B	HR	RBI	BB	SO	SB	CS	AVG_OBP_SLG	TAv	BABIP	BRR	FRAA	WARP
2010	BAL	MLB	24	621	76	25	5	19	69	23	119	7	7	.284/.325/.442	.266	.328	2.4	CF(149): 5.7	3.7
2011	BAL	MLB	25	618	68	26	2	25	83	29	113	12	4	.280/.319/.466	.285	.304	2.7	CF(148): -1.5	3.7
2012	BAL	MLB	26	697	103	39	3	32	82	34	126	16	7	.287/.334/.505	.297	.313	1.6	CF(162): 6.4	5.2
2013	*BAL*	*MLB*	*27*	*639*	*78*	*28*	*4*	*23*	*84*	*33*	*124*	*12*	*6*	*.275/.323/.454*	*.274*	*.311*	*0*	*CF 6*	*3.5*

Had it not been for Baltimore's improbable winning season and postseason appearance, Jones may have continued on as one of the most underrated players in baseball. Instead, he garnered a Gold Glove and several down-ballot MVP votes after essentially matching his 2011 performance in many categories. The athletic Jones is a true five-tool player—and five-category player, for the fantasy crowd—a veritable Swiss Army knife of baseball goodness who possesses quick wrists and better defense than certain metrics would imply. More of the same is to be expected in 2013, and that's a good thing.

Manny Machado 3B
Born: **7/6/1992** Age: **20**
Bats: **R** Throws: **R** Height: **6' 4"**
Weight: **185** Breakout: **14%**
Improve: **47%** Collapse: **4%**
Attrition: **12%** MLB: **90%**
Comparables:
Adrian Beltre,Robin Yount,Edgar Renteria

YEAR	TEAM	LVL	AGE	PA	R	2B	3B	HR	RBI	BB	SO	SB	CS	AVG_OBP_SLG	TAv	BABIP	BRR	FRAA	WARP
2011	DEL	A	18	170	24	8	2	6	24	23	25	3	1	.276/.376/.483	.272	.296	-0.3	SS(22): 0.9	0.5
2011	FRD	A+	18	260	24	12	3	5	26	22	48	8	5	.245/.308/.384	.284	.286	1.6	SS(52): -0.8	1.5
2012	BOW	AA	19	459	60	26	5	11	59	48	70	13	4	.266/.352/.438	.283	.297	0.9	SS(87): -5.1, 3B(2): -0.0	1.9
2012	BAL	MLB	19	202	24	8	3	7	26	9	38	2	0	.262/.294/.445	.261	.293	-0.3	3B(51): 0.6	0.5
2013	*BAL*	*MLB*	*20*	*257*	*28*	*12*	*2*	*7*	*30*	*16*	*51*	*4*	*1*	*.250/.299/.410*	*.252*	*.287*	*0.2*	*SS 2, 3B 0*	*1.0*

Machado began April at Low-A Delmarva but found himself the starting third baseman for the big club by August—quite the leap, even for one of the top prospects in baseball. Despite immediate success, expect Machado's 2013 to be more struggles than triumphs. He has little left to learn in the minors, but he is still capable of being exploited by big-league pitchers with full arsenals and the smarts to find his weaknesses. It'll be a "learn on the job" situation for Machado, who has excellent raw hitting tools and projects to be a great player once he adjusts to the game's highest level. While he had been a shortstop in the minors, expect the transition to third to be permanent; the team has J.J. Hardy locked up for two more years, and most expected Machado to slide over to the hot corner at some point anyway.

Nick Markakis RF
Born: **11/17/1983** Age: **29**
Bats: **L** Throws: **L** Height: **6' 2"**
Weight: **200** Breakout: **3%**
Improve: **39%** Collapse: **5%**
Attrition: **8%** MLB: **98%**
Comparables:
Al Kaline,Ron Fairly,Floyd Robinson

YEAR	TEAM	LVL	AGE	PA	R	2B	3B	HR	RBI	BB	SO	SB	CS	AVG_OBP_SLG	TAv	BABIP	BRR	FRAA	WARP
2010	BAL	MLB	26	709	79	45	3	12	60	73	93	7	2	.297/.370/.436	.278	.331	-0.8	RF(159): -2.4	2.5
2011	BAL	MLB	27	716	72	31	1	15	73	62	75	12	3	.284/.351/.406	.271	.300	0.3	RF(157): -3.0, 1B(3): 0.0	1.2
2012	BAL	MLB	28	471	59	28	3	13	54	42	51	1	1	.298/.363/.471	.292	.310	0	RF(102): -6.6	1.2
2013	*BAL*	*MLB*	*29*	*493*	*64*	*28*	*1*	*12*	*53*	*50*	*69*	*5*	*2*	*.285/.359/.438*	*.281*	*.313*	*-0.5*	*RF -0, 1B -0*	*2.1*

Now at the peak of the aging curve, Markakis really is what he is at this point: a one-time potential superstar who topped out as a complementary piece. His core ratios have remained steady for years, aside from a spike in HR/FB from 8.8 percent in 2009-11 to 12.6 percent in 2012. That appears to be a mirage, however, as Markakis isn't squaring the ball up any differently and is driving it the same modest distance as usual.

Expect him to settle back down in 2013. Scouts have always liked his defense more than the numbers do, but at some point, the numbers have to count for something, and he isn't getting any younger. Thumb surgery sidelined Markakis at the end of the season, but he said he would have been able to play had the O's made the World Series, so there should be no lingering issues.

Nate McLouth **OF**
Born: **10/28/1981** Age: **31**
Bats: **L** Throws: **R** Height: **6' 0"**
Weight: **180** Breakout: **0%**
Improve: **38%** Collapse: **5%**
Attrition: **12%** MLB: **90%**
Comparables:
Bobby Higginson,Rusty Greer,Wally Moon

YEAR	TEAM	LVL	AGE	PA	R	2B	3B	HR	RBI	BB	SO	SB	CS	AVG_OBP_SLG	TAv	BABIP	BRR	FRAA	WARP
2010	GWN	AAA	28	151	18	1	0	6	18	19	21	7	0	.234/.342/.383	.265	.238	0	CF(32): 2.8	0.8
2010	ATL	MLB	28	288	30	12	1	6	24	33	57	7	2	.190/.298/.322	.227	.221	3.4	CF(71): -1.7, LF(7): -0.2	-0.1
2011	ATL	MLB	29	321	35	12	2	4	16	44	52	4	2	.228/.344/.333	.253	.270	2.6	CF(55): -0.5, LF(26): -1.0	0.2
2012	NOR	AAA	30	209	29	5	2	10	33	18	26	5	0	.244/.325/.461	.257	.231	2.9	CF(22): -0.5, RF(10): -1.8	0.2
2012	BAL	MLB	30	236	35	12	1	7	18	22	43	12	1	.268/.342/.435	.278	.306	4.2	LF(55): -1.5, CF(6): -0.0	0.9
2012	PIT	MLB	30	62	4	2	0	0	2	5	18	0	0	.140/.210/.175	.148	.205	0.5	LF(9): -0.5, CF(4): 0.2	-0.7
2013	*BAL*	*MLB*	*31*	*316*	*44*	*14*	*1*	*11*	*35*	*33*	*57*	*8*	*2*	*.242/.331/.417*	*.261*	*.264*	*0.7*	*CF -1, LF 0*	*0.9*

While speaking with Orioles officials, we were told of a plot the team hatched last offseason that involved kidnapping and blackmailing Doc Brown, chloroforming their newly signed outfielder, and traveling back to the year 2007 to swap McLouths. Stranger yet is that his 2007 stats still wound up being really good. (This was meant to be off the record, but we felt the information too important not to divulge.) McLouth did seem to recapture some of the magic he possessed in his Pittsburgh days, but a repeat in 2013 seems unlikely. His home-run rate was a function of the hitter-friendly park and some luck; his raw power isn't what it used to be. He can still hit, run, and field a little, but McLouth is best suited as a fourth outfielder these days.

Yamaico Navarro **INF**
Born: **10/31/1987** Age: **25**
Bats: **R** Throws: **R** Height: **6' 0"**
Weight: **170** Breakout: **10%**
Improve: **53%** Collapse: **6%**
Attrition: **17%** MLB: **99%**
Comparables:
Daniel Descalso,Dave Hansen,Bob Bailey

YEAR	TEAM	LVL	AGE	PA	R	2B	3B	HR	RBI	BB	SO	SB	CS	AVG_OBP_SLG	TAv	BABIP	BRR	FRAA	WARP
2010	PME	AA	22	378	49	19	3	8	55	42	53	16	5	.274/.360/.422	.274	.305	0.4	SS(66): -6.7, 3B(22): 1.0	1.5
2010	PAW	AAA	22	59	8	4	0	3	6	5	6	2	1	.283/.345/.528	.311	.273	1.1	SS(11): -1.0, 3B(2): -0.2	0.6
2010	BOS	MLB	22	46	4	0	0	0	5	2	17	0	0	.143/.174/.143	.130	.222	0.2	SS(15): -0.3, 3B(4): 0.1	-0.4
2011	OMA	AAA	23	101	11	3	1	2	9	7	18	3	4	.272/.317/.391	.229	.311	-0.9	SS(12): -0.1, 2B(1): -0.1	-0.2
2011	PAW	AAA	23	149	25	8	2	5	13	17	25	3	2	.258/.362/.469	.283	.286	0.4	3B(7): -0.1, RF(7): 1.7	0.6
2011	BOS	MLB	23	40	6	2	0	1	3	3	9	0	0	.216/.275/.351	.224	.259	0.6	3B(11): -0.5, LF(3): 0.0	0.1
2011	KCA	MLB	23	26	2	1	0	0	6	2	5	0	0	.304/.346/.348	.293	.368	0	3B(5): -0.1, SS(1): -0.2	0.1
2012	IND	AAA	24	257	41	14	3	9	35	32	41	9	4	.279/.366/.491	.286	.303	0.5	3B(32): -0.3, 2B(11): 1.5	1.4
2012	PIT	MLB	24	56	4	0	0	1	4	5	13	0	2	.160/.232/.220	.177	.189	0.1	LF(8): -0.2, SS(3): -0.1	-0.4
2013	*BAL*	*MLB*	*25*	*250*	*29*	*10*	*1*	*7*	*28*	*22*	*51*	*6*	*3*	*.243/.312/.393*	*.250*	*.280*	*-0.1*	*3B 0, SS -1*	*0.5*

Pittsburgh acquired Navarro on the eve of the 2011 Rule 5 draft from Kansas City for two minor leaguers. The reaction to the trade favored the Pirates. Navarro seemed destined to become a solid utility infielder thanks to his defensive flexibility and a modicum of power. But that didn't happen. In fact, Navarro rarely played for the Pirates in the majors despite a solid season at Indianapolis. Given Pittsburgh's surplus of utility-infielder types, they traded him to the Orioles in the offseason. With Baltimore he'll compete for a bench role and/or serve as organizational depth. His opportunity to capitalize on his potential may have passed.

Steve Pearce **1B**
Born: **4/13/1983** Age: **30**
Bats: **R** Throws: **R** Height: **6' 0"**
Weight: **210** Breakout: **1%**
Improve: **44%** Collapse: **2%**
Attrition: **7%** MLB: **85%**
Comparables:
Lyle Overbay,Olmedo Saenz,Don Baylor

YEAR	TEAM	LVL	AGE	PA	R	2B	3B	HR	RBI	BB	SO	SB	CS	AVG_OBP_SLG	TAv	BABIP	BRR	FRAA	WARP
2010	IND	AAA	27	158	25	14	2	3	15	24	27	7	2	.326/.435/.535	.318	.394	0.4	1B(24): -1.1, RF(5): 0.3	1.4
2010	PIT	MLB	27	38	4	2	1	0	5	7	6	0	0	.276/.395/.414	.304	.320	0.3	1B(11): 0.9	0.3
2011	PIT	MLB	28	105	8	2	0	1	10	7	21	0	0	.202/.260/.255	.189	.243	-0.4	1B(15): 0.3, 3B(10): -0.4	-0.8
2012	SWB	AAA	29	227	37	15	0	11	30	29	33	3	1	.318/.419/.568	.361	.336	-0.3	1B(42): -1.1, 3B(3): 0.1	2.2
2012	BAL	MLB	29	83	8	4	0	3	14	8	17	0	1	.254/.321/.437	.289	.283	0.1	LF(20): -0.2, RF(9): -0.6	0.4
2012	HOU	MLB	29	75	2	4	1	0	8	7	16	1	1	.254/.347/.349	.244	.327	0.1	1B(10): -0.5, RF(10): -1.0	-0.4
2012	NYA	MLB	29	30	6	0	0	1	4	5	8	0	0	.160/.300/.280	.225	.188	0.3	1B(9): 0.2	-0.1
2013	*BAL*	*MLB*	*30*	*250*	*28*	*12*	*1*	*8*	*31*	*24*	*52*	*2*	*1*	*.244/.325/.414*	*.260*	*.281*	*-0.4*	*1B -2, RF -0*	*0.2*

Once a top prospect in the Pirates organization, Pearce has been reduced to a hollow shell of his former self. In the past year, unbelievably, he's been mauled by a squirrel, ambushed on *The Jerry Springer Show*, and claimed off waivers *five times*. Okay, only that last one's true. It's telling that he was even discarded by the lowly Astros, which is like flunking out of fourth-grade remedial English as a high-school senior. He still shows patience and power at the minor-league level, but he has never been able to handle right-handed pitching in the bigs. Hitters who are lefty specialists don't get nearly the same job security as their pitching counterparts.

Omar Quintanilla MI
Born: **10/24/1981** Age: **31**
Bats: **L** Throws: **R** Height: **5' 10"**
Weight: **190** Breakout: **1%**
Improve: **45%** Collapse: **8%**
Attrition: **14%** MLB: **92%**
Comparables:
Mike Mordecai,Leo Cardenas,Jay Bell

YEAR	TEAM	LVL	AGE	PA	R	2B	3B	HR	RBI	BB	SO	SB	CS	AVG_OBP_SLG	TAv	BABIP	BRR	FRAA	WARP
2010	CSP	AAA	28	135	14	7	1	1	15	11	25	1	1	.252/.316/.353	.226	.305	0.6	SS(14): 1.9, 3B(12): 0.7	0.1
2011	ROU	AAA	29	234	46	9	4	5	25	23	33	3	1	.298/.369/.452	.287	.333	0	--	0.0
2011	TEX	MLB	29	23	3	0	1	0	2	0	9	0	0	.045/.045/.136	.108	.077	0.1	2B(5): -0.2, SS(3): 0.3	-0.3
2012	BUF	AAA	30	172	18	11	2	6	27	14	27	1	3	.282/.345/.494	.255	.309	1.1	SS(40): 2.4	0.7
2012	BAL	MLB	30	110	12	3	0	3	12	8	25	0	1	.232/.284/.354	.236	.274	-0.9	2B(32): 0.7, SS(7): 0.0	0.1
2012	NYN	MLB	30	80	13	5	0	1	4	8	17	0	0	.257/.350/.371	.263	.327	1.3	SS(23): 0.5, 2B(2): 0.0	0.5
2013	*BAL*	*MLB*	*31*	*250*	*24*	*11*	*1*	*4*	*23*	*19*	*59*	*1*	*1*	*.228/.291/.344*	*.224*	*.281*	*-0.5*	*SS -0, 2B 0*	*0.0*

Quintanilla is a classic glove-first, bat-second (or eighth?) middle infielder. He was overexposed as a starter for both the O's and Mets for stretches last season—situations neither team was thrilled to find themselves in. Quintanilla raised some eyebrows by reaching double-digit home runs in just under 350 at-bats between Triple-A and the majors last year, but that's the last thing you should expect to carry over this season. His raw power is nil. It's worth noting that he tested positive for performance-enhancers once before, although saying anything more would be pure speculation.

Nolan Reimold OF
Born: **10/12/1983** Age: **29**
Bats: **R** Throws: **R** Height: **6' 5"**
Weight: **215** Breakout: **3%**
Improve: **35%** Collapse: **0%**
Attrition: **4%** MLB: **90%**
Comparables:
Fred Lewis,Josh Willingham,Minnie Minoso

YEAR	TEAM	LVL	AGE	PA	R	2B	3B	HR	RBI	BB	SO	SB	CS	AVG_OBP_SLG	TAv	BABIP	BRR	FRAA	WARP
2010	NOR	AAA	26	401	52	12	0	10	37	54	61	9	2	.249/.366/.374	.259	.278	-1.2	LF(49): 0.5, 1B(29): -0.9	0.1
2010	BAL	MLB	26	131	9	5	0	3	14	12	26	0	0	.207/.282/.328	.212	.236	-0.9	LF(22): 0.1, RF(2): -0.0	-0.4
2011	NOR	AAA	27	161	16	6	0	6	22	18	43	2	1	.237/.329/.410	.284	.293	-0.7	LF(20): 4.3	0.6
2011	BAL	MLB	27	305	40	10	3	13	45	28	57	7	2	.247/.328/.453	.285	.264	0.3	LF(72): 2.6, RF(8): -0.4	1.5
2012	BAL	MLB	28	69	10	6	0	5	10	2	14	1	0	.313/.333/.627	.329	.333	0.6	LF(15): -0.0	0.5
2013	*BAL*	*MLB*	*29*	*250*	*32*	*10*	*1*	*10*	*33*	*27*	*50*	*4*	*1*	*.255/.341/.443*	*.278*	*.287*	*0.1*	*LF 1, 1B -0*	*1.2*

Finally getting a chance to begin a season with semi-regular playing time for the first time since a 2009 injury turned him into a year-and-a-half-long afterthought, Reimold managed to play just one month last season before succumbing to injury once again. It's a shame, too, because the one-time top prospect was successfully building upon a strong 2011 second half, seemingly poised to establish himself as a legitimate threat. Reimold's best asset is his above-average power, and a solid approach at the plate should make him a well-rounded hitter the next time he gets a chance to prove himself. Let's hope he doesn't have to wait another year and a half for that opportunity.

Brian Roberts 2B
Born: **10/9/1977** Age: **35**
Bats: **B** Throws: **R** Height: **5' 10"**
Weight: **175** Breakout: **0%**
Improve: **24%** Collapse: **13%**
Attrition: **18%** MLB: **81%**
Comparables:
Bernie Allen,Ray Durham,Lou Whitaker

YEAR	TEAM	LVL	AGE	PA	R	2B	3B	HR	RBI	BB	SO	SB	CS	AVG_OBP_SLG	TAv	BABIP	BRR	FRAA	WARP
2010	BAL	MLB	32	261	28	14	0	4	15	26	40	12	2	.278/.354/.391	.265	.319	0.7	2B(59): -4.2	0.4
2011	BAL	MLB	33	178	18	7	1	3	19	12	21	6	1	.221/.273/.331	.217	.236	2.2	2B(39): -0.5	-0.3
2012	BAL	MLB	34	74	2	0	0	0	5	5	12	1	1	.182/.233/.182	.183	.214	-0.3	2B(17): -1.1	-0.7
2013	*BAL*	*MLB*	*35*	*250*	*32*	*15*	*1*	*4*	*22*	*25*	*42*	*9*	*2*	*.260/.335/.388*	*.256*	*.300*	*0.7*	*2B -2*	*0.6*

They say that those who live in glass houses shouldn't throw stones. Perhaps they should also say, "Those with glass bones shouldn't play baseball." Roberts has shown a serious case of reverse *Unbreakable* syndrome over the past three years, making four 60-day DL trips and spending a grand total of 420 days on the shelf thanks to maladies as varied as concussions and a hip labrum tear, not to mention a few weeks with nagging injuries that didn't merit roster moves. Even in his brief time on the field last year, Roberts looked to be an absolute mess, and two of his biggest assets, speed and defense, may have declined to the point that he will no longer be a suitable starter even if he recovers from hip surgery.

Trayvon Robinson OF
Born: **9/1/1987** Age: **25**
Bats: **B** Throws: **R** Height: **5' 11"**
Weight: **200** Breakout: **12%**
Improve: **64%** Collapse: **9%**
Attrition: **17%** MLB: **96%**
Comparables:
Michael Saunders,Jim Landis,Austin Jackson

YEAR	TEAM	LVL	AGE	PA	R	2B	3B	HR	RBI	BB	SO	SB	CS	AVG_OBP_SLG	TAv	BABIP	BRR	FRAA	WARP
2010	CHT	AA	22	523	80	23	5	9	57	73	125	38	15	.300/.400/.438	.305	.393	2.3	CF(120): -10.3	3.5
2011	ABQ	AAA	23	416	70	9	6	26	71	45	122	8	6	.293/.375/.562	.314	.373	0	--	0.0
2011	SEA	MLB	23	155	12	12	0	2	14	8	61	1	0	.210/.250/.336	.228	.346	-0.8	LF(30): 0.1, CF(16): -1.4	-0.7
2012	TAC	AAA	24	381	50	18	2	9	41	34	85	19	5	.265/.331/.409	.257	.325	2.3	CF(47): 2.4, LF(16): 2.2	1.0
2012	SEA	MLB	24	164	16	4	1	3	12	14	43	6	3	.221/.294/.324	.259	.293	0.2	LF(46): 3.9	0.5
2013	*BAL*	*MLB*	*25*	*250*	*32*	*11*	*1*	*6*	*22*	*21*	*72*	*9*	*3*	*.237/.304/.368*	*.240*	*.315*	*0.5*	*LF 1, CF -1*	*0.2*

In the span of a year and a half, Robinson has gone from a player some considered nearly ready to be a second-division starter to one who could be had for punchless Robert Andino. He still has potential if he can improve his approach at the plate and make more contact, although at 25 years old, time is against him doing so. If nothing else, his speed and athleticism make him a solid defensive outfielder capable of roaming center, which he'll complement with steals and a modicum of patience and power. He figures to serve as a reserve outfielder for Baltimore this season.

Jonathan Schoop MI
Born: **10/6/1991** Age: **21**
Bats: **R** Throws: **R** Height: **6' 2"**
Weight: **187** Breakout: **3%**
Improve: **63%** Collapse: **7%**
Attrition: **10%** MLB: **97%**
Comparables:
Glenn Hubbard,Roberto Alomar,Bill Mazeroski

YEAR	TEAM	LVL	AGE	PA	R	2B	3B	HR	RBI	BB	SO	SB	CS	AVG_OBP_SLG	TAv	BABIP	BRR	FRAA	WARP
2010	BLU	Rk	18	148	16	11	1	2	16	12	14	1	1	.316/.365/.459	.302	.333	-3.5	SS(38): 0.7	0.9
2010	ORI	Rk	18	70	11	4	0	3	16	7	7	0	0	.250/.338/.467	.307	.240	1.3	SS(16): -2.1	0.5
2011	DEL	A	19	238	45	12	3	8	34	20	32	6	4	.316/.376/.514	.284	.337	0.2	SS(25): 1.1, 3B(10): -1.6	1.1
2011	FRD	A+	19	329	37	12	2	5	37	22	44	6	3	.271/.329/.375	.257	.304	0.8	2B(53): 1.0, SS(8): 1.4	0.8
2012	BOW	AA	20	555	68	24	1	14	56	50	103	5	3	.245/.324/.386	.263	.282	-3	2B(72): -5.1, SS(35): -4.9	-0.3
2013	*BAL*	*MLB*	*21*	*250*	*27*	*10*	*1*	*6*	*24*	*15*	*51*	*1*	*1*	*.234/.283/.364*	*.229*	*.271*	*-0.4*	*2B -2, SS 1*	*0.1*

With Machado now in Baltimore, Schoop takes up the mantle of top position prospect in the Orioles organization. He has an excellent arm and hands, but he may be just a tad light in terms of natural athleticism to really thrive at second base, where he's already moved from shortstop. Schoop has a good approach at the plate, and his gap power began its transition into actual power last year at Double-A. He could be an above-average power hitter by middle-infield standards and a big part of a competitive Baltimore club in a few years, though he'll be less valuable if he has to move to a corner.

Taylor Teagarden C
Born: **12/21/1983** Age: **29**
Bats: **R** Throws: **R** Height: **6' 2"**
Weight: **200** Breakout: **3%**
Improve: **36%** Collapse: **15%**
Attrition: **33%** MLB: **95%**
Comparables:
Rick Wilkins,Mickey Tettleton,Bobby Estalella

YEAR	TEAM	LVL	AGE	PA	R	2B	3B	HR	RBI	BB	SO	SB	CS	AVG_OBP_SLG	TAv	BABIP	BRR	FRAA	WARP
2010	FRI	AA	26	220	24	10	1	3	32	25	75	0	0	.242/.339/.353	.248	.384	-2.3	C(44): 0.5	0.4
2010	TEX	MLB	26	85	10	1	0	4	6	8	34	0	0	.155/.259/.338	.244	.212	0.6	C(28): -0.1	0.1
2011	ROU	AAA	27	173	30	4	3	12	22	21	52	0	0	.285/.376/.589	.320	.356	0	--	0.0
2011	TEX	MLB	27	36	3	2	0	0	2	2	13	0	0	.235/.278/.294	.223	.381	-1	C(14): -0.3	-0.1
2012	BAL	MLB	28	64	4	3	0	2	9	5	23	0	0	.158/.226/.316	.220	.219	-1.1	C(21): -0.5	-0.2
2013	*BAL*	*MLB*	*29*	*250*	*26*	*10*	*1*	*8*	*28*	*21*	*89*	*0*	*0*	*.204/.279/.361*	*.229*	*.289*	*-0.4*	*C -1*	*0.2*

You might not be able to tell by the paltry plate-appearance total, but Teagarden was Matt Wieters' sole backup after the All-Star break. Wieters was a workhorse, starting 81 percent of games and going as many as eight straight without a rest, and that may speak a bit to the lack of faith the Orioles had in TT as they made their playoff push. Teagarden was once a promising offensive prospect on his way to becoming a three-true-outcomes catcher in the mold of Mike Napoli. His hacktastic approach at the plate has proven prohibitive, though, and his power hasn't developed enough to offset it. He is still a great defender, putting him on-par with your average, run-of-the-mill backup backstop.

Jim Thome DH
Born: **8/27/1970** Age: **42**
Bats: **L** Throws: **R** Height: **6' 4"**
Weight: **250** Breakout: **0%**
Improve: **8%** Collapse: **21%**
Attrition: **25%** MLB: **69%**
Comparables:
Andres Galarraga,Hank Aaron,Ted Williams

YEAR	TEAM	LVL	AGE	PA	R	2B	3B	HR	RBI	BB	SO	SB	CS	AVG_OBP_SLG	TAv	BABIP	BRR	FRAA	WARP
2010	MIN	MLB	39	340	48	16	2	25	59	60	82	0	0	.283/.412/.627	.351	.310	-3.5	--	3.3
2011	CLE	MLB	40	82	11	4	0	3	10	11	23	0	0	.296/.390/.479	.312	.400	0.3	--	0.5
2011	MIN	MLB	40	242	21	12	0	12	40	35	69	0	0	.243/.351/.476	.296	.302	-3.8	--	0.5
2012	BAL	MLB	41	115	8	5	0	3	10	14	40	0	0	.257/.348/.396	.262	.397	-0.7	--	0.0
2012	PHI	MLB	41	71	9	2	0	5	15	8	21	0	0	.242/.338/.516	.296	.278	0.7	1B(4): -0.0	0.4
2013	*BAL*	*MLB*	*42*	*250*	*33*	*10*	*0*	*12*	*37*	*35*	*72*	*0*	*0*	*.237/.346/.458*	*.282*	*.293*	*-0.5*	*1B 0*	*1.1*

After signing with the National League's Phillies for a small salary and an even smaller playing-time expectation, Thome's quest for a World Series ring was all but a failure by the time July rolled around. He was an easy choice for Philadelphia to dump at the trade deadline. His time in Baltimore was limited by injuries of his own, but his still prodigious power was on display whenever he stepped up to the plate in the much more fitting role of designated hitter. Should he decide to keep playing, Thome remains a cheap, capable DH with excellent pop.

Danny Valencia 3B
Born: **9/19/1984** Age: **28**
Bats: **R** Throws: **R** Height: **6' 3"**
Weight: **220** Breakout: **0%**
Improve: **46%** Collapse: **2%**
Attrition: **5%** MLB: **86%**
Comparables:
Jose Castillo,Joe Crede,Ray Knight

YEAR	TEAM	LVL	AGE	PA	R	2B	3B	HR	RBI	BB	SO	SB	CS	AVG_OBP_SLG	TAv	BABIP	BRR	FRAA	WARP
2010	ROC	AAA	25	202	22	15	0	0	24	14	34	2	0	.292/.348/.373	.250	.358	-1.2	3B(45): -1.5	0.1
2010	MIN	MLB	25	322	30	18	1	7	40	20	46	2	0	.311/.351/.448	.272	.345	-1.6	3B(81): 3.4	1.5
2011	MIN	MLB	26	608	63	28	2	15	72	40	102	2	6	.246/.294/.383	.247	.275	-1.4	3B(147): -6.3	-0.5
2012	PAW	AAA	27	53	3	3	0	1	8	3	12	0	2	.306/.358/.429	.281	.389	-0.9	3B(9): 1.1	0.2
2012	ROC	AAA	27	284	30	17	1	7	37	15	40	1	2	.250/.289/.399	.229	.270	0.8	3B(46): 0.6	-0.5
2012	BOS	MLB	27	29	1	0	0	1	4	0	6	0	0	.143/.138/.250	.163	.136	0	3B(10): -0.3	-0.3
2012	MIN	MLB	27	132	13	6	1	2	17	3	32	0	1	.198/.212/.310	.184	.242	0.1	3B(34): 0.7	-0.9
2013	*BAL*	*MLB*	*28*	*291*	*29*	*14*	*1*	*8*	*34*	*17*	*54*	*1*	*1*	*.254/.298/.401*	*.246*	*.288*	*-0.7*	*3B -2*	*0.0*

A deck chair added to the Boston Titanic from Minnesota in early August, Valencia didn't do much to endear himself to Red Sox fans. He was traded to Baltimore for cash considerations in the offseason. Hitting left-handed pitching is the sum total of Valencia's abilities. That would be fine if not for his lackluster defense, which makes finding a spot for him on the bench somewhere between difficult and self-defeating.

Matt Wieters **C**

Born: **5/21/1986** Age: **27**
Bats: **B** Throws: **R** Height: **6' 6"**
Weight: **225** Breakout: **2%**
Improve: **46%** Collapse: **6%**
Attrition: **14%** MLB: **95%**

Comparables:
Don Pavletich, Victor Martinez, Miguel Montero

YEAR	TEAM	LVL	AGE	PA	R	2B	3B	HR	RBI	BB	SO	SB	CS	AVG_OBP_SLG	TAv	BABIP	BRR	FRAA	WARP
2010	BAL	MLB	24	502	37	22	1	11	55	47	94	0	1	.249/.319/.377	.249	.287	-0.8	C(126): -1.0	1.7
2011	BAL	MLB	25	551	72	28	0	22	68	48	84	1	0	.262/.328/.450	.268	.276	-2.2	C(132): 3.1, 1B(1): -0.1	3.0
2012	BAL	MLB	26	593	67	27	1	23	83	60	112	3	0	.249/.329/.435	.270	.274	-6	C(134): -2.2	2.1
2013	*BAL*	*MLB*	*27*	*549*	*62*	*25*	*1*	*18*	*70*	*51*	*105*	*1*	*0*	*.260/.330/.426*	*.266*	*.294*	*-0.8*	*C -1, 1B -0*	*2.7*

Little-known fact outside of Baltimore's clubhouse: Wieters and Jones made a bet in camp last year to see who could more closely approximate their 2011 stats. Okay, that was a lie, but it sure as heck looks like it, doesn't it? Wieters is holding steady, meaning he has yet to take that next step forward into the realm of catching's elite. But he is a very adept hitter with some upside still remaining. Though he's middle-of-the-road overall defensively, thanks mostly to average framing skills, he was the best in baseball at blocking pitches last year, saving four runs, and second-best at controlling the running game, where he saved five more.

PITCHERS

Jake Arrieta

Born: **3/6/1986** Age: **27**
Bats: **R** Throws: **R** Height: **6' 5"** Weight: **225**
Breakout: **24%** Improve: **60%** Collapse: **20%**
Attrition: **18%** MLB: **87%**

Comparables:
Noah Lowry, Chad Billingsley, Micah Owings

YEAR	TEAM	LVL	AGE	W	L	SV	G	GS	IP	H	HR	BB	SO	BB9	SO9	GB%	BABIP	WHIP	ERA	FIP	FRA	WARP
2010	NOR	AAA	24	6	2	0	12	11	73	48	3	34	64	4.2	7.9	52%	.237	1.12	1.85	3.55	4.79	0.4
2010	BAL	MLB	24	6	6	0	18	18	100^1	106	9	48	52	4.3	4.7	44%	.289	1.53	4.66	4.73	5.09	0.5
2011	BAL	MLB	25	10	8	0	22	22	119^1	115	21	59	93	4.4	7.0	48%	.272	1.46	5.05	5.37	6.27	-0.8
2012	NOR	AAA	26	5	4	0	10	10	56	46	3	28	54	4.5	8.7	48%	.287	1.32	4.02	3.64	5.06	0.2
2012	BAL	MLB	26	3	9	0	24	18	114^2	122	16	35	109	2.7	8.6	46%	.320	1.37	6.20	4.01	4.61	1.0
2013	*BAL*	*MLB*	*27*	*7*	*7*	*0*	*20*	*20*	*113*	*111*	*15*	*50*	*95*	*3.9*	*7.6*	*45%*	*.293*	*1.42*	*4.63*	*4.57*	*5.03*	*0.4*

Arrieta had an amazing 2012 season—if you only look at the peripherals. Unfortunately, the surface numbers were horrendous, bad enough that it's tough to chalk it up to mere luck. Arrieta has terrific stuff—two 94-mph fastballs and three plus secondary offerings—but he doesn't seem to trust that stuff the way he should. He has a tendency to aim instead of pitch when he gets in a jam, and that manifested itself in the form of a 57 percent LOB percentage last year. The O's have a lot of rotation options, so continued struggles could earn Arrieta another demotion, but he is extremely talented and equally hard-working, so it would be no surprise if 2013 is his breakout year and he becomes the club's ace.

Luis Ayala

Born: **1/12/1978** Age: **35**
Bats: **R** Throws: **R** Height: **6' 3"** Weight: **190**
Breakout: **20%** Improve: **50%** Collapse: **38%**
Attrition: **12%** MLB: **70%**

Comparables:
Masa Kobayashi, Bobby Tiefenauer, Bryan Corey

YEAR	TEAM	LVL	AGE	W	L	SV	G	GS	IP	H	HR	BB	SO	BB9	SO9	GB%	BABIP	WHIP	ERA	FIP	FRA	WARP
2010	ABQ	AAA	32	1	3	4	14	0	14	14	1	7	10	4.5	6.4	50%	.277	1.50	4.50	4.80	5.72	0.1
2010	CSP	AAA	32	1	1	0	4	0	7^1	8	2	0	4	0.0	4.9	54%	.250	1.10	4.93	6.05	7.17	-0.1
2010	RNO	AAA	32	0	6	0	18	0	26^1	38	1	11	17	3.8	5.8	52%	.398	1.86	7.87	4.38	4.44	0.7
2011	SWB	AAA	33	0	0	0	3	0	5	6	0	0	7	0.0	12.6	67%	.444	1.20	1.80	0.44	2.53	0.1
2011	NYA	MLB	33	2	2	0	52	0	56	51	5	20	39	3.2	6.3	52%	.282	1.27	2.09	4.22	5.27	0.0
2012	BAL	MLB	34	5	5	1	66	0	75	81	7	14	51	1.7	6.1	50%	.303	1.27	2.64	3.62	3.72	1.1
2013	*BAL*	*MLB*	*35*	*3*	*1*	*1*	*53*	*0*	61^2	*66*	*8*	*18*	*43*	*2.7*	*6.3*	*47%*	*.302*	*1.36*	*4.65*	*4.37*	*5.06*	*0.1*

After resurrecting his career in 2011 with the Yankees, Ayala has managed to become a league-average reliever, though he's received some surface-stat luck. He managed to cut his walk rate practically in half last season, but issuing so few free passes seems unsustainable. A good portion of his resurgence can be attributed to the flip-flopping of his two- and four-seam fastball usage beginning in 2011, generating more grounders with heavy reliance on the sinker (48 percent last year). Despite his mediocre peripherals, the Orioles picked up Ayala's option this offseason.

Zach Braddock

Born: **8/23/1987** Age: **25**
Bats: **L** Throws: **L** Height: **6' 3"** Weight: **230**
Breakout: **25%** Improve: **54%** Collapse: **26%**
Attrition: **7%** MLB: **85%**

Comparables:
Tom Hall,Andrew Sisco,Hong-Chih Kuo

YEAR	TEAM	LVL	AGE	W	L	SV	G	GS	IP	H	HR	BB	SO	BB9	SO9	GB%	BABIP	WHIP	ERA	FIP	FRA	WARP
2010	NAS	AAA	22	0	0	1	11	0	16	10	1	9	28	5.1	15.8	53%	.310	1.19	4.50	2.96	3.92	0.4
2010	MIL	MLB	22	1	2	0	46	0	33^{2}	29	1	19	41	5.1	11.0	35%	.318	1.43	2.94	2.93	2.98	0.6
2011	WIS	A	23	0	0	0	2	2	4^{2}	0	0	1	7	1.9	13.5	—	.000	0.21	0.00	1.00	1.09	0.0
2011	NAS	AAA	23	0	0	1	6	0	5^{2}	4	0	7	10	11.1	15.9	33%	.333	1.94	4.76	3.96	4.96	0.0
2011	MIL	MLB	23	0	1	0	25	0	17^{1}	16	2	11	18	5.7	9.3	33%	.286	1.56	7.27	4.67	5.54	-0.2
2013	*BAL*	*MLB*	*25*	*2*	*1*	*1*	*42*	*0*	*34^{2}*	*30*	*4*	*18*	*41*	*4.6*	*10.5*	*39%*	*.299*	*1.36*	*4.07*	*3.89*	*4.42*	*0.3*

Braddock was once a talented Brewers relieving prospect who profiled as a potential late-inning type. HIPAA laws prevent us from knowing the whole story, but he was released last May. There were whispers of personal issues, sleep disorder, anxiety, and tardiness, among other off-field issues that led to the Brewers and Braddock parting ways. He was once very gifted, with a high-rising, 93-mph heater and a biting slider, so the potential exists for him to help the Orioles if other issues are behind him.

Zach Britton

Born: **12/22/1987** Age: **25**
Bats: **L** Throws: **L** Height: **6' 4"** Weight: **195**
Breakout: **26%** Improve: **59%** Collapse: **14%**
Attrition: **9%** MLB: **92%**

Comparables:
Aaron Laffey,Steve Avery,Sean Marshall

YEAR	TEAM	LVL	AGE	W	L	SV	G	GS	IP	H	HR	BB	SO	BB9	SO9	GB%	BABIP	WHIP	ERA	FIP	FRA	WARP
2010	BOW	AA	22	7	3	0	15	14	87	76	4	28	68	2.9	7.0	64%	.276	1.20	2.48	3.46	4.82	0.4
2010	NOR	AAA	22	3	4	0	12	12	66^{1}	63	3	23	56	3.1	7.6	64%	.303	1.30	2.99	3.28	4.70	0.4
2011	BOW	AA	23	0	2	0	3	3	11^{2}	14	3	2	15	1.5	11.6	44%	.355	1.37	5.40	4.95	6.95	-0.2
2011	NOR	AAA	23	0	1	0	1	1	5	3	0	1	3	1.8	5.4	50%	.214	0.80	1.80	2.64	3.43	0.1
2011	BAL	MLB	23	11	11	0	28	28	154^{1}	162	12	62	97	3.6	5.7	55%	.304	1.45	4.61	4.04	5.09	0.8
2012	BOW	AA	24	1	0	0	2	2	12	8	0	3	11	2.2	8.2	73%	.242	0.92	0.75	2.37	3.40	0.2
2012	NOR	AAA	24	4	2	0	9	9	51^{1}	49	5	20	37	3.5	6.5	56%	.278	1.34	4.91	4.15	5.83	-0.2
2012	BAL	MLB	24	5	3	0	12	11	60^{1}	61	6	32	53	4.8	7.9	61%	.311	1.54	5.07	4.27	5.14	0.2
2013	*BAL*	*MLB*	*25*	*5*	*6*	*0*	*15*	*15*	*84^{2}*	*89*	*10*	*36*	*60*	*3.9*	*6.3*	*59%*	*.300*	*1.48*	*4.81*	*4.59*	*5.23*	*0.1*

Britton missed the beginning of last season with an injury to the same (throwing) shoulder that ailed him in 2011, and upon return he once again underwhelmed. The issue with Britton isn't stuff, which is actually quite good—he throws 93 mph with an easy plus slider. The problem is the platoon split that the southpaw's repertoire generates: 3.21 xFIP against lefties, 4.51 xFIP vs. righties. (xFIP is a fielding-independent measure that assumes average luck on home runs per fly ball.) The resulting amalgamation is a mediocre starting pitcher. Britton needs to find a way to get righties out or the Orioles may decide he's better suited in a bullpen role, where he'd be deadly with carefully chosen matchups. He currently uses his sinker—the pitch with the single biggest platoon split in baseball—over 40 percent of the time against righties. If he were to rein that in and use more four-seamers and changeups? That could do the trick.

Dylan Bundy

Born: **11/15/1992** Age: **20**
Bats: **B** Throws: **R** Height: **6' 2"** Weight: **200**
Breakout: **44%** Improve: **78%** Collapse: **13%**
Attrition: **2%** MLB: **94%**

Comparables:
Bert Blyleven,Madison Bumgarner,Gary Nolan

YEAR	TEAM	LVL	AGE	W	L	SV	G	GS	IP	H	HR	BB	SO	BB9	SO9	GB%	BABIP	WHIP	ERA	FIP	FRA	WARP
2012	DEL	A	19	1	0	0	8	8	30	5	0	2	40	0.6	12.0	51%	.091	0.23	0.00	1.31	2.38	0.8
2012	FRD	A+	19	6	3	0	12	12	57	48	5	18	66	2.8	10.4	36%	.314	1.16	2.84	3.21	3.30	1.0
2012	BOW	AA	19	2	0	0	3	3	16^{2}	14	1	8	13	4.3	7.0	46%	.265	1.32	3.24	3.86	4.16	0.1
2012	BAL	MLB	19	0	0	0	2	0	1^{2}	1	0	1	0	5.4	0.0	20%	.200	1.20	0.00	4.85	6.09	0.0
2013	*BAL*	*MLB*	*20*	*2*	*2*	*0*	*8*	*8*	*35*	*33*	*5*	*15*	*33*	*3.8*	*8.4*	*42%*	*.298*	*1.38*	*4.40*	*4.46*	*4.79*	*0.3*

While pitching prospects are never a sure thing, they don't come with much higher praise than Bundy. In his first season as a professional, he scaled the organizational tree faster than a monkey in a flood, going from Low-A to the majors in a matter of months. He'll return to the high minors to begin this season but could be in Baltimore's rotation for good come 2014. His fastball is a bit straight, but it gets plenty of rise and comes in at 95 mph. He complements it with a plus curve, a developing changeup, and a slider. With clean mechanics and good makeup, the sky is the limit for Bundy.

Wei-Yin Chen

Born: **7/21/1985** Age: **27**
Bats: **L** Throws: **L** Height: **6' 1"** Weight: **175**
Breakout: **28%** Improve: **56%** Collapse: **26%**
Attrition: **12%** MLB: **88%**

Comparables:
Ryan Rowland-Smith,Phil Coke,Tom Sturdivant

YEAR	TEAM	LVL	AGE	W	L	SV	G	GS	IP	H	HR	BB	SO	BB9	SO9	GB%	BABIP	WHIP	ERA	FIP	FRA	WARP
2010	CHU	NPB	24	13	10	0	29	27	188	166	21	49	153	2.3	7.3	—	.268	1.14	2.87	3.73	4.05	0.0
2011	CHU	NPB	25	8	10	0	25	24	164^{2}	138	9	31	93	1.7	5.1	—	.257	1.03	2.68	0.00	0.00	0.0
2012	BAL	MLB	26	12	11	0	32	32	192^{2}	186	29	57	154	2.7	7.2	39%	.274	1.26	4.02	4.37	4.55	1.8
2013	*BAL*	*MLB*	*27*	*9*	*8*	*0*	*24*	*24*	*148*	*147*	*19*	*44*	*124*	*2.7*	*7.5*	*40%*	*.296*	*1.29*	*4.10*	*4.09*	*4.45*	*1.4*

While far less hyped than fellow Japanese import Yu Darvish, Wei-Yin Chen proved a capable mid-rotation pitcher for the Orioles. More importantly, he overcame many of the issues preseason prognosticators foresaw him having, such as regaining his stuff following 2011 groin and hamstring injuries. Chen remained healthy all year and his velocity was back to peak levels of sitting 92 mph and touching 95 by midseason. Combined with a solid change and a lesser-used curve, Chen should be able to maintain an above-average strikeout rate. His extreme fly-ball tendencies limit him to mid-rotation status, but his plus command and revitalized fastball and slider should make him effective every fifth day for the O's.

Miguel Gonzalez
Born: **5/27/1984** Age: **29**
Bats: **R** Throws: **R** Height: **6' 2"** Weight: **170**
Breakout: **16%** Improve: **39%** Collapse: **27%**
Attrition: **6%** MLB: **97%**
Comparables:
Steve Rogers, Freddy Garcia, Kevin Millwood

YEAR	TEAM	LVL	AGE	W	L	SV	G	GS	IP	H	HR	BB	SO	BB9	SO9	GB%	BABIP	WHIP	ERA	FIP	FRA	WARP
2010	SLM	A+	26	6	4	0	17	16	73^{1}	82	5	18	47	2.2	5.8	43%	.321	1.36	4.54	4.07	5.71	-0.2
2011	SLM	A+	27	0	1	0	2	2	5	5	0	2	4	3.6	7.2	—	.333	1.40	1.80	3.43	3.73	0.0
2011	PME	AA	27	0	5	0	15	6	46^{2}	55	4	19	45	3.7	8.7	—	.347	1.59	6.17	4.27	4.64	0.0
2011	PAW	AAA	27	0	1	0	1	1	5	2	1	2	5	3.6	9.0	—	.100	0.80	1.80	5.04	5.47	0.0
2012	NOR	AAA	28	3	2	1	14	6	44^{2}	22	1	10	53	2.0	10.7	42%	.208	0.72	1.61	1.75	2.58	1.1
2012	BAL	MLB	28	9	4	0	18	15	105^{1}	92	13	35	77	3.0	6.6	37%	.260	1.21	3.25	4.33	4.05	1.4
2013	*BAL*	*MLB*	*29*	*5*	*4*	*0*	*18*	*14*	82^{1}	*82*	*11*	*27*	*64*	*3.0*	*7.0*	*40%*	*.291*	*1.33*	*4.25*	*4.37*	*4.62*	*0.7*

If you predicted that Miguel Gonzalez would emerge to post a 3.25 ERA last season, you might have also predicted that Albert Pujols would quit baseball and turn into a purple-feathered half-tuna, half-Velociraptor creature. You also might want to see a psychiatrist. Still, here we are, and Gonzalez looks like he can be a solid starter. He has always had good command, and his stuff actually looked more than respectable last season: a high-rising 92-mph four-seamer, a brutal splitter, a hard slider with good tilt, a solid curve, and a sinker. Given his good pitchability, there are plenty of reasons to believe Gonzalez is for real, if not as a 3.25-ERA pitcher, as one capable of sitting in the low 4.00s.

Jason Hammel
Born: **9/2/1982** Age: **30**
Bats: **R** Throws: **R** Height: **6' 7"** Weight: **215**
Breakout: **6%** Improve: **32%** Collapse: **34%**
Attrition: **11%** MLB: **93%**
Comparables:
Curt Schilling, Jack McDowell, Brad Penny

YEAR	TEAM	LVL	AGE	W	L	SV	G	GS	IP	H	HR	BB	SO	BB9	SO9	GB%	BABIP	WHIP	ERA	FIP	FRA	WARP
2010	CSP	AAA	27	1	0	0	1	1	7	9	1	1	6	1.3	7.7	55%	.381	1.43	5.14	4.15	4.65	0.0
2010	COL	MLB	27	10	9	0	30	30	177^{2}	201	18	47	141	2.4	7.1	48%	.328	1.40	4.81	3.73	4.53	2.2
2011	COL	MLB	28	7	13	1	32	27	170^{1}	175	21	68	94	3.6	5.0	46%	.280	1.43	4.76	4.80	5.54	0.7
2012	FRD	A+	29	1	0	0	1	1	5	3	0	1	7	1.8	12.6	75%	.250	0.80	0.00	1.19	0.76	0.3
2012	BAL	MLB	29	8	6	0	20	20	118	104	9	42	113	3.2	8.6	54%	.291	1.24	3.43	3.24	3.54	2.7
2013	*BAL*	*MLB*	*30*	*7*	*6*	*0*	*18*	*18*	108^{2}	*112*	*13*	*33*	*84*	*2.7*	*6.9*	*47%*	*.302*	*1.33*	*4.29*	*4.12*	*4.66*	*0.8*

"Rocky Mountain High, my ass!" exclaimed Hammel as he stepped onto the plane to Baltimore last offseason. After barely striking out more batters than he walked in 2011, Hammel improved all of his core ratios with the Orioles, capitalizing on the promise he showed in 2009 and '10. Adding a sinker did wonders for his groundball rate, and he managed to add 1 mph and three inches of rise to his four-seamer in addition to sharper-looking breaking balls. That's not enough to explain striking out nearly a batter per inning, but he appears to be out of the doldrums he found himself in with Colorado and should be a solid middle-of-the-rotation starter going forward.

Tommy Hunter
Born: **7/3/1986** Age: **26**
Bats: **R** Throws: **R** Height: **6' 4"** Weight: **280**
Breakout: **23%** Improve: **65%** Collapse: **19%**
Attrition: **16%** MLB: **86%**
Comparables:
Dave Bush, Brad Radke, Justin Germano

YEAR	TEAM	LVL	AGE	W	L	SV	G	GS	IP	H	HR	BB	SO	BB9	SO9	GB%	BABIP	WHIP	ERA	FIP	FRA	WARP
2010	OKL	AAA	23	1	2	0	6	6	26^{2}	28	2	11	14	3.7	4.7	53%	.289	1.46	4.04	4.74	4.92	0.2
2010	TEX	MLB	23	13	4	0	23	22	128	126	21	33	68	2.3	4.8	42%	.255	1.24	3.73	4.96	5.31	0.4
2011	FRI	AA	24	0	0	0	1	0	4	3	1	1	5	2.2	11.2	56%	.250	1.00	4.50	5.63	4.84	0.0
2011	ROU	AAA	24	2	2	1	8	5	26^{2}	37	2	3	16	1.0	5.4	—	.361	1.50	5.06	4.01	4.36	0.0
2011	BAL	MLB	24	3	3	0	12	11	69^{1}	88	11	10	35	1.3	4.5	41%	.314	1.41	5.06	4.72	4.95	0.2
2011	TEX	MLB	24	1	1	0	8	0	15^{1}	12	1	5	10	2.9	5.9	57%	.239	1.11	2.93	3.58	4.06	0.2
2012	BOW	AA	25	1	0	1	2	1	10	3	0	1	6	0.9	5.4	59%	.111	0.40	0.00	2.30	3.26	0.1
2012	NOR	AAA	25	2	1	0	3	3	19^{1}	20	2	5	14	2.3	6.5	53%	.305	1.29	4.66	3.83	4.52	0.2
2012	BAL	MLB	25	7	8	0	33	20	133^{2}	161	32	27	77	1.8	5.2	48%	.298	1.41	5.45	5.70	6.13	-0.8
2013	*BAL*	*MLB*	*26*	*7*	*7*	*0*	*20*	*20*	115^{2}	*128*	*20*	*28*	*69*	*2.2*	*5.4*	*45%*	*.291*	*1.35*	*4.81*	*4.98*	*5.22*	*0.1*

Hunter spent 2012 bouncing between the rotation and the bullpen, and a swing role seems about all he's destined for. While he throws 93 mph, his secondary offerings are more about quantity than quality; he throws four other pitches (sinker, cutter, changeup, curve), but none induced whiffs on more than 21 percent of swings this year. To put their ineffectiveness in perspective, that's lower than a lot of pitchers' fastballs. This results in low strikeout rates and a reliance on pinpoint control, making Hunter a capable enough fifth starter, but he'll max out there unless he can find a way to induce more swings-and-misses.

Jim Johnson

Born: **6/27/1983** Age: **30**
Bats: **R** Throws: **R** Height: **6' 6"** Weight: **230**
Breakout: **26%** Improve: **47%** Collapse: **27%**
Attrition: **13%** MLB: **88%**

Comparables:
Bill Dailey,Mike Koplove,Brad Ziegler

YEAR	TEAM	LVL	AGE	W	L	SV	G	GS	IP	H	HR	BB	SO	BB9	SO9	GB%	BABIP	WHIP	ERA	FIP	FRA	WARP
2010	ORI	Rk	27	0	0	0	4	4	4	5	1	1	5	2.2	11.2	64%	.400	1.50	6.75	5.01	7.29	-0.1
2010	FRD	A+	27	0	0	0	2	0	3	6	0	0	1	0.0	3.0	69%	.462	2.00	3.00	2.74	3.86	0.0
2010	BOW	AA	27	0	0	0	4	1	5	2	1	0	6	0.0	10.8	67%	.167	0.40	1.80	3.56	4.93	0.0
2010	NOR	AAA	27	0	0	0	1	0	1	1	0	0	0	0.0	0.0	25%	.250	1.00	0.00	3.29	4.93	0.0
2010	BAL	MLB	27	1	1	1	26	0	26^{1}	32	2	5	22	1.7	7.5	51%	.345	1.41	3.42	3.05	4.43	0.3
2011	BAL	MLB	28	6	5	9	69	0	91	80	5	21	58	2.1	5.7	63%	.269	1.11	2.67	3.26	4.34	0.7
2012	BAL	MLB	29	2	1	51	71	0	68^{2}	55	3	15	41	2.0	5.4	64%	.251	1.02	2.49	3.21	4.02	0.7
2013	*BAL*	*MLB*	*30*	*3*	*1*	*18*	*53*	*0*	*59^{2}*	*58*	*6*	*17*	*41*	*2.6*	*6.2*	*53%*	*.287*	*1.26*	*3.66*	*3.99*	*3.98*	*0.8*

Since the save became an official statistic in 1969, only four pitchers have notched at least 40 saves while posting a lower strikeout rate than Johnson. He easily posted the lowest SO9 among pitchers with at least 20 saves last season, nearly a full strikeout per nine fewer than the next lowest: the Stay-Puft Marshmallow Man-sized mess that was Jose Valverde. Saying Johnson is not a prototypical closer would be like saying a hammer is not a prototypical power tool—it'll get the job done; it just won't be as flashy. Give Buck Showalter credit for giving Johnson the opportunity, because he dominated thanks to plus control and lots of groundballs. He generates grounders using a 95-mph sinker—yet another reason why he's an anomaly of a closer; pitchers rarely generate that kind of velocity on sinkers.

Steve Johnson

Born: **8/31/1987** Age: **25**
Bats: **R** Throws: **R** Height: **6' 2"** Weight: **200**
Breakout: **31%** Improve: **69%** Collapse: **14%**
Attrition: **16%** MLB: **89%**

Comparables:
John Ely,Wade Miller,Kyle Davies

YEAR	TEAM	LVL	AGE	W	L	SV	G	GS	IP	H	HR	BB	SO	BB9	SO9	GB%	BABIP	WHIP	ERA	FIP	FRA	WARP
2010	BOW	AA	22	7	8	0	28	28	145	144	24	78	128	4.8	7.9	28%	.312	1.53	5.09	5.59	6.32	-0.6
2011	BOW	AA	23	5	1	0	10	10	58^{1}	40	7	15	59	2.3	9.1	32%	.216	0.94	2.16	3.82	3.70	0.6
2011	NOR	AAA	23	2	7	0	17	17	87^{1}	101	7	47	63	4.8	6.5	26%	.305	1.69	5.56	4.59	5.48	-0.1
2012	NOR	AAA	24	4	8	0	19	14	91^{1}	66	7	31	86	3.1	8.5	30%	.244	1.06	2.86	3.49	4.84	0.4
2012	BAL	MLB	24	4	0	0	12	4	38^{1}	23	4	18	46	4.2	10.8	26%	.229	1.07	2.11	3.41	4.46	0.2
2013	*BAL*	*MLB*	*25*	*3*	*3*	*0*	*11*	*9*	*52^{1}*	*52*	*9*	*26*	*44*	*4.4*	*7.6*	*31%*	*.290*	*1.49*	*5.06*	*5.24*	*5.50*	*-0.1*

Previously in these pages we noted that Johnson "needs to be tried in middle relief." That's exactly what the Orioles did when they called him up last August—and it worked. He strikes out more batters than you'd expect from a guy who throws a straight fastball that barely reaches 90 mph, but his heater gets nice rise and makes hitters focus on multiple planes vs. the off-speed stuff. More than two feet separated his highest-rising fastballs and biggest-breaking curves last season, with sliders and changeups in between. Throwing his fastball two-thirds of the time may make those secondary offerings more effective, but also makes him an extreme fly-ball pitcher and susceptible to the long ball at Camden Yards. Johnson will need to improve his shaky control to stay successful, especially with regression expected in his gaudy strikeout rate. You can't have ducks on the pond if you're giving up a lot of home runs.

Brian Matusz

Born: **2/11/1987** Age: **26**
Bats: **L** Throws: **L** Height: **6' 5"** Weight: **190**
Breakout: **32%** Improve: **59%** Collapse: **12%**
Attrition: **21%** MLB: **93%**

Comparables:
Paul Maholm,Scott Olsen,Matt Maloney

YEAR	TEAM	LVL	AGE	W	L	SV	G	GS	IP	H	HR	BB	SO	BB9	SO9	GB%	BABIP	WHIP	ERA	FIP	FRA	WARP
2010	BAL	MLB	23	10	12	0	32	32	175^{2}	173	19	63	143	3.2	7.3	38%	.292	1.34	4.30	4.02	4.69	1.9
2011	FRD	A+	24	0	0	0	1	1	4	2	0	2	2	4.5	4.5	17%	.167	1.00	2.25	3.73	3.74	0.0
2011	BOW	AA	24	0	0	0	1	1	6	3	0	1	1	1.5	1.5	—	.150	0.67	0.00	3.58	3.89	0.0
2011	NOR	AAA	24	2	3	0	9	9	54^{2}	51	4	19	41	3.1	6.8	39%	.329	1.28	3.46	3.84	5.53	-0.1
2011	BAL	MLB	24	1	9	0	12	12	49^{2}	81	18	24	38	4.3	6.9	28%	.382	2.11	10.69	7.69	8.15	-1.4
2012	NOR	AAA	25	2	1	1	10	6	47	43	2	15	32	2.9	6.1	43%	.281	1.23	4.21	3.31	4.73	0.2
2012	BAL	MLB	25	6	10	0	34	16	98	112	15	41	81	3.8	7.4	43%	.319	1.56	4.87	4.64	4.62	0.6
2013	*BAL*	*MLB*	*26*	*5*	*6*	*0*	*18*	*18*	*93^{2}*	*99*	*14*	*34*	*78*	*3.3*	*7.5*	*39%*	*.307*	*1.43*	*4.81*	*4.57*	*5.23*	*0.2*

Improving on a season as dismal as Matusz's 2011 wasn't going to be hard, but Matusz was solid last season and downright good once he moved to the bullpen in August. He'll be tried again as a starter in 2013, with the pen always a fallback option. While his fastball topped 91 mph as a starter, that's still only lukewarm heat and below where he was in his prospect days. Aside from a changeup that some say is underwhelming, Matusz does have the repertoire of a starter, but he seems to lack the pitchability necessary to make his stuff work over multiple innings, as well as the work ethic to overcome this obstacle. His fastball sat near 93 mph in the bullpen and may serve him better in small bursts.

Daniel McCutchen
Born: **9/26/1982** Age: **30**
Bats: **R** Throws: **R** Height: **6' 3"** Weight: **210**
Breakout: **19%** Improve: **44%** Collapse: **21%**
Attrition: **18%** MLB: **80%**
Comparables:
Bobby Shantz, Sun-Woo Kim, Rick Langford

YEAR	TEAM	LVL	AGE	W	L	SV	G	GS	IP	H	HR	BB	SO	BB9	SO9	GB%	BABIP	WHIP	ERA	FIP	FRA	WARP
2010	PIT	MLB	27	2	5	0	28	9	67^2	83	13	28	38	3.7	5.1	38%	.298	1.64	6.12	5.81	5.84	-0.4
2011	PIT	MLB	28	5	3	0	73	0	84^2	87	7	33	47	3.5	5.0	42%	.293	1.42	3.72	4.27	4.73	-0.4
2012	BRD	A+	29	0	0	0	1	0	2	1	0	0	1	0.0	4.5	67%	.167	0.50	0.00	2.39	2.92	0.0
2012	IND	AAA	29	7	2	3	36	1	63^1	54	3	14	55	2.0	7.8	41%	.279	1.07	2.98	2.84	4.49	0.3
2012	PIT	MLB	29	0	1	0	1	0	0	1	1	1	0	—	—	%	—	—	—	0.00	3297.62	-0.2
2013	*BAL*	*MLB*	*30*	*2*	*1*	*0*	*18*	*3*	*34^2*	*38*	*6*	*11*	*22*	*2.9*	*5.8*	*39%*	*.294*	*1.42*	*5.12*	*5.13*	*5.56*	*-0.1*

The *other* McCutchen led the Pirates in relief innings in 2011 and posted a shiny ERA in the process. That's generally enough to secure a gig in the next year's bullpen, but not this time. Save for one appearance, in which he failed to record an out, McCutchen spent the entire 2012 season on the farm. He is not good enough to start or fill a meaningful relief role, leaving long relief as the best fit. Pittsburgh had seen enough by the end of the season, so he'll have to give it a go in Baltimore this year.

Darren O'Day
Born: **10/22/1982** Age: **30**
Bats: **R** Throws: **R** Height: **6' 5"** Weight: **220**
Breakout: **25%** Improve: **55%** Collapse: **27%**
Attrition: **10%** MLB: **95%**
Comparables:
Bobby Jenks, Jon Rauch, Greg McMichael

YEAR	TEAM	LVL	AGE	W	L	SV	G	GS	IP	H	HR	BB	SO	BB9	SO9	GB%	BABIP	WHIP	ERA	FIP	FRA	WARP
2010	TEX	MLB	27	6	2	0	72	0	62	43	5	12	45	1.7	6.5	39%	.220	0.89	2.03	3.47	4.25	0.5
2011	FRI	AA	28	0	0	0	1	1	1	1	1	0	1	0.0	9.0	—	.000	1.00	9.00	14.38	15.63	0.0
2011	ROU	AAA	28	1	0	1	17	1	20^1	16	2	4	26	1.8	11.5	—	.286	0.98	2.21	3.39	3.68	0.0
2011	TEX	MLB	28	0	1	0	16	0	16^2	17	7	5	18	2.7	9.7	37%	.238	1.32	5.40	7.62	7.17	-0.2
2012	BAL	MLB	29	7	1	0	69	0	67	49	6	14	69	1.9	9.3	36%	.251	0.94	2.28	2.91	2.73	1.4
2013	*BAL*	*MLB*	*30*	*3*	*1*	*1*	*52*	*0*	*48^1*	*43*	*6*	*13*	*44*	*2.3*	*8.3*	*44%*	*.282*	*1.14*	*3.38*	*3.80*	*3.67*	*0.8*

The Rangers' decision to designate O'Day for assignment last offseason was a peculiar one. The submariner's struggles appeared nothing more than a small-sample-size anomaly, though perhaps his injuries scared Texas off. In any case, Dan Duquette pounced and was handsomely rewarded with a quality high-leverage bullpen option. It's rare to see a pitcher with such a low arm slot and such a high strikeout rate, such an extreme fly-ball rate, or no actionable platoon split—much less all three!—but that's what the Orioles have in O'Day. His methods are unconventional, but damn does he get the job done.

Troy Patton
Born: **9/3/1985** Age: **27**
Bats: **B** Throws: **L** Height: **6' 2"** Weight: **185**
Breakout: **25%** Improve: **59%** Collapse: **16%**
Attrition: **10%** MLB: **92%**
Comparables:
J.D. Martin, Burt Hooton, Francisco Cordova

YEAR	TEAM	LVL	AGE	W	L	SV	G	GS	IP	H	HR	BB	SO	BB9	SO9	GB%	BABIP	WHIP	ERA	FIP	FRA	WARP
2010	NOR	AAA	24	8	11	0	25	25	136	144	15	43	89	2.8	5.9	41%	.295	1.38	4.43	4.54	5.43	0.0
2010	BAL	MLB	24	0	0	0	1	0	0^2	1	0	1	1	13.5	13.5	50%	.500	3.00	0.00	4.55	0.32	0.0
2011	NOR	AAA	25	4	1	0	17	2	44^1	44	0	12	30	2.4	6.1	40%	.319	1.26	1.83	2.83	4.24	0.2
2011	BAL	MLB	25	2	1	0	20	0	30	25	2	5	22	1.5	6.6	40%	.256	1.00	3.00	2.96	3.72	0.4
2012	BAL	MLB	26	1	0	0	54	0	55^2	45	5	12	49	1.9	7.9	50%	.256	1.02	2.43	3.21	3.37	1.0
2013	*BAL*	*MLB*	*27*	*2*	*2*	*0*	*19*	*5*	*44*	*46*	*6*	*13*	*30*	*2.8*	*6.1*	*41%*	*.291*	*1.35*	*4.60*	*4.50*	*5.00*	*0.1*

Finally getting a chance to spend an entire season in the majors, former top prospect Patton continued to build on his strong half-season in 2011. While his velocity isn't what it was in his prospect days—his fastball now averages a mere 90 mph—his deep repertoire is a remnant of his years as a starter. Patton throws five pitches, all for strikes, relying primarily on two fastballs and a slider, plus a changeup to righties and a lesser-used curve to lefties. He'll throw any pitch in any count, helping to compensate for that average velocity. Baltimore used him in the middle innings last year, but his ceiling may be as a setup man.

Stuart Pomeranz
Born: **12/17/1984** Age: **28**
Bats: **R** Throws: **R** Height: **6' 8"** Weight: **220**
Breakout: **27%** Improve: **44%** Collapse: **32%**
Attrition: **8%** MLB: **86%**
Comparables:
Ron Davis, Dan Wheeler, Bob James

YEAR	TEAM	LVL	AGE	W	L	SV	G	GS	IP	H	HR	BB	SO	BB9	SO9	GB%	BABIP	WHIP	ERA	FIP	FRA	WARP
2010	TUL	AA	25	1	6	18	51	0	49	57	5	20	53	3.7	9.7	46%	.361	1.57	3.67	3.62	4.32	0.5
2011	CHT	AA	26	0	0	0	2	0	1^1	3	0	3	2	20.2	13.5	—	.500	4.50	27.00	7.06	7.67	0.0
2012	BOW	AA	27	0	0	1	5	0	13^1	7	0	1	20	0.7	13.5	33%	.238	0.60	0.00	0.43	0.68	0.3
2012	NOR	AAA	27	0	0	2	5	0	10	2	0	2	15	1.8	13.5	38%	.125	0.40	0.00	0.76	1.95	0.3
2012	BAL	MLB	27	0	0	0	3	0	6	7	1	1	3	1.5	4.5	59%	.286	1.33	3.00	4.71	5.52	0.0
2013	*BAL*	*MLB*	*28*	*1*	*1*	*1*	*29*	*0*	*35*	*35*	*5*	*13*	*32*	*3.3*	*8.3*	*43%*	*.306*	*1.37*	*4.35*	*4.34*	*4.73*	*0.2*

The older brother of the more heralded Colorado pitcher Drew has traveled a tough road to the verge of relevance, only to have offseason surgery on his lower back that is expected to sideline him all of 2013. He was drafted back in 2003 and only made his MLB debut last year after being discarded by three teams, dealing with alcoholism and injuries, and spending some time in the independent leagues. Although his command is a bit loose, he keeps the walks down. His 94-95 mph heater and bat-missing 11-to-5 curve are both good enough to retire big-league hitters—and good enough to be worth a post-surgery rehab effort.

Joe Saunders

Born: **6/16/1981** Age: **32**
Bats: **L** Throws: **L** Height: **6' 4"** Weight: **210**
Breakout: **9%** Improve: **56%** Collapse: **29%**
Attrition: **10%** MLB: **87%**

Comparables:
Denny Neagle,Mark Redman,Jarrod Washburn

YEAR	TEAM	LVL	AGE	W	L	SV	G	GS	IP	H	HR	BB	SO	BB9	SO9	GB%	BABIP	WHIP	ERA	FIP	FRA	WARP
2010	ANA	MLB	29	6	10	0	20	20	120^{2}	135	14	45	64	3.4	4.8	44%	.304	1.49	4.62	4.64	4.87	0.6
2010	ARI	MLB	29	3	7	0	13	13	82^{2}	97	11	19	50	2.1	5.4	46%	.314	1.40	4.25	4.46	5.10	0.2
2011	ARI	MLB	30	12	13	0	33	33	212	210	29	67	108	2.8	4.6	46%	.271	1.31	3.69	4.74	5.39	-0.8
2012	DIA	Rk	31	0	1	0	1	1	4^{1}	3	0	5	7	10.4	14.5	80%	.200	1.85	6.23	4.61	3.86	0.1
2012	ARI	MLB	31	6	10	0	21	21	130	146	17	31	89	2.1	6.2	45%	.306	1.36	4.22	4.23	4.42	1.0
2012	BAL	MLB	31	3	3	0	7	7	44^{2}	49	4	8	23	1.6	4.6	42%	.302	1.28	3.63	3.72	3.95	0.5
2013	*BAL*	*MLB*	*32*	*9*	*9*	*0*	*24*	*24*	*149^{1}*	*163*	*23*	*46*	*82*	*2.8*	*5.0*	*46%*	*.292*	*1.40*	*4.86*	*5.03*	*5.28*	*-0.0*

Two years after being traded to the Diamondbacks along with Tyler Skaggs, Saunders was pushed out of their rotation to make room for the guy who was his accountabilibuddy on the trip over from Los Angeles . . . and wound up starting two playoff elimination games for the Orioles. That's quite a change of fortune for a guy who isn't even league average. While Saunders possesses plus control, his mediocre stuff means he struggles to strike batters out. He scrapped his slider (his least-used pitch) last season, but it had no noticeable effect on his numbers. He's a boring back-of-the-rotation pitcher.

Daniel Schlereth

Born: **5/9/1986** Age: **27**
Bats: **L** Throws: **L** Height: **6' 1"** Weight: **200**
Breakout: **37%** Improve: **55%** Collapse: **22%**
Attrition: **27%** MLB: **80%**

Comparables:
Dan Runzler,Alex Hinshaw,Jon Coutlangus

YEAR	TEAM	LVL	AGE	W	L	SV	G	GS	IP	H	HR	BB	SO	BB9	SO9	GB%	BABIP	WHIP	ERA	FIP	FRA	WARP
2010	DET	MLB	24	2	0	1	18	0	18^{2}	20	2	10	19	4.8	9.2	49%	.327	1.61	2.89	4.17	3.65	0.3
2011	TOL	AAA	25	1	0	0	8	0	11^{2}	6	0	5	18	3.9	13.9	53%	.333	0.94	0.77	1.44	0.80	0.4
2011	DET	MLB	25	2	2	0	49	0	49	36	6	31	44	5.7	8.1	42%	.238	1.37	3.49	5.06	5.94	-0.3
2012	LAK	A+	26	0	0	0	8	6	8	6	0	7	9	7.9	10.1	57%	.286	1.62	1.12	3.77	2.18	0.2
2012	TOL	AAA	26	0	0	0	3	0	1^{2}	3	0	4	2	21.6	10.8	33%	.500	4.20	10.80	7.96	7.33	-0.1
2012	DET	MLB	26	0	0	0	6	0	7	14	3	5	6	6.4	7.7	39%	.440	2.71	10.29	9.05	7.35	-0.2
2013	*BAL*	*MLB*	*27*	*2*	*1*	*0*	*31*	*0*	*34*	*30*	*4*	*20*	*37*	*5.4*	*9.8*	*48%*	*.297*	*1.48*	*4.37*	*4.32*	*4.75*	*0.2*

Schlereth was once considered the closer of the future for Arizona, but after three disappointing years for Detroit, he has moved on to the Orioles hoping to fulfill his promise. He has good stuff, with a 93-mph fastball (though that velocity has been on the decline) and a curveball that can miss some bats, but his control is so poor as to render him ineffective. He is reaching an age where gains in this department become increasingly unlikely, so unless he can do a 180 and fast, he'll be organizational depth.

Pedro Strop

Born: **6/13/1985** Age: **28**
Bats: **R** Throws: **R** Height: **6' 1"** Weight: **175**
Breakout: **25%** Improve: **53%** Collapse: **27%**
Attrition: **17%** MLB: **88%**

Comparables:
Jose Arredondo,Andrew Brown,Jesse Orosco

YEAR	TEAM	LVL	AGE	W	L	SV	G	GS	IP	H	HR	BB	SO	BB9	SO9	GB%	BABIP	WHIP	ERA	FIP	FRA	WARP
2010	OKL	AAA	25	1	2	13	39	0	42^{1}	32	1	14	57	3.0	12.1	55%	.307	1.09	1.91	2.19	2.24	1.6
2010	TEX	MLB	25	0	0	0	15	0	10^{2}	17	2	11	11	9.3	9.3	35%	.429	2.62	10.12	6.80	7.31	-0.3
2011	ROU	AAA	26	4	4	11	39	0	47^{2}	53	2	24	55	4.5	10.4	—	.381	1.62	3.59	3.59	3.91	0.0
2011	BAL	MLB	26	2	0	0	12	0	12^{1}	8	0	3	12	2.2	8.8	68%	.258	0.89	0.73	1.85	2.37	0.4
2011	TEX	MLB	26	0	1	0	11	0	9^{2}	7	0	7	9	6.5	8.4	52%	.259	1.45	3.72	3.68	3.39	0.2
2012	BAL	MLB	27	5	2	3	70	0	66^{1}	52	2	37	58	5.0	7.9	64%	.275	1.34	2.44	3.54	3.83	0.9
2013	*BAL*	*MLB*	*28*	*3*	*1*	*2*	*52*	*0*	*50*	*45*	*5*	*25*	*50*	*4.5*	*9.0*	*50%*	*.300*	*1.40*	*4.11*	*4.00*	*4.47*	*0.4*

Despite a sparkling ERA and the second-highest leverage index on the team last season, Strop seems unlikely to engage in a repeat performance unless he can improve his control. At least his sinker generates 73 percent groundballs, which mitigates some of that walk damage via double plays—12 percent of runners reaching first were doubled-up, and even that seems low. He's still got great stuff and additional strikeout upside. Both his two- and four-seam fastballs were up three ticks to an average of nearly 98 mph, which he complements with a swing-and-miss slider and a splitter that he primarily uses as a strikeout pitch to lefties. This all adds up to a good middle-innings option even without improvement, and there's closer upside here.

Chris Tillman

Born: **4/15/1988** Age: **25**
Bats: **R** Throws: **R** Height: **6' 6"** Weight: **210**
Breakout: **19%** Improve: **58%** Collapse: **19%**
Attrition: **16%** MLB: **93%**

Comparables:
Dillon Gee,Micah Owings,Homer Bailey

YEAR	TEAM	LVL	AGE	W	L	SV	G	GS	IP	H	HR	BB	SO	BB9	SO9	GB%	BABIP	WHIP	ERA	FIP	FRA	WARP
2010	NOR	AAA	22	11	7	0	21	21	121^{1}	120	10	30	94	2.2	7.0	39%	.301	1.24	3.34	3.60	4.48	0.9
2010	BAL	MLB	22	2	5	0	11	11	53^{2}	51	9	31	31	5.2	5.2	42%	.256	1.53	5.87	5.86	6.44	-0.2
2011	NOR	AAA	23	3	6	0	15	15	76^{1}	77	17	38	54	4.5	6.4	40%	.307	1.51	5.19	6.29	5.95	-0.3
2011	BAL	MLB	23	3	5	0	13	13	62	77	5	25	46	3.6	6.7	41%	.348	1.65	5.52	4.03	4.43	0.7
2012	BOW	AA	24	0	1	0	1	1	3^{1}	4	0	2	2	5.4	5.4	36%	.364	1.80	8.10	3.80	4.63	0.0
2012	NOR	AAA	24	8	8	0	16	15	89^{1}	85	5	30	92	3.0	9.3	51%	.323	1.29	3.63	2.93	3.95	0.9
2012	BAL	MLB	24	9	3	0	15	15	86	66	12	24	66	2.5	6.9	35%	.221	1.05	2.93	4.20	4.39	0.8
2013	*BAL*	*MLB*	*25*	*6*	*6*	*0*	*18*	*18*	*94^{1}*	*96*	*13*	*35*	*77*	*3.4*	*7.3*	*40%*	*.296*	*1.39*	*4.51*	*4.47*	*4.91*	*0.5*

Tillman finally broke his three-year cycle of preseason promise followed by offseason disappointment. Just when it became tempting to write the once bright-eyed ingenue off, Tillman delivered on his nearly forgotten potential, pushing his major-league ERA below 5.00 for the first time in his career. He worked hard last spring, and his fastball was up a full 3 mph from the 90 he threw in 2011. More importantly, however, Tillman took a step forward with his command. His extreme fly-ball nature limits his upside, but he boasts above-average stuff, and if his control gains are legitimate, he should be a quality mid-rotation pitcher for the Orioles.

Tsuyoshi Wada

Born: **2/21/1981** Age: **32**
Bats: **L** Throws: **R** Height: **6' 0"** Weight: **170**
Breakout: **22%** Improve: **65%** Collapse: **16%**
Attrition: **6%** MLB: **88%**

Comparables:
Pete Richert, Buddy Carlyle, Scott Downs

YEAR	TEAM	LVL	AGE	W	L	SV	G	GS	IP	H	HR	BB	SO	BB9	SO9	GB%	BABIP	WHIP	ERA	FIP	FRA	WARP
2010	FKU	NPB	29	17	8	0	26	26	169^1	145	11	55	169	2.9	9.0	—	.291	1.18	3.14	2.99	3.25	0.0
2011	FKU	NPB	30	16	5	0	26	26	184^2	145	7	40	168	1.9	8.2	—	.280	1.00	1.51	0.00	0.00	0.0
2012	NOR	AAA	31	0	1	0	1	1	2^2	6	1	4	1	13.5	3.4	39%	.417	3.75	20.25	11.78	68.46	0.0
2013	*BAL*	*MLB*	*32*	*2*	*2*	*0*	*5*	*5*	35^2	*35*	*5*	*12*	*32*	*3.0*	*8.1*	*45%*	*.303*	*1.32*	*4.15*	*4.24*	*4.51*	*0.3*

The O's surely didn't expect a Chen-like 4.02 ERA out of their "other" Japanese pitcher when they signed Wada last offseason, but they certainly expected more than two minor-league innings. Injuries abruptly ended Wada's 2012 campaign, and he underwent Tommy John surgery in May; he should return early this season. The Japanese-born lefty is definitely of the crafty variety, working with an unexceptional fastball in the 85-88 mph range. Instead, he relies on plus command and deception to attack hitters. In an ideal world one would call Wada a fifth starter, but he may be more suited to a swingman role. One scout compared him to Hisanori Takahashi in this regard.

Randy Wolf

Born: **8/22/1976** Age: **36**
Bats: **L** Throws: **L** Height: **6' 1"** Weight: **205**
Breakout: **19%** Improve: **47%** Collapse: **17%**
Attrition: **7%** MLB: **70%**

Comparables:
Mike Cuellar, John Tudor, Jarrod Washburn

YEAR	TEAM	LVL	AGE	W	L	SV	G	GS	IP	H	HR	BB	SO	BB9	SO9	GB%	BABIP	WHIP	ERA	FIP	FRA	WARP
2010	MIL	MLB	33	13	12	0	34	34	215^2	213	29	87	142	3.6	5.9	41%	.275	1.39	4.17	4.87	4.83	3.0
2011	MIL	MLB	34	13	10	0	33	33	212^1	214	23	66	134	2.8	5.7	40%	.286	1.32	3.69	4.26	4.74	1.3
2012	BAL	MLB	35	2	0	0	5	2	15^1	17	2	7	8	4.1	4.7	42%	.312	1.57	5.28	5.26	5.16	0.0
2012	MIL	MLB	35	3	10	0	25	24	142^1	179	21	45	96	2.8	6.1	46%	.340	1.57	5.69	4.78	5.62	0.2
2013	*BAL*	*MLB*	*36*	*8*	*8*	*0*	*22*	*22*	137^2	*145*	*20*	*47*	*91*	*3.1*	*5.9*	*41%*	*.293*	*1.40*	*4.79*	*4.79*	*5.20*	*0.1*

While Wolf posted an awful ERA last season—the worst of his 14-year major league career—rest assured, Team Wolf, he's not an awful pitcher; he's still the merely bad pitcher he has been for the past few years. Some bad luck combined with an influx of capable youngsters in Milwaukee got him shipped to the AL for the first time in his career last September, but some team desperate for veteran leadership figures to give him a shot . . . next offseason. Tommy John surgery has already ended his 2013 before it began.

LINEOUTS

HITTERS

PLAYER	TEAM	LVL	AGE	PA	R	2B	3B	HR	RBI	BB	SO	SB-CS	AVG/OBP/SLG	TAv	BABIP	BRR	FRAA	WARP
2B R. Adams	NOR	AAA	25	264	26	18	0	4	20	27	60	2-2	.224/.312/.353	.239	.284	0.7	2B(39): -3.7	-0.5
INF B. Davis	NOR	AAA	28	390	33	17	4	3	38	25	61	6-0	.251/.299/.346	.246	.293	0	SS(76): 1.4, 2B(7): 0.4	0.9
	DEL	A	20	465	53	16	2	0	25	51	91	29-9	.252/.342/.302	.267	.322	2.6	CF(91): -3.5, LF(2): -0.1	1.3
CF G. Davis	FRD	A+	20	97	11	1	1	0	4	12	25	8-1	.256/.358/.293	.275	.368	1.1	CF(15): -0.4, LF(3): -0.4	0.3
INF N. Delmonico	DEL	A	19	393	49	22	0	11	54	47	73	8-1	.249/.351/.411	.292	.286	-1.5	1B(51): -3.0, 2B(31): 2.5	1.4
3B J. Esposito	DEL	A	21	512	52	13	2	5	51	26	113	8-3	.209/.260/.277	.205	.262	-0.9	3B(110): -6.2	-3.0
OF J. Miller	BOW	AA	27	153	12	5	0	4	17	18	64	2-1	.195/.288/.323	.244	.328	0.8	CF(24): 4.0, RF(17): 0.1	0.2
	NOR	AAA	27	211	20	10	1	8	21	27	95	3-1	.196/.308/.397	.258	.346	-1.1	RF(35): 1.2, CF(5): 0.2	0.0
C R. Paulino	NOR	AAA	31	164	13	9	1	1	15	13	25	0-0	.287/.341/.380	.213	.336	-4.4	C(21): -0.4	-0.9
	BAL	MLB	31	64	5	3	0	0	5	1	9	0-0	.254/.266/.302	.170	.296	0.2	C(11): 0.3	-0.5
3B B. Waring	BOW	AA	26	222	38	16	1	11	30	27	56	2-0	.276/.389/.551	.314	.336	-0.2	1B(28): -0.1, 3B(3): -0.1	0.8
	NOR	AAA	26	270	44	12	0	13	33	23	86	0-1	.248/.337/.466	.264	.326	0.2	3B(36): 1.5, 1B(7): 0.0	0.6

The possibility still exists that **Ryan Adams** turns into a bat-first keystoner or utility player, but he'll have to battle back from a poor 2012 and an amphetamine-related suspension. **Blake Davis** is mere organizational depth, unable to do enough with the bat to warrant being anything more than a roster's 25th man, though his defensive flexibility helps him on that score. Still the fastest player in the system, **Glynn Davis** needs a lot of work at the plate if he hopes to be a major-league starter. **Nick Delmonico** is a bit raw and not especially toolsy, but he has a high baseball IQ, good makeup, and the potential to be a high-quality hitter. He played third base in high school, but moved to second and first last year. **Jason Esposito** has the potential to be a great defensive third-sacker, and while he has power upside, some scouts question his swing mechanics and his ultimate ability to hit. **Jai Miller**'s power waned while his strikeouts exploded—not a good combination for a three-true-outcomes hitter whose strikeouts were already a major concern. There's no skill more apt to keep a poor player employed than the ability to squat behind the plate and while **Ronny Paulino** isn't especially talented, he's a catcher, so he'll have a job as organizational depth for a few more years. The power is still there, but the defensively challenged **Brandon Waring** hasn't improved his plate discipline enough as he's climbed the ladder to make people believe he can be a major-league regular.

PITCHERS

PLAYER	TEAM	LVL	AGE	W	L	SV	IP	H	HR	BB	SO	BB9	SO9	GB%	BABIP	WHIP	ERA	FIP	FRA	WARP
M. Belfiore	BOW	AA	23	5	1	2	47^1	43	2	21	50	4.0	9.5	42%	.318	1.35	2.85	3.41	3.55	0.6
P. Bridwell	DEL	A	20	5	9	0	114^1	122	15	63	71	5.0	5.6	44%	.300	1.62	5.98	6.09	6.87	-1.3
R. Bundy	BOW	AA	22	2	11	0	80^2	98	7	35	64	3.9	7.1	42%	.345	1.65	6.25	4.34	5.23	-0.1
O. Drake	BOW	AA	25	1	1	0	18	8	1	4	15	2.0	7.5	71%	.146	0.67	1.5	3.09	4.23	0
D. Eveland	NOR	AAA	28	5	5	0	84	82	4	28	55	3.0	5.9	53%	.285	1.31	2.79	3.65	4.71	0.3
	BAL	MLB	28	0	1	0	32^1	32	3	13	18	3.6	5.0	49%	.274	1.39	4.73	4.81	5.97	-0.2
K. Gausman	ABE	A-	21	0	0	0	6	1	0	0	5	0.0	7.5	.357	.071	0.17	0	1.67	2.85	0.1
	FRD	A+	21	0	1	0	9	10	3	1	8	1.0	8.0	.586	.269	1.22	6	6.27	8.35	-0.2
K. Gregg	BAL	MLB	34	3	2	0	43^2	50	6	24	37	4.9	7.6	48%	.338	1.69	4.95	4.99	5.91	-0.3
D. Klein	—	—	—	—	—	—	—	—	—	—	—	—	—	—	—	—	—	—	—	—
B. Kline	ABE	A-	20	0	0	0	12	12	1	4	12	3.0	9	47%	.355	1.33	4.5	3.42	3.72	0.2
T. McFarland	AKR	AA	23	8	2	0	60^1	61	1	4	12	1.8	6.1	59%	.328	1.21	2.69	2.80	3.77	0.7
	COH	AAA	23	8	6	0	102^2	112	9	33	55	2.9	4.8	55%	.301	1.41	4.82	4.22	6.61	0.2
J. Pineiro	ORI	Rk	33	0	0	0	12	9	0	1	10	0.8	7.5	59%	0.265	0.83	2.25	2.02	4.05	0
	NOR	AAA	33	1	0	0	12^1	10	0	0	9	0.0	6.6	57%	0.278	0.81	3.65	1.94	4.39	0.1
E. Rodriguez	DEL	A	19	5	7	0	107	103	4	30	73	2.5	6.1	53%	.289	1.24	3.70	3.68	4.86	0.5
J. Romero	BAL	MLB	36	0	0	0	4	7	1	1	1	2.2	2.2	37%	.333	2.00	6.75	6.55	7.43	-0.1
	SLN	MLB	36	0	0	0	8	14	3	2	5	2.2	5.6	48%	.367	2.00	10.12	7.89	7.32	-0.3
C. Schrader	FRD	A+	22	1	1	4	35	20	0	27	51	6.9	13.1	37%	.282	1.34	1.29	3.04	2.00	1.2
	BOW	AA	22	1	0	1	23	15	1	24	17	9.4	6.7	41%	.233	1.70	2.74	5.55	6.68	-0.4

Former first-rounder **Michael Belfiore**, traded to Baltimore for Josh Bell, looked sharp in his first turn at Double-A and in his first full-season as a reliever. Raw, athletic, and projectable, **Parker Bridwell** throws a quality sinker in the low to mid-90s, but as with many young pitchers, he'll need to improve his secondary offerings and command. Dylan's older brother **Robert Bundy** throws in the low 90s with a good breaker and a developing change, and might one day join his little bro in Baltimore's rotation. A shoulder injury limited **Oliver Drake** to three starts last season, so he'll look to get back on track in 2013. At this point in his career, **Dana Eveland** is mere organizational fodder, filling the role of mop-up man/spot starter/Triple-A mascot, which may be why he signed with the Hanhwa Eagles of the Korean Baseball Organization. The first college pitcher taken in the 2012 draft, **Kevin Gausman** has a ceiling as a number-one starter if he can develop his slider or curve to match his still-growing plus 94-mph fastball and near-plus change. Despite once being valued as a "proven closer," **Kevin Gregg** is now a proven liability. Despite approaching big-league readiness before his surgery, **Daniel Klein** missed the entire year with his *third* shoulder operation, and despite a starter's arsenal, his best shot with that shoulder is as a seventh- or eighth-inning reliever. Baltimore's second-round pick in 2012, **Branden Kline** is a power pitcher with a projectable low-90s fastball and a hard curve who could one day be a middle-of-the-rotation starter. A soft-throwing lefty who can get some movement and deception but whose secondary offerings aren't up to snuff, Rule 5 pick **T.J. McFarland** seems like a lefty specialist, but not likely a successful one. ⚾ It's been two years since **Joel Pineiro** has shown any signs of life and after recent shoulder surgery he will have to fight if he hopes to make it back to the major leagues. ⚾ More about control than power, **Eduardo Rodriguez** projects as a middle- or back-of-the-rotation pitcher with a merely average fastball but a good curve and average changeup. ⚾ It took very little to convince three separate teams to discard the once-effective **J.C. Romero** last year, so stick a fork in him. ⚾ Control remains a huge issue for **Clayton Schrader**, but his plus fastball and curve project him to a setup role if he can find a way to harness them.

MANAGER: BUCK SHOWALTER

YEAR	TEAM	W-L	Pythag +/-	Avg PC	100+ P	120+ P	QS	BQS	REL	REL w Zero R	IBB	PH	PH Avg	PH HR	SB2	CS2	SB3	CS3	SAC Att	SAC %	POS SAC	Squeeze	Swing	In Play
2010	BAL	34-23	1	197.4	56	56	43	3	144	106	20	30	.154	0	4	0	0	0	30	80.0%	24	0	78	26
2011	BAL	69-93	0	91.8	50	0	60	6	478	351	42	57	.309	1	7	5	0	0	41	65.9%	26	2	309	97
2012	BAL	93-69	1	95.6	66	1	78	6	492	415	36	69	.161	0	3	8	0	0	51	90.2%	42	1	282	102

Last season, the Orioles improved their 2011 record by an astounding 24 games with Showalter at the helm—a feat he's accomplished before, when the 1999 Diamondbacks improved by an MLB-record 35 games—and the team beat its Pythagorean expectation by 11 games. That's a feat he's never accomplished before. He has a neutral career record of Pythag-beating.

While some of that was luck, Showalter certainly helped steer the ship in the right direction. He created a great atmosphere in the clubhouse, especially with such a young club, commanding the respect of his players and getting the most out of them. He utilized his bullpen particularly well, ranking fifth in the AL in Leverage-Index Weighted ERA.

Showalter has been quite vocal over the last year about his willingness to take sabermetric thought into consideration. He may not take it to heart quite enough for some statistically minded fans—he ranked 13th in sac flies and 17th in intentional walks last year—but open-mindedness is still a desirable quality for a manager to have.

Boston Red Sox

2012: MY BLOODY VALENTINE

Between injuries, Bobby Valentine-induced melodrama, and disappointing seasons by key players, the Red Sox were mediocre for most of the year. After trading three of their star players to the Dodgers, they cratered, finishing with their worst record since the Johnson administration.

New manager Valentine didn't waste time losing the clubhouse. Two weeks into the season, he publicly called out Kevin Youkilis, one of the harder working and better-respected players on the team. Two days prior, Jacoby Ellsbury had broken up a double play and suffered shoulder subluxation, which is either a partial dislocation or a 1950s vacuum cleaner. Ellsbury missed 80 games (so probably not a vacuum cleaner). Turns out he was a trendsetter. Boston missed 1,587 man-games to injury, second most of any team since 2007, as far back as our data goes. We estimate those injuries cost Boston 7.9 WARP, the most in baseball by 1.4.

RED SOX PROSPECTUS

2012 W-L: 69-93, 5th in AL East

Pythag	.455	23rd	DER	.703	20th
RS/G	4.53	8th	B-Age	29.4	23rd
RA/G	4.98	27th	P-Age	28.5	20th
TAv	.259	15th	Salary	$175.2	2nd
BRR	3.8	11th	M$/MW	$7.93	30th
TAv-P	.268	22nd	DL Days	1587	3rd
FIP	4.37	26th	DL WARP	7.9	1st

Three-Year Park Factors	
Overall	105
HR/RH	105
HR/LH	94
AVG/RH	110
AVG/LH	108

Fenway Park (1912)
Att. % of Capacity: 100.2% (2nd)
Dim. 310, 379, 390, 380, 302

Even during Boston's down year, Fenway yielded the most doubles and second-highest BABIP in MLB.

The Red Sox might have weathered the storm had their pitching performed to expectations, but the staff finished 27th in FRA. So, no. Of the projected starting rotation, only one man finished with an FRA below 5.00 (Felix Doubront's 4.64), one's relationship with the club and fan base deteriorated so badly he was traded to Los Angeles at midseason, and one was sent to the bullpen. In Triple-A.

Ineffective drafting meant no reinforcements were available, so Boston set 29 starts on fire via Daisuke Matsuzaka's 6.79 FRA and Aaron Cook's 6.88 FRA. The culmination was the mega-trade: Josh Beckett, Carl Crawford, Nick Punto, Adrian Gonzalez, and over a quarter-billion dollars in guaranteed salaries to the Dodgers for four prospects and James Loney. When trading away three stars universally qualifies as the best move of the season, that tells you all you need to know.

2013: THE CURE

The Red Sox minor-league system isn't ready to produce top-flight prospects yet. A wave is on the way, but it'll be another season or two before the system bears fruit worth eating, so the team once again turned to free agency to fill holes on the roster. The replacements for Beckett, Crawford, and Gonzalez don't have the same name recognition, but being an upgrade on that group's meager 2012 on-field production shouldn't be a problem. With some health and astute additions, the Sox are poised to surprise some folks in 2013.

The blockbuster with the Dodgers opened holes on Boston's roster that hadn't seen the light of day in a decade. To fill them, GM Ben Cherington has focused on flexing and flexibility. With $250 million off the books, Boston can afford to pay a bit more now to avoid keeping older, potentially less productive players rostered for longer-term commitments. The three-year contracts offered to Mike Napoli and Shane Victorino represent buying low on former All-Stars while avoiding long-term risk. Should the curse of Carl Crawford strike and either Victorino or Napoli fail to produce, the Red Sox will be disappointed, but won't face a franchise-altering crisis.

Whether or not Ellsbury's disappointing 2012 season was due to after-effects of injury, his performance has simultaneously made it very difficult to evaluate his suitability for a long-term contract (how many years do you give a guy who put up TAvs of .186, .320, and .244 over the last three seasons?) and both hurt and confused his trade value. He may not be in Boston long-term, but the Red Sox recognized his increased incentive for a productive final season under team control and have avoided trading him.

For the next two seasons the offense will revolve around an aging designated hitter coming off a severe Achilles tendon injury. That sounds insane but a 36-year-old David Ortiz was one of the three best hitters in baseball before getting hurt in mid-July. Even 80 percent of last season's production (on a rate basis) would give Boston a lineup centerpiece. If not, it's only two years and fans are spared the retina-searing image of Ortiz in pinstripes. Health from Dustin Pedroia and Will Middlebrooks, who must handle his first full season as a starter at third base, will provide further strength to the lineup and allow for growing pains at shortstop—where Jose Iglesias's limp bat may get most of the playing time—and catcher, where prospect Ryan Lavarnway figures to get the majority of work, despite a down 2012 season.

Improvement from the starting pitching will depend on many of the same players responsible for sinking last year's team. Jon Lester's descent into mediocrity is the chief concern, but the team is also counting on Clay Buchholz keeping the feel of his changeup for months at a time and for John Lackey to perform post-Tommy John surgery like he did pre-Boston. Faced with that, you'd have re-signed Ortiz, too.

THE STATE OF THE ORGANIZATION: SONIC YOUTH

The minor-league system is a year or two away from a full-blown talent tide. Matt Barnes, Xander Bogaerts, and Jackie Bradley Jr. have All-Star potential and play up-the-middle positions, while the deal with L.A. brought pitching prospects in addition to salary relief.

It's entirely conceivable that by 2014 the Red Sox could field a lineup consisting of Bogaerts, Bradley, Middlebrooks, Lavarnway, Iglesias, and some combination of Ryan Kalish and Bryce Brentz, all 26 or younger and cost-controlled. The pitching side of things features Barnes, Allan Webster, and Rubby De La Rosa, with some lesser talents on the way as well. Boston isn't awash in All-Star quality talent, but filling out the roster cheaply with productive players gives the Sox the ability to re-sign players like Pedroia, Ellsbury, and Lester and to supplement the roster with—should they so desire—high-cost free agent additions. Boston's farm system and newfound financial flexibility have the club poised to build the next great Red Sox team. Or at least the next Red Sox team that won't make you feel dirty rooting for them.

HITTERS

Xander Bogaerts **SS**
Born: **10/1/1992** Age: **20**
Bats: **R** Throws: **R** Height: **6' 4"**
Weight: **175** Breakout: **19%**
Improve: **60%** Collapse: **3%**
Attrition: **12%** MLB: **85%**
Comparables:
Tony Conigliaro,Justin Upton,B.J. Upton

YEAR	TEAM	LVL	AGE	PA	R	2B	3B	HR	RBI	BB	SO	SB	CS	AVG_OBP_SLG	TAv	BABIP	BRR	FRAA	WARP
2011	GRN	A	18	296	38	14	2	16	45	25	71	1	3	.260/.324/.509	.277	.291	0	--	0.0
2012	SLM	A+	19	435	59	27	3	15	64	43	85	4	4	.302/.378/.505	.260	.353	-1.6	SS(37): -6.6	-0.4
2012	PME	AA	19	97	12	10	0	5	17	1	21	1	1	.326/.351/.598	.243	.373	-1.4	SS(4): 1.5	0.0
2013	*BOS*	*MLB*	*20*	*250*	*26*	*12*	*1*	*8*	*32*	*15*	*61*	*0*	*0*	*.250/.301/.421*	*.253*	*.301*	*-0.4*	*SS 1*	*0.9*

The next great Red Sox prospect doesn't mean the next great Red Sox player, but to paraphrase Hall and Oates, Xander Bogaerts can make Red Sox fans' dreams come true. Oh, sure, there are some things Bogaerts doesn't do well. Flying, for instance, or time travel. But on a baseball field there isn't much he can't handle. The 20-year-old shortstop has already seen success in Double-A, showing elite bat speed, plus-plus power potential, and athleticism to spare. Plate discipline is a small-sample nitpick, and some people question whether he can stick at shortstop, but his bat will play either way. Bogaerts is slated for Portland, and if he continues to progress, Triple-A or even a September call-up is possible.

Jackie Bradley **CF**
Born: **4/19/1990** Age: **23**
Bats: **L** Throws: **R** Height: **5' 11"**
Weight: **180** Breakout: **3%**
Improve: **56%** Collapse: **4%**
Attrition: **8%** MLB: **93%**
Comparables:
Ryan Kalish,Johnny Briggs,Lee Mazzilli

YEAR	TEAM	LVL	AGE	PA	R	2B	3B	HR	RBI	BB	SO	SB	CS	AVG_OBP_SLG	TAv	BABIP	BRR	FRAA	WARP
2012	SLM	A+	22	304	53	26	2	3	34	52	40	16	6	.359/.480/.526	.333	.407	0.3	CF(27): 0.4, RF(1): -0.1	1.2
2012	PME	AA	22	271	37	16	2	6	29	35	49	8	3	.271/.373/.437	.308	.316	-2.2	CF(5): -0.6	-0.1
2013	*BOS*	*MLB*	*23*	*250*	*31*	*12*	*1*	*4*	*22*	*29*	*51*	*5*	*2*	*.250/.347/.377*	*.261*	*.304*	*0*	*CF -1, RF -0*	*0.7*

Many things stick out about Bradley, from his tremendous plate discipline to his plus bat speed and excellent makeup, but perhaps the most intriguing aspect of his game is his defense in center field. He doesn't possess otherworldly speed, but his instincts are so good that the end-product would be above average in the majors right now. While he has some trouble against left-handers and his production tailed off at the end of the year, neither is particularly unusual for players in their first full year in pro ball. If Jacoby Ellsbury leaves town, Bradley will be the expected replacement. A major-league debut in 2013 isn't out of the question.

Bryce Brentz OF
Born: 12/30/1988 Age: 24
Bats: R Throws: R Height: 6' 2"
Weight: 180 Breakout: 8%
Improve: 54% Collapse: 5%
Attrition: 11% MLB: 94%
Comparables:
Ron Swoboda, Ben Oglivie, Rusty Torres

YEAR	TEAM	LVL	AGE	PA	R	2B	3B	HR	RBI	BB	SO	SB	CS	AVG_OBP_SLG	TAv	BABIP	BRR	FRAA	WARP
2010	LOW	A-	21	286	28	14	4	5	39	21	76	5	4	.198/.261/.340	.228	.260	-1.2	RF(44): 1.2, CF(17): 0.3	-0.1
2011	GRN	A	22	186	43	10	3	11	36	14	35	2	2	.359/.414/.647	.352	.403	0	--	0.0
2011	SLM	A+	22	321	48	15	1	19	58	26	80	1	1	.274/.336/.531	.287	.311	0	--	0.0
2012	PME	AA	23	504	62	30	1	17	76	40	130	7	5	.296/.355/.478	.288	.377	-2.9	RF(21): 0.9	0.3
2013	*BOS*	*MLB*	*24*	*250*	*23*	*11*	*1*	*6*	*27*	*14*	*76*	*1*	*1*	*.223/.268/.361*	*.223*	*.297*	*-0.3*	*RF -0, CF -0*	*-0.5*

When the Red Sox traded Josh Reddick last offseason it may have been with the knowledge that Brentz was on the way. Like Reddick, Brentz has plus bat speed and serious power for someone his size, but often he just hacks up there. Pitch recognition is one of those tough-to-teach things. Some guys pick it up; some don't. If Brentz can, then he has All-Star potential. If not, like Reddick, he'll probably be starting for a different team before long.

Garin Cecchini 3B
Born: 4/20/1991 Age: 22
Bats: L Throws: R Height: 6' 3"
Weight: 200 Breakout: 8%
Improve: 59% Collapse: 5%
Attrition: 14% MLB: 96%
Comparables:
Hank Blalock, Matt Dominguez, Bob Bailey

YEAR	TEAM	LVL	AGE	PA	R	2B	3B	HR	RBI	BB	SO	SB	CS	AVG_OBP_SLG	TAv	BABIP	BRR	FRAA	WARP
2011	LOW	A-	20	133	21	12	1	3	23	17	19	12	2	.298/.398/.500	.380	.337	0.4	3B(14): -0.7	0.9
2012	GRN	A	21	526	84	38	4	4	62	61	90	51	6	.305/.394/.433	.265	.371	7.9	3B(40): 0.1	1.2
2013	*BOS*	*MLB*	*22*	*250*	*27*	*12*	*1*	*3*	*20*	*20*	*60*	*15*	*3*	*.230/.295/.327*	*.222*	*.296*	*1.9*	*3B 1*	*-0.1*

2011 was Cecchini's first pro "season": only 32 games book-ended by injuries, recovery from an ACL tear and a wrist fracture. Last season Cecchini found health and showed off the power, strong arm, and ability to take a walk that enticed the Red Sox to give him a $1.3 million signing bonus. As those attributes would lead you to believe, Cecchini does most things well. The holes in his game—problems with breaking pitches, adjusting to the speed of third base—are centered around his lack of experience, and his elite athleticism gives hope he'll figure that stuff out. He has All-Star potential, though much can go wrong on the trip from Greenville, South Carolina, to Boston.

Pedro Ciriaco INF
Born: 9/27/1985 Age: 27
Bats: R Throws: R Height: 6' 1"
Weight: 170 Breakout: 2%
Improve: 39% Collapse: 17%
Attrition: 13% MLB: 95%
Comparables:
Wilton Guerrero, Garry Templeton, Tony Pena

YEAR	TEAM	LVL	AGE	PA	R	2B	3B	HR	RBI	BB	SO	SB	CS	AVG_OBP_SLG	TAv	BABIP	BRR	FRAA	WARP
2010	IND	AAA	24	126	19	9	1	0	6	2	21	5	1	.281/.290/.372	.233	.337	1.5	SS(31): -1.6	0.3
2010	RNO	AAA	24	376	44	15	7	6	51	10	53	14	3	.259/.277/.392	.225	.285	2.3	SS(84): 4.7, 2B(3): -0.3	0.8
2010	PIT	MLB	24	6	3	1	1	0	1	0	3	0	0	.500/.500/1.000	.500	.000	-1	SS(1): 0.0	0.1
2011	IND	AAA	25	289	31	7	3	2	24	5	49	13	7	.231/.243/.300	.207	.272	0.8	SS(32): -2.1, 2B(10): -2.2	-1.0
2011	PIT	MLB	25	34	4	2	1	0	6	1	6	2	1	.303/.324/.424	.272	.370	-1.1	SS(7): 0.7, 3B(2): 0.0	0.2
2012	PAW	AAA	26	289	41	13	2	4	21	6	49	14	8	.301/.318/.406	.257	.351	-1.1	SS(33): 4.8, 2B(17): 0.8	1.0
2012	BOS	MLB	26	272	33	15	2	2	19	8	47	16	3	.293/.315/.390	.249	.352	0.7	3B(35): 3.0, 2B(16): 0.1	1.1
2013	*BOS*	*MLB*	*27*	*274*	*31*	*13*	*3*	*3*	*21*	*6*	*51*	*12*	*4*	*.265/.282/.366*	*.227*	*.313*	*1*	*SS -0, 3B 0*	*0.1*

Ciriaco is a bright red lichen on a tree trunk. It's beautiful, but lichen can't bloom unless the tree is ill. Ciriaco played for Boston not because he played well, but because the Red Sox ailed. Lacking patience and power, he played on the basis of a flukey hot start and Bobby Valentine's grasping any straw that might pull the team from its tailspin. For a while, it sort of worked. Ciriaco put up an 806 OPS in July, but from August on hit only .274/.299/.368. Ciriaco crushed the Yankees, hitting .415/.436/.566 against them in 14 games, eliciting calls for his statue to be erected on Yawkey Way, but that's not who he is. He's Triple-A filler, so if he shows up in Boston this year you'll know winter didn't go well.

Sean Coyle 2B
Born: 1/17/1992 Age: 21
Bats: R Throws: R Height: 5' 9"
Weight: 175 Breakout: 3%
Improve: 54% Collapse: 8%
Attrition: 17% MLB: 96%
Comparables:
Roberto Alomar, Ken Hubbs, Luis Castillo

YEAR	TEAM	LVL	AGE	PA	R	2B	3B	HR	RBI	BB	SO	SB	CS	AVG_OBP_SLG	TAv	BABIP	BRR	FRAA	WARP
2011	GRN	A	19	466	77	27	7	14	64	60	110	20	6	.247/.362/.464	.286	.303	0	--	0.0
2012	SLM	A+	20	484	60	31	2	9	63	29	116	16	0	.249/.316/.391	.243	.317	1.3	2B(39): 1.0	0.3
2013	*BOS*	*MLB*	*21*	*250*	*26*	*11*	*1*	*5*	*21*	*11*	*70*	*3*	*0*	*.216/.262/.331*	*.214*	*.285*	*0.2*	*2B -1*	*-0.4*

Everyone compares Coyle to Dustin Pedroia. We are even doing it in the course of saying others shouldn't do it. Of course they are discrete sentient carbon-based life forms, so there's that, but mostly Coyle is a Single-A second baseman who had a mediocre season. Coyle (like Pedroia) has shocking power for a player his size and can handle second base. After a rough start he attributed to over-swinging, Coyle hit .297/.355/.451 during the second half. Cutting down on his prodigious strikeout totals will be the order of the day as he enters Double-A, likely sometime in 2013.

Stephen Drew SS

Born: **3/16/1983** Age: **30**
Bats: **L** Throws: **R** Height: **6' 1"**
Weight: **190** Breakout: **2%**
Improve: **47%** Collapse: **2%**
Attrition: **3%** MLB: **90%**

Comparables:
Miguel Tejada,Jhonny Peralta,Carlos Guillen

YEAR	TEAM	LVL	AGE	PA	R	2B	3B	HR	RBI	BB	SO	SB	CS	AVG_OBP_SLG	TAv	BABIP	BRR	FRAA	WARP
2010	ARI	MLB	27	633	83	33	12	15	61	62	108	10	5	.278/.352/.458	.287	.321	2.5	SS(147): -1.7	4.6
2011	ARI	MLB	28	354	44	21	5	5	45	30	74	4	4	.252/.317/.396	.257	.313	1.4	SS(84): -2.5	0.9
2012	ARI	MLB	29	155	17	8	1	2	12	19	35	0	1	.193/.290/.311	.223	.242	0.1	SS(36): -3.8	-0.6
2012	OAK	MLB	29	172	21	5	0	5	16	18	41	1	1	.250/.326/.382	.267	.306	-0.7	SS(39): -0.3	0.6
2013	*BOS*	*MLB*	*30*	*320*	*39*	*17*	*4*	*8*	*33*	*28*	*58*	*3*	*2*	*.262/.326/.426*	*.265*	*.301*	*-0.2*	*SS -4*	*1.2*

Drew was a valuable player from age 24 to 27, providing rare power at the plate without selling out the defensive side of the ball. But bouts of inconsistency hampered his potential to ascend to the next level. A fractured ankle mercifully ended an empty 2011 campaign in which his bat took a vow of silence, and last season Drew performed like a man who was still injured, hastening his exile from Arizona. Despite a warmer reception with a playoff-bound Oakland team, his batting line provided little evidence that Drew has righted the ship. He signed a one-year deal with the Red Sox, whose fans have always been so kind to his family.

Jacoby Ellsbury CF

Born: **9/11/1983** Age: **29**
Bats: **L** Throws: **L** Height: **6' 2"**
Weight: **185** Breakout: **0%**
Improve: **42%** Collapse: **3%**
Attrition: **10%** MLB: **95%**

Comparables:
Johnny Damon,Coco Crisp,Shane Victorino

YEAR	TEAM	LVL	AGE	PA	R	2B	3B	HR	RBI	BB	SO	SB	CS	AVG_OBP_SLG	TAv	BABIP	BRR	FRAA	WARP
2010	BOS	MLB	26	83	10	4	0	0	5	4	9	7	1	.192/.241/.244	.186	.217	1.1	CF(13): 0.7, LF(6): 0.1	-0.3
2011	BOS	MLB	27	729	119	46	5	32	105	52	98	39	15	.321/.376/.552	.320	.336	3.2	CF(154): 11.3	7.5
2012	BOS	MLB	28	323	43	18	0	4	26	19	43	14	3	.271/.313/.370	.244	.304	3.7	CF(73): -0.4	0.2
2013	*BOS*	*MLB*	*29*	*389*	*55*	*19*	*3*	*8*	*37*	*27*	*51*	*24*	*6*	*.287/.340/.428*	*.270*	*.311*	*2.3*	*CF -0, LF 0*	*1.8*

Last year marked the second lost season in the last three for Ellsbury. One week in, his shoulder met Jeff Keppinger breaking up a double play, and Ellsbury missed eighty games. After returning, the swing that propelled him to a second-place MVP finish in 2011 wasn't right and he had his worst year at the plate. This will be Ellsbury's walk year, and given worries over his up-and-down production and the uncompromising nature of his agent (Scott Boras), a long-term deal seems unlikely. The MVP-quality talent is there but so is the injury-risk.

Jonny Gomes LF

Born: **11/22/1980** Age: **32**
Bats: **R** Throws: **R** Height: **6' 2"**
Weight: **225** Breakout: **1%**
Improve: **22%** Collapse: **9%**
Attrition: **13%** MLB: **88%**

Comparables:
Andre Thornton,John Jaha,Gil Hodges

YEAR	TEAM	LVL	AGE	PA	R	2B	3B	HR	RBI	BB	SO	SB	CS	AVG_OBP_SLG	TAv	BABIP	BRR	FRAA	WARP
2010	CIN	MLB	29	571	77	24	3	18	86	39	123	5	3	.266/.327/.431	.273	.311	2.6	LF(128): -8.1	1.3
2011	CIN	MLB	30	265	30	8	0	11	31	38	74	5	3	.211/.336/.399	.276	.255	-3.5	LF(54): -0.8	0.4
2011	WAS	MLB	30	107	11	4	1	3	12	10	31	2	0	.204/.299/.366	.245	.267	1.3	LF(19): 0.1, RF(11): 0.1	0.3
2012	OAK	MLB	31	333	46	10	0	18	47	44	104	3	1	.262/.377/.491	.321	.348	-1.8	LF(39): 0.6, RF(3): 0.3	2.2
2013	*BOS*	*MLB*	*32*	*321*	*40*	*14*	*1*	*13*	*43*	*31*	*87*	*4*	*2*	*.239/.326/.430*	*.269*	*.296*	*-0.2*	*LF -0, RF 0*	*1.0*

He may have only spent a single season in green and gold, but Gomes fit the Oakland environment like he was born there, and not just because he grew up in nearby Petaluma. Gomes was happy to support the local squad that advanced to the semifinal round of the Little League World Series, but his greatest joy was in raking the yard with AL left-handers. Gomes received a 400 percent annual raise to play the next two seasons in Boston, where Fenway Park should highlight his strengths well enough to cover for the expected regression as he comes off a career-best season. The Red Sox can limit his defensive exposure to their tiny left-field pasture as well as create platoon-favorable situations at the plate.

Mauro Gomez 1B

Born: **9/7/1984** Age: **28**
Bats: **R** Throws: **R** Height: **6' 3"**
Weight: **230** Breakout: **5%**
Improve: **45%** Collapse: **3%**
Attrition: **26%** MLB: **92%**

Comparables:
Mike Jacobs,Mike Diaz,Jake Fox

YEAR	TEAM	LVL	AGE	PA	R	2B	3B	HR	RBI	BB	SO	SB	CS	AVG_OBP_SLG	TAv	BABIP	BRR	FRAA	WARP
2010	MIS	AA	25	559	67	42	2	16	80	46	122	1	2	.281/.354/.471	.295	.345	-3.7	1B(125): -7.4	1.6
2011	GWN	AAA	26	557	76	34	2	24	90	38	131	6	2	.304/.356/.522	.296	.364	0	--	0.0
2012	PAW	AAA	27	426	65	34	1	24	74	35	88	1	0	.310/.371/.589	.300	.348	0	1B(44): 1.2, 3B(7): -0.8	1.7
2012	BOS	MLB	27	111	14	5	2	2	17	8	26	0	0	.275/.324/.422	.258	.347	1.5	1B(16): 1.4, 3B(9): -0.3	0.3
2013	*BOS*	*MLB*	*28*	*250*	*27*	*15*	*1*	*9*	*34*	*17*	*61*	*0*	*0*	*.260/.314/.452*	*.267*	*.314*	*-0.4*	*1B -3, 3B -0*	*0.2*

Signed before the season as a minor-league free agent, Gomez spent much of 2012 raking for Triple-A Pawtucket (960 OPS). Then Adrian Gonzalez became He Who Can Get Boston Out From Under Josh Beckett and Carl Crawford, and Gomez got the call. James Loney came the other way, but since James Loney hit like James Loney with a colony of monkeys living on his face, Gomez was pressed into service. He proved surprisingly adequate. He can play first base defensively and shows good power, but struck out roughly once a game during his minor-league career, a trend that figures to continue in the bigs. That inability to make contact limits his ceiling. Better Than James Loney is fine, but it's not what a contending team should settle for.

Brock Holt **MI**

Born: **6/11/1988** Age: **25**
Bats: **L** Throws: **R** Height: **5' 11"**
Weight: **165** Breakout: **6%**
Improve: **62%** Collapse: **5%**
Attrition: **18%** MLB: **95%**

Comparables:
Chin-lung Hu,Dickie Thon,Eduardo Nunez

YEAR	TEAM	LVL	AGE	PA	R	2B	3B	HR	RBI	BB	SO	SB	CS	AVG_OBP_SLG	TAv	BABIP	BRR	FRAA	WARP
2010	BRD	A+	22	218	31	12	1	1	27	19	30	6	6	.351/.412/.438	.306	.409	0	--	0.0
2011	ALT	AA	23	579	62	30	9	1	40	50	85	18	10	.288/.356/.387	.259	.340	0	2B(66): 2.1, SS(24): -0.2	0.9
2012	ALT	AA	24	432	52	24	6	2	43	40	51	11	11	.322/.389/.432	.286	.364	-1.4	SS(87): 2.3	2.3
2012	IND	AAA	24	106	13	7	0	1	7	9	9	5	2	.432/.476/.537	.352	.465	1.1	2B(11): 1.3, SS(9): 0.4	1.4
2012	PIT	MLB	24	72	6	2	1	0	3	4	14	0	0	.292/.329/.354	.242	.365	-0.8	2B(14): 0.2	-0.1
2013	*BOS*	*MLB*	*25*	*250*	*28*	*13*	*2*	*2*	*20*	*17*	*44*	*6*	*3*	*.273/.325/.375*	*.247*	*.322*	*-0.2*	*SS 1, 2B 0*	*0.8*

Remember David Eckstein? Of course you do. Holt might be the closest thing around these days. He's short and gritty, hits for average, and shows a knack for getting on base. The difference is that Eckstein got a chance to start at shortstop in the majors. Holt hasn't had that chance, and doesn't figure to get it any time soon with Drew on the roster. Holt has options left, so if he can't catch on as a utility man, he'll get to know Interstate 95, which will take him into and out of Pawtucket.

Jose Iglesias **SS**

Born: **1/5/1990** Age: **23**
Bats: **R** Throws: **R** Height: **6' 0"**
Weight: **175** Breakout: **5%**
Improve: **42%** Collapse: **12%**
Attrition: **22%** MLB: **90%**

Comparables:
Lenny Faedo,Andres Blanco,Edgar Renteria

YEAR	TEAM	LVL	AGE	PA	R	2B	3B	HR	RBI	BB	SO	SB	CS	AVG_OBP_SLG	TAv	BABIP	BRR	FRAA	WARP
2010	PME	AA	20	236	29	10	3	0	13	8	49	5	2	.285/.318/.357	.238	.364	4.3	SS(55): -8.3	0.1
2011	PAW	AAA	21	387	35	9	0	1	31	21	58	12	4	.235/.285/.269	.203	.279	-0.5	SS(74): 5.4	-0.5
2011	BOS	MLB	21	6	3	0	0	0	0	0	2	0	0	.333/.333/.333	.229	.500	-0.6	SS(8): -0.2	-0.1
2012	PAW	AAA	22	396	46	9	1	1	23	27	46	12	3	.266/.318/.306	.220	.299	0.6	SS(77): 14.3	0.9
2012	BOS	MLB	22	77	5	2	0	1	2	4	16	1	0	.118/.200/.191	.152	.137	0.9	SS(24): 1.0	-0.4
2013	*BOS*	*MLB*	*23*	*250*	*25*	*9*	*1*	*2*	*17*	*12*	*45*	*5*	*1*	*.243/.284/.319*	*.218*	*.287*	*0.3*	*SS -0*	*0.0*

Jose Iglesias can't hit. He can't he can't he can't. But oh *wow* can he field. That's the book on the 22-year-old Cuban shortstop: The glove is legit. Iglesias shows great range, a strong arm, quick reflexes, incredible fluidity, soft hands, amazing body control, and the ability to turn water into wine. Scouts hurried to grade his fielding an 80 (the highest possible using the 20-80 scale). Hitting is a different story. He brings good bat speed and quick wrists to the plate—which *could* translate into gap power if only he could put the barrel on the ball more frequently—and his plate patience has improved (though it's still not what you'd call above average). None of that has translated to on-field production. He's still young, with time to improve, but whether the Red Sox can wait for him is an open question.

Ryan Kalish **OF**

Born: **3/28/1988** Age: **25**
Bats: **L** Throws: **L** Height: **6' 1"**
Weight: **215** Breakout: **9%**
Improve: **69%** Collapse: **4%**
Attrition: **12%** MLB: **97%**

Comparables:
Felix Pie,Rondell White,Dusty Baker

YEAR	TEAM	LVL	AGE	PA	R	2B	3B	HR	RBI	BB	SO	SB	CS	AVG_OBP_SLG	TAv	BABIP	BRR	FRAA	WARP
2010	PME	AA	22	183	35	9	1	8	29	28	21	13	1	.293/.411/.527	.321	.298	1	RF(18): 0.1, LF(14): 1.0	1.6
2010	PAW	AAA	22	160	22	9	1	5	18	14	32	12	2	.294/.361/.476	.289	.349	3	CF(21): 4.1, LF(7): 0.7	1.6
2010	BOS	MLB	22	179	26	11	1	4	24	12	38	10	1	.252/.305/.405	.254	.303	2	CF(38): 1.8, LF(12): 0.4	0.9
2011	PAW	AAA	23	96	9	6	0	0	9	8	20	4	3	.209/.271/.279	.209	.265	-1	CF(15): 3.3	-0.1
2012	PAW	AAA	24	126	18	5	0	4	14	13	30	7	2	.261/.336/.414	.243	.321	0.2	CF(20): -1.4	-0.3
2012	BOS	MLB	24	103	12	3	0	0	5	6	26	3	2	.229/.272/.260	.197	.310	-0.1	CF(20): 0.3, RF(9): 0.2	-0.6
2013	*BOS*	*MLB*	*25*	*250*	*33*	*12*	*1*	*6*	*23*	*20*	*53*	*12*	*3*	*.252/.315/.392*	*.251*	*.303*	*0.9*	*CF 0, RF -0*	*0.6*

Kalish was the next big thing in Red Sox outfield prospects back in 2010 when he hit .294/.382/.502 across Double-A and Triple-A as a 22-year-old. But that was a billion injuries ago. Over the last two seasons Kalish partially tore his labrum (shoulder muscle), required surgery for a bulging disk in his neck, and then finished the job on his labrum and needed surgery for that as well. Culling anything from his stats over that time is pointless; he has about half a season's worth of plate appearances scattered over five levels. When on the field Kalish demonstrates excellent athleticism, good plate discipline, above-average power, and plus makeup. If he can find his health, he should reach his ceiling as a starter on a championship-level team. But Kalish hasn't demonstrated that health is a tool he possesses.

Ryan Lavarnway **C**

Born: **8/7/1987** Age: **25**
Bats: **R** Throws: **R** Height: **6' 5"**
Weight: **225** Breakout: **2%**
Improve: **52%** Collapse: **2%**
Attrition: **12%** MLB: **86%**

Comparables:
Ed Herrmann,Josh Donaldson,Matt Wieters

YEAR	TEAM	LVL	AGE	PA	R	2B	3B	HR	RBI	BB	SO	SB	CS	AVG_OBP_SLG	TAv	BABIP	BRR	FRAA	WARP
2010	SLM	A+	22	360	66	18	0	14	63	44	62	1	0	.289/.395/.487	.309	.325	-0.7	C(37): -0.1	3.0
2010	PME	AA	22	190	25	9	0	8	39	26	42	0	0	.285/.399/.494	.294	.343	1	C(16): -0.3	1.2
2011	PME	AA	23	239	35	5	0	14	38	25	47	0	0	.284/.360/.510	.295	.298	0	--	0.0
2011	PAW	AAA	23	264	40	18	0	18	55	32	60	1	1	.295/.390/.612	.308	.327	-2	C(25): -0.1	1.3
2011	BOS	MLB	23	43	5	2	0	2	8	4	10	0	0	.231/.302/.436	.283	.259	-0.4	C(8): 0.1	0.1
2012	PAW	AAA	24	367	52	22	0	8	43	40	62	1	0	.295/.376/.439	.270	.340	-5.2	C(71): -1.1	1.2
2012	BOS	MLB	24	166	11	8	0	2	12	11	41	0	0	.157/.211/.248	.174	.196	-0.2	C(28): -0.2	-1.4
2013	*BOS*	*MLB*	*25*	*250*	*27*	*13*	*0*	*8*	*30*	*24*	*57*	*0*	*0*	*.242/.320/.404*	*.257*	*.289*	*-0.5*	*C -1*	*0.8*

After mashing in the winter leagues, Lavarnway struggled with the bat at Triple-A and in the majors. The demands of the position often cause catchers to develop later than other position players, so his offensive dip may have been due to concentration on defense. Still, last season represented the first time Lavarnway slugged under .487 since his first taste of pro ball in 2008. Oddly, the knock against him has never been the stick, but the mitt, and in that arena Lavarnway grew at least by leaps if not bounds. Though he may never be a great defensive catcher, saying he can play the position at the major-league level will no longer get you laughed out of a room full of scouts.

Will Middlebrooks 3B

Born: **9/9/1988** Age: **24**
Bats: **R** Throws: **R** Height: **6' 5"**
Weight: **200** Breakout: **4%**
Improve: **59%** Collapse: **8%**
Attrition: **15%** MLB: **99%**

Comparables:
Gil McDougald, Juan Francisco, Gary Gaetti

YEAR	TEAM	LVL	AGE	PA	R	2B	3B	HR	RBI	BB	SO	SB	CS	AVG_OBP_SLG	TAv	BABIP	BRR	FRAA	WARP
2010	SLM	A+	21	481	69	31	2	12	70	35	121	5	3	.276/.335/.439	.278	.358	1.2	3B(106): 13.6	3.6
2011	PME	AA	22	397	54	25	1	18	80	21	95	6	0	.302/.345/.520	.290	.363	0	--	0.0
2011	PAW	AAA	22	60	4	0	0	2	8	3	18	3	1	.161/.200/.268	.174	.189	0.5	3B(14): -0.3	-0.5
2012	PAW	AAA	23	100	18	3	1	9	27	7	18	3	1	.333/.380/.677	.379	.333	-1.6	3B(21): -2.1	1.1
2012	BOS	MLB	23	286	34	14	0	15	54	13	70	4	1	.288/.325/.509	.278	.335	-0.2	3B(72): 4.2	1.5
2013	*BOS*	*MLB*	*24*	*250*	*30*	*12*	*1*	*11*	*35*	*13*	*65*	*3*	*1*	*.258/.299/.452*	*.261*	*.311*	*-0.1*	*3B 0*	*0.6*

It was an eventful year for Middlebrooks, who started the year a newbie in Triple-A and ended it as the third baseman for the Red Sox. Middlebrooks is a player of obvious skills and just as obvious deficiencies. He's big, strong, and athletic, with a good arm and plus bat-speed that gives him above-average power, as owners of broken-windowed cars parked across from the Green Monster can attest. Despite all that, his lack of patience—evidenced from his Delmon Young-esque walk rate—will supposedly limit his ceiling. However, last season he saw a perfectly acceptable 3.88 pitches per plate appearance, above the major-league average of 3.82. His chance to prove critics (including PECOTA) wrong should come in 2013 if he's recovered from the fractured wrist he suffered in August.

Daniel Nava LF

Born: **2/22/1983** Age: **30**
Bats: **B** Throws: **L** Height: **5' 11"**
Weight: **200** Breakout: **0%**
Improve: **44%** Collapse: **4%**
Attrition: **11%** MLB: **95%**

Comparables:
Johnny Grubb, John Milner, Bobby Kielty

YEAR	TEAM	LVL	AGE	PA	R	2B	3B	HR	RBI	BB	SO	SB	CS	AVG_OBP_SLG	TAv	BABIP	BRR	FRAA	WARP
2010	PAW	AAA	27	325	41	16	1	10	48	28	64	4	2	.289/.375/.458	.291	.343	0.3	RF(38): 2.0, LF(36): 5.6	2.5
2010	BOS	MLB	27	188	23	14	1	1	26	19	46	1	1	.242/.351/.360	.253	.333	-0.3	LF(54): -3.3	0.2
2011	PAW	AAA	28	522	69	27	2	10	48	70	88	10	3	.268/.372/.406	.273	.311	2.6	LF(67): 3.3, RF(1): 0.0	1.3
2012	PAW	AAA	29	120	20	7	1	4	18	16	15	1	1	.313/.425/.525	.339	.333	-0.1	LF(15): -0.6, RF(3): 0.1	0.8
2012	BOS	MLB	29	317	38	21	0	6	33	37	63	3	0	.243/.352/.390	.269	.295	2.1	LF(76): -5.2, RF(4): -0.0	0.7
2013	*BOS*	*MLB*	*30*	*297*	*36*	*16*	*1*	*5*	*28*	*31*	*62*	*3*	*1*	*.250/.346/.386*	*.263*	*.305*	*-0.2*	*LF -1, RF -0*	*0.6*

One of the most unlikely stories in baseball, Nava made his way to Boston after being cut by, in order, his college team, an independent-league team, and to complete the set, the Red Sox. Not invited to spring training, Nava garnered a call-up on the strength of hitting .313/.425/.525 in 29 games for Triple-A Pawtucket. He then hit .298/.429/.489 in 29 games for Boston before hurting his wrist. He experienced soreness during the rest of the season and missed 41 games. The injury and the resulting sporadic playing time predictably hurt his production, but when healthy he turned out to be a surprisingly good hitter. He'll never be an All-Star, but he knows the strike zone and can pop the occasional extra-base hit. In the field he passes the eye test and gets good marks from other metrics even if FRAA isn't a believer.

David Ortiz DH

Born: **11/18/1975** Age: **37**
Bats: **L** Throws: **L** Height: **6' 5"**
Weight: **230** Breakout: **1%**
Improve: **28%** Collapse: **8%**
Attrition: **20%** MLB: **80%**

Comparables:
Billy Williams, Edgar Martinez, Carlos Delgado

YEAR	TEAM	LVL	AGE	PA	R	2B	3B	HR	RBI	BB	SO	SB	CS	AVG_OBP_SLG	TAv	BABIP	BRR	FRAA	WARP
2010	BOS	MLB	34	606	86	36	1	32	102	82	145	0	1	.270/.370/.529	.304	.313	-4.1	1B(4): -0.1	3.1
2011	BOS	MLB	35	605	84	40	1	29	96	78	83	1	1	.309/.398/.554	.311	.321	-5.1	1B(2): -0.1	2.7
2012	BOS	MLB	36	383	65	26	0	23	60	56	51	0	1	.318/.415/.611	.343	.316	-3.4	1B(7): 0.1	3.0
2013	*BOS*	*MLB*	*37*	*404*	*52*	*22*	*1*	*18*	*60*	*51*	*77*	*1*	*1*	*.263/.357/.485*	*.291*	*.288*	*-0.9*	*1B 0*	*2.2*

Whether due to a newfound commitment to fitness, new hitting mechanics, or full recovery from a tendon-sheath injury to his left wrist sustained way back in 2008, Ortiz arrested his moribund Aprils of the last few seasons by, as Ben Lindbergh put it on the website, "making much more contact, and [...] hitting it harder." The only number going the wrong way for Ortiz is his age, as he walked more (on average), hit for more power, and even went the other way with more frequency, taking advantage of the exaggerated shifts thrown at him by opposing managers. Had he finished with enough plate appearances to qualify, Ortiz would have had the highest slugging percentage and second highest on-base percentage in baseball. Signed to a two-year deal, he'll have at least that to work on his Hall of Fame case.

Dustin Pedroia 2B
Born: **8/17/1983** Age: **29**
Bats: **R** Throws: **R** Height: **5' 10"**
Weight: **180** Breakout: **0%**
Improve: **37%** Collapse: **3%**
Attrition: **3%** MLB: **95%**
Comparables:
Jarrett Hoffpauir,Ian Kinsler,Roberto Alomar

YEAR	TEAM	LVL	AGE	PA	R	2B	3B	HR	RBI	BB	SO	SB	CS	AVG_OBP_SLG	TAv	BABIP	BRR	FRAA	WARP
2010	BOS	MLB	26	351	53	24	1	12	41	37	38	9	1	.288/.367/.493	.294	.291	1.3	2B(75): -7.2	1.6
2011	BOS	MLB	27	731	102	37	3	21	91	86	85	26	8	.307/.387/.474	.299	.325	1.4	2B(159): 1.9	4.7
2012	BOS	MLB	28	623	81	39	3	15	65	48	60	20	6	.290/.347/.449	.281	.300	-0.6	2B(139): -8.6	1.7
2013	*BOS*	*MLB*	*29*	*607*	*84*	*37*	*2*	*15*	*64*	*56*	*59*	*19*	*5*	*.294/.362/.452*	*.286*	*.304*	*0.8*	*2B -3*	*3.7*

Pedroia's down year (by his standards) was due to a torn adductor muscle in his thumb suffered in early May and aggravated later in the month. He played through it before finally hitting the DL in July. After returning, the laser show resumed to the tune of .318/.372/.508 for the rest of the season. As for his gold glove defense (as opposed to Gold Glove defense), Pedroia still passes the eye test and nine out of 10 metrics agree, even if FRAA was the dissenter. He fractured his finger with three games left in the season, but even though the Red Sox were 23 games out of first place, he played the final two, going 4-for-11 with two doubles. Whether that was gutty or stupid depends on your point of view, but in the maelstrom of disappointment, ego, and blood-in-the-water media coverage that was the Red Sox' 2012, it made a point. When he's on the field, Pedroia is the centerpiece of the franchise. Now if only he can stay healthy.

Scott Podsednik OF
Born: **3/18/1976** Age: **37**
Bats: **L** Throws: **L** Height: **6' 1"**
Weight: **185** Breakout: **2%**
Improve: **27%** Collapse: **7%**
Attrition: **31%** MLB: **80%**
Comparables:
Stan Javier,Lou Piniella,Frank Baumholtz

YEAR	TEAM	LVL	AGE	PA	R	2B	3B	HR	RBI	BB	SO	SB	CS	AVG_OBP_SLG	TAv	BABIP	BRR	FRAA	WARP
2010	KCA	MLB	34	435	46	8	6	5	44	29	57	30	12	.310/.353/.400	.267	.347	-1.1	LF(92): 5.9, CF(1): 0.0	1.5
2010	LAN	MLB	34	160	17	6	1	1	7	11	26	5	3	.262/.312/.336	.227	.311	2	LF(37): 2.8, CF(5): -0.0	0.3
2011	LEH	AAA	35	59	4	6	1	0	0	3	15	2	0	.245/.286/.396	.232	.342	0	--	0.0
2011	LVG	AAA	35	71	12	2	2	0	6	10	9	3	0	.254/.366/.356	.272	.294	1	CF(6): 0.3	0.2
2012	LEH	AAA	36	85	13	1	0	0	4	8	12	6	1	.197/.282/.211	.204	.234	2	CF(6): -0.7, RF(4): -0.2	-0.2
2012	PAW	AAA	36	102	10	2	1	1	11	8	13	4	2	.281/.330/.360	.264	.308	0.8	LF(9): -0.7, CF(5): 0.0	0.1
2012	BOS	MLB	36	216	19	7	0	1	12	6	35	8	2	.302/.322/.352	.242	.358	1.6	LF(31): -0.0, CF(23): -1.0	-0.1
2013	*BOS*	*MLB*	*37*	*250*	*30*	*10*	*2*	*2*	*18*	*16*	*39*	*12*	*4*	*.275/.322/.356*	*.238*	*.316*	*0.9*	*LF 1, CF -0*	*0.2*

That Podsednik ended up in Boston was strange. That he did it twice approached creepy. After losing the spring battle with Juan Pierre for the last spot on the Phillies bench, the former White Sox spark plug found himself playing for the Triple-A Lehigh Valley Iron Pigs. His play matched the effort level you expect with "Iron Pigs" emblazoned on your chest (493 OPS). But an injury blizzard blanketed the Red Sox outfield and Boston needed warm bodies. Podsednik soon found himself in Boston, where, shock of shocks, he crushed the ball! Just kidding. No ball crushing, but Podsednik ended up with an 893 OPS primarily due to a .434 BABIP. He went to Arizona in a deadline trade, but when the Diamondbacks optioned him to Triple-A he refused the assignment, became a free agent, and re-signed with Boston. The return trip wasn't as kind, (574 OPS), and the Podfather will likely be looking at another minor-league deal for 2013.

David Ross C
Born: **3/19/1977** Age: **36**
Bats: **R** Throws: **R** Height: **6' 3"**
Weight: **205** Breakout: **1%**
Improve: **14%** Collapse: **14%**
Attrition: **18%** MLB: **78%**
Comparables:
Carl Sawatski,Jorge Posada,Jason Varitek

YEAR	TEAM	LVL	AGE	PA	R	2B	3B	HR	RBI	BB	SO	SB	CS	AVG_OBP_SLG	TAv	BABIP	BRR	FRAA	WARP
2010	ATL	MLB	33	145	15	13	2	2	28	20	28	0	1	.289/.392/.479	.295	.359	-1.9	C(56): 0.6	1.1
2011	ATL	MLB	34	170	14	7	0	6	23	16	51	0	1	.263/.333/.428	.273	.358	-3.2	C(49): 0.8	0.7
2012	ATL	MLB	35	196	18	7	0	9	23	18	60	1	0	.256/.321/.449	.275	.330	-2	C(54): -0.0	0.8
2013	*BOS*	*MLB*	*36*	*250*	*29*	*12*	*1*	*7*	*29*	*29*	*67*	*1*	*0*	*.243/.333/.407*	*.262*	*.311*	*-0.4*	*C 1*	*1.2*

Ross is what happens when a sure thing turns out to be unsure. His return to the Braves never seemed in doubt until the ink dried on a two-year deal with the Red Sox. There is some risk involved in giving Ross a multi-year deal. Older catchers don't tend to age well, nor do hitters who dabble in the three true outcomes. Still, Ross has been the best reserve catcher in the league for a few years now, and deserves a chance to spread his wings.

Jarrod Saltalamacchia C
Born: **5/2/1985** Age: **28**
Bats: **B** Throws: **R** Height: **6' 5"**
Weight: **235** Breakout: **11%**
Improve: **50%** Collapse: **8%**
Attrition: **17%** MLB: **96%**
Comparables:
Hector Villanueva,Kelly Shoppach,Rick Wilkins

YEAR	TEAM	LVL	AGE	PA	R	2B	3B	HR	RBI	BB	SO	SB	CS	AVG_OBP_SLG	TAv	BABIP	BRR	FRAA	WARP
2010	OKL	AAA	25	270	37	11	2	11	33	25	60	1	0	.244/.328/.445	.259	.281	-1.6	C(55): -0.1	0.7
2010	BOS	MLB	25	25	2	3	0	0	1	6	4	0	0	.158/.360/.316	.252	.200	0.3	C(6): 0.0, 1B(1): -0.0	0.1
2010	TEX	MLB	25	5	0	0	0	0	1	0	1	0	0	.200/.200/.200	.148	.250	0	C(1): -0.0	0.0
2011	BOS	MLB	26	386	52	23	3	16	56	24	119	1	0	.235/.288/.450	.252	.304	-1.2	C(101): -2.0	0.4
2012	BOS	MLB	27	448	55	17	1	25	59	38	139	0	1	.222/.288/.454	.265	.265	-0.4	C(104): 0.5, 1B(1): -0.0	1.5
2013	*BOS*	*MLB*	*28*	*409*	*44*	*19*	*1*	*15*	*52*	*35*	*124*	*1*	*1*	*.228/.297/.406*	*.247*	*.298*	*-0.7*	*C -1, 1B -0*	*1.1*

Known as "Salty," because pronouncing—let alone spelling—"Saltalamacchia" is not a fit pursuit for man nor beast nor copy editor, Saltalamacchia posted an OPS within four points of his 2011 number. The similarities don't end there. For the second season in a row, he wore down as the season went on, hitting .195/.276/.390 after June 1. His Isolated Power remained high (an impressive .232), but his inability to hit for average and hacktastic approach make him a one-trick pony at the plate. That's not necessarily a huge problem: Salty's journey to league-average-ness may be odd, but he gets there eventually.

Ryan Sweeney OF

Born: 2/20/1985 Age: 28
Bats: L Throws: L Height: 6' 5"
Weight: 225 Breakout: 1%
Improve: 47% Collapse: 14%
Attrition: 27% MLB: 86%

Comparables:
Lyman Bostock,Russ Adams,Terry Puhl

YEAR	TEAM	LVL	AGE	PA	R	2B	3B	HR	RBI	BB	SO	SB	CS	AVG_OBP_SLG	TAv	BABIP	BRR	FRAA	WARP
2010	OAK	MLB	25	331	41	20	2	1	36	24	41	1	1	.294/.342/.383	.266	.333	0.5	RF(80): -0.6, CF(1): 0.0	0.7
2011	OAK	MLB	26	299	34	11	3	1	25	33	48	1	1	.265/.346/.341	.258	.319	-3.2	LF(41): -0.0, CF(34): 1.1	0.4
2012	BOS	MLB	27	219	22	19	2	0	16	12	43	0	0	.260/.303/.373	.238	.327	0.2	RF(49): 2.2, CF(19): -0.2	-0.1
2013	*BOS*	*MLB*	*28*	*250*	*24*	*15*	*2*	*3*	*25*	*20*	*38*	*2*	*1*	*.283/.342/.396*	*.262*	*.326*	*-0.3*	*RF 1, CF 0*	*0.8*

Expected to be the left-handed part of a right-field platoon with Cody Ross, Sweeney got off to a hot start that kept him in the lineup through most of April, though his early 962 OPS was assisted by an over-the-top .468 BABIP. Sweeney managed a powerless 536 OPS (with .256 BABIP) through July, shedding playing time as he went. A fractured finger then put him down for the rest of the season. A candidate to be non-tendered, Sweeney's above-average defense and acceptable mediocrity against left-handers should get him a bench seat somewhere.

Blake Swihart C

Born: 4/3/1992 Age: 21
Bats: B Throws: R Height: 6' 2"
Weight: 175 Breakout: 3%
Improve: 52% Collapse: 16%
Attrition: 20% MLB: 93%

Comparables:
Del Crandall,Johnny Bench,Buck Martinez

YEAR	TEAM	LVL	AGE	PA	R	2B	3B	HR	RBI	BB	SO	SB	CS	AVG_OBP_SLG	TAv	BABIP	BRR	FRAA	WARP
2012	GRN	A	20	378	44	17	4	7	53	26	68	6	2	.262/.307/.395	.225	.300	0.4	C(24): -0.5	-0.3
2013	*BOS*	*MLB*	*21*	*250*	*21*	*10*	*1*	*4*	*23*	*11*	*64*	*1*	*0*	*.218/.252/.325*	*.206*	*.275*	*-0.2*	*C -0*	*-0.5*

Switch-hitting catchers drafted out of high school might take the longest to develop of any player type, and Swihart is no exception. He's dripping with talent, but mastering the defensive intricacies of catching while maintaining two swings and learning the ins-and-outs of pro ball is time-consuming stuff. As of now nothing says he can't catch at the big-league level, but Swihart has the bat (plus hit tool, power, smooth swing from both sides of the plate) to play elsewhere if catching proves too much.

Shane Victorino OF

Born: 11/30/1980 Age: 32
Bats: B Throws: R Height: 5' 10"
Weight: 190 Breakout: 2%
Improve: 46% Collapse: 1%
Attrition: 12% MLB: 94%

Comparables:
Jody Gerut,Johnny Damon,Coco Crisp

YEAR	TEAM	LVL	AGE	PA	R	2B	3B	HR	RBI	BB	SO	SB	CS	AVG_OBP_SLG	TAv	BABIP	BRR	FRAA	WARP
2010	PHI	MLB	29	648	84	26	10	18	69	53	79	34	6	.259/.327/.429	.267	.273	5.8	CF(143): 4.3	3.8
2011	PHI	MLB	30	586	95	27	16	17	61	55	63	19	3	.279/.355/.491	.311	.292	5.4	CF(130): 5.1	5.3
2012	LAN	MLB	31	235	26	12	2	2	15	18	31	15	2	.245/.316/.351	.257	.278	0.5	LF(48): 6.4, CF(8): 0.0	1.0
2012	PHI	MLB	31	431	46	17	5	9	40	35	49	24	4	.261/.324/.401	.272	.278	2	CF(101): -0.9	1.7
2013	*BOS*	*MLB*	*32*	*611*	*83*	*30*	*9*	*13*	*60*	*50*	*73*	*29*	*6*	*.273/.339/.432*	*.270*	*.292*	*3.7*	*CF -4, LF 0*	*2.5*

Victorino returned to the Dodgers, who'd lost him in the Rule 5 draft in 2002 and again in 2004, via a deadline deal that sent Josh Lindblom, Ethan Martin, and Stefan Jarrin to Philadelphia. His line in Los Angeles was no better than the crummy collective that had manned left field prior to his arrival, but his speed and defense didn't suffer, and his struggles were confined to his work against righties. It was inevitable that some general manager would overpay for him, and Cherington won the sweepstakes with a three-year, $39 million deal.

PITCHERS

Alfredo Aceves

Born: 12/8/1982 Age: 30
Bats: R Throws: R Height: 6' 4" Weight: 220
Breakout: 19% Improve: 46% Collapse: 22%
Attrition: 9% MLB: 83%

Comparables:
Steve Karsay,Jeff Fulchino,Kameron Loe

YEAR	TEAM	LVL	AGE	W	L	SV	G	GS	IP	H	HR	BB	SO	BB9	SO9	GB%	BABIP	WHIP	ERA	FIP	FRA	WARP
2010	TRN	AA	27	0	0	0	4	3	8	10	1	1	7	1.1	7.9	44%	.375	1.38	5.62	3.61	4.98	0.0
2010	SWB	AAA	27	0	0	0	3	2	3^2	4	0	5	4	12.2	9.7	33%	.333	2.43	7.30	6.80	6.13	0.0
2010	NYA	MLB	27	3	0	1	10	0	12	10	1	4	2	3.0	1.5	50%	.200	1.17	3.00	5.05	6.19	-0.1
2011	PAW	AAA	28	0	1	0	2	2	8	6	0	4	6	4.5	6.8	36%	.364	1.25	5.62	3.61	5.26	0.0
2011	BOS	MLB	28	10	2	2	55	4	114	84	8	42	80	3.3	6.3	41%	.231	1.11	2.61	4.07	4.49	0.9
2012	BOS	MLB	29	2	10	25	69	0	84	80	11	31	75	3.3	8.0	40%	.290	1.32	5.36	4.28	5.17	0.2
2013	*BOS*	*MLB*	*30*	*3*	*2*	*8*	*49*	*3*	*79*	*74*	*9*	*25*	*59*	*2.8*	*6.8*	*42%*	*.278*	*1.25*	*3.90*	*4.14*	*4.24*	*1.1*

Aceves was a loser in the Fort Myers reality show *Who Wants to Be a Starter?* but was immediately pressed into closer duty when perpetually injured Andrew Bailey got injured. While closing games, the moody reliever experienced an uptick in velocity, his four-seam fastball jumping from 93 to 95 mph on average. Great, right? No. Speed brought with it a drop in groundballs and a rise in home runs, neither conducive to holding late leads. When Bailey returned, the Red Sox tried to use Aceves in a multi-inning role, but he chafed at losing the prestige position and clashed with Valentine. His likely role in 2013 is as a long reliever.

Scott Atchison

Born: **3/29/1976** Age: **37**
Bats: **R** Throws: **R** Height: **6' 3"** Weight: **200**
Breakout: **27%** Improve: **52%** Collapse: **37%**
Attrition: **16%** MLB: **86%**

Comparables:
Larry Andersen, Mike Jackson, Joe Borowski

YEAR	TEAM	LVL	AGE	W	L	SV	G	GS	IP	H	HR	BB	SO	BB9	SO9	GB%	BABIP	WHIP	ERA	FIP	FRA	WARP
2010	PAW	AAA	34	1	0	0	11	0	13^{1}	13	0	5	17	3.4	11.5	49%	.351	1.35	4.06	1.86	2.35	0.4
2010	BOS	MLB	34	2	3	0	43	1	60	58	9	19	41	2.8	6.2	48%	.268	1.28	4.50	4.63	5.22	0.0
2011	PAW	AAA	35	6	2	5	36	1	61^{1}	50	5	9	72	1.3	10.6	46%	.295	0.96	2.64	2.58	3.47	0.6
2011	BOS	MLB	35	1	0	1	17	0	30^{1}	31	0	6	17	1.8	5.0	46%	.320	1.22	3.26	2.73	3.53	0.6
2012	PAW	AAA	36	0	0	0	2	1	2	3	1	0	2	0.0	9.0	57%	.333	1.50	13.50	7.66	9.49	-0.1
2012	BOS	MLB	36	2	1	0	42	0	51^{1}	42	2	9	36	1.6	6.3	57%	.261	0.99	1.58	2.68	3.61	0.8
2013	*BOS*	*MLB*	*37*	*2*	*1*	*0*	*27*	*1*	41^{2}	*42*	*4*	*12*	*33*	*2.6*	*7.1*	*46%*	*.303*	*1.30*	*3.98*	*3.73*	*4.32*	*0.5*

A minor-league free agent, Atchison re-signed with Boston both because of opportunity in the bullpen and Massachusetts General Hospital. You see, Atchison's daughter suffers from a rare condition called thrombocytopenia-absent radius (TAR), marked by an absence of radius bones (one of two bones in your forearm, but you knew that). The former 49th-round pick was surprisingly effective, finishing fourth on the team in pWARP, a comment both on how good Atchison was and on how bad everyone else was. He doesn't wow you with stuff and was a bit hit-lucky, but he avoids walks and keeps the ball in the park. Despite missing two months with a UCL sprain (he returned in mid-September to throw 5 1/3 scoreless), Atchison is likely to land in Boston's bullpen again in 2013.

Andrew Bailey

Born: **5/31/1984** Age: **29**
Bats: **R** Throws: **R** Height: **6' 4"** Weight: **240**
Breakout: **22%** Improve: **47%** Collapse: **33%**
Attrition: **11%** MLB: **92%**

Comparables:
Aaron Heilman, Rich Gossage, Nick Masset

YEAR	TEAM	LVL	AGE	W	L	SV	G	GS	IP	H	HR	BB	SO	BB9	SO9	GB%	BABIP	WHIP	ERA	FIP	FRA	WARP
2010	SAC	AAA	26	0	0	0	1	1	0^{2}	3	0	0	1	0.0	12.9	%	.750	4.29	25.71	0.73	4.30	0.0
2010	OAK	MLB	26	1	3	25	47	0	49	34	3	13	42	2.4	7.7	39%	.237	0.96	1.47	2.92	2.93	0.9
2011	SAC	AAA	27	0	0	0	4	0	4	3	0	1	3	2.2	6.8	—	.250	1.00	0.00	4.53	4.93	0.0
2011	OAK	MLB	27	0	4	24	42	0	41^{2}	34	3	12	41	2.6	8.9	38%	.272	1.10	3.24	2.89	2.90	0.9
2012	RSX	Rk	28	0	0	0	2	2	2	2	0	1	4	4.5	18.0	50%	.500	1.50	0.00	2.43	-0.15	0.1
2012	PME	AA	28	0	0	0	1	0	1	3	0	0	2	0.0	18.0	50%	.750	3.00	9.00	-0.80	-6.21	0.1
2012	PAW	AAA	28	0	0	0	3	0	3^{1}	1	0	0	4	0.0	10.8	57%	.143	0.30	0.00	0.76	2.21	0.1
2012	BOS	MLB	28	1	1	6	19	0	15^{1}	21	2	8	14	4.7	8.2	33%	.380	1.89	7.04	4.48	5.35	0.0
2013	*BOS*	*MLB*	*29*	*2*	*1*	*16*	*37*	*0*	*36*	*32*	*4*	*13*	*35*	*3.2*	*8.8*	*42%*	*.290*	*1.24*	*3.54*	*3.78*	*3.85*	*0.6*

Forgetting that smart teams don't buy closers, they make them, the Red Sox panicked after Jonathan Papelbon bolted for Philadelphia and gave up Josh Reddick and two minor leaguers for the A's oft-injured fireballer Bailey. The results were predictable: Bailey got injured. A ligament in his thumb went snappy-snap and the resultant surgery put him on the shelf for the majority of the Valentine Era. When he returned in mid-August the season was effectively over. The good news is Bailey's average velocity was still around 95 mph, so there is no reason to think that he can't be the late-inning guy Boston acquired him to be, at least until he gets hurt again.

Daniel Bard

Born: **6/25/1985** Age: **28**
Bats: **R** Throws: **R** Height: **6' 5"** Weight: **215**
Breakout: **32%** Improve: **60%** Collapse: **25%**
Attrition: **12%** MLB: **86%**

Comparables:
David Aardsma, Rich Gossage, Ramon Ramirez

YEAR	TEAM	LVL	AGE	W	L	SV	G	GS	IP	H	HR	BB	SO	BB9	SO9	GB%	BABIP	WHIP	ERA	FIP	FRA	WARP
2010	BOS	MLB	25	1	2	3	73	0	74^{2}	45	6	30	76	3.6	9.2	47%	.215	1.00	1.93	3.34	3.32	1.2
2011	BOS	MLB	26	2	9	1	70	0	73	46	5	24	74	3.0	9.1	54%	.224	0.96	3.33	2.99	3.49	1.3
2012	PAW	AAA	27	3	2	0	31	1	32	31	2	29	32	8.2	9.0	56%	.322	1.88	7.03	5.63	7.20	-0.7
2012	BOS	MLB	27	5	6	0	17	10	59^{1}	60	9	43	38	6.5	5.8	45%	.285	1.74	6.22	6.32	6.95	-0.7
2013	*BOS*	*MLB*	*28*	*3*	*2*	*1*	*53*	*3*	66^{2}	*55*	*7*	*31*	*70*	*4.2*	*9.5*	*49%*	*.283*	*1.29*	*3.65*	*3.86*	*3.96*	*1.1*

What can one say about Bard that hasn't already been said about a five-car pile-up on the interstate? The beginning of the end was September 2011, when, like the rest of the team, Bard completely fell apart. Moving to the starting rotation last spring didn't help matters as first Bard's control abandoned him, then his velocity did: His average fastball was down 4.5 mph. The end result was a Rick Ankiel-like mess. Three months in Triple-A didn't fix anything, nor did returning to the bullpen, nor did being called back to Boston in late August. Maybe Bard isn't hiding an injury, so maybe if he fixes his mechanics, maybe his velocity and command return, but those are a lot of maybes.

Matt Barnes

Born: **6/17/1990** Age: **23**
Bats: **R** Throws: **R** Height: **6' 5"** Weight: **205**
Breakout: **31%** Improve: **68%** Collapse: **13%**
Attrition: **10%** MLB: **91%**

Comparables:
Scott Mathieson,Matt Garza,Johnny Cueto

YEAR	TEAM	LVL	AGE	W	L	SV	G	GS	IP	H	HR	BB	SO	BB9	SO9	GB%	BABIP	WHIP	ERA	FIP	FRA	WARP
2012	GRN	A	22	2	0	0	5	5	26^{2}	12	0	4	42	1.4	14.2	60%	.240	0.60	0.34	0.99	1.14	1.0
2012	SLM	A+	22	5	5	0	20	20	93	85	6	25	91	2.4	8.8	47%	.315	1.18	3.58	3.33	3.58	0.9
2013	*BOS*	*MLB*	*23*	*2*	*3*	*0*	*7*	*7*	34^{2}	*35*	*4*	*14*	*31*	*3.7*	*7.9*	*47%*	*.310*	*1.43*	*4.65*	*4.12*	*5.06*	*0.2*

Boston hasn't produced a top starting pitcher since Clay Buchholz in 2007, so Barnes isn't just a sip of water in the desert, he's a mirage come to life. Boston's first-round pick in 2011, Barnes has an easy delivery that pumps the ball in the mid-90s with excellent sink in the lower half of the zone. He keeps hitters off-balance with a good breaking ball and an average changeup, both with above-average potential. After five starts with just one run allowed in the Sally League, Boston moved him up to High-A, where he continued to pitch well. If he can improve his fastball command, don't be surprised to see Barnes reach the upper minors before the year is out.

Pedro Beato

Born: **10/27/1986** Age: **26**
Bats: **R** Throws: **R** Height: **6' 5"** Weight: **220**
Breakout: **24%** Improve: **48%** Collapse: **26%**
Attrition: **18%** MLB: **83%**

Comparables:
Gary Glover,Bill Stafford,Jeff Russell

YEAR	TEAM	LVL	AGE	W	L	SV	G	GS	IP	H	HR	BB	SO	BB9	SO9	GB%	BABIP	WHIP	ERA	FIP	FRA	WARP
2010	BOW	AA	23	4	0	16	43	0	59^{2}	49	4	19	50	2.9	7.5	45%	.264	1.14	2.11	3.66	4.32	0.6
2011	BUF	AAA	24	1	0	0	1	0	1^{1}	2	0	1	0	6.8	0.0	50%	.333	2.25	0.00	5.49	7.14	0.0
2011	NYN	MLB	24	2	1	0	60	0	67	59	5	27	39	3.6	5.2	50%	.260	1.28	4.30	4.19	5.00	-0.3
2012	SLU	A+	25	0	0	0	3	0	4	2	0	1	4	2.2	9.0	44%	.222	0.75	0.00	2.14	1.94	0.1
2012	BUF	AAA	25	4	4	0	24	1	37	32	7	11	27	2.7	6.6	47%	.240	1.16	4.14	5.21	6.48	-0.5
2012	PAW	AAA	25	0	0	1	4	0	5	1	0	4	7	7.2	12.6	38%	.125	1.00	0.00	2.76	3.46	0.1
2012	BOS	MLB	25	1	0	0	4	0	7^{2}	6	0	3	7	3.5	8.2	65%	.300	1.17	4.70	2.79	4.31	0.1
2012	NYN	MLB	25	0	0	0	7	0	4^{1}	5	1	2	5	4.2	10.4	31%	.333	1.62	10.38	5.21	5.06	0.0
2013	*BOS*	*MLB*	*26*	*1*	*0*	*0*	*27*	*0*	33^{1}	*38*	*5*	*14*	*18*	*3.8*	*5.0*	*47%*	*.301*	*1.57*	*5.70*	*5.33*	*6.19*	*-0.3*

Beato's fastball is fine if not spectacular, and that's about it. The prize for not releasing Kelly Shoppach outright, Beato's ability to harness his breaking stuff will be the key to his ability to pitch in the majors long-term. If his history is any guide, don't be optimistic.

Craig Breslow

Born: **8/8/1980** Age: **32**
Bats: **L** Throws: **L** Height: **6' 0"** Weight: **190**
Breakout: **30%** Improve: **56%** Collapse: **24%**
Attrition: **7%** MLB: **94%**

Comparables:
John Grabow,Bobby Seay,Pedro Feliciano

YEAR	TEAM	LVL	AGE	W	L	SV	G	GS	IP	H	HR	BB	SO	BB9	SO9	GB%	BABIP	WHIP	ERA	FIP	FRA	WARP
2010	OAK	MLB	29	4	4	5	75	0	74^{2}	53	9	29	71	3.5	8.6	31%	.226	1.10	3.01	3.88	4.27	0.3
2011	OAK	MLB	30	0	2	0	67	0	59^{1}	69	4	21	44	3.2	6.7	40%	.342	1.52	3.79	3.62	3.63	0.7
2012	ARI	MLB	31	2	0	0	40	0	43^{1}	38	5	13	42	2.7	8.7	43%	.277	1.18	2.70	3.67	4.09	0.4
2012	BOS	MLB	31	1	0	0	23	0	20	14	0	9	19	4.1	8.6	52%	.269	1.15	2.70	2.65	3.13	0.4
2013	*BOS*	*MLB*	*32*	*3*	*1*	*1*	*54*	*0*	52^{1}	*48*	*6*	*20*	*47*	*3.4*	*8.1*	*40%*	*.287*	*1.30*	*3.86*	*4.04*	*4.20*	*0.7*

The rare LOOGY who can get right-handed hitters out as well (RLOOGYWCGRHHOAW?), the Connecticut native and Yale graduate returned to Boston from Arizona for the perpetually about-to-be-traded Matt Albers. Although he can get wild (around the plate, not at parties, where he's frequently found in the kitchen talking to the host's cat), Breslow gets strikeouts and somehow keeps the ball in the yard despite a mediocre groundball rate. Last season, right-handed hitters got him for .037 of TAv more than lefties, but that was mostly because he held down lefties more than usual. If Breslow can continue to keep the ball in the yard while minimizing walks, he can be a valuable back-of-the-bullpen arm.

Drake Britton

Born: **5/22/1989** Age: **24**
Bats: **L** Throws: **L** Height: **6' 3"** Weight: **200**
Breakout: **29%** Improve: **60%** Collapse: **20%**
Attrition: **15%** MLB: **91%**

Comparables:
Brad Halsey,Sean Marshall,Sean West

YEAR	TEAM	LVL	AGE	W	L	SV	G	GS	IP	H	HR	BB	SO	BB9	SO9	GB%	BABIP	WHIP	ERA	FIP	FRA	WARP
2010	GRN	A	21	2	3	0	21	21	75^{2}	69	5	23	78	2.7	9.3	50%	.296	1.22	2.97	3.32	4.45	1.2
2011	SLM	A+	22	1	13	0	26	26	97^{2}	111	12	55	89	5.1	8.2	—	.334	1.70	6.91	4.88	5.30	0.0
2012	SLM	A+	23	3	5	0	10	8	45	42	5	19	42	3.8	8.4	51%	.282	1.36	5.80	4.50	6.38	-0.6
2012	PME	AA	23	4	7	0	16	16	84^{2}	86	3	38	76	4.0	8.1	49%	.331	1.46	3.72	3.25	3.67	0.4
2013	*BOS*	*MLB*	*24*	*1*	*3*	*0*	*7*	*7*	32^{2}	*36*	*4*	*18*	*23*	*4.9*	*6.5*	*44%*	*.311*	*1.66*	*5.68*	*5.04*	*6.17*	*-0.1*

After enduring a 2010 season in the Carolina League that the word "disastrous" fails to adequately describe, the big, strong lefty rebounded to post his most promising season yet. His big fastball from the left side is the draw here, and while he throws a curve, changeup, and slider, none are plus pitches. Unless that changes, his future is in the bullpen, but the Sox are keeping him in the rotation until he proves he can't handle it. He'll likely start the season back in Double-A, but continued success will move him quickly.

Clay Buchholz

Born: **8/14/1984** Age: **28**
Bats: **L** Throws: **R** Height: **6' 4"** Weight: **190**
Breakout: **15%** Improve: **44%** Collapse: **26%**
Attrition: **9%** MLB: **92%**

Comparables:
Tom Gorzelanny,Joe Saunders,Mark Mulder

YEAR	TEAM	LVL	AGE	W	L	SV	G	GS	IP	H	HR	BB	SO	BB9	SO9	GB%	BABIP	WHIP	ERA	FIP	FRA	WARP
2010	PAW	AAA	25	0	0	0	1	1	3^{2}	4	1	1	2	2.4	4.9	58%	.273	1.35	4.86	7.35	7.44	0.0
2010	BOS	MLB	25	17	7	0	28	28	173^{2}	142	9	67	120	3.5	6.2	52%	.261	1.20	2.33	3.58	4.40	1.8
2011	BOS	MLB	26	6	3	0	14	14	82^{2}	76	10	31	60	3.4	6.5	51%	.264	1.29	3.48	4.38	4.68	0.8
2012	PAW	AAA	27	0	0	0	1	1	2^{1}	1	0	2	3	7.7	11.6	60%	.200	1.29	0.00	3.16	2.41	0.1
2012	BOS	MLB	27	11	8	0	29	29	189^{1}	187	25	64	129	3.0	6.1	49%	.284	1.33	4.56	4.60	5.50	-0.3
2013	*BOS*	*MLB*	*28*	*8*	*9*	*0*	*24*	*24*	*147^{2}*	*142*	*16*	*54*	*114*	*3.3*	*6.9*	*49%*	*.288*	*1.32*	*4.07*	*4.16*	*4.42*	*1.8*

Through May 21, batters were hitting .330/.417/.537 against Buchholz, resulting in an ERA approaching 8.00. From then on (not counting his last disastrous start in New York), Buchholz pitched to a sub-3.00 ERA through grounders, strikeouts, and limiting walks. That's the problem with Buchholz: He looks good if you just overlook the bad stuff. The key to Clay is his changeup. When it's on, the grounders come and the fastball plays up for strikeouts. When it isn't, hitters sit on the straight fastball and crush it. Losing the change isn't always the problem though; sometimes it's health, sometimes it's mechanics. To be the guy Boston signed long term, Buchholz has to drop the selective endpoints, stay healthy, and pitch well all the time. PECOTA might not be optimistic, but we are.

Chris Carpenter

Born: **12/26/1985** Age: **27**
Bats: **R** Throws: **R** Height: **6' 5"** Weight: **220**
Breakout: **17%** Improve: **57%** Collapse: **21%**
Attrition: **8%** MLB: **91%**

Comparables:
Jim Clancy,Kip Wells,Roger Craig

YEAR	TEAM	LVL	AGE	W	L	SV	G	GS	IP	H	HR	BB	SO	BB9	SO9	GB%	BABIP	WHIP	ERA	FIP	FRA	WARP
2011	TEN	AA	25	1	1	1	10	0	12^{1}	10	2	4	6	2.9	4.4	20%	.300	1.14	4.38	5.66	3.75	0.1
2011	IOW	AAA	25	2	3	1	22	0	30^{1}	32	3	23	28	6.8	8.3	62%	.281	1.81	6.53	5.79	8.77	-0.2
2011	CHN	MLB	25	0	0	0	10	0	9^{2}	12	1	7	8	6.5	7.4	47%	.355	1.97	2.79	4.86	4.25	0.0
2012	RSX	Rk	26	0	0	0	2	1	2	1	0	1	1	4.5	4.5	67%	.167	1.00	4.50	3.93	8.40	-0.1
2012	GRN	A	26	0	0	0	2	2	2	1	0	1	4	4.5	18.0	67%	.333	1.00	4.50	2.58	1.82	0.1
2012	PME	AA	26	0	0	0	1	1	2	2	0	0	3	0.0	13.5	60%	.400	1.00	4.50	0.20	-4.08	0.0
2012	PAW	AAA	26	1	0	4	16	0	15^{2}	7	1	8	17	4.6	9.8	49%	.176	0.96	1.15	3.35	4.12	0.1
2012	BOS	MLB	26	1	0	0	8	0	6	7	1	10	2	15.0	3.0	59%	.286	2.83	9.00	9.55	8.03	-0.2
2013	*BOS*	*MLB*	*27*	*1*	*2*	*0*	*13*	*5*	*32^{2}*	*36*	*4*	*19*	*23*	*5.2*	*6.4*	*52%*	*.307*	*1.66*	*5.63*	*5.13*	*6.11*	*-0.1*

No, not that one. Carpenter is the going rate for a two-time World Series-winning GM, having come over from the Cubs in exchange for Theo Epstein's decampment to the Windy City. At this point it's the only thing to recommend him, but that's not to say there's nothing else there. The reliever has a live arm (he's hit 100 before), but excessive walks and injuries have robbed him of his prospect status. Carpenter has options left, so he can be stashed in Triple-A while the Red Sox play wait and see.

Aaron Cook

Born: **2/8/1979** Age: **34**
Bats: **R** Throws: **R** Height: **6' 4"** Weight: **215**
Breakout: **6%** Improve: **45%** Collapse: **29%**
Attrition: **18%** MLB: **86%**

Comparables:
Brad Penny,Joaquin Andujar,Bob Purkey

YEAR	TEAM	LVL	AGE	W	L	SV	G	GS	IP	H	HR	BB	SO	BB9	SO9	GB%	BABIP	WHIP	ERA	FIP	FRA	WARP
2010	TUL	AA	31	1	1	0	2	2	10^{2}	8	1	3	10	2.5	8.4	43%	.259	1.03	2.52	3.36	4.18	0.1
2010	COL	MLB	31	6	8	0	23	23	127^{2}	147	11	52	62	3.7	4.4	59%	.307	1.56	5.08	4.57	5.58	0.2
2011	TUL	AA	32	0	1	0	3	3	14	16	1	3	13	1.9	8.4	61%	.346	1.36	5.79	3.09	3.52	0.2
2011	CSP	AAA	32	1	0	0	2	2	14^{2}	13	2	2	5	1.2	3.1	62%	.229	1.02	5.52	5.28	6.81	0.2
2011	COL	MLB	32	3	10	0	18	17	97	127	9	37	48	3.4	4.5	56%	.345	1.69	6.03	4.51	5.13	0.8
2012	PAW	AAA	33	3	0	0	6	6	37^{1}	33	1	12	16	2.9	3.9	61%	.258	1.21	2.41	3.61	4.61	0.0
2012	BOS	MLB	33	4	11	0	18	18	94	117	15	21	20	2.0	1.9	59%	.288	1.47	5.65	5.40	6.88	-1.1
2013	*BOS*	*MLB*	*34*	*5*	*7*	*0*	*17*	*17*	*92^{2}*	*109*	*10*	*27*	*40*	*2.6*	*3.9*	*57%*	*.308*	*1.47*	*5.03*	*4.61*	*5.47*	*0.1*

Cook is a fire extinguisher on the 20th floor of a building engulfed in flames: It's there if you need it, but if you need it, you're probably already screwed. Cook's status in Boston was a placeholder for a better starting pitcher who didn't materialize. The offseason is a chance to find that pitcher, though, so if Cook is starting in Boston this season the front office didn't do its job or somebody got hurt. Cook stands out for more than general lousiness. His 1.91 SO9 is the second lowest for a starting pitcher since the DH was instituted in 1973, right behind the decidedly mortal Larry Pashnick's 1.81 for the Tigers in 1982.

Rubby De La Rosa

Born: **3/4/1989** Age: **24**
Bats: **R** Throws: **R** Height: **6' 2"** Weight: **185**
Breakout: **27%** Improve: **59%** Collapse: **18%**
Attrition: **14%** MLB: **94%**

Comparables:
Sean Gallagher, Bob Welch, Tyson Ross

YEAR	TEAM	LVL	AGE	W	L	SV	G	GS	IP	H	HR	BB	SO	BB9	SO9	GB%	BABIP	WHIP	ERA	FIP	FRA	WARP
2010	GRL	A	21	4	1	6	14	5	59^{1}	49	3	17	55	2.6	8.3	56%	.284	1.11	3.19	3.52	4.54	0.4
2010	CHT	AA	21	3	1	0	8	8	51	38	1	21	39	3.7	6.9	60%	.264	1.16	1.41	3.40	4.21	0.9
2011	CHT	AA	22	2	2	0	8	8	40	30	1	19	52	4.3	11.7	—	.290	1.23	2.92	2.61	2.83	0.0
2011	LAN	MLB	22	4	5	0	13	10	60^{2}	54	6	31	60	4.6	8.9	49%	.306	1.40	3.71	3.83	4.79	0.1
2012	DOD	Rk	23	0	0	0	1	1	3	1	0	0	3	0.0	9.0	83%	.167	0.33	0.00	2.38	2.65	0.1
2012	RCU	A+	23	1	0	0	3	2	9	4	0	3	9	3.0	9.0	65%	.200	0.78	0.00	2.81	-0.21	0.1
2012	CHT	AA	23	0	0	0	2	0	1	3	0	1	0	9.0	0.0	33%	.500	4.00	27.00	6.14	7.96	0.0
2012	LAN	MLB	23	0	0	0	1	0	0^{2}	0	0	2	0	27.0	0.0	%	.000	3.00	27.00	12.14	13.31	-0.1
2013	*BOS*	*MLB*	*24*	*1*	*2*	*0*	*8*	*5*	*34*	*35*	*4*	*17*	*28*	*4.4*	*7.3*	*50%*	*.304*	*1.50*	*4.80*	*4.58*	*5.22*	*0.1*

De La Rosa was acquired in the mega-trade with the Dodgers that made half of all Red Sox T-shirts obsolete, but is far better than your usual return for unwanted salary. He's still raw, but can miss bats with a plus-plus fastball that can reach the upper 90s. What makes him especially intriguing is his deceptive changeup. The speed differential and consistent release point between that and the fastball can cause batters to swing up to three times while waiting for the thing to cross the plate. De La Rosa broke out in Double-A Chattanooga in 2011, striking out 52 in 40 innings and ending the season with modest success in the Dodgers rotation. Shortly thereafter he underwent Tommy John surgery and missed the majority of 2012. It's unclear where he slots in with the Red Sox. He has options remaining so some time in Triple-A probably wouldn't hurt.

Ryan Dempster

Born: **5/3/1977** Age: **36**
Bats: **R** Throws: **R** Height: **6' 3"** Weight: **215**
Breakout: **22%** Improve: **51%** Collapse: **25%**
Attrition: **20%** MLB: **84%**

Comparables:
Bert Blyleven, Jose Contreras, Esteban Loaiza

YEAR	TEAM	LVL	AGE	W	L	SV	G	GS	IP	H	HR	BB	SO	BB9	SO9	GB%	BABIP	WHIP	ERA	FIP	FRA	WARP
2010	CHN	MLB	33	15	12	0	34	34	215^{1}	198	25	86	208	3.6	8.7	50%	.294	1.32	3.85	4.02	4.55	2.3
2011	CHN	MLB	34	10	14	0	34	34	202^{1}	211	23	82	191	3.6	8.5	46%	.324	1.45	4.80	3.87	4.61	2.0
2012	CHN	MLB	35	5	5	0	16	16	104	81	9	27	83	2.3	7.2	43%	.242	1.04	2.25	3.47	3.86	1.8
2012	TEX	MLB	35	7	3	0	12	12	69	74	10	25	70	3.3	9.1	47%	.330	1.43	5.09	4.03	4.50	0.8
2013	*BOS*	*MLB*	*36*	*8*	*9*	*0*	*24*	*24*	*145*	*142*	*16*	*52*	*132*	*3.2*	*8.2*	*47%*	*.306*	*1.34*	*4.13*	*3.89*	*4.49*	*1.7*

After more than 14 seasons in the National League, Dempster announced his presence in the AL last summer with a rocky 12-start stint for Texas. He'll be staying in the junior circuit after signing a two-year deal with Boston this offseason. One of baseball's more reliable pitchers since rejoining the starting ranks in 2008, Dempster logged 200-plus innings in four consecutive seasons until notching just under 180 frames last year. Despite his struggles in Texas, the righty had one of his better seasons. Entering his age-36 campaign, he has yet to show signs of slowing down. Although he doesn't overwhelm with velocity—mostly working at 88-92 mph—he consistently posts strikeout rates north of 20 percent. There's some concern that Dempster's numbers will suffer in a full season in the AL and Fenway, but expect a reliable mid-rotation starting pitcher.

Felix Doubront

Born: **10/23/1987** Age: **25**
Bats: **L** Throws: **L** Height: **6' 3"** Weight: **165**
Breakout: **35%** Improve: **62%** Collapse: **13%**
Attrition: **12%** MLB: **92%**

Comparables:
J.P. Howell, Marc Rzepczynski, Brian Matusz

YEAR	TEAM	LVL	AGE	W	L	SV	G	GS	IP	H	HR	BB	SO	BB9	SO9	GB%	BABIP	WHIP	ERA	FIP	FRA	WARP
2010	PME	AA	22	4	0	0	8	8	43	39	0	17	38	3.6	8.0	44%	.325	1.30	2.51	2.92	3.75	0.9
2010	PAW	AAA	22	4	3	0	9	8	37	36	1	16	34	3.9	8.3	56%	.340	1.41	3.16	3.43	3.86	0.6
2010	BOS	MLB	22	2	2	2	12	3	25	27	3	10	23	3.6	8.3	46%	.316	1.48	4.32	4.09	4.06	0.4
2011	LOW	A-	23	0	0	0	1	1	2	0	0	0	4	0.0	18.0	—	.000	0.00	0.00	-0.64	-0.69	0.0
2011	PME	AA	23	1	0	0	1	1	5	4	0	0	9	0.0	16.2	—	.400	0.80	1.80	-0.19	-0.21	0.0
2011	PAW	AAA	23	2	5	0	18	16	70^{1}	65	10	26	61	3.3	7.8	48%	.270	1.29	4.22	4.54	6.10	-0.3
2011	BOS	MLB	23	0	0	1	11	0	10^{1}	12	1	8	6	7.0	5.2	46%	.344	1.94	6.10	5.48	7.37	-0.2
2012	BOS	MLB	24	11	10	0	29	29	161	162	24	71	167	4.0	9.3	45%	.313	1.45	4.86	4.33	4.64	1.4
2013	*BOS*	*MLB*	*25*	*6*	*9*	*0*	*23*	*23*	*119*	*124*	*15*	*51*	*104*	*3.9*	*7.8*	*45%*	*.312*	*1.47*	*4.89*	*4.38*	*5.32*	*0.5*

Doubront is a case of damning with faint praise. His 2012 season was a huge step forward from his 2011, though that's the difference between mere adequacy and massive disappointment. The lefty made it through a full season in the rotation, posting the highest strikeout rate of any Red Sox starter, but again, on a staff that vastly underperformed. Doubront's problem is inefficiency. He averages more than four pitches per plate appearance, the 16th most of any pitcher in baseball (minimum 1,000 pitches thrown). Thus, he rarely lasts deep into a game: 29 starts, none longer than seven innings. Attacking the strike zone could fix that, but might mean fewer strikeouts. He's a back-of-the rotation guy with potential to move up a slot or two.

Joel Hanrahan

Born: **10/6/1981** Age: **31**
Bats: **R** Throws: **R** Height: **6' 5"** Weight: **245**
Breakout: **19%** Improve: **36%** Collapse: **20%**
Attrition: **7%** MLB: **95%**

Comparables:
Lee Smith,Kiko Calero,Frank Francisco

YEAR	TEAM	LVL	AGE	W	L	SV	G	GS	IP	H	HR	BB	SO	BB9	SO9	GB%	BABIP	WHIP	ERA	FIP	FRA	WARP
2010	BRD	A+	28	0	0	0	2	0	2	0	0	0	3	0.0	13.5	—	.000	0.00	0.00	0.44	0.47	0.0
2010	PIT	MLB	28	4	1	6	72	0	69^2	58	6	26	100	3.4	12.9	43%	.329	1.21	3.62	2.65	2.69	1.9
2011	PIT	MLB	29	1	4	40	70	0	68^2	56	1	16	61	2.1	8.0	54%	.282	1.05	1.83	2.15	3.01	1.3
2012	PIT	MLB	30	5	2	36	63	0	59^2	40	8	36	67	5.4	10.1	40%	.225	1.27	2.72	4.49	3.51	0.6
2013	*BOS*	*MLB*	*31*	*3*	*1*	*30*	*55*	*0*	*52^2*	*45*	*5*	*22*	*62*	*3.8*	*10.5*	*42%*	*.307*	*1.28*	*3.51*	*3.33*	*3.82*	*0.9*

Boston acquired Hanrahan in December to fill the ninth-inning hole left by Papelbon's departure and Bailey's durability woes. Hanrahan boasts an impressive strikeout rate and, in 2012, an impressive walk rate, in a really bad way. In the trade's aftermath, Pittsburgh pitching coach Ray Searage suggested the control woes stemmed from a foot injury, some slight mechanical inconsistencies, and decreased save opportunities. If he's right about all of that—and if Boston can avoid the last part—then the hard-throwing Hanrahan figures to be up to the task of nailing down the ninth and raising his free-agent stock in the process. But that's a lot to be right about.

Chris Hernandez

Born: **12/14/1988** Age: **24**
Bats: **L** Throws: **L** Height: **6' 2"** Weight: **185**
Breakout: **25%** Improve: **60%** Collapse: **26%**
Attrition: **16%** MLB: **90%**

Comparables:
Matt Harrison,John Lannan,Casey Coleman

YEAR	TEAM	LVL	AGE	W	L	SV	G	GS	IP	H	HR	BB	SO	BB9	SO9	GB%	BABIP	WHIP	ERA	FIP	FRA	WARP
2011	SLM	A+	22	10	7	0	25	25	127^1	112	8	51	80	3.6	5.7	—	.272	1.28	3.18	4.13	4.49	0.0
2012	PME	AA	23	4	8	0	18	18	103^2	102	7	36	60	3.1	5.2	56%	.286	1.33	3.13	4.08	5.64	0.2
2012	PAW	AAA	23	1	4	0	8	7	42^2	40	4	17	30	3.6	6.3	43%	.279	1.34	3.59	4.31	4.86	0.1
2013	*BOS*	*MLB*	*24*	*2*	*3*	*0*	*7*	*7*	*36*	*41*	*5*	*15*	*21*	*3.7*	*5.2*	*48%*	*.304*	*1.55*	*5.44*	*5.09*	*5.91*	*-0.1*

Sometimes it feels like there are two groups of pitchers, those who know how to pitch and those who have immense physical gifts for it. Hernandez is a charter member of the first group, but will never be admitted to the second. He spots his upper-80s fastball where you would spot an upper-80s fastball if you had to face pro hitters: anywhere but the middle of the plate. Batters are kept off-balance with a few breaking pitches, none of which is better than average. He has All-Star makeup, but unless middle relievers get more recognition, it'll probably be the only thing All-Star about him.

Rich Hill

Born: **3/11/1980** Age: **33**
Bats: **L** Throws: **L** Height: **6' 6"** Weight: **220**
Breakout: **16%** Improve: **50%** Collapse: **19%**
Attrition: **18%** MLB: **79%**

Comparables:
Kaz Ishii,Matt Young,Stephen Randolph

YEAR	TEAM	LVL	AGE	W	L	SV	G	GS	IP	H	HR	BB	SO	BB9	SO9	GB%	BABIP	WHIP	ERA	FIP	FRA	WARP
2010	MEM	AAA	30	4	3	0	23	4	46	35	5	30	47	5.9	9.2	44%	.265	1.41	4.30	5.43	6.68	-0.4
2010	PAW	AAA	30	3	1	0	19	6	53	45	3	29	55	4.9	9.3	49%	.307	1.40	3.74	4.10	4.77	0.0
2010	BOS	MLB	30	1	0	0	6	0	4	5	0	1	3	2.2	6.8	57%	.357	1.50	0.00	2.30	3.04	0.1
2011	PAW	AAA	31	1	0	1	10	0	16	8	1	5	18	2.8	10.1	41%	.115	0.81	1.12	2.92	4.70	0.1
2011	BOS	MLB	31	0	0	0	9	0	8	3	0	3	12	3.4	13.5	36%	.214	0.75	0.00	1.56	2.50	0.2
2012	RSX	Rk	32	0	1	0	2	1	1^1	0	0	2	3	13.5	20.2	1.%	.000	1.50	13.50	3.43	4.88	0.0
2012	GRN	A	32	0	0	0	2	2	2	2	0	0	5	0.0	22.5	67%	.667	1.00	4.50	-1.42	-0.77	0.0
2012	SLM	A+	32	0	0	0	3	3	4	1	0	1	8	2.2	18.0	1.%	.200	0.50	0.00	0.89	-0.89	0.0
2012	PME	AA	32	0	0	0	1	0	1	1	0	0	1	0.0	9.0	33%	.333	1.00	0.00	1.20	-1.71	0.0
2012	PAW	AAA	32	1	0	0	8	0	8	3	1	2	10	2.2	11.2	50%	.133	0.62	1.12	3.03	3.91	0.1
2012	BOS	MLB	32	1	0	0	25	0	19^2	17	0	11	21	5.0	9.6	43%	.333	1.42	1.83	2.59	3.40	0.3
2013	*BOS*	*MLB*	*33*	*2*	*1*	*0*	*22*	*3*	*33*	*31*	*4*	*21*	*31*	*5.8*	*8.5*	*42%*	*.297*	*1.58*	*5.00*	*4.81*	*5.43*	*0.1*

The Milton, Massachusetts, native moved to the bullpen upon his homecoming in 2011 and was lights out before his left elbow gave out, requiring Tommy John surgery. Hill returned in late April and was effective against right- and left-handed batters, showing a slight reverse platoon split. Injuries reared up again in early June, though, as he strained the flexor tendon in his left forearm, keeping him out until September. When healthy, Hill can be a valuable LOOGY who can face the occasional right-handed hitter, but it's the health caveat that is troubling. He is a free agent, so if he returns, he'll slot into the middle of Boston's pen.

John Lackey

Born: **10/23/1978** Age: **34**
Bats: **R** Throws: **R** Height: **6' 7"** Weight: **245**
Breakout: **12%** Improve: **36%** Collapse: **32%**
Attrition: **8%** MLB: **83%**

Comparables:
Bronson Arroyo,John Thomson,Bartolo Colon

YEAR	TEAM	LVL	AGE	W	L	SV	G	GS	IP	H	HR	BB	SO	BB9	SO9	GB%	BABIP	WHIP	ERA	FIP	FRA	WARP
2010	BOS	MLB	31	14	11	0	33	33	215	233	18	72	156	3.0	6.5	46%	.319	1.42	4.40	3.81	4.70	1.5
2011	PAW	AAA	32	0	0	0	1	1	5^2	3	1	0	4	0.0	6.4	53%	.143	0.53	1.59	4.12	5.11	0.0
2011	BOS	MLB	32	12	12	0	28	28	160	203	20	56	108	3.2	6.1	42%	.339	1.62	6.41	4.74	5.21	0.6
2013	*BOS*	*MLB*	*34*	*2*	*2*	*0*	*6*	*6*	*35*	*37*	*4*	*11*	*26*	*2.7*	*6.7*	*45%*	*.311*	*1.37*	*4.62*	*4.14*	*5.03*	*0.2*

After playing his part in the ignominious chicken-and-beer clubhouse narrative that allegedly explains the collapse of the 2011 Red Sox, Lackey had the good sense to have Tommy John surgery and miss the Valentine Era. Now healthy, or at least with his elbow healed, he'll attempt to recapture the skills that once made him a top-of-the-rotation starter. Chief among them, an ability to throw all three of his pitches for strikes. PECOTA and the rest of Red Sox Nation will believe it when they see it.

Jon Lester

Born: **1/7/1984** Age: **29**
Bats: **L** Throws: **L** Height: **6' 5"** Weight: **240**
Breakout: **12%** Improve: **42%** Collapse: **24%**
Attrition: **7%** MLB: **94%**

Comparables:
Rich Hill,CC Sabathia,Erik Bedard

YEAR	TEAM	LVL	AGE	W	L	SV	G	GS	IP	H	HR	BB	SO	BB9	SO9	GB%	BABIP	WHIP	ERA	FIP	FRA	WARP
2010	BOS	MLB	26	19	9	0	32	32	208	167	14	83	225	3.6	9.7	54%	.289	1.20	3.25	3.10	4.37	3.0
2011	BOS	MLB	27	15	9	0	31	31	191^{2}	166	20	75	182	3.5	8.5	51%	.286	1.26	3.47	3.86	4.58	1.9
2012	BOS	MLB	28	9	14	0	33	33	205^{1}	216	25	68	166	3.0	7.3	51%	.312	1.38	4.82	4.06	5.07	1.1
2013	*BOS*	*MLB*	*29*	*10*	*10*	*0*	*29*	*29*	*180^{1}*	*164*	*17*	*60*	*171*	*3.0*	*8.5*	*49%*	*.301*	*1.24*	*3.51*	*3.53*	*3.81*	*3.5*

Boston's nominal ace, Lester's slip from the front of the rotation continued in 2012. His strikeout rate dropped for the fourth year in a row and his homer rate rose. He endured a particularly rough stretch in July when he gave up 25 runs in 18 1/3 innings over four starts, but even if you buy the lost mechanics argument and don't count that against his season totals, his ERA is still an un-ace-like 4.09. The scary thing is Lester isn't doing anything particularly different. His pitch mix and velocity are about the same; the only thing different is the results. He has one more season and what was previously thought to be a no-brainer team option left on his contract, but another season like 2012 could be Lester's last in Boston. Maybe the return of former pitching coach John Farrell as manager will help.

Daisuke Matsuzaka

Born: **9/13/1980** Age: **32**
Bats: **R** Throws: **R** Height: **6' 1"** Weight: **185**
Breakout: **17%** Improve: **55%** Collapse: **27%**
Attrition: **8%** MLB: **70%**

Comparables:
Bob Gibson,Chris Young,Matt Clement

YEAR	TEAM	LVL	AGE	W	L	SV	G	GS	IP	H	HR	BB	SO	BB9	SO9	GB%	BABIP	WHIP	ERA	FIP	FRA	WARP
2010	BOS	MLB	29	9	6	0	25	25	153^{2}	137	13	74	133	4.3	7.8	35%	.284	1.37	4.69	4.02	5.05	0.8
2011	BOS	MLB	30	3	3	0	8	7	37^{1}	32	4	23	26	5.5	6.3	32%	.248	1.47	5.30	4.99	5.91	-0.1
2012	SLM	A+	31	0	1	0	1	1	4	6	2	0	3	0.0	6.8	40%	.308	1.50	6.75	8.39	17.47	0.0
2012	PME	AA	31	0	0	0	1	1	4^{2}	3	0	2	7	3.9	13.5	38%	.375	1.07	1.93	1.49	-0.38	0.0
2012	PAW	AAA	31	1	3	0	11	11	51	42	6	17	41	3.0	7.2	38%	.247	1.16	3.18	4.37	5.54	0.2
2012	BOS	MLB	31	1	7	0	11	11	45^{2}	58	11	20	41	3.9	8.1	41%	.336	1.71	8.28	5.89	6.79	-0.5
2013	*BOS*	*MLB*	*32*	*3*	*4*	*0*	*10*	*10*	*55^{1}*	*53*	*6*	*26*	*48*	*4.3*	*7.8*	*38%*	*.294*	*1.43*	*4.49*	*4.28*	*4.88*	*0.5*

The bloom is fully off the rose. Matsuzaka returned from Tommy John surgery seemingly a worse pitcher than he had been before going under the knife in mid-2011. Even when he's on, Dice-K is infuriating, seemingly refusing to throw strikes until forced to lob a cookie. With six years worth of data, we say it's less a game plan and more an inability to pitch. Fortunately, his six-year, $52 million contract (plus $52.1 million posting fee) is mercifully over, and Matsuzaka will head into the great wide open that is free agency. Some say a cushy spot in a pitcher-friendly National League park could do Matsuzaka good, but it's been four seasons since he posted an ERA below 4.50 and five since he came anywhere near 200 innings, so color us skeptical.

Andrew Miller

Born: **5/21/1985** Age: **28**
Bats: **L** Throws: **L** Height: **6' 8"** Weight: **210**
Breakout: **20%** Improve: **49%** Collapse: **32%**
Attrition: **28%** MLB: **86%**

Comparables:
Dennis Rasmussen,Fernando Valenzuela,Ken Kravec

YEAR	TEAM	LVL	AGE	W	L	SV	G	GS	IP	H	HR	BB	SO	BB9	SO9	GB%	BABIP	WHIP	ERA	FIP	FRA	WARP
2010	JUP	A+	25	1	1	0	3	3	15^{2}	8	0	15	23	8.6	13.2	47%	.250	1.46	1.72	3.56	3.97	0.2
2010	JAX	AA	25	1	8	0	18	18	85^{1}	98	6	61	66	6.4	7.0	49%	.338	1.86	6.01	5.07	5.66	-0.5
2010	FLO	MLB	25	1	5	0	9	7	32^{2}	51	6	26	28	7.2	7.7	42%	.409	2.36	8.54	6.26	6.07	-0.4
2011	PAW	AAA	26	3	3	0	13	12	65^{2}	42	2	35	61	4.8	8.4	50%	.242	1.17	2.47	3.51	4.23	0.4
2011	BOS	MLB	26	6	3	0	17	12	65	77	8	41	50	5.7	6.9	49%	.332	1.82	5.54	5.15	5.46	0.2
2012	GRN	A	27	0	0	0	2	1	2	2	0	0	3	0.0	13.5	50%	.000	1.00	0.00	2.08	-0.94	0.0
2012	PAW	AAA	27	0	0	1	10	0	11	4	1	14	23	11.5	18.8	53%	.214	1.64	5.73	4.25	4.83	0.0
2012	BOS	MLB	27	3	2	0	53	0	40^{1}	28	3	20	51	4.5	11.4	43%	.269	1.19	3.35	3.12	3.45	0.6
2013	*BOS*	*MLB*	*28*	*2*	*3*	*0*	*18*	*7*	*43^{1}*	*46*	*5*	*25*	*36*	*5.3*	*7.4*	*50%*	*.319*	*1.65*	*5.44*	*4.77*	*5.91*	*-0.1*

A former sixth-overall pick, Miller found extended big-league success for the first time last season in an inning-or-less, LOOGY-type role. The New And Improved Miller came from two things: an increased velocity (his average fastball hit almost 96 mph) and ditching his curveball for an effective slider. With the new repertoire, Miller struck out over 30 percent of the hitters he faced while dropping his walk rate to a career low. Two years after essentially being cut by the Marlins, Miller looks to have more of a career in front of him than college teammate Bard, who at the time was putting up a 1.93 ERA in 74 2/3 innings for an 88-win Boston team. How strange is baseball?

Clayton Mortensen

Born: 4/10/1985 **Age:** 28
Bats: R **Throws:** R **Height:** 6' 5" **Weight:** 185
Breakout: 28% **Improve:** 61% **Collapse:** 20%
Attrition: 17% **MLB:** 85%

Comparables:
Frank Castillo,Vicente Padilla,Enrique Gonzalez

YEAR	TEAM	LVL	AGE	W	L	SV	G	GS	IP	H	HR	BB	SO	BB9	SO9	GB%	BABIP	WHIP	ERA	FIP	FRA	WARP
2010	OAK	MLB	25	0	0	0	1	1	6	6	1	2	7	3.0	10.5	35%	.312	1.33	4.50	3.88	5.13	0.0
2011	CSP	AAA	26	2	8	0	15	15	64	104	13	29	54	4.1	7.6	39%	.419	2.08	9.42	6.19	6.06	1.0
2011	COL	MLB	26	2	4	0	16	6	58^1	55	9	24	30	3.7	4.6	54%	.257	1.35	3.86	5.31	5.94	-0.4
2012	PME	AA	27	0	0	0	1	0	1	3	0	1	0	9.0	0.0	50%	.500	4.00	18.00	6.20	896.25	0.0
2012	PAW	AAA	27	5	3	2	24	0	37^2	21	3	15	36	3.6	8.6	56%	.194	0.96	1.91	3.79	4.87	0.1
2012	BOS	MLB	27	1	1	0	26	0	42	32	7	19	41	4.1	8.8	45%	.238	1.21	3.21	4.69	5.90	-0.2
2013	*BOS*	*MLB*	*28*	*2*	*3*	*0*	*14*	*6*	*49*	*54*	*7*	*19*	*32*	*3.6*	*5.9*	*52%*	*.300*	*1.49*	*5.27*	*4.91*	*5.73*	*-0.1*

Boston dumped Marco Scutaro's salary on the Rockies, and got a strikeout-per-inning reliever in return in Mortensen during his brief stint. That was surprising, as Mortensen is known more for his groundball skills and mediocre velocity. A lack of strikeouts was always the thing that held him back. Whether he can repeat the feat in another go-around in Boston is a legitimate question. He is out of options and the Sox bullpen is like a toy store the night before Christmas; he may not get the chance.

Henry Owens

Born: 7/21/1992 **Age:** 20
Bats: L **Throws:** L **Height:** 6' 7" **Weight:** 190
Breakout: 42% **Improve:** 66% **Collapse:** 20%
Attrition: 14% **MLB:** 92%

Comparables:
Mike McCormick,David Clyde,Mike McQueen

YEAR	TEAM	LVL	AGE	W	L	SV	G	GS	IP	H	HR	BB	SO	BB9	SO9	GB%	BABIP	WHIP	ERA	FIP	FRA	WARP
2012	GRN	A	19	12	5	0	23	22	101^2	100	10	47	130	4.2	11.5	38%	.350	1.45	4.87	3.86	3.43	1.6
2013	*BOS*	*MLB*	*20*	*2*	*3*	*0*	*7*	*7*	33^1	*34*	*4*	*18*	*32*	*4.9*	*8.6*	*39%*	*.317*	*1.57*	*5.20*	*4.46*	*5.66*	*0.0*

Owens fits snugly in the part of your prospect suitcase that says "projectable lefty." He's tall and strong and projects to get stronger, though if he gets much taller he may have to switch sports. He can hit the mid-90s with a fastball, can drop a mean curve on you, and has only some idea where it's all going—not surprising considering his age and size. His strikeout rate is a thing of beauty and the scouts like the way he throws free and easy and hides the ball at the same time. There's a lot to dream on here, but for now it's only dreaming.

Vicente Padilla

Born: 9/27/1977 **Age:** 35
Bats: R **Throws:** R **Height:** 6' 1" **Weight:** 230
Breakout: 19% **Improve:** 35% **Collapse:** 24%
Attrition: 9% **MLB:** 87%

Comparables:
Jerry Koosman,Mark Langston,Orlando Hernandez

YEAR	TEAM	LVL	AGE	W	L	SV	G	GS	IP	H	HR	BB	SO	BB9	SO9	GB%	BABIP	WHIP	ERA	FIP	FRA	WARP
2010	SBR	A+	32	0	0	0	3	3	10^2	6	0	1	10	0.8	8.4	70%	.222	0.65	0.84	2.14	2.58	0.3
2010	ABQ	AAA	32	0	1	0	1	1	5^2	8	2	0	5	0.0	7.9	29%	.316	1.40	6.32	6.39	6.68	0.0
2010	LAN	MLB	32	6	5	0	16	16	95	79	14	24	84	2.3	8.0	42%	.250	1.08	4.07	4.23	5.10	0.3
2011	RCU	A+	33	0	0	0	4	4	6^1	4	0	1	5	1.4	7.1	—	.235	0.79	1.42	3.32	3.61	0.0
2011	LAN	MLB	33	0	0	3	9	0	8^2	7	0	5	9	5.2	9.3	68%	.318	1.38	4.15	2.65	3.89	0.0
2012	BOS	MLB	34	4	1	1	56	0	50	59	7	15	51	2.7	9.2	45%	.366	1.48	4.50	3.91	4.32	0.4
2013	*BOS*	*MLB*	*35*	*2*	*2*	*1*	*19*	*4*	37^1	*39*	*5*	*13*	*29*	*3.1*	*6.9*	*46%*	*.305*	*1.39*	*4.68*	*4.43*	*5.09*	*0.2*

Valentine's reliance on Padilla in high-leverage situations might have made sense on isolated occasions, but over the whole season it bordered on ridiculous. Padilla lived in the strike zone, meaning that while his strikeout and walk rates were good, when he got hit it was often hard. He had problems with home runs and batters got to him for an 845 OPS on the season, including hitting .337/.406/.616 from July on. While Padilla avoided the injuries that had plagued him in previous seasons, that is no guarantee his health will stay that way. The Red Sox can do better now that Padilla is a free agent.

Anthony Ranaudo

Born: 9/9/1989 **Age:** 23
Bats: R **Throws:** R **Height:** 6' 8" **Weight:** 231
Breakout: 27% **Improve:** 56% **Collapse:** 21%
Attrition: 14% **MLB:** 90%

Comparables:
Art Mahaffey,Jaret Wright,Ross Detwiler

YEAR	TEAM	LVL	AGE	W	L	SV	G	GS	IP	H	HR	BB	SO	BB9	SO9	GB%	BABIP	WHIP	ERA	FIP	FRA	WARP
2011	GRN	A	21	4	1	0	10	10	46	35	4	16	50	3.1	9.8	—	.272	1.11	3.33	3.79	4.12	0.0
2011	SLM	A+	21	5	5	0	16	16	81	80	6	30	67	3.3	7.4	—	.314	1.36	4.33	3.98	4.33	0.0
2012	PME	AA	22	1	3	0	9	9	37^2	41	4	27	27	6.5	6.5	36%	.311	1.81	6.69	5.54	9.18	-0.2
2013	*BOS*	*MLB*	*23*	*1*	*3*	*0*	*7*	*7*	32^2	*37*	*5*	*18*	*21*	*4.9*	*5.9*	*41%*	*.310*	*1.69*	*5.89*	*5.56*	*6.40*	*-0.2*

What Ranaudo does should work. He was lights out in college, and in the Cape. He's big, strong, and his plus velocity gets swings and misses. But mechanical inconsistencies coupled with injuries have resulted in a pitcher who is less than the sum of his parts. To date he has moved through the system based on potential and age more than anything he's shown since Boston drafted him. Some have speculated his future lies in the back of the bullpen, but he'll need to show much improvement in Double-A to even meet that modest forecast.

Junichi Tazawa
Born: **6/6/1986** Age: **27**
Bats: **R** Throws: **R** Height: **6' 0"** Weight: **180**
Breakout: **21%** Improve: **52%** Collapse: **25%**
Attrition: **13%** MLB: **90%**
Comparables:
Billy O'Dell, Taylor Buchholz, Carlos Villanueva

YEAR	TEAM	LVL	AGE	W	L	SV	G	GS	IP	H	HR	BB	SO	BB9	SO9	GB%	BABIP	WHIP	ERA	FIP	FRA	WARP
2011	SLM	A+	25	0	1	0	6	6	19^1	20	4	6	13	2.8	6.1	—	.276	1.34	6.05	5.97	6.49	0.0
2011	PME	AA	25	3	2	0	8	2	23	20	3	7	27	2.7	10.6	—	.283	1.17	4.70	3.93	4.27	0.0
2011	PAW	AAA	25	1	1	0	8	0	14^1	14	1	3	19	1.9	11.9	35%	.364	1.19	2.51	2.12	3.79	0.1
2011	BOS	MLB	25	0	0	0	3	0	3	3	1	1	4	3.0	12.0	12%	.286	1.33	6.00	5.73	3.58	0.0
2012	PAW	AAA	26	3	2	4	25	0	42^1	34	2	17	56	3.6	11.9	49%	.308	1.20	2.55	2.33	3.04	0.9
2012	BOS	MLB	26	1	1	1	37	0	44	37	1	5	45	1.0	9.2	49%	.303	0.95	1.43	1.77	2.61	1.2
2013	*BOS*	*MLB*	*27*	*2*	*1*	*0*	*30*	*0*	*41*	*41*	*5*	*12*	*36*	*2.6*	*7.9*	*43%*	*.307*	*1.28*	*4.05*	*3.91*	*4.40*	*0.4*

By WARP, Tazawa was as valuable to the Red Sox in 2012 as Lester. Now fully recovered from 2010 Tommy John surgery, Tazawa began the year in Triple-A but was quickly called up for the first of three tours in Boston. His fastball velocity has risen since his recovery, averaging 94.5 mph, and he pairs it with a brutal split. Add the occasional curveball or slider to keep hitters off-balance, and you get a young pitcher who dominated major-league hitters last season. He should be a strong contributor in a seventh- or eighth-inning role next season, and if Bailey goes down and Hanrahan doesn't rebound, don't be surprised if the bullpen door opens in the ninth and Tazawa emerges.

Koji Uehara
Born: **4/3/1975** Age: **38**
Bats: **R** Throws: **R** Height: **6' 2"** Weight: **190**
Breakout: **24%** Improve: **40%** Collapse: **32%**
Attrition: **9%** MLB: **81%**
Comparables:
Hoyt Wilhelm, Rick Aguilera, John Smoltz

YEAR	TEAM	LVL	AGE	W	L	SV	G	GS	IP	H	HR	BB	SO	BB9	SO9	GB%	BABIP	WHIP	ERA	FIP	FRA	WARP
2010	BOW	AA	35	0	0	0	2	2	2	1	0	1	1	4.5	4.5	60%	.200	1.00	0.00	3.86	4.71	0.1
2010	NOR	AAA	35	0	0	0	2	0	2	2	0	0	1	0.0	4.5	29%	.286	1.00	0.00	2.29	3.07	0.0
2010	BAL	MLB	35	1	2	13	43	0	44	37	5	5	55	1.0	11.2	25%	.294	0.95	2.86	2.37	3.22	1.0
2011	BAL	MLB	36	1	1	0	43	0	47	25	6	8	62	1.5	11.9	31%	.194	0.70	1.72	2.59	3.29	0.8
2011	TEX	MLB	36	1	2	0	22	0	18	13	5	1	23	0.5	11.5	36%	.200	0.78	4.00	4.28	4.23	0.1
2012	ROU	AAA	37	0	0	0	3	0	3	3	0	0	4	0.0	12.0	29%	.429	1.00	0.00	1.00	-1.92	0.1
2012	TEX	MLB	37	0	0	1	37	0	36	20	4	3	43	0.8	10.8	33%	.200	0.64	1.75	2.35	3.77	0.6
2013	*BOS*	*MLB*	*38*	*2*	*1*	*0*	*20*	*3*	*37^1*	*33*	*4*	*8*	*39*	*1.9*	*9.4*	*34%*	*.293*	*1.11*	*3.15*	*3.15*	*3.42*	*0.9*

Uehara's stuff is as straightforward as it gets; he's a two-pitch reliever, mixing his upper-80s fastball and low-80s splitter about evenly. The Japanese import has been one of baseball's most effective setup men over the last three seasons, posting a 2.36 ERA with nearly 11 strikeouts per walk. Uehara's dominance comes from both his strike-throwing ability and devastating splitter. While most split-finger specialists struggle to throw it for a strike, Uehara keeps hitters off-balance by moving it in and out of the zone as he pleases. His lack of overpowering velocity renders him homer-prone when he misses over the plate. He surrendered nine round-trippers in 54 innings with Texas in 2011-12. The 38-year-old righty should remain a usable reliever as long as his splitter remains a wipeout offering.

Allen Webster
Born: **2/10/1990** Age: **23**
Bats: **R** Throws: **R** Height: **6' 4"** Weight: **185**
Breakout: **23%** Improve: **56%** Collapse: **27%**
Attrition: **11%** MLB: **95%**
Comparables:
Art Mahaffey, Ross Detwiler, Jaret Wright

YEAR	TEAM	LVL	AGE	W	L	SV	G	GS	IP	H	HR	BB	SO	BB9	SO9	GB%	BABIP	WHIP	ERA	FIP	FRA	WARP
2010	GRL	A	20	12	9	0	26	23	131^1	119	6	53	114	3.6	7.8	50%	.297	1.31	2.88	3.91	5.00	0.6
2011	RCU	A+	21	5	2	0	9	9	54	46	2	21	62	3.5	10.3	—	.317	1.24	2.33	3.53	3.83	0.0
2011	CHT	AA	21	6	3	0	18	17	91	101	7	36	73	3.6	7.2	—	.332	1.51	5.04	4.15	4.51	0.0
2012	CHT	AA	22	6	8	0	27	22	121^2	120	1	57	117	4.2	8.7	60%	.329	1.45	3.55	3.15	3.41	1.2
2012	PME	AA	22	0	1	0	2	2	9	13	1	4	12	4.0	12.0	64%	.444	1.89	8.00	3.98	3.69	0.0
2013	*BOS*	*MLB*	*23*	*1*	*3*	*0*	*6*	*6*	*32^2*	*37*	*4*	*17*	*23*	*4.6*	*6.3*	*41%*	*.314*	*1.64*	*5.76*	*4.94*	*6.26*	*-0.2*

That the Red Sox were able to convince the Dodgers to take on a quarter-billion dollars in future salary was amazing. That they did it while receiving Webster (and others!) in return was astounding. That they did all of that while Ned Colletti got a contract extension is . . . happily not the province of this comment. Webster's slider and changeup both grade out higher than his mid-90s sinking fastball, which gets both grounders and swings and misses. We mean that in a good way. He needs to refine his fastball command, though in fairness, commanding a pitch with that much natural sink isn't the kind of thing you take care of in an afternoon after mowing the lawn. The Red Sox are hoping to see him in Boston next season if not sooner.

LINEOUTS

HITTERS

PLAYER	TEAM	LVL	AGE	PA	R	2B	3B	HR	RBI	BB	SO	SB-CS	AVG/OBP/SLG	TAv	BABIP	BRR	FRAA	WARP
OF A. Hassan	PAW	AAA	24	380	39	13	0	7	46	55	70	1-1	.256/.377/.365	.263	.305	-3.6	LF(52): 3.8, RF(28): -0.3	0.3
OF J. Hazelbaker	PME	AA	24	488	77	21	6	19	64	35	114	33-11	.273/.338/.479	.224	.328	4.7	LF(14): 1.7, RF(9): -1.0	0.2
OF B. Jacobs	SLM	A+	21	487	62	30	0	13	61	39	128	17-9	.252/.322/.410	.189	.324	1.5	LF(35): -0.9, CF(6): 0.4	-1.0
OF J. Linares	PME	AA	27	238	34	17	1	8	33	22	30	0-1	.333/.403/.538	.310	.356	-2.1	CF(6): 0.7, RF(5): 0.4	0.5
	PAW	AAA	27	216	24	11	1	8	29	7	36	0-0	.297/.321/.480	.274	.321	-3.6	RF(35): -1.0, LF(2): 0.1	-0.1
SS D. Marrero	LOW	A-	21	284	45	14	3	2	24	34	48	24-6	.268/.358/.374	.274	.325	2.5	SS(25): 0.2	1.0
1B T. Shaw	SLM	A+	22	423	69	31	3	16	73	59	81	11-2	.305/.411/.545	.355	.354	1.9	1B(31): 1.5, 3B(5): 0.2	2.2
	PME	AA	22	133	13	13	0	3	12	21	34	1-1	.227/.353/.427	.188	.297	-0.1	1B(6): 0.3	-0.2
UT D. Sutton	GWN	AAA	29	164	19	10	2	0	15	20	24	2-3	.270/.374/.372	.282	.322	0.9	2B(9): -1.3, 3B(2): -0.0	0.0
	PIT	MLB	29	79	10	8	1	1	7	4	26	0-1	.243/.278/.419	.256	.354	0.2	LF(13): 0.0, RF(8): -0.2	-0.1
	TBA	MLB	29	51	2	4	0	0	6	2	16	0-0	.271/.314/.354	.246	.406	0.1	3B(11): 0.6, 2B(6): 0.1	0.1
SS J. Vinicio	GRN	A	18	278	37	9	3	3	32	13	56	24-11	.277/.320/.371	.245	.342	2.2	SS(28): -0.9	0.4

Alex Hassan can take a walk, but beyond that the hit tool and athleticism to play regularly simply aren't there. ⚾ **Jeremy Hazelbaker** will take a walk and has range in the outfield, but the holes in his swing will prevent him from a full-time gig in the bigs. ⚾ A toolsy and athletic former running back, **Brandon Jacobs** has yet to turn those assets into performance on the field. ⚾ After three seasons in the system, Cuban defector **Juan Carlos Linares** has shown that he has some power and defensive ability, but not much else. ⚾ Boston's first-round pick in 2012, **Deven Marrero** has the tools to stick at short, and a line-drive bat to move through the system quickly. ⚾ **Travis Shaw** used power and advanced plate discipline to force himself into the prospect conversation with a 957 OPS in Single-A, but the hype train slowed a bit after a promotion to Double-A exposed a lack of tools. ⚾ **Drew Sutton**'s bat makes him a nice bit of organizational infield depth, but he has yet to find an organization willing to give him a long-term look in the majors. ⚾ Three years into his pro career, **Jose Vinicio** still shows the tools and lack of polish at shortstop that you'd expect from an international free agent signed at the age of 16. Which, fortunately, he was.

PITCHERS

PLAYER	TEAM	LVL	AGE	W	L	SV	IP	H	HR	BB	SO	BB9	SO9	GB%	BABIP	WHIP	ERA	FIP	FRA	WARP
T. Buttrey	RSX	Rk	19	0	0	0	5	5	0	1	5	1.8	9.0	40%	.500	1.20	1.80	2.63	3.49	0
A. Carter	CHR	AAA	26	4	6	2	62^{2}	71	6	22	54	3.2	7.8	53%	.335	1.48	4.60	3.83	5.33	0.0
G. Godfrey	SAC	AAA	27	9	2	1	104	98	8	26	60	2.2	5.2	39%	.281	1.19	3.29	4.52	5.85	0.2
	OAK	MLB	27	0	4	0	21	26	4	10	10	4.3	4.3	28%	.310	1.71	6.43	6.43	7.09	-0.6
B. Johnson	LOW	A-	22	0	0	0	5^{2}	2	0	1	4	1.6	6.4	93%	.143	0.53	0	2.45	3.78	0
K. Kaminska	JAX	AA	23	6	3	1	49^{1}	70	9	9	42	1.6	7.7	47%	.370	1.60	5.11	4.48	4.50	0.2
C. Kukuk	RSX	Rk	19	2	0	0	10	3	0	3	16	2.7	14.4	47%	.158	0.60	0.90	1.73	2.64	0.2
P. Light	LOW	A-	21	0	2	0	30^{1}	27	1	5	30	1.5	8.9	53%	.325	1.05	2.37	2.38	2.85	0.6
B. Workman	SLM	A+	23	7	7	0	113^{2}	104	10	20	107	1.6	8.5	47%	.297	1.09	3.40	3.20	4.15	0.3
	PME	AA	23	3	1	0	25	23	2	5	23	1.8	8.3	38%	.296	1.12	3.96	3.00	3.08	0.0

Ty Buttrey, a big, projectable power pitcher, is like a lottery ticket: They pan out sometimes, and when they do it can be a beautiful thing. At 19 years old, he has lots of development left. ⚾ **Anthony Carter** has seen his control improve with experience and he still dials his fastball up to the upper 90s, which got him protected on the 40-man roster; his slider and change are still far from being plus pitches. ⚾ **Graham Godfrey** was competing for a rotation spot out of spring training last year, but he has since been passed on the depth chart by a half-dozen starters, and the missed opportunity could seal his fate as a Triple-A mainstay who shuttles to Boston as the need arises. ⚾ First-round pick **Brian Johnson** commands multiple pitches and should move quickly through the system, but none of them are anything spectacular, so neither is his ceiling. ⚾ Finesse artist **Kyle Kaminska** had a successful stint in the Arizona Fall League before the Pirates sent him to Boston as a PTBNL for ex-prospect Zach Stewart. ⊘ Despite some impressive velocity from the left side, at this point in his career **Cody Kukuk**'s most interesting attribute is that his last name could be infinite. ⊘ If you re-arrange the letters in "**Pat Light**" you can spell "work in progress." Also "Phat Guilt." ⊘ A plus fastball moved **Brandon Workman** up the ranks to Double-A, where he'll have to improve his secondary offerings to avoid ending up in the bullpen.

MANAGER: JOHN FARRELL

To place the blame for Boston's 69-win season solely on the shoulders of now former manager Bobby Valentine would be foolish. But so would ignoring his negative impact on the team, both in his dealings with players and the media. The Red Sox didn't ignore that impact, so Valentine's tenure was short. His replacement is the less divisive if still unproven former Blue Jays manager John Farrell. The Red Sox tried to get Farrell last season, but were rebuffed by Toronto (rumor has it the Jays demanded Clay Buchholz in return). Approached again after a 73-win season with a year remaining on Farrell's contract, Toronto acquiesced, sending the skipper to Boston for infielder Mike Aviles.

Farrell's Blue Jays were near the top of the American League in intentional walks and in getting caught stealing. The Yunel Escobar eyeblack scandal was handled less than deftly, but Farrell's positive working relationship with GM Ben Cherington dates back to his time as Red Sox pitching coach in 2007-10. That plus his previous successes working with Red Sox starters Jon Lester and Buchholz were too good to pass up.

In the end a manager's credo should be similar to a doctor's: First, do no harm. Farrell's time in Toronto may fall just short of that, but his public pronouncements since his hiring, prior experience in Boston, and familiarity with the keystones of the Red Sox starting rotation are all ticks in his favor. His tenure will be defined by the players the front office puts on the field, not the self-created drama off of it, and that is already a step in the right direction.

Chicago White Sox

2012: BEAUTY BEFORE AGE

Ace starter Jake Peavy, slugger Adam Dunn, and enigmatic outfielder Alex Rios bounced back from disastrous 2011 campaigns to help lead the White Sox back into contention, while the emergence of Chris Sale and formerly anonymous rookie Jose Quintana helped hold together an injury-riddled rotation. The Sox held the division lead most of the summer but the magic ran out when the Tigers ran them down in September.

Peavy, Dunn, and Rios, along with still-productive franchise icon Paul Konerko, earned $52.5 million in 2011 but collectively produced like replacement players, totaling -0.1 WARP between them. Last year, however, Peavy was healthy and pitched like an ace, Dunn launched 40 bombs, Rios rediscovered his power-speed mojo, and Konerko (when healthy) continued to defy Father Time. The result: a combined 11 WARP at a cost of $55.5 million—more than half the team's payroll. Sale toted his lefty heat from the bullpen to the rotation with great success, while free-talent find Quintana provided unexpected production. Good thing too, as shoulder woes shelved starter John Danks in May, and serial underachiever Gavin Floyd ate fewer innings than usual due to recurring elbow issues. The ever-aggressive Sox bought low on veterans Kevin Youkilis, Brett Myers, and Francisco Liriano to patch roster holes in-season, with varying success.

In the end, however, the White Sox couldn't hold off a Detroit squad that had bigger paychecks and more talent. Given Chicago's aging core and lack of impact players in the pipeline, expect that to become a refrain.

WHITE SOX PROSPECTUS

2012 W-L: 85-77, 2nd in AL Central

Pythag	.547	9th	DER	.712	11th
RS/G	4.62	7th	B-Age	30.1	27th
RA/G	4.17	13th	P-Age	27.4	7th
TAv	.266	8th	Salary	$110.6	9th
BRR	1.0	15th	M$/MW	$2.31	12th
TAv-P	.257	11th	DL Days	498	30th
FIP	4.18	22nd	DL WARP	2.6	21st

Three-Year Park Factors	
Overall	102
HR/RH	117
HR/LH	115
AVG/RH	112
AVG/LH	112

U.S. Cellular Field (1991)
Att. % of Capacity: 59.8% (21st)
Dim. 330, 377, 400, 372, 335

Only the fans at Yankee Stadium and Miller Park saw more home runs than the denizens of The Cell.

2013: GROWING OLD, NOT UP

Assuming good health, a rotation featuring Peavy, Sale, Danks, and Floyd should be more than enough to keep the White Sox in contention. However, the heart of the lineup will almost certainly regress, and unless a few young veterans take unexpected steps forward, the Sox will find themselves looking up at the Tigers yet again.

The White Sox wasted little time in re-upping Peavy for two more years. They expect productive seasons from Danks and Floyd, and they're counting on Sale to solidify his place in the upper echelon of AL starters. If all those wishes come true, Chicago's rotation can square off with anyone's. However, Peavy has had one healthy season in the last four, and Danks and Floyd are coming off recent arm woes. Sale's delivery has long given scouts the vapors, and last year his workload increased by 120 innings. The smart money would be on at least one of them breaking down.

Even if they stay healthy—the Sox training staff has a tremendous reputation for keeping pitchers in the game—they'll need to pitch even better than they did last year to overcome what may be a less productive offense. Konerko is 36 and can't keep dodging the aging curve forever. Dunn is an old, bad-bodied 33, and struggled down the stretch. Rios is only 31 and more athletic, but the only thing consistent about him is his inconsistency. A.J. Pierzynski provided Silver Slugger production last season, but the Sox can't expect similar production from their catchers this year.

Unfortunately, you're as likely to find a lineup spot where the White Sox will improve as you are a good single malt at Applebee's. True, slugging left fielder Dayan Viciedo has youth and talent on his side, and may yet learn to stop making outs at an alarming rate. But center fielder Alejandro De Aza has reached his modest peak, as has shortstop Alexei Ramirez. Gordon Beckham continues to look like a lost tourist in the batter's box, and there's little money available to improve on the modest production Chicago received from Youkilis last year. Add it up, and odds are the Sox will struggle to score runs equal to last year's moderate pace.

Meanwhile, the Tigers are celebrating the return of Victor Martinez and the arrival of Torii Hunter. Their other highly paid players are young up-and-comers named Verlander, Cabrera, and Fielder. The White Sox *could* go all Buster Douglas on them, but on paper, this doesn't look like a fair fight.

STATE OF THE ORGANIZATION: TALENT SEARCH

Highly regarded Rick Hahn takes over at GM from recently promoted executive VP Kenny Williams, but the organization's commitment to competing every single season is unlikely to change. To win another championship, the White Sox need to develop a few cheap, home-grown stars, since a maddening inability to put fannies in seats limits revenue and the talent money can buy.

Hahn has long been on every prospective-GM shortlist, so the White Sox kicked Williams upstairs to keep his long-time assistant in the fold. Hahn had a hand in nearly all deals in the past, and Williams will retain oversight or input on all major decisions, so it's unlikely the South Siders will experience a lurching change in philosophy.

Part of that philosophy has been to never punt on a season. Williams has been pilloried for hollowing out the farm system, using it as a change purse to procure veterans to edge the club into contention. The current dearth of top-flight prospects reflects this, and the Sox (like all teams) would benefit from developing some home-grown talent to fill out their mid-market payroll. However, the club's unique position makes a complete tear-down and rebuild of the Houston variety hard to envision.

Last year, the White Sox were in contention into late September, yet saw their attendance dip below 2 million, 24th in the majors. Meanwhile, the Cubs suffered through a 100-loss season and saw a similar drop, but still drew their usual 900,000 more fans than the Sox—a fact that must infuriate the White Sox brain trust. Theo Epstein can afford to preach patience while the Cubs rebuild, safe in the knowledge that the Wrigley Field mystique guarantees them a reasonable revenue floor. Should the Sox attempt the same thing, they might draw smaller crowds than a Naperville zoning board meeting. Improving the farm system will definitely help the White Sox; figuring out a way to convince Chicagoans that watching a team win in Armour Square beats watching one lose in Wrigleyville would help even more.

HITTERS

Bryan Anderson **C**
Born: **12/16/1986** Age: **26**
Bats: **L** Throws: **R** Height: **6' 2"**
Weight: **200** Breakout: **4%**
Improve: **39%** Collapse: **4%**
Attrition: **15%** MLB: **87%**
Comparables:
Johnny Edwards,Brian Schneider,Bill Nahorodny

YEAR	TEAM	LVL	AGE	PA	R	2B	3B	HR	RBI	BB	SO	SB	CS	AVG_OBP_SLG	TAv	BABIP	BRR	FRAA	WARP
2010	MEM	AAA	23	302	39	12	0	12	42	27	54	0	0	.270/.343/.448	.259	.299	0.6	C(75): 0.1	1.4
2010	SLN	MLB	23	35	1	2	0	0	4	1	7	0	0	.281/.314/.344	.242	.346	0	C(8): -0.1	0.0
2011	MEM	AAA	24	378	39	19	0	8	37	36	76	1	1	.281/.357/.409	.272	.340	0	--	0.0
2012	MEM	AAA	25	392	35	12	1	6	35	36	89	0	0	.225/.302/.317	.320	.281	-3.1	C(24): 0.0	0.7
2012	SLN	MLB	25	14	2	1	0	0	0	1	6	1	0	.250/.357/.333	.201	.500	0.2	C(2): -0.0, 1B(1): 0.1	0.0
2013	*CHA*	*MLB*	*26*	*250*	*24*	*10*	*1*	*6*	*27*	*19*	*61*	*0*	*0*	*.229/.295/.360*	*.227*	*.282*	*-0.3*	*C -0, 1B -0*	*0.2*

Once considered the Cardinals' catcher-in-waiting, Anderson's game has gone sour on the shelf watching the Cardinals indulge their fetish for veteran catch-and-throw types to caddy for the indestructible Yadier Molina. Once the Cards finally used an in-house option they went with strong-armed Tony Cruz, leaving Anderson to cool his heels for another hot summer in Memphis. His recent numbers haven't been pretty for a catcher whose bat needs to overcome an unsavory defensive reputation, but Anderson's solid batting eye leads to enough walks to inspire hope he can meet the minimal offensive requirements of a backup backstop. The White Sox picked him up last fall as cheap Pierzynski insurance, so he might finally get his chance on the South Side.

Keon Barnum **1B**
Born: **1/16/1993** Age: **20**
Bats: **L** Throws: **L** Height: **6' 6"**
Weight: **225** Breakout: **--%**
Improve: **--%** Collapse: **--%**
Attrition: **--%** MLB: **--%**
Comparables:
--

YEAR	TEAM	LVL	AGE	PA	R	2B	3B	HR	RBI	BB	SO	SB	CS	AVG_OBP_SLG	TAv	BABIP	BRR	FRAA	WARP
2012	BRI	RK	19	49	6	1	0	3	8	5	13	0	0	.279/.347/.512	.289	.321	0	--	0.0

Big, left-handed power hitters with a lot of strikeouts are like congressmen. It's easy to criticize them in general, but everyone loves the one from their own town. Massive teen Barnum signed quickly and immediately showcased his power, blasting three home runs in his first four games. He struggled in August after returning from six weeks on the disabled list, but no long-term impact is expected from the shoulder injury. While his hit skill projects as below-average, his power skills are more than enough to overcome that weakness and an above-average bat at first base is expected when he's fully developed.

Gordon Beckham 2B

Born: **9/16/1986** Age: **26**
Bats: **R** Throws: **R** Height: **6' 1"**
Weight: **190** Breakout: **6%**
Improve: **49%** Collapse: **1%**
Attrition: **16%** MLB: **93%**

Comparables:
Luis Valbuena,Justin Turner,Warren Morris

YEAR	TEAM	LVL	AGE	PA	R	2B	3B	HR	RBI	BB	SO	SB	CS	AVG_OBP_SLG	TAv	BABIP	BRR	FRAA	WARP
2010	CHA	MLB	23	498	58	25	2	9	49	37	92	4	6	.252/.317/.378	.253	.297	-0.2	2B(126): -1.1	1.4
2011	CHA	MLB	24	557	60	23	0	10	44	35	111	5	3	.230/.296/.337	.242	.276	0.3	2B(149): 6.7	0.4
2012	CHA	MLB	25	582	62	24	0	16	60	40	89	5	4	.234/.296/.371	.248	.254	-0.9	2B(149): -0.5	0.4
2013	*CHA*	*MLB*	*26*	*542*	*61*	*27*	*1*	*14*	*60*	*40*	*96*	*5*	*4*	*.253/.319/.403*	*.253*	*.284*	*-1.1*	*2B -2*	*1.2*

Different hitting coach, same results for Beckham. The organization knew Beckham's mechanics were bent before he was drafted in 2008, but took him early in the first round anyway. The lure of great talent (and staggering college stats) made Beckham an obvious pick for the Pale Hose, with the expectation that whatever was wrong could be fixed. But whether due to physical limitations, personality quirks, a lack of seasoning in the minors, or the wrong hitting coaches, Beckham hasn't shown the ability to make adjustments. The book on how to exploit his weaknesses still reads as true today as it did in 2010, and more pitchers have read it. He has average range afield, though he flashes evidence that he could possibly become above average and he almost never makes a miscue. As a replacement-level ballplayer, only the lack of other legitimate options gives him job security heading into 2013.

Jordan Danks CF

Born: **8/7/1986** Age: **26**
Bats: **L** Throws: **R** Height: **6' 5"**
Weight: **210** Breakout: **3%**
Improve: **53%** Collapse: **5%**
Attrition: **9%** MLB: **93%**

Comparables:
Jeffrey Leonard,Brian Anderson,Dan Dobbek

YEAR	TEAM	LVL	AGE	PA	R	2B	3B	HR	RBI	BB	SO	SB	CS	AVG_OBP_SLG	TAv	BABIP	BRR	FRAA	WARP
2010	CHR	AAA	23	502	62	27	3	8	42	41	151	15	6	.245/.309/.373	.236	.342	3.7	CF(83): -8.3, LF(16): 1.2	-0.6
2011	CHR	AAA	24	535	65	24	6	14	65	57	155	18	4	.257/.344/.425	.245	.356	1.6	CF(76): 6.4, RF(1): -0.0	0.8
2012	CHR	AAA	25	264	37	17	1	8	30	44	66	6	3	.317/.428/.514	.326	.418	-0.1	CF(44): 2.7, RF(2): 0.1	2.0
2012	CHA	MLB	25	75	12	1	0	1	4	6	16	3	1	.224/.280/.284	.207	.269	-0.6	LF(21): 0.0, CF(14): -0.4	-0.4
2013	*CHA*	*MLB*	*26*	*250*	*27*	*11*	*1*	*5*	*26*	*23*	*70*	*7*	*2*	*.238/.312/.372*	*.237*	*.316*	*0.4*	*CF -1, LF 0*	*0.1*

For the first time since he blew up the Arizona Fall League following the 2009 season, Danks looked like he could end up as a starting position player last year. None have ever questioned his defense or drive, but until he made changes to his approach, his natural talent at the plate was obscured by his strikeouts. Showing renewed discipline and toning down the whiffs just enough led to some genuinely star-quality performances at Triple-A. With all three outfield positions on the major-league roster filled, he'll be forced to show he can do it again at Triple-A. If he keeps it up, the team will be forced to find time for him somehow.

Alejandro De Aza CF

Born: **4/11/1984** Age: **29**
Bats: **L** Throws: **L** Height: **6' 1"**
Weight: **190** Breakout: **0%**
Improve: **36%** Collapse: **2%**
Attrition: **9%** MLB: **96%**

Comparables:
Jackie Brandt,Ryan Spilborghs,Amos Otis

YEAR	TEAM	LVL	AGE	PA	R	2B	3B	HR	RBI	BB	SO	SB	CS	AVG_OBP_SLG	TAv	BABIP	BRR	FRAA	WARP
2010	CHR	AAA	26	358	53	21	4	5	49	29	60	16	3	.302/.366/.440	.278	.355	4.4	LF(37): 0.3, CF(25): -0.4	1.7
2010	CHA	MLB	26	32	7	3	0	0	2	1	4	2	1	.300/.323/.400	.249	.346	0.1	CF(9): -0.7, RF(5): 0.1	-0.1
2011	CHR	AAA	27	435	64	29	5	9	37	33	72	22	11	.322/.378/.494	.298	.373	1.7	LF(48): 0.2, CF(5): -0.4	1.7
2011	CHA	MLB	27	171	29	11	3	4	23	17	34	12	5	.329/.400/.520	.344	.404	1.6	RF(31): 0.7, CF(19): 1.4	2.1
2012	CHA	MLB	28	585	81	29	6	9	50	47	109	26	12	.281/.349/.410	.278	.339	2.9	CF(125): -0.5, LF(11): 0.0	2.3
2013	*CHA*	*MLB*	*29*	*503*	*70*	*26*	*5*	*10*	*48*	*43*	*96*	*23*	*10*	*.280/.349/.429*	*.270*	*.330*	*0.9*	*CF 2, LF -0*	*2.3*

Sometimes, a career minor-leaguer shocks the world by performing well when given a big-league chance. In De Aza's case, it was almost expected. He seemingly spent his early 20s dealing with ankle injuries, then—as a prospect whose expiration date had passed—had to do more to prove himself. The White Sox were a team with high-priced outfielders and always trying to contend, so De Aza kept doing his thing in the high minors. A flurry to finish the 2011 season helped convince the Sox they didn't need to spend money on an outfielder, and his 2012 stats looked remarkably like his major-league equivalencies from the previous three seasons at Triple-A. He also filled a lineup void, getting on base enough to be a good leadoff hitter for a team that had nothing resembling such. Everything about his performance the past four seasons suggests a carbon-copy 2013 season is as likely as not.

Adam Dunn 1B

Born: **11/9/1979** Age: **33**
Bats: **L** Throws: **R** Height: **6' 7"**
Weight: **285** Breakout: **2%**
Improve: **28%** Collapse: **5%**
Attrition: **7%** MLB: **85%**

Comparables:
Jack Clark,Carlos Pena,Jack Cust

YEAR	TEAM	LVL	AGE	PA	R	2B	3B	HR	RBI	BB	SO	SB	CS	AVG_OBP_SLG	TAv	BABIP	BRR	FRAA	WARP
2010	WAS	MLB	30	648	85	36	2	38	103	77	199	0	1	.260/.356/.536	.307	.329	-5.4	1B(153): -6.1	2.3
2011	CHA	MLB	31	496	36	16	0	11	42	75	177	0	1	.159/.292/.277	.218	.240	-6.5	1B(35): -2.3, RF(2): -0.1	-3.1
2012	CHA	MLB	32	649	87	19	0	41	96	105	222	2	1	.204/.333/.468	.288	.246	-2.4	1B(52): -0.8, LF(5): 0.1	1.6
2013	*CHA*	*MLB*	*33*	*579*	*79*	*21*	*1*	*30*	*88*	*90*	*182*	*1*	*1*	*.222/.348/.457*	*.279*	*.282*	*-1.2*	*1B -2, LF -0*	*1.9*

Five seasons since 1950 exist in which a batter hit 40 or more home runs and tallied fewer WARP than Dunn did in 2012; each required substantial negative FRAA contributions and none had a lower

VORP total. Given Dunn's fielding limitations, this could be the worst 40-homer season ever, or would be had he been forced to don a glove every game, rather than in just about a third of them. That he drew 105 walks and still accomplished this feat adds to its uniqueness. The news gets worse for those concerned that he's due $30 million over the next two seasons: He hit just .190/.314/.424 from May 15 onward. The silver lining is that his power and plate discipline are still intact. Also on the "plus" side, he missed tying Mark Reynolds's record for most strikeouts in a season by one, though we feel compelled to put scare quotes around "plus."

Tyler Flowers **C**

Born: **1/24/1986** Age: **27**
Bats: **R** Throws: **R** Height: **6' 5"**
Weight: **245** Breakout: **1%**
Improve: **53%** Collapse: **4%**
Attrition: **12%** MLB: **94%**

Comparables:
Kelly Shoppach, Mike Napoli, Cliff Johnson

YEAR	TEAM	LVL	AGE	PA	R	2B	3B	HR	RBI	BB	SO	SB	CS	AVG_OBP_SLG	TAv	BABIP	BRR	FRAA	WARP
2010	CHR	AAA	24	412	43	22	2	16	53	55	121	2	1	.220/.335/.434	.264	.284	-2.3	C(93): -0.1	1.8
2010	CHA	MLB	24	15	2	0	0	0	0	4	5	0	0	.091/.333/.091	.197	.167	0.4	C(7): -0.0	0.0
2011	CHR	AAA	25	270	36	8	0	15	32	39	84	2	0	.261/.390/.500	.289	.350	-2.3	C(36): -1.3	0.7
2011	CHA	MLB	25	129	13	5	1	5	16	14	38	0	1	.209/.310/.409	.262	.261	0.2	C(31): -0.3, 1B(3): 0.2	0.5
2012	CHA	MLB	26	153	19	6	0	7	13	12	56	2	1	.213/.296/.412	.239	.301	-0.4	C(49): -0.8, 1B(2): -0.1	0.1
2013	*CHA*	*MLB*	*27*	*250*	*30*	*10*	*1*	*10*	*33*	*31*	*78*	*1*	*0*	*.222/.335/.414*	*.263*	*.296*	*-0.3*	*C -1, 1B 0*	*1.1*

In 2012 Flowers cemented his role as a catcher, a full season as understudy for Chicago's other rag-armed backstop helping him grow in the mental aspects needed to handle a major-league staff. That was the silver lining in last year's dark clouds, as Flowers didn't grow much as a hitter, despite the opportunity. He seemed to lose any clue he had at the plate, resulting in a strikeout rate exceeding even Dunn's worst. The hope has always been that he'd provide enough offense that the team wouldn't miss a beat when A.J. Pierzynski aged out. At his present level of performance, Flowers makes an above-average backup catcher, but no more.

Courtney Hawkins **CF**

Born: **11/12/1993** Age: **19**
Bats: **R** Throws: **R** Height: **6' 4"**
Weight: **220** Breakout: **0%**
Improve: **68%** Collapse: **32%**
Attrition: **32%** MLB: **100%**

Comparables:
Ed Kranepool, Wayne Causey, Robin Yount

YEAR	TEAM	LVL	AGE	PA	R	2B	3B	HR	RBI	BB	SO	SB	CS	AVG_OBP_SLG	TAv	BABIP	BRR	FRAA	WARP
2012	BRI	Rk	18	159	25	8	1	3	16	7	37	8	2	.272/.314/.401	.679	.339	0	CF(1): -0.1	0.1
2012	KAN	A	18	72	11	5	2	4	15	4	17	3	2	.308/.352/.631	.442	.356	-0.6	CF(9): 0.6	1.0
2013	*CHA*	*MLB*	*19*	*250*	*37*	*10*	*1*	*10*	*29*	*12*	*63*	*10*	*6*	*.242/.281/.430*	*.243*	*.283*	*0.3*	*CF -0, LF 0*	*0.3*

Everybody loves a good backflip, and Hawkins was eager to please, flipping his way into prospect lovers' hearts with his pre-draft athletic displays, then following that up with impressive on-the-field production after he signed. Hawkins already shows a mature body, with some concerns that his good weight could blossom into bad weight as he ages. He has good speed for his size, but is unlikely to remain in center field, putting more pressure on his bat to carry the . . . weight. With plus bat speed and strength, Hawkins projects to hit for above-average power, giving him the necessary ingredient for a thumping corner outfielder.

Orlando Hudson **2B**

Born: **12/12/1977** Age: **35**
Bats: **B** Throws: **R** Height: **6' 1"**
Weight: **190** Breakout: **1%**
Improve: **27%** Collapse: **10%**
Attrition: **16%** MLB: **81%**

Comparables:
Adam Kennedy, Tony Graffanino, Mark Ellis

YEAR	TEAM	LVL	AGE	PA	R	2B	3B	HR	RBI	BB	SO	SB	CS	AVG_OBP_SLG	TAv	BABIP	BRR	FRAA	WARP
2010	MIN	MLB	32	559	80	24	5	6	37	50	87	10	3	.268/.338/.372	.255	.312	2.4	2B(123): 6.4	1.8
2011	SDN	MLB	33	454	54	15	3	7	43	49	84	19	3	.246/.329/.352	.256	.293	2.7	2B(114): 1.2	0.7
2012	CHA	MLB	34	152	10	3	3	2	17	12	24	3	1	.197/.262/.307	.206	.225	0.4	3B(29): 1.5, 2B(11): 0.3	-0.3
2012	SDN	MLB	34	131	11	0	5	1	11	8	27	3	2	.211/.260/.317	.223	.263	1.7	2B(33): -0.6	-0.2
2013	*CHA*	*MLB*	*35*	*302*	*37*	*13*	*3*	*6*	*28*	*28*	*52*	*7*	*2*	*.261/.332/.389*	*.251*	*.300*	*0.7*	*2B -2, 3B -0*	*0.7*

Recent Hall-of-Famers Roberto Alomar and Ryne Sandberg combined for a barely positive WARP after their age 33 seasons. So, it would be little surprise if a merely average career hitter (.260 TAv) like "O-Dog" didn't have anything left at age 34. Playing second base can do that to a guy's knees. Hudson shook off a handful of wobbly games afield at the hot corner last year, slightly upgrading his value by adding another position to his résumé. But he's unlikely to finish 2013 with a job unless he bucks the trend of aging keystoners and slows his offensive decline.

Dan Johnson **1B**

Born: **8/10/1979** Age: **33**
Bats: **L** Throws: **R** Height: **6' 3"**
Weight: **210** Breakout: **0%**
Improve: **24%** Collapse: **2%**
Attrition: **8%** MLB: **94%**

Comparables:
Lance Berkman, Paul Konerko, Todd Helton

YEAR	TEAM	LVL	AGE	PA	R	2B	3B	HR	RBI	BB	SO	SB	CS	AVG_OBP_SLG	TAv	BABIP	BRR	FRAA	WARP
2010	DUR	AAA	30	426	66	19	0	30	95	75	71	0	0	.303/.436/.624	.337	.305	-3.5	3B(36): 3.5, LF(22): -1.2	3.9
2010	TBA	MLB	30	140	15	3	0	7	23	25	27	1	0	.198/.343/.414	.277	.188	0.1	1B(13): -0.7, 3B(6): -0.1	0.3
2011	DUR	AAA	31	395	52	23	0	13	52	58	65	0	1	.273/.382/.459	.296	.304	0	--	0.0
2011	TBA	MLB	31	91	7	1	0	2	4	6	18	0	0	.119/.187/.202	.141	.125	0.2	1B(21): 1.2, 3B(3): 0.0	-1.0
2012	CHR	AAA	32	589	77	21	1	28	85	94	94	1	0	.267/.388/.492	.280	.272	0.2	1B(72): -3.1, 3B(10): 0.4	0.7
2012	CHA	MLB	32	31	8	1	0	3	6	9	3	0	0	.364/.548/.818	.453	.312	0.4	1B(3): 0.0	0.7
2013	*CHA*	*MLB*	*33*	*250*	*35*	*8*	*0*	*13*	*39*	*37*	*47*	*0*	*0*	*.249/.366/.484*	*.291*	*.257*	*-0.4*	*1B -2, 3B -0*	*1.0*

For the second consecutive season, Johnson's contribution came down to a single game, and the last one of the year at that. His three-homer exclamation point in 2012 lacked the playoff implications of his 2011 finale (which kept the Rays alive), but served as a reminder of how much power he has. Far worse players than Johnson have received more chances, and the fact that he has pushed himself to become viable in an emergency at third base is evidence of his drive. The position also adds value to his relatively strong bat.

Jeff Keppinger **INF**

Born: **4/21/1980** Age: **33**
Bats: **R** Throws: **R** Height: **6' 1"**
Weight: **185** Breakout: **2%**
Improve: **25%** Collapse: **5%**
Attrition: **17%** MLB: **84%**

Comparables:
Billy Goodman,Harvey Kuenn,Edgardo Alfonzo

YEAR	TEAM	LVL	AGE	PA	R	2B	3B	HR	RBI	BB	SO	SB	CS	AVG_OBP_SLG	TAv	BABIP	BRR	FRAA	WARP
2010	HOU	MLB	30	575	62	34	1	6	59	51	36	4	1	.288/.351/.393	.264	.298	-1.7	2B(126): 10.9, SS(12): -1.5	2.7
2011	HOU	MLB	31	169	22	9	0	4	20	4	7	0	1	.307/.320/.436	.255	.299	0.3	2B(38): 1.2	0.5
2011	SFN	MLB	31	230	17	11	0	2	15	8	17	0	0	.255/.285/.333	.228	.266	-1.5	2B(55): -2.5	-0.9
2012	TBA	MLB	32	418	46	15	1	9	40	24	31	1	0	.325/.367/.439	.294	.332	-0.6	3B(50): -0.5, 2B(27): 0.2	2.2
2013	*CHA*	*MLB*	*33*	*393*	*45*	*18*	*1*	*7*	*38*	*26*	*31*	*1*	*1*	*.283/.333/.402*	*.252*	*.289*	*-0.6*	*2B -2, 3B -0*	*0.6*

For a second straight season, the Rays got huge value from a bargain corner infielder whose last name started with K. Last year, Keppinger did what he always does—mash lefties, hardly ever walk or strike out—only he did it better than ever, and just for fun he hit right-handers, too (.302/.352/.403). Keppinger plugged holes for the Rays at third, first base, and DH—too bad there was only one of him. Like Casey Kotchman before him, he may have had an anomalous year, but you only need one of those to put yourself out of the Rays' financial reach. Keppinger's career .288 batting average—while about as empty as possible—made him alluring enough for the hot-corner-challenged White Sox to ink him to a multi-year deal instead of meeting the hefty price tag on a full season of Kevin Youkilis.

Paul Konerko **1B**

Born: **3/5/1976** Age: **37**
Bats: **R** Throws: **R** Height: **6' 3"**
Weight: **220** Breakout: **0%**
Improve: **28%** Collapse: **8%**
Attrition: **11%** MLB: **80%**

Comparables:
George Brett,Stan Musial,Rafael Palmeiro

YEAR	TEAM	LVL	AGE	PA	R	2B	3B	HR	RBI	BB	SO	SB	CS	AVG_OBP_SLG	TAv	BABIP	BRR	FRAA	WARP
2010	CHA	MLB	34	631	89	30	1	39	111	72	110	0	1	.312/.393/.584	.337	.326	-3.3	1B(125): -5.7	5.2
2011	CHA	MLB	35	639	69	25	0	31	105	77	89	1	1	.300/.388/.517	.317	.304	-6	1B(111): -8.8	2.4
2012	CHA	MLB	36	598	66	22	0	26	75	56	83	0	0	.298/.371/.486	.300	.312	-3.4	1B(105): -5.9	1.6
2013	*CHA*	*MLB*	*37*	*570*	*75*	*23*	*1*	*26*	*85*	*60*	*94*	*1*	*0*	*.277/.361/.484*	*.290*	*.294*	*-1*	*1B -2*	*2.2*

On June 3, Konerko's hitting was excellent (.366/.445/.617 with a .363 TAv) and the White Sox had a two-and-a-half-game lead in the American League Central. He had a minor procedure on his left wrist, returned quickly, and finished the season hitting just .263/.332/.417 after his return, while the White Sox finished three games out. While it's too facile to blame the team's collapse on its most important player the past three seasons, Paulie did set a high bar with a .327 TAv in 2010-11, not to mention his hot start. For him to suddenly turn into James Loney at the plate was a rude shock the team couldn't overcome. Lest too much blame be tossed his way, Konerko's season totals were still very good, and wrist surgery immediately following the season suggests his struggles were physical. Good health should result in another solid season.

Jose Lopez **3B**

Born: **11/24/1983** Age: **29**
Bats: **R** Throws: **R** Height: **6' 1"**
Weight: **205** Breakout: **2%**
Improve: **50%** Collapse: **8%**
Attrition: **18%** MLB: **92%**

Comparables:
Brooks Robinson,Dan Meyer,Terry Tiffee

YEAR	TEAM	LVL	AGE	PA	R	2B	3B	HR	RBI	BB	SO	SB	CS	AVG_OBP_SLG	TAv	BABIP	BRR	FRAA	WARP
2010	SEA	MLB	26	622	49	29	0	10	58	23	66	3	2	.239/.270/.339	.221	.254	-3.5	3B(142): 19.9	1.8
2011	NWO	AAA	27	135	24	9	0	9	30	6	12	2	0	.400/.430/.688	.369	.387	0	--	0.0
2011	COL	MLB	27	129	10	4	0	2	8	3	15	2	0	.208/.233/.288	.193	.222	-0.6	3B(29): 0.3, 2B(11): -0.6	-1.1
2011	FLO	MLB	27	113	13	8	0	6	13	4	13	0	0	.226/.259/.472	.265	.205	1	3B(10): -0.7, 2B(9): -0.2	0.1
2012	CHR	AAA	28	55	7	5	0	1	10	6	8	0	0	.306/.382/.469	.254	.350	0.4	3B(6): 0.4, 2B(3): -0.8	0.0
2012	CHA	MLB	28	24	2	1	0	0	0	1	6	0	0	.217/.250/.261	.175	.294	-1.3	3B(11): 0.1, 1B(3): -0.0	-0.3
2012	CLE	MLB	28	224	16	13	0	4	28	8	35	0	1	.249/.272/.366	.239	.277	-1.9	3B(39): -0.7, 1B(10): 0.2	-0.2
2013	*CHA*	*MLB*	*29*	*250*	*27*	*14*	*0*	*8*	*32*	*11*	*29*	*1*	*1*	*.270/.305/.437*	*.255*	*.276*	*-0.5*	*3B 1, 2B -0*	*0.5*

Lopez is a baffling case. He hit .330/.372/.544 in 711 career Triple-A plate appearances, knocked 25 home runs in the 2009 major-league season, and twice posted an above-average TAv. But various teams have given him almost two full seasons of playing time since 2009, during which he has been an utter failure at the plate. He was once considered a good defensive second baseman, but is now limited to the corners except in an emergency. At this juncture, it will take some good breaks for him to earn any more chances to revive his big-league career.

Jared Mitchell **CF**
Born: **10/13/1988** Age: **24**
Bats: **L** Throws: **L** Height: **6' 1"**
Weight: **205** Breakout: **5%**
Improve: **51%** Collapse: **6%**
Attrition: **11%** MLB: **89%**

Comparables:
Joe Benson, Rick Monday, Jimmy Wynn

YEAR	TEAM	LVL	AGE	PA	R	2B	3B	HR	RBI	BB	SO	SB	CS	AVG_OBP_SLG	TAv	BABIP	BRR	FRAA	WARP
2011	WNS	A+	22	541	74	31	8	9	58	52	183	14	6	.222/.304/.377	.238	.336	0	--	0.0
2012	BIR	AA	23	408	51	13	12	10	54	62	126	20	5	.240/.368/.440	.304	.350	0.1	CF(60): -0.5, LF(6): -1.0	1.8
2012	CHR	AAA	23	141	18	11	1	1	13	16	53	1	1	.231/.329/.364	.252	.397	1.6	LF(18): -0.9, CF(15): -2.6	-0.3
2013	*CHA*	*MLB*	*24*	*250*	*31*	*8*	*2*	*7*	*24*	*26*	*87*	*6*	*2*	*.209/.301/.361*	*.232*	*.307*	*0.7*	*CF -1, LF -0*	*0.0*

At this point, any good news about Mitchell will be welcome, so here's some: Some of the raw tools that made him a first-round pick in 2009 showed up in Double-A last year, and his walk rate was fantastic. Mitchell has speed, a center fielder's range, power enough for moderate home-run numbers, and plenty of extra-base hits. However, he won't hit enough to be a starter if he doesn't figure out how to make better contact. Given his other tools, making enough contact to hit .250 would make him an asset. Of course, in the context of his recent past, even playing his way into a reserve role would be great news.

Brent Morel **3B**
Born: **4/21/1987** Age: **26**
Bats: **R** Throws: **R** Height: **6' 3"**
Weight: **220** Breakout: **3%**
Improve: **39%** Collapse: **9%**
Attrition: **18%** MLB: **90%**

Comparables:
Brooks Robinson, Mike Dela Hoz, Joe Crede

YEAR	TEAM	LVL	AGE	PA	R	2B	3B	HR	RBI	BB	SO	SB	CS	AVG_OBP_SLG	TAv	BABIP	BRR	FRAA	WARP
2010	BIR	AA	23	203	25	13	1	2	30	14	36	5	5	.326/.378/.440	.305	.395	-0.7	3B(48): 0.5	1.6
2010	CHR	AAA	23	324	40	24	4	8	34	13	50	3	0	.320/.343/.503	.294	.356	0.9	3B(63): 1.6, SS(17): -0.4	2.8
2010	CHA	MLB	23	70	9	3	0	3	7	4	17	2	0	.231/.271/.415	.230	.261	0.8	3B(20): -0.7	0.0
2011	CHA	MLB	24	444	44	18	1	10	41	22	57	5	4	.245/.287/.366	.246	.262	-0.9	3B(125): -1.3	0.1
2012	CHR	AAA	25	132	12	4	0	1	10	8	28	0	0	.194/.242/.250	.189	.242	0.4	3B(21): 4.4	-0.4
2012	CHA	MLB	25	125	14	2	0	0	5	7	39	4	1	.177/.225/.195	.175	.270	0.1	3B(33): -0.2	-0.8
2013	*CHA*	*MLB*	*26*	*250*	*26*	*11*	*1*	*6*	*26*	*13*	*47*	*3*	*1*	*.255/.297/.387*	*.240*	*.293*	*-0.2*	*3B -1, SS -0*	*0.0*

Morel was theoretically recovered from his back injury (a lumbar strain) in early August, but his bat never got going. When healthy, he is a capable defender at the hot corner, and should supply enough power to support limited batting average and on-base capabilities. Now three seasons removed from raking at Birmingham and Charlotte in 2010, he will need to re-prove himself in the minors before anyone offers him a starting job again. Back problems can be persistent and tricky, so it's no sure thing he'll ever be 100 percent again, and anything less puts his chances to increase his service time in jeopardy.

Josh Phegley **C**
Born: **2/12/1988** Age: **25**
Bats: **R** Throws: **R** Height: **5' 11"**
Weight: **215** Breakout: **8%**
Improve: **37%** Collapse: **13%**
Attrition: **17%** MLB: **99%**

Comparables:
Don Slaught, Tony Pena, Joe Azcue

YEAR	TEAM	LVL	AGE	PA	R	2B	3B	HR	RBI	BB	SO	SB	CS	AVG_OBP_SLG	TAv	BABIP	BRR	FRAA	WARP
2010	WNS	A+	22	99	16	3	0	3	12	7	22	0	0	.292/.340/.427	.267	.354	0.8	C(20): 0.1	0.5
2010	BIR	AA	22	79	7	4	0	2	13	2	22	0	0	.292/.308/.431	.248	.373	0.5	C(10): 0.3	0.3
2011	BIR	AA	23	394	43	21	2	7	50	23	61	1	2	.242/.292/.368	.212	.271	-1.9	C(43): -0.3	-0.6
2011	CHR	AAA	23	90	9	4	0	2	6	8	18	0	0	.241/.326/.367	.232	.288	0.1	C(16): -0.1	0.0
2012	CHR	AAA	24	421	40	22	1	6	48	20	60	3	0	.266/.306/.373	.214	.299	0.1	C(73): 2.0	-0.1
2013	*CHA*	*MLB*	*25*	*250*	*23*	*11*	*1*	*6*	*27*	*11*	*49*	*0*	*0*	*.243/.283/.370*	*.224*	*.281*	*-0.4*	*C -0*	*0.1*

Phegley changed several aspects of his game last year. On defense, thanks to full health, he cut down passed balls, while continuing to throw out almost half of would-be base thieves. On offense, a more aggressive approach cut down on all of his three-true-outcome rates: strikeouts, walks, and homers. Catchers often develop late, and many players who've had long careers as starting catchers have been less advanced at age 24 than Phegley. Of course, he'll need to keep making changes to improve, and there are no guarantees.

Alexei Ramirez **SS**
Born: **9/22/1981** Age: **31**
Bats: **R** Throws: **R** Height: **6' 3"**
Weight: **175** Breakout: **0%**
Improve: **30%** Collapse: **6%**
Attrition: **8%** MLB: **96%**

Comparables:
Alvin Dark, Jack Wilson, Cristian Guzman

YEAR	TEAM	LVL	AGE	PA	R	2B	3B	HR	RBI	BB	SO	SB	CS	AVG_OBP_SLG	TAv	BABIP	BRR	FRAA	WARP
2010	CHA	MLB	28	626	83	29	2	18	70	27	82	13	8	.282/.313/.431	.265	.300	6.2	SS(156): 20.6	5.9
2011	CHA	MLB	29	684	81	31	2	15	70	51	84	7	5	.269/.328/.399	.254	.288	1.4	SS(155): 7.3	2.6
2012	CHA	MLB	30	621	59	24	4	9	73	16	77	20	7	.265/.287/.364	.234	.290	1.6	SS(158): 7.7	1.4
2013	*CHA*	*MLB*	*31*	*596*	*69*	*24*	*2*	*16*	*65*	*32*	*80*	*13*	*6*	*.272/.314/.409*	*.250*	*.289*	*-0.2*	*SS -1*	*2.0*

Fans have stopped worrying about his bat until temperatures reach the 80s. True to form, Ramirez had a sustained good stretch in the middle of the season last year, hitting .309/.329/.457 between May 27 and September 7. As an above-average shortstop who covers a lot of ground and has done a great job at reducing his errors over the years, the bar for his bat is pretty low, but last season, his cold streaks were positively Siberian, and he drew only 14 unintentional walks. He'll need to rebound to career norms to earn the approximately $9 million per year he'll make for the next three seasons.

Alex Rios RF

Born: **2/18/1981** Age: **32**
Bats: **R** Throws: **R** Height: **6' 6"**
Weight: **210** Breakout: **2%**
Improve: **38%** Collapse: **6%**
Attrition: **13%** MLB: **79%**

Comparables:
Brian Jordan,Carl Furillo,Juan Encarnacion

YEAR	TEAM	LVL	AGE	PA	R	2B	3B	HR	RBI	BB	SO	SB	CS	AVG_OBP_SLG	TAv	BABIP	BRR	FRAA	WARP
2010	CHA	MLB	29	617	89	29	3	21	88	38	93	34	14	.284/.334/.457	.270	.306	0	CF(143): 3.8, LF(1): 0.1	3.2
2011	CHA	MLB	30	570	64	22	2	13	44	27	68	11	6	.227/.265/.348	.217	.237	2.1	CF(143): -1.2	-1.2
2012	CHA	MLB	31	640	93	37	8	25	91	26	92	23	6	.304/.334/.516	.300	.323	6.1	RF(156): 9.4	4.6
2013	*CHA*	*MLB*	*32*	*587*	*71*	*29*	*4*	*18*	*70*	*33*	*93*	*22*	*7*	*.268/.313/.433*	*.257*	*.294*	*1.5*	*RF 2, CF 1*	*1.9*

In September, Rios said, "I really don't want to talk about last year," meaning 2011. Instead, he let his bat do the talking, putting up the third-best WARP among right fielders and instantly made the millions he's due appear to be a reasonable salary. Though he set a career high for home runs and is unlikely to contribute as much WARP again, his rebound was accompanied by solid peripherals and makes his terrible 2011 look like a fluke.

Carlos Sanchez MI

Born: **6/29/1992** Age: **21**
Bats: **B** Throws: **R** Height: **6' 0"**
Weight: **175** Breakout: **2%**
Improve: **63%** Collapse: **6%**
Attrition: **8%** MLB: **97%**

Comparables:
Robin Yount,Jose Lopez,Edgar Renteria

YEAR	TEAM	LVL	AGE	PA	R	2B	3B	HR	RBI	BB	SO	SB	CS	AVG_OBP_SLG	TAv	BABIP	BRR	FRAA	WARP
2011	KAN	A	19	294	44	10	1	1	27	15	49	7	8	.288/.341/.345	.256	.349	1.2	2B(45): -2.1, SS(10): -2.7	0.2
2012	WNS	A+	20	416	58	14	6	1	42	31	64	19	10	.315/.374/.395	.258	.373	-0.7	2B(18): 2.5, SS(12): 1.0	0.3
2012	BIR	AA	20	133	17	9	1	0	13	10	22	7	5	.370/.424/.462	.319	.449	-1.1	2B(9): -1.0, SS(7): 0.7	0.4
2013	*CHA*	*MLB*	*21*	*250*	*27*	*9*	*2*	*3*	*19*	*11*	*53*	*5*	*3*	*.257/.298/.346*	*.226*	*.313*	*-0.2*	*2B -1, SS 0*	*0.0*

Sanchez burst onto the prospect scene last year and has a chance to vault over many of the guys rated above him this year. His slick glove at second base and on-base skills will give him much value despite limited power potential and a penchant for running into far too many outs for someone with his speed. He has been tried on the left side of the infield, which is tempting based on his strong arm, but it's not out of the question that he supplants Beckham at the keystone late this season. More likely, a spot will be made for him somewhere early in the 2014 campaign.

Blake Tekotte CF

Born: **5/24/1987** Age: **26**
Bats: **L** Throws: **R** Height: **6' 0"**
Weight: **175** Breakout: **4%**
Improve: **60%** Collapse: **6%**
Attrition: **9%** MLB: **95%**

Comparables:
Irv Noren,Curtis Granderson,Tony Gonzalez

YEAR	TEAM	LVL	AGE	PA	R	2B	3B	HR	RBI	BB	SO	SB	CS	AVG_OBP_SLG	TAv	BABIP	BRR	FRAA	WARP
2010	LEL	A+	23	241	41	17	1	8	27	36	46	22	8	.310/.419/.522	.342	.369	-0.5	CF(58): -9.4	1.8
2010	SAN	AA	23	301	44	8	7	10	37	26	63	6	9	.250/.323/.444	.283	.289	1.4	CF(61): 0.7, LF(2): -0.2	2.1
2011	SAN	AA	24	498	77	27	2	19	67	67	108	36	12	.285/.393/.498	.334	.343	-1.5	CF(56): -3.0	2.3
2011	SDN	MLB	24	40	1	1	1	0	1	4	21	2	1	.176/.263/.265	.204	.462	-0.1	CF(7): -0.7, LF(3): -0.0	-0.2
2012	TUC	AAA	25	347	38	20	2	9	26	18	92	9	8	.243/.284/.402	.239	.312	0.5	CF(48): 0.7, LF(14): -1.6	0.1
2012	SDN	MLB	25	15	0	0	0	0	0	0	4	1	0	.133/.133/.133	.083	.182	-0.3	LF(2): -0.0, RF(1): -0.1	-0.3
2013	*CHA*	*MLB*	*26*	*250*	*36*	*10*	*2*	*8*	*25*	*20*	*69*	*12*	*5*	*.232/.300/.397*	*.241*	*.293*	*0.5*	*CF -2, LF -0*	*0.0*

Tekotte, the Padres' third-round pick in 2008, has a broad base of skills that were supposed to have gotten him to the big leagues in short order. Except for a few cups of coffee, that hasn't happened. Last year he abandoned his patient approach and swung at everything, failing to hit most of it despite playing his home games at the bandbox that is Tucson's Kino Veterans Memorial Stadium. Our earlier comparisons of Tekotte to Jeremy Reed seemed unflattering, but they may have been wildly optimistic. A fresh start with the White Sox could help, but probably not.

Trayce Thompson CF

Born: **3/15/1991** Age: **22**
Bats: **R** Throws: **R** Height: **6' 4"**
Weight: **195** Breakout: **3%**
Improve: **64%** Collapse: **1%**
Attrition: **6%** MLB: **97%**

Comparables:
Matt Kemp,Adam Jones,Rick Monday

YEAR	TEAM	LVL	AGE	PA	R	2B	3B	HR	RBI	BB	SO	SB	CS	AVG_OBP_SLG	TAv	BABIP	BRR	FRAA	WARP
2010	KAN	A	19	235	28	13	3	8	31	21	69	6	4	.229/.305/.433	.266	.301	1	CF(57): 2.6	0.9
2011	KAN	A	20	597	95	36	2	24	87	60	172	8	4	.241/.329/.457	.277	.309	-1.4	CF(98): 2.6, RF(13): -0.8	1.9
2012	WNS	A+	21	510	77	28	5	22	90	45	144	18	3	.254/.325/.486	.278	.316	1.5	CF(36): 1.7, RF(4): -0.1	1.2
2012	BIR	AA	21	58	10	1	1	3	6	8	16	2	0	.280/.379/.520	.336	.355	-0.5	CF(13): -1.3, RF(1): -0.1	0.5
2013	*CHA*	*MLB*	*22*	*250*	*28*	*9*	*1*	*10*	*32*	*18*	*83*	*3*	*1*	*.212/.272/.398*	*.230*	*.276*	*0.2*	*CF -3, RF -0*	*-0.3*

Promotion to Double-A in 2013 will be the big test for Thompson, who already had some small-sample-size success there in 2012. It can't be said that there are no weaknesses in Thompson's game: He is unlikely to stay in center field, hit for a good batting average, or even get on base as much as hoped for from a corner outfielder. His power seems all but certain to outweigh those potential weaknesses. If he passes the test this year against more advanced pitching, expect a nice, long career in the major leagues.

Steve Tolleson UT

Born: **11/1/1983** Age: **29**
Bats: **R** Throws: **R** Height: **6' 0"**
Weight: **190** Breakout: **5%**
Improve: **40%** Collapse: **6%**
Attrition: **19%** MLB: **96%**

Comparables:
Carlos Guillen,Adam Rosales,Eric Bruntlett

YEAR	TEAM	LVL	AGE	PA	R	2B	3B	HR	RBI	BB	SO	SB	CS	AVG_OBP_SLG	TAv	BABIP	BRR	FRAA	WARP
2010	SAC	AAA	26	339	52	17	3	9	43	37	50	8	2	.332/.409/.503	.324	.371	1.1	SS(54): -5.6, 3B(13): 0.7	3.0
2010	OAK	MLB	26	53	5	3	0	1	4	4	9	0	0	.286/.340/.408	.303	.333	0	SS(11): -0.8, 3B(6): -0.2	0.3
2011	SAC	AAA	27	209	29	6	0	5	19	31	37	8	2	.274/.388/.394	.284	.321	0	--	0.0
2011	TUC	AAA	27	348	48	21	2	4	36	29	56	16	3	.276/.340/.394	.240	.322	-1.8	3B(23): 0.5, SS(14): 0.5	-0.2
2012	NOR	AAA	28	193	15	8	0	1	21	23	32	3	2	.278/.358/.346	.255	.328	-2.7	SS(30): -0.1, 3B(4): -0.4	0.0
2012	BAL	MLB	28	76	4	3	0	2	6	4	17	1	0	.183/.227/.310	.190	.212	0.1	3B(12): 1.3, LF(7): 0.0	-0.4
2013	*CHA*	*MLB*	*29*	*250*	*32*	*11*	*1*	*6*	*23*	*22*	*50*	*8*	*2*	*.250/.319/.384*	*.245*	*.294*	*0.5*	*SS -2, 3B -0*	*0.3*

Tolleson has received scarcely more than a passing glance by a big-league manager in his time in baseball, instead spending most of the past five seasons at Triple-A trying to prove that he can be a useful bench cog. He has good patience and a sound enough approach at the plate, but his hit tool is questionable. He has played everywhere but catcher and first base in his career and was primarily a shortstop last year, so his best chance at a major-league career will be as a utilityman.

Dayan Viciedo LF

Born: **3/10/1989** Age: **24**
Bats: **R** Throws: **R** Height: **6' 0"**
Weight: **230** Breakout: **4%**
Improve: **48%** Collapse: **5%**
Attrition: **9%** MLB: **97%**

Comparables:
Willie Horton,Rick Reichardt,Adam Lind

YEAR	TEAM	LVL	AGE	PA	R	2B	3B	HR	RBI	BB	SO	SB	CS	AVG_OBP_SLG	TAv	BABIP	BRR	FRAA	WARP
2010	CHR	AAA	21	363	42	15	0	20	47	11	78	1	1	.274/.306/.493	.250	.298	-1	1B(59): 0.1, 3B(26): 1.0	0.2
2010	CHA	MLB	21	106	17	7	0	5	13	2	25	1	0	.308/.321/.519	.296	.365	-0.5	3B(23): -1.6, 1B(7): -0.1	0.3
2011	CHR	AAA	22	505	60	28	0	20	78	45	83	2	1	.296/.364/.491	.270	.324	2.7	RF(51): -4.4, 1B(9): 0.0	0.4
2011	CHA	MLB	22	113	11	3	0	1	6	9	23	1	0	.255/.327/.314	.239	.321	0.1	RF(21): -2.2, 1B(4): -0.1	-0.2
2012	CHA	MLB	23	543	64	18	1	25	78	28	120	0	2	.255/.300/.444	.266	.286	-1.4	LF(131): -1.6	0.6
2013	*CHA*	*MLB*	*24*	*460*	*53*	*19*	*1*	*19*	*65*	*24*	*99*	*1*	*1*	*.264/.310/.451*	*.264*	*.300*	*-0.8*	*LF 2, RF -0*	*1.2*

Any time a 23-year-old can hold his own for an entire major-league season, that's good. Bristling with raw power, Viciedo jacked 25 home runs, which may end up being a low-water mark for him over the next decade. But he paid a price in on-base percentage and strikeouts. All told, the excitement around him is still based primarily on projections; he wasn't much of a contributor last year, despite the home runs. Not particularly adept with the leather, he did make the transition to left field well enough that there's not likely to be talk of replacing him. He won't even be arbitration-eligible until 2015, so Sox fans can expect to follow his growth as a hitter through much of his prime.

Keenyn Walker CF

Born: **8/12/1990** Age: **22**
Bats: **B** Throws: **R** Height: **6' 4"**
Weight: **195** Breakout: **9%**
Improve: **59%** Collapse: **3%**
Attrition: **13%** MLB: **94%**

Comparables:
Grady Sizemore,Nelson Mathews,Gary Geiger

YEAR	TEAM	LVL	AGE	PA	R	2B	3B	HR	RBI	BB	SO	SB	CS	AVG_OBP_SLG	TAv	BABIP	BRR	FRAA	WARP
2011	GRF	Rk	20	72	16	7	1	0	9	7	17	11	5	.333/.431/.483	.349	.455	-1.4	CF(9): -2.4, RF(1): 0.2	0.2
2011	KAN	A	20	180	25	1	2	0	15	14	64	10	4	.228/.296/.259	.226	.374	1.5	RF(21): 0.0, CF(14): 1.1	0.0
2012	KAN	A	21	320	53	15	5	1	39	50	93	39	11	.282/.395/.387	.287	.425	9.6	CF(67): 1.6	2.1
2012	WNS	A+	21	168	31	7	1	3	16	24	50	17	4	.238/.345/.364	.251	.341	0.3	CF(11): 1.1, LF(2): -0.1	0.2
2013	*CHA*	*MLB*	*22*	*250*	*31*	*7*	*1*	*3*	*16*	*24*	*86*	*16*	*5*	*.202/.281/.290*	*.208*	*.307*	*1.4*	*CF -1, RF 0*	*-0.6*

Walker was playing for Central Arizona College in 2011. Though he signed early and got his career going that year, considering how little time he's had in full-season baseball, his improvement over the course of the 2012 season was enough to generate serious excitement. For example, his on-base percentage for June and July in Low-A (his last two months before being promoted) was over .450. He stole a base every other game on the season and improved his ability to use his speed on defense. The low contact rate and lack of in-game power can't be ignored, as they will cap his upside. But he's making adjustments so quickly at the plate that the organization is optimistic that he'll improve in both areas, possibly developing average power.

Dewayne Wise OF

Born: **2/24/1978** Age: **35**
Bats: **L** Throws: **L** Height: **6' 0"**
Weight: **195** Breakout: **0%**
Improve: **26%** Collapse: **13%**
Attrition: **19%** MLB: **81%**

Comparables:
Gary Ward,Bobby Thomson,Devon White

YEAR	TEAM	LVL	AGE	PA	R	2B	3B	HR	RBI	BB	SO	SB	CS	AVG_OBP_SLG	TAv	BABIP	BRR	FRAA	WARP
2010	LEH	AAA	32	146	17	11	5	4	13	8	27	2	2	.270/.315/.511	.273	.311	-1	CF(17): 0.3, RF(8): 0.8	0.8
2010	TOR	MLB	32	118	20	3	2	3	14	4	29	4	0	.250/.282/.393	.225	.312	1.3	CF(18): 0.9, RF(17): -0.4	0.4
2011	LVG	AAA	33	144	28	10	3	4	19	6	21	8	3	.338/.382/.549	.275	.376	0.2	CF(11): 1.5, RF(3): 0.7	0.6
2011	FLO	MLB	33	72	6	2	0	0	5	3	21	4	2	.239/.278/.269	.216	.340	-0.2	CF(25): 1.7, LF(10): 0.0	0.0
2011	TOR	MLB	33	32	4	0	1	2	2	0	15	2	0	.125/.125/.375	.181	.133	0.3	CF(12): 0.5, LF(3): -0.1	-0.1
2012	SWB	AAA	34	85	17	7	0	4	10	9	16	2	0	.329/.400/.579	.322	.375	-0.3	CF(11): 0.9, LF(5): 0.2	0.8
2012	CHA	MLB	34	176	20	7	1	5	22	9	40	12	4	.258/.295/.405	.264	.306	0.4	CF(34): 0.9, LF(10): 0.0	0.4
2012	NYA	MLB	34	63	11	3	1	3	8	2	12	7	0	.262/.286/.492	.269	.283	1.4	LF(43): -0.5, RF(7): 0.0	0.4
2013	*CHA*	*MLB*	*35*	*250*	*34*	*10*	*3*	*7*	*24*	*12*	*57*	*12*	*4*	*.245/.289/.405*	*.237*	*.291*	*1.5*	*CF 0, LF -0*	*0.3*

Wise is a fan favorite in Chicago—robbing a home run to preserve Mark Buehrle's perfecto in 2009 will do that. He hustles, flashes some leather at all three outfield spots, and hits righties enough to keep his head above the zero WARP mark. In an odd turn of events, he hit an unexpectedly high number of home runs for the Yankees in a very small sample size, giving him a TAv higher than that of Raul Ibanez, who, well, did the same thing on a much bigger stage.

PITCHERS

Dylan Axelrod

Born: **7/30/1985** Age: **27**
Bats: **R** Throws: **R** Height: **6' 1"** Weight: **195**
Breakout: **28%** Improve: **52%** Collapse: **21%**
Attrition: **16%** MLB: **90%**

Comparables:
Carl Erskine, Vida Blue, Brandon McCarthy

YEAR	TEAM	LVL	AGE	W	L	SV	G	GS	IP	H	HR	BB	SO	BB9	SO9	GB%	BABIP	WHIP	ERA	FIP	FRA	WARP
2010	WNS	A+	24	8	3	0	23	13	99^{1}	95	2	12	84	1.1	7.6	46%	.296	1.08	1.99	2.40	3.53	2.3
2010	BIR	AA	24	0	1	0	2	2	10	8	0	3	8	2.7	7.2	47%	.267	1.10	2.70	2.69	3.80	0.2
2011	BIR	AA	25	3	2	0	11	9	59^{1}	52	1	14	57	2.1	8.6	39%	.286	1.11	3.34	2.46	3.41	0.4
2011	CHR	AAA	25	6	1	0	15	15	91^{1}	74	2	21	75	2.1	7.4	47%	.290	1.04	2.27	2.70	3.54	1.0
2011	CHA	MLB	25	1	0	0	4	3	18^{2}	18	1	9	19	4.3	9.2	43%	.327	1.45	2.89	3.33	3.61	0.3
2012	CHR	AAA	26	7	5	0	16	16	97	81	8	31	92	2.9	8.5	38%	.283	1.15	2.88	3.35	4.37	1.0
2012	CHA	MLB	26	2	2	0	14	7	51	56	8	21	40	3.7	7.1	45%	.304	1.51	5.47	4.99	5.30	0.2
2013	*CHA*	*MLB*	*27*	*4*	*4*	*0*	*14*	*11*	*69^{2}*	*73*	*9*	*25*	*53*	*3.2*	*6.8*	*43%*	*.302*	*1.40*	*4.67*	*4.43*	*5.08*	*0.2*

As a rare "crafty righty," Axelrod's margin for error is low and his potential to make a roster if he can't hold a rotation spot is limited, as teams prefer to fill bullpen slots with fire-breathers who can dominate a single inning instead of traditional "swing men." In the minors, Axelrod had superior control, leading to excellent results. To stay in the majors, he's going to need to resume those strike-throwing ways and hope for the best. Nibbling with his five pitches—as he did in 2012—just compounds his problems.

Simon Castro

Born: **4/9/1988** Age: **25**
Bats: **R** Throws: **R** Height: **6' 6"** Weight: **210**
Breakout: **30%** Improve: **57%** Collapse: **18%**
Attrition: **28%** MLB: **91%**

Comparables:
Taylor Buchholz, Ty Taubenheim, Brett Cecil

YEAR	TEAM	LVL	AGE	W	L	SV	G	GS	IP	H	HR	BB	SO	BB9	SO9	GB%	BABIP	WHIP	ERA	FIP	FRA	WARP
2010	SAN	AA	22	7	6	0	24	23	129^{2}	107	8	36	107	2.5	7.4	50%	.266	1.10	2.91	3.30	4.16	0.8
2010	POR	AAA	22	0	1	0	2	2	10^{1}	16	1	6	6	5.2	5.2	48%	.366	2.14	7.86	5.43	6.41	-0.1
2011	SAN	AA	23	5	6	0	16	16	89^{1}	95	9	16	73	1.6	7.4	38%	.329	1.24	4.33	3.79	3.67	1.4
2011	TUC	AAA	23	2	2	0	6	6	25^{2}	37	5	18	21	6.3	7.4	32%	.362	2.14	10.17	6.78	7.70	0.0
2012	BRI	Rk	24	0	0	0	1	1	2	3	0	0	0	0.0	0.0	62%	.375	1.50	4.50	3.70	6.11	0.0
2012	BIR	AA	24	6	4	0	15	15	90	89	4	21	72	2.1	7.2	49%	.304	1.22	3.70	2.92	3.62	0.8
2012	CHR	AAA	24	1	1	0	5	5	25	32	2	6	16	2.2	5.8	56%	.361	1.52	4.32	3.88	4.90	0.1
2013	*CHA*	*MLB*	*25*	*2*	*2*	*0*	*6*	*6*	*35*	*38*	*6*	*13*	*25*	*3.4*	*6.4*	*44%*	*.303*	*1.48*	*5.32*	*5.11*	*5.79*	*-0.1*

Castro remains a scouting-report prospect, as opposed to someone who has posted imposing numbers. He uses his legs and large frame to generate good fastball velocity, which he easily sustains deep into games. His slider makes him highly effective against right-handed batters, and his changeup might yet come around with more coaching and experience. Doubters point out that he is often injured (two more disabled-list stints in 2012 after shoulder problems in 2011). He also struggles against lefties: Even those at Double-A hit him hard. He simply doesn't generate the bat-missing stuff expected of highly regarded 24-year-old prospects in Double-A. Castro will get another season or two to refine his game as a starter before a team decides to see what he can do in the pen.

Jesse Crain

Born: **7/5/1981** Age: **31**
Bats: **R** Throws: **R** Height: **6' 2"** Weight: **215**
Breakout: **31%** Improve: **54%** Collapse: **19%**
Attrition: **10%** MLB: **89%**

Comparables:
Mike Jackson, Fernando Rodney, Josh Kinney

YEAR	TEAM	LVL	AGE	W	L	SV	G	GS	IP	H	HR	BB	SO	BB9	SO9	GB%	BABIP	WHIP	ERA	FIP	FRA	WARP
2010	MIN	MLB	28	1	1	1	71	0	68	53	5	27	62	3.6	8.2	41%	.262	1.18	3.04	3.41	4.09	0.7
2011	CHA	MLB	29	8	3	1	67	0	65^{1}	50	7	31	70	4.3	9.6	36%	.269	1.24	2.62	3.73	3.43	1.0
2012	CHR	AAA	30	0	0	0	2	2	2	0	0	0	3	0.0	13.5	%	.000	0.00	0.00	1.66	3.06	0.1
2012	CHA	MLB	30	2	3	0	51	0	48	29	5	23	60	4.3	11.2	39%	.229	1.08	2.44	3.40	2.83	0.8
2013	*CHA*	*MLB*	*31*	*2*	*1*	*1*	*44*	*0*	*42^{2}*	*38*	*5*	*19*	*43*	*4.1*	*9.2*	*41%*	*.290*	*1.33*	*3.91*	*4.04*	*4.24*	*0.5*

Crain has done enough already in two seasons to make his $13 million contract money well spent, and the team gets another year as a bonus. As the Orioles showed, winning with a great, deep bullpen and little else is possible. Pitchers acting like good closers in the seventh and eighth innings—as Crain has done, posting the best SO9 of any Sock with real innings—is the key to this strategy. His July shoulder strain resulted in some lost velocity upon his return, but he was still exceptionally effective, and the team is optimistic that he'll be back to 100 percent for this season. While there's no easy-to-follow template for relief-pitcher success, Crain's career has been an exemplar of what can be done, augmenting his excellent velocity by expanding and refining his repertoire over the years. It's never safe to predict continued success for a reliever, but with good health, Crain's as likely as any to realize it.

John Danks

Born: **4/15/1985** Age: **28**
Bats: **L** Throws: **L** Height: **6' 2"** Weight: **215**
Breakout: **13%** Improve: **44%** Collapse: **22%**
Attrition: **10%** MLB: **91%**

Comparables:
Josh Johnson,Mark Mulder,Joe Saunders

YEAR	TEAM	LVL	AGE	W	L	SV	G	GS	IP	H	HR	BB	SO	BB9	SO9	GB%	BABIP	WHIP	ERA	FIP	FRA	WARP
2010	CHA	MLB	25	15	11	0	32	32	213	189	18	70	162	3.0	6.8	46%	.274	1.22	3.72	3.67	4.20	3.2
2011	CHR	AAA	26	1	0	0	2	2	9	9	2	2	6	2.0	6.0	47%	.294	1.22	2.00	5.46	4.02	0.1
2011	CHA	MLB	26	8	12	0	27	27	170^{1}	182	19	46	135	2.4	7.1	46%	.313	1.34	4.33	3.86	4.21	2.3
2012	CHR	AAA	27	0	0	0	1	1	4	4	0	1	1	2.2	2.2	53%	.267	1.25	2.25	3.41	12.76	0.0
2012	CHA	MLB	27	3	4	0	9	9	53^{2}	57	7	23	30	3.9	5.0	46%	.282	1.49	5.70	4.97	5.22	0.1
2013	*CHA*	*MLB*	*28*	*4*	*4*	*0*	*11*	*11*	68^{2}	*67*	*8*	*22*	*55*	*2.9*	*7.2*	*44%*	*.294*	*1.30*	*4.02*	*4.07*	*4.37*	*0.7*

Opening Day starter Danks was among the best-paid players on Chicago's roster and—with Mark Buehrle's departure—could've been considered the team's most indispensable player entering 2012. Yet his season was quickly brushed aside. Struggles in spring training continued into the season before he finally admitted to shoulder pain, which eventually led to surgery to repair multiple maladies. Last season proved that the team can compete without him, but he's expected to be ready for the start of this season. Perhaps in 2013 both Danks and the White Sox can be significant.

Gavin Floyd

Born: **1/27/1983** Age: **30**
Bats: **R** Throws: **R** Height: **6' 7"** Weight: **240**
Breakout: **4%** Improve: **31%** Collapse: **30%**
Attrition: **12%** MLB: **94%**

Comparables:
Roy Oswalt,John Lackey,Adam Wainwright

YEAR	TEAM	LVL	AGE	W	L	SV	G	GS	IP	H	HR	BB	SO	BB9	SO9	GB%	BABIP	WHIP	ERA	FIP	FRA	WARP
2010	CHA	MLB	27	10	13	0	31	31	187^{1}	199	14	58	151	2.8	7.3	51%	.325	1.37	4.08	3.43	4.14	2.9
2011	CHA	MLB	28	12	13	0	31	30	193^{2}	180	22	45	151	2.1	7.0	46%	.278	1.16	4.37	3.85	4.47	1.8
2012	CHA	MLB	29	12	11	0	29	29	168	166	22	63	144	3.4	7.7	48%	.299	1.36	4.29	4.41	4.81	1.5
2013	*CHA*	*MLB*	*30*	*9*	*8*	*0*	*25*	*25*	152^{2}	*149*	*19*	*47*	*125*	*2.7*	*7.4*	*45%*	*.295*	*1.28*	*4.08*	*4.10*	*4.44*	*1.5*

Even with full disclosure from pitcher and pitching coach, discerning when an injury began seriously affecting a pitcher's game is tricky. Going by results, Floyd's first-ever stint on the disabled list possibly traced back to an elbow injury that began bothering him on July 1. From then until he returned from a second DL stint on September 12, he started nine games and struck out a mere 29 batters in 48 1/3 innings, with an average fastball velocity under 92 mph. Sandwiching this disastrous span, Floyd struck out 115 batters in 119 2/3 innings, held batters to a stellar .202/.272/.298 in his final five starts, and added almost a full tick to his velocity. He has a well-earned reputation for being inconsistent, so nobody's going to count on this flurry to vault him to greater feats, but with good health he should resume eating innings with tantalizing flashes of great stuff.

Deunte Heath

Born: **8/8/1985** Age: **27**
Bats: **R** Throws: **R** Height: **6' 5"** Weight: **215**
Breakout: **30%** Improve: **51%** Collapse: **19%**
Attrition: **9%** MLB: **87%**

Comparables:
Barry Latman,Grant Jackson,Kelvim Escobar

YEAR	TEAM	LVL	AGE	W	L	SV	G	GS	IP	H	HR	BB	SO	BB9	SO9	GB%	BABIP	WHIP	ERA	FIP	FRA	WARP
2010	BIR	AA	24	2	4	2	39	0	57^{2}	49	4	32	84	5.0	13.1	43%	.357	1.40	3.12	3.25	3.25	1.2
2011	CHR	AAA	25	4	7	1	30	16	102^{2}	98	12	62	117	5.4	10.3	41%	.314	1.56	4.73	4.41	5.00	0.4
2012	CHR	AAA	26	4	3	3	36	4	67	47	4	20	74	2.7	9.9	34%	.253	1.00	1.48	2.80	3.35	1.3
2012	CHA	MLB	26	0	0	0	3	0	2	1	1	1	1	4.5	4.5	20%	.000	1.00	4.50	10.05	11.60	-0.1
2013	*CHA*	*MLB*	*27*	*1*	*1*	*0*	*17*	*2*	33^{1}	*35*	*5*	*17*	*28*	*4.7*	*7.5*	*45%*	*.308*	*1.59*	*5.46*	*5.00*	*5.94*	*-0.2*

Heath has improved his control both on and off the field, and now profiles as a good middle reliever with no concerns about his organization cutting him for indiscretions (as the Braves did in 2010). He relies primarily on high heat and a good slider, though taking a little off his fastball has allowed him to cut his walk rate drastically. Major leaguers are likely to have more success than Triple-A batters did, especially in hitting for power against him, but he should already be good enough to keep a bullpen job. There's potential for further progress here—including an outside chance of returning to a starting role—if he can find a third pitch he can trust.

Erik Johnson

Born: **12/30/1989** Age: **23**
Bats: **R** Throws: **R** Height: **6' 4"** Weight: **240**
Breakout: **28%** Improve: **60%** Collapse: **17%**
Attrition: **13%** MLB: **91%**

Comparables:
Livan Hernandez,Justin Germano,Kyle Drabek

YEAR	TEAM	LVL	AGE	W	L	SV	G	GS	IP	H	HR	BB	SO	BB9	SO9	GB%	BABIP	WHIP	ERA	FIP	FRA	WARP
2011	GRF	Rk	21	0	0	0	2	0	2	4	0	1	2	4.5	9.0	14%	.571	2.50	4.50	5.28	4.89	0.0
2012	KAN	A	22	2	2	0	9	9	43	39	3	19	39	4.0	8.2	49%	.290	1.35	2.30	4.14	4.41	0.9
2012	WNS	A+	22	4	3	0	8	8	49^{1}	43	0	10	48	1.8	8.8	49%	.305	1.07	2.74	2.11	1.52	0.8
2013	*CHA*	*MLB*	*23*	*2*	*2*	*0*	*6*	*6*	33^{1}	*37*	*5*	*16*	*23*	*4.3*	*6.4*	*45%*	*.307*	*1.60*	*5.62*	*5.21*	*6.11*	*-0.2*

If Johnson's entire season had gone like his eight starts with the Winston-Salem Dash, his name would be in discussions of the best pitching prospects in the game today. His fastball reaches the mid-90s with a slider as a second good pitch. Before his promotion to High-A, his control wasn't where it needed to be, but he pounded the strike zone to great effect for the Dash. If Johnson retains the improved control, he'll soon be ready to join a major-league rotation, with development of his dodgy changeup determining whether he's a fifth starter or something more.

Nathan Jones
Born: **1/28/1986** Age: **27**
Bats: **R** Throws: **R** Height: **6' 6"** Weight: **185**
Breakout: **27%** Improve: **48%** Collapse: **17%**
Attrition: **14%** MLB: **88%**
Comparables:
Joe Price,J.C. Romero,Sean Henn

YEAR	TEAM	LVL	AGE	W	L	SV	G	GS	IP	H	HR	BB	SO	BB9	SO9	GB%	BABIP	WHIP	ERA	FIP	FRA	WARP
2010	WNS	A+	24	11	6	0	28	28	152^{1}	176	10	56	109	3.3	6.4	47%	.335	1.52	4.08	4.17	5.16	0.6
2011	BIR	AA	25	2	3	12	42	0	63^{1}	58	3	27	67	3.8	9.5	53%	.337	1.34	3.27	3.18	3.47	0.8
2012	CHA	MLB	26	8	0	0	65	0	71^{2}	67	4	32	65	4.0	8.2	48%	.317	1.38	2.39	3.34	4.11	0.8
2013	*CHA*	*MLB*	*27*	*2*	*2*	*0*	*22*	*6*	*50*	*55*	*7*	*27*	*39*	*4.8*	*7.1*	*44%*	*.316*	*1.62*	*5.48*	*5.08*	*5.95*	*-0.3*

Is that why they call it relief pitching? With the pressure of refining his game lifted upon moving to the bullpen, Jones thrived. His four-seam fastball is regularly three-digit, and while the slider isn't as good as hoped from a breaking pitch backing such high velocity, it comes in 10 miles per hour slower and breaks. Focusing on just two pitches should allow him to maintain his effectiveness over the years as his velocity declines with age, and if he can keep his walk rate low, he has the stuff to pitch high-leverage innings.

Charles Leesman
Born: **3/10/1987** Age: **26**
Bats: **L** Throws: **L** Height: **6' 5"** Weight: **210**
Breakout: **25%** Improve: **55%** Collapse: **18%**
Attrition: **21%** MLB: **79%**
Comparables:
Horacio Ramirez,Chase Wright,Jim Parque

YEAR	TEAM	LVL	AGE	W	L	SV	G	GS	IP	H	HR	BB	SO	BB9	SO9	GB%	BABIP	WHIP	ERA	FIP	FRA	WARP
2010	WNS	A+	23	9	4	0	17	17	84^{2}	98	6	44	39	4.7	4.1	55%	.314	1.68	5.10	5.35	6.71	-0.9
2010	BIR	AA	23	5	2	0	11	11	63^{2}	47	1	20	51	2.8	7.2	56%	.261	1.05	2.68	3.07	4.43	0.4
2011	BIR	AA	24	10	7	0	27	27	152	150	4	83	113	4.9	6.7	63%	.309	1.53	4.03	4.06	5.29	0.0
2012	CHR	AAA	25	12	10	0	26	26	135	129	8	52	103	3.5	6.9	54%	.303	1.34	2.47	3.67	4.97	0.6
2013	*CHA*	*MLB*	*26*	*2*	*3*	*0*	*7*	*7*	38^{1}	*44*	*6*	*20*	*22*	*4.6*	*5.1*	*53%*	*.306*	*1.67*	*5.94*	*5.65*	*6.46*	*-0.4*

Though Leesman kept his Triple-A ERA down by pitching much better with runners on base than with them empty, he walks too many batters for someone with relatively pedestrian stuff. The news isn't all bad: He works his sinker and changeup low in the zone, generates plenty of groundballs, and shuts down the running game, turning more than his share of baserunners into double-play outs. His arsenal works equally well against both sides, and his low-90s velocity isn't poor for a lefty. He is already better than many fifth starters, and any further improvement in his control could solidify a role in a major-league rotation.

Francisco Liriano
Born: **10/26/1983** Age: **29**
Bats: **L** Throws: **L** Height: **6' 3"** Weight: **215**
Breakout: **13%** Improve: **45%** Collapse: **29%**
Attrition: **6%** MLB: **89%**
Comparables:
Rich Hill,Jonathan Sanchez,Erik Bedard

YEAR	TEAM	LVL	AGE	W	L	SV	G	GS	IP	H	HR	BB	SO	BB9	SO9	GB%	BABIP	WHIP	ERA	FIP	FRA	WARP
2010	MIN	MLB	26	14	10	0	31	31	191^{2}	184	9	58	201	2.7	9.4	56%	.331	1.26	3.62	2.62	3.44	4.3
2011	MIN	MLB	27	9	10	0	26	24	134^{1}	125	14	75	112	5.0	7.5	49%	.290	1.49	5.09	4.58	5.33	0.0
2012	CHA	MLB	28	3	2	0	12	11	56^{2}	54	7	32	58	5.1	9.2	42%	.307	1.52	5.40	4.46	4.91	0.3
2012	MIN	MLB	28	3	10	0	22	17	100	89	12	55	109	4.9	9.8	47%	.296	1.44	5.31	4.20	5.25	0.4
2013	*CHA*	*MLB*	*29*	*8*	*8*	*0*	*24*	*24*	134^{2}	*129*	*17*	*61*	*134*	*4.1*	*8.9*	*46%*	*.306*	*1.40*	*4.38*	*4.21*	*4.76*	*0.9*

It's often unfair to stereotype a general manager, but Francisco Liriano is a "Kenny Williams player" if ever there was one. Described in these pages as a "once-per-generation" talent after his 2006 debut, Liriano's talent went dormant. Williams picked up sleepers like Liriano at rock-bottom trade prices and trusted his baseball people to revive their performance. While the gamble didn't pay off for the White Sox last year, Liriano remains one to watch for the same traits that made him enticing as a trade target. His stuff remains intact. His fastballs and slider retain their velocity and his two varieties of changeup are baffling. Physical ailments have hurt his control and command. During two healthy seasons, Liriano issued fewer than three free passes per nine innings; now he's walking five per nine. Expect any progress he makes toward lowering that statistic to bring his ERA down with it.

Jhan Marinez
Born: **8/12/1988** Age: **24**
Bats: **R** Throws: **R** Height: **6' 2"** Weight: **165**
Breakout: **27%** Improve: **63%** Collapse: **13%**
Attrition: **9%** MLB: **93%**
Comparables:
Ed Whitson,John Rocker,Wesley Wright

YEAR	TEAM	LVL	AGE	W	L	SV	G	GS	IP	H	HR	BB	SO	BB9	SO9	GB%	BABIP	WHIP	ERA	FIP	FRA	WARP
2010	JUP	A+	21	0	1	4	21	1	25^{1}	12	1	14	44	5.0	15.7	33%	.300	1.03	1.42	2.25	1.81	0.9
2010	JAX	AA	21	1	0	6	15	0	16^{2}	9	1	7	20	3.8	10.8	44%	.229	0.96	2.16	3.03	3.64	0.2
2010	FLO	MLB	21	1	1	0	4	0	2^{2}	3	1	3	3	10.1	10.1	38%	.286	2.25	6.75	9.11	16.34	-0.3
2011	JAX	AA	22	3	8	3	56	0	58	47	7	42	74	6.5	11.5	48%	.231	1.53	3.57	4.55	3.88	0.4
2012	CHR	AAA	23	4	2	4	40	0	63	39	5	30	65	4.3	9.3	37%	.224	1.10	2.86	3.75	5.54	-0.2
2012	CHA	MLB	23	0	0	0	2	0	2^{2}	2	0	2	1	6.8	3.4	50%	.250	1.50	0.00	4.55	6.49	0.0
2013	*CHA*	*MLB*	*24*	*1*	*0*	*1*	*26*	*0*	*34*	*31*	*5*	*20*	*34*	*5.2*	*9.0*	*40%*	*.292*	*1.48*	*4.72*	*4.88*	*5.13*	*0.0*

Last year was an exciting year of development for "Max-effort Marinez." He blows batters away with his upper-90s heat and a slider that can embarrass. Most important, given his past, is a walk rate under one per two innings. At his current skill level, he should be an effective one-inning reliever, and any additional progress at finding the strike zone could make that inning come later and later.

Nestor Molina
Born: **1/9/1989** Age: **24**
Bats: **R** Throws: **R** Height: **6' 2"** Weight: **179**
Breakout: **23%** Improve: **50%** Collapse: **17%**
Attrition: **9%** MLB: **83%**
Comparables:
Carl Erskine,Joe Landrum,Brandon Lyon

YEAR	TEAM	LVL	AGE	W	L	SV	G	GS	IP	H	HR	BB	SO	BB9	SO9	GB%	BABIP	WHIP	ERA	FIP	FRA	WARP
2010	LNS	A	21	8	2	4	37	2	76^{2}	64	4	20	61	2.3	7.2	60%	.268	1.10	3.17	3.48	5.43	0.1
2010	DUN	A+	21	0	0	0	2	0	4^{1}	7	0	0	3	0.0	6.3	56%	.407	1.63	2.09	2.04	3.81	0.1
2011	DUN	A+	22	10	3	0	21	18	108^{1}	102	8	14	115	1.2	9.6	50%	.312	1.07	2.58	2.64	3.22	1.0
2011	NHP	AA	22	2	0	0	5	5	22	12	0	2	33	0.8	13.5	—	.267	0.64	0.41	0.68	0.74	0.0
2012	BIR	AA	23	6	10	0	22	21	122^{2}	156	7	26	84	1.9	6.2	46%	.359	1.48	4.26	3.20	3.54	1.3
2012	CHR	AAA	23	0	1	0	1	1	4	9	2	1	4	2.2	9.0	44%	.500	2.50	13.50	8.41	9.00	-0.2
2013	*CHA*	*MLB*	*24*	*1*	*2*	*0*	*10*	*4*	*34^{2}*	*43*	*6*	*12*	*21*	*3.1*	*5.5*	*48%*	*.319*	*1.57*	*5.86*	*5.28*	*6.37*	*-0.3*

Molina may be a converted third baseman, but he shows some of the best command in the game. It remains an open question whether that will be enough to keep him in a rotation, however, as only his fastball and split-finger pitch are above average. His changeup and slider showed much less improvement than hoped last year. The word is that the tendinitis he suffered isn't anything serious, but he didn't show enough to earn a promotion this year, and if he doesn't figure out how to baffle Double-A hitters early in 2013, his stock will plummet like one of his splitters.

Brett Myers
Born: **8/17/1980** Age: **32**
Bats: **R** Throws: **R** Height: **6' 5"** Weight: **240**
Breakout: **12%** Improve: **38%** Collapse: **38%**
Attrition: **20%** MLB: **88%**
Comparables:
Nate Robertson,Larry Jansen,Erik Hanson

YEAR	TEAM	LVL	AGE	W	L	SV	G	GS	IP	H	HR	BB	SO	BB9	SO9	GB%	BABIP	WHIP	ERA	FIP	FRA	WARP
2010	HOU	MLB	29	14	8	0	33	33	223^{2}	212	20	66	180	2.7	7.2	50%	.288	1.24	3.14	3.58	4.14	3.3
2011	HOU	MLB	30	7	14	0	34	33	216	226	31	57	160	2.4	6.7	49%	.293	1.31	4.46	4.23	5.12	-0.3
2012	CHA	MLB	31	3	4	0	35	0	34^{2}	30	4	9	21	2.3	5.5	49%	.252	1.12	3.12	4.20	5.03	0.1
2012	HOU	MLB	31	0	4	19	35	0	30^{2}	35	4	6	20	1.8	5.9	57%	.304	1.34	3.52	4.31	5.29	0.0
2013	*CHA*	*MLB*	*32*	*4*	*4*	*1*	*21*	*10*	*76^{2}*	*81*	*12*	*23*	*57*	*2.7*	*6.6*	*48%*	*.295*	*1.35*	*4.70*	*4.65*	*5.11*	*0.1*

Myers accepted relegation to seventh- and eighth-inning duty with more class than some other former closers and turned in a fine season in various bullpen roles. While his strikeout rate is barely half what it was in 2007, the velocity on both his fastballs improved by 3 mph last year, and he demonstrated the best control of his career, so his strikeout-to-walk ratio was better than his career norm. Durable when used as a starting pitcher, Myers has reached 190 innings six times in his career. With a $7 million difference between his option cost and buyout price, Myers may be more valuable filling out the back of the rotation.

Brian Omogrosso
Born: **4/26/1984** Age: **29**
Bats: **R** Throws: **R** Height: **6' 5"** Weight: **230**
Breakout: **41%** Improve: **59%** Collapse: **19%**
Attrition: **15%** MLB: **79%**
Comparables:
Sean Henn,Jim Gott,Tyler Yates

YEAR	TEAM	LVL	AGE	W	L	SV	G	GS	IP	H	HR	BB	SO	BB9	SO9	GB%	BABIP	WHIP	ERA	FIP	FRA	WARP
2011	BIR	AA	27	0	2	2	31	0	43	36	2	16	53	3.3	11.1	51%	.339	1.21	2.51	2.77	2.74	0.6
2011	CHR	AAA	27	1	1	0	11	1	22^{1}	24	1	8	19	3.2	7.7	56%	.280	1.43	4.03	3.19	4.20	0.1
2012	CHR	AAA	28	0	2	9	33	0	47^{1}	43	3	12	59	2.3	11.2	47%	.318	1.16	4.56	2.38	3.31	0.8
2012	CHA	MLB	28	0	0	0	17	0	21	20	3	9	18	3.9	7.7	35%	.283	1.38	2.57	4.47	3.32	0.4
2013	*CHA*	*MLB*	*29*	*1*	*0*	*1*	*25*	*0*	*34*	*34*	*5*	*17*	*30*	*4.4*	*8.0*	*45%*	*.305*	*1.51*	*5.04*	*4.85*	*5.48*	*-0.1*

Omogrosso uses one of the highest leg kicks in the game today, making him entertaining to watch. While he worked exclusively out of the bullpen in 2012, he frequently logged multiple-inning outings. As injuries recede into his past, he could audition for a rotation spot. His mid-90s four-seamer is complemented by a slider, curve, and changeup, each of which can look very good at times, but those times are too far apart to generate much excitement about his future. If he can kick the inconsistency, he could surprise.

Jake Peavy
Born: **5/31/1981** Age: **32**
Bats: **R** Throws: **R** Height: **6' 2"** Weight: **195**
Breakout: **10%** Improve: **30%** Collapse: **43%**
Attrition: **16%** MLB: **88%**
Comparables:
John Lackey,Chris Carpenter,Josh Beckett

YEAR	TEAM	LVL	AGE	W	L	SV	G	GS	IP	H	HR	BB	SO	BB9	SO9	GB%	BABIP	WHIP	ERA	FIP	FRA	WARP
2010	CHA	MLB	29	7	6	0	17	17	107	98	13	34	93	2.9	7.8	43%	.279	1.23	4.63	3.98	4.60	1.0
2011	BIR	AA	30	0	0	0	2	2	4^{1}	9	0	1	4	2.1	8.3	—	.500	2.31	6.23	2.15	2.34	0.0
2011	CHR	AAA	30	1	1	0	4	4	24^{2}	21	3	1	26	0.4	9.5	46%	.250	0.89	3.65	2.83	4.12	0.3
2011	CHA	MLB	30	7	7	0	19	18	111^{2}	117	10	24	95	1.9	7.7	40%	.317	1.26	4.92	3.25	4.01	1.7
2012	CHA	MLB	31	11	12	0	32	32	219	191	27	49	194	2.0	8.0	37%	.272	1.10	3.37	3.69	4.01	3.1
2013	*CHA*	*MLB*	*32*	*11*	*9*	*0*	*26*	*26*	*169^{1}*	*160*	*21*	*47*	*156*	*2.5*	*8.3*	*42%*	*.296*	*1.23*	*3.69*	*3.80*	*4.01*	*2.5*

Peavy is becoming a better pitcher with age. He throws more strikes, and batters are swinging at more of his offerings outside the zone and fewer inside it. Of course, his fastball velocity is down at least 4 mph from his early years, so there's no longer the anticipation of a no-hitter whenever he takes the mound. Much has been made of his so-called "improvement" in 2012, but in many ways he was the same pitcher, with similar FRAs and strikeout-to-walk ratios in each season. Expect more of the same in 2013, with the ERA correcting slightly upward given neutral luck.

Jake Petricka

Born: **6/5/1988** Age: **25**
Bats: **R** Throws: **R** Height: **6' 6"** Weight: **170**
Breakout: **32%** Improve: **62%** Collapse: **18%**
Attrition: **20%** MLB: **93%**

Comparables:
Jaret Wright,Sean Henn,Brad Hennessey

YEAR	TEAM	LVL	AGE	W	L	SV	G	GS	IP	H	HR	BB	SO	BB9	SO9	GB%	BABIP	WHIP	ERA	FIP	FRA	WARP
2010	BRI	Rk	22	2	4	0	8	8	34^2	25	1	7	38	1.8	9.9	62%	.266	0.92	2.85	2.50	4.25	0.3
2010	KAN	A	22	0	1	0	9	0	9^2	13	0	8	10	7.4	9.3	71%	.371	2.16	3.71	4.25	4.88	0.0
2011	BRI	Rk	23	0	0	0	2	1	4	4	0	0	5	0.0	11.2	—	.444	1.00	0.00	1.28	1.39	0.0
2011	KAN	A	23	3	1	0	8	8	41^2	39	0	13	48	2.8	10.4	51%	.358	1.25	2.81	2.16	3.20	1.0
2011	WNS	A+	23	4	7	0	13	13	67^2	71	3	26	46	3.5	6.1	—	.302	1.43	4.39	3.73	4.06	0.0
2012	WNS	A+	24	5	5	0	19	19	82^2	93	2	46	84	5.0	9.1	63%	.376	1.68	5.33	3.45	4.29	0.6
2012	BIR	AA	24	3	3	0	10	10	57^2	63	7	35	27	5.5	4.2	51%	.298	1.70	5.46	5.61	6.95	-1.1
2013	*CHA*	*MLB*	*25*	*2*	*3*	*0*	*8*	*8*	37^2	*44*	*6*	*22*	*24*	*5.4*	*5.9*	*52%*	*.316*	*1.77*	*6.38*	*5.75*	*6.94*	*-0.5*

Petricka is exactly the sort of player new GM Rick Hahn could use as trade bait. Highly regarded for his ability to throw hard, go deep in games, and generate groundballs, with a curve and change that are considered to have plus potential, he makes scouts salivate but hasn't shown the hoped-for performance. Of course, two years from now, after a guy like this has lost his shine, he'd be exactly the sort of player the White Sox might acquire, expecting their coaching staff to fix the flaws, like Petricka's terrible control. In short, he could turn things around at any time, but he does need to start throwing strikes to have value, no matter how good the scouting reports are.

Jose Quintana

Born: **1/24/1989** Age: **24**
Bats: **L** Throws: **L** Height: **6' 1"** Weight: **170**
Breakout: **23%** Improve: **66%** Collapse: **22%**
Attrition: **8%** MLB: **98%**

Comparables:
Aaron Laffey,Zach Duke,Steve Avery

YEAR	TEAM	LVL	AGE	W	L	SV	G	GS	IP	H	HR	BB	SO	BB9	SO9	GB%	BABIP	WHIP	ERA	FIP	FRA	WARP
2010	YAN	Rk	21	3	1	1	15	0	23^1	14	0	8	32	3.1	12.4	66%	.243	0.94	2.32	2.18	4.26	0.2
2010	CSC	A	21	0	1	0	5	3	15^1	11	1	10	12	5.9	7.1	62%	.227	1.37	4.71	4.97	7.55	-0.4
2011	TAM	A+	22	10	2	1	30	12	102	86	5	28	88	2.5	7.8	—	.289	1.12	2.91	3.15	3.43	0.0
2012	BIR	AA	23	1	3	0	9	9	48^2	43	1	14	41	2.6	7.6	55%	.299	1.17	2.77	2.59	2.57	0.5
2012	CHA	MLB	23	6	6	0	25	22	136^1	142	14	42	81	2.8	5.3	49%	.299	1.35	3.76	4.18	4.72	0.9
2013	*CHA*	*MLB*	*24*	*6*	*6*	*0*	*25*	*16*	105^1	*111*	*13*	*36*	*72*	*3.1*	*6.1*	*49%*	*.299*	*1.39*	*4.58*	*4.46*	*4.98*	*0.4*

Bursting onto the scene from nowhere, Quintana posted a 2.04 ERA through July 5, baffling hitters who saw his fastball, cutter, and curve combination for the first time. After the All-Star Game, he had a 5.01 ERA as he allowed too many hits and homers, and even his previously great control slipped to merely average. It's his turn to make adjustments, and as he lacks the raw stuff to blow hitters away, his best chance to return to adequacy will be to find another trick to add to his bag. To that end, it's important to remember that he didn't get promoted to Double-A until 2012, so he may be more likely than most to find such useful tricks as he makes up some of the courses he skipped. Meanwhile, he has the confidence that comes from a string of successful outings, something many young pitchers never acquire.

Addison Reed

Born: **12/27/1988** Age: **24**
Bats: **L** Throws: **R** Height: **6' 5"** Weight: **215**
Breakout: **22%** Improve: **52%** Collapse: **24%**
Attrition: **17%** MLB: **96%**

Comparables:
Jerry Blevins,Dave LaRoche,Josh Spence

YEAR	TEAM	LVL	AGE	W	L	SV	G	GS	IP	H	HR	BB	SO	BB9	SO9	GB%	BABIP	WHIP	ERA	FIP	FRA	WARP
2010	GRF	Rk	21	1	0	1	13	2	30	17	1	6	44	1.8	13.2	40%	.289	0.77	1.80	2.28	3.88	0.8
2011	KAN	A	22	0	0	0	4	0	8	4	0	1	11	1.1	12.4	47%	.235	0.62	1.12	1.15	1.88	0.3
2011	WNS	A+	22	2	0	1	15	0	28^1	21	1	4	39	1.3	12.4	—	.294	0.88	1.59	1.57	1.71	0.0
2011	BIR	AA	22	0	1	2	13	0	20^2	10	0	6	33	2.6	14.4	33%	.267	0.77	0.87	1.13	1.90	0.6
2011	CHR	AAA	22	0	0	2	11	0	21^1	8	2	3	28	1.3	11.8	27%	.100	0.52	1.27	2.25	4.55	0.1
2011	CHA	MLB	22	0	0	0	6	0	7^1	10	1	1	12	1.2	14.7	20%	.474	1.50	3.68	1.97	3.33	0.2
2012	CHA	MLB	23	3	2	29	62	0	55	57	6	18	54	2.9	8.8	33%	.323	1.36	4.75	3.59	3.83	0.8
2013	*CHA*	*MLB*	*24*	*2*	*1*	*11*	*33*	*1*	*44*	*40*	*5*	*14*	*48*	*2.9*	*9.8*	*37%*	*.303*	*1.23*	*3.65*	*3.45*	*3.97*	*0.6*

Quick quiz: Who was the closer for the 2012 White Sox? (Chicagoans, don't shout out the answer.) You didn't really just guess Bobby Jenks did you? Reed didn't allow any runs until May 13, when he made up for lost time quickly, allowing the Royals to put up a crooked number (six) in a non-save situation. And while he breathes fire, converts a good percentage of save opportunities, and looks like a great closer, the fact that batters hit .291/.345/.475 in 45 innings from that date onward is disconcerting. He also struck out only 40 batters in that span while walking 15. The Sox are much less worried about him than fans and analysts. They are moving forward with the expectation that excellent command of his heat (and his show-me slider and change) will return in 2013.

Santos Rodriguez

Born: **1/2/1988** Age: **25**
Bats: **L** Throws: **L** Height: **6' 6"** Weight: **180**
Breakout: **27%** Improve: **50%** Collapse: **25%**
Attrition: **9%** MLB: **91%**

Comparables:
Dave LaRoche,B.J. Ryan,Dan Runzler

YEAR	TEAM	LVL	AGE	W	L	SV	G	GS	IP	H	HR	BB	SO	BB9	SO9	GB%	BABIP	WHIP	ERA	FIP	FRA	WARP
2011	WNS	A+	23	2	3	2	40	5	62	70	4	33	49	4.8	7.1	—	.337	1.66	3.77	4.23	4.60	0.0
2012	BIR	AA	24	2	4	8	37	0	64	33	6	33	60	4.6	8.4	33%	.175	1.03	2.81	4.08	4.94	-0.1
2012	CHR	AAA	24	0	0	0	5	0	7^{1}	7	0	2	9	2.5	11.0	40%	.350	1.23	3.68	1.52	1.31	0.3
2013	*CHA*	*MLB*	*25*	*1*	*0*	*1*	*22*	*0*	*33^{2}*	*31*	*4*	*21*	*35*	*5.7*	*9.5*	*40%*	*.300*	*1.55*	*4.89*	*4.54*	*5.32*	*-0.0*

Relief-pitching prospects coming off their age-24 seasons in Double-A are a poor demographic to mine for future stars, but Rodriguez warrants consideration. He only tossed 44 1/3 innings of full-season ball before 2011, between spending a long time in rookie leagues and dealing with various health concerns. Two full seasons haven't miraculously cured his control issues nor turned his secondary pitches into plus offerings, but he still throws ridiculously hard for a lefty, and allowing a hit every other inning last year in Double-A gives an indication of just how unhittable he could be if he makes progress on any front.

Chris Sale

Born: **3/30/1989** Age: **24**
Bats: **L** Throws: **L** Height: **6' 7"** Weight: **180**
Breakout: **33%** Improve: **66%** Collapse: **13%**
Attrition: **11%** MLB: **96%**

Comparables:
Clayton Kershaw,Clay Buchholz,Fernando Valenzuela

YEAR	TEAM	LVL	AGE	W	L	SV	G	GS	IP	H	HR	BB	SO	BB9	SO9	GB%	BABIP	WHIP	ERA	FIP	FRA	WARP
2010	WNS	A+	21	0	0	0	4	0	4	3	0	2	4	4.5	9.0	46%	.273	1.25	2.25	2.91	4.59	0.0
2010	CHR	AAA	21	0	0	0	7	0	6^{1}	3	2	4	15	5.7	21.4	60%	.250	1.11	2.86	4.56	2.47	0.2
2010	CHA	MLB	21	2	1	4	21	0	23^{1}	15	2	10	32	3.9	12.3	52%	.271	1.07	1.93	2.70	3.55	0.4
2011	CHA	MLB	22	2	2	8	58	0	71	52	6	27	79	3.4	10.0	52%	.264	1.11	2.79	3.16	3.44	1.3
2012	CHA	MLB	23	17	8	0	30	29	192	167	19	51	192	2.4	9.0	46%	.294	1.14	3.05	3.22	3.53	3.6
2013	*CHA*	*MLB*	*24*	*9*	*5*	*4*	*59*	*15*	*146^{2}*	*123*	*16*	*44*	*163*	*2.7*	*10.0*	*46%*	*.294*	*1.14*	*3.05*	*3.30*	*3.32*	*3.3*

Sale's season was the 20th-best, based on pitcher WARP, by a White Sox hurler since 1950, and the seventh-best WARP-per-inning for a White Sox starting pitcher in that span. An early-season MRI gave everyone a scare—prompting a relief outing and discussion of a full-time move to the bullpen—but the results came back clean. Predictably for a pitcher increasing his workload to career highs after a season in relief, Sale wore down as the summer wore on, his velocity and effectiveness dipping, allowing batters an OPS over 790 after August 1. If Sale had a textbook delivery, there would be minimal concern about the innings, but he doesn't: Terms like "elbow drag," "Inverted W," and "terrifying" are bandied about. It's a tightrope he's walking, because that funky delivery allows his sinker-slider combination to erase left-handed batters, and his changeup has become good enough that righties no longer look forward to facing him, either.

Hector Santiago

Born: **12/16/1987** Age: **25**
Bats: **R** Throws: **L** Height: **6' 1"** Weight: **210**
Breakout: **33%** Improve: **55%** Collapse: **22%**
Attrition: **13%** MLB: **83%**

Comparables:
Greg Holland,Jon Meloan,Emiliano Fruto

YEAR	TEAM	LVL	AGE	W	L	SV	G	GS	IP	H	HR	BB	SO	BB9	SO9	GB%	BABIP	WHIP	ERA	FIP	FRA	WARP
2010	WNS	A+	22	4	5	2	37	1	60^{2}	63	4	19	61	2.8	9.0	39%	.330	1.35	4.15	3.34	3.30	1.7
2011	WNS	A+	23	2	3	0	8	8	44	38	7	14	43	2.9	8.8	—	.272	1.18	3.68	4.50	4.89	0.0
2011	BIR	AA	23	7	5	0	15	15	83^{1}	71	4	39	74	4.2	8.0	54%	.326	1.32	3.56	3.70	5.54	-0.1
2011	CHA	MLB	23	0	0	0	2	0	5^{1}	1	0	1	2	1.7	3.4	60%	.067	0.38	0.00	2.87	3.06	0.1
2012	CHR	AAA	24	1	0	0	3	3	14^{2}	9	0	6	13	3.7	8.0	51%	.257	1.02	0.00	2.61	3.41	0.3
2012	CHA	MLB	24	4	1	4	42	4	70^{1}	54	10	40	79	5.1	10.1	39%	.259	1.34	3.33	4.65	4.84	0.3
2013	*CHA*	*MLB*	*25*	*2*	*2*	*1*	*27*	*5*	*55^{2}*	*54*	*8*	*31*	*53*	*5.1*	*8.5*	*41%*	*.303*	*1.54*	*4.91*	*4.83*	*5.34*	*0.0*

Santiago has had a screwy career so far, to say the least. He generates enough velocity to be an interesting arm without the screwball, but his multiple other breaking-ball offerings don't show the same promise. His fastball-scroogie combo showed enough that manager Robin Ventura anointed him the closer to start the season, despite the fact that he'd been moved into the rotation in the minors. He failed spectacularly as the April closer, and was moved into middle relief, where he thrived until demoted to make room for Liriano. Again used as a starter in the minors, he showed enough in four September starts with the big club to be in the mix for a rotation spot in 2013.

Leyson Septimo

Born: **7/7/1985** Age: **27**
Bats: **L** Throws: **L** Height: **6' 2"** Weight: **195**
Breakout: **36%** Improve: **57%** Collapse: **26%**
Attrition: **23%** MLB: **87%**

Comparables:
Ray Newman,Rod Scurry,B.J. Ryan

YEAR	TEAM	LVL	AGE	W	L	SV	G	GS	IP	H	HR	BB	SO	BB9	SO9	GB%	BABIP	WHIP	ERA	FIP	FRA	WARP
2010	MOB	AA	24	2	2	4	26	0	28^{1}	16	1	23	37	7.3	11.8	46%	.259	1.38	4.13	3.88	3.92	0.3
2010	RNO	AAA	24	0	1	0	16	0	17	15	2	30	20	15.9	10.6	49%	.289	2.65	11.12	8.76	8.16	-0.3
2011	BIR	AA	25	2	1	0	22	0	26^{1}	23	1	16	38	5.5	13.0	49%	.209	1.48	4.10	3.08	2.66	0.5
2011	MOB	AA	25	2	1	0	21	0	29^{2}	20	1	25	22	7.6	6.7	43%	.206	1.52	6.37	5.40	9.20	-0.5
2012	CHR	AAA	26	2	1	1	24	0	34^{1}	16	1	20	43	5.2	11.3	48%	.208	1.05	1.31	2.87	3.40	0.6
2012	CHA	MLB	26	0	2	0	21	0	14^{1}	8	3	6	14	3.8	8.8	46%	.147	0.98	5.02	5.28	7.98	-0.3
2013	*CHA*	*MLB*	*27*	*1*	*0*	*0*	*29*	*0*	*33*	*29*	*4*	*25*	*35*	*6.8*	*9.4*	*45%*	*.291*	*1.62*	*5.23*	*4.93*	*5.68*	*-0.2*

Septimo is an exciting prospect, despite being somewhat advanced in age. He began as a toolsy outfielder in the Diamondbacks organization, then epitomized wildness after switching to the mound in 2008. Since claiming him on waivers, the Sox have been able to get him to throw more strikes at the expense of a little velocity (he hasn't hit triple digits recently, but still throws very hard for a lefty), and the resulting performance improvements last year all but insure he'll at least make the team. His upside beyond that is limited only by how much more progress he can make at improving his control.

Scott Snodgress
Born: **9/20/1989** Age: **23**
Bats: **L** Throws: **L** Height: **6' 6"** Weight: **210**
Breakout: **31%** Improve: **74%** Collapse: **14%**
Attrition: **12%** MLB: **96%**
Comparables:
Jo-Jo Reyes, Jason Jennings, Tom Gorzelanny

YEAR	TEAM	LVL	AGE	W	L	SV	G	GS	IP	H	HR	BB	SO	BB9	SO9	GB%	BABIP	WHIP	ERA	FIP	FRA	WARP
2011	GRF	Rk	21	3	3	0	16	12	59^1	61	5	17	68	2.6	10.3	52%	.333	1.31	3.34	4.00	4.20	1.3
2012	KAN	A	22	3	3	0	19	19	99	86	4	49	84	4.5	7.6	40%	.286	1.36	3.64	4.10	4.70	1.2
2012	WNS	A+	22	4	0	0	8	8	42	26	2	15	44	3.2	9.4	54%	.225	0.98	1.50	3.05	2.53	0.6
2013	*CHA*	*MLB*	*23*	*2*	*3*	*0*	*7*	*7*	36^2	*41*	*6*	*21*	*24*	*5.2*	*6.0*	*44%*	*.304*	*1.70*	*6.07*	*5.74*	*6.59*	*-0.4*

Snodgress has a deceptive motion with lots of arms and legs, leading most observers to predict a future in the bullpen. His fastball can reach 95 and his curve is a good secondary offering. If he gets his changeup going, talk of relieving should wane, as he has shown a decent ability to maintain his velocity throughout starts, though he's been limited to five or six innings most outings. As with teammate Johnson, it's tempting to make too much out of his stats in eight starts after the promotion last year, when everything was working for him. Hitting spots reduced his walk rate and made him much less hittable, allowing fewer hits and generating more strikeouts.

Matt Thornton
Born: **9/15/1976** Age: **36**
Bats: **L** Throws: **L** Height: **6' 7"** Weight: **235**
Breakout: **19%** Improve: **35%** Collapse: **51%**
Attrition: **6%** MLB: **90%**
Comparables:
Brian Fuentes, Billy Wagner, Arthur Rhodes

YEAR	TEAM	LVL	AGE	W	L	SV	G	GS	IP	H	HR	BB	SO	BB9	SO9	GB%	BABIP	WHIP	ERA	FIP	FRA	WARP
2010	CHA	MLB	33	5	4	8	61	0	60^2	41	3	20	81	3.0	12.0	41%	.286	1.01	2.67	2.11	2.75	1.5
2011	CHA	MLB	34	2	5	3	62	0	59^2	60	3	21	63	3.2	9.5	49%	.326	1.36	3.32	2.66	2.77	1.6
2012	CHA	MLB	35	4	10	3	74	0	65	63	4	17	53	2.4	7.3	55%	.317	1.23	3.46	3.14	4.02	0.7
2013	*CHA*	*MLB*	*36*	*3*	*1*	*2*	*60*	*0*	*56*	*49*	*5*	*17*	*62*	*2.8*	*10.0*	*48%*	*.304*	*1.18*	*3.15*	*3.06*	*3.42*	*1.2*

Following three straight seasons of allowing about one baserunner per inning, Thornton turned in his second just-okay season in a row last year. His velocity was down a tick, and throwing more strikes didn't make up for the resultant loss of strikeouts. Perhaps more significantly, his breaking pitch has slowed down enough that Brooks Baseball is now categorizing it as a curve instead of the wipeout slider he showed in the past. With no health problems, there's concern that Thornton's 2012 performance represents the pitcher he has become, with little chance of transforming back to previous levels of dominance.

Donnie Veal
Born: **9/18/1984** Age: **28**
Bats: **L** Throws: **L** Height: **6' 5"** Weight: **240**
Breakout: **36%** Improve: **61%** Collapse: **23%**
Attrition: **28%** MLB: **88%**
Comparables:
Neal Musser, Ken Kravec, Bill Murphy

YEAR	TEAM	LVL	AGE	W	L	SV	G	GS	IP	H	HR	BB	SO	BB9	SO9	GB%	BABIP	WHIP	ERA	FIP	FRA	WARP
2010	IND	AAA	25	3	2	0	9	9	49^2	42	3	23	41	4.2	7.4	45%	.277	1.31	4.35	4.18	5.41	0.0
2011	PIR	Rk	26	0	0	0	1	1	1^2	1	0	2	3	10.8	16.2	—	.333	1.80	5.40	5.22	5.67	0.0
2011	BRD	A+	26	0	1	0	7	4	19^1	17	1	6	18	2.8	8.4	—	.296	1.19	2.79	3.60	3.91	0.0
2011	ALT	AA	26	0	1	0	4	0	4^2	9	3	0	3	0.0	5.8	64%	.385	1.93	7.71	10.48	6.03	0.0
2011	IND	AAA	26	0	0	0	7	0	6^1	5	0	7	7	9.9	9.9	50%	.286	1.89	5.68	4.82	4.66	0.0
2012	CHR	AAA	27	7	3	2	35	0	52	40	0	23	61	4.0	10.6	56%	.305	1.21	2.08	2.43	2.83	1.1
2012	CHA	MLB	27	0	0	1	24	0	13	5	0	4	19	2.8	13.2	39%	.192	0.69	1.38	1.05	1.09	0.4
2013	*CHA*	*MLB*	*28*	*2*	*1*	*0*	*21*	*3*	33^1	*33*	*5*	*20*	*30*	*5.4*	*8.0*	*46%*	*.300*	*1.58*	*5.24*	*5.15*	*5.69*	*-0.1*

Veal has a lot to prove before he can be relied upon, but he represents a demographic of player who is a worthwhile risk: those less than two years removed from Tommy John surgery. He hadn't figured things out in 2011, and the Pirates gave up on him. But the before-surgery skills that made him a top prospect as a starting pitcher shone through in the bullpen after the White Sox signed him last year. His sinker-curve combination is highly effective against batters on both sides of the plate, and he has good velocity for a lefty. Veal has a chance to be an important part of the bullpen as long as he can avoid additional injuries.

LINEOUTS

HITTERS

PLAYER	TEAM	LVL	AGE	PA	R	2B	3B	HR	RBI	BB	SO	SB-CS	AVG/OBP/SLG	TAv	BABIP	BRR	FRAA	WARP
C M. Blanke	WNS	A+	23	373	46	24	0	10	50	27	66	0-0	.240/.303/.399	.247	.268	1.4	C(24): -0.4	0.0
2B J. DeMichele	BRI	Rk	21	52	7	4	3	2	9	3	8	3-0	.348/.412/.696	.362	.389	0	--	0.0
	KAN	A	21	256	30	12	7	5	29	19	54	5-4	.261/.319/.436	.227	.320	-0.3	2B(16): -0.2	-0.2
C H. Gimenez	CHR	AAA	29	418	50	22	2	14	57	37	89	2-1	.259/.324/.440	.249	.303	-0.1	C(41): -0.4, 1B(14): -0.1	0.1
	CHA	MLB	29	11	1	0	0	0	1	0	3	0-0	.455/.455/.455	.344	.625	0.2	C(3): -0.0, LF(1): -0.0	0.1
OF G. Golson	CHR	AAA	26	480	67	29	7	6	52	17	114	20-2	.276/.309/.412	.237	.356	7.2	RF(37): 4.7, CF(28): 0.4	0.6
SS T. Manzella	HUN	AA	29	252	22	7	0	1	28	27	57	3-4	.252/.336/.298	.257	.335	-1.8	SS(44): 2.3	0.9
SS T. Saladino	BIR	AA	22	509	71	15	4	4	39	75	91	38-8	.237/.359/.321	.249	.289	4.7	SS(67): 6.0, 2B(16): -1.5	1.7
	CHR	AAA	22	55	9	2	0	0	6	4	16	1-0	.224/.296/.265	.185	.333	1.2	SS(14): -0.0, 2B(1): 0.1	-0.2
SS A. Sanchez	OKL	AAA	28	398	48	13	1	5	45	40	25	7-3	.320/.390/.407	.185	.330	0	SS(13): -1.0, 2B(8): -0.4	-0.5
SS M. Semien	WNS	A+	21	487	80	31	5	14	59	55	97	11-5	.273/.362/.471	.324	.323	-1.6	SS(31): 3.3, 2B(8): -0.2	2.3
LF B. Shoemaker	WNS	A+	25	332	61	23	0	13	59	30	54	2-1	.331/.422/.549	.406	.370	-0.7	LF(20): 1.3	1.8
	BIR	AA	25	240	30	12	1	4	26	45	59	2-1	.254/.408/.392	.339	.346	-1.5	LF(31): 1.6, RF(2): 0.3	1.4
OF B. Short	WNS	A+	23	49	4	2	0	0	7	8	13	0-1	.297/.417/.351	.260	.423	0.4	—	0
	BIR	AA	23	44	5	2	0	0	1	2	7	1-0	.214/.250/.262	.190	.257	0.1	—	-0.3
	CHR	AAA	23	7	0	0	0	0	2	0	1	0-0	.333/.429/.333	.220	.400	0	RF(2): -0.2	0
3B J. Silverio	WNS	A+	21	286	36	20	3	8	51	15	67	4-4	.243/.285/.433	.201	.292	-0.6	3B(20): -1.6, RF(1): 0.0	-0.4
C K. Smith	KAN	A	24	379	48	26	0	7	60	25	62	0-1	.282/.344/.421	.285	.324	-1.6	C(56): 0.0	1.8
	WNS	A+	24	86	8	4	2	3	23	5	17	0-0	.273/.314/.494	.284	.300	0.1	C(8): -0.1	0.1
1B A. Wilkins	BIR	AA	23	502	68	28	1	17	69	63	94	6-4	.239/.335/.425	.283	.266	-1.9	1B(68): -4.8, 3B(3): -0.2	0.2

There were too many gross points to **Michael Blanke**'s 2012 season—he repeated the same level and his offense stagnated below par, and he assassinated fewer potential base thieves on defense, a performance unlikely to make Dan Aykroyd shout, "Popcorn!" Third-round pick **Joey DeMichele** hasn't emerged as a prospect yet, and doesn't have the first-round pedigree of former big-leaguer Todd Walker, but that's the sort of offense-first infielder mold the team is hoping he can fit into. Staying healthy has always been Mission Impossible for **Hector Gimenez**, but when all the parts are working, he has an elite gun and can be disguised as an almost adequate hitter. **Greg Golson** was traded for cash, and that's about the only thing he has in common with Babe Ruth. He and Wise would form a nice center-field platoon for a contending team in the International League. **Tommy Manzella** remains such a slick fielder at shortstop that he may get more major-league playing time before he's done, despite an inability to hit. **Tyler Saladino** posted 74 fewer points of OPS in the second half last year at Double-A, a disturbing in-season trend, but he maintains the potential to be a good leadoff hitter and shortstop. **Angel Sanchez** plays shortstop defense at a major-league level and bunts well, but his bat is light enough that he should only be a backup for a team blessed with middle infielders who are prone to stay healthy. Only seven players with 100 or more plate appearances in the Carolina League had a higher TAv than **Marcus Semien** and all were older than he. Even if he makes the likely move away from shortstop, the bat will play. As a 25-year-old corner outfielder with moderate power, **Brady Shoemaker** isn't much of a prospect, but he got a late start so he may have more room to grow than others his age. Time is short for **Brandon Short** to carve out a major-league career as a fourth outfielder, as injuries derailed his 2012 season. **Juan Silverio** came back from an early injury by slugging .541 in 61 May at-bats, teasing that he'd figured it out, but the rest of the season was a train wreck on both offense and defense, putting his future in doubt. **Kevan Smith** is on track to become an average catcher, with no real standout skills or weaknesses. **Andy Wilkins** is on track to become a below-average first baseman, having popped 40 home runs over the past two seasons while showing much better contact skills than his pre-draft expectations augured.

PITCHERS

PLAYER	TEAM	LVL	AGE	W	L	SV	IP	H	HR	BB	SO	BB9	SO9	GB%	BABIP	WHIP	ERA	FIP	FRA	WARP
C. Beck	GRF	Rk	21	4	3	0	40^{1}	51	3	12	36	2.7	8.0	47%	.387	1.56	4.69	4.51	5.43	0.5
B. Bruney	CHR	AAA	30	2	3	11	37	22	1	13	37	3.2	9.0	34%	.226	0.95	1.70	2.64	2.87	0.9
	CHA	MLB	30	1	0	0	1	0	0	2	2	18.0	18.0	%	.000	2.00	0.00	5.05	3.51	0.0
J. Gray	MIN	MLB	30	6	1	0	52	58	9	22	26	3.8	4.5	42%	.280	1.54	5.71	5.80	7.09	-1.0
D. Moskos	CHR	AAA	26	1	1	2	20^{1}	26	2	14	21	6.2	9.3	43%	.393	1.97	4.43	4.44	4.40	0.2
T. Reckling	SBR	A+	23	0	1	0	6^{2}	6	0	15	5	20.2	6.8	45%	.300	3.15	18.9	11.31	36.22	-0.2
D. Remenowsky	BIR	AA	26	1	3	3	46	21	1	22	54	4.3	10.6	43%	.215	0.93	2.15	2.51	3.16	0.8
	CHR	AAA	26	2	1	1	21	26	3	5	21	2.1	9.0	36%	.377	1.48	3.86	3.73	4.73	0.1
A. Rienzo	WNS	A+	23	3	0	0	25	17	0	7	31	2.5	11.2	45%	.293	0.96	1.08	1.75	0.87	0.3
	BIR	AA	23	4	3	0	71^{2}	56	2	33	72	4.1	9.0	45%	.274	1.24	3.27	2.92	2.61	1.5
S. Sanchez	BIR	AA	26	1	1	0	23^{1}	17	2	17	12	6.6	4.6	55%	.217	1.46	4.24	5.80	8.15	-0.8

Chris Beck struggled in his last college season and slid to the second round. He has good size, velocity, control, and has shown mastery of three off-speed offerings at times. **Brian Bruney** dealt with a velocity drop by learning enough about pitching to carve up Triple-A batters and earn another promotion. He promptly tore a labrum in his hip, casting doubt on his future. **Jeff Gray** and his 33 career Triple-A saves will try to help attract fans for the Charlotte Knights, who had the second-lowest attendance in the International League last year. Who says parent clubs never do anything for their affiliates. Former fourth pick **Daniel Moskos** was designated for assignment by the Pirates and outrighted to Triple-A by the White Sox. Even the good side of his reverse platoon split, right-handed batters, only makes him good enough to be a "fourth lefty," a role that doesn't exist. **Trevor Reckling** was once the Angels' top pitching prospect, and even last spring we ranked him the 17th-best prospect in the system, but he'd been heading backward since 2009 and missed much of 2011 with a sprained elbow; 15 walks in 6 innings at High-A got the lefty released in May. **Dan Remenowsky**'s previously pinpoint control abandoned him last year, without which his chances of making the bigs are nil. Blah blah blah "mid-90s fastball" blah blah blah "breaking ball needs work" blah blah blah "future may be in relief" but **Andre Rienzo**'s slurve was working better last year, and right-handed batters had no success against him. Hardly a top prospect, **Salvador Sanchez** formerly made a Double-A All-Star team as an outfielder, but the long, lanky, Dominican is now using his strong arm from the mound, and is regarded enough to earn a ticket to the Arizona Fall League.

MANAGER: ROBIN VENTURA

YEAR	TEAM	W-L	Pythag +/-	Avg PC	100+ P	120+ P	QS	BQS	REL	REL w Zero R	IBB	PH	PH Avg	PH HR	SB2	CS2	SB3	CS3	SAC Att	SAC %	POS SAC	Squeeze	Swing	In Play
2012	CHA	85-77	1	98.8	91	6	86	4	466	381	29	63	.135	1	2	1	0	1	45	80.0%	34	0	317	88

The hiring of Ventura, who had never run a clubhouse at any level, was met with a certain amount of skepticism, but the former third baseman wound up as a Manager of the Year finalist in his first season at the helm. The link between Ventura's leadership and bounce-back seasons from Adam Dunn, Alex Rios, and Jake Peavy is more likely one of correlation than causation, but there's no denying an improved atmosphere surrounded the club. His low-key approach was a welcome change from the cloud of drama that surrounded Ozzie Guillen, and his charges seemed to respond to it. Ventura communicates well, demands accountability, and earns respect from his players—traits far more important to success than game-day tactical wizardry. Whether he's among the best skippers in the league is a question that only time can answer, but Ventura has already proven he isn't among the worst.

Chicago Cubs

2012: THE GONG SHOW

The first year of the Theo Epstein era was all about the future at the expense of the present, as the Cubs tried to acquire as much young talent as they could and lost 101 games in the process.

Epstein sold off almost every veteran player who wasn't nailed down or on the disabled list, but his predecessor, Jim Hendry, was notable for his fondness of nails and handed out the no-trade clauses liberally. That explains how Alfonso Soriano stuck around even though the Cubs found an interested suitor at the trade deadline.

The on-field result was pretty much what you would expect: The 2012 Cubs were bad at pitching and hitting, as a handful of serviceable players (notably Starlin Castro, Matt Garza, and a surprisingly competent Jeff Samardzija) were not enough to keep this collection of misfit toys working.

CUBS PROSPECTUS

2012 W-L: 61-101, 5th in NL Central

Pythag	.403	28th	DER	.709	15th
RS/G	3.78	28th	B-Age	27.8	11th
RA/G	4.69	24th	P-Age	27.9	15th
TAv	.242	29th	Salary	$97.7	12th
BRR	5.8	7th	M$/MW	$7.83	29th
TAv-P	.268	22nd	DL Days	753	20th
FIP	4.50	27th	DL WARP	1.7	26th

Three-Year Park Factors	
Overall	104
HR/RH	112
HR/LH	103
AVG/RH	106
AVG/LH	99

Wrigley Field (1914)
Att. % of Capacity: 86.5% (9th)
Dim. 355, 368, 400, 368, 353

Venerable Wrigley Field was 18th in home runs last year, though the Cubs lineup had lots to do with that.

2013: DEAL OR NO DEAL

The North Siders will probably avoid losing 100 again, and there's a chance they could claw their way close to .500, but this is not the sort of team that can be fixed in one offseason, and the new regime seems willing to wait.

Anthony Rizzo matriculating to Chicago at first base helped, but this is still a lineup with some holes in it. The well-paid remnants of Soriano are hardly anyone's idea of an ideal clean-up hitter, and while guys like Darwin Barney, Nate Schierholtz, Ian Stewart, and David DeJesus might have their uses, they are not going to make anyone forget the 1927 Yankees. Or even the 2008 Cubs.

The club does have some prospects at its two greatest positions of need—third base and center field—but none that figure to make an impact in 2013.

In the starting rotation, Chicago has Garza and a bunch of question marks, and if you start considering health and trade value, even Garza is a question. The team managed to get a look at some young arms at the end of 2012, but results were mixed at best. Samardzija is coming off a strong year, but also one that was out of character for him, and the history of baseball is littered with as many one-hit wonders as pop music.

The Cubs didn't figure to be big sellers this offseason. Frankly, there's little left to sell. Epstein told the *Chicago Tribune*, "It's [not] the type of offseason where we have a ton of fits with 25 of the 29 other clubs. We'll pursue everything, but, realistically, our fits might be narrower this year, [which would] give us more time to focus on the free-agent market." That doesn't mean the Cubs were looking to stand pat—they very nearly dealt Carlos Marmol for Dan Haren until they reportedly backed off due to medical concerns about Haren—but a Dodgers- or Blue Jays-style blockbuster didn't appear to be in the cards.

Epstein also doesn't figure to make splashy free-agent signings any time soon. "We'll try to be disciplined," he told the *Tribune* early in the offseason, and "keep in mind we're not only trying to build for 2013, but we want to make sure we have a very solid future as well." Signing Scott Baker is a good example of the sort of deal the Cubs will be looking to make in the immediate future. The right-hander has some upside, but risk—in this case, injury—keeps his salary commitment low. Baker is the kind of player the Cubs can flip for yet more young talent at the trade deadline if he gets off to a good start.

STATE OF THE ORGANIZATION: AMERICA'S GOT TALENT

The first year of the Epstein administration has seen the Cubs following through on a commitment to rebuilding through player development, but there's still a long way to go.

There's a saying: We may be through with the past, but the past ain't through with us. Epstein and his top lieutenant, general manager Jed Hoyer, inherited a team that had a weak farm system due to weak draft position, some big whiffs at the top of the draft, and trades. The team has done about as much to rebuild as one could ask in a year, but had to start at the bottom, so while the Cubs have more young talent than in the recent past, almost all of it is too young to contribute to the big-league team any time soon.

Epstein has also taken steps toward increasing the size of what had been one of the smallest front offices in the game. The moves that have gotten the most attention have involved an embrace of analytics, with the Cubs signing a big deal with Bloomberg Sports to provide them with data. Less heralded but perhaps more significant, the Cubs have hired a bevy of new scouts in all aspects of the game—amateur, pro, international, and major league. Creating scouting depth is a critical part of any plan that involves significant investment in building through player development.

So the early returns are encouraging, but it's going to take time before the results show up at Wrigley Field and in the standings. And while Epstein and Co. seem to be doing a lot of things right, Cubs fans are cautioned to remember that baseball is hard, and even a good process isn't guaranteed to mean good results. It sure beats a bad process, though.

HITTERS

Albert Almora **CF**
Born: **4/16/1994** Age: **19**
Bats: **R** Throws: **R** Height: **6' 2"**
Weight: **170** Breakout: **0%**
Improve: **71%** Collapse: **29%**
Attrition: **29%** MLB: **100%**
Comparables:
Wayne Causey,Robin Yount,Ed Kranepool

YEAR	TEAM	LVL	AGE	PA	R	2B	3B	HR	RBI	BB	SO	SB	CS	AVG_OBP_SLG	TAv	BABIP	BRR	FRAA	WARP
2012	CUB	Rk	18	80	18	5	1	1	13	2	8	5	1	.347/.363/.480	.290	.368	0.4	CF(14): -0.1	0.0
2012	BOI	A-	18	65	9	7	0	1	6	0	5	0	1	.292/.292/.446	.251	.305	-3.3	CF(15): 2.0	0.0
2013	*CHN*	*MLB*	*19*	*250*	*20*	*10*	*1*	*4*	*23*	*8*	*56*	*2*	*1*	*.213/.240/.313*	*.199*	*.259*	*-0.1*	*CF -0*	*-0.6*

The first draft pick of the Theo Epstein era is a good indication the Cubs aren't trying to rush their plans. Almora's tools project to be average to plus across the board: He has the potential to be a strong defensive outfielder and his swing projects to deliver power as he fills out. Almora is more than just a collection of tools, as he shows tremendous feel for the game, which could not only help his physical gifts reach their projections, but could push them beyond expectations.

Javier Baez **SS**
Born: **12/1/1992** Age: **20**
Bats: **R** Throws: **R** Height: **6' 1"**
Weight: **180** Breakout: **24%**
Improve: **63%** Collapse: **3%**
Attrition: **12%** MLB: **85%**
Comparables:
Tony Conigliaro,Alex Rodriguez,B.J. Upton

YEAR	TEAM	LVL	AGE	PA	R	2B	3B	HR	RBI	BB	SO	SB	CS	AVG_OBP_SLG	TAv	BABIP	BRR	FRAA	WARP
2012	PEO	A	19	235	41	10	5	12	33	9	48	20	3	.333/.383/.596	.320	.378	5.2	SS(37): 2.7	2.1
2012	DAY	A+	19	86	9	3	1	4	13	5	21	4	2	.188/.244/.400	.155	.200	-0.9	SS(8): -0.9	-0.6
2013	*CHN*	*MLB*	*20*	*250*	*31*	*9*	*2*	*10*	*31*	*8*	*69*	*11*	*3*	*.227/.263/.407*	*.235*	*.273*	*1.5*	*SS 1*	*0.7*

Baez, already a top prospect, bolstered his stock considerably by tearing up the Midwest League. That he faltered in a short stint in High-A ball shouldn't dim his luster. Even in Dayton, Baez managed to flash a lot of power for someone who's only 19. Chicago ought to be patient with one of its best prospects: Even though the big club seems dismal at the moment, the Cubs are deep enough at shortstop that they shouldn't feel much pressure to rush Baez. The biggest question mark is whether and when the Cubs will ease him off short to third base. He certainly has the arm to play at shortstop, but his range is limited enough that once he starts to fill out a bit more he may not be able to stick there.

Darwin Barney **2B**
Born: **11/8/1985** Age: **27**
Bats: **R** Throws: **R** Height: **5' 11"**
Weight: **180** Breakout: **5%**
Improve: **33%** Collapse: **7%**
Attrition: **17%** MLB: **92%**
Comparables:
Jeff Treadway,Andres Blanco,Tommy Helms

YEAR	TEAM	LVL	AGE	PA	R	2B	3B	HR	RBI	BB	SO	SB	CS	AVG_OBP_SLG	TAv	BABIP	BRR	FRAA	WARP
2010	IOW	AAA	24	510	72	24	4	2	49	23	52	11	3	.299/.333/.378	.251	.330	-3.2	SS(111): 0.7, 2B(2): -0.3	1.5
2010	CHN	MLB	24	85	12	4	0	0	2	6	12	0	0	.241/.294/.291	.218	.284	2.7	SS(11): 0.4, 2B(10): -0.0	0.5
2011	CHN	MLB	25	570	66	23	6	2	43	22	67	9	2	.276/.313/.353	.238	.310	3.1	2B(134): 7.7, SS(5): 0.2	0.8
2012	CHN	MLB	26	588	73	26	4	7	44	33	58	6	1	.254/.299/.354	.235	.273	6.6	2B(155): 11.1, SS(3): 0.2	1.8
2013	*CHN*	*MLB*	*27*	*549*	*57*	*24*	*4*	*6*	*45*	*26*	*65*	*6*	*2*	*.261/.302/.360*	*.240*	*.285*	*0.3*	*2B -3, SS 0*	*0.6*

Raymond Chandler once said, "From 30 feet away she looked like a lot of class. From 10 feet away she looked like something made up to be seen from 30 feet away." And that's the sort of ballplayer Barney is. From a distance he's got impressive-looking batting averages for a middle infielder, but up close his lack of secondary offensive skills means that he profiles as a bench player or utility guy, not a starter for a contender. His reputation as a defender is sterling but overstated: He looks flashy, but when you look at how many plays he actually makes, he's very good, but not superlative.

Brian Bogusevic OF
Born: 2/18/1984 Age: 29
Bats: L Throws: L Height: 6' 4"
Weight: 220 Breakout: 4%
Improve: 29% Collapse: 6%
Attrition: 19% MLB: 81%
Comparables:
Abraham Nunez, Mike Vento, Pat Kelly

YEAR	TEAM	LVL	AGE	PA	R	2B	3B	HR	RBI	BB	SO	SB	CS	AVG_OBP_SLG	TAv	BABIP	BRR	FRAA	WARP
2010	ROU	AAA	26	575	91	26	2	13	57	67	108	23	1	.277/.365/.414	.275	.330	5.7	LF(51): 0.6, 1B(32): -4.1	2.8
2010	HOU	MLB	26	31	5	3	0	0	3	3	12	1	1	.179/.258/.286	.172	.312	0.6	LF(7): 0.5, CF(3): -0.1	-0.1
2011	OKL	AAA	27	254	27	11	5	3	35	30	49	20	3	.261/.362/.399	.272	.323	0	--	0.0
2011	HOU	MLB	27	182	22	14	1	4	15	15	40	4	2	.287/.348/.457	.259	.355	-0.5	RF(40): 0.7, LF(13): 0.4	0.3
2012	HOU	MLB	28	404	39	9	2	7	28	41	96	15	4	.203/.297/.299	.229	.257	1	RF(104): 1.0, CF(20): -0.5	-0.7
2013	*CHN*	*MLB*	*29*	*335*	*36*	*14*	*1*	*7*	*33*	*33*	*78*	*10*	*2*	*.230/.312/.354*	*.243*	*.287*	*0.8*	*RF 0, CF -0*	*0.3*

Bogusevic's fourth season of full-time position-player duty was a clunker, but he still delivered some value via his walk rate, baserunning, and decent fielding, the last aided by his ex-pitcher's arm. A first-round pick by the Astros out of Tulane in 2005, Bogusevic made it to Double-A as a pitcher before switching to the outfield in 2008, when he was 24. For context, Rick Ankiel, that crazy long-shot story, transitioned to the outfield at 25. Bogusevic's late start on learning to hit means he's aged out of his chance to be a starter in the major leagues, but he has enough tools to bounce around as a reserve—either on a bench or in Triple-A—for a few years.

Tony Campana OF
Born: 5/30/1986 Age: 27
Bats: L Throws: L Height: 5' 9"
Weight: 165 Breakout: 1%
Improve: 38% Collapse: 3%
Attrition: 8% MLB: 90%
Comparables:
Alex Sanchez, Nook Logan, Willy Taveras

YEAR	TEAM	LVL	AGE	PA	R	2B	3B	HR	RBI	BB	SO	SB	CS	AVG_OBP_SLG	TAv	BABIP	BRR	FRAA	WARP
2010	TEN	AA	24	550	76	22	5	0	39	44	82	48	20	.319/.375/.384	.272	.376	1.2	CF(119): -1.4, LF(14): -0.4	2.6
2011	IOW	AAA	25	129	27	8	2	0	9	6	23	8	1	.342/.383/.442	.312	.423	0.3	CF(6): -0.2, LF(1): -0.0	0.2
2011	CHN	MLB	25	155	24	3	0	1	6	8	30	24	2	.259/.303/.301	.218	.321	4.2	LF(34): 0.1, CF(29): -0.6	0.1
2012	IOW	AAA	26	165	24	2	1	1	4	12	34	18	7	.280/.338/.329	.233	.358	2.8	CF(26): -1.1, LF(3): 0.4	-0.1
2012	CHN	MLB	26	192	26	6	0	0	5	11	43	30	3	.264/.308/.299	.227	.351	3.9	CF(54): -1.6, LF(11): -0.1	-0.1
2013	*CHN*	*MLB*	*27*	*250*	*34*	*9*	*1*	*2*	*16*	*15*	*51*	*24*	*5*	*.257/.305/.332*	*.228*	*.312*	*2.6*	*CF -2, LF -0*	*0.0*

For many years, Cubs fans have not understood what a fast baseball player looks like. This is an unfortunate consequence of the team's quixotic drive to build a low-OBP slugging offense out of free agency, but it's meant that fans have mislabeled a rather motley assortment of players—from Ryan Theriot to Starlin Castro to the dried-up husk calling itself Alfonso Soriano—as speedy. So Cubs fans have a somewhat irrational devotion to Campana on account of his actually being fast, although the idea that his speed can be compared to phenom speedster Billy Hamilton is one that should only occur after about three too many Old Styles. The trouble with Campana is that he hits for the emptiest .260 batting average in creation, which means that no matter how fast he can run, he's nothing like an asset.

Jeimer Candelario 3B
Born: 11/24/1993 Age: 19
Bats: B Throws: R Height: 6' 2"
Weight: 180 Breakout: 0%
Improve: 16% Collapse: 84%
Attrition: 84% MLB: 100%
Comparables:
Ed Kranepool, Robin Yount, Wayne Causey

YEAR	TEAM	LVL	AGE	PA	R	2B	3B	HR	RBI	BB	SO	SB	CS	AVG_OBP_SLG	TAv	BABIP	BRR	FRAA	WARP
2011	DB2	Rk	17	305	50	16	2	5	53	50	42	4	4	.337/.443/.478	.331	.382	0	--	0.0
2012	BOI	A-	18	310	34	14	0	6	47	26	55	2	1	.281/.345/.396	.278	.327	0.7	3B(54): 1.9, 1B(2): -0.0	1.8
2013	*CHN*	*MLB*	*19*	*250*	*20*	*9*	*1*	*5*	*24*	*13*	*66*	*0*	*0*	*.205/.245/.309*	*.199*	*.261*	*-0.3*	*3B 2, 1B -0*	*-0.9*

A solid year in Boise has kept Candelario's stock as a well-regarded prospect intact. It was the first time Candelario played in the U.S. after an impressive showing in the Dominican Summer League, and the Cubs showed a lot of faith by putting him in the Northwest League, dominated by older college players. He didn't disappoint, hitting better than the league average and demonstrating encouraging signs of power. The big worry about Candelario is that he may be destined to play first base, but even there he might have the bat to make it. He's years away from that, though.

Adrian Cardenas 2B
Born: 10/10/1987 Age: 25
Bats: L Throws: R Height: 6' 1"
Weight: 205 Breakout: 2%
Improve: 44% Collapse: 12%
Attrition: 15% MLB: 94%
Comparables:
Ronnie Belliard, Jerry Hairston, Ken Boswell

YEAR	TEAM	LVL	AGE	PA	R	2B	3B	HR	RBI	BB	SO	SB	CS	AVG_OBP_SLG	TAv	BABIP	BRR	FRAA	WARP
2010	MID	AA	22	236	36	15	0	3	32	33	23	4	6	.345/.448/.469	.334	.381	-2.3	3B(26): -4.6, 2B(16): 1.2	1.9
2010	SAC	AAA	22	231	30	8	1	1	21	17	28	2	2	.267/.317/.329	.234	.299	-0.4	2B(39): -1.7, 3B(19): -1.7	-0.4
2011	SAC	AAA	23	545	70	28	4	5	51	47	56	13	6	.314/.374/.418	.282	.344	0	--	0.0
2012	IOW	AAA	24	282	30	22	4	3	32	33	32	5	0	.300/.381/.461	.290	.330	1.6	2B(30): -3.2, 3B(7): -0.4	0.7
2012	CHN	MLB	24	67	5	6	0	0	2	7	13	0	0	.183/.269/.283	.206	.234	0	2B(12): -0.5, LF(3): -0.1	-0.3
2013	*CHN*	*MLB*	*25*	*250*	*24*	*13*	*1*	*3*	*24*	*23*	*38*	*2*	*1*	*.253/.325/.367*	*.248*	*.288*	*-0.3*	*2B -1, 3B -0*	*0.3*

Cardenas had a top-prospect label on him at one point, and he was the prize for the A's in the deal that sent Joe Blanton to Philadelphia. Fast-forward a few years, and Cardenas was waived by Oakland and picked up by a Cubs team that was going nowhere. He hit well in Triple-A for Iowa in his third season at the level, but wasn't able to deliver on that during his brief stint in the majors. The Cubs don't have a lot of players much better than Cardenas capable of playing both second and third, but they probably have plenty who are better at one or the other, so it'll be hard for him to find playing time. He still has a shot as a utility player.

Welington Castillo C

Born: **4/24/1987** Age: **26**
Bats: **R** Throws: **R** Height: **5' 11"**
Weight: **210** Breakout: **3%**
Improve: **45%** Collapse: **5%**
Attrition: **14%** MLB: **91%**

Comparables:
Geovany Soto,Johnny Bench,Johnny Romano

YEAR	TEAM	LVL	AGE	PA	R	2B	3B	HR	RBI	BB	SO	SB	CS	AVG_OBP_SLG	TAv	BABIP	BRR	FRAA	WARP
2010	IOW	AAA	23	272	35	17	1	13	59	19	58	0	2	.255/.325/.498	.262	.284	-1.2	C(68): -1.3	1.0
2010	CHN	MLB	23	21	3	4	0	1	5	1	7	0	0	.300/.333/.650	.339	.417	-0.2	C(5): 0.1	0.3
2011	IOW	AAA	24	251	38	9	0	15	35	20	57	0	0	.286/.351/.524	.369	.321	-0.9	C(18): -0.4	1.0
2011	CHN	MLB	24	13	0	0	0	0	0	0	4	0	0	.154/.154/.154	.128	.222	-0.2	C(4): -0.1	-0.1
2012	IOW	AAA	25	176	22	6	0	6	22	23	37	0	0	.260/.375/.425	.270	.305	0.2	C(24): -0.4	0.4
2012	CHN	MLB	25	190	16	11	0	5	22	17	51	0	0	.265/.337/.418	.266	.348	-0.6	C(49): -1.4, 1B(1): -0.0	0.5
2013	*CHN*	*MLB*	*26*	*250*	*28*	*12*	*1*	*10*	*34*	*21*	*64*	*0*	*0*	*.244/.316/.432*	*.264*	*.295*	*-0.5*	*C -0, 1B -0*	*1.2*

"Beef" was once the heir apparent to Geovany Soto, whom the Cubs dealt to the Rangers at the trading deadline last year. Castillo kept up his end of the bargain, hitting well for his position in Triple-A and the majors. He faces competition from Steve Clevenger, a converted infielder whose offense has been disappointing even for the position, but who managed to beat out Castillo for playing time in 2012 by virtue of being a left-handed hitter. Castillo has a strong arm but otherwise has a defensive reputation that is mixed at best.

Starlin Castro SS

Born: **3/24/1990** Age: **23**
Bats: **R** Throws: **R** Height: **6' 1"**
Weight: **190** Breakout: **4%**
Improve: **48%** Collapse: **6%**
Attrition: **12%** MLB: **96%**

Comparables:
Jose Reyes,Barry Larkin,Wil Cordero

YEAR	TEAM	LVL	AGE	PA	R	2B	3B	HR	RBI	BB	SO	SB	CS	AVG_OBP_SLG	TAv	BABIP	BRR	FRAA	WARP
2010	TEN	AA	20	121	20	8	5	1	20	9	11	4	5	.376/.429/.569	.330	.412	-0.7	SS(26): -0.8	1.0
2010	CHN	MLB	20	506	53	31	5	3	41	29	71	10	8	.300/.347/.408	.258	.346	0.6	SS(122): -2.0	1.6
2011	CHN	MLB	21	715	91	36	9	10	66	35	96	22	9	.307/.341/.432	.270	.344	0.3	SS(158): 2.8	3.3
2012	CHN	MLB	22	691	78	29	12	14	78	36	100	25	13	.283/.323/.430	.265	.315	1.2	SS(162): -0.5	3.0
2013	*CHN*	*MLB*	*23*	*654*	*82*	*33*	*8*	*12*	*62*	*34*	*91*	*19*	*10*	*.289/.329/.427*	*.268*	*.321*	*0.2*	*SS 0*	*3.6*

It's easy to forget how young Castro is—he's been in the majors for three seasons now, but is still about five years from his expected peak as a hitter. He has an unearned reputation as a poor defensive player at shortstop because of errors, but looking at the number of plays he makes would suggest he's a roughly average fielder at one of the most demanding positions on the field. The Cubs have him signed through 2019 on a deal that could end up being a bargain for the team, something that's hard to say about a seven-year deal. As the Cubs rebuild, he's one of the guys they want to build around.

Steve Clevenger C

Born: **4/5/1986** Age: **27**
Bats: **L** Throws: **R** Height: **6' 1"**
Weight: **195** Breakout: **1%**
Improve: **41%** Collapse: **10%**
Attrition: **17%** MLB: **97%**

Comparables:
Milt May,Rick Cerone,Darrin Fletcher

YEAR	TEAM	LVL	AGE	PA	R	2B	3B	HR	RBI	BB	SO	SB	CS	AVG_OBP_SLG	TAv	BABIP	BRR	FRAA	WARP
2010	TEN	AA	24	294	37	24	0	5	47	20	28	0	6	.317/.369/.461	.272	.340	-2.2	C(68): -1.4, 3B(1): 0.0	1.3
2011	TEN	AA	25	351	42	27	3	5	39	35	39	1	0	.295/.363/.449	.232	.321	-1.5	C(29): -0.1, 1B(2): -0.2	-0.4
2011	IOW	AAA	25	97	9	3	1	3	15	9	7	1	0	.407/.454/.570	.319	.410	0.2	C(11): 0.0	0.5
2011	CHN	MLB	25	5	1	1	0	0	0	0	0	0	0	.250/.400/.500	.352	.250	0.3	C(2): -0.0	0.1
2012	CHN	MLB	26	215	16	12	0	1	16	16	39	0	1	.201/.260/.276	.179	.245	-1.7	C(51): -0.0, 1B(9): 0.2	-1.3
2013	*CHN*	*MLB*	*27*	*250*	*22*	*13*	*1*	*4*	*25*	*17*	*40*	*1*	*1*	*.241/.295/.355*	*.231*	*.273*	*-0.6*	*C -0, 1B -0*	*0.2*

Clevenger was drafted as a shortstop and started off as a second baseman in the Cubs' system before a manager convinced him that he had a better chance of making it to the majors if he donned the tools of ignorance. It seems to have worked, as Clevenger got a five-plate-appearance cup of coffee in 2011 and spent almost all of 2012 with the big club. With Soto shipped off to the Rangers, Clevenger figures to spend 2013 in Chicago too, battling Castillo for playing time behind the dish.

David DeJesus RF

Born: **12/20/1979** Age: **33**
Bats: **L** Throws: **L** Height: **6' 0"**
Weight: **190** Breakout: **1%**
Improve: **31%** Collapse: **6%**
Attrition: **8%** MLB: **91%**

Comparables:
Joe Inglett,Willie Harris,Bobby Murcer

YEAR	TEAM	LVL	AGE	PA	R	2B	3B	HR	RBI	BB	SO	SB	CS	AVG_OBP_SLG	TAv	BABIP	BRR	FRAA	WARP
2010	KCA	MLB	30	394	46	23	3	5	37	34	47	3	3	.318/.384/.443	.288	.355	-1.6	RF(70): -1.0, CF(19): 0.2	1.7
2011	OAK	MLB	31	506	60	20	5	10	46	45	86	4	3	.240/.323/.376	.265	.274	1.5	RF(116): 7.3, CF(8): -1.0	1.5
2012	CHN	MLB	32	582	76	28	8	9	50	61	89	7	8	.263/.350/.403	.273	.301	3	RF(99): -2.9, CF(50): -1.0	1.0
2013	*CHN*	*MLB*	*33*	*532*	*65*	*24*	*5*	*11*	*52*	*47*	*81*	*6*	*5*	*.265/.339/.406*	*.265*	*.296*	*-1*	*RF 1, CF 0*	*1.6*

After the Cubs traded Sammy Sosa, right field turned into a parade of mediocrities at Wrigley Field, featuring cringe-inducing flirtations with Jeromy Burnitz, Jacque Jones, the corpse of

Cliff Floyd, and even a brief stint by an inanimate carbon rod named Jake Fox. Oddly, both for the position and the exceedingly hacktastic Cubs, they eventually settled upon using the position as a source of mostly reliable on-base percentage without much pop, first from Kosuke Fukudome and now from DeJesus. The current resident has a very reasonable contract with only one year remaining, plus a favorable club option, so his biggest value to the Cubs may be as trade bait.

Marco Hernandez SS
Born: 9/6/1992 Age: 20
Bats: L Throws: R Height: 6' 1"
Weight: 170 Breakout: 16%
Improve: 40% Collapse: 10%
Attrition: 21% MLB: 84%

Comparables:
Jose Oquendo, Ted Kazanski, Robin Yount

YEAR	TEAM	LVL	AGE	PA	R	2B	3B	HR	RBI	BB	SO	SB	CS	AVG_OBP_SLG	TAv	BABIP	BRR	FRAA	WARP
2011	CUB	Rk	18	233	39	16	5	2	42	16	29	9	7	.333/.375/.486	.302	.370	-2	SS(29): -1.1, 2B(12): -1.1	1.2
2012	PEO	A	19	171	18	2	3	2	12	9	40	2	1	.210/.249/.299	.218	.263	-0.8	SS(25): 4.8	0.0
2012	BOI	A-	19	283	39	12	4	5	38	10	36	8	3	.286/.310/.416	.263	.313	-1.3	SS(58): -4.2	0.4
2013	*CHN*	*MLB*	*20*	*250*	*22*	*8*	*2*	*4*	*19*	*6*	*62*	*2*	*1*	*.203/.224/.301*	*.188*	*.252*	*0*	*SS 2, 2B -0*	*-0.6*

Hernandez looks at first glance like the archetypal useful glove-first shortstop, but he might be a little more than that. The first question, though, is whether he'll be able to put everything together to reach even that modest potential. He doesn't have the frame to hit for serious power, but he isn't destined to be some slap-hitting groundball machine either. He has a line-drive swing that could give him a decent average and modest doubles power, and given his fielding potential, that may be all he needs. He's rangy and has a strong arm, but he'll need to cut down on his errors to be the player he can be.

Brett Jackson CF
Born: 8/2/1988 Age: 24
Bats: L Throws: R Height: 6' 3"
Weight: 210 Breakout: 4%
Improve: 53% Collapse: 5%
Attrition: 10% MLB: 88%

Comparables:
Jimmy Wynn, Joe Benson, Rick Monday

YEAR	TEAM	LVL	AGE	PA	R	2B	3B	HR	RBI	BB	SO	SB	CS	AVG_OBP_SLG	TAv	BABIP	BRR	FRAA	WARP
2010	DAY	A+	21	312	56	19	8	6	38	43	63	12	7	.316/.421/.517	.331	.397	3.9	CF(62): 4.4	4.1
2010	TEN	AA	21	268	47	13	6	6	28	30	63	18	4	.276/.366/.465	.281	.352	2	RF(25): -2.7, CF(20): 1.1	1.0
2011	TEN	AA	22	297	45	10	3	10	32	45	74	15	6	.256/.373/.443	.216	.323	0.6	CF(19): -2.2, RF(4): -0.4	-0.6
2011	IOW	AAA	22	215	39	13	2	10	26	28	64	6	1	.297/.388/.551	.257	.402	1.2	CF(23): 0.7	0.3
2012	IOW	AAA	23	467	66	22	12	15	47	47	158	27	5	.256/.338/.479	.279	.372	-0.2	CF(51): -4.0, RF(8): 0.5	0.4
2012	CHN	MLB	23	142	14	6	1	4	9	22	59	0	3	.175/.303/.342	.240	.298	-1.3	CF(39): 0.9	0.0
2013	*CHN*	*MLB*	*24*	*250*	*34*	*9*	*3*	*7*	*24*	*26*	*81*	*10*	*3*	*.212/.301/.376*	*.243*	*.297*	*1.2*	*CF -1, RF -0*	*0.3*

There are a lot of things to like about Jackson, and one to really hate. He's able to take walks, hit for power, and with a solid line-drive swing he's able to do very well with balls hit into play. The problem is that he strikes out like he's trying to pick up women at a convent. Jackson absolutely needs to cut down on the strikeouts in order to hit for average, because it's not like there's a heck of a lot of room for his BABIP to grow. While there are worries that he may have to move to an outfield corner eventually, so far the Cubs have mainly stuck with him in center field. That lowers the level of offense he needs to be a valuable contributor, but not by so much that he can keep swinging and missing at his current pace.

Junior Lake SS
Born: 3/27/1990 Age: 23
Bats: R Throws: R Height: 6' 4"
Weight: 215 Breakout: 6%
Improve: 49% Collapse: 8%
Attrition: 11% MLB: 96%

Comparables:
Felix Mantilla, Derek Jeter, Jim Fregosi

YEAR	TEAM	LVL	AGE	PA	R	2B	3B	HR	RBI	BB	SO	SB	CS	AVG_OBP_SLG	TAv	BABIP	BRR	FRAA	WARP
2010	DAY	A+	20	447	56	18	4	9	46	35	99	13	9	.264/.329/.398	.268	.323	-1.6	SS(106): 8.3, 3B(12): 0.0	2.8
2011	DAY	A+	21	216	39	11	4	6	34	6	49	19	4	.315/.336/.498	.280	.384	0	--	0.0
2011	TEN	AA	21	262	41	10	2	6	17	13	60	19	2	.248/.300/.380	.192	.307	2.1	SS(33): 3.5	0.1
2012	TEN	AA	22	448	56	26	3	10	50	35	105	21	12	.279/.341/.432	.297	.353	-0.4	SS(57): 3.8, 3B(19): 1.2	2.6
2013	*CHN*	*MLB*	*23*	*250*	*28*	*10*	*1*	*5*	*23*	*14*	*68*	*9*	*3*	*.228/.277/.355*	*.227*	*.293*	*0.5*	*SS 2, 3B 0*	*0.5*

There's no truth to the rumor that Kevin Goldstein left Baseball Prospectus for a major-league job just to keep people from asking him about Lake. And by "no truth" we mean "some truth"—some Cubs fans are excited about Lake well out of proportion to his abilities. He has a lot of tools. The question is whether he can deploy them in the majors. His offense took great steps forward at Double-A in 2012, but he still has problems with strikeouts, and his bat isn't ready for the majors. Whether Lake can stick at shortstop is an important question that remains to be answered.

Joe Mather 4C

Born: **7/23/1982** Age: **30**
Bats: **R** Throws: **R** Height: **6' 5"**
Weight: **215** Breakout: **1%**
Improve: **37%** Collapse: **5%**
Attrition: **6%** MLB: **96%**

Comparables:
Gus Bell,Lee Maye,Dave May

YEAR	TEAM	LVL	AGE	PA	R	2B	3B	HR	RBI	BB	SO	SB	CS	AVG_OBP_SLG	TAv	BABIP	BRR	FRAA	WARP
2010	MEM	AAA	27	376	55	18	4	10	46	37	74	6	4	.275/.350/.442	.272	.327	-0.7	RF(89): -2.3, CF(10): -0.7	1.1
2010	SLN	MLB	27	64	7	4	0	0	3	2	11	1	1	.217/.242/.283	.176	.265	-0.1	CF(14): -0.8, RF(7): -0.1	-0.7
2011	CSP	AAA	28	234	36	14	1	6	31	18	39	3	0	.321/.363/.483	.286	.357	2.5	RF(21): 1.7, CF(8): -0.1	1.0
2011	GWN	AAA	28	70	13	5	0	1	4	8	14	2	1	.258/.343/.387	.260	.319	0	--	0.0
2011	ATL	MLB	28	83	4	4	0	1	9	6	23	0	1	.213/.272/.307	.216	.294	-0.7	RF(21): -1.1, LF(4): -0.0	-0.4
2012	CHN	MLB	29	243	18	11	0	5	19	14	46	5	2	.209/.256/.324	.208	.239	0.8	CF(28): 1.5, LF(25): 0.4	-0.9
2013	*CHN*	*MLB*	*30*	*250*	*27*	*11*	*1*	*8*	*29*	*19*	*53*	*4*	*2*	*.230/.293/.392*	*.242*	*.263*	*-0.1*	*RF -0, CF -0*	*0.1*

Mather is the sort of player every team has, many need to use at some point, and only the desperate rely upon heavily. Which is of course why he played 103 games for the Cubs in 2012. He's primarily a corner outfielder (whom the Cubs inexplicably deployed at third base and center field) who can't hit his way out of the paper bags of the Pacific Coast League, much less the ones in the majors. And he was too old for prospect status several years, not to mention teams, ago.

Dioner Navarro C

Born: **2/9/1984** Age: **29**
Bats: **B** Throws: **R** Height: **5' 10"**
Weight: **205** Breakout: **0%**
Improve: **39%** Collapse: **10%**
Attrition: **19%** MLB: **94%**

Comparables:
Ken Retzer,Jason Phillips,Lenny Webster

YEAR	TEAM	LVL	AGE	PA	R	2B	3B	HR	RBI	BB	SO	SB	CS	AVG_OBP_SLG	TAv	BABIP	BRR	FRAA	WARP
2010	DUR	AAA	26	169	19	9	0	2	21	23	25	3	0	.284/.389/.390	.290	.330	0.6	C(35): -0.0	1.5
2010	TBA	MLB	26	142	11	5	0	1	7	12	20	0	1	.194/.270/.258	.201	.223	-4.9	C(46): 0.7	-0.6
2011	LAN	MLB	27	202	13	6	1	5	17	20	35	0	0	.193/.276/.324	.228	.210	-1.5	C(54): 0.1	-0.2
2012	LOU	AAA	28	240	24	12	0	5	32	23	24	0	0	.319/.382/.449	.296	.332	-3.5	C(44): -0.4	1.4
2012	CIN	MLB	28	73	6	3	1	2	12	2	12	0	0	.290/.306/.449	.255	.321	0.9	C(21): -0.2	0.4
2013	*CHN*	*MLB*	*29*	*250*	*25*	*11*	*1*	*5*	*25*	*19*	*34*	*1*	*0*	*.248/.311/.374*	*.245*	*.266*	*-0.4*	*C -1*	*0.6*

Navarro was once a top prospect, but his star faded along the way and he turned into a journeyman. He has problems hitting for average, and even when he does he lacks enough pop or plate discipline to leverage it into a good batting line. He had a good defensive reputation early in his career, but not anymore. The Dodgers ended his second go-round with the team in 2011 for concerns about his work ethic, including a lack of perceived effort on blocking balls in the dirt. With Castillo in the fold, the Cubs can relegate Navarro to a backup role that hides most of those deficiencies.

Anthony Rizzo 1B

Born: **8/8/1989** Age: **23**
Bats: **L** Throws: **L** Height: **6' 4"**
Weight: **220** Breakout: **3%**
Improve: **62%** Collapse: **3%**
Attrition: **6%** MLB: **94%**

Comparables:
Willie McCovey,Prince Fielder,Eddie Murray

YEAR	TEAM	LVL	AGE	PA	R	2B	3B	HR	RBI	BB	SO	SB	CS	AVG_OBP_SLG	TAv	BABIP	BRR	FRAA	WARP
2010	SLM	A+	20	135	26	12	0	5	20	16	32	3	0	.248/.338/.479	.279	.300	1.7	1B(24): -0.3	0.7
2010	PME	AA	20	467	66	30	0	20	80	45	100	7	1	.263/.338/.481	.284	.303	-3	1B(107): 8.1	2.4
2011	TUC	AAA	21	413	64	34	1	26	101	43	89	7	6	.331/.404/.652	.361	.369	0.1	1B(56): 3.2	3.6
2011	SDN	MLB	21	153	9	8	1	1	9	21	46	2	1	.141/.281/.242	.219	.210	-2.3	1B(45): -2.3	-1.2
2012	IOW	AAA	22	284	48	18	2	23	62	23	52	2	2	.342/.405/.696	.339	.357	-3.4	1B(42): 7.9	2.0
2012	CHN	MLB	22	368	44	15	0	15	48	27	62	3	2	.285/.342/.463	.283	.310	-0.3	1B(85): -0.7	1.1
2013	*CHN*	*MLB*	*23*	*375*	*47*	*19*	*1*	*17*	*54*	*31*	*85*	*4*	*2*	*.257/.324/.470*	*.280*	*.292*	*-0.5*	*1B -5*	*0.5*

Many Cubs fans were hoping to see the team open up its pocketbook last offseason and sign one of the two available division rivals, Albert Pujols or Prince Fielder, to play first base. Instead, the Cubs got their first baseman by trading Andrew Cashner to the Padres for Rizzo after the latter's disappointing major-league debut in San Diego. Rizzo demolished Triple-A and held his own in his second stint in the majors. Given his youth and the dearth of outstanding National League first basemen not named Votto, Rizzo could be an All-Star for years. He probably won't hit for the kind of average he did in 2012, but he should hit for more power to make up the difference.

Dave Sappelt OF

Born: **1/2/1987** Age: **26**
Bats: **R** Throws: **R** Height: **5' 10"**
Weight: **195** Breakout: **5%**
Improve: **43%** Collapse: **8%**
Attrition: **12%** MLB: **90%**

Comparables:
Magglio Ordonez,Walt Williams,Alex Ochoa

YEAR	TEAM	LVL	AGE	PA	R	2B	3B	HR	RBI	BB	SO	SB	CS	AVG_OBP_SLG	TAv	BABIP	BRR	FRAA	WARP
2010	LYN	A+	23	77	7	5	0	0	4	5	15	6	4	.282/.338/.352	.261	.357	-0.4	CF(19): -0.4	0.2
2010	CAR	AA	23	372	53	19	8	9	62	31	46	15	13	.361/.416/.548	.343	.394	-3.6	CF(78): 6.4, LF(9): -0.0	4.7
2010	LOU	AAA	23	115	12	8	3	1	8	6	13	4	1	.324/.365/.481	.261	.362	-1.9	CF(30): 1.7	0.3
2011	LOU	AAA	24	336	40	16	3	7	29	30	39	4	4	.313/.377/.458	.264	.339	-2.1	CF(35): -1.3, LF(9): 0.4	-0.1
2011	CIN	MLB	24	118	14	8	0	0	5	7	17	1	1	.243/.289/.318	.224	.289	0.5	LF(31): 1.5, CF(4): 0.1	-0.2
2012	IOW	AAA	25	550	50	26	4	7	54	36	73	15	6	.266/.314/.376	.242	.296	1.6	RF(50): -1.9, CF(21): -0.7	-0.3
2012	CHN	MLB	25	78	8	6	0	2	8	7	9	0	0	.275/.351/.449	.270	.293	0.3	RF(20): 0.9, LF(3): -0.0	0.4
2013	*CHN*	*MLB*	*26*	*250*	*29*	*12*	*2*	*4*	*22*	*15*	*40*	*5*	*3*	*.261/.309/.384*	*.248*	*.294*	*-0.1*	*RF 0, CF -1*	*0.2*

The Cubs picked up Sappelt as a spare piece when they dealt Sean Marshall to the Reds for Travis Wood, but he's a useful one in a limited role. His bat is credible enough to make him a fourth outfielder, given that he can play a decent center field. With the crowded outfield situation in Chicago, though, he may have to bide his time waiting for a chance even to do that.

Nate Schierholtz RF

Born: **2/15/1984** Age: **29**
Bats: **L** Throws: **R** Height: **6' 2"**
Weight: **205** Breakout: **3%**
Improve: **56%** Collapse: **2%**
Attrition: **6%** MLB: **93%**

Comparables:
Magglio Ordonez,Alex Rios,Kevin Mench

YEAR	TEAM	LVL	AGE	PA	R	2B	3B	HR	RBI	BB	SO	SB	CS	AVG_OBP_SLG	TAv	BABIP	BRR	FRAA	WARP
2010	SFN	MLB	26	252	34	13	3	3	17	20	38	4	5	.242/.311/.366	.246	.278	1.1	RF(109): 1.5	0.5
2011	SFN	MLB	27	362	42	22	1	9	41	21	61	7	4	.278/.326/.430	.284	.315	1.5	RF(96): -1.3, LF(8): 0.4	1.4
2012	PHI	MLB	28	73	5	4	0	1	5	5	10	0	0	.273/.319/.379	.260	.304	-0.1	RF(27): -0.7, CF(7): -0.2	0.0
2012	SFN	MLB	28	196	15	4	5	5	16	18	36	3	2	.251/.321/.417	.282	.287	-1.5	RF(52): -0.7	0.3
2013	*CHN*	*MLB*	*29*	*274*	*30*	*14*	*2*	*7*	*33*	*18*	*45*	*4*	*2*	*.264/.317/.429*	*.263*	*.293*	*-0.2*	*RF 0, LF 0*	*0.7*

Schierholtz signed on as another veteran presence for the young Cubs. He has enjoyed short bursts of success as a part-time player for the Giants over the past two seasons, interspersed with periods of extravagant offensive struggle, including the brief interregnum last year between his inclusion in the deadline-day Hunter Pence trade to the Phillies and his season-ending fractured toe. It's clear Schierholtz is never going to deliver on the promise of his two 900-plus OPS seasons in Triple-A back in 2007-08. A fast runner who isn't a good baserunner, a mediocre fielder with a good arm, Schierholtz is a place-holder for a rebuilding team.

Jorge Soler RF

Born: **2/25/1992** Age: **21**
Bats: **R** Throws: **R** Height: **6' 4"**
Weight: **205** Breakout: **3%**
Improve: **53%** Collapse: **11%**
Attrition: **15%** MLB: **96%**

Comparables:
Roberto Clemente,Ron Fairly,Ed Kirkpatrick

YEAR	TEAM	LVL	AGE	PA	R	2B	3B	HR	RBI	BB	SO	SB	CS	AVG_OBP_SLG	TAv	BABIP	BRR	FRAA	WARP
2012	CUB	Rk	20	61	14	2	0	2	10	6	13	8	0	.241/.328/.389	.252	.282	0	--	0.0
2012	PEO	A	20	88	14	5	0	3	15	6	6	4	1	.338/.398/.512	.295	.338	0.2	RF(7): -0.1	0.1
2013	*CHN*	*MLB*	*21*	*250*	*27*	*10*	*1*	*5*	*24*	*14*	*53*	*11*	*2*	*.229/.279/.344*	*.225*	*.272*	*1.3*	*RF 0*	*-0.2*

The Cubs have committed to a long-term rebuilding effort by developing young talent, so it's not surprising they were the team that raced to sign a promising amateur from overseas right before MLB instituted draconian new rules on international spending. Pay more attention to the nine years the Cubs gave him than the $30 million. Soler's numbers at Peoria were very encouraging, but he's still young and raw. His tools are exciting, and if he puts it all together he should be a fun player to watch. That's an if, though, and one Cubs fans shouldn't expect a ready answer to. There's almost no chance Soler sees Chicago any time in 2013 outside of the "Road to Wrigley" minor-league game.

Alfonso Soriano LF

Born: **1/7/1976** Age: **37**
Bats: **R** Throws: **R** Height: **6' 2"**
Weight: **195** Breakout: **2%**
Improve: **23%** Collapse: **9%**
Attrition: **18%** MLB: **77%**

Comparables:
Champ Summers,George Foster,John Lowenstein

YEAR	TEAM	LVL	AGE	PA	R	2B	3B	HR	RBI	BB	SO	SB	CS	AVG_OBP_SLG	TAv	BABIP	BRR	FRAA	WARP
2010	CHN	MLB	34	548	67	40	3	24	79	45	123	5	1	.258/.322/.496	.284	.295	2	LF(134): -6.4	1.9
2011	CHN	MLB	35	508	50	27	1	26	88	27	113	2	1	.244/.289/.469	.258	.266	0.8	LF(128): -8.0	-0.2
2012	CHN	MLB	36	615	68	33	2	32	108	44	153	6	2	.262/.322/.499	.278	.303	-3	LF(145): 7.9	2.4
2013	*CHN*	*MLB*	*37*	*558*	*67*	*28*	*1*	*26*	*79*	*39*	*133*	*6*	*2*	*.240/.297/.449*	*.261*	*.273*	*-0.2*	*LF -2*	*1.1*

Soriano has had two really bad years in Chicago, three pretty good years and exactly one year when it might have seemed like he was actually worth the ridiculous amount of money the Cubs are paying him. Given the amount he still has coming—$18 million this year and the same in 2014—and his disappointing production, it's surprising that the real impediment to trading him so far hasn't been a lack of interested teams but Soriano's refusal to waive his no-trade clause. Odds are he'll be good enough not to be a boat anchor for a Cubs team that isn't going anywhere anyway, but it's hard to see that through the haze of dollar signs.

Ian Stewart 3B

Born: **4/5/1985** Age: **28**
Bats: **L** Throws: **R** Height: **6' 4"**
Weight: **215** Breakout: **4%**
Improve: **38%** Collapse: **1%**
Attrition: **7%** MLB: **73%**

Comparables:
Wilson Betemit,Howard Johnson,Jeff Larish

YEAR	TEAM	LVL	AGE	PA	R	2B	3B	HR	RBI	BB	SO	SB	CS	AVG_OBP_SLG	TAv	BABIP	BRR	FRAA	WARP
2010	COL	MLB	25	441	54	14	2	18	61	45	110	5	2	.256/.338/.443	.268	.308	1.4	3B(115): 3.2	2.8
2011	CSP	AAA	26	195	29	10	1	14	42	22	51	1	0	.275/.359/.591	.282	.308	-0.1	3B(28): -2.3	0.4
2011	COL	MLB	26	136	14	6	1	0	6	14	37	3	2	.156/.243/.221	.169	.224	-0.4	3B(42): -0.7	-1.0
2012	CHN	MLB	27	202	16	5	2	5	17	21	46	0	3	.201/.292/.335	.221	.242	-0.5	3B(52): -2.5	-0.7
2013	*CHN*	*MLB*	*28*	*250*	*30*	*9*	*1*	*10*	*33*	*26*	*68*	*3*	*2*	*.223/.312/.417*	*.258*	*.272*	*-0.3*	*3B 1*	*0.6*

The Cubs picked up Stewart hoping he could get over the wrist troubles that led to a miserable 2011. The idea was for him to do that on the field, though, not under a surgeon's knife. During the All-Star break, doctors removed a piece of bone in Stewart's wrist that they believed was causing him nerve problems, an injury that had gone unnoticed during several previous MRIs. An optimistic view is that with the bone removed and his wrist healed Stewart is ready for the comeback campaign that didn't happen in 2012. The Cubs were willing to bet $2 million on that proposition. That, plus another $500,000 in incentives, is what they signed Stewart for after non-tendering him.

Matthew Szczur OF

Born: **7/20/1989** Age: **23**
Bats: **R** Throws: **R** Height: **6' 2"**
Weight: **195** Breakout: **2%**
Improve: **44%** Collapse: **7%**
Attrition: **10%** MLB: **95%**

Comparables:
Darin Erstad,Coco Crisp,Luis Melendez

YEAR	TEAM	LVL	AGE	PA	R	2B	3B	HR	RBI	BB	SO	SB	CS	AVG_OBP_SLG	TAv	BABIP	BRR	FRAA	WARP
2010	BOI	A-	20	82	17	9	0	0	8	6	11	1	0	.397/.450/.521	.321	.468	-1.9	CF(5): -0.0, LF(4): -0.5	0.5
2011	PEO	A	21	298	55	15	1	5	27	21	28	17	5	.314/.366/.431	.295	.335	0.1	CF(19): 2.7, RF(4): -0.7	0.9
2011	DAY	A+	21	182	20	7	2	5	19	5	20	7	0	.260/.283/.410	.234	.268	0	--	0.0
2012	DAY	A+	22	352	68	19	4	2	34	47	50	38	12	.295/.394/.407	.335	.344	5	CF(13): -0.4, RF(1): -0.2	1.5
2012	TEN	AA	22	158	24	7	4	2	6	14	29	4	2	.210/.285/.357	.230	.250	2.9	CF(13): 0.6, RF(9): 1.3	0.3
2013	*CHN*	*MLB*	*23*	*250*	*31*	*11*	*2*	*3*	*18*	*20*	*50*	*14*	*4*	*.231/.298/.339*	*.230*	*.279*	*1.2*	*CF -0, RF 0*	*0.0*

Physically gifted but underdeveloped as a baseball player because of a devotion to college football (a tune all too familiar to Cubs fans), Szczur hit well in his second season at High-A but struggled after a promotion to Double-A. Inexperience aside, Szczur has been old for his level whenever he's had success, and some aspects of aging aren't about experience, they're about body. An old 23—he was born a few weeks too late for us to call him a 24-year-old—he has a limited window in which to put it all together.

Luis Valbuena UT

Born: **11/30/1985** Age: **27**
Bats: **L** Throws: **R** Height: **5' 11"**
Weight: **195** Breakout: **2%**
Improve: **47%** Collapse: **10%**
Attrition: **18%** MLB: **88%**

Comparables:
Rich Rollins,Todd Zeile,Adam Rosales

YEAR	TEAM	LVL	AGE	PA	R	2B	3B	HR	RBI	BB	SO	SB	CS	AVG_OBP_SLG	TAv	BABIP	BRR	FRAA	WARP
2010	COH	AAA	24	119	23	8	1	6	20	19	21	2	0	.312/.424/.604	.329	.338	0.6	SS(10): 0.2, 3B(7): -0.7	1.3
2010	CLE	MLB	24	310	22	12	0	2	24	28	61	1	2	.193/.273/.258	.204	.238	-1.4	2B(71): 2.6, 3B(9): -0.2	-0.7
2011	COH	AAA	25	472	64	22	0	17	75	46	96	6	3	.302/.372/.476	.294	.355	0	--	0.0
2011	CLE	MLB	25	44	4	0	0	1	1	1	9	1	0	.209/.227/.279	.183	.242	0.4	2B(11): -0.8, LF(2): -0.1	-0.3
2012	IOW	AAA	26	246	38	17	1	8	31	28	50	1	1	.303/.378/.507	.286	.352	1.2	SS(26): 1.6, 2B(6): -0.0	1.0
2012	CHN	MLB	26	303	26	20	0	4	28	36	55	0	2	.219/.310/.340	.234	.260	-0.5	3B(82): -0.5, 2B(5): -0.2	-0.2
2013	*CHN*	*MLB*	*27*	*269*	*28*	*13*	*1*	*6*	*28*	*25*	*52*	*2*	*1*	*.241/.314/.381*	*.248*	*.280*	*-0.5*	*3B 0, 2B -0*	*0.4*

As Loki asked Nick Fury in "The Avengers," "How desperate are you that you call on such lost creatures to defend you?" The answer here is the same as it was there: very desperate. Valbuena has bounced around to several clubs in his career, and he's too old for the prospect label to apply without smirking. But after the Cubs ran through plans A through U at third base, they turned to V, and he rewarded them with the sort of subtle mediocrity that teams like the 2012 Cubs often find useful.

Christian Villanueva 3B

Born: **6/19/1991** Age: **22**
Bats: **R** Throws: **R** Height: **6' 0"**
Weight: **160** Breakout: **5%**
Improve: **49%** Collapse: **3%**
Attrition: **11%** MLB: **97%**

Comparables:
Carlos Baerga,Howard Johnson,Gene Freese

YEAR	TEAM	LVL	AGE	PA	R	2B	3B	HR	RBI	BB	SO	SB	CS	AVG_OBP_SLG	TAv	BABIP	BRR	FRAA	WARP
2010	RNG	Rk	19	210	30	14	1	2	35	13	42	6	2	.314/.367/.431	.313	.390	0.4	3B(51): -0.6	1.6
2011	HIC	A	20	529	78	30	3	17	84	37	86	32	6	.278/.338/.465	.301	.300	3.7	3B(94): 12.1, SS(2): 0.2	4.7
2012	DAY	A+	21	95	14	5	0	4	9	10	24	5	2	.250/.337/.452	.180	.304	-0.1	3B(9): 1.2	0.1
2012	MYR	A+	21	425	45	19	1	10	59	24	83	9	9	.285/.356/.421	.268	.338	-2.4	3B(69): -4.4, 2B(4): 0.6	0.6
2013	*CHN*	*MLB*	*22*	*250*	*27*	*10*	*1*	*7*	*28*	*11*	*57*	*5*	*2*	*.233/.281/.376*	*.235*	*.275*	*0*	*3B 4, 2B -0*	*0.4*

Acquired from the Rangers for Ryan Dempster, Villanueva is an impressive defender who can do some damage at the plate as well. He's unlikely to be a star in the big leagues, and he's not the typical slugging third baseman, but he profiles to hit for average in the majors with decent on-base and slugging. Scouts credit him with a mature approach, and if he does well at Double-A it could be a short jump to the majors.

Josh Vitters 3B

Born: **8/27/1989** Age: **23**
Bats: **R** Throws: **R** Height: **6' 3"**
Weight: **200** Breakout: **6%**
Improve: **68%** Collapse: **2%**
Attrition: **9%** MLB: **96%**

Comparables:
Lonnie Chisenhall,Fernando Tatis,Hank Blalock

YEAR	TEAM	LVL	AGE	PA	R	2B	3B	HR	RBI	BB	SO	SB	CS	AVG_OBP_SLG	TAv	BABIP	BRR	FRAA	WARP
2010	DAY	A+	20	120	16	8	0	3	13	8	22	4	1	.291/.350/.445	.309	.341	0.4	3B(21): -3.3	0.5
2010	TEN	AA	20	228	28	12	0	7	26	13	41	2	0	.223/.289/.383	.222	.244	-0.6	3B(58): -5.5	-0.9
2011	TEN	AA	21	488	56	28	2	14	81	22	54	4	10	.283/.322/.448	.234	.290	-0.3	3B(43): -6.0, 1B(14): -0.7	-0.9
2012	IOW	AAA	22	452	54	32	2	17	68	30	77	6	3	.304/.356/.513	.319	.337	0	3B(61): -0.6, 1B(4): -0.2	2.0
2012	CHN	MLB	22	109	7	2	0	2	5	7	33	2	0	.121/.193/.202	.152	.154	-0.7	3B(29): -1.0	-1.3
2013	*CHN*	*MLB*	*23*	*250*	*26*	*11*	*1*	*8*	*29*	*12*	*54*	*3*	*2*	*.230/.275/.388*	*.236*	*.264*	*-0.4*	*3B -1, 1B -0*	*-0.2*

Vitters was a raw high school hitter the Cubs loved for his sweet swing, but the third pick of the 2007 draft stalled out as his ability to swing the bat wasn't paired up with an ability to see the ball. It seemed like he was finally back on track with a much-improved second season at Double-A and then an eye-popping year at Triple-A Iowa, but in 109 plate appearances with the big club he was barely able to keep his slugging above the Mendoza line. The Cubs have no heir apparent at third base, and they aren't going anywhere in 2013, so they can give Vitters another chance to show he can put it together for them.

Daniel Vogelbach 1B
Born: **12/17/1992** Age: **20**
Bats: **L** Throws: **R** Height: **6' 1"**
Weight: **250** Breakout: **21%**
Improve: **69%** Collapse: **3%**
Attrition: **13%** MLB: **91%**
Comparables:
Mickey Mantle, Justin Upton, Tony Conigliaro

YEAR	TEAM	LVL	AGE	PA	R	2B	3B	HR	RBI	BB	SO	SB	CS	AVG_OBP_SLG	TAv	BABIP	BRR	FRAA	WARP
2012	CUB	Rk	19	115	16	12	2	7	31	12	14	1	0	.324/.391/.686	.349	.317	-1.9	1B(21): -1.0	0.0
2012	BOI	A-	19	168	23	9	1	10	31	23	34	0	1	.322/.423/.608	.352	.364	0.1	1B(29): -3.3	1.2
2013	*CHN*	*MLB*	*20*	*250*	*28*	*9*	*1*	*11*	*34*	*18*	*65*	*0*	*0*	*.222/.279/.416*	*.244*	*.254*	*-0.3*	*1B -2*	*0.0*

A second-round pick in 2011, Vogelbach has one significant obstacle in his path to the big leagues: He's already a first baseman at the age of 19. In order to overcome that he's going to have to hit the baseball so hard it begs for mercy. Tearing apart short-season A-ball like a velociraptor falling upon an apatosaurus carcass is certainly a good start, but he has a long way to go from here.

PITCHERS

Scott Baker
Born: **9/19/1981** Age: **31**
Bats: **R** Throws: **R** Height: **6' 5"** Weight: **215**
Breakout: **12%** Improve: **47%** Collapse: **27%**
Attrition: **13%** MLB: **94%**
Comparables:
Freddy Garcia, Aaron Harang, Javier Vazquez

YEAR	TEAM	LVL	AGE	W	L	SV	G	GS	IP	H	HR	BB	SO	BB9	SO9	GB%	BABIP	WHIP	ERA	FIP	FRA	WARP
2010	MIN	MLB	28	12	9	0	29	29	170^{1}	186	23	43	148	2.3	7.8	37%	.323	1.34	4.49	3.93	4.11	2.1
2011	MIN	MLB	29	8	6	0	23	21	134^{2}	126	15	32	123	2.1	8.2	35%	.297	1.17	3.14	3.48	4.16	1.6
2012	FTM	A+	30	0	0	0	1	1	0^{1}	2	0	0	0	0.0	0.0	%	.667	6.00	54.00	3.39	3.69	0.0
2013	*CHN*	*MLB*	*31*	*2*	*2*	*0*	*7*	*7*	38^{2}	*35*	*5*	*9*	*34*	*2.2*	*7.8*	*37%*	*.290*	*1.15*	*3.58*	*3.82*	*3.89*	*0.5*

For some reason, the Twins were never satisfied with Baker. He was somewhat fragile, but he was also a mid-rotation starter with good control who struck out plenty of hitters. Minnesota seemed annoyed in 2011 when Baker started to complain about his elbow. He finally had surgery to clean it out, and surgeons discovered a previously undiagnosed torn UCL. Oops. Baker underwent ligament replacement and missed all of 2012. He doesn't figure to be ready to pitch until May, but still represents a good value for Chicago, which signed him for just $5.5 million plus incentives. Best-case scenario, Baker is the sort of mid-rotation innings sponge the Cubs lacked last year—and a decent shot at that is well-worth the sticker price.

Jason Berken
Born: **11/27/1983** Age: **29**
Bats: **R** Throws: **R** Height: **6' 1"** Weight: **205**
Breakout: **22%** Improve: **53%** Collapse: **13%**
Attrition: **8%** MLB: **76%**
Comparables:
Doc Medich, Jeff Karstens, Ron Reed

YEAR	TEAM	LVL	AGE	W	L	SV	G	GS	IP	H	HR	BB	SO	BB9	SO9	GB%	BABIP	WHIP	ERA	FIP	FRA	WARP
2010	BAL	MLB	26	3	3	0	41	0	62^{1}	64	5	19	45	2.7	6.5	49%	.307	1.33	3.03	3.56	4.28	0.7
2011	NOR	AAA	27	0	1	0	5	4	18	20	1	7	16	3.5	8.0	40%	.348	1.50	3.50	3.51	4.08	0.2
2011	BAL	MLB	27	1	2	0	40	0	47	63	10	21	41	4.0	7.9	42%	.353	1.79	5.36	5.49	5.36	0.0
2012	NOR	AAA	28	5	6	0	26	26	144	160	10	39	98	2.4	6.1	44%	.323	1.38	3.50	3.62	5.01	0.3
2012	BAL	MLB	28	0	0	0	1	0	1	6	2	1	0	9.0	0.0	33%	.571	7.00	18.00	32.05	20.87	-0.3
2012	CHN	MLB	28	0	3	0	4	4	18^{2}	23	3	6	11	2.9	5.3	51%	.312	1.55	4.82	5.17	5.29	0.1
2013	*CHN*	*MLB*	*29*	*3*	*3*	*0*	*25*	*7*	62^{2}	*66*	*8*	*21*	*44*	*3.0*	*6.3*	*45%*	*.309*	*1.38*	*4.88*	*4.46*	*5.30*	*-0.2*

Berken's career has been plagued with injuries: Tommy John surgery, a torn labrum, frayed rotator cuff . . . He started 2012 with a hamstring injury, but it didn't last long enough to keep him from pitching during the season, moving back into a starting role after a conversion to middle relief. Now that he's healthy, the thing that's holding Berken back is a lack of discernible pitching ability. Moving him back to the bullpen may be the best hope to salvage any kind of value from him.

Michael Bowden
Born: **9/9/1986** Age: **26**
Bats: **R** Throws: **R** Height: **6' 4"** Weight: **215**
Breakout: **22%** Improve: **52%** Collapse: **23%**
Attrition: **20%** MLB: **90%**
Comparables:
Carlos Rosa, Billy Loes, Steven Shell

YEAR	TEAM	LVL	AGE	W	L	SV	G	GS	IP	H	HR	BB	SO	BB9	SO9	GB%	BABIP	WHIP	ERA	FIP	FRA	WARP
2010	PAW	AAA	23	6	4	1	31	16	105^{2}	84	13	37	77	3.2	6.6	25%	.238	1.14	3.66	4.54	5.16	0.0
2010	BOS	MLB	23	0	1	0	14	0	15^{1}	20	2	4	13	2.3	7.6	27%	.383	1.57	4.70	3.83	5.70	-0.1
2011	PAW	AAA	24	3	3	16	41	0	52^{2}	43	5	18	61	3.1	10.4	37%	.276	1.16	2.73	3.24	4.75	0.4
2011	BOS	MLB	24	0	0	0	14	0	20	19	3	11	17	4.9	7.7	29%	.271	1.50	4.05	4.96	3.95	0.3
2012	IOW	AAA	25	3	2	2	23	0	32^{2}	19	2	17	35	4.7	9.6	46%	.205	1.10	2.76	3.88	4.79	0.3
2012	BOS	MLB	25	0	0	0	2	0	3	2	1	1	3	3.0	9.0	57%	.167	1.00	3.00	6.38	5.79	0.0
2012	CHN	MLB	25	0	0	0	30	0	36^{2}	30	4	16	29	3.9	7.1	39%	.252	1.25	2.95	4.36	4.84	0.1
2013	*CHN*	*MLB*	*26*	*2*	*1*	*0*	*24*	*3*	42^{2}	*39*	*5*	*15*	*33*	*3.2*	*7.0*	*36%*	*.282*	*1.27*	*4.05*	*4.23*	*4.40*	*0.3*

When Bowden was drafted, his most promising attribute was his curveball. Now the curve is gone and so is most of Bowden's promise. He's moved into a relief role and had some success, but not enough to stick with the Red Sox, who let him go to free up roster space. A low BABIP in 2012 masked unimpressive peripherals, which doesn't give much hope for Bowden to flourish in his new role.

Alberto Cabrera

Born: **10/25/1988** Age: **24**
Bats: **R** Throws: **R** Height: **6' 5"** Weight: **210**
Breakout: **33%** Improve: **54%** Collapse: **29%**
Attrition: **13%** MLB: **90%**

Comparables:
Darrell Jackson,Kevin Gross,Tom Bradley

YEAR	TEAM	LVL	AGE	W	L	SV	G	GS	IP	H	HR	BB	SO	BB9	SO9	GB%	BABIP	WHIP	ERA	FIP	FRA	WARP
2010	DAY	A+	21	7	5	0	18	17	93^1	92	6	26	90	2.5	8.7	52%	.321	1.26	3.28	3.21	4.51	0.4
2010	TEN	AA	21	0	4	0	10	9	42^2	57	1	24	35	5.1	7.4	50%	.373	1.90	6.32	3.95	5.05	0.2
2011	TEN	AA	22	6	2	0	9	9	48^2	60	4	21	34	3.9	6.3	41%	.295	1.66	5.36	4.40	5.80	0.1
2011	IOW	AAA	22	3	6	0	19	17	88^2	118	11	53	67	5.4	6.8	48%	.378	1.93	6.60	5.78	6.75	-0.1
2012	TEN	AA	23	2	1	5	23	0	35^2	30	2	10	45	2.5	11.4	51%	.315	1.12	2.52	2.19	2.43	1.0
2012	IOW	AAA	23	2	0	0	13	0	19^1	29	4	4	29	1.9	13.5	51%	.472	1.71	4.19	4.29	4.12	0.4
2012	CHN	MLB	23	1	1	0	25	0	21^2	16	1	18	27	7.5	11.2	43%	.288	1.57	5.40	3.87	4.15	0.1
2013	*CHN*	*MLB*	*24*	*1*	*2*	*0*	*13*	*5*	*35*	*37*	*5*	*18*	*26*	*4.7*	*6.8*	*45%*	*.312*	*1.57*	*5.61*	*5.11*	*6.10*	*-0.4*

Cabrera was drafted because of his ability to throw the ball hard, but that's not enough to succeed against higher-level hitters without the sort of secondary pitches Cabrera has yet to develop. A conversion to relief pitching has reduced emphasis on the lack of diversity in his pitches. The Cubs called him up because they were having one of those seasons, but he didn't cover himself in glory in his brief stint in the majors.

Shawn Camp

Born: **11/18/1975** Age: **37**
Bats: **R** Throws: **R** Height: **6' 1"** Weight: **205**
Breakout: **21%** Improve: **48%** Collapse: **43%**
Attrition: **26%** MLB: **85%**

Comparables:
Mike Timlin,Guillermo Mota,LaTroy Hawkins

YEAR	TEAM	LVL	AGE	W	L	SV	G	GS	IP	H	HR	BB	SO	BB9	SO9	GB%	BABIP	WHIP	ERA	FIP	FRA	WARP
2010	TOR	MLB	34	4	3	2	70	0	72^1	71	8	18	46	2.2	5.7	52%	.284	1.23	2.99	4.13	4.73	0.2
2011	TOR	MLB	35	6	3	1	67	0	66^1	79	3	22	32	3.0	4.3	55%	.332	1.52	4.21	3.95	4.29	0.6
2012	CHN	MLB	36	3	6	2	80	0	77^2	79	7	21	54	2.4	6.3	48%	.294	1.29	3.59	3.73	4.37	0.5
2013	*CHN*	*MLB*	*37*	*4*	*1*	*1*	*70*	*0*	*69^2*	*67*	*7*	*20*	*48*	*2.6*	*6.2*	*52%*	*.297*	*1.25*	*4.03*	*3.99*	*4.38*	*0.4*

Camp spent a few years as a journeyman middle reliever, settling in with the Blue Jays until they decided they didn't want him anymore and let him go to free agency. He signed with the Mariners in the offseason, but they released him in spring training (where he didn't even pitch badly, although that doesn't matter) to make room for younger players. The Cubs snapped him up and he did just fine, so they signed him for another year of dependable, low-value middle relieving. This is not exactly the stuff of Hollywood blockbusters, but a guy who can get big-league hitters out reasonably often is nice to have around.

Lendy Castillo

Born: **4/8/1989** Age: **24**
Bats: **R** Throws: **R** Height: **6' 2"** Weight: **170**
Breakout: **26%** Improve: **53%** Collapse: **22%**
Attrition: **21%** MLB: **78%**

Comparables:
Will Cunnane,Larry Sherry,Marcos Carvajal

YEAR	TEAM	LVL	AGE	W	L	SV	G	GS	IP	H	HR	BB	SO	BB9	SO9	GB%	BABIP	WHIP	ERA	FIP	FRA	WARP
2010	PHL	Rk	21	3	1	0	13	6	44^2	33	2	18	51	3.6	10.3	36%	.256	1.14	2.21	3.28	3.96	0.6
2010	WPT	A-	21	0	0	0	1	1	5	3	0	2	3	3.6	5.4	40%	.200	1.00	0.00	3.47	4.74	0.0
2011	LWD	A	22	4	2	0	21	2	46	37	1	16	46	3.1	9.0	46%	.260	1.15	2.54	3.18	3.30	0.7
2012	CUB	Rk	23	0	0	0	4	4	13	7	0	3	16	2.1	11.1	57%	.190	0.77	0.69	2.61	3.27	0.4
2012	DAY	A+	23	0	0	0	1	1	4	3	0	1	4	2.2	9.0	36%	.273	1.00	0.00	2.14	0.05	0.0
2012	TEN	AA	23	0	0	0	2	2	3	3	0	2	2	6.0	6.0	67%	.333	1.67	3.00	3.81	6.62	0.0
2012	CHN	MLB	23	0	1	0	13	0	16	24	2	12	13	6.8	7.3	38%	.379	2.25	7.88	5.95	6.93	-0.4
2013	*CHN*	*MLB*	*24*	*1*	*1*	*0*	*13*	*3*	*35^1*	*35*	*5*	*18*	*28*	*4.7*	*7.0*	*41%*	*.300*	*1.50*	*5.11*	*4.98*	*5.55*	*-0.2*

Sometimes players make it to the majors before their time, and the results aren't pretty. Castillo was a converted shortstop who was on the Cubs' major-league roster more because of the way the Rule 5 draft works than because of his ability to contribute, or even the Cubs' need for pitching. A left groin strain might have actually helped him stick with the team, as it used up some days without requiring him to use a big-league roster spot. Castillo has thrown exactly three innings above High-A and below the majors, so, having secured his rights by keeping him in Chicago all year, the Cubs will likely dispatch him to the farm for some much-needed experience.

Jaye Chapman

Born: **5/22/1987** Age: **26**
Bats: **R** Throws: **R** Height: **6' 1"** Weight: **180**
Breakout: **18%** Improve: **41%** Collapse: **29%**
Attrition: **24%** MLB: **89%**

Comparables:
Dewey Robinson,Luis Perdomo,Bill Campbell

YEAR	TEAM	LVL	AGE	W	L	SV	G	GS	IP	H	HR	BB	SO	BB9	SO9	GB%	BABIP	WHIP	ERA	FIP	FRA	WARP
2010	MYR	A+	23	0	1	2	10	0	12^{2}	10	1	7	21	5.0	14.9	52%	.321	1.34	5.67	2.78	2.60	0.4
2010	MIS	AA	23	1	4	0	36	1	50^{1}	60	1	25	53	4.5	9.5	46%	.381	1.69	5.19	3.21	4.19	0.4
2011	MIS	AA	24	1	0	2	9	0	14	5	1	5	16	3.2	10.3	—	.138	0.71	0.64	3.02	3.28	0.0
2011	GWN	AAA	24	2	3	2	43	1	54^{1}	40	5	26	61	4.3	10.1	—	.267	1.21	2.98	3.62	3.94	0.0
2012	TEN	AA	25	0	0	0	2	0	2	0	0	0	2	0.0	9.0	50%	.000	0.00	0.00	1.14	-0.67	0.0
2012	GWN	AAA	25	3	6	7	40	0	53^{2}	46	3	29	60	4.9	10.1	41%	.307	1.40	3.52	3.27	5.00	0.1
2012	IOW	AAA	25	0	2	0	8	0	9^{1}	11	0	7	10	6.8	9.6	48%	.379	1.93	7.71	3.77	3.17	0.3
2012	CHN	MLB	25	0	1	0	14	0	12	8	0	10	12	7.5	9.0	50%	.286	1.50	3.75	3.64	3.54	0.2
2013	*CHN*	*MLB*	*26*	*1*	*0*	*0*	*29*	*0*	*36*	*34*	*4*	*19*	*32*	*4.7*	*8.0*	*41%*	*.304*	*1.45*	*4.72*	*4.45*	*5.13*	*-0.1*

The Cubs picked up Chapman from the Braves with Arodys Vizcaino as part of their effort to sell off every usable piece they could at the trade deadline—in this case Reed Johnson and Paul Maholm—and they almost immediately put him into service in the majors. Chapman pitched well for 12 innings, but the Cubs should be cautious about expecting him to maintain that level of performance going forward. His minor-league numbers are pedestrian and his fastball sits in the high 80s.

Casey Coleman

Born: **7/3/1987** Age: **25**
Bats: **L** Throws: **R** Height: **6' 1"** Weight: **185**
Breakout: **27%** Improve: **53%** Collapse: **19%**
Attrition: **10%** MLB: **76%**

Comparables:
Jim Abbott,Zach Jackson,Chris Narveson

YEAR	TEAM	LVL	AGE	W	L	SV	G	GS	IP	H	HR	BB	SO	BB9	SO9	GB%	BABIP	WHIP	ERA	FIP	FRA	WARP
2010	IOW	AAA	22	10	7	0	20	20	117^{1}	106	10	35	59	2.7	4.5	57%	.256	1.20	4.07	4.63	5.53	1.3
2010	CHN	MLB	22	4	2	0	12	8	57	56	3	25	27	3.9	4.3	48%	.277	1.42	4.11	4.26	4.81	0.6
2011	IOW	AAA	23	5	2	0	12	12	74	69	11	22	54	2.7	6.6	45%	.277	1.23	3.65	5.15	5.47	0.5
2011	CHN	MLB	23	3	9	0	19	17	84^{1}	102	10	46	75	4.9	8.0	45%	.350	1.75	6.40	4.54	5.25	0.3
2012	IOW	AAA	24	2	4	0	13	11	58	53	4	25	52	3.9	8.1	48%	.299	1.34	4.34	4.17	5.14	1.0
2012	CHN	MLB	24	0	2	0	17	1	24^{1}	37	5	12	16	4.4	5.9	43%	.372	2.01	7.40	5.97	6.85	-0.5
2013	*CHN*	*MLB*	*25*	*3*	*4*	*0*	*9*	*9*	*50*	*51*	*6*	*21*	*31*	*3.7*	*5.6*	*49%*	*.295*	*1.42*	*4.83*	*4.78*	*5.25*	*-0.1*

Some guys get a reputation as being "pitchers, not just throwers," and Coleman is one of those guys. The trouble is that he's been unable to translate that into success in the major leagues. Even on a seriously pitching-deficient Cubs team, Coleman was moved to relief work and got utterly torched in the process. It remains to be seen whether he'll be given another shot at achieving the dream of being a back-of-the-rotation starter. The Cubs would be wise to stick with the transition to middle relief.

Gerardo Concepcion

Born: **2/29/1992** Age: **21**
Bats: **L** Throws: **L** Height: **6' 2"** Weight: **176**
Breakout: **25%** Improve: **47%** Collapse: **8%**
Attrition: **5%** MLB: **90%**

Comparables:
Ryan Feierabend,Mike McCormick,Chuck Stobbs

YEAR	TEAM	LVL	AGE	W	L	SV	G	GS	IP	H	HR	BB	SO	BB9	SO9	GB%	BABIP	WHIP	ERA	FIP	FRA	WARP
2012	PEO	A	20	2	6	0	12	12	52^{1}	70	6	30	28	5.2	4.8	—	.346	1.91	7.39	5.61	6.09	0.0
2013	*CHN*	*MLB*	*21*	*2*	*2*	*0*	*8*	*6*	*36^{2}*	*35*	*4*	*15*	*27*	*3.7*	*6.7*	*46%*	*.293*	*1.36*	*4.42*	*4.37*	*4.80*	*0.1*

Signed out of Cuba, Concepcion is still very raw, and 12 games in the low minors isn't enough to tell us much of anything about how well he'll transition to the majors. What we know isn't kind, though: It's never exactly good news when a guy walks more hitters than he strikes out. The scouting reports haven't been any kinder than his stats, with some already talking about a move to relief pitching for the young lefty.

Manuel Corpas

Born: **12/3/1982** Age: **30**
Bats: **R** Throws: **R** Height: **6' 4"** Weight: **210**
Breakout: **30%** Improve: **51%** Collapse: **36%**
Attrition: **14%** MLB: **88%**

Comparables:
Ken Sanders,Matt Guerrier,Geoff Geary

YEAR	TEAM	LVL	AGE	W	L	SV	G	GS	IP	H	HR	BB	SO	BB9	SO9	GB%	BABIP	WHIP	ERA	FIP	FRA	WARP
2010	COL	MLB	27	3	5	10	56	0	62^{1}	66	7	22	47	3.2	6.8	44%	.301	1.41	4.62	4.21	5.09	0.2
2012	IOW	AAA	29	0	2	0	19	0	33^{2}	30	4	9	19	2.4	5.1	47%	.237	1.16	4.01	5.24	7.58	-0.2
2012	CHN	MLB	29	0	2	0	48	0	46^{2}	50	7	16	28	3.1	5.4	46%	.289	1.41	5.01	5.24	5.25	-0.2
2013	*CHN*	*MLB*	*30*	*2*	*1*	*1*	*38*	*0*	*43^{2}*	*43*	*5*	*12*	*31*	*2.5*	*6.4*	*49%*	*.294*	*1.25*	*4.13*	*4.09*	*4.49*	*0.2*

Corpas lost 2011 to Tommy John surgery, and though his arm is healthy enough to pitch again, it doesn't seem to have returned to what passed for form to begin with. Perhaps most troubling for Corpas is that leaving Colorado didn't seem to cut down on the home runs he allows. There's some reason to think he'll bounce back from his 2012 campaign, but little reason to think he can be a significant contributor going forward.

Rafael Dolis

Born: **1/10/1988** Age: **25**
Bats: **R** Throws: **R** Height: **6' 5"** Weight: **215**
Breakout: **24%** Improve: **52%** Collapse: **19%**
Attrition: **11%** MLB: **95%**

Comparables:
David Nied,Ron Bryant,Bill Stafford

YEAR	TEAM	LVL	AGE	W	L	SV	G	GS	IP	H	HR	BB	SO	BB9	SO9	GB%	BABIP	WHIP	ERA	FIP	FRA	WARP
2010	DAY	A+	22	4	5	0	14	13	71	63	3	30	48	3.8	6.1	64%	.262	1.31	2.92	3.98	5.78	-0.6
2010	TEN	AA	22	5	4	0	12	12	55^{1}	65	3	27	45	4.4	7.3	56%	.354	1.66	4.07	3.98	5.05	0.7
2011	TEN	AA	23	8	5	17	51	4	72^{2}	61	2	35	48	4.3	5.9	64%	.281	1.32	3.22	3.91	4.90	0.3
2011	CHN	MLB	23	0	0	0	1	0	1^{1}	0	0	1	1	6.8	6.8	1.%	.000	0.75	0.00	3.74	4.45	0.0
2012	CUB	Rk	24	1	1	0	5	0	5^{2}	7	0	2	5	3.2	7.9	80%	.267	1.59	6.35	3.67	-0.76	0.1
2012	TEN	AA	24	0	0	0	2	0	2	2	0	0	2	0.0	9.0	67%	.333	1.00	0.00	2.64	-2.09	0.1
2012	IOW	AAA	24	0	1	3	13	0	14^{1}	15	1	6	14	3.8	8.8	46%	.350	1.47	2.51	3.87	4.10	0.2
2012	CHN	MLB	24	2	4	4	34	0	38	40	5	23	24	5.4	5.7	47%	.297	1.66	6.39	5.64	7.72	-0.9
2013	*CHN*	*MLB*	*25*	*2*	*2*	*1*	*18*	*4*	*37*	*37*	*5*	*19*	*23*	*4.6*	*5.5*	*51%*	*.293*	*1.51*	*5.27*	*5.25*	*5.72*	*-0.3*

Dolis is a converted shortstop with a nice sinker that produces a lot of groundballs, but little else has worked for him in the majors. The Cubs briefly tried him as part of their College of Closers after Carlos Marmol's early-season implosion, but he pitched so poorly that he got dispatched to the minors. If he can figure out how to miss bats he may get another shot to prove he's a closer of the future, but he has to do better than a K-to-BB ratio of just barely over one.

Scott Feldman

Born: **2/7/1983** Age: **30**
Bats: **L** Throws: **R** Height: **6' 7"** Weight: **230**
Breakout: **29%** Improve: **64%** Collapse: **11%**
Attrition: **11%** MLB: **87%**

Comparables:
Mel Parnell,Jeff Francis,Joe Saunders

YEAR	TEAM	LVL	AGE	W	L	SV	G	GS	IP	H	HR	BB	SO	BB9	SO9	GB%	BABIP	WHIP	ERA	FIP	FRA	WARP
2010	OKL	AAA	27	0	0	0	1	0	4	5	2	0	3	0.0	6.8	39%	.273	1.25	4.50	8.58	8.37	-0.1
2010	TEX	MLB	27	7	11	0	29	22	141^{1}	181	18	45	75	2.9	4.8	43%	.327	1.60	5.48	4.70	5.08	0.9
2011	FRI	AA	28	1	0	0	2	2	9	5	0	2	8	2.0	8.0	46%	.273	0.78	3.00	2.27	2.83	0.1
2011	ROU	AAA	28	2	1	0	8	8	40^{2}	48	5	9	24	2.0	5.3	—	.316	1.40	4.43	4.94	5.37	0.0
2011	TEX	MLB	28	2	1	0	11	2	32	25	3	10	22	2.8	6.2	63%	.239	1.09	3.94	4.03	4.81	0.2
2012	TEX	MLB	29	6	11	0	29	21	123^{2}	139	14	32	96	2.3	7.0	42%	.318	1.38	5.09	3.77	4.65	1.7
2013	*CHN*	*MLB*	*30*	*5*	*6*	*0*	*23*	*15*	*100^{1}*	*97*	*12*	*30*	*65*	*2.7*	*5.9*	*47%*	*.290*	*1.27*	*4.19*	*4.36*	*4.55*	*0.5*

Feldman pounds the strike zone with his low-90s sinker-cutter combination and can gobble innings in a starting or long-relief role. When his sinker and cutter are sharp, he can eat up bats and induce grounders with the best of them. He showed that during his dominant postseason performance out of the bullpen in 2011. However, both fastballs were often flat in last year's starting role, leading to a 5.09 ERA. Feldman's curveball and splitter are pedestrian but play up when the fastball quality is there. In the end, what you see is what you get: a sturdy, replacement-level, back-end rotation arm.

Kyuji Fujikawa

Born: **7/21/1980** Age: **32**
Bats: **L** Throws: **R** Height: **6' 1"** Weight: **185**
Breakout: **25%** Improve: **54%** Collapse: **30%**
Attrition: **5%** MLB: **93%**

Comparables:
Damaso Marte,Brian Fuentes,Billy Wagner

YEAR	TEAM	LVL	AGE	W	L	SV	G	GS	IP	H	HR	BB	SO	BB9	SO9	GB%	BABIP	WHIP	ERA	FIP	FRA	WARP
2010	HNS	NPB	29	3	4	28	58	0	62^{2}	47	7	20	81	2.9	11.6	—	.278	1.07	2.01	3.06	3.33	0.0
2011	HNS	NPB	30	3	3	41	56	0	51	25	2	13	80	2.3	14.1	—	—	0.75	1.24	—	—	—
2012	HNS	NPB	31	2	2	24	48	0	47^{1}	34	1	15	58	2.8	11	—	—	1.03	1.32	—	—	—
2013	*CHN*	*MLB*	*32*	*2*	*1*	*2*	*37*	*0*	*40*	*28*	*4*	*13*	*54*	*2.9*	*12.1*	*46%*	*.297*	*1.02*	*2.51*	*2.78*	*2.73*	*1.0*

The Cubs have had problems spelling relief M-A-R-M-O-L, so they went overseas to get an insurance plan. A closer in Japan, Fujikawa is ticketed as a set-up man in Chicago, but the Cubs could move him into the most prominent bullpen job if Marmol gets traded or starts 2013 like he did 2012. The Cubs prized Fujikawa for his durability, even though his age may be viewed as a concern. He caused a bit of a stir in the media by commenting that he didn't care if the Cubs, who don't like no-trade clauses, trade him eventually, but comments like that made through an interpreter should probably be taken with a grain of salt.

Matt Garza

Born: **11/11/1983** Age: **29**
Bats: **R** Throws: **R** Height: **6' 5"** Weight: **215**
Breakout: **12%** Improve: **49%** Collapse: **20%**
Attrition: **4%** MLB: **95%**

Comparables:
Adam Wainwright,Gavin Floyd,John Lackey

YEAR	TEAM	LVL	AGE	W	L	SV	G	GS	IP	H	HR	BB	SO	BB9	SO9	GB%	BABIP	WHIP	ERA	FIP	FRA	WARP
2010	TBA	MLB	26	15	10	1	33	32	204^{2}	193	28	63	150	2.8	6.6	37%	.272	1.25	3.91	4.39	4.94	0.6
2011	CHN	MLB	27	10	10	0	31	31	198	186	14	63	197	2.9	9.0	48%	.306	1.26	3.32	2.92	3.36	3.7
2012	CHN	MLB	28	5	7	0	18	18	103^{2}	90	15	32	96	2.8	8.3	50%	.271	1.18	3.91	4.21	5.53	-0.3
2013	*CHN*	*MLB*	*29*	*6*	*6*	*0*	*17*	*17*	*103^{1}*	*88*	*12*	*32*	*88*	*2.8*	*7.7*	*43%*	*.280*	*1.16*	*3.56*	*3.94*	*3.87*	*1.3*

Garza was acquired when then-general manager Jim Hendry dismantled much of what remained of his farm system in a last-ditch effort to save his job. It didn't work. Hendry got fired anyway, and now Garza looks out of place on a Cubs team trying to build around the sort of young players Chicago traded to get Garza in the first place. The Cubs weren't in a rush to deal him again, though, preferring to be patient and hope for an increased return from teams looking for rotation help at the deadline. Unfortunately for Chicago, patience isn't always a virtue: Midseason injuries scuttled trade talks and ended Garza's season. The Cubs could try again or they could hold on to Garza as the ace of an otherwise uninspiring pitching staff.

Edwin Jackson
Born: **9/9/1983** Age: **29**
Bats: **R** Throws: **R** Height: **6' 4"** Weight: **205**
Breakout: **20%** Improve: **45%** Collapse: **22%**
Attrition: **7%** MLB: **93%**
Comparables:
Jeff Niemann, Brad Penny, Gavin Floyd

YEAR	TEAM	LVL	AGE	W	L	SV	G	GS	IP	H	HR	BB	SO	BB9	SO9	GB%	BABIP	WHIP	ERA	FIP	FRA	WARP
2010	ARI	MLB	26	6	10	0	21	21	134^{1}	141	13	60	104	4.0	7.0	52%	.316	1.50	5.16	4.27	4.89	0.6
2010	CHA	MLB	26	4	2	0	11	11	75	73	8	18	77	2.2	9.2	48%	.308	1.21	3.24	3.14	3.54	1.5
2011	CHA	MLB	27	7	7	0	19	19	121^{2}	134	8	39	97	2.9	7.2	49%	.333	1.42	3.92	3.28	3.78	2.0
2011	SLN	MLB	27	5	2	0	13	12	78	91	8	23	51	2.7	5.9	42%	.325	1.46	3.58	3.98	4.25	0.8
2012	WAS	MLB	28	10	11	0	31	31	189^{2}	173	23	58	168	2.8	8.0	48%	.278	1.22	4.03	3.89	4.67	1.2
2013	*CHN*	*MLB*	*29*	*9*	*10*	*0*	*26*	*26*	*164^{2}*	*154*	*19*	*53*	*132*	*2.9*	*7.2*	*45%*	*.297*	*1.26*	*4.03*	*4.06*	*4.38*	*1.1*

Jackson's been everywhere, man. He's crossed the deserts bare, man. He's breathed the mountain air, man. Of travel he's had his share, man. The Cubs will be the eighth uniform in his collection. An Army brat born in West Germany and raised there and in the state of Georgia, the worldly Jackson employs an excellent fastball-slider tandem, and he has come a long way over the past three years, cutting down on his walks and posting a career-high strikeout rate in 2012. Jackson's mediocre changeup leaves him vulnerable to left-handed batters, rendering him more of a mid-rotation workhorse than a front-line starter, but with a clean bill of health dating back to 2004, his durability is unassailable.

Chang-Yong Lim
Born: **6/4/1976** Age: **37**
Bats: **R** Throws: **R** Height: **6' 0"** Weight: **175**
Breakout: **21%** Improve: **44%** Collapse: **39%**
Attrition: **12%** MLB: **87%**
Comparables:
Joe Borowski, Trever Miller, Todd Worrell

YEAR	TEAM	LVL	AGE	W	L	SV	G	GS	IP	H	HR	BB	SO	BB9	SO9	GB%	BABIP	WHIP	ERA	FIP	FRA	WARP
2010	YKL	NPB	34	1	2	35	53	0	55^{2}	32	3	16	53	2.6	8.6	—	.207	0.86	1.45	2.76	3.00	0.0
2011	YKL	NPB	35	4	2	32	65	0	62^{1}	40	2	22	69	3.2	10	—	—	1.00	2.17	—	—	—
2012	YKL	NPB	36	0	0	0	9	0	7	6	0	2	7	2.6	9	—	—	1.14	0	—	—	—
2013	*CHN*	*MLB*	*37*	*2*	*1*	*2*	*39*	*0*	*38*	*33*	*4*	*14*	*37*	*3.3*	*8.9*	*46%*	*.299*	*1.23*	*3.76*	*3.73*	*4.09*	*0.3*

Lim is a signing for the future, if a rather odd one. At 36, he's old for a relief pitcher, period, much less one who's never played in the United States. But Lim is rehabbing from Tommy John surgery, and thus isn't even expected to pitch in the majors until 2014. The Cubs are hedging their bets, though, giving Lim a minor-league deal with no guaranteed roster spot but heavily laden with incentives. Lim hails from Korea, but has been pitching in Japan since 2008. This wasn't his first chance to pitch in the U.S.: The Samsung Lions posted him back in 2002, but the Korean team decided the winning bid of $650,000 was too low to let Lim go.

Rodrigo Lopez
Born: **12/14/1975** Age: **37**
Bats: **R** Throws: **R** Height: **6' 2"** Weight: **185**
Breakout: **12%** Improve: **41%** Collapse: **21%**
Attrition: **20%** MLB: **75%**
Comparables:
Kevin Tapani, Preacher Roe, Ramon Ortiz

YEAR	TEAM	LVL	AGE	W	L	SV	G	GS	IP	H	HR	BB	SO	BB9	SO9	GB%	BABIP	WHIP	ERA	FIP	FRA	WARP
2010	ARI	MLB	34	7	16	0	33	33	200	227	37	56	116	2.5	5.2	40%	.287	1.41	4.99	5.24	5.70	-1.0
2011	GWN	AAA	35	6	1	0	9	9	59	59	2	14	44	2.1	6.7	—	.310	1.24	2.59	3.00	3.26	0.0
2011	CHN	MLB	35	6	6	0	26	16	97^{2}	116	18	29	54	2.7	5.0	43%	.302	1.48	4.42	5.33	5.38	-0.5
2012	IOW	AAA	36	2	5	0	18	15	73^{1}	84	8	26	55	3.2	6.8	41%	.330	1.50	5.28	4.69	5.28	0.5
2012	CHN	MLB	36	0	1	0	4	0	6^{1}	8	0	5	2	7.1	2.8	35%	.308	2.05	5.68	5.35	5.18	0.0
2013	*CHN*	*MLB*	*37*	*2*	*3*	*0*	*7*	*7*	*40*	*45*	*7*	*12*	*23*	*2.7*	*5.2*	*42%*	*.304*	*1.42*	*5.49*	*5.22*	*5.96*	*-0.4*

In some parts of Europe, the sight of a single magpie is considered a signal that misfortune is about to befall you. On a pitching staff, the sight of Lopez should be considered a signal that something bad has already happened. He's a dependably bad pitcher who can give you a fair amount of innings so long as you don't care one whit about the results. Teams with designs on contending, respectability, or just not giving up runs are advised to seek better options.

Dillon Maples
Born: **5/9/1992** Age: **21**
Bats: **R** Throws: **R** Height: **6' 3"** Weight: **195**
Breakout: **34%** Improve: **54%** Collapse: **20%**
Attrition: **4%** MLB: **70%**
Comparables:
Camilo Pascual, Brent Knackert, Bob Miller

YEAR	TEAM	LVL	AGE	W	L	SV	G	GS	IP	H	HR	BB	SO	BB9	SO9	GB%	BABIP	WHIP	ERA	FIP	FRA	WARP
2012	CUB	Rk	20	0	1	0	6	4	10^{1}	6	0	10	12	8.7	10.5	69%	.250	1.55	4.35	5.83	4.95	0.2
2013	*CHN*	*MLB*	*21*	*1*	*0*	*1*	*19*	*0*	*33^{1}*	*37*	*5*	*22*	*20*	*6.0*	*5.5*	*46%*	*.311*	*1.78*	*6.50*	*5.93*	*7.06*	*-0.6*

Maples dropped to the 14th round of the 2011 draft because of signability concerns and his commitment to football. The Cubs talked him off the gridiron by signing him for $2.5 million in the last draft in which such spending was possible. Yes, the Cubs signed a football player to pitch: Please try to contain your shock. An elbow injury kept Maples in extended spring training for much of the 2012 season and limited his work the rest of the year. He has a plus fastball and a strong 12-6 curve, but he lacks polish in all areas and has poor command. He has a lot of potential, but there are significant doubts he'll ever be able to reach it.

Carlos Marmol
Born: **10/14/1982** Age: **30**
Bats: **R** Throws: **R** Height: **6' 3"** Weight: **215**
Breakout: **24%** Improve: **43%** Collapse: **37%**
Attrition: **13%** MLB: **94%**
Comparables:
Brad Lidge,Jason Bulger,Derrick Turnbow

YEAR	TEAM	LVL	AGE	W	L	SV	G	GS	IP	H	HR	BB	SO	BB9	SO9	GB%	BABIP	WHIP	ERA	FIP	FRA	WARP
2010	CHN	MLB	27	2	3	38	77	0	77^{2}	40	1	52	138	6.0	16.0	33%	.293	1.18	2.55	2.04	1.58	2.7
2011	CHN	MLB	28	2	6	34	75	0	74	54	5	48	99	5.8	12.0	41%	.295	1.38	4.01	3.51	4.06	0.9
2012	IOW	AAA	29	0	0	0	2	0	2	1	0	2	4	9.0	18.0	67%	.333	1.50	0.00	2.67	-2.55	0.1
2012	CHN	MLB	29	3	3	20	61	0	55^{1}	40	4	45	72	7.3	11.7	41%	.290	1.54	3.42	4.02	4.29	0.4
2013	*CHN*	*MLB*	*30*	*3*	*1*	*22*	*59*	*0*	57^{2}	*35*	*4*	*34*	*80*	*5.3*	*12.5*	*38%*	*.274*	*1.19*	*2.86*	*3.10*	*3.10*	*1.2*

Batters can't figure out where Marmol's pitches are going. Then again, neither can he. That gives him low home-run rates and gaudy strikeout numbers, but it also means that he issues an impressive number of free passes. At one point the Cubs lost patience waiting for him to find the strike zone and demoted him from the closer's role. And then the rest of the bullpen reminded the team it had few other acceptable options. Marmol came within a hair's breadth of being traded to the Angels, and it's possible the Cubs could try to deal him again.

Marcos Mateo
Born: **4/18/1984** Age: **29**
Bats: **R** Throws: **R** Height: **6' 2"** Weight: **220**
Breakout: **41%** Improve: **59%** Collapse: **15%**
Attrition: **16%** MLB: **79%**
Comparables:
Milt Wilcox,Ike Delock,Don Elston

YEAR	TEAM	LVL	AGE	W	L	SV	G	GS	IP	H	HR	BB	SO	BB9	SO9	GB%	BABIP	WHIP	ERA	FIP	FRA	WARP
2010	CUB	Rk	26	0	0	0	1	0	1	0	0	0	1	0.0	9.0	1.%	.000	0.00	0.00	2.26	4.47	0.0
2010	TEN	AA	26	0	0	4	17	1	20^{2}	23	2	3	29	1.3	12.6	53%	.362	1.26	2.17	2.27	2.67	0.7
2010	IOW	AAA	26	0	1	0	8	0	12^{2}	12	0	4	15	2.8	10.6	53%	.333	1.26	4.96	2.17	3.35	0.3
2010	CHN	MLB	26	0	1	0	21	0	21^{2}	20	6	9	26	3.7	10.8	39%	.275	1.34	5.82	5.69	6.88	-0.4
2011	IOW	AAA	27	1	3	2	16	0	18^{1}	20	3	10	18	4.9	8.8	38%	.241	1.64	6.87	5.91	9.13	-0.2
2011	CHN	MLB	27	1	2	0	23	0	23	24	2	10	25	3.9	9.8	36%	.361	1.48	4.30	3.25	3.80	0.3
2013	*CHN*	*MLB*	*29*	*2*	*1*	*1*	*32*	*0*	36^{2}	*35*	*5*	*15*	*30*	*3.7*	*7.4*	*44%*	*.297*	*1.38*	*4.79*	*4.56*	*5.20*	*-0.1*

Mateo missed 2012 after Tommy John surgery, the latest in a string of injuries that have sidelined him. He has impressive stuff, with a high-90s fastball and a slider that gets rave reviews from scouts. The only people who like his repertoire more are major-league hitters, who show their appreciation by clubbing the everloving hell out of whatever he throws their way.

Trey McNutt
Born: **8/2/1989** Age: **23**
Bats: **R** Throws: **R** Height: **6' 5"** Weight: **220**
Breakout: **25%** Improve: **61%** Collapse: **24%**
Attrition: **8%** MLB: **96%**
Comparables:
Art Mahaffey,Doug Waechter,Richard Dotson

YEAR	TEAM	LVL	AGE	W	L	SV	G	GS	IP	H	HR	BB	SO	BB9	SO9	GB%	BABIP	WHIP	ERA	FIP	FRA	WARP
2010	PEO	A	20	6	0	0	13	13	59^{2}	43	0	24	70	3.6	10.6	47%	.293	1.12	1.51	2.57	3.29	1.5
2010	DAY	A+	20	4	0	0	9	9	41	29	3	9	49	2.0	10.8	40%	.264	0.93	2.63	2.80	3.20	1.0
2010	TEN	AA	20	0	1	0	3	3	15^{2}	21	2	4	13	2.3	7.5	47%	.346	1.59	5.73	4.15	4.60	0.2
2011	TEN	AA	21	5	6	0	23	22	95	120	5	39	65	3.7	6.2	49%	.369	1.67	4.55	4.01	5.07	0.6
2012	TEN	AA	22	9	8	0	34	17	95	93	12	45	66	4.3	6.3	45%	.270	1.45	4.26	5.04	6.25	-0.5
2013	*CHN*	*MLB*	*23*	*2*	*3*	*0*	*10*	*7*	35^{2}	*36*	*5*	*17*	*26*	*4.2*	*6.7*	*44%*	*.296*	*1.46*	*5.08*	*4.99*	*5.52*	*-0.1*

McNutt's status as a top prospect in the Cubs system didn't survive the jump to Double-A, where he has struggled for two seasons now. Once thought to show potential as a starter, he seems ticketed for the bullpen, where his hard fastball and power curve might have a chance to shine in spite of his pedestrian command.

Blake Parker
Born: **6/19/1985** Age: **28**
Bats: **R** Throws: **R** Height: **6' 4"** Weight: **225**
Breakout: **29%** Improve: **51%** Collapse: **29%**
Attrition: **18%** MLB: **86%**
Comparables:
Cecilio Guante,Antonio Osuna,Jorge Julio

YEAR	TEAM	LVL	AGE	W	L	SV	G	GS	IP	H	HR	BB	SO	BB9	SO9	GB%	BABIP	WHIP	ERA	FIP	FRA	WARP
2010	TEN	AA	25	0	1	5	13	0	17	11	0	6	25	3.2	13.2	62%	.262	1.00	2.65	1.50	1.96	0.9
2010	IOW	AAA	25	1	4	2	35	0	49^{1}	52	9	28	42	5.1	7.7	46%	.312	1.62	4.75	6.02	7.87	-0.7
2011	TEN	AA	26	1	2	3	16	0	24	20	1	13	20	4.9	7.5	41%	.385	1.38	4.12	3.93	6.39	-0.1
2011	IOW	AAA	26	3	3	4	37	0	51^{1}	37	5	27	60	4.7	10.5	47%	.234	1.25	2.81	4.41	2.93	0.7
2012	IOW	AAA	27	1	1	6	21	0	23^{2}	16	3	6	22	2.3	8.4	41%	.224	0.93	3.42	4.21	4.80	0.2
2012	CHN	MLB	27	0	0	0	7	0	6	10	3	5	6	7.5	9.0	38%	.389	2.50	6.00	10.14	6.92	-0.2
2013	*CHN*	*MLB*	*28*	*1*	*1*	*0*	*29*	*0*	*37*	*32*	*5*	*18*	*36*	*4.4*	*8.7*	*48%*	*.291*	*1.34*	*4.24*	*4.47*	*4.60*	*0.1*

Parker was drafted to work one side of the battery but has ended up on the other, moving from catcher to pitcher in 2007. He pitched well enough at Triple-A in 2011-12 to merit a look in the bullpen, but two extended DL stints with elbow injuries curtailed his chance to prove himself in the majors. Given his minor-league numbers and attractive fastball, Parker will probably get another chance to pitch in relief if he can get healthy again.

Zach Putnam

Born: **7/3/1987** Age: **25**
Bats: **R** Throws: **R** Height: **6' 3"** Weight: **225**
Breakout: **30%** Improve: **55%** Collapse: **15%**
Attrition: **12%** MLB: **83%**

Comparables:
Jensen Lewis,Osiris Matos,Jose Ascanio

YEAR	TEAM	LVL	AGE	W	L	SV	G	GS	IP	H	HR	BB	SO	BB9	SO9	GB%	BABIP	WHIP	ERA	FIP	FRA	WARP
2010	AKR	AA	22	4	1	3	20	7	51^1	58	2	9	41	1.6	7.2	45%	.335	1.31	3.86	2.80	3.85	0.9
2010	COH	AAA	22	0	1	0	17	0	24^1	20	2	7	24	2.6	8.9	46%	.257	1.11	3.33	3.25	4.08	0.5
2011	COH	AAA	23	6	3	9	44	0	69	61	6	23	68	3.0	8.9	—	.284	1.22	3.65	3.44	3.74	0.0
2011	CLE	MLB	23	1	1	0	8	0	7^1	10	1	0	9	0.0	11.0	35%	.409	1.36	6.14	3.20	2.90	0.2
2012	CSP	AAA	24	3	4	12	49	0	60^2	73	5	27	49	4.0	7.3	46%	.351	1.65	4.15	4.51	5.20	0.9
2012	COL	MLB	24	0	0	0	2	0	2	3	0	1	0	4.5	0.0	50%	.375	2.00	0.00	4.64	7.30	0.0
2013	*CHN*	*MLB*	*25*	*2*	*1*	*1*	*25*	*2*	*37^1*	*36*	*4*	*12*	*30*	*3.0*	*7.3*	*47%*	*.305*	*1.30*	*4.27*	*3.95*	*4.64*	*0.1*

Putnam, Cleveland's fifth-round pick in 2008, went to the Rockies in a January 2012 trade for Kevin Slowey. He started strong but struggled to throw strikes from June to season's end, walking 21 batters over his final 40 1/3 innings at Triple-A. He works with a low-90s fastball and a splitter that generates grounders. The University of Michigan product made a few starts earlier in his career but has spent the last two seasons working exclusively out of the bullpen, which is where his future lies. The Cubs picked him up on waivers in early November, then promptly non-tendered him.

Brooks Raley

Born: **6/29/1988** Age: **25**
Bats: **L** Throws: **L** Height: **6' 4"** Weight: **185**
Breakout: **27%** Improve: **64%** Collapse: **18%**
Attrition: **15%** MLB: **61%**

Comparables:
Luke French,Joe Saunders,Abe Alvarez

YEAR	TEAM	LVL	AGE	W	L	SV	G	GS	IP	H	HR	BB	SO	BB9	SO9	GB%	BABIP	WHIP	ERA	FIP	FRA	WARP
2010	DAY	A+	22	8	6	0	27	27	136^1	151	9	43	97	2.8	6.4	45%	.322	1.42	3.50	3.91	4.88	0.2
2011	TEN	AA	23	8	10	0	26	25	136^1	170	16	45	80	3.0	5.3	44%	.309	1.58	4.22	4.71	4.98	0.8
2012	TEN	AA	24	2	2	0	8	8	48^2	47	2	12	29	2.2	5.4	46%	.291	1.21	3.51	3.47	4.26	0.4
2012	IOW	AAA	24	4	8	0	14	14	82	87	7	28	69	3.1	7.6	51%	.321	1.40	3.62	4.23	4.82	0.6
2012	CHN	MLB	24	1	2	0	5	5	24^1	33	7	11	16	4.1	5.9	43%	.317	1.81	8.14	6.92	7.82	-0.6
2013	*CHN*	*MLB*	*25*	*3*	*4*	*0*	*10*	*10*	*54^1*	*59*	*8*	*21*	*32*	*3.5*	*5.2*	*44%*	*.300*	*1.47*	*5.38*	*5.10*	*5.84*	*-0.4*

When Garza went to the disabled list, the Cubs turned to Raley to take his spot in the rotation. Raley did a tremendous amount of damage before being shut down upon hitting his innings limit, giving up seven home runs in only 24 1/3 innings. The Cubs have to hope his poor performance is related to the rapid promotion, and that a more patient approach might allow him to better adjust to the majors. He has a mix of four pitches, with his changeup the featured offering in his repertoire.

Chris Rusin

Born: **10/22/1986** Age: **26**
Bats: **L** Throws: **L** Height: **6' 3"** Weight: **185**
Breakout: **26%** Improve: **60%** Collapse: **15%**
Attrition: **25%** MLB: **77%**

Comparables:
Zach Jackson,Chris Seddon,Matt Chico

YEAR	TEAM	LVL	AGE	W	L	SV	G	GS	IP	H	HR	BB	SO	BB9	SO9	GB%	BABIP	WHIP	ERA	FIP	FRA	WARP
2010	DAY	A+	23	4	3	0	20	17	91	79	6	15	84	1.5	8.3	64%	.292	1.03	3.36	3.17	5.14	0.0
2010	TEN	AA	23	2	1	0	4	4	19	21	0	4	15	1.9	7.1	64%	.344	1.32	1.89	2.60	3.44	0.5
2011	TEN	AA	24	3	2	0	15	15	76	80	5	16	49	1.9	5.8	55%	.286	1.26	3.91	3.70	5.25	0.3
2011	IOW	AAA	24	5	2	0	11	9	62^2	70	8	14	46	2.0	6.6	53%	.327	1.34	4.02	4.69	6.01	0.0
2012	TEN	AA	25	0	0	0	1	1	3	0	0	0	1	0.0	3.0	50%	.000	0.00	0.00	2.48	-1.71	0.0
2012	IOW	AAA	25	8	9	0	25	25	140^1	146	17	53	94	3.4	6.0	53%	.291	1.42	4.55	5.20	6.37	0.5
2012	CHN	MLB	25	2	3	0	7	7	29^2	38	4	11	21	3.3	6.4	47%	.354	1.65	6.37	4.89	4.95	0.3
2013	*CHN*	*MLB*	*26*	*3*	*5*	*0*	*12*	*12*	*63*	*65*	*9*	*22*	*41*	*3.2*	*5.8*	*53%*	*.294*	*1.37*	*4.98*	*4.80*	*5.41*	*-0.2*

Rusin got a brief taste of the majors in a massive roster shuffling that left Raley ineligible to be called up from Iowa, and he managed to come back for an extended audition in September. He might be in the mix to make a Cubs rotation that looks to be thin on talent, but Rusin's stuff looks a lot more like that of a lefty reliever than a credible starting pitcher.

James Russell

Born: **1/8/1986** Age: **27**
Bats: **L** Throws: **L** Height: **6' 5"** Weight: **200**
Breakout: **27%** Improve: **66%** Collapse: **17%**
Attrition: **16%** MLB: **83%**

Comparables:
Bud Daley,Don Gross,Cliff Fannin

YEAR	TEAM	LVL	AGE	W	L	SV	G	GS	IP	H	HR	BB	SO	BB9	SO9	GB%	BABIP	WHIP	ERA	FIP	FRA	WARP
2010	IOW	AAA	24	0	0	0	5	0	11	11	5	4	10	3.3	8.2	41%	.222	1.36	5.73	9.04	8.30	-0.3
2010	CHN	MLB	24	1	1	0	57	0	49	55	11	11	42	2.0	7.7	32%	.291	1.35	4.96	5.23	5.09	0.0
2011	CHN	MLB	25	1	6	0	64	5	67^2	76	12	14	43	1.9	5.7	40%	.290	1.33	4.12	4.74	4.60	0.2
2012	CHN	MLB	26	7	1	2	77	0	69^1	67	5	23	55	3.0	7.1	40%	.293	1.30	3.25	3.53	3.22	1.1
2013	*CHN*	*MLB*	*27*	*3*	*1*	*1*	*67*	*0*	*60^2*	*63*	*10*	*17*	*42*	*2.5*	*6.3*	*38%*	*.296*	*1.31*	*4.85*	*4.80*	*5.28*	*-0.3*

Russell has flirted with starting from time to time but has mostly stuck as a reliever, and was one of the few bright spots in the Cubs relief corps in 2012. A lefty but not a LOOGY, he pitches unconventionally, featuring a slider as his most common pitch. He also has more pitches to choose from than most relievers, with a two- and four-seam fastball, a cutter, a curve, and a changeup. Briefly a part of the College of Closers, he looks more like a middle- or long-relief guy in the future.

Jeff Samardzija

Born: **1/23/1985** Age: **28**
Bats: **R** Throws: **R** Height: **6' 6"** Weight: **225**
Breakout: **25%** Improve: **57%** Collapse: **26%**
Attrition: **12%** MLB: **78%**

Comparables:
Don Gullett, Dustin Nippert, Carlos Torres

YEAR	TEAM	LVL	AGE	W	L	SV	G	GS	IP	H	HR	BB	SO	BB9	SO9	GB%	BABIP	WHIP	ERA	FIP	FRA	WARP
2010	CHN	MLB	25	2	2	0	7	3	19^{1}	21	4	20	9	9.3	4.2	30%	.262	2.12	8.38	8.28	8.24	-0.4
2011	CHN	MLB	26	8	4	0	75	0	88	64	5	50	87	5.1	8.9	43%	.253	1.30	2.97	3.63	3.87	0.9
2012	CHN	MLB	27	9	13	0	28	28	174^{2}	157	20	56	180	2.9	9.3	46%	.296	1.22	3.81	3.59	4.19	2.5
2013	*CHN*	*MLB*	*28*	*7*	*6*	*0*	*48*	*15*	*131*	*116*	*16*	*57*	*114*	*3.9*	*7.8*	*43%*	*.288*	*1.32*	*4.16*	*4.35*	*4.52*	*0.6*

The only thing more baffling about Samardzija than his last name is how he went from being a bullpen failure to a credible setup man to one of the few bright spots in the Cubs starting rotation. Samardzija, called "Shark" by people who would rather not navigate that minefield, has always had an impressive fastball. He just had no idea where it was going, and his secondary pitches lacked polish. It's an open question which Samardzija shows up this year, the capable starter or the middling-to-poor pitcher he's been in the past. Given his history, nobody should be surprised whatever he does.

Miguel Socolovich

Born: **7/24/1986** Age: **26**
Bats: **R** Throws: **R** Height: **6' 2"** Weight: **175**
Breakout: **32%** Improve: **64%** Collapse: **14%**
Attrition: **18%** MLB: **80%**

Comparables:
Kevin Correia, Romulo Sanchez, A.J. Murray

YEAR	TEAM	LVL	AGE	W	L	SV	G	GS	IP	H	HR	BB	SO	BB9	SO9	GB%	BABIP	WHIP	ERA	FIP	FRA	WARP
2011	BIR	AA	24	0	0	1	5	0	7	0	0	2	7	2.6	9.0	60%	.000	0.29	0.00	2.16	4.91	0.0
2011	CHR	AAA	24	3	2	1	29	2	48	46	2	25	63	4.7	11.8	40%	.312	1.48	3.94	2.72	2.29	1.1
2012	IOW	AAA	25	0	0	0	3	0	3^{1}	3	1	0	5	0.0	13.5	50%	.286	0.90	5.40	4.57	6.38	-0.1
2012	NOR	AAA	25	4	0	2	28	0	52	33	4	14	52	2.4	9.0	45%	.223	0.90	1.90	3.14	4.23	0.4
2012	BAL	MLB	25	0	0	0	6	0	10^{1}	11	2	6	6	5.2	5.2	40%	.273	1.65	6.97	6.14	5.15	0.0
2012	CHN	MLB	25	0	0	0	6	0	6	4	1	3	6	4.5	9.0	31%	.200	1.17	4.50	4.80	4.66	0.0
2013	*CHN*	*MLB*	*26*	*1*	*0*	*1*	*23*	*0*	36^{2}	*34*	*5*	*17*	*29*	*4.1*	*7.1*	*43%*	*.288*	*1.39*	*4.62*	*4.78*	*5.02*	*-0.1*

Socolovich is the least interesting type of player in the majors: a replacement-level middle reliever. Even very good teams are sometimes called upon to press such a player into service in the lineup or the starting rotation, but replacement level is awfully low for middle relievers. If you're giving significant playing time to a 0.0-WARP sixth-inning guy, something has gone wrong somewhere along the way.

Arodys Vizcaino

Born: **11/13/1990** Age: **22**
Bats: **R** Throws: **R** Height: **6' 1"** Weight: **190**
Breakout: **26%** Improve: **62%** Collapse: **15%**
Attrition: **6%** MLB: **92%**

Comparables:
Ralph Terry, Jeff Russell, Trevor Cahill

YEAR	TEAM	LVL	AGE	W	L	SV	G	GS	IP	H	HR	BB	SO	BB9	SO9	GB%	BABIP	WHIP	ERA	FIP	FRA	WARP
2010	ROM	A	19	9	4	0	14	14	71^{2}	63	1	9	68	1.1	8.5	43%	.294	1.00	2.38	2.31	3.10	1.7
2010	MYR	A+	19	0	0	0	3	3	13^{2}	16	1	3	11	2.0	7.2	41%	.333	1.39	4.60	3.62	4.49	0.1
2011	LYN	A+	20	2	2	0	9	9	40^{1}	31	3	10	37	2.2	8.3	43%	.232	1.02	2.45	3.11	3.82	0.5
2011	MIS	AA	20	2	3	0	11	8	49^{2}	44	3	18	55	3.3	10.0	—	.313	1.25	3.81	3.15	3.42	0.0
2011	GWN	AAA	20	1	0	0	6	0	7	7	1	0	8	0.0	10.3	—	.316	1.00	1.29	2.81	3.05	0.0
2011	ATL	MLB	20	1	1	0	17	0	17^{1}	16	1	9	17	4.7	8.8	34%	.306	1.44	4.67	3.51	3.30	0.2
2013	*CHN*	*MLB*	*22*	*2*	*2*	*0*	*11*	*6*	36^{1}	*36*	*5*	*15*	*28*	*3.8*	*6.9*	*41%*	*.300*	*1.41*	*4.82*	*4.69*	*5.24*	*-0.1*

Vizcaino looked ticketed for greatness as a starter at one point, but needs of the big-league club in Atlanta and injury pushed him to be a tweener, and odds are he'll end up as a reliever. He missed all of 2012 thanks to Tommy John surgery, and while he was recovering he was shipped to the Cubs in the deadline deal that sent Maholm and Johnson to the Braves. How quickly and how well he bounces back will play a big part in determining what happens with him. He has an impressive fastball that sits in the mid-90s and a big, sexy curve to go with it, but his lack of command means he can't take full advantage of his weapons.

Travis Wood

Born: **2/6/1987** Age: **26**
Bats: **R** Throws: **L** Height: **6' 0"** Weight: **175**
Breakout: **27%** Improve: **59%** Collapse: **23%**
Attrition: **21%** MLB: **96%**

Comparables:
Micah Owings, Noah Lowry, Homer Bailey

YEAR	TEAM	LVL	AGE	W	L	SV	G	GS	IP	H	HR	BB	SO	BB9	SO9	GB%	BABIP	WHIP	ERA	FIP	FRA	WARP
2010	LOU	AAA	23	5	6	0	16	16	100	86	9	24	99	2.2	8.9	45%	.287	1.10	3.06	3.32	4.26	1.6
2010	CIN	MLB	23	5	4	0	17	17	102^{2}	85	9	26	86	2.3	7.5	32%	.259	1.08	3.51	3.45	3.78	2.2
2011	LOU	AAA	24	2	3	0	10	10	52^{1}	64	6	17	47	2.9	8.1	44%	.449	1.55	5.33	4.02	3.84	0.5
2011	CIN	MLB	24	6	6	0	22	18	106	118	10	40	76	3.4	6.5	36%	.324	1.49	4.84	4.03	4.49	0.6
2012	IOW	AAA	25	3	3	0	7	7	41^{1}	48	5	11	39	2.4	8.5	42%	.369	1.43	4.57	4.22	5.31	0.4
2012	CHN	MLB	25	6	13	0	26	26	156	133	25	54	119	3.1	6.9	37%	.244	1.20	4.27	4.89	5.39	1.0
2013	*CHN*	*MLB*	*26*	*8*	*9*	*0*	*23*	*23*	136^{2}	*124*	*16*	*45*	*106*	*3.0*	*7.0*	*39%*	*.286*	*1.24*	*4.05*	*4.16*	*4.40*	*0.9*

Wood had a breakout season in 2010 that looks more distant each passing year. While the Cubs would like to see him start showing the sort of promise he had back in his big year with the Reds, it might serve everyone better to start viewing him in terms of what he is rather than what he might have been. He's a young, cheap starting option and he's left-handed. Guys like Wood might grow on trees but they're not the sort of trees the Cubs have had much luck harvesting in recent years. He won't win a championship on his own, but plenty of teams have missed their chance at the playoffs for lack of a guy like Wood at the back of their rotation.

LINEOUTS

HITTERS

PLAYER	TEAM	LVL	AGE	PA	R	2B	3B	HR	RBI	BB	SO	SB-CS	AVG/OBP/SLG	TAv	BABIP	BRR	FRAA	WARP
UT A. Amezaga	IOW	AAA	34	439	65	17	2	6	42	37	60	12-3	.274/.336/.372	.225	.308	2.4	SS(31): -1.1, 2B(26): 3.7	-0.2
C J. Boscan	GWN	AAA	32	250	22	12	0	3	23	19	59	1-0	.189/.264/.284	.209	.242	1.7	C(27): 0.0	0.2
	ATL	MLB	32	10	0	0	0	0	2	0	1	0-0	.200/.200/.200	.140	.222	0	C(6): -0.0	-0.1
2B Z. DeVoss	PEO	A	21	581	88	24	7	6	38	82	118	35-16	.249/.382/.370	.315	.319	0.6	2B(77): -14.1	1.2
RF R. Golden	PEO	A	20	28	1	0	0	0	0	1	9	1-0	.192/.250/.192	.170	.294	0.3	- 0.1	0
CF J. Ha	TEN	AA	21	529	63	28	3	6	47	50	96	11-5	.273/.352/.385	.251	.331	2.4	CF(62): 2.3, RF(16): -1.1	1.4
INF D. Hernandez	IOW	AAA	28	170	10	9	1	2	13	9	20	1-0	.241/.278/.348	.211	.261	-2.2	3B(20): -0.5, 2B(14): -2.9	-1.1
1B B. LaHair	CHN	MLB	29	380	42	17	0	16	40	39	124	4-2	.259/.334/.450	.276	.358	0.2	1B(58): -6.6, RF(34): 0.9	0.0
SS E. Maysonet	NAS	AAA	30	259	20	13	2	3	19	16	43	2-1	.208/.268/.320	.218	.239	-0.2	SS(35): -5.7, 3B(3): 0.1	-0.8
	MIL	MLB	30	66	7	1	1	1	4	3	9	1-0	.250/.297/.350	.241	.280	-1.2	SS(18): 1.3, 2B(3): 0.0	0.0
INF M. Tolbert	IOW	AAA	30	375	38	16	1	1	13	34	66	9-5	.240/.313/.304	.229	.295	3.1	SS(44): -3.1, 2B(16): 1.2	-0.1

Alfredo Amezaga has a weak bat, but he can play seven positions, and he even pitched a perfect third of an inning in Triple-A last year. ⚾ Veteran backstop **J.C. Boscan** is an organizational soldier with one marketable skill: his ability to control the running game. ⚾ **Zeke DeVoss** has hit well for his level but is still a long way from the majors. ⚾ **Reggie Golden** missed most of 2012 with a torn ACL, but should recover from surgery in time for spring training. ⚾ A rangy center fielder signed out of South Korea, **Jae-Hoon Ha** receives raves for his defense but his bat lags behind. ⚾ **Diory Hernandez** is getting better at using a bindle stick but no better at using a bat. ⚾ **Bryan LaHair**, 2012's most improbable All-Star thanks to an out-of-nowhere first half and a weak crop of NL first basemen, made a smart move by grabbing a two-year, $4.5 million deal to play in Japan for the Softbank Hawks. ⚾ Injuries gave punchless shortstop **Edwin Maysonet** another big-league shot last year in Milwaukee, but the veteran played his way back to Triple-A faster than you can say, "Hey, doesn't his name sound like a French term for a small house?" ⚾ **Matt Tolbert** has fallen, and he can't get up.

PITCHERS

PLAYER	TEAM	LVL	AGE	W	L	SV	IP	H	HR	BB	SO	BB9	SO9	GB%	BABIP	WHIP	ERA	FIP	FRA	WARP
P. Blackburn	CUB	Rk	18	2	0	0	20^2	23	2	7	13	3.0	5.7	69%	.250	1.45	3.48	5.39	13.22	-0.1
A. Carpenter	LVG	AAA	27	6	3	0	74^2	83	10	19	56	2.3	6.8	51%	.315	1.37	3.38	4.75	5.36	0.5
	TOR	MLB	27	0	0	0	9	7	4	6	9	6.0	9.0	24%	.143	1.44	5.00	8.82	7.70	-0.2
J. Conway	—	—	—	—	—	—	—	—	—	—	—	—	—	—	—	—	—	—	—	—
C. Gutierrez	ROC	AAA	24	2	3	0	62^1	60	2	31	57	4.5	8.2	63%	.302	1.46	4.62	3.46	6.00	-0.4
P. Johnson	BOI	A-	21	0	0	0	8	10	0	3	12	3.4	13.5	58%	.526	1.62	4.5	1.45	1.99	0.4
	CUB	Rk	21	0	0	0	3	4	0	0	2	0	6	50%	.500	1.33	0	3.04	0.33	0
J. Lewis	RNO	AAA	28	7	2	4	56^2	50	7	20	43	3.2	6.8	36%	.257	1.24	3.65	4.92	5.65	0.1
R. McNeil	CUB	Rk	18	1	0	0	20	19	1	10	18	4.5	8.1	56%	.188	1.45	1.35	4.88	5.95	0.1
D. Rhee	TEN	AA	23	9	8	0	142^1	168	18	51	78	3.2	4.9	54%	.309	1.54	4.81	4.96	6.63	-0.3
R. Rowland-Smith	IOW	AAA	29	3	6	0	77^2	75	6	41	62	4.8	7.2	34%	.296	1.49	3.94	4.81	4.65	1.0
D. Underwood	CUB	Rk	17	0	1	0	8^2	7	1	6	7	6.2	7.3	67%	.222	1.50	5.19	6.68	5.88	0
B. Wells	PEO	A	19	3	2	1	44	48	0	12	36	2.5	7.4	62%	.345	1.36	3.27	2.81	4.31	0.5
D. Willis	CIN	MLB	29	1	6	0	75^2	78	6	37	57	4.4	6.8	57%	.310	1.52	5.00	4.06	4.82	1.0
A. Zych	DAY	A+	21	3	3	6	36^2	32	0	7	36	1.7	8.8	44%	.327	1.06	3.19	2.17	1.57	0.7
	TEN	AA	21	2	1	0	24^2	26	1	12	28	4.4	10.2	52%	.368	1.54	4.38	3.23	4.07	0.4

A supplemental first-round pick out of Heritage High School in Northern California, **Paul Blackburn** profiles as a mid-rotation starter. **Andrew Carpenter** is a low-velocity sinker-slider guy who doesn't walk or strike anyone out in the minors, but has done a whole bunch of both while also giving up numerous long balls in brief stints in the majors. **Joshua Conway** slid in the draft due to Tommy John surgery, letting the Cubs nab him in the fourth round late rounds. Former Twins first-rounder **Carlos Gutierrez** and his big-league-ready sinker were waived in October after he underwent arthroscopic shoulder surgery in July, and the Cubs snatched him up. **Pierce Johnson** has top-of-the-rotation stuff but is injury prone, causing him to drop to the supplemental round of the draft. **Jensen Lewis** was an effective reliever for a few years with the Indians, but he hasn't seen the majors since 2010 and his minor-league numbers since aren't particularly inspiring. A raw high school arm with good velocity, **Ryan McNeil** passed up a commitment to Long Beach State to play for the Cubs. **Dae-Eun Rhee** hasn't been the pitcher the Cubs expected him to be since coming back from 2008 Tommy John surgery. **Ryan Rowland-Smith** pitched so poorly he got lit up even in the cavernous Safeco Field, but a conversion to relief may be what he needs. The Cubs were able to lure **Duane Underwood** away from a commitment to Georgia with an over-slot $1.05 million bonus. **Benjamin Wells** was derailed by Tommy John surgery and has missed significant time the past two seasons. One-time fan favorite **Dontrelle Willis** hung up his cleats last July, but in the offseason signed a rather minor minor-league deal; the lack of an invite to big-league camp lessens the chances the D-Train will be elevated. A college closer, **Anthony Zych** needs to work on locating his fastball and improving his secondary pitches to make it to the majors.

MANAGER: DALE SVEUM

YEAR	TEAM	W-L	Pythag +/-	Avg PC	100+ P	120+ P	QS	BQS	REL	REL w Zero R	IBB	PH	PH Avg	PH HR	SB2	CS2	SB3	CS3	SAC Att	SAC %	POS SAC	Squeeze	Swing	In Play
2012	CHN	61-101	0	92.5	44	0	73	1	493	363	36	273	.244	6	24	7	0	0	75	64.0%	19	2	316	97

It would be unfair to judge Sveum on his team's record. He was given a roster that couldn't have been expected to contend, and even that was stripped down to the frame at the trade deadline. For the most part, Sveum was able to find the difficult ground between a Bobby Valentine-style blowup and throwing in the towel altogether. (That is, for the most part—his most notable blowup was a fight with umpire Larry Vanover for "eyeballing our dugout.") It helps that he has the support of management, which isn't expecting him to squeeze blood from a stone.

Cincinnati Reds

2012: A BIG RED PITCHING MACHINE

Rebounding from a 79-83 season, Dusty Baker's team claimed their second NL Central title in three years before being ousted by the Giants in an agonizing five-game Division Series in which they squandered a 2-0 lead built on the road. That aside, they produced their highest win total since the 1976 Big Red Machine's 102, and owned at least a share of first place for all but five days after May 23, not including the All-Star break. They pulled away to finish in first place by nine games, the widest margin of any division winner in 2012.

Despite ranking third in the NL in home runs, with seven players reaching double-digit totals, this was no offensive juggernaut. Hamstrung by a .208/.254/.327 line from the leadoff spot, the Reds ranked just ninth in scoring. Their 669 runs marked their lowest total since 1997, when they still played in Riverfront Stadium, and their .253 True Average and .315 on-base percentage both ranked 12th. Instead, they won with pitching and defense, leading the league in fewest runs allowed—fewer than any full-season Cincy squad since 1975—and ranking fourth in defensive efficiency.

The Reds' five-man rotation accounted for all but one stray start, with four starters reaching 200 innings. Johnny Cueto emerged as a Cy Young candidate, Mat Latos lived up to his end of last winter's blockbuster, Homer Bailey finally delivered on the promise he showed as a prospect, Bronson Arroyo pared 20 homers off his ledger from 2011, and Mike Leake was basically league average from the fifth spot once you account for his outstanding hitting. While the rotation ranked fourth in ERA (3.64) and quality-start rate (60 percent), the relief corps was even better, with the league's lowest ERA (2.65) and rate of allowing inherited runners to score (22.7 percent). The loss of free-agent signee Ryan Madson to Tommy John surgery had the potential to destabilize the bullpen, but fill-in closer Aroldis Chapman brought his flamethrower and singed 15.3 batters to a crisp per nine innings behind a capable setup corps.

REDS PROSPECTUS

2012 W-L: 97-65, 1st in NL Central

Pythag	.558	8th	DER	.712	11th
RS/G	4.13	21st	B-Age	28.8	20th
RA/G	3.63	2nd	P-Age	27.2	5th
TAv	.253	25th	Salary	$87.8	18th
BRR	-1.8	17th	M$/MW	$1.54	4th
TAv-P	.246	4th	DL Days	694	24th
FIP	3.77	7th	DL WARP	4.5	11th

Three-Year Park Factors	
Overall	107
HR/RH	120
HR/LH	125
AVG/RH	101
AVG/LH	105

Great American Ball Park (2003)
Att. % of Capacity: 68.5% (15th)
Dim. 328, 379, 404, 370, 325

It's not enough to impact the park factors, but Great American Ball Park yielded 94 fewer runs in 2012.

2013: FAVORITES, IF NOT CHOO-INS

The Reds go into the year as, at worst, co-favorites in the NL Central. At this writing, the 2013 team doesn't look drastically different from the 2012 one, though changes are in store. Cincinnati plans to open a rotation spot for Chapman, leaving the closer duties to late-season acquisition Jonathan Broxton, who's no longer as dominant as he was in his Dodgers days. The lineup will hopefully including more of Joey Votto, who missed seven weeks in the second half while enduring two surgeries on his left knee. Shin-Soo Choo, coming off a .373 OBP figures to provide a huge upgrade at the leadoff spot.

Which starter Chapman will replace remains to be seen; Leake is most likely on the bubble, though some cost savings could be found in absorbing part of Arroyo's $11.5 million salary in the wake of a rebound that could make him palatable to another club. Despite the durability of last year's starters, additional depth will likely be needed. The 4-by-200 feat was unseen since the 2005-06 White Sox, while the last NL team before that was, ominously enough, Baker's 2003 Cubs (Mark Prior, Kerry Wood, Carlos Zambrano, and Matt Clement), not all of whom remained free from longer-term harm, to say the least.

Todd Frazier, who put together a credible Rookie of the Year campaign as a 26-year-old while covering ably for the absences of Votto and Scott Rolen when they were on the DL, will man third base. Choo, acquired in a three-way trade that sent the disappointing Drew Stubbs to Cleveland, will play center field despite only eight starts there at the major-league level, and only one since 2006. Framed by Jay Bruce (who played 35 games in center in 2008) and the re-signed Ryan Ludwick, that outfield should provide pop, but its defense likely won't do the pitching staff many favors. Choo is in his final year before free agency (with $3.5 million of his $4.9 million paid by Cleveland), and the Reds hope he can bridge the gap to speedster Billy Hamilton, who began his conversion from shortstop to center field in the Arizona Fall League after stealing a record 155 bases in 2012.

STATE OF THE ORGANIZATION: TIGHT UNTIL TV MONEY COMES

Though the $87.8 million payroll was the highest in franchise history by about $7 million, it only ranked 18th in the majors and was the lowest of the five NL playoff teams. That reflects the strong player-development work done by the front office during the otherwise unhappy Dan O'Brien and Wayne Krivsky years, which preceded Walt Jocketty's ascension in 2008. The team's three most valuable pitchers (Cueto, Bailey, and Chapman) and five of its six most valuable hitters (Votto, Bruce, Frazier, Ryan Hanigan, and Zack Cozart) are all homegrown players still in their club-control years; Latos, who was acquired by trading homegrown products, is club-controlled as well.

That kind of player development is crucial for a small-market team, though it remains to be seen the extent to which that core can hold together. The Reds get $30 million a year in television rights, and their payroll situation should improve considerably when they're able to tap into the gamewide TV windfall, but that won't happen until after 2016. Votto signed a monster 10-year, $225 million extension in April 2012 that will keep him in Cincinnati through 2023, while Brandon Phillips inked a $72.5 million extension through 2017 around the same time, then stumbled through an ominously blah season. Bruce is signed through 2016, Cueto and Chapman through 2014.

At this writing, the 2013 payroll looks as though it might breach $100 million with the retentions of Ludwick (two years and $15 million) and Broxton (three years and $21 million). Arroyo, Choo, and Nick Masset—whose $3.1 million salary is likely a write-off due to a shoulder injury—come off the books after this season, and Votto effectively takes a $7 million pay cut as he transitions from his old deal to his new one, so this near-$100 million level isn't one that's expected to last even if the Reds don't take steps to pare it by Opening Day.

HITTERS

Tucker Barnhart C
Born: **1/7/1991** Age: **22**
Bats: **B** Throws: **R** Height: **5' 9"**
Weight: **175** Breakout: **3%**
Improve: **57%** Collapse: **3%**
Attrition: **12%** MLB: **97%**
Comparables:
Orlando Mercado,Alex Trevino,Charlie Moore

YEAR	TEAM	LVL	AGE	PA	R	2B	3B	HR	RBI	BB	SO	SB	CS	AVG_OBP_SLG	TAv	BABIP	BRR	FRAA	WARP
2010	BIL	Rk	19	131	17	9	0	0	12	18	25	4	1	.306/.412/.387	.329	.395	0	C(35): 1.6	1.9
2011	DYT	A	20	372	47	24	2	3	43	37	59	2	1	.273/.344/.387	.260	.320	0	--	0.0
2012	BAK	A+	21	231	26	12	1	4	22	29	45	0	2	.278/.371/.409	.293	.340	-5.9	C(47): 0.4	1.0
2012	PEN	AA	21	142	10	4	1	2	12	11	22	1	1	.200/.262/.292	.212	.226	1.5	C(13): -0.2	0.1
2013	*CIN*	*MLB*	*22*	*250*	*22*	*9*	*1*	*4*	*22*	*19*	*58*	*0*	*0*	*.216/.277/.321*	*.216*	*.266*	*-0.3*	*C 0*	*0.0*

Barnhart, a former 10th-round pick out of the same Indiana high school that produced Lance Lynn and Drew Storen, has good plate discipline but little power. Barnhart did almost all of his damage from the left side of the plate last year, and three of his six homers came in a six-game stretch in June. Behind the dish, he shows a strong arm (44 percent caught stealing in nearly 300 minor-league attempts) and solid catching mechanics.

Jay Bruce RF
Born: **4/3/1987** Age: **26**
Bats: **L** Throws: **L** Height: **6' 4"**
Weight: **225** Breakout: **3%**
Improve: **56%** Collapse: **3%**
Attrition: **7%** MLB: **94%**
Comparables:
David Justice,Frank Robinson,Manny Ramirez

YEAR	TEAM	LVL	AGE	PA	R	2B	3B	HR	RBI	BB	SO	SB	CS	AVG_OBP_SLG	TAv	BABIP	BRR	FRAA	WARP
2010	CIN	MLB	23	573	80	23	5	25	70	58	136	5	4	.281/.353/.493	.288	.334	-0.7	RF(146): 23.0	5.0
2011	CIN	MLB	24	664	84	27	2	32	97	71	158	8	7	.256/.341/.474	.276	.297	3.6	RF(155): -2.4	1.7
2012	CIN	MLB	25	633	89	35	5	34	99	62	155	9	3	.252/.327/.514	.285	.283	-4.2	RF(154): 10.5	2.7
2013	*CIN*	*MLB*	*26*	*601*	*80*	*25*	*3*	*30*	*91*	*56*	*143*	*8*	*4*	*.253/.326/.482*	*.282*	*.287*	*-0.5*	*RF 6*	*3.3*

Bruce's monster age-23 campaign in 2010 created unrealistic expectations. He is a premier power hitter who doesn't get on base or make contact all that well. He has overcome his earlier struggles against lefties but relies heavily on his home park, gaining nearly 200 OPS points there over his career. Defensive metrics are split on his abilities in right field, while human observers seem to like his glove and arm. Normally a good runner, Bruce slipped last year—he stole bases at an excellent rate but didn't take the extra base on balls in play as often, or with as much success, as he had in 2010-11. Bruce is a solid middle-of-the-order presence who should provide good value for the duration of his contract, which will pay him $42 million through 2016, when he will be just 29 years old.

Sean Buckley 1B
Born: 9/3/1989 Age: 23
Bats: R Throws: R Height: 6' 5"
Weight: 220 Breakout: 5%
Improve: 58% Collapse: 11%
Attrition: 21% MLB: 84%
Comparables:
Rich Murray,Bud Zipfel,Lee Stevens

YEAR	TEAM	LVL	AGE	PA	R	2B	3B	HR	RBI	BB	SO	SB	CS	AVG_OBP_SLG	TAv	BABIP	BRR	FRAA	WARP
2011	BIL	Rk	21	258	38	11	3	14	41	23	73	6	4	.289/.372/.551	.324	.364	-0.8	3B(20): -6.3	0.7
2012	DYT	A	22	469	46	28	1	14	68	33	139	1	2	.244/.307/.413	.276	.326	-2.9	1B(18): -1.0, LF(2): -0.1	-0.3
2013	*CIN*	*MLB*	*23*	*250*	*23*	*8*	*1*	*8*	*29*	*12*	*88*	*1*	*0*	*.197/.241/.346*	*.209*	*.270*	*-0.3*	*1B -0, 3B -0*	*-1.1*

The son of Reds senior director of amateur scouting Chris Buckley was taken in the sixth round of the 2011 draft out of St. Petersburg College (Bryan LaHair, Nick Masset). He played some third base in rookie ball but moved to first base last year. Buckley's power is real, but unless he improves his approach enough to display it consistently in games, he could say his last goodbye before long.

Emmanuel Burriss 2B
Born: 1/17/1985 Age: 28
Bats: B Throws: R Height: 6' 1"
Weight: 205 Breakout: 0%
Improve: 28% Collapse: 9%
Attrition: 12% MLB: 88%
Comparables:
Chris Getz,Juan Bonilla,Glenn Beckert

YEAR	TEAM	LVL	AGE	PA	R	2B	3B	HR	RBI	BB	SO	SB	CS	AVG_OBP_SLG	TAv	BABIP	BRR	FRAA	WARP
2010	FRE	AAA	25	305	32	11	2	0	22	19	29	11	5	.282/.326/.337	.237	.304	1	SS(36): -1.9, 2B(33): 0.0	0.2
2010	SFN	MLB	25	5	3	0	0	0	0	0	1	0	0	.400/.400/.400	.296	.500	0.2	2B(5): -0.1	0.0
2011	FRE	AAA	26	206	31	8	1	2	10	22	19	24	5	.297/.386/.389	.289	.323	1	2B(13): -2.0, SS(6): 0.2	0.3
2011	SFN	MLB	26	152	14	1	0	0	4	6	17	11	3	.204/.253/.212	.197	.233	0.6	2B(39): 1.3, SS(9): -0.4	-0.7
2012	FRE	AAA	27	120	12	7	2	0	3	11	12	5	0	.274/.342/.377	.270	.302	-0.9	2B(6): 0.3, LF(5): 0.1	0.1
2012	SFN	MLB	27	150	15	1	0	0	7	10	25	5	3	.213/.270/.221	.193	.259	1.4	2B(37): -2.7, 3B(6): -0.1	-0.9
2013	*CIN*	*MLB*	*28*	*250*	*31*	*8*	*1*	*3*	*18*	*16*	*34*	*13*	*4*	*.247/.302/.333*	*.230*	*.271*	*1*	*2B -2, SS -0*	*-0.1*

Burriss was a below-replacement-level player yet again last year with the Giants. The Reds, needing to replace negative-WARP machine Wilson Valdez, signed Burriss to a minor-league deal, and while his versatility in the field and above-average speed might allow him to stick around as an injury replacement or a pinch-running option when rosters expand, his noodle stick makes that his ceiling. Meanwhile, Valdez went to San Francisco, so the Giants won't have to miss Burriss.

Miguel Cairo INF
Born: 5/4/1974 Age: 39
Bats: R Throws: R Height: 6' 2"
Weight: 220 Breakout: 0%
Improve: 24% Collapse: 19%
Attrition: 21% MLB: 70%
Comparables:
Lou Piniella,Felipe Alou,B.J. Surhoff

YEAR	TEAM	LVL	AGE	PA	R	2B	3B	HR	RBI	BB	SO	SB	CS	AVG_OBP_SLG	TAv	BABIP	BRR	FRAA	WARP
2010	CIN	MLB	36	226	30	12	0	4	28	17	30	4	0	.290/.353/.410	.276	.320	0.2	3B(37): -4.6, 1B(14): -0.5	0.6
2011	CIN	MLB	37	276	33	8	2	8	33	18	36	3	4	.265/.330/.412	.265	.279	0.1	3B(58): 2.1, 2B(13): 1.3	1.1
2012	CIN	MLB	38	156	9	7	2	1	13	4	20	4	0	.187/.212/.280	.183	.208	0.8	1B(24): 1.6, 3B(13): -0.6	-0.7
2013	*CIN*	*MLB*	*39*	*250*	*24*	*10*	*2*	*4*	*24*	*13*	*38*	*4*	*1*	*.240/.290/.353*	*.232*	*.266*	*0.2*	*3B -0, 1B 0*	*-0.1*

On August 18, Cairo homered off the Cubs' Jeff Samardzija. It was Cairo's 13th jack in a Reds uniform; all have come at home. Aside from that one shining moment, he did nothing last year. As will happen to 38-year-olds, he saw every aspect of his game deteriorate to the point of uselessness. Only the presence of teammate Wilson Valdez kept him from being the worst infielder in Cincinnati.

Shin-Soo Choo RF
Born: 7/13/1982 Age: 30
Bats: L Throws: L Height: 6' 0"
Weight: 205 Breakout: 4%
Improve: 51% Collapse: 2%
Attrition: 9% MLB: 96%
Comparables:
J.D. Drew,Bobby Abreu,Luke Scott

YEAR	TEAM	LVL	AGE	PA	R	2B	3B	HR	RBI	BB	SO	SB	CS	AVG_OBP_SLG	TAv	BABIP	BRR	FRAA	WARP
2010	CLE	MLB	27	646	81	31	2	22	90	83	118	22	7	.300/.401/.484	.318	.347	-1.3	RF(142): -4.2	5.5
2011	CLE	MLB	28	358	37	11	3	8	36	36	78	12	5	.259/.344/.390	.271	.317	1.2	RF(85): 3.6	1.2
2012	CLE	MLB	29	686	88	43	2	16	67	73	150	21	7	.283/.373/.441	.296	.353	-0.4	RF(154): 0.2	3.1
2013	*CIN*	*MLB*	*30*	*579*	*77*	*28*	*4*	*19*	*75*	*64*	*128*	*17*	*6*	*.276/.368/.463*	*.294*	*.333*	*0.8*	*RF -1*	*3.4*

A rough 2011 both on and off the field left Choo chomping at the bit to return to his 2009-10 levels. Although he hit six fewer home runs than his career-high 22 in 2010, a career-high 43 doubles helped offset the dip. Also, as a leadoff hitter, power wasn't as critical for Choo as it had been in '09-10, when he primarily hit third or fourth. Choo's walk rate isn't what it was back then, but even his current 10 percent mark is a huge upgrade over what Dusty Baker would have put at the top of the order had the Reds not traded for Choo.

Mike Costanzo 3B
Born: 9/9/1983 Age: 29
Bats: L Throws: R Height: 6' 4"
Weight: 215 Breakout: 5%
Improve: 43% Collapse: 4%
Attrition: 7% MLB: 83%
Comparables:
Jack Howell,Sean Berry,Yurendell de Caster

YEAR	TEAM	LVL	AGE	PA	R	2B	3B	HR	RBI	BB	SO	SB	CS	AVG_OBP_SLG	TAv	BABIP	BRR	FRAA	WARP
2010	CAR	AA	26	351	47	21	2	11	50	33	84	7	0	.270/.352/.459	.288	.338	0.9	3B(56): 2.1, 1B(34): -0.4	2.1
2011	CAR	AA	27	291	43	18	5	8	36	33	68	2	3	.271/.351/.475	.283	.335	0	--	0.0
2011	LOU	AAA	27	173	15	6	0	5	26	14	59	1	1	.216/.277/.353	.249	.298	-1.3	3B(23): 3.8, 1B(11): -0.3	0.2
2012	LOU	AAA	28	358	41	18	1	9	38	43	79	0	4	.262/.355/.412	.265	.324	-2.4	3B(55): -4.2, 1B(13): 1.6	0.3
2012	CIN	MLB	28	21	0	0	0	0	2	1	10	0	0	.056/.095/.056	.103	.100	0	1B(2): -0.0	-0.3
2013	*CIN*	*MLB*	*29*	*250*	*26*	*9*	*1*	*8*	*30*	*21*	*73*	*1*	*0*	*.221/.291/.380*	*.240*	*.285*	*-0.4*	*3B -1, 1B -1*	*-0.2*

Taken one pick before Chase Headley in the second round of the 2005 draft, Costanzo is a third baseman who doesn't hit for enough power to offset his inability to make contact. He has hit more than 15 homers once in eight seasons (2007 at Double-A) and owns a career .430 SLG in the minors, which is a tough sell when you strike out every fourth plate appearance. He showed nothing in his cameo of a big-league debut and may not get many more shots. At least his name isn't Costanza, so you can't call him "Can't Stand Ya."

Zack Cozart SS

Born: 8/12/1985 Age: 27
Bats: R Throws: R Height: 6' 1"
Weight: 195 Breakout: 3%
Improve: 44% Collapse: 11%
Attrition: 14% MLB: 95%

Comparables:
Juan Uribe,Ronny Cedeno,Dickie Thon

YEAR	TEAM	LVL	AGE	PA	R	2B	3B	HR	RBI	BB	SO	SB	CS	AVG_OBP_SLG	TAv	BABIP	BRR	FRAA	WARP
2010	LOU	AAA	24	610	91	30	4	17	67	40	107	30	4	.255/.309/.416	.245	.285	3.9	SS(141): 5.8	2.5
2011	LOU	AAA	25	350	57	26	2	7	32	23	51	9	2	.310/.357/.467	.283	.348	1.9	SS(44): 2.0	1.4
2011	CIN	MLB	25	38	6	0	0	2	3	0	6	0	0	.324/.324/.486	.250	.345	-0.3	SS(11): 1.6	0.2
2012	CIN	MLB	26	600	72	33	4	15	35	31	113	4	0	.246/.288/.399	.243	.282	2.2	SS(138): 3.0	1.4
2013	*CIN*	*MLB*	*27*	*477*	*58*	*23*	*2*	*14*	*50*	*24*	*91*	*10*	*2*	*.248/.290/.405*	*.246*	*.279*	*1*	*SS -0*	*1.6*

A slick defensive shortstop, Cozart flashes occasional power and is a good baserunner but has few other offensive skills. He struggled mightily with runners on (559 OPS in 190 PA) last year. Twenty homers in a season isn't out of the question—Kevin Elster once hit 24—but even if that happens, it won't be pretty. Still, Cozart's glove is strong enough to keep him gainfully employed for the next decade. He'll be more valuable in real life than in fantasy, which is fine with him because fantasy doesn't pay the bills.

Jason Donald UT

Born: 9/4/1984 Age: 28
Bats: R Throws: R Height: 6' 2"
Weight: 195 Breakout: 4%
Improve: 46% Collapse: 5%
Attrition: 8% MLB: 92%

Comparables:
Elliot Johnson,Bobby Crosby,Jim Fregosi

YEAR	TEAM	LVL	AGE	PA	R	2B	3B	HR	RBI	BB	SO	SB	CS	AVG_OBP_SLG	TAv	BABIP	BRR	FRAA	WARP
2010	COH	AAA	25	165	27	10	2	2	17	21	33	10	2	.277/.394/.423	.259	.350	2.5	2B(28): 1.3, SS(9): 0.2	0.8
2010	CLE	MLB	25	325	39	19	3	4	24	22	70	5	1	.253/.312/.378	.256	.320	3.2	SS(47): -0.3, 2B(41): -0.7	1.1
2011	COH	AAA	26	201	32	12	0	4	15	19	33	7	3	.310/.397/.448	.301	.365	0	--	0.0
2011	CLE	MLB	26	143	13	6	1	1	8	7	35	3	2	.318/.364/.402	.289	.423	0.2	2B(19): -2.4, SS(16): -0.6	0.6
2012	COH	AAA	27	296	46	18	3	6	31	30	58	5	5	.277/.365/.441	.261	.337	-1.6	SS(14): 0.7, LF(3): -0.0	0.2
2012	CLE	MLB	27	135	18	2	1	2	11	5	40	4	0	.202/.246/.282	.212	.274	0.6	3B(12): -0.6, SS(10): -0.7	-0.6
2013	*CIN*	*MLB*	*28*	*250*	*29*	*11*	*2*	*5*	*22*	*17*	*61*	*5*	*2*	*.243/.306/.372*	*.244*	*.306*	*0.2*	*SS -1, 2B 0*	*0.5*

Donald has fully transitioned into life as "former prospect Jason Donald" and he appears to be doing so with some aplomb. He hit the ball well in Triple-A, but couldn't get things going in his three separate stints with the big club. With the infield spoken for, Donald tried some outfield last year, and he could definitely bring some value as the short side of a platoon. He has a 775 OPS against lefties in his career, compared to just 618 against righties. That said, his offensive skills play much better when he's manning a middle-infield rather than a corner-outfield spot. He came downstate in the same trade that made Choo a Red.

Juan Duran LF

Born: 9/2/1991 Age: 21
Bats: R Throws: R Height: 6' 8"
Weight: 205 Breakout: 3%
Improve: 45% Collapse: 10%
Attrition: 18% MLB: 77%

Comparables:
Johnny Callison,Jeff Burroughs,Gene Stephens

YEAR	TEAM	LVL	AGE	PA	R	2B	3B	HR	RBI	BB	SO	SB	CS	AVG_OBP_SLG	TAv	BABIP	BRR	FRAA	WARP
2010	BIL	Rk	18	221	23	10	1	6	25	19	71	2	3	.244/.308/.393	.266	.344	-2.3	RF(37): -5.2, LF(8): 0.4	-0.4
2011	DYT	A	19	404	48	21	2	16	71	34	152	1	4	.264/.329/.463	.269	.405	0	--	0.0
2012	BAK	A+	20	458	47	16	2	12	57	26	151	3	2	.237/.286/.370	.246	.333	-1.9	LF(59): -3.3, CF(1): -0.0	-0.8
2013	*CIN*	*MLB*	*21*	*250*	*19*	*8*	*1*	*6*	*25*	*10*	*92*	*0*	*0*	*.188/.223/.302*	*.189*	*.271*	*-0.3*	*LF -2, RF -0*	*-1.5*

Duran has serious raw power but an approach that keeps him from using it. He has struck out one-third of the time in more than 1,400 minor-league plate appearances. The Reds spent $2 million to sign him as a 16-year-old out of the Dominican Republic in 2008, but the results haven't come. A hamstring issue in spring training delayed the start of his 2012 campaign, after which he was dominated by pitchers in the hitter-friendly California League. There are concerns about Duran's defense, instincts, and makeup. Something this raw should come with plenty of wasabi and soy sauce.

Todd Frazier 4C

Born: 2/12/1986 Age: 27
Bats: R Throws: R Height: 6' 4"
Weight: 220 Breakout: 6%
Improve: 45% Collapse: 3%
Attrition: 7% MLB: 92%

Comparables:
Chase Headley,Kevin Mitchell,David Freese

YEAR	TEAM	LVL	AGE	PA	R	2B	3B	HR	RBI	BB	SO	SB	CS	AVG_OBP_SLG	TAv	BABIP	BRR	FRAA	WARP
2010	LOU	AAA	24	538	71	32	4	17	66	45	127	14	4	.258/.334/.448	.265	.318	2.6	LF(79): 6.9, 3B(35): -0.4	2.1
2011	LOU	AAA	25	359	47	18	1	15	46	34	82	17	4	.260/.340/.467	.291	.302	1.1	3B(22): 2.4, 1B(15): 0.9	1.6
2011	CIN	MLB	25	121	17	5	0	6	15	7	27	1	0	.232/.289/.438	.268	.253	1.3	3B(27): -0.9, LF(4): -0.0	0.5
2012	CIN	MLB	26	465	55	26	6	19	67	36	103	3	2	.273/.331/.498	.284	.316	0.1	3B(73): -1.4, 1B(39): -0.1	1.7
2013	*CIN*	*MLB*	*27*	*401*	*50*	*19*	*2*	*17*	*55*	*31*	*96*	*9*	*2*	*.247/.311/.450*	*.269*	*.288*	*0.6*	*3B -0, 1B -0*	*1.1*

A supersub we compared to Scott Brosius and Michael Cuddyer in last year's book, Frazier covered third base for an injured Scott Rolen in May and June, and first base for an injured Joey Votto in July and August. Frazier was consistent at the plate all season before fading in September, which may have cost him the NL Rookie of the Year award. He isn't young and he doesn't have a position, but the ability to hit and play all four corners makes him useful in a supporting role—sort of a baseball version of Bruno Kirby.

Brodie Greene 2B

Born: **9/25/1987** Age: **25**
Bats: **R** Throws: **R** Height: **6' 2"**
Weight: **195** Breakout: **6%**
Improve: **36%** Collapse: **15%**
Attrition: **32%** MLB: **93%**

Comparables:
Chuck Cottier,Johnny O'Brien,Mike Richardt

YEAR	TEAM	LVL	AGE	PA	R	2B	3B	HR	RBI	BB	SO	SB	CS	AVG_OBP_SLG	TAv	BABIP	BRR	FRAA	WARP
2010	LYN	A+	22	297	38	11	1	1	20	22	50	8	3	.269/.329/.330	.256	.324	1	SS(46): -1.6, 2B(8): 0.5	1.1
2011	BAK	A+	23	556	79	21	6	14	79	41	75	36	9	.287/.344/.436	.255	.312	3.4	2B(32): 2.0, SS(32): -2.2	1.0
2012	PEN	AA	24	496	46	22	3	3	46	43	70	12	4	.244/.319/.329	.251	.281	0.1	2B(39): 3.2	0.5
2013	*CIN*	*MLB*	*25*	*250*	*23*	*9*	*1*	*3*	*22*	*13*	*47*	*7*	*2*	*.223/.268/.317*	*.209*	*.260*	*0.6*	*2B -1, SS -0*	*-0.4*

A fourth-round pick in 2010 out of Texas A&M, Greene displayed a broad base of skills in 2011 that disappeared last year at Double-A, where he was old for the level. Only the plate discipline remained. Although he has played shortstop in the past, he is better suited to second base, where he spent the vast majority of his time in 2012. It's difficult to get excited about a second baseman who showed no offensive game as a 24-year-old at Double-A.

Billy Hamilton CF

Born: **9/9/1990** Age: **22**
Bats: **B** Throws: **R** Height: **6' 2"**
Weight: **160** Breakout: **10%**
Improve: **56%** Collapse: **6%**
Attrition: **14%** MLB: **97%**

Comparables:
Rance Mulliniks,B.J. Upton,Jeff Blauser

YEAR	TEAM	LVL	AGE	PA	R	2B	3B	HR	RBI	BB	SO	SB	CS	AVG_OBP_SLG	TAv	BABIP	BRR	FRAA	WARP
2010	BIL	Rk	19	316	61	13	10	2	24	28	56	48	9	.318/.385/.456	.336	.391	11.6	2B(55): 10.9, SS(13): -0.2	5.6
2011	DYT	A	20	610	99	18	9	3	50	52	133	103	20	.278/.340/.360	.252	.360	0	--	0.0
2012	BAK	A+	21	392	79	18	9	1	30	50	70	104	21	.323/.413/.439	.290	.404	15.8	SS(58): 5.0	3.8
2012	PEN	AA	21	213	33	4	5	1	15	36	43	51	16	.286/.406/.383	.267	.371	3.8	SS(18): 0.2	0.8
2013	*CIN*	*MLB*	*22*	*250*	*40*	*8*	*3*	*2*	*14*	*23*	*59*	*38*	*8*	*.233/.304/.328*	*.231*	*.301*	*4.9*	*SS 3, 2B 0*	*1.1*

Hamilton's ridiculous speed and equally ridiculous aggressiveness allowed him to take advantage of minor-league teams with limited talent and set what is believed to be a professional record for stolen bases. He won't be able to treat big-leaguers like Little Leaguers, though. The pitchers are quicker to the plate and have better pickoff moves, and teams can execute at every position. Hamilton moved from shortstop to center field last year and didn't immediately take to his new position. Center takes more than raw speed, though he does have a good chance to succeed there. The real question will be his bat. If he can hit major-league pitching enough to bring his speed into the equation, he'll be a monster. But if his bat plays more like Dee Gordon's, his speed will be handcuffed and his game will be one-dimensional. Again, he's got a good shot, but success is not a given.

Ryan Hanigan C

Born: **8/16/1980** Age: **32**
Bats: **R** Throws: **R** Height: **6' 1"**
Weight: **200** Breakout: **1%**
Improve: **28%** Collapse: **9%**
Attrition: **26%** MLB: **94%**

Comparables:
Carlos Ruiz,Paul Lo Duca,Jason Kendall

YEAR	TEAM	LVL	AGE	PA	R	2B	3B	HR	RBI	BB	SO	SB	CS	AVG_OBP_SLG	TAv	BABIP	BRR	FRAA	WARP
2010	LOU	AAA	29	52	6	3	0	0	2	4	6	0	0	.239/.327/.304	.220	.275	0.4	C(8): -0.1	0.0
2010	CIN	MLB	29	243	25	11	0	5	40	33	21	0	0	.300/.405/.429	.295	.313	-1.4	C(68): -0.6	1.8
2011	CIN	MLB	30	304	27	6	0	6	31	35	32	0	0	.267/.356/.357	.269	.285	0.9	C(89): -1.9	1.2
2012	CIN	MLB	31	371	25	14	0	2	24	44	37	0	0	.274/.365/.338	.256	.302	0.4	C(109): -0.2	1.7
2013	*CIN*	*MLB*	*32*	*335*	*36*	*11*	*1*	*6*	*33*	*37*	*40*	*0*	*0*	*.265/.353/.369*	*.262*	*.285*	*-0.6*	*C -0*	*1.6*

Hanigan is patient at the plate, especially against left-handers, against whom he has more than twice as many walks as strikeouts in his career. His power is in the Paul Bako/Gary Bennett range, which is to say nonexistent. Hanigan is a good defender with a strong arm—he caught 48 percent of potential basestealers last year, leading NL catchers, and is at 40 percent for his career. Pressed into starting duty because Devin Mesoraco wasn't ready, Hanigan is best suited to a backup role, where he is an asset.

Jack Hannahan 3B

Born: **3/4/1980** Age: **33**
Bats: **L** Throws: **R** Height: **6' 3"**
Weight: **210** Breakout: **3%**
Improve: **38%** Collapse: **11%**
Attrition: **23%** MLB: **86%**

Comparables:
Todd Zeile,Vance Law,Rico Petrocelli

YEAR	TEAM	LVL	AGE	PA	R	2B	3B	HR	RBI	BB	SO	SB	CS	AVG_OBP_SLG	TAv	BABIP	BRR	FRAA	WARP
2010	PAW	AAA	30	128	15	8	0	4	12	17	27	2	0	.255/.359/.436	.274	.304	0.5	3B(27): 8.5, 2B(3): 0.0	1.4
2010	TAC	AAA	30	264	32	9	1	5	33	34	55	1	0	.228/.333/.344	.248	.279	-1.2	2B(34): 1.8, 3B(19): 4.5	0.8
2011	CLE	MLB	31	366	38	16	2	8	40	38	80	2	1	.250/.331/.387	.264	.308	-0.8	3B(104): 15.9, 1B(8): 0.2	2.6
2012	CLE	MLB	32	318	23	16	0	4	29	27	63	0	2	.244/.312/.341	.246	.299	-0.9	3B(95): 10.7, SS(7): 0.1	1.0
2013	*CIN*	*MLB*	*33*	*310*	*31*	*13*	*1*	*7*	*31*	*30*	*77*	*1*	*1*	*.223/.301/.352*	*.236*	*.280*	*-0.5*	*3B 1, 2B -0*	*0.0*

Basic supply and demand is at work when a career .248 True Average hitter is being heavily pursued by multiple clubs. Hannahan is a glove-first option who has experienced an upturn with the bat in the last two years, moving from awful to something that can be hidden in the nine hole, as long as he's picking everything at third. The vagaries of small samples have done a number on his splits, too, as he crushed lefties and struggled against righties in 2011 only to fail so miserably last year against lefties (481 OPS in 81 plate appearances) that his 712 against righties looked excellent by comparison. Remember: His glove earns him his plate appearances.

Chris Heisey **OF**
Born: **12/14/1984** Age: **28**
Bats: **R** Throws: **R** Height: **6' 1"**
Weight: **225** Breakout: **0%**
Improve: **48%** Collapse: **6%**
Attrition: **16%** MLB: **91%**
Comparables:
Steve Henderson,Wes Covington,Cliff Floyd

YEAR	TEAM	LVL	AGE	PA	R	2B	3B	HR	RBI	BB	SO	SB	CS	AVG_OBP_SLG	TAv	BABIP	BRR	FRAA	WARP
2010	LOU	AAA	25	89	6	3	0	4	13	7	23	2	0	.241/.307/.430	.247	.283	0.1	CF(11): -0.8, RF(9): -0.7	0.1
2010	CIN	MLB	25	226	33	10	1	8	21	16	57	1	2	.254/.324/.433	.267	.312	2.2	LF(38): 0.4, RF(26): 0.1	1.1
2011	CIN	MLB	26	308	44	9	1	18	50	19	78	6	1	.254/.309/.487	.287	.283	0.5	LF(88): 0.4, CF(18): -0.3	1.2
2012	CIN	MLB	27	375	44	16	5	7	31	18	81	6	3	.265/.315/.401	.248	.328	-1.9	LF(61): 3.8, CF(36): -0.3	0.3
2013	*CIN*	*MLB*	*28*	*339*	*45*	*13*	*2*	*13*	*40*	*21*	*82*	*5*	*2*	*.250/.306/.431*	*.262*	*.295*	*0.1*	*LF 1, CF -1*	*1.0*

Heisey's power disappeared last year, his ISO dropping nearly 100 points from a 2011 season that defied his minor-league track record. He hit more grounders last year, but even the balls he hit in the air didn't leave the yard as often as they had in the past. Heisey did most of his damage in July and August, contributing little outside of those two months. He has atrocious plate discipline but can play all three outfield positions and is an adequate defender, which makes him a capable—if limited—role player.

Ryan LaMarre **CF**
Born: **11/21/1988** Age: **24**
Bats: **R** Throws: **L** Height: **6' 3"**
Weight: **205** Breakout: **2%**
Improve: **54%** Collapse: **2%**
Attrition: **15%** MLB: **95%**
Comparables:
Torii Hunter,Jerry Mumphrey,Jerry Morales

YEAR	TEAM	LVL	AGE	PA	R	2B	3B	HR	RBI	BB	SO	SB	CS	AVG_OBP_SLG	TAv	BABIP	BRR	FRAA	WARP
2010	DYT	A	21	263	44	11	0	5	29	21	53	18	7	.282/.372/.396	.273	.347	2.5	CF(31): 0.6, RF(26): 2.1	1.4
2011	BAK	A+	22	503	78	17	3	6	47	42	97	52	14	.279/.347/.371	.272	.339	0.8	CF(50): 2.4, RF(9): 2.1	1.3
2012	PEN	AA	23	558	68	22	3	5	32	60	119	30	10	.263/.356/.353	.270	.339	0.6	CF(37): -2.7	1.0
2013	*CIN*	*MLB*	*24*	*250*	*32*	*9*	*1*	*4*	*19*	*16*	*62*	*14*	*4*	*.224/.285/.329*	*.221*	*.283*	*1.2*	*CF -1, RF 0*	*-0.3*

LaMarre is an athletic center fielder who runs well but is lacking in offensive skills. He makes poor contact and has shown no signs of the power expected from him when the Reds took him in the second round of the 2010 draft. Tools only get you so far in life, and right now LaMarre looks like a fourth or fifth outfielder at best.

Ryan Ludwick **LF**
Born: **7/13/1978** Age: **34**
Bats: **R** Throws: **L** Height: **6' 4"**
Weight: **215** Breakout: **0%**
Improve: **28%** Collapse: **7%**
Attrition: **20%** MLB: **93%**
Comparables:
Jerry Lynch,Ben Oglivie,Luke Scott

YEAR	TEAM	LVL	AGE	PA	R	2B	3B	HR	RBI	BB	SO	SB	CS	AVG_OBP_SLG	TAv	BABIP	BRR	FRAA	WARP
2010	SDN	MLB	31	239	19	7	0	6	26	24	57	0	1	.211/.301/.330	.234	.257	0	RF(58): 3.0	-0.1
2010	SLN	MLB	31	312	44	20	2	11	43	24	64	0	3	.281/.343/.484	.303	.325	-3	RF(67): 3.9, CF(5): 0.2	2.2
2011	PIT	MLB	32	133	14	5	0	2	11	19	37	0	0	.232/.341/.330	.268	.324	-0.2	LF(22): -1.0, RF(13): 0.5	0.0
2011	SDN	MLB	32	420	42	18	0	11	64	32	87	1	1	.238/.301/.373	.249	.277	-2.2	LF(95): -6.4, RF(1): -0.1	-1.0
2012	CIN	MLB	33	472	53	28	1	26	80	42	97	0	1	.275/.346/.531	.290	.299	-0.3	LF(108): -1.5	1.8
2013	*CIN*	*MLB*	*34*	*461*	*56*	*21*	*1*	*21*	*66*	*38*	*107*	*1*	*1*	*.254/.322/.460*	*.276*	*.291*	*-1.1*	*LF -0, RF -0*	*1.6*

Still recovering from the effects of Petco Park, which he claimed affected his swing, Ludwick had a 694 OPS through June 6. The next day, he knocked two homers, beginning a 57-game stretch in which he hit 19 of his 26 home runs. His OPS during that binge was 360 points higher than before and after it. Ludwick found his stroke again in the playoffs, which is good because if he isn't hitting—as he wasn't in the previous year and a half—he has no value.

Donald Lutz **1B**
Born: **2/6/1989** Age: **24**
Bats: **L** Throws: **R** Height: **6' 5"**
Weight: **230** Breakout: **9%**
Improve: **39%** Collapse: **6%**
Attrition: **7%** MLB: **96%**
Comparables:
Rick Reichardt,Todd Hollandsworth,Luis Gonzalez

YEAR	TEAM	LVL	AGE	PA	R	2B	3B	HR	RBI	BB	SO	SB	CS	AVG_OBP_SLG	TAv	BABIP	BRR	FRAA	WARP
2010	BIL	Rk	21	233	36	10	4	7	28	21	45	6	2	.286/.364/.478	.340	.338	2.2	1B(28): -0.4, LF(5): -0.8	2.1
2011	DYT	A	22	506	85	23	3	20	75	34	125	5	4	.301/.358/.492	.290	.375	0	--	0.0
2012	BAK	A+	23	277	42	18	3	17	51	19	71	7	2	.265/.325/.561	.315	.301	0.5	LF(20): -2.9, 1B(19): -0.7	1.2
2012	PEN	AA	23	165	17	5	1	5	15	13	32	1	3	.242/.315/.389	.278	.277	-2.2	LF(13): 1.2, 1B(4): 0.5	0.2
2013	*CIN*	*MLB*	*24*	*250*	*26*	*9*	*2*	*9*	*32*	*13*	*68*	*2*	*1*	*.220/.265/.395*	*.233*	*.263*	*-0.1*	*LF -1, 1B -3*	*-0.6*

Lutz is an oldish first base/left field type out of Germany who focused on hockey in his youth before turning to baseball. He is a very large man who can hit the ball a long way against inferior pitching, as he did in the Arizona Fall League after a solid regular-season campaign that was interrupted mid-summer by a strained oblique incurred while swinging the bat. The power is nice, but Lutz plays a position that demands more than he can offer. Good velocity will beat him, and the higher he advances, the more of that he will see.

Devin Mesoraco C
Born: 6/19/1988 Age: 25
Bats: R Throws: R Height: 6' 2"
Weight: 220 Breakout: 4%
Improve: 63% Collapse: 1%
Attrition: 8% MLB: 92%
Comparables:
Buster Posey,Joe Torre,Miguel Montero

YEAR	TEAM	LVL	AGE	PA	R	2B	3B	HR	RBI	BB	SO	SB	CS	AVG_OBP_SLG	TAv	BABIP	BRR	FRAA	WARP
2010	LYN	A+	22	181	24	11	2	10	31	19	29	2	2	.335/.417/.620	.351	.361	-0.4	C(31): 0.7	2.4
2010	CAR	AA	22	212	42	11	3	13	31	18	37	1	0	.294/.368/.594	.329	.307	0.6	C(49): -0.1	2.8
2010	LOU	AAA	22	58	5	3	0	3	13	6	14	0	1	.231/.310/.462	.298	.257	-0.4	C(17): 0.3	0.6
2011	LOU	AAA	23	499	60	36	2	15	71	52	83	1	1	.289/.371/.484	.272	.325	-0.5	C(63): 1.8	1.3
2011	CIN	MLB	23	53	5	3	0	2	6	3	10	0	0	.180/.226/.360	.207	.184	-0.4	C(16): -0.1	-0.2
2012	CIN	MLB	24	184	17	8	0	5	14	17	33	1	1	.212/.288/.352	.232	.234	-0.3	C(52): 0.9	0.2
2013	*CIN*	*MLB*	*25*	*250*	*29*	*12*	*1*	*10*	*34*	*21*	*49*	*1*	*0*	*.247/.314/.442*	*.266*	*.272*	*-0.4*	*C -0*	*1.2*

When the Reds let Ramon Hernandez walk and traded Yasmani Grandal to San Diego, it was to clear a path for former first-round pick Mesoraco. A preseason favorite for Rookie of the Year honors, he instead reminded us how difficult it is to be a big-league catcher. He didn't hit and was below average in throwing out baserunners. He missed time with a concussion and was suspended in August for bumping an umpire. The good news is that Mesoraco is young and talented, and he isn't the first catcher to stumble out of the gate. He may never hit for much average, but the power should come.

Kristopher Negron UT
Born: 2/1/1986 Age: 27
Bats: R Throws: R Height: 6' 1"
Weight: 180 Breakout: 6%
Improve: 45% Collapse: 15%
Attrition: 19% MLB: 95%
Comparables:
Alex Gonzalez,Charlie Neal,Lyle Luttrell

YEAR	TEAM	LVL	AGE	PA	R	2B	3B	HR	RBI	BB	SO	SB	CS	AVG_OBP_SLG	TAv	BABIP	BRR	FRAA	WARP
2010	CAR	AA	24	547	79	19	6	11	41	51	97	34	9	.272/.358/.409	.273	.317	4.8	SS(120): 9.8	4.7
2011	LOU	AAA	25	465	54	16	4	9	45	22	102	11	1	.216/.269/.338	.213	.260	3.8	SS(37): -3.1, 2B(23): -1.7	-0.9
2012	LOU	AAA	26	319	34	13	2	6	20	22	77	17	3	.218/.287/.342	.207	.276	4.3	3B(17): 3.3, SS(16): -0.1	0.1
2012	CIN	MLB	26	5	2	0	0	0	0	1	2	0	0	.250/.400/.250	.351	.500	0	CF(1): -0.0	0.1
2013	*CIN*	*MLB*	*27*	*250*	*30*	*8*	*2*	*6*	*22*	*14*	*63*	*9*	*2*	*.215/.271/.345*	*.221*	*.262*	*1.3*	*SS -0, 2B 0*	*0.0*

Negron can play anywhere on the infield or outfield but doesn't hit. He has no power and less plate discipline. He's an excellent basestealer, succeeding on 84 percent of his attempts in seven minor-league seasons. A right ACL injury ended Negron's season in July and eventually required surgery. Assuming he's healthy, he can resume his quest to become the new Wilson Valdez.

Xavier Paul OF
Born: 2/25/1985 Age: 28
Bats: L Throws: R Height: 5' 10"
Weight: 205 Breakout: 1%
Improve: 39% Collapse: 11%
Attrition: 23% MLB: 91%
Comparables:
Marty Cordova,Kevin McReynolds,Rondell White

YEAR	TEAM	LVL	AGE	PA	R	2B	3B	HR	RBI	BB	SO	SB	CS	AVG_OBP_SLG	TAv	BABIP	BRR	FRAA	WARP
2010	ABQ	AAA	25	250	46	20	1	12	38	18	41	7	3	.325/.384/.579	.285	.354	2.2	LF(21): 1.2, CF(18): -1.6	1.4
2010	LAN	MLB	25	133	16	8	1	0	11	8	24	3	1	.231/.277/.314	.222	.286	1.2	LF(23): -0.5, RF(14): -0.2	-0.2
2011	LAN	MLB	26	11	0	0	0	0	0	0	5	0	0	.273/.273/.273	.189	.500	0.1	LF(5): 0.0, RF(1): -0.0	0.0
2011	PIT	MLB	26	251	30	6	5	2	20	13	57	16	6	.254/.293/.349	.245	.328	-0.5	RF(69): -1.8, LF(22): -0.9	-0.3
2012	SYR	AAA	27	237	30	16	1	8	44	19	41	6	3	.315/.376/.512	.284	.360	-0.7	LF(22): 0.5, RF(13): -1.6	0.6
2012	CIN	MLB	27	96	8	5	1	2	7	9	18	4	2	.314/.379/.465	.279	.379	-1.1	LF(17): -1.1, RF(1): -0.1	0.1
2013	*CIN*	*MLB*	*28*	*250*	*29*	*12*	*2*	*7*	*28*	*16*	*55*	*8*	*3*	*.260/.309/.414*	*.255*	*.307*	*0.5*	*LF -1, RF -0*	*0.5*

Signed by Cincinnati in July after the Nationals released him from their Triple-A club, Paul is a prototypical reserve outfielder. He is best on the corners but can play center in a pinch. He has poor plate discipline and is useless against left-handers. He runs well but is not an efficient basestealer. Paul wasn't the worst outfielder named Xavier to be released by the Nats last July, so there's that.

Brandon Phillips 2B
Born: 6/28/1981 Age: 32
Bats: R Throws: R Height: 6' 1"
Weight: 205 Breakout: 0%
Improve: 45% Collapse: 4%
Attrition: 8% MLB: 94%
Comparables:
Freddy Sanchez,Mark Ellis,Orlando Hudson

YEAR	TEAM	LVL	AGE	PA	R	2B	3B	HR	RBI	BB	SO	SB	CS	AVG_OBP_SLG	TAv	BABIP	BRR	FRAA	WARP
2010	CIN	MLB	29	687	100	33	5	18	59	46	83	16	12	.275/.332/.430	.266	.293	4.9	2B(152): 5.2	3.4
2011	CIN	MLB	30	674	94	38	2	18	82	44	85	14	9	.300/.353/.457	.280	.322	6.4	2B(148): -6.7	2.5
2012	CIN	MLB	31	623	86	30	1	18	77	28	79	15	2	.281/.321/.429	.257	.298	2.1	2B(146): -4.8	0.3
2013	*CIN*	*MLB*	*32*	*595*	*79*	*27*	*3*	*18*	*65*	*35*	*83*	*14*	*6*	*.267/.316/.428*	*.263*	*.282*	*0.2*	*2B -3*	*2.1*

Phillips' power has been in steady decline since he knocked 30 homers in 2007. Formerly an elite baserunner, he now is just very good. He has never drawn 50 walks in a season. Phillips has a strong defensive reputation, having won three Gold Glove awards, although some metrics like his work more than others do. He plays 140-plus games every year and hasn't been on the disabled list since 2008. Downward trends in power and plate discipline remove some of the luster of the six-year, $72.5 million extension he signed with the Reds in April 2012. Still, Phillips plays every day and should have a few good seasons left in him.

Denis Phipps **OF**

Born: **7/22/1985** Age: **27**
Bats: **R** Throws: **R** Height: **6' 4"**
Weight: **210** Breakout: **1%**
Improve: **48%** Collapse: **4%**
Attrition: **10%** MLB: **91%**

Comparables:
Dave Henderson,Roberto Kelly,Ray Sadler

YEAR	TEAM	LVL	AGE	PA	R	2B	3B	HR	RBI	BB	SO	SB	CS	AVG_OBP_SLG	TAv	BABIP	BRR	FRAA	WARP
2010	LYN	A+	24	103	23	10	1	8	21	10	19	9	1	.333/.398/.720	.375	.348	0.1	CF(24): 1.4	1.8
2010	CAR	AA	24	411	44	22	3	4	35	32	86	8	9	.228/.296/.336	.227	.286	-3.1	RF(66): -6.5, CF(36): 2.4	-1.3
2011	CAR	AA	25	338	53	22	5	7	38	27	83	10	6	.328/.382/.502	.304	.425	0	--	0.0
2011	LOU	AAA	25	173	30	12	2	5	26	13	41	4	1	.380/.428/.576	.318	.487	1.8	CF(21): -0.5, RF(4): 0.4	1.5
2012	LOU	AAA	26	398	48	19	0	15	45	33	103	4	2	.221/.293/.401	.247	.266	1.1	CF(62): 3.0, RF(8): -0.6	0.6
2012	CIN	MLB	26	11	4	1	0	1	2	1	4	0	0	.300/.364/.700	.331	.400	0.2	CF(1): 0.0, RF(1): -0.1	0.1
2012	CIN	MLB	26	11	4	1	0	1	2	1	4	0	0	.300/.364/.700	.331	.400	0.2	LF(2): 0.2	0.1
2013	*CIN*	*MLB*	*27*	*250*	*27*	*11*	*1*	*8*	*30*	*15*	*68*	*3*	*1*	*.230/.281/.395*	*.240*	*.284*	*-0.1*	*CF -1, RF -0*	*0.1*

Phipps is oldish, has marginal power, and can play all three outfield spots. The power comes in streaks—eight of his 18 homers last year came in August. He is an impatient hitter who has struck out more than three times as often as he's walked in more than 3,000 minor-league plate appearances. That and the career 727 OPS in the minors are limiting factors. If everything breaks right, Phipps could eke out a living as a fifth outfielder. More likely, he'll serve as an insurance policy at Triple-A, just a phone call and a plane ride away.

Henry Rodriguez **2B**

Born: **2/9/1990** Age: **23**
Bats: **B** Throws: **R** Height: **5' 11"**
Weight: **150** Breakout: **7%**
Improve: **54%** Collapse: **7%**
Attrition: **11%** MLB: **94%**

Comparables:
DJ LeMahieu,Ryne Sandberg,Aurelio Rodriguez

YEAR	TEAM	LVL	AGE	PA	R	2B	3B	HR	RBI	BB	SO	SB	CS	AVG_OBP_SLG	TAv	BABIP	BRR	FRAA	WARP
2010	DYT	A	20	547	76	37	3	14	78	22	70	33	13	.307/.340/.473	.298	.334	-0.1	2B(118): -6.0, SS(6): -0.0	3.0
2011	BAK	A+	21	254	37	17	0	8	44	14	35	12	7	.340/.378/.513	.305	.372	0.7	2B(31): -2.8, 3B(3): 0.2	0.9
2011	CAR	AA	21	312	39	19	1	5	37	25	43	18	3	.302/.367/.432	.282	.342	0	--	0.0
2012	PEN	AA	22	144	19	6	0	2	15	9	18	3	0	.348/.385/.439	.331	.386	0.9	3B(8): 0.1, 2B(1): 0.0	0.4
2012	LOU	AAA	22	221	23	10	0	3	20	6	35	5	4	.244/.264/.333	.198	.278	-1	3B(24): 3.3, 2B(14): 0.2	-0.6
2012	CIN	MLB	22	16	0	1	0	0	2	2	2	0	0	.214/.312/.286	.205	.250	0	2B(2): -0.0	0.0
2012	CIN	MLB	22	16	0	1	0	0	2	2	2	0	0	.214/.312/.286	.205	.250	0	3B(1): -0.0	0.0
2013	*CIN*	*MLB*	*23*	*250*	*25*	*11*	*1*	*6*	*26*	*6*	*46*	*6*	*3*	*.249/.266/.375*	*.225*	*.282*	*0*	*2B -2, 3B 0*	*-0.2*

Not to be mistaken for the former big-league outfielder who made the All-Star team as an Expo in 1996, or for the fireballing Nationals reliever, this Henry Rodriguez is a diminutive, switch-hitting second baseman. He doesn't walk or strike out much, pops the occasional double, and can get sloppy on defense. Rodriguez has work to do if he wants fans to throw candy bars onto the field in his honor.

Yorman Rodriguez **OF**

Born: **8/15/1992** Age: **20**
Bats: **R** Throws: **R** Height: **6' 3"**
Weight: **184** Breakout: **28%**
Improve: **56%** Collapse: **5%**
Attrition: **19%** MLB: **83%**

Comparables:
Clete Boyer,Bobby Delgreco,Al Kaline

YEAR	TEAM	LVL	AGE	PA	R	2B	3B	HR	RBI	BB	SO	SB	CS	AVG_OBP_SLG	TAv	BABIP	BRR	FRAA	WARP
2010	BIL	Rk	17	184	25	8	3	2	39	8	30	12	2	.339/.367/.456	.335	.400	1.4	RF(24): -0.7, CF(13): -0.3	1.9
2011	DYT	A	18	310	38	10	4	7	40	25	84	20	8	.254/.318/.393	.248	.337	0	--	0.0
2012	DYT	A	19	277	35	17	3	6	44	12	61	7	5	.271/.307/.430	.290	.332	1.6	RF(15): -1.7	0.0
2012	BAK	A+	19	94	7	4	0	0	7	3	39	4	0	.156/.181/.200	.171	.269	1.3	RF(18): -1.5, CF(3): 0.2	-0.8
2013	*CIN*	*MLB*	*20*	*250*	*20*	*9*	*1*	*4*	*22*	*5*	*76*	*4*	*1*	*.201/.219/.302*	*.186*	*.269*	*0.2*	*RF -1, CF -0*	*-1.5*

The good news is that Rodriguez spent his second year in full-season ball at age 19. The bad news is that he still swings at everything. Coming off a shoulder injury in 2011, he started at High-A, where he was overmatched before being sent to extended spring training in May. He enjoyed better success after resurfacing in the Midwest League toward the end of June. Signed out of Venezuela in 2008 for $2.5 million, Rodriguez has some speed and raw power that plays more in batting practice than in games. He has excellent range and a strong arm in right field, but his routes and baserunning aren't great. Despite the abundant tools, this could take a while and might never get finished.

Scott Rolen **3B**

Born: **4/4/1975** Age: **38**
Bats: **R** Throws: **R** Height: **6' 5"**
Weight: **245** Breakout: **0%**
Improve: **23%** Collapse: **21%**
Attrition: **18%** MLB: **73%**

Comparables:
Art Howe,Sid Gordon,Melvin Mora

YEAR	TEAM	LVL	AGE	PA	R	2B	3B	HR	RBI	BB	SO	SB	CS	AVG_OBP_SLG	TAv	BABIP	BRR	FRAA	WARP
2010	CIN	MLB	35	537	66	34	3	20	83	50	82	1	2	.285/.358/.497	.292	.302	-2.3	3B(130): 11.6	4.0
2011	CIN	MLB	36	269	31	20	2	5	36	10	36	1	0	.242/.279/.397	.246	.262	0.1	3B(63): 1.3	0.4
2012	CIN	MLB	37	330	26	17	2	8	39	30	62	2	1	.245/.318/.398	.246	.282	-0.1	3B(87): -0.3	0.2
2013	*CIN*	*MLB*	*38*	*299*	*31*	*16*	*1*	*8*	*35*	*23*	*48*	*2*	*1*	*.254/.321/.411*	*.261*	*.281*	*-0.4*	*3B 0*	*0.7*

If you saw Rolen toward the beginning of his career, you might find it difficult to watch the end. He had an 898 OPS in his twenties and appeared to be on a collision course with Cooperstown. Then injuries—mostly back and left shoulder—came along and his OPS has slipped to 791 in his thirties. He was a great fielder and a very good hitter in his prime, which seems like a lifetime ago. Rolen could still end up in the Hall of Fame. There isn't much difference between him and Ron Santo, although the back end of Rolen's career is what folks are likely to remember. That's unfortunate, because the front end was pretty darned special.

Gabriel Rosa **3B**
Born: **7/2/1993** Age: **19**
Bats: **R** Throws: **R** Height: **6' 5"**
Weight: **185** Breakout: **0%**
Improve: **46%** Collapse: **54%**
Attrition: **54%** MLB: **100%**
Comparables:
Robin Yount,Ed Kranepool,Wayne Causey

YEAR	TEAM	LVL	AGE	PA	R	2B	3B	HR	RBI	BB	SO	SB	CS	AVG_OBP_SLG	TAv	BABIP	BRR	FRAA	WARP
2011	RED	Rk	18	118	17	5	3	2	10	8	28	6	3	.245/.314/.406	.249	.312	0	--	0.0
2012	BIL	Rk	18	80	8	6	0	0	5	1	25	2	0	.179/.188/.256	.184	.259	1.2	3B(10): 0.3, SS(7): 0.8	0.0
2013	*CIN*	*MLB*	*19*	*250*	*16*	*8*	*1*	*3*	*20*	*8*	*81*	*2*	*0*	*.170/.199/.249*	*.162*	*.237*	*-0.1*	*3B -0, SS 0*	*-1.7*

Rosa was taken in the second round of the 2011 draft out of Puerto Rico. He is rangy and athletic, and possesses an enticing power-speed combination, although his plate discipline needs work. A third baseman for now, he profiles as a corner outfielder. Rosa has fewer than 200 professional plate appearances under his belt and was shut down in July with wrist and hip injuries. Refining his game through experience and finding a defensive position are priorities, not necessarily in that order.

Neftali Soto **1B**
Born: **2/28/1989** Age: **24**
Bats: **R** Throws: **R** Height: **6' 3"**
Weight: **180** Breakout: **9%**
Improve: **56%** Collapse: **4%**
Attrition: **23%** MLB: **97%**
Comparables:
Mike Ivie,Adrian Gonzalez,Brandon Snyder

YEAR	TEAM	LVL	AGE	PA	R	2B	3B	HR	RBI	BB	SO	SB	CS	AVG_OBP_SLG	TAv	BABIP	BRR	FRAA	WARP
2010	LYN	A+	21	565	73	33	2	21	73	32	105	0	0	.268/.320/.460	.272	.301	-3.3	1B(91): -5.4, C(10): 0.2	0.1
2011	CAR	AA	22	414	70	19	3	30	76	25	96	0	1	.272/.329/.575	.293	.286	0	--	0.0
2012	LOU	AAA	23	512	55	30	0	14	59	41	116	2	1	.245/.312/.400	.231	.298	-4.8	1B(93): 11.6, RF(1): -0.1	-0.4
2013	*CIN*	*MLB*	*24*	*250*	*25*	*11*	*1*	*9*	*32*	*13*	*61*	*0*	*0*	*.231/.274/.399*	*.237*	*.270*	*-0.4*	*1B -3, C 0*	*-0.7*

A third-round pick in 2007, Soto has been slow to develop. The trouble is plate discipline. Last year marked the first time in four full minor-league seasons that he drew more than 32 walks. He is strong, has good bat speed, and can drive the ball to all fields, although the power went into hiding last year—especially down the stretch, when he hit just one home run over his final 35 games. Soto has a strong arm but does little else in the field and is strictly a first baseman. Getting out from under Votto's shadow would help, as would an improved approach at the plate.

Joey Votto **1B**
Born: **9/10/1983** Age: **29**
Bats: **L** Throws: **R** Height: **6' 4"**
Weight: **220** Breakout: **6%**
Improve: **69%** Collapse: **1%**
Attrition: **4%** MLB: **97%**
Comparables:
Adrian Gonzalez,Mark Teixeira,Miguel Cabrera

YEAR	TEAM	LVL	AGE	PA	R	2B	3B	HR	RBI	BB	SO	SB	CS	AVG_OBP_SLG	TAv	BABIP	BRR	FRAA	WARP
2010	CIN	MLB	26	648	106	36	2	37	113	91	125	16	5	.324/.424/.600	.347	.361	-1.2	1B(148): 2.3	6.8
2011	CIN	MLB	27	719	101	40	3	29	103	110	129	8	6	.309/.416/.531	.322	.349	-3.9	1B(160): 14.2	6.3
2012	CIN	MLB	28	475	59	44	0	14	56	94	85	5	3	.337/.474/.567	.347	.404	-3.4	1B(109): 4.4	5.0
2013	*CIN*	*MLB*	*29*	*497*	*72*	*28*	*2*	*22*	*76*	*69*	*96*	*6*	*3*	*.300/.401/.534*	*.326*	*.340*	*-0.7*	*1B 3*	*4.2*

How intimidating a hitter is Votto? Surgery to repair a torn left meniscus cost him a month and a half after the All-Star break, and he still led the NL in walks and OBP. He is an elite offensive performer when healthy and handles lefties just fine. Votto's power disappeared down the stretch—his last homer came on June 24 and he was shut out over his final 167 plate appearances. The Reds signed him to a 10-year, $225 million deal with a full no-trade clause in April 2012. They will spend most of that time hoping that his knee and other body parts are okay. He is a stud, but with $157 million guaranteed from his age 34 to 40 seasons, this could turn into a Todd Helton contract. Then again, Helton gave his team a lot of great years.

Kyle Waldrop **OF**
Born: **11/26/1991** Age: **21**
Bats: **L** Throws: **L** Height: **6' 4"**
Weight: **190** Breakout: **3%**
Improve: **54%** Collapse: **11%**
Attrition: **15%** MLB: **95%**
Comparables:
Carl Crawford,Ed Kirkpatrick,Roberto Clemente

YEAR	TEAM	LVL	AGE	PA	R	2B	3B	HR	RBI	BB	SO	SB	CS	AVG_OBP_SLG	TAv	BABIP	BRR	FRAA	WARP
2011	BIL	Rk	19	293	38	22	9	5	29	10	65	4	4	.273/.305/.471	.286	.340	-1.4	RF(49): -3.0	-0.1
2012	DYT	A	20	469	59	21	6	8	50	38	77	10	6	.284/.346/.421	.251	.328	0.7	RF(16): -0.0, LF(7): 0.3	-0.2
2013	*CIN*	*MLB*	*21*	*250*	*20*	*9*	*2*	*5*	*24*	*11*	*63*	*2*	*1*	*.214/.248/.328*	*.204*	*.265*	*-0.1*	*RF -1, LF -0*	*-1.0*

Not to be confused with the eponymous Twins right-hander, this Waldrop is a former 12th-round pick who has tools and is young but hasn't produced yet. A two-sport star in high school (he played safety and wide receiver), he draws praise for bat speed that is supposed to generate power, although he and the Reds are still waiting for that to happen. Waldrop improved as the season progressed, but struggled against lefties. Can he translate his tools into usable baseball skills? Magic 8 Ball says: Ask again later.

Jesse Winker LF
Born: **8/17/1993** Age: **19**
Bats: **L** Throws: **L** Height: **6' 4"**
Weight: **200** Breakout: **0%**
Improve: **63%** Collapse: **37%**
Attrition: **37%** MLB: **100%**
Comparables:
Robin Yount,Wayne Causey,Ed Kranepool

YEAR	TEAM	LVL	AGE	PA	R	2B	3B	HR	RBI	BB	SO	SB	CS	AVG_OBP_SLG	TAv	BABIP	BRR	FRAA	WARP
2012	BIL	Rk	18	275	42	16	3	5	35	40	50	1	3	.338/.443/.500	.321	.414	-2.9	LF(26): 2.9, RF(16): -2.9	1.2
2013	*CIN*	*MLB*	*19*	*250*	*24*	*8*	*1*	*5*	*20*	*20*	*67*	*0*	*0*	*.197/.264/.301*	*.204*	*.253*	*-0.3*	*LF -1, RF -0*	*-1.0*

Taken in the supplemental first round of last year's draft as compensation for Ramon Hernandez, Winker had a great pro debut. Rookie-league numbers are not always reliable, and the Pioneer League is oriented toward offense, but as a kid out of high school, Winker fared well against older competition. He showed a good approach, finishing eighth in the circuit in walks despite being one of its youngest players. He hits the ball hard to all fields and has power to the pull side. Winkler doesn't run well and has a thick lower half. He projects as a left fielder or first baseman.

Ryan Wright 2B
Born: **3/12/1981** Age: **31**
Bats: **R** Throws: **R** Height: **6' 1"**
Weight: **195** Breakout: **0%**
Improve: **36%** Collapse: **0%**
Attrition: **13%** MLB: **67%**
Comparables:
Eddie Leon,Dickie Thon,Tito Fuentes

YEAR	TEAM	LVL	AGE	PA	R	2B	3B	HR	RBI	BB	SO	SB	CS	AVG_OBP_SLG	TAv	BABIP	BRR	FRAA	WARP
2011	BIL	Rk	29	182	28	11	2	7	32	9	27	6	1	.298/.348/.522	.306	.311	0.2	2B(30): 0.9	1.1
2012	DYT	A	30	429	53	27	6	5	50	32	51	14	1	.285/.343/.424	.251	.316	1.6	2B(21): 0.8	-0.2
2012	BAK	A+	30	102	17	5	2	5	16	2	17	3	1	.271/.284/.521	.293	.273	1	2B(15): 0.7	0.5
2013	*CIN*	*MLB*	*31*	*250*	*23*	*10*	*2*	*6*	*26*	*10*	*52*	*3*	*1*	*.223/.257/.352*	*.216*	*.258*	*0.3*	*2B -1*	*-0.3*

Wright, a tools-challenged second baseman, makes contact and is a high-percentage basestealer who draws praise for his instincts. The fifth-round pick in 2011 played all over the infield and outfield during his college career at Louisville. Such versatility could pay off, as his upside is that of a utility player. According to his college bio, his hobbies include "hanging out" and he likes to eat pizza and chicken, providing further evidence that he is capable of doing many things.

PITCHERS

Jose Arredondo
Born: **3/30/1984** Age: **29**
Bats: **R** Throws: **R** Height: **6' 1"** Weight: **175**
Breakout: **25%** Improve: **45%** Collapse: **29%**
Attrition: **15%** MLB: **88%**
Comparables:
Tug McGraw,Jason Frasor,Jesse Orosco

YEAR	TEAM	LVL	AGE	W	L	SV	G	GS	IP	H	HR	BB	SO	BB9	SO9	GB%	BABIP	WHIP	ERA	FIP	FRA	WARP
2011	CAR	AA	27	1	0	0	6	0	7^2	4	0	4	11	4.7	12.9	—	.286	1.04	2.35	2.00	2.18	0.0
2011	LOU	AAA	27	1	1	0	6	0	8	6	0	2	10	2.2	11.2	72%	.333	1.00	2.25	1.49	2.35	0.2
2011	CIN	MLB	27	4	4	0	53	0	53	43	5	31	48	5.3	8.2	44%	.271	1.40	3.23	4.28	4.87	0.0
2012	CIN	MLB	28	6	2	1	66	0	61	50	7	34	62	5.0	9.1	47%	.270	1.38	2.95	4.32	4.47	0.4
2013	*CIN*	*MLB*	*29*	*3*	*1*	*1*	*57*	*0*	*55*	*44*	*6*	*24*	*55*	*4.0*	*9.0*	*46%*	*.281*	*1.24*	*3.63*	*3.93*	*3.95*	*0.7*

Arredondo is the unusual right-hander who eats lefties for lunch (not literally; cannibalism is wrong), gaining more than 50 points of OBP against them and more than 120 points of SLG for his career. The former shortstop's command is inconsistent, which may help explain why he's used primarily in low-leverage situations. He doesn't throw as hard as he did when he first came up with the Angels, before 2010 Tommy John surgery, but he gets the job done and is a handy guy to have in middle relief.

Bronson Arroyo
Born: **2/24/1977** Age: **36**
Bats: **R** Throws: **R** Height: **6' 5"** Weight: **195**
Breakout: **25%** Improve: **52%** Collapse: **23%**
Attrition: **21%** MLB: **78%**
Comparables:
Braden Looper,Bret Saberhagen,Paul Byrd

YEAR	TEAM	LVL	AGE	W	L	SV	G	GS	IP	H	HR	BB	SO	BB9	SO9	GB%	BABIP	WHIP	ERA	FIP	FRA	WARP
2010	CIN	MLB	33	17	10	0	33	33	215^2	188	29	59	121	2.5	5.0	44%	.239	1.15	3.88	4.64	5.31	0.7
2011	CIN	MLB	34	9	12	0	32	32	199	227	46	45	108	2.0	4.9	40%	.278	1.37	5.07	5.68	6.06	-1.1
2012	CIN	MLB	35	12	10	0	32	32	202	209	26	35	129	1.6	5.7	43%	.286	1.21	3.74	4.13	4.42	2.4
2013	*CIN*	*MLB*	*36*	*11*	*9*	*0*	*27*	*27*	*172*	*167*	*28*	*41*	*107*	*2.2*	*5.6*	*42%*	*.277*	*1.21*	*4.23*	*4.79*	*4.60*	*0.9*

Arroyo is incredibly durable, having made at least 29 starts every year since 2004. After leading the NL in homers allowed in 2011, he returned to career norms last season and saw the rest of his game follow. His already-excellent control improved, compensating for a lack of dominance—he hasn't cracked 6 K/9 since 2008. Left-handed hitters have hit him like Matt Kemp during that same period, while righties have hit him like Yuniesky Betancourt. Nothing Arroyo does is pretty; he just goes out there, works a lot of innings, and gets more guys out than you think he should. For a right-hander whose fastball sits in the mid- to high-80s, that's not bad.

Homer Bailey

Born: **5/3/1986** Age: **27**
Bats: **R** Throws: **R** Height: **6' 4"** Weight: **200**
Breakout: **24%** Improve: **62%** Collapse: **17%**
Attrition: **8%** MLB: **92%**

Comparables:
Dave Bush, Gavin Floyd, Matt Garza

YEAR	TEAM	LVL	AGE	W	L	SV	G	GS	IP	H	HR	BB	SO	BB9	SO9	GB%	BABIP	WHIP	ERA	FIP	FRA	WARP
2010	DYT	A	24	0	1	0	1	1	4	4	0	1	5	2.2	11.2	36%	.364	1.25	6.75	1.86	2.75	0.1
2010	LOU	AAA	24	2	0	0	4	3	19	15	0	5	15	2.4	7.1	45%	.283	1.05	2.37	2.66	3.66	0.4
2010	CIN	MLB	24	4	3	0	19	19	109	109	11	40	100	3.3	8.3	44%	.315	1.37	4.46	3.77	3.91	2.0
2011	LOU	AAA	25	2	1	0	6	6	30	34	1	6	22	1.8	6.6	39%	.326	1.33	3.00	2.80	4.10	0.2
2011	CIN	MLB	25	9	7	0	22	22	132	136	18	33	106	2.2	7.2	41%	.296	1.28	4.43	4.02	4.88	0.8
2012	CIN	MLB	26	13	10	0	33	33	208	206	26	52	168	2.2	7.3	46%	.290	1.24	3.68	4.01	4.11	2.8
2013	*CIN*	*MLB*	*27*	*11*	*9*	*0*	*28*	*28*	*167^2*	*159*	*22*	*49*	*139*	*2.6*	*7.5*	*44%*	*.297*	*1.24*	*3.99*	*4.12*	*4.34*	*1.5*

The overall seventh pick in 2004, Bailey has been slow to develop but showed signs of becoming the pitcher the Reds envisioned last year. After having each of the previous two seasons truncated by shoulder injuries, he made all of his starts in 2012, showing improved command. Bailey finished strong, including a September 28 no-hitter at Pittsburgh and a seven-inning, 10-strikeout performance against the Giants in Game Three of the NLDS. His OPS against was more than 300 points higher at home than on the road. If he can solve that, he'll be a solid mid-rotation innings-eater for years to come.

Jonathan Broxton

Born: **6/16/1984** Age: **29**
Bats: **R** Throws: **R** Height: **6' 5"** Weight: **300**
Breakout: **24%** Improve: **49%** Collapse: **35%**
Attrition: **14%** MLB: **95%**

Comparables:
Michael Wuertz, Francisco Rodriguez, Brian Wilson

YEAR	TEAM	LVL	AGE	W	L	SV	G	GS	IP	H	HR	BB	SO	BB9	SO9	GB%	BABIP	WHIP	ERA	FIP	FRA	WARP
2010	LAN	MLB	26	5	6	22	64	0	62^1	64	4	28	73	4.0	10.5	46%	.366	1.48	4.04	3.04	3.24	0.8
2011	ABQ	AAA	27	0	0	0	2	2	2	2	0	1	5	4.5	22.5	—	.667	1.50	4.50	0.28	0.31	0.0
2011	LAN	MLB	27	1	2	7	14	0	12^2	15	2	9	10	6.4	7.1	42%	.317	1.89	5.68	5.60	4.55	-0.1
2012	CIN	MLB	28	3	3	4	25	0	22^1	20	1	3	20	1.2	8.1	49%	.306	1.03	2.82	2.46	2.65	0.6
2012	KCA	MLB	28	1	2	23	35	0	35^2	36	1	14	25	3.5	6.3	58%	.321	1.40	2.27	3.35	4.75	0.0
2013	*CIN*	*MLB*	*29*	*3*	*1*	*20*	*48*	*0*	*46^1*	*36*	*4*	*16*	*54*	*3.1*	*10.6*	*49%*	*.299*	*1.11*	*2.92*	*3.03*	*3.17*	*1.0*

Acquired at the trade deadline from Kansas City, Broxton set up Aroldis Chapman down the stretch and showed enough that the Reds re-signed him to a three-year, $21 million deal after the season. This allows Cincinnati to see if a) Chapman can handle starting and b) Broxton can handle closing again. The latter was a dominant closer in 2009 before slipping the following year and missing most of 2011 because of elbow surgery to repair an injury sustained but not disclosed the previous season. His fastball has lost a few ticks since the surgery, but he added a cutter in late August that helped him rediscover the ability to miss bats. The Reds are betting that he can sustain that into the future.

Aroldis Chapman

Born: **2/28/1988** Age: **25**
Bats: **L** Throws: **L** Height: **6' 5"** Weight: **195**
Breakout: **31%** Improve: **57%** Collapse: **16%**
Attrition: **8%** MLB: **94%**

Comparables:
Dave Righetti, Sam McDowell, Herb Score

YEAR	TEAM	LVL	AGE	W	L	SV	G	GS	IP	H	HR	BB	SO	BB9	SO9	GB%	BABIP	WHIP	ERA	FIP	FRA	WARP
2010	LOU	AAA	22	9	6	8	39	13	95^2	77	7	52	125	4.9	11.8	47%	.314	1.35	3.57	3.42	4.06	1.7
2010	CIN	MLB	22	2	2	0	15	0	13^1	9	0	5	19	3.4	12.8	70%	.333	1.05	2.03	1.38	2.58	0.4
2011	CAR	AA	23	1	1	0	5	2	7^1	5	1	6	11	7.4	13.5	—	.308	1.50	6.14	4.53	4.93	0.0
2011	LOU	AAA	23	0	1	0	4	1	5^2	9	0	2	9	3.2	14.3	44%	.500	1.94	11.12	1.12	1.87	0.3
2011	CIN	MLB	23	4	1	1	54	0	50	24	2	41	71	7.4	12.8	54%	.242	1.30	3.60	3.25	4.42	0.4
2012	CIN	MLB	24	5	5	38	68	0	71^2	35	4	23	122	2.9	15.3	37%	.252	0.81	1.51	1.59	1.94	2.5
2013	*CIN*	*MLB*	*25*	*4*	*2*	*3*	*22*	*8*	*59*	*41*	*5*	*28*	*76*	*4.3*	*11.6*	*46%*	*.289*	*1.17*	*3.02*	*3.15*	*3.29*	*1.3*

Already an elite power pitcher, Chapman ratcheted his game up to absurd levels, striking out 44 percent of batters he faced while cutting his walk rate in half and becoming one of baseball's best closers. Lefties had a 330 OPS against him last year, which is about what big-league pitchers hit. He works consistently in the upper-90s, sometimes higher. An injury to Ryan Madson kept the Reds from moving Chapman to the rotation in 2012, but the re-signing of Broxton suggests they may try again this year. Chapman is a completely different kind of pitcher, but as Byung-Hyun Kim reminded us a decade ago, the transition isn't guaranteed to succeed. If it works, Chapman could be a beast. If not, there will be plenty of second-guessing.

Tony Cingrani

Born: **7/5/1989** Age: **23**
Bats: **L** Throws: **L** Height: **6' 5"** Weight: **200**
Breakout: **22%** Improve: **58%** Collapse: **27%**
Attrition: **12%** MLB: **97%**

Comparables:
Brian Matusz, Scott Kazmir, Scott Olsen

YEAR	TEAM	LVL	AGE	W	L	SV	G	GS	IP	H	HR	BB	SO	BB9	SO9	GB%	BABIP	WHIP	ERA	FIP	FRA	WARP
2011	BIL	Rk	21	3	2	0	13	13	51^1	35	1	6	80	1.1	14.0	49%	.356	0.80	1.75	1.83	2.43	1.5
2012	BAK	A+	22	5	1	0	10	10	56^2	39	2	13	71	2.1	11.3	44%	.280	0.92	1.11	2.46	2.10	1.5
2012	PEN	AA	22	5	3	0	16	15	89^1	59	7	39	101	3.9	10.2	44%	.260	1.10	2.12	3.24	3.76	1.1
2012	CIN	MLB	22	0	0	0	3	0	5	4	1	2	9	3.6	16.2	64%	.300	1.20	1.80	3.34	2.72	0.1
2013	*CIN*	*MLB*	*23*	*3*	*2*	*0*	*8*	*8*	*42*	*35*	*5*	*16*	*44*	*3.5*	*9.4*	*44%*	*.293*	*1.24*	*3.76*	*3.80*	*4.09*	*0.5*

Cingrani has posted huge minor-league strikeout numbers thanks to a low-90s fastball with movement and a changeup with what Kevin Goldstein referred to as "very good arm speed and fade." A fringy slider probably keeps him from being a rotation option, but the two-pitch approach could serve him well in relief. Then again, if Cingrani develops a decent breaking ball, he becomes very interesting.

Andrew Cisco

Born: **7/29/1991** Age: **21**
Bats: **L** Throws: **R** Height: **6' 1"** Weight: **205**
Breakout: **23%** Improve: **58%** Collapse: **10%**
Attrition: **7%** MLB: **73%**

Comparables:
Ray Sadecki,Ken Brett,Mark Littell

YEAR	TEAM	LVL	AGE	W	L	SV	G	GS	IP	H	HR	BB	SO	BB9	SO9	GB%	BABIP	WHIP	ERA	FIP	FRA	WARP
2012	BIL	Rk	20	4	1	0	15	15	58^{1}	60	4	7	45	1.1	6.9	46%	.316	1.15	3.39	4.14	4.86	0.7
2013	*CIN*	*MLB*	*21*	*2*	*3*	*0*	*8*	*8*	33^{2}	*40*	*6*	*19*	*15*	*5.0*	*4.0*	*43%*	*.308*	*1.76*	*6.78*	*6.32*	*7.37*	*-0.7*

A sixth-round pick in 2010, Cisco finally made his professional debut last year following 2011 Tommy John surgery, and he showed great control. The grandson of former big-league pitcher and pitching coach Galen Cisco, he works with a low-90s fastball, curve, and sinking changeup. He draws praise for his command and polished approach, both of which will serve him well in full-season ball.

Carlos Contreras

Born: **1/8/1991** Age: **22**
Bats: **R** Throws: **R** Height: **6' 1"** Weight: **165**
Breakout: **23%** Improve: **43%** Collapse: **38%**
Attrition: **20%** MLB: **71%**

Comparables:
Reggie Harris,Ryan Wagner,Phil Paine

YEAR	TEAM	LVL	AGE	W	L	SV	G	GS	IP	H	HR	BB	SO	BB9	SO9	GB%	BABIP	WHIP	ERA	FIP	FRA	WARP
2011	BIL	Rk	20	2	1	0	18	0	36	35	5	23	38	5.8	9.5	34%	.299	1.61	5.00	6.31	5.97	0.1
2012	DYT	A	21	0	1	16	40	0	50^{2}	29	6	19	51	3.4	9.1	46%	.183	0.95	3.20	4.18	5.59	0.0
2012	BAK	A+	21	1	0	4	9	0	10	9	1	5	12	4.5	10.8	67%	.276	1.40	2.70	4.21	4.13	0.2
2013	*CIN*	*MLB*	*22*	*1*	*0*	*1*	*25*	*0*	35^{1}	*35*	*5*	*19*	*27*	*4.9*	*6.8*	*43%*	*.296*	*1.54*	*5.47*	*5.12*	*5.95*	*-0.4*

Contreras moved to the bullpen full time in 2011 and impressed in his full-season debut last year at two levels. He was particularly tough against right-handers, who hit .125 against him at Dayton and struck out three times as often as they got hits. It isn't wise to expect much out of A-ball relievers who stand 6-foot-nothing, but the Reds liked Contreras enough to add him to the 40-man in November.

Daniel Corcino

Born: **8/26/1990** Age: **22**
Bats: **R** Throws: **R** Height: **6' 0"** Weight: **165**
Breakout: **22%** Improve: **60%** Collapse: **19%**
Attrition: **10%** MLB: **84%**

Comparables:
Kyle Davies,Richard Dotson,Ryan Tucker

YEAR	TEAM	LVL	AGE	W	L	SV	G	GS	IP	H	HR	BB	SO	BB9	SO9	GB%	BABIP	WHIP	ERA	FIP	FRA	WARP
2010	BIL	Rk	19	1	3	0	9	9	39^{2}	38	2	17	31	3.9	7.0	51%	.296	1.39	3.40	4.59	5.91	-0.1
2010	DYT	A	19	1	1	0	6	6	31^{1}	31	1	15	29	4.3	8.3	56%	.319	1.47	4.31	3.90	4.14	0.5
2011	DYT	A	20	11	7	0	26	26	139^{1}	128	10	34	156	2.2	10.1	—	.314	1.16	3.42	2.96	3.22	0.0
2012	PEN	AA	21	8	8	0	26	26	143^{1}	111	9	65	126	4.1	7.9	41%	.261	1.23	3.01	3.69	4.86	0.7
2013	*CIN*	*MLB*	*22*	*2*	*2*	*0*	*7*	*7*	35^{2}	*36*	*5*	*18*	*25*	*4.4*	*6.3*	*43%*	*.295*	*1.49*	*5.23*	*5.13*	*5.69*	*-0.2*

Corcino sometimes draws comparisons to Johnny Cueto because of their similar stature, background, organization, and arm strength. He throws with a lot of effort, which leads to control problems, and he tends to leave pitches up in the zone. Corcino's secondary stuff is still in development, and an eventual move to the bullpen could be in his future, depending on how well that goes. The Reds were very aggressive in having him skip High-A last year, and despite the sharp—and unsurprising—decline in K/BB that accompanied the jump, he met the challenge.

Johnny Cueto

Born: **2/15/1986** Age: **27**
Bats: **R** Throws: **R** Height: **5' 11"** Weight: **220**
Breakout: **22%** Improve: **57%** Collapse: **20%**
Attrition: **5%** MLB: **94%**

Comparables:
Noah Lowry,Jeff Niemann,Matt Garza

YEAR	TEAM	LVL	AGE	W	L	SV	G	GS	IP	H	HR	BB	SO	BB9	SO9	GB%	BABIP	WHIP	ERA	FIP	FRA	WARP
2010	CIN	MLB	24	12	7	0	31	31	185^{2}	181	19	56	138	2.7	6.7	44%	.290	1.28	3.64	4.00	4.39	2.3
2011	LOU	AAA	25	0	2	0	4	4	14^{1}	19	1	6	13	3.8	8.2	50%	.318	1.74	6.28	3.59	3.35	0.1
2011	CIN	MLB	25	9	5	0	24	24	156	123	8	47	104	2.7	6.0	55%	.249	1.09	2.31	3.42	4.09	1.2
2012	CIN	MLB	26	19	9	0	33	33	217	205	15	49	170	2.0	7.1	50%	.296	1.17	2.78	3.31	4.14	3.2
2013	*CIN*	*MLB*	*27*	*11*	*9*	*0*	*28*	*28*	174^{2}	*153*	*20*	*47*	*144*	*2.4*	*7.4*	*45%*	*.283*	*1.15*	*3.61*	*3.85*	*3.92*	*2.4*

After battling shoulder issues throughout 2011, Cueto stayed healthy last year and had his best season to date. He does two things that are remarkable. First, he ignores the fact that Great American Ball Park is a bandbox. He has pitched better at home over the last three years than away. Bailey would do well to pick his brain about that. Second, he eliminates the running game. Would-be thieves were 1-for-10 against Cueto in 2012 and are 14-for-42 in his career. Thanks to a great pickoff move, he hasn't allowed a steal of second base since September 2010. Cueto throws strikes, keeps the ball down, and gives his team a good chance to win every time he takes the mound. He is especially tough in day games.

Amir Garrett

Born: **5/3/1992** Age: **21**
Bats: **L** Throws: **L** Height: **6' 6"** Weight: **210**
Breakout: **26%** Improve: **56%** Collapse: **16%**
Attrition: **6%** MLB: **74%**

Comparables:
Wade Blasingame,Bruce Robbins,Dan Schneider

YEAR	TEAM	LVL	AGE	W	L	SV	G	GS	IP	H	HR	BB	SO	BB9	SO9	GB%	BABIP	WHIP	ERA	FIP	FRA	WARP
2012	BIL	Rk	20	0	0	0	2	2	6	4	0	1	5	1.5	7.5	93%	.286	0.83	0.00	3.77	4.36	0.1
2012	CIN	Rk	20	0	2	0	7	5	14	14	1	12	13	7.7	8.4	65%	.303	1.86	5.79	6.45	8.36	-0.1
2013	*CIN*	*MLB*	*21*	*1*	*1*	*0*	*14*	*2*	*33^{1}*	*38*	*6*	*22*	*18*	*5.8*	*4.9*	*49%*	*.308*	*1.80*	*6.74*	*6.44*	*7.33*	*-0.6*

Garrett is perhaps better known as a forward for the St. John's basketball team, where he averaged 7.4 points per game as a freshman before pitching 20 innings last summer. The Reds took Garrett in the 22nd round of the 2011 draft out of a Nevada high school and signed him to a deal with a huge bonus that also allows him to pursue his collegiate hoop dreams. Tall, lanky, and raw, he has huge athleticism and upside but is very much a project.

Ismael Guillon

Born: **2/13/1992** Age: **21**
Bats: **L** Throws: **L** Height: **6' 4"** Weight: **185**
Breakout: **26%** Improve: **59%** Collapse: **8%**
Attrition: **6%** MLB: **76%**

Comparables:
Jim Maloney,David Clyde,Mark Davis

YEAR	TEAM	LVL	AGE	W	L	SV	G	GS	IP	H	HR	BB	SO	BB9	SO9	GB%	BABIP	WHIP	ERA	FIP	FRA	WARP
2010	RED	Rk	18	3	3	0	12	10	57	39	1	23	73	3.6	11.5	—	.292	1.09	3.32	3.13	3.41	0.0
2011	BIL	Rk	19	3	6	0	15	15	63	78	11	46	61	6.6	8.7	41%	.369	1.97	6.57	7.00	7.11	-0.1
2012	BIL	Rk	20	4	1	0	11	10	51	39	1	24	63	4.2	11.1	39%	.309	1.24	2.29	3.75	3.27	1.4
2012	DYT	A	20	2	0	0	4	4	24^{2}	22	2	7	27	2.6	9.9	41%	.323	1.18	2.55	3.07	3.55	0.4
2013	*CIN*	*MLB*	*21*	*2*	*3*	*0*	*7*	*7*	*34*	*36*	*5*	*22*	*25*	*5.9*	*6.6*	*38%*	*.307*	*1.71*	*6.09*	*5.58*	*6.62*	*-0.5*

Signed out of Venezuela in 2008, Guillon features a low-90s fastball and generates strikeouts with a plus changeup. He showed improved command last year but remains a work in progress. With fewer than 200 professional innings to his credit, and the vast majority of those in rookie leagues, he needs more reps at higher levels before we know what he is.

J.J. Hoover

Born: **8/13/1987** Age: **25**
Bats: **R** Throws: **R** Height: **6' 4"** Weight: **215**
Breakout: **35%** Improve: **64%** Collapse: **11%**
Attrition: **11%** MLB: **96%**

Comparables:
Bill Slayback,Aaron Crow,Steve Busby

YEAR	TEAM	LVL	AGE	W	L	SV	G	GS	IP	H	HR	BB	SO	BB9	SO9	GB%	BABIP	WHIP	ERA	FIP	FRA	WARP
2010	MYR	A+	22	11	6	0	24	24	132^{2}	126	7	35	118	2.4	8.0	43%	.299	1.21	3.26	3.24	3.76	2.0
2010	MIS	AA	22	3	1	0	4	4	20^{2}	15	1	15	34	6.5	14.8	27%	.350	1.45	3.48	2.90	3.06	0.6
2011	MIS	AA	23	2	5	1	31	12	87	65	5	28	86	2.9	8.9	—	.262	1.07	2.48	3.18	3.46	0.0
2011	GWN	AAA	23	1	1	1	12	2	18^{2}	12	0	12	31	5.8	14.9	—	.308	1.29	3.38	1.84	2.00	0.0
2012	LOU	AAA	24	4	0	13	30	0	37	15	1	12	55	2.9	13.4	32%	.185	0.73	1.22	1.59	2.68	0.7
2012	CIN	MLB	24	1	0	1	28	0	30^{2}	17	2	13	31	3.8	9.1	27%	.195	0.98	2.05	3.23	3.83	0.4
2013	*CIN*	*MLB*	*25*	*2*	*2*	*0*	*14*	*5*	*37^{1}*	*34*	*5*	*15*	*33*	*3.6*	*8.1*	*39%*	*.295*	*1.31*	*4.32*	*4.38*	*4.70*	*0.2*

British people call vacuum cleaners hoovers, after the once-dominant brand. Vacuum cleaners pick things up off the ground, but this Hoover—acquired from the Braves in April for Juan Francisco—propels them into the air. His extreme fly-ball tendencies could be dangerous in Cincinnati, although they weren't last year. The former starter, who moved to the bullpen in 2011, allowed just three hits over his final 12 appearances, including the postseason. He is a useful arm who can work in a variety of roles and whose arsenal might be better suited to a more forgiving home ballpark.

Mat Latos

Born: **12/9/1987** Age: **25**
Bats: **R** Throws: **R** Height: **6' 7"** Weight: **225**
Breakout: **12%** Improve: **44%** Collapse: **31%**
Attrition: **13%** MLB: **99%**

Comparables:
Jered Weaver,Daniel Hudson,Felix Hernandez

YEAR	TEAM	LVL	AGE	W	L	SV	G	GS	IP	H	HR	BB	SO	BB9	SO9	GB%	BABIP	WHIP	ERA	FIP	FRA	WARP
2010	SDN	MLB	22	14	10	0	31	31	184^{2}	150	16	50	189	2.4	9.2	46%	.273	1.08	2.92	3.03	3.51	3.1
2011	SDN	MLB	23	9	14	0	31	31	194^{1}	168	16	62	185	2.9	8.6	45%	.284	1.18	3.47	3.13	3.65	2.3
2012	CIN	MLB	24	14	4	0	33	33	209^{1}	179	25	64	185	2.8	8.0	47%	.266	1.16	3.48	3.90	4.63	2.4
2013	*CIN*	*MLB*	*25*	*12*	*8*	*0*	*29*	*29*	*178^{2}*	*150*	*21*	*47*	*163*	*2.4*	*8.2*	*44%*	*.279*	*1.10*	*3.19*	*3.69*	*3.46*	*3.5*

Latos moved from the most pitcher-friendly ballpark in MLB to one of the least, and yet his numbers remained virtually unchanged. Of the 25 homers he allowed, 18 came at home. Of those, all but three came with the bases empty, thus limiting the damage. His overall numbers at GABP were slightly better than on the road. After starting out slowly for his new team, Latos dominated in the second half. He has been worked hard for someone his age, and last year he showed a curious tendency to wear down in the middle innings that hadn't surfaced before. Assuming the workload doesn't come back to bite him, Latos should remain at the front of a big-league rotation for the foreseeable future.

Mike Leake

Born: **11/12/1987** Age: **25**
Bats: **R** Throws: **R** Height: **6' 2"** Weight: **185**
Breakout: **18%** Improve: **42%** Collapse: **23%**
Attrition: **16%** MLB: **95%**

Comparables:
Justin Germano,Scott Baker,David Huff

YEAR	TEAM	LVL	AGE	W	L	SV	G	GS	IP	H	HR	BB	SO	BB9	SO9	GB%	BABIP	WHIP	ERA	FIP	FRA	WARP
2010	CIN	MLB	22	8	4	0	24	22	138^1	158	19	49	91	3.2	5.9	51%	.314	1.50	4.23	4.70	5.65	1.2
2011	LOU	AAA	23	0	1	0	2	1	7^1	12	3	0	5	0.0	6.1	60%	.333	1.64	9.82	7.19	8.41	-0.1
2011	CIN	MLB	23	12	9	0	29	26	167^2	159	23	38	118	2.0	6.3	49%	.270	1.17	3.86	4.19	4.95	1.0
2012	CIN	MLB	24	8	9	0	30	30	179	201	26	41	116	2.1	5.8	50%	.306	1.35	4.58	4.47	5.05	2.0
2013	*CIN*	*MLB*	*25*	*10*	*8*	*0*	*25*	*25*	*153^2*	*151*	*22*	*36*	*107*	*2.1*	*6.3*	*48%*	*.294*	*1.22*	*4.22*	*4.37*	*4.59*	*0.9*

Instead of building on his sophomore campaign, Leake reverted to the more hittable version of himself that showed up as a rookie. He is always around the plate and has no platoon splits, but last year he forgot how to pitch at home. His rough second half is disappointing, although hardly cause for alarm. Leake's fastball barely cracks 90 mph, so his command must be impeccable if he is to succeed. Limiting walks is a good first step, but making better pitches in the strike zone is the key to reaching his ceiling, which is roughly Arroyo.

Sam LeCure

Born: **5/4/1984** Age: **29**
Bats: **R** Throws: **R** Height: **6' 2"** Weight: **205**
Breakout: **16%** Improve: **51%** Collapse: **18%**
Attrition: **8%** MLB: **94%**

Comparables:
Dustin Nippert,Bill Singer,Tim Belcher

YEAR	TEAM	LVL	AGE	W	L	SV	G	GS	IP	H	HR	BB	SO	BB9	SO9	GB%	BABIP	WHIP	ERA	FIP	FRA	WARP
2010	LOU	AAA	26	8	3	0	15	15	98	98	8	23	87	2.1	8.0	54%	.323	1.23	3.67	3.46	5.10	0.3
2010	CIN	MLB	26	2	5	0	15	6	48	50	6	25	37	4.7	6.9	46%	.306	1.56	4.50	5.06	5.12	0.1
2011	LOU	AAA	27	0	1	1	4	0	6^2	5	1	2	6	2.7	8.1	70%	.300	1.05	1.35	4.29	3.75	0.0
2011	CIN	MLB	27	2	1	0	43	4	77^2	57	10	21	73	2.4	8.5	47%	.236	1.00	3.71	3.75	4.20	0.8
2012	CIN	MLB	28	3	3	0	48	0	57^1	46	3	23	61	3.6	9.6	48%	.289	1.20	3.14	2.94	3.45	1.1
2013	*CIN*	*MLB*	*29*	*3*	*2*	*0*	*23*	*5*	*52^2*	*47*	*7*	*18*	*44*	*3.1*	*7.6*	*44%*	*.288*	*1.24*	*3.96*	*4.28*	*4.30*	*0.4*

Whatever LeProblem was, LeCure solved it on moving to the bullpen. The former fourth-round pick became a key part of Baker's bullpen last year, particularly toward the end. LeCure held batters to a 505 OPS in the second half and worked four scoreless innings in the NLDS. He didn't allow a homer after May 24—no small feat given his home park. LeCure doesn't throw hard, but features a starter's arsenal that keeps hitters guessing. There is nothing sexy about his game except the results, which in the end are all that matter.

Kyle Lotzkar

Born: **10/24/1989** Age: **23**
Bats: **L** Throws: **R** Height: **6' 5"** Weight: **200**
Breakout: **28%** Improve: **61%** Collapse: **25%**
Attrition: **23%** MLB: **97%**

Comparables:
Arthur Rhodes,Scott Olsen,Danny Duffy

YEAR	TEAM	LVL	AGE	W	L	SV	G	GS	IP	H	HR	BB	SO	BB9	SO9	GB%	BABIP	WHIP	ERA	FIP	FRA	WARP
2010	BIL	Rk	20	2	0	0	4	4	20	8	1	2	33	0.9	14.9	50%	.212	0.50	0.45	1.78	3.29	0.5
2010	RED	Rk	20	1	1	0	8	6	24^1	20	1	12	27	4.4	10.0	—	.317	1.32	3.33	4.91	5.34	0.0
2011	DYT	A	21	3	2	0	14	14	66^2	51	8	25	72	3.4	9.7	—	.264	1.14	4.32	4.56	4.96	0.0
2012	BAK	A+	22	3	0	0	5	5	26^1	22	2	10	27	3.4	9.2	39%	.286	1.22	2.39	4.00	3.32	0.7
2012	PEN	AA	22	4	6	0	18	17	86^1	77	12	53	96	5.5	10.0	38%	.295	1.51	5.21	4.92	5.47	0.3
2013	*CIN*	*MLB*	*23*	*2*	*2*	*0*	*7*	*7*	*36^1*	*33*	*5*	*18*	*35*	*4.4*	*8.7*	*39%*	*.297*	*1.39*	*4.70*	*4.55*	*5.11*	*0.1*

The 53rd overall pick in 2007, Lotzkar has seen his progress slowed by injuries. He missed part of 2008 with a fractured elbow caused by bad mechanics. Then he missed all of the following season thanks to Tommy John surgery—a result of by trying to pitch with said fractured elbow. He stayed healthy enough last year to break 70 innings for the first time in his career, and the lack of experience showed in his poor control. Lotzkar works with a mid-90s fastball, but concerns about his arm and ability to change speeds could force a shift to the bullpen.

Sean Marshall

Born: **8/30/1982** Age: **30**
Bats: **L** Throws: **L** Height: **6' 8"** Weight: **220**
Breakout: **37%** Improve: **67%** Collapse: **15%**
Attrition: **9%** MLB: **85%**

Comparables:
Willie Hernandez,Hong-Chih Kuo,Ryan Madson

YEAR	TEAM	LVL	AGE	W	L	SV	G	GS	IP	H	HR	BB	SO	BB9	SO9	GB%	BABIP	WHIP	ERA	FIP	FRA	WARP
2010	CHN	MLB	27	7	5	1	80	0	74^2	58	3	25	90	3.0	10.8	53%	.294	1.11	2.65	2.30	2.74	1.8
2011	CHN	MLB	28	6	6	5	78	0	75^2	66	1	17	79	2.0	9.4	60%	.312	1.10	2.26	1.83	2.55	1.8
2012	CIN	MLB	29	5	5	9	73	0	61	55	3	16	74	2.4	10.9	56%	.325	1.16	2.51	2.28	2.73	1.5
2013	*CIN*	*MLB*	*30*	*4*	*2*	*4*	*66*	*0*	*60*	*50*	*6*	*16*	*61*	*2.3*	*9.2*	*51%*	*.293*	*1.09*	*2.97*	*3.27*	*3.22*	*1.3*

When a pitcher isn't effective in one role, try him in another. After flailing as a starter for years, Marshall moved to the bullpen in 2009 and has shined. He throws strikes and is durable: He's one of three pitchers to work more than 70 games each of the last three years and he hasn't been on the DL since 2006. He's tough on left-handed batters, although last year righties gave him trouble, posting an OPS more than 300 points higher than that of southpaws. There was no change in Marshall's approach against righties, so this could be a blip. Still, it's worth noting, as his ability to handle right-handed hitters determines whether he's a setup man or a LOOGY. His track record suggests the former, but be mindful of last year's differential.

Nick Masset
Born: **5/17/1982** Age: **31**
Bats: **R** Throws: **R** Height: **6' 5"** Weight: **240**
Breakout: **28%** Improve: **56%** Collapse: **25%**
Attrition: **9%** MLB: **94%**
Comparables:
Juan Rincon,Aaron Heilman,Greg McMichael

YEAR	TEAM	LVL	AGE	W	L	SV	G	GS	IP	H	HR	BB	SO	BB9	SO9	GB%	BABIP	WHIP	ERA	FIP	FRA	WARP
2010	CIN	MLB	28	4	4	2	82	0	76^2	64	7	33	85	3.9	10.0	47%	.291	1.27	3.40	3.41	3.57	1.4
2011	CIN	MLB	29	3	6	1	75	0	70^1	76	5	31	62	4.0	7.9	52%	.332	1.52	3.71	3.52	4.45	0.5
2012	CIN	Rk	30	0	0	0	2	2	2	0	0	0	5	0.0	22.5	—	.000	0.00	0.00	-0.62	-1.12	0.1
2012	DYT	A	30	0	0	0	1	1	1	1	0	0	0	0.0	0.0	67%	.333	1.00	0.00	3.35	3.64	0.0
2012	LOU	AAA	30	0	1	0	6	2	6^2	7	0	3	9	4.1	12.1	67%	.389	1.50	8.10	2.26	5.37	0.0
2013	*CIN*	*MLB*	*31*	*2*	*1*	*1*	*42*	*0*	*38^2*	*33*	*4*	*13*	*37*	*3.1*	*8.5*	*49%*	*.294*	*1.19*	*3.45*	*3.64*	*3.75*	*0.6*

Signed to a two-year deal in January 2012 to avoid arbitration, the previously durable Masset tried to rehab a shoulder issue that began dogging him in spring training, but he never joined the big club and eventually required surgery in September. A hard thrower with spotty command before the injury, Masset made at least 70 appearances every year from 2009 to 2011, but now is a huge question mark, even as the Reds owe him $3.1 million this season.

Logan Ondrusek
Born: **2/13/1985** Age: **28**
Bats: **R** Throws: **R** Height: **6' 9"** Weight: **230**
Breakout: **28%** Improve: **55%** Collapse: **26%**
Attrition: **18%** MLB: **77%**
Comparables:
Ronald Belisario,Mike Schultz,Sean Green

YEAR	TEAM	LVL	AGE	W	L	SV	G	GS	IP	H	HR	BB	SO	BB9	SO9	GB%	BABIP	WHIP	ERA	FIP	FRA	WARP
2010	LOU	AAA	25	0	1	1	14	0	19^2	21	0	3	14	1.4	6.4	55%	.350	1.22	4.11	2.63	3.70	0.2
2010	CIN	MLB	25	5	0	0	60	0	58^2	49	7	20	39	3.1	6.0	50%	.241	1.18	3.68	4.35	4.80	0.2
2011	CIN	MLB	26	5	5	0	66	0	61^1	55	6	28	41	4.1	6.0	51%	.257	1.35	3.23	4.40	5.31	-0.2
2012	LOU	AAA	27	0	1	0	3	0	4	8	1	4	5	9.0	11.2	60%	.500	3.00	9.00	6.91	6.63	-0.1
2012	CIN	MLB	27	5	2	2	63	0	54^2	51	8	31	39	5.1	6.4	44%	.265	1.50	3.46	5.48	5.66	-0.3
2013	*CIN*	*MLB*	*28*	*3*	*1*	*1*	*57*	*0*	*54^2*	*50*	*7*	*21*	*39*	*3.5*	*6.4*	*48%*	*.278*	*1.30*	*4.17*	*4.59*	*4.53*	*0.3*

Ondrusek is a physically large man but not an overpowering pitcher. He lives on the margins with walk and strikeout totals that tarnish the shiny ERAs of his first three seasons. He is durable, having appeared in 60 games or more in each of those seasons, although he faded after the All-Star break for the second straight year. Considering his hard sinker, cutter, and curve, it seems like Ondrusek should be better than he is. The ability to soak innings in middle relief has value, but his continued inability to miss bats is cause for concern.

Curtis Partch
Born: **2/13/1987** Age: **26**
Bats: **R** Throws: **R** Height: **6' 6"** Weight: **227**
Breakout: **23%** Improve: **61%** Collapse: **25%**
Attrition: **35%** MLB: **84%**
Comparables:
Claudio Vargas,Rick Matula,Bill Pulsipher

YEAR	TEAM	LVL	AGE	W	L	SV	G	GS	IP	H	HR	BB	SO	BB9	SO9	GB%	BABIP	WHIP	ERA	FIP	FRA	WARP
2010	LYN	A+	23	7	11	0	28	24	132	165	11	45	96	3.1	6.5	56%	.350	1.59	4.98	4.22	5.09	0.3
2010	CAR	AA	23	0	1	0	1	1	3	7	2	2	1	6.0	3.0	64%	.417	3.00	21.00	14.39	16.25	-0.3
2011	BAK	A+	24	6	11	0	21	21	121^2	161	14	28	93	2.1	6.9	53%	.366	1.55	5.25	4.90	5.39	0.9
2011	CAR	AA	24	2	2	0	7	7	39	55	3	13	33	3.0	7.6	—	.397	1.74	6.92	3.85	4.18	0.0
2012	BAK	A+	25	0	0	2	7	0	12	7	1	3	15	2.2	11.2	71%	.222	0.83	1.50	3.15	2.88	0.3
2012	PEN	AA	25	7	4	6	45	4	70^1	75	7	33	64	4.2	8.2	48%	.332	1.54	4.73	4.20	7.20	0.1
2013	*CIN*	*MLB*	*26*	*2*	*2*	*0*	*11*	*5*	*34^2*	*40*	*6*	*16*	*18*	*4.1*	*4.8*	*48%*	*.309*	*1.61*	*6.19*	*5.80*	*6.73*	*-0.5*

Taken in the 26th round of the 2007 draft out of Merced College (Brian Fuentes, former Reds reliever Brad "The Animal" Lesley), Partch is a converted starter who went from being one of the most hittable pitchers in the minors to merely below average after moving to the bullpen. He pitched well in the Arizona Fall League, and the Reds responded by adding him to the 40-man roster.

Josh Ravin
Born: **1/21/1988** Age: **25**
Bats: **R** Throws: **R** Height: **6' 5"** Weight: **220**
Breakout: **34%** Improve: **60%** Collapse: **17%**
Attrition: **15%** MLB: **85%**
Comparables:
Matt Clement,Jason Schmidt,Carlos Hernandez

YEAR	TEAM	LVL	AGE	W	L	SV	G	GS	IP	H	HR	BB	SO	BB9	SO9	GB%	BABIP	WHIP	ERA	FIP	FRA	WARP
2010	RED	Rk	22	1	0	0	2	2	8	5	0	4	7	4.5	7.9	—	.238	1.12	3.38	4.38	4.76	0.0
2010	DYT	A	22	2	6	0	12	12	56^1	68	4	28	43	4.5	6.9	39%	.358	1.71	4.80	4.82	4.74	0.6
2010	LYN	A+	22	2	1	0	5	5	26	19	2	12	25	4.2	8.7	42%	.246	1.19	2.08	4.10	4.62	0.2
2011	BAK	A+	23	2	8	0	19	19	95^2	79	13	59	93	5.6	8.7	43%	.306	1.44	4.61	6.09	4.95	1.0
2011	CAR	AA	23	0	2	0	6	6	28	30	2	23	21	7.4	6.8	—	.333	1.89	7.07	5.31	5.77	0.0
2012	BAK	A+	24	0	0	0	3	0	3	4	1	2	4	6.0	12.0	46%	.300	2.00	6.00	7.48	6.01	0.0
2012	PEN	AA	24	1	3	0	20	0	24	23	3	20	22	7.5	8.2	51%	.288	1.79	5.25	5.56	6.57	-0.2
2013	*CIN*	*MLB*	*25*	*2*	*2*	*0*	*10*	*6*	*34*	*35*	*6*	*22*	*23*	*5.8*	*6.0*	*40%*	*.296*	*1.69*	*6.12*	*6.08*	*6.65*	*-0.5*

Ravin, a fifth-round pick in 2006 out of the same high school that gave us Dwight Evans and Mike Moustakas, has been slow to develop. In seven professional seasons, he has worked 52 innings above A-ball, with a 6.23 ERA. He has struggled with control throughout his career (6.0 BB/9), and a move to the bullpen—albeit one delayed until mid-June by an oblique injury—didn't help. Ravin made up for lost time in the Arizona Fall League, where he threw strikes in a tiny sample.

Todd Redmond

Born: **5/17/1985** Age: **28**
Bats: **R** Throws: **R** Height: **6' 4"** Weight: **215**
Breakout: **28%** Improve: **67%** Collapse: **17%**
Attrition: **17%** MLB: **80%**

Comparables:
Scott Bankhead, Adam Eaton, Virgil Vasquez

YEAR	TEAM	LVL	AGE	W	L	SV	G	GS	IP	H	HR	BB	SO	BB9	SO9	GB%	BABIP	WHIP	ERA	FIP	FRA	WARP
2010	GWN	AAA	25	9	10	0	28	28	162^{2}	156	21	44	142	2.4	7.9	36%	.287	1.23	4.26	4.05	5.09	0.9
2011	GWN	AAA	26	10	8	0	28	27	169^{2}	152	18	47	142	2.5	7.5	—	.280	1.17	2.92	3.91	4.25	0.0
2012	GWN	AAA	27	6	6	0	18	18	105^{2}	107	11	28	96	2.4	8.2	33%	.309	1.28	3.58	3.55	4.88	0.7
2012	LOU	AAA	27	2	5	0	8	7	43	43	7	11	40	2.3	8.4	36%	.297	1.26	3.77	4.25	6.03	0.0
2012	CIN	MLB	27	0	1	0	1	1	3^{1}	7	1	5	2	13.5	5.4	33%	.429	3.60	10.80	10.34	7.36	-0.1
2013	*CIN*	*MLB*	*28*	*2*	*3*	*0*	*7*	*7*	*41^{2}*	*42*	*7*	*12*	*32*	*2.6*	*6.9*	*36%*	*.292*	*1.29*	*4.75*	*4.71*	*5.16*	*-0.0*

On August 18, in the second game of a doubleheader at home against the Cubs, Redmond made his big-league debut. That kept the Reds from becoming the first team since the 2003 Mariners to use only five starting pitchers in a season. The minor-league veteran is durable and consistent, having made at least 24 starts and pitched at least 145 innings in each of his first seven full seasons. Acquired from Atlanta last July for Paul Janish, Redmond is big but doesn't throw hard, possessing what Kevin Goldstein called "plus-plus command of sub-standard stuff." He projects as a fifth starter or long reliever at best.

Salvatore Romano

Born: **10/12/1993** Age: **19**
Bats: **L** Throws: **R** Height: **6' 6"** Weight: **220**
Breakout: **13%** Improve: **82%** Collapse: **18%**
Attrition: **18%** MLB: **61%**

Comparables:
Mike McCormick, Lew Krausse, David Clyde

YEAR	TEAM	LVL	AGE	W	L	SV	G	GS	IP	H	HR	BB	SO	BB9	SO9	GB%	BABIP	WHIP	ERA	FIP	FRA	WARP
2012	BIL	Rk	18	5	6	0	15	15	64^{1}	74	1	23	52	3.2	7.3	60%	.353	1.51	5.32	4.23	5.51	0.7
2013	*CIN*	*MLB*	*19*	*2*	*3*	*0*	*7*	*7*	*33^{1}*	*40*	*6*	*21*	*14*	*5.6*	*3.9*	*49%*	*.310*	*1.82*	*6.94*	*6.59*	*7.54*	*-0.7*

The Reds went well above slot in signing Romano, a 23rd-round pick in 2011. Physically imposing, Romano held his own in the Pioneer League (the ERA looks high but was roughly league average) despite being one of its younger competitors. His fastball touches 94 mph and he backs it with a curve, although the changeup needs work—lefties hit .337 against him last year. A developing sinker led to plenty of groundball outs, which is a good thing for any pitcher, especially one in the Reds organization.

Alfredo Simon

Born: **5/8/1981** Age: **32**
Bats: **R** Throws: **R** Height: **6' 7"** Weight: **230**
Breakout: **27%** Improve: **50%** Collapse: **19%**
Attrition: **11%** MLB: **71%**

Comparables:
Gary Glover, Dave Giusti, D.J. Houlton

YEAR	TEAM	LVL	AGE	W	L	SV	G	GS	IP	H	HR	BB	SO	BB9	SO9	GB%	BABIP	WHIP	ERA	FIP	FRA	WARP
2010	NOR	AAA	29	1	1	0	4	3	17	15	1	5	14	2.6	7.4	55%	.280	1.18	1.59	3.47	3.63	0.3
2010	BAL	MLB	29	4	2	17	49	0	49^{1}	54	10	22	37	4.0	6.8	48%	.291	1.54	4.93	5.64	6.57	-0.6
2011	BOW	AA	30	1	0	0	4	4	18	15	1	6	20	3.0	10.0	41%	.292	1.17	3.00	3.08	2.58	0.5
2011	BAL	MLB	30	4	9	0	23	16	115^{2}	128	15	40	83	3.1	6.5	43%	.317	1.45	4.90	4.45	4.45	1.0
2012	CIN	MLB	31	3	2	1	36	0	61	65	2	22	52	3.2	7.7	56%	.337	1.43	2.66	3.23	3.49	1.1
2013	*CIN*	*MLB*	*32*	*3*	*2*	*0*	*29*	*6*	*65^{1}*	*64*	*9*	*22*	*52*	*3.0*	*7.2*	*45%*	*.297*	*1.30*	*4.58*	*4.41*	*4.97*	*0.1*

Claimed off waivers from Baltimore in April, Simon enjoyed unprecedented success at the big-league level with the Reds. After closing for the Orioles in 2010 (in a Shawn Chacon sort of way), he moved to the rotation the following year and continued to pitch like Chacon. Last year, back in relief, the huge Dominican threw more first-pitch strikes than in the past. He also—thanks at least in part to increased reliance on a mid-90s sinker—generated more grounders, which served him well at Great American Ball Park. Simon may never get another chance to close but showed enough working in garbage time to earn another look as a seventh- or eighth-inning guy.

Robert Stephenson

Born: **2/24/1993** Age: **20**
Bats: **R** Throws: **R** Height: **6' 3"** Weight: **190**
Breakout: **49%** Improve: **76%** Collapse: **10%**
Attrition: **4%** MLB: **85%**

Comparables:
Madison Bumgarner, Catfish Hunter, Milt Pappas

YEAR	TEAM	LVL	AGE	W	L	SV	G	GS	IP	H	HR	BB	SO	BB9	SO9	GB%	BABIP	WHIP	ERA	FIP	FRA	WARP
2012	BIL	Rk	19	1	0	0	7	7	30^{2}	22	2	8	37	2.3	10.9	56%	.267	0.98	2.05	3.75	3.62	0.8
2012	DYT	A	19	2	4	0	8	8	34^{1}	32	4	15	35	3.9	9.2	41%	.308	1.37	4.19	4.40	6.08	0.0
2013	*CIN*	*MLB*	*20*	*2*	*3*	*0*	*8*	*8*	*35^{1}*	*36*	*5*	*19*	*27*	*4.7*	*6.9*	*44%*	*.301*	*1.54*	*5.48*	*5.12*	*5.95*	*-0.2*

Stephenson, taken with the 27th pick in 2011, features a fastball that runs in the mid-90s and a power curve that can be inconsistent at times. He has simple mechanics and clean arm action, leading to good command and control for his age. The Reds went over slot to sign Stephenson away from a University of Washington commitment. He needs to gain experience and stay healthy, but with his stuff and feel for pitching, he has the upside of a front-line starter.

Nicholas Travieso
Born: **1/31/1994** Age: **19**
Bats: **R** Throws: **R** Height: **6' 3"** Weight: **215**
Breakout: **9%** Improve: **89%** Collapse: **11%**
Attrition: **11%** MLB: **39%**
Comparables:
Rick Wise,Bob Miller,Jim Bethke

YEAR	TEAM	LVL	AGE	W	L	SV	G	GS	IP	H	HR	BB	SO	BB9	SO9	GB%	BABIP	WHIP	ERA	FIP	FRA	WARP
2012	CIN	Rk	18	0	2	0	8	8	21	20	3	5	14	2.1	6.0	42%	.333	1.19	4.71	5.90	9.01	0.0
2013	*CIN*	*MLB*	*19*	*0*	*0*	*0*	*12*	*0*	*33^{1}*	*39*	*6*	*21*	*17*	*5.7*	*4.6*	*45%*	*.308*	*1.79*	*6.73*	*6.41*	*7.31*	*-0.5*

The Reds took Travieso with the 14th pick last year out of a Florida high school. His fastball sits in the mid-90s and has been clocked as high as 98 mph. He also features a late-breaking slider and works down in the zone. He has good mound presence and feel but needs to improve his command, which is not surprising given his lack of experience. Travieso's changeup shows promise but he sometimes leaves it up. His delivery is clean, with BP pitching mechanics expert Doug Thorburn praising his torque (aids velocity) and momentum (aids movement), while expressing some concern over his balance (aids command). Travieso, primarily a reliever until his senior year in high school, just needs to log innings and keep refining his game.

Pedro Villarreal
Born: **12/9/1987** Age: **25**
Bats: **R** Throws: **R** Height: **6' 2"** Weight: **215**
Breakout: **40%** Improve: **59%** Collapse: **21%**
Attrition: **28%** MLB: **85%**
Comparables:
Yorman Bazardo,Chris Reitsma,Joe Kennedy

YEAR	TEAM	LVL	AGE	W	L	SV	G	GS	IP	H	HR	BB	SO	BB9	SO9	GB%	BABIP	WHIP	ERA	FIP	FRA	WARP
2011	BAK	A+	23	4	3	0	10	10	58	68	9	8	41	1.2	6.4	40%	.333	1.31	4.34	5.07	4.89	0.7
2011	CAR	AA	23	7	4	0	17	17	91^{2}	92	11	20	68	2.0	6.7	—	.284	1.22	4.42	4.27	4.64	0.0
2012	PEN	AA	24	1	2	0	6	6	35^{1}	31	2	6	26	1.5	6.6	46%	.267	1.05	3.57	3.00	4.68	0.2
2012	LOU	AAA	24	3	12	0	20	20	113^{1}	129	9	32	81	2.5	6.4	40%	.322	1.42	4.61	3.69	4.80	0.3
2012	CIN	MLB	24	0	0	0	1	0	1	0	0	0	1	0.0	9.0	%	.000	0.00	0.00	1.14	1.52	0.0
2013	*CIN*	*MLB*	*25*	*2*	*3*	*0*	*8*	*8*	*40^{2}*	*44*	*6*	*14*	*23*	*3.2*	*5.2*	*41%*	*.296*	*1.44*	*5.42*	*5.02*	*5.89*	*-0.3*

Villareal, a former seventh-round pick out of Howard College in Texas, has been used primarily as a starter in the minors. His career 4.35 ERA and 6.4 K/9 over five seasons are about as exciting as buying socks at K-mart. But pitching staffs, like socks, sometimes get holes in them. And when they do, isn't it nice to know that you can pop on down and grab yourself a Villareal?

LINEOUTS

HITTERS

PLAYER	TEAM	LVL	AGE	PA	R	2B	3B	HR	RBI	BB	SO	SB-CS	AVG/OBP/SLG	TAv	BABIP	BRR	FRAA	WARP
C N. Ashley	RAY	Rk	27	53	6	3	0	1	5	7	6	2-0	.333/.434/.467	.333	.368	0.4	C(5): 0.1	0.5
	DUR	AAA	27	130	18	6	1	5	13	15	25	1-1	.245/.357/.455	.257	.275	-0.5	C(11): -0.2	-0.1
CF T. Bowe	DYT	A	21	100	8	1	2	0	2	12	19	12-1	.186/.286/.244	.327	.239	3.4	CF(4): 0.7	0.5
	BAK	A+	21	433	65	13	2	3	39	45	72	58-28	.314/.391/.383	.279	.377	4.1	CF(55): -9.4, LF(10): 3.1	1.5
MI R. Bueno	DRD	Rk	19	149	25	4	3	2	10	25	14	12-3	.233/.374/.367	.272	.250	0.2	—	0.0
OF J. Fellhauer	PEN	AA	24	399	50	20	2	4	41	54	54	6-4	.314/.409/.420	.297	.362	3.4	RF(28): 0.8, LF(5): 0.5	1.1
UT W. Harris	LOU	AAA	34	279	22	13	0	3	20	23	52	4-3	.224/.295/.312	.233	.269	-0.6	LF(23): 1.0, 2B(18): 3.2	0.0
	CIN	MLB	34	48	5	4	0	0	2	3	8	1-1	.114/.170/.205	.152	.139	-0.3	2B(7): 0.3, LF(1): -0.1	-0.4
3B M. Hessman	OKL	AAA	34	492	73	19	0	35	78	40	136	0-1	.231/.301/.512	.227	.244	-2.6	1B(28): 1.1	-0.5
MI D. Lohman	BAK	A+	23	575	80	23	3	14	70	60	108	34-9	.257/.353/.401	.273	.301	3.4	2B(50): 3.1, SS(48): -6.3	1.5
3B T. Mattair	BAK	A+	23	550	73	31	3	19	82	50	119	3-6	.274/.344/.465	.292	.324	-1.8	3B(73): 1.4, 1B(15): 1.9	2.0
3B S. Mejias-Brean	BIL	Rk	21	203	35	12	2	8	40	21	29	6-0	.313/.389/.536	.246	.336	0	3B(8): 1.1	0.0
C C. Miller	LOU	AAA	36	313	20	8	0	7	29	57	46	2-1	.235/.386/.354	.249	.259	-3	C(65): 0.5	0.7
1B B. Mills	PEN	AA	25	232	21	14	1	10	31	20	38	2-1	.272/.343/.495	.276	.289	-2.7	1B(20): 1.2, RF(1): -0.0	-0.2
	COH	AAA	25	138	13	4	0	7	21	7	34	0-0	.197/.239/.394	.194	.202	0	1B(9): -0.8	-0.7
SS J. Perez	DYT	A	20	555	64	27	8	9	51	51	88	24-14	.253/.336/.398	.260	.290	1.2	SS(31): -1.3	0.7
CF J. Reynoso	CIN	Rk	19	205	37	7	3	2	16	6	23	30-9	.311/.328/.411	.000	.337	5.2	CF(22): 0.4, RF(1): 0.1	0.7
OF S. Selsky	DYT	A	22	246	27	11	3	3	26	12	49	5-1	.281/.322/.395	.272	.343	0.3	LF(7): 0.2, CF(4): -0.5	-0.1
	BAK	A+	22	307	52	21	3	15	48	26	62	13-2	.348/.420/.618	.351	.402	1	RF(45): 1.0	2.6
OF J. Silva	DYT	A	21	465	58	24	3	8	42	69	109	25-12	.271/.380/.413	.258	.351	1.3	LF(20): 3.4, CF(7): 0.2	0.8
3B D. Vidal	BAK	A+	22	137	20	7	0	7	21	13	26	3-0	.281/.358/.512	.318	.303	-0.8	3B(25): 0.2	1.0
	PEN	AA	22	377	42	21	1	11	39	28	90	0-2	.230/.294/.397	.225	.277	-1	3B(29): -3.6	-0.6

Nevin Ashley lost almost three months to a broken hand last year but returned to Triple-A in late July and posted the first 800-plus OPS of his career, reviving his pulse as a legit catching prospect. A short, speedy center fielder who draws a few walks, **Theo Bowe** could become a spare part at the big-league level if everything breaks right. **Ronald Bueno** is a small, switch-hitting middle infielder from the Dominican Republic who has walked in 15 percent of his 680 career plate appearances, all in rookie ball. **Josh Fellhauer** was old for his level last year and has no power, but he controls the strike zone and can play all three outfield spots. By far the most successful of 1999's 24th-round draft picks, **Willie Harris** has parlayed being a nice guy who plays multiple positions and draws the occasional walk into a 12-year career. **Mike Hessman** has outhomered Todd Helton as a pro, 384 to 380, with the difference being that all but 14 of Hessman's home runs have come in the minors or Japan. Taken one pick ahead of Addison Reed in the 2010 draft, **Devin Lohman** can play on either side of second base and shows good secondary skills on offense, although he struggled against right-handers last year. A former second-round pick who showed little power in his first four minor-league seasons, third baseman **Travis Mattair** popped a few homers in the cozy California League but was old for the circuit. Taken in the eighth round last year, **Seth Mejias-Brean** is a good defensive third baseman who showed power in his professional debut, albeit as a college player in the six-runs-per-game Pioneer League. A study in persistence, **Corky Miller** re-signed with the Reds in the hope of playing that elusive 200th big-league game after spending all of 2012 at Triple-A Louisville. Taken one pick ahead of Jason Heyward in the 2007 draft, **Beau Mills** stalled out in the Indians organization and has spent parts of the last four seasons in Double-A. **Juan Perez** split time between second base and shortstop in junior college, sticking at shortstop as a pro and showing just enough offense to remain interesting for now. After spending two seasons in the Dominican Summer League, center fielder **Jhonatan Reynoso** made his stateside debut and tied for the Arizona League lead in stolen bases. **Steve Selsky**, a corner outfielder, put up crazy numbers after being promoted to the California League toward the end of June and will need to produce at every level to remain on the proverbial radar. **Juan Silva** displayed good on-base skills in his full-season debut, but he did almost all of his damage in June and August. **David Vidal** is a third baseman out of Puerto Rico who has some power but whose unrefined approach at the plate was exploited in Double-A.

PITCHERS

PLAYER	TEAM	LVL	AGE	W	L	SV	IP	H	HR	BB	SO	BB9	SO9	GB%	BABIP	WHIP	ERA	FIP	FRA	WARP
T. Crabbe	BAK	A+	24	5	2	0	57^2	46	5	15	60	2.3	9.4	43%	.268	1.06	3.28	3.64	3.63	1.7
	PEN	AA	24	3	6	0	86^1	81	9	66	93	6.9	9.7	39%	.321	1.70	4.90	4.74	5.34	0.1
J. Freeman	PEN	AA	25	4	7	16	68	49	7	16	68	2.1	9.0	46%	.244	0.96	2.91	3.23	3.06	0.8
D. Langfield	BIL	Rk	21	3	0	0	37	27	1	17	54	4.1	13.1	45%	.448	1.19	2.68	3.65	1.94	0.5
C. Rogers	BAK	A+	22	6	4	0	111^1	113	11	29	88	2.3	7.1	52%	.309	1.28	3.15	4.35	5.02	1.4
	PEN	AA	22	3	1	0	31^2	27	3	6	23	1.7	6.5	46%	.264	1.04	1.99	3.49	2.82	0.0
J. Smith	BAK	A+	24	9	8	0	147	143	15	46	140	2.8	8.6	44%	.308	1.29	3.80	4.36	4.53	2.0
M. Wiley	BIL	RK	22	3	2	9	18^1	13	3	6	26	2.9	12.8	57%	.350	1.04	2.45	5.04	11.42	-0.3
L. Van Mil	AKR	AA	27	1	1	0	46^1	34	2	11	40	2.1	7.8	48%	.250	0.97	1.94	2.75	3.50	0.7

Tim Crabbe couldn't find the plate at Double-A, pitched better after being demoted to the California League in mid-July, and capped the year with six mediocre starts in the Arizona Fall League. Strike-throwing **Justin Freeman** became nearly unhittable in his second year at Double-A, which is out of line with his four previous minor-league seasons. **Dan Langfield**, drafted out of the University of Memphis in the third round last year, throws hard but has spotty command and could end up in the bullpen. **Chad Rogers**—who hails from the same college that produced Keith Foulke and Juan Pierre—is a short right-hander who throws strikes but doesn't miss many bats. Durable **Josh Smith** has good command, puts the ball past hitters, and handled the California League just fine, although he was old for the circuit. **Loek Van Mil**, a right-hander out of the Netherlands, is taller than Patrick Ewing and probably a better pitcher. **M.O. Wiley**, a 28th-round pick in 2012, finished second in the Pioneer League in saves and racked plenty of strikeouts but was old for the level.

MANAGER: DUSTY BAKER

YEAR	TEAM	W-L	Pythag +/-	Avg PC	100+ P	120+ P	QS	BQS	REL	REL w Zero R	IBB	PH	PH Avg	PH HR	SB2	CS2	SB3	CS3	SAC Att	SAC %	POS SAC	Squeeze	Swing	In Play
2010	CIN	91-71	1	195.5	158	157	111	5	501	408	64	512	.236	20	14	5	0	2	200	75.0%	68	6	322	99
2011	CIN	79-83	1	95.5	67	2	90	7	502	398	47	240	.286	8	12	6	0	1	110	78.2%	39	2	377	131
2012	CIN	97-65	1	97.4	74	1	98	6	425	365	33	201	.269	2	14	2	0	1	119	65.5%	33	2	310	97

For the second time in three years, Dusty Baker led the Reds to an NL Central championship. Both times he finished second in Manager of the Year voting and his team was eliminated in the NLDS. Baker suffered a mild stroke in September that kept him from seeing his team clinch the division, but he was back in the dugout for the playoffs. Days after the Reds were eliminated by the Giants, Baker signed a two-year contract extension.

In spring training, when closer Ryan Madson blew out his elbow and required season-ending Tommy John surgery, plans to move Aroldis Chapman into the rotation were scrapped. This year, with Jonathan Broxton in the fold, Baker again plans to move Chapman. The risk is that the hard-throwing young left-hander may not be able to handle the increased workload. And Baker carries a reputation from his days with the Cubs as someone who, if he trusts you, will work you. The most curious aspect of Baker's style, however, is his fondness for inappropriate leadoff men. The top spot in the Reds' lineup produced an MLB-worst .254 OBP last year, and in five years at the helm in Cincinnati, Baker has gotten a pathetic .306 OBP from his leadoff hitters. The trade of Drew Stubbs for Shin-Soo Choo and his .381 OBP removes the temptation for Baker to let Stubbs drop silverware all over the floor when he's supposed to be setting the table.

Baker sometimes needs saving from his own curious strategic moves, but he must be doing something right. His players swear by him, and he has a .525 winning percentage and five first-place finishes in his 19 years as a manager.

Cleveland Indians

2012: BAD IN EVERY WAY POSSIBLE

It's difficult to summon enough willful ignorance to claim the Indians' 2012 season was anything other than an abject failure. On May 28, everyone in the AL Central was looking up at Cleveland. Despite a negative run differential, it was their 33rd consecutive day in first place . . . and it would be their last. The next day, they lost 8-2 to Kansas City. The Indians won 41 of their remaining 114 games (a .360 winning percentage) to finish with the second-worst record in the American League. Only the utter futility of the Twins saved Cleveland from last place.

INDIANS PROSPECTUS

2012 W-L: 68-94, 4th in AL Central

Pythag	.390	29th	DER	.700	23rd
RS/G	4.12	22nd	B-Age	27.8	11th
RA/G	5.22	29th	P-Age	27.8	13th
TAv	.259	15th	Salary	$66.9	24th
BRR	-1.1	16th	M$/MW	$2.75	18th
TAv-P	.278	29th	DL Days	813	16th
FIP	4.35	25th	DL WARP	1.6	27th

Three-Year Park Factors	
Overall	99
HR/RH	88
HR/LH	102
AVG/RH	98
AVG/LH	107

Progressive Field (1994)
Att. % of Capacity: 45.6% (29th)
Dim. 325, 370, 405, 375, 325

Here's an odd bit of triples trivia: Progressive yielded just one three-bagger to a righty hitter all season.

The Indians spent $9.25 million on Casey Kotchman, Derek Lowe, and Johnny Damon, who combined for -1.3 WARP. Yes, negative. Supposed staff aces, or at least the local versions of such, Justin Masterson and Ubaldo Jimenez, took big steps backwards. Masterson's walk rate and homers allowed rose (though most of his peripheral stats stayed close to his successful 2011 season rates), and Jimenez . . . well, everything Jimenez touched fell apart: walks, strikeouts, homers, groundball rate, this sentence.

Despite the promise of one of the youngest rosters in the American League and a 32 percent bump in payroll, the Indians didn't take the leap. Instead, they managed the dual embarrassment of being both bad offensively (22nd in runs scored) and at run-prevention (29th).

2013: A SHORTAGE OF TALENT

If everything breaks right (as opposed to just breaks) the 2013 Indians could win some games in a weak division. They have young talent in Jimenez, Masterson, Carlos Santana, Asdrubal Cabrera, and Michael Brantley. Full seasons of Jason Kipnis and Lonnie Chisenhall could help, as could the sly stylings of Zack McAllister. But there are big problems. None of these players are without serious and fair questions as to their ability to produce. Some have more than one that must be answered affirmatively, further muddying their productive waters. While all have the potential to be above-average players, none is a star with the potential exception of Santana (courtesy of Santa Colletti). Star-power balances out weak spots on the roster, in effect positively answering one or more of the above player questions. But the Indians just don't have that five-plus win player, so to succeed they need all of the above—or at least an extreme majority—to succeed. That just isn't very likely.

But suppose it happens. For the Indians to succeed, Cleveland's front office must have proficiently filled out the remainder of the roster. That sounds simple, but last season the Indians had 29 different players contribute negative WARP. Many of those were bit players or minor leaguers up briefly and then sent down, but not all. Ten hitters received over 100 plate appearances and registered negative WARP, while four pitchers threw 50 innings and achieved same. That Cleveland was forced to repeatedly play those players speaks to a lack of depth. Put another way, the Indians don't have nearly enough even average players, players who can competently step in and not immediately hurt the team. A team with star power up front might be able to overcome that. The Indians are not that team.

The farm system isn't likely to contribute more than a few relievers to the 2013 squad either, so cross that off your "Places to look for help" list. The possibility of trading shortstop Cabrera the way outfielder Shin-Soo Choo was dealt exists. While such moves would replenish the lacking talent level down on the farm, the major-league roster would sorely miss them. But maybe that doesn't matter as it hardly seems likely the Indians are playing to win in 2013.

Within the sabermetric community, there has been a reaction against the idea of success windows. We can't predict baseball well enough to tell with certainty whether a team will win 75 or 90 games the next season, says the anti-window theory, so tearing down or building up a team based on existing talent and age patterns is futile. That may be true and the 2013 Indians may yet be champions, but when taking all the different factors into account, it's difficult to see the Indians as contenders in 2013.

THE STATE OF THE ORGANIZATION: NOT MUCH HELP COMING

Billy Beane and a few other GMs have improved their teams based on what we now see as sabermetric orthodoxy. The Indians, one of the select few when it came to smarty-pants teams, pioneered long-term contracts to arbitration-eligible players. It's now common practice, but the deals John Hart gave to Jim Thome and Manny Ramirez before they hit free agency are what allowed the Indians to keep star players at below market prices for more years than an organization with Cleveland's meager means normally could. Back in those heady days of early sabermetrics, being the smartest guy in the room gave you an advantage over other teams. Now just about every team is the smartest guy in the room—it's a big room—so the advantage is, if not gone, at least significantly muted.

This leveling of the playing field has brought, for the most part, the haves up to the level of the have-nots. It has placed more emphasis on acquiring talent through trades and the draft, routes the Indians have mostly failed at in recent years. Right now, the Tribe's minor-league system is a tale of two players, and neither of them is 19 yet. Trades to increase the talent base in the upper minors may be coming, but even there the Indians have a poor track record. Look at what they got for Cliff Lee and CC Sabathia. Actually, maybe you'd better not. It's an old story, but to get better the Indians are going to have to draft better and hold on to the star players they develop. Until they do so, they'll be fighting over a spot on the couch in the AL Central basement.

HITTERS

Mike Aviles **SS**
Born: **3/13/1981** Age: **32**
Bats: **R** Throws: **R** Height: **5' 11"**
Weight: **205** Breakout: **2%**
Improve: **33%** Collapse: **5%**
Attrition: **14%** MLB: **94%**
Comparables:
Pete Orr,Cristian Guzman,Alvin Dark

YEAR	TEAM	LVL	AGE	PA	R	2B	3B	HR	RBI	BB	SO	SB	CS	AVG_OBP_SLG	TAv	BABIP	BRR	FRAA	WARP
2010	OMA	AAA	29	75	8	3	1	1	8	4	10	0	0	.271/.320/.386	.241	.305	0.1	SS(14): -0.1, 2B(1): -0.0	0.1
2010	KCA	MLB	29	448	63	16	3	8	32	20	49	14	5	.304/.335/.413	.262	.327	1.5	2B(87): 3.9, SS(13): 0.2	1.9
2011	OMA	AAA	30	150	21	8	2	9	25	6	17	6	4	.307/.329/.586	.387	.291	0	SS(8): 1.1	0.8
2011	BOS	MLB	30	107	17	6	0	2	8	4	17	4	2	.317/.340/.436	.272	.361	-0.2	3B(22): 0.6, SS(8): 0.8	0.5
2011	KCA	MLB	30	202	14	11	3	5	31	9	27	10	2	.222/.261/.395	.229	.231	-1.7	3B(24): 1.0, 2B(20): -0.8	-0.4
2012	BOS	MLB	31	546	57	28	0	13	60	23	77	14	6	.250/.282/.381	.244	.269	3.5	SS(128): 0.4, 2B(2): -0.0	1.1
2013	*CLE*	*MLB*	*32*	*470*	*52*	*22*	*2*	*10*	*47*	*20*	*73*	*14*	*5*	*.260/.293/.388*	*.247*	*.288*	*0.6*	*SS -1, 2B -0*	*1.1*

Ten years ago a player with Aviles's stats wouldn't have made it through the season as a backup, but that era is gone. In this climate of diminished offense and weak shortstops, Aviles has value. Rescued from the Royals and dropped into the Red Sox starting lineup, Aviles showed average (read: valuable) defensive skills with occasional pop—his 13 homers were tied for 10th by a shortstop. An anemic walk rate throughout his career, consistently 4 percent, severely hampers his offense. Aviles lost his starting gig in mid-September when the Red Sox took a look at Jose Iglesias, and he was traded to Toronto for manager John Farrell. Yes, for a manager. He was then flipped to Cleveland with Yan Gomes for lefty reliever Esmil Rogers. At least that trade was for a player.

Michael Brantley **CF**
Born: **5/15/1987** Age: **26**
Bats: **L** Throws: **L** Height: **6' 3"**
Weight: **200** Breakout: **3%**
Improve: **47%** Collapse: **8%**
Attrition: **16%** MLB: **92%**
Comparables:
Mark Kotsay,Johnny Groth,Jeremy Reed

YEAR	TEAM	LVL	AGE	PA	R	2B	3B	HR	RBI	BB	SO	SB	CS	AVG_OBP_SLG	TAv	BABIP	BRR	FRAA	WARP
2010	COH	AAA	23	316	54	13	2	4	29	34	28	13	5	.319/.392/.425	.276	.337	4.3	CF(45): 4.5, LF(24): 1.0	2.3
2010	CLE	MLB	23	325	38	9	3	3	22	22	38	10	2	.246/.296/.327	.229	.271	3.5	CF(65): -1.6, LF(7): -0.9	0.1
2011	CLE	MLB	24	496	63	24	4	7	46	34	76	13	5	.266/.318/.384	.253	.303	0.5	LF(66): -2.8, CF(52): -1.5	0.1
2012	CLE	MLB	25	609	63	37	4	6	60	53	56	12	9	.288/.348/.402	.274	.310	2.7	CF(144): -11.4	0.9
2013	*CLE*	*MLB*	*26*	*550*	*66*	*25*	*3*	*6*	*44*	*45*	*69*	*17*	*6*	*.269/.330/.371*	*.256*	*.297*	*0.6*	*CF -1, LF -0*	*1.3*

As the 26-year-old continues to develop, he distances himself further from Matt LaPorta as the prize of the CC Sabathia trade with Milwaukee. A lot of Brantley's surplus value over replacement was generated in a big July. He hit half of his six home runs that month with a gaudy 934 OPS in 101 plate appearances. In no other month did he top 768 with his OPS nor exceed .400 in slugging. He still carried a reasonable 715 OPS in the other five months spanning 508 plate appearances. To be fair, he's not a slugger, but that didn't stop the Indians from deploying him in the fourth and fifth slots in the order for 89 of his 149 games played. His walk and strikeout rates are better suited in the top two lineup slots, not run-producing ones.

Asdrubal Cabrera SS
Born: **11/13/1985** Age: **27**
Bats: **B** Throws: **R** Height: **6' 1"**
Weight: **180** Breakout: **1%**
Improve: **58%** Collapse: **7%**
Attrition: **8%** MLB: **90%**
Comparables:
Steve Tolleson,Stephen Drew,John Valentin

YEAR	TEAM	LVL	AGE	PA	R	2B	3B	HR	RBI	BB	SO	SB	CS	AVG_OBP_SLG	TAv	BABIP	BRR	FRAA	WARP
2010	CLE	MLB	24	425	39	16	1	3	29	25	60	6	4	.276/.326/.346	.248	.318	0.7	SS(95): -2.7	1.1
2011	CLE	MLB	25	667	87	32	3	25	92	44	119	17	5	.273/.332/.460	.286	.302	2.4	SS(151): -19.0	2.0
2012	CLE	MLB	26	616	70	35	1	16	68	52	99	9	4	.270/.338/.423	.267	.303	3.3	SS(136): 2.5	2.4
2013	*CLE*	*MLB*	*27*	*589*	*74*	*30*	*2*	*13*	*58*	*45*	*100*	*12*	*4*	*.272/.335/.411*	*.269*	*.309*	*0*	*SS -6*	*2.6*

With a quick look at two lines above, you might note a marked difference between Cabrera in 2011 and last year thanks to nine fewer home runs and 24 fewer RBIs. But a closer look reveals drastic improvement in FRAA, leading to an overall improvement in WARP, favoring 2012 despite the offensive decline. Whether he leans closer to 2011 or 2012 for the next few years, or has everything break right and sets his career-best bar even higher than 2011, the Indians have a middle infielder in his prime at the center of their nucleus. That said, some trade rumors have swirled. The Indians would have a great asset to dangle at a tough-to-fill position and Cabrera would likely fetch a mint. On the other hand, it's a tough-to-fill position.

Ezequiel Carrera OF
Born: **6/11/1987** Age: **26**
Bats: **L** Throws: **L** Height: **5' 11"**
Weight: **185** Breakout: **3%**
Improve: **64%** Collapse: **6%**
Attrition: **14%** MLB: **92%**
Comparables:
Josh Anderson,Rudy Law,Tony Gwynn

YEAR	TEAM	LVL	AGE	PA	R	2B	3B	HR	RBI	BB	SO	SB	CS	AVG_OBP_SLG	TAv	BABIP	BRR	FRAA	WARP
2010	COH	AAA	23	183	19	7	3	1	16	12	34	11	3	.286/.324/.385	.250	.336	-2.4	CF(48): 7.6	1.0
2010	TAC	AAA	23	243	24	6	2	0	18	20	32	9	5	.268/.329/.315	.236	.303	-0.8	CF(40): 1.4, LF(22): -0.6	0.1
2011	COH	AAA	24	377	63	8	3	2	25	39	53	35	4	.287/.371/.348	.266	.337	0	--	0.0
2011	CLE	MLB	24	226	27	8	3	0	14	16	35	10	5	.243/.301/.312	.223	.293	0.1	CF(55): -3.7, LF(9): -0.7	-0.8
2012	COH	AAA	25	438	65	19	6	6	42	29	60	26	7	.294/.345/.419	.225	.332	2	CF(37): 2.2	-0.3
2012	CLE	MLB	25	158	20	6	3	2	11	8	35	8	1	.272/.312/.395	.250	.342	1.7	LF(36): 2.5, CF(15): 1.6	0.4
2013	*CLE*	*MLB*	*26*	*250*	*29*	*9*	*3*	*2*	*18*	*16*	*45*	*11*	*3*	*.249/.302/.340*	*.233*	*.294*	*1*	*CF 0, LF 0*	*0.2*

Carrera is a speedy Swiss Army knife, capable of manning left, center, or right, better deployed as a defensive replacement/pinch runner than in your lineup daily. Neither of his major-league samples is large enough to make sweeping judgments, but his inability to bring his minor-league strikeout-to-walk rate with him has made it tough for him to display his best asset: speed. Contact is a must for guys like him to get the most out of their skill set.

Lonnie Chisenhall 3B
Born: **10/4/1988** Age: **24**
Bats: **L** Throws: **R** Height: **6' 2"**
Weight: **200** Breakout: **7%**
Improve: **60%** Collapse: **3%**
Attrition: **10%** MLB: **95%**
Comparables:
Neil Walker,Steve Garvey,Andy Marte

YEAR	TEAM	LVL	AGE	PA	R	2B	3B	HR	RBI	BB	SO	SB	CS	AVG_OBP_SLG	TAv	BABIP	BRR	FRAA	WARP
2010	AKR	AA	21	524	81	22	3	17	84	46	77	3	0	.278/.357/.450	.284	.303	-0.8	3B(96): -3.9	2.2
2011	COH	AAA	22	292	45	15	3	7	45	28	47	0	1	.267/.353/.431	.274	.300	0	--	0.0
2011	CLE	MLB	22	223	27	13	0	7	22	8	49	1	0	.255/.284/.415	.253	.299	-0.3	3B(58): 4.0	0.7
2012	COH	AAA	23	126	16	12	0	4	17	4	22	0	0	.314/.341/.517	.252	.351	0.6	3B(13): 1.5	0.4
2012	CLE	MLB	23	151	16	6	1	5	16	8	27	2	1	.268/.311/.430	.269	.300	-1	3B(30): -0.3	0.3
2013	*CLE*	*MLB*	*24*	*250*	*26*	*12*	*1*	*8*	*30*	*13*	*50*	*1*	*0*	*.254/.299/.409*	*.256*	*.291*	*-0.3*	*3B -0*	*0.4*

Chisenhall only played 73 games between Triple-A and the majors, but all in all it was a worthwhile season. The 24-year-old former top prospect still has work to do, but he improved in virtually every rate statistic after a rough debut in 2011. He struggles mightily against lefties and could end up a platoon player if he doesn't start advancing in that realm quickly. The problems against southpaws make it difficult to see the dreams of hitting .300 that his swing elicits becoming reality. However, he is on the right side of 25 with fewer than 400 big-league plate appearances under his belt, so it would be foolish to tag any of his skills as set in stone, especially someone with his minor-league pedigree.

Juan Diaz SS
Born: **12/12/1988** Age: **24**
Bats: **B** Throws: **R** Height: **6' 5"**
Weight: **200** Breakout: **5%**
Improve: **42%** Collapse: **10%**
Attrition: **20%** MLB: **94%**
Comparables:
Ted Martinez,Phil Linz,Dale Berra

YEAR	TEAM	LVL	AGE	PA	R	2B	3B	HR	RBI	BB	SO	SB	CS	AVG_OBP_SLG	TAv	BABIP	BRR	FRAA	WARP
2010	HDS	A+	21	276	39	8	3	7	41	19	45	8	2	.295/.345/.433	.267	.335	-0.3	SS(69): -2.5	1.0
2010	KIN	A+	21	238	17	7	1	1	19	15	51	2	2	.271/.311/.326	.230	.339	-2.7	SS(63): 0.3	0.4
2011	AKR	AA	22	569	64	24	4	9	60	40	116	9	2	.255/.310/.368	.259	.310	-2.1	SS(88): 4.6	1.6
2012	AKR	AA	23	405	51	24	2	11	52	25	95	1	3	.259/.309/.423	.260	.318	-1.7	SS(80): 9.6	1.7
2012	COH	AAA	23	76	12	5	0	2	11	4	18	0	0	.306/.342/.458	.241	.385	-0.5	SS(10): 1.9	0.1
2012	CLE	MLB	23	17	4	0	0	0	0	1	5	0	0	.267/.353/.267	.166	.400	0.2	SS(5): -0.3	-0.1
2013	*CLE*	*MLB*	*24*	*250*	*21*	*10*	*1*	*4*	*24*	*11*	*62*	*1*	*0*	*.230/.267/.336*	*.219*	*.289*	*-0.3*	*SS 2*	*0.2*

The scouting report about his bat reads: "great fielder." In other words, Diaz's offense is lacking, but there are worse fates in pro baseball than being a glove-first shortstop, especially one who is still relatively young. Diaz would love to end up with former Indian John McDonald's career as a light-hitting utility infielder. While he may not have the glove of McDonald, he should have a bit more bat, though still below average.

Yan Gomes C
Born: 7/19/1987 Age: 25
Bats: R Throws: R Height: 6' 3"
Weight: 215 Breakout: 4%
Improve: 47% Collapse: 6%
Attrition: 20% MLB: 90%
Comparables:
Jerry Willard,Jarrod Saltalamacchia,Jesus Flores

YEAR	TEAM	LVL	AGE	PA	R	2B	3B	HR	RBI	BB	SO	SB	CS	AVG_OBP_SLG	TAv	BABIP	BRR	FRAA	WARP
2010	DUN	A+	22	247	37	21	1	9	40	9	64	0	0	.275/.313/.489	.266	.344	0.9	C(55): 0.0	1.0
2011	NHP	AA	23	309	34	18	1	13	51	25	75	0	0	.250/.317/.464	.263	.292	0	--	0.0
2012	LVG	AAA	24	335	44	29	1	13	59	25	72	4	0	.328/.380/.557	.289	.392	-4	C(24): 0.1, 3B(22): -1.2	1.1
2012	TOR	MLB	24	111	9	4	0	4	13	6	32	0	0	.204/.264/.367	.238	.246	-1	1B(20): 0.4, C(9): -0.1	-0.2
2013	*CLE*	*MLB*	*25*	*250*	*25*	*12*	*0*	*8*	*30*	*13*	*70*	*1*	*0*	*.235/.281/.391*	*.244*	*.297*	*-0.4*	*C -0, 1B 0*	*0.3*

Gomes came to Cleveland in November, along with Aviles, in a deal that sent reliever Esmil Rogers to Toronto. Gomes's chief virtue is his ability to play multiple positions, albeit none of them very well. He's a below-average hitter with above-average pop and a mild traditional batting split that favors left-handed pitching.

Travis Hafner DH
Born: 6/3/1977 Age: 36
Bats: L Throws: R Height: 6' 4"
Weight: 240 Breakout: 0%
Improve: 22% Collapse: 18%
Attrition: 20% MLB: 84%
Comparables:
Ryan Klesko,David Justice,Cliff Floyd

YEAR	TEAM	LVL	AGE	PA	R	2B	3B	HR	RBI	BB	SO	SB	CS	AVG_OBP_SLG	TAv	BABIP	BRR	FRAA	WARP
2010	CLE	MLB	33	462	46	29	0	13	50	51	94	2	1	.278/.374/.449	.303	.332	-2.1	--	2.4
2011	CLE	MLB	34	368	41	16	0	13	57	36	78	0	0	.280/.361/.449	.292	.332	-1.2	--	1.2
2012	CLE	MLB	35	263	23	6	2	12	34	32	47	0	0	.228/.346/.438	.289	.233	-1.6	--	0.7
2013	*CLE*	*MLB*	*36*	*270*	*32*	*11*	*0*	*8*	*32*	*28*	*57*	*0*	*0*	*.245/.337/.406*	*.271*	*.289*	*-0.5*	*--*	*0.9*

While not performing at the near-MVP levels of the mid-2000s, Hafner had shown some usefulness at the dish over the last four years with an 814 OPS, 54 home runs, and 91 RBIs in 1,472 plate appearances. The problem is that a full-time player should log about 2,300 plate appearances in a four-year span. Pronk's body simply hasn't cooperated with him, but left-handed power like his will find a job and collect a major-league paycheck until he hangs 'em up for good.

Jason Kipnis 2B
Born: 4/3/1987 Age: 26
Bats: L Throws: R Height: 6' 0"
Weight: 185 Breakout: 7%
Improve: 63% Collapse: 1%
Attrition: 15% MLB: 97%
Comparables:
Ian Kinsler,Scott Sizemore,Marcus Giles

YEAR	TEAM	LVL	AGE	PA	R	2B	3B	HR	RBI	BB	SO	SB	CS	AVG_OBP_SLG	TAv	BABIP	BRR	FRAA	WARP
2010	KIN	A+	23	237	33	12	3	6	31	24	46	2	3	.300/.387/.478	.298	.359	0.8	2B(45): -2.6	1.4
2010	AKR	AA	23	355	63	20	5	10	43	31	61	7	1	.311/.383/.502	.300	.358	0.9	2B(75): 4.0	3.0
2011	COH	AAA	24	400	65	16	9	12	55	44	72	12	1	.280/.362/.484	.290	.318	0	--	0.0
2011	CLE	MLB	24	150	24	9	1	7	19	11	34	5	0	.272/.333/.507	.294	.312	0	2B(36): -1.5	0.7
2012	CLE	MLB	25	672	86	22	4	14	76	67	109	31	7	.257/.335/.379	.264	.291	3.3	2B(146): -8.6	0.9
2013	*CLE*	*MLB*	*26*	*527*	*69*	*22*	*4*	*13*	*52*	*45*	*100*	*15*	*4*	*.258/.329/.404*	*.266*	*.299*	*1.3*	*2B 5*	*3.0*

When his hit streak reached 10 games on May 6, Kipnis saw his OPS rise to 917 and the Indians began licking their chops. It looked like their budding star second baseman was picking up right where his 36-game cup of coffee from 2011 left off. Then from May 7 on, he hit a mere .248 with a 672 OPS in 556 plate appearances. His skills didn't collapse: Kipnis maintained his 10 percent walk and 16 percent strikeout rates throughout the season. His issue was a power outage. After posting a 21 percent home-run-to-fly-ball rate in that brief debut, he sank to 10 percent last year. Worse yet, his volume of fly balls was just 30 percent—super-charged by a 40 percent mark in April—and he didn't reach 30 after June. No injury was documented, so perhaps the dip is due to sophomore adjusting. It's time for the 26-year-old to counter opposing pitchers.

Casey Kotchman 1B
Born: 2/22/1983 Age: 30
Bats: L Throws: L Height: 6' 4"
Weight: 220 Breakout: 0%
Improve: 29% Collapse: 2%
Attrition: 7% MLB: 86%
Comparables:
Norm Larker,Mark Grace,Conor Jackson

YEAR	TEAM	LVL	AGE	PA	R	2B	3B	HR	RBI	BB	SO	SB	CS	AVG_OBP_SLG	TAv	BABIP	BRR	FRAA	WARP
2010	SEA	MLB	27	457	37	20	1	9	51	35	57	0	0	.217/.280/.336	.222	.229	-3.7	1B(116): -2.8	-2.0
2011	TBA	MLB	28	563	44	24	2	10	48	48	66	2	2	.306/.378/.422	.304	.335	-4.4	1B(146): -2.2	1.9
2012	CLE	MLB	29	500	46	12	0	12	55	26	49	3	0	.229/.280/.333	.222	.233	-6.1	1B(137): 8.5	-1.2
2013	*CLE*	*MLB*	*30*	*482*	*48*	*21*	*1*	*10*	*52*	*35*	*53*	*2*	*1*	*.257/.320/.376*	*.258*	*.271*	*-0.7*	*1B 5*	*0.8*

Sometimes fans and analysts can get a bit hung up on BABIP and lean on it as the primary reason for a performance, whether good or bad. Those folks will miss positive adjustments or legitimate flaws in a player's game and never see the assumed regression. Kotchman's 2011 wasn't one of those cases. Everything in his game was virtually the same, save a career-high .335 BABIP that was fueling his .306 batting average, also a career high. If he couldn't maintain that, he wasn't going to stay a .300-hitter. Turns out he couldn't. In fact, he didn't just regress to his career norm, he skipped right past that and posted a .233 BABIP in 2012, causing his average to sink to a paltry .229 for the Tribe.

Matt LaPorta **1B**

Born: **1/8/1985** Age: **28**
Bats: **R** Throws: **R** Height: **6' 3"**
Weight: **215** Breakout: **1%**
Improve: **42%** Collapse: **7%**
Attrition: **13%** MLB: **92%**

Comparables:
Steve Pearce, Don Baylor, Hank Blalock

YEAR	TEAM	LVL	AGE	PA	R	2B	3B	HR	RBI	BB	SO	SB	CS	AVG_OBP_SLG	TAv	BABIP	BRR	FRAA	WARP
2010	COH	AAA	25	81	7	4	0	5	16	12	10	0	1	.362/.457/.638	.333	.370	-1	LF(10): -1.0, 1B(7): 0.2	0.6
2010	CLE	MLB	25	425	41	15	1	12	41	46	82	0	0	.221/.306/.362	.241	.250	-2.7	1B(93): -12.5, LF(7): -1.1	-2.0
2011	CLE	MLB	26	385	34	23	1	11	53	23	87	1	0	.247/.299/.412	.269	.293	-5.6	1B(97): -5.3	-0.9
2012	COH	AAA	27	434	56	19	1	19	62	44	81	0	3	.264/.350/.472	.247	.285	-1.1	1B(21): -0.7, LF(9): 0.1	-0.6
2012	CLE	MLB	27	60	2	2	0	1	5	1	17	0	0	.241/.267/.328	.205	.325	0.1	1B(11): -0.3	-0.4
2013	*CLE*	*MLB*	*28*	*250*	*27*	*11*	*1*	*8*	*31*	*21*	*52*	*0*	*0*	*.242/.313/.410*	*.264*	*.277*	*-0.5*	*1B 1, LF -0*	*0.4*

LaPorta was a highly touted prospect out of the University of Florida who ended up as the centerpiece for the aforementioned Sabathia trade. A power bat, LaPorta crushed the minors to the tune of a 941 OPS and 51 home runs in 956 plate appearances before his debut. That is a home-run pace of 35 per 650 plate appearances, and while you couldn't expect all of that to translate immediately, a reasonable facsimile would've been sufficient. Instead, LaPorta has yet to hit his 35th big-league home run despite logging 1,068 plate appearances across parts of four seasons. There is a glimmer of hope left for the former seventh-overall pick, but that once sky-high ceiling has caved in on LaPorta and the Indians.

Brent Lillibridge **UT**

Born: **9/18/1983** Age: **29**
Bats: **R** Throws: **R** Height: **6' 0"**
Weight: **185** Breakout: **2%**
Improve: **37%** Collapse: **8%**
Attrition: **13%** MLB: **86%**

Comparables:
Luis Aguayo, Gil McDougald, Jose Valentin

YEAR	TEAM	LVL	AGE	PA	R	2B	3B	HR	RBI	BB	SO	SB	CS	AVG_OBP_SLG	TAv	BABIP	BRR	FRAA	WARP
2010	CHR	AAA	26	206	26	8	0	4	16	17	46	19	3	.270/.335/.378	.255	.341	2.5	SS(36): 0.9, 2B(9): 0.7	0.8
2010	CHA	MLB	26	101	19	5	2	2	16	3	36	5	3	.224/.248/.378	.212	.333	0.1	2B(24): 0.4, CF(6): -0.1	-0.2
2011	CHA	MLB	27	216	38	5	1	13	29	17	62	10	6	.258/.340/.505	.298	.310	1.8	RF(43): 0.7, 1B(20): 0.7	1.4
2012	BOS	MLB	28	16	0	0	0	0	0	0	5	0	0	.125/.125/.125	.093	.182	-0.7	RF(4): 0.2, CF(3): -0.2	-0.3
2012	CHA	MLB	28	70	10	1	0	0	2	4	26	7	2	.175/.232/.190	.181	.289	1.4	1B(20): 0.1, LF(16): -0.2	-0.3
2012	CLE	MLB	28	123	15	5	0	3	8	7	40	6	0	.216/.276/.342	.249	.300	0.9	SS(21): -2.9, 3B(12): -0.2	-0.2
2013	*CLE*	*MLB*	*29*	*250*	*30*	*9*	*1*	*6*	*22*	*18*	*72*	*13*	*4*	*.219/.286/.342*	*.231*	*.289*	*1.4*	*SS -0, 3B -0*	*0.1*

So that's what happened to Kipnis's home-run-to-fly-ball rate. Lillibridge stole it and used it in 2011. After just 298 plate appearances of utter nothingness, split almost evenly from 2008-10, Lillibridge went berzerk in 2011 with an out-of-nowhere 13 home runs. The 845 OPS was 220 points higher than his previous career high. You'll be shocked to learn that it didn't last. His 2012 was right in line with his first three seasons, yet he still amassed a career high of 102 games played, likely due to the fact that he played every position but the battery.

Francisco Lindor **SS**

Born: **11/14/1993** Age: **19**
Bats: **B** Throws: **R** Height: **6' 0"**
Weight: **175** Breakout: **0%**
Improve: **62%** Collapse: **38%**
Attrition: **38%** MLB: **100%**

Comparables:
Ed Kranepool, Wayne Causey, Robin Yount

YEAR	TEAM	LVL	AGE	PA	R	2B	3B	HR	RBI	BB	SO	SB	CS	AVG_OBP_SLG	TAv	BABIP	BRR	FRAA	WARP
2012	LKC	A	18	568	83	24	3	6	42	61	78	27	12	.257/.352/.355	.244	.295	4.2	SS(18): 1.1	0.5
2013	*CLE*	*MLB*	*19*	*250*	*26*	*9*	*1*	*2*	*17*	*18*	*54*	*6*	*3*	*.217/.281/.296*	*.217*	*.270*	*0*	*SS -0*	*0.0*

The stats alone might leave you wanting, but when you consider the fact that Lindor was an 18-year-old who needed just five games in Low-A before handling a full-season assignment last year, things begin to crystalize a bit more. Of course, considering his youth only makes his 11 percent walk and 13 percent strikeout rates that much more impressive. Given how far away he is, this is all more dream than actualization, but Lindor is a first-division shortstop in the making, with a superstar ceiling. His amazing glove at a premium position will make his offensive output play up, but at his peak he can be a .285 batting average/.375 on-base percentage guy with gap power and good speed. It will be fun to watch him develop.

Lou Marson **C**

Born: **6/26/1986** Age: **27**
Bats: **R** Throws: **R** Height: **6' 2"**
Weight: **200** Breakout: **5%**
Improve: **37%** Collapse: **16%**
Attrition: **20%** MLB: **96%**

Comparables:
Brian Downing, Gregg Zaun, Jim Essian

YEAR	TEAM	LVL	AGE	PA	R	2B	3B	HR	RBI	BB	SO	SB	CS	AVG_OBP_SLG	TAv	BABIP	BRR	FRAA	WARP
2010	COH	AAA	24	147	19	7	1	4	14	22	24	5	0	.202/.327/.371	.244	.219	1.1	C(36): 0.1	0.5
2010	CLE	MLB	24	294	29	15	0	3	22	26	55	8	1	.195/.274/.286	.217	.234	0.8	C(87): -0.8	0.6
2011	CLE	MLB	25	272	26	9	2	1	19	24	68	4	2	.230/.300/.296	.220	.312	0.1	C(78): 0.0	0.1
2012	CLE	MLB	26	235	27	8	2	0	13	36	44	4	2	.226/.348/.287	.241	.289	0.1	C(69): -1.1	0.0
2013	*CLE*	*MLB*	*27*	*250*	*25*	*11*	*1*	*2*	*20*	*28*	*54*	*4*	*1*	*.232/.323/.321*	*.244*	*.293*	*0*	*C -1*	*0.7*

Credit where it is due: Marson is improving. He is on an upward trajectory over the last three years. Unfortunately, it isn't much of a bar to clear. When you consider that his slugging percentage hasn't topped .300 in any of his three seasons as a backup catcher, you understand what we are dealing with here. Good receivers can enjoy long, satisfying careers in the big leagues and many of them even transition into management immediately after they retire. Marson is already a millionaire, and if he can show any improvement with the bat, he will stick around to become a multimillionaire.

Tyler Naquin CF
Born: **4/24/1991** Age: **22**
Bats: **L** Throws: **R** Height: **6' 3"**
Weight: **175** Breakout: **8%**
Improve: **58%** Collapse: **9%**
Attrition: **22%** MLB: **96%**
Comparables:
Paul Blair,Joe Lovitto,Gary Geiger

YEAR	TEAM	LVL	AGE	PA	R	2B	3B	HR	RBI	BB	SO	SB	CS	AVG_OBP_SLG	TAv	BABIP	BRR	FRAA	WARP
2012	MHV	A-	21	161	22	11	2	0	13	17	26	4	3	.270/.379/.380	.305	.333	0.2	CF(13): 3.6	0.8
2013	*CLE*	*MLB*	*22*	*250*	*23*	*9*	*1*	*2*	*16*	*16*	*66*	*3*	*1*	*.196/.258/.270*	*.200*	*.262*	*-0.2*	*CF 0*	*-0.8*

Some were shocked to see the Indians grab Naquin in the middle of the first round last year, higher than expected. Such a high draft position puts the onus on the player to live up to the expectations inherent in the slot. Naquin's best tools enhance his defensive game with a great arm and above-average speed, and yet there is concern about whether he can become a legitimate center fielder. Without question, his offensive profile plays best in center because he simply doesn't have the power for a corner-outfield role. On the right team, one loaded with power at other positions, perhaps Naquin could pass in right since he has the arm for it.

Thomas Neal OF
Born: **8/17/1987** Age: **25**
Bats: **R** Throws: **R** Height: **6' 3"**
Weight: **225** Breakout: **8%**
Improve: **42%** Collapse: **5%**
Attrition: **31%** MLB: **91%**
Comparables:
Ken Griffey,Jamie Hoffmann,Tony Tarasco

YEAR	TEAM	LVL	AGE	PA	R	2B	3B	HR	RBI	BB	SO	SB	CS	AVG_OBP_SLG	TAv	BABIP	BRR	FRAA	WARP
2010	RIC	AA	22	585	69	40	1	12	69	46	94	11	5	.291/.361/.440	.297	.337	0	LF(108): -4.3, RF(12): 1.6	2.9
2011	FRE	AAA	23	239	35	13	3	2	25	13	50	7	6	.295/.351/.409	.250	.375	0.2	LF(38): -0.6, CF(3): 0.6	-0.2
2012	AKR	AA	24	470	77	24	1	12	51	46	71	11	8	.314/.400/.467	.318	.355	-0.2	RF(49): 3.1, LF(25): 2.8	3.3
2012	CLE	MLB	24	24	2	1	0	0	2	0	6	0	0	.217/.250/.261	.168	.294	0	LF(6): 0.1, RF(2): -0.2	-0.3
2013	*CLE*	*MLB*	*25*	*250*	*25*	*12*	*1*	*5*	*26*	*15*	*51*	*3*	*2*	*.253/.312/.374*	*.254*	*.304*	*-0.4*	*LF -1, RF 0*	*0.3*

Neal's prospect status was inflated by a huge season in the California League back in 2009, a league that artificially inflates opinions of prospects as often as the state it resides in artificially inflates body parts of celebrities. He came back down to earth the next year, though it wasn't exactly a catastrophic fall. Neal is a toolsy player capable of being a legitimate fourth outfielder. None of his skills on their own will wow you, but the combination is something worthwhile.

Dorssys Paulino SS
Born: **11/21/1994** Age: **18**
Bats: **R** Throws: **R** Height: **6' 1"**
Weight: **175** Breakout: **0%**
Improve: **69%** Collapse: **31%**
Attrition: **31%** MLB: **100%**
Comparables:
Wayne Causey,Robin Yount,Robin Yount

YEAR	TEAM	LVL	AGE	PA	R	2B	3B	HR	RBI	BB	SO	SB	CS	AVG_OBP_SLG	TAv	BABIP	BRR	FRAA	WARP
2012	CLE	Rk	17	188	42	14	6	6	30	15	31	9	1	.355/.404/.610	.339	.404	0	SS(1): -0.0	0.0
2012	MHV	A-	17	62	5	5	0	1	8	3	14	2	1	.271/.306/.407	.237	.341	0.4	SS(8): -0.8	-0.1
2013	*CLE*	*MLB*	*18*	*250*	*23*	*9*	*1*	*4*	*21*	*9*	*74*	*8*	*2*	*.198/.229/.297*	*.193*	*.262*	*0.9*	*SS -0*	*-0.5*

Like Lindor, Paulino is a teenager. In fact, he's a year younger—turning 18 last fall. The top of the Indians' system is rich with this pair of potential star-level players, but they are so far away that projecting with any confidence is near impossible. Paulino could end up with four average-to-above tools, including a hit tool that some scouts tab as a future 70. He projects for more power than Lindor, too, with our own Jason Parks seeing the potential for 10-15 home runs at his peak. With Kipnis and Cabrera as the current double-play duo, the team needn't rush these two future studs, but it sure is nice to dream on the potential of an even better duo knocking on the door in the late 2010s.

Cord Phelps 2B
Born: **1/23/1987** Age: **26**
Bats: **B** Throws: **R** Height: **6' 3"**
Weight: **200** Breakout: **7%**
Improve: **49%** Collapse: **1%**
Attrition: **16%** MLB: **93%**
Comparables:
Danny Richar,Luis Valbuena,Warren Morris

YEAR	TEAM	LVL	AGE	PA	R	2B	3B	HR	RBI	BB	SO	SB	CS	AVG_OBP_SLG	TAv	BABIP	BRR	FRAA	WARP
2010	AKR	AA	23	218	25	8	3	2	23	15	29	1	4	.296/.347/.397	.268	.337	-1.2	2B(52): -5.5	0.0
2010	COH	AAA	23	273	41	20	4	6	31	24	39	3	2	.317/.386/.506	.299	.357	-3	2B(65): -2.7	1.4
2011	COH	AAA	24	434	51	25	4	14	63	51	89	3	6	.294/.376/.492	.299	.348	0	--	0.0
2011	CLE	MLB	24	80	10	2	1	1	6	8	17	1	0	.155/.241/.254	.190	.189	0.7	2B(20): -2.3	-0.6
2012	COH	AAA	25	582	82	34	3	16	62	71	94	9	4	.276/.368/.451	.254	.311	-1.8	2B(55): -8.9	-0.8
2012	CLE	MLB	25	34	2	0	0	1	5	1	10	0	0	.212/.235/.303	.204	.273	0.2	2B(5): -0.2, SS(1): 0.1	-0.2
2013	*CLE*	*MLB*	*26*	*250*	*24*	*11*	*2*	*5*	*26*	*22*	*48*	*2*	*1*	*.245/.315/.372*	*.254*	*.290*	*-0.2*	*2B -2, SS 0*	*0.5*

He beat Kipnis to the majors by a couple of weeks, but unfortunately you can't call dibs for being first. Kipnis has taken firm hold of the second-base job while Phelps was left behind and spent the entire year in Triple-A—save a September cup of coffee, during which he did not impress. He has dabbled with third base and been successful, so perhaps his best bet is to become the short end of the platoon with Chisenhall and mash lefties every couple of days. As a switch-hitter, he has hit better against righties in the minors, yet held his own against lefties, with power being the only difference. Phelps has enough talent to be a big leaguer, but not a regular on a team looking to contend.

Mark Reynolds INF
Born: **8/3/1983** Age: **29**
Bats: **R** Throws: **R** Height: **6' 3"**
Weight: **220** Breakout: **7%**
Improve: **50%** Collapse: **2%**
Attrition: **9%** MLB: **93%**
Comparables:
Cecil Fielder,Jim Thome,Fred McGriff

YEAR	TEAM	LVL	AGE	PA	R	2B	3B	HR	RBI	BB	SO	SB	CS	AVG_OBP_SLG	TAv	BABIP	BRR	FRAA	WARP
2010	ARI	MLB	26	596	79	17	2	32	85	83	211	7	4	.198/.320/.433	.263	.257	1.5	3B(142): -0.9, 1B(5): 0.0	1.7
2011	BAL	MLB	27	620	84	27	1	37	86	75	196	6	4	.221/.323/.483	.284	.266	-2.3	3B(114): -14.7, 1B(44): 0.2	0.8
2012	BAL	MLB	28	538	65	26	0	23	69	73	159	1	3	.221/.335/.429	.270	.282	-1.8	1B(108): -13.8, 3B(15): -1.3	-1.0
2013	*CLE*	*MLB*	*29*	*523*	*70*	*20*	*1*	*27*	*76*	*63*	*174*	*7*	*4*	*.220/.321/.445*	*.277*	*.286*	*-0.8*	*3B -3, 1B -1*	*1.3*

Mark Reynolds strikes out. A lot. He's not particularly adept at third (though scouts liked his play at first down the stretch after Baltimore shifted him), but at least he always had power. Call him a one-trick pony in the spirit of Chumbawamba; unfortunately, his rendition of "Tubthumping" was lackluster in 2012. For the second season in a row, he started the season ice-cold, and this time the cold snap lasted longer. Reynolds failed to reach double-digit dingers until August. He exploded after that, so was it bad hitting, bad luck, or an aversion to early-season cold weather? It probably wasn't the cold: by May Baltimore averaged highs of 82 degrees and lows of a balmy 65. Scouts say his power is still there. If they're right, Reynolds could find his way back over 30 homers in Cleveland this year.

Luigi Rodriguez CF
Born: **11/13/1992** Age: **20**
Bats: **B** Throws: **R** Height: **6' 0"**
Weight: **160** Breakout: **22%**
Improve: **62%** Collapse: **3%**
Attrition: **16%** MLB: **83%**
Comparables:
Bobby Delgreco,Mike Trout,Ken Griffey

YEAR	TEAM	LVL	AGE	PA	R	2B	3B	HR	RBI	BB	SO	SB	CS	AVG_OBP_SLG	TAv	BABIP	BRR	FRAA	WARP
2011	IND	Rk	18	103	18	6	2	3	14	5	19	12	5	.379/.408/.579	.334	.440	0	--	0.0
2011	LKC	A	18	148	10	4	2	0	5	14	36	6	5	.250/.320/.311	.231	.340	0	--	0.0
2012	LKC	A	19	521	75	21	5	11	48	50	133	24	9	.268/.338/.406	.210	.350	6.1	CF(16): -1.6, RF(3): 0.2	0.0
2013	*CLE*	*MLB*	*20*	*250*	*27*	*8*	*1*	*4*	*19*	*16*	*79*	*6*	*2*	*.206/.257/.309*	*.210*	*.287*	*0.2*	*CF -2, RF -0*	*-0.8*

Another undeveloped youngster for the Indians, Luigi Rodriguez doesn't have nearly the upside of Lindor or Paulino. He wasn't a complete flop in his full-season assignment, but his 26 percent strikeout rate was concerning, especially from a defense-first center fielder who doesn't do enough with the bat to carry so much swing-and-miss. The Indians will continue to challenge him in hopes of tapping some potential and molding into him into a top-of-the-order center fielder instead of one more suited for batting eighth or ninth.

Ronny Rodriguez SS
Born: **4/17/1992** Age: **21**
Bats: **R** Throws: **R** Height: **6' 1"**
Weight: **170** Breakout: **3%**
Improve: **57%** Collapse: **9%**
Attrition: **17%** MLB: **98%**
Comparables:
Garry Templeton,Wil Cordero,Jim Fregosi

YEAR	TEAM	LVL	AGE	PA	R	2B	3B	HR	RBI	BB	SO	SB	CS	AVG_OBP_SLG	TAv	BABIP	BRR	FRAA	WARP
2011	LKC	A	19	394	41	28	7	11	42	13	83	10	7	.246/.274/.449	.238	.286	0	--	0.0
2012	CAR	A+	20	483	67	20	4	19	66	19	88	7	7	.264/.300/.452	.268	.289	-2.8	SS(27): 4.6, 2B(19): 4.2	1.3
2013	*CLE*	*MLB*	*21*	*250*	*24*	*9*	*1*	*8*	*30*	*7*	*60*	*2*	*1*	*.229/.254/.383*	*.230*	*.266*	*-0.2*	*SS 1, 2B -0*	*0.3*

Nice power for his size and age, but there isn't much else to Rodriguez's offensive game. Thankfully, the power alone may be enough to carry him offensively, when matched with the defense value of his great arm. There is still debate about whether he profiles as an eventual shortstop or second baseman, though obviously sticking at the former would give him a lot more leeway at the dish. His overly aggressive approach stunts his potential for batting average, especially since right-handers eat him alive. Lefties, meanwhile, don't stand a chance against him. This is becoming a running theme with the team's prospects: He is still far off, leaving a lot unanswered at this early point. Cleaning up his approach against righties should be his first order of business, though.

Carlos Santana C
Born: **4/8/1986** Age: **27**
Bats: **B** Throws: **R** Height: **6' 0"**
Weight: **190** Breakout: **2%**
Improve: **56%** Collapse: **5%**
Attrition: **8%** MLB: **99%**
Comparables:
Brian McCann,Joe Ferguson,Chris Iannetta

YEAR	TEAM	LVL	AGE	PA	R	2B	3B	HR	RBI	BB	SO	SB	CS	AVG_OBP_SLG	TAv	BABIP	BRR	FRAA	WARP
2010	COH	AAA	24	246	39	14	1	13	51	45	39	6	0	.316/.451/.597	.329	.340	1.7	C(45): 0.6	3.0
2010	CLE	MLB	24	192	23	13	0	6	22	37	29	3	0	.260/.401/.467	.316	.277	-0.1	C(40): 0.6	2.1
2011	CLE	MLB	25	658	84	35	2	27	79	97	133	5	3	.239/.351/.457	.287	.263	-1.8	C(95): -1.9, 1B(66): 1.5	2.9
2012	CLE	MLB	26	609	72	27	2	18	76	91	101	3	5	.252/.365/.420	.290	.278	-1.9	C(100): -0.7, 1B(21): 0.0	3.2
2013	*CLE*	*MLB*	*27*	*583*	*74*	*28*	*2*	*21*	*76*	*88*	*109*	*5*	*3*	*.249/.364/.439*	*.292*	*.278*	*-0.9*	*C -1, 1B 2*	*4.1*

Some fans assume if a guy isn't on the disabled list, he is playing at 100 percent health. For catchers that may be true for the first week in April. After that, expect them to be playing hurt. Santana posted an 863 OPS in April. Then a concussion and back troubles were among the reported ailments plaguing him in May and

June when he labored to a meager 592 OPS. With a cleaner bill of health the rest of the way, he posted an 872 OPS in the final 80 games of the year. The Indians do their best to protect Santana with spells at first base and DH. He isn't enough of a value-add behind the dish that they feel compelled to play him there, so expect those spells to continue. Eventually he may become a full-time first baseman; his offensive profile is rich enough to carry that position.

Grady Sizemore CF
Born: **8/2/1982** Age: **30**
Bats: **L** Throws: **L** Height: **6' 3"**
Weight: **200** Breakout: **6%**
Improve: **53%** Collapse: **4%**
Attrition: **3%** MLB: **98%**
Comparables:
Curtis Granderson,Bernie Williams,Fred Lynn

YEAR	TEAM	LVL	AGE	PA	R	2B	3B	HR	RBI	BB	SO	SB	CS	AVG_OBP_SLG	TAv	BABIP	BRR	FRAA	WARP
2010	CLE	MLB	27	140	15	6	2	0	13	9	35	4	2	.211/.271/.289	.205	.287	1.7	CF(32): -3.9	-0.6
2011	CLE	MLB	28	295	34	21	1	10	32	18	85	0	2	.224/.285/.422	.250	.284	-0.7	CF(56): -3.8	-0.2
2013	*CLE*	*MLB*	*30*	*250*	*35*	*12*	*2*	*9*	*28*	*26*	*54*	*6*	*3*	*.242/.330/.429*	*.273*	*.280*	*0.1*	*CF -0*	*1.1*

Oh, what could've been! It doesn't matter if your team's biggest rival is on the losing end, no one who truly enjoys baseball likes to see a star cut down by injury before he even hits his prime. Sizemore was the best center fielder in baseball in 2005-08 and he has been a shell of himself since, relegated to 210 games of barely league-average production in four years, including missing all of 2012. Another microfracture surgery last fall puts his 2013 in doubt and the 30-year-old Sizemore is now staring down the barrel of one of the all-time "what could've been" careers.

Drew Stubbs CF
Born: **10/4/1984** Age: **28**
Bats: **R** Throws: **R** Height: **6' 5"**
Weight: **200** Breakout: **0%**
Improve: **41%** Collapse: **6%**
Attrition: **9%** MLB: **87%**
Comparables:
Bob Brower,Luis Terrero,Adolfo Phillips

YEAR	TEAM	LVL	AGE	PA	R	2B	3B	HR	RBI	BB	SO	SB	CS	AVG_OBP_SLG	TAv	BABIP	BRR	FRAA	WARP
2010	CIN	MLB	25	583	91	19	6	22	77	55	168	30	6	.255/.329/.444	.270	.330	9.2	CF(147): 6.4	4.1
2011	CIN	MLB	26	681	92	22	3	15	44	63	205	40	10	.243/.321/.364	.248	.343	4.9	CF(157): -3.1	0.6
2012	CIN	MLB	27	544	75	13	2	14	40	42	166	30	7	.213/.277/.333	.221	.290	3.8	CF(134): -8.7	-1.6
2013	*CLE*	*MLB*	*28*	*540*	*74*	*18*	*2*	*13*	*48*	*48*	*157*	*31*	*7*	*.232/.305/.360*	*.246*	*.310*	*3.3*	*CF 1*	*1.4*

Stubbs offers a tantalizing combination of power, speed, and center-field defense—although the metrics and his reputation don't align well on that last point. Unfortunately, he cannot hit baseballs. Stubbs is Mike Cameron's evil twin. He hasn't hit right-handers at all over the last two years, and for his career he strikes out more often than Adam Dunn, Ryan Howard, or Carlos Pena. A left abdomen strain cost Stubbs three weeks in June, and he slumped badly toward the end, posting a 388 OPS over his final 47 regular-season games. Stubbs's defensive reputation will keep him around a while longer, but eventually his inability to make contact will offset his usefulness in the field. Landing in Cleveland was a godsend, as the Indians are in a position to take a chance on him without incident.

Nick Swisher RF
Born: **11/25/1980** Age: **32**
Bats: **B** Throws: **L** Height: **6' 0"**
Weight: **210** Breakout: **2%**
Improve: **27%** Collapse: **4%**
Attrition: **6%** MLB: **91%**
Comparables:
Roger Maris,Reggie Smith,Trot Nixon

YEAR	TEAM	LVL	AGE	PA	R	2B	3B	HR	RBI	BB	SO	SB	CS	AVG_OBP_SLG	TAv	BABIP	BRR	FRAA	WARP
2010	NYA	MLB	29	635	91	33	3	29	89	58	139	1	2	.288/.359/.511	.301	.335	-1	RF(134): 10.1, 1B(6): 0.0	4.6
2011	NYA	MLB	30	635	81	30	0	23	85	95	125	2	2	.260/.374/.449	.289	.295	-0.3	RF(141): 2.9, 1B(11): -0.2	3.0
2012	NYA	MLB	31	624	75	36	0	24	93	77	141	2	3	.272/.364/.473	.290	.324	-0.7	RF(109): 8.8, 1B(41): 3.8	3.7
2013	*CLE*	*MLB*	*32*	*588*	*70*	*28*	*1*	*21*	*76*	*74*	*133*	*2*	*2*	*.247/.346/.430*	*.280*	*.291*	*-1.3*	*RF 3, 1B -0*	*2.6*

Players don't come much more consistent than Swisher, who's played between 148 and 157 games for seven straight seasons, posting a TAv between .289 and .301 and a WARP between 3.0 and 4.9 in every one except his BABIP-bitten 2008. Unfortunately, his October play has been just as predictably poor: in 181 postseason plate appearances, he's hit roughly like Adam Dunn did in 2011, posting a .169/.283/.305 line. Normally we're not ones to throw around the "C" words—"clutch" and "choke"—but in a sample size that large, Swisher's struggles might actually mean something. The Indians decided that what Swisher, who played college baseball at Ohio State, does during the first six months of the season will suit them over the next four years.

Tony Wolters INF
Born: **6/9/1992** Age: **21**
Bats: **L** Throws: **R** Height: **5' 11"**
Weight: **165** Breakout: **3%**
Improve: **53%** Collapse: **9%**
Attrition: **14%** MLB: **96%**
Comparables:
Glenn Hubbard,Bill Mazeroski,Tim Foli

YEAR	TEAM	LVL	AGE	PA	R	2B	3B	HR	RBI	BB	SO	SB	CS	AVG_OBP_SLG	TAv	BABIP	BRR	FRAA	WARP
2011	MHV	A-	19	313	50	10	3	1	20	30	49	19	4	.292/.385/.363	.276	.353	0	--	0.0
2012	CAR	A+	20	537	66	30	8	8	58	36	104	5	9	.260/.320/.404	.275	.314	-2.2	SS(23): 0.9, 2B(20): 1.8	0.6
2013	*CLE*	*MLB*	*21*	*250*	*24*	*10*	*2*	*4*	*20*	*12*	*63*	*1*	*1*	*.217/.259/.326*	*.213*	*.273*	*-0.3*	*2B -1, SS 0*	*-0.3*

This will blow your mind, but here is yet *another* Indians prospect who can't drink legally, making him both promising and difficult to accurately project. Wolters doesn't have near the upside of the others so it's a matter of determining whether he becomes a solid 22nd-25th guy or the 26th guy who pinballs between Columbus and Cleveland. Let's get him to Columbus first. He is a utility infielder with your classic "sum is greater than the whole of the parts" profile because he "plays the game the right way." What he lacks in skill, he makes up for intangibles. Clichés are born out of truths, so while we've heard these tags placed on countless guys before, we've also seen what those guys can become in the big leagues.

PITCHERS

Matt Albers

Born: **1/20/1983** Age: **30**
Bats: **L** Throws: **R** Height: **6' 1"** Weight: **225**
Breakout: **53%** Improve: **69%** Collapse: **16%**
Attrition: **6%** MLB: **90%**

Comparables:
John Franco,Javier Lopez,Jeff Fassero

YEAR	TEAM	LVL	AGE	W	L	SV	G	GS	IP	H	HR	BB	SO	BB9	SO9	GB%	BABIP	WHIP	ERA	FIP	FRA	WARP
2010	BAL	MLB	27	5	3	0	62	0	75^{2}	78	6	34	49	4.0	5.8	58%	.303	1.48	4.52	4.21	5.41	0.0
2011	PAW	AAA	28	0	0	0	2	0	3	1	0	0	2	0.0	6.0	38%	.125	0.33	0.00	1.90	3.81	0.0
2011	BOS	MLB	28	4	4	0	56	0	64^{2}	62	7	31	68	4.3	9.5	48%	.309	1.44	4.73	4.04	4.72	0.5
2012	ARI	MLB	29	1	1	0	23	0	21	16	3	7	19	3.0	8.1	60%	.241	1.10	2.57	4.33	4.82	-0.1
2012	BOS	MLB	29	2	0	0	40	0	39^{1}	30	6	15	25	3.4	5.7	56%	.218	1.14	2.29	4.98	5.92	-0.3
2013	*CLE*	*MLB*	*30*	*2*	*1*	*1*	*45*	*0*	*50*	*48*	*5*	*22*	*40*	*4.0*	*7.2*	*51%*	*.292*	*1.40*	*4.22*	*4.22*	*4.59*	*0.3*

Cleveland's affinity for groundball pitchers found a new muse in Albers this offseason. Albers cooks his sinker with gas, averaging 94 mph with late movement that coaxes a steady stream of grounders from opposing batters. He had his most successful season in 2012, with a 20 percent drop in both hits and walks allowed that anchored his stingy run-prevention across both leagues. The net result was an ERA that eclipsed his previous best by more than a run.

Cody Allen

Born: **11/22/1988** Age: **24**
Bats: **R** Throws: **R** Height: **6' 2"** Weight: **210**
Breakout: **33%** Improve: **61%** Collapse: **24%**
Attrition: **13%** MLB: **91%**

Comparables:
Fernando Cabrera,Chris Ray,Joe Smith

YEAR	TEAM	LVL	AGE	W	L	SV	G	GS	IP	H	HR	BB	SO	BB9	SO9	GB%	BABIP	WHIP	ERA	FIP	FRA	WARP
2011	LKC	A	22	2	0	0	7	0	17	10	0	5	28	2.6	14.8	—	.303	0.88	0.00	0.95	1.03	0.0
2011	MHV	A-	22	3	1	0	14	0	33^{2}	21	1	9	42	2.4	11.2	—	.256	0.89	2.14	2.32	2.53	0.0
2011	KIN	A+	22	0	0	0	1	0	3	1	0	0	3	0.0	9.0	41%	.250	0.33	0.00	1.23	6.19	0.0
2011	AKR	AA	22	0	0	0	1	0	1	3	0	0	2	0.0	18.0	25%	.750	3.00	18.00	-0.59	1.00	0.1
2012	CAR	A+	23	0	0	0	2	0	4	1	0	0	8	0.0	18.0	60%	.200	0.25	0.00	-0.61	0.00	0.2
2012	AKR	AA	23	0	0	1	5	0	7^{2}	2	1	0	10	0.0	11.7	27%	.071	0.26	1.17	2.29	2.83	0.2
2012	COH	AAA	23	3	2	2	24	0	31^{2}	22	3	9	35	2.6	9.9	42%	.244	0.98	2.27	3.03	2.97	0.5
2012	CLE	MLB	23	0	1	0	27	0	29	29	2	15	27	4.7	8.4	42%	.329	1.52	3.72	3.63	4.07	0.1
2013	*CLE*	*MLB*	*24*	*1*	*1*	*0*	*28*	*0*	*36*	*32*	*4*	*14*	*37*	*3.4*	*9.2*	*42%*	*.294*	*1.27*	*3.60*	*3.76*	*3.92*	*0.5*

Allen started 2012 at High-A and finished it in the majors, where he found a fair bit of success immediately. He works with two easy-plus pitches: a 95-mph fastball with good rise and a ridiculously hard 85-mph curveball with a lot of bite. His fastball-heavy approach means he gives up a lot of fly balls, and he still has some control and command issues to work out, but Allen certainly has the stuff to be a closer one day. It's possible he finds himself working high-leverage innings as soon as this season.

Scott Barnes

Born: **9/5/1987** Age: **25**
Bats: **L** Throws: **L** Height: **6' 5"** Weight: **185**
Breakout: **41%** Improve: **69%** Collapse: **17%**
Attrition: **9%** MLB: **93%**

Comparables:
Jake McGee,Glen Perkins,Marc Rzepczynski

YEAR	TEAM	LVL	AGE	W	L	SV	G	GS	IP	H	HR	BB	SO	BB9	SO9	GB%	BABIP	WHIP	ERA	FIP	FRA	WARP
2010	AKR	AA	22	6	11	0	26	26	138	126	15	58	127	3.8	8.3	44%	.285	1.33	5.22	4.39	5.34	0.5
2011	AKR	AA	23	1	0	0	2	2	11	5	0	2	17	1.6	13.9	60%	.250	0.64	1.64	0.86	1.91	0.4
2011	COH	AAA	23	7	4	0	16	15	88	80	12	34	90	3.5	9.2	—	.292	1.30	3.68	4.23	4.59	0.0
2012	COH	AAA	24	2	3	2	31	3	52	37	1	23	67	4.0	11.6	44%	.288	1.15	3.98	2.39	3.30	0.9
2012	CLE	MLB	24	0	0	0	16	0	19	17	1	7	16	3.3	7.6	39%	.291	1.26	4.26	3.63	4.08	0.2
2013	*CLE*	*MLB*	*25*	*2*	*2*	*0*	*12*	*5*	*34^{2}*	*33*	*4*	*15*	*31*	*4.0*	*8.0*	*40%*	*.292*	*1.38*	*4.32*	*4.21*	*4.70*	*0.2*

Barnes made the transition from starter to reliever last May, and he projects to be a pretty good one: nearly ready for the show at present. He won't overpower anyone with his fastball, which sits in the low-90s, but he features a hard, plus slider and a quality changeup that should allow him to retire batters from both sides of the plate. His 2012 sips of coffee could turn into gulps this year, and it wouldn't surprise to see him working the seventh or eighth innings for the Tribe within a year or two.

Trevor Bauer

Born: **1/17/1991** Age: **22**
Bats: **R** Throws: **R** Height: **6' 2"** Weight: **175**
Breakout: **26%** Improve: **58%** Collapse: **17%**
Attrition: **8%** MLB: **93%**

Comparables:
Phil Hughes,Kerry Wood,Matt Cain

YEAR	TEAM	LVL	AGE	W	L	SV	G	GS	IP	H	HR	BB	SO	BB9	SO9	GB%	BABIP	WHIP	ERA	FIP	FRA	WARP
2011	VIS	A+	20	0	1	0	3	3	9	7	1	4	17	4.0	17.0	44%	.353	1.22	3.00	2.95	2.93	0.4
2011	MOB	AA	20	1	1	0	4	4	16^{2}	20	2	8	26	4.3	14.0	43%	.333	1.68	7.56	3.55	6.27	0.1
2012	MOB	AA	21	7	1	0	8	8	48^{1}	33	1	26	60	4.8	11.2	48%	.296	1.22	1.68	2.67	2.83	1.0
2012	RNO	AAA	21	5	1	0	14	14	82	74	8	35	97	3.8	10.6	46%	.315	1.33	2.85	3.85	3.75	1.0
2012	ARI	MLB	21	1	2	0	4	4	16^{1}	14	2	13	17	7.2	9.4	48%	.273	1.65	6.06	5.22	6.34	-0.2
2013	*CLE*	*MLB*	*22*	*3*	*2*	*0*	*8*	*8*	43^{2}	*38*	*5*	*21*	*48*	*4.3*	*10.0*	*45%*	*.297*	*1.33*	*3.80*	*3.93*	*4.13*	*0.6*

A cerebral pitcher who takes pride in his advanced knowledge of the craft, Bauer's unusual conditioning regimen and his complicated approach have stirred the witch's brew of proper pitching development. Bauer's in-depth knowledge of biomechanics has the potential to raise his ceiling if he approaches the game with an open mind, but his delivery has a lot of holes for a guy who spends so much time honing it. Thus far he has struggled to repeat his complex motion on a consistent basis. Bauer treats every at-bat as an individual chess match. With a plethora of breaking balls in addition to a signature pitch that he calls a "reverse slider," he has a tendency to overcomplicate matters when forming a game plan. This Lincecum understudy might benefit by simplifying things in the short term, and then advancing his approach once he has better command of his athletic talents.

Carlos Carrasco

Born: **3/21/1987** Age: **26**
Bats: **R** Throws: **R** Height: **6' 4"** Weight: **215**
Breakout: **27%** Improve: **50%** Collapse: **26%**
Attrition: **26%** MLB: **98%**

Comparables:
Micah Owings,Homer Bailey,Boof Bonser

YEAR	TEAM	LVL	AGE	W	L	SV	G	GS	IP	H	HR	BB	SO	BB9	SO9	GB%	BABIP	WHIP	ERA	FIP	FRA	WARP
2010	COH	AAA	23	10	6	0	25	25	150^{1}	139	16	46	133	2.8	8.0	49%	.291	1.23	3.65	3.96	5.39	0.7
2010	CLE	MLB	23	2	2	0	7	7	44^{2}	47	6	14	38	2.8	7.7	57%	.318	1.37	3.83	4.10	4.56	0.2
2011	AKR	AA	24	0	0	0	1	1	3^{2}	4	1	3	3	7.4	7.4	—	.273	1.91	9.82	8.59	9.34	0.0
2011	CLE	MLB	24	8	9	0	21	21	124^{2}	130	15	40	85	2.9	6.1	51%	.293	1.36	4.62	4.32	5.03	0.0
2013	*CLE*	*MLB*	*26*	*2*	*2*	*0*	*6*	*6*	34^{2}	*36*	*5*	*12*	*28*	*3.1*	*7.1*	*46%*	*.299*	*1.38*	*4.59*	*4.50*	*4.99*	*0.1*

Before Tommy John surgery sidelined him for the entire 2012 regular season, Carrasco was on his way to becoming a solid second or third starter. He'd been improving the control that gave him issues early in his professional career, and his plus stuff was allowing him to miss bats at the major-league level. Carrasco comes armed with a 93-mph fastball that he can add some sink to and a bouquet of quality off-speed offerings, including a changeup, slider, and curve. Pitchers returning from ligament replacement often take a year or two to regain all their velocity and effectiveness, however, so give Carrasco a break if he struggles a bit this year.

Jeanmar Gomez

Born: **2/10/1988** Age: **25**
Bats: **R** Throws: **R** Height: **6' 4"** Weight: **170**
Breakout: **29%** Improve: **48%** Collapse: **19%**
Attrition: **28%** MLB: **93%**

Comparables:
Jeff Manship,Anthony Swarzak,Pat Misch

YEAR	TEAM	LVL	AGE	W	L	SV	G	GS	IP	H	HR	BB	SO	BB9	SO9	GB%	BABIP	WHIP	ERA	FIP	FRA	WARP
2010	COH	AAA	22	8	8	0	20	20	116	129	16	42	78	3.3	6.1	45%	.308	1.47	5.20	4.85	6.41	-0.4
2010	CLE	MLB	22	4	5	0	11	11	57^{2}	73	7	22	34	3.4	5.3	47%	.330	1.65	4.68	4.69	5.22	-0.1
2011	MHV	A-	23	0	0	0	1	1	4	5	0	0	3	0.0	6.8	—	.357	1.25	2.25	1.86	2.03	0.0
2011	COH	AAA	23	10	7	0	21	21	137^{2}	123	8	49	107	3.2	7.0	—	.287	1.25	2.55	3.61	3.93	0.0
2011	CLE	MLB	23	5	3	0	11	10	58^{1}	73	6	15	31	2.3	4.8	53%	.325	1.51	4.47	4.16	4.68	0.4
2012	COH	AAA	24	6	5	0	11	11	69^{1}	75	6	17	54	2.2	7.0	55%	.319	1.33	4.41	3.50	5.55	0.0
2012	CLE	MLB	24	5	8	0	20	17	90^{2}	95	15	34	47	3.4	4.7	50%	.271	1.42	5.96	5.42	6.19	-0.8
2013	*CLE*	*MLB*	*25*	*5*	*6*	*0*	*16*	*16*	90^{1}	*100*	*12*	*31*	*57*	*3.1*	*5.7*	*47%*	*.302*	*1.45*	*4.97*	*4.69*	*5.40*	*-0.1*

What do you call a season in which Gomez posts 20 wins and a 3.00 ERA? Unlikely. (Little League would have also been an acceptable answer.) Gomez is not very good by major-league standards. He relies heavily on a 90-mph sinker, utilizing a changeup and slider to change speeds. He generates plenty of groundballs, but the praise pretty much stops there. His control is fringe-average, and he doesn't generate many strikeouts. His minor-league numbers in that regard are okay, and his stuff, while far from dominating, does indicate he's better than a 4.7-SO9 pitcher. If he can manage even a decent impression of those minor-league numbers while in Cleveland, he could still prove to be a usable fifth starter.

Nick Hagadone

Born: **1/1/1986** Age: **27**
Bats: **L** Throws: **L** Height: **6' 6"** Weight: **230**
Breakout: **37%** Improve: **68%** Collapse: **16%**
Attrition: **11%** MLB: **77%**

Comparables:
Bill Murphy,Dustin Richardson,Mark McLemore

YEAR	TEAM	LVL	AGE	W	L	SV	G	GS	IP	H	HR	BB	SO	BB9	SO9	GB%	BABIP	WHIP	ERA	FIP	FRA	WARP
2010	KIN	A+	24	1	3	0	10	10	37^{2}	28	2	29	45	6.9	10.7	49%	.286	1.51	2.39	4.02	4.25	0.5
2010	AKR	AA	24	2	2	1	19	7	48	44	5	34	44	6.4	8.2	44%	.273	1.62	4.50	5.07	5.91	0.0
2011	AKR	AA	25	2	1	0	12	0	22^{2}	14	0	7	24	2.8	9.5	36%	.262	0.93	1.59	2.22	2.29	0.5
2011	COH	AAA	25	4	3	4	34	0	48^{1}	42	5	15	53	2.8	9.9	—	.282	1.18	3.35	3.32	3.61	0.0
2011	CLE	MLB	25	1	0	0	9	0	11	4	0	6	11	4.9	9.0	33%	.167	0.91	4.09	2.97	3.66	0.2
2012	COH	AAA	26	0	0	0	5	0	7^{1}	4	0	1	7	1.2	8.6	31%	.308	0.68	0.00	1.66	1.32	0.1
2012	CLE	MLB	26	1	0	1	27	0	25^{1}	26	4	15	26	5.3	9.2	37%	.310	1.62	6.39	4.82	5.21	0.0
2013	*CLE*	*MLB*	*27*	*2*	*1*	*0*	*18*	*4*	*33^{2}*	*31*	*4*	*20*	*32*	*5.3*	*8.6*	*46%*	*.296*	*1.51*	*4.51*	*4.63*	*4.91*	*0.1*

Hagadone has a big, solid pitching frame and a power arm, boasting a 95-mph fastball with rise and an 83-mph, bat-missing slider. That's certainly the stuff to succeed, potentially as a late-inning reliever, but he needs to work on his command and approach. He tends to pitch up in the zone, even when he's ahead in the count, and throws pitches that batters can put a good swing on. There's nothing wrong with him mechanically, but doing a better job repeating those mechanics could help him out. He's not a great athlete, which could make that a bit difficult, but the upside is there. Hagadone is merely a work-in-progress at the moment.

Trey Haley

Born: **6/21/1990** Age: **23**
Bats: **R** Throws: **R** Height: **6' 4"** Weight: **180**
Breakout: **32%** Improve: **68%** Collapse: **19%**
Attrition: **12%** MLB: **77%**

Comparables:
Whammy Douglas,Jim O'Toole,Jim Nelson

YEAR	TEAM	LVL	AGE	W	L	SV	G	GS	IP	H	HR	BB	SO	BB9	SO9	GB%	BABIP	WHIP	ERA	FIP	FRA	WARP
2010	LKC	A	20	5	11	0	27	26	116	122	13	86	97	6.7	7.5	50%	.317	1.79	5.97	5.95	7.12	-1.6
2011	IND	Rk	21	0	0	0	2	1	3	0	0	0	4	0.0	12.0	—	.000	0.00	0.00	1.70	1.85	0.0
2011	LKC	A	21	0	0	1	8	2	12^{2}	5	0	8	17	5.7	12.1	—	.208	1.03	2.84	3.04	3.31	0.0
2011	KIN	A+	21	1	1	1	19	0	28^{2}	25	1	17	27	5.3	8.5	80%	.296	1.47	3.77	3.89	3.49	0.3
2012	CLE	Rk	22	1	0	0	4	0	6	8	0	2	10	3.0	15.0	83%	.417	1.67	7.50	2.04	1.15	0.3
2012	CAR	A+	22	0	0	2	12	0	17^{1}	8	0	6	16	3.1	8.3	69%	.178	0.81	1.04	3.27	3.13	0.3
2012	AKR	AA	22	3	1	0	9	0	15^{1}	10	0	11	23	6.5	13.5	70%	.333	1.37	1.76	2.94	3.15	0.3
2013	*CLE*	*MLB*	*23*	*1*	*2*	*0*	*11*	*5*	*31*	*34*	*4*	*25*	*19*	*7.2*	*5.7*	*51%*	*.301*	*1.90*	*6.68*	*6.07*	*7.26*	*-0.6*

Haley only reached Double-A in the second half of 2012, but some believe he could be ready to join the big boys in Cleveland this year. He walks a lot of batters (and always will) due to some mechanical issues, but he has the stuff to retire major leaguers. He works in the mid- to high-90s with his fastball and complements it with a curveball that is tops among all Indians prospects. The control issues will prevent him from ever becoming a top-notch reliever, but he has the upside of a seventh- or eighth-inning type.

Frank Herrmann

Born: **5/30/1984** Age: **29**
Bats: **L** Throws: **R** Height: **6' 5"** Weight: **220**
Breakout: **23%** Improve: **52%** Collapse: **25%**
Attrition: **20%** MLB: **82%**

Comparables:
Billy Traber,Justin Hampson,David Wells

YEAR	TEAM	LVL	AGE	W	L	SV	G	GS	IP	H	HR	BB	SO	BB9	SO9	GB%	BABIP	WHIP	ERA	FIP	FRA	WARP
2010	COH	AAA	26	3	0	2	19	0	28^{2}	15	0	8	22	2.5	6.9	47%	.200	0.80	0.31	2.59	3.58	0.5
2010	CLE	MLB	26	0	1	1	40	0	44^{2}	48	6	9	24	1.8	4.8	37%	.286	1.28	4.03	4.46	5.07	-0.1
2011	COH	AAA	27	0	0	0	9	0	10^{2}	13	1	4	12	3.4	10.1	—	.387	1.59	5.91	3.33	3.62	0.0
2011	CLE	MLB	27	4	0	0	40	0	56^{1}	71	7	16	34	2.6	5.4	33%	.327	1.54	5.11	4.32	4.41	0.4
2012	COH	AAA	28	2	2	8	42	0	52^{2}	58	8	15	58	2.6	9.9	40%	.355	1.39	4.78	3.84	5.10	0.1
2012	CLE	MLB	28	0	0	0	15	0	19^{1}	12	1	4	14	1.9	6.5	40%	.212	0.83	2.33	2.89	3.42	0.3
2013	*CLE*	*MLB*	*29*	*1*	*1*	*0*	*27*	*0*	*35^{1}*	*38*	*4*	*10*	*22*	*2.5*	*5.7*	*39%*	*.299*	*1.35*	*4.41*	*4.28*	*4.79*	*0.1*

Each time Herrmann has appeared in the pages of a Baseball Prospectus annual, mention is made of his Harvard diploma, so we promise not to bring it up this year. Oops. Never mind. It's actually not fair, because Herrmann has more going for him than an Ivy League education; he's on the verge of becoming a capable middle reliever. Herrmann has always had a great arm, capable of sitting comfortably at 95 mph with his fastball, but until last year, he was vulnerable when behind in the count and hitters sat on the heater. Last year, he added a curveball that has the makings of a very effective pitch, which should give him an alternative to his splitter to throw in tough counts. Herrmann is smart and athletic and seems capable of taking the next step toward being a quality middle-innings arm.

David Huff
Born: **8/22/1984** Age: **28**
Bats: **B** Throws: **L** Height: **6' 3"** Weight: **215**
Breakout: **27%** Improve: **66%** Collapse: **17%**
Attrition: **13%** MLB: **89%**
Comparables:
Dustin Moseley,Cha Seung Baek,Daniel McCutchen

YEAR	TEAM	LVL	AGE	W	L	SV	G	GS	IP	H	HR	BB	SO	BB9	SO9	GB%	BABIP	WHIP	ERA	FIP	FRA	WARP
2010	COH	AAA	25	8	2	0	12	12	74^{1}	84	8	21	52	2.5	6.3	42%	.310	1.41	4.36	4.22	5.13	0.8
2010	CLE	MLB	25	2	11	0	15	15	79^{2}	101	14	34	37	3.8	4.2	38%	.310	1.69	6.21	5.80	5.49	-0.3
2011	COH	AAA	26	9	3	0	18	18	107	111	10	30	66	2.5	5.6	—	.292	1.32	3.87	4.12	4.47	0.0
2011	CLE	MLB	26	2	6	0	11	10	50^{2}	55	6	17	36	3.0	6.4	35%	.292	1.42	4.09	4.19	4.32	0.9
2012	AKR	AA	27	0	0	0	1	1	4	1	0	1	3	2.2	6.8	56%	.111	0.50	0.00	2.45	3.84	0.1
2012	COH	AAA	27	7	6	0	24	22	134	155	27	34	79	2.3	5.3	38%	.293	1.41	4.97	5.40	7.27	-0.2
2012	CLE	MLB	27	3	1	0	6	4	26^{2}	30	5	5	19	1.7	6.4	40%	.298	1.31	3.38	4.73	5.40	0.1
2013	*CLE*	*MLB*	*28*	*4*	*4*	*0*	*11*	*11*	62^{2}	*68*	*9*	*19*	*40*	*2.7*	*5.7*	*41%*	*.295*	*1.39*	*4.82*	*4.70*	*5.24*	*-0.0*

What do you call a pitcher with a 96-mph fastball, a hammer curve, and plus control? Stephen Strasburg. That's called misdirection. Huff, on the other hand, doesn't have much deception working for him, he's just trying to be major-league relevant. He does have solid control on his side, but his heavy four-seam usage results in tons of fly balls, and his lack of a wipe-out pitch means he doesn't strike out enough batters to compensate. Throwing the fastball two-thirds of the time at least leaves hitters off-balance when he throws his changeup, slider, or curve, but it also leaves them ample opportunity to make contact. Huff's strong major-league ERA last year was largely luck-driven; he'll be up and down from the minors quite a bit over the next few years.

Ubaldo Jimenez
Born: **1/22/1984** Age: **29**
Bats: **R** Throws: **R** Height: **6' 5"** Weight: **210**
Breakout: **11%** Improve: **48%** Collapse: **21%**
Attrition: **7%** MLB: **93%**
Comparables:
A.J. Burnett,Kevin Appier,Carlos Zambrano

YEAR	TEAM	LVL	AGE	W	L	SV	G	GS	IP	H	HR	BB	SO	BB9	SO9	GB%	BABIP	WHIP	ERA	FIP	FRA	WARP
2010	COL	MLB	26	19	8	0	33	33	221^{2}	164	10	92	214	3.7	8.7	50%	.271	1.15	2.88	3.13	3.79	4.4
2011	CLE	MLB	27	4	4	0	11	11	65^{1}	68	7	27	62	3.7	8.5	48%	.318	1.45	5.10	3.89	4.59	0.6
2011	COL	MLB	27	6	9	0	21	21	123	118	10	51	118	3.7	8.6	48%	.312	1.37	4.46	3.55	4.39	1.8
2012	CLE	MLB	28	9	17	0	31	31	176^{2}	190	25	95	143	4.8	7.3	40%	.309	1.61	5.40	5.02	5.08	0.5
2013	*CLE*	*MLB*	*29*	*11*	*8*	*0*	*27*	*27*	163^{1}	*144*	*13*	*70*	*152*	*3.8*	*8.4*	*49%*	*.291*	*1.30*	*3.61*	*3.66*	*3.93*	*2.3*

Jimenez's 2012 season was so bad that it wouldn't be a surprise to see him go on *Intentional Talk* and declare that it was all one big "Got Heeeeeeem!" Good peripherals led many to declare his inflated 2011 ERA bad luck, but there was nothing ambiguous about Ubaldo's 2012; he was just bad. His velocity continued its precipitous decline, dropping from nearly 98 mph in 2009 to just over 93 mph last season, dragging his strikeout rate to a career low. His mechanics were a complete mess, which explains some of the velocity fall-off, but more importantly, it led to severe control issues. Jimenez still has it in him to be a very good pitcher, but he'll need to work hard to get his delivery back to where it was.

Corey Kluber
Born: **4/10/1986** Age: **27**
Bats: **R** Throws: **R** Height: **6' 5"** Weight: **215**
Breakout: **32%** Improve: **67%** Collapse: **14%**
Attrition: **18%** MLB: **87%**
Comparables:
Brad Mills,Rick VandenHurk,Felipe Paulino

YEAR	TEAM	LVL	AGE	W	L	SV	G	GS	IP	H	HR	BB	SO	BB9	SO9	GB%	BABIP	WHIP	ERA	FIP	FRA	WARP
2010	AKR	AA	24	2	2	0	5	5	26^{1}	38	0	10	21	3.4	7.2	41%	.418	1.83	3.76	3.13	3.19	0.7
2010	SAN	AA	24	6	6	0	22	21	122^{2}	121	7	40	136	2.9	10.0	42%	.342	1.31	3.45	2.90	3.35	2.3
2010	COH	AAA	24	1	1	0	2	2	11	10	1	6	8	4.9	6.5	30%	.310	1.45	3.27	5.20	6.61	-0.1
2011	COH	AAA	25	7	11	0	27	27	150^{2}	153	19	70	143	4.2	8.5	—	.314	1.48	5.56	4.53	4.92	0.0
2011	CLE	MLB	25	0	0	0	3	0	4^{1}	6	0	3	5	6.2	10.4	40%	.400	2.08	8.31	4.22	3.26	0.1
2012	COH	AAA	26	11	7	0	21	21	125^{1}	121	9	49	128	3.5	9.2	48%	.316	1.36	3.59	3.34	4.06	0.5
2012	CLE	MLB	26	2	5	0	12	12	63	76	9	18	54	2.6	7.7	46%	.342	1.49	5.14	4.24	4.81	0.2
2013	*CLE*	*MLB*	*27*	*4*	*5*	*0*	*14*	*14*	77^{2}	*82*	*10*	*32*	*68*	*3.7*	*7.8*	*42%*	*.315*	*1.48*	*5.04*	*4.36*	*5.47*	*-0.2*

Kluber is coming off his rookie season, during which he found moderate success, at least in terms of peripherals. He leaned much more heavily on a two-seamer after previously being primarily a four-seam guy, which made him more effective at the bottom of the strike zone while generating more grounders than ever before. Of course, with this switch to the two-seamer, his secondary stuff needs to be sharper to generate whiffs. His slider has shown this ability at times, but the key to his success may ultimately be improving a changeup that is still in the developmental stages. He'll also need to find consistency from the stretch—something he's struggled with at times in the minors. If he can do this, he could be a solid fourth starter.

Chen Lee
Born: **10/21/1986** Age: **26**
Bats: **R** Throws: **R** Height: **6' 0"** Weight: **175**
Breakout: **28%** Improve: **48%** Collapse: **25%**
Attrition: **18%** MLB: **88%**
Comparables:
Roberto Novoa,Rich Thompson,Antonio Osuna

YEAR	TEAM	LVL	AGE	W	L	SV	G	GS	IP	H	HR	BB	SO	BB9	SO9	GB%	BABIP	WHIP	ERA	FIP	FRA	WARP
2010	AKR	AA	23	5	4	0	44	0	72^{2}	59	6	22	82	2.7	10.2	48%	.275	1.11	3.22	3.25	3.79	1.2
2011	AKR	AA	24	2	1	0	23	0	39^{2}	27	1	11	56	2.5	12.7	58%	.325	0.96	2.50	2.20	2.71	1.0
2011	COH	AAA	24	4	0	1	21	0	31^{2}	26	2	12	43	3.4	12.2	—	.343	1.20	2.27	2.57	2.80	0.0
2012	COH	AAA	25	2	0	0	5	0	7	5	1	1	8	1.3	10.3	71%	.250	0.86	2.57	3.16	4.85	0.0
2013	*CLE*	*MLB*	*26*	*1*	*0*	*1*	*21*	*0*	35^{1}	*32*	*4*	*14*	*35*	*3.5*	*9.0*	*47%*	*.299*	*1.31*	*3.99*	*3.88*	*4.34*	*0.3*

Lee stood a good chance of being promoted to Cleveland's bullpen last year before going down in April and requiring Tommy John surgery. He has put up video-game numbers at nearly every level, and he has good, if not top-notch, stuff to back it up. He throws a fastball in the low-to-mid-90s, touching 96, which he pairs with a plus slider and good pitchability to generate plenty of strikeouts. He'll need to rebound from surgery at Triple-A this season and may have to wait until 2014 for his call-up.

Justin Masterson

Born: **3/22/1985** Age: **28**
Bats: **R** Throws: **R** Height: **6' 7"** Weight: **250**
Breakout: **15%** Improve: **57%** Collapse: **23%**
Attrition: **10%** MLB: **97%**

Comparables:
Matt Garza,Dean Chance,Brandon Webb

YEAR	TEAM	LVL	AGE	W	L	SV	G	GS	IP	H	HR	BB	SO	BB9	SO9	GB%	BABIP	WHIP	ERA	FIP	FRA	WARP
2010	CLE	MLB	25	6	13	0	34	29	180	197	14	73	140	3.7	7.0	60%	.324	1.50	4.70	3.90	4.24	2.3
2011	CLE	MLB	26	12	10	0	34	33	216	211	11	65	158	2.7	6.6	56%	.302	1.28	3.21	3.32	3.67	3.8
2012	CLE	MLB	27	11	15	0	34	34	206^{1}	212	18	88	159	3.8	6.9	57%	.309	1.45	4.93	4.11	5.29	0.0
2013	*CLE*	*MLB*	*28*	*12*	*10*	*0*	*30*	*30*	*183^{1}*	*177*	*16*	*69*	*150*	*3.4*	*7.4*	*56%*	*.301*	*1.34*	*3.98*	*3.83*	*4.32*	*1.8*

After an apparent breakout season in 2011, Masterson took a step back last year. Despite the disparity of nearly a full run between his ERA and Fielding Independent Pitching (FIP), we can't simply point to bad luck given the kind of pitcher he is: a sinker/slider side-armer with an extreme platoon split. Masterson has struggled at times with runners on base, and that was a big part of the problem last year. In fact, the only years it hasn't been a problem are those when he faced less than his fair share of lefties with runners on, and last year teams stacked lineups with more lefties than ever before (59 percent). The sequencing of hits is usually random, for the most part, but for a pitcher who struggles against a particular type of hitter, trouble is bound to occur when those hitters are clustered together.

Zach McAllister

Born: **12/8/1987** Age: **25**
Bats: **R** Throws: **R** Height: **6' 7"** Weight: **240**
Breakout: **17%** Improve: **45%** Collapse: **20%**
Attrition: **21%** MLB: **93%**

Comparables:
David Huff,Juan Nicasio,Scott Baker

YEAR	TEAM	LVL	AGE	W	L	SV	G	GS	IP	H	HR	BB	SO	BB9	SO9	GB%	BABIP	WHIP	ERA	FIP	FRA	WARP
2011	COH	AAA	23	12	3	0	25	25	154^{2}	155	11	31	128	1.8	7.4	—	.308	1.20	3.32	3.22	3.50	0.0
2011	CLE	MLB	23	0	1	0	4	4	17^{2}	26	1	7	14	3.6	7.1	43%	.403	1.87	6.11	3.40	4.33	0.2
2012	COH	AAA	24	5	2	0	11	11	63^{1}	59	5	19	52	2.7	7.4	40%	.307	1.23	2.98	3.54	3.55	0.2
2012	CLE	MLB	24	6	8	0	22	22	125^{1}	133	19	38	110	2.7	7.9	41%	.304	1.36	4.24	4.20	4.65	0.6
2013	*CLE*	*MLB*	*25*	*6*	*7*	*0*	*19*	*19*	*106^{2}*	*114*	*14*	*33*	*75*	*2.8*	*6.3*	*44%*	*.302*	*1.38*	*4.62*	*4.43*	*5.02*	*0.3*

At this time last year, McAllister was a mere afterthought in Cleveland's fifth-starter discussion. Following a strong 2012 campaign, he now appears to be a legitimate fourth starter. He trailed off toward the end of the year—3.7 K/BB from May to July; 2.9 K/BB from August on—but he showed more than enough to be a capable rotation cog. His fastball was up to 93 mph in 2012. He combines it with a plus changeup that gets 10 miles per hour of separation, a good slider, and a cutter to generate his fair share of strikeouts. Combined with above-average command, McAllister has a solid back-end profile.

Chris Perez

Born: **7/1/1985** Age: **27**
Bats: **R** Throws: **R** Height: **6' 5"** Weight: **230**
Breakout: **31%** Improve: **50%** Collapse: **35%**
Attrition: **18%** MLB: **89%**

Comparables:
Vinnie Pestano,Andrew Brown,Jeff Stevens

YEAR	TEAM	LVL	AGE	W	L	SV	G	GS	IP	H	HR	BB	SO	BB9	SO9	GB%	BABIP	WHIP	ERA	FIP	FRA	WARP
2010	CLE	MLB	24	2	2	23	63	0	63	40	4	28	61	4.0	8.7	37%	.222	1.08	1.71	3.51	3.93	0.7
2011	CLE	MLB	25	4	7	36	64	0	59^{2}	46	5	26	39	3.9	5.9	31%	.234	1.21	3.32	4.30	5.48	-0.2
2012	CLE	MLB	26	0	4	39	61	0	57^{2}	49	6	16	59	2.5	9.2	41%	.270	1.13	3.59	3.29	3.49	0.9
2013	*CLE*	*MLB*	*27*	*3*	*1*	*31*	*53*	*0*	*50^{2}*	*41*	*5*	*21*	*52*	*3.6*	*9.2*	*38%*	*.273*	*1.21*	*3.43*	*3.67*	*3.72*	*0.8*

Watching an extreme fly-ball pitcher with control issues, we always feel like we're waiting for the other shoe to drop. Perez's stuff was never in question save for a small velocity drop in 2011, which seemed a contributing factor to his strikeout plummet, but he regained most of the velocity last year and his strikeouts returned. The thing that has kept him in the ninth inning, though, despite the fly ball/lackluster control profile, was a stubborn BABIP that has thus far refused to regress to the mean. Being more aggressive in the zone with his four-seamer last year led to a drastically reduced walk rate. Should that prove sustainable, as some insiders believe, Perez will remain an effective high-leverage option even if the BABIP suddenly decides to be more social and join those belonging to MLB's other pitchers.

Vinnie Pestano

Born: **2/20/1985** Age: **28**
Bats: **R** Throws: **R** Height: **6' 1"** Weight: **200**
Breakout: **30%** Improve: **60%** Collapse: **28%**
Attrition: **15%** MLB: **90%**

Comparables:
Rafael Soriano,Michael Gonzalez,Jose Veras

YEAR	TEAM	LVL	AGE	W	L	SV	G	GS	IP	H	HR	BB	SO	BB9	SO9	GB%	BABIP	WHIP	ERA	FIP	FRA	WARP
2010	AKR	AA	25	1	1	3	14	0	13^{1}	12	1	2	18	1.4	12.2	47%	.333	1.05	2.71	2.08	2.81	0.4
2010	COH	AAA	25	1	2	14	43	0	46^{1}	35	1	14	59	2.7	11.5	54%	.297	1.06	1.56	2.00	2.98	1.4
2010	CLE	MLB	25	0	0	1	5	0	5	4	0	5	8	9.0	14.4	30%	.400	1.80	3.60	2.85	1.71	0.2
2011	CLE	MLB	26	1	2	2	67	0	62	41	5	24	84	3.5	12.2	40%	.269	1.05	2.32	2.71	2.90	1.3
2012	CLE	MLB	27	3	3	2	70	0	70	53	7	24	76	3.1	9.8	41%	.263	1.10	2.57	3.37	3.41	1.0
2013	*CLE*	*MLB*	*28*	*3*	*1*	*1*	*59*	*0*	*58^{2}*	*48*	*5*	*22*	*66*	*3.4*	*10.2*	*46%*	*.291*	*1.20*	*3.18*	*3.18*	*3.46*	*1.1*

Pestano is the rare sidearmer whose pitch movement charts don't look like they obviously belong to a guy who throws from that arm angle. Once essentially a submariner, Pestano enjoyed success when he raised his arm up a bit (and he raised it slightly again this year). He generates tons of strikeouts using a 93-mph heater (which he can also sink and cut) and a hard curve. He's below-average in terms of groundballs—rare for a side-armer—but with all the whiffs he generates, he's more than capable of late-inning work. The one issue is an extreme platoon split, though the Indians will occasionally pull him when a lefty is up with runners on to prevent damage. He was their top choice to close had Perez missed time to start 2012, but it seems unlikely he'd succeed in such a role long-term.

Bryan Shaw
Born: **11/8/1987** Age: **25**
Bats: **B** Throws: **R** Height: **6' 2"** Weight: **210**
Breakout: **30%** Improve: **62%** Collapse: **12%**
Attrition: **12%** MLB: **94%**
Comparables:
Steve Comer,Alejandro Pena,Jon Huber

YEAR	TEAM	LVL	AGE	W	L	SV	G	GS	IP	H	HR	BB	SO	BB9	SO9	GB%	BABIP	WHIP	ERA	FIP	FRA	WARP
2010	MOB	AA	22	4	9	2	33	13	101^{1}	102	4	43	75	3.8	6.7	56%	.309	1.43	4.26	3.99	5.00	-0.2
2011	MOB	AA	23	3	1	7	15	0	20^{2}	15	1	8	15	3.5	6.5	54%	.222	1.11	0.87	3.65	6.11	-0.1
2011	RNO	AAA	23	1	0	9	16	0	17^{2}	14	4	4	15	2.0	7.6	—	.222	1.02	4.58	6.05	6.57	0.0
2011	ARI	MLB	23	1	0	0	33	0	28^{1}	30	2	8	24	2.5	7.6	60%	.333	1.34	2.54	3.49	3.62	0.3
2012	RNO	AAA	24	0	0	2	8	0	8	6	0	2	10	2.2	11.2	47%	.316	1.00	2.25	1.92	1.54	0.3
2012	ARI	MLB	24	1	6	2	64	0	59^{1}	60	4	24	41	3.6	6.2	57%	.309	1.42	3.49	3.95	4.74	0.0
2013	*CLE*	*MLB*	*25*	*2*	*2*	*0*	*33*	*3*	*47*	*49*	*5*	*19*	*33*	*3.7*	*6.2*	*53%*	*.297*	*1.44*	*4.62*	*4.39*	*5.02*	*0.1*

Shaw studied at the Mariano Rivera school of relief pitching, where he learned to rely heavily on a mid-90s cut fastball that darts late in the flight path. The pitch has also been dubbed a sinker due to the vertical qualities of its late life, but semantics aside, Shaw uses the pitch's subtle movement to generate a bevy of grounders. He will mix in an occasional breaking ball, particularly with two strikes against right-handed batters, but the cutter dominates Shaw's strategy, thanks to his impressive repetition of solid mechanics. Somewhere, Rivera is smiling.

Kevin Slowey
Born: **5/4/1984** Age: **29**
Bats: **R** Throws: **R** Height: **6' 4"** Weight: **205**
Breakout: **20%** Improve: **38%** Collapse: **19%**
Attrition: **5%** MLB: **91%**
Comparables:
Ricky Nolasco,Scott Baker,James Shields

YEAR	TEAM	LVL	AGE	W	L	SV	G	GS	IP	H	HR	BB	SO	BB9	SO9	GB%	BABIP	WHIP	ERA	FIP	FRA	WARP
2010	MIN	MLB	26	13	6	0	30	28	155^{2}	172	21	29	116	1.7	6.7	29%	.308	1.29	4.45	3.95	3.83	2.7
2011	FTM	A+	27	0	1	0	4	4	12	9	1	1	9	0.8	6.8	50%	.182	0.83	3.75	3.22	8.71	-0.1
2011	ROC	AAA	27	1	2	0	7	7	38	44	3	5	29	1.2	6.9	29%	.340	1.29	3.55	3.53	3.40	0.7
2011	MIN	MLB	27	0	8	0	14	8	59^{1}	78	10	5	34	0.8	5.2	33%	.330	1.40	6.67	4.51	4.68	0.4
2012	COH	AAA	28	3	3	0	8	8	49	52	7	13	34	2.4	6.2	39%	.288	1.33	5.14	4.48	6.02	0.0
2013	*CLE*	*MLB*	*29*	*2*	*2*	*0*	*7*	*7*	*36*	*38*	*5*	*7*	*28*	*1.6*	*7.0*	*36%*	*.303*	*1.24*	*4.18*	*4.03*	*4.54*	*0.3*

Once upon a time, Slowey was a sabermetric darling for the Twins. His moderate strikeout rates affirmed his soft-throwing nature, but pinpoint command kept his FIP at better-than-average levels. While he still fits that profile, his FIP may not be a reasonable standard by which to judge him anymore; he has struggled mightily with runners on base over the past few seasons, both in the majors and the minors. The problem is that Slowey works much too quickly from the stretch, loses some command, and essentially becomes a one-pitch pitcher. He is also said to be very stubborn in his thinking and difficult to work with, which might make it difficult to make the kind of changes necessary to turn his career around.

Joe Smith
Born: **3/22/1984** Age: **29**
Bats: **R** Throws: **R** Height: **6' 3"** Weight: **205**
Breakout: **24%** Improve: **46%** Collapse: **30%**
Attrition: **24%** MLB: **92%**
Comparables:
Matt Lindstrom,Mel Rojas,Manny Delcarmen

YEAR	TEAM	LVL	AGE	W	L	SV	G	GS	IP	H	HR	BB	SO	BB9	SO9	GB%	BABIP	WHIP	ERA	FIP	FRA	WARP
2010	COH	AAA	26	2	1	2	20	0	23	17	0	10	19	3.9	7.4	64%	.266	1.17	1.96	2.94	3.84	0.3
2010	CLE	MLB	26	2	2	0	53	0	40	30	4	24	32	5.4	7.2	57%	.239	1.35	3.83	4.62	4.77	0.0
2011	AKR	AA	27	0	0	0	4	0	3^{2}	1	0	2	7	4.9	17.2	75%	.250	0.82	2.45	1.23	2.48	0.1
2011	CLE	MLB	27	3	3	0	71	0	67	52	1	21	45	2.8	6.0	58%	.258	1.09	2.01	2.94	3.67	0.9
2012	CLE	MLB	28	7	4	0	72	0	67	53	4	25	53	3.4	7.1	60%	.253	1.16	2.96	3.45	4.34	0.4
2013	*CLE*	*MLB*	*29*	*3*	*1*	*1*	*63*	*0*	*57*	*50*	*5*	*23*	*47*	*3.6*	*7.4*	*57%*	*.278*	*1.27*	*3.55*	*3.90*	*3.86*	*0.8*

Smith looks like a traditional low-arm-slot pitcher, throwing a sinker-slider combo and thriving on lots of groundballs and enough strikeouts to make him a very effective ROOGY. Over the past two years, however, Smith has found a way to become relatively successful against lefties, ratcheting up his usage totals in the process. While the secret is far from a traditional four-seamer, Smith has utilized this second fastball far more often vs. lefties of late, using it 250 percent more frequently than the two-seamer this year. Given the extreme platoon split associated with two-seamers, should that usage pattern continue, Smith will remain a capable mid- to late-inning option.

Josh Tomlin

Born: **10/19/1984** Age: **28**
Bats: **R** Throws: **R** Height: **6' 2"** Weight: **190**
Breakout: **13%** Improve: **45%** Collapse: **26%**
Attrition: **8%** MLB: **93%**

Comparables:
Dave Bush,Bill Monbouquette,Denny McLain

YEAR	TEAM	LVL	AGE	W	L	SV	G	GS	IP	H	HR	BB	SO	BB9	SO9	GB%	BABIP	WHIP	ERA	FIP	FRA	WARP
2010	COH	AAA	25	8	4	0	20	17	107^1	83	11	33	80	2.8	6.7	40%	.238	1.08	2.68	4.11	4.99	0.9
2010	CLE	MLB	25	6	4	0	12	12	73	72	10	19	43	2.3	5.3	32%	.274	1.25	4.56	4.55	5.29	-0.2
2011	CLE	MLB	26	12	7	0	26	26	165^1	157	24	21	89	1.1	4.8	40%	.253	1.08	4.25	4.31	4.74	1.1
2012	CLE	MLB	27	5	8	0	21	16	103^1	126	18	25	56	2.2	4.9	43%	.309	1.46	6.36	5.04	5.93	-0.8
2013	*CLE*	*MLB*	*28*	*6*	*6*	*0*	*17*	*17*	*101^2*	*104*	*15*	*22*	*67*	*2.0*	*5.9*	*39%*	*.282*	*1.24*	*4.18*	*4.45*	*4.54*	*0.7*

The 2012 season was not kind to Tomlin, who gave up a lot of runs before being moved to the bullpen and ultimately requiring Tommy John surgery—a surgery that will cost him most, if not all, of the coming season. When healthy, Tomlin is much better than indicated by his 2012 ERA—which was compromised by some bad luck with hit sequencing. Tomlin's excellent command is his only appreciable skill, which can leave him open to disaster when he's not spot on with it. When at his controlly best, he's a more-than-adequate back-end starter—a career path he'll try to pick back up when he returns in 2014.

Blake Wood

Born: **8/8/1985** Age: **27**
Bats: **R** Throws: **R** Height: **6' 6"** Weight: **240**
Breakout: **33%** Improve: **49%** Collapse: **25%**
Attrition: **21%** MLB: **67%**

Comparables:
Bob Grim,Juan Gutierrez,A.J. Murray

YEAR	TEAM	LVL	AGE	W	L	SV	G	GS	IP	H	HR	BB	SO	BB9	SO9	GB%	BABIP	WHIP	ERA	FIP	FRA	WARP
2010	OMA	AAA	24	2	1	5	12	0	16^2	12	0	7	12	3.8	6.5	56%	.250	1.14	2.16	3.40	4.08	0.3
2010	KCA	MLB	24	1	3	0	51	0	49^2	54	6	22	31	4.0	5.6	51%	.300	1.53	5.07	4.76	5.98	-0.4
2011	OMA	AAA	25	0	0	0	3	0	5	2	0	0	6	0.0	10.8	—	.222	0.40	0.00	1.38	1.50	0.0
2011	KCA	MLB	25	5	3	1	55	0	69^2	66	5	32	62	4.1	8.0	55%	.303	1.41	3.75	3.72	4.68	0.3
2013	*CLE*	*MLB*	*27*	*1*	*1*	*1*	*30*	*0*	*34^2*	*35*	*4*	*14*	*27*	*3.7*	*7.0*	*48%*	*.300*	*1.43*	*4.52*	*4.35*	*4.91*	*0.1*

Another member of the Royals 2012 Tommy John Quartet, Wood was shelved in spring training with elbow soreness and finally had the surgery in late May. When healthy, his fastball lived in the mid-90s, and once he learned how to apply some movement to the pitch, his strikeouts increased appreciably. Waived in November as the Royals set their 40-man roster, he was claimed by the Indians.

LINEOUTS

HITTERS

PLAYER	TEAM	LVL	AGE	PA	R	2B	3B	HR	RBI	BB	SO	SB-CS	AVG/OBP/SLG	TAv	BABIP	BRR	FRAA	WARP
1B J. Aguilar	CAR	A+	22	427	63	25	2	12	58	45	91	0-1	.277/.365/.454	.272	.333	-2.6	1B(34): 0.8	0.2
	AKR	AA	22	87	12	6	0	3	13	13	24	0-0	.292/.402/.500	.324	.391	-1.3	1B(12): 1.3	0.4
OF M. Carson	ROC	AAA	30	469	64	28	2	14	53	37	106	9-5	.282/.347/.457	.264	.345	5.1	RF(76): 0.5, CF(10): -1.6	1.2
	MIN	MLB	30	69	3	1	0	0	4	2	21	0-0	.227/.246/.242	.226	.326	-0.4	LF(15): -0.1, RF(9): -0.6	-0.2
C C. Chen	AKR	AA	23	459	62	30	1	5	43	56	101	6-3	.308/.394/.426	.296	.400	-3.6	1B(46): 2.2, C(7): 0.1	1.4
OF T. Fedroff	AKR	AA	25	239	27	9	5	3	22	30	33	5-6	.305/.396/.443	.290	.351	-4.3	CF(38): -3.4	0.0
	COH	AAA	25	304	52	14	5	9	32	31	45	9-0	.325/.393/.517	.290	.360	1.1	LF(13): 0.5, CF(10): -0.7	0.6
3B J. Martinez	CLR	Rk	19	211	31	14	3	7	39	16	44	4-0	.347/.393/.563	.324	.413	-0.3	—	0.0
OF D. McClure	CLE	Rk	18	107	15	4	0	1	12	11	19	2-1	.211/.305/.289	.219	.250	-0.2	LF(2): -0.1	0.0
1B M. McDade	NHP	AA	23	429	44	16	0	15	49	43	85	1-0	.275/.354/.437	.254	.317	-4.6	1B(27): 2.6	-0.6
	LVG	AAA	23	79	9	3	1	2	18	7	11	0-0	.338/.392/.493	.291	.373	-0.7	1B(8): -0.2	0.0
C A. Monsalve	LKC	A	20	313	36	17	1	7	36	23	35	1-2	.265/.324/.406	.294	.279	-1.4	C(9): 0.1	0.2
	CAR	A+	20	126	10	4	0	1	6	7	17	1-0	.233/.280/.293	.235	.263	-0.9	C(15): 0.1	-0.6
2B J. Ramirez	LKC	A	19	313	54	13	4	3	27	24	26	15-6	.354/.403/.462	.335	.378	-2.3	2B(10): 1.7, SS(1): 0.1	0.5
OF A. Santander	CLE	Rk	17	176	27	15	1	4	32	13	37	6-3	.305/.381/.494	.018	.374	-0.5	LF(1): 0.1, RF(1): -0.1	-0.1
OF L. Washington	LKC	A	20	32	8	1	0	0	1	6	8	0-3	.440/.562/.480	.271	.647	-0.4	—	0.0
	CAR	A+	20	15	2	0	0	0	1	1	3	0-0	.071/.133/.071	-.063	.091	-0.4	—	-0.3

Jesus Aguilar made it through the Rule 5 draft, giving the Indians more time to see if this 23-year-old's power is going to develop enough to fulfill the needs of first base. Short on bodies in late August, the Twins added 30-year-old **Matt Carson** to the 40 man and gave him 69 plate appearances. He signed with Cleveland and will try to escape the Columbus outfield at some point. **Chun-Hsiu Chen** could've shown more improvement in his repeat of Double-A to get on the fast track toward being Santana's backup, but there are some tools here and Marson hasn't exactly set an unreachable bar. The Indians might be more impressed with **Tim Fedroff**'s 2012 numbers if he hadn't repeated both Double-A and Triple-A, the former for a third time, though he did massively improve in his second go-round in Columbus. **Jorge Martinez** shifted from shortstop to third base last year and finally mastered the Rookie League in his third attempt. A third try at a league might be more damning if he weren't just 20 years old. When you see multi-sport athletes like **D'vone McClure** at their best, it's impossible not to salivate at what could be, but actually molding these mounds of clay into ballplayers is almost never easy, and they quickly learn that the hardest thing in sports is hitting a bending baseball with a wooden stick. **Mike McDade** possesses legitimate power against right-handed pitchers, but lack of athleticism—and, thus, defensive versatility—could make it difficult for him to find a home on a major-league bench. Ho-hum, another raw prospect for the Indians: **Alex Monsalve** has the tools and athleticism to be a viable backstop, but we're still waiting to see it on the field with some consistency. Although his subpar arm has talent evaluators putting him at second base for the future, **Jose Ramirez** is yet another Latin infielder under 21 who could develop into a legitimate starter thanks to an excellent full-season debut. **Anthony Santander** had an impressive debut by just about any standard, but considering that he was a 17-year-old posting an 874 OPS in his 43-game stint adds to the intrigue. Hip surgery cost **LeVon Washington** most of 2012, and he's been much more promise than payoff to date; yet at 21 and with elite speed, he still has some leeway on the prospect-o-meter.

PITCHERS

PLAYER	TEAM	LVL	AGE	W	L	SV	IP	H	HR	BB	SO	BB9	SO9	GB%	BABIP	WHIP	ERA	FIP	FRA	WARP
A. Adams	—	—	—	—	—	—	—	—	—	—	—	—	—	—	—	—	—	—	—	—
S. Armstrong	CAR	A+	21	1	3	1	43^{2}	31	0	23	52	4.7	10.7	42%	.307	1.24	2.06	3.00	3.57	0.5
	AKR	AA	21	1	0	3	20^{1}	12	0	12	22	5.3	9.7	39%	.261	1.18	0.89	2.96	1.86	0.5
D. Baker	CLE	Rk	20	0	1	0	24	24	1	15	30	5.6	11.2	58%	.364	1.62	4.12	4.29	4.34	0.1
M. Brown	CLE	Rk	18	2	0	0	27^{2}	20	3	10	26	3.3	8.5	15%	.273	1.08	3.58	4.99	5.90	0.0
T. House	CAR	A+	22	2	0	0	25	17	1	6	26	2.2	9.4	56%	.246	0.92	1.44	2.91	1.15	0.0
	AKR	AA	22	8	5	0	124^{1}	114	7	44	90	3.2	6.5	53%	.285	1.27	3.98	3.72	4.78	0.8
D. Howard	CLE	Rk	19	1	7	0	41	65	3	18	35	4.0	7.7	65%	.393	2.02	7.90	5.16	6.80	0.2
K. Lovegrove	CLE	Rk	17	0	2	0	21	28	1	9	18	3.9	7.7	57%	.143	1.76	6.00	4.71	4.29	0.1
J. Martinez	RNO	AAA	29	10	11	0	155^{1}	206	15	49	99	2.8	5.7	53%	.359	1.64	5.39	4.73	5.86	0.9
	ARI	MLB	29	0	0	0	1	2	0	0	1	0.0	9.0	25%	.500	2.00	9.00	1.14	1.99	0.0
F. Martinez Mesa	SBR	A+	22	0	5	0	22^{2}	26	2	32	23	12.7	9.1	54%	.353	2.56	10.72	7.70	11.25	0.0
F. Nieve	ABQ	AAA	29	7	9	0	119^{1}	162	19	38	107	2.9	8.1	45%	.365	1.68	5.96	5.07	7.26	0.0
D. Salazar	CAR	A+	22	1	2	0	53^{2}	46	3	19	53	3.2	8.9	43%	.297	1.21	2.68	3.20	3.37	0.0
	AKR	AA	22	4	0	0	34	25	1	8	23	2.1	6.1	47%	.240	0.97	1.85	2.94	3.18	0.5
C. Seddon	COH	AAA	28	11	5	0	123	112	16	27	108	2.0	7.9	35%	.283	1.13	3.44	3.80	4.90	0.7
	CLE	MLB	28	1	1	0	34^{1}	35	2	13	18	3.4	4.7	41%	.289	1.40	3.67	3.89	4.15	0.3
J. Sisco	MHV	A-	20	1	6	0	77	81	6	30	45	3.5	5.3	48%	.300	1.44	5.03	4.58	7.60	-0.3
F. Sterling	CLE	Rk	19	3	0	2	21^{2}	14	0	7	31	2.9	12.9	39%	.323	0.97	1.66	2.62	1.44	0.8
	LKC	A	19	4	8	1	93	104	15	40	71	3.9	6.9	43%	.303	1.55	6.58	5.57	9.69	0.0
R. Tejeda	COH	AAA	30	0	0	0	1	3	1	0	1	0	9	0	.500	3	18	14.16	10.52	-0.1

Shoulder surgery kept **Austin Adams** off the mound in 2012, so he'll have to rebound in 2013 in order to restore any prospect luster. **Shawn Armstrong** throws a high-90s fastball with a plus slider, and could get a shot in Cleveland this year due to the stuff, but he'll struggle unless he can refine his control. **Dylan Baker** flashes three pitches that could be above-average, but like many young pitchers, he needs to work on his changeup and his command, the two things that will determine his role as either back-end starter or reliever. 2012 second-rounder **Mitch Brown** has solid stuff with a low-90s fastball, power curve, and cutter. He has a long road ahead, but he could be a mid-rotation starter if he can ease concerns with command and pitchability. **T.J. House** impressed enough late in the year and in the AFL to secure a spot on the 40-man, improving his changeup and command of his solid if unspectacular four-pitch mix. The Tribe's 2011 second-round pick, **Dillon Howard**, disappointed in his debut last year, but his fastball/change-up combo and big frame give him the upside to be a mid-rotation starter. **Kieran Lovegrove** is a projectable pitcher with a tall frame and room to fill out, working in the mid-90s with a quality slider and developing changeup. **Joe Martinez** has posted impressive walk rates all the way up the minor-league ladder, but failure to miss bats doomed him in the killing fields of the PCL, an ominous indicator of his odds of survival in Cleveland. As high-risk as they come, **Fabio Martinez Mesa** has been an absolute mess of injuries, mechanical issues, and awful command since 2010, when he showed a lot of potential. **Fernando Nieve** has spent 12 pro seasons trying to carve out a career, but he's only managed a few big-league cups of coffee, and the hill only gets steeper to climb from here. **Danny Salazar** impressed in his first full season post Tommy John surgery, and his fastball and slider both project plus. **Chris Seddon** was described in these pages as organizational filler, but now he is off to fill an organization in the Korean Baseball Organization. **Jake Sisco** isn't among the Tribe's top pitching prospects and struggled mightily last year, but he has some projection with a fastball/slider combo that could wind up plus/plus. **Felix Sterling** has a power arm, but he had a down 2012, is high risk, and is quite a ways from reaching his potential, which is likely as a reliever. One-time closer candidate **Robinson Tejeda** has been effective as recently as 2010, but he spent most of 2012 injured and as a free agent. He'll need to reprove himself.

MANAGER: TERRY FRANCONA

YEAR	TEAM	W-L	Pythag +/–	Avg PC	100+ P	120+ P	QS	BQS	REL	REL w Zero R	IBB	PH	PH Avg	PH HR	SB2	CS2	SB3	CS3	SAC Att	SAC %	POS SAC	Squeeze	Swing	In Play
2010	BOS	89-73	0.547	205.6	159	157	105	5	443	348	60	234	.26	4	11	2	1	1	76	86.8%	56	0	340	108
2011	BOS	90-72	0.584	96.8	78	4	71	5	443	359	11	83	.175	2	9	1	0	1	33	72.7%	24	0	366	122

After a year off in the broadcast booth to recharge his batteries (Boston does nothing if not kill your battery power), Francona signed on to restart his managerial career with the Indians. Cleveland's reason for interest in Francona is obvious; two World Series wins during arguably the most successful run in Boston Red Sox history makes for an impressive résumé. Francona's interest in Cleveland is harder to figure, but it's where his biggest strengths, fierce loyalty to his players and an ability to bring people together towards a common goal, show themselves.

Even in his first managerial stop in Philadelphia, as media and fan opinion turned increasingly hostile toward the team and him in general (he's told of having his tires routinely slashed), he held the team together. That former-Phillie Curt Schilling thought highly enough of Francona to reroute himself from his preferred team, the Yankees, to its arch rival speaks volumes (as opposed to Schilling himself, who lets his actions speak for him). Once in Boston, Francona showed his loyalty both to his players and to the front office. One example: Despite rookie Dustin Pedroia's April OPS of 500 and in the face of intense media and fan scrutiny, he continued playing the kid. Francona's patience was rewarded as Pedroia won Rookie of the Year that season and MVP the next. It's this steady-handedness and ability to see the long view that will be especially relevant as Francona helps old friends Mark Shapiro and Chris Antonetti rebuild Cleveland's roster.

Colorado Rockies

2012: ROCK SLIDE

Injuries and ill-advised free-agent signings sabotaged the Rockies' season. A few young, homegrown players showed promise, but not enough for the team to be competitive after April, especially given the complete collapse of the starting rotation. Front-office changes contributed to manager Jim Tracy's decision to resign at season's end.

ROCKIES PROSPECTUS

2012 W-L: 64-98, 5th in NL West

Pythag	.423	25th	DER	.675	30th
RS/G	4.68	6th	B-Age	28.1	15th
RA/G	5.49	30th	P-Age	28.1	18th
TAv	.256	20th	Salary	$80.2	22nd
BRR	4.5	8th	M$/MW	$4.33	25th
TAv-P	.279	30th	DL Days	1185	9th
FIP	4.63	30th	DL WARP	5.8	4th

Three-Year Park Factors	
Overall	**113**
HR/RH	**115**
HR/LH	**122**
AVG/RH	**121**
AVG/LH	**124**

Coors Field (1995)
Att. % of Capacity: 64.4% (18th)
Dim. 347, 390, 415, 375, 350

With 1,009 runs, Coors fell just 25 short of doubling up Safeco, and yielded a .345 BABIP last season.

On May 2, the Rockies were 12-12. After an off day, they lost at home against Atlanta in extra innings and saw their record permanently slip below .500. They were beaten badly at Coors Field (tying for worst home record in the National League) and worse away from it. Although Colorado was third among National League teams in runs scored, much of that was a Rocky Mountain mirage—when adjusted for altitude, their mundane .256 TAv ranked only 10th, and their 5.22 team ERA was the worst in baseball since 2004.

Shortstop Troy Tulowitzki and catcher Ramon Hernandez spent most of the season on the disabled list. Todd Helton continued to age more like vinegar than wine. Free-agent signing Michael Cuddyer hit like the platoon outfielder he really is. Only one pitcher—Reds castoff Jeff Francis—worked 100 innings (and he worked only 113 after joining the club in June).

There were bright spots. Hernandez's injury opened the door for Wilin Rosario, who performed well at the plate if not behind it. Fellow homegrown players Chris Nelson and Dexter Fowler stepped up their games, while newcomer Tyler Colvin rediscovered his power stroke—at least in games played above 5,000 feet.

The team experimented with a four-man rotation and a strict 75-pitch count, but, according to the *Denver Post,* Tracy was never comfortable with the idea. At season's end, the man who received an "indefinite"extension in February walked away from his post, saying, "I really don't feel that I am the right man for the job any longer"after front-office changes reportedly caused him to feel like he was always looking over his shoulder.

Others wondered if the right man had left Denver. Was this disaster of a season all Tracy's fault, or did the problems start at higher levels of management? Either way, the results were miserable and so were the fans.

2013: SEE WHAT STICKS

New skipper Walt Weiss must learn to work with players and front-office personnel alike. Key players must return to health and/or sustain newly established levels of performance. Fans must be patient as it all unfolds in sometimes painful fashion.

With Tracy and hitting coach Carney Lansford replaced by Weiss and Colorado folk hero Dante Bichette, questions abound. Will the new on-field staff mesh with the front office? Can they coax better performances and health out of their players?

Tulowitzki is an impact player if healthy. Rosario might be if he improves his defense. Nelson and Fowler need to build on their breakout performances. Both are young enough to do so, but neither comes without risk. If Nelson can't repeat, Nolan Arenado could be this year's Rosario, although there are questions about Arenado's readiness and upside.

Carlos Gonzalez is an exciting ballplayer, but not the MVP threat he appeared to be in 2010. Helton is all but finished and Cuddyer's contract is unmovable. Given the team's uneven batting talent, Bichette will have his work cut out for him.

The pitching side is even less settled. Can Jhoulys Chacin return to the levels he flashed in the first half of 2011? Can Jorge de la Rosa stay on the field and be the front-line starter the Rockies thought they were getting when they extended his contract? Which, if any, of the young pitchers will establish themselves as legitimate big-leaguers who can help now and into the future?

For a team that should be rebuilding, there are too many old and injury-prone guys on the roster. Talent is on the way, but the brightest probably won't make a significant difference this year. The Rockies will spend the summer evaluating—deciding which players can be part of the next contending team, which are chips to acquire more of the same, and which must be jettisoned for lack of utility in either capacity.

This promises to be a long season in Denver. Fans should hope for hot starts from a few movable veterans, a return to health for Tulowitzki and Chacin, and the continued development of Rosario et al. And remember that good things come to those who wait. Sometimes.

STATE OF THE ORGANIZATION: IT'S THE PITCHING, STUPID

Colorado has some solid building blocks, but like a $99 Lego set, this is going to take some time to assemble. A few high-end arms would help. So would a field staff and a front office that can prove they're singing from the same hymnal.

Assuming Rosario stays behind the plate and Tulowitzki stays healthy, the Rockies are in good shape up the middle. Trevor Story gives them the luxury of a second young legitimate shortstop on the way. Lesser second-base options provide additional depth. Fowler is an asset in center field, and 2012 first-rounder David Dahl is being groomed as a potential successor. He could be special.

In left field, Gonzalez is solid and his game suits Coors Field well. Right field looks less promising, with Cuddyer, Colvin, and a slew of future fourth outfielders in the minors. Still, if hitters like Garrett Atkins and Brad Hawpe could make it work at Coors Field, maybe Corey Dickerson or Kyle Parker can do the same for a few years. Nelson had a nice season at the hot corner and Arenado is talented, though questions remain about both.

That all may add up to a productive lineup, but the Rockies won't compete until they develop something more than a chuck-and-duck pitching staff. Unfortunately, there are no impact arms in the system. The ballpark obviously creates unique problems, but with the possible exceptions of Chacin and Drew Pomeranz, there are no front-line starters here or on the horizon. Notice we say possible exceptions: Chacin and Pomeranz aren't exactly Seaver and Koosman, but they're the best the team has. Strength up the middle is great, but without good arms to complement it, the Rockies will continue to look up at their NL West competitors.

Throughout the Rockies' existence, the club has struggled to develop pitchers. Limitations inherent in playing at altitude notwithstanding, the organization must find a way to solve this. The four-man rotation with the 75-pitch limit may not have worked, but at least it suggested a willingness to try unconventional methods. If that failed experiment leads to something that helps future pitching staffs, then it will have been worth the trouble. Otherwise, folks will have a lot of explaining to do.

HITTERS

Nolan Arenado 3B

Born: **4/16/1991** Age: **22**
Bats: **R** Throws: **R** Height: **6' 2"**
Weight: **205** Breakout: **5%**
Improve: **54%** Collapse: **2%**
Attrition: **10%** MLB: **99%**

Comparables:
Matt Dominguez, Glenn Hoffman, Edgardo Alfonzo

YEAR	TEAM	LVL	AGE	PA	R	2B	3B	HR	RBI	BB	SO	SB	CS	AVG_OBP_SLG	TAv	BABIP	BRR	FRAA	WARP
2010	ASH	A	19	400	45	41	1	12	65	19	52	1	3	.308/.344/.520	.282	.333	-3.3	3B(81): -6.6	1.4
2011	MOD	A+	20	583	82	32	3	20	122	47	53	2	1	.298/.349/.487	.316	.293	1.1	3B(75): -4.1	2.6
2012	TUL	AA	21	573	55	36	1	12	56	39	58	0	2	.285/.337/.428	.256	.296	-5.2	3B(105): 23.0	3.6
2013	*COL*	*MLB*	*22*	*250*	*25*	*15*	*1*	*7*	*31*	*12*	*35*	*0*	*0*	*.270/.308/.434*	*.242*	*.288*	*-0.4*	*3B 5*	*0.6*

Arenado, the Rockies top prospect entering 2012 and one of the best third-base prospects in baseball, fell short of lofty expectations at Double-A. He made contact and drove some gappers but showed little home-run power. A strong start and finish surrounded a stretch from May to July when his offensive game disappeared. Arenado was not recalled in September due to concerns about his maturity and the fact that he wasn't already on the 40-man roster. He isn't always quick to make adjustments, which could be a problem at the big-league level, where he will spend time this year. There still is a lot to like, although earlier hype levels may have been higher than warranted.

Charlie Blackmon OF

Born: **7/1/1986** Age: **26**
Bats: **L** Throws: **L** Height: **6' 4"**
Weight: **200** Breakout: **3%**
Improve: **58%** Collapse: **8%**
Attrition: **14%** MLB: **95%**

Comparables:
Bryan Petersen, Josh Anderson, Shane Victorino

YEAR	TEAM	LVL	AGE	PA	R	2B	3B	HR	RBI	BB	SO	SB	CS	AVG_OBP_SLG	TAv	BABIP	BRR	FRAA	WARP
2010	TUL	AA	24	381	53	22	4	11	55	32	43	19	7	.297/.362/.484	.304	.311	1.8	CF(71): -4.4, LF(4): 0.1	2.4
2011	CSP	AAA	25	272	49	19	4	10	49	19	34	12	5	.337/.393/.572	.306	.356	0.8	RF(30): 0.9, LF(2): -0.0	1.1
2011	COL	MLB	25	102	9	1	0	1	8	3	8	5	1	.255/.277/.296	.189	.270	-0.5	LF(25): -1.2, CF(2): -0.0	-0.8
2012	TRI	A-	25	69	8	5	0	1	3	7	10	3	0	.237/.348/.373	.336	.271	-1	CF(9): -0.6, LF(1): 0.0	0.5
2012	CSP	AAA	25	264	55	18	4	5	34	29	42	10	0	.303/.385/.482	.275	.350	1.9	CF(49): -1.9, LF(3): -0.1	0.9
2012	COL	MLB	25	121	15	8	0	2	9	4	17	1	2	.283/.325/.407	.241	.319	1	RF(17): -0.0, LF(15): 1.6	0.3
2013	*COL*	*MLB*	*26*	*250*	*32*	*13*	*2*	*5*	*25*	*17*	*38*	*8*	*2*	*.276/.330/.421*	*.252*	*.305*	*0.6*	*CF -2, LF -0*	*0.3*

Blackmon first surfaced with the Rockies in 2011 to replace a then-slumping Dexter Fowler and promptly fractured his right foot while rounding second base. He added 15 pounds before last season while rehabbing and tweaked his stance—adopting more of a crouch, lowering the back elbow, and incorporating his lower half—in an effort to add power. It didn't help. Neither did the turf toe in his left big toe coming out of spring training. Blackmon makes contact and runs well. The 2008 second-round pick out of Georgia Tech has been a center fielder in the minors but can play the corners as well and profiles more as a fourth outfielder.

Andrew Brown OF
Born: **9/10/1984** Age: **28**
Bats: **R** Throws: **R** Height: **6' 1"**
Weight: **185** Breakout: **0%**
Improve: **62%** Collapse: **3%**
Attrition: **9%** MLB: **92%**
Comparables:
George Foster,Greg Vaughn,Richie Zisk

YEAR	TEAM	LVL	AGE	PA	R	2B	3B	HR	RBI	BB	SO	SB	CS	AVG_OBP_SLG	TAv	BABIP	BRR	FRAA	WARP
2010	SFD	AA	25	407	65	17	1	22	63	41	98	1	2	.291/.371/.526	.298	.344	-1.5	1B(36): -0.1, RF(32): -0.1	2.3
2011	MEM	AAA	26	428	67	12	3	20	73	56	105	4	4	.284/.382/.501	.304	.340	0	--	0.0
2011	SLN	MLB	26	22	1	1	0	0	3	0	8	0	0	.182/.182/.227	.139	.286	0.4	RF(7): -0.0	-0.2
2012	CSP	AAA	27	438	81	33	4	24	98	37	100	3	1	.308/.364/.597	.306	.350	-2.1	LF(49): 0.9, RF(38): 0.3	2.1
2012	COL	MLB	27	126	14	7	0	5	11	12	34	2	2	.232/.302/.429	.246	.280	-1.2	RF(23): 1.0, LF(12): 0.2	0.3
2013	*COL*	*MLB*	*28*	*250*	*30*	*12*	*1*	*11*	*36*	*20*	*67*	*1*	*0*	*.259/.322/.472*	*.266*	*.316*	*-0.3*	*RF -0, LF -1*	*0.5*

Brown is a minor-league veteran whom the Rockies claimed off waivers from St. Louis in October 2011. He isn't young but he hits the occasional homer and draws enough walks to keep pitchers honest. Used primarily as a corner outfielder last year, Brown also has experience at both infield corners. His OPS at Security Service Field in Colorado Springs was 370 points higher than away from it. Brown is younger and cheaper than Michael Cuddyer, and probably not much worse.

Tyler Colvin OF
Born: **9/5/1985** Age: **27**
Bats: **L** Throws: **L** Height: **6' 4"**
Weight: **210** Breakout: **3%**
Improve: **45%** Collapse: **8%**
Attrition: **10%** MLB: **94%**
Comparables:
Rhyne Hughes,Shawn Green,Willie Kirkland

YEAR	TEAM	LVL	AGE	PA	R	2B	3B	HR	RBI	BB	SO	SB	CS	AVG_OBP_SLG	TAv	BABIP	BRR	FRAA	WARP
2010	CHN	MLB	24	394	60	18	5	20	56	30	100	6	1	.254/.316/.500	.275	.296	1.2	RF(59): 1.3, LF(52): -0.4	1.5
2011	IOW	AAA	25	212	32	12	6	7	32	5	55	1	1	.256/.270/.478	.208	.312	-0.2	LF(5): -0.4, RF(5): -0.1	-0.3
2011	CHN	MLB	25	222	17	8	3	6	20	14	58	0	0	.150/.204/.306	.184	.175	1.2	RF(44): 1.7, LF(9): -0.0	-1.0
2012	COL	MLB	26	452	62	27	10	18	72	21	117	7	3	.290/.327/.531	.273	.364	1.3	RF(59): 0.2, CF(38): 3.0	1.1
2013	*COL*	*MLB*	*27*	*382*	*45*	*18*	*6*	*16*	*53*	*22*	*95*	*4*	*2*	*.256/.302/.471*	*.249*	*.303*	*0.5*	*RF 0, CF -0*	*0.5*

The good news is that Colvin, acquired from the Cubs in December 2011 for fellow disappointment Ian Stewart, hit more line drives and returned to his rookie level of offensive production. The bad news is that his plate discipline has gone from bad to worse. Once pitchers figure out that they don't have to throw Colvin strikes, he'll scuffle again. In fact, it may have started to happen. Last season, his ISO dropped from .321 in the first half to .176 in the second. Small samples or not, those are troubling trends. Primarily a right fielder, Colvin also saw action in center field and at first base last year.

Michael Cuddyer RF
Born: **3/27/1979** Age: **34**
Bats: **R** Throws: **R** Height: **6' 3"**
Weight: **220** Breakout: **0%**
Improve: **40%** Collapse: **8%**
Attrition: **14%** MLB: **89%**
Comparables:
Albert Belle,Andy Pafko,Moises Alou

YEAR	TEAM	LVL	AGE	PA	R	2B	3B	HR	RBI	BB	SO	SB	CS	AVG_OBP_SLG	TAv	BABIP	BRR	FRAA	WARP
2010	MIN	MLB	31	675	93	37	5	14	81	58	93	7	3	.271/.336/.417	.265	.298	1.9	1B(84): -7.1, RF(66): -1.2	0.6
2011	MIN	MLB	32	584	70	29	2	20	70	48	95	11	1	.284/.346/.459	.294	.312	0.1	RF(77): -6.1, 1B(46): 1.6	2.1
2012	COL	MLB	33	394	53	30	2	16	58	32	78	8	3	.260/.317/.489	.280	.287	1.2	RF(74): -2.9, 1B(25): -0.8	1.1
2013	*COL*	*MLB*	*34*	*409*	*50*	*22*	*3*	*14*	*54*	*34*	*69*	*6*	*2*	*.276/.341/.465*	*.273*	*.305*	*0.3*	*RF -1, 1B -1*	*1.2*

The Rockies' signing of Cuddyer to a three-year, $31.5 million deal raised eyebrows when it happened in December 2011, four months shy of his 33rd birthday. After a 98-loss season, it looks even worse. Cuddyer's offensive skill set is best suited to the bottom of the order, and he struggles to hit right-handed pitching. A right oblique strain that he termed "beyond frustrating" limited him to nine plate appearances from August 1 to season's end. If healthy, his best role is that of a platoon corner outfielder on a contending team. Cuddyer, cited by younger players as a positive influence and someone who is "always willing to help," is a more expensive version of Scott Hairston.

Charlie Culberson 2B
Born: **4/10/1989** Age: **24**
Bats: **R** Throws: **R** Height: **6' 2"**
Weight: **200** Breakout: **5%**
Improve: **50%** Collapse: **4%**
Attrition: **16%** MLB: **87%**
Comparables:
Tommy Hinzo,Dick Green,Jose Castillo

YEAR	TEAM	LVL	AGE	PA	R	2B	3B	HR	RBI	BB	SO	SB	CS	AVG_OBP_SLG	TAv	BABIP	BRR	FRAA	WARP
2010	SJO	A+	21	551	80	28	4	16	71	33	99	25	7	.290/.343/.457	.282	.334	1.1	2B(127): -1.9	2.8
2011	RIC	AA	22	587	69	34	2	10	56	22	129	14	4	.259/.293/.382	.244	.320	1.1	2B(104): -4.2	-0.2
2012	CSP	AAA	23	128	17	11	1	2	12	1	18	6	2	.336/.344/.488	.263	.377	1.1	2B(28): 2.5	0.6
2012	FRE	AAA	23	380	53	14	6	10	53	20	76	8	2	.236/.283/.396	.241	.272	1.7	2B(79): -0.8	-0.2
2012	SFN	MLB	23	23	0	0	0	0	1	0	7	0	0	.136/.136/.136	.097	.200	0.4	2B(6): -0.4	-0.3
2013	*COL*	*MLB*	*24*	*250*	*24*	*12*	*2*	*5*	*26*	*8*	*56*	*5*	*1*	*.251/.279/.380*	*.220*	*.304*	*0.4*	*2B -2*	*-0.3*

Culberson, a supplemental first-round pick of the Giants in 2007, came to Colorado last July in the Marco Scutaro trade. He played second base exclusively in 2010-12 but also has experience at shortstop and third base, neither of which he played well. A free swinger (.311 OBP in 2,704 career minor-league plate appearances) with doubles power (.122 ISO), his upside is that of utility infielder. Given his offensive and defensive limitations, even that might be a stretch.

David Dahl CF

Born: **4/1/1994** Age: **19**
Bats: **L** Throws: **R** Height: **6' 3"**
Weight: **185** Breakout: **0%**
Improve: **66%** Collapse: **34%**
Attrition: **34%** MLB: **100%**

Comparables:
Robin Yount,Wayne Causey,Ed Kranepool

YEAR	TEAM	LVL	AGE	PA	R	2B	3B	HR	RBI	BB	SO	SB	CS	AVG_OBP_SLG	TAv	BABIP	BRR	FRAA	WARP
2012	GJR	Rk	18	306	62	22	10	9	57	21	42	12	7	.379/.423/.625	.422	.420	-0.5	CF(7): -1.0	0.5
2013	*COL*	*MLB*	*19*	*250*	*38*	*9*	*1*	*7*	*21*	*12*	*65*	*18*	*10*	*.222/.263/.364*	*.207*	*.272*	*0.7*	*CF -1*	*-0.6*

Reading Rookie League numbers is like reading tea leaves, only less accurate. That being said, Dahl more than held his own—he led the Pioneer League in total bases—against older competition after being taken with the 10th pick overall in the 2012 draft out of an Alabama high school. Dahl, who has been compared to Andy Van Slyke, among others, has great hands that allow him to make hard contact to the gaps. He is fast, although he must learn to use that speed on the bases and in center field. We'll know more after he plays full-season ball, but the early returns point to his being a future stud.

Corey Dickerson LF

Born: **5/22/1989** Age: **24**
Bats: **L** Throws: **R** Height: **6' 3"**
Weight: **210** Breakout: **4%**
Improve: **55%** Collapse: **6%**
Attrition: **11%** MLB: **99%**

Comparables:
Billy Williams,Ivan Calderon,Tommy Brown

YEAR	TEAM	LVL	AGE	PA	R	2B	3B	HR	RBI	BB	SO	SB	CS	AVG_OBP_SLG	TAv	BABIP	BRR	FRAA	WARP
2010	CAS	Rk	21	308	54	22	9	13	61	28	51	12	6	.348/.414/.634	.356	.392	1.5	LF(55): -3.9, CF(2): 0.3	3.3
2011	ASH	A	22	435	78	27	5	32	87	39	99	9	6	.282/.356/.629	.297	.296	1	LF(37): -2.4, RF(11): 0.5	1.3
2012	MOD	A+	23	270	43	24	4	9	43	25	42	9	5	.338/.396/.583	.362	.373	1.4	RF(26): -0.0, LF(11): 1.3	2.8
2012	TUL	AA	23	290	40	16	3	13	38	18	51	7	3	.274/.322/.504	.277	.293	1.7	LF(57): -6.7	0.0
2013	*COL*	*MLB*	*24*	*250*	*31*	*12*	*3*	*11*	*36*	*15*	*55*	*4*	*2*	*.260/.306/.481*	*.254*	*.291*	*0.1*	*LF -4, RF -0*	*0.0*

The Rockies popped Dickerson in the eighth round of the 2010 draft, and all he has done is hit. This is good, because it's all he can do. He has the Bubba Trammell skill set. After posting crazy numbers in his first full season—thanks in large part to his home park, where he hit 26 of 32 homers—Dickerson followed that with another solid showing. The power is real, and he killed lefties last year. He looks like a future platoon left fielder, with maybe a few seasons as a regular thrown in as well, à la Trammell or Kevin Mench.

Dexter Fowler CF

Born: **3/22/1986** Age: **27**
Bats: **B** Throws: **R** Height: **6' 5"**
Weight: **190** Breakout: **11%**
Improve: **62%** Collapse: **3%**
Attrition: **16%** MLB: **96%**

Comparables:
Lloyd Moseby,Tom Tresh,Cole Gillespie

YEAR	TEAM	LVL	AGE	PA	R	2B	3B	HR	RBI	BB	SO	SB	CS	AVG_OBP_SLG	TAv	BABIP	BRR	FRAA	WARP
2010	CSP	AAA	24	124	23	10	4	2	13	17	27	1	0	.340/.435/.566	.296	.442	0.7	CF(24): 1.3	1.0
2010	COL	MLB	24	505	73	20	14	6	36	57	104	13	7	.260/.347/.410	.255	.328	3.1	CF(120): -0.9	1.2
2011	CSP	AAA	25	114	17	6	1	2	9	15	24	2	1	.237/.345/.381	.214	.296	-0.1	CF(22): -0.1	-0.5
2011	COL	MLB	25	563	84	35	15	5	45	68	130	12	9	.266/.363/.432	.275	.354	7.1	CF(122): 9.9	4.0
2012	COL	MLB	26	530	72	18	11	13	53	68	128	12	5	.300/.389/.474	.284	.390	2.2	CF(131): -10.7	1.3
2013	*COL*	*MLB*	*27*	*518*	*67*	*25*	*10*	*8*	*49*	*61*	*116*	*13*	*6*	*.274/.364/.429*	*.264*	*.344*	*0.6*	*CF -7*	*1.1*

Fowler finally survived an entire season without being shipped back to Triple-A for a few weeks to learn something. He is equally adept from either side of the plate and draws enough walks to be useful at the top of a lineup, although his raw speed hasn't translated into consistent base-stealing success. Fowler takes pride in his ability to reach base and last year added power to his game, at least in the first half, when he hit 11 of his 13 home runs before being slowed by back, ankle, and wrist issues. Whether or not the power returns, he remains a potent table-setter who should continue to thrive in that role for some time.

Jason Giambi 1B

Born: **1/8/1971** Age: **42**
Bats: **L** Throws: **R** Height: **6' 4"**
Weight: **240** Breakout: **0%**
Improve: **8%** Collapse: **17%**
Attrition: **22%** MLB: **67%**

Comparables:
Hank Aaron,Edgar Martinez,Darrell Evans

YEAR	TEAM	LVL	AGE	PA	R	2B	3B	HR	RBI	BB	SO	SB	CS	AVG_OBP_SLG	TAv	BABIP	BRR	FRAA	WARP
2010	COL	MLB	39	222	17	9	0	6	35	35	47	2	0	.244/.378/.398	.268	.289	-0.3	1B(37): -0.8	0.3
2011	COL	MLB	40	152	20	6	0	13	32	17	45	0	0	.260/.355/.603	.320	.284	0.1	1B(23): 0.2	1.0
2012	COL	MLB	41	113	7	4	0	1	8	20	24	0	0	.225/.372/.303	.240	.288	-0.3	1B(13): -0.2	-0.3
2013	*COL*	*MLB*	*42*	*250*	*32*	*9*	*1*	*10*	*34*	*34*	*56*	*1*	*0*	*.238/.358/.435*	*.269*	*.274*	*-0.3*	*1B -1*	*0.6*

Giambi still has patience at the plate, but his other offensive skills disappeared last year. He missed most of the second half due first to a "viral syndrome" and then to a hernia that required offseason surgery. He finished the season on a 2-for-21 run, with his last extra-base hit coming on June 9. Giambi has expressed a desire to resume his quest for 430 homers but the body may not be willing. Perhaps in an effort to hedge his bets, he interviewed for the Rockies managerial vacancy.

Carlos Gonzalez LF

Born: **10/17/1985** Age: **27**
Bats: **L** Throws: **L** Height: **6' 2"**
Weight: **205** Breakout: **5%**
Improve: **51%** Collapse: **5%**
Attrition: **5%** MLB: **98%**

Comparables:
Scott Hairston,Allen Craig,Wes Covington

YEAR	TEAM	LVL	AGE	PA	R	2B	3B	HR	RBI	BB	SO	SB	CS	AVG_OBP_SLG	TAv	BABIP	BRR	FRAA	WARP
2010	COL	MLB	24	636	111	34	9	34	117	40	135	26	8	.336/.376/.598	.315	.384	3.9	LF(63): -3.2, CF(57): 2.7	5.3
2011	COL	MLB	25	542	92	27	3	26	92	48	105	20	5	.295/.363/.526	.291	.326	0.5	LF(61): -2.2, RF(34): -0.7	2.4
2012	COL	MLB	26	579	89	31	5	22	85	56	115	20	5	.303/.371/.510	.284	.352	1	LF(131): -5.3	1.3
2013	*COL*	*MLB*	*27*	*538*	*75*	*28*	*5*	*23*	*78*	*42*	*111*	*18*	*5*	*.298/.356/.517*	*.286*	*.342*	*1.6*	*LF -5, CF -0*	*2.4*

CarGo's MVP-caliber 2010 campaign is looking more and more like the outlier. He started strong last year but struggled in the second half when Troy Tulowitzki was out of the lineup ("I am getting pitched to differently," he told the *Denver Post's* Troy Renck in September). The death of his grandfather in Venezuela and a nagging left hamstring injury may have been contributing factors. His defense in left field isn't as good as you'd expect from a former center fielder, and for his career, Gonzalez loses nearly 300 OPS points away from Coors Field. He hits lefties well enough to be a solid everyday player and is in his physical prime. Expect more of the same for the next few years.

Ramon Hernandez C

Born: **5/20/1976** Age: **37**
Bats: **R** Throws: **R** Height: **6' 1"**
Weight: **220** Breakout: **0%**
Improve: **20%** Collapse: **8%**
Attrition: **14%** MLB: **75%**

Comparables:
Tom Lampkin,Sherm Lollar,Ron Hassey

YEAR	TEAM	LVL	AGE	PA	R	2B	3B	HR	RBI	BB	SO	SB	CS	AVG_OBP_SLG	TAv	BABIP	BRR	FRAA	WARP
2010	CIN	MLB	34	352	30	18	1	7	48	29	49	0	0	.297/.364/.428	.274	.332	-1.5	C(91): 3.3, 1B(5): -0.1	2.5
2011	CIN	MLB	35	328	28	13	0	12	36	23	41	0	0	.282/.341/.446	.264	.291	-3.4	C(82): 1.0, 1B(1): -0.1	1.4
2012	COL	MLB	36	196	16	10	0	5	28	6	32	0	1	.217/.247/.353	.208	.235	-3.3	C(46): -0.6, 1B(2): -0.0	-1.0
2013	*COL*	*MLB*	*37*	*250*	*27*	*11*	*1*	*6*	*27*	*17*	*33*	*0*	*0*	*.269/.327/.405*	*.243*	*.288*	*-0.4*	*C 0, 1B 0*	*0.7*

The Rockies traded incumbent backstop Chris Iannetta to the Angels at the end of November 2011. That same day, Colorado signed the older and more expensive Hernandez to a two-year deal. Last year, as will happen to 36-year-olds who squat and take foul balls off the body for a living, he did not play often or well. Hernandez missed 42 games from late-May to mid-July with a left hand strain that kept him from gripping the bat properly, then in September ruptured a tendon in his left thigh, which required season-ending surgery. Hernandez may not have much baseball left in him, but he has $3.2 million guaranteed coming his way, which will buy plenty of ice packs.

Jonathan Herrera INF

Born: **11/3/1984** Age: **28**
Bats: **B** Throws: **R** Height: **5' 10"**
Weight: **150** Breakout: **5%**
Improve: **35%** Collapse: **12%**
Attrition: **15%** MLB: **89%**

Comparables:
Ramon Santiago,Scott Fletcher,Mike Bordick

YEAR	TEAM	LVL	AGE	PA	R	2B	3B	HR	RBI	BB	SO	SB	CS	AVG_OBP_SLG	TAv	BABIP	BRR	FRAA	WARP
2010	CSP	AAA	25	260	30	6	1	2	17	27	29	3	3	.261/.335/.324	.235	.283	-0.6	SS(46): 8.1, 2B(10): -1.1	0.9
2010	COL	MLB	25	257	34	6	2	1	21	25	36	2	2	.284/.352/.342	.245	.330	0.4	2B(57): 5.5, 3B(16): -0.5	0.8
2011	COL	MLB	26	320	28	5	1	3	14	28	40	4	4	.242/.313/.299	.228	.273	-0.7	2B(62): 0.2, SS(21): -0.4	-0.7
2012	COL	MLB	27	251	29	9	1	3	12	16	39	4	1	.262/.317/.351	.229	.306	0.9	SS(42): -1.5, 2B(19): -0.2	-0.5
2013	*COL*	*MLB*	*28*	*253*	*28*	*8*	*2*	*3*	*21*	*20*	*35*	*3*	*2*	*.264/.327/.354*	*.230*	*.293*	*-0.1*	*2B -0, SS 0*	*0.1*

After spending much of 2011 starting at second base for Colorado and being overmatched by big-league pitching, Herrera settled into a utility role last year. He mainly played shortstop, and although he didn't commit many errors, he also didn't get to many balls. Herrera missed the end of May and most of June due to a right hamstring strain. He also landed on the DL in August with a left wrist infection "caused by his watch." Herrera isn't a threat at the plate, in the field, or on the bases. He is no better or worse than Alberto Gonzalez. Investing money for his family now would be advisable. So would investing in a new watch.

Rosell Herrera INF

Born: **10/16/1992** Age: **20**
Bats: **B** Throws: **R** Height: **6' 4"**
Weight: **180** Breakout: **9%**
Improve: **21%** Collapse: **37%**
Attrition: **44%** MLB: **92%**

Comparables:
Wayne Causey,Jose Oquendo,Ted Kazanski

YEAR	TEAM	LVL	AGE	PA	R	2B	3B	HR	RBI	BB	SO	SB	CS	AVG_OBP_SLG	TAv	BABIP	BRR	FRAA	WARP
2011	CAS	Rk	18	275	38	6	8	6	34	27	62	5	4	.284/.361/.449	.261	.358	-1.5	SS(27): -0.7, 3B(13): -1.3	0.0
2012	ASH	A	19	237	22	8	2	1	26	21	49	6	3	.202/.271/.272	.204	.255	0.7	3B(28): -0.6, SS(27): 2.6	-0.4
2012	TRI	A-	19	211	30	6	2	1	30	14	34	7	3	.284/.332/.351	.292	.335	1.6	SS(39): 4.6	1.5
2013	*COL*	*MLB*	*20*	*250*	*23*	*8*	*2*	*3*	*18*	*14*	*65*	*2*	*1*	*.210/.254/.295*	*.185*	*.274*	*-0.1*	*SS 2, 3B 0*	*-0.8*

The biggest point working in Herrera's favor is his youth. He didn't hit at Asheville, where everyone hits, but showed signs of life after being demoted to the Northwest League. The nominal switch-hitter struggled from the right side at both stops. He split time between shortstop and third base at the higher level, playing only the former back in short-season ball. He won't stay at short and may not stay on the infield at all due to "poor actions and hands." Herrera is a big kid, and the power is expected to come, but the timetable is fuzzy.

DJ LeMahieu **2B**
Born: **7/13/1988** Age: **24**
Bats: **R** Throws: **R** Height: **6' 5"**
Weight: **205** Breakout: **4%**
Improve: **44%** Collapse: **9%**
Attrition: **14%** MLB: **90%**
Comparables:
William Bergolla,Erick Aybar,Joaquin Arias

YEAR	TEAM	LVL	AGE	PA	R	2B	3B	HR	RBI	BB	SO	SB	CS	AVG_OBP_SLG	TAv	BABIP	BRR	FRAA	WARP
2010	DAY	A+	21	600	63	24	5	2	73	29	61	15	7	.314/.343/.386	.269	.343	0.3	2B(64): 3.7, 3B(39): 2.8	3.0
2011	TEN	AA	22	202	32	15	2	2	27	11	22	4	3	.358/.386/.492	.329	.389	-1.1	3B(16): -0.7, 2B(11): 1.0	0.7
2011	IOW	AAA	22	247	23	7	1	3	23	14	27	5	5	.286/.328/.366	.268	.308	0.1	3B(12): -0.2, 2B(7): 1.3	0.4
2011	CHN	MLB	22	62	3	2	0	0	4	1	12	0	0	.250/.262/.283	.196	.312	-0.7	2B(15): -0.7, 3B(11): -0.0	-0.2
2012	CSP	AAA	23	280	33	14	2	1	31	23	29	13	6	.314/.368/.396	.250	.348	-0.9	2B(38): 1.5, 3B(6): 0.3	0.2
2012	COL	MLB	23	247	26	12	4	2	22	13	42	1	2	.297/.332/.410	.253	.353	2.6	2B(67): 6.9, 3B(9): -0.2	1.2
2013	*COL*	*MLB*	*24*	*259*	*29*	*11*	*2*	*3*	*22*	*12*	*38*	*5*	*3*	*.290/.324/.394*	*.238*	*.328*	*-0.1*	*2B 1, 3B 0*	*0.4*

Acquired from the Cubs in December 2011, LeMahieu started the season at Triple-A before joining the big club toward the end of May. The former second-round pick out of Louisiana State floundered in a reserve role, returned to the minors for a month, then was recalled for good on July 17. Shortly thereafter he became the Rockies' everyday second baseman, where he produced at the plate and played solid defense. LeMahieu's minor-league track record is spotty, but he responded well to regular playing time and could be useful as a stopgap solution at second or eventually in a utility role.

Matt McBride **OF**
Born: **5/23/1985** Age: **28**
Bats: **R** Throws: **R** Height: **6' 3"**
Weight: **215** Breakout: **1%**
Improve: **44%** Collapse: **6%**
Attrition: **13%** MLB: **89%**
Comparables:
Kevin Bass,Troy O'Leary,Jeff Francoeur

YEAR	TEAM	LVL	AGE	PA	R	2B	3B	HR	RBI	BB	SO	SB	CS	AVG_OBP_SLG	TAv	BABIP	BRR	FRAA	WARP
2010	AKR	AA	25	404	54	25	1	17	64	30	62	0	2	.283/.351/.499	.293	.301	1.6	RF(34): 2.2, 1B(33): 0.7	2.3
2010	COH	AAA	25	127	16	6	0	4	11	5	17	0	0	.269/.294/.420	.232	.280	-1.4	LF(13): 1.9, 1B(12): -0.2	-0.3
2011	AKR	AA	26	346	50	24	4	14	53	30	44	3	0	.297/.359/.535	.302	.306	-0.2	1B(34): -1.1, RF(19): -0.6	1.0
2012	CSP	AAA	27	469	73	42	6	10	87	19	47	0	1	.344/.365/.535	.281	.360	0.1	RF(42): 1.2, 1B(32): 2.0	1.3
2012	COL	MLB	27	81	8	2	0	2	11	1	17	0	0	.205/.222/.308	.168	.233	0.4	RF(12): 0.1, 1B(8): -1.0	-0.9
2013	*COL*	*MLB*	*28*	*250*	*26*	*14*	*2*	*7*	*32*	*11*	*41*	*0*	*0*	*.272/.309/.443*	*.246*	*.299*	*-0.3*	*RF -0, 1B -1*	*-0.1*

Taken in the second round of the 2006 draft by the Indians as a catcher, McBride still gets behind the dish a few times a year but is mainly a first baseman/corner outfielder now. He came over in the July 2011 Ubaldo Jimenez trade and features a limited offensive skill set: decent batting average, some doubles, not many walks. He's sort of a weaker-hitting, right-handed version of Robert Fick.

Chris Nelson **3B**
Born: **9/3/1985** Age: **27**
Bats: **R** Throws: **R** Height: **6' 0"**
Weight: **175** Breakout: **5%**
Improve: **46%** Collapse: **7%**
Attrition: **14%** MLB: **85%**
Comparables:
Hector Lopez,Ray Knight,Ray Jablonski

YEAR	TEAM	LVL	AGE	PA	R	2B	3B	HR	RBI	BB	SO	SB	CS	AVG_OBP_SLG	TAv	BABIP	BRR	FRAA	WARP
2010	CSP	AAA	24	356	60	15	3	12	55	29	53	7	3	.313/.376/.492	.281	.344	-1.1	SS(52): -2.2, 2B(23): -1.5	1.6
2010	COL	MLB	24	27	7	1	0	0	0	1	4	1	0	.280/.308/.320	.196	.333	1.7	2B(4): -0.1, 3B(4): -0.1	0.1
2011	CSP	AAA	25	315	52	20	5	11	65	17	48	3	3	.329/.366/.547	.297	.357	-1	SS(24): 3.6, 2B(16): -1.6	1.6
2011	COL	MLB	25	189	20	10	1	4	16	7	35	3	1	.250/.280/.383	.216	.289	0.7	2B(29): -2.6, 3B(24): 0.9	-0.6
2012	CSP	AAA	26	54	12	4	1	0	8	2	12	1	1	.294/.333/.412	.253	.385	-0.1	3B(9): 0.3, 2B(2): 0.2	0.1
2012	COL	MLB	26	377	45	21	3	9	53	27	84	2	1	.301/.352/.458	.270	.374	1.3	3B(92): -9.9, 2B(21): 0.8	0.4
2013	*COL*	*MLB*	*27*	*348*	*38*	*17*	*2*	*9*	*42*	*21*	*69*	*3*	*2*	*.281/.327/.434*	*.251*	*.329*	*-0.2*	*3B -1, 2B -1*	*0.5*

Drafted as a shortstop in the first round in 2004, Nelson has been slow to develop. He spent most of last season at third base, where he hit enough for the position but didn't play great defense. Nelson landed on the DL in mid-July due to an irregular heartbeat that he attributed to "too much caffeine, dehydration, and stress." After returning to the lineup three weeks later, he hit .345 with power over his final 53 games. His minor-league record suggests this is a small-sample fluke, but Nelson is at the right age for a sudden leap forward, although he never will be a coffee achiever.

Rafael Ortega **CF**
Born: **5/15/1991** Age: **22**
Bats: **L** Throws: **R** Height: **6' 0"**
Weight: **160** Breakout: **8%**
Improve: **55%** Collapse: **6%**
Attrition: **16%** MLB: **97%**
Comparables:
Rowland Office,Chet Lemon,Bobby Tolan

YEAR	TEAM	LVL	AGE	PA	R	2B	3B	HR	RBI	BB	SO	SB	CS	AVG_OBP_SLG	TAv	BABIP	BRR	FRAA	WARP
2010	CAS	Rk	19	322	69	17	3	7	45	28	42	23	9	.358/.416/.510	.337	.398	1	CF(68): 4.4	3.9
2011	ASH	A	20	519	77	26	8	9	66	28	90	32	19	.294/.335/.438	.229	.344	0	CF(76): -1.8	-0.3
2012	MOD	A+	21	556	81	23	8	8	60	46	93	36	18	.283/.344/.410	.288	.329	3.6	CF(88): 3.6	3.6
2012	COL	MLB	21	6	0	0	0	0	0	1	2	1	0	.500/.667/.500	.447	.000	0.1	CF(1): 0.0	0.1
2013	*COL*	*MLB*	*22*	*250*	*30*	*9*	*2*	*3*	*18*	*13*	*54*	*11*	*6*	*.240/.281/.340*	*.206*	*.294*	*0.4*	*CF -4, RF -0*	*-1.1*

Ortega is an athletic outfielder who possesses good speed and a strong arm. An impatient hitter in the past, he tightened his strike zone last year while moving up a level. Ortega is an unrefined baserunner but a plus defender in center field. He received his first look with the big club in late September due to the Rockies' need for healthy bodies and the fact that he had been playing in the instructional league in Arizona while other minor leaguers had called it a season. He is smallish—according to Carlos Gonzalez, "He looks like he's 10"—and probably won't be back in the big leagues for a while.

Jordan Pacheco 3B

Born: **1/30/1986** Age: **27**
Bats: **R** Throws: **R** Height: **6' 2"**
Weight: **190** Breakout: **0%**
Improve: **50%** Collapse: **6%**
Attrition: **18%** MLB: **95%**

Comparables:
Bob Aspromonte,Terry Tiffee,Dan Meyer

YEAR	TEAM	LVL	AGE	PA	R	2B	3B	HR	RBI	BB	SO	SB	CS	AVG_OBP_SLG	TAv	BABIP	BRR	FRAA	WARP
2010	MOD	A+	24	460	59	27	3	5	70	54	36	5	6	.321/.413/.444	.314	.343	1.5	C(71): -0.7	4.4
2010	TUL	AA	24	91	11	5	0	1	19	6	6	1	1	.333/.409/.436	.293	.352	0.5	C(20): 0.3	0.8
2011	CSP	AAA	25	411	57	21	3	3	50	30	48	2	2	.278/.343/.377	.236	.308	2.1	C(53): -0.8, 3B(3): 0.2	0.1
2011	COL	MLB	25	88	5	1	0	2	14	3	9	0	0	.286/.318/.369	.235	.301	-0.6	1B(13): -0.2, 3B(7): -0.1	-0.3
2012	CSP	AAA	26	74	10	4	0	3	10	3	5	1	0	.433/.479/.627	.347	.441	0.6	3B(10): -1.5, C(4): -0.1	0.4
2012	COL	MLB	26	505	51	32	3	5	54	22	61	7	2	.309/.341/.421	.252	.344	0.6	3B(82): -4.5, 1B(43): -3.4	-0.8
2013	*COL*	*MLB*	*27*	*433*	*42*	*22*	*2*	*6*	*45*	*25*	*52*	*2*	*1*	*.286/.335/.400*	*.244*	*.313*	*-0.5*	*3B 1, C -0*	*0.3*

Pacheco is a contact hitter who has a short stroke and marginal secondary skills, which means that he must maintain a high batting average to have value. He caught a lot in the minors but as a rookie mainly played the corner infield spots, where his lack of power is more of an issue. His defense at third caused the Rockies to send him back to Triple-A eight games into the season for a three-week "tuneup." It improved as the season progressed and he became less tentative with experience. Pacheco hits lefties well and could be useful in a platoon role, particularly if he moves back behind the plate.

Kyle Parker RF

Born: **9/30/1989** Age: **23**
Bats: **R** Throws: **R** Height: **6' 1"**
Weight: **200** Breakout: **5%**
Improve: **61%** Collapse: **10%**
Attrition: **5%** MLB: **96%**

Comparables:
Jesse Barfield,Domonic Brown,Wladimir Balentien

YEAR	TEAM	LVL	AGE	PA	R	2B	3B	HR	RBI	BB	SO	SB	CS	AVG_OBP_SLG	TAv	BABIP	BRR	FRAA	WARP
2011	ASH	A	21	516	75	23	1	21	95	48	133	2	0	.285/.367/.483	.260	.355	-4.6	RF(67): -0.7	-0.2
2012	MOD	A+	22	463	86	18	6	23	73	66	88	1	2	.308/.415/.562	.363	.346	-0.3	RF(59): -5.4	3.4
2013	*COL*	*MLB*	*23*	*250*	*28*	*9*	*2*	*9*	*33*	*22*	*63*	*0*	*0*	*.249/.319/.431*	*.250*	*.300*	*-0.2*	*RF -1*	*0.2*

Parker, Colorado's first-round pick in 2010 out of Clemson, improved on a strong pro debut last year, increasing his power and cutting his K/BB in half while moving up a level. A pitched ball broke his hand in the season's second game, causing him to miss 33 games. His power was slow to return. Parker's slugging percentage didn't climb above .400 for good until June 12, after which he abused California League pitchers, knocking 16 homers in his final 55 games. A torn ligament in his left thumb at season's end required surgery, keeping him out of the Arizona Fall League. Parker must hit at every level, as he is strictly a corner outfielder.

Wilin Rosario C

Born: **2/23/1989** Age: **24**
Bats: **R** Throws: **R** Height: **6' 0"**
Weight: **200** Breakout: **2%**
Improve: **57%** Collapse: **14%**
Attrition: **18%** MLB: **99%**

Comparables:
Earl Williams,Matt Nokes,Johnny Bench

YEAR	TEAM	LVL	AGE	PA	R	2B	3B	HR	RBI	BB	SO	SB	CS	AVG_OBP_SLG	TAv	BABIP	BRR	FRAA	WARP
2010	TUL	AA	21	297	42	13	1	19	52	21	57	1	0	.285/.341/.552	.297	.296	-1	C(67): -1.3	2.5
2011	TUL	AA	22	426	52	15	3	21	48	19	91	1	2	.249/.284/.457	.256	.272	-0.6	C(57): -0.7	0.8
2011	COL	MLB	22	57	6	3	1	3	8	2	20	0	0	.204/.228/.463	.226	.250	-1	C(14): -0.1	0.0
2012	COL	MLB	23	426	67	19	0	28	71	25	99	4	5	.270/.312/.530	.274	.289	-1.4	C(105): 0.6, 3B(3): -0.0	1.9
2013	*COL*	*MLB*	*24*	*358*	*47*	*16*	*2*	*21*	*59*	*19*	*86*	*2*	*2*	*.266/.307/.512*	*.268*	*.295*	*-0.5*	*C -0, 1B -0*	*1.9*

Rosario delivered on his power potential as a rookie, leading the Rockies in homers despite starting the season at Triple-A. Other aspects of his game are less refined. He has a strong arm, but led MLB catchers in passed balls (21 on the season, including four in one game) and errors. Player and team made improving his play behind the dish a priority over the offseason, but even if Rosario can't clean up his defensive game, he'll stick around with that bat. If he continues to improve his plate discipline as in the second half of 2012, he could be dangerous.

Josh Rutledge MI

Born: **4/21/1989** Age: **24**
Bats: **R** Throws: **R** Height: **6' 2"**
Weight: **190** Breakout: **6%**
Improve: **51%** Collapse: **3%**
Attrition: **11%** MLB: **97%**

Comparables:
Stephen Drew,Nomar Garciaparra,Jim Fregosi

YEAR	TEAM	LVL	AGE	PA	R	2B	3B	HR	RBI	BB	SO	SB	CS	AVG_OBP_SLG	TAv	BABIP	BRR	FRAA	WARP
2011	MOD	A+	22	523	91	33	9	9	71	41	91	16	3	.348/.414/.517	.365	.417	-1	SS(66): -6.2	3.5
2012	TUL	AA	23	379	57	27	3	13	35	14	69	14	4	.306/.338/.508	.315	.345	1.8	SS(52): -3.9, 2B(19): -0.9	2.0
2012	COL	MLB	23	291	37	20	5	8	37	9	54	7	0	.274/.306/.469	.256	.315	-0.3	SS(57): -3.6, 2B(7): -0.3	0.0
2013	*COL*	*MLB*	*24*	*307*	*39*	*17*	*3*	*9*	*34*	*12*	*60*	*7*	*1*	*.282/.319/.454*	*.256*	*.327*	*0.8*	*SS 1, 2B -0*	*1.4*

Building on a strong second half in 2011, Rutledge posted solid numbers at Double-A before being recalled to the big club after the All-Star break. He has decent power for a middle infielder but hasn't controlled the strike zone at any level. Until he learns to do so, pitchers will exploit this. Rutledge mostly played shortstop due to Tulowitzki's extended absence, but his arm is better suited to second base in the long run.

Omir Santos **C**

Born: **4/29/1981** Age: **32**
Bats: **R** Throws: **R** Height: **6' 1"**
Weight: **215** Breakout: **1%**
Improve: **26%** Collapse: **12%**
Attrition: **25%** MLB: **95%**

Comparables:
Tony Pena,Tom Pagnozzi,Chris Heintz

YEAR	TEAM	LVL	AGE	PA	R	2B	3B	HR	RBI	BB	SO	SB	CS	AVG_OBP_SLG	TAv	BABIP	BRR	FRAA	WARP
2010	BIN	AA	29	64	5	3	0	1	8	4	7	0	0	.138/.206/.241	.190	.140	0.5	C(15): -0.3, 1B(1): -0.0	-0.3
2011	TOL	AAA	30	163	12	5	0	2	16	3	29	0	0	.245/.259/.318	.223	.285	0	C(27): -0.4	-0.1
2011	DET	MLB	30	22	1	0	0	0	0	0	4	0	0	.227/.227/.227	.199	.278	-0.2	C(10): -0.1	-0.1
2012	CSP	AAA	31	123	12	9	0	2	21	2	17	0	0	.311/.320/.437	.235	.347	-0.7	C(34): 0.3	0.1
2012	TOL	AAA	31	89	7	7	1	0	9	2	17	0	1	.310/.315/.417	.248	.371	-0.7	C(19): 0.3	0.0
2012	DET	MLB	31	10	0	0	0	0	1	0	1	0	0	.125/.111/.125	.083	.125	0	C(3): -0.0	-0.2
2013	*COL*	*MLB*	*32*	*250*	*23*	*12*	*1*	*4*	*25*	*10*	*41*	*0*	*0*	*.261/.297/.378*	*.224*	*.295*	*-0.4*	*C -0, 1B -0*	*0.2*

Santos has been playing professionally since 2001 and he's drawn as many as 20 walks twice in a season. Before last year, his best batting average was .275, in his second pro season. He hit 10 homers at Double-A back in 2005. He isn't a great defensive catcher. Santos is one of four Yankees 21st-round picks ever to play in the big leagues, the most notable being Jim Deshaies. Santos is sort of Miguel Olivo without the power. And persistent. Very persistent.

Trevor Story **SS**

Born: **11/15/1992** Age: **20**
Bats: **R** Throws: **R** Height: **6' 2"**
Weight: **175** Breakout: **19%**
Improve: **52%** Collapse: **5%**
Attrition: **17%** MLB: **81%**

Comparables:
Alex Rodriguez,Edgar Renteria,B.J. Upton

YEAR	TEAM	LVL	AGE	PA	R	2B	3B	HR	RBI	BB	SO	SB	CS	AVG_OBP_SLG	TAv	BABIP	BRR	FRAA	WARP
2011	CAS	Rk	18	210	37	8	2	6	28	26	41	13	1	.268/.364/.436	.262	.313	2.2	SS(23): -1.8, 3B(10): 0.7	0.8
2012	ASH	A	19	548	96	43	6	18	63	60	121	15	3	.277/.367/.505	.266	.335	4.1	SS(76): 11.5, 3B(19): 1.5	3.0
2013	*COL*	*MLB*	*20*	*250*	*29*	*10*	*2*	*7*	*25*	*19*	*70*	*4*	*1*	*.223/.288/.375*	*.221*	*.288*	*0.4*	*SS 2, 3B 0*	*0.2*

The Rockies picked Story in the supplemental first round of the 2011 draft out of a Texas high school and went well over slot to sign him. Story's full-season debut couldn't have been much better, although he received help from cozy McCormick Field in Asheville, where his OPS was 185 points higher than on the road. The high strikeout total is mitigated by the high walk total, although he'll need to make better contact at higher levels. Story has time to iron out whatever flaws exist in his game. He projects to be at least a solid regular at a premium position.

Troy Tulowitzki **SS**

Born: **10/10/1984** Age: **28**
Bats: **R** Throws: **R** Height: **6' 4"**
Weight: **215** Breakout: **1%**
Improve: **38%** Collapse: **0%**
Attrition: **4%** MLB: **100%**

Comparables:
Robin Yount,Nomar Garciaparra,Hanley Ramirez

YEAR	TEAM	LVL	AGE	PA	R	2B	3B	HR	RBI	BB	SO	SB	CS	AVG_OBP_SLG	TAv	BABIP	BRR	FRAA	WARP
2010	COL	MLB	25	529	89	32	3	27	95	48	78	11	2	.315/.381/.568	.307	.327	0.3	SS(122): 5.3	5.6
2011	COL	MLB	26	606	81	36	2	30	105	59	79	9	3	.302/.372/.544	.301	.305	-1.8	SS(140): -2.8	3.7
2012	COL	MLB	27	203	33	8	2	8	27	19	19	2	2	.287/.360/.486	.272	.284	1	SS(47): 0.6	1.1
2013	*COL*	*MLB*	*28*	*275*	*39*	*14*	*2*	*13*	*42*	*27*	*40*	*5*	*2*	*.299/.370/.528*	*.296*	*.311*	*-0.1*	*SS 1*	*2.4*

Tulowitzki is a perennial MVP candidate when healthy, which isn't often enough. Over the past five seasons he has averaged 113 games and 477 plate appearances, missing extended periods due to thigh, thumb, and wrist injuries. Last year his big-league season ended with the month of May due to a left groin issue that required surgery after he aggravated it while running the bases in June during a rehab assignment. Colorado owes Tulowitzki at least $144 million over the next nine seasons. If he returns to 2009-11 levels, that's not a problem. But if he can't stay on the field, his contract could hamstring the Rockies for years to come. Or maybe it will groin them.

Ryan Wheeler **INF**

Born: **7/10/1988** Age: **24**
Bats: **L** Throws: **R** Height: **6' 5"**
Weight: **220** Breakout: **7%**
Improve: **54%** Collapse: **2%**
Attrition: **12%** MLB: **93%**

Comparables:
Aramis Ramirez,Brandon Laird,Ken McMullen

YEAR	TEAM	LVL	AGE	PA	R	2B	3B	HR	RBI	BB	SO	SB	CS	AVG_OBP_SLG	TAv	BABIP	BRR	FRAA	WARP
2010	VIS	A+	21	506	62	25	2	9	57	35	98	3	1	.284/.341/.404	.273	.344	-3.7	3B(104): -9.1, 1B(7): -0.5	0.7
2010	MOB	AA	21	73	8	3	0	3	10	5	16	0	0	.254/.315/.433	.233	.292	0.4	3B(22): 0.4, 1B(1): -0.0	-0.1
2011	MOB	AA	22	531	69	30	2	16	89	45	102	3	4	.294/.358/.465	.278	.343	-3.8	3B(48): -0.6, 1B(11): -0.3	0.5
2012	RNO	AAA	23	399	56	27	4	15	90	26	67	3	1	.351/.388/.572	.319	.388	0.5	3B(20): 0.1, 1B(14): -0.7	1.3
2012	ARI	MLB	23	119	11	6	1	1	10	9	22	1	0	.239/.294/.339	.236	.287	-0.1	3B(23): -2.2, 1B(4): 0.2	-0.3
2013	*COL*	*MLB*	*24*	*250*	*25*	*12*	*2*	*6*	*30*	*13*	*53*	*1*	*0*	*.270/.310/.420*	*.242*	*.320*	*-0.2*	*3B 1, 1B -1*	*0.1*

Wheeler has split time between the infield corners in the minors, and Arizona's acquisition of Josh Bell had the ripple effect of Wheeler having to learn left field in order to fit his bat into the Triple-A lineup. Much of Wheeler's value is tied to his batting average, and though he pasted the ball all over Reno, a major-league call-up served as a harsh reality check. The good news is that opportunities at the corners are more plentiful in Colorado than they were in Arizona and that if any ballpark can make Wheeler look as good as Reno did, it's Coors Field.

Tim Wheeler OF
Born: **1/21/1988** Age: **25**
Bats: **L** Throws: **R** Height: **6' 5"**
Weight: **205** Breakout: **14%**
Improve: **57%** Collapse: **7%**
Attrition: **23%** MLB: **94%**
Comparables:
Ken Griffey,Ollie Brown,Glenn Braggs

YEAR	TEAM	LVL	AGE	PA	R	2B	3B	HR	RBI	BB	SO	SB	CS	AVG_OBP_SLG	TAv	BABIP	BRR	FRAA	WARP
2010	MOD	A+	22	592	88	21	6	12	63	60	114	22	8	.249/.340/.384	.260	.296	2.9	CF(124): 3.4, RF(7): -0.1	1.9
2011	TUL	AA	23	637	105	28	6	33	86	59	142	21	12	.287/.365/.535	.309	.329	-2.4	CF(82): -9.7	1.3
2012	CSP	AAA	24	415	67	27	4	2	37	29	69	7	7	.303/.357/.412	.245	.366	-1.2	RF(31): -5.1, LF(28): -2.2	-1.1
2013	*COL*	*MLB*	*25*	*250*	*31*	*11*	*2*	*6*	*24*	*17*	*55*	*6*	*3*	*.249/.306/.391*	*.231*	*.299*	*0*	*CF -2, RF -0*	*-0.3*

After leading the Texas League with 33 homers in 2011, Wheeler pulled a reverse Chase Headley and hit just two last year in the hitter-friendly PCL. April surgery to repair a hamate bone in his right wrist cost him a month and may have been a factor. Even before the drop in home runs, scouts didn't expect him to have elite power at the big-league level. He did make better contact than in the past. Wheeler mostly played center field in 2010 and 2011 before spending more time at the corners last year. He isn't young, and if he doesn't stay in center, the lack of power could be a limiting factor. He is starting to look like a fourth outfielder.

Eric Young OF
Born: **5/25/1985** Age: **28**
Bats: **B** Throws: **R** Height: **5' 11"**
Weight: **180** Breakout: **1%**
Improve: **56%** Collapse: **5%**
Attrition: **11%** MLB: **90%**
Comparables:
Kenny Lofton,Billy North,Michael Bourn

YEAR	TEAM	LVL	AGE	PA	R	2B	3B	HR	RBI	BB	SO	SB	CS	AVG_OBP_SLG	TAv	BABIP	BRR	FRAA	WARP
2010	CSP	AAA	25	142	20	5	1	1	9	15	32	10	0	.252/.340/.333	.237	.330	2	2B(20): 0.8, CF(6): -0.4	0.3
2010	COL	MLB	25	189	26	5	1	0	8	17	32	17	6	.244/.312/.285	.220	.300	2.4	2B(35): 4.0, LF(10): -0.1	0.2
2011	CSP	AAA	26	275	61	18	9	2	28	39	36	17	1	.363/.454/.552	.313	.416	3.8	CF(23): -2.2, 2B(11): -0.4	1.4
2011	COL	MLB	26	229	34	4	3	0	10	26	38	27	4	.247/.342/.298	.225	.304	4	LF(35): -1.6, 2B(7): -0.6	-0.4
2012	COL	MLB	27	196	36	7	2	4	15	13	31	14	2	.316/.377/.448	.278	.367	5.1	CF(15): 1.8, RF(11): -0.7	1.2
2013	*COL*	*MLB*	*28*	*250*	*35*	*9*	*3*	*3*	*19*	*23*	*45*	*20*	*4*	*.266/.343/.375*	*.246*	*.316*	*2.5*	*LF -0, CF -0*	*0.6*

Out of minor-league options and with the burden of occasionally having to play second base removed, Young saw his offensive game blossom in 2012. He has been an efficient base stealer throughout his professional career and gets on base just often enough to make that matter. Young was enjoying a strong second half last year when a left rib cage muscle strain ended his season on August 20. Once healthy, the workout- and diet-conscious Young will resume his pursuit of a career as a fourth or fifth outfielder.

PITCHERS

Tyler Anderson
Born: **12/30/1989** Age: **23**
Bats: **L** Throws: **L** Height: **6' 5"** Weight: **215**
Breakout: **32%** Improve: **67%** Collapse: **15%**
Attrition: **13%** MLB: **93%**
Comparables:
John Lannan,Eric Milton,Bud Smith

YEAR	TEAM	LVL	AGE	W	L	SV	G	GS	IP	H	HR	BB	SO	BB9	SO9	GB%	BABIP	WHIP	ERA	FIP	FRA	WARP
2012	ASH	A	22	12	3	0	20	20	120^{1}	102	5	28	81	2.1	6.1	54%	.270	1.08	2.47	3.55	4.42	2.3
2013	*COL*	*MLB*	*23*	*2*	*3*	*0*	*6*	*6*	*35*	*41*	*5*	*15*	*18*	*3.8*	*4.7*	*48%*	*.319*	*1.61*	*6.11*	*5.31*	*6.64*	*-0.4*

Anderson, the Rockies' first-round pick in 2011 out of the University of Oregon, is a finesse pitcher who relies on command and who has little margin for error. He generated a lot of groundballs in his pro debut, which served him well at the pitchers' nightmare that is Asheville. Anderson's strikeout rate was well below league average, as it will be at every level. Lack of dominance limits his upside, but he is polished and figures to slot at the back of a rotation before long. When he does reach the big leagues, he will join Mike Morgan, Greg Maddux, and Matt DeWitt as the fourth pitcher from his high school to have done so.

Jayson Aquino
Born: **11/22/1992** Age: **20**
Bats: **L** Throws: **L** Height: **6' 2"** Weight: **170**
Breakout: **25%** Improve: **43%** Collapse: **50%**
Attrition: **43%** MLB: **95%**
Comparables:
Bruce Robbins,Mike McCormick,Chris Zachary

YEAR	TEAM	LVL	AGE	W	L	SV	G	GS	IP	H	HR	BB	SO	BB9	SO9	GB%	BABIP	WHIP	ERA	FIP	FRA	WARP
2011	DCK	Rk	18	8	2	0	14	14	89^{2}	55	1	22	80	2.2	8.0	—	.227	0.86	1.30	2.34	2.54	0.0
2012	DRO	Rk	19	6	1	0	9	9	65	45	1	9	74	1.2	10.2	1.%	.667	0.83	1.52	1.59	-0.32	1.6
2012	GJR	Rk	19	4	0	0	7	7	43^{1}	32	2	11	36	2.3	7.5	57%	.246	0.99	1.87	4.34	3.89	0.3
2013	*COL*	*MLB*	*20*	*1*	*1*	*0*	*5*	*2*	*34*	*39*	*5*	*19*	*24*	*5.1*	*6.5*	*47%*	*.328*	*1.70*	*6.26*	*5.38*	*6.80*	*-0.4*

Signed out of the Dominican Republic in 2009, Aquino features a low-90s fastball and a changeup, but he needs work on his breaking ball. The lanky lefty's command is ahead of his stuff. The Rockies have been slow to bring him along, keeping him in the Dominican Summer League for two full seasons and part of another before his promotion to the Pioneer League last July. Aquino is a long way away, but the combination of command and projection makes him worth watching.

Matt Belisle

Born: **6/6/1980** Age: **33**
Bats: **R** Throws: **R** Height: **6' 5"** Weight: **225**
Breakout: **22%** Improve: **36%** Collapse: **33%**
Attrition: **15%** MLB: **86%**

Comparables:
Dan Giese, Jon Rauch, Roy Face

YEAR	TEAM	LVL	AGE	W	L	SV	G	GS	IP	H	HR	BB	SO	BB9	SO9	GB%	BABIP	WHIP	ERA	FIP	FRA	WARP
2010	COL	MLB	30	7	5	1	76	0	92	84	7	16	91	1.6	8.9	49%	.309	1.09	2.93	2.70	3.78	1.8
2011	COL	MLB	31	10	4	0	74	0	72	77	5	14	58	1.8	7.2	55%	.327	1.26	3.25	3.04	4.24	0.9
2012	COL	MLB	32	3	8	3	80	0	80	91	5	18	69	2.0	7.8	52%	.340	1.36	3.71	3.01	3.59	1.3
2013	*COL*	*MLB*	*33*	*4*	*1*	*2*	*69*	*0*	*73^{2}*	*76*	*8*	*15*	*59*	*1.9*	*7.2*	*49%*	*.322*	*1.24*	*4.11*	*3.62*	*4.47*	*0.7*

Belisle tied for the MLB lead in appearances last year and is one of four pitchers to get into at least 70 games each of the past three seasons. In April, Colorado brass expressed a desire to limit Belisle's workload to maximize his effectiveness. Pitching coach Bob Apodaca wanted to keep him under 70 innings, but when the Rockies rotation imploded, that didn't happen. Perhaps not coincidentally, Belisle faded in the second half, with his ERA more than tripling and opponents gaining 150 points of SLG against him. Belisle's overall numbers look solid, especially considering his home park, but that fade is worrisome.

Rafael Betancourt

Born: **4/29/1975** Age: **38**
Bats: **R** Throws: **R** Height: **6' 3"** Weight: **215**
Breakout: **27%** Improve: **42%** Collapse: **25%**
Attrition: **9%** MLB: **78%**

Comparables:
Tom Henke, Trevor Hoffman, John Smoltz

YEAR	TEAM	LVL	AGE	W	L	SV	G	GS	IP	H	HR	BB	SO	BB9	SO9	GB%	BABIP	WHIP	ERA	FIP	FRA	WARP
2010	COL	MLB	35	5	1	1	72	0	62^{1}	52	9	8	89	1.2	12.9	28%	.303	0.96	3.61	2.51	3.60	1.0
2011	COL	MLB	36	2	0	8	68	0	62^{1}	46	7	8	73	1.2	10.5	31%	.262	0.87	2.89	2.50	3.33	1.2
2012	COL	MLB	37	1	4	31	60	0	57^{2}	53	6	12	57	1.9	8.9	36%	.292	1.13	2.81	3.14	3.24	1.3
2013	*COL*	*MLB*	*38*	*3*	*1*	*15*	*58*	*0*	*53^{1}*	*46*	*6*	*12*	*58*	*2.1*	*9.9*	*33%*	*.308*	*1.11*	*3.23*	*3.16*	*3.51*	*1.1*

Last year, we said that Betancourt "could close games if given the opportunity." The control artist, who owns the highest K/BB of any pitcher in MLB history (minimum 500 games), did just that after Colorado traded Huston Street. Despite breaking double digits in walks for the first time since 2009, Betancourt worked the ninth inning as well as he had worked the eighth. The extreme fly-ball pitcher remains immune to Coors Field, owning a 3.32 ERA there in 125 appearances. Betancourt is in the twilight of his career, and slippage in dominance is a concern, but he pitches 60 games a year and is good at what he does.

Chad Bettis

Born: **4/26/1989** Age: **24**
Bats: **R** Throws: **R** Height: **6' 2"** Weight: **193**
Breakout: **30%** Improve: **63%** Collapse: **22%**
Attrition: **29%** MLB: **88%**

Comparables:
Carlos Rosa, Vance Worley, Troy Patton

YEAR	TEAM	LVL	AGE	W	L	SV	G	GS	IP	H	HR	BB	SO	BB9	SO9	GB%	BABIP	WHIP	ERA	FIP	FRA	WARP
2010	ASH	A	21	2	0	0	3	3	18^{2}	14	1	3	17	1.4	8.2	43%	.260	0.91	0.96	2.89	4.08	0.4
2010	TRI	A-	21	4	1	0	10	9	48^{1}	44	0	10	39	1.9	7.3	63%	.282	1.12	1.12	2.49	4.07	0.3
2011	MOD	A+	22	12	5	0	27	27	169^{2}	142	10	45	184	2.4	9.8	53%	.272	1.10	3.34	3.49	3.54	2.4
2013	*COL*	*MLB*	*24*	*2*	*3*	*0*	*6*	*6*	*35^{2}*	*39*	*5*	*14*	*25*	*3.5*	*6.3*	*49%*	*.317*	*1.48*	*5.30*	*4.80*	*5.76*	*-0.1*

When healthy, Bettis features a power fastball/slider combination that misses bats. Colorado's second-round pick in 2010 out of Texas Tech missed all of last year due to what began in March as "triceps tightness" and ended with more questions than answers. Instead of developing his off-speed stuff against better hitters, he spent 2012 rehabbing. If he improves at changing speeds, Bettis could be a mid-rotation starter. Otherwise, the two pitches already in his arsenal should make the former college closer an effective late-inning reliever. All of this assumes that his shoulder cooperates, which is far from given.

Rex Brothers

Born: **12/18/1987** Age: **25**
Bats: **L** Throws: **L** Height: **6' 1"** Weight: **205**
Breakout: **26%** Improve: **53%** Collapse: **28%**
Attrition: **13%** MLB: **91%**

Comparables:
Rob Dibble, Daniel Schlereth, Taylor Tankersley

YEAR	TEAM	LVL	AGE	W	L	SV	G	GS	IP	H	HR	BB	SO	BB9	SO9	GB%	BABIP	WHIP	ERA	FIP	FRA	WARP
2010	MOD	A+	22	0	2	3	33	0	37	20	0	19	43	4.6	10.5	56%	.235	1.05	2.68	2.95	4.35	0.4
2010	TUL	AA	22	2	1	4	24	0	23	14	2	18	27	7.0	10.6	56%	.226	1.39	3.91	4.43	5.43	0.0
2011	CSP	AAA	23	3	2	0	25	0	28	29	2	15	45	4.8	14.5	53%	.417	1.57	2.89	3.10	3.56	0.6
2011	COL	MLB	23	1	2	1	48	0	40^{2}	33	4	20	59	4.4	13.1	46%	.326	1.30	2.88	2.85	2.91	0.7
2012	CSP	AAA	24	0	0	1	4	0	5^{1}	3	0	3	13	5.1	21.9	33%	.500	1.12	1.69	0.48	0.00	0.4
2012	COL	MLB	24	8	2	0	75	0	67^{2}	63	5	37	83	4.9	11.0	48%	.343	1.48	3.86	3.33	3.58	1.1
2013	*COL*	*MLB*	*25*	*3*	*1*	*1*	*64*	*0*	*61^{1}*	*49*	*6*	*29*	*76*	*4.2*	*11.1*	*48%*	*.318*	*1.28*	*3.65*	*3.41*	*3.97*	*1.0*

Brothers, a hard-throwing southpaw, made the big club out of spring training but was banished to Triple-A in May to fix his mechanics as well as his mental approach. Two weeks later he returned and was nearly unhittable in June. Then he hit a stretch where he allowed at least one run in six of eight appearances. As in his rookie campaign, Brothers was tough with men on base. He remained effective against lefties, but right-handed batters had much better success against him last year than in 2011. Brothers has quality stuff but must reduce his platoon split (an effective changeup might help) and gain consistency if he is to take the next step and become a big-league closer.

Edwar Cabrera

Born: **10/20/1987** Age: **25**
Bats: **L** Throws: **L** Height: **6' 1"** Weight: **160**
Breakout: **39%** Improve: **64%** Collapse: **12%**
Attrition: **10%** MLB: **91%**

Comparables:
Brian Matusz,Jeff Francis,J.A. Happ

YEAR	TEAM	LVL	AGE	W	L	SV	G	GS	IP	H	HR	BB	SO	BB9	SO9	GB%	BABIP	WHIP	ERA	FIP	FRA	WARP
2010	TRI	A-	22	1	8	0	14	14	73^1	71	2	24	87	2.9	10.7	56%	.354	1.30	3.07	2.73	3.19	1.1
2011	ASH	A	23	4	2	0	13	13	86	77	10	18	110	1.9	11.5	48%	.280	1.10	3.14	3.32	3.51	2.1
2011	MOD	A+	23	4	1	0	13	13	81	78	8	23	107	2.6	11.9	51%	.331	1.25	3.56	3.48	3.11	1.9
2012	TUL	AA	24	8	4	0	15	15	98	65	15	23	82	2.1	7.5	48%	.198	0.90	2.94	4.39	4.93	0.7
2012	CSP	AAA	24	3	1	0	6	6	31^2	26	6	12	39	3.4	11.1	53%	.270	1.20	3.41	4.99	5.64	0.3
2012	COL	MLB	24	0	2	0	2	2	5^2	9	3	7	5	11.1	7.9	48%	.333	2.82	11.12	11.96	10.18	-0.2
2013	*COL*	*MLB*	*25*	*2*	*3*	*0*	*7*	*7*	*42^2*	*44*	*7*	*19*	*37*	*4.0*	*7.7*	*46%*	*.314*	*1.47*	*5.34*	*4.93*	*5.80*	*-0.1*

Cabrera has been a strikeout machine in the minors thanks to a great changeup. His fastball has good sinking action, although he struggled to command it in his cameo with the Rockies last year. There isn't much upside here, but if Cabrera gains consistency with his sinker and slider in the zone, he could slot into the back of a big-league rotation sooner rather than later.

Jhoulys Chacin

Born: **1/7/1988** Age: **25**
Bats: **R** Throws: **R** Height: **6' 4"** Weight: **215**
Breakout: **23%** Improve: **59%** Collapse: **21%**
Attrition: **12%** MLB: **96%**

Comparables:
Matt Cain,Tim Hudson,Ubaldo Jimenez

YEAR	TEAM	LVL	AGE	W	L	SV	G	GS	IP	H	HR	BB	SO	BB9	SO9	GB%	BABIP	WHIP	ERA	FIP	FRA	WARP
2010	CSP	AAA	22	3	2	0	7	7	35^2	27	1	17	34	4.3	8.6	70%	.283	1.23	1.51	3.64	3.93	0.9
2010	COL	MLB	22	9	11	0	28	21	137^1	114	10	61	138	4.0	9.0	47%	.285	1.27	3.28	3.57	4.79	1.3
2011	COL	MLB	23	11	14	0	31	31	194	168	20	87	150	4.0	7.0	57%	.262	1.31	3.62	4.20	5.01	1.8
2012	MOD	A+	24	0	1	0	1	1	2^1	7	0	0	1	0.0	3.9	33%	.583	3.00	19.29	2.96	4.78	0.0
2012	TUL	AA	24	0	1	0	2	2	9	9	1	2	7	2.0	7.0	64%	.296	1.22	6.00	3.84	7.42	-0.2
2012	CSP	AAA	24	1	1	0	2	2	13^2	10	1	5	5	3.3	3.3	62%	.205	1.10	2.63	4.98	7.18	0.0
2012	COL	MLB	24	3	5	0	14	14	69	80	10	32	45	4.2	5.9	40%	.311	1.62	4.43	5.19	5.40	0.9
2013	*COL*	*MLB*	*25*	*5*	*5*	*0*	*15*	*15*	*86^2*	*80*	*9*	*36*	*71*	*3.8*	*7.3*	*54%*	*.296*	*1.34*	*4.38*	*4.16*	*4.76*	*0.7*

Chacin appeared to break out in the first half of 2011, then struggled after the All-Star break and didn't find himself again until August of last year. Demoted to Triple-A on May 1 after five starts, Chacin revealed that his arm had been hurting since spring training. The Rockies instead placed him on the DL due to a nerve impingement in his right pectoral area. Four months later, he returned to the big-league rotation with improved velocity. He also ditched his curveball for a slider that put less stress on the pectoral muscle. Chacin gave up a lot of fly balls and struggled against lefties in 2012, two areas in which he must improve to succeed.

Tyler Chatwood

Born: **12/16/1989** Age: **23**
Bats: **R** Throws: **R** Height: **6' 1"** Weight: **185**
Breakout: **16%** Improve: **56%** Collapse: **19%**
Attrition: **13%** MLB: **88%**

Comparables:
Greg Maddux,Geremi Gonzalez,Gary Gentry

YEAR	TEAM	LVL	AGE	W	L	SV	G	GS	IP	H	HR	BB	SO	BB9	SO9	GB%	BABIP	WHIP	ERA	FIP	FRA	WARP
2010	RCU	A+	20	8	3	0	14	13	81^1	71	6	36	70	4.0	7.7	64%	.294	1.32	1.77	4.37	4.75	0.9
2010	ARK	AA	20	4	6	0	12	12	68^1	72	3	27	36	3.6	4.7	53%	.303	1.45	3.82	3.96	5.28	-0.4
2010	SLC	AAA	20	1	0	0	1	1	5^2	9	1	0	3	0.0	4.7	39%	.364	1.58	6.32	4.81	4.22	0.1
2011	SLC	AAA	21	1	2	0	4	4	16	21	2	11	11	6.2	6.2	47%	.353	2.00	5.06	6.47	6.88	0.1
2011	ANA	MLB	21	6	11	0	27	25	142	166	14	71	74	4.5	4.7	48%	.325	1.67	4.75	4.93	5.65	-1.1
2012	TUL	AA	22	1	1	0	4	4	24	17	2	7	22	2.6	8.2	67%	.242	1.00	3.00	3.41	4.06	0.4
2012	CSP	AAA	22	0	2	0	9	9	37^1	52	2	19	31	4.6	7.5	59%	.394	1.90	5.79	4.39	4.98	1.0
2012	COL	MLB	22	5	6	1	19	12	64^2	74	9	33	41	4.6	5.7	58%	.308	1.65	5.43	5.21	6.19	-0.3
2013	*COL*	*MLB*	*23*	*4*	*7*	*0*	*16*	*16*	*84*	*97*	*11*	*44*	*52*	*4.7*	*5.6*	*51%*	*.326*	*1.68*	*6.09*	*5.24*	*6.61*	*-0.8*

Chatwood, the Angels' 2008 second-round pick, came to Colorado in the Iannetta trade. He battled command issues and showed little growth from his rookie season. Part of the problem was that he kept bouncing from level to level and from role to role. When he returned to the big club for good in August, it was in his more familiar starting role and he pitched well. If Chatwood continues to attack hitters the way he did at the end of 2012, he could be effective at the back of a rotation, although it might not happen right away.

Jorge De La Rosa

Born: **4/5/1981** Age: **32**
Bats: **L** Throws: **L** Height: **6' 2"** Weight: **215**
Breakout: **15%** Improve: **65%** Collapse: **16%**
Attrition: **5%** MLB: **84%**

Comparables:
Steve Carlton,Ted Lilly,David Cone

YEAR	TEAM	LVL	AGE	W	L	SV	G	GS	IP	H	HR	BB	SO	BB9	SO9	GB%	BABIP	WHIP	ERA	FIP	FRA	WARP
2010	CSP	AAA	29	1	2	0	3	3	14^{2}	17	1	4	15	2.4	9.2	59%	.372	1.43	5.51	3.24	5.06	0.4
2010	COL	MLB	29	8	7	0	20	20	121^{2}	105	15	55	113	4.1	8.4	54%	.278	1.32	4.22	4.33	5.27	0.8
2011	COL	MLB	30	5	2	0	10	10	59	48	4	22	52	3.4	7.9	46%	.267	1.19	3.51	3.33	4.07	0.8
2012	GJR	Rk	31	0	0	0	1	1	3	3	0	0	5	0.0	15.0	29%	.429	1.00	0.00	1.10	-4.77	0.0
2012	MOD	A+	31	0	0	0	2	2	5^{2}	7	0	3	7	4.8	11.1	65%	.412	1.76	4.76	2.93	2.45	0.3
2012	TUL	AA	31	0	0	0	2	2	5	8	0	3	5	5.4	9.0	53%	.471	2.20	9.00	3.08	4.02	0.1
2012	CSP	AAA	31	0	1	0	2	2	6^{2}	9	3	3	5	4.1	6.8	38%	.286	1.80	9.45	9.82	10.05	-0.2
2012	COL	MLB	31	0	2	0	3	3	10^{2}	17	5	2	6	1.7	5.1	36%	.300	1.78	9.28	8.67	8.02	-0.3
2013	*COL*	*MLB*	*32*	*2*	*3*	*0*	*7*	*7*	*37*	*35*	*4*	*15*	*35*	*3.7*	*8.6*	*47%*	*.316*	*1.36*	*4.61*	*3.93*	*5.01*	*0.2*

After undergoing Tommy John surgery in June 2011, De La Rosa had a long road back to the big leagues. He made a few rehab starts in May and June but was shut down as a precautionary measure because of "forearm tightness." In September, he reached 94 mph with his fastball during a rehab start and said, "I am throwing normal, throwing all my pitches. I am feeling strong with no pain. I am ready." De La Rosa's three starts for the big club were horrible, but at least he was out there. He has given the Rockies 13 starts and a 4.39 ERA for $19.5 million during the first two years of a contract that culminates in an $11 million player option for 2013.

Edgmer Escalona

Born: **10/6/1986** Age: **26**
Bats: **R** Throws: **R** Height: **6' 5"** Weight: **215**
Breakout: **31%** Improve: **51%** Collapse: **16%**
Attrition: **17%** MLB: **83%**

Comparables:
Warner Madrigal,Shawn Kelley,Mike Henneman

YEAR	TEAM	LVL	AGE	W	L	SV	G	GS	IP	H	HR	BB	SO	BB9	SO9	GB%	BABIP	WHIP	ERA	FIP	FRA	WARP
2010	CSP	AAA	23	3	5	1	57	0	69	66	17	32	74	4.2	9.7	37%	.274	1.42	6.00	6.21	6.76	0.1
2010	COL	MLB	23	0	0	0	5	0	6	4	0	4	2	6.0	3.0	30%	.200	1.33	1.50	4.44	4.01	0.1
2011	CSP	AAA	24	3	1	1	34	0	39^{2}	35	4	11	40	2.5	9.1	33%	.264	1.16	3.18	4.14	4.59	0.7
2011	COL	MLB	24	0	0	0	14	0	25^{2}	17	3	7	14	2.5	4.9	37%	.187	0.94	1.75	4.24	4.61	0.3
2012	CSP	AAA	25	3	3	5	32	0	40	37	2	17	40	3.8	9.0	44%	.315	1.35	2.92	3.67	3.23	1.3
2012	COL	MLB	25	0	1	0	22	0	22^{1}	23	5	7	21	2.8	8.5	37%	.286	1.34	6.04	5.24	5.78	-0.1
2013	*COL*	*MLB*	*26*	*1*	*1*	*0*	*30*	*0*	*37*	*36*	*6*	*13*	*31*	*3.3*	*7.6*	*41%*	*.298*	*1.33*	*4.63*	*4.69*	*5.04*	*0.1*

Escalona enjoyed his second straight strong season at Colorado Springs but didn't fare as well in multiple stints with the big club. Demoted to Triple-A in May after seven appearances, the right-hander from Venezuela returned in August and was hammered in two more outings before being shut down for a month with right elbow inflammation and an 11.88 ERA. Escalona, who backs a mid-90s fastball with a hard slider, pitched much better after coming off the DL in September. Health-permitting, he should have value in middle relief.

Jeff Francis

Born: **1/8/1981** Age: **32**
Bats: **L** Throws: **L** Height: **6' 6"** Weight: **220**
Breakout: **12%** Improve: **66%** Collapse: **24%**
Attrition: **8%** MLB: **87%**

Comparables:
John Smiley,Mark Buehrle,Odalis Perez

YEAR	TEAM	LVL	AGE	W	L	SV	G	GS	IP	H	HR	BB	SO	BB9	SO9	GB%	BABIP	WHIP	ERA	FIP	FRA	WARP
2010	TUL	AA	29	0	0	0	2	2	11^{2}	11	1	2	5	1.5	3.8	55%	.270	1.11	1.54	4.20	5.38	0.0
2010	CSP	AAA	29	0	0	0	1	1	3	1	0	1	3	3.0	9.0	33%	.167	0.67	0.00	2.58	2.95	0.1
2010	COL	MLB	29	4	6	0	20	19	104^{1}	119	11	23	67	2.0	5.8	50%	.320	1.36	5.00	3.91	4.89	1.3
2011	KCA	MLB	30	6	16	0	31	31	183	224	19	39	91	1.9	4.5	49%	.316	1.44	4.82	4.14	4.93	0.6
2012	LOU	AAA	31	3	6	0	12	12	77^{1}	84	6	18	65	2.1	7.6	53%	.336	1.32	3.72	3.22	4.73	0.3
2012	COL	MLB	31	6	7	0	24	24	113	145	15	22	76	1.8	6.1	52%	.341	1.48	5.58	4.31	4.52	1.6
2013	*COL*	*MLB*	*32*	*7*	*9*	*0*	*23*	*23*	*127^{2}*	*150*	*17*	*30*	*81*	*2.1*	*5.7*	*47%*	*.328*	*1.40*	*5.17*	*4.37*	*5.62*	*-0.0*

After being released by the Reds on June 4, Francis signed with the Rockies, who originally took him with the ninth pick of the 2002 draft. Despite his late arrival, he led the club in innings pitched with the lowest total by a team leader since 1891. That would be during the Benjamin Harrison administration, for those keeping score. Shoulder injuries have slowed Francis' fastball, but he set a good example for young Rockies pitchers by getting ahead in counts and keeping hitters off-balance. Francis has been vulnerable to right-handed batters in recent years but is a strike-throwing machine against lefties, who haven't drawn a walk off him since August 2011.

Will Harris

Born: **8/28/1984** Age: **28**
Bats: **R** Throws: **R** Height: **6' 5"** Weight: **225**
Breakout: **21%** Improve: **38%** Collapse: **36%**
Attrition: **7%** MLB: **87%**

Comparables:
Heath Bell,Ron Davis,Mike Schooler

YEAR	TEAM	LVL	AGE	W	L	SV	G	GS	IP	H	HR	BB	SO	BB9	SO9	GB%	BABIP	WHIP	ERA	FIP	FRA	WARP
2011	MOD	A+	26	3	2	0	33	0	47	45	4	21	55	4.0	10.5	44%	.217	1.40	5.55	4.06	3.72	0.7
2012	TUL	AA	27	2	1	1	31	0	34^{1}	26	2	12	46	3.1	12.1	53%	.307	1.11	2.62	2.49	2.88	0.8
2012	CSP	AAA	27	2	0	0	13	0	17^{2}	9	0	1	20	0.5	10.2	64%	.214	0.57	1.02	1.57	2.49	0.6
2012	COL	MLB	27	1	1	0	20	0	17^{2}	27	3	6	19	3.1	9.7	36%	.400	1.87	8.15	4.38	6.00	-0.1
2013	*COL*	*MLB*	*28*	*2*	*1*	*0*	*31*	*0*	*37*	*36*	*5*	*13*	*36*	*3.2*	*8.7*	*48%*	*.320*	*1.33*	*4.38*	*4.06*	*4.76*	*0.2*

Harris, taken by the Rockies in the ninth round of the 2006 draft out of Louisiana State, has been a hit-prevention machine in six minor-league seasons despite pitching in tough environments. He was anything but that in his first shot at the big leagues. Lefties hit him hard, and righties hit him harder. Harris, who attended the same high school as Xavier Paul, features a low-90s fastball and a slow curve. As a right-hander with so-so velocity, his command must be outstanding—as it has been in the minors—for him to succeed.

Wilton Lopez
Born: **7/19/1983** Age: **29**
Bats: **R** Throws: **R** Height: **6' 1"** Weight: **200**
Breakout: **29%** Improve: **54%** Collapse: **27%**
Attrition: **21%** MLB: **85%**
Comparables:
Dave Schmidt, Brandon Lyon, Chris Reitsma

YEAR	TEAM	LVL	AGE	W	L	SV	G	GS	IP	H	HR	BB	SO	BB9	SO9	GB%	BABIP	WHIP	ERA	FIP	FRA	WARP
2010	ROU	AAA	26	2	1	0	3	0	5	8	0	0	2	0.0	3.6	55%	.400	1.60	5.40	2.78	4.38	0.1
2010	HOU	MLB	26	5	2	1	68	0	67	66	4	5	50	0.7	6.7	56%	.305	1.06	2.96	2.61	3.58	0.9
2011	HOU	MLB	27	2	6	0	73	0	71	72	6	18	56	2.3	7.1	57%	.307	1.27	2.79	3.40	3.71	0.8
2012	OKL	AAA	28	0	0	0	2	0	2	4	2	0	1	0.0	4.5	70%	.250	2.00	13.50	15.67	74.93	-0.2
2012	HOU	MLB	28	6	3	10	64	0	66^1	61	4	8	54	1.1	7.3	57%	.297	1.04	2.17	2.74	3.81	0.8
2013	*COL*	*MLB*	*29*	*3*	*1*	*3*	*57*	*0*	*57^2*	*64*	*7*	*11*	*39*	*1.8*	*6.1*	*55%*	*.327*	*1.31*	*4.62*	*4.00*	*5.02*	*0.2*

Ignoring when he was pitching hurt early in 2011, Lopez has posted Eckersley-esque walk rates the past three seasons, and uses much the same playbook as the Hall of Famer. No one has mused about using Lopez in the rotation, but he has three quality pitches, all centered around a groundball-inducing sinking two-seam fastball. When needed, he can chuck the four-seamer in the mid-90s, and his changeup worked particularly well in 2012, a fact to which left-handed hitters will attest. Unlike Eck, his mix of pitches makes stealing a terrible risk: four allowed and five thieves caught so far. Acquired from Houston in December, Lopez gives the Rockies a durable arm whose ability to keep the ball down should serve him well in setting up Betancourt.

Tyler Matzek
Born: **10/19/1990** Age: **22**
Bats: **L** Throws: **L** Height: **6' 4"** Weight: **210**
Breakout: **35%** Improve: **57%** Collapse: **17%**
Attrition: **13%** MLB: **85%**
Comparables:
Franklin Morales, Rich Harden, Pete Falcone

YEAR	TEAM	LVL	AGE	W	L	SV	G	GS	IP	H	HR	BB	SO	BB9	SO9	GB%	BABIP	WHIP	ERA	FIP	FRA	WARP
2010	ASH	A	19	5	1	0	18	18	89^1	62	6	62	88	6.2	8.9	40%	.259	1.39	2.92	4.65	5.91	0.0
2011	ASH	A	20	5	4	0	12	12	64	45	3	50	74	7.0	10.4	42%	.295	1.48	4.36	4.26	5.84	0.5
2011	MOD	A+	20	0	3	0	10	10	33	34	5	46	37	12.5	10.1	42%	.307	2.42	9.82	8.04	6.05	0.2
2012	MOD	A+	21	6	8	0	28	28	142^1	134	7	95	153	6.0	9.7	44%	.322	1.61	4.62	4.41	4.74	1.6
2013	*COL*	*MLB*	*22*	*2*	*4*	*0*	*9*	*9*	*43^1*	*44*	*6*	*32*	*36*	*6.6*	*7.5*	*40%*	*.318*	*1.75*	*6.05*	*5.55*	*6.57*	*-0.4*

Matzek, the Rockies' first-round pick in 2009, recorded a career high in innings and lowered (!) his walk rate to 6.0 per 9 innings. Mechanical issues have affected his control and velocity in the past, with things getting so bad in 2011 that he left his team for a stretch to try to work out the kinks with his former high school pitching coach. Matzek's fastball command could be better, and he sometimes forgets about his secondary pitches, but he drew praise for an improved mental approach last year. As with many young pitchers, consistency is an issue, such as when he walked eight batters in four innings on June 4 after walking five over his previous three starts. The stuff is there, but this could take a while.

Juan Nicasio
Born: **8/31/1986** Age: **26**
Bats: **R** Throws: **R** Height: **6' 4"** Weight: **200**
Breakout: **28%** Improve: **59%** Collapse: **20%**
Attrition: **19%** MLB: **98%**
Comparables:
Kevin Millwood, Scott Baker, Jordan Zimmermann

YEAR	TEAM	LVL	AGE	W	L	SV	G	GS	IP	H	HR	BB	SO	BB9	SO9	GB%	BABIP	WHIP	ERA	FIP	FRA	WARP
2011	TUL	AA	24	5	1	0	9	9	56^2	48	3	10	63	1.6	10.0	43%	.320	1.02	2.22	2.37	2.21	1.2
2011	COL	MLB	24	4	4	0	13	13	71^2	73	8	18	58	2.3	7.3	47%	.304	1.27	4.14	3.62	4.17	1.3
2012	COL	MLB	25	2	3	0	11	11	58	72	7	22	54	3.4	8.4	41%	.376	1.62	5.28	4.03	4.66	0.8
2013	*COL*	*MLB*	*26*	*3*	*4*	*0*	*9*	*9*	*53^1*	*58*	*7*	*17*	*42*	*2.8*	*7.1*	*44%*	*.329*	*1.41*	*4.92*	*4.29*	*5.35*	*0.1*

Nicasio made good on his vow to return from a broken neck sustained when he was hit by a line drive in August 2011. His fastball ran in the mid-90s, same as before the injury, but his change and slider continued to be inconsistent. Nicasio pitched a gem in his season debut at Houston and again at Dodger Stadium about five weeks later, but his other nine starts ranged from passable to awful. His season ended early again, this time because of an injury sustained in June that required microfracture surgery a month later to remove four bone chips underneath the left kneecap. He is expected to be ready for spring training. Wavering command of secondary pitches may make him a better fit for the bullpen.

Adam Ottavino
Born: **11/22/1985** Age: **27**
Bats: **R** Throws: **R** Height: **6' 6"** Weight: **230**
Breakout: **30%** Improve: **51%** Collapse: **18%**
Attrition: **19%** MLB: **82%**
Comparables:
Ramon A. Ramirez,Steve Busby,Kevin Hart

YEAR	TEAM	LVL	AGE	W	L	SV	G	GS	IP	H	HR	BB	SO	BB9	SO9	GB%	BABIP	WHIP	ERA	FIP	FRA	WARP
2010	MEM	AAA	24	5	3	0	9	9	47^{2}	43	5	12	43	2.3	8.1	51%	.286	1.15	3.96	4.09	4.43	0.8
2010	SLN	MLB	24	0	2	0	5	3	22^{1}	37	5	9	12	3.6	4.8	37%	.381	2.06	8.46	6.15	5.81	-0.2
2011	MEM	AAA	25	7	8	0	26	25	141	154	14	71	120	4.5	7.7	—	.329	1.60	4.85	5.07	5.52	0.0
2012	CSP	AAA	26	0	0	0	13	0	19^{2}	22	2	7	25	3.2	11.4	44%	.364	1.47	3.20	3.51	3.34	0.6
2012	COL	MLB	26	5	1	0	53	0	79	76	9	34	81	3.9	9.2	49%	.313	1.39	4.56	3.90	4.37	0.9
2013	*COL*	*MLB*	*27*	*2*	*2*	*1*	*28*	*4*	*59^{2}*	*63*	*8*	*26*	*49*	*3.9*	*7.4*	*45%*	*.322*	*1.49*	*5.32*	*4.61*	*5.78*	*-0.2*

Ottavino is a converted starter who saw his strikeout rate soar in his new role. The Cardinals' first-round pick in 2006 was used primarily in low-leverage situations after being claimed on waivers by the Rockies in April. He had no trouble with Coors Field and, except for a three-game stretch in mid-September that caused his ERA to jump more than a full run, pitched well in the second half. Shoulder issues and inconsistent off-speed stuff have held him back in the past, but he had good health for a second straight year, and changing speeds is less of a concern out of the bullpen. If his arm continues to hold up, he could have a nice career as a reliever.

Josh Outman
Born: **9/14/1984** Age: **28**
Bats: **L** Throws: **L** Height: **6' 2"** Weight: **185**
Breakout: **21%** Improve: **52%** Collapse: **25%**
Attrition: **15%** MLB: **85%**
Comparables:
Manny Parra,Britt Burns,Steve Carlton

YEAR	TEAM	LVL	AGE	W	L	SV	G	GS	IP	H	HR	BB	SO	BB9	SO9	GB%	BABIP	WHIP	ERA	FIP	FRA	WARP
2011	SAC	AAA	26	8	3	0	17	17	78^{1}	77	7	47	72	5.4	8.3	—	.310	1.58	3.91	4.98	5.42	0.0
2011	OAK	MLB	26	3	5	0	13	9	58^{1}	62	4	23	35	3.5	5.4	42%	.302	1.46	3.70	3.94	3.90	0.5
2012	MOD	A+	27	0	0	0	1	1	1	0	0	0	1	0.0	9.0	1.%	.000	0.00	0.00	1.81	2.52	0.0
2012	TUL	AA	27	2	5	0	14	11	69^{1}	64	4	30	71	3.9	9.2	54%	.330	1.36	3.63	3.41	3.84	0.9
2012	CSP	AAA	27	0	0	0	2	0	2	1	0	0	1	0.0	4.5	83%	.167	0.50	0.00	2.67	4.93	0.0
2012	COL	MLB	27	1	3	0	27	7	40^{2}	47	7	20	40	4.4	8.9	49%	.339	1.65	8.19	4.88	5.41	0.1
2013	*COL*	*MLB*	*28*	*3*	*4*	*0*	*19*	*10*	*58*	*60*	*7*	*23*	*46*	*3.5*	*7.2*	*44%*	*.319*	*1.43*	*4.86*	*4.37*	*5.28*	*0.2*

Outman, who came to the Rockies with Moscoso in the Seth Smith deal, throws hard for a lefty. The problem is that his pitches either catch too much plate or not enough. He missed the start of 2012 due to a right oblique strain incurred as a result of food poisoning and, uh, the various bodily functions it induces. When healthy, he pitched better out of the bullpen than as a starter and wasn't intimidated by Coors Field. Outman has been much more effective against lefties (514 OPS) than righties (837 OPS) in his brief big-league tenure. If a team had him work one inning at a time, throwing only fastballs and sliders, he might have a career.

Drew Pomeranz
Born: **11/22/1988** Age: **24**
Bats: **R** Throws: **L** Height: **6' 6"** Weight: **230**
Breakout: **28%** Improve: **65%** Collapse: **15%**
Attrition: **11%** MLB: **95%**
Comparables:
Brett Cecil,Matt Garza,Wade Davis

YEAR	TEAM	LVL	AGE	W	L	SV	G	GS	IP	H	HR	BB	SO	BB9	SO9	GB%	BABIP	WHIP	ERA	FIP	FRA	WARP
2011	KIN	A+	22	3	2	0	15	15	77	56	2	32	95	3.7	11.1	52%	.299	1.14	1.87	2.39	2.89	1.6
2011	AKR	AA	22	0	1	0	3	3	14	10	1	6	17	3.9	10.9	26%	.227	1.14	2.57	3.20	4.23	0.1
2011	TUL	AA	22	1	0	0	2	2	10	2	0	0	7	0.0	6.3	17%	.000	0.20	0.00	1.98	2.79	0.1
2011	COL	MLB	22	2	1	0	4	4	18^{1}	19	0	5	13	2.5	6.4	50%	.328	1.31	5.40	2.56	3.14	0.5
2012	TUL	AA	23	0	0	0	1	1	4	4	0	1	4	2.2	9.0	61%	.308	1.25	0.00	2.78	-8.78	0.0
2012	CSP	AAA	23	4	4	0	9	9	46^{2}	52	2	20	46	3.9	8.9	56%	.347	1.54	2.51	3.54	4.46	1.2
2012	COL	MLB	23	2	9	0	22	22	96^{2}	97	14	46	83	4.3	7.7	45%	.289	1.48	4.93	4.85	5.03	1.2
2013	*COL*	*MLB*	*24*	*5*	*7*	*0*	*19*	*19*	*90*	*88*	*11*	*38*	*79*	*3.8*	*7.9*	*47%*	*.313*	*1.40*	*4.65*	*4.30*	*5.05*	*0.6*

Pomeranz, a first-round pick of the Indians in 2010 who came over in the Jimenez trade, saw his rookie season sabotaged by injury and inconsistency. Bad mechanics in spring caused a dip in velocity and led to a May 11 demotion to Triple-A. Recalled again in July, he followed two brilliant starts with more inefficiency, averaging 18.4 pitches per inning over his final 15 starts. Minor arm (left thumb, forearm, and biceps) and leg (right hip and quad) ailments dogged him throughout the year. Pomeranz has terrific stuff but must keep his mechanics clean, gain consistency with his secondary pitches, and resolve at-bats more quickly if he is to succeed.

Daniel Rosenbaum
Born: **10/10/1987** Age: **25**
Bats: **R** Throws: **L** Height: **6' 2"** Weight: **210**
Breakout: **33%** Improve: **59%** Collapse: **19%**
Attrition: **21%** MLB: **91%**
Comparables:
Carl Pavano,Tobi Stoner,Mitchell Boggs

YEAR	TEAM	LVL	AGE	W	L	SV	G	GS	IP	H	HR	BB	SO	BB9	SO9	GB%	BABIP	WHIP	ERA	FIP	FRA	WARP
2011	POT	A+	23	6	5	0	20	19	132	113	4	41	108	2.8	7.4	58%	.285	1.17	2.59	3.08	4.36	0.9
2011	HAR	AA	23	3	1	0	6	6	39^{1}	27	0	11	27	2.5	6.2	76%	.222	0.97	2.29	3.03	4.66	0.1
2012	HAR	AA	24	8	10	0	26	26	155^{1}	164	8	39	99	2.3	5.7	62%	.315	1.31	3.94	3.41	4.83	1.1
2013	*COL*	*MLB*	*25*	*2*	*4*	*0*	*8*	*8*	*45^{2}*	*53*	*6*	*19*	*25*	*3.7*	*5.0*	*55%*	*.321*	*1.58*	*5.87*	*5.06*	*6.38*	*-0.4*

Selected in this offseason's Rule 5 draft, Rosenbaum overcomes fringy velocity with a sharp cutter, good curveball, and excellent control—a skill set that reminds some evaluators of another former Nationals prospect, Tommy Milone. Coors Field is not an ideal landing spot for the lefty's contact-dependent style, but he generates abundant groundballs and should have an opportunity to secure a spot in Colorado's fluid rotation. With a 5.8 K/9 in nearly 200 innings above A-ball, Rosenbaum won't ever be more than a fourth starter, but at a cost of $50,000, he was a nice find for Dan O'Dowd.

Jonathan Sanchez
Born: **11/19/1982** Age: **30**
Bats: **L** Throws: **L** Height: **6' 1"** Weight: **200**
Breakout: **31%** Improve: **60%** Collapse: **16%**
Attrition: **17%** MLB: **86%**
Comparables:
Rudy May, Rich Hill, Jorge De La Rosa

YEAR	TEAM	LVL	AGE	W	L	SV	G	GS	IP	H	HR	BB	SO	BB9	SO9	GB%	BABIP	WHIP	ERA	FIP	FRA	WARP
2010	SFN	MLB	27	13	9	0	34	33	193^1	142	21	96	205	4.5	9.5	41%	.252	1.23	3.07	4.03	4.09	2.2
2011	SJO	A+	28	0	0	0	1	1	2^2	6	1	2	3	6.8	10.1	–	.500	3.00	20.25	8.83	9.59	0.0
2011	FRE	AAA	28	1	0	0	2	2	11	10	1	5	13	4.1	10.6	35%	.360	1.36	3.27	3.97	4.07	0.2
2011	SFN	MLB	28	4	7	0	19	19	101^1	80	9	66	102	5.9	9.1	45%	.272	1.44	4.26	4.27	4.64	0.3
2012	OMA	AAA	29	1	1	0	3	3	13^1	14	5	7	13	4.7	8.8	30%	.257	1.58	6.75	8.39	9.47	-0.4
2012	COL	MLB	29	0	3	0	3	3	11^1	17	3	9	9	7.1	7.1	33%	.389	2.29	9.53	7.37	7.76	-0.2
2012	KCA	MLB	29	1	6	0	12	12	53^1	65	8	44	36	7.4	6.1	42%	.322	2.04	7.76	6.40	6.79	-0.8
2013	*COL*	*MLB*	*30*	*4*	*5*	*0*	*14*	*14*	*73^2*	*69*	*10*	*38*	*71*	*4.7*	*8.7*	*42%*	*.308*	*1.46*	*4.98*	*4.58*	*5.42*	*0.1*

Like Oliver Perez and Dontrelle Willis before him, Sanchez is left-handed and used to be good. Colorado acquired Sanchez in July but shut him down after three starts due to left biceps inflammation that previously had cost him five weeks in May and June. Sanchez doesn't throw as hard as he once did, and his walk rate keeps rising while his whiff rate keeps falling. Last year he added allowing hits and homers to his increasingly volatile bag of tricks. Sanchez hasn't been effective against right-handed hitters since 2010, so maybe he can reinvent himself as a reliever à la Perez. The other option is to keep riding the D-Train into oblivion.

Rob Scahill
Born: **2/15/1987** Age: **26**
Bats: **L** Throws: **R** Height: **6' 3"** Weight: **220**
Breakout: **18%** Improve: **52%** Collapse: **12%**
Attrition: **18%** MLB: **88%**
Comparables:
Michael O'Connor, Tom Gorzelanny, Brian Burres

YEAR	TEAM	LVL	AGE	W	L	SV	G	GS	IP	H	HR	BB	SO	BB9	SO9	GB%	BABIP	WHIP	ERA	FIP	FRA	WARP
2010	MOD	A+	23	10	7	0	27	27	156	173	9	59	140	3.4	8.1	48%	.342	1.49	4.73	4.02	5.11	1.2
2011	TUL	AA	24	12	11	0	27	26	160^2	164	12	60	104	3.4	5.8	48%	.307	1.39	3.92	4.27	4.96	0.8
2012	CSP	AAA	25	9	11	0	29	29	152	168	11	74	159	4.4	9.4	54%	.355	1.59	5.68	4.11	5.15	3.2
2012	COL	MLB	25	0	0	0	6	0	8^2	7	0	3	4	3.1	4.2	50%	.269	1.15	1.04	3.25	3.76	0.2
2013	*COL*	*MLB*	*26*	*3*	*4*	*0*	*10*	*10*	*53*	*59*	*6*	*25*	*38*	*4.2*	*6.5*	*49%*	*.328*	*1.57*	*5.63*	*4.65*	*6.12*	*-0.3*

Scahill, an eighth-round pick of the Rockies in 2009 out of Bradley University (Hall of Fame outfielder Kirby Puckett, former Rockies right-hander Bryan Rekar), works with a mid-90s fastball that sinks and generates groundballs. He hasn't enjoyed much success as a starter in the minors. If he doesn't improve his ability to change speeds, he could have a future in the bullpen.

LINEOUTS

HITTERS

PLAYER	TEAM	LVL	AGE	PA	R	2B	3B	HR	RBI	BB	SO	SB-CS	AVG/OBP/SLG	TAv	BABIP	BRR	FRAA	WARP
SS C. Adames	MOD	A+	20	485	59	21	7	2	54	47	82	4-2	.280/.352/.378	.272	.338	4.2	SS(90): -2.0	1.8
OF D. Cleary	ASH	A	22	277	47	13	2	4	35	30	43	14-7	.304/.389/.426	.281	.358	0.1	CF(47): 6.3, LF(4): -0.2	1.7
	MOD	A+	22	279	42	11	3	2	32	19	56	9-6	.277/.322/.368	.259	.342	-0.1	LF(36): -1.8, CF(9): 1.4	0.2
2B M. Dilone	DRO	Rk	18	261	45	19	6	1	37	30	24	15-7	.319/.396/.469	.305	.348	-0.4	–	0.0
RF K. Matthes	TUL	AA	25	368	44	18	2	17	40	22	80	6-2	.214/.273/.432	.248	.228	-1.4	RF(77): -4.5	-0.7
1B H. Riggins	ASH	A	22	379	63	23	0	19	76	37	104	8-5	.302/.388/.546	.300	.385	-2.4	1B(57): 0.3	1.4
C W. Rodriguez	GJR	Rk	18	183	26	14	1	2	27	13	23	1-1	.319/.370/.452	.292	.359	0	C(4): 0.1	0.2
C W. Swanner	ASH	A	20	372	60	24	1	16	61	38	101	3-2	.302/.385/.529	.307	.392	0.1	C(66): 2.4	2.0
OF M. White	GJR	Rk	18	203	30	5	3	4	18	29	72	6-5	.200/.322/.335	.263	.316	-1.6	LF(3): -0.1, CF(2): 0.2	-0.1

Christhian Adames, out of the Dominican Republic, is a solid defensive shortstop with passable on-base skills but no power or usable speed. **Delta Cleary**, the Rockies' 37th-round pick in 2008, has been slow to develop but enjoyed a strong season at two levels last year and actually performed much better on the road during his stay in hitter-friendly Asheville. **Miguel Dilone**, son of the former outfielder with the same name, has shown good on-base skills in two seasons but is very young and has yet to see action on the North American continent. **Kent Matthes**, the Rockies' fourth-round pick in 2009 out of the University of Alabama, is an old-for-his-level corner outfielder whose power declined and plate discipline remained atrocious on advancing to Double-A before a strained oblique ended his season in July. **Harold Riggins**, the Rockies' seventh-round pick in 2011 out of North Carolina State, has power to all fields but doesn't make enough contact and missed the season's final month due to a thumb injury. **Wilfredo Rodriguez** was Colorado's seventh-round pick in 2012 and held his own in his pro debut as one of the Pioneer League's younger players. **William Swanner**, a 15th-round pick in 2010, showed good power in his full-season debut (and it wasn't because of his home park), but questions about his ability to make contact and his defense behind the plate persist. **Max White**, the Rockies' second-round pick in 2012, is an athletic center fielder who is fast but whose raw approach at the plate caused him to be overmatched by older pitchers in his pro debut.

PITCHERS

PLAYER	TEAM	LVL	AGE	W	L	SV	IP	H	HR	BB	SO	BB9	SO9	GB%	BABIP	WHIP	ERA	FIP	FRA	WARP
C. Bergman	MOD	A+	24	16	5	0	162^2	161	16	37	121	2.0	6.7	41%	.295	1.22	3.65	4.34	4.96	1.6
A. Bibens-Dirkx	SYR	AAA	27	0	3	1	46^2	57	4	16	41	3.1	7.9	49%	.363	1.56	5.59	3.74	4.98	0.2
R. Brewer	ASH	A	24	1	3	3	60^1	38	5	15	76	2.2	11.3	45%	.241	0.88	2.09	3.03	3.61	1.8
E. Butler	GJR	Rk	21	7	1	0	67^2	59	1	13	55	1.7	7.3	60%	.287	1.06	2.13	3.58	1.85	0.5
I. Froneberger	MOD	A+	23	7	4	10	76	67	1	39	78	4.6	9.2	48%	.312	1.39	2.84	3.55	3.56	1.5
J. Gardner	TUL	AA	24	8	8	1	138^1	129	13	39	99	2.5	6.4	60%	.265	1.21	3.97	4.18	5.42	0.0
A. Jorgenson	MOD	A+	26	1	0	16	29	23	1	7	41	2.2	12.7	39%	.314	1.03	1.86	2.26	1.96	1.1
L. Kensing	BRD	A+	29	1	1	0	5^1	1	0	4	1	6.8	1.7	71%	.071	0.94	1.69	5.27	11.66	-0.1
	ALT	AA	29	2	0	1	17^2	18	1	6	14	3.1	7.1	39%	.309	1.36	4.58	3.37	3.44	0.4
	IND	AAA	29	0	0	0	11	8	1	5	10	4.1	8.2	50%	.226	1.18	4.09	4.16	5.68	-0.1
J. Manship	ROC	AAA	27	6	3	0	80^1	79	5	35	52	3.9	5.8	55%	.311	1.42	2.91	4.02	5.33	0.1
	MIN	MLB	27	0	0	0	21^2	29	4	7	12	2.9	5.0	50%	.338	1.66	7.89	5.45	6.71	-0.3
J. Marquez	TAC	AAA	27	4	8	0	76^2	108	10	34	45	4.0	5.3	45%	.356	1.85	6.69	5.67	6.05	-0.2
M. McClendon	NAS	AAA	27	4	3	5	43	40	2	18	27	3.8	5.7	53%	.286	1.35	4.19	4.48	5.55	0.0
	MIL	MLB	27	0	0	0	14	20	1	5	4	3.2	2.6	54%	.339	1.79	6.43	5.21	6.18	-0.1
N. Schmidt	TUL	AA	26	5	3	0	82	74	9	15	73	1.6	8.0	43%	.284	1.09	3.29	3.66	4.11	1.1
	CSP	AAA	26	7	3	0	65	80	5	31	47	4.3	6.5	47%	.352	1.71	5.68	4.79	6.65	1.0
P. Tago	TRI	A-	19	2	7	0	72^1	68	4	39	37	4.9	4.6	59%	.269	1.48	5.47	5.05	7.23	-1.4
J. Williamson	TUL	AA	26	3	2	1	43^1	36	1	24	53	5.0	11.0	44%	.337	1.38	1.87	3.28	3.87	0.5
D. Winkler	ASH	A	22	11	10	0	145^1	152	16	47	136	2.9	8.4	43%	.322	1.37	4.46	4.56	5.20	1.7

Christian Bergman led the California League in wins, but Colorado's 24th-round pick in 2010 was old for the circuit and had trouble putting the ball past hitters. **Austin Bibens-Dirkx** has improved his control, and following a good showing in the Venezuelan Winter League, he has a shot to emerge as a useful big leaguer. **Russell Brewer**, the Rockies' 31st-round pick in 2010, dominated younger hitters despite pitching half his games in a bandbox and was especially tough on righties. **Eddie Butler**, taken by the Rockies out of Vanderbilt in the supplemental first round last year, pitched well in an offense-enhanced league in his debut, but he hasn't shown the ability to strike out batters despite good velocity and may eventually move to the bullpen. **Isaiah Froneberger**, Colorado's fourth-round pick in 2007, enjoyed his best season as a pro but was old for his level and has command issues. **Joe Gardner**, another part of the Jimenez deal, works with a low-90s sinker that induces a steady diet of grounders, but lackluster secondary pitches leave him vulnerable to left-handed hitters and may force a move to the bullpen. **Adam Jorgenson** took advantage of younger hitters—especially right-handers—in the California League for two months and change before a shoulder injury sabotaged his second half. Former second-round pick **Logan Kensing** hasn't pitched in the big leagues since 2009 but provides Triple-A depth to be used in the event of, say, consecutive doubleheaders or assorted post-apocalyptic needs. **Jeff Manship** has pitched in very small parts of four seasons with the Twins; can work as a starter or a reliever; and is the owner of a 3.47 career minor-league ERA, a 6.20 big-league ERA, and one of the all-time great last names. **Jeff Marquez** is a minor-league veteran who has had a couple cups of coffee but whose ineffectiveness in nearly 400 Triple-A innings trumps his status as a former first-round pick in the quest for that elusive third cup. After two years of relative success, **Mike McClendon**'s annual sinkerball clinic didn't go so well in Milwaukee last year, but the big righty is a handy guy to stash in Triple-A should an unforeseen bullpen emergency arise. **Nick Schmidt**, the Padres' first-round pick in 2007, came to Colorado in the Street trade and remained healthy enough to break triple digits in innings for the first time in his career but was hit hard in his initial exposure to Triple-A. **Peter Tago** has a good build and a loose arm but so far is more projection than production, working with a hard sinking fastball that misses the plate too often and bats not often enough. **Joey Williamson** went 22–3 from 2007 to 2009 before retiring at age 24, then returned in 2011 and could find a home in a big-league bullpen or provide insurance at Triple-A. **Daniel Winkler**, Colorado's 20th-round pick in 2011, has fringy stuff but survived in a tough hitting environment last year thanks to a good sinker and the ability to throw strikes.

MANAGER: WALT WEISS

Colorado signed former shortstop Walt Weiss to a one-year deal in November, replacing Jim Tracy, who left at season's end. Given Tracy's clash with a front office that wanted things done a specific way, it made sense for the team to hire someone more likely to buy in. Weiss, having served as a special assistant to Dan O'Dowd in the mid-aughties, fits the bill. He spent last season coaching the Regis Jesuit High School baseball team, and lest people snigger about his lack of clubhouse experience, press clippings were careful to note that he led the Raiders to Colorado's Class 5A semifinals. Weiss has a reputation for being quiet and reserved but is an intense competitor who cites Tony La Russa and Bobby Cox, for whom he played, as strong influences. Weiss has emphasized the importance of communication, being "real," and gaining the trust of players, which is often more important than a game-honed store of tactical wizardry—a fact borne out by the success of similarly inexperienced skippers Robin Ventura and Mike Matheny last year. Former Expos manager Tom Runnels will be on hand to dispense grizzled advice, while new hitting coach Dante Bichette will focus on getting his charges to produce away from Coors Field—an amusing thought, seeing as Bichette owns a career OPS 200 points higher at home than on the road.

Detroit Tigers

2012: BRIDESMAIDS

What happens with the best car on the track gets a shot of nitroglycerine? A team loaded with superstar talent signed Prince Fielder in the winter, revving up expectations, especially in a weak division. Detroit expected to run away with the Central and be legitimate World Series contenders, and a 9-3 start at the green flag fueled the fire. A 13-16 May left the Tigers at 24-27, but they topped .500 for good on July 7. They chased down the White Sox on September 25 and held on for good. So despite taking the long route, they ended up meeting expectations after all. A dynamic pitching staff then carried them to the World Series.

Lost in the shuffle of Miguel Cabrera's Triple Crown season was the fact that Justin Verlander essentially repeated his MVP and Cy Young season with a less fortunate win-loss record, Fielder transitioned to the AL brilliantly, Austin Jackson and Max Scherzer broke out, and Doug Fister's post-trade run from 2011 was legitimate. All of that superstar production allowed the Tigers to sustain a bevy of black holes: up the middle in the infield, two more on the corners in the outfield (save Andy Dirks' star turn as a part-timer, which was stunted by injury), and yet another at DH.

TIGERS PROSPECTUS

2012 W-L: 88-74, 1st in AL Central

Pythag	.537	12th	DER	.693	26th
RS/G	4.48	11th	B-Age	27.9	13th
RA/G	4.14	11th	P-Age	27.6	9th
TAv	.268	6th	Salary	$133.0	5th
BRR	-9.8	28th	M$/MW	$3.03	20th
TAv-P	.255	7th	DL Days	822	15th
FIP	3.58	2nd	DL WARP	4.7	9th

Three-Year Park Factors	
Overall	103
HR/RH	100
HR/LH	101
AVG/RH	105
AVG/LH	109

Comerica Park (2000)
Att. % of Capacity: 90.6% (5th)
Dim. 345, 370, 420, 365, 330

The Tigers offense kept spacious Comerica in the middle of the pack in homers and sixth in BABIP.

2013: POLE POSITION

Detroit rolls into the season in much the same enviable position as this time last year. This team is in full-throttle win-now mode and its moves will continue to reflect as much for the foreseeable future.

The champagne was barely dry in San Francisco's locker room before the World Series runners-up had already filled two of their biggest holes. Victor Martinez, whose injury spurred the Fielder signing, will return to fill a chasm at DH, a position for which only the Texas Rangers received less production in 2012. Meanwhile, Torii Hunter will plug the right-field gap. A full season of Omar Infante should also yield their best second-base production since Placido Polanco in 2009. And the team is hoping that regression from 2012's hitting stars will be offset by a return to prominence for Alex Avila and Jhonny Peralta, as well as a full season of Dirks.

The presence of Hunter and Infante also ameliorates the biggest team weakness: defense. Hunter relieves some of the burden on Jackson, and Infante could play without a glove and still add to the team's defensive output, compared to what the keystone has yielded recently. On the mound, there is still growth potential for Scherzer and volume potential for Fister, who was limited to 162 innings last year. That the Tigers could have such an effortless upgrade is no doubt a scary proposition for the rest of the American League.

The back end of the bullpen will feature at least one new face since the stopper, Jose Valverde, has left to seek new employment. At press time, rumors were swirling about who might fill the role, whether from within or via free agency.

The win-now mentality is why trade rumors continually swirl around 24-year-old Rick Porcello and the Tigers' top prospect, Nick Castellanos. Of the Tigers' key players, all are on the right side of 30 except for Martinez and Hunter, and the team made the World Series without either of them. When the guys on the short list for best pitcher and best hitter in all of baseball are on your roster, you're going to compete. When you surround them with other bona-fide stars, you're going to be a World Series frontrunner.

STATE OF THE ORGANIZATION: PIT ROAD

The earliest Detroit's stars can begin leaving is 2015 (Verlander and Scherzer) while the offensive core is intact until at least 2016. After over a decade of futility, from the early '90s to the mid-'00s, the team is now looking at the potential for a decade of prominence. The farm system is thin on depth, but the top guys carry high ceilings. There is also a group of tough-to-project youngsters in the system who could come of age just as the core starts to break up. If enough of them emerge as blue-chip prospects in the next year or two, they might bridge the gap nicely and lead to another bout of sustained success, or be moved to fortify the 2014-15 clubs. GM Dave Dombrowski and owner Mike Illitch have never been afraid to deal tomorrow's potential for today's certainty.

Dombrowski built this team from the bottom up starting in 2002. Should he last until his contract is up at the end of 2015, he will have had ample time to bring home a title. He is backed by a large pocketbook from Illitch, the Detroit lifer and pizza magnate who owns Little Caesar's. Illitch, 83, is desperate for a trip to victory lane, which no doubt makes Dombrowski's job somewhat easier when it comes to talent acquisition, but tougher considering the mounting pressure after a pair of pennants in the last seven years, but no championships.

A major advantage for the Tigers was nixed by the latest collective-bargaining agreement, as new rules now prevent teams from paying over slot. The Tigers can no longer freely throw Illitch's wallet at premium draftees who drop out of the first round because of signability concerns, health, or college plans. That advantage netted them Cameron Maybin, Porcello, and—most notably—Castellanos. (Unfortunately they weren't able to strike one final time in 2011, arguably the deepest first round ever, because their pick went to Boston after Detroit signed Victor Martinez.)

Power arms flood their system, but pitching development is the biggest "if" in baseball. The team will get a pick in the first round for the first time since 2010, perfect timing on the heels of trading three prospects in the Infante-Anibal Sanchez last July. A strong pick and careful development of their raw arms into blue chips will be the key to sustained success.

HITTERS

Alex Avila **C**
Born: **1/29/1987** Age: **26**
Bats: **L** Throws: **R** Height: **6' 0"**
Weight: **210** Breakout: **5%**
Improve: **46%** Collapse: **4%**
Attrition: **12%** MLB: **97%**
Comparables:
Chris Iannetta, Ed Bailey, Darrell Porter

YEAR	TEAM	LVL	AGE	PA	R	2B	3B	HR	RBI	BB	SO	SB	CS	AVG_OBP_SLG	TAv	BABIP	BRR	FRAA	WARP
2010	DET	MLB	23	333	28	12	0	7	31	36	71	2	2	.228/.316/.340	.231	.278	-2.7	C(98): -1.9	0.1
2011	DET	MLB	24	551	63	33	4	19	82	73	131	3	1	.295/.389/.506	.318	.366	2.8	C(133): 1.3, 3B(1): -0.1	6.0
2012	DET	MLB	25	434	42	21	2	9	48	61	104	2	0	.243/.352/.384	.260	.312	-1.4	C(113): -2.7	1.3
2013	*DET*	*MLB*	*26*	*432*	*52*	*20*	*2*	*13*	*51*	*53*	*102*	*2*	*1*	*.256/.350/.424*	*.273*	*.316*	*-0.4*	*C -1, 3B -0*	*2.4*

While all catchers take a beating behind the dish, Avila was listed as day-to-day with one ailment or another right from the start of the season, and he hit the disabled list for a spell in June. These nagging injuries noticeably sapped his power, resulting in a 10 percent drop in fly-ball rate to a career-low 30 percent, depressing his home-run total and slugging percentage. Even with his 2011 plate-appearance allotment, he would have hit only 11 home runs. His core skills remained intact, allowing him to be valuable to the team despite the severe power outage. A healthy Avila in 2013 will look a lot more like the 2011 version who made the All-Star team.

Quintin Berry **OF**
Born: **11/21/1984** Age: **28**
Bats: **L** Throws: **L** Height: **6' 1"**
Weight: **175** Breakout: **2%**
Improve: **50%** Collapse: **7%**
Attrition: **16%** MLB: **82%**
Comparables:
Mike Huff, Alex Cole, Adam Greenberg

YEAR	TEAM	LVL	AGE	PA	R	2B	3B	HR	RBI	BB	SO	SB	CS	AVG_OBP_SLG	TAv	BABIP	BRR	FRAA	WARP
2010	REA	AA	25	285	35	10	2	2	25	33	50	23	6	.210/.304/.294	.220	.246	1	CF(51): -1.1, LF(15): -1.5	-0.5
2010	SAN	AA	25	124	11	1	1	1	8	10	28	4	2	.209/.290/.264	.198	.268	0.5	LF(20): -2.5, CF(9): -1.4	-0.9
2011	CAR	AA	26	378	64	16	1	6	41	52	83	40	7	.297/.399/.409	.293	.384	0	--	0.0
2012	TOL	AAA	27	187	18	8	0	0	11	22	46	19	3	.270/.368/.321	.252	.377	0.3	CF(34): 0.7	0.2
2012	DET	MLB	27	330	44	10	6	2	29	25	80	21	0	.258/.330/.354	.253	.348	1.5	LF(64): 0.9, CF(22): 1.9	0.7
2013	*DET*	*MLB*	*28*	*274*	*33*	*9*	*3*	*2*	*18*	*22*	*66*	*16*	*2*	*.231/.302/.316*	*.224*	*.300*	*2.5*	*LF 0, CF -1*	*-0.1*

By season's end it became clear why Berry was a 27-year-old rookie. The Tigers were fortunate that he essentially mirrored his Triple-A production; most players experience some degradation upon arrival. He gave the team a speed element they were lacking, but the gains were more than offset by a punchless bat that featured a strikeout almost 25 percent of the time. Contact is a must when speed is your meal ticket, but Berry was among the worst on the team at putting bat on ball—a weakness the opposition exploited. Berry saw the second-most pitches in the zone on the team.

Brennan Boesch RF
Born: **4/12/1985** Age: **28**
Bats: **L** Throws: **L** Height: **6' 5"**
Weight: **235** Breakout: **1%**
Improve: **50%** Collapse: **4%**
Attrition: **17%** MLB: **94%**
Comparables:
Alex Rios,Xavier Nady,Joe Mather

YEAR	TEAM	LVL	AGE	PA	R	2B	3B	HR	RBI	BB	SO	SB	CS	AVG_OBP_SLG	TAv	BABIP	BRR	FRAA	WARP
2010	TOL	AAA	25	66	6	3	1	3	17	4	17	2	1	.379/.455/.621	.342	.500	-1.4	RF(13): -0.6, CF(1): 0.0	0.5
2010	DET	MLB	25	512	49	26	3	14	67	40	99	7	1	.256/.320/.416	.265	.297	-2.8	RF(79): 0.3, LF(44): 1.2	1.3
2011	DET	MLB	26	472	75	25	1	16	54	35	83	5	3	.283/.341/.458	.285	.315	-1.1	LF(57): 0.4, RF(51): 2.1	1.7
2012	DET	MLB	27	503	52	22	2	12	54	26	104	6	3	.240/.286/.372	.237	.284	1.1	RF(121): -4.6	-1.1
2013	*DET*	*MLB*	*28*	*466*	*51*	*22*	*3*	*14*	*56*	*32*	*94*	*6*	*2*	*.258/.315/.418*	*.258*	*.300*	*-0.1*	*RF -2, LF 1*	*0.8*

Doing less with more is never the way to go, yet that crystallizes Boesch's 2012 season. He regressed in every significant category, whether you are into back-of-the-baseball-card numbers or sabermetrics. Beating the ball into the ground half the time was bad enough, but pairing that with a career-worst 5 percent walk rate turned Boesch into a left-handed Jeff Francoeur. The front office still loves his power and his ability to hang in against lefties, but it will take a small miracle to get him 503 plate appearances again this year.

Miguel Cabrera 3B
Born: **4/18/1983** Age: **30**
Bats: **R** Throws: **R** Height: **6' 5"**
Weight: **240** Breakout: **1%**
Improve: **41%** Collapse: **1%**
Attrition: **7%** MLB: **98%**
Comparables:
George Brett,Eddie Mathews,Alex Rodriguez

YEAR	TEAM	LVL	AGE	PA	R	2B	3B	HR	RBI	BB	SO	SB	CS	AVG_OBP_SLG	TAv	BABIP	BRR	FRAA	WARP
2010	DET	MLB	27	648	111	45	1	38	126	89	95	3	3	.328/.420/.622	.352	.336	-1.4	1B(148): -4.3	6.6
2011	DET	MLB	28	688	111	48	0	30	105	108	89	2	1	.344/.448/.586	.355	.365	-2.7	1B(152): -11.8	5.9
2012	DET	MLB	29	697	109	40	0	44	139	66	98	4	1	.330/.393/.606	.332	.331	-5.5	3B(154): -2.3, 1B(2): -0.0	6.1
2013	*DET*	*MLB*	*30*	*653*	*95*	*37*	*2*	*34*	*109*	*72*	*104*	*3*	*1*	*.314/.392/.564*	*.327*	*.333*	*-0.9*	*3B -4, 1B 1*	*5.3*

The doomsday scenario of Cabrera moving to third base didn't come close to playing out as naysayers predicted. Instead of performing so badly at third that his offense would tank and he would have to move back to first, Cabrera kept his head above water in the field (and then some, depending on your metric of choice) en route to a Triple Crown and his first MVP award. Given that he had his lowest True Average in three years, we could see an *upturn* in his overall production next year—which is a scary thought. He truly is a legend in the making, and the only remaining question seems to be how on earth was he not invited to the 2008 and 2009 All-Star Games?

Ramon Cabrera C
Born: **11/5/1989** Age: **23**
Bats: **B** Throws: **R** Height: **5' 8"**
Weight: **202** Breakout: **10%**
Improve: **49%** Collapse: **6%**
Attrition: **16%** MLB: **90%**
Comparables:
Tim McCarver,Joe Azcue,Alex Trevino

YEAR	TEAM	LVL	AGE	PA	R	2B	3B	HR	RBI	BB	SO	SB	CS	AVG_OBP_SLG	TAv	BABIP	BRR	FRAA	WARP
2010	WVA	A	20	372	49	14	4	1	40	22	42	3	4	.269/.312/.342	.245	.301	-2	C(89): -0.9	0.3
2011	BRD	A+	21	379	46	25	4	3	53	38	29	5	1	.343/.410/.471	.312	.361	0	--	0.0
2012	ALT	AA	22	428	47	22	2	3	50	39	44	0	3	.276/.342/.367	.240	.305	-1.9	C(67): -0.1	-0.2
2013	*DET*	*MLB*	*23*	*250*	*19*	*10*	*2*	*2*	*22*	*13*	*39*	*0*	*0*	*.246/.285/.335*	*.219*	*.281*	*-0.3*	*C -0*	*-0.1*

You won't believe it, but this is Alex Cabrera's son. Despite having slugger in the bloodlines, the younger Cabrera's best skill is his excellent bat control. He offers little in the way of power, or any other tool. Most of his defensive attributes grade out as average, except for his weak arm. Short, stocky, switch-hitting, singles-dependent catchers usually waste away in the minors. Maybe Cabrera can do his father proud and become the new Brayan Pena.

Nick Castellanos RF
Born: **3/4/1992** Age: **21**
Bats: **R** Throws: **R** Height: **6' 5"**
Weight: **195** Breakout: **3%**
Improve: **51%** Collapse: **9%**
Attrition: **25%** MLB: **98%**
Comparables:
Aramis Ramirez,Brooks Robinson,Kevin Bell

YEAR	TEAM	LVL	AGE	PA	R	2B	3B	HR	RBI	BB	SO	SB	CS	AVG_OBP_SLG	TAv	BABIP	BRR	FRAA	WARP
2011	WMI	A	19	562	65	36	3	7	76	45	130	3	2	.312/.367/.436	.306	.402	-5.2	3B(40): -6.7	0.3
2012	LAK	A+	20	243	37	17	3	3	32	22	42	3	2	.405/.461/.553	.374	.486	0.2	3B(34): 0.8	2.3
2012	ERI	AA	20	341	35	15	1	7	25	14	76	5	4	.264/.296/.382	.218	.322	-3.7	RF(25): -1.7, 3B(11): -2.9	-1.5
2013	*DET*	*MLB*	*21*	*250*	*22*	*11*	*1*	*5*	*27*	*10*	*65*	*1*	*1*	*.254/.285/.376*	*.232*	*.325*	*-0.3*	*3B -0, RF 0*	*-0.2*

Pitchers couldn't get Castellanos out in High-A last year. He went hitless only five times in a 55-game run, never in back-to-back games, and in two of the five he reached via walk. He was brought up to Double-A, and some fans were clamoring for him to come all the way to the big-league club. The chorus grew louder after he hit .311 in his first two months at Double-A Erie, but his 791 OPS was a far cry from the 1014 of High-A. His walk rate evaporated to just 2 percent in that span, down from 9. He stumbled to the finish (.189/.250/.246 in 132 plate appearances spanning August and three games in September) and then looked worn out in the Arizona Fall League as well, though his tools remained evident. The team's system is thin, but Castellanos isn't the Tigers' top prospect just by virtue of that fact; he would be atop many organizational lists regardless of their depth. Blocked at third by Cabrera, his future position isn't set, but the Tigers have had him playing right field lately.

Tyler Collins **OF**
Born: 6/6/1990 Age: 23
Bats: L Throws: L Height: 6' 0"
Weight: 205 Breakout: 5%
Improve: 49% Collapse: 8%
Attrition: 11% MLB: 94%
Comparables:
Tim Raines,Dave Collins,Mike Lum

YEAR	TEAM	LVL	AGE	PA	R	2B	3B	HR	RBI	BB	SO	SB	CS	AVG_OBP_SLG	TAv	BABIP	BRR	FRAA	WARP
2011	ONE	A-	21	178	28	10	1	8	31	10	17	6	1	.313/.360/.534	.300	.307	0	--	0.0
2012	LAK	A+	22	542	68	35	5	7	66	58	64	20	3	.290/.371/.429	.291	.319	0.9	LF(57): -0.4, RF(25): 2.4	2.1
2013	*DET*	*MLB*	*23*	*250*	*25*	*11*	*2*	*5*	*26*	*19*	*44*	*4*	*1*	*.244/.303/.373*	*.239*	*.280*	*0.3*	*LF -1, RF 0*	*0.0*

Collins is a prospect of note in the thin system, with an already advanced approach at the dish. The organization sees some more power developing, too. How much remains to be seen, but somewhere in the 12-15 home-run range seems most likely. His profile would work best as a center fielder, but he doesn't quite have the defensive chops required for the position. His hit tool and speed will have to be enough to sustain him at a corner outfield position. He has every-day upside and should end up as no worse than a fourth outfielder-platoon type.

Andy Dirks **OF**
Born: 1/24/1986 Age: 27
Bats: L Throws: L Height: 6' 1"
Weight: 195 Breakout: 4%
Improve: 53% Collapse: 10%
Attrition: 16% MLB: 96%
Comparables:
Juan Rivera,Omar Infante,Lou Montanez

YEAR	TEAM	LVL	AGE	PA	R	2B	3B	HR	RBI	BB	SO	SB	CS	AVG_OBP_SLG	TAv	BABIP	BRR	FRAA	WARP
2010	ERI	AA	24	434	64	20	2	11	46	35	59	19	4	.278/.345/.425	.277	.304	1.3	LF(58): -2.5, CF(36): -1.6	1.9
2010	TOL	AAA	24	93	14	10	1	4	17	3	12	3	0	.375/.402/.648	.344	.403	0.6	LF(12): 2.9, CF(10): 0.6	1.6
2011	TOL	AAA	25	172	30	8	1	7	24	12	28	12	2	.325/.368/.522	.266	.355	0.6	CF(20): 2.2, LF(6): 1.3	0.8
2011	DET	MLB	25	235	34	13	0	7	28	11	36	5	2	.251/.296/.406	.245	.273	-0.4	LF(38): 2.7, RF(22): 0.6	0.0
2012	DET	MLB	26	344	56	18	5	8	35	23	53	1	1	.322/.370/.487	.302	.365	2	LF(59): -1.0, RF(24): -2.1	1.3
2013	*DET*	*MLB*	*27*	*323*	*41*	*16*	*3*	*9*	*34*	*18*	*54*	*8*	*2*	*.279/.323/.435*	*.265*	*.311*	*0.7*	*LF 1, RF -0*	*1.1*

There is danger in smooshing two half-seasons together and assuming the result will be the same if you give a player a full season of playing time, but that's what we have to go on with Dirks. He flopped at first in 2011, but excelled last year, resulting in a nice, 579-plate-appearance "season." With his improvements, Dirks should get the first crack at playing time and relegate Boesch to second fiddle in the left side of a left-field platoon. With the addition of Torii Hunter and return of Victor Martinez, there's no need to bat Dirks second, though Jim Leyland may see value in having Dirks there against righties, with Hunter handling duties against southpaws. He should be a boon to the bottom third of the lineup. Either way, Leyland's lineup has some flexibility thanks to Dirks's emergence.

Prince Fielder **1B**
Born: 5/9/1984 Age: 29
Bats: L Throws: R Height: 6' 0"
Weight: 275 Breakout: 7%
Improve: 64% Collapse: 2%
Attrition: 4% MLB: 96%
Comparables:
Jeff Bagwell,Miguel Cabrera,Frank Thomas

YEAR	TEAM	LVL	AGE	PA	R	2B	3B	HR	RBI	BB	SO	SB	CS	AVG_OBP_SLG	TAv	BABIP	BRR	FRAA	WARP
2010	MIL	MLB	26	714	94	25	0	32	83	114	138	1	0	.261/.401/.471	.297	.291	-6.2	1B(160): 1.1	3.2
2011	MIL	MLB	27	692	95	36	1	38	120	107	106	1	1	.299/.415/.566	.325	.306	-3.3	1B(159): -0.7	4.4
2012	DET	MLB	28	690	83	33	1	30	108	85	84	1	0	.313/.412/.528	.326	.321	-8.2	1B(159): 0.9	4.1
2013	*DET*	*MLB*	*29*	*649*	*93*	*28*	*2*	*32*	*103*	*87*	*111*	*1*	*1*	*.286/.394/.525*	*.317*	*.305*	*-0.9*	*1B -4*	*4.0*

There was concern coming into the year that Fielder's move from Miller Park to Comerica Park would cause degradation in his numbers. There was a dip, though it wasn't nearly as sharp as some anticipated. His 1015 OPS in his new digs wasn't too far from the 1096 he put up at home in 2011, but all of the difference was manifested in slugging percentage and a six-homer difference from two years ago to last year. Was it the park, or was he simply better in 2011? Spray charts of the two seasons show that all but one of his home homers would have cleared the fences in Detroit, too. The simple fact is that he remains a superstar and his power plays anywhere.

Daniel Fields **CF**
Born: 1/23/1991 Age: 22
Bats: L Throws: R Height: 6' 2"
Weight: 201 Breakout: 7%
Improve: 61% Collapse: 5%
Attrition: 18% MLB: 96%
Comparables:
David Green,Grady Sizemore,Roger Cedeno

YEAR	TEAM	LVL	AGE	PA	R	2B	3B	HR	RBI	BB	SO	SB	CS	AVG_OBP_SLG	TAv	BABIP	BRR	FRAA	WARP
2010	LAK	A+	19	438	33	13	6	8	47	55	119	8	9	.240/.344/.371	.267	.329	-2.6	CF(101): -5.2	1.2
2010	LAK	A+	19	438	33	13	6	8	47	55	119	8	9	.240/.344/.371	.267	.329	-2.6	CF(1): 0.0	1.2
2011	LAK	A+	20	495	57	14	4	8	46	49	133	4	4	.220/.308/.326	.213	.297	-1.1	CF(53): -0.2	-1.0
2012	LAK	A+	21	267	31	11	4	1	26	19	55	14	7	.266/.318/.357	.274	.335	2.3	CF(35): -2.6, LF(1): -0.1	0.3
2012	ERI	AA	21	122	13	4	0	2	7	13	21	9	1	.264/.352/.358	.290	.310	1.2	LF(10): 0.4, CF(1): 0.0	0.3
2013	*DET*	*MLB*	*22*	*250*	*23*	*8*	*2*	*4*	*22*	*18*	*69*	*5*	*3*	*.218/.278/.319*	*.217*	*.291*	*0.2*	*CF -2, LF 0*	*-0.6*

Tools and youth remain firmly on Fields's side. The 22-year-old rebounded enough from a dismal 2011 campaign that he ended up getting promoted to Double-A, where he acquitted himself well in a short spell. Strikeouts have been an issue throughout Fields's pro career, but he took a major step forward last year, cutting his rate down to 20 percent after back-to-back seasons at 27. With time still on his side and tools hanging out of every pocket, Fields is still viewed by the organization as a prospect, but it is time for him to start turning the dreams into reality. The team has been aggressive with him throughout, but he should spend all of 2013 in Double-A, barring a major breakout.

Avisail Garcia OF

Born: 6/12/1991 **Age:** 22
Bats: R **Throws:** R **Height:** 6' 5"
Weight: 230 **Breakout:** 6%
Improve: 51% **Collapse:** 2%
Attrition: 9% **MLB:** 95%

Comparables:
Jose Guillen,Claudell Washington,Roberto Clemente

YEAR	TEAM	LVL	AGE	PA	R	2B	3B	HR	RBI	BB	SO	SB	CS	AVG_OBP_SLG	TAv	BABIP	BRR	FRAA	WARP
2010	WMI	A	19	524	58	17	4	4	63	20	113	20	4	.281/.316/.356	.248	.358	-2.7	RF(120): 2.8	-0.2
2011	LAK	A+	20	515	53	16	6	11	56	18	132	14	5	.264/.297/.389	.261	.339	0.8	RF(55): -2.6	0.1
2012	LAK	A+	21	287	47	8	5	8	36	11	57	14	4	.289/.324/.447	.292	.335	2.4	RF(42): -1.6, CF(2): 0.4	1.2
2012	ERI	AA	21	226	31	9	3	6	22	7	38	9	4	.312/.345/.465	.266	.357	1.7	CF(24): 1.0	0.6
2012	DET	MLB	21	51	7	0	0	0	3	3	10	0	2	.319/.373/.319	.245	.405	0.1	RF(18): -0.5, LF(2): 0.1	0.0
2013	*DET*	*MLB*	*22*	*250*	*23*	*8*	*2*	*5*	*25*	*4*	*62*	*6*	*2*	*.247/.264/.357*	*.220*	*.310*	*0.6*	*RF -0, CF 0*	*-0.4*

Garcia held his own last year in limited time given his age and the fact that he skipped Triple-A after just 55 games in Double-A. However, he is not a fully developed prospect and the organization wants him playing daily, so if he doesn't win a job in spring training, he'll be sent down. He bears a striking resemblance to Cabrera, but the Tigers would be over the moon if he delivered 75 percent of the MVP's average output. That would make him approximately a 25-home-run hitter with 30 doubles, 90 runs batted in, and 75 runs scored. Even 60 percent would suffice.

Tyler Gibson CF

Born: 6/17/1993 **Age:** 20
Bats: L **Throws:** R **Height:** 6' 3"
Weight: 190 **Breakout:** 20%
Improve: 50% **Collapse:** 6%
Attrition: 26% **MLB:** 82%

Comparables:
Wayne Causey,Ed Kirkpatrick,Bobby Delgreco

YEAR	TEAM	LVL	AGE	PA	R	2B	3B	HR	RBI	BB	SO	SB	CS	AVG_OBP_SLG	TAv	BABIP	BRR	FRAA	WARP
2012	TGR	Rk	19	221	30	6	2	2	16	30	68	18	7	.167/.295/.253	.210	.250	0.9	LF(28): 1.4, CF(24): -1.0	-0.8
2013	*DET*	*MLB*	*20*	*250*	*26*	*6*	*1*	*3*	*15*	*17*	*89*	*8*	*4*	*.161/.222/.242*	*.170*	*.241*	*0.7*	*LF -1, CF -1*	*-1.8*

A quick glance above probably has you wondering why we are even talking (or writing, in our case, and reading, in yours) about Gibson, but he is just one of many examples across professional baseball of why the numbers don't always tell the story. He moved from shortstop in high school to center field as a pro. His speed will sustain him out there while he learns the finer points of manning the big garden. The real work is at the dish, where his approach is a mess. He is extremely raw. Nevertheless, the organization sees big power down the line to go with his raw speed. His contact ability must take a major step forward in 2013 to retain his prospect status.

Bryan Holaday C

Born: 11/19/1987 **Age:** 25
Bats: R **Throws:** R **Height:** 6' 1"
Weight: 205 **Breakout:** 11%
Improve: 47% **Collapse:** 9%
Attrition: 15% **MLB:** 99%

Comparables:
Cam Carreon,Bill Freehan,Charlie Moore

YEAR	TEAM	LVL	AGE	PA	R	2B	3B	HR	RBI	BB	SO	SB	CS	AVG_OBP_SLG	TAv	BABIP	BRR	FRAA	WARP
2010	LAK	A+	22	188	14	8	0	3	12	21	43	0	0	.220/.337/.327	.233	.283	-0.9	C(32): -0.3	-0.1
2010	LAK	A+	22	188	14	8	0	3	12	21	43	0	0	.220/.337/.327	.233	.283	-0.9	C(1): -0.0	-0.1
2011	ERI	AA	23	371	35	18	0	7	42	27	76	6	1	.242/.304/.361	.234	.291	0	--	0.0
2012	TOL	AAA	24	282	18	12	1	2	25	22	43	2	0	.240/.312/.320	.241	.280	-1.1	C(64): 0.8	0.3
2012	DET	MLB	24	13	3	1	0	0	0	0	2	0	0	.250/.250/.333	.204	.300	1.1	C(6): -0.0	0.1
2013	*DET*	*MLB*	*25*	*250*	*23*	*10*	*1*	*4*	*23*	*17*	*50*	*0*	*0*	*.233/.293/.339*	*.228*	*.278*	*-0.2*	*C -0*	*0.3*

Trading Rob Brantly to the Marlins in July and letting Gerald Laird sign with the Braves: two signs that the Tigers have confidence that Holaday can back up Avila. The team likes Holaday's work behind the dish. The fact that he can hit some against lefties makes him a perfect caddy for Avila (career 682 OPS vs. LHP). Holaday will be given a legitimate shot to make the backup slot his own. If that doesn't work, the Tigers will have to acquire an external solution: Victor Martinez is not seen as an option behind the dish under any circumstances.

Torii Hunter OF

Born: 7/18/1975 **Age:** 37
Bats: R **Throws:** R **Height:** 6' 3"
Weight: 225 **Breakout:** 1%
Improve: 22% **Collapse:** 12%
Attrition: 13% **MLB:** 81%

Comparables:
Bobby Abreu,Larry Walker,Dave Winfield

YEAR	TEAM	LVL	AGE	PA	R	2B	3B	HR	RBI	BB	SO	SB	CS	AVG_OBP_SLG	TAv	BABIP	BRR	FRAA	WARP
2010	ANA	MLB	34	646	76	36	0	23	90	61	106	9	12	.281/.354/.464	.300	.307	-4.9	CF(98): -0.7, RF(46): 3.6	4.4
2011	ANA	MLB	35	649	80	24	2	23	82	62	125	5	7	.262/.336/.429	.283	.297	-1	RF(136): 0.4, CF(1): 0.1	2.2
2012	ANA	MLB	36	584	81	24	1	16	92	38	133	9	1	.313/.365/.451	.289	.389	5.1	RF(134): 0.9	3.3
2013	*DET*	*MLB*	*37*	*562*	*68*	*26*	*3*	*19*	*72*	*47*	*111*	*9*	*5*	*.276/.341/.447*	*.278*	*.319*	*-0.6*	*RF 0, CF 0*	*2.4*

It was pretty easy to mock the Angels for vastly overpaying for Hunter—even he admitted he would have signed for much less. But Hunter's 30s were kind to investors, and judging by TAv he gave the Angels four of the five best offensive seasons of his career. Hunter's excellent 2012 campaign has some factors that make us skeptical of a repeat, especially at age 37. The fact of the matter is that he needn't hold himself to such a high standard, nor should he assume the Tigers will either, as he comes in to replace the 30th-ranked right-field production by OPS and UZR. Even a return to his 2011 production with steady, league-average defense would be leaps and bounds above what the Tigers got out of their 2012 group.

Omar Infante 2B

Born: **12/26/1981** Age: **31**
Bats: **R** Throws: **R** Height: **6' 1"**
Weight: **180** Breakout: **1%**
Improve: **33%** Collapse: **4%**
Attrition: **12%** MLB: **95%**

Comparables:
Red Schoendienst,Skip Schumaker,Freddy Sanchez

YEAR	TEAM	LVL	AGE	PA	R	2B	3B	HR	RBI	BB	SO	SB	CS	AVG_OBP_SLG	TAv	BABIP	BRR	FRAA	WARP
2010	ATL	MLB	28	506	65	15	3	8	47	29	62	7	6	.321/.359/.416	.271	.355	-0.9	2B(65): 2.0, 3B(28): -0.1	2.5
2011	FLO	MLB	29	640	55	24	8	7	49	34	67	4	2	.276/.315/.382	.262	.298	-1.7	2B(146): 21.6	3.5
2012	DET	MLB	30	241	27	7	5	4	20	9	23	7	2	.257/.283/.385	.242	.269	0.3	2B(61): 0.7, 3B(6): -0.3	-0.1
2012	MIA	MLB	30	347	42	23	2	8	33	12	42	10	1	.287/.312/.442	.264	.307	4.6	2B(83): 3.5	1.9
2013	*DET*	*MLB*	*31*	*563*	*65*	*24*	*6*	*10*	*53*	*28*	*66*	*9*	*3*	*.286/.322/.410*	*.257*	*.306*	*0.6*	*2B 7, 3B 0*	*2.7*

Despite delivering a paltry 668 OPS as a Tiger in 64 games, for this team Infante was actually a massive upgrade at second base even before you consider the benefits of his defensive value. Prior to the July 24 trade that brought him from Miami, second base was a black hole in Detroit: Ryan Raburn fell off the map completely and Ramon Santiago was overstretched as a full-time player. Infante brings a capable bat and—more importantly—a steady glove, to an infield defense known for its bats. Anibal Sanchez was the major draw of the trade, but having Infante for the remainder of 2012 plus all of 2013 sealed it for the Tigers.

Austin Jackson CF

Born: **2/1/1987** Age: **26**
Bats: **R** Throws: **R** Height: **6' 2"**
Weight: **185** Breakout: **4%**
Improve: **62%** Collapse: **4%**
Attrition: **7%** MLB: **96%**

Comparables:
Chris Young,Lloyd Moseby,B.J. Upton

YEAR	TEAM	LVL	AGE	PA	R	2B	3B	HR	RBI	BB	SO	SB	CS	AVG_OBP_SLG	TAv	BABIP	BRR	FRAA	WARP
2010	DET	MLB	23	675	103	34	10	4	41	47	170	27	6	.293/.345/.400	.271	.396	4.7	CF(149): 2.9	3.7
2011	DET	MLB	24	668	90	22	11	10	45	56	181	22	5	.249/.317/.374	.250	.340	0.7	CF(152): 5.6	1.3
2012	DET	MLB	25	617	103	29	10	16	66	67	134	12	9	.300/.377/.479	.307	.371	2.6	CF(137): 8.6	5.4
2013	*DET*	*MLB*	*26*	*591*	*74*	*25*	*9*	*10*	*55*	*51*	*148*	*17*	*6*	*.272/.338/.411*	*.265*	*.353*	*1.3*	*CF 2*	*2.5*

Jackson's well-publicized removal of a cumbersome leg kick at the plate paid immediate dividends in the form of a breakout season slowed only by the strained abdominal muscle that cost him 21 games. The cleaner approach gave him more balance, which aided a massive power boost and a significant drop in strikeouts. He slashed his strikeout rate from 27 percent to 22. Meanwhile, his improved discipline was reflected in a career-best 4.15 pitches per plate appearance, tying him with Michael Bourn for the best among leadoff hitters. While his hot rookie season bred many skeptics thanks to the glaring holes in his swing, those holes are shrinking. This growth was built on change and maturation, suggesting we may not yet have seen Jackson's best work.

Dixon Machado SS

Born: **2/22/1992** Age: **21**
Bats: **R** Throws: **R** Height: **6' 1"**
Weight: **140** Breakout: **7%**
Improve: **55%** Collapse: **11%**
Attrition: **13%** MLB: **89%**

Comparables:
Ted Kazanski,Ruben Tejada,Jose Oquendo

YEAR	TEAM	LVL	AGE	PA	R	2B	3B	HR	RBI	BB	SO	SB	CS	AVG_OBP_SLG	TAv	BABIP	BRR	FRAA	WARP
2010	TGR	Rk	18	183	22	4	3	0	11	14	27	12	3	.261/.315/.321	.263	.307	0.6	SS(43): -1.5	0.8
2011	WMI	A	19	491	47	1	2	0	28	46	77	25	5	.235/.314/.247	.240	.285	3.5	SS(36): 2.1	0.6
2012	LAK	A+	20	490	59	16	1	2	37	51	61	23	5	.195/.283/.252	.230	.223	0.7	SS(81): -9.6	-1.2
2013	*DET*	*MLB*	*21*	*250*	*27*	*8*	*1*	*2*	*16*	*16*	*51*	*10*	*3*	*.207/.260/.283*	*.196*	*.248*	*1*	*SS 0*	*-0.4*

The statistics are ones only a mother could love, yet the Detroit front office still sees the 21-year-old as a prospect of note. Machado is an elite defender with great speed, and despite the tepid production, his approach at the dish is actually quite solid. He has walked in 10 percent of his plate appearances as a pro while striking out in 14 percent, so he isn't getting the bat knocked out of his hands. The organization wants to see Machado add strength to his wiry frame because he wears down during the season, only adding to his offensive woes.

Victor Martinez DH

Born: **12/23/1978** Age: **34**
Bats: **B** Throws: **R** Height: **6' 3"**
Weight: **210** Breakout: **0%**
Improve: **36%** Collapse: **4%**
Attrition: **17%** MLB: **86%**

Comparables:
Rusty Staub,Sean Casey,Nomar Garciaparra

YEAR	TEAM	LVL	AGE	PA	R	2B	3B	HR	RBI	BB	SO	SB	CS	AVG_OBP_SLG	TAv	BABIP	BRR	FRAA	WARP
2010	BOS	MLB	31	538	64	32	1	20	79	40	52	1	0	.302/.351/.493	.293	.303	-4.3	C(110): -0.6, 1B(14): 1.5	3.1
2011	DET	MLB	32	595	76	40	0	12	103	46	51	1	0	.330/.380/.470	.297	.343	-3.5	C(26): -0.4, 1B(6): 0.3	2.5
2013	*DET*	*MLB*	*34*	*250*	*28*	*13*	*1*	*6*	*31*	*20*	*28*	*0*	*0*	*.294/.352/.442*	*.280*	*.311*	*-0.3*	*C -0, 1B -0*	*1.3*

In essence, the first offseason addition for the Tigers was their own stud designated hitter: Martinez is slated to return from injury in 2013. He likely slots back into the five hole, instantly improving the team's 671 OPS from that lineup spot, which ranked 29th in baseball last year. His torn ACL spurred the signing of Fielder, but the real joy was the long-term outlook of having Cabrera, Fielder, and Martinez manning the heart of the order. Martinez spent a mere 26 games behind the plate in 2011 before his ACL injury, so don't be surprised to see that number dwindle to zero. The organization views him as its primary designated hitter. Period. He may swap out with Fielder to give him a semi-off day here and there, but Laird's departure wasn't meant to open a slot for Martinez as a backup catcher.

James McCann C

Born: **6/13/1990** Age: **23**
Bats: **R** Throws: **R** Height: **6' 3"**
Weight: **210** Breakout: **12%**
Improve: **51%** Collapse: **16%**
Attrition: **22%** MLB: **89%**

Comparables:
Joe Azcue, Javier Valentin, Terry Humphrey

YEAR	TEAM	LVL	AGE	PA	R	2B	3B	HR	RBI	BB	SO	SB	CS	AVG_OBP_SLG	TAv	BABIP	BRR	FRAA	WARP
2012	LAK	A+	22	177	24	10	0	0	20	10	29	3	0	.287/.345/.350	.297	.346	-0.8	C(30): 0.3	0.9
2012	ERI	AA	22	230	15	12	0	2	19	8	44	2	2	.200/.227/.282	.181	.240	-2.2	C(28): 0.3	-0.8
2013	*DET*	*MLB*	*23*	*250*	*20*	*10*	*1*	*3*	*21*	*8*	*56*	*1*	*0*	*.224/.254/.319*	*.204*	*.276*	*-0.2*	*C -0*	*-0.4*

McCann is a defense-first catcher who draws most of his prospect value by virtue of his organization. His position helps, of course, but he might not draw as much attention in most farm systems as a glove-only catcher. One can carve out quite a living as an exceptional defensive catcher, so that will continue to be the focus for McCann, with hopes that his gap power can develop into something a bit more substantial. His cleanest path to the majors would be to continue to hone his strong defense behind the dish and focus all of his hitting efforts on southpaws, because Avila—the incumbent in the majors—struggles against same-sided pitchers.

Steven Moya RF

Born: **9/8/1991** Age: **21**
Bats: **L** Throws: **R** Height: **6' 7"**
Weight: **220** Breakout: **4%**
Improve: **59%** Collapse: **10%**
Attrition: **19%** MLB: **97%**

Comparables:
Sammy Sosa, Gene Stephens, Lloyd Moseby

YEAR	TEAM	LVL	AGE	PA	R	2B	3B	HR	RBI	BB	SO	SB	CS	AVG_OBP_SLG	TAv	BABIP	BRR	FRAA	WARP
2010	TGR	Rk	18	144	12	5	2	2	11	6	64	0	0	.190/.229/.299	.189	.338	0.7	RF(39): 0.3, LF(1): -0.1	-0.8
2011	WMI	A	19	337	38	10	1	13	39	12	127	1	1	.204/.234/.362	.188	.288	0	RF(25): -0.7	-1.0
2012	WMI	A	20	258	28	14	3	9	47	11	59	5	3	.288/.319/.481	.277	.345	-2.7	RF(38): -2.4	-0.2
2013	*DET*	*MLB*	*21*	*250*	*20*	*8*	*2*	*6*	*25*	*6*	*92*	*1*	*1*	*.196/.214/.317*	*.188*	*.281*	*0*	*RF -2, LF -0*	*-1.6*

In the midst of a breakout season, Moya's run was cut short by Tommy John surgery. Contact has been a problem throughout Moya's pro career. Let's put it this way: He has had strikeout rates that would make Adam Dunn blush—44 and 38 percent in 2010 and 2011. Before the injury, though, he had cut it down to 23 percent. His walk rate has held steady at 4 percent in each of the last three years, but the organization sees potential for more. His power is the draw, and if he can harness it in his 6-foot-7 frame, he should shoot up the prospect lists.

Gustavo Nunez SS

Born: **2/8/1988** Age: **25**
Bats: **B** Throws: **R** Height: **5' 11"**
Weight: **170** Breakout: **7%**
Improve: **56%** Collapse: **5%**
Attrition: **23%** MLB: **97%**

Comparables:
Desi Relaford, Kim Batiste, Neifi Perez

YEAR	TEAM	LVL	AGE	PA	R	2B	3B	HR	RBI	BB	SO	SB	CS	AVG_OBP_SLG	TAv	BABIP	BRR	FRAA	WARP
2010	LAK	A+	22	572	66	13	6	2	33	21	93	33	8	.222/.257/.281	.205	.257	4.5	SS(122): 8.1	-0.5
2010	LAK	A+	22	572	66	13	6	2	33	21	93	33	8	.222/.257/.281	.205	.257	4.5	SS(1): -0.0	-0.5
2011	LAK	A+	23	294	46	10	7	3	18	25	40	14	10	.304/.368/.431	.344	.349	0.3	SS(24): -2.6	1.2
2011	ERI	AA	23	131	13	3	0	2	8	5	27	4	3	.215/.252/.289	.192	.261	0	--	0.0
2013	*DET*	*MLB*	*25*	*250*	*28*	*8*	*3*	*3*	*17*	*9*	*50*	*11*	*5*	*.226/.257/.317*	*.203*	*.269*	*0.9*	*SS 2*	*-0.1*

Nunez was a Rule 5 selection of the Pirates in 2011, was then scooped up off of waivers by the Diamondbacks after the 2012 season, and has since been returned to the Tigers. He is a slick fielder and a poor hitter who missed most of the 2012 season following ankle surgery. A busted wheel is a bad sign for a player whose value is largely tied to his speed, particularly one who stole bases at just a 65 percent clip prior to the injury. Limited to 14 games a year ago, he has a mere 41 contests at Double-A, meaning he will need some seasoning in the high minors before being considered for even a utility role in the majors.

Brayan Pena C

Born: **1/7/1982** Age: **31**
Bats: **B** Throws: **R** Height: **6' 0"**
Weight: **235** Breakout: **2%**
Improve: **31%** Collapse: **12%**
Attrition: **18%** MLB: **87%**

Comparables:
Michel Hernandez, Johnny Estrada, Brian Harper

YEAR	TEAM	LVL	AGE	PA	R	2B	3B	HR	RBI	BB	SO	SB	CS	AVG_OBP_SLG	TAv	BABIP	BRR	FRAA	WARP
2010	KCA	MLB	28	174	11	10	0	1	19	12	27	2	0	.253/.306/.335	.225	.295	-0.2	C(47): 0.4	0.2
2011	KCA	MLB	29	240	17	11	0	3	24	12	24	0	0	.248/.287/.338	.223	.261	-1.8	C(67): -1.5	-0.2
2012	KCA	MLB	30	226	16	10	1	2	25	9	24	0	1	.236/.262/.321	.208	.253	-2	C(52): -0.7, 1B(3): -0.0	-1.0
2013	*DET*	*MLB*	*31*	*250*	*24*	*12*	*1*	*5*	*25*	*14*	*31*	*1*	*1*	*.256/.301/.378*	*.239*	*.274*	*-0.3*	*C -0, 1B 0*	*0.5*

Pena's calling card when he arrived in KC read: receiver with limited defensive skill but the ability to get on base. Four consecutive years of declining on-base percentage have laid the latter half of that perception to rest. Regarding the former, he got marginally better at blocking pitches in the dirt, but his defense remains extremely rough. Runners took notice, attempting 52 steals against Pena in just 417 defensive innings. He nabbed just under a quarter of them. With Perez healthy, and less expensive options in the fold to fill the backup role for the Royals, Pena was brought in to contend for the backup job behind Avila in Detroit. If he had any ability against left-handed pitchers, he would have an inside track on the job. Alas.

Jhonny Peralta **SS**

Born: **5/28/1982** Age: **31**
Bats: **R** Throws: **R** Height: **6' 3"**
Weight: **215** Breakout: **1%**
Improve: **37%** Collapse: **9%**
Attrition: **7%** MLB: **87%**

Comparables:
Miguel Tejada,Juan Uribe,Carlos Guillen

YEAR	TEAM	LVL	AGE	PA	R	2B	3B	HR	RBI	BB	SO	SB	CS	AVG_OBP_SLG	TAv	BABIP	BRR	FRAA	WARP
2010	CLE	MLB	28	373	37	23	2	7	43	32	69	1	0	.246/.308/.389	.262	.284	-5.6	3B(91): 4.8	1.3
2010	DET	MLB	28	242	23	7	0	8	38	21	34	0	0	.253/.314/.396	.262	.263	-0.6	SS(46): 0.6, 3B(9): -0.6	0.8
2011	DET	MLB	29	576	68	25	3	21	86	40	95	0	2	.299/.345/.478	.287	.325	-1.9	SS(145): 2.0, 1B(1): -0.0	3.4
2012	DET	MLB	30	585	58	32	3	13	63	49	105	1	2	.239/.305/.384	.244	.275	-0.8	SS(149): -6.0	0.3
2013	*DET*	*MLB*	*31*	*548*	*56*	*27*	*3*	*15*	*65*	*41*	*104*	*1*	*1*	*.258/.315/.413*	*.258*	*.297*	*-0.9*	*SS -6, 3B 0*	*1.6*

After an excellent 2011 campaign, Peralta regressed to his 2009-10 levels. The doubles that had turned into home runs couldn't handle success and went back to life as doubles. He also shifted a large chunk of his fly balls into groundballs, many of which were turned into outs, resulting in a career-low 127 hits. Despite the downturn, he is easily worth his $6 million option, especially in a paper-thin free-agent market at the position. The Tigers wasted no time bringing him back. He has averaged 48 extra-base hits the last four years, with no more than 49 and no fewer than 47, but the distribution between the doubles and home runs seems to bounce around. The Tigers would gladly trade some doubles on Tuesday for some home runs today.

Ryan Raburn **LF**

Born: **4/17/1981** Age: **32**
Bats: **R** Throws: **R** Height: **6' 1"**
Weight: **185** Breakout: **14%**
Improve: **37%** Collapse: **4%**
Attrition: **21%** MLB: **90%**

Comparables:
Woodie Held,Robby Thompson,Jeff Kent

YEAR	TEAM	LVL	AGE	PA	R	2B	3B	HR	RBI	BB	SO	SB	CS	AVG_OBP_SLG	TAv	BABIP	BRR	FRAA	WARP
2010	DET	MLB	29	410	54	25	1	15	62	27	92	2	2	.280/.340/.474	.284	.333	1.7	LF(73): 0.5, RF(20): 0.2	2.1
2011	DET	MLB	30	418	53	22	2	14	49	21	114	1	1	.256/.297/.432	.262	.324	-0.1	2B(56): -3.7, LF(52): 3.4	1.0
2012	TOL	AAA	31	66	8	2	0	4	12	5	15	1	0	.250/.318/.483	.191	.268	0.3	2B(6): -0.3, LF(3): 0.3	-0.1
2012	DET	MLB	31	222	14	14	0	1	12	13	53	1	1	.171/.226/.254	.175	.224	-0.3	2B(32): -1.0, LF(30): -0.1	-2.0
2013	*DET*	*MLB*	*32*	*257*	*28*	*12*	*1*	*8*	*32*	*17*	*64*	*2*	*1*	*.248/.304/.421*	*.254*	*.302*	*-0.3*	*2B -0, LF 1*	*0.6*

The Tigers probably got so used to Raburn's slow starts and hot finishes that they weren't as concerned with his 420 OPS through May as you might expect. He was demoted to Triple-A for half of June and posted an 809 OPS in 10 games after returning. Business as usual, right? Not quite. He sputtered through another 19 games the rest of the season with a 448 OPS, effectively ending his career as a Detroit Tiger. He has shown enough in his previous 500 games that his throwaway 2012 season likely won't preclude him from finding work somewhere.

Ramon Santiago **MI**

Born: **8/31/1979** Age: **33**
Bats: **B** Throws: **R** Height: **6' 0"**
Weight: **175** Breakout: **2%**
Improve: **29%** Collapse: **5%**
Attrition: **19%** MLB: **98%**

Comparables:
Alan Bannister,Pete Runnels,Bobby Avila

YEAR	TEAM	LVL	AGE	PA	R	2B	3B	HR	RBI	BB	SO	SB	CS	AVG_OBP_SLG	TAv	BABIP	BRR	FRAA	WARP
2010	DET	MLB	30	367	38	9	1	3	22	30	56	2	2	.262/.337/.325	.249	.308	0.1	SS(85): 5.9, 2B(25): -0.1	1.8
2011	DET	MLB	31	294	29	11	3	5	30	17	38	0	0	.260/.311/.384	.247	.283	1.3	2B(74): -2.4, SS(27): 3.4	0.7
2012	DET	MLB	32	259	19	7	1	2	17	20	39	1	0	.206/.283/.272	.199	.239	0.9	2B(71): 2.2, SS(20): -1.1	-1.1
2013	*DET*	*MLB*	*33*	*250*	*25*	*8*	*2*	*4*	*23*	*18*	*41*	*1*	*0*	*.250/.317/.354*	*.236*	*.280*	*-0.1*	*2B 0, SS -1*	*0.3*

Santiago had been a positive-value player for a couple of years because he was an up-the-middle defensive asset with a bat that didn't hurt too much. His production was something that would earn him the distinction of "a good little player." Last year saw his production at the plate tumble: He had a .199 True Average in 259 plate appearances, baseball's worst for anyone with 250 or more. His fielding remained above average, but it needed to be at his 2010 level (5.8 fielding runs above average) to carry that bad a bat. Considering how far afield his bat strayed from his own norm, we can reasonably expect a return in 2013 to something like the ~.250 True Average level he enjoyed in 2009-11.

Austin Schotts **CF**

Born: **9/16/1993** Age: **19**
Bats: **R** Throws: **R** Height: **6' 0"**
Weight: **180** Breakout: **0%**
Improve: **65%** Collapse: **35%**
Attrition: **35%** MLB: **100%**

Comparables:
Robin Yount,Wayne Causey,Ed Kranepool

YEAR	TEAM	LVL	AGE	PA	R	2B	3B	HR	RBI	BB	SO	SB	CS	AVG_OBP_SLG	TAv	BABIP	BRR	FRAA	WARP
2012	TGR	Rk	18	177	31	11	1	3	21	12	41	15	4	.310/.360/.452	.212	.395	0.8	CF(6): -0.6	-0.1
2013	*DET*	*MLB*	*19*	*250*	*29*	*8*	*1*	*4*	*17*	*10*	*71*	*12*	*4*	*.196/.232/.299*	*.188*	*.255*	*1.4*	*CF -0*	*-1.0*

Schotts is a 2012 draftee who impressed in his short time in the organization. He profiles as a leadoff type, with premiere speed and a hit tool that carries some potential. Though he was a shortstop in high school, the Tigers always intended to make him a center fielder. While his arm isn't extraordinary, his speed paired with experience at the position should result in an above-average defender. He struck out in nearly a quarter of his plate appearances while walking just 6 percent of the time, but many see more patience coming with time. His aggressive approach worked for him from a production standpoint, but it will be tougher to sustain that kind of strikeout-to-walk ratio at higher levels while still maintaining an 800-plus OPS.

Eugenio Suarez SS
Born: **7/18/1991** Age: **21**
Bats: **B** Throws: **R** Height: **6' 0"**
Weight: **155** Breakout: **3%**
Improve: **62%** Collapse: **8%**
Attrition: **12%** MLB: **96%**
Comparables:
Ed Brinkman,Jim Fregosi,Alan Trammell

YEAR	TEAM	LVL	AGE	PA	R	2B	3B	HR	RBI	BB	SO	SB	CS	AVG_OBP_SLG	TAv	BABIP	BRR	FRAA	WARP
2011	ONE	A-	19	229	37	11	5	5	24	18	43	9	5	.250/.323/.426	.258	.295	0	--	0.0
2012	WMI	A	20	604	82	34	5	6	67	65	116	21	9	.288/.380/.409	.282	.356	-4	SS(77): 0.1, 2B(7): 0.4	1.7
2013	*DET*	*MLB*	*21*	*250*	*27*	*10*	*2*	*4*	*20*	*18*	*65*	*3*	*1*	*.226/.290/.331*	*.225*	*.295*	*0*	*SS -1, 2B -0*	*0.1*

The club was thrilled with the 21-year-old Suarez's breakout season at West Michigan. He doesn't have the tools that prospect hounds fawn over, but he is putting up the results to make them take notice. He has the glove to stick at short, too, which only adds to his prospect status. His presence in the top 10 for the organization is no doubt related to the dearth of big-ticket talent in the system, but he is a legitimate prospect. Like a lot of the second-tier talent in the organization, he is a long way out, adding uncertainty to his long-term projection.

Danry Vasquez OF
Born: **1/8/1994** Age: **19**
Bats: **L** Throws: **R** Height: **6' 4"**
Weight: **169** Breakout: **0%**
Improve: **69%** Collapse: **31%**
Attrition: **31%** MLB: **100%**
Comparables:
Robin Yount,Wayne Causey,Ed Kranepool

YEAR	TEAM	LVL	AGE	PA	R	2B	3B	HR	RBI	BB	SO	SB	CS	AVG_OBP_SLG	TAv	BABIP	BRR	FRAA	WARP
2011	TGR	Rk	17	224	25	8	1	2	30	7	34	3	2	.272/.306/.350	.235	.314	-0.2	RF(43): -3.6	-0.9
2012	WMI	A	18	112	5	3	0	1	7	7	20	0	0	.162/.218/.222	.177	.185	1.3	LF(14): 0.7	-0.3
2012	ONE	A-	18	311	36	16	2	2	35	13	45	6	4	.311/.341/.401	.293	.361	-1.3	LF(24): -2.8, RF(2): 0.1	0.3
2013	*DET*	*MLB*	*19*	*250*	*17*	*9*	*1*	*3*	*21*	*4*	*61*	*1*	*0*	*.214/.229/.298*	*.184*	*.268*	*-0.2*	*LF -1, RF -0*	*-1.6*

The Tigers tested the 18-year-old Vasquez with a full-season assignment, but he sputtered in his first month there. They acted quickly and moved him down to Low-A, where he found his footing immediately. He got a built-in month off because the New York-Penn League didn't start until mid-June. The organization believes Vasquez will be a legitimate hitter and is eager to see what kind of power can develop as his 6-foot-3 frame fills out. This an organization known for aggressively promoting prospects, but given his struggles with such aggression in 2012, perhaps the Tigers will temper their eagerness with Vasquez.

Delmon Young LF
Born: **9/14/1985** Age: **27**
Bats: **R** Throws: **R** Height: **6' 4"**
Weight: **200** Breakout: **5%**
Improve: **47%** Collapse: **4%**
Attrition: **11%** MLB: **91%**
Comparables:
Xavier Nady,Lance Niekro,Hal Morris

YEAR	TEAM	LVL	AGE	PA	R	2B	3B	HR	RBI	BB	SO	SB	CS	AVG_OBP_SLG	TAv	BABIP	BRR	FRAA	WARP
2010	MIN	MLB	24	613	77	46	1	21	112	28	81	5	4	.298/.333/.493	.292	.312	-2.5	LF(149): -11.7	1.8
2011	DET	MLB	25	178	28	5	1	8	32	5	30	0	0	.274/.298/.458	.275	.286	1.1	LF(40): -2.8	0.4
2011	MIN	MLB	25	325	26	16	0	4	32	18	55	1	0	.266/.305/.357	.237	.310	-0.9	LF(75): -2.8	-0.7
2012	DET	MLB	26	608	54	27	1	18	74	20	112	0	2	.267/.296/.411	.252	.299	-3.5	LF(31): -1.2	-0.9
2013	*DET*	*MLB*	*27*	*553*	*58*	*27*	*3*	*16*	*68*	*24*	*97*	*3*	*2*	*.279/.315/.434*	*.263*	*.314*	*-1*	*LF -0*	*1.3*

His ALCS and World Series weren't enough to keep Delmon "Yankee Killer" Young in Detroit for another year. He leaves as the franchise's postseason home-run leader with eight. He was the freest of swingers last year, offering at 59 percent of the pitches that came his way. In fact, he has been third or higher in that category in five of his six full seasons, twice leading the majors. Expect more of the same. Forever.

PITCHERS

Al Alburquerque
Born: **6/10/1986** Age: **27**
Bats: **R** Throws: **R** Height: **6' 1"** Weight: **195**
Breakout: **31%** Improve: **58%** Collapse: **36%**
Attrition: **20%** MLB: **95%**
Comparables:
Francisco Rodriguez,Anthony Slama,David Robertson

YEAR	TEAM	LVL	AGE	W	L	SV	G	GS	IP	H	HR	BB	SO	BB9	SO9	GB%	BABIP	WHIP	ERA	FIP	FRA	WARP
2011	TOL	AAA	25	0	0	0	4	0	4^2	5	0	2	10	3.9	19.3	20%	.600	1.50	1.93	0.88	-0.15	0.2
2011	DET	MLB	25	6	1	0	41	0	43^1	21	0	29	67	6.0	13.9	58%	.250	1.15	1.87	2.12	2.10	1.3
2012	LAK	A+	26	0	0	0	4	3	3^1	5	1	1	9	2.7	24.3	%	.800	1.80	5.40	2.79	2.35	0.1
2012	TOL	AAA	26	1	0	0	9	0	10^2	9	1	4	18	3.4	15.2	43%	.364	1.22	1.69	2.41	3.09	0.2
2012	DET	MLB	26	0	0	0	8	0	13^1	6	0	8	18	5.4	12.1	67%	.222	1.05	0.68	2.15	2.51	0.4
2013	*DET*	*MLB*	*27*	*2*	*1*	*1*	*29*	*0*	*35^2*	*28*	*3*	*18*	*46*	*4.6*	*11.5*	*50%*	*.303*	*1.30*	*3.43*	*3.23*	*3.72*	*0.6*

Alburquerque's slider has officially been labeled NSFW by the government. Three Downriver fans were fired for watching GIFs of it on their lunch break. The 86-88 mph breaker is easily one of the best in baseball. Of Alburquerque's 85 strikeouts as a major leaguer, 74 of them have ended on a slider, even though the hitters have known it was coming. He throws the pitch nearly 60 percent of the time, the third-highest rate in baseball over the last two years (among relievers with 50 or more innings). Alburquerque is one of several closer candidates in the Detroit bullpen, though his candidacy is more of the dark-horse variety since he needs to clear the health hurdle first. He missed most of 2012 after elbow surgery.

Duane Below
Born: **11/15/1985** Age: **27**
Bats: **L** Throws: **L** Height: **6' 4"** Weight: **220**
Breakout: **40%** Improve: **69%** Collapse: **19%**
Attrition: **7%** MLB: **76%**
Comparables:
Travis Blackley, Luis Martinez, Jason Vargas

YEAR	TEAM	LVL	AGE	W	L	SV	G	GS	IP	H	HR	BB	SO	BB9	SO9	GB%	BABIP	WHIP	ERA	FIP	FRA	WARP
2010	ERI	AA	24	7	12	0	28	28	126	137	17	37	103	2.6	7.4	45%	.304	1.38	4.93	4.43	5.10	0.9
2011	TOL	AAA	25	9	4	0	18	18	115	99	12	37	83	2.9	6.5	44%	.274	1.18	3.13	4.25	4.96	0.2
2011	DET	MLB	25	0	2	0	14	2	29	28	2	11	14	3.4	4.3	53%	.263	1.34	4.34	4.23	4.66	0.2
2012	TOL	AAA	26	1	2	0	4	4	17^1	24	3	12	7	6.2	3.6	46%	.350	2.08	6.23	6.68	8.52	-0.3
2012	DET	MLB	26	2	1	0	27	1	46^1	49	6	8	29	1.6	5.6	43%	.297	1.23	3.88	4.06	5.27	0.0
2013	*DET*	*MLB*	*27*	*3*	*2*	*0*	*13*	*7*	*44^2*	*50*	*6*	*18*	*30*	*3.6*	*6.1*	*41%*	*.308*	*1.52*	*5.30*	*4.81*	*5.76*	*-0.1*

Home runs remain an issue for Below and may have led to his demotion from the big club in mid-August. He gave up five in six appearances from July 3 to August 13 after having allowed only one in 21 appearances prior to that. The issue continued in Triple-A as he allowed three in four starts spanning 17 innings to close out the season. He has more control than command, so he stays in the zone and avoids walks, but he doesn't have the kind of stuff that can live in the zone without getting hammered. He will likely vacillate between Detroit and Toledo as a 25th-26th man type, papering over injuries in the bullpen, grabbing a spot start here and there, or being the first arm up when a doubleheader follows a 15-inning game.

Joaquin Benoit
Born: **7/26/1977** Age: **35**
Bats: **R** Throws: **R** Height: **6' 4"** Weight: **220**
Breakout: **19%** Improve: **46%** Collapse: **34%**
Attrition: **16%** MLB: **85%**
Comparables:
Moe Drabowsky, Kazuhiro Sasaki, Lee Smith

YEAR	TEAM	LVL	AGE	W	L	SV	G	GS	IP	H	HR	BB	SO	BB9	SO9	GB%	BABIP	WHIP	ERA	FIP	FRA	WARP
2010	DUR	AAA	32	0	1	2	8	0	9^2	8	2	3	17	2.8	15.8	45%	.333	1.13	2.78	3.39	3.62	0.2
2010	TBA	MLB	32	1	2	1	63	0	60^1	30	6	11	75	1.6	11.2	39%	.192	0.68	1.34	2.40	2.99	1.1
2011	DET	MLB	33	4	3	2	66	0	61	47	5	17	63	2.5	9.3	40%	.273	1.05	2.95	3.00	3.78	0.8
2012	DET	MLB	34	5	3	2	73	0	71	59	14	22	84	2.8	10.6	38%	.269	1.14	3.68	4.22	4.25	0.7
2013	*DET*	*MLB*	*35*	*3*	*1*	*2*	*62*	*0*	*59^1*	*49*	*7*	*21*	*67*	*3.1*	*10.2*	*38%*	*.288*	*1.17*	*3.23*	*3.54*	*3.51*	*1.2*

Below's home-run issues were nothing compared to Benoit's. Benoit tied the record for the most outings with two or more home runs allowed in the 2000s with four. He and five others share that dubious distinction. He separated himself from them by having a worthwhile season. All four outings came in a horrid span from June 30 to August 9, causing speculation that Benoit was not fully healthy at the time. While always a fly-ball pitcher, Benoit has not been bitten by the home-run bug this severely since he transferred into the bullpen. The alarming decrease in his infield-fly-ball rate over the last two years suggests that batters are making better contact, but his home-run-per-fly-ball rate of 18 percent is nearly double anything we have seen from him in the last six years. Expect a regression there and don't be surprised to see Benoit as a serious contender for the team's open closer role.

Phil Coke
Born: **7/19/1982** Age: **30**
Bats: **L** Throws: **L** Height: **6' 2"** Weight: **210**
Breakout: **36%** Improve: **66%** Collapse: **13%**
Attrition: **10%** MLB: **75%**
Comparables:
Jeremy Affeldt, Mike Cuellar, Don Mossi

YEAR	TEAM	LVL	AGE	W	L	SV	G	GS	IP	H	HR	BB	SO	BB9	SO9	GB%	BABIP	WHIP	ERA	FIP	FRA	WARP
2010	DET	MLB	27	7	5	2	74	1	64^2	67	2	26	53	3.6	7.4	38%	.335	1.44	3.76	3.20	3.62	1.0
2011	TOL	AAA	28	0	0	0	1	1	5^1	8	0	2	6	3.4	10.1	41%	.471	1.88	5.06	2.11	2.30	0.2
2011	DET	MLB	28	3	9	1	48	14	108^2	118	5	40	69	3.3	5.7	45%	.317	1.45	4.47	3.60	4.30	1.1
2012	DET	MLB	29	2	3	1	66	0	54	71	5	18	51	3.0	8.5	50%	.388	1.65	4.00	3.42	3.56	0.9
2013	*DET*	*MLB*	*30*	*4*	*2*	*1*	*48*	*4*	*58^2*	*60*	*6*	*20*	*48*	*3.0*	*7.3*	*45%*	*.312*	*1.37*	*4.26*	*3.92*	*4.63*	*0.5*

If you looked at Coke's 2012 regular-season numbers and then someone told you that he would emerge as the team's most reliable reliever—and even become their closer in the playoffs—you would probably call that person some names not fit for print in this publication. Alas, that is exactly how the 2012 season played out. Coke allowed just one run in 10 outings, striking out 12 and walking a pair in a dominating October for the AL champs. The carryover impact for Coke seems to be minimal, though—he is pretty far down the list of closer candidates for 2013. The lefty-as-a-closer stigma may be playing a role, but it's more likely the pesky old "we don't want our closer yielding a 1050 OPS to right-handers" bias at play. Coke has always had trouble against righties and was especially poor against them last year.

Casey Crosby
Born: **9/17/1988** Age: **24**
Bats: **R** Throws: **L** Height: **6' 6"** Weight: **200**
Breakout: **32%** Improve: **63%** Collapse: **17%**
Attrition: **19%** MLB: **92%**
Comparables:
Edwin Jackson, Juan Mateo, Tyler Clippard

YEAR	TEAM	LVL	AGE	W	L	SV	G	GS	IP	H	HR	BB	SO	BB9	SO9	GB%	BABIP	WHIP	ERA	FIP	FRA	WARP
2010	TGR	Rk	21	0	1	0	3	3	12^1	21	1	4	10	2.9	7.3	53%	.444	2.03	8.78	3.91	6.19	-0.2
2011	ERI	AA	22	9	7	0	25	25	131^2	122	11	77	121	5.3	8.3	—	.312	1.51	4.10	4.53	4.92	0.0
2012	TOL	AAA	23	7	9	0	22	22	125^2	112	12	65	112	4.7	8.0	50%	.284	1.41	4.01	4.17	5.54	-0.2
2012	DET	MLB	23	1	1	0	3	3	12^1	15	2	11	9	8.0	6.6	51%	.351	2.11	9.49	6.37	10.33	-0.4
2013	*DET*	*MLB*	*24*	*3*	*2*	*0*	*7*	*7*	*39*	*41*	*5*	*22*	*31*	*5.0*	*7.1*	*48%*	*.306*	*1.61*	*5.34*	*4.97*	*5.80*	*-0.2*

When is it relatively easy to overlook a walk rate approaching 5.0? When the pitcher in question is a left-hander who throws 95–96 mph with a quality curveball and progressing changeup. Crosby is a power lefty who misses bats and generates grounders, but he lacks the command and control necessary to be a reliable starter. Age is still on his side, and given his vast upside, the organization will leave him as a starter for the foreseeable future. If for some reason the ability to find the zone never clicks, he has the fallback of becoming a high-leverage reliever.

Octavio Dotel

Born: **11/25/1973** Age: **39**
Bats: **R** Throws: **R** Height: **6' 1"** Weight: **220**
Breakout: **11%** Improve: **38%** Collapse: **48%**
Attrition: **8%** MLB: **80%**

Comparables:
Tom Gordon, Jesse Orosco, Rudy Seanez

YEAR	TEAM	LVL	AGE	W	L	SV	G	GS	IP	H	HR	BB	SO	BB9	SO9	GB%	BABIP	WHIP	ERA	FIP	FRA	WARP
2010	COL	MLB	36	0	1	0	8	0	5^{1}	6	1	4	6	6.8	10.1	28%	.294	1.88	5.06	5.54	5.15	0.0
2010	LAN	MLB	36	1	1	1	19	0	18^{2}	11	3	11	21	5.3	10.1	35%	.186	1.18	3.38	4.71	5.45	-0.2
2010	PIT	MLB	36	2	2	21	41	0	40	35	5	17	48	3.8	10.8	32%	.300	1.30	4.28	3.83	4.84	0.2
2011	SLN	MLB	37	3	3	2	29	0	24^{2}	16	1	5	32	1.8	11.7	37%	.259	0.85	3.28	1.53	2.71	0.4
2011	TOR	MLB	37	2	1	1	36	0	29^{1}	20	5	12	30	3.7	9.2	29%	.205	1.09	3.68	4.66	5.36	-0.1
2012	DET	MLB	38	5	3	1	57	0	58	50	3	12	62	1.9	9.6	43%	.301	1.07	3.57	2.25	2.70	1.4
2013	*DET*	*MLB*	*39*	*3*	*1*	*1*	*51*	*0*	*47^{2}*	*41*	*5*	*19*	*56*	*3.5*	*10.6*	*38%*	*.294*	*1.25*	*3.60*	*3.41*	*3.92*	*0.7*

Dotel is known for having played on a lot of teams. He's been on seven in the last four years. 2013 will be the first time since 2009 that he will start the season on the same team he ended the last one with. As interesting as his Rolodex is (13 cities in 14 seasons), we needn't forget that he is also a very good pitcher. He continues to miss tons of bats, and his four-year decline in walk rate culminated in last year's career-best 1.9 BB9 mark. With 109 career saves and 22 as recently as 2010, Dotel will no doubt be given consideration for the role this spring.

Doug Fister

Born: **2/4/1984** Age: **29**
Bats: **L** Throws: **R** Height: **6' 9"** Weight: **210**
Breakout: **15%** Improve: **61%** Collapse: **17%**
Attrition: **10%** MLB: **93%**

Comparables:
Joe Saunders, Odalis Perez, Mark Buehrle

YEAR	TEAM	LVL	AGE	W	L	SV	G	GS	IP	H	HR	BB	SO	BB9	SO9	GB%	BABIP	WHIP	ERA	FIP	FRA	WARP
2010	TAC	AAA	26	0	0	0	1	1	4	4	0	0	3	0.0	6.8	50%	.333	1.00	4.50	2.08	3.37	0.1
2010	SEA	MLB	26	6	14	0	28	28	171	187	13	32	93	1.7	4.9	47%	.302	1.28	4.11	3.61	4.30	0.6
2011	DET	MLB	27	8	1	0	11	10	70^{1}	54	4	5	57	0.6	7.3	51%	.245	0.84	1.79	2.52	3.17	1.5
2011	SEA	MLB	27	3	12	0	21	21	146	139	7	32	89	2.0	5.5	47%	.284	1.17	3.33	3.31	4.08	1.2
2012	TOL	AAA	28	0	0	0	1	1	4	2	0	1	5	2.2	11.2	44%	.222	0.75	0.00	1.41	2.23	0.1
2012	DET	MLB	28	10	10	0	26	26	161^{2}	156	15	37	137	2.1	7.6	53%	.296	1.19	3.45	3.37	4.20	2.0
2013	*DET*	*MLB*	*29*	*11*	*6*	*0*	*23*	*23*	*147^{2}*	*156*	*16*	*30*	*98*	*1.8*	*6.0*	*47%*	*.302*	*1.26*	*4.09*	*3.89*	*4.45*	*1.4*

Sometimes the notion comes along that a player needs a change of scenery to excel. Fister wasn't exactly in that category, though he seems to have benefited from being moved in a trade from Seattle in July 2011. The 6-foot-8 Fister was seen as a soft-tossing control artist before coming alive as a Tiger and striking out 21 percent of the batters he faced down the stretch that year. Most of those gains were written off due to favorable schedule, but Fister proved his critics wrong in 2012 by nearly matching that rate, fanning 20 percent of the batters he faced in 162 innings. While his entire repertoire has experienced a bump in effectiveness, the biggest improvement has come from the curveball. He is generating a lot more swings-and-misses with the pitch, giving him the confidence to throw it more often (career-high 20 percent in 2012). The only thing missing from his season was health. He struggled with intercostal and groin injuries during the season. A healthy Fister gives the Tigers one of the best third starters in all of baseball.

Rick Porcello

Born: **12/27/1988** Age: **24**
Bats: **R** Throws: **R** Height: **6' 6"** Weight: **200**
Breakout: **17%** Improve: **47%** Collapse: **39%**
Attrition: **32%** MLB: **94%**

Comparables:
Scott Baker, Tommy Hunter, Jesse Litsch

YEAR	TEAM	LVL	AGE	W	L	SV	G	GS	IP	H	HR	BB	SO	BB9	SO9	GB%	BABIP	WHIP	ERA	FIP	FRA	WARP
2010	TOL	AAA	21	1	2	0	4	4	28	24	0	10	19	3.2	6.1	65%	.296	1.21	3.21	3.11	4.60	0.1
2010	DET	MLB	21	10	12	0	27	27	162^{2}	188	18	38	84	2.1	4.6	51%	.307	1.39	4.92	4.28	5.19	0.0
2011	DET	MLB	22	14	9	0	31	31	182	210	18	46	104	2.3	5.1	54%	.316	1.41	4.75	4.09	4.60	1.2
2012	DET	MLB	23	10	12	0	31	31	176^{1}	226	16	44	107	2.2	5.5	55%	.344	1.53	4.59	3.86	4.82	1.1
2013	*DET*	*MLB*	*24*	*11*	*8*	*0*	*27*	*27*	*158^{2}*	*178*	*18*	*39*	*93*	*2.2*	*5.3*	*54%*	*.308*	*1.37*	*4.54*	*4.24*	*4.94*	*0.7*

A 24-year-old with four full seasons of near-league-average work makes Porcello a valuable commodity. But as a highly touted prospect who had his best season in his rookie year and hasn't pitched below a 4.50 ERA since, Porcello gets viewed as something nearing a bust in some circles. Those in the know will tell you he is anything but, and many believe he has multiple levels of untapped potential. Some of that may require the proverbial change of scenery to emerge because Porcello is an elite groundball artist on a team horribly ill-equipped to turn those into outs. This is a major reason why his sabermetric figures are often much better than his ERA. There is still star potential here.

Luke Putkonen
Born: **5/10/1986** Age: **27**
Bats: **R** Throws: **R** Height: **6' 7"** Weight: **200**
Breakout: **24%** Improve: **56%** Collapse: **23%**
Attrition: **26%** MLB: **76%**
Comparables:
Carl Pavano,Marty Bystrom,Jay Tibbs

YEAR	TEAM	LVL	AGE	W	L	SV	G	GS	IP	H	HR	BB	SO	BB9	SO9	GB%	BABIP	WHIP	ERA	FIP	FRA	WARP
2010	LAK	A+	24	9	7	0	27	26	152^2	144	8	44	87	2.6	5.1	49%	.284	1.23	3.18	3.96	5.29	-0.8
2011	LAK	A+	25	2	6	0	18	8	65	77	10	18	52	2.5	7.2	50%	.343	1.46	5.54	4.76	6.14	-0.3
2011	ERI	AA	25	1	7	0	11	11	52^1	68	8	22	23	3.8	4.0	—	.312	1.72	7.57	5.89	6.41	0.0
2012	TOL	AAA	26	3	3	0	24	2	56^2	68	3	20	46	3.2	7.3	49%	.366	1.55	4.92	3.33	4.84	0.1
2012	DET	MLB	26	0	2	1	12	0	16	19	0	8	10	4.5	5.6	54%	.352	1.69	3.94	3.30	4.44	0.1
2013	*DET*	*MLB*	*27*	*2*	*2*	*0*	*9*	*4*	*32^2*	*41*	*5*	*15*	*15*	*4.0*	*4.2*	*50%*	*.317*	*1.70*	*6.21*	*5.65*	*6.76*	*-0.4*

Putkonen labored in the minors longer than you'd expect a 6-foot-6 righty with a mid-90s fastball to hang around, even after the Tigers finally decided that relief was his future. Upon conversion to the bullpen, his strikeout rate instantly surged, a common phenomenon, but the 7.3-per-nine rate in 57 Triple-A innings wasn't particularly special and he didn't bring much of it with him in a 16-innning major-league stint. He's a fastball-reliant arm who can't even consistently rely on his fastball. His curveball has flashes of usefulness, but command of his heater should be first, second, and third on his list of priorities.

Bruce Rondon
Born: **12/9/1990** Age: **22**
Bats: **R** Throws: **R** Height: **6' 3"** Weight: **190**
Breakout: **14%** Improve: **44%** Collapse: **32%**
Attrition: **9%** MLB: **86%**
Comparables:
Ambiorix Burgos,Matt Anderson,Boone Logan

YEAR	TEAM	LVL	AGE	W	L	SV	G	GS	IP	H	HR	BB	SO	BB9	SO9	GB%	BABIP	WHIP	ERA	FIP	FRA	WARP
2010	TGR	Rk	19	0	0	15	24	0	25^2	11	1	14	26	4.9	9.1	54%	.194	0.97	0.70	4.21	4.76	0.0
2010	LAK	A+	19	0	0	2	4	0	6^2	2	1	2	7	2.7	9.4	43%	.077	0.60	1.34	4.18	4.59	0.0
2011	WMI	A	20	2	2	19	41	0	40	22	0	34	61	7.7	13.7	59%	.379	1.40	2.03	3.23	2.57	0.4
2012	LAK	A+	21	1	0	15	22	0	23^1	12	1	10	34	3.9	13.1	58%	.244	0.94	1.93	2.45	2.27	0.5
2012	ERI	AA	21	0	1	12	21	0	21^2	15	1	9	23	3.7	9.6	52%	.264	1.11	0.83	3.48	3.45	0.3
2012	TOL	AAA	21	1	0	2	9	0	8	5	1	7	9	7.9	10.1	62%	.200	1.50	2.25	5.16	5.31	0.0
2013	*DET*	*MLB*	*22*	*1*	*1*	*1*	*31*	*0*	*33^2*	*33*	*4*	*19*	*32*	*5.1*	*8.5*	*50%*	*.307*	*1.54*	*4.92*	*4.54*	*5.35*	*-0.0*

For an organization thought to be thin on talent, the upper levels of the Tigers system still generates plenty of interested talk. Whether it is Castellanos popping up in every other trade rumor or Rondon being hinted at as the next closer, the team's top prospects are on the tip of many tongues. Rondon's 32 percent strikeout rate in 92 minor-league innings as a 21-year-old is bound to draw attention. That is a figure reserved for elites in the majors, though of the 14 who achieved it last year, none were near Rondon's 15 percent career walk rate. Only four guys were in double digits, and of those only Ernesto Frieri was a closer. Rondon is a hulking mass of triple-digit fastballs and has been closing since 2010, so the role itself wouldn't be new, but will a guy with all of eight innings at Triple-A and legitimate control issues be closing out the ninth inning for the Tigers in Minnesota on April 1? Hard to imagine.

Anibal Sanchez
Born: **2/27/1984** Age: **29**
Bats: **R** Throws: **R** Height: **6' 1"** Weight: **205**
Breakout: **14%** Improve: **42%** Collapse: **22%**
Attrition: **6%** MLB: **95%**
Comparables:
John Maine,John Lackey,Gavin Floyd

YEAR	TEAM	LVL	AGE	W	L	SV	G	GS	IP	H	HR	BB	SO	BB9	SO9	GB%	BABIP	WHIP	ERA	FIP	FRA	WARP
2010	FLO	MLB	26	13	12	0	32	32	195	192	10	70	157	3.2	7.2	47%	.305	1.34	3.55	3.35	3.77	3.3
2011	FLO	MLB	27	8	9	0	32	32	196^1	187	20	64	202	2.9	9.3	46%	.310	1.28	3.67	3.31	3.82	2.8
2012	DET	MLB	28	4	6	0	12	12	74^2	81	8	15	57	1.8	6.9	47%	.313	1.29	3.74	3.64	4.30	0.8
2012	MIA	MLB	28	5	7	0	19	19	121	119	12	33	110	2.5	8.2	49%	.308	1.26	3.94	3.47	3.83	1.5
2013	*DET*	*MLB*	*29*	*12*	*7*	*0*	*26*	*26*	*159^2*	*163*	*18*	*51*	*132*	*2.8*	*7.4*	*46%*	*.307*	*1.34*	*4.19*	*3.97*	*4.55*	*1.4*

The prize of a deadline deal with the Marlins, Sanchez took a few starts to find his footing in the American League, but then threw to a 2.15 ERA over 54 innings in his final eight starts. He carried that success into the playoffs, netting a 1.77 ERA in 20 innings across three starts. Injuries plagued the early part of his career, but he strung together a trio of 195-inning seasons at the perfect time. There is significant value in an arm that can miss plenty of bats while keeping the ball on the ground for 30-plus games a season.

Max Scherzer
Born: **7/27/1984** Age: **28**
Bats: **R** Throws: **R** Height: **6' 4"** Weight: **220**
Breakout: **25%** Improve: **65%** Collapse: **16%**
Attrition: **8%** MLB: **96%**
Comparables:
Hideo Nomo,Josh Beckett,Jake Peavy

YEAR	TEAM	LVL	AGE	W	L	SV	G	GS	IP	H	HR	BB	SO	BB9	SO9	GB%	BABIP	WHIP	ERA	FIP	FRA	WARP
2010	TOL	AAA	25	2	0	0	2	2	15	4	0	2	17	1.2	10.2	48%	.121	0.40	0.60	1.42	2.36	0.5
2010	DET	MLB	25	12	11	0	31	31	195^2	174	20	70	184	3.2	8.5	42%	.297	1.25	3.50	3.68	4.23	2.5
2011	DET	MLB	26	15	9	0	33	33	195	207	29	56	174	2.6	8.0	42%	.314	1.35	4.43	4.18	4.74	0.9
2012	DET	MLB	27	16	7	0	32	32	187^2	179	23	60	231	2.9	11.1	39%	.333	1.27	3.74	3.22	3.52	3.8
2013	*DET*	*MLB*	*28*	*12*	*7*	*0*	*27*	*27*	*163^2*	*153*	*20*	*52*	*174*	*2.8*	*9.6*	*43%*	*.309*	*1.25*	*3.80*	*3.62*	*4.13*	*2.3*

Reason number 4,281,930 Why ERAs Alone Can Misinform: Scherzer's didn't get below 5.00 until June 28, perhaps leading some to believe that his outing that day was the "turning point" of his season. Well, when you give up 9 percent of your entire year's earned-run total in your first outing (seven of 78), in fewer than three innings, it will take a while to work it off. Scherzer's 3.22 FIP for the year tells the story of how great he was on the whole, and if he can tame his violent delivery for 32 starts, avoiding the meltdown outing every fifth or sixth time out, then a truly special season will be the end result, complete with Cy Young consideration.

Drew Smyly

Born: **6/13/1989** Age: **24**
Bats: **L** Throws: **L** Height: **6' 4"** Weight: **190**
Breakout: **32%** Improve: **75%** Collapse: **10%**
Attrition: **7%** MLB: **97%**

Comparables:
Cole Hamels, John Danks, James McDonald

YEAR	TEAM	LVL	AGE	W	L	SV	G	GS	IP	H	HR	BB	SO	BB9	SO9	GB%	BABIP	WHIP	ERA	FIP	FRA	WARP
2011	LAK	A+	22	7	3	0	14	14	80^1	71	1	21	77	2.4	8.6	46%	.378	1.15	2.58	2.53	3.31	0.7
2011	ERI	AA	22	4	3	0	8	7	45^2	32	1	15	53	3.0	10.4	—	.287	1.03	1.18	2.42	2.64	0.0
2012	TOL	AAA	23	0	2	0	7	7	17^2	22	3	8	25	4.1	12.7	35%	.413	1.70	6.11	4.06	4.79	0.2
2012	DET	MLB	23	4	3	0	23	18	99^1	93	12	33	94	3.0	8.5	42%	.295	1.27	3.99	3.78	4.28	1.3
2013	*DET*	*MLB*	*24*	*6*	*4*	*0*	*16*	*16*	*77*	*75*	*9*	*25*	*74*	*2.9*	*8.6*	*42%*	*.306*	*1.30*	*4.09*	*3.77*	*4.44*	*0.9*

Many pegged Smyly for a 2012 cup of coffee at best after a solid debut season in pro ball that ended in Double-A. Instead, he threw 99 strong innings for the big club, including 18 starts. Pitching with more of a high-80s fastball in the minors, Smyly impressed with his heater averaging 92 mph in the majors. Smyly's debut would be considered a resounding success under any circumstance, but considering the fact that he had just 126 innings of pro ball under his belt (including 46 at Double-A), he ended up one of the most pleasant rookie surprises in the league. He will have to be ready for double duty again in 2013, as he could find himself locking down the back end of the rotation or a key bullpen role.

Jake Thompson

Born: **1/31/1994** Age: **19**
Bats: **R** Throws: **R** Height: **6' 5"** Weight: **235**
Breakout: **--%** Improve: **--%** Collapse: **--%**
Attrition: **--%** MLB: **--%**

Comparables:
--

YEAR	TEAM	LVL	AGE	W	L	SV	G	GS	IP	H	HR	BB	SO	BB9	SO9	GB%	BABIP	WHIP	ERA	FIP	FRA	WARP
2012	TGR	Rk	18	1	2	0	7	7	28^1	14	1	10	31	3.2	9.8	—	.206	0.85	1.91	2.53	3.12	0.0

This second-round high schooler out of Texas was actually the first pick in 2012 for the Tigers because their first-round pick was lost in the Fielder signing. The big right-hander brings a solid three-pitch arsenal with him, highlighted by a low-90s fastball with great sink. The curveball and changeup need still need work, but at age 19 that is hardly a knock on him. The curve has more potential of the two, though neither projects to a plus pitch at this point. Thompson has a mid-rotation ceiling, which doesn't require a ton of projection, given that the size and fastball are already in place.

Jose Valverde

Born: **3/24/1978** Age: **35**
Bats: **R** Throws: **R** Height: **6' 5"** Weight: **255**
Breakout: **17%** Improve: **43%** Collapse: **43%**
Attrition: **16%** MLB: **78%**

Comparables:
Brendan Donnelly, Al Reyes, Jason Isringhausen

YEAR	TEAM	LVL	AGE	W	L	SV	G	GS	IP	H	HR	BB	SO	BB9	SO9	GB%	BABIP	WHIP	ERA	FIP	FRA	WARP
2010	DET	MLB	32	2	4	26	60	0	63	41	5	32	63	4.6	9.0	54%	.231	1.16	3.00	3.75	4.96	0.2
2011	DET	MLB	33	2	4	49	75	0	72^1	52	5	34	69	4.2	8.6	44%	.247	1.19	2.24	3.59	3.74	1.0
2012	DET	MLB	34	3	4	35	71	0	69	59	3	27	48	3.5	6.3	36%	.264	1.25	3.78	3.57	4.00	0.8
2013	*DET*	*MLB*	*35*	*3*	*1*	*31*	*61*	*0*	*60^2*	*52*	*6*	*24*	*59*	*3.6*	*8.8*	*42%*	*.283*	*1.26*	*3.55*	*3.73*	*3.86*	*0.9*

Valverde will be dancing off of another mound in 2013 as his Tigers tenure ends with a whimper—a very public whimper in the form of a 30.00 ERA in four postseason performances. That came on the heels of his worst season yet in terms of core skills. His dwindling strikeout rate tumbled this time from 8.6 SO9 in 2011 to just 6.3 last year. His strikeout rate is on a seven-year slide from his 12.6 peak in 2006, and Valverde found out how difficult it is to survive with only half the stuff.

Justin Verlander

Born: **2/20/1983** Age: **30**
Bats: **R** Throws: **R** Height: **6' 6"** Weight: **225**
Breakout: **8%** Improve: **32%** Collapse: **37%**
Attrition: **17%** MLB: **94%**

Comparables:
Jake Peavy, A.J. Burnett, Roger Clemens

YEAR	TEAM	LVL	AGE	W	L	SV	G	GS	IP	H	HR	BB	SO	BB9	SO9	GB%	BABIP	WHIP	ERA	FIP	FRA	WARP
2010	DET	MLB	27	18	9	0	33	33	224^1	190	14	71	219	2.8	8.8	42%	.286	1.16	3.37	2.94	3.28	5.3
2011	DET	MLB	28	24	5	0	34	34	251	174	24	57	250	2.0	9.0	42%	.236	0.92	2.40	3.03	3.53	5.0
2012	DET	MLB	29	17	8	0	33	33	238^1	192	19	60	239	2.3	9.0	43%	.273	1.06	2.64	2.90	3.33	4.7
2013	*DET*	*MLB*	*30*	*16*	*6*	*0*	*29*	*29*	*203^1*	*174*	*18*	*56*	*205*	*2.5*	*9.1*	*41%*	*.289*	*1.13*	*2.98*	*3.16*	*3.24*	*4.8*

Perhaps we aren't past the "Age of Winlightenment" when it comes to handing out Cy Young awards. Verlander put together a season on par with the 2011 campaign that had netted him both the Cy Young and MVP awards, but this time with a 17-8 record instead of the gaudy 24-5 from the year before. The eventual winner, David Price, had a tremendous season in his own right, but it wasn't really better than Verlander's in any discernible way, save the fact that he reached the 20-win plateau. The result isn't a travesty by any stretch, but had Verlander netted wins in three of the four no-decisions where he went at least seven innings and allowed two or fewer runs, you can bet that he would've won his second straight Cy Young.

Brayan Villarreal

Born: **5/10/1987** Age: **26**
Bats: **R** Throws: **R** Height: **6' 1"** Weight: **170**
Breakout: **30%** Improve: **55%** Collapse: **12%**
Attrition: **19%** MLB: **96%**

Comparables:
Francisco Cruceta,Jose Rijo,Antonio Bastardo

YEAR	TEAM	LVL	AGE	W	L	SV	G	GS	IP	H	HR	BB	SO	BB9	SO9	GB%	BABIP	WHIP	ERA	FIP	FRA	WARP
2011	TOL	AAA	24	3	5	0	17	10	66	65	6	29	40	4.0	5.5	43%	.323	1.42	5.05	5.02	6.69	-0.5
2011	DET	MLB	24	1	1	0	16	0	16	21	3	10	14	5.6	7.9	42%	.367	1.94	6.75	5.62	6.70	-0.2
2012	TOL	AAA	25	0	0	1	8	0	14	5	1	7	22	4.5	14.1	71%	.200	0.86	1.29	2.66	2.56	0.4
2012	DET	MLB	25	3	5	0	50	0	54^{2}	38	3	28	66	4.6	10.9	32%	.276	1.21	2.63	2.94	3.56	1.0
2013	*DET*	*MLB*	*26*	*3*	*2*	*0*	*20*	*5*	*45*	*44*	*6*	*21*	*42*	*4.2*	*8.5*	*41%*	*.302*	*1.43*	*4.62*	*4.47*	*5.02*	*0.2*

Looking at his composite line, it is hard to quibble with anything the Tigers got from Villarreal last year, but he wore down in the dog days. There was some right-elbow inflammation in mid-August that may have been the primary cause. He had 13 walks in his first 33 innings through July, which is a passable 3.5 rate when you are striking out 11.7 per game. In the final two months, he walked 15 in 22 innings. That 6.1 rate is unacceptable on any level. His 3-mph spike in fastball velocity from 2011, combined with his strong slider, make him a deadly weapon out of the bullpen for the Tigers.

Adam Wilk

Born: **12/9/1987** Age: **25**
Bats: **L** Throws: **L** Height: **6' 3"** Weight: **180**
Breakout: **19%** Improve: **65%** Collapse: **15%**
Attrition: **8%** MLB: **87%**

Comparables:
Tommy Milone,Randy Tomlin,Zach Duke

YEAR	TEAM	LVL	AGE	W	L	SV	G	GS	IP	H	HR	BB	SO	BB9	SO9	GB%	BABIP	WHIP	ERA	FIP	FRA	WARP
2010	LAK	A+	22	9	5	0	24	24	143^{2}	139	8	19	100	1.2	6.3	41%	.290	1.10	3.01	3.25	4.53	0.3
2010	ERI	AA	22	2	0	0	3	3	23^{2}	10	1	5	14	1.9	5.3	40%	.167	0.63	1.14	3.49	4.39	0.2
2011	TOL	AAA	23	8	6	0	18	18	102^{2}	105	15	14	76	1.2	6.7	36%	.271	1.16	3.24	4.15	5.07	0.2
2011	DET	MLB	23	0	0	0	5	0	13^{1}	14	3	3	10	2.0	6.8	27%	.268	1.27	5.40	5.16	5.45	0.0
2012	TOL	AAA	24	7	11	0	24	24	149^{2}	123	13	28	128	1.7	7.7	40%	.258	1.01	2.77	3.14	4.36	1.0
2012	DET	MLB	24	0	3	0	3	3	11	21	4	3	7	2.5	5.7	42%	.415	2.18	8.18	7.32	6.53	-0.1
2013	*DET*	*MLB*	*25*	*4*	*3*	*0*	*9*	*9*	*51^{1}*	*57*	*7*	*12*	*31*	*2.1*	*5.5*	*38%*	*.293*	*1.33*	*4.60*	*4.47*	*5.00*	*0.2*

Wilk is more pitchability than stuff, but his left-handedness and pinpoint control keep him relevant. With 252 innings of excellent Triple-A work under his belt, he doesn't have anything left to prove there, but there isn't a clear path to innings for him with Detroit yet either. He is a prototypical swing man/long man who can go four innings for a starter who leaves after one with an injury, or he can close out a 12-2 shellacking for a handful innings, saving the team's late-inning relievers. He should learn the quickest route from Toledo to Detroit this year.

LINEOUTS

HITTERS

PLAYER	TEAM	LVL	AGE	PA	R	2B	3B	HR	RBI	BB	SO	SB-CS	AVG/OBP/SLG	TAv	BABIP	BRR	FRAA	WARP
C C. Casali	WMI	A	23	206	25	12	0	8	25	27	18	2-1	.288/.402/.500	.276	.283	-0.8	C(27): -0.9	0.6
	LAK	A+	23	179	18	13	0	1	18	11	28	0-0	.250/.322/.350	.246	.298	-2.8	C(28): 0.3	0.2
2B H. Castro	TGR	Rk	18	216	24	14	2	1	21	10	25	15-3	.311/.343/.420	.286	.347	-1.3	2B(48): 1.5	0.9
1B D. Green	WMI	A	23	253	34	16	0	9	38	23	39	0-3	.306/.381/.502	.298	.331	-2.1	1B(6): 0.0	0.3
	LAK	A+	23	156	16	11	2	3	36	7	25	2-0	.348/.410/.518	.327	.407	-1.8	--	0.8
OF B. Guez	ERI	AA	25	107	22	4	0	3	11	20	17	4-2	.308/.481/.474	.350	.356	0.9	RF(7): 0.3, LF(3): -0.1	0.6
	TOL	AAA	25	340	43	20	6	6	37	33	76	11-6	.284/.379/.455	.271	.365	-2.6	RF(54): 1.0, LF(13): -0.3	0.1
OF D. Kelly	TOL	AAA	32	85	8	2	0	1	12	12	17	4-1	.233/.341/.301	.195	.291	-1	3B(11): 1.3, CF(2): -0.1	-0.2
	DET	MLB	32	127	14	2	1	1	7	14	22	2-0	.186/.276/.248	.201	.222	1.6	RF(35): 0.2, LF(18): -0.4	-0.5
2B J. Kobernus	HAR	AA	24	366	41	10	2	1	19	19	57	42-11	.282/.325/.333	.236	.333	5	2B(65): 4.2	0.9
2B H. Perez	LAK	A+	21	479	50	11	4	5	44	24	70	27-4	.261/.298/.338	.237	.296	-1.1	2B(78): 1.7, SS(11): -0.9	-0.6
2B D. Travis	ONE	A-	21	107	17	2	2	3	11	8	10	3-1	.280/.352/.441	.276	.284	0	--	0.0
1B A. Westlake	WMI	A	23	518	56	35	2	9	69	47	105	4-1	.249/.320/.391	.256	.303	1.9	1B(59): -0.0	0.1
INF D. Worth	TOL	AAA	26	255	30	15	2	5	24	31	58	10-5	.264/.364/.421	.262	.335	-1.3	2B(22): -3.0, SS(19): 1.3	0.2
	DET	MLB	26	90	9	3	0	0	3	13	23	0-0	.216/.330/.257	.232	.308	-1.4	2B(31): -2.3, 3B(5): -0.1	-0.7

Curt Casali gives the Tigers yet another young backstop of some note; his offensive profile is highlighted by great strike-zone knowledge and a bit of pop. **Harold Castro**'s debut in the States was a resounding success, but even the aggressive Tigers know that his promising bat is years from contributing. Excitement for **Dean Green**'s strong offensive season is tempered by his age (23) and the fact that his best defensive position is "hitter." If the Tigers need an outfielder in a pinch this year, they may turn to 25-year-old **Ben Guez**, who is more org guy than prospect at this point, but could hold his own for a spell, thanks to a solid eye. **Don Kelly** was Jim Leyland's favorite Swiss Army knife 25th man, but his production last year was too scanty to hold onto a 40-man roster spot. **Jeff Kobernus** is a Rule 5 pickup who was initially selected by Boston and then traded over. He is a super-speedy contact hitter who has a future, though at 25 his prospect status is waning a bit as he heads to Triple-A for the first time. **Hernan Perez** has an exceptional glove, so exceptional that he jumped from High-A to the majors for a brief turn. The progress of his bat will determine his future. **Devon Travis** was given a six-figure bonus as a 13th-rounder out of Florida State, and while his size (5-foot-9) doesn't wow scouts, he does a lot of things well on the diamond. One to watch. The third-round draft position of **Aaron Westlake** keeps him on the radar, but the 24-year-old hasn't exactly torn up the low minors—could be a late bloomer, but even then the ceiling isn't high. **Danny Worth** shuttled between Detroit and Toledo five different times in 2012 and should probably expect more of the same in 2013.

PITCHERS

PLAYER	TEAM	LVL	AGE	W	L	SV	IP	H	HR	BB	SO	BB9	SO9	GB%	BABIP	WHIP	ERA	FIP	FRA	WARP
T. Bell	SLC	AAA	25	1	6	0	37	62	7	24	19	5.8	4.6	41%	.390	2.32	8.27	7.13	9.33	-0.7
E. Briceno	ONE	A-	20	4	3	0	57^2	60	3	22	30	3.4	4.7	50%	.298	1.42	5.15	4.48	6.34	0.1
A. Burgos	LAK	A+	21	8	10	0	121^1	115	6	88	78	6.5	5.8	47%	.311	1.67	4.90	5.07	7.28	-0.3
T. Collier	WMI	A	22	9	8	0	124^2	112	5	37	84	2.7	6.1	49%	.288	1.20	2.74	3.54	4.60	1.0
E. De La Rosa	ONE	A-	21	4	4	0	72^2	66	3	35	54	4.3	6.7	44%	.286	1.39	3.10	4.08	4.93	-0.2
D. Downs	TOL	AAA	27	0	2	0	29^1	25	0	8	33	2.5	10.1	53%	.325	1.12	2.15	1.73	2.52	0.8
	DET	MLB	27	2	1	0	20^2	18	1	9	20	3.9	8.7	45%	.309	1.31	3.48	3.19	3.44	0.4
L. Ehlers	TGR	Rk	20	0	0	0	16^1	9	0	3	16	1.7	8.8	59%	.231	0.73	1.10	2.39	3.84	0.2
S. Hill	LVG	AAA	31	9	2	0	89^2	115	10	22	52	2.2	5.2	53%	.340	1.53	4.52	4.93	6.86	0.4
	TOR	MLB	31	1	0	0	3	0	0	2	0	6.0	0.0	89%	.000	0.67	0.00	5.05	7.68	-0.1
M. Hoffman	TOL	AAA	23	1	2	0	46^1	55	4	16	32	3.1	6.2	40%	.325	1.53	3.69	4.19	5.44	-0.2
K. Lobstein	MNT	AA	22	8	7	0	144	140	12	69	129	4.3	8.1	43%	.311	1.45	4.06	3.91	4.46	0.3
L. Marte	TOL	AAA	25	3	2	2	24^1	20	1	10	27	3.7	10.0	35%	.292	1.23	3.70	2.71	3.05	0.5
	DET	MLB	25	1	0	0	22^1	19	4	9	19	3.6	7.7	31%	.250	1.25	2.82	5.02	5.33	0.1
J. Ortega	TOL	AAA	23	5	8	1	62^2	76	4	51	68	7.3	9.8	51%	.393	2.03	5.74	4.35	4.92	0.1
	DET	MLB	23	0	0	0	2^2	3	1	1	4	3.4	13.5	38%	.286	1.50	3.38	6.05	7.45	-0.1
B. Paulino	—	—	—	—	—	—	—	—	—	—	—	—	—	—	—	—	—	—	—	—
M. Robertson	ONE	A-	22	0	4	0	48	42	2	20	33	3.8	6.2	53%	.270	1.29	4.69	3.81	5.41	-0.1
J. Rogers	ONE	A-	21	2	1	3	23^2	20	0	12	28	4.6	10.6	60%	.200	1.35	2.28	2.61	1.75	0.2
D. VerHagen	LAK	A+	21	0	3	0	27	20	0	14	17	4.7	5.7	78%	.348	1.26	3.67	4.02	3.22	0.0

In 2001, *Baseball America* named **Trevor Bell** the nation's best 14-year-old, except 14-year-olds aren't far from outdoing him now and he likely won't be facing any 14-year-olds in Toledo. **Endrys Briceno** was part of an exciting short-season rotation, and while his results were unspectacular, there is promise in the 6-foot-4, 160-pound frame thanks to a low-90s fastball and his incrementally improving secondary stuff. Youth is on his side, but **Alex Burgos** lost any semblance of command and control in 2012, resulting in a dismal season. **Thomas Collier** is a sinker-slider type with an okay changeup, paired with some above-average command, resulting in a back-end-starter ceiling. **Edgar De La Rosa** was part of that short-season rotation, and the 6-foot-6 righty has the velocity you would expect from such a frame, but he's still searching for the command needed to get the most out of the pitch. **Darin Downs** showed how fungible relievers can be. After 10 years and 16 stops in the minors, he emerged as a 27-year-old to give the Tigers 21 quality bullpen innings, but don't be surprised if he's back down for year 11 and stop 17 in 2013. The Tigers got **Logan Ehlers** in the 20th round, two years after Toronto saw him as an eighth round pick. His advanced feel for pitching, combined with the organization's tendency to push, could accelerate Ehlers's path. ⚾ **Shawn Hill** went from the independent Atlantic League to the Blue Jays bullpen in a little more than three months, making his first major-league appearance since 2010 at the tail end of the season, and he'll likely ply his trade in Triple-A in 2013. ⚾ **Matt Hoffman** is slated to start his third season in Triple-A, but the good news is that he is left-handed and 24, so he has at least 10 more years of leash to figure it out and become a viable LOOGY. ⚾ The Mets took **Kyle Lobstein** from the Rays in the Rule 5 draft, then traded him to Detroit. The Rays could lose 10 Lobsteins without batting an eye, but with the Tigers he can be an asset as a lefty swing man. ⚾ There are three guys named **Luis Marte** currently in pro ball, though only the righty reliever for the Tigers has made the majors, and he'll likely put in an appearance there again in 2013. ⚾ **Jose Ortega** is a 24-year-old with a high-90s heater and little idea of where it will go. ⚾ Shoulder issues cost **Brenny Paulino** all of 2012, but he remains an arm the organization is extremely high on, especially as a 20-year-old with mid-90s heat. ⚾ **Montreal Robertson** has shown mid- to high-90s velocity in short spurts, leading many to believe that his future is in the bullpen, though the Tigers want to see if they can make him a starter. ⚾ Meanwhile, **Joe Rogers** has been tabbed as a reliever and threw 24 innings out of the pen last year, but many believe he has the ability to start at some point. ⚾ **Drew VerHagen** is one of five Vanderbilt products the Tigers have drafted in the last two seasons. His mid-90s heater is intriguing, but he hasn't developed anything of note to go with it.

MANAGER: JIM LEYLAND

YEAR	TEAM	W-L	Pythag +/-	Avg PC	100+ P	120+ P	QS	BQS	REL	REL w Zero R	IBB	PH	PH Avg	PH HR	SB2	CS2	SB3	CS3	SAC Att	SAC %	POS SAC	Squeeze	Swing	In Play
2010	DET	81-81	1	198.7	161	159	100	4	416	317	58	242	.214	4	1	8	0	0	118	88.1%	100	4	344	109
2011	DET	95-67	1	98.2	78	9	90	3	421	337	34	79	.300	5	1	3	0	0	72	79.2%	57	3	305	105
2012	DET	88-74	1	98.3	79	8	90	4	420	326	35	67	.236	0	4	0	0	1	48	87.5%	35	0	273	94

It wasn't the fourth straight season of .500 or better ball that kept the firing squad at bay for Leyland, but the second straight division title and second AL pennant in seven years that earned him his reprieve. Leyland has the look and feel of an old-school manager due in large part to the 20-30 daily Marlboros he sucks down, not to mention his penchant for bunting despite his team lacking the speed needed to make that strategy at all productive. The Tigers have had the second-most sacrifice bunts in the AL during his tenure and easily carry the lowest stolen-base total, sitting 103 below the 13th-place Indians. Where Leyland excels is in that most intangible aspect of a manager's job: player management. His 25 men are behind him without question, as evidenced by his star player Miguel Cabrera's behavior toward a fan: While signing autographs late in the season, as the team was struggling to meet lofty expectations, Cabrera didn't take kindly to a fan's "Fire Leyland" sign and confiscated it.

The label "player's manager" implies favoritism toward veterans, but that is not the case with Leyland. He embraces rookies and will place them in critical spots without hesitation. Leyland's lineup construction draws the most negative attention. Some dislike his policy of simply replacing hitters in the lineup with subs without shuffling the batting order. Just because Don Kelly is giving Cabrera the day off doesn't mean he should be hitting third, too. Expectations remain high in Detroit, where Leyland has been for nearly a decade. With Leyland approaching 70, his next dud of a season could be his last, but there is no way anyone can label his time with the Tigers a failure. He has taken this team from perennial loser to two World Series appearances, and will helm a World Series favorite in 2013.

Houston Astros

2012: THIS OLD HOUSE

New owner Jim Crane knew he was buying a fixer-upper in the Astros, and 2012 was just as ugly as a house in severe disrepair. There would be no quick fixes and no surprises as the team posted its second consecutive 100-loss season.

George C. Marshall once said, "When a thing is done, it's done. Don't look back. Look forward to your next objective." Marshall's advice aptly describes 2012 for Houston as the team plowed stoically ahead through 107 losses and a last-place finish, below even the 61-101 Cubs. Even the most ardent Astros fan knew 2012 would be hard on the eyes given the state of the organization that Crane purchased in November 2011. That didn't give new general manager Jeff Luhnow much time to begin rebuilding.

ASTROS PROSPECTUS

2012 W-L: 55-107, 6th in NL Central

Pythag	.361	30th	DER	.693	26th
RS/G	3.60	30th	B-Age	26.5	2nd
RA/G	4.90	26th	P-Age	27.1	3rd
TAv	.241	30th	Salary	$60.8	27th
BRR	-7.0	25th	M$/MW	$7.40	28th
TAv-P	.271	24th	DL Days	747	22nd
FIP	4.31	24th	DL WARP	0.7	28th

Three-Year Park Factors	
Overall	103
HR/RH	109
HR/LH	107
AVG/RH	102
AVG/LH	100

Minute Maid Park (2000)
Att. % of Capacity: 48.5% (28th)
Dim. 315, 362, 435, 373, 326

In a fitting tribute to the Astros' disastrous season, Minute Maid Park yielded a devilish 666 runs in 2012.

The organization reached its breaking point after years of questionable contracts and trades had left Houston with just a handful of enviable assets. Despite Luhnow's acumen from his successful days in St. Louis, he could not reverse that course overnight. Rather than try to patch the gaping holes on the organizational depth chart, Luhnow took to his job less like Bob Vila and more like casino-magnate Steve Wynn, demolishing the crumbling edifice to make way for something shinier and better. The end result is a 2013 payroll without a single long-term commitment, substantial investment in the amateur draft as well as the international market, and an ongoing overhaul of organizational personnel—all items Luhnow laid out in a personal letter to season-ticket holders in August and reiterated when announcing the hiring of new manager Bo Porter.

"The point of this year was to set up the foundation," Luhnow wrote. "Now I think we've got almost the entire foundation set up. Obviously, the major league staff is another key piece to it as well as finishing off the front office staff. Now we've got to figure out where we add strategically to improve results in 2013."

2013: RENOVATION REALITIES

A five-year plan is tough to sell to fans, but it is unlikely that 2013 will be much different from 2012. The talent level on the field should be a step above what the organization had in 2012, but so will the level of competition as the Astros move to the American League West.

Given how hard the organization worked to purge itself of toxic assets, don't expect a shopping spree or even a cosmetic paint job until the underlying structural renovation is complete. For the most part, the team has resisted the temptation to dip into the cesspool of overpriced free agents for instant fixes, but do look for Houston to add players via free agency who can act as stopgaps to buy more time for the rest of the organization to continue taking shape, similar to what both Oakland and Tampa Bay have done in the last decade.

The roster saw so many changes last season that the equipment staff could have switched to Velcro-ing name plates to the uniforms rather than stitching them. The 40-man roster at season's end had 24 different players acquired either via trade or free agency, but the 2013 version should see more stability due to the simple fact the team is nearly tapped out of tradable assets.

The strength of the team should be its infield, with Jose Altuve, Jed Lowrie, and a promising Matt Dominguez leading the way. Justin Maxwell's career has been sidetracked by his fragility, but he showed a bit of his long-forgotten potential last season. Fans should also start to see some additional returns on past trades as players such as moundsmen Jarred Cosart, Brett Oberholtzer, and Paul Clemens could see time in the majors.

As any contractor knows, the shiniest appliances, the best paint, and the fanciest fixtures won't do much for a house with rotting beams. The old regime too often played for the now, despite all signs pointing in the opposite direction. Astros fans could very well be in for another 100-loss season, but the overarching goal is to further develop a foundation of talent to build on.

STATE OF THE ORGANIZATION: TRADING SPACES

To move any organization forward, everyone must be on the same page. Tearing down the rotting structure means tearing apart previous axioms to begin anew. Luhnow has assembled a diverse front-office staff that combines both analytical and scouting skills. His goal is to reshape the Astros in the image of the Cardinals organization he came from. The Cardinals played most of the 2012 postseason with seven homegrown players in their lineup, a situation Luhnow would love for the Astros to emulate in the future.

To achieve that, Houston must stockpile talent in the pipeline and develop it. Luhnow refined this technique while in St. Louis. The first three drafts he oversaw (2005-07) yielded 24 major-league players, the highest total in MLB during those years, and Cardinals minor-league affiliates won five championships during his tenure. St. Louis affiliates had the best overall record in minor-league baseball just two seasons ago. The Astros organization shows glimmers in that direction: Last season, six of the eight affiliates finished at or above .500, three advanced to the postseason, and the High-A affiliate won the California League championship. The 417-347 record compiled by the stateside squads was the best record in baseball, attesting to the organization's improved depth of talent and commitment to instilling a winning culture.

Acquiring the right talent is only one step in developing major-league prospects. Organizations must also have the right people to identify a winning process for developing that talent and an effective way to proliferate that process throughout the organization. The amount of organizational turnover in Houston, from top to bottom, is both staggering and unique. Normally, a team with chronically poor performance (below .500 in five of the last six years) can stockpile strong prospects, but it was just two years ago that BP's Kevin Goldstein—since hired by Luhnow to run Houston's pro scouting department—ranked this farm system as the worst in all of baseball.

The Astros start with a fresh slate in a new league after 51 seasons of playing in the senior circuit. Things are headed in the right direction for the organization as the demolition portion of the project is complete.

HITTERS

Jose Altuve **2B**

Born: **5/6/1990** Age: **23**
Bats: **R** Throws: **R** Height: **5' 8"**
Weight: **170** Breakout: **2%**
Improve: **52%** Collapse: **4%**
Attrition: **6%** MLB: **87%**

Comparables:
Paul Molitor,Jose Lopez,Steve Sax

YEAR	TEAM	LVL	AGE	PA	R	2B	3B	HR	RBI	BB	SO	SB	CS	AVG_OBP_SLG	TAv	BABIP	BRR	FRAA	WARP
2010	LEX	A	20	434	75	15	3	11	45	33	49	39	14	.308/.360/.445	.310	.325	5.7	2B(90): -3.6, 3B(1): -0.0	3.4
2010	LNC	A+	20	127	18	5	2	4	22	9	17	3	4	.276/.331/.457	.253	.292	1	2B(26): -0.3, 3B(1): -0.0	0.3
2011	LNC	A+	21	238	38	13	7	5	34	19	26	19	9	.408/.451/.606	.509	.443	-0.5	2B(3): -0.5	0.2
2011	CCH	AA	21	153	21	9	3	5	25	7	14	5	5	.361/.388/.569	.322	.373	0	--	0.0
2011	HOU	MLB	21	234	26	10	1	2	12	5	29	7	3	.276/.297/.357	.234	.309	-2.2	2B(55): -0.3	-0.6
2012	HOU	MLB	22	630	80	34	4	7	37	40	74	33	11	.290/.340/.399	.269	.321	4.2	2B(146): 6.8	3.3
2013	*HOU*	*MLB*	*23*	*514*	*66*	*23*	*3*	*9*	*44*	*27*	*70*	*25*	*10*	*.275/.317/.390*	*.258*	*.301*	*1*	*2B -2, 3B 0*	*1.6*

The haters can point out that Altuve's second half was disappointing, a red flag for a young player, from whom constant growth is expected. Also, he barely survived against right-handed pitching. But there were so many positives for this diminutive keystoner who won't turn 23 until May. He had the seventh-best TAv of qualifying second basemen. He had the 20th-best strikeout rate among all qualifying batters, battered lefties enough to compensate for struggles against northpaws, had a positive BRR thanks to 33 stolen bases and good baserunning, and posted a very good FRAA total. All told, a very well-rounded set of contributions. His size perpetually limits expectations, but even slight improvements in his game—the most likely a rediscovery of some of the power he showed in the minors—will make him one player who legitimately qualifies for the star he wears on his cap.

Brandon Barnes **CF**

Born: **5/15/1986** Age: **27**
Bats: **R** Throws: **R** Height: **6' 3"**
Weight: **210** Breakout: **1%**
Improve: **46%** Collapse: **5%**
Attrition: **12%** MLB: **92%**

Comparables:
Roberto Kelly,Ray Sadler,Dave Henderson

YEAR	TEAM	LVL	AGE	PA	R	2B	3B	HR	RBI	BB	SO	SB	CS	AVG_OBP_SLG	TAv	BABIP	BRR	FRAA	WARP
2010	LNC	A+	24	538	81	31	5	27	80	37	122	14	3	.269/.324/.517	.279	.303	0.6	RF(113): -2.5, CF(11): 1.0	2.0
2011	CCH	AA	25	224	25	13	0	7	27	14	42	6	3	.286/.335/.453	.270	.327	0	--	0.0
2011	OKL	AAA	25	263	34	13	5	8	27	29	69	5	1	.197/.294/.402	.238	.242	0	--	0.0
2012	CCH	AA	26	183	30	20	0	7	31	14	42	7	2	.317/.377/.567	.303	.385	0.7	CF(10): 0.7, RF(1): -0.0	0.6
2012	OKL	AAA	26	263	51	19	1	5	38	23	49	14	4	.323/.383/.477	.346	.388	4	CF(14): 1.3, LF(2): 0.2	1.3
2012	HOU	MLB	26	105	8	3	0	1	7	5	29	1	1	.204/.250/.265	.192	.279	0.2	CF(32): 1.9, RF(5): -0.3	-0.2
2013	*HOU*	*MLB*	*27*	*250*	*27*	*12*	*1*	*7*	*28*	*15*	*67*	*5*	*2*	*.232/.281/.385*	*.239*	*.290*	*0.3*	*CF -1, RF -0*	*0.1*

Barnes showed enough last year to get protected on the 40-man roster. In 2011 he was so lost at the plate in Triple-A that he was sent back to Double-A, and then played in Sydney over the winter. But he didn't stay down under in 2012, instead earning promotions first to Triple-A, then to Houston when Schafer went down. A true center fielder, Barnes is too old to be considered a prospect, but his moderate power and speed combine with his glove to make him a useful bench cog.

Bobby Borchering 3B
Born: **10/25/1990** Age: **22**
Bats: **B** Throws: **R** Height: **6' 4"**
Weight: **200** Breakout: **5%**
Improve: **60%** Collapse: **1%**
Attrition: **9%** MLB: **96%**
Comparables:
Joel Guzman, Ron Swoboda, Greg Luzinski

YEAR	TEAM	LVL	AGE	PA	R	2B	3B	HR	RBI	BB	SO	SB	CS	AVG_OBP_SLG	TAv	BABIP	BRR	FRAA	WARP
2010	SBN	A	19	588	74	31	2	15	74	54	128	1	1	.270/.343/.423	.277	.331	-3.6	3B(84): -16.2	0.5
2011	VIS	A+	20	590	80	29	3	24	92	49	162	4	1	.267/.332/.469	.305	.337	1.3	1B(36): -1.4, 3B(29): -3.2	1.5
2012	VIS	A+	21	344	47	23	1	18	60	28	96	0	2	.277/.340/.534	.313	.338	-1.5	RF(36): -7.1, LF(24): -0.1	0.8
2012	CCH	AA	21	109	11	5	1	4	18	10	36	1	1	.189/.275/.389	.236	.246	-0.2	3B(5): -0.0	0.0
2012	MOB	AA	21	82	4	0	0	2	8	3	27	0	1	.130/.183/.208	.046	.167	-0.5	LF(6): -0.7	-0.7
2013	*HOU*	*MLB*	*22*	*250*	*24*	*9*	*1*	*9*	*30*	*15*	*78*	*0*	*0*	*.211/.261/.368*	*.228*	*.274*	*-0.4*	*3B -0, LF -0*	*-0.5*

Acquired for Chris Johnson, who went to the same high school, Borchering piques interest anew as a prospect thanks to the Astros' decision to return him to his prep position: third base. He retains the exciting power potential from both sides of the plate that made him a first-round pick in 2009, but needs to improve in two areas: He needs to strike out less than 30 percent of the time and upgrade his defense to something resembling average. It's unlikely he'll be able to do both this year, given the humbling he endured at Double-A, but he's just entering his age-22 season, so he's still young for his level.

Jason Castro C
Born: **6/18/1987** Age: **26**
Bats: **L** Throws: **R** Height: **6' 4"**
Weight: **205** Breakout: **3%**
Improve: **50%** Collapse: **4%**
Attrition: **14%** MLB: **94%**
Comparables:
Don Pavletich, Jorge Posada, Bill Freehan

YEAR	TEAM	LVL	AGE	PA	R	2B	3B	HR	RBI	BB	SO	SB	CS	AVG_OBP_SLG	TAv	BABIP	BRR	FRAA	WARP
2010	ROU	AAA	23	244	31	7	0	4	26	32	34	1	1	.265/.365/.355	.252	.301	-0.7	C(54): -0.1	1.0
2010	HOU	MLB	23	217	26	8	1	2	8	22	41	0	0	.205/.286/.287	.212	.250	-0.2	C(67): -0.1	0.0
2012	HOU	MLB	25	295	29	15	2	6	29	31	61	0	0	.257/.334/.401	.260	.309	-0.3	C(78): -1.6	0.4
2013	*HOU*	*MLB*	*26*	*250*	*25*	*10*	*1*	*5*	*25*	*26*	*49*	*0*	*0*	*.240/.321/.362*	*.248*	*.285*	*-0.3*	*C -0*	*0.8*

Castro lived up to expectations offensively, checking in with the 17th-best TAv among catchers who had 295 or more plate appearances in 2012. He showed above-average walk and strikeout rates, and with a .294 TAv against right-handed pitchers was particularly adept against the side he was supposed to thrive against. Considering both wild pitches and passed balls, he let a ton of balls get past him and was inept at deterring or apprehending would-be base thieves. Still young, he is expected to bring his defense back to speed as his knee injuries recede into the past. If health solves Castro's defensive woes, the Astros are set behind the plate for the next few years, but that's a big "if."

Carlos Correa SS
Born: **9/22/1994** Age: **18**
Bats: **R** Throws: **R** Height: **6' 5"**
Weight: **190** Breakout: **0%**
Improve: **64%** Collapse: **36%**
Attrition: **36%** MLB: **100%**
Comparables:
Robin Yount, Wayne Causey, Wayne Causey

YEAR	TEAM	LVL	AGE	PA	R	2B	3B	HR	RBI	BB	SO	SB	CS	AVG_OBP_SLG	TAv	BABIP	BRR	FRAA	WARP
2012	AST	Rk	17	163	23	11	1	2	9	7	36	5	1	.232/.270/.355	.126	.291	0	SS(1): -0.3	-0.1
2013	*HOU*	*MLB*	*18*	*250*	*29*	*8*	*1*	*3*	*14*	*13*	*76*	*15*	*4*	*.179/.226/.260*	*.179*	*.245*	*1.8*	*SS 0*	*-0.8*

The scouting reports on Correa contain all the superstar buzzwords associated with young talents like him, and to suggest anything short of a Hall-of-Fame career would be a buzz kill. His stats weren't special, but rookie-ball numbers are all but meaningless—at least he improved somewhat as the season went on. For players this far away, possible stumbling blocks are revealed in what the scouts don't emphasize; for Correa, his "hit tool" (ability to make consistent hard contact) is barely nascent, his power has a long way to go, and his size may force him to the hot corner. His power potential is massive, especially for an infielder. His arm draws raves, which should help delay any positional move and make third base an easy shift if necessary. His progress will be scrutinized in 2013, with his ability to translate his great bat speed into hits and homers watched most closely.

Delino DeShields 2B
Born: **8/16/1992** Age: **20**
Bats: **R** Throws: **R** Height: **5' 10"**
Weight: **188** Breakout: **16%**
Improve: **54%** Collapse: **5%**
Attrition: **19%** MLB: **83%**
Comparables:
Wayne Causey, Clete Boyer, Bill Mazeroski

YEAR	TEAM	LVL	AGE	PA	R	2B	3B	HR	RBI	BB	SO	SB	CS	AVG_OBP_SLG	TAv	BABIP	BRR	FRAA	WARP
2010	GRV	Rk	17	73	11	6	1	0	8	5	18	5	1	.313/.361/.433	.293	.429	0.9	CF(15): -0.5	0.4
2011	LEX	A	18	541	73	17	2	9	48	52	118	30	11	.220/.305/.322	.242	.271	4.5	2B(93): -5.6	-0.4
2012	LEX	A	19	523	96	22	5	10	52	70	108	83	14	.298/.401/.439	.280	.373	9.6	2B(90): -1.5	2.4
2012	LNC	A+	19	114	17	2	3	2	9	13	23	18	5	.237/.336/.381	.344	.288	2	2B(11): -3.0	0.4
2013	*HOU*	*MLB*	*20*	*250*	*33*	*7*	*1*	*4*	*17*	*20*	*68*	*19*	*5*	*.207/.275/.304*	*.213*	*.272*	*2.2*	*2B -2, CF -0*	*-0.3*

Beware the illusory success of players repeating a level and having good seasons, but be excited about the 2012 DeShields had. His father ("Bop") had a .375 on-base percentage and 42 steals as a 21-year-old rookie second baseman. Lil Bop's speedy conversion to the keystone (from center field), and equally speedy baserunning suggest he could see similar success. Junior has the short, powerful physique of the running back he was in high school. He already shows the base-stealing savvy to convert his impact speed into more baserunning runs than his father—who stole 463 bases—did. He also has the strength to tally double-digit homers in his prime. Lancaster should inflate his stats early this year, which could mean he'll face Double-A pitching before he turns 21 in August. With only two seasons of full-season ball and two as a second baseman, DeShields needs polish, but the organization's worries are now about how they'll get him on the field with Altuve, not about whether his repeat Single-A season was a fluke.

Matt Dominguez 3B
Born: **8/28/1989** Age: **23**
Bats: **R** Throws: **R** Height: **6' 2"**
Weight: **205** Breakout: **7%**
Improve: **62%** Collapse: **5%**
Attrition: **13%** MLB: **96%**
Comparables:
George Brett,Adrian Beltre,Blake DeWitt

YEAR	TEAM	LVL	AGE	PA	R	2B	3B	HR	RBI	BB	SO	SB	CS	AVG_OBP_SLG	TAv	BABIP	BRR	FRAA	WARP
2010	JAX	AA	20	577	61	34	2	14	81	56	96	0	2	.252/.337/.411	.285	.286	0	3B(145): 4.5	4.0
2011	NWO	AAA	21	356	47	18	1	12	55	24	50	0	1	.258/.312/.431	.253	.270	0	--	0.0
2011	FLO	MLB	21	48	2	4	0	0	2	2	8	0	0	.244/.292/.333	.205	.297	-1.6	3B(16): -0.4	-0.4
2012	NWO	AAA	22	315	27	14	0	7	46	23	31	0	1	.234/.291/.357	.332	.239	-2.9	3B(18): -0.1	0.5
2012	OKL	AAA	22	177	21	10	0	2	23	11	21	0	0	.298/.347/.398	.269	.329	0.8	3B(17): 0.8	0.3
2012	HOU	MLB	22	113	14	2	2	5	16	4	17	0	0	.284/.310/.477	.264	.299	-2.8	3B(31): 0.2	0.1
2013	*HOU*	*MLB*	*23*	*250*	*24*	*11*	*1*	*6*	*28*	*15*	*43*	*0*	*0*	*.242/.292/.384*	*.245*	*.269*	*-0.4*	*3B -2*	*0.0*

For the second year in a row, the Astros finished the season with a surprisingly adequate performance at third base from a young, prospect-y player. Last year's edition was Dominguez, the bounty from the Carlos Lee trade. That the team was able to get a slick-fielding prospect who was believed to have good power potential was a testament both to some creative negotiating (the Astros paid all but a tiny portion of Lee's salary) and to Dominguez's awful struggles in Triple-A in the Marlins' system. As with Jimmy Paredes in 2011, the good numbers Dominguez posted in the big leagues are fluky. But it's possible that his defense is good enough to make him an average all-around third baseman, and he's young enough that there's still a chance for significant growth.

Jacob Elmore MI
Born: **6/15/1987** Age: **26**
Bats: **R** Throws: **R** Height: **5' 11"**
Weight: **180** Breakout: **4%**
Improve: **49%** Collapse: **7%**
Attrition: **12%** MLB: **97%**
Comparables:
Emmanuel Burriss,Jason Bartlett,Dave Chalk

YEAR	TEAM	LVL	AGE	PA	R	2B	3B	HR	RBI	BB	SO	SB	CS	AVG_OBP_SLG	TAv	BABIP	BRR	FRAA	WARP
2010	MOB	AA	23	462	64	16	2	2	31	58	56	25	13	.278/.372/.345	.282	.315	3.8	2B(79): -2.7, SS(38): -2.9	2.7
2011	MOB	AA	24	458	58	19	1	3	41	54	65	15	11	.270/.362/.349	.294	.309	0.1	2B(51): 5.0, P(1): -0.0	1.8
2012	RNO	AAA	25	511	95	30	9	1	73	74	54	32	8	.344/.442/.465	.285	.386	0.4	SS(28): -1.1, 2B(20): -0.4	1.0
2012	ARI	MLB	25	73	1	4	0	0	7	5	6	0	0	.191/.247/.250	.190	.210	0.8	SS(17): 0.4, 2B(5): 0.1	-0.1
2013	*HOU*	*MLB*	*26*	*250*	*30*	*10*	*2*	*2*	*18*	*26*	*39*	*10*	*4*	*.251/.332/.339*	*.253*	*.293*	*0.4*	*SS 0, 2B 0*	*0.9*

Elmore's 2012 season serves as a cautionary tale of how bandbox ballparks can skew the perception of a player. He had established himself in the Diamondbacks system as a guy with little power but a bit of speed who could take a walk or three. Then a PCL tour magnified his offensive output. Elmore topped his best full-season batting average by 66 points and added an extra dose of doubles. The end result was an OPS 200 points higher than his previous apex, a performance that helped to earn him a big-league call-up in August. Lacking talent depth, the Astros had little to lose by plucking him off waivers. After all, Elmore did draw 20 more walks than he had strikeouts, so his "breakout" season wasn't totally skewed up.

Marwin Gonzalez SS
Born: **3/14/1989** Age: **24**
Bats: **B** Throws: **R** Height: **6' 2"**
Weight: **186** Breakout: **6%**
Improve: **41%** Collapse: **5%**
Attrition: **17%** MLB: **83%**
Comparables:
Bucky Dent,Yuniesky Betancourt,Pedro Lopez

YEAR	TEAM	LVL	AGE	PA	R	2B	3B	HR	RBI	BB	SO	SB	CS	AVG_OBP_SLG	TAv	BABIP	BRR	FRAA	WARP
2010	DAY	A+	21	96	7	3	0	0	5	7	13	7	1	.271/.326/.306	.244	.311	1.4	1B(11): -0.9, LF(4): -0.1	-0.1
2010	TEN	AA	21	330	24	11	3	4	41	17	40	6	4	.246/.285/.341	.223	.269	-3.5	SS(89): 8.7, CF(1): -0.2	0.5
2011	TEN	AA	22	239	29	18	1	2	20	17	27	4	2	.301/.359/.421	.228	.335	0.3	SS(18): -1.4, 2B(6): 0.4	-0.1
2011	IOW	AAA	22	226	24	12	1	2	19	16	21	3	1	.274/.326/.376	.224	.292	-2	SS(25): 1.9	-0.1
2012	HOU	MLB	23	219	21	13	0	2	12	13	29	3	3	.234/.280/.327	.217	.264	-3.1	SS(47): 0.0, 3B(14): 0.4	-0.5
2013	*HOU*	*MLB*	*24*	*250*	*24*	*11*	*1*	*3*	*21*	*13*	*40*	*4*	*2*	*.237/.279/.336*	*.221*	*.269*	*-0.1*	*SS 0, 3B 0*	*0.1*

When his ankle is fully healthy, Gonzalez wows some observers with his defense, but posts mediocre metrics and leaves others unimpressed. He's willing to play multiple positions and makes consistent contact, but is still a notch below the offensive requirements for a good utilityman. He only stuck on the roster all last season because he was a Rule 5 draftee. Offering little in the way of power, patience, or speed, his chances of sticking as a regular someday will depend on meaningless batting average and finding a manager who is convinced by his defensive prowess. Alternately, waiting around for Jed Lowrie to get injured is another proven way to get playing time.

Tyler Greene SS
Born: **8/17/1983** Age: **29**
Bats: **R** Throws: **R** Height: **6' 3"**
Weight: **190** Breakout: **2%**
Improve: **43%** Collapse: **10%**
Attrition: **12%** MLB: **92%**
Comparables:
Robby Thompson,Keith Ginter,Ike Brown

YEAR	TEAM	LVL	AGE	PA	R	2B	3B	HR	RBI	BB	SO	SB	CS	AVG_OBP_SLG	TAv	BABIP	BRR	FRAA	WARP
2010	MEM	AAA	26	385	67	21	5	9	34	32	89	12	5	.284/.349/.456	.284	.351	0.9	SS(82): 0.5	2.5
2010	SLN	MLB	26	122	14	3	1	2	10	13	24	2	0	.221/.328/.327	.255	.266	1.6	SS(22): -0.9, 2B(15): -0.3	0.5
2011	MEM	AAA	27	303	53	19	2	14	43	37	75	19	2	.323/.422/.579	.342	.407	0	--	0.0
2011	SLN	MLB	27	121	22	5	0	1	11	13	31	11	0	.212/.322/.288	.237	.292	1.7	2B(25): -1.2, SS(20): 0.3	0.3
2012	HOU	MLB	28	133	18	6	0	7	11	6	39	3	2	.246/.278/.460	.252	.296	0.3	SS(34): -1.3, 2B(4): -0.2	0.0
2012	SLN	MLB	28	197	16	9	2	4	19	13	56	9	2	.218/.272/.358	.234	.289	0.4	2B(55): -0.4, SS(9): 0.1	0.0
2013	*HOU*	*MLB*	*29*	*268*	*35*	*10*	*2*	*7*	*26*	*21*	*73*	*10*	*2*	*.231/.300/.379*	*.248*	*.295*	*1.2*	*SS 0, 2B 1*	*1.0*

Greene may be a replacement-level player so far in his career, but he's the sort of 0-WARP guy who can help a team, even if his power barrage with Houston shouldn't be expected again. He has played almost nowhere but shortstop in the minors, so being used as a utilityman in the majors has hurt his fielding metrics. And while he won't ever be confused with fellow Georgia Tech alumnus Nomar Garciaparra against left-handed pitching, he's not an automatic out. He'll never have the on-base or righty-hitting skills to warrant a bigger role, but as an average-fielding shortstop with a little pop who can hit one hand of pitcher, he can be a cog in the machinery of a good team.

Robbie Grossman CF
Born: **9/16/1989** Age: **23**
Bats: **B** Throws: **L** Height: **6' 2"**
Weight: **190** Breakout: **6%**
Improve: **50%** Collapse: **5%**
Attrition: **13%** MLB: **90%**
Comparables:
Reggie Smith,Ryan Kalish,Bob Coluccio

YEAR	TEAM	LVL	AGE	PA	R	2B	3B	HR	RBI	BB	SO	SB	CS	AVG_OBP_SLG	TAv	BABIP	BRR	FRAA	WARP
2010	BRD	A+	20	562	84	29	3	4	50	66	118	15	8	.245/.340/.345	.249	.308	0	--	0.0
2011	BRD	A+	21	616	127	34	2	13	56	104	111	24	10	.294/.418/.451	.312	.351	0	--	0.0
2012	ALT	AA	22	417	59	20	4	7	36	59	78	9	10	.266/.378/.406	.281	.325	-0.1	CF(84): -13.5	0.3
2012	CCH	AA	22	160	22	8	2	3	11	18	43	4	1	.267/.371/.422	.175	.367	0.9	CF(5): 0.2, LF(4): 0.0	-0.1
2013	*HOU*	*MLB*	*23*	*250*	*29*	*10*	*1*	*5*	*22*	*26*	*64*	*3*	*2*	*.226/.314/.350*	*.241*	*.291*	*-0.3*	*CF -5, RF -0*	*-0.3*

Grossman's 2012 could be considered somewhat of a failure, possibly taking him off the track to a starting job. His home runs, stolen bases, and all his rate stats were down, while strikeouts were up. He did little to suggest he'll be able to stay in center field (as opposed to moving to right). The glass-half-full outlook focuses on the oft-underappreciated on-base skill. Only six players in professional ball have drawn more walks over the past two seasons than Grossman, a list that includes Joey Votto, Jose Bautista, and Prince Fielder. Double-A is supposed to be the biggest test for prospects, and despite the statistical slippage, Grossman passed, getting on base more than 37 percent of the time. Whether he can regain lost power and speed will determine his upside, but he's on track to become a contributor.

Che-Hsuan Lin CF
Born: **9/21/1988** Age: **24**
Bats: **R** Throws: **R** Height: **6' 1"**
Weight: **180** Breakout: **1%**
Improve: **43%** Collapse: **4%**
Attrition: **9%** MLB: **94%**
Comparables:
Gerald Young,Adrian Brown,Richie Ashburn

YEAR	TEAM	LVL	AGE	PA	R	2B	3B	HR	RBI	BB	SO	SB	CS	AVG_OBP_SLG	TAv	BABIP	BRR	FRAA	WARP
2010	PME	AA	21	543	88	17	4	2	34	72	63	26	12	.275/.386/.343	.268	.315	3.2	CF(114): 15.8, RF(4): 0.6	4.7
2011	PME	AA	22	161	23	5	2	0	11	20	14	12	3	.268/.373/.333	.264	.298	0	--	0.0
2011	PAW	AAA	22	378	49	11	1	2	25	38	51	16	4	.235/.325/.293	.223	.271	-1.3	CF(54): 4.4, RF(8): 0.4	-0.4
2012	PAW	AAA	23	445	42	11	5	2	30	42	65	15	4	.247/.323/.316	.224	.290	-1.9	CF(75): -2.1, RF(19): 2.3	-0.9
2012	BOS	MLB	23	12	1	0	0	0	0	0	5	0	0	.250/.250/.250	.176	.429	0	RF(6): -0.2, CF(3): -0.1	-0.2
2013	*HOU*	*MLB*	*24*	*250*	*28*	*8*	*2*	*2*	*17*	*24*	*42*	*8*	*2*	*.234/.315/.312*	*.235*	*.276*	*0.6*	*CF -1, RF 0*	*0.0*

If Lin could hit like he fields, he'd be a perennial All-Star. Alas, there are no signs he can. While he is disciplined at the plate, he has no power and a hit tool that's weak at best, with little room for improvement. As such, he's best suited as a defensive replacement. Removed from Boston's 40-man roster during the offseason, he should find it somewhat easier to make it as the 25th man in Houston, where Martinez (J.D.) and/or Martinez (Fernando) may frequently need replacing in late innings.

Jed Lowrie SS
Born: **4/17/1984** Age: **29**
Bats: **B** Throws: **R** Height: **6' 1"**
Weight: **180** Breakout: **3%**
Improve: **30%** Collapse: **4%**
Attrition: **9%** MLB: **97%**
Comparables:
Brendan Harris,Stephen Drew,John Valentin

YEAR	TEAM	LVL	AGE	PA	R	2B	3B	HR	RBI	BB	SO	SB	CS	AVG_OBP_SLG	TAv	BABIP	BRR	FRAA	WARP
2010	BOS	MLB	26	197	31	14	0	9	24	25	25	1	1	.287/.381/.526	.317	.292	0.2	2B(28): 1.5, SS(23): -1.7	1.7
2011	BOS	MLB	27	341	40	14	4	6	36	23	60	1	1	.252/.303/.382	.250	.289	1.9	SS(49): -1.4, 3B(33): 2.9	0.6
2012	HOU	MLB	28	387	43	18	0	16	42	43	65	2	0	.244/.331/.438	.279	.257	0.6	SS(93): 5.5	2.8
2013	*HOU*	*MLB*	*29*	*358*	*38*	*17*	*2*	*10*	*42*	*36*	*68*	*2*	*1*	*.243/.323/.403*	*.262*	*.277*	*-0.3*	*SS -1, 3B 0*	*1.4*

At the break, Lowrie was showing the world why he was such a highly regarded prospect with the Red Sox. He had arguably the best offensive stats among shortstops in the National League, a positive FRAA, and—most importantly, given his history—had played in 78 of 80 games after the start to his season was delayed slightly by a thumb injury. But, alas, a combination of badly sprained ankle and nerve damage in his leg led to a two-month gap in his season. Continuing the theme from his pre-Astros days, Lowrie was also ineffective upon his return.

The talent is there and when he's 100 percent, he's a force to be reckoned with in the middle infield. But reaching 341 plate appearances was a performance bonus milestone in his last contract, making it clear nobody expects 100 percent playing time.

Fernando Martinez LF
Born: **10/10/1988** Age: **24**
Bats: **L** Throws: **R** Height: **6' 2"**
Weight: **205** Breakout: **4%**
Improve: **48%** Collapse: **6%**
Attrition: **9%** MLB: **98%**
Comparables:
Travis Snider,Rick Reichardt,Willie Horton

YEAR	TEAM	LVL	AGE	PA	R	2B	3B	HR	RBI	BB	SO	SB	CS	AVG_OBP_SLG	TAv	BABIP	BRR	FRAA	WARP
2010	BUF	AAA	21	287	39	16	0	12	33	17	65	1	0	.253/.316/.455	.252	.290	-0.8	RF(50): 1.9, CF(12): -1.9	0.0
2010	NYN	MLB	21	22	1	0	0	0	2	1	5	0	1	.167/.273/.167	.199	.214	-0.2	LF(6): -0.0, RF(2): -0.1	-0.1
2011	BUF	AAA	22	250	29	11	0	8	30	18	60	0	0	.260/.329/.417	.281	.318	-2.2	RF(27): -2.5, LF(1): -0.1	-0.1
2011	NYN	MLB	22	23	3	2	0	1	2	1	7	0	0	.227/.261/.455	.255	.286	0.4	RF(3): -0.1, LF(1): -0.0	0.0
2012	OKL	AAA	23	373	55	23	2	13	62	24	85	1	2	.314/.367/.507	.289	.384	4.1	LF(9): -0.7, RF(9): 0.8	0.6
2012	HOU	MLB	23	130	12	7	1	6	14	6	34	0	1	.237/.300/.466	.277	.278	0.2	LF(31): -0.0, RF(6): -0.6	0.1
2013	*HOU*	*MLB*	*24*	*250*	*27*	*12*	*1*	*9*	*32*	*13*	*61*	*1*	*0*	*.242/.298/.423*	*.260*	*.286*	*-0.4*	*LF -1, RF -0*	*0.5*

Six long years ago, Martinez was roaming center field in Binghamton, and his bat speed had scouts gushing about his potential to hit for average and power someday. The Mets waived goodbye to their former phenom after the 2011 season, and expectations are much lower in his new organization. Given his long injury history, Martinez's foot speed is a thing of the past (along with any thoughts of playing center field), but some of his much-publicized bat speed did show up in both Triple-A and Houston last year. He's in the right place to have a chance to earn playing time, and his spring training will determine how soon that happens.

J.D. Martinez LF
Born: **8/21/1987** Age: **25**
Bats: **R** Throws: **R** Height: **6' 4"**
Weight: **200** Breakout: **10%**
Improve: **57%** Collapse: **1%**
Attrition: **11%** MLB: **92%**
Comparables:
Brandon Jones,Billy Williams,Hal McRae

YEAR	TEAM	LVL	AGE	PA	R	2B	3B	HR	RBI	BB	SO	SB	CS	AVG_OBP_SLG	TAv	BABIP	BRR	FRAA	WARP
2010	LEX	A	22	393	83	31	3	15	64	33	55	3	0	.362/.434/.598	.346	.399	-2.1	RF(64): 0.7	4.2
2010	CCH	AA	22	207	24	9	1	3	25	15	42	2	2	.302/.359/.407	.265	.375	-2.1	RF(27): -2.8, LF(15): 1.0	0.2
2011	CCH	AA	23	370	50	25	1	13	72	42	55	1	0	.338/.414/.546	.330	.367	0	--	0.0
2011	HOU	MLB	23	226	29	13	0	6	35	13	48	0	1	.274/.319/.423	.255	.325	-2.4	LF(51): -0.3, RF(1): -0.0	-0.1
2012	OKL	AAA	24	95	6	6	0	0	4	4	17	0	1	.233/.263/.300	.076	.284	-1.6	LF(4): -1.1	-0.4
2012	HOU	MLB	24	439	34	14	3	11	55	40	96	0	2	.241/.311/.375	.235	.290	-4.2	LF(100): -11.3	-2.4
2013	*HOU*	*MLB*	*25*	*383*	*39*	*17*	*2*	*10*	*44*	*27*	*83*	*1*	*1*	*.251/.308/.395*	*.251*	*.299*	*-0.6*	*LF -3, RF -0*	*0.1*

In the "you pick the punch line" contest, the Astros sent Martinez, then the team's RBI leader, to the minors on August 10. Martinez has always had a scouts-defying swing, and has had to over-produce to earn his chances. So the fact that his walk and home-run rates (in addition to his RBIs) remained about the same in 2012 wasn't enough, given that his production of base hits (especially doubles) dropped. He didn't do anything during his demotion to inspire confidence, and with nothing to offer defensively or on the basepaths, his career has started down the path of the "Brett Wallace Express" to Quadruple-A.

Justin Maxwell CF
Born: **11/6/1983** Age: **29**
Bats: **R** Throws: **R** Height: **6' 6"**
Weight: **235** Breakout: **7%**
Improve: **56%** Collapse: **6%**
Attrition: **11%** MLB: **91%**
Comparables:
Jonathan Van Every,Don Lock,Dale Murphy

YEAR	TEAM	LVL	AGE	PA	R	2B	3B	HR	RBI	BB	SO	SB	CS	AVG_OBP_SLG	TAv	BABIP	BRR	FRAA	WARP
2010	SYR	AAA	26	272	34	17	0	6	21	35	75	16	7	.287/.386/.439	.275	.395	2.6	CF(59): 3.9, RF(5): 0.1	2.2
2010	WAS	MLB	26	131	16	6	0	3	12	25	43	5	1	.144/.305/.288	.232	.200	1.1	RF(28): 1.1, CF(20): 0.7	0.3
2011	SWB	AAA	27	204	36	8	1	16	35	26	72	11	2	.260/.358/.588	.322	.337	1.9	LF(18): 3.5, CF(14): 0.5	2.2
2012	HOU	MLB	28	352	46	13	3	18	53	32	114	9	4	.229/.304/.460	.268	.292	1.3	CF(59): 2.8, LF(38): 1.2	1.5
2013	*HOU*	*MLB*	*29*	*281*	*37*	*10*	*1*	*11*	*34*	*32*	*92*	*12*	*4*	*.219/.315/.404*	*.261*	*.298*	*1*	*CF 0, LF 0*	*1.0*

As with Greene, Maxwell was another highly regarded 2005 college hitter, graduating from the University of Maryland, where he, um, got injured a lot and slid to the fourth round. Not much has changed in the ensuing years, as he still demonstrates five-tool talent in a body that suggests huge power potential. These looks belie the fragility of the athlete, as he continues to rack up the disabled list days year after year. The positive spin on the injuries is that there's a lot more untapped upside than with most players his age, as his power stats from last year indicate.

Jiovanni Mier SS
Born: **8/26/1990** Age: **22**
Bats: **R** Throws: **R** Height: **6' 3"**
Weight: **180** Breakout: **9%**
Improve: **55%** Collapse: **5%**
Attrition: **15%** MLB: **96%**
Comparables:
Rick Auerbach,Alan Trammell,Dick Schofield

YEAR	TEAM	LVL	AGE	PA	R	2B	3B	HR	RBI	BB	SO	SB	CS	AVG_OBP_SLG	TAv	BABIP	BRR	FRAA	WARP
2010	LEX	A	19	573	83	31	1	2	53	63	107	15	7	.235/.326/.314	.248	.295	5	SS(128): 4.9	3.0
2011	LEX	A	20	257	39	14	0	5	29	37	58	6	2	.245/.354/.380	.270	.308	0.9	SS(47): 2.9	1.0
2011	LNC	A+	20	248	35	7	1	2	23	29	54	5	3	.233/.335/.306	.225	.301	-0.1	SS(19): 1.6	0.2
2012	LNC	A+	21	204	28	9	1	3	25	29	34	6	3	.292/.396/.409	.344	.348	0.5	SS(24): 1.4	1.5
2013	*HOU*	*MLB*	*22*	*250*	*25*	*9*	*1*	*3*	*17*	*23*	*63*	*3*	*1*	*.199/.274/.279*	*.207*	*.260*	*-0.3*	*SS 1*	*-0.1*

The offensive environment in Lancaster is fantastic and the sample size was small, so Mier's batting exploits last year look sexy, but can't be dwelled upon too much. This former first-rounder from California is moving well after returning from a hamstring injury sustained in early 2012, and as a slick-fielding shortstop, will still become a seductive prospect even if he can't hit like Derek Jeter. He did take strides last year toward Jeterdom by improving his patience and strikeout rate, and if he consolidates those gains this year—and stays healthy—he could get back on track to becoming a model shortstop.

Telvin Nash OF

Born: **2/20/1991** Age: **22**
Bats: **R** Throws: **R** Height: **6' 2"**
Weight: **230** Breakout: **5%**
Improve: **62%** Collapse: **1%**
Attrition: **4%** MLB: **99%**

Comparables:
Adam Dunn,Darryl Strawberry,Jose Canseco

YEAR	TEAM	LVL	AGE	PA	R	2B	3B	HR	RBI	BB	SO	SB	CS	AVG_OBP_SLG	TAv	BABIP	BRR	FRAA	WARP
2010	GRV	Rk	19	227	30	12	1	12	39	25	64	1	1	.265/.350/.515	.302	.331	1.5	LF(51): -5.2	0.9
2011	LEX	A	20	316	41	16	0	14	37	40	103	2	0	.269/.373/.485	.289	.379	-1.6	1B(31): 0.3, LF(11): 0.1	1.0
2012	LNC	A+	21	449	61	19	0	29	75	47	198	0	1	.224/.316/.494	.278	.351	-1.5	LF(24): -1.6, 1B(6): -0.1	0.0
2013	*HOU*	*MLB*	*22*	*250*	*27*	*7*	*0*	*11*	*33*	*21*	*105*	*0*	*0*	*.186/.262/.372*	*.227*	*.277*	*-0.4*	*LF -2, 1B -1*	*-0.7*

To shamelessly steal a comment from an online reader, "Nash is the Billy Hamilton of strikeouts." He also hits a lot of homers, even considering Lancaster's home park, which inflates power numbers more than any other minor-league stadium. But few expect him to make enough contact to advance steadily. The question is whether he can make the adjustments needed to advance at all, or whether the whiffs will steal his chance at a career.

Jimmy Paredes OF

Born: **11/25/1988** Age: **24**
Bats: **B** Throws: **R** Height: **6' 2"**
Weight: **200** Breakout: **17%**
Improve: **54%** Collapse: **1%**
Attrition: **21%** MLB: **92%**

Comparables:
Jorge Orta,Pedro Garcia,Rod Carew

YEAR	TEAM	LVL	AGE	PA	R	2B	3B	HR	RBI	BB	SO	SB	CS	AVG_OBP_SLG	TAv	BABIP	BRR	FRAA	WARP
2010	CSC	A	21	434	59	24	6	5	48	18	82	36	10	.282/.312/.408	.286	.339	5.2	2B(71): -3.0, SS(16): -1.0	2.6
2010	LEX	A	21	154	24	10	1	3	17	7	25	14	1	.299/.331/.442	.281	.345	3.7	2B(34): 2.3	1.3
2011	CCH	AA	22	407	69	22	4	10	41	15	84	29	12	.270/.300/.426	.246	.322	0	--	0.0
2011	HOU	MLB	22	179	16	8	2	2	18	9	47	5	4	.286/.320/.393	.254	.383	0.6	3B(46): -2.6	0.1
2012	OKL	AAA	23	536	92	28	7	13	59	22	101	37	10	.318/.348/.477	.315	.375	1.5	2B(23): 0.5, CF(9): -0.8	1.1
2012	HOU	MLB	23	82	7	1	1	0	3	6	21	2	1	.189/.244/.230	.193	.255	0.6	RF(15): -0.3, 2B(5): 0.3	-0.5
2013	*HOU*	*MLB*	*24*	*250*	*31*	*10*	*2*	*5*	*21*	*9*	*61*	*12*	*3*	*.251/.280/.371*	*.236*	*.312*	*1.2*	*2B 0, 3B -0*	*0.3*

Without diminishing the hard, humbling work Paredes has done to improve himself, his story is the sort in which a player-development staff can take great pride. He's always going to be a bit of a hack-and-slash hitter—never drawing a ton of walks and striking out more than you'd want—but his second-half Triple-A stats showed across-the-board improvements, with 20 extra-base hits and nine walks in 170 at-bats, with only 32 strikeouts. The biggest change, though, was his move from second base to center field. While this raises the bar for offense, he wasn't making it at second. The development staff is convinced he'll become a very good defensive center fielder. He's probably already as good as many utility players, and could end up starter-quality if the hard work and coaching pay off again.

Carlos Pena 1B

Born: **5/17/1978** Age: **35**
Bats: **L** Throws: **L** Height: **6' 3"**
Weight: **225** Breakout: **2%**
Improve: **21%** Collapse: **15%**
Attrition: **13%** MLB: **97%**

Comparables:
Jeff Bagwell,Ken Phelps,Mickey Tettleton

YEAR	TEAM	LVL	AGE	PA	R	2B	3B	HR	RBI	BB	SO	SB	CS	AVG_OBP_SLG	TAv	BABIP	BRR	FRAA	WARP
2010	TBA	MLB	32	582	64	18	0	28	84	87	158	5	1	.196/.325/.407	.277	.222	0.5	1B(142): -6.4	1.1
2011	CHN	MLB	33	606	72	27	3	28	80	101	161	2	2	.225/.357/.462	.289	.267	0.1	1B(153): -0.2	1.6
2012	TBA	MLB	34	600	72	17	2	19	61	87	182	2	3	.197/.330/.354	.266	.264	-4.5	1B(153): -2.5	-0.3
2013	*HOU*	*MLB*	*35*	*565*	*73*	*19*	*2*	*26*	*78*	*84*	*165*	*3*	*2*	*.210/.338/.423*	*.276*	*.259*	*-0.9*	*1B -0*	*1.3*

It seemed like a great idea to bring the beloved Pena back to Tampa Bay on a one-year deal worth $7.25 million (which made him the team's highest-paid position player). Instead, he had the worst season of his career, undershooting his projected TAv by 30 points. Pena's slowing bat finally lost him his starting job for a while late in the year, but the damage was done: Pena was a prime culprit in the theft of the Rays' playoff dreams. He'll cost the Astros less than $2 million for the first four months, at which point the team will almost certainly trade him if he's doing well, or consider releasing him (and likely avoiding some performance bonuses) if not.

Carlos Perez C

Born: **10/27/1990** Age: **22**
Bats: **R** Throws: **R** Height: **6' 1"**
Weight: **193** Breakout: **2%**
Improve: **50%** Collapse: **3%**
Attrition: **8%** MLB: **98%**

Comparables:
Yadier Molina,Charlie Moore,Alex Trevino

YEAR	TEAM	LVL	AGE	PA	R	2B	3B	HR	RBI	BB	SO	SB	CS	AVG_OBP_SLG	TAv	BABIP	BRR	FRAA	WARP
2010	AUB	A-	19	278	44	11	8	2	41	34	41	7	3	.298/.400/.438	.299	.354	-1.2	C(44): 0.7	2.1
2011	LNS	A	20	429	58	17	6	3	41	37	74	6	2	.256/.320/.355	.241	.304	0	--	0.0
2012	LNS	A	21	319	48	22	5	5	40	35	38	3	2	.275/.358/.447	.261	.298	1.4	C(18): 0.6	0.4
2012	LNC	A+	21	97	11	6	1	0	10	6	17	0	1	.318/.368/.409	.247	.394	0.2	C(11): 0.3	0.5
2013	*HOU*	*MLB*	*22*	*250*	*21*	*9*	*2*	*3*	*23*	*19*	*53*	*0*	*0*	*.222/.285/.325*	*.224*	*.270*	*-0.2*	*C 0*	*0.2*

Score (another) one for Jeff Luhnow, picking up a very good catching prospect on the sly. Perez is not high on prospect lists yet, due to repeating Single-A after a disappointing 2011. But he profiles as an average defensive catcher, and won his team's MVP award three straight years in short-season ball. While his High-A stats were inflated by an unsustainable BABIP, he makes solid contact, which should make for solid average. With more than 10 percent of his at-bats resulting in extra-base hits last year, he is developing the average power scouts expect. Though catchers develop more slowly than prospects at other positions, Perez appears on track to league-average hitterhood, i.e. well above average for a catcher. Not all the talent grabs Luhnow has made will turn out, but plenty will, and he's getting guys with lots of potential in exchange for scraps.

Rio Ruiz 3B
Born: **5/22/1994** Age: **19**
Bats: **L** Throws: **R** Height: **6' 4"**
Weight: **195** Breakout: **0%**
Improve: **60%** Collapse: **40%**
Attrition: **40%** MLB: **100%**
Comparables:
Robin Yount, Wayne Causey, Ed Kranepool

YEAR	TEAM	LVL	AGE	PA	R	2B	3B	HR	RBI	BB	SO	SB	CS	AVG_OBP_SLG	TAv	BABIP	BRR	FRAA	WARP
2012	AST	Rk	18	97	13	8	2	0	11	12	22	2	0	.271/.361/.412	.311	.365	0	3B(6): 0.7	0.5
2012	GRV	Rk	18	55	8	3	1	1	7	4	10	0	0	.220/.291/.380	.135	.256	0.8	3B(3): 0.3	-0.1
2013	*HOU*	*MLB*	*19*	*250*	*18*	*8*	*1*	*3*	*20*	*15*	*72*	*1*	*0*	*.183/.235/.263*	*.184*	*.247*	*-0.2*	*3B 0*	*-1.4*

In high school, Ruiz was a star quarterback and his mid-90s velocity as a pitcher had scouts slavering. Undaunted by his injury history, the Astros were able to talk him out of college by offering first-round money after he slid to the fourth round. The tools are there for a plus hitter with plus power and plus defense, but he's still plus-plus raw. You see, football and a fastball won't do much to help him at the hot corner.

Domingo Santana RF
Born: **8/5/1992** Age: **20**
Bats: **R** Throws: **R** Height: **6' 6"**
Weight: **200** Breakout: **37%**
Improve: **75%** Collapse: **2%**
Attrition: **11%** MLB: **90%**
Comparables:
Justin Upton, Tony Conigliaro, Mickey Mantle

YEAR	TEAM	LVL	AGE	PA	R	2B	3B	HR	RBI	BB	SO	SB	CS	AVG_OBP_SLG	TAv	BABIP	BRR	FRAA	WARP
2010	LWD	A	17	202	27	10	0	3	16	29	76	5	6	.182/.325/.297	.255	.314	-1.4	RF(40): -1.3, LF(1): -0.2	-0.2
2010	WPT	A-	17	214	28	9	0	5	20	23	73	4	4	.237/.336/.366	.252	.361	-2.7	RF(45): 5.6	0.4
2011	LEX	A	18	76	13	4	0	5	21	6	15	1	0	.382/.447/.662	.360	.438	-0.9	RF(16): -2.0	0.6
2011	LWD	A	18	391	45	29	4	7	32	26	120	4	1	.269/.345/.434	.312	.390	-1.9	RF(34): -3.8	1.2
2012	LNC	A+	19	525	87	26	6	23	97	55	148	7	1	.302/.385/.536	.324	.397	-0.6	RF(73): -3.1	2.1
2013	*HOU*	*MLB*	*20*	*250*	*24*	*9*	*1*	*7*	*28*	*19*	*89*	*1*	*0*	*.208/.278/.352*	*.232*	*.303*	*-0.3*	*RF -2, LF -0*	*-0.4*

Baseball is a game of adjustments, and while Santana was making minor adjustments last year, he was spared making any major ones. Lancaster is one of the most hitter-friendly environs in all baseball, and he was allowed to hang out there all summer and build confidence. The staff and coaches believe this was in Santana's best interest, but it could lead to early-season disappointment this year, as he tries to jump the much taller Double-A hurdle. The biggest adjustment he'll have to make is getting the bat on the ball against better stuff. His enormous power potential gives him great upside, even if the other aspects of his game are unlikely to develop into assets.

Jonathan Singleton 1B
Born: **9/18/1991** Age: **21**
Bats: **L** Throws: **L** Height: **6' 3"**
Weight: **215** Breakout: **4%**
Improve: **59%** Collapse: **8%**
Attrition: **15%** MLB: **98%**
Comparables:
Travis Snider, Freddie Freeman, Clint Hurdle

YEAR	TEAM	LVL	AGE	PA	R	2B	3B	HR	RBI	BB	SO	SB	CS	AVG_OBP_SLG	TAv	BABIP	BRR	FRAA	WARP
2010	LWD	A	18	450	64	25	2	14	77	62	74	9	7	.290/.399/.479	.325	.330	-1.4	1B(102): 6.4	4.1
2011	CLR	A+	19	382	48	14	0	9	47	56	83	3	3	.284/.387/.412	.247	.352	-2.3	1B(24): 0.2, LF(12): 0.2	-0.4
2011	LNC	A+	19	148	20	9	1	4	16	14	40	0	0	.333/.405/.512	.377	.448	0.2	1B(15): -0.1	0.7
2012	CCH	AA	20	555	94	27	4	21	79	88	131	7	2	.284/.396/.497	.282	.350	0.9	1B(34): 0.3, LF(9): 0.2	0.1
2013	*HOU*	*MLB*	*21*	*250*	*28*	*10*	*1*	*8*	*30*	*31*	*64*	*1*	*0*	*.235/.330/.394*	*.263*	*.294*	*-0.4*	*1B -6, LF -0*	*-0.3*

Singleton may still be in pre-launch status, but expect all systems to be "go" soon. While he won't be confused with Kevin Durant, he should provide excitement in Oklahoma City this summer. Singleton combines the sort of patience and power that could lead to on-base-percentage and slugging-percentage titles in his future. He hasn't figured out how to hit hard lefties, and he'll need to for elite offensive stats, but he likely has a year of Triple-A and six MLB seasons before he hits his prime. On defense he doesn't project as elite, but 2013 is only his age-21 season. With adequate height for a first baseman, good hand-eye coordination, and a great work ethic, he has a shot to become a decent fielder by the time he reaches full orbit.

Chris Snyder C
Born: **2/12/1981** Age: **32**
Bats: **R** Throws: **R** Height: **6' 5"**
Weight: **240** Breakout: **3%**
Improve: **36%** Collapse: **11%**
Attrition: **20%** MLB: **85%**
Comparables:
Darren Daulton, Duke Sims, Johnny Romano

YEAR	TEAM	LVL	AGE	PA	R	2B	3B	HR	RBI	BB	SO	SB	CS	AVG_OBP_SLG	TAv	BABIP	BRR	FRAA	WARP
2010	ARI	MLB	29	234	22	8	0	10	32	36	61	0	0	.231/.352/.426	.267	.280	-1.6	C(61): -0.2	1.2
2010	PIT	MLB	29	142	12	1	0	5	16	16	33	0	0	.169/.268/.298	.199	.184	-1.7	C(40): 0.4	-0.3
2011	PIT	MLB	30	119	13	3	0	3	17	17	23	0	1	.271/.376/.396	.289	.315	-0.6	C(33): 0.5	1.0
2012	HOU	MLB	31	258	23	8	0	7	24	33	70	0	0	.176/.295/.308	.216	.222	-0.5	C(72): -1.1, 1B(1): -0.0	-0.6
2013	*HOU*	*MLB*	*32*	*250*	*29*	*8*	*0*	*9*	*29*	*33*	*65*	*0*	*0*	*.211/.324/.375*	*.253*	*.256*	*-0.5*	*C 0, 1B -0*	*1.0*

Snyder was a good gamble for the pittance the Astros committed to paying him. He had always hit left-handed pitching hard and played average defense. His career batting line would have made him better than some starting catchers, and would have given him the 17th-best OPS among catchers with 300 or more plate appearances in 2012. He should have been just the sort of veteran to help Castro acclimate. But good gambles don't always work out, and though Snyder will likely sign on as a backup again this year after the Astros declined his $4 million option, more playing time is only in the cards if Castro goes down with a midseason injury.

George Springer CF
Born: **9/19/1989** Age: **23**
Bats: **R** Throws: **R** Height: **6' 4"**
Weight: **205** Breakout: **4%**
Improve: **59%** Collapse: **7%**
Attrition: **9%** MLB: **94%**
Comparables:
B.J. Upton,Andruw Jones,Rick Monday

YEAR	TEAM	LVL	AGE	PA	R	2B	3B	HR	RBI	BB	SO	SB	CS	AVG_OBP_SLG	TAv	BABIP	BRR	FRAA	WARP
2012	LNC	A+	22	500	101	18	10	22	82	56	131	28	6	.316/.398/.557	.369	.404	9.9	CF(75): -1.3	6.0
2012	CCH	AA	22	81	8	3	0	2	5	6	25	4	2	.219/.287/.342	.190	.304	1.5	CF(7): -0.3, RF(3): -0.3	-0.2
2013	*HOU*	*MLB*	*23*	*250*	*32*	*8*	*2*	*8*	*26*	*19*	*78*	*7*	*2*	*.224/.288/.381*	*.243*	*.297*	*0.8*	*CF -2, RF -0*	*0.2*

Springer's nascent career is the sort people dreamed about for Maxwell, another five-tool right-handed college outfielder with massive power potential. Unlike Maxwell, Springer has remained healthy, and getting 500 plate appearances—the home ones in the jet streams of Lancaster—did nothing to slow down his flight to the majors. The holes in his swing—which have always been a concern—were exploited by Double-A pitching, and without adjustment could limit his ability to make consistent contact against high-level pitching. The team believes in him as a center fielder, but swapped him and Grossman in right at times to get a look at each player in both positions.

Jonathan Villar SS
Born: **5/2/1991** Age: **22**
Bats: **B** Throws: **R** Height: **6' 2"**
Weight: **195** Breakout: **9%**
Improve: **40%** Collapse: **3%**
Attrition: **36%** MLB: **97%**
Comparables:
Jeff Blauser,Jay Bell,Jhonny Peralta

YEAR	TEAM	LVL	AGE	PA	R	2B	3B	HR	RBI	BB	SO	SB	CS	AVG_OBP_SLG	TAv	BABIP	BRR	FRAA	WARP
2010	LWD	A	19	420	61	18	4	2	36	26	103	38	13	.272/.323/.358	.258	.355	6.1	SS(99): 0.0	2.4
2010	LNC	A+	19	143	18	6	2	3	19	12	50	7	2	.225/.296/.372	.224	.342	0.1	SS(31): -1.8	-0.2
2011	LNC	A+	20	207	26	7	4	4	26	25	56	20	6	.259/.353/.414	.091	.350	0	SS(3): -0.2	-0.3
2011	CCH	AA	20	367	52	16	2	10	26	29	100	14	6	.231/.301/.386	.238	.301	0	--	0.0
2012	CCH	AA	21	377	54	7	2	11	50	35	87	39	8	.261/.336/.396	.238	.319	3.6	SS(32): 4.6	1.0
2013	*HOU*	*MLB*	*22*	*250*	*31*	*8*	*1*	*4*	*18*	*15*	*75*	*15*	*4*	*.210/.264/.311*	*.210*	*.283*	*1.7*	*SS 2*	*0.2*

Villar's 2012 report card is similar to 2011: young for his league, improved walk and strikeout rates, cut errors substantially, still showing all the tools that make him exciting. Not so exiting was the end of his season, as he deserved detention for punching a door and injuring his hand. Like Mier, he's no Derek Jeter in the batter's box, but he is expected to stay at shortstop and he can run like the wind. Villar has star potential even without hitting like an all-time great.

Brett Wallace 1B
Born: **8/26/1986** Age: **26**
Bats: **L** Throws: **R** Height: **6' 3"**
Weight: **250** Breakout: **5%**
Improve: **47%** Collapse: **3%**
Attrition: **16%** MLB: **85%**
Comparables:
Ryan Doumit,Mat Gamel,Bryan LaHair

YEAR	TEAM	LVL	AGE	PA	R	2B	3B	HR	RBI	BB	SO	SB	CS	AVG_OBP_SLG	TAv	BABIP	BRR	FRAA	WARP
2010	LVG	AAA	23	423	64	24	1	18	61	27	83	1	1	.301/.361/.509	.265	.345	-0.2	1B(76): -0.7	0.4
2010	HOU	MLB	23	159	14	6	1	2	13	8	50	0	0	.222/.296/.319	.236	.326	0.2	1B(48): 1.5	0.3
2011	OKL	AAA	24	126	16	10	0	1	24	15	28	1	0	.356/.437/.481	.328	.456	0	--	0.0
2011	HOU	MLB	24	378	37	22	0	5	29	36	91	1	1	.259/.334/.369	.244	.339	-3.9	1B(96): 7.7	-0.4
2012	OKL	AAA	25	351	54	16	0	16	57	27	87	0	1	.300/.379/.506	.361	.370	-3.7	1B(10): -0.8, 3B(9): 0.3	0.7
2012	HOU	MLB	25	254	24	10	1	9	24	18	73	0	0	.253/.323/.424	.263	.331	-1.3	1B(58): -0.3, 3B(8): -0.3	0.0
2013	*HOU*	*MLB*	*26*	*314*	*32*	*14*	*1*	*9*	*37*	*22*	*85*	*0*	*0*	*.242/.310/.392*	*.252*	*.310*	*-0.6*	*1B -3, 3B -0*	*-0.3*

Twenty-seven first basemen (primary position) had 250 plate appearances and a .260 or higher TAv in 2012. That Wallace was barely among that group suggests he wasn't overly disappointing compared to his peers and borders on starter-quality at the position. But 2012 was a terrible season for first basemen. Also, the changes Wallace made in his approach that allowed him to pummel Triple-A pitching for over 170 PA seemed to be countered by adjustments from the pitching universe down the stretch: He had just 14 hits and 26 strikeouts in his final 82 PA. Despite weight loss, Wallace doesn't contribute anywhere but the batter's box: sub-par at first base and a nightmare at third. He's likely to get some playing time until Singleton proves that Triple-A can't contain him, but to become more than a pinch-hitter Wallace will have to do more with this chance than be a top-30 hitter among a terrible first-base crop.

PITCHERS

Hector Ambriz

Born: **5/24/1984** Age: **29**
Bats: **L** Throws: **R** Height: **6' 3"** Weight: **235**
Breakout: **19%** Improve: **66%** Collapse: **15%**
Attrition: **10%** MLB: **87%**

Comparables:
Mike Smithson, Mike Gosling, John Tudor

YEAR	TEAM	LVL	AGE	W	L	SV	G	GS	IP	H	HR	BB	SO	BB9	SO9	GB%	BABIP	WHIP	ERA	FIP	FRA	WARP
2010	COH	AAA	26	0	0	0	7	0	8	9	0	1	15	1.1	16.9	42%	.474	1.25	1.12	-0.08	0.53	0.5
2010	CLE	MLB	26	0	2	0	34	0	48^{1}	68	10	17	37	3.2	6.9	43%	.365	1.76	5.59	5.32	5.32	-0.1
2012	COH	AAA	28	0	1	1	20	1	33	29	3	17	25	4.6	6.8	54%	.274	1.39	3.55	4.37	5.57	0.0
2012	OKL	AAA	28	1	1	2	18	0	24^{1}	28	1	11	18	4.1	6.7	53%	.351	1.60	3.33	4.20	4.42	0.2
2012	HOU	MLB	28	1	1	0	18	0	19^{1}	14	0	11	22	5.1	10.2	52%	.292	1.29	4.19	2.88	3.02	0.4
2013	*HOU*	*MLB*	*29*	*1*	*0*	*0*	*25*	*0*	*34*	*38*	*5*	*13*	*26*	*3.4*	*7.0*	*43%*	*.313*	*1.49*	*5.14*	*4.73*	*5.58*	*-0.1*

The final pitch in the National League Astros history was a straight-as-a-rope, right-down-the-middle, 94-mph fastball from Ambriz to Bryan LaHair that resulted in a game-winning single. Originally a soft-tossing starter drafted out of UCLA in 2006, Ambriz throws harder since converting to the bullpen in 2010, but his two fastballs and slider don't have enough variance to fool anyone. Though protected on the 40-man roster, he is unlikely to become more than the answer to an obscure Astros trivia question.

Xavier Cedeno

Born: **8/26/1986** Age: **26**
Bats: **L** Throws: **L** Height: **6' 2"** Weight: **165**
Breakout: **40%** Improve: **64%** Collapse: **21%**
Attrition: **18%** MLB: **86%**

Comparables:
Bud Daley, Leo Kiely, Jeremy Horst

YEAR	TEAM	LVL	AGE	W	L	SV	G	GS	IP	H	HR	BB	SO	BB9	SO9	GB%	BABIP	WHIP	ERA	FIP	FRA	WARP
2011	CCH	AA	24	5	6	0	23	19	111^{2}	98	8	45	110	3.6	8.9	—	.290	1.28	3.95	3.68	4.00	0.0
2011	OKL	AAA	24	2	3	0	12	3	26	32	2	8	27	2.8	9.3	—	.375	1.54	6.23	3.63	3.95	0.0
2011	HOU	MLB	24	0	0	0	3	0	1^{2}	7	2	0	0	0.0	0.0	27%	.556	4.20	27.00	18.59	22.33	-0.3
2012	OKL	AAA	25	2	0	1	22	0	27^{2}	27	0	9	25	2.9	8.1	58%	.318	1.30	2.28	3.05	1.90	0.6
2012	HOU	MLB	25	0	1	1	44	0	31	30	3	14	36	4.1	10.5	52%	.321	1.42	3.77	3.52	4.06	0.3
2013	*HOU*	*MLB*	*26*	*2*	*1*	*1*	*38*	*0*	33^{1}	*37*	*5*	*14*	*23*	*3.9*	*6.1*	*50%*	*.303*	*1.55*	*5.51*	*5.03*	*5.99*	*-0.3*

Cedeno doesn't throw hard, and so far his offerings to right-handed batters may as well have "hit me" stitched on them, but he gives lefties fits. He hits the lower outside corner with his fastball and his breaking pitches look the same . . . until they're not. Some end up in the dirt and *still* draw swings. Cedeno is young enough that he could surprise and pick up a trick against righties, but without velocity, it's likely his peak value will be as a LOOGY.

Paul Clemens

Born: **2/14/1988** Age: **25**
Bats: **R** Throws: **R** Height: **6' 5"** Weight: **180**
Breakout: **33%** Improve: **64%** Collapse: **10%**
Attrition: **14%** MLB: **86%**

Comparables:
Amaury Telemaco, Jack Fisher, Joe Presko

YEAR	TEAM	LVL	AGE	W	L	SV	G	GS	IP	H	HR	BB	SO	BB9	SO9	GB%	BABIP	WHIP	ERA	FIP	FRA	WARP
2010	ROM	A	22	2	0	1	8	0	19	11	1	8	16	3.8	7.6	36%	.196	1.00	1.42	3.79	4.52	0.1
2010	MYR	A+	22	0	4	2	27	8	75^{2}	83	5	28	65	3.3	7.7	49%	.333	1.47	3.69	3.74	4.35	0.5
2011	CCH	AA	23	2	1	0	5	5	30^{2}	23	3	12	26	3.5	7.6	—	.233	1.14	2.35	4.13	4.49	0.0
2011	MIS	AA	23	6	5	0	20	20	108^{2}	103	8	44	93	3.6	7.7	—	.299	1.35	3.73	3.90	4.24	0.0
2011	OKL	AAA	23	0	1	0	1	1	4^{2}	4	1	6	6	11.6	11.6	—	.273	2.14	15.43	7.85	8.54	0.0
2012	CCH	AA	24	3	2	0	7	7	41^{2}	41	7	11	37	2.4	8.0	42%	.291	1.25	3.46	4.62	6.52	0.1
2012	OKL	AAA	24	8	8	0	20	20	101^{2}	145	16	32	68	2.8	6.0	42%	.375	1.74	6.73	5.38	7.64	0.0
2013	*HOU*	*MLB*	*25*	*1*	*3*	*0*	*9*	*5*	32^{2}	*40*	*6*	*17*	*19*	*4.6*	*5.3*	*43%*	*.315*	*1.74*	*6.48*	*5.99*	*7.05*	*-0.5*

Originally in the Braves system and part of the haul for Michael Bourn, Clemens (no relation) once struck out 16 in a high-school game. The standard assumption is that he should be close to being able to hold down a major-league bullpen slot, but so far he has allowed a 7.11 ERA to Triple-A hitters in 106 1/3 innings. He has been controlling his breaking pitches better than in the past, and his fastball still reaches the mid-90s. But the organization had to demote him last year to help rally his confidence at Double-A. Barring a miracle turnaround, he's not close to having an impact in the majors.

Francisco Cordero

Born: **5/11/1975** Age: **38**
Bats: **R** Throws: **R** Height: **6' 4"** Weight: **245**
Breakout: **34%** Improve: **50%** Collapse: **32%**
Attrition: **15%** MLB: **83%**

Comparables:
Stu Miller, Tim Worrell, David Weathers

YEAR	TEAM	LVL	AGE	W	L	SV	G	GS	IP	H	HR	BB	SO	BB9	SO9	GB%	BABIP	WHIP	ERA	FIP	FRA	WARP
2010	CIN	MLB	35	6	5	40	75	0	72^{2}	68	5	36	59	4.5	7.3	44%	.294	1.43	3.84	3.95	4.43	0.8
2011	CIN	MLB	36	5	3	37	68	0	69^{2}	49	6	22	42	2.8	5.4	50%	.214	1.02	2.45	3.98	4.27	0.4
2012	HOU	MLB	37	0	3	0	6	0	5	13	2	4	5	7.2	9.0	41%	.550	3.40	19.80	9.34	7.65	-0.2
2012	TOR	MLB	37	3	5	2	41	0	34^{1}	48	7	14	26	3.7	6.8	41%	.366	1.81	5.77	5.49	5.31	0.0
2013	*HOU*	*MLB*	*38*	*2*	*1*	*12*	*44*	*0*	41^{2}	*39*	*4*	*18*	*36*	*4.0*	*7.8*	*44%*	*.295*	*1.39*	*4.08*	*4.02*	*4.43*	*0.4*

Cordero failed as a closer in two different countries last year and looked overwhelmed by the task of adapting his repertoire to his lessened velocity. He ended the season with shoulder problems, so he may have been pitching in pain all season long. That will be the hope (along with hopes that he'll be fully recovered) of whatever team takes a chance on him as a free agent this year. As bad as he looked, he'll be lucky to get a major-league contract with incentives.

While he has the mental makeup teams want in pressure situations, he has let left-handers on base at a .362 clip in his career, so expectations that he can be more than a role-player should be kept in check.

Jarred Cosart
Born: **5/25/1990** Age: **23**
Bats: **R** Throws: **R** Height: **6' 4"** Weight: **180**
Breakout: **24%** Improve: **62%** Collapse: **22%**
Attrition: **10%** MLB: **92%**
Comparables:
Jaret Wright,Vin Mazzaro,Jerome Williams

YEAR	TEAM	LVL	AGE	W	L	SV	G	GS	IP	H	HR	BB	SO	BB9	SO9	GB%	BABIP	WHIP	ERA	FIP	FRA	WARP
2010	LWD	A	20	7	3	0	14	14	71^1	60	3	16	77	2.0	9.7	59%	.298	1.07	3.79	2.80	4.23	0.5
2011	CLR	A+	21	9	8	0	20	19	108	98	7	43	79	3.6	6.6	53%	.326	1.31	3.92	4.18	5.46	0.0
2011	CCH	AA	21	1	2	0	7	7	36^1	33	4	13	22	3.2	5.4	—	.246	1.27	4.71	4.67	5.08	0.0
2012	CCH	AA	22	5	5	0	15	15	87	83	3	38	68	3.9	7.0	63%	.300	1.39	3.52	3.72	4.20	0.4
2012	OKL	AAA	22	1	2	0	6	5	27^2	26	0	13	24	4.2	7.8	57%	.325	1.41	2.60	3.45	2.55	0.3
2013	*HOU*	*MLB*	*23*	*1*	*3*	*0*	*6*	*6*	*33^1*	*36*	*4*	*17*	*23*	*4.5*	*6.3*	*53%*	*.301*	*1.57*	*5.28*	*4.91*	*5.74*	*-0.1*

Cosart continues to blow away scouts, his blazing fastball actually being among the fastest in the Arizona Fall League and his groundball rate leading to great expectations when he is eventually backed by a top-quality defensive infield. The time he missed was due to a blister that isn't expected to impact his future. By focusing a bit more on velocity, Cosart raised both his strikeouts and walks last year, and he will need to rein in the wildness if he wants to blow away major-league hitters someday.

Rhiner Cruz
Born: **11/1/1986** Age: **26**
Bats: **R** Throws: **R** Height: **6' 3"** Weight: **205**
Breakout: **36%** Improve: **50%** Collapse: **32%**
Attrition: **34%** MLB: **88%**
Comparables:
Ken Robinson,Tom Davey,Butch Metzger

YEAR	TEAM	LVL	AGE	W	L	SV	G	GS	IP	H	HR	BB	SO	BB9	SO9	GB%	BABIP	WHIP	ERA	FIP	FRA	WARP
2010	SLU	A+	23	0	5	6	51	0	75^1	62	6	53	66	6.3	7.9	43%	.270	1.53	3.47	5.31	6.53	-1.1
2011	SLU	A+	24	2	1	0	8	0	13	9	1	6	18	4.2	12.5	40%	.400	1.15	2.77	3.47	1.18	0.3
2011	BIN	AA	24	3	2	7	36	0	58^2	43	4	39	51	6.0	7.8	42%	.250	1.40	4.14	4.81	6.17	0.0
2012	OKL	AAA	25	0	0	0	2	0	1^2	1	0	1	3	5.4	16.2	50%	.500	1.20	5.40	3.67	2.84	0.0
2012	HOU	MLB	25	1	1	0	52	0	55	65	8	29	46	4.7	7.5	40%	.339	1.71	6.05	5.05	5.46	-0.2
2013	*HOU*	*MLB*	*26*	*1*	*0*	*0*	*30*	*0*	*41*	*42*	*6*	*26*	*32*	*5.7*	*7.0*	*42%*	*.296*	*1.66*	*5.74*	*5.44*	*6.24*	*-0.4*

Cruz can be positively embarrassing—sometimes to batters, sometimes to himself. On the rare occasions this hard-throwing righty is in control of his fastball and slider, he works the bottom of the strike zone and makes it impossible for batters to make hard contact from either side of the plate. Most days, however, he overthrows early in the count and misses; then if he manages to tone it down and throw strikes, they're inferior offerings that aren't major-league ready. The first instance is what kept him on the roster all year and will get him another year of much-needed instruction in Triple-A.

Sam Demel
Born: **10/23/1985** Age: **27**
Bats: **R** Throws: **R** Height: **6' 1"** Weight: **205**
Breakout: **18%** Improve: **47%** Collapse: **41%**
Attrition: **26%** MLB: **75%**
Comparables:
Jon Link,Scott Sullivan,Boone Logan

YEAR	TEAM	LVL	AGE	W	L	SV	G	GS	IP	H	HR	BB	SO	BB9	SO9	GB%	BABIP	WHIP	ERA	FIP	FRA	WARP
2010	SAC	AAA	24	2	0	6	22	0	28^2	22	1	9	28	2.8	8.8	50%	.273	1.08	1.25	3.13	3.83	0.4
2010	ARI	MLB	24	2	1	2	37	0	37	42	5	12	33	2.9	8.0	53%	.325	1.46	5.35	4.13	5.83	-0.2
2011	RNO	AAA	25	0	2	1	11	0	10^2	11	1	5	9	4.2	7.6	—	.303	1.50	5.06	5.00	5.44	0.0
2011	ARI	MLB	25	2	2	0	34	0	25^2	31	4	13	15	4.6	5.3	59%	.329	1.71	4.21	5.60	6.82	-0.6
2012	RNO	AAA	26	1	4	1	56	0	66^1	60	11	22	75	3.0	10.2	60%	.293	1.24	4.07	4.60	4.70	0.6
2012	ARI	MLB	26	0	1	0	1	0	1	2	0	1	0	9.0	0.0	60%	.400	3.00	9.00	6.14	5.63	0.0
2013	*HOU*	*MLB*	*27*	*2*	*1*	*0*	*33*	*0*	*34^2*	*33*	*4*	*14*	*32*	*3.7*	*8.3*	*53%*	*.296*	*1.37*	*4.34*	*4.07*	*4.71*	*0.2*

For those pitchers who do not profile in the top half of a major-league rotation or the back end of a bullpen, an annual goal is to simply secure a big-league paycheck for as much of the season as possible. In that regard, Demel's career is going backwards, with a three-year decline in innings pitched in the bigs that culminated in the single frame that he tossed in Arizona last season. Demel pitched admirably in Reno, with the best strikeout-to-walk ratio of his career, although a case of gopheritis sabotaged his ERA. Signed by the Astros, Demel has a chance to crack the Opening Day roster in Houston, though a poor spring would further extend his tour of the Pacific Coast League.

John Ely
Born: **5/13/1986** Age: **27**
Bats: **R** Throws: **R** Height: **6' 3"** Weight: **200**
Breakout: **29%** Improve: **66%** Collapse: **15%**
Attrition: **22%** MLB: **88%**
Comparables:
Gavin Floyd,Kyle Davies,Armando Galarraga

YEAR	TEAM	LVL	AGE	W	L	SV	G	GS	IP	H	HR	BB	SO	BB9	SO9	GB%	BABIP	WHIP	ERA	FIP	FRA	WARP
2010	ABQ	AAA	24	5	4	0	13	13	68	70	10	29	56	3.8	7.4	48%	.299	1.46	6.22	5.26	5.75	0.8
2010	LAN	MLB	24	4	10	0	18	18	100	105	12	40	76	3.6	6.8	47%	.310	1.45	5.49	4.41	5.28	-0.3
2011	ABQ	AAA	25	7	8	0	25	25	144^1	178	21	44	99	2.7	6.2	—	.326	1.54	5.99	5.36	5.83	0.0
2011	LAN	MLB	25	0	1	0	5	1	12^2	12	2	7	13	5.0	9.2	44%	.294	1.50	4.26	4.65	4.85	0.0
2012	ABQ	AAA	26	14	7	0	27	27	168^2	150	18	36	165	1.9	8.8	53%	.281	1.10	3.20	3.81	3.82	0.9
2012	LAN	MLB	26	0	2	0	2	0	2^2	6	0	4	3	13.5	10.1	64%	.545	3.75	20.25	6.51	5.43	0.0
2013	*HOU*	*MLB*	*27*	*2*	*3*	*0*	*7*	*7*	*42^2*	*43*	*6*	*17*	*35*	*3.5*	*7.3*	*49%*	*.295*	*1.39*	*4.60*	*4.58*	*5.00*	*0.2*

Ely had a magical run to begin his Dodgers career back in 2010—a 2.54 ERA and six quality starts out of seven—but he's been rocked for a 7.79 ERA in 69 1/3 innings in his dozen big-league appearances since then. The Dodgers gave up on him becoming anything more than organizational depth, despite the fact that he's been killing it at Triple-A recently. Thanks to an improved fastball-changeup combo, he won the Pacific Coast League's Pitcher of the Year honors. The Astros master plan of cornering the market on "crafty righties" is unlikely to result in fans up I-45 worrying anytime soon, but Ely has been durable, and someone has to start the 162 games Houston plays.

Josh Fields

Born: **8/19/1985** Age: **27**
Bats: **R** Throws: **R** Height: **6' 1"** Weight: **185**
Breakout: **34%** Improve: **51%** Collapse: **38%**
Attrition: **27%** MLB: **73%**

Comparables:
Scott Strickland,Jim Miller,David Aardsma

YEAR	TEAM	LVL	AGE	W	L	SV	G	GS	IP	H	HR	BB	SO	BB9	SO9	GB%	BABIP	WHIP	ERA	FIP	FRA	WARP
2010	WTN	AA	24	1	1	6	21	0	28^{2}	19	0	18	28	5.6	8.8	53%	.253	1.29	3.14	3.32	4.09	0.3
2011	PME	AA	25	3	0	1	9	0	17^{1}	10	2	10	25	5.2	13.0	—	.258	1.15	3.12	3.93	4.27	0.0
2011	WTN	AA	25	1	2	3	20	0	26	17	0	19	26	6.6	9.0	—	.258	1.38	2.77	3.96	4.30	0.0
2011	TAC	AAA	25	0	0	0	9	0	13	11	2	13	13	9.0	9.0	39%	.241	1.85	6.23	6.78	8.86	-0.1
2012	PME	AA	26	3	3	8	32	0	44^{2}	30	4	16	59	3.2	11.9	47%	.248	1.03	2.62	2.87	2.63	0.9
2012	PAW	AAA	26	1	0	4	10	0	13^{2}	8	0	2	19	1.3	12.5	37%	.296	0.73	0.00	0.82	0.42	0.6
2013	*HOU*	*MLB*	*27*	*1*	*0*	*1*	*25*	*0*	*34^{1}*	*31*	*4*	*18*	*35*	*4.6*	*9.2*	*44%*	*.295*	*1.42*	*4.35*	*4.25*	*4.73*	*0.2*

Fields was expected to be a quick-to-the-majors pick as a first-round reliever in the 2008 draft. Drafted again as a Rule 5 pick from the Red Sox, he's likely to bring his upper-90s heat and knee-buckling curve to the majors this year. The Astros coaching staff will work on release point consistency to help keep his walk rate at an acceptable level, as it was—for the first time—last year.

Michael Foltynewicz

Born: **10/7/1991** Age: **21**
Bats: **R** Throws: **R** Height: **6' 5"** Weight: **200**
Breakout: **30%** Improve: **64%** Collapse: **15%**
Attrition: **12%** MLB: **86%**

Comparables:
Joe Coleman,Bob Friend,Tommy Boggs

YEAR	TEAM	LVL	AGE	W	L	SV	G	GS	IP	H	HR	BB	SO	BB9	SO9	GB%	BABIP	WHIP	ERA	FIP	FRA	WARP
2011	LEX	A	19	5	11	0	26	26	134	149	10	51	88	3.4	5.9	45%	.331	1.49	4.97	4.48	5.35	0.8
2012	LEX	A	20	14	4	0	27	27	152	145	11	62	125	3.7	7.4	49%	.298	1.36	3.14	4.20	4.67	2.0
2013	*HOU*	*MLB*	*21*	*1*	*5*	*0*	*9*	*9*	*44*	*52*	*7*	*25*	*23*	*5.0*	*4.6*	*45%*	*.306*	*1.75*	*6.34*	*5.93*	*6.89*	*-0.6*

A power arm from a cold-weather state, Foltynewicz repeated at Lexington in 2012. The velocity returned for Folty, who was again touching the mid-90s on occasion, as he had in high school. He is labelled as durable, but he wasn't the same pitcher in the second half, with his control abandoning him and his pitches getting up in the zone. He needs that power sink: Fewer groundballs is bad news for a guy who could use more.

Lucas Harrell

Born: **6/3/1985** Age: **28**
Bats: **B** Throws: **R** Height: **6' 3"** Weight: **210**
Breakout: **14%** Improve: **47%** Collapse: **30%**
Attrition: **19%** MLB: **92%**

Comparables:
Mike Hampton,Tommy John,Roberto Hernandez

YEAR	TEAM	LVL	AGE	W	L	SV	G	GS	IP	H	HR	BB	SO	BB9	SO9	GB%	BABIP	WHIP	ERA	FIP	FRA	WARP
2010	CHR	AAA	25	10	10	0	26	26	137^{2}	141	11	61	84	4.0	5.5	51%	.294	1.47	4.58	4.55	5.91	-0.5
2010	CHA	MLB	25	1	0	0	8	3	24	34	2	17	15	6.4	5.6	53%	.376	2.12	4.88	5.01	4.80	0.3
2011	CHR	AAA	26	7	3	0	13	12	74^{1}	67	6	26	56	3.1	6.8	61%	.286	1.25	3.27	3.87	4.54	0.2
2011	OKL	AAA	26	5	2	0	9	9	52^{1}	42	0	24	38	4.1	6.5	—	.268	1.26	1.72	3.82	4.15	0.0
2011	CHA	MLB	26	0	0	0	3	0	5	11	0	1	5	1.8	9.0	60%	.550	2.40	7.20	1.66	1.71	0.2
2011	HOU	MLB	26	0	2	0	6	2	13	12	0	7	10	4.8	6.9	55%	.286	1.46	3.46	3.30	4.38	0.1
2012	HOU	MLB	27	11	11	0	32	32	193^{2}	185	13	78	140	3.6	6.5	58%	.289	1.36	3.76	3.79	5.09	0.7
2013	*HOU*	*MLB*	*28*	*5*	*11*	*0*	*23*	*23*	*127^{2}*	*135*	*13*	*58*	*82*	*4.1*	*5.8*	*55%*	*.301*	*1.52*	*4.77*	*4.60*	*5.19*	*0.3*

Harrell—arguably the "ace" of the pitching-poor Astros—ate innings while posting the 32nd-best FIP among 88 qualifying pitchers, shocking all but his immediate family by the improvements in his game. While he is deceptive to hitters, there's little in the way of trickery to his approach; he added a tick to his heavy sinker and everything he does feeds off that one pitch, moving it around the zone, occasionally mixing in a variety of other offerings to keep batters honest or to put them away when they sit on the sinker. He's been particularly baffling to left-handed hitters, who often succeed against righties who work down in the zone, just not Harrell. With success will come a wave of batter adjustments, but nothing about Harrell's peripherals suggest that 2012 was a fluke. The organization will be happy with another year of him eating innings, and happier still when the day comes that he's no longer the ace of the staff.

Philip Humber
Born: **12/21/1982** Age: **30**
Bats: **R** Throws: **R** Height: **6' 4"** Weight: **210**
Breakout: **12%** Improve: **39%** Collapse: **36%**
Attrition: **17%** MLB: **87%**
Comparables:
Kevin Millwood,Tim Stauffer,Nate Robertson

YEAR	TEAM	LVL	AGE	W	L	SV	G	GS	IP	H	HR	BB	SO	BB9	SO9	GB%	BABIP	WHIP	ERA	FIP	FRA	WARP
2010	OMA	AAA	27	5	6	0	21	20	118^2	131	17	20	80	1.5	6.1	48%	.297	1.27	4.47	4.75	5.94	0.0
2010	KCA	MLB	27	2	1	0	8	1	21^2	22	1	7	16	2.9	6.6	44%	.304	1.34	4.15	3.28	3.55	0.4
2011	CHR	AAA	28	0	0	0	1	1	5	7	1	1	5	1.8	9.0	35%	.375	1.60	7.20	4.44	4.85	0.0
2011	CHA	MLB	28	9	9	0	28	26	163	151	14	41	116	2.3	6.4	48%	.275	1.18	3.75	3.62	3.86	2.3
2012	BIR	AA	29	1	0	0	1	1	6	2	0	0	5	0.0	7.5	40%	.133	0.33	1.50	1.48	3.27	0.1
2012	CHR	AAA	29	0	1	0	2	2	6^1	8	1	4	4	5.7	5.7	36%	.333	1.89	5.68	5.84	5.68	0.0
2012	CHA	MLB	29	5	5	0	26	16	102	113	23	44	85	3.9	7.5	36%	.294	1.54	6.44	5.72	5.72	-0.1
2013	*HOU*	*MLB*	*30*	*4*	*8*	*0*	*18*	*18*	*103*	*107*	*15*	*35*	*76*	*3.1*	*6.7*	*42%*	*.292*	*1.38*	*4.60*	*4.64*	*5.00*	*0.4*

It was the feel-good story of the early season when the likable former first-round pick retired 27 straight Mariners to log the 21st perfect game in history. The hangover from the good time set in immediately—nine earned runs allowed in a five-inning start—and the headache throbbed all season as Humber's slop resulted in a 7.39 ERA in 87 2/3 post-*perfecto* innings for the White Sox. A demotion to the bullpen didn't help, either; his ERA was 8.36 during 10 games in the pen. Optimists remember 2011, when Humber's solid peripherals supported his fine results, and point to how elbow issues landed him on the disabled list last June. But the continued struggles upon his return, the lack of follow-up surgery, and him saying his arm "feels great" suggest the stint on the disabled list may have been due to a case of inflamed ERA, rather than something that can be corrected medically. The last "sixth starter" from the White Sox to join the Astros was Harrell, and the 'stros would feel good if they have half as much success revitalizing Humber's career.

Dallas Keuchel
Born: **1/1/1988** Age: **25**
Bats: **L** Throws: **L** Height: **6' 4"** Weight: **200**
Breakout: **35%** Improve: **64%** Collapse: **13%**
Attrition: **8%** MLB: **80%**
Comparables:
Zach Jackson,Luke French,Clayton Richard

YEAR	TEAM	LVL	AGE	W	L	SV	G	GS	IP	H	HR	BB	SO	BB9	SO9	GB%	BABIP	WHIP	ERA	FIP	FRA	WARP
2010	LNC	A+	22	5	8	0	19	18	120^2	129	10	25	97	1.9	7.2	64%	.321	1.28	3.36	3.87	5.66	0.9
2010	CCH	AA	22	2	6	0	9	9	53^2	59	2	11	36	1.8	6.0	52%	.328	1.30	4.69	2.99	4.71	0.3
2011	CCH	AA	23	9	7	0	20	20	127^2	116	9	27	76	1.9	5.4	—	.270	1.12	3.17	3.83	4.17	0.0
2011	OKL	AAA	23	1	1	0	7	7	36	52	5	12	15	3.0	3.8	—	.353	1.78	7.50	5.76	6.26	0.0
2012	OKL	AAA	24	6	4	0	16	16	92^1	92	5	20	50	1.9	4.9	59%	.291	1.21	3.90	3.94	4.80	0.0
2012	HOU	MLB	24	3	8	0	16	16	85^1	93	14	39	38	4.1	4.0	54%	.277	1.55	5.27	5.78	6.97	-0.8
2013	*HOU*	*MLB*	*25*	*3*	*7*	*0*	*13*	*13*	77^1	*87*	*11*	*28*	*40*	*3.2*	*4.7*	*54%*	*.294*	*1.48*	*5.13*	*5.10*	*5.58*	*-0.2*

When "knows how to pitch" runs up against "not enough skill (yet)" something has to give. In this case, Keuchel did the giving. Despite a fortunate .277 BABIP, his ERA was unsatisfactory, and he didn't even do a good job of getting left-handed batters out. Searching for a silver lining to his dark debut? Note that 21 of his 56 runs allowed came in just three outings—two at Milwaukee and one at Arizona—all three in good hitters parks against teams that hit southpaws well. Of course, one of his reputed strengths is his mental game, which is supposed to help him avoid getting massacred when he doesn't have his best stuff. Time will tell whether he'll be able to make that happen.

Chia-Jen Lo
Born: **4/7/1986** Age: **27**
Bats: **R** Throws: **R** Height: **6' 0"** Weight: **185**
Breakout: **42%** Improve: **58%** Collapse: **28%**
Attrition: **26%** MLB: **75%**
Comparables:
David Aardsma,Ray Narleski,Scott Strickland

YEAR	TEAM	LVL	AGE	W	L	SV	G	GS	IP	H	HR	BB	SO	BB9	SO9	GB%	BABIP	WHIP	ERA	FIP	FRA	WARP
2010	CCH	AA	24	0	1	0	7	0	15	9	0	10	13	6.0	7.8	39%	.220	1.27	1.80	3.64	3.94	0.2
2011	LEX	A	25	0	0	0	2	0	2	2	1	2	3	9.0	13.5	—	.250	2.00	13.50	10.03	10.90	0.0
2012	AST	Rk	26	0	1	0	8	5	11	5	0	2	11	1.6	9.0	54%	.179	0.64	0.00	2.25	3.68	0.1
2012	LNC	A+	26	0	0	0	11	0	19	14	1	4	20	1.9	9.5	49%	.300	0.95	1.42	3.18	3.57	0.3
2013	*HOU*	*MLB*	*27*	*1*	*1*	*1*	*17*	*2*	34^1	*32*	*4*	*18*	*33*	*4.7*	*8.7*	*44%*	*.295*	*1.45*	*4.53*	*4.37*	*4.92*	*0.1*

Lo has good stuff—a sinking fastball and several breaking pitches—and the polish and mental toughness one would expect from a veteran of international competition. He carved up advanced hitters in the Arizona Fall League, indicating he's likely not far from being ready to contribute to a major-league bullpen despite his lack of American professional experience. That's assuming his arm stays intact long enough for that to happen.

Jordan Lyles

Born: **10/19/1990** Age: **22**
Bats: **R** Throws: **R** Height: **6' 5"** Weight: **210**
Breakout: **24%** Improve: **63%** Collapse: **16%**
Attrition: **10%** MLB: **92%**

Comparables:
Michael Bowden, Zack Greinke, Hayden Penn

YEAR	TEAM	LVL	AGE	W	L	SV	G	GS	IP	H	HR	BB	SO	BB9	SO9	GB%	BABIP	WHIP	ERA	FIP	FRA	WARP
2010	CCH	AA	19	7	9	0	21	20	127	133	10	35	115	2.5	8.1	45%	.327	1.32	3.12	3.33	4.01	1.6
2010	ROU	AAA	19	0	3	0	6	6	31^{2}	48	2	11	22	3.1	6.2	52%	.397	1.86	5.39	4.25	4.27	0.4
2011	OKL	AAA	20	3	3	0	12	10	62^{1}	64	4	17	42	2.5	6.1	—	.317	1.30	3.61	4.33	4.71	0.0
2011	HOU	MLB	20	2	8	0	20	15	94	107	14	26	67	2.5	6.4	44%	.307	1.41	5.36	4.49	5.28	0.1
2012	OKL	AAA	21	5	0	0	7	7	40^{2}	41	2	8	33	1.8	7.3	59%	.331	1.20	3.54	3.71	4.79	0.0
2012	HOU	MLB	21	5	12	0	25	25	141^{1}	159	20	42	99	2.7	6.3	55%	.302	1.42	5.09	4.57	5.07	0.7
2013	*HOU*	*MLB*	*22*	*4*	*10*	*0*	*20*	*20*	116^{2}	*129*	*16*	*39*	*85*	*3.0*	*6.6*	*46%*	*.308*	*1.44*	*5.09*	*4.53*	*5.54*	*-0.2*

Sometimes velocity is over-emphasized, but Lyles is a pitcher who might benefit greatly if he could somehow throw his four-seam fastball another mile per hour faster. The separation between that fastball and his sinker and breaking pitches often isn't quite enough to disrupt the timing of hitters consistently. He has had some good stretches, and started to really look good at the end of last season, allowing a sub-.300 on-base percentage over his last 10 starts. He throws strikes and works a smart game, is responsive to coaching, and he has the size to make it easy to believe he could find a little more velocity. Until he does, his upside will likely be limited to stretches of good pitching interlaced with enough bad ones to disappoint.

Lance McCullers

Born: **10/2/1993** Age: **19**
Bats: **L** Throws: **R** Height: **6' 2"** Weight: **190**
Breakout: **11%** Improve: **85%** Collapse: **15%**
Attrition: **15%** MLB: **71%**

Comparables:
Lew Krausse, Mike McCormick, David Clyde

YEAR	TEAM	LVL	AGE	W	L	SV	G	GS	IP	H	HR	BB	SO	BB9	SO9	GB%	BABIP	WHIP	ERA	FIP	FRA	WARP
2012	AST	Rk	18	0	1	0	4	4	11	10	0	2	12	1.6	9.8	—	.312	1.09	1.64	1.80	1.95	0.0
2012	GRV	Rk	18	0	3	0	4	4	15	10	2	10	17	6.0	10.2	56%	.227	1.33	4.80	5.37	7.75	-0.2
2013	*HOU*	*MLB*	*19*	*1*	*4*	*0*	*7*	*7*	30^{2}	*38*	*5*	*22*	*16*	*6.3*	*4.6*	*46%*	*.312*	*1.94*	*7.17*	*6.43*	*7.79*	*-0.6*

Don't let the name limit expectations: McCullers may have learned the nuances of the game from his father and have baseball in his blood. He may even have the same power arm with a good curve and lack of control, but that doesn't dictate that Junior's ceiling is a moderately successful relief career like his dad's. Sure, there have been whispers that his imperfect mechanics will land him in the bullpen, but he had one of the best two-pitch combos in the draft for a high schooler. His fastball is almost as good as anyone's and his curve has great potential. He's not close to ready: His control is more off than on, and he's had little cause to use his changeup. He'll need that pitch to thrive as a starter. Senior made the majors at the precocious age of 21, but control issues almost immediately relegated him to the bullpen. The Astros will be patient with his kid and they won't give up on him as a starter lightly.

Joe Musgrove

Born: **12/4/1992** Age: **20**
Bats: **R** Throws: **R** Height: **6' 6"** Weight: **230**
Breakout: **54%** Improve: **73%** Collapse: **16%**
Attrition: **5%** MLB: **45%**

Comparables:
Joe Moeller, Vida Blue, Jim Waugh

YEAR	TEAM	LVL	AGE	W	L	SV	G	GS	IP	H	HR	BB	SO	BB9	SO9	GB%	BABIP	WHIP	ERA	FIP	FRA	WARP
2011	BLJ	Rk	18	0	1	0	8	7	21^{2}	17	1	4	16	1.7	6.6	54%	.267	0.97	4.57	3.93	6.94	-0.1
2011	BLU	Rk	18	1	0	0	1	0	3	2	0	1	2	3.0	6.0	43%	.286	1.00	0.00	3.45	5.12	0.0
2012	BLU	Rk	19	0	0	0	2	1	8	5	0	0	9	0.0	10.1	68%	.263	0.62	1.12	1.82	3.95	0.2
2012	GRV	Rk	19	0	1	0	4	0	9	14	0	4	10	4.0	10.0	31%	.483	2.00	7.00	2.81	-0.15	0.3
2013	*HOU*	*MLB*	*20*	*1*	*2*	*0*	*10*	*4*	*31*	*38*	*5*	*20*	*16*	*5.9*	*4.8*	*45%*	*.314*	*1.90*	*7.01*	*6.20*	*7.62*	*-0.5*

Until the shoulder injury that cost him most of the 2012 season, Musgrove had it all going for him: size, velocity (which he usually tempered by sinking his fastballs), easy delivery, projectability, and at least two viable breaking pitches, including a hard-breaking curve. He had been picked in the first round of the 2011 draft by the Blue Jays, 46th overall. He came back after the injury, and the Astros think he has put it behind him. But it's difficult not to worry about a guy after his drafting organization gave up on him, and who ended up only pitching a few innings in a rookie league when he was expected to be a starter at Single-A. Still, the upside is unmistakable.

Bud Norris

Born: **3/2/1985** Age: **28**
Bats: **R** Throws: **R** Height: **6' 1"** Weight: **220**
Breakout: **25%** Improve: **61%** Collapse: **22%**
Attrition: **23%** MLB: **86%**

Comparables:
Ervin Santana, John Patterson, Ian Snell

YEAR	TEAM	LVL	AGE	W	L	SV	G	GS	IP	H	HR	BB	SO	BB9	SO9	GB%	BABIP	WHIP	ERA	FIP	FRA	WARP
2010	ROU	AAA	25	1	0	0	3	3	14^{2}	16	1	6	14	3.7	8.6	41%	.349	1.50	3.06	3.79	4.06	0.3
2010	HOU	MLB	25	9	10	0	27	27	153^{2}	151	18	77	158	4.5	9.3	45%	.314	1.48	4.92	4.19	4.49	1.4
2011	HOU	MLB	26	6	11	0	31	31	186	177	24	70	176	3.4	8.5	42%	.294	1.33	3.77	3.99	4.32	1.7
2012	OKL	AAA	27	1	0	0	1	1	5	3	2	3	7	5.4	12.6	18%	.111	1.20	3.60	7.87	8.03	0.0
2012	HOU	MLB	27	7	13	0	29	29	168^{1}	165	23	66	165	3.5	8.8	41%	.301	1.37	4.65	4.27	4.50	1.7
2013	*HOU*	*MLB*	*28*	*6*	*11*	*0*	*24*	*24*	137^{2}	*134*	*19*	*58*	*132*	*3.8*	*8.7*	*44%*	*.303*	*1.40*	*4.56*	*4.34*	*4.96*	*0.7*

The overall result in 2012 was a slight backslide from Norris's league average-ish 2011 season, but—typical of Norris—it tantalized with its promise. When fully healthy, Norris seemed in better control of his stuff, and he was doing a good job of spotting his sinker behind his four-seam fastball and slider. He used his change less, which was just as well, as it still doesn't fool lefties. But one really has to selectively pick endpoints (as in first nine and final seven starts) to be tantalized, as the portion of the season sandwiched in the middle was foul indeed. The question of whether he's the average pitcher his overall results keep indicating or something better is no closer to being answered than it was before last season.

Rudy Owens
Born: **12/18/1987** Age: **25**
Bats: **L** Throws: **L** Height: **6' 4"** Weight: **225**
Breakout: **24%** Improve: **63%** Collapse: **16%**
Attrition: **15%** MLB: **80%**
Comparables:
Tommy Milone, Elizardo Ramirez, Zach Duke

YEAR	TEAM	LVL	AGE	W	L	SV	G	GS	IP	H	HR	BB	SO	BB9	SO9	GB%	BABIP	WHIP	ERA	FIP	FRA	WARP
2010	ALT	AA	22	12	6	0	26	26	150	124	11	23	132	1.4	7.9	48%	.297	0.98	2.46	3.11	4.05	1.9
2011	IND	AAA	23	9	7	0	21	21	112^{1}	129	10	32	71	2.6	5.7	44%	.313	1.43	5.05	4.14	5.08	0.2
2012	IND	AAA	24	8	5	0	19	19	117^{1}	112	12	25	85	1.9	6.5	42%	.280	1.17	3.14	3.83	4.58	0.6
2012	OKL	AAA	24	2	3	0	8	8	45^{2}	43	7	14	23	2.8	4.5	40%	.228	1.25	4.34	5.83	9.67	0.0
2013	*HOU*	*MLB*	*25*	*2*	*4*	*0*	*8*	*8*	45^{2}	*49*	*7*	*14*	*30*	*2.8*	*5.9*	*42%*	*.292*	*1.38*	*4.83*	*4.80*	*5.24*	*0.1*

Owens doesn't throw hard at his best, but last year he reclaimed most of the velocity he'd lost in 2011, and his mechanics also recovered, and with them his sub-2.0 walks-per-nine-innings ratio. That rebound corroborates the story told before he was included in the Wandy Rodriguez trade, that 2011 was the result of pitching in pain. However, in Oklahoma City, everything went bad again. The current story is that the downturn was just shell shock from the better hitting environment. Houston is hoping for a strong showing in spring training and that Owens will need only a short Triple-A refresher before being ready to be yet another back-of-the-rotation starter for the big club.

Fernando Rodriguez
Born: **6/18/1984** Age: **29**
Bats: **R** Throws: **R** Height: **6' 4"** Weight: **215**
Breakout: **43%** Improve: **62%** Collapse: **15%**
Attrition: **17%** MLB: **84%**
Comparables:
Jim Gott, Tyler Yates, Dennys Reyes

YEAR	TEAM	LVL	AGE	W	L	SV	G	GS	IP	H	HR	BB	SO	BB9	SO9	GB%	BABIP	WHIP	ERA	FIP	FRA	WARP
2011	OKL	AAA	27	2	3	2	16	0	24	16	2	11	33	4.1	12.4	—	.280	1.12	1.50	3.62	3.93	0.0
2011	HOU	MLB	27	2	3	0	47	0	52^{1}	51	6	30	57	5.2	9.8	38%	.333	1.55	3.96	4.20	4.80	0.3
2012	HOU	MLB	28	2	10	0	71	0	70^{1}	68	10	34	78	4.4	10.0	38%	.312	1.45	5.37	4.26	3.52	1.0
2013	*HOU*	*MLB*	*29*	*2*	*2*	*0*	*38*	*4*	56^{1}	*58*	*8*	*28*	*49*	*4.6*	*7.9*	*39%*	*.306*	*1.53*	*5.07*	*4.80*	*5.51*	*-0.1*

Rodriguez actually threw a little harder last year than in the past as he moved further from his former role as a starting pitcher. But it did him no good: His peripherals were similar to 2011 (belying a huge illusory increase in ERA), with a bit lower walk rate and a few more balls leaving the yard. He misses enough bats, but to become more than filler he needs to tune his control to the point where he's walking fewer than four batters per nine innings.

Nick Tropeano
Born: **8/27/1990** Age: **22**
Bats: **R** Throws: **R** Height: **6' 5"** Weight: **205**
Breakout: **29%** Improve: **63%** Collapse: **14%**
Attrition: **8%** MLB: **90%**
Comparables:
Chris Tillman, Trevor Cahill, Hayden Penn

YEAR	TEAM	LVL	AGE	W	L	SV	G	GS	IP	H	HR	BB	SO	BB9	SO9	GB%	BABIP	WHIP	ERA	FIP	FRA	WARP
2011	TCV	A-	20	3	2	0	12	12	53^{1}	42	1	21	63	3.5	10.6	—	.301	1.18	2.36	2.48	2.70	0.0
2012	LEX	A	21	6	4	0	15	14	87^{1}	77	3	26	97	2.7	10.0	49%	.323	1.18	2.78	2.77	3.48	2.4
2012	LNC	A+	21	6	3	0	12	12	70^{2}	72	8	21	69	2.7	8.8	43%	.325	1.32	3.31	4.35	4.76	0.6
2013	*HOU*	*MLB*	*22*	*1*	*3*	*0*	*7*	*7*	38^{2}	*40*	*5*	*17*	*31*	*3.9*	*7.1*	*44%*	*.304*	*1.48*	*4.94*	*4.60*	*5.37*	*0.0*

Tropeano is a name to remember. He was seemingly born with a great changeup, and his delivery and mental game are also considered top-tier. Even with a good slider and very good control, because of velocity deficiencies (he was lucky to hit 92 once per outing) he was thought of as a right-handed Dallas Keuchel, a pitcher for whom everything would have to be perfect to succeed. All that changed in 2012, as dedication to adding strength over the offseason pushed his typical fastball velocity into the low 90s.

Jose Veras
Born: **10/20/1980** Age: **32**
Bats: **R** Throws: **R** Height: **6' 7"** Weight: **235**
Breakout: **22%** Improve: **39%** Collapse: **33%**
Attrition: **10%** MLB: **94%**
Comparables:
Troy Percival, Jeff Nelson, Armando Benitez

YEAR	TEAM	LVL	AGE	W	L	SV	G	GS	IP	H	HR	BB	SO	BB9	SO9	GB%	BABIP	WHIP	ERA	FIP	FRA	WARP
2010	NWO	AAA	29	1	1	2	24	0	29^{1}	34	2	15	37	4.6	11.4	42%	.395	1.67	4.61	3.48	3.79	0.5
2010	FLO	MLB	29	3	3	0	48	0	48	32	5	29	54	5.4	10.1	42%	.241	1.27	3.75	4.09	4.44	0.2
2011	PIT	MLB	30	2	4	1	79	0	71	54	6	34	79	4.3	10.0	39%	.264	1.24	3.80	3.47	3.52	0.9
2012	MIL	MLB	31	5	4	1	72	0	67	61	5	40	79	5.4	10.6	46%	.322	1.51	3.63	3.63	3.95	0.7
2013	*HOU*	*MLB*	*32*	*3*	*1*	*1*	*61*	*0*	59^{1}	*50*	*7*	*30*	*65*	*4.6*	*9.9*	*42%*	*.286*	*1.36*	*3.89*	*4.06*	*4.23*	*0.7*

Armed with a fastball that can reach the mid-90s and a knee-buckling slow curve, Veras has always had the stuff to make batters look silly. If only those pesky hitters would stop stubbornly waiting him out and making him throw strikes, he could lower his execrable walk rate and really do some damage. There are worse relievers around, and Veras is a leading contender to catch lightning in a bottle one season, fleetingly improve his command, and put in a dominant 50-inning stretch. The Astros will become the sixth team with a Leyden jar attached to a kite string in the past five years.

Alex White

Born: **8/29/1988** Age: **24**
Bats: **R** Throws: **R** Height: **6' 4"** Weight: **215**
Breakout: **28%** Improve: **61%** Collapse: **24%**
Attrition: **26%** MLB: **87%**

Comparables:
Hayden Penn,Alex Cobb,Garrett Richards

YEAR	TEAM	LVL	AGE	W	L	SV	G	GS	IP	H	HR	BB	SO	BB9	SO9	GB%	BABIP	WHIP	ERA	FIP	FRA	WARP
2010	KIN	A+	21	2	3	0	8	8	44	32	4	19	41	3.9	8.4	56%	.237	1.16	2.86	4.02	4.68	0.3
2010	AKR	AA	21	8	7	0	18	17	106^2	91	8	27	76	2.3	6.4	59%	.254	1.11	2.28	3.73	4.51	1.4
2011	TUL	AA	22	1	1	0	4	4	16^1	10	1	1	10	0.6	5.5	38%	.267	0.67	1.65	3.32	7.17	0.0
2011	COH	AAA	22	1	0	0	4	4	23^2	19	1	5	28	1.9	10.6	—	.295	1.01	1.90	2.31	2.51	0.0
2011	CLE	MLB	22	1	0	0	3	3	15	14	3	9	13	5.4	7.8	57%	.268	1.53	3.60	5.73	6.09	-0.2
2011	COL	MLB	22	2	4	0	7	7	36^1	48	12	16	24	4.0	5.9	45%	.313	1.76	8.42	7.62	7.77	-0.9
2012	CSP	AAA	23	3	4	0	11	11	60^2	54	3	23	45	3.4	6.7	55%	.280	1.27	3.71	4.06	4.91	1.0
2012	COL	MLB	23	2	9	0	23	20	98	114	13	51	64	4.7	5.9	56%	.310	1.68	5.51	5.27	6.20	0.1
2013	*HOU*	*MLB*	*24*	*3*	*8*	*0*	*17*	*17*	90^1	*94*	*14*	*39*	*65*	*3.9*	*6.4*	*52%*	*.287*	*1.47*	*5.09*	*5.07*	*5.53*	*-0.0*

In his first full season in the Rockies organization after coming over from Cleveland in the Ubaldo Jimenez trade, White proved less hittable and less susceptible to the long ball but struggled to throw strikes and miss bats. Recalled from Triple-A in early May, he was sent back toward the end of June thanks to poor command. The 2009 first-round pick features a heavy two-seam fastball that induces grounders, much like former Colorado right-hander Aaron Cook, but sometimes relies too much on his slider. In short, he's much the same pitcher he was in his University of North Carolina days, and the Astros will be the third organization to attempt to get him to make the refinements he needs (read: throwing the ball over the plate and trusting his stuff) to translate his abundant talent into major-league results.

Asher Wojciechowski

Born: **12/21/1988** Age: **24**
Bats: **R** Throws: **R** Height: **6' 5"** Weight: **235**
Breakout: **26%** Improve: **57%** Collapse: **27%**
Attrition: **35%** MLB: **83%**

Comparables:
Juan Gutierrez,Troy Patton,Anthony Swarzak

YEAR	TEAM	LVL	AGE	W	L	SV	G	GS	IP	H	HR	BB	SO	BB9	SO9	GB%	BABIP	WHIP	ERA	FIP	FRA	WARP
2011	DUN	A+	22	11	9	0	25	22	130^1	156	15	31	96	2.1	6.6	48%	.324	1.43	4.70	4.22	4.80	0.6
2012	DUN	A+	23	7	3	0	18	18	93^1	91	3	22	76	2.1	7.3	46%	.320	1.21	3.57	3.05	3.52	1.4
2012	CCH	AA	23	2	2	0	8	8	43^2	30	0	14	34	2.9	7.0	44%	.236	1.01	2.06	3.03	3.28	0.3
2013	*HOU*	*MLB*	*24*	*1*	*3*	*0*	*7*	*7*	36^1	*39*	*5*	*14*	*24*	*3.5*	*6.0*	*45%*	*.300*	*1.48*	*5.00*	*4.82*	*5.44*	*0.0*

Viewed through the lens of TINSTAPP, Wojciechowski looks like a better pitching prospect than most think he is now. If that seems illogical, the point is that he pitched very well in 2012, but is not highly regarded because he was old for his leagues and doesn't throw 100 miles per hour. He does have good sink on his fastball, decent velocity, a working slider, and a changeup that has improved to the point where lefties aren't hitting him any better than righties. In a bit of an oddity, he generates only an average amount of groundballs, yet has managed to keep the ball in the park. Stranger still, he has allowed a higher-than-typical batting average on grounders allowed, leading to low groundout-to-fly-out ratios. His delivery doesn't seem to call for that, so expect a regression to normal home run and groundout-to-fly-out rates. How much his home-run suppression regresses will determine his future more than his age will.

Wesley Wright

Born: **1/28/1985** Age: **28**
Bats: **R** Throws: **L** Height: **6' 0"** Weight: **180**
Breakout: **27%** Improve: **53%** Collapse: **30%**
Attrition: **18%** MLB: **83%**

Comparables:
John Ennis,Ike Delock,Pedro Viola

YEAR	TEAM	LVL	AGE	W	L	SV	G	GS	IP	H	HR	BB	SO	BB9	SO9	GB%	BABIP	WHIP	ERA	FIP	FRA	WARP
2010	ROU	AAA	25	4	1	0	15	14	69^2	76	8	33	41	4.3	5.3	46%	.301	1.56	4.65	5.49	6.09	0.5
2010	HOU	MLB	25	1	2	0	14	4	33	37	6	13	29	3.5	7.9	45%	.320	1.52	5.73	5.17	5.81	-0.2
2011	OKL	AAA	26	3	1	2	39	3	65^1	49	4	23	52	3.2	7.2	—	.246	1.10	2.07	4.18	4.54	0.0
2011	HOU	MLB	26	0	0	0	21	0	12	6	1	5	11	3.8	8.2	57%	.185	0.92	1.50	3.49	4.05	0.1
2012	HOU	MLB	27	2	2	1	77	0	52^1	45	4	17	54	2.9	9.3	57%	.289	1.18	3.27	3.38	4.54	0.2
2013	*HOU*	*MLB*	*28*	*2*	*2*	*1*	*29*	*4*	37^2	*35*	*5*	*17*	*35*	*4.1*	*8.3*	*47%*	*.292*	*1.39*	*4.46*	*4.42*	*4.85*	*0.2*

Time to pull out the big red LOOGY stamp and decorate Wright's baseball card. In a concession that 155 previous games of data were indeed telling the tale, experiments with Wright in various other roles ended in 2012. He pitched less than a full inning 46 times and held lefty batters to a .209 TAv, 15th-best among pitchers with 133 or more plate appearances against that side. As usual, he wasn't very effective against righties, but expect the sinker-slider combo to return and continue to make the left-handed batting population want to spit in 2013.

LINEOUTS

HITTERS

PLAYER	TEAM	LVL	AGE	PA	R	2B	3B	HR	RBI	BB	SO	SB-CS	AVG/OBP/SLG	TAv	BABIP	BRR	FRAA	WARP
C C. Corporan	OKL	AAA	28	229	35	15	0	6	31	15	46	2-0	.286/.349/.447	.196	.340	0.2	C(15): -0.0	0.1
	HOU	MLB	28	85	5	2	0	4	13	4	19	0-1	.269/.310/.449	.252	.304	-0.2	C(24): 0.5	0.3
OF T. Crowe	COH	AAA	28	152	20	7	1	3	12	17	24	8-3	.250/.336/.386	.271	.280	-1.6	RF(9): 0.8, LF(3): -0.1	0.0
	SLC	AAA	28	181	26	10	3	0	16	15	28	10-6	.301/.354/.399	.253	.355	-1.2	CF(27): 1.2, RF(3): 0.1	0.0
UT M. Downs	OKL	AAA	28	102	14	2	0	3	15	8	20	3-2	.267/.343/.389	.189	.309	0.6	2B(3): -0.1, 1B(1): 0.0	0.0
	HOU	MLB	28	191	15	4	1	8	16	8	38	2-4	.202/.253/.371	.221	.212	-1.1	1B(25): 0.7, 3B(18): 0.5	-0.2
SS N. Fontana	LEX	A	21	222	37	9	1	2	25	65	44	12-2	.225/.464/.338	.301	.302	3.5	SS(45): -1.8	1.6
1B N. Freiman	SAN	AA	25	581	80	31	1	24	105	49	95	0-2	.298/.370/.502	.299	.324	-8.4	1B(94): -4.7	0.2
OF M. Krauss	MOB	AA	24	434	75	29	2	15	61	73	91	6-4	.283/.416/.509	.337	.339	-2.7	LF(38): 1.4, RF(17): -2.5	2.0
	OKL	AAA	24	66	3	0	0	0	2	6	20	1-1	.123/.203/.123	.155	.184	-0.2	RF(2): 0.1, LF(2): 0.3	-0.2
3B B. Laird	SWB	AAA	24	550	54	31	2	15	77	34	103	1-0	.254/.307/.414	.236	.289	-2.8	3B(69): -6.8, 1B(39): 0.3	-1.6
	HOU	MLB	24	37	2	1	0	1	4	2	8	0-0	.257/.297/.371	.259	.308	0.1	3B(8): 0.3, 1B(4): -0.2	0.0
RF A. Ovando	GRV	Rk	18	247	34	13	2	6	35	22	67	0-0	.287/.350/.444	.248	.384	-0.2	RF(13): 0.0	-0.3
OF A. Wates	CCH	AA	23	409	58	16	4	7	48	31	71	17-11	.304/.375/.429	.264	.360	-0.5	LF(19): 0.5, CF(7): -0.7	0.2

Carlos Corporan's throwing arm rebounded after a down year in 2011, which—combined with his surprising success at the plate—earned him a 40-man roster spot, but he's a fungible backup catcher. **Trevor Crowe** was a first-round pick in 2005 and had promising seasons in both 2006 and 2008, but he was never able to solve major-league pitching, though he retains enough speed and defensive ability that he should stick around the game as a backup outfielder for a while. The retooled swing that **Matt Downs** unveiled in 2011 was exploited mercilessly last year, and even a willingness to play wherever needed wasn't enough to make him an asset. While **Nolan Fontana** remains at shortstop, the Astros have quality depth at the key position; his pitch recognition and plate discipline were astonishingly good and should help him progress. **Nate Freiman**, the Padres' eighth-round pick in 2009 out of Duke and a Rule 5 pick for Houston, is an enormous human being who can hit the ball a long way but has trouble with good fastballs. The two most important skills a player can have are getting on base and slugging, yet somehow guys like **Marc Krauss** get the "one-dimensional" label applied; he's a bit too old to be much of a prospect, but it would be far from shocking if he did develop into a useful major leaguer. For all the gains the organization has made in improving the talent base, there are still signs—such as **Brandon Laird** making the 40-man roster—that the lean years aren't quite past. In his senior year of high school, er, make that his second year in the Appalachian League, monster power lefty outfielder **Ariel Ovando** took some steps forward, and though he's fallen out of favor after getting $2.6 million to sign in 2010, there's still a lot of time for him to figure things out. The Crawfish Boxes blog voted **Austin Wates** Best Prospect Twitter Account To Follow even though he lacks extra-base pop, true center-field range, or stolen base efficiency, which means he's barely a prospect.

PITCHERS

PLAYER	TEAM	LVL	AGE	W	L	SV	IP	H	HR	BB	SO	BB9	SO9	GB%	BABIP	WHIP	ERA	FIP	FRA	WARP
J. Armstrong	—	—	—	—	—	—	—	—	—	—	—	—	—	—	—	—	—	—	—	—
J. De Leon	LNC	A+	24	2	9	6	87^2	116	11	44	60	4.5	6.2	38%	.350	1.83	7.70	5.72	6.96	0.1
E. Del Rosario	OKL	AAA	26	4	1	1	41^1	43	5	20	18	4.4	3.9	49%	.267	1.52	5.01	5.96	13.96	-0.8
	HOU	MLB	26	0	0	0	19	34	1	7	11	3.3	5.2	39%	.434	2.16	9.00	4.08	4.50	0.1
C. Devenski	KAN	A	21	6	5	2	61^2	63	8	19	54	2.8	7.9	42%	.304	1.33	4.23	4.58	5.30	0.4
	LEX	A	21	2	2	0	29^1	23	1	16	38	4.9	11.7	46%	.333	1.33	3.07	3.27	4.13	0.5
S. Escalona	—	—	—	—	—	—	—	—	—	—	—	—	—	—	—	—	—	—	—	—
C. Fick	MEM	AAA	26	1	1	2	42^1	49	6	13	20	2.8	4.3	60%	.291	1.46	4.68	5.56	7.85	-0.2
	HOU	MLB	26	0	1	0	23	24	4	17	17	6.7	6.7	51%	.299	1.78	4.30	6.40	6.25	-0.2
	SLN	MLB	26	0	0	0	1^2	3	0	1	0	5.4	0.0	12%	.375	2.40	5.40	4.94	5.04	0.0
A. Gillingham	ASH	A	22	6	8	0	123	122	5	28	83	2.0	6.1	64%	.302	1.22	3.66	3.81	5.65	1.8
E. Gonzalez	CSP	AAA	29	3	3	0	46^2	54	5	11	40	2.1	7.7	46%	.331	1.39	5.40	4.37	5.15	0.8
	HOU	MLB	29	3	1	0	25	23	3	8	18	2.9	6.5	47%	.263	1.24	5.04	4.22	5.15	0.2
A. Houser	GRV	Rk	19	3	4	0	58	53	1	23	54	3.6	8.4	60%	.312	1.31	4.19	3.51	3.96	0.0
B. Oberholtzer	CCH	AA	22	5	3	0	77	81	11	21	68	2.5	7.9	54%	.304	1.32	4.21	4.23	5.06	0.0
	OKL	AAA	22	5	7	0	89^2	105	13	19	69	1.9	6.9	41%	.324	1.38	4.52	4.71	5.33	0.4
D. Rollins	LEX	A	22	1	3	0	31	27	5	9	25	2.6	7.3	49%	.262	1.16	3.48	5.13	6.19	0.0
	LNS	A	22	6	1	0	77^2	64	2	36	75	4.2	8.7	44%	.298	1.29	2.78	3.22	3.41	0.6
J. Valdez	OKL	AAA	29	0	5	21	43^2	53	5	12	59	2.5	12.2	48%	.378	1.49	4.95	3.35	1.43	1.5
	HOU	MLB	29	0	0	0	12	12	1	8	10	6.0	7.5	54%	.289	1.67	2.25	4.55	3.68	0.2
V. Velasquez	TCV	A-	20	4	1	0	45^2	37	2	17	51	3.4	10.1	44%	.299	1.18	3.35	2.98	3.62	0.2
B. Walters	KAN	A	22	3	3	0	72	61	6	18	69	2.2	8.6	46%	.279	1.10	2.88	3.70	4.13	1.3
	LNC	A+	22	3	3	0	39	49	8	15	34	3.5	7.8	45%	.336	1.64	7.62	6.04	7.26	0.0
	WNS	A+	22	1	3	0	25^2	38	3	4	24	1.4	8.4	43%	.407	1.64	7.01	3.85	4.66	0.1

When healthy, **Jack Armstrong** is aptly named, and has good potential, but so far, the pitcher most often mentioned with him isn't Jack Armstrong Sr., but rather Tommy John. ⚾ **Jorge De Leon** may still be working out the kinks after switching from shortstop, and pitching for the JetHawks is thankless at best, but he was taken off the 40-man roster after posting an ERA that could be the model number on a Boeing product. ⚾ Touted as always having fantastic control in the minors in last year's book, **Enerio Del Rosario** lost even that distinction in 2012, and is now going to require some fantastic luck to accrue more service time. ⚾ **Chris Devenski** threw a no-hitter with one walk and 16 strikeouts in his final start of the season, significantly raising the stock of this former shortstop/former reliever obtained in the Brett Myers trade. ⚾ Before missing last season with Tommy John surgery, **Sergio Escalona** had finally settled in as a useful LOOGY, and once his confidence in his rebuilt arm returns (and with it his command), he should again be adequate in that role. ⚾ As Luhnow tries to get the band back together, **Chuckie Fick** can handle the pyrotechnics; he was drafted by the Cardinals in 2007 while Luhnow was vice president of scouting. ⚾ **Alex Gillingham** is a control artist who lacks a strikeout pitch but who managed to allow one stingy home run in 66 2/3 innings at Asheville's unforgiving McCormick Field last year. ⚾ **Edgar Gonzalez** has 350 innings of replacement-level work in his career so far, serving as a reminder—by contrast—of just how valuable good starting pitchers are. ⚾ A second-round pick in 2011, **Adrian Houser** really utilized his repeat stint in rookie ball, refining control on both his sharp curve and his heavy fastball that makes up for substandard velocity with good movement. ⚾ **Brett Oberholtzer** is still young, but since coming over from Atlanta he's discovered that a lot more fly balls leave the park in the Southern and Pacific Coast Leagues. If he keeps throwing strikes, he could become a fifth starter. ⚾ **David Rollins** isn't a high-upside prospect, but if he can keep refining his pitches and keep them down in the zone while continuing the strike-throwing, he could develop into a rotation asset someday. ⚾ **Jose Valdez** can top 95 mph semi-regularly, but the Astros let him go, and there was so little demand for him that they were able to bring him back on a minor-league deal. ⚾ Power righty **Vincent Velasquez** took the standard 18 month "vacation" for Tommy John surgery, and the return was about as positive as possible, as he showed full arm strength, both breaking pitches intact, and none of the wobbly control often accompanying injury returnees. ⚾ **Blair Walters** throws a sinker, but it couldn't sink fast enough to avoid High-A bats, and if he doesn't figure out another trick, his pitches won't be the only thing sunk.

MANAGER: BRAD MILLS

YEAR	TEAM	W-L	Pythag +/-	Avg PC	100+ P	120+ P	QS	BQS	REL	REL w Zero R	IBB	PH	PH Avg	PH HR	SB2	CS2	SB3	CS3	SAC Att	SAC %	POS SAC	Squeeze	Swing	In Play
2010	HOU	76-86	0	199.6	161	158	112	4	508	400	76	556	.224	6	10	4	0	0	200	84.0%	72	12	298	84
2011	HOU	56-106	0	100.3	88	3	80	8	503	378	59	278	.263	6	20	1	0	2	112	73.2%	48	2	318	87
2012	HOU	55-107	0	94.1	61	0	73	2	541	405	40	260	.242	6	12	2	1	2	77	80.5%	22	3	343	97

"In order to score runs you have to get on base," Porter said in an interview with FanGraphs when he was coaching third base for the Nationals last summer. "I want to make sure that the guys at the top of the lineup are able to get on base at a high percentage." While much has been said about Porter's character, leadership, and work ethic, answering the most fundamental offensive question with commentary about on-base percentage got him noticed by the forward-thinking Astros. He has the analytical bent that should allow him to play nice with the sabermetrically inclined front office, and has shown—in his time managing in the minors and coaching in the majors—a willingness to adapt.

Only time will determine how frequently he tinkers with things such as defensive positioning, pitch sequencing, and creative offensive options (atypical stolen-base attempts, bunting, etc.). While he may not be Lisa Simpson in *MoneyBART*, there's every expectation that whatever Porter tries will be based on the organization's best analysis, and expect that things *will* be tried. From a public-facing perspective, he has a high level of intensity and garners the respect of people inside and outside the game. While managers are virtually never heard to decline job offers at this level, Porter's résumé is so perfect that he was on the fast track to some managerial post, and he would have been given a different chance if he didn't want the Houston challenge. So, the introduction is written to a hero's journey: Only time will tell if Bo Porter can rally the troops—a la Aragorn—by exhorting, "Stand! Men of the West!" en route to reviving the kingdom so long in disarray.

Kansas City Royals

2012: STUNTED PROCESS

At the dawn of the sixth year of Dayton Moore's tenure as the Royals GM, hopes were high. "The Process," a term used by Moore himself in an attempt to calm fans anxious for success, should have been on the verge of success. The first wave of an outstanding farm system had arrived the previous season, and the Royals were poised to advance their cause in a mediocre American League Central. Yet hope quickly morphed into despair.

The Royals stumbled out of the gate and lost 14 of their first 17 games in 2012. This wasn't an ordinary slow start: the Kansas City nine failed in style, losing 12 consecutive games, including their first 10 at home. While the Royals were scuffling to win games, some key players were going down with severe injuries. Catcher Salvador Perez tore the meniscus in his right knee in February and was lost until July. Closer Joakim Soria had Tommy John surgery in March and was quickly followed into Dr. Lewis Yocum's operating room by starters Danny Duffy and Felipe Paulino. By the time the Royals filled out their ligament-replacement punch card (buy four, get the fifth one free!), they were at the bottom of the standings. The rotation was thin to begin with; losing two of the club's better starters was difficult to weather. The staff finished with a 4.65 FRA, an improvement from the previous season, but still in the lower half of the league.

ROYALS PROSPECTUS

2012 W-L: 72-90, 3rd in AL Central

Pythag	.454	24th	DER	.689	28th
RS/G	4.17	20th	B-Age	26.1	1st
RA/G	4.60	23rd	P-Age	27.7	10th
TAv	.254	24th	Salary	$64.4	25th
BRR	-4.4	20th	M$/MW	$2.18	10th
TAv-P	.272	26th	DL Days	1074	11th
FIP	4.13	19th	DL WARP	3.0	17th

Three-Year Park Factors	
Overall	102
HR/RH	100
HR/LH	93
AVG/RH	106
AVG/LH	107

Kauffman Stadium (1973)
Att. % of Capacity: 57.4% (24th)
Dim. 330, 387, 410, 387, 330

The Royals hope maturing hitters and revamped hitting philosophies will improve The K's homer rate.

The rotation was expected to scuffle along, but the Royals were supposed to have the bats to keep offensive pace with the league. Yet their .254 TAv was the second worst rate in the AL. Continuing the hallmark of Royals teams in the Moore era, the lineup was stocked with hitters who mostly refused to accept a free pass. Their collective 6.6 percent walk rate was the worst in baseball. And when they did reach base, they weren't efficient with their baserunning. They finished with a -4.4 BRr and inspired the Twitter hashtag of #RoyalsFreeOut.

Despite the offensive shortcomings, there were positives. One year after leading all left fielders with 6.5 WARP, Alex Gordon followed up with 4.3 WARP. Billy Butler has been the Royals' most consistent hitter the last several seasons, coming close to reaching a .300 TAv each year since 2009. Last year, he added a little more power to his hitting arsenal, posting a career high .197 ISO and a .304 TAv. The bullpen, thought by outside observers to be in dire straits without the sidelined Soria, thrived with Jonathan Broxton, Kelvin Herrera, and Greg Holland in the late innings. The Kansas City bullpen threw 561 innings last summer, second highest total in baseball. That three of the Royals' top four pitchers ranked by WARP were relievers (Holland, Herrera, and Tim Collins) underscored the value of the pen.

It wasn't enough. Six years into Moore's Process, in a season in which there was supposed to be important progress, the Royals improved by a single win. The failure to get better damned the Royals to their 27th consecutive season on the sidelines in October, the longest postseason drought in professional sports.

2013: THE PROCESS DELAYED

Now entering its seventh season, Moore's Process comes under increased scrutiny, and with good reason. While the injuries of 2012 were unfortunate, the real reason the Royals have failed to make inroads in a perpetually weak Central Division can be found in their failure to parlay a bountiful farm system into solid, major-league talent. The cold, hard fact is Moore's front office has yet to draft and develop a single impact player.

With a limited budget and little help on the immediate horizon, the Royals figure to roll into 2013 with the same set of position players they had planned to open with in 2012. Their offensive success will depend on improvement from their young corner-infield tandem. The hyped dynamic duo of Eric Hosmer and Mike Moustakas blitzed through the minors, yet have failed to make their mark at the major-league level. Hosmer finished with a -0.2 WARP and Moustakas chimed in with a respectable 2.7 thanks mostly to his glove work. For the Royals to rebound offensively, the corner infield pair will have to more than double their collective output from 2012.

While the Royals will wait for their young bats to develop, they don't have that luxury with their rotation. Surgery for Duffy and Paulino will prevent their two best starters from taking the mound until midseason. And absent decent options knocking on the big-league door, the Royals have little choice but to cast the net far and wide looking for rotation help. It was this urgency that led them to re-sign midseason acquisition Jeremy Guthrie, trade for Ervin Santana, and pull off one of the blockbuster trades of the winter in sending prospects Wil Myers and Jake Odorizzi to Tampa Bay for James Shields and Wade Davis.

It's not lost on Moore's growing cavalcade of critics that his best players—Gordon and Butler—were drafted and largely developed by the previous regime. Injuries and assorted struggles have delayed the Process. Now Moore hopes that 2013 will be to his young team what 2012 should have been: a clear step forward. In that sense, the heat is on. If the Royals stumble again in April, or if Hosmer and Moustakas continue to struggle with major-league pitching, The Process may not survive its seventh season.

STATE OF THE ORGANIZATION: THE PROCESS AS CRUTCH

The Royals are aware their window of opportunity is open. Key players are signed long-term, with the hitting stalwart Butler under contract through 2014 with a 2015 club option and Gordon inked through the 2015 season. Youngsters like Perez and Alcides Escobar are under club-friendly deals that bought out their arbitration years, leaving Moustakas and Hosmer as the two key every-day players yet to commit. No surprise, as both are clients of the Boras Corp. Of course, none of that really matters if neither can consistently produce with the bat.

Moore has often repeated the mantra "home grown"—the majority of his major-league club must be drafted and developed by his support staff or the Royals can't compete with the financial realities of baseball stacked against them. The mantra has become a crutch, a way of explaining a lack of progress. While the Royals spent 2011 and 2012 promoting young players to the majors with gusto, organizational depth remains but now it's in the lower minors. With the gap in the wave of prospects, Moore has opted to deal his two prospects closest to reaching the bigs, Myers and Odorizzi, for major-league talent.

In light of the recent successes of the Orioles, Athletics, and Nationals, three teams that were entrenched in last place in their respective divisions as recently as four seasons ago, yet managed to play meaningful October baseball last year, Moore is under great pressure to produce results. His actions this offseason illustrate his depth of understanding. The danger is he may be sacrificing long-term results for the short-term gain. The Royals will be an improved club in 2013, but even with the overhaul, doubts remain whether they can contend.

If Moore can't strike pitching gold, the Process will be doomed to further delay. The Royals will settle into a comfortable stride on the treadmill of mediocrity, and Moore will be searching for employment.

HITTERS

Tony Abreu **INF**

Born: **11/13/1984** Age: **28**
Bats: **B** Throws: **R** Height: **5' 10"**
Weight: **200** Breakout: **1%**
Improve: **36%** Collapse: **8%**
Attrition: **14%** MLB: **87%**

Comparables:
Orlando Miller, Juan Uribe, Alex Gonzalez

YEAR	TEAM	LVL	AGE	PA	R	2B	3B	HR	RBI	BB	SO	SB	CS	AVG_OBP_SLG	TAv	BABIP	BRR	FRAA	WARP
2010	RNO	AAA	25	102	17	7	1	2	21	4	21	2	0	.351/.386/.511	.283	.431	0.5	SS(11): -0.1, 2B(8): -0.0	0.7
2010	ARI	MLB	25	201	16	11	1	1	13	4	47	2	1	.233/.244/.316	.187	.295	0.7	3B(20): 0.7, SS(15): -0.2	-0.8
2011	RNO	AAA	26	529	83	26	5	10	72	30	84	12	7	.292/.335/.429	.265	.329	0	--	0.0
2012	OMA	AAA	27	453	60	36	5	9	73	14	69	7	2	.322/.347/.492	.319	.365	3	SS(64): -3.9, 2B(4): 1.0	3.0
2012	KCA	MLB	27	74	5	2	1	1	15	2	13	0	0	.257/.284/.357	.225	.298	-2.4	2B(11): -0.4, 3B(6): 0.3	-0.4
2013	*KCA*	*MLB*	*28*	*250*	*23*	*14*	*2*	*5*	*27*	*7*	*50*	*2*	*1*	*.266/.289/.397*	*.240*	*.315*	*-0.1*	*SS -2, 2B -0*	*0.3*

Once upon a time, Abreu projected as the second baseman-in-waiting for the Dodgers behind Jeff Kent. His myriad injuries and hacktastic approach derailed those plans. These days, he's the most utility of utility players, playing three infield positions while continuing to swing at anything inside his current area code. A switch-hitter, he's better from the right side of the plate. However, his lack of discipline is present no matter where he digs in.

Billy Butler DH

Born: **4/18/1986** Age: **27**
Bats: **R** Throws: **R** Height: **6' 2"**
Weight: **240** Breakout: **2%**
Improve: **52%** Collapse: **7%**
Attrition: **11%** MLB: **95%**

Comparables:
Ron Blomberg,Todd Helton,Gaby Sanchez

YEAR	TEAM	LVL	AGE	PA	R	2B	3B	HR	RBI	BB	SO	SB	CS	AVG_OBP_SLG	TAv	BABIP	BRR	FRAA	WARP
2010	KCA	MLB	24	678	77	45	0	15	78	69	78	0	0	.318/.388/.469	.298	.341	-4.6	1B(127): 0.5	3.0
2011	KCA	MLB	25	673	74	44	0	19	95	66	95	2	1	.291/.361/.461	.287	.316	-4.1	1B(11): -0.9	1.5
2012	KCA	MLB	26	679	72	32	1	29	107	54	111	2	1	.313/.373/.510	.304	.341	-4.8	1B(20): -0.2	2.6
2013	*KCA*	*MLB*	*27*	*637*	*75*	*37*	*2*	*20*	*84*	*55*	*90*	*1*	*1*	*.297/.360/.471*	*.291*	*.322*	*-1.1*	*1B 0*	*3.2*

They call him Country Breakfast. The Royals had long desired their designated hitter to hit for more power and Butler finally obliged. He traded his prodigious doubles numbers for the long ball, offsetting a career low in two-baggers with a career high in home runs. His 23 percent line-drive rate was the highest of his career, but his 19.9 percent HR/FB rate suggests he won't replicate the power surge in 2013. Still, there's plenty of value here. Butler is among the more selective hitters in the game, offering at just under 60 percent of all pitches in the strike zone last year. Hitting in the heart of the order, he brought home 19 percent of all baserunners, the sixth-best rate among qualified batters. The man is asked to do one thing: hit. He does it extremely well.

Lorenzo Cain CF

Born: **4/13/1986** Age: **27**
Bats: **R** Throws: **R** Height: **6' 3"**
Weight: **200** Breakout: **4%**
Improve: **51%** Collapse: **8%**
Attrition: **14%** MLB: **94%**

Comparables:
Will Venable,Bobby Tolan,Ellis Burks

YEAR	TEAM	LVL	AGE	PA	R	2B	3B	HR	RBI	BB	SO	SB	CS	AVG_OBP_SLG	TAv	BABIP	BRR	FRAA	WARP
2010	HUN	AA	24	280	45	6	6	3	18	34	52	21	2	.324/.407/.434	.303	.400	3.6	CF(59): 1.8	2.5
2010	NAS	AAA	24	100	13	5	3	0	9	11	17	5	1	.299/.380/.425	.255	.366	1.3	CF(22): 2.4	0.6
2010	MIL	MLB	24	158	17	11	1	1	13	9	28	7	1	.306/.348/.415	.280	.370	1.9	CF(38): 1.7, RF(1): 0.0	1.2
2011	OMA	AAA	25	549	84	28	7	16	81	40	102	16	6	.312/.380/.497	.300	.366	1.6	CF(39): -0.2, RF(10): -1.2	1.3
2011	KCA	MLB	25	23	4	1	0	0	1	1	4	0	0	.273/.304/.318	.217	.333	0.3	RF(4): -0.3, CF(2): -0.2	-0.1
2012	KCA	MLB	26	244	27	9	2	7	31	15	56	10	0	.266/.316/.419	.267	.319	0.7	CF(50): 2.1, RF(9): 0.6	1.1
2013	*KCA*	*MLB*	*27*	*250*	*32*	*11*	*3*	*5*	*23*	*17*	*51*	*10*	*2*	*.267/.321/.398*	*.258*	*.322*	*1.4*	*CF -1, RF -0*	*0.8*

Part of the Zack Greinke bounty, Cain was supposed to anchor center field in 2012. As they say, the best laid plans . . . Cain went down with a groin strain in the season's opening week, then injured a hip flexor while on a minor-league rehab assignment. He returned in July but was sidelined again in September with a hamstring injury. Incurring three lower-body injuries in a single season isn't the best way for a speedy outfielder to spend his summer. Fair or not, he now wears the injury-prone tag. When healthy, Cain flashes positive speed, but his swing gets long at times. His bat projects to the lower third of the batting order.

Orlando Calixte SS

Born: **2/3/1992** Age: **21**
Bats: **R** Throws: **R** Height: **6' 0"**
Weight: **160** Breakout: **3%**
Improve: **57%** Collapse: **9%**
Attrition: **17%** MLB: **97%**

Comparables:
Jack Heidemann,Robin Yount,Jim Fregosi

YEAR	TEAM	LVL	AGE	PA	R	2B	3B	HR	RBI	BB	SO	SB	CS	AVG_OBP_SLG	TAv	BABIP	BRR	FRAA	WARP
2011	KNC	A	19	317	19	5	1	3	31	20	70	11	4	.208/.256/.263	.188	.259	0	--	0.0
2012	KNC	A	20	254	31	13	4	10	34	21	44	2	5	.241/.303/.465	.288	.256	-2.6	SS(8): 0.2	-0.1
2012	WIL	A+	20	278	38	17	4	4	28	15	65	8	3	.281/.326/.426	.246	.360	1.5	SS(52): 8.6	1.4
2013	*KCA*	*MLB*	*21*	*250*	*24*	*10*	*2*	*6*	*26*	*11*	*63*	*2*	*1*	*.228/.263/.370*	*.221*	*.279*	*-0.1*	*SS 3*	*0.4*

Signed for $1 million as an 18-year-old in the Dominican Republic, Calixte has been equal parts exciting and frustrating. He started to make noise and move up in prospect rankings with a breakout performance in Kane County. He led the Cougars in home runs the first half of the season before earning a promotion to High-A Wilmington. His swing packs a wallop, but gets long at times. His approach is swing first and ask questions later. The Royals are working on his pitch recognition so he can harness that power for good and not evil. A strong arm, he remains raw defensively, but his footwork and positioning have improved.

Christian Colon MI

Born: **5/14/1989** Age: **24**
Bats: **R** Throws: **R** Height: **6' 2"**
Weight: **180** Breakout: **2%**
Improve: **33%** Collapse: **4%**
Attrition: **8%** MLB: **93%**

Comparables:
Bobby Valentine,Roger Metzger,Bob Heise

YEAR	TEAM	LVL	AGE	PA	R	2B	3B	HR	RBI	BB	SO	SB	CS	AVG_OBP_SLG	TAv	BABIP	BRR	FRAA	WARP
2010	WIL	A+	21	271	38	12	2	3	30	13	33	2	4	.278/.325/.380	.239	.305	-0.6	SS(60): 4.8	0.9
2011	NWA	AA	22	568	69	14	2	8	61	46	51	17	7	.257/.325/.342	.222	.271	-1.5	SS(64): 4.4, 2B(10): 0.5	0.1
2012	NWA	AA	23	315	33	9	2	5	27	31	27	12	6	.289/.364/.392	.268	.305	-2.6	SS(45): -0.6, 2B(17): 0.0	0.6
2013	*KCA*	*MLB*	*24*	*250*	*27*	*10*	*1*	*3*	*19*	*15*	*31*	*5*	*2*	*.250/.300/.339*	*.227*	*.273*	*0*	*SS 1, 2B -0*	*0.3*

Selected fourth overall in the 2010 draft, Colon was promoted to Triple-A in early August, but fouled a ball off his face, injuring his right eye. The injury sidelined him for the rest of the season, but when he recovered he played winter ball in Puerto Rico. He has good pitch recognition, strong instincts, and an above-average contact rate. The Royals have kept him mostly at shortstop, but lack of range will probably force him to the other side of the bag. It's worth trying as he's blocked by Alcides Escobar and the Royals are looking for a solid, regular second baseman.

Jarrod Dyson OF

Born: **8/15/1984** Age: **28**
Bats: **L** Throws: **R** Height: **5' 10"**
Weight: **160** Breakout: **2%**
Improve: **52%** Collapse: **5%**
Attrition: **14%** MLB: **90%**

Comparables:
Scott Podsednik,Dave Collins,Michael Bourn

YEAR	TEAM	LVL	AGE	PA	R	2B	3B	HR	RBI	BB	SO	SB	CS	AVG_OBP_SLG	TAv	BABIP	BRR	FRAA	WARP
2010	WIL	A+	25	52	7	6	2	0	9	1	9	5	1	.327/.340/.531	.297	.400	0.8	CF(12): 1.7	0.7
2010	OMA	AAA	25	219	33	10	1	1	19	16	32	13	3	.272/.323/.349	.252	.311	0.1	CF(46): 7.1	1.3
2010	KCA	MLB	25	65	11	4	2	1	5	6	16	9	1	.211/.286/.404	.251	.275	0	CF(15): 1.5	0.3
2011	OMA	AAA	26	369	69	10	3	3	26	35	47	38	2	.279/.356/.357	.277	.320	3.6	CF(13): -1.4, LF(9): 2.0	1.1
2011	KCA	MLB	26	53	8	1	0	0	3	7	14	11	1	.205/.308/.227	.193	.290	2.4	CF(17): 0.4	0.1
2012	OMA	AAA	27	71	12	3	3	0	5	4	5	7	1	.333/.373/.476	.367	.362	2.7	CF(10): 0.6	1.2
2012	KCA	MLB	27	330	52	8	5	0	9	30	56	30	5	.260/.328/.322	.242	.318	6.2	CF(88): 9.0	1.8
2013	*KCA*	*MLB*	*28*	*281*	*38*	*11*	*3*	*2*	*17*	*23*	*51*	*29*	*5*	*.251/.316/.343*	*.236*	*.301*	*4.3*	*CF 2, LF 0*	*0.9*

A 50th-round selection in 2006, Dyson figured to get passed on the outfield depth chart by Cain. Opportunity knocked when Cain couldn't stay healthy. With limited power, Dyson could gain value if he draws more walks, because once he reaches base, he's insanely dangerous. He has attempted to swipe a base in 31 percent of his opportunities. More impressive, he's touched home exactly half the times he's been on base in his career. Defensively, Dyson struggles reading the ball off the bat, getting late jumps and taking some interesting routes to the ball. At least he has the speed to recover.

Alcides Escobar SS

Born: **12/16/1986** Age: **26**
Bats: **R** Throws: **R** Height: **6' 2"**
Weight: **185** Breakout: **7%**
Improve: **44%** Collapse: **9%**
Attrition: **26%** MLB: **95%**

Comparables:
Brendan Ryan,Bill Russell,Erick Aybar

YEAR	TEAM	LVL	AGE	PA	R	2B	3B	HR	RBI	BB	SO	SB	CS	AVG_OBP_SLG	TAv	BABIP	BRR	FRAA	WARP
2010	MIL	MLB	23	552	57	14	10	4	41	36	70	10	4	.235/.288/.326	.218	.264	1	SS(138): -0.0, RF(2): -0.0	-0.2
2011	KCA	MLB	24	598	69	21	8	4	46	25	73	26	9	.254/.290/.343	.239	.285	0.7	SS(158): 0.9	0.5
2012	KCA	MLB	25	648	68	30	7	5	52	27	100	35	5	.293/.331/.390	.253	.344	1.6	SS(155): -12.3	0.8
2013	*KCA*	*MLB*	*26*	*599*	*64*	*24*	*7*	*6*	*50*	*26*	*84*	*26*	*6*	*.272/.309/.371*	*.241*	*.305*	*3.2*	*SS -1, RF -0*	*1.8*

Known for his glove, Escobar surprised with his bat in 2012, finishing in the middle of the shortstop pack when ranked by TAv. A savvy baserunner, he's always a threat to steal and knows when to take the extra base. He attempted more sacrifice bunts than any other Royal. Defensively, Escobar is among the best at moving to his right, but last season his range was so diminished scouts were whispering he somehow lost a step. The arm remains strong as ever, but he can get lazy with his footwork, which can lead to errant throws.

Irving Falu INF

Born: **6/6/1983** Age: **30**
Bats: **B** Throws: **R** Height: **6' 0"**
Weight: **180** Breakout: **2%**
Improve: **27%** Collapse: **13%**
Attrition: **18%** MLB: **79%**

Comparables:
Chris Stynes,Craig Wilson,Lou Klimchock

YEAR	TEAM	LVL	AGE	PA	R	2B	3B	HR	RBI	BB	SO	SB	CS	AVG_OBP_SLG	TAv	BABIP	BRR	FRAA	WARP
2010	OMA	AAA	27	552	75	14	6	1	46	42	39	15	4	.272/.325/.330	.237	.291	5.7	SS(81): 11.4, 2B(36): -3.0	2.0
2011	OMA	AAA	28	437	50	10	9	2	47	35	47	21	11	.301/.358/.390	.279	.335	0.3	RF(16): 0.4, SS(12): -1.9	0.5
2012	OMA	AAA	29	406	69	22	3	7	50	28	41	21	6	.329/.375/.463	.294	.354	3.7	3B(24): -0.7, SS(22): -5.1	1.6
2012	KCA	MLB	29	91	14	6	1	0	7	4	9	0	2	.341/.371/.435	.276	.382	0.1	2B(14): -0.1, SS(5): -0.1	0.5
2013	*KCA*	*MLB*	*30*	*250*	*28*	*10*	*3*	*2*	*18*	*14*	*31*	*9*	*4*	*.270/.310/.360*	*.239*	*.301*	*0.6*	*SS -0, 2B -0*	*0.3*

The Good Soldier. Falu opened 2012 in Triple-A, the fourth consecutive season he started the year in Omaha. He finally got the call in May and made the most of his limited opportunity. Falu can fill in at second, short, or third. He has never walked much at any stop in his long minor-league career and he has limited power, so PECOTA reflects the effect increased playing time would have on his slash line. He can be useful to the Royals in a cost-controlled, utility-infielder sort of way.

Jeff Francoeur RF

Born: **1/8/1984** Age: **29**
Bats: **R** Throws: **R** Height: **6' 6"**
Weight: **220** Breakout: **3%**
Improve: **51%** Collapse: **6%**
Attrition: **10%** MLB: **90%**

Comparables:
Alex Rios,Jim Northrup,Ruben Sierra

YEAR	TEAM	LVL	AGE	PA	R	2B	3B	HR	RBI	BB	SO	SB	CS	AVG_OBP_SLG	TAv	BABIP	BRR	FRAA	WARP
2010	NYN	MLB	26	447	43	16	2	11	54	29	76	8	2	.237/.293/.369	.248	.259	-2.2	RF(118): -7.2	0.0
2010	TEX	MLB	26	56	9	2	0	2	11	1	5	0	1	.340/.357/.491	.306	.340	0	RF(13): -0.4, LF(2): -0.1	0.3
2011	KCA	MLB	27	656	77	47	4	20	87	37	123	22	10	.285/.329/.476	.281	.323	-2.7	RF(152): 6.8	3.4
2012	KCA	MLB	28	603	58	26	3	16	49	34	119	4	7	.235/.287/.378	.231	.272	-2	RF(145): -18.0, CF(3): -0.4	-3.0
2013	*KCA*	*MLB*	*29*	*577*	*61*	*30*	*3*	*15*	*66*	*29*	*102*	*9*	*6*	*.257/.302/.406*	*.249*	*.291*	*-0.6*	*RF 0, CF -0*	*0.6*

When we left Francoeur and his biggest fan, Dayton Moore, they were celebrating Francoeur's best season in the bigs with a two-year deal. But a movie's ending is only happy if you know where to stop the screenplay. In the sequel, Frenchy betrayed Moore's undying faith with a complete failure of a season, putting himself on the list of worst every-day players in 2012. Always a free swinger, Francoeur continued a three-year trend of offering at more than 40 percent of pitches outside the strike zone. Defensively, his range was abysmal and he often took questionable outfield routes. The lone bright spot was his arm, which saved some runs. Most troubling of all, the Royals insisted on playing him every day, blocking uber-prospect Wil Myers. Looks like they're set to repeat the crime in 2013. Shame.

Chris Getz **2B**
Born: **8/30/1983** Age: **29**
Bats: **L** Throws: **R** Height: **6' 1"**
Weight: **185** Breakout: **1%**
Improve: **35%** Collapse: **3%**
Attrition: **5%** MLB: **94%**

Comparables:
Cookie Rojas,Steve Sax,Dave Cash

YEAR	TEAM	LVL	AGE	PA	R	2B	3B	HR	RBI	BB	SO	SB	CS	AVG_OBP_SLG	TAv	BABIP	BRR	FRAA	WARP
2010	KCA	MLB	26	248	23	9	0	0	18	19	28	15	2	.237/.302/.277	.215	.270	1.8	2B(64): -6.8, 3B(2): -0.2	-1.0
2011	KCA	MLB	27	429	50	6	3	0	26	30	45	21	7	.255/.313/.287	.230	.288	1.1	2B(110): 4.0, SS(4): 0.2	-0.1
2012	KCA	MLB	28	210	22	10	3	0	17	11	17	9	3	.275/.312/.360	.240	.299	3.2	2B(61): -3.7	0.0
2013	*KCA*	*MLB*	*29*	*250*	*27*	*10*	*2*	*2*	*19*	*18*	*29*	*11*	*3*	*.263/.320/.344*	*.240*	*.290*	*1.1*	*2B -2, SS -0*	*0.3*

Each spring, the Royals come up with a bizarre plan for a player. In 2011, the idea was for Butler to steal at least 10 bases. Last year, it was Getz hitting for more power. Really. The same Getz who had a grand total of 42 extra-base hits in 1,099 plate appearances. Funny thing, Getz did punch a few more doubles and finished with a career high in slugging, but we're tilting at windmills here. His high grit factor couldn't keep him off the DL and injuries limited him to his fewest plate appearances in a season as a Royal. His manager surely missed him as a player who does all the little things. Not surprisingly, he finished second on the club with nine sac-bunt attempts and led the team in percentage of productive outs. The Royals tout his "exceptional" defense. Don't buy it. His range is limited to the point he's slightly below average.

Johnny Giavotella **2B**
Born: **7/10/1987** Age: **25**
Bats: **R** Throws: **R** Height: **5' 9"**
Weight: **185** Breakout: **2%**
Improve: **40%** Collapse: **13%**
Attrition: **17%** MLB: **95%**

Comparables:
Jemile Weeks,Rich McKinney,Roberto Alomar

YEAR	TEAM	LVL	AGE	PA	R	2B	3B	HR	RBI	BB	SO	SB	CS	AVG_OBP_SLG	TAv	BABIP	BRR	FRAA	WARP
2010	NWA	AA	22	597	92	35	5	9	65	61	67	13	7	.322/.392/.460	.290	.351	-1.7	2B(139): -0.4	3.7
2011	OMA	AAA	23	503	67	34	2	9	72	40	57	9	5	.338/.390/.481	.299	.367	0.6	2B(33): 2.1, LF(2): -0.4	1.2
2011	KCA	MLB	23	187	20	9	4	2	21	6	32	5	2	.247/.273/.376	.231	.288	-0.6	2B(46): -0.0	-0.2
2012	OMA	AAA	24	418	67	20	2	10	71	46	40	7	1	.323/.404/.472	.313	.339	0.3	2B(50): -3.4, 3B(4): 0.3	1.9
2012	KCA	MLB	24	189	21	7	1	1	15	8	35	3	0	.238/.270/.304	.213	.290	0.3	2B(45): -4.8	-1.1
2013	*KCA*	*MLB*	*25*	*258*	*29*	*12*	*2*	*3*	*22*	*17*	*40*	*4*	*1*	*.271/.323/.383*	*.253*	*.310*	*0.1*	*2B -1, 3B -0*	*0.6*

Coming off a presidential election, it makes sense to poll Royals fans "Getz or Giavotella?" at second base. Giavotella has had a pair of limited auditions in the majors but has yet to translate his Triple-A success to Kansas City. Fastballs eat him up, and because he's intent on looking for the heater, he becomes vulnerable to off-speed stuff, particularly on pitches breaking outside the strike zone. It's frustrating because for the second consecutive season he has shown strong plate discipline in the minors, yet when called to the big club, his patience disappears. He doesn't further his cause by playing second base with the grace and urgency of a three-toed sloth. Giavotella is running out of time to prove he can be a productive major leaguer.

Alex Gordon **LF**
Born: **2/10/1984** Age: **29**
Bats: **L** Throws: **R** Height: **6' 3"**
Weight: **220** Breakout: **3%**
Improve: **38%** Collapse: **0%**
Attrition: **3%** MLB: **86%**

Comparables:
Luke Scott,Tom Tresh,Gary Roenicke

YEAR	TEAM	LVL	AGE	PA	R	2B	3B	HR	RBI	BB	SO	SB	CS	AVG_OBP_SLG	TAv	BABIP	BRR	FRAA	WARP
2010	OMA	AAA	26	321	59	20	3	14	44	51	72	7	2	.315/.439/.577	.335	.386	0.4	LF(56): 3.0, RF(7): -0.7	3.7
2010	KCA	MLB	26	281	34	10	0	8	20	34	62	1	5	.215/.315/.355	.250	.254	-3.3	LF(55): 3.0, 3B(10): -1.0	0.5
2011	KCA	MLB	27	688	101	45	4	23	87	67	139	17	8	.303/.376/.502	.312	.358	3	LF(148): 9.8, 1B(7): 0.1	6.5
2012	KCA	MLB	28	721	93	51	5	14	72	73	140	10	5	.294/.368/.455	.288	.356	0	LF(160): 9.2	4.3
2013	*KCA*	*MLB*	*29*	*671*	*81*	*38*	*3*	*19*	*82*	*73*	*143*	*11*	*5*	*.269/.354/.442*	*.281*	*.324*	*-0.6*	*LF 7, 3B -0*	*3.7*

Proving 2011 wasn't a fluke, Gordon posted his second consecutive season of 4-plus WARP. He lost a bit of his home-run swagger, but traded the bombs for gap power, clubbing a career high in doubles. Perhaps some of that power transfer came via his approach at the dish. As leadoff hitter for 81 games, he stated on record that he was more selective in order to get on base. His BABIP remained high, but he came by that number honestly, as he was lacing line drives a quarter of the time he put the ball in play. Drafted as a third baseman, Gordon continues to play exceptional defense in left, flashing plus range, leading the league in outfield assists, and finishing atop the positional leaderboard in FRAA. Gordon is quietly becoming one of the most complete players in the game.

Brett Hayes **C**
Born: **2/13/1984** Age: **29**
Bats: **R** Throws: **R** Height: **6' 2"**
Weight: **205** Breakout: **2%**
Improve: **29%** Collapse: **10%**
Attrition: **10%** MLB: **97%**

Comparables:
Chris Widger,Andy Etchebarren,Jesse Gonder

YEAR	TEAM	LVL	AGE	PA	R	2B	3B	HR	RBI	BB	SO	SB	CS	AVG_OBP_SLG	TAv	BABIP	BRR	FRAA	WARP
2010	NWO	AAA	26	63	7	3	0	1	5	2	9	0	0	.220/.258/.322	.208	.245	0.8	C(16): 0.4	0.0
2010	FLO	MLB	26	83	6	6	1	2	6	6	26	0	0	.208/.265/.390	.220	.286	-0.8	C(24): 0.3	0.0
2011	FLO	MLB	27	144	19	9	0	5	16	11	39	0	0	.231/.291/.415	.259	.291	-0.5	C(49): 0.8, RF(1): -0.0	0.6
2012	NWO	AAA	28	63	9	4	0	3	8	3	13	0	0	.356/.397/.576	.319	.419	0	C(4): 0.1	0.0
2012	MIA	MLB	28	118	7	6	0	0	3	4	49	1	0	.202/.229/.254	.168	.354	-0.1	C(33): 1.4	-0.6
2013	*KCA*	*MLB*	*29*	*250*	*23*	*12*	*1*	*5*	*25*	*14*	*67*	*1*	*0*	*.228/.273/.358*	*.222*	*.292*	*-0.3*	*C 1, 1B -0*	*0.2*

A glove-first backup catcher, Hayes lost his job in Miami when the Marlins nabbed Rob Brantly. His biggest accomplishment of 2012 turned out to be spotting a gunman walking on the Florida Turnpike. Hayes is a decent blocker and an average thrower, having gunned down 26 percent of would-be base stealers. Those skills led the Royals to claim him on waivers in November.

Eric Hosmer 1B
Born: **10/24/1989** Age: **23**
Bats: **L** Throws: **L** Height: **6' 5"**
Weight: **230** Breakout: **4%**
Improve: **58%** Collapse: **5%**
Attrition: **10%** MLB: **92%**
Comparables:
James Loney, Al Oliver, Billy Butler

YEAR	TEAM	LVL	AGE	PA	R	2B	3B	HR	RBI	BB	SO	SB	CS	AVG_OBP_SLG	TAv	BABIP	BRR	FRAA	WARP
2010	WIL	A+	20	375	48	29	6	7	51	44	39	11	1	.354/.434/.545	.340	.387	-3.7	1B(79): -3.2	2.7
2010	NWA	AA	20	211	39	14	3	13	35	15	27	3	1	.313/.365/.615	.312	.310	1.1	1B(52): 2.9	2.2
2011	OMA	AAA	21	118	21	5	0	3	15	19	16	3	0	.439/.525/.582	.474	.500	-0.1	1B(9): 0.2	1.2
2011	KCA	MLB	21	563	66	27	3	19	78	34	82	11	5	.293/.334/.465	.281	.314	1	1B(127): -7.0	0.8
2012	KCA	MLB	22	598	65	22	2	14	60	56	95	16	1	.232/.304/.359	.242	.255	1.3	1B(148): 5.2, RF(3): -0.2	-0.2
2013	*KCA*	*MLB*	*23*	*561*	*66*	*27*	*3*	*17*	*71*	*42*	*86*	*10*	*2*	*.276/.331/.444*	*.272*	*.300*	*0.8*	*1B -3, RF -0*	*1.0*

We haven't seen a sophomore slump this bad since the Stone Roses. Hosmer took a step back in nearly every facet of his game. Hitting coach Kevin Seitzer preached taking the ball to the opposite field, yet Hosmer became intent on pulling the ball. When Hosmer got out in front of pitches, he would roll his wrists and hit weak grounders right into the teeth of an unfriendly defensive shift. His groundball rate went up almost 5 percentage points and his BABIP and power suffered. What should be troubling to the Royals was that he never recovered his form at the plate, even briefly. Hosmer's struggles (among others) ultimately cost Seitzer his job. The Royals are now among the teams using dual hitting coaches. We will see if one of the two new guys can set the beleaguered first baseman on track.

David Lough OF
Born: **1/20/1986** Age: **27**
Bats: **L** Throws: **L** Height: **6' 0"**
Weight: **180** Breakout: **3%**
Improve: **47%** Collapse: **5%**
Attrition: **20%** MLB: **92%**
Comparables:
Mike Kingery, Mel Clark, Alex Ochoa

YEAR	TEAM	LVL	AGE	PA	R	2B	3B	HR	RBI	BB	SO	SB	CS	AVG_OBP_SLG	TAv	BABIP	BRR	FRAA	WARP
2010	OMA	AAA	24	531	65	15	12	11	58	40	72	14	5	.280/.336/.437	.271	.298	0.9	LF(56): 2.6, CF(53): -0.7	2.4
2011	OMA	AAA	25	516	87	26	11	9	65	36	49	14	8	.318/.367/.482	.267	.335	-0.8	LF(27): 0.6, RF(5): -0.3	0.3
2012	OMA	AAA	26	544	69	19	11	10	69	25	65	26	4	.275/.317/.420	.279	.296	5.2	RF(56): 13.5, CF(21): 1.1	2.8
2012	KCA	MLB	26	65	9	2	1	0	2	4	9	1	0	.237/.292/.305	.213	.275	0	CF(12): -0.1, RF(5): -0.6	-0.2
2013	*KCA*	*MLB*	*27*	*250*	*25*	*10*	*4*	*4*	*23*	*12*	*40*	*8*	*2*	*.245/.288/.366*	*.231*	*.274*	*1.1*	*RF 1, CF -0*	*0.0*

Lough's slash numbers took a step back as his walk rate tumbled and fewer line drives found the gaps in Triple-A outfields. His plus talent is speed, which is useful in center but wasted in his inability or unwillingness to accept a free pass. He continues to profile as a fourth outfielder, but has slipped in the organizational depth chart. He could be the next Mitch Maier, but more than likely he's the next Kit Pellow.

Adalberto Mondesi SS
Born: **7/27/1995** Age: **17**
Bats: **S** Throws: **R** Height: **6' 1"**
Weight: **165** Breakout: **0%**
Improve: **65%** Collapse: **35%**
Attrition: **35%** MLB: **100%**
Comparables:
Ed Kranepool, Wayne Causey, Robin Yount

YEAR	TEAM	LVL	AGE	PA	R	2B	3B	HR	RBI	BB	SO	SB	CS	AVG_OBP_SLG	TAv	BABIP	BRR	FRAA	WARP
2012	IDA	Rk	16	232	35	7	2	3	30	19	65	11	2	.290/.346/.386	.328	.399	1	SS(9): 0.5	0.5
2013	*KCA*	*MLB*	*17*	*250*	*28*	*8*	*1*	*3*	*15*	*11*	*67*	*14*	*4*	*.193/.230/.274*	*.182*	*.251*	*1.7*	*SS 1*	*-0.7*

Raul's son was the youngest player in the Pioneer League last summer, and more than held his own thanks to a premium set of tools and a tremendous feel for the game. With legit shortstop skills and precocious bat-to-ball ability, Mondesi has star potential if everything comes together. The Royals are suddenly flush with shortstop prospects in the low minors, and Mondesi may have the highest upside of the bunch.

Adam Moore C
Born: **5/8/1984** Age: **29**
Bats: **R** Throws: **R** Height: **6' 4"**
Weight: **220** Breakout: **1%**
Improve: **27%** Collapse: **9%**
Attrition: **16%** MLB: **93%**
Comparables:
Mike Rabelo, Tony Eusebio, Terry Steinbach

YEAR	TEAM	LVL	AGE	PA	R	2B	3B	HR	RBI	BB	SO	SB	CS	AVG_OBP_SLG	TAv	BABIP	BRR	FRAA	WARP
2010	TAC	AAA	26	142	18	8	1	3	15	7	24	1	0	.321/.359/.463	.296	.374	0	C(31): -0.1	1.0
2010	SEA	MLB	26	218	12	6	0	4	15	8	63	0	1	.195/.230/.283	.189	.257	-0.9	C(59): -0.7	-1.0
2011	SEA	MLB	27	6	0	1	0	0	0	0	2	0	0	.167/.167/.333	.152	.250	0	C(2): -0.0	-0.1
2012	OMA	AAA	28	135	18	8	0	3	22	14	24	2	0	.296/.381/.443	.260	.344	-1.1	C(20): -0.3	0.1
2012	TAC	AAA	28	94	10	5	0	3	11	5	14	0	0	.209/.247/.372	.199	.211	0.5	C(20): -0.4	-0.1
2012	KCA	MLB	28	12	1	1	0	1	2	1	3	0	0	.182/.250/.545	.275	.143	0	C(3): -0.0	0.0
2013	*KCA*	*MLB*	*29*	*250*	*24*	*11*	*1*	*6*	*26*	*14*	*55*	*0*	*0*	*.242/.289/.368*	*.234*	*.291*	*-0.4*	*C -1*	*0.4*

A surprise waiver claim from the Seattle organization, Moore was the fourth catcher on the Royals 40-man roster. Once upon a time he held promise as a power-hitting backstop, but now he feels like organizational filler. The Royals are a reactionary team. They lost their top two catchers last year in spring training and had to go outside the organization for the disaster known as Humberto Quintero. So they've decided to stock their roster with surplus catching. Don't confuse surplus with quality.

Mike Moustakas **3B**
Born: **9/11/1988** Age: **24**
Bats: **L** Throws: **R** Height: **6' 0"**
Weight: **230** Breakout: **7%**
Improve: **68%** Collapse: **4%**
Attrition: **9%** MLB: **96%**
Comparables:
Richie Hebner,Eric Chavez,Neil Walker

YEAR	TEAM	LVL	AGE	PA	R	2B	3B	HR	RBI	BB	SO	SB	CS	AVG_OBP_SLG	TAv	BABIP	BRR	FRAA	WARP
2010	NWA	AA	21	298	58	25	0	21	76	26	42	0	1	.347/.421/.687	.348	.352	-0.3	3B(61): 5.7	4.5
2010	OMA	AAA	21	236	36	16	0	15	48	8	25	2	0	.293/.318/.564	.295	.276	-0.3	3B(52): 1.2	2.0
2011	OMA	AAA	22	250	38	15	1	10	44	19	44	1	1	.287/.347/.498	.270	.314	0	3B(23): 1.7	0.6
2011	KCA	MLB	22	365	26	18	1	5	30	22	51	2	0	.263/.309/.367	.251	.296	-1	3B(89): 1.3	0.6
2012	KCA	MLB	23	614	69	34	1	20	73	39	124	5	2	.242/.296/.412	.254	.274	-2.6	3B(149): 16.8	2.7
2013	*KCA*	*MLB*	*24*	*541*	*59*	*30*	*2*	*18*	*70*	*31*	*95*	*3*	*1*	*.261/.308/.438*	*.261*	*.288*	*-0.6*	*3B 3*	*1.6*

Together with Hosmer, Moustakas was supposed to form the Royals' Dynamic Duo. Instead they got Sleepy Sophs. On the positive side, Moustakas flashed a home-run stroke that has many scouts believing he'll hit for more power than Hosmer. He looks for pitches away and with an uppercut swing generates loft and power. However, his "grip it and rip it" approach is sometimes too aggressive, chasing after high heat and elevating his strikeout rate to uncomfortably high levels. His offensive production took a nosedive in the second half thanks to assorted bumps and bruises. His glove work was outstanding despite plate woes. He proved especially adept at covering the line, robbing a number of extra-base hits, and emerged as one of the top defensive third basemen in the league.

Xavier Nady **OF**
Born: **11/14/1978** Age: **34**
Bats: **R** Throws: **R** Height: **6' 3"**
Weight: **215** Breakout: **1%**
Improve: **16%** Collapse: **16%**
Attrition: **23%** MLB: **88%**
Comparables:
Leon Wagner,Todd Hollandsworth,Raul Mondesi

YEAR	TEAM	LVL	AGE	PA	R	2B	3B	HR	RBI	BB	SO	SB	CS	AVG_OBP_SLG	TAv	BABIP	BRR	FRAA	WARP
2010	CHN	MLB	31	347	33	13	0	6	33	17	85	0	0	.256/.306/.353	.229	.326	1.9	1B(52): -0.2, RF(23): -2.3	-0.8
2011	ARI	MLB	32	223	26	11	0	4	35	10	46	2	0	.248/.287/.359	.239	.294	-0.3	1B(52): -1.6, LF(10): -0.1	-0.6
2012	FRE	AAA	33	99	13	5	0	6	18	7	20	0	0	.270/.343/.528	.248	.286	-0.4	LF(7): -1.0, 1B(5): -0.0	-0.4
2012	SFN	MLB	33	57	6	3	1	1	7	6	13	0	0	.240/.333/.400	.245	.306	0.4	LF(16): -0.2	0.0
2012	WAS	MLB	33	109	6	3	0	3	6	7	24	1	0	.157/.211/.275	.164	.173	0.2	LF(24): -1.4, RF(15): -0.1	-1.2
2013	*KCA*	*MLB*	*34*	*250*	*25*	*12*	*1*	*7*	*29*	*14*	*53*	*1*	*0*	*.252/.302/.395*	*.245*	*.299*	*-0.3*	*1B -1, LF 0*	*0.0*

Nady's professional baseball career began in 2000, and when he signed a minor-league contract with the Royals in December, he'd become a member of his ninth organization. It's safe to call Nady a journeyman, and his career is hanging on by a thread. He's not noted for his glove and is best served playing first base, though he can fake it in the outfield. Unfortunately for him, his defensive limitations put a great deal of pressure on his bat. That's bad news for a guy whose TAv hasn't been north of .250 since 2008.

Salvador Perez **C**
Born: **5/10/1990** Age: **23**
Bats: **R** Throws: **R** Height: **6' 4"**
Weight: **230** Breakout: **5%**
Improve: **48%** Collapse: **6%**
Attrition: **8%** MLB: **95%**
Comparables:
Hank Conger,Russ Nixon,Ted Simmons

YEAR	TEAM	LVL	AGE	PA	R	2B	3B	HR	RBI	BB	SO	SB	CS	AVG_OBP_SLG	TAv	BABIP	BRR	FRAA	WARP
2010	WIL	A+	20	396	35	21	1	7	53	18	38	1	1	.290/.328/.411	.268	.308	-3.1	C(84): 0.7	1.8
2011	NWA	AA	21	309	35	14	0	9	43	16	30	0	1	.283/.329/.427	.244	.290	-0.4	C(43): -0.4	0.2
2011	KCA	MLB	21	158	20	8	2	3	21	7	20	0	0	.331/.361/.473	.305	.362	-1.5	C(39): -0.4	1.1
2012	OMA	AAA	22	53	11	2	0	0	7	2	5	0	0	.340/.365/.380	.249	.378	-0.6	C(8): 0.0	0.0
2012	KCA	MLB	22	305	38	16	0	11	39	12	27	0	0	.301/.328/.471	.274	.299	-1.8	C(74): -1.6	1.7
2013	*KCA*	*MLB*	*23*	*285*	*28*	*15*	*1*	*7*	*34*	*11*	*33*	*0*	*0*	*.289/.317/.430*	*.264*	*.305*	*-0.4*	*C -1*	*1.3*

It's rare that a 22-year-old with less than a full season in the majors could be thought of as a team leader, but that's exactly how the Royals view Perez. Pitchers love the game-calling skills of this stalwart defensive catcher, while runners fear his lethal arm. A torn meniscus in spring training sidelined him until the All-Star break, but he still managed to lead the majors in runners picked off. He also threw out 42 percent of all would-be thieves, tops among catchers with at least 1,000 stolen-base opportunities against. For the second consecutive season he has also shown surprising ability with the bat. Another in a long line of free-swinging Royals hitters, he seldom misses his pitch and flashes progressive power. The Royals are fortunate to have one of the best young catchers in the game signed to an extremely club-friendly extension with options through 2019.

Manny Pina **C**
Born: **6/5/1987** Age: **26**
Bats: **R** Throws: **R** Height: **6' 1"**
Weight: **230** Breakout: **4%**
Improve: **42%** Collapse: **5%**
Attrition: **21%** MLB: **93%**
Comparables:
Joe Ginsberg,Ron Hodges,Ramon Hernandez

YEAR	TEAM	LVL	AGE	PA	R	2B	3B	HR	RBI	BB	SO	SB	CS	AVG_OBP_SLG	TAv	BABIP	BRR	FRAA	WARP
2010	NWA	AA	23	302	39	16	0	7	44	24	37	0	0	.259/.321/.398	.231	.274	-1.4	C(82): -1.3	0.3
2010	OMA	AAA	23	60	5	2	0	2	5	3	7	0	0	.218/.271/.364	.210	.217	-0.4	C(17): -0.1	-0.2
2011	OMA	AAA	24	259	34	13	0	5	25	34	37	0	0	.238/.364/.371	.277	.266	0.5	C(23): -0.7	0.5
2011	KCA	MLB	24	15	2	2	0	0	0	1	2	0	0	.214/.267/.357	.180	.250	-0.5	C(4): -0.1	-0.1
2012	NWA	AA	25	162	9	3	0	5	20	24	24	0	0	.260/.389/.397	.254	.279	-3.3	C(30): -0.4	0.3
2012	KCA	MLB	25	2	0	0	0	0	0	0	0	0	0	.000/.000/.000	.004	.000	0	C(1): -0.0	0.0
2013	*KCA*	*MLB*	*26*	*250*	*23*	*11*	*1*	*5*	*26*	*20*	*42*	*0*	*0*	*.233/.303/.355*	*.236*	*.262*	*-0.4*	*C -1*	*0.4*

A solid defender in his own right, Pina is destined for backup status behind the more accomplished Perez. Like his counterpart, he suffered a torn meniscus in spring training. After undergoing surgery, he finished the season healthy in Double-A. The last two years, he has made strides in pitch recognition, which has pushed his OBP to above-average levels in the minors, but he's still a work in progress at the plate. If he's to offer value as a backup, he'll need to remain patient once he gets his shot at big-league pitching.

Derrick Robinson OF

Born: **9/28/1987** Age: **25**
Bats: **B** Throws: **L** Height: **6' 0"**
Weight: **170** Breakout: **5%**
Improve: **53%** Collapse: **2%**
Attrition: **14%** MLB: **90%**

Comparables:
Alan Bannister,Vince Coleman,Stan Javier

YEAR	TEAM	LVL	AGE	PA	R	2B	3B	HR	RBI	BB	SO	SB	CS	AVG_OBP_SLG	TAv	BABIP	BRR	FRAA	WARP
2010	NWA	AA	22	570	74	26	8	2	48	45	86	50	17	.286/.345/.380	.252	.336	-0.5	CF(125): 8.8, LF(9): 0.0	1.8
2011	NWA	AA	23	483	56	6	2	1	25	46	87	55	15	.251/.323/.282	.195	.311	4.1	CF(54): 4.1, LF(14): 1.6	-0.7
2012	OMA	AAA	24	488	73	12	3	2	28	50	84	23	9	.268/.344/.325	.253	.325	-1.5	LF(75): 0.2, CF(3): -0.1	0.2
2013	*KCA*	*MLB*	*25*	*250*	*29*	*8*	*2*	*1*	*14*	*16*	*51*	*17*	*5*	*.234/.283/.299*	*.210*	*.290*	*1.7*	*LF 0, CF -0*	*-0.5*

Speed merchant Robinson had his usual successful campaign as a basestealer, but there's little else to his game that projects as major-league quality. The Royals seem to have thousands of players like Robinson: a speedy outfielder with no power and a poor approach at the plate that limits his ability to get on base.

Bubba Starling CF

Born: **8/3/1992** Age: **20**
Bats: **R** Throws: **R** Height: **6' 5"**
Weight: **180** Breakout: **23%**
Improve: **64%** Collapse: **3%**
Attrition: **16%** MLB: **86%**

Comparables:
Mickey Mantle,Ken Griffey,Justin Upton

YEAR	TEAM	LVL	AGE	PA	R	2B	3B	HR	RBI	BB	SO	SB	CS	AVG_OBP_SLG	TAv	BABIP	BRR	FRAA	WARP
2012	BNC	Rk	19	234	35	8	2	10	33	28	70	10	1	.275/.371/.485	.279	.372	1.7	CF(20): 1.0	0.8
2013	*KCA*	*MLB*	*20*	*250*	*22*	*7*	*1*	*7*	*26*	*15*	*84*	*1*	*0*	*.191/.243/.322*	*.201*	*.259*	*-0.1*	*CF -0*	*-0.8*

If you want to freak out a Royals fan, point out that Starling turned 20 last August while playing for Burlington in the Appalachian League, while Bryce Harper turned 20 just four days after his rookie season ended for the Washington Nationals. Breathe. While Harper has long been a baseball prodigy, Starling didn't begin playing baseball year-round until he was under contract with the Royals. The organization moved him slowly, rebuilding his swing in extended spring training before sending him to Burlington at the end of June. He showed plenty of power, but scouts feel he can be exploited with inside fastballs or off-speed pitches away. A rangy center fielder, Starling has the instincts and ability to excel defensively. The Royals will continue to bring him along with care.

PITCHERS

Jason Adam

Born: **8/4/1991** Age: **21**
Bats: **R** Throws: **R** Height: **6' 5"** Weight: **225**
Breakout: **29%** Improve: **65%** Collapse: **13%**
Attrition: **5%** MLB: **89%**

Comparables:
Jordan Lyles,Hayden Penn,Dan Petry

YEAR	TEAM	LVL	AGE	W	L	SV	G	GS	IP	H	HR	BB	SO	BB9	SO9	GB%	BABIP	WHIP	ERA	FIP	FRA	WARP
2011	KNC	A	19	6	9	0	21	21	104^{1}	94	9	25	76	2.2	6.6	—	.266	1.14	4.23	3.92	4.26	0.0
2012	WIL	A+	20	7	12	0	27	27	158	148	18	36	123	2.1	7.0	46%	.284	1.16	3.53	4.24	4.82	0.7
2013	*KCA*	*MLB*	*21*	*2*	*3*	*0*	*7*	*7*	37^{2}	*44*	*6*	*14*	*20*	*3.4*	*4.9*	*44%*	*.305*	*1.55*	*5.67*	*5.32*	*6.17*	*-0.3*

Local product Adam pitched for his high-school team just 20 minutes from Kauffman Stadium. A 2010 fifth-rounder, he combines a three-quarter arm slot with a high leg kick for maximum deception. Plenty of positivity surrounds his makeup as he pitched extremely well in Wilmington, while lackluster offense and poor defense behind him conspired to prevent the results he deserved. Adam features a fastball and curve combo, but his change has developed into his strongest pitch. Look for this sleeper as a prospect to make great strides as he moves up to the Texas League.

Nathan Adcock

Born: **2/25/1988** Age: **25**
Bats: **R** Throws: **R** Height: **6' 6"** Weight: **220**
Breakout: **31%** Improve: **57%** Collapse: **16%**
Attrition: **13%** MLB: **98%**

Comparables:
Mike Hampton,Todd Burns,Ned Garver

YEAR	TEAM	LVL	AGE	W	L	SV	G	GS	IP	H	HR	BB	SO	BB9	SO9	GB%	BABIP	WHIP	ERA	FIP	FRA	WARP
2010	BRD	A+	22	11	7	0	27	26	141^{1}	131	8	38	113	2.4	7.2	—	.288	1.20	3.38	3.53	3.83	0.0
2011	KCA	MLB	23	1	1	1	24	3	60^{1}	63	5	26	36	3.9	5.4	56%	.297	1.48	4.62	4.39	5.69	0.0
2012	OMA	AAA	24	8	6	0	19	18	99^{1}	116	5	30	60	2.7	5.4	56%	.333	1.47	5.53	4.23	5.42	0.4
2012	KCA	MLB	24	0	3	0	12	2	34^{2}	37	4	13	22	3.4	5.7	51%	.306	1.44	2.34	4.49	4.97	0.0
2013	*KCA*	*MLB*	*25*	*2*	*3*	*0*	*16*	*7*	57^{2}	*65*	*7*	*25*	*33*	*3.9*	*5.1*	*50%*	*.306*	*1.56*	*5.38*	*4.93*	*5.85*	*-0.3*

A former Rule 5 pick from the Pittsburgh organization, Adcock is your prototypical pitch-to-contact arm who relies on keeping the ball down in the zone to find success. He doesn't have enough separation in the velocity between his fastball and off-speed pitches to sneak a pitch by a hungry hitter, so he has to rely on location to be effective. Part of the I-29 brigade that blazed a trail between Kansas City and Omaha in 2012, his value lies in his versatility. He can start or come out of the bullpen. Besides, as the Royals can attest, it's always useful to keep an emergency starter around.

Noel Arguelles
Born: **1/12/1990** Age: **23**
Bats: **L** Throws: **L** Height: **6' 4"** Weight: **215**
Breakout: **33%** Improve: **64%** Collapse: **18%**
Attrition: **12%** MLB: **90%**
Comparables:
Dave Williams, Jimmy Gobble, John Lannan

YEAR	TEAM	LVL	AGE	W	L	SV	G	GS	IP	H	HR	BB	SO	BB9	SO9	GB%	BABIP	WHIP	ERA	FIP	FRA	WARP
2011	WIL	A+	21	4	5	0	21	21	104	93	6	24	64	2.1	5.5	36%	.281	1.12	3.20	3.59	5.15	0.0
2012	NWA	AA	22	4	14	0	25	25	119^1	146	12	66	59	5.0	4.4	44%	.324	1.78	6.41	5.31	6.58	-0.4
2013	*KCA*	*MLB*	*23*	*1*	*3*	*0*	*7*	*7*	*34^2*	*44*	*5*	*18*	*13*	*4.7*	*3.4*	*41%*	*.310*	*1.79*	*6.64*	*5.88*	*7.22*	*-0.6*

After signing with the Royals, Arguelles missed all of 2010 due to surgery to repair a torn labrum. The team brought him back to action slowly in 2011. Last year, the shoulder appeared sound and he made a full complement of starts. Sadly, quantity did not equal quality as he struggled through most of his trips to the mound. A lefty who lacks a power fastball and relies on location, his K/BB ratio was turned upside down. In 15 of his 25 Double-A starts he struck out two or fewer batters. His velocity, which dropped to the mid-80s following his surgery, rebounded to the lower 90s. Royals scouts remain optimistic that he'll learn to trust his shoulder and harness his control. They invested a bunch of cash in the Cuban defector. They'll remain patient.

Francisley Bueno
Born: **3/5/1981** Age: **32**
Bats: **L** Throws: **L** Height: **6' 0"** Weight: **200**
Breakout: **31%** Improve: **53%** Collapse: **25%**
Attrition: **11%** MLB: **95%**
Comparables:
Gary Lucas, Brian Gordon, Mike Maddux

YEAR	TEAM	LVL	AGE	W	L	SV	G	GS	IP	H	HR	BB	SO	BB9	SO9	GB%	BABIP	WHIP	ERA	FIP	FRA	WARP
2012	OMA	AAA	31	1	4	6	35	0	55^2	43	5	15	54	2.4	8.7	49%	.260	1.04	2.75	3.86	5.17	0.2
2012	KCA	MLB	31	1	1	0	18	0	17^1	16	0	2	7	1.0	3.6	59%	.271	1.04	1.56	2.76	3.92	0.2
2013	*KCA*	*MLB*	*32*	*1*	*0*	*0*	*26*	*0*	*35*	*37*	*4*	*11*	*23*	*2.9*	*5.9*	*45%*	*.296*	*1.37*	*4.49*	*4.31*	*4.88*	*0.1*

Bueno features five pitches, but his fastball barely tops 90 mph. Showcasing the variety in his repertoire, he busts the slider in toward left-handed hitters and favors his change against righties. Nevertheless, he's another reliever who has difficulty missing bats. The Royals tried to use him in what you would think would be a favorable platoon split, but his lack of deception seemed to negate his potential LOOGY status. He was better against hitters from the right side.

Bruce Chen
Born: **6/19/1977** Age: **36**
Bats: **L** Throws: **L** Height: **6' 3"** Weight: **215**
Breakout: **13%** Improve: **35%** Collapse: **28%**
Attrition: **8%** MLB: **85%**
Comparables:
Ted Lilly, Mike Cuellar, Jeff Fassero

YEAR	TEAM	LVL	AGE	W	L	SV	G	GS	IP	H	HR	BB	SO	BB9	SO9	GB%	BABIP	WHIP	ERA	FIP	FRA	WARP
2010	OMA	AAA	33	0	1	0	3	3	20^2	13	0	5	20	2.2	8.7	45%	.255	0.87	1.30	2.38	3.02	0.6
2010	KCA	MLB	33	12	7	1	33	23	140^1	136	17	57	98	3.7	6.3	35%	.275	1.38	4.17	4.51	4.27	1.6
2011	NWA	AA	34	0	1	0	1	1	2	5	0	0	2	0.0	9.0	22%	.556	2.50	18.00	1.38	4.19	0.0
2011	OMA	AAA	34	0	0	0	2	2	9	11	3	1	8	1.0	8.0	29%	.312	1.33	6.00	7.01	6.17	0.0
2011	KCA	MLB	34	12	8	0	25	25	155	152	18	50	97	2.9	5.6	37%	.278	1.30	3.77	4.42	4.88	1.2
2012	KCA	MLB	35	11	14	0	34	34	191^2	215	33	47	140	2.2	6.6	34%	.304	1.37	5.07	4.68	4.70	1.9
2013	*KCA*	*MLB*	*36*	*9*	*11*	*0*	*28*	*28*	*160*	*168*	*23*	*51*	*114*	*2.9*	*6.4*	*36%*	*.294*	*1.37*	*4.65*	*4.60*	*5.06*	*0.6*

Chen went fishing for a multi-year deal during the last couple of offseasons. A solid 2011, when he outpaced his peripherals, earned him a two-year deal from Moore. It wasn't surprising he stumbled. A fly-ball pitcher for his entire career, his line-drive rate saw an increase for four consecutive years and his home-run rate traversed back into red-flag territory. He pitched around the plate and kept his walk rate down, but hitters had little difficulty making contact. His previous success was thanks to the deception of varying his arm slot, but last year that deception wasn't worth much. The Royals would love to trade him, but there's little market for a 36-year-old lefty who doesn't miss bats and is owed $4.5 million in his one remaining year.

Louis Coleman
Born: **4/4/1986** Age: **27**
Bats: **R** Throws: **R** Height: **6' 5"** Weight: **200**
Breakout: **26%** Improve: **46%** Collapse: **44%**
Attrition: **26%** MLB: **93%**
Comparables:
Vinnie Pestano, Jason Motte, Pat Neshek

YEAR	TEAM	LVL	AGE	W	L	SV	G	GS	IP	H	HR	BB	SO	BB9	SO9	GB%	BABIP	WHIP	ERA	FIP	FRA	WARP
2010	NWA	AA	24	2	1	6	21	1	51^2	31	5	14	55	2.4	9.6	35%	.213	0.87	2.09	3.23	4.04	0.8
2010	OMA	AAA	24	5	2	1	21	0	40^1	31	2	11	48	2.5	10.7	36%	.296	1.04	2.23	3.04	2.88	1.1
2011	OMA	AAA	25	0	1	2	6	0	7	4	0	4	16	5.1	20.6	%	.333	1.14	3.86	0.93	-0.53	0.2
2011	KCA	MLB	25	1	4	1	48	0	59^2	44	9	26	64	3.9	9.7	33%	.246	1.17	2.87	4.34	4.03	0.6
2012	OMA	AAA	26	0	2	3	11	1	19^2	13	1	8	26	3.7	11.9	28%	.267	1.07	3.20	2.90	3.29	0.5
2012	KCA	MLB	26	0	0	0	42	0	51	41	10	26	65	4.6	11.5	22%	.270	1.31	3.71	4.63	5.09	-0.2
2013	*KCA*	*MLB*	*27*	*2*	*1*	*0*	*34*	*0*	*51^2*	*43*	*6*	*20*	*59*	*3.4*	*10.3*	*34%*	*.287*	*1.20*	*3.41*	*3.59*	*3.71*	*0.9*

With a three-quarter delivery, Coleman features a fastball-slider combo that is murder on right-handed hitters. He held them to .210/.329/.395 last summer. Against lefties, he'll toss in an occasional changeup to keep them on their toes, but his arm slot gives them ample opportunity to measure the pitch. His whiff rate is exceptional against right-handed batters when he can keep the pitch on the outer half of the plate, but he doesn't miss near as many bats against lefties. Control was his calling card in the minors, but has been elusive since his promotion to the bigs. He remains an extremely useful cog in a solid bullpen.

Tim Collins

Born: **8/21/1989** Age: **23**
Bats: **L** Throws: **L** Height: **5' 8"** Weight: **170**
Breakout: **27%** Improve: **52%** Collapse: **26%**
Attrition: **18%** MLB: **94%**

Comparables:
Sparky Lyle,Andrew Sisco,Chris Sale

YEAR	TEAM	LVL	AGE	W	L	SV	G	GS	IP	H	HR	BB	SO	BB9	SO9	GB%	BABIP	WHIP	ERA	FIP	FRA	WARP
2010	MIS	AA	20	0	0	2	6	0	8	4	1	3	14	3.4	15.8	33%	.273	0.88	1.12	2.64	2.86	0.2
2010	NHP	AA	20	1	0	9	35	0	43	27	4	16	73	3.3	15.3	38%	.295	1.00	2.51	2.29	2.69	1.3
2010	OMA	AAA	20	2	1	4	15	0	20^{1}	9	0	8	21	3.5	9.3	36%	.180	0.84	1.33	2.70	3.06	0.5
2011	KCA	MLB	21	4	4	0	68	0	67	52	5	48	60	6.4	8.1	42%	.261	1.49	3.63	4.48	4.66	0.3
2012	KCA	MLB	22	5	4	0	72	0	69^{2}	55	8	34	93	4.4	12.0	43%	.297	1.28	3.36	3.42	3.76	1.0
2013	*KCA*	*MLB*	*23*	*3*	*1*	*1*	*57*	*0*	*60*	*49*	*6*	*31*	*72*	*4.7*	*10.8*	*41%*	*.297*	*1.33*	*3.63*	*3.65*	*3.95*	*0.9*

Collins added almost a full mile per hour to his heater and some lateral movement to his curve, yet improved his control and accelerated his strikeout rate to an elite level. Manager Ned Yost leaned heavily on his bullpen and Collins threw the second-most innings among the Royals relief corps. The workload didn't faze him: he added rather than lost velocity the final two months of the season. He was his most effective when pitching on no rest, striking out 24 batters and walking just one in such games. The Royals have tried to leverage a platoon split to their advantage with the lefty, but Collins has always been better against right-handed batters: they hit just .196/.293/.333 against him in 160 plate appearances last year.

Aaron Crow

Born: **11/10/1986** Age: **26**
Bats: **R** Throws: **R** Height: **6' 4"** Weight: **190**
Breakout: **30%** Improve: **61%** Collapse: **10%**
Attrition: **16%** MLB: **95%**

Comparables:
Len Barker,Andrew Bailey,Mike Boddicker

YEAR	TEAM	LVL	AGE	W	L	SV	G	GS	IP	H	HR	BB	SO	BB9	SO9	GB%	BABIP	WHIP	ERA	FIP	FRA	WARP
2010	WIL	A+	23	2	3	0	7	7	44	51	6	6	53	1.2	10.8	54%	.378	1.30	5.93	3.25	4.81	0.2
2010	NWA	AA	23	7	7	0	22	22	119^{1}	130	13	59	90	4.5	6.8	64%	.315	1.58	5.66	4.71	6.43	-0.8
2011	KCA	MLB	24	4	4	0	57	0	62	55	8	31	65	4.5	9.4	53%	.290	1.39	2.76	4.14	4.10	0.7
2012	KCA	MLB	25	3	1	2	73	0	64^{2}	54	4	22	65	3.1	9.0	53%	.298	1.18	3.48	2.91	4.01	0.7
2013	*KCA*	*MLB*	*26*	*3*	*2*	*1*	*29*	*5*	*52^{2}*	*52*	*6*	*21*	*48*	*3.7*	*8.2*	*53%*	*.307*	*1.39*	*4.27*	*4.05*	*4.64*	*0.4*

With a 95-mph fastball and a wicked slider, Crow enjoyed a consistent season coming out of the pen for the Royals. In many ways, he's an ideal reliever, possessing a high strikeout rate, solid control, and a sinking fastball that leads to a groundball rate over 50 percent. Crow was drafted as a starter, but moved to the bullpen when he struggled in the rotation in the minors. The Royals are always in the market for starting pitching, so it's natural to consider their right-hander. However, given his comfort and success in his current role, it's probably best for everyone if he sticks with short relief.

Wade Davis

Born: **9/7/1985** Age: **27**
Bats: **R** Throws: **R** Height: **6' 6"** Weight: **220**
Breakout: **21%** Improve: **56%** Collapse: **19%**
Attrition: **11%** MLB: **85%**

Comparables:
Micah Owings,Jeff Niemann,Noah Lowry

YEAR	TEAM	LVL	AGE	W	L	SV	G	GS	IP	H	HR	BB	SO	BB9	SO9	GB%	BABIP	WHIP	ERA	FIP	FRA	WARP
2010	TBA	MLB	24	12	10	0	29	29	168	165	24	62	113	3.3	6.1	40%	.272	1.35	4.07	4.76	5.02	0.4
2011	TBA	MLB	25	11	10.	0	29	29	184	190	23	63	105	3.1	5.1	38%	.280	1.38	4.45	4.70	4.46	0.6
2012	TBA	MLB	26	3	0	0	54	0	70^{1}	48	5	29	87	3.7	11.1	40%	.264	1.09	2.43	2.73	2.74	1.6
2013	*KCA*	*MLB*	*27*	*4*	*4*	*0*	*20*	*11*	*75^{2}*	*76*	*9*	*28*	*56*	*3.3*	*6.7*	*42%*	*.293*	*1.38*	*4.38*	*4.38*	*4.76*	*0.5*

Davis's velocity dropped in 2011, which puzzled and annoyed adherents all season long. Whether that decline or the glut of starters prompted the Rays to move him to the bullpen—which Davis accepted stoically (he does everything stoically)—it certainly did the trick. All of Davis's pitches gained a couple miles an hour in 2012, with his four-seamer averaging almost 95 mph, and he added a cutter. Davis threw 70-plus innings with a 2.43 ERA (and 2.74 FIP), forming a late-inning, lefty-righty power duo with Jake McGee. Shipped to Kansas City in the James Shields-Wil Myers blockbuster, Davis will return to starting. The Royals will bank on his velocity, increased strikeout rate, and overall success translating back to the rotation. Under contract with team options through 2017, he is the key player in the trade for the Royals.

Danny Duffy

Born: **12/21/1988** Age: **24**
Bats: **L** Throws: **L** Height: **6' 4"** Weight: **200**
Breakout: **31%** Improve: **72%** Collapse: **13%**
Attrition: **8%** MLB: **88%**

Comparables:
James McDonald,Scott Olsen,Eric Surkamp

YEAR	TEAM	LVL	AGE	W	L	SV	G	GS	IP	H	HR	BB	SO	BB9	SO9	GB%	BABIP	WHIP	ERA	FIP	FRA	WARP
2010	IDA	Rk	21	0	1	0	2	2	6	4	0	0	6	0.0	9.0	56%	.250	0.67	1.50	2.48	4.19	0.2
2010	ROY	Rk	21	0	0	0	2	2	2^{2}	2	0	1	4	3.3	13.3	60%	.400	1.11	3.33	2.40	2.25	0.1
2010	WIL	A+	21	0	0	0	3	3	14	8	2	7	18	4.5	11.6	43%	.214	1.07	2.57	4.41	5.76	0.0
2010	NWA	AA	21	5	2	0	7	7	39^{2}	38	3	9	41	2.0	9.3	47%	.353	1.18	2.95	2.77	3.45	1.5
2011	OMA	AAA	22	3	1	0	8	8	42	37	5	10	48	2.1	10.3	33%	.111	1.12	3.43	3.97	2.03	0.4
2011	KCA	MLB	22	4	8	0	20	20	105^{1}	119	15	51	87	4.4	7.4	40%	.329	1.61	5.64	4.86	4.77	0.6
2012	KCA	MLB	23	2	2	0	6	6	27^{2}	26	2	18	28	5.9	9.1	33%	.329	1.59	3.90	3.91	4.34	0.3
2013	*KCA*	*MLB*	*24*	*2*	*3*	*0*	*7*	*7*	*37^{1}*	*38*	*4*	*16*	*33*	*4.0*	*8.0*	*40%*	*.312*	*1.46*	*4.69*	*4.11*	*5.10*	*0.2*

Many observers thought Duffy was injured when he struggled with command in a short outing the start after throwing 113 pitches at the end of April. Adding fuel to the fire were Moore's comments that the club knew its left-hander would eventually need Tommy John surgery. But Duffy had been throwing with a partial tear in his UCL for several years and the team did follow accepted medical protocol when diagnosing the injury. Whatever the cause, the result is that he is another of the parade of Royals pitchers who landed in the operating room for the procedure. His rehab program has begun and he appears on target to return late in the 2013 season. The best-case scenario would have him contributing in 2014.

Chris Dwyer

Born: **4/10/1988** Age: **25**
Bats: **R** Throws: **L** Height: **6' 3"** Weight: **210**
Breakout: **35%** Improve: **67%** Collapse: **13%**
Attrition: **23%** MLB: **86%**

Comparables:
Adam Ottavino,Kevin Hart,Jimmy Barthmaier

YEAR	TEAM	LVL	AGE	W	L	SV	G	GS	IP	H	HR	BB	SO	BB9	SO9	GB%	BABIP	WHIP	ERA	FIP	FRA	WARP
2010	WIL	A+	22	6	3	0	15	15	84^1	79	3	33	93	3.5	9.9	47%	.328	1.33	2.99	2.91	3.75	1.3
2010	NWA	AA	22	2	1	0	4	4	17^2	11	2	10	20	5.1	10.2	37%	.220	1.19	3.05	4.08	5.10	0.3
2011	NWA	AA	23	8	10	0	27	27	141^1	124	14	78	126	5.0	8.0	41%	.277	1.43	5.60	4.67	4.43	1.4
2012	NWA	AA	24	5	8	0	17	16	85^2	79	13	44	71	4.6	7.5	40%	.269	1.44	5.25	5.28	7.33	-0.2
2012	OMA	AAA	24	3	4	0	9	9	50^1	73	10	24	33	4.3	5.9	45%	.366	1.93	6.97	6.43	7.56	-0.2
2013	*KCA*	*MLB*	*25*	*2*	*3*	*0*	*8*	*8*	*41^1*	*45*	*6*	*21*	*31*	*4.6*	*6.8*	*41%*	*.307*	*1.59*	*5.46*	*5.11*	*5.93*	*-0.2*

Dwyer was officially booted from the prospect train in 2012. He was "promoted" to Triple-A midseason when the Royals demoted foundering prospect Mike Montgomery, because there's a rule you can't have two derailed prospects pitching for the same team. Dwyer certainly didn't deserve the move to Omaha and predictably struggled when facing more accomplished hitters. He has a plus curve, but has trouble throwing it for strikes. That leads to an overreliance on his fastball, which International League hitters feasted on. The clock is ticking.

Jeremy Guthrie

Born: **4/8/1979** Age: **34**
Bats: **R** Throws: **R** Height: **6' 2"** Weight: **205**
Breakout: **8%** Improve: **36%** Collapse: **27%**
Attrition: **12%** MLB: **82%**

Comparables:
John Thomson,Bronson Arroyo,Cory Lidle

YEAR	TEAM	LVL	AGE	W	L	SV	G	GS	IP	H	HR	BB	SO	BB9	SO9	GB%	BABIP	WHIP	ERA	FIP	FRA	WARP
2010	BAL	MLB	31	11	14	0	32	32	209^1	193	25	50	119	2.1	5.1	43%	.254	1.16	3.83	4.41	4.99	1.1
2011	BAL	MLB	32	9	17	0	34	32	208	213	26	66	130	2.9	5.6	41%	.285	1.34	4.33	4.52	5.09	0.9
2012	MOD	A+	33	0	0	0	1	1	4	3	0	1	4	2.2	9.0	64%	.273	1.00	0.00	2.56	2.86	0.2
2012	COL	MLB	33	3	9	0	19	15	90^2	122	21	31	45	3.1	4.5	43%	.318	1.69	6.35	6.41	6.60	-0.7
2012	KCA	MLB	33	5	3	0	14	14	91	84	9	19	56	1.9	5.5	41%	.268	1.13	3.16	3.79	4.53	0.8
2013	*KCA*	*MLB*	*34*	*9*	*10*	*0*	*26*	*26*	*159^2*	*167*	*21*	*45*	*92*	*2.6*	*5.2*	*42%*	*.284*	*1.33*	*4.54*	*4.60*	*4.94*	*0.7*

The Royals turned lemons into lemonade. Jonathan Sanchez left Kansas City while Guthrie left Colorado. Both men had struggled mightily, were designated for assignment, then swapped for each other. Here's where the stories diverge. Sanchez continued to struggle before shutting down for the season with a sore arm. Guthrie rejuvenated his career with the Royals. Freed from Coors Field, he sliced his home-run rate in half and found his control. His home-run-per-fly-ball rate topped 18 percent in Colorado, vs. 8 percent for the Royals. Sometimes it's that simple. Guthrie's age and need to pitch to contact make a sustainable repeat unlikely. However, his performance in Kansas City convinced Moore to bring him back for three years at $25 million.

Kelvin Herrera

Born: **12/31/1989** Age: **23**
Bats: **R** Throws: **R** Height: **5' 11"** Weight: **190**
Breakout: **25%** Improve: **45%** Collapse: **29%**
Attrition: **10%** MLB: **93%**

Comparables:
Brandon McCarthy,Scott Elarton,Cloyd Boyer

YEAR	TEAM	LVL	AGE	W	L	SV	G	GS	IP	H	HR	BB	SO	BB9	SO9	GB%	BABIP	WHIP	ERA	FIP	FRA	WARP
2010	BUR	A	20	2	3	0	8	8	41^1	38	2	15	40	3.3	8.7	51%	.321	1.28	4.36	3.68	4.45	0.5
2011	WIL	A+	21	2	1	1	8	0	14^2	8	1	2	12	1.2	7.4	59%	.148	0.68	0.61	2.89	2.76	0.2
2011	NWA	AA	21	4	0	7	23	0	36	22	4	6	40	1.5	10.0	72%	.271	0.78	1.75	3.18	3.55	0.5
2011	OMA	AAA	21	1	0	6	14	0	17	12	1	7	18	3.7	9.5	68%	.158	1.12	2.12	3.67	2.91	0.2
2011	KCA	MLB	21	0	1	0	2	0	2	2	1	0	0	0.0	0.0	38%	.143	1.00	13.50	11.06	15.99	-0.2
2012	KCA	MLB	22	4	3	3	76	0	84^1	79	4	21	77	2.2	8.2	57%	.312	1.19	2.35	2.65	3.26	1.6
2013	*KCA*	*MLB*	*23*	*3*	*2*	*1*	*41*	*3*	*60^2*	*61*	*6*	*18*	*49*	*2.7*	*7.3*	*52%*	*.304*	*1.31*	*3.99*	*3.76*	*4.34*	*0.7*

After rocketing through four levels in 2011, Herrera kept the moving trucks at bay in '12, spending the entire year with the big club. It's as if he enters the game with a flamethrower attached to his arm: His average fastball velocity of 97.4 mph was the highest in the AL and second only to Aroldis Chapman in MLB. He uses the fastball to jump ahead and then finishes off hitters with a filthy changeup. When foes actually put the ball in play, it's frequently on the ground. The Royals bullpen is flush with quality arms, and Herrera may be at the head of the class. Closer material to be sure.

Luke Hochevar

Born: **9/15/1983** Age: **29**
Bats: **R** Throws: **R** Height: **6' 6"** Weight: **220**
Breakout: **20%** Improve: **45%** Collapse: **20%**
Attrition: **10%** MLB: **87%**

Comparables:
Jeremy Bonderman, Nate Robertson, Scott Richmond

YEAR	TEAM	LVL	AGE	W	L	SV	G	GS	IP	H	HR	BB	SO	BB9	SO9	GB%	BABIP	WHIP	ERA	FIP	FRA	WARP
2010	OMA	AAA	26	0	0	0	2	2	5	3	0	1	4	1.8	7.2	43%	.214	0.80	1.80	3.18	2.75	0.2
2010	KCA	MLB	26	6	6	0	18	17	103	110	9	37	76	3.2	6.6	46%	.312	1.43	4.81	3.90	4.66	0.7
2011	KCA	MLB	27	11	11	0	31	31	198	192	23	62	128	2.8	5.8	51%	.275	1.28	4.68	4.32	5.01	0.6
2012	KCA	MLB	28	8	16	0	32	32	185^1	202	27	61	144	3.0	7.0	44%	.315	1.42	5.73	4.58	5.36	0.5
2013	*KCA*	*MLB*	*29*	*9*	*11*	*0*	*28*	*28*	*163^1*	*172*	*20*	*51*	*116*	*2.8*	*6.4*	*47%*	*.302*	*1.36*	*4.64*	*4.31*	*5.05*	*0.6*

The inside joke in Kansas City is Hochevar is *this close* to turning the corner. Right. The Royals have been slow to admit that the only overall number-one draft pick in franchise history was a bust. Hochevar has become the poster boy for the organization's inability to develop starting pitching. Pitching coach Dave Eiland thinks he has too many pitches in his repertoire and should eliminate his cut fastball. Would it surprise you to learn that was his best pitch last season? To put his horribleness in historical terms, Hochevar has the third-worst ERA of all time among starters who have thrown at least 750 innings in their career. That corner he's going to turn? It leads to either the bullpen or Triple-A. The sooner the Royals decide to move on, the better.

Greg Holland

Born: **11/20/1985** Age: **27**
Bats: **R** Throws: **R** Height: **5' 11"** Weight: **200**
Breakout: **32%** Improve: **51%** Collapse: **40%**
Attrition: **16%** MLB: **94%**

Comparables:
Al Hrabosky, Steve Bedrosian, Vinnie Pestano

YEAR	TEAM	LVL	AGE	W	L	SV	G	GS	IP	H	HR	BB	SO	BB9	SO9	GB%	BABIP	WHIP	ERA	FIP	FRA	WARP
2010	OMA	AAA	24	3	3	3	36	0	56^2	40	3	30	60	4.8	9.5	46%	.248	1.23	3.81	3.74	4.77	0.6
2010	KCA	MLB	24	0	1	0	15	0	18^2	23	3	8	23	3.9	11.1	36%	.377	1.66	6.75	3.96	5.07	0.0
2011	OMA	AAA	25	2	0	2	13	0	21^2	13	1	11	27	4.6	11.2	38%	.125	1.11	2.08	3.41	2.82	0.3
2011	KCA	MLB	25	5	1	4	46	0	60	37	3	19	74	2.8	11.1	45%	.250	0.93	1.80	2.24	2.85	1.4
2012	NWA	AA	26	0	1	0	2	2	2	1	0	0	3	0.0	13.5	75%	.250	0.50	0.00	0.28	2.32	0.1
2012	KCA	MLB	26	7	4	16	67	0	67	58	2	34	91	4.6	12.2	47%	.346	1.37	2.96	2.24	2.08	2.2
2013	*KCA*	*MLB*	*27*	*2*	*1*	*5*	*47*	*0*	*58^2*	*51*	*5*	*25*	*66*	*3.8*	*10.1*	*45%*	*.307*	*1.28*	*3.44*	*3.34*	*3.74*	*1.0*

Moved into the closer role with the midseason trade of Jonathan Broxton to Cincinnati, Holland made the transition from the eighth to ninth inning with ease. He features mostly a fastball-slider combo, but will show a curve from time to time. The heater clocks in around 96 mph, the slider at 86 mph, and his curve at 76 mph to give the hitters plenty to think about while digging into the box. His overall numbers were down a bit from 2011, but he pitched through the first part of April with a rib injury suffered in spring training that eventually sent him to the DL. From his return on May 12 to the end of the season, he had a 2.08 ERA and a 12 SO9. He looks like the replacement for Joakim Soria.

John Lamb

Born: **7/10/1990** Age: **22**
Bats: **L** Throws: **L** Height: **6' 5"** Weight: **200**
Breakout: **41%** Improve: **58%** Collapse: **14%**
Attrition: **25%** MLB: **86%**

Comparables:
Ryan Feierabend, Jaime Garcia, Jon Niese

YEAR	TEAM	LVL	AGE	W	L	SV	G	GS	IP	H	HR	BB	SO	BB9	SO9	GB%	BABIP	WHIP	ERA	FIP	FRA	WARP
2010	BUR	A	19	2	3	0	8	8	40	26	2	17	43	3.8	9.7	38%	.253	1.08	1.58	3.61	3.79	0.8
2010	WIL	A+	19	6	3	0	13	13	74^2	59	1	15	90	1.8	10.8	50%	.315	0.99	1.45	1.89	2.82	2.1
2010	NWA	AA	19	2	1	0	7	7	33	37	2	13	26	3.5	7.1	45%	.310	1.52	5.45	3.84	5.40	0.3
2011	NWA	AA	20	1	2	0	8	8	35	33	3	13	22	3.3	5.7	47%	.347	1.31	3.09	4.43	4.87	0.3
2012	IDA	Rk	21	0	1	0	2	2	7^1	9	2	2	8	2.5	9.8	46%	.350	1.50	7.36	6.62	6.31	0.0
2012	ROY	Rk	21	0	0	0	4	4	5^2	6	0	2	6	3.2	9.5	46%	.364	1.41	6.35	3.32	4.41	0.2
2013	*KCA*	*MLB*	*22*	*2*	*3*	*0*	*7*	*7*	*33^1*	*36*	*4*	*16*	*24*	*4.3*	*6.5*	*43%*	*.309*	*1.57*	*5.32*	*4.76*	*5.79*	*-0.1*

Another of the group of Royals power lefty prospects who have experienced serious setbacks. For Lamb, it was Tommy John surgery in 2011 and a slower-than-expected recovery. He hurt his foot while conditioning and had to wear a protective boot, further delaying his return. He finally made six starts in rookie league, throwing a total of 13 innings as the club eased him back to the mound. The Royals insist Lamb will report to spring training with no limitations, which is good news given the recent struggles of a number of the team's pitching prospects. He figures to return to Double-A and the top of Kansas City's pitching prospect pecking order.

Luis Mendoza

Born: **10/31/1983** Age: **29**
Bats: **R** Throws: **R** Height: **6' 4"** Weight: **235**
Breakout: **25%** Improve: **65%** Collapse: **21%**
Attrition: **14%** MLB: **83%**

Comparables:
Frank Lary, Dock Ellis, David Pauley

YEAR	TEAM	LVL	AGE	W	L	SV	G	GS	IP	H	HR	BB	SO	BB9	SO9	GB%	BABIP	WHIP	ERA	FIP	FRA	WARP
2010	OMA	AAA	26	10	9	0	24	22	131^2	145	13	32	59	2.2	4.0	51%	.295	1.34	4.10	4.86	5.93	-0.1
2010	KCA	MLB	26	0	1	0	4	0	4	10	4	3	1	6.8	2.2	38%	.353	3.25	22.50	17.80	19.22	-0.6
2011	OMA	AAA	27	12	5	2	33	18	144^1	126	5	54	81	3.4	5.1	44%	.343	1.25	2.18	4.38	4.39	0.8
2011	KCA	MLB	27	2	0	0	2	2	14^2	11	0	5	7	3.1	4.3	46%	.239	1.09	1.23	3.54	4.08	0.2
2012	KCA	MLB	28	8	10	0	30	25	166	176	15	59	104	3.2	5.6	54%	.310	1.42	4.23	4.23	4.94	0.5
2013	*KCA*	*MLB*	*29*	*6*	*8*	*0*	*24*	*18*	*119^2*	*138*	*13*	*41*	*66*	*3.1*	*5.0*	*49%*	*.312*	*1.49*	*5.06*	*4.54*	*5.50*	*-0.1*

Mendoza is a pitch-to-contact starter who depends on team defense to save him from the precipice of the big inning. He relies on his sinker yet switches to his curve once he jumps ahead of the batter. He keeps the ball in the infield and his home-run rate manageable. His strikeout rate has always been underwhelming, which is why he's a longshot to repeat even his middling performance from 2012. If he's in the rotation for the Royals in 2013, you'll know their offseason plan of adding starting pitching was unsuccessful.

Guillermo Moscoso
Born: **11/14/1983** Age: **29**
Bats: **R** Throws: **R** Height: **6' 2"** Weight: **200**
Breakout: **16%** Improve: **48%** Collapse: **20%**
Attrition: **5%** MLB: **93%**
Comparables:
Don Drysdale,Shaun Marcum,Alex Fernandez

YEAR	TEAM	LVL	AGE	W	L	SV	G	GS	IP	H	HR	BB	SO	BB9	SO9	GB%	BABIP	WHIP	ERA	FIP	FRA	WARP
2010	OKL	AAA	26	7	7	0	23	22	123^1	142	17	49	107	3.6	7.8	36%	.327	1.55	5.18	4.93	5.77	0.8
2010	TEX	MLB	26	0	0	0	1	0	0^2	2	0	2	2	27.0	27.0	%	.000	6.00	27.00	10.55	9.11	0.0
2011	SAC	AAA	27	3	3	0	9	8	46^1	41	3	16	52	3.1	10.1	—	.309	1.23	3.88	3.42	3.71	0.0
2011	OAK	MLB	27	8	10	0	23	21	128	102	14	38	74	2.7	5.2	27%	.221	1.09	3.38	4.26	5.25	-0.7
2012	CSP	AAA	28	8	6	0	18	18	98^1	127	14	26	85	2.4	7.8	44%	.364	1.56	6.13	4.58	5.25	0.7
2012	COL	MLB	28	3	2	0	23	3	50	67	8	19	47	3.4	8.5	35%	.378	1.72	6.12	4.54	5.28	0.4
2013	*KCA*	*MLB*	*29*	*4*	*5*	*0*	*18*	*13*	*80*	*83*	*10*	*25*	*61*	*2.9*	*6.9*	*35%*	*.298*	*1.35*	*4.50*	*4.24*	*4.89*	*0.5*

The Royals claimed Moscoso on waivers in November from Colorado, where he'd gone in the trade that sent Seth Smith to Oakland last winter. His fastball sits in the low 90s but has good movement. Following up on a strong rookie campaign in the A's rotation, he bounced back and forth last year between Colorado Springs and Denver, and between starting and relieving. Moscoso was hit hard regardless of level or role, with spotty command forcing him to work behind in the count too often with the big club. He could develop into a serviceable swing man, but at his age, he'd better do it now.

Felipe Paulino
Born: **10/5/1983** Age: **29**
Bats: **R** Throws: **R** Height: **6' 3"** Weight: **270**
Breakout: **13%** Improve: **42%** Collapse: **29%**
Attrition: **9%** MLB: **86%**
Comparables:
Melido Perez,Ray Culp,Len Barker

YEAR	TEAM	LVL	AGE	W	L	SV	G	GS	IP	H	HR	BB	SO	BB9	SO9	GB%	BABIP	WHIP	ERA	FIP	FRA	WARP
2010	CCH	AA	26	0	0	0	1	1	4	2	0	1	3	2.2	6.8	40%	.200	0.75	0.00	2.42	4.23	0.0
2010	HOU	MLB	26	1	9	0	19	14	91^2	95	4	46	83	4.5	8.1	45%	.332	1.54	5.11	3.47	4.46	1.2
2011	COL	MLB	27	0	4	0	18	0	14^2	23	3	7	14	4.3	8.6	51%	.455	2.05	7.36	5.18	5.69	0.0
2011	KCA	MLB	27	4	6	0	21	20	124^2	123	10	48	119	3.5	8.6	46%	.327	1.37	4.11	3.54	3.94	1.8
2012	NWA	AA	28	1	0	0	3	3	13^1	12	3	4	14	2.7	9.4	47%	.257	1.20	4.05	5.01	5.06	0.2
2012	KCA	MLB	28	3	1	0	7	7	37^2	31	3	15	39	3.6	9.3	44%	.283	1.22	1.67	3.21	3.52	0.8
2013	*KCA*	*MLB*	*29*	*3*	*3*	*0*	*9*	*9*	*50*	*52*	*6*	*20*	*46*	*3.7*	*8.3*	*44%*	*.322*	*1.45*	*4.64*	*4.12*	*5.04*	*0.2*

Too bad they don't have those frequent-customer punch cards for Tommy John surgery like they do at your favorite sandwich shop. Because if they did, Paulino's operation would have been free. Paulino was hands down the best Royals starting pitcher through his nine starts, and his removal from the rotation crunched a team already light on starting pitching. Paulino has a violent delivery that made him a ticking time bomb for this type of injury. Like Duffy, the best-case scenario would have him making a few starts at the end of 2013 before contributing in 2014.

Ervin Santana
Born: **1/10/1983** Age: **30**
Bats: **R** Throws: **R** Height: **6' 3"** Weight: **185**
Breakout: **11%** Improve: **34%** Collapse: **32%**
Attrition: **16%** MLB: **85%**
Comparables:
Nate Robertson,Devern Hansack,Gil Meche

YEAR	TEAM	LVL	AGE	W	L	SV	G	GS	IP	H	HR	BB	SO	BB9	SO9	GB%	BABIP	WHIP	ERA	FIP	FRA	WARP
2010	ANA	MLB	27	17	10	0	33	33	222^2	221	27	73	169	3.0	6.8	37%	.289	1.32	3.92	4.25	4.01	2.0
2011	ANA	MLB	28	11	12	0	33	33	228^2	207	26	72	178	2.8	7.0	45%	.272	1.22	3.38	4.03	4.68	0.5
2012	ANA	MLB	29	9	13	0	30	30	178	165	39	61	133	3.1	6.7	45%	.241	1.27	5.16	5.58	6.22	-2.1
2013	*KCA*	*MLB*	*30*	*9*	*10*	*0*	*25*	*25*	*162^2*	*162*	*23*	*49*	*130*	*2.7*	*7.2*	*41%*	*.291*	*1.30*	*4.31*	*4.34*	*4.68*	*1.1*

Santana has always struggled to maintain his arm slot within games and over stretches of starts. Losing it in 2012 nearly lost him his rotation spot. By July, Angels manager Mike Scioscia had diagnosed the problem: Santana was getting too far on top of his pitches, flattening out his fastball while robbing his slider of velocity and telegraphing pitch type. The adjustments seemed to take, and in August and most of September he was probably the Angels' best starter. Then he got bombed in his final start of the year; three teams clinched a postseason berth and a fourth clinched at least a tie with the outcome of the game, but the Angels, alas, were not one of them. The Angels declined his 2013 option and dealt him to the pitching-starved Royals. He'll slot into the rotation, keeping warm a spot for either Duffy or Paulino when they're fully recovered in 2014.

James Shields

Born: **12/20/1981** Age: **31**
Bats: **R** Throws: **R** Height: **6' 5"** Weight: **220**
Breakout: **17%** Improve: **45%** Collapse: **31%**
Attrition: **12%** MLB: **92%**

Comparables:
Curt Schilling,Dan Haren,Josh Beckett

YEAR	TEAM	LVL	AGE	W	L	SV	G	GS	IP	H	HR	BB	SO	BB9	SO9	GB%	BABIP	WHIP	ERA	FIP	FRA	WARP
2010	TBA	MLB	28	13	15	0	34	33	203^1	246	34	51	187	2.3	8.3	42%	.341	1.46	5.18	4.21	4.43	2.0
2011	TBA	MLB	29	16	12	0	33	33	249^1	195	26	65	225	2.3	8.1	47%	.258	1.04	2.82	3.45	3.96	2.3
2012	TBA	MLB	30	15	10	0	33	33	227^2	208	25	58	223	2.3	8.8	53%	.292	1.17	3.52	3.42	4.43	0.8
2013	*KCA*	*MLB*	*31*	*12*	*11*	*0*	*29*	*29*	*199*	*202*	*24*	*44*	*165*	*2.0*	*7.4*	*46%*	*.306*	*1.24*	*4.00*	*3.77*	*4.35*	*2.1*

The durable Shields has thrown the fourth-most innings in baseball since 2009. His 2012 stats ranged near those of his dominant 2011, save a regressive groundball rate and concomitant rise in BABIP. Therein lies the difference, perhaps, between an elite ace and an estimable number two? Yet Shields ended the year with probably the best game of his career: a 15-strikeout two-hitter for the Rays against the Orioles on October 2 that reasserted his ace ability. (He lost on a solo homer; the 94 game score was the highest ever by a losing pitcher.) Shields's strike-out and walk rates were better than David Price's last year. Acquired by the Royals in a polarizing deal the week following the Winter Meetings—for prospects Myers and Jake Odorizzi—Shields immediately heads to the front of Kansas City's rotation.

Will Smith

Born: **7/10/1989** Age: **23**
Bats: **R** Throws: **L** Height: **6' 6"** Weight: **235**
Breakout: **30%** Improve: **60%** Collapse: **9%**
Attrition: **11%** MLB: **85%**

Comparables:
Justin Germano,Alex White,Liam Hendriks

YEAR	TEAM	LVL	AGE	W	L	SV	G	GS	IP	H	HR	BB	SO	BB9	SO9	GB%	BABIP	WHIP	ERA	FIP	FRA	WARP
2010	RCU	A+	20	2	2	0	6	6	37^1	36	4	13	31	3.1	7.5	47%	.296	1.31	4.58	4.51	5.87	0.1
2010	WIL	A+	20	4	1	0	8	8	54^2	48	6	4	51	0.7	8.4	53%	.278	0.95	2.80	3.24	4.30	0.5
2010	ARK	AA	20	1	2	0	4	4	18^2	33	3	9	8	4.3	3.9	47%	.400	2.25	7.22	6.01	6.84	-0.2
2010	SLC	AAA	20	2	4	0	9	9	53	65	6	20	40	3.4	6.8	45%	.341	1.60	5.60	4.68	5.36	0.2
2011	NWA	AA	21	13	9	0	27	27	161^1	171	13	45	108	2.5	6.0	43%	.300	1.34	3.85	4.03	5.04	1.1
2012	OMA	AAA	22	4	4	0	15	15	89^2	104	8	22	74	2.2	7.4	44%	.341	1.41	3.61	3.98	4.37	0.2
2012	KCA	MLB	22	6	9	0	16	16	89^2	111	12	33	59	3.3	5.9	43%	.340	1.61	5.32	4.61	4.99	0.4
2013	*KCA*	*MLB*	*23*	*5*	*7*	*0*	*16*	*16*	*92^1*	*109*	*13*	*32*	*58*	*3.1*	*5.7*	*44%*	*.316*	*1.52*	*5.38*	*4.81*	*5.85*	*-0.4*

In the move to the majors, Smith left his pinpoint control in Triple-A. While trying to adjust, he started leaving too many pitches in the middle of the zone. He comes by that BABIP honestly: 23 percent of all balls in play were classified as line drives. Control will continue to be key to any success as his fastball struggles to hit 90 mph and he lacks a plus pitch that can cause hitters to swing and miss. If he eventually sticks in the majors, it will be in the back of the rotation, although he could be used out of the bullpen as a long reliever and emergency starter.

Everett Teaford

Born: **5/15/1984** Age: **29**
Bats: **L** Throws: **L** Height: **6' 0"** Weight: **155**
Breakout: **20%** Improve: **66%** Collapse: **12%**
Attrition: **7%** MLB: **88%**

Comparables:
Doug Rau,Glen Perkins,Bud Black

YEAR	TEAM	LVL	AGE	W	L	SV	G	GS	IP	H	HR	BB	SO	BB9	SO9	GB%	BABIP	WHIP	ERA	FIP	FRA	WARP
2010	NWA	AA	26	14	3	0	27	12	99	91	7	32	113	2.9	10.3	46%	.314	1.24	3.36	2.87	4.25	2.3
2010	OMA	AAA	26	0	1	0	1	1	4^2	8	2	1	4	1.9	7.7	39%	.375	1.91	13.40	8.05	7.67	0.0
2011	OMA	AAA	27	3	2	0	16	3	35	23	5	11	33	2.8	8.5	39%	.226	0.97	3.34	4.78	3.18	0.2
2011	KCA	MLB	27	2	1	1	26	3	44	36	8	14	28	2.9	5.7	46%	.226	1.14	3.27	5.18	5.77	-0.1
2012	OMA	AAA	28	4	0	0	7	6	33	24	2	8	25	2.2	6.8	42%	.247	0.97	1.09	3.76	4.11	0.4
2012	KCA	MLB	28	1	4	0	18	5	61^1	68	11	21	35	3.1	5.1	45%	.294	1.45	4.99	5.36	6.15	-0.5
2013	*KCA*	*MLB*	*29*	*2*	*3*	*0*	*18*	*7*	*57^2*	*62*	*9*	*20*	*36*	*3.2*	*5.7*	*40%*	*.295*	*1.44*	*4.95*	*5.02*	*5.38*	*0.0*

Teaford features a low-90s fastball, but stays in the zone and possesses a higher-than-average contact rate. Used primarily as a mop-up reliever and spot starter, he came into the game in the fourth inning or earlier in seven of his 13 relief appearances. With the Royals hurting for starters, he took five turns in the rotation, but didn't distinguish himself and couldn't lock down a permanent spot. His control is a positive, but his home-run rate will ultimately keep him in the swing-man role or exclusively in the bullpen.

Yordano Ventura

Born: **6/3/1991** Age: **22**
Bats: **R** Throws: **R** Height: **6' 0"** Weight: **140**
Breakout: **24%** Improve: **59%** Collapse: **16%**
Attrition: **6%** MLB: **92%**

Comparables:
Jake Peavy,Alex Fernandez,Chris Tillman

YEAR	TEAM	LVL	AGE	W	L	SV	G	GS	IP	H	HR	BB	SO	BB9	SO9	GB%	BABIP	WHIP	ERA	FIP	FRA	WARP
2010	ROY	Rk	19	4	2	0	14	6	52^2	49	3	17	58	2.9	9.9	51%	.348	1.25	3.24	3.93	4.55	0.4
2011	KNC	A	20	4	6	0	19	19	84^1	82	8	24	88	2.6	9.4	—	.327	1.26	4.27	3.54	3.85	0.0
2012	ROY	Rk	21	0	0	0	1	1	3^2	3	0	1	7	2.5	17.2	60%	.400	1.09	2.45	1.38	1.59	0.2
2012	WIL	A+	21	3	5	0	16	16	76^1	66	7	28	98	3.3	11.6	43%	.314	1.23	3.30	3.31	3.51	1.1
2012	NWA	AA	21	1	2	0	6	6	29^1	23	1	13	25	4.0	7.7	52%	.275	1.23	4.60	3.76	3.97	0.2
2013	*KCA*	*MLB*	*22*	*2*	*2*	*0*	*7*	*6*	*33^2*	*35*	*4*	*16*	*28*	*4.4*	*7.6*	*45%*	*.312*	*1.54*	*5.16*	*4.51*	*5.61*	*-0.0*

With one of the best fastballs in the Royals system, Ventura overmatched hitters in High-A before earning a promotion to the Texas League. It also earned him an appearance in Kansas City in July as the starter for the World Team in the Futures Game. Local fans got to witness firsthand his heater, which lives in the mid-90s and can tickle triple digits on occasion. He also features a breathtaking curve. The issue here is consistency. He failed to make it through the fourth inning in six of his starts for Wilmington. His size, lack of consistency, and the ability to air out his fastball means he could profile as a late-inning reliever.

Ryan Verdugo
Born: 4/10/1987 Age: 26
Bats: L Throws: L Height: 6' 1" Weight: 195
Breakout: 36% Improve: 67% Collapse: 10%
Attrition: 6% MLB: 97%
Comparables:
Ken Kravec,Michael Dunn,Dustin Richardson

YEAR	TEAM	LVL	AGE	W	L	SV	G	GS	IP	H	HR	BB	SO	BB9	SO9	GB%	BABIP	WHIP	ERA	FIP	FRA	WARP
2010	AUG	A	23	4	1	1	22	0	32	26	0	14	50	3.9	14.1	49%	.377	1.25	2.25	1.71	2.35	1.0
2010	SJO	A+	23	4	0	0	22	1	30^{2}	15	3	19	44	5.6	12.9	44%	.226	1.11	1.47	3.99	4.09	0.6
2011	RIC	AA	24	8	6	0	25	25	130^{1}	115	14	63	133	4.4	9.2	35%	.298	1.37	4.35	4.31	5.12	0.1
2012	OMA	AAA	25	12	4	0	27	24	136^{2}	114	19	67	118	4.4	7.8	36%	.251	1.32	3.75	5.30	5.93	0.2
2012	KCA	MLB	25	0	1	0	1	1	1^{2}	8	1	2	2	10.8	10.8	46%	.700	6.00	32.40	12.05	8.08	-0.1
2013	*KCA*	*MLB*	*26*	*2*	*3*	*0*	*14*	*6*	*43*	*42*	*6*	*23*	*39*	*4.8*	*8.1*	*39%*	*.298*	*1.52*	*4.89*	*4.80*	*5.31*	*0.1*

The third piece of the infamous Melky Cabrera-Jonathan Sanchez trade, Verdugo has struggled with command throughout his career. He has compensated with a plus slider that is a true strikeout pitch—at least in the lower levels of the minors. As he has progressed up the ladder, the good qualities of his stuff have been lost in the translation. That's ultimately what will hold him in the minors.

Chris Volstad
Born: 9/23/1986 Age: 26
Bats: R Throws: R Height: 6' 9" Weight: 230
Breakout: 40% Improve: 81% Collapse: 10%
Attrition: 14% MLB: 77%
Comparables:
Tim Stauffer,Jeff Karstens,Justin Germano

YEAR	TEAM	LVL	AGE	W	L	SV	G	GS	IP	H	HR	BB	SO	BB9	SO9	GB%	BABIP	WHIP	ERA	FIP	FRA	WARP
2010	NWO	AAA	23	1	0	0	3	3	17	13	1	9	13	4.8	6.9	63%	.250	1.29	3.18	4.41	5.39	0.1
2010	FLO	MLB	23	12	9	0	30	30	175	187	17	60	102	3.1	5.2	49%	.298	1.41	4.58	4.37	5.12	0.5
2011	NWO	AAA	24	1	1	0	3	3	18^{1}	20	1	9	14	4.4	6.9	—	.339	1.58	4.42	4.44	4.82	0.0
2011	FLO	MLB	24	5	13	0	29	29	165^{2}	187	23	49	117	2.7	6.4	54%	.310	1.42	4.89	4.29	5.03	-0.1
2012	IOW	AAA	25	3	5	0	12	12	71^{1}	86	7	19	52	2.4	6.6	61%	.339	1.47	5.17	4.45	5.28	0.4
2012	CHN	MLB	25	3	12	0	21	21	111^{1}	137	16	43	61	3.5	4.9	52%	.315	1.62	6.31	5.15	5.53	0.0
2013	*KCA*	*MLB*	*26*	*6*	*8*	*0*	*21*	*21*	117^{2}	*136*	*16*	*37*	*65*	*2.9*	*4.9*	*53%*	*.306*	*1.47*	*5.10*	*4.81*	*5.54*	*-0.1*

Some players are better defined by what they aren't than what they are. For the Cubs, what Volstad wasn't was Carlos Zambrano. The Cubs didn't miss Zambrano's feuding (and sometimes outright fist-fighting) with other players and managers. They didn't miss what Zambrano did in 2012 for the Marlins, either. But Volstad leaves a lot to be desired as a pitcher in his own right — a change of scenery from Miami to Chicago did nothing to improve upon what he does on the field, to the point where even a club as desperate for starting pitching as the Cubs let him linger in the minors for nearly half of the season. The Cubs apparently decided that having gotten rid of Zambrano, they could now get rid of Volstad, who is now with the even more pitching-starved Royals.

Dan Wheeler
Born: 12/10/1977 Age: 35
Bats: R Throws: R Height: 6' 4" Weight: 220
Breakout: 24% Improve: 55% Collapse: 26%
Attrition: 7% MLB: 83%
Comparables:
Tyler Walker,Joel Peralta,Shawn Camp

YEAR	TEAM	LVL	AGE	W	L	SV	G	GS	IP	H	HR	BB	SO	BB9	SO9	GB%	BABIP	WHIP	ERA	FIP	FRA	WARP
2010	TBA	MLB	32	2	4	3	64	0	48^{1}	36	7	16	46	3.0	8.6	36%	.232	1.08	3.35	4.08	3.92	0.4
2011	PAW	AAA	33	0	0	0	3	0	4^{2}	3	1	2	7	3.9	13.5	%	.333	1.07	1.93	4.31	-0.02	0.1
2011	BOS	MLB	33	2	2	0	47	0	49^{1}	47	7	8	39	1.5	7.1	33%	.272	1.11	4.38	3.81	4.96	0.3
2012	COH	AAA	34	3	3	5	36	0	42^{2}	38	4	13	30	2.7	6.3	38%	.264	1.20	2.32	4.10	6.13	-0.2
2012	CLE	MLB	34	0	0	0	12	0	12^{1}	17	3	7	2	5.1	1.5	42%	.286	1.95	8.76	7.59	8.73	-0.5
2013	*KCA*	*MLB*	*35*	*2*	*1*	*0*	*38*	*0*	36^{1}	*34*	*5*	*10*	*28*	*2.5*	*6.9*	*36%*	*.274*	*1.22*	*3.90*	*4.27*	*4.24*	*0.4*

Once the closer for the Astros and Rays and one of the more underrated relievers in baseball, Wheeler's career may be winding down. He was excellent as recently as 2010 and very good as recently as 2011, but he took a bit of a nosedive in 2012, spending most of the season in the minors. His stuff was way down, and he never had exceptional secondary offerings to begin with. He used to be a good strike-thrower with command of his fastball to both sides of plate, but he lost a bit of that in 2012. It seems the years of pitching 70-plus games are starting to catch up him. The Royals have rolled the dice on broken relievers in the past, and have inked Wheeler to a minor-league deal.

Kyle Zimmer
Born: 9/13/1991 Age: 21
Bats: R Throws: R Height: 6' 4" Weight: 215
Breakout: 31% Improve: 66% Collapse: 13%
Attrition: 9% MLB: 86%
Comparables:
Kevin Kobel,Bob Friend,Tommy Boggs

YEAR	TEAM	LVL	AGE	W	L	SV	G	GS	IP	H	HR	BB	SO	BB9	SO9	GB%	BABIP	WHIP	ERA	FIP	FRA	WARP
2012	ROY	Rk	20	1	0	0	3	3	10	5	0	0	13	0.0	11.7	—	.250	0.50	0.90	1.78	1.93	0.0
2012	KNC	A	20	2	3	0	6	6	29^{2}	34	1	8	29	2.4	8.8	63%	.370	1.42	2.43	3.05	5.15	-0.1
2013	*KCA*	*MLB*	*21*	*1*	*3*	*0*	*6*	*6*	32^{1}	*40*	*5*	*16*	*15*	*4.5*	*4.3*	*46%*	*.312*	*1.74*	*6.38*	*5.77*	*6.94*	*-0.5*

Zimmer was the fifth pick in 2012 and signed for a $3.5 million bonus just three days after the draft. He opened with the Royals' rookie team in Arizona before moving to Low-A Kane

County. He throws his fastball in the mid-90s and is developing a plus curve with a ferocious 12-to-6 break, and scouts feel his changeup has the potential to be an above-average pitch as well. He underwent surgery to remove loose bodies from his elbow in mid-August. Given the Royals' experience with elbow issues in 2012, you can't blame fans for holding their breath. They were assured the procedure was minor and he is on track to be ready for the 2013 season. Exhale.

LINEOUTS

HITTERS

PLAYER	TEAM	LVL	AGE	PA	R	2B	3B	HR	RBI	BB	SO	SB-CS	AVG/OBP/SLG	TAv	BABIP	BRR	FRAA	WARP
SS H. Arteaga	BNC	Rk	18	262	40	13	3	2	29	9	31	7-3	.274/.313/.380	.262	.304	0.9	SS(22): 0.5	0.4
RF J. Bonifacio	KNC	A	19	448	54	20	6	10	61	30	84	6-3	.282/.336/.432	.283	.333	-1.9	RF(13): -0.1	0.1
3B C. Cuthbert	WIL	A+	19	517	47	18	0	7	59	37	80	6-3	.240/.296/.322	.237	.274	-4.5	3B(97): -4.9	-1.2
MI K. Diekroeger	BNC	Rk	21	222	21	6	1	8	33	18	60	5-0	.208/.275/.366	.297	.252	1.5	2B(11): 0.2, SS(4): 0.2	0.5
CF B. Eibner	WIL	A+	23	486	60	26	5	15	53	57	165	5-2	.196/.299/.388	.260	.280	-1	CF(89): -4.9	0.2
LF B. Fletcher	WIL	A+	23	272	27	15	0	5	25	19	51	5-2	.289/.353/.411	.258	.346	-0.1	1B(31): 2.5, LF(12): -1.0	-0.1
	NWA	AA	23	280	32	11	2	10	34	15	96	6-3	.256/.318/.433	.276	.367	-0.1	LF(40): -2.3	0.1
C C. Gallagher	BNC	Rk	19	139	13	10	0	3	15	10	16	1-3	.276/.331/.425	.173	.294	-2.6	C(16): -0.4	-0.8
RF E. Hernandez	IDA	Rk	17	267	30	10	4	0	34	14	66	2-0	.208/.256/.280	.181	.283	0.4	RF(15): 1.0	-0.4
SS J. Lopez	KNC	A	19	288	30	9	2	0	16	14	43	14-4	.222/.271/.272	.224	.265	1.8	SS(13): -0.7	-0.3
OF W. Taveras	—	—	—	—	—	—	—	—	—	—	—	—	—	—	—	—	—	—
INF M. Tejada	NOR	AAA	38	151	10	5	0	0	18	11	16	1-0	.259/.325/.296	.220	.289	-0.4	3B(28): -0.6, SS(3): -0.5	-0.5
UT B. Wood	CSP	AAA	27	438	56	28	1	10	64	28	97	2-0	.259/.313/.409	.237	.315	-0.3	3B(35): -0.2, 2B(18): 1.9	0.2

Humberto Arteaga was signed for $1.1. million as part of the Royals' effort to build up shortstop depth in the low minors, and like many Venezuelan shortstops, he has an exceptional glove and suspect bat. The younger brother of Emilio, **Jorge Bonifacio** has a violent swing, but also the ability to make exceptional contact, squaring the ball up and hitting for plus power. As the youngest player in the Carolina League, **Cheslor Cuthbert** faced on-the-field setbacks for the first time, but he has the type of makeup to move forward in a likely return to High-A in 2013. Drafted by the Rays in the second round in 2009, **Kenny Diekroeger**'s stock drop in three years at Stanford. The Royals nabbed him in the fourth round in 2012, projecting him to parlay his athleticism into defensive versatility. **Brett Eibner** was drafted as a two-way player out of Arkansas in 2010 and pushed to pursue the power potential he flashed in 2011, only to sputter in 2012. **Brian Fletcher** showed his power as he split the season between High-A and Double-A, but his plate discipline and pitch recognition need to improve for him to make a serious impact in a deep system. Injuries have gotten in the way of **Cameron Gallagher**'s development, but his ability to make contact and his defensive skills behind the plate have gotten notice. A $3 million international bonus baby, **Elier Hernandez** struggled in his first taste of professional ball, but scouts rave about his bat speed and believe that once he adapts, the power will come around. Drafted in the 16th round in 2011 but paid second-round money, **Jack Lopez** is touted as a strong defender with the ability to make contact at the plate, but he needs to develop a little pop in his bat. Signed by the Royals in December, **Willy Taveras** last played in the majors in 2010 and last posted a positive WARP in 2008. Six-time All-Star, one-time MVP, and one-time liar to federal investigators in the PED probe, **Miguel Tejada** signed a one-year minor-league deal that could be worth $1.5 million if he makes the majors and collects performance bonuses. **Brandon Wood** was a first-round pick in 2003 and hit 43 homers at High-A in 2005 but never learned how to make contact and has seen his career collapse faster than you can say Chad Hermansen.

PITCHERS

PLAYER	TEAM	LVL	AGE	W	L	SV	IP	H	HR	BB	SO	BB9	SO9	GB%	BABIP	WHIP	ERA	FIP	FRA	WARP
M. Almonte	DRY	Rk	19	6	1	0	50	34	2	8	46	1.4	8.3	—	.251	0.84	1.44	2.62	1.89	0.6
	ROY	Rk	19	2	1	0	27	22	0	5	28	1.7	9.3	50%	.295	1.00	2.33	3.30	3.30	0.7
G. Billo	WIL	A+	21	5	4	0	60	55	4	20	56	3.0	8.4	44%	.298	1.25	4.35	3.49	4.42	0.3
B. Brickhouse	KNC	A	20	3	3	0	51^1	50	3	23	40	4.0	7.0	60%	.292	1.42	5.61	4.13	7.18	-0.1
D. Joseph	PEN	AA	24	4	2	13	30^1	13	1	8	46	2.4	13.6	65%	.208	0.69	0.89	1.43	0.91	0.9
	LOU	AAA	24	4	1	5	22	22	0	9	22	3.7	9.0	53%	.344	1.41	2.86	2.39	3.47	0.3
T. Melville	NWA	AA	22	2	1	0	23^1	27	4	15	19	5.8	7.3	36%	.324	1.80	7.71	6.19	7.28	-0.1
C. Rodgers	BNC	Rk	18	3	1	0	48^1	40	2	16	25	3.0	4.7	58%	.316	1.16	2.05	4.32	3.97	0.0
S. Selman	IDA	Rk	21	5	4	0	60^1	45	1	22	89	3.3	13.3	70%	.336	1.11	2.09	2.79	3.19	1.8
A. Severino	SYR	AAA	27	3	0	3	48	37	5	36	43	6.8	8.1	45%	.256	1.52	2.81	5.16	5.53	-0.1
G. Sherrill	SEA	MLB	35	0	0	0	1^1	6	2	1	0	6.8	0.0	56%	.571	5.25	27.00	24.80	21.16	-0.3
K. Smith	KNC	A	19	4	3	0	67^1	62	3	20	87	2.7	11.6	43%	.360	1.22	2.94	2.28	0.74	0.4

Miguel Almonte impressed in the Fall Instructional League, showcasing a 92-95 mph fastball with late life, a sharp curve, and an above-average change. He has the raw stuff to have a breakout season. The 2011 Midwest League Pitcher of the Year, **Greg Billo** underwent Tommy John surgery in July and hopefully did not leave his exceptional control on the operating table. **Bryan Brickhouse** can bring the heat, induce groundballs, and rack up strikeout numbers, but struggled with shoulder soreness in 2012 and saw his innings limited as a result. Questionable mechanics and a violent delivery don't help **Donnie Joseph**'s command, but a southpaw who throws in the mid-90s with a groundball rate greater than 50 percent and a strikeout rate of one per inning will always pique interest. Former prospect **Timothy Melville** took two years to pass the High-A test at Wilmington, then was alternately rocked and injured in Double-A. A third-round pick in 2012 who signed for $700,000, **Colin Rodgers** enjoyed a solid debut for Wilmington with a curve that grades as above average and a low-90s fastball. **Sam Selman** was the Royals' second-round pick in 2012, and his mid-90s fastball and developing slider got him the Pioneer League Pitcher of the Year title, though the Royals would rather he got a better changeup. Signed to a minor-league pact by the Royals last November, **Atahualpa Severino** is a diminutive southpaw with solid stuff but fringy control. Lefties hit 1.000/1.000/1.750 against **George Sherrill**, who got to face only four of them—and six righties—for a reason. The plan for 2011 fourth-round pick **Kyle Smith** was to pitch in the Pioneer League last summer, but a dominant debut where he struck out 11 in five innings prompted the Royals to move him and his curveball to Low-A Kane County.

MANAGER: NED YOST

YEAR	TEAM	W-L	Pythag +/-	Avg PC	100+ P	120+ P	QS	BQS	REL	REL w Zero R	IBB	PH	PH Avg	PH HR	SB2	CS2	SB3	CS3	SAC Att	SAC %	POS SAC	Squeeze	Swing	In Play
2010	KCA	55-72	0	192.8	126	125	68	7	332	257	50	104	.214	4	12	4	1	2	90	77.8%	60	0	281	78
2011	KCA	71-91	0	96.9	74	0	75	5	420	339	42	36	.152	1	23	8	0	2	75	84.0%	58	2	399	113
2012	KCA	72-90	0	90.5	55	0	69	4	500	411	44	55	.208	3	22	4	1	0	42	66.7%	27	1	334	97

Yost made his managerial bones in Milwaukee piloting a young, developing Brewers club, but was cut loose when the pressure of the pennant race became too much for him to handle. On the surface, it doesn't look like he's learned much from his first go-round on the managerial carousel.

He adores the sacrifice bunt the way one nostalgically remembers their first love. Perhaps that's why he calls for sacrifice bunts in the first inning and often attempts it with runners on first and second with nobody out, despite the Run Expectancy Matrix saying you don't gain an edge by giving up an out in that situation. You do crazy things for love.

Yost plays the platoon splits when going to his bullpen, even when there's evidence a certain platoon advantage doesn't exist. He also went to his bullpen more often than any manager in 2012, but with one of the worst rotations in the game, that was understandable. Still, most of his moves were automatic, predictable, and lacked imagination. When the Royals started slow in 2012 there were rumblings for his job, but Dayton Moore stood by his man. This year, with Moore's own job now on the line, it's unlikely the GM will show as much patience.

Los Angeles Angels of Anaheim

2012: TOTAL MAKEOVER

Has any team in our lifetimes been so desperate to make the postseason? Like a high-school student trying to get a prom date, the Angels underwent a total makeover—and still missed the prom. The Angels turned over almost their entire front office, signed two stars for more than $300 million before the season began, and at the trade deadline swapped the bulk of their farm system's upside for Zack Greinke. They also added a rookie who produced the best season in franchise history and made personnel upgrades at catcher and closer, yet still managed only three wins more than in 2011.

The additions of Albert Pujols, Mike Trout, Chris Iannetta, and Kendrys Morales gave the Angels the best offense in baseball, by True Average, and the team's defensive efficiency was tops in the American League. Surprisingly, it was the rotation—which included the previous year's second-, sixth-, and seventh-place Cy Young finishers—that doomed the Angels to third place. Jered Weaver was great but missed time. C.J. Wilson was healthy but collapsed in the second half. Dan Haren and fourth-starter Ervin Santana combined to allow nearly 50 more runs than PECOTA had projected. After the first week of the season, the Angels were never within two games of first place, the standings a continual reminder that there are no sure things when it comes to pitching.

In the end, was the Angels' problem that they weren't quite desperate enough? They started Trout in Triple-A, after all, letting Vernon Wells kick over the bulk of April's games in left field. After calling up Trout late in April, they actually outplayed the Rangers by four games, and were just a half-game worse than the division-champion Athletics. Alas, the decision to retain or reassign was taken out of the Angels' hands by the illness that felled Trout for most of spring training. The "what if" possibility probably never was.

Attendance, meanwhile, dropped for the second year in a row, despite the splashy signings and the jolt provided by Trout. The Angels hadn't drawn so few fans since 2003. After missing the playoffs again, they could be looking at even lower turnstile results. It's not just the prom, then: A makeover doesn't always make someone dateable.

ANGELS PROSPECTUS

2012 W-L: 89-73, 3rd in AL West

Pythag	.544	11th	DER	.723	1st
RS/G	4.73	4th	B-Age	28.7	19th
RA/G	4.31	16th	P-Age	29.8	27th
TAv	.283	1st	Salary	$155.0	4th
BRR	14.5	1st	M$/MW	$3.50	22nd
TAv-P	.266	21st	DL Days	752	21st
FIP	4.21	23rd	DL WARP	2.7	20th

Three-Year Park Factors	
Overall	94
HR/RH	94
HR/LH	92
AVG/RH	100
AVG/LH	95

Angel Stadium (1966)
Att. % of Capacity: 82.2% (11th)
Dim. 333, 386, 404, 386, 333

It's pretty clear that sluggers will overlook the Angels' park if enough dollars are dangled before them.

2013: SO CLOSE, TRY AGAIN

The Angels enter 2013 hoping to repeat much of the previous season's third-place performance. That team was a scant six wins worse than the league's best record, so the Angels don't need to consider a tear-down effort, despite missing the postseason for a third year in a row. They entered the offseason controlling the rights to every relevant member of the 2012 club's offense except Torii Hunter and Maicer Izturis. The departure of Hunter was, for the big-budget Angels, an opportunity, as they replaced his $18.5 million salary with a $25 million annual commitment to Josh Hamilton.

With three of their five starting pitchers hitting free agency or under undesirable club options, the Angels faced a paradox: They had a chance to purge themselves of the previous season's goats, but would be left with a severe pitching shortage. ("The food here is terrible, and such small portions, "Woody Allen might conclude.)

Meanwhile, some offensive regression can certainly be expected. Pujols's aging curve has been a dependable southbound line. Trout's season was so good that even an MVP-level follow-up could be inferior to his rookie campaign by three or four wins. As a unit the lineup stayed in great health, with just one lengthy injury (to Iannetta). No team can depend on such good health.

STATE OF THE ORGANIZATION: WIN NOW

The sacrifices required in the Angels' pursuit of a 2012 postseason berth could severely strain the team's ability to improve itself in the future—though they also helped the Angels build a big-league core that will stay together, and stay in a decent age window, for at least a few more years.

Pujols and Wilson each deferred loads of money in 2012 so the Angels could sign the other. Both players are due a raise in 2013, and bigger salary jumps in 2014 and beyond. The Angels spent a bit more than $150 million in 2012, and have already committed $110 million for seven players in 2015. It's hard to know where owner Arte Moreno's payroll limits are, and he has blown past them in the past to add players he covets when they've been available. But, assuming there is a limit well short of Dodgers/Yankees territory, the Angels will be hard-pressed to undertake any expensive renovations.

The inexpensive variety are also not likely to be an option. Trades for Haren (in 2010), Ernesto Frieri (in May 2012), and Greinke (at the 2012 trade deadline) have gutted the system. So too did the signings of Wilson and Pujols; the Angels' first pick didn't come until the third round in June, and the strategy of drafting advanced college kids who could move quickly to bolster the system comes at the expense of upside. There's one legit prospect in the system: Kaleb Cowart. The importance of the 2013-14 window is clear.

The Angels turned over much of their scouting and player development system in 2010 and '11. It's too soon to evaluate the new regime, which has shown a single-minded focus on college athletes in its first two drafts. The organization also took a hit just after the season ended when organizational elder Tom Kotchman resigned. Kotchman had been both a successful scout and short-season manager for the Angels for decades.

HITTERS

Erick Aybar **SS**
Born: **1/14/1984** Age: **29**
Bats: **B** Throws: **R** Height: **5' 11"**
Weight: **180** Breakout: **7%**
Improve: **44%** Collapse: **1%**
Attrition: **10%** MLB: **93%**

Comparables:
Rafael Furcal,Jason Bartlett,Brendan Ryan

YEAR	TEAM	LVL	AGE	PA	R	2B	3B	HR	RBI	BB	SO	SB	CS	AVG_OBP_SLG	TAv	BABIP	BRR	FRAA	WARP
2010	ANA	MLB	26	589	69	18	4	5	29	35	81	22	8	.253/.306/.330	.242	.289	5.7	SS(135): -2.5	1.7
2011	ANA	MLB	27	605	71	33	8	10	59	31	68	30	6	.279/.322/.421	.276	.301	4.4	SS(142): 3.3	3.7
2012	ANA	MLB	28	554	67	31	5	8	45	22	61	20	4	.290/.324/.416	.281	.316	1.2	SS(139): -5.6	2.4
2013	*ANA*	*MLB*	*29*	*530*	*63*	*24*	*6*	*6*	*43*	*25*	*66*	*20*	*5*	*.274/.315/.385*	*.256*	*.299*	*2*	*SS -7*	*1.7*

The Angels extended Aybar for four years on April 19, when he was hitting .190/.227/.262. Looked like a pretty slick extend-low moment for the Angels, but Aybar made them sweat a bit, as one month later he was hitting .197/.221/.250. Those six weeks polluted his seasonal line, but he ended up bettering the career-high TAv he put up in 2011. Aybar relies on a high BABIP to provide value, but he's not nearly so volatile as many similar players: He has enough power to homer without changing his approach, and enough speed to beat out 30 infield hits each year. FRAA knocks his glove work, but the Angels dispute that assessment more vigorously than most.

Peter Bourjos **CF**
Born: **3/31/1987** Age: **26**
Bats: **R** Throws: **R** Height: **6' 2"**
Weight: **185** Breakout: **2%**
Improve: **58%** Collapse: **7%**
Attrition: **17%** MLB: **94%**

Comparables:
Adam Jones,Rocco Baldelli,Ellis Burks

YEAR	TEAM	LVL	AGE	PA	R	2B	3B	HR	RBI	BB	SO	SB	CS	AVG_OBP_SLG	TAv	BABIP	BRR	FRAA	WARP
2010	SLC	AAA	23	455	85	13	12	13	52	24	78	27	5	.314/.363/.498	.297	.358	7.2	CF(96): 3.5, LF(4): 0.5	4.3
2010	ANA	MLB	23	193	19	6	4	6	15	6	40	10	3	.204/.237/.381	.228	.228	1.1	CF(51): 2.0	0.5
2011	ANA	MLB	24	552	72	26	11	12	43	32	124	22	9	.271/.327/.438	.284	.338	5.6	CF(147): -7.1	2.5
2012	ANA	MLB	25	195	27	7	0	3	19	15	44	3	1	.220/.291/.315	.235	.274	1.4	CF(90): 8.0	1.2
2013	*ANA*	*MLB*	*26*	*259*	*30*	*10*	*4*	*6*	*26*	*13*	*58*	*9*	*3*	*.250/.299/.397*	*.256*	*.299*	*1.1*	*CF 0, LF -0*	*0.9*

Given his glove—it can't be said enough that he's a generational talent in the outfield—how badly can Bourjos hit before he's a worse option than Vernon Wells? As it turns out, worse than .220/.291/.315, which left him with 1.2 WARP to Wells's 0.8. That's not to say Bourjos's season wasn't an undercarriage-scraping speed bump, and his inability to lay off or hit low breaking balls sounds like many a washout's sob story. But he did make some positive steps in his approach: He swung at fewer pitches outside the zone, and he made contact with more pitches inside it. He got two starts, and 15 plate appearances, in the last two months of the season, so it's clear the glove alone won't be enough for Mike Scioscia—no matter how generationally good it is.

Kole Calhoun OF

Born: 10/14/1987 **Age:** 25
Bats: L **Throws:** L **Height:** 5' 11"
Weight: 200 **Breakout:** 6%
Improve: 55% **Collapse:** 6%
Attrition: 10% **MLB:** 97%

Comparables:
Jim Nettles, Carl Yastrzemski, Ruppert Jones

YEAR	TEAM	LVL	AGE	PA	R	2B	3B	HR	RBI	BB	SO	SB	CS	AVG_OBP_SLG	TAv	BABIP	BRR	FRAA	WARP
2010	ORM	Rk	22	247	43	14	4	7	42	39	45	3	1	.292/.412/.505	.344	.344	1.1	RF(57): 0.4, LF(1): -0.0	2.6
2011	SBR	A+	23	594	94	36	6	22	99	73	96	20	10	.324/.410/.547	.329	.362	0	--	0.0
2012	SLC	AAA	24	463	79	30	7	14	73	44	88	12	3	.298/.369/.507	.275	.346	5.6	CF(47): 5.4, RF(28): -1.0	2.1
2012	ANA	MLB	24	25	2	1	0	0	1	2	6	1	0	.174/.240/.217	.180	.235	0.5	RF(14): 0.2, LF(4): -0.0	-0.1
2013	*ANA*	*MLB*	*25*	*250*	*25*	*10*	*2*	*5*	*26*	*21*	*62*	*3*	*1*	*.226/.294/.359*	*.242*	*.283*	*0.2*	*RF -1, CF -0*	*0.1*

When the Angels called Calhoun up in July, the flight from Reno to Newark required three transfers; Calhoun landed but his equipment bag didn't. Calhoun's trip from eighth-round pick to big leaguer went considerably more smoothly, as the Angels twice skipped him past a level, and he made his major-league debut not even two years after he was drafted. Salt Lake has produced some outlandish batting lines in the past, but offense was down there (and in the PCL generally) and Calhoun's numbers were the best on his team. Once considered a corner outfielder at best, he played center field 52 times for the Bees. That extra merit badge should get him plenty of flights back and forth as the sixth outfielder that the Angels stash in Triple-A. He got four such trips in 2012.

Alberto Callaspo 3B

Born: 4/19/1983 **Age:** 30
Bats: B **Throws:** R **Height:** 5' 10"
Weight: 195 **Breakout:** 1%
Improve: 37% **Collapse:** 3%
Attrition: 8% **MLB:** 93%

Comparables:
Edgardo Alfonzo, Maicer Izturis, Jeff Keppinger

YEAR	TEAM	LVL	AGE	PA	R	2B	3B	HR	RBI	BB	SO	SB	CS	AVG_OBP_SLG	TAv	BABIP	BRR	FRAA	WARP
2010	ANA	MLB	27	228	21	8	0	2	13	12	13	2	2	.249/.291/.315	.223	.256	1.8	3B(54): 4.8, LF(1): -0.0	0.4
2010	KCA	MLB	27	373	40	19	2	8	43	19	29	3	1	.275/.308/.410	.260	.278	-1.3	3B(76): -0.4, 2B(11): -1.0	0.9
2011	ANA	MLB	28	536	54	23	0	6	46	58	48	8	1	.288/.366/.375	.275	.310	-1	3B(129): 14.1	3.6
2012	ANA	MLB	29	520	55	20	0	10	53	56	59	4	3	.252/.331/.361	.271	.268	1.8	3B(131): 2.9	2.5
2013	*ANA*	*MLB*	*30*	*492*	*48*	*22*	*2*	*7*	*50*	*40*	*49*	*4*	*2*	*.270/.328/.380*	*.266*	*.287*	*-0.4*	*3B -2, 2B -0*	*1.2*

Since Jerry Dipoto took over as GM, the Angels have signed three position players to long extensions, signed two free agents to massive long-term deals, and handed full-time jobs to two players who aren't even arbitration eligible yet. That means two-thirds of the Angels' lineup is set for *2015*. But what about third base? Callaspo might reasonably wonder whether he has played himself up to the level of Howie Kendrick and Aybar, both of whom have produced fewer WARP in the past two seasons than he has. Callaspo set a career high in unintentional walks and continued to rate very well on advanced defensive metrics (though ours liked him more a year earlier). Alas, he's 29, which makes it more difficult to decide whether this is part of his growth or the end of his peak.

Hank Conger C

Born: 1/29/1988 **Age:** 25
Bats: B **Throws:** R **Height:** 6' 2"
Weight: 220 **Breakout:** 4%
Improve: 49% **Collapse:** 3%
Attrition: 11% **MLB:** 93%

Comparables:
Todd Zeile, Ted Simmons, Thurman Munson

YEAR	TEAM	LVL	AGE	PA	R	2B	3B	HR	RBI	BB	SO	SB	CS	AVG_OBP_SLG	TAv	BABIP	BRR	FRAA	WARP
2010	SLC	AAA	22	452	56	26	2	11	49	55	58	0	2	.300/.384/.463	.297	.325	-1.3	C(81): -1.4	3.1
2010	ANA	MLB	22	34	2	1	1	0	5	5	9	0	0	.172/.294/.276	.224	.250	-0.1	C(10): -0.1	-0.1
2011	SLC	AAA	23	114	14	4	0	5	26	12	18	0	0	.300/.375/.490	.304	.325	-1.2	C(13): -0.1	0.5
2011	ANA	MLB	23	197	14	8	0	6	19	17	37	0	0	.209/.282/.356	.244	.231	0.3	C(56): -0.5	0.2
2012	SLC	AAA	24	288	48	17	0	10	42	19	49	2	0	.295/.347/.473	.278	.329	2	C(47): 0.6	1.4
2012	ANA	MLB	24	22	0	0	0	0	1	1	0	0	0	.167/.238/.167	.165	.158	-0.2	C(7): 0.1	-0.2
2013	*ANA*	*MLB*	*25*	*250*	*25*	*11*	*1*	*6*	*28*	*20*	*47*	*0*	*0*	*.243/.306/.382*	*.254*	*.275*	*-0.4*	*C -1*	*0.9*

Conger posted his lowest OPS in three tries in the PCL, and if the losing margin was small, it showed up in the most troubling place: a walk rate that dropped from 12.2 percent in 2010 to 6.5 percent in 2012, and 5.6 percent in the second half. Conger's stalled development can't be blamed on just one factor. He is in exactly the wrong organization for a player with his skills, sure, but he also hasn't hit in the majors, doesn't have much durability, and throws poorly. But no matter which cause he himself focuses on, it would be a shame to see him sacrifice part of what made him special—his hitting approach—in an effort to force his way back up.

Scott Cousins OF

Born: 1/22/1985 **Age:** 28
Bats: L **Throws:** L **Height:** 6' 2"
Weight: 195 **Breakout:** 1%
Improve: 36% **Collapse:** 6%
Attrition: 18% **MLB:** 85%

Comparables:
Chris Aguila, Trent Oeltjen, Joel Youngblood

YEAR	TEAM	LVL	AGE	PA	R	2B	3B	HR	RBI	BB	SO	SB	CS	AVG_OBP_SLG	TAv	BABIP	BRR	FRAA	WARP
2010	NWO	AAA	25	451	74	20	5	14	49	32	78	12	4	.285/.339/.461	.284	.323	-2.8	CF(50): -5.4, RF(40): 4.4	2.0
2010	FLO	MLB	25	38	2	2	2	0	2	1	13	0	0	.297/.316/.459	.260	.458	-0.7	CF(8): 0.5, RF(3): -0.0	0.1
2011	FLO	MLB	26	58	5	1	0	1	4	6	21	1	1	.135/.224/.212	.182	.200	0	RF(12): 0.3, CF(5): 0.2	-0.3
2012	NWO	AAA	27	262	36	13	2	7	36	24	58	14	3	.296/.364/.459	.300	.365	1.6	RF(15): -1.9	0.3
2012	MIA	MLB	27	92	7	4	1	1	3	4	24	1	1	.163/.200/.267	.163	.213	-0.3	CF(18): 0.4, RF(12): -0.2	-0.7
2013	*ANA*	*MLB*	*28*	*250*	*25*	*10*	*2*	*5*	*25*	*14*	*63*	*6*	*2*	*.230/.277/.356*	*.235*	*.290*	*0.6*	*RF -0, CF -0*	*0.0*

Cousins may always be remembered for his home-plate collision with Buster Posey in May 2011, but the University of San Francisco product has the tools to emerge as a strong reserve outfielder and add a batch of less-grisly memories to the bank. Claimed by the Blue Jays in mid-October and the Mariners in early November before finally ending up with the Angels later the same month, Cousins is an excellent corner outfielder and has sufficient range to handle center. Together with a steady output at Triple-A New Orleans last year, that profile could land him his first extended stay in the majors at the age of 28, though he's on the wrong team if he hopes to start.

Kaleb Cowart 3B
Born: 6/2/1992 Age: 21
Bats: B Throws: R Height: 6' 4"
Weight: 190 Breakout: 3%
Improve: 63% Collapse: 8%
Attrition: 17% MLB: 98%
Comparables:
Ron Santo,Bob Bailey,Adrian Beltre

YEAR	TEAM	LVL	AGE	PA	R	2B	3B	HR	RBI	BB	SO	SB	CS	AVG_OBP_SLG	TAv	BABIP	BRR	FRAA	WARP
2011	ORM	Rk	19	319	49	12	3	7	40	25	81	11	4	.283/.345/.420	.268	.363	0	--	0.0
2012	CDR	A	20	290	42	16	3	9	54	22	44	9	4	.293/.348/.479	.285	.319	2.2	3B(17): 1.4	0.6
2012	SBR	A+	20	316	48	15	4	7	49	45	67	5	3	.259/.366/.426	.267	.316	-0.9	3B(15): 3.4	0.6
2013	*ANA*	*MLB*	*21*	*250*	*23*	*9*	*1*	*5*	*25*	*18*	*65*	*2*	*1*	*.218/.275/.339*	*.231*	*.275*	*-0.1*	*3B 2*	*0.0*

The best reason not to extend Callaspo was this 20-year-old holding his own in High-A in 2012. Cowart, a 2010 first-round pick, has just enough of each tool to be exciting, and the Angels hope he's the every-day third baseman by 2014. Scouts worry his long swing from the left side could be a liability as he faces higher-level velocity. The splits don't show it yet: Cowart hit .293 and slugged .408 against left-handers in 2012, and .269/.470 against right-handers.

C.J. Cron 1B
Born: 1/5/1990 Age: 23
Bats: R Throws: R Height: 6' 5"
Weight: 235 Breakout: 5%
Improve: 55% Collapse: 8%
Attrition: 9% MLB: 87%
Comparables:
Jim Spencer,Tony Horton,Joe Pepitone

YEAR	TEAM	LVL	AGE	PA	R	2B	3B	HR	RBI	BB	SO	SB	CS	AVG_OBP_SLG	TAv	BABIP	BRR	FRAA	WARP
2011	ORM	Rk	21	159	30	5	1	13	41	10	34	0	0	.308/.371/.629	.326	.320	0	--	0.0
2012	SBR	A+	22	557	73	32	2	27	123	17	72	3	4	.293/.327/.516	.355	.295	-5	1B(22): -1.2	0.9
2013	*ANA*	*MLB*	*23*	*250*	*24*	*10*	*1*	*9*	*32*	*3*	*49*	*0*	*0*	*.241/.257/.409*	*.243*	*.262*	*-0.4*	*1B -2*	*-0.4*

The day that the Angels signed Albert Pujols, 2011 first-round pick C.J. Cron became every Angels fan's trade bait of choice. One complication: Cron hasn't done enough to plump his value. While leading the California League in RBIs and finishing second in home runs, he was just 80th in OBP and 23rd in slugging, and he committed 19 errors in part-time play at first base. He resembles the High-A version of Mark Trumbo (.283/.329/.553 as a 22-year-old) more than anything. That cuts both ways; Trumbo's story turned out great, but he wasn't considered much of a prospect at the time. Cron probably shouldn't be, either.

Tommy Field SS
Born: 2/22/1987 Age: 26
Bats: R Throws: R Height: 5' 10"
Weight: 175 Breakout: 5%
Improve: 60% Collapse: 5%
Attrition: 24% MLB: 90%
Comparables:
Oswaldo Navarro,Ed Jurak,Bob Johnson

YEAR	TEAM	LVL	AGE	PA	R	2B	3B	HR	RBI	BB	SO	SB	CS	AVG_OBP_SLG	TAv	BABIP	BRR	FRAA	WARP
2010	MOD	A+	23	543	84	21	7	15	72	66	114	16	5	.284/.396/.466	.307	.344	1	SS(121): -1.5	4.6
2011	TUL	AA	24	544	77	22	3	17	61	53	108	9	4	.271/.357/.439	.249	.316	0.4	2B(59): 3.9, SS(19): -0.5	0.5
2011	COL	MLB	24	51	4	0	0	0	3	3	14	0	0	.271/.314/.271	.207	.382	0.7	SS(15): 1.1, RF(1): 0.0	0.0
2012	CSP	AAA	25	494	74	31	6	8	49	41	76	4	0	.246/.315/.400	.232	.279	3.8	SS(99): 2.3	0.4
2012	COL	MLB	25	3	0	0	0	0	0	1	1	0	0	.000/.333/.000	.179	.000	-0.1	2B(1): -0.0	0.0
2013	*ANA*	*MLB*	*26*	*250*	*26*	*9*	*2*	*4*	*20*	*19*	*59*	*2*	*1*	*.209/.279/.321*	*.226*	*.258*	*0*	*SS -1, 2B -0*	*0.1*

Field, the Rockies' 24th-round pick in 2008 out of Texas State (alma mater of Paul Goldschmidt and Scott Linebrink), has beaten the odds already by getting into 18 big-league games. The Angels' incumbent undersized utility man, Maicer Izturis, signed with Toronto early in the offseason, so Dipoto plucked this similarly small middle infielder off waivers. Field showed some pop in 2010-11, but the power disappeared after his promotion to hitter-friendly Colorado Springs in 2012. He could have a future as a utility infielder—as could any number of players with identical skills. If the diminutive Field sticks, he will be called "scrappy."

Randal Grichuk OF
Born: 8/13/1991 Age: 21
Bats: R Throws: R Height: 6' 2"
Weight: 195 Breakout: 3%
Improve: 52% Collapse: 9%
Attrition: 16% MLB: 98%
Comparables:
Lloyd Moseby,Ruben Sierra,Delmon Young

YEAR	TEAM	LVL	AGE	PA	R	2B	3B	HR	RBI	BB	SO	SB	CS	AVG_OBP_SLG	TAv	BABIP	BRR	FRAA	WARP
2010	ANG	Rk	18	52	7	3	2	4	10	3	9	0	0	.327/.365/.714	.402	.333	-0.9	RF(8): -0.3	0.6
2010	CDR	A	18	214	41	19	4	7	36	9	50	4	0	.292/.329/.530	.310	.359	0.9	RF(51): -0.2	1.6
2011	CDR	A	19	131	12	7	4	2	13	6	29	0	1	.230/.267/.402	.224	.280	0	--	0.0
2011	SBR	A+	19	57	13	4	2	1	6	0	13	0	0	.283/.316/.491	.268	.350	0	--	0.0
2012	SBR	A+	20	575	79	30	9	18	71	23	92	16	6	.298/.335/.488	.277	.329	3.4	RF(14): 1.4, CF(10): 1.5	1.3
2013	*ANA*	*MLB*	*21*	*250*	*23*	*11*	*2*	*7*	*28*	*4*	*60*	*2*	*1*	*.236/.251/.379*	*.232*	*.281*	*0.1*	*RF -1, CF -0*	*-0.3*

Grichuk has been around so long, and been linked to Mike Trout (who went one pick later) for so long, that he's got the sheen of disappointment muddying his image. But he was only 20 in 2012, and playing in a league where the average hitter was two years older. He stayed healthy for the first time and managed a pretty good batting line. (Just

Available on NOOK Video Starting 11/13/12
Julie's NOOK
Disney · PIXAR
BRAVE
THE
HOBBIT
J.R.R. TOLKIEN
75TH ANNIVERSARY
NOOK HD+
World's Lightest and
Lowest-Priced Full HD 9" Tablet*
NOOK HD
World's Best
7" Media Tablet
NOOK.com
Compared to devices available in the U.S. market as of October 8, 2012.
NOOK is a registered trademark of barnesandnoble.com llc or its affiliates. Screen images simulated. Content sold separately.
Brave © 2012 Disney/Pixar. All Rights Reserved. Rated PG.

pretty good: The Cal League's average hitter provided a 770 OPS.) Fifteen high-schoolers besides Grichuk were taken in the first round in 2009. One is Trout, but eight of the 15 have played no higher than High-A at this point, which means Grichuk isn't behind the curve. Yet.

Josh Hamilton OF

Born: **5/21/1981** Age: **32**
Bats: **L** Throws: **L** Height: **6' 5"**
Weight: **240** Breakout: **0%**
Improve: **28%** Collapse: **4%**
Attrition: **7%** MLB: **97%**

Comparables:
Andruw Jones,Willie Mays,Ken Griffey

YEAR	TEAM	LVL	AGE	PA	R	2B	3B	HR	RBI	BB	SO	SB	CS	AVG_OBP_SLG	TAv	BABIP	BRR	FRAA	WARP
2010	TEX	MLB	29	571	95	40	3	32	100	43	95	8	1	.359/.411/.633	.352	.390	0.9	LF(92): 3.7, CF(40): -1.5	7.9
2011	TEX	MLB	30	538	80	31	5	25	94	39	93	8	1	.298/.346/.536	.304	.317	-2	LF(85): 2.8, CF(35): 0.6	3.5
2012	TEX	MLB	31	636	103	31	2	43	128	60	162	7	4	.285/.354/.577	.307	.320	1.8	CF(95): -2.1, LF(82): 0.6	3.9
2013	*ANA*	*MLB*	*32*	*578*	*75*	*29*	*3*	*25*	*84*	*42*	*125*	*8*	*2*	*.280/.336/.490*	*.296*	*.321*	*0.1*	*LF 2, CF 0*	*3.9*

An entire book could be written about Hamilton's last calendar year. The highlights are as follows: February alcohol incident, historic first two months of the regular season, sudden fade down the stretch, capped by signing with a division rival. The 32-year-old outfielder slugged his way through May, posting an inhuman .360/.420/.764 slash line with 21 home runs in 207 plate appearances. In his last 429 trips, he dropped off to a mortal .245/.322/.487. For much of the second half, Hamilton was wildly flailing and saw his strikeout rate jump from 17.3 percent in 2011 to 25.5 percent last season. The true Hamilton lies somewhere in the middle. He's a legendarily talented player, aggressive to a fault at times and hounded by nagging injuries. Despite the peaks and valleys of 2012, he is an elite player. The question is how much longer he'll hold up, and whether he's part of the Angels' next run of success or an expensive impediment to it.

Brendan Harris INF

Born: **8/26/1980** Age: **32**
Bats: **R** Throws: **R** Height: **6' 2"**
Weight: **200** Breakout: **1%**
Improve: **36%** Collapse: **13%**
Attrition: **14%** MLB: **86%**

Comparables:
Scott Spiezio,Ramon Vazquez,Felipe Lopez

YEAR	TEAM	LVL	AGE	PA	R	2B	3B	HR	RBI	BB	SO	SB	CS	AVG_OBP_SLG	TAv	BABIP	BRR	FRAA	WARP
2010	ROC	AAA	29	258	31	14	1	4	29	14	41	1	0	.233/.295/.353	.220	.266	-1	3B(23): -1.9, SS(21): -1.6	-0.9
2010	MIN	MLB	29	120	11	3	0	1	4	9	23	0	0	.157/.233/.213	.180	.188	1.2	3B(27): 0.2, SS(11): -1.2	-0.5
2011	NOR	AAA	30	565	50	21	2	10	50	37	87	2	2	.225/.282/.331	.224	.251	2.5	SS(32): 0.3, 2B(26): -4.5	-0.6
2012	CSP	AAA	31	424	73	33	4	9	63	52	44	2	3	.317/.407/.507	.298	.334	2.3	3B(64): -3.4, 2B(9): 0.1	2.3
2013	*ANA*	*MLB*	*32*	*250*	*21*	*11*	*1*	*4*	*24*	*17*	*49*	*0*	*0*	*.232/.292/.336*	*.240*	*.275*	*-0.4*	*3B -1, SS -0*	*-0.1*

Harris, last seen doing nothing for the Twins in 2010, had fun at the expense of PCL pitchers last year. He has experience all over the infield but mostly played third base in 2012. Once upon a time, the Cubs drafted Harris two slots ahead of Ryan Howard and three ahead of C.J. Wilson. That same year, they drafted Mark Prior three slots ahead of Mark Teixeira. On the bright side, Harris's career has lasted longer than Prior's.

Chris Iannetta C

Born: **4/8/1983** Age: **30**
Bats: **R** Throws: **R** Height: **6' 1"**
Weight: **230** Breakout: **4%**
Improve: **48%** Collapse: **6%**
Attrition: **15%** MLB: **94%**

Comparables:
Johnny Romano,Dick Dietz,Chris Snyder

YEAR	TEAM	LVL	AGE	PA	R	2B	3B	HR	RBI	BB	SO	SB	CS	AVG_OBP_SLG	TAv	BABIP	BRR	FRAA	WARP
2010	CSP	AAA	27	76	17	7	0	5	21	10	10	0	0	.349/.453/.698	.334	.354	0.7	C(15): -0.1, 1B(1): -0.0	1.0
2010	COL	MLB	27	223	20	6	1	9	27	30	48	1	0	.197/.318/.383	.236	.212	-1.4	C(51): 0.6, 1B(3): 0.0	0.1
2011	COL	MLB	28	426	51	17	1	14	55	70	89	6	3	.238/.370/.414	.267	.276	-1	C(105): -0.1, 1B(2): -0.0	1.9
2012	ANA	MLB	29	253	27	6	1	9	26	29	60	1	3	.240/.332/.398	.269	.288	0.1	C(78): -0.5	1.2
2013	*ANA*	*MLB*	*30*	*276*	*34*	*10*	*1*	*10*	*33*	*35*	*65*	*2*	*1*	*.226/.337/.405*	*.274*	*.266*	*-0.5*	*C 0, 1B 0*	*1.7*

Surprise! Iannetta's defense was an issue, and if not quite the drama that Napoli & Mathis was, certainly a distraction. Iannetta actually does the basics capably, but Scioscia's concern for his backstops has always gone beyond mere pitch-blocking and throwing. Iannetta's inability to work effectively with his pitchers led to at least two sit-downs, one of which involved GM Dipoto. None of that stopped Scioscia from playing his better hitter, though, and Iannetta matched the second-best TAv of his career. He agreed to a three-year extension two days after the regular season ended. If you really want to turn a ballgame into a soap opera, you might note that Iannetta has become a pretty good bet to outlast Scioscia in the organization.

Luis Jimenez 3B

Born: **1/18/1988** Age: **25**
Bats: **R** Throws: **R** Height: **6' 2"**
Weight: **205** Breakout: **16%**
Improve: **54%** Collapse: **8%**
Attrition: **17%** MLB: **95%**

Comparables:
Brent Morel,Chris Johnson,Aramis Ramirez

YEAR	TEAM	LVL	AGE	PA	R	2B	3B	HR	RBI	BB	SO	SB	CS	AVG_OBP_SLG	TAv	BABIP	BRR	FRAA	WARP
2010	CDR	A	22	184	32	15	5	2	38	11	27	6	2	.292/.339/.476	.291	.338	2.2	3B(30): 3.3	1.8
2010	RCU	A+	22	344	52	31	4	12	43	13	43	15	8	.286/.323/.522	.290	.296	3.6	3B(47): 1.2	2.8
2011	ARK	AA	23	541	62	40	1	18	94	27	72	15	6	.290/.335/.486	.273	.303	0.9	3B(68): -3.7	1.1
2012	SLC	AAA	24	517	78	38	2	16	85	19	70	17	7	.309/.334/.495	.269	.331	-0.3	3B(101): 13.1	3.3
2013	*ANA*	*MLB*	*25*	*250*	*25*	*14*	*1*	*5*	*26*	*7*	*47*	*6*	*2*	*.242/.266/.377*	*.236*	*.275*	*0.3*	*3B 1*	*0.1*

Neither snow nor rain nor level nor ballpark can disrupt Jimenez's batting statistics. In four levels over the past three seasons, his OPS has reliably landed between .800 and .850. He doesn't strike out, he leads every team he's on in doubles, he's not particularly flashy nor reliable as a defender, and he'd rather not walk if that's okay with you. Without a spectacular offensive season, he won't have a full-time job handed to him, and he has never played a game in the United States anywhere but third base, so he doesn't bring much utility. He'll be lucky to get a pinch-hitting appearance or two before Cowart passes him on the organizational depth chart.

Howard Kendrick 2B

Born: **7/12/1983** Age: **29**
Bats: **R** Throws: **R** Height: **5' 11"**
Weight: **210** Breakout: **2%**
Improve: **51%** Collapse: **5%**
Attrition: **10%** MLB: **98%**

Comparables:
Felipe Lopez,Brandon Phillips,Ryne Sandberg

YEAR	TEAM	LVL	AGE	PA	R	2B	3B	HR	RBI	BB	SO	SB	CS	AVG_OBP_SLG	TAv	BABIP	BRR	FRAA	WARP
2010	ANA	MLB	26	658	67	41	4	10	75	28	94	14	4	.279/.313/.407	.268	.313	-2.7	2B(143): -10.4, 1B(15): 0.1	1.5
2011	ANA	MLB	27	583	86	30	6	18	63	33	119	14	6	.285/.338/.464	.286	.338	0.9	2B(108): 0.4, LF(23): -2.5	2.2
2012	ANA	MLB	28	594	57	32	3	8	67	29	115	14	6	.287/.325/.400	.265	.347	4.2	2B(143): 8.9, 1B(2): 0.0	3.0
2013	*ANA*	*MLB*	*29*	*556*	*59*	*31*	*4*	*11*	*60*	*26*	*103*	*13*	*5*	*.278/.318/.413*	*.269*	*.326*	*0.3*	*2B 1, LF 0*	*2.6*

The offseason buzz was all about how Kendrick—batting in front of Pujols—would get such a steady supply of fastballs that he'd finally win that batting title, the one we've mentioned in four of his previous BP annual comments (with increasing irony). The anticlimactic truth: Kendrick spent only 21 games batting in the two-hole, and when he did, he hit an un-buzzworthy .273/.297/.420. Still, after another strong second half—Kendrick has gained more than 50 points of OPS after the break in his career—he has plenty to brag about. Among second basemen, only Dustin Pedroia and Robinson Cano have a higher TAv in the past two years. FRAA finally bought into his defensive gains, which propelled him to a career-high WARP.

Taylor Lindsey 2B

Born: **12/2/1991** Age: **21**
Bats: **L** Throws: **R** Height: **6' 1"**
Weight: **195** Breakout: **3%**
Improve: **55%** Collapse: **8%**
Attrition: **12%** MLB: **96%**

Comparables:
Dalton Jones,Tim Foli,Bill Mazeroski

YEAR	TEAM	LVL	AGE	PA	R	2B	3B	HR	RBI	BB	SO	SB	CS	AVG_OBP_SLG	TAv	BABIP	BRR	FRAA	WARP
2010	ANG	Rk	18	211	26	12	6	0	18	12	33	8	3	.284/.325/.407	.286	.337	1	2B(45): 2.5	1.2
2011	ORM	Rk	19	307	64	28	6	9	46	13	46	10	4	.362/.394/.593	.330	.407	0	--	0.0
2012	SBR	A+	20	589	79	26	6	9	58	29	66	8	6	.289/.328/.408	.270	.313	-4.1	2B(23): 0.9	-0.4
2013	*ANA*	*MLB*	*21*	*250*	*19*	*10*	*2*	*3*	*21*	*6*	*47*	*1*	*0*	*.228/.250/.319*	*.212*	*.267*	*-0.2*	*2B -1*	*-0.5*

After batting better than .500 in his last two high-school seasons, .364 in short-season Orem in 2011, and .471 in big-league spring training in 2012, Lindsey finally heard that old "failing at his job seven out of 10 times" aphorism. The Angels skipped him past the Midwest League, putting him (briefly) on a faster pace than his highly touted draft classmate Kaleb Cowart. But despite the favors of the California League, Lindsey required twice as many plate appearances to match his 2011 counting stats. He was the second-youngest player on his team, so he earns a trophy for participation, but he is not very athletic and his arm is only adequate for second base. He will have to hit—really hit—to make an impact, and hopes that he could develop like a left-handed Kendrick are fading.

Albert Pujols 1B

Born: **1/16/1980** Age: **33**
Bats: **R** Throws: **R** Height: **6' 4"**
Weight: **230** Breakout: **1%**
Improve: **25%** Collapse: **3%**
Attrition: **7%** MLB: **96%**

Comparables:
Ted Kluszewski,Todd Helton,Lance Berkman

YEAR	TEAM	LVL	AGE	PA	R	2B	3B	HR	RBI	BB	SO	SB	CS	AVG_OBP_SLG	TAv	BABIP	BRR	FRAA	WARP
2010	SLN	MLB	30	700	115	39	1	42	118	103	76	14	4	.312/.414/.596	.340	.297	3.5	1B(157): 14.5	9.2
2011	SLN	MLB	31	651	105	29	0	37	99	61	58	9	1	.299/.366/.541	.312	.277	-0.9	1B(146): 13.3, 3B(7): 0.4	5.2
2012	ANA	MLB	32	670	85	50	0	30	105	52	76	8	1	.285/.343/.516	.307	.282	-3.2	1B(120): 6.8, 3B(3): -0.0	3.7
2013	*ANA*	*MLB*	*33*	*626*	*94*	*35*	*1*	*34*	*104*	*73*	*73*	*10*	*2*	*.299/.384/.554*	*.330*	*.290*	*0*	*1B 9, 3B 0*	*6.3*

PECOTA already wasn't a fan of the 10-year, $240 million contract the Angels gave Pujols. Over the life of the deal, it forecast 29 WARP for the first baseman; assuming $5 million per win and a generous 7 percent inflation, Pujols would be "worth" about $170 million. Having produced 3.7 WARP in 2012, he's now behind on two counts: nearly two and a half wins below expectations through year one, and now a lousier bet to uphold the other nine years of PECOTA's forecast (which, it should be noted, still expects him to lead the league in WARP in 2013). Pujols's career-low TAv marked a fourth consecutive year of decline. His career-low unintentional-walk rate is half what it was three years ago. Even his defense, while still good, is declining—from 31 runs above average in 2007 to seven runs in 2012. He's still one of the three best first basemen in the game, so it's not time to panic yet. But it will be, sooner than the Angels hoped.

Andrew Romine SS

Born: **12/24/1985** Age: **27**
Bats: **B** Throws: **R** Height: **6' 2"**
Weight: **190** Breakout: **2%**
Improve: **42%** Collapse: **19%**
Attrition: **22%** MLB: **93%**

Comparables:
Bill Russell,Al Pedrique,Phil Linz

YEAR	TEAM	LVL	AGE	PA	R	2B	3B	HR	RBI	BB	SO	SB	CS	AVG_OBP_SLG	TAv	BABIP	BRR	FRAA	WARP
2010	ARK	AA	24	453	55	15	4	3	34	50	66	21	9	.282/.361/.366	.272	.321	6.2	SS(103): 12.3	4.3
2010	ANA	MLB	24	12	0	0	0	0	0	0	4	0	0	.091/.091/.091	.083	.143	0.2	SS(4): -0.0	-0.1
2011	SLC	AAA	25	438	67	9	2	4	35	45	87	23	6	.281/.363/.346	.252	.355	0	SS(42): 1.6, 2B(15): 1.3	1.0
2011	ANA	MLB	25	18	2	0	0	0	0	1	6	1	0	.125/.176/.125	.164	.200	0.1	SS(7): 0.4, 3B(3): -0.0	-0.1
2012	SLC	AAA	26	388	57	11	7	4	39	24	46	23	10	.285/.336/.390	.263	.317	5	SS(56): -2.0, 3B(10): -0.4	1.7
2012	ANA	MLB	26	21	2	0	0	0	1	3	3	1	0	.412/.500/.412	.352	.500	0.2	SS(8): 0.2, 3B(1): -0.0	0.2
2013	*ANA*	*MLB*	*27*	*250*	*28*	*8*	*2*	*1*	*16*	*16*	*51*	*11*	*4*	*.236/.290/.303*	*.228*	*.288*	*0.8*	*SS 1, 3B -0*	*0.4*

When the Angels signed Aybar to a four-year extension, it appeared to be bad news for anybody on the middle-infield depth chart. But it might have been a blessing for Romine, who was never going to hit enough to earn a starting job, but who can walk, run, and certainly field well enough to challenge for a utility/bench role. That role is up for grabs, as Aybar's extension allowed the Angels to trade Jean Segura midseason. Romine is a very good defensive shortstop, but at Triple-A the Angels started him semi-regularly at third and second base to increase his utility to the big club.

J.B. Shuck OF

Born: **6/18/1987** Age: **26**
Bats: **L** Throws: **L** Height: **6' 0"**
Weight: **195** Breakout: **3%**
Improve: **55%** Collapse: **9%**
Attrition: **18%** MLB: **92%**

Comparables:
Mike Felder,Shannon Stewart,Chris Stynes

YEAR	TEAM	LVL	AGE	PA	R	2B	3B	HR	RBI	BB	SO	SB	CS	AVG_OBP_SLG	TAv	BABIP	BRR	FRAA	WARP
2010	CCH	AA	23	435	52	14	2	2	28	46	56	9	9	.298/.372/.360	.280	.344	-1.5	LF(53): -2.3, CF(46): -4.7	1.2
2010	ROU	AAA	23	156	15	2	2	0	7	16	15	7	3	.273/.346/.317	.259	.304	-2.2	CF(35): -7.5	-0.4
2011	OKL	AAA	24	419	60	11	7	0	30	56	30	20	11	.297/.398/.367	.284	.323	0	--	0.0
2011	HOU	MLB	24	92	9	2	1	0	3	11	7	2	0	.272/.359/.321	.243	.297	-0.2	RF(15): -0.0, CF(9): 0.7	0.0
2012	OKL	AAA	25	358	49	11	3	0	33	39	20	12	8	.298/.374/.352	.245	.316	3	LF(15): -0.0, CF(4): -0.2	-0.2
2013	*ANA*	*MLB*	*26*	*250*	*26*	*8*	*2*	*1*	*17*	*21*	*33*	*5*	*3*	*.261/.322/.325*	*.250*	*.298*	*-0.2*	*LF -1, CF -1*	*0.1*

Shuck has the hustle, personality, and baseball intellect to make him a "lifer." If he was a smidgen better at baseball, he'd not only be worthy of a bench spot, but perhaps a leadoff job. Unfortunately, the combined shortfall of being not quite fast enough, not quite rangy enough to be a full-time center fielder, and having almost no power is too much to overcome. He does have a very good batting eye, and has improved his contact rate to be among the best, but all that means is he'll spend a few more years working to remain among baseball's on-field personnel. He signed with the Angels in early November, when left-handed outfield depth seemed like a necessity; the addition of Hamilton a month later, though, probably made him grumble. "Shucks," he might have said. Or not.

Mike Trout CF

Born: **8/7/1991** Age: **21**
Bats: **R** Throws: **R** Height: **6' 2"**
Weight: **200** Breakout: **6%**
Improve: **63%** Collapse: **6%**
Attrition: **16%** MLB: **99%**

Comparables:
Ken Griffey,Jason Heyward,Justin Upton

YEAR	TEAM	LVL	AGE	PA	R	2B	3B	HR	RBI	BB	SO	SB	CS	AVG_OBP_SLG	TAv	BABIP	BRR	FRAA	WARP
2010	CDR	A	18	368	76	19	7	6	39	46	52	45	9	.362/.452/.526	.347	.418	7.2	CF(78): -2.2, LF(2): 0.1	5.3
2010	RCU	A+	18	232	30	9	2	4	19	27	33	11	6	.306/.384/.434	.319	.341	2.3	CF(58): -3.7, LF(3): 0.2	2.3
2011	ARK	AA	19	412	82	18	13	11	38	45	76	33	10	.326/.414/.544	.329	.390	4.1	CF(51): -1.0, LF(1): -0.0	2.6
2011	ANA	MLB	19	135	20	6	0	5	16	9	30	4	0	.220/.281/.390	.264	.247	0.8	CF(13): 0.9, RF(13): -0.3	0.4
2012	SLC	AAA	20	93	21	4	5	1	13	11	16	6	1	.403/.467/.623	.383	.476	-0.3	CF(8): -1.1, LF(3): 0.4	0.9
2012	ANA	MLB	20	639	129	27	8	30	83	67	139	49	5	.326/.399/.564	.357	.383	8.7	CF(110): 6.1, LF(67): 2.7	9.1
2013	*ANA*	*MLB*	*21*	*542*	*85*	*22*	*6*	*18*	*62*	*48*	*117*	*35*	*7*	*.289/.357/.473*	*.302*	*.342*	*4.4*	*CF -3, LF 0*	*4.1*

Readers of last year's annual saw this sentence: "Pay no attention to his forecast—there aren't enough [comparables] for PECOTA to get a good read." That was about Jamie Moyer, and the problem was age; we stand behind PECOTA's projection for Trout in 2013, but his age and performance are similarly unique. The best 20-year-old ever was Alex Rodriguez at 8.3 WARP; Trout produced 9.1—not including 0.9 from three weeks at Salt Lake. (His 90th percentile projection was 1.8 WARP.) Cabrera won the Triple Crown, but Trout nearly pulled off this far more impressive trifecta: He led the majors in True Average, was third in baserunning runs, and was fifth in defensive runs saved, according to the +/- system. Baseball is a game of adjustments—"I tell people, relax, the 1-for-30s are coming," his dad told a reporter in August—but so far Trout has adjusted just fine. The first time he saw a starting pitcher in a game, he hit .295 with 35 strikeouts and seven walks; he was far better the second time up, and by the third trip he was hitting .393 with 17 walks and 17 strikeouts.

Mark Trumbo **4C**

Born: **1/16/1986** Age: **27**
Bats: **R** Throws: **R** Height: **6' 5"**
Weight: **220** Breakout: **13%**
Improve: **59%** Collapse: **2%**
Attrition: **3%** MLB: **96%**

Comparables:
Wes Covington,Willie Horton,Albert Belle

YEAR	TEAM	LVL	AGE	PA	R	2B	3B	HR	RBI	BB	SO	SB	CS	AVG_OBP_SLG	TAv	BABIP	BRR	FRAA	WARP
2010	SLC	AAA	24	595	103	29	5	36	122	58	126	3	4	.301/.371/.577	.316	.335	-2.9	1B(97): -0.1, RF(22): 3.4	4.2
2010	ANA	MLB	24	16	2	0	0	0	2	1	8	0	0	.067/.125/.067	.068	.143	0.5	1B(6): 0.1, RF(1): -0.0	-0.2
2011	ANA	MLB	25	573	65	31	1	29	87	25	120	9	4	.254/.291/.477	.280	.274	1.3	1B(149): 2.1, RF(10): -0.1	1.9
2012	ANA	MLB	26	586	66	19	3	32	95	36	153	4	5	.268/.317/.491	.290	.316	-3.5	LF(66): -0.3, RF(35): -2.4	1.3
2013	*ANA*	*MLB*	*27*	*548*	*69*	*23*	*2*	*28*	*83*	*31*	*134*	*5*	*3*	*.259/.305/.477*	*.281*	*.296*	*-0.8*	*1B -3, LF 0*	*1.7*

After all the ups and downs (965 first-half OPS, 630 second-half), Trumbo ended 2012 within the margin of BABIP of his 2011 season, suggesting he's neither the MVP candidate Scioscia trumpeted nor the deeply flawed free-swinger statheads dismiss. He's still a free-swinger: The early-season chatter about his improving patience was just the hope of spring. He swung at 38 percent of pitches outside the zone, a small improvement from 2011 but also the 20th-highest rate in baseball among batters who saw a minimum of 1,000 pitches. If he can cut it a few more percentage points, he may be onto something, but endless tinkering can spiral into madness. In the second half, the Angels worried he was thinking himself into a deeper and deeper hole. At this point, it might be best for him (and everybody) to realize what he is: a good hitter, playing positions where good hitters are useful, if not special.

Vernon Wells **LF**

Born: **12/8/1978** Age: **34**
Bats: **R** Throws: **R** Height: **6' 2"**
Weight: **230** Breakout: **0%**
Improve: **22%** Collapse: **17%**
Attrition: **18%** MLB: **97%**

Comparables:
Jay Payton,Eric Byrnes,Al Oliver

YEAR	TEAM	LVL	AGE	PA	R	2B	3B	HR	RBI	BB	SO	SB	CS	AVG_OBP_SLG	TAv	BABIP	BRR	FRAA	WARP
2010	TOR	MLB	31	646	79	44	3	31	88	50	84	6	4	.273/.331/.515	.286	.272	-0.6	CF(151): -3.7	3.6
2011	ANA	MLB	32	529	60	15	4	25	66	20	86	9	4	.218/.248/.412	.247	.214	-1.4	LF(111): 8.1, CF(12): 0.0	0.6
2012	ANA	MLB	33	262	36	9	0	11	29	16	35	3	1	.230/.279/.403	.256	.226	3.1	LF(69): 4.6, CF(6): -0.4	0.8
2013	*ANA*	*MLB*	*34*	*304*	*34*	*13*	*1*	*10*	*37*	*17*	*44*	*5*	*2*	*.249/.291/.411*	*.261*	*.260*	*0.1*	*LF 3, CF -1*	*1.1*

Wells showed up to spring training with a surprise: He had been working with well-regarded hitting instructor Rudy Jaramillo and had rebuilt his swing almost from scratch. "I finally have a load in my swing, which will be fun," he said, pledging to get more power from a shorter swing and laying off bad pitches. Great plan! Until, oh, almost immediately upon starting game action that spring, he scrapped that approach and reverted to his old one. We used to say Wells wasn't a bad player, just an overpaid one; now we'll say he's not a totally worthless player, just a bad one. He's got enough power to be a useful pinch-hitter, can play center field in a pinch, and that's about it. Even a platoon is probably out of the question. He has an uninspiring .250/.305/.453 line against lefties the past three years. Two years, $42 million left.

Travis Witherspoon **CF**

Born: **4/16/1989** Age: **24**
Bats: **R** Throws: **R** Height: **6' 3"**
Weight: **190** Breakout: **3%**
Improve: **57%** Collapse: **0%**
Attrition: **6%** MLB: **94%**

Comparables:
Shane Mack,Dave Martinez,Bruce Boisclair

YEAR	TEAM	LVL	AGE	PA	R	2B	3B	HR	RBI	BB	SO	SB	CS	AVG_OBP_SLG	TAv	BABIP	BRR	FRAA	WARP
2010	ORM	Rk	21	323	57	11	3	10	45	24	73	20	0	.309/.357/.472	.317	.371	5.6	CF(74): 2.7	3.7
2011	CDR	A	22	450	60	16	4	12	42	36	103	44	9	.245/.312/.394	.246	.298	0	--	0.0
2011	SBR	A+	22	74	15	4	0	1	10	5	14	2	2	.279/.338/.382	.256	.340	0	--	0.0
2012	SBR	A+	23	306	52	10	5	7	27	33	52	25	7	.319/.399/.470	.481	.374	0.7	CF(11): 1.4	1.6
2012	ARK	AA	23	235	28	9	2	6	21	24	54	9	4	.202/.286/.351	.258	.242	-0.3	CF(45): 0.6	0.3
2013	*ANA*	*MLB*	*24*	*250*	*29*	*8*	*1*	*5*	*21*	*16*	*66*	*8*	*2*	*.215/.268/.329*	*.224*	*.272*	*0.9*	*CF -3*	*-0.4*

The toolsy center fielder had his breakout campaign and reached the level of his incompetence in the same season. In his second exposure to the California League, his power played up and he torched the league with a .374 batting average on balls in play, echoing his strong 2010 season, when he was repeating in the high-offense Pioneer League. All that progress vanished after a June promotion to Arkansas, as the swing-and-miss in his game returned and his speed failed to spook superior defenders. He'll get another shot at conquering Double-A in 2013, but, on the verge of turning 24, he has all of Bourjos's faults with only a fraction of the success.

PITCHERS

R.J. Alvarez

Born: **6/8/1991** Age: **22**
Bats: **R** Throws: **R** Height: **6' 2"** Weight: **180**
Breakout: **17%** Improve: **45%** Collapse: **35%**
Attrition: **21%** MLB: **77%**

Comparables:
Reggie Harris,Phil Paine,Ryan Wagner

YEAR	TEAM	LVL	AGE	W	L	SV	G	GS	IP	H	HR	BB	SO	BB9	SO9	GB%	BABIP	WHIP	ERA	FIP	FRA	WARP
2012	CDR	A	21	3	2	0	23	0	27^{1}	22	2	11	38	3.6	12.5	56%	.250	1.21	3.29	3.28	1.81	0.2
2013	*ANA*	*MLB*	*22*	*1*	*0*	*1*	*24*	*0*	33^{2}	*36*	*4*	*16*	*26*	*4.2*	*6.8*	*46%*	*.306*	*1.53*	*5.11*	*4.63*	*5.55*	*-0.2*

When they signed Pujols and Wilson, the Angels also bought themselves an extra day of paid vacation in mid-June. On day two of the draft, with the 112th overall pick, they finally got to Alvarez, a college reliever with a mid-90s fastball and a hard, effective slider, but so-so command and a jerky, wide-open pitching motion. Alvarez reflected the Angels' draft strategy of picking college players who would give the system some quick depth, and he is expected to advance rapidly. Fun note: In 37 fielding chances in college, he committed nine errors.

Cameron Bedrosian

Born: **10/2/1991** Age: **21**
Bats: **R** Throws: **R** Height: **6' 1"** Weight: **205**
Breakout: **35%** Improve: **62%** Collapse: **11%**
Attrition: **8%** MLB: **83%**

Comparables:
Jon Garland, Gene Nelson, Gil Meche

YEAR	TEAM	LVL	AGE	W	L	SV	G	GS	IP	H	HR	BB	SO	BB9	SO9	GB%	BABIP	WHIP	ERA	FIP	FRA	WARP
2012	CDR	A	20	3	11	0	21	21	82^{2}	91	5	52	48	5.7	5.2	47%	.319	1.73	6.31	5.15	9.54	-0.3
2013	*ANA*	*MLB*	*21*	*1*	*3*	*0*	*8*	*8*	*31^{1}*	*38*	*4*	*20*	*14*	*5.6*	*4.0*	*45%*	*.307*	*1.84*	*6.65*	*5.88*	*7.23*	*-0.6*

Nearly two years after being drafted in the first round, Steve's son finally made his full-season debut in May. He threw 4 1/3 hitless innings before reaching his pitch count in that first start, but that was as good as it got. His ERA in his next 20 starts? A non-angelic 6.66. The mid-90s velocity returned, but his control didn't. Walks weren't the end of the story: He also threw 15 wild pitches and hit eight batters in 82 innings. The few nights he got his curve over, he was unhittable, so the Angels are optimistic he will take a big step forward this year.

Joe Blanton

Born: **12/11/1980** Age: **32**
Bats: **R** Throws: **R** Height: **6' 4"** Weight: **245**
Breakout: **16%** Improve: **41%** Collapse: **32%**
Attrition: **20%** MLB: **81%**

Comparables:
Larry Jansen, Kevin Tapani, Rodrigo Lopez

YEAR	TEAM	LVL	AGE	W	L	SV	G	GS	IP	H	HR	BB	SO	BB9	SO9	GB%	BABIP	WHIP	ERA	FIP	FRA	WARP
2010	LWD	A	29	0	0	0	1	1	2	0	0	0	2	0.0	9.0	1.%	.000	0.00	0.00	1.53	2.90	0.0
2010	REA	AA	29	0	1	0	2	2	8	9	2	2	5	2.2	5.6	53%	.176	1.38	5.62	6.11	7.97	0.0
2010	PHI	MLB	29	9	6	0	29	28	175^{2}	206	27	43	134	2.2	6.9	43%	.321	1.42	4.82	4.36	4.80	0.6
2011	LWD	A	30	0	0	0	1	1	1	0	0	0	0	0.0	0.0	33%	.000	0.00	0.00	3.53	4.57	0.0
2011	PHI	MLB	30	1	2	0	11	8	41^{1}	52	5	9	35	2.0	7.6	58%	.362	1.48	5.01	3.60	4.19	0.1
2012	LAN	MLB	31	2	4	0	10	10	57^{2}	66	7	16	51	2.5	8.0	49%	.343	1.42	4.99	3.78	4.57	0.5
2012	PHI	MLB	31	8	9	0	21	20	133^{1}	141	22	18	115	1.2	7.8	45%	.296	1.19	4.59	4.03	4.21	0.8
2013	*ANA*	*MLB*	*32*	*7*	*8*	*0*	*22*	*22*	*131*	*143*	*18*	*30*	*98*	*2.0*	*6.7*	*45%*	*.306*	*1.31*	*4.45*	*4.18*	*4.83*	*0.1*

After missing most of 2011 due to elbow impingement, Blanton returned to regular duty and put up one of the season's stranger pitching lines, with the league's third-lowest walk rate accompanied by its second-highest homer rate. Even given that odd combination, his ERA was far above what his peripherals would have suggested, in part because he was pummeled with men in scoring position (.300/.343/.480, driven by a searing .348 BABIP). Blanton is not a bad back-of-the-rotation starter, but if anything, he throws too many strikes, or at least too many on the fat part of the plate. Throwing 200 innings would be his best contribution to an Angels postseason run; hopefully they'll have better options for the October rotation.

Sean Burnett

Born: **9/17/1982** Age: **30**
Bats: **L** Throws: **L** Height: **6' 2"** Weight: **200**
Breakout: **38%** Improve: **60%** Collapse: **14%**
Attrition: **5%** MLB: **89%**

Comparables:
Craig Breslow, Pedro Feliciano, Dave Righetti

YEAR	TEAM	LVL	AGE	W	L	SV	G	GS	IP	H	HR	BB	SO	BB9	SO9	GB%	BABIP	WHIP	ERA	FIP	FRA	WARP
2010	WAS	MLB	27	1	7	3	73	0	63	52	3	20	62	2.9	8.9	56%	.280	1.14	2.14	2.76	2.87	1.3
2011	WAS	MLB	28	5	5	4	69	0	56^{2}	54	6	21	33	3.3	5.2	56%	.268	1.32	3.81	4.48	5.14	-0.1
2012	WAS	MLB	29	1	2	2	70	0	56^{2}	58	4	12	57	1.9	9.1	60%	.331	1.24	2.38	2.84	3.12	1.0
2013	*ANA*	*MLB*	*30*	*3*	*1*	*3*	*59*	*0*	*49^{1}*	*44*	*5*	*17*	*43*	*3.1*	*7.9*	*52%*	*.283*	*1.25*	*3.47*	*3.81*	*3.77*	*0.6*

In two of the past three seasons, Burnett has been one of the best relievers in baseball, and he throws left-handed to boot. Those two seasons sandwiched one of the age's most mysterious outliers, as he lost nearly four strikeouts per nine while allowing more walks and home runs. What's particularly vexing is how hard it is to explain the 2011 drop. He wasn't hurt, so far as we know (though note his recent bone-spur-removal surgery). His fastball velocity was actually a career high, and he had better control (by rate of pitches in the zone). Being unable to explain it means being unable to say that those struggles won't reappear, but perhaps that's being too gloomy. The Angels got a pitcher who gets groundballs, makes batters chase, and has just turned 30 for a mere $8 million over two years. Odds aren't bad that he turns out to be the best reliever in that bullpen.

David Carpenter

Born: **9/1/1987** Age: **25**
Bats: **R** Throws: **R** Height: **6' 4"** Weight: **180**
Breakout: **33%** Improve: **57%** Collapse: **24%**
Attrition: **11%** MLB: **84%**

Comparables:
Billy Koch, Edgmer Escalona, Mauro Zarate

YEAR	TEAM	LVL	AGE	W	L	SV	G	GS	IP	H	HR	BB	SO	BB9	SO9	GB%	BABIP	WHIP	ERA	FIP	FRA	WARP
2011	SBR	A+	23	0	1	11	25	0	29	23	1	9	36	2.8	11.2	—	.310	1.10	0.93	2.95	3.21	0.0
2011	ARK	AA	23	1	0	5	19	0	18^{2}	12	0	5	16	2.4	7.7	67%	.273	0.91	0.00	2.63	3.63	0.3
2012	SLC	AAA	24	0	0	1	15	0	19^{2}	10	2	8	14	3.7	6.4	49%	.157	0.92	2.75	4.94	6.90	-0.1
2012	ANA	MLB	24	1	2	0	28	0	39^{2}	42	6	17	28	3.9	6.4	45%	.300	1.49	4.76	4.89	5.34	-0.3
2013	*ANA*	*MLB*	*25*	*1*	*0*	*0*	*27*	*0*	*34^{2}*	*34*	*4*	*15*	*27*	*3.8*	*7.1*	*49%*	*.295*	*1.42*	*4.53*	*4.44*	*4.92*	*-0.1*

"Stuff doesn't match his stats" isn't something you tend to hear at the major-league level. If a pitcher's stats continue to shine in the bigs, nobody cares about his stuff. If the stats don't hold? That's why this qualifier is important when talking about minor-league relief prospects like Carpenter. His 0.57 ERA between High-A and Double-A in 2011 looks good, but his sinker-slider combo lacks the velocity for the upper levels. More troubling than his mediocre big-league stats are the mediocre Triple-A stats: Pretty ERA aside, he missed few bats in Salt Lake and saw his grounder-to-fly ratio drop from 2.10 in 2011 to 1.20.

Scott Downs
Born: **3/17/1976** Age: **37**
Bats: **L** Throws: **L** Height: **6' 3"** Weight: **210**
Breakout: **17%** Improve: **56%** Collapse: **34%**
Attrition: **9%** MLB: **83%**
Comparables:
Mike Stanton, Brian Shouse, Buddy Groom

YEAR	TEAM	LVL	AGE	W	L	SV	G	GS	IP	H	HR	BB	SO	BB9	SO9	GB%	BABIP	WHIP	ERA	FIP	FRA	WARP
2010	TOR	MLB	34	5	5	0	67	0	61^{1}	47	3	14	48	2.1	7.0	59%	.256	0.99	2.64	3.00	3.62	0.9
2011	SBR	A+	35	1	1	0	2	1	2	5	0	1	1	4.5	4.5	—	.500	3.00	9.00	4.45	4.84	0.0
2011	ANA	MLB	35	6	3	1	60	0	53^{2}	39	3	15	35	2.5	5.9	64%	.218	1.01	1.34	3.32	4.25	0.2
2012	ANA	MLB	36	1	1	9	57	0	45^{2}	43	3	17	32	3.4	6.3	61%	.282	1.31	3.15	3.62	4.61	0.0
2013	*ANA*	*MLB*	*37*	*3*	*1*	*2*	*48*	*0*	*41^{2}*	*38*	*3*	*12*	*32*	*2.7*	*7.0*	*58%*	*.283*	*1.21*	*3.30*	*3.46*	*3.59*	*0.6*

Scioscia has never been big on carrying a lefty specialist. In 13 years with Scioscia as manager, only four lefties have pitched at least 40 games for the Angels while averaging less than an inning per appearance: Mike Holtz, in Scioscia's first year; J.C. Romero, who rewarded Scioscia with a 6.70 ERA; Brian Fuentes, who doesn't fit the form, as he was actually the closer; and Downs, the exception that proves the rule. Lefties have slugged .250 or worse against Downs in each of the past three seasons. Increasingly, Scioscia uses him for matchups instead of full innings, but he'll never limit Downs to mere LOOGY work. In 2012 Downs matched his career high with nine saves.

Barry Enright
Born: **3/30/1986** Age: **27**
Bats: **R** Throws: **R** Height: **6' 4"** Weight: **220**
Breakout: **32%** Improve: **66%** Collapse: **10%**
Attrition: **18%** MLB: **82%**
Comparables:
Sidney Ponson, David Huff, Doug Waechter

YEAR	TEAM	LVL	AGE	W	L	SV	G	GS	IP	H	HR	BB	SO	BB9	SO9	GB%	BABIP	WHIP	ERA	FIP	FRA	WARP
2010	MOB	AA	24	4	1	0	14	14	93^{2}	81	9	15	83	1.4	8.0	40%	.281	1.02	2.88	3.50	4.48	1.5
2010	ARI	MLB	24	6	7	0	17	17	99	97	20	29	49	2.6	4.5	37%	.248	1.27	3.91	5.65	5.68	0.4
2011	RNO	AAA	25	9	5	0	21	21	122^{2}	127	20	42	86	3.1	6.3	—	.291	1.38	5.21	5.65	6.14	0.0
2011	ARI	MLB	25	1	4	0	7	7	37^{2}	50	11	15	21	3.6	5.0	40%	.307	1.73	7.41	6.95	7.19	-0.6
2012	RNO	AAA	26	8	6	0	21	21	110^{1}	118	19	51	72	4.2	5.9	38%	.294	1.53	5.87	6.04	10.87	-0.1
2012	SLC	AAA	26	5	1	0	8	8	52^{2}	42	3	19	30	3.2	5.1	37%	.247	1.16	2.73	4.46	6.18	0.2
2012	ANA	MLB	26	0	0	0	3	0	3^{2}	7	1	1	0	2.5	0.0	26%	.333	2.18	14.73	7.41	9.11	-0.2
2013	*ANA*	*MLB*	*27*	*3*	*3*	*0*	*9*	*9*	*50*	*55*	*8*	*15*	*30*	*2.8*	*5.3*	*40%*	*.289*	*1.40*	*4.93*	*4.98*	*5.36*	*-0.2*

Every team picks up spare veteran starters to stock the Triple-A rotation. Usually they just fill innings, though in case of catastrophe an appearance with the big-league club could happen. Dipoto has skewed younger than most with his rotation fillers: Eric Hurley, Brad Mills, Greg Smith, and now Enright. The Angels picked him up during the waiver-trade period, and he cut three runs from his ERA despite leaving his poor peripherals intact. Enright's guts and guile seem to have topped out in Double-A, but Dipoto knows him well from his time in Arizona, so if he's vouching for the guy it's not irrelevant.

Ernesto Frieri
Born: **7/19/1985** Age: **27**
Bats: **R** Throws: **R** Height: **6' 3"** Weight: **200**
Breakout: **19%** Improve: **71%** Collapse: **13%**
Attrition: **8%** MLB: **92%**
Comparables:
Dick Selma, Francisco Cruceta, Tyler Clippard

YEAR	TEAM	LVL	AGE	W	L	SV	G	GS	IP	H	HR	BB	SO	BB9	SO9	GB%	BABIP	WHIP	ERA	FIP	FRA	WARP
2010	POR	AAA	24	3	1	17	34	0	37^{2}	14	2	18	49	4.3	11.7	20%	.164	0.85	1.43	3.27	3.69	0.5
2010	SDN	MLB	24	1	1	0	33	0	31^{2}	18	2	17	41	4.8	11.7	24%	.235	1.11	1.71	2.95	2.86	0.6
2011	TUC	AAA	25	1	0	0	4	0	3^{1}	3	0	2	5	5.4	13.5	25%	.500	1.50	2.70	2.58	2,07	0.1
2011	SDN	MLB	25	1	2	0	59	0	63	51	3	34	76	4.9	10.9	24%	.312	1.35	2.71	3.25	2.77	1.1
2012	ANA	MLB	26	4	2	23	56	0	54^{1}	26	7	26	80	4.3	13.3	27%	.188	0.96	2.32	3.49	3.50	0.9
2012	SDN	MLB	26	1	0	0	11	0	11^{2}	9	2	4	18	3.1	13.9	27%	.292	1.11	2.31	3.82	3.90	0.0
2013	*ANA*	*MLB*	*27*	*3*	*1*	*4*	*54*	*0*	*55^{1}*	*46*	*6*	*23*	*60*	*3.7*	*9.7*	*30%*	*.282*	*1.25*	*3.64*	*3.69*	*3.96*	*0.6*

By the time Frieri allowed a hit as an Angel, he had faced 52 batters. By the time he allowed a run, he had pitched 26 innings. Nobody makes pitching look as simple as Frieri does: He throws almost all fastballs, nearly all aimed at the same quadrant, up and away to lefties and up and in to righties. There's some downside to this relentlessness. He had the third-lowest groundball rate in baseball (minimum 50 innings), and the lack of a different look makes his wild ones comparably easy to take. But every pitcher has imperfections, few have the ability to blow hitters away like Frieri.

Steven Geltz

Born: 11/1/1987 **Age:** 25
Bats: **R** Throws: **R** Height: **5' 11"** Weight: **170**
Breakout: **24%** Improve: **43%** Collapse: **29%**
Attrition: **13%** MLB: **89%**

Comparables:
Fernando Cabrera,Sammy Gervacio,Jim York

YEAR	TEAM	LVL	AGE	W	L	SV	G	GS	IP	H	HR	BB	SO	BB9	SO9	GB%	BABIP	WHIP	ERA	FIP	FRA	WARP
2010	RCU	A+	22	3	1	2	22	0	34	20	4	10	51	2.6	13.5	43%	.242	0.88	3.44	3.41	3.26	0.8
2010	ARK	AA	22	1	0	0	16	0	18^2	9	0	16	36	7.7	17.3	35%	.346	1.34	2.41	2.05	2.88	0.4
2011	ARK	AA	23	3	3	0	32	0	46^2	31	5	14	67	2.7	12.9	22%	.286	0.96	3.09	2.86	2.50	1.0
2011	SLC	AAA	23	0	0	0	2	0	1^2	4	0	2	1	10.8	5.4	40%	.800	3.60	21.60	6.18	6.94	0.0
2012	ARK	AA	24	3	0	6	21	0	25^1	13	0	6	37	2.1	13.1	31%	.250	0.75	0.36	1.19	1.38	0.8
2012	SLC	AAA	24	0	1	5	25	0	33^2	29	4	14	33	3.7	8.8	34%	.284	1.28	5.08	4.68	6.16	0.1
2012	ANA	MLB	24	0	0	0	2	0	2	2	0	3	1	13.5	4.5	29%	.286	2.50	4.50	6.55	6.86	-0.1
2013	*ANA*	*MLB*	*25*	*1*	*1*	*1*	*27*	*0*	*35^1*	*30*	*4*	*17*	*40*	*4.3*	*10.3*	*35%*	*.299*	*1.33*	*3.79*	*3.85*	*4.12*	*0.3*

In 2008, just after going undrafted out of the University of Buffalo, Geltz signed with the Angels and joined their rookie-ball team in Arizona. Check his player page online and you'll see Geltz's SO9: 27.0. Sure, it was only 2 1/3 innings, but in the slow climb from undrafted free agent to the majors, Geltz has always struck batters out: 12.3 per nine in short-season ball, 11.3 in High-A, 13.9 in Double-A. He's a short righty, so instead of hopelessly trying to achieve downhill plane, he throws almost uphill, giving his four-seam fastball "rise." That trajectory also makes him one of the most extreme fly-ball pitchers in the sport, and Geltz will allow more home runs than a high-leverage reliever should. His first half, in Arkansas, was the best stretch of his career; his second half, in Salt Lake, was the worst.

Tommy Hanson

Born: 8/28/1986 **Age:** 26
Bats: **R** Throws: **R** Height: **6' 7"** Weight: **220**
Breakout: **24%** Improve: **56%** Collapse: **19%**
Attrition: **16%** MLB: **98%**

Comparables:
Josh Beckett,Yovani Gallardo,Ervin Santana

YEAR	TEAM	LVL	AGE	W	L	SV	G	GS	IP	H	HR	BB	SO	BB9	SO9	GB%	BABIP	WHIP	ERA	FIP	FRA	WARP
2010	ATL	MLB	23	10	11	0	34	34	202^2	182	14	56	173	2.5	7.7	43%	.286	1.17	3.33	3.33	3.90	3.3
2011	ATL	MLB	24	11	7	0	22	22	130	106	17	46	142	3.2	9.8	41%	.268	1.17	3.60	3.64	4.16	0.7
2012	GWN	AAA	25	1	0	0	1	1	5	3	0	2	5	3.6	9.0	50%	.250	1.00	0.00	2.36	2.10	0.0
2012	ATL	MLB	25	13	10	0	31	31	174^2	183	27	71	161	3.7	8.3	42%	.314	1.45	4.48	4.61	4.96	-0.2
2013	*ANA*	*MLB*	*26*	*8*	*8*	*0*	*24*	*24*	*140^1*	*125*	*16*	*42*	*134*	*2.7*	*8.6*	*40%*	*.285*	*1.19*	*3.49*	*3.67*	*3.79*	*1.9*

Hanson spent last offseason reworking his delivery to prevent shoulder damage. Mission accomplished, as he remained healthy throughout the year. If baseball were only about staying healthy you could call Hanson's season a success. Unfortunately, his performance worsened across the board: His peripherals declined, his outings shortened, and his start-to-start quality became more erratic. It's easy to wonder if the mechanical change led to a deterioration of stuff, but blaming the injuries seems like a more reasonable explanation. Hanson was supposed to become a franchise cornerstone in Atlanta. Traded to the Angels for reliever Jordan Walden, he'll try to rebuild his career in Anaheim.

LaTroy Hawkins

Born: 12/21/1972 **Age:** 40
Bats: **R** Throws: **R** Height: **6' 6"** Weight: **220**
Breakout: **23%** Improve: **44%** Collapse: **17%**
Attrition: **11%** MLB: **71%**

Comparables:
Darren Oliver,David Weathers,Mike Timlin

YEAR	TEAM	LVL	AGE	W	L	SV	G	GS	IP	H	HR	BB	SO	BB9	SO9	GB%	BABIP	WHIP	ERA	FIP	FRA	WARP
2010	BRR	Rk	37	0	0	0	2	2	3^2	4	0	0	5	0.0	12.2	60%	.400	1.08	2.43	1.55	2.50	0.2
2010	NAS	AAA	37	0	0	1	4	0	6^1	4	0	0	1	0.0	1.4	52%	.190	0.63	0.00	3.27	4.76	0.1
2010	MIL	MLB	37	0	3	0	18	0	16	21	2	6	18	3.4	10.1	48%	.413	1.69	8.44	3.98	5.97	-0.1
2011	BRV	A+	38	0	0	0	3	0	3^2	6	1	0	5	0.0	12.3	—	.500	1.64	4.91	4.21	4.57	0.0
2011	NAS	AAA	38	0	0	0	2	0	1^1	1	0	2	1	13.5	6.8	67%	.333	2.25	0.00	6.78	4.04	0.0
2011	MIL	MLB	38	3	1	0	52	0	48^1	50	1	10	28	1.9	5.2	63%	.297	1.24	2.42	2.73	3.93	0.5
2012	SBR	A+	39	0	0	0	1	0	1	2	1	0	2	0.0	18.0	33%	.500	2.00	9.00	12.81	11.79	0.0
2012	SLC	AAA	39	0	0	0	2	1	2	1	0	1	1	4.5	4.5	50%	.167	1.00	0.00	4.17	4.17	0.0
2012	ANA	MLB	39	2	3	1	48	0	42	45	5	13	23	2.8	4.9	58%	.292	1.38	3.64	4.43	5.42	-0.3
2013	*ANA*	*MLB*	*40*	*2*	*1*	*1*	*42*	*0*	*38^2*	*39*	*4*	*11*	*27*	*2.5*	*6.3*	*52%*	*.294*	*1.28*	*3.75*	*4.00*	*4.08*	*0.3*

While pitching for eight teams in the past eight years, Hawkins has provided a lesson on a relief pitcher's small-sample volatility. The Astros loved the guy who struck out 7.5 per nine innings with a 1.71 ERA; the Orioles have already forgotten the guy who struck out 5.0 per nine with a 5.71 ERA. Through it all, Hawkins has a 3.61 ERA, 5.8 SO9 and 2.5 BB9, just about a perfect model for his 2012 performance as an Angel. He's 40, but he still averaged 92 mph with his heat and he has learned in the past two years to be a groundballer. Whoever signs him knows what they're getting, even if they have no idea what they'll actually get.

Jason Isringhausen

Born: **9/7/1972** Age: **40**
Bats: **R** Throws: **R** Height: **6' 4"** Weight: **235**
Breakout: **25%** Improve: **61%** Collapse: **24%**
Attrition: **9%** MLB: **66%**

Comparables:
Keiichi Yabu,Don McMahon,Jose Mesa

YEAR	TEAM	LVL	AGE	W	L	SV	G	GS	IP	H	HR	BB	SO	BB9	SO9	GB%	BABIP	WHIP	ERA	FIP	FRA	WARP
2011	NYN	MLB	38	3	3	7	53	0	46^{2}	36	6	24	44	4.6	8.5	41%	.240	1.29	4.05	4.39	4.72	0.0
2012	ANA	MLB	39	3	2	0	50	0	45^{2}	44	7	19	31	3.7	6.1	46%	.262	1.38	4.14	4.93	5.76	-0.5
2013	*ANA*	*MLB*	*40*	*2*	*1*	*3*	*44*	*0*	*39*	*38*	*5*	*18*	*31*	*4.1*	*7.2*	*45%*	*.287*	*1.43*	*4.52*	*4.66*	*4.91*	*-0.1*

"[The] part of baseball I enjoy is that adrenaline," Isringhausen told a reporter in September. "I don't always get it pitching the fifth or sixth inning. It's not the same. I wasn't bred that way and I'm not wired that way." That was a problem, because even in a shaky bullpen like the one in Anaheim, Isringhausen isn't a late-innings option anymore. He did earn a bit more of Scioscia's trust around the All-Star break, but 76 percent of his outings were in less-than-average leverage. His adrenaline-based explanation for his 92 ERA+ doesn't hold up, at least on first glance. In his dozen highest-leverage opportunities, he allowed seven runs (including three home runs) in 8 1/3 innings. Better explanation: He's old, on his fourth ulnar collateral ligament, and barely hanging onto 90 mph.

Kevin Jepsen

Born: **7/26/1984** Age: **28**
Bats: **R** Throws: **R** Height: **6' 4"** Weight: **230**
Breakout: **19%** Improve: **43%** Collapse: **30%**
Attrition: **18%** MLB: **90%**

Comparables:
Manny Delcarmen,Brandon Medders,Mark Eichhorn

YEAR	TEAM	LVL	AGE	W	L	SV	G	GS	IP	H	HR	BB	SO	BB9	SO9	GB%	BABIP	WHIP	ERA	FIP	FRA	WARP
2010	ANA	MLB	25	2	4	0	68	0	59	54	2	29	61	4.4	9.3	56%	.327	1.41	3.97	3.00	3.81	0.4
2011	SLC	AAA	26	1	3	7	24	0	28^{1}	32	4	8	20	2.5	6.4	49%	.349	1.41	4.45	5.05	5.04	0.3
2011	ANA	MLB	26	1	2	0	16	0	13	21	2	9	6	6.2	4.2	56%	.380	2.31	7.62	6.45	5.94	-0.2
2012	SLC	AAA	27	2	2	2	23	0	25	18	1	9	35	3.2	12.6	39%	.321	1.08	3.24	2.47	3.27	0.7
2012	ANA	MLB	27	3	2	2	49	0	44^{2}	39	3	12	38	2.4	7.7	37%	.293	1.14	3.02	3.16	4.03	0.3
2013	*ANA*	*MLB*	*28*	*2*	*1*	*1*	*43*	*0*	39^{2}	*38*	*3*	*16*	*37*	*3.6*	*8.5*	*51%*	*.310*	*1.34*	*3.71*	*3.53*	*4.03*	*0.4*

Jepsen's nightmarish 2011 season spilled into 2012, and after a month he was optioned to Triple-A to make room for Frieri. The reliever who returned in July was Scioscia's best in the second half, with a 1.67 ERA from the time of his call-up on. Jepsen throws hard and he boosted his fastball velocity to a career-best 96.6 mph during the second half. Extra heat also showed up in his cutter, a 92-mph beast that got a tremendous whiff rate but rarely followed Jepsen's directions to the plate. If he can regain the control of that pitch from 2010, he'll regain his future-closer tag.

Ryan Madson

Born: **8/28/1980** Age: **32**
Bats: **L** Throws: **R** Height: **6' 7"** Weight: **200**
Breakout: **28%** Improve: **53%** Collapse: **31%**
Attrition: **5%** MLB: **96%**

Comparables:
Pedro Feliciano,Hideki Okajima,Willie Hernandez

YEAR	TEAM	LVL	AGE	W	L	SV	G	GS	IP	H	HR	BB	SO	BB9	SO9	GB%	BABIP	WHIP	ERA	FIP	FRA	WARP
2010	CLR	A+	29	0	1	0	2	0	2	1	1	0	3	0.0	13.5	40%	.000	0.50	4.50	6.94	7.54	-0.1
2010	REA	AA	29	0	0	0	1	0	2	2	0	0	1	0.0	4.5	33%	.333	1.00	0.00	3.86	2.50	0.1
2010	LEH	AAA	29	0	0	0	2	0	1^{2}	1	0	2	2	10.6	10.6	75%	.250	1.76	5.29	4.47	7.05	-0.1
2010	PHI	MLB	29	6	2	5	55	0	53	42	4	13	64	2.2	10.9	52%	.288	1.04	2.55	2.63	2.63	1.2
2011	CLR	A+	30	0	0	0	1	1	1	0	0	0	1	0.0	9.0	—	.000	0.00	0.00	4.39	4.77	0.0
2011	PHI	MLB	30	4	2	32	62	0	60^{2}	54	2	16	62	2.4	9.2	52%	.315	1.15	2.37	2.22	2.57	1.4
2013	*ANA*	*MLB*	*32*	*2*	*1*	*16*	*38*	*0*	*37*	*33*	*3*	*9*	*37*	*2.1*	*8.9*	*49%*	*.299*	*1.13*	*2.86*	*2.98*	*3.11*	*0.8*

Talk about bad timing. Madson almost signed a four-year, $44 million deal with the Phillies in January before they went out and got Jonathan Papelbon. The Reds then inked Madson to a one-year, $8.5 million deal with a mutual option for 2013. He got hurt in spring training, had Tommy John surgery in April, and never pitched for his new team. The Angels signed him in November to a one-year, $3.5 million deal with performance and roster bonuses. He's a safe gamble for the Angels, who would like to have a famous closer but who don't strictly need one, thanks to the emergence of Frieri. When healthy, Madson is a near-elite reliever who showed the ability to close in 2011. Freakin' Papelbon.

Nick Maronde

Born: **9/5/1989** Age: **23**
Bats: **B** Throws: **L** Height: **6' 4"** Weight: **205**
Breakout: **30%** Improve: **67%** Collapse: **13%**
Attrition: **8%** MLB: **92%**

Comparables:
Matt Garza,Larry Dierker,Frank Castillo

YEAR	TEAM	LVL	AGE	W	L	SV	G	GS	IP	H	HR	BB	SO	BB9	SO9	GB%	BABIP	WHIP	ERA	FIP	FRA	WARP
2011	ORM	Rk	21	5	0	0	11	11	46^{1}	36	5	15	50	2.9	9.7	—	.274	1.10	2.14	4.63	5.03	0.0
2012	ANG	Rk	22	0	1	0	3	3	8	3	0	2	9	2.2	10.1	67%	.111	0.62	1.12	3.25	4.79	0.1
2012	SBR	A+	22	3	1	0	10	10	59^{1}	40	4	14	60	2.1	9.1	40%	.240	0.91	1.82	3.38	2.96	0.4
2012	ARK	AA	22	3	2	0	7	5	32^{1}	39	1	3	21	0.8	5.8	34%	.349	1.30	3.34	2.75	3.36	0.3
2012	ANA	MLB	22	0	0	0	12	0	6	6	0	3	7	4.5	10.5	41%	.353	1.50	1.50	2.21	1.53	0.1
2013	*ANA*	*MLB*	*23*	*2*	*2*	*0*	*11*	*5*	*35*	*36*	*4*	*12*	*28*	*3.0*	*7.1*	*41%*	*.300*	*1.35*	*4.19*	*4.11*	*4.55*	*0.1*

Maronde ended 2011 pitching in the short-season Pioneer League playoffs. He ended 2012 as the Angels' September surprise, a lefty relief ace. As a starter, Maronde has excellent fastball command to both sides of the plate, and to lefties and righties alike, with mid-90s velocity. His slider has yet to pass the test against higher-level righties, and he telegraphs his changeup. He could largely ignore both flaws in his short big-league relief appearances. For that reason, his September performance was misleading. The real Maronde has both considerably more upside and more question marks.

Brad Mills
Born: **3/5/1985** Age: **28**
Bats: **R** Throws: **L** Height: **6' 1"** Weight: **185**
Breakout: **25%** Improve: **71%** Collapse: **13%**
Attrition: **10%** MLB: **84%**
Comparables:
Anibal Sanchez,Edwin Jackson,Armando Galarraga

YEAR	TEAM	LVL	AGE	W	L	SV	G	GS	IP	H	HR	BB	SO	BB9	SO9	GB%	BABIP	WHIP	ERA	FIP	FRA	WARP
2010	LVG	AAA	25	8	6	0	20	20	112^{1}	118	15	43	100	3.4	8.0	43%	.310	1.43	4.97	4.74	5.61	1.0
2010	TOR	MLB	25	1	0	0	7	3	22^{1}	20	2	13	18	5.2	7.3	41%	.281	1.48	5.64	4.48	4.97	0.1
2011	LVG	AAA	26	11	9	0	24	24	157^{1}	161	20	39	136	2.2	7.8	43%	.310	1.27	4.00	4.55	4.64	2.2
2011	TOR	MLB	26	1	2	0	5	4	18^{1}	23	4	12	18	5.9	8.8	34%	.345	1.91	9.82	6.23	6.86	-0.3
2012	SLC	AAA	27	5	10	0	21	19	109	133	13	40	67	3.3	5.5	45%	.331	1.59	5.86	5.23	6.09	0.4
2012	ANA	MLB	27	1	0	0	1	1	5	3	0	0	6	0.0	10.8	33%	.250	0.60	0.00	0.65	1.16	0.2
2013	*ANA*	*MLB*	*28*	*2*	*3*	*0*	*8*	*8*	*43^{1}*	*43*	*5*	*16*	*35*	*3.4*	*7.2*	*43%*	*.296*	*1.37*	*4.36*	*4.19*	*4.73*	*0.1*

"Sorry, the phone is cutting out. Did you say you'll give us bad pills for Jeff Mathis? Because, yeah, okay, we'll definitely take it, no take-backs!" The Angels actually got back an undersized lefty who throws strikes, keeps his fastball high and his changeup low, and simply doesn't throw hard enough to earn a permanent spot on a big-league staff. Mills did get one start in July when injuries nipped the Angels rotation, and he was great—just not great enough to prevent a demotion after the game, back to Salt Lake, where he had a 7.23 ERA at home. That could bode poorly now that he has been traded to Anaheim for Kendrys Morales.

Garrett Richards
Born: **5/27/1988** Age: **25**
Bats: **R** Throws: **R** Height: **6' 4"** Weight: **215**
Breakout: **36%** Improve: **57%** Collapse: **15%**
Attrition: **19%** MLB: **92%**
Comparables:
Vin Mazzaro,Mitch Talbot,Ross Detwiler

YEAR	TEAM	LVL	AGE	W	L	SV	G	GS	IP	H	HR	BB	SO	BB9	SO9	GB%	BABIP	WHIP	ERA	FIP	FRA	WARP
2010	CDR	A	22	8	4	0	19	19	108^{1}	92	6	34	108	2.8	9.0	59%	.295	1.16	3.41	3.36	4.75	0.9
2010	RCU	A+	22	4	1	0	7	7	34^{2}	38	4	9	41	2.3	10.6	54%	.325	1.35	3.89	3.73	4.26	0.9
2011	ARK	AA	23	12	2	0	22	21	143	123	10	40	103	2.5	6.5	49%	.277	1.14	3.15	3.85	3.91	1.5
2011	ANA	MLB	23	0	2	0	7	3	14	16	4	7	9	4.5	5.8	43%	.286	1.64	5.79	6.99	6.99	-0.2
2012	SLC	AAA	24	7	3	0	14	14	77	87	5	35	65	4.1	7.6	52%	.349	1.58	4.21	4.42	4.10	0.9
2012	ANA	MLB	24	4	3	1	30	9	71	77	7	34	47	4.3	6.0	47%	.308	1.56	4.69	4.57	5.13	-0.3
2013	*ANA*	*MLB*	*25*	*4*	*6*	*0*	*14*	*14*	*81^{2}*	*85*	*9*	*33*	*58*	*3.6*	*6.4*	*49%*	*.303*	*1.45*	*4.71*	*4.42*	*5.11*	*-0.2*

The conventional wisdom had Richards as the Angels' second- or third-best prospect heading into 2012, but Kevin Goldstein wasn't so confident. "Richards doesn't have a plus secondary pitch, which allows hitters to sit on the fastball and prevents him from racking up the kind of strikeout totals his velocity would suggest," he wrote, ranking him seventh in the system with the upside of a fourth-starter. Goldstein was right. Richards's fastball had, by far, the best whiff rate among Angels starters, but it wasn't enough to keep him in the rotation, or guarantee him a turn in this year's. His walk rate in the minors was 2.4 per nine going into the season; it was 4.2 between Salt Lake and Anaheim. Nobody ever said the higher levels weren't harder.

Jason Vargas
Born: **2/2/1983** Age: **30**
Bats: **L** Throws: **L** Height: **6' 1"** Weight: **215**
Breakout: **26%** Improve: **62%** Collapse: **10%**
Attrition: **9%** MLB: **91%**
Comparables:
Denny Neagle,Joe Saunders,Jeff Francis

YEAR	TEAM	LVL	AGE	W	L	SV	G	GS	IP	H	HR	BB	SO	BB9	SO9	GB%	BABIP	WHIP	ERA	FIP	FRA	WARP
2010	SEA	MLB	27	9	12	0	31	31	192^{2}	187	18	54	116	2.5	5.4	37%	.272	1.25	3.78	3.91	3.91	1.7
2011	SEA	MLB	28	10	13	0	32	32	201	205	22	59	131	2.6	5.9	39%	.285	1.31	4.25	4.12	3.96	2.2
2012	SEA	MLB	29	14	11	0	33	33	217^{1}	201	35	55	141	2.3	5.8	42%	.254	1.18	3.85	4.64	5.28	-0.3
2013	*ANA*	*MLB*	*30*	*10*	*11*	*0*	*29*	*29*	*183*	*185*	*23*	*45*	*119*	*2.2*	*5.9*	*38%*	*.283*	*1.25*	*4.01*	*4.27*	*4.36*	*1.1*

In last year's annual, we suggested—hoped? noted whimsically?—that "a little extra torso twist on his leg kick" might turn Vargas into something better. Alas. Vargas's small velocity bump didn't make a difference and the pitcher was, but for a slight improvement in walk rate and a few extra long balls sailing away, a perfect match for Jason Vargas Now And Forever. There's nothing wrong with that, and heaven help the teams that don't have a couple Vargases around. But note that when pitching away from the pitcher-friendly expanse of Safeco, his career ERA is 1.74 runs higher. The move to Anaheim could be detrimental.

Jered Weaver
Born: **10/4/1982** Age: **30**
Bats: **R** Throws: **R** Height: **6' 8"** Weight: **215**
Breakout: **4%** Improve: **33%** Collapse: **33%**
Attrition: **14%** MLB: **92%**
Comparables:
Chris Young,Josh Beckett,Shaun Marcum

YEAR	TEAM	LVL	AGE	W	L	SV	G	GS	IP	H	HR	BB	SO	BB9	SO9	GB%	BABIP	WHIP	ERA	FIP	FRA	WARP
2010	ANA	MLB	27	13	12	0	34	34	224^{1}	187	23	54	233	2.2	9.3	38%	.276	1.07	3.01	3.02	3.27	4.5
2011	ANA	MLB	28	18	8	0	33	33	235^{2}	182	20	56	198	2.1	7.6	34%	.250	1.01	2.41	3.24	3.31	4.0
2012	ANA	MLB	29	20	5	0	30	30	188^{2}	147	20	45	142	2.1	6.8	37%	.241	1.02	2.81	3.70	4.41	1.0
2013	*ANA*	*MLB*	*30*	*10*	*8*	*0*	*25*	*25*	*165^{1}*	*143*	*17*	*40*	*149*	*2.2*	*8.1*	*35%*	*.275*	*1.11*	*2.98*	*3.46*	*3.23*	*3.3*

The first year of the Jered Weaver Hometown Discount couldn't have gone better for all involved, except perhaps Scott Boras and Weaver's great-grandkids. He was headed for free agency this winter and a potential $150 million payday. Instead, the Angels locked him down for $85 million. His decision to stay in his cozy home ballpark—particularly cozy and homey for the Southern Californian—and in front of the best outfield defense in the league helped him win 20 games for the first time, lead the league in WHIP, and produce . . . 1.0 WARP? Really? None of the Wins Above Replacement models, including ours, knows what to do with Weaver, who doesn't strike out all that many batters and allows copious flyballs. Should he get no credit for his defense and ballpark (in which he has a career 2.66 ERA)? How should we account for his ability to thrive in a team effort, which almost certainly accounts for much of his success?

Jerome Williams

Born: **12/4/1981** Age: **31**
Bats: **R** Throws: **R** Height: **6' 4"** Weight: **240**
Breakout: **17%** Improve: **48%** Collapse: **20%**
Attrition: **13%** MLB: **87%**

Comparables:
Kevin Correia,Vida Blue,Gene Conley

YEAR	TEAM	LVL	AGE	W	L	SV	G	GS	IP	H	HR	BB	SO	BB9	SO9	GB%	BABIP	WHIP	ERA	FIP	FRA	WARP
2011	SLC	AAA	29	7	2	0	11	10	73^2	78	10	15	60	1.8	7.3	51%	.280	1.26	3.91	4.69	4.74	0.8
2011	ANA	MLB	29	4	0	0	10	6	44	45	6	15	28	3.1	5.7	51%	.291	1.36	3.68	4.65	5.70	-0.4
2012	SBR	A+	30	1	0	0	2	2	11	11	1	1	9	0.8	7.4	69%	.294	1.09	3.27	3.90	1.84	0.0
2012	SLC	AAA	30	0	1	0	2	2	8	13	1	0	8	0.0	9.0	43%	.444	1.62	7.88	3.29	4.84	0.2
2012	ANA	MLB	30	6	8	1	32	15	137^2	139	17	35	98	2.3	6.4	54%	.293	1.26	4.58	4.10	5.06	-0.4
2013	*ANA*	*MLB*	*31*	*5*	*6*	*0*	*24*	*14*	*111*	*116*	*14*	*31*	*76*	*2.6*	*6.1*	*49%*	*.296*	*1.33*	*4.40*	*4.31*	*4.78*	*0.1*

Unfortunately, you'll never go broke betting against miracles. Williams followed up his can-you-believe-this-guy-is-even-here 2011 with a small step back. His ERA caught up to his peripherals and the Angels gave his innings to the famous names (Wilson, Greinke) more befitting their big-budget self-image. Williams throws a good cutter to righties and a good sinker to lefties, but he's skittish around the strike zone and needs to command all four of his pitches to succeed. The good news is that his peripherals improved, though massive home-road splits raise the question of how much to credit Anaheim's spacious outfield. He's a solid backup plan, but if he's in the rotation to start the year it means the Angels front office had a disappointing offseason or somebody got hurt.

C.J. Wilson

Born: **11/18/1980** Age: **32**
Bats: **L** Throws: **L** Height: **6' 2"** Weight: **210**
Breakout: **15%** Improve: **61%** Collapse: **17%**
Attrition: **7%** MLB: **85%**

Comparables:
Warren Spahn,Whitey Ford,David Cone

YEAR	TEAM	LVL	AGE	W	L	SV	G	GS	IP	H	HR	BB	SO	BB9	SO9	GB%	BABIP	WHIP	ERA	FIP	FRA	WARP
2010	TEX	MLB	29	15	8	0	33	33	204	161	10	93	170	4.1	7.5	50%	.266	1.25	3.35	3.53	4.35	2.4
2011	TEX	MLB	30	16	7	0	34	34	223^1	191	16	74	206	3.0	8.3	51%	.287	1.19	2.94	3.28	4.21	2.9
2012	ANA	MLB	31	13	10	0	34	34	202^1	181	19	91	173	4.0	7.7	50%	.281	1.34	3.83	4.00	4.43	1.3
2013	*ANA*	*MLB*	*32*	*11*	*10*	*0*	*30*	*30*	*183*	*156*	*13*	*69*	*167*	*3.4*	*8.2*	*50%*	*.287*	*1.23*	*3.38*	*3.43*	*3.68*	*2.7*

Shortly after signing with the Angels, Wilson pointed out to a reporter that he led the AL in road ERA in 2011. Stat-savvy players like Wilson, who can talk intelligently about park factors, are rare. Unfortunately, he's as prone to small-sample conclusions as we are. Despite escaping the hitter-friendly Ballpark at Arlington, Wilson's ERA (and everything else, including home runs) went the wrong direction in 2012. Wilson isn't a bat-misser, but his cutter and slider have good bite and are hard to square up. The issue is strikes, and his 61 percent strike rate is an impediment. Only five AL starters (minimum 140 innings) threw fewer strikes than Wilson in 2012, and the five combined for a 5.18 ERA. Getting back to 63 percent, Wilson's 2011 rate, doesn't sound like much, but it would put him in better company.

LINEOUTS

HITTERS

PLAYER	TEAM	LVL	AGE	PA	R	2B	3B	HR	RBI	BB	SO	SB-CS	AVG/OBP/SLG	TAv	BABIP	BRR	FRAA	WARP
LF Z. Borenstein	CDR	A	21	327	42	25	3	11	50	27	60	13-5	.266/.339/.485	.290	.300	0.9	LF(10): 0.3, RF(3): -0.3	0.6
MI C. Bushyhead	ORM	Rk	22	143	17	6	3	0	15	15	20	2-1	.289/.370/.388	.308	.343	-0.3	SS(3): -0.3, 2B(2): 0.3	0.2
INF J. Cantu	SLC	AAA	30	90	12	5	0	4	22	2	11	0-0	.291/.300/.488	.232	.288	-1.2	2B(8): -0.5, 3B(6): -0.9	-0.4
CF C. Clarke	ORM	Rk	20	221	34	11	0	3	26	31	51	11-1	.271/.388/.384	.301	.360	1.4	RF(12): -1.0, CF(9): 0.3	0.2
	CDR	A	20	307	38	9	2	6	27	22	79	11-3	.190/.276/.305	.219	.242	2	CF(18): 0.0	-0.1
C J. Hester	SLC	AAA	28	105	7	4	2	3	13	9	32	0-1	.217/.282/.402	.218	.288	-1.2	C(20): -0.3	-0.2
	ANA	MLB	28	95	14	1	0	3	4	8	25	0-0	.212/.287/.329	.241	.263	-1	C(38): -0.2	-0.2
1B P. McAnulty	ARK	AA	31	170	26	5	0	10	27	25	31	0-2	.279/.400/.529	.335	.290	-2.1	1B(22): -1.5	0.6
	SLC	AAA	31	326	44	23	1	15	56	48	73	1-2	.247/.359/.502	.276	.280	0.2	1B(5): -0.5, LF(3): -0.3	0.4
OF J. Moore	—	—	—	—	—	—	—	—	—	—	—	—	—	—	—	—	—	—
C C. Ramirez	ARK	AA	24	323	29	12	1	2	23	33	55	4-0	.204/.312/.276	.252	.245	-1.1	C(66): -1.2	1.0
INF L. Rodriguez	TAC	AAA	32	422	49	18	1	12	51	50	41	5-3	.296/.389/.452	.298	.306	3	2B(60): 0.1, 1B(13): -0.2	1.9
2B A. Yarbrough	CDR	A	20	257	35	12	9	0	27	10	20	9-2	.287/.320/.410	.244	.312	0.7	2B(5): -0.8	0.0

23rd-rounder **Zachary Borenstein**'s numbers at Cedar Rapids were quite similar to top prospect Kaleb Cowart's, but Borenstein is two years older and limited defensively, though his top PECOTA comp *is* Carl Yastrzemski. **Caleb Bushyhead**, in case you wonder, keeps his hair cropped short. "Why do you sign **Jorge Cantu** if you don't want a .291/.300/.488 hitter?" Cantu probably wondered aloud in the third person, after the Angels released him in April when he hit .291/.300/.488 in Triple-A. How many of **Chevy Clarke**'s 19,974 Twitter followers will stick with him when he's out of the game? The 2010 first-rounder is a .222/.308/.362 hitter in three minor-league seasons, so we may not wait long to find out. Of the seven players who have caught for Scioscia in the past five years, **John Hester** has the third-best OPS+, but even this one-time Triple-A masher is a lousy bat now. **Paul McAnulty** once again provided organizational slugging, but his real value is as a mentor to Angels prospects (Trout lived next door in Salt Lake), even going so far as to take on a semi-official role as player-coach in Arkansas midway through the season; his future as a full-time coach is imminent. Hip surgery cost toolsy **Jeremy Moore** a year of at-bats, game action and (presumably) development, though good for him spending it on the major-league DL, earning a year of service time and a major-league salary. Classic O. Henry twist: Just as **Carlos Ramirez**'s defense started getting raves within the organization—a prerequisite for Angels backstops—his bat disappeared. Dependable Triple-A infield bat **Luis Rodriguez** joins a messy competition for the Angels' utility spot, but his age and unaccomplished major-league peregrinations are marks against him. The organization has turned over the front office and scouting department in recent years, but **Alex Yarbrough** is a classic Angels prospect: an undersized, switch-hitting middle infielder who can run a bit, doesn't strike out, and expresses his modest pop via line drives in the gaps.

PITCHERS

PLAYER	TEAM	LVL	AGE	W	L	SV	IP	H	HR	BB	SO	BB9	SO9	GB%	BABIP	WHIP	ERA	FIP	FRA	WARP
B. Cassevah	SLC	AAA	26	4	1	10	46^{1}	60	3	19	28	3.7	5.4	52%	.348	1.71	6.22	4.59	5.83	0.1
	ANA	MLB	26	1	0	0	5	5	2	6	2	10.8	3.6	60%	.167	2.20	7.20	11.65	11.33	-0.4
E. Jimenez	CDR	A	20	7	5	0	97^{1}	113	4	19	59	1.8	5.5	46%	.355	1.36	3.51	3.50	5.09	0.0
M. Kohn	—	—	—	—	—	—	—	—	—	—	—	—	—	—	—	—	—	—	—	—
J. Reyes	IND	AAA	27	6	2	0	54	51	5	13	43	2.2	7.2	43%	.280	1.19	2.67	3.55	4.63	0.2
M. Russell	SBR	A+	23	6	12	0	133	200	26	41	83	2.8	5.6	42%	.367	1.81	7.11	6.19	10.62	-0.2
A. Schugel	ARK	AA	23	6	8	0	140^{1}	117	9	55	109	3.5	7.0	41%	.275	1.23	2.89	3.86	4.27	0.7
M. Shoemaker	SLC	AAA	25	11	10	0	176^{2}	229	25	45	124	2.3	6.3	42%	.350	1.55	5.65	4.95	5.63	1.3
A. Taylor	ARK	AA	25	2	4	2	41	44	4	14	39	3.1	8.6	42%	.317	1.41	4.61	3.89	3.96	0.3
	ANA	MLB	25	0	0	0	2^{1}	3	0	4	0	15.4	0.0	30%	.300	3.00	11.57	8.19	7.01	-0.1
D. Tillman	SBR	A+	23	1	1	8	24	10	0	14	31	5.2	11.6	50%	.192	1.00	1.88	3.36	2.35	0.5

Extreme sinkerballer **Bobby Cassevah**'s surprise emergence as Scioscia's favorite bullpen toy didn't survive contact with 2012, as his awful peripherals caught up to him, and losing his manager's faith in a very brief stint in the majors was followed by losing his manager's faith in Triple-A. A strike-throwing lefty who keeps the ball down, **Eswarlin Jimenez** earned a promotion in his first year stateside, and as a 20-year-old he struck out 14 and walked one in three Cal League starts. If control is the last thing to return after Tommy John surgery, **Michael Kohn** is in luck, because he never had any. **Jo-Jo Reyes** is just what Dipoto looks for in small pickups: Not too old and throws strikes, though the Angels would surely prefer a pitcher whose career-best ERA is lower than 5.57. **Max Russell**'s fringy stuff (high-80s heat) didn't play in the California League, as hitters shrank the strike zone and took away his groundball tendencies. He'll need another pitch—maybe a cutter—to keep moving up. **A.J. Schugel** was a junior-college third baseman who couldn't hit, so the Angels drafted him in the 25th round as a pitcher, and his stuff—mid-90s fastball, over-the-top curve and advanced change—and success have made him the fastest-moving pitcher in their 2010 draft class. The transition from Arkansas to Salt Lake—the most extreme parks in the Angels' system—is hell on pitchers like **Matt Shoemaker**, who don't miss bats, and whose raw numbers might actually improve in pitcher-friendly Anaheim, if he could only get there. A conversion to relief did wonders for **Andrew Taylor**'s walk rate, but he struggles to hide the ball and throws 60-70 percent sliders, not good enough to fool big-league lefties yet. **Daniel Tillman** has the stuff to be a power reliever, but fringy control gave way to catastrophe in Arkansas, and after walking a batter per inning he was demoted midseason to Inland Empire, where a brilliant July turned into a wild August, in which he walked nine in eight innings.

MANAGER: MIKE SCIOSCIA

YEAR	TEAM	W-L	Pythag +/-	Avg PC	100+ P	120+ P	QS	BQS	REL	REL w Zero R	IBB	PH	PH Avg	PH HR	SB2	CS2	SB3	CS3	SAC Att	SAC %	POS SAC	Squeeze	Swing	In Play
2010	ANA	80-82	0	204.3	162	160	108	6	410	325	66	172	.174	0	14	10	0	3	140	72.9%	100	6	400	125
2011	ANA	86-76	1	101.0	98	11	98	8	386	313	34	75	.154	2	18	4	1	1	78	80.8%	59	1	417	144
2012	ANA	89-73	1	97.4	87	4	91	3	444	365	20	68	.203	2	12	4	1	2	72	88.9%	60	3	419	132

For the third year in a row, Scioscia's season ended after game 162, but during that stretch his Angels have averaged 85 wins and improved each season. That leaves Scioscia in a sort of managerial purgatory: He hasn't managed a team into a necessary rebuilding, but he has failed to meet expectations for a big-market franchise that figures it should be the division's default frontrunner. Mediocre baseball has a habit of turning a manager's characteristics into a caricature, and Scioscia's foibles—his sacrifice bunting, his slash-and-dash offenses, and his preference for defense behind the plate—start to look more indicting.

That's particularly true now that he's working under a new boss, and his first season under Jerry Dipoto exposed some cracks in his manager-for-life status. "The communication between Scioscia and Dipoto is strained, and their relationship has teetered throughout the season and neared a breaking point," Ken Rosenthal reported in late September. He detailed Scioscia's frustrated reaction after Dipoto fired hitting coach and friend-of-Scioscia Mickey Hatcher, Scioscia's contentious relationship with assistant GM Scott Servais, and Scioscia's resistance to advanced statistics prepared by the front office.

Scioscia still has many years left on his $50 million contract—six years, according to reports—and he remains a shrewd manager respected throughout the game for his attention to in-game details, his ability to evaluate talent and his communication skills when dealing with the press and public. Yes, he led the league in sacrifice bunts, again. Yes, his hitters had the AL's third-lowest gap between batting average and on-base percentage. But many teams would love to have Scioscia at the helm, and Arte Moreno will hope and pray that a return to the postseason in 2013 prevents him from having to fire the only manager he has ever employed.

Los Angeles Dodgers

2012: WHO WANTS TO BE A MILLIONAIRE?

In the dying days of the Frank McCourt era, with the team still in bankruptcy, general manager Ned Colletti filled out his roster with midpriced veterans signed to back-loaded two-year deals and cut-rate solutions at left field and catcher. While it looked like the Dodgers had brought a spork to a knife fight, the franchise's record-setting $2.15 billion sale to the Magic Johnson/Stan Kasten-fronted Guggenheim Partners just before Opening Day heralded a new era. The team somewhat miraculously bolted to a 32-15 start, then lingered in contention through the remainder of the first half despite a deluge of injuries that included losing Matt Kemp for two months. The Dodgers—pardon the expression—went for broke in the second half, but faded out of contention.

The new owners, who had already begun flexing their financial muscle via an extension for Andre Ethier and the signing of Cuban defector Yasiel Puig, allowed Colletti to upgrade the roster by spending cash like he was firing it out of a T-shirt cannon. Not only did reinforcements—Hanley Ramirez, Shane Victorino, Brandon League, Joe Blanton, Adrian Gonzalez, and Josh Beckett—arrive, but when the dust had settled, the Dodgers had taken on nearly $300 million in post-2012 contract commitments with only a negligible discount, providing the Red Sox with the equivalent of a TARP bailout via a late-August blockbuster. Despite the upgrades, the team went just 30-27 from August 1 onward, their offense continuing to sputter as the Giants left them in the dust in the NL West race, and a wild card berth slowly slipped away.

Injuries were a major part of the 2012 club's story, as they ranked fourth in the majors in DL days (1,598), seventh in WARP lost (5.2). Beyond that, though, with the exception of Beckett and League, most of the reinforcements and replacements failed to play up to their potential, with Gonzalez and Victorino doing alarming impressions of James Loney and Juan Rivera.

DODGERS PROSPECTUS

2012 W-L: 86-76, 2nd in NL West

Pythag	.529	14th	DER	.717	6th
RS/G	3.93	26th	B-Age	30.5	28th
RA/G	3.69	4th	P-Age	29.2	24th
TAv	.256	20th	Salary	$97.6	14th
BRR	-3.7	18th	M$/MW	$2.25	11th
TAv-P	.249	5th	DL Days	1415	4th
FIP	3.68	5th	DL WARP	5.4	6th

Three-Year Park Factors	
Overall	94
HR/RH	97
HR/LH	94
AVG/RH	94
AVG/LH	99

Dodger Stadium (1962)
Att. % of Capacity: 73.3% (12th)
Dim. 330, 385, 395, 385, 330

This venerable pitcher's park is a good fit for Zack Greinke, and L.A. is a good place to spend $150 million.

2013: LET'S MAKE A DEAL

It's a whole new ballgame for the Dodgers, who are stepping out of an era marked by the contrast between the McCourts' personal extravagance—especially when it came to legal fees—and penny-pinching when it came to roster management, draft and international spending. Suddenly, the Dodgers are threatening to become a cartoon version of the Yankees during the height of the Steinbrenner era. If there's anything scarier than Colletti's cut-rate solutions, it's Colletti with a blank check.

Driven by a new TV deal with Fox Sports that will pay them at least $6 billion in rights fees over the next 25 years, the 2013 Dodgers had blown past the 2010 Yankees' record-setting $213 million payroll by Christmas 2012 thanks to Zack Greinke's six-year, $147 million deal.

Where the Yankees have been able to support their massive payrolls with revenues that come with annual postseason appearances, the Dodgers haven't been to the playoffs since 2009. With name-brand solutions at so many spots around the diamond, they certainly ought to contend in the NL West, but with the world champion Giants, retooling Diamondbacks, and rapidly rebuilding Padres all set to provide their share of challenges (you can forget the Rockies), the Dodgers are hardly guaranteed a postseason berth.

STATE OF THE ORGANIZATION: THE $64 (MILLION) DOLLAR QUESTION

Including Carl Crawford, who had just undergone Tommy John surgery when he was included in the Boston trade and therefore has yet to play for the team, the Dodgers have $315.5 million tied up in their starting outfield through 2018, a figure that doesn't include the $42 million committed to Puig. And any position shifting of the four is complicated by the $127 million remaining on Gonzalez's deal. All of those salaries are on the books through at least 2017.

Even with all of the money taken on, a farm system that was already in the lower half of the majors due to the McCourt regime's skimping on draft and international bonuses took a significant hit with the trades of Nathan Eovaldi, Allen Webster, Ethan Martin, and Josh Lindblom—not to mention Rubby de la Rosa, with all of 61 2/3 major-league innings under his belt—in the various deadline deals. While Colletti doggedly held onto pitcher Zach Lee, he had been surpassed by Webster as the team's top prospect before the latter was included in the Boston trade.

So for the foreseeable future, the Dodger Way will be to use money to spackle over every crack and fill every hole. At least the signings of Puig and Korean southpaw Hyun-jin Ryu, for whom the Dodgers paid $25.7 million for the right to negotiate what turned out to be a six-year, $36 million contract, indicate a renewed interest in the international market, long neglected during the McCourt era. Unfortunately, the newest Collective Bargaining Agreement will limit the team's international and draft spending going forward, leaving it to continue spending silly money on major-league talent, much of which inevitably won't deliver, because that's what free agents on the wrong side of 30 tend to do.

The good news is that there's almost no way the team will fail to retain Clayton Kershaw, who has one more year of club control after his 2013 deal expires; the bad news is that Greinke's contract will raise the salary bar for Kershaw.

Not making the playoffs in 2013 wouldn't be disastrous for the Dodgers, 2012 Marlins style, but when some of these contracts inevitably sour in the coming years, will they have enough space in Chavez Ravine to bury them, and enough willingness to throw good money after bad?

HITTERS

Bobby Abreu OF

Born: **3/11/1974** Age: **39**
Bats: **L** Throws: **R** Height: **6' 1"**
Weight: **220** Breakout: **0%**
Improve: **16%** Collapse: **5%**
Attrition: **8%** MLB: **72%**

Comparables:
Luis Gonzalez,Moises Alou,Johnny Grubb

YEAR	TEAM	LVL	AGE	PA	R	2B	3B	HR	RBI	BB	SO	SB	CS	AVG_OBP_SLG	TAv	BABIP	BRR	FRAA	WARP
2010	ANA	MLB	36	667	88	41	1	20	78	87	132	24	10	.255/.352/.435	.298	.296	-6.1	RF(93): -6.5, LF(41): -3.2	2.2
2011	ANA	MLB	37	585	54	30	1	8	60	78	113	21	5	.253/.353/.365	.278	.310	0	LF(18): -2.8, RF(10): -1.0	1.1
2012	ANA	MLB	38	27	1	3	0	0	5	2	5	0	0	.208/.259/.333	.206	.250	-0.8	LF(6): 0.1, RF(1): -0.0	-0.2
2012	LAN	MLB	38	230	28	8	1	3	19	35	51	6	2	.246/.361/.344	.264	.319	-0.2	LF(46): -0.9, RF(1): 0.1	0.2
2013	*LAN*	*MLB*	*39*	*310*	*36*	*15*	*1*	*6*	*31*	*38*	*63*	*10*	*3*	*.248/.341/.371*	*.267*	*.302*	*0.3*	*LF 0, RF -0*	*1.0*

Released by the Angels on April 28 to make room for Mike Trout, Abreu quickly found work with the Dodgers and carved a niche as their regular left fielder with a hot May (.318/.430/.424 in 79 PA). The returns diminished predictably enough. Shane Victorino's late-July arrival cost Abreu his roster spot, and he spent August cooling his heels—and a sprained ankle—in Albuquerque before returning as a pinch-hitter in September. Even with his fading power, his keen plate discipline and remaining speed could find him continued employment in a reserve role, extending the coda on a criminally underappreciated career.

Alex Castellanos OF

Born: **8/4/1986** Age: **26**
Bats: **R** Throws: **R** Height: **6' 0"**
Weight: **180** Breakout: **5%**
Improve: **54%** Collapse: **4%**
Attrition: **12%** MLB: **98%**

Comparables:
Jeff Kent,Geronimo Pena,Sean Rodriguez

YEAR	TEAM	LVL	AGE	PA	R	2B	3B	HR	RBI	BB	SO	SB	CS	AVG_OBP_SLG	TAv	BABIP	BRR	FRAA	WARP
2010	PMB	A+	23	517	62	35	7	13	58	38	112	19	9	.270/.339/.462	.294	.328	0.2	RF(123): 5.9, LF(1): 0.0	2.5
2010	PMB	A+	23	517	62	35	7	13	58	38	112	19	9	.270/.339/.462	.294	.328	0.2	RF(2): -0.0	2.5
2011	CHT	AA	24	143	30	14	4	4	23	15	24	4	1	.322/.406/.603	.339	.365	0	--	0.0
2011	SFD	AA	24	391	72	21	4	19	62	24	94	10	1	.319/.379/.562	.316	.387	0	--	0.0
2012	ABQ	AAA	25	407	74	25	7	17	52	46	85	16	8	.328/.420/.590	.374	.390	2.3	2B(17): -0.1, 3B(7): -0.3	1.7
2012	LAN	MLB	25	25	3	0	1	1	3	0	8	0	0	.174/.200/.391	.209	.200	-0.9	LF(11): -0.1, RF(4): 0.2	-0.2
2013	*LAN*	*MLB*	*26*	*250*	*28*	*10*	*2*	*8*	*29*	*17*	*68*	*6*	*3*	*.232/.298/.394*	*.256*	*.293*	*0.2*	*2B 0, RF -0*	*0.6*

A strong 2011 showing, both before and after he was acquired from St. Louis in the Rafael Furcal deal, put this 2008 10th-rounder on the prospect map despite advanced age, and Castellanos built upon that in 2012. Despite missing most of May with a hamstring injury, he tore up Triple-A pitching and significantly improved his plate discipline. Just as significantly, he returned to the infield for the first time since 2009 and held his own, playing second base until late July, then shifting to third. The irony is that in his brief call-up in late May and early June, the Dodgers used him solely in the outfield despite myriad injuries to their infielders. Castellanos isn't particularly athletic but he has a strong arm (hands, not so much), above-average speed, and power that profiles better as an infielder than at an outfield corner. With the latter route blocked in LA, he'll continue refining his game in Triple-A.

Brian Cavazos-Galvez OF
Born: **5/17/1987** Age: **26**
Bats: **R** Throws: **R** Height: **6' 1"**
Weight: **215** Breakout: **6%**
Improve: **57%** Collapse: **7%**
Attrition: **9%** MLB: **96%**
Comparables:
Alex Johnson, Glenn Wilson, Willie Smith

YEAR	TEAM	LVL	AGE	PA	R	2B	3B	HR	RBI	BB	SO	SB	CS	AVG_OBP_SLG	TAv	BABIP	BRR	FRAA	WARP
2010	GRL	A	23	513	76	43	4	16	77	12	60	43	13	.318/.345/.520	.310	.338	-1	CF(43): -0.4, LF(26): 1.2	4.3
2011	CHT	AA	24	440	60	27	5	14	61	12	63	13	11	.277/.311/.470	.261	.296	0	--	0.0
2012	RCU	A+	25	54	14	2	1	3	11	2	4	4	2	.346/.370/.596	.319	.333	0.5	--	0.0
2012	CHT	AA	25	87	11	3	0	4	11	6	17	5	0	.167/.233/.359	.331	.155	0.8	1B(4): -0.1, LF(3): -0.1	0.2
2012	ABQ	AAA	25	187	33	11	3	7	32	5	24	1	1	.354/.376/.567	.302	.378	1.2	LF(10): 0.0, 1B(1): -0.0	0.2
2013	*LAN*	*MLB*	*26*	*250*	*28*	*12*	*1*	*7*	*28*	*5*	*48*	*9*	*3*	*.250/.268/.398*	*.244*	*.280*	*0.7*	*LF -1, RF -0*	*0.1*

After leveling off at Double-A in 2011, Cavazos-Galvez—a 2009 12th-round pick whose father was a Dodgers reliever—struggled to a .167/.233/.359 April that pushed him back to High-A. While he hit well enough in the offensive havens of Rancho Cucamonga and later Albuquerque to recover some forward momentum, an ankle sprain cost him a month; he played in just half a dozen Rookie League games after July 20. Cavazos-Galvez has tremendous bat speed and a strong arm, but he's still a hacker with a poor approach at the plate, minimal defensive value, and a crowd of younger players behind him in the Dodgers chain.

Bobby Coyle OF
Born: **3/6/1989** Age: **24**
Bats: **L** Throws: **L** Height: **6' 2"**
Weight: **215** Breakout: **9%**
Improve: **58%** Collapse: **4%**
Attrition: **22%** MLB: **94%**
Comparables:
Marc Newfield, Steve Brye, Joe Rudi

YEAR	TEAM	LVL	AGE	PA	R	2B	3B	HR	RBI	BB	SO	SB	CS	AVG_OBP_SLG	TAv	BABIP	BRR	FRAA	WARP
2010	OGD	Rk	21	249	38	16	1	4	52	10	29	7	1	.316/.347/.443	.281	.348	-1.4	RF(14): -2.1, LF(13): -1.0	0.3
2011	GRL	A	22	416	42	16	1	9	44	30	68	3	2	.250/.303/.368	.235	.279	0	--	0.0
2012	RCU	A+	23	213	34	17	2	8	32	11	18	3	1	.378/.408/.602	.278	.386	1.1	LF(5): -0.5, RF(3): -0.3	0.1
2013	*LAN*	*MLB*	*24*	*250*	*20*	*10*	*1*	*4*	*24*	*8*	*52*	*0*	*0*	*.230/.255/.333*	*.218*	*.273*	*-0.3*	*LF -1, RF -0*	*-0.7*

A 10th-round 2010 pick out of Fresno State, Coyle struggled in his intro to full-season ball in 2011 and didn't make his 2012 debut until May 29. When he did, he lit up the California League like a pinball machine, and kept the hot streak going in a late-season promotion to the Southern League. Coyle has good pitch-recognition skills and the potential for average or better power, but he isn't as good as his numbers suggest. The scouting consensus is that he won't have enough bat to carry left field as a regular, and is more likely a fourth outfielder in the long run.

Carl Crawford LF
Born: **8/5/1981** Age: **31**
Bats: **L** Throws: **L** Height: **6' 3"**
Weight: **215** Breakout: **0%**
Improve: **35%** Collapse: **5%**
Attrition: **16%** MLB: **85%**
Comparables:
Felipe Alou, Moises Alou, Del Ennis

YEAR	TEAM	LVL	AGE	PA	R	2B	3B	HR	RBI	BB	SO	SB	CS	AVG_OBP_SLG	TAv	BABIP	BRR	FRAA	WARP
2010	TBA	MLB	28	657	110	30	13	19	90	46	104	47	10	.307/.356/.495	.310	.342	4.9	LF(147): 10.1	6.6
2011	BOS	MLB	29	538	65	29	7	11	56	23	104	18	6	.255/.289/.405	.247	.299	3	LF(127): 2.6	0.6
2012	BOS	MLB	30	125	23	10	2	3	19	3	22	5	0	.282/.306/.479	.267	.319	0.8	LF(30): -1.4	0.0
2013	*LAN*	*MLB*	*31*	*250*	*33*	*10*	*3*	*5*	*22*	*15*	*43*	*14*	*4*	*.268/.316/.400*	*.266*	*.308*	*1.6*	*LF 4*	*1.3*

Coming off his nightmare first season in Boston, Crawford underwent surgery to repair cartilage in his left wrist in January. Initially, the Red Sox explained he had begun experiencing soreness during his offseason hitting workouts, but by Opening Day, it emerged that he'd dealt with wrist pain for years and had received painkilling injections to manage the problem in 2011. Just as he was nearing game-readiness in mid-April, he sprained his left UCL, and didn't make his season debut until July 16. When it became apparent his elbow was a problem and the Sox were going nowhere, he shut it down and opted for Tommy John surgery in late August, and two days later, the Sox miraculously unloaded him—and every last dollar remaining on his seven-year, $142 million contract—on the Dodgers as part of the Nick Punto blockbuster. The change of scenery out of Boston's fishbowl should help, and there's a chance he could be ready for Opening Day, but the difference between the guy at his peak who put up a stellar walk year and the guy who will debut in Dodger blue may be nontrivial.

Luis Cruz INF
Born: **2/10/1984** Age: **29**
Bats: **R** Throws: **R** Height: **6' 2"**
Weight: **210** Breakout: **4%**
Improve: **42%** Collapse: **6%**
Attrition: **14%** MLB: **89%**
Comparables:
Yuniesky Betancourt, Craig Reynolds, Tony Kubek

YEAR	TEAM	LVL	AGE	PA	R	2B	3B	HR	RBI	BB	SO	SB	CS	AVG_OBP_SLG	TAv	BABIP	BRR	FRAA	WARP
2010	NAS	AAA	26	518	54	29	3	10	68	15	56	0	0	.281/.309/.414	.244	.298	2.1	SS(124): 2.8, 3B(4): 0.2	1.7
2010	MIL	MLB	26	17	2	0	1	0	1	0	2	0	0	.235/.235/.353	.181	.267	-0.2	SS(5): -0.2	-0.1
2011	ROU	AAA	27	286	34	15	1	9	34	10	40	2	1	.273/.301/.433	.248	.292	0	--	0.0
2012	ABQ	AAA	28	305	46	31	3	8	46	13	34	1	2	.318/.348/.529	.230	.337	1.4	SS(16): -2.6, 3B(1): 0.2	-0.1
2012	LAN	MLB	28	296	26	20	0	6	40	9	34	2	1	.297/.322/.431	.272	.320	1.4	3B(51): 1.1, SS(24): -1.9	1.2
2013	*LAN*	*MLB*	*29*	*264*	*23*	*14*	*1*	*4*	*25*	*8*	*37*	*1*	*1*	*.250/.278/.361*	*.235*	*.275*	*-0.6*	*SS 0, 3B 0*	*0.3*

Eleven years after beginning his professional career, six years after playing in the All-Star Futures Game, and two years after fading from the major-league scene, Cruz went from organizational fodder to folk hero. He tore up Albuquerque, then arrived in Los Angeles on July 2, just before Dee Gordon went down, shifted to third base upon Hanley Ramirez's arrival, and hit well enough not only to maintain his spot but to become a crowd favorite. Cruz doesn't have much patience at the plate, but he's a contact hitter with enough gap power and versatility to give himself a chance to stick around if the hits fall.

A.J. Ellis **C**

Born: **4/9/1981** Age: **32**
Bats: **R** Throws: **R** Height: **6' 3"**
Weight: **225** Breakout: **2%**
Improve: **32%** Collapse: **11%**
Attrition: **11%** MLB: **89%**

Comparables:
Scott Hatteberg,Bill Freehan,Sherm Lollar

YEAR	TEAM	LVL	AGE	PA	R	2B	3B	HR	RBI	BB	SO	SB	CS	AVG_OBP_SLG	TAv	BABIP	BRR	FRAA	WARP
2010	ABQ	AAA	29	76	11	5	1	0	7	13	12	1	0	.262/.395/.377	.249	.320	-0.6	C(18): 0.6	0.3
2010	LAN	MLB	29	128	6	5	0	0	16	14	18	0	0	.278/.363/.324	.259	.330	-1.8	C(43): 0.0	0.4
2011	ABQ	AAA	30	248	36	15	0	2	28	50	23	0	1	.304/.467/.418	.330	.338	0	--	0.0
2011	LAN	MLB	30	103	8	1	1	2	11	14	16	0	1	.271/.392/.376	.285	.313	-1	C(29): -0.2	0.4
2012	LAN	MLB	31	505	44	20	1	13	52	65	107	0	0	.270/.373/.414	.287	.329	-3.8	C(131): -0.0	3.0
2013	*LAN*	*MLB*	*32*	*394*	*41*	*14*	*1*	*6*	*36*	*50*	*77*	*0*	*0*	*.247/.353/.348*	*.265*	*.300*	*-0.6*	*C 0*	*2.0*

The Dodgers' decision to let Rod Barajas walk—something he himself is unaccustomed to, of course—opened the door for Ellis to become a major-league regular for the first time at age 31, and the decision paid off handsomely. He flashed newfound power and showed that his walk rate wasn't entirely a function of batting in front of the pitcher, drawing unintentional passes in 8.7 percent of his PA batting eighth, 14.5 percent elsewhere. Unfortunately, Don Mattingly squandered that revelation by keeping him at the bottom of the lineup two-thirds of the time. Ellis did fade late in the season, and underwent surgery to repair a torn meniscus in his left knee, but it's clear he's a keeper, one who should be under club control for most of his remaining shelf life.

Mark Ellis **2B**

Born: **6/6/1977** Age: **36**
Bats: **R** Throws: **R** Height: **5' 11"**
Weight: **185** Breakout: **0%**
Improve: **33%** Collapse: **10%**
Attrition: **20%** MLB: **73%**

Comparables:
Howie Clark,Damion Easley,Tony Graffanino

YEAR	TEAM	LVL	AGE	PA	R	2B	3B	HR	RBI	BB	SO	SB	CS	AVG_OBP_SLG	TAv	BABIP	BRR	FRAA	WARP
2010	OAK	MLB	33	492	45	24	0	5	49	40	56	7	6	.291/.358/.381	.283	.321	-1.1	2B(116): 3.3	2.7
2011	COL	MLB	34	286	34	13	0	6	25	14	43	7	3	.274/.317/.392	.237	.307	2.4	2B(64): -0.3	-0.3
2011	OAK	MLB	34	233	21	11	1	1	16	8	32	7	2	.217/.253/.290	.213	.249	0.7	2B(59): 4.8, 1B(2): 0.1	-0.1
2012	LAN	MLB	35	464	62	21	1	7	31	40	70	5	0	.258/.333/.364	.261	.296	-1.4	2B(110): 0.9	0.9
2013	*LAN*	*MLB*	*36*	*449*	*50*	*19*	*1*	*7*	*36*	*30*	*69*	*8*	*3*	*.243/.302/.342*	*.242*	*.273*	*-0.1*	*2B -1, 1B 0*	*0.6*

Signed to a backloaded two-year, $8.75 million deal, Ellis rebounded from a down 2011 to give the Dodgers exactly what they might have expected: steady defense at the keystone combined with modest on-base skills but minimal power. He missed seven weeks when a collision with the Cardinals' Tyler Greene caused such severe swelling in his left calf that emergency surgery may have saved his leg. An effective hitter against lefties (.306/.355/.449 in 397 PA from 2010-12), he has become a drag on the offense against righties (.250/.315/.331 in 1,078 PA during that span), not to mention increasingly fragile (fewer than 125 games every year since 2007). And now he's a year older and more expensive.

Gorman Erickson **C**

Born: **3/11/1988** Age: **25**
Bats: **B** Throws: **R** Height: **6' 5"**
Weight: **220** Breakout: **11%**
Improve: **47%** Collapse: **7%**
Attrition: **16%** MLB: **98%**

Comparables:
Greg Myers,Tom Satriano,Glenn Borgmann

YEAR	TEAM	LVL	AGE	PA	R	2B	3B	HR	RBI	BB	SO	SB	CS	AVG_OBP_SLG	TAv	BABIP	BRR	FRAA	WARP
2010	GRL	A	22	299	32	13	3	2	27	34	45	3	0	.215/.309/.310	.233	.251	-1.2	C(84): 0.7	0.2
2011	RCU	A+	23	273	37	16	4	6	40	41	42	3	2	.305/.408/.491	.316	.346	0	--	0.0
2011	CHT	AA	23	157	18	8	0	7	26	11	22	1	0	.275/.329/.479	.272	.281	0	--	0.0
2012	CHT	AA	24	328	25	15	1	3	25	44	56	1	2	.234/.345/.328	.265	.282	0	C(28): -0.3	0.0
2013	*LAN*	*MLB*	*25*	*250*	*21*	*9*	*1*	*2*	*19*	*21*	*54*	*0*	*0*	*.207/.277/.288*	*.217*	*.256*	*-0.4*	*C 0*	*0.0*

After a breakout 2011, Erickson looked like a nice little sleeper in an organization desperately thin at catcher, an impressive turnaround following his glacial pace through the low minors. In repeating at Chattanooga, however, "Griff" took steps backward on both sides of the ball. Offensively, while he maintained his plate discipline, his power dissipated, and he was eaten alive by righties, a marked contrast to a strong showing against them in 2011. He fared better against lefties in a smaller sample size. Defensively, his caught-stealing rate sank from 30 percent to 21.

Andre Ethier RF

Born: **4/10/1982** Age: **31**
Bats: **L** Throws: **L** Height: **6' 3"**
Weight: **205** Breakout: **1%**
Improve: **40%** Collapse: **5%**
Attrition: **2%** MLB: **93%**

Comparables:
Vladimir Guerrero,Shawn Green,Michael Cuddyer

YEAR	TEAM	LVL	AGE	PA	R	2B	3B	HR	RBI	BB	SO	SB	CS	AVG_OBP_SLG	TAv	BABIP	BRR	FRAA	WARP
2010	LAN	MLB	28	585	71	33	1	23	82	59	102	2	1	.292/.364/.493	.312	.322	0.1	RF(132): -7.7, 1B(1): -0.0	3.2
2011	LAN	MLB	29	551	67	30	0	11	62	58	103	0	1	.292/.368/.421	.291	.348	-2.2	RF(126): 1.3	1.9
2012	LAN	MLB	30	618	79	36	1	20	89	50	124	2	2	.284/.351/.460	.305	.333	-0.4	RF(146): -8.6, CF(1): 0.1	2.3
2013	*LAN*	*MLB*	*31*	*568*	*67*	*31*	*1*	*19*	*75*	*54*	*106*	*2*	*2*	*.275/.350/.456*	*.295*	*.312*	*-1.2*	*RF -2, CF -0*	*3.0*

Following an offseason cleanup of his right knee, Ethier bolted from the gate, hitting .324/.381/.569 through the end of May to help the Dodgers overcome the absence of Matt Kemp. Naturally, the team used this time to buy high, announcing Ethier's five-year, $85 million extension in early June. The right fielder's production regressed considerably the rest of the way, and as much as ever, he struggled against left-handed pitching (606 OPS) to the point of becoming a true liability; his 239 PA against southpaws were 52 more than in any other season. His defense declined as well, according to most major metrics. Relative to the likes of Crawford, Jayson Werth, and Matt Holliday, Ethier's deal is reasonable, but tying up an expensive and incomplete player on the wrong side of 30 is never a sound tactic. He needs a platoon partner, and badly.

Tim Federowicz C

Born: **8/5/1987** Age: **25**
Bats: **R** Throws: **R** Height: **6' 0"**
Weight: **200** Breakout: **15%**
Improve: **42%** Collapse: **12%**
Attrition: **26%** MLB: **95%**

Comparables:
Alan Ashby,Marc Hill,Jimmie Coker

YEAR	TEAM	LVL	AGE	PA	R	2B	3B	HR	RBI	BB	SO	SB	CS	AVG_OBP_SLG	TAv	BABIP	BRR	FRAA	WARP
2010	SLM	A+	22	457	47	34	1	4	61	43	86	1	1	.253/.327/.371	.251	.312	-1.4	C(75): -0.8	0.7
2011	PME	AA	23	382	46	20	0	8	52	32	63	1	0	.277/.338/.407	.261	.312	0	--	0.0
2011	ABQ	AAA	23	102	17	7	0	6	17	15	20	0	0	.325/.431/.627	.357	.356	0	--	0.0
2011	LAN	MLB	23	16	0	0	0	0	1	2	4	0	0	.154/.312/.154	.206	.222	-0.1	C(7): 0.1	0.0
2012	ABQ	AAA	24	475	71	34	1	11	76	52	91	0	1	.294/.371/.461	.225	.347	-2.8	C(23): 0.2	0.0
2012	LAN	MLB	24	4	0	0	0	0	0	1	2	0	0	.333/.500/.333	.362	.000	0	C(2): -0.0	0.1
2013	*LAN*	*MLB*	*25*	*250*	*21*	*12*	*0*	*3*	*23*	*20*	*62*	*0*	*0*	*.221/.287/.320*	*.230*	*.284*	*-0.5*	*C -0*	*0.2*

When Federowicz was acquired from Boston in a three-way deal at the 2011 trading deadline—the one that sent Trayvon Robinson to Seattle—Ned Colletti's stated intention was to pair him with A.J. Ellis in 2012 as part of a cheap catching tandem. Instead, "FedEx" spent virtually the entire season at Albuquerque as Ellis broke out. Defense is Federowicz's calling card, and he improved at blocking the ball while gunning down 39 percent of stolen-base attempts. With Ellis having grabbed the starting job, the Dodgers can either let FedEx serve as the understudy in the bigs or keep him in Triple-A, overnighting him to the majors if the need arises.

Adrian Gonzalez 1B

Born: **5/8/1982** Age: **31**
Bats: **L** Throws: **L** Height: **6' 3"**
Weight: **225** Breakout: **2%**
Improve: **32%** Collapse: **6%**
Attrition: **7%** MLB: **98%**

Comparables:
Todd Helton,Eddie Murray,Mark Teixeira

YEAR	TEAM	LVL	AGE	PA	R	2B	3B	HR	RBI	BB	SO	SB	CS	AVG_OBP_SLG	TAv	BABIP	BRR	FRAA	WARP
2010	SDN	MLB	28	692	87	33	0	31	101	93	114	0	0	.298/.393/.511	.326	.322	-5	1B(159): 8.8	6.4
2011	BOS	MLB	29	715	108	45	3	27	117	74	119	1	0	.338/.410/.548	.318	.380	-8.1	1B(156): 8.9, RF(2): -0.2	4.5
2012	BOS	MLB	30	527	63	37	0	15	86	31	81	0	0	.300/.343/.469	.286	.329	-0.5	1B(115): 12.5, RF(18): -1.1	2.6
2012	LAN	MLB	30	157	12	10	1	3	22	11	29	2	0	.297/.344/.441	.286	.351	-2.8	1B(36): 1.5	0.4
2013	*LAN*	*MLB*	*31*	*649*	*84*	*31*	*1*	*27*	*94*	*69*	*117*	*1*	*0*	*.286/.366/.487*	*.307*	*.316*	*-1.1*	*1B 5, RF -0*	*4.3*

Gonzalez's first year under his seven-year, $154 million extension didn't go smoothly. The only one of Boston's 13 highest-paid players to avoid the disabled list, he was surprisingly punchless in the first half (.283/.329/.416, 6 HR). A second-half surge eased concerns about his surgically repaired right shoulder, and after his shocking inclusion in the late-August blockbuster, he tagged a three-run homer off Josh Johnson in his Dodgers debut. Alas, he homered just twice more the rest of the year, both in a September 23 game after his offensively challenged team's playoff hopes drained away. Assuming he can iron out the kinks, he could become one of the team's most marketable players in Hispanic-heavy L.A., but three straight seasons of declining WARP bodes ominously for the remainder of his deal.

Dee Gordon SS

Born: **4/22/1988** Age: **25**
Bats: **L** Throws: **R** Height: **6' 0"**
Weight: **150** Breakout: **5%**
Improve: **66%** Collapse: **3%**
Attrition: **14%** MLB: **96%**

Comparables:
Erick Aybar,Alcides Escobar,Luis Aparicio

YEAR	TEAM	LVL	AGE	PA	R	2B	3B	HR	RBI	BB	SO	SB	CS	AVG_OBP_SLG	TAv	BABIP	BRR	FRAA	WARP
2010	CHT	AA	22	614	86	17	10	2	39	40	89	53	20	.277/.329/.355	.255	.321	4	SS(133): -12.4	1.5
2011	ABQ	AAA	23	313	51	10	6	0	24	18	40	30	4	.333/.373/.410	.280	.382	0	--	0.0
2011	LAN	MLB	23	233	34	9	2	0	11	7	27	24	7	.304/.325/.362	.252	.345	3	SS(54): -2.4	0.6
2012	LAN	MLB	24	330	38	9	2	1	17	20	62	32	10	.228/.280/.281	.223	.281	2.3	SS(79): -4.1	-0.5
2013	*LAN*	*MLB*	*25*	*295*	*37*	*10*	*2*	*2*	*18*	*14*	*50*	*23*	*7*	*.251/.290/.323*	*.232*	*.296*	*2.1*	*SS -1*	*0.6*

Despite his speed and raw athleticism, Gordon didn't come close to living up to the late-2011 showing that nabbed him the position of starting shortstop and leadoff hitter. His lack of strength and failure to command the strike zone were easily exploited by opposing pitchers, but he was nonetheless allowed to take 280 plate appearances atop the lineup, hitting .217/.269/.271 before a torn ligament in his right thumb mercifully sent him to the disabled list on July 5. Gordon's work afield—particularly his throwing—was erratic, with both Defensive Runs Saved (-14) and Ultimate Zone Rating (-13) particularly down on him. The arrival of Ramirez and the emergence of Cruz may mean Gordon's future lies elsewhere; second base in Albuquerque may be a possibility for 2013.

Tony Gwynn **OF**

Born: **10/4/1982** Age: **30**
Bats: **L** Throws: **R** Height: **6' 0"**
Weight: **195** Breakout: **0%**
Improve: **47%** Collapse: **9%**
Attrition: **13%** MLB: **92%**

Comparables:
Nyjer Morgan,Alfredo Amezaga,Darryl Hamilton

YEAR	TEAM	LVL	AGE	PA	R	2B	3B	HR	RBI	BB	SO	SB	CS	AVG_OBP_SLG	TAv	BABIP	BRR	FRAA	WARP
2010	SDN	MLB	27	339	30	9	3	3	20	41	50	17	4	.204/.304/.287	.230	.236	1.2	CF(105): -9.0	-0.8
2011	LAN	MLB	28	340	37	12	6	2	22	23	61	22	6	.256/.308/.353	.251	.311	2.9	LF(109): 1.9, CF(12): 0.4	0.7
2012	ABQ	AAA	29	79	12	4	1	0	7	8	12	4	1	.338/.416/.426	.243	.411	-0.3	LF(2): -0.3, CF(1): -0.2	-0.3
2012	LAN	MLB	29	277	29	8	4	0	17	16	52	13	6	.232/.276/.293	.215	.290	0	CF(53): -0.6, LF(38): 3.0	-0.4
2013	*LAN*	*MLB*	*30*	*285*	*33*	*9*	*3*	*2*	*19*	*23*	*48*	*13*	*4*	*.244/.308/.321*	*.240*	*.287*	*1.2*	*CF 0, LF 0*	*0.4*

His name is one of the more blatant cases of false advertising in baseball history, but that doesn't mean Tony the Younger lacks uses. During his seven-year career, Gwynn has hit an unplayable .238/.306/.310 as a starter or non-pinch-hitting substitute but .305/.372/.405 in 147 PA as pinch-hitter. Whether it's the mindset or having a manager pick his spots, Gwynn has legitimate value in that role. Between that and above-average defense, he was much more deserving of a roster spot than Abreu or Juan Uribe down the stretch, yet he was outrighted off the roster in early August and wasn't even called up in September. Via yet another of Colletti's backloaded two-year deals, Gwynn is signed for $1.15 million, but the Dodgers may be paying for someone else to roster him.

Jerry Hairston **UT**

Born: **5/29/1976** Age: **37**
Bats: **R** Throws: **R** Height: **5' 11"**
Weight: **190** Breakout: **1%**
Improve: **30%** Collapse: **8%**
Attrition: **12%** MLB: **72%**

Comparables:
Orlando Cabrera,Roberto Alomar,Tony Fernandez

YEAR	TEAM	LVL	AGE	PA	R	2B	3B	HR	RBI	BB	SO	SB	CS	AVG_OBP_SLG	TAv	BABIP	BRR	FRAA	WARP
2010	SDN	MLB	34	476	53	13	2	10	50	31	54	9	6	.244/.299/.353	.248	.255	-0.3	SS(62): 3.3, 2B(47): -1.5	1.1
2011	MIL	MLB	35	138	18	10	0	1	7	11	16	1	0	.274/.348/.379	.253	.308	1.6	2B(27): 1.6, CF(11): 0.3	0.6
2011	WAS	MLB	35	238	25	11	1	4	24	22	30	2	2	.268/.342/.385	.265	.296	1.2	3B(44): -3.1, LF(22): 0.9	0.2
2012	LAN	MLB	36	267	19	13	1	4	26	23	27	1	2	.273/.342/.387	.269	.292	-0.4	3B(32): 2.7, 2B(30): -0.9	1.4
2013	*LAN*	*MLB*	*37*	*274*	*31*	*12*	*1*	*4*	*24*	*19*	*37*	*4*	*2*	*.253/.313/.364*	*.252*	*.276*	*-0.5*	*2B -0, 3B -0*	*0.5*

Signed to a two-year, $6 million deal, Hairston was a godsend for the injury-ravaged Dodgers early in the season, hitting .377/.447/.507 through May while playing plenty of second and third base. When he missed time in May with a hamstring injury, it counted as a crisis. Alas, playing through left hip impingement caused by a torn labrum took its toll on both his offense and defense. He concealed his condition until mid-August, but wound up needing season-ending surgery. Under best-case scenarios, Hairston should be ready for spring training, and while he's unlikely to recapture his early-2012 hot streak, he has evolved into a better hitter than most utilitymen, and could spot as a platoon-mate for Crawford or Ethier should the Dodgers take those two outfielders' shortcomings seriously.

Elian Herrera **UT**

Born: **2/1/1985** Age: **28**
Bats: **B** Throws: **R** Height: **6' 0"**
Weight: **190** Breakout: **2%**
Improve: **56%** Collapse: **8%**
Attrition: **11%** MLB: **94%**

Comparables:
Bump Wills,Craig Biggio,Ray Durham

YEAR	TEAM	LVL	AGE	PA	R	2B	3B	HR	RBI	BB	SO	SB	CS	AVG_OBP_SLG	TAv	BABIP	BRR	FRAA	WARP
2010	CHT	AA	25	365	44	11	4	2	38	47	71	31	10	.258/.354/.341	.262	.315	-0.5	LF(38): 0.1, 2B(24): -1.6	0.8
2010	ABQ	AAA	25	59	8	0	1	0	8	10	9	1	1	.229/.362/.271	.236	.282	-0.2	2B(9): 0.4, LF(8): 0.7	0.1
2011	CHT	AA	26	449	69	17	6	3	35	58	103	33	11	.278/.370/.378	.272	.367	0	--	0.0
2012	ABQ	AAA	27	297	50	20	10	3	40	17	47	11	7	.341/.381/.520	.304	.400	0.6	SS(5): -1.0, 3B(3): -0.4	0.2
2012	LAN	MLB	27	214	26	10	1	1	17	23	50	4	2	.251/.340/.332	.254	.338	1.6	LF(22): 1.2, 3B(20): -0.8	0.4
2013	*LAN*	*MLB*	*28*	*250*	*28*	*10*	*2*	*2*	*17*	*22*	*57*	*9*	*4*	*.237/.309/.324*	*.242*	*.304*	*0.4*	*2B -0, 3B -0*	*0.3*

Signed out of the Dominican Republic in 2003, Herrera toiled in the minors for nine years without landing on the major-league radar, but versatility, a hot start at Albuquerque and Mark Ellis's injury propelled him to the Dodgers in mid-May. He started hot (.305/.407/.390 in 124 PA through June 17) before pitchers caught up to him, but hit .183/.247/.256 the rest of the way while bouncing around the diamond and back to Triple-A a couple of times. Decent on-base skills—particularly against lefties—and the ability to play second, third, and all three outfield positions with competence make him a reasonable choice as a utilityman, though redundant in the presence of Hairston.

Matt Kemp CF

Born: 9/23/1984 Age: 28
Bats: R Throws: R Height: 6' 4''
Weight: 215 Breakout: 0%
Improve: 58% Collapse: 3%
Attrition: 6% MLB: 99%

Comparables:
Dale Murphy,Willie Mays,Duke Snider

YEAR	TEAM	LVL	AGE	PA	R	2B	3B	HR	RBI	BB	SO	SB	CS	AVG_OBP_SLG	TAv	BABIP	BRR	FRAA	WARP
2010	LAN	MLB	25	668	82	25	6	28	89	53	170	19	15	.249/.310/.450	.279	.295	-1.8	CF(158): -9.0	2.0
2011	LAN	MLB	26	689	115	33	4	39	126	74	159	40	11	.324/.399/.586	.350	.380	4.6	CF(159): -8.3	8.3
2012	LAN	MLB	27	449	74	22	2	23	69	40	103	9	4	.303/.367/.538	.322	.354	0.7	CF(105): -7.2	3.3
2013	*LAN*	*MLB*	*28*	*474*	*67*	*21*	*3*	*21*	*67*	*39*	*112*	*18*	*7*	*.282/.344/.488*	*.302*	*.335*	*0.8*	*CF -4*	*3.3*

Kemp signed an eight-year, $160 million extension in November 2011, before the spending really got crazy, and after having nearly won MVP honors in 2011, he looked as though he might lock up the 2012 trophy early, batting .359/.446/.726 before a left hamstring strain sidelined him in mid-May. He returned too quickly, reinjured the leg, and wound up playing just two games over a two-month span during which the team went 24-29 while eking out 3.4 runs per game. Upon returning, Kemp couldn't match his early showing—no one could—but his production nosedived after an August 28 outfield-wall collision in Colorado. Worse than initially feared, the torn shoulder labrum required surgery and could delay his spring training and cut into his power. The good news is that when teammates Gonzalez and Ramirez underwent similar surgeries on their non-throwing shoulders, they combined to average 26 homers and a .195 isolated power the following season.

Adam Kennedy INF

Born: 1/10/1976 Age: 37
Bats: L Throws: R Height: 6' 2''
Weight: 195 Breakout: 0%
Improve: 51% Collapse: 12%
Attrition: 15% MLB: 81%

Comparables:
Geoff Blum,Denny Walling,Brooks Robinson

YEAR	TEAM	LVL	AGE	PA	R	2B	3B	HR	RBI	BB	SO	SB	CS	AVG_OBP_SLG	TAv	BABIP	BRR	FRAA	WARP
2010	WAS	MLB	34	389	43	16	1	3	31	37	44	14	2	.249/.327/.327	.250	.274	-2.1	2B(86): 1.4, 1B(50): 0.0	0.2
2011	SEA	MLB	35	409	36	23	1	7	38	22	67	8	2	.234/.277/.355	.234	.266	0.4	1B(36): 0.8, 2B(34): 2.1	-0.1
2012	LAN	MLB	36	201	22	8	1	2	16	23	33	1	1	.262/.345/.357	.272	.304	0.2	3B(39): 3.1, 2B(16): 0.4	1.0
2013	*LAN*	*MLB*	*37*	*250*	*24*	*11*	*1*	*3*	*22*	*18*	*40*	*5*	*1*	*.247/.304/.337*	*.241*	*.284*	*0.2*	*2B -1, 3B 0*	*0.2*

No longer able to hack it as a regular, Kennedy turned in a useful season as a bench player, spotting occasionally at third or second base against righties without ever getting an extended look, even amid the Biblical slew of injuries that befell the Dodgers' infielders. Despite missing six weeks in the second half with a recurrent groin strain that ended his season in early September, he ranked second on the team with 33 pinch-hit appearances, and hit righties well enough that he should find part-time work again.

Joc Pederson CF

Born: 4/21/1992 Age: 21
Bats: L Throws: L Height: 6' 2''
Weight: 185 Breakout: 4%
Improve: 60% Collapse: 8%
Attrition: 16% MLB: 98%

Comparables:
Curt Flood,Thad Bosley,Rick Manning

YEAR	TEAM	LVL	AGE	PA	R	2B	3B	HR	RBI	BB	SO	SB	CS	AVG_OBP_SLG	TAv	BABIP	BRR	FRAA	WARP
2011	OGD	Rk	19	310	54	20	2	11	64	36	54	24	5	.353/.429/.568	.314	.403	0.7	LF(26): -2.5, RF(14): 0.8	1.3
2011	GRL	A	19	60	4	0	0	0	1	7	9	2	0	.160/.288/.160	.183	.195	0	--	0.0
2012	RCU	A+	20	499	96	26	4	18	70	51	81	26	14	.313/.396/.516	.376	.350	6.2	CF(12): -2.3, LF(5): -0.5	1.7
2013	*LAN*	*MLB*	*21*	*250*	*30*	*10*	*1*	*5*	*21*	*18*	*58*	*8*	*3*	*.229/.290/.349*	*.239*	*.279*	*0.3*	*CF -1, LF -1*	*0.0*

Pederson, who got second-round money after being drafted in the 11th round in 2010, emerged as the Dodgers' top positional prospect in 2012, putting up strong numbers at a young age in a hitter-friendly league, and demonstrating a high baseball IQ and serious #want to go with his tools and skills. All five tools have the potential to be average or better. He has a compact stroke with legitimate power, and an advanced, grind-it-out approach at the plate. While he can handle center, he profiles better as a left fielder because of the limitations of his speed and arm. The total package translates into a player with a chance to be an above-average regular or better, though finding an opening in the Dodgers outfield will be another matter. He'll move up to Double-A in 2013.

Yasiel Puig OF

Born: 12/7/1990 Age: 22
Bats: R Throws: R Height: 6' 4''
Weight: 215 Breakout: 5%
Improve: 53% Collapse: 12%
Attrition: 20% MLB: 97%

Comparables:
Gary Thomasson,Keith Hernandez,Cliff Floyd

YEAR	TEAM	LVL	AGE	PA	R	2B	3B	HR	RBI	BB	SO	SB	CS	AVG_OBP_SLG	TAv	BABIP	BRR	FRAA	WARP
2012	RCU	A+	21	59	10	2	0	1	4	6	8	7	4	.327/.407/.423	.199	.372	0	RF(3): -0.3	-0.2
2013	*LAN*	*MLB*	*22*	*250*	*30*	*9*	*1*	*4*	*21*	*14*	*60*	*18*	*8*	*.224/.272/.329*	*.226*	*.278*	*0.9*	*RF -0*	*-0.2*

In what seemed like an overreaction both to years of neglecting the international market in the McCourt era and to the looming cap on international spending, the Dodgers signed this Cuban defector to a record-setting seven-year, $42 million deal—more than Yoenis Cespedes or Jorge Soler received. Considered the fastest player in Cuban baseball, Puig is a five-tool guy with plus raw power, plus speed, and a plus arm, with names like Vladimir Guerrero and Giancarlo Stanton thrown about—perhaps haphazardly—as comps. He hit well during limited playing time in August despite being out of shape and not having played competitively in over a year. Puig will go to camp with the big-league club in the spring, but the Dodgers will likely keep him in the minors all year, particularly with no opening in their outfield.

Nick Punto **3B**
Born: **11/8/1977** Age: **35**
Bats: **B** Throws: **R** Height: **5' 10"**
Weight: **190** Breakout: **2%**
Improve: **35%** Collapse: **11%**
Attrition: **21%** MLB: **83%**
Comparables:
Bobby Avila,Jamey Carroll,Solly Hemus

YEAR	TEAM	LVL	AGE	PA	R	2B	3B	HR	RBI	BB	SO	SB	CS	AVG_OBP_SLG	TAv	BABIP	BRR	FRAA	WARP
2010	MIN	MLB	32	288	24	11	1	1	20	28	50	6	2	.238/.313/.302	.240	.289	-1.3	3B(48): 4.2, SS(31): -1.0	1.0
2011	SLN	MLB	33	166	21	8	4	1	20	25	21	1	1	.278/.387/.421	.291	.319	1.8	2B(44): 2.2, SS(8): -0.3	1.4
2012	BOS	MLB	34	148	14	6	0	1	10	19	33	5	0	.200/.301/.272	.206	.258	-0.2	3B(26): 2.0, 2B(15): -0.7	-0.3
2012	LAN	MLB	34	43	6	1	0	0	0	6	9	1	0	.286/.390/.314	.276	.385	0.5	2B(11): 0.7, 3B(5): -0.0	0.4
2013	*LAN*	*MLB*	*35*	*250*	*25*	*9*	*1*	*1*	*18*	*28*	*46*	*6*	*1*	*.232/.320/.302*	*.235*	*.280*	*0.5*	*2B -1, 3B 1*	*0.2*

Aided by small sample sizes, the hand of Tony La Russa picking his spots, and the OBP bounce that comes with batting eighth in the NL (he had a 1/10 strikeout-to-walk-ratio there in 2011), Punto finagled a two-year, $3 million deal from the Red Sox last winter. Predictably, he regressed, proving a poor substitute for the injured Dustin Pedroia and Kevin Youkilis, and putting up his worst numbers since 2007. Sent to the Dodgers in the blockbuster, he fared slightly better, but on a team that has Hairston, Uribe, Gordon, and Herrera either under contract or club control, it's unclear how little Nicky fits in.

Hanley Ramirez **SS**
Born: **12/23/1983** Age: **29**
Bats: **R** Throws: **R** Height: **6' 4"**
Weight: **230** Breakout: **2%**
Improve: **48%** Collapse: **1%**
Attrition: **7%** MLB: **98%**
Comparables:
George Brett,David Wright,Chipper Jones

YEAR	TEAM	LVL	AGE	PA	R	2B	3B	HR	RBI	BB	SO	SB	CS	AVG_OBP_SLG	TAv	BABIP	BRR	FRAA	WARP
2010	FLO	MLB	26	619	92	28	2	21	76	64	93	32	10	.300/.378/.475	.301	.327	1.2	SS(140): -9.9	4.1
2011	FLO	MLB	27	385	55	16	0	10	45	44	66	20	10	.243/.333/.379	.255	.275	1.2	SS(86): -8.7	0.2
2012	LAN	MLB	28	272	30	11	2	10	44	17	60	7	3	.271/.324/.450	.276	.319	1.8	SS(57): -3.4, 3B(8): 0.0	1.2
2012	MIA	MLB	28	395	49	18	2	14	48	37	72	14	4	.246/.322/.428	.267	.271	3.4	3B(90): -12.7	0.1
2013	*LAN*	*MLB*	*29*	*571*	*80*	*26*	*1*	*21*	*75*	*55*	*100*	*24*	*9*	*.278/.355/.460*	*.298*	*.308*	*0.8*	*SS -6, 3B -3*	*3.5*

Desperate for offense in late July, the Dodgers traded for Ramirez and agreed to absorb the $31.5 million remaining on the final two years of his deal, a move that looks like small beer next to the salary they took on via the monster Red Sox trade. Despite the shorter timeframe, the Dodgers have taken on considerable risk. Ramirez was terrible at both third and short, according to multiple metrics, and his bat didn't fully rebound after a down 2011 caused by left shoulder woes that required offseason surgery. In Miami, he resisted the move to third base to accommodate Jose Reyes and showed a lack of maturity when he punched an electric fan in the dugout, requiring stitches. He missed time due to an infection when he didn't take his medication, an absence that precipitated the trade. In happier surroundings in Los Angeles, another year removed from surgery, and still on the right side of 30, a further rebound isn't out of the question, but it's hardly a given.

Juan Rivera **LF**
Born: **7/3/1978** Age: **34**
Bats: **R** Throws: **R** Height: **6' 3"**
Weight: **230** Breakout: **1%**
Improve: **39%** Collapse: **6%**
Attrition: **18%** MLB: **87%**
Comparables:
Ross Gload,Wally Joyner,Nomar Garciaparra

YEAR	TEAM	LVL	AGE	PA	R	2B	3B	HR	RBI	BB	SO	SB	CS	AVG_OBP_SLG	TAv	BABIP	BRR	FRAA	WARP
2010	ANA	MLB	32	455	53	20	0	15	52	33	58	2	2	.252/.312/.409	.267	.261	-1.5	LF(83): 2.9, RF(25): 0.9	1.7
2011	LAN	MLB	33	246	24	12	1	5	46	21	35	2	1	.274/.333/.406	.281	.299	-2	LF(32): 0.6, 1B(17): -1.1	0.4
2011	TOR	MLB	33	275	22	11	0	6	28	22	41	3	2	.243/.305/.360	.230	.265	0.8	LF(24): -1.7, 1B(21): -0.2	-0.7
2012	LAN	MLB	33	339	30	14	0	9	47	18	35	1	3	.244/.286/.375	.245	.245	1.4	1B(54): -0.7, LF(37): -0.8	-0.4
2013	*LAN*	*MLB*	*34*	*357*	*37*	*15*	*0*	*11*	*42*	*23*	*50*	*2*	*2*	*.247/.300/.390*	*.257*	*.260*	*-0.9*	*LF 1, 1B -0*	*0.6*

Rivera lives up to the "RBI Machine" tag that is so often attached to him. For the second straight year, he drove in precisely 17.1 percent of baserunners, a rate that placed him in the upper 20 percent among hitters with at least 200 plate appearances. Unfortunately, the other holes in his game were glaringly apparent. He didn't hit lefties as well as advertised (.260/.312/.433), didn't hit righties at all (.232/.269/.335) and failed to provide a sound alternative to the meager production the Dodgers got from Loney or their other left fielders. The Dodgers declined his $4 million option; he'll be lucky to get half that elsewhere.

Kyle Russell **OF**
Born: **6/27/1986** Age: **27**
Bats: **L** Throws: **L** Height: **6' 6"**
Weight: **195** Breakout: **7%**
Improve: **44%** Collapse: **1%**
Attrition: **7%** MLB: **90%**
Comparables:
Mitchell Page,Ryan Klesko,Dan Pasqua

YEAR	TEAM	LVL	AGE	PA	R	2B	3B	HR	RBI	BB	SO	SB	CS	AVG_OBP_SLG	TAv	BABIP	BRR	FRAA	WARP
2010	SBR	A+	24	239	42	11	4	16	53	32	64	8	3	.354/.455/.692	.396	.458	0.4	RF(40): 2.1, CF(6): 0.1	3.9
2010	CHT	AA	24	308	36	23	3	10	28	29	113	3	2	.245/.321/.462	.269	.377	0.1	RF(66): 0.6, CF(6): 0.0	1.3
2011	CHT	AA	25	447	61	29	4	19	69	45	144	5	1	.259/.342/.497	.283	.356	0	--	0.0
2012	CHT	AA	26	277	38	18	1	11	44	41	69	4	2	.262/.379/.493	.292	.322	-0.3	LF(17): -1.4, RF(7): 0.6	0.2
2013	*LAN*	*MLB*	*27*	*250*	*28*	*10*	*1*	*9*	*32*	*22*	*85*	*2*	*1*	*.218/.293/.397*	*.252*	*.297*	*-0.2*	*RF -1, LF -0*	*0.2*

The Texas Wind Machine—so named for his long swing, penchant for strikeouts, and University of Texas pedigree—made considerably more contact in 2012 than in years past, cutting his strikeout rate below 25 percent when it had never been below 31 percent in his entire pro career. Alas, he also did two stints on the disabled list for an oblique strain and was shelved for the season in late July. Russell has 80 raw power, a good arm, and decent speed, but he's not getting any younger, and the holes in his swing—and complete helplessness against left-handers—significantly limit his ceiling.

Skip Schumaker UT
Born: **2/3/1980** Age: **33**
Bats: **L** Throws: **R** Height: **5' 11"**
Weight: **195** Breakout: **3%**
Improve: **31%** Collapse: **4%**
Attrition: **15%** MLB: **98%**
Comparables:
Red Schoendienst, Bobby Avila, Mark Loretta

YEAR	TEAM	LVL	AGE	PA	R	2B	3B	HR	RBI	BB	SO	SB	CS	AVG_OBP_SLG	TAv	BABIP	BRR	FRAA	WARP
2010	SLN	MLB	30	529	66	18	1	5	42	43	64	5	3	.265/.328/.338	.247	.294	-0.4	2B(123): 2.3, RF(12): 0.9	1.2
2011	SLN	MLB	31	400	34	19	0	2	38	27	50	0	2	.283/.333/.351	.251	.321	-1.2	2B(95): 1.5, RF(30): 0.2	0.2
2012	SLN	MLB	32	304	37	14	4	1	28	27	50	1	1	.276/.339/.368	.255	.332	-1	2B(61): -0.0, CF(14): -0.1	0.4
2013	*LAN*	*MLB*	*33*	*308*	*32*	*13*	*1*	*3*	*24*	*24*	*45*	*2*	*1*	*.268/.326/.349*	*.254*	*.307*	*-0.5*	*2B 1, CF -0*	*0.9*

Schumaker remains as gritty and adaptable as ever, willing to pitch in defensively all over the field and smack a few line drives against right-handed pitching. He's a liability with the glove at second base, hasn't slugged over .400 during the Obama administration, is hopeless against lefties, and was supplanted in St. Louis's super-sub role by the arrival of the more capable Matt Carpenter. Traded to the Dodgers for Jake Lemmerman, he's not a bad fit for a platoon with Mark Ellis, but the Dodgers are awash in spare infielders, so his leash may not be long.

Corey Seager SS
Born: **4/27/1994** Age: **19**
Bats: **L** Throws: **R** Height: **6' 4"**
Weight: **195** Breakout: **0%**
Improve: **67%** Collapse: **33%**
Attrition: **33%** MLB: **100%**
Comparables:
Ed Kranepool, Wayne Causey, Robin Yount

YEAR	TEAM	LVL	AGE	PA	R	2B	3B	HR	RBI	BB	SO	SB	CS	AVG_OBP_SLG	TAv	BABIP	BRR	FRAA	WARP
2012	OGD	Rk	18	202	34	9	2	8	33	21	33	8	2	.309/.383/.520	.278	.336	2.8	SS(33): -7.5	0.1
2013	*LAN*	*MLB*	*19*	*250*	*20*	*8*	*1*	*5*	*24*	*12*	*68*	*1*	*0*	*.193/.235/.301*	*.200*	*.242*	*-0.2*	*SS -1*	*-0.6*

The younger but bigger brother of the Mariners' Kyle Seager was chosen 18th in the 2012 draft out of a North Carolina high school, and signed for an above-slot $2.35 million bonus. He sparkled in his professional debut, putting up good numbers as one of the youngest players in a hitter-friendly league. Seager is lean and athletic with very good bat speed, a knack for contact, and potentially above-average power. In the field he has quick hands, good footwork, and a strong arm that should play well at third base given the strong likelihood that he winds up there. Overall, he's easily one of the Dodgers' top prospects, and while he's years away from the majors, he's worth getting excited about.

Blake Smith RF
Born: **12/9/1987** Age: **25**
Bats: **L** Throws: **R** Height: **6' 3"**
Weight: **225** Breakout: **9%**
Improve: **51%** Collapse: **6%**
Attrition: **18%** MLB: **95%**
Comparables:
Earl Robinson, Ron Swoboda, Carl Everett

YEAR	TEAM	LVL	AGE	PA	R	2B	3B	HR	RBI	BB	SO	SB	CS	AVG_OBP_SLG	TAv	BABIP	BRR	FRAA	WARP
2010	GRL	A	22	493	77	28	2	19	76	49	135	2	3	.281/.363/.488	.296	.366	-0.2	RF(103): 5.6	3.4
2011	RCU	A+	23	329	59	24	0	16	63	32	83	3	2	.294/.359/.539	.301	.354	0	--	0.0
2012	CHT	AA	24	531	69	29	4	13	65	64	134	14	6	.267/.358/.432	.276	.348	-0.8	RF(39): 3.5, CF(4): 0.1	1.3
2013	*LAN*	*MLB*	*25*	*250*	*25*	*10*	*1*	*7*	*28*	*19*	*77*	*2*	*1*	*.220/.283/.365*	*.239*	*.293*	*-0.3*	*RF -0, CF 0*	*0.0*

A second-round 2009 pick out of Cal, Smith rebounded from a season interrupted by a sports hernia and asserted his place as one of the Dodgers' better position prospects. Even so, his season wasn't an unqualified success; after earning All-Star honors in the first half, he hit just .236/.323/.359 from July 1 on. Smith does have real pop, but his long swing continues to leave him prone to strikeouts, and there remains concern about how well his aggressive approach will play against better pitching. He's got a great arm—many scouts preferred him as a pitcher coming out of college—and the mound is always a backup plan if his career as an outfielder stalls.

Matt Treanor C
Born: **3/3/1976** Age: **37**
Bats: **R** Throws: **R** Height: **6' 1"**
Weight: **205** Breakout: **4%**
Improve: **27%** Collapse: **7%**
Attrition: **21%** MLB: **72%**
Comparables:
Rick Dempsey, Chad Kreuter, Johnny Roseboro

YEAR	TEAM	LVL	AGE	PA	R	2B	3B	HR	RBI	BB	SO	SB	CS	AVG_OBP_SLG	TAv	BABIP	BRR	FRAA	WARP
2010	TEX	MLB	34	272	22	6	1	5	27	22	43	1	2	.211/.287/.308	.221	.233	-1.8	C(81): -1.0	0.0
2011	KCA	MLB	35	230	24	6	0	3	21	33	49	2	2	.226/.351/.306	.261	.287	-2.3	C(65): -1.3	0.5
2011	TEX	MLB	35	12	0	0	0	0	1	1	4	0	0	.000/.083/.000	.087	.000	0	C(7): 0.1	-0.2
2012	LAN	MLB	36	122	11	3	1	2	10	14	29	1	1	.175/.281/.282	.223	.216	-1.8	C(35): 0.2	-0.5
2013	*LAN*	*MLB*	*37*	*250*	*23*	*7*	*1*	*3*	*20*	*24*	*56*	*2*	*1*	*.205/.292/.285*	*.222*	*.254*	*-0.5*	*C -0*	*0.1*

Treanor's still a member of the International Brotherhood of Backup Catchers, but just barely. Even by his own meager standards, he failed to hit a lick, and threw out just 25 percent of would-be base thieves. The Dodgers can't afford to run A.J. Ellis into the ground as they did in 2012, so it's hardly a surprise that they'll turn elsewhere for backup help, having declined a $950,000 option on Treanor's services.

Juan Uribe SS

Born: **7/22/1979** Age: **33**
Bats: **R** Throws: **R** Height: **6' 0"**
Weight: **230** Breakout: **5%**
Improve: **31%** Collapse: **11%**
Attrition: **18%** MLB: **90%**

Comparables:
Tony Batista, Ken Caminiti, Sean Berry

YEAR	TEAM	LVL	AGE	PA	R	2B	3B	HR	RBI	BB	SO	SB	CS	AVG_OBP_SLG	TAv	BABIP	BRR	FRAA	WARP
2010	SFN	MLB	30	575	64	24	2	24	85	45	92	1	2	.248/.310/.440	.263	.256	-2.5	SS(103): -5.0, 3B(26): 0.9	2.1
2011	LAN	MLB	31	295	21	12	0	4	28	17	60	2	0	.204/.264/.293	.204	.245	0.5	3B(59): 0.6, 2B(18): -1.4	-1.3
2012	LAN	MLB	32	179	15	9	0	2	17	13	37	0	1	.191/.258/.284	.197	.234	1.6	3B(46): 2.3, SS(1): -0.1	-0.3
2013	*LAN*	*MLB*	*33*	*250*	*24*	*11*	*1*	*7*	*28*	*16*	*50*	*1*	*1*	*.235/.288/.379*	*.247*	*.268*	*-0.4*	*3B 1, SS -0*	*0.4*

Two-thirds of the way through his three-year, $21 million deal, Uribe has already taken his seat alongside Jason Schmidt and Andruw Jones among Colletti's biggest boondoggles. Again, injuries kept him out of the lineup. This time, left wrist inflammation robbed him of his power and reduced him to the role of not-so-innocent bystander. He got just 92 plate appearances upon coming off the DL on June 11, raising the question of why the Dodgers bothered to keep him on the roster at all. The bet here is that the Dodgers cut bait by Opening Day.

Jesmuel Valentin SS

Born: **5/12/1994** Age: **19**
Bats: **S** Throws: **R** Height: **5' 11"**
Weight: **174** Breakout: **0%**
Improve: **58%** Collapse: **42%**
Attrition: **42%** MLB: **100%**

Comparables:
Ed Kranepool, Robin Yount, Wayne Causey

YEAR	TEAM	LVL	AGE	PA	R	2B	3B	HR	RBI	BB	SO	SB	CS	AVG_OBP_SLG	TAv	BABIP	BRR	FRAA	WARP
2012	DOD	Rk	18	197	34	6	2	2	18	35	24	5	2	.211/.352/.316	.249	.229	-0.8	SS(5): -0.1	0.0
2013	*LAN*	*MLB*	*19*	*250*	*26*	*7*	*1*	*2*	*14*	*17*	*73*	*10*	*4*	*.176/.235/.243*	*.184*	*.241*	*0.6*	*SS 0*	*-0.6*

The son of former major-league infielder Jose Valentin was chosen 51st in the 2012 draft out of the Puerto Rico Baseball Academy and High School, where he played second base alongside overall top pick Carlos Correa. Bypassing a scholarship to Louisiana State University—a mistake in the eyes of some—he signed for the recommended slot bonus of $984,700. A natural righty who has only been switch-hitting for a couple of years, Valentin's bag of tools includes a strong, accurate arm with a quick release, above-average range, average speed, and a line-drive approach. He struggled at the plate in his professional debut, however, showing stiff swing mechanics and swinging late on fastballs and over off-speed pitches. He'll need time to mature, particularly on the offensive side.

Scott Van Slyke OF

Born: **7/24/1986** Age: **26**
Bats: **R** Throws: **R** Height: **6' 6"**
Weight: **220** Breakout: **7%**
Improve: **52%** Collapse: **7%**
Attrition: **11%** MLB: **91%**

Comparables:
Josh Kroeger, Alex Rios, Paul O'Neill

YEAR	TEAM	LVL	AGE	PA	R	2B	3B	HR	RBI	BB	SO	SB	CS	AVG_OBP_SLG	TAv	BABIP	BRR	FRAA	WARP
2010	SBR	A+	23	209	34	12	2	9	35	17	39	3	1	.307/.370/.534	.313	.348	-0.1	RF(42): -2.2, LF(2): 0.0	1.2
2010	CHT	AA	23	241	28	7	3	4	29	18	37	4	2	.235/.301/.350	.223	.266	-0.8	RF(52): -2.0, LF(10): 1.8	-0.5
2011	CHT	AA	24	529	81	45	4	20	92	65	100	6	5	.348/.427/.595	.348	.406	0	--	0.0
2012	ABQ	AAA	25	411	68	34	1	18	67	46	64	5	3	.327/.404/.578	.370	.354	-0.8	RF(8): -1.3, 1B(7): -0.7	0.4
2012	LAN	MLB	25	57	4	2	0	2	7	2	14	1	0	.167/.196/.315	.186	.184	0.8	RF(12): 0.5, LF(10): 0.1	-0.3
2013	*LAN*	*MLB*	*26*	*250*	*25*	*11*	*1*	*7*	*29*	*17*	*55*	*1*	*1*	*.235/.290/.387*	*.251*	*.274*	*-0.3*	*RF -1, 1B -0*	*0.1*

Scouts have never been enamored of the tools of this son of a longtime former major leaguer, who was drafted in the 14th round by the Dodgers in 2005. His power is nothing special for his position, and he doesn't run well. Even so, Van Slyke earned the Dodgers Minor League Player of the Year honors with a breakout 2011, and while he did taste the majors in 2012 when the injury bug bit, the weakness of the team's solutions at left field and first base suggested he deserved a longer look. Now blocked at all three positions by players under long-term contract, his last remaining chance with the Dodgers may hinge on a slow recovery for Crawford or a niche role as Ethier's platoon partner. Don't hold your breath.

PITCHERS

Steve Ames

Born: **3/15/1988** Age: **25**
Bats: **R** Throws: **R** Height: **6' 2"** Weight: **205**
Breakout: **26%** Improve: **48%** Collapse: **22%**
Attrition: **8%** MLB: **93%**

Comparables:
Adam Wainwright, Rich Thompson, Antonio Osuna

YEAR	TEAM	LVL	AGE	W	L	SV	G	GS	IP	H	HR	BB	SO	BB9	SO9	GB%	BABIP	WHIP	ERA	FIP	FRA	WARP
2010	DOD	Rk	22	0	0	0	3	0	3	2	0	0	4	0.0	12.0	—	.286	0.67	0.00	1.59	3.29	0.1
2010	GRL	A	22	0	2	16	23	0	28^{1}	21	0	3	44	1.0	14.0	49%	.375	0.85	2.54	0.82	2.37	1.0
2011	RCU	A+	23	0	0	9	15	0	15^{1}	10	1	2	28	1.2	16.4	—	.310	0.78	1.17	1.54	1.67	0.0
2011	CHT	AA	23	2	2	5	28	0	32^{2}	32	3	11	41	3.0	11.3	—	.349	1.32	2.48	3.00	3.26	0.0
2012	CHT	AA	24	3	3	18	54	0	63^{1}	52	2	13	72	1.8	10.2	35%	.306	1.03	1.56	1.90	1.26	1.8
2013	*LAN*	*MLB*	*25*	*2*	*1*	*2*	*33*	*0*	*38^{2}*	*33*	*4*	*12*	*41*	*2.9*	*9.5*	*41%*	*.305*	*1.17*	*3.34*	*3.36*	*3.63*	*0.4*

A 17th-round 2009 pick out of Gonzaga, Ames has put up double-digit strikeout rates out of the bullpen at every stop in the Dodgers chain. Even so, scouts aren't as impressed by his stuff—a low-90s fastball/slider combo—as his numbers, which isn't to say that they don't see a major-league future for a guy with good command who changes speeds and pounds the strike zone relentlessly. He's a middle reliever in the making, one who will likely wait his turn at Albuquerque in 2013.

Josh Beckett

Born: **5/15/1980** Age: **33**
Bats: **R** Throws: **R** Height: **6' 6"** Weight: **225**
Breakout: **18%** Improve: **52%** Collapse: **18%**
Attrition: **25%** MLB: **84%**

Comparables:
Chris Carpenter,Kelvim Escobar,John Smoltz

YEAR	TEAM	LVL	AGE	W	L	SV	G	GS	IP	H	HR	BB	SO	BB9	SO9	GB%	BABIP	WHIP	ERA	FIP	FRA	WARP
2010	PAW	AAA	30	0	0	0	2	2	8	7	2	1	7	1.1	7.9	38%	.227	1.00	4.50	5.17	5.59	0.0
2010	BOS	MLB	30	6	6	0	21	21	127^2	151	20	45	116	3.2	8.2	47%	.338	1.54	5.78	4.51	5.17	0.6
2011	BOS	MLB	31	13	7	0	30	30	193	146	21	52	175	2.4	8.2	42%	.245	1.03	2.89	3.61	4.13	2.4
2012	BOS	MLB	32	5	11	0	21	21	127^1	131	16	38	94	2.7	6.6	42%	.292	1.33	5.23	4.22	5.36	0.5
2012	LAN	MLB	32	2	3	0	7	7	43	43	5	14	38	2.9	8.0	51%	.302	1.33	2.93	3.86	3.64	0.3
2013	*LAN*	*MLB*	*33*	*11*	*7*	*0*	*27*	*27*	*164^1*	*139*	*17*	*39*	*152*	*2.1*	*8.3*	*45%*	*.286*	*1.08*	*3.05*	*3.41*	*3.32*	*2.6*

Beckett, already in the heel role after the fried chicken and beer revelations from 2011, didn't do his reputation any favors when he played golf on an offday in May after being scratched from a start with a stiff latissimus dorsi. Whether or not he really was the problem for Bobby Valentine that many reports suggested, his uneven performance fit into a career-long pattern reminiscent of the oft-injured Bret Saberhagen: healthy and effective during odd-numbered years, less so in even-numbered ones. Relocation from Boston and the AL East to Los Angeles and the NL West appears to have helped his cause, but he's far from the pitcher he was in 2007, having lost 4.2 miles per hour off his average fastball, now at 92. Further reinvention isn't out of the question, but even with the calendar showing another odd-numbered year, the chances of him living up to his contract are slim.

Ronald Belisario

Born: **12/31/1982** Age: **30**
Bats: **R** Throws: **R** Height: **6' 4"** Weight: **235**
Breakout: **24%** Improve: **52%** Collapse: **29%**
Attrition: **9%** MLB: **88%**

Comparables:
Ramon Ramirez,Jason Isringhausen,Mel Rojas

YEAR	TEAM	LVL	AGE	W	L	SV	G	GS	IP	H	HR	BB	SO	BB9	SO9	GB%	BABIP	WHIP	ERA	FIP	FRA	WARP
2010	LAN	MLB	27	3	1	2	59	0	55^1	52	6	19	38	3.1	6.2	63%	.275	1.28	5.04	4.34	4.76	-0.1
2012	RCU	A+	29	0	1	0	2	1	3	6	0	0	1	0.0	3.0	79%	.429	2.00	12.00	3.15	3.25	0.0
2012	ABQ	AAA	29	0	0	0	2	0	1^2	2	0	2	0	10.8	0.0	86%	.286	2.40	0.00	7.27	1260.12	-0.1
2012	LAN	MLB	29	8	1	1	68	0	71	47	3	29	69	3.7	8.7	65%	.243	1.07	2.54	3.14	3.95	0.4
2013	*LAN*	*MLB*	*30*	*3*	*1*	*1*	*54*	*0*	*53^1*	*44*	*5*	*19*	*46*	*3.1*	*7.8*	*55%*	*.280*	*1.17*	*3.33*	*3.76*	*3.61*	*0.6*

After two years of substance abuse, legal, and immigration problems, Belisario finally got his life and his paperwork in order, and after serving a 25-game suspension for a violation of the Joint Drug Agreement, joined the Dodgers in early May. With his two-seamer—thrown a remarkable 83 percent of the time—still firing at 95 mph, he quickly pitched his way into high-leverage duty. Working 81 appearances, he reeled off a carbon copy of his breakout 2009 campaign, save for allowing a few more inherited runners to score. He smothered righties, and if he couldn't do the same to lefties, his overall 558 OPS allowed testified to his dominance. If he can keep his nose clean, he'll be part of the Dodgers' late-game plan again in 2013.

Chad Billingsley

Born: **7/29/1984** Age: **28**
Bats: **R** Throws: **R** Height: **6' 2"** Weight: **240**
Breakout: **20%** Improve: **70%** Collapse: **13%**
Attrition: **6%** MLB: **88%**

Comparables:
Anibal Sanchez,John Maine,Noah Lowry

YEAR	TEAM	LVL	AGE	W	L	SV	G	GS	IP	H	HR	BB	SO	BB9	SO9	GB%	BABIP	WHIP	ERA	FIP	FRA	WARP
2010	LAN	MLB	25	12	11	0	31	31	191^2	176	8	69	171	3.2	8.0	51%	.301	1.28	3.57	3.10	3.32	3.6
2011	LAN	MLB	26	11	11	0	32	32	188	189	14	84	152	4.0	7.3	47%	.306	1.45	4.21	3.80	4.24	1.6
2012	LAN	MLB	27	10	9	0	25	25	149^2	148	11	45	128	2.7	7.7	47%	.308	1.29	3.55	3.38	3.79	2.5
2013	*LAN*	*MLB*	*28*	*9*	*7*	*0*	*23*	*23*	*135^2*	*120*	*10*	*46*	*121*	*3.1*	*8.0*	*47%*	*.303*	*1.23*	*3.61*	*3.39*	*3.93*	*1.0*

A .343 BABIP, lousy offensive support, and a 4-9 won-loss record masked Billingsley's first-half rebound. During that 104 2/3-inning span, he struck out 8.6 per nine and walked 2.9, and all he had to show for it was a lousy 4.30 ERA and an angry mob of frustrated fans hoping he'd be traded. Instead, Billingsley went on the disabled list for an inflamed flexor tendon, and when he returned 15 days later, his luck began evening out: 6-0 with a 1.80 ERA and a .243 BABIP over his next seven turns despite striking out just 5.6 per nine. Alas, he hit the DL in late August with a sprained UCL, and while a platelet-rich plasma injection didn't help him recover in time to return to active duty, he was pain-free and touching 94 mph in a simulated game in late October, forestalling Tommy John surgery at least for the moment. If his elbow can hold together and he can replicate his 2012 form, he's the Dodgers' number-two starter behind Kershaw, but those are big ifs.

Chris Capuano
Born: **8/19/1978** Age: **34**
Bats: **L** Throws: **L** Height: **6' 4"** Weight: **220**
Breakout: **16%** Improve: **51%** Collapse: **13%**
Attrition: **12%** MLB: **85%**
Comparables:
Ted Lilly,Bruce Hurst,John Smiley

YEAR	TEAM	LVL	AGE	W	L	SV	G	GS	IP	H	HR	BB	SO	BB9	SO9	GB%	BABIP	WHIP	ERA	FIP	FRA	WARP
2010	BRV	A+	31	2	0	0	3	3	14^2	12	1	0	17	0.0	10.4	39%	.289	0.82	1.22	2.01	3.14	0.3
2010	NAS	AAA	31	1	1	0	4	4	25	21	0	4	16	1.4	5.8	44%	.259	1.00	1.80	2.90	3.61	0.7
2010	MIL	MLB	31	4	4	0	24	9	66	65	9	21	54	2.9	7.4	44%	.290	1.30	3.95	4.24	4.74	0.6
2011	NYN	MLB	32	11	12	0	33	31	186	198	27	53	168	2.6	8.1	44%	.311	1.35	4.55	4.01	4.36	1.5
2012	LAN	MLB	33	12	12	0	33	33	198^1	188	25	54	162	2.5	7.4	43%	.284	1.22	3.72	3.99	4.19	1.6
2013	*LAN*	*MLB*	*34*	*11*	*9*	*0*	*29*	*29*	*166^2*	*156*	*21*	*43*	*140*	*2.3*	*7.5*	*43%*	*.297*	*1.20*	*3.85*	*3.93*	*4.18*	*0.8*

Signed to a backloaded two-year, $10 million deal last winter, this two-time Tommy John surgery survivor lived up to his end of the bargain, staying healthy and pitching more than in any season since 2006. His strikeout rate was right around his career mark, his walk and home-run rates a bit better. That said, he clearly ran out of gas late in the year, with a 5.98 ERA, two homers per nine and just 4.2 strikeouts per nine over his last eight starts. He could probably use a bit of extra rest now and then, but even with his salary doubling to $6 million in the final year of his deal, he's a good back-rotation filler as long as he's healthy.

Todd Coffey
Born: **9/9/1980** Age: **32**
Bats: **R** Throws: **R** Height: **6' 5"** Weight: **240**
Breakout: **19%** Improve: **43%** Collapse: **34%**
Attrition: **13%** MLB: **92%**
Comparables:
Vinnie Chulk,Bruce Sutter,Matt Wise

YEAR	TEAM	LVL	AGE	W	L	SV	G	GS	IP	H	HR	BB	SO	BB9	SO9	GB%	BABIP	WHIP	ERA	FIP	FRA	WARP
2010	NAS	AAA	29	0	0	0	1	0	1	0	0	0	1	0.0	9.0	1.%	.000	0.00	0.00	1.58	1.87	0.0
2010	MIL	MLB	29	2	4	0	69	0	62^1	65	8	23	56	3.3	8.1	49%	.310	1.41	4.76	4.23	4.47	0.5
2011	WAS	MLB	30	5	1	0	69	0	59^2	55	4	20	46	3.0	6.9	44%	.279	1.26	3.62	3.38	3.83	0.4
2012	RCU	A+	31	0	1	0	2	2	2	3	0	0	1	0.0	4.5	57%	.429	1.50	4.50	2.81	4.07	0.0
2012	LAN	MLB	31	1	0	0	23	0	19^1	17	1	9	18	4.2	8.4	61%	.302	1.34	4.66	3.65	4.02	0.1
2013	*LAN*	*MLB*	*32*	*2*	*1*	*0*	*44*	*0*	*38^2*	*34*	*4*	*11*	*33*	*2.5*	*7.6*	*51%*	*.295*	*1.17*	*3.42*	*3.69*	*3.72*	*0.4*

Dodgers fans yearning for a supersized reliever to fill the Jonathan Broxton-shaped voids in their hearts quickly got their fill of Coffey. The massive redhead's sprints from the bullpen were the most entertaining part of his game. He was hit hard by righties in his limited stint, the latest chapter in his up-and-down career. He did two stretches on the disabled list, one for knee inflammation and the other for elbow soreness that wound up requiring Tommy John surgery in mid-July. The Dodgers declined his $2.5 million option.

Scott Elbert
Born: **8/13/1985** Age: **27**
Bats: **L** Throws: **L** Height: **6' 2"** Weight: **210**
Breakout: **37%** Improve: **60%** Collapse: **22%**
Attrition: **16%** MLB: **82%**
Comparables:
Don Carman,Mark McLemore,J.P. Howell

YEAR	TEAM	LVL	AGE	W	L	SV	G	GS	IP	H	HR	BB	SO	BB9	SO9	GB%	BABIP	WHIP	ERA	FIP	FRA	WARP
2010	ABQ	AAA	24	1	1	0	9	9	43^1	46	4	34	45	7.1	9.4	47%	.339	1.85	4.99	5.20	5.63	0.7
2010	LAN	MLB	24	0	0	0	1	0	0^2	1	0	3	0	40.5	0.0	%	.333	6.00	13.50	16.61	28.59	-0.2
2011	ABQ	AAA	25	2	0	3	13	0	14^1	13	1	9	16	5.7	10.0	—	.316	1.53	5.02	4.55	4.95	0.0
2011	LAN	MLB	25	0	1	2	47	0	33^1	27	1	14	34	3.8	9.2	43%	.292	1.23	2.43	2.69	2.94	0.5
2012	CHT	AA	26	0	0	0	3	0	2	0	0	0	6	0.0	27.0	—	.000	0.00	0.00	-2.86	-0.75	0.1
2012	LAN	MLB	26	1	1	0	43	0	32^2	27	3	13	29	3.6	8.0	37%	.276	1.22	2.20	3.84	4.30	0.0
2013	*LAN*	*MLB*	*27*	*3*	*2*	*0*	*35*	*3*	*37^2*	*31*	*4*	*16*	*40*	*3.8*	*9.4*	*42%*	*.298*	*1.25*	*3.55*	*3.73*	*3.86*	*0.3*

While he's never lived up to the expectations that came with being drafted in the first round by the Dodgers in the interval between Billingsley and Kershaw, Elbert finally found a niche as a reliever. That said, he's been somewhat miscast as a specialist given basically even platoon splits. Elbert's success owes plenty to the development of his slider as a reliable swing-and-miss complement to his 91-94 mph heater. The pitch has its costs, though: Elbow inflammation sent him to the disabled list on July 26, and he made just four more appearances before undergoing surgery to remove scar tissue. He should be good to go for 2013, and it wouldn't be a surprise to see him work toward higher-leverage duty.

Stephen Fife
Born: **10/4/1986** Age: **26**
Bats: **R** Throws: **R** Height: **6' 4"** Weight: **210**
Breakout: **46%** Improve: **77%** Collapse: **12%**
Attrition: **11%** MLB: **75%**
Comparables:
Troy Patton,Robert Ray,Brad Penny

YEAR	TEAM	LVL	AGE	W	L	SV	G	GS	IP	H	HR	BB	SO	BB9	SO9	GB%	BABIP	WHIP	ERA	FIP	FRA	WARP
2010	PME	AA	23	8	6	0	26	26	136^1	144	11	46	82	3.0	5.4	49%	.283	1.39	4.75	4.33	5.28	0.9
2011	CHT	AA	24	3	0	0	6	6	33^2	36	2	15	25	4.0	6.7	—	.312	1.51	4.01	4.02	4.37	0.0
2011	PME	AA	24	11	4	0	19	18	103^1	107	7	37	70	3.2	6.1	—	.306	1.39	3.66	4.18	4.55	0.0
2012	ABQ	AAA	25	11	7	0	25	24	135^1	157	13	44	93	2.9	6.2	51%	.326	1.49	4.66	4.74	5.84	0.4
2012	LAN	MLB	25	0	2	0	5	5	26^2	25	2	12	20	4.1	6.8	46%	.291	1.39	2.70	4.19	3.93	0.4
2013	*LAN*	*MLB*	*26*	*3*	*3*	*0*	*10*	*10*	*54^2*	*55*	*6*	*19*	*37*	*3.1*	*6.0*	*50%*	*.298*	*1.34*	*4.46*	*4.32*	*4.84*	*-0.1*

A third-round 2008 pick acquired from the Red Sox in the Trayvon Robinson deal, Fife survived the perils of pitching at Albuquerque. Of course, the Dodgers scored a whopping 1.7 runs per game for him in his starts, three of which came in late

July and early August, and the other two in mid-September, when they were stalling for time with Kershaw's hip. Fife isn't blessed with outstanding stuff, but he has good command of a 90ish sinker, curve, and cutter. He projects as a middle reliever, but with the Dodgers staff getting crowded by high-priced acquisitions, it's more likely he spends another summer in Albuquerque, waiting for another calamity to befall a starter.

Onelki Garcia

Born: 8/2/1989 **Age:** 23
Bats: L **Throws:** L **Height:** 6' 3" **Weight:** 220
Breakout: --% **Improve:** --% **Collapse:** --%
Attrition: --% **MLB:** --%
Comparables:
--

YEAR	TEAM	LVL	AGE	W	L	SV	G	GS	IP	H	HR	BB	SO	BB9	SO9	GB%	BABIP	WHIP	ERA	FIP	FRA	WARP
2012	RCU	A+	22	0	0	0	1	1	2	0	0	0	4	0	18	—	0	0	0	-0.19	-0.2	0
2012	MSS	WNT	22	0	0	0	2	2	4	4	0	2	2	4.5	4.5	—	.286	1.5	2.25	4.42	4.81	0
2012	MAY	WNT	22	0	1	0	3	3	10^{1}	15	0	3	9	2.6	7.8	—	.405	1.74	4.35	2.33	2.99	0

Garcia, a Cuban defector, was said to be demanding a $7 million signing bonus in the 2012 draft, but the Dodgers secured him via a third-round pick and an under-slot $382,000 bonus. That's quite a bargain given the apparent package: a power-pitcher build and good command of a 91-95 mph fastball, sinker, swing-and miss curve, and developing changeup. He pitched in just two minor-league games, including a Double-A playoff game for Chattanooga (not reflected in the stats above), but made quite an impression by striking out 11 of the 15 hitters he faced. The Dodgers sent him to the AFL for more work, but biceps and oblique injuries limited him to two appearances. What the Dodgers have here is an open question, but at less than 1 percent of their investment in Puig, Garcia's a bargain.

Garrett Gould

Born: 7/19/1991 **Age:** 21
Bats: R **Throws:** R **Height:** 6' 5" **Weight:** 190
Breakout: 32% **Improve:** 69% **Collapse:** 13%
Attrition: 6% **MLB:** 87%
Comparables:
Catfish Hunter,Hayden Penn,Dan Petry

YEAR	TEAM	LVL	AGE	W	L	SV	G	GS	IP	H	HR	BB	SO	BB9	SO9	GB%	BABIP	WHIP	ERA	FIP	FRA	WARP
2010	OGD	Rk	18	1	4	0	13	13	57^{2}	68	4	20	52	3.1	8.1	55%	.338	1.53	4.06	4.17	5.72	0.7
2011	GRL	A	19	11	6	0	27	24	123^{2}	102	8	37	104	2.7	7.6	—	.263	1.12	2.40	3.47	3.77	0.0
2012	RCU	A+	20	5	10	0	27	23	130	140	19	54	123	3.7	8.5	38%	.317	1.49	5.75	5.14	6.12	0.5
2013	*LAN*	*MLB*	*21*	*2*	*3*	*0*	*7*	*7*	35^{2}	*36*	*5*	*17*	*25*	*4.3*	*6.4*	*41%*	*.304*	*1.51*	*5.16*	*5.05*	*5.61*	*-0.4*

The California League is a notoriously tough one for pitchers, and those with command insecurities tend to ease their foot off the gas to avoid the longball. That appears to be what happened with Gould, a 2009 second-round pick who broke out in 2011 but got splattered all over Rancho and the rest of the circuit in 2012. Gould profiles as a future third or fourth starter, with a clean delivery and a body that offers projection, and he augments his fastball with a plus curveball and a changeup that's at least average. In short, he's a much better arm than the numbers indicate, if not a frontliner.

Zack Greinke

Born: 10/21/1983 **Age:** 29
Bats: R **Throws:** R **Height:** 6' 3" **Weight:** 190
Breakout: 14% **Improve:** 41% **Collapse:** 19%
Attrition: 1% **MLB:** 96%
Comparables:
Ben Sheets,Dan Haren,Josh Beckett

YEAR	TEAM	LVL	AGE	W	L	SV	G	GS	IP	H	HR	BB	SO	BB9	SO9	GB%	BABIP	WHIP	ERA	FIP	FRA	WARP
2010	KCA	MLB	26	10	14	0	33	33	220	219	18	55	181	2.2	7.4	47%	.306	1.25	4.17	3.31	4.04	2.9
2011	BRV	A+	27	0	0	0	1	1	3	1	0	0	4	0.0	12.0	—	.167	0.33	0.00	0.72	0.78	0.0
2011	NAS	AAA	27	0	1	0	2	2	7^{2}	10	1	2	9	2.3	10.6	56%	.333	1.57	4.70	3.91	3.84	0.1
2011	MIL	MLB	27	16	6	0	28	28	171^{2}	161	19	45	201	2.4	10.5	49%	.319	1.20	3.83	2.95	3.90	3.3
2012	ANA	MLB	28	6	2	0	13	13	89^{1}	80	11	26	78	2.6	7.9	45%	.279	1.19	3.53	3.84	4.54	0.4
2012	MIL	MLB	28	9	3	0	21	21	123	120	7	28	122	2.0	8.9	55%	.326	1.20	3.44	2.58	3.51	2.9
2013	*LAN*	*MLB*	*29*	*13*	*8*	*0*	*30*	*30*	185^{1}	*154*	*14*	*41*	*186*	*2.0*	*9.0*	*44%*	*.299*	*1.05*	*2.84*	*2.84*	*3.09*	*3.5*

For the third year in a row, Greinke's ERA didn't conform to his sexier FIP, and the culprit is the same each year: a ridiculously high BABIP when runners are in scoring position. That figure since 2010 is now .357, compared to .308 with the bases empty. There comes a point when we must take that seriously and ask whether Greinke's catchers are calling bad pitches, or whether Greinke himself tries to get cute when in trouble. But that point is well down the road. For now, we're talking about a sample of just 353 batted balls, a typical half-season. Such fluky results due to sequencing might have lowered Greinke's price given a more conservative market, but the Dodgers showed no hesitation in making him the highest-paid pitcher in the game in terms of average annual value via a six-year, $147 million contract that contains an opt-out clause after three years.

Javy Guerra
Born: 10/31/1985 **Age:** 27
Bats: R **Throws:** R **Height:** 6' 1" **Weight:** 205
Breakout: 24% **Improve:** 50% **Collapse:** 31%
Attrition: 14% **MLB:** 89%
Comparables:
Terry Adams, Kevin Jepsen, Mike Timlin

YEAR	TEAM	LVL	AGE	W	L	SV	G	GS	IP	H	HR	BB	SO	BB9	SO9	GB%	BABIP	WHIP	ERA	FIP	FRA	WARP
2010	DOD	Rk	24	0	1	0	2	0	2	2	1	0	3	0.0	13.5	—	.250	1.00	4.50	9.26	7.43	-0.1
2010	CHT	AA	24	2	0	5	28	0	27	24	1	22	27	7.3	9.0	59%	.311	1.70	2.33	4.42	5.42	0.0
2011	CHT	AA	25	1	0	3	14	0	17	8	1	5	15	2.6	7.9	—	.175	0.76	1.06	3.19	3.47	0.0
2011	LAN	MLB	25	2	2	21	47	0	46^{2}	37	2	18	38	3.5	7.3	44%	.261	1.18	2.31	3.27	4.33	0.3
2012	RCU	A+	26	0	0	0	2	2	2	1	0	0	1	0.0	4.5	71%	.143	0.50	4.50	2.81	-6.91	0.0
2012	ABQ	AAA	26	0	0	0	3	0	4^{1}	7	0	1	3	2.1	6.2	23%	.412	1.85	8.31	2.97	-1.65	0.1
2012	LAN	MLB	26	2	3	8	45	0	45	44	1	23	37	4.6	7.4	50%	.321	1.49	2.60	3.38	3.63	0.5
2013	*LAN*	*MLB*	*27*	*2*	*1*	*10*	*43*	*0*	*42^{2}*	*38*	*4*	*20*	*36*	*4.1*	*7.7*	*44%*	*.298*	*1.36*	*3.99*	*4.14*	*4.34*	*0.1*

A late-bloomer who came out of nowhere to claim the Dodgers' closer role in mid-2011, Guerra had a difficult time writing a follow-up, mainly because he kept getting hurt. Though he avoided the nightmare scenario when a Brian McCann line drive hit his jaw on April 25, he tore his right lateral meniscus trying to avoid the shot. Pitching through the injury, he soon lost the ninth inning job to Kenley Jansen, and just as he was settling into a setup role, he finally underwent surgery to repair the knee. His misfortunes continued upon returning, as an oblique strain wiped out his final month, and he underwent arthroscopic shoulder surgery in early November to clean up bursitis in his AC joint. He should be ready to roll in time for spring training, and figures to be part of the setup crew again.

Matt Guerrier
Born: 8/2/1978 **Age:** 34
Bats: R **Throws:** R **Height:** 6' 4" **Weight:** 195
Breakout: 12% **Improve:** 32% **Collapse:** 35%
Attrition: 6% **MLB:** 87%
Comparables:
Ramon Hernandez, Mike Henneman, Mike Timlin

YEAR	TEAM	LVL	AGE	W	L	SV	G	GS	IP	H	HR	BB	SO	BB9	SO9	GB%	BABIP	WHIP	ERA	FIP	FRA	WARP
2010	MIN	MLB	31	5	7	1	74	0	71	56	7	22	42	2.8	5.3	48%	.231	1.10	3.17	4.20	5.41	-0.2
2011	LAN	MLB	32	4	3	1	70	0	66^{1}	59	4	25	50	3.4	6.8	41%	.271	1.27	4.07	3.40	4.31	0.2
2012	RCU	A+	33	0	0	0	5	3	5	3	0	0	5	0.0	9.0	61%	.231	0.60	3.60	1.81	-0.28	0.1
2012	LAN	MLB	33	0	2	0	16	0	14	8	3	7	9	4.5	5.8	39%	.139	1.07	3.86	6.35	6.60	-0.3
2013	*LAN*	*MLB*	*34*	*2*	*1*	*1*	*40*	*0*	*38^{1}*	*33*	*4*	*12*	*29*	*2.9*	*6.8*	*45%*	*.270*	*1.18*	*3.47*	*3.98*	*3.78*	*0.3*

Guerrier's three-year, $12 million deal looked like a bad idea the moment it was signed in December 2010—money that could have been better spent to retain Russell Martin, let's recall—and looks even worse now that he missed most of the 2012 season with elbow inflammation. When Guerrier did pitch, during the season's first two weeks and its final month, he was lousy. He'll make $4.75 million in 2013, and likely be no more than the fourth or fifth most important righty in the bullpen after Brandon League, Kenley Jansen, Belisario, and Guerra. Nice work if you can get it.

Aaron Harang
Born: 5/9/1978 **Age:** 35
Bats: R **Throws:** R **Height:** 6' 8" **Weight:** 260
Breakout: 23% **Improve:** 42% **Collapse:** 19%
Attrition: 8% **MLB:** 83%
Comparables:
Freddy Garcia, Bartolo Colon, Ryan Glynn

YEAR	TEAM	LVL	AGE	W	L	SV	G	GS	IP	H	HR	BB	SO	BB9	SO9	GB%	BABIP	WHIP	ERA	FIP	FRA	WARP
2010	LOU	AAA	32	0	2	0	2	2	11	14	1	2	10	1.6	8.2	38%	.361	1.45	9.00	3.47	4.61	0.1
2010	CIN	MLB	32	6	7	0	22	20	111^{2}	139	16	38	82	3.1	6.6	38%	.338	1.59	5.32	4.63	5.01	0.6
2011	LEL	A+	33	0	1	0	1	1	4	5	0	1	7	2.2	15.8	—	.556	1.50	6.75	1.20	1.31	0.0
2011	SDN	MLB	33	14	7	0	28	28	170^{2}	175	20	58	124	3.1	6.5	43%	.302	1.37	3.64	4.14	4.47	-0.2
2012	LAN	MLB	34	10	10	0	31	31	179^{2}	167	14	85	131	4.3	6.6	41%	.277	1.40	3.61	4.18	4.51	0.6
2013	*LAN*	*MLB*	*35*	*9*	*9*	*0*	*27*	*27*	*154^{1}*	*157*	*19*	*47*	*119*	*2.7*	*7.0*	*40%*	*.308*	*1.32*	*4.40*	*4.17*	*4.79*	*-0.4*

A season pitching for the Padres in spacious Petco Park helped paint Harang's comeback from forearm and back woes in the most flattering light, so he figured to be one of the riskier bets among Colletti's backloaded two-year deals. Like Capuano, Harang survived the season intact, with his highest totals of innings and starts since 2007. More often than not, he kept the Dodgers in the game, partly because he got very lucky in the home-run department, with a 6.3 percent home-run-to-fly-ball rate, well below his Petco and career marks (9.3 and 10.3 percent, respectively). With a whole lot of regression on his horizon, his salary jumps from $3 million to $7 million in 2013, with a $2 million buyout on a $7 million option as well, meaning that he'll be tougher to move than Capuano should the Dodgers stock their rotation more fully.

Kenley Jansen
Born: 9/30/1987 **Age:** 25
Bats: B **Throws:** R **Height:** 6' 6" **Weight:** 255
Breakout: 20% **Improve:** 41% **Collapse:** 23%
Attrition: 10% **MLB:** 93%
Comparables:
Jonathan Broxton, David Robertson, Francisco Rodriguez

YEAR	TEAM	LVL	AGE	W	L	SV	G	GS	IP	H	HR	BB	SO	BB9	SO9	GB%	BABIP	WHIP	ERA	FIP	FRA	WARP
2010	SBR	A+	22	1	1	0	11	0	18	15	0	6	28	3.0	14.0	51%	.385	1.17	1.50	1.62	1.61	0.8
2010	CHT	AA	22	4	0	8	22	0	27	14	0	17	50	5.7	16.7	32%	.318	1.15	1.67	1.57	0.90	1.4
2010	LAN	MLB	22	1	0	4	25	0	27	12	0	15	41	5.0	13.7	36%	.231	1.00	0.67	1.85	1.76	0.9
2011	CHT	AA	23	0	1	0	5	0	6	2	1	3	9	4.5	13.5	—	.111	0.83	4.50	3.97	4.32	0.0
2011	LAN	MLB	23	2	1	5	51	0	53^{2}	30	3	26	96	4.4	16.1	29%	.297	1.04	2.85	1.71	1.41	1.5
2012	LAN	MLB	24	5	3	25	65	0	65	33	6	22	99	3.0	13.7	33%	.221	0.85	2.35	2.44	2.74	1.3
2013	*LAN*	*MLB*	*25*	*3*	*1*	*10*	*52*	*0*	*56^{2}*	*33*	*4*	*22*	*87*	*3.5*	*13.8*	*36%*	*.289*	*0.97*	*1.82*	*2.21*	*1.98*	*1.8*

Jansen couldn't match his record-setting strikeout rate from 2011, but his cutter still ranked among the game's toughest-to-hit pitches, and he remained dominant. He held batters to a .146/.230/.274 line and took over the full-time closer role from a struggling Guerra in late April. Alas, the cardiac arrhythmia that sidelined him for four weeks in 2011 resurfaced again, and he wound up spending three weeks on the DL in late August and September, a stretch during which the Dodgers' playoff hopes faded for good. After the season, he underwent a surgical ablation to correct the problem. With the Dodgers re-signing League—who took over closer chores in Jansen's absence—to an expensive and unnecessary contract, the plan is for Jansen to return to a setup role, where at least he'll be able to pitch multiple innings when the occasion dictates.

Clayton Kershaw

Born: **3/19/1988** Age: **25**
Bats: **L** Throws: **L** Height: **6' 4"** Weight: **215**
Breakout: **30%** Improve: **64%** Collapse: **16%**
Attrition: **11%** MLB: **96%**

Comparables:
Francisco Liriano,David Price,Rich Harden

YEAR	TEAM	LVL	AGE	W	L	SV	G	GS	IP	H	HR	BB	SO	BB9	SO9	GB%	BABIP	WHIP	ERA	FIP	FRA	WARP
2010	LAN	MLB	22	13	10	0	32	32	204^{1}	160	13	81	212	3.6	9.3	42%	.275	1.18	2.91	3.15	3.29	3.8
2011	LAN	MLB	23	21	5	0	33	33	233^{1}	174	15	54	248	2.1	9.6	45%	.269	0.98	2.28	2.44	2.83	6.2
2012	LAN	MLB	24	14	9	0	33	33	227^{2}	170	16	63	229	2.5	9.1	49%	.262	1.02	2.53	2.93	3.32	4.1
2013	*LAN*	*MLB*	*25*	*13*	*7*	*0*	*28*	*28*	191^{1}	*144*	*14*	*59*	*196*	*2.8*	*9.2*	*45%*	*.281*	*1.07*	*2.62*	*3.03*	*2.85*	*4.1*

Kershaw rolled another Clayton Kershaw season off the assembly line, and were it not for a drop in offensive support (4.0 runs per game) and the narrative arc of R.A. Dickey, he probably would have claimed a second straight Cy Young Award. As it was, he still led the league in ERA and came within one strikeout of the league lead as well. He'd have captured that title for sure—as well as the innings one—were it not for late-season right hip impingement that limited him to one start from September 12 through 27. The good news is that he closed the season strong, with a pair of eight-inning starts, and didn't need surgery for what was initially feared to be a torn acetabular labrum. Kershaw still has one more year of club control after the coming year, when he'll earn $11 million. With the cost of long-term contracts only rising—along with the Dodgers' payroll—the team would do well to lock him up before another market-setting deal comes along.

Brandon League

Born: **3/16/1983** Age: **30**
Bats: **R** Throws: **R** Height: **6' 3"** Weight: **210**
Breakout: **27%** Improve: **55%** Collapse: **26%**
Attrition: **15%** MLB: **90%**

Comparables:
Brandon Lyon,Matt Lindstrom,Tony Pena

YEAR	TEAM	LVL	AGE	W	L	SV	G	GS	IP	H	HR	BB	SO	BB9	SO9	GB%	BABIP	WHIP	ERA	FIP	FRA	WARP
2010	SEA	MLB	27	9	7	6	70	0	79	67	7	27	56	3.1	6.4	63%	.256	1.19	3.42	3.88	5.86	-1.0
2011	SEA	MLB	28	1	5	37	65	0	61^{1}	56	3	10	45	1.5	6.6	58%	.279	1.08	2.79	2.82	3.77	0.6
2012	LAN	MLB	29	2	1	6	28	0	27^{1}	17	0	14	27	4.6	8.9	58%	.258	1.13	2.30	2.81	2.79	0.5
2012	SEA	MLB	29	0	5	9	46	0	44^{2}	48	1	19	27	3.8	5.4	48%	.322	1.50	3.63	3.40	3.64	0.4
2013	*LAN*	*MLB*	*30*	*3*	*1*	*20*	*65*	*0*	65^{2}	*56*	*5*	*19*	*55*	*2.7*	*7.5*	*57%*	*.290*	*1.15*	*3.27*	*3.38*	*3.56*	*0.7*

After joining the Proven Closer club in Seattle in 2011, League pitched himself out of the role by the end of May. Even so, the Dodgers traded two prospects, center fielder Leon Landry and pitcher Logan Bawcom, for League in late July, and after a few more hiccups, set about ironing out his delivery to prevent him from pulling to the side in mid-pitch, thus dragging his arm behind him. The changes took hold, and from August 21 through the end of the season, League allowed just one run and eight hits while striking out 22 in 22 1/3 innings, taking over closer chores from the sidelined Jansen along the way. Colletti's natural response was to shower him with silly money. He'll go to camp as the closer, but the chances of him staving off Jansen during the three-year life of his deal aren't high.

Zach Lee

Born: **9/13/1991** Age: **21**
Bats: **R** Throws: **R** Height: **6' 5"** Weight: **190**
Breakout: **27%** Improve: **57%** Collapse: **13%**
Attrition: **3%** MLB: **91%**

Comparables:
Larry Dierker,Hayden Penn,Jordan Lyles

YEAR	TEAM	LVL	AGE	W	L	SV	G	GS	IP	H	HR	BB	SO	BB9	SO9	GB%	BABIP	WHIP	ERA	FIP	FRA	WARP
2011	GRL	A	19	9	6	0	24	24	109	101	9	32	91	2.6	7.5	—	.280	1.22	3.47	3.84	4.17	0.0
2012	RCU	A+	20	2	3	0	12	12	55^{1}	60	9	10	52	1.6	8.5	48%	.316	1.27	4.55	4.65	4.31	0.4
2012	CHT	AA	20	4	3	0	13	13	65^{2}	69	6	22	51	3.0	7.0	48%	.313	1.39	4.25	3.83	4.66	0.4
2013	*LAN*	*MLB*	*21*	*2*	*2*	*0*	*8*	*8*	37^{1}	*37*	*5*	*12*	*27*	*2.9*	*6.5*	*46%*	*.300*	*1.31*	*4.46*	*4.46*	*4.85*	*-0.1*

The 2010 first-rounder leveled off after a strong professional debut, in part due to a groin strain that sidelined him for three weeks in May. Lee did pitch well enough to earn a midseason promotion/reprieve from the Cal League and closed the season on a roll, allowing just six runs in 36 innings over his last six starts. Scouts still love his athleticism, but his profile is based more on pitchability and a broad arsenal—a 91-94 mph sinking fastball, a plus slider, a decent curve, and a changeup with the potential to be average—than outstanding stuff. For that reason, his ceiling tops out as a third or fourth starter barring a breakthrough, though his floor is high. He could be ready for an audition in Los Angeles late in 2013.

Ted Lilly

Born: **1/4/1976** Age: **37**
Bats: **L** Throws: **L** Height: **6' 2"** Weight: **195**
Breakout: **7%** Improve: **29%** Collapse: **12%**
Attrition: **11%** MLB: **89%**

Comparables:
David Wells,Whitey Ford,Mike Mussina

YEAR	TEAM	LVL	AGE	W	L	SV	G	GS	IP	H	HR	BB	SO	BB9	SO9	GB%	BABIP	WHIP	ERA	FIP	FRA	WARP
2010	PEO	A	34	1	0	0	1	1	7	3	0	1	9	1.3	11.6	40%	.200	0.57	1.29	1.47	1.99	0.3
2010	IOW	AAA	34	0	0	0	1	1	4	1	1	1	4	2.2	9.0	56%	.000	0.50	2.25	5.58	5.81	0.0
2010	CHN	MLB	34	3	8	0	18	18	117	104	19	29	89	2.2	6.8	31%	.249	1.14	3.69	4.49	4.45	1.6
2010	LAN	MLB	34	7	4	0	12	12	76^{2}	61	13	15	77	1.8	9.0	33%	.244	0.99	3.52	4.01	3.92	0.8
2011	LAN	MLB	35	12	14	0	33	33	192^{2}	172	28	51	158	2.4	7.4	35%	.260	1.16	3.97	4.18	4.14	1.1
2012	RCU	A+	36	0	1	0	4	4	11	10	3	2	7	1.6	5.7	34%	.222	1.09	5.73	6.63	20.15	0.0
2012	LAN	MLB	36	5	1	0	8	8	48^{2}	36	3	19	31	3.5	5.7	45%	.224	1.13	3.14	3.96	4.12	0.3
2013	*LAN*	*MLB*	*37*	*5*	*3*	*0*	*12*	*12*	*68^{1}*	*58*	*9*	*16*	*58*	*2.1*	*7.7*	*36%*	*.269*	*1.08*	*3.31*	*3.92*	*3.60*	*0.8*

If anyone needed a reminder of Lilly's advancing age, they got it in 2012 as injuries slowed him down and then wiped out his season. A stiff neck put him behind schedule in spring training and he opened the year on the disabled list. He was outstanding through his first five starts, pitching to a 1.41 ERA, but scuffled through his next three, then went on the DL with shoulder inflammation in late May. He wasn't initially expected to be out long, but his timetable kept getting pushed back until he finally had arthroscopic surgery to clean up his labrum in mid-September. As of November he had begun throwing again, and the hope is that he can reclaim his spot in the rotation for the final year of his three-year, $33 million deal.

Matt Magill

Born: **11/10/1989** Age: **23**
Bats: **R** Throws: **R** Height: **6' 4"** Weight: **190**
Breakout: **41%** Improve: **61%** Collapse: **21%**
Attrition: **32%** MLB: **93%**

Comparables:
Edinson Volquez,Juan Morillo,Tyler Clippard

YEAR	TEAM	LVL	AGE	W	L	SV	G	GS	IP	H	HR	BB	SO	BB9	SO9	GB%	BABIP	WHIP	ERA	FIP	FRA	WARP
2010	GRL	A	20	7	4	2	24	20	126^{1}	87	13	52	135	3.7	9.6	44%	.252	1.10	3.28	4.16	4.89	0.6
2011	RCU	A+	21	11	5	0	26	21	139^{1}	156	15	52	126	3.4	8.1	—	.334	1.49	4.33	4.70	5.11	0.0
2012	CHT	AA	22	11	8	0	26	26	146^{1}	127	8	61	168	3.8	10.3	49%	.312	1.28	3.75	2.87	3.17	0.7
2013	*LAN*	*MLB*	*23*	*2*	*2*	*0*	*7*	*7*	*37^{2}*	*34*	*5*	*17*	*32*	*4.1*	*7.7*	*43%*	*.295*	*1.37*	*4.40*	*4.58*	*4.78*	*-0.1*

A 31st-round 2008 pick, Magill had never gotten much attention as a prospect prior to 2012 because his stuff was considered fringy, but thanks to a significantly improved changeup, he took a big step forward to fill the organizational void left by the trades of Rubby de la Rosa, Allen Webster, Nathan Eovaldi, and Ethan Martin. He led the Southern League in strikeouts and K rate, and cut his home-run rate in half thanks to an increased groundball rate and the move to the more pitcher-friendly league. Added to the 40-man roster this winter, he could get his first big-league look in 2013.

Aaron Miller

Born: **9/18/1987** Age: **25**
Bats: **L** Throws: **L** Height: **6' 4"** Weight: **200**
Breakout: **34%** Improve: **53%** Collapse: **23%**
Attrition: **19%** MLB: **85%**

Comparables:
Donnie Veal,J.A. Happ,Cliff Lee

YEAR	TEAM	LVL	AGE	W	L	SV	G	GS	IP	H	HR	BB	SO	BB9	SO9	GB%	BABIP	WHIP	ERA	FIP	FRA	WARP
2010	SBR	A+	22	6	4	0	19	17	101^{2}	76	6	48	99	4.2	8.8	42%	.261	1.22	2.92	4.12	4.41	1.2
2010	CHT	AA	22	1	4	0	6	6	23	28	3	18	22	7.0	8.6	41%	.368	2.00	7.04	5.52	6.45	-0.1
2011	DOD	Rk	23	1	0	0	1	0	2	1	0	1	3	4.5	13.5	—	.250	1.00	0.00	2.87	3.12	0.0
2011	RCU	A+	23	3	2	0	10	6	34	37	2	18	30	4.8	7.9	—	.347	1.62	3.97	4.63	5.03	0.0
2012	CHT	AA	24	6	6	0	25	25	121^{1}	117	10	71	110	5.3	8.2	42%	.316	1.55	4.45	4.36	6.11	0.4
2013	*LAN*	*MLB*	*25*	*2*	*2*	*0*	*7*	*7*	*36*	*34*	*4*	*18*	*31*	*4.6*	*7.7*	*40%*	*.300*	*1.45*	*4.68*	*4.42*	*5.08*	*-0.2*

A 2009 supplemental first-round pick out of Baylor (where he was a two-way player), Miller lost much of 2011 to a sports hernia that went undiagnosed until late in the year and eventually required surgery. He stayed healthy in 2012, but battled command problems. With those problems exacerbated by a lack of defensive support, his ERA stayed well above 4.00 from his third start to the end of the season even in a pitcher-friendly environment. Miller has low-90s velocity, with secondary stuff—a slider with true plus potential and a changeup with good sink—that still needs work. A shift to the bullpen may be in his future, though his .227/.348/.347 line against lefties suggests he won't be a shutdown LOOGY.

Chris Reed

Born: **5/20/1990** Age: **23**
Bats: **L** Throws: **L** Height: **6' 5"** Weight: **195**
Breakout: **23%** Improve: **59%** Collapse: **22%**
Attrition: **21%** MLB: **96%**

Comparables:
Andrew Oliver,J.P. Howell,Lynn McGlothen

YEAR	TEAM	LVL	AGE	W	L	SV	G	GS	IP	H	HR	BB	SO	BB9	SO9	GB%	BABIP	WHIP	ERA	FIP	FRA	WARP
2011	RCU	A+	21	0	1	0	3	3	7	9	1	4	9	5.1	11.6	—	.421	1.86	7.71	5.38	5.85	0.0
2012	RCU	A+	22	1	4	0	7	6	35	25	1	14	38	3.6	9.8	58%	.280	1.11	3.09	3.30	2.99	0.2
2012	CHT	AA	22	0	4	0	12	11	35^{1}	31	2	20	29	5.1	7.4	61%	.286	1.44	4.84	4.28	5.50	-0.3
2013	*LAN*	*MLB*	*23*	*2*	*2*	*0*	*9*	*8*	*37*	*34*	*4*	*16*	*31*	*3.9*	*7.6*	*51%*	*.299*	*1.35*	*4.21*	*4.23*	*4.58*	*0.1*

A 2011 first-rounder who converted to the rotation after closing at Stanford, Reed battled shoulder soreness and a blister problem in his first full season, and put together an uneven performance. He racked up strikeouts at Rancho but battled control problems at Chattanooga, with his rate stats moving in the wrong directions. The jury is still out as to whether Reed can stick in the rotation, as his pitches are better in shorter bursts, and at times he tends to overthrow and lose his delivery. Still, he has a very good feel for pitching. At worst he's a late-game reliever down the road.

Steven Rodriguez

Born: **4/16/1991** Age: **22**
Bats: **L** Throws: **L** Height: **6' 4"** Weight: **215**
Breakout: **26%** Improve: **63%** Collapse: **21%**
Attrition: **6%** MLB: **83%**

Comparables:
Terry Forster,Masanori Murakami,Tim Collins

YEAR	TEAM	LVL	AGE	W	L	SV	G	GS	IP	H	HR	BB	SO	BB9	SO9	GB%	BABIP	WHIP	ERA	FIP	FRA	WARP
2012	GRL	A	21	0	0	2	6	0	6	4	0	0	10	0.0	15.0	67%	.333	0.67	0.00	0.02	-2.50	0.3
2012	CHT	AA	21	1	0	3	15	0	13^2	7	0	6	22	4.0	14.5	46%	.269	0.95	1.32	1.46	0.79	0.5
2012	LAN	MLB	21	0	1	0	11	0	6^2	3	0	4	6	5.4	8.1	44%	.188	1.05	1.35	3.14	2.01	0.1
2013	*LAN*	*MLB*	*22*	*3*	*1*	*0*	*47*	*0*	*38^2*	*31*	*4*	*14*	*42*	*3.3*	*9.8*	*46%*	*.295*	*1.15*	*3.13*	*3.46*	*3.40*	*0.6*

A University of Florida reliever chosen with the 82nd pick (second round) of the 2012 draft, Rodriguez (nicknamed Paco) signed for slot value ($610,800), and after dominating in brief stops at two levels became the first member of his draft class to reach the majors. Unfazed by the heat of the playoff race, he fared reasonably well in September as the bullpen's second lefty, allowing just one out of 12 inherited runners to score. Rodriguez has a deceptive delivery, good command, and enough stuff that he should escape the LOOGY typecasting, with closing and starting both possibilities. His 2013 destination may hinge on who else the Dodgers bring in as a lefty reliever; it wouldn't be a surprise if he breaks camp with the big club—or winds up back in Chattanooga.

Hyun-Jin Ryu

Born: **3/25/1987** Age: **26**
Bats: **L** Throws: **L** Height: **6' 3"** Weight: **215**
Breakout: **--%** Improve: **--%** Collapse: **--%**
Attrition: **--%** MLB: **--%**

Comparables:
--

The Dodgers paid a $25.7 million posting fee for the rights to this portly portsider from South Korea, then signed him to a six-year, $36 million contract. Pitching for the Hanwha Eagles of the KBO, Ryu was the MVP and Rookie of the Year at age 19 and an All-Star in all seven of his years, with five strikeout titles. Even so, exactly what the Dodgers have gotten for their money is a mystery, though the consensus appears to be something around an MLB-ready mid-rotation starter. Ryu throws a four-pitch mix with a 90-ish fastball that he can push to 94–95 mph, a plus changeup (his best pitch), a slider, and a curve. His delivery is relatively sound and offers some deception, while outstanding command helps his pitches play up, though he does have a fly-ball tendency. He had Tommy John surgery while in high school, but has been largely healthy as a pro save for a fatigue issue that sent him to the bullpen for a spell in 2011. Expect him to start the year behind Kershaw and Greinke in the Dodgers rotation.

Shawn Tolleson

Born: **1/19/1988** Age: **25**
Bats: **R** Throws: **R** Height: **6' 3"** Weight: **215**
Breakout: **22%** Improve: **53%** Collapse: **26%**
Attrition: **14%** MLB: **90%**

Comparables:
Jim Hoey,Sammy Gervacio,Antonio Osuna

YEAR	TEAM	LVL	AGE	W	L	SV	G	GS	IP	H	HR	BB	SO	BB9	SO9	GB%	BABIP	WHIP	ERA	FIP	FRA	WARP
2010	OGD	Rk	22	1	1	17	26	0	28^2	17	1	5	39	1.6	12.2	65%	.237	0.77	0.63	2.24	4.19	0.8
2011	GRL	A	23	1	0	10	14	0	15	8	0	4	33	2.4	19.8	—	.421	0.80	0.00	-0.24	-0.26	0.0
2011	RCU	A+	23	2	0	3	5	0	9^2	2	1	3	17	2.8	15.8	—	.067	0.52	0.93	2.71	2.95	0.0
2011	CHT	AA	23	4	2	12	38	0	44^1	42	2	11	55	2.2	11.2	—	.360	1.20	1.62	2.29	2.49	0.0
2012	CHT	AA	24	0	0	5	11	0	13	8	2	4	19	2.8	13.2	58%	.250	0.92	1.38	3.14	2.68	0.3
2012	ABQ	AAA	24	0	1	0	8	0	9^1	8	1	1	15	1.0	14.5	43%	.350	0.96	4.82	2.17	1.15	0.3
2012	LAN	MLB	24	3	1	0	40	0	37^2	30	4	20	39	4.8	9.3	42%	.271	1.33	4.30	4.12	4.19	0.0
2013	*LAN*	*MLB*	*25*	*2*	*1*	*0*	*35*	*0*	*38^2*	*31*	*4*	*15*	*41*	*3.5*	*9.6*	*47%*	*.291*	*1.18*	*3.36*	*3.59*	*3.66*	*0.4*

Tolleson dominated hitters at every stop save for a couple of hiccups in Albuquerque, and he found his way to the Dodgers bullpen in early June. Despite scuffling initially, he stuck around and pitched reasonably well in low-leverage duty. He dominated righty hitters (.152/.244/.241 in 92 PA) but was smoked by lefties (.316/.426/.561 in 68 PA), suggesting that while his combination of a 92-95 mph fastball and 84-88 mph cutter works well enough against same-side hitters, he'll have to come up with another pitch in order to get the lefties out, or risk trying to make his way through life as a ROOGY.

Josh Wall

Born: **1/21/1987** Age: **26**
Bats: **R** Throws: **R** Height: **6' 7"** Weight: **218**
Breakout: **20%** Improve: **50%** Collapse: **36%**
Attrition: **26%** MLB: **80%**

Comparables:
Jason Johnson,Dan Wright,Shawn Sedlacek

YEAR	TEAM	LVL	AGE	W	L	SV	G	GS	IP	H	HR	BB	SO	BB9	SO9	GB%	BABIP	WHIP	ERA	FIP	FRA	WARP
2010	GRL	A	23	9	7	0	26	26	153	144	11	68	151	4.0	8.9	47%	.309	1.39	4.24	4.18	4.97	0.6
2011	CHT	AA	24	4	5	1	51	0	68^2	72	6	27	57	3.5	7.5	—	.320	1.44	3.93	4.09	4.45	0.0
2012	ABQ	AAA	25	2	1	28	55	0	53^2	50	7	20	52	3.4	8.7	45%	.284	1.30	4.53	4.65	4.74	0.4
2012	LAN	MLB	25	1	0	0	7	0	5^2	3	1	1	4	1.6	6.4	40%	.143	0.71	4.76	5.08	6.31	0.0
2013	*LAN*	*MLB*	*26*	*2*	*2*	*0*	*14*	*4*	*35^1*	*36*	*5*	*17*	*24*	*4.4*	*6.0*	*42%*	*.302*	*1.53*	*5.38*	*5.12*	*5.84*	*-0.5*

A second-round 2005 pick out of a Louisiana high school, Wall has taken his own sweet time climbing the ladder, at times battling to keep his big limbs in sync during his delivery and dealing with a 96-99 mph fastball that tends to straighten out at higher velocities. He offsets that heater primarily with an above-average slider, a decent curve, and a fringy changeup. Wall's season in Triple-A was uneven, as he alternated dreadful stretches with dominant ones, with his home park a factor in the former. He served three brief stints with the big club and found similar trouble in one late-August shellacking at Coors Field. He'll have to learn to survive at altitude, because his fate appears to be to wait around in Albuquerque for a bullpen opening, though he has the stuff for a late-game role down the road.

Chris Withrow
Born: **4/1/1989** Age: **24**
Bats: **R** Throws: **R** Height: **6' 4"** Weight: **195**
Breakout: **35%** Improve: **65%** Collapse: **17%**
Attrition: **14%** MLB: **95%**
Comparables:
Jim Gott,Ken Holtzman,Edwin Jackson

YEAR	TEAM	LVL	AGE	W	L	SV	G	GS	IP	H	HR	BB	SO	BB9	SO9	GB%	BABIP	WHIP	ERA	FIP	FRA	WARP
2010	CHT	AA	21	4	9	0	27	27	129^{2}	146	13	69	120	4.8	8.3	40%	.340	1.66	5.97	4.69	5.61	0.8
2011	CHT	AA	22	6	6	0	25	25	128^{2}	111	8	75	130	5.2	9.1	—	.307	1.45	4.20	3.96	4.30	0.0
2012	CHT	AA	23	3	3	2	22	7	60	52	3	36	64	5.4	9.6	53%	.306	1.47	4.65	3.56	4.88	0.1
2013	*LAN*	*MLB*	*24*	*2*	*2*	*0*	*9*	*6*	*36*	*34*	*4*	*18*	*31*	*4.6*	*7.8*	*42%*	*.307*	*1.46*	*4.77*	*4.42*	*5.18*	*-0.2*

Withrow has battled injuries and control problems during his time in the Dodgers chain, spending so long in Chattanooga—three seasons and change—that he could run for mayor. The locals would need a tolerance for control problems and inefficiency, however, since difficulty repeating his delivery has caused the 2007 first-rounder to struggle to harness his mid-to-high-90s heat and a power curve that has the potential to be a plus pitch. After six weeks of starting and a month on the shelf with a pectoral injury, he moved to the bullpen and found better results more due to a drop in BABIP than a decreased walk rate. His future lies in the late innings.

Jamey Wright
Born: **12/24/1974** Age: **38**
Bats: **R** Throws: **R** Height: **6' 7"** Weight: **230**
Breakout: **24%** Improve: **42%** Collapse: **41%**
Attrition: **15%** MLB: **80%**
Comparables:
Steve Reed,Jason Grimsley,Roberto Hernandez

YEAR	TEAM	LVL	AGE	W	L	SV	G	GS	IP	H	HR	BB	SO	BB9	SO9	GB%	BABIP	WHIP	ERA	FIP	FRA	WARP
2010	SAC	AAA	35	1	0	1	10	0	14	23	2	9	16	5.8	10.3	48%	.477	2.29	9.00	5.08	6.31	-0.1
2010	CLE	MLB	35	1	2	0	18	0	21^{1}	25	1	9	9	3.8	3.8	61%	.312	1.59	5.48	4.36	5.32	-0.1
2010	SEA	MLB	35	0	1	0	28	0	37	30	2	16	19	3.9	4.6	65%	.248	1.24	3.41	4.10	4.82	-0.1
2011	SEA	MLB	36	2	3	1	60	0	68^{1}	61	6	30	48	4.0	6.3	58%	.279	1.33	3.16	4.33	5.43	-0.5
2012	LAN	MLB	37	5	3	0	66	0	67^{2}	72	2	30	54	4.0	7.2	69%	.324	1.51	3.72	3.43	4.51	0.0
2013	*LAN*	*MLB*	*38*	*3*	*1*	*1*	*55*	*0*	*62^{2}*	*57*	*5*	*26*	*47*	*3.7*	*6.8*	*58%*	*.297*	*1.34*	*4.11*	*3.98*	*4.47*	*-0.0*

Wright may be the ultimate grinder among pitchers, the poor man's Mike Morgan. A 17-year veteran who has never once reached the playoffs or received any accolades, he has bounced from team to team to team, showing up in spring training on non-roster invitations for seven straight years and finding work at the major-league level each time. He broke camp with the Dodgers thanks to a slew of preseason injuries, and while most of his work was in low-leverage duty, he didn't shame himself in higher-leverage work. He wound up posting career bests in strikeout, unintentional walk, groundball, and home-run rates, maxing out all $500,000 worth of appearance-based incentive bonuses in his contract along the way. The combination should be enough to land him another job, though you can bet he'll probably have to sing for his supper once again.

LINEOUTS

HITTERS

PLAYER	TEAM	LVL	AGE	PA	R	2B	3B	HR	RBI	BB	SO	SB-CS	AVG/OBP/SLG	TAv	BABIP	BRR	FRAA	WARP
CF M. Angle	ABQ	AAA	26	447	62	18	5	5	47	41	82	13-3	.303/.376/.412	.267	.370	5.7	CF(29): -2.4	0.4
INF E. Gonzalez	BRD	A+	22	178	17	9	1	4	20	25	42	3-3	.216/.335/.372	.221	.272	-0.1	3B(7): 0.4, 2B(3): 0.4	0.1
	ALT	AA	22	167	10	6	1	2	15	14	42	1-3	.196/.274/.291	.219	.260	-0.7	3B(13): 0.6, 2B(13): -0.4	-0.5
3B D. McPherson	CHR	AAA	31	260	35	12	0	12	47	28	83	2-1	.253/.335/.463	.253	.338	-2.3	3B(21): -0.2, 1B(2): 0.1	-0.2
	IND	AAA	31	86	10	4	1	5	15	9	32	1-0	.299/.372/.571	.310	.450	-0.3	RF(9): 0.9, 3B(4): 0.3	0.6
C T. Ogle	GRL	A	21	71	10	1	0	3	7	6	16	0-0	.210/.310/.371	.218	.233	0.4	C(3): -0.0	-0.1
SS J. Sellers	LAN	MLB	26	50	6	3	1	1	2	5	14	0-0	.205/.286/.386	.246	.276	0	SS(9): -0.0, 3B(7): 0.0	0.0
C E. Smith	OGD	Rk	21	302	55	17	7	3	55	33	32	2-1	.336/.417/.492	.222	.366	0.4	C(5): -0.1	0.0
MI R. Ynoa	CHT	AA	24	493	58	23	4	0	37	58	70	23-8	.278/.364/.352	.281	.330	2	SS(20): 0.9, 2B(16): -0.5	1.3

Matt Angle has speed to burn on both sides of the ball, not to mention a good arm, but his lack of power means he'll never be more than a bench player at the major-league level. ⊘ The smallish **Elevys Gonzalez** does a lot of things decently and few things well, making him a potential utility infielder. ⊘ Former top prospect **Dallas McPherson** never panned out in the majors due to back woes and a long swing; still knocking around as organizational depth, he can hope to match his 42 homers at Albuquerque from when it was a Marlins affiliate back in 2008. Catcher **Tyler Ogle** has solid power and contact skills, with a good eye for the strike zone; defensively, there are doubts about his arm strength, though he threw out 28 percent of would-be base thieves. The window of opportunity may be closing for **Justin Sellers**, who missed the rest of 2012 with a back injury after a mid-May tumble into the stands to catch a foul ball. **Eric Smith**, a converted middle infielder, has taken to catching quickly, showing soft hands and a strong arm as well as a good approach at the plate. Switch-hitting Dominican **Rafael Ynoa** has plodded through the Dodgers system, but has developed decent on-base skills as well as capability at both middle-infield positions.

PITCHERS

PLAYER	TEAM	LVL	AGE	W	L	SV	IP	H	HR	BB	SO	BB9	SO9	GB%	BABIP	WHIP	ERA	FIP	FRA	WARP
J. Dominguez	GRL	A	21	4	3	4	72	77	4	47	78	5.9	9.8	45%	.351	1.72	5.25	4.07	4.37	0.6
J. Martin	GRL	A	22	4	5	0	77^{2}	63	4	48	78	5.6	9.0	62%	.284	1.43	4.29	4.06	5.84	0.4
R. Patterson	CHT	AA	25	7	1	0	70^{1}	70	2	32	71	4.1	9.1	42%	.329	1.45	3.07	2.94	1.42	1.8
R. Rasmussen	JUP	A+	23	4	7	0	87^{2}	83	6	36	75	3.7	7.7	46%	.300	1.36	3.90	3.84	4.16	0.0
	CCH	AA	23	4	4	0	54^{1}	58	6	18	44	3.0	7.3	47%	.319	1.40	4.80	4.15	5.39	-0.3
J. Redding	RCU	A+	24	9	7	0	130^{1}	149	10	48	102	3.3	7.0	49%	.333	1.51	4.42	4.56	5.09	0.6
A. Sanchez	RCU	A+	22	6	12	0	130	157	26	51	103	3.5	7.1	46%	.327	1.60	6.58	6.12	9.02	-0.4
A. Santiago	RCU	A+	22	5	3	0	86^{1}	69	6	27	96	2.8	10.0	46%	.289	1.11	3.96	3.68	2.97	1.0
	CHT	AA	22	1	2	0	26	21	1	13	26	4.5	9.0	49%	.286	1.31	2.77	3.49	4.83	0.2
J. Solano	CHT	AA	22	3	0	0	62^{2}	58	4	17	60	2.4	8.6	46%	.315	1.20	2.73	2.92	2.80	0.8

Dominican righty **Jose Dominguez** has the stuff to succeed in a bullpen role but his control still needs work; he'll start the season on a 25-game suspension for a violation of baseball's drug policy. Acquired from the Orioles in a trade for Dana Eveland, **Jarret Martin** is a 6-foot-4 lefty with a fastball that can reach 97 mph, but his breaking ball and changeup are below average, and difficulty repeating his delivery leads to control problems. Not to be confused with the public relations guru who fathered the tape-measure home run, **Red Patterson** switched to the bullpen in 2012 and made the Southern League All-Star team. In the good news is bad news department, undersized lefty **Rob Rasmussen**'s changeup was working about as well as his fastball and slider last year . . . but none was working particularly well. A rough quartet of starts in Chattanooga led to **Jon Michael Redding** repeating the hitter-friendly Cal League for the third straight year, suggesting that his less-than-overpowering arsenal won't be enough in the upper minors. **Angel Sanchez** sparkled in his first stateside season in 2011 but couldn't keep the ball in the park in 2012. Drafted out of Puerto Rico in 2007, **Andres Santiago** spent his age 17-20 seasons in Rookie ball, but he's begun missing bats with an impressive regularity over the last two seasons. **Javier Solano** may be shorter than his listed 6 feet and lacking a high ceiling, but he nonetheless has the stuff to wind up in a major-league bullpen.

MANAGER: DON MATTINGLY

YEAR	TEAM	W-L	Pythag +/-	Avg PC	100+ P	120+ P	QS	BQS	REL	REL w Zero R	IBB	PH	PH Avg	PH HR	SB2	CS2	SB3	CS3	SAC Att	SAC %	POS SAC	Squeeze	Swing	In Play
2011	LAN	82-79	1	97.8	66	3	94	4	461	369	48	229	.199	4	17	9	1	0	101	80.2%	46	2	360	118
2012	LAN	86-76	1	96.2	66	0	93	5	506	426	62	241	.281	2	10	2	1	3	122	73.0%	40	2	329	97

Mattingly has been a calming presence for a team that has seen its share of tumult and distraction over the past two seasons, but his tactical shortcomings severely compromise whatever positive leadership qualities he brings to the dugout and the clubhouse. As in his rookie season, he again burned too many outs on one-run strategies for an offense-strapped club to survive. The Dodgers ranked second in the league in sacrifice attempts, fifth in position-player sacrifices, tied for fourth in hit-

and-run plays and sixth in stolen-base attempts. Unlike in 2011, their baserunning was a net negative, falling from +4.0 (and +3.4 on steals) to -3.7 (and -2.0 on steals).

Worse, Mattingly struggled with the fundamental concept of the batting order, using Dee Gordon (.280 OBP) in the leadoff spot 62 times despite the fact that it clearly wasn't working. Mattingly got the league's worst performance from his leadoff and number-two hitters combined (.237/.304/.322) and couldn't figure out how to get A.J. Ellis (.373 OBP) above the seventh spot in the order for more than 21 games, but at the same time he hit James Loney (.302 OBP) higher than seventh in 69 games, and Juan Rivera (.286 OBP) in 66. Injuries or no, it's no wonder the team ranked 13th in the NL in scoring. Mattingly's bullpen handling was laudable despite turnover from Javy Guerra to Kenley Jansen to Brandon League as closer, and he got good mileage out of shaky starters Chris Capuano and Aaron Harang. On the other hand, he did lead the league in intentional walks issued (62) as well as the highest number of such walks that backfired en route to a multi-run inning (15). Twice that happened against the Giants in the season's final four weeks when Mattingly passed Angel Pagan only to have the game broken open by Marco Scutaro—one of those in the loss that eliminated the Dodgers on the season's penultimate day, in case you needed confirmation of the negative cost of such maneuvers.

Miami Marlins

2012: THE KILLING FIELD(S)

Eight days after the Marlins' season-ending loss to the Mets, the team's Facebook feed featured a photo of the sun setting in the background of the new ballpark and a caption asking fans to share their best memories from the inaugural season. Some commenters reminisced about their favorite victories, but many instead released their most fervid vitriol, decrying the state of the Marlins as the sun set on a 69-93 campaign, their worst in 13 years.

The dismal performance might have been acceptable for a low-budget team in the midst of a rebuilding process, but neither description was supposed to fit the Marlins any longer. President of baseball operations Larry Beinfest promised to raise the team's payroll from $57 million to more than $85 million, and then surpassed that target by doling out $191 million in multi-year contracts over five days, pushing the 2012 books into nine figures. His reward: a three-game dip in the standings and a second consecutive last-place finish.

MARLINS PROSPECTUS

2012 W-L: 69-93, 5th in NL East

Pythag	.421	26th	DER	.700	23rd
RS/G	3.76	29th	B-Age	28.2	16th
RA/G	4.47	21st	P-Age	28.7	21st
TAv	.248	28th	Salary	$101.6	10th
BRR	13.3	2nd	M$/MW	$4.32	24th
TAv-P	.261	16th	DL Days	626	26th
FIP	3.94	15th	DL WARP	2.5	22nd

Three-Year Park Factors	
Overall	100
HR/RH	92
HR/LH	89
AVG/RH	97
AVG/LH	98

Marlins Park (2012)
Att. % of Capacity: 73.2% (13th)
Dim. 344, 386, 418, 392, 335

The park's first season saw few homers, lots of triples, lefty-righty balance, and liberal use of pastels.

Meanwhile, embattled owner Jeffrey Loria and president David Samson strove to turn the Marlins into an esteemed organization, one able to compete for attention with the star-studded, neighboring Heat of the NBA. As part of the stadium deal, they dropped the Florida tag to make the franchise Miami's own. They chose their new manager, Ozzie Guillen, for his ability to reach out to the city's Hispanic community. And, after years of profiteering from revenue-sharing dollars, they briefly loosened Beinfest's purse strings to enable the acquisition of elite free agents. Their reward: a season bookended by a public-relations disaster late in spring training, when Guillen enraged Cuban-Americans by expressing love for Fidel Castro, and the Facebook fiasco, which served to give swindled fans an opportunity to voice their displeasure.

2013: THEY WERE EXPENDABLE

On November 13, the Marlins traded Jose Reyes, Josh Johnson, Mark Buehrle, John Buck, and Emilio Bonifacio to the Blue Jays for Yunel Escobar, Jeff Mathis, and a flock of prospects. The 12-player deal was panned on Twitter timelines nationwide—by fans of the Marlins and of baseball, by remaining superstar Giancarlo Stanton and his teammate Ricky Nolasco—with everyone bashing the architects of the team's latest fire sale, which later sent Escobar on to Tampa Bay. Gone are the fruits of the previous offseason's spending spree, and along with them any hope of a playoff run this year. Left are the state-of-the-art facility, a $2.4 billion mortgage for taxpayers, and dejected supporters lamenting their financing of the world's most expensive aquarium.

For all of the reputation-wrecking fury that it stirred, the November purge that shaved the player payroll to less than $25 million was a shrewd baseball move. Beinfest shed two backloaded contracts and infused talented players into an already impressive pipeline, conceding that his team's short-term future was gloomy, but assembling pieces that could brighten it. Unfortunately, the fans in Miami, after being fed the bill for the new ballpark and teased with a short-lived foray into the high-payroll domain, are unlikely to have the patience to endure a perpetual wait for tomorrow.

Despite a lackluster product, 2,219,444 fans came to Marlins Park, the team's highest aggregate attendance since the 1997 championship season and the first time since 2005 that Miami was not the National League's caboose in per-game ticket sales. But the 44.2 percent attendance hike from

2011, the largest such increase in the majors, still ranked as a disappointment compared to the new-stadium boosts other franchises have enjoyed since the turn of the century. In fact, even with that bump, the Marlins posted the worst first-year total of the 14-team lot. That is damning evidence of a dispassionate fan base, in a market where the professional basketball franchise just won a world championship and the local university's baseball program has produced as many Most Valuable Player award-winners as the major-league team.

STATE OF THE ORGANIZATION: APOCALYPSE NOW

For Loria and Samson, who value revenues over rings, the latest rebuild is a bump in the road, and the owners' approximately $120 million investment in the new ballpark will be recouped through revenue-sharing payouts regardless of attendance. That is the nature of the business, and Loria and Samson are experts at sacrificing their own integrity to game the system. Moreover, while cries for the franchise to be sold are loud now, the owners can point to the team's 877–904 record during their tenure—the sixth-best ledger in the senior circuit over that 11-season span—and rest assured that when the farm system's latest crops ripen, interested fans will return.

Jose Fernandez and Justin Nicolino will soon fill the shoes of Johnson and Buehrle. Shortstop Adeiny Hechavarria lacks Reyes's bat and wheels, but his fielding prowess is undeniable. Christian Yelich and Jacob Realmuto are high-ceiling hitters who could fortify a potent, Stanton-led lineup. And those blue-chip prospects are merely the most esteemed in a hopper that Beinfest and his evaluators have consistently kept well stocked.

Beinfest and Miami's coaches, led by first-year manager Mike Redmond, are now tasked with gauging their existing talent and pondering how the players may jell into a contender. In an era of multibillion-dollar television contracts and in an increasingly competitive division, the Marlins' boom-and-bust cycle will continue trending toward ephemeral successes and elongated droughts, such as the ongoing one, now at nine years and counting with no end in sight. This truism influenced the decision to push the restart button again, to postpone the window of competition until a more complete roster can be assembled.

But after a season of window dressing, fans are well aware that the emperors—like Redmond during a slump-busting batting practice session in 2003—have no clothes. New ballpark or not, the team, with a TV deal worth just $18 million annually, is a relative pauper, one that can enjoy prolonged booms only if its owners' priorities change. Loria and Samson, who still face a Securities and Exchange Commission investigation into the financing of Marlins Park, have asked for patience while cashing paychecks.

HITTERS

Rob Brantly **C**
Born: **7/14/1989** Age: **23**
Bats: **L** Throws: **R** Height: **6' 3"**
Weight: **205** Breakout: **3%**
Improve: **49%** Collapse: **6%**
Attrition: **10%** MLB: **96%**

Comparables:
Mike Sweeney,Russ Nixon,Tim McCarver

YEAR	TEAM	LVL	AGE	PA	R	2B	3B	HR	RBI	BB	SO	SB	CS	AVG_OBP_SLG	TAv	BABIP	BRR	FRAA	WARP
2010	WMI	A	20	217	26	10	1	1	21	23	22	2	2	.255/.350/.335	.253	.283	-1.7	C(55): 0.9	0.7
2011	WMI	A	21	317	42	16	1	7	44	24	39	2	2	.303/.366/.440	.307	.331	-2.1	C(26): -0.3	0.8
2011	LAK	A+	21	155	16	6	0	3	18	5	17	0	0	.219/.239/.322	.215	.223	-0.8	C(14): -0.0	-0.1
2012	ERI	AA	22	195	16	16	1	3	24	12	17	0	3	.311/.359/.461	.324	.329	0.3	C(11): -0.2	0.5
2012	NWO	AAA	22	54	7	4	0	2	11	1	9	0	0	.365/.389/.558	.313	.415	-0.3	C(7): -0.1	0.3
2012	TOL	AAA	22	139	11	4	0	0	6	7	25	0	0	.254/.295/.285	.163	.311	1	C(26): -0.7	-1.1
2012	MIA	MLB	22	113	14	8	0	3	8	13	16	1	1	.290/.372/.460	.296	.321	0.6	C(28): 0.0	0.9
2013	*MIA*	*MLB*	*23*	*250*	*22*	*12*	*1*	*3*	*24*	*16*	*41*	*1*	*0*	*.251/.301/.355*	*.241*	*.288*	*-0.5*	*C -0*	*0.5*

An athletic catcher with a smooth swing and excellent contact-hitting skills, Brantly came over from the Tigers in the Anibal Sanchez deal and took over the every-day catching responsibilities in short order. Brantly's mature approach, both in the batter's box and in the squat, impressed the Marlins during his three-month stint last year, and he figures to remain the team's primary backstop this season, ahead of newly acquired Jeff Mathis. Brantly's home-run ceiling lies somewhere in the low teens, but his polish may help him push Jacob Realmuto to be the team's catcher of the future. In the worst-case scenario, he'll give the Marlins one of the best overall backups in the league, or a fine trading chip.

Chris Coghlan **OF**
Born: **6/18/1985** Age: **28**
Bats: **L** Throws: **R** Height: **6' 1"**
Weight: **205** Breakout: **2%**
Improve: **49%** Collapse: **6%**
Attrition: **25%** MLB: **92%**

Comparables:
Martin Prado,Bill Sample,Bernard Gilkey

YEAR	TEAM	LVL	AGE	PA	R	2B	3B	HR	RBI	BB	SO	SB	CS	AVG_OBP_SLG	TAv	BABIP	BRR	FRAA	WARP
2010	FLO	MLB	25	400	60	20	3	5	28	33	84	10	3	.268/.335/.383	.265	.336	4.3	LF(90): -1.9	1.3
2011	NWO	AAA	26	68	11	4	0	1	7	8	5	3	1	.245/.358/.377	.266	.240	0	--	0.0
2011	FLO	MLB	26	298	33	20	1	5	22	22	49	7	6	.230/.296/.368	.243	.263	-2.3	CF(65): 3.0	0.0
2012	NWO	AAA	27	368	42	21	3	7	31	46	44	10	2	.284/.375/.435	.302	.309	0.5	LF(12): -0.7, RF(9): 0.3	0.5
2012	MIA	MLB	27	105	10	1	0	1	10	9	12	0	2	.140/.212/.183	.157	.146	0.7	LF(21): 1.0, CF(13): -0.6	-1.0
2013	*MIA*	*MLB*	*28*	*250*	*30*	*12*	*2*	*4*	*22*	*22*	*38*	*5*	*2*	*.263/.331/.382*	*.262*	*.299*	*0*	*CF -0, LF 0*	*0.7*

Coghlan burst onto the scene by hitting .321 in his first tour of the majors and taking home the 2009 National League Rookie of the Year award. Skeptics who pointed to his unsustainable BABIP have since been vindicated. It is now safe to call Coghlan's decorated debut a fluke. He was demoted to Triple-A in early June, despite the fact that a spate of Marlins' injuries should have created ample opportunities for him to contribute. Now battling for a spot on the organizational depth chart, Coghlan needs to separate himself in spring training or he may struggle to resurface as more than a fifth outfielder.

Zack Cox 3B

Born: **5/9/1989** Age: **24**
Bats: **L** Throws: **R** Height: **6' 1"**
Weight: **215** Breakout: **7%**
Improve: **54%** Collapse: **2%**
Attrition: **11%** MLB: **93%**

Comparables:
Aramis Ramirez, Ken McMullen, Larry Parrish

YEAR	TEAM	LVL	AGE	PA	R	2B	3B	HR	RBI	BB	SO	SB	CS	AVG_OBP_SLG	TAv	BABIP	BRR	FRAA	WARP
2011	PMB	A+	22	180	22	8	0	3	20	11	29	2	2	.335/.380/.439	.290	.388	0	--	0.0
2011	SFD	AA	22	389	54	19	0	10	48	29	69	0	1	.293/.355/.432	.276	.338	0	--	0.0
2012	JAX	AA	23	106	14	6	1	1	13	10	27	0	0	.253/.321/.368	.304	.338	-1.4	3B(12): 1.1	0.5
2012	MEM	AAA	23	316	27	23	0	9	30	12	63	1	0	.254/.294/.421	.311	.295	-3.5	3B(14): -0.0	0.4
2013	*MIA*	*MLB*	*24*	*250*	*21*	*12*	*1*	*5*	*26*	*11*	*61*	*0*	*0*	*.231/.268/.352*	*.228*	*.288*	*-0.3*	*3B 0*	*-0.3*

The Cardinals made Cox—a polished college third baseman—their first-round pick in 2010, even though they knew that their hot-corner incumbent, David Freese, could block the University of Arkansas product down the road. Freese's development into an All-Star made Cox expendable at the trade deadline, allowing Larry Beinfest to nab him for contract-year setup man Edward Mujica. Cox has yet to solve the upper minors, but he projects as a potential glove-first regular and could get a taste of the majors this summer.

Derek Dietrich MI

Born: **7/18/1989** Age: **23**
Bats: **L** Throws: **R** Height: **6' 2"**
Weight: **200** Breakout: **5%**
Improve: **44%** Collapse: **10%**
Attrition: **10%** MLB: **96%**

Comparables:
Alex Gonzalez, Derek Jeter, Jim Fregosi

YEAR	TEAM	LVL	AGE	PA	R	2B	3B	HR	RBI	BB	SO	SB	CS	AVG_OBP_SLG	TAv	BABIP	BRR	FRAA	WARP
2010	HUD	A-	20	198	33	12	2	3	20	11	42	2	2	.279/.340/.419	.281	.348	-0.7	SS(32): -4.8	0.4
2011	BGR	A	21	538	73	34	4	22	81	38	128	5	7	.277/.346/.502	.305	.331	0	SS(33): -3.7	0.7
2012	PCH	A+	22	417	49	21	9	10	58	25	78	4	2	.282/.343/.468	.270	.329	3.7	SS(16): -2.9, 2B(8): -1.3	0.3
2012	MNT	AA	22	146	22	7	1	4	17	7	36	0	1	.271/.324/.429	.209	.340	0.3	2B(10): 0.2	0.0
2013	*MIA*	*MLB*	*23*	*250*	*22*	*10*	*2*	*5*	*26*	*9*	*65*	*1*	*1*	*.228/.268/.356*	*.228*	*.288*	*-0.2*	*SS -1, 2B -0*	*0.0*

This 2010 second-rounder from Georgia Tech calibrated his age to his level by hitting his way out of High-A Port Charlotte (where he was named team MVP) in late July. Dietrich offers good power, and it's nice to have a lefty-hitting middle infielder, but he will have to do something about his poor walk and walk-to-strikeout rates if he is to make himself into a viable prospect. His promotion to Double-A came with a move from shortstop to second base, largely because the Rays thought his power bat projected better there (and because Hak-Ju Lee owned shortstop). Acquired for Yunel Escobar at the Winter Meetings, Dietrich will need to show that he can support his power with patience to emerge as the Marlins' second or third baseman of the future.

Greg Dobbs 4C

Born: **7/2/1978** Age: **34**
Bats: **L** Throws: **R** Height: **6' 2"**
Weight: **205** Breakout: **2%**
Improve: **34%** Collapse: **7%**
Attrition: **17%** MLB: **79%**

Comparables:
Pedro Feliz, Tim Wallach, Tony Batista

YEAR	TEAM	LVL	AGE	PA	R	2B	3B	HR	RBI	BB	SO	SB	CS	AVG_OBP_SLG	TAv	BABIP	BRR	FRAA	WARP
2010	LEH	AAA	32	70	10	3	1	2	9	7	12	2	0	.210/.290/.387	.248	.229	-0.4	RF(11): -0.2, 3B(4): 0.1	0.1
2010	PHI	MLB	32	176	13	7	0	5	15	12	39	1	1	.196/.251/.331	.204	.227	0.3	3B(36): -3.7, 1B(2): -0.0	-0.8
2011	FLO	MLB	33	439	38	23	0	8	49	22	83	0	0	.275/.311/.389	.251	.325	-1.9	3B(100): -4.6, 1B(4): 0.3	-0.4
2012	MIA	MLB	33	342	26	13	2	5	39	14	53	4	2	.285/.313/.386	.255	.321	-2.4	3B(35): -4.5, LF(21): -1.1	-0.8
2013	*MIA*	*MLB*	*34*	*341*	*32*	*15*	*1*	*7*	*36*	*17*	*64*	*2*	*1*	*.254/.292/.370*	*.242*	*.294*	*-0.3*	*3B -2, RF -0*	*-0.1*

A versatile bench player who can handle any of the four corner positions but is miscast as an every-day third baseman, Dobbs was exposed when pressed into regular duty by the rash of injuries that struck the Marlins roster. He started 97 games, 52 of them in the five- or six-hole of Ozzie Guillen's batting order—where his .255 TAv sagged the team's run output—and 30 of them at the hot corner, where his -5.6 FRAA was detrimental to Miami's pitchers. The two-year deal Dobbs signed last January guarantees him a spot on the 2013 bench, and he may again find more playing time than the Marlins would like.

Adeiny Hechavarria SS

Born: **4/15/1989** Age: **24**
Bats: **R** Throws: **R** Height: **6' 0"**
Weight: **180** Breakout: **3%**
Improve: **41%** Collapse: **7%**
Attrition: **22%** MLB: **94%**

Comparables:
Phil Linz, Cristian Guzman, Anderson Hernandez

YEAR	TEAM	LVL	AGE	PA	R	2B	3B	HR	RBI	BB	SO	SB	CS	AVG_OBP_SLG	TAv	BABIP	BRR	FRAA	WARP
2011	NHP	AA	22	502	58	22	6	6	46	25	78	19	13	.235/.275/.347	.216	.267	0	--	0.0
2011	LVG	AAA	22	116	16	6	2	2	11	8	21	1	2	.389/.431/.537	.302	.471	1.2	SS(17): -3.6	0.5
2012	LVG	AAA	23	490	78	20	6	6	63	38	86	8	2	.312/.363/.424	.248	.371	2.3	SS(74): 7.0, 2B(7): 1.7	1.5
2012	TOR	MLB	23	137	10	8	0	2	15	4	32	0	0	.254/.280/.365	.228	.323	0.1	3B(18): 0.9, SS(17): -0.8	-0.1
2013	*MIA*	*MLB*	*24*	*250*	*23*	*10*	*2*	*2*	*18*	*12*	*53*	*2*	*1*	*.243/.278/.322*	*.225*	*.301*	*0*	*SS 1, 3B 0*	*0.2*

Hechavarria entered last year as a glove-first shortstop with a career .255 batting average, but the batter-friendly confines of the Pacific Coast League helped him post a career-best .312/.363/.424 line at Triple-A Las Vegas. Scouts acknowledge improvement in his approach, but still question whether he'll ever be more than a nine-hole hitter in the major leagues. His defense is another story, however, as he has been lauded as one of the game's premier defensive shortstops since signing with Toronto in 2010. The Blue Jays traded him to Miami in November, where he is expected to take over for the departed Jose Reyes as the every-day shortstop.

Gorkys Hernandez CF

Born: **9/7/1987** Age: **25**
Bats: **R** Throws: **R** Height: **6' 1"**
Weight: **185** Breakout: **11%**
Improve: **42%** Collapse: **3%**
Attrition: **21%** MLB: **94%**

Comparables:
Angel Pagan,Michael Bourn,Dave Collins

YEAR	TEAM	LVL	AGE	PA	R	2B	3B	HR	RBI	BB	SO	SB	CS	AVG_OBP_SLG	TAv	BABIP	BRR	FRAA	WARP
2010	ALT	AA	22	414	45	11	4	2	26	33	95	17	3	.266/.330/.334	.247	.347	2.5	CF(92): -5.4	0.5
2011	IND	AAA	23	475	48	25	9	1	40	35	91	21	9	.283/.348/.392	.270	.357	4.6	CF(83): -0.3, RF(3): 0.3	1.4
2012	IND	AAA	24	281	43	11	2	2	25	34	64	13	7	.257/.353/.346	.258	.341	1.5	LF(37): 6.1, CF(17): 3.2	1.7
2012	MIA	MLB	24	147	16	2	3	3	11	12	37	5	2	.212/.288/.341	.223	.272	-0.2	CF(35): -0.3, LF(1): -0.0	-0.2
2012	PIT	MLB	24	26	2	0	0	0	2	1	5	2	0	.083/.154/.083	.113	.105	0.6	LF(13): 1.0, RF(6): -0.0	-0.2
2013	*MIA*	*MLB*	*25*	*250*	*28*	*9*	*2*	*2*	*17*	*18*	*59*	*9*	*3*	*.238/.301/.326*	*.235*	*.306*	*0.7*	*CF -0, LF 0*	*0.1*

Once a toolsy outfielder perennially mentioned in trade talks, Hernandez is now with his fourth organization, and the prospect shine has officially come off. Acquired from the Pirates in the Gaby Sanchez deal at the trade deadline, Hernandez failed to produce enough to warrant consideration for a full-time gig with the Marlins in 2013. Though he is a plus defender at all three outfield positions, his offensive value is limited to his wheels. That one-dimensional skill won't ever suffice for more than a reserve-outfielder/pinch-runner role on a contender.

Austin Kearns OF

Born: **5/20/1980** Age: **33**
Bats: **R** Throws: **R** Height: **6' 4"**
Weight: **240** Breakout: **4%**
Improve: **34%** Collapse: **9%**
Attrition: **17%** MLB: **88%**

Comparables:
Jose Cruz Jr.,John Lowenstein,Gary Roenicke

YEAR	TEAM	LVL	AGE	PA	R	2B	3B	HR	RBI	BB	SO	SB	CS	AVG_OBP_SLG	TAv	BABIP	BRR	FRAA	WARP
2010	CLE	MLB	30	342	42	18	1	8	42	34	78	4	1	.272/.354/.419	.273	.341	1.1	LF(69): 2.9, RF(14): 0.6	1.7
2010	NYA	MLB	30	119	13	3	0	2	7	12	38	0	0	.235/.345/.324	.247	.355	0.3	LF(22): 1.1, RF(18): -0.1	0.2
2011	CLE	MLB	31	174	18	5	1	2	7	18	48	0	4	.200/.302/.287	.224	.280	0.8	LF(36): 1.6, RF(19): 0.3	-0.1
2012	MIA	MLB	32	175	21	6	0	4	16	22	44	2	1	.245/.366/.367	.256	.323	0.5	LF(21): 4.4, RF(12): 2.4	0.8
2013	*MIA*	*MLB*	*33*	*250*	*25*	*9*	*1*	*4*	*24*	*27*	*61*	*2*	*1*	*.225/.323/.329*	*.246*	*.291*	*-0.4*	*LF 1, RF 0*	*0.3*

Kearns cracked the Marlins roster as a fourth outfielder in April, but his most salient contribution may have been an ill-timed hamstring strain that sidelined him in late May and impelled Beinfest to pull the trigger on the Justin Ruggiano trade. Ruggiano's emergence ate into Kearns's playing time when he returned in June. He'll likely need to settle for another minor-league deal and endure a second straight roster-spot competition in whichever camp he lands. At press time he was still a free agent.

Carlos Lee 1B

Born: **6/20/1976** Age: **37**
Bats: **R** Throws: **R** Height: **6' 3"**
Weight: **265** Breakout: **0%**
Improve: **29%** Collapse: **11%**
Attrition: **13%** MLB: **74%**

Comparables:
Rusty Staub,Moises Alou,Mike Sweeney

YEAR	TEAM	LVL	AGE	PA	R	2B	3B	HR	RBI	BB	SO	SB	CS	AVG_OBP_SLG	TAv	BABIP	BRR	FRAA	WARP
2010	HOU	MLB	34	649	67	29	1	24	89	37	59	3	3	.246/.291/.417	.245	.238	-1.2	LF(133): -13.9, 1B(19): -0.5	-1.7
2011	HOU	MLB	35	653	66	38	4	18	94	59	60	4	3	.275/.342/.446	.289	.279	-3.9	LF(80): -6.3, 1B(79): 6.5	2.4
2012	HOU	MLB	36	277	24	15	1	5	29	19	17	0	0	.287/.336/.411	.258	.292	-3.5	1B(65): -2.9	-0.9
2012	MIA	MLB	36	338	29	12	0	4	48	39	32	3	0	.243/.328/.325	.250	.256	1.3	1B(80): 0.7	0.1
2013	*MIA*	*MLB*	*37*	*587*	*61*	*27*	*2*	*16*	*69*	*41*	*58*	*3*	*2*	*.262/.314/.406*	*.265*	*.267*	*-0.8*	*1B -1, LF -2*	*0.8*

Imported from the Astros on July 4, when the Marlins were 38-42 but still had a puncher's chance to compete, Lee predictably did nothing to stem the tide, contributing half a season of replacement-level work. The portly Panamanian has 358 home runs to his name, but his power has eroded with age, and El Caballo's glove is now barely passable at first base, let alone in left field, where he used to prance. That puts even more pressure on his fading bat. Lee should find a taker willing to offer a short-term hitch, but he is no longer worthy of a full-time role.

Joe Mahoney 1B

Born: **2/1/1987** Age: **26**
Bats: **L** Throws: **L** Height: **6' 7"**
Weight: **240** Breakout: **4%**
Improve: **52%** Collapse: **3%**
Attrition: **6%** MLB: **82%**

Comparables:
Mike Ivie,Lamar Johnson,Tony Horton

YEAR	TEAM	LVL	AGE	PA	R	2B	3B	HR	RBI	BB	SO	SB	CS	AVG_OBP_SLG	TAv	BABIP	BRR	FRAA	WARP
2010	FRD	A+	23	299	37	18	0	9	49	22	56	5	3	.299/.360/.465	.304	.350	-3	1B(69): -0.3, LF(3): 0.0	1.3
2010	BOW	AA	23	209	30	12	2	9	29	17	39	8	1	.319/.378/.545	.319	.364	-0.4	1B(42): 2.4, LF(10): 0.7	1.7
2011	BOW	AA	24	355	43	24	5	11	67	25	84	7	2	.289/.344/.502	.333	.349	0.6	1B(53): -1.1, LF(2): 0.0	2.1
2012	NOR	AAA	25	536	54	29	1	10	56	35	95	4	2	.265/.319/.389	.243	.308	-1	1B(102): 5.9, LF(1): 0.1	-0.5
2012	BAL	MLB	25	4	0	0	0	0	0	0	0	0	0	.000/.000/.000	.015	.000	0	1B(2): -0.1	-0.1
2013	*MIA*	*MLB*	*26*	*250*	*25*	*12*	*1*	*6*	*28*	*14*	*55*	*2*	*1*	*.256/.301/.395*	*.253*	*.307*	*-0.1*	*1B -2, LF -0*	*-0.2*

Originally drafted by Baltimore in 2010, Mahoney is quickly approaching the age where he no longer really qualifies as a "prospect." He certainly looks the part of a major-league masher, but despite his size and the countless scouting reports that have been filed over the years about his "power upside," Mahoney has yet to translate that upside into production. . . and there's no guarantee that he ever will. Just because you're tall doesn't mean you automatically hit for power; just ask Michael Jordan. If Mahoney hopes to carve out a career as a big league first baseman, he'll need to find the power that everyone expects from him.

Jake Marisnick CF

Born: **3/30/1991** Age: **22**
Bats: **R** Throws: **R** Height: **6' 5"**
Weight: **200** Breakout: **12%**
Improve: **58%** Collapse: **4%**
Attrition: **20%** MLB: **97%**

Comparables:
David Green, Bobby Tolan, Thad Bosley

YEAR	TEAM	LVL	AGE	PA	R	2B	3B	HR	RBI	BB	SO	SB	CS	AVG_OBP_SLG	TAv	BABIP	BRR	FRAA	WARP
2010	BLJ	Rk	19	142	17	12	0	3	14	13	18	14	1	.287/.379/.459	.312	.317	-0.1	CF(34): 0.9	1.5
2010	LNS	A	19	143	16	8	2	1	12	9	37	9	2	.220/.294/.339	.219	.297	1.8	CF(29): 4.5, LF(2): 0.5	0.4
2011	LNS	A	20	523	68	27	6	14	77	43	91	37	8	.320/.392/.496	.308	.371	0	--	0.0
2012	DUN	A+	21	306	41	18	7	6	35	26	55	10	5	.263/.349/.451	.277	.309	-0.7	CF(42): 3.1	1.4
2012	NHP	AA	21	247	25	11	3	2	15	11	45	14	4	.233/.286/.336	.292	.278	2.3	CF(20): 0.9	1.0
2013	*MIA*	*MLB*	*22*	*250*	*27*	*10*	*2*	*3*	*18*	*12*	*60*	*8*	*2*	*.212/.262/.315*	*.216*	*.267*	*0.8*	*CF -1, LF 0*	*-0.4*

Toronto's third-round pick in 2009, Marisnick was aggressively promoted to Double-A in July despite struggling with timing and hitting just .263/.349/.451 in the Florida State League. Predictably, his struggles continued against more advanced pitching. Four of his tools—speed, arm, power, and defense—grade as average or better, but the development of his hit tool will determine whether Marisnick becomes a star. After being dealt to Miami in November, he was scheduled to join top prospects Christian Yelich and Marcell Ozuna in Double-A Jacksonville's outfield.

Jeff Mathis C

Born: **3/31/1983** Age: **30**
Bats: **R** Throws: **R** Height: **6' 1"**
Weight: **200** Breakout: **5%**
Improve: **31%** Collapse: **18%**
Attrition: **24%** MLB: **93%**

Comparables:
Pat Corrales, A.J. Hinch, Andy Etchebarren

YEAR	TEAM	LVL	AGE	PA	R	2B	3B	HR	RBI	BB	SO	SB	CS	AVG_OBP_SLG	TAv	BABIP	BRR	FRAA	WARP
2010	ANA	MLB	27	218	19	6	1	3	18	6	59	3	0	.195/.219/.278	.194	.253	0.8	C(67): 1.1	-0.3
2011	ANA	MLB	28	281	18	12	0	3	22	15	75	1	2	.174/.225/.259	.190	.233	-0.8	C(91): 0.2	-1.2
2012	TOR	MLB	29	227	25	13	0	8	27	9	68	1	0	.218/.249/.393	.221	.279	-1.7	C(66): -1.1, P(2): -0.0	-0.2
2013	*MIA*	*MLB*	*30*	*250*	*22*	*9*	*1*	*5*	*22*	*16*	*70*	*2*	*1*	*.201/.258/.308*	*.208*	*.257*	*-0.3*	*C -0*	*-0.3*

After a disastrous 2011 wherein Mathis hit a meager .174/.225/.259 with a .190 True Average, there was really only one direction his production could go. Then again, the same could have been (and probably was) said after he hit .195/.219/.278 in 2010. Fortunately for Mathis and the Blue Jays, the 29-year-old veteran experienced a perverted kind of renaissance at the plate, establishing career highs with a .218 batting average, .393 slugging average, and .221 TAv in addition to his best on-base percentage since 2009. A -1.2 FRAA put a dent in Mathis's rapidly diminishing reputation as a defense-first backstop, however. Despite all of his inadequacies, Toronto inked Mathis to a two-year, $3 million contract extension in August. Perhaps realizing their mistake, the Blue Jays then jettisoned him to Miami in November.

Kevin Mattison CF

Born: **9/20/1985** Age: **27**
Bats: **L** Throws: **L** Height: **6' 1"**
Weight: **180** Breakout: **2%**
Improve: **51%** Collapse: **9%**
Attrition: **20%** MLB: **88%**

Comparables:
Luis Terrero, Choo Freeman, Shane Mack

YEAR	TEAM	LVL	AGE	PA	R	2B	3B	HR	RBI	BB	SO	SB	CS	AVG_OBP_SLG	TAv	BABIP	BRR	FRAA	WARP
2010	JUP	A+	24	397	46	13	4	3	29	22	87	44	10	.218/.274/.301	.225	.276	4.4	CF(85): 6.2, RF(2): 0.3	0.3
2010	JUP	A+	24	397	46	13	4	3	29	22	87	44	10	.218/.274/.301	.225	.276	4.4	CF(2): -0.0	0.3
2010	JAX	AA	24	51	10	4	1	0	1	4	10	4	0	.222/.275/.356	.221	.270	1.7	LF(15): 2.0, RF(3): -0.0	0.2
2011	JAX	AA	25	591	87	17	16	8	49	58	127	38	16	.260/.353/.406	.324	.330	2.1	CF(53): 6.4, RF(3): -0.1	3.4
2012	NWO	AAA	26	539	80	23	6	13	41	44	145	26	12	.241/.310/.394	.223	.315	5.8	CF(31): 2.0	0.5
2012	MIA	MLB	26	5	0	0	0	0	0	0	2	0	0	.000/.000/.000	.005	.000	0	LF(1): -0.0	-0.1
2013	*MIA*	*MLB*	*27*	*250*	*32*	*9*	*3*	*4*	*18*	*15*	*67*	*16*	*6*	*.215/.269/.328*	*.219*	*.279*	*1.7*	*CF -1, LF 0*	*-0.2*

A speedster out of UNC-Asheville, Mattison made a cameo in May before returning to New Orleans when the Marlins brought in Ruggiano. Given his sky-high strikeout rate and lack of power, even plus speed and a good glove in center won't save Mattison from a career on the fringe. After going 0-for-5 in May, Mattison will need another chance to join Ty Wigginton and Tony Campana as the only Asheville Bulldogs who can boast a hit in the major leagues.

Logan Morrison LF

Born: **8/25/1987** Age: **25**
Bats: **L** Throws: **L** Height: **6' 4"**
Weight: **235** Breakout: **8%**
Improve: **48%** Collapse: **1%**
Attrition: **6%** MLB: **95%**

Comparables:
Gary Matthews, Roy Foster, Mike Greenwell

YEAR	TEAM	LVL	AGE	PA	R	2B	3B	HR	RBI	BB	SO	SB	CS	AVG_OBP_SLG	TAv	BABIP	BRR	FRAA	WARP
2010	NWO	AAA	22	293	36	17	4	6	45	48	35	1	2	.307/.431/.487	.317	.340	-1.5	1B(49): 0.2, LF(19): 1.0	2.0
2010	FLO	MLB	22	287	43	20	7	2	18	41	51	0	1	.283/.390/.447	.298	.351	1.8	LF(62): -1.8	2.1
2011	FLO	MLB	23	525	54	25	4	23	72	54	99	2	1	.247/.330/.468	.289	.265	-2.4	LF(119): -2.9, 1B(1): -0.1	1.6
2012	MIA	MLB	24	334	30	15	1	11	36	31	58	1	0	.230/.308/.399	.249	.248	-0.8	LF(59): -3.9, 1B(21): 2.4	-0.4
2013	*MIA*	*MLB*	*25*	*352*	*39*	*17*	*3*	*10*	*44*	*38*	*61*	*1*	*0*	*.255/.341/.433*	*.282*	*.285*	*-0.2*	*LF 0, 1B -1*	*1.5*

Shelved for much of the summer by a torn patellar tendon in his right knee, Morrison played in only 93 games, leaving him plenty of time to entertain Twitter followers with posts about body parts and functions and drinking Four Loko. Injuries have done their part in stunting the former top prospect's development, but Morrison's immaturity has not helped, and the June 2011 dismissal of hitting coach John Mallee—which Morrison, to the organization's displeasure, publicly panned—left his approach in disarray. With Gaby Sanchez in Pittsburgh, first base is there for Morrison's taking. He has to stay on the field and return to the patient, sweet-swinging ways that got his career off to such a promising start.

Marcell Ozuna RF

Born: **11/12/1990** Age: **22**
Bats: **R** Throws: **R** Height: **6' 3"**
Weight: **190** Breakout: **3%**
Improve: **64%** Collapse: **1%**
Attrition: **4%** MLB: **98%**

Comparables:
Miguel Cabrera, Jay Bruce, Tony Conigliaro

YEAR	TEAM	LVL	AGE	PA	R	2B	3B	HR	RBI	BB	SO	SB	CS	AVG_OBP_SLG	TAv	BABIP	BRR	FRAA	WARP
2010	JAM	A-	19	293	53	11	2	21	60	17	94	3	1	.267/.317/.556	.290	.329	1.5	RF(49): 4.2, CF(8): 0.4	2.0
2011	GRB	A	20	552	87	28	5	23	71	46	121	17	2	.266/.330/.482	.273	.308	0	--	0.0
2012	JUP	A+	21	539	89	27	2	24	95	44	116	8	3	.266/.328/.476	.314	.301	1.6	RF(74): 11.9, CF(11): -0.9	4.2
2013	*MIA*	*MLB*	*22*	*250*	*26*	*9*	*1*	*11*	*34*	*12*	*78*	*0*	*0*	*.220/.258/.404*	*.240*	*.273*	*-0.3*	*RF 1, CF -0*	*0.1*

Doubt Ozuna's pop at your own peril. The 21-year-old isn't exactly the second coming of Giancarlo Stanton, but he paced the pitcher-friendly Florida State League with 24 home runs and ranked fourth in the circuit in slugging. Ozuna is a prototypical right fielder, with light-tower power and a plus arm. He'll need to continue honing his approach to maintain an acceptable batting average and strikeout rate in the upper minors. If he makes those adjustments, that will put him a year or two away from giving the Marlins one of the most fearsome sets of corner outfielders in the league.

Noah Perio 2B

Born: **11/14/1991** Age: **21**
Bats: **L** Throws: **R** Height: **6' 1"**
Weight: **170** Breakout: **3%**
Improve: **51%** Collapse: **9%**
Attrition: **13%** MLB: **94%**

Comparables:
Bill Mazeroski, Dalton Jones, Tim Foli

YEAR	TEAM	LVL	AGE	PA	R	2B	3B	HR	RBI	BB	SO	SB	CS	AVG_OBP_SLG	TAv	BABIP	BRR	FRAA	WARP
2010	JAM	A-	18	246	30	10	0	0	31	17	25	7	0	.258/.316/.302	.236	.290	2.2	SS(33): -1.4, 2B(16): 3.7	0.4
2011	GRB	A	19	519	76	30	3	6	52	19	64	15	6	.295/.323/.406	.254	.327	0	--	0.0
2012	JUP	A+	20	502	50	22	2	1	40	27	68	6	4	.248/.293/.311	.233	.286	-0.7	2B(80): -0.8	-0.8
2013	*MIA*	*MLB*	*21*	*250*	*20*	*9*	*1*	*1*	*16*	*9*	*50*	*0*	*0*	*.216/.247/.282*	*.198*	*.264*	*-0.3*	*2B -2, SS 0*	*-0.9*

Picks from the 39th round of the draft seldom reach the Show, but Perio—who slid to the third day because of what was perceived to be a strong football commitment—might join Kenny Rogers and Bryan LaHair among notable players who beat the odds. He scuffled in his first tour of High-A, but was young for the Florida State League and still has time to tone down his swing-happy ways. With gap power, plus athleticism, and quality defense at the keystone, Perio could become a middling starter or a top reserve. Expect him to return to Jupiter to begin the 2013 season, and go step-by-step up the ladder as he refines his approach.

Bryan Petersen OF

Born: **4/9/1986** Age: **27**
Bats: **L** Throws: **R** Height: **6' 1"**
Weight: **205** Breakout: **9%**
Improve: **44%** Collapse: **7%**
Attrition: **24%** MLB: **90%**

Comparables:
Jim Dwyer, Randy Ready, Jim Delsing

YEAR	TEAM	LVL	AGE	PA	R	2B	3B	HR	RBI	BB	SO	SB	CS	AVG_OBP_SLG	TAv	BABIP	BRR	FRAA	WARP
2010	NWO	AAA	24	368	47	13	2	5	27	34	63	5	4	.255/.332/.354	.252	.298	0.4	LF(31): 0.9, RF(29): 5.2	1.3
2010	FLO	MLB	24	25	1	0	0	0	2	1	6	0	0	.083/.120/.083	.093	.111	0.2	LF(5): -0.0, RF(1): -0.0	-0.4
2011	NWO	AAA	25	286	47	21	0	11	26	36	41	6	5	.351/.434/.569	.346	.386	0	--	0.0
2011	FLO	MLB	25	241	18	13	3	2	10	26	49	7	1	.265/.357/.387	.275	.333	-1.3	CF(42): -2.9, LF(22): -0.7	0.8
2012	NWO	AAA	26	271	45	8	2	3	28	20	43	8	7	.321/.380/.407	.270	.375	-0.9	LF(6): -0.7, RF(5): 0.7	0.0
2012	MIA	MLB	26	273	29	9	3	0	17	25	58	8	2	.195/.272/.257	.201	.255	0.7	LF(51): -1.2, CF(20): -1.5	-1.7
2013	*MIA*	*MLB*	*27*	*291*	*31*	*11*	*2*	*2*	*20*	*24*	*59*	*6*	*3*	*.232/.304/.318*	*.234*	*.287*	*0.1*	*LF -1, CF -1*	*-0.2*

After emerging as a passable replacement during the 2011 season, Petersen earned a second look in 2012. Unfortunately, his bid for an encore quickly turned into a flop, with the new ballpark sapping his already mediocre pop and exposing his fringy range in center field. Petersen is a tweener, even by reserve standards, with a fifth-outfielder bat and insufficient versatility to compensate. He'll face long odds to make the major-league roster out of spring training, and a return trip to New Orleans is the most likely outcome.

Juan Pierre LF

Born: **8/14/1977** Age: **35**
Bats: **L** Throws: **L** Height: **6' 0"**
Weight: **175** Breakout: **2%**
Improve: **23%** Collapse: **13%**
Attrition: **19%** MLB: **83%**

Comparables:
Manny Mota, Dave Roberts, Peanuts Lowrey

YEAR	TEAM	LVL	AGE	PA	R	2B	3B	HR	RBI	BB	SO	SB	CS	AVG_OBP_SLG	TAv	BABIP	BRR	FRAA	WARP
2010	CHA	MLB	32	734	96	18	3	1	47	45	47	68	18	.275/.341/.316	.242	.294	8.6	LF(149): 5.3	1.5
2011	CHA	MLB	33	711	80	17	4	2	50	43	41	27	17	.279/.329/.327	.243	.294	10	LF(155): -10.3	-0.8
2012	PHI	MLB	34	439	59	10	6	1	25	23	27	37	7	.307/.351/.371	.272	.327	2.7	LF(107): 2.9	1.7
2013	*MIA*	*MLB*	*35*	*467*	*56*	*13*	*4*	*0*	*27*	*26*	*34*	*31*	*10*	*.278/.328/.327*	*.240*	*.291*	*2.5*	*LF 1*	*0.5*

Signed to a minor-league deal by the Phillies last January, Pierre turned in his best batting average and on-base percentage since 2009 and the most efficient stolen-base rate of his career. All of that is good news; the bad news is that Pierre's 2012 output represents his offensive ceiling as a speedy left fielder without a whit of thump, and the rebuilding Marlins are one of the few teams that would still consider him an every-day player. Pierre's perch at the top of Mike Redmond's batting order makes him a steal-oriented asset in fantasy, and his $1.6 million contract makes him a cost-effective placeholder for Miami, where he roamed center field from 2003-05. The award bonuses in his new pact—$25,000 for a Silver Slugger Award, $100,000 for being named league or World Series MVP—are Beinfest's version of high comedy.

Placido Polanco 3B
Born: **10/10/1975** Age: **37**
Bats: **R** Throws: **R** Height: **5' 11"**
Weight: **190** Breakout: **1%**
Improve: **34%** Collapse: **6%**
Attrition: **14%** MLB: **75%**
Comparables:
Carlos Baerga,Wade Boggs,Chris Gomez

YEAR	TEAM	LVL	AGE	PA	R	2B	3B	HR	RBI	BB	SO	SB	CS	AVG_OBP_SLG	TAv	BABIP	BRR	FRAA	WARP
2010	PHI	MLB	34	602	76	27	2	6	52	32	47	5	0	.298/.339/.386	.264	.312	1.9	3B(123): 7.8, 2B(12): 1.3	2.9
2011	PHI	MLB	35	523	46	14	0	5	50	42	44	3	0	.277/.335/.339	.254	.292	-2	3B(118): 12.7, 2B(1): -0.0	1.9
2012	PHI	MLB	36	328	28	15	0	2	19	18	25	0	0	.257/.302/.327	.241	.274	-2	3B(80): 5.2	0.3
2013	*MIA*	*MLB*	*37*	*349*	*35*	*14*	*1*	*2*	*25*	*20*	*30*	*2*	*0*	*.270/.315/.338*	*.246*	*.289*	*-0.2*	*3B 4, 2B -0*	*0.7*

Polanco returned to Philadelphia in 2010 and failed to recapture the magic from his first stint as a Phillie or the time he spent with the Tigers in between. Stretched offensively as a third baseman anyway, his age caught up to him, robbing him of some speed and the ability to make firm, useful contact. That, in turn, sapped his batting average and rendered him a well-below-average asset. The Marlins signed him to a cheap one-year deal in the hope that there's something left in the tank.

Jacob Realmuto C
Born: **3/18/1991** Age: **22**
Bats: **R** Throws: **R** Height: **6' 2"**
Weight: **190** Breakout: **3%**
Improve: **56%** Collapse: **3%**
Attrition: **10%** MLB: **97%**
Comparables:
Yadier Molina,Alex Trevino,Charlie Moore

YEAR	TEAM	LVL	AGE	PA	R	2B	3B	HR	RBI	BB	SO	SB	CS	AVG_OBP_SLG	TAv	BABIP	BRR	FRAA	WARP
2011	GRB	A	20	381	46	16	3	12	49	26	78	13	6	.287/.347/.454	.277	.341	0	--	0.0
2012	JUP	A+	21	499	63	16	0	8	46	37	64	13	5	.256/.319/.345	.280	.279	-1	C(66): 0.5	1.5
2013	*MIA*	*MLB*	*22*	*250*	*22*	*9*	*1*	*4*	*24*	*14*	*51*	*2*	*1*	*.223/.271/.322*	*.222*	*.263*	*-0.2*	*C -0, 1B 0*	*0.0*

Realmuto struggled in the Florida State League's cavernous parks, but did little to dim his overall prospect stock. A converted shortstop, Realmuto combines a 70-grade arm with rapidly improving blocking skills behind the plate and leadership qualities that have received high marks. He also has solid hit and power tools and good speed for a catcher. All-around contributors are seldom found at the position, making Realmuto one of the most intriguing prospects in the system and a potential All-Star down the line. He'll begin 2013 in Double-A, where the more amiable hitting environments of the Southern League should fuel a rebound in his offensive numbers.

Avery Romero INF
Born: **5/11/1993** Age: **20**
Bats: **R** Throws: **R** Height: **6' 0"**
Weight: **195** Breakout: **34%**
Improve: **60%** Collapse: **7%**
Attrition: **38%** MLB: **89%**
Comparables:
Adrian Beltre,Ted Kazanski,Wayne Causey

YEAR	TEAM	LVL	AGE	PA	R	2B	3B	HR	RBI	BB	SO	SB	CS	AVG_OBP_SLG	TAv	BABIP	BRR	FRAA	WARP
2012	MRL	Rk	19	139	8	6	0	3	15	10	21	0	1	.223/.309/.347	.311	.242	0	3B(5): -0.0, 2B(1): -0.2	0.1
2013	*MIA*	*MLB*	*20*	*250*	*18*	*8*	*1*	*2*	*20*	*14*	*63*	*2*	*1*	*.200/.247/.273*	*.196*	*.258*	*-0.2*	*3B 0, 2B -0*	*-1.0*

A third-round steal from St. Augustine, Romero signed for $700,000. Scouts rave about his hit tool, and he showed passable defense at second base, though he may fit better at third, where his glove and hands could make him a plus fielder. Romero boasts good raw power, and his next challenge will be translating that batting-practice pop into games. After debuting in the Gulf Coast League and only appearing in seven games for Short-Season Jamestown, Romero will either head back to the New York-Penn League or advance to Low-A Greensboro to begin the year. Some evaluators believe he has a star-level ceiling if all breaks right.

Justin Ruggiano OF
Born: **4/12/1982** Age: **31**
Bats: **R** Throws: **R** Height: **6' 3"**
Weight: **205** Breakout: **0%**
Improve: **38%** Collapse: **7%**
Attrition: **10%** MLB: **96%**
Comparables:
Preston Wilson,Jim Edmonds,Rick Ankiel

YEAR	TEAM	LVL	AGE	PA	R	2B	3B	HR	RBI	BB	SO	SB	CS	AVG_OBP_SLG	TAv	BABIP	BRR	FRAA	WARP
2010	DUR	AAA	28	507	77	31	0	15	70	42	129	24	6	.287/.357/.453	.265	.371	-2.8	RF(62): 2.2, CF(38): 3.0	1.9
2011	DUR	AAA	29	190	29	13	1	7	34	20	42	12	2	.304/.378/.518	.306	.370	0	--	0.0
2011	TBA	MLB	29	111	11	4	0	4	13	4	26	1	1	.248/.273/.400	.262	.289	-1.7	LF(27): 1.5, RF(6): 0.0	0.2
2012	OKL	AAA	30	138	21	13	1	5	29	18	24	5	3	.325/.409/.581	.465	.367	0.7	CF(5): 0.5, LF(4): 0.4	1.2
2012	MIA	MLB	30	320	38	23	1	13	36	29	84	14	8	.312/.374/.535	.314	.401	0.2	CF(52): 3.0, LF(31): -1.1	2.3
2013	*MIA*	*MLB*	*31*	*278*	*34*	*14*	*1*	*8*	*33*	*21*	*75*	*9*	*4*	*.256/.316/.418*	*.266*	*.327*	*0.2*	*CF 1, LF 0*	*1.1*

A minor-league free agent last offseason, Ruggiano was busy shelling Pacific Coast League pitching for the Astros affiliate in Oklahoma City when a decimated Marlins outfield sent Beinfest scouring for a stopgap. The 30-year-old Ruggiano came over for minor-league catcher Jobduan Morales and picked up right where he left off in Triple-A. Major-league pitchers eventually found ways to exploit Ruggiano's unpolished approach, but he showed enough to stick as a fourth outfielder with an average glove and a knack for hitting southpaws. Ruggiano's long-term role is probably on the short end of a platoon, but it's fair to say that Miami's scouting department found a useful player at a low cost.

Alfredo Silverio OF

Born: **5/6/1987** Age: **26**
Bats: **R** Throws: **R** Height: **6' 1"**
Weight: **205** Breakout: **10%**
Improve: **51%** Collapse: **13%**
Attrition: **19%** MLB: **92%**

Comparables:
Willie McGee, Jim Fairey, Brian McRae

YEAR	TEAM	LVL	AGE	PA	R	2B	3B	HR	RBI	BB	SO	SB	CS	AVG_OBP_SLG	TAv	BABIP	BRR	FRAA	WARP
2010	SBR	A+	23	417	66	27	6	12	43	18	63	17	7	.292/.322/.486	.306	.318	0.1	LF(45): 1.9, RF(27): -0.0	3.2
2011	CHT	AA	24	572	90	42	18	16	85	30	91	11	12	.306/.340/.542	.292	.340	0	--	0.0
2013	*MIA*	*MLB*	*26*	*250*	*27*	*11*	*1*	*4*	*21*	*8*	*52*	*6*	*2*	*.234/.258/.350*	*.224*	*.276*	*0.3*	*LF -2, RF -0*	*-0.6*

Following a breakout year in the Southern League, Silverio ranked seventh on our Dodgers prospect list and figured to get at least a major-league look in 2012, but his season was a nightmare and he never made it into a game. A January car accident in the Dominican Republic left him with a concussion as well as neck, elbow, and shoulder injuries. Post-concussion symptoms as well as Tommy John surgery on his throwing elbow kept him on the shelf all year. When healthy, Silverio has an impressive collection of tools, but despite his raw speed, he's not a good baserunner, and his defensive skills profile better in right field than center. The Marlins plucked him in the Rule 5 draft, and he has a chance to stick in the majors if he can top Coghlan, Hernandez, and Petersen for a reserve outfielder role.

Donovan Solano 2B

Born: **12/17/1987** Age: **25**
Bats: **R** Throws: **R** Height: **5' 11"**
Weight: **185** Breakout: **2%**
Improve: **41%** Collapse: **9%**
Attrition: **18%** MLB: **97%**

Comparables:
Luis Rivas, Ed Romero, Larry Brown

YEAR	TEAM	LVL	AGE	PA	R	2B	3B	HR	RBI	BB	SO	SB	CS	AVG_OBP_SLG	TAv	BABIP	BRR	FRAA	WARP
2010	MEM	AAA	22	344	41	12	1	4	27	11	35	2	1	.255/.282/.333	.226	.274	1.3	SS(69): 3.8, 2B(14): 0.6	0.5
2011	SFD	AA	23	104	5	7	0	2	10	3	16	0	0	.228/.250/.356	.205	.253	0	--	0.0
2011	MEM	AAA	23	258	22	21	1	1	23	19	35	2	0	.284/.336/.397	.258	.325	0	--	0.0
2012	NWO	AAA	24	160	14	7	1	0	14	10	27	4	0	.262/.327/.326	.289	.322	-0.3	2B(7): 1.3, SS(2): -0.0	0.3
2012	MIA	MLB	24	316	29	11	3	2	28	21	58	7	0	.295/.342/.375	.262	.357	1.6	2B(57): 3.6, 3B(10): -0.3	1.1
2013	*MIA*	*MLB*	*25*	*258*	*23*	*10*	*2*	*2*	*21*	*13*	*44*	*3*	*0*	*.257/.299/.338*	*.237*	*.303*	*0.2*	*2B -0, SS -0*	*0.3*

After seven-plus seasons in the minors, Solano—who signed as a minor-league free agent last offseason—earned a ticket to the bigs in mid-May and held his own when pressed into regular duty by the Infante trade. The diminutive Colombian is a contact hitter with a reliable glove. While he'll never post sexy counting stats, he can be a second-division starter or a quality reserve infielder. Just ask Braves righty Kris Medlen, who allowed only six homers in 138 innings but served up both of Solano's 2012 shots in a single outing on September 25, producing one of the best @cantpredictball nuggets of the season.

Jesus Solorzano OF

Born: **8/8/1990** Age: **22**
Bats: **R** Throws: **R** Height: **6' 1"**
Weight: **190** Breakout: **8%**
Improve: **54%** Collapse: **3%**
Attrition: **11%** MLB: **90%**

Comparables:
Norm Miller, George Bell, Carl Yastrzemski

YEAR	TEAM	LVL	AGE	PA	R	2B	3B	HR	RBI	BB	SO	SB	CS	AVG_OBP_SLG	TAv	BABIP	BRR	FRAA	WARP
2011	MRL	Rk	20	214	34	13	4	3	31	13	30	18	7	.299/.355/.454	.278	.337	2.2	CF(41): -1.9	0.9
2012	JAM	A-	21	235	36	13	3	8	27	17	49	7	6	.314/.374/.519	.293	.372	-2	LF(23): 1.2, RF(19): -1.7	0.5
2013	*MIA*	*MLB*	*22*	*250*	*23*	*9*	*1*	*5*	*22*	*8*	*70*	*7*	*4*	*.206/.236/.315*	*.203*	*.266*	*0.1*	*CF -2, LF -0*	*-1.1*

Solorzano was a bit old for Low-A Jamestown, but if you forgive the age and look at his skills, you see a high-ceiling, full-toolbox center fielder. The Venezuelan already boasts impressive contact ability, plenty of untapped raw power in his swing, and a plus arm. He is developing reads in the outfield. Miami figures to be aggressive with Solorzano, and he may not want to get too comfortable in Jupiter, because a promotion to Jacksonville could come midseason. If Solorzano adjusts to those challenges quickly, he might push for a big-league role by the middle of next year.

Giancarlo Stanton RF

Born: **11/8/1989** Age: **23**
Bats: **R** Throws: **R** Height: **6' 6"**
Weight: **235** Breakout: **5%**
Improve: **62%** Collapse: **4%**
Attrition: **6%** MLB: **98%**

Comparables:
Phil Plantier, Eddie Mathews, Darryl Strawberry

YEAR	TEAM	LVL	AGE	PA	R	2B	3B	HR	RBI	BB	SO	SB	CS	AVG_OBP_SLG	TAv	BABIP	BRR	FRAA	WARP
2010	JAX	AA	20	240	42	13	2	21	52	44	53	1	0	.312/.445/.729	.392	.331	0	RF(46): 2.6, LF(5): 0.2	4.2
2010	FLO	MLB	20	396	45	21	1	22	59	34	123	5	2	.259/.326/.507	.286	.330	-1.3	RF(98): 9.6	2.7
2011	FLO	MLB	21	601	79	30	5	34	87	70	166	5	5	.262/.356/.537	.311	.314	-2.5	RF(142): 11.3, CF(1): 0.0	4.8
2012	MIA	MLB	22	501	75	30	1	37	86	46	143	6	2	.290/.361/.608	.332	.344	0.4	RF(117): 7.2	5.2
2013	*MIA*	*MLB*	*23*	*493*	*73*	*24*	*2*	*31*	*85*	*48*	*136*	*5*	*2*	*.267/.344/.543*	*.312*	*.314*	*-0.5*	*RF 2, LF -0*	*4.0*

Few baseball events light up Twitter timelines quite like Stanton home runs, which range from moonshots across the Georgia border to missiles that reach the bleachers at Mach 1. Despite logging his first big fly of the season on April 29 and playing in only 123 games, Stanton set a career high with 37 homers, good for second in the National League. And unlike fellow 80-grade sluggers such as Adam Dunn and Miguel Cabrera, Stanton is a defensive asset, worth 7.2 FRAA in right field last year. With a modest dip in his strikeout rate and uptick in his walk rate—both plausible improvements considering his age—Stanton could contend for Most Valuable Player honors in the near future.

Christian Yelich CF
Born: **12/5/1991** Age: **21**
Bats: **L** Throws: **R** Height: **6' 5"**
Weight: **189** Breakout: **4%**
Improve: **72%** Collapse: **5%**
Attrition: **29%** MLB: **99%**
Comparables:
Adam Jones, Vada Pinson, Willie Mays

YEAR	TEAM	LVL	AGE	PA	R	2B	3B	HR	RBI	BB	SO	SB	CS	AVG_OBP_SLG	TAv	BABIP	BRR	FRAA	WARP
2011	GRB	A	19	521	73	32	1	15	77	55	102	32	5	.312/.388/.484	.304	.373	0	--	0.0
2012	JUP	A+	20	447	76	29	5	12	48	49	85	20	6	.330/.404/.519	.379	.397	2.9	CF(69): -4.9, LF(6): -0.1	4.5
2013	*MIA*	*MLB*	*21*	*250*	*26*	*11*	*2*	*6*	*27*	*19*	*64*	*5*	*1*	*.248/.304/.386*	*.254*	*.313*	*0.3*	*CF 0, LF -0*	*0.6*

There aren't many chinks in Yelich's offensive armor, and any doubters who remained were likely silenced when the former first-round pick tore up the Florida State League, ranking second in batting average and leading the circuit in slugging by nearly 40 points. Defensively, though, Yelich must continue honing his reads in the outfield, especially because his 40-grade arm will relegate him to left. A potential perennial .300 hitter with 25-homer power and the smarts to steal 20 bases, Yelich could debut this summer and become a household name thereafter.

PITCHERS

Henderson Alvarez
Born: **4/18/1990** Age: **23**
Bats: **R** Throws: **R** Height: **6' 2"** Weight: **195**
Breakout: **27%** Improve: **59%** Collapse: **14%**
Attrition: **9%** MLB: **85%**
Comparables:
Greg Reynolds, Jesse Litsch, Kyle Kendrick

YEAR	TEAM	LVL	AGE	W	L	SV	G	GS	IP	H	HR	BB	SO	BB9	SO9	GB%	BABIP	WHIP	ERA	FIP	FRA	WARP
2010	DUN	A+	20	8	7	0	23	21	112^{1}	137	10	27	78	2.2	6.3	52%	.337	1.46	4.33	4.11	5.29	-0.1
2011	DUN	A+	21	0	1	0	2	2	8^{1}	11	0	1	4	1.1	4.3	59%	.344	1.44	6.48	3.51	5.37	0.1
2011	NHP	AA	21	8	4	0	15	14	88	81	7	17	66	1.7	6.8	—	.286	1.11	2.86	3.66	3.98	0.0
2011	TOR	MLB	21	1	3	0	10	10	63^{2}	64	8	8	40	1.1	5.7	55%	.281	1.13	3.53	4.00	5.04	0.2
2012	TOR	MLB	22	9	14	0	31	31	187^{1}	216	29	54	79	2.6	3.8	58%	.291	1.44	4.85	5.13	6.38	-1.4
2013	*MIA*	*MLB*	*23*	*6*	*12*	*0*	*27*	*27*	152^{2}	*163*	*17*	*39*	*79*	*2.3*	*4.7*	*51%*	*.301*	*1.33*	*4.55*	*4.38*	*4.94*	*-0.2*

For a pitcher who specializes in generating groundballs, Alvarez gave up an unusual number of home runs last year. Of the 24 American League pitchers with at least 75 innings pitched and 50 percent of batted balls being hit on the ground, Alvarez was among the nine to average more than one home run per nine innings. He throws a heavy, low-to-mid-90s fastball, but batters didn't have much trouble with it last year, hitting .293/.339/.498 in 307 at bats. Alvarez's secondary offerings are less impressive, though he does have good deception on his changeup. He was traded to Miami in November's blockbuster deal with the Blue Jays, and is expected to occupy one of the top three slots in the Marlins rotation this year.

Austin Brice
Born: **6/19/1992** Age: **21**
Bats: **R** Throws: **R** Height: **6' 5"** Weight: **205**
Breakout: **43%** Improve: **63%** Collapse: **23%**
Attrition: **10%** MLB: **91%**
Comparables:
Sandy Koufax, Jim Palmer, Dick Drott

YEAR	TEAM	LVL	AGE	W	L	SV	G	GS	IP	H	HR	BB	SO	BB9	SO9	GB%	BABIP	WHIP	ERA	FIP	FRA	WARP
2010	MRL	Rk	18	0	1	0	6	0	8^{1}	7	0	7	8	7.6	8.7	56%	.280	1.69	4.34	4.83	6.63	-0.3
2011	MRL	Rk	19	6	0	0	11	9	48^{2}	32	2	33	55	6.1	10.2	46%	.272	1.34	2.96	4.10	6.07	-0.2
2012	GRB	A	20	8	6	3	25	19	109^{2}	96	13	68	122	5.6	10.0	43%	.304	1.50	4.35	4.95	5.92	0.7
2013	*MIA*	*MLB*	*21*	*1*	*3*	*0*	*9*	*6*	34^{2}	*33*	*4*	*23*	*30*	*5.9*	*7.9*	*42%*	*.307*	*1.60*	*5.21*	*4.96*	*5.67*	*-0.3*

A two-sport athlete in high school, Brice was too busy making moves on the soccer field and web gems at shortstop to learn how to pitch. But the Marlins saw an outstanding arm, selected him in the ninth round of the 2010 draft, and were soon treated to a solidly built right-hander with a power fastball and a hammer curve. His control is steadily improving, and continuing that trend through the upper minors will be his primary hurdle. If he develops a changeup to go along with his plus fastball-curveball tandem, Brice could be a number-two starter.

Arquimedes Caminero
Born: **6/16/1987** Age: **26**
Bats: **R** Throws: **R** Height: **6' 5"** Weight: **185**
Breakout: **18%** Improve: **38%** Collapse: **23%**
Attrition: **15%** MLB: **87%**
Comparables:
Stan Belinda, Dale Willis, Bryce Florie

YEAR	TEAM	LVL	AGE	W	L	SV	G	GS	IP	H	HR	BB	SO	BB9	SO9	GB%	BABIP	WHIP	ERA	FIP	FRA	WARP
2010	GRB	A	23	5	2	3	48	0	74^{2}	55	4	34	97	4.1	11.7	51%	.283	1.19	3.01	3.27	3.88	1.3
2011	MRL	Rk	24	0	0	0	1	0	1	2	0	1	2	9.0	18.0	33%	.667	3.00	9.00	2.42	0.26	0.1
2012	JUP	A+	25	1	0	1	19	0	20^{2}	12	0	9	27	3.9	11.8	42%	.250	1.02	0.44	2.52	2.23	0.5
2012	JAX	AA	25	0	0	2	12	0	17^{2}	16	0	10	17	5.1	8.7	50%	.320	1.47	3.06	2.92	2.54	0.4
2013	*MIA*	*MLB*	*26*	*1*	*0*	*1*	*25*	*0*	35^{2}	*32*	*4*	*20*	*35*	*5.2*	*8.9*	*44%*	*.307*	*1.46*	*4.55*	*4.38*	*4.95*	*-0.1*

The most philosophical pitcher in the minors, Arquimedes Walker—if you'll pardon the Spanglish—may not be much of a thinker, but his upper-90s heat could one day land him a big-league relief gig. Caminero solved High-A in 2012, and he held his own in a brief promotion to Double-A Jacksonville, recording nearly a strikeout per inning. The bad news: He turns 26 in June and still lacks control and a reliable off-speed pitch. Solving one of those issues would make him a serviceable middle reliever; fixing both could turn him into an electric setup man. But Arquimedes needs his "Eureka!" moment to come soon, because there are younger, more-polished arms chasing him up the ladder.

Jose Ceda
Born: **1/28/1987** Age: **26**
Bats: **R** Throws: **R** Height: **6' 5"** Weight: **275**
Breakout: **35%** Improve: **63%** Collapse: **18%**
Attrition: **20%** MLB: **86%**
Comparables:
Rich Gossage,Juan Morillo,Robert Coello

YEAR	TEAM	LVL	AGE	W	L	SV	G	GS	IP	H	HR	BB	SO	BB9	SO9	GB%	BABIP	WHIP	ERA	FIP	FRA	WARP
2010	GRB	A	23	0	0	0	7	0	8	7	2	1	5	1.1	5.6	54%	.208	1.00	4.50	6.28	7.02	-0.2
2010	JAX	AA	23	4	1	6	27	0	32^{1}	18	2	20	45	5.6	12.5	38%	.250	1.18	1.39	3.54	3.30	0.6
2010	FLO	MLB	23	0	0	0	8	0	8^{2}	8	1	11	9	11.4	9.3	29%	.304	2.19	5.19	6.68	5.53	-0.1
2011	NWO	AAA	24	3	1	24	36	0	39^{2}	30	1	13	53	2.9	12.0	—	.299	1.08	1.36	2.50	2.71	0.0
2011	FLO	MLB	24	0	1	0	17	0	20^{1}	16	1	12	21	5.3	9.3	40%	.278	1.38	4.43	3.34	3.37	0.3
2013	*MIA*	*MLB*	*26*	*2*	*1*	*0*	*31*	*0*	*36^{2}*	*31*	*3*	*19*	*36*	*4.7*	*8.7*	*40%*	*.298*	*1.38*	*4.11*	*3.85*	*4.47*	*0.1*

Ceda is a big man with a big fastball, big control problems, and now a big injury history. After dealing with a torn shoulder labrum in 2009, Ceda underwent Tommy John surgery last April, and he'll head to extended spring training when he's ready to return to the mound this spring. Assuming Ceda fully recovers his 98-mph cheese, he'll need only a semblance of an idea where the ball is going to warrant consideration for a late-inning role by summertime. But without a consistent feel for his slider and at least average control, the closer ceiling once considered attainable is likely out of reach.

Steve Cishek
Born: **6/18/1986** Age: **27**
Bats: **R** Throws: **R** Height: **6' 6"** Weight: **200**
Breakout: **46%** Improve: **66%** Collapse: **23%**
Attrition: **10%** MLB: **86%**
Comparables:
Jesse Orosco,Jared Burton,Joe Smith

YEAR	TEAM	LVL	AGE	W	L	SV	G	GS	IP	H	HR	BB	SO	BB9	SO9	GB%	BABIP	WHIP	ERA	FIP	FRA	WARP
2010	JUP	A+	24	0	6	4	26	0	35	29	0	19	28	4.9	7.2	52%	.271	1.37	2.83	3.98	4.38	0.0
2010	JAX	AA	24	3	1	2	22	0	31^{1}	30	0	10	34	2.9	9.8	41%	.348	1.28	4.31	2.65	2.46	1.0
2010	FLO	MLB	24	0	0	0	3	0	4^{1}	1	0	1	3	2.1	6.2	46%	.091	0.46	0.00	2.41	3.60	0.1
2011	NWO	AAA	25	1	1	0	15	0	23	18	1	12	19	4.7	7.4	—	.262	1.30	2.35	4.52	4.92	0.0
2011	FLO	MLB	25	2	1	3	45	0	54^{2}	45	1	19	55	3.1	9.1	57%	.291	1.17	2.63	2.43	2.93	0.9
2012	MIA	MLB	26	5	2	15	68	0	63^{2}	54	3	29	68	4.1	9.6	54%	.302	1.30	2.69	3.26	3.12	0.8
2013	*MIA*	*MLB*	*27*	*3*	*1*	*5*	*49*	*0*	*57^{1}*	*48*	*4*	*23*	*52*	*3.6*	*8.2*	*49%*	*.292*	*1.24*	*3.63*	*3.50*	*3.95*	*0.5*

Sidewinders who can hold their own against opposite-handed hitters are a rare breed, but Cishek showed that he has that uncommon DNA, stepping in for Heath Bell when the beleaguered ninth-inning man needed a break from his high-stress role. Despite his low arm angle, Cishek can touch 94 mph with his fastball, and the righty complements that uncanny heat with a changeup and slider that each induced a whiff rate above 14 percent last season. With only a modest cut to his walk rate, Cishek could blossom into one of the senior circuit's best setup men, and Bell's departure opened the door for him to earn save opportunities in the near term.

Adam Conley
Born: **5/24/1990** Age: **23**
Bats: **L** Throws: **L** Height: **6' 4"** Weight: **185**
Breakout: **23%** Improve: **59%** Collapse: **19%**
Attrition: **24%** MLB: **96%**
Comparables:
Danny Duffy,Jon Niese,Andrew Oliver

YEAR	TEAM	LVL	AGE	W	L	SV	G	GS	IP	H	HR	BB	SO	BB9	SO9	GB%	BABIP	WHIP	ERA	FIP	FRA	WARP
2011	MRL	Rk	21	0	0	0	2	0	2	1	0	0	2	0.0	9.0	33%	.333	0.50	0.00	1.42	3.55	0.0
2012	GRB	A	22	7	3	0	14	14	74^{1}	58	4	24	84	2.9	10.2	57%	.289	1.10	2.78	3.07	3.44	0.2
2012	JUP	A+	22	4	2	0	12	12	52^{2}	59	0	19	51	3.2	8.7	56%	.366	1.48	4.44	2.60	2.56	0.9
2013	*MIA*	*MLB*	*23*	*2*	*3*	*0*	*7*	*7*	*36^{2}*	*35*	*4*	*16*	*31*	*3.9*	*7.7*	*50%*	*.310*	*1.38*	*4.35*	*4.24*	*4.73*	*0.1*

College pitchers don't often have much projection left, but this wiry Washington State product could buck that rule. Conley showed a plus changeup and an average slider during his first full minor-league campaign. While his fastball hovered in the low-90s, he could tap into more velocity down the road. The southpaw should join the Double-A Jacksonville rotation out of spring training, and is on track to settle in as a dependable third or fourth starter for the Marlins toward the end of next year.

Grant Dayton
Born: **11/25/1987** Age: **25**
Bats: **L** Throws: **L** Height: **6' 3"** Weight: **200**
Breakout: **31%** Improve: **57%** Collapse: **24%**
Attrition: **6%** MLB: **87%**
Comparables:
Terry Forster,Mike Zagurski,Ryan Rowland-Smith

YEAR	TEAM	LVL	AGE	W	L	SV	G	GS	IP	H	HR	BB	SO	BB9	SO9	GB%	BABIP	WHIP	ERA	FIP	FRA	WARP
2010	MRL	Rk	22	0	0	1	1	0	1	0	0	0	1	0.0	9.0	1.%	.000	0.00	0.00	1.51	2.77	0.0
2010	JAM	A-	22	1	1	1	17	0	28^{2}	18	0	15	23	4.7	7.2	51%	.240	1.15	1.25	3.44	5.23	0.0
2011	GRB	A	23	7	1	5	49	0	71^{2}	59	5	24	99	3.0	12.4	—	.323	1.16	2.89	2.89	3.14	0.0
2012	JUP	A+	24	2	5	2	31	6	60	48	1	18	71	2.7	10.6	38%	.303	1.10	2.10	2.24	2.33	1.1
2012	JAX	AA	24	2	1	0	7	0	13	12	2	4	19	2.8	13.2	47%	.333	1.23	4.15	3.14	4.39	0.1
2013	*MIA*	*MLB*	*25*	*1*	*1*	*1*	*20*	*2*	*37*	*34*	*4*	*16*	*34*	*3.9*	*8.4*	*42%*	*.306*	*1.34*	*4.08*	*4.06*	*4.44*	*0.1*

If you like peripherals, then Dayton is your man. The Auburn grad and 11th-round 2010 pick started slowly for a big-program college senior, but the Marlins tweaked his mechanics and were rewarded with significantly improved control. Armed with the tandem of a plus fastball and slider, Dayton is now on the fast track to the majors and could make his debut before the end of the season. He has the stuff to push Michael Dunn for lefty setup work once he gets the call.

Michael Dunn

Born: **5/23/1985** Age: **28**
Bats: **L** Throws: **L** Height: **6' 2"** Weight: **195**
Breakout: **26%** Improve: **44%** Collapse: **27%**
Attrition: **5%** MLB: **86%**

Comparables:
Mark Davis,Frank Dipino,Neal Cotts

YEAR	TEAM	LVL	AGE	W	L	SV	G	GS	IP	H	HR	BB	SO	BB9	SO9	GB%	BABIP	WHIP	ERA	FIP	FRA	WARP
2010	GWN	AAA	25	2	0	7	38	0	47^{1}	31	1	25	64	4.8	12.2	43%	.278	1.18	1.52	2.57	2.39	1.5
2010	ATL	MLB	25	2	0	0	25	0	19	15	1	17	27	8.1	12.8	32%	.326	1.68	1.89	3.63	4.53	0.2
2011	FLO	MLB	26	5	6	0	72	0	63	51	9	31	68	4.4	9.7	40%	.268	1.30	3.43	4.26	4.62	-0.2
2012	NWO	AAA	27	1	1	0	12	0	17^{2}	19	0	7	24	3.6	12.2	47%	.422	1.47	4.58	2.14	1.19	0.6
2012	MIA	MLB	27	0	3	1	60	0	44	49	3	29	47	5.9	9.6	36%	.357	1.77	4.91	3.86	3.69	0.5
2013	*MIA*	*MLB*	*28*	*3*	*1*	*1*	*55*	*0*	*50^{2}*	*43*	*5*	*27*	*54*	*4.7*	*9.5*	*39%*	*.306*	*1.37*	*4.01*	*3.95*	*4.36*	*0.2*

One of two active major leaguers from the College of Southern Nevada—the other is Bryce Harper—Dunn offers plus velocity for a lefty, but the strides he took in posting a 4.20 strikeout-to-walk ratio during the second half of 2011 turned out to be a mirage. With a hard slider as his primary off-speed pitch, Dunn's success in retiring fellow lefties has surprisingly wavered, preventing him from nailing down a late-inning role even when Randy Choate was sent to the Dodgers. Absent improvement in his control or against like-handed batters, Dunn is best relegated to middle-inning work—which isn't what the Marlins had in mind when they picked him up in the Dan Uggla deal two years ago.

Nathan Eovaldi

Born: **2/13/1990** Age: **23**
Bats: **R** Throws: **R** Height: **6' 4"** Weight: **195**
Breakout: **17%** Improve: **59%** Collapse: **18%**
Attrition: **7%** MLB: **89%**

Comparables:
Joe Magrane,Ricky Bones,Jerome Williams

YEAR	TEAM	LVL	AGE	W	L	SV	G	GS	IP	H	HR	BB	SO	BB9	SO9	GB%	BABIP	WHIP	ERA	FIP	FRA	WARP
2010	DOD	Rk	20	0	1	0	3	3	8^{1}	6	0	4	10	4.3	10.8	—	.316	1.20	4.34	3.65	4.97	0.1
2010	OGD	Rk	20	1	0	0	1	1	5	3	0	0	4	0.0	7.2	71%	.324	0.60	1.80	2.98	5.40	0.2
2010	SBR	A+	20	3	5	0	16	14	85	99	3	33	58	3.5	6.1	50%	.354	1.55	4.45	4.13	4.50	1.1
2011	CHT	AA	21	6	5	0	20	19	103	76	3	46	99	4.0	8.7	—	.264	1.18	2.62	3.16	3.44	0.0
2011	LAN	MLB	21	1	2	0	10	6	34^{2}	28	2	20	23	5.2	6.0	45%	.263	1.38	3.63	4.32	5.11	0.0
2012	CHT	AA	22	2	2	0	9	8	35	30	2	13	30	3.3	7.7	61%	.296	1.23	3.09	3.46	4.63	0.5
2012	LAN	MLB	22	1	6	0	10	10	56^{1}	63	5	20	34	3.2	5.4	49%	.319	1.47	4.15	4.15	4.78	0.0
2012	MIA	MLB	22	3	7	0	12	12	63	70	5	27	44	3.9	6.3	45%	.316	1.54	4.43	4.20	5.00	0.3
2013	*MIA*	*MLB*	*23*	*4*	*8*	*0*	*18*	*18*	*95*	*99*	*9*	*41*	*59*	*3.9*	*5.6*	*47%*	*.308*	*1.48*	*4.82*	*4.48*	*5.24*	*-0.3*

Many Marlins fans were disappointed when Eovaldi headlined the return package for Hanley Ramirez, but the former 11th-round pick flashed mid-rotation potential during his second tour of big-league duty. Eovaldi's command needs work, but his fastball and slider are quality offerings and his changeup is steadily coming along. After enduring his worst month of the season in August, a six-start stretch marred by more walks than strikeouts, Eovaldi bounced back with a much-improved 3.38 K/BB ratio in September, and he will look to build off of that finish while competing for a rotation spot in spring training.

Jose Fernandez

Born: **7/31/1992** Age: **20**
Bats: **R** Throws: **R** Height: **6' 4"** Weight: **215**
Breakout: **40%** Improve: **75%** Collapse: **16%**
Attrition: **2%** MLB: **94%**

Comparables:
Bert Blyleven,Felix Hernandez,Gary Nolan

YEAR	TEAM	LVL	AGE	W	L	SV	G	GS	IP	H	HR	BB	SO	BB9	SO9	GB%	BABIP	WHIP	ERA	FIP	FRA	WARP
2011	MRL	Rk	18	0	0	0	1	1	2	1	0	1	3	4.5	13.5	80%	.200	1.00	0.00	1.92	3.38	0.1
2011	JAM	A-	18	0	1	0	1	1	2^{1}	4	0	3	4	11.6	15.4	—	.667	3.00	19.29	5.08	5.52	0.0
2012	GRB	A	19	7	0	0	14	14	79	51	2	18	99	2.1	11.3	47%	.282	0.87	1.59	2.16	2.14	1.8
2012	JUP	A+	19	7	1	0	11	11	55	38	0	17	59	2.8	9.7	46%	.270	1.00	1.96	2.34	2.62	0.2
2013	*MIA*	*MLB*	*20*	*2*	*3*	*0*	*7*	*7*	*38*	*32*	*3*	*15*	*38*	*3.6*	*9.0*	*45%*	*.302*	*1.25*	*3.58*	*3.41*	*3.89*	*0.5*

If Fernandez isn't already among the elite pitching prospects, he'll be there soon enough. The Cuban-born northpaw breezed through Low-A and High-A last season, recording a 4.51 K/BB along the way, and with three plus pitches—a fastball, curveball, and slider—at his disposal, Fernandez shouldn't find many roadblocks in Jacksonville. In addition to his world-class arsenal, Fernandez has plus makeup and excellent feel, attributes that have impressed coaches at every stage of his career, leading some to project him as a legitimate number-one starter. Though another full year of minor-league development wouldn't hurt, if the Marlins enjoy an unexpectedly good first half, Fernandez could provide reinforcements for the rotation this summer.

Brian Flynn

Born: **4/19/1990** Age: **23**
Bats: **L** Throws: **L** Height: **6' 9"** Weight: **239**
Breakout: **31%** Improve: **68%** Collapse: **16%**
Attrition: **17%** MLB: **95%**

Comparables:
Felix Doubront, Matt Harrison, Abe Alvarez

YEAR	TEAM	LVL	AGE	W	L	SV	G	GS	IP	H	HR	BB	SO	BB9	SO9	GB%	BABIP	WHIP	ERA	FIP	FRA	WARP
2011	WMI	A	21	7	2	0	13	13	67^{2}	58	3	23	57	3.1	7.6	43%	.314	1.20	3.46	3.45	5.05	0.1
2012	LAK	A+	22	8	4	0	18	18	102	113	5	32	84	2.8	7.4	46%	.341	1.42	3.71	3.41	4.36	0.7
2012	ERI	AA	22	0	1	0	1	1	5	8	1	2	3	3.6	5.4	42%	.389	2.00	9.00	5.80	7.16	-0.1
2012	JAX	AA	22	3	0	0	8	8	45	48	3	13	32	2.6	6.4	47%	.315	1.36	3.80	3.72	4.94	0.0
2013	*MIA*	*MLB*	*23*	*2*	*4*	*0*	*8*	*8*	*41^{2}*	*45*	*5*	*16*	*26*	*3.4*	*5.6*	*44%*	*.310*	*1.47*	*5.02*	*4.66*	*5.46*	*-0.3*

Selected by the Tigers in the 11th round of the 2011 draft and shipped to the Marlins in the Sanchez-Infante trade, the towering southpaw found a repeatable set of mechanics last year and saw his fastball tick up into the mid-90s. Flynn's off-speed offerings remain a work in progress, but if he can maintain the strides he took in 2012, he'll project as a back-end starter or setup man. Refinements to his changeup and slider, on the other hand, could turn Flynn into a middle-of-the-rotation horse. His plus makeup bolsters the glass-half-full outlook on his future.

Brad Hand

Born: **3/20/1990** Age: **23**
Bats: **L** Throws: **L** Height: **6' 4"** Weight: **200**
Breakout: **27%** Improve: **73%** Collapse: **16%**
Attrition: **16%** MLB: **96%**

Comparables:
J.P. Howell, Tom Gorzelanny, Jo-Jo Reyes

YEAR	TEAM	LVL	AGE	W	L	SV	G	GS	IP	H	HR	BB	SO	BB9	SO9	GB%	BABIP	WHIP	ERA	FIP	FRA	WARP
2010	JUP	A+	20	8	8	0	26	26	140^{2}	153	10	49	134	3.1	8.6	48%	.345	1.44	3.33	3.61	5.21	-0.5
2010	JAX	AA	20	1	0	0	1	1	6	3	0	3	4	4.5	6.0	47%	.196	1.00	3.00	3.55	3.58	0.3
2011	JUP	A+	21	0	1	0	1	1	5	5	1	5	4	9.0	7.2	—	.286	2.00	7.20	7.39	8.03	0.0
2011	JAX	AA	21	11	4	0	19	18	108^{2}	90	11	50	71	4.1	5.9	36%	.249	1.29	3.40	4.72	4.32	1.2
2011	FLO	MLB	21	1	8	0	12	12	60	53	10	35	38	5.2	5.7	30%	.240	1.47	4.20	5.69	6.54	-0.8
2012	NWO	AAA	22	11	7	0	27	27	148^{1}	129	15	75	141	4.6	8.6	44%	.289	1.38	4.00	4.60	5.47	1.1
2012	MIA	MLB	22	0	1	0	1	1	3^{2}	6	1	6	3	14.7	7.4	50%	.385	3.27	17.18	9.95	8.66	-0.2
2013	*MIA*	*MLB*	*23*	*2*	*5*	*0*	*10*	*10*	*53^{1}*	*52*	*6*	*29*	*39*	*4.8*	*6.6*	*44%*	*.299*	*1.52*	*4.99*	*4.83*	*5.43*	*-0.3*

Jerry Seinfeld would have you believe that Hand is tough to get, but major-league hitters haven't gotten the memo. Hand has a good curveball, but his erratic fastball command results in an abundance of hitters' counts, and that prevents him from utilizing the deuce. Miami's newly acquired arms pushed Hand further down an already crowded depth chart, and he's likely to return to New Orleans for more seasoning. There's fourth-starter upside here, with better control and a more polished changeup, but Brad is gonna need more hand to convince the Marlins to give him another shot.

Chris Hatcher

Born: **1/12/1985** Age: **28**
Bats: **B** Throws: **R** Height: **6' 3"** Weight: **205**
Breakout: **30%** Improve: **53%** Collapse: **32%**
Attrition: **10%** MLB: **83%**

Comparables:
Darren Holmes, Carlos Muniz, Luis Vizcaino

YEAR	TEAM	LVL	AGE	W	L	SV	G	GS	IP	H	HR	BB	SO	BB9	SO9	GB%	BABIP	WHIP	ERA	FIP	FRA	WARP
2010	JAX	AA	25	1	0	0	1	0	1	0	0	0	1	0.0	9.0	%	.000	0.00	0.00	1.39	1.67	-0.2
2011	JAX	AA	26	2	1	6	42	0	47^{1}	32	2	19	57	3.6	10.8	48%	.283	1.08	1.90	2.65	2.36	0.6
2011	FLO	MLB	26	0	0	0	11	0	10^{1}	14	2	4	8	3.5	7.0	53%	.353	1.74	6.97	5.12	5.88	-0.2
2012	NWO	AAA	27	1	0	11	37	0	47	33	1	15	45	2.9	8.6	33%	.262	1.02	0.77	3.11	1.17	1.1
2012	MIA	MLB	27	0	0	0	11	0	14^{2}	17	3	6	10	3.7	6.1	37%	.304	1.57	4.30	5.86	6.48	-0.2
2013	*MIA*	*MLB*	*28*	*2*	*1*	*0*	*31*	*0*	*37^{2}*	*34*	*4*	*13*	*32*	*3.2*	*7.7*	*41%*	*.297*	*1.27*	*3.85*	*3.92*	*4.18*	*0.2*

From Kenley Jansen to Sean Doolittle, converting middling position prospects into flame-throwing relievers is all the rage these days, and Hatcher—a former arm-first catcher—is hoping to follow in the footsteps of his fellow converts. The righty made quick work of Double-A and Triple-A, but has sputtered in two cups of coffee at the major-league level as his inadequate secondary-pitch command enabled hitters to sit dead red. With more experience and better feel for his slider or changeup, Hatcher has the heat to become a Jason-Motte-like, late-inning force. He already has the facial-hair down pat.

Andrew Heaney

Born: **6/5/1991** Age: **22**
Bats: **L** Throws: **L** Height: **6' 2"** Weight: **155**
Breakout: **26%** Improve: **43%** Collapse: **23%**
Attrition: **20%** MLB: **87%**

Comparables:
Buddy Carlyle, Ryan Feierabend, Brad Hand

YEAR	TEAM	LVL	AGE	W	L	SV	G	GS	IP	H	HR	BB	SO	BB9	SO9	GB%	BABIP	WHIP	ERA	FIP	FRA	WARP
2012	MRL	Rk	21	0	0	0	2	2	7	7	0	2	9	2.6	11.6	42%	.368	1.29	2.57	2.15	2.04	0.3
2012	GRB	A	21	1	2	0	4	4	20	25	0	4	21	1.8	9.4	54%	.373	1.45	4.95	2.23	1.78	0.3
2013	*MIA*	*MLB*	*22*	*1*	*3*	*0*	*7*	*7*	*35^{1}*	*37*	*4*	*17*	*24*	*4.3*	*6.2*	*45%*	*.311*	*1.54*	*5.26*	*4.76*	*5.72*	*-0.3*

Almost indisputably the top-ranked college southpaw in the 2012 draft, Heaney led the NCAA with 140 strikeouts but slipped to ninth overall, where the Marlins plucked him for $2.6 million. Heaney pitched well in six starts, four of them at Low-A Greensboro. Armed with solid stuff and outstanding pitchability, Heaney is on the fast track to the majors, with a chance to earn a rotation spot by 2014. He won't blow many big-league hitters away, and should settle in as a third or fourth starter long-term. If his slight build holds up, Heaney will be a valuable asset in short order.

Chad James

Born: **1/23/1991** Age: **22**
Bats: **L** Throws: **L** Height: **6' 4"** Weight: **185**
Breakout: **26%** Improve: **42%** Collapse: **27%**
Attrition: **20%** MLB: **87%**

Comparables:
Joel Davis,Arthur Rhodes,Brad Hand

YEAR	TEAM	LVL	AGE	W	L	SV	G	GS	IP	H	HR	BB	SO	BB9	SO9	GB%	BABIP	WHIP	ERA	FIP	FRA	WARP
2010	GRB	A	19	5	10	0	24	24	114^1	116	3	65	105	5.1	8.3	50%	.339	1.58	5.12	3.87	5.50	0.1
2011	JUP	A+	20	5	15	0	27	27	149^1	173	12	51	124	3.1	7.5	43%	.361	1.50	3.80	3.84	4.84	-0.2
2012	JUP	A+	21	6	10	0	24	23	114^2	138	9	50	80	3.9	6.3	43%	.340	1.64	4.87	4.54	5.05	-0.7
2013	*MIA*	*MLB*	*22*	*1*	*4*	*0*	*8*	*8*	*37^1*	*42*	*4*	*21*	*23*	*5.0*	*5.5*	*43%*	*.320*	*1.68*	*5.95*	*5.05*	*6.47*	*-0.6*

James took a discouraging step backward last year, watching his walk rate increase and his strikeout rate diminish in a repeat stint at High-A Jupiter. Mechanical alterations to make his delivery less violent-looking may have been the culprit. The onetime top prospect now faces a crossroads. A solid performance at Double-A, which remains possible thanks to his plus stuff from the left side, would restore his place near the top of the organization's list of arms. A poor one could push James off the radar.

Dan Jennings

Born: **4/17/1987** Age: **26**
Bats: **L** Throws: **L** Height: **6' 4"** Weight: **190**
Breakout: **44%** Improve: **56%** Collapse: **30%**
Attrition: **23%** MLB: **90%**

Comparables:
Tim Davis,Bill Lee,Terry Forster

YEAR	TEAM	LVL	AGE	W	L	SV	G	GS	IP	H	HR	BB	SO	BB9	SO9	GB%	BABIP	WHIP	ERA	FIP	FRA	WARP
2010	JAX	AA	23	4	2	0	37	0	52^2	49	0	26	44	4.4	7.5	62%	.320	1.42	2.56	3.20	4.32	0.5
2011	JAX	AA	24	4	1	2	21	0	25^2	26	1	11	29	3.9	10.2	63%	.333	1.44	3.16	2.84	3.04	0.5
2011	NWO	AAA	24	1	3	2	24	0	30^2	34	3	17	27	5.0	7.9	—	.344	1.66	7.04	4.96	5.39	0.0
2012	NWO	AAA	25	1	3	2	42	0	51^2	48	2	16	48	2.8	8.4	60%	.315	1.24	3.14	3.24	2.50	0.9
2012	MIA	MLB	25	1	0	0	22	0	19	18	2	11	8	5.2	3.8	46%	.254	1.53	1.89	5.72	6.55	-0.4
2013	*MIA*	*MLB*	*26*	*1*	*1*	*0*	*29*	*0*	*36^1*	*36*	*3*	*16*	*27*	*4.0*	*6.7*	*53%*	*.313*	*1.45*	*4.61*	*4.11*	*5.01*	*-0.1*

Jennings walked the ballpark during his occasional promotions to the majors last year, but the wildness was uncharacteristic for the lefty. A starter at the University of Nebraska, Jennings moved to the bullpen in 2009, making better use of a his two-pitch set, which involves a low-90s fastball and an above-average slider. He'll have to outpitch the team's other upper-minors arms to earn a roster spot out of spring training, but Jennings has the talent to emerge as a situational lefty by the end of the year.

Tom Koehler

Born: **6/29/1986** Age: **27**
Bats: **R** Throws: **R** Height: **6' 4"** Weight: **225**
Breakout: **38%** Improve: **67%** Collapse: **8%**
Attrition: **16%** MLB: **79%**

Comparables:
Brandon Claussen,Philip Humber,Sam LeCure

YEAR	TEAM	LVL	AGE	W	L	SV	G	GS	IP	H	HR	BB	SO	BB9	SO9	GB%	BABIP	WHIP	ERA	FIP	FRA	WARP
2010	JAX	AA	24	16	2	0	28	28	158^2	140	11	46	145	2.6	8.2	42%	.288	1.17	2.61	3.48	3.73	2.7
2011	NWO	AAA	25	12	7	0	28	28	150^1	144	18	79	116	4.7	6.9	—	.283	1.48	4.97	5.47	5.95	0.0
2012	NWO	AAA	26	12	11	0	28	27	151	154	15	61	138	3.6	8.2	47%	.319	1.42	4.17	4.46	5.52	-0.3
2012	MIA	MLB	26	0	1	0	8	1	13^1	15	4	2	13	1.4	8.8	24%	.297	1.27	5.40	5.54	6.59	-0.2
2013	*MIA*	*MLB*	*27*	*2*	*4*	*0*	*9*	*9*	*48^1*	*48*	*6*	*19*	*36*	*3.5*	*6.7*	*43%*	*.302*	*1.38*	*4.60*	*4.50*	*5.00*	*-0.1*

Called up to the majors when rosters expanded, Koehler threw strikes and whiffed nearly a batter per inning, but could not keep the ball in the yard. He turns 27 in June, and will face steep odds to earn a roster spot out of spring training. At this stage of his career, what you see is what you get, and what you see is a low-ceiling pitcher who needs a big ballpark to hold down a job.

Wade LeBlanc

Born: **8/7/1984** Age: **28**
Bats: **L** Throws: **L** Height: **6' 4"** Weight: **215**
Breakout: **16%** Improve: **48%** Collapse: **27%**
Attrition: **15%** MLB: **87%**

Comparables:
Eric Milton,Jeff Francis,Cliff Lee

YEAR	TEAM	LVL	AGE	W	L	SV	G	GS	IP	H	HR	BB	SO	BB9	SO9	GB%	BABIP	WHIP	ERA	FIP	FRA	WARP
2010	POR	AAA	25	0	1	0	2	2	10	13	1	1	15	0.9	13.5	48%	.429	1.40	7.20	2.18	3.02	0.3
2010	SDN	MLB	25	8	12	0	26	25	146	157	24	51	110	3.1	6.8	36%	.304	1.42	4.25	4.83	4.69	1.2
2011	TUC	AAA	26	9	1	0	17	17	106^2	108	8	28	92	2.4	7.8	40%	.338	1.27	4.30	3.85	3.99	2.4
2011	SDN	MLB	26	5	6	0	14	14	79^2	84	7	28	51	3.2	5.8	35%	.306	1.41	4.63	3.95	4.02	0.9
2012	NWO	AAA	27	5	5	0	16	16	98^2	91	10	20	91	1.8	8.3	47%	.287	1.12	3.74	3.78	4.99	0.7
2012	MIA	MLB	27	2	5	0	25	9	68^2	71	7	19	43	2.5	5.6	38%	.299	1.31	3.67	4.08	4.27	0.8
2013	*MIA*	*MLB*	*28*	*4*	*7*	*0*	*15*	*15*	*89*	*87*	*11*	*26*	*68*	*2.6*	*6.8*	*40%*	*.299*	*1.27*	*4.09*	*4.16*	*4.45*	*0.4*

An extreme fly-ball pitcher who logged the eighth-lowest groundball rate in the National League last year, LeBlanc has had the good fortune of pitching in two of the senior circuit's friendliest stadiums: Petco Park and the Marlins' new yard. His improvement in 2012 was driven largely by a drop in his walk rate and a greater reliance on sinkers and cutters rather than four-seam fastballs. LeBlanc's changeup is his bread-and-butter offering and the source of his success against right-handed batters. Despite his occasional struggles with like-handed batters, LeBlanc is a serviceable swingman or fifth starter in the Marlins' pitcher-friendly ballpark. With Josh Johnson and Mark Buehrle now in Toronto, he could be in line for a rotation spot out of the gate.

Justin Nicolino

Born: **11/22/1991** Age: **21**
Bats: **L** Throws: **L** Height: **6' 4"** Weight: **160**
Breakout: **28%** Improve: **49%** Collapse: **8%**
Attrition: **5%** MLB: **91%**

Comparables:
Ryan Feierabend,Mike McCormick,Frank Tanana

YEAR	TEAM	LVL	AGE	W	L	SV	G	GS	IP	H	HR	BB	SO	BB9	SO9	GB%	BABIP	WHIP	ERA	FIP	FRA	WARP
2011	LNS	A	19	1	1	0	3	3	8^2	11	0	2	9	2.1	9.3	—	.393	1.50	3.12	1.98	2.15	0.0
2011	VAN	A-	19	5	1	0	12	9	52^1	28	0	11	64	1.9	11.0	57%	.231	0.75	1.03	1.85	2.59	1.5
2012	LNS	A	20	10	4	0	28	22	124^1	112	6	21	119	1.5	8.6	55%	.314	1.07	2.46	2.69	2.74	1.0
2013	*MIA*	*MLB*	*21*	*1*	*3*	*0*	*8*	*6*	*37*	*36*	*4*	*14*	*29*	*3.4*	*7.0*	*49%*	*.305*	*1.35*	*4.29*	*4.17*	*4.66*	*0.1*

Nicolino was a member of Lansing's prospect-studded starting rotation that also featured top arms Aaron Sanchez and Noah Syndergaard. Nicolino has the lowest ceiling of the former Blue-Jays trio, but is also the safest bet to reach the big leagues. Scouts rave about his pitchability, but he isn't a soft-tosser by any means. His fastball lives in the low 90s, which is a tick better than average from the left side. His bread-and-butter pitch is a plus changeup that he'll throw in any count. What sets him apart from other pitchers his age is how he commands his three-pitch repertoire: He can deliver any pitch to any part of the zone with ease.

Ricky Nolasco

Born: **12/13/1982** Age: **30**
Bats: **R** Throws: **R** Height: **6' 3"** Weight: **230**
Breakout: **8%** Improve: **44%** Collapse: **19%**
Attrition: **8%** MLB: **92%**

Comparables:
Dan Haren,Shane Reynolds,James Shields

YEAR	TEAM	LVL	AGE	W	L	SV	G	GS	IP	H	HR	BB	SO	BB9	SO9	GB%	BABIP	WHIP	ERA	FIP	FRA	WARP
2010	FLO	MLB	27	14	9	0	26	26	157^2	169	24	33	147	1.9	8.4	42%	.316	1.28	4.51	3.89	4.15	2.4
2011	FLO	MLB	28	10	12	0	33	33	206	244	20	44	148	1.9	6.5	47%	.331	1.40	4.67	3.50	4.18	1.3
2012	MIA	MLB	29	12	13	0	31	31	191	214	18	47	125	2.2	5.9	49%	.310	1.37	4.48	3.92	4.27	1.6
2013	*MIA*	*MLB*	*30*	*8*	*12*	*0*	*29*	*29*	*174^2*	*169*	*19*	*33*	*141*	*1.7*	*7.3*	*43%*	*.305*	*1.16*	*3.66*	*3.57*	*3.98*	*1.7*

A native of Corona, California, Nolasco could have used a few Coronas to help him through the 2012 campaign. Once an extreme fly-ball pitcher, too often snakebitten by home runs, Nolasco gradually altered his pitch selection to induce more groundballs. But his new mix also contributed to a precipitous decline in strikeouts. And that, in turn, was responsible for much of the righty's plight last season, because Miami's infield defense—particularly with Dobbs at third—ranked among the league's worst. Without a rebound in his strikeout rate, Nolasco won't ever be more than a league-average starter. He'll need to devise a new recipe for drawing whiffs to entice prospective suitors this winter.

Edgar Olmos

Born: **4/12/1990** Age: **23**
Bats: **L** Throws: **L** Height: **6' 6"** Weight: **180**
Breakout: **29%** Improve: **70%** Collapse: **22%**
Attrition: **18%** MLB: **95%**

Comparables:
Pete Falcone,Matt Perisho,Jerry Reuss

YEAR	TEAM	LVL	AGE	W	L	SV	G	GS	IP	H	HR	BB	SO	BB9	SO9	GB%	BABIP	WHIP	ERA	FIP	FRA	WARP
2010	GRB	A	20	3	9	0	25	25	117^1	122	9	59	108	4.5	8.3	47%	.331	1.54	4.37	4.60	5.56	0.2
2011	JUP	A+	21	4	17	0	28	28	127^2	167	13	81	101	5.7	7.1	45%	.378	1.94	6.63	5.27	6.38	-0.8
2012	JUP	A+	22	1	5	0	24	13	89^1	83	5	48	78	4.8	7.9	35%	.305	1.47	4.33	4.22	4.14	0.6
2012	JAX	AA	22	0	1	0	9	1	16^2	8	0	16	13	8.6	7.0	51%	.186	1.44	0.54	4.46	5.07	0.2
2013	*MIA*	*MLB*	*23*	*1*	*3*	*0*	*9*	*6*	*34^1*	*36*	*4*	*21*	*24*	*5.6*	*6.4*	*41%*	*.311*	*1.66*	*5.67*	*5.15*	*6.16*	*-0.4*

The Marlins tried to brighten Olmos's dimming prospect bulb by converting him into a reliever, but the southpaw's control issues followed him to the bullpen. Olmos still features the live, projectable arm that once put him in the conversation with the organization's best pitching prospects, but he turns 23 in April, and hopes for a breakthrough wane with each passing year.

Juan Oviedo

Born: **8/14/1983** Age: **29**
Bats: **R** Throws: **R** Height: **6' 3"** Weight: **190**
Breakout: **17%** Improve: **35%** Collapse: **33%**
Attrition: **20%** MLB: **86%**

Comparables:
Jeff Zimmerman,Dan Wheeler,Dave Veres

YEAR	TEAM	LVL	AGE	W	L	SV	G	GS	IP	H	HR	BB	SO	BB9	SO9	GB%	BABIP	WHIP	ERA	FIP	FRA	WARP
2010	FLO	MLB	26	4	3	30	68	0	65	62	5	21	71	2.9	9.8	54%	.329	1.28	3.46	2.89	3.45	1.2
2011	FLO	MLB	27	1	4	36	68	0	64^1	57	8	21	55	2.9	7.7	35%	.268	1.21	4.06	3.93	4.42	0.2
2012	JUP	A+	28	0	1	0	2	2	2^2	1	0	1	2	3.4	6.8	50%	.125	0.75	3.38	3.02	4.78	0.0
2012	NWO	AAA	28	0	0	0	1	0	0^1	1	0	1	0	27.0	0.0	%	.500	6.00	0.00	12.67	815.71	0.0
2013	*MIA*	*MLB*	*29*	*2*	*1*	*20*	*40*	*0*	*38^1*	*33*	*4*	*12*	*33*	*2.7*	*7.9*	*42%*	*.287*	*1.17*	*3.43*	*3.77*	*3.73*	*0.5*

The reliever formerly known as Leo Nunez missed the entire 2012 season—first because of a suspension for faking his identity, then because he required Tommy John surgery—a poorly timed hiatus because he was set to hit the free agent market this winter. Since Oviedo went under the knife in July, he will miss at least the first two months of the 2013 campaign, and he is unlikely to be in the mix for saves wherever he lands in the second half. An incentive-laden deal with a club option for the 2014 season may be Oviedo's best bet this winter.

Zach Phillips

Born: **9/21/1986** Age: **26**
Bats: **L** Throws: **L** Height: **6' 2"** Weight: **200**
Breakout: **34%** Improve: **58%** Collapse: **25%**
Attrition: **10%** MLB: **92%**

Comparables:
Jeremy Affeldt,Jonny Venters,Lenny DiNardo

YEAR	TEAM	LVL	AGE	W	L	SV	G	GS	IP	H	HR	BB	SO	BB9	SO9	GB%	BABIP	WHIP	ERA	FIP	FRA	WARP
2010	FRI	AA	23	0	0	4	12	0	16^{2}	9	0	5	23	2.7	12.4	49%	.257	0.84	1.08	1.32	2.03	0.5
2010	OKL	AAA	23	3	2	1	33	1	50^{1}	50	1	29	40	5.2	7.2	56%	.325	1.57	3.22	4.04	4.55	0.8
2011	NOR	AAA	24	1	1	1	14	0	13^{2}	12	0	7	7	4.6	4.6	52%	.333	1.39	2.63	3.75	3.94	0.1
2011	ROU	AAA	24	1	3	3	33	0	44^{2}	50	3	21	38	4.2	7.7	—	.333	1.59	4.43	4.43	4.82	0.0
2011	BAL	MLB	24	0	0	0	10	0	8	6	1	2	8	2.2	9.0	39%	.227	1.00	1.12	3.44	2.48	0.1
2012	NOR	AAA	25	2	2	7	42	0	54	56	1	22	45	3.7	7.5	50%	.331	1.44	3.17	3.07	3.79	0.6
2012	BAL	MLB	25	0	0	0	6	0	6	7	2	3	5	4.5	7.5	35%	.278	1.67	6.00	7.21	6.86	-0.1
2013	*MIA*	*MLB*	*26*	*1*	*1*	*0*	*28*	*0*	*36*	*35*	*3*	*17*	*27*	*4.2*	*6.7*	*49%*	*.301*	*1.43*	*4.45*	*4.20*	*4.84*	*-0.1*

Phillips received his second cup of coffee in as many years last season, but he has done little in those appearances—or in the minors, for that matter—to prove he can be anything more than a low-leverage reliever. He throws a standard three-pitch mix—90-mph fastball, curveball, changeup—but among them lacks both a high-velocity offering and a true swing-and-miss pitch. Throw in below-average control, and you have a player whose prospects don't look particularly strong. A reliever cannot live on groundballs alone.

Alejandro Ramos

Born: **9/20/1986** Age: **26**
Bats: **R** Throws: **R** Height: **5' 11"** Weight: **210**
Breakout: **28%** Improve: **49%** Collapse: **30%**
Attrition: **12%** MLB: **87%**

Comparables:
Jose Valverde,Fernando Cabrera,Michael Kohn

YEAR	TEAM	LVL	AGE	W	L	SV	G	GS	IP	H	HR	BB	SO	BB9	SO9	GB%	BABIP	WHIP	ERA	FIP	FRA	WARP
2010	GRB	A	23	3	7	28	49	0	58^{1}	40	3	32	78	4.9	12.0	52%	.291	1.23	3.70	3.42	3.67	1.0
2011	JUP	A+	24	1	4	25	49	0	50^{2}	37	2	19	71	3.4	12.6	46%	.308	1.11	1.78	2.52	2.21	0.6
2012	JAX	AA	25	3	3	21	55	0	68^{2}	36	3	21	89	2.8	11.7	47%	.224	0.83	1.44	2.04	2.75	1.3
2012	MIA	MLB	25	0	0	0	11	0	9^{1}	8	2	4	13	3.9	12.5	32%	.300	1.29	3.86	4.74	5.15	0.0
2013	*MIA*	*MLB*	*26*	*2*	*1*	*2*	*32*	*0*	*38*	*29*	*3*	*17*	*44*	*4.0*	*10.5*	*45%*	*.299*	*1.22*	*3.31*	*3.25*	*3.59*	*0.5*

Generously listed at 5-foot-10, Ramos toed a big-league rubber for the first time last summer and promptly struck out the side on 13 pitches. The Texas Tech product features a plus slider that flashes plus-plus break at times, and he pairs that sweeping offering with a fastball that ticked up to 94 last season after looking fringy in the past. With Mujica now in St. Louis, there is an opening for a middle-relief righty in Miami's bullpen, and Ramos will head to spring training with a chance to seize it. If he maintains the newfound fastball velocity and sharpens his command, Ramos could find setup work down the line.

Evan Reed

Born: **12/31/1985** Age: **27**
Bats: **R** Throws: **R** Height: **6' 5"** Weight: **225**
Breakout: **29%** Improve: **56%** Collapse: **16%**
Attrition: **13%** MLB: **86%**

Comparables:
Bill Slayback,J.C. Romero,Marcos Mateo

YEAR	TEAM	LVL	AGE	W	L	SV	G	GS	IP	H	HR	BB	SO	BB9	SO9	GB%	BABIP	WHIP	ERA	FIP	FRA	WARP
2010	FRI	AA	24	1	1	5	30	0	39	35	0	13	34	3.0	7.8	50%	.310	1.23	1.62	2.43	3.60	0.5
2010	JAX	AA	24	0	0	0	1	0	1^{2}	1	0	1	1	5.3	5.3	50%	.250	1.18	0.00	3.97	4.71	0.0
2010	OKL	AAA	24	1	0	0	1	0	2	1	1	0	2	0.0	9.0	40%	.000	0.50	4.50	8.08	8.69	0.0
2011	MRL	Rk	25	0	0	0	8	3	8^{2}	15	0	0	11	0.0	11.4	33%	.467	1.73	3.12	0.88	2.27	0.2
2011	JUP	A+	25	0	1	0	11	0	15^{2}	9	0	10	13	5.7	7.5	43%	.357	1.21	4.02	3.84	3.77	0.0
2012	JAX	AA	26	3	1	12	27	0	34^{2}	24	1	11	43	2.9	11.2	45%	.297	1.01	2.34	1.99	2.15	0.8
2012	NWO	AAA	26	2	3	1	23	0	32^{2}	43	2	16	27	4.4	7.4	50%	.369	1.81	7.16	4.28	5.78	0.0
2013	*MIA*	*MLB*	*27*	*1*	*0*	*1*	*27*	*0*	*36*	*36*	*4*	*17*	*27*	*4.2*	*6.8*	*44%*	*.310*	*1.47*	*4.73*	*4.56*	*5.14*	*-0.2*

Half of the Marlins' end (along with Omar Poveda) of the Jorge Cantu swap with the Rangers in 2010, Reed underwent Tommy John surgery that September, and then was added to the 40-man roster to protect him from the Rule 5 Draft. The big-bodied righty solved Double-A early in 2012, but hit a roadblock when promoted to New Orleans for the second half. He turned 27 in December, so he'll head to Jupiter in February with his prospect clock ticking. A below-average athlete, Reed gets by with a 91–95 mph fastball and a middling slider. Reed could nab an Opening Day bullpen gig or put himself in line for a midseason promotion by impressing the coaching staff this spring.

Alex Sanabia

Born: **9/8/1988** Age: **24**
Bats: **R** Throws: **R** Height: **6' 3"** Weight: **165**
Breakout: **19%** Improve: **55%** Collapse: **26%**
Attrition: **26%** MLB: **89%**

Comparables:
Luis Mendoza,Jesse Litsch,Chris Volstad

YEAR	TEAM	LVL	AGE	W	L	SV	G	GS	IP	H	HR	BB	SO	BB9	SO9	GB%	BABIP	WHIP	ERA	FIP	FRA	WARP
2010	JAX	AA	21	5	1	0	14	14	84^{1}	59	2	16	65	1.7	6.9	47%	.238	0.89	2.03	2.83	3.35	2.0
2010	NWO	AAA	21	1	0	0	2	2	14	9	0	3	5	1.9	3.2	48%	.205	0.86	1.29	3.51	5.30	0.1
2010	FLO	MLB	21	5	3	0	15	12	72^{1}	74	6	16	47	2.0	5.8	39%	.289	1.24	3.73	3.67	3.68	1.2
2011	MRL	Rk	22	0	0	0	3	3	8	5	0	0	5	0.0	5.6	85%	.150	0.62	0.00	2.54	4.94	0.1
2011	JUP	A+	22	0	2	0	2	2	11	13	2	0	1	0.0	0.8	—	.244	1.18	5.73	5.84	6.35	0.0
2011	NWO	AAA	22	0	3	0	4	4	21^{2}	35	4	3	13	1.2	5.4	—	.387	1.75	7.89	5.68	6.17	0.0
2011	FLO	MLB	22	0	0	0	3	2	11	13	2	3	8	2.5	6.5	32%	.314	1.45	3.27	4.72	3.99	0.1
2012	MRL	Rk	23	0	0	0	1	1	3	4	0	0	3	0.0	9.0	60%	.400	1.33	0.00	1.43	-5.16	0.0
2012	NWO	AAA	23	6	7	0	17	17	88^{2}	92	11	24	63	2.4	6.4	41%	.293	1.31	4.06	4.74	5.98	0.5
2013	*MIA*	*MLB*	*24*	*2*	*3*	*0*	*7*	*7*	37^{1}	*37*	*4*	*11*	*22*	*2.8*	*5.4*	*42%*	*.291*	*1.31*	*4.25*	*4.30*	*4.62*	*0.1*

Sanabia impressed the Marlins during a three-month big-league stint in 2010, when he was barely old enough to enjoy the Miami nightlife, throwing strikes and fooling his fair share of batters with a plus changeup. But he suffered elbow soreness throughout the 2011 season, and slipped down the depth chart when Beinfest reeled in Eovaldi and Jacob Turner in midseason trades last year. The righty lacks the oomph on his fastball or the bite on his breaking pitches to ever emerge as more than a fifth starter or swingman, but he's an excellent option as far as Triple-A depth goes, and should compete alongside the aforementioned higher-ceiling arms for a major-league spot in spring training.

Jacob Turner

Born: **5/21/1991** Age: **22**
Bats: **R** Throws: **R** Height: **6' 6"** Weight: **210**
Breakout: **30%** Improve: **63%** Collapse: **21%**
Attrition: **11%** MLB: **87%**

Comparables:
Michael Bowden,Jair Jurrjens,Troy Patton

YEAR	TEAM	LVL	AGE	W	L	SV	G	GS	IP	H	HR	BB	SO	BB9	SO9	GB%	BABIP	WHIP	ERA	FIP	FRA	WARP
2010	WMI	A	19	2	3	0	11	10	54	53	4	9	51	1.5	8.5	44%	.301	1.15	3.67	3.24	4.32	0.7
2010	LAK	A+	19	4	2	0	13	13	61^{1}	53	3	14	51	2.1	7.5	48%	.294	1.09	2.94	3.44	4.06	0.6
2011	ERI	AA	20	3	5	0	17	17	113^{2}	102	9	32	90	2.5	7.1	—	.278	1.18	3.48	3.89	4.22	0.0
2011	TOL	AAA	20	1	0	0	3	3	17^{1}	15	1	3	20	1.6	10.4	46%	.311	1.04	3.12	2.20	3.93	0.3
2011	DET	MLB	20	0	1	0	3	3	12^{2}	17	3	4	8	2.8	5.7	43%	.318	1.66	8.53	6.06	6.63	-0.1
2012	LAK	A+	21	1	2	0	4	4	21^{2}	17	1	7	17	2.9	7.1	53%	.267	1.11	1.66	3.53	3.62	0.2
2012	NWO	AAA	21	2	0	0	5	5	27^{1}	27	2	12	16	4.0	5.3	42%	.291	1.43	1.98	4.76	4.71	0.2
2012	TOL	AAA	21	4	2	0	10	10	62^{2}	52	2	24	40	3.4	5.7	56%	.265	1.21	3.16	3.54	4.96	-0.1
2012	DET	MLB	21	1	1	0	3	3	12^{1}	17	4	7	7	5.1	5.1	53%	.302	1.95	8.03	7.83	9.12	-0.3
2012	MIA	MLB	21	1	4	0	7	7	42^{2}	33	5	9	29	1.9	6.1	45%	.220	0.98	3.38	3.93	4.53	0.2
2013	*MIA*	*MLB*	*22*	*3*	*6*	*0*	*14*	*14*	71^{1}	*69*	*8*	*23*	*49*	*2.9*	*6.2*	*46%*	*.291*	*1.30*	*4.13*	*4.25*	*4.49*	*0.3*

Unsatisfied with Turner's preparedness for a playoff run, the Tigers sent their top pitching prospect to Miami, and the 21-year-old fared well down the stretch. One cause for concern, however, is Turner's middling strikeout rate, an Achilles heel that would be forgivable based on his youth if it weren't one that has followed him throughout his professional career. Turner has an array of quality pitches, but no single offering that consistently grades out above 60 on the 20-80 scouting scale, so he'll always be somewhat reliant on deception and guile. That still makes Turner a solid mid-rotation starter, but scouts who previously thought he might grow into an ace are unlikely to see those lofty hopes fulfilled.

Jose Urena

Born: **9/12/1991** Age: **21**
Bats: **R** Throws: **R** Height: **6' 4"** Weight: **172**
Breakout: **31%** Improve: **69%** Collapse: **12%**
Attrition: **8%** MLB: **87%**

Comparables:
Tommy Boggs,Kevin Kobel,Dan Petry

YEAR	TEAM	LVL	AGE	W	L	SV	G	GS	IP	H	HR	BB	SO	BB9	SO9	GB%	BABIP	WHIP	ERA	FIP	FRA	WARP
2011	JAM	A-	19	4	7	0	15	15	72^{2}	74	4	29	48	3.6	5.9	48%	.262	1.42	4.33	4.08	5.12	0.3
2012	GRB	A	20	9	6	2	27	22	138^{1}	143	13	29	101	1.9	6.6	49%	.306	1.24	3.38	3.99	4.97	0.7
2013	*MIA*	*MLB*	*21*	*1*	*3*	*0*	*7*	*6*	36^{2}	*40*	*5*	*15*	*20*	*3.7*	*4.9*	*45%*	*.304*	*1.50*	*5.24*	*5.11*	*5.70*	*-0.3*

It's hard to say what's scarier about Urena—that he already possesses 98-mph gas, or that his skinny frame suggests there is more in the tank. The righty's results, most notably a 17.7 percent strikeout rate for Low-A Greensboro in 2011, have yet to match his premium velocity, largely because his off-speed offerings lag light-years behind his heater. Urena could take off if the Marlins move him to the bullpen, with a chance to develop into one of the league's elite closers, but the organization is unwilling to overlook his top-of-the-rotation ceiling as a starter. He should move up to High-A Jacksonville in 2013, where the Florida State League will provide him with a cushy environment in which to hone his secondary pitches. The progress Urena makes there will dictate his long-term role.

Ryan Webb

Born: **2/5/1986** Age: **27**
Bats: **R** Throws: **R** Height: **6' 7"** Weight: **215**
Breakout: **37%** Improve: **58%** Collapse: **15%**
Attrition: **18%** MLB: **81%**

Comparables:
Steve Ontiveros, Jon Huber, Derek Lowe

YEAR	TEAM	LVL	AGE	W	L	SV	G	GS	IP	H	HR	BB	SO	BB9	SO9	GB%	BABIP	WHIP	ERA	FIP	FRA	WARP
2010	POR	AAA	24	1	0	1	17	0	20^{2}	12	1	5	23	2.2	10.0	65%	.229	0.82	0.87	2.71	2.37	0.6
2010	SDN	MLB	24	3	1	0	54	0	59	64	1	19	44	2.9	6.7	62%	.335	1.41	2.90	2.85	3.09	1.1
2011	MRL	Rk	25	0	0	0	1	1	2	2	0	0	2	0.0	9.0	—	.400	1.00	0.00	1.42	1.54	0.0
2011	JUP	A+	25	1	0	0	3	1	3^{1}	4	0	3	3	8.1	8.1	62%	.500	2.10	2.70	4.29	6.67	0.0
2011	FLO	MLB	25	2	4	0	53	0	50^{2}	48	2	20	31	3.6	5.5	62%	.289	1.34	3.20	3.59	4.61	-0.1
2012	NWO	AAA	26	2	0	0	3	0	5^{2}	3	0	1	1	1.6	1.6	78%	.167	0.71	1.59	3.84	4.01	0.0
2012	MIA	MLB	26	4	3	0	65	0	60^{1}	72	2	20	44	3.0	6.6	53%	.350	1.52	4.03	3.30	3.16	0.8
2013	*MIA*	*MLB*	*27*	*3*	*1*	*1*	*54*	*0*	55^{2}	*57*	*4*	*17*	*39*	*2.8*	*6.3*	*51%*	*.314*	*1.33*	*4.12*	*3.65*	*4.48*	*0.1*

Webb broke into a middle-relief role with the Padres in 2009, relying heavily on a mid-90s fastball with plus movement to generate groundball outs. He has maintained that skill through parts of four major-league seasons, but he's shown few signs of further development, failing to either miss more bats or tone down his walk rate. Though Webb does employ a slider more than 30 percent of the time, it's a fringy offering that serves as a change-of-pace tool, not as a wipeout whiff-inducer. All of those factors are likely to limit his ceiling to middle relief.

Carlos Zambrano

Born: **6/1/1981** Age: **32**
Bats: **B** Throws: **R** Height: **6' 6"** Weight: **270**
Breakout: **13%** Improve: **50%** Collapse: **27%**
Attrition: **11%** MLB: **84%**

Comparables:
Vicente Padilla, Jaret Wright, Doug Davis

YEAR	TEAM	LVL	AGE	W	L	SV	G	GS	IP	H	HR	BB	SO	BB9	SO9	GB%	BABIP	WHIP	ERA	FIP	FRA	WARP
2010	CUB	Rk	29	0	0	0	1	0	1	0	0	0	1	0.0	9.0	1.%	.000	0.00	0.00	2.26	3.59	0.0
2010	IOW	AAA	29	0	0	0	3	0	4	6	0	1	4	2.2	9.0	57%	.429	1.75	6.75	3.08	3.52	0.2
2010	CHN	MLB	29	11	6	0	36	20	129^{2}	119	7	69	117	4.8	8.1	45%	.301	1.45	3.33	3.74	4.16	2.4
2011	PEO	A	30	0	0	0	1	1	4	3	0	3	4	6.8	9.0	—	.333	1.50	0.00	3.61	3.92	0.0
2011	CHN	MLB	30	9	7	0	24	24	145^{2}	154	19	56	101	3.5	6.2	46%	.299	1.44	4.82	4.56	5.20	0.7
2012	MIA	MLB	31	7	10	0	35	20	132^{1}	123	9	75	95	5.1	6.5	51%	.284	1.50	4.49	4.51	5.32	0.1
2013	*MIA*	*MLB*	*32*	*5*	*9*	*0*	*21*	*21*	120^{2}	*109*	*9*	*50*	*97*	*3.7*	*7.3*	*47%*	*.297*	*1.31*	*3.88*	*3.80*	*4.22*	*0.9*

The Marlins reeled "Big Z" in from the Cubs for Chris Volstad in January 2012, hoping that a change of scenery pairing him with his friend Ozzie Guillen would keep Zambrano's emotions in check. Zambrano did stay on his best behavior for much of the year, but he posted his highest walk rate since 2002 and was moved to the bullpen in late July. The righty now becomes a free agent for the first time in his career, at the usually still-ripe age of 31, but with nearly 2,000 innings on his right shoulder, he may not have much left.

LINEOUTS

HITTERS

PLAYER	TEAM	LVL	AGE	PA	R	2B	3B	HR	RBI	BB	SO	SB-CS	AVG/OBP/SLG	TAv	BABIP	BRR	FRAA	WARP
2B A. Barnes	GRB	A	22	566	76	36	3	12	65	59	61	9-2	.318/.401/.481	.309	.343	0.1	2B(54): 1.1, C(5): 0.1	2.0
SS Y. Cabrera	STO	A+	21	239	26	9	2	3	21	16	68	2-2	.232/.293/.332	.229	.322	-0.2	SS(48): -7.5	-1.0
1B M. Canha	JUP	A+	23	478	65	24	3	6	68	54	75	1-3	.293/.382/.411	.291	.339	-3.1	1B(61): -0.5, 3B(10): -0.4	0.9
OF A. Dean	MRL	Rk	18	182	15	11	0	2	15	24	35	2-2	.223/.337/.338	.346	.272	0.4	CF(4): -0.1, LF(1): -0.0	0.2
INF N. Green	NWO	AAA	33	237	44	16	1	12	47	15	36	2-2	.344/.397/.599	.290	.367	-1.6	2B(8): 0.2, SS(3): -0.6	0.1
	MIA	MLB	33	24	1	3	0	0	1	0	6	0-0	.174/.208/.304	.183	.235	-0.2	3B(3): 0.0, 2B(2): 0.1	-0.1
OF A. Greenberg	MIA	MLB	31	1	0	0	0	0	0	0	1	0-0	.000/.000/.000	0	0	0	—	0.0
RF K. Jensen	JAX	AA	24	521	70	21	2	24	84	69	162	1-1	.234/.338/.452	.265	.304	2.2	RF(71): 1.8	1.2
OF M. Main	MRL	Rk	23	51	10	2	1	0	7	4	4	1-2	.340/.392/.426	.305	.372	0.1	CF(10): 0.3	0.4
	JAM	A-	23	180	18	8	1	2	20	14	18	5-5	.276/.339/.374	.280	.299	-1.5	RF(18): 0.1, CF(7): 0.8	0.5
C K. Skipworth	JAX	AA	22	468	59	16	2	21	63	36	143	1-1	.217/.285/.414	.251	.268	-0.9	C(68): 1.0	0.8
LF J. Smolinski	JAX	AA	23	500	71	24	3	7	42	78	74	9-4	.257/.388/.382	.321	.298	4.8	LF(69): 2.5, RF(1): -0.0	3.7
INF G. Velazquez	NWO	AAA	32	461	52	15	1	4	42	49	50	6-8	.312/.391/.384	.288	.347	0.8	SS(27): -1.4, 2B(3): 0.6	0.9
	MIA	MLB	32	57	2	1	0	0	2	1	11	0-0	.232/.246/.250	.177	.289	1.5	3B(17): 0.3	0.0

After serving primarily as a catcher for Arizona State, **Austin Barnes** successfully transitioned to second base during the second half of last year, but expectations stemming from his offensive performance in the Sally League should be tempered because he was old for the level. Miami's reward for eating $5 million of Heath Bell's remaining salary, **Yordy Cabrera** is a Florida native with plenty of tools but no results to match. **Mark Canha** enjoyed an impressive year in Jupiter and has good power from the right side, but he's a spotty fielder at first and in left, and is most likely a reserve in the long run. A fourth-round pick last June, **Austin Dean** has outstanding bat speed and could become an impact hitter if he tames an overly aggressive approach. A fringy big leaguer, **Nick Green** tore up the Pacific Coast League, but he contributed nothing in limited major-league duty and was non-tendered in October. In one of the season's best stories, **Adam Greenberg** returned to the majors for a single plate appearance against R.A. Dickey Oct. 2, and he'll now look for camp opportunities to revive his career this spring. Come for the power, stay for the—well, that's the problem; **Kyle Jensen**'s plate approach is unrefined, and he has no defensive position, so the Quad-A label will be tough to shed even after an impressive showing in the Arizona Fall League. **Michael Main** flamed out as a pitcher in the Rangers and Giants organizations, but the two-way high school star has intriguing tools and is relishing the chance to revive his career in the outfield. The Marlins aggressively promoted **Kyle Skipworth** to Double-A in 2011, and while the former first-rounder has displayed good pop, his whiff-prone approach remains a hindrance through two years in Jacksonville. **Jake Smolinski**'s mature approach doesn't compensate for his lack of athleticism and tools, rendering him an "org. guy" in most evaluators' eyes. Like Green, **Gil Velazquez** played well in New Orleans and earned a few looks in the big-league infield when injuries struck, but his poor showing got him booted off the 40-man roster in October.

PITCHERS

PLAYER	TEAM	LVL	AGE	W	L	SV	IP	H	HR	BB	SO	BB9	SO9	GB%	BABIP	WHIP	ERA	FIP	FRA	WARP
J. Albaladejo	RNO	AAA	29	5	3	25	56^{2}	46	8	23	60	3.7	9.5	36%	.268	1.22	3.65	4.76	5.06	0.3
	ARI	MLB	29	0	0	0	3	5	1	0	2	0.0	6.0	25%	.364	1.67	9.00	7.14	7.64	-0.1
M. Brady	JUP	A+	25	2	4	22	53^{1}	54	4	7	64	1.2	10.8	36%	.347	1.14	3.38	2.42	2.57	1.0
A. DeSclafani	LNS	A	22	11	3	0	123	145	3	25	92	1.8	6.7	58%	.367	1.38	3.37	2.85	2.57	0.5
M. Hope	JAM	A-	20	3	4	0	71^{1}	72	1	27	53	3.4	6.7	54%	.327	1.39	2.90	3.33	4.68	0.0
C. Lowell	GRB	A	21	5	5	0	109^{2}	90	9	59	117	4.8	9.6	53%	.288	1.36	4.35	4.37	5.43	0.3
J. Maine	SWB	AAA	31	8	5	0	79^{2}	76	7	31	66	3.5	7.5	49%	.287	1.34	4.97	3.96	5.57	-0.2
	IOW	AAA	27	4	2	5	34^{1}	21	1	13	29	3.4	7.6	57%	.213	0.99	2.88	3.75	4.44	0.4
	CHN	MLB	27	1	1	0	20^{2}	17	2	12	26	5.2	11.3	25%	.300	1.40	4.79	4.20	4.23	0.1
	CLE	MLB	27	1	2	0	6	13	1	3	6	4.5	9.0	35%	.545	2.67	10.50	5.21	6.90	-0.1
S. McGough	RCU	A+	22	3	5	5	47^{1}	45	3	26	48	4.9	9.1	46%	.313	1.50	3.99	4.38	4.08	0.5
O. Poveda	JAX	AA	24	6	3	0	70^{2}	84	5	23	53	2.9	6.8	58%	.325	1.51	4.71	3.58	4.04	0.4
	NWO	AAA	24	4	3	0	60^{2}	65	11	34	61	5.0	9.0	46%	.315	1.63	4.90	5.74	7.13	0.0
J. Smith	LOU	AAA	26	3	3	13	56^{2}	67	2	16	36	2.5	5.7	53%	.340	1.46	4.76	3.35	5.17	-0.2
N. Wittgren	JAM	A-	21	0	2	11	24^{2}	24	0	4	34	1.5	12.4	50%	.000	1.14	1.46	1.18	-4.13	0.2

Jonathan Albaladejo returned stateside after a year in Japan, and the International League record-holder for saves was able to survive a full season in the closer role for Reno despite nerve-racking levels of walks and homers allowed. A 24th-rounder from Cal in 2009, **Michael Brady** will be 26 on Opening Day and spent the 2012 campaign in High-A, but his peripherals out of the bullpen are difficult to ignore. Drafted out of Florida in 2011, **Anthony DeSclafani** was expected to move quickly through the Blue Jays organization, and he'll be on a similar timetable with the Marlins. Armed with an above-average fastball and curve, **Mason Hope** was a sleeper in an elite Oklahoma prep class in 2011, but he'll emerge as a legitimate prospect if he can improve his strikeout rate. Wichita State's Friday starter two years ago, **Charlie Lowell** has good velocity from the left side, but his fringy control might be more easily addressed in a relief role. **John Maine** showed signs of being a quality starter in 2007, but he has undergone two shoulder surgeries since then and last pitched in the bigs in 2010. **Scott McGough** came over with Eovaldi in the Hanley Ramirez deal, and has seventh-inning stuff if he can slash his walk rate. Plucked from the Rangers for Jorge Cantu in 2010, **Omar Poveda** fanned a batter per inning at Triple-A, but is nothing more than a depth starter in a saturated system. Former sixth-round pick

Jordan Smith didn't have a strikeout pitch in four seasons as a starter and hasn't found one in three seasons as a reliever, averaging 5.8 SO9 for his career in more than 500 innings. ⚾ A ninth-round senior-sign out of Purdue, **Nick Wittgren** offers plus command of a three-pitch mix and could shoot up the system if he's moved to the bullpen.

MANAGER: MIKE REDMOND

Following a trend set by the Cardinals (Mike Matheny) and White Sox (Robin Ventura) of hiring managers with no major-league coaching experience, the Marlins chose Redmond to be their fourth Opening Day skipper in as many years. The 41-year-old former backup catcher played seven seasons in Miami, became a fan favorite, and won a World Series ring in 2003. Redmond gained coaching experience during a two-year stint in the Blue Jays farm system—steering Low-A Lansing to a then-record 77 wins and earning Midwest League Manager of the Year honors in 2011 before moving up to High-A Dunedin last year—but he is also only three years removed from lacing up his cleats, a factor that should enable him to relate to a youthful squad and serve as a mentor to the team's young pitchers.

We don't yet have data on which to gauge Redmond's particular style, but his knowledge of the game and positive relationship with the Miami community make him an ideal candidate to succeed Ozzie Guillen, who alienated fans with his comments about Cuban leader Fidel Castro last April. Retaining some of Guillen's traits—such as his willingness to base bullpen decisions on performance rather than shoehorn pitchers into predetermined roles—would serve Redmond well. The Marlins are likely to be patient while their new manager learns the big-league ropes. As long as Redmond stays in Jeffrey Loria's good graces, he should outlive his three most recent predecessors and have a chance to develop the players on the next good Marlins team.

Milwaukee Brewers

2012: LAST CALL

The defending National League Central champions, buoyed by the additions of Aramis Ramirez and Norichika Aoki, managed to fill the Prince-sized hole in their lineup and field the circuit's highest-scoring offense. However, much of that good work was undone by a bullpen that frequently resembled a Superfund site, and a late-season surge couldn't quite lift the Brewers back into the playoffs.

If only the Brewers could have sued the league to end games after eight innings, they would have been playing in October. Milwaukee held the lead going into the ninth 83 times last year, a total surpassed by only the Nationals (89), Cardinals (86), Giants (84), and Braves (84)—but not the Reds (81). Yet the back of the bullpen, primarily John Axford and Francisco Rodriguez, gave away 11 of those games. Looked at another way, the Brewers blew over 14 percent of the games they led entering the ninth, compared to 5 percent for the rest of the National League. If Milwaukee had held onto those late leads at the same rate as their competitors, they would have won seven more games and cruised into the wild-card game ahead of the Cardinals.

Their bullpen woes helped put the Brewers 15 games back at the trade deadline, when they traded ace starter Zack Greinke for a trio of prospects and plugged their depleted rotation with a handful of young arms. Surprisingly, the kids held their own, the bullpen cleaned up its act, and the Brewers put together a 24-6 run that brought them to the edge of contention and spawned optimism for 2013.

2013: TOP SHELF

With Ryan Braun heading up what should be virtually the same lineup that ran roughshod last season, the Brewers will put up plenty of crooked numbers, unless manager Ron Roenicke chooses to bunt his way out of them. However, the departures of Greinke and Shaun Marcum leave Yovani Gallardo as the only returning veteran starter. Milwaukee's season will depend greatly on how well general manager Doug Melvin can fill out the rotation and retool the bullpen.

BREWERS PROSPECTUS

2012 W-L: 83-79, 3rd in NL Central

Pythag	.527	15th	DER	.687	29th
RS/G	4.79	3rd	B-Age	29.1	22nd
RA/G	4.52	22nd	P-Age	29.0	23rd
TAv	.265	10th	Salary	$97.7	13th
BRR	1.7	13th	M$/MW	$2.45	13th
TAv-P	.259	15th	DL Days	772	17th
FIP	3.87	13th	DL WARP	3.6	14th

Three-Year Park Factors	
Overall	106
HR/RH	131
HR/LH	123
AVG/RH	109
AVG/LH	107

Miller Park (2001)
Att. % of Capacity: 83.4% (10th)
Dim. 344, 371, 400, 374, 345

Brewers hit eight more homers than opponents in baseball's second-most homerific ballpark last season.

The Greinke trade wasn't the only reason the Brewers had to hustle to find starters last year. Injuries to Marcum and Chris Narveson, alongside Randy Wolf's summer-long face plant, forced the Brewers into creative solutions to find starting pitchers. Both veteran swingman Marco Estrada and unheralded rookie Mike Fiers found success despite their marginal stuff, though it's an open question whether they can bear up to a full season's workload. Top prospects Wily Peralta, Tyler Thornburg, and Mark Rogers have snootier pedigrees and more high-octane arsenals, but have only 17 big-league starts among them. Other than Gallardo, Milwaukee's in-house options are akin to a David Lynch film: uneven, inscrutable, but with an outside shot at greatness.

As for the bullpen, Brewers fans have to hope Axford's strong finish portends an end to Milwaukee's *Twilight Zone* ninth innings. Jim Henderson, a similarly lanky, hard-throwing free-talent find, will get a chance to prove last year's production wasn't a fluke. Beyond them it will be an open casting call, and given the variable production and high expense of signing a veteran reliever, that's not necessarily a bad thing. Melvin has spent the last year stockpiling hard-throwing young castoffs like Michael Olmsted, Arcenio Leon, and Los Dos De Los Santoses (Fautino and Miguel), which is as good a plan as any.

If the pitching can improve even a little, the Brewers offense should be more than enough to carry them into contention. Braun remains the primary antagonist of every pitcher's nightmares, while the surprising Aoki provides Milwaukee with a spark plug at the top of the order. The ageless Ramirez and Corey Hart, newly installed at first base, will provide ample thump in the heart of the order. A bounce-back season from Rickie Weeks would make up for the likely regression of Jonathan Lucroy and Carlos Gomez. The lineup continues to have a noticeable starboard-side lean, but there's little reason to think the Brewers won't find themselves atop offensive leaderboards again this year, and if the pitching comes together, they'll be in for an exciting September.

STATE OF THE ORGANIZATION: TAPPING THE DRAFT

After years spent struggling to abet Braun and Prince Fielder with the pitching they deserved, Melvin's two-year lease on Greinke and Marcum paid off in a division championship in 2011. However, the young talent they surrendered in those deals, particularly Alcides Escobar, Jake Odorizzi, and Brett Lawrie, weren't fully recouped by last summer's Greinke trade. Combined with a series of troublingly unproductive drafts, this has left the system short on blue-chip talent beyond shortstop Jean Segura.

Since taking Braun at the top of their 2005 draft, the Brewers haven't gotten much from their premium picks. Of the 11 first-round or supplemental picks they've used through 2011, those who have seen significant time in the majors (Lawrie, Matt LaPorta, and Jeremy Jeffress) or are knocking on the doorstep (Odorizzi) have been dealt away. Those that remain have ranged from somewhat disappointing to heartbreaking, including Taylor Jungmann and Jed Bradley, the twin first rounders from 2011 who didn't exactly light it up in High-A last year.

More concerning this season is the probable need to find a free agent starter or two, and as Brewers fans still suffering from Post-Suppan Stress Disorder can attest, that is not Melvin's strength. Thankfully there's money to spend, as there are no albatross contracts on the books and owner Mark Attanasio has shown an admirable willingness to invest in his team. While the Brewers have enough offense under contract to stay competitive for the next few years, the system will need a major influx of talent to keep the boiler well-fed.

HITTERS

Norichika Aoki RF
Born: 1/5/1982 Age: 31
Bats: L Throws: R Height: 5' 10"
Weight: 170 Breakout: 0%
Improve: 38% Collapse: 9%
Attrition: 20% MLB: 93%
Comparables:
Matt Lawton,Tony Gwynn,Floyd Robinson

YEAR	TEAM	LVL	AGE	PA	R	2B	3B	HR	RBI	BB	SO	SB	CS	AVG_OBP_SLG	TAv	BABIP	BRR	FRAA	WARP
2012	MIL	MLB	30	588	81	37	4	10	50	43	55	30	8	.288/.355/.433	.283	.304	2.1	RF(107): 3.6, CF(19): -2.3	2.5
2013	*MIL*	*MLB*	*31*	*511*	*70*	*26*	*3*	*8*	*47*	*40*	*51*	*26*	*7*	*.298/.362/.424*	*.275*	*.315*	*1.8*	*RF 1, CF -0*	*2.3*

The Brewers seemed surprised to sign Aoki last season, when GM Doug Melvin reportedly "put in a bid on him just to see what would happen." More surprising still was the player who emerged once the former NPB batting champ earned regular playing time. Far from the aging, punchless import most scouts expected, Aoki demonstrated extra-base power, stole 30 bases, and sparked the Brewers lineup from the leadoff spot during their late-season surge. His swing isn't easy on the eyes, but Aoki's tremendous hand-eye coordination helps him make hard contact, hang in well against lefties, and avoid strikeouts at a rate that would make Ichiro proud. At 31, he's already stretched in center field. His future is in right, where his average power is less than ideal but his glove is an asset. Signed for a relative song through 2014, Aoki may lose some of his power as the league catches on to him, but so far Milwaukee's casual investment has turned out A-OK.

Jeff Bianchi SS
Born: 10/5/1986 Age: 26
Bats: R Throws: R Height: 5' 11"
Weight: 190 Breakout: 8%
Improve: 55% Collapse: 9%
Attrition: 27% MLB: 93%
Comparables:
Diory Hernandez,Anderson Hernandez,Bert Campaneris

YEAR	TEAM	LVL	AGE	PA	R	2B	3B	HR	RBI	BB	SO	SB	CS	AVG_OBP_SLG	TAv	BABIP	BRR	FRAA	WARP
2011	NWA	AA	24	499	63	23	2	2	48	39	85	20	5	.259/.320/.333	.249	.313	-0.7	2B(38): 0.7, SS(20): 1.6	0.6
2012	HUN	AA	25	85	11	4	0	0	6	6	11	3	1	.351/.398/.403	.287	.409	-0.5	SS(16): 0.5	0.5
2012	NAS	AAA	25	278	33	13	1	5	19	22	48	11	5	.317/.374/.438	.299	.376	1.6	SS(48): 3.4	2.1
2012	MIL	MLB	25	76	8	2	0	3	9	4	13	0	0	.188/.230/.348	.217	.185	0.6	SS(14): 0.5, 3B(6): -0.1	-0.1
2013	*MIL*	*MLB*	*26*	*250*	*27*	*11*	*1*	*5*	*26*	*14*	*50*	*8*	*2*	*.253/.299/.378*	*.234*	*.295*	*0.5*	*SS 1, 2B -0*	*0.5*

An oft-injured former top prospect in the Royals system, Bianchi took advantage of Milwaukee's season-long shortstop disaster to revive his sputtering career. Finally healthy, Bianchi spent much of last year in the upper minors rediscovering his compact, line-drive stroke, hitting for average, and earning a late-season audition with the big club. He doesn't have the range or arm to project as an every-day shortstop, but a combination of soft hands, solid fundamentals, and good instincts makes him playable there in a pinch. He could grow into a second-division starter at the keystone, but it's more likely he'll spend his career paying dues to the International Brotherhood of Utility Infielders.

Ryan Braun **LF**

Born: **11/17/1983** Age: **29**
Bats: **R** Throws: **R** Height: **6' 2"**
Weight: **210** Breakout: **2%**
Improve: **50%** Collapse: **1%**
Attrition: **0%** MLB: **94%**

Comparables:
Jason Bay,Ryan Raburn,Matt Holliday

YEAR	TEAM	LVL	AGE	PA	R	2B	3B	HR	RBI	BB	SO	SB	CS	AVG_OBP_SLG	TAv	BABIP	BRR	FRAA	WARP
2010	MIL	MLB	26	684	101	45	1	25	103	56	105	14	3	.304/.365/.501	.297	.331	5	LF(153): 3.9	4.7
2011	MIL	MLB	27	629	109	38	6	33	111	58	93	33	6	.332/.397/.597	.341	.350	0.2	LF(147): 2.2	5.8
2012	MIL	MLB	28	677	108	36	3	41	112	63	128	30	7	.319/.391/.595	.332	.346	0.7	LF(151): 2.1	6.1
2013	*MIL*	*MLB*	*29*	*626*	*95*	*35*	*4*	*33*	*101*	*49*	*113*	*22*	*5*	*.303/.366/.551*	*.315*	*.329*	*1.9*	*LF 3*	*5.5*

Now *that's* how you silence your critics. Braun entered last season as both the reigning National League MVP and a suspected PED user, dodging a lengthy suspension only through what some viewed as a chain-of-custody technicality. In response, Braun let his game do the talking by setting career highs in home runs and WARP, stealing 30 bases, playing solid defense, and essentially matching his numbers from 2011 despite the absence of Prince Fielder. Clearly this proves that Braun was never a PED user, or is still a PED user, or that PEDs don't necessarily lead to improved performance, depending on your personal prejudices. The only thing beyond debate is that Braun is a Hall-worthy talent at his peak, with speed, power, durability, athleticism that's likely to age well, and a contract that will keep him in Milwaukee until 2020 but won't pay him superstar wages until 2016. What could be more valuable than that?

Clint Coulter **C**

Born: **7/30/1993** Age: **19**
Bats: **R** Throws: **R** Height: **6' 4"**
Weight: **210** Breakout: **0%**
Improve: **61%** Collapse: **39%**
Attrition: **39%** MLB: **100%**

Comparables:
Robin Yount,Wayne Causey,Ed Kranepool

YEAR	TEAM	LVL	AGE	PA	R	2B	3B	HR	RBI	BB	SO	SB	CS	AVG_OBP_SLG	TAv	BABIP	BRR	FRAA	WARP
2012	BRR	Rk	18	214	37	3	3	5	33	37	40	3	5	.302/.439/.444	.322	.365	-0.5	C(6): 0.2	0.0
2013	*MIL*	*MLB*	*19*	*250*	*24*	*8*	*1*	*5*	*21*	*17*	*70*	*5*	*4*	*.196/.256/.301*	*.196*	*.255*	*-0.4*	*C 0*	*-0.4*

Milwaukee's top pick in the 2012 draft, Coulter made an impressive Rookie League debut. An imposing physical presence with significant power potential and a strong arm, the 19-year-old catcher displayed a smooth swing and an unexpectedly advanced plate approach. He's raw defensively, allowing a raft of passed balls and struggling to throw out runners, but the organization believes he has the skills and makeup necessary to learn the position. His bat will likely play even if he has to change positions, but if he can stay behind the dish, Coulter could grow into a monster.

Kentrail Davis **RF**

Born: **6/29/1988** Age: **25**
Bats: **L** Throws: **R** Height: **5' 10"**
Weight: **195** Breakout: **20%**
Improve: **52%** Collapse: **13%**
Attrition: **26%** MLB: **92%**

Comparables:
Rusty Torres,Al Luplow,Tito Francona

YEAR	TEAM	LVL	AGE	PA	R	2B	3B	HR	RBI	BB	SO	SB	CS	AVG_OBP_SLG	TAv	BABIP	BRR	FRAA	WARP
2010	WIS	A	22	290	44	26	5	3	46	31	36	3	1	.335/.428/.518	.327	.383	-1.6	RF(60): 2.1, CF(1): 0.1	2.4
2010	BRV	A+	22	150	20	2	5	0	17	17	28	8	2	.244/.380/.341	.257	.316	0.4	CF(31): -1.6	0.3
2011	BRV	A+	23	565	76	19	8	8	46	37	97	33	8	.245/.317/.361	.241	.287	0	--	0.0
2012	HUN	AA	24	498	55	22	7	7	41	54	121	19	11	.274/.357/.404	.293	.363	-0.7	RF(80): -0.1	1.7
2013	*MIL*	*MLB*	*25*	*250*	*25*	*11*	*2*	*4*	*25*	*19*	*65*	*5*	*2*	*.233/.302/.360*	*.233*	*.303*	*0.2*	*RF -1, CF -0*	*-0.3*

When Davis first appeared in these pages back in 2010, we expressed fear that "he won't have the range for center, the arm for right, the on-base skills for the top of the order, or the power to be a run-producer." Since then, Davis has done precious little to extinguish any one those doubts. His recent exile to right field makes it even less likely his bat can carry his glove. His Double-A debut did about as much to jumpstart his career as a Double-A battery. If Davis doesn't develop some home-run power soon, he won't have a career.

Khris Davis **LF**

Born: **12/21/1987** Age: **25**
Bats: **R** Throws: **R** Height: **6' 1"**
Weight: **195** Breakout: **7%**
Improve: **44%** Collapse: **1%**
Attrition: **8%** MLB: **95%**

Comparables:
Chase Headley,Ben Grieve,Steve Kemp

YEAR	TEAM	LVL	AGE	PA	R	2B	3B	HR	RBI	BB	SO	SB	CS	AVG_OBP_SLG	TAv	BABIP	BRR	FRAA	WARP
2010	WIS	A	22	555	86	26	4	22	72	77	120	17	10	.280/.399/.499	.309	.334	-5	LF(87): 10.0	4.4
2011	BRV	A+	23	371	50	21	1	15	68	51	70	10	5	.309/.415/.533	.328	.350	0	--	0.0
2011	HUN	AA	23	136	10	7	1	2	16	10	23	0	0	.210/.272/.331	.173	.240	-0.1	LF(12): -1.0	-0.6
2012	HUN	AA	24	154	23	9	0	8	23	20	33	2	2	.383/.484/.641	.331	.471	-1.1	LF(19): 4.0	1.1
2012	NAS	AAA	24	140	23	12	0	4	24	20	27	1	0	.310/.414/.522	.361	.360	-0.2	LF(20): -3.0, RF(2): -0.1	1.0
2013	*MIL*	*MLB*	*25*	*250*	*30*	*10*	*1*	*10*	*34*	*24*	*66*	*2*	*1*	*.240/.327/.431*	*.265*	*.293*	*-0.4*	*LF -1, RF -0*	*0.6*

Davis has frequently been disparaged as a bat-only prospect, but after he put up video-game numbers in the upper minors last year, scouts had best start taking that bat seriously. The former Cal State Fullerton star thrived while facing the more advanced pitchers many thought would expose his long swing, drawing more walks and amping up his power numbers in the process. His weak arm and poor foot speed limit him to left field, but it's not like he's Greg Luzinski out there. If Davis can duplicate his success this year at Triple-A his bat might just be able to carry him.

Mat Gamel **1B**
Born: **7/26/1985** Age: **27**
Bats: **L** Throws: **R** Height: **6' 1"**
Weight: **215** Breakout: **2%**
Improve: **33%** Collapse: **6%**
Attrition: **15%** MLB: **78%**
Comparables:
Matthew Brown,Jeff Clement,Juan Miranda

YEAR	TEAM	LVL	AGE	PA	R	2B	3B	HR	RBI	BB	SO	SB	CS	AVG_OBP_SLG	TAv	BABIP	BRR	FRAA	WARP
2010	NAS	AAA	24	359	54	24	0	13	67	38	64	3	1	.309/.393/.511	.301	.355	-3	3B(72): -7.4, RF(4): -0.1	2.0
2010	MIL	MLB	24	17	1	1	0	0	1	1	8	0	0	.200/.294/.267	.195	.429	0.2	3B(3): -0.2, LF(1): -0.0	-0.1
2011	NAS	AAA	25	545	90	29	0	28	96	46	84	2	0	.310/.372/.540	.330	.326	-1.4	1B(39): -0.3, 3B(12): -0.8	1.5
2011	MIL	MLB	25	27	1	1	0	0	2	1	4	0	0	.115/.148/.154	.097	.136	0	3B(3): -0.1, 1B(2): -0.1	-0.4
2012	MIL	MLB	26	75	10	2	1	1	6	4	15	3	0	.246/.293/.348	.227	.296	1.3	1B(20): -1.7, 3B(1): -0.0	-0.3
2013	*MIL*	*MLB*	*27*	*250*	*29*	*12*	*1*	*8*	*32*	*22*	*64*	*1*	*0*	*.258/.327/.435*	*.263*	*.322*	*-0.2*	*1B -0, 3B 0*	*0.4*

The fondest dream of all understudies is to step into a leading role, while their greatest fear is to flub their lines and botch their big chance. Gamel has spent years burnishing his minor-league batting credentials while waiting in the wings, but when he finally heard his big cue—*"Exit the Prince"*—everything went wrong. Instead of providing the inexpensive lefty power the Brewers badly needed, Gamel struggled at the plate before his season was cut short in early May by a torn ACL. In his absence, Corey Hart settled in for what might be a long stay at first base, further clouding Gamel's future. Already 27 and with little defensive value, Gamel may soon run out of chances to prove he can handle a role more challenging than Quad-A Slugger.

Scooter Gennett **2B**
Born: **5/1/1990** Age: **23**
Bats: **L** Throws: **R** Height: **5' 10"**
Weight: **164** Breakout: **5%**
Improve: **54%** Collapse: **8%**
Attrition: **8%** MLB: **89%**
Comparables:
Rod Carew,Wilton Guerrero,Rennie Stennett

YEAR	TEAM	LVL	AGE	PA	R	2B	3B	HR	RBI	BB	SO	SB	CS	AVG_OBP_SLG	TAv	BABIP	BRR	FRAA	WARP
2010	WIS	A	20	525	87	39	4	9	55	31	91	14	4	.309/.355/.463	.290	.364	-0.5	2B(107): 0.1, SS(13): 0.6	3.6
2011	BRV	A+	21	601	74	20	6	9	51	27	69	11	10	.300/.334/.406	.259	.326	0	--	0.0
2012	HUN	AA	22	573	66	30	2	5	44	28	71	11	5	.293/.330/.385	.273	.328	-2.7	2B(90): 4.6	1.3
2013	*MIL*	*MLB*	*23*	*250*	*22*	*12*	*1*	*5*	*26*	*6*	*50*	*2*	*1*	*.254/.276/.374*	*.223*	*.299*	*-0.2*	*2B -0, SS 0*	*-0.1*

Everybody loves to root for the underdog, and Gennett's short stature, manic energy, and aggressive approach have earned him a legion of fans. Unfortunately, the young infielder's numbers have declined at each stop of his minor-league journey. Gennett has an unquestioned ability to make solid contact, but he rarely walks, has limited power and even less speed, is merely adequate at the keystone, and can't play shortstop. His plus hit tool will only take him so far, and no amount of squinting will make him Dustin Pedroia. Gennett is still young enough to develop more power or refine his approach, but his current profile matches Aaron Miles—a similarly pint-sized infielder with good contact skills, a low walk rate, and an indifferent glove. Of course, Miles has managed to earn millions over nine major-league seasons, so you never know.

Caleb Gindl **OF**
Born: **8/31/1988** Age: **24**
Bats: **L** Throws: **L** Height: **5' 10"**
Weight: **205** Breakout: **4%**
Improve: **47%** Collapse: **1%**
Attrition: **12%** MLB: **91%**
Comparables:
Tony Tarasco,Tito Francona,Chad Curtis

YEAR	TEAM	LVL	AGE	PA	R	2B	3B	HR	RBI	BB	SO	SB	CS	AVG_OBP_SLG	TAv	BABIP	BRR	FRAA	WARP
2010	HUN	AA	21	534	61	33	1	9	60	55	78	10	5	.272/.352/.406	.280	.306	-3.5	RF(74): -9.3, CF(50): 2.0	1.3
2011	NAS	AAA	22	538	84	23	5	15	60	63	93	6	5	.307/.390/.472	.304	.357	2.1	RF(37): 1.9, CF(13): -1.9	1.3
2012	NAS	AAA	23	498	54	27	5	12	50	37	98	4	1	.261/.317/.423	.243	.306	1.2	RF(50): 3.2, CF(22): -0.4	-0.1
2013	*MIL*	*MLB*	*24*	*250*	*25*	*12*	*1*	*6*	*28*	*18*	*53*	*2*	*1*	*.244/.301/.389*	*.239*	*.289*	*-0.2*	*RF -2, CF -0*	*-0.2*

Gindl struggled early on during his second spin through the Pacific Coast League, a fairly common occurrence when a prospect used to yearly promotions suddenly plateaus in the high minors. He recovered in the second half, posting a .291/.347/.486 line that may earn him a shot at a big-league backup role. Longer on production than tools, Gindl generates incongruous lefty power from his compact frame, makes contact, isn't allergic to ball four, and has a strong arm that fits well in right field. He has worked hard to improve his outfield play, but he remains a tweener who's stretched in center field and doesn't swing quite enough lumber for right.

Carlos Gomez **CF**
Born: **12/4/1985** Age: **27**
Bats: **R** Throws: **R** Height: **6' 5"**
Weight: **215** Breakout: **1%**
Improve: **51%** Collapse: **6%**
Attrition: **11%** MLB: **94%**
Comparables:
Bobby Tolan,Ken Boyer,Aaron Rowand

YEAR	TEAM	LVL	AGE	PA	R	2B	3B	HR	RBI	BB	SO	SB	CS	AVG_OBP_SLG	TAv	BABIP	BRR	FRAA	WARP
2010	MIL	MLB	24	318	38	11	3	5	24	17	72	18	3	.247/.298/.357	.231	.313	4.2	CF(75): -8.3, LF(5): -0.0	-0.3
2011	MIL	MLB	25	258	37	11	3	8	24	15	64	16	2	.225/.276/.403	.244	.273	0	CF(86): 7.1	1.0
2012	MIL	MLB	26	452	72	19	4	19	51	20	98	37	6	.260/.305/.463	.267	.296	4.4	CF(128): 2.0	2.0
2013	*MIL*	*MLB*	*27*	*388*	*55*	*16*	*4*	*10*	*37*	*20*	*90*	*25*	*5*	*.247/.296/.399*	*.239*	*.295*	*3.4*	*CF 4, LF -0*	*1.2*

Last spring, we predicted Gomez might very well put up an unexpectedly valuable season despite his obvious talents having long been undermined by his indiscriminate plate approach. Chalk one up for the crystal ball, as last year Gomez used a combination of strong speed, top-notch defense, and surprising thump to earn the starting gig in center and help power the Brewers through their unexpected stretch run. Gomez remains as hacktastic as they come, offering at more pitches than any NL regular, posting walk-to-strikeout ratios near the league bottom, and constantly swinging for the fences—essentially doing everything he can to avoid taking advantage of his speed. His sudden power surge doesn't seem like a fluke, however, as power is often the last tool to develop and last year's home-run-per-fly-ball ratio isn't ridiculously unsustainable. Gomez will be an acceptable starter as long as he can run down fly balls and launch a few over the fence, but if the power goes away, his value leaves with it.

Hector Gomez SS
Born: **3/5/1988** Age: **25**
Bats: **R** Throws: **R** Height: **6' 3"**
Weight: **180** Breakout: **6%**
Improve: **50%** Collapse: **10%**
Attrition: **22%** MLB: **94%**

Comparables:
Mariano Duncan,Greg Gagne,Ed Brinkman

YEAR	TEAM	LVL	AGE	PA	R	2B	3B	HR	RBI	BB	SO	SB	CS	AVG_OBP_SLG	TAv	BABIP	BRR	FRAA	WARP
2010	TRI	A-	22	75	8	2	1	2	7	5	15	0	3	.246/.297/.391	.316	.288	-1.6	SS(11): 1.4	0.6
2011	TUL	AA	23	453	46	23	6	14	50	19	94	16	4	.235/.272/.416	.211	.270	1.7	SS(60): 3.5	0.0
2011	COL	MLB	23	7	1	0	0	0	0	1	2	0	0	.333/.429/.333	.242	.500	0.5	SS(2): 0.0	0.1
2012	BRV	A+	24	85	9	3	1	1	8	4	19	0	0	.105/.179/.211	.116	.123	0.5	SS(9): 1.4	-0.3
2013	*MIL*	*MLB*	*25*	*250*	*27*	*10*	*2*	*4*	*19*	*10*	*66*	*7*	*2*	*.213/.249/.325*	*.198*	*.272*	*0.7*	*SS -0, 2B -0*	*-0.5*

Frequent injuries and a maddening inability to reach first base have plagued Gomez throughout his career. A former top prospect in the Rockies system, Gomez is a true shortstop with soft hands and more power than your average futility infielder, but at 25 and with a career on-base percentage of .275 in the high minors, he'll likely spend the next few years filed in a folder labeled "organizational depth."

Alex Gonzalez SS
Born: **2/15/1977** Age: **36**
Bats: **R** Throws: **R** Height: **6' 0"**
Weight: **215** Breakout: **2%**
Improve: **22%** Collapse: **4%**
Attrition: **18%** MLB: **72%**

Comparables:
Greg Gagne,Dickie Thon,Juan Castro

YEAR	TEAM	LVL	AGE	PA	R	2B	3B	HR	RBI	BB	SO	SB	CS	AVG_OBP_SLG	TAv	BABIP	BRR	FRAA	WARP
2010	ATL	MLB	33	292	27	17	2	6	38	14	53	0	2	.240/.291/.386	.229	.276	-1.1	SS(72): 5.5	0.5
2010	TOR	MLB	33	348	47	25	1	17	50	17	65	1	0	.259/.296/.497	.273	.274	-0.6	SS(85): 10.4	3.4
2011	ATL	MLB	34	593	59	27	1	15	56	22	126	2	0	.241/.270/.372	.228	.285	-1.3	SS(149): 10.8	1.1
2012	MIL	MLB	35	89	8	4	0	4	15	6	15	1	1	.259/.326/.457	.273	.274	0.2	SS(24): -0.3	0.4
2013	*MIL*	*MLB*	*36*	*250*	*26*	*12*	*1*	*8*	*28*	*11*	*51*	*1*	*0*	*.238/.277/.394*	*.230*	*.269*	*-0.4*	*SS 2*	*0.5*

Few major-league players are as dedicated to making outs as Gonzalez. A torn ACL last May forced the superannuated shortstop to end his season with an on-base percentage above .300 for the first time in a half-decade, a number that was sure to fall as the season progressed. On the flip side, Gonzalez remains a slick defender who can turn grounders into outs at a rate that rivals a Yankees fan's fictionalized projection of Derek Jeter. When Gonzalez is able to unleash his boom stick and launch double-digit home runs, as he has the last few years, the good outweighs the bad and he earns his keep. As stopgap shortstops go, Gonzalez is a reasonable low-risk, low-reward bet and may still have the skills to play a role in some contender's infield.

Taylor Green INF
Born: **11/2/1986** Age: **26**
Bats: **L** Throws: **R** Height: **6' 0"**
Weight: **200** Breakout: **2%**
Improve: **38%** Collapse: **20%**
Attrition: **29%** MLB: **90%**

Comparables:
Jeff Baisley,Ryan Rohlinger,Freddy Sandoval

YEAR	TEAM	LVL	AGE	PA	R	2B	3B	HR	RBI	BB	SO	SB	CS	AVG_OBP_SLG	TAv	BABIP	BRR	FRAA	WARP
2010	HUN	AA	23	451	51	29	1	13	81	45	67	0	2	.260/.341/.438	.272	.283	2	3B(102): 6.7, 1B(3): -0.1	2.7
2011	NAS	AAA	24	487	74	36	1	22	88	55	72	1	0	.336/.413/.583	.335	.360	1.3	3B(36): -5.6, 2B(9): -0.1	1.7
2011	MIL	MLB	24	37	2	3	0	0	1	0	6	0	0	.270/.270/.351	.218	.323	0.6	2B(7): 0.1, 3B(5): 0.0	0.0
2012	NAS	AAA	25	313	24	17	0	7	29	28	57	1	3	.273/.345/.408	.276	.321	-2	3B(40): -0.7, 2B(9): 1.0	0.5
2012	MIL	MLB	25	117	8	7	0	3	14	10	24	0	0	.184/.265/.340	.221	.205	-0.6	1B(18): 0.4, 3B(12): -0.1	-0.5
2013	*MIL*	*MLB*	*26*	*250*	*26*	*13*	*1*	*8*	*30*	*18*	*49*	*0*	*0*	*.246/.307/.407*	*.246*	*.280*	*-0.5*	*3B -0, 1B -0*	*0.1*

Milwaukee's lineup leans more right than a Utah primary voter, so the Brewers would love to see Green's lefty bat mature. Unfortunately, the young infielder hasn't built on his breakout 2011 season, looking overmatched in limited big-league action and taking a step back during a lackluster Triple-A campaign. A patient hitter with below-average power for an infield corner and a subpar glove at the keystone, Green demonstrated even less pop last season while his walk and strikeout rates moved in the wrong direction. The organization loves his makeup and is willing to write off last year's struggles as a bump in the road, hoping Green can become a solid insurance policy for the injury-prone Aramis Ramirez and Rickie Weeks, or a contributor at first base. The odds against him becoming a long-term starter are high, but as a former late-round draft pick, Green has already proven he can exceed expectations.

Corey Hart 1B
Born: **3/24/1982** Age: **31**
Bats: **R** Throws: **R** Height: **6' 7"**
Weight: **235** Breakout: **3%**
Improve: **36%** Collapse: **9%**
Attrition: **14%** MLB: **85%**

Comparables:
Ben Broussard,Orlando Cepeda,Glenn Davis

YEAR	TEAM	LVL	AGE	PA	R	2B	3B	HR	RBI	BB	SO	SB	CS	AVG_OBP_SLG	TAv	BABIP	BRR	FRAA	WARP
2010	MIL	MLB	28	614	91	34	4	31	102	45	140	7	6	.283/.340/.525	.294	.324	2	RF(141): -8.7	2.4
2011	MIL	MLB	29	551	80	25	4	26	63	51	114	7	6	.285/.356/.510	.296	.323	-1.4	RF(126): 1.5	2.1
2012	MIL	MLB	30	622	91	35	4	30	83	44	151	5	0	.270/.334/.507	.283	.318	-0.7	1B(103): 0.8, RF(53): -2.7	1.3
2013	*MIL*	*MLB*	*31*	*571*	*72*	*30*	*4*	*24*	*81*	*39*	*126*	*8*	*4*	*.266/.324/.478*	*.278*	*.305*	*-0.3*	*RF 2, 1B -0*	*2.2*

Hart's midseason move from right field was certainly an aesthetic success, as the lanky Kentuckian looks much better stretching for errant throws at first base than he does almost, but not quite, chasing down long fly balls. Hart's declining outfield range was threatening to erode much of the value his power bat provides. The move helped in the standings as well, covering for Gamel's failure to launch and freeing up a spot for Aoki's superior glove and on-base acumen. Hart's mediocre on-base percentage and right-handedness make him a less-than-ideal first sacker, and he now has a higher offensive bar to clear, but a healthy Hart should launch 25 bombs—more than enough to earn his keep.

Jonathan Lucroy C

Born: **6/13/1986** Age: **27**
Bats: **R** Throws: **R** Height: **6' 1"**
Weight: **190** Breakout: **5%**
Improve: **31%** Collapse: **11%**
Attrition: **22%** MLB: **94%**

Comparables:
John Wockenfuss,Keith Moreland,Mike Lieberthal

YEAR	TEAM	LVL	AGE	PA	R	2B	3B	HR	RBI	BB	SO	SB	CS	AVG_OBP_SLG	TAv	BABIP	BRR	FRAA	WARP
2010	NAS	AAA	24	83	8	4	0	2	11	3	14	0	0	.237/.265/.363	.230	.266	0.2	C(21): -0.6	0.4
2010	MIL	MLB	24	297	24	9	0	4	26	18	44	4	2	.253/.300/.329	.217	.287	1.5	C(75): 1.1	0.3
2011	MIL	MLB	25	468	45	16	1	12	59	29	99	2	1	.265/.312/.391	.245	.317	2.2	C(132): -2.1	1.0
2012	MIL	MLB	26	346	46	17	4	12	58	22	44	4	1	.320/.368/.513	.300	.338	-2.3	C(88): -2.3	1.9
2013	*MIL*	*MLB*	*27*	*354*	*40*	*15*	*2*	*10*	*41*	*22*	*62*	*3*	*1*	*.273/.322/.419*	*.257*	*.307*	*-0.1*	*C -0*	*1.5*

You never know what sort of nastiness you'll encounter when reaching under a hotel bed in Los Angeles. In Lucroy's case it was something called a "boxer's fracture," caused when his wife accidentally knocked a suitcase onto his hand as he groped for a lost sock. The freak injury cost Lucroy two months of the season and a puncher's chance at an All-Star berth, but the Brewers catcher managed to bookend his bad break with an offensive breakout. When healthy, Lucroy cut down on his strikeouts, walked more, made more frequent contact, and started driving the ball. Even better, the twin klaxons of imminent regression—BABIP and home runs per fly ball—saw only modest inflation, meaning there's good reason to think most of Lucroy's improvement is sustainable. He won't need to match his 2012 numbers to remain among the league's better-hitting catchers, and he gets good marks for his work behind the dish. Signed to a club-friendly contract through 2016 with a reasonable club option thereafter, Lucroy should provide the Brewers with solid production on the cheap for the foreseeable future—exactly what every small-market team needs.

Martin Maldonado C

Born: **8/16/1986** Age: **26**
Bats: **R** Throws: **R** Height: **6' 2"**
Weight: **225** Breakout: **6%**
Improve: **42%** Collapse: **10%**
Attrition: **15%** MLB: **94%**

Comparables:
Jeff Mathis,Johnny Roseboro,Adam Moore

YEAR	TEAM	LVL	AGE	PA	R	2B	3B	HR	RBI	BB	SO	SB	CS	AVG_OBP_SLG	TAv	BABIP	BRR	FRAA	WARP
2010	HUN	AA	23	123	9	6	0	2	12	9	24	0	2	.252/.347/.369	.235	.304	-0.7	C(34): -0.2	0.2
2010	NAS	AAA	23	201	19	9	0	7	26	14	45	0	1	.253/.305/.425	.253	.287	-4.7	C(52): 1.5	0.5
2011	HUN	AA	24	241	24	13	0	3	34	19	56	2	1	.264/.349/.370	.304	.344	-0.3	C(21): 0.2	0.8
2011	NAS	AAA	24	160	23	5	0	8	25	16	21	0	0	.321/.410/.537	.355	.330	-1.3	C(18): -0.3	0.9
2011	MIL	MLB	24	1	0	0	0	0	0	0	1	0	0	.000/.000/.000	.015	.000	0	C(3): -0.0	0.0
2012	NAS	AAA	25	138	10	6	0	4	13	9	37	0	2	.198/.270/.347	.256	.241	0.5	C(26): 0.2	0.5
2012	MIL	MLB	25	256	22	9	0	8	30	17	56	1	1	.266/.321/.408	.257	.320	1.8	C(69): 0.9, 1B(4): -0.0	0.9
2013	*MIL*	*MLB*	*26*	*250*	*28*	*10*	*1*	*8*	*30*	*16*	*60*	*1*	*1*	*.241/.300/.401*	*.242*	*.283*	*-0.5*	*C 0, 1B 0*	*0.6*

Maldonado has long been known for his peerless defensive chops, but when Milwaukee lost Lucroy for an extended spell last summer, the long-time minor-league receiver surprised everyone by helping out in the batter's box. He didn't hit for average, and with a long swing that leads to high strikeout rates, he never will. But Maldonado demonstrated enough home-run pop to show he can survive at the bottom of a major-league lineup. He controls the running game with a strong, accurate arm, blocks pitches well, and earns plaudits for his game-calling skills, while his wicked cool nickname—"Machete"—gains him bonus points with Milwaukee's legion of Danny Trejo fans. All that points to a long career as a backup backstop, but if Maldonado can show his gains at the plate are real, he could spend a few seasons working full-time.

Nyjer Morgan CF

Born: **7/2/1980** Age: **32**
Bats: **L** Throws: **L** Height: **6' 1"**
Weight: **175** Breakout: **1%**
Improve: **41%** Collapse: **4%**
Attrition: **11%** MLB: **80%**

Comparables:
Dave Martinez,Stan Javier,Kenny Lofton

YEAR	TEAM	LVL	AGE	PA	R	2B	3B	HR	RBI	BB	SO	SB	CS	AVG_OBP_SLG	TAv	BABIP	BRR	FRAA	WARP
2010	WAS	MLB	30	577	60	17	7	0	24	40	88	34	17	.253/.319/.314	.235	.304	4.9	CF(134): 1.6	0.7
2011	MIL	MLB	31	429	61	20	6	4	37	19	70	13	4	.304/.357/.421	.266	.362	4.4	CF(94): 4.8, RF(20): 0.9	2.2
2012	MIL	MLB	31	322	44	5	3	3	16	20	63	12	5	.239/.302/.308	.217	.296	1.6	CF(53): 0.9, RF(27): -0.5	-0.8
2013	*MIL*	*MLB*	*32*	*324*	*41*	*11*	*3*	*4*	*25*	*20*	*58*	*16*	*6*	*.267/.326/.367*	*.242*	*.312*	*1*	*CF 1, RF 0*	*0.6*

With a subpar walk rate and little power, Morgan's offensive value is extraordinarily dependant on the vagaries of his batting average on balls in play. When his BABIP climbs above .350, as it did in 2011, he's a speedy table setter with above-average range in the center pasture; when it plummets, as it did last year, he's a serial out-maker, pinch-runner, and defensive replacement. How Morgan's colorful demeanor is perceived has often seemed similarly pegged to his performance, careening from energizing to off-putting and back again—until last season, when Morgan set a major-league record for consecutive plate appearances without an RBI and lost his place in the lineup, yet was still uniformly praised for his clubhouse presence and professionalism. That can only help his future prospects. Organizations will be more likely to sign him as a veteran fourth outfielder with upside if they're not afraid he'll become a distraction. If he gets enough playing time, T. Plush could very well ride the BABIP train back to the big time.

Hunter Morris 1B
Born: **10/7/1988** Age: **24**
Bats: **L** Throws: **R** Height: **6' 3"**
Weight: **200** Breakout: **3%**
Improve: **58%** Collapse: **8%**
Attrition: **21%** MLB: **99%**
Comparables:
Brandon Allen, Orlando Cepeda, Greg Walker

YEAR	TEAM	LVL	AGE	PA	R	2B	3B	HR	RBI	BB	SO	SB	CS	AVG_OBP_SLG	TAv	BABIP	BRR	FRAA	WARP
2010	WIS	A	21	314	38	19	4	9	44	20	58	7	2	.251/.306/.436	.257	.286	-0.2	1B(58): -2.4, LF(12): -2.1	-0.2
2011	BRV	A+	22	531	75	28	5	19	67	18	84	7	3	.271/.299/.461	.253	.289	0	--	0.0
2012	HUN	AA	23	571	77	40	6	28	113	40	117	2	1	.303/.357/.563	.322	.342	0	1B(96): -8.3	2.0
2013	*MIL*	*MLB*	*24*	*250*	*28*	*12*	*2*	*11*	*36*	*10*	*62*	*1*	*0*	*.250/.284/.459*	*.251*	*.290*	*-0.2*	*1B -5, LF -0*	*-0.5*

Milwaukee's best power prospect by a country mile, Morris survived the jump to Double-A with his slugging credentials intact. The former Auburn first baseman paced the Southern League in home runs and slugging percentage, and more importantly demonstrated a better approach that led to a few more walks. He's a poor defender already clinging to the bottom rung of the defensive spectrum and will always have a lot of swing-and-miss in his game, so he'll need to rake to have a future. If he keeps launching moon shots while showing more patience at the plate, he may just become the lefty power bat the Brewers sorely need.

Donnie Murphy INF
Born: **3/10/1983** Age: **30**
Bats: **R** Throws: **R** Height: **5' 11"**
Weight: **195** Breakout: **2%**
Improve: **54%** Collapse: **9%**
Attrition: **6%** MLB: **95%**
Comparables:
Brooks Conrad, Dan Uggla, Alfonso Soriano

YEAR	TEAM	LVL	AGE	PA	R	2B	3B	HR	RBI	BB	SO	SB	CS	AVG_OBP_SLG	TAv	BABIP	BRR	FRAA	WARP
2010	NWO	AAA	27	224	31	12	1	12	35	16	41	0	0	.277/.335/.519	.301	.294	0.7	SS(51): 1.5	2.1
2010	FLO	MLB	27	47	9	6	1	3	16	2	19	0	0	.318/.348/.705	.346	.500	0	SS(4): 0.0, 3B(4): 0.1	0.5
2011	FLO	MLB	28	100	10	4	1	2	9	4	21	0	0	.185/.240/.315	.195	.214	0.6	SS(18): 0.1, 3B(15): 0.4	-0.3
2012	NWO	AAA	29	125	21	6	0	13	25	14	28	1	0	.302/.400/.726	.407	.288	-2.4	SS(3): 0.1, 2B(2): -0.0	0.1
2012	MIA	MLB	29	129	13	6	2	3	12	9	35	1	1	.216/.281/.379	.236	.278	-0.8	3B(22): -2.8, 2B(13): -0.0	-0.6
2013	*MIL*	*MLB*	*30*	*250*	*30*	*11*	*2*	*12*	*37*	*16*	*70*	*1*	*0*	*.235/.296/.458*	*.259*	*.280*	*-0.1*	*SS -1, 3B -0*	*0.7*

A second-division utility man with above-average pop for the role, Murphy can play shortstop but brings few other assets to the table. The Marlins outrighted him in October but the Brewers scooped him up, allowing him to compete for a backup infield role. If he can earn a job with the big club, Murphy will keep one impressive streak alive: Riverside Poly High School has had at least one alumnus appear in the majors every season since the debut of Bobby Bonds in 1968. Murphy will have to bridge the gap to Miami outfield prospect Jake Marisnick.

Aramis Ramirez 3B
Born: **6/25/1978** Age: **35**
Bats: **R** Throws: **R** Height: **6' 2"**
Weight: **215** Breakout: **1%**
Improve: **28%** Collapse: **7%**
Attrition: **14%** MLB: **94%**
Comparables:
Chipper Jones, Mark DeRosa, Mike Lowell

YEAR	TEAM	LVL	AGE	PA	R	2B	3B	HR	RBI	BB	SO	SB	CS	AVG_OBP_SLG	TAv	BABIP	BRR	FRAA	WARP
2010	CHN	MLB	32	507	61	21	1	25	83	34	90	0	0	.241/.294/.452	.258	.245	-4	3B(118): -8.0	0.2
2011	CHN	MLB	33	626	80	35	1	26	93	43	69	1	1	.306/.361/.510	.302	.308	-5.3	3B(145): -14.5	2.0
2012	MIL	MLB	34	630	92	50	3	27	105	44	82	9	2	.300/.360/.540	.308	.310	-2.4	3B(143): -4.0	3.8
2013	*MIL*	*MLB*	*35*	*591*	*75*	*32*	*2*	*26*	*87*	*45*	*93*	*4*	*1*	*.276/.340/.490*	*.284*	*.289*	*-0.7*	*3B -5*	*2.3*

Consistency, thy nickname is A-Ram. Over the last decade, Ramirez has posted a .294/.355/.526 line and averaged 28 home runs and 98 RBIs per season—numbers similar to those he put up last year, and virtually *every* season since his last year in Pittsburgh. Signed to a reasonable three-year deal to help fill the Prince Fielder power vacuum, Ramirez responded by pacing the National League with 80 extra-base hits (tying Braun) while showing better-than-expected agility and sure hands at the hot corner. He doesn't strike out much for a power hitter, often shortening up with two strikes or when he needs to make contact to drive in a run, and despite a series of nagging injuries he continues to reach the 500-plate-appearance threshold. As Ramirez enters his mid-30s, it's fair to wonder how long he'll keep this up. But we're not quite ready to bet against him.

Yadiel Rivera SS
Born: **5/2/1992** Age: **21**
Bats: **R** Throws: **R** Height: **6' 3"**
Weight: **175** Breakout: **3%**
Improve: **53%** Collapse: **11%**
Attrition: **18%** MLB: **95%**
Comparables:
Ken Hubbs, Ed Brinkman, Jack Heidemann

YEAR	TEAM	LVL	AGE	PA	R	2B	3B	HR	RBI	BB	SO	SB	CS	AVG_OBP_SLG	TAv	BABIP	BRR	FRAA	WARP
2010	BRR	Rk	18	218	22	8	1	0	23	9	72	6	2	.209/.245/.257	.158	.321	-0.2	SS(51): 3.9	-0.6
2011	HEL	Rk	19	349	47	14	7	8	38	14	91	7	3	.248/.285/.406	.243	.320	-0.2	SS(51): 10.5	1.2
2011	WIS	A	19	111	6	2	1	1	5	4	34	0	0	.194/.224/.262	.200	.279	0	SS(12): -1.2	-0.3
2012	WIS	A	20	506	60	26	5	12	49	26	119	7	3	.247/.290/.402	.241	.304	1.5	SS(86): 1.1	0.5
2013	*MIL*	*MLB*	*21*	*250*	*20*	*8*	*1*	*5*	*23*	*7*	*82*	*1*	*0*	*.192/.216/.304*	*.179*	*.260*	*-0.2*	*SS 2*	*-0.8*

True shortstops who can do some damage at the plate are few and far between, but Milwaukee may have something in Rivera. He's a defensive whiz with good instincts, a rifle arm, and excellent range, projecting as a premium defender in the big leagues. At the plate he's hardly distinguishable from every other young middle infielder, with piles of strikeouts, few walks, and an insatiable appetite for off-speed stuff he can't reach. What sets him apart is his size and swing, which portend the possibility of untapped raw power. Rivera will have a future if he improves his pitch recognition and begins to unleash more of his batting-practice power during games, something the Brewers will give him ample opportunity to do.

Victor Roache OF
Born: 9/17/1991 Age: 21
Bats: R Throws: R Height: 6' 1"
Weight: 200 Breakout: --%
Improve: --% Collapse: --%
Attrition: --% MLB: --%
Comparables:
--

An outfielder out of Georgia Southern, Roache led Division I with 30 home runs in his breakout 2011 season, but a badly broken wrist in 2012 lowered his draft stock. The Brewers were happy to snag him late in the first round, and Roache spent the summer rehabbing and preparing for his professional debut. Wrist injuries are always a concern for power hitters. None of his other tools stands out, but if Roache can recover the thunder in his bat he profiles as a prototypical right fielder.

Logan Schafer CF
Born: 9/8/1986 Age: 26
Bats: L Throws: L Height: 6' 2"
Weight: 180 Breakout: 7%
Improve: 60% Collapse: 6%
Attrition: 10% MLB: 97%
Comparables:
Ken Landreaux,Paul Blair,Andy Dirks

YEAR	TEAM	LVL	AGE	PA	R	2B	3B	HR	RBI	BB	SO	SB	CS	AVG_OBP_SLG	TAv	BABIP	BRR	FRAA	WARP
2011	HUN	AA	24	211	31	9	4	0	19	17	25	10	5	.302/.368/.392	.281	.348	2.4	CF(16): 0.4	0.5
2011	NAS	AAA	24	194	31	13	2	5	23	17	18	5	3	.331/.401/.521	.334	.345	0.7	CF(23): -0.2	1.4
2011	MIL	MLB	24	5	1	0	0	0	0	1	1	0	0	.333/.500/.333	.285	.500	0	RF(1): -0.0, CF(1): -0.0	0.0
2012	NAS	AAA	25	513	72	23	9	11	40	29	72	16	7	.278/.332/.438	.284	.307	3.1	CF(81): 9.6	2.4
2012	MIL	MLB	25	25	3	1	2	0	5	1	3	0	1	.304/.320/.522	.297	.333	0	CF(5): 0.3, LF(2): 0.1	0.2
2013	*MIL*	*MLB*	*26*	*250*	*32*	*11*	*3*	*6*	*25*	*14*	*45*	*8*	*4*	*.259/.309/.418*	*.248*	*.289*	*0.4*	*CF -2, LF -0*	*0.4*

Schafer arrived in Milwaukee last September sporting the complete fourth-outfielder accessory kit—lefty bat, contact-oriented approach, gap power, and enough range to play a credible center field—and managed to impress the big club enough to earn a long look this spring. A former third-round pick, Schafer is more well-rounded than toolsy, and his first full season in Triple-A did nothing to make us think he's primed for a breakout. Nevertheless, true center fielders who don't let major-league pitchers knock the bat out of their hands and aren't useless against lefties can make a place for themselves, something Schafer will soon get a chance to do.

Jean Segura SS
Born: 3/17/1990 Age: 23
Bats: R Throws: L Height: 6' 0"
Weight: 160 Breakout: 3%
Improve: 40% Collapse: 13%
Attrition: 17% MLB: 92%
Comparables:
Rance Mulliniks,Erick Aybar,Osvaldo Martinez

YEAR	TEAM	LVL	AGE	PA	R	2B	3B	HR	RBI	BB	SO	SB	CS	AVG_OBP_SLG	TAv	BABIP	BRR	FRAA	WARP
2010	CDR	A	20	581	89	24	12	10	79	45	72	50	10	.313/.363/.464	.298	.340	5.1	2B(128): 25.5	7.3
2011	SBR	A+	21	202	26	9	4	3	21	15	26	18	6	.281/.337/.422	.264	.312	0	--	0.0
2012	ARK	AA	22	414	50	10	5	7	40	23	57	33	13	.294/.346/.404	.307	.329	2.4	SS(65): 4.8, 2B(2): -0.0	3.3
2012	ANA	MLB	22	3	0	0	0	0	0	0	2	0	0	.000/.000/.000	.251	.000	-0.1	SS(1): 0.1	0.0
2012	MIL	MLB	22	163	19	4	3	0	14	13	21	7	1	.264/.321/.331	.234	.305	0.9	SS(43): -2.7	-0.1
2013	*MIL*	*MLB*	*23*	*250*	*32*	*9*	*3*	*5*	*22*	*13*	*43*	*13*	*3*	*.263/.304/.387*	*.239*	*.298*	*1.5*	*SS -1, 2B 1*	*0.6*

Segura came to Milwaukee last summer in the Greinke trade, and the Brewers wasted little time measuring their new top prospect against major-league competition. A tremendous raw athlete with excellent speed and surprising strength, Segura has outstanding bat speed and a knack for hard contact, with the potential for double-digit home runs, a high batting average, and 30 steals at his peak. In the field, Segura is still learning shortstop and lacks a cannon arm, but he's made strides to improve his range and flexibility, leading many scouts to think he can be at least adequate there. He struggled at the plate early in his big-league stint, but seemed to adjust his approach as the season wore on, with positive results. Segura is far from a finished product and would benefit from some Triple-A seasoning, but Brewers fans are already dreaming of All-Star Games to come.

Yorvit Torrealba C
Born: 7/19/1978 Age: 34
Bats: R Throws: R Height: 6' 0"
Weight: 200 Breakout: 1%
Improve: 23% Collapse: 17%
Attrition: 23% MLB: 86%
Comparables:
Lenny Webster,Milt May,Bo Diaz

YEAR	TEAM	LVL	AGE	PA	R	2B	3B	HR	RBI	BB	SO	SB	CS	AVG_OBP_SLG	TAv	BABIP	BRR	FRAA	WARP
2010	SDN	MLB	31	363	31	14	0	7	37	33	67	7	5	.271/.343/.378	.269	.321	1.6	C(92): -0.6	2.3
2011	TEX	MLB	32	419	40	27	1	7	37	20	65	0	2	.273/.306/.399	.240	.310	-4.8	C(97): 0.1	0.0
2012	MIL	MLB	33	6	0	0	0	0	0	1	2	0	0	.000/.167/.000	.097	.000	0	C(2): -0.0	-0.1
2012	TEX	MLB	33	182	16	8	0	3	12	14	31	1	1	.236/.302/.342	.240	.271	-3.7	C(48): 0.3	-0.2
2012	TOR	MLB	33	30	3	0	0	1	2	2	7	0	0	.214/.267/.321	.213	.250	0.3	C(9): 0.1, 1B(1): -0.0	0.0
2013	*MIL*	*MLB*	*34*	*250*	*26*	*12*	*0*	*5*	*25*	*16*	*48*	*2*	*1*	*.255/.309/.379*	*.240*	*.297*	*-0.6*	*C -0, 1B -0*	*0.5*

Have shin guards, will travel. Torrealba plied his trade in three major-league cities last season, deploying his usual mélange of solid backstoppery and clubhouse alchemy to cover the taste of his increasingly modest offensive achievements. Viewed as a steady hand with young pitchers, the aging Venezuelan will likely spend a few more years talking softly, carrying a small stick, and earning his pay in ways that won't do much to help your fantasy team but are greatly prized by major-league organizations.

Rickie Weeks **2B**
Born: **9/13/1982** Age: **30**
Bats: **R** Throws: **R** Height: **5' 11"**
Weight: **215** Breakout: **0%**
Improve: **47%** Collapse: **3%**
Attrition: **9%** MLB: **91%**
Comparables:
Keith Ginter,Kelly Johnson,Dan Uggla

YEAR	TEAM	LVL	AGE	PA	R	2B	3B	HR	RBI	BB	SO	SB	CS	AVG_OBP_SLG	TAv	BABIP	BRR	FRAA	WARP
2010	MIL	MLB	27	754	112	32	4	29	83	76	184	11	4	.269/.366/.464	.288	.332	5.5	2B(159): -3.1	4.0
2011	MIL	MLB	28	515	77	26	2	20	49	50	107	9	2	.269/.350/.468	.283	.310	2.6	2B(115): 0.3	2.5
2012	MIL	MLB	29	677	85	29	4	21	63	74	169	16	3	.230/.328/.400	.264	.285	-1.2	2B(152): -13.8	-0.1
2013	*MIL*	*MLB*	*30*	*604*	*85*	*25*	*4*	*22*	*71*	*60*	*145*	*12*	*3*	*.247/.339/.435*	*.274*	*.298*	*0.7*	*2B -9*	*2.2*

While his overall numbers show Weeks struggled through a tough season at the plate and in the field, it's more accurate to say he struggled through a tough half-season. The longtime Brewers second baseman arrived at parties during the All-Star break dressed as a sub-Mendozan, but rebounded to post a .261/.343/.457 second-half line—numbers perfectly consistent with his career averages. His early-season swoon coincided with a less aggressive plate approach and an altered batting stance that may have been caused by toughing out the lingering effects of his nasty 2011 ankle injury. Whatever the reason, Weeks eventually righted the ship and unleashed his normal mix of patience and power during Milwaukee's stretch run. More distressing was his terrible glovework, as Weeks showed little range and played down to his woeful (and frequently undeserved) defensive reputation. The Brewers had best hope this, too, was injury-related, since a Weeks who can't play a reasonable second base will provide far more value to fantasy teams than to his real one.

PITCHERS

John Axford
Born: **4/1/1983** Age: **30**
Bats: **R** Throws: **R** Height: **6' 6"** Weight: **195**
Breakout: **27%** Improve: **49%** Collapse: **33%**
Attrition: **12%** MLB: **94%**
Comparables:
Derrick Turnbow,Michael Wuertz,Juan Cruz

YEAR	TEAM	LVL	AGE	W	L	SV	G	GS	IP	H	HR	BB	SO	BB9	SO9	GB%	BABIP	WHIP	ERA	FIP	FRA	WARP
2010	NAS	AAA	27	3	2	2	12	0	13^1	14	0	5	19	3.4	12.9	53%	.412	1.43	2.03	1.85	1.85	0.6
2010	MIL	MLB	27	8	2	24	50	0	58	42	1	27	76	4.2	11.8	50%	.308	1.19	2.48	2.16	2.37	1.7
2011	MIL	MLB	28	2	2	46	74	0	73^2	59	4	25	86	3.1	10.5	50%	.289	1.14	1.95	2.38	2.96	1.6
2012	MIL	MLB	29	5	8	35	75	0	69^1	61	10	39	93	5.1	12.1	48%	.307	1.44	4.67	4.10	4.06	0.5
2013	*MIL*	*MLB*	*30*	*3*	*1*	*35*	*66*	*0*	*67*	*53*	*7*	*31*	*79*	*4.2*	*10.6*	*45%*	*.302*	*1.25*	*3.61*	*3.59*	*3.93*	*0.8*

If they were to analyze Milwaukee's 2012 outbreak of Bullpen Dropsy, forensic epidemiologists would have little difficulty identifying Axford as Patient Zero. The Brewers closer maintained his frequently overpowering stuff, but struggled with his command and had difficulty throwing his curveball for strikes, making it easier for hitters to sit on his fastball. The resultant swelling of his home-run and walk rates led to a disastrous series of blown saves culminating in a brief dismissal from ninth-inning duties. On the plus side, Axford rebounded down the stretch, and his fastball can still dent walls and generate enough strikeouts to overcome his always-iffy walk rate. As with most flamethrowers of his ilk, he's likely to toggle from dominance to combustibility and back again for years to come.

Burke Badenhop
Born: **2/8/1983** Age: **30**
Bats: **R** Throws: **R** Height: **6' 6"** Weight: **220**
Breakout: **34%** Improve: **54%** Collapse: **25%**
Attrition: **14%** MLB: **85%**
Comparables:
Tony Pena,Brad Ziegler,Casey Janssen

YEAR	TEAM	LVL	AGE	W	L	SV	G	GS	IP	H	HR	BB	SO	BB9	SO9	GB%	BABIP	WHIP	ERA	FIP	FRA	WARP
2010	NWO	AAA	27	0	1	0	12	1	16	16	0	7	9	3.9	5.1	60%	.302	1.44	2.81	4.33	3.84	0.3
2010	FLO	MLB	27	2	5	1	53	0	67^2	62	5	21	47	2.8	6.3	59%	.277	1.23	3.99	3.70	5.01	0.4
2011	NWO	AAA	28	1	1	1	11	0	14^2	20	1	7	10	4.3	6.1	—	.365	1.84	6.75	4.94	5.37	0.0
2011	FLO	MLB	28	2	3	1	50	0	63^2	65	1	24	51	3.4	7.2	61%	.327	1.40	4.10	2.92	3.12	1.3
2012	TBA	MLB	29	3	2	0	66	0	62^1	63	6	12	42	1.7	6.1	55%	.284	1.20	3.03	3.58	4.22	0.3
2013	*MIL*	*MLB*	*30*	*2*	*1*	*1*	*49*	*0*	*57*	*56*	*7*	*17*	*42*	*2.6*	*6.7*	*55%*	*.300*	*1.27*	*4.24*	*4.22*	*4.61*	*0.2*

Badenhop wasn't quite the groundball machine he had been in 2011, but he was close enough (52.9 percent, down from 58.5). His HR/FB rate rose along with his pitches, to 12 percent from 2.4 (it had been just under 9.0 for two seasons prior). Nonetheless, as a generally low-leverage reliever offering multiple-innings capacity and a 3.58 FIP, he was yet another reason why the Rays boasted one of the best and most cost-effective bullpens in baseball. Traded to the Brewers for Raul Mondesi Jr., Badenhop's brand of veteran competence can only help Milwaukee's struggling bullpen.

Jed Bradley

Born: **6/12/1990** Age: **23**
Bats: **L** Throws: **L** Height: **6' 5"** Weight: **224**
Breakout: **33%** Improve: **64%** Collapse: **18%**
Attrition: **13%** MLB: **89%**

Comparables:
John Lannan, Brian Bohanon, Jimmy Gobble

YEAR	TEAM	LVL	AGE	W	L	SV	G	GS	IP	H	HR	BB	SO	BB9	SO9	GB%	BABIP	WHIP	ERA	FIP	FRA	WARP
2012	BRV	A+	22	5	10	0	20	20	107^1	136	9	43	60	3.6	5.0	52%	.338	1.67	5.53	4.74	7.04	-0.5
2013	*MIL*	*MLB*	*23*	*1*	*3*	*0*	*6*	*6*	*34^1*	*41*	*6*	*16*	*17*	*4.1*	*4.5*	*48%*	*.314*	*1.67*	*6.54*	*5.88*	*7.11*	*-0.7*

Short of blowing out his elbow, things could hardly have gone worse in Bradley's pro debut. The former first-round pick suffered through an April groin injury, then struggled with his mechanics and couldn't get anyone out. A power lefty with prototypical size, when he's right Bradley can dominate with a low-90s fastball and plus slider, but the maddening inconsistency he displayed at Georgia Tech continued to plague him last year. The organization mercifully pulled the plug on his season after a run of disastrous July starts, citing fatigue, but his head likely needed the timeout as much as his arm. Bradley may still own the tools to build a big league career, but right now they're scattered around the garage.

Fautino De Los Santos

Born: **2/15/1986** Age: **27**
Bats: **R** Throws: **R** Height: **6' 3"** Weight: **225**
Breakout: **25%** Improve: **55%** Collapse: **35%**
Attrition: **21%** MLB: **87%**

Comparables:
Bob James, John Wetteland, Rafael Soriano

YEAR	TEAM	LVL	AGE	W	L	SV	G	GS	IP	H	HR	BB	SO	BB9	SO9	GB%	BABIP	WHIP	ERA	FIP	FRA	WARP
2011	MID	AA	25	0	0	3	8	0	9^1	8	1	4	15	3.9	14.5	—	.350	1.29	2.89	2.84	3.09	0.0
2011	SAC	AAA	25	0	0	0	15	0	19^2	18	0	12	21	5.5	9.6	—	.340	1.53	1.83	3.48	3.78	0.0
2011	OAK	MLB	25	3	2	0	34	0	33^1	27	4	17	43	4.6	11.6	40%	.291	1.32	4.32	3.57	4.49	0.2
2012	NAS	AAA	26	1	0	0	11	0	13^2	17	0	4	17	2.6	11.2	34%	.421	1.54	1.98	2.28	1.91	0.4
2012	SAC	AAA	26	1	3	0	28	0	36	49	2	16	43	4.0	10.8	48%	.427	1.81	7.25	3.50	4.37	0.5
2012	OAK	MLB	26	0	0	0	6	0	3	7	0	3	3	9.0	9.0	43%	.500	3.33	3.00	4.05	4.29	0.0
2013	*MIL*	*MLB*	*27*	*2*	*1*	*1*	*33*	*0*	*37*	*33*	*4*	*15*	*42*	*3.7*	*10.3*	*44%*	*.320*	*1.30*	*4.06*	*3.55*	*4.41*	*0.2*

De Los Santos came to the Brewers in the George Kottaras trade last summer, giving him the opportunity to frustrate yet another organization. He's a perpetual tease, drawing your eye with his alluring mid-90s fastball and darting slider, then driving you away with his continual lack of production. De Los Santos racks up the strikeouts and his walk rate isn't terrible for a power reliever, but lack of command leaves him far more hittable than someone with his arsenal should be. Given Milwaukee's bullpen mess he should get another long look this spring and could become the new Jose Veras.

Miguel De Los Santos

Born: **7/10/1988** Age: **24**
Bats: **L** Throws: **L** Height: **6' 2"** Weight: **170**
Breakout: **34%** Improve: **65%** Collapse: **16%**
Attrition: **16%** MLB: **86%**

Comparables:
Sid Fernandez, Scott Elbert, Balor Moore

YEAR	TEAM	LVL	AGE	W	L	SV	G	GS	IP	H	HR	BB	SO	BB9	SO9	GB%	BABIP	WHIP	ERA	FIP	FRA	WARP
2011	RNG	Rk	22	0	0	0	1	1	3	4	0	1	7	3.0	21.0	—	.667	1.67	3.00	1.70	1.85	0.0
2011	MYR	A+	22	6	3	0	13	12	63^2	46	2	28	97	4.0	13.7	32%	.362	1.16	3.82	1.91	3.17	1.2
2011	FRI	AA	22	1	3	0	6	6	28	27	4	17	38	5.5	12.2	12%	.348	1.57	8.04	4.45	4.53	0.1
2012	FRI	AA	23	3	2	0	26	4	58^2	54	8	34	70	5.2	10.7	33%	.311	1.50	5.22	4.41	4.09	0.4
2013	*MIL*	*MLB*	*24*	*2*	*2*	*0*	*11*	*5*	*36^1*	*31*	*5*	*20*	*43*	*5.0*	*10.7*	*35%*	*.312*	*1.41*	*4.49*	*4.27*	*4.88*	*0.1*

A series of maneuvers last summer designed to add Jurickson Profar to the Rangers roster exposed De Los Santos to waivers, and the Brewers were happy to spend a few bucks to add the young lefty to their stockpile of potential bullpen saints. This De Los Santos lives off his Bugs Bunny changeup, a seriously wicked screwball offering that's delivered with arm action indistinguishable from his fastball. Minor-league hitters have treated it like kryptonite, striking out nearly a third of the time, but De Los Santos's lack of fastball command has led to worrisome walk rates and a rash of gopher balls. His velocity has climbed into the low-90s since his move to the bullpen, and if he can learn to locate his fastball he could ride his wipeout change to the big leagues. That's a big if, of course, but one that's well worth betting a few bucks on.

Marco Estrada

Born: **7/5/1983** Age: **29**
Bats: **R** Throws: **R** Height: **6' 1"** Weight: **180**
Breakout: **14%** Improve: **45%** Collapse: **19%**
Attrition: **3%** MLB: **95%**

Comparables:
Dennis Leonard, Ted Higuera, Shaun Marcum

YEAR	TEAM	LVL	AGE	W	L	SV	G	GS	IP	H	HR	BB	SO	BB9	SO9	GB%	BABIP	WHIP	ERA	FIP	FRA	WARP
2010	NAS	AAA	26	1	2	0	7	7	40	30	1	11	33	2.5	7.4	42%	.257	1.02	3.15	3.08	4.28	0.7
2010	MIL	MLB	26	0	0	0	7	1	11^1	14	3	6	13	4.8	10.3	32%	.314	1.76	9.53	6.11	6.77	-0.2
2011	MIL	MLB	27	4	8	0	43	7	92^2	83	11	29	88	2.8	8.5	43%	.287	1.21	4.08	3.64	4.51	0.7
2012	NAS	AAA	28	0	0	0	2	2	8	7	0	5	5	5.6	5.6	32%	.280	1.50	1.12	4.29	5.06	0.0
2012	MIL	MLB	28	5	7	0	29	23	138^1	129	18	29	143	1.9	9.3	37%	.298	1.14	3.64	3.39	4.09	2.0
2013	*MIL*	*MLB*	*29*	*6*	*5*	*0*	*33*	*15*	*109^1*	*102*	*15*	*32*	*98*	*2.6*	*8.1*	*42%*	*.299*	*1.22*	*4.06*	*4.07*	*4.41*	*0.8*

Chris Narveson's injury last April forced Estrada into the starting rotation, and the Brewers were so impressed with the results that his days as a swingman may be at an end. No one will ever describe Estrada's stuff as "electric," but the former Nats farmhand maintains excellent command of his low-90s fastball, has a serviceable curveball, and mixes in a solid changeup that keeps lefties honest. It's a mixture that results in more swinging strikes than expected, few free passes, and lots of fly balls. That last part isn't generally a good fit for Miller Park, and Estrada's effectiveness will vary along with his home-run rate. So long as he can keep runners off the bases when those inevitable long flies come around, he'll provide mid-rotation production at bargain-basement prices.

Mike Fiers
Born: **6/15/1985** Age: **28**
Bats: **R** Throws: **R** Height: **6' 4"** Weight: **200**
Breakout: **20%** Improve: **47%** Collapse: **30%**
Attrition: **4%** MLB: **94%**
Comparables:
Len Barker,Dennis Leonard,Tim Belcher

YEAR	TEAM	LVL	AGE	W	L	SV	G	GS	IP	H	HR	BB	SO	BB9	SO9	GB%	BABIP	WHIP	ERA	FIP	FRA	WARP
2010	BRV	A+	25	4	8	0	17	15	93^{1}	78	6	23	94	2.2	9.1	43%	.281	1.08	3.47	3.35	4.04	0.6
2010	HUN	AA	25	1	1	1	10	4	31^{2}	28	3	9	36	2.6	10.2	43%	.305	1.17	3.69	3.48	3.98	0.4
2011	HUN	AA	26	5	3	5	22	8	61^{1}	42	7	14	63	2.1	9.2	51%	.311	0.91	2.64	3.52	3.15	0.8
2011	NAS	AAA	26	8	0	0	12	10	64^{2}	41	4	22	69	3.1	9.6	44%	.217	0.97	1.11	3.61	4.47	0.6
2011	MIL	MLB	26	0	0	0	2	0	2	2	0	3	2	13.5	9.0	40%	.400	2.50	0.00	5.49	1.17	0.0
2012	NAS	AAA	27	1	3	0	10	10	55	49	6	18	49	2.9	8.0	42%	.278	1.22	4.42	4.45	4.82	0.3
2012	MIL	MLB	27	9	10	0	23	22	127^{2}	125	12	36	135	2.5	9.5	34%	.319	1.26	3.74	3.14	3.41	3.1
2013	*MIL*	*MLB*	*28*	*7*	*6*	*0*	*19*	*19*	*108^{1}*	*97*	*13*	*33*	*106*	*2.8*	*8.8*	*41%*	*.299*	*1.20*	*3.80*	*3.72*	*4.13*	*1.2*

Fiers has spent several years polishing his sterling minor-league numbers but drawing yawns from the scouting community, as most observers expected big-league hitters to treat his straight upper-80s fastball the way Sonny Liston treated sparring partners. But when injuries forced Fiers into the Milwaukee rotation last May, the former 22nd-round pick shocked the world by posting a 1.80 ERA in his first 80 innings and striking out a batter per inning before fading badly down the stretch. Fiers doesn't hand out free passes, overcomes his lack of velocity by hiding the ball well during his deceptive over-the-top delivery, and uses a great changeup, a cutter, and a big, looping curve to keep hitters off-balance. Perhaps the league caught onto his tricks as the season wore on, yet he was still able to get batters to swing and miss—his strikeout rate was actually higher down the stretch. Fiers induced groundballs at a lower rate than any other National League starter last year, so home runs will always be a concern, but he seems to get the most out of his marginal stuff. He's no ace, but if Fiers can keep the ball in the park and continue to avoid ball four, he'll be an asset at the back of the rotation.

Drew Gagnon
Born: **6/26/1990** Age: **23**
Bats: **R** Throws: **R** Height: **6' 5"** Weight: **195**
Breakout: **31%** Improve: **60%** Collapse: **16%**
Attrition: **14%** MLB: **86%**
Comparables:
Dan Haren,Collin Balester,Jeanmar Gomez

YEAR	TEAM	LVL	AGE	W	L	SV	G	GS	IP	H	HR	BB	SO	BB9	SO9	GB%	BABIP	WHIP	ERA	FIP	FRA	WARP
2011	HEL	Rk	21	0	3	1	8	7	19	25	1	10	27	4.7	12.8	49%	.439	1.84	8.05	4.02	4.18	0.5
2012	WIS	A	22	6	1	0	14	14	82^{2}	67	6	19	65	2.1	7.1	46%	.258	1.04	2.83	3.52	4.78	0.4
2012	BRV	A+	22	1	2	0	11	11	67	56	3	18	49	2.4	6.6	41%	.275	1.10	2.82	3.54	4.19	0.4
2013	*MIL*	*MLB*	*23*	*2*	*3*	*0*	*7*	*7*	*38^{1}*	*41*	*6*	*16*	*26*	*3.8*	*6.2*	*42%*	*.304*	*1.48*	*5.42*	*5.13*	*5.89*	*-0.3*

Gagnon's full-season debut was a success, as the Long Beach State alum did enough in the Midwest League to earn a midseason promotion to High-A. Long and lean, Gagnon's three-pitch mix (a low-90s fastball with decent movement, a curveball, and a changeup) doesn't wow anyone, but he throws strikes and manages to keep the ball in the yard. His limited ability to miss bats means he's at best a swingman-in-waiting, but at least he has the organization paying attention to what he can do, rather than what he can't.

Yovani Gallardo
Born: **2/27/1986** Age: **27**
Bats: **R** Throws: **R** Height: **6' 3"** Weight: **210**
Breakout: **26%** Improve: **63%** Collapse: **16%**
Attrition: **4%** MLB: **95%**
Comparables:
Daisuke Matsuzaka,Josh Beckett,Pedro Martinez

YEAR	TEAM	LVL	AGE	W	L	SV	G	GS	IP	H	HR	BB	SO	BB9	SO9	GB%	BABIP	WHIP	ERA	FIP	FRA	WARP
2010	MIL	MLB	24	14	7	0	31	31	185	178	12	75	200	3.6	9.7	45%	.324	1.37	3.84	3.05	3.31	6.1
2011	MIL	MLB	25	17	10	0	33	33	207^{1}	193	27	59	207	2.6	9.0	48%	.291	1.22	3.52	3.56	4.27	3.1
2012	MIL	MLB	26	16	9	0	33	33	204	185	26	81	204	3.6	9.0	49%	.290	1.30	3.66	3.98	4.55	2.2
2013	*MIL*	*MLB*	*27*	*11*	*9*	*0*	*29*	*29*	*177^{2}*	*152*	*21*	*59*	*185*	*3.0*	*9.4*	*45%*	*.300*	*1.19*	*3.59*	*3.65*	*3.90*	*2.3*

Gallardo was at his best last year when the Brewers needed him most, winning six straight starts after the Greinke trade left him as the undisputed staff leader and finishing with an 8-1 record during Milwaukee's improbable stretch run. The right-hander continues to rack up strikeouts at an elite level, using his four-pitch arsenal to keep hitters guessing and cutting them down with high fastballs or sliders away. A few too many walks and long ones have kept him from becoming the perennial Cy Young candidate some predicted, yet Gallardo is still only 27, has never lost time due to a sore arm, and won't earn an eight-figure salary until 2014. If the Brewers can ever manage to field something resembling a defense behind him, there may still be time for their young ace to take a great leap forward.

Tom Gorzelanny
Born: **7/12/1982** Age: **30**
Bats: **L** Throws: **L** Height: **6' 3"** Weight: **210**
Breakout: **29%** Improve: **58%** Collapse: **13%**
Attrition: **14%** MLB: **88%**
Comparables:
Chris Narveson,Bob Lemon,Steve Carlton

YEAR	TEAM	LVL	AGE	W	L	SV	G	GS	IP	H	HR	BB	SO	BB9	SO9	GB%	BABIP	WHIP	ERA	FIP	FRA	WARP
2010	CHN	MLB	27	7	9	1	29	23	136^{1}	136	11	68	119	4.5	7.9	43%	.309	1.50	4.09	3.95	4.54	1.5
2011	SYR	AAA	28	0	1	0	1	1	4	5	1	1	3	2.2	6.8	31%	.333	1.50	9.00	6.49	10.53	-0.2
2011	WAS	MLB	28	4	6	0	30	15	105	102	15	33	95	2.8	8.1	38%	.292	1.29	4.03	4.16	4.27	0.7
2012	WAS	MLB	29	4	2	1	45	1	72	65	7	30	62	3.8	7.8	43%	.283	1.32	2.88	4.01	4.12	0.6
2013	*MIL*	*MLB*	*30*	*3*	*3*	*0*	*23*	*9*	*68^{1}*	*63*	*9*	*27*	*61*	*3.6*	*8.0*	*42%*	*.297*	*1.32*	*4.46*	*4.31*	*4.85*	*0.2*

Converted to full-time relief after splitting his appearances between the rotation and the bullpen in 2011, Gorzelanny actually deepened his repertoire, using his curveball more than ever. The results were largely positive—and if you forgive a two-inning, six-run clunker on April 19, his ERA for the season would have been 2.19. Those kind of results are incongruous with Gorzelanny's skill set and potential, but the Brewers bet two years and $6 million that he can do it again.

John Hellweg

Born: **10/29/1988** Age: **24**
Bats: **R** Throws: **R** Height: **6' 10"** Weight: **210**
Breakout: **34%** Improve: **63%** Collapse: **20%**
Attrition: **17%** MLB: **91%**

Comparables:
Barry Latman, John Pacella, Joey Jay

YEAR	TEAM	LVL	AGE	W	L	SV	G	GS	IP	H	HR	BB	SO	BB9	SO9	GB%	BABIP	WHIP	ERA	FIP	FRA	WARP
2010	CDR	A	21	2	4	16	41	0	43^2	20	2	45	66	9.3	13.6	50%	.216	1.49	4.32	4.55	5.59	-0.1
2011	SBR	A+	22	6	4	0	28	14	89^1	75	2	59	113	5.9	11.4	—	.340	1.50	3.73	4.20	4.56	0.0
2012	ARK	AA	23	5	10	0	21	21	119^2	105	8	60	88	4.5	6.6	56%	.289	1.38	3.38	4.51	5.30	0.1
2012	HUN	AA	23	2	1	0	7	2	20	16	0	15	17	6.8	7.7	69%	.296	1.55	2.70	3.84	3.98	0.3
2013	*MIL*	*MLB*	*24*	*2*	*2*	*0*	*13*	*4*	*35*	*34*	*5*	*24*	*29*	*6.1*	*7.4*	*49%*	*.301*	*1.65*	*5.70*	*5.46*	*6.20*	*-0.4*

Long known for his fastball, height, and ridiculous walk rates, Hellweg came to Milwaukee last summer in the Greinke deal. His height giveth, allowing him to throw his mid-90s heater on a steep downward plane and generate tons of groundballs. It also taketh away, as he often struggles to get Mt. Hellweg moving in a repeatable way, leading to variable release points and loss of command. Hellweg's walk rate has gone down since he moved to the rotation two years ago, but so has his strikeout rate, and with a power curve and changeup that haven't become plus offerings, his future may be in the bullpen. Few prospects have a wider range of likely outcomes, from frontline starter to closer to middle reliever to washout, and Hellweg's season will be one of the year's more interesting stories.

Jim Henderson

Born: **10/21/1982** Age: **30**
Bats: **L** Throws: **R** Height: **6' 6"** Weight: **190**
Breakout: **27%** Improve: **52%** Collapse: **14%**
Attrition: **4%** MLB: **81%**

Comparables:
Jack Taschner, Damaso Marte, Charlie Manning

YEAR	TEAM	LVL	AGE	W	L	SV	G	GS	IP	H	HR	BB	SO	BB9	SO9	GB%	BABIP	WHIP	ERA	FIP	FRA	WARP
2011	HUN	AA	28	4	1	5	22	0	30^2	22	4	8	39	2.3	11.4	53%	.207	0.98	2.64	3.53	2.33	0.4
2011	NAS	AAA	28	3	1	0	20	0	30^1	24	4	23	30	6.8	8.9	21%	.138	1.55	5.93	5.89	3.42	0.3
2012	NAS	AAA	29	4	3	15	35	0	48	36	2	22	56	4.1	10.5	35%	.297	1.21	1.69	3.37	3.16	1.1
2012	MIL	MLB	29	1	3	3	36	0	30^2	26	1	13	45	3.8	13.2	44%	.352	1.27	3.52	1.99	2.96	0.8
2013	*MIL*	*MLB*	*30*	*2*	*1*	*3*	*30*	*0*	*37*	*32*	*5*	*17*	*38*	*4.1*	*9.2*	*41%*	*.296*	*1.32*	*4.09*	*4.28*	*4.45*	*0.2*

Perhaps the final Expos draftee ever to make his big-league debut, Henderson spent a decade kicking around the bus leagues before last year's Milwaukee bullpen implosion finally gave him his shot—and unlike, say, Lance Zawadzki or Luke Montz, he may stick around awhile. Like bullpen mate Axford, Henderson is a well-traveled Canuck with a big fastball and spotty control that's caused him to walk nearly five batters per nine innings in the high minors. When he commands his fastball and can throw his sharp-breaking slider anywhere near the strike zone, as he did last year, he can punch out batters at a breathtaking rate. That should be enough to earn him a set-up job, though his ability to keep it will depend on his ability to avoid ball four.

Livan Hernandez

Born: **2/20/1975** Age: **38**
Bats: **R** Throws: **R** Height: **6' 3"** Weight: **245**
Breakout: **10%** Improve: **42%** Collapse: **20%**
Attrition: **17%** MLB: **71%**

Comparables:
Woody Williams, Rick Reuschel, Brian Moehler

YEAR	TEAM	LVL	AGE	W	L	SV	G	GS	IP	H	HR	BB	SO	BB9	SO9	GB%	BABIP	WHIP	ERA	FIP	FRA	WARP
2010	WAS	MLB	35	10	12	0	33	33	211^2	216	16	64	114	2.7	4.8	40%	.287	1.32	3.66	3.98	4.45	2.6
2011	WAS	MLB	36	8	13	0	29	29	175^1	199	16	46	99	2.4	5.1	43%	.313	1.40	4.47	3.92	4.33	1.9
2012	ATL	MLB	37	1	1	1	18	0	31	40	5	8	19	2.3	5.5	41%	.337	1.55	4.94	4.78	4.97	0.0
2012	MIL	MLB	37	3	0	0	26	0	36^1	44	10	8	29	2.0	7.2	45%	.315	1.43	7.68	5.86	6.72	-0.4
2013	*MIL*	*MLB*	*38*	*4*	*4*	*0*	*17*	*10*	74^1	*84*	*11*	*22*	*47*	*2.6*	*5.7*	*43%*	*.318*	*1.42*	*5.09*	*4.75*	*5.53*	*-0.4*

After 474 career starts, the deathless one toed the rubber in a relief role last year for the first time in 16 years. Improved walk and strikeout rates indicate that his stuff played up when coming out of the bullpen … okay, we'll stop. Obviously the words "stuff" and "played up" deserve quotation marks, and while the thought of Hernandez reaching the end of the line leaves a hollow spot in all of our souls, we're going to have to face it. Whatever voodoo allowed him to retire hitters with a fastball that wouldn't raise eyebrows in a school zone has likely run its course. While there's some value in having a rubber-armed swingman on the roster, a contender should find a better option, and a pretender should find a younger option. Fun fact: Livan will almost certainly retire with a higher career batting average than Dave Duncan.

Taylor Jungmann

Born: **12/18/1989** Age: **23**
Bats: **R** Throws: **R** Height: **6' 7"** Weight: **220**
Breakout: **21%** Improve: **57%** Collapse: **12%**
Attrition: **9%** MLB: **86%**

Comparables:
Brett Myers,Seth Greisinger,Carl Pavano

YEAR	TEAM	LVL	AGE	W	L	SV	G	GS	IP	H	HR	BB	SO	BB9	SO9	GB%	BABIP	WHIP	ERA	FIP	FRA	WARP
2012	BRV	A+	22	11	6	0	26	26	153	159	7	46	99	2.7	5.8	56%	.311	1.34	3.53	3.81	4.72	-0.1
2013	*MIL*	*MLB*	*23*	*2*	*3*	*0*	*7*	*7*	*40*	*45*	*6*	*16*	*23*	*3.6*	*5.2*	*51%*	*.310*	*1.54*	*5.82*	*5.20*	*6.32*	*-0.5*

Milwaukee's first pick in the 2011 draft, Jungmann has ideal size, a smooth delivery, and decent velocity, but didn't miss many bats in his minor-league debut. He was effective but far from dominant in the pitcher-friendly Florida State League, working his low-90s fastball down in the zone to generate plenty of groundballs, few home runs, and not many strikeouts. Jungmann's slurvy breaking pitch and changeup are works in progress, but he throws strikes and doesn't beat himself. It's early, but so far, Jungmann profiles as more of an innings-eater than an ace.

Brandon Kintzler

Born: **8/1/1984** Age: **28**
Bats: **R** Throws: **R** Height: **5' 11"** Weight: **185**
Breakout: **25%** Improve: **53%** Collapse: **27%**
Attrition: **8%** MLB: **84%**

Comparables:
Dave Schmidt,Justin Duchscherer,Juan Oviedo

YEAR	TEAM	LVL	AGE	W	L	SV	G	GS	IP	H	HR	BB	SO	BB9	SO9	GB%	BABIP	WHIP	ERA	FIP	FRA	WARP
2010	HUN	AA	25	1	0	10	20	0	22^1	11	0	1	23	0.4	9.3	60%	.200	0.54	0.40	1.59	3.10	0.5
2010	NAS	AAA	25	3	0	6	22	0	26^2	19	1	6	21	2.0	7.1	65%	.237	0.94	2.36	3.28	4.54	0.3
2010	MIL	MLB	25	0	1	0	7	0	7^1	10	2	4	9	4.9	11.0	75%	.444	1.91	7.36	5.83	5.78	-0.1
2011	NAS	AAA	26	0	0	0	1	0	1	0	0	0	2	0.0	18.0	—	.000	0.00	0.00	-0.22	-0.24	0.0
2011	MIL	MLB	26	1	1	0	9	0	14^2	14	3	3	15	1.8	9.2	60%	.275	1.16	3.68	4.22	5.10	-0.1
2012	BRV	A+	27	0	1	0	6	0	6	7	0	3	9	4.5	13.5	53%	.467	1.67	3.00	1.89	-1.56	0.2
2012	HUN	AA	27	0	2	9	31	0	35^2	35	1	12	20	3.0	5.0	63%	.306	1.32	3.28	3.56	4.56	0.2
2012	NAS	AAA	27	0	1	0	8	0	11^2	8	0	2	11	1.5	8.5	69%	.276	0.86	1.54	2.29	2.66	0.2
2012	MIL	MLB	27	3	0	0	14	0	16^2	18	1	7	14	3.8	7.6	51%	.340	1.50	3.78	3.50	3.89	0.2
2013	*MIL*	*MLB*	*28*	*2*	*1*	*1*	*31*	*0*	*38*	*36*	*5*	*12*	*33*	*2.7*	*7.9*	*54%*	*.304*	*1.25*	*4.17*	*4.12*	*4.53*	*0.2*

Kintzler returned from a year lost to elbow surgery and something called Valgus Extension Overload (or what a layman might call "a sore elbow caused by the unnatural stress of throwing a baseball really, really hard") to prove he was healthy and earn a September call-up. While his ability to throw a low-90s fastball and a usable slider differentiates him considerably from the masses, it's not particularly remarkable for a middle reliever. Given the state of Milwaukee's bullpen he may well earn a roster spot this spring, and the laws of probability say he's as likely as anyone to randomly post 50 solid innings—or pitch his way back to Nashville.

Kameron Loe

Born: **9/10/1981** Age: **31**
Bats: **R** Throws: **R** Height: **6' 9"** Weight: **240**
Breakout: **24%** Improve: **55%** Collapse: **30%**
Attrition: **9%** MLB: **85%**

Comparables:
Ramiro Mendoza,Justin Duchscherer,Dave Schmidt

YEAR	TEAM	LVL	AGE	W	L	SV	G	GS	IP	H	HR	BB	SO	BB9	SO9	GB%	BABIP	WHIP	ERA	FIP	FRA	WARP
2010	NAS	AAA	28	4	3	0	10	10	62^2	57	6	19	39	2.7	5.6	60%	.263	1.21	3.16	4.68	5.46	0.3
2010	MIL	MLB	28	3	5	0	53	0	58^1	54	6	15	46	2.3	7.1	60%	.281	1.18	2.78	3.74	4.31	0.5
2011	MIL	MLB	29	4	7	1	72	0	72	65	4	16	61	2.0	7.6	64%	.293	1.12	3.50	2.77	4.09	0.5
2012	MIL	MLB	30	6	5	2	70	0	68^1	78	9	20	55	2.6	7.2	59%	.319	1.43	4.61	4.25	5.34	0.0
2013	*MIL*	*MLB*	*31*	*3*	*2*	*2*	*47*	*3*	*65*	*63*	*8*	*17*	*50*	*2.4*	*6.9*	*56%*	*.298*	*1.23*	*4.10*	*4.05*	*4.46*	*0.4*

A sinkerballer named Loe shouldn't have any trouble remembering where he needs to locate his pitches, but last season the towering right-hander kept making mistakes up in the zone. The inevitable result: more home runs and hits allowed and a drop in the groundball rate that has made him a valuable bullpen workhorse. Loe's struggles were amplified down the stretch and he struggled to retire lefties, a combination that made it easy for Milwaukee to cut ties with him at season's end. He still misses a lot of bats, and if he can work out his mechanical kinks and stay on top of his sinker, Loe should continue his worm-killing ways well into his thirties.

Jorge Lopez

Born: **2/10/1993** Age: **20**
Bats: **R** Throws: **R** Height: **6' 5"** Weight: **165**
Breakout: **45%** Improve: **60%** Collapse: **31%**
Attrition: **5%** MLB: **76%**

Comparables:
Jim Waugh,Dick Calmus,Bob Miller

YEAR	TEAM	LVL	AGE	W	L	SV	G	GS	IP	H	HR	BB	SO	BB9	SO9	GB%	BABIP	WHIP	ERA	FIP	FRA	WARP
2011	BRR	Rk	18	0	0	0	4	4	12	13	0	3	10	2.2	7.5	44%	.222	1.33	2.25	3.45	5.31	0.0
2012	BRR	Rk	19	1	3	2	7	3	25^1	27	2	12	20	4.3	7.1	54%	.289	1.54	5.33	5.48	6.13	0.1
2012	DBW	Rk	19	0	1	0	5	3	22^2	22	0	10	26	4.0	10.3	—	.344	1.41	4.76	2.72	0.00	0.5
2013	*MIL*	*MLB*	*20*	*0*	*0*	*0*	*9*	*0*	*33^1*	*39*	*6*	*21*	*20*	*5.7*	*5.5*	*46%*	*.317*	*1.80*	*6.83*	*6.23*	*7.42*	*-0.7*

You're as likely to divine the future by studying chicken entrails or coffee grounds as you are from a surgical dissection of Rookie League numbers, so let's just say it's all about projection with Lopez. A lanky 20-year-old who figures to add velocity and stamina as he fills out, Lopez can already reach the low-90s with his fastball and can flash a solid curveball. All he needs to do to reach the bigs is stay healthy, command his fastball, develop secondary stuff, master the art of pitch sequencing, translate his tools into production, and learn how to retire Joey Votto. No pressure, son.

Santo Manzanillo

Born: **12/20/1988** Age: **24**
Bats: **R** Throws: **R** Height: **6' 1"** Weight: **190**
Breakout: **27%** Improve: **72%** Collapse: **16%**
Attrition: **14%** MLB: **77%**
Comparables:
Ron Law,Fernando Arroyo,Ken Clay

YEAR	TEAM	LVL	AGE	W	L	SV	G	GS	IP	H	HR	BB	SO	BB9	SO9	GB%	BABIP	WHIP	ERA	FIP	FRA	WARP
2011	BRV	A+	22	1	0	10	28	0	41^{1}	31	2	14	43	3.0	9.4	—	.259	1.09	1.52	3.03	3.29	0.0
2011	HUN	AA	22	0	1	7	20	0	20^{1}	13	2	12	19	5.3	8.4	41%	.235	1.23	2.21	4.63	3.31	0.1
2012	BRR	Rk	23	0	1	0	2	0	2^{2}	4	0	0	2	0.0	6.8	75%	.500	1.50	10.12	2.88	0.82	0.1
2012	WIS	A	23	2	1	0	4	0	6	5	1	5	2	7.5	3.0	40%	.211	1.67	7.50	7.35	11.16	-0.3
2012	HUN	AA	23	0	4	1	12	0	13^{1}	13	2	10	10	6.8	6.8	44%	.282	1.73	6.07	5.84	7.16	-0.3
2013	*MIL*	*MLB*	*24*	*1*	*0*	*1*	*21*	*0*	33^{1}	*39*	*6*	*21*	*19*	*5.7*	*5.1*	*44%*	*.312*	*1.79*	*6.71*	*6.29*	*7.29*	*-0.8*

Manzanillo is lucky to be alive after being thrown from his Hummer while driving to the Brewers academy in San Pedro de Macoris shortly after the 2011 season, separating his shoulder. The young right-hander has spent most of the last year not quite recovering his health, posting a few minor-league innings and working in the Arizona Fall League before coming up sore yet again in winter ball. If he ever bounces back, opposing batters had best strap themselves in, as Manzanillo has long had trouble controlling his triple-digit heater, and a long layoff can't have helped.

Shaun Marcum

Born: **12/14/1981** Age: **31**
Bats: **R** Throws: **R** Height: **6' 1"** Weight: **195**
Breakout: **11%** Improve: **36%** Collapse: **28%**
Attrition: **12%** MLB: **94%**
Comparables:
Roy Oswalt,Freddy Garcia,Bronson Arroyo

YEAR	TEAM	LVL	AGE	W	L	SV	G	GS	IP	H	HR	BB	SO	BB9	SO9	GB%	BABIP	WHIP	ERA	FIP	FRA	WARP
2010	TOR	MLB	28	13	8	0	31	31	195^{1}	181	24	43	165	2.0	7.6	39%	.279	1.15	3.64	3.71	4.19	3.2
2011	MIL	MLB	29	13	7	0	33	33	200^{2}	175	22	57	158	2.6	7.1	40%	.262	1.16	3.54	3.70	4.39	2.5
2012	WIS	A	30	1	0	0	3	3	12^{2}	9	1	3	10	2.1	7.1	41%	.222	0.95	2.84	3.51	4.02	0.1
2012	MIL	MLB	30	7	4	0	21	21	124	116	16	41	109	3.0	7.9	37%	.280	1.27	3.70	4.14	4.44	1.0
2013	*MIL*	*MLB*	*31*	*8*	*7*	*0*	*20*	*20*	122^{1}	*109*	*16*	*32*	*106*	*2.4*	*7.8*	*40%*	*.282*	*1.15*	*3.68*	*3.95*	*4.00*	*1.5*

Watching Marcum pitch can be a joy, as the human-scaled right-hander consistently distracts the Goliaths facing him with an array of off-speed junk before jamming them with his mid-80s heater—the pitching equivalent of Otter telling Greg Marmalard to look at his thumb before cold-cocking him. If only Marcum could embody our bully-revenge fantasies more frequently, he'd be a wealthier man. To no one's surprise, Marcum missed two months with a barking elbow last summer, leaving his career total of 200-inning seasons stuck at one. When healthy, he's a valuable mid-rotation starter whose extreme fly-ball tendencies would play best in a larger ballpark, but he'll have to shed his reputation for fragility in order to earn the big bucks his talent and productivity otherwise deserve.

Chris Narveson

Born: **12/20/1981** Age: **31**
Bats: **L** Throws: **L** Height: **6' 4"** Weight: **205**
Breakout: **16%** Improve: **54%** Collapse: **16%**
Attrition: **13%** MLB: **81%**
Comparables:
Chris Oxspring,Gary Peters,Jason Jennings

YEAR	TEAM	LVL	AGE	W	L	SV	G	GS	IP	H	HR	BB	SO	BB9	SO9	GB%	BABIP	WHIP	ERA	FIP	FRA	WARP
2010	MIL	MLB	28	12	9	0	37	28	167^{2}	172	21	59	137	3.2	7.4	41%	.301	1.38	4.99	4.25	4.65	2.7
2011	MIL	MLB	29	11	8	0	30	28	161^{2}	160	17	65	126	3.6	7.0	44%	.292	1.39	4.45	4.03	4.93	1.0
2012	MIL	MLB	30	1	1	0	2	2	9	10	2	4	5	4.0	5.0	41%	.267	1.56	7.00	6.25	7.37	-0.2
2013	*MIL*	*MLB*	*31*	*2*	*2*	*0*	*7*	*7*	*37*	*36*	*5*	*13*	*30*	*3.1*	*7.2*	*42%*	*.298*	*1.33*	*4.59*	*4.39*	*4.99*	*0.0*

It's been a good story so far. Saddled with marginal lefty stuff and a name seemingly designed to be shouted by an angry sitcom boss—"Narveson! Get in here!"—a young starter toils away in the minors for a full decade before improbably earning his shot, posts two credible seasons in a big-league rotation, then suffers a season-ending shoulder injury that clouds his future. Can he bounce back? Will he still have the moxie to retire major-league hitters with a mid-80s fastball and three unremarkable off-speed pitches, fulfilling his fifth-starter dreams? Tune in this spring to find out.

Jimmy Nelson

Born: **6/5/1989** Age: **24**
Bats: **R** Throws: **R** Height: **6' 7"** Weight: **245**
Breakout: **27%** Improve: **57%** Collapse: **18%**
Attrition: **18%** MLB: **93%**
Comparables:
Pete Smith,Freddy Garcia,Shawn Hillegas

YEAR	TEAM	LVL	AGE	W	L	SV	G	GS	IP	H	HR	BB	SO	BB9	SO9	GB%	BABIP	WHIP	ERA	FIP	FRA	WARP
2010	HEL	Rk	21	2	0	3	12	0	26^{2}	30	2	13	33	4.4	11.1	61%	.363	1.61	3.71	3.95	4.94	0.4
2011	WIS	A	22	8	9	0	26	25	146	146	9	65	120	4.0	7.4	48%	.292	1.45	4.38	3.98	4.93	0.2
2012	BRV	A+	23	4	4	0	13	13	81^{1}	63	3	25	77	2.8	8.5	61%	.273	1.08	2.21	3.09	2.63	0.0
2012	HUN	AA	23	2	4	0	10	10	46	34	2	37	42	7.2	8.2	57%	.256	1.54	3.91	4.49	4.61	0.4
2013	*MIL*	*MLB*	*24*	*2*	*2*	*0*	*8*	*5*	35^{1}	*36*	*5*	*18*	*28*	*4.7*	*7.2*	*52%*	*.305*	*1.53*	*5.34*	*4.98*	*5.81*	*-0.3*

Nelson's year was really more of a half-Nelson, as the beefy right-hander shone while outpitching the more pedigreed Jungmann and Bradley in High-A, then lost his feel for the strike zone after a midseason promotion to Huntsville. A hulking presence on the mound, Nelson gets great mileage out of a heavy low-90s sinker that hitters continually beat into the ground, and his slider is much more than a show-me pitch. Whether he grows into a durable mid-rotation starter depends on his fleeting control, as those triumphant two months as a Brevard County Manatee represent the only time his walk rate was anywhere near acceptable. He'll get another chance to pass the Double-A exam this summer.

Michael Olmsted
Born: **5/2/1987** Age: **26**
Bats: **R** Throws: **R** Height: **6' 7"** Weight: **245**
Breakout: **35%** Improve: **52%** Collapse: **18%**
Attrition: **20%** MLB: **89%**
Comparables:
John Wetteland,Robert Coello,Ugueth Urbina

YEAR	TEAM	LVL	AGE	W	L	SV	G	GS	IP	H	HR	BB	SO	BB9	SO9	GB%	BABIP	WHIP	ERA	FIP	FRA	WARP
2011	RSX	Rk	24	1	0	2	3	0	4	1	0	1	4	2.2	9.0	38%	.125	0.50	0.00	2.17	4.67	0.0
2011	GRN	A	24	1	0	4	18	0	28^1	17	0	9	44	2.9	14.0	—	.321	0.92	1.59	1.59	1.72	0.0
2012	SLM	A+	25	0	2	16	33	0	39^1	25	1	8	61	1.8	14.0	33%	.289	0.84	2.29	1.38	0.91	1.4
2012	PME	AA	25	1	2	3	14	0	20	11	0	7	31	3.2	13.9	39%	.268	0.90	0.00	1.30	0.90	0.6
2013	*MIL*	*MLB*	*26*	*1*	*1*	*1*	*30*	*0*	*37^1*	*32*	*5*	*16*	*42*	*3.8*	*10.0*	*40%*	*.309*	*1.28*	*4.05*	*3.98*	*4.40*	*0.2*

A massive right-hander with mid-90s heat and a wipeout slider, Olmsted has resurrected his career after Tommy John surgery, a stint in the Japanese minor leagues, and months kicking around California backlots before Boston gave him a second chance. Since making his way back onto the map, Olmsted's walk-to-strikeout ratio has been off the charts, and when the Red Sox couldn't find a place for him on the 40-man roster last fall, the Brewers swooped in and signed him. His Gossage-like mound presence and unflappable demeanor can only help him, and if he can work the same tricks against Triple-A hitters this year, Milwaukee may have found another power arm to help cure its bullpen woes.

Manny Parra
Born: **10/30/1982** Age: **30**
Bats: **L** Throws: **L** Height: **6' 4"** Weight: **205**
Breakout: **35%** Improve: **63%** Collapse: **12%**
Attrition: **16%** MLB: **85%**
Comparables:
Casey Fossum,Steve Carlton,Bob Lemon

YEAR	TEAM	LVL	AGE	W	L	SV	G	GS	IP	H	HR	BB	SO	BB9	SO9	GB%	BABIP	WHIP	ERA	FIP	FRA	WARP
2010	MIL	MLB	27	3	10	0	42	16	122	135	18	63	129	4.6	9.5	48%	.337	1.62	5.02	4.53	4.54	1.7
2011	WIS	A	28	1	0	0	1	0	2	0	0	0	4	0.0	18.0	—	.000	0.00	0.00	-0.64	-0.70	0.0
2011	NAS	AAA	28	0	1	0	7	1	10^1	12	0	5	8	4.4	7.0	67%	.333	1.65	6.10	3.69	5.46	0.0
2012	MIL	MLB	29	2	3	0	62	0	58^2	62	3	35	61	5.4	9.4	49%	.345	1.65	5.06	3.66	3.69	0.8
2013	*MIL*	*MLB*	*30*	*2*	*2*	*0*	*26*	*4*	*45*	*46*	*6*	*20*	*41*	*4.0*	*8.2*	*49%*	*.324*	*1.46*	*4.90*	*4.44*	*5.33*	*-0.2*

Parra returned from back and shoulder complaints that cost him all of 2011, proving his lefty heat and four-pitch variety pack were still intact. Also intact was the miserable walk rate that has perpetually undercut his stuff and bedeviled the organization for years. Before his latest injuries there had been some hope that moving him to the pen would help cure his free-pass addiction, but that treatment has proven ineffective. Parra was reasonably successful against lefty hitters last season, and an optimist who chooses to ignore his career platoon splits could envision him as a future LOOGY. That's a far cry from the rotation stalwart many hoped he would become.

Ariel Pena
Born: **5/20/1989** Age: **24**
Bats: **R** Throws: **R** Height: **6' 4"** Weight: **186**
Breakout: **26%** Improve: **61%** Collapse: **21%**
Attrition: **20%** MLB: **92%**
Comparables:
Mike Campbell,Kip Wells,Ryan Dempster

YEAR	TEAM	LVL	AGE	W	L	SV	G	GS	IP	H	HR	BB	SO	BB9	SO9	GB%	BABIP	WHIP	ERA	FIP	FRA	WARP
2010	CDR	A	21	7	5	0	18	18	103	93	7	60	88	5.2	7.7	46%	.285	1.49	3.76	4.74	5.57	0.2
2010	RCU	A+	21	0	1	0	3	3	10^1	10	0	13	8	11.4	7.0	38%	.345	2.23	8.74	5.97	8.47	-0.3
2011	SBR	A+	22	10	6	0	27	27	151^2	154	10	81	180	4.8	10.7	—	.358	1.55	4.45	4.18	4.54	0.0
2011	SLC	AAA	22	0	0	0	1	1	4	7	0	4	3	9.0	6.8	53%	.467	2.75	2.25	5.28	5.10	0.1
2012	ARK	AA	23	6	6	0	19	19	114^1	95	14	42	111	3.3	8.7	43%	.264	1.20	2.99	4.06	4.34	0.8
2012	HUN	AA	23	0	2	0	7	7	32^1	40	5	23	29	6.4	8.1	43%	.385	1.95	7.24	5.96	7.80	-0.4
2013	*MIL*	*MLB*	*24*	*2*	*3*	*0*	*7*	*7*	*37^2*	*39*	*6*	*21*	*29*	*5.1*	*7.0*	*41%*	*.305*	*1.59*	*5.73*	*5.40*	*6.23*	*-0.4*

While it's true Pena has by far the best control of any pitcher who came to Milwaukee in the Greinke deal, that only means he's a little more tame than Hellweg. The willowy Dominican has long struggled to fill the strike zone, although he made progress commanding his low-90s fastball and plus slider last year. Stop us if you've heard this one before, but if he can improve his command, develop his changeup, and learn to work lower in the zone, he could become a mid-rotation starter. If not, he'll likely earn his pension in middle relief.

Wily Peralta
Born: **5/8/1989** Age: **24**
Bats: **R** Throws: **R** Height: **6' 3"** Weight: **240**
Breakout: **32%** Improve: **61%** Collapse: **20%**
Attrition: **20%** MLB: **86%**
Comparables:
Denny Bautista,Edwin Jackson,Juan Mateo

YEAR	TEAM	LVL	AGE	W	L	SV	G	GS	IP	H	HR	BB	SO	BB9	SO9	GB%	BABIP	WHIP	ERA	FIP	FRA	WARP
2010	BRV	A+	21	6	3	0	19	17	105	102	5	40	75	3.4	6.4	54%	.298	1.35	3.86	3.94	4.77	-0.3
2010	HUN	AA	21	2	3	0	8	8	42^1	43	5	24	29	5.1	6.2	54%	.297	1.58	3.62	5.54	6.46	-0.2
2011	HUN	AA	22	9	7	0	21	21	119^2	106	9	48	117	3.6	8.8	50%	.267	1.29	3.46	3.63	4.98	0.4
2011	NAS	AAA	22	2	0	0	5	5	31	21	0	11	40	3.2	11.6	50%	.274	1.03	2.03	2.36	2.31	0.9
2012	NAS	AAA	23	7	11	0	28	28	146^2	154	9	78	143	4.8	8.8	54%	.352	1.58	4.66	4.29	4.65	1.0
2012	MIL	MLB	23	2	1	0	6	5	29	24	0	11	23	3.4	7.1	57%	.304	1.21	2.48	2.69	3.12	0.6
2013	*MIL*	*MLB*	*24*	*3*	*4*	*0*	*11*	*11*	*61*	*60*	*8*	*29*	*51*	*4.3*	*7.6*	*49%*	*.310*	*1.47*	*5.00*	*4.66*	*5.44*	*-0.2*

The Battleship Peralta steamed into Milwaukee harbor last September, firing mid-90s broadsides that usually found their target and pummeling opposing hitters into submission. It was an impressive debut, especially when you consider the burly right-hander had spent the summer doing little in Triple-A to put to rest longstanding concerns about his lack of command

and consistent inconsistency. Peralta's heavy sinker often finds infielders' gloves and is a big-league pitch, as is a slider that can be hell-on-wheels against righties. His changeup is another story, and one month spent filling the zone doesn't exactly prove his control problems are behind him. The Brewers will give him every chance to earn a role with the big club this spring, and if he continues to hit his spots he can be a solid contributor in the middle of the rotation.

Francisco Rodriguez

Born: **1/7/1982** Age: **31**
Bats: **R** Throws: **R** Height: **6' 1"** Weight: **195**
Breakout: **30%** Improve: **51%** Collapse: **19%**
Attrition: **5%** MLB: **93%**

Comparables:
Frank Francisco,Mike Jackson,Jeff Montgomery

YEAR	TEAM	LVL	AGE	W	L	SV	G	GS	IP	H	HR	BB	SO	BB9	SO9	GB%	BABIP	WHIP	ERA	FIP	FRA	WARP
2010	NYN	MLB	28	4	2	25	53	0	57^{1}	45	3	21	67	3.3	10.5	44%	.294	1.15	2.20	2.65	2.63	1.3
2011	MIL	MLB	29	4	0	0	31	0	29	23	1	10	33	3.1	10.2	52%	.289	1.14	1.86	2.20	2.55	0.7
2011	NYN	MLB	29	2	2	23	42	0	42^{2}	44	3	16	46	3.4	9.7	53%	.342	1.41	3.16	3.02	3.34	0.6
2012	MIL	MLB	30	2	7	3	78	0	72	65	8	31	72	3.9	9.0	42%	.294	1.33	4.38	3.87	4.70	0.2
2013	*MIL*	*MLB*	*31*	*4*	*2*	*8*	*68*	*0*	*67*	*54*	*7*	*26*	*76*	*3.5*	*10.2*	*44%*	*.296*	*1.19*	*3.37*	*3.45*	*3.66*	*1.0*

Baseball can be a fickle mistress. When a misguided arbitration offer kept Rodriguez on the Brewers roster for 2012, the organization was criticized for its extravagance in paying closer money for a reliever who would merely be setting up John Axford. The Brewers were hailed as visionaries, however, after Rodriguez took the reins from a struggling Axford and saved not only the bullpen but Milwaukee's season—or at least that would have been the case if K-Rod hadn't turned into a pumpkin at exactly the same time. Rodriguez maintained his low-90s velocity and posted his typically enviable walk and strikeout rates, but batters had a much easier time making contact and hit twice as many home runs—poor harbingers for his future. Only 31 but with a lot of miles on his arm, K-Rod was a risky bet for the Brewers even before his September arrest for domestic abuse.

Mark Rogers

Born: **1/30/1986** Age: **27**
Bats: **R** Throws: **R** Height: **6' 3"** Weight: **226**
Breakout: **22%** Improve: **52%** Collapse: **23%**
Attrition: **20%** MLB: **84%**

Comparables:
Robinson Tejeda,Vinegar Bend Mizell,Aaron Sele

YEAR	TEAM	LVL	AGE	W	L	SV	G	GS	IP	H	HR	BB	SO	BB9	SO9	GB%	BABIP	WHIP	ERA	FIP	FRA	WARP
2010	HUN	AA	24	6	8	0	24	24	111^{2}	86	3	69	111	5.6	8.9	56%	.276	1.39	3.71	3.76	4.54	1.8
2010	NAS	AAA	24	0	0	0	1	1	4^{1}	3	0	3	3	6.3	6.3	61%	.231	1.40	2.09	4.28	4.45	0.2
2010	MIL	MLB	24	0	0	0	4	2	10	2	0	3	11	2.7	9.9	52%	.095	0.50	1.80	2.11	2.34	0.3
2011	BRR	Rk	25	0	0	0	5	3	13	13	1	5	11	3.5	7.6	51%	.316	1.38	4.85	4.83	4.46	0.3
2011	BRV	A+	25	0	3	0	5	5	16^{1}	22	4	15	17	8.3	9.4	—	.333	2.27	9.37	7.61	8.27	0.0
2011	NAS	AAA	25	0	2	0	5	5	15	21	1	22	12	13.2	7.2	44%	.625	2.87	13.20	7.45	10.48	-0.2
2012	NAS	AAA	26	6	6	0	18	18	95^{1}	92	13	49	74	4.6	7.0	43%	.288	1.48	4.72	5.59	6.34	-0.7
2012	MIL	MLB	26	3	1	0	7	7	39	36	5	14	41	3.2	9.5	44%	.298	1.28	3.92	3.85	3.96	0.8
2013	*MIL*	*MLB*	*27*	*3*	*4*	*0*	*11*	*11*	*52*	*48*	*7*	*26*	*45*	*4.4*	*7.9*	*48%*	*.295*	*1.41*	*4.69*	*4.72*	*5.10*	*0.1*

If there's one thing you can't question about Rogers, it's his determination. The former top pick has an injury history longer and more unfortunate than the *Dune* director's cut, yet last year he overcame his latest ailment (carpal tunnel surgery), a stimulant suspension, and a forgettable half-season at Triple-A to contribute a solid string of starts with the big club. The Brewers then shut him down because of innings limitations, and therein lies the question: How much can he pitch without winding up on the shelf? History would answer "not much," and when you factor in his still-unsolved control issues, it's clear his mid-90s heat will play best in the bullpen, if at all.

Josh Stinson

Born: **3/14/1988** Age: **25**
Bats: **R** Throws: **R** Height: **6' 5"** Weight: **210**
Breakout: **16%** Improve: **50%** Collapse: **28%**
Attrition: **15%** MLB: **89%**

Comparables:
Dan Serafini,George Susce,Ron Bryant

YEAR	TEAM	LVL	AGE	W	L	SV	G	GS	IP	H	HR	BB	SO	BB9	SO9	GB%	BABIP	WHIP	ERA	FIP	FRA	WARP
2010	BIN	AA	22	9	3	1	32	14	110^{1}	108	7	50	68	4.1	5.5	51%	.292	1.43	4.24	4.42	5.33	0.3
2010	BUF	AAA	22	2	2	0	4	4	28	22	5	8	21	2.6	6.8	52%	.218	1.07	2.57	4.97	5.84	0.0
2011	BIN	AA	23	4	3	6	27	2	47^{1}	46	1	16	39	3.0	7.4	48%	.286	1.31	3.99	3.30	3.03	0.5
2011	BUF	AAA	23	3	7	0	13	13	61^{2}	77	7	33	32	4.8	4.7	44%	.353	1.78	7.44	5.33	6.64	-0.5
2011	NYN	MLB	23	0	2	1	14	0	13	14	1	7	8	4.8	5.5	48%	.317	1.62	6.92	4.38	6.16	-0.2
2012	HUN	AA	24	11	9	1	29	24	145^{1}	167	7	71	91	4.4	5.6	55%	.328	1.64	3.16	4.21	4.54	1.8
2012	MIL	MLB	24	0	0	0	6	1	9^{1}	7	1	5	3	4.8	2.9	47%	.207	1.29	0.96	5.49	5.46	0.0
2013	*MIL*	*MLB*	*25*	*2*	*3*	*0*	*15*	*7*	*50^{1}*	*55*	*7*	*24*	*31*	*4.3*	*5.6*	*48%*	*.309*	*1.57*	*5.67*	*5.21*	*6.17*	*-0.6*

Stinson capped a rather somnambulant campaign in the Huntsville rotation with a surprise September call-up, even earning a start against the Padres on the last day of the season. It may be his last big-league start, however, as the low-90s fastball and flat slider he delivers from a low-three-quarters slot doesn't fool that many Double-A batters, let alone the world's best. It will take a whole lot of Lake Louie Milk Stout to drown the sorrows of Brewers fans if Stinson ever wins a rotation job, but there's an outside chance he could carve out a niche as a ROOGY.

Tyler Thornburg
Born: **9/29/1988** Age: **24**
Bats: **R** Throws: **R** Height: **6' 0"** Weight: **185**
Breakout: **33%** Improve: **61%** Collapse: **12%**
Attrition: **6%** MLB: **97%**
Comparables:
Luis Tiant, Josh Beckett, Johnny Cueto

YEAR	TEAM	LVL	AGE	W	L	SV	G	GS	IP	H	HR	BB	SO	BB9	SO9	GB%	BABIP	WHIP	ERA	FIP	FRA	WARP
2011	WIS	A	22	7	0	0	12	12	68^{2}	49	3	25	76	3.3	10.0	47%	.263	1.08	1.57	2.98	3.99	0.2
2011	BRV	A+	22	3	6	0	12	12	68	45	5	33	84	4.4	11.1	—	.256	1.15	3.57	3.51	3.81	0.0
2012	HUN	AA	23	8	1	0	13	13	75	57	6	24	71	2.9	8.5	41%	.250	1.08	3.00	3.33	4.23	1.1
2012	NAS	AAA	23	2	3	0	8	8	37^{2}	38	1	13	42	3.1	10.0	53%	.359	1.35	3.58	2.98	3.21	0.5
2012	MIL	MLB	23	0	0	0	8	3	22	24	8	7	20	2.9	8.2	45%	.271	1.41	4.50	7.14	6.54	-0.1
2013	*MIL*	*MLB*	*24*	*3*	*3*	*0*	*10*	*8*	*45^{1}*	*42*	*7*	*17*	*45*	*3.4*	*8.9*	*44%*	*.300*	*1.29*	*4.30*	*4.35*	*4.67*	*0.3*

Thornburg began last season by dominating in his first taste of the high minors, finished it in Milwaukee, and in the process demonstrated how valuable his arm can be. Short in stature but long on stuff, Thornburg has a heater that can reach the mid-90s, a changeup and curveball that are more than just distractions, and an odd delivery that hides the ball well. He's a fly-ball pitcher who may struggle to keep the ball in the park, but he limits the damage by keeping his walks in check. Pitchers his size will always have their durability questioned, and his stuff might play up in a relief role, but Thornburg has proven he can survive a starter's workload and profiles as a solid contributor at the back of the rotation.

LINEOUTS

HITTERS

PLAYER	TEAM	LVL	AGE	PA	R	2B	3B	HR	RBI	BB	SO	SB-CS	AVG/OBP/SLG	TAv	BABIP	BRR	FRAA	WARP
SS O. Arcia	—	—	—	—	—	—	—	—	—	—	—	—	—	—	—	—	—	—
CF M. Haniger	WIS	A	21	58	9	4	0	1	8	7	13	1-0	.286/.379/.429	.262	.361	0.9	CF(9): -0.7	0.2
CF J. Prince	HUN	AA	24	596	74	28	3	7	55	74	107	41-18	.251/.346/.360	.262	.301	1.5	CF(96): -11.7, SS(1): 0.1	0.0
CF D. Richardson	—	—	—	—	—	—	—	—	—	—	—	—	—	—	—	—	—	—

Dominican shortstop prodigy **Orlando Arcia** broke his ankle in May and never made it back on the field, postponing his much-anticipated stateside debut until this year. ⊘ Supplemental first-rounder **Mitch Haniger** tore up his knee before he could tear up the Midwest League last summer, but now that he's healthy, we'll soon see if he can deliver on his power potential. ⊘ The fastest thing ever to come out of Sulphur, Louisiana, **Josh Prince** moved from shortstop to center field and flew back onto prospect radars by drawing walks, stealing bases, and raking in the Arizona Fall League; adding to his glove collection may help him grow into a speedy super-utility player. ⊘ You have to respect **D'Vontrey Richardson**, as the toolsy outfielder and former Florida State quarterback decided the minor-league grind wasn't for him and followed his bliss back to school; the Brewers stand at the ready if he chooses to come back and give it another go.

PITCHERS

PLAYER	TEAM	LVL	AGE	W	L	SV	IP	H	HR	BB	SO	BB9	SO9	GB%	BABIP	WHIP	ERA	FIP	FRA	WARP
N. Bucci	BRV	A+	21	2	2	0	31^{2}	25	3	15	37	4.3	10.5	31%	.253	1.26	1.99	3.99	2.95	0.3
H. Burgos	BRV	A+	24	2	1	0	41^{1}	21	1	6	41	1.3	8.9	48%	.202	0.65	0.87	2.23	1.94	0.4
	HUN	AA	24	6	1	0	83^{1}	68	3	28	77	3.0	8.3	49%	.292	1.15	1.94	2.88	3.31	1.3
	NAS	AAA	24	2	2	0	46^{1}	39	4	15	35	2.9	6.8	41%	.257	1.17	2.91	4.31	4.56	0.2
V. Chulk	NAS	AAA	33	3	0	1	25^{2}	17	2	9	25	3.2	8.8	43%	.227	1.01	1.75	3.78	4.87	0.1
	MIL	MLB	33	1	0	0	9	17	0	4	10	4.0	10.0	27%	.500	2.33	10.00	2.25	2.42	0.3
F. De La Cruz	IOW	AAA	28	1	6	0	94^{2}	91	6	58	57	5.5	5.4	49%	.279	1.57	3.80	5.22	5.92	0.4
T. Dillard	MIL	MLB	28	0	2	0	37	45	3	14	29	3.4	7.1	54%	.353	1.59	4.38	3.84	3.70	0.5
D. Goforth	WIS	A	23	10	8	0	150^{2}	154	16	63	93	3.8	5.6	50%	.291	1.44	4.66	4.93	7.04	-0.7
A. Leon	CCH	AA	25	3	2	2	63^{2}	60	6	33	58	4.7	8.2	53%	.302	1.46	4.38	4.38	6.14	-0.3
D. Magnifico	HEL	Rk	21	0	3	0	21^{2}	21	2	15	25	6.2	10.4	63%	.328	1.66	5.82	5.40	5.82	0.2
J. Sanchez	HUN	AA	24	3	2	11	45^{1}	34	2	13	41	2.6	8.1	50%	.248	1.04	1.59	2.97	3.04	0.8
	NAS	AAA	24	4	1	0	26^{1}	23	0	9	23	3.1	7.9	58%	.303	1.22	1.71	2.94	3.19	0.3
C. Scarpetta	—	—	—	—	—	—	—	—	—	—	—	—	—	—	—	—	—	—	—	—

Canadian right-hander **Nick Bucci** worked his way back from early-season arm woes to post solid numbers in High-A; the club loves his makeup and expects him to produce more than you'd expect from his fringe-average stuff. ⚾ The organization's minor-league pitcher of the year, **Hiram Burgos** used a five-pitch assortment to dominate at three stops and earn a spot on the 40-man roster; if he can work his low-velo magic again at Triple-A, he could get a look later this summer. ⚾ Three years removed from his last major-league appearance, **Vinnie Chulk** popped up in the Milwaukee relief corps last May and stuck around for a few minutes, which tells you all you need to know about the Brewers' bullpen woes. ⚾ Fireballing reliever **Frankie De La Cruz** is back with the Brewers after spending a year in Iowa and Taiwan; with little control of his high-90s heater, he's a bullpen option, but not a particularly good one. ⚾ **Tim Dillard** can induce enough double-play grounders with his mid-80s sinker to get filed somewhere between bullpen filler and bullpen beef, although managers that let him face too many lefties deserve the indigestion that's sure to follow. ⚾ Not to be confused with the well-respected Cabarrus County horticulture agent, hard-throwing **David Goforth** spent his full-season debut hoping his career could take root, but inconsistent secondary stuff and a low strikeout rate have so far stunted his growth. ⚾ Stout fireballer **Arcenio Leon** offers mid-90s heat and a wipeout slider but rarely has a clue where either pitch is going; if he can somehow develop a little control, he could help out in middle relief. ⚾ Radar-gun enthusiast **Damien Magnifico** draws gasps with his triple-digit heater, but his lack of command and subpar secondary pitches reveal the magician's hand. ⚾ Minor-league closer **Jesus Sanchez** keeps his walks down with excellent command of a low-90s fastball, and he flashes a solid changeup; as with every biped they can get their mitts on, the Brewers will give him a look for the bullpen this spring. ⚾ Curveball *artista* **Cody Scarpetta** underwent Tommy John surgery last summer and won't be able to get back on the prospect trail until midseason at least.

MANAGER: RON ROENICKE

YEAR	TEAM	W-L	Pythag +/-	Avg PC	100+ P	120+ P	QS	BQS	REL	REL w Zero R	IBB	PH	PH Avg	PH HR	SB2	CS2	SB3	CS3	SAC Att	SAC %	POS SAC	Squeeze	Swing	In Play
2011	MIL	96-66	1	99.3	85	2	98	7	434	342	16	257	.222	5	12	5	0	3	117	82.1%	54	5	297	109
2012	MIL	83-79	1	97.1	84	0	85	3	512	370	20	315	.223	4	24	5	0	2	129	71.3%	60	8	356	90

There's a lot to like about Roenicke, especially where his job counts the most. He kept a steady hand on the tiller during both Milwaukee's first-half struggles and its improbable stretch run. Players respect him and respond to his go-go-gadget offensive approach. He tempers his desire to run the bases when his charges won't succeed, and lets them loose when they will. He eschews the intentional walk. But seriously, something has to be done about all those bunts. Excluding pitchers, the Brewers laid down 25 percent more sacrifices than any other National League team, and Roenicke's boys led the league with eight squeezes—only Crazy Ozzie called for even half that many. It's one thing to take the bat away from, say, Edwin Maysonet, but when you're asking Corey Hart to lay one down, it's time for an intervention. Outs are almost always more valuable than bases, especially in the context of Milwaukee's power-packed lineup, and while it may seem like small beer, a few runs lost here and there may someday cost the Brewers a pennant.

Minnesota Twins

2012: DOOMED TO FAIL

A large number of things went right for the last-place Twins in 2012, especially in terms of improved health by key position players, but none of those things could overcome the fact that the philosophy underpinning the team is rotten to the core.

TWINS PROSPECTUS

2012 W-L: 66-96, 5th in AL Central

Pythag	.419	27th	DER	.706	18th
RS/G	4.33	16th	B-Age	28.9	21st
RA/G	5.14	28th	P-Age	27.7	10th
TAv	.259	15th	Salary	$100.4	11th
BRR	4.5	9th	M$/MW	$5.00	27th
TAv-P	.276	28th	DL Days	702	23rd
FIP	4.61	28th	DL WARP	2.5	23rd

Three-Year Park Factors	
Overall	101
HR/RH	110
HR/LH	93
AVG/RH	112
AVG/LH	104

Target Field (2010)
Att. % of Capacity: 86.8% (8th)
Dim. 339, 377, 404, 367, 328

Three years into its existence, Target Field remains a worst-case scenario for Joe Mauer's home-run totals.

When people get heavily invested in any political philosophy, they tend to take it to its logical extreme. Thus are the disciples of Ayn Rand and Karl Marx born and grow insufferable. These extreme systems prove woefully inadequate when encountering the realities of human nature and the real world. That's why, despite the fervor of Randian and Marxist aficionados, neither vision has actually been realized in any country, ever. Serious people understand that any ideology is doomed if rigidly followed to its logical extreme.

And so it goes for the Minnesota Twins, who are fervently devoted to the idea that strike-throwing soft-tossers who pitch to contact will be their saviors, and are true believers in the gospel of limiting walks. They tried to find the next Brad Radke, but found only the next Nick Blackburn. The Twins were the only team in the majors to strike out fewer than 1,000 batters, and finished more than 150 punchouts behind the next worst team. The club was led in strikeouts by a man they traded in July (Francisco Liriano), and he was the only Twin to strike out more than 100. Relying on suspect defense went about as well as you'd expect: The Twins allowed more runs than any team save the Rockies and Indians.

It's a shame that the failure of Minnesota's run prevention overshadowed the rest of the club's season, when so many things went right. Joe Mauer played 147 games and led the American League in on-base percentage. Denard Span and Justin Morneau both shook off devastating concussion symptoms from 2011 and made tentative steps toward regaining their form. Josh Willingham and Ryan Doumit proved to be excellent free-agent signings, wildly exceeding expectations. Trevor Plouffe and Ben Revere emerged as potential long-term solutions at third base and center field, respectively. But the only thing that truly mattered was that the Twins' formerly vaunted pitching and defense let them down completely.

2013: DROUGHT CONTINUES

The saddest thing about the Twins' 2012 is that it's nearly impossible to find ways in which things could get *better* in 2013. The pitchers they have aren't suddenly going to start striking batters out, the offense doesn't appear to have much growing room, and there's very little in the way of big-league-ready help in the minors.

On the mound, things figure to be just as bad as they were in 2012. The only major-league-quality pitchers with whom the Twins ended the season were starter Scott Diamond—probably a number-four starter on most good teams—and relievers Glen Perkins and Jared Burton. Scott Baker, the only member of the rotation who did *not* subscribe to the club's strikeout-fearing dogma, has left to pursue his Tommy John recovery with the Cubs. Unless four top free-agent pitchers walk through that clubhouse door, the Twins figure to open 2013 with one of the worst pitching staffs in the majors.

That more or less does them in, but for completeness' sake: The offense was hardly bad last year, but now Span and Revere have been traded for pitching. Plouffe could take another step forward, but one has to assume Willingham will take at least an equal step back, and it's probably too much to ask for a repeat of the level of health Mauer and Morneau enjoyed in 2012. Matching the 701 runs they scored in 2012 seems the most anyone can hope for, and the current crop of pitchers is going to give up many more than that.

Finally, there's no significant help on the way up. Pitcher Kyle Gibson made an impressive return from Tommy John surgery and could make his big-league debut this season, but everyone else of note is at least a year away. It figures to be another long summer in Minnesota (and not in the good, staving-off-a-northern-winter way).

STATE OF THE ORGANIZATION: TURNING OVER AN OLD LEAF

Generations have passed since the last time the Twins made as many big changes as they've made this offseason, jettisoning seemingly every member of the coaching staff except pitching coach Rick Anderson and manager Ron Gardenhire. Of course, given that they're filling virtually every hole internally, and that Anderson, Gardenhire, and former and current GM Terry Ryan survived the purge, it's entirely possible that the more things change, the more they'll stay the same. Still, the front-office shakeup is a testament to how impatient the club's owners and fans are growing with the team. Even the long-hallowed tenets of Nordic stoicism and "Minnesota Nice" have their limits.

Sadly, patience is exactly what fans and executives will need. The impact prospects in the system are years away. Miguel Sano, Aaron Hicks, Byron Buxton, Eddie Rosario, and newly acquired Travor May could be All-Stars . . . sometime after 2014. Former first-rounder Alex Wimmers had his Tommy John surgery delayed by almost a full season by the club, and Joe Benson will have to demonstrate that he is healthy and effective after a season lost to a wrist injury. The team has acknowledged it needs to add big arms through the draft, but that won't help in the short term.

With a thin big-league club and so little help on the way, the front office needs to recognize that, if everything goes perfectly, the next competitive Twins team is at least two years off. With that in mind, the Twins would do well to move every veteran they can who is worth more now than he will be then: Morneau and Willingham, at the least, and very likely Perkins and Burton.

This team needs to be torn down to its foundations. Sadly, there's little indication the front office comprehends this; Ryan has indicated that more coaching and front-office changes are likely if he doesn't see improvement *this season*—a turnaround that would be both unwise to attempt and (very likely) impossible to achieve. Further, despite their move away from strike-throwers at the amateur level, the Twins seem likely to once again be looking for "affordable" pitchers to fill out the suspect rotation. Almost by definition these will be guys who eat innings, limit walks, and are completely incapable of striking anybody out. So even though they've lost faith, the Twins are still stuck with the same doomed strategy.

HITTERS

Oswaldo Arcia **RF**
Born: **5/9/1991** Age: **22**
Bats: **B** Throws: **R** Height: **6' 1"**
Weight: **210** Breakout: **3%**
Improve: **63%** Collapse: **1%**
Attrition: **6%** MLB: **98%**
Comparables:
Jeff Francoeur,Tony Conigliaro,Miguel Cabrera

YEAR	TEAM	LVL	AGE	PA	R	2B	3B	HR	RBI	BB	SO	SB	CS	AVG_OBP_SLG	TAv	BABIP	BRR	FRAA	WARP
2010	ELZ	Rk	19	283	47	21	7	14	51	19	67	4	4	.375/.426/.672	.385	.466	0.6	CF(41): -2.7, RF(30): 1.2	4.2
2011	BLT	A	20	81	18	8	1	5	18	9	16	2	2	.352/.420/.704	.368	.392	0	--	0.0
2011	FTM	A+	20	227	27	14	2	8	32	9	53	1	1	.263/.300/.460	.279	.312	0	RF(25): -2.1	0.2
2012	FTM	A+	21	235	22	16	3	7	31	23	45	1	3	.309/.376/.517	.308	.361	0.3	RF(35): 1.7	1.4
2012	NBR	AA	21	299	54	20	5	10	67	28	62	3	2	.328/.398/.557	.350	.392	1.4	RF(41): -1.8, CF(4): -0.1	2.7
2013	*MIN*	*MLB*	*22*	*250*	*26*	*11*	*3*	*8*	*31*	*16*	*66*	*0*	*0*	*.253/.304/.426*	*.256*	*.317*	*-0.2*	*RF 0, CF -0*	*0.5*

Arcia turned some heads with a strong start to 2011, and after a full recovery from midseason elbow surgery, he did more than that in 2012, batting .320/.388/.539 between High-A and Double-A. The most encouraging signs were the sharp increase in his walk rate, from 5.6 percent to 9.6 percent, and that he did it while slightly *lowering* his strikeout rate. Arcia is probably ready to start 2013 in Triple-A, and with a good showing there, could debut in Minnesota in late 2013 if some of the Twins' current outfielders are dealt.

Joe Benson **OF**
Born: **3/5/1988** Age: **25**
Bats: **R** Throws: **R** Height: **6' 2"**
Weight: **205** Breakout: **5%**
Improve: **61%** Collapse: **3%**
Attrition: **7%** MLB: **99%**
Comparables:
Rick Monday,Jose Cruz Jr.,Reggie Sanders

YEAR	TEAM	LVL	AGE	PA	R	2B	3B	HR	RBI	BB	SO	SB	CS	AVG_OBP_SLG	TAv	BABIP	BRR	FRAA	WARP
2010	FTM	A+	22	96	16	11	1	4	13	8	21	5	0	.294/.375/.588	.346	.350	1	CF(19): -0.5, RF(2): 0.1	1.0
2010	NBR	AA	22	423	65	20	7	23	49	39	115	14	9	.251/.336/.527	.297	.301	2.4	CF(52): -1.0, RF(41): 1.3	3.6
2011	NBR	AA	23	472	69	28	4	16	67	56	109	13	9	.285/.388/.495	.299	.353	2.8	CF(45): 5.3, RF(5): -0.2	2.5
2011	MIN	MLB	23	74	3	6	1	0	2	3	21	2	2	.239/.270/.352	.229	.340	-1.5	LF(11): -1.0, RF(7): 0.9	-0.3
2012	NBR	AA	24	157	13	6	1	3	20	13	43	4	3	.184/.268/.305	.223	.242	-2.1	RF(14): -1.3, CF(10): 1.8	-0.5
2012	ROC	AAA	24	108	9	3	2	2	8	11	27	4	0	.179/.269/.316	.206	.224	0.8	CF(22): -0.9	-0.5
2013	*MIN*	*MLB*	*25*	*250*	*30*	*11*	*2*	*8*	*29*	*20*	*72*	*8*	*4*	*.224/.296/.393*	*.246*	*.290*	*0.3*	*CF -1, RF -0*	*0.3*

Considered a better prospect than Ben Revere not so long ago, Benson saw his game fall apart on every level in 2012. While Revere established himself as a passable regular, Benson batted .202/.288/.336 across four minor-league levels and battled a severely limiting wrist injury. With Revere and Denard Span gone, Benson will get a chance—perhaps the first chance—at winning the starting center-field job. But at age 25 and with outfielders Arcia, Aaron Hicks, and possibly, eventually, Byron Buxton on the climb behind him, this feels very much like a last-chance sort of year for Benson.

Drew Butera **C**

Born: **8/9/1983** Age: **29**
Bats: **R** Throws: **R** Height: **6' 2"**
Weight: **195** Breakout: **2%**
Improve: **34%** Collapse: **12%**
Attrition: **20%** MLB: **93%**

Comparables:
Junior Ortiz,Rick Cerone,J. C. Martin

YEAR	TEAM	LVL	AGE	PA	R	2B	3B	HR	RBI	BB	SO	SB	CS	AVG_OBP_SLG	TAv	BABIP	BRR	FRAA	WARP
2010	MIN	MLB	26	155	12	6	1	2	13	4	25	0	0	.197/.237/.296	.194	.222	-0.3	C(47): 0.1	-0.2
2011	MIN	MLB	27	254	19	9	1	2	23	11	42	0	0	.167/.210/.239	.163	.194	-1.8	C(93): 0.6	-1.7
2012	MIN	MLB	28	122	7	6	0	1	5	9	26	0	0	.198/.270/.279	.207	.250	0.2	C(41): 0.3, P(1): -0.0	-0.2
2013	*MIN*	*MLB*	*29*	*250*	*21*	*11*	*1*	*3*	*22*	*13*	*46*	*0*	*0*	*.216/.267/.318*	*.209*	*.250*	*-0.2*	*C -0, LF -0*	*-0.3*

Butera might be the worst active hitter in the major leagues, but upon his 91st plate appearance of 2012, he added an honor that beats that. He has now had over 500 big-league plate appearances, and among all non-pitchers in baseball history who have reached that mark, Butera's career 497 OPS is the 25th-lowest. That puts him at third-lowest among all players to have played a game *since 1920*. This is history Butera is making here! Thankfully for the Twins, Joe Mauer and Ryan Doumit splitting the catching duties reduces his impact.

Byron Buxton **CF**

Born: **12/18/1993** Age: **19**
Bats: **R** Throws: **R** Height: **6' 2"**
Weight: **188** Breakout: **0%**
Improve: **67%** Collapse: **33%**
Attrition: **33%** MLB: **100%**

Comparables:
Robin Yount,Wayne Causey,Ed Kranepool

YEAR	TEAM	LVL	AGE	PA	R	2B	3B	HR	RBI	BB	SO	SB	CS	AVG_OBP_SLG	TAv	BABIP	BRR	FRAA	WARP
2012	ELZ	Rk	18	87	16	6	1	1	6	8	15	7	0	.286/.368/.429	.411	.344	0.2	CF(3): -0.1	0.1
2012	TWI	Rk	18	102	17	4	3	4	14	11	26	4	3	.216/.324/.466	.267	.259	0	--	0.0
2013	*MIN*	*MLB*	*19*	*250*	*32*	*8*	*1*	*3*	*15*	*13*	*68*	*18*	*6*	*.196/.242/.285*	*.190*	*.256*	*1.9*	*CF -0*	*-0.9*

Maybe the best pure talent in the 2012 draft, Buxton looked predictably raw in his first 189 professional plate appearances. He showed good power and walked in 10 percent of his trips to the plate, though, and there's a lot to like here. Buxton is a *long* way off—at least three full years—but it'll be three years of heaven for prospect wonks, as we wait to find out if he turns into the next Andre Dawson or the next Shawn Abner . . . or the next one of dozens of immensely talented prospects who *dream* of the kind of career Shawn Abner had.

Jamey Carroll **INF**

Born: **2/18/1974** Age: **39**
Bats: **R** Throws: **R** Height: **5' 10"**
Weight: **170** Breakout: **0%**
Improve: **19%** Collapse: **10%**
Attrition: **22%** MLB: **70%**

Comparables:
Barry Larkin,Red Schoendienst,Craig Counsell

YEAR	TEAM	LVL	AGE	PA	R	2B	3B	HR	RBI	BB	SO	SB	CS	AVG_OBP_SLG	TAv	BABIP	BRR	FRAA	WARP
2010	LAN	MLB	36	414	48	15	1	0	23	51	64	12	4	.291/.379/.339	.284	.349	2.9	SS(69): 6.0, 2B(48): 2.3	3.4
2011	LAN	MLB	37	510	52	14	6	0	17	47	58	10	0	.290/.359/.347	.267	.332	1.6	2B(81): 4.3, SS(66): -6.7	1.8
2012	MIN	MLB	38	537	65	18	1	1	40	52	65	9	5	.268/.343/.317	.248	.306	0.5	2B(66): 1.1, 3B(44): 0.1	1.2
2013	*MIN*	*MLB*	*39*	*499*	*48*	*17*	*4*	*1*	*37*	*46*	*75*	*9*	*3*	*.268/.341/.327*	*.245*	*.313*	*0.4*	*2B -2, SS 0*	*1.0*

The list of players who were first productive in the major leagues at age 32 and were still productive at 38 is not a long one, and the list of middle infielders about whom you can say that may have only one name on it. For Jamey Carroll, it's been a really interesting second half of a career that never had a first half. It has to stop sometime, but there's no real reason to think that'll happen in 2013. He is signed cheaply and the team holds a similarly cheap 2014 option. As such, if your favorite contender finds itself in need of a second baseman, it could do a lot worse than a late-season deal for Carroll.

Ryan Doumit **C**

Born: **4/3/1981** Age: **32**
Bats: **B** Throws: **R** Height: **6' 2"**
Weight: **215** Breakout: **5%**
Improve: **36%** Collapse: **12%**
Attrition: **15%** MLB: **91%**

Comparables:
Gus Triandos,Michael Barrett,Ramon Hernandez

YEAR	TEAM	LVL	AGE	PA	R	2B	3B	HR	RBI	BB	SO	SB	CS	AVG_OBP_SLG	TAv	BABIP	BRR	FRAA	WARP
2010	PIT	MLB	29	456	42	22	1	13	45	41	87	1	0	.251/.331/.406	.252	.290	-3.2	C(100): 4.0, RF(18): 0.2	0.9
2011	PIT	MLB	30	236	17	12	1	8	30	16	35	0	1	.303/.353/.477	.289	.331	-2.6	C(60): 0.1	1.1
2012	MIN	MLB	31	528	56	34	1	18	75	29	98	0	0	.275/.320/.461	.273	.306	1.9	C(59): 0.3, LF(16): 1.1	1.8
2013	*MIN*	*MLB*	*32*	*439*	*47*	*23*	*1*	*13*	*55*	*29*	*78*	*1*	*0*	*.266/.321/.431*	*.263*	*.299*	*-0.7*	*C 1, LF 0*	*1.8*

Doumit, thanks to the designated-hitter rule, had his fullest, healthiest season, with career highs in games and plate appearances. He wasn't quite as effective with the bat as he had been in 2011, but he was still potent. Unfortunately, the bat is about all he has. Doumit shifted gamely around the field in 2012, logging 56 games at catcher, 16 in left, six in right, and even three innings at first base—four positions and he doesn't seem particularly comfortable or adept at any of them. The Twins signed him to a reasonable two-year extension midway through the season, and if there's a contender this July who could use a DH vs. southpaws who can double as backup or third-string catcher, Doumit should be on the move.

Brian Dozier INF

Born: **5/15/1987** Age: **26**
Bats: **R** Throws: **R** Height: **6' 0"**
Weight: **190** Breakout: **4%**
Improve: **50%** Collapse: **6%**
Attrition: **20%** MLB: **93%**

Comparables:
Sean Kazmar,Angel Sanchez,Ed Romero

YEAR	TEAM	LVL	AGE	PA	R	2B	3B	HR	RBI	BB	SO	SB	CS	AVG_OBP_SLG	TAv	BABIP	BRR	FRAA	WARP
2010	BLT	A	23	170	24	7	1	0	17	16	16	6	1	.278/.341/.338	.252	.304	2.1	SS(32): 1.8, 3B(3): -0.1	0.9
2010	FTM	A+	23	410	44	11	1	5	42	44	41	10	4	.274/.349/.354	.249	.291	-0.9	SS(65): -7.4, 3B(14): -1.2	0.1
2011	FTM	A+	24	218	32	11	5	2	22	27	20	13	4	.322/.423/.472	.285	.350	0.2	SS(11): 1.0, 2B(7): 0.7	0.6
2011	NBR	AA	24	351	60	22	7	7	34	28	46	11	7	.318/.384/.502	.265	.357	2.1	SS(33): -4.6, 2B(10): -1.0	0.1
2012	ROC	AAA	25	200	15	11	1	2	17	14	34	3	2	.232/.286/.337	.205	.270	-0.4	SS(38): -0.3, 2B(4): -1.0	-0.8
2012	MIN	MLB	25	340	33	11	1	6	33	16	58	9	2	.234/.271/.332	.229	.267	-2.2	SS(83): 4.6	0.3
2013	*MIN*	*MLB*	*26*	*315*	*35*	*12*	*2*	*5*	*25*	*19*	*52*	*8*	*3*	*.240/.289/.341*	*.226*	*.272*	*0.4*	*SS 1, 2B -0*	*0.4*

Dozier came into 2012 unfairly hyped as the next big thing by the Twins and by the local media after they saw his A) beautiful, flowing blond hair, and B) breakout 2011 split across two levels. Nobody thought to mention that he was high on the age curve: 24 years old at High-A. He was promoted in May and installed as the every-day shortstop through August, but fell out of favor because of terrible plate discipline, inability to make solid contact, and defensive struggles. The Twins demoted him back to Rochester, where he began transitioning to second base with the hope that he can play there regularly, or at least be a passable utility infielder.

Eduardo Escobar INF

Born: **1/5/1989** Age: **24**
Bats: **B** Throws: **R** Height: **5' 11"**
Weight: **165** Breakout: **6%**
Improve: **49%** Collapse: **9%**
Attrition: **22%** MLB: **92%**

Comparables:
Dave Hilton,Barry Evans,Pat Kelly

YEAR	TEAM	LVL	AGE	PA	R	2B	3B	HR	RBI	BB	SO	SB	CS	AVG_OBP_SLG	TAv	BABIP	BRR	FRAA	WARP
2010	WNS	A+	21	408	57	18	8	3	39	23	76	8	5	.285/.322/.402	.259	.340	-0.8	SS(87): 5.4	2.2
2010	BIR	AA	21	216	22	8	3	3	22	9	35	3	0	.262/.287/.376	.255	.296	-0.2	SS(49): 3.9	1.3
2011	CHR	AAA	22	536	55	23	4	4	49	27	104	13	8	.266/.303/.354	.229	.327	-2.5	SS(62): 2.8, 2B(19): 0.3	-0.3
2011	CHA	MLB	22	7	0	0	0	0	0	0	1	0	0	.286/.286/.286	.196	.333	0	SS(3): 0.1, 2B(2): -0.0	0.0
2012	ROC	AAA	23	151	19	3	3	1	9	8	26	3	1	.217/.259/.304	.195	.259	0.8	3B(15): -3.9, SS(9): -1.2	-1.1
2012	CHA	MLB	23	97	14	4	1	0	3	9	23	2	0	.207/.281/.276	.210	.281	0.5	3B(22): 0.3, 2B(6): -0.4	-0.3
2012	MIN	MLB	23	49	4	0	0	0	6	2	8	1	0	.227/.271/.227	.194	.270	0.2	2B(8): 0.6, SS(6): 0.4	-0.1
2013	*MIN*	*MLB*	*24*	*250*	*24*	*9*	*2*	*2*	*18*	*11*	*51*	*4*	*2*	*.238/.275/.322*	*.214*	*.290*	*0.2*	*SS 2, 3B -0*	*-0.1*

Throughout the minor leagues, Escobar—the biggest of the small pieces that came over from the White Sox in the Francisco Liriano trade in July—was touted as a fantastic defensive shortstop who couldn't hit a lick. That certainly held true as he got his first real taste of the big leagues in 2012, in both Chicago and Minneapolis. Escobar is entering his age-24 season, and owns a .312 minor-league OBP to go with a .278 big-league one (in just 178 plate appearances). We can't name a lot of examples of players who were hopeless in the minors but who suddenly figured it out in the majors. Escobar's glove and versatility will likely make him a useful utility guy, but anything more will require a big, almost unprecedented leap forward.

Pedro Florimon Jr. SS

Born: **12/10/1986** Age: **26**
Bats: **B** Throws: **R** Height: **6' 3"**
Weight: **180** Breakout: **8%**
Improve: **59%** Collapse: **9%**
Attrition: **29%** MLB: **90%**

Comparables:
U.L. Washington,Robert Andino,Jay Bell

YEAR	TEAM	LVL	AGE	PA	R	2B	3B	HR	RBI	BB	SO	SB	CS	AVG_OBP_SLG	TAv	BABIP	BRR	FRAA	WARP
2010	FRD	A+	23	252	32	10	4	4	33	20	52	8	5	.288/.365/.423	.265	.361	1.4	SS(66): 4.2	2.1
2010	BOW	AA	23	134	16	3	0	1	12	11	31	4	1	.183/.248/.233	.207	.233	1.3	SS(37): -2.7	-0.3
2011	BOW	AA	24	520	53	27	4	8	60	51	114	15	12	.267/.344/.396	.277	.336	-1.7	SS(95): 6.4, 2B(1): -0.0	2.5
2011	BAL	MLB	24	10	1	1	0	0	2	1	6	0	0	.125/.222/.250	.233	.500	0.1	SS(4): 0.1	0.1
2012	NBR	AA	25	127	11	4	0	2	8	11	28	7	1	.283/.347/.372	.259	.361	0.7	SS(22): 2.7	0.7
2012	ROC	AAA	25	345	38	16	2	3	27	23	89	6	7	.251/.308/.344	.219	.341	4	SS(65): 6.7	0.4
2012	MIN	MLB	25	150	16	5	2	1	10	10	30	3	1	.219/.272/.307	.216	.274	1.6	SS(43): 0.9	0.0
2013	*MIN*	*MLB*	*26*	*250*	*24*	*10*	*2*	*3*	*20*	*16*	*61*	*5*	*3*	*.233/.288/.329*	*.220*	*.299*	*-0.1*	*SS 2, 2B 0*	*0.3*

Florimon went into 2013 as the odds-on favorite to win the Opening Day job at shortstop. This makes sense because he's a wispy defensive specialist who is 26 years old, had a .318 OBP at New Britain and Rochester last year, and logged a 579 OPS in 150 plate appearances for the Twins, and because Ron Gardenhire does love his wispy middle infielders. Florimon did play relatively under control in the field throughout 2012, committing 19 errors in 156 games across three levels and maintaining his excellent range, so he could prove a decent enough stopgap until the Twins manage to develop or trade for someone better.

Aaron Hicks **CF**

Born: **10/2/1989** Age: **23**
Bats: **B** Throws: **R** Height: **6' 3"**
Weight: **185** Breakout: **5%**
Improve: **51%** Collapse: **4%**
Attrition: **12%** MLB: **92%**

Comparables:
Johnny Briggs,Ryan Kalish,Bob Coluccio

YEAR	TEAM	LVL	AGE	PA	R	2B	3B	HR	RBI	BB	SO	SB	CS	AVG_OBP_SLG	TAv	BABIP	BRR	FRAA	WARP
2010	BLT	A	20	518	86	27	6	8	49	88	112	21	11	.279/.400/.428	.310	.358	5.5	CF(91): 4.9, RF(12): 2.2	5.8
2011	FTM	A+	21	528	79	31	5	5	38	78	110	17	9	.242/.354/.368	.263	.308	3.9	CF(50): 3.8	1.6
2012	NBR	AA	22	563	100	21	11	13	61	79	116	32	11	.286/.384/.460	.286	.348	8.1	CF(84): 0.1, LF(3): 0.2	2.8
2013	*MIN*	*MLB*	*23*	*250*	*31*	*9*	*3*	*4*	*20*	*29*	*61*	*9*	*4*	*.234/.324/.356*	*.243*	*.300*	*0.6*	*CF -1, RF 0*	*0.3*

When the Twins drafted Hicks in 2008, scouts and stat wonks both salivated over his physical tools and patience. But after three seasons in the Twins system, Hicks seemed too patient, letting hittable pitches go by, and seemed to stagnate physically. But at New Britain Hicks thrived, reaching double digits in doubles, triples, and homers—setting professional bests in the latter two—and showing he hasn't gone all Tim Beckham on us yet. He has tremendous speed and defensive range, and plays a plus center field with a dangerous arm, so if he can hit even a little, he figures to be an above-average player. With Span and Revere moving on, Hicks is in the mix for a big-league outfield job, whether he wins it out of spring training or comes up partway through the season.

Max Kepler **OF**

Born: **2/10/1993** Age: **20**
Bats: **L** Throws: **L** Height: **6' 5"**
Weight: **180** Breakout: **19%**
Improve: **51%** Collapse: **6%**
Attrition: **21%** MLB: **85%**

Comparables:
Al Kaline,Ed Kirkpatrick,Bobby Delgreco

YEAR	TEAM	LVL	AGE	PA	R	2B	3B	HR	RBI	BB	SO	SB	CS	AVG_OBP_SLG	TAv	BABIP	BRR	FRAA	WARP
2011	ELZ	Rk	18	221	29	11	3	1	24	23	54	1	1	.262/.347/.366	.258	.355	0	--	0.0
2012	ELZ	Rk	19	269	40	16	5	10	49	27	33	7	0	.297/.387/.539	.331	.309	0.3	CF(11): -0.4, LF(6): 1.1	0.9
2013	*MIN*	*MLB*	*20*	*250*	*20*	*9*	*2*	*4*	*24*	*13*	*57*	*0*	*0*	*.207/.255/.314*	*.204*	*.251*	*-0.1*	*CF -1, LF -0*	*-0.9*

Kepler is far enough away from the majors that he might ordinarily rate only a lineout in this book, except that he may have the most unique and fascinating background of any active pro. Born and raised in Germany, Kepler signed the biggest contract ever given to a European player. His Texan mother and Polish father were both professional ballet dancers. Oh, and the baseball? He signed forever ago, but is still just 20 years old, and his considerable promise finally started to turn into numbers in 2012. Kepler should get his first real full season of pro work in 2013 and is worth watching simply for the oddity, though he could well end up being pretty good at this game.

Darin Mastroianni **OF**

Born: **8/26/1985** Age: **27**
Bats: **R** Throws: **R** Height: **6' 0"**
Weight: **190** Breakout: **6%**
Improve: **49%** Collapse: **3%**
Attrition: **20%** MLB: **90%**

Comparables:
Jerry Mumphrey,Shannon Stewart,Eric Young

YEAR	TEAM	LVL	AGE	PA	R	2B	3B	HR	RBI	BB	SO	SB	CS	AVG_OBP_SLG	TAv	BABIP	BRR	FRAA	WARP
2010	NHP	AA	24	617	101	25	7	4	46	77	96	46	10	.301/.389/.398	.284	.356	4.8	CF(127): -1.9	4.2
2011	NHP	AA	25	198	29	8	3	1	13	22	24	14	3	.254/.342/.355	.252	.286	0	--	0.0
2011	LVG	AAA	25	364	63	18	6	2	23	40	54	20	7	.276/.358/.389	.258	.327	0.3	CF(40): -1.1, LF(5): 0.5	0.6
2011	TOR	MLB	25	3	0	0	0	0	0	0	1	0	0	.000/.000/.000	.101	.000	0	CF(1): -0.0	0.0
2012	ROC	AAA	26	85	10	2	2	0	11	5	14	10	1	.346/.393/.423	.280	.422	1.9	LF(13): 0.2, 2B(5): 0.6	0.6
2012	MIN	MLB	26	186	22	3	2	3	17	18	45	21	3	.252/.328/.350	.256	.328	1.2	RF(34): 1.0, LF(25): -0.1	0.5
2013	*MIN*	*MLB*	*27*	*250*	*32*	*9*	*2*	*2*	*17*	*22*	*51*	*18*	*4*	*.252/.320/.337*	*.240*	*.312*	*2.2*	*CF -1, RF 0*	*0.2*

The fourth outfielder on a 96-loss team will never get a ton of attention, but as fourth outfielders go, Mastroianni has the makings of a very good one. His excellent foot speed makes him useful both on the bases and at any outfield position, and while he didn't exactly set the world ablaze with his bat in 2012, he has shown solid on-base abilities in the minors. He may find himself stretched into a starting role, but if Benson or Hicks wins the center-field job and Mastroianni can fill in across the outfield—whether in Minnesota or elsewhere—he can be awfully useful.

Joe Mauer **C**

Born: **4/19/1983** Age: **30**
Bats: **L** Throws: **R** Height: **6' 6"**
Weight: **235** Breakout: **0%**
Improve: **49%** Collapse: **6%**
Attrition: **6%** MLB: **96%**

Comparables:
Bill Freehan,Victor Martinez,Ted Simmons

YEAR	TEAM	LVL	AGE	PA	R	2B	3B	HR	RBI	BB	SO	SB	CS	AVG_OBP_SLG	TAv	BABIP	BRR	FRAA	WARP
2010	MIN	MLB	27	584	88	43	1	9	75	65	53	1	4	.327/.402/.469	.304	.348	4.4	C(112): -1.6	5.3
2011	MIN	MLB	28	333	38	15	0	3	30	32	38	0	0	.287/.360/.368	.267	.319	-1.4	C(52): -0.3, 1B(18): 2.5	1.2
2012	MIN	MLB	29	641	81	31	4	10	85	90	88	8	4	.319/.416/.446	.304	.364	-1.9	C(74): -1.6, 1B(30): -2.1	3.0
2013	*MIN*	*MLB*	*30*	*542*	*66*	*28*	*2*	*12*	*65*	*67*	*60*	*4*	*2*	*.316/.402/.460*	*.305*	*.341*	*-0.9*	*C -1, 1B -0*	*4.2*

After a year of injuries, low batting averages, and no power to speak of, Mauer was essentially his old self in 2012, putting up offensive numbers across the board that are roughly in line with his career averages. Any thought of his becoming the power hitter he briefly resembled in 2009 (28 HR, .587 SLG) is long gone by now, but 2012 showed that he remains an elite talent in virtually every other way. Unfortunately, he caught in barely half of his games, and Mauer at first base or DH (or maybe, eventually, other positions) will become an increasingly common sight over the remaining six years of his contract. That's not a good thing for his overall value. But boy, can he hit a baseball.

Levi Michael **MI**

Born: **2/9/1991** Age: **22**
Bats: **B** Throws: **R** Height: **5' 11"**
Weight: **180** Breakout: **5%**
Improve: **61%** Collapse: **3%**
Attrition: **8%** MLB: **96%**

Comparables:
Derrel Thomas,Glenn Hubbard,Lou Whitaker

YEAR	TEAM	LVL	AGE	PA	R	2B	3B	HR	RBI	BB	SO	SB	CS	AVG_OBP_SLG	TAv	BABIP	BRR	FRAA	WARP
2012	FTM	A+	21	512	58	14	4	2	38	56	82	6	0	.246/.339/.311	.260	.295	-2.6	2B(48): 0.5, SS(36): 0.5	0.8
2013	*MIN*	*MLB*	*22*	*250*	*24*	*8*	*2*	*3*	*19*	*20*	*54*	*0*	*0*	*.222/.292/.309*	*.216*	*.272*	*-0.1*	*2B -1, SS -0*	*-0.3*

Widely believed to be the best college middle infielder in the 2011 draft, Michael was picked to address an organizational weakness. Instead, he only compounded that weakness in his minor-league debut, posting a 650 OPS and spending more time at second base than shortstop. If he can't hit enough or play short well enough to play regularly, his only path to the majors would be as a utility infielder.

Justin Morneau **1B**

Born: **5/15/1981** Age: **32**
Bats: **L** Throws: **R** Height: **6' 5"**
Weight: **235** Breakout: **3%**
Improve: **30%** Collapse: **2%**
Attrition: **8%** MLB: **91%**

Comparables:
Kent Hrbek,Eddie Murray,Mike Sweeney

YEAR	TEAM	LVL	AGE	PA	R	2B	3B	HR	RBI	BB	SO	SB	CS	AVG_OBP_SLG	TAv	BABIP	BRR	FRAA	WARP
2010	MIN	MLB	29	348	53	25	1	18	56	50	62	0	0	.345/.437/.618	.362	.385	-3.1	1B(77): -1.1	3.8
2011	MIN	MLB	30	288	19	16	0	4	30	19	44	0	0	.227/.285/.333	.221	.257	-1.7	1B(56): -5.2	-2.0
2012	MIN	MLB	31	570	63	26	2	19	77	49	102	1	0	.267/.333/.440	.274	.294	-4.2	1B(99): -4.0	0.2
2013	*MIN*	*MLB*	*32*	*481*	*58*	*26*	*2*	*17*	*65*	*50*	*77*	*0*	*0*	*.274/.352/.465*	*.285*	*.297*	*-0.7*	*1B -4*	*1.4*

While he's a far cry from where he was before his debilitating concussion in 2010, Morneau's ability to make it through a full season without a recurrence of his symptoms was a major victory. If only that were his only problem. Let's not forget four surgeries (neck, foot, knee, and wrist) since January 2011 and that he is going to be 32 in May. Minnesota would love to unload him to make way for Chris Parmelee, but there doesn't figure to be a lot of interest in a player who carries so much injury risk and is making $14 million. The Twins will probably have to make do and hope that more time removed from his trauma will bring back the former MVP.

Chris Parmelee **1B**

Born: **2/24/1988** Age: **25**
Bats: **L** Throws: **L** Height: **6' 2"**
Weight: **230** Breakout: **1%**
Improve: **63%** Collapse: **1%**
Attrition: **11%** MLB: **93%**

Comparables:
Joey Votto,Justin Morneau,Mike Carp

YEAR	TEAM	LVL	AGE	PA	R	2B	3B	HR	RBI	BB	SO	SB	CS	AVG_OBP_SLG	TAv	BABIP	BRR	FRAA	WARP
2010	FTM	A+	22	93	9	2	1	2	17	13	11	0	1	.338/.430/.463	.320	.373	-0.5	1B(13): 1.3, RF(2): -0.1	0.5
2010	NBR	AA	22	463	51	25	2	6	44	43	70	3	2	.275/.346/.389	.265	.319	-2	1B(72): 8.4, RF(36): 1.2	1.5
2011	NBR	AA	23	610	76	30	5	13	83	68	94	0	1	.287/.366/.436	.318	.322	-0.8	1B(57): 1.9, RF(12): -0.3	2.1
2011	MIN	MLB	23	88	8	6	0	4	14	12	13	0	0	.355/.443/.592	.361	.390	-0.3	1B(20): 1.6	1.0
2012	ROC	AAA	24	282	45	17	1	17	49	51	52	1	1	.338/.457/.645	.326	.373	-2.5	1B(55): 9.5	2.5
2012	MIN	MLB	24	210	18	10	2	5	20	13	52	0	0	.229/.290/.380	.236	.287	-0.5	1B(38): 0.2, RF(18): -0.6	-0.5
2013	*MIN*	*MLB*	*25*	*254*	*28*	*12*	*2*	*7*	*31*	*24*	*50*	*0*	*0*	*.272/.345/.432*	*.274*	*.318*	*-0.3*	*1B -2, RF -0*	*0.4*

Gardenhire wanted to hand Parmelee an every-day job on the basis of 88 great at-bats in September 2011 and a strong spring training last year, but the 24-year-old with no experience above Double-A understandably flopped out of the gate. A 512 OPS through May 15 got him demoted to Rochester, where he raked and earned promotions in June, July, and August, during which he mostly sat on the bench and lost out on the reps he'll need to develop into Morneau's eventual replacement. A comparatively strong September (750 OPS) has him in the mix for the right-field job.

Josmil Pinto **C**

Born: **3/31/1989** Age: **24**
Bats: **R** Throws: **R** Height: **6' 0"**
Weight: **230** Breakout: **5%**
Improve: **38%** Collapse: **5%**
Attrition: **11%** MLB: **94%**

Comparables:
Jeff Torborg,Bill Freehan,Joe Azcue

YEAR	TEAM	LVL	AGE	PA	R	2B	3B	HR	RBI	BB	SO	SB	CS	AVG_OBP_SLG	TAv	BABIP	BRR	FRAA	WARP
2010	BLT	A	21	392	60	21	1	10	54	32	67	2	3	.225/.298/.378	.247	.250	-0.6	C(66): -0.7, 3B(1): -0.0	0.3
2011	FTM	A+	22	236	21	11	1	5	32	12	36	1	0	.262/.305/.389	.210	.293	-0.4	C(21): -0.7	-0.5
2012	FTM	A+	23	393	45	22	2	12	51	39	63	0	0	.295/.361/.473	.294	.326	-2.6	C(40): -0.7	1.5
2012	NBR	AA	23	52	8	4	1	2	9	4	10	0	0	.298/.365/.553	.332	.343	0.2	--	0.2
2013	*MIN*	*MLB*	*24*	*250*	*23*	*11*	*1*	*6*	*28*	*14*	*54*	*0*	*0*	*.228/.275/.369*	*.227*	*.266*	*-0.3*	*C -0*	*0.0*

Pinto was a surprising addition to the 40-man roster early this offseason. He'll turn 24 before the season starts and has played just 12 games above Single-A. He hit fairly well in that brief sample and his second trip through High-A in 2012, but he was the DH in nearly half of his 105 games, suggesting (despite improved passed ball, error, and caught-stealing rates when he did catch) that the organization still doesn't view his defense as a strength. The team must see some possibility that Pinto can provide value as a hitter, something he'll have the opportunity to show in New Britain and, if it goes well there, in Rochester this season.

Trevor Plouffe 3B
Born: **6/15/1986** Age: **27**
Bats: **R** Throws: **R** Height: **6' 3"**
Weight: **200** Breakout: **6%**
Improve: **48%** Collapse: **3%**
Attrition: **7%** MLB: **88%**

Comparables:
Hank Blalock, Pete Ward, Chase Headley

YEAR	TEAM	LVL	AGE	PA	R	2B	3B	HR	RBI	BB	SO	SB	CS	AVG_OBP_SLG	TAv	BABIP	BRR	FRAA	WARP
2010	ROC	AAA	24	445	53	22	4	15	49	27	90	5	5	.244/.296/.430	.250	.272	0.4	SS(91): -10.2, 3B(7): 0.1	0.5
2010	MIN	MLB	24	44	7	1	0	2	6	0	14	0	0	.146/.143/.317	.173	.154	0.3	SS(9): 0.0, 2B(2): 0.0	-0.3
2011	ROC	AAA	25	220	33	11	3	15	33	21	39	3	1	.312/.384/.635	.339	.319	-2.1	SS(25): 6.3, 2B(9): -1.1	2.5
2011	MIN	MLB	25	320	47	18	1	8	31	25	71	3	3	.238/.305/.392	.259	.286	-0.7	SS(45): -5.9, 2B(17): -1.3	0.1
2012	MIN	MLB	26	465	56	19	1	24	55	37	92	1	3	.235/.301/.455	.266	.244	-2.6	3B(95): -2.3, RF(15): -0.7	0.3
2013	*MIN*	*MLB*	*27*	*433*	*57*	*19*	*2*	*18*	*53*	*32*	*92*	*3*	*2*	*.242/.305/.439*	*.261*	*.268*	*-0.6*	*3B 0, SS -2*	*1.1*

For a month in 2012, from June 2 to July 1, Plouffe could do no wrong at the plate. He batted .333/.395/.784, belting 13 home runs in just 114 plate appearances. Unfortunately, he sandwiched that between a dreadful .163/.261/.347 in the first two months and a .221/.275/.351 in the final three, with 11 homers combined in those 351 plate appearances. Plouffe clearly has excellent power, but doesn't have excellent patience at the best of times. When things go poorly, he tends to get overly swing-happy. He'll be given every opportunity to recapture some of that June magic and become the third baseman of the future, but the Twins plan to bring in some competition and/or a backup plan in case he's more like the Danny Valencia of 2012.

Eddie Rosario 2B
Born: **9/28/1991** Age: **21**
Bats: **L** Throws: **R** Height: **6' 1"**
Weight: **170** Breakout: **3%**
Improve: **55%** Collapse: **9%**
Attrition: **16%** MLB: **97%**

Comparables:
Tim Foli, Glenn Hubbard, Bill Mazeroski

YEAR	TEAM	LVL	AGE	PA	R	2B	3B	HR	RBI	BB	SO	SB	CS	AVG_OBP_SLG	TAv	BABIP	BRR	FRAA	WARP
2010	TWI	Rk	18	213	34	9	2	5	26	16	28	22	5	.294/.348/.438	.298	.323	1.3	CF(34): 1.9, LF(10): -0.2	1.6
2011	ELZ	Rk	19	298	71	9	9	21	60	27	60	17	6	.337/.397/.670	.349	.370	0	--	0.0
2012	BLT	A	20	429	60	32	4	12	70	31	69	11	11	.296/.345/.490	.275	.329	0.1	2B(13): -0.0, CF(4): -0.1	0.6
2013	*MIN*	*MLB*	*21*	*250*	*25*	*11*	*1*	*6*	*26*	*11*	*56*	*5*	*3*	*.231/.265/.364*	*.223*	*.275*	*-0.1*	*2B -1, CF -0*	*-0.3*

Rosario has split his time more or less equally between second base and the outfield, but given that he has the athleticism to handle second and the Twins have an overabundance of candidates for the outfield, the keystone seems like the clearest path forward. Rosario suffered a midseason injury and fell apart over the last month or two, but ended at a still-solid .299/.347/.499. He has the tools to hit for a solid average, get on base, hit 20 or more home runs and steal 20 or more bases, which—should he stick at second—would probably get him to some All-Star Games. He, like most fun things on this team, is at least a full year away.

Miguel Sano 3B
Born: **5/11/1993** Age: **20**
Bats: **R** Throws: **R** Height: **6' 4"**
Weight: **195** Breakout: **24%**
Improve: **68%** Collapse: **3%**
Attrition: **14%** MLB: **89%**

Comparables:
Justin Upton, Mickey Mantle, Tony Conigliaro

YEAR	TEAM	LVL	AGE	PA	R	2B	3B	HR	RBI	BB	SO	SB	CS	AVG_OBP_SLG	TAv	BABIP	BRR	FRAA	WARP
2010	TWI	Rk	17	161	23	14	0	4	19	10	43	2	2	.291/.338/.466	.288	.382	-2.7	3B(21): -1.6, SS(16): 0.5	0.7
2011	ELZ	Rk	18	293	58	18	7	20	59	23	77	5	4	.292/.352/.637	.318	.339	0	--	0.0
2012	BLT	A	19	553	75	28	4	28	100	80	144	8	3	.258/.373/.521	.247	.307	2	3B(22): 2.9, 1B(1): -0.1	0.3
2013	*MIN*	*MLB*	*20*	*250*	*26*	*9*	*1*	*9*	*31*	*22*	*80*	*0*	*0*	*.208/.281/.378*	*.233*	*.273*	*-0.3*	*3B 2, SS 0*	*0.1*

After three minor-league seasons and a documentary about his signing (*Pelotero*; it's good, watch it), Sano remains one of the brightest prospects in the minor leagues. In his first full season of action, he saw his batting average plummet, but led the Midwest League in homers by nine and walks by 11—at just 19 years old. His strikeout rate remained high and he seems to have already outgrown third base (his 42 errors speak both to his lack of interest in defense and his awkwardness in the field). He's still in line to be an All-Star regardless of whether he ends up at an outfield corner or at first base, and the Twins would do well to begin that transition soon. He'll probably split 2013 between Fort Myers and New Britain, and figures to debut sometime in 2014.

Josh Willingham LF
Born: **2/17/1979** Age: **34**
Bats: **R** Throws: **R** Height: **6' 3"**
Weight: **215** Breakout: **2%**
Improve: **30%** Collapse: **2%**
Attrition: **15%** MLB: **93%**

Comparables:
Pat Burrell, Milton Bradley, Bob Allison

YEAR	TEAM	LVL	AGE	PA	R	2B	3B	HR	RBI	BB	SO	SB	CS	AVG_OBP_SLG	TAv	BABIP	BRR	FRAA	WARP
2010	WAS	MLB	31	450	54	19	2	16	56	67	85	8	0	.268/.389/.459	.299	.304	1.4	LF(108): -9.2	2.1
2011	OAK	MLB	32	563	69	26	0	29	98	56	150	4	1	.246/.332/.477	.305	.287	-0.3	LF(96): -3.0	2.9
2012	MIN	MLB	33	615	85	30	1	35	110	76	141	3	2	.260/.366/.524	.312	.287	0.9	LF(119): 4.8	4.5
2013	*MIN*	*MLB*	*34*	*567*	*75*	*26*	*2*	*25*	*81*	*66*	*129*	*5*	*2*	*.251/.352/.466*	*.289*	*.289*	*-0.4*	*LF -1*	*2.9*

The poor man's Michael Cuddyer ended up being the Michael Cuddyer of Michael Cuddyer's dreams. Coming to Minnesota on an eminently reasonable three-year, $21 million deal to replace the departing Cuddyer (or Jason Kubel), Willingham found that the right-handed-pull-hitter-friendly Target Field suited his right-handed, pull-hitting tendencies. He set career highs in WARP, VORP, TAv, games, plate appearances, runs, home runs, RBIs, and walks, and even managed his second career FRAA above zero. At 34, it's all downhill from here, but the Twins can reasonably hope that for the next two years, the downward slope will be a slight one.

PITCHERS

Jose Berrios

Born: **5/27/1994** Age: **19**
Bats: **R** Throws: **R** Height: **6' 1"** Weight: **187**
Breakout: **19%** Improve: **59%** Collapse: **41%**
Attrition: **41%** MLB: **54%**

Comparables:
Rick Wise,Von McDaniel,Lew Krausse

YEAR	TEAM	LVL	AGE	W	L	SV	G	GS	IP	H	HR	BB	SO	BB9	SO9	GB%	BABIP	WHIP	ERA	FIP	FRA	WARP
2012	ELZ	Rk	18	2	0	0	3	3	14	8	1	1	22	0.6	14.1	46%	.333	0.64	1.29	1.91	5.81	0.0
2012	TWI	Rk	18	1	0	4	8	1	16^{2}	7	0	3	27	1.6	14.6	—	.219	0.60	1.08	0.73	0.80	0.0
2013	*MIN*	*MLB*	*19*	*1*	*3*	*0*	*6*	*6*	*31*	*39*	*5*	*21*	*16*	*6.1*	*4.6*	*45%*	*.318*	*1.93*	*7.06*	*6.30*	*7.67*	*-0.7*

If you saw the YouTube video of Berrios and his friends and family watching him get drafted last summer and it didn't make you smile, man, there's no hope for you. There's plenty of hope for Berrios, on the other hand, a sandwich-round pick out of Bayamon, Puerto Rico. He throws in the low- to mid-90s, with a lot of potential to develop a plus curve or changeup down the line. The Twins have made a concerted effort to pick hard-throwers with high ceilings in their last two drafts, and Berrios looks like the best of that bunch. He'll still only be 18 when the season gets going, so he has a long way to go. But striking out 49 batters in his first 30 professional innings while walking only four is a pretty good way to start.

Nick Blackburn

Born: **2/24/1982** Age: **31**
Bats: **R** Throws: **R** Height: **6' 5"** Weight: **240**
Breakout: **11%** Improve: **38%** Collapse: **33%**
Attrition: **20%** MLB: **86%**

Comparables:
Tomo Ohka,Bill Wegman,Brian Moehler

YEAR	TEAM	LVL	AGE	W	L	SV	G	GS	IP	H	HR	BB	SO	BB9	SO9	GB%	BABIP	WHIP	ERA	FIP	FRA	WARP
2010	MIN	MLB	28	10	12	0	28	26	161	194	25	40	68	2.2	3.8	52%	.305	1.45	5.42	5.04	6.07	-0.9
2011	MIN	MLB	29	7	10	0	26	26	148^{1}	183	19	54	76	3.3	4.6	55%	.317	1.60	4.49	4.87	5.34	0.0
2012	ROC	AAA	30	3	1	0	7	7	36^{2}	42	2	9	11	2.2	2.7	60%	.310	1.39	2.70	4.00	5.85	-0.1
2012	MIN	MLB	30	4	9	0	19	19	98^{2}	143	23	26	42	2.4	3.8	47%	.330	1.71	7.39	6.05	6.88	-1.7
2013	*MIN*	*MLB*	*31*	*4*	*9*	*0*	*19*	*19*	*107^{2}*	*129*	*16*	*28*	*51*	*2.3*	*4.3*	*49%*	*.308*	*1.46*	*5.27*	*4.96*	*5.73*	*-0.5*

After confusingly strong years in 2008 and 2009, Blackburn and his strategy of never missing the strike zone or a bat embarked on a slow slide that seemed to bottom out in 2012, ending with his removal from the Twins 40-man roster. He is owed $5.5 million by the Twins in 2013, so the odds we've seen the last of him are slim to none, but the trend over the last few years—walks up, homers up, groundballs down, strikeouts still largely non-existent—make it highly unlikely we'll see a renaissance at age 31 or beyond.

Alex Burnett

Born: **7/26/1987** Age: **25**
Bats: **R** Throws: **R** Height: **6' 1"** Weight: **220**
Breakout: **36%** Improve: **65%** Collapse: **16%**
Attrition: **14%** MLB: **91%**

Comparables:
Brandon League,Jon Huber,Alberto Arias

YEAR	TEAM	LVL	AGE	W	L	SV	G	GS	IP	H	HR	BB	SO	BB9	SO9	GB%	BABIP	WHIP	ERA	FIP	FRA	WARP
2010	ROC	AAA	22	0	2	2	14	0	19^{2}	26	1	8	18	3.7	8.2	46%	.391	1.73	5.48	3.34	4.44	0.2
2010	MIN	MLB	22	2	2	0	41	0	47^{2}	52	6	23	37	4.3	7.0	48%	.322	1.57	5.29	4.70	5.09	0.1
2011	ROC	AAA	23	0	0	1	4	0	3^{2}	5	1	1	3	2.5	7.4	46%	.400	1.64	7.36	5.96	6.51	-0.1
2011	MIN	MLB	23	2	5	0	66	0	50^{2}	50	4	21	33	3.7	5.9	47%	.289	1.40	5.51	4.50	5.72	-0.5
2012	MIN	MLB	24	4	4	0	67	0	71^{2}	71	4	26	36	3.3	4.5	53%	.279	1.35	3.52	3.98	4.54	0.3
2013	*MIN*	*MLB*	*25*	*3*	*1*	*0*	*57*	*0*	*58*	*62*	*7*	*23*	*37*	*3.6*	*5.7*	*45%*	*.299*	*1.47*	*4.84*	*4.68*	*5.26*	*-0.1*

We're as flummoxed by Burnett as the rest of you. He throws hard enough, but doesn't strike anybody out. For two seasons, he posted the 5.00 ERA you would expect, but last year did a better job of keeping balls on the ground. So even as his strikeout rate dropped for the second straight season, his results were pretty phenomenal. Burnett led the Twins in relief innings, stranded runners at an above-average rate, and had a sparkling ERA. Obviously, if current trends continue, he's unlikely to repeat this success, and there is a real danger of the Twins signing him to an unwise contract extension to buy out his arbitration years.

Jared Burton

Born: **6/2/1981** Age: **32**
Bats: **R** Throws: **R** Height: **6' 6"** Weight: **225**
Breakout: **20%** Improve: **39%** Collapse: **38%**
Attrition: **13%** MLB: **95%**

Comparables:
Matt Wise,Aaron Heilman,Jeff Russell

YEAR	TEAM	LVL	AGE	W	L	SV	G	GS	IP	H	HR	BB	SO	BB9	SO9	GB%	BABIP	WHIP	ERA	FIP	FRA	WARP
2010	LOU	AAA	29	3	2	4	33	0	38	29	4	16	34	3.8	8.1	42%	.234	1.18	2.61	4.21	5.02	0.0
2010	CIN	MLB	29	0	0	0	4	0	3^{1}	0	0	0	1	0.0	2.7	44%	.000	0.00	0.00	2.51	2.51	0.1
2011	RED	Rk	30	0	1	0	3	3	4	7	1	0	6	0.0	13.5	—	.500	1.75	9.00	4.62	5.02	0.0
2011	LOU	AAA	30	2	0	0	11	0	13	12	1	5	11	3.5	7.6	50%	.333	1.31	4.15	4.39	5.96	-0.1
2011	CIN	MLB	30	0	0	0	6	0	4^{2}	6	1	3	3	5.8	5.8	41%	.312	1.93	3.86	6.42	5.74	-0.1
2012	MIN	MLB	31	3	2	5	64	0	62	41	5	16	55	2.3	8.0	48%	.220	0.92	2.18	3.34	3.87	0.8
2013	*MIN*	*MLB*	*32*	*2*	*1*	*2*	*41*	*0*	*42^{1}*	*40*	*4*	*15*	*36*	*3.3*	*7.6*	*46%*	*.288*	*1.31*	*4.01*	*3.79*	*4.36*	*0.4*

An astute pickup for GM Terry Ryan, Burton rebounded from two injury-wrecked years after having established himself as a quality reliever with the Reds in 2007-09. From June 12 through July 29, Burton made 16 appearances, each of an inning or more (16 2/3 innings total) without giving up a single run. He's not likely to put up a 2.18 ERA again, but he's a cheap, high-quality short reliever who may draw some interest on the trade market in July or August.

Matt Capps

Born: **9/3/1983** Age: **29**
Bats: **R** Throws: **R** Height: **6' 3"** Weight: **245**
Breakout: **23%** Improve: **42%** Collapse: **30%**
Attrition: **19%** MLB: **85%**

Comparables:
John Habyan, Brandon Lyon, Todd Coffey

YEAR	TEAM	LVL	AGE	W	L	SV	G	GS	IP	H	HR	BB	SO	BB9	SO9	GB%	BABIP	WHIP	ERA	FIP	FRA	WARP
2010	MIN	MLB	26	2	0	16	27	0	27	24	1	8	21	2.7	7.0	55%	.303	1.19	2.00	2.86	3.58	0.4
2010	WAS	MLB	26	3	3	26	47	0	46	51	5	9	38	1.8	7.4	49%	.313	1.30	2.74	3.45	3.62	0.5
2011	MIN	MLB	27	4	7	15	69	0	65^{2}	66	10	13	34	1.8	4.7	43%	.263	1.20	4.25	4.78	5.74	-0.5
2012	FTM	A+	28	1	0	0	2	1	2	1	0	0	1	0.0	4.5	29%	.143	0.50	0.00	2.39	4.72	0.0
2012	MIN	MLB	28	1	4	14	30	0	29^{1}	28	5	4	18	1.2	5.5	45%	.247	1.09	3.68	4.44	5.13	0.0
2013	*MIN*	*MLB*	*29*	*2*	*1*	*8*	*37*	*0*	*35^{2}*	*37*	*5*	*8*	*27*	*2.0*	*6.7*	*42%*	*.296*	*1.26*	*4.09*	*4.18*	*4.45*	*0.3*

Glory be, the Twins are mercifully done with Capps, who they gave up a potential All-Star catcher to acquire in 2010 and whose presence was a constant reminder of the trials and tribulations of the Bill Smith era. While Wilson Ramos, the catcher in question, has struggled with injury—not to mention a frightening kidnapping—in the wake of the deal, he remains just 25 and will be the starter in Washington through 2016, while Capps gave Minnesota 93 competent innings. The club then compounded the trade mistake by forgoing a draft pick and re-signing Capps for another season. Now coming off of a strained rotator cuff, which he had tried to pitch through, Capps will look for a one-year deal as a set-up man.

Kevin Correia

Born: **8/24/1980** Age: **32**
Bats: **R** Throws: **R** Height: **6' 4"** Weight: **200**
Breakout: **14%** Improve: **36%** Collapse: **32%**
Attrition: **15%** MLB: **78%**

Comparables:
Tomo Ohka, Kyle Lohse, John Burkett

YEAR	TEAM	LVL	AGE	W	L	SV	G	GS	IP	H	HR	BB	SO	BB9	SO9	GB%	BABIP	WHIP	ERA	FIP	FRA	WARP
2010	SDN	MLB	29	10	10	0	28	26	145	152	20	64	115	4.0	7.1	50%	.302	1.49	5.40	4.74	5.46	-1.1
2011	PIT	MLB	30	12	11	0	27	26	154	175	24	39	77	2.3	4.5	47%	.292	1.39	4.79	4.82	5.75	-0.6
2012	PIT	MLB	31	12	11	0	32	28	171	176	20	46	89	2.4	4.7	54%	.274	1.30	4.21	4.48	5.27	-0.6
2013	*MIN*	*MLB*	*32*	*6*	*11*	*0*	*23*	*23*	*131^{1}*	*151*	*19*	*42*	*77*	*2.9*	*5.3*	*47%*	*.306*	*1.47*	*5.06*	*4.87*	*5.50*	*-0.3*

In a surreal late-season moment, Pittsburgh manager Clint Hurdle informed the media that the Pirates had attempted to trade Correia at the deadline, but that 20 teams replied with variations of "No thanks." Apparently nobody checked in with Minnesota, who proceeded to court Correia with great gusto and saw fit to reward him for having a right arm and being the pitching-to-contactiest guy around (his 4.6 SO9 ranks last among righty starters) with a two-year, $10 million contract. With a little hard work and a lot of luck, he just might fare better than Jason Marquis did last year in Target Field.

Samuel Deduno

Born: **7/2/1983** Age: **29**
Bats: **R** Throws: **R** Height: **6' 4"** Weight: **190**
Breakout: **14%** Improve: **49%** Collapse: **18%**
Attrition: **11%** MLB: **90%**

Comparables:
Tom Phoebus, Daniel Cabrera, Bob Gibson

YEAR	TEAM	LVL	AGE	W	L	SV	G	GS	IP	H	HR	BB	SO	BB9	SO9	GB%	BABIP	WHIP	ERA	FIP	FRA	WARP
2010	TRI	A-	26	0	2	0	4	4	16^{1}	18	0	5	20	2.8	11.0	59%	.409	1.41	5.52	2.13	3.61	0.2
2010	CSP	AAA	26	3	1	0	6	6	30^{2}	20	3	18	29	5.3	8.5	64%	.218	1.24	2.93	5.21	5.41	0.3
2010	COL	MLB	26	0	0	0	4	0	2^{2}	3	1	1	3	3.4	10.1	38%	.286	1.50	3.38	6.86	8.59	-0.1
2011	TUC	AAA	27	4	6	0	40	12	105^{1}	101	2	58	85	5.0	7.3	54%	.328	1.51	3.93	4.27	4.52	1.4
2011	SDN	MLB	27	0	0	0	2	0	3	5	0	3	4	9.0	12.0	90%	.500	2.67	3.00	3.33	1.55	0.1
2012	ROC	AAA	28	1	2	0	9	9	42	27	2	22	46	4.7	9.9	64%	.235	1.17	2.14	3.44	4.83	0.1
2012	MIN	MLB	28	6	5	0	15	15	79	69	10	53	57	6.0	6.5	59%	.266	1.54	4.44	5.45	6.53	-0.7
2013	*MIN*	*MLB*	*29*	*3*	*5*	*0*	*20*	*12*	*69^{2}*	*65*	*7*	*41*	*59*	*5.3*	*7.6*	*56%*	*.293*	*1.52*	*4.66*	*4.58*	*5.06*	*0.2*

Deduno was a minor-league free agent the Twins were simply using to fill out the Rochester roster, but when every single member of the Opening Day rotation ended up either hurt or sent packing, the Twins turned to the 28-year-old rookie. Improbably, and despite walking 20 and striking out 19 in 29 innings, Deduno won three of his first five starts and had a 2.48 ERA, raising hopes across Twins Territory. Reality, being a real bitch, reasserted itself in start number six, and he posted a 5.58 ERA with 33 walks and 38 strikeouts in 50 innings over his last 10 games. Blessed and cursed with ridiculous movement on his fastball, Deduno has no earthly idea where it will go on any given pitch, except that it will probably stay in and around the Rochester area for most of 2013, as he signed another minor-league contract.

Cole DeVries

Born: **2/12/1985** Age: **28**
Bats: **R** Throws: **R** Height: **6' 3"** Weight: **185**
Breakout: **29%** Improve: **66%** Collapse: **20%**
Attrition: **12%** MLB: **90%**

Comparables:
Larry Christenson, Reggie Cleveland, Jeff Karstens

YEAR	TEAM	LVL	AGE	W	L	SV	G	GS	IP	H	HR	BB	SO	BB9	SO9	GB%	BABIP	WHIP	ERA	FIP	FRA	WARP
2010	NBR	AA	25	1	5	1	39	2	68^{1}	87	10	25	63	3.3	8.3	45%	.353	1.64	5.80	4.65	5.46	-0.2
2010	ROC	AAA	25	0	3	0	9	3	23^{1}	26	2	14	24	5.4	9.3	45%	.348	1.72	5.79	4.15	4.89	0.1
2011	NBR	AA	26	0	0	9	15	0	27^{2}	17	3	5	33	1.6	10.7	39%	.138	0.80	2.28	2.98	4.51	0.1
2011	ROC	AAA	26	4	2	0	30	2	62^{1}	74	4	18	42	2.6	6.1	39%	.345	1.48	3.90	3.59	5.22	0.1
2012	ROC	AAA	27	3	5	0	12	12	70	75	7	10	50	1.3	6.4	37%	.306	1.21	4.37	3.50	4.23	0.7
2012	MIN	MLB	27	5	5	0	17	16	87^{2}	88	16	18	58	1.8	6.0	33%	.258	1.21	4.11	4.85	5.28	0.3
2013	*MIN*	*MLB*	*28*	*3*	*4*	*1*	*28*	*9*	*81^{1}*	*95*	*12*	*27*	*50*	*3.0*	*5.5*	*41%*	*.309*	*1.50*	*5.42*	*4.88*	*5.90*	*-0.5*

Pretty much the Platonic ideal of a Twins pitcher, DeVries is right-handed, throws around 90 mph, never walks anybody, doesn't strike out many, and lets his defense make plays behind him. That doesn't sound like much, but for a team desperate for anyone to soak up innings, he proved a godsend until cracked ribs ended his season in September. DeVries debuted at 27 and doesn't have any room to grow, so this was probably his high-water mark. Still, the Minnesota native and math teacher-doppelganger will be healthy and get a chance to win one of the many open spots in the rotation in spring training, where everyone will try to ignore the fact that he's essentially Nick Blackburn, except with fly balls.

Scott Diamond

Born: **7/30/1986** Age: **26**
Bats: **L** Throws: **L** Height: **6' 4"** Weight: **215**
Breakout: **37%** Improve: **63%** Collapse: **14%**
Attrition: **15%** MLB: **84%**

Comparables:
Jose Rosado,Paul Maholm,Zach Duke

YEAR	TEAM	LVL	AGE	W	L	SV	G	GS	IP	H	HR	BB	SO	BB9	SO9	GB%	BABIP	WHIP	ERA	FIP	FRA	WARP
2010	MIS	AA	23	4	6	0	17	17	102^{1}	113	4	39	90	3.4	7.9	56%	.356	1.49	3.52	3.34	4.05	1.1
2010	GWN	AAA	23	4	1	0	10	10	56^{1}	53	2	15	33	2.4	5.3	53%	.291	1.21	3.36	3.43	5.07	0.2
2011	ROC	AAA	24	4	14	0	23	23	123	158	11	36	90	2.6	6.6	51%	.342	1.58	5.56	3.84	5.02	0.4
2011	MIN	MLB	24	1	5	0	7	7	39	51	3	17	19	3.9	4.4	48%	.338	1.74	5.08	4.39	4.35	0.4
2012	ROC	AAA	25	4	1	0	6	6	34^{2}	35	1	7	26	1.8	6.8	49%	.321	1.21	2.60	2.73	3.93	0.4
2012	MIN	MLB	25	12	9	0	27	27	173	184	17	31	90	1.6	4.7	54%	.292	1.24	3.54	3.89	4.94	0.3
2013	*MIN*	*MLB*	*26*	*6*	*11*	*0*	*23*	*23*	*136*	*158*	*15*	*42*	*80*	*2.8*	*5.3*	*51%*	*.317*	*1.48*	*5.03*	*4.38*	*5.46*	*-0.3*

Diamond is the latest in a line of classically Twins-style pitchers: It doesn't seem like what they do should work at the big-league level, but it does, at least for a while. The problem is that the line includes such flashes in the pan as Joe Mays, Carlos Silva, and Blackburn; he who lives by the ball in play tends, eventually, to die by the ball in play. Diamond is not likely to maintain a 3.54 ERA, or belong at or near the top of any kind of respectable rotation. He did post a league-low walks per nine in 2012, though, and anyone who can do that and keep the ball in the park has value. Diamond's value is just likely to be much closer to the fourth-starter variety than the second starter he looked like in 2012.

Brian Duensing

Born: **2/22/1983** Age: **30**
Bats: **L** Throws: **L** Height: **6' 1"** Weight: **205**
Breakout: **21%** Improve: **61%** Collapse: **15%**
Attrition: **14%** MLB: **83%**

Comparables:
Paul Maholm,Johnny Antonelli,Chris Oxspring

YEAR	TEAM	LVL	AGE	W	L	SV	G	GS	IP	H	HR	BB	SO	BB9	SO9	GB%	BABIP	WHIP	ERA	FIP	FRA	WARP
2010	MIN	MLB	27	10	3	0	53	13	130^{2}	122	11	35	78	2.4	5.4	54%	.272	1.20	2.62	3.82	4.92	0.8
2011	MIN	MLB	28	9	14	0	32	28	161^{2}	193	21	52	115	2.9	6.4	46%	.330	1.52	5.23	4.31	4.85	0.7
2012	MIN	MLB	29	4	12	0	55	11	109	126	10	27	69	2.2	5.7	48%	.319	1.40	5.12	3.77	4.51	0.9
2013	*MIN*	*MLB*	*30*	*5*	*6*	*0*	*36*	*14*	*104*	*114*	*12*	*31*	*64*	*2.7*	*5.5*	*48%*	*.306*	*1.40*	*4.56*	*4.36*	*4.96*	*0.4*

The Twins' 2013 rotation is about as open as they come, but several years of data suggest that Duensing's career as a starting pitcher should probably be over. As a reliever in 2012, Duensing faced 231 batters and put up a 3.44 ERA, with only one home run allowed; as a starter, he faced 241 batters and put up a 6.92 ERA, surrendering nine homers. In his career, Duensing has thrown about 2.5 times as many innings as a starter than as a reliever, but has given up six times as many homers. The starting thing just isn't working. He can be exceptionally useful as a set-up man, having held left-handed hitters to a 560 career OPS (678 in 2012) while getting torched by righties to the tune of an 830 OPS (808 in 2012).

Casey Fien

Born: **10/21/1983** Age: **29**
Bats: **R** Throws: **R** Height: **6' 3"** Weight: **195**
Breakout: **17%** Improve: **41%** Collapse: **27%**
Attrition: **18%** MLB: **79%**

Comparables:
Julio Mateo,Jeff Gray,Dave Veres

YEAR	TEAM	LVL	AGE	W	L	SV	G	GS	IP	H	HR	BB	SO	BB9	SO9	GB%	BABIP	WHIP	ERA	FIP	FRA	WARP
2010	TOL	AAA	26	3	3	8	44	0	62^{1}	54	8	13	44	1.9	6.4	41%	.256	1.08	2.60	4.22	5.24	-0.1
2010	DET	MLB	26	0	0	0	2	0	2^{2}	4	2	0	0	0.0	0.0	42%	.200	1.50	10.12	12.80	15.07	-0.2
2011	AST	Rk	27	1	0	0	2	0	2	1	0	0	3	0.0	13.5	50%	.250	0.50	0.00	0.42	1.23	0.1
2011	OKL	AAA	27	2	2	3	21	0	24^{1}	28	7	8	24	3.0	8.9	—	.309	1.48	4.81	6.54	7.11	0.0
2012	ROC	AAA	28	2	5	9	33	0	46	39	5	14	42	2.7	8.2	33%	.274	1.15	4.30	3.66	4.73	0.2
2012	MIN	MLB	28	2	1	0	35	0	35	25	3	9	32	2.3	8.2	26%	.229	0.97	2.06	3.19	3.74	0.4
2013	*MIN*	*MLB*	*29*	*1*	*1*	*0*	*28*	*0*	*35^{2}*	*35*	*5*	*11*	*29*	*2.8*	*7.3*	*37%*	*.293*	*1.30*	*4.18*	*4.32*	*4.55*	*0.2*

After an elbow strain knocked him out for most of 2011, Fien (pronounced Feen) didn't even make last year's book. Not that 28-year-old relievers with 14 innings of major-league experience forced to sign minor-league deals are typically worthy of an entry, mind you, and his omission seemed fairly justified through the first three months of the season as Fien did little to distinguish himself at Rochester. But with a promotion in July, Fien ripped off the best three months of his career and forced himself into the team's bullpen plans for 2013 as one of the few guys on the staff who can reliably strike batters out. An extreme fly-ball pitcher, Fien is perfectly suited for the spacious Target Field and will be making around the league minimum for the next three years. He can't be trusted to repeat his ridiculous performance, but should be a perfectly serviceable part of the club's bullpen.

Kyle Gibson

Born: 10/23/1987 Age: 25
Bats: R Throws: R Height: 6' 7" Weight: 210
Breakout: 19% Improve: 55% Collapse: 16%
Attrition: 20% MLB: 89%

Comparables:
Taylor Buchholz, Juan Nicasio, Jason Windsor

YEAR	TEAM	LVL	AGE	W	L	SV	G	GS	IP	H	HR	BB	SO	BB9	SO9	GB%	BABIP	WHIP	ERA	FIP	FRA	WARP
2010	FTM	A+	22	4	1	0	7	7	43^1	33	2	12	40	2.5	8.3	69%	.260	1.04	1.87	3.16	4.08	0.4
2010	NBR	AA	22	7	5	0	16	16	93	91	5	22	77	2.1	7.5	54%	.308	1.22	3.68	3.24	4.28	0.9
2010	ROC	AAA	22	0	0	0	3	3	15^2	12	0	5	9	2.9	5.2	57%	.245	1.08	1.72	3.29	4.50	0.1
2011	ROC	AAA	23	3	8	0	18	18	95^1	109	11	27	91	2.5	8.6	59%	.361	1.43	4.81	3.71	4.49	0.8
2012	TWI	Rk	24	0	0	0	9	7	14^2	9	1	4	16	2.5	9.8	63%	.235	0.89	2.45	2.96	4.59	0.0
2012	FTM	A+	24	0	0	0	2	2	7	6	1	1	7	1.3	9.0	45%	.263	1.00	2.57	4.11	4.04	0.0
2012	ROC	AAA	24	0	2	0	2	2	6^2	11	1	1	10	1.4	13.5	45%	.526	1.80	9.45	2.56	4.46	0.1
2013	*MIN*	*MLB*	*25*	*2*	*3*	*0*	*7*	*7*	*34^2*	*38*	*4*	*12*	*25*	*3.2*	*6.5*	*53%*	*.310*	*1.44*	*4.84*	*4.30*	*5.26*	*0.1*

The Twins' 2009 first-round pick had put together a somewhat underwhelming minor-league career heading into September 2011, when it got worse: Gibson had Tommy John surgery. But he came back strong in late 2012, then impressed in the Arizona Fall League, showing a greater ability to strike hitters out than he had before, and worked his way back to number five on to our list of the team's top-10 prospects. He may be a future third starter; for 2013, he'll get plenty of chances to be the Twins' number five, though more likely in May or June than April due to the lingering injury concerns.

Deolis Guerra

Born: 4/17/1989 Age: 24
Bats: R Throws: R Height: 6' 6" Weight: 245
Breakout: 18% Improve: 56% Collapse: 24%
Attrition: 21% MLB: 92%

Comparables:
Dan Haren, Bobby J. Jones, Jeff Suppan

YEAR	TEAM	LVL	AGE	W	L	SV	G	GS	IP	H	HR	BB	SO	BB9	SO9	GB%	BABIP	WHIP	ERA	FIP	FRA	WARP
2010	NBR	AA	21	2	10	0	19	19	102^1	127	14	37	67	3.3	5.9	40%	.344	1.60	6.25	5.03	5.95	-0.7
2010	ROC	AAA	21	0	3	0	5	4	25	35	5	8	18	2.9	6.5	51%	.357	1.72	6.84	5.53	5.76	0.0
2011	NBR	AA	22	8	7	1	37	10	95	102	11	28	95	2.7	9.0	40%	.271	1.37	5.59	3.93	2.68	1.4
2012	NBR	AA	23	2	0	1	7	0	12^2	5	0	1	15	0.7	10.7	53%	.158	0.47	0.71	1.31	2.00	0.3
2012	ROC	AAA	23	2	3	0	29	0	57^1	59	7	21	56	3.3	8.8	46%	.327	1.40	4.87	3.99	4.83	0.2
2013	*MIN*	*MLB*	*24*	*1*	*2*	*0*	*11*	*3*	*32^2*	*40*	*5*	*15*	*19*	*4.0*	*5.2*	*42%*	*.313*	*1.65*	*6.11*	*5.40*	*6.64*	*-0.4*

The last remnant of the regrettable 2008 trade that sent Johan Santana to the Mets, Guerra's first four years in the Twins system were rough enough that some in his position would have retired by now; his excellent stuff didn't translate into missed bats, which meant an ERA consistently above 5.00. The team moved him to the bullpen midway through 2011 and it's been a different story. In 2012, Guerra finally resembled a pitcher who might make a contribution someday, pitching exclusively out of the bullpen and striking out 71 in 70 innings between Double-A and Triple-A with just 22 walks and seven homers allowed. Now 24 and out of options, Guerra will have every opportunity to capture a bullpen spot in 2013.

Rich Harden

Born: 11/30/1981 Age: 31
Bats: L Throws: R Height: 6' 2" Weight: 195
Breakout: 17% Improve: 54% Collapse: 22%
Attrition: 19% MLB: 89%

Comparables:
Steve Carlton, Jorge De La Rosa, David Cone

YEAR	TEAM	LVL	AGE	W	L	SV	G	GS	IP	H	HR	BB	SO	BB9	SO9	GB%	BABIP	WHIP	ERA	FIP	FRA	WARP
2010	OKL	AAA	28	0	2	0	5	5	23^1	21	3	8	34	3.1	13.1	50%	.327	1.24	3.86	3.50	3.98	0.6
2010	TEX	MLB	28	5	5	0	20	18	92	91	18	62	75	6.1	7.3	34%	.274	1.66	5.58	6.28	6.63	-0.5
2011	SAC	AAA	29	0	0	0	2	2	7^2	3	1	3	12	3.5	14.1	—	.154	0.78	3.52	3.52	3.83	0.0
2011	OAK	MLB	29	4	4	0	15	15	82^2	87	17	31	91	3.4	9.9	34%	.315	1.43	5.12	4.73	4.82	0.2
2013	*MIN*	*MLB*	*31*	*2*	*3*	*0*	*7*	*7*	*35*	*31*	*5*	*16*	*38*	*4.1*	*9.9*	*37%*	*.295*	*1.35*	*4.16*	*4.26*	*4.52*	*0.3*

Harden hasn't pitched at all since 2011, hasn't topped 100 innings since 2009, and has logged more than 150 exactly once, as a bright-eyed 22-year-old in 2004. But even with diminishing stuff and vanishing hopes of ever being able to put it to use over a full season, his consistent ability to miss bats means he's probably got a few years to go before he stops being enticing to some team, at some price. The Twins bought the lottery ticket this year, and will have until July 31 to decide whether he's got enough left to earn a roster spot. After that, Harden can opt out and become a free agent if he's still in the minors.

Liam Hendriks

Born: 2/10/1989 Age: 24
Bats: R Throws: R Height: 6' 2" Weight: 200
Breakout: 22% Improve: 63% Collapse: 22%
Attrition: 16% MLB: 92%

Comparables:
Junichi Tazawa, Bryan Augenstein, Mike Leake

YEAR	TEAM	LVL	AGE	W	L	SV	G	GS	IP	H	HR	BB	SO	BB9	SO9	GB%	BABIP	WHIP	ERA	FIP	FRA	WARP
2010	BLT	A	21	2	1	0	6	6	34	16	0	4	39	1.1	10.3	51%	.203	0.59	1.32	1.76	2.56	1.1
2010	FTM	A+	21	6	3	0	13	12	74^2	63	2	8	66	1.0	8.0	54%	.278	0.95	1.93	2.38	3.40	1.1
2011	NBR	AA	22	8	2	0	16	15	90	85	5	18	81	1.8	8.1	44%	.326	1.14	2.70	3.03	3.52	1.5
2011	ROC	AAA	22	4	4	0	9	9	49^1	52	0	3	30	0.5	5.5	44%	.314	1.11	4.56	2.32	4.20	0.4
2011	MIN	MLB	22	0	2	0	4	4	23^1	29	3	6	16	2.3	6.2	47%	.347	1.50	6.17	4.13	4.91	0.1
2012	ROC	AAA	23	9	3	0	16	16	106^1	76	5	28	82	2.4	6.9	46%	.240	0.98	2.20	3.04	4.16	0.9
2012	MIN	MLB	23	1	8	0	16	16	85^1	106	17	26	50	2.7	5.3	42%	.313	1.55	5.59	5.52	5.96	-0.7
2013	*MIN*	*MLB*	*24*	*4*	*7*	*0*	*17*	*17*	*98^2*	*107*	*13*	*28*	*66*	*2.6*	*6.0*	*46%*	*.303*	*1.36*	*4.63*	*4.43*	*5.03*	*0.3*

The story of Hendriks's career so far: He started 18 games before picking up his first win, last September 19. It's been an exceptionally tough big-league road for Hendriks, who has given up about a homer and two-thirds per nine MLB innings. But he's only 23 and has a long, solid record in the minor leagues, where home runs have never been a problem, so he'll get plenty of chances to earn a rotation spot in 2013. Hendriks is already fifth all-time among Australian-born pitchers in games started, and could move up to second with a full year's worth this season.

Trevor May

Born: 9/23/1989 Age: 23
Bats: R Throws: R Height: 6' 6" Weight: 215
Breakout: 24% Improve: 51% Collapse: 21%
Attrition: 18% MLB: 92%

Comparables:
Ken Cloude, Rick VandenHurk, Gio Gonzalez

YEAR	TEAM	LVL	AGE	W	L	SV	G	GS	IP	H	HR	BB	SO	BB9	SO9	GB%	BABIP	WHIP	ERA	FIP	FRA	WARP
2010	LWD	A	20	7	3	0	11	11	65	51	3	20	92	2.8	12.7	42%	.337	1.09	2.91	2.27	2.61	2.3
2010	CLR	A+	20	5	5	0	16	14	70	53	7	61	90	7.8	11.6	42%	.291	1.63	5.01	4.99	5.11	0.2
2011	CLR	A+	21	10	8	0	27	27	151^{1}	121	8	67	208	4.0	12.4	37%	.364	1.24	3.63	2.75	3.27	1.9
2012	REA	AA	22	10	13	0	28	28	149^{2}	139	22	78	151	4.7	9.1	43%	.292	1.45	4.87	4.88	5.34	0.2
2013	*MIN*	*MLB*	*23*	*2*	*4*	*0*	*8*	*8*	*41^{1}*	*41*	*6*	*26*	*40*	*5.7*	*8.8*	*39%*	*.311*	*1.63*	*5.29*	*5.04*	*5.75*	*-0.2*

May's inclusion in the Revere trade turned it from a head-scratcher to a clear win for Ryan. May's stock rose quickly after he struck out 12.4 batters per nine innings at Clearwater in 2011, but took a dive along with his command and control last year as he was promoted to Double-A. He remains a big kid with a big fastball, however, something that's in very short supply in Minnesota, and will need work to improve his mechanics and mental approach if he's going to make it as a starter. He will almost certainly start the season at New Britain, but a trip to Rochester, and maybe even to the Twin Cities, isn't unrealistic for the 23-year-old.

Alex Meyer

Born: 1/3/1990 Age: 23
Bats: R Throws: R Height: 6' 10" Weight: 220
Breakout: 32% Improve: 63% Collapse: 14%
Attrition: 15% MLB: 91%

Comparables:
Homer Bailey, Tyler Clippard, Chris Tillman

YEAR	TEAM	LVL	AGE	W	L	SV	G	GS	IP	H	HR	BB	SO	BB9	SO9	GB%	BABIP	WHIP	ERA	FIP	FRA	WARP
2012	HAG	A	22	7	4	0	18	18	90	68	4	34	107	3.4	10.7	54%	.292	1.13	3.10	3.01	3.57	2.1
2012	POT	A+	22	3	2	0	7	7	39	29	2	11	32	2.5	7.4	53%	.252	1.03	2.31	3.41	3.99	1.0
2013	*MIN*	*MLB*	*23*	*1*	*3*	*0*	*7*	*7*	*34*	*35*	*4*	*16*	*28*	*4.3*	*7.3*	*48%*	*.306*	*1.51*	*4.95*	*4.49*	*5.38*	*0.0*

Most 6-foot-9 products of the University of Kentucky are one-and-dones for coach John Calipari's basketball team, but Meyer uses his towering frame to generate 98-mph fastballs, which he pairs with a sharp slider. Plucked from the Nationals in the Span deal in November, Meyer gives the Twins system a much-needed power arm, though his future role is unclear. Meyer's changeup lags well behind his fastball and slider, and his long-levered mechanics can grow unwieldy, so while he has a second-starter ceiling, he is more likely to become a ninth-inning stalwart. If Meyer moves to the bullpen, he could make his debut sometime this summer; given the dearth of high-upside starters in Minnesota, though, expect him to spend 2013 in the upper minors before getting a rotation look next spring.

Lester Oliveros

Born: 5/28/1988 Age: 25
Bats: R Throws: R Height: 6' 1" Weight: 225
Breakout: 37% Improve: 60% Collapse: 24%
Attrition: 10% MLB: 89%

Comparables:
Warner Madrigal, Sam Demel, Cecilio Guante

YEAR	TEAM	LVL	AGE	W	L	SV	G	GS	IP	H	HR	BB	SO	BB9	SO9	GB%	BABIP	WHIP	ERA	FIP	FRA	WARP
2010	LAK	A+	22	0	1	9	20	0	19	13	0	6	24	2.8	11.4	50%	.325	1.00	1.89	2.17	2.53	0.4
2010	ERI	AA	22	1	2	14	24	0	25^{1}	20	3	21	36	7.5	12.8	42%	.279	1.62	4.98	4.78	5.31	0.1
2011	ERI	AA	23	2	0	0	10	0	17	11	0	4	28	2.1	14.8	—	.367	0.88	0.53	1.00	1.09	0.0
2011	ROC	AAA	23	0	0	0	2	0	3	2	1	0	4	0.0	12.0	50%	.250	0.67	3.00	4.90	2.37	0.1
2011	TOL	AAA	23	1	3	5	22	0	28	37	7	17	26	5.5	8.4	52%	.407	1.93	6.43	6.45	7.57	-0.4
2011	DET	MLB	23	0	0	0	9	0	8	8	0	4	4	4.5	4.5	63%	.296	1.50	5.62	3.56	4.41	0.0
2011	MIN	MLB	23	0	0	0	10	0	13^{1}	13	0	7	9	4.7	6.1	38%	.325	1.50	4.05	3.29	4.27	0.1
2012	NBR	AA	24	1	1	2	13	0	19	10	0	7	16	3.3	7.6	45%	.213	0.89	1.42	2.62	3.46	0.3
2012	ROC	AAA	24	1	2	6	19	0	29^{1}	24	2	8	35	2.5	10.7	39%	.306	1.09	3.07	2.48	2.89	0.8
2012	MIN	MLB	24	0	0	0	1	0	1^{2}	1	0	1	1	5.4	5.4	20%	.200	1.20	5.40	3.65	3.99	0.0
2013	*MIN*	*MLB*	*25*	*1*	*0*	*0*	*28*	*0*	*34*	*34*	*4*	*17*	*30*	*4.4*	*8.0*	*42%*	*.308*	*1.49*	*4.71*	*4.46*	*5.12*	*0.0*

Acquired for Delmon Young in 2011, Oliveros only pitched one and two-thirds innings last year but was still more valuable than the Twins' former outfielder in that at least his performance wasn't tinged with anti-Semitism. Oliveros had finally shown signs of harnessing his big fastball, but a torn UCL and Tommy John surgery in late August mean that he probably won't pitch at all in 2013. He was non-tendered, and the Twins will almost certainly bring him back as a minor-league free agent.

Carl Pavano

Born: **1/8/1976** Age: **37**
Bats: **R** Throws: **R** Height: **6' 6"** Weight: **250**
Breakout: **11%** Improve: **52%** Collapse: **21%**
Attrition: **16%** MLB: **79%**

Comparables:
Bob Tewksbury,Bartolo Colon,Paul Byrd

YEAR	TEAM	LVL	AGE	W	L	SV	G	GS	IP	H	HR	BB	SO	BB9	SO9	GB%	BABIP	WHIP	ERA	FIP	FRA	WARP
2010	MIN	MLB	34	17	11	0	32	32	221	227	24	37	117	1.5	4.8	53%	.281	1.19	3.75	3.98	4.96	0.3
2011	MIN	MLB	35	9	13	0	33	33	222	262	23	40	102	1.6	4.1	53%	.306	1.36	4.30	4.14	4.69	1.1
2012	FTM	A+	36	0	0	0	2	2	5	4	1	0	3	0.0	5.4	44%	.200	0.80	1.80	4.79	4.87	0.0
2012	MIN	MLB	36	2	5	0	11	11	63	80	9	8	33	1.1	4.7	43%	.329	1.40	6.00	4.33	5.57	-0.3
2013	*MIN*	*MLB*	*37*	*4*	*6*	*0*	*13*	*13*	*81^{1}*	*93*	*10*	*16*	*46*	*1.8*	*5.1*	*48%*	*.307*	*1.34*	*4.64*	*4.26*	*5.04*	*0.2*

The Twins re-signed Carl Pavano and his mustache at a premium rate in 2011 because they expected them to continue to be workhorses who could throw 200 innings or more while getting by striking out fewer than five batters per nine innings. Neither of those things happened, obviously, as anyone who was not former-GM Bill Smith could have predicted. With a bum shoulder (that they suggested the Twins training staff failed to diagnose properly), Pavano and his mustache were limited to only 63 innings last year. They won't get a multi-year deal this time around, but assuming their shoulder is healed and velocity recovers, Pavano and his mustache could still be good enough to fill a fourth-starter spot. It probably won't be on the Twins, but they could, and probably will, do worse.

Mike Pelfrey

Born: **1/14/1984** Age: **29**
Bats: **R** Throws: **R** Height: **6' 8"** Weight: **250**
Breakout: **27%** Improve: **55%** Collapse: **23%**
Attrition: **10%** MLB: **86%**

Comparables:
Pat Hentgen,Jon Garland,Darrell Rasner

YEAR	TEAM	LVL	AGE	W	L	SV	G	GS	IP	H	HR	BB	SO	BB9	SO9	GB%	BABIP	WHIP	ERA	FIP	FRA	WARP
2010	NYN	MLB	26	15	9	1	34	33	204	213	12	68	113	3.0	5.0	51%	.300	1.38	3.66	3.85	4.24	1.8
2011	NYN	MLB	27	7	13	0	34	33	193^{2}	220	21	65	105	3.0	4.9	48%	.301	1.47	4.74	4.43	5.13	-0.7
2012	NYN	MLB	28	0	0	0	3	3	19^{2}	24	0	4	13	1.8	5.9	54%	.353	1.42	2.29	2.42	2.44	0.7
2013	*MIN*	*MLB*	*29*	*2*	*3*	*0*	*7*	*7*	*41^{1}*	*48*	*4*	*14*	*22*	*3.0*	*4.8*	*50%*	*.312*	*1.48*	*4.91*	*4.41*	*5.34*	*-0.0*

Pelfrey had Tommy John surgery on May 1 and was non-tendered by the Mets, and keeping with a theme, the Twins were compelled to offer the righty who doesn't strike anyone out a chance to help the club set the modern record for fewest strikeouts in a season. Not that Pelfrey's a bad pitcher! In fact, he has been a solid mid-rotation starter in two of his four full seasons. But the combination of his groundball tendencies, the recovery from TJS, and Minnesota's suspect middle-infield defense could get ugly.

Glen Perkins

Born: **3/2/1983** Age: **30**
Bats: **L** Throws: **L** Height: **6' 1"** Weight: **210**
Breakout: **20%** Improve: **60%** Collapse: **15%**
Attrition: **12%** MLB: **88%**

Comparables:
John Smiley,Howie Pollet,Denny Neagle

YEAR	TEAM	LVL	AGE	W	L	SV	G	GS	IP	H	HR	BB	SO	BB9	SO9	GB%	BABIP	WHIP	ERA	FIP	FRA	WARP
2010	ROC	AAA	27	4	9	0	26	24	124	160	14	36	98	2.6	7.1	46%	.352	1.58	5.81	4.17	4.95	0.7
2010	MIN	MLB	27	1	1	0	13	1	21^{2}	29	3	5	14	2.1	5.8	53%	.361	1.57	5.82	4.80	5.36	0.0
2011	ROC	AAA	28	0	0	0	2	1	3	4	0	0	2	0.0	6.0	60%	.400	1.33	0.00	1.90	3.58	0.1
2011	MIN	MLB	28	4	4	2	65	0	61^{2}	55	2	21	65	3.1	9.5	52%	.323	1.23	2.48	2.45	2.40	1.6
2012	MIN	MLB	29	3	1	16	70	0	70^{1}	57	8	16	78	2.0	10.0	44%	.278	1.04	2.56	3.12	3.55	1.0
2013	*MIN*	*MLB*	*30*	*3*	*3*	*2*	*35*	*5*	*55^{2}*	*62*	*7*	*16*	*38*	*2.6*	*6.2*	*44%*	*.309*	*1.40*	*4.75*	*4.33*	*5.17*	*0.1*

Say it with me: Closers are not born, they are made. It is a role, not a position. Rinse, lather, repeat. Take virtually any good reliever, and he can do just fine finishing up games. Perkins follows in a long Twins tradition that includes Rick Aguilera, Eddie Guardado, Mike Trombley, Joe Nathan, and Jon Rauch, failed starters all who found a higher calling at the end of Twins games (let us not speak of LaTroy Hawkins, for he totally ruins this theory). Not that we should sell Perkins short. In 2010, he was considering filing a grievance against the club for how it handled his shoulder injury, and two years later, he's a tremendously valuable weapon on the back end, making less than $4 million to be one of the 10 best closers in baseball.

Ryan Pressly

Born: **12/15/1988** Age: **24**
Bats: **R** Throws: **R** Height: **6' 4"** Weight: **175**
Breakout: **27%** Improve: **54%** Collapse: **23%**
Attrition: **21%** MLB: **85%**

Comparables:
Chad Durbin,Brian Williams,Marcelino Lopez

YEAR	TEAM	LVL	AGE	W	L	SV	G	GS	IP	H	HR	BB	SO	BB9	SO9	GB%	BABIP	WHIP	ERA	FIP	FRA	WARP
2010	GRN	A	21	5	7	0	26	24	113^{2}	110	9	43	96	3.4	7.6	49%	.310	1.35	3.72	4.13	5.51	0.0
2011	SLM	A+	22	6	11	0	26	26	130	125	9	53	72	3.7	5.0	—	.272	1.37	4.50	4.55	4.94	0.0
2012	SLM	A+	23	5	3	0	20	12	76	86	9	26	61	3.1	7.2	50%	.329	1.47	6.28	4.50	6.84	-0.1
2012	PME	AA	23	2	2	0	14	0	27^{2}	23	2	10	21	3.3	6.8	45%	.262	1.19	2.93	3.71	4.38	0.2
2013	*MIN*	*MLB*	*24*	*1*	*3*	*0*	*9*	*5*	*32*	*39*	*5*	*18*	*17*	*5.1*	*4.8*	*46%*	*.312*	*1.78*	*6.40*	*5.86*	*6.95*	*-0.5*

The Red Sox turned Pressly, an 11th-round pick in 2007, into a reliever last year, and the early returns were encouraging. After scuffling in both 2011 and 2012 at High-A Salem, he moved up to Double-A Portland and pitched well in 27 2/3 innings over 14 games. The Twins took him with the fourth pick in the Rule 5 draft, and he's essentially an archetypal Rule 5 pick: They have only a handful of successful relief innings to go on, but they're taking a chance that his 94-mph fastball and power curve can be enough to make him a late-inning reliever. Pressly is a longshot to stay on the roster all year, but the Twins have rung the bell a few times with Rule 5 picks, and if he impresses them enough, they can offer the Sox a little something for the right to send Pressly down.

Tyler Robertson

Born: **12/23/1987** Age: **25**
Bats: **L** Throws: **L** Height: **6' 6"** Weight: **220**
Breakout: **36%** Improve: **57%** Collapse: **16%**
Attrition: **11%** MLB: **84%**

Comparables:
John Dopson, Jim Kaat, Dave Hamilton

YEAR	TEAM	LVL	AGE	W	L	SV	G	GS	IP	H	HR	BB	SO	BB9	SO9	GB%	BABIP	WHIP	ERA	FIP	FRA	WARP
2011	NBR	AA	23	10	3	16	55	0	89^2	87	6	29	88	2.9	8.8	53%	.307	1.29	3.61	3.39	3.93	0.7
2012	ROC	AAA	24	2	2	2	33	0	28^2	26	2	13	33	4.1	10.4	62%	.307	1.36	3.77	3.12	3.35	0.6
2012	MIN	MLB	24	2	2	0	40	0	25	21	4	14	26	5.0	9.4	54%	.258	1.40	5.40	4.85	5.58	-0.3
2013	*MIN*	*MLB*	*25*	*1*	*2*	*0*	*18*	*3*	*33*	*39*	*5*	*15*	*21*	*4.2*	*5.7*	*50%*	*.314*	*1.64*	*5.84*	*5.26*	*6.35*	*-0.4*

The 2006 third-round pick was as impressive as possible for a reliever in his big-league debut, striking out the side against the White Sox on June 26. Unfortunately, things got pretty rough after that. Small-sample-size warnings abound, but Robertson held the 72 fellow lefties that he faced in the big leagues to a .190/.268/.317 line, while the 37 righties who faced him collectively went .290/.436/.484. He has an extremely strong slider that dominates left-handed hitters, but even a LOOGY generally ends up facing righties at least half the time, so he'll need to find a way to get them out to stick around.

Josh Roenicke

Born: **8/4/1982** Age: **30**
Bats: **R** Throws: **R** Height: **6' 4"** Weight: **200**
Breakout: **23%** Improve: **57%** Collapse: **28%**
Attrition: **18%** MLB: **83%**

Comparables:
Jesus Colome, Brandon Medders, Danys Baez

YEAR	TEAM	LVL	AGE	W	L	SV	G	GS	IP	H	HR	BB	SO	BB9	SO9	GB%	BABIP	WHIP	ERA	FIP	FRA	WARP
2010	LVG	AAA	27	9	1	1	36	0	59^1	61	7	25	54	3.8	8.2	49%	.314	1.45	3.64	4.66	5.84	0.4
2010	TOR	MLB	27	1	0	0	16	0	19	18	1	13	18	6.2	8.5	55%	.298	1.63	5.68	4.21	4.69	0.1
2011	CSP	AAA	28	0	1	0	23	0	30^2	30	3	7	22	2.1	6.5	53%	.310	1.21	3.52	4.40	4.20	0.6
2011	LVG	AAA	28	1	3	0	16	0	22^1	25	3	15	20	6.0	8.1	50%	.353	1.79	6.04	6.02	7.89	-0.1
2011	COL	MLB	28	0	0	0	19	0	16^2	14	1	7	12	3.8	6.5	46%	.277	1.26	3.78	3.77	3.89	0.2
2012	COL	MLB	29	4	2	1	63	0	88^2	85	9	43	54	4.4	5.5	51%	.276	1.44	3.25	4.76	5.76	-0.2
2013	*MIN*	*MLB*	*30*	*2*	*1*	*1*	*48*	*0*	64^2	*65*	*7*	*29*	*52*	*4.0*	*7.2*	*48%*	*.300*	*1.44*	*4.49*	*4.34*	*4.88*	*0.2*

After several false starts, Roenicke finally stuck in the big leagues for an entire season. His ERA for the Rockies was shiny in 2012 thanks to a staff-high eight unearned runs, but the peripherals told a different story: too many walks, not enough strike-outs. His fastball is hard but straight, and when his breaking ball flattens . . . well, Giancarlo Stanton pounded one for the longest home run in MLB since 2009. Hitters had greater success against Roenicke in the second half, a trend that is likely to continue due to a lack of both stuff and command.

Anthony Slama

Born: **1/6/1984** Age: **29**
Bats: **R** Throws: **R** Height: **6' 4"** Weight: **200**
Breakout: **20%** Improve: **45%** Collapse: **40%**
Attrition: **21%** MLB: **94%**

Comparables:
Frank Francisco, Mark Wohlers, Michael Wuertz

YEAR	TEAM	LVL	AGE	W	L	SV	G	GS	IP	H	HR	BB	SO	BB9	SO9	GB%	BABIP	WHIP	ERA	FIP	FRA	WARP
2010	ROC	AAA	26	2	2	17	54	0	65^1	41	5	32	74	4.4	10.2	46%	.243	1.12	2.21	3.54	4.18	0.7
2010	MIN	MLB	26	0	1	0	5	0	4^2	6	1	5	5	9.6	9.6	27%	.357	2.36	7.71	6.90	4.78	0.0
2011	ROC	AAA	27	3	2	1	27	0	37	27	4	16	42	3.9	10.2	41%	.258	1.16	2.92	3.91	3.66	0.5
2011	MIN	MLB	27	0	0	0	2	0	2^1	0	0	2	3	7.7	11.6	25%	.000	0.86	0.00	3.06	2.05	0.1
2012	TWI	Rk	28	0	0	0	2	0	2^2	2	0	1	3	3.4	10.1	33%	.333	1.12	3.38	2.31	2.09	0.1
2012	ROC	AAA	28	1	0	14	31	0	36^1	26	1	18	56	4.5	13.9	43%	.329	1.21	1.24	1.92	1.73	1.4
2013	*MIN*	*MLB*	*29*	*2*	*1*	*1*	*29*	*0*	35^1	*29*	*3*	*18*	*42*	*4.6*	*10.6*	*43%*	*.302*	*1.35*	*3.67*	*3.45*	*3.99*	*0.5*

Slama has emerged as the pet cause célèbre of the Twins blogosphere. He's been stuck in Triple-A for parts of four years, and there, despite lacking real overpowering stuff, he has struck out 191 batters in 154 1/3 innings and posted a 2.27 ERA. Nonetheless, his major-league experience has been limited to seven innings, none of them coming in service of a 2012 bullpen that badly needed help. He certainly should get a serious look in 2013, but if he hasn't yet, who's to say when, or whether, he ever will?

Anthony Swarzak

Born: **9/10/1985** Age: **27**
Bats: **R** Throws: **R** Height: **6' 5"** Weight: **210**
Breakout: **30%** Improve: **72%** Collapse: **6%**
Attrition: **8%** MLB: **90%**

Comparables:
Doug Drabek, Mike Grace, Jeff Karstens

YEAR	TEAM	LVL	AGE	W	L	SV	G	GS	IP	H	HR	BB	SO	BB9	SO9	GB%	BABIP	WHIP	ERA	FIP	FRA	WARP
2010	ROC	AAA	24	5	12	0	22	22	111^2	143	14	38	69	3.1	5.6	36%	.333	1.62	6.20	4.84	6.29	-1.0
2011	ROC	AAA	25	2	1	0	6	6	32^1	35	3	7	25	1.9	7.0	37%	.291	1.30	3.90	3.55	4.77	0.2
2011	MIN	MLB	25	4	7	0	27	11	102	111	9	26	55	2.3	4.9	40%	.296	1.34	4.32	4.07	4.52	0.8
2012	MIN	MLB	26	3	6	0	44	5	96^2	106	15	31	62	2.9	5.8	44%	.298	1.42	5.03	4.74	5.57	-0.3
2013	*MIN*	*MLB*	*27*	*3*	*5*	*0*	*24*	*11*	83^2	*96*	*11*	*27*	*47*	*2.9*	*5.0*	*38%*	*.304*	*1.47*	*5.10*	*4.75*	*5.54*	*-0.2*

Cut from the same cloth the Twins should have burned after making Brad Radke, Swarzak is a command righty who can't miss bats, with a low-90s fastball, fly-ball tendencies, and almost no upside. It's been five years since he was a real prospect, so the Twins are finally trying to turn him into a reliever and getting mediocre results for their efforts. If Twins fans didn't love Bradke so much to this day, they'd curse the reign of soft-tossing terror he hath wrought. Swarzak will be part of the uninspiring middle-relief corps the Twins trot out on Opening Day as part of what will probably be an eight-man bullpen.

Caleb Thielbar

Born: **1/31/1987** Age: **26**
Bats: **L** Throws: **R** Height: **6' 1"** Weight: **200**
Breakout: **30%** Improve: **44%** Collapse: **40%**
Attrition: **33%** MLB: **88%**

Comparables:
Scott Schoeneweis,Will McEnaney,Donnie Moore

YEAR	TEAM	LVL	AGE	W	L	SV	G	GS	IP	H	HR	BB	SO	BB9	SO9	GB%	BABIP	WHIP	ERA	FIP	FRA	WARP
2010	HEL	Rk	23	0	0	0	9	0	14^{2}	16	2	0	9	0.0	5.5	47%	.311	1.09	3.67	4.53	6.16	-0.1
2010	WIS	A	23	0	2	3	30	0	53	65	6	14	43	2.4	7.3	42%	.331	1.49	5.60	4.25	5.93	-0.3
2011	FTM	A+	24	1	0	0	3	1	7^{1}	1	0	5	5	6.1	6.1	61%	.000	0.82	0.00	4.07	4.76	0.0
2012	FTM	A+	25	1	1	1	7	0	12^{1}	4	0	2	16	1.5	11.7	36%	.160	0.49	0.00	1.77	1.93	0.4
2012	NBR	AA	25	2	0	4	16	0	25	18	1	3	26	1.1	9.4	52%	.262	0.84	1.80	2.00	2.28	0.7
2012	ROC	AAA	25	3	1	1	25	1	40^{1}	42	5	16	32	3.6	7.1	44%	.301	1.44	3.57	4.45	5.39	0.0
2013	*MIN*	*MLB*	*26*	*1*	*0*	*1*	*20*	*0*	33^{2}	*39*	*5*	*14*	*20*	*3.6*	*5.4*	*44%*	*.309*	*1.56*	*5.63*	*5.19*	*6.12*	*-0.3*

After being cut by the Brewers at the end of 2010, Thielbar, a Minnesota native, latched on with the independent St. Paul Saints and impressed enough there in 2011 that the crosstown Twins picked him up toward the end of the season. He had a wild and highly successful 2012, his work across three levels impressing the Twins enough for them to add him to the 40-man. His peripherals got predictably worse as he climbed the ladder, though, and his 2-1 strikeout-to-walk ratio and five homers allowed don't suggest immediate success at the next level. He might be a better story than pitcher at this point, but it's an awfully good story.

Esmerling Vasquez

Born: **11/7/1983** Age: **29**
Bats: **R** Throws: **R** Height: **6' 2"** Weight: **200**
Breakout: **30%** Improve: **56%** Collapse: **20%**
Attrition: **17%** MLB: **79%**

Comparables:
Danys Baez,Ruddy Lugo,Steve Bedrosian

YEAR	TEAM	LVL	AGE	W	L	SV	G	GS	IP	H	HR	BB	SO	BB9	SO9	GB%	BABIP	WHIP	ERA	FIP	FRA	WARP
2010	RNO	AAA	26	0	0	0	1	0	1	1	0	0	1	0.0	9.0	33%	.333	1.00	0.00	1.58	2.36	0.0
2010	ARI	MLB	26	1	6	0	57	0	53^{2}	46	6	38	55	6.4	9.2	33%	.296	1.57	5.20	4.97	5.80	-0.4
2011	RNO	AAA	27	2	2	0	23	0	27^{2}	26	3	21	26	6.8	8.5	—	.287	1.70	6.18	5.92	6.43	0.0
2011	ARI	MLB	27	1	1	0	31	0	30^{1}	27	2	13	20	3.9	5.9	36%	.269	1.32	4.15	4.21	4.78	0.0
2012	ROC	AAA	28	9	6	0	31	8	100^{1}	74	8	39	98	3.5	8.8	38%	.265	1.13	2.78	3.62	4.65	0.6
2012	MIN	MLB	28	0	2	0	6	6	31^{2}	32	2	19	14	5.4	4.0	34%	.286	1.61	5.68	4.88	5.90	-0.2
2013	*MIN*	*MLB*	*29*	*2*	*2*	*0*	*29*	*3*	50^{2}	*48*	*5*	*29*	*40*	*5.1*	*7.2*	*40%*	*.292*	*1.52*	*4.78*	*4.62*	*5.19*	*0.0*

Stop us if you've heard this before: The Twins were desperate for anyone who could soak up innings late in 2012, so much so that they started looking for Allan Anderson and Les Straker's phone numbers. Enter Vasquez, the former top prospect of the Texas Rangers, who at least had something of a pedigree to dream on, even though he's 28 and has a 4.59 ERA in five seasons at Triple-A. He got six starts, walked more batters than he struck out, and, shockingly, was not retained. He'll trade off his name and youthful exploits for one more summer on somebody's Triple-A roster, refusing to admit what many of us have had to, that he peaked too early.

Kyle Waldrop

Born: **10/27/1985** Age: **27**
Bats: **R** Throws: **R** Height: **6' 6"** Weight: **215**
Breakout: **46%** Improve: **62%** Collapse: **19%**
Attrition: **15%** MLB: **85%**

Comparables:
Franquelis Osoria,Chuck Crim,Wayne Granger

YEAR	TEAM	LVL	AGE	W	L	SV	G	GS	IP	H	HR	BB	SO	BB9	SO9	GB%	BABIP	WHIP	ERA	FIP	FRA	WARP
2010	ROC	AAA	24	5	3	2	59	0	87^{2}	89	5	20	60	2.1	6.2	63%	.303	1.24	2.57	3.59	4.71	0.3
2011	ROC	AAA	25	5	5	3	56	0	79	84	7	18	44	2.1	5.0	64%	.316	1.29	3.87	4.11	5.68	-0.3
2011	MIN	MLB	25	1	0	0	7	0	11	10	1	6	5	4.9	4.1	77%	.237	1.45	5.73	4.97	5.01	0.0
2012	FTM	A+	26	0	0	0	4	0	4	2	0	1	5	2.2	11.2	33%	.222	0.75	0.00	1.64	-1.13	0.1
2012	ROC	AAA	26	0	0	4	24	0	35	35	1	13	16	3.3	4.1	75%	.291	1.37	3.34	3.90	6.74	-0.5
2012	MIN	MLB	26	0	1	0	17	0	21^{1}	27	2	6	7	2.5	3.0	73%	.329	1.55	2.53	4.87	5.46	-0.1
2013	*MIN*	*MLB*	*27*	*1*	*0*	*0*	*24*	*0*	*34*	*39*	*4*	*12*	*16*	*3.1*	*4.2*	*58%*	*.304*	*1.50*	*5.12*	*4.85*	*5.57*	*-0.2*

Waldrop was drafted in the first round by the Twins way back in 2004. The story since then has been dominated by two themes: injury, including shoulder surgery that cost him all of 2008, and an inability to miss bats, both pre- and post-injury. Waldrop's minor-league strikeout rate is just 5.7 per nine innings, lower still in the upper levels, and in 21 1/3 big-league innings in 2012, he struck out just one for every three innings. That's unacceptably low, even by Twins standards.

P.J. Walters

Born: **3/12/1985** Age: **28**
Bats: **R** Throws: **R** Height: **6' 5"** Weight: **200**
Breakout: **32%** Improve: **70%** Collapse: **14%**
Attrition: **17%** MLB: **80%**

Comparables:
Luke Hochevar, Nate Robertson, Colby Lewis

YEAR	TEAM	LVL	AGE	W	L	SV	G	GS	IP	H	HR	BB	SO	BB9	SO9	GB%	BABIP	WHIP	ERA	FIP	FRA	WARP
2010	MEM	AAA	25	8	5	0	19	18	108^2	106	12	30	106	2.5	8.8	38%	.311	1.25	3.81	4.12	3.94	2.4
2010	SLN	MLB	25	2	0	0	7	3	30	32	5	10	22	3.0	6.6	43%	.293	1.40	6.00	4.81	5.79	-0.3
2011	LVG	AAA	26	1	3	0	7	7	29	44	4	16	26	5.0	8.1	35%	.382	2.07	8.38	5.75	4.61	0.5
2011	MEM	AAA	26	7	4	0	17	17	103^1	105	9	42	87	3.7	7.6	—	.316	1.42	4.27	4.80	5.22	0.0
2011	SLN	MLB	26	0	0	0	4	0	4	3	1	2	3	4.5	6.8	39%	.167	1.25	9.00	6.24	9.79	-0.2
2011	TOR	MLB	26	0	0	0	1	0	1	0	0	1	1	9.0	9.0	%	.000	1.00	0.00	4.06	4.43	0.0
2012	ROC	AAA	27	3	3	0	14	14	58^1	67	7	15	47	2.3	7.3	43%	.337	1.41	4.01	3.93	5.18	0.3
2012	MIN	MLB	27	2	5	0	12	12	61^2	71	12	22	42	3.2	6.1	43%	.307	1.51	5.69	5.43	5.89	-0.3
2013	*MIN*	*MLB*	*28*	*2*	*5*	*0*	*12*	*12*	*59^2*	*65*	*9*	*23*	*46*	*3.5*	*7.0*	*46%*	*.310*	*1.48*	*5.20*	*4.78*	*5.65*	*-0.2*

Injuries to what seemed like most of the Twins staff forced 27-year-old journeyman Walters into the starting rotation for about a third of a season. In his first four starts, Walters threw 27 innings with a 2.96 ERA, including a complete-game, eight-strikeout performance on May 22. Beginner's luck? In his remaining eight, Walters threw 34 1/3 innings with a 7.86 ERA sandwiched around a 60-day DL stint with shoulder inflammation. He's neither nearly as good nor quite as bad as all that, but with a knack for serving up the home-run ball and an uninspiring K/BB rate, a 2013 Twins season that sees Walters as anything more than a long reliever figures to be a very long one.

Alex Wimmers

Born: **11/1/1988** Age: **24**
Bats: **L** Throws: **R** Height: **6' 3"** Weight: **195**
Breakout: **33%** Improve: **61%** Collapse: **18%**
Attrition: **12%** MLB: **90%**

Comparables:
Scott Elbert, Gerry Arrigo, Jonathan Sanchez

YEAR	TEAM	LVL	AGE	W	L	SV	G	GS	IP	H	HR	BB	SO	BB9	SO9	GB%	BABIP	WHIP	ERA	FIP	FRA	WARP
2010	FTM	A+	21	2	0	0	4	4	15^2	6	0	5	23	2.9	13.2	44%	.200	0.70	0.57	1.46	2.93	0.4
2011	TWI	Rk	22	0	0	0	1	0	1	0	0	1	1	9.0	9.0	50%	.000	1.00	0.00	4.42	4.66	0.0
2011	FTM	A+	22	2	3	1	12	4	40^2	28	5	22	39	4.9	8.6	28%	.180	1.23	4.20	4.84	6.79	-0.3
2012	TWI	Rk	23	0	1	0	1	1	0^2	4	0	1	0	13.5	0.0	40%	.800	7.50	40.50	7.93	15.03	-0.1
2012	NBR	AA	23	0	0	0	1	1	4^1	6	1	2	3	4.2	6.2	—	.333	1.85	4.15	6.20	6.74	0.0
2013	*MIN*	*MLB*	*24*	*1*	*2*	*0*	*10*	*5*	*33^2*	*33*	*4*	*19*	*33*	*4.9*	*8.7*	*41%*	*.307*	*1.52*	*4.81*	*4.48*	*5.22*	*0.1*

So much for that. The 2010 first-rounder was considered a safe pick who would move quickly through the Twins organization and wind up a perfectly capable mid-rotation starter. Instead, he developed the yips in his first outing of 2011 and lost almost the entire season. Then he was diagnosed with a partially torn elbow ligament last year, which the Twins tried to treat with rest and rehabilitation (as they seem to always do). Alas, it deteriorated and Wimmers went under the knife in August. He'll miss all of this season and will go into 2014 as a 25-year-old who has pitched a grand total of four-and-a-third innings above A-ball.

Tim Wood

Born: **11/16/1982** Age: **30**
Bats: **R** Throws: **R** Height: **6' 1"** Weight: **180**
Breakout: **26%** Improve: **50%** Collapse: **34%**
Attrition: **18%** MLB: **85%**

Comparables:
Tim Crabtree, Bill Dailey, Luis Aponte

YEAR	TEAM	LVL	AGE	W	L	SV	G	GS	IP	H	HR	BB	SO	BB9	SO9	GB%	BABIP	WHIP	ERA	FIP	FRA	WARP
2010	NWO	AAA	27	0	1	0	14	0	14	19	4	4	12	2.6	7.7	52%	.326	1.64	6.43	6.44	7.46	-0.3
2010	FLO	MLB	27	0	1	1	26	0	27^2	33	2	15	10	4.9	3.3	42%	.304	1.73	5.53	4.95	5.19	-0.1
2011	IND	AAA	28	2	0	23	40	0	44^1	32	1	12	32	2.4	6.5	51%	.172	0.99	2.84	2.90	4.27	0.3
2011	ROU	AAA	28	0	0	1	4	0	4^2	9	1	3	2	5.8	3.9	—	.471	2.57	9.64	7.64	8.30	0.0
2011	PIT	MLB	28	0	3	0	13	0	8	8	1	8	2	9.0	2.2	36%	.259	2.00	5.62	7.12	8.40	-0.3
2012	IND	AAA	29	6	6	21	54	0	70	55	3	23	67	3.0	8.6	47%	.267	1.11	2.19	2.83	3.56	1.0
2013	*MIN*	*MLB*	*30*	*1*	*1*	*1*	*30*	*0*	*34^1*	*36*	*4*	*14*	*22*	*3.8*	*5.7*	*49%*	*.292*	*1.46*	*4.72*	*4.66*	*5.13*	*0.0*

Wood has logged 58 innings over three seasons in the big leagues, and the results haven't been good. His recent minor-league performance has been solid, though, especially since the start of 2011. The 30-year-old will never be a relief ace, but did get nearly a strikeout per inning in Triple-A in 2012, and the Twins signed him to a minor-league deal in November, then added him to the 40-man two weeks later, with the idea that he could be a better bullpen option than the chaff they were stuck trotting out there in 2012.

Vance Worley

Born: **9/25/1987** Age: **25**
Bats: **R** Throws: **R** Height: **6' 3"** Weight: **230**
Breakout: **16%** Improve: **47%** Collapse: **18%**
Attrition: **24%** MLB: **90%**

Comparables:
Jason Windsor, Dillon Gee, Brett Cecil

YEAR	TEAM	LVL	AGE	W	L	SV	G	GS	IP	H	HR	BB	SO	BB9	SO9	GB%	BABIP	WHIP	ERA	FIP	FRA	WARP
2010	REA	AA	22	9	4	0	19	19	112^2	114	9	36	83	2.9	6.6	47%	.309	1.33	3.19	3.96	4.14	1.7
2010	LEH	AAA	22	1	3	0	8	8	45^1	46	3	10	36	2.0	7.2	52%	.314	1.24	3.77	3.29	4.05	0.3
2010	PHI	MLB	22	1	1	0	5	2	13	8	1	4	12	2.8	8.3	51%	.206	0.92	1.38	3.18	3.30	0.3
2011	LEH	AAA	23	5	2	0	9	9	50^2	41	5	12	50	2.1	8.9	—	.271	1.05	2.31	3.37	3.67	0.0
2011	PHI	MLB	23	11	3	0	25	21	131^2	116	10	46	119	3.1	8.1	42%	.283	1.23	3.01	3.29	3.83	1.6
2012	PHI	MLB	24	6	9	0	23	23	133	154	12	47	107	3.2	7.2	47%	.341	1.51	4.20	3.90	4.14	1.2
2013	*MIN*	*MLB*	*25*	*5*	*8*	*0*	*18*	*18*	*106^2*	*117*	*12*	*38*	*74*	*3.2*	*6.3*	*45%*	*.310*	*1.45*	*4.89*	*4.34*	*5.31*	*-0.0*

The trade of Worley and May to the Twins in early December for Revere catapulted Worley from a forgotten man in an excellent rotation to perhaps the top man in a very poor one. He gets a fair number of strikeouts, avoids walks at about an average rate, and generally keeps the ball in the park. Worley isn't a savior, but at just 25 and under team control for the next five seasons, he's a good start toward a rebuilt rotation that *could* be respectable by 2014 or 2015.

LINEOUTS

HITTERS

PLAYER	TEAM	LVL	AGE	PA	R	2B	3B	HR	RBI	BB	SO	SB-CS	AVG/OBP/SLG	TAv	BABIP	BRR	FRAA	WARP
3B S. Burroughs	ROC	AAA	31	240	23	14	0	1	18	16	25	2-0	.271/.326/.348	.205	.303	0.4	1B(23): 0.1, 3B(9): -0.1	-0.8
	MIN	MLB	31	18	0	1	0	0	1	1	3	0-0	.118/.167/.176	.119	.143	0	3B(3): 0.1, 1B(1): 0.0	-0.2
1B J. Clement	IND	AAA	28	459	58	35	2	16	57	41	101	1-0	.276/.340/.486	.261	.329	-3.3	1B(52): 0.3	-0.2
	PIT	MLB	28	24	1	1	0	0	1	2	7	0-0	.136/.208/.182	.165	.200	0	1B(1): 0.0	-0.2
OF B. Dinkelman	ROC	AAA	28	279	32	13	3	4	32	26	46	5-5	.252/.336/.378	.228	.296	1.3	LF(21): -1.1, 2B(9): 0.8	-0.7
C E. Fryer	IND	AAA	26	176	14	7	0	0	10	10	38	1-0	.204/.257/.247	.178	.264	0.8	C(31): -0.4, LF(7): -0.4	-1.1
3B T. Harrison	ELZ	Rk	19	253	39	12	4	5	27	24	51	3-0	.301/.383/.461	.295	.367	-2.5	3B(23): -4.4	-0.1
OF C. Herrmann	NBR	AA	24	558	91	25	1	10	61	58	89	2-1	.276/.350/.392	.271	.315	1.4	C(64): 0.2, LF(21): -2.1	1.6
	MIN	MLB	24	19	0	0	0	0	1	1	5	0-0	.056/.105/.056	.072	.077	0	C(3): -0.0, LF(2): -0.1	-0.4
CF A. Morales	FTM	A+	22	420	56	8	5	7	35	45	115	12-3	.220/.310/.328	.257	.298	-0.1	CF(81): 8.9	1.8
MI T. Nishioka	ROC	AAA	27	431	42	18	1	2	34	32	53	7-7	.258/.315/.324	.221	.293	-1.5	2B(72): -3.5, SS(15): 0.9	-1.6
	MIN	MLB	27	14	0	0	0	0	1	1	1	0-0	.000/.071/.000	.071	.000	0	2B(3): -0.2	-0.2
INF R. Olmedo	CHR	AAA	31	310	24	15	1	0	19	27	42	9-3	.273/.340/.335	.242	.322	0.9	SS(32): -0.5, 2B(15): 2.5	0.3
	CHA	MLB	31	42	8	2	0	0	1	0	9	0-0	.244/.244/.293	.205	.312	-0.2	3B(10): 0.0, SS(5): 0.0	-0.1
SS J. Polanco	ELZ	Rk	18	204	35	15	2	5	27	20	26	6-3	.318/.388/.514	.299	.340	-1.3	2B(14): 2.4, SS(5): -0.0	0.6
MI D. Santana	FTM	A+	21	547	70	21	9	8	60	29	77	17-11	.286/.329/.410	.277	.322	-1.4	SS(63): -3.7, 2B(25): 0.2	0.8
OF C. Thomas	ROC	AAA	28	426	47	22	5	12	47	27	109	15-4	.232/.281/.405	.216	.288	-0.4	CF(82): -13.8, RF(4): 1.8	-2.7
	MIN	MLB	28	29	2	1	0	1	4	0	16	0-0	.143/.172/.286	.152	.273	0	RF(9): 0.0, CF(1): 0.1	-0.2

It's been a rocky ride for **Sean Burroughs**, BP's number-three prospect of 2002, and the MLB leg of it may have come to an end with his 2-for-18 performance with the Twins in 2012. ⚾ **Jeff Clement**, the former third-overall pick, returned to the majors for the first time since 2010, but his slow bat and lack of position will land him in Rochester for most or all of 2013. ⚾ **Brian Dinkelman**: At least his name was memorable. Dinkelman . . . heh. ⚾ **Eric Fryer** can do whatever the organization asks him to do—except hit big-league pitching. ⚾ **Travis Harrison**, a 2011 sandwich-round pick, has the misfortune of being the positionless player with an excellent bat that's just not nearly as excellent as Miguel Sano's. ⚾ Having shown impressive on-base skills in the minors, there's a good chance **Chris Herrmann** has a future in the big leagues as a fourth outfielder/third-string catcher. ⚾ **Angel Morales** has gotten progressively worse in each of his three seasons at Fort Myers, and is quickly running out of time. ⚾ **Tsuyoshi Nishioka** agreed to forego about $3.25 million in exchange for a release from his contract to return to Japan. Here's hoping he resurrects his career and is remembered more for that classy move than as a cautionary tale. ⚾ **Ray Olmedo** can cover several positions and is probably still good enough at shortstop that he's worth starting at Triple-A. ⚾ A rare middle-infield prospect in this system, **Jorge Polanco** broke out in a huge way in the Appalachian League, but is only 19 and will have to prove himself in full-season ball this year. ⚾ **Daniel Santana** is a bit error-prone at both second and short and has never played above High-A, but the Twins liked his improved bat enough to use a 40-man slot on him. ⚾ **Clete Thomas** was picked up off of waivers, hit a homer in his first at-bat, and struck out in 55.2 percent of his plate appearances, which is seventh worst in history among players who came to the plate at least 20 times.

PITCHERS

PLAYER	TEAM	LVL	AGE	W	L	SV	IP	H	HR	BB	SO	BB9	SO9	GB%	BABIP	WHIP	ERA	FIP	FRA	WARP
M. Boer	BLT	A	22	2	2	0	27^2	26	1	10	20	3.3	6.5	52%	.294	1.30	3.58	3.46	3.49	0.0
	FTM	A+	22	7	10	0	111	147	15	32	66	2.6	5.4	42%	.344	1.61	6.41	5.02	6.47	-0.6
H. Boyd	ELZ	Rk	19	2	5	0	58	63	7	23	36	3.6	5.6	54%	.293	1.48	2.95	5.48	7.07	0.3
B. Hermsen	FTM	A+	22	1	0	0	23	16	1	5	12	2.0	4.7	49%	.211	0.91	0.78	3.70	4.54	0.2
	NBR	AA	22	11	6	0	139^2	145	12	25	75	1.6	4.8	45%	.286	1.22	3.22	3.89	4.66	0.6
P. Hernandez	BIR	AA	23	7	2	0	68^2	68	6	18	37	2.4	4.8	46%	.276	1.25	2.75	3.99	4.09	0.3
	CHA	MLB	23	0	1	0	4	12	3	1	2	2.2	4.5	41%	.474	3.25	18.00	12.55	13.00	-0.3
M. Maloney	ROC	AAA	28	0	4	0	24	46	5	7	16	2.6	6.0	41%	.423	2.21	9.38	5.78	6.84	0.0
	MIN	MLB	28	1	0	0	11	17	2	1	5	0.8	4.1	42%	.349	1.64	8.18	5.05	5.07	0.0
L. Perdomo	NBR	AA	28	4	4	2	39^1	27	0	16	43	3.7	9.8	48%	.273	1.09	2.75	2.31	3.17	0.7
	ROC	AAA	28	4	1	7	33^1	27	4	6	25	1.6	6.8	51%	.232	0.99	2.43	3.76	4.84	0.2
	MIN	MLB	28	0	0	0	17	15	0	12	8	6.4	4.2	50%	.268	1.59	3.18	4.58	6.53	-0.3
A. Salcedo	FTM	A+	21	0	1	0	25^1	33	1	15	14	5.3	5.0	55%	.352	1.89	6.39	4.70	6.09	0.0
M. Tonkin	BLT	A	22	3	0	6	39	29	1	9	53	2.1	12.2	52%	.313	0.97	1.38	1.74	0.42	1.3
	FTM	A+	22	1	1	6	30^1	24	2	11	44	3.3	13.1	37%	.324	1.15	2.97	2.64	2.74	0.7

The Twins hoped for more from **Madison Boer**, a second-round pick who's gone bad; he could still turn out okay, 'cause his fastball will play, but he's no longer such a young lad. Don't let the ERA fool you: Hard-throwing **Hudson Boyd**, a sandwich-round pick in 2011, had a terrible debut at Elizabethton, not missing any bats and allowing 33 runs in 58 innings. Another command righty who doesn't miss bats, **B.J. Hermsen** generates good sink and a lot of grounders and will probably see time in Minnesota (and get knocked around something fierce) before this season mercifully ends. Part of the "haul" from the Francisco Liriano trade, **Pedro Hernandez** is a short command lefty in the Eddie Guardado mold who could make it in short relief. **Matt Maloney** was knocked all over the Twin Cities, then all over Rochester, and then it turned out he was pitching with a bum elbow; after Tommy John surgery, he might still get a shot at the back end of somebody's rotation. **Luis Perdomo**'s 17 big-league innings included 12 walks, but his minor-league 2012 numbers suggest a pitcher who could be of some value in the back of the Twins pen, or someone's. Righty **Adrian Salcedo** is a classic Twins starter in development—with a low-90s fastball and more talent at avoiding walks than collecting strikeouts—but will only turn 22 early in the 2013 season, and still has a long way to go. A hard thrower, **Michael Tonkin** made a leap last year and really began missing bats; he has an outside chance to wind up in Minnesota before the year is out.

MANAGER: RON GARDENHIRE

YEAR	TEAM	W-L	Pythag +/-	Avg PC	100+ P	120+ P	QS	BQS	REL	REL w Zero R	IBB	PH	PH Avg	PH HR	SB2	CS2	SB3	CS3	SAC Att	SAC %	POS SAC	Squeeze	Swing	In Play
2010	MIN	94-68	1	187.1	157	155	105	6	465	377	38	150	.156	4	8	5	0	0	100	86.0%	76	2	272	101
2011	MIN	63-99	0	95.2	66	2	80	9	457	340	37	87	.175	0	6	4	0	2	52	86.5%	45	1	361	135
2012	MIN	66-96	0	88.0	29	0	62	3	499	390	43	59	.260	0	24	3	0	1	52	73.1%	37	1	384	108

All the changes to his coaching staff may indicate that Gardenhire is finally on the hot seat in Minnesota after 11 seasons. That would really be a shame. It's not that Gardy is some kind of tactical genius. He's not. He orders steals fairly often and at a good rate, and has, historically at least, proven good at managing his bullpen, even if he has a tendency to ride his go-to arms a little hard. But he balances his strong points by refusing to platoon players who have needed it, insisting on carrying extra pitchers, and occasionally forgetting players who are on his bench for a week or more at a time. So he's comfortably blah on the field. He may not earn the club extra wins, but he doesn't cost them much either.

Where Gardenhire excels is in the clubhouse, where he remains popular and has successfully minimized squabbles among his players. We tend to downplay this part of a manager's job, but players spend almost every day and night together for more than six months, and without careful management of their personalities, locker rooms can become toxic environments. That may or may not matter to the performance on the field, but players do talk to one another. And when hometown stars want to extend their stays for below market value, or free agents weigh competitive offers, having a respected, beloved, and stable manager in place can tip the balance in the Twins' favor. Gardenhire deserves recognition for that.

New York Mets

2012: SORRY

The most important Mets news of 2012 was made off the field as the ownership group began to rise from the Bernie Madoff-related grave it had fallen into. Between the lines, the team's performance was solid but uninspiring, driven by a wealth of useful players but very few stars.

Financial news is often far from scintillating. We might prefer to focus on whether general manager Sandy Alderson hit on his second-round pick, but the team getting its books in order is more meaningful for the future of the franchise. Majority owners Fred Wilpon and Saul Katz settled a $1 billion suit for about 15 percent of that amount and sold minority shares of the team. This allowed them to retain control while infusing the franchise with over $200 million in cash, which allowed them to pay back loans to Bank of America and Major League Baseball.

Meanwhile, the on-field product was respectable but simply lacked the top-end talent to make a realistic run at the playoffs. David Wright and Cy Young Award-winner R.A. Dickey were excellent, but that Daniel Murphy—a merely solid player—finished third on the squad in WARP illustrates the thin upper-crust of the roster. That said, many 2012 teams engaged in rebuilding projects while fielding a significantly worse team than the Mets, who wound up just under .500 in BP's third-order adjusted standings, which take account of underlying player performance and adjust for schedule strength.

METS PROSPECTUS

2012 W-L: 74-88, 4th in NL East

Pythag	.460	20th	DER	.710	14th
RS/G	4.01	25th	B-Age	27.7	8th
RA/G	4.38	19th	P-Age	30.1	28th
TAv	.255	22nd	Salary	$94.5	16th
BRR	6.7	5th	M$/MW	$3.19	21st
TAv-P	.258	13th	DL Days	916	13th
FIP	3.97	17th	DL WARP	2.8	19th

Three-Year Park Factors	
Overall	99
HR/RH	109
HR/LH	107
AVG/RH	96
AVG/LH	97

Citi Field (2009)
Att. % of Capacity: 67.1% (17th)
Dim. 335, 385, 408, 398, 330

Citi Field continues to play as a solid homer park, but is tough otherwise for hitters, especially righties.

2013: PATIENCE

Expectations for 2013 should be measured on the same scale as 2012: hope for respectability, wish for high-upside talent in the draft, and dream on the occasional heart-lifting individual performance on the field. Whatever shape the Opening Day roster winds up taking, 2013 must be viewed as a middle year in a long-term project to completely rebuild the health of what should be one of the marquee franchises in baseball.

Middles can be dull—*The Two Towers* was the least compelling of Peter Jackson's *Lord of the Rings* trilogy—but the possibility for excitement is not wiped out completely. With no legitimate shot at a World Series ring to rule them all, the focus for Mets fans will turn to enjoying the stars the team does have to offer, as well as potential future stars such as Matt Harvey, who dominated in a short stint late in 2012, Zack Wheeler, who is in line for a late-2013 promotion of his own, and Travis d'Arnaud, who headlined the blockbuster trade of Dickey to Toronto and could be starting by the All-Star break.

A team in the Mets' position typically looks to flip anybody who will not be part of the next good squad for young players with upside, as they did with Dickey. Of course, if the Mets had a stockpile of talent to deal, they would also have a stockpile of talent to put on the field. Having signed Wright to an extension and traded Dickey, there does not appear to be much else for the Mets to sell off. Thus, Alderson, amateur scouting chief Paul DePodesta, and the rest of the draft team must do better than previous regimes at selecting future stars. Former GMs Steve Phillips, Jim Duquette, and Omar Minaya combined to draft one excellent player (Wright) in 13 first rounds, including sandwich picks. In all those drafts, they managed exactly four players in the second round who even made the majors.

STATE OF THE ORGANIZATION: CLUE

The Mets operate in a metropolitan area of 20 million souls. What they ought to be doing is throwing their financial heft around to supplement a home-grown core with hole-filling free-agent stars, as a certain other New York team is wont to do. With the debt situation under control and the Shadow of Madoff slowly receding, a light flickers in the gloom that has persisted since 2009. The franchise is on the path to recovery and has every opportunity to be a menace to the rest of the league soon.

Models for the Mets to follow in accomplishing this task abound, with the nearest being just miles away in a general northwesterly direction. The Yankees have been adding pricey outside ballers like Alex Rodriguez and Randy Johnson to their Jeter-Pettitte-Rivera-Posada-Cano core for close to two decades now. The Mets can also look to their own recent past: the 2007-09 team featured the home-grown Wright and Jose Reyes, dual import Carloses (Beltran and Delgado), and Johan Santana. The latter represents what a team can accomplish with both money and a farm system: Win the bidding for a star player in trade, then sign him to a long-term extension. The Mets are about to regain the financial wherewithal to make moves that teams in places like Oakland and San Diego can only watch with envy.

By all appearances, the team is in good hands. There are three ex-general managers in the Mets front office (the aforementioned Alderson and DePodesta along with former Blue Jays honcho J.P. Ricciardi), all of whom are comfortable with the new world order that requires a blend of scouting and statistical acumen. The team also employs the well-respected John Ricco, who was interim GM for 25 days in 2010 and has a strong background in contract-compliance and statistical/financial analysis. The (relatively) new collective bargaining agreement's limits on draft and international spending will not let the Mets take shortcuts in the amateur markets, but the overall advantage of financial brawn is not likely to be eliminated any time soon. Some of Minaya's questionable decisions and, even more importantly, those of Wilpon and Katz left the Mets in a shambles, but the reordering of the franchise's fortunes proceeds apace.

HITTERS

Mike Baxter **OF**
Born: **12/7/1984** Age: **28**
Bats: **L** Throws: **R** Height: **6' 1"**
Weight: **190** Breakout: **0%**
Improve: **49%** Collapse: **5%**
Attrition: **14%** MLB: **91%**
Comparables:
Bob Hazle, Trot Nixon, Bobby Higginson

YEAR	TEAM	LVL	AGE	PA	R	2B	3B	HR	RBI	BB	SO	SB	CS	AVG_OBP_SLG	TAv	BABIP	BRR	FRAA	WARP
2010	POR	AAA	25	552	89	30	10	18	72	58	78	22	10	.301/.385/.517	.313	.329	0.4	RF(57): -1.9, 1B(46): -0.2	3.4
2010	SDN	MLB	25	9	0	0	0	0	1	0	2	0	0	.125/.111/.125	.083	.143	0	1B(1): -0.0	-0.1
2011	BUF	AAA	26	71	4	0	2	1	7	5	19	1	0	.188/.257/.297	.171	.250	0.1	RF(7): -0.8, LF(5): -0.5	-0.7
2011	NYN	MLB	26	40	6	2	1	1	4	5	9	0	0	.235/.350/.441	.278	.292	-0.3	RF(10): -1.0, LF(3): 0.1	0.1
2012	NYN	MLB	27	211	26	14	2	3	17	25	45	5	3	.263/.365/.413	.286	.331	3.1	RF(45): -0.9, LF(18): -0.1	0.8
2013	*NYN*	*MLB*	*28*	*250*	*28*	*12*	*2*	*6*	*27*	*23*	*52*	*6*	*3*	*.248/.328/.398*	*.264*	*.297*	*0.1*	*RF -0, LF -0*	*0.6*

Pop songs and fringe ballplayers: both need hooks if they're going to be successful. Baxter's hook is that he hit .458/.559/.708 in 34 pinch-hit appearances. He won't do that every year, but if managers can platoon him as strictly as Terry Collins did in 2012, he could be a minor asset to a National League team, much like Eagle Eye Cherry's "Save Tonight" is a minor asset to every senior prom since 1999.

John Buck **C**
Born: **7/7/1980** Age: **32**
Bats: **R** Throws: **R** Height: **6' 4"**
Weight: **230** Breakout: **6%**
Improve: **31%** Collapse: **6%**
Attrition: **16%** MLB: **90%**
Comparables:
Ozzie Virgil, Gus Triandos, Gene Oliver

YEAR	TEAM	LVL	AGE	PA	R	2B	3B	HR	RBI	BB	SO	SB	CS	AVG_OBP_SLG	TAv	BABIP	BRR	FRAA	WARP
2010	TOR	MLB	30	437	53	25	0	20	66	16	111	0	0	.281/.314/.489	.281	.335	1	C(112): -1.1	2.9
2011	FLO	MLB	31	530	41	15	1	16	57	54	115	0	1	.227/.316/.367	.246	.268	-0.3	C(135): -2.0	0.6
2012	MIA	MLB	31	398	29	15	1	12	41	49	103	0	0	.192/.297/.347	.232	.235	-0.9	C(104): 3.3	0.5
2013	*NYN*	*MLB*	*32*	*400*	*43*	*16*	*1*	*13*	*46*	*33*	*102*	*0*	*0*	*.225/.295/.385*	*.248*	*.273*	*-0.7*	*C -0*	*1.2*

Buck is a good man. He puts food on the table for his wife and twin boys, and he rescues elderly women when their cars flip over in Broward County. But he's no longer a good baseball player, and the Marlins were on the hook for $6 million for another year of a human legend and a baseball lemon. Buck's offensive numbers predictably tumbled with the move to Miami in 2011, and they were felled further by the new ballpark, which sent his batting average plummeting through the Mendoza line. Our hero was involved in both of the Blue Jays' major trades over the winter, moving from Miami in the Jose Reyes-Mark Buehrle-Josh Johnson deal and then coming to Queens in the R.A. Dickey swap. He could start, but with Travis d'Arnaud breathing down his neck, his time is short.

Gavin Cecchini SS

Born: 12/22/1993 Age: 19
Bats: R Throws: R Height: 6' 2"
Weight: 180 Breakout: 0%
Improve: 65% Collapse: 35%
Attrition: 35% MLB: 100%

Comparables:
Ed Kranepool,Wayne Causey,Robin Yount

YEAR	TEAM	LVL	AGE	PA	R	2B	3B	HR	RBI	BB	SO	SB	CS	AVG_OBP_SLG	TAv	BABIP	BRR	FRAA	WARP
2012	KNG	Rk	18	212	21	9	2	1	22	18	43	5	4	.246/.311/.330	.285	.309	0.7	SS(14): -2.0	0.1
2013	*NYN*	*MLB*	*19*	*250*	*15*	*8*	*1*	*2*	*18*	*11*	*74*	*0*	*0*	*.179/.218/.238*	*.175*	*.249*	*-0.3*	*SS 0*	*-1.3*

If you think you've already read about Cecchini, it's because his brother Garin is a well-regarded third baseman in the Red Sox system. Gavin's profile is classic coach's kid (which he is—dad was his head coach at powerhouse Louisiana high school Barbe): the sum is greater than the parts, baseball smarts abound, etc. He was the 12th-overall pick, though, so he's not David Eckstein. The consensus is that Cecchini has all the tools and instincts to stay at shortstop and be an asset in the field at the major-league level. The open question is whether he has enough pop to keep the bat from being knocked out of his hands as he moves up the ladder.

Darrell Ceciliani CF

Born: 6/22/1990 Age: 23
Bats: L Throws: L Height: 6' 2"
Weight: 220 Breakout: 7%
Improve: 44% Collapse: 5%
Attrition: 13% MLB: 91%

Comparables:
Milt Cuyler,Roger Cedeno,Dave Martinez

YEAR	TEAM	LVL	AGE	PA	R	2B	3B	HR	RBI	BB	SO	SB	CS	AVG_OBP_SLG	TAv	BABIP	BRR	FRAA	WARP
2010	BRO	A-	20	303	56	19	12	2	35	24	56	21	14	.351/.407/.531	.331	.431	3.5	CF(68): 6.7	4.5
2011	SAV	A	21	488	62	23	4	4	40	52	96	25	8	.259/.351/.361	.285	.327	1.3	CF(65): 3.8	1.9
2012	SLU	A+	22	99	19	6	1	1	10	10	13	2	0	.329/.402/.459	.272	.375	0.2	CF(12): -0.4	0.2
2013	*NYN*	*MLB*	*23*	*250*	*27*	*10*	*1*	*2*	*16*	*16*	*64*	*8*	*4*	*.225/.279/.306*	*.219*	*.298*	*0.2*	*CF -1*	*-0.4*

By reaching High-A, Ceciliani has already gone farther than you would expect from someone who wasn't drafted out of high school. He's been bothered repeatedly by hamstring issues, however, and players who make the entirely reasonable decision to work their family ranch rather than play on travel teams need all the development time they can get. If he can't get on the field, he can't learn to actualize his speed and become the nice fourth outfielder he's always dreamed of being.

Ronny Cedeno MI

Born: 2/2/1983 Age: 30
Bats: R Throws: R Height: 6' 1"
Weight: 190 Breakout: 2%
Improve: 50% Collapse: 2%
Attrition: 10% MLB: 89%

Comparables:
Alvin Dark,Dickie Thon,Dave Concepcion

YEAR	TEAM	LVL	AGE	PA	R	2B	3B	HR	RBI	BB	SO	SB	CS	AVG_OBP_SLG	TAv	BABIP	BRR	FRAA	WARP
2010	PIT	MLB	27	502	42	29	3	8	38	23	106	12	3	.256/.293/.382	.242	.315	0.7	SS(136): -5.4	0.2
2011	PIT	MLB	28	454	43	25	3	2	32	30	93	2	5	.249/.297/.339	.228	.313	1.7	SS(125): 9.3, 2B(1): 0.1	1.1
2012	NYN	MLB	29	186	18	11	1	4	22	17	35	0	1	.259/.332/.410	.257	.307	0.1	2B(28): -0.5, SS(27): -1.5	0.1
2013	*NYN*	*MLB*	*30*	*250*	*24*	*11*	*1*	*4*	*23*	*16*	*55*	*3*	*2*	*.235/.285/.347*	*.233*	*.286*	*-0.3*	*SS 1, 2B -0*	*0.4*

Cedeno had his best season with the stick, helped by Collins picking his spots: He got more plate time against lefties than righties on the year. He did manage two weeks as a starter, replacing Ruben Tejada after the latter went down with an injury in May. Unfortunately, Cedeno couldn't stay healthy himself—he hit the disabled list in late May with a strained calf. By the time he came back, Tejada was nearly ready to return. "Second-division starter" would be generous for a player of Cedeno's ilk, but two teams last year actually got worse production at second base than Cedeno's .226 career TAv.

Collin Cowgill OF

Born: 5/22/1986 Age: 27
Bats: R Throws: L Height: 5' 10"
Weight: 185 Breakout: 3%
Improve: 44% Collapse: 11%
Attrition: 23% MLB: 93%

Comparables:
Craig Gentry,Lynn Jones,Kevin Thompson

YEAR	TEAM	LVL	AGE	PA	R	2B	3B	HR	RBI	BB	SO	SB	CS	AVG_OBP_SLG	TAv	BABIP	BRR	FRAA	WARP
2010	MOB	AA	24	577	89	34	4	16	83	57	73	25	9	.285/.367/.464	.289	.308	-3	RF(80): -0.8, CF(38): 2.1	3.2
2011	RNO	AAA	25	456	95	24	8	13	70	51	63	30	3	.354/.430/.554	.341	.397	0	--	0.0
2011	ARI	MLB	25	100	8	3	0	1	9	8	28	4	2	.239/.300/.304	.230	.333	-1.3	LF(18): 2.3, CF(10): -0.3	-0.1
2012	SAC	AAA	26	285	33	17	1	4	37	20	50	8	2	.254/.312/.373	.322	.298	-0.3	CF(8): 0.4, LF(4): 0.6	0.6
2012	OAK	MLB	26	116	10	2	0	1	9	11	27	3	4	.269/.336/.317	.242	.351	-1.1	LF(16): 1.0, CF(15): -0.4	0.1
2013	*NYN*	*MLB*	*27*	*250*	*29*	*10*	*1*	*5*	*21*	*18*	*52*	*6*	*3*	*.239/.298/.354*	*.244*	*.288*	*0.1*	*CF -1, LF 0*	*0.2*

Cowgill had a logjam of outfielders ahead of him in Oakland, but a winter trade to the Mets may give him his first clear shot at playing time. With lefty-swinging Baxter, Lucas Duda, and Kirk Nieuwenhuis around and Terry Collins's propensity to platoon, Cowgill should at least find himself a job-share, and he could start at any of the three outfield spots. He's short and underpowered for a corner, but he'd make a lovely fourth outfielder on a good team.

Travis d'Arnaud C
Born: **2/10/1989** Age: **24**
Bats: **R** Throws: **R** Height: **6' 3"**
Weight: **195** Breakout: **5%**
Improve: **48%** Collapse: **9%**
Attrition: **18%** MLB: **98%**
Comparables:
Jesus Flores,Johnny Bench,Javy Lopez

YEAR	TEAM	LVL	AGE	PA	R	2B	3B	HR	RBI	BB	SO	SB	CS	AVG_OBP_SLG	TAv	BABIP	BRR	FRAA	WARP
2010	DUN	A+	21	292	36	20	1	6	38	20	63	3	1	.259/.321/.411	.263	.320	-2.4	C(58): -1.0	1.0
2011	NHP	AA	22	466	72	33	1	21	78	33	100	4	2	.311/.371/.542	.308	.365	0	--	0.0
2012	LVG	AAA	23	303	45	21	2	16	52	19	59	1	1	.333/.380/.595	.304	.374	0.1	C(48): 0.4, 1B(2): -0.1	2.2
2013	*NYN*	*MLB*	*24*	*250*	*26*	*11*	*1*	*9*	*32*	*14*	*62*	*0*	*0*	*.243/.288/.408*	*.252*	*.291*	*-0.4*	*C -0, 1B -0*	*0.8*

D'Arnaud missed the second half of the year with a left knee sprain, but he did enough in the first two months of the season to solidify his status as the game's best catching prospect. It would be easy to attribute d'Arnaud's power spike to the thin air of the Pacific Coast League, but 2012 marked the second consecutive year that his slugging percentage and home-run rates had increased. The only thing d'Arnaud has left to prove in the minor leagues is that he can stay healthy—he's averaged just 95 games per season since 2009. He has a shot at an Opening Day start, though a first half call-up is more likely.

Ike Davis 1B
Born: **3/22/1987** Age: **26**
Bats: **L** Throws: **L** Height: **6' 5"**
Weight: **230** Breakout: **3%**
Improve: **46%** Collapse: **4%**
Attrition: **13%** MLB: **98%**
Comparables:
Don Mincher,Mark Teixeira,Joey Votto

YEAR	TEAM	LVL	AGE	PA	R	2B	3B	HR	RBI	BB	SO	SB	CS	AVG_OBP_SLG	TAv	BABIP	BRR	FRAA	WARP
2010	NYN	MLB	23	601	73	33	1	19	71	72	138	3	2	.264/.351/.440	.288	.321	0.2	1B(146): 5.1	3.1
2011	NYN	MLB	24	149	20	8	1	7	25	17	31	0	0	.302/.383/.543	.323	.344	1.7	1B(36): 1.0	1.4
2012	NYN	MLB	25	584	66	26	0	32	90	61	141	0	2	.227/.308/.462	.270	.246	-2.7	1B(148): 3.0	1.0
2013	*NYN*	*MLB*	*26*	*462*	*57*	*21*	*1*	*21*	*66*	*51*	*109*	*1*	*1*	*.249/.332/.457*	*.284*	*.288*	*-1*	*1B -4*	*1.0*

Davis's 2012 was reminiscent of those old Tony Batista seasons where the home runs make you perk up right before the on-base percentage lets you back down. Talk of Davis's nightlife habits surfaced simultaneously with trade rumors in September, but rebuilding teams don't get anywhere by trading young, cheap players at the nadir of their value. Unless there's a real problem in his behavior, he's a bounce-back candidate: He swings at the pitches that power hitters should swing at, takes his walks, hits the ball in the air, and has consistently shown plenty of pop, including posting the 18th-best isolated slugging in baseball last year.

Matt Den Dekker CF
Born: **8/10/1987** Age: **25**
Bats: **L** Throws: **L** Height: **6' 2"**
Weight: **205** Breakout: **5%**
Improve: **61%** Collapse: **6%**
Attrition: **13%** MLB: **96%**
Comparables:
Derek Bell,Lloyd Moseby,Jason Repko

YEAR	TEAM	LVL	AGE	PA	R	2B	3B	HR	RBI	BB	SO	SB	CS	AVG_OBP_SLG	TAv	BABIP	BRR	FRAA	WARP
2011	SLU	A+	23	302	54	19	8	6	36	24	65	12	5	.296/.362/.494	.312	.369	1.8	CF(26): -2.2	1.0
2011	BIN	AA	23	314	49	13	3	11	32	27	91	12	5	.235/.312/.426	.254	.305	1.3	CF(39): -2.2	0.2
2012	BIN	AA	24	268	47	21	4	8	29	20	64	10	7	.340/.397/.563	.311	.429	2.1	CF(34): -1.5, RF(1): -0.1	1.2
2012	BUF	AAA	24	317	37	10	4	9	47	14	90	11	2	.220/.256/.373	.211	.279	4	CF(68): -2.8	-0.9
2013	*NYN*	*MLB*	*25*	*250*	*31*	*10*	*2*	*6*	*22*	*13*	*75*	*9*	*3*	*.229/.274/.367*	*.233*	*.304*	*0.7*	*CF -1, RF 0*	*0.1*

The reports on den Dekker's defense are excellent, as he is able to use his speed to run down balls that lesser athletes cannot. Said speed also plays on the bases, but the question is whether he'll make enough contact in the majors to put those jets to productive use. His impatience and tendency to expand the hitting zone, which may be seen as a symptom of his overall testicles-to-the-wall approach, are reflected in his walk and strikeout numbers above. If he's whiffing 150 times a year against Double-A and Triple-A pitchers, how is he going to fare against Roy Halladay and Cliff Lee?

Lucas Duda OF
Born: **2/3/1986** Age: **27**
Bats: **L** Throws: **R** Height: **6' 5"**
Weight: **255** Breakout: **3%**
Improve: **54%** Collapse: **5%**
Attrition: **7%** MLB: **96%**
Comparables:
Matt Joyce,Roger Maris,Austin Kearns

YEAR	TEAM	LVL	AGE	PA	R	2B	3B	HR	RBI	BB	SO	SB	CS	AVG_OBP_SLG	TAv	BABIP	BRR	FRAA	WARP
2010	BIN	AA	24	197	30	17	0	6	34	29	27	1	0	.286/.413/.503	.309	.312	0.5	LF(35): 1.9, 1B(9): -0.2	1.3
2010	BUF	AAA	24	298	44	23	2	17	53	31	57	0	0	.314/.391/.610	.321	.347	0.6	LF(60): -4.3, 1B(5): 0.4	2.0
2010	NYN	MLB	24	92	11	6	0	4	13	6	22	0	0	.202/.261/.417	.250	.220	0.7	LF(24): -1.4	0.0
2011	BUF	AAA	25	157	22	8	0	10	24	23	27	0	0	.302/.414/.597	.318	.309	-0.6	RF(10): -0.5, LF(8): -1.3	0.7
2011	NYN	MLB	25	347	38	21	3	10	50	33	57	1	0	.292/.370/.482	.308	.326	-3.8	1B(43): 1.2, RF(42): -2.3	1.3
2012	BUF	AAA	26	107	12	4	0	3	8	10	21	0	0	.260/.327/.396	.270	.301	-1	LF(17): -0.5, RF(4): 0.2	0.2
2012	NYN	MLB	26	459	43	15	0	15	57	51	120	1	0	.239/.329/.389	.259	.301	-5.2	RF(81): -6.9, LF(24): -0.5	-1.5
2013	*NYN*	*MLB*	*27*	*438*	*51*	*20*	*1*	*16*	*58*	*44*	*97*	*1*	*0*	*.251/.333/.433*	*.277*	*.293*	*-0.6*	*RF -0, LF -1*	*1.4*

Zip-a-Dee's WARP scores in 2011 and 2012 show the two poles for a player who hurts his team on the bases and in the field: hit and have modest value or don't hit and be a horrible sinkhole. Duda struggles with the low pitch. Major league pitchers being what they are, and major league advance scouting being what it is, you can guess where Duda was pitched in 2012. The ability to recognize the problem and adjust back will be key to Duda returning to a semblance of his 2011 self. (Apologies to readers who have been waiting all comment for a *Big Lebowski* joke. Not happening.)

Phillip Evans **SS**
Born: 9/10/1992 Age: 20
Bats: R Throws: R Height: 5' 11"
Weight: 185 Breakout: 9%
Improve: 24% Collapse: 35%
Attrition: 42% MLB: 93%
Comparables:
Robin Yount,Jose Oquendo,Ted Kazanski

YEAR	TEAM	LVL	AGE	PA	R	2B	3B	HR	RBI	BB	SO	SB	CS	AVG_OBP_SLG	TAv	BABIP	BRR	FRAA	WARP
2012	BRO	A-	19	329	32	8	1	5	29	31	48	2	0	.252/.328/.337	.275	.285	1.6	SS(57): -4.3	1.0
2013	*NYN*	*MLB*	*20*	*250*	*20*	*8*	*1*	*4*	*23*	*13*	*60*	*0*	*0*	*.207/.248/.301*	*.205*	*.256*	*-0.3*	*SS 1*	*-0.3*

Don't let Evans's 15th-round-pick status fool you: The Mets were willing to give him $650,000 to buy him out of his commitment to San Diego State. The bonus provides a more sensible starting point for expectations of Evans's future. That said, while he is a shortstop for now, Evans's thick lower body has led to little belief that he'll be anything but a second baseman if he reaches the majors. Even moving across the keystone is likely to leave Evans needing to be an offense-first prospect, which itself means that he's going to have to overcome some physical limitations, most notably the T-Rex arms that give him little in the way of plate coverage.

Wilmer Flores **INF**
Born: 8/6/1991 Age: 21
Bats: R Throws: R Height: 6' 4"
Weight: 175 Breakout: 2%
Improve: 47% Collapse: 25%
Attrition: 28% MLB: 98%
Comparables:
Brooks Robinson,Ron Santo,Derrell Griffith

YEAR	TEAM	LVL	AGE	PA	R	2B	3B	HR	RBI	BB	SO	SB	CS	AVG_OBP_SLG	TAv	BABIP	BRR	FRAA	WARP
2010	SAV	A	18	307	30	18	2	7	44	23	37	2	1	.278/.344/.433	.299	.300	-0.5	SS(65): -1.3	2.6
2010	SLU	A+	18	290	32	18	1	4	40	9	40	2	4	.300/.326/.415	.247	.339	0.4	SS(66): -3.4	0.9
2010	SLU	A+	18	290	32	18	1	4	40	9	40	2	4	.300/.326/.415	.247	.339	0.4	SS(1): -0.0	0.9
2011	SLU	A+	19	559	52	26	2	9	81	27	68	2	2	.269/.309/.380	.274	.291	-1.9	SS(55): 5.1	1.3
2012	SLU	A+	20	272	31	12	0	10	42	18	30	3	2	.289/.336/.463	.266	.286	-3	3B(38): -0.5, 2B(1): -0.0	0.0
2012	BIN	AA	20	275	37	18	2	8	33	20	30	0	0	.311/.361/.494	.258	.326	-1.8	3B(23): -2.9, 2B(20): 0.8	-0.2
2013	*NYN*	*MLB*	*21*	*250*	*23*	*11*	*1*	*6*	*28*	*10*	*43*	*0*	*0*	*.249/.279/.382*	*.240*	*.276*	*-0.4*	*3B -1, SS -0*	*0.1*

Flores is a prototypical "been around forever!" guy: When you appear briefly in the South Atlantic League in your age-16 season, you have leeway to take your time. Flores was still young for his leagues in 2012, but this time, it was less an excuse for merely decent performance than an additional reason to be happy about a .494 slugging percentage in Double-A. The Mets finally admitted that Flores isn't a shortstop last year: He split his time evenly between second and third at Binghamton after manning the hot corner almost exclusively at St. Lucie. Settling into his long-term defensive home should be good for Flores except insofar as that home is already occupied by David Wright in Queens. Big leaguers don't do roommates.

Scott Hairston **OF**
Born: 5/25/1980 Age: 33
Bats: R Throws: R Height: 6' 1"
Weight: 205 Breakout: 0%
Improve: 31% Collapse: 11%
Attrition: 9% MLB: 94%
Comparables:
Dusty Baker,Benny Ayala,Jim Rice

YEAR	TEAM	LVL	AGE	PA	R	2B	3B	HR	RBI	BB	SO	SB	CS	AVG_OBP_SLG	TAv	BABIP	BRR	FRAA	WARP
2010	SDN	MLB	30	336	34	10	0	10	36	31	69	6	1	.210/.295/.346	.254	.236	-0.7	LF(71): -0.4, CF(19): 0.7	0.4
2011	NYN	MLB	31	145	20	8	1	7	24	11	34	1	1	.235/.303/.470	.274	.264	-0.5	RF(15): -0.5, CF(10): 0.1	0.3
2012	NYN	MLB	32	398	52	25	3	20	57	19	83	8	2	.263/.299/.504	.287	.287	0	LF(59): -4.6, RF(48): 2.4	1.4
2013	*NYN*	*MLB*	*33*	*323*	*39*	*15*	*1*	*13*	*43*	*20*	*70*	*6*	*2*	*.244/.296/.437*	*.267*	*.274*	*0.2*	*LF 0, RF 0*	*1.1*

Hairston has never been prone to graciously accepting ball four, but he set a new low in 2012. Not that the Mets are complaining. On balance, Hairston had his best year with the bat since 2008. If he's used properly (Collins ensured that half of Hairston's plate appearances were against lefties) and stays healthy, Hairston can be a useful reserve/platoon partner for years yet. "Stays healthy" is probably the harder part—Hairston's injury history is as long as the rap sheet of a tertiary character on *The Sopranos*.

Reese Havens **2B**
Born: 10/20/1986 Age: 26
Bats: L Throws: R Height: 6' 2"
Weight: 195 Breakout: 6%
Improve: 54% Collapse: 7%
Attrition: 21% MLB: 97%
Comparables:
Sean Rodriguez,Billy Grabarkewitz,Bobby Grich

YEAR	TEAM	LVL	AGE	PA	R	2B	3B	HR	RBI	BB	SO	SB	CS	AVG_OBP_SLG	TAv	BABIP	BRR	FRAA	WARP
2010	SLU	A+	23	65	9	2	1	3	7	8	18	0	1	.281/.369/.509	.283	.361	-0.8	2B(13): 0.2	0.3
2010	BIN	AA	23	75	12	2	1	6	12	6	15	0	2	.338/.400/.662	.358	.362	-0.5	2B(16): 4.4	1.3
2011	BIN	AA	24	242	37	15	1	6	26	27	59	2	0	.289/.372/.455	.289	.372	1.4	2B(33): -2.0	0.7
2012	BIN	AA	25	390	41	14	0	10	39	58	113	1	1	.215/.340/.351	.244	.296	-3	2B(63): -5.4	-1.0
2013	*NYN*	*MLB*	*26*	*250*	*29*	*8*	*1*	*8*	*26*	*25*	*76*	*0*	*0*	*.215/.299/.366*	*.244*	*.285*	*-0.4*	*2B -2*	*0.2*

Speaking of staying healthy, the "PA" column above is the key one for Havens. While his tools do not cause scouts to moan in ecstasy, Havens has enough bat to be an average-to-above-average second baseman at the highest level if he can only stay on the field. Especially worrisome is that aside from surgery to correct rib-tip syndrome, Havens' problems have not been of the freak-injury type. It may be time to start rooting for Havens to have a productive career rather than expecting it to happen.

Juan Lagares **CF**

Born: **3/17/1989** Age: **24**
Bats: **R** Throws: **R** Height: **6' 2"**
Weight: **175** Breakout: **3%**
Improve: **37%** Collapse: **2%**
Attrition: **6%** MLB: **97%**

Comparables:
Jose Cardenal,Brian McRae,Jay Johnstone

YEAR	TEAM	LVL	AGE	PA	R	2B	3B	HR	RBI	BB	SO	SB	CS	AVG_OBP_SLG	TAv	BABIP	BRR	FRAA	WARP
2010	SAV	A	21	307	42	13	9	5	39	7	44	18	2	.300/.321/.459	.311	.337	3.9	LF(38): 2.7, CF(20): 0.8	3.5
2010	SLU	A+	21	137	16	5	0	2	16	2	18	7	3	.233/.250/.316	.203	.257	0.6	CF(25): 1.4, RF(12): -1.1	0.0
2011	SLU	A+	22	335	51	15	6	7	49	21	47	5	6	.338/.380/.494	.283	.379	0	LF(18): 0.5, CF(5): 0.9	0.8
2011	BIN	AA	22	170	21	11	3	2	22	5	29	10	2	.370/.391/.512	.355	.439	1.2	RF(15): 1.1, LF(10): 1.3	1.7
2012	BIN	AA	23	548	69	29	6	4	48	37	93	21	10	.283/.334/.389	.258	.337	3.3	CF(61): 11.6, RF(30): 3.6	3.1
2013	*NYN*	*MLB*	*24*	*250*	*27*	*11*	*2*	*3*	*19*	*9*	*52*	*7*	*3*	*.248/.275/.352*	*.231*	*.300*	*0.5*	*CF 1, RF 0*	*0.1*

The Mets believe that Lagares can develop into a good center fielder. If he did, it would go a long way toward helping him have a major-league career, as his patience at the plate is modest and his power is even modest-er. The good news is that Lagares has the tools to play the position—what's holding him back right now is reads and routes, skills that are at least theoretically acquirable by the time-honored method of playing center field a lot. Theoretically. Anyone who plays Frisbee with dogs knows that some creatures simply have a better innate sense of physics than others.

Zach Lutz **3B**

Born: **6/3/1986** Age: **27**
Bats: **R** Throws: **R** Height: **6' 2"**
Weight: **222** Breakout: **1%**
Improve: **46%** Collapse: **2%**
Attrition: **13%** MLB: **94%**

Comparables:
Ian Stewart,Troy Glaus,Josh Fields

YEAR	TEAM	LVL	AGE	PA	R	2B	3B	HR	RBI	BB	SO	SB	CS	AVG_OBP_SLG	TAv	BABIP	BRR	FRAA	WARP
2010	BIN	AA	24	263	42	14	0	17	42	33	63	0	2	.289/.388/.578	.312	.329	-2.3	3B(57): -6.9	1.1
2011	BUF	AAA	25	250	38	12	0	11	31	27	70	0	0	.295/.380/.500	.302	.388	0.1	3B(24): 0.3, 1B(12): 0.0	1.0
2012	BUF	AAA	26	294	34	16	1	10	35	42	75	0	0	.299/.410/.496	.304	.391	-2.4	3B(51): -6.0, 1B(9): -1.1	0.6
2012	NYN	MLB	26	11	1	0	0	0	0	0	5	0	0	.091/.091/.091	.040	.167	0.2	1B(1): 0.0	-0.3
2013	*NYN*	*MLB*	*27*	*250*	*29*	*10*	*1*	*10*	*33*	*25*	*72*	*0*	*0*	*.240/.323/.424*	*.271*	*.305*	*-0.5*	*3B -1, 1B -0*	*0.6*

Lutz is a beefy corner infielder with a bat and bad defense who wears a double-ear-flap helmet at the plate. That kind of thing has its uses. Not the helmet part. The part where Lutz can back up Wright at third and Davis at first (or even platoon with Davis as necessary), pinch-hit against lefty relievers, maybe designatedly hit in American League parks, and generally make himself useful for the minimum salary. The Mets can go buy that on the market or they can use what they already have on hand. Seeing as how they finished 24 games out of first in 2012, this choice is no choice at all.

Daniel Murphy **2B**

Born: **4/1/1985** Age: **28**
Bats: **L** Throws: **R** Height: **6' 3"**
Weight: **205** Breakout: **2%**
Improve: **55%** Collapse: **4%**
Attrition: **6%** MLB: **95%**

Comparables:
Robinson Cano,Aaron Hill,Jose Vidro

YEAR	TEAM	LVL	AGE	PA	R	2B	3B	HR	RBI	BB	SO	SB	CS	AVG_OBP_SLG	TAv	BABIP	BRR	FRAA	WARP
2011	NYN	MLB	26	423	49	28	2	6	49	24	42	5	5	.320/.362/.448	.281	.345	-3.3	1B(52): 0.1, 3B(28): -0.5	1.2
2012	NYN	MLB	27	612	62	40	3	6	65	36	82	10	2	.291/.332/.403	.266	.329	3.7	2B(137): -1.5, 1B(12): -0.3	1.7
2013	*NYN*	*MLB*	*28*	*537*	*56*	*32*	*2*	*10*	*59*	*35*	*74*	*7*	*3*	*.280/.328/.417*	*.271*	*.308*	*-0.4*	*2B -2, 1B -0*	*2.0*

Murphy's batting line doesn't jump off the page, but here are the last names of some second basemen he outhit in 2012: Phillips, Weeks (two of them), Kinsler, Kendrick. Adequate defense, adequate hitting, and adequate health, mixed with some eye of newt and a troll tooth or two, results in a useful ballplayer for the league minimum. However, an arbitration paycheck and Evans, Flores, and Havens on the farm might spell a midseason trade to a contending team that finds itself staring into the abyss of a .220 TAv at the keystone.

Kirk Nieuwenhuis **CF**

Born: **8/7/1987** Age: **25**
Bats: **L** Throws: **R** Height: **6' 4"**
Weight: **215** Breakout: **6%**
Improve: **61%** Collapse: **4%**
Attrition: **7%** MLB: **98%**

Comparables:
Chili Davis,Dave Henderson,Curtis Granderson

YEAR	TEAM	LVL	AGE	PA	R	2B	3B	HR	RBI	BB	SO	SB	CS	AVG_OBP_SLG	TAv	BABIP	BRR	FRAA	WARP
2010	BIN	AA	22	433	81	35	2	16	60	30	93	13	7	.289/.339/.510	.294	.340	-0.1	CF(91): 16.7	4.3
2010	BUF	AAA	22	133	10	8	1	2	17	11	39	0	0	.225/.293/.358	.233	.312	0.2	CF(30): -3.7	-0.1
2011	BUF	AAA	23	221	33	17	2	6	14	32	59	5	2	.298/.403/.505	.284	.407	0.6	CF(36): -1.4, RF(2): -0.1	0.7
2012	NYN	MLB	24	314	40	12	1	7	28	25	98	4	4	.252/.315/.376	.253	.358	-0.3	CF(50): 4.2, LF(23): -0.5	0.8
2013	*NYN*	*MLB*	*25*	*254*	*30*	*11*	*1*	*6*	*24*	*19*	*74*	*4*	*2*	*.235/.296/.374*	*.244*	*.313*	*-0.2*	*CF -1, LF -0*	*0.2*

It's less remarkable that Nieuwenhuis was bestowed with the altogether obvious "Captain Kirk" moniker than that Kirks Gibson, Rueter, Saarloos, or even Dressendorfer before him had not already claimed it. The adequacy of Nieuwenhuis's speed to cover center was already in doubt before he tore his plantar fascia in August after being demoted to Triple-A, a demotion that came because he hit .130/.193/.234 after June 15. (Arbitrary endpoint fully acknowledged.) He's young yet, but Nieuwenhuis is going to have to hit a lot of baseballs a lot farther if he can't play center. At least he's handsome.

Brandon Nimmo CF

Born: **3/27/1993** Age: **20**
Bats: **L** Throws: **R** Height: **6' 4"**
Weight: **185** Breakout: **20%**
Improve: **62%** Collapse: **3%**
Attrition: **17%** MLB: **86%**

Comparables:
Ed Kirkpatrick,Ken Griffey,Justin Upton

YEAR	TEAM	LVL	AGE	PA	R	2B	3B	HR	RBI	BB	SO	SB	CS	AVG_OBP_SLG	TAv	BABIP	BRR	FRAA	WARP
2012	BRO	A-	19	321	41	20	2	6	40	46	78	1	5	.248/.372/.406	.279	.328	1.2	CF(52): 5.8	1.7
2013	*NYN*	*MLB*	*20*	*250*	*25*	*8*	*1*	*5*	*21*	*21*	*79*	*0*	*0*	*.192/.266/.306*	*.214*	*.263*	*-0.4*	*CF -2*	*-0.6*

Nimmo's advanced approach at the plate is extremely impressive in light of his age and his background: He comes out of Wyoming, a state where the only baseball option is American Legion ball. (Though it's worth noting that an American Legion team plays more games in a season than a typical high school squad.) In other ways, though, Nimmo's tools are ahead of his skills—he has plus speed, for instance, but is still learning the orienteering skills needed to track down fly balls. His stolen-base numbers say all you need to know about how well he's reading pitchers. He's also delightfully small-town. His manager in Brooklyn had to threaten Nimmo with sprints to get him to stop saying "sir."

Cesar Puello CF

Born: **4/1/1991** Age: **22**
Bats: **R** Throws: **R** Height: **6' 3"**
Weight: **195** Breakout: **15%**
Improve: **59%** Collapse: **4%**
Attrition: **21%** MLB: **96%**

Comparables:
Curt Flood,Carlos Gomez,Thad Bosley

YEAR	TEAM	LVL	AGE	PA	R	2B	3B	HR	RBI	BB	SO	SB	CS	AVG_OBP_SLG	TAv	BABIP	BRR	FRAA	WARP
2010	SAV	A	19	469	80	22	1	1	34	32	82	45	10	.292/.368/.359	.286	.353	9.1	RF(103): 3.1	3.8
2011	SLU	A+	20	488	67	21	5	10	50	18	103	19	9	.259/.313/.397	.239	.311	1	RF(30): -0.5, CF(23): 3.8	0.3
2012	SLU	A+	21	252	36	17	4	4	21	7	58	19	2	.260/.328/.423	.250	.333	2.7	CF(27): 2.1, RF(13): 2.3	0.8
2013	*NYN*	*MLB*	*22*	*250*	*25*	*10*	*1*	*3*	*20*	*8*	*67*	*13*	*3*	*.212/.261/.303*	*.210*	*.278*	*1.3*	*RF 0, CF 0*	*-0.5*

Puello's low plate-appearance total is explained by a broken hamate bone in May. This is unfortunate on at least two levels. First, while every prospect needs reps, those, like Puello, who need to work on actualizing their tools (in Puello's case, great speed and good power potential) need those reps critically. Second, one might worry about a hand injury cutting off Puello's power development just as it was beginning to bear fruit in his stat line. Puello's ability to play the premium defensive position in center rather than the less critical right field will, as with every prospect ever, be a significant determinant of his future value.

Anthony Recker C

Born: **8/29/1983** Age: **29**
Bats: **R** Throws: **R** Height: **6' 3"**
Weight: **240** Breakout: **2%**
Improve: **36%** Collapse: **14%**
Attrition: **21%** MLB: **99%**

Comparables:
Rick Wilkins,Jim Pagliaroni,Stan Lopata

YEAR	TEAM	LVL	AGE	PA	R	2B	3B	HR	RBI	BB	SO	SB	CS	AVG_OBP_SLG	TAv	BABIP	BRR	FRAA	WARP
2010	SAC	AAA	26	276	36	18	2	10	42	22	62	0	1	.288/.346/.496	.290	.348	-0.3	C(69): 1.1, 1B(1): 0.0	2.4
2011	SAC	AAA	27	412	61	24	1	16	48	56	81	7	5	.287/.388/.501	.308	.328	0	--	0.0
2011	OAK	MLB	27	21	3	1	0	0	0	4	7	0	0	.176/.333/.235	.240	.300	-0.3	C(5): 0.1	-0.1
2012	SAC	AAA	28	229	29	7	0	9	29	28	56	3	1	.265/.358/.435	.204	.326	-1.4	C(13): -0.2, LF(2): -0.0	-0.3
2012	CHN	MLB	28	21	1	1	0	1	4	2	2	0	0	.167/.286/.389	.236	.133	-0.1	C(5): 0.1, 1B(1): -0.0	0.0
2012	OAK	MLB	28	37	3	1	0	0	0	4	13	0	0	.129/.250/.161	.178	.222	0.4	C(12): -0.2	-0.1
2013	*NYN*	*MLB*	*29*	*250*	*26*	*9*	*1*	*7*	*27*	*22*	*70*	*1*	*0*	*.224/.296/.369*	*.245*	*.287*	*-0.3*	*C -0, LF 0*	*0.6*

It's too bad, but Recker's name is sadly not descriptive of what he does to major-league pitching. It works all right as a description of what major-league pitching does to him, though. Unfortunately for Recker's hopes of being a backup catcher, this seems equally true on defense as on offense—to be an effective catch-and-throw type you have to actually catch and throw, which doesn't seem to be Recker's game. With Buck on board and D'Arnaud coming to a major-league field near you sooner rather than later, Recker's window for a big-league job is appropriately small.

Kelly Shoppach C

Born: **4/29/1980** Age: **33**
Bats: **R** Throws: **R** Height: **6' 1"**
Weight: **220** Breakout: **1%**
Improve: **32%** Collapse: **9%**
Attrition: **19%** MLB: **87%**

Comparables:
Johnny Bench,Todd Hundley,Mickey Tettleton

YEAR	TEAM	LVL	AGE	PA	R	2B	3B	HR	RBI	BB	SO	SB	CS	AVG_OBP_SLG	TAv	BABIP	BRR	FRAA	WARP
2010	TBA	MLB	30	187	17	8	0	5	17	20	71	0	0	.196/.308/.342	.249	.313	-1.2	C(55): -1.0	0.3
2011	TBA	MLB	31	253	23	3	0	11	22	19	79	0	0	.176/.268/.339	.223	.212	-0.6	C(86): -0.8	-0.1
2012	BOS	MLB	32	158	16	12	2	5	17	11	62	1	0	.250/.327/.471	.274	.411	-2.9	C(46): -0.2	0.4
2012	NYN	MLB	32	87	7	2	0	3	10	5	27	0	0	.203/.276/.342	.238	.265	0.1	C(27): -0.5	0.0
2013	*NYN*	*MLB*	*33*	*250*	*29*	*10*	*1*	*9*	*30*	*21*	*86*	*0*	*0*	*.210/.301/.387*	*.251*	*.291*	*-0.4*	*C -1*	*0.8*

Shoppach's calling cards are his power, especially against lefties, his whiffs (he struck out at a higher rate than Adam Dunn in 2012), and his excellent 2008 season. Warm, fuzzy memories of Cleveland aside, Shoppach should be able to leverage his skills into some backup or job-share gigs for a few more years. One would be forgiven for hoping that he winds up with Boston one more time—not many players have a chance to be traded three times by one team.

Ruben Tejada SS
Born: **10/27/1989** Age: **23**
Bats: **R** Throws: **R** Height: **6' 0"**
Weight: **185** Breakout: **3%**
Improve: **43%** Collapse: **11%**
Attrition: **23%** MLB: **93%**
Comparables:
J.J. Hardy,Rudy Meoli,Gary Sutherland

YEAR	TEAM	LVL	AGE	PA	R	2B	3B	HR	RBI	BB	SO	SB	CS	AVG_OBP_SLG	TAv	BABIP	BRR	FRAA	WARP
2010	BUF	AAA	20	244	25	11	0	1	16	14	36	1	3	.280/.322/.344	.228	.319	0.6	SS(58): 3.8, 2B(7): 0.1	0.5
2010	NYN	MLB	20	255	28	12	0	1	15	22	38	2	2	.213/.305/.282	.220	.250	2.2	2B(50): 0.4, SS(28): -0.3	0.0
2011	BUF	AAA	21	231	26	7	3	3	21	19	30	4	2	.246/.314/.353	.233	.274	1.3	SS(41): -2.1, 2B(1): 0.1	-0.2
2011	NYN	MLB	21	376	31	15	1	0	36	35	50	5	1	.284/.360/.335	.269	.331	1.8	2B(55): 1.0, SS(41): -0.7	1.7
2012	NYN	MLB	22	501	53	26	0	1	25	27	73	4	4	.289/.333/.351	.260	.339	2.7	SS(112): -4.6	1.5
2013	*NYN*	*MLB*	*23*	*471*	*45*	*21*	*1*	*4*	*40*	*33*	*72*	*4*	*3*	*.261/.320/.344*	*.249*	*.298*	*-0.9*	*SS -2, 2B -1*	*1.1*

So-called "secondary" skills on offense (whether that be power, walks, base-stealing, getting hit by pitches, or being really good at drawing catcher's interference) are great, but if you're a shortstop who can put up a .289 batting average and play non-awful defense, you can make some money without them. Tejada gets good marks for maturity, polish, and all those other not-tools words, though Collins was reportedly miffed that Tejada dared to show up merely *on time* for spring training rather than reporting early. With Tejada still cheap and the Mets' best shortstop prospect having just been drafted in 2012, Collins might do well not to run Tejada out of town because of a day or two of workouts in February.

Justin Turner INF
Born: **11/23/1984** Age: **28**
Bats: **R** Throws: **R** Height: **6' 1"**
Weight: **210** Breakout: **2%**
Improve: **43%** Collapse: **7%**
Attrition: **9%** MLB: **94%**
Comparables:
Billy Goodman,Roberto Alomar,Jarrett Hoffpauir

YEAR	TEAM	LVL	AGE	PA	R	2B	3B	HR	RBI	BB	SO	SB	CS	AVG_OBP_SLG	TAv	BABIP	BRR	FRAA	WARP
2010	BUF	AAA	25	348	58	22	1	11	35	24	38	5	3	.333/.387/.516	.301	.348	-0.5	2B(49): -2.1, SS(21): -2.9	2.0
2010	NOR	AAA	25	95	11	8	0	1	8	9	13	2	0	.250/.319/.381	.247	.282	-0.3	2B(16): 3.2, 3B(2): 0.0	0.4
2010	BAL	MLB	25	9	0	0	0	0	0	0	3	0	0	.000/.000/.000	.009	.000	0	2B(3): -0.1, SS(1): -0.0	-0.2
2010	NYN	MLB	25	9	1	1	0	0	0	1	0	0	0	.125/.222/.250	.179	.125	0	2B(3): -0.1, 3B(1): 0.0	0.0
2011	NYN	MLB	26	487	49	30	0	4	51	39	59	7	2	.260/.334/.356	.252	.292	0.9	2B(78): 2.4, 3B(36): -2.7	0.5
2012	NYN	MLB	27	185	20	13	1	2	19	9	24	1	1	.269/.319/.392	.270	.301	0.6	2B(14): -0.3, 3B(11): -0.3	0.3
2013	*NYN*	*MLB*	*28*	*250*	*28*	*14*	*1*	*4*	*22*	*19*	*34*	*3*	*1*	*.260/.325/.375*	*.261*	*.288*	*-0.3*	*2B -2, 3B -0*	*0.6*

A list of Turner's virtues as a utilityman: He makes the league minimum; he's halfway decent with the bat; he's perfectly willing to give any position the ol' college try; and he used Carly Rae Jepsen's smash hit "Call Me Maybe" as his walkup music. A list of Turner's deficiencies: Nobody makes the minimum forever; halfway decent isn't all-the-way decent; the "college try" isn't worth much in the big leagues because the pitchers are a hell of a lot tougher than they were at Fullerton; and "Call Me Maybe" is ... well, there's not actually anything bad to say about "Call Me Maybe." As with Lutz, a team with low expectations should not be overly concerned about doing better than Turner on the bench.

Jordany Valdespin UT
Born: **12/23/1987** Age: **25**
Bats: **L** Throws: **R** Height: **6' 1"**
Weight: **190** Breakout: **2%**
Improve: **45%** Collapse: **14%**
Attrition: **21%** MLB: **96%**
Comparables:
Chris Valaika,Josh Barfield,Jose Castillo

YEAR	TEAM	LVL	AGE	PA	R	2B	3B	HR	RBI	BB	SO	SB	CS	AVG_OBP_SLG	TAv	BABIP	BRR	FRAA	WARP
2010	SLU	A+	22	288	40	16	3	6	33	8	45	13	10	.289/.321/.437	.259	.324	0.5	2B(33): 0.6, SS(23): -2.2	1.1
2010	SLU	A+	22	288	40	16	3	6	33	8	45	13	10	.289/.321/.437	.259	.324	0.5	2B(2): 0.0	1.1
2010	BIN	AA	22	117	8	8	0	0	8	2	23	4	2	.232/.241/.304	.183	.286	0.6	2B(28): -2.1	-0.8
2011	BIN	AA	23	441	62	24	3	15	51	21	68	33	14	.297/.341/.483	.285	.325	-0.3	SS(40): -2.1, 2B(7): -0.6	0.8
2011	BUF	AAA	23	113	7	8	0	2	9	4	25	4	4	.280/.304/.411	.236	.346	-0.9	SS(14): -0.8, 2B(3): 0.2	-0.2
2012	BUF	AAA	24	163	22	2	1	5	23	10	22	10	8	.285/.331/.411	.257	.304	1.4	2B(21): -1.8, CF(14): -0.1	0.3
2012	NYN	MLB	24	206	28	9	1	8	26	10	44	10	3	.241/.286/.424	.264	.273	0.2	LF(21): -0.5, 2B(16): -0.2	0.5
2013	*NYN*	*MLB*	*25*	*250*	*36*	*10*	*1*	*7*	*23*	*9*	*51*	*15*	*7*	*.246/.279/.392*	*.242*	*.281*	*0.5*	*2B -0, SS -0*	*0.4*

Valdespin was slapped with the "out of control" label a while ago, and it shows up most critically in his batting numbers. Despite being heavily platooned by Collins, Valdespin exhibited no discipline at the plate. Weirdly, he actually swung at fewer pitches than the league average, but he did it backwards: He both swung out of the zone and took in the zone more often than his colleagues. Sometimes aggressiveness works out, though, as in his first big-league hit, a three-run pinch-hit homer off of Jonathan Papelbon, or in the other four pinch-hit dingers he managed on the season. He does play pretty much any position, for what that's worth.

David Wright 3B
Born: **12/20/1982** Age: **30**
Bats: **R** Throws: **R** Height: **6' 1"**
Weight: **210** Breakout: **1%**
Improve: **44%** Collapse: **1%**
Attrition: **13%** MLB: **96%**
Comparables:
Eric Chavez,Scott Rolen,Ron Santo

YEAR	TEAM	LVL	AGE	PA	R	2B	3B	HR	RBI	BB	SO	SB	CS	AVG_OBP_SLG	TAv	BABIP	BRR	FRAA	WARP
2010	NYN	MLB	27	670	87	36	3	29	103	69	161	19	11	.283/.354/.503	.304	.335	0.1	3B(155): -0.8	5.3
2011	NYN	MLB	28	447	60	23	1	14	61	52	97	13	2	.254/.345/.427	.284	.302	-2.1	3B(101): -10.9, SS(1): -0.0	0.6
2012	NYN	MLB	29	670	91	41	2	21	93	81	112	15	10	.306/.391/.492	.312	.347	1	3B(155): 1.0, SS(1): -0.0	5.7
2013	*NYN*	*MLB*	*30*	*588*	*78*	*31*	*2*	*20*	*77*	*67*	*124*	*16*	*7*	*.278/.361/.462*	*.297*	*.328*	*-0.3*	*3B -1, SS -0*	*3.5*

It's clear now, if it wasn't before, that Wright isn't the seven-WARP player he was for three of his age-22 through -25 seasons, but there's little shame in that. Six more five-WARP years puts him at Chipper Jones' career value, for instance, and nobody thinks Jones isn't a Hall of Famer. He's also in the discussion for best third baseman in the game with Miguel Cabrera (assuming he stays at third) and Evan Longoria (assuming he stays healthy). Add in that Wright's medical history is essentially limited to his 2009 concussion and a 2011 stress fracture in his back and it seemed a no-brainer to keep him in a Mets uniform into his mid-30s.

PITCHERS

Tim Byrdak

Born: **10/31/1973** Age: **39**
Bats: **L** Throws: **L** Height: **6' 0"** Weight: **190**
Breakout: **22%** Improve: **40%** Collapse: **55%**
Attrition: **5%** MLB: **83%**

Comparables:
Arthur Rhodes,Ron Mahay,Mike Remlinger

YEAR	TEAM	LVL	AGE	W	L	SV	G	GS	IP	H	HR	BB	SO	BB9	SO9	GB%	BABIP	WHIP	ERA	FIP	FRA	WARP
2010	ROU	AAA	36	0	0	0	2	1	2	1	0	2	1	9.0	4.5	33%	.167	1.50	4.50	5.58	6.66	0.0
2010	HOU	MLB	36	2	2	0	64	0	38^{2}	40	4	20	29	4.7	6.8	31%	.308	1.55	3.49	4.50	4.61	0.1
2011	NYN	MLB	37	2	1	1	72	0	37^{2}	34	3	19	47	4.5	11.2	42%	.316	1.41	3.82	3.13	2.80	0.5
2012	NYN	MLB	38	2	2	0	56	0	30^{2}	18	2	18	34	5.3	10.0	39%	.229	1.17	4.40	3.63	4.11	0.0
2013	*NYN*	*MLB*	*39*	*3*	*1*	*1*	*66*	*0*	*37*	*30*	*4*	*18*	*37*	*4.4*	*9.1*	*41%*	*.280*	*1.30*	*3.87*	*4.06*	*4.20*	*0.2*

It's now been eight years since Byrdak returned to the big leagues from independent baseball and he's mostly had a successful run of LOOGYdom. Just once in those eight years did Byrdak pitch more innings than games, and he's done well enough with his slider-throwing ways to get a new one-year contract each season (though he's had to sign minor-league deals, later purchased by the big squad, a couple of times). If this is sounding like a eulogy, it's because it might well be: Byrdak tore the anterior capsule in his throwing shoulder in August. Other pitchers who have suffered the injury include Chris Young, Johan Santana, Dallas Braden, Chien-Ming Wang, and Mark Prior. None of these players were 38 when they incurred their injuries. Wish Byrdak well if he wants to try to come back from this, but don't get your hopes up.

Joel Carreno

Born: **3/7/1987** Age: **26**
Bats: **R** Throws: **R** Height: **6' 1"** Weight: **190**
Breakout: **24%** Improve: **42%** Collapse: **22%**
Attrition: **21%** MLB: **91%**

Comparables:
Greg Harris,Mike Moore,Ken Holtzman

YEAR	TEAM	LVL	AGE	W	L	SV	G	GS	IP	H	HR	BB	SO	BB9	SO9	GB%	BABIP	WHIP	ERA	FIP	FRA	WARP
2010	DUN	A+	23	9	6	0	27	25	137^{2}	147	8	30	173	2.0	11.3	44%	.383	1.29	3.73	2.59	2.87	3.8
2011	NHP	AA	24	7	9	0	24	23	134^{2}	100	12	68	152	4.5	10.2	—	.276	1.25	3.41	4.09	4.45	0.0
2011	TOR	MLB	24	1	0	0	11	0	15^{2}	11	1	4	14	2.3	8.0	54%	.250	0.96	1.15	2.87	3.19	0.3
2012	NHP	AA	25	2	4	0	17	7	53^{2}	43	4	19	58	3.2	9.7	41%	.281	1.16	3.86	3.13	3.33	0.7
2012	LVG	AAA	25	2	5	0	10	8	36^{1}	50	7	27	30	6.7	7.4	43%	.371	2.12	8.92	6.91	8.38	0.1
2012	TOR	MLB	25	0	2	0	11	2	22	22	7	14	16	5.7	6.5	40%	.250	1.64	6.14	7.64	8.86	-0.7
2013	*NYN*	*MLB*	*26*	*2*	*3*	*0*	*13*	*7*	44^{1}	*43*	*6*	*19*	*38*	*3.8*	*7.7*	*41%*	*.307*	*1.41*	*4.72*	*4.53*	*5.13*	*-0.1*

Carreno was one of several pitchers to take a turn at filling the void at the back of the Blue Jays rotation last year, making a pair of unimpressive starts. He relies on a heavy, low-90s fastball and inconsistent secondary pitches to get batters to swing and miss, and his control has declined since reaching Double-A in 2011. The Mets signed him as a minor-league free agent after the season.

Robert Carson

Born: **1/23/1989** Age: **24**
Bats: **L** Throws: **L** Height: **6' 4"** Weight: **220**
Breakout: **24%** Improve: **56%** Collapse: **25%**
Attrition: **12%** MLB: **87%**

Comparables:
Sean Burnett,Jason Dickson,Horacio Ramirez

YEAR	TEAM	LVL	AGE	W	L	SV	G	GS	IP	H	HR	BB	SO	BB9	SO9	GB%	BABIP	WHIP	ERA	FIP	FRA	WARP
2010	SLU	A+	21	7	5	0	17	16	86^{1}	98	5	33	69	3.4	7.2	47%	.341	1.52	4.17	3.91	4.60	0.7
2010	BIN	AA	21	1	6	0	10	10	48^{2}	68	7	23	30	4.3	5.5	47%	.367	1.87	8.32	5.54	7.05	-0.6
2011	BIN	AA	22	4	11	0	25	24	128^{1}	154	14	55	91	3.9	6.4	35%	.355	1.63	5.05	4.77	5.22	0.3
2012	BIN	AA	23	1	2	9	31	0	35^{2}	45	2	15	37	3.8	9.3	36%	.377	1.68	4.79	3.12	2.19	1.2
2012	BUF	AAA	23	0	0	1	10	0	15^{2}	16	1	6	15	3.4	8.6	36%	.349	1.40	1.72	3.22	3.29	0.3
2012	NYN	MLB	23	0	0	0	17	0	13^{1}	13	2	4	5	2.7	3.4	37%	.250	1.27	4.72	5.69	5.81	-0.2
2013	*NYN*	*MLB*	*24*	*1*	*2*	*0*	*13*	*5*	34^{2}	*40*	*5*	*17*	*19*	*4.5*	*4.9*	*47%*	*.315*	*1.65*	*5.93*	*5.45*	*6.45*	*-0.6*

Carson is a big, powerful man who made the transition to relief last year and should have a shot at Byrdak's job this season. He can bring the heat, averaging 95 mph on the fastball, but he doesn't have much idea where it's going, and his secondary stuff (slider, theoretical change) needs work. But hey, did you notice that he's a big, powerful lefty who throws 95? Those guys tend to get chances after chances just in case they ever figure out how to harness their stuff.

Josh Edgin

Born: **12/17/1986** Age: **26**
Bats: **L** Throws: **L** Height: **6' 2"** Weight: **225**
Breakout: **24%** Improve: **39%** Collapse: **43%**
Attrition: **22%** MLB: **86%**

Comparables:
Jose Mijares,Scott Maine,Paul Assenmacher

YEAR	TEAM	LVL	AGE	W	L	SV	G	GS	IP	H	HR	BB	SO	BB9	SO9	GB%	BABIP	WHIP	ERA	FIP	FRA	WARP
2010	KNG	Rk	23	0	1	3	18	0	31^{2}	28	2	12	41	3.4	11.6	63%	.330	1.26	2.84	3.28	4.40	0.3
2010	SAV	A	23	0	0	0	2	0	3	3	0	0	5	0.0	15.0	54%	.231	1.00	0.00	0.19	2.52	0.1
2011	SAV	A	24	1	0	16	24	0	31	14	0	10	41	2.9	11.9	65%	.229	0.77	0.87	1.85	0.98	1.0
2011	SLU	A+	24	2	1	11	25	0	35	30	2	13	35	3.3	9.0	51%	.350	1.23	2.06	3.33	3.84	0.3
2012	BIN	AA	25	0	0	2	6	0	6^{1}	5	1	2	5	2.8	7.1	79%	.222	1.11	1.42	4.62	4.99	0.0
2012	BUF	AAA	25	3	2	1	35	0	37	34	0	18	40	4.4	9.7	43%	.324	1.41	3.89	2.54	2.96	0.7
2012	NYN	MLB	25	1	2	0	34	0	25^{2}	19	5	10	30	3.5	10.5	41%	.233	1.13	4.56	4.73	5.60	-0.2
2013	*NYN*	*MLB*	*26*	*2*	*1*	*1*	*32*	*0*	*37^{2}*	*32*	*4*	*16*	*38*	*3.8*	*9.2*	*49%*	*.296*	*1.27*	*3.81*	*3.84*	*4.14*	*0.2*

Edgin appears to be Carson's main rival for the top lefty role in the 2013 bullpen. He was drafted in the 30th round and was already 23 at the time, so calling him a longshot to ever appear in the big leagues was probably charitable. If he was going to come at all, he had to come fast, and that's exactly what he did—Edgin pitched at two levels in 2011 and three in 2012, culminating in a big-league stint. He has a stocky build and a classic LOOGY delivery, as his front foot goes more toward the left-hand batter's box than the plate. He also has 94-mph heat and a slider. He does drop down a bit to throw the slide piece, so it's going to have to be a very good pitch to survive his telegraphing of it.

Jeurys Familia

Born: **10/10/1989** Age: **23**
Bats: **R** Throws: **R** Height: **6' 4"** Weight: **185**
Breakout: **30%** Improve: **59%** Collapse: **25%**
Attrition: **15%** MLB: **96%**

Comparables:
Edinson Volquez,Mike Pelfrey,Ross Detwiler

YEAR	TEAM	LVL	AGE	W	L	SV	G	GS	IP	H	HR	BB	SO	BB9	SO9	GB%	BABIP	WHIP	ERA	FIP	FRA	WARP
2010	SLU	A+	20	6	9	0	24	24	121	117	7	74	137	5.5	10.2	46%	.357	1.58	5.58	4.13	4.56	0.8
2011	SLU	A+	21	1	1	0	6	6	36^{1}	21	1	8	36	2.0	8.9	49%	.178	0.80	1.49	2.51	3.40	0.3
2011	BIN	AA	21	4	4	0	17	17	87^{2}	85	10	35	96	3.6	9.9	37%	.336	1.37	3.49	4.17	4.78	0.8
2012	BUF	AAA	22	9	9	0	28	28	137	145	8	73	128	4.8	8.4	55%	.333	1.59	4.73	3.73	4.72	0.3
2012	NYN	MLB	22	0	0	0	8	1	12^{1}	10	0	9	10	6.6	7.3	48%	.303	1.54	5.84	3.70	4.12	0.1
2013	*NYN*	*MLB*	*23*	*2*	*4*	*0*	*10*	*10*	*50^{2}*	*49*	*6*	*26*	*41*	*4.7*	*7.3*	*48%*	*.303*	*1.48*	*4.89*	*4.66*	*5.32*	*-0.2*

Familia's unreliable secondary pitches and poor control (much less command) have had scouts and observers pointing toward the bullpen for years, where not having to pitch multiple times through the order would allow him to rely on (and thus perhaps harness) his 96-mph fastball. One can dream a dream that Familia would even add a few ticks to said heater. The Mets have so far resisted the temptation to change his role, which is the right call for a team without present World Series ambitions. As long as Familia can handle the possibility of failure mentally and emotionally, his upside as a starter is so high that it's worth letting him take his lumps until it becomes obvious that he won't be able to hack it in the rotation.

Frank Francisco

Born: **9/11/1979** Age: **33**
Bats: **R** Throws: **R** Height: **6' 3"** Weight: **250**
Breakout: **21%** Improve: **46%** Collapse: **37%**
Attrition: **12%** MLB: **84%**

Comparables:
Kiko Calero,Brian Sikorski,Skip Lockwood

YEAR	TEAM	LVL	AGE	W	L	SV	G	GS	IP	H	HR	BB	SO	BB9	SO9	GB%	BABIP	WHIP	ERA	FIP	FRA	WARP
2010	TEX	MLB	30	6	4	2	56	0	52^{2}	49	5	18	60	3.1	10.3	40%	.321	1.27	3.76	3.09	3.46	1.0
2011	DUN	A+	31	0	1	0	5	0	5	6	2	4	6	7.2	10.8	50%	.444	2.00	10.80	8.59	12.58	-0.2
2011	TOR	MLB	31	1	4	17	54	0	50^{2}	49	7	18	53	3.2	9.4	40%	.300	1.32	3.55	3.83	3.33	0.8
2012	BIN	AA	32	0	0	1	5	0	4^{2}	6	0	1	4	1.9	7.7	38%	.375	1.50	3.86	2.13	3.34	0.1
2012	NYN	MLB	32	1	3	23	48	0	42^{1}	47	5	21	47	4.5	10.0	33%	.339	1.61	5.53	3.94	3.73	0.5
2013	*NYN*	*MLB*	*33*	*3*	*1*	*17*	*51*	*0*	*46^{2}*	*37*	*5*	*16*	*53*	*3.0*	*10.3*	*37%*	*.295*	*1.13*	*3.10*	*3.35*	*3.37*	*0.7*

Transitioning to the National League is different for relievers than for starters: You almost never bat, and you're more likely to face pinch-hitters than pitchers while you're on the mound. Still, one should not have expected Francisco to see his walks jump as they did. He hasn't lost velocity (his fastball averages 94–95 mph) and he's a good bounce-back candidate, but it's not clear that the Mets need a $6 million closer. The number of scenarios in which Francisco finishes the year in some city other than New York likely exceed those in which he's saving September games for the Mets.

Michael Fulmer

Born: **3/15/1993** Age: **20**
Bats: **R** Throws: **R** Height: **6' 4"** Weight: **200**
Breakout: **52%** Improve: **80%** Collapse: **9%**
Attrition: **3%** MLB: **86%**

Comparables:
Madison Bumgarner,Catfish Hunter,Milt Pappas

YEAR	TEAM	LVL	AGE	W	L	SV	G	GS	IP	H	HR	BB	SO	BB9	SO9	GB%	BABIP	WHIP	ERA	FIP	FRA	WARP
2011	MTS	Rk	18	0	1	0	4	3	5^{1}	9	0	4	10	6.8	16.9	50%	.643	2.44	10.12	2.48	2.17	0.3
2012	SAV	A	19	7	6	0	21	21	108^{1}	92	6	38	101	3.2	8.4	42%	.284	1.20	2.74	3.65	3.50	2.0
2013	*NYN*	*MLB*	*20*	*2*	*3*	*0*	*7*	*7*	*35^{2}*	*36*	*5*	*17*	*26*	*4.1*	*6.6*	*41%*	*.302*	*1.47*	*5.03*	*4.99*	*5.46*	*-0.2*

Fulmer, a 2011 sandwich pick, was the third-youngest pitcher in the South Atlantic League, but he owes his excellent results more to a fastball that overmatched the competition than to his overall pitching profile. The slider and change both need work, in other words. The Mets were well aware of that, however, and put Fulmer at Savannah specifically so he could work with pitching coach Frank Viola and join a rotation that featured three college-drafted starters. He's smart and coachable, so if his body can master the secondary pitches, Fulmer is a good bet to make the adjustments necessary to succeed at higher levels.

Dillon Gee

Born: **4/28/1986** Age: **27**
Bats: **R** Throws: **R** Height: **6' 2"** Weight: **205**
Breakout: **27%** Improve: **63%** Collapse: **15%**
Attrition: **14%** MLB: **87%**
Comparables:
Noah Lowry,Armando Galarraga,Edwin Jackson

YEAR	TEAM	LVL	AGE	W	L	SV	G	GS	IP	H	HR	BB	SO	BB9	SO9	GB%	BABIP	WHIP	ERA	FIP	FRA	WARP
2010	BUF	AAA	24	13	8	0	28	28	161^{1}	174	23	41	165	2.3	9.2	45%	.332	1.33	4.97	4.10	4.73	1.7
2010	NYN	MLB	24	2	2	0	5	5	33	25	2	15	17	4.1	4.6	49%	.225	1.21	2.18	4.23	4.79	0.0
2011	BUF	AAA	25	1	1	0	2	2	11^{2}	7	1	5	8	3.9	6.2	53%	.158	1.03	4.63	4.52	4.30	0.0
2011	NYN	MLB	25	13	6	0	30	27	160^{2}	150	18	71	114	4.0	6.4	49%	.270	1.38	4.43	4.62	5.21	-0.1
2012	NYN	MLB	26	6	7	0	17	17	109^{2}	108	12	29	97	2.4	8.0	52%	.302	1.25	4.10	3.75	4.14	1.5
2013	*NYN*	*MLB*	*27*	*5*	*7*	*0*	*17*	*17*	*103^{1}*	*94*	*12*	*33*	*85*	*2.9*	*7.4*	*45%*	*.290*	*1.23*	*3.95*	*4.02*	*4.30*	*0.6*

Gee throws five pitches on any count to either lefties or righties. Not one of the pitches grades out better than average, but that's why we play the games instead of simulating them from PITCHf/x data: Gee's whole is greater than the sum of his parts because of the unpredictability he presents to hitters. A note of caution, though: Gee had a good first half in 2011 before falling apart in the second. In 2012, he never got the chance to collapse as he went under the knife for artery replacement surgery to decrease the chance of repeated blood clots in his shoulder. He received a clean bill of health in late August, but the doctor's note failed to take a position on whether he's a solid mid-rotation starter or a replacement-level player. Always passing the buck, doctors.

Darin Gorski

Born: **10/6/1987** Age: **25**
Bats: **L** Throws: **L** Height: **6' 5"** Weight: **210**
Breakout: **34%** Improve: **57%** Collapse: **19%**
Attrition: **19%** MLB: **74%**
Comparables:
Jo-Jo Reyes,Randy Wolf,Travis Blackley

YEAR	TEAM	LVL	AGE	W	L	SV	G	GS	IP	H	HR	BB	SO	BB9	SO9	GB%	BABIP	WHIP	ERA	FIP	FRA	WARP
2010	SAV	A	22	6	8	3	25	18	114	125	12	43	109	3.4	8.6	39%	.335	1.47	4.58	4.38	5.43	-0.7
2011	SLU	A+	23	11	3	1	27	21	138^{2}	109	11	29	140	1.9	9.1	42%	.257	1.00	2.08	3.18	4.33	1.0
2012	BIN	AA	24	9	8	0	25	24	139^{2}	128	20	50	118	3.2	7.6	35%	.276	1.27	4.00	4.53	5.46	0.1
2013	*NYN*	*MLB*	*25*	*2*	*3*	*0*	*8*	*7*	*40^{1}*	*41*	*6*	*18*	*30*	*3.9*	*6.6*	*37%*	*.295*	*1.45*	*5.12*	*4.99*	*5.57*	*-0.3*

Gorski doesn't have velocity, projection, or upside, he's already 25, and his excellent component stats at High-A dipped to nothing-special status at Double-A. On the other hand, he's a lefty and he shares an alma mater—Kutztown University—with Ryan Vogelsong, so we can't count him out.

Matt Harvey

Born: **3/27/1989** Age: **24**
Bats: **R** Throws: **R** Height: **6' 5"** Weight: **210**
Breakout: **33%** Improve: **63%** Collapse: **8%**
Attrition: **7%** MLB: **97%**
Comparables:
Chad Billingsley,Ian Kennedy,Matt Cain

YEAR	TEAM	LVL	AGE	W	L	SV	G	GS	IP	H	HR	BB	SO	BB9	SO9	GB%	BABIP	WHIP	ERA	FIP	FRA	WARP
2011	SLU	A+	22	8	2	0	14	14	76	67	5	24	92	2.8	10.9	48%	.333	1.20	2.37	2.85	3.60	1.0
2011	BIN	AA	22	5	3	0	12	12	59^{2}	58	4	23	64	3.5	9.7	53%	.330	1.36	4.53	3.44	4.00	0.6
2012	BUF	AAA	23	7	5	0	20	20	110	97	9	48	112	3.9	9.2	46%	.295	1.32	3.68	3.66	4.70	0.2
2012	NYN	MLB	23	3	5	0	10	10	59^{1}	42	5	26	70	3.9	10.6	41%	.262	1.15	2.73	3.34	3.88	1.3
2013	*NYN*	*MLB*	*24*	*4*	*5*	*0*	*14*	*14*	*76*	*63*	*8*	*29*	*78*	*3.4*	*9.2*	*45%*	*.294*	*1.20*	*3.49*	*3.66*	*3.80*	*1.0*

Harvey made his much-anticipated debut in 2012 and did not disappoint, posting strikeout numbers that border on ridiculous for a rookie starter, including 11 whiffs in 5 1/3 innings in his first game. He comes over the top with heat that averages 95 and has the ability to leave the pitch up in the zone without getting hurt, as his fastball managed a whiff rate on par with those of Gio Gonzalez and Neftali Feliz. The future is not only bright, it is now.

Jeremy Hefner

Born: **3/11/1986** Age: **27**
Bats: **R** Throws: **R** Height: **6' 5"** Weight: **215**
Breakout: **31%** Improve: **70%** Collapse: **8%**
Attrition: **16%** MLB: **85%**
Comparables:
Dustin Moseley,Mike Grace,Ismael Valdez

YEAR	TEAM	LVL	AGE	W	L	SV	G	GS	IP	H	HR	BB	SO	BB9	SO9	GB%	BABIP	WHIP	ERA	FIP	FRA	WARP
2010	SAN	AA	24	11	8	0	28	28	167^{2}	156	11	51	115	2.7	6.2	42%	.287	1.23	2.95	3.66	4.35	1.1
2011	TUC	AAA	25	9	7	0	28	28	157^{1}	178	21	61	120	3.5	6.9	43%	.325	1.52	4.98	5.21	5.35	1.3
2012	BUF	AAA	26	5	2	0	10	9	61^{2}	55	4	10	37	1.5	5.4	48%	.266	1.05	2.77	3.29	4.58	0.2
2012	NYN	MLB	26	4	7	0	26	13	93^{2}	110	9	18	62	1.7	6.0	46%	.319	1.37	5.09	3.70	4.26	0.8
2013	*NYN*	*MLB*	*27*	*4*	*6*	*0*	*15*	*15*	*88^{1}*	*90*	*11*	*27*	*61*	*2.7*	*6.2*	*42%*	*.302*	*1.32*	*4.43*	*4.35*	*4.82*	*-0.0*

Hefner hit a home run in his first big-league win, but the fan who caught the ball demanded Johan Santana's autograph rather than Hefner's own in trade. Baseball players probably learn their place in the hierarchy fairly quickly, but that still seems an unnecessarily harsh reminder. Hefner's walk rate was surprisingly low for someone who worked out of the zone as much as he did, and his slightly elevated BABIP raises the question of whether he got unlucky or his stuff simply isn't good enough to avoid being hammered. Fortunately, the Mets have enough pitching that they shouldn't have to find out the answer in high-leverage situations.

Cory Mazzoni
Born: 10/19/1989 Age: 23
Bats: R Throws: R Height: 6' 2" Weight: 190
Breakout: 31% Improve: 61% Collapse: 12%
Attrition: 13% MLB: 85%
Comparables:
Justin Germano,Vance Worley,Liam Hendriks

YEAR	TEAM	LVL	AGE	W	L	SV	G	GS	IP	H	HR	BB	SO	BB9	SO9	GB%	BABIP	WHIP	ERA	FIP	FRA	WARP
2011	BRO	A-	21	1	0	0	6	1	6	5	0	2	10	3.0	15.0	43%	.714	1.17	0.00	2.03	-0.04	0.3
2011	SLU	A+	21	1	1	0	6	0	7	7	1	1	8	1.3	10.3	58%	.364	1.14	2.57	3.39	5.34	0.0
2012	SLU	A+	22	5	1	0	12	12	63^{2}	64	3	16	48	2.3	6.8	39%	.310	1.26	3.25	3.30	3.81	0.3
2012	BIN	AA	22	5	5	0	14	14	80^{2}	90	9	20	56	2.2	6.2	43%	.312	1.36	4.46	4.08	5.13	0.7
2013	*NYN*	*MLB*	*23*	*2*	*3*	*0*	*7*	*7*	*38^{2}*	*40*	*5*	*13*	*27*	*3.0*	*6.3*	*41%*	*.303*	*1.37*	*4.69*	*4.49*	*5.10*	*-0.1*

Mazzoni has received plaudits for his smooth delivery, and he does bring a hard fastball, but his questionable secondary stuff and relatively small stature mark him as a likely reliever. It's too early to fully consign him to that fate, though: His back-of-the-rotation upside is still in play. He'll need to miss more bats if he wants to reach that ceiling. The list of right-handed pitchers without size who succeed despite striking out six men per nine in the minors is shorter than, well, than the pitchers themselves.

Collin McHugh
Born: 6/19/1987 Age: 26
Bats: R Throws: R Height: 6' 3" Weight: 195
Breakout: 30% Improve: 53% Collapse: 21%
Attrition: 19% MLB: 90%
Comparables:
Ken Holtzman,Marco Estrada,Gil Meche

YEAR	TEAM	LVL	AGE	W	L	SV	G	GS	IP	H	HR	BB	SO	BB9	SO9	GB%	BABIP	WHIP	ERA	FIP	FRA	WARP
2010	SAV	A	23	7	8	1	28	20	132^{1}	139	7	38	129	2.6	8.8	59%	.339	1.34	3.33	3.40	4.32	1.0
2011	SLU	A+	24	1	2	1	9	6	35^{2}	47	3	14	39	3.5	9.8	57%	.310	1.71	6.31	3.56	3.65	0.3
2011	BIN	AA	24	8	2	2	18	16	93^{1}	78	2	32	100	3.1	9.6	48%	.373	1.18	2.89	2.83	2.61	1.7
2012	BIN	AA	25	5	5	0	12	12	74^{2}	63	4	17	65	2.0	7.8	48%	.278	1.07	2.41	3.04	3.39	1.4
2012	BUF	AAA	25	2	4	0	13	13	73^{2}	60	8	29	70	3.5	8.6	50%	.256	1.21	3.42	3.93	4.94	0.4
2012	NYN	MLB	25	0	4	0	8	4	21^{1}	27	5	8	17	3.4	7.2	39%	.328	1.64	7.59	6.00	6.59	-0.2
2013	*NYN*	*MLB*	*26*	*2*	*4*	*0*	*11*	*9*	*56*	*56*	*7*	*22*	*44*	*3.6*	*7.1*	*49%*	*.307*	*1.40*	*4.78*	*4.43*	*5.20*	*-0.2*

McHugh throws five average pitches with good command, but was victimized by the league after his debut start against Colorado to the tune of 21 runs in 14 1/3 innings. His fastball averages just 91, though he gets a surprising number of swings-and-misses with it given the velocity. If McHugh isn't a starter, though, it's unclear what he is. Do five average pitches play out of the bullpen any better than they do in the rotation? In other words, McHugh isn't Familia, for whom the benefits of eliminating mediocre pitches from the repertoire are obvious.

Jenrry Mejia
Born: 10/11/1989 Age: 23
Bats: R Throws: R Height: 6' 1" Weight: 205
Breakout: 19% Improve: 56% Collapse: 25%
Attrition: 10% MLB: 91%
Comparables:
Charlie Haeger,Vin Mazzaro,Jerome Williams

YEAR	TEAM	LVL	AGE	W	L	SV	G	GS	IP	H	HR	BB	SO	BB9	SO9	GB%	BABIP	WHIP	ERA	FIP	FRA	WARP
2010	MTS	Rk	20	0	0	0	1	1	3	4	0	1	3	3.0	9.0	89%	.444	1.67	3.00	2.51	3.61	0.1
2010	SLU	A+	20	0	0	0	1	1	4	1	0	0	7	0.0	15.8	83%	.167	0.25	0.00	-0.06	1.94	0.2
2010	BIN	AA	20	2	0	0	6	6	27^{1}	19	0	14	26	4.6	8.6	66%	.268	1.21	1.32	2.99	3.70	0.6
2010	BUF	AAA	20	0	0	0	1	1	8	5	1	1	9	1.1	10.1	71%	.250	0.75	1.12	3.42	4.35	0.1
2010	NYN	MLB	20	0	4	0	33	3	39	46	3	20	22	4.6	5.1	61%	.319	1.69	4.62	4.75	4.65	0.2
2011	BUF	AAA	21	1	2	0	5	5	28^{1}	16	1	14	21	4.4	6.7	42%	.209	1.06	2.86	3.91	5.12	0.0
2012	SLU	A+	22	1	0	0	2	2	11	7	1	2	8	1.6	6.5	55%	.200	0.82	2.45	3.67	5.08	0.1
2012	BIN	AA	22	0	0	0	2	2	8	11	1	3	8	3.4	9.0	62%	.435	1.75	5.62	3.95	4.44	-0.1
2012	BUF	AAA	22	3	4	0	26	10	73^{2}	75	4	24	39	2.9	4.8	56%	.291	1.34	3.54	3.82	5.68	-0.4
2012	NYN	MLB	22	1	2	0	5	3	16	20	2	9	8	5.1	4.5	68%	.327	1.81	5.62	5.45	5.99	-0.1
2013	*NYN*	*MLB*	*23*	*2*	*2*	*0*	*14*	*6*	*37*	*36*	*4*	*16*	*26*	*3.9*	*6.3*	*57%*	*.296*	*1.41*	*4.50*	*4.50*	*4.89*	*-0.0*

Mejia posted good groundball numbers in his return from Tommy John surgery, but he didn't miss bats at Buffalo. The Mets called him up anyway in September and gave him two relief appearances and three starts (two bad, one decent). Mejia, who is short-ish and solidly built, pumped his fastball in at 95, with a little extra in relief. Scouts were calling Mejia a future reliever long before he went under the knife and the lost development time and questions about whether his body can handle the rigors of 200 innings per year only give that analysis more force. He should be a filthy setup man or closer, though.

Akeel Morris
Born: 11/14/1992 Age: 20
Bats: R Throws: R Height: 6' 2" Weight: 170
Breakout: 48% Improve: 70% Collapse: 10%
Attrition: 4% MLB: 81%
Comparables:
Jim Waugh,Catfish Hunter,Sandy Koufax

YEAR	TEAM	LVL	AGE	W	L	SV	G	GS	IP	H	HR	BB	SO	BB9	SO9	GB%	BABIP	WHIP	ERA	FIP	FRA	WARP
2010	MTS	Rk	17	1	1	0	8	6	24^{2}	13	0	17	28	6.2	10.2	45%	.217	1.21	2.19	3.55	4.63	0.1
2011	KNG	Rk	18	3	2	0	11	11	51^{1}	30	5	38	61	6.7	10.7	—	.210	1.32	3.86	5.07	5.51	0.0
2012	KNG	Rk	19	0	6	2	11	6	38^{1}	38	7	22	50	5.2	11.7	43%	.323	1.57	7.98	5.50	7.74	0.3
2013	*NYN*	*MLB*	*20*	*1*	*2*	*0*	*9*	*6*	*34*	*34*	*5*	*23*	*28*	*6.2*	*7.4*	*42%*	*.311*	*1.69*	*5.82*	*5.49*	*6.33*	*-0.5*

A fascinating project, Morris is a skinny guy from the Virgin Islands with a live fastball and little else, including control. His delivery is a max-effort, just-chuck-the-ball-hard mess of arms and legs and head-snaps and who even knows what else. The last major-league pitcher from the Virgin Islands was Al McBean in 1970. Morris has the arm to be the next one, but he's a long, *long* way away.

Jon Niese

Born: **10/27/1986** Age: **26**
Bats: **L** Throws: **L** Height: **6' 5"** Weight: **215**
Breakout: **26%** Improve: **56%** Collapse: **15%**
Attrition: **16%** MLB: **94%**

Comparables:
Dontrelle Willis, Dallas Braden, Matt Maloney

YEAR	TEAM	LVL	AGE	W	L	SV	G	GS	IP	H	HR	BB	SO	BB9	SO9	GB%	BABIP	WHIP	ERA	FIP	FRA	WARP
2010	BUF	AAA	23	0	0	0	1	1	6	8	1	0	3	0.0	4.5	46%	.333	1.33	3.00	4.46	5.28	0.0
2010	NYN	MLB	23	9	10	0	30	30	173^2	192	20	62	148	3.2	7.7	48%	.324	1.46	4.20	4.13	4.51	2.2
2011	NYN	MLB	24	11	11	0	27	26	157^1	178	14	44	138	2.5	7.9	55%	.333	1.41	4.40	3.33	3.72	2.6
2012	NYN	MLB	25	13	9	0	30	30	190^1	174	22	49	155	2.3	7.3	49%	.272	1.17	3.40	3.85	4.21	2.7
2013	*NYN*	*MLB*	*26*	*8*	*10*	*0*	*26*	*26*	*156^2*	*151*	*17*	*45*	*131*	*2.6*	*7.5*	*50%*	*.307*	*1.25*	*3.97*	*3.80*	*4.31*	*0.8*

Niese cut his ERA by a full run without moving the needle on his component stats, his velocity, his movement, or anything else beyond the fact that he threw his cutter as his second pitch instead of his fourth in terms of frequency. The cutter alone was very likely not responsible for a 68-point drop in BABIP, especially since Niese used a very similar pitch mix in 2010. With or without the BABIP Kraken on his side, Niese is a nice mid-rotation lefty who won't blow anyone away with either his stuff or his contract, which maxes out at $9 million guaranteed money in 2016 before two option years at $10 million and $11 million.

Bobby Parnell

Born: **9/8/1984** Age: **28**
Bats: **R** Throws: **R** Height: **6' 5"** Weight: **200**
Breakout: **23%** Improve: **58%** Collapse: **24%**
Attrition: **14%** MLB: **91%**

Comparables:
Chris Resop, Nick Masset, Carlos Villanueva

YEAR	TEAM	LVL	AGE	W	L	SV	G	GS	IP	H	HR	BB	SO	BB9	SO9	GB%	BABIP	WHIP	ERA	FIP	FRA	WARP
2010	BUF	AAA	25	1	1	4	24	0	41^1	36	3	17	42	3.7	9.2	66%	.289	1.28	4.14	3.51	5.52	0.0
2010	NYN	MLB	25	0	1	0	41	0	35	41	1	8	33	2.1	8.5	58%	.374	1.40	2.83	2.28	2.83	0.7
2011	SLU	A+	26	0	0	0	1	1	1	0	0	1	0	9.0	0.0	—	.000	1.00	0.00	6.39	6.94	0.0
2011	BUF	AAA	26	0	0	1	8	0	8	7	1	2	11	2.2	12.4	41%	.375	1.12	3.38	2.86	8.05	-0.2
2011	NYN	MLB	26	4	6	6	60	0	59^1	60	4	27	64	4.1	9.7	55%	.327	1.47	3.64	3.18	3.25	1.0
2012	NYN	MLB	27	5	4	7	74	0	68^2	65	4	20	61	2.6	8.0	63%	.302	1.24	2.49	3.03	3.61	1.1
2013	*NYN*	*MLB*	*28*	*3*	*1*	*4*	*60*	*0*	*61^2*	*57*	*6*	*22*	*55*	*3.2*	*8.1*	*52%*	*.307*	*1.28*	*3.79*	*3.75*	*4.12*	*0.4*

Parnell has gone from a groundballing righty out of the bullpen to a ridiculously groundballing righty out of the bullpen. His sinking fastball averages 96–97 mph, he has no career platoon split (though in a rigorous analysis, we would regress that split significantly toward the league average given his relatively small number of batters faced so far), and he is, as you might expect, not susceptible to the home run. Closers are made, not born, and Parnell stands ready for his initiation.

Elvin Ramirez

Born: **10/10/1987** Age: **25**
Bats: **R** Throws: **R** Height: **6' 4"** Weight: **210**
Breakout: **25%** Improve: **53%** Collapse: **20%**
Attrition: **6%** MLB: **92%**

Comparables:
Jim Britton, Juan Cruz, Dickie Noles

YEAR	TEAM	LVL	AGE	W	L	SV	G	GS	IP	H	HR	BB	SO	BB9	SO9	GB%	BABIP	WHIP	ERA	FIP	FRA	WARP
2010	SLU	A+	22	4	3	0	49	0	73^1	56	0	43	65	5.3	8.0	49%	.271	1.35	4.17	3.79	4.49	0.4
2010	BIN	AA	22	0	1	0	3	0	6^2	5	2	6	7	8.1	9.4	41%	.200	1.64	4.03	7.84	6.41	0.0
2012	BIN	AA	24	0	1	1	8	0	13	7	0	7	16	4.8	11.1	37%	.233	1.08	1.38	2.36	2.90	0.3
2012	BUF	AAA	24	3	1	1	33	0	42	26	2	25	41	5.4	8.8	46%	.224	1.21	2.36	3.75	4.42	0.2
2012	NYN	MLB	24	0	1	0	20	0	21^1	24	1	20	22	8.4	9.3	42%	.390	2.06	5.48	4.50	4.25	0.1
2013	*NYN*	*MLB*	*25*	*1*	*0*	*0*	*26*	*0*	*35*	*34*	*4*	*21*	*26*	*5.5*	*6.7*	*47%*	*.298*	*1.58*	*5.10*	*5.00*	*5.55*	*-0.4*

Ramirez has been a solid bullpen piece for five years now, continually introducing changes to his approach to compensate for declining fastball velocity. In 2011, he threw more sliders at the expense of his fastball; in 2012, he cut the slider back and went much heavier on changeups. One might worry about nibbling, however: Ramirez threw the seventh-fewest pitches in the strike zone of any pitcher with 50 or more innings last year. If Ramirez has a good month or two to start 2013, Sandy Alderson and company might do well to find one of America's suckers born every minute and flip him for a youngster.

Ramon Ramirez

Born: **8/31/1981** Age: **31**
Bats: **R** Throws: **R** Height: **6' 0"** Weight: **200**
Breakout: **37%** Improve: **65%** Collapse: **22%**
Attrition: **9%** MLB: **94%**

Comparables:
Jesse Orosco, Jason Isringhausen, Eddie Watt

YEAR	TEAM	LVL	AGE	W	L	SV	G	GS	IP	H	HR	BB	SO	BB9	SO9	GB%	BABIP	WHIP	ERA	FIP	FRA	WARP
2010	BOS	MLB	28	0	3	2	44	0	42^1	39	6	16	31	3.4	6.6	36%	.264	1.30	4.46	4.56	5.38	-0.1
2010	SFN	MLB	28	1	0	1	25	0	27	13	1	11	15	3.7	5.0	39%	.152	0.89	0.67	3.70	3.73	0.2
2011	SFN	MLB	29	3	3	4	66	0	68^2	54	3	26	66	3.4	8.7	51%	.277	1.17	2.62	2.91	3.34	0.6
2012	SLU	A+	30	0	0	0	2	1	2	5	0	0	0	0.0	0.0	55%	.455	2.50	13.50	3.39	3.69	0.0
2012	BUF	AAA	30	0	1	0	1	0	0^2	4	0	1	0	13.5	0.0	50%	.667	7.50	40.50	7.66	815.71	0.0
2012	NYN	MLB	30	3	4	1	58	0	63^2	58	4	35	52	4.9	7.4	47%	.292	1.46	4.24	3.97	4.11	0.5
2013	*NYN*	*MLB*	*31*	*3*	*1*	*1*	*58*	*0*	*60*	*50*	*5*	*24*	*53*	*3.6*	*7.9*	*44%*	*.280*	*1.22*	*3.36*	*3.72*	*3.65*	*0.7*

Ramirez lost 2011 to a shoulder injury after being taken in the Rule 5 Draft by Washington, and he suddenly finds himself 25 and needing to show something to make a case for his career. Not many pitchers post a Triple-A walk rate like Ramirez did and get called up anyway, and those that do tend to fare exactly as Ramirez did in 2012: poorly. The BABIP looks ugly, but when you're dealing with a pitcher who obviously has no idea where the baseball is going, that's just as likely to be caused by accidentally grooved fastballs as by the poor fortune of dinks and bloops.

Jon Rauch

Born: **9/27/1978** Age: **34**
Bats: **R** Throws: **R** Height: **6' 11"** Weight: **290**
Breakout: **19%** Improve: **44%** Collapse: **35%**
Attrition: **7%** MLB: **86%**

Comparables:
Keith Foulke, Joe Hoerner, LaTroy Hawkins

YEAR	TEAM	LVL	AGE	W	L	SV	G	GS	IP	H	HR	BB	SO	BB9	SO9	GB%	BABIP	WHIP	ERA	FIP	FRA	WARP
2010	MIN	MLB	31	3	1	21	59	0	57^2	61	3	14	46	2.2	7.2	38%	.320	1.30	3.12	2.91	2.90	1.2
2011	TOR	MLB	32	5	4	11	53	0	52	56	11	14	36	2.4	6.2	36%	.276	1.35	4.85	5.29	5.14	0.0
2012	NYN	MLB	33	3	7	4	73	0	57^2	45	7	12	42	1.9	6.6	38%	.222	0.99	3.59	3.93	3.87	0.4
2013	*NYN*	*MLB*	*34*	*3*	*1*	*4*	*57*	*0*	*51^2*	*46*	*6*	*12*	*43*	*2.1*	*7.4*	*38%*	*.285*	*1.14*	*3.42*	*3.74*	*3.72*	*0.6*

The contrast between Rauch's stuff (fastball that averages 91-92, good but not exactly Randy Johnson–like slider) and his size will never cease to amaze, but he is what he is: a solid bullpen piece who will limit walks and benefit from a good outfield defense. His high release point, contributed to by both his over-the-top motion and his height, causes homers to be a bugaboo, but the benefit for fans is the potential for the curiosity of a 1:1 walk-to-homer ratio. The second highlight of any right-thinking Mets fan's year, after Santana's no-hitter, was obviously Rauch pitching to Jose Altuve.

Johan Santana

Born: **3/13/1979** Age: **34**
Bats: **L** Throws: **L** Height: **6' 1"** Weight: **210**
Breakout: **18%** Improve: **55%** Collapse: **13%**
Attrition: **9%** MLB: **92%**

Comparables:
Ted Lilly, Mike Cuellar, Andy Pettitte

YEAR	TEAM	LVL	AGE	W	L	SV	G	GS	IP	H	HR	BB	SO	BB9	SO9	GB%	BABIP	WHIP	ERA	FIP	FRA	WARP
2010	NYN	MLB	31	11	9	0	29	29	199	179	16	55	144	2.5	6.5	37%	.272	1.18	2.98	3.56	3.80	3.5
2011	SLU	A+	32	0	0	0	2	2	5	5	0	0	5	0.0	9.0	—	.357	1.00	1.80	1.99	2.16	0.0
2012	BRO	A-	33	0	0	0	1	1	3	1	0	1	3	3.0	9.0	29%	.143	0.67	0.00	2.33	4.68	0.0
2012	NYN	MLB	33	6	9	0	21	21	117	117	17	39	111	3.0	8.5	35%	.301	1.33	4.85	4.13	4.20	1.6
2013	*NYN*	*MLB*	*34*	*5*	*5*	*0*	*14*	*14*	*86*	*77*	*10*	*21*	*73*	*2.2*	*7.6*	*39%*	*.287*	*1.14*	*3.33*	*3.75*	*3.62*	*1.2*

Did you hear that the Mets finally threw a no-hitter? No? Well, they did. Santana tossed the gem on June 1, then missed about a month from July to August with an ankle sprain before finishing the year on the disabled list with back inflammation. Santana is not what he was, and he has almost no chance of being worth his $25.5 million salary in 2013. While he struck out batters at his best rate since leaving Minnesota, he also posted his worst walk rate since becoming a full-time starter. Even more alarmingly, after a career spent keeping his BABIPs at .285 or less (frequently much less), he finished worse than the league average in 2012. Were he simply a 33-year-old former great, one might guess at bad luck or bad defense. As a 33-year-old former great coming off a major shoulder injury and less able to find the strike zone than ever before, one suspects a more sinister and lasting cause. All of that said, Santana still has talent sufficient to be a number-three starter, and if the Mets are willing to eat his salary, a contending team might take him on that basis.

Chris Schwinden

Born: **9/22/1986** Age: **26**
Bats: **R** Throws: **R** Height: **6' 4"** Weight: **215**
Breakout: **27%** Improve: **53%** Collapse: **27%**
Attrition: **27%** MLB: **89%**

Comparables:
Jim McGlothlin, Doug Drabek, Cory Luebke

YEAR	TEAM	LVL	AGE	W	L	SV	G	GS	IP	H	HR	BB	SO	BB9	SO9	GB%	BABIP	WHIP	ERA	FIP	FRA	WARP
2011	BIN	AA	24	0	0	0	2	0	3	2	0	0	5	0.0	15.0	33%	.333	0.67	0.00	0.08	1.10	0.1
2011	BUF	AAA	24	8	8	0	26	26	145^2	138	14	48	134	3.0	8.3	34%	.303	1.28	3.95	3.84	4.60	0.9
2011	NYN	MLB	24	0	2	0	4	4	21	23	1	6	17	2.6	7.3	41%	.314	1.38	4.71	2.99	3.56	0.3
2012	BUF	AAA	25	8	6	0	21	19	106^2	102	7	30	92	2.5	7.8	38%	.301	1.24	2.70	3.19	4.08	1.4
2012	COH	AAA	25	1	2	0	3	3	15^1	16	4	6	5	3.5	2.9	39%	.226	1.43	5.87	7.07	29.71	0.0
2012	LVG	AAA	25	0	1	0	1	1	3	8	1	1	2	3.0	6.0	27%	.500	3.00	21.00	7.67	8.11	0.0
2012	SWB	AAA	25	0	1	0	1	1	4	8	0	1	2	2.2	4.5	50%	.444	2.25	6.75	2.91	3.62	0.1
2012	NYN	MLB	25	0	1	0	3	2	8^2	15	4	3	1	3.1	1.0	52%	.289	2.08	12.46	9.94	11.57	-0.4
2013	*NYN*	*MLB*	*26*	*3*	*4*	*0*	*10*	*10*	*53*	*56*	*7*	*16*	*39*	*2.8*	*6.6*	*39%*	*.310*	*1.36*	*4.71*	*4.35*	*5.12*	*-0.2*

Despite having options remaining, Schwinden was designated for assignment no fewer than four times in 2012, making a circuit of organized baseball, moving from the Mets to the Blue Jays to the Indians to the Yankees before coming back to the Mets, only to be outrighted to Triple-A three days later. All of those teams wanted him enough at some point to put in a claim, but nobody wanted him enough to keep him once they needed that 40-man spot for someone else. Schwinden is a righty who throws 90 and is perfectly capable of getting bashed around in Coors on short notice. You can safely forget about him as soon as you turn the page, but four DFAs and an outright assignment in one year are worth noting.

Noah Syndergaard

Born: 8/29/1992 Age: 20
Bats: L Throws: R Height: 6' 6" Weight: 200
Breakout: 36% Improve: 62% Collapse: 26%
Attrition: 17% MLB: 93%

Comparables:
Chris Zachary,Bruce Robbins,Mike McCormick

YEAR	TEAM	LVL	AGE	W	L	SV	G	GS	IP	H	HR	BB	SO	BB9	SO9	GB%	BABIP	WHIP	ERA	FIP	FRA	WARP
2011	BLU	Rk	18	4	0	0	7	5	32	23	1	11	37	3.1	10.4	52%	.255	1.06	1.41	2.91	4.46	0.3
2011	LNS	A	18	0	0	0	2	2	9	8	0	2	9	2.0	9.0	—	.320	1.11	3.00	2.03	2.20	0.0
2011	VAN	A-	18	1	2	0	4	4	18	15	0	5	22	2.5	11.0	52%	.326	1.11	2.00	2.00	2.80	0.6
2012	LNS	A	19	8	5	1	27	19	103^{2}	81	3	31	122	2.7	10.6	58%	.299	1.08	2.60	2.36	1.87	0.4
2013	*NYN*	*MLB*	*20*	*2*	*2*	*0*	*9*	*7*	*36^{2}*	*34*	*4*	*17*	*32*	*4.1*	*7.9*	*49%*	*.302*	*1.39*	*4.46*	*4.26*	*4.84*	*0.1*

A tall, lean righty from suburban Dallas, Syndergaard separated himself from Lansing rotation-mates Justin Nicolino and Aaron Sanchez by showcasing the pitching staff's best combination of stuff and feel. At 20, Syndergaard already owns an above-average upper-90s fastball and a plus, mid-80s changeup. Like Nicolino and Sanchez, Syndergaard was held back early in the year, tag-teaming with Anthony DeSclafani to pitch three- and four-inning outings before being extended further as the season wore on. Syndergaard had emerged as the top pitching prospect in the Blue Jays organization before coming to the Mets in the Dickey trade, and his combination of stuff and polish could grease the rails of an accelerated ascent to the big leagues, perhaps as early as 2014.

Domingo Tapia

Born: 12/16/1991 Age: 21
Bats: R Throws: R Height: 6' 5" Weight: 186
Breakout: 30% Improve: 68% Collapse: 13%
Attrition: 7% MLB: 87%

Comparables:
Tommy Boggs,Dave McNally,Dan Petry

YEAR	TEAM	LVL	AGE	W	L	SV	G	GS	IP	H	HR	BB	SO	BB9	SO9	GB%	BABIP	WHIP	ERA	FIP	FRA	WARP
2010	MTS	Rk	18	4	3	0	10	10	47	49	0	10	29	1.9	5.6	54%	.338	1.26	3.45	3.42	5.56	-0.3
2011	KNG	Rk	19	5	5	0	11	11	50	50	3	16	30	2.9	5.4	—	.288	1.32	3.78	4.38	4.76	0.0
2011	BRO	A-	19	1	0	0	1	1	6	5	0	0	6	0.0	9.0	50%	.312	0.83	0.00	1.36	2.34	0.2
2012	SAV	A	20	6	5	0	20	19	108^{2}	92	2	32	101	2.7	8.4	64%	.291	1.14	3.98	3.06	4.60	0.6
2013	*NYN*	*MLB*	*21*	*2*	*3*	*0*	*7*	*7*	*35^{2}*	*38*	*5*	*16*	*22*	*4.2*	*5.6*	*53%*	*.306*	*1.53*	*5.36*	*5.13*	*5.83*	*-0.4*

Tapia is a 6'5" drink of water with a triple-digit right arm who has always flashed surprisingly good control numbers for a teenager with that kind of heat. Last year saw him finally convert the rocket fuel into whiffs, as he leaped from striking out a pedestrian 5.4 men per nine in rookie ball to 8.4 in Single-A. That kind of improvement in a single year while skipping a level at age 20 is special. While he may not develop the kind of breaking pitch a starter needs, his vicious fastball (which oh by the way is a sinker) and improving change are probably good enough to play in any major-league bullpen.

Carlos Torres

Born: 10/22/1982 Age: 30
Bats: R Throws: R Height: 6' 2" Weight: 190
Breakout: 14% Improve: 44% Collapse: 24%
Attrition: 21% MLB: 91%

Comparables:
Jack Sanford,Andy Messersmith,Tim Belcher

YEAR	TEAM	LVL	AGE	W	L	SV	G	GS	IP	H	HR	BB	SO	BB9	SO9	GB%	BABIP	WHIP	ERA	FIP	FRA	WARP
2010	CHR	AAA	27	9	9	0	27	25	160^{1}	125	13	71	140	4.0	7.9	48%	.257	1.22	3.42	3.98	4.80	0.8
2010	CHA	MLB	27	0	1	0	5	1	13^{2}	23	2	9	13	5.9	8.6	31%	.447	2.34	8.56	5.02	5.24	0.0
2012	CSP	AAA	29	5	4	0	14	13	61	62	6	25	59	3.7	8.7	48%	.329	1.43	3.98	4.29	5.09	1.2
2012	COL	MLB	29	5	3	0	31	0	53	49	2	26	42	4.4	7.1	46%	.299	1.42	5.26	3.74	4.35	0.7
2013	*NYN*	*MLB*	*30*	*3*	*3*	*0*	*15*	*8*	*56*	*49*	*6*	*24*	*50*	*3.9*	*8.0*	*47%*	*.294*	*1.32*	*3.93*	*4.09*	*4.27*	*0.3*

Torres should have called it a season after his July 29 outing against the Reds, when he owned a 1.50 ERA in 18 innings and opponents had a 463 OPS against him. Then August and September happened. He had similar results in previous cups of coffee. Torres was a 2004 15th-round pick of the White Sox and spent 2011 in Japan. He isn't young, doesn't throw hard, and hasn't established himself yet. Still, with his experience and ability to start or relieve, he's not a bad guy to stash at Triple-A just in case.

Zack Wheeler

Born: 5/30/1990 Age: 23
Bats: R Throws: R Height: 6' 5" Weight: 185
Breakout: 23% Improve: 59% Collapse: 22%
Attrition: 15% MLB: 92%

Comparables:
Chad Billingsley,Vinegar Bend Mizell,Sean Gallagher

YEAR	TEAM	LVL	AGE	W	L	SV	G	GS	IP	H	HR	BB	SO	BB9	SO9	GB%	BABIP	WHIP	ERA	FIP	FRA	WARP
2010	AUG	A	20	3	3	0	21	13	58^{2}	47	0	38	70	5.8	10.7	63%	.320	1.45	3.99	3.44	4.25	0.4
2011	SJO	A+	21	7	5	0	16	16	88	74	7	47	98	4.8	10.0	—	.293	1.38	3.99	4.50	4.89	0.0
2011	SLU	A+	21	2	2	0	6	6	27	26	0	5	31	1.7	10.3	27%	.467	1.15	2.00	1.87	3.37	0.1
2012	BIN	AA	22	10	6	0	19	19	116	92	2	43	117	3.3	9.1	48%	.300	1.16	3.26	2.80	3.44	1.6
2012	BUF	AAA	22	2	2	0	6	6	33	23	2	16	31	4.4	8.5	48%	.250	1.18	3.27	3.61	4.51	0.1
2013	*NYN*	*MLB*	*23*	*2*	*3*	*0*	*7*	*7*	*38*	*33*	*4*	*18*	*36*	*4.3*	*8.7*	*48%*	*.299*	*1.34*	*4.05*	*4.09*	*4.40*	*0.2*

If Harvey is the number-one young pitcher in the Mets organization, then Wheeler is number 1A. Or maybe vice versa. Choosing between the two doesn't matter, but it's a fun parlor game. Wheeler's ETA is 2013, though Collins has called the chances that he makes the Mets out of spring training "slim," and rightfully so. While Wheeler has advanced mechanics for such a young pitcher, resulting in a mid-90s fastball and a slow curve along with a slider and change, his fastball command can still use fine-tuning. Still, if there's any young pitcher who understands the importance of command, it's Wheeler: Few young pitchers, especially those with his overpowering stuff, manage to develop the baseball intelligence and understanding of how to manage an at-bat that Wheeler has. Wheeler is going to be good. If he can put together the physical tools with the existing aptitude, he can be great.

Chris Young
Born: 5/25/1979 Age: 34
Bats: R Throws: R Height: 6' 11" Weight: 260
Breakout: 9% Improve: 39% Collapse: 34%
Attrition: 14% MLB: 78%

Comparables:
Livan Hernandez, Russ Ortiz, Brad Penny

YEAR	TEAM	LVL	AGE	W	L	SV	G	GS	IP	H	HR	BB	SO	BB9	SO9	GB%	BABIP	WHIP	ERA	FIP	FRA	WARP
2010	SAN	AA	31	0	1	0	1	1	0^{2}	2	0	4	1	51.4	12.9	%	.000	8.57	64.29	17.46	19.62	-0.1
2010	POR	AAA	31	0	0	0	2	2	6^{1}	2	1	2	4	2.9	5.7	35%	.062	0.63	1.43	5.33	5.32	0.1
2010	SDN	MLB	31	2	0	0	4	4	20	10	1	11	15	4.9	6.8	32%	.164	1.05	0.90	3.91	3.41	0.3
2011	NYN	MLB	32	1	0	0	4	4	24	12	3	11	22	4.1	8.2	21%	.155	0.96	1.88	4.29	4.11	0.3
2012	SLU	A+	33	1	0	0	3	3	17	17	1	2	7	1.1	3.7	26%	.286	1.12	3.18	3.86	4.62	0.1
2012	BUF	AAA	33	0	0	0	1	1	6	2	0	3	2	4.5	3.0	32%	.105	0.83	0.00	3.99	5.17	0.0
2012	NYN	MLB	33	4	9	0	20	20	115	119	16	36	80	2.8	6.3	25%	.287	1.35	4.15	4.54	4.16	1.5
2013	*NYN*	*MLB*	*34*	*5*	*6*	*0*	*16*	*16*	*88*	*82*	*12*	*35*	*64*	*3.6*	*6.5*	*30%*	*.275*	*1.32*	*4.24*	*4.71*	*4.61*	*0.2*

Young and Rauch are quite a pair of high-altitude, low-velocity righties. Where Rauch is a fly-ball pitcher, Young is an extreme fly-ball pitcher, but historically he has suppressed hits on balls in play, and his strikeout rate is solid. These characteristics don't make Young *good*, but they let him survive as a starting major-league pitcher. Given his injury history and his established status as a back-end guy, he can likely be had cheaply by anyone with a fetish for tall righties, Ivy League grads, or people who write theses on race in America. And if you like all three? Well, boy howdy.

LINEOUTS

HITTERS

PLAYER	TEAM	LVL	AGE	PA	R	2B	3B	HR	RBI	BB	SO	SB-CS	AVG/OBP/SLG	TAv	BABIP	BRR	FRAA	WARP
C J. Centeno	BIN	AA	22	313	29	12	2	0	35	23	43	1-1	.285/.337/.342	.241	.331	-2.2	C(59): -0.5	0.2
SS B. Hicks	SAC	AAA	26	383	61	26	3	18	61	47	115	5-4	.244/.350/.506	.168	.316	0.3	SS(18): 2.9, 2B(7): 0.4	-0.4
	OAK	MLB	26	70	8	5	0	3	7	6	31	1-0	.172/.243/.391	.223	.267	-0.9	SS(19): -0.1, 2B(1): 0.0	-0.3
OF J. Hoffmann	NOR	AAA	27	427	49	19	2	11	44	54	74	9-2	.254/.347/.407	.262	.286	-0.6	LF(41): 5.2, RF(30): -0.0	0.3
2B D. Muno	SLU	A+	23	352	36	16	2	6	39	50	53	19-3	.280/.387/.412	.279	.321	-1.7	2B(40): -6.0, SS(13): -0.4	0.0
C K. Plawecki	BRO	A-	21	252	26	8	0	7	27	25	24	0-0	.250/.345/.384	.229	.250	-0.5	C(8): 0.0, 1B(1): -0.0	-0.1
SS M. Reynolds	SAV	A	21	179	18	8	0	3	13	12	26	5-1	.259/.335/.367	.548	.290	0.1	SS(3): -0.1	0.4
3B A. Rodriguez	SAV	A	20	352	41	21	1	16	59	29	71	1-0	.274/.336/.497	.282	.305	-3.3	3B(59): 1.3, 1B(6): 0.5	1.2
	SLU	A+	20	163	19	5	0	8	24	8	30	1-0	.242/.288/.431	.228	.252	0.8	3B(27): -0.5, 1B(3): -0.3	-0.4
INF J. Satin	BUF	AAA	27	527	72	25	1	14	60	77	109	3-4	.286/.391/.442	.273	.346	-0.6	1B(67): 0.1, 2B(34): 1.4	0.9
SS W. Tovar	SLU	A+	20	256	31	17	1	1	23	29	17	12-7	.284/.377/.385	.286	.303	1.5	SS(39): 0.3	1.3
	BIN	AA	20	217	20	11	2	0	27	11	22	2-1	.254/.308/.332	.215	.280	1	SS(48): 0.7	0.2
RF C. Vaughn	SLU	A+	23	535	73	25	3	23	69	65	114	21-4	.243/.351/.463	.278	.274	-0.1	RF(71): 8.1, LF(12): 0.5	2.0

Baseball teams always need catchers, especially ones who hit lefty, and catchers can take time to develop, so keep an eye out for **Juan Centeno** as a 29-year-old rookie in 2019. **Brandon Hicks** has decent power for a shortstop but swinging for the fences has a price, and a player with 42 strikeouts in his first 98 big-league plate appearances is not making a strong case for more. **Jamie Hoffmann** is a hard worker who plays good defense and has an inkling of power and speed, so, given the Mets' weakness in the outfield, he signed on with the right team. **Daniel Muno** is a Fresno State alumnus who took a ton of walks in High-A but got busted for a PED, costing him development time that, as a 23-year-old, he didn't have the luxury of wasting. **Kevin Plawecki** is a 2012 sandwich pick from Purdue with fantastic contact skills, only a modest likelihood to add power, and a defensive package that, outside of a mediocre arm, will easily permit him to stay at catcher. **Matthew Reynolds** was an excellent defensive third baseman at Arkansas whom the Mets took with their second-round pick and immediately moved to short, though he's likely a utility man in the long run. **Aderlin Rodriguez** is a thick third baseman who has significant power potential but needs to work on his plate approach and defensive skills. **Josh Satin** plays first, second, and third, and takes mighty, chopping hacks at the baseball that have given very solid results in the minors. **Wilfredo Tovar**'s glove at short will give him every opportunity to prove he can hit enough to stick around the majors, and if (*if*) he can replicate his High-A line over most of a year at Double-A as a 21-year-old, he'll be well on his way. Yep, **Cory Vaughn** is Greg's son, and the rediscovery of his power stroke in the Florida State League was impressive, but the strikeouts are so high that projecting any kind of big-league contact skills is difficult.

PITCHERS

PLAYER	TEAM	LVL	AGE	W	L	SV	IP	H	HR	BB	SO	BB9	SO9	GB%	BABIP	WHIP	ERA	FIP	FRA	WARP
M. Acosta	BUF	AAA	31	0	1	0	28	24	1	4	25	1.3	8.0	47%	.287	1.00	2.25	2.26	2.99	0.6
	NYN	MLB	31	1	3	1	47^{1}	48	7	25	46	4.8	8.7	40%	.304	1.54	6.46	4.89	6.31	-0.6
G. Burke	BOW	AA	29	1	0	14	29^{1}	21	0	4	20	1.2	6.1	62%	.228	0.85	1.53	2.35	3.10	0.4
	NOR	AAA	29	2	1	3	35^{1}	25	1	11	30	2.8	7.6	68%	.245	1.02	1.53	2.85	3.80	0.4
R. Fraser	SLU	A+	23	3	2	2	30^{1}	30	1	7	18	2.1	5.3	54%	.299	1.22	2.08	3.53	4.60	0.2
	BIN	AA	23	2	2	4	33^{2}	29	1	13	25	3.5	6.7	61%	.269	1.25	3.48	3.44	4.61	0.3
G. Germen	SLU	A+	24	3	0	0	26^{2}	25	3	8	21	2.7	7.1	56%	.289	1.24	3.04	4.18	5.86	-0.1
	BIN	AA	24	8	12	0	119^{2}	127	11	33	97	2.5	7.3	51%	.314	1.34	4.59	3.70	4.85	1.1
J. Hampson	BUF	AAA	32	4	3	4	65^{2}	63	5	22	59	3.0	8.1	50%	.304	1.29	2.33	3.36	4.75	0.1
	NYN	MLB	32	0	0	0	10	6	0	5	4	4.5	3.6	68%	.214	1.10	1.80	3.84	4.37	0.0
B. Holt	BIN	AA	25	2	1	1	47^{2}	43	3	28	42	5.3	7.9	36%	.292	1.49	3.40	4.15	3.90	0.6
J. Kaplan	BIN	AA	26	3	0	1	26	35	1	8	24	2.8	8.3	48%	.410	1.65	3.12	2.89	2.87	0.6
M. Koch	BRO	A-	21	0	2	0	23^{1}	25	1	7	19	2.7	7.3	48%	.324	1.37	5.01	3.55	5.15	0.0
R. Montero	SAV	A	21	6	3	0	71^{1}	61	4	8	54	1.0	6.8	37%	.260	0.97	2.52	3.17	3.40	1.2
	SLU	A+	21	5	2	0	50^{2}	35	2	11	56	2.0	9.9	41%	.270	0.91	2.13	2.47	2.79	1.1
C.J. Nitkowski	BIN	AA	39	0	0	0	4^{2}	1	0	4	8	7.7	15.4	67%	.167	1.07	0.00	2.99	1.35	0.2
	BUF	AAA	39	0	2	1	14^{1}	24	1	8	13	5.0	8.2	52%	.451	2.23	7.53	3.93	4.86	0.0
G. Peavey	BIN	AA	23	8	8	0	144	169	18	37	84	2.3	5.2	45%	.320	1.43	5.06	4.53	6.14	0.3
H. Robles	BRO	A-	21	6	1	0	72^{2}	47	0	10	66	1.2	8.2	53%	.245	0.78	1.11	2.09	3.25	0.8
A. Rodriguez	BIN	AA	24	2	3	1	72^{2}	58	13	21	77	2.6	9.5	28%	.249	1.09	3.22	4.40	5.06	0.6
J. Urbina	KNG	Rk	19	1	0	0	12^{1}	9	0	16	18	11.7	13.1	.308	.346	2.03	5.11	4.67	6.95	0.0
	BRO	A-	19	0	0	0	5	4	0	3	5	5.4	9	.429	.286	1.40	3.60	3.13	3.61	0.1
L. Verrett	SAV	A	22	3	2	0	64^{2}	57	7	9	67	1.3	9.3	48%	.279	1.02	3.06	3.47	4.63	0.0
	SLU	A+	22	2	0	0	38^{2}	30	4	4	26	0.9	6.1	46%	.226	0.88	2.09	3.70	4.37	0.4

Non-tendered after a brutal year, **Manny Acosta** signed with the Yomiuri Giants in Japan. **Greg Burke** is 30 and signed a minor-league deal in November, but was added to the 40-man in advance of the Rule 5 draft. Throw out all reports on him prior to 2012, though, because he became a submariner last year. **Ryan Fraser** throws hard, and he converted to relief in 2012, but he didn't have the kind of strikeout rate you'd want to see from a 23-year-old reliever in High-A. **Gonzalez Germen** didn't sign out of the Dominican Republic until he was 20, but he has nice component stats (nearly 4:1 strikeout-to-walk ratio in the minors) and he's on the 40-man so youneverknow. An 82-mph cutter and a slightly unusual delivery that doesn't quite merit the adjective "funky" are what **Justin Hampson** has to offer, which explains why the Mets outrighted him after the season. Former first-round pick and top prospect **Bradley Holt** finally reached Triple-A last year as a reliever, but he still has not found the strike zone since 2009. **Jeffrey Kaplan** is a hittable reliever without a lot of stuff who has yet to reach Triple-A despite keeping the ball in the yard, avoiding the free pass, and recording a reasonable number of strikeouts. **Matthew Koch**, the Mets' 2012 third-round pick after being co-closer at Louisville, features a hard but flat fastball and poor secondary stuff, but the Mets might profitably try him as a starter, if for no other reason than to give him more time to improve his pitches. **Rafael Montero** is a small Dominican right-hander who, despite not signing until he was 20, has excellent control of a low-90s fastball and sharp slider which he has put to good use in rising through six levels in just two years. **C.J. Nitkowski** is a curiosity, but a fun one: After four years in Japan and Korea and one year not playing at all, he signed a minor-league deal with the Mets, struck out almost 10 per nine, and walked over five and a half. He's funny on Twitter. **Greg Peavey** is a command 'n' control starboardsider whose fastball reportedly hit 90 when he was 14 and goes in the low 90s these days. **Hansel Robles** had incredible results in Brooklyn and has only allowed three homers in 235 1/3 innings as a professional, but as a short righty without above-average stuff, he might consider getting his real estate license in his spare time. **Armando Rodriguez** moved to Double-A and the bullpen in 2012, with the main benefit being cutting a walk per nine out of his results. There is some junk in his trunk, which is not the worst thing in the world for a pitcher. **Juan Urbina** is a skinny lefty who got demoted after just three innings in Brooklyn, then shut down after 12 1/3 more in Kingsport, but he's also Ugueth's son. **Logan Verrett** has command, control, a 90-mph fastball, an 11:13 homer-to-walk ratio, and seven times as many strikeouts as free passes.

MANAGER: TERRY COLLINS

YEAR	TEAM	W-L	Pythag +/-	Avg PC	100+ P	120+ P	QS	BQS	REL	REL w Zero R	IBB	PH	PH Avg	PH HR	SB2	CS2	SB3	CS3	SAC Att	SAC %	POS SAC	Squeeze	Swing	In Play
2011	NYN	77-85	0	95.7	63	6	84	7	514	398	48	306	.203	8	16	4	1	0	102	72.5%	35	2	347	114
2012	NYN	74-88	0	95.5	69	2	101	1	505	380	29	322	.240	10	13	3	0	0	82	79.3%	20	4	321	108

A team without a deep pool of star talent has to have a manager who can maximize the tools at his disposal. While we have yet to find a good way to measure the power of motivation and happy feelings engendered by a top battle commander, we can ask whether the players were put in a position to succeed. Mets hitters had the platoon advantage 61 percent of the time in 2012, fourth-most in the National League, and pitchers had the advantage at a slightly above-league-average rate. This doesn't end any analysis, but it serves as an indication that Collins is thinking about his players and their limitations and strengths. He also displayed an understanding of what might be called basic sabermetric tenets, ordering a well-below-average number of intentional walks and having his position players sacrifice a mere 19 times all season. (Where about 42 percent of the league's sacrifices came from non-pitchers, fewer than 30 percent of Collins's did.)

On the intangible side of the ledger, Collins is not the devastatingly intense manager he was in Anaheim over a decade ago. He has learned to modulate his energy and focus it in a positive direction. Collins now gets raves for his optimism and enthusiasm, attributes that, so long as they do not spill over into yapping-chihuahua territory, any leader would like to hear associated with his name.

New York Yankees

2012: THE OLD MAN DOWN THE ROAD

The Bronx Bombers fought off Father Time by living up to their nickname, slugging their opponents into submission and then sealing the deal with a strong bullpen. After blowing a 10-game AL East lead, they hung on to beat Baltimore by two games, earning a chance to take home a 28th World Series title. But then Father Time caught up with them—not just with Alex Rodriguez, who could barely play, but to his teammates, as well, who cratered in the postseason.

YANKEES PROSPECTUS

2012 W-L: 95-67, 1st in AL East

Pythag	.586	2nd	DER	.704	19th
RS/G	4.96	2nd	B-Age	33.0	30th
RA/G	4.12	10th	P-Age	30.4	30th
TAv	.279	2nd	Salary	$211.8	1st
BRR	-6.5	23rd	M$/MW	$4.28	23rd
TAv-P	.258	13th	DL Days	1596	2nd
FIP	3.93	14th	DL WARP	7.5	2nd

Three-Year Park Factors	
Overall	104
HR/RH	103
HR/LH	126
AVG/RH	103
AVG/LH	109

Yankee Stadium (2009)
Att. % of Capacity: 86.9% (7th)
Dim. 318, 399, 408, 385, 314

Lefty hitters hit 139 home runs at Yankee Stadium in 2012, 38 more than at any other big-league park.

The Yankees featured the oldest pitching staff in the AL and by far the oldest batters in baseball; the team's postseason roster was the eighth-oldest in postseason history. Collectively, those bats showed few signs of age until October, finishing the regular season second in the majors with a .279 TAv. Led by a near-MVP-caliber campaign from Robinson Cano—at 29, the second-youngest regular in the lineup—another solid season from Nick Swisher, and a birthdate-defying offensive renaissance by 38-year-old Derek Jeter, the Yankees scored almost five runs per game in a league that averaged under 4.5.

A higher percentage of the Yankees' runs (48.4 percent) scored via the home run than did any other team's, but they hit so many homers—the most in franchise history and the seventh-most of all time—and put so many men on via the walk that their reliance on the big blow was a help, not a hindrance. That performance at the plate, coupled with a convincing comeback by Andy Pettitte, a successful first AL season for Hiroki Kuroda, a midseason trade for a resurgent Ichiro Suzuki, and the late-inning efforts of David Robertson and Rafael Soriano, who stepped up with an injured Mariano Rivera out after April, propelled the Yankees to the league's best record (and the +136 run differential to back it up).

However, the season ended on a sour note. Detroit swept New York out of the ALCS after the Yankees barely squeaked by Baltimore in the Division Series. The Yanks scored a mere 22 runs in nine games, batting .188/.254/.303, as Swisher, Cano, Curtis Granderson, and a secretly injured A-Rod went a combined 14-for-125.

2013: WHO'LL STOP THE REIGN?

The Yankees opened their offseason by re-signing or importing some of the oldest players on the market—Rivera, Pettitte, Kuroda, Ichiro, and Kevin Youkilis—while watching a series of free agents in whom they'd had interest accept offers from other teams. The players under (big) contract remain talented enough to compete, but the holes in the roster are increasingly tough to ignore. Without a concerted effort to get younger or the million-dollar bills to paper over the cracks, the Yankees could succumb to natural causes before any significant in-house assistance arrives.

As we went to press, the Yankees lineup contained almost as many question marks (to put it charitably) as it did dependable players, with Chris Stewart, Eduardo Nunez, and Chris Dickerson slated for roster slots. Whether they plug those positions before Opening Day or not, it's unusual for the Yankees to wait well into the winter without lining up an established player at every position.

In an article at Baseball Prospectus last September (URL: bbp.cx/a/18232), Colin Wyers found that a team as old as the Yankees would be expected to win three fewer games per season over the next five years than an average-aged team with the same 2012 winning percentage. Although the Yankees have thus far managed to avoid a serious decline and to sustain their success through spending, the roster's advanced age leaves the team susceptible to the sort of mass extinction event that wiped out the dinosaurs (and the Philadelphia Phillies). That downward spiral could take the form of an epidemic of injuries, a simultaneous slowing of swings and loss of stuff, or a further breakdown in the team's already shoddy defense (a skill that tends to peak early in most players' professional lives). The return of Brett Gardner to the lineup—an actual sub-30 starter, at least until August—should help the Yankees fend off those fates.

But we shouldn't overstate our dire predictions for the Bombers based on how impotent they looked the last time we saw them and how many of their players experienced the '70s. Each of the four previous times that the Yankees were swept out of the postseason, they responded by reaching the World Series the following year. That doesn't mean they're destined to do it again in 2013, but it is a reminder that an ignominious end in October isn't necessarily a symptom of a long-term ailment.

THE STATE OF THE ORGANIZATION: FORTUNATE SONS

The Yankees' ills are nothing that couldn't be cured with one of their customary cash infusions. But the team's newfound fiscal restraint—while not an obstacle to long-term contention—could make for a difficult transition period from an organization that spent freely on free agents to one that spends more responsibly and makes a commitment to promoting from within—at least until its luxury-tax rate resets.

The one time Brian Cashman took the podium at the MLB Winter Meetings, it was to announce not a high-profile player acquisition, but another injury to A-Rod. The next day, the GM dropped the line "beggars can't be choosers" when discussing the Yankees' outlook for free agency, which would have sounded even more incongruous than it did if the Pirates, of all teams, hadn't just lured catcher Russell Martin to Pittsburgh with a two-year, $17 million offer the Yankees couldn't or wouldn't match.

All of this uncharacteristic penny-pinching stems from the Steinbrenner sons' desire to get the Yankees' payroll below the $189 million luxury-tax threshold by 2014. According to BP's Maury Brown, the Yankees have accounted for 91 percent of the league-wide luxury-tax penalties paid since 2003. If they achieve their payroll goal, they won't pay any additional tax on their 2014 total, and any future overage charges will be levied at the rate assessed for first-time offenders. Couple that with corresponding reductions in taxation rates on revenue-sharing rebates, and we're talking serious savings.

Of course, Yankees fans are used to talking about titles, not tax rates, and there's no telling how patient they'll be with the Steinbrothers' attempt to economize, especially since it beggars belief that their pinstriped profit machine can't make money with payrolls as high as they've had in the past. Perennial contenders can't stay that way without annual injections of new talent, and while the Yankees have plenty of promising players on the farm, not many of them are major-league ready.

It's not a coincidence that the Yankees, historically baseball's most successful franchise, have also long been its wealthiest. As player salaries and payrolls rise across baseball, led by the new ownership of the Dodgers, the sport's traditional top spenders are temporarily bucking the trend. Barring a buzzer-beating spending spree, the Bombers will fail to start a season with baseball's highest payroll for the first time since 1998. The Yankees won't forsake their financial advantage for long, but in the short term, they're running the risk of a damaging lull between titles.

HITTERS

David Adams INF

Born: **5/15/1987** Age: **26**
Bats: **R** Throws: **R** Height: **6' 3"**
Weight: **190** Breakout: **7%**
Improve: **51%** Collapse: **2%**
Attrition: **20%** MLB: **94%**

Comparables:
Danny Richar, Luis Valbuena, Warren Morris

YEAR	TEAM	LVL	AGE	PA	R	2B	3B	HR	RBI	BB	SO	SB	CS	AVG_OBP_SLG	TAv	BABIP	BRR	FRAA	WARP
2010	TRN	AA	23	173	31	15	3	3	32	18	31	5	2	.309/.393/.507	.335	.373	3.8	2B(36): 2.6	2.6
2011	YAN	Rk	24	64	13	9	0	1	11	5	10	2	1	.429/.469/.643	.351	.489	0.4	2B(15): 1.2	0.9
2011	TAM	A+	24	57	6	3	0	0	4	4	8	0	2	.308/.368/.365	.268	.364	0	--	0.0
2012	TRN	AA	25	383	44	23	0	8	48	38	53	3	1	.306/.385/.450	.344	.336	-0.9	2B(15): 0.3, 3B(10): 1.0	1.5
2013	*NYA*	*MLB*	*26*	*250*	*25*	*13*	*1*	*6*	*28*	*19*	*51*	*1*	*0*	*.253/.317/.392*	*.254*	*.300*	*-0.4*	*2B 1, 3B 0*	*0.7*

Adams first made himself known to Yankees fans as the man who sabotaged a 2010 trade for Cliff Lee by fracturing his ankle at an inopportune time, but he might soon distinguish himself for something other than getting hurt. In light of A-Rod's latest injury and the banged-up body of Kevin Youkilis, Adams's shift from full-time second baseman to part-time third baseman last season might turn out to be his ticket to the big leagues as early as 2013. His ankle woes have limited him to an average of 51 games over the past three seasons, but he hit well in Double-A and the Arizona Fall League and should continue to make decent contact and draw the odd walk in the majors if he can stay on his feet.

Zoilo Almonte OF

Born: **6/10/1989** Age: **24**
Bats: **B** Throws: **R** Height: **6' 0"**
Weight: **165** Breakout: **4%**
Improve: **54%** Collapse: **4%**
Attrition: **9%** MLB: **94%**

Comparables:
Dick Sharon,Leon Durham,Sixto Lezcano

YEAR	TEAM	LVL	AGE	PA	R	2B	3B	HR	RBI	BB	SO	SB	CS	AVG_OBP_SLG	TAv	BABIP	BRR	FRAA	WARP
2010	CSC	A	21	255	33	13	2	10	35	21	65	7	6	.278/.340/.485	.311	.342	-0.2	RF(39): 0.7, CF(12): 0.6	2.0
2010	TAM	A+	21	264	26	10	3	3	26	23	65	8	1	.261/.326/.366	.246	.347	-1.4	RF(64): 4.0	0.1
2011	TAM	A+	22	296	38	15	3	12	54	31	60	14	4	.293/.368/.514	.300	.335	0	--	0.0
2011	TRN	AA	22	191	23	11	1	3	23	14	45	4	1	.251/.309/.377	.240	.320	0	--	0.0
2012	TRN	AA	23	451	64	23	1	21	70	25	103	15	4	.277/.322/.487	.301	.319	2.2	RF(32): 0.6, CF(3): -0.3	1.1
2013	*NYA*	*MLB*	*24*	*250*	*28*	*10*	*1*	*9*	*31*	*13*	*71*	*4*	*1*	*.234/.276/.403*	*.240*	*.291*	*0.1*	*RF -1, CF -0*	*0.0*

Hamstring spasms forced the 23-year-old Almonte to miss April, but after making it to Trenton in May, the switch-hitter stayed healthy and showed good power with poor plate discipline, striking out four times for every walk. That offensive profile probably won't play in an outfield corner in the majors, so Almonte will have to find room on a roster as a switch-hitting reserve. That means he's another Melky Mesa, more or less, but at least he's a year and a half younger.

Tyler Austin RF

Born: **9/6/1991** Age: **21**
Bats: **R** Throws: **R** Height: **6' 3"**
Weight: **200** Breakout: **4%**
Improve: **61%** Collapse: **6%**
Attrition: **14%** MLB: **99%**

Comparables:
Ruben Sierra,Justin Upton,Andruw Jones

YEAR	TEAM	LVL	AGE	PA	R	2B	3B	HR	RBI	BB	SO	SB	CS	AVG_OBP_SLG	TAv	BABIP	BRR	FRAA	WARP
2011	YAN	Rk	19	89	13	8	1	3	22	5	16	11	0	.390/.438/.622	.347	.460	1.2	1B(10): -1.0, 3B(6): 0.1	0.9
2011	STA	A-	19	112	16	10	1	3	14	10	23	7	0	.323/.402/.542	.395	.389	0.4	3B(18): 1.5, 1B(1): 0.1	1.6
2012	CSC	A	20	309	69	22	5	14	54	37	68	17	2	.320/.405/.598	.415	.380	3.3	RF(19): -1.3, 1B(2): -0.0	2.1
2012	TAM	A+	20	148	20	13	1	2	23	12	28	6	0	.321/.385/.478	.278	.394	0.1	RF(10): 1.2	0.1
2013	*NYA*	*MLB*	*21*	*250*	*29*	*11*	*1*	*9*	*31*	*16*	*69*	*6*	*1*	*.243/.297/.413*	*.253*	*.306*	*0.8*	*RF 0, 3B 0*	*0.4*

Austin hasn't stopped hitting since the Yankees somehow snagged and bagged him in the 13th round in 2010 for a bargain $130,000 bonus. His 2012 season may have been the best by any Yankees prospect. In his full-season debut, the right-handed hitter tore up the Sally League, surrendered some power but preserved his high average in Tampa, and reached Trenton a few days before his 21st birthday. Drafted as a catcher and shuttled between infield corners at first, last season he found a home in right field (where he has an above-average arm), a position at which the Yankees could use reinforcements. And he did all that despite missing three weeks in June after a concussion from being hit in the head with a pitch. Austin is at best an average runner and defender, and his bat will have a high bar to clear in right, but his advanced offensive skills and smarts should continue to carry him.

Dante Bichette 3B

Born: **9/26/1992** Age: **20**
Bats: **R** Throws: **R** Height: **6' 2"**
Weight: **215** Breakout: **26%**
Improve: **58%** Collapse: **6%**
Attrition: **30%** MLB: **89%**

Comparables:
Ted Kazanski,Adrian Beltre,Wayne Causey

YEAR	TEAM	LVL	AGE	PA	R	2B	3B	HR	RBI	BB	SO	SB	CS	AVG_OBP_SLG	TAv	BABIP	BRR	FRAA	WARP
2011	YAN	Rk	18	240	33	17	3	3	47	30	41	3	3	.342/.446/.505	.316	.410	-0.9	3B(49): -4.1	1.6
2012	CSC	A	19	522	67	24	3	3	46	44	94	3	4	.248/.322/.331	.290	.305	-0.1	3B(45): 2.5	1.1
2013	*NYA*	*MLB*	*20*	*250*	*19*	*9*	*1*	*4*	*22*	*15*	*65*	*0*	*0*	*.207/.262/.301*	*.205*	*.268*	*-0.4*	*3B 1*	*-0.9*

Bichette was the Yankees' first pick in the 2011 amateur draft, and he looked the part in his initial exposure to pro pitching after his signing. However, his first full season didn't produce the same positive reports. He failed to hit for average or power, showing a tendency to chase breaking balls outside the zone, struggling to square up good velocity, and looking uncomfortable at the plate. He was young for the league, the jump from the GCL to the Sally League is a big one, and he has a good chance to stick at third, so there's still hope here, but 2012 was a setback for sure.

Robinson Cano 2B

Born: **10/22/1982** Age: **30**
Bats: **L** Throws: **R** Height: **6' 1"**
Weight: **205** Breakout: **0%**
Improve: **40%** Collapse: **3%**
Attrition: **7%** MLB: **95%**

Comparables:
Ian Kinsler,Chase Utley,Brandon Phillips

YEAR	TEAM	LVL	AGE	PA	R	2B	3B	HR	RBI	BB	SO	SB	CS	AVG_OBP_SLG	TAv	BABIP	BRR	FRAA	WARP
2010	NYA	MLB	27	696	103	41	3	29	109	57	77	3	2	.319/.381/.534	.310	.326	0.1	2B(158): -0.5	5.4
2011	NYA	MLB	28	681	104	46	7	28	118	38	96	8	2	.302/.349/.533	.309	.316	2.8	2B(157): 6.0	5.5
2012	NYA	MLB	29	697	105	48	1	33	94	61	96	3	2	.313/.379/.550	.318	.326	-1.7	2B(154): 8.0	6.4
2013	*NYA*	*MLB*	*30*	*652*	*79*	*40*	*3*	*24*	*92*	*40*	*85*	*4*	*2*	*.293/.342/.491*	*.292*	*.307*	*-1*	*2B -1*	*4.4*

So all-encompassing was the Mike Trout-Miguel Cabrera MVPocalypse that Cano, whose WARP trailed Trout's but beat out Cabrera's, couldn't sniff a second-place vote. Thanks to that snub and an 0-for-29 postseason slump, his season ended with a whimper. Still, Cano solidified his stardom by setting career highs in every important offensive category and winning a Gold Glove that didn't make anyone angry. At 30, Cano's best may already be behind him, but another standout season would set him up for a free-agent payday that likely has agent Scott Boras salivating. Cano seems to share Derek Jeter's durability gene—he hasn't missed more than a day due to injury in any season since 2006—and his athleticism and improved walk rate bode well for a graceful decline, but the steep historical aging curve for second basemen should give potential employers pause. The Yankees have every incentive to retain their homegrown star, but Brian

Cashman saw Chuck Knoblauch go south after his age-30 season and has watched his warnings about re-signing Alex Rodriguez prove prescient. Don't be surprised if he no-sells the initial offseason bluster from Boras and pursues a prudent approach.

Russ Canzler 1B

Born: **4/11/1986** Age: **27**
Bats: **R** Throws: **R** Height: **6' 3"**
Weight: **220** Breakout: **1%**
Improve: **39%** Collapse: **10%**
Attrition: **12%** MLB: **89%**

Comparables:
Jeff Baker,Wilson Betemit,Gil Hodges

YEAR	TEAM	LVL	AGE	PA	R	2B	3B	HR	RBI	BB	SO	SB	CS	AVG_OBP_SLG	TAv	BABIP	BRR	FRAA	WARP
2010	TEN	AA	24	411	68	28	4	21	66	46	95	5	4	.287/.377/.566	.317	.339	-0.5	3B(64): -1.2, 1B(28): -0.2	3.3
2011	DUR	AAA	25	549	78	40	4	18	83	67	129	5	2	.314/.401/.530	.320	.396	0	--	0.0
2011	TBA	MLB	25	5	0	0	0	0	1	1	1	0	0	.333/.400/.333	.357	.333	0	--	0.1
2012	COH	AAA	26	539	68	36	3	22	79	46	128	2	4	.265/.328/.487	.229	.314	-0.1	LF(22): 1.7, 1B(16): -0.9	-0.9
2012	CLE	MLB	26	97	9	3	0	3	11	4	22	0	0	.269/.299/.398	.257	.324	-0.8	LF(11): 0.0, 1B(8): 0.1	0.1
2013	*NYA*	*MLB*	*27*	*250*	*28*	*12*	*1*	*10*	*34*	*18*	*67*	*1*	*1*	*.243/.299/.440*	*.261*	*.294*	*-0.4*	*1B -2, LF -0*	*0.2*

Canzler has been something of a minor-league journeyman, spending nine seasons at 10 stops across three organizations. He is hoping to parlay a three-year power surge of 61 home runs—two-thirds of which came at Triple-A—into a major-league job that will allow him to trade the "journeyman" tag for one that says, "late bloomer." Of course, as a 30th-round draft pick, he has already beat the odds with his 102 major-league plate appearances, and at age 27 he will likely get at least another shot to switch labels. He had a busy winter, claimed off waivers from Cleveland by Toronto, then claimed back by Cleveland, then claimed by New York, where he could be a right-handed bench piece and back-up first baseman.

Francisco Cervelli C

Born: **3/6/1986** Age: **27**
Bats: **R** Throws: **R** Height: **6' 2"**
Weight: **210** Breakout: **6%**
Improve: **35%** Collapse: **16%**
Attrition: **22%** MLB: **98%**

Comparables:
Luis Martinez,Charlie Moore,Rob Johnson

YEAR	TEAM	LVL	AGE	PA	R	2B	3B	HR	RBI	BB	SO	SB	CS	AVG_OBP_SLG	TAv	BABIP	BRR	FRAA	WARP
2010	NYA	MLB	24	317	27	11	3	0	38	33	42	1	1	.271/.359/.335	.250	.316	-2.5	C(89): 1.0, 3B(2): -0.0	0.7
2011	NYA	MLB	25	137	17	4	0	4	22	9	29	4	1	.266/.324/.395	.259	.315	0.2	C(41): -0.0, 3B(2): -0.0	0.4
2012	SWB	AAA	26	417	43	15	2	2	39	39	82	6	0	.246/.341/.316	.247	.308	-2.8	C(82): 1.1	0.6
2012	NYA	MLB	26	2	1	0	0	0	0	1	0	0	0	.000/.500/.000	.275	.000	0.2	C(3): -0.0	0.0
2013	*NYA*	*MLB*	*27*	*250*	*25*	*10*	*1*	*4*	*23*	*19*	*48*	*2*	*1*	*.249/.320/.353*	*.245*	*.295*	*-0.2*	*C -0, 3B -0*	*0.7*

The Yankees' trade for Chris Stewart on the last day of 2012 spring training limited former big-league backup catcher Francisco Cervelli to three plate appearances in the majors, and his .316 slugging percentage at Triple-A didn't make a convincing argument for more. On the bright side, he still has the best head of hair in the organization. As we went to press, the catching picture remained murky for New York and Cervelli's fate may be determined less by his own attributes and more by how much Austin Romine can contribute.

Matt Diaz LF

Born: **3/3/1978** Age: **35**
Bats: **R** Throws: **R** Height: **6' 1"**
Weight: **215** Breakout: **1%**
Improve: **25%** Collapse: **14%**
Attrition: **26%** MLB: **78%**

Comparables:
Cesar Cedeno,Marlon Anderson,Shane Mack

YEAR	TEAM	LVL	AGE	PA	R	2B	3B	HR	RBI	BB	SO	SB	CS	AVG_OBP_SLG	TAv	BABIP	BRR	FRAA	WARP
2010	ATL	MLB	32	244	27	17	2	7	31	13	44	3	1	.250/.302/.438	.266	.282	0.7	LF(63): 2.4	0.9
2011	ATL	MLB	33	37	2	1	0	0	1	1	8	1	0	.286/.297/.314	.206	.357	-0.3	RF(9): 0.3, LF(3): -0.2	-0.2
2011	PIT	MLB	33	231	14	12	1	0	19	11	44	4	2	.259/.303/.324	.228	.324	-0.8	RF(45): -4.0, LF(15): -0.5	-1.2
2012	ATL	MLB	34	118	10	6	0	2	13	9	21	0	0	.222/.280/.333	.226	.256	-1.3	LF(19): 0.6, RF(6): 0.3	-0.3
2013	*NYA*	*MLB*	*35*	*250*	*26*	*11*	*1*	*6*	*27*	*15*	*55*	*4*	*2*	*.252/.306/.385*	*.250*	*.304*	*-0.1*	*LF 0, RF -0*	*0.3*

Diaz was once known as a lefty masher, but his stock has slipped over the past two years. An infected thumb ended his season in July, but even before the ailment, Diaz couldn't hitchhike his way up to replacement level. He has not shown his trademark power since 2010 and he turns 35 before Opening Day. The Yankees signed him to a minor-league deal in December in their search for some right-handed power for their all-lefty outfield.

Brett Gardner LF

Born: **8/24/1983** Age: **29**
Bats: **L** Throws: **L** Height: **5' 11"**
Weight: **185** Breakout: **1%**
Improve: **37%** Collapse: **5%**
Attrition: **13%** MLB: **91%**

Comparables:
Dale Mitchell,Shannon Stewart,Bip Roberts

YEAR	TEAM	LVL	AGE	PA	R	2B	3B	HR	RBI	BB	SO	SB	CS	AVG_OBP_SLG	TAv	BABIP	BRR	FRAA	WARP
2010	NYA	MLB	26	569	97	20	7	5	47	79	101	47	9	.277/.383/.379	.277	.340	8.7	LF(123): 5.6, CF(44): 0.4	4.3
2011	NYA	MLB	27	588	87	19	8	7	36	60	93	49	13	.259/.345/.369	.256	.303	7.7	LF(149): 13.0, CF(18): 0.8	2.9
2012	NYA	MLB	28	37	7	2	0	0	3	5	7	2	2	.323/.417/.387	.295	.417	0.7	LF(15): -0.2	0.2
2013	*NYA*	*MLB*	*29*	*250*	*32*	*8*	*3*	*3*	*20*	*29*	*44*	*20*	*5*	*.258/.350/.365*	*.260*	*.307*	*2.2*	*LF 3, CF 0*	*1.1*

Through his first nine games, Gardner was on track for another season of stealing, slap-hitting, and sporadic swinging, with an on-base percentage high enough to make his low slugging percentage acceptable. But a slow-healing April 17 elbow injury essentially scotched his season, eventually requiring surgery in late July. When he returned in September, the long layoff and the addition of Ichiro made him a more versatile version of Herb Washington, relegated to a replacement role with few appearances at the plate. He reprised that part in the playoffs, though he did earn a pair of ALCS starts when a frustrated Joe Girardi cast around for anyone capable of making contact.

Gardner should be back at full strength this season, which he might spend in center field. It's not clear how well a player with his unusual profile projects long term, but Gardner should be able to approximate his 2010-11 production at age 29.

Curtis Granderson CF

Born: **3/16/1981** Age: **32**
Bats: **L** Throws: **R** Height: **6' 2"**
Weight: **185** Breakout: **0%**
Improve: **29%** Collapse: **1%**
Attrition: **8%** MLB: **97%**

Comparables:
Andruw Jones,Fred Lynn,Howard Johnson

YEAR	TEAM	LVL	AGE	PA	R	2B	3B	HR	RBI	BB	SO	SB	CS	AVG_OBP_SLG	TAv	BABIP	BRR	FRAA	WARP
2010	NYA	MLB	29	528	76	17	7	24	67	53	116	12	2	.247/.324/.468	.281	.277	3.2	CF(134): 1.8	3.3
2011	NYA	MLB	30	691	136	26	10	41	119	85	169	25	10	.262/.364/.552	.311	.295	4.8	CF(155): -12.9	4.6
2012	NYA	MLB	31	684	102	18	4	43	106	75	195	10	3	.232/.319/.492	.285	.260	2	CF(157): -10.0	2.4
2013	*NYA*	*MLB*	*32*	*644*	*97*	*22*	*7*	*31*	*85*	*68*	*154*	*15*	*5*	*.244/.328/.469*	*.279*	*.278*	*1.6*	*CF 1*	*3.6*

Twenty-four of the 25 least-valuable 40-homer seasons since 1950 were posted by designated hitters or players at corner positions. The other one was Granderson's 2012. Historically, center fielders who hit 40 homers have been worth about seven wins, but the stats say Granderson is a center fielder only in name. For the second straight season, his FRAA ranked second-worst among AL center fielders, and the apologist's excuse from 2011—that left fielder Gardner had bogarted his fly balls—didn't sound so convincing with Gardner replaced by range-averse Raul Ibanez. Granderson's offense made up for his defensive flaws, though he batted everywhere in the order but ninth, as if Girardi couldn't figure out what kind of hitter he had. Since his first season in New York, Granderson has morphed from a borderline platoon player with power into a three-true-outcomes type who can hold his own against lefties, lead the league in homers, and go 10 games between singles. Whether he recovers some of those singles or not, Granderson will have to keep hitting homers to command a big contract at the end of the year, since a healthy Gardner might make him a center fielder only in memory as soon as this spring.

Angelo Gumbs 2B

Born: **10/13/1992** Age: **20**
Bats: **R** Throws: **R** Height: **6' 1"**
Weight: **175** Breakout: **20%**
Improve: **50%** Collapse: **5%**
Attrition: **18%** MLB: **76%**

Comparables:
B.J. Upton,Wayne Causey,Clete Boyer

YEAR	TEAM	LVL	AGE	PA	R	2B	3B	HR	RBI	BB	SO	SB	CS	AVG_OBP_SLG	TAv	BABIP	BRR	FRAA	WARP
2011	STA	A-	18	220	32	11	4	3	29	20	57	11	7	.264/.332/.406	.243	.353	-1.9	2B(27): 1.0	0.1
2012	CSC	A	19	278	40	14	3	7	36	18	60	26	3	.272/.320/.432	.253	.328	2.9	2B(21): 3.1	0.8
2013	*NYA*	*MLB*	*20*	*250*	*28*	*8*	*1*	*6*	*23*	*11*	*76*	*13*	*4*	*.203/.237/.327*	*.202*	*.265*	*1.6*	*2B 1, SS 0*	*-0.4*

In 2010, the Yankees drafted Gumbs one round after shortstop Cito Culver (his double-play partner for the past three seasons), but since then, the two have flip-flopped in prospect status: Culver is on the verge of being a bust and Gumbs has seen his stock rise. Gumbs, one of the system's toolsiest players, has great bat speed and good foot speed, which he used to steal bases at a high rate of success last year before an injured elbow ended his season in June. He needs to simplify his swing and improve his plate discipline to unlock his hit tool's full potential, but he'll play the whole season at age 20, which should give him the time to do it. He's already become a better defender at second, though some have suggested he might make more sense in center.

Slade Heathcott CF

Born: **9/28/1990** Age: **22**
Bats: **L** Throws: **L** Height: **6' 2"**
Weight: **190** Breakout: **7%**
Improve: **56%** Collapse: **5%**
Attrition: **15%** MLB: **93%**

Comparables:
Gary Thomasson,Keith Hernandez,Ken Harrelson

YEAR	TEAM	LVL	AGE	PA	R	2B	3B	HR	RBI	BB	SO	SB	CS	AVG_OBP_SLG	TAv	BABIP	BRR	FRAA	WARP
2010	CSC	A	19	351	48	16	3	2	30	42	101	15	10	.258/.358/.352	.276	.379	4	CF(75): -6.9	1.6
2011	CSC	A	20	237	36	11	4	4	16	19	57	6	7	.271/.342/.419	.266	.353	0	--	0.0
2012	TAM	A+	21	243	38	16	2	5	27	20	66	17	4	.307/.378/.470	.255	.421	1.2	CF(6): 0.7, LF(1): 0.1	0.2
2013	*NYA*	*MLB*	*22*	*250*	*29*	*9*	*1*	*4*	*19*	*20*	*81*	*8*	*3*	*.209/.278/.317*	*.216*	*.299*	*0.3*	*CF -2, LF 0*	*-0.6*

Recovery from shoulder surgery (his second since being drafted) kept Heathcott out until June, but his play in 60 games for Tampa and subsequent white-hot .388/.494/.612 showing in the Arizona Fall League reminded evaluators why the Yankees picked him in the first round in 2009. The 22-year-old has some work to do on his swing, but his speed and defense are special, and he always devotes his maximum effort on the field (which can come back to bite him *à la* Aaron Rowand). Heathcott has already overcome not only previous injuries but also an alcohol problem and unhappy home, which should give him the mental strength to allow his five-tool potential to flourish, provided his body cooperates.

Derek Jeter SS

Born: **6/26/1974** Age: **39**
Bats: **R** Throws: **R** Height: **6' 4"**
Weight: **195** Breakout: **0%**
Improve: **19%** Collapse: **12%**
Attrition: **23%** MLB: **71%**

Comparables:
Alan Trammell,Barry Larkin,Maury Wills

YEAR	TEAM	LVL	AGE	PA	R	2B	3B	HR	RBI	BB	SO	SB	CS	AVG_OBP_SLG	TAv	BABIP	BRR	FRAA	WARP
2010	NYA	MLB	36	739	111	30	3	10	67	63	106	18	5	.270/.340/.370	.246	.307	2.6	SS(151): -13.3	0.8
2011	NYA	MLB	37	607	84	24	4	6	61	46	81	16	6	.297/.355/.388	.271	.336	-2.7	SS(122): -10.1	1.0
2012	NYA	MLB	38	740	99	32	0	15	58	45	90	9	4	.316/.362/.429	.274	.347	-1.3	SS(135): -6.1	2.5
2013	*NYA*	*MLB*	*39*	*669*	*79*	*26*	*2*	*9*	*57*	*49*	*100*	*14*	*5*	*.281/.338/.374*	*.258*	*.319*	*0.1*	*SS -11*	*1.6*

It's rare enough for someone Jeter's age to play a full season at shortstop, let alone hit well while doing it; as Mike Axisa of *River Ave. Blues* observed last October, Hall of Famers Rogers Hornsby and Luke Appling were the only full-time shortstops 38 or older to have qualified for a batting title as at least league-average hitters before Jeter joined that exclusive club in 2012. And he did it with plenty of plate appearances to spare: Jeter equaled his career high in games played, led the league in PA, and had his highest TAv since 2009. As usual, Jeter rarely hit the ball in the air—only Ben Revere had a higher groundball rate—but he recovered some of his lost power, and not only did he destroy south-paws, he held his own against right-handers, who had made him look like Luis Sojo in the previous two seasons. He also swung more often without sacrificing much contact, posting career-low walk and strikeout rates. Jeter fractured his ankle in the ALCS, but that shouldn't prevent him from another attempt at boldly going where only Hornsby and Appling have gone before at age 39.

Corban Joseph **2B**

Born: **10/28/1988** Age: **24**
Bats: **L** Throws: **R** Height: **6' 1"**
Weight: **168** Breakout: **3%**
Improve: **37%** Collapse: **2%**
Attrition: **7%** MLB: **90%**

Comparables:
Gordon Beckham,Travis Denker,Marcus Giles

YEAR	TEAM	LVL	AGE	PA	R	2B	3B	HR	RBI	BB	SO	SB	CS	AVG_OBP_SLG	TAv	BABIP	BRR	FRAA	WARP
2010	TAM	A+	21	437	52	27	3	6	52	43	74	5	8	.302/.382/.436	.289	.361	-2.3	2B(85): -7.9, 3B(6): 1.0	1.1
2010	TRN	AA	21	130	11	6	4	0	13	15	33	1	0	.216/.305/.342	.261	.300	-1	2B(31): 2.4	0.1
2011	TRN	AA	22	564	75	38	8	5	58	59	104	4	3	.277/.353/.415	.271	.339	0	--	0.0
2012	TRN	AA	23	102	9	4	0	2	6	15	13	0	0	.314/.412/.430	.338	.347	0.7	2B(5): -0.3	0.4
2012	SWB	AAA	23	386	50	25	2	13	56	53	57	0	1	.266/.366/.474	.281	.285	2.6	2B(69): 7.0	2.3
2013	*NYA*	*MLB*	*24*	*250*	*29*	*12*	*1*	*6*	*26*	*24*	*51*	*0*	*0*	*.244/.320/.396*	*.254*	*.286*	*-0.4*	*2B -1, 3B 0*	*0.6*

Unlike Adams, who was drafted one round before him in 2008, Joseph doesn't have the range or arm strength to play on the left side of second, which makes his path past Triple-A murky as long as Cano remains in the Bronx. However, he showed enough power and plate discipline after his June arrival in the International League to look like a second-division starter candidate for a team with no star second baseman, which could translate to a trade.

Melky Mesa **CF**

Born: **1/31/1987** Age: **26**
Bats: **R** Throws: **R** Height: **6' 2"**
Weight: **190** Breakout: **9%**
Improve: **53%** Collapse: **5%**
Attrition: **7%** MLB: **99%**

Comparables:
Casper Wells,Duke Snider,Ray Lankford

YEAR	TEAM	LVL	AGE	PA	R	2B	3B	HR	RBI	BB	SO	SB	CS	AVG_OBP_SLG	TAv	BABIP	BRR	FRAA	WARP
2010	TAM	A+	23	507	81	21	9	19	74	44	129	31	9	.260/.341/.475	.297	.324	6.1	CF(110): 8.9, RF(2): -0.2	5.1
2011	TRN	AA	24	433	58	24	4	9	46	36	129	18	13	.251/.329/.404	.256	.353	0	--	0.0
2012	TRN	AA	25	371	60	18	1	14	46	29	75	17	3	.277/.344/.464	.265	.318	6	CF(24): 0.6	1.2
2012	SWB	AAA	25	133	19	8	1	9	21	7	43	5	1	.230/.271/.524	.277	.270	0.2	CF(29): -1.0	0.4
2012	NYA	MLB	25	2	0	0	0	0	1	0	0	0	0	.500/.500/.500	.350	.500	-0.9	CF(1): -0.0	-0.1
2013	*NYA*	*MLB*	*26*	*250*	*31*	*10*	*1*	*11*	*33*	*16*	*72*	*8*	*2*	*.229/.285/.421*	*.252*	*.281*	*0.9*	*CF -2, RF -0*	*0.4*

Mesa has power and seemed to conquer his strikeout woes in his second season in Trenton, but they returned with a vengeance in his first exposure to Scranton. The outfielder posted a six-plus strikeout-to-walk ratio in his first 33 games in the International League, which doesn't bode well for his odds of hitting at higher levels. Age 26 is a little old to expect Mesa to stop missing the ball, so while he might see some playing time in 2013, pinch-running right past third base in his September debut might turn out to be one of his most memorable major-league moments.

Jayson Nix **UT**

Born: **8/26/1982** Age: **30**
Bats: **R** Throws: **R** Height: **6' 0"**
Weight: **195** Breakout: **4%**
Improve: **46%** Collapse: **7%**
Attrition: **9%** MLB: **90%**

Comparables:
Sean Berry,Rob Mackowiak,Brandon Inge

YEAR	TEAM	LVL	AGE	PA	R	2B	3B	HR	RBI	BB	SO	SB	CS	AVG_OBP_SLG	TAv	BABIP	BRR	FRAA	WARP
2010	CHA	MLB	27	57	3	1	0	1	5	7	12	0	0	.163/.268/.245	.188	.194	0.2	3B(16): -0.9, 2B(3): -0.1	-0.4
2010	CLE	MLB	27	306	29	14	0	13	29	13	75	1	2	.234/.283/.422	.257	.270	0.3	3B(40): 0.3, 2B(25): -0.5	1.0
2011	LVG	AAA	28	182	30	12	2	8	29	14	38	3	0	.270/.341/.515	.287	.305	1	3B(9): 2.7, SS(8): -0.2	1.3
2011	TOR	MLB	28	151	15	5	1	4	16	12	42	4	1	.169/.245/.309	.206	.209	1.6	3B(41): 3.4, 2B(4): 0.1	0.2
2012	NYA	MLB	29	202	24	13	0	4	18	14	53	6	3	.243/.306/.384	.236	.325	-0.9	3B(29): 1.3, SS(18): -0.8	-0.1
2013	*NYA*	*MLB*	*30*	*250*	*30*	*11*	*0*	*9*	*29*	*19*	*63*	*5*	*2*	*.222/.290/.391*	*.243*	*.263*	*0*	*3B -0, 2B 0*	*0.3*

Take note, Eduardo Nunez: this is what a utility infielder looks like. After being promoted in mid-May, Nix split time between four positions, playing all of them well. However, he didn't hit, though he has shown non-negligible power in past seasons. Nix is best in moderation, and with the left side of the Yankees infield a combined 75 years old, Jeter recovering from a fractured ankle, and Rodriguez expected to be out until August while he recovers from offseason hip surgery, the Yankees will want to find a backup with a better bat in case of additional extended absences.

Eduardo Nunez **UT**

Born: **6/15/1987** Age: **26**
Bats: **R** Throws: **R** Height: **6' 1"**
Weight: **155** Breakout: **4%**
Improve: **43%** Collapse: **6%**
Attrition: **19%** MLB: **96%**

Comparables:
Brendan Ryan,Barry Larkin,Erick Aybar

YEAR	TEAM	LVL	AGE	PA	R	2B	3B	HR	RBI	BB	SO	SB	CS	AVG_OBP_SLG	TAv	BABIP	BRR	FRAA	WARP
2010	SWB	AAA	23	506	55	25	3	4	50	32	60	23	5	.289/.339/.381	.251	.323	1.3	SS(100): -4.6, 3B(11): -1.7	1.1
2010	NYA	MLB	23	53	12	1	0	1	7	3	2	5	0	.280/.321/.360	.235	.277	0.7	3B(15): -0.6, SS(11): 0.5	0.1
2011	NYA	MLB	24	338	38	18	2	5	30	22	37	22	6	.265/.313/.385	.246	.287	0.5	SS(50): -4.2, 3B(40): -1.1	0.1
2012	SWB	AAA	25	172	18	4	0	2	16	7	28	16	3	.227/.256/.288	.189	.259	2.3	SS(33): 0.1	-0.5
2012	NYA	MLB	25	100	14	4	1	1	11	6	12	11	2	.292/.330/.393	.275	.312	1	SS(16): -0.2, 3B(9): 0.1	0.5
2013	*NYA*	*MLB*	*26*	*250*	*29*	*11*	*1*	*4*	*23*	*15*	*33*	*15*	*3*	*.261/.307/.371*	*.242*	*.286*	*1.7*	*SS -1, 3B -0*	*0.5*

May 10 was a microcosm of Nunez's 2012 season: He started at third base against southpaw David Price and went 2-for-2 with a walk and two steals, but he also committed two errors. As soon as the Yankees got a lead, he was removed from the game and replaced by Nix. The next day, he was demoted to Triple-A despite a .294 average and a .356 OBP, which tells you most of what you need to know about his defense. Nunez lacks the glove of a true super-sub, so he's trying to pioneer the position of bat-first utility guy. The problem is that he has neither the patience nor the power to pull that off at any position, and there's a reason why the part he wants to play wasn't pioneered earlier.

Alex Rodriguez **3B**
Born: **7/27/1975** Age: **37**
Bats: **R** Throws: **R** Height: **6' 4"**
Weight: **230** Breakout: **0%**
Improve: **23%** Collapse: **8%**
Attrition: **15%** MLB: **80%**

Comparables:
Chipper Jones,Ken Caminiti,Casey Blake

YEAR	TEAM	LVL	AGE	PA	R	2B	3B	HR	RBI	BB	SO	SB	CS	AVG_OBP_SLG	TAv	BABIP	BRR	FRAA	WARP
2010	NYA	MLB	34	595	74	29	2	30	125	59	98	4	3	.270/.341/.506	.297	.274	-0.5	3B(124): 5.4	4.9
2011	NYA	MLB	35	428	67	21	0	16	62	47	80	4	1	.276/.362/.461	.286	.311	2	3B(89): 5.0	2.8
2012	NYA	MLB	36	529	74	17	1	18	57	51	116	13	1	.272/.353/.430	.280	.323	-1.6	3B(81): -4.0	1.2
2013	*NYA*	*MLB*	*37*	*478*	*64*	*20*	*1*	*21*	*67*	*50*	*99*	*8*	*2*	*.261/.347/.460*	*.287*	*.294*	*0.2*	*3B -1*	*2.4*

In the seven seasons preceding the signing of his current contract, which runs roughly from 2008 to eternity, Rodriguez averaged 159 games. In the five seasons since, he's averaged 124. The problem isn't only how often he's been hurt, but how poorly he's played when "healthy": A graph of his TAv and WARP since 2007 looks roughly like a plot of *American Idol's* plummeting ratings. Before a slider from Felix Hernandez broke his hand on July 24, A-Rod's descent seemed to have slowed, but he slugged a meager .369 in 28 games following his September return, looking particularly helpless against right-handers, who struck him out a third of the time. October was worse: 27 playoff plate appearances, 12 Ks, a spot on the bench, and calls for a trade to the Marlins. Girardi's lack of confidence bodes ill for the five seasons remaining on the 37-year-old future Hall of Famer's contract, but it's nothing compared to the torn hip labrum diagnosed in December. After surgery, he's not expected back until after the All-Star break.

Austin Romine **C**
Born: **11/22/1988** Age: **24**
Bats: **R** Throws: **R** Height: **6' 1"**
Weight: **220** Breakout: **3%**
Improve: **33%** Collapse: **6%**
Attrition: **8%** MLB: **94%**

Comparables:
Bill Freehan,Jeff Torborg,Joe Azcue

YEAR	TEAM	LVL	AGE	PA	R	2B	3B	HR	RBI	BB	SO	SB	CS	AVG_OBP_SLG	TAv	BABIP	BRR	FRAA	WARP
2010	TRN	AA	21	497	61	31	0	10	69	37	94	2	0	.268/.326/.402	.261	.319	-3.2	C(106): -1.0	1.6
2011	TRN	AA	22	373	43	13	0	6	47	32	60	2	2	.286/.351/.378	.262	.331	0	--	0.0
2011	NYA	MLB	22	20	2	0	0	0	0	1	5	0	0	.158/.200/.158	.129	.214	-0.2	C(8): -0.1	-0.2
2012	SWB	AAA	23	71	6	2	0	3	9	8	10	0	0	.213/.296/.393	.199	.200	-0.4	C(11): 0.0	-0.3
2013	*NYA*	*MLB*	*24*	*250*	*23*	*11*	*0*	*6*	*28*	*14*	*54*	*0*	*0*	*.238/.282/.369*	*.233*	*.280*	*-0.5*	*C -1*	*0.2*

Romine got a cup of coffee in 2011 and might have been the backup catcher in 2012 had it not been for the bulging discs that sidelined him from spring training until late August. After returning, he posted a sub-700 OPS in 49 games across three minor-league levels and the Arizona Fall League, showing good plate discipline but little pop. Behind the plate, he has a good reputation as a receiver, but his arm is only okay. He could contend for playing time behind the plate this season, provided he can avoid a third straight year with back problems, though he'll likely start the season in Triple-A.

Gary Sanchez **C**
Born: **12/2/1992** Age: **20**
Bats: **R** Throws: **R** Height: **6' 3"**
Weight: **220** Breakout: **25%**
Improve: **68%** Collapse: **3%**
Attrition: **12%** MLB: **89%**

Comparables:
Alex Rodriguez,Tony Conigliaro,Mickey Mantle

YEAR	TEAM	LVL	AGE	PA	R	2B	3B	HR	RBI	BB	SO	SB	CS	AVG_OBP_SLG	TAv	BABIP	BRR	FRAA	WARP
2010	YAN	Rk	17	136	25	11	0	6	36	11	28	1	1	.353/.425/.597	.366	.424	-0.5	C(18): -0.2	1.6
2010	STA	A-	17	60	8	2	0	2	7	3	16	1	1	.278/.339/.426	.308	.361	-0.1	C(12): -0.3	0.6
2011	CSC	A	18	343	49	16	1	17	52	36	93	2	1	.256/.335/.485	.277	.308	0	--	0.0
2012	CSC	A	19	289	44	19	0	13	56	22	65	11	4	.297/.353/.517	.312	.348	-1.6	C(14): -0.3	0.6
2012	TAM	A+	19	185	21	10	1	5	29	10	41	4	0	.279/.330/.436	.268	.341	-0.4	C(11): -0.2	0.0
2013	*NYA*	*MLB*	*20*	*250*	*26*	*10*	*0*	*10*	*31*	*9*	*74*	*2*	*1*	*.228/.260/.394*	*.233*	*.285*	*-0.2*	*C -0*	*0.3*

Comparisons between the Yankees' top catching prospect and Jesus Montero are old hat, but there's a reason why they won't go away: Almost any compliment or complaint made about Montero as he hit his way through the Yankees system applies equally well to Sanchez. The latter is a better athlete, but that hasn't translated into better performance behind the plate, since an apparent indifference toward defense is among the many concerns about his makeup. Like Montero, Sanchez may stick at catcher until he makes the majors, but his catching career likely won't last much longer than that. Fortunately for the Yankees, a position switch won't erase his value, since the right-handed hitter's prospect buzz is all about the bat. Sanchez recovered from a homerless April to show expected improvement in his second season in Charleston and earn a promotion to Tampa in July, where he held his own offensively despite being one of only two age-19 players in the Florida State League.

Chris Stewart C

Born: **2/19/1982** Age: **31**
Bats: **R** Throws: **R** Height: **6' 5"**
Weight: **215** Breakout: **2%**
Improve: **28%** Collapse: **11%**
Attrition: **14%** MLB: **87%**

Comparables:
Jim Essian,Bill Fahey,Bob Boone

YEAR	TEAM	LVL	AGE	PA	R	2B	3B	HR	RBI	BB	SO	SB	CS	AVG_OBP_SLG	TAv	BABIP	BRR	FRAA	WARP
2010	POR	AAA	28	309	31	14	2	7	39	30	38	1	0	.248/.337/.395	.260	.263	0.8	C(76): 0.7, 1B(7): -0.6	1.5
2010	SDN	MLB	28	0	0	0	0	0	0	0	0	0	0	--	—	.000	0	1B(1): 0.0, C(1): -0.0	0.0
2011	FRE	AAA	29	112	9	5	0	0	10	11	16	3	1	.221/.312/.274	.216	.262	0.2	C(19): 0.6, 1B(1): -0.0	0.0
2011	SFN	MLB	29	183	20	8	0	3	10	16	18	0	0	.204/.283/.309	.226	.213	0.2	C(63): 1.0, 1B(3): 0.0	0.5
2012	NYA	MLB	30	157	15	8	0	1	13	10	21	2	0	.241/.292/.319	.236	.273	0.9	C(54): -0.4	0.2
2013	*NYA*	*MLB*	*31*	*250*	*25*	*12*	*0*	*4*	*24*	*20*	*36*	*2*	*0*	*.237/.305/.350*	*.238*	*.260*	*-0.3*	*C 0, 1B -0*	*0.6*

Concerns about depleted catching depth due to Romine's back injury caused the Yankees to trade reliever George Kontos to the Giants for Stewart on the final day of spring training. Kontos established himself as a dependable reliever on a World Series team, but Stewart wasn't entirely without value, despite his unsightly slash lines. Like Russell Martin and Eli Whiteside—raise your hand if you're starting to sense a pattern—Stewart is a strong receiver, saving 13 runs through framing in fewer than 400 innings behind the plate. Unfortunately, his bat also belongs to the Whiteside school. Despite his age, Stewart is under team control through 2016 and won't make much more than the major-league minimum this season, which should give the incumbent the inside track in the battle for backup duties.

Ichiro Suzuki OF

Born: **10/22/1973** Age: **39**
Bats: **L** Throws: **R** Height: **6' 0"**
Weight: **170** Breakout: **0%**
Improve: **21%** Collapse: **13%**
Attrition: **23%** MLB: **72%**

Comparables:
Kenny Lofton,Bob Boyd,So Taguchi

YEAR	TEAM	LVL	AGE	PA	R	2B	3B	HR	RBI	BB	SO	SB	CS	AVG_OBP_SLG	TAv	BABIP	BRR	FRAA	WARP
2010	SEA	MLB	36	732	74	30	3	6	43	45	86	42	9	.315/.359/.394	.287	.353	2.2	RF(160): -0.8	3.5
2011	SEA	MLB	37	721	80	22	3	5	47	39	69	40	7	.272/.310/.335	.244	.295	8.9	RF(151): -18.0	-1.3
2012	NYA	MLB	38	240	28	13	1	5	27	5	21	14	5	.322/.340/.454	.277	.337	-1.3	RF(39): -2.0, LF(35): 0.3	0.2
2012	SEA	MLB	38	423	49	15	5	4	28	17	40	15	2	.261/.288/.353	.235	.279	2	RF(93): 5.6	0.4
2013	*NYA*	*MLB*	*39*	*634*	*79*	*24*	*3*	*8*	*52*	*31*	*72*	*31*	*7*	*.291/.327/.382*	*.254*	*.317*	*3.1*	*RF 3, LF 0*	*1.7*

When the Yankees traded for Ichiro, he had a .261/.288/.353 line and what would have been the lowest BABIP of his career; the team's intention was to replace some of the speed and defense that was lost when Gardner went down, not to upgrade offensively. Expectations status: exceeded. The first sight of Suzuki in something other than a Seattle uniform was strange, but once the newness wore off, fans quickly rediscovered vintage Ichiro. Whether his revival owed to the invigoration of leaving the last-place Mariners or simply to playing home games in Yankee Stadium instead of Safeco Field (he hit .359/.385/.564 in the Bronx), Ichiro continued to surge after August (.362/.376/.486) while playing both outfield corners, and he was one of the few Yankees who didn't disappear at the plate in October. That made the Yankees forget he was 39, so they re-signed him for two more years. Maybe they were just trying to extend their commitment to aging former Mariners outfielders whose last names start with I.

Mark Teixeira 1B

Born: **4/11/1980** Age: **33**
Bats: **B** Throws: **R** Height: **6' 4"**
Weight: **220** Breakout: **0%**
Improve: **24%** Collapse: **2%**
Attrition: **9%** MLB: **94%**

Comparables:
Edgar Martinez,Paul Konerko,Todd Helton

YEAR	TEAM	LVL	AGE	PA	R	2B	3B	HR	RBI	BB	SO	SB	CS	AVG_OBP_SLG	TAv	BABIP	BRR	FRAA	WARP
2010	NYA	MLB	30	712	113	36	0	33	108	93	122	0	1	.256/.365/.481	.294	.268	-2.2	1B(149): 13.6	4.7
2011	NYA	MLB	31	684	90	26	1	39	111	76	110	4	1	.248/.341/.494	.297	.239	-3.3	1B(147): -1.3	1.7
2012	NYA	MLB	32	524	66	27	1	24	84	54	83	2	1	.251/.332/.475	.298	.250	-3.5	1B(119): 8.1	2.5
2013	*NYA*	*MLB*	*33*	*524*	*70*	*26*	*1*	*25*	*79*	*60*	*90*	*2*	*1*	*.259/.352/.485*	*.296*	*.270*	*-0.9*	*1B 3*	*2.7*

Sabermetricians often belittle batting average in response to the traditional fan's unhealthy attachment to it, but while average doesn't work well on its own as an evaluation tool, it sometimes tells a story in concert with other stats. Teixeira, a .295 hitter in the five seasons prior to his arrival in New York, has been a .263 hitter since, and the 10-point difference between his before and after True Averages can be attributed mostly to missing singles. Like Jason Giambi before him, Teixeira has watched those singles vanish into the shift but decided that it wouldn't behoove him to drop down the occasional bunt as a deterrent. The good news is that unlike Giambi, Teixeira is a Gold Glove-caliber fielder, which should help him hold on to his value, assuming last season's lingering calf strain doesn't portend a repeat of Giambi's chronic leg problems.

Mason Williams CF

Born: **8/21/1991** Age: **21**
Bats: **L** Throws: **R** Height: **6' 1"**
Weight: **150** Breakout: **4%**
Improve: **58%** Collapse: **10%**
Attrition: **16%** MLB: **97%**

Comparables:
Jay Johnstone,Thad Bosley,Curt Flood

YEAR	TEAM	LVL	AGE	PA	R	2B	3B	HR	RBI	BB	SO	SB	CS	AVG_OBP_SLG	TAv	BABIP	BRR	FRAA	WARP
2011	STA	A-	19	298	42	11	6	3	31	20	41	28	12	.349/.395/.468	.325	.399	2.3	CF(46): 4.4	2.7
2012	CSC	A	20	311	55	19	4	8	28	21	33	19	9	.304/.359/.489	.271	.319	0.9	CF(18): 0.3	0.6
2012	TAM	A+	20	86	13	3	0	3	7	3	14	1	4	.277/.302/.422	.321	.303	0.1	CF(4): 0.1	0.2
2013	*NYA*	*MLB*	*21*	*250*	*33*	*10*	*2*	*6*	*22*	*9*	*53*	*10*	*6*	*.241/.271/.377*	*.226*	*.277*	*0.1*	*CF -2*	*-0.3*

For better or worse, a few of the Yankees' most promising prospects come matched with easy comps to promising prospects of the past. In the case of Williams, the 2010 fourth-rounder who enjoyed a breakout year at Charleston and Tampa until a dislocated shoulder ended it in July, the name most often invoked isn't that of his last-namesake, Bernie, but rather Austin Jackson, who five years ago played the same position for the same team at the same age. While you'd never guarantee a particular prospect will become a top-10 player in the majors—which Jackson was last season—Williams stacks up well, boasting the same sort of hit tool, speed, and plus defense in center that make Jackson special. Scouts are split on whether his thin build contains the strength necessary to hit for power at the highest level. Which side of that debate you stand on determines whether you think Williams is a future average player or a future star; either way, the Yankees would be thrilled to see another homegrown hitter make good.

Kevin Youkilis **3B**
Born: **3/15/1979** Age: **34**
Bats: **R** Throws: **R** Height: **6' 2"**
Weight: **220** Breakout: **1%**
Improve: **37%** Collapse: **3%**
Attrition: **4%** MLB: **93%**
Comparables:
Ron Cey, Eddie Mathews, Chipper Jones

YEAR	TEAM	LVL	AGE	PA	R	2B	3B	HR	RBI	BB	SO	SB	CS	AVG_OBP_SLG	TAv	BABIP	BRR	FRAA	WARP
2010	BOS	MLB	31	435	77	26	5	19	62	58	67	4	1	.307/.411/.564	.345	.327	1.7	1B(101): -1.8, 3B(2): 0.1	4.4
2011	BOS	MLB	32	517	68	32	2	17	80	68	100	3	0	.258/.373/.459	.291	.296	0.5	3B(112): -1.7, 1B(6): 0.4	2.3
2012	BOS	MLB	33	165	25	7	1	4	14	14	39	0	0	.233/.315/.377	.248	.288	0.1	3B(33): -0.6, 1B(13): -0.1	-0.2
2012	CHA	MLB	33	344	47	8	1	15	46	37	69	0	0	.236/.346/.425	.271	.257	1.8	3B(78): -1.7, 1B(13): -0.4	1.1
2013	*NYA*	*MLB*	*34*	*483*	*62*	*23*	*2*	*19*	*68*	*55*	*100*	*3*	*1*	*.263/.362/.466*	*.296*	*.300*	*-0.6*	*3B -3, 1B 1*	*2.6*

White Sox fans got the entire gamut of Youkilis in a half season. He received a hero's welcome when he hit .319/.415/.551 and drove in 18 runs in his first few weeks in Chicago and looked to take a clubhouse leadership role. Then he left a game with an upset stomach and missed time with ailments to his hamstring, ankle, knee, forearm, and knee again. Would his offensive production remain high if he were protected from the dangers of fielding by becoming a full-time designated hitter? Possibly, but even the injury-impacted statistics he generates are good enough to be above-average. He's there to keep the hot corner warm until A-Rod returns, or to be insurance in case of the likely setbacks in Rodriguez's recovery.

PITCHERS

David Aardsma
Born: **12/27/1981** Age: **31**
Bats: **R** Throws: **R** Height: **6' 4"** Weight: **210**
Breakout: **25%** Improve: **63%** Collapse: **19%**
Attrition: **9%** MLB: **92%**
Comparables:
Paul Shuey, Jeff Nelson, Jose Veras

YEAR	TEAM	LVL	AGE	W	L	SV	G	GS	IP	H	HR	BB	SO	BB9	SO9	GB%	BABIP	WHIP	ERA	FIP	FRA	WARP
2010	SEA	MLB	28	0	6	31	53	0	49^2	33	5	25	49	4.5	8.9	41%	.231	1.17	3.44	4.01	4.80	-0.1
2011	TAC	AAA	29	0	1	0	5	0	4	8	1	4	5	9.0	11.2	31%	.500	3.00	15.75	8.28	7.86	-0.1
2012	YAN	Rk	30	0	0	0	3	3	5	3	0	1	7	1.8	12.6	58%	.250	0.80	0.00	1.23	2.05	0.2
2012	STA	A-	30	0	1	0	1	1	0^2	4	1	1	1	13.5	13.5	43%	.500	7.50	27.00	24.33	5.05	0.0
2012	TAM	A+	30	0	0	0	1	1	1	0	0	1	0	9.0	0.0	%	.000	1.00	0.00	6.39	8.22	0.0
2012	NYA	MLB	30	0	0	0	1	0	1	1	1	1	1	9.0	9.0	67%	.000	2.00	9.00	17.05	14.72	-0.1
2013	*NYA*	*MLB*	*31*	*2*	*1*	*1*	*34*	*1*	34^2	*30*	*4*	*18*	*37*	*4.7*	*9.5*	*38%*	*.287*	*1.39*	*4.06*	*4.12*	*4.41*	*0.4*

As they did with Jon Lieber in 2003, the Yankees signed a damaged Aardsma several months after he underwent Tommy John surgery, knowing he'd spend the season rehabbing from the procedure. The former Mariners closer made it back in time to pitch a single September inning, and the team exercised his $500,000 option for 2013, hoping for a full second season at little more than the major-league minimum. When healthy—which he hasn't been since 2010—Aardsma depended on a mid-90s fastball to rack up enough strikeouts to survive all the walks and fly balls he allowed. If his hip and elbow surgeries have robbed his four-seamer of some speed, he'll have to rely more heavily on his rarely seen slider and splitter to succeed.

Manny Banuelos
Born: **3/13/1991** Age: **22**
Bats: **L** Throws: **L** Height: **6' 0"** Weight: **155**
Breakout: **35%** Improve: **56%** Collapse: **15%**
Attrition: **17%** MLB: **82%**
Comparables:
Rich Harden, Jaime Garcia, Jon Niese

YEAR	TEAM	LVL	AGE	W	L	SV	G	GS	IP	H	HR	BB	SO	BB9	SO9	GB%	BABIP	WHIP	ERA	FIP	FRA	WARP
2010	YAN	Rk	19	0	0	0	2	2	5	1	0	3	6	5.4	10.8	60%	.100	0.80	1.80	2.91	4.52	0.0
2010	TAM	A+	19	0	3	0	10	10	44^1	38	1	14	62	2.8	12.6	44%	.348	1.17	2.23	1.95	2.54	1.3
2010	TRN	AA	19	0	1	0	3	3	15^1	15	2	8	17	4.7	10.0	63%	.338	1.50	3.53	4.41	5.54	-0.1
2011	TRN	AA	20	4	5	0	20	20	95^1	94	7	52	94	4.9	8.9	—	.331	1.53	3.59	4.22	4.58	0.0
2011	SWB	AAA	20	2	2	0	7	7	34^1	36	2	19	31	5.0	8.1	46%	.303	1.60	4.19	3.94	6.20	-0.3
2012	SWB	AAA	21	0	2	0	6	6	24	29	2	10	22	3.8	8.2	43%	.360	1.62	4.50	3.78	5.33	0.0
2013	*NYA*	*MLB*	*22*	*2*	*3*	*0*	*7*	*7*	33^2	*35*	*5*	*17*	*27*	*4.5*	*7.1*	*44%*	*.302*	*1.55*	*5.21*	*5.04*	*5.67*	*0.0*

Banuelos made only six starts for Scranton before being shut down with what Yankees VP of baseball ops Mark Newman initially termed a "bone bruise," confidently predicting, "He'll recover from this." Technically, Newman was correct—the elbow injury didn't prove fatal. But by October, the bone bruise had turned into something more serious, and Banuelos became the latest Tommy John surgery survivor. Even after the injury, the southpaw remains the team's best starting-pitcher prospect, thanks to his three quality pitches and history of missing bats, though he'll have to refine his command to fulfill his potential as a solid starter. He won't get a chance to do that until 2014, at which point he'll have to overcome almost two full seasons of lost development time and try to build his arm back up to the point that he can make it to the 130-inning mark for the first time.

Dellin Betances
Born: **3/23/1988** Age: **25**
Bats: **R** Throws: **R** Height: **6' 9"** Weight: **260**
Breakout: **29%** Improve: **59%** Collapse: **22%**
Attrition: **18%** MLB: **91%**
Comparables:
Radhames Liz,Dennis Leonard,Jason Bere

YEAR	TEAM	LVL	AGE	W	L	SV	G	GS	IP	H	HR	BB	SO	BB9	SO9	GB%	BABIP	WHIP	ERA	FIP	FRA	WARP
2010	TAM	A+	22	8	1	0	14	14	71	43	1	19	88	2.4	11.2	43%	.251	0.87	1.77	2.07	2.64	1.9
2010	TRN	AA	22	0	0	0	3	3	14^{1}	10	3	3	20	1.9	12.6	42%	.212	0.91	3.78	4.13	4.22	0.3
2011	TRN	AA	23	4	6	0	21	21	105^{1}	86	7	55	115	4.7	9.8	—	.288	1.34	3.42	3.91	4.25	0.0
2011	SWB	AAA	23	0	3	0	4	4	21	16	2	15	27	6.4	11.6	29%	.242	1.48	5.14	4.19	5.40	-0.1
2011	NYA	MLB	23	0	0	0	2	1	2^{2}	1	0	6	2	20.2	6.8	14%	.143	2.62	6.75	9.44	11.29	-0.1
2012	TRN	AA	24	3	4	0	11	10	56^{2}	73	4	30	53	4.8	8.4	41%	.394	1.82	6.51	4.15	5.49	0.3
2012	SWB	AAA	24	3	5	0	16	16	74^{2}	71	9	69	71	8.3	8.6	43%	.298	1.88	6.39	5.84	7.30	-1.8
2013	*NYA*	*MLB*	*25*	*2*	*3*	*0*	*8*	*8*	*37*	*37*	*5*	*24*	*34*	*5.9*	*8.3*	*41%*	*.300*	*1.66*	*5.59*	*5.06*	*6.07*	*-0.2*

Control problems, shoulder problems, and an iffy third pitch: Betances checks all the boxes marked "bullpen guy." The righty's climb up the minor-league ladder hit a loose rung last season, as he walked more than eight batters per nine in Scranton and saw his formerly robust strikeout rate dip under a K per inning before he was sent back down to Double-A in late June. Even after the demotion, he struggled to throw strikes until shoulder tendinitis brought his season out behind the barn and shot it in August. Betances still throws hard, but he's a bad athlete and has had trouble repeating his delivery at the best of times. Even if he stays healthy in 2013, we've likely seen the last of him as a starter.

Jose Campos
Born: **7/27/1992** Age: **20**
Bats: **R** Throws: **R** Height: **6' 5"** Weight: **195**
Breakout: **51%** Improve: **80%** Collapse: **10%**
Attrition: **3%** MLB: **85%**
Comparables:
Catfish Hunter,Madison Bumgarner,Milt Pappas

YEAR	TEAM	LVL	AGE	W	L	SV	G	GS	IP	H	HR	BB	SO	BB9	SO9	GB%	BABIP	WHIP	ERA	FIP	FRA	WARP
2011	EVE	A-	18	5	5	0	14	14	81^{1}	66	4	13	85	1.4	9.4	52%	.259	0.97	2.32	2.79	4.34	1.2
2012	CSC	A	19	3	0	0	5	5	24^{2}	20	2	8	26	2.9	9.5	43%	.269	1.14	4.01	3.62	3.85	0.0
2013	*NYA*	*MLB*	*20*	*2*	*3*	*0*	*6*	*6*	*33*	*37*	*5*	*16*	*21*	*4.3*	*5.8*	*45%*	*.299*	*1.60*	*5.76*	*5.35*	*6.26*	*-0.2*

Yankees fans distraught over the announcement that Michael Pineda would miss the rest of the season had exactly two days to think "At least we still have Jose Campos!" before the then-19-year-old right-hander's disastrous fifth Sally League start of the season, in which he allowed eight runs on seven hits and three walks in 2 2/3 innings. Instead of making his next start, the *other* pitcher acquired in the Montero trade was placed on the DL with elbow inflammation, after which he pitched no more than Pineda. Campos's first four starts were as dominant as his 14 in the Northwest League the previous season, and his stuff backs up the stats: precocious command of a mid-90s fastball, a power curve, and a promising changeup. However, he didn't pitch in instructs and Yankees sources won't offer much more than confirmation that the elbow is still attached to his arm. In other words, his health continues to be a concern.

Joba Chamberlain
Born: **9/23/1985** Age: **27**
Bats: **R** Throws: **R** Height: **6' 3"** Weight: **240**
Breakout: **17%** Improve: **52%** Collapse: **27%**
Attrition: **8%** MLB: **92%**
Comparables:
Tim Belcher,Len Barker,Andrew Bailey

YEAR	TEAM	LVL	AGE	W	L	SV	G	GS	IP	H	HR	BB	SO	BB9	SO9	GB%	BABIP	WHIP	ERA	FIP	FRA	WARP
2010	NYA	MLB	24	3	4	3	73	0	71^{2}	71	6	22	77	2.8	9.7	46%	.327	1.30	4.40	2.95	3.57	1.3
2011	NYA	MLB	25	2	0	0	27	0	28^{2}	23	3	7	24	2.2	7.5	60%	.267	1.05	2.83	3.58	4.58	0.2
2012	YAN	Rk	26	0	0	0	3	3	4	0	0	0	6	0.0	13.5	88%	.000	0.00	0.00	0.43	3.11	0.1
2012	TAM	A+	26	0	1	0	3	3	4	3	1	1	1	2.2	2.2	58%	.182	1.00	2.25	6.89	15.54	0.0
2012	TRN	AA	26	1	0	0	1	0	1^{1}	1	0	0	3	0.0	20.2	%	.333	0.75	0.00	-1.30	-4.98	0.1
2012	NYA	MLB	26	1	0	0	22	0	20^{2}	26	3	6	22	2.6	9.6	46%	.371	1.55	4.35	3.97	3.86	0.3
2013	*NYA*	*MLB*	*27*	*2*	*1*	*0*	*36*	*0*	35^{2}	*33*	*4*	*13*	*36*	*3.3*	*9.2*	*48%*	*.304*	*1.29*	*3.82*	*3.73*	*4.15*	*0.5*

Chamberlain's career has been so star-crossed and injury-interrupted that a November tweet about stubbing his toe briefly caused concern. Chamberlain quickly tweeted again to reassure his followers, using the self-aware hashtag #bubblewrappedjoba. At times, Kevlar seemed more appropriate, but when we went to press Chamberlain was healthy (who knows what's befallen him since?). He recovered fully from June 2011 Tommy John surgery and the ankle operation that followed his trampoline catastrophe last March. By the time he reached a major-league mound last August, Chamberlain was throwing as hard as he had pre-injuries, and only lousy luck on balls in play prevented his ERA from looking as impressive as his peripherals. Perhaps 2013 will be his happiest season since the heady days of 2007, but we wouldn't blame the Yankees if they forbade him from making any excess movements in the meantime.

Cody Eppley

Born: **10/8/1985** Age: **27**
Bats: **R** Throws: **R** Height: **6' 6"** Weight: **205**
Breakout: **19%** Improve: **42%** Collapse: **41%**
Attrition: **26%** MLB: **83%**

Comparables:
Blaine Boyer, Josh Lueke, Warren Brusstar

YEAR	TEAM	LVL	AGE	W	L	SV	G	GS	IP	H	HR	BB	SO	BB9	SO9	GB%	BABIP	WHIP	ERA	FIP	FRA	WARP
2010	BAK	A+	24	2	0	6	14	0	18	9	0	1	24	0.5	12.0	80%	.231	0.56	0.00	1.40	1.06	0.9
2010	FRI	AA	24	1	1	9	19	0	22^{2}	12	0	9	27	3.6	10.7	79%	.231	0.93	1.19	1.98	3.05	0.5
2010	OKL	AAA	24	2	1	1	18	0	28^{2}	32	3	13	31	4.1	9.7	53%	.360	1.57	4.08	4.14	4.77	0.5
2011	ROU	AAA	25	4	2	10	43	0	55^{1}	51	3	34	55	5.5	8.9	—	.306	1.54	3.90	4.40	4.78	0.0
2011	TEX	MLB	25	1	1	0	10	0	9	11	3	5	6	5.0	6.0	55%	.286	1.78	8.00	8.06	9.37	-0.2
2012	SWB	AAA	26	0	0	2	7	0	9^{1}	3	0	1	13	1.0	12.5	82%	.176	0.43	0.00	0.69	2.16	0.2
2012	NYA	MLB	26	1	2	0	59	0	46	46	3	17	32	3.3	6.3	64%	.303	1.37	3.33	3.61	4.12	0.4
2013	*NYA*	*MLB*	*27*	*2*	*1*	*0*	*34*	*0*	*35^{2}*	*35*	*4*	*13*	*31*	*3.3*	*7.8*	*56%*	*.299*	*1.36*	*4.24*	*4.01*	*4.61*	*0.3*

Eppley, whom the Yankees plucked off waivers from the Rangers on Opening Day, was the right-handed half of the team's league of extraordinary side-arming specialists. He faced 3.3 batters per outing, the fewest of any right-handed AL reliever with at least 30 total innings, and like lefty counterpart Clay Rapada, dominated same-handed hitters but got his comeuppance against opposite-siders. Also like Rapada, Eppley throws a sinker that gets grounders approximately 70 percent of the time it's put in play, but Eppley throws his about twice as often—on roughly four out of every five pitches. That means fewer strikeouts, but the highest groundball rate of any AL reliever not named Jim Johnson.

Freddy Garcia

Born: **10/6/1976** Age: **36**
Bats: **R** Throws: **R** Height: **6' 5"** Weight: **250**
Breakout: **25%** Improve: **53%** Collapse: **23%**
Attrition: **28%** MLB: **81%**

Comparables:
Cory Lidle, Esteban Loaiza, Kevin Millwood

YEAR	TEAM	LVL	AGE	W	L	SV	G	GS	IP	H	HR	BB	SO	BB9	SO9	GB%	BABIP	WHIP	ERA	FIP	FRA	WARP
2010	CHA	MLB	33	12	6	0	28	28	157	171	23	45	89	2.6	5.1	42%	.290	1.38	4.64	4.74	4.96	0.8
2011	SWB	AAA	34	1	0	0	1	0	4	8	1	1	0	2.2	0.0	44%	.412	2.25	4.50	7.24	8.27	-0.1
2011	NYA	MLB	34	12	8	0	26	25	146^{2}	152	16	45	96	2.8	5.9	39%	.292	1.34	3.62	4.15	4.33	1.9
2012	NYA	MLB	35	7	6	0	30	17	107^{1}	112	18	35	89	2.9	7.5	42%	.297	1.37	5.20	4.63	4.78	0.4
2013	*NYA*	*MLB*	*36*	*6*	*6*	*0*	*18*	*18*	*100*	*106*	*14*	*29*	*70*	*2.6*	*6.3*	*41%*	*.295*	*1.35*	*4.48*	*4.49*	*4.87*	*0.7*

Glance at Garcia's nearly even mix of starts and relief appearances and you might conclude he was a classic swing man, pitching in, so to speak, wherever he was most needed. To a certain extent, he was, but his role changes were as much about hiding him where he could do the least damage as they were about putting him where he could be of the most help. The righty's move to the pen was a response to his four disastrous April starts, and while he pitched better in relief, his innings were low leverage. He had his moments filling in for Andy Pettitte and CC Sabathia as a starter in June and July, but his days as a useful arm are about at an end, barring a move to a more forgiving fly-ball park.

Ty Hensley

Born: **7/30/1993** Age: **19**
Bats: **R** Throws: **R** Height: **6' 5"** Weight: **220**
Breakout: **8%** Improve: **90%** Collapse: **10%**
Attrition: **10%** MLB: **54%**

Comparables:
Rick Wise, Jim Bethke, Bob Miller

YEAR	TEAM	LVL	AGE	W	L	SV	G	GS	IP	H	HR	BB	SO	BB9	SO9	GB%	BABIP	WHIP	ERA	FIP	FRA	WARP
2012	YAN	Rk	18	1	2	0	5	4	12	8	1	7	14	5.2	10.5	71%	.143	1.25	3.00	4.43	3.99	0.0
2013	*NYA*	*MLB*	*19*	*0*	*0*	*0*	*12*	*0*	*31*	*38*	*5*	*21*	*16*	*6.1*	*4.8*	*46%*	*.312*	*1.92*	*7.07*	*6.30*	*7.69*	*-0.3*

The Yankees selected a high-school pitcher with their first pick in the 2012 draft, taking the right-handed Hensley out of Oklahoma. He was all set to sign for slot value ($1.6 million) when an MRI revealed a shoulder "abnormality"—thus far asymptomatic—that lowered his leverage, but he got a deal done for $1.2 million in time to get his first taste of the Gulf Coast League. Hensley's fastball can touch the mid-90s, and he has a good 12-to-6 curve, but he'll have to improve his command and develop the changeup he didn't need to succeed as a prep player.

Phil Hughes

Born: **6/24/1986** Age: **27**
Bats: **R** Throws: **R** Height: **6' 6"** Weight: **240**
Breakout: **38%** Improve: **67%** Collapse: **15%**
Attrition: **5%** MLB: **95%**

Comparables:
Juan Marichal, Dan Haren, Jered Weaver

YEAR	TEAM	LVL	AGE	W	L	SV	G	GS	IP	H	HR	BB	SO	BB9	SO9	GB%	BABIP	WHIP	ERA	FIP	FRA	WARP
2010	NYA	MLB	24	18	8	0	31	29	176^{1}	162	25	58	146	3.0	7.5	36%	.273	1.25	4.19	4.22	5.12	1.3
2011	STA	A-	25	0	0	0	1	1	4^{1}	3	1	1	7	2.1	14.5	33%	.250	0.92	2.08	3.83	2.03	0.2
2011	TRN	AA	25	1	0	0	2	2	9^{2}	6	0	4	11	3.7	10.2	—	.261	1.03	1.86	2.38	2.58	0.0
2011	NYA	MLB	25	5	5	0	17	14	74^{2}	84	9	27	47	3.3	5.7	34%	.304	1.49	5.79	4.61	4.68	0.7
2012	NYA	MLB	26	16	13	0	32	32	191^{1}	196	35	46	165	2.2	7.8	33%	.286	1.26	4.19	4.51	4.54	1.7
2013	*NYA*	*MLB*	*27*	*9*	*9*	*0*	*26*	*26*	*150^{2}*	*145*	*20*	*43*	*135*	*2.6*	*8.0*	*37%*	*.291*	*1.25*	*3.86*	*3.99*	*4.20*	*2.2*

If Yankees fans could only forget that Hughes was ever expected to be an ace, they might be happier with him. After his injury-plagued disaster of a 2011 season, league average should have been something to celebrate. The righty avoided the DL, recorded a career-high innings total and career-best walk and strikeout rates, and finished the season as the embodiment of a league-average pitcher despite his awful April (18 runs in four starts and 16 innings). As a scary fly-ball guy in a scary fly-ball stadium, Hughes is a bad fit for his ballpark. He tied for the second-most homers allowed in the majors, including 22 at home (though he surprisingly had a higher ERA on the road).

Hiroki Kuroda

Born: **2/10/1975** Age: **38**
Bats: **R** Throws: **R** Height: **6' 2"** Weight: **190**
Breakout: **11%** Improve: **28%** Collapse: **24%**
Attrition: **12%** MLB: **78%**
Comparables:
Early Wynn,Derek Lowe,Greg Maddux

YEAR	TEAM	LVL	AGE	W	L	SV	G	GS	IP	H	HR	BB	SO	BB9	SO9	GB%	BABIP	WHIP	ERA	FIP	FRA	WARP
2010	LAN	MLB	35	11	13	0	31	31	196^{1}	180	15	48	159	2.2	7.3	53%	.283	1.16	3.39	3.29	3.87	1.9
2011	LAN	MLB	36	13	16	0	32	32	202	196	24	49	161	2.2	7.2	46%	.287	1.21	3.07	3.75	3.99	2.0
2012	NYA	MLB	37	16	11	0	33	33	219^{2}	205	25	51	167	2.1	6.8	53%	.281	1.17	3.32	3.81	4.56	2.1
2013	*NYA*	*MLB*	*38*	*11*	*10*	*0*	*27*	*27*	*180^{2}*	*182*	*23*	*44*	*131*	*2.2*	*6.5*	*50%*	*.290*	*1.25*	*3.98*	*4.14*	*4.33*	*2.1*

Paying for wins from free-agent starters is a good way to waste money, but it worked out well for the Yankees in Kuroda's case. Several of last offseason's available starters signed for more money and more years, but only Yu Darvish and Sabathia contributed more to their teams. Kuroda claimed in an October interview that he has "never enjoyed pitching," but Yankees fans enjoyed watching him pitch as he combined a career-best park-adjusted ERA with career highs in starts and innings, despite being 37 and leaving both the National League and a bigger ballpark behind. Two strong postseason starts only sweetened the deal. It took a 50 percent raise to keep Kuroda in pinstripes for a second season, but another one-year commitment made sense, even for $15 million.

Boone Logan

Born: **8/13/1984** Age: **28**
Bats: **R** Throws: **L** Height: **6' 6"** Weight: **225**
Breakout: **24%** Improve: **49%** Collapse: **30%**
Attrition: **13%** MLB: **86%**
Comparables:
Chris Ray,Kerry Ligtenberg,Tim Stoddard

YEAR	TEAM	LVL	AGE	W	L	SV	G	GS	IP	H	HR	BB	SO	BB9	SO9	GB%	BABIP	WHIP	ERA	FIP	FRA	WARP
2010	SWB	AAA	25	0	1	0	14	0	21^{1}	18	1	4	23	1.7	9.7	46%	.304	1.03	2.11	2.59	3.44	0.3
2010	NYA	MLB	25	2	0	0	51	0	40	34	3	20	38	4.5	8.6	48%	.290	1.35	2.92	3.70	4.66	0.2
2011	NYA	MLB	26	5	3	0	64	0	41^{2}	43	4	13	46	2.8	9.9	45%	.331	1.34	3.46	3.33	3.25	0.7
2012	NYA	MLB	27	7	2	1	80	0	55^{1}	48	6	28	68	4.6	11.1	40%	.311	1.37	3.74	3.62	3.56	0.7
2013	*NYA*	*MLB*	*28*	*3*	*1*	*1*	*61*	*0*	*46^{1}*	*43*	*5*	*18*	*48*	*3.6*	*9.4*	*46%*	*.304*	*1.33*	*4.01*	*3.70*	*4.36*	*0.5*

Logan wasn't necessarily the Yankees' most effective southpaw—Rapada held lefties to a more anemic line—but he was by far the most trusted and frequently deployed one, not to mention the one who wasn't a complete liability against righties. Deprived of Pedro Feliciano's services, Girardi simply forced Logan to fill the same role, summoning him a league-leading 80 times. Logan still walks too many batters, but over the past two seasons, he's altered his performance in other ways, dramatically increasing his slider use at the expense of his sinker and four-seamer, and becoming one of just a handful of pitchers who throw the pitch more than 50 percent of the time. Fewer sinkers means fewer groundballs, but more sliders means more strikeouts, and so far, the trade-off seems to be working well.

Derek Lowe

Born: **6/1/1973** Age: **40**
Bats: **R** Throws: **R** Height: **6' 7"** Weight: **230**
Breakout: **20%** Improve: **45%** Collapse: **12%**
Attrition: **6%** MLB: **79%**
Comparables:
Kevin Brown,Rick Reuschel,Woody Williams

YEAR	TEAM	LVL	AGE	W	L	SV	G	GS	IP	H	HR	BB	SO	BB9	SO9	GB%	BABIP	WHIP	ERA	FIP	FRA	WARP
2010	ATL	MLB	37	16	12	0	33	33	193^{2}	204	18	61	136	2.8	6.3	59%	.307	1.37	4.00	3.92	5.01	1.2
2011	ATL	MLB	38	9	17	0	34	34	187	212	14	70	137	3.4	6.6	60%	.327	1.51	5.05	3.67	4.25	2.0
2012	CLE	MLB	39	8	10	0	21	21	119	156	8	45	41	3.4	3.1	60%	.333	1.69	5.52	4.44	5.03	0.1
2012	NYA	MLB	39	1	1	1	17	0	23^{2}	24	2	6	14	2.3	5.3	55%	.289	1.27	3.04	3.72	4.28	0.3
2013	*NYA*	*MLB*	*40*	*7*	*9*	*0*	*23*	*23*	*131^{1}*	*150*	*15*	*43*	*75*	*3.0*	*5.1*	*59%*	*.311*	*1.47*	*4.87*	*4.52*	*5.30*	*0.3*

For the first six weeks of the season, Lowe made it look like spamming sinkers and leading the league in groundball rate was a viable strategy for surviving a strikeout rate straight out of the Deadball Era. An 8.80 ERA in his next 12 starts suggested otherwise. Released by the Indians in August, Lowe fled back to the warm embrace of the bullpen, this time in the Bronx, where he was adequate as a middle-inning arm. His stated desire to return to the rotation this season seems career-suicidal. Lowe's sinker still does what it's designed to do—as he put it last March, "Without it, I'm working at McDonald's supersizing your value meal." But even with it, he's less likely to succeed as a starter than to ask you if you want fries with that. (After all, he's already made $110 million over the course of his career.)

Brett Marshall

Born: **3/22/1990** Age: **23**
Bats: **R** Throws: **R** Height: **6' 1"** Weight: **195**
Breakout: **25%** Improve: **58%** Collapse: **17%**
Attrition: **13%** MLB: **86%**
Comparables:
Shairon Martis,Collin Balester,Jeanmar Gomez

YEAR	TEAM	LVL	AGE	W	L	SV	G	GS	IP	H	HR	BB	SO	BB9	SO9	GB%	BABIP	WHIP	ERA	FIP	FRA	WARP
2010	YAN	Rk	20	0	0	0	2	1	8	6	0	4	8	4.5	9.0	52%	.261	1.25	2.25	3.38	3.72	0.2
2010	CSC	A	20	4	2	0	13	13	72	52	2	22	56	2.8	7.0	54%	.240	1.03	2.50	3.29	4.48	0.2
2010	TAM	A+	20	0	0	0	1	1	4	5	0	0	6	0.0	13.5	41%	.296	1.25	4.50	0.44	2.58	0.3
2011	TAM	A+	21	9	7	0	27	26	140^{1}	142	6	48	114	3.1	7.3	—	.328	1.35	3.78	3.43	3.73	0.0
2012	TRN	AA	22	13	7	0	27	27	158^{1}	151	15	53	120	3.0	6.8	51%	.292	1.29	3.52	4.09	5.27	0.4
2013	*NYA*	*MLB*	*23*	*2*	*3*	*0*	*7*	*7*	*38*	*43*	*6*	*18*	*23*	*4.3*	*5.5*	*47%*	*.297*	*1.61*	*5.76*	*5.46*	*6.26*	*-0.3*

Even looking only at his road line, Marshall moved up from Tampa to Trenton in his fifth professional season without taking much of a step back statistically, which is always a win. The 2008 sixth-rounder features a lively low-90s fastball that he can place where he wants, and a good changeup that he disguises well and throws 10 or more miles per hour slower. His slider and curve are less exciting. Everything sinks, so Marshall gets grounders, and while calling him an option for the middle of a major-league rotation might be a stretch, he could be ready to take over a spot toward the end of one in 2014.

Jim Miller
Born: **4/28/1982** Age: **31**
Bats: **R** Throws: **R** Height: **6' 2"** Weight: **200**
Breakout: **29%** Improve: **48%** Collapse: **43%**
Attrition: **7%** MLB: **93%**
Comparables:
David Riske, Mel Rojas, Jeff Reardon

YEAR	TEAM	LVL	AGE	W	L	SV	G	GS	IP	H	HR	BB	SO	BB9	SO9	GB%	BABIP	WHIP	ERA	FIP	FRA	WARP
2010	NOR	AAA	28	1	0	0	33	0	57^2	60	9	18	53	2.8	8.3	35%	.313	1.35	4.84	4.42	5.33	0.0
2011	CSP	AAA	29	8	5	24	65	0	72	93	7	21	73	2.6	9.1	43%	.397	1.58	5.25	4.10	4.55	1.2
2011	COL	MLB	29	0	0	0	6	0	7	3	0	4	5	5.1	6.4	25%	.150	1.00	2.57	3.28	4.95	0.0
2012	SAC	AAA	30	0	3	6	16	0	19^1	15	0	4	21	1.9	9.8	44%	.269	0.98	2.79	2.11	0.26	0.6
2012	OAK	MLB	30	2	1	0	33	0	48^2	39	6	27	44	5.0	8.1	37%	.252	1.36	2.59	4.69	4.00	0.4
2013	*NYA*	*MLB*	*31*	*2*	*1*	*0*	*32*	*0*	*43^2*	*42*	*6*	*17*	*40*	*3.6*	*8.3*	*38%*	*.295*	*1.36*	*4.24*	*4.32*	*4.61*	*0.4*

The 28-year-old right-hander received his first extended look in a major-league uniform, reaping the advantage of a top-tier Oakland defense to keep runs off the board despite his surrendering a slew of base runners via the free pass. Miller had honed his command over the past few years in the minor leagues but the progress failed to translate to the majors, and the Yankees might be in for a rude awakening if Miller is unable to locate his targets with more consistency and/or his BABIP suffers inevitable regression.

Mark Montgomery
Born: **8/30/1990** Age: **22**
Bats: **R** Throws: **R** Height: **6' 0"** Weight: **205**
Breakout: **39%** Improve: **56%** Collapse: **15%**
Attrition: **4%** MLB: **94%**
Comparables:
Pedro Martinez, Billy McCool, Francisco Rodriguez

YEAR	TEAM	LVL	AGE	W	L	SV	G	GS	IP	H	HR	BB	SO	BB9	SO9	GB%	BABIP	WHIP	ERA	FIP	FRA	WARP
2011	CSC	A	20	0	0	14	22	0	24^1	17	0	11	41	4.1	15.2	—	.327	1.15	1.85	1.64	1.78	0.0
2011	STA	A-	20	0	0	1	4	0	4	3	0	2	10	4.5	22.5	20%	.600	1.25	2.25	1.36	3.07	0.1
2012	TAM	A+	21	4	1	14	31	0	40^1	23	0	16	61	3.6	13.6	56%	.287	0.97	1.34	1.78	0.64	1.4
2012	TRN	AA	21	3	1	1	15	0	24	12	1	6	38	2.2	14.2	34%	.239	0.75	1.88	1.33	2.02	0.7
2013	*NYA*	*MLB*	*22*	*1*	*1*	*1*	*26*	*0*	*36*	*29*	*4*	*15*	*46*	*3.7*	*11.4*	*45%*	*.300*	*1.23*	*3.34*	*3.34*	*3.63*	*0.6*

College closers tend to move quickly after going pro, and Montgomery, the Yankees' top relief prospect, might be the minor leaguer most likely to make the team in 2013. The 2011 11th-rounder's stature, strikeout rates, career minor-league home runs allowed (one), rapid rise through the system, and high socks have elicited David Robertson comps, although his breaking ball of choice is a slider, not a curve. That might mean more noticeable platoon splits. Because of his height, Montgomery's fastball can be flat-planed, but it's still a plus pitch, and the slider would miss bats in the majors right now. Neither Robertson nor Montgomery has the overpowering fastball the classic closer profile calls for, but the two of them together could give the Yankees an enviable under-30 late-inning duo.

Ivan Nova
Born: **1/12/1987** Age: **26**
Bats: **R** Throws: **R** Height: **6' 5"** Weight: **225**
Breakout: **32%** Improve: **69%** Collapse: **18%**
Attrition: **23%** MLB: **90%**
Comparables:
Mitch Talbot, Joe Blanton, Wade Davis

YEAR	TEAM	LVL	AGE	W	L	SV	G	GS	IP	H	HR	BB	SO	BB9	SO9	GB%	BABIP	WHIP	ERA	FIP	FRA	WARP
2010	SWB	AAA	23	12	3	0	23	23	145	135	10	48	115	3.0	7.1	53%	.298	1.26	2.86	3.64	4.50	0.8
2010	NYA	MLB	23	1	2	0	10	7	42	44	4	17	26	3.6	5.6	51%	.294	1.45	4.50	4.33	5.44	0.1
2011	SWB	AAA	24	1	2	0	3	3	16	16	3	2	18	1.1	10.1	46%	.282	1.12	3.38	3.80	4.73	0.0
2011	NYA	MLB	24	16	4	0	28	27	165^1	163	13	57	98	3.1	5.3	54%	.283	1.33	3.70	4.04	4.78	0.8
2012	NYA	MLB	25	12	8	0	28	28	170^1	194	28	56	153	3.0	8.1	46%	.331	1.47	5.02	4.55	4.87	0.6
2013	*NYA*	*MLB*	*26*	*8*	*9*	*0*	*24*	*24*	*148*	*157*	*19*	*53*	*106*	*3.2*	*6.4*	*50%*	*.304*	*1.42*	*4.69*	*4.51*	*5.10*	*0.6*

It was a strange season for Nova, whose ugly ERA wiped out the good feelings surrounding his strong 2011 season. The 26-year-old may have been burned by bad luck, as evidenced by his elevated BABIP and home-run-per-fly-ball rate (his Fair Run Average was essentially unchanged), but to borrow from Branch Rickey, bad luck can also be the residue of design. Pitching coach Larry Rothschild encouraged Nova to mix in more breaking balls to get hitters guessing, and he did up his curve and slider rates, but opposing batters still recorded a .360 TAv against his four-seamer, as well as 12 of his 28 home runs allowed. (Five more homers came against the changeup, which he threw only 81 times.) Nova did some time on the 15-day DL in August for rotator-cuff inflammation, which could have been connected to his iffy command, though he failed to show any convincing improvement after his return. Whatever the explanation, David Phelps displaced him on the rotation depth chart (and the postseason roster) before the dust settled.

Andy Pettitte
Born: **6/15/1972** Age: **41**
Bats: **L** Throws: **L** Height: **6' 6"** Weight: **225**
Breakout: **14%** Improve: **51%** Collapse: **31%**
Attrition: **11%** MLB: **69%**
Comparables:
Mike Mussina, Jamie Moyer, Steve Carlton

YEAR	TEAM	LVL	AGE	W	L	SV	G	GS	IP	H	HR	BB	SO	BB9	SO9	GB%	BABIP	WHIP	ERA	FIP	FRA	WARP
2010	NYA	MLB	38	11	3	0	21	21	129	123	13	41	101	2.9	7.0	46%	.291	1.27	3.28	3.81	4.32	1.7
2012	TAM	A+	40	0	0	0	2	2	7	4	0	0	5	0.0	6.4	63%	.211	0.57	1.29	1.96	1.28	0.1
2012	TRN	AA	40	0	1	0	1	1	5	7	0	1	3	1.8	5.4	55%	.350	1.60	5.40	2.60	2.20	0.0
2012	SWB	AAA	40	0	1	0	1	1	5	8	0	2	5	3.6	9.0	41%	.471	2.00	5.40	2.36	3.15	0.1
2012	NYA	MLB	40	5	4	0	12	12	75^1	65	8	21	69	2.5	8.2	56%	.278	1.14	2.87	3.43	4.06	1.2
2013	*NYA*	*MLB*	*41*	*3*	*3*	*0*	*9*	*9*	*54^1*	*55*	*6*	*18*	*43*	*2.9*	*7.1*	*49%*	*.300*	*1.33*	*4.06*	*4.05*	*4.41*	*0.7*

Maybe taking 2011 off helped heal the wear and tear of two decades of professional pitching. Pettitte's comeback didn't begin until mid-May, and a fibula fractured by a batted ball cost him July, August, and the first half of September, but when he was on the mound, he pitched better than he had for the better part of a decade (despite a slightly slower fastball). Pettitte returns in 2013 on a $12 million, one-year deal. The list of left-handed starters who've succeeded at age 41 isn't a long one, but that doesn't mean Pettitte won't make that list a little longer this season; we wouldn't have projected him to be this well preserved 15, 10, or even five years ago, but pitchers who've succeeded at age 40 have mostly remained effective the following year.

David Phelps

Born: **10/9/1986** Age: **26**
Bats: **R** Throws: **R** Height: **6' 3"** Weight: **185**
Breakout: **23%** Improve: **59%** Collapse: **22%**
Attrition: **20%** MLB: **95%**

Comparables:
Johnny Cueto,Homer Bailey,Noah Lowry

YEAR	TEAM	LVL	AGE	W	L	SV	G	GS	IP	H	HR	BB	SO	BB9	SO9	GB%	BABIP	WHIP	ERA	FIP	FRA	WARP
2010	TRN	AA	23	6	0	0	14	14	88^{1}	63	2	23	84	2.3	8.6	49%	.264	0.97	2.04	2.60	3.41	1.7
2010	SWB	AAA	23	4	2	0	12	11	70^{1}	76	4	13	57	1.7	7.3	44%	.317	1.27	3.07	3.01	3.74	1.3
2011	YAN	Rk	24	1	1	0	2	2	7	4	0	1	5	1.3	6.4	67%	.190	0.71	0.00	2.42	4.58	0.1
2011	SWB	AAA	24	6	6	0	18	18	107^{1}	115	11	26	90	2.2	7.5	36%	.335	1.31	3.19	3.73	3.92	0.5
2012	TAM	A+	25	0	0	0	2	2	5^{1}	7	0	1	5	1.7	8.4	53%	.467	1.50	0.00	2.08	1.74	0.1
2012	TRN	AA	25	1	0	0	1	1	6^{2}	1	0	1	11	1.4	14.9	70%	.100	0.30	0.00	0.35	-0.13	0.0
2012	SWB	AAA	25	1	0	0	1	1	6^{2}	4	0	3	7	4.1	9.4	29%	.235	1.05	0.00	2.41	2.64	0.1
2012	NYA	MLB	25	4	4	0	33	11	99^{2}	81	14	38	96	3.4	8.7	45%	.258	1.19	3.34	4.27	4.84	0.7
2013	*NYA*	*MLB*	*26*	*4*	*4*	*0*	*17*	*12*	77^{2}	*80*	*11*	*27*	*60*	*3.2*	*6.9*	*46%*	*.298*	*1.39*	*4.50*	*4.54*	*4.89*	*0.5*

Phelps made the team out of spring training and spent the season up and down and in and out of the rotation. As one would expect, he posted better peripherals in the pen, but not by much, missing bats even as a starter. His velocity isn't impressive—his four-seamer averaged just under 92 mph—but he uses five pitches with regularity, giving batters lots of different looks. The 2008 14th-rounder may not go on to become much more than this, but "this" is a player in his 20s who works cheap, which isn't a description met by many members of the Yankees' ancient, expensive roster.

Michael Pineda

Born: **1/18/1989** Age: **24**
Bats: **R** Throws: **R** Height: **6' 8"** Weight: **260**
Breakout: **29%** Improve: **68%** Collapse: **6%**
Attrition: **7%** MLB: **97%**

Comparables:
Matt Cain,Tommy Hanson,Daniel Hudson

YEAR	TEAM	LVL	AGE	W	L	SV	G	GS	IP	H	HR	BB	SO	BB9	SO9	GB%	BABIP	WHIP	ERA	FIP	FRA	WARP
2010	WTN	AA	21	8	1	0	13	13	77	67	1	17	78	2.0	9.1	45%	.306	1.09	2.22	2.35	2.84	2.3
2010	TAC	AAA	21	3	3	0	12	12	62^{1}	54	9	17	76	2.5	11.0	41%	.290	1.14	4.77	3.98	4.41	1.0
2011	SEA	MLB	22	9	10	0	28	28	171	133	18	55	173	2.9	9.1	39%	.258	1.10	3.74	3.46	3.77	2.2
2013	*NYA*	*MLB*	*24*	*2*	*2*	*0*	*6*	*6*	*36*	*32*	*5*	*12*	*34*	*2.9*	*8.5*	*42%*	*.282*	*1.23*	*3.67*	*4.12*	*3.99*	*0.6*

Most fears about low velocity early in the year are unfounded: The radar readings rise along with the temperature. Then there's Pineda. He arrived at camp out of shape and struggled in six starts while topping out in the low-90s. A trip to the disabled list led to a late-April diagnosis of a shoulder labrum tear. Three months later, Cashman, who'd stuck his neck out by dealing his top hitting prospect (Montero) for Pineda, called the deal "a massive decision gone wrong." Since there was no accompanying damage to Pineda's rotator cuff, there's still a chance for him to pay off, but he won't be back until midseason at the earliest. Even if he takes the Anibal Sanchez route to recovery (Sanchez had a similar surgery in 2007), it could be years before Pineda's fully himself again. And with but a single major-league season on his résumé, it's unclear what self that really is.

Jose A. Ramirez

Born: **1/21/1990** Age: **23**
Bats: **R** Throws: **R** Height: **6' 2"** Weight: **155**
Breakout: **27%** Improve: **59%** Collapse: **17%**
Attrition: **13%** MLB: **92%**

Comparables:
Ross Detwiler,Chris Carpenter,Jeanmar Gomez

YEAR	TEAM	LVL	AGE	W	L	SV	G	GS	IP	H	HR	BB	SO	BB9	SO9	GB%	BABIP	WHIP	ERA	FIP	FRA	WARP
2010	CSC	A	20	6	5	0	22	21	115	106	3	42	105	3.3	8.2	49%	.301	1.29	3.60	3.37	3.83	1.3
2011	CSC	A	21	5	7	0	15	15	79	84	9	32	74	3.6	8.4	—	.329	1.47	4.90	4.50	4.89	0.0
2011	TAM	A+	21	0	5	0	6	6	24^{1}	35	3	11	25	4.1	9.2	—	.400	1.89	8.14	4.42	4.80	0.0
2012	TAM	A+	22	7	6	0	21	18	98^{2}	92	7	30	94	2.7	8.6	45%	.295	1.24	3.19	3.47	3.58	0.2
2013	*NYA*	*MLB*	*23*	*2*	*3*	*0*	*6*	*6*	*33*	*37*	*5*	*17*	*22*	*4.5*	*6.0*	*45%*	*.299*	*1.62*	*5.81*	*5.38*	*6.31*	*-0.2*

Ramirez saw his prospect status suffer after his first try at taming Tampa in 2011 ended in a hard-luck 8.00-plus ERA and a trip back to Charleston, but his second attempt last season went smoothly. He showed improved control and continued to miss bats and get grounders. The 23-year-old right-hander has a low-90s fastball that can spike at 96, which he complements with a well-developed changeup and slider. His past injury issues and slight frame will likely make him a reliever in the long term, but his feel for the changeup and ability to throw strikes give him at least some chance to start.

Clay Rapada
Born: **3/9/1981** Age: **32**
Bats: **R** Throws: **L** Height: **6' 6"** Weight: **200**
Breakout: **24%** Improve: **41%** Collapse: **32%**
Attrition: **10%** MLB: **95%**
Comparables:
Jason Frasor,Felix Rodriguez,Santiago Casilla

YEAR	TEAM	LVL	AGE	W	L	SV	G	GS	IP	H	HR	BB	SO	BB9	SO9	GB%	BABIP	WHIP	ERA	FIP	FRA	WARP
2010	OKL	AAA	29	1	2	2	50	0	59^{1}	32	1	21	61	3.2	9.3	50%	.215	0.89	1.82	3.01	3.84	1.2
2010	TEX	MLB	29	0	0	0	13	0	9	6	2	7	5	7.0	5.0	33%	.160	1.44	4.00	7.16	6.38	-0.2
2011	NOR	AAA	30	0	1	1	26	0	20^{2}	24	1	4	20	1.7	8.7	50%	.364	1.35	3.92	2.80	2.54	0.2
2011	BAL	MLB	30	2	0	0	32	0	16^{1}	14	3	7	18	3.9	9.9	36%	.268	1.29	6.06	4.53	4.47	0.1
2012	NYA	MLB	31	3	0	0	70	0	38^{1}	29	2	17	38	4.0	8.9	47%	.278	1.20	2.82	3.15	3.67	0.4
2013	*NYA*	*MLB*	*32*	*2*	*1*	*1*	*48*	*0*	*35*	*32*	*4*	*16*	*34*	*4.1*	*8.7*	*45%*	*.291*	*1.36*	*3.98*	*4.11*	*4.32*	*0.4*

Rapada pitched to just 2.5 percent of the batters faced by the Yankees staff last season and was relegated to low-leverage work by incumbent Logan, but when he was on the mound, he played the part of a LOOGY to perfection. He averaged 2.2 batters faced per appearance, making his the shortest outings of any AL reliever who lasted at least 30 innings, but he limited lefties to a .194 TAv and boasts a .183 multi-year mark against them. The price of suppressing southpaws is complete carnage at the hands of righties, who've hit Rapada over the course of his career like Mike Trout hit the rest of the league last season. Girardi deftly limited the damage, arranging for the platoon advantage in a major-league-leading 74 percent of the side-armer's plate appearances. Rapada is not the next Jesse Orosco—that long-lived lefty wasn't limited to LOOGY duty until he turned 40—but one successful season for a pitcher with his skill set can mean a long major-league life. Not bad for a guy who went undrafted, was released by the Orioles, and wasn't signed by the Yankees until the day before pitchers and catchers reported.

Mariano Rivera
Born: **11/29/1969** Age: **43**
Bats: **R** Throws: **R** Height: **6' 3"** Weight: **185**
Breakout: **47%** Improve: **54%** Collapse: **21%**
Attrition: **22%** MLB: **64%**
Comparables:
Mike Timlin,Trevor Hoffman,Hoyt Wilhelm

YEAR	TEAM	LVL	AGE	W	L	SV	G	GS	IP	H	HR	BB	SO	BB9	SO9	GB%	BABIP	WHIP	ERA	FIP	FRA	WARP
2010	NYA	MLB	40	3	3	33	61	0	60	39	2	11	45	1.6	6.8	52%	.222	0.83	1.80	2.78	4.09	1.1
2011	NYA	MLB	41	1	2	44	64	0	61^{1}	47	3	8	60	1.2	8.8	48%	.275	0.90	1.91	2.23	2.95	1.5
2012	NYA	MLB	42	1	1	5	9	0	8^{1}	6	0	2	8	2.2	8.6	46%	.273	0.96	2.16	1.85	2.14	0.2
2013	*NYA*	*MLB*	*43*	*2*	*1*	*29*	*40*	*0*	*38^{1}*	*31*	*4*	*7*	*38*	*1.6*	*8.9*	*51%*	*.274*	*0.99*	*2.40*	*3.12*	*2.60*	*1.2*

Rivera is back. He signed for one year, $10 million, after mulling retirement following a May fly-shagging incident left him with a torn ACL and meniscus, cutting his 2012 season short. Rivera's only concession to advancing age, aside from his receding hairline, has been a decrease in his counting stats, which dipped deeper than ever before in 2012. Until the ACL tear, increasingly careful handling kept him off the DL from 2004-11—a span during which his ERA only once rose above 2.00. Rivera's cutter was averaging just over 91 miles per hour before his injury, but that was attributed to his usual cold-weather start. No one would be shocked if the 43-year-old channeled Hoyt Wilhelm and continued to defy Father Time, but even if Rivera's reckoning comes in 2013, we can console ourselves with the knowledge that we won't have to watch him endure the indignity of a lengthy decline phase.

David Robertson
Born: **4/9/1985** Age: **28**
Bats: **R** Throws: **R** Height: **6' 0"** Weight: **195**
Breakout: **37%** Improve: **55%** Collapse: **34%**
Attrition: **15%** MLB: **94%**
Comparables:
Michael Gonzalez,Jose Valverde,Francisco Rodriguez

YEAR	TEAM	LVL	AGE	W	L	SV	G	GS	IP	H	HR	BB	SO	BB9	SO9	GB%	BABIP	WHIP	ERA	FIP	FRA	WARP
2010	NYA	MLB	25	4	5	1	64	0	61^{1}	59	5	33	71	4.8	10.4	43%	.335	1.50	3.82	3.55	3.94	1.0
2011	NYA	MLB	26	4	0	1	70	0	66^{2}	40	1	35	100	4.7	13.5	48%	.289	1.12	1.08	1.88	0.90	2.4
2012	SWB	AAA	27	0	0	0	2	1	2	0	0	0	2	0.0	9.0	50%	.000	0.00	0.00	1.16	2.30	0.1
2012	NYA	MLB	27	2	7	2	65	0	60^{2}	52	5	19	81	2.8	12.0	45%	.331	1.17	2.67	2.44	2.90	1.5
2013	*NYA*	*MLB*	*28*	*3*	*1*	*1*	*56*	*0*	*53*	*41*	*5*	*23*	*71*	*3.9*	*12.0*	*47%*	*.303*	*1.21*	*2.89*	*3.05*	*3.15*	*1.3*

Robertson's 2012 was a regression only in the sense that his one-home-run-per-season rate from the previous year was unsustainable. The right-hander met or surpassed any realistic expectations, matching his career strikeout rate, cutting his walk rate by roughly two free passes per nine, and rating as one of baseball's 10 most valuable bullpen arms by WARP for the second straight season. Robertson's high-spin fastball has the most vertical movement of any pitch classified as a cutter by Brooks Baseball, and his extremely long stride makes his modest fastball play up. The combination of a cutter that appears to be rising and an effective velocity that outstrips his radar-gun readings makes many batters too surprised to swing, which could explain why Robertson has recorded the second-highest percentage of called strikes (called strikes/total strikes) among the 300-plus pitchers who've faced at least 1,000 batters over the past five seasons. A mid-May oblique strain ended Robertson's cameo as closer, limiting him to two measly saves, but more ninth-inning outings probably lie ahead.

CC Sabathia

Born: **7/21/1980** Age: **32**
Bats: **L** Throws: **L** Height: **6' 8"** Weight: **290**
Breakout: **16%** Improve: **67%** Collapse: **19%**
Attrition: **7%** MLB: **87%**

Comparables:
John Smiley,Johan Santana,Cliff Lee

YEAR	TEAM	LVL	AGE	W	L	SV	G	GS	IP	H	HR	BB	SO	BB9	SO9	GB%	BABIP	WHIP	ERA	FIP	FRA	WARP
2010	NYA	MLB	29	21	7	0	34	34	237^2	209	20	74	197	2.8	7.5	52%	.281	1.19	3.18	3.51	3.93	3.9
2011	NYA	MLB	30	19	8	0	33	33	237^1	230	17	61	230	2.3	8.7	49%	.318	1.23	3.00	2.91	3.60	4.4
2012	NYA	MLB	31	15	6	0	28	28	200	184	22	44	197	2.0	8.9	50%	.288	1.14	3.38	3.29	3.74	3.5
2013	*NYA*	*MLB*	*32*	*12*	*8*	*0*	*26*	*26*	*183^2*	*164*	*17*	*45*	*172*	*2.2*	*8.4*	*48%*	*.292*	*1.14*	*3.10*	*3.27*	*3.37*	*4.2*

Sabathia didn't surrender his ace status last season, but he did lose his aura of invincibility. After five straight seasons without a start sacrificed to injury, he spent two stints on the disabled list—one for the first arm injury of his major-league career. A bone spur was removed arthroscopically from his elbow shortly after the Yankees' elimination from the ALCS. CC was also a little less effective when ostensibly healthy, allowing a career-high home-run rate, thanks largely to a more fly-ball-prone slider. He also lost roughly 1.5 mph from his four-seam fastball. Despite all that, Sabathia's WARP says he was by far the team's most valuable pitcher. The question is how much the bone spur had to do with his decline and, in turn, how much his mileage and advancing age had to do with the bone spur. The four seasons and many millions of dollars remaining on Sabathia's contract will likely encourage the Yankees to be more conservative with his workloads going forward.

Rafael Soriano

Born: **12/19/1979** Age: **33**
Bats: **R** Throws: **R** Height: **6' 2"** Weight: **230**
Breakout: **18%** Improve: **47%** Collapse: **38%**
Attrition: **8%** MLB: **91%**

Comparables:
Mike Adams,J.J. Putz,Joaquin Benoit

YEAR	TEAM	LVL	AGE	W	L	SV	G	GS	IP	H	HR	BB	SO	BB9	SO9	GB%	BABIP	WHIP	ERA	FIP	FRA	WARP
2010	TBA	MLB	30	3	2	45	64	0	62^1	36	4	14	57	2.0	8.2	32%	.199	0.80	1.73	2.77	3.21	1.0
2011	TAM	A+	31	0	1	0	2	2	2^1	4	1	0	1	0.0	3.9	—	.375	1.71	11.57	8.10	8.81	0.0
2011	SWB	AAA	31	1	0	0	2	0	2	1	1	0	2	0.0	9.0	80%	.000	0.50	4.50	7.74	8.89	-0.1
2011	NYA	MLB	31	2	3	2	42	0	39^1	33	4	18	36	4.1	8.2	36%	.276	1.30	4.12	4.00	4.90	0.2
2012	NYA	MLB	32	2	1	42	69	0	67^2	55	6	24	69	3.2	9.2	38%	.274	1.17	2.26	3.27	3.27	1.3
2013	*NYA*	*MLB*	*33*	*3*	*1*	*18*	*57*	*0*	*55*	*44*	*6*	*19*	*60*	*3.0*	*9.8*	*36%*	*.276*	*1.14*	*3.05*	*3.47*	*3.31*	*1.3*

In the long run, there's no reliever like Mariano Rivera, but Soriano pulled off a fairly convincing imitation, delivering a season that but for a few walks wouldn't have looked out of place on the back of Rivera's baseball card. Soriano simplified his approach, abandoning his cutter and leaning heavily on his slider, which accounted for 44 percent of his pitches, perhaps a few too many. After an August blown save in which Soriano threw five consecutive sliders—the last of which ended up in the seats—Rivera reminded him that his fastball was the foundation of his success. Still, not every flamethrower who once threw 75 percent fastballs successfully reinvents himself when his velocity fades: Soriano's adaptability bodes well for his future . . . elsewhere. Despite his relationship with Rivera, the 33-year-old opted out of his contract in search of a big-money, multi-year deal.

Josh Spence

Born: **1/22/1988** Age: **25**
Bats: **L** Throws: **L** Height: **6' 2"** Weight: **170**
Breakout: **26%** Improve: **55%** Collapse: **26%**
Attrition: **6%** MLB: **85%**

Comparables:
Jose Mijares,Ryan Rowland-Smith,Mike Zagurski

YEAR	TEAM	LVL	AGE	W	L	SV	G	GS	IP	H	HR	BB	SO	BB9	SO9	GB%	BABIP	WHIP	ERA	FIP	FRA	WARP
2010	PDR	Rk	22	0	0	0	1	0	1	1	0	0	3	0.0	27.0	50%	.500	1.00	0.00	-1.74	-0.93	0.1
2010	FTW	A	22	2	2	0	7	3	17	14	2	6	31	3.2	16.4	44%	.419	1.18	3.71	2.73	3.57	0.5
2010	EUG	A-	22	0	0	0	2	2	6	4	1	1	8	1.5	12.0	67%	.273	0.83	1.50	3.48	4.06	0.0
2011	SAN	AA	23	3	1	0	35	0	47^1	29	4	11	42	2.1	8.0	33%	.298	0.85	1.71	3.46	3.70	0.3
2011	SDN	MLB	23	0	2	0	40	0	29^2	14	2	19	31	5.8	9.4	38%	.174	1.11	2.73	3.90	4.16	0.0
2012	TUC	AAA	24	4	2	0	31	4	49^1	48	4	20	36	3.6	6.6	43%	.280	1.38	4.20	4.54	5.67	0.4
2012	SDN	MLB	24	0	1	0	11	0	10^1	13	1	5	10	4.4	8.7	30%	.375	1.74	4.35	3.91	3.20	0.1
2013	*NYA*	*MLB*	*25*	*2*	*1*	*0*	*28*	*2*	*35*	*32*	*5*	*15*	*35*	*3.9*	*8.9*	*41%*	*.290*	*1.35*	*4.08*	*4.34*	*4.43*	*0.4*

Spence is a finesse lefty from Australia by way of Arizona State who throws sinkers and sliders. He works in the low-80s and, when going well, gets hitters to chase the slider out of the zone. Guys learned to take that pitch toward the end of 2011, and Spence spent most of last year at Triple-A searching for a backup plan. While pitching in the Arizona Fall League he was claimed by the Yankees off waivers from the Padres, which seems backwards, but isn't.

Nik Turley

Born: **9/11/1989** Age: **23**
Bats: **L** Throws: **L** Height: **6' 7"** Weight: **230**
Breakout: **28%** Improve: **71%** Collapse: **18%**
Attrition: **19%** MLB: **96%**

Comparables:
J.P. Howell,Felix Doubront,Jo-Jo Reyes

YEAR	TEAM	LVL	AGE	W	L	SV	G	GS	IP	H	HR	BB	SO	BB9	SO9	GB%	BABIP	WHIP	ERA	FIP	FRA	WARP
2010	YAN	Rk	20	0	2	0	3	2	10^2	11	0	2	9	1.7	7.6	47%	.289	1.21	0.84	2.39	4.42	0.1
2010	STA	A-	20	4	4	0	12	12	61^2	57	0	29	47	4.2	6.9	47%	.318	1.39	4.38	3.46	4.50	0.5
2011	CSC	A	21	4	6	0	15	15	82^1	70	8	21	82	2.3	9.0	—	.277	1.11	2.51	3.86	4.19	0.0
2011	TAM	A+	21	0	0	0	2	2	7^1	11	1	1	5	1.2	6.1	—	.385	1.64	6.14	4.62	5.02	0.0
2012	TAM	A+	22	9	5	0	23	21	112	97	7	44	116	3.5	9.3	49%	.308	1.26	2.89	3.55	3.34	0.1
2012	TRN	AA	22	1	0	0	1	1	5	8	0	1	1	1.8	1.8	43%	.381	1.80	5.40	4.00	5.01	0.0
2013	*NYA*	*MLB*	*23*	*2*	*3*	*0*	*6*	*6*	*32^2*	*36*	*5*	*18*	*24*	*4.8*	*6.6*	*44%*	*.308*	*1.64*	*5.74*	*5.37*	*6.24*	*-0.2*

Turley wasn't selected until the 1,502nd pick in the 2008 draft, but he subsequently skipped the Mormon mission that had tainted perceptions of his signability. Almost five years later, and with Banuelos on the shelf until 2014, Turley—no relation to "Bullet Bob"—is the system's most promising southpaw. Despite his 6'6" frame, Turley doesn't throw especially hard, but he commands his fastball and rounds out his pitches with a projectable curve, a more advanced changeup, and a Pettitte-esque pickoff move. After setting a career-high innings total and earning three September starts (two in the postseason) for Trenton, he was added to the 40-man roster and projects as a back-of-the-rotation arm.

Adam Warren
Born: **8/25/1987** Age: **25**
Bats: **R** Throws: **R** Height: **6' 3"** Weight: **215**
Breakout: **21%** Improve: **42%** Collapse: **18%**
Attrition: **26%** MLB: **92%**
Comparables:
Jeff Manship, Mitch Talbot, Kevin Mulvey

YEAR	TEAM	LVL	AGE	W	L	SV	G	GS	IP	H	HR	BB	SO	BB9	SO9	GB%	BABIP	WHIP	ERA	FIP	FRA	WARP
2010	TAM	A+	22	7	5	0	15	15	81	72	2	17	67	1.9	7.4	59%	.275	1.10	2.22	2.95	3.90	0.6
2010	TRN	AA	22	4	2	0	10	10	54^1	49	2	16	59	2.7	9.8	48%	.303	1.20	3.15	2.72	3.13	1.3
2011	SWB	AAA	23	6	8	0	27	27	152^1	145	13	53	111	3.1	6.6	41%	.287	1.30	3.60	4.09	4.97	0.0
2012	SWB	AAA	24	7	8	0	26	26	152^2	167	11	46	107	2.7	6.3	49%	.319	1.40	3.71	3.68	5.06	-0.6
2012	NYA	MLB	24	0	0	0	1	1	2^1	8	2	2	1	7.7	3.9	29%	.500	4.29	23.14	15.90	9.59	-0.1
2013	*NYA*	*MLB*	*25*	*3*	*3*	*0*	*9*	*9*	*49^1*	*54*	*7*	*17*	*33*	*3.2*	*6.0*	*49%*	*.301*	*1.45*	*4.83*	*4.74*	*5.25*	*0.2*

Warren went one-and-done in his first taste of the majors, taking one of the injured Sabathia's starts and pitching so poorly that the next one went to Phelps. The fourth-round pick from 2009 has neither standout stuff nor standout stats, working off a low-90s fastball with an assortment of vanilla off-speed weapons. He's as close to a finished product as pitching prospects come: When we say he repeated Triple-A in 2012, we mean he *really* repeated it, with a déjà-vu all over again stat line. Warren might be a back-of-the-rotation arm somewhere, but probably not New York. He did win a Gold Glove, ostensibly awarded to the best fielding pitcher in the (full-season) minor leagues. Maybe he can make it back to the majors as a utility guy.

LINEOUTS

HITTERS

PLAYER	TEAM	LVL	AGE	PA	R	2B	3B	HR	RBI	BB	SO	SB-CS	AVG/OBP/SLG	TAv	BABIP	BRR	FRAA	WARP
OF C. Dickerson	SWB	AAA	30	321	57	24	4	7	25	49	73	17-3	.316/.417/.515	.342	.403	4.5	CF(30): 1.8, LF(13): -1.4	3.0
	NYA	MLB	30	17	5	0	0	2	5	3	5	3-0	.286/.412/.714	.353	.286	-0.1	LF(18): -0.3, RF(5): -0.1	0.2
LF R. Flores	TAM	A+	20	583	83	29	7	6	39	54	85	24-9	.302/.370/.420	.295	.348	3.6	LF(25): 1.6, CF(12): 0.4	1.9
OF A. Jones	NYA	MLB	35	269	27	7	0	14	34	28	71	0-0	.197/.294/.408	.260	.212	-1.4	LF(47): -1.9, RF(23): -1.0	-0.1
3B C. McGehee	NYA	MLB	29	59	9	3	0	1	6	5	10	0-0	.151/.220/.264	.194	.163	-0.3	3B(12): -1.2, 1B(8): -0.2	-0.5
	PIT	MLB	29	293	27	13	1	8	35	24	60	1-1	.230/.297/.377	.251	.266	-1.4	1B(77): 2.6, 3B(9): 0.0	0.0

Speed, ability to play all three outfield positions, and competence against right-handed pitching make **Chris Dickerson** a useful spare part in the majors, but he didn't get much time there, instead having his best offensive season in the minors, largely free of the struggles vs. southpaws that made him a part-time player. **Ramon Flores's** polished approach at the plate earned him a promotion to Trenton before his 21st birthday, but long term, he's a subpar left fielder or first baseman without the power needed to maintain prospect status at those positions. This season, the tweener type will be the Yankees' fourth-best Double-A outfielder behind the trio of Austin, Mason Williams, and Slade Heathcott, which will be good preparation for a future of being the fourth-best outfielder on every upper-level team he plays for. **Andruw Jones** will take his big bat against lefties and decent defense to Japan in 2013. After A-Rod went down with a fractured hand, the Yankees traded Chad Qualls to Pittsburgh for **Casey McGehee**, but in light of how McGehee hit over the final two months of the season, Cashman might have been better off asking Qualls to play third. McGehee is now off to Japan for the foreseeable future.

PITCHERS

PLAYER	TEAM	LVL	AGE	W	L	SV	IP	H	HR	BB	SO	BB9	SO9	GB%	BABIP	WHIP	ERA	FIP	FRA	WARP
C. Cabral	—	—	—	—	—	—	—	—	—	—	—	—	—	—	—	—	—	—	—	—
P. Feliciano	YAN	Rk	35	0	0	0	4	2	0	1	5	2.2	11.2	67%	.222	0.75	0	1.68	0.99	0.1
	STA	A-	35	0	0	0	3	3	1	0	2	0	6	36%	.200	1.00	3.00	6.33	6.17	0
	TAM	A+	35	0	0	0	1	4	0	0	1	0	9	17%	.667	4.00	18.0	1.39	-1.72	0
	TRN	AA	35	0	0	0	1^{1}	0	0	2	2	13.5	13.5	50%	0	1.50	0	4.70	4.04	0
D. Herndon	PHI	MLB	26	0	1	0	7^{2}	10	1	1	8	1.2	9.4	54%	.391	1.43	4.70	3.14	3.54	0.1
R. Igarashi	LVG	AAA	33	1	1	4	21	10	0	3	28	1.3	12.0	44%	.222	0.62	1.29	1.43	2.08	0.7
	SWB	AAA	33	4	3	10	36^{2}	30	1	18	55	4.4	13.5	54%	.341	1.31	2.45	2.07	2.00	1.1
	NYA	MLB	33	0	0	0	3	4	0	3	3	9.0	9.0	50%	.400	2.33	12.00	4.05	4.03	0.0
	TOR	MLB	33	0	0	0	1	5	0	2	2	18.0	18.0	33%	.833	7.00	36.00	5.05	3.61	0.1
F. Rondon	TRN	AA	24	5	0	1	63^{2}	56	6	39	70	5.5	9.9	43%	.297	1.49	3.96	4.07	4.23	0.4

Lefty reliever **Cesar Cabral** struck out 12 and walked two in 11 1/3 innings last March, making a strong case for inclusion on the Opening Day roster, but he suffered a stress fracture in his elbow late in the exhibition schedule, which ended his season and allowed Rapada to make the team instead. ⚾ After two seasons spent trying to avoid and then trying to recover from rotator cuff surgery, lefty reliever **Pedro Feliciano**'s bank account contains the best evidence that he ever spent time with the team. ⚾ **David Herndon** made five April appearances for the Phillies before his elbow went pop in mid-June. The Yankees preemptively added him to the middle-inning mix on a minor-league deal in November, hoping that he'd make a quicker recovery than Aardsma did. ⚾ Right-handed reliever **Ryota Igarashi** baffles minor-league hitters, but his 95-mph fastball is flat and he hands out walks more freely than Oprah does cars, including five more in four innings for the Yankees and Blue Jays last season. ⚾ After adding 24-year-old **Francisco Rondon** to the 40-man, the Yankees can rest secure in the knowledge that if Logan, Rapada, Spence, and Cabral are all abducted by left-handed-reliever-loving aliens, they'll still have a southpaw on the premises, albeit one who's never walked fewer than five batters per nine innings.

MANAGER: JOE GIRARDI

YEAR	TEAM	W-L	Pythag +/-	Avg PC	100+ P	120+ P	QS	BQS	REL	REL w Zero R	IBB	PH	PH Avg	PH HR	SB2	CS2	SB3	CS3	SAC Att	SAC %	POS SAC	Squeeze	Swing	In Play
2010	NYA	95-67	1	194.2	160	157	105	3	431	349	74	190	.167	4	9	4	1	0	96	93.8%	78	0	362	110
2011	NYA	97-65	1	95.7	69	2	84	6	465	404	43	54	.196	0	21	3	1	1	54	83.3%	38	0	357	94
2012	NYA	95-67	1	97.9	84	3	82	7	485	409	32	129	.148	4	16	3	0	0	50	86.0%	40	0	321	88

Girardi showed some signs of strain as his team's lead disappeared down the stretch, snapping at a heckler during a postgame press gaggle in August and inviting a beat writer who asked one too many questions about CC Sabathia's health into his office for a closed-door shouting match in September. However, while his normally calm façade showed some cracks, Girardi held his team together despite the strain of injuries to prominent players and the Orioles' improbable pursuit. In most respects, Girardi was a middle-of-the-pack tactical manager, doing little to earn either the admiration or the ire of backseat sabermetric skippers—despite the much-maligned binder he sometimes consults before moves, he's not a stathead at heart. He did a good job of leveraging his relievers and swapping in arms to replace injured pitchers, but the team's fossilized roster meant he didn't have to concern himself with too many moving parts. The one respect in which he stood out was his use of pinch-hitters: the Yankees' 129 just barely trailed first-place Tampa Bay's 135 and more than doubled the third-place total of the Orioles. That was emblematic of Girardi's dogged pursuit of the platoon advantage: The success of role players and situational relievers like Eric Chavez, Raul Ibanez, Cody Eppley, and Clay Rapada owed much to their manager's scrupulous attention to matchups. One could argue that his handling of the lineup in October smacked of desperation, but passivity would have been just as unpopular, and unlikely to alter the outcome.

Oakland Athletics

2012: ANIMAL HOUSE

Aside from Peter Brand's computer, everyone had the A's projected for the bottom half of the AL West standings, but a season-long frat party re-ignited the baseball fever that had been dormant in the east bay for the past half-dozen years. The A's went 33-13 down the stretch, culminated by a three-game sweep of the Rangers to steal the division crown on the final day of the season, but the modern-day nightmare of playoff disappointments returned when Oakland ran into the brick wall of Justin Verlander in Game Five of the ALDS.

ATHLETICS PROSPECTUS

2012 W-L: 94-68, 1st in AL West

Pythag	.568	6th	DER	.721	3rd
RS/G	4.40	14th	B-Age	27.7	8th
RA/G	3.79	6th	P-Age	27.7	10th
TAv	.266	8th	Salary	$54.0	29th
BRR	1.3	14th	M$/MW	$0.89	1st
TAv-P	.256	10th	DL Days	1209	8th
FIP	3.84	10th	DL WARP	4.1	12th

Three-Year Park Factors	
Overall	**95**
HR/RH	**87**
HR/LH	**101**
AVG/RH	**96**
AVG/LH	**100**

O.co Coliseum (1968)
Att. % of Capacity: 59.1% (22nd)
Dim. 330, 362, 400, 362, 330

Oakland's park is tough for hitters, but last year A's lefties outhomered opposing lefties 46-21 at home.

The A's relied on a familiar blend of pitching, patience, and power in their emergence from baseball's second division. The rotation was anchored by freshmen, with more than half of their games started by rookies in 2012. Offseason trades paid immediate dividends, with 60 starts coming from new arrivals Tommy Milone and Jarrod Parker. Those starts combined with the relief work of Ryan Cook produced almost 50 VORP for less than $1.5 million. Bolstered by fielders who ranked third in the major leagues in Defensive Efficiency, the young arms of Oakland posted the second-best ERA in the American League.

The Athletics' batters established a new AL record for strikeouts, with a top-tier walk rate that resulted from seeing the most pitches per plate appearance in baseball, an ode to the take-and-rake philosophy that personified the great Oakland lineups of the past. Power returned to the Coliseum after a four-year run of bottom-feeding the league home-run ranks, and, despite the departure of 2011 home-run leader Josh Willingham, the A's returned to their fence-clearing roots with 195 bombs, led by newcomers Josh Reddick and Yoenis Cespedes. The team took advantage of strategic platooning to maximize the output of their supporting cast, but the greatest weakness was a low batting average that was fueled by excessive strikeouts and the highest fly-ball frequency in the majors.

2013: NO COUNTRY FOR OLD MEN

Despite the division crown, the A's will enter the season as the middle child in the reformatted AL West. They lack the affluence and star-power of the Angels or Rangers, but take note that the Athletics' 2012 run differential was right in line with the powerhouse clubs in the division, and most of Oakland's young roster is still riding the chair lift up the performance curve.

Chris Young is new in Oaktown and the outfield is locked and loaded, though the associated loss of Cliff Pennington weakens an infield that has already been the Achilles heel of the team, where the shortstop position has been a revolving door of under-performance. The stability of Oakland's lineup is strongly dependent on the right side of the dirt, where youngsters Jemile Weeks and Chris Carter have the upside to hit in the top half of a major-league lineup, though each player's maddening inconsistencies at the plate have already resulted in return trips to Sacramento. Scott Sizemore will be ready to seize the second-base job if Weeks falters in the spring, but the wild card is former first-rounder Grant Green, an ultimate tweener whose bat profiles light at a corner but strong up the middle, and whose 2012 résumé includes 10 or more games spent at five different positions.

The pitching depth will allow the A's to cover for potential losses incurred due to injury or trade. The staff lacks a true ace, but might have a half-dozen guys who'd fit comfortably in the middle of a contender's rotation, with enough in-house options to stoke the competitive fires of the incumbents and support the safe development of their young pitchers' workloads. Oakland might start the season as an 80-to-85-win team on paper, but management's approach to the season is dynamic, and if the first third of the schedule presents an opportunity for contention, Billy Beane and Co. will spend the summer addressing the needs to make another run.

STATE OF THE ORGANIZATION: MONEYBALL . . . CONTINUED

The cross-bay Giants are blocking the driveway to San Jose, and with nothing having changed in the four years since Bud Selig appointed his special task force to catalyze the situation, A's owner Lew Wolff might reconsider the organization's efforts to secure a new stadium within its current zip code. Local fans have grown weary of the pattern of parting with the best players when costs become prohibitive, a trend that extends throughout the franchise's history, from Jimmie Foxx and Lefty Grove to Reggie Jackson and Mark McGwire, and which recently has been extended to players who are still years from free agency. Fans don't buy the jersey of a favorite A's player, they rent it.

The Oakland franchise is driven by financial efficiency, and the philosophy that once refused to tie half the payroll to Jason Giambi's bat is still intact, and possibly bolstered by the disastrous results of its long-term investment in Eric Chavez. The move for Cespedes was a tangent to that strategy, and the A's previous pursuit of Aroldis Chapman suggests that they have an inside track on scouting the Cuban market. In the effort to curb the team's injury-checkered history, the A's appear to have devised a development plan that emphasizes mechanical efficiency for pitchers, and they have displayed an affinity for identifying pitchers from other organizations that fit into their system with minimal transitional adjustment, further fueling the player-development machine. Beane is active on the trade front, and a savvy negotiator can be deadly when loaded with a stockpile of arms.

First-round shortstop Addison Russell had an explosive debut, helping to justify Oakland's decision to make him its first high-school selection in the top round of the draft since the Jeremy Bonderman pick that sent chairs flying back in 2002. A string of 75-80-win seasons has kept the Athletics outside the draft's single-digit picks, challenging the coaching staff to overcome a deficiency of impact bats in the system, with much riding on 2010 first-rounder Michael Choice. With only one guaranteed year remaining on Young's contract, his Oakland future likely hinges on the ability of Choice to be ready for the majors by late 2013—and that'll be a challenge with the only club that still shares grass with an NFL team: During the last third of the season, Raiders games make the Coliseum outfield look like Carl Spackler is exterminating gophers.

HITTERS

Daric Barton **1B**
Born: **8/16/1985** Age: **27**
Bats: **L** Throws: **R** Height: **6' 1"**
Weight: **205** Breakout: **2%**
Improve: **44%** Collapse: **3%**
Attrition: **5%** MLB: **99%**
Comparables:
Mark Grace,Terry Crowley,Mike Hargrove

YEAR	TEAM	LVL	AGE	PA	R	2B	3B	HR	RBI	BB	SO	SB	CS	AVG_OBP_SLG	TAv	BABIP	BRR	FRAA	WARP
2010	OAK	MLB	24	686	79	33	5	10	57	110	102	7	3	.273/.393/.405	.302	.316	2.1	1B(157): 3.6	4.4
2011	SAC	AAA	25	75	10	2	0	0	4	14	16	0	0	.197/.347/.230	.228	.267	0	--	0.0
2011	OAK	MLB	25	280	27	13	0	0	21	39	47	2	1	.212/.325/.267	.235	.260	1.6	1B(65): 2.2	-0.3
2012	SAC	AAA	26	336	49	14	3	8	35	66	53	7	1	.255/.411/.425	.302	.286	1.5	1B(22): -1.4, 3B(1): -0.0	0.3
2012	OAK	MLB	26	136	8	7	0	1	6	22	32	1	0	.204/.338/.292	.247	.275	0	1B(43): -0.8	-0.2
2013	*OAK*	*MLB*	*27*	*250*	*30*	*11*	*1*	*4*	*22*	*36*	*43*	*2*	*1*	*.238/.352/.364*	*.266*	*.276*	*-0.1*	*1B -2*	*0.2*

Barton is the lone remnant from the 2004 trade that sent Mark Mulder to St. Louis, the move that produced the baseball-transaction equivalent of "Six Degrees of Kevin Bacon." His trademark patience is impressive, particularly since his light bat offers little incentive for big-league pitchers to avoid the strike zone. Barton's career Isolated Power is just .122, a mark that leaves much to be desired from the power-saturated demands of the cold corner. The 27-year old Barton is only two years removed from a team-leading WARP total, so there could still be some gas left in his player-development tank, but the gap between who he is and who he could be is shrinking fast.

Chris Carter **1B**
Born: **12/18/1986** Age: **26**
Bats: **R** Throws: **R** Height: **6' 5"**
Weight: **245** Breakout: **1%**
Improve: **44%** Collapse: **3%**
Attrition: **11%** MLB: **99%**
Comparables:
Jonny Gomes,Boog Powell,Erubiel Durazo

YEAR	TEAM	LVL	AGE	PA	R	2B	3B	HR	RBI	BB	SO	SB	CS	AVG_OBP_SLG	TAv	BABIP	BRR	FRAA	WARP
2010	SAC	AAA	23	551	92	29	2	31	94	73	138	1	1	.258/.368/.529	.303	.301	0.2	1B(96): -7.3, LF(23): 1.2	2.3
2010	OAK	MLB	23	78	8	1	0	3	7	7	21	1	0	.186/.256/.329	.227	.213	-0.8	LF(22): -1.2	-0.3
2011	SAC	AAA	24	344	55	18	2	18	72	42	85	5	1	.274/.366/.530	.303	.321	0	--	0.0
2011	OAK	MLB	24	46	2	0	0	0	0	2	20	0	0	.136/.174/.136	.117	.250	-0.1	1B(11): -0.3	-0.7
2012	SAC	AAA	25	324	48	19	1	12	53	38	74	5	1	.279/.367/.486	.278	.332	0.6	1B(14): -0.8	0.1
2012	OAK	MLB	25	260	38	12	0	16	39	39	83	0	0	.239/.350/.514	.317	.295	-1.3	1B(55): 0.5	1.4
2013	*OAK*	*MLB*	*26*	*252*	*31*	*10*	*1*	*12*	*36*	*28*	*74*	*1*	*0*	*.227/.317/.435*	*.273*	*.279*	*-0.3*	*1B -6, LF -0*	*0.0*

Carter is a living testament to the theory of the hot hand and streaky performance, alternating bouts of complete inadequacy with torrid stretches when his bat carries the offense. The roller-coaster ride began with a 2010 debut that saw him go hitless in his first 33 at-bats, stirring up Dan Johnson nightmares for the Oakland faithful; another big plummet was 2011's pitcher-esque 310 OPS over 46 plate appearances. In 2012 he finally delivered on his fence-clearing potential with a summer hot flash before disaster struck down the stretch and he collected splinters during the push to the playoffs. He has the upside to be the best right-handed masher to man first base in Oakland since Mark McGwire, but Carter could just as easily find himself back in Sacramento if he continues the Jekyll-and-Hyde act at the plate.

Yoenis Cespedes **OF**

Born: **10/18/1985** Age: **27**
Bats: **R** Throws: **R** Height: **5' 11"**
Weight: **200** Breakout: **2%**
Improve: **55%** Collapse: **7%**
Attrition: **7%** MLB: **99%**

Comparables:
Chris Heisey,Wes Covington,Ryan Braun

YEAR	TEAM	LVL	AGE	PA	R	2B	3B	HR	RBI	BB	SO	SB	CS	AVG_OBP_SLG	TAv	BABIP	BRR	FRAA	WARP
2012	OAK	MLB	26	540	70	25	5	23	82	43	102	16	4	.292/.356/.505	.322	.326	-0.2	LF(56): -1.3, CF(48): -0.4	4.3
2013	*OAK*	*MLB*	*27*	*449*	*59*	*19*	*3*	*20*	*64*	*30*	*84*	*11*	*3*	*.275/.329/.481*	*.293*	*.299*	*0.8*	*LF 0, CF 0*	*2.9*

Cespedes was an online celebrity before he played a game in Oakland, thanks to a low-budget promotional video that went Gangnam-style viral. There was no question about his athleticism, with a power-speed combination that invoked the previously unmentionable comp of Bo Jackson, but there was plenty of doubt surrounding Cespedes's skill level. Most thought he would need some minor-league seasoning, but Cespedes broke camp with the team and never looked back. A hand injury shelved him in May, but he broke loose upon his return in June and saved his greatest power display for the season's final month. In a rookie season that was dripping with upside, flashing elite potential, Cespedes received down-ballot recognition for the AL MVP Award. As he enters his prime, a fan-base that is dying for a new stadium will be dreaming of vaulted ceilings in the House that Yoenis Built.

Michael Choice **CF**

Born: **11/10/1989** Age: **23**
Bats: **R** Throws: **R** Height: **6' 1"**
Weight: **215** Breakout: **2%**
Improve: **62%** Collapse: **5%**
Attrition: **6%** MLB: **94%**

Comparables:
Mel Hall,Ruppert Jones,Andruw Jones

YEAR	TEAM	LVL	AGE	PA	R	2B	3B	HR	RBI	BB	SO	SB	CS	AVG_OBP_SLG	TAv	BABIP	BRR	FRAA	WARP
2010	VAN	A-	20	121	20	10	2	7	26	15	43	6	1	.284/.392/.627	.354	.423	-1.7	CF(29): 0.1	1.3
2011	STO	A+	21	542	79	28	1	30	82	61	134	9	5	.285/.376/.542	.331	.336	0.2	CF(57): 4.8	3.1
2012	MID	AA	22	402	59	15	2	10	58	33	88	5	1	.287/.356/.423	.306	.352	0.6	CF(30): -1.3	0.7
2013	*OAK*	*MLB*	*23*	*250*	*27*	*10*	*1*	*9*	*31*	*17*	*70*	*2*	*1*	*.234/.292/.400*	*.252*	*.292*	*-0.1*	*CF -2, RF 0*	*0.3*

After a torrid 2011 campaign that culminated with his thrashing of the Arizona Fall League, Choice entered 2012 rated as the top bat in the system. The former top-10 pick with game-ready power was on the fast track to Oakland, aiming to make an impact as soon as 2013. Then his power mysteriously disappeared somewhere in Midland, and just when Choice started to right the ship midsummer, a fractured hand shelved him for the last six weeks of the minor-league season. It was his first professional encounter with adversity, and how he responds to disappointment could determine whether he can be the Choice of a new generation of Athletics baseball.

Coco Crisp **CF**

Born: **11/1/1979** Age: **33**
Bats: **B** Throws: **R** Height: **5' 11"**
Weight: **185** Breakout: **1%**
Improve: **30%** Collapse: **9%**
Attrition: **15%** MLB: **92%**

Comparables:
Reed Johnson,Robin Yount,Johnny Damon

YEAR	TEAM	LVL	AGE	PA	R	2B	3B	HR	RBI	BB	SO	SB	CS	AVG_OBP_SLG	TAv	BABIP	BRR	FRAA	WARP
2010	OAK	MLB	30	328	51	14	4	8	38	30	49	32	3	.279/.342/.438	.293	.307	5.7	CF(73): 2.1	2.9
2011	OAK	MLB	31	583	69	27	5	8	54	41	65	49	9	.264/.314/.379	.263	.284	4.3	CF(133): 6.9	2.4
2012	OAK	MLB	32	508	68	25	7	11	46	45	64	39	4	.259/.325/.418	.273	.280	3.4	CF(97): 2.6, LF(16): -0.8	2.0
2013	*OAK*	*MLB*	*33*	*492*	*68*	*21*	*5*	*8*	*40*	*41*	*68*	*38*	*6*	*.257/.319/.385*	*.258*	*.280*	*5.5*	*CF 0, LF 0*	*2.0*

Crisp was a lightning rod of intrigue in 2012. He battled a litany of medical ailments throughout the year, missing time for everything from inner-ear infections to pink eye, but Coco's presence was felt even when he was absent from the lineup. He was the instigator of the playful nostalgia of a B-rate '80s flick that made the "Bernie Lean" a fan craze and hip-hop rallying cry for an Athletics team that rose from the dead to contend. Crisp has more pop than the stereotypical speed demon and has hit particularly well at the Coliseum during his career. He has helped to re-brand a team that was perceived as reluctant on the basepaths, with a 90 percent success rate on stolen-base attempts that makes him worthy of the green light.

Josh Donaldson **3B**

Born: **12/8/1985** Age: **27**
Bats: **R** Throws: **R** Height: **6' 1"**
Weight: **220** Breakout: **8%**
Improve: **42%** Collapse: **3%**
Attrition: **7%** MLB: **89%**

Comparables:
Chase Headley,Eric Chavez,Kevin Mitchell

YEAR	TEAM	LVL	AGE	PA	R	2B	3B	HR	RBI	BB	SO	SB	CS	AVG_OBP_SLG	TAv	BABIP	BRR	FRAA	WARP
2010	SAC	AAA	24	348	52	14	1	18	67	45	79	3	1	.238/.343/.476	.260	.264	-3.3	C(67): 1.2, 3B(8): -0.0	1.5
2010	OAK	MLB	24	34	1	1	0	1	4	2	12	0	0	.156/.206/.281	.176	.211	0.1	C(7): -0.1, 1B(2): -0.0	-0.1
2011	SAC	AAA	25	503	79	28	0	17	70	51	100	13	4	.261/.344/.439	.272	.301	0	--	0.0
2012	SAC	AAA	26	234	38	12	2	13	45	23	34	5	2	.335/.402/.598	.379	.350	-0.1	C(9): 0.2, 3B(3): -0.7	1.1
2012	OAK	MLB	26	294	34	16	0	9	33	14	61	4	1	.241/.289/.398	.258	.278	0.6	3B(71): 5.5, C(3): -0.0	1.4
2013	*OAK*	*MLB*	*27*	*253*	*29*	*11*	*1*	*10*	*33*	*19*	*56*	*2*	*1*	*.243/.304/.424*	*.266*	*.278*	*-0.1*	*3B 0, C -0*	*0.9*

Donaldson made the transition to the hot corner from behind the plate with surprising ease, displaying a penchant for getting his uniform dirty on diving stops down the line, and he was not shy about cutting off Oakland shortstops on shots in the hole. The glove work helped to cover for a bat that went quiet in the majors despite his laying waste to Triple-A pitching, but the A's may have found an internal answer to the third-base conundrum if Donaldson's skills at the plate and in the field can coalesce in the bigs. He has at least earned an extended opportunity to prove that his bat can stick, in which case the A's would reap some late value on the trade that sent Rich Harden to the Cubs in the summer of '08.

Grant Green **UT**

Born: **9/27/1987** Age: **25**
Bats: **R** Throws: **R** Height: **6' 4"**
Weight: **180** Breakout: **8%**
Improve: **52%** Collapse: **0%**
Attrition: **10%** MLB: **95%**

Comparables:
Jeff Stone,Delmon Young,Darryl Motley

YEAR	TEAM	LVL	AGE	PA	R	2B	3B	HR	RBI	BB	SO	SB	CS	AVG_OBP_SLG	TAv	BABIP	BRR	FRAA	WARP
2010	STO	A+	22	606	107	39	6	20	87	38	117	9	5	.318/.367/.520	.304	.372	2.1	SS(116): -13.1, 2B(1): -0.0	3.8
2011	MID	AA	23	587	76	33	1	9	62	39	119	6	8	.291/.343/.408	.264	.355	0	--	0.0
2012	SAC	AAA	24	562	73	28	6	15	75	33	75	13	9	.296/.338/.458	.283	.320	1.8	LF(20): 1.6, CF(11): -0.2	1.1
2013	*OAK*	*MLB*	*25*	*250*	*27*	*11*	*2*	*6*	*24*	*10*	*50*	*3*	*1*	*.250/.282/.383*	*.245*	*.291*	*-0.2*	*SS -1, LF 0*	*0.3*

Green was a human Swiss Army knife for the River Cats, playing 10 or more games at five positions, including second, third, short, left and center field (basically everything left of the 3.5 hole). Green offers the contact skills that were sorely lacking from the Oakland lineup last season, and while his positional versatility opens up playing-time opportunities, one can imagine how asking a rookie to play multiple defensive positions could distract from the development of a player who is still learning how to realize his potential at the plate. On the other hand, claiming the super-utility role might be Green's clearest path to playing time in Bob Melvin's lineup.

Miles Head **3B**

Born: **5/2/1991** Age: **22**
Bats: **R** Throws: **R** Height: **6' 1"**
Weight: **215** Breakout: **3%**
Improve: **51%** Collapse: **3%**
Attrition: **12%** MLB: **98%**

Comparables:
Travis Fryman,Brett Lawrie,Roy Howell

YEAR	TEAM	LVL	AGE	PA	R	2B	3B	HR	RBI	BB	SO	SB	CS	AVG_OBP_SLG	TAv	BABIP	BRR	FRAA	WARP
2010	LOW	A-	19	272	21	16	2	1	35	30	36	1	1	.240/.337/.341	.255	.280	-0.6	1B(64): -1.0	-0.1
2011	GRN	A	20	298	61	25	1	15	53	30	53	4	2	.338/.409/.612	.342	.376	0	--	0.0
2011	SLM	A+	20	259	27	12	1	7	29	20	56	0	2	.254/.328/.405	.256	.306	0	--	0.0
2012	STO	A+	21	294	57	23	6	18	56	23	55	3	0	.382/.433/.715	.392	.431	-0.5	3B(41): -1.2, 1B(6): 0.9	3.5
2012	MID	AA	21	234	25	9	2	5	28	16	75	0	1	.272/.338/.404	.296	.398	-0.4	3B(18): -2.1, 1B(1): -0.0	0.1
2013	*OAK*	*MLB*	*22*	*250*	*23*	*10*	*2*	*6*	*28*	*14*	*66*	*0*	*0*	*.234/.282/.374*	*.241*	*.295*	*-0.2*	*3B 0, 1B -2*	*-0.2*

Initially considered an afterthought in the trade that sent Andrew Bailey to the Red Sox, Head took a giant leap forward in his development last season that triggered a similar vault to his prospect status. He made a mockery of Stockton for the first half of the minor-league season but then took his lumps when promoted to Double-A, a repeat of the pattern that he exhibited in his first jump to the California League. The pattern suggests that Head might need extra time to adjust to new levels of competition, a trend that could slow his development pace at the higher levels, but the 21-year old has time on his side.

Brandon Inge **3B**

Born: **5/19/1977** Age: **36**
Bats: **R** Throws: **R** Height: **6' 0"**
Weight: **190** Breakout: **1%**
Improve: **23%** Collapse: **16%**
Attrition: **28%** MLB: **75%**

Comparables:
Davey Johnson,Jose Valentin,Robin Ventura

YEAR	TEAM	LVL	AGE	PA	R	2B	3B	HR	RBI	BB	SO	SB	CS	AVG_OBP_SLG	TAv	BABIP	BRR	FRAA	WARP
2010	DET	MLB	33	580	47	28	5	13	70	54	134	4	3	.247/.321/.397	.258	.305	-4.1	3B(144): 9.3	2.2
2011	TOL	AAA	34	126	18	4	0	7	19	17	30	0	0	.287/.389/.519	.285	.338	-1	3B(17): 2.9	0.6
2011	DET	MLB	34	303	29	10	2	3	23	24	74	1	1	.197/.265/.283	.201	.256	0.4	3B(99): 9.2	-0.3
2012	DET	MLB	35	20	2	1	0	1	2	0	6	0	0	.100/.100/.300	.134	.077	0.1	2B(6): 0.3, 3B(2): 0.0	-0.1
2012	OAK	MLB	35	311	31	13	0	11	52	24	85	0	1	.226/.286/.389	.244	.279	0.7	3B(74): 3.1	0.6
2013	*OAK*	*MLB*	*36*	*323*	*32*	*11*	*1*	*8*	*32*	*28*	*86*	*1*	*1*	*.210/.287/.343*	*.234*	*.266*	*-0.5*	*3B -1, 2B -0*	*-0.3*

The offensive demands of third basemen are dwindling, as a position that was once considered an offensive juggernaut commensurate with the other corners has been heavily downgraded in recent years, which explains how a hitless wonder with a glove like Inge's can carve out a 12-year career in the majors. The voters for the Gold Glove award felt that Inge's defensive exploits merited serious consideration for the 2012 hardware despite his playing only half a season at the position, but he could have been Brooks Robinson on defense and his anemic offense would have kept his WARP in the red.

George Kottaras **C**

Born: **5/16/1983** Age: **30**
Bats: **L** Throws: **R** Height: **6' 1"**
Weight: **190** Breakout: **2%**
Improve: **49%** Collapse: **7%**
Attrition: **10%** MLB: **92%**

Comparables:
John Baker,Chris Snyder,Johnny Romano

YEAR	TEAM	LVL	AGE	PA	R	2B	3B	HR	RBI	BB	SO	SB	CS	AVG_OBP_SLG	TAv	BABIP	BRR	FRAA	WARP
2010	MIL	MLB	27	250	24	12	1	9	26	33	44	2	0	.203/.305/.396	.261	.209	-4.6	C(61): -0.9, 1B(2): -0.0	0.2
2011	NAS	AAA	28	118	19	8	1	4	21	16	29	0	1	.343/.432/.559	.314	.449	0	C(11): 0.4	0.4
2011	MIL	MLB	28	123	15	6	1	5	17	10	26	0	1	.252/.311/.459	.262	.284	0	C(36): 0.0	0.4
2012	MIL	MLB	29	116	10	4	0	3	12	29	24	0	0	.209/.409/.360	.281	.254	-0.3	C(27): -0.6, 1B(6): -0.1	0.4
2012	OAK	MLB	29	93	10	2	1	6	19	8	24	0	0	.212/.280/.471	.273	.218	-0.5	C(27): 0.6	0.3
2013	*OAK*	*MLB*	*30*	*250*	*28*	*11*	*1*	*8*	*28*	*31*	*56*	*1*	*0*	*.222/.319/.388*	*.261*	*.259*	*-0.3*	*C -0, 1B -0*	*1.1*

Acquired from the Brewers late in the summer, Kottaras provided a buffer for catcher-of-the-future Derek Norris in the wake of the Kurt Suzuki trade. Kottaras's left-handed bat will keep him employed as long as he can handle the defensive duties at catcher, and his career walk rate of 13 percent will endear him to saber-savvy ballclubs even as his contact ability deteriorates. His batting average has already played a game of chicken with the Mendoza line. Kottaras took a free pass in more than one-fourth of his Milwaukee plate appearances in 2012, and the sudden disappearance of walks upon arriving in Oakland was a testament to the fluctuations that are inherent with small sample sizes.

Jefry Marte **3B**

Born: **6/21/1991** Age: **22**
Bats: **R** Throws: **R** Height: **6' 2"**
Weight: **187** Breakout: **6%**
Improve: **58%** Collapse: **3%**
Attrition: **9%** MLB: **98%**

Comparables:
Bob Bailey, Dan Driessen, Glenn Hoffman

YEAR	TEAM	LVL	AGE	PA	R	2B	3B	HR	RBI	BB	SO	SB	CS	AVG_OBP_SLG	TAv	BABIP	BRR	FRAA	WARP
2010	SAV	A	19	366	40	19	4	6	44	30	65	4	5	.264/.335/.401	.285	.314	0.3	3B(80): 1.0	1.9
2011	SLU	A+	20	537	56	22	2	7	55	41	86	14	2	.248/.313/.346	.243	.285	-0.8	3B(53): -1.0	-0.2
2012	BIN	AA	21	513	61	20	3	9	58	43	76	9	5	.251/.322/.366	.220	.282	-0.4	3B(84): -5.7, 1B(5): -0.3	-1.6
2013	*OAK*	*MLB*	*22*	*250*	*22*	*10*	*1*	*4*	*23*	*15*	*51*	*3*	*1*	*.220/.269/.323*	*.224*	*.262*	*0*	*3B -0, 1B 0*	*-0.4*

Marte was once a highly regarded prospect and is now merely regarded. Warily. The Mets have worked with him on his plate discipline, but the effects of such teaching are nearly invisible in his stat line: Walk rate and isolated power aren't improving, and while he is striking out less, his batting average hasn't changed because of a decline in BABIP. Factor in poor defense at third (though his error rate is improving) and it's fair to wonder, no matter how young Marte is, how exactly he's going to conjure up a major-league career. Shipped to Oakland in the offseason, Marte is out from under the shadow of David Wright and now has a clearer path to a future job at the hot corner, though his odds of landing such a gig remain slim.

Scott Moore **UT**

Born: **11/17/1983** Age: **29**
Bats: **L** Throws: **R** Height: **6' 3"**
Weight: **195** Breakout: **2%**
Improve: **38%** Collapse: **3%**
Attrition: **10%** MLB: **91%**

Comparables:
Jim Ray Hart, Bill Melton, Rico Petrocelli

YEAR	TEAM	LVL	AGE	PA	R	2B	3B	HR	RBI	BB	SO	SB	CS	AVG_OBP_SLG	TAv	BABIP	BRR	FRAA	WARP
2010	NOR	AAA	26	253	34	9	1	11	45	21	47	2	3	.280/.348/.476	.284	.310	-1.5	3B(34): -4.0, 2B(14): -0.6	0.6
2010	BAL	MLB	26	96	8	2	0	3	10	8	19	3	0	.209/.274/.337	.224	.231	0.3	2B(22): -0.4, 1B(10): 0.2	-0.2
2011	IOW	AAA	27	425	60	19	4	9	53	48	79	3	1	.295/.380/.444	.297	.348	0.5	1B(16): -0.2, 3B(11): -1.6	0.8
2012	OKL	AAA	28	291	47	26	1	10	54	35	51	3	3	.318/.410/.555	.408	.362	0.8	3B(10): -0.5, LF(3): -0.7	1.1
2012	HOU	MLB	28	228	23	11	0	9	26	16	56	0	1	.259/.330/.448	.269	.309	-1.6	3B(28): -1.7, 1B(19): -0.1	0.2
2013	*OAK*	*MLB*	*29*	*250*	*27*	*11*	*1*	*8*	*30*	*20*	*57*	*2*	*1*	*.239/.309/.402*	*.259*	*.282*	*-0.4*	*3B -1, 1B -0*	*0.4*

As a high-schooler, Moore elicited comparisons to Chipper Jones. After he was taken eighth overall in 2002, he quickly moved from his high-school position (shortstop) to Chipper's. He spent three seasons in the Cubs farm system, successful but stuck behind Aramis Ramirez. After the 2007 season he was traded for Steve Trachsel. His 2008–11 seasons were forgettable, slipping him from prospect to journeyman, but he seemed to remember how to hit in Oklahoma last year, forcing the Astros to promote him. He'll never be mistaken for Mr. Jones again, but third basemen who bat left-handed are a rarity. Moore has learned to wear many gloves in his travels and showed enough batting chops last year to hold a spot on the big-league bench. In 2013 he'll try to do the same in Oakland.

Brandon Moss **UT**

Born: **9/16/1983** Age: **29**
Bats: **L** Throws: **R** Height: **6' 1"**
Weight: **210** Breakout: **5%**
Improve: **45%** Collapse: **8%**
Attrition: **17%** MLB: **85%**

Comparables:
Adam LaRoche, Mike Jacobs, Ryan Klesko

YEAR	TEAM	LVL	AGE	PA	R	2B	3B	HR	RBI	BB	SO	SB	CS	AVG_OBP_SLG	TAv	BABIP	BRR	FRAA	WARP
2010	IND	AAA	26	556	73	32	2	22	96	42	118	12	7	.266/.329/.470	.262	.305	-2.9	RF(77): -10.4, LF(17): 1.0	-0.3
2010	PIT	MLB	26	27	2	1	0	0	2	1	6	0	0	.154/.185/.192	.115	.200	-0.6	RF(5): -0.2, LF(2): -0.0	-0.4
2011	LEH	AAA	27	506	66	31	1	23	80	62	127	4	6	.275/.368/.509	.299	.334	0	--	0.0
2011	PHI	MLB	27	6	0	0	0	0	0	0	2	0	0	.000/.000/.000	.054	.000	0	RF(1): 0.1	-0.2
2012	SAC	AAA	28	224	32	11	1	15	33	22	40	4	0	.286/.371/.582	.364	.289	-0.5	LF(4): -0.3, RF(3): 0.2	0.6
2012	OAK	MLB	28	296	48	18	0	21	52	26	90	1	1	.291/.358/.596	.336	.359	-0.3	1B(55): -3.0, RF(13): 0.2	2.1
2013	*OAK*	*MLB*	*29*	*254*	*29*	*11*	*1*	*9*	*33*	*20*	*64*	*2*	*1*	*.240/.304/.425*	*.263*	*.288*	*-0.2*	*1B -1, RF 0*	*0.4*

Meet the premier benefactor from Melvin's penchant for the platoon. The left-handed-hitting Moss cracked a 1000 OPS against right-handed pitchers, and he was strategically employed to perfection, carrying the platoon advantage in 79 percent of his plate appearances. The minor-league veteran has slugged Triple-A pitching for the past five years, and he started the 2012 season with 15 bombs in his first two months with Sacramento, so his Ruthian ratio of a homer every 12.6 at-bats in the majors was not completely out of left field. Moss may have been a dormant volcano who suddenly exploded in 2012, but there is no telling when or if Mount Moss will erupt again.

Hiroyuki Nakajima SS

Born: **7/31/1982** Age: **30**
Bats: **R** Throws: **R** Height: **5' 11"**
Weight: **185** Breakout: **--%**
Improve: **--%** Collapse: **--%**
Attrition: **--%** MLB: **--%**

Comparables:
--

YEAR	TEAM	LVL	AGE	PA	R	2B	3B	HR	RBI	BB	SO	SB	CS	AVG_OBP_SLG	TAv	BABIP	BRR	FRAA	WARP
2010	SEI	NPB	27	579	80	33	3	20	93	52	97	15	5	.314/.385/.511	—	—	—	—	—
2011	SEI	NPB	28	633	82	27	1	16	100	44	93	21	2	.297/.354/.433	—	—	—	—	—
2012	SEI	NPB	29	567	69	29	1	13	74	52	76	7	6	.311/.382/.451	—	—	—	—	—

Nakajima went through Nippon Professional Baseball's posting system a year ago, but failed to reach an agreement with the New York Yankees and returned to Japan for the 2012 season. His second attempt to play stateside was more successful, as the international free agent no longer required a posting fee to secure his services, and the A's committed $6.5 million for Nakajima to play shortstop in Oakland for the next two seasons. The multimillion-dollar question is whether the bat will translate to this side of the Pacific, thrilling the Oakland crowds with the swagger of his bat-flip on home runs, or if he will follow in the offensively empty footsteps of fellow NPB middle-infielders Kaz Matsui and Tsuyoshi Nishioka.

Derek Norris C

Born: **2/14/1989** Age: **24**
Bats: **R** Throws: **R** Height: **6' 1"**
Weight: **210** Breakout: **5%**
Improve: **30%** Collapse: **15%**
Attrition: **19%** MLB: **95%**

Comparables:
Chris Iannetta,Charles Johnson,Darrell Porter

YEAR	TEAM	LVL	AGE	PA	R	2B	3B	HR	RBI	BB	SO	SB	CS	AVG_OBP_SLG	TAv	BABIP	BRR	FRAA	WARP
2010	POT	A+	21	399	67	19	0	12	49	89	94	6	3	.235/.423/.419	.309	.302	-0.8	C(75): 1.6	4.3
2011	HAR	AA	22	423	75	17	1	20	46	77	117	13	4	.210/.367/.446	.300	.251	1.2	C(70): 0.8	3.1
2012	SAC	AAA	23	246	39	14	2	9	38	21	41	5	1	.271/.329/.477	.265	.287	-0.7	C(17): -0.5	0.3
2012	OAK	MLB	23	232	19	8	1	7	34	21	66	5	1	.201/.276/.349	.231	.255	0	C(58): 0.0	-0.2
2013	*OAK*	*MLB*	*24*	*250*	*29*	*9*	*1*	*8*	*29*	*32*	*67*	*4*	*1*	*.213/.317/.376*	*.260*	*.265*	*0.1*	*C -0*	*1.1*

The 23-year-old rookie announced his presence with authority, nailing a walk-off, three-run home run against the cross-bay Giants in just his third major-league game, and Norris quickly captured the affection of the green-collar Oakland fans with his various permutations of facial-hair. Norris has followed a very deliberate path to the majors, hitting every rung on the minor-league ladder and ascending exactly one level per season for six consecutive years. The 2012 season was the first of his career in which Norris played his home games in more than one city, and the A's will give him every opportunity to set up a permanent residence in the Bay Area.

Matthew Olson 1B

Born: **3/29/1994** Age: **19**
Bats: **L** Throws: **R** Height: **6' 5"**
Weight: **236** Breakout: **0%**
Improve: **63%** Collapse: **37%**
Attrition: **37%** MLB: **100%**

Comparables:
Robin Yount,Ed Kranepool,Wayne Causey

YEAR	TEAM	LVL	AGE	PA	R	2B	3B	HR	RBI	BB	SO	SB	CS	AVG_OBP_SLG	TAv	BABIP	BRR	FRAA	WARP
2012	ATH	Rk	18	197	29	16	1	8	41	16	46	0	0	.282/.345/.520	.290	.336	1	1B(6): -0.7	0.0
2013	*OAK*	*MLB*	*19*	*250*	*24*	*8*	*1*	*8*	*26*	*13*	*68*	*1*	*0*	*.203/.247/.342*	*.217*	*.246*	*-0.2*	*1B -0*	*-0.1*

Olson was the third high-school position player selected by the A's among the first 50 picks of the draft, and his selection virtually cemented that a remodeled strategy was guiding Oakland's selections on draft day, perhaps influenced by the new rules set forth in the Collective Bargaining Agreement. Olson is a large human whose listed weight of 236 pounds tips the scales more than any other player among the first 60 picks. A two-way player in high school, if he fails to develop as a hitter, there's always the option to follow the Sean Doolittle path from first base to the mound.

Andy Parrino UT

Born: **10/31/1985** Age: **27**
Bats: **B** Throws: **R** Height: **6' 1"**
Weight: **180** Breakout: **2%**
Improve: **43%** Collapse: **15%**
Attrition: **14%** MLB: **92%**

Comparables:
Denis Menke,Dick McAuliffe,Craig Stansberry

YEAR	TEAM	LVL	AGE	PA	R	2B	3B	HR	RBI	BB	SO	SB	CS	AVG_OBP_SLG	TAv	BABIP	BRR	FRAA	WARP
2010	SAN	AA	24	492	70	28	4	11	49	68	115	4	2	.246/.361/.415	.292	.312	1.7	SS(43): -5.7, 2B(26): 2.6	3.1
2011	SAN	AA	25	179	28	7	1	9	32	22	40	3	1	.303/.388/.539	.382	.349	-0.6	SS(23): 0.2, LF(1): -0.0	1.6
2011	TUC	AAA	25	178	26	13	1	3	24	16	25	2	1	.327/.399/.484	.298	.364	0.9	SS(22): 1.3, 2B(13): 0.8	1.2
2011	SDN	MLB	25	55	3	1	0	0	4	9	17	1	0	.182/.327/.205	.251	.286	-0.1	3B(11): 0.7, SS(4): 0.2	0.2
2012	TUC	AAA	26	265	43	23	3	1	32	25	49	6	2	.328/.400/.464	.275	.409	1.1	SS(29): 4.1, 2B(8): -0.3	1.3
2012	SDN	MLB	26	138	9	5	0	1	6	17	35	1	0	.207/.316/.276	.231	.284	-0.4	SS(26): -0.1, 2B(15): -0.5	0.1
2013	*OAK*	*MLB*	*27*	*250*	*26*	*11*	*1*	*4*	*23*	*26*	*63*	*2*	*1*	*.231/.319/.351*	*.248*	*.299*	*-0.1*	*SS 0, 2B 0*	*0.7*

Parrino, the Padres' 26th-round pick in 2007 out of LeMoyne College (Tom Browning, Jim Deshaies), is a middle infielder but has done everything except catch in his six professional seasons. He doesn't make a lot of contact but draws a few walks and knocks a few doubles. If everything breaks right, Parrino could have Geoff Blum's career, minus the awesome hair. The A's picked him up from San Diego in the Tyson Ross deal and quickly proclaimed him "in the mix" for the shortstop job.

Josh Reddick **RF**
Born: **2/19/1987** Age: **26**
Bats: **L** Throws: **R** Height: **6' 3"**
Weight: **180** Breakout: **4%**
Improve: **44%** Collapse: **6%**
Attrition: **10%** MLB: **93%**
Comparables:
Johnny Callison,John Bowker,Steve Pearce

YEAR	TEAM	LVL	AGE	PA	R	2B	3B	HR	RBI	BB	SO	SB	CS	AVG_OBP_SLG	TAv	BABIP	BRR	FRAA	WARP
2010	PAW	AAA	23	481	59	28	4	18	65	25	73	4	7	.266/.305/.466	.271	.283	0.3	CF(88): -2.7, RF(13): -0.6	2.1
2010	BOS	MLB	23	63	5	3	1	1	5	1	15	1	0	.194/.206/.323	.203	.239	0.4	RF(15): -0.0, CF(6): 0.4	-0.2
2011	PAW	AAA	24	231	37	9	1	14	36	33	39	4	1	.230/.333/.508	.265	.207	-0.6	CF(21): -1.6, RF(15): 1.1	0.3
2011	BOS	MLB	24	278	41	18	3	7	28	19	50	1	2	.280/.327/.457	.284	.318	0.6	RF(56): 4.9, LF(21): 1.4	1.7
2012	OAK	MLB	25	673	85	29	5	32	85	55	151	11	1	.242/.305/.463	.277	.269	1.9	RF(136): 3.3, CF(14): 0.6	2.6
2013	*OAK*	*MLB*	*26*	*573*	*64*	*26*	*5*	*21*	*74*	*40*	*120*	*6*	*3*	*.243/.297/.428*	*.264*	*.274*	*0*	*RF 1, CF -0*	*1.7*

Reddick was the main cog in the Bailey trade, and while his counterpart spent the first four months of the season in Boston's infirmary, Reddick was busy establishing himself in the middle of the Oakland lineup. He was the A's top fence-clearing threat, becoming the club's first player to crack 30 homers since 2008, and Reddick continued to build on his patience and pitch-recognition skills. He is evolving the finer elements of his game, and Reddick is on a three-year trend of increasing walk rates and rising levels of pitches per plate appearance. Most impressive was the quality of his defense, which included 15 outfield kills that ranked as the third-highest total in baseball. Despite the laundry list of positives, Reddick ended the season on a sour note when his bat fell down the rabbit hole in early September, where it remained hidden throughout the postseason.

Daniel Robertson **INF**
Born: **3/22/1994** Age: **19**
Bats: **R** Throws: **R** Height: **6' 1"**
Weight: **190** Breakout: **0%**
Improve: **64%** Collapse: **36%**
Attrition: **36%** MLB: **100%**
Comparables:
Ed Kranepool,Wayne Causey,Robin Yount

YEAR	TEAM	LVL	AGE	PA	R	2B	3B	HR	RBI	BB	SO	SB	CS	AVG_OBP_SLG	TAv	BABIP	BRR	FRAA	WARP
2012	ATH	Rk	18	127	25	10	2	4	22	16	15	2	0	.297/.405/.554	.328	.302	0	SS(1): 0.1	0.0
2012	VER	A-	18	104	9	2	0	1	8	7	31	1	1	.181/.238/.234	.146	.258	0.2	SS(14): 0.7, 3B(1): 0.0	-0.5
2013	*OAK*	*MLB*	*19*	*250*	*18*	*7*	*1*	*2*	*18*	*10*	*76*	*5*	*2*	*.181/.216/.247*	*.175*	*.250*	*0.3*	*SS 0, 3B 0*	*-1.0*

It could be a one-year blip, but the selection of Robertson marked just the second time in 34 years that the A's used their top two draft picks on prep players. Though he was listed as a shortstop on draft day, whispers of an impending move to third base indicate that Robertson and 2012 top pick Addison Russell could share the left side of the future Oakland infield if all of the dominoes fall into place. Robertson coasted through the Rookie League before he hit a speed bump in short-season ball, though at his age the performance is less important than the process. Rough stretches can reveal weaknesses to be addressed through coaching, and a player's resolve is tested through adversity and his response to failure.

Adam Rosales **INF**
Born: **5/20/1983** Age: **30**
Bats: **R** Throws: **R** Height: **6' 2"**
Weight: **195** Breakout: **1%**
Improve: **54%** Collapse: **0%**
Attrition: **4%** MLB: **89%**
Comparables:
Dickie Thon,Jay Bell,Carlos Guillen

YEAR	TEAM	LVL	AGE	PA	R	2B	3B	HR	RBI	BB	SO	SB	CS	AVG_OBP_SLG	TAv	BABIP	BRR	FRAA	WARP
2010	OAK	MLB	27	279	31	8	2	7	31	19	65	2	2	.271/.321/.400	.281	.335	0	2B(47): -1.2, SS(14): -0.1	1.4
2011	SAC	AAA	28	164	23	5	1	3	22	13	32	1	1	.265/.323/.374	.247	.313	0	--	0.0
2011	OAK	MLB	28	68	5	0	0	2	8	4	13	0	0	.098/.162/.197	.152	.083	0.2	SS(7): -0.3, 3B(6): -0.6	-0.7
2012	SAC	AAA	29	310	46	21	1	8	47	26	57	4	2	.280/.340/.451	.326	.319	1.2	SS(19): -1.9, 2B(4): 0.8	1.6
2012	OAK	MLB	29	111	12	5	0	2	8	11	24	0	0	.222/.297/.333	.236	.270	-0.8	2B(21): -1.8, SS(11): 0.1	-0.3
2013	*OAK*	*MLB*	*30*	*250*	*25*	*11*	*1*	*5*	*25*	*18*	*51*	*2*	*1*	*.235/.297/.361*	*.247*	*.279*	*-0.2*	*SS -0, 2B -1*	*0.4*

Rosales has been filling the A's' reserve-infielder needs for three seasons, and though he lacks the offensive profile or the defensive chops for full-time work, a system that is startlingly thin at shortstop may press him into an expanded role. His minor-league profile paints the picture of an offensive force in the middle of the diamond, with a career slash line of .286/.358/.477 in more than 2,000 at bats and an OPS in excess of 800 at every level of the minors. At 29, Rosales is essentially the shortstop equivalent of Kila Ka'aihue (who departed for Arizona in November).

Addison Russell **SS**
Born: **1/23/1994** Age: **19**
Bats: **R** Throws: **R** Height: **6' 1"**
Weight: **185** Breakout: **0%**
Improve: **71%** Collapse: **29%**
Attrition: **29%** MLB: **100%**
Comparables:
Ed Kranepool,Wayne Causey,Robin Yount

YEAR	TEAM	LVL	AGE	PA	R	2B	3B	HR	RBI	BB	SO	SB	CS	AVG_OBP_SLG	TAv	BABIP	BRR	FRAA	WARP
2012	ATH	Rk	18	121	29	4	5	6	29	14	23	9	1	.415/.488/.717	.405	.494	3.5	SS(20): -2.9	0.0
2012	BUR	A	18	66	8	4	2	0	9	5	12	5	1	.310/.369/.448	.316	.383	1.6	SS(9): -0.2	0.7
2012	VER	A-	18	57	9	2	2	1	7	4	13	2	0	.340/.386/.509	.357	.436	0.1	SS(9): -0.0	0.5
2013	*OAK*	*MLB*	*19*	*250*	*27*	*8*	*2*	*5*	*21*	*13*	*69*	*5*	*1*	*.216/.259/.330*	*.220*	*.279*	*0.6*	*SS 0*	*0.3*

Russell must have made quite an impression on the Oakland brass, becoming the highest-drafted high-school player by the A's since Eric Chavez was selected number 10 overall in 1998. Russell has the tools to stay at short and eventually fill the club's greatest need on the diamond, and if his introductory performance is any indication, then the young shortstop could be the rare high-school player who moves quickly. He cracked a 1000 OPS in 55 games across three different stops in his professional debut. He has quick hands that will allow him to barrel-up fastballs, but pitch recognition will dictate the pace of his ascent as he faces healthy diets of secondary stuff during his minor-league climb.

Scott Sizemore INF
Born: **1/4/1985** Age: **28**
Bats: **R** Throws: **R** Height: **6' 1"**
Weight: **185** Breakout: **1%**
Improve: **48%** Collapse: **3%**
Attrition: **14%** MLB: **91%**
Comparables:
Jayson Nix,Dave Hollins,Bob Bailey

YEAR	TEAM	LVL	AGE	PA	R	2B	3B	HR	RBI	BB	SO	SB	CS	AVG_OBP_SLG	TAv	BABIP	BRR	FRAA	WARP
2010	TOL	AAA	25	342	49	23	1	9	37	31	77	2	2	.298/.379/.472	.284	.374	-0.3	2B(41): -1.0, 3B(11): 0.5	1.7
2010	DET	MLB	25	163	19	7	0	3	14	15	40	0	0	.224/.296/.336	.227	.287	1.5	2B(40): -1.4, 3B(6): -0.1	-0.3
2011	TOL	AAA	26	92	17	7	1	2	15	12	19	3	1	.408/.495/.605	.383	.518	-0.4	2B(15): -0.9	0.9
2011	DET	MLB	26	74	8	1	0	0	4	10	19	1	1	.222/.329/.238	.240	.318	0.3	2B(17): 1.4	0.1
2011	OAK	MLB	26	355	42	21	1	11	52	43	93	4	2	.249/.345/.433	.292	.322	3.2	3B(91): -7.3, 2B(1): 0.0	1.3
2013	*OAK*	*MLB*	*28*	*250*	*30*	*11*	*1*	*6*	*24*	*26*	*63*	*3*	*1*	*.241/.327/.382*	*.262*	*.305*	*-0.3*	*3B -2, 2B -1*	*0.4*

The A's acquired Sizemore in exchange for David Purcey in May 2011, and after his strong half-season in green-n-gold, the team penciled him in as the 2012 third baseman. But then the baseball gods continued their assault on people named Sizemore. Scott was eliminated from hot-corner consideration before he could see a pitch, suffering a torn ACL while doing infield drills on the first day of spring-training workouts, and he spent the entire year rehabbing from the injury. The A's are now hoping to use him as an option at multiple infield positions, as Sizemore satisfies the organizational fondness for patience with an ability to dial long distance on occasion. His injury recovery will likely dictate his role on the team.

Seth Smith OF
Born: **9/30/1982** Age: **30**
Bats: **L** Throws: **L** Height: **6' 4"**
Weight: **210** Breakout: **1%**
Improve: **50%** Collapse: **1%**
Attrition: **6%** MLB: **96%**
Comparables:
Rico Carty,Billy Williams,Milton Bradley

YEAR	TEAM	LVL	AGE	PA	R	2B	3B	HR	RBI	BB	SO	SB	CS	AVG_OBP_SLG	TAv	BABIP	BRR	FRAA	WARP
2010	COL	MLB	27	398	55	19	5	17	52	35	67	2	1	.246/.314/.469	.262	.256	-0.5	LF(71): 4.8, RF(33): 0.3	1.2
2011	COL	MLB	28	533	67	32	9	15	59	46	93	10	2	.284/.347/.483	.276	.320	2	RF(107): 0.3, LF(25): -0.5	1.0
2012	OAK	MLB	29	441	55	23	2	14	52	50	98	2	2	.240/.333/.420	.284	.285	1.5	LF(57): 2.4, RF(13): -0.5	1.8
2013	*OAK*	*MLB*	*30*	*433*	*49*	*21*	*3*	*13*	*53*	*44*	*84*	*5*	*1*	*.250/.329/.423*	*.275*	*.285*	*0.1*	*RF -1, LF -0*	*1.6*

Smith was employed in a manner that emphasized his strengths, with Melvin using the Moss approach: 82 percent of Smith's plate appearances came against right-handed pitchers. The strategy helped mask Smith's overall decline in his first season away from the thin air of Denver, and though his home-run rate was minimally impacted by the move, he sorely missed the expansive outfield that had gifted him with so many doubles and triples. The incentive to walk is diminished when playing at altitude, and Smith made the necessary adjustments to appease Oakland management by posting his highest walk rate in three years.

Max Stassi C
Born: **3/15/1991** Age: **22**
Bats: **R** Throws: **R** Height: **5' 11"**
Weight: **205** Breakout: **5%**
Improve: **53%** Collapse: **4%**
Attrition: **15%** MLB: **92%**
Comparables:
Rich Gedman,Jerry Grote,Bill Freehan

YEAR	TEAM	LVL	AGE	PA	R	2B	3B	HR	RBI	BB	SO	SB	CS	AVG_OBP_SLG	TAv	BABIP	BRR	FRAA	WARP
2010	KNC	A	19	465	54	21	1	13	51	45	141	3	3	.229/.312/.380	.254	.314	-2.3	C(96): -0.3	1.8
2011	STO	A+	20	139	22	6	0	2	19	16	22	1	1	.231/.331/.331	.288	.268	0.6	--	0.4
2012	STO	A+	21	360	48	18	0	15	45	27	83	3	1	.268/.331/.468	.285	.304	-1.7	C(51): -1.3	0.9
2013	*OAK*	*MLB*	*22*	*250*	*21*	*9*	*1*	*6*	*26*	*15*	*73*	*0*	*0*	*.202/.257/.323*	*.217*	*.264*	*-0.4*	*C -1*	*-0.2*

Stassi looked like a steal when he slipped to the A's in the fourth round of the 2009 draft, but after 155 games of 700 OPS baseball in the low minors, fans began to detect the suspicious scent that kept the other 29 teams from pouncing on the talented backstop. The offensive promise that fueled the hype machine finally began to show itself in 2012, as Stassi had his most potent season in his second tour of the California League. A career-long battle with injuries continued, limiting him to just 84 games split between catcher and DH. Various ailments have restricted him to a mere 66 games behind the dish over the last two years.

Michael Taylor OF
Born: **12/19/1985** Age: **27**
Bats: **R** Throws: **R** Height: **6' 6"**
Weight: **255** Breakout: **2%**
Improve: **34%** Collapse: **8%**
Attrition: **21%** MLB: **84%**
Comparables:
Tom Brunansky,Bobby Kielty,Michael Restovich

YEAR	TEAM	LVL	AGE	PA	R	2B	3B	HR	RBI	BB	SO	SB	CS	AVG_OBP_SLG	TAv	BABIP	BRR	FRAA	WARP
2010	SAC	AAA	24	523	79	26	6	6	78	51	92	16	5	.272/.350/.392	.259	.328	1	RF(98): -3.1, CF(22): -0.8	0.7
2011	SAC	AAA	25	400	51	16	0	16	64	46	80	14	5	.272/.360/.456	.283	.310	0	--	0.0
2011	OAK	MLB	25	35	4	0	0	1	1	5	11	0	0	.200/.314/.300	.268	.278	0.1	RF(8): 0.6, LF(3): -0.1	0.1
2012	SAC	AAA	26	543	81	31	1	12	67	86	105	18	3	.287/.405/.441	.308	.349	4.7	RF(37): -5.7, CF(1): -0.1	0.7
2012	OAK	MLB	26	21	2	1	0	0	0	0	10	0	0	.143/.143/.190	.106	.273	0.4	RF(4): 0.3, LF(2): -0.0	-0.2
2013	*OAK*	*MLB*	*27*	*250*	*25*	*10*	*1*	*4*	*24*	*26*	*57*	*5*	*1*	*.234/.316/.346*	*.250*	*.296*	*0.3*	*RF -1, LF -0*	*0.2*

Taylor has spent enough time in Sacramento to run for office, and though his stagnation has taken the luster off his projection, he has quietly made significant strides at the plate in successive seasons with the River Cats. Something clicked for the massive outfielder, and his walk rate skyrocketed above 15 percent, complemented by a high contact-rate, doubles power, and efficiency on the basepaths. It will be difficult for Taylor to seize a spot in an Oakland outfield that is teeming with talent—with more on the way—but the 27-year-old has a small window of opportunity to convert his skills into a major-league gig.

Jemile Weeks 2B

Born: **1/26/1987** Age: **26**
Bats: **B** Throws: **R** Height: **5' 10"**
Weight: **160** Breakout: **4%**
Improve: **43%** Collapse: **5%**
Attrition: **14%** MLB: **91%**

Comparables:
Luis Rodriguez,Aaron Hill,Kevin Frandsen

YEAR	TEAM	LVL	AGE	PA	R	2B	3B	HR	RBI	BB	SO	SB	CS	AVG_OBP_SLG	TAv	BABIP	BRR	FRAA	WARP
2010	MID	AA	23	312	43	14	7	3	33	28	37	11	6	.267/.340/.403	.259	.298	0.4	2B(67): 1.6	1.1
2011	SAC	AAA	24	217	30	6	4	3	22	29	32	10	4	.321/.417/.446	.310	.373	0	--	0.0
2011	OAK	MLB	24	437	50	26	8	2	36	21	62	22	11	.303/.340/.421	.289	.350	1.3	2B(96): 4.1	2.7
2012	SAC	AAA	25	51	5	4	0	0	10	6	8	1	0	.333/.412/.422	.186	.405	0.2	2B(7): -0.1	-0.3
2012	OAK	MLB	25	511	54	15	8	2	20	50	70	16	5	.221/.305/.304	.234	.256	-1.4	2B(113): -8.5	-1.1
2013	*OAK*	*MLB*	*26*	*473*	*54*	*21*	*6*	*3*	*34*	*35*	*70*	*16*	*7*	*.253/.313/.356*	*.248*	*.289*	*1.2*	*2B -4*	*0.8*

Je-Green-mile entered the season with a 15 percent collapse rate, the highest mark PECOTA had projected for the regulars in Oakland's lineup, and those one-in-six odds came to fruition as Weeks's bat went into hibernation for the summer. The sophomore slump may have been magnified given his magnificent rookie campaign, which featured a BABIP-fueled offensive spike that was out of line with his minor-league numbers. Weeks showed professionalism when he received an August demotion, acknowledging that he had work to do in order to earn his starting job, and the mature approach and positive attitude could help Weeks regain his status as Oakland's long-term solution at the keystone.

Chris Young CF

Born: **9/5/1983** Age: **29**
Bats: **R** Throws: **R** Height: **6' 3"**
Weight: **190** Breakout: **3%**
Improve: **45%** Collapse: **0%**
Attrition: **8%** MLB: **88%**

Comparables:
Ken Henderson,Carlos Beltran,Grady Sizemore

YEAR	TEAM	LVL	AGE	PA	R	2B	3B	HR	RBI	BB	SO	SB	CS	AVG_OBP_SLG	TAv	BABIP	BRR	FRAA	WARP
2010	ARI	MLB	26	664	94	33	0	27	91	74	145	28	7	.257/.341/.452	.278	.296	2.7	CF(156): 4.9	4.2
2011	ARI	MLB	27	659	89	38	3	20	71	80	139	22	9	.236/.331/.420	.273	.275	5.3	CF(155): -5.9	2.0
2012	ARI	MLB	28	363	36	24	0	14	41	36	79	8	3	.231/.311/.434	.261	.263	-0.1	CF(87): -0.5	0.9
2013	*OAK*	*MLB*	*29*	*402*	*49*	*20*	*1*	*13*	*48*	*43*	*92*	*12*	*4*	*.230/.313/.406*	*.263*	*.271*	*0.5*	*CF 2*	*1.6*

Young's bat caught fire for the first two weeks of the season, but a separated right shoulder knocked him out of the lineup for a month, and he was a shell of his pre-injury self upon his return. He hit just .206 from May through the end of the season, and also battled a right thigh strain that kept him out of the starting lineup for the final month. Traded to Oakland in the offseason, Young now finds himself as a small fish in a crowded outfield, but he could thrive in a new environment with the alleviated pressure of lowered expectations, though he will have to overcome the difficult transition from the fly-ball haven of Chase Field to the pop-up hell that is the Coliseum.

PITCHERS

Jeremy Accardo

Born: **12/18/1981** Age: **31**
Bats: **R** Throws: **R** Height: **6' 2"** Weight: **200**
Breakout: **26%** Improve: **48%** Collapse: **34%**
Attrition: **10%** MLB: **87%**

Comparables:
Lou Pote,Brandon Medders,Luis Aponte

YEAR	TEAM	LVL	AGE	W	L	SV	G	GS	IP	H	HR	BB	SO	BB9	SO9	GB%	BABIP	WHIP	ERA	FIP	FRA	WARP
2010	LVG	AAA	28	3	2	24	42	0	44	52	1	15	26	3.1	5.3	52%	.340	1.52	3.48	3.79	4.75	0.6
2010	TOR	MLB	28	0	1	0	5	0	6^2	12	0	3	3	4.1	4.1	44%	.444	2.25	8.10	3.95	4.43	0.1
2011	NOR	AAA	29	1	1	2	26	0	33^1	26	1	11	27	3.0	7.3	54%	.233	1.11	2.16	3.09	2.54	0.4
2011	BAL	MLB	29	3	3	0	31	0	37^2	43	5	18	23	4.3	5.5	39%	.317	1.62	5.73	5.08	5.14	0.0
2012	COH	AAA	30	0	2	4	13	0	16^1	12	0	7	16	3.9	8.8	63%	.279	1.16	2.76	2.67	3.16	0.2
2012	SAC	AAA	30	1	0	2	7	0	7^2	7	0	3	4	3.5	4.7	48%	.280	1.30	1.17	4.19	4.21	0.1
2012	CLE	MLB	30	0	0	0	26	0	35^1	38	3	16	28	4.1	7.1	48%	.333	1.53	4.58	3.92	4.38	0.2
2012	OAK	MLB	30	0	0	0	1	0	2	4	0	0	1	0.0	4.5	33%	.444	2.00	9.00	2.05	3.26	0.1
2013	*OAK*	*MLB*	*31*	*2*	*1*	*0*	*32*	*0*	39^1	*41*	*4*	*16*	*27*	*3.8*	*6.1*	*48%*	*.302*	*1.46*	*4.50*	*4.37*	*4.89*	*-0.0*

In a classic example of the misplaced value tied to the closer title, Accardo keeps hanging on despite diminished stuff and lackluster performances by riding the coattails of his 2007 save totals. His numbers are below average across the board, and though his fastball-splitter-sinker arsenal invokes thoughts of a groundball-machine, Accardo's career grounder rates are a poor endorsement for such an approach. He has notched only one major-league save over the past four years, yet it appears that his career track is still hinging on the visual distraction of the one major outlier on his performance record.

Brett Anderson

Born: **2/1/1988** Age: **25**
Bats: **L** Throws: **L** Height: **6' 5"** Weight: **235**
Breakout: **19%** Improve: **65%** Collapse: **15%**
Attrition: **8%** MLB: **97%**

Comparables:
John Candelaria, Dallas Braden, Jaime Garcia

YEAR	TEAM	LVL	AGE	W	L	SV	G	GS	IP	H	HR	BB	SO	BB9	SO9	GB%	BABIP	WHIP	ERA	FIP	FRA	WARP
2010	ATH	Rk	22	0	0	0	2	2	6	11	0	0	6	0.0	9.0	44%	.611	1.83	3.00	2.76	2.86	0.2
2010	SAC	AAA	22	1	0	0	3	3	13^{1}	19	0	3	12	2.0	8.1	51%	.422	1.65	4.06	2.68	3.11	0.5
2010	OAK	MLB	22	7	6	0	19	19	112^{1}	112	6	22	75	1.8	6.0	55%	.294	1.19	2.80	3.18	3.37	1.9
2011	OAK	MLB	23	3	6	0	13	13	83^{1}	86	8	25	61	2.7	6.6	59%	.306	1.33	4.00	4.00	5.15	0.1
2012	STO	A+	24	0	0	0	1	1	2	4	0	0	0	0.0	0.0	60%	.400	2.00	9.00	5.31	5.94	0.0
2012	SAC	AAA	24	1	1	0	5	5	23^{1}	27	4	5	18	1.9	6.9	51%	.324	1.37	4.24	5.12	4.93	0.0
2012	OAK	MLB	24	4	2	0	6	6	35	29	1	7	25	1.8	6.4	61%	.272	1.03	2.57	2.67	3.40	0.5
2013	*OAK*	*MLB*	*25*	*2*	*3*	*0*	*8*	*8*	43^{2}	*43*	*4*	*11*	*34*	*2.2*	*7.0*	*53%*	*.297*	*1.22*	*3.61*	*3.59*	*3.92*	*0.6*

Once the shining prince of the Oakland pitching corps, Anderson missed the majority of the season recovering from his 2011 Tommy John surgery. He came back in September and pitched effectively down the stretch, joining an all-rookie rotation during the playoff chase and then shutting down Detroit for six-plus innings to notch the win in his first career postseason appearance. The son of a former Division I head baseball coach, Anderson is in a great system to nurture his pitching development and bring him back safely from injury. The left-hander's velocity was back to pre-injury levels and his pitch command was within range. Anderson is poised to reclaim his spot near the top of the pecking order in the Oakland rotation.

Grant Balfour

Born: **12/30/1977** Age: **35**
Bats: **R** Throws: **R** Height: **6' 3"** Weight: **195**
Breakout: **20%** Improve: **54%** Collapse: **27%**
Attrition: **15%** MLB: **82%**

Comparables:
Kiko Calero, Brendan Donnelly, J.J. Putz

YEAR	TEAM	LVL	AGE	W	L	SV	G	GS	IP	H	HR	BB	SO	BB9	SO9	GB%	BABIP	WHIP	ERA	FIP	FRA	WARP
2010	PCH	A+	32	0	1	0	2	2	1^{2}	2	0	3	2	15.9	10.6	—	.400	2.94	10.59	6.38	6.90	0.0
2010	TBA	MLB	32	2	1	0	57	0	55^{1}	43	3	17	56	2.8	9.1	30%	.274	1.08	2.28	2.65	2.52	1.4
2011	SAC	AAA	33	0	0	0	1	0	1	2	0	1	0	9.0	0.0	—	.400	3.00	9.00	6.78	7.37	0.0
2011	OAK	MLB	33	5	2	2	62	0	62	44	8	20	59	2.9	8.6	39%	.232	1.03	2.47	3.80	4.31	0.2
2012	OAK	MLB	34	3	2	24	75	0	74^{2}	41	4	28	72	3.4	8.7	36%	.201	0.92	2.53	2.98	3.93	0.6
2013	*OAK*	*MLB*	*35*	*3*	*2*	*7*	*61*	*0*	*60*	*46*	*5*	*23*	*64*	*3.4*	*9.7*	*38%*	*.270*	*1.14*	*2.72*	*3.30*	*2.96*	*1.4*

The image that is memory-stamped from the Athletics' thrilling run to the playoffs was the sight of Balfour emerging from the bullpen in the ninth inning with Metallica's "One" blasting over the stadium speakers while the rabid fans in the right-field stands rode the arm-powered bicycle in frenzy. It was a nightly ritual during the crux of the season, Melvin calling Balfour's name to finish five consecutive games in a five-day span to end the regular season, the right-hander converting every opportunity. Formerly a one-trick pony who relied exclusively on his mid-90s fastball, Balfour has slowly increased the use of his slider over the past five years, nodding to the breaking ball more than 40 percent of the time against right-handed batters. Lefties retain the luxury of sitting dead-red on heat.

Travis Blackley

Born: **11/4/1982** Age: **30**
Bats: **L** Throws: **L** Height: **6' 4"** Weight: **205**
Breakout: **23%** Improve: **57%** Collapse: **13%**
Attrition: **19%** MLB: **68%**

Comparables:
Jerry Reuss, Lenny DiNardo, Kurt Birkins

YEAR	TEAM	LVL	AGE	W	L	SV	G	GS	IP	H	HR	BB	SO	BB9	SO9	GB%	BABIP	WHIP	ERA	FIP	FRA	WARP
2010	STO	A+	27	0	0	0	2	2	5	3	0	0	2	0.0	3.6	38%	.188	0.60	1.80	2.93	3.90	0.1
2010	BUF	AAA	27	0	0	0	4	0	6^{1}	6	2	7	4	10.0	5.7	48%	.211	2.06	8.57	9.48	11.35	-0.4
2010	SAC	AAA	27	2	1	0	15	4	35^{2}	31	2	22	35	5.5	8.8	39%	.308	1.48	2.52	4.37	3.85	0.5
2012	FRE	AAA	29	3	0	1	4	3	23^{1}	13	1	3	19	1.2	7.3	56%	.200	0.69	0.39	2.98	3.42	0.6
2012	OAK	MLB	29	6	4	0	24	15	102^{2}	91	10	30	69	2.6	6.0	48%	.261	1.18	3.86	3.93	4.44	0.6
2012	SFN	MLB	29	0	0	0	4	0	5	7	0	2	2	3.6	3.6	52%	.333	1.80	9.00	3.54	5.46	-0.1
2013	*OAK*	*MLB*	*30*	*3*	*4*	*0*	*23*	*10*	76^{2}	*77*	*9*	*30*	*54*	*3.5*	*6.3*	*44%*	*.290*	*1.40*	*4.43*	*4.49*	*4.82*	*0.2*

Blackley and Balfour formed an intimidating tandem of Aussies in the Oakland bullpen—that is, when Blackley was not being called upon to fill a slot in the starting rotation. The left-hander was claimed off of waivers from the Giants in May, after which he admirably filled the swingman role for Melvin to plug-and-play as needed. Blackley's lack of a glaring platoon split kept him on the mound vs. left- and right-handed batters alike, effectively mixing a wide array of pitches to keep batters honest on both sides of the plate. Hitters had a difficult time identifying the southpaw's patterns of pitch selection, with Blackley calling upon each of five different pitches at least 14 percent of the time.

Jerry Blevins

Born: **9/6/1983** Age: **29**
Bats: **L** Throws: **L** Height: **6' 7"** Weight: **175**
Breakout: **29%** Improve: **42%** Collapse: **41%**
Attrition: **21%** MLB: **93%**

Comparables:
Dan Plesac, Doug Slaten, Sparky Lyle

YEAR	TEAM	LVL	AGE	W	L	SV	G	GS	IP	H	HR	BB	SO	BB9	SO9	GB%	BABIP	WHIP	ERA	FIP	FRA	WARP
2010	OAK	MLB	26	2	1	1	63	0	48^{2}	54	7	18	46	3.3	8.5	39%	.318	1.48	3.70	4.20	4.38	0.2
2011	SAC	AAA	27	2	0	0	27	0	29^{2}	25	3	7	35	2.1	10.6	—	.293	1.08	4.85	3.55	3.86	0.0
2011	OAK	MLB	27	0	0	0	26	0	28^{1}	24	2	14	26	4.4	8.3	41%	.278	1.34	2.86	3.73	3.96	0.2
2012	OAK	MLB	28	5	1	1	63	0	65^{1}	45	7	25	54	3.4	7.4	39%	.224	1.07	2.48	4.16	4.32	0.2
2013	*OAK*	*MLB*	*29*	*3*	*1*	*0*	*52*	*0*	48^{1}	*44*	*5*	*16*	*45*	*3.1*	*8.3*	*42%*	*.288*	*1.25*	*3.63*	*3.68*	*3.95*	*0.5*

It is as convenient as it is inaccurate to blindly attribute an extreme BABIP to the ghost of "luck," and groundbreaking research by BP alum Mike Fast revealed that pitchers can have a measurable influence over balls in play. That said, Blevins has not demonstrated any particular affinity for suppressing BABIP in the past. All signs point to a fluke, and the odds of his repeating the outlier .230 BABIP of 2012 are exceedingly slim, but Blevins does have some inherent advantages in the battle against regression, including playing his home games in a pitcher-friendly ballpark and an Oakland defense that was one of the best in baseball.

Jesse Chavez

Born: **8/21/1983** Age: **29**
Bats: **R** Throws: **R** Height: **6' 3"** Weight: **170**
Breakout: **35%** Improve: **63%** Collapse: **18%**
Attrition: **11%** MLB: **79%**

Comparables:
Mark Guthrie, Doug Bird, Turk Farrell

YEAR	TEAM	LVL	AGE	W	L	SV	G	GS	IP	H	HR	BB	SO	BB9	SO9	GB%	BABIP	WHIP	ERA	FIP	FRA	WARP
2010	ATL	MLB	26	3	2	0	28	0	36^2	40	6	12	29	2.9	7.1	31%	.298	1.42	5.89	4.72	4.53	0.1
2010	KCA	MLB	26	2	3	0	23	0	26	29	5	11	16	3.8	5.5	41%	.279	1.54	5.88	5.59	5.45	-0.1
2011	OMA	AAA	27	2	4	16	45	0	57^2	63	6	16	54	2.5	8.4	47%	.371	1.37	3.75	4.10	3.99	0.4
2011	KCA	MLB	27	0	0	0	4	0	7^2	12	3	5	8	5.9	9.4	58%	.391	2.22	10.57	8.02	10.73	-0.4
2012	LVG	AAA	28	8	5	1	19	17	95	90	10	20	86	1.9	8.1	48%	.294	1.16	3.98	3.89	4.61	1.4
2012	SAC	AAA	28	0	0	1	2	1	10	8	0	2	9	1.8	8.1	45%	.276	1.00	1.80	2.47	3.08	0.4
2012	OAK	MLB	28	0	0	0	4	0	3^1	9	1	1	3	2.7	8.1	44%	.533	3.00	18.90	6.95	8.14	-0.1
2012	TOR	MLB	28	1	1	0	9	2	21^1	25	6	10	27	4.2	11.4	36%	.333	1.64	8.44	5.86	7.08	-0.3
2013	*OAK*	*MLB*	*29*	*2*	*2*	*0*	*23*	*4*	*49*	*49*	*7*	*16*	*42*	*3.0*	*7.6*	*42%*	*.292*	*1.33*	*4.21*	*4.32*	*4.57*	*0.2*

The hard-throwing right-hander keeps getting chances thanks to a fastball that averages 95 mph, but he is currently on a three-year run of sub-replacement-level performance. He has a horrific tendency toward the long ball, and the control that he displayed in the minors has yet to materialize at the highest level. With a lifetime ERA of 5.99 over 177 innings, Chavez's career is hanging by a thread, and the few innings that he was allotted in Oakland did little to support the notion that the 29-year-old has a major-league future.

A.J. Cole

Born: **1/5/1992** Age: **21**
Bats: **R** Throws: **R** Height: **6' 5"** Weight: **180**
Breakout: **30%** Improve: **57%** Collapse: **15%**
Attrition: **4%** MLB: **91%**

Comparables:
Arodys Vizcaino, Hayden Penn, Jordan Lyles

YEAR	TEAM	LVL	AGE	W	L	SV	G	GS	IP	H	HR	BB	SO	BB9	SO9	GB%	BABIP	WHIP	ERA	FIP	FRA	WARP
2010	VER	A-	18	0	0	0	1	0	1	1	0	1	1	9.0	9.0	50%	.500	2.00	0.00	4.47	5.66	0.0
2011	HAG	A	19	4	7	0	20	18	89	87	6	24	108	2.4	10.9	39%	.340	1.25	4.04	2.85	2.54	3.1
2012	BUR	A	20	6	3	0	19	19	95^2	78	7	19	102	1.8	9.6	47%	.292	1.01	2.07	2.89	3.42	1.1
2012	STO	A+	20	0	7	0	8	8	38	60	7	10	31	2.4	7.3	37%	.405	1.84	7.82	5.60	5.63	0.1
2013	*OAK*	*MLB*	*21*	*2*	*3*	*0*	*8*	*8*	*38^2*	*41*	*5*	*15*	*30*	*3.6*	*7.0*	*41%*	*.305*	*1.46*	*4.79*	*4.49*	*5.21*	*-0.0*

Cole was widely regarded as the biggest prize in the prospect haul for Gio Gonzalez, though his youth meant high upside came paired with high risk. Trade-mates Tommy Milone and Brad Peacock battled for rotation spots in spring training while Cole punched a ticket to High-A Stockton, but two months later the young right-hander had compiled one of the highest ERAs in the California League, a beating that sent him slipping back a rung on the minor-league ladder. He rebounded gracefully with a strong showing against softer competition, but he will need to develop his secondary stuff in order to succeed against fastball-feasting hitters at the upper levels of the minors.

Bartolo Colon

Born: **5/24/1973** Age: **40**
Bats: **R** Throws: **R** Height: **6' 0"** Weight: **265**
Breakout: **13%** Improve: **31%** Collapse: **13%**
Attrition: **6%** MLB: **80%**

Comparables:
Don Sutton, Woody Williams, Greg Maddux

YEAR	TEAM	LVL	AGE	W	L	SV	G	GS	IP	H	HR	BB	SO	BB9	SO9	GB%	BABIP	WHIP	ERA	FIP	FRA	WARP
2011	NYA	MLB	38	8	10	0	29	26	164^1	172	21	40	135	2.2	7.4	45%	.305	1.29	4.00	3.86	4.45	1.7
2012	OAK	MLB	39	10	9	0	24	24	152^1	161	17	23	91	1.4	5.4	47%	.286	1.21	3.43	3.77	3.99	1.3
2013	*OAK*	*MLB*	*40*	*7*	*9*	*0*	*22*	*22*	*133^2*	*139*	*16*	*31*	*86*	*2.1*	*5.8*	*45%*	*.291*	*1.27*	*4.07*	*4.17*	*4.43*	*0.8*

Colon underwent an unprecedented stem-cell procedure in April 2010, one piece in the puzzle that produced his best season in seven years, interrupted by a 50-game suspension for a failed drug test in which he tested positive for synthetic testosterone. The A's were undeterred, giving Colon a 50 percent raise to $3 million, a relatively modest bargain that is the net result of his surprisingly effective season and the potentially artificial nature of said performance. The underlying ingredient to Colon's success was a career-best walk rate that was the lowest in the AL among starters with at least 150 innings pitched, though his strikes would have likely been hammered had the 15-year veteran not been able to average 93 mph on his fastball. It remains to be seen whether that velocity will carry over into the right-hander's age-40 season.

Ryan Cook
Born: 6/30/1987 Age: 26
Bats: R Throws: R Height: 6' 4" Weight: 200
Breakout: 16% Improve: 56% Collapse: 19%
Attrition: 9% MLB: 87%
Comparables:
Ernie Broglio,J.D. Durbin,Frankie De La Cruz

YEAR	TEAM	LVL	AGE	W	L	SV	G	GS	IP	H	HR	BB	SO	BB9	SO9	GB%	BABIP	WHIP	ERA	FIP	FRA	WARP
2010	VIS	A+	23	4	7	0	20	20	108^1	110	3	36	100	3.0	8.3	62%	.331	1.35	4.24	3.60	4.25	1.9
2010	MOB	AA	23	1	1	0	3	3	18^2	13	1	10	12	4.8	5.8	69%	.222	1.23	2.89	4.56	5.15	0.1
2010	RNO	AAA	23	0	0	0	1	1	5	7	1	2	5	3.6	9.0	31%	.400	1.80	10.80	6.58	7.55	0.0
2011	MOB	AA	24	1	4	13	34	0	44	28	2	14	50	2.9	10.2	59%	.292	0.95	2.25	2.72	3.77	0.3
2011	RNO	AAA	24	0	1	6	14	0	17	13	0	8	12	4.2	6.4	—	.283	1.24	2.12	3.96	4.30	0.0
2011	ARI	MLB	24	0	1	0	12	0	7^2	11	0	8	7	9.4	8.2	46%	.423	2.48	7.04	4.30	4.92	0.0
2012	OAK	MLB	25	6	2	14	71	0	73^1	42	4	27	80	3.3	9.8	48%	.220	0.94	2.09	2.84	3.00	1.1
2013	*OAK*	*MLB*	*26*	*2*	*2*	*2*	*26*	*5*	*49^2*	*48*	*5*	*22*	*37*	*4.0*	*6.8*	*49%*	*.291*	*1.42*	*4.44*	*4.35*	*4.83*	*0.1*

Cook was untouchable for the first two months of the season, pitching 23 innings of scoreless baseball before giving up his first run of the year on May 28. The goose eggs earned him a shot in the closer role, where he held down the fort for two months before hitting a poorly timed rough patch that coincided with Balfour's resurgence, effectively ending Cook's save opportunities. The hardest thrower on the team, with a fastball that averaged 96 mph, Cook joined forces with Balfour and Doolittle as the heat-seeking triumvirate that marched in to shorten games and close out Athletics' victories. The A's clearly won the reliever portion of the trade that pried Cook from Arizona, as he superseded the value of Craig Breslow for a fraction of the price.

Sean Doolittle
Born: 9/26/1986 Age: 26
Bats: L Throws: L Height: 6' 4" Weight: 210
Breakout: 37% Improve: 64% Collapse: 23%
Attrition: 10% MLB: 91%
Comparables:
Dan Plesac,Rob Dibble,Randy Myers

YEAR	TEAM	LVL	AGE	W	L	SV	G	GS	IP	H	HR	BB	SO	BB9	SO9	GB%	BABIP	WHIP	ERA	FIP	FRA	WARP
2011	ATH	Rk	24	0	0	0	1	0	1	0	0	1	2	9.0	18.0	1.%	.000	1.00	9.00	3.37	5.36	0.0
2012	STO	A+	25	0	0	0	6	0	10^1	5	0	2	21	1.7	18.3	50%	.357	0.68	0.87	0.91	-0.07	0.7
2012	MID	AA	25	0	0	1	8	0	11	2	0	4	19	3.3	15.5	47%	.118	0.55	0.82	1.19	2.43	0.2
2012	SAC	AAA	25	0	0	0	2	0	3^2	1	0	1	8	2.5	19.6	25%	.250	0.55	0.00	0.12	-0.26	0.2
2012	OAK	MLB	25	2	1	1	44	0	47^1	40	3	11	60	2.1	11.4	37%	.316	1.08	3.04	2.03	2.03	1.4
2013	*OAK*	*MLB*	*26*	*2*	*1*	*1*	*34*	*0*	*40^1*	*31*	*3*	*11*	*52*	*2.5*	*11.5*	*42%*	*.294*	*1.04*	*2.37*	*2.41*	*2.58*	*1.1*

In a season full of surprises, the most shocking development was the rocket-fueled ascension of Sean Doolittle. The former first-round pick—whose hitting career was derailed by multiple knee surgeries that cost him nearly two years of development at the plate—made the complicated transition from first base to the mound. All would be forgiven if Doolittle took a while to learn the nuances of pitching, but the southpaw needed just 26 minor-league innings to discover that he had a preternatural knack for it. By early June he was on a big-league mound, dominating the best hitters in the world. Doolittle led all Oakland relievers with a 31 percent strikeout rate, and his microscopic walk rate fueled a K-to-walk ratio of 5.5-to-one. The southpaw dominated with a mid-90s fastball that he threw 87 percent of the time, and though he was surprisingly vulnerable to left-handed batters in a small sample size, the reverse platoon split did minimal damage as Doolittle faced fellow lefties in just 35 percent of plate appearances.

Mike Ekstrom
Born: 8/30/1983 Age: 29
Bats: R Throws: R Height: 6' 1" Weight: 190
Breakout: 26% Improve: 50% Collapse: 20%
Attrition: 15% MLB: 85%
Comparables:
Terry Adams,Jeff Bennett,Dave Schmidt

YEAR	TEAM	LVL	AGE	W	L	SV	G	GS	IP	H	HR	BB	SO	BB9	SO9	GB%	BABIP	WHIP	ERA	FIP	FRA	WARP
2010	DUR	AAA	26	6	1	1	39	1	58	55	5	19	48	2.9	7.4	57%	.296	1.28	2.79	3.84	3.93	1.0
2010	TBA	MLB	26	0	1	0	15	0	16^1	12	0	9	10	5.0	5.5	38%	.255	1.29	3.31	3.84	5.43	0.0
2011	DUR	AAA	27	6	4	5	46	1	68^1	75	5	29	65	3.8	8.6	—	.347	1.52	4.35	3.60	3.92	0.0
2011	TBA	MLB	27	0	0	0	1	0	1	1	0	0	1	0.0	9.0	33%	.333	1.00	0.00	1.06	1.83	0.0
2012	CSP	AAA	28	3	1	1	43	0	57	47	0	18	57	2.8	9.0	59%	.293	1.14	2.53	2.77	3.38	1.6
2012	COL	MLB	28	0	0	0	15	0	15^2	21	1	2	9	1.1	5.2	49%	.333	1.47	6.32	3.20	3.43	0.4
2013	*OAK*	*MLB*	*29*	*1*	*1*	*0*	*27*	*0*	*35*	*35*	*4*	*13*	*26*	*3.2*	*6.6*	*52%*	*.295*	*1.37*	*4.23*	*4.31*	*4.60*	*0.1*

Ekstrom is one of two pitchers (Andrew Carpenter is the other) to have made at least one big-league appearance every year from 2008 to 2012 without pitching as many as 20 innings in any of them. He received a written warning from MLB last July advising him that he twice had taken too long warming up after entering a game and that he could be fined if he continued to violate Section 1(d) of Baseball's Pace of Game Regulations. So, even if no team needs him for 15 innings this year, at least Ekstrom will be known for something.

Sonny Gray
Born: 11/7/1989 Age: 23
Bats: R Throws: R Height: 6' 0" Weight: 200
Breakout: 24% Improve: 55% Collapse: 21%
Attrition: 13% MLB: 84%
Comparables:
Alex Sanabia,Greg Reynolds,Sean O'Sullivan

YEAR	TEAM	LVL	AGE	W	L	SV	G	GS	IP	H	HR	BB	SO	BB9	SO9	GB%	BABIP	WHIP	ERA	FIP	FRA	WARP
2011	ATH	Rk	21	0	1	0	1	1	2	4	0	0	2	0.0	9.0	43%	.571	2.00	4.50	2.37	2.07	0.1
2011	MID	AA	21	1	0	0	5	5	20	15	0	6	18	2.7	8.1	—	.278	1.05	0.45	2.48	2.69	0.0
2012	MID	AA	22	6	9	0	26	26	148	148	8	57	97	3.5	5.9	57%	.303	1.39	4.14	3.91	4.98	0.4
2012	SAC	AAA	22	0	0	0	1	1	4	10	0	1	2	2.2	4.5	45%	.500	2.75	9.00	4.17	4.34	0.1
2013	*OAK*	*MLB*	*23*	*2*	*3*	*0*	*7*	*7*	*38^1*	*42*	*5*	*16*	*22*	*3.9*	*5.2*	*51%*	*.297*	*1.52*	*5.06*	*5.00*	*5.50*	*-0.2*

Scouting reports often begin by noting his non-ideal size, but Gray's stable balance and 70-grade momentum result in a deep release point that more than compensates for any height disadvantage. Gray was unfazed by an ultra-aggressive assignment to Double-A just nine weeks after being selected in the first round of the 2011 draft, but the advanced competition caught up to him during his extended trial for Midland in 2012. He will likely stay on the advanced-placement track for pitchers, starting the 2013 season in Sacramento, where he will be within dreaming distance of the bright lights and expansive foul grounds of the Coliseum, with the only thing between him and the majors being a 90-mile stretch of Interstate-80.

A.J. Griffin

Born: **1/28/1988** Age: **25**
Bats: **R** Throws: **R** Height: **6' 6"** Weight: **215**
Breakout: **11%** Improve: **43%** Collapse: **28%**
Attrition: **12%** MLB: **98%**

Comparables:
Daniel Hudson, Jered Weaver, Dwight Gooden

YEAR	TEAM	LVL	AGE	W	L	SV	G	GS	IP	H	HR	BB	SO	BB9	SO9	GB%	BABIP	WHIP	ERA	FIP	FRA	WARP
2010	ATH	Rk	22	0	0	0	4	0	5	1	0	0	6	0.0	10.8	71%	.000	0.20	0.00	1.86	3.35	0.1
2010	VAN	A-	22	1	1	15	20	0	21^{1}	14	0	7	27	3.0	11.4	45%	.286	0.99	2.96	2.36	3.54	0.3
2011	BUR	A	23	4	0	0	8	8	52	36	2	5	46	0.9	8.0	37%	.195	0.79	1.56	2.49	3.21	0.2
2011	STO	A+	23	5	3	0	12	12	70^{2}	64	8	14	82	1.8	10.4	47%	.292	1.10	3.57	3.78	3.37	1.2
2011	MID	AA	23	2	3	0	6	6	32	39	6	11	20	3.1	5.6	—	.308	1.56	6.47	5.78	6.29	0.0
2011	SAC	AAA	23	0	1	0	1	1	6	6	1	2	8	3.0	12.0	—	.385	1.33	3.00	4.28	4.66	0.0
2012	MID	AA	24	3	1	0	7	7	43^{1}	31	4	7	44	1.5	9.1	43%	.250	0.88	2.49	3.00	4.15	0.1
2012	SAC	AAA	24	4	2	0	10	10	58^{2}	48	3	11	47	1.7	7.2	41%	.259	1.01	3.07	3.50	4.00	0.5
2012	OAK	MLB	24	7	1	0	15	15	82^{1}	74	10	19	64	2.1	7.0	38%	.264	1.13	3.06	3.80	4.20	0.8
2013	*OAK*	*MLB*	*25*	*5*	*5*	*0*	*20*	*13*	*85^{2}*	*79*	*9*	*21*	*69*	*2.3*	*7.2*	*41%*	*.280*	*1.18*	*3.39*	*3.69*	*3.68*	*1.3*

Griffin is a classic counterexample to the theory that downhill plane is the instigator of groundballs. The tall right-hander with a high arm slot and a steep curveball has a glaring tendency to surrender hits in the air. He was one of a handful of quick climbers in the Oakland pitching corps in 2012, soaring from Double-A to the majors by midsummer, and his stat line maintained its brilliance after the big-league promotion. Griffin kept runners off the bases with pinpoint command and a little help from the gloves behind him on batted balls, elements that will have to hold if his 90-mph fastball is to continue to play on the big stage.

Tommy Milone

Born: **2/16/1987** Age: **26**
Bats: **L** Throws: **L** Height: **6' 2"** Weight: **205**
Breakout: **23%** Improve: **48%** Collapse: **21%**
Attrition: **10%** MLB: **93%**

Comparables:
Dallas Braden, John Candelaria, Andy Sonnanstine

YEAR	TEAM	LVL	AGE	W	L	SV	G	GS	IP	H	HR	BB	SO	BB9	SO9	GB%	BABIP	WHIP	ERA	FIP	FRA	WARP
2010	HAR	AA	23	12	5	0	27	27	158	161	10	23	155	1.3	8.8	45%	.326	1.16	2.85	2.73	3.52	3.7
2011	SYR	AAA	24	12	6	0	24	24	148^{1}	137	9	16	155	1.0	9.4	40%	.326	1.03	3.22	2.28	3.24	2.3
2011	WAS	MLB	24	1	0	0	5	5	26	28	2	4	15	1.4	5.2	35%	.299	1.23	3.81	3.53	3.70	0.4
2012	OAK	MLB	25	13	10	0	31	31	190	207	24	36	137	1.7	6.5	40%	.310	1.28	3.74	3.88	4.29	1.6
2013	*OAK*	*MLB*	*26*	*7*	*9*	*0*	*24*	*24*	*143*	*153*	*16*	*32*	*103*	*2.0*	*6.5*	*40%*	*.306*	*1.29*	*4.12*	*3.89*	*4.48*	*0.8*

Milone has already exceeded expectations. A soft-tossing lefty with a quiet delivery and pinpoint command, he provided a team-leading 190 innings of quality pitching for a staff that was greener than Stomper's uniform. He is the prototypical back-of-the-rotation starter and exemplifies a tenet of Billy Beane's philosophy that strike-throwers generally have solid mechanics and are thus at lower risk for injury. Milone's ERA was deflated by 11 unearned runs, and his hittable stuff will leave him vulnerable to the vagaries of batted balls, but the southpaw can continue to collect a big-league paycheck and find work at the back of a rotation so long as he continues to keep his walk rate below 5 percent.

Pat Neshek

Born: **9/4/1980** Age: **32**
Bats: **B** Throws: **R** Height: **6' 4"** Weight: **210**
Breakout: **23%** Improve: **45%** Collapse: **30%**
Attrition: **18%** MLB: **89%**

Comparables:
Greg McMichael, Joe Hoerner, Don Aase

YEAR	TEAM	LVL	AGE	W	L	SV	G	GS	IP	H	HR	BB	SO	BB9	SO9	GB%	BABIP	WHIP	ERA	FIP	FRA	WARP
2010	FTM	A+	29	0	0	0	2	0	2	3	0	2	2	9.0	9.0	29%	.429	2.50	13.50	4.44	7.30	-0.1
2010	ROC	AAA	29	5	1	1	30	0	39^{1}	40	4	13	25	3.0	5.7	41%	.288	1.35	3.89	4.56	5.34	-0.1
2010	MIN	MLB	29	0	1	0	11	0	9	7	1	8	9	8.0	9.0	32%	.250	1.67	5.00	5.49	7.57	-0.2
2011	TUC	AAA	30	1	2	3	24	0	26^{1}	29	5	10	13	3.4	4.4	48%	.224	1.48	4.10	6.40	9.03	-0.3
2011	SDN	MLB	30	1	1	0	25	0	24^{2}	19	4	22	20	8.0	7.3	30%	.231	1.66	4.01	6.28	6.72	-0.7
2012	NOR	AAA	31	3	2	11	35	0	44	42	1	7	49	1.4	10.0	42%	.345	1.11	2.66	1.77	2.79	1.0
2012	OAK	MLB	31	2	1	0	24	0	19^{2}	10	3	6	16	2.7	7.3	35%	.137	0.81	1.37	4.47	5.10	0.0
2013	*OAK*	*MLB*	*32*	*2*	*1*	*0*	*32*	*0*	*35*	*33*	*4*	*15*	*28*	*3.8*	*7.3*	*39%*	*.283*	*1.37*	*4.25*	*4.37*	*4.62*	*0.1*

More than three years removed from Tommy John surgery, the old sidewinder's stuff finally returned to pre-injury levels. Neshek's velocity gained three clicks from the previous season, with his fastball averaging 90-mph on the gun for the first time since 2008. Command was his greatest asset at his peak, but his 2010-11 walk rate was indicative of a pitcher who could not find his signature delivery on a consistent basis. The right-hander rediscovered his release point in 2012. Oakland was convinced of Neshek's resurgence, handing him just under a million bucks to keep his submarine docked at the marina in Jack London Square.

Jordan Norberto
Born: 12/8/1986 Age: 26
Bats: L Throws: L Height: 6' 1" Weight: 195
Breakout: 52% Improve: 59% Collapse: 23%
Attrition: 13% MLB: 91%
Comparables:
Mark Lowe,Danny Frisella,Rod Scurry

YEAR	TEAM	LVL	AGE	W	L	SV	G	GS	IP	H	HR	BB	SO	BB9	SO9	GB%	BABIP	WHIP	ERA	FIP	FRA	WARP
2010	RNO	AAA	23	3	0	4	21	0	29^{1}	25	2	19	38	5.8	11.7	49%	.319	1.50	3.07	3.82	3.70	0.9
2010	ARI	MLB	23	0	2	0	33	0	20	16	3	22	15	9.9	6.8	40%	.241	1.90	5.85	6.86	6.66	-0.6
2011	RNO	AAA	24	6	2	1	41	0	48^{2}	46	1	26	54	4.8	10.0	—	.341	1.48	4.25	3.62	3.93	0.0
2011	SAC	AAA	24	0	0	1	6	0	8^{1}	6	1	4	10	4.3	10.8	—	.263	1.20	1.08	4.38	4.76	0.0
2011	OAK	MLB	24	0	0	0	6	0	6^{2}	8	0	7	4	9.4	5.4	39%	.348	2.25	8.10	5.46	6.34	-0.1
2012	SAC	AAA	25	0	0	0	1	0	1	0	0	0	2	0.0	18.0	%	.000	0.00	0.00	-0.33	0.23	0.0
2012	OAK	MLB	25	4	1	1	39	0	52	37	5	22	46	3.8	8.0	47%	.232	1.13	2.77	3.85	3.82	0.5
2013	*OAK*	*MLB*	*26*	*2*	*1*	*1*	*32*	*0*	*34^{2}*	*33*	*4*	*21*	*32*	*5.4*	*8.3*	*40%*	*.296*	*1.56*	*4.79*	*4.67*	*5.21*	*-0.1*

Norberto kept umpires busy in the minor leagues as he piled up walks and strikeouts like they were going out of style, but he enjoyed his longest stretch in the majors in 2012 with solid results. He pitched a single frame in the minors and otherwise stuck with the big club all season until shoulder tendonitis prematurely ended his campaign in mid-August. Much like fellow southpaw Blevins, Norberto was the beneficiary of an ultra-low BABIP that was out of line with his career numbers, though Norberto's intimidation factor is increased by a thick beard from the Sergio Romo school of facial fuzz.

Jarrod Parker
Born: 11/24/1988 Age: 24
Bats: R Throws: R Height: 6' 2" Weight: 195
Breakout: 30% Improve: 69% Collapse: 14%
Attrition: 13% MLB: 95%
Comparables:
Ervin Santana,Justin Verlander,Travis Wood

YEAR	TEAM	LVL	AGE	W	L	SV	G	GS	IP	H	HR	BB	SO	BB9	SO9	GB%	BABIP	WHIP	ERA	FIP	FRA	WARP
2011	MOB	AA	22	11	8	0	26	26	130^{2}	112	7	55	112	3.8	7.7	55%	.237	1.28	3.79	3.80	4.54	1.1
2011	ARI	MLB	22	0	0	0	1	1	5^{2}	4	0	1	1	1.6	1.6	45%	.200	0.88	0.00	3.17	3.75	0.1
2012	SAC	AAA	23	1	0	0	4	4	20^{2}	22	2	6	21	2.6	9.1	55%	.345	1.35	2.18	3.76	3.84	0.3
2012	OAK	MLB	23	13	8	0	29	29	181^{1}	166	11	63	140	3.1	6.9	45%	.290	1.26	3.47	3.38	3.79	1.9
2013	*OAK*	*MLB*	*24*	*7*	*9*	*0*	*23*	*23*	*134^{1}*	*130*	*13*	*50*	*107*	*3.4*	*7.2*	*47%*	*.296*	*1.34*	*3.94*	*3.98*	*4.28*	*1.1*

Chalk up another success story for Dr. James Andrews, as Parker's return from Tommy John surgery was a rousing success, and he quickly regained the stuff that made him a top prospect. The hardest-throwing starter on staff, Parker routinely cracks 95 mph on the radar gun, and he offsets the heat with a late-fading changeup that comes in 12 mph slower than the fastball. He maintained velocity throughout the season and peaked in September, which bodes well for his development curve. Parker's advanced command of both pitches allows him to upset batter timing. His deceptive approach flies under the radar, and he mixes in a slider to keep right-handed batters honest with two strikes.

Brad Peacock
Born: 2/2/1988 Age: 25
Bats: R Throws: R Height: 6' 2" Weight: 175
Breakout: 32% Improve: 62% Collapse: 16%
Attrition: 26% MLB: 92%
Comparables:
Brett Myers,Hayden Penn,Marco Estrada

YEAR	TEAM	LVL	AGE	W	L	SV	G	GS	IP	H	HR	BB	SO	BB9	SO9	GB%	BABIP	WHIP	ERA	FIP	FRA	WARP
2010	POT	A+	22	4	9	0	19	18	103^{1}	109	11	25	118	2.2	10.3	50%	.343	1.30	4.44	3.35	3.96	1.7
2010	HAR	AA	22	2	2	0	7	7	38^{2}	33	5	22	30	5.1	7.0	41%	.252	1.42	4.65	5.20	6.06	0.1
2011	HAR	AA	23	10	2	0	16	14	98^{2}	62	4	23	129	2.1	11.8	40%	.279	0.86	2.01	2.08	3.12	1.6
2011	SYR	AAA	23	5	1	0	9	9	48	36	5	24	48	4.5	9.0	34%	.288	1.25	3.19	4.22	3.90	0.2
2011	WAS	MLB	23	2	0	0	3	2	12	7	0	6	4	4.5	3.0	32%	.184	1.08	0.75	3.83	3.98	0.0
2012	SAC	AAA	24	12	9	0	28	25	134^{2}	147	16	66	139	4.4	9.3	35%	.342	1.58	6.01	4.73	5.72	0.3
2013	*OAK*	*MLB*	*25*	*2*	*3*	*0*	*8*	*8*	*42^{2}*	*45*	*6*	*19*	*31*	*4.1*	*6.6*	*42%*	*.297*	*1.51*	*5.09*	*4.91*	*5.54*	*-0.2*

Peacock was supposed to be the relatively safe bet in the deal that sent Gonzalez to Washington, serving as the middle ground between the safe, low-ceiling of Milone and the risk/reward gamble of Cole, but Peacock's flight to major-league relevance never got off the ground. He was expected to contend for a rotation spot out of spring training, but was unable to rebound from a rough Cactus League showing and spent 2012 toiling in the PCL. The former 41st-round pick is accustomed to long odds, so his disappointing season was merely a detour on his long journey toward the middle.

Chris Resop
Born: 11/4/1982 Age: 30
Bats: R Throws: R Height: 6' 4" Weight: 225
Breakout: 25% Improve: 64% Collapse: 14%
Attrition: 8% MLB: 86%
Comparables:
Steve Karsay,Don Elston,Matt Wise

YEAR	TEAM	LVL	AGE	W	L	SV	G	GS	IP	H	HR	BB	SO	BB9	SO9	GB%	BABIP	WHIP	ERA	FIP	FRA	WARP
2010	MIS	AA	27	0	0	0	2	2	4^{1}	5	0	1	2	2.1	4.2	56%	.312	1.40	4.19	3.15	4.95	0.2
2010	GWN	AAA	27	6	3	0	15	15	82	53	4	32	91	3.5	10.0	50%	.258	1.04	2.09	2.95	3.72	1.6
2010	ATL	MLB	27	0	0	0	1	0	2	5	0	3	2	13.5	9.0	22%	.556	4.00	22.50	5.61	5.61	0.0
2010	PIT	MLB	27	0	0	0	22	0	19	10	1	10	24	4.7	11.4	40%	.214	1.05	1.89	2.84	2.89	0.3
2011	PIT	MLB	28	5	4	1	76	0	69^{2}	73	8	30	79	3.9	10.2	38%	.344	1.48	4.39	3.64	3.66	0.6
2012	PIT	MLB	29	1	4	1	61	0	73^{2}	81	6	24	46	2.9	5.6	52%	.298	1.43	3.91	4.00	4.36	0.4
2013	*OAK*	*MLB*	*30*	*3*	*2*	*1*	*43*	*4*	*63^{1}*	*60*	*6*	*25*	*55*	*3.5*	*7.8*	*44%*	*.292*	*1.34*	*3.93*	*3.88*	*4.27*	*0.5*

After years spent as a sabermetrics *cause célèbre* with great peripherals and bad results, Resop posted worse component measures but had a good ERA. Go figure. This isn't a case where a pitcher made the decision to swap strikeouts for weak contact; Resop allowed a similar number of hits and home runs as he had in prior seasons. There's a risk that the strikeouts are gone for good and that Resop's hittability issues will wash him out of the league. If they don't, Resop is a good middle reliever to have around until he gets expensive. Then you go out and find a cheaper model. Lather, rinse, Resop.

Evan Scribner
Born: **7/19/1985** Age: **27**
Bats: **R** Throws: **R** Height: **6' 4"** Weight: **190**
Breakout: **20%** Improve: **39%** Collapse: **44%**
Attrition: **22%** MLB: **88%**
Comparables:
Blaine Boyer, Rich Thompson, Fernando Salas

YEAR	TEAM	LVL	AGE	W	L	SV	G	GS	IP	H	HR	BB	SO	BB9	SO9	GB%	BABIP	WHIP	ERA	FIP	FRA	WARP
2010	SAN	AA	24	4	5	16	57	0	66	51	6	15	81	2.0	11.0	47%	.288	1.00	2.59	2.81	2.96	1.3
2011	TUC	AAA	25	2	3	10	28	0	28^{2}	27	2	12	27	3.8	8.5	30%	.310	1.36	4.71	4.06	5.14	0.4
2011	SDN	MLB	25	0	0	0	10	0	14	18	1	4	10	2.6	6.4	42%	.347	1.57	7.07	3.35	5.56	-0.2
2012	SAC	AAA	26	3	0	8	26	0	35^{2}	26	4	10	38	2.5	9.6	39%	.250	1.01	3.03	3.83	4.74	0.3
2012	OAK	MLB	26	2	0	1	30	0	35^{1}	30	2	12	30	3.1	7.6	40%	.269	1.19	2.55	3.10	3.79	0.4
2013	*OAK*	*MLB*	*27*	*2*	*1*	*0*	*32*	*0*	*38*	*34*	*4*	*12*	*37*	*2.9*	*8.7*	*38%*	*.289*	*1.22*	*3.48*	*3.57*	*3.78*	*0.5*

Scribner has proven himself in the bush leagues with a sub-3.00 ERA covering more than 300 innings on the farm. His dominance of the strike zone is evident in a career K-to-walk ratio of 4.5-to-one. He finds himself in the system of a Western Division franchise for the third time in his six years as a professional, and he capped his most successful season with a couple of scoreless innings in the ALDS against the Tigers. Scribner may not have the velocity to guarantee second chances, but he has the confidence in his curveball to unleash the bender in any count, keeping opposing batters from sitting on his mild-mannered fastball.

Dan Straily
Born: **12/1/1988** Age: **24**
Bats: **R** Throws: **R** Height: **6' 3"** Weight: **220**
Breakout: **35%** Improve: **60%** Collapse: **11%**
Attrition: **6%** MLB: **95%**
Comparables:
Johnny Cueto, Carlos Carrasco, Garrett Olson

YEAR	TEAM	LVL	AGE	W	L	SV	G	GS	IP	H	HR	BB	SO	BB9	SO9	GB%	BABIP	WHIP	ERA	FIP	FRA	WARP
2010	KNC	A	21	10	7	0	28	28	148	138	13	61	149	3.7	9.1	46%	.316	1.34	4.32	4.12	4.77	1.5
2011	STO	A+	22	11	9	0	28	26	160^{2}	160	10	40	154	2.2	8.6	50%	.305	1.24	3.87	3.85	4.19	2.3
2012	MID	AA	23	3	4	0	14	14	85^{1}	70	6	23	108	2.4	11.4	44%	.312	1.09	3.38	2.65	2.93	0.5
2012	SAC	AAA	23	6	3	0	11	11	66^{2}	40	3	19	82	2.6	11.1	41%	.247	0.88	2.03	2.69	2.36	1.0
2012	OAK	MLB	23	2	1	0	7	7	39^{1}	36	11	16	32	3.7	7.3	31%	.225	1.32	3.89	6.43	5.82	-0.2
2013	*OAK*	*MLB*	*24*	*4*	*5*	*0*	*13*	*13*	*72^{1}*	*69*	*9*	*28*	*63*	*3.5*	*7.8*	*42%*	*.290*	*1.34*	*4.20*	*4.24*	*4.57*	*0.4*

Straily was perhaps the greatest prospect breakout of the 2012 season. A pitcher who failed to crack anyone's rankings of the organization's top prospects, Straily came out of nowhere to lead the minor leagues in strikeouts, cruising through the upper levels over the first four months of the season, adding yet another young gun to the A's weapons cabinet. He fits the mold of Oakland's pitching-development system, with efficient mechanics that support advanced pitch command, allowing his low-90s fastball and sharp slider to play up a notch. If anything, Straily caught too much plate, and big-league sluggers greeted him with 11 homers in fewer than 40 innings. Straily's rookie hazing was surprisingly gentle, given that each of his empathetic staff-mates had been paddled within the past few months. Despite the encouraging indicators, Oakland's extraordinary pitching depth means that Straily will have to battle stiff competition to claim a spot in the rotation.

Andrew Werner
Born: **2/25/1987** Age: **26**
Bats: **L** Throws: **L** Height: **6' 3"** Weight: **215**
Breakout: **28%** Improve: **58%** Collapse: **12%**
Attrition: **14%** MLB: **89%**
Comparables:
Dallas Braden, Paul Maholm, Matt Maloney

YEAR	TEAM	LVL	AGE	W	L	SV	G	GS	IP	H	HR	BB	SO	BB9	SO9	GB%	BABIP	WHIP	ERA	FIP	FRA	WARP
2011	FTW	A	24	2	6	0	12	12	68	70	4	13	52	1.7	6.9	63%	.322	1.22	3.44	3.21	4.04	0.5
2011	LEL	A+	24	5	2	0	13	13	68^{1}	72	1	13	55	1.7	7.2	—	.329	1.24	3.03	3.23	3.52	0.0
2012	SAN	AA	25	4	8	0	18	18	103	107	6	25	89	2.2	7.8	68%	.332	1.28	3.23	3.12	3.76	1.3
2012	TUC	AAA	25	1	2	0	4	4	23^{1}	26	1	6	20	2.3	7.7	58%	.333	1.37	5.79	3.28	4.27	0.0
2012	SDN	MLB	25	2	3	0	8	8	40^{1}	45	5	14	35	3.1	7.8	54%	.328	1.46	5.58	4.13	4.47	0.1
2013	*OAK*	*MLB*	*26*	*3*	*4*	*0*	*11*	*11*	*60^{1}*	*63*	*7*	*19*	*45*	*2.8*	*6.7*	*56%*	*.303*	*1.36*	*4.34*	*4.16*	*4.72*	*0.2*

The Padres signed Werner out of a tryout camp in 2010. He joined the big club in August, thanks to a lack of suitable alternatives within the organization, and made four good starts, followed by four terrible ones. Werner doesn't throw hard but keeps the ball around the plate and in the yard. Traded to the A's in November, he is the quintessential generic lefty.

LINEOUTS

HITTERS

PLAYER	TEAM	LVL	AGE	PA	R	2B	3B	HR	RBI	BB	SO	SB-CS	AVG/OBP/SLG	TAv	BABIP	BRR	FRAA	WARP
1B A. Aliotti	MID	AA	24	531	72	29	1	10	76	68	129	0-0	.292/.385/.426	.254	.384	-0.6	1B(37): 1.2	0.0
OF B. Crocker	BUR	A	22	470	56	19	2	6	53	39	109	17-10	.268/.347/.369	.260	.347	0	RF(27): 0.5, CF(27): 2.1	0.1
UT C. Crumbliss	MID	AA	25	605	94	21	6	10	45	120	98	24-8	.257/.414/.391	.255	.302	2.5	LF(34): 1.6, CF(4): -0.3	0.4
RF V. De La Cruz	ATH	Rk	18	148	25	5	3	3	17	11	43	2-1	.230/.291/.378	.242	.311	2.2	RF(24): 0.3, LF(1): 0.2	0.1
C S. Hill	MEM	AAA	27	331	52	16	0	17	52	25	74	0-1	.266/.326/.488	.260	.297	1.4	1B(10): 0.0, 3B(8): -0.6	0.2
	SLN	MLB	27	10	1	1	0	0	0	0	3	0-0	.200/.200/.300	.248	.286	0	1B(1): -0.0	0.0
C L. Montz	NWO	AAA	28	420	55	14	0	29	74	45	101	1-3	.222/.310/.495	.275	.219	1.5	1B(20): -1.2, C(4): 0.0	0.2
SS D. Perez	ARK	AA	22	460	51	14	3	6	36	44	98	15-8	.214/.293/.307	.243	.265	4.4	SS(50): 6.9, 2B(48): -2.6	1.1
OF S. Peterson	MID	AA	24	205	27	11	3	2	23	44	47	9-3	.274/.441/.420	.305	.380	2.4	LF(12): -1.1, RF(4): 0.3	0.5
	SAC	AAA	24	157	36	7	1	7	23	23	31	4-3	.389/.484/.618	.395	.473	1.8	LF(8): -0.4, RF(5): -0.7	0.8
CF A. Shipman	BUR	A	20	427	40	12	4	0	32	60	86	11-11	.206/.319/.261	.247	.266	-3.8	CF(52): -2.0, RF(11): -0.2	-0.8
INF E. Sogard	SAC	AAA	26	180	29	5	2	5	22	23	17	11-3	.331/.417/.484	.309	.348	0.9	2B(16): 4.1, 3B(2): 0.3	1.3
	OAK	MLB	26	108	8	3	1	2	7	5	17	2-0	.167/.206/.275	.186	.181	0.2	SS(15): 1.2, 3B(14): 0.2	-0.3

Anthony Aliotti lacks the classic power profile for first base, but the spray hitter is gradually learning to pull the ball with more authority and his discerning eye allows him to embrace the concept of selective aggression. **Bobby Crocker** has potential speed and power in his game, though the power forgot to show up for his first full season in the pros. **Conner Crumbliss** has walked 120 or more times in two of the past three seasons, and he has cracked a .400 OBP at every stop of his minor-league career. With the versatility to play second base or the outfield, Crumbliss is on a straight-line trajectory to Oakland in 2014. **Vicmal De La Cruz** could not repeat his eye-opening Dominican Summer League numbers, but disappointment in his 35-game performance should be tempered by realizing he is an 18-year old adjusting to life in a foreign country. Minor-league masher **Steven Hill** is only notionally a catcher, but having been plucked by Oakland in the minor-league Rule 5 draft last fall, he may finally be able to hit his way into the DH league. After 10 minor-league seasons, **Luke Montz** has played all over the country and all over the diamond (C, 1B, LF, RF, DH in 2012 alone) hoping the glimmers of power he displays might turn into a big-league job one of these days. In July 2011, **Darwin Perez** was hitting .318/.413/.424 as a 21-year-old shortstop in offensive sinkhole Arkansas, but his numbers dissolved after that, and the wrong half followed him into 2012. **Shane Peterson** had the obscene walk rate that is common in the Oakland system, and the 24-year old enjoyed the best 38 games of his professional life in his second go-around with the River Cats. **Aaron Shipman** has tools that are not translating into games, from inefficiency on the basepaths to an empty batting average, and his green-collar walk rate is offset by a weak bat that has yet to clear a fence in 691 minor-league plate appearances. **Eric Sogard**'s minor-league track record is covered with doubles and walks, blending the ingredients into a career OBP of .382 in the minors, but those skills have yet to materialize in the majors.

PITCHERS

PLAYER	TEAM	LVL	AGE	W	L	SV	IP	H	HR	BB	SO	BB9	SO9	GB%	BABIP	WHIP	ERA	FIP	FRA	WARP
R. Alcantara	BUR	A	19	6	11	0	102^{2}	119	12	38	57	3.3	5.0	53%	.323	1.53	5.08	5.07	7.05	-0.9
A. Carignan	OAK	MLB	25	1	1	0	9^{2}	8	0	10	8	9.3	7.4	46%	.308	1.86	4.66	4.49	6.38	-0.2
P. Figueroa	SAC	AAA	26	0	2	1	44^{2}	35	1	18	40	3.6	8.1	48%	.272	1.19	2.62	3.58	3.80	0.6
	OAK	MLB	26	0	0	0	21^{2}	16	2	15	14	6.2	5.8	42%	.241	1.43	3.32	5.03	5.59	-0.3
I. Krol	STO	A+	21	1	7	0	86^{1}	95	13	24	79	2.5	8.2	46%	.315	1.38	5.21	4.88	5.10	1.2
A. Leon	SAC	AAA	23	3	0	0	35^{2}	26	4	15	31	3.8	7.8	52%	.239	1.15	1.77	4.82	4.55	0.3
G. Olson	BUF	AAA	28	4	7	0	122^{1}	133	11	53	107	3.9	7.9	46%	.326	1.52	4.63	3.93	4.61	0.3
	NYN	MLB	28	0	0	0	0^{1}	3	0	1	0	27.0	0.0	25%	.750	12.00	108.00	12.14	5.16	0.0
J. Simmons	MID	AA	25	1	2	1	48^{1}	41	3	14	37	2.6	6.9	36%	.261	1.14	3.35	3.67	3.85	0.3
J. Thomas	SWB	AAA	28	2	1	1	57^{1}	49	3	20	49	3.1	7.7	51%	.286	1.20	3.45	3.23	3.87	0.5
	BOS	MLB	28	0	0	0	4^{2}	10	0	2	4	3.9	7.7	33%	.556	2.57	7.71	3.26	3.80	0.1
	NYA	MLB	28	0	0	0	3	2	1	1	3	3.0	9.0	25%	.143	1.00	9.00	6.38	6.03	-0.1
M. Ynoa	VER	A-	20	1	3	0	20^{2}	20	2	16	19	7.0	8.3	24%	.295	1.74	6.97	5.51	6.30	0.1

Raul Alcantara arrived via the Andrew Bailey trade and immediately cracked the system's top-10 prospects, according to Kevin Goldstein, but the pitch command that was the foundation for his lofty status escaped Alcantara last year, and the pitches that did cross the plate rarely missed bats. ⊘ **Andrew Carignan** underwent Tommy John surgery in June, and a successful rehab could have him back on the mound at some point in the second half of the season. ⊘ **Pedro Figueroa** walked more batters than he struck out in his major-league debut, but left-handed pitchers with 96-mph sinkers don't grow on trees, and he will be given plenty of chances to stick despite a spotty track record in the minors. ⊘ **Ian Krol** rebounded from a lost season to reach Double-A, and though his control numbers are a positive sign for the health of his elbow, opposing batters had no problem squaring up his strikes. ⊘ **Arnold Leon** was a hidden gem from the Mexican League before the prospect's career was derailed in 2010 by Tommy John surgery, and his first full season back on the mound was a triumph that finished just one step away from the majors. ⊘ **Garrett Olson** posted a 108.00 ERA in 2012, though FIP reveals that he didn't pitch anywhere near that poorly: a 12.14 mark is much more appropriate. ⊘ **James Simmons** began his career in Double-A at the age of 20, and five years later the former first-rounder was back in Midland, making his comeback from the right-shoulder surgery that derailed his career. ⊘ **Justin Thomas** makes a brief cameo every couple of years, and his bitter cup of coffee from last season will likely be his only taste of the majors until he resurfaces in 2014. ⊘ **Michael Ynoa** quadrupled his career total for innings pitched in 2012, though the former wunderkind labored through his scant 30 innings. The A's could not bear the thought of releasing him into the wild, adding Ynoa to the 40-man roster to protect him from the Rule 5 draft.

MANAGER: BOB MELVIN

YEAR	TEAM	W-L	Pythag +/-	Avg PC	100+ P	120+ P	QS	BQS	REL	REL w Zero R	IBB	PH	PH Avg	PH HR	SB2	CS2	SB3	CS3	SAC Att	SAC %	POS SAC	Squeeze	Swing	In Play
2011	OAK	47-52	0	100.4	51	1	55	3	282	220	9	30	.276	2	19	2	0	0	38	78.9%	28	0	229	63
2012	OAK	94-68	1	92.5	52	0	90	4	462	386	34	93	.231	3	33	5	0	1	43	74.4%	31	0	307	76

The Athletics were one of the two most shocking teams in 2012, and unlike the extra-inning anomaly in Baltimore, the A's had the run differential to back up their lofty record. Melvin piloted the A's to a script-worthy sprint to the finish, battling head to head with the heavily favored Rangers to take the division crown. For his efforts, Melvin was awarded the prize for AL Manager of the Year. Though the public is privy to just a fraction of the skipper's skills, Melvin's strategic use of his roster effectively married the A's long-term goals with a winning culture in the clubhouse.

He was careful with his young pitching staff: Not a single starter exceeded 120 pitches in a ballgame, passing the baton to a shutdown bullpen. Oakland's depth in the relief corps was bolstered by pitchers who were not limited to platoon roles, giving Melvin the freedom to ride the hot hand in critical situations. Roles were reversed on offense, and he successfully employed an effective platoon rotation to maximize his batter output. Melvin oversaw a well-rounded club, including a field unit that finished with the third-ranked defensive efficiency in baseball, just two points behind the leaders. He successfully navigated through a high-pressure season, moving past the PED suspension of Bartolo Colon without missing a beat, and he confidently utilized the organizational pitching depth by trusting that a gang of rookies had been well-prepared by the player-development machine.

Philadelphia Phillies

2012: NO TIME TO LOSE

The Phillies only got about two-thirds of the inning allotment they had grown accustomed to from Roy Halladay, making it far more difficult for the pitching to paper over the ineptitude of the offense, which had to make do with a combined 654 plate appearances from Chase Utley and Ryan Howard. The bullpen was among the league leaders in strikeouts, but also home runs allowed, meaning the relievers threw away far too many games, most of which seemed to be started by Cliff Lee.

The best season at the plate ended up coming from the catcher, the regular who plays the least, so the impact of Carlos Ruiz's star turn was muted. Otherwise, the Phillies regulars tended to be hurting (Utley, Howard, Placido Polanco), aging (Utley, Howard, Polanco, Jimmy Rollins), or Juan Pierre.

Seeing their season was a lost cause, Philadelphia traded valuable chips such as Hunter Pence and Shane Victorino to bolster a dried-up farm system. Almost predictably, the team then went 35-24 over the final two months because why not? It still wasn't enough. The Phillies missed the expanded playoffs by seven games, but the strong finish did leave them with a .500 record.

The horde of fireballers to emerge in the bullpen was an unexpected treat that could bode well for the future if they can keep the ball in the park. Unfortunately, the lost season didn't foster any emerging talents on the offensive side as Dominic Brown and John Mayberry failed to establish themselves as the foundation for the next contending team in Philadelphia.

2013: HEALTHY=WEALTHY AND WISE

The Phils did add some youth to the lineup by trading for 25-year-old center fielder Ben Revere, but immediately cancelled that youth out by also trading for 36-year-old Michael Young. This team is reliant upon old stars Utley and Howard staying healthy, especially with an outfield in flux and Ruiz on the sidelines for 25 games with an amphetamine suspension. In other words, it is still all about the pitching. If they don't get 640 or more innings from their Big Three—Halladay, Lee, and Cole Hamels—the Phillies can't even begin to dream of contention.

PHILLIES PROSPECTUS

2012 W-L: 81-81, 3rd in NL East

Pythag	.503	17th	DER	.702	21st
RS/G	4.22	19th	B-Age	31.3	29th
RA/G	4.20	14th	P-Age	29.2	24th
TAv	.263	13th	Salary	$172.1	3rd
BRR	-9.7	27th	M$/MW	$4.90	26th
TAv-P	.262	19th	DL Days	1303	6th
FIP	3.76	6th	DL WARP	6.5	3rd

Three-Year Park Factors	
Overall	95
HR/RH	114
HR/LH	107
AVG/RH	104
AVG/LH	97

Citizens Bank Park (2004)
Att. % of Capacity: 100.8% (1st)
Dim. 329, 374, 401, 369, 330

C.B.P. is still a nice place to go deep, especially for righties, but plays more neutral than in its early days.

The rotation is obviously top-heavy because, short of putting Justin Verlander and David Price in the four and five spots, virtually anyone will be overshadowed by these three studs. That said, the back end is sturdy with Kyle Kendrick and John Lannan, plus capable minor-league reinforcements. So the need for the 640-plus innings isn't because the Phillies would struggle to find replacements, but because the Big Three is where Philly's star power lies, and that power needs to carry the lagging offense.

Health is important for any team, but when your club's driving force is a handful of guys who are all—save Hamels—well on the wrong side of 30, it becomes paramount. There are contending teams who can survive a significant injury or two, as the Reds did with Joey Votto or the Nationals did with Jayson Werth and Michael Morse last year. The 2013 Phillies will not be one of those teams.

STATE OF THE ORGANIZATION: WINDOW DRESSING

The Phillies have unquestionably been one of the most successful organizations of the 2000s, with a run of five straight division titles that ended last year, just two sub-.500 seasons, two World Series appearances, and their 2008 title. The window isn't closed yet, but they have been passed by divisional foes Washington and Atlanta, making it harder to see how this team gets back on top with its core group. The farm system has some exciting young talent, but most of it, especially the hitting, is quite some time away. Still, while the batters of note are mostly dreams at this point, their upside is significant.

If you are a Phillies fan the unsettling potential in this situation is that the front office could have its head turned by a strong start or a good midsummer run and start flipping minor-league talent to patch holes on the big club and keep the window cracked open a bit longer. Just ask fans in Houston how that works out. Ideally, Phillies management will see this team for what it is and, barring a surprising and sustained bid for contention, realize that once again moving veteran parts in July is the best move. You can never have too much talent on the farm.

Meanwhile, the bills due on some onerous contracts could make some players more difficult to move. Rollins is 34 and owed at least $22.5 million. Howard, 33, still has an astonishing $105 million coming to him from the five-year extension that kicked in last year. Lee is still elite entering his age-34 season, but he's owed $25 million a year for the next three years, plus a $12.5 million buyout of a $27.5 million option for 2016. Jonathan Papelbon is a mere lad at 32, but $39 million is an awful lot to owe a relief pitcher, even a good one. The Phillies are presumably happy to have locked up Hamels, but what are the odds they'll stay happy as his six-year, $144 million deal ages?

Arms like Tyler Cloyd, who made his debut last year, Jonathan Pettibone, and Brody Colvin are ready or soon will be, with Colvin carrying the loftiest ceiling among them. Jesse Biddle is the one to watch, though. The 21-year-old blue-chip lefty may be ready to take Lannan's place in 2014. The needed reinforcements for the offense are further out and require patience. Dylan Cozens, Maikel Franco, Larry Greene, and Roman Quinn could make up two-thirds of an outfield and the left side of an infield in the future, but they will be a combined 79 years old in 2013, and when you're dividing by four, that isn't very old. Catcher Tommy Joseph is the best offensive prospect on the verge and may allow the team to let Ruiz walk after 2013.

HITTERS

Cody Asche 3B

Born: **6/30/1990** Age: **23**
Bats: **L** Throws: **R** Height: **6' 2"**
Weight: **180** Breakout: **6%**
Improve: **71%** Collapse: **3%**
Attrition: **6%** MLB: **96%**

Comparables:
Steve Garvey, Aurelio Rodriguez, Fernando Tatis

YEAR	TEAM	LVL	AGE	PA	R	2B	3B	HR	RBI	BB	SO	SB	CS	AVG_OBP_SLG	TAv	BABIP	BRR	FRAA	WARP
2011	WPT	A-	21	268	14	11	0	2	19	24	50	0	3	.192/.273/.264	.232	.234	-1.7	2B(37): 3.5	0.0
2012	CLR	A+	22	270	31	13	3	2	25	12	37	10	2	.349/.378/.447	.270	.399	-0.3	3B(44): -2.8	-0.1
2012	REA	AA	22	289	42	20	3	10	47	22	56	1	1	.300/.360/.513	.311	.348	-1.5	3B(53): 1.7	1.9
2013	*PHI*	*MLB*	*23*	*250*	*22*	*11*	*1*	*5*	*26*	*11*	*56*	*1*	*1*	*.242/.278/.367*	*.232*	*.293*	*-0.2*	*3B -0, 2B 0*	*-0.1*

Asche enjoyed a breakout season by responding well to an aggressive assignment to High-A. He also acquitted himself well in Double-A before heading west for a strong showing in the Arizona Fall League, which he led in doubles. At 23, the college product should earn a Triple-A assignment to start the season and could reasonably wind up in Philly at some point during the season, though it should be noted that defense is easily the biggest hole in his game, and the Phillies will want him to work on that.

Domonic Brown RF

Born: **9/3/1987** Age: **25**
Bats: **L** Throws: **L** Height: **6' 6"**
Weight: **205** Breakout: **5%**
Improve: **58%** Collapse: **1%**
Attrition: **5%** MLB: **95%**

Comparables:
Don Baylor, Andre Ethier, Gary Matthews

YEAR	TEAM	LVL	AGE	PA	R	2B	3B	HR	RBI	BB	SO	SB	CS	AVG_OBP_SLG	TAv	BABIP	BRR	FRAA	WARP
2010	REA	AA	22	271	50	16	3	15	47	29	51	12	6	.318/.397/.602	.330	.353	-1.2	RF(61): 3.9	2.8
2010	LEH	AAA	22	118	15	6	1	5	21	8	23	5	1	.346/.397/.561	.331	.405	1.8	RF(25): -0.4, LF(3): -0.1	1.2
2010	PHI	MLB	22	70	8	3	0	2	13	5	24	2	1	.210/.257/.355	.241	.282	-0.1	RF(15): 0.9	0.1
2011	LEH	AAA	23	174	22	6	0	3	15	28	33	12	4	.261/.391/.370	.281	.311	0	--	0.0
2011	PHI	MLB	23	210	28	10	1	5	19	25	35	3	1	.245/.333/.391	.279	.276	2.8	RF(52): -4.3	0.2
2012	LEH	AAA	24	239	33	13	2	5	28	17	42	4	6	.286/.335/.432	.209	.331	-1.3	LF(16): 1.1, CF(7): -0.3	-0.5
2012	PHI	MLB	24	212	21	11	2	5	26	21	34	0	0	.235/.316/.396	.254	.260	-3.5	RF(38): -0.7, LF(28): 1.1	-0.2
2013	*PHI*	*MLB*	*25*	*250*	*29*	*12*	*1*	*8*	*31*	*21*	*50*	*4*	*2*	*.258/.323/.430*	*.270*	*.295*	*-0.2*	*RF -1, LF -0*	*0.7*

Consistently labeled as a prime "change-of-scenery" trade candidate, Brown spent another disappointing season split between a modest Triple-A stint and an equally ho-hum third of a season with the big club. Now 25, his career is at a crossroads. As a post-hype prospect, he's on the verge of becoming either a late-bloomer or a bust. The Phillies are in transition following last year's trades of Hunter Pence and Shane Victorino, and Brown has a prime chance to prove himself. It's worth noting that he hasn't yet amassed 500 big-league plate appearances, meaning we aren't close to a meaningful sample with which to judge him as a major leaguer.

Zach Collier OF
Born: **9/8/1990** Age: **22**
Bats: **L** Throws: **L** Height: **6' 3"**
Weight: **185** Breakout: **7%**
Improve: **54%** Collapse: **5%**
Attrition: **18%** MLB: **96%**
Comparables:
David Green,Chet Lemon,Bobby Tolan

YEAR	TEAM	LVL	AGE	PA	R	2B	3B	HR	RBI	BB	SO	SB	CS	AVG_OBP_SLG	TAv	BABIP	BRR	FRAA	WARP
2011	LWD	A	20	471	50	24	6	1	36	40	99	35	13	.255/.328/.349	.266	.328	2.4	CF(49): 3.4, LF(26): -1.5	1.0
2012	CLR	A+	21	319	39	13	3	6	32	26	60	11	3	.269/.333/.399	.276	.315	-1.2	CF(56): -4.7, LF(3): -0.4	0.2
2013	*PHI*	*MLB*	*22*	*250*	*25*	*9*	*1*	*4*	*21*	*13*	*62*	*10*	*4*	*.216/.263/.316*	*.213*	*.272*	*0.7*	*CF -1, LF -1*	*-0.6*

Collier's season was shortened by a 50-game amphetamine suspension, though he followed it up with a nice 78-game stint in High-A that showed incremental improvements on his 2011. He then had an even nicer 19-game run in the Arizona Fall League, where he was among the league leaders in batting average and OPS. Collier fits an organizational philosophy that strongly favors ultra-talented, athletic outfielders who carry significant upside should they reach the potential of their raw tools. The Phillies figure that if one of their gaggle of such players breaks through, it'll all be worth it. Collier may not be the most likely to succeed, but there's plenty to like about him.

Maikel Franco 3B
Born: **8/26/1992** Age: **20**
Bats: **R** Throws: **R** Height: **6' 2"**
Weight: **180** Breakout: **28%**
Improve: **62%** Collapse: **5%**
Attrition: **29%** MLB: **90%**
Comparables:
Ted Kazanski,Adrian Beltre,Wayne Causey

YEAR	TEAM	LVL	AGE	PA	R	2B	3B	HR	RBI	BB	SO	SB	CS	AVG_OBP_SLG	TAv	BABIP	BRR	FRAA	WARP
2010	PHL	Rk	17	217	23	11	2	2	29	16	46	0	0	.222/.293/.330	.250	.279	-4.1	3B(54): -0.5	0.0
2011	LWD	A	18	67	6	2	0	1	6	1	15	0	0	.123/.149/.200	.135	.143	0	3B(11): -0.4	-0.6
2011	WPT	A-	18	229	19	17	1	2	38	25	30	0	0	.287/.367/.411	.284	.327	-2.2	3B(17): 1.3	0.3
2012	LWD	A	19	554	70	32	3	14	84	38	80	3	1	.280/.336/.439	.298	.306	0.7	3B(108): -13.0	1.6
2013	*PHI*	*MLB*	*20*	*250*	*20*	*10*	*1*	*5*	*25*	*10*	*61*	*0*	*0*	*.211/.245/.326*	*.208*	*.258*	*-0.4*	*3B -1*	*-0.9*

Philadelphia has an impressive group of third-base prospects, but none of them is ready to take the reins, so Michael Young was brought in as a one-year stopgap. Franco has the highest ceiling of the group, though he is a long way away. His defensive skills are evident, but it's his offense that could make him a star. He has an aggressive approach, but it's controlled aggression, so he avoids too much swing-and-miss. His power showed up in a big way last year with 49 extra-base hits, and many scouts see him developing even more. With the defense in place, he is left to focus on turning the raw hit and power tools into the plus assets they can be.

Kevin Frandsen 3B
Born: **5/24/1982** Age: **31**
Bats: **R** Throws: **R** Height: **6' 1"**
Weight: **185** Breakout: **0%**
Improve: **36%** Collapse: **4%**
Attrition: **16%** MLB: **96%**
Comparables:
Red Schoendienst,Ryan Theriot,Placido Polanco

YEAR	TEAM	LVL	AGE	PA	R	2B	3B	HR	RBI	BB	SO	SB	CS	AVG_OBP_SLG	TAv	BABIP	BRR	FRAA	WARP
2010	PAW	AAA	28	71	9	3	0	2	4	5	3	2	0	.258/.338/.403	.243	.241	0.4	SS(10): -0.3, 2B(4): -0.2	0.0
2010	SLC	AAA	28	155	25	9	1	1	12	7	19	2	1	.277/.348/.380	.247	.311	1.4	3B(18): 1.5, 2B(9): -0.7	0.3
2010	ANA	MLB	28	173	24	11	0	0	14	9	10	2	0	.250/.294/.319	.244	.267	-0.3	3B(43): -0.3, 2B(4): 0.0	0.3
2011	LEH	AAA	29	322	32	13	3	4	40	11	31	10	3	.303/.356/.412	.272	.322	0	--	0.0
2012	LEH	AAA	30	418	38	34	0	1	33	14	31	2	4	.302/.337/.396	.210	.323	0.9	2B(29): 0.2, 1B(6): -0.5	-0.6
2012	PHI	MLB	30	210	24	10	3	2	14	9	18	0	1	.338/.383/.451	.303	.366	-1.9	3B(52): -2.7	0.8
2013	*PHI*	*MLB*	*31*	*250*	*26*	*13*	*1*	*3*	*21*	*10*	*27*	*1*	*1*	*.260/.305/.364*	*.244*	*.279*	*-0.5*	*3B -0, 2B -1*	*0.1*

Frandsen has been a great example of how small samples can deliver varied performance without any discernible skill change. He spent a year in the minors in between, but his 2010 and 2012 seasons are on opposite ends of the production spectrum. Even though the better one is more recent, he's still a journeyman utility player, not someone in the midst of a career rebirth. He is best deployed against left-handed pitchers in very limited doses. Any extended playing time for Frandsen will mean something has gone very wrong for the Phillies.

Freddy Galvis SS
Born: **11/14/1989** Age: **23**
Bats: **B** Throws: **R** Height: **5' 11"**
Weight: **170** Breakout: **7%**
Improve: **52%** Collapse: **6%**
Attrition: **10%** MLB: **83%**
Comparables:
Edgardo Alfonzo,Alexi Amarista,Manny Lee

YEAR	TEAM	LVL	AGE	PA	R	2B	3B	HR	RBI	BB	SO	SB	CS	AVG_OBP_SLG	TAv	BABIP	BRR	FRAA	WARP
2010	REA	AA	20	545	58	16	4	5	48	30	89	15	4	.233/.274/.311	.215	.269	4.3	SS(138): 10.7	0.9
2011	REA	AA	21	464	63	22	4	8	35	28	68	19	11	.273/.326/.400	.272	.308	-0.4	SS(46): 5.0	1.1
2011	LEH	AAA	21	126	15	6	1	0	8	3	18	4	2	.298/.315/.364	.240	.350	0	--	0.0
2012	PHI	MLB	22	200	14	15	1	3	24	7	29	0	0	.226/.254/.363	.217	.253	0.7	2B(55): 3.2, SS(5): 0.7	-0.2
2013	*PHI*	*MLB*	*23*	*250*	*24*	*11*	*1*	*3*	*21*	*9*	*45*	*7*	*3*	*.231/.262/.331*	*.215*	*.267*	*0.3*	*2B 0, SS -0*	*-0.1*

When discussing Galvis's hitting, it's worth noting that he has an excellent glove. The prototypical eight-spot hitter found himself in the Opening Day lineup for the Phillies last year because of Chase Utley's injury. He started off horribly, with a 519 OPS in April, before posting a more tolerable 705 in May. Soon thereafter, he was popped for banned substances and hit with a 50-game suspension. Even when that ended, a fractured back kept him out the rest of the year. It'd be foolish to think he was flailing in April, took something illegal, and then became useful in

May. He is better than that first month and maybe as good as his second at his peak. Galvis will never be much of an offensive force. He's best deployed as a defensive replacement all around the infield.

Tyson Gillies CF
Born: **10/31/1988** Age: **24**
Bats: **L** Throws: **R** Height: **6' 3"**
Weight: **195** Breakout: **2%**
Improve: **45%** Collapse: **1%**
Attrition: **10%** MLB: **90%**
Comparables:
Rowland Office,Torii Hunter,Alejandro De Aza

YEAR	TEAM	LVL	AGE	PA	R	2B	3B	HR	RBI	BB	SO	SB	CS	AVG_OBP_SLG	TAv	BABIP	BRR	FRAA	WARP
2010	REA	AA	21	113	15	2	1	2	6	5	24	2	2	.238/.283/.333	.220	.287	0.3	CF(26): 0.7	0.0
2012	REA	AA	23	311	59	13	8	4	24	18	52	8	6	.304/.369/.453	.270	.362	1.7	CF(48): -1.6	0.8
2013	*PHI*	*MLB*	*24*	*250*	*26*	*9*	*2*	*3*	*20*	*11*	*58*	*4*	*2*	*.236/.285/.340*	*.230*	*.294*	*0*	*CF -2*	*-0.2*

Once a real prospect, Gillies has played a mere 106 games in three years since coming over in the Cliff Lee trade. Injuries have completely derailed his career and cut into his once-80-grade speed. In the past, he had projected as a legitimate leadoff hitter at a premium position, displaying patience at the plate and using his incredible wheels to track down anything and everything in center field. At 24, his prospect status hasn't entirely evaporated, but it's running dry after three busted seasons. If he doesn't start the season in Lehigh Valley with the Triple-A club, he should get there eventually, but with Ben Revere in town, Gillies's future likely isn't in Philadelphia.

Larry Greene LF
Born: **2/10/1993** Age: **20**
Bats: **L** Throws: **R** Height: **6' 1"**
Weight: **235** Breakout: **19%**
Improve: **51%** Collapse: **5%**
Attrition: **28%** MLB: **85%**
Comparables:
Wayne Causey,Bobby Delgreco,Ed Kirkpatrick

YEAR	TEAM	LVL	AGE	PA	R	2B	3B	HR	RBI	BB	SO	SB	CS	AVG_OBP_SLG	TAv	BABIP	BRR	FRAA	WARP
2012	WPT	A-	19	303	36	22	0	2	26	41	78	1	2	.272/.373/.381	.257	.378	-0.4	LF(59): 4.4	0.5
2013	*PHI*	*MLB*	*20*	*250*	*19*	*9*	*1*	*3*	*21*	*19*	*83*	*0*	*0*	*.185/.249/.272*	*.194*	*.269*	*-0.4*	*LF -1*	*-1.4*

This hulking mass of a man was all set to terrorize ball-carriers in the SEC with a commitment to play linebacker at Alabama, but the Phillies lured him to baseball with a cool million dollars. Now he's expected to develop into a player who will treat baseballs the way he'd been planning to treat Auburn running backs. Greene has raw power that some project as future 80-grade. The question is, will it develop? That power manifested itself more in doubles than home runs last year, but Greene has the potential to become a three-true-outcomes stud in the middle of the lineup.

Cesar Hernandez 2B
Born: **5/23/1990** Age: **23**
Bats: **B** Throws: **R** Height: **5' 11"**
Weight: **160** Breakout: **3%**
Improve: **55%** Collapse: **4%**
Attrition: **9%** MLB: **84%**
Comparables:
Jose Lopez,Bip Roberts,Emilio Bonifacio

YEAR	TEAM	LVL	AGE	PA	R	2B	3B	HR	RBI	BB	SO	SB	CS	AVG_OBP_SLG	TAv	BABIP	BRR	FRAA	WARP
2010	WPT	A-	20	287	36	13	2	0	23	26	27	32	6	.325/.394/.392	.301	.364	1.6	2B(65): 0.1	2.6
2011	CLR	A+	21	452	47	7	4	4	37	23	80	23	10	.268/.306/.333	.254	.322	0.6	2B(54): 4.6	0.8
2012	REA	AA	22	450	50	26	11	2	51	27	67	16	12	.304/.345/.436	.302	.358	0.2	2B(81): 3.3	2.3
2012	LEH	AAA	22	129	13	4	1	0	6	4	11	5	3	.248/.270/.298	.245	.270	0.8	2B(13): 0.4	0.1
2013	*PHI*	*MLB*	*23*	*250*	*28*	*10*	*2*	*2*	*17*	*10*	*44*	*10*	*5*	*.251/.283/.336*	*.226*	*.295*	*0.5*	*2B -2*	*-0.1*

Hernandez has handled some aggressive assignments with aplomb, though he wasn't quite ready for Triple-A last year. He looked good in Double-A, though, smacking the ball all over the place and cleaning up his approach from High-A in 2011, resulting in a 3 percentage-point improvement in his strikeout rate. His speed was evident when he used his gap power for 26 doubles and 11 triples, but the horrid 16-for-28 stolen-base rate shows that his baserunning instincts need work. Hernandez's defense is fine. He just needs to continue honing his offense and he could find himself succeeding Utley.

Ryan Howard 1B
Born: **11/19/1979** Age: **33**
Bats: **L** Throws: **L** Height: **6' 5"**
Weight: **240** Breakout: **2%**
Improve: **29%** Collapse: **7%**
Attrition: **7%** MLB: **87%**
Comparables:
Willie Stargell,Dick Allen,Carlos Pena

YEAR	TEAM	LVL	AGE	PA	R	2B	3B	HR	RBI	BB	SO	SB	CS	AVG_OBP_SLG	TAv	BABIP	BRR	FRAA	WARP
2010	PHI	MLB	30	620	87	23	5	31	108	59	157	1	1	.276/.353/.505	.295	.332	-8.3	1B(139): -3.3	1.6
2011	PHI	MLB	31	644	81	30	1	33	116	75	172	1	0	.253/.346/.488	.306	.303	-9.4	1B(149): 0.2	1.6
2012	PHI	MLB	32	292	28	11	0	14	56	25	99	0	0	.219/.295/.423	.251	.287	-4	1B(67): -3.5	-1.0
2013	*PHI*	*MLB*	*33*	*348*	*47*	*14*	*1*	*19*	*55*	*35*	*99*	*1*	*0*	*.248/.329/.489*	*.288*	*.298*	*-0.4*	*1B -2*	*1.2*

Once a three-true-outcomes guy himself, Howard has seen his walk rate fade considerably since 2007, when it peaked at 16.5 percent. Most of that is because his intentional walks have dropped precipitously from the mid-30s to no higher than 17 since 2008. Howard had better make some adjustments if he wants to have any chance of living up to the rest of his massive contract. Even his 2010-11 performance wouldn't be worth anywhere near the $20 million he'll make this year, let alone the $25 million he is slated to collect annually, 2014-16. At least Phillies fans are reasonable and measured in their response to players.

Jiwan James CF
Born: **4/11/1989** Age: **24**
Bats: **B** Throws: **R** Height: **6' 5"**
Weight: **180** Breakout: **6%**
Improve: **51%** Collapse: **4%**
Attrition: **23%** MLB: **88%**

Comparables:
Jim Pyburn,Bobby Gene Smith,Jarvis Tatum

YEAR	TEAM	LVL	AGE	PA	R	2B	3B	HR	RBI	BB	SO	SB	CS	AVG_OBP_SLG	TAv	BABIP	BRR	FRAA	WARP
2010	LWD	A	21	617	85	26	6	5	64	35	132	33	20	.270/.322/.365	.270	.341	0.8	CF(137): -5.6	2.2
2011	CLR	A+	22	577	76	26	6	4	38	40	120	31	16	.268/.327/.363	.272	.339	0.9	CF(58): -3.4, RF(1): -0.1	0.8
2012	REA	AA	23	416	55	14	5	6	31	21	115	8	8	.249/.291/.360	.267	.335	4.6	CF(54): -3.6, RF(20): 1.8	0.9
2013	*PHI*	*MLB*	*24*	*250*	*26*	*9*	*2*	*3*	*17*	*9*	*69*	*8*	*5*	*.220/.252/.308*	*.207*	*.291*	*0*	*CF -3, RF 0*	*-1.0*

Yet another of the toolsy-but-raw outfielders in the Philadelphia system, James is on the wrong end of that spectrum; his upside is fading rapidly. He was passed over in the 2011 Rule 5 draft and followed that up with another unimpressive performance in the minors. Now 24 years old, he is looking at a potential repeat of Double-A, quickly moving from what could be to what could've been.

Tommy Joseph C
Born: **7/16/1991** Age: **21**
Bats: **R** Throws: **R** Height: **6' 2"**
Weight: **220** Breakout: **1%**
Improve: **62%** Collapse: **13%**
Attrition: **18%** MLB: **97%**

Comparables:
Rene Lachemann,Johnny Bench,Joe Torre

YEAR	TEAM	LVL	AGE	PA	R	2B	3B	HR	RBI	BB	SO	SB	CS	AVG_OBP_SLG	TAv	BABIP	BRR	FRAA	WARP
2010	AUG	A	18	473	46	22	1	16	68	26	116	0	0	.236/.291/.401	.249	.286	-3.8	C(65): -0.6, 1B(10): 0.2	0.4
2011	SJO	A+	19	560	80	33	2	22	95	29	102	1	0	.270/.317/.471	.264	.295	0	--	0.0
2012	REA	AA	20	114	12	8	0	3	10	9	32	0	1	.250/.327/.420	.244	.333	-0.4	C(18): -0.5, 1B(2): -0.1	0.0
2012	RIC	AA	20	335	32	16	0	8	38	25	64	0	3	.260/.313/.391	.272	.300	-2.5	C(43): -0.3, 1B(12): -0.8	0.9
2013	*PHI*	*MLB*	*21*	*250*	*22*	*10*	*0*	*7*	*28*	*11*	*68*	*0*	*0*	*.217/.256/.359*	*.222*	*.269*	*-0.5*	*C -0, 1B -0*	*-0.2*

The prize of the Hunter Pence deal, Joseph enjoyed the hitter's haven that is the California League, where at one point he hit eight home runs in six road games in Stockton and Lancaster. Unsurprisingly, he saw his power fade upon the move to Reading. The Eastern League represents a higher level and an ERA nearly a full run lower, so don't read too much into the slippage. That said, defense figures to be Joseph's calling card in the majors. He spends some time at first base, but his catching skills have advanced enough that he shouldn't have to worry about his bat carrying another position.

Erik Kratz C
Born: **6/15/1980** Age: **33**
Bats: **R** Throws: **R** Height: **6' 5"**
Weight: **255** Breakout: **0%**
Improve: **27%** Collapse: **13%**
Attrition: **21%** MLB: **92%**

Comparables:
Ramon Castro,Gene Oliver,Carlton Fisk

YEAR	TEAM	LVL	AGE	PA	R	2B	3B	HR	RBI	BB	SO	SB	CS	AVG_OBP_SLG	TAv	BABIP	BRR	FRAA	WARP
2010	IND	AAA	30	274	30	22	1	9	41	32	54	1	2	.274/.384/.496	.273	.323	-1.3	C(63): 1.2, 1B(3): 0.0	1.3
2010	PIT	MLB	30	36	2	0	0	0	1	2	9	0	0	.118/.167/.118	.129	.160	-0.9	C(9): 0.1	-0.4
2011	LEH	AAA	31	409	56	19	0	15	53	38	72	2	0	.288/.372/.466	.292	.322	0	--	0.0
2011	PHI	MLB	31	6	0	1	0	0	0	0	1	0	0	.333/.333/.500	.294	.400	-0.1	C(1): 0.0	0.1
2012	LEH	AAA	32	141	17	10	0	8	30	10	20	0	0	.266/.326/.540	.295	.250	-1.1	C(15): -0.4	0.4
2012	PHI	MLB	32	157	14	9	0	9	26	11	34	0	0	.248/.306/.504	.292	.257	-1.4	C(41): 0.7	1.3
2013	*PHI*	*MLB*	*33*	*250*	*29*	*12*	*0*	*10*	*31*	*19*	*56*	*0*	*0*	*.231/.299/.416*	*.256*	*.262*	*-0.5*	*C 0, 1B -0*	*1.0*

Kratz is a journeyman catcher who finally got a shot at some serious playing time in the majors. There he displayed some big power consistent with the power he had demonstrated at Triple-A. Old catcher skills coming to the fore or simply good fortune in a pair of small samples? Almost certainly the latter. If the Phillies plan to use Kratz as the starter while Carlos Ruiz serves his suspension for amphetamines, then he'll be exposed. That is, unless he has suddenly acquired the ability to hit home runs on 20 percent of his fly balls. Spoiler alert: He hasn't.

Michael Martinez UT
Born: **9/16/1982** Age: **30**
Bats: **B** Throws: **R** Height: **5' 10"**
Weight: **145** Breakout: **2%**
Improve: **25%** Collapse: **4%**
Attrition: **19%** MLB: **84%**

Comparables:
Matt Tolbert,Larvell Blanks,Granny Hamner

YEAR	TEAM	LVL	AGE	PA	R	2B	3B	HR	RBI	BB	SO	SB	CS	AVG_OBP_SLG	TAv	BABIP	BRR	FRAA	WARP
2010	HAR	AA	27	387	41	14	6	8	37	20	54	15	9	.253/.295/.393	.257	.276	1.9	2B(83): -1.9, CF(12): 1.9	1.1
2010	SYR	AAA	27	135	16	7	0	3	19	3	20	8	3	.325/.351/.452	.270	.362	2.2	CF(17): -2.3, SS(11): 1.5	0.7
2011	PHI	MLB	28	234	25	5	2	3	24	18	35	3	0	.196/.258/.282	.224	.220	1.7	3B(26): -1.0, 2B(19): 0.7	-0.4
2012	LEH	AAA	29	122	12	4	2	2	15	10	12	3	1	.271/.331/.402	.273	.281	-0.8	2B(5): 1.3, SS(3): -0.3	0.1
2012	PHI	MLB	29	122	10	3	0	2	7	5	21	0	0	.174/.208/.252	.171	.196	0.4	2B(16): -1.9, 3B(10): 0.7	-0.7
2013	*PHI*	*MLB*	*30*	*250*	*27*	*9*	*2*	*4*	*21*	*13*	*42*	*5*	*2*	*.228/.271/.337*	*.224*	*.255*	*0.2*	*2B -1, 3B 0*	*-0.1*

The pint-sized former Rule 5 pick is technically a success in that he remained with the team for the year he was drafted, and he even stuck around for part of the following year. But he hit .188 in 356 at-bats during those two years, the lowest of any NL player with at least 350 at-bats. That suggests that success is a relative term. The glove-only Martinez was retained on a minor-league deal and may get a chance to launch another assault on the Mendoza line as a utility player.

John Mayberry OF
Born: **12/21/1983** Age: **29**
Bats: **R** Throws: **R** Height: **6' 7"**
Weight: **230** Breakout: **4%**
Improve: **47%** Collapse: **0%**
Attrition: **9%** MLB: **86%**
Comparables:
Scott Hairston,George Hendrick,Matt Carson

YEAR	TEAM	LVL	AGE	PA	R	2B	3B	HR	RBI	BB	SO	SB	CS	AVG_OBP_SLG	TAv	BABIP	BRR	FRAA	WARP
2010	LEH	AAA	26	547	75	25	1	15	65	39	111	20	3	.267/.330/.412	.265	.316	0.8	RF(64): 1.4, LF(49): 5.3	1.9
2010	PHI	MLB	26	13	4	0	0	2	6	1	4	0	1	.333/.385/.833	.402	.333	-1.1	RF(3): -0.1, CF(2): -0.0	0.1
2011	LEH	AAA	27	122	16	8	0	4	15	5	23	2	0	.265/.287/.442	.243	.289	0	--	0.0
2011	PHI	MLB	27	296	37	17	1	15	49	26	55	8	3	.273/.341/.513	.306	.293	-0.4	CF(32): -0.1, LF(21): 0.2	1.8
2012	PHI	MLB	28	479	53	24	0	14	46	34	111	1	0	.245/.301/.395	.262	.296	-2.6	LF(70): 4.2, CF(58): 0.5	1.0
2013	*PHI*	*MLB*	*29*	*414*	*49*	*19*	*1*	*16*	*54*	*30*	*98*	*6*	*2*	*.247/.306/.427*	*.267*	*.290*	*0*	*CF -0, LF -0*	*1.3*

Mayberry couldn't build upon his 2011 success despite being given a full season of playing time. Everything in his game collapsed: He needed 186 more plate appearances to hit one fewer home run and draw just eight more walks. Weak contact did him in as he saw a 10 percent rise in groundball rate and a 12 percent dip in fly-ball rate. He had to leg out 21 infield hits just to hit the paltry .245 he ended up with, and that accounted for 12.2 percent of his hits, third-most in the National League. Mayberry did hit lefties to the tune of an 811 OPS, compared to 626 against right-handers, so perhaps a platoon is in his immediate future.

Laynce Nix OF
Born: **10/30/1980** Age: **32**
Bats: **L** Throws: **L** Height: **6' 2"**
Weight: **220** Breakout: **1%**
Improve: **30%** Collapse: **8%**
Attrition: **15%** MLB: **88%**
Comparables:
Glenn Davis,Eric Karros,Richie Zisk

YEAR	TEAM	LVL	AGE	PA	R	2B	3B	HR	RBI	BB	SO	SB	CS	AVG_OBP_SLG	TAv	BABIP	BRR	FRAA	WARP
2010	CIN	MLB	29	182	16	11	2	4	18	15	39	0	1	.291/.350/.455	.275	.361	-0.1	LF(50): -0.8, CF(4): -0.0	0.9
2011	WAS	MLB	30	351	38	15	1	16	44	23	82	2	2	.250/.299/.451	.280	.284	-1.6	LF(73): -2.6, RF(12): -0.3	0.7
2012	PHI	MLB	31	127	13	10	0	3	16	12	42	0	0	.246/.315/.412	.272	.357	-1.3	LF(18): 0.1, RF(10): 0.0	0.2
2013	*PHI*	*MLB*	*32*	*250*	*27*	*13*	*1*	*9*	*33*	*18*	*63*	*1*	*1*	*.243/.298/.430*	*.261*	*.291*	*-0.5*	*LF 0, RF 0*	*0.6*

Perhaps Nix could be Mayberry's platoon partner. Nix has developed into a worthwhile league-average part-timer against right-handers over the last four years, bringing some useful power for an average of about 250 plate appearances per year. Last year was his least productive offensively, but it was also his smallest sample. Teams have learned how to deploy Nix. It's just a matter of finding his platoon partner—and Mayberry seems like an excellent candidate.

Cameron Perkins 4C
Born: **9/27/1990** Age: **22**
Bats: **R** Throws: **R** Height: **6' 6"**
Weight: **195** Breakout: **7%**
Improve: **49%** Collapse: **7%**
Attrition: **13%** MLB: **92%**
Comparables:
Tookie Gilbert,Joe Rudi,Bob Hale

YEAR	TEAM	LVL	AGE	PA	R	2B	3B	HR	RBI	BB	SO	SB	CS	AVG_OBP_SLG	TAv	BABIP	BRR	FRAA	WARP
2012	WPT	A-	21	293	31	23	1	1	38	14	41	5	2	.304/.352/.407	.304	.352	0.5	1B(18): 1.2, 3B(10): -0.0	1.5
2013	*PHI*	*MLB*	*22*	*250*	*17*	*10*	*1*	*3*	*21*	*6*	*62*	*1*	*0*	*.208/.233/.294*	*.192*	*.264*	*-0.3*	*1B -0, 3B -0*	*-1.4*

Perkins differs from the super-athletic, tools-laden profiles often found in the Philly system. He's a polished college draftee with some upside to go, tied almost entirely to his bat. His aggressive approach could be exposed as a negative as the competition improves, but that's a facet of his game he can improve. The Phillies drafted Perkins as a third baseman, but last year he played three of the four corners at Williamsport.

Andrew Pullin 2B
Born: **9/25/1993** Age: **19**
Bats: **L** Throws: **R** Height: **6' 1"**
Weight: **190** Breakout: **0%**
Improve: **57%** Collapse: **43%**
Attrition: **43%** MLB: **100%**
Comparables:
Robin Yount,Ed Kranepool,Wayne Causey

YEAR	TEAM	LVL	AGE	PA	R	2B	3B	HR	RBI	BB	SO	SB	CS	AVG_OBP_SLG	TAv	BABIP	BRR	FRAA	WARP
2012	PHL	Rk	18	160	16	10	0	2	13	12	32	3	5	.321/.403/.436	.220	.406	-0.1	2B(4): 1.3	0.0
2013	*PHI*	*MLB*	*19*	*250*	*23*	*8*	*1*	*3*	*18*	*11*	*76*	*9*	*7*	*.180/.217/.259*	*.176*	*.245*	*-0.3*	*2B 0*	*-1.4*

A fifth-round pick, Pullin is being transitioned from the outfield to second base, and if that works, his prospect value will be much greater. He's an advanced hitter, especially for a player coming out of high school, and while the power will never be special, there is some development to tap into that could result in solid pop, especially for a second baseman. Thoughts on his overall potential vary, but there is little disagreement about the notion that he can hit. An interesting side note about Pullin is that he was a switch-pitcher in high school, so if for some reason the hitting doesn't pan out, he has a secondary route to explore. Maybe two of them, one with each hand.

Roman Quinn SS
Born: **5/14/1993** Age: **20**
Bats: **B** Throws: **R** Height: **5' 11"**
Weight: **170** Breakout: **15%**
Improve: **39%** Collapse: **15%**
Attrition: **28%** MLB: **83%**
Comparables:
B.J. Upton,Jose Oquendo,Ted Kazanski

YEAR	TEAM	LVL	AGE	PA	R	2B	3B	HR	RBI	BB	SO	SB	CS	AVG_OBP_SLG	TAv	BABIP	BRR	FRAA	WARP
2012	WPT	A-	19	309	56	9	11	1	23	28	61	30	6	.281/.370/.408	.325	.357	7.3	SS(55): -7.0	2.5
2013	*PHI*	*MLB*	*20*	*250*	*28*	*7*	*2*	*3*	*16*	*13*	*73*	*11*	*3*	*.198/.251/.287*	*.202*	*.271*	*1.4*	*SS -1*	*-0.4*

Tabbed as the fastest player in the 2011 draft, Quinn is an emerging middle-infield prospect the Phillies feel has enough upside in his bat to become a first-division, top-of-the-order hitter. They will leave him at shortstop as long as they can, though if he doesn't fully develop there, center field is a real option. For obvious reasons, his skills and potential positions have led to comparisons with both Michael Bourn and Jimmy Rollins. A breakout in his full-season debut would have him shooting up prospect lists for 2014.

Ben Revere **CF**
Born: **5/3/1988** Age: **25**
Bats: **L** Throws: **R** Height: **5' 10"**
Weight: **170** Breakout: **6%**
Improve: **46%** Collapse: **3%**
Attrition: **11%** MLB: **94%**
Comparables:
Miguel Dilone,Steve Hovley,J.B. Shuck

YEAR	TEAM	LVL	AGE	PA	R	2B	3B	HR	RBI	BB	SO	SB	CS	AVG_OBP_SLG	TAv	BABIP	BRR	FRAA	WARP
2010	NBR	AA	22	406	44	10	4	1	23	32	41	36	13	.305/.372/.363	.279	.340	3	CF(76): 4.3, LF(14): 0.2	2.9
2010	MIN	MLB	22	30	1	0	0	0	2	2	5	0	1	.179/.233/.179	.146	.217	-0.2	CF(5): -0.2, LF(3): 0.1	-0.4
2011	ROC	AAA	23	141	15	3	1	1	9	6	11	8	2	.303/.338/.364	.242	.325	0.4	CF(22): 2.9, LF(2): -0.1	0.2
2011	MIN	MLB	23	481	56	9	5	0	30	26	41	34	9	.267/.310/.309	.230	.293	8	CF(89): -2.7, LF(13): 0.7	-0.3
2012	ROC	AAA	24	101	9	1	0	0	6	4	6	6	2	.330/.360/.340	.252	.348	1.6	CF(12): 0.8, LF(6): 0.6	0.3
2012	MIN	MLB	24	553	70	13	6	0	32	29	54	40	9	.294/.333/.342	.245	.325	10	RF(84): 2.4, CF(39): -1.2	1.1
2013	*PHI*	*MLB*	*25*	*534*	*65*	*15*	*4*	*4*	*36*	*28*	*60*	*33*	*9*	*.273/.315/.343*	*.243*	*.300*	*3.4*	*CF -0, RF 0*	*0.9*

Ben Revere is fast. How fast? He's so fast, he got into Cool Papa Bell's bed before Bell could turn out the light. He's so fast that he covers the two-thirds of the Earth Garry Maddox can't be bothered to take care of. He's so fast, he got traded before this book was published and we had to re-write this comment. Revere broke out in a big way in 2012, thanks in no small part to his terrific baserunning and defense. He also legged out 43 infield hits, more than anyone else in baseball. Playing mostly right field, in spite of his terrible throwing arm, Revere proved valuable thanks to his phenomenal range, which will only play up in Philadelphia as the new Phillies center fielder.

Jimmy Rollins **SS**
Born: **11/27/1978** Age: **34**
Bats: **B** Throws: **R** Height: **5' 9"**
Weight: **170** Breakout: **1%**
Improve: **17%** Collapse: **11%**
Attrition: **20%** MLB: **92%**
Comparables:
Orlando Cabrera,Alan Trammell,Marco Scutaro

YEAR	TEAM	LVL	AGE	PA	R	2B	3B	HR	RBI	BB	SO	SB	CS	AVG_OBP_SLG	TAv	BABIP	BRR	FRAA	WARP
2010	PHI	MLB	31	394	48	16	3	8	41	40	32	17	1	.243/.320/.374	.262	.246	0.3	SS(87): -3.5	1.2
2011	PHI	MLB	32	631	87	22	2	16	63	58	59	30	8	.268/.338/.399	.279	.275	-0.1	SS(138): 1.1	3.5
2012	PHI	MLB	33	699	102	33	5	23	68	62	96	30	5	.250/.316/.427	.274	.262	5.3	SS(156): -8.5	3.0
2013	*PHI*	*MLB*	*34*	*643*	*86*	*30*	*4*	*16*	*62*	*51*	*74*	*28*	*5*	*.249/.311/.397*	*.257*	*.258*	*3.3*	*SS -1*	*2.9*

Rollins started off his 30s with a couple of subpar seasons, but has bounced back the last two years with a pair of solid performances across the board, including a power surge in 2012. While he is a lesser Rollins than the stud he was in his 20s, this version remains mighty effective by virtually any measure. He tied Starlin Castro as baseball's best shortstop, according to WARP, and his True Average was bested only by Ian Desmond, Jose Reyes, and Erick Aybar among qualifying shortstops, and tied by Derek Jeter. A shortstop of his caliber who can be relied upon for 600-plus plate appearances a year is extremely valuable, even when he isn't posting OPS totals north of 800. Rollins is aging gracefully after that two-year blip, and he has a good chance to continue doing so.

Darin Ruf **1B**
Born: **7/28/1986** Age: **26**
Bats: **R** Throws: **R** Height: **6' 4"**
Weight: **220** Breakout: **2%**
Improve: **48%** Collapse: **4%**
Attrition: **12%** MLB: **95%**
Comparables:
Adrian Gonzalez,Mark Teixeira,Eddie Murray

YEAR	TEAM	LVL	AGE	PA	R	2B	3B	HR	RBI	BB	SO	SB	CS	AVG_OBP_SLG	TAv	BABIP	BRR	FRAA	WARP
2010	LWD	A	23	141	25	7	3	4	17	21	23	3	2	.330/.443/.548	.363	.382	2	1B(30): -0.7	1.7
2010	CLR	A+	23	406	45	34	2	5	50	26	87	2	2	.277/.338/.421	.257	.351	-2.8	1B(55): 0.6, LF(4): 0.1	-0.1
2010	CLR	A+	23	406	45	34	2	5	50	26	87	2	2	.277/.338/.421	.257	.351	-2.8	1B(2): 0.0	-0.1
2011	CLR	A+	24	554	72	43	1	17	82	56	95	0	1	.308/.388/.506	.337	.351	-1.8	1B(29): 1.5, LF(3): -0.3	2.0
2012	REA	AA	25	584	93	32	1	38	104	65	102	2	0	.317/.408/.620	.369	.325	-2.7	1B(87): -3.9, LF(22): -2.8	4.8
2012	PHI	MLB	25	37	4	2	1	3	10	2	12	0	0	.333/.351/.727	.378	.400	-0.3	LF(6): -0.4, 1B(3): 0.1	0.4
2013	*PHI*	*MLB*	*26*	*250*	*29*	*13*	*1*	*10*	*35*	*19*	*57*	*0*	*0*	*.256/.323/.461*	*.280*	*.295*	*-0.4*	*1B -4, LF -0*	*0.4*

Ruf was a college draftee in 2009 who was always old for his level, making it tough to get excited about his otherwise quality performances at each stop. Then he made everyone take notice last year with 38 home runs in Double-A, good enough to lead the minor leagues. Of course, it still came as a 25-year-old and thus wasn't as impressive as Mike Olt hitting 10 fewer as a 23-year old at the same level. Ruf still projects as a slugging minor leaguer with a chance at some cups of coffee in the majors, where every pitch has a wrinkle. But he wouldn't be the first minor-league slugger to fail to translate a gaudy home-run total to the top level. It should say something that in the midst of his huge season, he wasn't promoted to Triple-A. On the other hand, he did get 12 games of java with the big club in September, during which he smacked three homers.

Carlos Ruiz C

Born: **1/22/1979** Age: **34**
Bats: **R** Throws: **R** Height: **5' 11"**
Weight: **205** Breakout: **1%**
Improve: **32%** Collapse: **9%**
Attrition: **16%** MLB: **90%**

Comparables:
Paul Lo Duca,Ron Hassey,Smoky Burgess

YEAR	TEAM	LVL	AGE	PA	R	2B	3B	HR	RBI	BB	SO	SB	CS	AVG_OBP_SLG	TAv	BABIP	BRR	FRAA	WARP
2010	PHI	MLB	31	433	43	28	1	8	53	55	54	0	1	.302/.400/.447	.298	.335	-4.6	C(118): 0.8	3.3
2011	PHI	MLB	32	472	49	23	0	6	40	48	48	1	0	.283/.371/.383	.288	.308	-1.7	C(128): 0.7, 3B(1): -0.0	3.0
2012	PHI	MLB	33	421	56	32	0	16	68	29	50	4	0	.325/.394/.540	.331	.339	-1.5	C(106): 2.5	4.9
2013	*PHI*	*MLB*	*34*	*406*	*46*	*22*	*0*	*9*	*43*	*41*	*50*	*2*	*1*	*.268/.354/.405*	*.274*	*.288*	*-0.7*	*C 1*	*2.5*

On the heels of an amazing season, Ruiz was suspended for the first 25 games of 2013 after testing positive for the banned amphetamine Adderall. How much the drug may have impacted his breakthrough is unknown. He had established himself as one of the top catchers in the game offensively in 2010-11, but nobody expected this kind of surge from a 33-year-old. Known for his keen eye, even when accounting for the intentional walks common to eight-hole hitters in the National League, Ruiz actually saw his walk rate drop to a career-low 5 percent. Those extra at-bats were turned into hits, including huge increases in Ruiz's rate of hitting doubles and home runs. Ruiz's success will likely be attributed in part to the drugs, but did the banned stimulant yield better contact? It is more likely that the confluence of these events (of his making, mind you) has simply worked against him to form an easy and unfortunate narrative.

Brian Schneider C

Born: **11/26/1976** Age: **36**
Bats: **L** Throws: **R** Height: **6' 2"**
Weight: **210** Breakout: **1%**
Improve: **24%** Collapse: **10%**
Attrition: **28%** MLB: **87%**

Comparables:
Ron Hassey,Tom Lampkin,Johnny Roseboro

YEAR	TEAM	LVL	AGE	PA	R	2B	3B	HR	RBI	BB	SO	SB	CS	AVG_OBP_SLG	TAv	BABIP	BRR	FRAA	WARP
2010	PHI	MLB	33	147	17	4	1	4	15	19	25	0	0	.240/.345/.384	.252	.271	1.3	C(46): -0.6	0.5
2011	PHI	MLB	34	139	11	4	0	2	9	11	35	0	0	.176/.246/.256	.187	.225	-1.5	C(40): -0.1	-0.9
2012	PHI	MLB	35	98	9	5	0	2	7	5	15	0	0	.225/.289/.348	.219	.250	0.3	C(29): -0.1	0.0
2013	*PHI*	*MLB*	*36*	*250*	*25*	*10*	*0*	*5*	*24*	*22*	*43*	*0*	*0*	*.228/.301/.344*	*.235*	*.256*	*-0.4*	*C 0*	*0.5*

Schneider is the backupiest of backup catchers. Unfortunately for him, he isn't getting that mid-to-late-30s power surge common in catchers, and while suitable behind the dish, his usefulness is wearing ever thinner. If his 13-year career does come to a close, he will no doubt be happy with how it played out. And if for some reason he isn't, he can wipe his tears with some of his more than $22 million in career earnings.

Chase Utley 2B

Born: **12/17/1978** Age: **34**
Bats: **L** Throws: **R** Height: **6' 2"**
Weight: **200** Breakout: **0%**
Improve: **37%** Collapse: **8%**
Attrition: **10%** MLB: **97%**

Comparables:
Brian Roberts,George Brett,Joe Morgan

YEAR	TEAM	LVL	AGE	PA	R	2B	3B	HR	RBI	BB	SO	SB	CS	AVG_OBP_SLG	TAv	BABIP	BRR	FRAA	WARP
2010	PHI	MLB	31	511	75	20	2	16	65	63	63	13	2	.275/.387/.445	.305	.288	2	2B(114): 8.1	5.3
2011	PHI	MLB	32	454	54	21	6	11	44	39	47	14	0	.259/.344/.425	.287	.269	0.9	2B(100): 8.5	2.9
2012	PHI	MLB	33	362	48	15	2	11	45	43	43	11	1	.256/.365/.429	.292	.261	2.9	2B(81): 4.1	2.7
2013	*PHI*	*MLB*	*34*	*365*	*48*	*15*	*2*	*13*	*48*	*37*	*54*	*10*	*1*	*.261/.359/.449*	*.290*	*.276*	*1.2*	*2B -3*	*2.3*

The Utley of the last two years is likely the one we should expect to see the rest of the way, at least in terms of ceiling with his rate statistics. As with Rollins, this isn't necessarily a bad thing, but it feels that way because of the player Utley used to be. Though teammates Howard and Rollins won MVP awards in 2006 and '07, Utley was the Phillies' best player both years. Hardware or not, Utley has been one of the top players of his generation, and the skills are intact for him to ease into the twilight of his career. Health is a major concern after three years of 115 games or fewer, but the 1:1 strikeout-to-walk ratio and capable power keep him among the best at his position per plate appearance. A pair of sub-.270 BABIP seasons might also be some misfortune ready to regress, though that number has been declining yearly since 2007, so perhaps his days of .300 BABIP are behind him.

Sebastian Valle C

Born: **7/24/1990** Age: **22**
Bats: **R** Throws: **L** Height: **6' 2"**
Weight: **170** Breakout: **5%**
Improve: **56%** Collapse: **4%**
Attrition: **9%** MLB: **94%**

Comparables:
Joe Pepitone,Rich Gedman,Andres Mora

YEAR	TEAM	LVL	AGE	PA	R	2B	3B	HR	RBI	BB	SO	SB	CS	AVG_OBP_SLG	TAv	BABIP	BRR	FRAA	WARP
2010	LWD	A	19	485	51	28	1	16	74	27	101	3	2	.255/.301/.430	.260	.295	-1.3	C(108): 3.1	2.3
2011	CLR	A+	20	365	34	19	2	5	40	13	84	0	0	.284/.312/.394	.246	.360	-0.6	C(39): 0.4	0.6
2012	REA	AA	21	329	31	13	1	13	45	11	83	0	2	.261/.280/.435	.253	.308	-2.8	C(63): -1.0	0.4
2012	LEH	AAA	21	82	7	2	0	4	13	2	31	0	1	.218/.232/.397	.301	.289	0.4	C(9): -0.1	0.3
2013	*PHI*	*MLB*	*22*	*250*	*22*	*10*	*1*	*8*	*29*	*6*	*72*	*0*	*0*	*.221/.240/.368*	*.216*	*.276*	*-0.5*	*C -0*	*-0.1*

Valle is racing Joseph to the majors to succeed Ruiz, who becomes a free agent after 2013. Valle has an edge defensively, but he trails Joseph by a good bit with the bat, especially considering that Joseph is a year younger. Possibly having to choose between two plum catching prospects is unquestionably an enviable position for the Phillies, though they may still have to sign a 2014 stopgap while their two prizes continue to ripen. Valle is still green with the bat and needs to work on his approach, which is far too aggressive. He walks in about 3 percent of his plate appearances and strikes out about a quarter of the time, suggesting that he would be eaten alive by big-league pitching. His power and defense give him a lofty upside, but the risk remains significant with an approach so lacking.

Michael Young 3B
Born: **10/19/1976** Age: **36**
Bats: **R** Throws: **R** Height: **6' 2"**
Weight: **200** Breakout: **1%**
Improve: **35%** Collapse: **14%**
Attrition: **17%** MLB: **79%**
Comparables:
Mike Sweeney,Rondell White,Rich Aurilia

YEAR	TEAM	LVL	AGE	PA	R	2B	3B	HR	RBI	BB	SO	SB	CS	AVG_OBP_SLG	TAv	BABIP	BRR	FRAA	WARP
2010	TEX	MLB	33	718	99	36	3	21	91	50	115	4	2	.284/.330/.444	.267	.311	2.7	3B(155): -8.6	2.1
2010	TEX	MLB	33	718	99	36	3	21	91	50	115	4	2	.284/.330/.444	.267	.311	2.7	3B(155): -8.6	2.1
2011	TEX	MLB	34	689	88	41	6	11	106	47	78	6	2	.338/.380/.474	.292	.367	0.7	3B(40): -0.4, 1B(36): -3.6	2.4
2011	TEX	MLB	34	689	88	41	6	11	106	47	78	6	2	.338/.380/.474	.292	.367	0.7	3B(40): -0.4, 1B(36): -3.6	2.4
2012	TEX	MLB	35	651	79	27	3	8	67	33	70	2	2	.277/.312/.370	.239	.299	-1.6	1B(41): 0.2, 3B(25): -1.3	-1.5
2012	TEX	MLB	35	651	79	27	3	8	67	33	70	2	2	.277/.312/.370	.239	.299	-1.6	1B(41): 0.2, 3B(25): -1.3	-1.5
2013	*PHI*	*MLB*	*36*	*619*	*70*	*30*	*2*	*11*	*59*	*39*	*96*	*4*	*2*	*.277/.322/.396*	*.262*	*.314*	*-0.7*	*3B -2, 1B -1*	*1.1*

Often dubbed "Mr. Ranger" by fans and media alike, Young heads to Philadelphia after 13 seasons in Texas. Although Young and the Rangers produced their share of offseason drama in recent years, the infielder departs Texas as the franchise's all-time hits leader. Sentimental value aside, the trade should give Young an opportunity to continue seeing every-day at-bats. It's no secret that Young is no longer the offensive force he was in his prime. However, on the heels of a resurgent 2011, few could have predicted last season's collapse. There's no doubt the veteran has lost some of the bat speed that made him so comfortable in the box as a perennial batting-title contender. But even with Young at 36, coming off a dreadful season, it wouldn't be wise to write him off at the plate.

PITCHERS

Mike Adams
Born: **7/29/1978** Age: **34**
Bats: **R** Throws: **R** Height: **6' 6"** Weight: **195**
Breakout: **13%** Improve: **35%** Collapse: **47%**
Attrition: **4%** MLB: **94%**
Comparables:
J.J. Putz,Heath Bell,Rich Gossage

YEAR	TEAM	LVL	AGE	W	L	SV	G	GS	IP	H	HR	BB	SO	BB9	SO9	GB%	BABIP	WHIP	ERA	FIP	FRA	WARP
2010	SAN	AA	31	0	0	0	1	0	1	0	0	0	1	0.0	9.0	%	.000	0.00	0.00	1.17	1.70	0.0
2010	SDN	MLB	31	4	1	0	70	0	66^{2}	48	2	23	73	3.1	9.9	41%	.271	1.07	1.75	2.34	2.79	1.2
2011	SDN	MLB	32	3	1	1	48	0	48	26	2	9	49	1.7	9.2	46%	.202	0.73	1.12	2.06	2.70	0.8
2011	TEX	MLB	32	2	3	1	27	0	25^{2}	18	3	5	25	1.8	8.8	46%	.231	0.90	2.10	3.22	4.25	0.3
2012	TEX	MLB	33	5	3	1	61	0	52^{1}	56	4	17	45	2.9	7.7	48%	.327	1.39	3.27	3.47	3.56	1.0
2013	*PHI*	*MLB*	*34*	*3*	*1*	*1*	*58*	*0*	54^{2}	*42*	*5*	*13*	*57*	*2.2*	*9.4*	*45%*	*.280*	*1.01*	*2.58*	*3.02*	*2.81*	*1.2*

A significant velocity decline led to a severe performance decline for Adams in 2012. His ERA, WHIP, and walk rate skyrocketed while his strikeout rate plummeted. A possible cause emerged during the offseason when Adams admitted to dealing with thoracic outlet syndrome for almost the entire season. He underwent surgery for the condition in October. The Phillies obviously aren't too worried about his recovery: He made his health problem public at the press conference announcing his two-year, $12 million dollar contract with Philadelphia. Coming into 2012, the only reliever better than Adams from 2008-11 was Mariano Rivera. With a healthy Adams, Antonio Bastardo, and Jonathan Papelbon, the Phillies have a dynamic late-inning trio.

Phillippe Aumont
Born: **1/7/1989** Age: **24**
Bats: **R** Throws: **R** Height: **6' 8"** Weight: **255**
Breakout: **23%** Improve: **58%** Collapse: **17%**
Attrition: **17%** MLB: **87%**
Comparables:
Dennys Reyes,Len Barker,Larry Sherry

YEAR	TEAM	LVL	AGE	W	L	SV	G	GS	IP	H	HR	BB	SO	BB9	SO9	GB%	BABIP	WHIP	ERA	FIP	FRA	WARP
2010	CLR	A+	21	2	5	1	16	10	72^{1}	74	6	42	77	5.2	9.6	44%	.361	1.60	4.48	4.38	4.60	0.4
2010	REA	AA	21	1	6	0	11	11	49^{2}	55	4	38	38	6.9	6.9	50%	.365	1.87	7.42	5.53	6.36	-0.2
2011	REA	AA	22	1	5	4	25	0	31	23	2	11	41	3.2	11.9	62%	.250	1.10	2.32	2.76	1.99	0.4
2011	LEH	AAA	22	1	0	3	18	0	22^{2}	21	0	14	37	5.6	14.7	—	.412	1.54	3.18	2.09	2.27	0.0
2012	LEH	AAA	23	3	1	15	41	0	44^{1}	34	3	34	59	6.9	12.0	58%	.303	1.53	4.26	4.01	4.93	0.1
2012	PHI	MLB	23	0	1	2	18	0	14^{2}	10	0	9	14	5.5	8.6	76%	.244	1.30	3.68	3.27	2.98	0.2
2013	*PHI*	*MLB*	*24*	*1*	*2*	*1*	*18*	*4*	35^{2}	*33*	*4*	*20*	*32*	*4.9*	*8.0*	*49%*	*.300*	*1.47*	*4.76*	*4.55*	*5.18*	*-0.2*

Unable to tame Aumont's mid-90s sinker or power curveball with any measure of consistency, the Phillies are beginning to wonder if his closer-level potential will ever bear fruit. He can and will be a major-league reliever, but if he's going to get the most out of that incredible stuff and be trusted in high-leverage situations, he needs to iron out his command issues. His mechanics are awkward: He is unnecessarily hunched over for someone of his stature, making it difficult to repeat his delivery. At 24, there's still time for Aumont, and when he demolishes the middle three of a big-league lineup on 10 pitches, striking out two—as he did to the Rockies on September 7—it's easy to envision him as a premier shutdown closer.

Antonio Bastardo

Born: **9/21/1985** Age: **27**
Bats: **R** Throws: **L** Height: **6' 0"** Weight: **195**
Breakout: **28%** Improve: **64%** Collapse: **19%**
Attrition: **8%** MLB: **95%**

Comparables:
Mario Soto, Rafael Soriano, Tyler Clippard

YEAR	TEAM	LVL	AGE	W	L	SV	G	GS	IP	H	HR	BB	SO	BB9	SO9	GB%	BABIP	WHIP	ERA	FIP	FRA	WARP
2010	CLR	A+	24	0	0	0	3	0	3	3	0	0	6	0.0	18.0	50%	.500	1.00	0.00	-0.56	0.33	0.1
2010	LEH	AAA	24	1	1	3	20	0	17^1	12	0	6	27	3.1	14.0	43%	.324	1.04	2.08	1.21	1.78	0.6
2010	PHI	MLB	24	2	0	0	25	0	18^2	19	1	9	26	4.3	12.5	35%	.375	1.50	4.34	2.78	2.11	0.6
2011	PHI	MLB	25	6	1	8	64	0	58	28	6	26	70	4.0	10.9	27%	.179	0.93	2.64	3.27	3.26	0.7
2012	PHI	MLB	26	2	5	1	65	0	52	40	7	26	81	4.5	14.0	30%	.306	1.27	4.33	3.39	3.58	0.7
2013	*PHI*	*MLB*	*27*	*3*	*1*	*2*	*59*	*0*	*49^2*	*38*	*6*	*19*	*59*	*3.5*	*10.6*	*34%*	*.286*	*1.15*	*3.23*	*3.54*	*3.51*	*0.6*

Bastardo is an excellent example of the volatility experienced by relievers in their small sample sets. Skills-wise he was actually a bit better in 2012, adding more than 5 ticks to his strikeout rate, up to 36 percent, while maintaining his walk rate. But his left-on-base percentage and BABIP bounced back to league-average, so his ERA jumped from 2.64 to 4.33. Alas, next-level metrics suggest he probably deserved something closer to the 3.44 average of the two years in each of the individual seasons. It wasn't all misfortune, though. Bastardo's home-run rate increased in 2012, though all those big flies came in a three-month period from June to August, yielding a 6.75 ERA in 27 innings. He had a 1.78 ERA in the 25 homer-less innings that bookended his season.

Jesse Biddle

Born: **10/22/1991** Age: **21**
Bats: **L** Throws: **L** Height: **6' 5"** Weight: **225**
Breakout: **23%** Improve: **47%** Collapse: **8%**
Attrition: **6%** MLB: **86%**

Comparables:
Mark Davis, Oliver Perez, Ryan Feierabend

YEAR	TEAM	LVL	AGE	W	L	SV	G	GS	IP	H	HR	BB	SO	BB9	SO9	GB%	BABIP	WHIP	ERA	FIP	FRA	WARP
2010	PHL	Rk	18	3	1	0	9	9	33^1	35	2	9	41	2.4	11.1	44%	.333	1.32	4.32	2.82	4.72	0.2
2010	WPT	A-	18	1	0	0	3	3	10^1	5	0	11	9	9.6	7.9	48%	.200	1.55	2.62	5.51	7.40	-0.1
2011	LWD	A	19	7	8	0	25	24	133	104	5	66	124	4.5	8.4	45%	.281	1.28	2.98	3.71	3.86	1.0
2012	CLR	A+	20	10	6	0	26	26	142^2	129	10	54	151	3.4	9.5	41%	.308	1.28	3.22	3.43	4.07	1.6
2013	*PHI*	*MLB*	*21*	*2*	*4*	*0*	*9*	*9*	*44^1*	*43*	*6*	*23*	*35*	*4.6*	*7.1*	*41%*	*.302*	*1.49*	*4.97*	*4.94*	*5.40*	*-0.4*

The trade of Trevor May clears the way for Biddle to assume the top spot in the organization's prospect rankings for 2013. The local product has put up excellent results in each of his full-season campaigns, and last year his skills jumped forward, too. His velocity is inconsistent, topping out in the low-90s, which is great for a lefty. Meanwhile his secondary stuff has always been advanced for his age and there are stretches of time when he is working with three above-average pitches. As Biddle continues to refine his command, his upside is to have three consistently plus pitches. With that, he could lead the next wave of pitching talent into Philadelphia as a front-line starter.

Tyler Cloyd

Born: **5/16/1987** Age: **26**
Bats: **R** Throws: **R** Height: **6' 4"** Weight: **190**
Breakout: **33%** Improve: **64%** Collapse: **18%**
Attrition: **24%** MLB: **78%**

Comparables:
Daniel Barone, Jeff D'Amico, Doug Waechter

YEAR	TEAM	LVL	AGE	W	L	SV	G	GS	IP	H	HR	BB	SO	BB9	SO9	GB%	BABIP	WHIP	ERA	FIP	FRA	WARP
2010	CLR	A+	23	4	3	0	35	4	69^1	85	8	16	67	2.1	8.7	39%	.354	1.46	5.32	3.78	4.66	0.3
2010	REA	AA	23	1	1	0	2	1	9	5	3	1	6	1.0	6.0	33%	.083	0.67	4.00	6.69	7.40	-0.2
2011	CLR	A+	24	3	1	0	13	5	39^1	31	3	7	39	1.6	8.9	54%	.220	0.97	2.75	3.01	3.41	0.2
2011	REA	AA	24	6	3	0	18	17	106^2	101	7	15	99	1.3	8.4	46%	.323	1.09	2.78	3.03	3.04	1.6
2012	REA	AA	25	3	0	0	4	4	25	22	1	3	20	1.1	7.2	41%	.292	1.00	1.80	2.60	3.60	0.2
2012	LEH	AAA	25	12	1	0	22	22	142	105	14	38	93	2.4	5.9	46%	.230	1.01	2.35	4.02	6.19	-0.2
2012	PHI	MLB	25	2	2	0	6	6	33	33	8	7	30	1.9	8.2	35%	.275	1.21	4.91	5.29	5.42	0.0
2013	*PHI*	*MLB*	*26*	*3*	*4*	*0*	*16*	*9*	*66^1*	*69*	*10*	*20*	*42*	*2.8*	*5.7*	*43%*	*.297*	*1.35*	*4.84*	*4.80*	*5.26*	*-0.5*

Cloyd looked like he might be in line to slide into the fifth-starter job in 2013 after a fantastic 2012 that started in Double-A and ended up in the majors. But the signing of John Lannan drops Kyle Kendrick into that job, and Kendrick is basically an older, more refined version of Cloyd. Often working high-80s with spurts in the low-90s, Cloyd has never been viewed as a prospect despite production that might be worthy of such acclaim. In addition to the unimpressive velocity, his secondary stuff is merely okay. He succeeds with touch and feel, pounding the zone and placing the ball where he wants it. Given that approach, you would be right to assume that when he misses, he gets hammered.

Brody Colvin

Born: **8/14/1990** Age: **22**
Bats: **R** Throws: **R** Height: **6' 4"** Weight: **195**
Breakout: **19%** Improve: **50%** Collapse: **25%**
Attrition: **15%** MLB: **80%**

Comparables:
Edwin Jackson, Jamey Wright, Bill Pulsipher

YEAR	TEAM	LVL	AGE	W	L	SV	G	GS	IP	H	HR	BB	SO	BB9	SO9	GB%	BABIP	WHIP	ERA	FIP	FRA	WARP
2010	LWD	A	19	6	8	0	27	27	138	138	7	42	120	2.7	7.8	52%	.311	1.30	3.39	3.56	4.35	1.0
2011	CLR	A+	20	3	8	0	22	21	116^2	131	10	42	78	3.2	6.0	48%	.311	1.48	4.71	4.50	5.34	0.1
2012	CLR	A+	21	5	6	0	23	18	105^1	113	5	51	93	4.4	7.9	47%	.353	1.56	4.27	3.93	4.78	0.7
2012	REA	AA	21	1	4	0	7	7	32^2	43	6	23	16	6.3	4.4	36%	.333	2.02	11.02	7.64	9.51	-1.0
2013	*PHI*	*MLB*	*22*	*1*	*4*	*0*	*8*	*8*	*41*	*45*	*6*	*21*	*25*	*4.5*	*5.6*	*45%*	*.309*	*1.60*	*5.78*	*5.42*	*6.29*	*-0.7*

More maybe than yes at this point, Colvin labored through an uneven 2012, including buckling under the pressure of a promotion to Double-A in late July. Inconsistent mechanics spur his troubles: His command and control have regressed every year as a pro, resulting in an ugly 10 percent walk rate for his career. He has swing-and-miss stuff when his fastball, curveball, and changeup are all working, but those instances are rare. The chorus of scouts and analysts who had Colvin's future in the bullpen from the jump is growing louder, though for now there's no reason for the Phillies not to keep working with him as a starter.

Justin De Fratus

Born: **10/21/1987** Age: **25**
Bats: **B** Throws: **R** Height: **6' 5"** Weight: **220**
Breakout: **19%** Improve: **53%** Collapse: **13%**
Attrition: **8%** MLB: **95%**
Comparables:
Pete Filson,Steve Comer,Gary Glover

YEAR	TEAM	LVL	AGE	W	L	SV	G	GS	IP	H	HR	BB	SO	BB9	SO9	GB%	BABIP	WHIP	ERA	FIP	FRA	WARP
2010	CLR	A+	22	2	0	15	29	0	40^{1}	31	1	11	43	2.5	9.6	55%	.303	1.04	1.79	2.59	3.11	0.8
2010	REA	AA	22	1	0	6	20	0	24^{2}	17	2	5	28	1.8	10.2	43%	.255	0.89	2.19	2.75	3.73	0.4
2011	REA	AA	23	4	0	8	23	0	34^{1}	28	1	14	43	3.7	11.3	61%	.286	1.22	2.10	2.77	1.42	0.6
2011	LEH	AAA	23	2	3	7	28	0	41	35	3	11	56	2.4	12.3	—	.330	1.12	3.73	2.48	2.70	0.0
2011	PHI	MLB	23	1	0	0	5	0	4	1	0	3	3	6.8	6.8	50%	.100	1.00	2.25	4.49	5.24	0.0
2012	PHL	Rk	24	0	0	0	2	1	2	1	0	0	3	0.0	13.5	75%	.250	0.50	0.00	0.43	2.83	0.1
2012	CLR	A+	24	0	0	0	2	1	2	2	0	0	1	0.0	4.5	50%	.333	1.00	0.00	2.39	2.94	0.1
2012	LEH	AAA	24	0	1	3	17	0	21^{2}	15	2	3	22	1.2	9.1	55%	.245	0.83	2.49	2.74	3.29	0.3
2012	PHI	MLB	24	0	0	0	13	0	10^{2}	7	0	5	8	4.2	6.8	52%	.226	1.12	3.38	3.04	3.59	0.1
2013	*PHI*	*MLB*	*25*	*1*	*1*	*0*	*30*	*0*	*36^{2}*	*37*	*4*	*14*	*27*	*3.4*	*6.5*	*49%*	*.302*	*1.38*	*4.62*	*4.29*	*5.02*	*-0.2*

An elbow injury robbed De Fratus of most of the 2012 season, but he was excellent for 22 innings in Triple-A before an uneventful 11 with Philadelphia in September. Despite De Fratus posting some gaudy minor-league numbers and having plenty of experience closing games, the general consensus is that his ceiling is as a setup man, not as Papelbon's successor.

Kenneth Giles

Born: **9/20/1990** Age: **22**
Bats: **R** Throws: **R** Height: **6' 3"** Weight: **190**
Breakout: **16%** Improve: **48%** Collapse: **30%**
Attrition: **10%** MLB: **84%**
Comparables:
Tex Clevenger,Len Barker,Edwin Nunez

YEAR	TEAM	LVL	AGE	W	L	SV	G	GS	IP	H	HR	BB	SO	BB9	SO9	GB%	BABIP	WHIP	ERA	FIP	FRA	WARP
2011	PHL	Rk	20	1	1	0	3	0	4^{2}	6	1	3	7	5.8	13.5	50%	.444	1.93	5.79	5.78	5.38	0.0
2012	LWD	A	21	3	3	5	29	6	67^{1}	54	5	44	86	5.9	11.5	44%	.299	1.46	3.61	4.22	4.08	0.4
2012	CLR	A+	21	1	0	3	10	0	14^{2}	10	1	6	25	3.7	15.3	32%	.300	1.09	3.07	2.10	1.33	0.6
2013	*PHI*	*MLB*	*22*	*1*	*1*	*1*	*17*	*2*	*36*	*32*	*4*	*19*	*37*	*4.8*	*9.1*	*42%*	*.305*	*1.42*	*4.55*	*4.17*	*4.95*	*-0.2*

Like the batters he's facing, Giles rarely knows where his mid-90s heat is going, especially when he runs it up near 99. Sometimes that works. Thirty percent of the professional batters to face him have whiffed, including an eye-popping 38 percent in his 14 innings to close out the season in High-A. The 14 percent walk rate is the obvious opportunity area for Giles: His command desperately needs to improve as he faces a higher caliber of competition. He is a successful thrower for now since he can overpower the competition in the low minors, but he needs to become more of a pitcher to maximize his potential and emerge as a closer candidate.

Mitch Gueller

Born: **11/10/1993** Age: **19**
Bats: **R** Throws: **R** Height: **6' 4"** Weight: **210**
Breakout: **19%** Improve: **57%** Collapse: **43%**
Attrition: **43%** MLB: **57%**
Comparables:
Rick Wise,Lew Krausse,Von McDaniel

YEAR	TEAM	LVL	AGE	W	L	SV	G	GS	IP	H	HR	BB	SO	BB9	SO9	GB%	BABIP	WHIP	ERA	FIP	FRA	WARP
2012	PHL	Rk	18	1	5	0	8	6	27^{1}	26	0	12	19	4.0	6.3	29%	.571	1.39	5.27	3.36	3.80	0.1
2013	*PHI*	*MLB*	*19*	*1*	*3*	*0*	*7*	*7*	*33^{2}*	*37*	*5*	*21*	*22*	*5.6*	*5.7*	*44%*	*.312*	*1.73*	*6.21*	*5.70*	*6.75*	*-0.7*

Part of a pair of 2012 supplemental-round draftees, Gueller is extremely raw, building off a low-90s fastball, but so far little else. His curveball is inconsistent, thanks to a lack of command, and his changeup is underdeveloped because he didn't really need it in high school. He has mid-rotation upside that's a long way from being realized, but it's built on a solid foundation, especially for a teenager.

Roy Halladay

Born: **5/14/1977** Age: **36**
Bats: **R** Throws: **R** Height: **6' 7"** Weight: **230**
Breakout: **21%** Improve: **50%** Collapse: **23%**
Attrition: **11%** MLB: **88%**
Comparables:
Hiroki Kuroda,Greg Maddux,Chris Carpenter

YEAR	TEAM	LVL	AGE	W	L	SV	G	GS	IP	H	HR	BB	SO	BB9	SO9	GB%	BABIP	WHIP	ERA	FIP	FRA	WARP
2010	PHI	MLB	33	21	10	0	33	33	250^{2}	231	24	30	219	1.1	7.9	53%	.290	1.04	2.44	3.03	3.62	4.4
2011	PHI	MLB	34	19	6	0	32	32	233^{2}	208	10	35	220	1.3	8.5	53%	.298	1.04	2.35	2.17	2.80	4.9
2012	CLR	A+	35	0	0	0	1	1	3	3	0	0	4	0.0	12.0	56%	.333	1.00	0.00	0.73	1.07	0.2
2012	PHI	MLB	35	11	8	0	25	25	156^{1}	155	18	36	132	2.1	7.6	45%	.301	1.22	4.49	3.73	4.33	1.1
2013	*PHI*	*MLB*	*36*	*8*	*8*	*0*	*22*	*22*	*151*	*134*	*14*	*22*	*132*	*1.3*	*7.8*	*51%*	*.296*	*1.03*	*2.86*	*3.09*	*3.11*	*2.7*

Halladay is begging the league to underestimate him for 2013 after he looked mortal for the first time in seven seasons. A balky back cost him all of June and half of July, and when he came back he wasn't especially good, though he did show glimpses of his normal brilliance. He gave up way too many hits and an alarming number of them cleared the fence, and then his shoulder started acting up in September. Is an offseason enough for Halladay to heal or is the mid-30s super-ace finally starting to show cracks? It's worth a bet on the former since even a diminished Halladay posted a 3.7 strikeout-to-walk ratio that many pitchers would sell their Phiten necklaces for. The idea that he is no longer a sure-fire Cy Young candidate has to be considered, but there's no need to make one year into a trend.

Cole Hamels

Born: **12/27/1983** Age: **29**
Bats: **L** Throws: **L** Height: **6' 4"** Weight: **195**
Breakout: **14%** Improve: **49%** Collapse: **28%**
Attrition: **8%** MLB: **93%**

Comparables:
Odalis Perez, Harvey Haddix, Mike Mussina

YEAR	TEAM	LVL	AGE	W	L	SV	G	GS	IP	H	HR	BB	SO	BB9	SO9	GB%	BABIP	WHIP	ERA	FIP	FRA	WARP
2010	PHI	MLB	26	12	11	0	33	33	208^{2}	185	26	61	211	2.6	9.1	47%	.289	1.18	3.06	3.70	3.80	4.0
2011	PHI	MLB	27	14	9	0	32	31	216	169	19	44	194	1.8	8.1	55%	.255	0.99	2.79	3.02	3.67	2.3
2012	PHI	MLB	28	17	6	0	31	31	215^{1}	190	24	52	216	2.2	9.0	45%	.290	1.12	3.05	3.35	3.62	3.8
2013	*PHI*	*MLB*	*29*	*10*	*11*	*0*	*28*	*28*	*184^{1}*	*158*	*21*	*38*	*169*	*1.9*	*8.2*	*46%*	*.285*	*1.06*	*3.11*	*3.47*	*3.38*	*2.6*

After rumors swirled for months about potential trades involving Hamels, the Phillies did the smart thing and locked up their ace—although that implies they have only one ace. Hamels is in the midst of churning out one 200-plus-inning masterpiece after another, and since he's still on the right side of 30, it's reasonable to expect that to continue. The southpaw fanned a career-high 25 percent of the batters he faced in 2012, with only a slight uptick in his walk rate. The only thing missing is a Cy Young Award, but never mind the whole National League, it's enough of a challenge to be the best pitcher on the Phillies.

Jeremy Horst

Born: **10/1/1985** Age: **27**
Bats: **L** Throws: **L** Height: **6' 4"** Weight: **220**
Breakout: **37%** Improve: **61%** Collapse: **23%**
Attrition: **16%** MLB: **74%**

Comparables:
Jimmy Gobble, Omar Daal, Troy Cate

YEAR	TEAM	LVL	AGE	W	L	SV	G	GS	IP	H	HR	BB	SO	BB9	SO9	GB%	BABIP	WHIP	ERA	FIP	FRA	WARP
2010	LYN	A+	24	0	2	0	11	0	14^{2}	17	1	4	17	2.4	10.4	44%	.364	1.43	4.29	3.00	3.30	0.3
2010	CAR	AA	24	3	2	0	27	0	43	35	1	9	46	1.9	9.6	48%	.291	1.02	2.09	2.18	2.35	1.5
2010	LOU	AAA	24	1	0	0	6	2	14^{1}	17	0	5	12	3.1	7.6	40%	.327	1.54	2.52	2.87	4.11	0.3
2011	LOU	AAA	25	1	4	0	36	0	51^{1}	41	2	14	42	2.5	7.4	46%	.275	1.07	2.81	3.04	4.12	0.5
2011	CIN	MLB	25	0	0	0	12	0	15^{1}	18	2	6	9	3.5	5.3	39%	.308	1.57	2.93	4.69	4.93	0.1
2012	LEH	AAA	26	2	1	2	26	0	38^{1}	43	3	18	32	4.2	7.5	45%	.339	1.59	2.11	4.07	3.45	0.4
2012	PHI	MLB	26	2	0	0	32	0	31^{1}	21	1	14	40	4.0	11.5	46%	.290	1.12	1.15	2.43	2.89	0.6
2013	*PHI*	*MLB*	*27*	*1*	*1*	*0*	*28*	*0*	*37^{1}*	*36*	*5*	*14*	*30*	*3.5*	*7.2*	*43%*	*.302*	*1.36*	*4.58*	*4.46*	*4.98*	*-0.2*

Horst has all the makings of a LOOGY, as lefties managed a pathetic 441 OPS against him last year compared to a 658 mark for righties, but he was having so much success in his mostly second-half stint with the Phillies that they decided to push him a bit. He went at least an inning in 21 of his 32 outings and pitched more than an inning in nine of those, yielding a 1.05 ERA in his multi-inning outings. What is shaping up to be a deep bullpen for Philly will likely prevent that same usage pattern for Horst. Instead, he'll be summoned to thwart key lefties in the middle innings.

Kyle Kendrick

Born: **8/26/1984** Age: **28**
Bats: **R** Throws: **R** Height: **6' 4"** Weight: **210**
Breakout: **25%** Improve: **67%** Collapse: **15%**
Attrition: **16%** MLB: **89%**

Comparables:
Brian Lawrence, Mike Grace, Bobby J. Jones

YEAR	TEAM	LVL	AGE	W	L	SV	G	GS	IP	H	HR	BB	SO	BB9	SO9	GB%	BABIP	WHIP	ERA	FIP	FRA	WARP
2010	PHI	MLB	25	11	10	0	33	31	180^{2}	199	26	49	84	2.4	4.2	45%	.284	1.37	4.73	4.91	5.68	-0.1
2011	PHI	MLB	26	8	6	0	34	15	114^{2}	110	14	30	59	2.4	4.6	46%	.261	1.22	3.22	4.52	5.47	-0.7
2012	PHI	MLB	27	11	12	0	37	25	159^{1}	154	20	49	116	2.8	6.6	48%	.278	1.27	3.90	4.37	4.69	1.0
2013	*PHI*	*MLB*	*28*	*6*	*9*	*0*	*30*	*20*	*129*	*130*	*17*	*35*	*74*	*2.4*	*5.2*	*47%*	*.285*	*1.28*	*4.49*	*4.58*	*4.88*	*-0.4*

It was bleak for Kendrick back in 2008, when he posted horrible baseline skills and even worse results. But the 23-year-old was resilient and now he's a 28-year old veteran on the heels of two strong seasons rounding out the Phillies starting rotation. Low on pure stuff, Kendrick has survived on a control-first approach paired with a strikeout rate that skyrocketed nicely from 12 to 17 percent last year. His primary flaw is the home-run bug. Despite a rate of better than one per game, he has survived with sub-4.00 ERAs each of the past two seasons, but pulling the trifecta with the same skill set would be a real magic trick. Even if he does fall in line closer to where you would expect someone with his skills to be, as a fifth starter the bar is low: He has margin for error between where he's been and what's acceptable.

John Lannan

Born: **9/27/1984** Age: **28**
Bats: **L** Throws: **L** Height: **6' 5"** Weight: **215**
Breakout: **12%** Improve: **45%** Collapse: **17%**
Attrition: **14%** MLB: **80%**

Comparables:
Andy Pettitte, John Rheinecker, Clayton Richard

YEAR	TEAM	LVL	AGE	W	L	SV	G	GS	IP	H	HR	BB	SO	BB9	SO9	GB%	BABIP	WHIP	ERA	FIP	FRA	WARP
2010	HAR	AA	25	1	4	0	7	7	40^{2}	49	3	10	28	2.2	6.2	51%	.342	1.45	4.20	3.97	4.41	0.6
2010	WAS	MLB	25	8	8	0	25	25	143^{1}	175	14	49	71	3.1	4.5	51%	.319	1.56	4.65	4.49	5.07	0.4
2011	WAS	MLB	26	10	13	0	33	33	184^{2}	194	15	76	106	3.7	5.2	57%	.296	1.46	3.70	4.25	5.25	-0.8
2012	SYR	AAA	27	9	11	0	24	24	148^{2}	164	16	50	86	3.0	5.2	57%	.304	1.44	4.30	4.43	6.52	-0.9
2012	WAS	MLB	27	4	1	0	6	6	32^{2}	33	0	14	17	3.9	4.7	59%	.303	1.44	4.13	3.75	3.58	0.6
2013	*PHI*	*MLB*	*28*	*4*	*7*	*0*	*16*	*16*	*92^{2}*	*93*	*10*	*30*	*56*	*2.9*	*5.5*	*54%*	*.296*	*1.33*	*4.47*	*4.37*	*4.85*	*-0.3*

Assigned the unenviable task of supplanting Stephen Strasburg in the Nationals rotation last September, Lannan responded by allowing two or fewer runs in three of his four starts. The lefty walks too many and strikes out too few to be a dependable starter for a contender, but his ability to induce grounders makes him a decent swingman for a good defensive team—which the 2012 Nationals were but the 2013 Phillies don't figure to be.

Cliff Lee

Born: **8/30/1978** Age: **34**
Bats: **L** Throws: **L** Height: **6' 4"** Weight: **190**
Breakout: **16%** Improve: **54%** Collapse: **17%**
Attrition: **10%** MLB: **93%**

Comparables:
Andy Pettitte,Mike Mussina,Mike Cuellar

YEAR	TEAM	LVL	AGE	W	L	SV	G	GS	IP	H	HR	BB	SO	BB9	SO9	GB%	BABIP	WHIP	ERA	FIP	FRA	WARP
2010	TAC	AAA	31	0	0	0	1	1	6	3	0	0	4	0.0	6.0	44%	.188	0.50	0.00	2.25	3.56	0.1
2010	SEA	MLB	31	8	3	0	13	13	103^{2}	92	5	6	89	0.5	7.7	41%	.283	0.95	2.34	2.13	2.50	2.3
2010	TEX	MLB	31	4	6	0	15	15	108^{2}	103	11	12	96	1.0	8.0	43%	.292	1.06	3.98	2.96	3.74	2.0
2011	PHI	MLB	32	17	8	0	32	32	232^{2}	197	18	42	238	1.6	9.2	49%	.291	1.03	2.40	2.57	3.05	5.1
2012	PHI	MLB	33	6	9	0	30	30	211	207	26	28	207	1.2	8.8	46%	.309	1.11	3.16	3.17	3.36	3.9
2013	*PHI*	*MLB*	*34*	*10*	*10*	*0*	*26*	*26*	*185^{1}*	*167*	*17*	*25*	*164*	*1.2*	*8.0*	*44%*	*.301*	*1.03*	*2.90*	*3.03*	*3.15*	*3.1*

Lee would probably rather hear someone's bad-beat poker story than any of his fellow pitchers griping about being saddled with a no-decision after a well-pitched outing. Merriam-Webster needs a new phrase for what Lee went through in 2012 because "bad luck" is insufficient to describe his 15 no-decisions. As strong as ever, Lee paced all of baseball with a 7.4 strikeout-to-walk ratio and 1.2-per-nine walk rate while continuing a five-year incremental gain in velocity. Lee's fine-wine transformation makes the $75 million he is guaranteed over the next three years a lot more palatable for the Phillies, as even a downturn in velocity won't rob him of his effectiveness. His game is built on the movement of the sinker, not the speed of it, which is merely a bonus. Lee remains one of the most underrated aces in the game, thanks in large part to sharing a clubhouse with Hamels and Halladay.

Ethan Martin

Born: **6/6/1989** Age: **24**
Bats: **R** Throws: **R** Height: **6' 3"** Weight: **195**
Breakout: **34%** Improve: **63%** Collapse: **17%**
Attrition: **18%** MLB: **96%**

Comparables:
Shawn Chacon,Dan Cortes,Carlos Marmol

YEAR	TEAM	LVL	AGE	W	L	SV	G	GS	IP	H	HR	BB	SO	BB9	SO9	GB%	BABIP	WHIP	ERA	FIP	FRA	WARP
2010	SBR	A+	21	9	14	0	25	22	113^{1}	120	10	81	105	6.4	8.3	44%	.338	1.77	6.35	5.36	5.72	0.4
2011	RCU	A+	22	4	4	0	16	9	55	65	8	37	61	6.1	10.0	—	.365	1.85	7.36	5.91	6.43	0.0
2011	CHT	AA	22	5	3	2	21	3	40^{1}	31	3	29	43	6.5	9.6	—	.277	1.49	4.02	4.30	4.67	0.0
2012	CHT	AA	23	8	6	0	20	20	118	89	5	61	112	4.7	8.5	44%	.273	1.27	3.58	3.42	4.17	0.7
2012	REA	AA	23	5	0	0	7	7	39^{2}	29	3	18	35	4.1	7.9	45%	.243	1.18	3.18	3.78	4.32	0.3
2013	*PHI*	*MLB*	*24*	*2*	*3*	*0*	*7*	*7*	*38*	*36*	*5*	*22*	*32*	*5.3*	*7.5*	*41%*	*.297*	*1.52*	*5.06*	*4.96*	*5.51*	*-0.4*

Martin finally took large steps toward the second-starter ceiling he's been tabbed with for years. Control and consistency are the big issues, and while he still walked 4.5 batters per nine innings, that was a major improvement from the 6.5 per nine he walked in 2011. He has two plus-potential pitches, a mid-90s heater and a quality slider that has taken the place of his curveball. The former Dodgers first-round pick (he came in the Shane Victorino deal last year) also shows potential for an average changeup, but if that doesn't develop, his future will be in the bullpen. Martin drew positive reviews for being more of a pitcher last year. There is work to be done, but 2012 was progress.

Jonathan Papelbon

Born: **11/23/1980** Age: **32**
Bats: **R** Throws: **R** Height: **6' 5"** Weight: **225**
Breakout: **28%** Improve: **45%** Collapse: **35%**
Attrition: **5%** MLB: **96%**

Comparables:
Mike Adams,John Wetteland,Robb Nen

YEAR	TEAM	LVL	AGE	W	L	SV	G	GS	IP	H	HR	BB	SO	BB9	SO9	GB%	BABIP	WHIP	ERA	FIP	FRA	WARP
2010	BOS	MLB	29	5	7	37	65	0	67	57	7	28	76	3.8	10.2	40%	.287	1.27	3.90	3.48	3.24	1.5
2011	BOS	MLB	30	4	1	31	63	0	64^{1}	50	3	10	87	1.4	12.2	38%	.309	0.93	2.94	1.57	1.87	2.3
2012	PHI	MLB	31	5	6	38	70	0	70	56	8	18	92	2.3	11.8	44%	.296	1.06	2.44	2.94	3.17	1.2
2013	*PHI*	*MLB*	*32*	*4*	*2*	*30*	*63*	*0*	*64*	*48*	*6*	*15*	*76*	*2.1*	*10.7*	*39%*	*.290*	*0.99*	*2.41*	*2.75*	*2.62*	*1.5*

The first year of his lofty four-year, $50 million dollar contract (which can vest into a fifth for a total of $63 million) was a success despite some skill deterioration from 2011. Does Papelbon have three (maybe four) more years in him, though? It's tough to know, but even if he does, the Phillies shouldn't have paid him this much to be the guinea pigs, especially with some of the big relief arms in their system already matriculating their way toward the majors. This is a no-upside deal for the team, and a tinge of downside may already be poking through in the form of Papelbon's home-run rate in Citizen's Bank Park. It led to a career-worst 1.0 allowed per nine innings, and if that's the start of growing a trend, it's going to get ugly in a hurry.

Jonathan Pettibone

Born: **7/19/1990** Age: **22**
Bats: **L** Throws: **R** Height: **6' 6"** Weight: **200**
Breakout: **28%** Improve: **49%** Collapse: **16%**
Attrition: **10%** MLB: **84%**

Comparables:
Leo Kiely,Dick Ellsworth,Jerry Reuss

YEAR	TEAM	LVL	AGE	W	L	SV	G	GS	IP	H	HR	BB	SO	BB9	SO9	GB%	BABIP	WHIP	ERA	FIP	FRA	WARP
2011	CLR	A+	20	10	11	0	27	27	161	149	5	34	115	1.9	6.4	43%	.268	1.14	2.96	3.11	4.04	1.1
2012	REA	AA	21	9	7	0	19	19	117^{1}	115	9	27	81	2.1	6.2	53%	.290	1.21	3.30	3.64	3.76	1.5
2012	LEH	AAA	21	4	1	0	7	7	42^{1}	31	0	22	32	4.7	6.8	53%	.254	1.25	2.55	3.20	4.16	0.5
2013	*PHI*	*MLB*	*22*	*2*	*4*	*0*	*8*	*8*	*45^{1}*	*47*	*6*	*18*	*26*	*3.6*	*5.1*	*48%*	*.291*	*1.43*	*4.91*	*4.96*	*5.34*	*-0.4*

More advanced than some of his fellow Philadelphia prospects with higher upsides, Pettibone has been able to move through the system briskly thanks to a command-oriented approach that allows his solid but far from overpowering arsenal to play up a bit. At 6'5", he's built like the proverbial workhorse starter, and while his ceiling is stretched as a number three in a perfect world, his floor as a back-end starter is within view. Pettibone will get some more seasoning in Triple-A and figures to get a look should the Phillies need reinforcements during the season.

Julio Rodriguez

Born: 8/29/1990 Age: 22
Bats: R Throws: R Height: 6' 5" Weight: 195
Breakout: 26% Improve: 56% Collapse: 24%
Attrition: 8% MLB: 91%

Comparables:
Andy Benes,Tom Griffin,Vinegar Bend Mizell

YEAR	TEAM	LVL	AGE	W	L	SV	G	GS	IP	H	HR	BB	SO	BB9	SO9	GB%	BABIP	WHIP	ERA	FIP	FRA	WARP
2011	CLR	A+	20	16	7	0	27	27	156^{2}	102	13	56	168	3.2	9.7	32%	.248	1.01	2.76	3.64	4.11	0.8
2012	REA	AA	21	7	7	0	29	22	134	121	14	76	136	5.1	9.1	31%	.301	1.47	4.23	4.70	4.26	1.3
2013	*PHI*	*MLB*	*22*	*2*	*3*	*0*	*8*	*6*	*39^{1}*	*35*	*5*	*21*	*38*	*4.8*	*8.7*	*36%*	*.296*	*1.42*	*4.70*	*4.52*	*5.11*	*-0.2*

The lack of stuff worthy of the numbers Rodriguez had been posting through 2011 finally caught up to him in his first trip through the advanced minors. He didn't completely fall on his face, still fanning quite a few, but the hits and walks soared, leveling out the expectations among those who simply saw the loud results and assumed the best. It's hardly slanderous to say that Rodriguez has always profiled as a fourth starter at best. It's time for him to adjust to the tougher competition and continue working toward that ceiling. Developing impeccable command of his average stuff will be the best route.

B.J. Rosenberg

Born: 9/17/1985 Age: 27
Bats: R Throws: R Height: 6' 3" Weight: 215
Breakout: 18% Improve: 56% Collapse: 27%
Attrition: 16% MLB: 85%

Comparables:
Gordie Richardson,Brandon Gomes,Bobby Ayala

YEAR	TEAM	LVL	AGE	W	L	SV	G	GS	IP	H	HR	BB	SO	BB9	SO9	GB%	BABIP	WHIP	ERA	FIP	FRA	WARP
2011	REA	AA	25	5	7	2	39	14	109^{1}	114	11	38	103	3.1	8.5	51%	.313	1.39	4.28	4.10	4.68	0.3
2012	REA	AA	26	1	0	3	5	0	8	5	1	2	10	2.2	11.2	42%	.091	0.88	1.12	3.08	3.99	0.1
2012	LEH	AAA	26	4	2	0	20	6	54	49	4	16	63	2.7	10.5	50%	.333	1.20	2.00	2.84	3.19	0.7
2012	PHI	MLB	26	1	2	0	22	1	25	18	4	14	24	5.0	8.6	41%	.226	1.28	6.12	5.22	5.85	-0.3
2013	*PHI*	*MLB*	*27*	*2*	*2*	*0*	*18*	*4*	*38*	*35*	*5*	*15*	*35*	*3.6*	*8.4*	*46%*	*.302*	*1.31*	*4.24*	*4.25*	*4.61*	*-0.0*

More fine work at the minor-league level earned the 27-year-old a major-league opportunity. Alas, it didn't go so well as Rosenberg struggled with walks and home runs. Working at 95-96 mph consistently will afford the right-hander more chances to erase those memories, though an already deep pen and the signing of Mike Adams cuts into the likelihood that Rosenberg will be a part of the Phillies' Opening Day roster.

Michael Schwimer

Born: 2/19/1986 Age: 27
Bats: R Throws: R Height: 6' 9" Weight: 240
Breakout: 29% Improve: 43% Collapse: 45%
Attrition: 20% MLB: 85%

Comparables:
Vinnie Pestano,Josh Roenicke,Bob James

YEAR	TEAM	LVL	AGE	W	L	SV	G	GS	IP	H	HR	BB	SO	BB9	SO9	GB%	BABIP	WHIP	ERA	FIP	FRA	WARP
2010	REA	AA	24	5	3	11	32	0	40	34	5	14	58	3.2	13.1	43%	.342	1.20	3.60	3.29	3.77	1.0
2010	LEH	AAA	24	2	2	0	16	0	20	16	1	7	18	3.2	8.1	42%	.259	1.15	1.35	3.34	3.03	0.4
2011	LEH	AAA	25	9	1	10	47	0	68	51	4	22	86	2.9	11.4	–	.287	1.07	1.85	2.49	2.70	0.0
2011	PHI	MLB	25	1	1	0	12	0	14^{1}	15	2	7	16	4.4	10.0	28%	.342	1.53	5.02	4.25	5.23	-0.1
2012	LEH	AAA	26	2	1	6	15	0	18^{1}	17	2	5	19	2.5	9.3	52%	.300	1.20	3.93	3.49	5.08	0.1
2012	PHI	MLB	26	2	1	0	35	0	34^{1}	30	3	16	36	4.2	9.4	32%	.300	1.34	4.46	3.75	3.64	0.3
2013	*PHI*	*MLB*	*27*	*2*	*1*	*1*	*33*	*0*	*37^{2}*	*32*	*4*	*14*	*41*	*3.5*	*9.7*	*43%*	*.302*	*1.23*	*3.66*	*3.52*	*3.97*	*0.2*

Deception aided by his gargantuan frame helps Schwimer's low-90s heater play up and cause fits for batters. Unfortunately, he makes things easier on hitters with free passes that lead to trouble. Throw in a severe fly-ball lean in the wrong park for such an ailment, and it's hard to see Schwimer as much more than a low-leverage, middle-inning reliever.

Michael Stutes

Born: 9/4/1986 Age: 26
Bats: R Throws: R Height: 6' 2" Weight: 185
Breakout: 22% Improve: 60% Collapse: 17%
Attrition: 10% MLB: 88%

Comparables:
Ron Schueler,Barry Latman,Francisco Rosario

YEAR	TEAM	LVL	AGE	W	L	SV	G	GS	IP	H	HR	BB	SO	BB9	SO9	GB%	BABIP	WHIP	ERA	FIP	FRA	WARP
2010	REA	AA	23	3	0	2	25	0	35^{2}	28	2	21	37	5.3	9.3	39%	.260	1.37	3.78	4.37	3.58	0.8
2010	LEH	AAA	23	4	1	1	28	0	40^{2}	29	5	23	42	5.1	9.3	37%	.250	1.28	3.10	4.59	5.18	-0.2
2011	LEH	AAA	24	2	1	1	7	0	10	9	0	4	14	3.6	12.6	–	.391	1.30	1.80	1.64	1.78	0.0
2011	PHI	MLB	24	6	2	0	57	0	62	49	7	28	58	4.1	8.4	35%	.256	1.24	3.63	4.04	3.96	0.3
2012	PHI	MLB	25	0	0	0	6	0	5^{2}	7	0	4	5	6.4	7.9	20%	.350	1.94	6.35	3.49	3.40	0.1
2013	*PHI*	*MLB*	*26*	*1*	*1*	*0*	*29*	*0*	*36^{2}*	*33*	*5*	*17*	*31*	*4.1*	*7.6*	*41%*	*.288*	*1.36*	*4.48*	*4.67*	*4.87*	*-0.2*

A promising debut in 2011 landed Stutes on the 2012 Opening Day roster, but it was short-lived: A right-shoulder injury cost him most of the season. He managed six outings before hitting the shelf, the last of them on April 21. Arthroscopic surgery was done on the shoulder to clean it out, and Stutes began throwing again in late September. He is expected to be ready for spring training.

Shane Watson
Born: 8/13/1993 Age: 19
Bats: R Throws: R Height: 6' 5" Weight: 200
Breakout: 18% Improve: 64% Collapse: 36%
Attrition: 36% MLB: 45%
Comparables:
Rick Wise, Von McDaniel, Lew Krausse

YEAR	TEAM	LVL	AGE	W	L	SV	G	GS	IP	H	HR	BB	SO	BB9	SO9	GB%	BABIP	WHIP	ERA	FIP	FRA	WARP
2012	PHL	Rk	18	0	1	0	5	3	7	5	0	1	8	1.3	10.3	57%	.286	0.86	1.29	2.01	5.44	0.0
2013	*PHI*	*MLB*	*19*	*1*	*4*	*0*	*7*	*7*	*33^1*	*39*	*5*	*21*	*17*	*5.6*	*4.6*	*45%*	*.312*	*1.78*	*6.59*	*6.02*	*7.16*	*-0.8*

The Phillies made Watson their first pick of 2012 in the supplemental round and signed him away from a commitment to USC. Watson is a tall, projectable righty who can run it up to the mid-90s, though he often works closer to 91-92 with plenty of life. He complements the fastball with a sharp 12-to-6 curveball that has plus potential as well. There's a lot of upside here for sure, but a teenager this far away is also rife with risk.

Austin Wright
Born: 9/26/1989 Age: 23
Bats: L Throws: L Height: 6' 5" Weight: 235
Breakout: 26% Improve: 71% Collapse: 16%
Attrition: 17% MLB: 95%
Comparables:
J.P. Howell, Felix Doubront, Jo-Jo Reyes

YEAR	TEAM	LVL	AGE	W	L	SV	G	GS	IP	H	HR	BB	SO	BB9	SO9	GB%	BABIP	WHIP	ERA	FIP	FRA	WARP
2011	LWD	A	21	1	2	0	7	7	33^2	29	2	9	41	2.4	11.0	47%	.356	1.13	2.67	2.67	2.92	0.6
2011	WPT	A-	21	3	1	0	8	7	34^2	30	1	13	44	3.4	11.4	41%	.327	1.24	3.38	2.41	2.54	0.8
2012	CLR	A+	22	11	5	0	27	25	147^2	147	11	60	133	3.7	8.1	48%	.315	1.40	3.47	3.92	4.83	0.7
2013	*PHI*	*MLB*	*23*	*2*	*4*	*0*	*8*	*8*	*43^1*	*44*	*6*	*19*	*33*	*4.0*	*6.9*	*44%*	*.305*	*1.45*	*4.97*	*4.79*	*5.40*	*-0.4*

This big, strapping southpaw has a future, but it will most likely come as a reliever with an outside shot of being a back-end starter. While not overwhelming, Wright's repertoire shows promise, and the continued development of his changeup will determine his ultimate path. He handled his first full-season assignment well, all things considered, and will get a crack at the high minors in 2013.

LINEOUTS

HITTERS

PLAYER	TEAM	LVL	AGE	PA	R	2B	3B	HR	RBI	BB	SO	SB-CS	AVG/OBP/SLG	TAv	BABIP	BRR	FRAA	WARP
OF A. Altherr	LWD	A	21	471	65	27	6	8	50	38	102	25-8	.252/.319/.402	.283	.310	3.7	CF(52): 9.5, LF(21): 3.1	3.4
RF D. Cozens	PHL	Rk	18	183	24	11	2	5	24	21	44	8-2	.255/.341/.441	.232	.321	0	RF(4): -0.2	-0.1
RF K. Dugan	LWD	A	21	498	83	33	2	12	60	48	122	5-1	.300/.387/.470	.330	.391	0.5	RF(77): 2.9, 1B(17): -2.6	3.4
3B J. Fields	ABQ	AAA	29	561	96	32	5	13	71	59	116	9-4	.322/.392/.488	.284	.394	-1	3B(13): -1.0, 1B(8): -0.0	0.2
3B Z. Green	PHL	Rk	18	183	20	13	1	3	21	8	43	2-2	.284/.333/.426	.076	.363	-0.1	3B(4): 0.2	-0.3
CF E. Inciarte	SBN	A	21	264	36	16	5	1	30	31	31	18-4	.293/.375/.422	.282	.332	0.2	CF(14): 0.3	0.2
	VIS	A+	21	279	46	12	5	1	17	22	32	28-8	.319/.377/.419	.294	.361	2.9	CF(20): 1.2, LF(18): 1.8	1.4
C G. Lino	DEL	A	19	227	28	13	0	4	18	16	64	1-1	.218/.282/.340	.214	.293	0.9	C(47): -0.1	-0.7
	LWD	A	19	148	16	10	0	3	14	14	33	0-2	.227/.311/.371	.237	.281	0.8	C(35): -0.8	0.2
CF J. Mitchell	SAC	AAA	27	474	75	15	11	6	38	54	104	15-7	.252/.345/.386	.287	.322	4.5	CF(31): -0.5, LF(2): -0.1	1.2
UT P. Orr	LEH	AAA	33	332	43	13	2	4	33	23	53	16-2	.258/.314/.354	.202	.301	3.2	3B(17): 1.1, SS(5): 1.2	0.3
	PHI	MLB	33	57	6	5	1	0	7	1	18	3-1	.315/.327/.444	.273	.472	-1.2	2B(13): -0.1, 3B(4): 0.0	0.2
C H. Quintero	NAS	AAA	32	100	9	8	0	1	12	1	21	0-0	.263/.283/.379	.245	.324	-0.2	C(19): -0.2	0.3
	KCA	MLB	32	144	7	12	0	1	19	4	28	0-1	.232/.257/.341	.215	.282	-2.6	C(43): 0.4	-0.3
3B M. Walding	WPT	A-	19	292	33	10	3	1	31	31	66	5-2	.233/.326/.308	.255	.309	1.2	3B(51): -1.1	0.3

Aaron Altherr, another high-upside, raw outfielder, sputtered in his first go in the Sally League in 2011, but bounced back with a solid second tour. ⚾ Powerful **Dylan Cozens** is one of the best bats from the team's 2012 draft, but there's a first-baseman's mitt with his name on it. ⚾ **Kelly Dugan**—stop us if you've heard this—is a toolsy outfielder who doesn't do any one thing extremely well, but has a nice package of skills and could wind up as a solid major-leaguer. ⚾ **Josh Fields** is five years removed from his 23-homer rookie season and has just 106 MLB games played since then, none in the past two years. ⚾ **Zach Green** isn't quite as big as Cozens at 6'3", but he too is built for success. He'll have to hit more after moving from short to third. ⚾ **Ender Inciarte**'s bat was resuscitated in the California League, as the contact skills that marked his teen years returned to spark his prospect candle. ⚾ **Gabriel Lino** still hasn't shown he can hit, and his plate discipline suffered last year, but he continues to hint at power and, if nothing else, could have a future as a backup catcher thanks to excellent defense. ⚾ **Jermaine Mitchell** appeared to be on the verge of a big-league look in Oakland after a fine 2011, but 27 is a bad age at which to stumble in the minors, which he did last year. ⚾ **Pete Orr** has spent parts of seven seasons in Triple-A and parts of seven seasons in the majors, and 2012 figures to be the eighth for both. ⚾ The Ruiz suspension could give **Humberto Quintero** and his anemic bat a shot at an Opening Day roster spot, and maybe even a start. ⚾ **Mitch Walding** debuted in short-season as he transitions from shortstop to third base. He has both the offensive potential and defensive chops to handle the move, but he is far from a finished product.

PITCHERS

PLAYER	TEAM	LVL	AGE	W	L	SV	IP	H	HR	BB	SO	BB9	SO9	GB%	BABIP	WHIP	ERA	FIP	FRA	WARP
J. Diekman	LEH	AAA	25	1	1	7	26^{2}	19	0	13	37	4.4	12.5	58%	.322	1.20	1.69	2.07	1.49	0.7
	PHI	MLB	25	1	1	0	27^{1}	25	1	20	35	6.6	11.5	55%	.333	1.65	3.95	3.58	3.47	0.4
P. Garner	CLR	A+	23	7	9	0	134	135	9	63	91	4.2	6.1	51%	.295	1.48	4.84	4.45	5.02	0.3
T. Knigge	CLR	A+	23	4	1	9	44^{2}	26	0	11	45	2.2	9.1	48%	.234	0.83	0.60	2.12	2.29	1.1
	REA	AA	23	0	0	2	24^{2}	25	1	12	25	4.4	9.1	61%	.343	1.50	2.92	3.28	3.65	0.4
H. Milner	LWD	A	21	6	3	0	62^{2}	52	6	22	47	3.2	6.8	39%	.260	1.18	2.59	4.43	4.55	0.3
Z. Miner	TOL	AAA	30	2	0	2	36	23	3	20	16	5.0	4.0	46%	.182	1.19	2.50	5.10	6.13	-0.3
A. Morgan	CLR	A+	22	4	10	0	123	103	7	28	140	2.0	10.2	45%	.307	1.07	3.29	2.59	2.97	2.1
	REA	AA	22	4	1	0	35^{2}	34	2	11	29	2.8	7.3	39%	.323	1.26	3.53	3.23	3.51	0.4
M. Robles	WTN	AA	23	2	2	0	50^{2}	36	2	41	50	7.3	8.9	43%	.260	1.52	4.09	4.29	6.22	-0.2
	TAC	AAA	23	0	3	0	21	22	3	22	19	9.4	8.1	32%	.322	2.10	9.86	7.14	10.21	-0.4
J. Savery	LEH	AAA	26	1	1	2	23^{1}	27	3	9	26	3.5	10.0	45%	.353	1.54	4.24	3.89	5.18	0.1
	PHI	MLB	26	1	2	0	25	26	4	8	16	2.9	5.8	46%	.278	1.36	5.40	5.02	4.95	-0.2
R. Valdes	LEH	AAA	34	1	2	3	30	26	3	2	41	0.6	12.3	35%	.338	0.93	2.70	1.92	3.02	0.7
	PHI	MLB	34	3	2	0	31	18	3	5	35	1.5	10.2	25%	.214	0.74	2.90	2.62	2.99	0.6

Jake Diekman, unique as a hard-throwing lefty side-armer, misses a lot of bats, but he also misses the strike zone a lot. ⚾ **Perci Garner** was finally healthy enough for a full season of work. The next step is ironing out the mechanics to tap into his power potential. ⚾ **Tyler Knigge** faced his toughest competition and put up his best season of work. He hopes to continue that success in Triple-A with a possible chance at big league time in 2013 as well. ⚾ **Hoby Milner** is a polished college product from the University of Texas who impressed in 68 innings of pro ball after 72 with the Longhorns. His future is likely as a reliever, but the Phillies have him starting for now. ⚾ It's been three years since ground-ball pitcher **Zach Miner** worked in the majors as a useful swingman for the Tigers. ⚾ **Adam Morgan** doesn't have a huge ceiling beyond perhaps fifth starter, but the polished lefty from Alabama is moving quickly and putting up results. ⚾ With 96 walks in 104 innings over the past two seasons, all the strikeout stuff and left-handedness in the world won't save **Mauricio Robles**. ⚾ Former first-rounder **Joe Savery** seems to have finally honed in on a role after vacillating between hitting and pitching, but he could be in big trouble if 2012's home run issues aren't fixed fast. ⚾ Despite the bevy of young, live arms contending for bullpen spots, veteran **Raul Valdes** was perhaps the best of the bunch and his left-handedness will likely keep him around for an encore in 2013.

MANAGER: CHARLIE MANUEL

YEAR	TEAM	W-L	Pythag +/-	Avg PC	100+ P	120+ P	QS	BQS	REL	REL w Zero R	IBB	PH	PH Avg	PH HR	SB2	CS2	SB3	CS3	SAC Att	SAC %	POS SAC	Squeeze	Swing	In Play
2010	PHI	97-65	1	196.7	159	157	106	9	452	362	84	538	.188	16	20	3	0	2	140	68.6%	38	2	279	101
2011	PHI	102-60	1	98.0	86	10	107	7	394	308	41	259	.236	4	15	3	0	0	91	74.7%	28	0	276	105
2012	PHI	81-81	1	97.7	80	2	99	8	439	340	33	268	.206	5	28	3	0	0	102	80.4%	47	2	277	94

With his paunch and grizzled look, Manuel is straight out of central casting for baseball managers. It turns out he has been the right man for the part, with some great results in his 11 years. He has just one sub-.500 record in his credits, the 2002 Indians going 39-47 before he was shown the door. Manuel has spent his 60s winning 56 percent of his games with the Phillies. His charges are fourth in baseball in stolen bases during his eight-year tenure despite being just 11th in attempts. Having Davey Lopes as a coach in 2007-10 helped, but the success rate has stayed above 80 percent in the two years since Lopes left. Bunting has never been a major part of Manuel's game: Throughout his tenure, the Phillies have been below league average for sacrifice bunts every year except 2012.

Manuel has been blessed with excellent starting pitching, and he leaves them out there to do their thing, resisting an urge to tinker just for the sake of tinkering. During his years in the Phillies dugout, Philadelphia has logged the most starting-pitcher innings in the NL and third-most in all of baseball. Even during a rough 2012, Manuel realized that his best chance was to let his horses work, and they threw a league-high 1,033 innings. With another veteran team on tap in Philly, expect to see more of the same from Manuel. With his paunch and grizzled look, does he look like the kind of guy who tries to fix what ain't broken?

Pittsburgh Pirates

2012: SEPTEMBER STUMBLE

Pittsburgh entered September with nine more wins than losses, yet for the second straight year the Pirates mangled the chance to end their 19-year streak without a winning season. This time, the bullpen, a strength throughout the season, fell apart. The constant losing over the season's final weeks zapped the goodwill an active trade deadline created and overshadowed a number of notable individual seasons—including an MVP-caliber campaign from Andrew McCutchen—all while pushing the worst losing streak in sports to 20 years.

Neal Huntington's bunch had the finish line in sight. In a few short weeks, the Pirates would have had their first winning season since the days of Jim Leyland, Doug Drabek, and Barry Bonds. But the ghosts of failures past haunted the club in September by turning a normally reliable relief staff into proverbial gas cans. The Pirates bullpen posted a 4.82 ERA from September on after entering the month at 2.99. They earned seven of their 19 losses on the season, and blew five of their 14 save chances. This wasn't just the work of dogsbody arms in the bigs because of expanded rosters, either. Reliable veteran arms Joel Hanrahan, Jason Grilli, and Chris Resop got in on the fireworks as often as anyone.

PIRATES PROSPECTUS

2012 W-L: 79-83, 4th in NL Central

Pythag	.484	18th	DER	.714	10th
RS/G	4.02	23rd	B-Age	27.5	6th
RA/G	4.16	12th	P-Age	30.3	29th
TAv	.253	25th	Salary	$51.9	30th
BRR	-4.2	19th	M$/MW	$1.27	3rd
TAv-P	.255	7th	DL Days	609	27th
FIP	3.97	17th	DL WARP	0.7	30th

Three-Year Park Factors	
Overall	101
HR/RH	92
HR/LH	111
AVG/RH	92
AVG/LH	99

PNC Park (2001)
Att. % of Capacity: 68.2% (16th)
Dim. 325, 389, 399, 375, 320

PNC was 26th in homers, which wasn't unusual. It was also 27th in BABIP, which was out of character.

This was also not the act of a vengeful regression god. The Pirates had outperformed their Pythagorean record, but not egregiously. Huntington had to wonder what might have been as he watched the Pirates' American League doppelganger, the Orioles, reach the postseason.

It wasn't all on Huntington. He had done things general managers of winning teams do. At the deadline, he had acquired Wandy Rodriguez from a division rival, and he tried beefing up the offense by adding bats Gaby Sanchez and Travis Snider. He talked about building the best possible playoff roster as September approached. But the Pirates' September disaster meant they never got to use that roster.

2013: UP IN ARMS

Will the third time be the charm? Huntington's big offseason addition, Russell Martin, should close an organizational hole that has festered since the Jason Kendall trade in 2004. With a number of solid players in place and a few impact youngsters on the way, autumn baseball could be relevant again in Pittsburgh as soon as this season.

So long as the Pirates have McCutchen, second baseman Neil Walker, and third baseman Pedro Alvarez, they have the makings of a solid lineup. Surrounding those players with quality teammates has proven difficult. Huntington took a step in the right direction by snatching Martin from the Yankees on a two-year deal. Martin figures to outperform Rod Barajas by default, but his real value could come from handling the pitching staff, which is in transition.

Veterans A.J. Burnett and Rodriguez are back. Otherwise, this is a relatively inexperienced bunch. Kevin Correia and Jeff Karstens aren't around anymore, leaving youngsters Kyle McPherson, Justin Wilson, and Jeff Locke in charge until top prospects Gerrit Cole and Jameson Taillon arrive. Having a top defender like Martin behind the plate should ease the transition from the minors to the majors. If all goes well, Pittsburgh could emulate Oakland and compete with a rotation of greenhorns.

THE STATE OF THE ORGANIZATION: GOOD TALENT, STRANGE PRACTICES

Huntington's return for another season would not be a surprise if not for some controversial late-season developments. The club announced his return during the Pirates' downfall and shortly after details surfaced about Pittsburgh holding bizarre, military-style workouts for its prospects. The Pirates have improved their talent level and their on-field results under Huntington, improving from 57 wins in 2010 to 72 and 79 the last two years, but you can only flirt with even a low-level celebration for so long. Huntington may need the Pirates to break through that magic 81-win barrier to keep his job.

The Pirates were fading when news broke concerning military-style boot camps for the Pirates' prospects. A leaked email from assistant general manager Kyle Stark made matters worse. Stark wrote that the Pirates needed players who dream big, play with reckless abandon, and love each other. Harmless rhetoric, except Stark sprinkled in ill-received references to hippies, Boy Scouts, and Hells Angels.

The worst part about the boot camps is the potential downside. Ignoring the injury risk, the camps angered players and agents alike. This could be a topic that comes up during later contract negotiations, and that will affect how the Pirates do business. Under Huntington, the club has shown an eagerness to lock up young talent to team-friendly deals. Putting the players through "Hell Week" may negatively affect their willingness to stick around.

Magnifying the oddness of the training regimens is that Pittsburgh has some of the best prospects in the land. First-round pick Mark Appel didn't sign, but the Pirates have three pitchers who could develop into front-of-the-rotation starters: Cole, Taillon, and Luis Heredia. On the position-player side, the Pirates have a number of international signings with high ceilings, such as Starling Marte, Alen Hanson, and Gregory Polanco. Selecting twice within the first 14 picks in the 2013 draft should keep the system strong in spite of graduations.

The poor second halves and odd developmental choices have obscured the things Huntington has excelled at—securing young talent, finding cheap veteran help, and refusing to yield or rush prospects for short-term gain. Those are the earmarks of a good organization. Many of the success stories of 2012 had Huntington's fingerprints all over them. Walker moved to second base on his watch; Burnett came to Pittsburgh in an opportunistic buy-low trade; and Huntington drafted Alvarez and signed Garrett Jones to a minor-league deal. Then there's McCutchen, whom Huntington inked to a lengthy extension during the season. As is often the case, the Bucs' rise did less to raise Huntington's stock than their fall hurt it. If the losses and dirty laundry continue piling up, the Pirates may have no choice but to let someone else benefit from Huntington's solid work.

HITTERS

Stetson Allie 1B
Born: **3/13/1991** Age: **22**
Bats: **R** Throws: **R** Height: **6' 3"**
Weight: **220** Breakout: **10%**
Improve: **53%** Collapse: **6%**
Attrition: **15%** MLB: **89%**
Comparables:
Norm Miller, Tookie Gilbert, Ken Harrelson

YEAR	TEAM	LVL	AGE	PA	R	2B	3B	HR	RBI	BB	SO	SB	CS	AVG_OBP_SLG	TAv	BABIP	BRR	FRAA	WARP
2012	PIR	Rk	21	173	23	6	2	3	19	21	50	2	0	.213/.314/.340	.230	.299	-1.1	1B(19): -0.9, 3B(9): -0.2	-0.8
2013	*PIT*	*MLB*	*22*	*250*	*18*	*7*	*1*	*4*	*21*	*15*	*82*	*1*	*0*	*.169/.221/.260*	*.180*	*.236*	*-0.2*	*1B -1, 3B 0*	*-1.7*

Allie made two appearances as a pitcher last season, got two outs, and walked eight batters. The Pirates called time out and sent Allie to extended spring training. Conditions did not improve, and Pittsburgh announced in June that Allie would become a third baseman. Allie had familiarity with the hot corner, having played there in high school, though he soon slid across the diamond to the cold corner. His numbers as a hitter were horrible, of course. The parallels between his hitting and pitching are hard to ignore. In both cases, there's a lot of raw power potential and little usability. The Pirates knew Allie was a huge risk when they selected him. This is just an effort to salvage value.

Pedro Alvarez 3B
Born: **2/6/1987** Age: **26**
Bats: **L** Throws: **R** Height: **6' 4"**
Weight: **235** Breakout: **4%**
Improve: **36%** Collapse: **8%**
Attrition: **20%** MLB: **97%**
Comparables:
Ian Stewart, Troy Glaus, Josh Fields

YEAR	TEAM	LVL	AGE	PA	R	2B	3B	HR	RBI	BB	SO	SB	CS	AVG_OBP_SLG	TAv	BABIP	BRR	FRAA	WARP
2010	IND	AAA	23	278	42	15	4	13	53	32	68	4	4	.277/.366/.533	.301	.335	-2.2	3B(61): 6.2	2.3
2010	PIT	MLB	23	386	42	21	1	16	64	37	119	0	0	.256/.326/.461	.268	.341	-1.3	3B(94): 0.4	1.5
2011	IND	AAA	24	148	16	5	1	5	19	22	42	0	1	.256/.365/.432	.303	.342	-0.8	3B(20): 1.9	0.8
2011	PIT	MLB	24	262	18	9	1	4	19	24	80	1	0	.191/.272/.289	.196	.272	-2	3B(66): 5.0	-0.8
2012	PIT	MLB	25	586	64	25	1	30	85	57	180	1	0	.244/.317/.467	.276	.308	0.5	3B(145): -4.7	1.5
2013	*PIT*	*MLB*	*26*	*498*	*57*	*20*	*2*	*20*	*67*	*47*	*151*	*1*	*1*	*.234/.308/.424*	*.264*	*.301*	*-0.7*	*3B 3*	*1.7*

Scouts regarded Alvarez as a well-rounded hitter coming out of Vanderbilt. He had a knack for contact, tremendous raw strength, and a mature approach at the plate. Alvarez's offensive profile has boiled down to the three true outcomes since reaching the majors, with strikeouts, walks, and home runs accounting for nearly half of his career plate appearances. His chronic contact woes stem from poor pitch recognition and pitch tracking. Alvarez is helpless against left-handers and off-speed pitches alike. He can hit a fastball a long way down the right-field line, and he takes a walk often enough to provide above-average production. The Pirates envisioned something special, but the imperfect Alvarez is merely a good, albeit frustrating, hitter.

Rod Barajas **C**
Born: **9/5/1975** Age: **37**
Bats: **R** Throws: **R** Height: **6' 3"**
Weight: **250** Breakout: **0%**
Improve: **23%** Collapse: **12%**
Attrition: **17%** MLB: **78%**
Comparables:
Damian Miller,Henry Blanco,Gary Carter

YEAR	TEAM	LVL	AGE	PA	R	2B	3B	HR	RBI	BB	SO	SB	CS	AVG_OBP_SLG	TAv	BABIP	BRR	FRAA	WARP
2010	LAN	MLB	34	72	9	3	0	5	13	5	15	0	0	.297/.361/.578	.348	.311	-0.7	C(23): 0.1	0.9
2010	NYN	MLB	34	267	30	11	0	12	34	8	39	0	0	.225/.263/.414	.244	.219	-3	C(73): -0.1	0.3
2011	LAN	MLB	35	336	29	13	0	16	47	22	71	0	0	.230/.287/.430	.257	.244	-4	C(88): 0.3	0.5
2012	PIT	MLB	36	361	29	11	0	11	31	29	69	0	0	.206/.283/.343	.236	.224	-1.9	C(99): -0.4, 1B(1): -0.0	-0.5
2013	*PIT*	*MLB*	*37*	*334*	*35*	*13*	*0*	*12*	*40*	*16*	*62*	*0*	*0*	*.224/.269/.385*	*.239*	*.239*	*-0.6*	*C -0, 1B 0*	*0.7*

The Pirates' decision to fill their catching void with Barajas worked out wonderfully for National League basestealers. Barajas allowed 93 stolen bases on 99 attempts, good for the worst caught-stealing rate since 1950. You might think Barajas made up for his poor throwing by hitting well, but he didn't. The public research on framing suggests he is below-average at that, too. So what did Barajas bring to the table? Supposedly he had a positive psychological impact on A.J. Burnett and the other pitchers. The quantitative must overshadow the qualitative at some point. If your catcher's only utility is serving as a backstop therapist, it might be time to invest in a sports psychologist.

Clint Barmes **SS**
Born: **3/6/1979** Age: **34**
Bats: **R** Throws: **R** Height: **6' 2"**
Weight: **205** Breakout: **1%**
Improve: **25%** Collapse: **7%**
Attrition: **15%** MLB: **81%**
Comparables:
Geoff Blum,Jorge Velandia,Alex Gonzalez

YEAR	TEAM	LVL	AGE	PA	R	2B	3B	HR	RBI	BB	SO	SB	CS	AVG_OBP_SLG	TAv	BABIP	BRR	FRAA	WARP
2010	COL	MLB	31	432	43	21	0	8	50	35	66	3	2	.235/.305/.351	.234	.263	2.1	2B(88): -0.6, SS(47): 4.0	0.7
2011	HOU	MLB	32	495	47	27	0	12	39	38	88	3	1	.244/.312/.386	.247	.279	-2	SS(122): 5.5	1.3
2012	PIT	MLB	33	493	34	16	1	8	45	20	106	0	2	.229/.272/.321	.216	.280	2	SS(141): 9.1, 1B(1): -0.0	0.1
2013	*PIT*	*MLB*	*34*	*464*	*46*	*21*	*1*	*11*	*46*	*24*	*91*	*4*	*2*	*.231/.279/.360*	*.233*	*.264*	*-0.8*	*SS 5, 2B 0*	*1.2*

In an effort to improve their defense, the Pirates signed Barmes to a two-year deal. He delivered with the glove and rated as the second-best defensive shortstop in the National League, according to FRAA. That's a good thing too, because every aspect of Barmes's offensive game went backward. He struck out, walked, and hit for power at career-worst rates. Granted, Barmes had previously spent his career hitting at the offense-friendly establishments in Denver and Houston, but this is beyond park factors. Teams without elite shortstops must choose between creating more runs at the plate or more outs in the field. The Pirates chose to make more outs; boy, did they ever.

Barrett Barnes **CF**
Born: **7/29/1991** Age: **21**
Bats: **R** Throws: **R** Height: **6' 1"**
Weight: **195** Breakout: **--%**
Improve: **--%** Collapse: **--%**
Attrition: **--%** MLB: **--%**
Comparables:
--

YEAR	TEAM	LVL	AGE	PA	R	2B	3B	HR	RBI	BB	SO	SB	CS	AVG_OBP_SLG	TAv	BABIP	BRR	FRAA	WARP
2012	SCO	A-	20	153	16	6	0	5	24	17	21	10	6	.288/.401/.456	.305	.307	0	—	0.0

Barnes became the top pick in the Pirates draft class to sign after Mark Appel opted to return to Stanford. A product of Texas Tech, Barnes is not your usual low-beta collegiate. He boasts plus speed and more power potential than his frame initially indicates. The power may come in handy down the line, since Barnes's arm does not play in center field. A move to left field might have come regardless, given the presence of Andrew McCutchen. Barnes's professional debut ended prematurely after he suffered a stress fracture in his leg.

Josh Bell **3B**
Born: **8/14/1992** Age: **20**
Bats: **B** Throws: **R** Height: **6' 5"**
Weight: **195** Breakout: **26%**
Improve: **57%** Collapse: **5%**
Attrition: **20%** MLB: **84%**
Comparables:
Bobby Delgreco,Ed Kirkpatrick,Al Kaline

YEAR	TEAM	LVL	AGE	PA	R	2B	3B	HR	RBI	BB	SO	SB	CS	AVG_OBP_SLG	TAv	BABIP	BRR	FRAA	WARP
2012	WVA	A	19	66	6	5	0	1	11	2	21	1	0	.274/.288/.403	.205	.381	0	RF(12): -1.7	-0.4
2013	*PIT*	*MLB*	*20*	*250*	*19*	*9*	*1*	*4*	*22*	*10*	*76*	*2*	*1*	*.198/.232/.293*	*.195*	*.268*	*-0.1*	*RF -0*	*-1.2*

Bell tried his best to go undrafted in 2011. He sent out letters to each team in the weeks leading to the draft, informing them of his intent to attend the University of Texas, where his mom serves as a professor. The Pirates called Bell's bluff and lured him away from the academy with a $5 million signing bonus. Bell is a switch-hitter with the potential to hit for average and power from both sides. His hands are excellent, and he can drive the ball to all fields. Add in good athleticism and a plus arm and you have the template for a star right fielder. Bell just needs time to work on his craft in the minors. Unfortunately, his professional debut ended after he hurt his knee while running the bases.

Matt Curry **1B**

Born: **7/27/1988** Age: **24**
Bats: **L** Throws: **R** Height: **6' 2"**
Weight: **225** Breakout: **7%**
Improve: **51%** Collapse: **7%**
Attrition: **20%** MLB: **94%**

Comparables:
Joey Votto,Mike Jorgensen,Randy Johnson

YEAR	TEAM	LVL	AGE	PA	R	2B	3B	HR	RBI	BB	SO	SB	CS	AVG_OBP_SLG	TAv	BABIP	BRR	FRAA	WARP
2010	SCO	A-	21	240	36	14	0	7	29	39	47	7	5	.299/.423/.477	.343	.364	-1.4	1B(51): 0.8	2.2
2011	WVA	A	22	195	39	15	3	9	34	35	29	6	2	.361/.477/.671	.407	.392	-1.5	1B(31): -0.2	2.6
2011	ALT	AA	22	351	38	16	3	6	39	33	90	1	1	.242/.320/.374	.242	.315	-0.7	1B(59): 5.9	0.0
2012	ALT	AA	23	450	53	34	5	11	76	44	107	4	4	.285/.352/.480	.309	.357	-3.6	1B(84): 2.1	1.4
2013	*PIT*	*MLB*	*24*	*250*	*25*	*11*	*1*	*6*	*28*	*23*	*66*	*1*	*1*	*.230/.304/.379*	*.248*	*.292*	*-0.3*	*1B -4*	*-0.6*

You know the rule concerning first base prospects: In order to be prospects they have to hit—and hit and hit. Pittsburgh believed in Curry's bat enough to draft him twice. Last spring, the club worked with him to reduce how often he pulled off on the ball by shortening his leg kick. The tweak had no impact on his strikeout rate, which remained too high for an over-age prospect repeating a level. Curry's body is thick and unathletic, leaving him with no defensive home other than first base. A late-season promotion to Triple-A put him in position to reach the majors in 2013. It's unlikely he becomes more than a bench bat.

Chase d'Arnaud **SS**

Born: **1/21/1987** Age: **26**
Bats: **R** Throws: **R** Height: **6' 2"**
Weight: **200** Breakout: **8%**
Improve: **58%** Collapse: **6%**
Attrition: **26%** MLB: **91%**

Comparables:
Diory Hernandez,Brent Lillibridge,Miguel Tejada

YEAR	TEAM	LVL	AGE	PA	R	2B	3B	HR	RBI	BB	SO	SB	CS	AVG_OBP_SLG	TAv	BABIP	BRR	FRAA	WARP
2010	ALT	AA	23	607	91	33	9	6	48	56	102	33	7	.247/.330/.377	.285	.293	4.6	SS(115): -6.6, 2B(25): -1.5	4.0
2011	IND	AAA	24	321	43	12	6	4	37	23	53	20	4	.264/.328/.389	.238	.310	0.3	SS(28): -2.5, 2B(14): 2.6	0.1
2011	PIT	MLB	24	151	17	6	2	0	6	4	36	12	2	.217/.242/.287	.195	.287	3.4	SS(29): -1.7, 3B(12): 1.1	-0.3
2012	IND	AAA	25	427	63	24	4	6	38	37	93	34	5	.252/.325/.383	.246	.318	4	SS(77): -5.1, 2B(5): -0.9	0.4
2012	PIT	MLB	25	6	2	0	0	0	1	0	2	1	0	.000/.000/.000	.002	.000	0	2B(2): -0.0, SS(1): -0.0	-0.1
2013	*PIT*	*MLB*	*26*	*250*	*30*	*11*	*2*	*3*	*18*	*15*	*57*	*14*	*2*	*.224/.279/.337*	*.231*	*.277*	*2*	*SS -1, 2B 0*	*0.5*

The Pirates have a surplus of utility infielders, starting with d'Arnaud. After missing the first month of the season due to a concussion, he returned and battled through a tough stretch at Triple-A. It's possible the concussion was to blame for his sluggish hitting. He eventually earned a September promotion to the majors, where the Pirates put his speed to use by deploying him as a pinch runner. It wouldn't be surprising to see d'Arnaud spend more time in Indianapolis in 2013.

Ivan De Jesus **SS**

Born: **5/1/1987** Age: **26**
Bats: **R** Throws: **R** Height: **6' 0"**
Weight: **200** Breakout: **1%**
Improve: **35%** Collapse: **12%**
Attrition: **19%** MLB: **85%**

Comparables:
Eddie Miksis,Terry Shumpert,David Bell

YEAR	TEAM	LVL	AGE	PA	R	2B	3B	HR	RBI	BB	SO	SB	CS	AVG_OBP_SLG	TAv	BABIP	BRR	FRAA	WARP
2010	ABQ	AAA	23	580	89	33	2	7	70	32	81	6	1	.296/.334/.405	.246	.334	2.1	2B(114): -2.1, SS(19): -1.1	1.0
2011	ABQ	AAA	24	443	61	19	2	8	59	45	68	4	1	.310/.389/.432	.293	.358	0	--	0.0
2011	LAN	MLB	24	35	2	0	0	0	1	2	11	0	0	.188/.235/.188	.156	.286	0.4	2B(11): 0.5	-0.2
2012	ABQ	AAA	25	243	32	12	3	3	33	14	53	1	1	.295/.333/.415	.237	.366	-1	2B(14): -0.0, SS(4): -0.2	-0.2
2012	BOS	MLB	25	8	0	0	0	0	0	0	6	0	0	.000/.000/.000	.007	.000	0	2B(5): -0.2, 3B(1): -0.0	-0.1
2012	LAN	MLB	25	37	5	3	0	0	4	3	7	1	1	.273/.324/.364	.266	.333	-0.1	2B(7): 0.0, 3B(5): -0.0	0.1
2013	*PIT*	*MLB*	*26*	*250*	*22*	*11*	*1*	*1*	*17*	*12*	*55*	*1*	*0*	*.232/.271/.306*	*.217*	*.291*	*-0.3*	*2B -2, SS -0*	*-0.4*

At one point De Jesus was a top prospect with big-league bloodlines. Injuries and lack of opportunities have devalued his stock, to the extent that he passed through waivers unclaimed prior to being traded for the second time in six months. He shows off the bloodlines with technically sound defensive play at multiple infield positions. He doesn't have the skills profile to start at any of those positions, though, and that limits him to utility work. The Pirates have plenty of those types roaming around the upper minors, so De Jesus will have to work to earn a spot.

Alex Dickerson **1B**

Born: **5/26/1990** Age: **23**
Bats: **L** Throws: **L** Height: **6' 4"**
Weight: **235** Breakout: **6%**
Improve: **60%** Collapse: **7%**
Attrition: **10%** MLB: **81%**

Comparables:
John Ellis,Chris Marrero,Chris Chambliss

YEAR	TEAM	LVL	AGE	PA	R	2B	3B	HR	RBI	BB	SO	SB	CS	AVG_OBP_SLG	TAv	BABIP	BRR	FRAA	WARP
2011	SCO	A-	21	173	25	16	1	3	19	16	28	0	0	.313/.393/.493	.308	.364	0	--	0.0
2012	BRD	A+	22	541	65	31	3	13	90	39	93	12	7	.295/.353/.451	.235	.339	-1.8	1B(31): -1.5	-0.7
2013	*PIT*	*MLB*	*23*	*250*	*23*	*11*	*1*	*6*	*27*	*11*	*57*	*2*	*1*	*.236/.273/.366*	*.232*	*.282*	*-0.2*	*1B -1*	*-0.6*

As with Curry, Dickerson fails to meet the lofty offensive standards that come with playing first base. One of the best collegiate hitters available in the 2011 draft, Dickerson slipped to the third round in part due to a history of back problems. He brings a mature approach to the plate and uses the entire field, thanks to a good hit tool. The issue is power. He has average-to-above-average raw strength that has not translated to in-game results yet. Because he lacks the arm or range to play anywhere but first base, Dickerson's going to need some of that pop to show up during games if he's ever going to be a big-league regular.

Willy Garcia **OF**

Born: **9/4/1992** Age: **20**
Bats: **R** Throws: **R** Height: **6' 4"**
Weight: **177** Breakout: **24%**
Improve: **59%** Collapse: **4%**
Attrition: **21%** MLB: **86%**

Comparables:
Mickey Mantle,Alex Rodriguez,Ed Kirkpatrick

YEAR	TEAM	LVL	AGE	PA	R	2B	3B	HR	RBI	BB	SO	SB	CS	AVG_OBP_SLG	TAv	BABIP	BRR	FRAA	WARP
2011	PIR	Rk	18	201	26	9	4	5	35	11	49	7	5	.266/.323/.446	.253	.331	-1.4	CF(25): 0.0, RF(22): 2.5	0.1
2012	WVA	A	19	497	57	17	2	18	77	32	131	10	8	.240/.286/.403	.233	.292	-1.5	RF(50): -2.9, LF(49): 1.3	-1.3
2013	*PIT*	*MLB*	*20*	*250*	*21*	*8*	*1*	*7*	*25*	*8*	*81*	*2*	*2*	*.192/.220/.317*	*.197*	*.253*	*-0.2*	*RF -0, LF -1*	*-1.2*

West Virginia hosted many of the Pirates' most intriguing positional prospects last year, including Bell, Gregory Polanco, and Alen Hanson. Fans and evaluators flocking to see those talents also got exposure to Garcia. Another raw international signing, he looks like a right-fielder starter kit. His arm is strong and he has the potential to add more power as he fills out and redefines his plate approach. Plenty needs to happen for him to reach his upside, but he's young enough to hold out hope.

Matt Hague **1B**

Born: **8/20/1985** Age: **27**
Bats: **R** Throws: **R** Height: **6' 4"**
Weight: **225** Breakout: **3%**
Improve: **32%** Collapse: **8%**
Attrition: **11%** MLB: **93%**

Comparables:
Tony Muser,Ray Webster,Jason Phillips

YEAR	TEAM	LVL	AGE	PA	R	2B	3B	HR	RBI	BB	SO	SB	CS	AVG_OBP_SLG	TAv	BABIP	BRR	FRAA	WARP
2010	ALT	AA	24	581	90	30	0	15	86	61	62	3	6	.295/.378/.442	.296	.312	-1.8	1B(142): 8.5, 3B(1): -0.0	3.9
2011	IND	AAA	25	594	70	37	3	12	75	47	68	4	3	.309/.372/.457	.270	.334	-2	1B(82): 3.2, 3B(13): -0.3	0.5
2012	IND	AAA	26	399	41	13	0	4	54	26	50	3	1	.283/.332/.351	.240	.316	0.4	3B(41): -0.2, 1B(38): -1.1	-0.5
2012	PIT	MLB	26	74	5	2	0	0	7	3	14	1	0	.229/.270/.257	.187	.286	-0.6	1B(16): 1.5	-0.5
2013	*PIT*	*MLB*	*27*	*250*	*23*	*12*	*1*	*4*	*26*	*16*	*37*	*0*	*0*	*.256/.309/.368*	*.251*	*.286*	*-0.4*	*1B -3, 3B 0*	*-0.2*

Before fungible became an overused term in analytical circles, it was used to described non-elite right-handed batters who played a corner position. Were Hague in the league 10 years ago, chances are he would have received the tag at some point. He is a 27-year-old without a position. He lacks the power to play first base or the corner outfield and the defensive ability to play elsewhere. Pittsburgh gave Hague a look in the majors last season to uninspiring results. His 40-man roster spot is in peril heading forward.

Alen Hanson **SS**

Born: **10/22/1992** Age: **20**
Bats: **B** Throws: **R** Height: **6' 0"**
Weight: **152** Breakout: **13%**
Improve: **40%** Collapse: **4%**
Attrition: **13%** MLB: **72%**

Comparables:
Robin Yount,Edgar Renteria,B.J. Upton

YEAR	TEAM	LVL	AGE	PA	R	2B	3B	HR	RBI	BB	SO	SB	CS	AVG_OBP_SLG	TAv	BABIP	BRR	FRAA	WARP
2011	PIR	Rk	18	234	42	13	7	2	35	21	34	24	6	.263/.352/.429	.264	.307	2.3	SS(39): -5.4, 2B(12): -1.8	0.3
2012	WVA	A	19	558	99	33	13	16	62	55	105	35	19	.309/.381/.528	.315	.364	7.3	SS(91): -10.3	3.5
2013	*PIT*	*MLB*	*20*	*250*	*30*	*9*	*2*	*5*	*20*	*15*	*64*	*10*	*5*	*.219/.267/.347*	*.224*	*.271*	*0.6*	*SS -1, 2B -0*	*0.0*

One of those West Virginia draws, Hanson enjoyed a breakthrough campaign last year. Signed as a smallish, switch-hitting middle infielder out of the Dominican Republic in 2009, he always had plus speed and an easy line-drive-generating swing. His improved power stems from good hands, as he gets the bat into the hitting zone quickly and it stays there for a long time. He also has excellent hand-eye coordination and barrel awareness. The defensive outlook is less exciting. He continues to play shortstop but scouts think he lacks the actions and the arm to stick long-term. Even with a ceiling of an offensive-minded second baseman, Hanson is one of the best prospects in the system.

Josh Harrison **UT**

Born: **7/8/1987** Age: **25**
Bats: **R** Throws: **R** Height: **5' 9"**
Weight: **185** Breakout: **5%**
Improve: **50%** Collapse: **7%**
Attrition: **15%** MLB: **96%**

Comparables:
Jose Lind,Kevin Frandsen,Jose Lopez

YEAR	TEAM	LVL	AGE	PA	R	2B	3B	HR	RBI	BB	SO	SB	CS	AVG_OBP_SLG	TAv	BABIP	BRR	FRAA	WARP
2010	ALT	AA	22	585	74	33	3	4	75	32	52	19	7	.300/.343/.398	.282	.318	2.3	3B(94): -0.1, 2B(47): 5.6	4.2
2011	IND	AAA	23	254	35	15	2	5	23	15	28	13	5	.310/.365/.460	.293	.333	-0.7	3B(25): -3.0, 2B(17): 2.8	0.8
2011	PIT	MLB	23	204	21	13	2	1	16	3	24	4	1	.272/.281/.374	.232	.304	-0.7	3B(50): 3.9, 2B(6): 0.1	0.2
2012	PIT	MLB	24	276	34	9	5	3	16	10	37	7	3	.233/.279/.345	.235	.259	0.5	2B(27): -0.2, SS(25): -1.9	-0.3
2013	*PIT*	*MLB*	*25*	*266*	*29*	*13*	*2*	*3*	*22*	*9*	*34*	*7*	*2*	*.259/.291/.370*	*.242*	*.281*	*0.4*	*3B 1, 2B 0*	*0.4*

Figuring out why the Pirates like Harrison enough to keep him around is tough. His best skills are defensive flexibility and putting the bat on the ball, but both are undermined by the lack of other necessary qualities. Harrison isn't fit to play shortstop, though the Pirates play him there anyway. It's a bad sign when a player walking in 4 percent of his plate appearances is a sign of progress. In fact, his plate discipline is so miserable, it leaves him with below-average offensive production regardless of his batting average. Add in Harrison's upcoming 26th birthday, and the what-if game about his career will soon shift focus from the future to the past.

Garrett Jones RF

Born: **6/21/1981** Age: **32**
Bats: **L** Throws: **L** Height: **6' 5"**
Weight: **240** Breakout: **1%**
Improve: **28%** Collapse: **9%**
Attrition: **16%** MLB: **87%**

Comparables:
Xavier Nady,Ben Broussard,Glenn Davis

YEAR	TEAM	LVL	AGE	PA	R	2B	3B	HR	RBI	BB	SO	SB	CS	AVG_OBP_SLG	TAv	BABIP	BRR	FRAA	WARP
2010	PIT	MLB	29	654	64	34	1	21	86	53	123	7	3	.247/.306/.414	.251	.274	-3.1	1B(112): 2.1, RF(48): -0.3	0.2
2011	PIT	MLB	30	477	51	30	1	16	58	48	104	6	3	.243/.321/.433	.269	.283	-0.5	RF(90): 1.0, 1B(34): -1.6	0.7
2012	PIT	MLB	31	515	68	28	3	27	86	33	103	2	0	.274/.317/.516	.300	.293	-3.2	1B(72): -1.2, RF(66): -1.2	1.5
2013	*PIT*	*MLB*	*32*	*476*	*57*	*24*	*1*	*19*	*65*	*38*	*103*	*6*	*2*	*.249/.309/.445*	*.272*	*.281*	*-0.2*	*RF 1, 1B -3*	*1.2*

Clint Hurdle is the best thing to happen to Jones. In the two seasons the big lefty spent with the Pirates before Hurdle, he faced 67 percent right-handed pitchers, while since Hurdle's arrival two years ago, that rate has jumped to 85 percent. He is a platoon player through and through: Back when he faced left-handed pitchers, he hit them about as well as Manny Ramirez hit the cutoff man. Now, Jones's numbers look a lot better than they would otherwise. This isn't a knock on Jones, either. He's a useful player and a good hitter against righties. The extreme prejudice with which Hurdle uses him is refreshing.

Starling Marte OF

Born: **10/9/1988** Age: **24**
Bats: **R** Throws: **R** Height: **6' 2"**
Weight: **170** Breakout: **2%**
Improve: **59%** Collapse: **2%**
Attrition: **3%** MLB: **96%**

Comparables:
Junior Felix,Duke Snider,Matt Kemp

YEAR	TEAM	LVL	AGE	PA	R	2B	3B	HR	RBI	BB	SO	SB	CS	AVG_OBP_SLG	TAv	BABIP	BRR	FRAA	WARP
2010	BRD	A+	21	253	41	16	5	0	33	12	59	22	8	.315/.386/.432	.292	.424	0	--	0.0
2011	ALT	AA	22	572	91	38	8	12	50	22	100	24	12	.332/.370/.500	.317	.390	5.6	CF(91): 0.0	4.3
2012	IND	AAA	23	431	64	21	13	12	62	28	91	21	12	.286/.347/.500	.282	.344	-1.5	CF(59): 2.8, LF(14): 1.9	1.8
2012	PIT	MLB	23	182	18	3	6	5	17	8	50	12	5	.257/.300/.437	.261	.333	-1.2	LF(43): -2.1, CF(4): -0.0	-0.2
2013	*PIT*	*MLB*	*24*	*250*	*34*	*11*	*4*	*6*	*25*	*10*	*60*	*11*	*5*	*.262/.300/.425*	*.261*	*.321*	*0.9*	*CF -1, LF -0*	*0.7*

Marte's introduction to the majors included the good and bad sides of his aggressive nature. He homered on the first pitch he saw in the bigs, and showed off his ability to hit for power throughout his stay. But Marte also showed a tendency to swing and miss, fueling an unacceptable strikeout rate in the face of his paucity of walks. Swinging at bad pitches is a concern that dates back to his days on the farm. With all that said, Marte still managed to hit like a league-average batter. He has the tools to become an above-average corner outfielder; he just needs some additional refinement first.

Russell Martin C

Born: **2/15/1983** Age: **30**
Bats: **R** Throws: **R** Height: **5' 11"**
Weight: **230** Breakout: **1%**
Improve: **47%** Collapse: **6%**
Attrition: **9%** MLB: **92%**

Comparables:
Bill Freehan,Carlos Ruiz,Smoky Burgess

YEAR	TEAM	LVL	AGE	PA	R	2B	3B	HR	RBI	BB	SO	SB	CS	AVG_OBP_SLG	TAv	BABIP	BRR	FRAA	WARP
2010	LAN	MLB	27	387	45	13	0	5	26	48	61	6	2	.248/.347/.332	.257	.287	-0.2	C(93): -0.8	1.6
2011	NYA	MLB	28	476	57	17	0	18	65	50	81	8	2	.237/.324/.408	.253	.252	-0.7	C(125): -0.5, 3B(3): -0.0	1.4
2012	NYA	MLB	29	485	50	18	0	21	53	53	95	6	1	.211/.311/.403	.255	.222	1.1	C(128): -0.5	1.5
2013	*PIT*	*MLB*	*30*	*454*	*53*	*17*	*1*	*11*	*47*	*52*	*71*	*8*	*2*	*.242/.336/.373*	*.265*	*.268*	*-0.2*	*C -0, 3B 0*	*2.3*

According to his own spring training statements, Martin has reported to camp in the best shape of his life for five consecutive seasons. (By the time you read this, he may have made it six.) Whatever workout plan has made his annual proclamation so predictable has had the same effect on his on-field performance. Since his heyday as a hitter with the Dodgers, Martin has settled in as a slightly above-average offensive catcher, a slightly above-average thrower, and a slightly above-average blocker. However, he has distinguished himself to an even greater degree as a receiver. According to Max Marchi's estimates, Martin saved nearly 90 runs due to framing from 2008–12, the third most among backstops behind Jose Molina and Brian McCann. Some fans won't care about framing until it becomes a category in their fantasy leagues, but Martin's work with the glove meant more to the Yankees than his career-high home-run total, and figures to mean more still to the catching-starved Pirates.

Wyatt Mathisen C

Born: **12/30/1993** Age: **19**
Bats: **R** Throws: **R** Height: **6' 2"**
Weight: **205** Breakout: **0%**
Improve: **59%** Collapse: **41%**
Attrition: **41%** MLB: **100%**

Comparables:
Robin Yount,Ed Kranepool,Wayne Causey

YEAR	TEAM	LVL	AGE	PA	R	2B	3B	HR	RBI	BB	SO	SB	CS	AVG_OBP_SLG	TAv	BABIP	BRR	FRAA	WARP
2012	PIR	Rk	18	167	24	8	0	1	15	16	19	10	8	.295/.388/.374	.277	.328	0.6	C(5): 0.2	0.2
2013	*PIT*	*MLB*	*19*	*250*	*31*	*8*	*1*	*4*	*17*	*15*	*66*	*19*	*12*	*.186/.240/.278*	*.195*	*.238*	*0.1*	*C -0*	*-0.8*

You've heard of a projectable pitching prospect? Well, here's a projectable catching prospect. Mathisen didn't catch a lot in high school, but the Pirates took him in the second round because they think he's got a chance to stick behind the plate at the professional level. That belief starts with his athleticism and strong arm and continues with his potential to hit for average and power. Still, we're a few years from knowing whether Mathisen will be able to don the tools of ignorance in the majors.

Andrew McCutchen CF

Born: **10/10/1986** Age: **26**
Bats: **R** Throws: **R** Height: **5' 11"**
Weight: **190** Breakout: **4%**
Improve: **52%** Collapse: **5%**
Attrition: **7%** MLB: **95%**

Comparables:
Chet Lemon,Cesar Cedeno,Grady Sizemore

YEAR	TEAM	LVL	AGE	PA	R	2B	3B	HR	RBI	BB	SO	SB	CS	AVG_OBP_SLG	TAv	BABIP	BRR	FRAA	WARP
2010	PIT	MLB	23	653	94	35	5	16	56	70	89	33	10	.286/.365/.449	.291	.311	4.1	CF(152): -11.7	3.2
2011	PIT	MLB	24	678	87	34	5	23	89	89	126	23	10	.259/.364/.456	.297	.291	-2.8	CF(155): 9.4	4.5
2012	PIT	MLB	25	673	107	29	6	31	96	70	132	20	12	.327/.400/.553	.328	.375	-0.7	CF(156): -9.6	4.9
2013	*PIT*	*MLB*	*26*	*633*	*85*	*30*	*6*	*21*	*82*	*68*	*113*	*22*	*9*	*.279/.360/.469*	*.299*	*.312*	*0.9*	*CF -1*	*4.6*

In the movie *Charade*, Audrey Hepburn says to Cary Grant, "You know what's wrong with you? Nothing!" Imagine the movie with McCutchen in Grant's place and the statement remains apt. McCutchen signed a six-year extension in March with a club option for a seventh, then went out and made it look good, setting new career bests across the board and solidifying himself as one of the best players in the game. Here's the scary part: An increase in opposite-field home runs may be a sign he's gaining his grown-man strength. If so, one of the game's most dynamic players is about to get scarier. What's wrong with Andrew McCutchen? Nothing!

Michael McKenry C

Born: **3/4/1985** Age: **28**
Bats: **R** Throws: **R** Height: **5' 11"**
Weight: **200** Breakout: **12%**
Improve: **42%** Collapse: **12%**
Attrition: **21%** MLB: **89%**

Comparables:
Nick Hundley,Jorge Posada,Brad Davis

YEAR	TEAM	LVL	AGE	PA	R	2B	3B	HR	RBI	BB	SO	SB	CS	AVG_OBP_SLG	TAv	BABIP	BRR	FRAA	WARP
2010	CSP	AAA	25	384	44	23	1	10	49	32	77	1	1	.265/.331/.424	.239	.315	-4	C(94): 1.2	0.6
2010	COL	MLB	25	9	0	0	0	0	0	1	5	0	0	.000/.111/.000	.045	.000	-0.1	C(2): -0.0	-0.2
2011	PAW	AAA	26	111	10	5	0	3	12	14	24	1	0	.274/.369/.421	.290	.333	-1.5	C(23): -0.3	0.4
2011	PIT	MLB	26	201	17	12	0	2	11	14	49	0	1	.222/.276/.322	.224	.290	-0.2	C(58): -0.4, 3B(1): -0.0	-0.3
2012	PIT	MLB	27	275	25	14	0	12	39	29	73	0	0	.233/.320/.442	.278	.278	-0.6	C(79): 1.4	1.6
2013	*PIT*	*MLB*	*28*	*254*	*26*	*12*	*1*	*7*	*27*	*21*	*64*	*0*	*0*	*.227/.294/.372*	*.246*	*.278*	*-0.5*	*C 0, 3B 0*	*0.8*

In *Baseball Prospectus 2012* we wrote, "A hitch in [McKenry's] swing limits his ability to make contact, so he relies on walks and the occasional extra-base hit." Sure enough, McKenry's 2012 season featured plenty of strikeouts, walks, and extra-base hits. McKenry's caught-stealing rate was nothing special, but compared to Barajas, he threw like Johnny Bench. The only reasons McKenry failed to overtake Barajas for more playing time were his apparent shortcomings as a defender and field general. An odd development, since McKenry owned a strong defensive reputation in the minors.

Jordy Mercer SS

Born: **8/27/1986** Age: **26**
Bats: **R** Throws: **R** Height: **6' 4"**
Weight: **191** Breakout: **7%**
Improve: **55%** Collapse: **6%**
Attrition: **24%** MLB: **92%**

Comparables:
Dickie Thon,Omar Infante,Zack Cozart

YEAR	TEAM	LVL	AGE	PA	R	2B	3B	HR	RBI	BB	SO	SB	CS	AVG_OBP_SLG	TAv	BABIP	BRR	FRAA	WARP
2010	ALT	AA	23	538	67	31	2	3	65	31	69	7	1	.282/.331/.373	.269	.320	0.9	3B(54): 0.5, 2B(49): 10.9	2.9
2011	ALT	AA	24	301	40	17	1	13	48	23	35	6	3	.268/.329/.487	.292	.260	-1.1	SS(49): -0.0	1.3
2011	IND	AAA	24	250	39	13	1	6	21	13	43	3	3	.239/.304/.385	.236	.271	1	2B(23): -1.9, SS(19): 1.8	0.0
2012	IND	AAA	25	236	28	14	1	4	27	20	45	3	5	.287/.357/.421	.287	.346	1.6	SS(25): 1.2, 3B(10): 0.7	1.4
2012	PIT	MLB	25	68	7	5	1	1	5	4	14	0	1	.210/.265/.371	.230	.250	0	SS(27): 0.4, 2B(7): 0.6	0.0
2013	*PIT*	*MLB*	*26*	*250*	*23*	*13*	*1*	*5*	*26*	*13*	*47*	*2*	*1*	*.240/.286/.365*	*.241*	*.275*	*-0.4*	*SS 1, 2B 0*	*0.5*

Mercer came up in early July and stayed with the Pirates through the remainder of the season, though you're forgiven if you didn't notice. The tall shortstop got into 42 games, but made only 68 plate appearances. Granted, he didn't do a whole lot when he did get the chance to swing the bat. He is another victim of Pittsburgh's Harrison infatuation.

Gregory Polanco CF

Born: **9/14/1991** Age: **21**
Bats: **L** Throws: **L** Height: **6' 5"**
Weight: **170** Breakout: **3%**
Improve: **57%** Collapse: **8%**
Attrition: **14%** MLB: **97%**

Comparables:
Rick Manning,Thad Bosley,Curt Flood

YEAR	TEAM	LVL	AGE	PA	R	2B	3B	HR	RBI	BB	SO	SB	CS	AVG_OBP_SLG	TAv	BABIP	BRR	FRAA	WARP
2010	PIR	Rk	18	200	21	5	1	3	23	9	41	19	2	.202/.246/.287	.205	.243	1.3	RF(38): 2.7, CF(10): 1.4	0.0
2011	PIR	Rk	19	203	34	4	4	3	34	24	33	18	0	.237/.333/.361	.253	.268	0.9	CF(21): 8.7, RF(21): 2.8	1.3
2012	WVA	A	20	485	84	26	6	16	85	44	64	40	15	.325/.388/.522	.322	.352	6.3	CF(84): -4.6	3.6
2013	*PIT*	*MLB*	*21*	*250*	*26*	*8*	*2*	*5*	*23*	*13*	*59*	*10*	*3*	*.216/.257/.334*	*.220*	*.261*	*1.2*	*CF -1, RF -0*	*-0.3*

Polanco is another potential gem uncovered by the Pirates' international scouting efforts. Lean and long-limbed, Polanco is as projectable as they come. He has plus speed, but his defense needs sharpening. The most polished aspect of his game is his offense. He has a better understanding of the nuances of hitting than you would expect from someone with his age and background. He shows good bat speed along with natural loft to his swing. Polanco figures to develop into a threat to hit for average and power alike. Where he winds up in the outfield is up for debate, though there is a camp pegging him as a future center fielder. His ceiling is sky high, but he's a long way off.

Alex Presley LF

Born: **7/25/1985** Age: **27**
Bats: **L** Throws: **L** Height: **5' 10"**
Weight: **190** Breakout: **4%**
Improve: **51%** Collapse: **14%**
Attrition: **19%** MLB: **97%**

Comparables:
Tommy Davis,Ben Francisco,Lou Montanez

YEAR	TEAM	LVL	AGE	PA	R	2B	3B	HR	RBI	BB	SO	SB	CS	AVG_OBP_SLG	TAv	BABIP	BRR	FRAA	WARP
2010	ALT	AA	24	269	42	13	7	6	47	19	33	5	1	.350/.399/.533	.333	.385	-0.8	LF(53): 1.1, RF(12): 0.2	2.8
2010	IND	AAA	24	296	44	15	6	6	38	22	42	8	7	.294/.348/.460	.268	.329	2.7	CF(64): -1.0, LF(3): 0.2	1.3
2010	PIT	MLB	24	25	2	1	0	0	0	1	8	1	1	.261/.292/.304	.212	.400	-0.5	RF(8): -0.2, CF(4): -0.1	-0.2
2011	IND	AAA	25	376	58	18	5	8	41	28	54	22	8	.333/.388/.485	.278	.376	2.3	LF(44): 5.5, CF(12): 0.8	1.8
2011	PIT	MLB	25	231	27	12	6	4	20	13	40	9	3	.298/.339/.465	.279	.349	0.8	LF(48): -3.7, CF(5): -0.3	0.4
2012	IND	AAA	26	179	24	3	4	5	22	24	26	7	2	.307/.399/.477	.301	.341	-0.2	CF(19): -0.2, LF(14): -0.0	0.9
2012	PIT	MLB	26	370	46	14	7	10	25	18	72	9	7	.237/.279/.405	.240	.273	3.6	LF(81): 2.8, RF(8): -0.5	0.1
2013	*PIT*	*MLB*	*27*	*376*	*48*	*16*	*6*	*9*	*37*	*21*	*68*	*12*	*5*	*.266/.310/.420*	*.263*	*.303*	*0.8*	*LF -1, CF -1*	*0.9*

After beginning the season as the Pirates' left fielder, Presley slumped his way into a demotion, and then suffered a concussion. His luck turned around once he returned to the majors in June, and he hit .246/.295/.456 over the final four months. The power production is nice but Presley needs to show a consistent ability to get on base—whether it's via a better average or more walks. Presley seems likely to become a fourth outfielder.

Clint Robinson 1B

Born: **2/16/1985** Age: **28**
Bats: **L** Throws: **L** Height: **6' 6"**
Weight: **235** Breakout: **1%**
Improve: **49%** Collapse: **6%**
Attrition: **9%** MLB: **92%**

Comparables:
Don Baylor,Ryan Garko,Kent Hrbek

YEAR	TEAM	LVL	AGE	PA	R	2B	3B	HR	RBI	BB	SO	SB	CS	AVG_OBP_SLG	TAv	BABIP	BRR	FRAA	WARP
2010	NWA	AA	25	548	90	41	5	29	98	58	86	4	3	.335/.413/.625	.335	.360	-1.6	1B(83): 1.3, LF(1): 0.0	5.5
2011	OMA	AAA	26	572	86	35	0	23	100	58	88	2	1	.326/.399/.533	.328	.356	-2.5	1B(27): -1.0, LF(2): -0.2	1.3
2012	OMA	AAA	27	570	70	37	1	13	67	79	65	1	0	.292/.393/.452	.308	.315	0.2	1B(65): -3.2, LF(1): -0.0	1.9
2012	KCA	MLB	27	4	0	0	0	0	0	0	2	0	0	.000/.000/.000	.001	.000	0	--	-0.1
2013	*PIT*	*MLB*	*28*	*250*	*27*	*14*	*1*	*8*	*31*	*23*	*45*	*0*	*0*	*.262/.333/.435*	*.277*	*.294*	*-0.4*	*1B -2, LF -0*	*0.5*

His production slipped a bit in Triple-A, but Robinson finally got a cup of coffee for the Royals in 2012. His minor-league power has declined in the two previous seasons, which won't help his cause as he tries to crack the big-league roster. While his performance dropped, his approach stayed on an even keel. Still, his swing got long at times last summer and he really slumped in the second half. His defense at first base is considered below average. The Pirates have plenty of Quad-A types already in the cabinet and Robinson does nothing to differentiate himself from the bunch.

Gaby Sanchez 1B

Born: **9/2/1983** Age: **29**
Bats: **R** Throws: **R** Height: **6' 2"**
Weight: **225** Breakout: **4%**
Improve: **59%** Collapse: **13%**
Attrition: **14%** MLB: **93%**

Comparables:
Cesar Cedeno,Ryan Garko,Rafael Palmeiro

YEAR	TEAM	LVL	AGE	PA	R	2B	3B	HR	RBI	BB	SO	SB	CS	AVG_OBP_SLG	TAv	BABIP	BRR	FRAA	WARP
2010	FLO	MLB	26	643	72	37	3	19	85	57	101	5	0	.273/.341/.448	.276	.299	-1.4	1B(149): -4.9	1.3
2011	FLO	MLB	27	661	72	35	0	19	78	74	97	3	1	.266/.352/.427	.284	.287	-2.8	1B(153): 3.9	1.8
2012	NWO	AAA	28	144	20	7	0	5	18	22	23	2	2	.302/.431/.491	.242	.337	0.7	1B(9): 1.0	0.2
2012	MIA	MLB	28	196	12	10	0	3	17	12	36	1	0	.202/.250/.306	.199	.234	-0.2	1B(54): 5.4	-0.8
2012	PIT	MLB	28	130	18	6	0	4	13	13	20	0	0	.241/.323/.397	.242	.261	0.7	1B(41): 0.7	0.1
2013	*PIT*	*MLB*	*29*	*395*	*45*	*20*	*1*	*12*	*49*	*36*	*60*	*2*	*1*	*.257/.329/.423*	*.274*	*.276*	*-0.5*	*1B 0*	*0.9*

A year after making the All-Star team, Sanchez found himself back in the minors. Miami opted to acquire Carlos Lee, and later sold low on Sanchez to the Pirates. Despite the disappointing season, he still figures to have some value. A timeshare with Jones at first base makes a lot of sense, since Sanchez has a long history of punishing lefties. He'll probably never make another All-Star team, but he can help a club win games if used properly.

Tony Sanchez C

Born: **5/20/1988** Age: **25**
Bats: **R** Throws: **R** Height: **6' 1"**
Weight: **215** Breakout: **10%**
Improve: **41%** Collapse: **9%**
Attrition: **15%** MLB: **98%**

Comparables:
Charlie Moore,Bill Freehan,Joe Ginsberg

YEAR	TEAM	LVL	AGE	PA	R	2B	3B	HR	RBI	BB	SO	SB	CS	AVG_OBP_SLG	TAv	BABIP	BRR	FRAA	WARP
2010	BRD	A+	22	250	31	17	0	4	35	28	41	2	1	.314/.423/.454	.315	.377	0	--	0.0
2011	ALT	AA	23	469	46	14	1	5	44	47	76	5	5	.241/.340/.318	.243	.285	1	C(71): -0.5	0.0
2012	ALT	AA	24	162	22	14	1	0	17	18	33	1	1	.277/.370/.390	.295	.361	-2.2	C(31): 0.1	0.6
2012	IND	AAA	24	236	21	12	0	8	26	23	46	0	0	.233/.316/.408	.238	.260	-1.6	C(51): -0.5	-0.1
2013	*PIT*	*MLB*	*25*	*250*	*23*	*11*	*1*	*5*	*25*	*18*	*51*	*1*	*1*	*.229/.293/.344*	*.237*	*.271*	*-0.4*	*C -0*	*0.5*

In 2007, the Pirates selected Daniel Moskos instead of Matt Wieters. In 2008, Pittsburgh passed on Buster Posey to take Pedro Alvarez. In 2009, the Pirates finally picked a collegiate backstop. Sanchez never had the upside of Wieters or Posey. Rather, he appealed to the Pirates because of his modest price tag—they went overslot later on in the draft—and his safeness. Three-plus years later, Sanchez is still trying to break into the majors. He continues to get high marks for his makeup and defense, and all signs point to him becoming a field general in time, but he's nothing special at the plate. He might not be Wieters or Posey, but Sanchez could shore up the catching position starting at some point in 2013.

Jerry Sands **1B**
Born: **9/28/1987** Age: **25**
Bats: **R** Throws: **R** Height: **6' 5"**
Weight: **220** Breakout: **6%**
Improve: **45%** Collapse: **5%**
Attrition: **5%** MLB: **97%**
Comparables:
Chase Headley,Barry Bonds,Matt LaPorta

YEAR	TEAM	LVL	AGE	PA	R	2B	3B	HR	RBI	BB	SO	SB	CS	AVG_OBP_SLG	TAv	BABIP	BRR	FRAA	WARP
2010	GRL	A	22	287	48	16	3	18	46	40	61	14	2	.333/.434/.646	.367	.384	1.6	1B(41): 3.1, RF(19): 2.4	5.0
2010	CHT	AA	22	303	54	12	2	17	47	33	62	4	0	.270/.366/.529	.304	.294	3.6	LF(35): 3.4, 1B(21): -1.7	2.6
2011	ABQ	AAA	23	418	78	21	3	29	88	38	86	3	1	.278/.344/.586	.304	.282	0	--	0.0
2011	LAN	MLB	23	227	20	15	0	4	26	25	51	3	3	.253/.338/.389	.265	.319	1.5	LF(41): 0.9, RF(22): -0.7	0.6
2012	ABQ	AAA	24	522	84	17	4	26	107	59	106	1	0	.296/.375/.524	.335	.329	4.1	LF(14): -1.4, 1B(14): -0.7	1.3
2012	LAN	MLB	24	24	2	2	0	0	1	1	9	0	0	.174/.208/.261	.162	.286	0	LF(6): -0.1, 1B(1): 0.0	-0.2
2013	*PIT*	*MLB*	*25*	*250*	*29*	*10*	*1*	*10*	*34*	*23*	*60*	*2*	*0*	*.243/.315/.433*	*.269*	*.284*	*-0.1*	*LF -0, 1B -2*	*0.5*

Sands is a left fielder or first baseman without a bat that makes him playable at those positions. A subpar hit tool puts further emphasis on the translatability of his power potential. He's going to have to prove he can damage big-league pitchers in a hurry, otherwise his swing-and-miss tendencies and blah athletic profile will leave him labeled as a Quad-A slugger. Sands, like De Jesus, went from Los Angeles to Boston to Pittsburgh in two big trades five months apart, though Sands was the post-season PTBNL in the Dodgers-Sox blockbuster. He doesn't serve a purpose on the Pirates' roster, which already features too many just-okay outfield and first-base options.

Travis Snider **RF**
Born: **2/2/1988** Age: **25**
Bats: **L** Throws: **L** Height: **6' 1"**
Weight: **235** Breakout: **3%**
Improve: **52%** Collapse: **2%**
Attrition: **7%** MLB: **95%**
Comparables:
Wladimir Balentien,Willie Horton,Rico Carty

YEAR	TEAM	LVL	AGE	PA	R	2B	3B	HR	RBI	BB	SO	SB	CS	AVG_OBP_SLG	TAv	BABIP	BRR	FRAA	WARP
2010	NHP	AA	22	85	14	5	0	5	17	2	21	3	1	.296/.313/.543	.272	.345	-0.6	RF(13): -0.5, LF(2): 0.2	0.1
2010	TOR	MLB	22	319	36	20	0	14	32	21	79	6	3	.255/.304/.463	.264	.302	-3.9	LF(53): 0.1, RF(29): -1.5	0.0
2011	LVG	AAA	23	277	47	22	2	4	42	25	44	12	1	.327/.394/.480	.306	.383	-1.2	LF(19): 1.3, RF(4): -0.6	0.8
2011	TOR	MLB	23	202	23	14	0	3	30	11	56	9	3	.225/.269/.348	.216	.300	1.5	LF(44): -0.4, CF(6): -0.0	-0.4
2012	LVG	AAA	24	246	49	16	0	13	56	34	42	2	4	.335/.423/.598	.327	.363	0.5	LF(27): 1.4, RF(6): 0.2	1.6
2012	PIT	MLB	24	145	17	5	1	1	9	14	34	2	0	.250/.324/.328	.242	.326	0.5	RF(33): 0.6, LF(5): 0.2	0.0
2012	TOR	MLB	24	40	6	2	0	3	8	3	14	0	0	.250/.300/.556	.301	.300	0	LF(10): 0.6	0.3
2013	*PIT*	*MLB*	*25*	*250*	*29*	*13*	*1*	*8*	*31*	*19*	*65*	*4*	*2*	*.250/.310/.422*	*.264*	*.309*	*-0.1*	*LF -0, RF -0*	*0.6*

Another piece of the Pirates' deadline haul, Snider remains maddeningly inconsistent. In the three months he spent with Pittsburgh, he never played like the same player in any two of them. In July he looked like a power-dependent slugger. In August he hit for average and walked but the power disappeared. In September it wasn't apparent that Snider was a big-league hitter. Future months will definitely be like one of those three. Or something completely different.

Jose Tabata **LF**
Born: **8/12/1988** Age: **24**
Bats: **R** Throws: **R** Height: **6' 0"**
Weight: **220** Breakout: **1%**
Improve: **51%** Collapse: **4%**
Attrition: **9%** MLB: **96%**
Comparables:
Tony Gwynn,Terry Puhl,Roy White

YEAR	TEAM	LVL	AGE	PA	R	2B	3B	HR	RBI	BB	SO	SB	CS	AVG_OBP_SLG	TAv	BABIP	BRR	FRAA	WARP
2010	IND	AAA	21	252	42	13	2	3	19	23	35	25	6	.308/.378/.424	.280	.355	2.6	CF(39): -1.0, LF(15): 1.4	1.4
2010	PIT	MLB	21	441	61	21	4	4	35	28	57	19	7	.299/.346/.400	.263	.339	3.5	LF(93): 4.8, CF(13): -0.9	1.6
2011	PIT	MLB	22	382	53	18	1	4	21	40	61	16	7	.266/.349/.362	.250	.312	3	LF(76): 1.7, RF(15): -1.9	0.2
2012	IND	AAA	23	173	21	9	0	0	15	10	20	5	2	.297/.353/.354	.246	.338	0.7	CF(23): -0.0, RF(11): 1.8	0.5
2012	PIT	MLB	23	374	43	20	3	3	16	29	58	8	12	.243/.315/.348	.244	.287	-0.1	RF(77): -0.4, LF(32): 2.4	-0.2
2013	*PIT*	*MLB*	*24*	*382*	*47*	*18*	*2*	*4*	*30*	*29*	*59*	*14*	*7*	*.266/.327/.372*	*.257*	*.304*	*-0.2*	*LF 1, RF 0*	*0.8*

When the Pirates signed Tabata to a team-friendly extension, it seemed like a smart move. With a history of decent play and the potential to improve, the young outfielder appeared to be the kind of player you roll the dice on. But he missed September 2011 with a fractured hand, and he never got on track in 2012, struggling to make hard contact in both Pittsburgh and Indianapolis. The Pirates hope it's just a hiccup because Tabata is due $12.5 million through the 2016 season.

Neil Walker **2B**
Born: **9/10/1985** Age: **27**
Bats: **B** Throws: **R** Height: **6' 4"**
Weight: **215** Breakout: **2%**
Improve: **55%** Collapse: **4%**
Attrition: **8%** MLB: **91%**
Comparables:
Kelly Johnson,Jim Lefebvre,Chase Utley

YEAR	TEAM	LVL	AGE	PA	R	2B	3B	HR	RBI	BB	SO	SB	CS	AVG_OBP_SLG	TAv	BABIP	BRR	FRAA	WARP
2010	IND	AAA	24	189	25	18	2	6	26	19	31	10	1	.321/.394/.560	.307	.366	-0.6	2B(21): 0.7, LF(14): 1.8	1.6
2010	PIT	MLB	24	469	57	29	3	12	66	34	83	2	3	.296/.349/.462	.279	.340	-1.9	2B(105): -16.4, 3B(6): 0.1	0.7
2011	PIT	MLB	25	662	76	36	4	12	83	54	112	9	6	.273/.334/.408	.262	.315	1	2B(159): -5.9	0.8
2012	PIT	MLB	26	530	62	27	0	14	69	47	104	7	5	.280/.342/.426	.277	.326	-1.2	2B(125): -0.7	1.5
2013	*PIT*	*MLB*	*27*	*524*	*57*	*28*	*2*	*14*	*61*	*40*	*100*	*7*	*4*	*.265/.323/.419*	*.269*	*.305*	*-0.6*	*2B -6, LF 0*	*1.6*

Although back woes limited Walker down the stretch, his 2012 season was a successful one. He has now spent three seasons in the majors and solidified himself as a second baseman. His defense has improved, and his bat remains consistently above league-average. Past rumors had the Pirates interested in locking the native Yinzer into a long-term extension. Walker entered his arbitration years during the offseason, so if the Pirates are going to make a move it has to happen soon.

PITCHERS

Erik Bedard

Born: **3/5/1979** Age: **34**
Bats: **L** Throws: **L** Height: **6' 2"** Weight: **200**
Breakout: **19%** Improve: **59%** Collapse: **13%**
Attrition: **12%** MLB: **89%**
Comparables:
Steve Carlton,Kaz Ishii,Ted Lilly

YEAR	TEAM	LVL	AGE	W	L	SV	G	GS	IP	H	HR	BB	SO	BB9	SO9	GB%	BABIP	WHIP	ERA	FIP	FRA	WARP
2010	MRN	Rk	31	0	0	0	2	2	6^{2}	7	0	0	11	0.0	14.8	71%	.412	1.04	2.69	0.97	1.28	0.4
2010	TAC	AAA	31	0	0	0	1	1	4^{1}	3	0	3	3	6.3	6.3	54%	.231	1.40	0.00	4.28	5.09	0.0
2011	BOS	MLB	32	1	2	0	8	8	38	41	3	18	38	4.3	9.0	43%	.349	1.55	4.03	3.51	4.65	0.4
2011	SEA	MLB	32	4	7	0	16	16	91^{1}	77	11	30	87	3.0	8.6	42%	.270	1.17	3.45	3.74	4.14	0.6
2012	PIT	MLB	33	7	14	0	24	24	125^{2}	129	14	56	118	4.0	8.5	46%	.314	1.47	5.01	4.11	4.64	0.8
2013	*PIT*	*MLB*	*34*	*7*	*7*	*0*	*21*	*21*	*113*	*98*	*12*	*42*	*104*	*3.4*	*8.3*	*45%*	*.290*	*1.24*	*3.77*	*3.85*	*4.10*	*1.1*

Pittsburgh's decision to sign Bedard to a one-year deal looked smart for a while. Through his first six starts, he had a 2.65 ERA and 23 more strikeouts than walks. He left his seventh start with back spasms, returned a week later, and saw everything fall apart. In Bedard's final 17 starts, he allowed more than six runs per nine innings. Pittsburgh decided to move on at the end of August.

Victor Black

Born: **5/23/1988** Age: **25**
Bats: **R** Throws: **R** Height: **6' 4"** Weight: **185**
Breakout: **36%** Improve: **57%** Collapse: **22%**
Attrition: **10%** MLB: **85%**
Comparables:
Wesley Wright,Greg Holland,Emiliano Fruto

YEAR	TEAM	LVL	AGE	W	L	SV	G	GS	IP	H	HR	BB	SO	BB9	SO9	GB%	BABIP	WHIP	ERA	FIP	FRA	WARP
2010	WVA	A	22	0	0	0	2	2	4^{2}	3	1	5	8	9.6	15.3	33%	.250	1.70	9.57	6.72	6.96	-0.1
2011	WVA	A	23	2	1	1	22	0	29	30	0	16	23	5.0	7.1	55%	.297	1.59	5.28	3.80	5.16	0.0
2011	BRD	A+	23	1	0	0	5	0	6^{2}	8	1	4	5	5.4	6.8	—	.350	1.80	4.05	6.09	6.62	0.0
2012	ALT	AA	24	2	3	13	51	0	60	40	2	29	85	4.3	12.8	54%	.290	1.15	1.65	2.45	2.89	1.3
2013	*PIT*	*MLB*	*25*	*2*	*1*	*1*	*30*	*0*	*37*	*31*	*4*	*18*	*37*	*4.4*	*9.1*	*48%*	*.298*	*1.33*	*4.06*	*4.06*	*4.41*	*0.1*

The Pirates may have drafted Black as a starter out of Dallas Baptist University but they didn't wait long to move him to the bullpen. Nine starts, to be exact. It took until he reached Double-A for the transition to take, but it was worth the wait. He more than doubled his career appearances total and posted the second-best strikeout rate in the Eastern League. His fastball sits in the mid-90s and his slider is a worthy knockout pitch. Factor in the coolness of his name and Vic Black has the makings of a lockdown reliever. He still needs to tighten his control, but you could see him in the majors late in the 2013 season.

A.J. Burnett

Born: **1/3/1977** Age: **36**
Bats: **R** Throws: **R** Height: **6' 5"** Weight: **230**
Breakout: **24%** Improve: **55%** Collapse: **24%**
Attrition: **20%** MLB: **84%**
Comparables:
Jose Contreras,Sam Jones,Esteban Loaiza

YEAR	TEAM	LVL	AGE	W	L	SV	G	GS	IP	H	HR	BB	SO	BB9	SO9	GB%	BABIP	WHIP	ERA	FIP	FRA	WARP
2010	NYA	MLB	33	10	15	0	33	33	186^{2}	204	25	78	145	3.8	7.0	46%	.319	1.51	5.26	4.79	5.26	0.6
2011	NYA	MLB	34	11	11	0	33	32	190^{1}	190	31	83	173	3.9	8.2	51%	.294	1.43	5.15	4.81	5.50	-0.5
2012	BRD	A+	35	0	2	0	2	2	6^{1}	7	0	2	9	2.8	12.8	44%	.389	1.42	8.53	1.97	-0.08	0.0
2012	IND	AAA	35	0	1	0	1	1	4	7	2	4	0	9.0	0.0	41%	.333	2.75	11.25	12.66	14.02	-0.2
2012	PIT	MLB	35	16	10	0	31	31	202^{1}	189	18	62	180	2.8	8.0	58%	.294	1.24	3.51	3.57	3.80	3.1
2013	*PIT*	*MLB*	*36*	*10*	*11*	*0*	*30*	*30*	177^{2}	*160*	*19*	*62*	*161*	*3.2*	*8.2*	*50%*	*.300*	*1.25*	*3.97*	*3.82*	*4.32*	*1.0*

Pittsburgh's decision to buy low on Burnett paid off almost immediately. The enigmatic right-hander had his best season since 2008—that's pre-Yankees—according to FIP and FRA. Most of the improvement is being credited to a better state of mind. It sounds silly, and like something an earlier copy of this book would've trashed as a narrative, but it may be right. Remember the constant mound visits in New York? Or the idea that Burnett needed various veteran players around as a support system? Some players are just wired differently. Burnett might be one of those who needs certain niceties to perform.

Gerrit Cole

Born: **9/8/1990** Age: **22**
Bats: **R** Throws: **R** Height: **6' 5"** Weight: **220**
Breakout: **24%** Improve: **58%** Collapse: **14%**
Attrition: **7%** MLB: **96%**
Comparables:
Brandon McCarthy,Jake Peavy,Chris Tillman

YEAR	TEAM	LVL	AGE	W	L	SV	G	GS	IP	H	HR	BB	SO	BB9	SO9	GB%	BABIP	WHIP	ERA	FIP	FRA	WARP
2012	BRD	A+	21	5	1	0	13	13	67	53	5	21	69	2.8	9.3	51%	.267	1.10	2.55	3.38	3.63	0.0
2012	ALT	AA	21	3	6	0	12	12	59	54	2	23	60	3.5	9.2	50%	.315	1.31	2.90	2.88	3.61	0.7
2012	IND	AAA	21	1	0	0	1	1	6	6	0	1	7	1.5	10.5	31%	.375	1.17	4.50	1.32	2.80	0.2
2013	*PIT*	*MLB*	*22*	*2*	*2*	*0*	*7*	*7*	37^{2}	*34*	*4*	*14*	*33*	*3.3*	*7.9*	*47%*	*.296*	*1.26*	*3.97*	*3.94*	*4.31*	*0.3*

Cole, the number-one pick in the 2011 draft, has a chance to be special. His arm strength and raw stuff are as impressive as those of any pitcher in the minors. He regularly hits triple digits and his slider is already capable of serving as an out pitch. Factor in the big frame and his upside is ace-level. But there are reasons to believe he could fall short of that ceiling. Cole's command is inconsistent and his fastball has more zip than wiggle. His maturity continues to come under fire as well. He still has the tools to be a star even if he falls short of his promise.

Juan Cruz

Born: **10/15/1978** Age: **34**
Bats: **R** Throws: **R** Height: **6' 3"** Weight: **165**
Breakout: **12%** Improve: **31%** Collapse: **33%**
Attrition: **10%** MLB: **91%**

Comparables:
Jay Witasick,Troy Percival,Eric Plunk

YEAR	TEAM	LVL	AGE	W	L	SV	G	GS	IP	H	HR	BB	SO	BB9	SO9	GB%	BABIP	WHIP	ERA	FIP	FRA	WARP
2010	KCA	MLB	31	0	0	0	5	0	5^{1}	9	0	4	7	6.8	11.8	35%	.529	2.44	3.38	2.67	4.15	0.1
2011	PCH	A+	32	0	0	0	1	1	1	2	0	0	2	0.0	18.0	—	.667	2.00	0.00	2.39	2.60	0.0
2011	TBA	MLB	32	5	0	0	56	0	48^{2}	36	5	28	46	5.2	8.5	36%	.256	1.32	3.88	4.23	3.85	0.3
2012	ALT	AA	33	0	0	0	2	2	1^{1}	5	0	0	2	0.0	13.5	43%	.714	3.75	13.50	0.20	2.81	0.1
2012	PIT	MLB	33	1	1	3	43	0	35^{2}	39	3	19	33	4.8	8.3	39%	.346	1.63	2.78	4.23	4.08	0.3
2013	*PIT*	*MLB*	*34*	*2*	*1*	*1*	*43*	*0*	*37^{1}*	*31*	*4*	*18*	*38*	*4.3*	*9.1*	*36%*	*.294*	*1.31*	*3.84*	*4.00*	*4.17*	*0.2*

Not often does a team send a reliever with as many innings and an ERA as low as Cruz's packing, but Pittsburgh did just that in late August. Shoulder inflammation limited him in his last weeks with the club and may have sparked the release. Whatever the reason, other teams agreed with the Pirates and passed on him for the stretch run. Relievers capable of missing bats and hitting the mid-90s pitch until they can't do those things anymore. Cruz can, so he should be around for a few more years.

Brandon Cumpton

Born: **11/16/1988** Age: **24**
Bats: **R** Throws: **R** Height: **6' 3"** Weight: **198**
Breakout: **21%** Improve: **50%** Collapse: **22%**
Attrition: **23%** MLB: **77%**

Comparables:
Luis Mendoza,Kyle Kendrick,Anthony Ortega

YEAR	TEAM	LVL	AGE	W	L	SV	G	GS	IP	H	HR	BB	SO	BB9	SO9	GB%	BABIP	WHIP	ERA	FIP	FRA	WARP
2010	SCO	A-	21	0	1	0	4	3	10^{2}	8	0	5	6	4.2	5.0	59%	.235	1.21	2.52	3.75	5.28	0.0
2011	WVA	A	22	7	4	0	13	12	67	60	6	18	48	2.4	6.4	58%	.246	1.16	4.30	4.47	4.81	0.4
2011	BRD	A+	22	3	3	0	13	12	66^{1}	73	6	12	42	1.6	5.7	—	.307	1.28	3.66	4.11	4.47	0.0
2012	ALT	AA	23	12	11	0	27	27	152^{1}	149	9	46	88	2.7	5.2	60%	.289	1.28	3.84	4.02	5.20	1.2
2013	*PIT*	*MLB*	*24*	*2*	*3*	*0*	*8*	*8*	*42^{2}*	*44*	*5*	*14*	*23*	*3.1*	*4.8*	*54%*	*.291*	*1.38*	*4.88*	*4.63*	*5.31*	*-0.2*

A ninth-round pick out of Georgia Tech, Cumpton quickly reached Double-A in his second full professional season. Many within the industry felt he would wind up in the bullpen, and he still might. The Pirates have kept him in the rotation so far, however, and the results have been decent. He retains his velocity throughout starts, and his fastball can touch the mid-90s. His secondary pitches still lag behind, though his curveball is at least average. With more seasoning, Cumpton could turn into a respectable number four starter. He should start the season in Indianapolis.

Zack Dodson

Born: **7/23/1990** Age: **22**
Bats: **L** Throws: **L** Height: **6' 3"** Weight: **190**
Breakout: **24%** Improve: **44%** Collapse: **22%**
Attrition: **11%** MLB: **79%**

Comparables:
Ray Sadecki,Joel Davis,Sean Burnett

YEAR	TEAM	LVL	AGE	W	L	SV	G	GS	IP	H	HR	BB	SO	BB9	SO9	GB%	BABIP	WHIP	ERA	FIP	FRA	WARP
2010	SCO	A-	19	2	6	0	15	13	57^{2}	57	2	27	41	4.2	6.4	43%	.311	1.46	4.84	4.17	5.67	-0.2
2011	PIR	Rk	20	0	1	0	3	3	8^{2}	8	1	3	7	3.1	7.3	33%	.269	1.27	4.15	4.34	5.35	0.1
2011	WVA	A	20	6	4	0	13	13	66^{2}	61	3	15	46	2.0	6.2	56%	.294	1.14	2.57	3.59	4.08	0.8
2011	SCO	A-	20	0	1	0	4	4	17^{2}	22	2	4	13	2.0	6.6	—	.345	1.47	4.58	4.89	5.32	0.0
2012	WVA	A	21	6	6	0	21	21	100	111	12	40	67	3.6	6.0	44%	.304	1.51	4.86	5.21	6.45	-0.3
2013	*PIT*	*MLB*	*22*	*2*	*3*	*0*	*8*	*8*	*34^{2}*	*39*	*5*	*17*	*16*	*4.3*	*4.1*	*43%*	*.299*	*1.61*	*5.92*	*5.62*	*6.44*	*-0.5*

Few players in the organization had worse years than Dodson. The former fourth-round pick battled control hiccups and saw his statistics walk the wrong way. In addition, he failed a second substance abuse test, which earned him a 50-game suspension. The ban carries into the 2013 season and will cost Dodson developmental time that he, frankly, cannot afford to miss. He still has the potential to become a back-of-the-rotation starter, but factor in the regression and transgressions of his 2012 season and he's heading toward Non-Prospectsville.

Jason Grilli

Born: **11/11/1976** Age: **36**
Bats: **R** Throws: **R** Height: **6' 6"** Weight: **225**
Breakout: **31%** Improve: **46%** Collapse: **31%**
Attrition: **8%** MLB: **75%**

Comparables:
John Hiller,Tom Gordon,Troy Percival

YEAR	TEAM	LVL	AGE	W	L	SV	G	GS	IP	H	HR	BB	SO	BB9	SO9	GB%	BABIP	WHIP	ERA	FIP	FRA	WARP
2011	LEH	AAA	34	4	1	3	28	0	32^{2}	26	2	12	43	3.3	11.8	—	.308	1.16	1.93	2.59	2.82	0.0
2011	PIT	MLB	34	2	1	1	28	0	32^{2}	24	2	15	37	4.1	10.2	49%	.268	1.19	2.48	3.27	3.04	0.7
2012	PIT	MLB	35	1	6	2	64	0	58^{2}	45	7	22	90	3.4	13.8	32%	.309	1.14	2.91	2.85	2.55	1.4
2013	*PIT*	*MLB*	*36*	*3*	*1*	*1*	*50*	*0*	*49^{1}*	*38*	*4*	*19*	*56*	*3.6*	*10.3*	*42%*	*.296*	*1.16*	*3.13*	*3.14*	*3.41*	*0.8*

The former fourth-overall pick has been nails since joining Pittsburgh in 2011. Grilli has thrown more than 90 innings with a 3.43 strikeout-to-walk ratio and a sub-3 ERA. When discussions about the fungibility of middle relievers come up, so should Grilli's name. He went from out of work to being an above-average reliever in a heartbeat. The Pirates have shown the ability to identify scrapheap arms able to contribute immediately. Grilli is one of their badges of honor.

Luis Heredia

Born: **8/10/1994** Age: **18**
Bats: **R** Throws: **R** Height: **6' 7"** Weight: **205**
Breakout: **100%** Improve: **100%** Collapse: **0%**
Attrition: **0%** MLB: **56%**
Comparables:
Jim Derrington,Bob Miller

YEAR	TEAM	LVL	AGE	W	L	SV	G	GS	IP	H	HR	BB	SO	BB9	SO9	GB%	BABIP	WHIP	ERA	FIP	FRA	WARP
2011	PIR	Rk	16	1	2	0	12	11	30^1	28	3	19	23	5.6	6.8	37%	.291	1.55	4.75	5.46	7.46	-0.1
2012	SCO	A-	17	4	2	0	14	14	66^1	53	2	20	40	2.7	5.4	55%	.252	1.10	2.71	3.47	4.50	0.2
2013	*PIT*	*MLB*	*18*	*2*	*3*	*0*	*9*	*9*	*34^2*	*38*	*5*	*19*	*16*	*4.8*	*4.1*	*45%*	*.297*	*1.64*	*6.02*	*5.80*	*6.54*	*-0.5*

In August 2015, Heredia will finally be old enough to order a Penn Pilsner at PNC Park. Despite his youth, scouts rave about his maturity on and off the mound. His fastball presently tops out in the mid-90s, but he could gain a few ticks because of his size and easy arm action. There are some hitches in Heredia's game, most notably inconsistencies in release point and his breaking ball's spin. We're talking about a teenager here, so it's hard to expect perfection. If he continues on this developmental path, he could become an ace. But as always when dealing with teenage arms, be wary of attrition.

Clay Holmes

Born: **3/27/1993** Age: **20**
Bats: **R** Throws: **R** Height: **6' 6"** Weight: **230**
Breakout: **48%** Improve: **75%** Collapse: **13%**
Attrition: **6%** MLB: **74%**
Comparables:
Wally Bunker,Jim Waugh,Joe Moeller

YEAR	TEAM	LVL	AGE	W	L	SV	G	GS	IP	H	HR	BB	SO	BB9	SO9	GB%	BABIP	WHIP	ERA	FIP	FRA	WARP
2012	SCO	A-	19	5	3	0	13	13	59^1	35	1	29	34	4.4	5.2	58%	.204	1.08	2.28	4.12	5.66	-0.3
2013	*PIT*	*MLB*	*20*	*2*	*3*	*0*	*7*	*7*	*34^2*	*37*	*5*	*19*	*17*	*5.1*	*4.5*	*49%*	*.296*	*1.65*	*5.92*	*5.74*	*6.44*	*-0.5*

When evaluating pitchers, start with the body. Holmes is listed at 6-foot-6, 230 pounds, and he has the wide, tall, durable look down pat. The arsenal screams power starter. Both his fastball and his slider could develop into devastating offerings. Holmes struggled with his control during his professional debut, but there's no reason to panic yet. In a system full of intriguing arms, he has the potential to shoot up prospect lists in the near future.

Jared Hughes

Born: **7/4/1985** Age: **27**
Bats: **R** Throws: **R** Height: **6' 8"** Weight: **235**
Breakout: **29%** Improve: **68%** Collapse: **9%**
Attrition: **16%** MLB: **80%**
Comparables:
Ed Figueroa,Vicente Padilla,Miguel Asencio

YEAR	TEAM	LVL	AGE	W	L	SV	G	GS	IP	H	HR	BB	SO	BB9	SO9	GB%	BABIP	WHIP	ERA	FIP	FRA	WARP
2010	ALT	AA	24	12	8	0	30	23	150^2	166	15	41	120	2.4	7.2	58%	.317	1.37	4.42	4.10	4.30	1.9
2011	ALT	AA	25	3	4	0	13	11	61^2	62	2	18	33	2.6	4.8	55%	.255	1.30	4.09	4.03	5.17	-0.1
2011	IND	AAA	25	3	1	0	35	0	42^2	35	1	18	45	3.8	9.5	74%	.337	1.24	2.11	2.91	3.91	0.4
2011	PIT	MLB	25	0	1	0	12	0	11	9	1	4	10	3.3	8.2	69%	.258	1.18	4.09	3.45	3.71	0.1
2012	IND	AAA	26	0	0	0	2	0	2	1	0	1	3	4.5	13.5	50%	.250	1.00	0.00	1.66	2.34	0.0
2012	PIT	MLB	26	2	2	2	66	0	75^2	65	7	22	50	2.6	5.9	60%	.250	1.15	2.85	4.09	5.26	-0.3
2013	*PIT*	*MLB*	*27*	*3*	*3*	*0*	*30*	*6*	*60^2*	*60*	*7*	*21*	*37*	*3.1*	*5.5*	*54%*	*.290*	*1.34*	*4.68*	*4.52*	*5.09*	*-0.2*

Hughes is 1) a leftover from the Dave Littlefield administration and 2) a big, bulky right-hander with a low-90s sinker and slider combination. Unsurprisingly, he coaxes a high rate of groundballs and has some issues against left-handed batters. The appearance and substance of the package make Kameron Loe comparisons fair game. Hughes won't be the best reliever in any given bullpen, but if he's used correctly he can be an asset.

Jeff Karstens

Born: **9/24/1982** Age: **30**
Bats: **R** Throws: **R** Height: **6' 4"** Weight: **185**
Breakout: **11%** Improve: **34%** Collapse: **22%**
Attrition: **17%** MLB: **90%**
Comparables:
Jimmy Key,Brad Radke,Bob Friend

YEAR	TEAM	LVL	AGE	W	L	SV	G	GS	IP	H	HR	BB	SO	BB9	SO9	GB%	BABIP	WHIP	ERA	FIP	FRA	WARP
2010	IND	AAA	27	1	2	0	5	1	16	21	3	2	12	1.1	6.8	32%	.333	1.44	7.31	4.60	5.52	0.0
2010	PIT	MLB	27	3	10	0	26	19	122^2	146	21	27	72	2.0	5.3	43%	.309	1.41	4.92	4.84	5.14	0.1
2011	PIT	MLB	28	9	9	0	30	26	162^1	163	22	33	96	1.8	5.3	48%	.275	1.21	3.38	4.26	4.73	0.1
2012	ALT	AA	29	1	0	0	2	2	10	8	0	1	6	0.9	5.4	53%	.267	0.90	0.90	2.30	3.24	0.2
2012	IND	AAA	29	0	2	0	3	3	13^2	11	1	3	13	2.0	8.6	67%	.263	1.02	4.61	3.08	5.33	0.0
2012	PIT	MLB	29	5	4	0	19	15	90^2	89	8	15	66	1.5	6.6	40%	.287	1.15	3.97	3.36	4.02	1.0
2013	*PIT*	*MLB*	*30*	*5*	*6*	*0*	*17*	*17*	*94*	*92*	*12*	*20*	*60*	*2.0*	*5.8*	*43%*	*.288*	*1.20*	*3.97*	*4.22*	*4.31*	*0.6*

Over the last two seasons, Karstens has accumulated the statistics of a well-above-average starter in spite of lackluster stuff. Can he make it three-for-three? Karstens is, and always has been, a strike-thrower who survives by locating and mixing his pitches, including his curveball and straight changeup. An improvement against left-handed hitters, credited to a better change, was the key in 2012. There is some reason to doubt the sustainability of his breakthrough. He pitches from the third base side of the rubber and has a closed delivery, thus complicating his ability to throw inside against lefties. Eliminate one-third of the plate and big-league batters will feast. He'll need to keep those lefties honest if he wants to enjoy prolonged success.

Nicholas Kingham

Born: **11/8/1991** Age: **21**
Bats: **R** Throws: **R** Height: **6' 6"** Weight: **220**
Breakout: **27%** Improve: **59%** Collapse: **20%**
Attrition: **5%** MLB: **89%**

Comparables:
Dan Petry,Jordan Lyles,Hayden Penn

YEAR	TEAM	LVL	AGE	W	L	SV	G	GS	IP	H	HR	BB	SO	BB9	SO9	GB%	BABIP	WHIP	ERA	FIP	FRA	WARP
2010	PIR	Rk	18	0	0	0	2	0	3	3	0	0	2	0.0	6.0	78%	.333	1.00	0.00	2.17	4.67	0.0
2011	SCO	A-	19	6	2	0	15	15	71	63	5	15	47	1.9	6.0	—	.272	1.10	2.15	3.67	3.99	0.0
2012	WVA	A	20	6	8	0	27	27	127	115	15	36	117	2.6	8.3	50%	.286	1.19	4.39	4.34	4.97	1.4
2013	*PIT*	*MLB*	*21*	*2*	*3*	*0*	*8*	*8*	*36*	*37*	*5*	*15*	*25*	*3.8*	*6.2*	*46%*	*.297*	*1.43*	*5.03*	*4.87*	*5.47*	*-0.2*

The Pirates selected Kingham in the fourth round of the 2010 draft. A big right-hander from Nevada, he features a lively fastball that touches the mid-90s on occasion. His best secondary offering is the changeup, while his breaking pitch lags behind. Kingham projects to become a middle-of-the-rotation innings sponge because of his large frame, pitch selection, and strike-throwing tendencies.

Chris Leroux

Born: **4/14/1984** Age: **29**
Bats: **L** Throws: **R** Height: **6' 7"** Weight: **225**
Breakout: **28%** Improve: **52%** Collapse: **31%**
Attrition: **17%** MLB: **89%**

Comparables:
Jeff Fassero,Doug Slaten,Gary Lucas

YEAR	TEAM	LVL	AGE	W	L	SV	G	GS	IP	H	HR	BB	SO	BB9	SO9	GB%	BABIP	WHIP	ERA	FIP	FRA	WARP
2010	MRL	Rk	26	1	0	0	3	0	4	4	0	0	3	0.0	6.8	77%	.308	1.00	4.50	2.01	5.29	-0.1
2010	JUP	A+	26	0	0	0	2	0	2^{2}	2	0	1	0	3.3	0.0	30%	.200	1.11	3.33	5.66	6.69	-0.1
2010	NWO	AAA	26	0	3	1	21	0	22	26	2	7	20	2.9	8.2	51%	.358	1.50	6.95	4.17	5.04	0.2
2010	FLO	MLB	26	0	0	0	17	0	18	24	1	11	18	5.5	9.0	53%	.426	1.94	7.00	3.66	3.32	0.3
2010	PIT	MLB	26	0	1	0	6	0	4^{2}	4	0	3	4	5.8	7.7	50%	.286	1.50	5.79	3.32	2.79	0.1
2011	ALT	AA	27	1	2	0	5	0	7	9	2	0	6	0.0	7.7	31%	.214	1.29	2.57	5.84	8.06	-0.1
2011	IND	AAA	27	6	3	1	32	0	61	48	1	21	57	3.1	8.4	56%	.262	1.13	2.80	2.91	3.03	1.0
2011	PIT	MLB	27	1	1	0	23	0	25	26	0	7	24	2.5	8.6	42%	.333	1.32	2.88	2.03	2.99	0.5
2012	BRD	A+	28	0	1	0	1	1	3	2	0	1	2	3.0	6.0	75%	.250	1.00	3.00	3.06	0.16	0.0
2012	IND	AAA	28	4	0	0	21	7	63^{2}	52	6	14	56	2.0	7.9	54%	.263	1.04	3.11	3.66	4.60	0.4
2012	PIT	MLB	28	0	0	0	10	0	11^{1}	11	1	2	12	1.6	9.5	55%	.312	1.15	5.56	2.96	2.49	0.3
2013	*PIT*	*MLB*	*29*	*2*	*1*	*0*	*24*	*2*	37^{2}	*35*	*4*	*12*	*32*	*2.9*	*7.6*	*49%*	*.300*	*1.24*	*3.82*	*3.84*	*4.15*	*0.3*

Leroux entered the spring without options to spare. He reportedly incurred a pectoral strain, which appeared to be a convenient excuse for the Pirates to clear a roster logjam. But it wasn't. He missed the first three months of the season before returning. Pittsburgh removed him from the 40-man roster, though they later added him back. Leroux has a mid-90s fastball and slider combination that should be good enough to work in middle relief. If the tall Canuck goes on waivers again, expect another team to snatch him.

Jeff Locke

Born: **11/20/1987** Age: **25**
Bats: **L** Throws: **L** Height: **6' 2"** Weight: **215**
Breakout: **37%** Improve: **63%** Collapse: **12%**
Attrition: **16%** MLB: **80%**

Comparables:
Matt Chico,Scott Diamond,Sean West

YEAR	TEAM	LVL	AGE	W	L	SV	G	GS	IP	H	HR	BB	SO	BB9	SO9	GB%	BABIP	WHIP	ERA	FIP	FRA	WARP
2010	BRD	A+	22	9	3	0	17	17	86^{1}	82	6	14	83	1.5	8.7	—	.313	1.11	3.55	3.15	3.42	0.0
2010	ALT	AA	22	3	2	0	10	10	57^{2}	57	5	12	56	1.9	8.7	44%	.315	1.20	3.59	3.38	4.22	0.4
2011	ALT	AA	23	7	8	0	23	22	125	118	9	46	114	3.3	8.2	45%	.301	1.31	4.03	3.82	4.86	0.4
2011	IND	AAA	23	1	2	0	5	5	28^{1}	25	1	9	25	2.9	7.9	50%	.244	1.20	2.22	2.88	3.57	0.3
2011	PIT	MLB	23	0	3	0	4	4	16^{2}	21	3	10	5	5.4	2.7	39%	.305	1.86	6.48	6.71	7.43	-0.4
2012	IND	AAA	24	10	5	0	24	24	141^{2}	126	9	43	131	2.7	8.3	47%	.296	1.19	2.48	3.19	4.04	1.4
2012	PIT	MLB	24	1	3	0	8	6	34^{1}	36	6	11	34	2.9	8.9	50%	.312	1.37	5.50	4.48	5.46	-0.1
2013	*PIT*	*MLB*	*25*	*4*	*5*	*0*	*13*	*13*	*70*	*71*	*9*	*25*	*51*	*3.2*	*6.5*	*46%*	*.305*	*1.38*	*4.73*	*4.49*	*5.14*	*-0.2*

Acquired from the Braves in the Nate McLouth trade, Locke is still trying to break into the majors consistently. He's got one more option left, and the Pirates will probably send him to the minors to start the season. He throws a low-90s sinker, curveball, and changeup, and he projects to become a fourth or fifth starter. It's worth noting that Locke won his first career game against his old team by allowing one run over six innings despite walking five. Sometimes it pays to be lucky.

Vin Mazzaro

Born: **9/27/1986** Age: **26**
Bats: **R** Throws: **R** Height: **6' 4"** Weight: **220**
Breakout: **27%** Improve: **75%** Collapse: **13%**
Attrition: **14%** MLB: **89%**

Comparables:
Freddy Garcia,Kevin Mulvey,Mitch Talbot

YEAR	TEAM	LVL	AGE	W	L	SV	G	GS	IP	H	HR	BB	SO	BB9	SO9	GB%	BABIP	WHIP	ERA	FIP	FRA	WARP
2010	SAC	AAA	23	3	1	0	7	6	37^{1}	35	2	17	38	4.1	9.2	42%	.308	1.39	3.14	3.85	4.23	0.6
2010	OAK	MLB	23	6	8	0	24	18	122^{1}	127	19	50	79	3.7	5.8	46%	.281	1.45	4.27	5.10	6.18	-1.5
2011	OMA	AAA	24	7	2	0	22	22	123^{2}	140	9	60	107	4.4	7.8	54%	.358	1.62	4.29	4.65	3.76	1.1
2011	KCA	MLB	24	1	1	0	7	4	28^{1}	39	4	15	10	4.8	3.2	47%	.347	1.91	8.26	5.88	7.15	-0.7
2012	OMA	AAA	25	2	2	5	22	8	67	69	4	20	62	2.7	8.3	55%	.355	1.33	3.63	3.62	4.34	0.6
2012	KCA	MLB	25	4	3	0	18	6	44	55	3	19	26	3.9	5.3	48%	.354	1.68	5.73	4.25	4.98	0.3
2013	*PIT*	*MLB*	*26*	*3*	*3*	*0*	*15*	*9*	61^{1}	*60*	*6*	*20*	*44*	*3.0*	*6.4*	*48%*	*.299*	*1.31*	*4.22*	*4.02*	*4.59*	*0.2*

Mazzaro is a sinkerballer whose sinker doesn't have enough sink. He was better at keeping the ball down in the zone last year, but still sails too many pitches through the heart of the plate and pays a heavy price. The Royals were desperate for starting pitching last summer, yet Mazzaro made only six starts for Kansas City before being shipped to Pittsburgh during the offseason. That should tell you all you need to know about how teams view him.

James McDonald
Born: **10/19/1984** Age: **28**
Bats: **L** Throws: **R** Height: **6' 5"** Weight: **200**
Breakout: **17%** Improve: **51%** Collapse: **26%**
Attrition: **19%** MLB: **90%**
Comparables:
Sid Fernandez,J.A. Happ,Juan Pizarro

YEAR	TEAM	LVL	AGE	W	L	SV	G	GS	IP	H	HR	BB	SO	BB9	SO9	GB%	BABIP	WHIP	ERA	FIP	FRA	WARP
2010	DOD	Rk	25	0	0	0	2	2	5^{2}	3	0	3	8	4.7	12.6	—	.250	1.05	1.58	3.03	4.85	0.0
2010	ABQ	AAA	25	6	1	0	12	12	63^{1}	64	4	24	57	3.4	8.1	45%	.313	1.39	4.41	3.98	4.49	1.6
2010	LAN	MLB	25	0	1	0	4	1	7^{2}	11	1	5	7	5.9	8.2	27%	.400	2.09	8.22	4.93	4.79	-0.1
2010	PIT	MLB	25	4	5	0	11	11	64	59	3	24	61	3.4	8.6	33%	.311	1.30	3.52	2.93	3.30	1.3
2011	PIT	MLB	26	9	9	0	31	31	171	176	24	78	142	4.1	7.5	40%	.303	1.49	4.21	4.65	5.15	-0.2
2012	PIT	MLB	27	12	8	0	30	29	171	147	21	69	151	3.6	7.9	41%	.269	1.26	4.21	4.25	4.66	1.7
2013	*PIT*	*MLB*	*28*	*8*	*9*	*0*	*26*	*26*	*146^{1}*	*127*	*17*	*53*	*131*	*3.3*	*8.1*	*38%*	*.287*	*1.23*	*3.80*	*4.01*	*4.13*	*1.3*

On paper, McDonald's 2012 season looks like a repeat of his 2011. In reality, it had the chance to be more, much more. McDonald posted a strong first half, raising hopes about a new, higher celing, but he fell to earth. His final four appearances served as the thud. He allowed 20 hits, 18 runs, and six home runs in 12 innings. If fatigue is the cause, you have to wonder why; McDonald worked the same number of innings in both seasons. Expect performances worthy of a mid-rotation starter heading forward.

Kyle McPherson
Born: **11/11/1987** Age: **25**
Bats: **B** Throws: **R** Height: **6' 5"** Weight: **215**
Breakout: **28%** Improve: **53%** Collapse: **21%**
Attrition: **29%** MLB: **92%**
Comparables:
Kyle Lohse,Collin Balester,Andrew Carpenter

YEAR	TEAM	LVL	AGE	W	L	SV	G	GS	IP	H	HR	BB	SO	BB9	SO9	GB%	BABIP	WHIP	ERA	FIP	FRA	WARP
2011	BRD	A+	23	4	1	0	12	12	71^{2}	62	4	6	60	0.8	7.5	—	.278	0.95	2.89	3.03	3.29	0.0
2011	ALT	AA	23	8	5	0	16	16	89^{1}	75	7	21	82	2.1	8.3	34%	.287	1.07	3.02	3.37	3.42	1.1
2012	ALT	AA	24	3	5	0	9	9	48^{2}	54	5	5	46	0.9	8.5	35%	.338	1.21	4.07	3.14	3.73	0.8
2012	IND	AAA	24	0	1	0	3	3	18^{1}	11	1	4	17	2.0	8.3	40%	.213	0.82	0.98	2.67	3.68	0.3
2012	PIT	MLB	24	0	2	0	10	3	26^{1}	24	3	7	21	2.4	7.2	47%	.284	1.18	2.73	4.05	4.22	0.2
2013	*PIT*	*MLB*	*25*	*2*	*3*	*0*	*7*	*7*	*38*	*39*	*5*	*12*	*25*	*2.8*	*5.8*	*38%*	*.292*	*1.33*	*4.75*	*4.54*	*5.17*	*-0.1*

McPherson should be in contention for a rotation spot throughout the season. His fastball is his bread and butter. The pitch can touch the upper-90s and he commands it exceptionally well. His changeup is occasionally a good offering, and his curveball is usable, but not a pitch you want him to fall in love with during a game. McPherson took over for McDonald late in the season and showed that he belongs in the bigs. His upside is that of a third starter.

Mark Melancon
Born: **3/28/1985** Age: **28**
Bats: **R** Throws: **R** Height: **6' 3"** Weight: **215**
Breakout: **21%** Improve: **49%** Collapse: **26%**
Attrition: **14%** MLB: **88%**
Comparables:
Mark Eichhorn,Brandon Medders,Doug Corbett

YEAR	TEAM	LVL	AGE	W	L	SV	G	GS	IP	H	HR	BB	SO	BB9	SO9	GB%	BABIP	WHIP	ERA	FIP	FRA	WARP
2010	ROU	AAA	25	1	0	1	3	0	4^{1}	5	0	1	2	2.1	4.2	75%	.312	1.40	0.00	3.35	3.80	0.1
2010	SWB	AAA	25	6	1	6	40	0	56^{1}	63	5	31	58	5.0	9.3	56%	.365	1.67	3.68	4.20	4.64	0.2
2010	HOU	MLB	25	2	0	0	20	0	17^{1}	12	1	8	19	4.2	9.9	47%	.262	1.15	3.12	3.22	3.58	0.2
2010	NYA	MLB	25	0	0	0	2	0	4	7	1	0	3	0.0	6.8	44%	.400	1.75	9.00	4.80	5.55	0.0
2011	HOU	MLB	26	8	4	20	71	0	74^{1}	65	5	26	66	3.1	8.0	59%	.287	1.22	2.78	3.22	4.54	0.2
2012	PAW	AAA	27	0	0	11	21	0	21^{2}	15	0	3	27	1.2	11.2	63%	.278	0.83	0.83	1.36	2.35	0.6
2012	BOS	MLB	27	0	2	1	41	0	45	45	8	12	41	2.4	8.2	51%	.285	1.27	6.20	4.54	6.40	-0.3
2013	*PIT*	*MLB*	*28*	*3*	*1*	*5*	*48*	*0*	*53^{2}*	*45*	*5*	*16*	*48*	*2.7*	*8.0*	*54%*	*.285*	*1.14*	*3.37*	*3.52*	*3.66*	*0.7*

After a brutal start to his Red Sox career, Melancon went to Triple-A and smoothed his mechanics. Upon returning to the majors, he pitched well enough to serve as the centerpiece in the Joel Hanrahan trade. A bowling-ball sinker and curveball are the key pieces of Melancon's arsenal. While those pitches dice up righties, they have not been as effective against left-handers. The wide platoon split will keep Melancon from closing for the time being, though with some improvement on that front he could become the Pirates' ninth-inning man in due time.

Bryan Morris
Born: **3/28/1987** Age: **26**
Bats: **L** Throws: **R** Height: **6' 4"** Weight: **220**
Breakout: **18%** Improve: **44%** Collapse: **21%**
Attrition: **16%** MLB: **90%**
Comparables:
Wil Ledezma,Leo Kiely,Bill Henry

YEAR	TEAM	LVL	AGE	W	L	SV	G	GS	IP	H	HR	BB	SO	BB9	SO9	GB%	BABIP	WHIP	ERA	FIP	FRA	WARP
2010	BRD	A+	23	3	0	0	8	8	44^{2}	37	0	7	40	1.4	8.1	—	.282	0.98	0.60	2.25	2.45	0.0
2010	ALT	AA	23	6	4	0	19	16	89	87	9	31	84	3.1	8.5	52%	.293	1.33	4.25	4.03	4.77	0.7
2011	ALT	AA	24	3	4	3	35	6	78	72	2	33	64	3.8	7.4	62%	.311	1.35	3.35	3.41	4.32	0.9
2012	IND	AAA	25	2	2	5	46	0	81	76	8	17	79	1.9	8.8	58%	.296	1.15	2.67	3.12	4.35	0.6
2012	PIT	MLB	25	0	0	0	5	0	5	2	0	2	6	3.6	10.8	73%	.182	0.80	1.80	2.54	3.18	0.1
2013	*PIT*	*MLB*	*26*	*1*	*1*	*0*	*15*	*3*	*36^{1}*	*37*	*4*	*15*	*25*	*3.6*	*6.1*	*53%*	*.300*	*1.42*	*4.82*	*4.49*	*5.24*	*-0.2*

Remember the Jason Bay trade? Morris is the final piece of the Pirates' return still hanging around the system. He made his big-league debut last season, showing off a plus sinker and good slider combination. There are some concerns with Morris, notably his unwillingness to always trust his stuff, and in the past he's been known to throw across his body. If he buys into his own hype and stays healthy, he could turn into a closer, albeit not one of the elite ones. That won't be enough to vindicate the trade, but it's better than nothing.

Charlie Morton

Born: **11/12/1983** Age: **29**
Bats: **R** Throws: **R** Height: **6' 6"** Weight: **230**
Breakout: **25%** Improve: **59%** Collapse: **24%**
Attrition: **17%** MLB: **81%**

Comparables:
Dock Ellis, Runelvys Hernandez, Wandy Rodriguez

YEAR	TEAM	LVL	AGE	W	L	SV	G	GS	IP	H	HR	BB	SO	BB9	SO9	GB%	BABIP	WHIP	ERA	FIP	FRA	WARP
2010	IND	AAA	26	4	4	0	14	14	80	83	6	30	53	3.4	6.0	56%	.294	1.41	3.83	4.29	5.73	0.1
2010	PIT	MLB	26	2	12	0	17	17	79^{2}	112	15	26	59	2.9	6.7	48%	.353	1.73	7.57	5.32	6.06	-0.9
2011	PIT	MLB	27	10	10	0	29	29	171^{2}	186	6	77	110	4.0	5.8	61%	.320	1.53	3.83	3.74	4.67	0.7
2012	IND	AAA	28	0	0	0	1	1	7^{2}	6	0	1	8	1.2	9.4	—	.300	0.91	1.17	1.46	1.59	0.0
2012	PIT	MLB	28	2	6	0	9	9	50^{1}	62	5	11	25	2.0	4.5	58%	.317	1.45	4.65	4.21	5.27	-0.4
2013	*PIT*	*MLB*	*29*	*3*	*4*	*0*	*11*	*11*	*63*	*64*	*6*	*22*	*43*	*3.1*	*6.1*	*52%*	*.306*	*1.36*	*4.59*	*4.12*	*4.98*	*-0.1*

Morton gained popularity in 2011 after changing his mechanics to mimic Roy Halladay. The results that followed weren't as good as Halladay's. In fact, if you only looked at peripherals, they were horrible. But Morton did allow fewer runs to score than the average starter, so people were interested in how he'd perform moving forward. Unfortunately, he missed the start of the 2012 season following offseason hip labrum surgery. He returned quickly, made nine starts, and then headed back to the operating room for Tommy John surgery. He will be out through at least June, which means a true follow-up to his 2011 season might be on hold until 2014.

Andrew Oliver

Born: **12/3/1987** Age: **25**
Bats: **L** Throws: **L** Height: **6' 4"** Weight: **210**
Breakout: **37%** Improve: **60%** Collapse: **18%**
Attrition: **15%** MLB: **85%**

Comparables:
Donnie Veal, Kyle Weiland, J.A. Happ

YEAR	TEAM	LVL	AGE	W	L	SV	G	GS	IP	H	HR	BB	SO	BB9	SO9	GB%	BABIP	WHIP	ERA	FIP	FRA	WARP
2010	ERI	AA	22	6	4	0	14	14	77^{1}	74	7	25	70	2.9	8.2	41%	.305	1.28	3.61	3.74	4.32	1.1
2010	TOL	AAA	22	3	4	0	9	9	53	43	6	25	49	4.2	8.3	41%	.266	1.28	3.23	4.39	5.55	0.0
2010	DET	MLB	22	0	4	0	5	5	22	26	3	13	18	5.3	7.4	43%	.348	1.77	7.36	5.23	5.61	0.0
2011	TOL	AAA	23	8	12	0	26	26	147	149	15	80	143	4.9	8.8	35%	.317	1.56	4.71	4.33	5.22	0.1
2011	DET	MLB	23	0	1	0	2	2	9^{2}	11	3	8	5	7.4	4.7	27%	.258	1.97	6.52	9.16	10.09	-0.4
2012	TOL	AAA	24	5	9	0	28	19	118	103	7	88	112	6.7	8.5	44%	.294	1.62	4.88	4.34	5.46	0.0
2013	*PIT*	*MLB*	*25*	*2*	*3*	*0*	*8*	*8*	42^{1}	*39*	*5*	*21*	*36*	*4.5*	*7.6*	*41%*	*.293*	*1.41*	*4.59*	*4.52*	*4.99*	*-0.0*

Oliver actually regressed in his second go-round at Triple-A: Every stat of importance got worse except hits allowed per nine innings. His strikeout rate essentially held for all intents and purposes, but technically speaking it dipped a smidge. His problem is command and control. It is hard not to love his mid-90s fastball from the left side, but the biggest issue is that he seems to be using Apple Maps to find the strike zone. As a lefty with this kind of power arm, Oliver's leash will be longer than many. Now with the Pirates, expect him to start the 2013 season in the Triple-A rotation.

Stolmy Pimentel

Born: **2/1/1990** Age: **23**
Bats: **R** Throws: **R** Height: **6' 4"** Weight: **165**
Breakout: **31%** Improve: **62%** Collapse: **12%**
Attrition: **14%** MLB: **88%**

Comparables:
Dan Haren, Collin Balester, Jeanmar Gomez

YEAR	TEAM	LVL	AGE	W	L	SV	G	GS	IP	H	HR	BB	SO	BB9	SO9	GB%	BABIP	WHIP	ERA	FIP	FRA	WARP
2010	SLM	A+	20	9	11	0	26	26	128^{2}	120	11	42	102	2.9	7.1	47%	.291	1.26	4.06	4.03	4.89	0.7
2011	SLM	A+	21	6	4	0	11	10	51^{2}	50	8	16	35	2.8	6.1	—	.273	1.28	4.53	5.28	5.74	0.0
2011	PME	AA	21	0	9	0	15	15	50^{1}	75	8	23	30	4.1	5.4	—	.370	1.95	9.12	6.13	6.67	0.0
2012	PME	AA	22	6	7	0	22	22	115^{2}	115	9	42	86	3.3	6.7	51%	.297	1.36	4.59	3.87	5.41	0.0
2013	*PIT*	*MLB*	*23*	*2*	*3*	*0*	*7*	*7*	*36*	*38*	*5*	*15*	*22*	*3.7*	*5.5*	*43%*	*.299*	*1.46*	*5.20*	*5.03*	*5.65*	*-0.3*

Pimentel is that perfect Italian sports car: It's fast, looks amazing, and you look incredible in it, except that it never works right. You turn on the windshield wipers and the turn signal goes on. You close the door and the window falls out. You turn the ignition key and the engine explodes. That's Pimentel, a starting pitcher with perfect size, good fastball velocity, and no refinement whatsoever. A fresh start with the Pirates could help spark improvement, though with just one option year remaining, Pimentel will have to make more progress in 2013 than he had in previous years to avoid the bullpen.

Chad Qualls

Born: **8/17/1978** Age: **34**
Bats: **R** Throws: **R** Height: **6' 6"** Weight: **220**
Breakout: **18%** Improve: **46%** Collapse: **31%**
Attrition: **6%** MLB: **85%**

Comparables:
Scott Atchison, Jeff Shaw, Gene Garber

YEAR	TEAM	LVL	AGE	W	L	SV	G	GS	IP	H	HR	BB	SO	BB9	SO9	GB%	BABIP	WHIP	ERA	FIP	FRA	WARP
2010	ARI	MLB	31	1	4	12	43	0	38	61	5	15	34	3.6	8.1	57%	.415	2.00	8.29	4.29	4.54	0.2
2010	TBA	MLB	31	2	0	0	27	0	21	24	2	6	15	2.6	6.4	55%	.328	1.43	5.57	3.86	5.42	-0.1
2011	SDN	MLB	32	6	8	0	77	0	74^{1}	73	7	20	43	2.4	5.2	60%	.280	1.25	3.51	3.87	5.02	-0.5
2012	IND	AAA	33	0	0	0	1	1	1	0	0	0	3	0.0	27.0	—	.000	0.00	0.00	-2.84	0.22	0.1
2012	NYA	MLB	33	1	0	0	8	0	7^{1}	10	0	3	2	3.7	2.5	54%	.357	1.77	6.14	3.73	4.80	0.0
2012	PHI	MLB	33	1	1	0	35	0	31^{1}	39	7	9	19	2.6	5.5	56%	.308	1.53	4.60	5.69	6.40	-0.6
2012	PIT	MLB	33	0	0	0	17	0	13^{2}	14	0	2	6	1.3	4.0	60%	.280	1.17	6.59	2.70	3.75	0.1
2013	*PIT*	*MLB*	*34*	*3*	*1*	*1*	*61*	*0*	*54^{2}*	*52*	*6*	*12*	*41*	*1.9*	*6.7*	*55%*	*.298*	*1.17*	*3.73*	*3.79*	*4.06*	*0.4*

Qualls came to Pittsburgh in a junk-for-junk deadline swap that sent Casey McGehee to the Yankees. He still gets a good number of groundballs thanks to his low-90s sinker, but his Achilles heel is an ineffective slider. Formerly his out pitch, the slider doesn't have the same bite it used to. Until Qualls adjusts his arsenal to compensate, or tweaks his slider, he's unlikely to profile as anything more than a below-average middle reliever.

Wandy Rodriguez

Born: **1/18/1979** Age: **34**
Bats: **B** Throws: **L** Height: **6' 0"** Weight: **195**
Breakout: **17%** Improve: **40%** Collapse: **29%**
Attrition: **11%** MLB: **89%**

Comparables:
Roy Oswalt, Bartolo Colon, Kevin Millwood

YEAR	TEAM	LVL	AGE	W	L	SV	G	GS	IP	H	HR	BB	SO	BB9	SO9	GB%	BABIP	WHIP	ERA	FIP	FRA	WARP
2010	HOU	MLB	31	11	12	0	32	32	195	183	16	68	178	3.1	8.2	49%	.304	1.29	3.60	3.53	4.25	3.6
2011	CCH	AA	32	0	0	0	1	1	4	6	1	1	2	2.2	4.5	—	.385	1.75	2.25	6.38	6.93	0.0
2011	HOU	MLB	32	11	11	0	30	30	191	182	25	69	166	3.3	7.8	47%	.289	1.31	3.49	4.12	4.47	1.6
2012	HOU	MLB	33	7	9	0	21	21	130^{2}	134	13	32	89	2.2	6.1	52%	.287	1.27	3.79	3.85	4.40	1.0
2012	PIT	MLB	33	5	4	0	13	12	75	71	8	24	50	2.9	6.0	46%	.269	1.27	3.72	4.19	4.61	0.6
2013	*PIT*	*MLB*	*34*	*10*	*10*	*0*	*29*	*29*	*178*	*162*	*18*	*49*	*138*	*2.5*	*7.0*	*46%*	*.290*	*1.18*	*3.73*	*3.79*	*4.05*	*1.6*

After a few years spent on the trading block, Rodriguez must have felt relieved to finally get shipped out of Houston. Previously, teams had balked on acquiring him because of his contract. Rodriguez is a consistent, durable middle-of-the-rotation southpaw paid like a front-of-the-rotation staff anchor. The Pirates searched high and low for a veteran starter before netting Rodriguez for three prospects. Pittsburgh also agreed to pay him nearly $18 million of the $30 million remaining on his contract. Rodriguez pitched like himself for the Bucs down the stretch, and he could spend the next two seasons in Pittsburgh if he exercises a $14 million player option for 2014.

Zach Stewart

Born: **9/28/1986** Age: **26**
Bats: **R** Throws: **R** Height: **6' 3"** Weight: **205**
Breakout: **21%** Improve: **50%** Collapse: **27%**
Attrition: **23%** MLB: **94%**

Comparables:
Pat Misch, Reggie Cleveland, Doug Drabek

YEAR	TEAM	LVL	AGE	W	L	SV	G	GS	IP	H	HR	BB	SO	BB9	SO9	GB%	BABIP	WHIP	ERA	FIP	FRA	WARP
2010	NHP	AA	23	8	3	0	26	26	136^{1}	131	13	54	106	3.6	7.0	49%	.299	1.36	3.63	4.34	4.95	1.0
2011	NHP	AA	24	5	5	0	16	16	94^{1}	106	6	27	74	2.6	7.1	—	.339	1.41	4.20	3.56	3.87	0.0
2011	CHR	AAA	24	0	1	0	1	1	6^{1}	10	0	0	5	0.0	7.1	—	.435	1.58	4.26	1.66	1.80	0.0
2011	CHA	MLB	24	2	5	0	10	8	50^{2}	64	9	13	35	2.3	6.2	52%	.337	1.52	6.22	4.82	5.35	0.1
2011	TOR	MLB	24	0	1	0	3	3	16^{2}	26	2	5	10	2.7	5.4	46%	.421	1.86	4.86	4.50	5.21	0.0
2012	PAW	AAA	25	3	5	0	11	11	59^{1}	58	6	14	42	2.1	6.4	36%	.283	1.21	3.94	3.87	4.77	0.3
2012	BOS	MLB	25	0	2	0	2	2	5^{2}	17	4	0	3	0.0	4.8	47%	.500	3.00	22.24	11.69	10.07	-0.4
2012	CHA	MLB	25	1	2	0	18	1	30	41	10	4	16	1.2	4.8	54%	.298	1.50	6.00	6.71	8.02	-0.7
2013	*PIT*	*MLB*	*26*	*3*	*4*	*0*	*11*	*11*	*57^{1}*	*59*	*8*	*16*	*40*	*2.5*	*6.3*	*47%*	*.307*	*1.32*	*4.51*	*4.46*	*4.90*	*0.0*

The Red Sox valued Stewart as part of their return on Kevin Youkilis so much that they dealt him to the Pirates in the offseason for Kyle Kaminska. Stewart is Triple-A filler but pitched like Double-A filler in the majors at the end of last season. His best-case scenario is becoming a middle-relief option, though the stuff has always been better than the results and that's probably not changing any time soon.

Jameson Taillon

Born: **11/18/1991** Age: **21**
Bats: **R** Throws: **R** Height: **6' 7"** Weight: **225**
Breakout: **28%** Improve: **60%** Collapse: **15%**
Attrition: **4%** MLB: **89%**

Comparables:
Alex Fernandez, Jordan Lyles, Hayden Penn

YEAR	TEAM	LVL	AGE	W	L	SV	G	GS	IP	H	HR	BB	SO	BB9	SO9	GB%	BABIP	WHIP	ERA	FIP	FRA	WARP
2011	WVA	A	19	2	3	0	23	23	92^{2}	89	9	22	97	2.1	9.4	48%	.317	1.20	3.98	3.70	4.43	1.0
2012	BRD	A+	20	6	8	0	23	23	125	109	10	37	98	2.7	7.1	47%	.268	1.17	3.82	3.90	4.56	0.0
2012	ALT	AA	20	3	0	0	3	3	17	11	0	1	18	0.5	9.5	40%	.256	0.71	1.59	1.26	0.72	0.2
2013	*PIT*	*MLB*	*21*	*2*	*3*	*0*	*9*	*9*	*42^{1}*	*42*	*5*	*15*	*29*	*3.1*	*6.1*	*44%*	*.293*	*1.33*	*4.56*	*4.43*	*4.95*	*0.0*

As is the case with Cole, Taillon's numbers lag behind his stuff. Taillon has a big frame with long limbs, gets good extension, and pitches on a downhill plane. His fastball is plus and runs in on right-handed batters, and does so at speeds in the high-90s; it's easy heat. His power breaking ball should serve as his out pitch, though his changeup figures to be above average too. The biggest issues Taillon has to overcome are missing up in the zone and becoming overly reliant on his fastball. He reached Double-A late in the year. A late-season promotion to the majors is not out of the question.

Rick VandenHurk

Born: **5/22/1985** Age: **28**
Bats: **R** Throws: **R** Height: **6' 6"** Weight: **215**
Breakout: **24%** Improve: **75%** Collapse: **11%**
Attrition: **10%** MLB: **85%**

Comparables:
Luke Hochevar, Armando Galarraga, Edwin Jackson

YEAR	TEAM	LVL	AGE	W	L	SV	G	GS	IP	H	HR	BB	SO	BB9	SO9	GB%	BABIP	WHIP	ERA	FIP	FRA	WARP
2010	BAL	MLB	25	0	1	0	7	1	16^{1}	13	2	7	17	3.9	9.4	34%	.282	1.22	4.96	4.21	5.96	0.0
2010	FLO	MLB	25	0	0	0	2	0	1^{1}	3	0	1	1	6.8	6.8	43%	.429	3.00	6.75	3.86	3.67	0.0
2011	NOR	AAA	26	9	13	0	26	26	154^{1}	141	23	40	108	2.3	6.3	34%	.264	1.17	4.43	4.80	5.69	-0.3
2011	BAL	MLB	26	0	0	0	4	2	9	12	4	8	7	8.0	7.0	23%	.308	2.22	8.00	10.28	9.99	-0.3
2012	BRD	A+	27	1	0	0	1	1	6	8	1	1	5	1.5	7.5	45%	.368	1.50	6.00	4.39	9.38	0.0
2012	IND	AAA	27	13	5	0	21	19	123^{1}	112	8	35	113	2.6	8.2	48%	.294	1.19	2.92	3.29	4.58	1.2
2012	PIT	MLB	27	0	1	0	4	0	2^{2}	5	0	1	3	3.4	10.1	55%	.455	2.25	13.50	3.14	2.75	0.1
2013	*PIT*	*MLB*	*28*	*3*	*3*	*0*	*8*	*8*	46^{1}	*42*	*6*	*15*	*38*	*2.9*	*7.3*	*37%*	*.283*	*1.22*	*4.10*	*4.21*	*4.46*	*0.2*

Believe it or not, VandenHurk has appeared in the majors in six straight seasons. The Dutchman, who used to be something of a prospect, could be on his way to becoming a big-league staple. A change in delivery and arsenal sparked improved results, including a career-best groundball rate. VandenHurk now stands on the first base side of the rubber as a way of making up for his closed landing, and he throws a slider instead of a curveball. He's a bullpen sleeper in an organization suddenly overflowing with capable relief arms.

Zack Von Rosenberg

Born: **9/24/1990** Age: **22**
Bats: **R** Throws: **R** Height: **6' 6"** Weight: **205**
Breakout: **22%** Improve: **54%** Collapse: **23%**
Attrition: **15%** MLB: **83%**

Comparables:
Phil Huffman, Joe Moeller, Bob Wolcott

YEAR	TEAM	LVL	AGE	W	L	SV	G	GS	IP	H	HR	BB	SO	BB9	SO9	GB%	BABIP	WHIP	ERA	FIP	FRA	WARP
2011	WVA	A	20	5	9	0	27	25	125^{2}	143	19	23	114	1.6	8.2	38%	.348	1.32	5.73	4.47	5.34	0.6
2012	WVA	A	21	5	7	0	17	17	86^{2}	94	11	24	60	2.5	6.2	43%	.299	1.36	4.36	4.88	6.26	-0.1
2013	*PIT*	*MLB*	*22*	*2*	*3*	*0*	*7*	*7*	35^{1}	*41*	*6*	*14*	*18*	*3.5*	*4.6*	*40%*	*.305*	*1.53*	*5.81*	*5.58*	*6.32*	*-0.5*

The old aphorism says patience is a virtue. When it comes to Von Rosenberg, patience is a necessity. He started slowly again, this time by posting radar-gun readings in the 80s during the spring. He is a projectable arm, and velocity fluctuations are normal. You'd just rather those numbers go upward rather than downward. At his best he throws three pitches for strikes, and he did finish strong—throwing a complete game three-hitter in his final start. The frame and repertoire for future success are still here.

Tony Watson

Born: **5/30/1985** Age: **28**
Bats: **L** Throws: **L** Height: **6' 5"** Weight: **220**
Breakout: **33%** Improve: **64%** Collapse: **15%**
Attrition: **20%** MLB: **86%**

Comparables:
Rigo Beltran, Bryan Hickerson, Don Carman

YEAR	TEAM	LVL	AGE	W	L	SV	G	GS	IP	H	HR	BB	SO	BB9	SO9	GB%	BABIP	WHIP	ERA	FIP	FRA	WARP
2010	ALT	AA	25	6	4	2	34	9	111^{1}	82	11	24	105	1.9	8.5	36%	.240	0.95	2.67	3.54	4.36	1.0
2011	IND	AAA	26	3	3	0	26	1	34^{1}	24	2	11	35	2.9	9.2	38%	.271	1.02	2.36	3.09	4.10	0.3
2011	PIT	MLB	26	2	2	0	43	0	41	34	6	20	37	4.4	8.1	36%	.257	1.32	3.95	4.63	4.67	-0.1
2012	PIT	MLB	27	5	2	0	68	0	53^{1}	37	5	23	53	3.9	8.9	42%	.241	1.12	3.38	3.72	3.94	0.3
2013	*PIT*	*MLB*	*28*	*2*	*1*	*0*	*34*	*2*	46^{1}	*41*	*6*	*16*	*39*	*3.1*	*7.5*	*36%*	*.281*	*1.24*	*3.95*	*4.24*	*4.29*	*0.3*

Although Watson continue to appear best suited for lefty-on-lefty work, the Pirates allowed him to face more right-handers than lefties last season. The results weren't horrible. Watson uses a low-90 fastball, a mid-80s slider, and a mid-80s changeup, along with moxie and wits, to retire batters. The combination seems to be enough to fake it against the occasional right-hander, though his closed landing and to-the-side release point still make him appear to be a lefty thrasher waiting to happen.

Duke Welker

Born: **2/10/1986** Age: **27**
Bats: **R** Throws: **R** Height: **6' 8"** Weight: **220**
Breakout: **26%** Improve: **53%** Collapse: **23%**
Attrition: **26%** MLB: **78%**

Comparables:
Alan Hargesheimer, Don Carrithers, Miguel Batista

YEAR	TEAM	LVL	AGE	W	L	SV	G	GS	IP	H	HR	BB	SO	BB9	SO9	GB%	BABIP	WHIP	ERA	FIP	FRA	WARP
2010	WVA	A	24	1	1	5	20	0	22^{1}	16	0	24	25	9.7	10.1	54%	.281	1.79	3.63	4.65	6.46	-0.2
2010	BRD	A+	24	0	1	0	20	0	24^{1}	16	2	23	20	8.5	7.4	—	.209	1.60	3.70	5.82	6.33	0.0
2011	BRD	A+	25	3	5	6	36	0	52	33	2	25	41	4.3	7.1	—	.225	1.12	2.25	3.87	4.21	0.0
2011	ALT	AA	25	1	0	0	8	0	10	11	0	1	9	0.9	8.1	61%	.355	1.20	5.40	2.21	2.31	0.3
2012	ALT	AA	26	2	1	5	15	0	23^{1}	19	0	7	19	2.7	7.3	68%	.267	1.11	2.31	2.47	3.28	0.3
2012	IND	AAA	26	0	1	0	26	0	31^{2}	24	1	18	30	5.1	8.5	54%	.284	1.33	2.27	3.47	4.64	0.2
2013	*PIT*	*MLB*	*27*	*1*	*0*	*1*	*28*	*0*	34^{1}	*37*	*4*	*21*	*18*	*5.4*	*4.6*	*53%*	*.302*	*1.68*	*6.02*	*5.50*	*6.55*	*-0.7*

People think about power fastballs and the intimidation factor when they think about 6-foot-8 relievers named Duke. Welker does not disappoint. His fastball features plus-plus velocity and he shows the ability to locate it down in the zone. He will struggle with control occasionally, and this brings up the intimidating part of his game. He has hit a batter once every 15 innings throughout his minor-league career, the same rate as the 2012 big-league leader in hit batsmen, Ian Kennedy. Expect Welker to bring strikeouts, walks, groundballs, and bruises to the Steel City sometime soon.

Justin Wilson

Born: **8/18/1987** Age: **25**
Bats: **L** Throws: **L** Height: **6' 3"** Weight: **233**
Breakout: **29%** Improve: **48%** Collapse: **23%**
Attrition: **22%** MLB: **86%**
Comparables:
Cliff Lee,Andrew Miller,Kyle Weiland

YEAR	TEAM	LVL	AGE	W	L	SV	G	GS	IP	H	HR	BB	SO	BB9	SO9	GB%	BABIP	WHIP	ERA	FIP	FRA	WARP
2010	ALT	AA	22	11	8	0	27	26	142^{2}	109	4	71	134	4.5	8.5	53%	.268	1.26	3.09	3.49	4.38	1.1
2011	IND	AAA	23	10	8	3	30	21	124^{1}	121	12	67	94	4.8	6.8	48%	.287	1.51	4.13	4.69	6.32	-0.5
2012	IND	AAA	24	9	6	0	29	25	135^{2}	91	12	66	138	4.4	9.2	37%	.232	1.16	3.78	3.89	5.17	0.1
2012	PIT	MLB	24	0	0	0	8	0	4^{2}	10	0	3	7	5.8	13.5	25%	.625	2.79	1.93	2.06	2.97	0.1
2013	*PIT*	*MLB*	*25*	*3*	*3*	*0*	*9*	*9*	*46*	*42*	*5*	*21*	*37*	*4.2*	*7.2*	*46%*	*.286*	*1.37*	*4.43*	*4.37*	*4.81*	*0.1*

Wilson is another starting pitching prospect nearing the Show. A chunky southpaw, Wilson features a lively fastball and good-enough breaking ball. His command and third pitch are iffy, which limits his ceiling to that of a back-of-the-rotation starter. There's some thought that the Pirates will shift him to the bullpen, where his stuff would play up. For now, he remains a starter. Expect Wilson to make his big-league debut in 2013.

Mike Zagurski

Born: **1/27/1983** Age: **30**
Bats: **L** Throws: **L** Height: **6' 1"** Weight: **225**
Breakout: **26%** Improve: **59%** Collapse: **20%**
Attrition: **5%** MLB: **89%**
Comparables:
Xavier Hernandez,Arthur Rhodes,Paul Assenmacher

YEAR	TEAM	LVL	AGE	W	L	SV	G	GS	IP	H	HR	BB	SO	BB9	SO9	GB%	BABIP	WHIP	ERA	FIP	FRA	WARP
2010	LEH	AAA	27	2	3	3	52	0	52^{1}	44	3	27	71	4.6	12.2	48%	.319	1.36	3.27	2.99	3.30	1.1
2010	PHI	MLB	27	0	0	0	8	0	7	8	1	5	11	6.4	14.1	31%	.467	1.86	10.29	4.82	4.81	0.0
2011	LEH	AAA	28	4	0	11	46	0	54^{1}	43	3	27	63	4.5	10.4	—	.312	1.29	2.65	3.29	3.58	0.0
2011	PHI	MLB	28	0	0	0	4	0	3^{1}	4	1	3	4	8.1	10.8	50%	.333	2.10	5.40	7.19	5.42	0.0
2012	RNO	AAA	29	0	0	0	6	0	9	3	1	2	7	2.0	7.0	46%	.095	0.56	2.00	4.55	6.53	0.0
2012	ARI	MLB	29	0	0	0	45	0	37^{1}	37	5	19	34	4.6	8.2	43%	.308	1.50	5.54	4.66	4.41	0.2
2013	*PIT*	*MLB*	*30*	*2*	*1*	*0*	*40*	*0*	37^{2}	*31*	*4*	*16*	*39*	*3.9*	*9.3*	*44%*	*.295*	*1.27*	*3.91*	*3.78*	*4.25*	*0.2*

Zagurski was slugged to the tune of .463 in 2012, the highest rate on the Arizona pitching staff. Unsurprisingly, the Diamondbacks let Zagurski walk after that miserable performance, and he landed with the Pirates. The left-hander sticks to a two-pitch repertoire of fastballs and breaking pitches, trusting his 91-94 mph heater to get the job done nearly three-fourths of the time. He struggles with control because an inability to balance his bowling-ball frame leads to an inconsistent release point, and as such, his penchant for missed targets has been a consistent criticism in his scouting reports. If Zagurski can get in better shape, he could become a left-handed specialist.

LINEOUTS

HITTERS

PLAYER	TEAM	LVL	AGE	PA	R	2B	3B	HR	RBI	BB	SO	SB-CS	AVG/OBP/SLG	TAv	BABIP	BRR	FRAA	WARP
2B J. Cunningham	ALT	AA	22	415	43	19	3	6	45	37	111	3-3	.217/.300/.337	.239	.293	1.2	2B(88): 2.6	0.4
2B D. Herrera	PIR	Rk	18	227	41	11	4	7	27	18	41	11-4	.281/.341/.482	.260	.325	4	2B(52): 0.0	0.8
SS G. Ngoepe	BRD	A+	22	538	66	11	5	9	36	63	131	22-14	.232/.330/.338	.219	.304	2.4	SS(32): -1.6, 2B(3): 0.6	-0.1
1B J. Osuna	WVA	A	19	524	68	36	0	16	72	31	82	4-4	.280/.324/.454	.272	.304	-2.4	1B(88): 2.4	0.5
OF F. Pie	GWN	AAA	27	365	39	26	7	6	51	23	46	16-0	.285/.338/.459	.261	.313	1	RF(27): 0.8, LF(6): -0.9	0.2
OF M. Rojas	BRD	A+	22	546	61	12	12	6	51	35	107	16-8	.245/.303/.354	.263	.300	3.3	CF(30): -2.3, RF(5): 0.3	0.9
C A. Solis	SAN	AA	24	343	26	25	1	6	40	11	77	1-1	.283/.307/.419	.232	.352	-2.9	C(55): -0.4, 3B(1): -0.0	-0.4

Jarek Cunningham received some attention after more than half of his hits in 2011 went for extra bases. He spent 2012 at Double-A, where advanced pitchers exposed his loopy swing and poor pitch recognition. ⊘ Colombian **Dilson Herrera** does not run or defend well, limiting him to second base, but his bat speed and feel for hitting could get him to the majors. ⊘ As easy as it is to like **Gift Ngoepe**, the first black South African to sign a professional baseball contract, his story and attitude are better than his skill set. Ngoepe's ability to hit pitchers with average or better stuff is in serious doubt, and so is his big-league future. ⊘ **Jose Osuna** is a young outfielder-turned-first baseman with an idea at the plate and the ability to hit for some power. ⊘ Journeyman outfielder **Felix Pie** failed to make a big-league appearance for the first time since 2006. ⊘ **Mel Rojas**

Jr. turns 23 this season, his third professional campaign, and looks no more likely to fulfill his promise than he did on draft day. **Ali Solis** is a catch-and-throw guy without any offensive skills who will try to turn that into a career with the Pirates.

PITCHERS

PLAYER	TEAM	LVL	AGE	W	L	SV	IP	H	HR	BB	SO	BB9	SO9	GB%	BABIP	WHIP	ERA	FIP	FRA	WARP
T. Alderson	ALT	AA	23	5	4	3	84^{2}	89	7	26	62	2.8	6.6	47%	.309	1.36	4.25	4.02	4.51	0.8
N. Baker	ALT	AA	24	4	7	1	105^{2}	100	9	57	77	4.9	6.6	50%	.283	1.49	4.94	4.73	5.75	-0.5
C. Beck	LVG	AAA	27	2	0	18	48	39	2	13	24	2.4	4.5	47%	.242	1.08	1.31	4.08	4.58	0.7
	TOR	MLB	27	0	0	0	15^{2}	21	2	5	9	2.9	5.2	50%	.339	1.66	6.32	4.51	4.93	0.0
E. Cordier	GWN	AAA	26	1	1	0	24^{2}	27	1	21	15	7.7	5.5	51%	.347	1.95	4.38	5.14	7.02	-0.1
J. Inman	ALT	AA	24	2	2	3	51^{2}	45	2	19	36	3.3	6.3	57%	.269	1.24	3.83	3.41	4.68	0.4
P. Irwin	ALT	AA	25	4	7	0	104^{1}	97	7	17	83	1.5	7.2	53%	.296	1.09	2.93	3.40	3.90	0.8
	IND	AAA	25	3	0	0	21	20	1	7	28	3.0	12.0	47%	.365	1.29	2.57	2.25	2.75	0.7
R. Rowland	WVA	A	20	9	5	0	106^{1}	110	10	23	62	1.9	5.2	56%	.291	1.25	3.30	4.54	5.51	0.4
D. Slaten	IND	AAA	32	3	3	10	42^{2}	30	5	13	24	2.7	5.1	56%	.202	1.01	2.11	4.61	5.69	-0.1
	PIT	MLB	32	0	0	0	13	9	1	8	6	5.5	4.2	51%	.200	1.31	2.77	5.06	6.46	-0.2
H. Takahashi	ANA	MLB	37	0	3	0	42	39	6	10	41	2.1	8.8	37%	.284	1.17	4.93	3.67	4.24	0.2
	PIT	MLB	37	0	0	0	8^{1}	10	2	4	11	4.3	11.9	50%	.364	1.68	8.64	5.06	5.40	-0.1

Tim Alderson, once a hyped prospect, is bordering on irrelevancy. He spent most of last season in the bullpen or on the shelf with a sore elbow. **Nathan Baker** finds himself in the bullpen after walking the world as a starter. Baker could turn into a left-handed specialist if his control obliges. A move to the bullpen helped **Chad Beck** lower his hits and walks allowed, but it's hard to predict big-league success because he doesn't strike enough batters out. At one point a highly touted prospect, **Erik Cordier** continues to see his stock slide due to injuries. **Jeff Inman** still throws hard, and that gives him a chance to reach the majors as a reliever. Right-hander **Phil Irwin** is bland compared to the other arms in the system, but he could soon become a back-of-the-rotation starter thanks to good command and control. Pittsburgh nabbed **Robby Rowland**, a large, athletic strike-thrower, in exchange for letting Arizona keep Rule 5 pick Brett Lorin. **Doug Slaten** just needs one team to believe in his ability to retire left-handed batters in order to end his tour of the International League. The Pirates snatched up **Hisanori Takahashi** banking on some positive regression. He threw just eight innings for Pittsburgh with horrible results.

MANAGER: CLINT HURDLE

YEAR	TEAM	W-L	Pythag +/-	Avg PC	100+ P	120+ P	QS	BQS	REL	REL w Zero R	IBB	PH	PH Avg	PH HR	SB2	CS2	SB3	CS3	SAC Att	SAC %	POS SAC	Squeeze	Swing	In Play
2011	PIT	72-90	0	89.5	26	0	78	2	549	452	65	275	.201	1	13	3	0	2	110	76.4%	45	1	384	114
2012	PIT	79-83	0	90.4	42	0	83	2	483	398	30	266	.173	2	7	3	0	4	93	73.1%	35	2	271	94

Communication is paramount for managers. Communicating well with the players, the front office, the media, and sometimes the fans can make an average manager look better than he is. Hurdle purportedly is a good communicator. That's why his public shaming of Kevin Correia stood out. Hurdle's attempts to explain why Rod Barajas continued to play over Michael McKenry often failed to add up, too. But there is one thing to consider. Despite back-to-back collapses, the Pirates elected to keep Hurdle around. The manager always serves as a lightning rod for criticism or praise. The Pirates could have dumped Hurdle and blamed their second-half faults on his laissez-faire clubhouses, or his strategic decisions, or his hipster eyewear. They could have fingered Hurdle as the reason the Pirates were unable to produce a running game, or stop one on the defensive end. Heck, they coulda said whatever they wanted and people would've eaten it up because bloodlust was running high in Pittsburgh down the stretch. But they didn't. Instead, Hurdle will return for at least one more season as the club's manager. Maybe that speaks to Hurdle's communication skills more than anything else we have.

San Diego Padres

2012: DRAMA LLAMA DING DONG

Ownership and television contract drama overshadowed the action on the field, which started slowly, and the team was hit hard by injuries. By the end of the season, the youngsters got a chance to play and led the club to a strong finish, but 2012 was largely a lost season in San Diego.

Opening Day hadn't even arrived yet when new GM Josh Byrnes had sent first-base prospect Anthony Rizzo to the Cubs for electric but fragile right-hander Andrew Cashner and CEO Jeff Moorad had resigned. Once the season got underway, 42 percent of households in San Diego did without television broadcasts of Padres games, and then the team was sold again, this time to a group headed by the O'Malley family (of Dodgers fame) and local businessman Ron Fowler. This is a vast oversimplification of a complicated and convoluted situation. For a more detailed explanation, see Geoff Young's essay online at http://www.baseballprospectus.com/article.php?articleid=18561.

On the field, the Padres lost 12 of their first 15 games en route to a 34-53 first half that had them battling the Cubs, Rockies, and Astros for the first pick in the 2013 draft. By mid-May, only two members of the Padres' projected rotation—Clayton Richard and Edinson Volquez—hadn't been lost to injuries for the year, leaving a motley collection of not-quites, has-beens, and never-weres to start games.

With nothing to lose, the team called up the kids and let them play. Offseason acquisition Yasmani Grandal replaced an injured Nick Hundley behind the plate. Logan Forsythe and newcomer Alexi Amarista split time at second base. The all-but-forgotten Everth Cabrera took over at shortstop and ended up leading the National League in stolen bases.

Behind the youngsters and a resurgent Chase Headley, who survived trade rumors and became a legitimate MVP candidate, the Padres went 42-33 in the season's second half. They still only finished in fourth place, but for a team with minimal expectations and in apparent disarray, things could have been much worse.

2013: O RLY? YA RLY

With new ownership comes stability and the promise of money to spend on free agents and/or contract extensions. A core of strong, club-controlled talent (Alonso, Cashner, Cameron Maybin) is in place and figures to improve. This is an exciting team in a division that should be up for grabs, but health is key—particularly on the pitching side, where Anthony Bass, Casey Kelly, Cory Luebke, and Joe Wieland all missed large chunks of 2012.

A farm system that Kevin Goldstein rated as the best in baseball before last season has started to produce, and more talent is on its way. Kelly struggled in his debut but showed promise, Jedd Gyorko could see material playing time at second base, and southpaw Robbie Erlin should be in the picture at some point, assuming he stays healthy. Prized outfield prospect Rymer Liriano could make an appearance late in the season.

Still, questions abound: Can Headley repeat? How will Grandal hold up over an entire season? Will Carlos Quentin (who underwent another round of knee surgery in October) and Huston Street stay healthy enough to justify their contract extensions? Is Cabrera a legitimate big-league shortstop? What's up with the rotation? Jason Marquis and Eric Stults were great reclamation projects, but history suggests they cannot sustain their success.

PADRES PROSPECTUS

2012 W-L: 76-86, 4th in NL West

Pythag	.460	20th	DER	.716	7th
RS/G	4.02	23rd	B-Age	27.4	5th
RA/G	4.38	19th	P-Age	28.0	17th
TAv	.262	14th	Salary	$55.6	28th
BRR	6.7	6th	M$/MW	$1.54	5th
TAv-P	.271	24th	DL Days	1757	1st
FIP	4.15	20th	DL WARP	2.2	24th

Three-Year Park Factors	
Overall	93
HR/RH	99
HR/LH	79
AVG/RH	101
AVG/LH	95

Petco Park (2004)
Att. % of Capacity: 61.4% (19th)
Dim. 334, 367, 396, 382, 322

Shorter dimensions and a lower fence should benefit lefties, who hit an MLB-low 31 homers at Petco.

The Padres are moving the fences in 11–12 feet for 2013, mostly in right and right-center, but also a little in left-center, hoping to help their hitters. Such changes are not an automatic boost to a team's success, however: When the Mets did this prior to 2012, not only did the change fail to boost the Mets' offense, it also had a negative impact on their pitchers. They notched their lowest runs-scored total since Citi Field opened in 2009, and their pitchers allowed many more home runs at home. A less extreme home park could make it easier for the Padres to attract free-agent position players, while having the opposite effect on pitchers.

This is the best offensive core Bud Black has had since he became manager in 2007. With ownership issues in the rear-view mirror and an influx of good, young talent, the short-term prognosis is good. Unfortunately, barring a radical shift in TV negotiations, many fans in town will be unable to watch what should be an exciting team.

STATE OF THE ORGANIZATION: ONE DOES NOT SIMPLY EXPECT PEOPLE TO SHOW UP

The farm system is deep and the front office is full of smart people, but without a healthy fan base, these things mean nothing.

That system has the Padres poised for long-term success if they get the business side in order. The team is loaded behind the plate with youngsters Grandal and, further down, Austin Hedges. Third base and center field look good as well, while second base could be a strength if Gyorko sticks there. Shortstop is a concern. Cabrera might not be the answer, and the only hope on the horizon is Jace Peterson, who is several years away and whose upside might not be much higher than Cabrera's.

The organization boasts many promising young pitchers, but all are raw (Adys Portillo, Keyvius Sampson), fragile (Erlin, Kelly, Luebke, Wieland), or both (Cashner). If some of them find health and consistency, they could be dangerous, especially at Petco Park—assuming any dimension changes don't negate that advantage.

San Diego will never be a top destination for marquee free agents. Even with new owners and new money, the market doesn't bear that kind of spending, which makes drafting and developing talent crucial. The Padres must also get their games on local television to renew interest in the team. The opening of Petco Park in 2004 lit a spark that burned while the team was winning, but last year attendance slipped to 14th out of 16 National League teams. With ownership and broadcast issues overshadowing the actual baseball, local folks spent their time in other pursuits.

There is plenty of talent in the system and among the people making decisions in the front office. But if the Padres can't find a way to make the team accessible and relevant to San Diegans, such talent will be wasted on empty seats at the ballpark and televisions tuned to whichever Kardashian happens to be imploding at the moment.

HITTERS

Yonder Alonso 1B
Born: **4/8/1987** Age: **26**
Bats: **L** Throws: **R** Height: **6' 3"**
Weight: **240** Breakout: **5%**
Improve: **53%** Collapse: **5%**
Attrition: **10%** MLB: **96%**
Comparables:
Gaby Sanchez, Billy Butler, Todd Helton

YEAR	TEAM	LVL	AGE	PA	R	2B	3B	HR	RBI	BB	SO	SB	CS	AVG_OBP_SLG	TAv	BABIP	BRR	FRAA	WARP
2010	CAR	AA	23	121	19	5	0	3	13	19	16	4	2	.267/.388/.406	.269	.293	-1	1B(14): -0.2, LF(13): -1.0	0.2
2010	LOU	AAA	23	445	50	31	2	12	56	37	76	9	1	.296/.356/.470	.279	.340	-4.3	1B(81): -0.1, LF(17): -1.6	1.0
2010	CIN	MLB	23	29	2	2	0	0	3	0	10	0	0	.207/.207/.276	.166	.316	-0.3	1B(6): 0.7	-0.1
2011	LOU	AAA	24	409	46	24	4	12	56	46	60	6	5	.296/.374/.486	.269	.324	-0.6	LF(39): -5.2, 1B(13): 0.6	0.0
2011	CIN	MLB	24	98	9	4	0	5	15	10	21	0	0	.330/.398/.545	.309	.387	0.9	LF(16): -0.5, 1B(3): 0.1	0.6
2012	SDN	MLB	25	619	47	39	0	9	62	62	101	3	0	.273/.348/.393	.278	.318	-5.5	1B(149): 5.0	1.5
2013	*SDN*	*MLB*	*26*	*508*	*54*	*26*	*2*	*11*	*56*	*47*	*92*	*5*	*2*	*.265/.334/.404*	*.269*	*.308*	*-0.4*	*1B -6, LF -1*	*0.3*

Alonso came to San Diego in the December 2011 trade that sent Mat Latos to the Reds. The stocky, slow-footed native of Cuba features a smooth swing that doesn't generate much loft. He has never hit more than 17 homers in any professional season but has good knowledge of the strike zone and used Petco Park's large power alleys to maximum advantage, hitting 23 doubles there last year. He is a liability on the bases, and his glove work isn't great, although he improved as the season progressed. Alonso would be a perennial threat to hit .300 if not for a complete absence of foot speed. He profiles as a useful but not exciting cog in the mold of Lyle Overbay.

Alexi Amarista UT

Born: **4/6/1989** Age: **24**
Bats: **L** Throws: **R** Height: **5' 9"**
Weight: **150** Breakout: **2%**
Improve: **36%** Collapse: **10%**
Attrition: **13%** MLB: **89%**

Comparables:
Felix Millan,William Bergolla,Joaquin Arias

YEAR	TEAM	LVL	AGE	PA	R	2B	3B	HR	RBI	BB	SO	SB	CS	AVG_OBP_SLG	TAv	BABIP	BRR	FRAA	WARP
2010	RCU	A+	21	323	39	19	6	4	39	19	42	17	10	.303/.349/.448	.300	.340	-3.1	2B(68): 9.5	3.1
2010	ARK	AA	21	213	25	2	1	1	20	13	15	4	1	.288/.337/.325	.256	.305	1.3	2B(45): 0.2	0.7
2010	SLC	AAA	21	70	13	6	3	0	9	1	4	4	2	.400/.406/.585	.336	.413	0.2	2B(15): -0.4, SS(1): -0.0	0.6
2011	SLC	AAA	22	396	49	24	5	4	50	22	56	15	8	.292/.337/.419	.265	.333	-2	2B(36): 8.7, CF(16): -0.9	1.0
2011	ANA	MLB	22	56	2	3	1	0	5	2	8	0	0	.154/.182/.250	.168	.178	-1.2	2B(14): -1.0, LF(8): 0.0	-0.7
2012	SLC	AAA	23	83	11	6	2	0	12	3	6	1	0	.273/.289/.403	.227	.284	0.9	2B(8): -0.3, 3B(6): 1.0	-0.1
2012	TUC	AAA	23	51	6	1	0	1	6	1	6	3	0	.286/.300/.367	.260	.310	0.3	2B(2): -0.2	0.0
2012	ANA	MLB	23	0	1	0	0	0	0	0	0	0	0	--	—	.000	-0.2	--	0.0
2012	SDN	MLB	23	300	35	15	5	5	32	17	42	8	4	.240/.282/.385	.246	.265	2.8	2B(51): -3.3, LF(27): 0.7	0.1
2013	*SDN*	*MLB*	*24*	*289*	*30*	*13*	*3*	*3*	*21*	*13*	*44*	*8*	*3*	*.242/.278/.344*	*.231*	*.275*	*0.4*	*2B 1, SS 0*	*0.2*

Amarista was acquired in May as part of a trade that sent Ernesto Frieri to the Angels. The diminutive Venezuelan played six different positions, spending most of his time at second base. Amarista is an impatient hitter who makes contact and occasionally hits a ball farther than you think he should, although the power comes in streaks—four of his five homers came in the span of 12 plate appearances. He is a decent defender, has some usable speed, and profiles as a utility player.

John Baker C

Born: **1/20/1981** Age: **32**
Bats: **L** Throws: **R** Height: **6' 2"**
Weight: **220** Breakout: **1%**
Improve: **38%** Collapse: **12%**
Attrition: **11%** MLB: **87%**

Comparables:
Johnny Roseboro,Miguel Ojeda,Bob Brenly

YEAR	TEAM	LVL	AGE	PA	R	2B	3B	HR	RBI	BB	SO	SB	CS	AVG_OBP_SLG	TAv	BABIP	BRR	FRAA	WARP
2010	FLO	MLB	29	88	7	3	1	0	6	9	18	0	0	.218/.307/.282	.215	.283	1.2	C(21): -0.5	0.0
2011	FLO	MLB	30	16	0	0	0	0	1	2	3	0	0	.154/.267/.154	.173	.200	0	C(1): -0.0	-0.1
2012	SDN	MLB	31	214	17	8	0	0	14	20	41	2	1	.238/.310/.280	.229	.303	-1.9	C(56): 0.4	-0.5
2013	*SDN*	*MLB*	*32*	*250*	*25*	*11*	*1*	*4*	*23*	*25*	*52*	*1*	*0*	*.246/.326/.352*	*.253*	*.304*	*-0.4*	*C 0*	*0.9*

The good news is that Baker, who missed much of the previous two seasons with elbow issues that required Tommy John surgery in September 2010, stayed healthy all year. The bad news is that whatever offensive game he once possessed went MIA. His OPS over the last three years is 582, and he hasn't homered in a big-league game since September 4, 2009. Baker's defense behind the plate wasn't much better. That leaves "CHiPs" jokes and . . . well, just "CHiPs" jokes.

Kyle Blanks LF

Born: **9/11/1986** Age: **26**
Bats: **R** Throws: **R** Height: **6' 7"**
Weight: **270** Breakout: **5%**
Improve: **46%** Collapse: **6%**
Attrition: **15%** MLB: **98%**

Comparables:
Boog Powell,Brandon Allen,Bob Robertson

YEAR	TEAM	LVL	AGE	PA	R	2B	3B	HR	RBI	BB	SO	SB	CS	AVG_OBP_SLG	TAv	BABIP	BRR	FRAA	WARP
2010	SDN	MLB	23	120	14	6	1	3	15	15	46	1	0	.157/.283/.324	.239	.245	1.7	LF(30): -0.8, 1B(4): 0.1	0.0
2011	SAN	AA	24	201	33	16	3	4	27	17	41	3	0	.282/.353/.475	.294	.341	0.1	1B(14): 1.4, LF(1): 0.2	0.5
2011	TUC	AAA	24	152	36	12	2	11	35	16	37	0	1	.351/.421/.716	.307	.414	-0.4	1B(15): -0.6, LF(5): -0.1	0.3
2011	SDN	MLB	24	190	21	7	1	7	26	16	51	2	0	.229/.300/.406	.269	.281	0.5	LF(37): -0.3, 1B(13): 0.0	0.6
2012	SDN	MLB	25	6	0	0	0	0	0	1	2	0	0	.200/.333/.200	.237	.333	-0.2	LF(1): -0.0, 1B(1): -0.0	0.0
2013	*SDN*	*MLB*	*26*	*250*	*29*	*10*	*1*	*9*	*32*	*25*	*73*	*1*	*0*	*.230/.320/.410*	*.271*	*.299*	*-0.1*	*LF 0, 1B -2*	*0.5*

Blanks' explosive 2009 debut is a distant memory obscured by his inability to make consistent contact or stay healthy. April surgery to repair the labrum in his left (non-throwing) shoulder wrecked his 2012. When healthy, Blanks possesses power that plays anywhere. He is a first baseman who is athletic enough to patrol the outfield. At an age when he should be refining his game and gaining experience, Blanks is watching from the sidelines. His is a potential impact bat, but at some point the injuries could take their toll and remove that potential. The window is closing, if it hasn't closed already.

Everth Cabrera SS

Born: **11/17/1986** Age: **26**
Bats: **B** Throws: **R** Height: **5' 11"**
Weight: **175** Breakout: **5%**
Improve: **50%** Collapse: **8%**
Attrition: **27%** MLB: **92%**

Comparables:
Ivan Ochoa,Phil Linz,Brent Lillibridge

YEAR	TEAM	LVL	AGE	PA	R	2B	3B	HR	RBI	BB	SO	SB	CS	AVG_OBP_SLG	TAv	BABIP	BRR	FRAA	WARP
2010	SDN	MLB	23	241	22	6	3	1	22	19	54	10	6	.208/.279/.278	.200	.274	0.7	SS(61): -1.3, 2B(6): 0.1	-0.7
2011	TUC	AAA	24	278	52	12	4	2	15	29	40	29	8	.297/.370/.402	.272	.346	2.1	SS(41): 4.2	1.4
2011	SDN	MLB	24	9	1	0	0	0	0	1	3	2	0	.125/.222/.125	.318	.200	0.2	SS(2): 0.0	0.1
2012	TUC	AAA	25	159	27	9	1	0	15	12	28	15	0	.333/.389/.410	.275	.414	3.2	SS(14): -2.7, 3B(5): 0.1	0.7
2012	SDN	MLB	25	449	49	19	3	2	24	43	110	44	4	.246/.324/.324	.250	.336	6.2	SS(111): 6.1, 2B(6): -0.1	2.5
2013	*SDN*	*MLB*	*26*	*382*	*49*	*15*	*4*	*3*	*25*	*35*	*85*	*30*	*6*	*.245/.320/.335*	*.246*	*.311*	*3.9*	*SS 2, 2B 0*	*1.8*

The Padres took Cabrera from Colorado in the 2008 Rule 5 draft, and the speedy Nicaraguan enjoyed a fine rookie campaign despite jumping from Low-A ball. After two disappointing seasons, he resurfaced last May to replace the injured Jason Bartlett and helped revitalize a sluggish Padres offense. Cabrera's inability to consistently make contact and reach base limits his effectiveness at the top of a lineup. Still, despite spending the first six weeks at Triple-A, he led the National League in steals. The most memorable came on July 14, when he swiped home to tie the game with the Padres down to their final strike at Dodger Stadium while Kanley Jensen strolled behind the mound to collect his thoughts.

James Darnell **4C**

Born: **1/19/1987** Age: **26**
Bats: **R** Throws: **R** Height: **6' 3"**
Weight: **195** Breakout: **0%**
Improve: **52%** Collapse: **2%**
Attrition: **8%** MLB: **97%**

Comparables:
Puddin Head Jones,Chipper Jones,Jim Lefebvre

YEAR	TEAM	LVL	AGE	PA	R	2B	3B	HR	RBI	BB	SO	SB	CS	AVG_OBP_SLG	TAv	BABIP	BRR	FRAA	WARP
2010	SAN	AA	23	426	46	21	1	10	50	44	64	2	0	.265/.350/.408	.292	.297	-3	3B(95): -6.4	1.7
2011	SAN	AA	24	346	62	25	1	17	62	52	48	2	1	.333/.434/.604	.342	.348	-0.5	3B(36): -6.4	1.1
2011	TUC	AAA	24	155	20	4	0	6	17	16	30	0	0	.261/.344/.425	.249	.290	-1.6	3B(13): -1.5, LF(10): -0.8	-0.5
2011	SDN	MLB	24	52	2	2	0	1	7	5	7	1	0	.222/.294/.333	.195	.237	0.3	3B(12): -1.1, LF(3): 0.0	-0.3
2012	TUC	AAA	25	137	22	6	0	7	21	16	25	1	1	.267/.365/.500	.283	.279	-0.9	3B(18): 1.1, LF(8): -0.1	0.4
2012	SDN	MLB	25	19	1	1	0	1	1	2	2	0	0	.235/.316/.471	.239	.214	0	LF(4): -0.3, 3B(1): -0.1	0.0
2013	*SDN*	*MLB*	*26*	*250*	*27*	*11*	*1*	*7*	*30*	*25*	*49*	*1*	*0*	*.241/.323/.397*	*.266*	*.276*	*-0.3*	*3B -1, LF -0*	*0.6*

Taken in the second round of the 2008 draft, Darnell has hit at every level. Finding him a defensive home and keeping him healthy have been trickier. His natural position is third base, but he wasn't great with the glove and was blocked by Chase Headley, so he shifted to the outfield. Once there, Darnell injured his left (non-throwing) shoulder in his seventh game of the season while diving for a ball. The injury kept him out of action for the remainder of 2012, requiring surgery toward the end of August. Darnell's right-handed power will play in any ballpark, but time is not on his side.

Jaff Decker **OF**

Born: **2/23/1990** Age: **23**
Bats: **L** Throws: **L** Height: **5' 11"**
Weight: **190** Breakout: **6%**
Improve: **59%** Collapse: **6%**
Attrition: **10%** MLB: **94%**

Comparables:
Joe Lahoud,Jeremy Hermida,Austin Kearns

YEAR	TEAM	LVL	AGE	PA	R	2B	3B	HR	RBI	BB	SO	SB	CS	AVG_OBP_SLG	TAv	BABIP	BRR	FRAA	WARP
2010	LEL	A+	20	348	53	14	2	17	58	47	80	5	4	.262/.378/.500	.320	.306	-0.3	LF(77): 5.4, RF(1): -0.1	3.3
2011	SAN	AA	21	613	90	29	2	19	92	103	145	15	5	.236/.373/.417	.290	.291	-2	LF(64): 0.5, CF(2): 0.2	1.1
2012	SAN	AA	22	190	30	3	2	3	9	40	37	6	2	.184/.365/.293	.278	.224	-1.8	RF(32): 0.1, CF(5): -0.2	0.4
2013	*SDN*	*MLB*	*23*	*250*	*29*	*9*	*1*	*7*	*29*	*31*	*62*	*4*	*1*	*.217/.321/.376*	*.258*	*.265*	*0.1*	*LF -2, RF 0*	*0.4*

For the second time in three years, Decker missed a good chunk of the season due to injury. He hurt his foot at the end of May and missed six weeks. After returning for a handful of rookie-league games, he was shut down for good at the end of July. When he is right, Decker possesses a discriminating batting eye (too discriminating, according to some) and home-run power. The latter never appeared last year, perhaps because of the foot injury. He is an adequate corner outfielder whose future depends on his bat. If the power returns, he could have a career.

Chris Denorfia **OF**

Born: **7/15/1980** Age: **32**
Bats: **R** Throws: **R** Height: **6' 1"**
Weight: **195** Breakout: **1%**
Improve: **40%** Collapse: **8%**
Attrition: **15%** MLB: **92%**

Comparables:
Tito Francona,Carl Furillo,Juan Encarnacion

YEAR	TEAM	LVL	AGE	PA	R	2B	3B	HR	RBI	BB	SO	SB	CS	AVG_OBP_SLG	TAv	BABIP	BRR	FRAA	WARP
2010	POR	AAA	29	134	17	10	4	2	12	12	18	7	1	.306/.366/.504	.328	.343	0.4	LF(15): -0.6, RF(12): 1.6	1.5
2010	SDN	MLB	29	317	41	15	2	9	36	27	51	8	4	.271/.335/.433	.287	.300	1.9	CF(50): 1.8, LF(44): 0.1	2.4
2011	SDN	MLB	30	340	38	13	2	5	19	28	49	11	6	.277/.337/.381	.260	.314	0.7	RF(62): 0.8, LF(33): 0.3	0.5
2012	SDN	MLB	31	382	56	19	6	8	36	27	52	13	5	.293/.345/.451	.291	.323	2.8	RF(79): -4.7, LF(52): 0.8	1.7
2013	*SDN*	*MLB*	*32*	*351*	*43*	*16*	*3*	*6*	*32*	*24*	*56*	*10*	*4*	*.267/.320/.394*	*.263*	*.303*	*0.4*	*RF -0, LF -0*	*1.0*

Denorfia has overcome injuries that derailed the early portion of his career to become, in his 30s, a productive fourth outfielder/right-handed half of a platoon (his OPS is more than 230 points higher against lefties over the last two years). Once capable of playing all three outfield spots, he now stays on the corners except in emergencies. His defense has slipped even in the less demanding spots. Denorfia doesn't have blazing speed but is a heady baserunner who excelled at advancing on grounders in 2012. He is the ultimate role player. Earl Weaver would have loved him.

Logan Forsythe **2B**

Born: **1/14/1987** Age: **26**
Bats: **R** Throws: **R** Height: **6' 2"**
Weight: **205** Breakout: **5%**
Improve: **50%** Collapse: **1%**
Attrition: **16%** MLB: **93%**

Comparables:
Luis Valbuena,Bill Doran,Roberto Alomar

YEAR	TEAM	LVL	AGE	PA	R	2B	3B	HR	RBI	BB	SO	SB	CS	AVG_OBP_SLG	TAv	BABIP	BRR	FRAA	WARP
2010	SAN	AA	23	472	66	22	1	3	38	75	95	17	5	.253/.378/.337	.284	.327	1.3	2B(98): -5.0, 3B(2): 0.2	2.2
2011	TUC	AAA	24	218	41	12	0	8	34	33	50	8	4	.326/.445/.528	.330	.413	2.1	2B(19): -1.9, 3B(11): -0.4	1.2
2011	SDN	MLB	24	169	12	9	1	0	12	12	33	3	1	.213/.281/.287	.219	.269	0.7	3B(26): 1.4, 2B(23): -2.2	-0.5
2012	TUC	AAA	25	74	12	2	3	1	9	13	18	3	0	.259/.419/.448	.309	.359	-0.3	SS(5): 0.6, 3B(5): 0.1	0.6
2012	SDN	MLB	25	350	45	13	3	6	26	28	57	8	2	.273/.343/.390	.275	.316	0	2B(81): -3.4, SS(5): 0.1	0.8
2013	*SDN*	*MLB*	*26*	*322*	*33*	*14*	*2*	*5*	*30*	*31*	*67*	*7*	*2*	*.245/.329/.355*	*.258*	*.302*	*0.4*	*2B -2, 3B -0*	*0.9*

Forsythe, a supplemental first-round pick of the Padres in 2008, has good on-base skills and can play any infield position. A third baseman by trade, he has spent most of his big-league tenure at second, where he is less comfortable but adequate. He can be used at shortstop in a pinch but is exposed if left there for long. Surgery last March to repair a fractured sesamoid bone in his left foot kept him out until June. Once healthy, Forsythe hit much better at home than on the road, which, given Petco Park's reputation, is probably a small-sample fluke. He also gained 400 OPS points against left-handed pitchers. That and his versatility make Forsythe a useful role player.

Reymond Fuentes CF

Born: 2/12/1991 Age: 22
Bats: L Throws: L Height: 6' 1"
Weight: 160 Breakout: 10%
Improve: 57% Collapse: 5%
Attrition: 17% MLB: 95%

Comparables:
Thad Bosley,Bobby Tolan,Gary Geiger

YEAR	TEAM	LVL	AGE	PA	R	2B	3B	HR	RBI	BB	SO	SB	CS	AVG_OBP_SLG	TAv	BABIP	BRR	FRAA	WARP
2010	GRN	A	19	414	59	15	5	5	41	25	87	42	5	.270/.325/.377	.247	.334	1.3	CF(102): 1.2	0.6
2011	LEL	A+	20	573	84	15	9	5	45	44	117	41	14	.275/.342/.369	.255	.347	0	--	0.0
2012	SAN	AA	21	541	53	20	4	4	34	52	133	35	9	.218/.301/.302	.235	.292	3.2	CF(100): 8.1	1.0
2013	*SDN*	*MLB*	*22*	*250*	*27*	*8*	*2*	*2*	*15*	*16*	*70*	*12*	*2*	*.200/.256/.279*	*.202*	*.271*	*1.7*	*CF -3*	*-0.8*

Acquired in the December 2010 trade that sent Adrian Gonzalez to Boston, Fuentes needed a late surge to push his OBP and SLG north of .300. He is a gifted athlete with good bloodlines (Carlos Beltran is his cousin) but struggles to make contact and has no usable power. On the plus side, Fuentes has started to draw more walks and last year improved his base-stealing efficiency. The athleticism is real and he was young for his league, but right now he looks like a future fourth or fifth outfielder.

Jonathan Galvez 2B

Born: 1/18/1991 Age: 22
Bats: R Throws: R Height: 6' 3"
Weight: 175 Breakout: 8%
Improve: 57% Collapse: 3%
Attrition: 12% MLB: 96%

Comparables:
Ruben Gotay,Delino DeShields,Rod Carew

YEAR	TEAM	LVL	AGE	PA	R	2B	3B	HR	RBI	BB	SO	SB	CS	AVG_OBP_SLG	TAv	BABIP	BRR	FRAA	WARP
2010	FTW	A	19	466	64	19	3	10	49	58	121	18	7	.259/.360/.397	.270	.346	1.5	SS(106): -6.7, 2B(6): -0.6	1.9
2011	LEL	A+	20	545	84	36	5	13	86	41	123	37	9	.291/.355/.465	.283	.361	0	--	0.0
2012	SAN	AA	21	350	47	20	2	6	35	31	70	12	3	.292/.364/.426	.285	.359	-0.6	2B(52): 10.3, LF(3): 0.4	2.0
2013	*SDN*	*MLB*	*22*	*250*	*24*	*10*	*1*	*4*	*22*	*19*	*70*	*4*	*1*	*.218/.282/.325*	*.228*	*.292*	*0.1*	*2B 1, SS -0*	*0.3*

Galvez has hit at every level and possesses good power for a middle infielder. He runs well but is a poor defender who moved from shortstop to second base in 2011 and whose glove might not be good enough to stick there. Galvez spent last year as one of the Texas League's younger players. He didn't make his season debut until mid-May after spraining his right ankle in spring training, and he also missed a handful of games in June with a right hamstring injury. If he stays on the infield, his bat could carry him to the big leagues in a support role.

Yasmani Grandal C

Born: 11/8/1988 Age: 24
Bats: B Throws: R Height: 6' 3"
Weight: 205 Breakout: 5%
Improve: 39% Collapse: 10%
Attrition: 13% MLB: 98%

Comparables:
Ed Herrmann,Matt Wieters,Chris Iannetta

YEAR	TEAM	LVL	AGE	PA	R	2B	3B	HR	RBI	BB	SO	SB	CS	AVG_OBP_SLG	TAv	BABIP	BRR	FRAA	WARP
2011	BAK	A+	22	251	47	14	0	10	40	41	57	0	0	.296/.410/.510	.318	.359	-0.6	C(28): 0.1	1.6
2011	CAR	AA	22	172	20	15	0	4	26	13	39	0	1	.301/.360/.474	.288	.377	0	--	0.0
2012	TUC	AAA	23	235	40	18	0	6	35	37	35	0	0	.335/.443/.521	.321	.381	1	C(34): -0.8	1.7
2012	SDN	MLB	23	226	28	7	1	8	36	31	39	0	0	.297/.394/.469	.321	.333	-3.2	C(55): 0.3	1.8
2013	*SDN*	*MLB*	*24*	*250*	*29*	*11*	*1*	*7*	*31*	*31*	*50*	*0*	*0*	*.265/.360/.426*	*.288*	*.312*	*-0.3*	*C -0*	*1.8*

Acquired in the Latos trade, Grandal saw his timetable accelerated thanks to Nick Hundley's balky knee. The native of Cuba flashed power from both sides of the plate and exhibited a strong understanding of the strike zone for someone who had never faced big-league pitching. Behind the dish Grandal remains a work in progress, although he improved with experience. Now that the league knows who he is, the game of adjustments and counter-adjustments begins. Grandal's offense might slip some as a sophomore, but assuming he continues to develop offensively and defensively, the long-term outlook is bright. He is a first-division starting catcher in the making. A positive test for elevated testosterone levels will keep Grandal out of action until the end of May.

Jesus Guzman 4C

Born: 6/14/1984 Age: 29
Bats: R Throws: R Height: 6' 2"
Weight: 215 Breakout: 4%
Improve: 38% Collapse: 1%
Attrition: 7% MLB: 92%

Comparables:
Del Ennis,Moises Alou,Bob Watson

YEAR	TEAM	LVL	AGE	PA	R	2B	3B	HR	RBI	BB	SO	SB	CS	AVG_OBP_SLG	TAv	BABIP	BRR	FRAA	WARP
2010	FRE	AAA	26	492	66	28	1	18	72	38	68	6	4	.321/.376/.510	.301	.345	-0.8	3B(61): -4.6, LF(36): -1.2	2.4
2011	TUC	AAA	27	286	40	22	1	8	57	34	42	4	4	.332/.423/.529	.307	.374	-2.5	3B(31): -0.3, 1B(6): 0.1	1.0
2011	SDN	MLB	27	271	33	22	2	5	44	22	43	9	2	.312/.369/.478	.315	.360	2.2	1B(53): 1.3, LF(6): 0.4	1.8
2012	SDN	MLB	28	321	32	18	2	9	48	29	71	3	3	.247/.319/.418	.279	.297	0.8	LF(52): 1.0, 1B(19): 0.9	1.3
2013	*SDN*	*MLB*	*29*	*317*	*34*	*17*	*2*	*8*	*36*	*24*	*62*	*4*	*2*	*.268/.329/.417*	*.272*	*.315*	*-0.4*	*LF -0, 1B -2*	*0.7*

Guzman, a minor-league veteran given the opportunity to play in 2011, unsurprisingly saw his production drop in the encore but still proved useful. An indifferent defender, he has line-drive power that plays especially well against left-handers, against whom his career OPS is 200 points higher than against righties. Guzman has been immune to Petco Park, having hit better at home than on the road since joining the Padres. A capable fourth outfielder who can play the infield in a pinch, he should continue to produce at or near last season's levels for the next few years.

Jedd Gyorko 3B

Born: **9/23/1988** Age: **24**
Bats: **R** Throws: **R** Height: **5' 11"**
Weight: **195** Breakout: **5%**
Improve: **64%** Collapse: **5%**
Attrition: **9%** MLB: **97%**

Comparables:
Hank Blalock,Jim Ray Hart,Eric Chavez

YEAR	TEAM	LVL	AGE	PA	R	2B	3B	HR	RBI	BB	SO	SB	CS	AVG_OBP_SLG	TAv	BABIP	BRR	FRAA	WARP
2010	FTW	A	21	183	19	11	0	2	23	19	31	1	0	.284/.366/.389	.271	.341	-1.1	3B(27): 1.2, 2B(1): -0.1	0.5
2010	EUG	A-	21	115	16	6	0	5	18	9	26	1	1	.330/.383/.528	.356	.400	-0.8	3B(26): -1.1	1.5
2011	LEL	A+	22	382	78	35	2	18	74	38	64	11	3	.365/.429/.638	.358	.408	0	--	0.0
2011	SAN	AA	22	265	41	12	0	7	40	26	50	1	0	.288/.358/.428	.251	.337	0.8	3B(35): 0.5	0.5
2012	SAN	AA	23	149	18	4	0	6	17	17	27	1	1	.262/.356/.431	.241	.289	0.3	3B(16): 0.3, 2B(10): -0.9	0.0
2012	TUC	AAA	23	408	62	24	0	24	83	34	68	4	3	.328/.380/.588	.329	.344	-0.3	3B(46): 0.3, 2B(24): 4.1	3.7
2013	*SDN*	*MLB*	*24*	*250*	*27*	*10*	*1*	*9*	*32*	*18*	*57*	*1*	*0*	*.245/.303/.409*	*.261*	*.288*	*-0.4*	*3B 1, 2B 0*	*0.8*

Taken in the second round of the 2010 draft out of West Virginia, Gyorko is a pure hitter who combines an advanced understanding of the strike zone with line-drive power to all fields. He will knock a few home runs, though probably not as many as he did last year in the hitter-friendly PCL. With Chase Headley blocking his path to third base in San Diego, the Padres had Gyorko play some second base in 2012 with an eye toward getting his bat into the lineup sooner rather than later. He has a thick body and won't be a great defender at any position, but if he holds his own at the keystone corner and maintains his offensive skills, he could be an impact player starting now.

Chase Headley 3B

Born: **5/9/1984** Age: **29**
Bats: **B** Throws: **R** Height: **6' 3"**
Weight: **200** Breakout: **1%**
Improve: **44%** Collapse: **2%**
Attrition: **20%** MLB: **94%**

Comparables:
Eric Chavez,Rico Petrocelli,Jim Ray Hart

YEAR	TEAM	LVL	AGE	PA	R	2B	3B	HR	RBI	BB	SO	SB	CS	AVG_OBP_SLG	TAv	BABIP	BRR	FRAA	WARP
2010	SDN	MLB	26	674	77	29	3	11	58	56	139	17	5	.264/.327/.375	.266	.323	3.5	3B(158): 0.2	3.4
2011	SDN	MLB	27	439	43	28	1	4	44	52	92	13	2	.289/.374/.399	.288	.368	0.3	3B(107): -9.0	1.3
2012	SDN	MLB	28	699	95	31	2	31	115	86	157	17	6	.286/.376/.498	.324	.337	-2.4	3B(159): -7.3, 1B(1): -0.0	5.3
2013	*SDN*	*MLB*	*29*	*605*	*71*	*30*	*2*	*15*	*70*	*59*	*137*	*13*	*4*	*.268/.343/.418*	*.279*	*.330*	*0.4*	*3B 2, 1B 0*	*2.9*

With the help of new hitting coach Phil Plantier, Headley altered his mechanics to "generate more pull-side loft," according to MLB.com beat writer Corey Brock, and it paid off. Headley went from on-base machine to multi-dimensional offensive dynamo, especially in the second half. Petco Park continued to cut into his production, but to a much lesser degree than in the past. Headley plays a better third base than FRAA indicates and generally is a smart baserunner, although he got thrown out on the bases more than usual last year. Even with some expected slippage in power, 20–25 homers is a more reasonable baseline than the previously established 10–15. Headley is in his prime and is one of the best third basemen in baseball.

Austin Hedges C

Born: **8/18/1992** Age: **20**
Bats: **R** Throws: **R** Height: **6' 2"**
Weight: **190** Breakout: **18%**
Improve: **58%** Collapse: **4%**
Attrition: **16%** MLB: **89%**

Comparables:
Ivan Rodriguez,Ed Kranepool,Claudell Washington

YEAR	TEAM	LVL	AGE	PA	R	2B	3B	HR	RBI	BB	SO	SB	CS	AVG_OBP_SLG	TAv	BABIP	BRR	FRAA	WARP
2012	FTW	A	19	373	44	28	0	10	56	23	62	14	9	.279/.334/.451	.294	.312	-1.1	C(61): 0.6	2.0
2013	*SDN*	*MLB*	*20*	*250*	*24*	*10*	*1*	*6*	*25*	*11*	*62*	*5*	*3*	*.219/.260/.340*	*.223*	*.269*	*-0.2*	*C -0*	*0.2*

The Padres picked Hedges in the second round of the 2011 draft on the strength of defensive skills that are advanced beyond his age and experience. After being signed away from a commitment to UCLA, he added a surprisingly potent bat to his arsenal. If he keeps hitting like he did in his full-season debut at Fort Wayne, Hedges could advance more quickly than the typical high school catcher. His glove, arm, and ability to handle pitchers will get him to the big leagues and possibly keep him there for a long time. Anything he does at the plate is a bonus, but the early returns are promising.

Nick Hundley C

Born: **9/8/1983** Age: **29**
Bats: **R** Throws: **R** Height: **6' 2"**
Weight: **205** Breakout: **1%**
Improve: **35%** Collapse: **10%**
Attrition: **13%** MLB: **98%**

Comparables:
Eliezer Alfonzo,Gene Green,Mike Macfarlane

YEAR	TEAM	LVL	AGE	PA	R	2B	3B	HR	RBI	BB	SO	SB	CS	AVG_OBP_SLG	TAv	BABIP	BRR	FRAA	WARP
2010	SDN	MLB	26	307	33	18	2	8	43	25	66	0	5	.249/.308/.418	.274	.293	-5.6	C(76): -0.9	1.2
2011	SDN	MLB	27	308	34	16	5	9	29	22	74	1	1	.288/.347/.477	.305	.362	-0.1	C(76): -0.1	2.9
2012	SDN	MLB	28	225	14	7	1	3	22	15	56	0	3	.157/.219/.245	.174	.196	0.3	C(56): 1.7	-0.8
2013	*SDN*	*MLB*	*29*	*250*	*25*	*11*	*2*	*6*	*28*	*18*	*60*	*1*	*2*	*.233/.291/.382*	*.247*	*.284*	*-0.6*	*C 0*	*0.8*

Coming off a breakout 2011, Hundley signed a three-year extension in March. He then spent the season battling right-knee problems that destroyed his game and eventually required season-ending surgery in August to repair a torn meniscus. When healthy, Hundley generates power from the right side and isn't intimidated by Petco Park (two-thirds of his 33 career homers have come there). He has improved his defense and works well with pitchers. Making contact and getting on base are not part of his skill set, but the rest of his game is strong enough that he should start somewhere for a few years, assuming his knee is okay. With Grandal's suspension, Hundley's shot at redemption could come sooner rather than later.

Mark Kotsay **OF**

Born: **12/2/1975** Age: **37**
Bats: **L** Throws: **L** Height: **6' 1"**
Weight: **210** Breakout: **1%**
Improve: **35%** Collapse: **7%**
Attrition: **22%** MLB: **78%**

Comparables:
Moises Alou,Orlando Palmeiro,Jesus Alou

YEAR	TEAM	LVL	AGE	PA	R	2B	3B	HR	RBI	BB	SO	SB	CS	AVG_OBP_SLG	TAv	BABIP	BRR	FRAA	WARP
2010	CHA	MLB	34	359	30	17	2	8	31	32	36	1	3	.239/.306/.376	.238	.247	-4.1	1B(38): -1.1, RF(8): -0.6	-0.9
2011	MIL	MLB	35	255	18	13	1	3	31	21	27	3	0	.270/.329/.373	.256	.294	-0.8	RF(29): -1.0, LF(19): -1.7	-0.3
2012	SDN	MLB	36	156	9	8	0	2	14	11	14	0	2	.259/.314/.357	.250	.273	-0.1	LF(19): 0.7, RF(9): -0.1	0.2
2013	*SDN*	*MLB*	*37*	*250*	*22*	*11*	*1*	*3*	*23*	*18*	*30*	*2*	*1*	*.247/.301/.345*	*.240*	*.272*	*-0.4*	*RF 0, LF -0*	*0.0*

During Kotsay's first tenure with the Padres, he would have been a perfect fit for Petco Park. Unfortunately, he was traded just before the club moved downtown. Kotsay is cited as a positive influence on younger players, which counts for something, but he has been the living embodiment of "replacement level" for the last seven years. That isn't likely to change now, and if it does, at this stage in his career it won't be for the better.

Rymer Liriano **RF**

Born: **6/20/1991** Age: **22**
Bats: **R** Throws: **R** Height: **6' 1"**
Weight: **211** Breakout: **5%**
Improve: **54%** Collapse: **3%**
Attrition: **12%** MLB: **92%**

Comparables:
Sixto Lezcano,Faye Throneberry,Gus Bell

YEAR	TEAM	LVL	AGE	PA	R	2B	3B	HR	RBI	BB	SO	SB	CS	AVG_OBP_SLG	TAv	BABIP	BRR	FRAA	WARP
2010	FTW	A	19	201	21	11	1	2	20	10	54	11	6	.191/.236/.293	.201	.258	0.2	RF(37): -0.7, CF(13): 1.6	-0.6
2010	EUG	A-	19	225	35	13	6	0	12	17	53	17	7	.271/.335/.394	.279	.364	0.6	RF(36): 1.8, CF(16): -1.2	1.3
2010	LEL	A+	19	55	3	2	0	1	6	5	12	3	0	.220/.291/.320	.255	.270	0.1	RF(13): -0.2	0.0
2011	FTW	A	20	519	81	30	8	12	62	47	95	65	20	.319/.383/.499	.342	.373	-0.1	RF(30): -2.9, CF(5): 0.1	1.4
2011	LEL	A+	20	61	8	1	1	0	6	6	13	1	1	.127/.213/.182	.149	.167	0	--	0.0
2012	LEL	A+	21	314	41	22	2	5	41	21	69	22	7	.298/.360/.443	.237	.374	-1.5	RF(18): -0.5	-0.4
2012	SAN	AA	21	206	24	10	2	3	20	20	50	10	1	.251/.335/.377	.241	.331	1.9	RF(40): 1.6, CF(5): -0.2	0.3
2013	*SDN*	*MLB*	*22*	*250*	*27*	*11*	*2*	*3*	*20*	*12*	*71*	*14*	*5*	*.216/.259/.317*	*.215*	*.291*	*1.4*	*RF -2, CF -0*	*-0.6*

Scouts drool over Liriano's power potential, which isn't reflected in his actual output to date. He is learning to use his natural strength and to look for pitches to drive, but it has been a slow process. Liriano runs well and possesses a right fielder's arm. He showed flashes in the Arizona Fall League, where one veteran observer identified Liriano as having the circuit's best pure power. The next step is translating his batting-practice exploits into something that can impact games over the course of a season. When that happens, he could be a force in the heart of the order for a long time.

Cameron Maybin **CF**

Born: **4/4/1987** Age: **26**
Bats: **R** Throws: **R** Height: **6' 4"**
Weight: **210** Breakout: **1%**
Improve: **56%** Collapse: **7%**
Attrition: **17%** MLB: **93%**

Comparables:
Rocco Baldelli,Lloyd Moseby,Ellis Burks

YEAR	TEAM	LVL	AGE	PA	R	2B	3B	HR	RBI	BB	SO	SB	CS	AVG_OBP_SLG	TAv	BABIP	BRR	FRAA	WARP
2010	NWO	AAA	23	147	21	6	2	4	23	13	24	5	1	.338/.401/.508	.305	.385	2.4	CF(30): 2.9	1.6
2010	FLO	MLB	23	322	46	7	3	8	28	24	92	9	2	.234/.302/.361	.242	.312	2.9	CF(77): 7.2	1.4
2011	SDN	MLB	24	568	82	24	8	9	40	44	125	40	8	.264/.323/.393	.266	.331	7.2	CF(136): 7.5	2.8
2012	SDN	MLB	25	561	67	20	5	8	45	44	110	26	7	.243/.306/.349	.255	.293	2.9	CF(145): 3.4	1.2
2013	*SDN*	*MLB*	*26*	*530*	*67*	*20*	*5*	*10*	*46*	*43*	*124*	*22*	*6*	*.252/.317/.380*	*.259*	*.317*	*2.5*	*CF 1*	*2.0*

After a breakout campaign in 2011, Maybin slipped last year. He signed a five-year extension in March and hit a mammoth home run on Opening Day, then went dormant for three months. After the All-Star break, he cut down his strikeouts and added 70 points to his batting average. He hit much better at Petco Park than away from it, opposite of his split the previous season, suggesting a fluke. An excellent defensive center fielder who is fast and smart on the bases, Maybin is still young and learning his capabilities at the big-league level. He may never become the impact player once envisioned, but he is a solid all-around ballplayer best suited to the bottom of a lineup.

Jace Peterson **SS**

Born: **5/9/1990** Age: **23**
Bats: **L** Throws: **R** Height: **6' 1"**
Weight: **200** Breakout: **4%**
Improve: **42%** Collapse: **11%**
Attrition: **17%** MLB: **88%**

Comparables:
Alan Trammell,Toby Harrah,Kurt Stillwell

YEAR	TEAM	LVL	AGE	PA	R	2B	3B	HR	RBI	BB	SO	SB	CS	AVG_OBP_SLG	TAv	BABIP	BRR	FRAA	WARP
2011	EUG	A-	21	333	48	9	5	2	27	50	53	39	10	.243/.360/.333	.300	.290	3.7	SS(60): -1.9	2.3
2012	FTW	A	22	521	78	23	9	2	48	62	63	51	13	.286/.378/.392	.271	.328	6.6	SS(68): -1.3	1.6
2013	*SDN*	*MLB*	*23*	*250*	*30*	*8*	*2*	*1*	*14*	*22*	*53*	*16*	*5*	*.219/.290/.294*	*.221*	*.273*	*1.6*	*SS -2*	*0.0*

Peterson, taken 58th overall in 2011 out of McNeese State as compensation for losing Kevin Correia, displayed an enticing blend of on-base skills and base-stealing ability in his full-season debut. He has no power but draws praise for his athleticism and instincts. Although reports about his defense at shortstop are mixed, there are few viable options at that position in the Padres organization and he will have every opportunity to stick there. The former two-sport star (he was a cornerback in college) is behind the development curve but could move quickly now that he is focused on baseball.

Carlos Quentin — LF

Born: **8/28/1982** Age: **30**
Bats: **R** Throws: **R** Height: **6' 3"**
Weight: **235** Breakout: **2%**
Improve: **58%** Collapse: **1%**
Attrition: **6%** MLB: **100%**

Comparables:
Rocky Colavito,Billy Williams,Carl Yastrzemski

YEAR	TEAM	LVL	AGE	PA	R	2B	3B	HR	RBI	BB	SO	SB	CS	AVG_OBP_SLG	TAv	BABIP	BRR	FRAA	WARP
2010	CHA	MLB	27	527	73	25	2	26	87	50	83	2	2	.243/.342/.479	.284	.241	0.8	RF(104): -9.1	1.0
2011	CHA	MLB	28	483	53	31	0	24	77	34	84	1	1	.254/.340/.499	.302	.261	-0.7	RF(102): -4.4	1.5
2012	SDN	MLB	29	340	44	21	0	16	46	36	41	0	1	.261/.374/.504	.319	.252	-1.5	LF(69): -3.7, RF(3): -0.4	1.7
2013	*SDN*	*MLB*	*30*	*353*	*46*	*17*	*1*	*16*	*52*	*32*	*57*	*1*	*1*	*.251/.346/.473*	*.298*	*.257*	*-0.6*	*RF -0, LF -1*	*2.0*

The Padres acquired local product Quentin from the White Sox on New Year's Eve 2011 for a couple of minor-league arms. Right-knee surgery in spring training kept him from making his debut until May 28, but when he did, his impact was immediate. Quentin finished second on the team in home runs despite missing nearly half the season. The Padres, impressed with his work when healthy, signed him to a three-year extension in July. He is a liability on the bases and in the field, but his bat compensates. Quentin is in his prime, and the only question is how many games he can play. His career high is 131, and he had another round of knee surgery this winter.

Edinson Rincon — 3B

Born: **8/11/1990** Age: **22**
Bats: **R** Throws: **R** Height: **6' 2"**
Weight: **185** Breakout: **8%**
Improve: **54%** Collapse: **3%**
Attrition: **7%** MLB: **96%**

Comparables:
Carlos Baerga,Aurelio Rodriguez,Glenn Hoffman

YEAR	TEAM	LVL	AGE	PA	R	2B	3B	HR	RBI	BB	SO	SB	CS	AVG_OBP_SLG	TAv	BABIP	BRR	FRAA	WARP
2010	FTW	A	19	565	72	35	1	13	69	44	95	1	2	.250/.317/.399	.253	.285	-1.2	3B(106): -10.9	-0.2
2011	LEL	A+	20	340	54	24	1	8	50	32	59	1	1	.329/.394/.497	.310	.380	0	--	0.0
2012	SAN	AA	21	521	45	30	0	10	48	22	78	1	6	.291/.321/.413	.267	.327	-4	3B(62): -14.7, LF(22): -2.5	-1.5
2013	*SDN*	*MLB*	*22*	*250*	*20*	*12*	*1*	*5*	*25*	*9*	*54*	*0*	*0*	*.230/.260/.342*	*.223*	*.276*	*-0.5*	*3B -1, LF -0*	*-0.6*

Rincon is a line-drive machine with doubles power that could develop into home-run power as he matures. He doesn't draw walks or run well, and is an awful third baseman (career .844 fielding percentage in more than 300 minor-league games). The Padres tried sticking him in left field last year, but his best position is DH. If the power comes, Rincon could have a future in the American League.

Cory Spangenberg — 2B

Born: **3/16/1991** Age: **22**
Bats: **L** Throws: **R** Height: **6' 1"**
Weight: **185** Breakout: **6%**
Improve: **45%** Collapse: **4%**
Attrition: **7%** MLB: **96%**

Comparables:
Roberto Alomar,Mark Lewis,Derrel Thomas

YEAR	TEAM	LVL	AGE	PA	R	2B	3B	HR	RBI	BB	SO	SB	CS	AVG_OBP_SLG	TAv	BABIP	BRR	FRAA	WARP
2011	FTW	A	20	209	35	7	1	2	24	14	42	15	4	.286/.345/.365	.300	.359	0.4	2B(19): 0.1	0.7
2011	EUG	A-	20	121	20	10	0	1	20	31	15	10	4	.384/.545/.535	.387	.444	-1.5	2B(19): -1.3	1.1
2012	LEL	A+	21	426	53	12	8	1	40	26	72	27	9	.271/.324/.352	.227	.327	5.1	2B(22): -2.2	0.3
2013	*SDN*	*MLB*	*22*	*250*	*28*	*9*	*2*	*1*	*15*	*14*	*56*	*12*	*4*	*.221/.271/.292*	*.213*	*.279*	*1.1*	*2B -1*	*-0.3*

On the heels of a sparkling professional debut, expectations were high for Spangenberg entering 2012. Taken 10th overall in the 2011 draft, he figured to thrive in the hitter-friendly California League. That didn't happen. He runs well and is a decent enough second baseman, but his anticipated top-of-the-order skills never made more than a cameo in May. He was hit in the head by a ball during batting practice in June, which kept him out for a month. Good breaking balls gave him trouble, as did lefties. His future looks less bright now than it did a year ago, but he still has time to make the necessary adjustments and get back on the fast track.

Donavan Tate — OF

Born: **9/27/1990** Age: **22**
Bats: **R** Throws: **R** Height: **6' 4"**
Weight: **200** Breakout: **12%**
Improve: **54%** Collapse: **7%**
Attrition: **18%** MLB: **90%**

Comparables:
Willie Upshaw,Don Hahn,Norm Miller

YEAR	TEAM	LVL	AGE	PA	R	2B	3B	HR	RBI	BB	SO	SB	CS	AVG_OBP_SLG	TAv	BABIP	BRR	FRAA	WARP
2010	PDR	Rk	19	107	19	5	0	2	10	15	41	7	1	.222/.340/.344	.253	.383	0.4	CF(14): -1.0, RF(6): -0.4	0.0
2011	EUG	A-	20	155	24	8	4	0	20	25	32	17	5	.283/.406/.409	.257	.375	0.4	CF(20): -1.5	-0.1
2012	FTW	A	21	219	26	6	0	1	21	22	62	10	5	.207/.294/.254	.225	.298	1.9	CF(14): -1.5, LF(12): -0.4	-0.3
2012	LEL	A+	21	221	28	6	2	0	7	38	56	11	9	.247/.391/.303	.199	.361	0.4	CF(4): 0.1, LF(3): -0.1	-0.4
2013	*SDN*	*MLB*	*22*	*250*	*26*	*7*	*1*	*1*	*13*	*26*	*81*	*9*	*5*	*.178/.268/.233*	*.196*	*.270*	*0.1*	*CF -1, LF -0*	*-1.1*

The good news is that Tate, taken third overall in the 2009 draft, stayed healthy and unsuspended enough to play more than 40 games in a season for the first time in his career. The bad news is that aside from drawing walks, he displayed no usable offensive skills. He hasn't hit for average or power as a pro, and isn't a proficient basestealer despite his speed. It is too soon to call the hyper-athletic Tate a bust, but without significant, rapid improvement, that won't be true much longer.

Jeudy Valdez **SS**
Born: **5/5/1989** Age: **24**
Bats: **R** Throws: **R** Height: **5' 11"**
Weight: **185** Breakout: **3%**
Improve: **35%** Collapse: **9%**
Attrition: **21%** MLB: **93%**
Comparables:
Rafael Ramirez,Dale Berra,Ted Martinez

YEAR	TEAM	LVL	AGE	PA	R	2B	3B	HR	RBI	BB	SO	SB	CS	AVG_OBP_SLG	TAv	BABIP	BRR	FRAA	WARP
2010	FTW	A	21	590	81	34	3	10	76	43	115	34	14	.247/.306/.380	.248	.296	3.3	2B(119): -3.7, SS(11): -0.1	0.6
2011	LEL	A+	22	560	93	37	7	15	92	31	108	34	11	.295/.339/.481	.278	.346	0	--	0.0
2012	SAN	AA	23	507	52	24	2	12	46	21	126	13	7	.225/.273/.364	.225	.278	2.9	SS(95): -4.0	-0.2
2013	*SDN*	*MLB*	*24*	*250*	*26*	*10*	*1*	*4*	*19*	*8*	*69*	*6*	*3*	*.200/.233/.305*	*.199*	*.258*	*0.2*	*SS 1, 2B -0*	*-0.5*

A free swinger whose lack of discipline undermines a nice power-speed package, Valdez has been slow to convert his tools into skills. He has spent the last two seasons at shortstop but also has played more than 200 games at second base, where some observers believe his future lies. Which side of the bag he is on won't matter unless Valdez learns the difference between balls and strikes. Right-handers in particular gave him trouble last year, posting a better than 9-to-1 strikeout-to-walk ratio. Valdez's upside is that of a utility player, but he isn't there yet, although he made strides in the Arizona Fall League.

Will Venable **RF**
Born: **10/29/1982** Age: **30**
Bats: **L** Throws: **L** Height: **6' 3"**
Weight: **205** Breakout: **0%**
Improve: **40%** Collapse: **7%**
Attrition: **11%** MLB: **94%**
Comparables:
Gary Matthews,Cliff Floyd,George Hendrick

YEAR	TEAM	LVL	AGE	PA	R	2B	3B	HR	RBI	BB	SO	SB	CS	AVG_OBP_SLG	TAv	BABIP	BRR	FRAA	WARP
2010	SDN	MLB	27	445	60	11	7	13	51	45	128	29	7	.245/.324/.408	.273	.324	4	RF(89): 4.1, CF(25): 2.0	2.8
2011	TUC	AAA	28	64	14	3	2	3	11	5	13	3	0	.276/.328/.552	.267	.302	1.1	RF(14): -0.3	0.1
2011	SDN	MLB	28	411	49	14	7	9	44	31	92	26	3	.246/.310/.395	.274	.300	3.3	RF(91): 0.8, CF(14): -0.4	1.4
2012	SDN	MLB	29	470	62	26	8	9	45	41	94	24	6	.264/.335/.429	.281	.320	3.9	RF(114): 4.5, CF(21): -1.3	2.0
2013	*SDN*	*MLB*	*30*	*437*	*59*	*18*	*5*	*11*	*43*	*35*	*106*	*20*	*4*	*.247/.314/.406*	*.262*	*.306*	*2.7*	*RF 2, CF -0*	*1.6*

Venable did what he always does, which is flash each of the five tools in tantalizing fashion and have a nice season that seems disappointing in light of expectations created by those tantalizing tools. He is a plus defender in right field who can hold his own in center if needed. He is a graceful runner with long, easy strides and will take the extra base if he sees the opportunity. Venable wasn't the automatic out against lefties last year that he had been in the past, but he still profiles best as a platoon player. He continues to tighten his strike zone and make improvements to his game. Although his production will never match his athleticism, he is a useful player.

PITCHERS

Anthony Bass
Born: **11/1/1987** Age: **25**
Bats: **R** Throws: **R** Height: **6' 3"** Weight: **190**
Breakout: **16%** Improve: **36%** Collapse: **19%**
Attrition: **13%** MLB: **94%**
Comparables:
John Thomson,Jim McAndrew,Steve Rogers

YEAR	TEAM	LVL	AGE	W	L	SV	G	GS	IP	H	HR	BB	SO	BB9	SO9	GB%	BABIP	WHIP	ERA	FIP	FRA	WARP
2010	LEL	A+	22	8	7	0	27	27	132^{1}	124	9	20	109	1.4	7.4	54%	.292	1.09	3.13	3.45	4.49	1.9
2010	POR	AAA	22	0	1	0	1	1	5^{2}	7	1	3	3	4.7	4.7	40%	.316	1.75	7.89	6.92	6.36	-0.1
2011	SAN	AA	23	6	4	0	13	13	69^{2}	62	6	21	62	2.7	8.0	47%	.291	1.19	3.75	3.62	3.99	0.7
2011	TUC	AAA	23	1	0	0	1	1	5	6	0	0	3	0.0	5.4	77%	.353	1.20	1.80	3.18	3.05	0.2
2011	SDN	MLB	23	2	0	0	27	3	48^{1}	41	3	21	24	3.9	4.5	47%	.255	1.28	1.68	4.17	4.97	-0.1
2012	TUC	AAA	24	0	0	0	3	3	8	8	0	0	9	0.0	10.1	46%	.333	1.00	5.62	1.42	1.46	0.2
2012	SDN	MLB	24	2	8	1	24	15	97	89	10	39	80	3.6	7.4	50%	.281	1.32	4.73	4.06	5.15	-0.3
2013	*SDN*	*MLB*	*25*	*4*	*5*	*0*	*21*	*13*	*80*	*76*	*9*	*28*	*56*	*3.2*	*6.2*	*47%*	*.290*	*1.30*	*4.16*	*4.31*	*4.52*	*-0.0*

After working mostly in relief as a rookie, Bass moved into the Padres rotation last year. He started strong before getting hit hard toward the end of May and into June. Then shoulder inflammation sidelined him for two and a half months. He returned to the bullpen before making one final regrettable start to end the season. Bass has good enough stuff to succeed at the back of a rotation, assuming his arm cooperates. Otherwise, he could end up in middle relief.

Brad Boxberger
Born: **5/27/1988** Age: **25**
Bats: **R** Throws: **R** Height: **6' 3"** Weight: **200**
Breakout: **32%** Improve: **58%** Collapse: **17%**
Attrition: **11%** MLB: **88%**
Comparables:
Emiliano Fruto,Daniel Bard,Ugueth Urbina

YEAR	TEAM	LVL	AGE	W	L	SV	G	GS	IP	H	HR	BB	SO	BB9	SO9	GB%	BABIP	WHIP	ERA	FIP	FRA	WARP
2011	CAR	AA	23	1	2	4	30	0	34^{1}	16	2	13	57	3.4	14.9	—	.241	0.84	1.31	1.88	2.04	0.0
2011	LOU	AAA	23	1	2	7	25	0	27^{2}	16	2	15	36	4.9	11.7	50%	.222	1.12	2.93	3.20	4.87	0.0
2012	TUC	AAA	24	2	2	5	37	0	43^{1}	37	0	19	62	3.9	12.9	50%	.370	1.29	2.70	2.26	2.01	1.8
2012	SDN	MLB	24	0	0	0	24	0	27^{2}	22	3	18	33	5.9	10.7	40%	.297	1.45	2.60	4.33	4.51	-0.1
2013	*SDN*	*MLB*	*25*	*2*	*1*	*0*	*23*	*3*	*37^{2}*	*30*	*3*	*18*	*43*	*4.3*	*10.3*	*46%*	*.304*	*1.27*	*3.69*	*3.39*	*4.01*	*0.2*

Boxberger came from Cincinnati in the Latos trade. After starting the year at Tucson, he joined the big club for a couple of weeks in June, then for good at the end of July. A converted starter, Boxberger features a fastball in the low-90s, backing it with an average slider and changeup. If he learns to find the plate with greater frequency, he could develop into a setup man.

Brad Brach

Born: **4/12/1986** Age: **27**
Bats: **R** Throws: **R** Height: **6' 7"** Weight: **210**
Breakout: **22%** Improve: **41%** Collapse: **46%**
Attrition: **27%** MLB: **87%**

Comparables:
Tom Niedenfuer, Bob James, Rich Thompson

YEAR	TEAM	LVL	AGE	W	L	SV	G	GS	IP	H	HR	BB	SO	BB9	SO9	GB%	BABIP	WHIP	ERA	FIP	FRA	WARP
2010	LEL	A+	24	5	2	41	62	0	65^{2}	50	6	11	74	1.5	10.1	47%	.286	0.93	2.47	3.17	4.11	0.9
2011	SAN	AA	25	2	2	23	42	0	44	32	3	5	64	1.0	13.1	33%	.310	0.84	2.25	1.83	3.45	0.5
2011	TUC	AAA	25	1	3	11	25	0	27^{2}	28	1	7	30	2.3	9.8	52%	.422	1.27	3.90	2.84	2.99	0.6
2011	SDN	MLB	25	0	2	0	9	0	7	9	0	7	11	9.0	14.1	26%	.474	2.29	5.14	3.28	2.66	0.2
2012	TUC	AAA	26	2	1	3	10	0	9^{2}	11	0	1	5	0.9	4.7	44%	.344	1.24	2.79	2.94	3.51	0.2
2012	SDN	MLB	26	2	4	0	67	0	66^{2}	50	11	33	75	4.5	10.1	36%	.245	1.25	3.78	4.61	4.53	-0.3
2013	*SDN*	*MLB*	*27*	*3*	*1*	*0*	*54*	*0*	*55*	*46*	*6*	*20*	*59*	*3.2*	*9.7*	*40%*	*.296*	*1.19*	*3.35*	*3.56*	*3.64*	*0.5*

Brach already has done more than most 42nd-round picks do. He soaked up low-leverage innings as a rookie, getting plenty of strikeouts in the process thanks to a deceptive delivery that makes his low-90s fastball look harder than it is. The excellent control he exhibited in the minors hasn't translated to the big leagues, where hitters spit at pitches out of the zone rather than chase them. Brach gives up a lot of fly balls, which makes him susceptible to occasional bouts of gopheritis, even in the most forgiving of environments. He is a decent middle-relief option whose gaudy strikeout totals may fool some into believing he is more than that.

Andrew Cashner

Born: **9/11/1986** Age: **26**
Bats: **R** Throws: **R** Height: **6' 7"** Weight: **200**
Breakout: **26%** Improve: **60%** Collapse: **11%**
Attrition: **16%** MLB: **92%**

Comparables:
Mike Boddicker, Ernie Broglio, Andrew Bailey

YEAR	TEAM	LVL	AGE	W	L	SV	G	GS	IP	H	HR	BB	SO	BB9	SO9	GB%	BABIP	WHIP	ERA	FIP	FRA	WARP
2010	TEN	AA	23	3	1	0	6	6	36	22	1	13	42	3.2	10.5	54%	.253	0.97	2.75	2.50	3.58	0.9
2010	IOW	AAA	23	3	0	0	5	3	21	17	0	2	17	0.9	7.3	60%	.283	0.90	0.86	2.39	3.01	0.8
2010	CHN	MLB	23	2	6	0	53	0	54^{1}	55	8	30	50	5.0	8.3	52%	.301	1.56	4.80	5.06	5.39	0.1
2011	TEN	AA	24	0	1	0	3	3	2^{2}	3	0	0	6	0.0	20.2	1.%	.000	1.12	6.75	-1.19	1.27	0.1
2011	IOW	AAA	24	0	0	0	2	0	2	0	0	0	2	0.0	9.0	75%	.000	0.00	0.00	1.78	2.63	0.1
2011	CHN	MLB	24	0	0	0	7	1	10^{2}	3	1	4	8	3.4	6.8	56%	.077	0.66	1.69	3.84	4.29	0.1
2012	SAN	AA	25	2	0	0	3	3	14^{1}	10	0	3	22	1.9	13.8	52%	.345	0.91	1.88	1.26	-0.02	0.3
2012	TUC	AAA	25	0	1	0	3	3	9	8	0	2	8	2.0	8.0	54%	.308	1.11	3.00	2.55	1.98	0.3
2012	SDN	MLB	25	3	4	0	33	5	46^{1}	42	5	19	52	3.7	10.1	56%	.311	1.32	4.27	3.59	3.95	0.4
2013	*SDN*	*MLB*	*26*	*2*	*2*	*1*	*24*	*5*	*41^{1}*	*35*	*4*	*17*	*38*	*3.7*	*8.4*	*49%*	*.290*	*1.26*	*3.67*	*3.85*	*3.99*	*0.2*

Acquired from the Cubs before the season, Cashner wowed observers with a triple-digit fastball and biting slider. He started the year in the bullpen. Having missed five months in 2011 with a right rotator-cuff strain, his command was inconsistent. In June, the Padres sent Cashner to Triple-A so he could build arm strength and move into the big-league rotation. He spent the second half on the Tucson-San Diego shuttle, alternating brief healthy stretches with shoulder strains. Cashner's stuff can make hitters look silly, but the former college closer has yet to prove he can bear up to a starter's workload. His upside is enormous, as is his risk—which he managed to compound in the offseason by injuring himself with a knife on a hunting trip. He'll miss Opening Day.

Jose De Paula

Born: **3/4/1990** Age: **23**
Bats: **L** Throws: **L** Height: **6' 2"** Weight: **170**
Breakout: **29%** Improve: **74%** Collapse: **14%**
Attrition: **13%** MLB: **93%**

Comparables:
Bud Smith, Dick Ellsworth, Eric Milton

YEAR	TEAM	LVL	AGE	W	L	SV	G	GS	IP	H	HR	BB	SO	BB9	SO9	GB%	BABIP	WHIP	ERA	FIP	FRA	WARP
2010	FTW	A	20	8	5	0	20	14	85^{1}	71	7	20	69	2.1	7.3	43%	.268	1.07	3.27	3.83	5.19	0.7
2011	LEL	A+	21	10	5	0	26	23	112	129	4	37	87	3.0	7.0	—	.332	1.48	5.22	3.91	4.25	0.0
2013	*SDN*	*MLB*	*23*	*1*	*3*	*0*	*8*	*6*	*35^{1}*	*38*	*5*	*16*	*22*	*4.0*	*5.6*	*44%*	*.308*	*1.53*	*5.39*	*5.15*	*5.86*	*-0.5*

De Paula, a native of the Dominican Republic, missed all of 2012 because of visa issues that landed him on the restricted list. Used primarily as a starter throughout his career, he split time between the bullpen and rotation in the Dominican League over the winter and is expected to be back in action this year. De Paula features three quality pitches and a loose, easy delivery. The key for him now is to get repetitions to make up for lost development time.

Robert Erlin

Born: **10/8/1990** Age: **22**
Bats: **L** Throws: **L** Height: **6' 1"** Weight: **175**
Breakout: **29%** Improve: **58%** Collapse: **20%**
Attrition: **5%** MLB: **88%**

Comparables:
Dontrelle Willis, Greg Swindell, John Candelaria

YEAR	TEAM	LVL	AGE	W	L	SV	G	GS	IP	H	HR	BB	SO	BB9	SO9	GB%	BABIP	WHIP	ERA	FIP	FRA	WARP
2010	HIC	A	19	6	3	1	28	17	114^{2}	89	9	17	125	1.3	9.8	41%	.272	0.92	2.12	2.92	3.65	2.4
2011	MYR	A+	20	3	2	0	9	9	54^{2}	25	7	5	62	0.8	10.2	32%	.145	0.55	2.14	3.07	3.41	0.6
2011	FRI	AA	20	5	2	0	11	10	66^{2}	73	9	7	61	0.9	8.2	43%	.283	1.20	4.32	3.71	3.38	0.8
2011	SAN	AA	20	1	0	0	6	6	26	26	2	4	31	1.4	10.7	38%	.356	1.15	1.38	2.45	3.15	0.5
2012	PDR	Rk	21	0	2	0	3	3	8^{1}	7	0	2	8	2.2	8.6	69%	.077	1.08	2.16	3.18	4.69	0.1
2012	SAN	AA	21	3	1	0	11	11	52^{1}	53	6	14	72	2.4	12.4	40%	.353	1.28	2.92	2.99	2.83	1.3
2013	*SDN*	*MLB*	*22*	*2*	*2*	*0*	*8*	*6*	*38*	*34*	*4*	*12*	*36*	*2.8*	*8.5*	*40%*	*.300*	*1.21*	*3.81*	*3.62*	*4.14*	*0.2*

Erlin, acquired in the July 2011 trade that sent Mike Adams to Texas, lacks overpowering stuff but makes up for it with baseball intelligence and pinpoint control of a fastball, curve, and changeup. Last year he started strong at Double-A before being placed on the disabled list mid-May with elbow tendinitis. He made up for some of his lost time by pitching in the Arizona Fall League. Erlin worked on quickening his tempo, which he believes helps "sell" his off-speed stuff. He is very close to contributing at the big-league level and eventually could be a third starter.

Max Fried

Born: **12/31/1993** Age: **19**
Bats: **L** Throws: **L** Height: **6' 4"** Weight: **170**
Breakout: **9%** Improve: **89%** Collapse: **11%**
Attrition: **11%** MLB: **68%**
Comparables:
Jim Bethke,Bob Miller,Mike McCormick

YEAR	TEAM	LVL	AGE	W	L	SV	G	GS	IP	H	HR	BB	SO	BB9	SO9	GB%	BABIP	WHIP	ERA	FIP	FRA	WARP
2012	PDR	Rk	18	0	1	0	10	9	17^2	14	1	6	17	3.1	8.7	70%	.269	1.13	3.57	4.38	5.32	0.2
2013	*SDN*	*MLB*	*19*	*1*	*0*	*1*	*19*	*0*	33^2	*37*	*4*	*21*	*21*	*5.7*	*5.5*	*47%*	*.312*	*1.73*	*6.14*	*5.37*	*6.67*	*-0.7*

The Padres took Fried (pronounced "freed") with the seventh overall pick in 2012 out of a Southern California high school. The top left-hander in the draft features a fastball in the low-90s with arm-side run and backs it with a curve that has good downward break. He is athletic (played guard on his high school basketball team), has long arms and a clean delivery, and could add velocity as he grows into his body. The word that keeps surfacing is "projectability," which means that there is plenty of reason for excitement but also plenty of time to wait and see what happens.

Luke Gregerson

Born: **5/14/1984** Age: **29**
Bats: **L** Throws: **R** Height: **6' 4"** Weight: **200**
Breakout: **27%** Improve: **44%** Collapse: **36%**
Attrition: **22%** MLB: **95%**
Comparables:
Craig Breslow,Dan Plesac,Bill Bray

YEAR	TEAM	LVL	AGE	W	L	SV	G	GS	IP	H	HR	BB	SO	BB9	SO9	GB%	BABIP	WHIP	ERA	FIP	FRA	WARP
2010	SDN	MLB	26	4	7	2	80	0	78^1	47	8	18	89	2.1	10.2	48%	.215	0.83	3.22	2.89	3.96	0.5
2011	TUC	AAA	27	0	0	0	2	0	1^1	3	0	2	2	13.5	13.5	—	.600	3.75	20.25	5.28	5.74	0.0
2011	SDN	MLB	27	3	3	0	61	0	55^2	57	2	19	34	3.1	5.5	52%	.299	1.37	2.75	3.37	4.12	0.1
2012	SDN	MLB	28	2	0	9	77	0	71^2	57	7	21	72	2.6	9.0	53%	.262	1.09	2.39	3.40	3.25	1.0
2013	*SDN*	*MLB*	*29*	*4*	*2*	*4*	*67*	*0*	63^1	*50*	*5*	*18*	*64*	*2.5*	*9.1*	*51%*	*.286*	*1.07*	*2.82*	*3.06*	*3.06*	*1.0*

Last year we suggested that Gregerson needed to "rediscover the tilt on his slider" for continued success. He did, and the results were spectacular. He subtracted velocity, replacing it with more horizontal and vertical movement. He also leaned on the slider more than ever before, throwing it two-thirds of the time (three-quarters of the time against right-handers). Gregerson has all but abandoned his four-seam fastball in favor of the sinker. He closed some games while Huston Street was injured and will continue to be a late-inning option as long as his right arm allows him to keep spinning sliders.

Casey Kelly

Born: **10/4/1989** Age: **23**
Bats: **R** Throws: **R** Height: **6' 4"** Weight: **195**
Breakout: **32%** Improve: **61%** Collapse: **14%**
Attrition: **11%** MLB: **86%**
Comparables:
Justin Germano,Vance Worley,Liam Hendriks

YEAR	TEAM	LVL	AGE	W	L	SV	G	GS	IP	H	HR	BB	SO	BB9	SO9	GB%	BABIP	WHIP	ERA	FIP	FRA	WARP
2010	PME	AA	20	3	5	0	21	21	95	118	10	35	81	3.3	7.7	47%	.366	1.61	5.31	4.19	4.61	1.3
2011	SAN	AA	21	11	6	0	27	27	142^1	153	8	46	105	2.9	6.6	55%	.267	1.40	3.98	3.77	4.49	1.0
2012	PDR	Rk	22	0	1	0	3	3	9	10	0	0	7	0.0	7.0	33%	.333	1.11	4.00	3.15	4.58	0.2
2012	SAN	AA	22	0	1	0	3	3	16^2	11	1	3	18	1.6	9.7	45%	.244	0.84	3.78	2.62	3.51	0.1
2012	TUC	AAA	22	0	0	0	2	2	12	12	0	0	14	0.0	10.5	55%	.364	1.00	2.25	1.58	2.36	0.5
2012	SDN	MLB	22	2	3	0	6	6	29	39	5	10	26	3.1	8.1	57%	.366	1.69	6.21	4.83	5.14	0.0
2013	*SDN*	*MLB*	*23*	*2*	*3*	*0*	*7*	*7*	36^2	*37*	*4*	*13*	*26*	*3.1*	*6.4*	*48%*	*.304*	*1.36*	*4.60*	*4.26*	*5.00*	*-0.2*

The centerpiece of the Gonzalez trade, Kelly generated buzz in spring training and appeared poised to take a step or three forward. He fanned 14 and walked none in his first two starts at Triple-A, then incurred a right elbow ligament strain that kept him out for three and a half months. Kelly joined the big club toward the end of August and spun six scoreless innings in his debut before getting hit hard over his final five starts. With a low-90s fastball, plus curve, and average changeup, the athletic Kelly projects as a mid-rotation workhorse who could enjoy a long career if he stays healthy.

Tom Layne

Born: **11/2/1984** Age: **28**
Bats: **L** Throws: **L** Height: **6' 4"** Weight: **185**
Breakout: **19%** Improve: **47%** Collapse: **29%**
Attrition: **18%** MLB: **81%**
Comparables:
Willard Nixon,Eric DuBose,Mike Maddux

YEAR	TEAM	LVL	AGE	W	L	SV	G	GS	IP	H	HR	BB	SO	BB9	SO9	GB%	BABIP	WHIP	ERA	FIP	FRA	WARP
2010	MOB	AA	25	12	7	0	26	26	149^1	146	9	57	91	3.4	5.5	62%	.288	1.36	3.74	4.22	5.72	-0.1
2011	MOB	AA	26	2	0	0	3	3	17^2	16	1	6	14	3.1	7.1	50%	.333	1.25	2.55	3.65	1.63	0.2
2011	RNO	AAA	26	10	7	0	32	15	121^2	148	14	57	56	4.2	4.1	—	.315	1.68	6.21	5.91	6.43	0.0
2012	SAN	AA	27	0	5	1	32	2	35^2	31	2	16	36	4.0	9.1	64%	.305	1.32	3.28	3.34	5.15	0.5
2012	RNO	AAA	27	0	2	0	5	4	20	30	4	9	14	4.1	6.3	48%	.366	1.95	10.35	6.52	12.96	0.1
2012	TUC	AAA	27	0	3	0	5	5	22	28	4	15	19	6.1	7.8	56%	.348	1.95	7.77	6.76	8.76	0.0
2012	SDN	MLB	27	2	0	2	26	0	16^2	9	0	3	25	1.6	13.5	51%	.243	0.72	3.24	1.22	2.68	0.3
2013	*SDN*	*MLB*	*28*	*2*	*2*	*0*	*14*	*6*	35^2	*37*	*4*	*16*	*22*	*4.0*	*5.6*	*54%*	*.300*	*1.47*	*5.02*	*4.77*	*5.46*	*-0.4*

Acquired in May from Arizona, Layne joined the Padres in mid-August and fanned six of the first eight hitters he faced. He quickly worked his way into a seventh- and eighth-inning role, even getting the occasional save opportunity. Layne is a sinker-slider guy who relies more on deception than stuff. He is tough on lefties but was terrorized by righties last year at three levels–most notably at Triple-A, where they hit him like Ted Williams in his prime. This vulnerability makes Layne a LOOGY candidate at best, which isn't bad for a 26th-round pick.

Cory Luebke

Born: **3/4/1985** Age: **28**
Bats: **R** Throws: **L** Height: **6' 5"** Weight: **205**
Breakout: **17%** Improve: **68%** Collapse: **10%**
Attrition: **4%** MLB: **90%**

Comparables:
Jack McDowell,Kevin Millwood,Gavin Floyd

YEAR	TEAM	LVL	AGE	W	L	SV	G	GS	IP	H	HR	BB	SO	BB9	SO9	GB%	BABIP	WHIP	ERA	FIP	FRA	WARP
2010	SAN	AA	25	5	1	0	10	8	56^1	41	2	12	44	1.9	7.0	46%	.234	0.94	2.40	2.82	3.39	0.8
2010	POR	AAA	25	5	0	0	9	9	57^2	42	6	17	44	2.7	6.9	40%	.225	1.02	2.96	4.29	4.70	0.8
2010	SDN	MLB	25	1	1	0	4	3	17^2	17	3	6	18	3.1	9.2	47%	.292	1.30	4.08	4.46	5.18	0.0
2011	SDN	MLB	26	6	10	0	46	17	139^2	105	12	44	154	2.8	9.9	41%	.271	1.07	3.29	2.89	3.39	2.6
2012	SDN	MLB	27	3	1	0	5	5	31	28	1	8	23	2.3	6.7	49%	.276	1.16	2.61	2.85	3.62	0.3
2013	*SDN*	*MLB*	*28*	*2*	*2*	*0*	*10*	*6*	42^1	*38*	*4*	*13*	*35*	*2.7*	*7.6*	*45%*	*.292*	*1.21*	*3.78*	*3.70*	*4.11*	*0.2*

After a terrific rookie campaign, Luebke signed a four-year extension in spring training. Five starts into the new contract he blew out his elbow and ended up having Tommy John surgery on May 23. When healthy, Luebke features a low-90s fastball and sharp slider. He will pitch this year, but not as often or as well as the Padres had hoped. Assuming no complications, the long-term outlook remains promising.

Jason Marquis

Born: **8/21/1978** Age: **34**
Bats: **L** Throws: **R** Height: **6' 2"** Weight: **210**
Breakout: **26%** Improve: **54%** Collapse: **19%**
Attrition: **12%** MLB: **94%**

Comparables:
Jarrod Washburn,Ed Lopat,Mark Redman

YEAR	TEAM	LVL	AGE	W	L	SV	G	GS	IP	H	HR	BB	SO	BB9	SO9	GB%	BABIP	WHIP	ERA	FIP	FRA	WARP
2010	NAT	Rk	31	0	0	0	1	1	3	2	0	0	4	0.0	12.0	1.%	.333	0.67	0.00	0.84	3.43	0.1
2010	POT	A+	31	0	0	0	1	1	3^2	6	0	1	3	2.4	7.3	61%	.462	1.89	7.30	3.41	3.37	0.1
2010	HAR	AA	31	0	0	0	1	1	3^1	5	0	1	3	2.7	8.2	58%	.417	1.82	8.18	2.45	5.36	0.0
2010	SYR	AAA	31	0	0	0	2	2	11	7	2	3	11	2.5	9.0	78%	.200	0.91	4.09	4.75	5.77	0.0
2010	WAS	MLB	31	2	9	0	13	13	58^2	76	9	24	31	3.7	4.8	55%	.328	1.70	6.60	5.68	5.90	-0.2
2011	ARI	MLB	32	0	1	0	3	3	11^1	22	3	4	5	3.2	4.0	62%	.380	2.29	9.53	6.88	6.36	-0.3
2011	WAS	MLB	32	8	5	0	20	20	120^2	132	8	39	71	2.9	5.3	55%	.309	1.42	3.95	3.75	4.11	0.7
2012	NBR	AA	33	1	0	0	2	2	14	12	1	0	11	0.0	7.1	61%	.289	0.86	1.93	2.56	3.33	0.1
2012	SAN	AA	33	1	0	0	1	1	7	5	0	2	5	2.6	6.4	63%	.263	1.00	1.29	2.71	1.90	0.0
2012	MIN	MLB	33	2	4	0	7	7	34	52	9	14	12	3.7	3.2	55%	.352	1.94	8.47	7.28	7.16	-0.7
2012	SDN	MLB	33	6	7	0	15	15	93^2	94	14	28	79	2.7	7.6	53%	.287	1.30	4.04	4.32	5.09	0.3
2013	*SDN*	*MLB*	*34*	*6*	*9*	*0*	*22*	*22*	119^2	*120*	*12*	*40*	*74*	*3.0*	*5.6*	*53%*	*.298*	*1.34*	*4.45*	*4.27*	*4.83*	*-0.5*

Signed by the Padres at the end of May, Marquis bore scant resemblance to the human batting tee that had been released by the Twins a day earlier. Once in San Diego, he threw strikes and put balls past batters at rates not seen in his 13-year big-league career. He fractured his left wrist in August while attempting to field a line drive, ending his season. Everything about Marquis's resurgence screams fluke, but it may have bought him a few more looks despite his having been one of the least effective starting pitchers in baseball over the last three seasons.

Miles Mikolas

Born: **8/23/1988** Age: **24**
Bats: **R** Throws: **R** Height: **6' 6"** Weight: **220**
Breakout: **25%** Improve: **49%** Collapse: **24%**
Attrition: **24%** MLB: **87%**

Comparables:
Scott McGregor,Osiris Matos,Brandon League

YEAR	TEAM	LVL	AGE	W	L	SV	G	GS	IP	H	HR	BB	SO	BB9	SO9	GB%	BABIP	WHIP	ERA	FIP	FRA	WARP
2010	FTW	A	21	6	3	13	60	0	81^2	76	3	15	78	1.7	8.6	58%	.301	1.11	2.20	2.73	4.37	1.1
2011	LEL	A+	22	3	0	12	34	0	39^2	31	1	9	42	2.0	9.5	—	.288	1.01	1.13	3.07	3.34	0.0
2011	SAN	AA	22	1	0	9	28	0	32^1	29	0	6	27	1.7	7.5	58%	.200	1.08	1.67	2.26	2.72	0.6
2012	SAN	AA	23	1	1	4	12	0	12^1	16	0	3	11	2.2	8.0	46%	.410	1.54	2.92	2.23	3.07	0.3
2012	TUC	AAA	23	2	1	0	17	0	19^2	20	1	8	17	3.7	7.8	52%	.311	1.42	3.20	3.82	3.70	0.4
2012	SDN	MLB	23	2	1	0	25	0	32^1	32	4	15	23	4.2	6.4	55%	.280	1.45	3.62	4.90	6.17	-0.6
2013	*SDN*	*MLB*	*24*	*1*	*1*	*1*	*29*	*0*	36^2	*37*	*4*	*13*	*25*	*3.2*	*6.2*	*51%*	*.303*	*1.37*	*4.65*	*4.32*	*5.06*	*-0.3*

Mikolas might be best known for once eating a lizard in the bullpen during an Arizona Fall League game. He also is a strike thrower who pounds the bottom of the zone with sinkers and curves. He has experience closing games but projects as a middle reliever in the big leagues—that is, if hitters don't take too many bites out of him along the way.

Dustin Moseley

Born: **12/26/1981** Age: **31**
Bats: **R** Throws: **R** Height: **6' 5"** Weight: **215**
Breakout: **6%** Improve: **39%** Collapse: **34%**
Attrition: **17%** MLB: **88%**

Comparables:
Mark Clark, Kris Benson, Josh Fogg

YEAR	TEAM	LVL	AGE	W	L	SV	G	GS	IP	H	HR	BB	SO	BB9	SO9	GB%	BABIP	WHIP	ERA	FIP	FRA	WARP
2010	SWB	AAA	28	4	4	0	12	12	72^{2}	83	6	18	55	2.2	6.8	64%	.333	1.39	4.21	3.76	5.24	-0.3
2010	NYA	MLB	28	4	4	0	16	9	65^{1}	66	13	27	33	3.7	4.5	51%	.261	1.42	4.96	5.96	6.75	-0.6
2011	SDN	MLB	29	3	10	0	20	20	120	117	10	36	64	2.7	4.8	51%	.273	1.27	3.30	3.96	4.64	-0.2
2012	SDN	MLB	30	0	0	0	1	1	5	5	1	2	4	3.6	7.2	50%	.267	1.40	9.00	5.34	4.22	0.0
2013	*SDN*	*MLB*	*31*	*2*	*3*	*0*	*6*	*6*	*37*	*38*	*4*	*12*	*24*	*2.8*	*5.8*	*50%*	*.301*	*1.34*	*4.62*	*4.28*	*5.02*	*-0.3*

After a surprising 2011 campaign, Moseley made his first start last year on April 7 and survived five innings. He landed on the disabled list a day later, and had surgery to repair his right labrum and rotator cuff a few weeks later. At his best, Moseley serves up grounders and can work in a variety of roles, ideally low-leverage ones for a team hoping to contend.

Juan Oramas

Born: **5/11/1990** Age: **23**
Bats: **L** Throws: **L** Height: **5' 11"** Weight: **215**
Breakout: **25%** Improve: **56%** Collapse: **23%**
Attrition: **18%** MLB: **93%**

Comparables:
Scott Olsen, Andrew Oliver, Johnny Podres

YEAR	TEAM	LVL	AGE	W	L	SV	G	GS	IP	H	HR	BB	SO	BB9	SO9	GB%	BABIP	WHIP	ERA	FIP	FRA	WARP
2010	FTW	A	20	0	1	0	5	0	15	9	0	3	25	1.8	15.0	41%	.333	0.80	1.20	0.88	1.67	0.6
2010	LEL	A+	20	7	3	0	24	21	84	64	10	26	90	2.8	9.6	32%	.271	1.07	3.00	4.25	4.25	1.5
2011	SAN	AA	21	10	5	0	19	18	104^{2}	99	10	28	102	2.4	8.8	35%	.291	1.21	3.10	3.59	3.97	1.1
2011	TUC	AAA	21	0	1	0	1	1	3^{2}	7	3	1	4	2.5	9.8	—	.364	2.18	14.73	13.87	15.08	0.0
2012	SAN	AA	22	3	4	0	8	8	35^{1}	39	5	16	33	4.1	8.4	37%	.295	1.56	6.37	4.78	5.08	0.5
2013	*SDN*	*MLB*	*23*	*2*	*2*	*0*	*9*	*7*	*37^{1}*	*34*	*4*	*14*	*33*	*3.5*	*8.1*	*37%*	*.297*	*1.30*	*4.16*	*3.95*	*4.52*	*0.0*

A lefty who relies on command, Oramas saw his season end in mid-May because of a balky elbow that required Tommy John surgery in June. He is a fly-ball pitcher who features a fastball, downward curve, and changeup, varying his arm angle to keep hitters off-balance. The ability to add and subtract velocity on all of his pitches creates further deception. Oramas is expected to begin pitching in games in June, but as with all Tommy John survivors, his command isn't likely to reappear until much later.

Adys Portillo

Born: **12/21/1991** Age: **21**
Bats: **R** Throws: **R** Height: **6' 3"** Weight: **185**
Breakout: **34%** Improve: **64%** Collapse: **13%**
Attrition: **7%** MLB: **86%**

Comparables:
Tommy Boggs, Dave McNally, Jon Garland

YEAR	TEAM	LVL	AGE	W	L	SV	G	GS	IP	H	HR	BB	SO	BB9	SO9	GB%	BABIP	WHIP	ERA	FIP	FRA	WARP
2010	FTW	A	18	0	0	0	1	0	2	2	1	1	1	4.5	4.5	33%	.200	1.50	4.50	10.61	11.58	-0.1
2010	EUG	A-	18	2	6	0	14	14	62	55	2	40	62	5.8	9.0	54%	.312	1.53	4.79	4.08	5.09	-0.3
2011	FTW	A	19	3	11	0	23	20	82^{1}	89	10	55	97	6.0	10.6	39%	.356	1.75	7.11	4.70	5.93	-0.1
2012	FTW	A	20	6	6	0	18	18	91^{2}	54	3	45	81	4.4	8.0	44%	.210	1.08	1.87	3.58	4.21	1.0
2012	SAN	AA	20	2	5	0	8	8	35	34	4	25	26	6.4	6.7	46%	.280	1.69	7.20	5.85	8.04	-0.4
2013	*SDN*	*MLB*	*21*	*1*	*3*	*0*	*7*	*7*	*34^{1}*	*35*	*4*	*22*	*23*	*5.7*	*6.1*	*44%*	*.298*	*1.65*	*5.64*	*5.30*	*6.13*	*-0.6*

After three mostly disappointing seasons, Portillo showed better command of his mid-90s fastball and an improved breaking ball under the tutelage of former big-league pitcher Willie Blair, his pitching coach at Fort Wayne. The Venezuelan pitched well enough in the Midwest League to earn a promotion to Double-A in July. Not surprisingly, he struggled after skipping a level, walking three or more batters in all but one of his starts at San Antonio. The stuff is electric, and Portillo is young despite having been around seemingly forever. If his secondary pitches develop, he could be a front-line starter. If not, he could close games. Either way, we won't know for a while.

Clayton Richard

Born: **9/12/1983** Age: **29**
Bats: **L** Throws: **L** Height: **6' 6"** Weight: **245**
Breakout: **24%** Improve: **58%** Collapse: **18%**
Attrition: **12%** MLB: **83%**

Comparables:
John Rheinecker, Jason Vargas, Mike Maroth

YEAR	TEAM	LVL	AGE	W	L	SV	G	GS	IP	H	HR	BB	SO	BB9	SO9	GB%	BABIP	WHIP	ERA	FIP	FRA	WARP
2010	SDN	MLB	26	14	9	0	33	33	201^{2}	206	16	78	153	3.5	6.8	47%	.311	1.41	3.75	3.84	4.48	1.4
2011	SDN	MLB	27	5	9	0	18	18	99^{2}	104	8	38	53	3.4	4.8	52%	.294	1.42	3.88	4.18	4.64	0.0
2012	SDN	MLB	28	14	14	0	33	33	218^{2}	228	31	42	107	1.7	4.4	54%	.272	1.23	3.99	4.66	5.65	-1.9
2013	*SDN*	*MLB*	*29*	*9*	*11*	*0*	*27*	*27*	*167*	*166*	*17*	*48*	*104*	*2.6*	*5.6*	*51%*	*.296*	*1.28*	*4.22*	*4.14*	*4.58*	*-0.3*

Despite calling Petco Park home, Richard led National League pitchers in home runs allowed last year. On the road, hitters took him deep a little more often (24.7 PA/HR) than Carlos Beltran has homered throughout his career (25.0 PA/HR). Richard is a fly-ball pitcher without overpowering stuff, a combination that has served him well in San Diego, although this could change with the fences moving in for 2013 (his career ERA at Petco is 2.82; it's 4.99 at all other venues). Richard, a quick worker and fierce competitor, showed no ill effects from July 2011 shoulder surgery. He isn't a bad option at the back of a rotation, although the lack of dominance means his margin for error is slim in any ballpark.

Joseph Ross

Born: **5/21/1993** Age: **20**
Bats: **R** Throws: **R** Height: **6' 4"** Weight: **185**
Breakout: **51%** Improve: **78%** Collapse: **9%**
Attrition: **3%** MLB: **85%**

Comparables:
Dick Brodowski,Catfish Hunter,Milt Pappas

YEAR	TEAM	LVL	AGE	W	L	SV	G	GS	IP	H	HR	BB	SO	BB9	SO9	GB%	BABIP	WHIP	ERA	FIP	FRA	WARP
2011	PDR	Rk	18	0	0	0	1	0	1	2	0	0	0	0.0	0.0	60%	.400	2.00	0.00	7.37	8.80	0.0
2012	PDR	Rk	19	0	0	0	1	1	0^2	2	0	2	1	27.0	13.5	—	.693	6.00	13.50	10.38	20.16	-0.1
2012	FTW	A	19	0	2	0	6	6	27^1	33	2	11	27	3.6	8.9	46%	.378	1.61	6.26	3.53	4.74	0.0
2012	EUG	A-	19	0	2	0	8	8	26^2	16	1	9	28	3.0	9.4	62%	.238	0.94	2.03	2.84	4.20	0.2
2013	*SDN*	*MLB*	*20*	*2*	*3*	*0*	*8*	*8*	*35^1*	*36*	*4*	*18*	*27*	*4.6*	*6.8*	*47%*	*.307*	*1.53*	*5.16*	*4.67*	*5.61*	*-0.4*

The Padres took Tyson Ross's younger brother with the 25th pick in the 2011 draft. He got shelled in his full-season debut before making a few more starts, including six strong innings at West Michigan on May 4. Scratched from his next outing with right shoulder soreness, Ross ended up missing seven weeks. After an aborted rehab assignment at the end of June, he returned for good a month later and fared much better while rebuilding arm strength in the short-season Northwest League. When healthy, Ross works with a fastball-slider combination and a clean, easy delivery that gives him good command of both pitches.

Tyson Ross

Born: **4/22/1987** Age: **26**
Bats: **R** Throws: **R** Height: **6' 7"** Weight: **230**
Breakout: **28%** Improve: **65%** Collapse: **16%**
Attrition: **14%** MLB: **91%**

Comparables:
Freddy Garcia,Ricky Romero,Bartolo Colon

YEAR	TEAM	LVL	AGE	W	L	SV	G	GS	IP	H	HR	BB	SO	BB9	SO9	GB%	BABIP	WHIP	ERA	FIP	FRA	WARP
2010	SAC	AAA	23	2	1	0	6	6	25^1	22	1	13	30	4.6	10.7	63%	.362	1.38	3.56	3.74	4.33	0.6
2010	OAK	MLB	23	1	4	1	26	2	39^1	39	4	20	32	4.6	7.3	55%	.310	1.50	5.49	4.27	5.95	-0.5
2011	STO	A+	24	0	0	0	1	1	1	2	0	1	1	9.0	9.0	25%	.500	3.00	9.00	4.95	2.84	0.1
2011	SAC	AAA	24	3	2	0	9	9	36^2	52	5	22	34	5.4	8.3	—	.385	2.02	7.61	5.50	5.98	0.0
2011	OAK	MLB	24	3	3	0	9	6	36	33	1	13	24	3.2	6.0	49%	.299	1.28	2.75	3.17	3.69	0.4
2012	SAC	AAA	25	6	2	0	15	13	78^1	69	4	29	64	3.3	7.4	61%	.283	1.25	2.99	3.92	4.47	0.8
2012	OAK	MLB	25	2	11	0	18	13	73^1	96	7	37	46	4.5	5.6	52%	.360	1.81	6.50	4.75	5.56	-0.4
2013	*SDN*	*MLB*	*26*	*4*	*5*	*0*	*26*	*14*	*86^1*	*80*	*8*	*35*	*69*	*3.7*	*7.2*	*54%*	*.300*	*1.34*	*4.16*	*4.02*	*4.52*	*-0.0*

Ross, a 2008 second-round pick, has seen his development stalled by severe mechanical issues. He throws hard and draws praise for his makeup, but has what BP's pitching mechanics expert Doug Thorburn refers to as "zero momentum and a short stride," which hurts his perceived velocity and late movement on breaking pitches. Injuries (biceps in 2009, elbow in 2010, oblique in 2011) may have been a contributing factor, but that explanation doesn't get him any closer to resolving the underlying issues. Shipped to San Diego in November, Ross could spend time in the bullpen as well as the rotation. The jury is still out on whether he's best suited to the former, the latter, or neither.

Keyvius Sampson

Born: **1/6/1991** Age: **22**
Bats: **R** Throws: **R** Height: **6' 1"** Weight: **185**
Breakout: **25%** Improve: **59%** Collapse: **17%**
Attrition: **7%** MLB: **93%**

Comparables:
Alex Fernandez,Randall Delgado,Chris Tillman

YEAR	TEAM	LVL	AGE	W	L	SV	G	GS	IP	H	HR	BB	SO	BB9	SO9	GB%	BABIP	WHIP	ERA	FIP	FRA	WARP
2010	EUG	A-	19	3	3	0	10	10	43	35	4	17	58	3.6	12.1	49%	.320	1.21	3.56	3.32	4.95	0.0
2011	FTW	A	20	12	3	0	24	24	118	81	8	49	143	3.7	10.9	32%	.263	1.10	2.90	3.22	4.30	0.6
2012	SAN	AA	21	8	11	0	26	25	122^1	108	11	57	122	4.2	9.0	43%	.288	1.35	5.00	3.95	4.96	1.1
2013	*SDN*	*MLB*	*22*	*2*	*3*	*0*	*8*	*8*	*36^1*	*33*	*4*	*18*	*33*	*4.4*	*8.1*	*41%*	*.298*	*1.40*	*4.47*	*4.30*	*4.86*	*-0.1*

Sampson skipped a level after enjoying a strong full-season debut in the Midwest League in 2011. The aggressive promotion was intended to challenge Sampson and place him in an environment where he could develop his breaking ball. The results were mixed. Three times he worked six or more scoreless innings, but five times he allowed five runs or more (although only one of those came after June 1). His ERA away from pitcher-friendly Wolff Stadium was nearly four runs higher than at home. That he missed so many bats at Double-A is encouraging, but Sampson remains a work in progress whose ultimate role and timetable are uncertain.

Tim Stauffer

Born: **6/2/1982** Age: **31**
Bats: **R** Throws: **R** Height: **6' 2"** Weight: **225**
Breakout: **8%** Improve: **41%** Collapse: **33%**
Attrition: **14%** MLB: **87%**

Comparables:
Dave Goltz,Frank Sullivan,Frank Lary

YEAR	TEAM	LVL	AGE	W	L	SV	G	GS	IP	H	HR	BB	SO	BB9	SO9	GB%	BABIP	WHIP	ERA	FIP	FRA	WARP
2010	POR	AAA	28	0	0	0	6	5	17^2	24	0	7	8	3.6	4.1	59%	.343	1.75	4.58	3.87	4.69	0.2
2010	SDN	MLB	28	6	5	0	32	7	82^2	65	3	24	61	2.6	6.6	56%	.263	1.08	1.85	3.05	3.80	0.9
2011	SDN	MLB	29	9	12	0	31	31	185^2	180	20	53	128	2.6	6.2	54%	.282	1.25	3.73	4.00	4.87	0.6
2012	PDR	Rk	30	0	0	0	1	1	1	1	0	0	1	0.0	9.0	33%	.333	1.00	0.00	2.38	-2.18	0.0
2012	LEL	A+	30	0	1	0	4	4	13^1	15	0	2	11	1.4	7.4	49%	.341	1.27	3.38	2.61	-1.57	0.0
2012	TUC	AAA	30	0	1	0	2	2	8	10	1	1	2	1.1	2.2	54%	.333	1.38	3.38	5.17	6.75	0.0
2012	SDN	MLB	30	0	0	0	1	1	5	7	1	3	5	5.4	9.0	56%	.400	2.00	5.40	5.54	5.35	0.0
2013	*SDN*	*MLB*	*31*	*2*	*2*	*0*	*10*	*6*	*38^2*	*37*	*4*	*11*	*28*	*2.5*	*6.4*	*49%*	*.296*	*1.23*	*3.93*	*3.95*	*4.27*	*0.1*

After being overworked in 2011, the oft-injured Stauffer lost another season to arm trouble. A right elbow strain caused him to miss his first scheduled Opening Day start. A month and a half later, he worked five innings against the Nationals. The next day, he was back on the disabled list. He had surgery on the elbow at the end of August and became a free agent after the World Series. Stauffer has proven that when healthy, he is a solid mid-rotation starter. He also has proven that "when healthy" is the cruelest phrase in a pitcher's vocabulary.

Huston Street

Born: **8/2/1983** Age: **29**
Bats: **R** Throws: **R** Height: **6' 1"** Weight: **190**
Breakout: **21%** Improve: **47%** Collapse: **38%**
Attrition: **9%** MLB: **93%**

Comparables:
Sergio Romo,Robb Nen,Roberto Hernandez

YEAR	TEAM	LVL	AGE	W	L	SV	G	GS	IP	H	HR	BB	SO	BB9	SO9	GB%	BABIP	WHIP	ERA	FIP	FRA	WARP
2010	TUL	AA	26	0	0	0	2	1	1^1	1	0	1	2	6.9	13.8	33%	.333	1.54	0.00	2.40	1.35	0.1
2010	CSP	AAA	26	1	1	0	7	1	7	11	1	2	9	2.6	11.6	48%	.455	1.86	10.29	3.73	5.00	0.2
2010	COL	MLB	26	4	4	20	44	0	47^1	39	5	11	45	2.1	8.6	38%	.274	1.06	3.61	3.40	4.35	0.5
2011	CSP	AAA	27	0	0	0	2	0	2	0	0	0	2	0.0	9.0	50%	.000	0.00	0.00	1.78	2.86	0.1
2011	COL	MLB	27	1	4	29	62	0	58^1	62	10	9	55	1.4	8.5	38%	.317	1.22	3.86	3.85	4.32	0.8
2012	LEL	A+	28	0	0	0	2	2	2	1	1	1	1	4.5	4.5	50%	.000	1.00	9.00	10.81	36.96	0.0
2012	SDN	MLB	28	2	1	23	40	0	39	17	2	11	47	2.5	10.8	43%	.179	0.72	1.85	2.24	2.76	0.7
2013	*SDN*	*MLB*	*29*	*2*	*1*	*18*	*41*	*0*	*40^2*	*31*	*4*	*9*	*44*	*2.1*	*9.8*	*41%*	*.282*	*0.99*	*2.44*	*2.98*	*2.65*	*0.9*

Acquired from Colorado in December 2011, the strike-throwing Street pitched well for the Padres when he wasn't on the disabled list. He missed most of May with a right shoulder strain, and good chunks of August and September with a left-calf strain. Five of the eight runs he allowed last year came in his final three appearances, after the second DL stint. In between injuries, Street signed an extension that will keep him in San Diego at least through 2014, with a club option for 2015. Not every budget-conscious organization would allocate $14 million to a guy who hasn't worked as many as 60 innings in a season since 2009.

Eric Stults

Born: **12/9/1979** Age: **33**
Bats: **L** Throws: **L** Height: **6' 1"** Weight: **225**
Breakout: **16%** Improve: **52%** Collapse: **18%**
Attrition: **13%** MLB: **84%**

Comparables:
Bud Black,Bob Ojeda,Tommy Phelps

YEAR	TEAM	LVL	AGE	W	L	SV	G	GS	IP	H	HR	BB	SO	BB9	SO9	GB%	BABIP	WHIP	ERA	FIP	FRA	WARP
2010	HRO	NPB	30	6	10	0	21	0	124^1	149	23	46	87	3.3	6.3	—	.314	1.57	5.07	5.18	5.64	0.0
2011	CSP	AAA	31	4	4	1	52	0	68	76	11	16	69	2.1	9.1	36%	.318	1.35	4.63	4.56	3.00	1.6
2011	COL	MLB	31	0	0	0	6	0	12	11	4	4	7	3.0	5.2	29%	.189	1.25	6.00	7.41	9.01	-0.3
2012	CHR	AAA	32	1	1	0	5	5	28^2	25	0	10	26	3.1	8.2	42%	.316	1.22	2.20	2.39	1.06	0.4
2012	TUC	AAA	32	0	0	0	2	2	6^2	7	0	4	10	5.4	13.5	42%	.368	1.65	5.40	2.47	4.61	0.1
2012	CHA	MLB	32	0	0	0	2	1	6^2	6	0	4	4	5.4	5.4	57%	.286	1.50	2.70	4.10	3.91	0.1
2012	SDN	MLB	32	8	3	0	18	14	92^1	86	7	23	51	2.2	5.0	41%	.262	1.18	2.92	3.80	3.98	1.2
2013	*SDN*	*MLB*	*33*	*4*	*5*	*0*	*23*	*11*	*81^2*	*79*	*9*	*27*	*57*	*3.0*	*6.3*	*42%*	*.291*	*1.30*	*4.21*	*4.23*	*4.58*	*-0.2*

Another reclamation project that landed in a Padres rotation desperate for healthy arms, Stults pitched surprisingly well last year after being claimed off waivers from the White Sox in mid-May. The journeyman got hit hard his third time through a lineup and fared much better against lefties than righties, suggesting that the bullpen might be a more suitable home. Then again, his versatility is a chief selling point. Stults may never have a clearly defined role or stay in the big leagues for extended periods, but he's a good insurance policy just in case your entire pitching staff gets hurt. Again.

Joe Thatcher

Born: **10/4/1981** Age: **31**
Bats: **L** Throws: **L** Height: **6' 3"** Weight: **230**
Breakout: **20%** Improve: **48%** Collapse: **28%**
Attrition: **12%** MLB: **91%**

Comparables:
Pedro Feliciano,Arthur Rhodes,Sparky Lyle

YEAR	TEAM	LVL	AGE	W	L	SV	G	GS	IP	H	HR	BB	SO	BB9	SO9	GB%	BABIP	WHIP	ERA	FIP	FRA	WARP
2010	POR	AAA	28	0	1	0	6	0	5	6	0	3	3	5.4	5.4	65%	.353	1.80	3.60	4.78	4.42	0.0
2010	SDN	MLB	28	1	0	0	65	0	35	23	1	7	45	1.8	11.6	44%	.265	0.86	1.29	1.59	1.87	0.7
2011	LEL	A+	29	0	0	0	1	0	1	0	0	0	2	0.0	18.0	—	.000	0.00	0.00	-0.05	-0.05	0.0
2011	TUC	AAA	29	0	0	0	8	0	7^1	3	0	3	10	3.7	12.3	40%	.200	0.82	1.23	2.69	1.33	0.4
2011	SDN	MLB	29	0	0	0	18	0	10	8	1	7	9	6.3	8.1	43%	.259	1.50	4.50	4.59	4.73	-0.2
2012	LEL	A+	30	0	0	0	1	1	1	0	0	0	1	0.0	9.0	50%	.000	0.00	0.00	1.81	0.34	0.0
2012	SDN	MLB	30	1	4	1	55	0	31^2	30	2	14	39	4.0	11.1	45%	.337	1.39	3.41	3.10	2.17	0.5
2013	*SDN*	*MLB*	*31*	*3*	*2*	*1*	*65*	*0*	*38^1*	*32*	*3*	*12*	*41*	*2.9*	*9.6*	*48%*	*.307*	*1.17*	*3.23*	*3.02*	*3.51*	*0.5*

After missing most of 2011 recovering from left shoulder surgery, Thatcher stayed relatively healthy last year. He sat out August with a right knee issue that required surgery after the season, but for the most part he returned to the business of abusing left-handed batters. Thatcher's sidearm delivery makes it difficult for them to pick up the ball. Right-handers have no such trouble, limiting Thatcher to the role of LOOGY, albeit a good one.

Dale Thayer

Born: **12/17/1980** Age: **32**
Bats: **R** Throws: **R** Height: **6' 1"** Weight: **195**
Breakout: **20%** Improve: **49%** Collapse: **30%**
Attrition: **16%** MLB: **91%**

Comparables:
Luis Ayala,Jeff Shaw,Matt Guerrier

YEAR	TEAM	LVL	AGE	W	L	SV	G	GS	IP	H	HR	BB	SO	BB9	SO9	GB%	BABIP	WHIP	ERA	FIP	FRA	WARP
2010	DUR	AAA	29	4	1	3	46	0	60	68	3	25	55	3.8	8.2	49%	.338	1.55	3.45	3.56	4.58	0.6
2010	TBA	MLB	29	0	0	0	1	0	2	7	1	0	2	0.0	9.0	46%	.600	3.50	27.00	7.55	4.44	0.0
2011	BUF	AAA	30	4	3	21	54	0	71	54	8	15	66	1.9	8.4	54%	.233	0.97	2.66	3.52	3.93	0.6
2011	NYN	MLB	30	0	3	0	11	0	10^{1}	12	0	0	5	0.0	4.4	46%	.324	1.16	3.48	2.03	2.87	0.2
2012	TUC	AAA	31	0	0	0	7	0	8^{1}	2	0	2	5	2.2	5.4	50%	.091	0.48	0.00	3.19	2.99	0.2
2012	SDN	MLB	31	2	2	7	64	0	57^{2}	53	4	12	47	1.9	7.3	43%	.287	1.13	3.43	3.08	3.78	0.5
2013	*SDN*	*MLB*	*32*	*2*	*1*	*2*	*43*	*0*	*49*	*46*	*4*	*13*	*39*	*2.4*	*7.1*	*46%*	*.297*	*1.20*	*3.56*	*3.47*	*3.87*	*0.3*

Thayer has a walrus-like mustache and a last name that rhymes with "slayer," making him an ideal choice to close games in Street's absence last May. The minor-league veteran features a mid-90s fastball, throws strikes, and isn't intimidated by situations. On June 20, his ERA was 6.27. Over his final 44 appearances it was 2.08, with opposing batters registering a 533 OPS against him. Thayer may or may not be a big-league closer—the qualifications are nebulous—but he did enough in his first extended stay to merit further looks in the late innings.

Nick Vincent

Born: **7/12/1986** Age: **26**
Bats: **R** Throws: **R** Height: **6' 1"** Weight: **175**
Breakout: **29%** Improve: **57%** Collapse: **17%**
Attrition: **14%** MLB: **84%**

Comparables:
Randor Bierd,Ted Davidson,Frank Smith

YEAR	TEAM	LVL	AGE	W	L	SV	G	GS	IP	H	HR	BB	SO	BB9	SO9	GB%	BABIP	WHIP	ERA	FIP	FRA	WARP
2010	LEL	A+	23	4	0	0	48	1	81^{2}	60	7	23	76	2.5	8.4	44%	.248	1.02	1.87	4.01	4.50	0.9
2011	SAN	AA	24	8	2	3	66	0	79^{1}	54	6	20	89	2.3	10.1	38%	.265	0.93	2.27	2.99	3.91	0.7
2012	SAN	AA	25	1	0	0	9	0	9^{2}	4	0	0	15	0.0	14.0	50%	.222	0.41	1.86	0.49	1.07	0.4
2012	TUC	AAA	25	1	1	2	23	0	21^{2}	27	2	11	19	4.6	7.9	43%	.368	1.75	5.82	4.91	5.26	0.2
2012	SDN	MLB	25	2	0	0	27	0	26^{1}	19	2	7	28	2.4	9.6	39%	.254	0.99	1.71	2.91	3.79	0.2
2013	*SDN*	*MLB*	*26*	*2*	*1*	*0*	*30*	*0*	*37^{1}*	*34*	*4*	*14*	*33*	*3.3*	*8.1*	*42%*	*.296*	*1.28*	*4.04*	*3.95*	*4.39*	*-0.0*

A local product taken by the Padres in the 18th round of the 2008 draft, Vincent was one of Bud Black's more reliable options down the stretch, albeit mostly in low-leverage situations. Vincent barely reaches 90 mph with his fastball, relying more on movement. His margin for error is slim, but for a ninth or 10th guy on a staff, teams could do worse.

Edinson Volquez

Born: **7/3/1983** Age: **29**
Bats: **R** Throws: **R** Height: **6' 1"** Weight: **225**
Breakout: **15%** Improve: **42%** Collapse: **26%**
Attrition: **13%** MLB: **88%**

Comparables:
Daisuke Matsuzaka,Daniel Cabrera,Jack Sanford

YEAR	TEAM	LVL	AGE	W	L	SV	G	GS	IP	H	HR	BB	SO	BB9	SO9	GB%	BABIP	WHIP	ERA	FIP	FRA	WARP
2010	DYT	A	26	0	0	0	2	2	13	11	2	4	19	2.8	13.2	57%	.321	1.15	1.38	3.84	2.68	0.4
2010	LYN	A+	26	1	0	0	2	2	8	3	0	0	7	0.0	7.9	40%	.150	0.38	0.00	2.03	2.60	0.2
2010	LOU	AAA	26	3	0	0	4	4	23	11	1	8	21	3.1	8.2	41%	.175	0.83	1.96	3.20	3.93	0.3
2010	CIN	MLB	26	4	3	0	12	12	62^{2}	59	6	35	67	5.0	9.6	57%	.323	1.50	4.31	4.03	4.67	1.1
2011	LOU	AAA	27	4	2	0	13	13	87^{1}	72	5	29	83	3.0	8.6	53%	.265	1.16	2.37	3.21	4.17	0.7
2011	CIN	MLB	27	5	7	0	20	20	108^{2}	106	19	65	104	5.4	8.6	54%	.293	1.57	5.71	5.26	5.77	-1.0
2012	SDN	MLB	28	11	11	0	32	32	182^{2}	160	14	105	174	5.2	8.6	52%	.292	1.45	4.14	4.10	4.60	0.0
2013	*SDN*	*MLB*	*29*	*8*	*10*	*0*	*27*	*27*	*153^{2}*	*125*	*13*	*74*	*153*	*4.3*	*9.0*	*48%*	*.292*	*1.30*	*3.87*	*3.75*	*4.20*	*0.5*

Part of the Latos trade, Volquez was one of the few Padres starting pitchers to remain healthy all year. He made more than 20 starts in a season for the second time in his career and the first time since 2008. He also led the league in walks. Volquez has good stuff but nibbles and gets flustered when things don't go his way. If he improves his command and learns to keep his emotions in check, he could be a front-line starter. Unfortunately, he has shown little aptitude on either front in 122 big-league starts, so it's more likely that he'll remain an innings eater who periodically teases at something more.

Joe Wieland

Born: **1/21/1990** Age: **23**
Bats: **R** Throws: **R** Height: **6' 4"** Weight: **175**
Breakout: **30%** Improve: **61%** Collapse: **11%**
Attrition: **13%** MLB: **83%**

Comparables:
Joe Kennedy,Daryl Thompson,Liam Hendriks

YEAR	TEAM	LVL	AGE	W	L	SV	G	GS	IP	H	HR	BB	SO	BB9	SO9	GB%	BABIP	WHIP	ERA	FIP	FRA	WARP
2010	HIC	A	20	7	4	0	15	15	89	84	4	15	71	1.5	7.2	50%	.303	1.11	3.34	3.12	4.50	0.8
2010	BAK	A+	20	4	3	0	11	10	59	67	6	10	62	1.5	9.5	39%	.317	1.31	5.19	3.56	3.95	1.2
2011	MYR	A+	21	6	3	0	14	13	85^{2}	78	7	4	96	0.4	10.1	49%	.322	0.96	2.10	2.26	2.91	1.7
2011	FRI	AA	21	4	0	0	7	7	44	35	2	11	36	2.2	7.4	49%	.029	1.05	1.23	3.08	3.89	0.3
2011	SAN	AA	21	3	1	0	5	5	26	23	0	6	18	2.1	6.2	47%	.224	1.12	2.77	2.92	3.79	0.4
2012	TUC	AAA	22	0	1	0	2	2	7^{2}	10	0	2	11	2.3	12.9	52%	.476	1.57	3.52	1.58	2.12	0.4
2012	SDN	MLB	22	0	4	0	5	5	27^{2}	26	5	9	24	2.9	7.8	43%	.262	1.27	4.55	4.83	5.36	-0.1
2013	*SDN*	*MLB*	*23*	*2*	*3*	*0*	*6*	*6*	*37*	*37*	*4*	*12*	*27*	*3.0*	*6.6*	*44%*	*.301*	*1.32*	*4.45*	*4.12*	*4.83*	*-0.2*

Wieland, a fourth-round pick of the Rangers in 2008, came to San Diego in the Adams trade. Forced to the big club by a rash of injuries, Wieland held his own in five starts before injuring his elbow in May (he underwent Tommy John surgery toward the end of July). He features a low-90s fastball and decent secondary pitches (curve, changeup). The key to his success is command, which is the last thing to return after Tommy John surgery. If and when it does, Wieland slots as a third or fourth starter, but all bets are off until he actually throws again.

LINEOUTS

HITTERS

PLAYER	TEAM	LVL	AGE	PA	R	2B	3B	HR	RBI	BB	SO	SB-CS	AVG/OBP/SLG	TAv	BABIP	BRR	FRAA	WARP
SS J. Bartlett	SDN	MLB	32	98	8	5	0	0	4	12	27	0-0	.133/.240/.193	.168	.193	0.8	SS(27): -1.1	-0.6
OF T. Buck	OKL	AAA	28	71	9	4	0	1	6	5	8	0-0	.359/.414/.469	.332	.400	0.9	--	0.3
	HOU	MLB	28	81	7	5	1	0	6	6	18	0-0	.216/.284/.311	.212	.286	-0.1	LF(11): -0.2, RF(10): 1.3	-0.1
1B M. Clark	TUC	AAA	25	511	75	26	2	22	77	57	113	0-0	.290/.367/.506	.285	.338	-3.1	1B(85): -6.5, LF(1): -0.1	-0.1
OF C. Decker	SAN	AA	25	406	54	19	1	25	68	54	100	1-4	.263/.367/.540	.322	.296	-2.3	RF(27): -3.9, LF(26): -1.9	1.4
	TUC	AAA	25	121	12	7	0	4	13	11	27	0-0	.215/.298/.393	.242	.247	-0.5	LF(15): -1.1, 1B(6): 0.4	-0.2
C J. Hagerty	SAN	AA	24	286	30	12	0	7	30	35	51	0-0	.248/.346/.382	.265	.284	-0.3	C(43): 0.4	0.4
RF J. Hermida	TUC	AAA	28	170	21	7	0	3	22	15	43	1-0	.252/.318/.358	.200	.324	0.6	RF(28): -3.1	-1.2
	SDN	MLB	28	27	2	1	1	0	2	3	7	1-0	.250/.333/.375	.256	.353	-0.1	RF(6): 0.3, LF(1): -0.0	0.0
CF T. Jankowski	FTW	A	21	256	32	10	4	1	23	13	44	17-7	.282/.318/.370	.302	.337	1.4	CF(11): 1.1	0.6
1B T. Medica	LEL	A+	24	406	65	37	5	19	87	41	86	1-1	.330/.406/.623	.363	.387	0.9	1B(8): -0.1	0.6
SS G. Petit	COH	AAA	27	422	51	24	0	10	45	29	75	1-2	.260/.320/.403	.201	.297	-0.7	SS(27): 0.5, 3B(12): 1.4	-0.2
C R. Rivera	ROC	AAA	28	326	31	14	1	10	34	30	62	0-1	.226/.307/.385	.237	.255	-1.8	C(67): 2.2, 1B(6): -0.3	0.3
OF D. Robertson	TUC	AAA	26	553	70	28	4	2	38	48	58	18-8	.302/.371/.388	.260	.339	2.4	CF(62): 4.8, LF(26): 0.1	1.2
C E. Rodriguez	LEL	A+	26	353	37	13	0	13	36	19	100	2-1	.223/.269/.381	.233	.275	-3.3	C(17): 0.2	-0.6
	TUC	AAA	26	53	3	4	0	1	6	2	13	0-0	.180/.226/.320	.190	.222	0.7	C(12): 0.2	-0.1
	SDN	MLB	26	7	1	0	0	1	1	2	3	0-0	.200/.429/.800	.376	.000	0.2	C(2): -0.0	0.1
SS B. Weems	TUC	AAA	24	270	33	12	0	5	26	20	57	0-1	.241/.305/.351	.221	.293	-0.8	SS(49): -2.2, 3B(4): -0.3	-0.6

Jason Bartlett missed most of 2012 with a right knee strain that limited his ability to hurt the Padres on offense or on defense. **Travis Buck** appeared in 33 games last year for the Astros, who lost 107 games, are moving to a league that doesn't require its players to play in the field, and still couldn't use him; if he wasn't on the DL when you started reading this sentence, he probably is now. Taken by the Padres in the 12th round of the 2008 draft out of LSU, **Matt Clark** is an oldish first baseman who has cracked more than 20 homers in each of his four full professional seasons. The Padres took **Cody Decker** in the 22nd round of the 2009 draft out of UCLA and he has hit at every level; his ceiling is roughly that of Bubba Trammell. **Jason Hagerty** is an offense-first catcher who doesn't provide enough offense and who isn't particularly young. **Jeremy Hermida** made the Padres out of spring training, had surgery to repair a sports hernia in May, and then did nothing in two months at Triple-A before being released at the end of August. The Padres took **Travis Jankowski**, an athletic center fielder with good speed and makeup, 44th overall in 2012 out of Stony Brook; his pro-debut numbers aren't exciting, but it was the end of a long season and he finished strong. **Tommy Medica**, a 2010 14th-rounder out of Santa Clara University, is a converted catcher who has spent the last two seasons abusing younger California League pitchers. Primarily a shortstop, minor-league veteran **Gregorio Petit** can play any infield position and fail to hit at all of them. Journeyman catcher **Rene Rivera** owns a career 514 OPS in the big leagues, 710 OPS at Triple-A, and the distinction of having been taken seven picks ahead of J.J. Hardy in the 2001 draft. **Daniel Robertson** can hit a little and play all three outfield positions but has been old for his level every step of the way. **Eddy Rodriguez** is a catch-and-throw guy who homered in his first big-league at-bat off Johnny Cueto of the Reds, the team that originally signed Rodriguez, which is cool because he might not ever hit another. **Beamer Weems** is a gifted defensive shortstop who has trouble hitting baseballs and staying healthy.

PITCHERS

PLAYER	TEAM	LVL	AGE	W	L	SV	IP	H	HR	BB	SO	BB9	SO9	GB%	BABIP	WHIP	ERA	FIP	FRA	WARP
M. Andriese	LEL	A+	22	10	8	0	146	140	9	38	131	2.3	8.1	58%	.315	1.22	3.58	3.68	2.85	0.5
J. Barbato	FTW	A	19	6	1	3	73^1	52	4	31	84	3.8	10.3	42%	.265	1.13	1.84	3.12	3.58	1.3
Z. Eflin	PDR	Rk	18	0	1	0	7	9	0	3	4	3.9	5.1	—	.346	1.71	7.71	4.52	4.91	0
C. Hebner	FTW	A	21	7	7	1	109^2	108	5	50	110	4.1	9.0	41%	.337	1.44	5.01	3.41	4.31	0.4
M. Lollis	LEL	A+	21	0	7	0	58	77	8	29	50	4.5	7.8	45%	.384	1.83	6.83	5.69	7.62	0.0
	SAN	AA	21	1	5	0	35^1	39	4	15	36	3.8	9.2	47%	.326	1.53	5.86	4.16	5.68	0.0
R. Ohlendorf	PAW	AAA	29	4	3	0	52^2	57	5	15	37	2.6	6.3	39%	.310	1.37	4.61	4.30	5.50	-0.2
	SDN	MLB	29	4	4	0	48^2	62	7	24	39	4.4	7.2	33%	.340	1.77	7.77	4.94	4.55	0.1
S. O'Sullivan	LVG	AAA	24	9	3	0	89^1	77	5	23	44	2.3	4.4	48%	.258	1.12	2.72	4.35	5.76	0.6
	OMA	AAA	24	5	4	1	53^1	76	6	23	26	3.9	4.4	43%	.350	1.86	6.75	5.56	5.99	-0.4
M. Owings	SDN	MLB	29	0	2	0	9^2	8	1	5	7	4.7	6.5	50%	.259	1.34	2.79	4.89	5.85	-0.2
M. Palmer	TUC	AAA	33	6	9	0	98^2	120	3	42	64	3.8	5.8	47%	.346	1.64	5.66	4.28	5.22	1.1
	SDN	MLB	33	0	0	0	2	2	1	2	2	9.0	9.0	50%	.200	2.00	9.00	10.64	12.15	-0.1
K. Quackenbush	LEL	A+	23	3	2	27	57^2	42	1	22	70	3.4	10.9	50%	.301	1.11	0.94	2.76	1.11	1.4
C. Rearick	PCH	A+	24	2	3	20	45^1	35	0	15	59	3.0	11.7	38%	.307	1.10	1.79	1.92	0.22	1.6
	MNT	AA	24	2	1	2	24^2	22	4	8	26	2.9	9.5	44%	.269	1.22	4.38	4.36	5.25	0.0
D. Roach	LEL	A+	22	5	1	0	46^2	41	1	11	44	2.1	8.5	71%	.303	1.11	1.74	3.17	2.11	0.4
	SBR	A+	22	5	0	0	41^2	36	1	3	29	0.6	6.3	78%	.268	0.94	2.16	3.02	-0.19	0.0
B. Smith	LEL	A+	22	9	6	0	128^2	127	11	27	137	1.9	9.6	42%	.330	1.20	3.85	3.59	3.15	0.6
M. Stites	FTW	A	22	2	0	13	48^2	25	4	3	60	0.6	11.1	36%	.192	0.58	0.74	2.20	2.40	1.2
J. Suppan	SDN	MLB	37	2	3	0	30^2	34	4	13	7	3.8	2.1	58%	.265	1.53	5.28	5.65	6.18	-0.5
T. Weber	TOL	AAA	27	7	11	0	128^2	123	16	31	97	2.2	6.8	51%	.278	1.20	4.20	4.13	5.57	0.0
	DET	MLB	27	0	1	0	4	10	0	2	1	4.5	2.2	81%	.476	3.00	9.00	4.05	4.29	0.0
W. Weickel	PDR	Rk	18	1	3	0	14	16	0	6	12	3.9	7.7	.639	.389	1.57	4.50	3.95	5.00	0.3
K. Wells	TUC	AAA	35	2	4	0	50^2	60	4	26	22	4.6	3.9	61%	.320	1.70	4.80	5.42	7.26	-0.2
	SDN	MLB	35	2	4	0	37^1	41	6	20	19	4.8	4.6	48%	.285	1.63	4.58	5.90	5.97	-0.3
M. Wisler	FTW	A	19	5	4	0	114	95	1	28	113	2.2	8.9	46%	.302	1.08	2.53	2.35	2.87	1.3

Strike thrower **Matt Andriese** fared much better against right-handed batters than against lefties in his full-season debut. ⊘ The Padres selected **Johnny Barbato** in the sixth round of the 2010 draft; he moved to the bullpen last year and held right-handed hitters to a .139 batting average. ⊘ Taken with the 33rd pick overall in 2012 out of a Florida high school, **Zach Eflin** missed a month of his senior season with triceps tendonitis but was healthy enough to get some work in after signing. ⊘ **Cody Hebner**, taken in the fourth round of the 2011 draft, throws hard and started the season strong (3.43 ERA in 63 innings through June 11) before posting a 7.14 ERA the rest of the way. ⊘ **Matt Lollis** is a huge man with a huge arm that hasn't produced huge results. ⊘ The Padres signed **Ross Ohlendorf** in June because they needed innings real bad, and he gave them real bad innings. ⊘ Toronto purchased **Sean O'Sullivan**'s contract from Kansas City in June but, despite a sparkling ERA at Triple-A Las Vegas and the big-league club's pitching woes, he never threw a pitch for the Blue Jays before signing with his hometown Padres as a minor-league free agent in December. ⊘ **Micah Owings** made the Padres out of spring training, got into a handful of games as a reliever, hurt his elbow at the end of April, contemplated becoming a position player, and had season-ending surgery in July. ⊘ In nearly 700 PCL innings, **Matt Palmer** owns a career 4.86 ERA, which is high even for a hitter-friendly league and which might keep him from making his obligatory three big-league appearances in 2013. ⊘ **Kevin Quackenbush**, an eighth-round pick in 2011, has posted ridiculous numbers in two pro seasons with a low-90s fastball and good deception; after a strong Arizona Fall League showing, he could advance quickly. ⊘ **Chris Rearick**, a 41st-rounder in 2010, doesn't have electric stuff (low-90s fastball, low-80s slider), but he pitches with purpose and intelligence: He earned minor-league Best Relief Pitcher accolades from Tampa Bay, a trip to the AFL, and a December trade to the Padres. ⊘ Acquired from the Angels in the Amarista-Frieri trade, **Donn Roach** is an extreme groundball pitcher who throws strikes; shut down in July to limit his innings, he could be a serious sleeper. ⊘ The Padres' 14th-round pick in 2011 out of the University of Oklahoma, **Burch Smith** overcame a slow start (11 homers allowed in his first 13 starts, none in his last 13) to have a strong full-season debut that quelled talk of a move to the bullpen. ⊘ **Matthew Stites** throws hard and has good control; he didn't issue his first walk of the year until June 26 and didn't walk a right-handed batter all season. ⊘ After spending

2011 at Triple-A in the Royals organization, **Jeff Suppan** made three good starts for the Padres and three horrible ones, then was released in June to make room for the younger and worse Ohlendorf. ⊘ Claimed by the Padres off waivers from Detroit in August, **Thad Weber** is a finesse righty whose greatest asset is the ability to log innings. ⊘ Taken with the 55th pick in the 2012 draft out of a Florida high school, **Walker Weickel** is a tall, athletic right-hander who throws in the low- to mid-90s and has projection. ⊘ After having not pitched in the big leagues since 2009, **Kip Wells** became part of the Padres rotation toward the end of June ostensibly because Juan Eichelberger wasn't available. ⊘ **Matt Wisler**, who dropped to the seventh round in 2011 because of signability concerns coming out of an Ohio high school, finished third in the Midwest League in ERA in his full-season debut despite being one of the circuit's younger players.

MANAGER: BUD BLACK

YEAR	TEAM	W-L	Pythag +/-	Avg PC	100+ P	120+ P	QS	BQS	REL	REL w Zero R	IBB	PH	PH Avg	PH HR	SB2	CS2	SB3	CS3	SAC Att	SAC %	POS SAC	Squeeze	Swing	In Play
2010	SDN	90-72	1	189.6	162	160	116	2	499	431	102	556	.206	18	10	1	0	2	222	80.2%	108	2	359	97
2011	SDN	71-91	0	96.7	65	1	91	4	489	416	56	283	.160	2	21	2	2	0	86	72.1%	30	4	391	88
2012	SDN	76-86	0	92.2	49	1	75	5	529	449	48	278	.248	6	25	2	1	2	107	70.1%	42	1	396	88

Black's biggest challenge in 2012 was finding healthy players to send onto the field every day. Including DL stints and other injuries, the Padres lost 2,009 days last year, tied with the Yankees for most in baseball. Black was without the services of his projected starting catcher, shortstop, or left fielder for much of the season, while 15 different players took a turn in the rotation. Considering Jason Marquis, Ross Ohlendorf, Eric Stults, Jeff Suppan, Kip Wells, and Andrew Werner combined for more than a third of the club's starts, 76 wins and a fourth-place finish seem remarkable.

As in 2009, before San Diego's improbable run the following year, the team performed very well in the second half with Black letting the kids play and run wild. Optimists would say that he has the talent in place and is poised to guide his team to another surprise. Pessimists would note the "improbable" in "improbable run." The truth almost certainly lies somewhere between those two positions. Regardless, Black has the organization's confidence and will continue to lead the Padres wherever they go.

San Francisco Giants

2012: OOPS I DID IT AGAIN

A club that, outside of the starting rotation, bore little resemblance to the 2010 championship team fended off a late push by the newly rich and reinforced Dodgers, won the NL West, won three straight elimination games in back-to-back playoff series, and swept Detroit to win its second championship in three years.

As surprising as this World Series win was, *how* the Giants did it was perhaps more surprising. While the 2010 Giants relied on their pitching to carry a moribund offense, the bats drove the 2012 club. San Francisco posted a surprising .272 team True Average—just a single point behind league-leading St. Louis.

The hero, of course, was eventual NL MVP Buster Posey, who posted a .350 TAv while spending most of his time at the most punishing position on the diamond. But right behind him was an enhanced Melky Cabrera, who led the league in hitting and turned in a 5-WARP performance before being suspended for the rest of the year in mid-August for performance-enhancing drugs.

After the Melk Man went sour, general manager Brian Sabean captured lightning in a bottle again. In 2010 he claimed Cody Ross solely to ensure the outfielder didn't go to the Padres, and Ross went on to be the NLCS MVP. This time, Sabean picked up Marco Scutaro from the Rockies in a seemingly minor deadline deal, and *he* went on to become the 2012 NLCS MVP, going 14-for-28 in the series.

But that wasn't the only gaping hole San Francisco had to fill: The Giants also lost All-Star closer Brian Wilson in April after just two appearances. Skipper Bruce Bochy played the matchups and mixed and matched late-inning relievers, trying Santiago Casilla and his "closer stuff" and flirting with lefty-killer Javier Lopez in the closer role before settling on Sergio Romo and his physics-defying slider.

For most of the season the starting pitching, long the Giants' strength, was pretty mediocre, Matt Cain's perfect game against the Astros on June 13 standing out as a notable exception. The team's Fair Run Average was 11th in the NL, dragged down by Barry Zito and a broken Tim Lincecum—both of whom played huge roles in the Giants postseason run. See? Timing is everything!

GIANTS PROSPECTUS

2012 W-L: 94-68, 1st in NL West

Pythag	.546	10th	DER	.711	13th
RS/G	4.43	12th	B-Age	27.6	7th
RA/G	4.01	8th	P-Age	29.6	26th
TAv	.272	4th	Salary	$132.0	6th
BRR	4.3	10th	M$/MW	$2.61	16th
TAv-P	.265	20th	DL Days	882	14th
FIP	3.82	9th	DL WARP	3.7	13th

Three-Year Park Factors	
Overall	92
HR/RH	82
HR/LH	80
AVG/RH	96
AVG/LH	97

AT&T Park (2000)
Att. % of Capacity: 99.5% (3rd)
Dim. 339, 382, 399, 421, 309

Lefties hit 34 homers at AT&T Park in 2012, or three fewer than Barry Bonds hit there by himself in 2001.

2013: BABY, ONE MORE TIME?

The Giants are in an interesting place as an organization. On one hand, they have a solid core of young, homegrown players locked up or under control for the foreseeable future. That includes their two best starting pitchers, Cain and Madison Bumgarner, along with Posey, Pablo Sandoval, and youngsters Brandon Belt and Brandon Crawford. On the other hand, there are some big holes to fill, and no prospect cavalry will be cresting the hill anytime soon.

Freddy Sanchez and Aubrey Huff coming off the books helped give Sabean the leeway to re-sign Scutaro and Angel Pagan, for three and four years, respectively, and a combined $60 million, two-thirds of that to Pagan. Those signings create potential roadblocks for former first-rounders Joe Panik at second base and Gary Brown in center field, though neither figures to be an issue for a while. Panik likely won't be ready until 2014 and Brown is looking a little less lustrous after struggling in Double-A last year. He also won't be ready for the big leagues on Opening Day 2013.

Hunter Pence and Gregor Blanco will surround Pagan in the outfield, though the Giants will probably look for a platoon partner for the latter. Francisco Peguero, who struggled in a brief look last year, should get a chance at the role. Pence struggled in a Giants uniform, though he became an emotional leader in the October rallies. He's likely to bounce back to being the solid, non-superstar middle-of-the-order hitter he'd been before heading west.

The rotation is set for 2013—or is it? Lincecum, so dominant in his first two full big-league seasons, has struggled mightily for parts of the last three. And as effective as he was out of the pen in the playoffs, it seems unlikely that San Francisco would use him as a reliever out of spring training. If he were to struggle early, however, anything is possible—even a reliever making $22 million.

The closer role is still an open question. The Giants declined to gamble $8 million on Wilson's surgically repaired elbow and non-tendered him. One of the knocks on Romo has been his durability; would he be effective as a closer over a 162-game season? Heath Hembree, the closer-apparent, struggled last year in Triple-A and is no longer considered a lock for the job. Bochy may just have to play his hunches for another few months until an answer presents itself.

STATE OF THE ORGANIZATION: GIMME MORE

The Giants' farm system is thin—we ranked it 25th in 2012—but mostly for the right reason: graduations. In Game Four of the World Series, half of the 10 starting players were homegrown, and all of those players remain under team control in '13 and beyond.

One thing the Giants have been able to do consistently over the last several years is draft and develop big-league pitchers, and the system does have some intriguing arms: Chris Stratton, Kyle Crick, Clayton Blackburn, and the aforementioned Hembree all look like potential big-leaguers at this point.

When it comes to position players, though, the system is nearly bereft. After Brown and Panik, top Giants prospects tend to be coin-flip types such as first baseman Ricky Oropesa and catcher Andrew Susac, or raw tools guys such as outfielders Gustavo Cabrera and Mac Williamson.

The Giants will need a couple of these youngsters to hit if they hope to keep pace with the new-look Dodgers in the NL West. They'll also need to continue drafting shrewdly. Maybe the only downside to winning is the corresponding drop in draft order; the Giants will pick 27th in the 2013 draft.

One thing San Francisco won't have to worry about is who's running the show. Baseball's longest-tenured general manager, Sabean, will be back in 2013, as will skipper Bochy. The team also holds 2014 options for both men, and given San Francisco's recent run of phenomenal success, Giants fans should view that as a positive.

HITTERS

Joaquin Arias **UT**
Born: **9/21/1984** Age: **28**
Bats: **R** Throws: **R** Height: **6' 2"**
Weight: **170** Breakout: **2%**
Improve: **28%** Collapse: **11%**
Attrition: **15%** MLB: **79%**
Comparables:
Bert Campaneris,Jack Wilson,Cristian Guzman

YEAR	TEAM	LVL	AGE	PA	R	2B	3B	HR	RBI	BB	SO	SB	CS	AVG_OBP_SLG	TAv	BABIP	BRR	FRAA	WARP
2010	NYN	MLB	25	33	5	1	0	0	4	2	6	0	0	.200/.250/.233	.201	.250	-0.1	2B(13): -0.3, SS(2): -0.1	0.0
2010	TEX	MLB	25	101	18	5	1	0	9	2	17	1	0	.276/.290/.347	.230	.333	1.9	2B(25): -0.1, 1B(5): -0.2	0.3
2011	OMA	AAA	26	259	37	12	4	3	25	14	28	7	1	.232/.272/.353	.211	.250	0.5	3B(18): 1.5, SS(5): -0.7	-0.5
2012	FRE	AAA	27	74	14	5	0	2	17	3	11	0	1	.400/.432/.557	.336	.456	0	SS(16): -0.5	0.7
2012	SFN	MLB	27	344	30	13	5	5	34	13	44	5	1	.270/.304/.389	.250	.295	2.3	3B(74): 1.5, SS(50): -1.5	0.8
2013	*SFN*	*MLB*	*28*	*280*	*26*	*11*	*3*	*3*	*23*	*11*	*40*	*6*	*1*	*.252/.286/.344*	*.237*	*.285*	*0.8*	*SS -1, 3B 0*	*0.3*

Arias's journey to being a major-league contributor was a roller-coaster ride that was thoroughly covered by Ian Miller in his *Punk Hits* series back in September. He was a prospect the Rangers infamously chose as the player to be named later over Robinson Cano in the Alex Rodriguez blockbuster. Shoulder injuries derailed his development, and Sabean signed him to a minor-league contract last winter. Arias rewarded Sabean by serving as a valuable utility infielder who was especially effective against left-handed pitching. He's not going to be the above-average shortstop many expected him to become, but he has positioned himself well to stick around in a utility role for the foreseeable future.

Brandon Belt **1B**
Born: **4/20/1988** Age: **25**
Bats: **L** Throws: **L** Height: **6' 6"**
Weight: **220** Breakout: **1%**
Improve: **52%** Collapse: **2%**
Attrition: **8%** MLB: **97%**
Comparables:
John Olerud,Ike Davis,John Mayberry

YEAR	TEAM	LVL	AGE	PA	R	2B	3B	HR	RBI	BB	SO	SB	CS	AVG_OBP_SLG	TAv	BABIP	BRR	FRAA	WARP
2010	SJO	A+	22	333	62	28	4	10	62	58	50	18	7	.383/.497/.628	.386	.445	-2.1	1B(71): 4.6	5.3
2010	RIC	AA	22	201	26	11	6	9	40	22	34	2	1	.337/.417/.623	.369	.379	0	1B(36): 1.7, RF(5): 0.9	2.7
2010	FRE	AAA	22	61	11	4	0	4	10	13	15	2	0	.229/.393/.562	.324	.241	-0.7	RF(6): -0.6, 1B(5): 0.3	0.4
2011	FRE	AAA	23	212	32	12	0	8	32	42	47	4	4	.309/.448/.527	.310	.381	0.5	LF(14): 0.3, 1B(7): -0.7	0.8
2011	SFN	MLB	23	209	21	6	1	9	18	20	57	3	2	.225/.306/.412	.263	.273	0.1	LF(31): 0.6, 1B(31): -0.5	0.2
2012	SFN	MLB	24	472	47	27	6	7	56	54	106	12	2	.275/.360/.421	.304	.351	-0.6	1B(139): -2.4, LF(4): -0.1	2.3
2013	*SFN*	*MLB*	*25*	*404*	*48*	*20*	*3*	*10*	*47*	*47*	*91*	*8*	*3*	*.261/.350/.421*	*.284*	*.323*	*0.3*	*1B -5, LF -0*	*1.0*

The Giants' handling of Belt in 2011 and early last year frustrated many fans, which led to Twitter cries of #FreeBelt. He eventually asserted himself as the team's primary first baseman, but not before making mechanical adjustments to his swing in May.

Belt hits for less power than most of his counterparts at the position, but he helps offset that deficiency with strong on-base skills. A list of comparables that includes John Olerud serves as a reminder that not all All-Star first baseman are lumbering sluggers. If Belt is able to follow a similar career path to Olerud, then tweets of frustration will be replaced by the hashtag #Belted.

Gregor Blanco OF

Born: **12/12/1983** Age: **29**
Bats: **L** Throws: **L** Height: **6' 0"**
Weight: **170** Breakout: **5%**
Improve: **31%** Collapse: **7%**
Attrition: **27%** MLB: **85%**

Comparables:
Steve Hovley,Al Pilarcik,Mark Sweeney

YEAR	TEAM	LVL	AGE	PA	R	2B	3B	HR	RBI	BB	SO	SB	CS	AVG_OBP_SLG	TAv	BABIP	BRR	FRAA	WARP
2010	GWN	AAA	26	187	26	8	0	1	11	23	28	9	1	.286/.364/.357	.266	.321	2.4	CF(26): -2.6, RF(13): 0.3	0.7
2010	ATL	MLB	26	66	9	1	1	0	3	8	15	1	2	.310/.394/.362	.270	.419	0.8	CF(25): -0.1, LF(7): -0.0	0.4
2010	KCA	MLB	26	203	22	8	3	1	11	21	35	10	2	.274/.348/.369	.259	.333	0.4	CF(40): -5.5, RF(3): -0.1	0.2
2011	OMA	AAA	27	74	13	5	0	0	4	17	15	9	1	.196/.384/.286	.442	.268	0.4	LF(6): 0.5	0.6
2011	SYR	AAA	27	178	28	7	2	3	10	27	35	15	1	.203/.335/.343	.246	.245	2.2	LF(23): 3.1, CF(15): 0.5	0.4
2012	SFN	MLB	28	453	56	14	5	5	34	51	104	26	6	.244/.333/.344	.266	.318	5.5	RF(54): -1.2, LF(53): -2.5	1.2
2013	*SFN*	*MLB*	*29*	*356*	*43*	*11*	*3*	*2*	*23*	*43*	*74*	*18*	*4*	*.236/.332/.312*	*.247*	*.296*	*2*	*RF -0, CF -0*	*0.6*

Like Arias, Blanco was signed as a minor-league free agent last winter. Blanco broke camp with the Giants and served as a near-every-day player by playing all three outfield positions. On June 13, he made one of the most memorable plays of the 2012 season: Playing right field, he helped preserve Matt Cain's perfect game with a diving catch in deepest right-center, AT&T Park's "Triples Alley." His bat doesn't fit the corner-outfield mold, where he'll get most of his playing time if Pagan is healthy, but he is a plus defender and an efficient base stealer. Blanco's best role for a contending team would be as a fourth outfielder.

Gary Brown CF

Born: **9/28/1988** Age: **24**
Bats: **R** Throws: **R** Height: **6' 2"**
Weight: **190** Breakout: **1%**
Improve: **52%** Collapse: **3%**
Attrition: **7%** MLB: **97%**

Comparables:
Marquis Grissom,Tony Gwynn,Curt Flood

YEAR	TEAM	LVL	AGE	PA	R	2B	3B	HR	RBI	BB	SO	SB	CS	AVG_OBP_SLG	TAv	BABIP	BRR	FRAA	WARP
2011	SJO	A+	22	638	115	34	13	14	80	46	77	53	19	.336/.407/.519	.321	.369	0	--	0.0
2012	RIC	AA	23	610	73	32	2	7	42	40	87	33	18	.279/.347/.385	.282	.318	3.6	CF(113): -2.4, LF(6): -0.0	3.0
2013	*SFN*	*MLB*	*24*	*250*	*29*	*11*	*1*	*3*	*18*	*13*	*49*	*9*	*4*	*.238/.293/.330*	*.235*	*.286*	*0.2*	*CF -2, LF -0*	*-0.1*

Brown made a splash in his professional debut at High-A. He appeared to be on the fast track to patrolling center field at AT&T as the Giants' long-term answer at the position. He was solid—but not spectacular—in Double-A last year, which has resulted in tempered expectations. Brown, whose makeup is lauded, has plus speed and uses it to play above-average defense at a premium position. His future role is dependent on the development of his hit tool. If it develops to be average, he can be an every-day center fielder. If it doesn't, he'll be a fourth outfielder.

Brandon Crawford SS

Born: **1/21/1987** Age: **26**
Bats: **L** Throws: **R** Height: **6' 3"**
Weight: **215** Breakout: **7%**
Improve: **54%** Collapse: **5%**
Attrition: **20%** MLB: **94%**

Comparables:
Toby Harrah,Diory Hernandez,Chris Speier

YEAR	TEAM	LVL	AGE	PA	R	2B	3B	HR	RBI	BB	SO	SB	CS	AVG_OBP_SLG	TAv	BABIP	BRR	FRAA	WARP
2010	RIC	AA	23	342	43	12	3	7	22	39	77	4	1	.241/.341/.375	.268	.303	0	SS(75): 20.5	3.7
2011	SJO	A+	24	69	14	5	1	3	15	9	13	0	0	.322/.412/.593	.340	.372	0	--	0.0
2011	FRE	AAA	24	118	13	5	1	1	9	9	20	5	2	.234/.291/.327	.216	.276	-0.8	SS(12): 1.1	0.0
2011	SFN	MLB	24	220	22	5	2	3	21	23	31	1	3	.204/.288/.296	.213	.228	0.4	SS(65): 0.4	-0.3
2012	SFN	MLB	25	476	44	26	3	4	45	33	95	1	4	.248/.304/.349	.248	.307	0.5	SS(139): 13.1	2.5
2013	*SFN*	*MLB*	*26*	*402*	*38*	*17*	*2*	*5*	*35*	*32*	*79*	*3*	*2*	*.233/.298/.337*	*.240*	*.279*	*-0.6*	*SS 4, 3B -0*	*1.3*

As a pre-arbitration-eligible player, Crawford provides the Giants a cheap every-day regular at a demanding defensive position. He is a slick fielder who can turn eye-catching double plays and get to balls in the hole that many of his peers can't touch. After an erratic start to the season, Crawford tightened up his glove work by cutting down miscues on routine plays. His bat currently profiles in the bottom third of an NL lineup, but he did rank 12th in TAv out of 22 shortstops who had 400 or more plate appearances, and he did improve his slash line across the board in the second half.

Chris Dominguez LF

Born: **11/22/1986** Age: **26**
Bats: **R** Throws: **R** Height: **6' 4"**
Weight: **215** Breakout: **7%**
Improve: **50%** Collapse: **4%**
Attrition: **14%** MLB: **93%**

Comparables:
John Boccabella,Rip Repulski,Larry Stahl

YEAR	TEAM	LVL	AGE	PA	R	2B	3B	HR	RBI	BB	SO	SB	CS	AVG_OBP_SLG	TAv	BABIP	BRR	FRAA	WARP
2010	AUG	A	23	608	85	32	4	21	101	35	133	14	7	.272/.327/.456	.288	.323	-0.3	3B(134): 4.7	4.8
2011	SJO	A+	24	279	40	10	1	11	40	18	73	8	2	.291/.337/.465	.274	.364	0	--	0.0
2011	RIC	AA	24	313	35	22	2	7	45	9	78	1	5	.244/.272/.403	.244	.302	-1	3B(61): -4.1	-0.5
2012	RIC	AA	25	197	17	9	0	2	19	7	50	3	0	.223/.254/.303	.178	.292	3	LF(43): 0.6, 3B(3): -0.6	-1.0
2012	FRE	AAA	25	178	15	11	0	3	25	2	47	1	2	.247/.264/.362	.197	.323	-1.4	LF(31): -2.3, RF(3): -0.1	-0.9
2013	*SFN*	*MLB*	*26*	*250*	*20*	*10*	*1*	*5*	*24*	*7*	*70*	*2*	*1*	*.211/.239/.323*	*.210*	*.274*	*-0.4*	*3B 0, LF -0*	*-0.8*

Dominguez was drafted as a third baseman, but he played left field almost exclusively last year. He has a big body, but not necessarily a bad one. Dominguez isn't very athletic, and that will reduce the odds of him succeeding at his new position, but he has a strong arm and plus power. While his approach and suspect hit tool limit the utility of his pop, he could get a look in the majors if he is able to improve those facets of his offensive game. That's a big if.

Adam Duvall **3B**
Born: **9/4/1988** Age: **24**
Bats: **R** Throws: **R** Height: **6' 2"**
Weight: **205** Breakout: **6%**
Improve: **53%** Collapse: **5%**
Attrition: **12%** MLB: **96%**
Comparables:
Gil McDougald, Josh Bell, Hank Blalock

YEAR	TEAM	LVL	AGE	PA	R	2B	3B	HR	RBI	BB	SO	SB	CS	AVG_OBP_SLG	TAv	BABIP	BRR	FRAA	WARP
2010	SLO	A-	21	217	30	10	1	4	18	14	45	2	3	.245/.315/.370	.259	.295	-1.3	2B(26): 6.9, 3B(17): -0.6	1.0
2011	AUG	A	22	510	69	30	4	22	87	59	98	4	4	.285/.385/.527	.325	.320	0.1	3B(73): -2.5	2.9
2012	SJO	A+	23	598	101	24	4	30	100	47	116	8	2	.258/.327/.487	.270	.274	2.5	3B(48): -3.7	0.6
2013	*SFN*	*MLB*	*24*	*250*	*24*	*9*	*1*	*8*	*30*	*14*	*61*	*0*	*0*	*.219/.273/.376*	*.241*	*.258*	*-0.3*	*3B 3, 2B 0*	*0.4*

Duvall has hit for considerable power in the low minors in consecutive seasons. That power is his calling card: He may possess enough pop to smack 25-plus home runs in the majors in the future. The tradeoff is that he doesn't project to hit for much average. He's currently a third baseman, but not overly athletic. He has good instincts, so there is a non-zero chance that he can stick at the hot corner. If forced to move across the diamond, he'll be a second-division player.

Conor Gillaspie **3B**
Born: **7/18/1987** Age: **25**
Bats: **L** Throws: **R** Height: **6' 2"**
Weight: **195** Breakout: **10%**
Improve: **50%** Collapse: **8%**
Attrition: **29%** MLB: **97%**
Comparables:
Ryan Rohlinger, Jeff Cirillo, Taylor Green

YEAR	TEAM	LVL	AGE	PA	R	2B	3B	HR	RBI	BB	SO	SB	CS	AVG_OBP_SLG	TAv	BABIP	BRR	FRAA	WARP
2010	RIC	AA	22	540	57	25	8	8	67	37	67	0	4	.287/.338/.420	.286	.318	0	3B(122): -3.2	2.8
2011	FRE	AAA	23	503	63	22	6	11	61	66	79	9	9	.297/.389/.453	.289	.339	-3	3B(65): 2.4, 1B(5): 0.3	1.3
2011	SFN	MLB	23	21	2	0	0	1	2	2	1	0	0	.263/.333/.421	.294	.235	0	3B(4): -0.2	0.1
2012	FRE	AAA	24	465	60	18	3	14	49	41	54	0	0	.281/.345/.441	.285	.291	-0.2	3B(57): -6.1, 1B(19): 0.1	0.8
2012	SFN	MLB	24	20	2	1	0	0	2	0	2	0	0	.150/.150/.200	.121	.167	0	3B(5): -0.3	-0.4
2013	*SFN*	*MLB*	*25*	*250*	*22*	*10*	*2*	*4*	*24*	*17*	*42*	*1*	*1*	*.243/.297/.351*	*.241*	*.279*	*-0.4*	*3B -1, 1B 0*	*-0.1*

Defensively, Gillaspie is limited to an infield corner. That's bad news for him because he simply doesn't have enough thunder in the stick or secondary offensive skills to profile as an every-day third baseman. Gillaspie isn't completely devoid of value: He makes a lot of contact, and is competent at taking walks. He is also cost-controlled since he is not eligible for arbitration until 2015. Those marketable attributes make him a potential up-and-down guy or bench bat.

Aubrey Huff **1B**
Born: **12/20/1976** Age: **36**
Bats: **L** Throws: **R** Height: **6' 5"**
Weight: **225** Breakout: **1%**
Improve: **33%** Collapse: **14%**
Attrition: **18%** MLB: **90%**
Comparables:
Kevin Millar, Mike Sweeney, Hideki Matsui

YEAR	TEAM	LVL	AGE	PA	R	2B	3B	HR	RBI	BB	SO	SB	CS	AVG_OBP_SLG	TAv	BABIP	BRR	FRAA	WARP
2010	SFN	MLB	33	668	100	35	5	26	86	83	91	7	0	.290/.385/.506	.312	.303	2.7	1B(100): 5.6, LF(46): 5.2	5.8
2011	SFN	MLB	34	579	45	27	1	12	59	47	90	5	3	.246/.306/.370	.261	.271	-4.7	1B(120): 7.0, RF(13): -0.9	-0.2
2012	SFN	MLB	35	95	7	4	0	1	7	16	12	0	0	.192/.326/.282	.250	.212	0.3	1B(15): 0.6, LF(5): 0.1	0.0
2013	*SFN*	*MLB*	*36*	*250*	*26*	*12*	*1*	*6*	*28*	*23*	*39*	*2*	*1*	*.249/.322/.395*	*.268*	*.274*	*-0.3*	*1B -0, RF 0*	*0.5*

Huff was a primary piece in the Giants' run to a championship in 2010, but the wearer of the famed "rally thong" has been a wreck since. Bochy blamed Huff's failings at the plate in 2011 on lackadaisical offseason training. Huff responded by rededicating himself to conditioning. He was rewarded with a further collapse of his bat. In addition to his struggles on the field, Huff also spent over 90 days on the disabled list for reasons ranging from battling an anxiety disorder to recovering from an ACL sprain incurred while jumping the dugout rail to celebrate Cain's perfect game. Huff's career has spanned more than a decade and it should probably come to an end with him retiring a champion.

Efrin Oropesa **1B**
Born: **12/15/1989** Age: **23**
Bats: **L** Throws: **R** Height: **6' 4"**
Weight: **225** Breakout: **7%**
Improve: **61%** Collapse: **10%**
Attrition: **19%** MLB: **82%**
Comparables:
Justin Huber, John Ellis, Chris Chambliss

YEAR	TEAM	LVL	AGE	PA	R	2B	3B	HR	RBI	BB	SO	SB	CS	AVG_OBP_SLG	TAv	BABIP	BRR	FRAA	WARP
2012	SJO	A+	22	583	70	30	3	16	98	59	150	1	1	.263/.338/.425	.287	.337	-4.1	1B(46): -0.1	0.8
2013	*SFN*	*MLB*	*23*	*250*	*21*	*10*	*1*	*5*	*24*	*18*	*73*	*0*	*0*	*.211/.269/.322*	*.223*	*.284*	*-0.3*	*1B -3*	*-1.0*

Better known as Ricky, Oropesa had a ho-hum pro debut. Drafted for his bat, the former USC Trojan failed to take advantage of the hitter-friendly California League. Oropesa is a poor athlete who is limited to first base. He has a fringy hit tool and his in-game power is closer to average than plus. He'll need to tap into more of his fence-clearing power if he hopes to reach the majors.

Angel Pagan CF
Born: 7/2/1981 Age: 31
Bats: B Throws: R Height: 6' 3"
Weight: 200 Breakout: 1%
Improve: 52% Collapse: 2%
Attrition: 6% MLB: 95%
Comparables:
Coco Crisp,Alex Rios,Vernon Wells

YEAR	TEAM	LVL	AGE	PA	R	2B	3B	HR	RBI	BB	SO	SB	CS	AVG_OBP_SLG	TAv	BABIP	BRR	FRAA	WARP
2010	NYN	MLB	29	633	80	31	7	11	69	44	97	37	9	.290/.340/.425	.277	.331	9.3	CF(94): 8.2, RF(33): -0.7	5.4
2011	NYN	MLB	30	532	68	24	4	7	56	44	62	32	7	.262/.322/.372	.259	.285	4	CF(121): 1.2	1.5
2012	SFN	MLB	30	659	95	38	15	8	56	48	97	29	7	.288/.338/.440	.290	.329	2.5	CF(151): 10.9	4.7
2013	*SFN*	*MLB*	*31*	*594*	*75*	*30*	*8*	*7*	*49*	*44*	*90*	*29*	*7*	*.271/.324/.396*	*.266*	*.308*	*3.3*	*CF 2, RF 0*	*2.8*

Pagan's name can be added to the list of savvy trade acquisitions by Sabean. The Giants shipped Andres Torres and Ramon Ramirez to the Mets to get him. Pagan was coming off a disappointing 2011 season in which he failed to build on his 2010 breakout. Last year, he reverted back to the good Pagan and enjoyed a career year at the plate, adding value with his efficient base stealing and by playing a premium defensive position. His above-average speed allows him to make tough plays in the field, but bad reads off the bat and occasional bad routes make him an inconsistent defender. The total package is very good, and one that is easy to underrate.

Joe Panik SS
Born: 10/30/1990 Age: 22
Bats: L Throws: R Height: 6' 2"
Weight: 193 Breakout: 4%
Improve: 68% Collapse: 3%
Attrition: 7% MLB: 97%
Comparables:
Sonny Jackson,Ruben Tejada,Bobby Valentine

YEAR	TEAM	LVL	AGE	PA	R	2B	3B	HR	RBI	BB	SO	SB	CS	AVG_OBP_SLG	TAv	BABIP	BRR	FRAA	WARP
2011	SLO	A-	20	304	49	10	3	6	54	28	25	13	5	.341/.401/.467	.307	.354	0	--	0.0
2012	SJO	A+	21	605	93	27	4	7	76	58	54	10	4	.297/.368/.402	.299	.317	4.4	SS(47): 3.0	1.7
2013	*SFN*	*MLB*	*22*	*250*	*23*	*11*	*1*	*1*	*18*	*17*	*37*	*0*	*0*	*.240/.295/.315*	*.234*	*.276*	*-0.3*	*SS 3*	*0.7*

Panik is the type of player who grows on scouts. He isn't loaded with tools, but is a gamer who gets the most out of what he has. His ceiling probably straddles the line between a first- and second-division starter. Though he is currently being developed as a shortstop, where he has decent actions and a fringy arm, the best bet is on him ending up at second base. Offensively, Panik makes contact at a high rate, but his power is limited to driving the ball to the gaps. He'll likely be tested this year with a Double-A assignment.

Francisco Peguero OF
Born: 6/1/1988 Age: 25
Bats: R Throws: R Height: 6' 0"
Weight: 195 Breakout: 9%
Improve: 61% Collapse: 8%
Attrition: 25% MLB: 99%
Comparables:
Roberto Clemente,Bob Gallagher,Jose Guillen

YEAR	TEAM	LVL	AGE	PA	R	2B	3B	HR	RBI	BB	SO	SB	CS	AVG_OBP_SLG	TAv	BABIP	BRR	FRAA	WARP
2010	SJO	A+	22	538	78	19	16	10	77	18	88	40	22	.329/.358/.488	.301	.382	1	CF(63): -3.8, RF(48): -4.7	3.2
2011	SJO	A+	23	76	12	2	0	2	9	7	8	4	0	.324/.387/.441	.294	.345	0	--	0.0
2011	RIC	AA	23	296	34	12	6	5	37	5	45	8	1	.309/.318/.446	.292	.346	0	RF(43): 0.6, CF(3): 0.6	0.9
2012	FRE	AAA	24	476	46	20	10	5	68	15	82	1	0	.272/.297/.394	.232	.319	-1.7	RF(59): 10.0, CF(19): -1.4	-0.4
2012	SFN	MLB	24	16	6	0	0	0	0	0	7	3	0	.188/.188/.188	.141	.333	0.1	LF(8): 0.2, RF(2): 0.3	-0.1
2013	*SFN*	*MLB*	*25*	*250*	*20*	*9*	*3*	*2*	*21*	*5*	*54*	*5*	*2*	*.246/.264/.332*	*.224*	*.307*	*0.5*	*RF 0, CF -1*	*-0.3*

Peguero has some tools, but he struggles with consistency. One day he'll look great and show off all of his skills, and the next he'll be a mess. He's currently an average defender in right field, but there is potential for him to become above average there. At the plate, he struggles with breaking balls, and as his walk rate would suggest, he's an aggressive hitter. If everything clicks he can be an every-day regular. If it doesn't, he may still have a major-league career as an extra outfielder.

Hunter Pence RF
Born: 4/13/1983 Age: 30
Bats: R Throws: R Height: 6' 5"
Weight: 220 Breakout: 0%
Improve: 38% Collapse: 6%
Attrition: 14% MLB: 94%
Comparables:
Corey Hart,Roberto Clemente,Andre Dawson

YEAR	TEAM	LVL	AGE	PA	R	2B	3B	HR	RBI	BB	SO	SB	CS	AVG_OBP_SLG	TAv	BABIP	BRR	FRAA	WARP
2010	HOU	MLB	27	658	93	29	3	25	91	41	105	18	9	.282/.325/.461	.280	.304	3.7	RF(155): 9.5	4.0
2011	HOU	MLB	28	432	49	26	3	11	62	30	86	7	1	.308/.356/.471	.297	.368	1.4	RF(100): -1.0	2.2
2011	PHI	MLB	28	236	35	12	2	11	35	26	38	1	1	.324/.394/.560	.342	.348	0.2	RF(53): -3.4	2.2
2012	PHI	MLB	29	440	59	15	2	17	59	37	85	4	2	.271/.336/.447	.281	.305	-0.3	RF(101): -8.5	0.3
2012	SFN	MLB	29	248	28	11	2	7	45	19	60	1	0	.219/.287/.384	.260	.261	0	RF(58): -0.2	0.0
2013	*SFN*	*MLB*	*30*	*642*	*74*	*29*	*4*	*20*	*79*	*48*	*121*	*9*	*5*	*.267/.323/.430*	*.279*	*.304*	*-0.4*	*RF 3*	*3.0*

Pence's motivational pre-game speeches received a great deal of coverage in the postseason, which is good for him because it diverted attention from his lackluster hitting. He was acquired at the trade deadline from the Phillies for Nate Schierholtz, Tommy Joseph, and Seth Rosin. He was expected to provide a jolt to the lineup, but he failed to do so. Unlike the team's 2011 trade acquisition, Carlos Beltran, Pence was not a half-year rental. He may look awkward at the plate, running, and essentially doing anything on a baseball diamond, but it's probably premature to view his struggles with the Giants as a sign of a total skills collapse. The Giants' decision to tender him suggests they believe he'll bounce back.

Brett Pill **1B**
Born: **9/9/1984** Age: **28**
Bats: **R** Throws: **R** Height: **6' 5"**
Weight: **210** Breakout: **1%**
Improve: **42%** Collapse: **4%**
Attrition: **11%** MLB: **90%**
Comparables:
Brad Fullmer,Michael Aubrey,Dick Kryhoski

YEAR	TEAM	LVL	AGE	PA	R	2B	3B	HR	RBI	BB	SO	SB	CS	AVG_OBP_SLG	TAv	BABIP	BRR	FRAA	WARP
2010	FRE	AAA	25	567	63	34	0	16	84	30	65	7	2	.275/.324/.433	.257	.289	-1.6	1B(126): -3.3, 3B(2): -0.0	-0.1
2011	FRE	AAA	26	576	82	36	3	25	107	25	54	6	6	.312/.341/.530	.287	.305	-1.5	1B(48): -2.9, 2B(43): -3.3	0.6
2011	SFN	MLB	26	53	7	3	2	2	9	2	8	0	1	.300/.321/.560	.310	.317	-0.3	1B(14): 1.0	0.3
2012	FRE	AAA	27	268	35	18	1	11	45	13	36	0	0	.285/.336/.500	.309	.294	-2.3	1B(41): -3.4, LF(2): 0.2	0.5
2012	SFN	MLB	27	114	10	3	0	4	11	6	19	1	0	.210/.265/.352	.219	.220	-1.4	1B(24): 2.4, LF(7): -0.0	-0.2
2013	*SFN*	*MLB*	*28*	*250*	*24*	*12*	*1*	*7*	*28*	*10*	*39*	*2*	*1*	*.243/.281/.389*	*.249*	*.264*	*-0.3*	*1B -6, 2B -0*	*-0.6*

Despite an underwhelming track record, Pill was able to sneak into Bochy's rotation at first base early last season, though he eventually played himself out of that role. Pill has seen time at first base, third base, and left field in the majors, and has also dabbled at second base in the minors. Unfortunately, when not playing first he looks like a first baseman masquerading as a utility player. Offensively, he has all the punch of a middle infielder and an aggressive approach that doesn't lend itself to drawing walks. Pill's profile isn't a good one and it leaves him fighting to stick around.

Buster Posey **C**
Born: **3/27/1987** Age: **26**
Bats: **R** Throws: **R** Height: **6' 2"**
Weight: **220** Breakout: **3%**
Improve: **44%** Collapse: **3%**
Attrition: **4%** MLB: **99%**
Comparables:
Yogi Berra,Joe Torre,Brian McCann

YEAR	TEAM	LVL	AGE	PA	R	2B	3B	HR	RBI	BB	SO	SB	CS	AVG_OBP_SLG	TAv	BABIP	BRR	FRAA	WARP
2010	FRE	AAA	23	208	31	13	2	6	32	28	30	1	1	.349/.451/.552	.340	.397	-2.5	C(32): 0.1, 1B(12): 1.7	2.5
2010	SFN	MLB	23	443	58	23	2	18	67	30	55	0	2	.305/.357/.505	.298	.315	-1.6	C(76): 0.4, 1B(30): -0.8	3.5
2011	SFN	MLB	24	185	17	5	0	4	21	18	30	3	0	.284/.368/.389	.271	.326	-1	C(41): -0.2, 1B(2): 0.0	0.8
2012	SFN	MLB	25	610	78	39	1	24	103	69	96	1	1	.336/.408/.549	.350	.368	-3.8	C(114): -0.5, 1B(29): -2.0	7.0
2013	*SFN*	*MLB*	*26*	*488*	*59*	*25*	*1*	*16*	*65*	*47*	*76*	*1*	*1*	*.295/.367/.471*	*.307*	*.323*	*-0.8*	*C 0, 1B -1*	*4.2*

A gruesome ankle injury ended Posey's 2011 season prematurely, and he exceeded even the most optimistic expectations when he returned to the field last year. He brought home some hardware for his efforts, most notably the NL MVP and the first batting title for an NL catcher since Ernie Lombardi's in 1942. He led the league in BVORP, finishing second overall to Mike Trout, while spending the bulk of his playing time at the most demanding defensive position, catcher. Posey doesn't control the running game as well as some of his peers, but he's not entirely to blame, and the rest of his defense, such as receiving and handling the staff, is sound. When Posey wasn't catching, Bochy often played him at first base, an approach that worked wonders to keep Posey's legs fresh.

Freddy Sanchez **2B**
Born: **12/21/1977** Age: **35**
Bats: **R** Throws: **R** Height: **6' 1"**
Weight: **200** Breakout: **0%**
Improve: **27%** Collapse: **14%**
Attrition: **29%** MLB: **86%**
Comparables:
Jorge Orta,Dane Iorg,Danny Cater

YEAR	TEAM	LVL	AGE	PA	R	2B	3B	HR	RBI	BB	SO	SB	CS	AVG_OBP_SLG	TAv	BABIP	BRR	FRAA	WARP
2010	SFN	MLB	32	479	55	22	1	7	47	32	68	3	1	.292/.342/.397	.267	.330	-2.1	2B(109): 1.4	1.9
2011	SFN	MLB	33	261	21	15	1	3	24	13	35	0	1	.289/.332/.397	.266	.327	0.5	2B(58): -6.4	0.0
2013	*SFN*	*MLB*	*35*	*250*	*25*	*12*	*1*	*2*	*20*	*12*	*38*	*1*	*1*	*.265/.304/.355*	*.248*	*.301*	*-0.4*	*2B -5*	*0.0*

Much of what you need to know about Sanchez is revealed in the injury history section of his Baseball Prospectus player page. He last appeared in a major-league game on June 10, 2011, though he did manage to get into three minor-league games last year. Sanchez underwent microdiscectomy surgery on his back in July. His recovery, and his lengthy list of injuries in recent years, makes accurately projecting his future performance difficult.

Hector Sanchez **C**
Born: **11/17/1989** Age: **23**
Bats: **B** Throws: **R** Height: **6' 0"**
Weight: **235** Breakout: **5%**
Improve: **55%** Collapse: **8%**
Attrition: **7%** MLB: **88%**
Comparables:
Charlie Moore,Rene Rivera,Wilson Ramos

YEAR	TEAM	LVL	AGE	PA	R	2B	3B	HR	RBI	BB	SO	SB	CS	AVG_OBP_SLG	TAv	BABIP	BRR	FRAA	WARP
2010	AUG	A	20	341	29	20	1	5	31	28	50	0	2	.274/.334/.394	.272	.311	-1.7	C(58): 1.4	1.8
2011	SJO	A+	21	228	31	14	1	11	58	11	49	0	1	.302/.338/.533	.289	.342	0	--	0.0
2011	FRE	AAA	21	168	15	9	0	1	26	13	22	0	1	.261/.315/.340	.212	.295	0	C(26): 0.7	-0.2
2011	SFN	MLB	21	34	0	2	0	0	1	3	6	0	0	.258/.324/.323	.225	.320	0.1	C(11): -0.0	0.0
2012	SFN	MLB	22	227	22	15	0	3	34	5	52	0	0	.280/.295/.390	.247	.349	-1.7	C(56): -1.1	-0.1
2013	*SFN*	*MLB*	*23*	*250*	*21*	*12*	*1*	*3*	*22*	*12*	*51*	*0*	*0*	*.242/.280/.338*	*.232*	*.293*	*-0.5*	*C 0*	*0.3*

Prior to earning backup-catcher duties, Sanchez had played in fewer than 50 games in the upper minors. With that in mind, struggles were to be expected. Giants fans bestowed the nickname "Hacktor" upon Sanchez due to his free swinging. Among batters who saw 800 or more pitches, Sanchez ranked 14th in swing rate at pitches outside the strike zone. Not all is bad with him, though, as he can barrel balls up and rip line drives. Further major-league seasoning may help Sanchez better determine which pitches he should drive and which he should take. Behind the plate, he won't find himself mentioned with the finest defenders. Overall, Sanchez is a capable, developing, cost-controlled backup catcher.

Pablo Sandoval 3B

Born: 8/11/1986 Age: 26
Bats: B Throws: R Height: 6' 0"
Weight: 240 Breakout: 1%
Improve: 48% Collapse: 2%
Attrition: 6% MLB: 99%

Comparables:
Puddin Head Jones,Edwin Encarnacion,Ryan Zimmerman

YEAR	TEAM	LVL	AGE	PA	R	2B	3B	HR	RBI	BB	SO	SB	CS	AVG_OBP_SLG	TAv	BABIP	BRR	FRAA	WARP
2010	SFN	MLB	23	616	61	34	3	13	63	47	81	3	2	.268/.323/.409	.260	.291	-1.4	3B(143): -4.7, 1B(11): -1.1	1.6
2011	SFN	MLB	24	466	55	26	3	23	70	32	63	2	4	.315/.357/.552	.324	.320	-1.7	3B(106): 7.9, 1B(6): 0.1	5.1
2012	SFN	MLB	25	442	59	25	2	12	63	38	59	1	1	.283/.342/.447	.294	.301	-0.5	3B(102): 8.2, 1B(3): 0.1	3.2
2013	*SFN*	*MLB*	*26*	*428*	*50*	*25*	*2*	*14*	*58*	*30*	*56*	*2*	*2*	*.295/.345/.477*	*.301*	*.312*	*-0.9*	*3B 3, 1B -0*	*3.0*

Sandoval was an afterthought in the 2010 postseason, but he etched his name in baseball lore by hitting three home runs in Game One of the 2012 World Series. Panda underwent surgery to have the hamate bone in his right wrist removed in 2011 and the left one last year. Happily for him, he no longer has any hamate bones to lose. Much is made of Sandoval's waistline, but he continues to defy logic by fielding the hot corner well. He's a free swinger, but he makes the approach work and saw his unintentional walk rate reach a career high last year. He started in the 2012 All-Star Game, and he should continue to play at a high level.

Marco Scutaro MI

Born: 10/30/1975 Age: 37
Bats: R Throws: R Height: 5' 11"
Weight: 185 Breakout: 0%
Improve: 28% Collapse: 20%
Attrition: 11% MLB: 78%

Comparables:
Willie Randolph,Eric Young,Mark Loretta

YEAR	TEAM	LVL	AGE	PA	R	2B	3B	HR	RBI	BB	SO	SB	CS	AVG_OBP_SLG	TAv	BABIP	BRR	FRAA	WARP
2010	BOS	MLB	34	695	92	38	0	11	56	53	71	5	4	.275/.333/.388	.259	.295	0.5	SS(132): 0.3, 2B(16): 0.6	3.0
2011	BOS	MLB	35	445	59	26	1	7	54	38	36	4	2	.299/.358/.423	.271	.312	2	SS(109): -0.7, 2B(2): 0.0	1.9
2012	COL	MLB	36	415	47	16	3	4	30	27	35	7	3	.271/.324/.361	.240	.287	0.9	2B(72): 4.9, SS(27): 3.1	0.9
2012	SFN	MLB	36	268	40	16	1	3	44	13	14	2	1	.362/.385/.473	.313	.366	0.7	2B(46): -3.6, 3B(15): 1.6	1.7
2013	*SFN*	*MLB*	*37*	*594*	*63*	*26*	*1*	*3*	*43*	*50*	*64*	*7*	*3*	*.261/.325/.335*	*.251*	*.285*	*-0.7*	*SS -0, 2B 1*	*1.8*

The Giants picked up Scutaro in a small deal with the Rockies a few days before the non-waiver trade deadline, and his outstanding play earned him the half-joking nickname "Blockbuster" from his teammates. Scutaro initially filled in for an injured Sandoval at third base before settling in as the team's every-day second baseman. He provided a spark to the lineup by using a high contact rate—the highest among players who saw more than 1,000 pitches—to rope line drives. He carried his sizzling regular-season finish into the playoffs, where he earned NLCS MVP honors, and closed the show by driving in the game-winning run of Game Four of the World Series.

Andrew Susac C

Born: 3/22/1990 Age: 23
Bats: R Throws: R Height: 6' 2"
Weight: 200 Breakout: 3%
Improve: 55% Collapse: 8%
Attrition: 20% MLB: 90%

Comparables:
Gary Carter,Steve Swisher,Lou Marson

YEAR	TEAM	LVL	AGE	PA	R	2B	3B	HR	RBI	BB	SO	SB	CS	AVG_OBP_SLG	TAv	BABIP	BRR	FRAA	WARP
2012	SJO	A+	22	426	58	16	3	9	52	55	100	1	1	.244/.351/.380	.263	.311	-0.7	C(37): -0.2	0.7
2013	*SFN*	*MLB*	*23*	*250*	*21*	*8*	*1*	*4*	*22*	*23*	*68*	*0*	*0*	*.205/.284/.303*	*.223*	*.272*	*-0.2*	*C -0*	*0.1*

The Giants' second-round pick in the 2011 draft, Susac made his pro debut in High-A last year. Not a mechanically sound defender at catcher, he displays poor footwork. That said, he's an above-average athlete at the position and has a chance to improve. He has good power but a poor approach at the plate. Susac has plenty of work to do, but there is enough here to be optimistic he can become a major leaguer.

Ryan Theriot MI

Born: 12/7/1979 Age: 33
Bats: R Throws: R Height: 6' 0"
Weight: 180 Breakout: 1%
Improve: 24% Collapse: 4%
Attrition: 22% MLB: 95%

Comparables:
Jerry Lumpe,Steve Sax,Mark Loretta

YEAR	TEAM	LVL	AGE	PA	R	2B	3B	HR	RBI	BB	SO	SB	CS	AVG_OBP_SLG	TAv	BABIP	BRR	FRAA	WARP
2010	CHN	MLB	30	412	45	10	2	1	21	19	46	16	6	.284/.320/.327	.235	.319	0.1	2B(66): -0.2, SS(29): -0.5	0.4
2010	LAN	MLB	30	228	27	5	0	1	8	22	28	4	3	.242/.323/.283	.240	.276	0.2	2B(53): -0.2	0.2
2011	SLN	MLB	31	483	46	26	1	1	47	29	41	4	6	.271/.321/.342	.238	.296	-1.6	SS(91): -5.5, 2B(35): 0.1	-0.2
2012	SFN	MLB	32	384	45	16	1	0	28	24	47	13	5	.270/.316/.321	.241	.308	1	2B(91): -7.8, LF(2): 0.0	-0.8
2013	*SFN*	*MLB*	*33*	*380*	*40*	*13*	*2*	*0*	*23*	*27*	*47*	*10*	*5*	*.264/.320/.314*	*.242*	*.298*	*-0.3*	*2B -3, SS -1*	*0.3*

You know that old joke: What do you call the guy who finished last in his class in med school? Doctor. Well, what do you call one of the worst players on a World Series winner? Champion. For the second year in a row, Theriot found himself getting more playing time than his ability warranted on a championship team. Theriot fails to distinguish himself at the keystone with his glove, and at the plate he offers no power and roughly league-average on-base skills. He is often described as a scrappy player, and his maximum-effort style of play endears him to teammates and managers. Being liked will only carry him so far, though, and if his skills erode even a little he'll be a man without a major-league job.

Andres Torres CF
Born: **1/26/1978** Age: **35**
Bats: **B** Throws: **R** Height: **5' 10"**
Weight: **200** Breakout: **2%**
Improve: **29%** Collapse: **9%**
Attrition: **16%** MLB: **79%**
Comparables:
Brady Anderson,Jose Cruz Jr.,Amos Otis

YEAR	TEAM	LVL	AGE	PA	R	2B	3B	HR	RBI	BB	SO	SB	CS	AVG_OBP_SLG	TAv	BABIP	BRR	FRAA	WARP
2010	SFN	MLB	32	570	84	43	8	16	63	56	128	26	7	.268/.343/.479	.284	.331	7.8	CF(84): 3.8, RF(43): 1.5	4.8
2011	FRE	AAA	33	62	10	2	2	4	11	6	13	1	0	.273/.355/.600	.328	.289	1	CF(7): 1.0	0.5
2011	SFN	MLB	33	398	50	24	1	4	19	42	95	19	6	.221/.312/.330	.248	.293	5.5	CF(106): 0.5, RF(4): 0.3	1.1
2012	NYN	MLB	34	434	47	17	7	3	35	52	90	13	5	.230/.327/.337	.251	.293	1.3	CF(124): 2.3	1.0
2013	*SFN*	*MLB*	*35*	*407*	*50*	*20*	*5*	*6*	*33*	*40*	*97*	*15*	*5*	*.234/.315/.367*	*.254*	*.299*	*1.5*	*CF 1, RF 0*	*1.2*

Be honest: If you hadn't already looked at Torres's stats above, how old would you have thought he was? Torres just jumped into national semi-prominence in 2010, yet he's already 35. He adds value on the bases and in center and will happily take a walk, but if he can't wring enough pop out of his slap-hitter's body to push his BABIP above the league average, his batting average won't be high enough to make him more than a reserve outfielder. At his age, late-bloomer or not, he's not a good bet to rebound, especially when you see calf, achilles, and hamstring strains in his injury history.

Wilson Valdez SS
Born: **5/20/1978** Age: **35**
Bats: **R** Throws: **R** Height: **6' 0"**
Weight: **170** Breakout: **1%**
Improve: **35%** Collapse: **5%**
Attrition: **17%** MLB: **77%**
Comparables:
John McDonald,Luis Figueroa,Luis Aparicio

YEAR	TEAM	LVL	AGE	PA	R	2B	3B	HR	RBI	BB	SO	SB	CS	AVG_OBP_SLG	TAv	BABIP	BRR	FRAA	WARP
2010	PHI	MLB	32	363	37	16	3	4	35	21	43	7	0	.258/.306/.360	.227	.287	2.9	SS(59): -2.0, 2B(42): -0.1	0.0
2011	PHI	MLB	33	300	39	14	4	1	30	18	41	3	3	.249/.294/.341	.230	.288	3.2	2B(45): 1.0, SS(25): -0.8	-0.4
2012	CIN	MLB	34	208	15	4	0	0	15	8	36	3	1	.206/.236/.227	.178	.252	0.5	SS(33): -5.0, 2B(22): -0.8	-1.8
2013	*SFN*	*MLB*	*35*	*250*	*20*	*9*	*2*	*0*	*17*	*15*	*36*	*4*	*2*	*.235/.282/.293*	*.222*	*.272*	*0.1*	*SS -1, 2B -0*	*-0.1*

At his best, Valdez is an anemic hitter. Last year with the Reds, he was not at his best, posting the lowest slugging percentage of any big-league hitter who amassed at least 200 plate appearances. He is not a great defender but plays multiple positions and can even pitch if needed—he won an epic 19-inning game as a Phillie in 2011. He is the new Manny Alexander, only with a worse glove and better control on the mound.

PITCHERS

Jeremy Affeldt
Born: **6/6/1979** Age: **34**
Bats: **L** Throws: **L** Height: **6' 5"** Weight: **230**
Breakout: **25%** Improve: **43%** Collapse: **36%**
Attrition: **14%** MLB: **83%**
Comparables:
Aaron Fultz,Alberto Castillo,Pedro Feliciano

YEAR	TEAM	LVL	AGE	W	L	SV	G	GS	IP	H	HR	BB	SO	BB9	SO9	GB%	BABIP	WHIP	ERA	FIP	FRA	WARP
2010	SJO	A+	31	0	0	0	2	2	3	2	0	1	4	3.0	12.0	43%	.286	1.00	0.00	2.07	1.46	0.2
2010	SFN	MLB	31	4	3	4	53	0	50	56	4	24	44	4.3	7.9	60%	.340	1.60	4.14	4.01	4.63	0.1
2011	SFN	MLB	32	3	2	3	67	0	61^{2}	47	5	24	54	3.5	7.9	63%	.244	1.15	2.63	3.66	4.26	0.1
2012	SFN	MLB	33	1	2	3	67	0	63^{1}	57	1	23	57	3.3	8.1	62%	.306	1.26	2.70	2.77	3.99	0.4
2013	*SFN*	*MLB*	*34*	*3*	*1*	*2*	*62*	*0*	*58^{1}*	*49*	*4*	*21*	*53*	*3.2*	*8.2*	*57%*	*.294*	*1.19*	*3.29*	*3.35*	*3.57*	*0.6*

Affeldt has been a key cog in the Giants bullpen for four years. He's a groundball-inducing machine that can miss bats at a solid rate. He's also a southpaw who has shown the ability to get out right-handed batters. That blend of skills was enough to convince the Giants to pounce fast in free agency and lock him up for three years and $18 million. Affeldt has never missed time due to an elbow or shoulder injury. When that's factored in with his consistent track record in groundball and strikeout rate, and his improving walk rate, Affeldt becomes a relatively projectable player at a position—relief pitcher—known for volatility.

Martin Agosta
Born: **4/7/1991** Age: **22**
Bats: **R** Throws: **R** Height: **6' 2"** Weight: **180**
Breakout: **28%** Improve: **51%** Collapse: **31%**
Attrition: **22%** MLB: **58%**
Comparables:
Onan Masaoka,Neil Allen,Joe Gilbert

YEAR	TEAM	LVL	AGE	W	L	SV	G	GS	IP	H	HR	BB	SO	BB9	SO9	GB%	BABIP	WHIP	ERA	FIP	FRA	WARP
2012	GIA	Rk	21	0	0	0	5	5	10^{2}	8	0	9	19	7.6	16.0	25%	.000	1.59	4.22	3.91	-3.11	0.3
2013	*SFN*	*MLB*	*22*	*1*	*0*	*1*	*15*	*0*	*34*	*36*	*4*	*21*	*24*	*5.6*	*6.3*	*44%*	*.316*	*1.69*	*5.75*	*5.17*	*6.25*	*-0.4*

The Giants used their second-round pick on Agosta last June. His fastball primarily resides in the 89-92 mph range. He can reach back for 94-95 mph on the heater, but he struggles to locate it in the strike zone when he does. Agosta throws both a slider and a cutter in the low-80s, and both have similar shape, but varying depth and bite. His changeup is in the rudimentary stages of development with Agosta sometimes slowing his arm to throw it. His future role is reliant on him further developing his change, which would give him three potentially average pitches. If the development staff is able to coax fastball command, he could fit a late-inning reliever profile.

Clayton Blackburn

Born: **1/6/1993** Age: **20**
Bats: **L** Throws: **R** Height: **6' 4"** Weight: **220**
Breakout: **37%** Improve: **64%** Collapse: **23%**
Attrition: **14%** MLB: **92%**

Comparables:
David Clyde,Bruce Robbins,Mike McCormick

YEAR	TEAM	LVL	AGE	W	L	SV	G	GS	IP	H	HR	BB	SO	BB9	SO9	GB%	BABIP	WHIP	ERA	FIP	FRA	WARP
2011	GIA	Rk	18	3	1	0	12	6	33^{1}	16	2	3	30	0.8	8.1	74%	.200	0.57	1.08	3.89	4.78	0.4
2012	AUG	A	19	8	4	0	22	22	131^{1}	116	3	18	143	1.2	9.8	60%	.315	1.02	2.54	2.29	3.03	2.9
2013	*SFN*	*MLB*	*20*	*2*	*2*	*0*	*7*	*7*	36^{2}	*36*	*4*	*14*	*28*	*3.3*	*6.9*	*54%*	*.304*	*1.35*	*4.35*	*4.24*	*4.73*	*-0.1*

Blackburn has used a plus 90-92 mph sinker with very good control to emerge as a legitimate prospect. His innings were limited last year by pitching as part of a six-man rotation for Low-A Augusta. Pitchers with good command and control are often able to put up gaudy numbers in the low minors, and Blackburn will be challenged facing more advanced hitters as he rises. Ceiling-wise, he could someday be the number-three man in a major-league rotation.

Madison Bumgarner

Born: **8/1/1989** Age: **23**
Bats: **R** Throws: **L** Height: **6' 6"** Weight: **225**
Breakout: **33%** Improve: **66%** Collapse: **12%**
Attrition: **4%** MLB: **93%**

Comparables:
Mat Latos,Steve Busby,Felix Hernandez

YEAR	TEAM	LVL	AGE	W	L	SV	G	GS	IP	H	HR	BB	SO	BB9	SO9	GB%	BABIP	WHIP	ERA	FIP	FRA	WARP
2010	SFN	MLB	20	7	6	0	18	18	111	119	11	26	86	2.1	7.0	46%	.314	1.31	3.00	3.68	4.00	1.8
2011	SFN	MLB	21	13	13	0	33	33	204^{2}	202	12	46	191	2.0	8.4	48%	.322	1.21	3.21	2.64	3.14	3.8
2012	SFN	MLB	22	16	11	0	32	32	208^{1}	183	23	49	191	2.1	8.3	49%	.276	1.11	3.37	3.54	4.13	2.1
2013	*SFN*	*MLB*	*23*	*11*	*9*	*0*	*28*	*28*	*177*	*157*	*15*	*41*	*149*	*2.1*	*7.6*	*45%*	*.294*	*1.12*	*3.19*	*3.31*	*3.47*	*2.2*

Among qualified pitchers, Bumgarner was the youngest to rank in the top 20 in ERA. He set a new career high in innings pitched last year, but the heavy workload may have taken a toll on him. He struggled down the stretch, and his troubles coincided with a drop in fastball velocity and fewer empty swings on his slider. His four-seam fastball velocity peaked in August at 92.3 mph, but bottomed out sitting under 91 mph in September and October. He ended the year on a high note, pitching a gem in Game Two of the World Series, and the Giants have to hope he'll carry that over to this year.

Matt Cain

Born: **10/1/1984** Age: **28**
Bats: **R** Throws: **R** Height: **6' 4"** Weight: **230**
Breakout: **23%** Improve: **64%** Collapse: **15%**
Attrition: **3%** MLB: **94%**

Comparables:
Scott Baker,Justin Verlander,Roy Oswalt

YEAR	TEAM	LVL	AGE	W	L	SV	G	GS	IP	H	HR	BB	SO	BB9	SO9	GB%	BABIP	WHIP	ERA	FIP	FRA	WARP
2010	SFN	MLB	25	13	11	0	33	33	223^{1}	181	22	61	177	2.5	7.1	38%	.252	1.08	3.14	3.67	4.23	2.1
2011	SFN	MLB	26	12	11	0	33	33	221^{2}	177	9	63	179	2.6	7.3	44%	.260	1.08	2.88	2.88	3.47	2.8
2012	SFN	MLB	27	16	5	0	32	32	219^{1}	177	21	51	193	2.1	7.9	41%	.259	1.04	2.79	3.44	3.69	3.1
2013	*SFN*	*MLB*	*28*	*12*	*9*	*0*	*28*	*28*	185^{2}	*152*	*15*	*51*	*154*	*2.5*	*7.5*	*40%*	*.274*	*1.09*	*2.96*	*3.42*	*3.22*	*2.8*

Last year was nothing short of remarkable for Cain. He signed the largest-ever contract for a right-handed pitcher, at the time, in April. In June, he tossed the 22nd perfect game in big-league history, and the first in the history of the Giants organization. His 14 strikeouts in that game tied Sandy Koufax for the most in a perfect game. Cain went on to start for the National League in the All-Star Game and capped the year by starting the World Series clincher, Game Four. Last year marked the sixth year in a row in which Cain topped 200 innings pitched. He has never been on the disabled list, and his ability to pile up quality innings makes him a front-line starter who has emerged as the Giants' ace.

Santiago Casilla

Born: **6/25/1980** Age: **33**
Bats: **R** Throws: **R** Height: **6' 1"** Weight: **220**
Breakout: **26%** Improve: **42%** Collapse: **40%**
Attrition: **13%** MLB: **91%**

Comparables:
Mike Jackson,Rudy Seanez,Mike Marshall

YEAR	TEAM	LVL	AGE	W	L	SV	G	GS	IP	H	HR	BB	SO	BB9	SO9	GB%	BABIP	WHIP	ERA	FIP	FRA	WARP
2010	FRE	AAA	30	0	0	2	4	0	4	2	0	2	7	4.5	15.8	43%	.286	1.00	0.00	2.33	0.89	0.2
2010	SFN	MLB	30	7	2	2	52	0	55^{1}	40	2	26	56	4.2	9.1	52%	.277	1.19	1.95	3.18	2.73	0.9
2011	SJO	A+	31	0	0	0	2	2	3	3	0	2	1	6.0	3.0	—	.300	1.67	0.00	5.28	5.74	0.0
2011	FRE	AAA	31	0	0	0	4	0	5	3	1	1	4	1.8	7.2	—	.182	0.80	1.80	5.98	6.50	0.0
2011	SFN	MLB	31	2	2	6	49	0	51^{2}	33	1	25	45	4.4	7.8	54%	.232	1.12	1.74	3.07	3.39	0.5
2012	SFN	MLB	32	7	6	25	73	0	63^{1}	55	8	22	55	3.1	7.8	55%	.254	1.22	2.84	4.18	4.86	-0.4
2013	*SFN*	*MLB*	*33*	*3*	*1*	*10*	*58*	*0*	56^{2}	*49*	*5*	*22*	*50*	*3.4*	*8.0*	*47%*	*.292*	*1.24*	*3.59*	*3.75*	*3.91*	*0.3*

Casilla was an integral part of the bullpen last year, and he ultimately led the team in saves. He leaned heavily on a pair of mid-to-upper-90s fastballs—a sinker and four-seamer—throwing them roughly 70 percent of the time. He complimented them with a pair of evenly used breaking balls: a curveball and a slider. The artist formerly known as Jairo Garcia finished the season with the best strikeout-to-walk ratio of his career, but not all was smooth sailing as he allowed the most home runs of his career as well. Casilla should once again be used in high-leverage situations out of the bullpen this year.

Kyle Crick

Born: **11/30/1992** Age: **20**
Bats: **L** Throws: **R** Height: **6' 5"** Weight: **220**
Breakout: **38%** Improve: **63%** Collapse: **22%**
Attrition: **15%** MLB: **92%**

Comparables:
David Clyde,Mike McQueen,Bruce Robbins

YEAR	TEAM	LVL	AGE	W	L	SV	G	GS	IP	H	HR	BB	SO	BB9	SO9	GB%	BABIP	WHIP	ERA	FIP	FRA	WARP
2011	GIA	Rk	18	1	0	0	7	0	7	9	0	8	8	10.3	10.3	71%	.412	2.43	6.43	5.94	5.45	0.1
2012	AUG	A	19	7	6	0	23	22	111^1	75	1	67	128	5.4	10.3	48%	.279	1.28	2.51	3.53	3.47	2.1
2013	*SFN*	*MLB*	*20*	*2*	*3*	*0*	*7*	*7*	*35^2*	*32*	*3*	*21*	*32*	*5.4*	*8.1*	*46%*	*.303*	*1.49*	*4.60*	*4.27*	*5.00*	*-0.2*

Crick's bread and butter is his fastball—a very good one with movement—but he is too reliant on the pitch. In addition to the heater, he throws a plus but inconsistent slider he sometimes struggles to command. His third pitch is an underdeveloped changeup that has a chance to become an average pitch. Crick is athletic and throws with a clean, repeatable delivery. If his slider becomes more consistent, and he trusts it, he could move quickly. That said, there is no need to rush him. He'll be tested this year by pitching in the hitter-friendly California League, and that could lead to poor numbers.

Chad Gaudin

Born: **3/24/1983** Age: **30**
Bats: **R** Throws: **R** Height: **5' 11"** Weight: **190**
Breakout: **32%** Improve: **60%** Collapse: **22%**
Attrition: **7%** MLB: **82%**

Comparables:
Joe Hesketh,Alejandro Pena,Andy McGaffigan

YEAR	TEAM	LVL	AGE	W	L	SV	G	GS	IP	H	HR	BB	SO	BB9	SO9	GB%	BABIP	WHIP	ERA	FIP	FRA	WARP
2010	NYA	MLB	27	1	2	0	30	0	48	46	11	20	33	3.8	6.2	40%	.250	1.38	4.50	6.21	7.20	-0.8
2010	OAK	MLB	27	0	2	0	12	0	17^1	27	5	5	20	2.6	10.4	36%	.415	1.85	8.83	5.87	4.90	0.0
2011	HAG	A	28	0	0	0	1	0	2	2	0	0	0	0.0	0.0	38%	.250	1.00	0.00	3.53	4.72	0.0
2011	POT	A+	28	0	0	0	1	1	1	0	0	0	0	0.0	0.0	67%	.000	0.00	0.00	3.23	4.42	0.0
2011	LVG	AAA	28	2	3	0	6	6	29^1	37	2	9	13	2.8	4.0	51%	.333	1.57	6.14	5.11	6.20	0.2
2011	SYR	AAA	28	0	2	0	6	2	12^1	17	0	3	14	2.2	10.2	60%	.400	1.62	4.38	1.94	3.44	0.1
2011	WAS	MLB	28	1	1	0	10	0	8^1	12	1	8	10	8.6	10.8	33%	.423	2.40	6.48	5.03	4.75	0.0
2012	MIA	MLB	29	4	2	0	46	0	69^1	72	6	26	57	3.4	7.4	43%	.314	1.41	4.54	3.87	4.20	0.4
2013	*SFN*	*MLB*	*30*	*2*	*1*	*0*	*34*	*2*	*54^1*	*50*	*5*	*20*	*47*	*3.3*	*7.8*	*46%*	*.303*	*1.30*	*4.06*	*3.77*	*4.41*	*-0.0*

Look out, Octavio Dotel! The ancient setup man set a major-league record when he signed with the Tigers, his 13th organization, last winter—but Gaudin, who will only be 30 on Opening Day, put a ninth uniform in his collection when he signed a minor-league contract with the Giants in December. A sinker-slider righty with experience in a variety of roles, Gaudin should be in line for a major-league bullpen job even if he doesn't stick with the Giants.

Heath Hembree

Born: **1/13/1989** Age: **24**
Bats: **R** Throws: **R** Height: **6' 5"** Weight: **210**
Breakout: **34%** Improve: **60%** Collapse: **19%**
Attrition: **14%** MLB: **93%**

Comparables:
Chris Ray,Wesley Wright,Ed Vande Berg

YEAR	TEAM	LVL	AGE	W	L	SV	G	GS	IP	H	HR	BB	SO	BB9	SO9	GB%	BABIP	WHIP	ERA	FIP	FRA	WARP
2010	GIA	Rk	21	0	0	3	12	0	11	9	0	0	22	0.0	18.0	60%	.400	0.82	0.82	0.26	1.60	0.5
2011	SJO	A+	22	0	0	21	26	0	24^2	16	1	12	44	4.4	16.1	—	.349	1.14	0.73	2.49	2.71	0.0
2011	RIC	AA	22	1	1	17	28	0	28^2	20	1	13	34	4.1	10.7	32%	.276	1.15	2.83	2.85	3.57	0.4
2012	SJO	A+	23	0	0	0	5	0	5	0	0	1	7	1.8	12.6	56%	.000	0.20	0.00	1.61	0.58	0.2
2012	FRE	AAA	23	1	1	15	39	0	38	29	2	20	36	4.7	8.5	41%	.250	1.29	4.74	4.35	4.48	0.3
2013	*SFN*	*MLB*	*24*	*2*	*1*	*2*	*38*	*0*	*37^1*	*31*	*3*	*17*	*36*	*4.1*	*8.6*	*42%*	*.294*	*1.30*	*3.79*	*3.68*	*4.12*	*0.1*

Hembree is a two-pitch reliever. Those two pitches are a plus fastball with big velocity and life, and a slider that is average to slightly better. He spent most of last year in Triple-A and is knocking on the door. Hembree could develop into a closer, but he is probably better suited serving as a set-up man.

Chris Heston

Born: **4/10/1988** Age: **25**
Bats: **R** Throws: **R** Height: **6' 5"** Weight: **185**
Breakout: **33%** Improve: **52%** Collapse: **17%**
Attrition: **29%** MLB: **92%**

Comparables:
Anthony Swarzak,Clayton Mortensen,Lance Broadway

YEAR	TEAM	LVL	AGE	W	L	SV	G	GS	IP	H	HR	BB	SO	BB9	SO9	GB%	BABIP	WHIP	ERA	FIP	FRA	WARP
2010	AUG	A	22	5	13	0	26	26	148^2	161	6	33	124	2.0	7.5	57%	.330	1.30	3.75	3.23	4.85	-0.2
2011	SJO	A+	23	12	4	0	24	24	151	144	10	40	131	2.4	7.8	—	.315	1.22	3.16	4.03	4.38	0.0
2012	RIC	AA	24	9	8	0	25	25	148^2	124	2	40	135	2.4	8.2	54%	.295	1.10	2.24	2.45	3.59	2.0
2013	*SFN*	*MLB*	*25*	*2*	*2*	*0*	*6*	*6*	*36^1*	*37*	*3*	*14*	*25*	*3.5*	*6.2*	*51%*	*.308*	*1.41*	*4.57*	*4.05*	*4.97*	*-0.2*

Heston serves as a cautionary tale of stats not telling the whole story about a prospect. He is the type of pitcher who succeeds throughout the minors but struggles in the majors. His numbers are glowing, but his fastball resides in the upper-80s and none of his secondary pitches grade out as average. All of his pitches—fastball, curveball, slider, and changeup—play up because he has excellent control of them. Heston has excellent pitchability, and he sequences well. He's nearly big-league ready, and could serve as an emergency starter. Ultimately, he could have a career in the bullpen.

Stephen Johnson
Born: **2/21/1991** Age: **22**
Bats: **R** Throws: **R** Height: **6' 5"** Weight: **205**
Breakout: **21%** Improve: **43%** Collapse: **37%**
Attrition: **21%** MLB: **71%**
Comparables:
Jon Warden,Ryan Wagner,Phil Paine

YEAR	TEAM	LVL	AGE	W	L	SV	G	GS	IP	H	HR	BB	SO	BB9	SO9	GB%	BABIP	WHIP	ERA	FIP	FRA	WARP
2012	GIA	Rk	21	0	0	0	2	0	2	1	0	2	2	9.0	9.0	—	.250	1.50	4.50	5.38	5.84	0.0
2012	SLO	A-	21	0	2	2	17	0	19^{1}	19	2	12	19	5.6	8.8	38%	.250	1.60	4.66	4.57	0.44	0.2
2013	*SFN*	*MLB*	*22*	*1*	*0*	*1*	*26*	*0*	*35^{1}*	*36*	*4*	*19*	*26*	*4.8*	*6.6*	*44%*	*.309*	*1.55*	*5.14*	*4.81*	*5.59*	*-0.4*

Out of Division II St. Edwards, Johnson was the Giants' sixth-round pick last year. He began his college career as a starter, but he flourished when he was shifted to the bullpen. His fastball velocity rose in the pen, and now sits in the mid-to-upper-90s and can reach triple digits. Beyond the fastball, Johnson also features an inconsistent, slurvy breaking ball. With some refining and development, he could be a late-inning reliever.

George Kontos
Born: **6/12/1985** Age: **28**
Bats: **R** Throws: **R** Height: **6' 4"** Weight: **215**
Breakout: **24%** Improve: **52%** Collapse: **30%**
Attrition: **21%** MLB: **80%**
Comparables:
Angel Guzman,Fernando Nieve,Chad Gaudin

YEAR	TEAM	LVL	AGE	W	L	SV	G	GS	IP	H	HR	BB	SO	BB9	SO9	GB%	BABIP	WHIP	ERA	FIP	FRA	WARP
2010	TAM	A+	25	0	1	0	5	2	10^{1}	7	0	3	8	2.6	7.0	41%	.241	0.97	2.62	2.76	3.61	0.1
2010	TRN	AA	25	0	2	0	17	0	32	30	2	11	28	3.1	7.9	44%	.310	1.28	3.38	3.45	4.64	0.0
2010	SWB	AAA	25	0	1	0	2	0	2^{2}	5	1	1	2	3.3	6.7	44%	.467	2.22	10.00	7.74	4.93	0.0
2011	SWB	AAA	26	4	4	2	40	4	89^{1}	72	12	26	91	2.6	9.2	35%	.246	1.10	2.62	3.89	5.10	-0.1
2011	NYA	MLB	26	0	0	0	7	0	6	4	1	3	6	4.5	9.0	20%	.214	1.17	3.00	4.73	4.41	0.0
2012	FRE	AAA	27	2	0	1	23	0	31^{2}	24	1	7	26	2.0	7.4	54%	.253	0.98	1.71	3.19	3.21	0.7
2012	SFN	MLB	27	2	1	0	44	0	43^{2}	34	3	12	44	2.5	9.1	50%	.263	1.05	2.47	2.84	3.72	0.4
2013	*SFN*	*MLB*	*28*	*2*	*1*	*0*	*31*	*0*	*42^{1}*	*37*	*4*	*16*	*37*	*3.4*	*7.8*	*42%*	*.289*	*1.25*	*3.87*	*3.81*	*4.20*	*0.1*

Not much was made of the Giants sending backup catcher Chris Stewart to the Yankees for a reliever who, save for a cup of coffee in 2011, was a six-year minor-league veteran. But Kontos proved to be a solid bullpen arm at Bochy's disposal last year. He primarily used two fastballs, a four-seam and sinker, plus a slider, to get hitters out. The slider was his put-away pitch, and he went to it often with two strikes regardless of the handedness of his opposition. His fastball-slider combination may leave him vulnerable against left-handed batters, but he was able to effectively neutralize them last year.

Tim Lincecum
Born: **6/15/1984** Age: **29**
Bats: **L** Throws: **R** Height: **6' 0"** Weight: **165**
Breakout: **11%** Improve: **37%** Collapse: **28%**
Attrition: **4%** MLB: **94%**
Comparables:
Rich Harden,Rich Hill,Erik Bedard

YEAR	TEAM	LVL	AGE	W	L	SV	G	GS	IP	H	HR	BB	SO	BB9	SO9	GB%	BABIP	WHIP	ERA	FIP	FRA	WARP
2010	SFN	MLB	26	16	10	0	33	33	212^{1}	194	18	76	231	3.2	9.8	50%	.310	1.27	3.43	3.18	3.93	2.6
2011	SFN	MLB	27	13	14	0	33	33	217	176	15	86	220	3.6	9.1	49%	.281	1.21	2.74	3.14	3.89	1.4
2012	SFN	MLB	28	10	15	0	33	33	186	183	23	90	190	4.4	9.2	47%	.309	1.47	5.18	4.22	4.79	-0.3
2013	*SFN*	*MLB*	*29*	*11*	*8*	*0*	*28*	*28*	*172^{2}*	*138*	*12*	*60*	*187*	*3.1*	*9.7*	*48%*	*.300*	*1.15*	*2.95*	*2.98*	*3.21*	*2.7*

Lincecum continued to strike out batters at a high rate, but that's essentially where the positives ended, at least in the regular season. He struggled with his command and control, and he lost more than 2 mph on his four-seam fastball, which caused many to conclude his unorthodox mechanics have caught up to him. There may be something to that, as John Shea of the *San Francisco Chronicle* quoted Sabean saying Lincecum needs to be "willing to accept the delivery he's going to use to be a successful pitcher." Sabean also mentioned that Lincecum will need to pitch more to contact. In addition to changing his mechanics, Lincecum was also tasked with putting on about five pounds in the offseason. He ended the year dominating out of the bullpen during the postseason, though he was no ordinary reliever, throwing at least two innings in all five of his appearances. Back in the rotation this year, he'll try to right the ship, and PECOTA (despite an alarming set of comps) thinks he can do it.

Javier Lopez
Born: **7/11/1977** Age: **35**
Bats: **L** Throws: **L** Height: **6' 5"** Weight: **220**
Breakout: **25%** Improve: **31%** Collapse: **42%**
Attrition: **15%** MLB: **85%**
Comparables:
Joe Beimel,Ricardo Rincon,Sparky Lyle

YEAR	TEAM	LVL	AGE	W	L	SV	G	GS	IP	H	HR	BB	SO	BB9	SO9	GB%	BABIP	WHIP	ERA	FIP	FRA	WARP
2010	PIT	MLB	32	2	2	0	50	0	38^{2}	39	2	18	22	4.2	5.1	60%	.303	1.47	2.79	4.19	5.27	-0.1
2010	SFN	MLB	32	2	0	0	27	0	19	11	0	2	16	0.9	7.6	67%	.216	0.68	1.42	1.74	2.56	0.3
2011	SFN	MLB	33	5	2	1	70	0	53	42	0	26	40	4.4	6.8	64%	.275	1.28	2.72	3.13	4.46	0.1
2012	SFN	MLB	34	3	0	7	70	0	36	37	1	14	28	3.5	7.0	60%	.318	1.42	2.50	3.11	2.94	0.4
2013	*SFN*	*MLB*	*35*	*3*	*1*	*3*	*56*	*0*	*37^{2}*	*34*	*2*	*15*	*28*	*3.5*	*6.6*	*57%*	*.294*	*1.28*	*3.71*	*3.60*	*4.03*	*0.2*

For better and for worse, Lopez reiterated that he is a true LOOGY. He dominated lefties, ranking 24th in TAv, .183, among pitchers who had 50 plate appearances or more against left-handed batters. Conversely, he had the second highest TAv, .366, against right-handed batters using the same qualifying criteria. The Giants learned their lesson from his overexposure to right-handed hitters in 2010 and 2011. He averaged 120.5 plate appearances against righties those seasons, and that was reduced to 56 last year. When used correctly, Lopez can be a bullpen asset who neutralizes left-handed hitters in high-leverage situations.

Jean Machi

Born: **2/1/1982** Age: **31**
Bats: **R** Throws: **R** Height: **6' 1"** Weight: **250**
Breakout: **36%** Improve: **48%** Collapse: **36%**
Attrition: **12%** MLB: **86%**

Comparables:
Tom Gorman, Rick Bauer, Roy Thomas

YEAR	TEAM	LVL	AGE	W	L	SV	G	GS	IP	H	HR	BB	SO	BB9	SO9	GB%	BABIP	WHIP	ERA	FIP	FRA	WARP
2010	IND	AAA	28	5	5	23	58	0	59^2	51	6	32	58	4.8	8.7	49%	.283	1.39	3.92	4.36	4.78	0.6
2011	FRE	AAA	29	1	1	0	3	0	4	5	0	0	6	0.0	13.5	22%	.556	1.25	9.00	0.78	1.02	0.2
2012	FRE	AAA	30	2	1	15	53	0	56^2	67	7	17	44	2.7	7.0	52%	.324	1.48	3.97	4.78	6.39	-0.2
2012	SFN	MLB	30	0	0	0	8	0	6^2	7	2	1	4	1.4	5.4	39%	.238	1.20	6.75	6.29	6.50	-0.1
2013	*SFN*	*MLB*	*31*	*2*	*1*	*0*	*35*	*0*	*37*	*35*	*4*	*15*	*27*	*3.7*	*6.6*	*49%*	*.295*	*1.36*	*4.36*	*4.36*	*4.74*	*-0.2*

Machi signed with the Phillies in 2000 and spent more than a decade in the minors playing for multiple organizations before savoring his first cup of joe last September. He throws a pair of fastballs in the 93-94 mph range on average, a slider, and a changeup. His fastball falls a few ticks short of earning him a flame-thrower label, and he doesn't strike out batters in bunches, but he does induce grounders at a high rate. He's struggled with his control at times during his minor-league journey, but if he continues to throw strikes as he has the past two years, he offers enough to be in the mix for a bullpen job.

Adalberto Mejia

Born: **6/20/1993** Age: **20**
Bats: **L** Throws: **L** Height: **6' 4"** Weight: **195**
Breakout: **28%** Improve: **57%** Collapse: **30%**
Attrition: **17%** MLB: **92%**

Comparables:
David Clyde, Mike McCormick, Bruce Robbins

YEAR	TEAM	LVL	AGE	W	L	SV	G	GS	IP	H	HR	BB	SO	BB9	SO9	GB%	BABIP	WHIP	ERA	FIP	FRA	WARP
2011	DSI	Rk	18	5	2	0	13	13	76	58	0	8	71	0.9	8.4	—	.272	0.87	1.42	1.76	1.91	0.0
2012	AUG	A	19	10	7	0	30	14	106^2	122	4	21	79	1.8	6.7	44%	.332	1.34	3.97	3.29	4.21	1.4
2013	*SFN*	*MLB*	*20*	*2*	*2*	*0*	*10*	*5*	*35^1*	*40*	*4*	*14*	*18*	*3.6*	*4.6*	*42%*	*.308*	*1.52*	*5.38*	*4.84*	*5.84*	*-0.5*

The Giants spent $350,000 to sign Mejia in 2011, and the early results suggest it was money well spent. Mejia made his stateside debut last year, when he was one of the youngest players in the South Atlantic League. He has a projectable frame that should allow him to add velocity to a fastball that already sits in the low-90s.

Jose Mijares

Born: **10/29/1984** Age: **28**
Bats: **L** Throws: **L** Height: **6' 1"** Weight: **230**
Breakout: **13%** Improve: **32%** Collapse: **42%**
Attrition: **7%** MLB: **83%**

Comparables:
Doug Slaten, Ron Flores, Jeff Calhoun

YEAR	TEAM	LVL	AGE	W	L	SV	G	GS	IP	H	HR	BB	SO	BB9	SO9	GB%	BABIP	WHIP	ERA	FIP	FRA	WARP
2010	ROC	AAA	25	0	0	0	2	0	1^2	6	1	1	2	5.3	10.6	33%	.625	4.12	26.47	10.35	8.00	-0.1
2010	MIN	MLB	25	1	1	0	47	0	32^2	34	4	9	28	2.5	7.7	32%	.309	1.32	3.31	3.84	3.87	0.4
2011	MIN	MLB	26	0	2	0	58	0	49	53	4	30	30	5.5	5.5	33%	.304	1.69	4.59	4.92	5.08	-0.2
2012	KCA	MLB	27	2	2	0	51	0	38^2	36	3	13	37	3.0	8.6	34%	.297	1.27	2.56	3.46	3.79	0.4
2012	SFN	MLB	27	1	0	0	27	0	17^2	14	0	8	20	4.1	10.2	39%	.304	1.25	2.55	2.23	1.93	0.4
2013	*SFN*	*MLB*	*28*	*4*	*1*	*1*	*68*	*0*	*51^2*	*45*	*4*	*19*	*46*	*3.3*	*7.9*	*39%*	*.290*	*1.23*	*3.55*	*3.53*	*3.86*	*0.3*

Mijares was in the midst of a solid season for the Royals last year, which made it surprising that the Giants were able to claim him off waivers in August at the cost of assuming the remainder of his one-year deal. He joined Lopez and Affeldt as left-handed relievers, and though he was less effective than Lopez against lefties, he was still quite good. He was better than Lopez against right-handers hitters—though that's a relative term: In spite of having a three-pitch mix (fastball, slider, and changeup) that should allow him to get right-handers out, Mijares has done so at a subpar level.

Guillermo Mota

Born: **7/25/1973** Age: **39**
Bats: **R** Throws: **R** Height: **6' 7"** Weight: **240**
Breakout: **22%** Improve: **42%** Collapse: **27%**
Attrition: **17%** MLB: **44%**

Comparables:
Tug McGraw, Jay Howell, Giovanni Carrara

YEAR	TEAM	LVL	AGE	W	L	SV	G	GS	IP	H	HR	BB	SO	BB9	SO9	GB%	BABIP	WHIP	ERA	FIP	FRA	WARP
2010	SFN	MLB	36	1	3	1	56	0	54	49	4	22	38	3.7	6.3	39%	.274	1.31	4.33	3.88	4.39	0.2
2011	SFN	MLB	37	2	2	1	52	0	80^1	71	10	30	77	3.4	8.6	42%	.285	1.26	3.81	3.89	4.35	0.0
2012	GIA	Rk	38	0	0	0	2	1	2^2	8	1	0	2	0.0	6.8	69%	.583	3.00	23.62	7.75	7.36	0.0
2012	FRE	AAA	38	0	0	0	4	0	6^1	8	1	2	3	2.8	4.3	46%	.333	1.58	4.26	6.19	7.55	-0.1
2012	SFN	MLB	38	0	1	0	26	0	20^2	24	3	8	24	3.5	10.5	37%	.389	1.55	5.23	4.15	4.26	0.1
2013	*SFN*	*MLB*	*39*	*2*	*1*	*1*	*32*	*0*	*37^2*	*34*	*4*	*14*	*30*	*3.4*	*7.2*	*43%*	*.292*	*1.27*	*3.81*	*4.10*	*4.14*	*0.1*

It's probably safe to say it was a wise move shifting Mota from shortstop to pitcher in the minors, as he's stuck around the majors for over a decade. Last year was a tough one for Mota. He served a 100-game suspension for testing positive for a banned substance, Clenbuterol. It was Mota's second drug-related suspension, and he claimed it was the result of taking a children's cough syrup. A third failed drug test would result in a lifetime ban, but that might be a moot point. Mota's fastball velocity has been sliding for years, and he may have reached the end of the line.

Joshua Osich

Born: **9/3/1988** Age: **24**
Bats: **L** Throws: **L** Height: **6' 4"** Weight: **235**
Breakout: **21%** Improve: **47%** Collapse: **20%**
Attrition: **16%** MLB: **92%**

Comparables:
Donnie Moore,Jake Woods,Joe Nuxhall

YEAR	TEAM	LVL	AGE	W	L	SV	G	GS	IP	H	HR	BB	SO	BB9	SO9	GB%	BABIP	WHIP	ERA	FIP	FRA	WARP
2012	SJO	A+	23	0	2	1	27	2	32^{1}	34	1	11	34	3.1	9.5	41%	.352	1.39	3.62	3.13	2.78	0.6
2013	*SFN*	*MLB*	*24*	*2*	*1*	*1*	*29*	*1*	*36^{2}*	*36*	*4*	*15*	*28*	*3.8*	*7.0*	*43%*	*.306*	*1.40*	*4.47*	*4.32*	*4.86*	*-0.2*

Osich, the team's sixth-round pick in the 2011 draft, fell largely due to health concerns that include a Tommy John surgery in his past. He made his pro debut last year and did the bulk of his work out of the bullpen. Osich is a big southpaw with a plus-velocity fastball, a very good changeup, and a slider. If he's kept in the pen, and stays healthy, he could climb through the system quickly.

Yusmeiro Petit

Born: **11/22/1984** Age: **28**
Bats: **R** Throws: **R** Height: **6' 2"** Weight: **250**
Breakout: **19%** Improve: **55%** Collapse: **13%**
Attrition: **13%** MLB: **91%**

Comparables:
Jeremy Bonderman,Tom Bradley,Erik Hanson

YEAR	TEAM	LVL	AGE	W	L	SV	G	GS	IP	H	HR	BB	SO	BB9	SO9	GB%	BABIP	WHIP	ERA	FIP	FRA	WARP
2010	TAC	AAA	25	4	2	0	24	6	59^{1}	54	9	16	55	2.4	8.3	25%	.280	1.18	4.86	4.56	4.51	0.9
2012	FRE	AAA	27	7	7	0	28	28	166^{2}	178	14	36	153	1.9	8.3	32%	.330	1.28	3.46	3.59	3.76	2.6
2012	SFN	MLB	27	0	0	0	1	1	4^{2}	7	0	4	1	7.7	1.9	41%	.412	2.36	3.86	5.28	4.58	0.0
2013	*SFN*	*MLB*	*28*	*3*	*3*	*0*	*11*	*7*	*48^{1}*	*44*	*6*	*13*	*41*	*2.4*	*7.7*	*33%*	*.292*	*1.19*	*3.72*	*3.92*	*4.05*	*0.2*

After spending 2011 outside of affiliated ball, Petit made a strong showing in the Venezuelan Winter League, which earned him a minor-league contract and a non-roster invite to Giants camp. He had an outstanding season in the hitter-friendly Pacific Coast League. Among qualifying pitchers, he ranked in the top five in innings pitched, ERA, and strikeouts and sixth in WHIP. Petit parlayed that success into a September call-up and one start. Be careful overvaluing his stats. That's been a common problem in the past. Petit is a right-handed pitcher with a fastball that sits under 90 mph. He's a cheap emergency starting-pitching option, and that's about it.

Sergio Romo

Born: **3/4/1983** Age: **30**
Bats: **R** Throws: **R** Height: **5' 11"** Weight: **185**
Breakout: **27%** Improve: **49%** Collapse: **30%**
Attrition: **7%** MLB: **96%**

Comparables:
John Wetteland,Jonathan Papelbon,Rafael Soriano

YEAR	TEAM	LVL	AGE	W	L	SV	G	GS	IP	H	HR	BB	SO	BB9	SO9	GB%	BABIP	WHIP	ERA	FIP	FRA	WARP
2010	SFN	MLB	27	5	3	0	68	0	62	46	6	14	70	2.0	10.2	37%	.261	0.97	2.18	2.98	2.93	1.0
2011	GIA	Rk	28	0	0	0	1	1	1	1	0	0	3	0.0	27.0	%	.000	1.00	0.00	-1.63	-0.43	0.1
2011	SFN	MLB	28	3	1	1	65	0	48	29	2	5	70	0.9	13.1	36%	.276	0.71	1.50	0.93	1.81	1.2
2012	SFN	MLB	29	4	2	14	69	0	55^{1}	37	5	10	63	1.6	10.2	50%	.239	0.85	1.79	2.74	2.86	0.7
2013	*SFN*	*MLB*	*30*	*3*	*2*	*4*	*60*	*0*	*49*	*35*	*4*	*10*	*57*	*1.8*	*10.5*	*38%*	*.279*	*0.91*	*2.03*	*2.55*	*2.20*	*1.4*

Romo has been one of the best set-up men in baseball for a few years, and he proved last year that he could carry his stellar work into the ninth inning. He isn't a classic overpowering closer. Instead, Romo relies on a filthy slider that he threw 58 percent of the time last year. His fastball doesn't have enough velocity to blow past hitters, but Romo knows how to effectively mix it in. A perfect example came on the final pitch of the World Series, when he froze Miguel Cabrera with a fastball right down the middle. He threw no changeups to right-handed batters, but he has it in his bag of tricks to get lefties out. With no platoon struggles, he should remain a reliable closer.

Dan Runzler

Born: **3/30/1985** Age: **28**
Bats: **L** Throws: **L** Height: **6' 5"** Weight: **235**
Breakout: **19%** Improve: **45%** Collapse: **34%**
Attrition: **3%** MLB: **82%**

Comparables:
Will Ohman,Jack Taschner,Neal Cotts

YEAR	TEAM	LVL	AGE	W	L	SV	G	GS	IP	H	HR	BB	SO	BB9	SO9	GB%	BABIP	WHIP	ERA	FIP	FRA	WARP
2010	GIA	Rk	25	0	0	0	1	1	2	0	0	0	4	0.0	18.0	—	.000	0.00	0.00	0.26	1.95	0.1
2010	SJO	A+	25	0	0	0	1	1	1	0	0	0	2	0.0	18.0	1.%	.000	0.00	0.00	-0.27	2.09	0.1
2010	FRE	AAA	25	0	1	0	6	0	7	8	0	4	5	5.1	6.4	59%	.364	1.71	3.86	3.87	4.98	0.1
2010	SFN	MLB	25	3	0	0	41	0	32^{2}	29	1	20	37	5.5	10.2	57%	.329	1.50	3.03	3.17	3.30	0.3
2011	FRE	AAA	26	2	3	0	17	10	52	47	2	32	59	5.5	10.2	57%	.314	1.52	3.98	4.03	4.68	0.4
2011	SFN	MLB	26	1	2	0	31	1	27^{1}	29	0	16	25	5.3	8.2	49%	.367	1.65	6.26	2.92	3.74	0.3
2012	SJO	A+	27	0	2	0	3	2	3	3	1	1	1	3.0	3.0	64%	.200	1.33	6.00	8.48	52.90	0.0
2012	FRE	AAA	27	0	2	1	29	0	27	36	2	14	33	4.7	11.0	42%	.447	1.85	6.00	3.85	4.40	0.3
2012	SFN	MLB	27	0	0	0	6	0	3^{2}	1	0	3	5	7.4	12.3	33%	.167	1.09	0.00	3.68	4.49	0.0
2013	*SFN*	*MLB*	*28*	*2*	*1*	*0*	*34*	*2*	*37*	*31*	*3*	*19*	*39*	*4.6*	*9.4*	*54%*	*.304*	*1.33*	*3.69*	*3.69*	*4.01*	*0.2*

A strained left latissimus dorsi muscle caused Runzler to miss a large chunk of 2012. The injury didn't require surgery, and rest seemed to do the trick as his stuff returned to pre-injury form when he got back to game action in June. Though the Giants experimented with Runzler starting in 2011, he's best suited for the bullpen because of his fastball-slider repertoire and his shaky control. Runzler's heater is a big-velocity pitch, sitting in the mid-90s, and earns swinging strikes commensurate with that speed. He's much better against left-handed hitters, but he's not helpless against right-handers. If he limits his walks, he's a big-league reliever.

Chris Stratton

Born: **8/22/1990** Age: **22**
Bats: **R** Throws: **R** Height: **6' 4"** Weight: **186**
Breakout: **22%** Improve: **54%** Collapse: **22%**
Attrition: **16%** MLB: **82%**
Comparables:
Dave Stieb,Jamey Wright,Bill Pulsipher

YEAR	TEAM	LVL	AGE	W	L	SV	G	GS	IP	H	HR	BB	SO	BB9	SO9	GB%	BABIP	WHIP	ERA	FIP	FRA	WARP
2012	SLO	A-	21	0	1	0	8	5	16^1	14	1	10	16	5.5	8.8	60%	.300	1.47	2.76	4.37	2.20	0.0
2013	*SFN*	*MLB*	*22*	*2*	*3*	*0*	*7*	*7*	*34^2*	*38*	*4*	*18*	*20*	*4.7*	*5.2*	*45%*	*.309*	*1.62*	*5.63*	*5.10*	*6.11*	*-0.6*

A former Mississippi State Bulldog, Stratton was the club's top draft pick last June. He throws two fastballs, a straight four-seamer at 91-93 mph and topping out at 96 mph, and a two-seamer a few ticks slower. He's willing to elevate the four-seam fastball for strikeouts. His repertoire also includes three secondary pitches, a slider, curveball, and changeup. All three have a chance to be average or better, and his arm action makes them tough to differentiate from his fastballs. The slider is the best of them, grading above-average to plus, but when hitters lay off it out of the zone, it leads to high pitch counts. Stratton is able to get downhill well, and throws with a loose, free, very easy arm action.

Eric Surkamp

Born: **7/16/1987** Age: **25**
Bats: **L** Throws: **L** Height: **6' 5"** Weight: **190**
Breakout: **44%** Improve: **68%** Collapse: **14%**
Attrition: **12%** MLB: **91%**
Comparables:
J.A. Happ,Marc Rzepczynski,J.P. Howell

YEAR	TEAM	LVL	AGE	W	L	SV	G	GS	IP	H	HR	BB	SO	BB9	SO9	GB%	BABIP	WHIP	ERA	FIP	FRA	WARP
2010	SJO	A+	22	4	2	0	17	17	101^1	79	5	22	108	2.0	9.6	43%	.289	1.00	3.11	3.07	4.34	1.7
2011	SJO	A+	23	1	0	0	1	1	6	4	0	1	5	1.5	7.5	—	.250	0.83	0.00	2.78	3.03	0.0
2011	RIC	AA	23	10	4	0	23	22	142^1	110	5	44	165	2.8	10.4	47%	.276	1.08	2.02	2.58	3.37	2.4
2011	SFN	MLB	23	2	2	0	6	6	26^2	32	1	17	13	5.7	4.4	36%	.333	1.84	5.74	4.64	4.61	0.0
2013	*SFN*	*MLB*	*25*	*2*	*2*	*0*	*6*	*6*	*36^2*	*34*	*3*	*15*	*32*	*3.7*	*7.9*	*43%*	*.309*	*1.35*	*4.10*	*3.75*	*4.46*	*0.0*

Surkamp entered 2012 ranked seventh on BP's Giants Top 11 Prospects list. Unfortunately, he failed to pitch in any games, and he underwent Tommy John surgery in late July. The southpaw didn't feature much in the way of velocity prior to the injury. Instead, Surkamp relied heavily on location and secondary pitches to rack up gaudy strikeout totals throughout his minor-league career. If his recovery doesn't hit a snag, he'll be pitching late this summer.

Ryan Vogelsong

Born: **7/22/1977** Age: **35**
Bats: **R** Throws: **R** Height: **6' 5"** Weight: **215**
Breakout: **16%** Improve: **35%** Collapse: **33%**
Attrition: **9%** MLB: **91%**
Comparables:
Doug Davis,Jose Contreras,Mark Langston

YEAR	TEAM	LVL	AGE	W	L	SV	G	GS	IP	H	HR	BB	SO	BB9	SO9	GB%	BABIP	WHIP	ERA	FIP	FRA	WARP
2011	FRE	AAA	33	2	0	0	2	2	11^1	8	1	5	17	4.0	13.5	36%	.308	1.15	1.59	3.25	3.59	0.1
2011	SFN	MLB	33	13	7	0	30	28	179^2	164	15	61	139	3.1	7.0	48%	.280	1.25	2.71	3.63	4.05	1.6
2012	FRE	AAA	34	1	0	0	2	2	10	9	0	4	12	3.6	10.8	48%	.360	1.30	1.80	2.47	2.58	0.4
2012	SFN	MLB	34	14	9	0	31	31	189^2	171	17	62	158	2.9	7.5	44%	.284	1.23	3.37	3.74	4.08	1.2
2013	*SFN*	*MLB*	*35*	*9*	*9*	*0*	*27*	*27*	*159^1*	*145*	*15*	*57*	*130*	*3.2*	*7.3*	*44%*	*.295*	*1.27*	*3.87*	*3.87*	*4.21*	*0.5*

After Vogelsong's improbable season in 2011, in which he bested both his FIP and FRA by significant margins, there was some thought regression would be harsh. That didn't end up being the case. Vogelsong improved his strikeout and walk rates, and he continued to outpitch the advanced metrics. He doesn't wow onlookers with any one offering, but he is able to sink and cut his fastball, and he further keeps batters guessing by mixing in a curveball and changeup. The Giants signed Vogelsong to a contract extension last January. He's guaranteed $5 million this year with a chance to earn up to another $300,000 by reaching various innings thresholds. The club also holds a $6.5 million option with a $300,000 buyout for 2014.

Brian Wilson

Born: **3/16/1982** Age: **31**
Bats: **R** Throws: **R** Height: **6' 3"** Weight: **205**
Breakout: **28%** Improve: **46%** Collapse: **24%**
Attrition: **8%** MLB: **93%**
Comparables:
Heath Bell,Michael Wuertz,J.J. Putz

YEAR	TEAM	LVL	AGE	W	L	SV	G	GS	IP	H	HR	BB	SO	BB9	SO9	GB%	BABIP	WHIP	ERA	FIP	FRA	WARP
2010	SFN	MLB	28	3	3	48	70	0	74^2	62	3	26	93	3.1	11.2	49%	.316	1.18	1.81	2.22	2.18	1.7
2011	SFN	MLB	29	6	4	36	57	0	55	50	2	31	54	5.1	8.8	55%	.312	1.47	3.11	3.30	3.48	0.5
2012	SFN	MLB	30	0	0	1	2	0	2	4	0	2	2	9.0	9.0	25%	.500	3.00	9.00	4.14	6.19	0.0
2013	*SFN*	*MLB*	*31*	*2*	*1*	*24*	*38*	*0*	*38^2*	*31*	*2*	*14*	*42*	*3.3*	*9.8*	*49%*	*.302*	*1.16*	*2.87*	*2.79*	*3.12*	*0.6*

The eccentric closer pitched just two times before undergoing Tommy John surgery on April 19. Wilson began his throwing program in late October and it's unclear whether he'll be ready for Opening Day. He was paid $8.5 million last year, and when he and the Giants couldn't come to an agreement, they deemed him too expensive to tender. Wilson flirted with danger in 2011, seeing his walk rate balloon and his strikeout rate dip below a batter per inning for the first time since 2007. His slip in effectiveness combined with recovery from surgery makes him a dicey gamble in 2013.

Barry Zito

Born: **5/13/1978** Age: **35**
Bats: **L** Throws: **L** Height: **6' 3"** Weight: **205**
Breakout: **20%** Improve: **54%** Collapse: **12%**
Attrition: **11%** MLB: **77%**

Comparables:
Bruce Chen,Mark Redman,Kaz Ishii

YEAR	TEAM	LVL	AGE	W	L	SV	G	GS	IP	H	HR	BB	SO	BB9	SO9	GB%	BABIP	WHIP	ERA	FIP	FRA	WARP
2010	SFN	MLB	32	9	14	0	34	33	199^{1}	184	20	84	150	3.8	6.8	38%	.279	1.34	4.15	4.28	4.47	1.4
2011	SJO	A+	33	2	1	0	3	3	21^{1}	15	2	5	19	2.1	8.0	—	.241	0.94	2.53	4.37	4.75	0.0
2011	FRE	AAA	33	2	0	0	3	3	17^{2}	10	1	5	17	2.5	8.7	49%	.167	0.85	2.55	3.44	4.46	0.2
2011	SFN	MLB	33	3	4	0	13	9	53^{2}	51	10	24	32	4.0	5.4	41%	.258	1.40	5.87	5.57	6.97	-1.1
2012	SFN	MLB	34	15	8	0	32	32	184^{1}	186	20	70	114	3.4	5.6	43%	.282	1.39	4.15	4.53	5.04	-0.6
2013	*SFN*	*MLB*	*35*	*8*	*9*	*0*	*24*	*24*	*139*	*130*	*14*	*56*	*97*	*3.7*	*6.3*	*40%*	*.289*	*1.34*	*4.24*	*4.32*	*4.60*	*-0.2*

While Zito's back-of-the-baseball-card stats last year were much better than in 2011, he was still a below-league-average starter. Zito doesn't miss many bats, but he reduced his walk rate to its lowest mark since 2004, which Zito fans will remember as his last really good year. He was at his stingiest with the free passes after the All-Star break, with a 2.31 BB9. In a postseason of surprises, Zito's stellar pitching may have been the biggest shocker. He kept the Giants season alive by throwing a gem and winning Game Five of the NLCS, and followed that up by winning Game One of the World Series. His contract remains a massive overpay, but he'll always have his 2012 postseason heroics to hang his hat on.

LINEOUTS

HITTERS

PLAYER	TEAM	LVL	AGE	PA	R	2B	3B	HR	RBI	BB	SO	SB-CS	AVG/OBP/SLG	TAv	BABIP	BRR	FRAA	WARP
SS E. Adrianza	RIC	AA	22	512	52	22	5	3	32	41	90	16-4	.220/.289/.310	.234	.266	-0.9	SS(117): -6.9	-0.7
2B R. Jones	SLO	A-	21	227	20	8	0	1	20	22	35	2-3	.227/.307/.283	.234	.267	0.5	2B(5): -0.5	0.0
OF R. Kieschnick	FRE	AAA	25	250	49	13	4	15	40	24	68	0-2	.306/.376/.604	.321	.376	0	LF(36): -1.6, RF(4): 0.1	1.6
OF S. McCall	GIA	RK	18	164	22	7	1	3	20	25	43	6-2	.246/.366/.377	.269	.337	0	LF(6): 0.2	0
SS N. Noonan	FRE	AAA	23	541	65	26	3	9	62	40	84	7-3	.296/.347/.416	.257	.338	-1.9	SS(75): -3.5, 3B(13): 1.8	0.5
OF J. Perez	RIC	AA	25	513	65	26	4	11	53	22	85	18-15	.302/.341/.441	.283	.349	2.4	RF(80): 2.2, CF(15): 0.6	2.9
C G. Quiroz	TAC	AAA	30	347	45	15	1	15	52	36	70	0-0	.278/.362/.483	.285	.315	0.2	C(74): -1.8	1.6
OF R. Rodriguez	SLO	A-	19	176	9	10	1	3	20	9	31	7-7	.235/.287/.364	.222	.273	-2.7	LF(9): -0.1	-0.6
1B A. Villalona	DGI	Rk	21	193	32	9	0	7	34	23	40	0-0	.303/.430/.497	.328	.364	0.8	--	0.0
OF J. Williamson	SLO	A-	21	126	22	8	0	7	25	6	19	0-0	.342/.392/.596	.297	.360	0.8	RF(14): -0.2	0.3

Ehire Adrianza is a good defender at shortstop, but has been unable to pack muscle onto his frame as once projected, and he struggles with the bat, pointing to a future as a utility infielder. **Ryan Jones** has an undersized second baseman profile, but he could fill in at shortstop or third base. He's a good baserunner who makes a lot of contact, and his feel for the game gives him a shot. **Roger Kieschnick**'s season was cut short due to injury, but in his time on the field he was able to show off his power at the dish. He was able to make up for some of his lost time by playing in the Dominican Winter League. If **Shilo McCall**'s pull-side power doesn't fully develop, he could be a bit of a tweener with not enough bat for a corner and not enough glove for center field. **Nick Noonan** isn't likely to live up to his sandwich-round selection, but he played all of the infield positions except first base for Fresno last year, and he could have a future as a utility infielder. **Juan Perez** was a late bloomer as an amateur, and because of that, he was a bit old for his level when he broke out offensively last year. A card-carrying member of the international Brotherhood of Back-Up Catchers, Triple-A Division, **Guillermo Quiroz** has posted positive WARP figures twice in parts of eight seasons in the majors: 0.1 both times. Thus far, **Rafael Rodriguez** has struggled to justify receiving the largest international bonus in Giants history ($2.55 million) in 2009. **Angel Villalona** played in actual baseball games for the first time in three years last season, but did so in the Dominican Republic while dealing with visa issues. **Jonathan "Mac" Williamson** was the team's third-round selection last June, and he brings corner power to the plate, but has questions to answer about his bat-to-ball skills.

PITCHERS

PLAYER	TEAM	LVL	AGE	W	L	SV	IP	H	HR	BB	SO	BB9	SO9	GB%	BABIP	WHIP	ERA	FIP	FRA	WARP
B. Bochy	RIC	AA	24	7	3	14	53^{1}	29	3	18	69	3.0	11.6	33%	.232	0.88	2.53	2.53	3.92	0.6
J. Dunning	RIC	AA	23	5	2	0	68	74	2	22	53	2.9	7.0	56%	.338	1.41	4.10	3.17	4.00	0.7
J. Dunnington	AUG	A	21	1	0	0	10	8	1	5	14	4.5	12.6	33%	0.304	1.3	4.5	3.58	4.69	0.1
	RIC	AA	21	0	0	0	15^{1}	12	0	8	18	4.7	10.6	36%	0.333	1.3	1.76	2.61	2.91	0.3
	SCO	WNT	21	0	1	0	9^{1}	13	0	4	14	3.9	13.5	-	0.52	1.82	6.75	2.21	2.4	0
S. Edlefsen	FRE	AAA	27	1	3	0	38	33	3	18	29	4.3	6.9	59%	.263	1.34	3.79	4.82	5.80	-0.1
	SFN	MLB	27	0	1	0	15^{1}	20	1	6	9	3.5	5.3	61%	.358	1.70	4.70	3.98	5.14	-0.3
E. Escobar	AUG	A	20	7	8	0	130^{2}	121	7	32	122	2.2	8.4	46%	.301	1.17	2.96	3.30	4.03	1.8
I. Gardeck	SLO	A-	21	2	2	0	30	22	0	24	45	7.2	13.5	58%	.328	1.53	4.20	2.83	3.09	0.6
C. Gloor	RIC	AA	25	4	5	0	105^{2}	99	7	29	74	2.5	6.3	43%	.290	1.21	2.81	3.54	4.29	1.1
C. Hensley	SFN	MLB	32	4	5	3	50^{2}	50	5	30	42	5.3	7.5	52%	.292	1.58	4.62	4.72	4.54	-0.3
M. Kickham	RIC	AA	23	11	10	0	150^{2}	119	8	75	137	4.5	8.2	55%	.275	1.29	3.05	3.61	4.38	1.1
S. Loux	FRE	AAA	32	4	1	0	32	23	0	5	22	1.4	6.2	55%	.250	0.88	1.41	2.85	3.44	0.7
	SFN	MLB	32	1	0	0	25^{1}	32	3	9	9	3.2	3.2	52%	.322	1.62	4.97	5.03	5.91	-0.5
C. Marlowe	AUG	A	22	1	9	2	83^{2}	66	5	59	86	6.3	9.3	48%	.282	1.49	4.20	4.60	5.26	0.2
D. Otero	FRE	AAA	27	5	5	0	62	70	4	8	45	1.2	6.5	57%	.332	1.26	2.90	3.58	4.39	0.7
	SFN	MLB	27	0	0	0	12^{1}	19	0	2	8	1.5	5.8	67%	.422	1.70	5.84	2.81	3.06	0.2
B. Penny	SFN	MLB	34	0	1	0	28	42	4	9	10	2.9	3.2	53%	.349	1.82	6.11	5.35	5.31	-0.3
S. Rosario	NWO	AAA	26	0	2	16	26	20	0	2	24	0.7	8.3	43%	.290	0.85	1.04	2.17	0.50	0.6
	MIA	MLB	26	0	0	0	3	8	0	0	2	0.0	6.0	60%	.533	2.67	18.00	1.80	2.95	0.1

The Giants selected **Brett Bochy**, who was recovering from April Tommy John surgery, in the 20th round of the 2010 draft, and he thrived closing for most of last year for Double-A Richmond. Yeah, he's the skipper's kid. **Jake Dunning** has successfully made the transition from shortstop to pitcher, and he has used a four-pitch mix—mid-90s fastball, curveball, slider, and changeup—to make the Giants 40-man roster. **Jacob Dunnington** relies on a fastball that tops out at 95 mph to rack up strikeouts, and he rode those whiffs to an Arizona Fall League assignment. Inducing groundballs is great, but **Steve Edlefsen** illustrates that it takes more than generating worm burners at a high rate to succeed on the mound. **Edwin Escobar** made substantial strides in throwing strikes with his swing-and-miss stuff. The organization added him to the 40-man roster to protect him from the Rule 5 draft. **Ian Gardeck** is an arm-strength guy with a wipeout slider who lacks control of either pitch. With work, he could become a late-inning reliever. **Chris Gloor** began last year in the bullpen and finished it starting. Despite a big build, he doesn't throw very hard, instead relying on locating all of his pitches. **Clay Hensley**'s pitch repertoire leaves little room for error, so if he hopes to stick in a big-league bullpen, he'll need to get his walk rate back under control. **Michael Kickham** is closer to realizing his fourth-starter potential after a solid year in Double-A. He's a big southpaw with plus velocity on his fastball, a slider, and a slant toward inducing grounders. If **Shane Loux** were a hitter his near-identical career walk and strikeout rates would be solid. Alas, he is not. **Christopher Marlowe** throws a good fastball that sits at 94-95 mph and has touched 96 mph, but his control isn't very good. **Danny Otero** avoids walks, but he caught too much plate in his limited big-league stint and was quite hittable. It's hard to fathom anyone giving 34-year-old **Brad Penny** a look in 2013 after he finished 2012 with a paltry 3.2 K/9 while pitching exclusively out of the bullpen. Between the middle of October and the end of December, **Sandy Rosario** was included in five transactions involving four organizations. He throws a fastball in the mid-to-upper-90s and backs it with a slider (his primary secondary offering), changeup, and curveball.

MANAGER: BRUCE BOCHY

YEAR	TEAM	W-L	Pythag +/-	Avg PC	100+ P	120+ P	QS	BQS	REL	REL w Zero R	IBB	PH	PH Avg	PH HR	SB2	CS2	SB3	CS3	SAC Att	SAC %	POS SAC	Squeeze	Swing	In Play
2010	SFN	92-70	1	198.8	161	161	119	4	476	402	116	438	.262	12	6	3	0	1	212	77.4%	58	0	264	85
2011	SFN	86-76	0	99.8	90	7	103	3	480	411	46	244	.212	4	7	6	2	3	86	79.1%	35	2	395	118
2012	SFN	94-68	1	100.0	91	3	93	6	526	440	42	214	.217	3	6	2	1	2	100	77.0%	35	0	382	123

After the Giants won their second World Series championship in the last three years, general manager Brian Sabean referred to Bochy as a Hall of Fame manager. When it's all said and done, he'll have a strong case, as he is just the 23rd man to have won multiple world championships. Bochy once again managed the club with a deft touch, juggling his bullpen nearly flawlessly, playing matchups, and shaking up the closer spot when necessary after losing Brian Wilson to injury. Bochy had the club running frequently, and they ranked sixth in the National League in stolen bases. He was rightfully criticized in *Baseball Prospectus 2012* for his inability to find a balance between youth and veterans. He did a much better job last year of trusting the club's youngsters while not losing sight of the importance of supplementing them with veterans. The results speak for themselves.

Seattle Mariners

2012: JURASSIC PARK

For the first time since his rookie season, Ichiro Suzuki played in the postseason. Alas, it wasn't with the Mariners, as the right fielder begged out of another losing season in Seattle and was traded to New York in July, ending an unforgettable—but, ultimately, unsuccessful—era in the Pacific Northwest.

For the fourth year in a row, the Mariners finished last in the American League in runs scored. Their expansive ballpark suppresses scoring, and this year the Mariners' home-road splits were almost enough to convince fans to feel some optimism about the bats Jack Zduriencik has collected. Seattle scored 100 more runs on the road, slugged 37 more home runs, and finished fifth in the American League in road scoring and eighth in road OPS. The Mariners' big offseason move—trading for phenom catcher/DH Jesus Montero—didn't change the offense much, but the Mariners' much smaller offseason move—trading for late-blooming catcher/DH John Jaso—did. Jaso had the highest OPS+ by a Mariner (minimum 100 plate appearances) since 2001, when Bret Boone and Edgar Martinez were MVP candidates.

Though the park suppressed Mariners bats, it wasn't the only—or even primary—culprit. Rather, former blue-chip prospects Justin Smoak and Dustin Ackley combined for a .292 OBP, topping a list of 11 Mariners who got at least 100 plate appearances with a sub-.300 OBP. After Jaso, the team's best OBP was .316. Adjusting for ballpark still leaves the Mariners with the worst True Average in the American League, and the lack of offense again doomed Seattle to last place. It was a much lonelier cellar than in previous years, as upstart Oakland escaped and left it to the Mariners alone.

MARINERS PROSPECTUS

2012 W-L: 75-87, 4th in AL West

Pythag	.477	19th	DER	.718	4th
RS/G	3.82	27th	B-Age	27.0	3rd
RA/G	4.02	9th	P-Age	27.9	15th
TAv	.252	27th	Salary	$84.8	20th
BRR	-8.1	26th	M$/MW	$2.70	17th
TAv-P	.261	16th	DL Days	559	29th
FIP	3.95	16th	DL WARP	0.7	29th

Three-Year Park Factors	
Overall	92
HR/RH	86
HR/LH	88
AVG/RH	92
AVG/LH	92

Safeco Field (1999)
Att. % of Capacity: 44.4% (30th)
Dim. 331, 378, 401, 381, 326

Safeco has gotten smaller – by as much as 17 feet in left center – but it'll likely remain a pitcher's park.

Unsurprisingly, hitting coach Chris Chambliss was fired after the season.

2013: WESTWORLD

The Mariners have two more seasons until Felix Hernandez could hit free agency, but 2013 doesn't look to be the year that the King gets his first postseason start, as the Mariners finished 2012 14 wins behind even the AL West's third-best team. On the bright side, the addition of the Houston Astros to the division should snap Seattle's three-season last-place streak.

The Mariners' austerity measures over the past three seasons have slimmed the roster to a very young, very affordable core. Seattle had the second-youngest offense in the AL in 2012, and that was with Ichiro and Chone Figgins on the roster. Their pitchers' age was closer to league average, but the bulk of their pitching talent was below the surface, mowing down Southern League batters. The three aces at Double-A Jackson—Danny Hultzen, James Paxton, and Taijuan Walker—had varying degrees of success, but each could see the big-league rotation in 2013 and each has the stuff to contribute immediately. Having three top pitching prospects gives any GM a giant slurp of optimism, but expecting all three to take leaps forward, stay healthy, and contribute immediately might be a bit much. With the bulk of the farm system's high-ceiling talent on the verge of matriculating, and the Felix-in-Seattle window potentially closing, the Mariners are finally in a position to start spending again.

They entered the offseason with about $23 million to play with just to match 2012, a margin that dropped to $15 million with the re-ups of Hisanori Iwakuma and Oliver Perez.

But, given the Mariners' payroll history, the 2012 version ($82 million) was artificially low. Should the Mariners decide that the next win might be the one that will get them to the postseason, they have the space to spend even more. The time might be now: Zduriencik told a beat writer in November that he anticipated a payroll increase. The Mariners were linked to Josh Hamilton and Mike Napoli early in the offseason, but Hamilton signed with the Angels and as we went to press Napoli did not appear headed for Seattle.

STATE OF THE ORGANIZATION: RISING SUN?

The Mariners have been disciplined for three years, and as a result have no bad contract beyond Figgins's 2013 salary. They also boast a farm system heavy on talent in the high minors. Financial flexibility doesn't win games, though, and they'll need to show they can take the next step by trading for or signing middle-of-the-order hitters.

Before the 2012 season, the Mariners were closely linked to 27-year-old free agent Prince Fielder, and Zduriencik publicly confirmed his pursuit. Fielder, though, told the *Seattle Times* later that the Mariners "weren't among his final list of choices." Whether they couldn't sign Fielder because they didn't pursue him with enough effort or because Seattle is an unattractive destination for free-agent hitters, the moral is the same: Top offense is going to be hard to get, and the Mariners must be ready to write the sort of check that can make a GM's palms sweat.

In pursuing Napoli early in the offseason, Seattle stressed the changing offensive environment. The fences will come in from right-center to the left-field corner, juicing home-run totals by 30 to 40 per year, according to the Mariners' math. BP's Colin Wyers looked at the changes and concluded that Safeco will still be solidly on the pitchers' side, but the Mariners would know best how much the ballpark dimensions have affected the pursuit of free agents in recent years. The Mariners' decision to sign sharp defenders, rather than power hitters, might not have been the sabermetric strategy it appeared so much as playing the hand that was dealt them.

If the Mariners can convince players to move to Seattle, the club will have the money to pay them. The team's cable contract leaves them far behind AL West rivals in Arlington and Anaheim, but there is a silver lining in the form of an opt-out after the 2015 season. The Mariners can safely count on that revenue stream in the future, giving Zduriencik the freedom to offer multi-year contracts, or take on another club's.

HITTERS

Dustin Ackley **2B**
Born: **2/26/1988** Age: **25**
Bats: **L** Throws: **R** Height: **6' 2"**
Weight: **190** Breakout: **1%**
Improve: **41%** Collapse: **11%**
Attrition: **16%** MLB: **95%**
Comparables:
Luis Valbuena, Blake DeWitt, Ian Kinsler

YEAR	TEAM	LVL	AGE	PA	R	2B	3B	HR	RBI	BB	SO	SB	CS	AVG_OBP_SLG	TAv	BABIP	BRR	FRAA	WARP
2010	WTN	AA	22	350	42	21	4	2	28	55	41	8	2	.263/.390/.384	.282	.301	1.3	2B(70): -6.4	1.2
2010	TAC	AAA	22	237	37	12	4	5	23	20	38	2	1	.274/.342/.439	.291	.314	1.6	2B(59): -10.1	0.7
2011	TAC	AAA	23	331	57	17	3	9	35	55	38	7	3	.303/.421/.487	.345	.324	-1.2	2B(35): -1.5	1.6
2011	SEA	MLB	23	376	39	16	7	6	36	40	79	6	0	.273/.348/.417	.299	.339	-0.5	2B(86): -1.7, 1B(1): -0.0	2.2
2012	SEA	MLB	24	668	84	22	2	12	50	59	124	13	3	.226/.294/.328	.241	.265	3.2	2B(142): -1.5, 1B(10): -0.2	-0.2
2013	*SEA*	*MLB*	*25*	*590*	*68*	*24*	*5*	*10*	*51*	*58*	*110*	*9*	*2*	*.242/.319/.361*	*.263*	*.286*	*0.7*	*2B -6, 1B -0*	*1.7*

On the surface, Ackley followed up a good year with a bad year, but that's not the whole story: He batted a paltry .242/.327/.311 after July 4, 2011, which makes his 2012 line look like less of a plot twist and more like the plot. Patience, one of Ackley's nicer attributes, is erroneously seen as a toggle-type skill, but young players often need to refine their patience to make it usable. Ackley's shows up in called third strikes and a stubborn refusal to adapt to umpires' strike zones. It's better to start with the eye and learn to deploy it than have no eye at all, though: Ackley's approach could still turn into a weapon. He's a clean defender, his speed plays well in games, and the power—10 home runs on the road—suggests a pretty good fantasy second baseman, if not a superstar, is going to come out of this package.

Robert Andino **INF**
Born: **4/25/1984** Age: **29**
Bats: **R** Throws: **R** Height: **6' 1"**
Weight: **195** Breakout: **8%**
Improve: **40%** Collapse: **2%**
Attrition: **12%** MLB: **87%**
Comparables:
John Castino, Andy Green, Julio Gotay

YEAR	TEAM	LVL	AGE	PA	R	2B	3B	HR	RBI	BB	SO	SB	CS	AVG_OBP_SLG	TAv	BABIP	BRR	FRAA	WARP
2010	NOR	AAA	26	588	72	30	4	13	76	29	110	16	3	.264/.305/.405	.248	.308	-1	SS(111): 8.7, 2B(21): -0.6	2.0
2010	BAL	MLB	26	66	6	4	0	2	6	3	13	1	1	.295/.333/.459	.258	.340	-0.3	2B(8): -0.4, SS(7): 0.1	0.0
2011	BAL	MLB	27	511	63	22	0	5	36	41	83	13	3	.263/.327/.344	.245	.311	1.9	2B(94): -6.2, SS(30): 5.6	0.6
2012	BAL	MLB	28	431	41	13	1	7	28	37	100	5	5	.211/.283/.305	.218	.266	0.6	2B(108): -1.8, 3B(15): -0.7	-1.3
2013	*SEA*	*MLB*	*29*	*422*	*40*	*16*	*1*	*5*	*33*	*30*	*91*	*8*	*3*	*.224/.284/.308*	*.231*	*.277*	*-0.1*	*2B -2, SS -0*	*0.0*

Among the 193 players with at least 400 plate appearances in 2012, Andino's TAv ranked 192nd. Put it this way: If Andino were a blind date, you wouldn't bail on dinner, but you probably wouldn't bring him home to meet mom. Andino—acquired by Seattle for Trayvon Robinson—really is the bare minimum a team can accept as a starting player. He gets bonus points for flexibility, for doing things other guys can't or won't, and has the ability play all around the diamond. That has value, but in a bench role, as someone you can call on (or just call) in a pinch.

Jason Bay **LF**
Born: **9/20/1978** Age: **34**
Bats: **R** Throws: **R** Height: **6' 3"**
Weight: **210** Breakout: **0%**
Improve: **31%** Collapse: **6%**
Attrition: **18%** MLB: **82%**
Comparables:
Fernando Tatis,Bob Nieman,Milton Bradley

YEAR	TEAM	LVL	AGE	PA	R	2B	3B	HR	RBI	BB	SO	SB	CS	AVG_OBP_SLG	TAv	BABIP	BRR	FRAA	WARP
2010	NYN	MLB	31	401	48	20	6	6	47	44	91	10	0	.259/.347/.402	.279	.329	1.9	LF(93): -8.3	1.1
2010	NYN	MLB	31	401	48	20	6	6	47	44	91	10	0	.259/.347/.402	.279	.329	1.9	LF(93): -8.3	1.1
2011	NYN	MLB	32	509	59	19	1	12	57	56	109	11	1	.245/.329/.374	.260	.295	0.6	LF(122): -1.6	0.5
2011	NYN	MLB	32	509	59	19	1	12	57	56	109	11	1	.245/.329/.374	.260	.295	0.6	LF(122): -1.6	0.5
2012	NYN	MLB	33	215	21	2	0	8	20	19	58	5	1	.165/.237/.299	.206	.185	0.2	LF(64): 5.5	-0.4
2012	NYN	MLB	33	215	21	2	0	8	20	19	58	5	1	.165/.237/.299	.206	.185	0.2	LF(64): 5.5	-0.4
2013	*SEA*	*MLB*	*34*	*267*	*32*	*9*	*1*	*9*	*32*	*31*	*66*	*6*	*1*	*.232/.325/.396*	*.276*	*.283*	*0.6*	*LF -0*	*1.1*

Bay's 2011 season looked bad at the time, but that's only because we had no idea what was going to happen in 2012. He started the year well enough, but broke a rib diving for a ball in late April. He hadn't been back for two weeks when he dived for another ball and slammed into the wall head-first, suffering his second concussion in the big leagues. (To add insult to injury, Jay Bruce motored around the bases for an inside-the-park home run.) In November, the Mets and Bay agreed on a buyout, and the Mariners picked him up for a million bucks. He's not obviously better than the fourth- and fifth-outfielders in the organization already, so he might need to prove himself in spring training to stick.

Mike Carp **1B**
Born: **6/30/1986** Age: **27**
Bats: **L** Throws: **R** Height: **6' 3"**
Weight: **210** Breakout: **2%**
Improve: **38%** Collapse: **9%**
Attrition: **15%** MLB: **82%**
Comparables:
Justin Huber,Travis Ishikawa,Juan Miranda

YEAR	TEAM	LVL	AGE	PA	R	2B	3B	HR	RBI	BB	SO	SB	CS	AVG_OBP_SLG	TAv	BABIP	BRR	FRAA	WARP
2010	TAC	AAA	24	463	67	17	1	29	76	41	93	1	2	.257/.333/.516	.299	.265	-2.2	1B(53): -2.1, LF(48): 6.8	3.0
2010	SEA	MLB	24	41	1	2	0	0	0	4	8	0	0	.189/.268/.243	.230	.241	-0.7	1B(9): -0.0, LF(1): -0.0	0.0
2011	TAC	AAA	25	286	55	14	0	21	64	28	50	6	2	.343/.411/.649	.366	.355	1.2	LF(21): 0.3, 1B(3): 0.5	2.3
2011	SEA	MLB	25	313	27	17	1	12	46	19	81	0	2	.276/.326/.466	.282	.343	-2.1	1B(34): -0.8, LF(27): -0.0	0.6
2012	TAC	AAA	26	154	13	8	0	2	17	12	31	1	3	.223/.286/.324	.225	.269	-0.8	1B(10): -0.3, LF(2): 0.3	-0.6
2012	SEA	MLB	26	189	17	6	0	5	20	21	46	1	0	.213/.312/.341	.240	.263	-1.4	LF(24): 0.9, 1B(23): -0.1	-0.3
2013	*SEA*	*MLB*	*27*	*250*	*28*	*10*	*1*	*9*	*31*	*21*	*60*	*1*	*1*	*.236/.310/.402*	*.268*	*.279*	*-0.5*	*1B -2, LF 0*	*0.4*

In 2011, Carp hit well enough against lefties, and overall, that he seemed poised to break out of platoon prison. In 2012, he hit so poorly against righties that the Mariners might exile him to a distant island instead. As it was, they batted him eighth in baseball's worst lineup. Carp injured his shoulder in the team's opener in Japan, the first of three stints on the disabled list. That gave him plenty of time to rehab in Tacoma, where, surprisingly, he was even worse than in Seattle. The best news is that his walk rate returned. The worst is that he has turned into a groundball machine, a losing strategy for a player whose only tool is second-deck power.

Joseph DeCarlo **3B**
Born: **9/13/1993** Age: **19**
Bats: **R** Throws: **R** Height: **5' 11"**
Weight: **205** Breakout: **0%**
Improve: **34-%** Collapse: **66%**
Attrition: **66%** MLB: **100%**
Comparables:
Robin Yount,Ed Kranepool,Wayne Causey

YEAR	TEAM	LVL	AGE	PA	R	2B	3B	HR	RBI	BB	SO	SB	CS	AVG_OBP_SLG	TAv	BABIP	BRR	FRAA	WARP
2012	MRN	Rk	18	223	29	12	3	4	31	31	47	0	2	.236/.368/.401	.276	.293	-0.3	3B(11): -0.2	0.0
2013	*SEA*	*MLB*	*19*	*250*	*20*	*7*	*1*	*3*	*18*	*24*	*72*	*1*	*1*	*.173/.256/.253*	*.202*	*.236*	*-0.3*	*3B 0*	*-0.2*

The Mariners didn't waste any time moving their second-round pick from shortstop, where DeCarlo was drafted, to third base, for which his body is better suited and where his arm will play. He has good strength, is mature physically, and led his Arizona League team in walks. But there's already a lot of swing-and-miss in his bat, and he'll need to add more power without adding more strikeouts if he's going to develop into a real prospect.

Eric Farris **UT**
Born: **3/3/1986** Age: **27**
Bats: **R** Throws: **R** Height: **5' 10"**
Weight: **180** Breakout: **13%**
Improve: **42%** Collapse: **9%**
Attrition: **21%** MLB: **89%**
Comparables:
Anderson Hernandez,Rennie Stennett,Kevin Sefcik

YEAR	TEAM	LVL	AGE	PA	R	2B	3B	HR	RBI	BB	SO	SB	CS	AVG_OBP_SLG	TAv	BABIP	BRR	FRAA	WARP
2010	NAS	AAA	24	249	28	9	1	2	15	9	25	14	2	.274/.306/.348	.229	.293	0.6	2B(59): 1.9	0.1
2011	NAS	AAA	25	594	70	26	5	6	55	32	70	21	7	.271/.317/.372	.261	.300	0.5	2B(44): -3.4, SS(7): 0.3	0.1
2011	MIL	MLB	25	1	0	0	0	0	0	0	0	0	0	.000/.000/.000	.016	.000	0	--	0.0
2012	NAS	AAA	26	528	63	21	1	7	31	27	56	35	13	.286/.329/.377	.254	.309	3.7	2B(73): -15.6, LF(11): 0.4	-0.5
2012	MIL	MLB	26	9	1	0	0	0	0	1	2	1	0	.125/.222/.125	.142	.167	0.3	2B(2): -0.0, LF(1): -0.0	-0.1
2013	*SEA*	*MLB*	*27*	*250*	*28*	*10*	*1*	*2*	*15*	*10*	*39*	*13*	*4*	*.233/.271/.305*	*.223*	*.268*	*1.1*	*2B 1, SS 0*	*0.2*

In three full seasons at Triple-A, Farris has learned to play enough different positions to qualify as a utility man, but he hasn't figured out upper-level pitching: His cumulative line in those three PCL-boosted seasons is just

.277/.321/.369. He did get his longest look in the big leagues in 2012, as a September call-up, but he's still looking for his first start in the majors. The Mariners have been known to give loads of at-bats to terrible hitters, but the only position at which Farris's glove plays up is second base—the position at which the Mariners are deepest.

Chone Figgins UT

Born: **1/22/1978** Age: **35**
Bats: **B** Throws: **R** Height: **5' 9"**
Weight: **180** Breakout: **0%**
Improve: **33%** Collapse: **10%**
Attrition: **18%** MLB: **83%**

Comparables:
Lenny Green,Dave Roberts,Tim Raines

YEAR	TEAM	LVL	AGE	PA	R	2B	3B	HR	RBI	BB	SO	SB	CS	AVG_OBP_SLG	TAv	BABIP	BRR	FRAA	WARP
2010	SEA	MLB	32	702	62	21	2	1	35	74	114	42	15	.259/.340/.306	.247	.314	2.2	2B(161): -16.9	-0.2
2011	SEA	MLB	33	313	24	11	1	1	15	21	42	11	6	.188/.241/.243	.200	.215	0.1	3B(80): 0.4, LF(2): 0.0	-1.1
2012	SEA	MLB	34	194	18	5	2	2	11	19	48	4	1	.181/.262/.271	.206	.237	-0.6	LF(38): -2.7, 3B(10): 0.6	-1.1
2013	*SEA*	*MLB*	*35*	*250*	*29*	*8*	*1*	*0*	*14*	*27*	*45*	*12*	*5*	*.236/.322/.290*	*.241*	*.287*	*0.5*	*3B -0, 2B -1*	*0.1*

Figgins spent yet another full season on the Mariners' active roster, but set a new low for playing time and started only nine games after July 1, and one in September. Just two players have a worse OPS over the past two seasons (minimum 300 PA), and his negative WARP per plate appearance has gotten worse each year in Seattle. He played some center field for the first time since 2006, which is the sort of thing that would help him land a job elsewhere if he had even one other marketable skill. The Mariners finally released Figgins in November.

Franklin Gutierrez CF

Born: **2/21/1983** Age: **30**
Bats: **R** Throws: **R** Height: **6' 3"**
Weight: **190** Breakout: **1%**
Improve: **37%** Collapse: **5%**
Attrition: **7%** MLB: **92%**

Comparables:
Jerry Mumphrey,Jacob Brumfield,Lee Maye

YEAR	TEAM	LVL	AGE	PA	R	2B	3B	HR	RBI	BB	SO	SB	CS	AVG_OBP_SLG	TAv	BABIP	BRR	FRAA	WARP
2010	SEA	MLB	27	629	61	25	3	12	64	50	137	25	3	.245/.303/.363	.259	.297	-0.7	CF(146): 1.7	1.8
2011	SEA	MLB	28	344	26	13	0	1	19	16	56	13	2	.224/.261/.273	.200	.266	0.9	CF(92): 4.7	-0.6
2012	TAC	AAA	29	72	11	5	0	2	8	8	13	0	1	.258/.333/.435	.284	.286	-0.2	CF(10): 1.2	0.4
2012	SEA	MLB	29	163	18	10	1	4	17	9	31	3	1	.260/.309/.420	.272	.302	-0.5	CF(38): 0.7	0.3
2013	*SEA*	*MLB*	*30*	*250*	*26*	*10*	*1*	*5*	*24*	*17*	*51*	*7*	*2*	*.241/.296/.355*	*.249*	*.286*	*0.6*	*CF 4*	*0.9*

Gutierrez's season started late because of a torn pectoral muscle, and was interrupted by a concussion suffered when a pickoff throw hit him in the face. When he could play, he had the best OPS+ of his career. It's hard to know what to make of that, given the sample size, a statement that's especially true when evaluating his defense. Gutierrez was the best center fielder in the game three years ago, but advanced metrics have gone south on him since then. If a single season of defensive data is inconclusive, then the half- and quarter-seasons Gutierrez has been playing might be worse than no data at all. He also has lost speed, as shown by his stolen-base attempts. Given his age, it may not return.

Raul Ibanez DH

Born: **6/2/1972** Age: **41**
Bats: **L** Throws: **R** Height: **6' 3"**
Weight: **220** Breakout: **0%**
Improve: **21%** Collapse: **7%**
Attrition: **21%** MLB: **66%**

Comparables:
Ken Griffey,Hank Sauer,Moises Alou

YEAR	TEAM	LVL	AGE	PA	R	2B	3B	HR	RBI	BB	SO	SB	CS	AVG_OBP_SLG	TAv	BABIP	BRR	FRAA	WARP
2010	PHI	MLB	38	636	75	37	5	16	83	68	108	4	3	.275/.349/.444	.279	.311	-0.2	LF(145): -16.8, 1B(1): 0.0	1.0
2011	PHI	MLB	39	575	65	31	1	20	84	33	106	2	0	.245/.289/.419	.261	.268	-0.6	LF(134): -4.2	0.0
2012	NYA	MLB	40	425	50	19	3	19	62	35	67	3	0	.240/.308/.453	.263	.243	0.7	LF(80): 0.7, RF(13): -1.1	0.4
2013	*SEA*	*MLB*	*41*	*429*	*45*	*20*	*2*	*13*	*51*	*35*	*83*	*2*	*1*	*.239/.302/.399*	*.264*	*.270*	*-0.3*	*LF -3, RF -0*	*0.9*

Ibanez was forced out of his comfortable DH platoon with the Yankees and into the outfield after an injury to left-fielder Brett Gardner. The bald veteran was little better than a living statue out there, but he endeared himself to Yankees fans by launching three improbable postseason homers. Those heroics aren't likely to carry over into his age-41 season. Against righties at home, Ibanez hit a home run every 11.1 at-bats, better than the career rate of the guy the original Yankee Stadium was built for, but he was next to useless against lefties and on the road. Joe Girardi got him the platoon advantage in 85 percent of his plate appearances—more than any other non-switch-hitter with at least 400 PA—but the other 15 percent, plus all the ones without the short porch, made him a roughly replacement-level player. He will be returning for his third stint as a Mariner. Perhaps familiarity will make Safeco more hospitable to his swing, since the dimensions won't.

John Jaso C

Born: **9/19/1983** Age: **29**
Bats: **L** Throws: **R** Height: **6' 3"**
Weight: **205** Breakout: **0%**
Improve: **49%** Collapse: **13%**
Attrition: **14%** MLB: **96%**

Comparables:
Mark Grace,John Olerud,Gail Hopkins

YEAR	TEAM	LVL	AGE	PA	R	2B	3B	HR	RBI	BB	SO	SB	CS	AVG_OBP_SLG	TAv	BABIP	BRR	FRAA	WARP
2010	TBA	MLB	26	404	57	18	3	5	44	59	39	4	0	.263/.372/.378	.277	.282	-0.7	C(96): -1.8, 1B(1): -0.0	2.1
2011	TBA	MLB	27	273	26	15	1	5	27	25	36	1	2	.224/.298/.354	.234	.244	0.7	C(82): -0.9	-0.1
2012	SEA	MLB	28	361	41	19	2	10	50	56	51	5	0	.276/.394/.456	.336	.298	0.1	C(43): -0.4	3.3
2013	*SEA*	*MLB*	*29*	*322*	*36*	*14*	*2*	*6*	*31*	*41*	*43*	*3*	*1*	*.248/.349/.373*	*.276*	*.273*	*-0.1*	*C -1, 1B -0*	*1.7*

Here's one for you: John Jaso's True Average in his first year as a Mariner was .336. Miguel Cabrera's True Average in 2012 was .332. Jaso dramatically changed his swing on the trip west from Tampa, getting out of his tight, punchy crouch into an upright, hands-high power posture—think Gregor Blanco, then think Adam Dunn. The results tracked the stances, and Jaso's power even proved Safeco-proof: his 877 OPS at home was more than 200 points better than the next best Mariner's. Jaso has an excellent batting eye, but was aggressive on pitches in the zone in 2012, leveraging favorable counts instead of waiting for a walk. Sure enough, his production bump was far greater on the first pitch (190 points of OPS better than his career split) or when he was ahead in the count (148 points) than when he was behind (56 points). He's a lousy bet to top Cabrera again, but PECOTA's 2013 projection for him would have been the Mariners' second-best hitter in 2012. Break out the M-V-P chants.

Munenori Kawasaki SS

Born: **6/3/1981** Age: **32**
Bats: **L** Throws: **R** Height: **6' 0"**
Weight: **165** Breakout: **4%**
Improve: **30%** Collapse: **6%**
Attrition: **19%** MLB: **97%**

Comparables:
Adam Everett,Luis Aparicio,Wilson Valdez

YEAR	TEAM	LVL	AGE	PA	R	2B	3B	HR	RBI	BB	SO	SB	CS	AVG_OBP_SLG	TAv	BABIP	BRR	FRAA	WARP
2010	FKU	NPB	29	662	74	27	5	4	53	43	86	30	11	.316/.368/.397	.275	.363	0	—	0
2011	FKU	NPB	30	639	71	14	9	1	37	36	84	31	10	.267/.308/.325	.229	.309	0	—	0
2012	*SEA*	MLB	31	115	13	1	0	0	7	8	18	2	2	.192/.257/.202	.187	.233	-0.8	SS(38): -2.0, 2B(9): 0.3	-0.8
2013	*SEA*	*MLB*	*32*	*250*	*22*	*8*	*2*	*0*	*17*	*14*	*35*	*6*	*3*	*.255/.301/.306*	*.235*	*.295*	*0.1*	*SS -2, 2B -0*	*0.3*

Kawasaki's story can be told in full because it's over and there won't be a sequel: Kawasaki wanted to play in the majors but only if he could play with his hero, Ichiro. He got an invite to Mariners spring training even though he didn't hit in Japan in 2011 as a 30-year-old. But he led all of baseball in batting average in spring training and made the team. Ichiro's team! What a story! And then he was unspeakably bad, knocking one extra-base hit all year. Among *pitchers* he would have been in the 65th percentile for slugging. But he was the smiliest Mariner, "often seen dancing or doing aerobics in the dugout," according to a local newspaper account. He was released in October.

Leon Landry OF

Born: **9/20/1989** Age: **23**
Bats: **L** Throws: **R** Height: **6' 0"**
Weight: **185** Breakout: **9%**
Improve: **47%** Collapse: **6%**
Attrition: **11%** MLB: **91%**

Comparables:
Rod Craig,Ruben Mateo,Rowland Office

YEAR	TEAM	LVL	AGE	PA	R	2B	3B	HR	RBI	BB	SO	SB	CS	AVG_OBP_SLG	TAv	BABIP	BRR	FRAA	WARP
2010	OGD	Rk	20	274	46	20	4	4	38	20	36	13	9	.349/.401/.510	.318	.395	-1.9	CF(61): -2.4	2.0
2011	GRL	A	21	552	59	21	11	4	41	37	67	28	12	.250/.307/.360	.235	.281	0	--	0.0
2012	HDS	A+	22	111	25	8	3	5	25	5	14	7	2	.385/.414/.663	.372	.407	0	CF(7): 0.2, LF(1): -0.0	0.5
2012	RCU	A+	22	376	63	26	15	8	51	14	52	20	9	.328/.358/.559	.318	.362	4.8	CF(11): -1.8, LF(4): -0.3	0.7
2013	*SEA*	*MLB*	*23*	*250*	*26*	*11*	*3*	*3*	*18*	*7*	*54*	*7*	*3*	*.226/.252/.329*	*.218*	*.274*	*0.5*	*CF -3, LF -0*	*-0.6*

Landry enjoyed a bounce-back season, and the Mariners liked him enough to snag him from the Dodgers in the Brandon League trade. He has just enough power to look great in the California League, where offense is cheap, particularly in High Desert: Landry hit .463/.511/.780 at home after joining the Mavericks. But most of that power is concentrated in triples and came in hitters parks, and a promotion to the Southern League this year could conservatively claim 200 points of OPS. Landry has the skills to be a fourth outfielder, with strong defense, good, though unrefined, speed, and a favorable platoon future, but there's not much of an offensive approach or raw power to dream on yet.

Alex Liddi 4C

Born: **8/14/1988** Age: **24**
Bats: **R** Throws: **R** Height: **6' 5"**
Weight: **230** Breakout: **7%**
Improve: **55%** Collapse: **13%**
Attrition: **19%** MLB: **98%**

Comparables:
Jim Thome,Bill Melton,Josh Bell

YEAR	TEAM	LVL	AGE	PA	R	2B	3B	HR	RBI	BB	SO	SB	CS	AVG_OBP_SLG	TAv	BABIP	BRR	FRAA	WARP
2010	WTN	AA	21	565	78	37	8	15	92	50	145	5	7	.281/.352/.476	.279	.364	-1.6	3B(121): 4.3, 1B(24): 1.9	3.3
2011	TAC	AAA	22	637	121	32	3	30	104	61	170	5	1	.259/.332/.488	.274	.312	3	3B(72): -1.5, SS(17): -0.3	1.7
2011	SEA	MLB	22	44	7	3	0	3	6	3	17	1	0	.225/.295/.525	.280	.300	0.8	3B(14): 0.0	0.2
2012	TAC	AAA	23	323	39	18	2	11	30	24	75	9	6	.270/.325/.456	.262	.325	-3.4	3B(27): -2.0, LF(21): 1.7	0.1
2012	SEA	MLB	23	126	8	4	1	3	10	9	49	2	1	.224/.278/.353	.231	.354	-1.2	3B(23): -0.7, LF(7): -0.2	-0.4
2013	*SEA*	*MLB*	*24*	*250*	*25*	*10*	*1*	*7*	*28*	*17*	*76*	*3*	*1*	*.221/.276/.370*	*.243*	*.293*	*-0.2*	*3B -2, 1B -0*	*-0.1*

Liddi's hot start tweaked the Mariners' hopes for him a bit, and in early May, when the Italian-born third baseman was hitting .293/.349/.431, Eric Wedge put Liddi in left field. He hadn't played an inning there since the old country, but it was a creative way to get a bat in the lineup. That batting line, unfortunately, was propped up by a .395 BABIP, and when it came to earth Liddi hit .155/.206/.276 the rest of the way. Liddi has one big-league tool—his raw power—but a terrible approach that seems endemic to the Mariners farm system. He played a lot more left field (and first base) in subsequent visits to Triple-A, but now it looks less like a way to get his bat in the lineup and more like a way to squeeze some value out of him as a four-corners utility option.

Jesus Montero C
Born: **11/28/1989** Age: **23**
Bats: **R** Throws: **R** Height: **6' 4"**
Weight: **235** Breakout: **5%**
Improve: **63%** Collapse: **3%**
Attrition: **8%** MLB: **91%**
Comparables:
Prince Fielder,Nick Evans,Kent Hrbek

YEAR	TEAM	LVL	AGE	PA	R	2B	3B	HR	RBI	BB	SO	SB	CS	AVG_OBP_SLG	TAv	BABIP	BRR	FRAA	WARP
2010	SWB	AAA	20	504	66	34	3	21	75	46	91	0	0	.289/.356/.517	.296	.323	-4	C(104): -1.5	3.4
2011	SWB	AAA	21	463	52	19	1	18	67	36	98	0	0	.288/.348/.467	.292	.336	-2.2	C(60): -1.0	1.6
2011	NYA	MLB	21	69	9	4	0	4	12	7	17	0	0	.328/.406/.590	.333	.400	-2.1	C(3): -0.0	0.3
2012	SEA	MLB	22	553	46	20	0	15	62	29	99	0	2	.260/.298/.386	.253	.292	-7	C(56): -0.6	-0.7
2013	*SEA*	*MLB*	*23*	*460*	*50*	*21*	*1*	*15*	*59*	*30*	*92*	*1*	*0*	*.264/.315/.428*	*.277*	*.302*	*-0.8*	*C -1*	*2.3*

Right-handed pitchers had their way with Montero, a new red flag for a player whose defense continues to insist he's a premature DHer. His minor-league splits don't show any particular vulnerability to righties, so it's nothing to get serious about yet, though he also probably never saw arm-side tailing fastballs quite as fast and quite as tailing in the minors. The Mariners gave him 56 games to prove he could be an adequate backstop, and he didn't: His passed-ball and wild-pitch rates were among the worst in the game, as was his pitch-framing, and he threw out only 17 percent of base thieves. A catcher is so much more valuable than a DH that a team might continue to give him some starts there, at the least keeping the option open. But he's never going to be credible as a catcher, and it might be time to let him focus on trying to rediscover the special in his bat.

Kendrys Morales 1B
Born: **6/20/1983** Age: **30**
Bats: **B** Throws: **R** Height: **6' 2"**
Weight: **225** Breakout: **2%**
Improve: **31%** Collapse: **9%**
Attrition: **23%** MLB: **93%**
Comparables:
Benny Ayala,Michael Morse,Orlando Cepeda

YEAR	TEAM	LVL	AGE	PA	R	2B	3B	HR	RBI	BB	SO	SB	CS	AVG_OBP_SLG	TAv	BABIP	BRR	FRAA	WARP
2010	ANA	MLB	27	211	29	5	0	11	39	12	31	0	1	.290/.346/.487	.309	.296	2.1	1B(51): 0.7	1.7
2012	ANA	MLB	29	522	61	26	1	22	73	31	116	0	1	.273/.320/.467	.298	.315	-2.5	1B(28): 0.5	1.8
2013	*SEA*	*MLB*	*30*	*386*	*46*	*19*	*1*	*16*	*55*	*26*	*77*	*1*	*1*	*.269/.322/.465*	*.292*	*.301*	*-1*	*1B -1*	*1.9*

The good news is that the broken ankle that cost Morales nearly two full seasons did not end his career, and it did not crush his value as a hitter. His .298 TAv was not only better than PECOTA forecast for him, it was better than PECOTA forecast for him in pre-injury 2010. It's tempting to blame some of Morales's lost power on the injury, as a pair of scouts in July did. "He's not getting any power off that back foot," one said while watching him bat left-handed. Perhaps: His isolated power (in a tiny, 70-PA sample) was 60 points higher from his normally weaker right side. But the more conservative and likely explanation is that Morales was never going to replicate his 2009 power. He's strong, but his approach tilts toward the line drive. So the ankle probably didn't diminish his abilities, much less end his career. On the eve of his age-30 season and free agency, the Angels traded him to Seattle.

Miguel Olivo C
Born: **7/15/1978** Age: **34**
Bats: **R** Throws: **R** Height: **6' 1"**
Weight: **230** Breakout: **1%**
Improve: **21%** Collapse: **10%**
Attrition: **22%** MLB: **93%**
Comparables:
Mark Parent,Elston Howard,Sal Fasano

YEAR	TEAM	LVL	AGE	PA	R	2B	3B	HR	RBI	BB	SO	SB	CS	AVG_OBP_SLG	TAv	BABIP	BRR	FRAA	WARP
2010	COL	MLB	31	427	55	17	6	14	58	27	117	7	4	.269/.315/.449	.251	.346	2.6	C(111): -0.2	2.2
2011	SEA	MLB	32	507	54	19	1	19	62	20	140	6	5	.224/.253/.388	.243	.270	-0.3	C(127): 1.6	0.7
2012	SEA	MLB	33	323	27	14	0	12	29	7	85	3	6	.222/.239/.381	.244	.266	0.7	C(73): 1.9	1.1
2013	*SEA*	*MLB*	*34*	*342*	*35*	*13*	*2*	*12*	*41*	*14*	*100*	*4*	*3*	*.223/.257/.383*	*.240*	*.281*	*-0.4*	*C 0*	*0.8*

Olivo swung at 43 percent of pitches outside the strike zone in 2012. If no pitcher ever threw a strike to him again, his swing rate would be a little below the median swing rate in baseball (46 percent). That's assuming Olivo wouldn't eventually wise up. Unfortunately, that might be exactly what you have to assume. Olivo's approach at the plate is so awful that you can't help cheering for it. Accompanying the inability to lay off pitches in the dirt is the inability to pull the trigger on pitches that are actually strikes. Olivo had the 116th-highest swing rate (minimum 500 pitches) on pitches that are *in* the zone. It's starting to feel like something special is happening here: His unthinkable 2011 OBP actually dropped 14 points in 2012, and as long as Olivo gets to keep playing—and he's still better than replacement level, so why not?—there's no telling how low it'll go. Our 10-year PECOTA forecast has him with a .158 OBP in 2021, which falls midway between the career marks of A.J. Burnett and Carl Pavano.

Carlos Peguero OF
Born: **2/22/1987** Age: **26**
Bats: **L** Throws: **L** Height: **6' 6"**
Weight: **245** Breakout: **4%**
Improve: **55%** Collapse: **3%**
Attrition: **6%** MLB: **98%**
Comparables:
Danny Tartabull,Jesse Barfield,Mike Marshall

YEAR	TEAM	LVL	AGE	PA	R	2B	3B	HR	RBI	BB	SO	SB	CS	AVG_OBP_SLG	TAv	BABIP	BRR	FRAA	WARP
2010	WTN	AA	23	553	86	23	5	23	73	56	178	7	9	.254/.341/.463	.276	.352	0.8	LF(66): 1.3, RF(34): 4.8	3.0
2011	TAC	AAA	24	258	44	15	2	13	47	15	82	8	0	.317/.364/.558	.313	.434	1.8	LF(15): -0.5, RF(12): -1.6	1.1
2011	SEA	MLB	24	155	14	3	2	6	19	8	54	0	1	.196/.252/.371	.231	.262	-0.4	LF(40): 2.1, RF(3): 0.1	0.0
2012	TAC	AAA	25	322	47	13	1	21	54	29	103	2	2	.285/.366/.562	.352	.369	-0.9	RF(45): 0.1, LF(18): -2.0	2.5
2012	SEA	MLB	25	57	2	2	1	2	7	1	28	0	0	.179/.193/.357	.210	.308	0.1	RF(11): 0.8, LF(2): 0.1	-0.1
2013	*SEA*	*MLB*	*26*	*250*	*27*	*8*	*1*	*10*	*32*	*17*	*92*	*2*	*1*	*.213/.275/.396*	*.248*	*.301*	*-0.1*	*LF 0, RF 0*	*0.3*

If you lower the minimum to 200 pitches seen, Olivo is no longer the hackingest batter in baseball. That top spot (at least among non-pitchers) becomes Peguero's. Few batters look as fearsome at the plate as Peguero, who is huge and knows how to leverage his swing for power, but he's got the approach of a guy determined to get his dollar's worth at the batting cages. In 56 plate appearances in Seattle, he walked once, and got ahead 2-0 only three times. Against lefties he's even worse: 2-for-21 with 13 Ks as a big leaguer. He did hit well in a second trip through the PCL—that OPS led his team—but even after the Mariners traded Ichiro in July, Casper Wells and Marcus Thames outranked him on the depth chart. Peguero is 26 this year, and the odds that he'll figure out the strike zone are getting longer than—well, they're getting long.

Brendan Ryan **SS**

Born: **3/26/1982** Age: **31**
Bats: **R** Throws: **R** Height: **6' 3"**
Weight: **195** Breakout: **0%**
Improve: **35%** Collapse: **12%**
Attrition: **15%** MLB: **94%**

Comparables:
Marco Scutaro,Alex Arias,Nick Punto

YEAR	TEAM	LVL	AGE	PA	R	2B	3B	HR	RBI	BB	SO	SB	CS	AVG_OBP_SLG	TAv	BABIP	BRR	FRAA	WARP
2010	SLN	MLB	28	486	50	19	3	2	36	33	60	11	4	.223/.279/.294	.219	.253	1.8	SS(139): 8.3	0.9
2011	SEA	MLB	29	494	51	19	3	3	39	34	87	13	3	.248/.313/.326	.250	.299	2.5	SS(123): 13.3	3.1
2012	SEA	MLB	30	470	42	19	3	3	31	44	98	11	5	.194/.277/.278	.225	.244	-0.9	SS(138): 12.0	1.4
2013	*SEA*	*MLB*	*31*	*446*	*42*	*18*	*3*	*3*	*33*	*32*	*78*	*11*	*4*	*.227/.290/.307*	*.232*	*.268*	*0.5*	*SS 6*	*1.4*

For fantasy purposes, Ryan is worthless and you can skip this comment. But for the Mariners' purposes, Ryan is probably the best defensive player at the most important defensive position in fair territory. In winning his first Fielding Bible award, he got nine of 10 first-place votes at his position, though leading all shortstops in UZR and +/- couldn't get him a Gold Glove. Ideally, the Mariners would convince Bud Selig to double the number of designated hitters permitted—instead, they pinch-hit for him 20 times in 2012—but his lack of offense does have the benefit of suppressing what he can ask for in arbitration. Ryan is one of the best bargains in the game, 555 OPS or not.

Michael Saunders **CF**

Born: **11/19/1986** Age: **26**
Bats: **L** Throws: **R** Height: **6' 5"**
Weight: **215** Breakout: **1%**
Improve: **62%** Collapse: **3%**
Attrition: **6%** MLB: **96%**

Comparables:
Tito Francona,Dusty Baker,Lloyd Moseby

YEAR	TEAM	LVL	AGE	PA	R	2B	3B	HR	RBI	BB	SO	SB	CS	AVG_OBP_SLG	TAv	BABIP	BRR	FRAA	WARP
2010	TAC	AAA	23	93	6	1	0	0	5	11	17	4	0	.200/.293/.213	.217	.250	0.9	LF(11): 0.5, CF(7): -0.6	0.0
2010	SEA	MLB	23	327	29	11	2	10	33	35	84	6	3	.211/.295/.367	.252	.260	-1	LF(77): 5.4, CF(14): -0.6	0.9
2011	TAC	AAA	24	291	51	11	3	7	38	50	71	10	3	.288/.415/.449	.319	.384	0.8	CF(35): 6.3, LF(12): 1.3	2.5
2011	SEA	MLB	24	179	16	5	0	2	8	12	56	6	2	.149/.207/.217	.164	.212	0.8	CF(46): 2.6, LF(12): 0.7	-1.0
2012	SEA	MLB	25	553	71	31	3	19	57	43	132	21	4	.247/.306/.432	.279	.297	1.5	CF(113): -4.7, LF(22): 0.5	1.6
2013	*SEA*	*MLB*	*26*	*471*	*54*	*18*	*3*	*12*	*48*	*42*	*121*	*14*	*4*	*.224/.295/.368*	*.251*	*.279*	*1.3*	*CF 2, LF 1*	*1.4*

A less-famous cousin of the Best Shape of My Life spring training story is the Best Swing of My Life. Saunders came to camp telling of his swing transformation: He'd spent the offseason working with a hitting coach, swinging a 60-ounce bat in cages, and focusing on getting more lower body into a short, compact swing. In this case, the results came. Saunders was less vulnerable to pitches away, and for the first time in his career he hit lefties, slugging .477 against southpaws after a .262 mark entering the season. He's stretched in center field but now has the bat to be average at a corner.

Kyle Seager **3B**

Born: **11/3/1987** Age: **25**
Bats: **L** Throws: **R** Height: **6' 1"**
Weight: **195** Breakout: **6%**
Improve: **60%** Collapse: **5%**
Attrition: **16%** MLB: **97%**

Comparables:
Taylor Green,Jeff Cirillo,Puddin Head Jones

YEAR	TEAM	LVL	AGE	PA	R	2B	3B	HR	RBI	BB	SO	SB	CS	AVG_OBP_SLG	TAv	BABIP	BRR	FRAA	WARP
2010	HDS	A+	22	643	126	40	3	14	74	71	94	13	12	.345/.421/.503	.319	.394	3.7	2B(102): 0.4, 3B(22): 1.0	6.5
2011	WTN	AA	23	299	33	25	1	4	37	26	38	8	5	.312/.381/.459	.295	.350	0	--	0.0
2011	TAC	AAA	23	117	24	8	2	3	17	11	12	3	1	.387/.444/.585	.343	.418	0.2	2B(9): -0.2, 3B(9): -0.6	1.2
2011	SEA	MLB	23	201	22	13	0	3	13	13	36	3	1	.258/.312/.379	.267	.303	-1.1	3B(42): 2.6, SS(10): -0.9	0.5
2012	SEA	MLB	24	651	62	35	1	20	86	46	110	13	5	.259/.316/.423	.273	.286	0.2	3B(138): -2.8, 2B(18): 1.5	2.3
2013	*SEA*	*MLB*	*25*	*534*	*63*	*27*	*2*	*11*	*51*	*39*	*95*	*7*	*4*	*.260/.318/.392*	*.267*	*.298*	*-0.7*	*3B -3, 2B -1*	*1.3*

If one Seattle hitter convinced the Mariners to adjust the dimensions at Safeco Field, it might have been Seager. On the road, the 2009 third-round pick hit .293/.324/.511 with 15 home runs. That's a star, about what Aramis Ramirez—who finished ninth in NL MVP voting—hit on the road in 2012. But at Safeco, Seager hit five home runs and slugged a Brendan Ryanesque .325. It's not just that he was better on the road; he seemed more enthusiastic about hitting on the road, drawing half as many walks when he was in ballparks that gave him a fighting chance against the outfield. With the fences moved in, now he can bring that enthusiasm home to the good folks of Seattle.

Justin Smoak **1B**

Born: **12/5/1986** Age: **26**
Bats: **B** Throws: **L** Height: **6' 5"**
Weight: **230** Breakout: **7%**
Improve: **54%** Collapse: **4%**
Attrition: **11%** MLB: **95%**

Comparables:
Keith Hernandez, Matt LaPorta, Ryan Garko

YEAR	TEAM	LVL	AGE	PA	R	2B	3B	HR	RBI	BB	SO	SB	CS	AVG_OBP_SLG	TAv	BABIP	BRR	FRAA	WARP
2010	OKL	AAA	23	66	10	6	0	2	5	16	8	0	0	.300/.470/.540	.339	.325	-0.2	1B(14): 0.2	0.6
2010	TAC	AAA	23	159	23	7	0	7	25	23	32	0	0	.271/.382/.481	.323	.309	-1.1	1B(39): -1.1	1.1
2010	SEA	MLB	23	122	11	4	0	5	14	8	34	0	0	.239/.287/.407	.246	.293	-0.3	1B(25): -0.9	-0.3
2010	TEX	MLB	23	275	29	10	0	8	34	38	57	1	0	.209/.316/.353	.240	.238	0.4	1B(69): 4.2	0.1
2011	SEA	MLB	24	489	38	24	0	15	55	55	105	0	0	.234/.323/.396	.276	.273	-3.1	1B(108): -6.1	0.0
2012	TAC	AAA	25	82	10	6	1	0	4	16	16	1	0	.242/.390/.364	.239	.320	0.6	1B(15): -0.1	-0.2
2012	SEA	MLB	25	535	49	14	0	19	51	49	111	1	0	.217/.290/.364	.236	.242	-2.5	1B(131): -8.8	-2.6
2013	*SEA*	*MLB*	*26*	*507*	*54*	*19*	*1*	*15*	*59*	*57*	*111*	*1*	*0*	*.226/.315/.377*	*.261*	*.265*	*-0.8*	*1B -5*	*-0.1*

In this space last year, we used not-quite-arbitrary endpoints to suggest that Smoak's problems were related to thumb injuries, and that he might actually be pretty good. Whoops! Smoak, the Mariners' cleanup hitter throughout the month of April, had the second-worst WARP in baseball in 2012. He's an odd sort of failure to watch, as he draws some walks, doesn't strike out too often, and managed 19 home runs; he just rarely hits anything hard. While the homers hint at the ability to damage a mistake, his doubles total is suspiciously low, and his .256 career BABIP is the 11th worst in baseball (minimum 1,000 plate appearances) during that three-year stretch. He was better in the second half, giving the Mariners one more offseason to talk themselves into feeling optimistic.

Eric Thames **OF**

Born: **11/10/1986** Age: **26**
Bats: **L** Throws: **R** Height: **6' 2"**
Weight: **205** Breakout: **7%**
Improve: **50%** Collapse: **5%**
Attrition: **15%** MLB: **97%**

Comparables:
Mike Carp, Mel Hall, Marty Cordova

YEAR	TEAM	LVL	AGE	PA	R	2B	3B	HR	RBI	BB	SO	SB	CS	AVG_OBP_SLG	TAv	BABIP	BRR	FRAA	WARP
2010	NHP	AA	23	573	95	25	6	27	104	50	121	8	5	.288/.373/.526	.307	.331	0.2	LF(99): 2.5	4.2
2011	LVG	AAA	24	241	38	25	4	7	45	23	41	5	2	.352/.423/.610	.383	.406	0	LF(25): 0.2, RF(4): -0.4	1.7
2011	TOR	MLB	24	394	58	24	5	12	37	23	88	2	1	.262/.313/.456	.267	.313	4.5	LF(52): -0.8, RF(27): 0.8	1.0
2012	LVG	AAA	25	231	31	15	3	6	32	26	42	1	1	.330/.407/.528	.290	.383	-1	LF(25): -0.2, RF(4): 0.2	0.7
2012	SEA	MLB	25	130	10	5	2	6	14	6	47	1	0	.220/.256/.439	.271	.300	-0.3	RF(35): 1.3, LF(1): 0.1	0.2
2012	TOR	MLB	25	160	17	7	1	3	11	9	40	0	1	.243/.287/.365	.229	.308	0.1	LF(43): 2.3	-0.1
2013	*SEA*	*MLB*	*26*	*343*	*35*	*15*	*3*	*10*	*40*	*22*	*86*	*2*	*1*	*.241/.298/.401*	*.262*	*.298*	*-0.2*	*LF -1, RF 0*	*0.8*

When you start feeling confident in advanced defensive metrics, go look at Thames, who is either an above-average left fielder (+4 runs in his 181-game career, according to us) or a considerably worse option than Bobby Abreu right now (-19, by John Dewan's +/- ratings). That's a big difference and it's a big deal in evaluating Thames, whose bat is just average for a corner. With an average glove, he's an every-day player on a second-division team, and perhaps the big half of a platoon on a contender; without it, he's quad-A. The consensus among those who watched him in Toronto, where he was frequently replaced for defense late in games, leans heavily toward the latter.

Carlos Triunfel **SS**

Born: **2/27/1990** Age: **23**
Bats: **R** Throws: **R** Height: **6' 0"**
Weight: **175** Breakout: **5%**
Improve: **39%** Collapse: **11%**
Attrition: **23%** MLB: **95%**

Comparables:
Robin Yount, Tito Fuentes, Dickie Thon

YEAR	TEAM	LVL	AGE	PA	R	2B	3B	HR	RBI	BB	SO	SB	CS	AVG_OBP_SLG	TAv	BABIP	BRR	FRAA	WARP
2010	WTN	AA	20	498	51	12	1	7	42	13	54	2	8	.257/.285/.332	.220	.275	-3.2	SS(126): -16.8, 2B(2): -0.3	-2.1
2011	WTN	AA	21	433	45	22	2	6	35	25	71	5	7	.281/.340/.392	.259	.330	0	--	0.0
2011	TAC	AAA	21	117	7	6	1	0	10	2	17	1	0	.279/.302/.351	.228	.326	-1.2	SS(20): 1.9, 2B(1): 0.0	0.0
2012	TAC	AAA	22	543	74	31	2	10	62	23	89	3	2	.260/.308/.391	.252	.297	1.8	SS(89): -0.7, 2B(22): -3.2	0.2
2012	SEA	MLB	22	24	2	2	0	0	3	1	4	0	0	.227/.261/.318	.218	.278	0.1	SS(7): -0.1, 2B(2): 0.2	0.0
2013	*SEA*	*MLB*	*23*	*250*	*19*	*10*	*1*	*3*	*21*	*6*	*46*	*0*	*0*	*.225/.253/.309*	*.218*	*.262*	*-0.4*	*SS -4, 2B -0*	*-0.5*

Back in 2007, no team was pushing prospects faster than the Mariners, and in the California League six of the 12 youngest players in the league played for Seattle's affiliate in High Desert. None was as young as Triunfel, who held his own— .288/.333/.356—as a 17-year-old. In the five years since, Triunfel has barely improved on that slash line, while the rest of the minors have gained on him in age. He finally made his big-league debut in 2012, but it was mostly another lost year: He commenced the predictable move off of shortstop, and showed a lousy approach against higher-level pitching. He's still young, but there's not a lot left to project here.

Casper Wells **OF**

Born: **11/23/1984** Age: **28**
Bats: **R** Throws: **R** Height: **6' 3"**
Weight: **210** Breakout: **0%**
Improve: **58%** Collapse: **3%**
Attrition: **11%** MLB: **93%**

Comparables:
Sixto Lezcano, Scott Hairston, Greg Vaughn

YEAR	TEAM	LVL	AGE	PA	R	2B	3B	HR	RBI	BB	SO	SB	CS	AVG_OBP_SLG	TAv	BABIP	BRR	FRAA	WARP
2010	TOL	AAA	25	430	56	22	6	21	46	34	111	7	8	.233/.309/.483	.261	.271	-0.6	CF(83): 0.6, RF(16): -0.2	1.2
2010	DET	MLB	25	99	14	6	1	4	17	6	19	0	1	.323/.364/.538	.325	.371	0.6	RF(29): -1.7, LF(8): -0.3	0.9
2011	DET	MLB	26	125	16	10	0	4	12	9	29	1	0	.257/.323/.451	.277	.312	-0.3	RF(51): 0.6, LF(6): 0.3	0.7
2011	SEA	MLB	26	116	14	1	0	7	15	9	42	2	2	.216/.310/.431	.292	.283	-0.4	LF(15): 1.4, RF(6): -0.2	0.7
2012	TAC	AAA	27	95	18	7	2	2	14	20	17	2	1	.239/.415/.479	.314	.283	0.9	RF(8): 0.9, LF(6): -0.6	0.7
2012	SEA	MLB	27	316	42	12	3	10	36	26	80	3	0	.228/.302/.396	.262	.282	-0.4	LF(52): 0.0, RF(25): -2.0	0.1
2013	*SEA*	*MLB*	*28*	*298*	*34*	*12*	*2*	*11*	*37*	*25*	*80*	*3*	*2*	*.229/.304/.409*	*.268*	*.282*	*-0.2*	*LF 1, RF 0*	*1.1*

It's easy to attribute plate discipline to choice, and it's frustrating to watch an overly aggressive hitter who seems to have no plan. But Wells shows how much this tool is out of the player's control: Against lefties, he walked in 13 percent of his plate appearances, an ultra-disciplined rate if he could do it all the time. Against righties, he walked in 4 percent of his trips, about the same as Delmon Young's career walk rate. Is he just a dummy half the time? Of course not. Plate discipline depends on the ability to pick up the ball from the pitcher's hand, identify it quickly, and adjust to the movement. Wells, alas, doesn't do those things when facing right-handers.

Mike Zunino **C**

Born: **3/25/1991** Age: **22**
Bats: **--** Throws: **--** Height: **6' 3"**
Weight: **215** Breakout: **3%**
Improve: **58%** Collapse: **1%**
Attrition: **6%** MLB: **99%**

Comparables:
Darrell Porter, Johnny Bench, Jesus Montero

YEAR	TEAM	LVL	AGE	PA	R	2B	3B	HR	RBI	BB	SO	SB	CS	AVG_OBP_SLG	TAv	BABIP	BRR	FRAA	WARP
2012	EVE	A-	21	133	29	10	0	10	35	18	26	1	0	.373/.474/.736	.357	.413	-0.3	C(17): 0.4	1.6
2012	WTN	AA	21	57	6	4	0	3	8	5	7	0	0	.333/.386/.588	.333	.333	0	C(3): -0.0	0.1
2013	*SEA*	*MLB*	*22*	*250*	*28*	*9*	*1*	*10*	*34*	*17*	*62*	*1*	*0*	*.235/.292/.417*	*.263*	*.272*	*-0.3*	*C -0*	*1.0*

The Mariners' third top-three pick in the past four years, Zunino fits in the same basket as Ackley and Danny Hultzen: advanced, low floor, considered a safe pick, and capable of contributing quickly. Zunino was torching Double-A within three months of his selection, launching talk that he could join Seattle sometime in 2013. He also threw out 43 percent of baserunners between two levels. The organization talks up his defense and ability to handle pitching staffs, a result of his work with an advanced collection of arms at the University of Florida, but he's not polished yet. A .288/.337/.463 line in the Arizona Fall League speaks well to his conditioning.

PITCHERS

Blake Beavan

Born: **1/17/1989** Age: **24**
Bats: **R** Throws: **R** Height: **6' 8"** Weight: **240**
Breakout: **20%** Improve: **54%** Collapse: **24%**
Attrition: **22%** MLB: **88%**

Comparables:
Kyle Kendrick, Tommy Hunter, Steve Kline

YEAR	TEAM	LVL	AGE	W	L	SV	G	GS	IP	H	HR	BB	SO	BB9	SO9	GB%	BABIP	WHIP	ERA	FIP	FRA	WARP
2010	FRI	AA	21	10	5	0	17	17	110	100	6	12	68	1.0	5.6	50%	.272	1.02	2.78	3.00	3.97	1.3
2010	WTN	AA	21	2	1	0	3	3	18	18	1	1	11	0.5	5.5	39%	.293	1.06	5.00	3.39	4.75	0.2
2010	TAC	AAA	21	2	2	0	7	7	40^{1}	56	6	8	22	1.8	4.9	37%	.354	1.59	6.48	5.17	4.99	0.4
2011	TAC	AAA	22	5	3	0	16	16	93	118	10	20	64	1.9	6.2	44%	.341	1.48	4.45	4.48	3.88	1.2
2011	SEA	MLB	22	5	6	0	15	15	97	106	13	15	42	1.4	3.9	39%	.280	1.25	4.27	4.49	5.09	-0.3
2012	TAC	AAA	23	4	0	0	6	6	38	39	3	9	15	2.1	3.6	42%	.277	1.26	2.61	4.77	4.87	0.2
2012	SEA	MLB	23	11	11	0	26	26	152^{1}	168	23	24	67	1.4	4.0	39%	.280	1.26	4.43	4.80	4.95	0.1
2013	*SEA*	*MLB*	*24*	*8*	*8*	*0*	*22*	*22*	135^{2}	*149*	*17*	*27*	*62*	*1.8*	*4.1*	*43%*	*.286*	*1.29*	*4.39*	*4.51*	*4.77*	*0.0*

As Beavan is learning, it's hard to keep both SO9 and ERA below 4.00—only six pitchers have done it in the past 15 years. It requires a good defense, a forgiving home ballpark, sterling walk rates—check, check, check—and the ability to keep balls in the yard. There's the rub for Beavan, who is in the 8th percentile for inducing groundballs. Beavan works up in the zone, where the strikeout pitchers live, but doesn't have the heat to get whiffs or the movement to break bats. He abandoned the not-good changeup he had been throwing, which limits optimism that he might solve left-handed batters, who hit like Jay Bruce against him last year.

Carter Capps

Born: **8/7/1990** Age: **22**
Bats: **R** Throws: **R** Height: **6' 6"** Weight: **220**
Breakout: **20%** Improve: **43%** Collapse: **18%**
Attrition: **5%** MLB: **92%**

Comparables:
Ambiorix Burgos, Huston Street, Francisco Rodriguez

YEAR	TEAM	LVL	AGE	W	L	SV	G	GS	IP	H	HR	BB	SO	BB9	SO9	GB%	BABIP	WHIP	ERA	FIP	FRA	WARP
2011	CLN	A	20	1	1	0	4	4	18	19	1	10	21	5.0	10.5	—	.383	1.61	6.00	3.75	4.07	0.0
2012	WTN	AA	21	2	3	19	38	0	50	40	2	12	72	2.2	13.0	44%	.317	1.04	1.26	1.56	0.11	1.8
2012	TAC	AAA	21	0	0	0	1	0	1^{1}	0	0	0	3	0.0	20.2	%	.000	0.00	0.00	-0.83	-1.91	0.1
2012	SEA	MLB	21	0	0	0	18	0	25	25	0	11	28	4.0	10.1	41%	.357	1.44	3.96	2.13	2.38	0.7
2013	*SEA*	*MLB*	*22*	*2*	*1*	*0*	*28*	*0*	36^{2}	*30*	*3*	*13*	*43*	*3.1*	*10.5*	*43%*	*.296*	*1.15*	*2.84*	*2.98*	*3.09*	*0.7*

Fail fast, they used to tell us in business school. Capps started four games after the Mariners drafted him, and that was that; they moved him to the bullpen and, in his first full season, he was the organization's Pitcher of the Year and spent the final two months getting whiffs in the big leagues. He's got a funky motion—the tall right-hander lunges more than he drives toward home, and he drops his whole body down for an unusually low release point, creating more "rise" than most pitchers' fastballs. His, incidentally, is 100 mph. There's all sorts of late-innings upside here, particularly considering that Capps is a converted catcher who is still fairly new to the position.

Andrew Carraway

Born: **9/4/1986** Age: **26**
Bats: **R** Throws: **R** Height: **6' 3"** Weight: **200**
Breakout: **31%** Improve: **64%** Collapse: **21%**
Attrition: **23%** MLB: **82%**

Comparables:
Justin Germano,Cory Luebke,Jeff Karstens

YEAR	TEAM	LVL	AGE	W	L	SV	G	GS	IP	H	HR	BB	SO	BB9	SO9	GB%	BABIP	WHIP	ERA	FIP	FRA	WARP
2010	HDS	A+	23	11	8	0	27	27	150^1	190	25	31	120	1.9	7.2	44%	.342	1.47	5.33	5.10	5.31	2.3
2011	WTN	AA	24	9	5	0	28	21	137^2	123	9	25	106	1.6	6.9	—	.280	1.08	3.66	3.38	3.67	0.0
2012	WTN	AA	25	4	0	0	7	7	38	37	1	7	32	1.7	7.6	36%	.327	1.16	2.61	2.43	1.92	0.4
2012	TAC	AAA	25	5	7	0	20	20	112	114	15	30	69	2.4	5.5	36%	.281	1.29	4.66	5.14	5.14	0.7
2013	*SEA*	*MLB*	*26*	*2*	*2*	*0*	*7*	*7*	*37^2*	*40*	*5*	*11*	*24*	*2.7*	*5.7*	*39%*	*.293*	*1.36*	*4.52*	*4.53*	*4.91*	*-0.0*

When Mariners brass talk about the pitching prospects incubating in the minors, they increasingly slip Carraway into the conversation. That's about 10 levels of optimism too many, but as a fifth starter in reserve he could have a future. Think of Carraway as a crafty lefty who happens to throw with his right hand: He survives thanks to a good changeup, command, and the ability to outsmart lesser hitters, and despite a mid-80s fastball. He's a fly-ball pitcher. In pitcher-friendly leagues, home runs haven't been a problem at all; in hitter-friendly environments, they're close to a deal-breaker, so count him among those watching closely to see how Safeco plays this year.

Edwin Diaz

Born: **3/22/1994** Age: **19**
Bats: **R** Throws: **R** Height: **6' 3"** Weight: **165**
Breakout: **9%** Improve: **89%** Collapse: **11%**
Attrition: **11%** MLB: **45%**

Comparables:
Rick Wise,Bob Miller,Jim Bethke

YEAR	TEAM	LVL	AGE	W	L	SV	G	GS	IP	H	HR	BB	SO	BB9	SO9	GB%	BABIP	WHIP	ERA	FIP	FRA	WARP
2012	MRN	Rk	18	2	1	0	9	1	19	12	2	17	20	8.1	9.5	67%	.333	1.53	5.21	7.11	496.90	0.0
2013	*SEA*	*MLB*	*19*	*1*	*0*	*1*	*31*	*0*	*31^1*	*37*	*4*	*21*	*15*	*6.1*	*4.4*	*45%*	*.306*	*1.86*	*6.54*	*5.91*	*7.11*	*-0.9*

The 2012 third-round pick is long and thin, with a mid-90s fastball and easy arm action. Find that in an 18-year-old and the rest is teachable, so now the Mariners get to try teaching him. Diaz was tremendously wild in his pro debut, walking nearly a batter per inning in the Arizona League and hitting every 18th batter for good measure. The secondary pitches aren't close, and the mechanics are all over the place, but he's got a mid-90s fastball and easy arm action and he's long and thin . . . you know how this works.

Charlie Furbush

Born: **4/11/1986** Age: **27**
Bats: **L** Throws: **L** Height: **6' 6"** Weight: **215**
Breakout: **30%** Improve: **70%** Collapse: **17%**
Attrition: **15%** MLB: **89%**

Comparables:
Mike Flanagan,Cliff Lee,Harvey Haddix

YEAR	TEAM	LVL	AGE	W	L	SV	G	GS	IP	H	HR	BB	SO	BB9	SO9	GB%	BABIP	WHIP	ERA	FIP	FRA	WARP
2010	LAK	A+	24	4	5	0	13	13	77	68	7	14	109	1.6	12.7	43%	.330	1.06	3.39	2.41	3.55	1.1
2010	ERI	AA	24	1	0	0	5	5	33^1	31	5	10	37	2.7	10.0	33%	.390	1.23	3.24	4.08	4.47	0.4
2010	TOL	AAA	24	3	4	0	9	9	48^2	59	9	16	37	3.0	6.8	44%	.333	1.54	6.28	5.16	6.82	-0.5
2011	TOL	AAA	25	5	3	0	10	9	54	35	7	16	61	2.7	10.2	39%	.230	0.94	3.17	3.61	5.12	0.3
2011	DET	MLB	25	1	3	0	17	2	32^1	36	5	14	26	3.9	7.2	45%	.341	1.55	3.62	5.04	5.73	-0.1
2011	SEA	MLB	25	3	7	0	11	10	53	61	11	16	41	2.7	7.0	43%	.309	1.45	6.62	5.29	5.60	-0.3
2012	TAC	AAA	26	1	0	0	7	0	10	7	1	3	13	2.7	11.7	33%	.261	1.00	3.60	3.27	4.10	0.1
2012	SEA	MLB	26	5	2	0	48	0	46^1	28	3	16	53	3.1	10.3	45%	.231	0.95	2.72	2.77	3.40	0.6
2013	*SEA*	*MLB*	*27*	*3*	*2*	*0*	*18*	*7*	*49^2*	*47*	*6*	*17*	*45*	*3.1*	*8.2*	*42%*	*.292*	*1.29*	*4.02*	*3.99*	*4.37*	*0.3*

America's left-handed batters managed a .147/.217/.187 line against Furbush in 2012, which, for perspective, is a worse line than they had against Javier Lopez in his best season against them. Lopez is a valuable pitcher and GMs are happy to pay him millions of dollars, but he's only *so* valuable and they only want to pay him *so* much money, which introduces the Furbush Paradox: The better Furbush does as a reliever, the easier it is to keep him in the pen; but the better he gets, the more valuable he *might* be as a starter. The Mariners will have to decide whether Furbush thrived in the bullpen because he improved or because he's particularly suited for that role. He was very effective against right-handers, too, which argues for the former; he added an extra mile on his fastball in relief, so that argues for the latter. The Mariners say they'll keep him in the bullpen in 2013.

Felix Hernandez

Born: **4/8/1986** Age: **27**
Bats: **R** Throws: **R** Height: **6' 4"** Weight: **235**
Breakout: **18%** Improve: **51%** Collapse: **20%**
Attrition: **2%** MLB: **97%**

Comparables:
Kevin Appier,Roger Clemens,Bill Singer

YEAR	TEAM	LVL	AGE	W	L	SV	G	GS	IP	H	HR	BB	SO	BB9	SO9	GB%	BABIP	WHIP	ERA	FIP	FRA	WARP
2010	SEA	MLB	24	13	12	0	34	34	249^2	194	17	70	232	2.5	8.4	55%	.263	1.06	2.27	3.01	3.94	2.6
2011	SEA	MLB	25	14	14	0	33	33	233^2	218	19	67	222	2.6	8.6	52%	.307	1.22	3.47	3.17	3.77	2.5
2012	SEA	MLB	26	13	9	0	33	33	232	209	14	56	223	2.2	8.7	51%	.308	1.14	3.06	2.79	3.33	3.6
2013	*SEA*	*MLB*	*27*	*14*	*8*	*0*	*29*	*29*	*202^2*	*171*	*14*	*57*	*193*	*2.5*	*8.6*	*53%*	*.289*	*1.13*	*2.80*	*3.04*	*3.04*	*4.2*

Hernandez had the best strikeout rate, the best walk rate, and the best home-run rate of his career, which is why nobody in Seattle is freaking out too much over his falling velocity. Hernandez's average fastball in 2012 was 92.1 mph, down from 93.3 a year earlier and 94.1 a year before that. But he has added a cutter, a hard one that matches his regular fastball velocity but gets more whiffs, more swings, and more fouls than his two- and four-seamers. "I wouldn't worry about fastball velocity," Dustin Pedroia told a reporter who was asking about Hernandez in August. "How about you only write good things, because there's not a bad thing you can say."

Danny Hultzen
Born: **11/28/1989** Age: **23**
Bats: **L** Throws: **L** Height: **6' 4"** Weight: **200**
Breakout: **25%** Improve: **62%** Collapse: **22%**
Attrition: **15%** MLB: **96%**
Comparables:
Adam Loewen,Clayton Kershaw,Scott Kazmir

YEAR	TEAM	LVL	AGE	W	L	SV	G	GS	IP	H	HR	BB	SO	BB9	SO9	GB%	BABIP	WHIP	ERA	FIP	FRA	WARP
2012	WTN	AA	22	8	3	0	13	13	75^1	38	2	32	79	3.8	9.4	49%	.203	0.93	1.19	2.79	3.00	0.5
2012	TAC	AAA	22	1	4	0	12	12	48^2	49	2	43	57	8.0	10.5	37%	.351	1.89	5.92	4.75	5.40	0.4
2013	*SEA*	*MLB*	*23*	*2*	*2*	*0*	*7*	*7*	*35*	*29*	*3*	*18*	*36*	*4.7*	*9.3*	*44%*	*.287*	*1.36*	*3.73*	*3.80*	*4.06*	*0.4*

Hultzen might be further from the Mariners' rotation now than he was one year ago, before he'd ever thrown a professional pitch. Hultzen wasn't merely bad in Triple-A, he was bad in the least predictable way. He'd walked 1.8 batters per nine in his final year in college, and that combination of control and command made him a sleeper for the Mariners' 2012 rotation—particularly after he smoked Double-A batters, with a 0.60 ERA in his final dozen starts. His control went south in the Pacific Coast League, and kept getting worse, with 14 walks in his final 7 2/3 innings over three starts. (The improved strikeout rate is also a bit deceptive, as he was facing many more batters per nine innings to earn those 10.5 Ks.) Hultzen's stuff is still solidly above average. The Mariners eased up on his innings in the second half, hoping that he'll improve once he makes the adjustment to pitching on four days rest, instead of the six he was used to in college.

Hisashi Iwakuma
Born: **4/12/1981** Age: **32**
Bats: **R** Throws: **R** Height: **6' 4"** Weight: **170**
Breakout: **10%** Improve: **39%** Collapse: **30%**
Attrition: **19%** MLB: **91%**
Comparables:
Matt Belisle,Frank Sullivan,Wilbur Wood

YEAR	TEAM	LVL	AGE	W	L	SV	G	GS	IP	H	HR	BB	SO	BB9	SO9	GB%	BABIP	WHIP	ERA	FIP	FRA	WARP
2010	RAK	NPB	29	10	9	0	28	28	201	184	11	36	153	1.6	6.9	—	.284	1.09	2.82	3.05	3.32	0.0
2011	RAK	NPB	30	6	7	0	17	17	119	106	6	19	90	1.4	6.8	—	.288	1.05	2.42	0.00	0.00	0.0
2012	SEA	MLB	31	9	5	2	30	16	125^1	117	17	43	101	3.1	7.3	54%	.282	1.28	3.16	4.30	4.90	-0.2
2013	*SEA*	*MLB*	*32*	*6*	*5*	*0*	*14*	*14*	*97^1*	*93*	*9*	*27*	*75*	*2.5*	*6.9*	*49%*	*.292*	*1.24*	*3.59*	*3.69*	*3.90*	*0.9*

Iwakuma spent three months pitching sporadically out of the bullpen before he got his first start on July 2. He was a career starter in Japan, so it's no surprise he was more comfortable in that role, and in 16 starts he had 2.65 ERA with an improved strikeout rate and peripherals that suggest he credibly fills a number-three slot. He no longer throws hard, but he'll miss enough bats thanks to his splitter. The split gets the highest swing rate of all his pitches, despite rarely appearing in the strike zone. The shoulder problems that sidelined Iwakuma in 2011 didn't follow him to the States, though the three months he spent in the bullpen kept his innings artificially low. The health history, and exceptional home-road splits, are red flags, but the Mariners still saw a bargain and re-signed him for two years and $14 million.

Shawn Kelley
Born: **4/26/1984** Age: **29**
Bats: **R** Throws: **R** Height: **6' 3"** Weight: **220**
Breakout: **17%** Improve: **39%** Collapse: **36%**
Attrition: **17%** MLB: **80%**
Comparables:
Mike Schooler,Dave Veres,Aaron Rakers

YEAR	TEAM	LVL	AGE	W	L	SV	G	GS	IP	H	HR	BB	SO	BB9	SO9	GB%	BABIP	WHIP	ERA	FIP	FRA	WARP
2010	TAC	AAA	26	0	0	1	3	0	3^2	1	0	3	6	7.3	14.6	50%	.167	1.08	4.86	2.77	4.44	0.0
2010	SEA	MLB	26	3	1	0	22	0	25	26	5	12	26	4.3	9.4	26%	.313	1.52	3.96	5.13	5.96	-0.3
2011	WTN	AA	27	0	1	0	3	2	3	4	0	0	3	0.0	9.0	—	.400	1.33	0.00	2.31	2.51	0.0
2011	TAC	AAA	27	1	0	0	12	0	14^2	11	3	6	15	3.7	9.2	15%	.300	1.16	1.84	5.62	2.66	0.3
2011	SEA	MLB	27	0	0	0	10	0	12^2	7	0	3	10	2.1	7.1	38%	.206	0.79	0.00	2.19	2.33	0.3
2012	TAC	AAA	28	2	0	6	14	0	20	9	0	4	25	1.8	11.2	43%	.214	0.65	0.90	1.77	1.47	0.8
2012	SEA	MLB	28	2	4	0	47	0	44^1	43	5	15	45	3.0	9.1	31%	.304	1.31	3.25	3.50	3.23	0.7
2013	*SEA*	*MLB*	*29*	*2*	*1*	*0*	*36*	*0*	*39^2*	*35*	*4*	*13*	*38*	*2.8*	*8.7*	*39%*	*.286*	*1.19*	*3.30*	*3.58*	*3.59*	*0.5*

In his second season since elbow surgery, Kelley regained most of the fastball velocity that had been slow to return in 2011, and he chipped in a solid season in mostly low-leverage roles. Kelley has never had great stuff, and he still doesn't, but except for 2010—which we might chalk up to the fraying elbow ligaments—he has been a reliable strike-thrower. Remove the six of his 15 walks in 2012 that were intentional, and he's got a 45-to-9 ratio with a punchout per inning. He earned more prestigious assignments as the season went on, and with a 2.53 post-surgery ERA, he is in line to get more.

Josh Kinney
Born: **3/31/1979** Age: **34**
Bats: **R** Throws: **R** Height: **6' 2"** Weight: **215**
Breakout: **16%** Improve: **38%** Collapse: **39%**
Attrition: **8%** MLB: **91%**
Comparables:
Joe Borowski,Akinori Otsuka,Dave Veres

YEAR	TEAM	LVL	AGE	W	L	SV	G	GS	IP	H	HR	BB	SO	BB9	SO9	GB%	BABIP	WHIP	ERA	FIP	FRA	WARP
2010	MEM	AAA	31	3	4	17	56	0	60	42	4	17	51	2.5	7.7	54%	.251	0.98	1.80	3.85	3.68	1.3
2011	CHR	AAA	32	6	3	14	49	0	61^2	49	2	17	66	2.5	9.6	57%	.289	1.07	2.77	2.59	3.14	0.8
2011	CHA	MLB	32	0	0	0	13	0	17^2	23	1	7	20	3.6	10.2	58%	.431	1.70	6.62	3.06	4.10	0.2
2012	TAC	AAA	33	1	0	3	27	0	36^2	37	0	11	38	2.7	9.3	48%	.363	1.31	2.70	2.74	2.22	1.1
2012	SEA	MLB	33	0	3	1	35	0	32	24	3	15	36	4.2	10.1	45%	.266	1.22	3.94	3.70	3.70	0.2
2013	*SEA*	*MLB*	*34*	*2*	*1*	*0*	*33*	*0*	*38^1*	*34*	*3*	*15*	*36*	*3.4*	*8.5*	*51%*	*.295*	*1.27*	*3.63*	*3.51*	*3.94*	*0.3*

Kinney signed a minor-league deal with the Mariners and ended up as a high-leverage reliever in September, but high-leverage with the Mariners isn't the same as on a contending team. Despite the seemingly significant major-league role, Kinney could easily play out the rest of his career with minor-league stints. Seventy percent of the pitches he throws have a bend on them, so he'll get strikeouts but struggle with control. This is particularly so for lefties, one in seven of whom have walked against Kinney in his career.

Lucas Luetge

Born: **3/24/1987** Age: **26**
Bats: **L** Throws: **L** Height: **6' 5"** Weight: **203**
Breakout: **44%** Improve: **58%** Collapse: **28%**
Attrition: **26%** MLB: **89%**

Comparables:
Bill Lee,Mark Lowe,Jeff Holly

YEAR	TEAM	LVL	AGE	W	L	SV	G	GS	IP	H	HR	BB	SO	BB9	SO9	GB%	BABIP	WHIP	ERA	FIP	FRA	WARP
2010	BRV	A+	23	1	1	0	16	1	35^{1}	36	1	10	21	2.5	5.4	54%	.307	1.30	2.29	3.55	4.79	-0.2
2010	HUN	AA	23	3	2	0	23	2	44	52	4	17	47	3.5	9.6	45%	.361	1.57	3.48	3.73	4.28	0.6
2011	HUN	AA	24	1	3	3	46	1	69	63	3	23	69	3.0	9.0	55%	.303	1.25	3.13	2.92	3.41	0.7
2012	SEA	MLB	25	2	2	2	63	0	40^{2}	37	3	24	38	5.3	8.4	49%	.304	1.50	3.98	3.98	3.78	0.2
2013	*SEA*	*MLB*	*26*	*1*	*1*	*0*	*29*	*0*	*34*	*35*	*4*	*16*	*25*	*4.2*	*6.5*	*45%*	*.300*	*1.50*	*4.75*	*4.67*	*5.17*	*-0.2*

The Mariners kept Luetge, a Rule 5 pick, on the active roster all season and got a pretty good specialist out of him: Lefties hit .193/.289/.241, while righties (895 OPS) were happier to see him. Against lefties, Luetge leans heavily on breaking pitches, and when he sneaks a two-seam fastball into the mix he gets whiffs. He's less confident throwing the breakers to righties, though, and they sit on a fastball that rarely tops 90. He didn't allow an earned run until his 26th outing, and his ERA was nearly 7.00 after that, though his underlying performance didn't change much. The combination of a bad second half and the emergence of Oliver Perez makes him inessential, but he's cheap.

Kevin Millwood

Born: **12/24/1974** Age: **38**
Bats: **R** Throws: **R** Height: **6' 5"** Weight: **230**
Breakout: **11%** Improve: **35%** Collapse: **22%**
Attrition: **11%** MLB: **75%**

Comparables:
John Burkett,Woody Williams,Early Wynn

YEAR	TEAM	LVL	AGE	W	L	SV	G	GS	IP	H	HR	BB	SO	BB9	SO9	GB%	BABIP	WHIP	ERA	FIP	FRA	WARP
2010	BAL	MLB	35	4	16	0	31	31	190^{2}	223	30	65	132	3.1	6.2	39%	.317	1.51	5.10	4.83	5.42	-0.1
2011	TRN	AA	36	1	0	0	1	1	7	1	0	4	3	5.1	3.9	—	.053	0.71	0.00	4.27	4.64	0.0
2011	PAW	AAA	36	5	1	0	13	13	73^{2}	79	7	25	66	3.1	8.1	42%	.380	1.41	4.28	3.74	4.92	0.2
2011	SWB	AAA	36	1	1	0	2	2	9	14	3	2	7	2.0	7.0	31%	.379	1.78	8.00	6.68	7.66	-0.3
2011	COL	MLB	36	4	3	0	9	9	54^{1}	58	9	8	36	1.3	6.0	46%	.290	1.21	3.98	4.26	5.02	0.5
2012	SEA	MLB	37	6	12	0	28	28	161	168	13	56	107	3.1	6.0	47%	.304	1.39	4.25	3.87	4.45	0.6
2013	*SEA*	*MLB*	*38*	*8*	*7*	*0*	*22*	*22*	125^{2}	*130*	*14*	*41*	*88*	*2.9*	*6.3*	*43%*	*.300*	*1.36*	*4.24*	*4.23*	*4.61*	*0.3*

In 2011, Millwood set a career best, walking only 1.3 batters per nine innings. In 2012, he returned to career norms. What's interesting is how little changed: Millwood threw 62.5 percent strikes in 2011, 62.7 in 2012. That's a difference of only one pitch per 100 in or out of the strike zone. The difference, it turns out, comes mostly on three-ball counts: In Colorado, hitters were swinging when they were ahead in the count; in Seattle, where a swing is more likely to produce an out and less likely to produce a home run, they sat back and let Millwood walk them. This effect might be real or it might just be a sample-size illusion, but the point is the same either way: Even focusing on peripherals can lead us astray when those peripherals suggest an old ballplayer has learned a new trick.

D.J. Mitchell

Born: **5/13/1987** Age: **26**
Bats: **R** Throws: **R** Height: **6' 1"** Weight: **160**
Breakout: **43%** Improve: **70%** Collapse: **21%**
Attrition: **11%** MLB: **75%**

Comparables:
Kris Benson,Jordan Tata,John Thomson

YEAR	TEAM	LVL	AGE	W	L	SV	G	GS	IP	H	HR	BB	SO	BB9	SO9	GB%	BABIP	WHIP	ERA	FIP	FRA	WARP
2010	TRN	AA	23	11	4	0	23	22	133	128	11	57	96	3.9	6.5	59%	.294	1.39	4.06	4.41	5.55	-0.8
2010	SWB	AAA	23	2	0	0	3	3	17^{2}	19	0	7	16	3.6	8.1	43%	.356	1.47	3.56	2.67	4.03	0.3
2011	SWB	AAA	24	13	9	0	28	24	161^{1}	155	10	63	112	3.5	6.2	47%	.288	1.35	3.18	3.99	5.22	-0.3
2012	SWB	AAA	25	6	4	0	15	14	85^{2}	85	8	29	72	3.0	7.6	51%	.308	1.33	5.04	3.92	5.62	-0.3
2012	TAC	AAA	25	3	2	0	8	8	48^{2}	41	4	19	33	3.5	6.1	44%	.250	1.23	2.96	4.61	4.43	0.3
2012	NYA	MLB	25	0	0	0	4	0	4^{2}	7	1	3	2	5.8	3.9	58%	.333	2.14	3.86	6.90	6.72	-0.1
2013	*SEA*	*MLB*	*26*	*3*	*3*	*0*	*8*	*8*	47^{1}	*48*	*5*	*20*	*31*	*3.7*	*5.8*	*52%*	*.288*	*1.42*	*4.47*	*4.53*	*4.86*	*-0.0*

It's not uncommon for groundball rates to disappear when sinkerballers move up the minor-league system, as advanced hitters do a better job of shrinking the strike zone and hammering mistakes. That's what has happened to Mitchell, a slight right-hander who went to Seattle in the Ichiro trade. After dropping with each promotion, his groundball rate reached a new low once he joined Tacoma, and while he'll limit fly balls enough to make it as a middle reliever in the big leagues, that's probably as much as one can wish for. The Mariners (like the Yankees before them) have kept him starting in the minors, but he doesn't have the sort of peripherals that will survive in a major-league rotation—even one that plays half its games in Seattle.

Hector Noesi
Born: **1/26/1987** Age: **26**
Bats: **R** Throws: **R** Height: **6' 4"** Weight: **200**
Breakout: **19%** Improve: **45%** Collapse: **28%**
Attrition: **27%** MLB: **96%**
Comparables:
Moose Haas, Reggie Cleveland, Josh Tomlin

YEAR	TEAM	LVL	AGE	W	L	SV	G	GS	IP	H	HR	BB	SO	BB9	SO9	GB%	BABIP	WHIP	ERA	FIP	FRA	WARP
2010	TAM	A+	23	5	2	0	8	8	43	35	3	6	53	1.3	11.1	42%	.291	0.95	2.72	2.44	3.05	1.1
2010	TRN	AA	23	8	4	0	17	16	98^{2}	90	7	18	86	1.6	7.8	38%	.304	1.09	3.10	3.15	4.05	1.1
2010	SWB	AAA	23	1	1	0	3	3	18^{2}	23	1	4	14	1.9	6.7	37%	.405	1.44	4.81	3.29	4.52	0.1
2011	SWB	AAA	24	1	1	0	6	5	24^{2}	28	0	9	17	3.3	6.2	40%	.333	1.50	3.28	3.20	4.25	0.1
2011	NYA	MLB	24	2	2	0	30	2	56^{1}	63	6	22	45	3.5	7.2	43%	.331	1.51	4.47	4.13	4.19	0.8
2012	TAC	AAA	25	2	6	0	11	11	64^{1}	80	7	22	55	3.1	7.7	40%	.349	1.59	5.74	4.49	5.36	0.3
2012	SEA	MLB	25	2	12	0	22	18	106^{2}	107	21	39	68	3.3	5.7	38%	.266	1.37	5.82	5.48	5.74	-0.9
2013	*SEA*	*MLB*	*26*	*6*	*5*	*0*	*24*	*16*	*102*	*106*	*13*	*33*	*76*	*3.0*	*6.7*	*39%*	*.297*	*1.37*	*4.44*	*4.34*	*4.82*	*0.0*

Michael Pineda missed the season, Jesus Montero scuffled at the plate, and Jose Campos was shut down by elbow soreness, but Noesi might have had the worst year of anyone involved in last winter's trade between Seattle and New York. He had the fourth-worst home-run rate in the majors (minimum 100 innings) despite pitching his home games at Petco Northwest. He lost his last nine decisions and his spot in the rotation. His stuff should play in the majors, particularly for a team that can support a fly-ball pitcher: He has a fastball that can reach the mid-90s, good stamina, and a solid changeup. What he lacks is a plan to put away hitters. After Noesi got ahead 0-2 in 2012, opponents still hit .319/.313/.702 against him, including five homers. Compare Noesi's OPS on an 0-2 count—1015—against the entire Seattle staff: 418. When batters are ahead, Noesi (974 OPS against) is no worse than the league average (977). An effective waste pitch might be the most important thing for him to develop next.

James Paxton
Born: **11/6/1988** Age: **24**
Bats: **L** Throws: **L** Height: **6' 5"** Weight: **220**
Breakout: **34%** Improve: **70%** Collapse: **13%**
Attrition: **8%** MLB: **90%**
Comparables:
J.P. Howell, Marc Rzepczynski, Eric Surkamp

YEAR	TEAM	LVL	AGE	W	L	SV	G	GS	IP	H	HR	BB	SO	BB9	SO9	GB%	BABIP	WHIP	ERA	FIP	FRA	WARP
2011	CLN	A	22	3	3	0	10	10	56	45	1	30	80	4.8	12.9	—	.358	1.34	2.73	2.40	2.60	0.0
2011	WTN	AA	22	3	0	0	7	7	39	28	2	13	51	3.0	11.8	—	.302	1.05	1.85	2.43	2.65	0.0
2012	WTN	AA	23	9	4	0	21	21	106^{1}	96	5	54	110	4.6	9.3	49%	.324	1.41	3.05	3.24	3.51	0.7
2013	*SEA*	*MLB*	*24*	*2*	*2*	*0*	*7*	*7*	*35*	*32*	*4*	*16*	*32*	*4.1*	*8.3*	*46%*	*.297*	*1.38*	*4.03*	*4.23*	*4.38*	*0.2*

Paxton's overall line looks like a wash, but a closer look shows two separate campaigns: before he spent five weeks on the disabled list for a knee injury, and after. In the first half, he struggled with walks and home runs, with a 4.50 FIP and a 3.88 ERA. After he returned healthy, the walks were under control, he didn't allow a home run in 60 innings, the FIP was 2.37, and the ERA 2.40. He has the best curveball in the Mariners system and was touching 95 even at the end of a long year, but his mechanics can get away from him and his command goes with them.

Oliver Perez
Born: **8/15/1981** Age: **31**
Bats: **L** Throws: **L** Height: **6' 4"** Weight: **210**
Breakout: **16%** Improve: **52%** Collapse: **15%**
Attrition: **14%** MLB: **82%**
Comparables:
Rudy May, Jack Harshman, Rick Sutcliffe

YEAR	TEAM	LVL	AGE	W	L	SV	G	GS	IP	H	HR	BB	SO	BB9	SO9	GB%	BABIP	WHIP	ERA	FIP	FRA	WARP
2010	SLU	A+	28	1	1	0	2	2	11^{2}	7	2	4	14	3.1	10.8	29%	.192	0.94	4.62	4.55	4.46	0.1
2010	BUF	AAA	28	0	0	0	2	2	11^{2}	10	2	7	10	5.4	7.7	44%	.250	1.45	2.31	6.11	6.00	-0.1
2010	NYN	MLB	28	0	5	0	17	7	46^{1}	54	9	42	37	8.2	7.2	36%	.317	2.07	6.80	7.01	6.92	-0.7
2011	HAR	AA	29	3	5	0	16	15	75^{2}	78	10	27	58	3.2	6.9	36%	.303	1.39	3.09	4.82	4.65	0.5
2012	TAC	AAA	30	2	2	1	22	0	31	33	4	19	42	5.5	12.2	41%	.382	1.68	4.65	4.47	4.43	0.5
2012	SEA	MLB	30	1	3	0	33	0	29^{2}	27	1	10	24	3.0	7.3	35%	.295	1.25	2.12	2.88	2.94	0.5
2013	*SEA*	*MLB*	*31*	*2*	*2*	*0*	*17*	*4*	*33^{2}*	*32*	*4*	*20*	*29*	*5.3*	*7.8*	*36%*	*.290*	*1.54*	*4.83*	*4.80*	*5.25*	*-0.2*

When last we saw Perez, in 2010, he had an 89-mph fastball and threw 57 percent of his pitches for strikes. After a year spent in Double-A with the Nationals, he signed with the Mariners, moved to the bullpen, junked the changeup, and was reborn. He showed off a 93-mph average fastball and 68 percent strikes in the majors in 2012. It's hard to draw many conclusions from 30 innings, and harder still from the splits within. But his control did dissolve a bit after August 1, and his effectiveness against righties is propped up by a BABIP plunge. Still, there's certainly enough heat on Perez's fastball and tilt on his slider to project an effective bullpen lefty. He's only 31, if you can believe it.

Stephen Pryor
Born: **7/23/1989** Age: **23**
Bats: **R** Throws: **R** Height: **6' 7"** Weight: **225**
Breakout: **48%** Improve: **62%** Collapse: **22%**
Attrition: **33%** MLB: **90%**
Comparables:
Rich Thompson,Ryan Perry,Ambiorix Burgos

YEAR	TEAM	LVL	AGE	W	L	SV	G	GS	IP	H	HR	BB	SO	BB9	SO9	GB%	BABIP	WHIP	ERA	FIP	FRA	WARP
2010	CLN	A	20	0	2	1	12	0	17	17	0	6	29	3.2	15.4	58%	.395	1.35	3.71	1.43	2.98	0.6
2010	EVE	A-	20	0	0	4	11	0	18^1	7	0	7	26	3.4	12.8	40%	.200	0.77	0.49	1.79	1.11	0.8
2011	HDS	A+	21	1	0	4	22	0	27	28	2	26	34	8.7	11.3	—	.371	2.00	7.67	5.51	5.99	0.0
2011	WTN	AA	21	2	1	6	17	0	22^2	9	0	7	27	2.8	10.7	—	.184	0.71	1.19	1.98	2.16	0.0
2012	HDS	A+	22	0	0	0	2	1	2^2	0	0	3	3	10.1	10.1	75%	.000	1.12	6.75	4.94	8.28	0.1
2012	WTN	AA	22	1	0	7	11	0	16	7	0	5	24	2.8	13.5	41%	.222	0.75	1.12	1.08	-0.22	0.7
2012	TAC	AAA	22	0	0	3	16	0	20	11	0	11	20	4.9	9.0	37%	.224	1.10	0.00	3.32	2.82	0.5
2012	SEA	MLB	22	3	1	0	26	0	23	22	5	13	27	5.1	10.6	39%	.288	1.52	3.91	5.22	5.88	-0.3
2013	*SEA*	*MLB*	*23*	*2*	*1*	*0*	*29*	*0*	*35^2*	*29*	*3*	*17*	*39*	*4.3*	*9.9*	*43%*	*.288*	*1.30*	*3.52*	*3.54*	*3.83*	*0.4*

The Mariners seemed to have an endless supply of pitchers like Pryor in 2012: 11 different relievers threw at least 20 innings, and the worst ERA among them was Steve Delabar's 4.17. Pryor was one of seven who struck out at least a batter per inning, and one of 10 making less than a million bucks. Relievers are so interchangeable! Not Pryor, though. Pryor is going to be a cut above the rest, perhaps as soon as the moment you finish this sentence. Besides high-90s heat, he's now throwing a low-90s cutter that has replaced his slider. Double-A and Triple-A hitters were helpless—not one squared him up enough to trot around the bases—and, after he joined the big-league bullpen, no Mariner (besides Delabar, who's gone now) had a better whiff rate on pitches inside the strike zone. His mistakes were less forgivable to major-league hitters and he still needs a pitch they'll chase. But plus-plus fastballs are 96 percent of high-leverage relief work, and Pryor's got one.

Erasmo Ramirez
Born: **5/2/1990** Age: **23**
Bats: **R** Throws: **R** Height: **6' 0"** Weight: **180**
Breakout: **31%** Improve: **57%** Collapse: **17%**
Attrition: **8%** MLB: **90%**
Comparables:
Tommy Hunter,Jair Jurrjens,Rick Porcello

YEAR	TEAM	LVL	AGE	W	L	SV	G	GS	IP	H	HR	BB	SO	BB9	SO9	GB%	BABIP	WHIP	ERA	FIP	FRA	WARP
2010	CLN	A	20	10	4	1	26	23	151^2	142	13	21	117	1.2	6.9	54%	.292	1.07	2.97	3.85	4.88	0.8
2011	WTN	AA	21	7	6	0	19	19	110^1	127	10	19	81	1.5	6.6	—	.322	1.32	4.73	3.75	4.08	0.0
2011	TAC	AAA	21	3	2	0	7	7	42^1	51	4	13	35	2.8	7.4	38%	.337	1.51	5.10	4.42	4.57	0.6
2012	TAC	AAA	22	6	3	0	15	15	77^1	81	5	18	58	2.1	6.8	48%	.299	1.28	3.72	3.86	4.49	0.9
2012	SEA	MLB	22	1	3	0	16	8	59	47	6	12	48	1.8	7.3	41%	.243	1.00	3.36	3.50	3.65	0.8
2013	*SEA*	*MLB*	*23*	*4*	*3*	*0*	*11*	*11*	*63^1*	*62*	*7*	*16*	*42*	*2.3*	*6.0*	*46%*	*.282*	*1.24*	*3.88*	*4.07*	*4.22*	*0.4*

The Mariners signed Ramirez out of Nicaragua five years ago, when he was a strike-thrower with unexciting arm strength. As he has moved up levels, he has bulked up and added velocity, and he debuted in Seattle in April as a strike-thrower with a fastball averaging 93-mph, sometimes hitting a few ticks higher. He saw action as a starter and as a reliever with the big club. As a starter, his ERA was worse but his peripherals weren't, and he has both the stamina and the changeup (lefties hit .207.260/.351 against him) to merit a shot in the Mariners rotation. As with many Mariners, the challenge is separating the performance from the park, and while the samples are small, the split isn't: 2.41 ERA at Safeco, 4.66 on the road.

Taijuan Walker
Born: **8/13/1992** Age: **20**
Bats: **R** Throws: **R** Height: **6' 5"** Weight: **195**
Breakout: **56%** Improve: **81%** Collapse: **8%**
Attrition: **2%** MLB: **92%**
Comparables:
Milt Pappas,Larry Dierker,Madison Bumgarner

YEAR	TEAM	LVL	AGE	W	L	SV	G	GS	IP	H	HR	BB	SO	BB9	SO9	GB%	BABIP	WHIP	ERA	FIP	FRA	WARP
2010	MRN	Rk	17	1	1	0	4	0	7	2	0	3	9	3.9	11.6	57%	.143	0.71	1.29	3.40	4.47	0.0
2011	CLN	A	18	6	5	0	18	18	96^2	69	4	39	113	3.6	10.5	—	.289	1.12	2.89	2.86	3.11	0.0
2012	WTN	AA	19	7	10	0	25	25	126^2	124	12	50	118	3.6	8.4	43%	.308	1.37	4.69	3.98	5.78	-0.1
2013	*SEA*	*MLB*	*20*	*2*	*2*	*0*	*7*	*7*	*34^2*	*34*	*4*	*14*	*28*	*3.7*	*7.4*	*43%*	*.294*	*1.39*	*4.42*	*4.30*	*4.80*	*0.0*

There's only one number here that screams "elite prospect," and it's the age: 19. Walker was 13 months younger than the next-youngest pitcher in the Southern League, and he held his own. Walker has added a high-80s cutter that splits the difference between his two plus pitches, a mid-70s curve and a mid-90s fastball. Through two months, he was so good (2.23 ERA) in Double-A that he might have forced the Mariners' hand, but a sluggish second half (6.01 after June 1) made it easier for them to keep him there. He recovered with two very strong starts in the playoffs. He'll still need to improve his command and keep his mechanics sound late in games, but his is an elite arm. A solid first half could put him in Seattle before his 21st birthday.

Tom Wilhelmsen
Born: **12/16/1983** Age: **29**
Bats: **R** Throws: **R** Height: **6' 7"** Weight: **230**
Breakout: **28%** Improve: **49%** Collapse: **26%**
Attrition: **9%** MLB: **87%**

Comparables:
Chris Resop,Nick Masset,Aaron Heilman

YEAR	TEAM	LVL	AGE	W	L	SV	G	GS	IP	H	HR	BB	SO	BB9	SO9	GB%	BABIP	WHIP	ERA	FIP	FRA	WARP
2011	WTN	AA	27	4	5	0	14	12	60^2	66	8	26	40	3.9	5.9	—	.302	1.52	5.49	5.33	5.80	0.0
2011	SEA	MLB	27	2	0	0	25	0	32^2	25	2	13	30	3.6	8.3	35%	.258	1.16	3.31	3.40	4.19	0.1
2012	SEA	MLB	28	4	3	29	73	0	79^1	59	5	29	87	3.3	9.9	48%	.266	1.11	2.50	2.84	2.95	1.3
2013	*SEA*	*MLB*	*29*	*3*	*2*	*6*	*34*	*4*	*60*	*52*	*6*	*23*	*56*	*3.5*	*8.3*	*43%*	*.282*	*1.26*	*3.52*	*3.78*	*3.82*	*0.7*

A video went around of Alexei Ramirez buckling at Wilhelmsen's curveball. The White Sox shortstop doesn't just flinch; he drops to a knee, raises one hand over his face, and turns his head down like he's just walked in on the sun . . . all before the pitch drops into the strike zone. Interestingly, if you just look at pitch results, you'd figure Wilhelmsen's curveball was good but not one of the best breaking balls in the game. But measuring the value of a pitch is complex, and Wilhelmsen's curve is part of a package that plays extremely well. Both of his fastballs, his changeup, and his curveball all got swinging strikes more than 10 percent of the time. He took over the closer's job in early June and had a 1.76 ERA from that point on.

LINEOUTS

HITTERS

PLAYER	TEAM	LVL	AGE	PA	R	2B	3B	HR	RBI	BB	SO	SB-CS	AVG/OBP/SLG	TAv	BABIP	BRR	FRAA	WARP
3B V. Catricala	TAC	AAA	23	507	58	23	1	10	60	37	88	4-2	.229/.292/.348	.228	.262	-3.2	3B(87): 2.0, LF(14): -1.4	-0.9
MI N. Franklin	WTN	AA	21	239	25	17	4	4	26	24	38	9-2	.322/.394/.502	.293	.378	-0.5	SS(11): 0.2, 2B(3): 0.3	0.4
	TAC	AAA	21	296	39	15	5	7	29	24	68	3-2	.243/.310/.416	.244	.301	0	2B(32): -2.3, SS(30): -0.3	-0.2
3B P. Kivlehan	EVE	A-	22	316	46	17	3	12	52	19	93	14-1	.301/.373/.511	.313	.412	0.5	3B(13): 0.2	0.7
UT J. Marder	HDS	A+	22	320	68	24	4	10	56	21	44	16-6	.360/.425/.583	.264	.396	0	2B(11): 1.2, LF(4): 0.1	0.2
3B F. Martinez	WTN	AA	21	402	55	16	1	2	23	43	85	27-7	.227/.315/.295	.271	.294	5.6	3B(19): 0.5, CF(1): -0.1	0.8
SS B. Miller	HDS	A+	22	473	89	33	5	11	56	52	79	19-6	.339/.412/.524	.292	.394	1.8	SS(13): 1.3	0.8
	WTN	AA	22	170	21	7	2	4	12	22	26	4-1	.320/.406/.476	.370	.364	-0.5	SS(9): -0.7	0.5
INF M. Peguero	PUL	Rk	18	256	30	11	2	0	24	12	32	3-1	.231/.269/.294	.197	.264	2.1	2B(30): 4.3, SS(15): 1.0	-0.5
OF G. Pimentel	CLN	A	19	398	37	18	0	9	51	19	115	5-2	.245/.289/.366	.281	.328	-1.9	LF(16): -1.3	-0.4
INF S. Proscia	HDS	A+	22	471	88	24	3	24	94	25	97	12-2	.333/.368/.567	.251	.377	6.8	3B(10): -0.9, 2B(3): -0.3	0.5
	WTN	AA	22	83	10	2	0	4	9	4	16	0-2	.211/.259/.395	.314	.214	-1	1B(5): 0.2	0.0
2B S. Romero	HDS	A+	23	276	47	19	3	11	51	13	35	6-2	.357/.391/.581	.347	.379	-0.8	2B(6): -0.0	0.2
	WTN	AA	23	240	38	15	4	12	50	14	37	6-3	.347/.392/.620	.320	.366	0.2	2B(8): -0.9	0.1

If the 400-point drop in his OPS is any indication, **Vinnie Catricala** is like a modern-day Columbus: He went looking for the Pacific Coast League but ended up crashing into a rock. **Nick Franklin**'s OPS against right-handers has been 350 points higher than against left-handers over the past three years, which isn't ideal but at least leans in the optimal direction. **Patrick Kivlehan** took four years off to play college football, picked up the baseball again his senior year, won the Big East triple crown, and was picked in the fourth round to play third base poorly, hit the stuffing out of the ball, and try to improve his pitch recognition. The detective peered down at the baseball, bruised almost beyond recognition where it lay motionless far beyond the outfield wall. "This was no accident," he said. "It was (**Jack**) **Marder**!" The upside portion of the Doug Fister trade showed his downside, as **Fernando Martinez**'s there-in-theory power continued to not show up in games and a balky hamstring cost him more than a month. It's been nothing but blue skies and line drives for second-round pick **Brad Miller**, who now has a .398 BABIP in the pros. 18-year-old **Martin Peguero** scuffled in short-season ball and moved off of shortstop, as expected, to second base, but it's still too early to say whether, when, and how his many tools will show up. Three years after the Mariners signed 70-power **Guillermo Pimentel** for $2 million, he lacks the plate discipline or all-fields approach he'll need to bring that power into games. The average High Desert player batted .303/.359/.497 in 2012, so seventh-rounder **Steven Proscia** hasn't answered as many questions as his own High-A line suggests. **Stefen Romero** has improved his line with each promotion, and the oversized second-baseman—a 12th-round pick two years ago—won the Southern League OPS crown by a hefty 77 points.

PITCHERS

PLAYER	TEAM	LVL	AGE	W	L	SV	IP	H	HR	BB	SO	BB9	SO9	GB%	BABIP	WHIP	ERA	FIP	FRA	WARP
M. Brazis	PUL	RK	22	1	0	2	8^1	1	0	0	19	0	20.5	—	.111	0.12	0	-0.86	-0.94	0
	CLN	A	22	1	0	5	19^1	10	1	5	32	2.3	14.9	20%	.333	0.78	0.93	1.64	0.42	0.2
D. Farquhar	NHP	AA	25	0	1	1	30^1	28	2	10	33	3.0	9.8	42%	.310	1.25	2.97	3.17	2.83	0.5
A. Fernandez	HDS	A+	22	2	5	0	88	89	6	14	79	1.4	8.1	52%	.315	1.17	3.68	3.59	2.68	0.1
	WTN	AA	22	4	3	0	76	74	6	24	55	2.8	6.5	56%	.298	1.29	3.32	3.71	4.63	0.1
B. Maurer	WTN	AA	21	9	2	0	137^2	133	4	48	117	3.1	7.6	48%	.327	1.31	3.20	3.00	3.08	0.7
Y. Medina	WTN	AA	23	5	5	5	69^1	63	5	35	77	4.5	10.0	55%	.317	1.41	3.25	3.59	3.08	1.0
T. Miller	CLN	A	21	7	7	0	120^2	120	11	17	84	1.3	6.3	45%	.283	1.14	3.36	3.72	4.26	0.4
	HDS	A+	21	1	2	0	29^2	29	0	7	29	2.1	8.8	43%	.358	1.21	2.73	2.57	1.77	0.1
B. Moran	WTN	AA	23	1	2	0	31^2	30	1	6	29	1.7	8.2	32%	.319	1.14	1.14	2.29	0.89	0.9
	TAC	AAA	23	3	3	2	37	23	6	12	53	2.9	12.9	33%	.236	0.95	3.89	3.88	3.95	0.6
C. Ruffin	TAC	AAA	23	0	5	1	70^2	75	8	35	54	4.5	6.9	38%	.300	1.56	5.99	5.22	5.42	0.1
D. Unsworth	EVE	A-	19	7	2	0	85^1	76	9	19	67	2.0	7.1	43%	.268	1.11	3.90	3.97	5.63	0.5

Matt Brazis, a 28th-round reliever with a good changeup and deceptive delivery, put up one of those amazing short-season lines: 8 innings, 19 strikeouts, one baserunner. **Danny Farquhar**, half of the Ichiro return, is an inconsistent sinkerballing longman who was traded three times and claimed off waivers twice within a 20-month span. Long lefty **Anthony Fernandez** has added velocity and a cutter to his command-and-makeup profile, putting him on the Mariners' depth chart, if not at the top of any prospect lists. **Brandon Maurer**'s stuff played a lot better when he escaped High Desert, and his ability to peck at the outer portions of the strike zone got him added to the 40-man roster after the season. For the first time since coming stateside, **Yoervis Medina** didn't pitch at three levels in a season, and the stability suited the hard-thrower. **Trevor Miller**, a 40th-rounder in the 2011 draft, might be a late-round steal after his secondary pitches took a step forward in 2012, but he'll have to survive a longer stint in the California League to prove it. **Brian Moran** has a deceptive delivery that should make for a good LOOGY; oddly, though, lefties bring out his wild side. **Chance Ruffin** spent the season in Triple-A, but all he needs is a chan—you thought we were going to say chance, right? No, he needs a good changeup, because lefties kill him. For now, the peak of South African baseball history is scratching out one hit against Roger Clemens in the 2006 WBC, but **Dylan Unsworth**—high 80s, movement, decent changeup—might change that in a few years.

MANAGER: ERIC WEDGE

YEAR	TEAM	W-L	Pythag +/-	Avg PC	100+ P	120+ P	QS	BQS	REL	REL w Zero R	IBB	PH	PH Avg	PH HR	SB2	CS2	SB3	CS3	SAC Att	SAC %	POS SAC	Squeeze	Swing	In Play
2011	SEA	67-95	0	99.7	83	6	94	10	351	272	27	49	.209	1	18	3	0	0	49	91.8%	44	2	322	90
2012	SEA	75-87	0	95.1	69	2	89	5	451	359	39	78	.235	1	9	2	1	0	48	75.0%	35	0	228	61

It's difficult to judge managerial performance during a bridge season like 2012. Many moves might look self-destructive through the narrow lens of the present, but fit a team's long-term goals and views of itself. The savvy Mariners fan had plenty to gripe about with Wedge's decisions: Chone Figgins got to hang around all year, and even start 24 games in the leadoff spot; Ichiro was the Mariners' number-three hitter for two months despite an OPS that started with a 6; too many opportunities for Miguel Olivo; too few for John Jaso. What's damning about those moves is that they hurt the Mariners in the short term and *also* seemed counterproductive in the long. None of the three veterans will be around for the next good Mariners team (or, probably, the next bad one); getting Jesus Montero and Jaso reps behind the dish, on the other hand, might have tangible effects. The optimistic take is that the Mariners hired a tough guy "field general" for a reason, and that the psychology of tough love is opaque. Perhaps the true value of such moves had to do with loyalty, or comportment, or sticking to a plan, or simply respecting elders.

Wedge did improve his statistical résumé a bit by outperforming his team's run differential for just the second time in his career. Entering the season, Wedge was nearly 30 games worse than Pythagoras would have calculated, one of the worst records in modern history, according to the manager research of Chris Jaffe. This year's team was a couple of wins better than expected. Wedge's most notable on-field tactic is leaving the pitcher in, but he was considerably more likely to walk to the mound in 2012. The previous season, he'd made just 351 pitching changes, a whopping 35 fewer than the next-lowest in the American League. He tacked an even 100 pitching changes onto that total in 2012, putting him in the lower half but no longer the extreme. That actually describes Wedge pretty well: in the lower half of managers, but not the extreme.

St. Louis Cardinals

2012: ALBERT WHO?

The 2011 World Series champions faced a daunting task last year, having to defend their crown without franchise icons Tony La Russa, Dave Duncan, and Albert Pujols for the first time in a decade. Despite injuries to veteran stars Chris Carpenter, Jaime Garcia, and Lance Berkman, rookie skipper Mike Matheny managed to lead the Cardinals to within one game of the World Series. While Pujols as the face of the franchise was missed, Pujols the player was successfully replaced by a crowd of home-grown talent who kept the organization's fortunes riding high.

CARDINALS PROSPECTUS

2012 W-L: 88-74, 2nd in NL Central

Pythag	.577	4th	DER	.702	21st
RS/G	4.72	5th	B-Age	29.4	23rd
RA/G	4.00	7th	P-Age	28.8	22nd
TAv	.273	3rd	Salary	$111.9	8th
BRR	-4.8	21st	M$/MW	$2.50	14th
TAv-P	.255	7th	DL Days	760	19th
FIP	3.66	4th	DL WARP	5.1	8th

Three-Year Park Factors	
Overall	99
HR/RH	100
HR/LH	104
AVG/RH	99
AVG/LH	104

Busch Stadium (2006)
Att. % of Capacity: 91.6% (4th)
Dim. 336, 375, 400, 375, 335

Draw your own conclusions: The .315 BABIP at Busch last year was third in MLB, up from 20th in 2011.

The original plan to replace Pujols involved installing the recently resurrected Berkman at first base and free-agent signee Carlos Beltran in right field. But, as Helmuth von Moltke the Elder—sort of the Branch Rickey of Prussia—noted, no plan survives contact with the enemy. When Berkman couldn't stay healthy, versatile Allen Craig stepped in admirably to claim the job. The lineup was littered with other happy stories, as Jon Jay and David Freese emerged as top-flight bats, Matt Holliday was a rock, and catcher Yadier Molina became a legitimate MVP candidate. All told, the post-Pujols Cardinals were the second-most potent offense in the National League, outscoring the 2011 squad in the process.

Ace starter Adam Wainwright made a triumphant return after a year lost to elbow surgery, just in time to anchor an injury-plagued rotation. Folk-hero Carpenter missed most of the year after losing a rib and some neck muscles to a horrifically invasive surgery, and Garcia sat out two months with his own shoulder woes. In response, the Cardinals were able to plug in home-grown replacements Lance Lynn and Joe Kelly to work alongside Wainwright, Jake Westbrook, and a resurgent Kyle Lohse. The result was a staff that not only gave up fewer runs than the 2011 champions, but placed fifth in the circuit.

The season ended on a sour note when the Cardinals couldn't finish off the Giants in the NLCS—an outcome they were perhaps owed after their own Rasputin-like performance in 2011—but the emergence of players like Craig, Freese, and Jay have kept expectations high for the coming season.

2013: GOING DEEP

With the same productive lineup returning and plenty of depth on hand to guard against injury, the Cardinals should continue to pummel opponents into submission. The health and effectiveness of their rotation will be the key to the season, but with a new wave of young power arms knocking on the door, the Cardinals should once again be in the thick of the NL Central race.

With the possible exceptions of Molina and Jay, no one in the St. Louis lineup played significantly above their true talent level last year. More worrying to the offense is the injury histories of Freese, Craig, and Beltran. However, the Cardinals have exceptional lineup depth and flexibility, inoculating them against injuries and ineffectiveness. Super-sub Matt Carpenter has proven to be a solid fill-in at all four corner positions, boppin' first baseman Matt Adams has already had a taste of the big leagues, and young outfield phenom Oscar Taveras is nearly ready to show off his otherworldly hit tool in Busch Stadium. Between them the Cardinals should be well-equipped to overcome even multiple injuries.

The middle infield is more of a mess, as the increasingly fragile and ineffective Rafael Furcal is slated to play shortstop alongside a slew of potential out-makers at the keystone. Last season the Cardinals wisely decided to go with defense down the stretch in the form of Pete Kozma and Daniel Descalso, and with so much thunder in the rest of the lineup, they can again afford to trade outs in the lineup for outs in the field.

GM John Mozeliak wisely allowed another team to overpay for the twilight of Lohse's career, leaving the Cardinals with a potentially stellar rotation of Wainwright, Carpenter, Garcia, Westbrook, and Lynn. But Garcia was shut down in October after trying to pitch through yet another injury, and Carpenter's health generally spawns more questions than a *Jeopardy* marathon. Yet here, too, the Cardinals have fall-back options in place. Rocket-armed youngsters Shelby Miller and Trevor Rosenthal both made dazzling debuts last season and could be plugged into the rotation as needed. Miller is an ace-in-waiting, while St. Louis could deploy Rosenthal's triple-digit heat as either a starter or a bullpen leviathan. Assuming a modicum of veteran health and a dollop of maturation from the young arms, the Cardinals rotation should be more than enough to keep them in contention.

The bullpen will again be anchored by flame-throwing closer Jason Motte, with Mitchell Boggs and Edward Mujica reprising the set-up roles they filled last year down the stretch. If Rosenthal and Miller aren't in the rotation, St. Louis could benefit from the Earl Weaver approach of stashing young starters in relief. Unlike recent years, the Cardinals should have a solid bullpen in April, rather than waiting for it to right itself in August.

THE STATE OF THE ORGANIZATION: A FERTILE FARM

With a roster filled with cost-controlled players and a farm system loaded with high-ceiling talent, the Cardinals can avoid handing out risky free-agent contracts, and are well-positioned to compete for the foreseeable future.

In addition to the departures of Pujols, La Russa, and Duncan, scouting director Jeff Luhnow left the organization after the 2011 season to become the general manager in Houston. The organization has greatly benefited from Luhnow's work, as evidenced by the 16 Cardinals draftees who took the field for last year's NLCS. New scouting director Dan Kantrovitz has big shoes to fill, but the early returns have been positive. The team's top pick in the 2011 draft, pitcher Michael Wacha, was virtually unhittable last summer and has vaulted far up numerous prospect lists.

The ability to churn out home-grown players keeps payroll down and helps the Cardinals avoid albatross contracts. With players like Wacha, Miller, Rosenthal, Taveras, second baseman Kolten Wong, and pitcher Carlos Martinez already in the pipeline, one of the best-run franchises in baseball looks set to continue its run as an annual contender for the National League pennant for years to come.

HITTERS

Matt Adams 1B

Born: **8/31/1988** Age: **24**
Bats: **L** Throws: **R** Height: **6' 4"**
Weight: **230** Breakout: **3%**
Improve: **54%** Collapse: **4%**
Attrition: **17%** MLB: **98%**

Comparables:
Justin Morneau, Orlando Cepeda, Brian R. Hunter

YEAR	TEAM	LVL	AGE	PA	R	2B	3B	HR	RBI	BB	SO	SB	CS	AVG_OBP_SLG	TAv	BABIP	BRR	FRAA	WARP
2010	QUD	A	21	510	71	41	0	22	88	33	78	5	1	.310/.361/.541	.316	.335	-1.7	1B(110): 1.9	3.2
2011	SFD	AA	22	513	80	23	2	32	101	40	90	0	1	.300/.357/.566	.305	.308	0	--	0.0
2012	MEM	AAA	23	276	41	22	0	18	50	15	57	3	1	.329/.362/.624	.280	.360	0.8	1B(11): 0.2	0.1
2012	SLN	MLB	23	91	8	6	0	2	13	5	24	0	0	.244/.286/.384	.228	.317	-1.6	1B(24): 0.4	-0.4
2013	*SLN*	*MLB*	*24*	*250*	*27*	*13*	*0*	*10*	*34*	*10*	*56*	*1*	*0*	*.259/.289/.445*	*.257*	*.296*	*-0.4*	*1B -4*	*-0.3*

Adams has little left to prove in the minors, but one obstacle after another has kept the Bunyanesque slugger from taking over the Cardinals first-base job. First it was Lance Berkman, whose 2011 resurgence earned him the job once Albert Pujols left for sunnier climes. Then it was Adams himself, who forgot to pack his boom stick when he got his shot in St. Louis after Berkman wrecked his knee. Sent back down to Memphis for more seasoning, Adams watched as Allen Craig took over at the cold corner and made his bat indispensable. Surgery to remove bone spurs in his elbow ended Adams's season. Adams doesn't walk enough to be a top-tier slugger, and his bat is his only tool, but his tremendous raw power and solid contact skills should make him an average big-league starter if fate hands him another chance.

Steve Bean C

Born: **9/15/1993** Age: **19**
Bats: **L** Throws: **R** Height: **6' 3"**
Weight: **190** Breakout: **0%**
Improve: **61%** Collapse: **39%**
Attrition: **39%** MLB: **100%**

Comparables:
Robin Yount, Wayne Causey, Ed Kranepool

YEAR	TEAM	LVL	AGE	PA	R	2B	3B	HR	RBI	BB	SO	SB	CS	AVG_OBP_SLG	TAv	BABIP	BRR	FRAA	WARP
2012	CRD	Rk	18	59	8	4	0	0	7	8	11	0	0	.320/.424/.400	.747	.410	0	C(1): -0.0	0.2
2012	JCY	Rk	18	95	6	4	0	1	5	15	32	2	0	.125/.263/.213	.181	.191	0	--	0.0
2013	*SLN*	*MLB*	*19*	*250*	*20*	*8*	*1*	*3*	*19*	*11*	*72*	*6*	*2*	*.186/.226/.265*	*.180*	*.249*	*0.6*	*C -0*	*-1.0*

The organization thinks this supplemental first-rounder from Rockwell, Texas, has the tools to become an above-average receiver both behind the plate and with the bat. As with all teenage catchers, Bean's catch-and-throw skills have a long way to go, but he has the athleticism and agility to learn the position. His bat is an open question, as he's not built like a slugger, and only time will tell whether he'll be able to clear the low offensive bar set for major-league catchers.

Carlos Beltran RF

Born: **4/24/1977** Age: **36**
Bats: **B** Throws: **R** Height: **6' 2"**
Weight: **215** Breakout: **0%**
Improve: **30%** Collapse: **3%**
Attrition: **11%** MLB: **88%**

Comparables:
Gary Sheffield,Lance Berkman,Larry Walker

YEAR	TEAM	LVL	AGE	PA	R	2B	3B	HR	RBI	BB	SO	SB	CS	AVG_OBP_SLG	TAv	BABIP	BRR	FRAA	WARP
2010	SLU	A+	33	57	5	5	0	0	5	7	6	0	0	.367/.446/.469	.318	.419	0.5	CF(10): 0.3	0.5
2010	NYN	MLB	33	255	21	11	3	7	27	30	39	3	1	.255/.341/.427	.280	.275	-2.7	CF(61): -1.3	0.9
2011	NYN	MLB	34	419	61	30	2	15	66	60	61	3	0	.289/.391/.513	.322	.310	-0.4	RF(91): -8.3	2.1
2011	SFN	MLB	34	179	17	9	4	7	18	11	27	1	2	.323/.369/.551	.322	.353	-0.1	RF(43): 0.1	1.2
2012	SLN	MLB	35	619	83	26	1	32	97	65	124	13	6	.269/.346/.495	.298	.291	-0.4	RF(132): -8.7, CF(8): -0.2	1.9
2013	*SLN*	*MLB*	*36*	*577*	*74*	*29*	*3*	*21*	*78*	*63*	*96*	*10*	*3*	*.274/.355/.466*	*.292*	*.299*	*0*	*RF -3, CF 0*	*3.0*

Signed to a reasonable two-year deal as part of the positional cascade to replace Pujols, Beltran took over in right field and put up another All-Star season. His perpetually balky knees have robbed him of the speed that helped make him a young superstar, but the thunder in his bat is still very real—it just takes more focus to bring it out. Beltran spent the year swinging from the heels, offering at more pitches and making less contact than ever before. His walk and strike-out rates are moving in the wrong direction, and pitchers have found they can get him out with off-speed junk out of the zone. Beltran still has the power to be an asset this year, but his declining on-base percentage and diminished range will continue to erode his value as he moves into his late-30s.

Lance Berkman 1B

Born: **2/10/1976** Age: **37**
Bats: **B** Throws: **L** Height: **6' 2"**
Weight: **220** Breakout: **0%**
Improve: **32%** Collapse: **8%**
Attrition: **12%** MLB: **83%**

Comparables:
Rafael Palmeiro,Stan Musial,Edgar Martinez

YEAR	TEAM	LVL	AGE	PA	R	2B	3B	HR	RBI	BB	SO	SB	CS	AVG_OBP_SLG	TAv	BABIP	BRR	FRAA	WARP
2010	HOU	MLB	34	358	39	16	1	13	49	60	70	3	2	.245/.372/.436	.290	.279	-0.5	1B(85): 1.4	1.5
2010	NYA	MLB	34	123	9	7	0	1	9	17	15	0	0	.255/.358/.349	.240	.289	0.4	1B(8): -0.7	-0.2
2011	SLN	MLB	35	587	90	23	2	31	94	92	93	2	6	.301/.412/.547	.341	.315	-1.7	RF(110): -10.0, 1B(21): 0.5	4.0
2012	SLN	MLB	36	97	12	7	1	2	7	14	19	2	0	.259/.381/.444	.296	.317	0	1B(23): -1.2	0.3
2013	*SLN*	*MLB*	*37*	*250*	*33*	*12*	*1*	*10*	*35*	*36*	*45*	*2*	*2*	*.269/.379/.471*	*.301*	*.300*	*-0.5*	*RF -0, 1B 0*	*1.5*

His triumphant 2011 season may have been the last loud encore of the Fat Elvis show, as Berkman's legs gave out from under him last season and limited him to 32 games. During his ever-diminishing periods of health he can likely still help out at the plate, with enough patience and power—especially from the left side—to hold down first base or a DH spot. The questions are whether his body will let him stay in the lineup long enough to produce, and whether Berkman wants to put himself through another season-long grind. Whichever team ultimately signs him to a short-term deal could be rewarded with another late-career hit, but each year that passes lengthens those odds.

Matt Carpenter UT

Born: **11/26/1985** Age: **27**
Bats: **L** Throws: **R** Height: **6' 4"**
Weight: **200** Breakout: **2%**
Improve: **47%** Collapse: **4%**
Attrition: **6%** MLB: **94%**

Comparables:
Dan Johnson,Mike Jorgensen,Alvin Davis

YEAR	TEAM	LVL	AGE	PA	R	2B	3B	HR	RBI	BB	SO	SB	CS	AVG_OBP_SLG	TAv	BABIP	BRR	FRAA	WARP
2010	PMB	A+	24	128	17	5	2	1	16	26	14	0	1	.283/.438/.404	.313	.318	-0.8	3B(28): 0.8	0.8
2010	SFD	AA	24	472	76	26	3	12	53	64	88	11	2	.316/.412/.487	.307	.377	3.2	3B(109): 14.7	6.2
2011	MEM	AAA	25	535	61	29	3	12	70	84	68	5	4	.300/.417/.463	.314	.328	0	--	0.0
2011	SLN	MLB	25	19	0	1	0	0	0	4	4	0	0	.067/.263/.133	.156	.091	-0.2	3B(5): 0.2	-0.2
2012	SLN	MLB	26	340	44	22	5	6	46	34	63	1	1	.294/.365/.463	.293	.346	-0.9	1B(44): -1.2, 3B(33): -0.9	0.8
2013	*SLN*	*MLB*	*27*	*259*	*27*	*13*	*2*	*5*	*29*	*28*	*51*	*1*	*1*	*.262/.346/.403*	*.269*	*.313*	*-0.2*	*3B 1, 1B -0*	*0.8*

After earning a spot on the big club during spring training, Carpenter spent the year as Mike Matheny's most valuable human multi-tool. Berkman and Craig laid up at the same time? Plug Carpenter in at first. Freese hurt again? Carpenter's a capable third baseman. Tired of that unsightly offensive hole at second base? Call the Carpenter! He always hit in the minors, but last year Carpenter proved his patience and line-drive stroke can play on the largest of stages. The Cardinals had him working out at second base over the winter so he can provide insurance at five positions, and with injury risks in each corner and no clear answer at the keystone, he should get plenty of action again this year. His on-base percentage last year was 85 points higher against right-handed pitching, so Carpenter may someday perfectly perform another function: platoon partner.

Adron Chambers CF

Born: **10/8/1986** Age: **26**
Bats: **L** Throws: **L** Height: **5' 11"**
Weight: **185** Breakout: **2%**
Improve: **62%** Collapse: **5%**
Attrition: **25%** MLB: **95%**

Comparables:
Jason McDonald,Rick Miller,Jeff Salazar

YEAR	TEAM	LVL	AGE	PA	R	2B	3B	HR	RBI	BB	SO	SB	CS	AVG_OBP_SLG	TAv	BABIP	BRR	FRAA	WARP
2010	SFD	AA	23	292	52	9	5	5	27	31	50	8	4	.282/.373/.417	.274	.332	4.5	CF(46): -4.6, LF(19): 0.3	1.6
2010	MEM	AAA	23	83	11	0	1	1	8	9	18	6	1	.290/.390/.362	.279	.373	0.9	LF(16): -0.1, CF(4): 0.1	0.4
2011	MEM	AAA	24	501	73	19	5	10	44	53	90	22	13	.277/.368/.415	.279	.328	0	--	0.0
2011	SLN	MLB	24	8	2	0	1	0	4	0	1	0	0	.375/.375/.625	.349	.429	-0.1	LF(6): -0.0, CF(5): 0.1	0.1
2012	MEM	AAA	25	419	60	17	2	3	44	51	80	13	4	.319/.405/.403	.317	.398	5.6	CF(16): 2.3	1.3
2012	SLN	MLB	25	62	4	0	2	0	4	5	18	2	1	.222/.300/.296	.220	.333	-0.2	CF(10): -0.3, LF(9): 0.3	-0.2
2013	*SLN*	*MLB*	*26*	*250*	*28*	*9*	*2*	*2*	*19*	*22*	*57*	*5*	*2*	*.246/.321/.337*	*.240*	*.314*	*0.4*	*CF -1, LF -0*	*0.1*

The speedy Chambers continues to get on base at an impressive rate in the high minors, and for the second year in a row the Cardinals chose to add his legs and glove to their postseason roster. The former Mississippi State defensive back has worked hard to smooth out his game and take better advantage of his speed, making fewer outs on the bases and taking better routes in center field. With a lefty bat, gap power, and a solid approach, Chambers looks to be a solid fourth outfielder, but with so much talent already on the field in St. Louis and in the pipeline behind him, he's unlikely to play every day.

Allen Craig 1B
Born: **7/18/1984** Age: **28**
Bats: **R** Throws: **R** Height: **6' 3"**
Weight: **210** Breakout: **2%**
Improve: **48%** Collapse: **3%**
Attrition: **17%** MLB: **93%**

Comparables:
Kendrys Morales, Mike Jacobs, Jake Fox

YEAR	TEAM	LVL	AGE	PA	R	2B	3B	HR	RBI	BB	SO	SB	CS	AVG_OBP_SLG	TAv	BABIP	BRR	FRAA	WARP
2010	MEM	AAA	25	350	57	24	2	14	81	34	59	1	0	.320/.395/.549	.315	.361	-1.2	LF(50): 0.5, 1B(33): 0.0	2.5
2010	SLN	MLB	25	124	12	7	0	4	18	9	26	0	1	.246/.298/.412	.260	.282	-0.7	RF(30): -1.2, LF(5): 0.1	0.1
2011	SLN	MLB	26	219	33	15	0	11	40	15	40	5	0	.315/.362/.555	.320	.344	1.6	LF(26): -0.5, RF(18): 0.5	2.0
2012	SLN	MLB	27	514	76	35	0	22	92	37	89	2	1	.307/.354/.522	.308	.334	-4	1B(90): -7.6, RF(23): -0.5	1.2
2013	*SLN*	*MLB*	*28*	*428*	*53*	*25*	*1*	*18*	*62*	*30*	*82*	*2*	*1*	*.284/.336/.490*	*.291*	*.315*	*-0.5*	*1B -3, RF -0*	*1.6*

Craig entered last season sporting both a World Series ring, earned in large part through his 2011 postseason heroics, and a limp, courtesy of offseason knee surgery. Once he got back on the field, he picked up where he left off at the plate, settled in at first base, and nearly had Cardinals fans asking themselves, "Albert who?" He put up slash stats that surpassed the Archangel Pujols, and posted a TAv in the same neighborhood. He can't afford to *live* in the same neighborhood, and that's exactly the point—Craig can provide reasonably similar offensive production for a few years despite a paycheck that's two digits shorter, allowing the Cardinals to address other issues with the savings. He makes more contact and draws fewer walks than your typical slugger, is adequate at best in the field, and has already reached his peak, so the only way Craig will improve is to finally stay healthy for a full season.

Tony Cruz C
Born: **8/18/1986** Age: **26**
Bats: **R** Throws: **R** Height: **6' 0"**
Weight: **205** Breakout: **8%**
Improve: **34%** Collapse: **8%**
Attrition: **20%** MLB: **96%**

Comparables:
Mike Lieberthal, Jonathan Lucroy, Hal Smith

YEAR	TEAM	LVL	AGE	PA	R	2B	3B	HR	RBI	BB	SO	SB	CS	AVG_OBP_SLG	TAv	BABIP	BRR	FRAA	WARP
2010	PMB	A+	23	202	21	16	1	1	25	19	33	0	2	.282/.348/.398	.263	.338	-2.5	C(43): 0.8	0.9
2010	SFD	AA	23	169	26	10	0	6	20	17	30	0	0	.289/.363/.477	.280	.325	-1.4	C(30): -0.0, 3B(2): 0.1	1.2
2011	MEM	AAA	24	164	13	5	1	4	25	11	31	0	1	.262/.315/.389	.246	.304	0	--	0.0
2011	SLN	MLB	24	72	8	5	0	0	6	6	13	0	1	.262/.333/.338	.253	.327	0	C(20): 0.0, 3B(3): 0.0	0.1
2012	SLN	MLB	25	131	11	9	1	1	11	3	19	0	1	.254/.267/.365	.222	.287	-0.8	C(46): 0.4, 1B(2): 0.0	-0.1
2013	*SLN*	*MLB*	*26*	*250*	*22*	*14*	*1*	*4*	*25*	*15*	*46*	*1*	*1*	*.249/.295/.365*	*.239*	*.292*	*-0.5*	*C 0, 3B -0*	*0.5*

Did you know that St. Louis actually had two catchers on their roster last summer? It's true! A full 28 times last year you may have tuned into the first inning of a Cardinals game and caught a glimpse of Cruz, the young, strong-armed converted third baseman who finally convinced the organization to stop ordering out for the Gerald Lairds of the world and try one of their own. Cruz has limited power and doesn't draw many walks, but did we mention he has a strong arm? When it comes to backup backstops, that's long been music to the organization's ears.

Daniel Descalso MI
Born: **10/19/1986** Age: **26**
Bats: **L** Throws: **R** Height: **5' 11"**
Weight: **190** Breakout: **4%**
Improve: **44%** Collapse: **1%**
Attrition: **12%** MLB: **87%**

Comparables:
Edgardo Alfonzo, Pete Rose, Kevin Russo

YEAR	TEAM	LVL	AGE	PA	R	2B	3B	HR	RBI	BB	SO	SB	CS	AVG_OBP_SLG	TAv	BABIP	BRR	FRAA	WARP
2010	MEM	AAA	23	531	86	32	3	9	71	47	48	8	4	.282/.350/.421	.273	.296	5	2B(116): -0.6, 1B(6): -0.6	2.3
2010	SLN	MLB	23	37	6	2	0	0	4	2	6	1	0	.265/.324/.324	.271	.321	0.7	3B(9): 0.1, SS(1): 0.0	0.2
2011	SLN	MLB	24	375	35	20	3	1	28	33	65	2	2	.264/.334/.353	.262	.323	-0.3	3B(117): -8.9, 2B(18): 0.5	0.1
2012	SLN	MLB	25	426	41	10	7	4	26	37	83	6	3	.227/.303/.324	.240	.279	4.7	2B(94): 3.8, SS(26): 1.7	0.7
2013	*SLN*	*MLB*	*26*	*390*	*38*	*17*	*3*	*4*	*34*	*31*	*68*	*4*	*2*	*.248/.313/.352*	*.245*	*.289*	*-0.1*	*2B 0, 3B -0*	*0.7*

Despite his abysmal year at the plate, Descalso was the best thing in the store for the Cardinals at second base last September, and the club reaped the benefit of his steady glove and timely hitting down the stretch and in the postseason. His numbers suffered from an abnormally low BABIP last year, but even at his best Descalso is a max-effort grinder with gap power and only moderate on-base skills. He can play a reasonable shortstop and fill in anywhere around the infield, meaning he's ideally suited for a utility role—a position he'll assume either immediately or at the dawning of the Kolten Wong Era.

David Freese **3B**
Born: **4/28/1983** Age: **30**
Bats: **R** Throws: **R** Height: **6' 3"**
Weight: **220** Breakout: **2%**
Improve: **40%** Collapse: **3%**
Attrition: **12%** MLB: **91%**
Comparables:
Ty Wigginton,Scott Rolen,Jeff Baker

YEAR	TEAM	LVL	AGE	PA	R	2B	3B	HR	RBI	BB	SO	SB	CS	AVG_OBP_SLG	TAv	BABIP	BRR	FRAA	WARP
2010	SLN	MLB	27	270	28	12	1	4	36	21	59	1	1	.296/.361/.404	.276	.376	1.6	3B(66): 1.4, 1B(1): 0.0	1.5
2011	SLN	MLB	28	363	41	16	1	10	55	24	75	1	0	.297/.350/.441	.276	.356	-3.3	3B(88): 0.3, 1B(5): -0.1	1.1
2012	SLN	MLB	29	567	70	25	1	20	79	57	122	3	3	.293/.372/.467	.290	.352	-3.4	3B(134): 1.1	2.5
2013	*SLN*	*MLB*	*30*	*492*	*57*	*22*	*1*	*16*	*63*	*40*	*110*	*2*	*1*	*.278/.344/.440*	*.280*	*.335*	*-0.8*	*3B 3, 1B -0*	*2.5*

So *that's* what happens when Freese stays (mostly) healthy for a full season. The 2011 World Series MVP avoided the DL despite a variety of nagging ailments and spent last year punishing National League pitching. More a hitter than a slugger, Freese maintains a high batting average by stinging copious hard grounders and line drives around the park, and when he does loft one it tends to leave the yard—his rate of 20 percent home runs per fly ball last year was among the circuit's highest. That's not likely to continue, but if he can continue to draw walks and play a capable third base, he'll provide great production. As pleasant as all that is, Freese is 30 and seems to have ankle ligaments made of spun sugar, so as he grows more expensive the Cardinals should already be planning their exit strategy.

Rafael Furcal **SS**
Born: **10/24/1977** Age: **35**
Bats: **B** Throws: **R** Height: **5' 9"**
Weight: **190** Breakout: **0%**
Improve: **34%** Collapse: **4%**
Attrition: **11%** MLB: **86%**
Comparables:
Cal Ripken Jr.,Jerry Hairston,Marco Scutaro

YEAR	TEAM	LVL	AGE	PA	R	2B	3B	HR	RBI	BB	SO	SB	CS	AVG_OBP_SLG	TAv	BABIP	BRR	FRAA	WARP
2010	LAN	MLB	32	428	66	23	7	8	43	40	60	22	4	.300/.366/.460	.303	.338	3.2	SS(93): 7.1	4.5
2011	LAN	MLB	33	152	15	4	0	1	12	11	21	5	3	.197/.272/.248	.217	.226	0.4	SS(36): 0.6	-0.3
2011	SLN	MLB	33	217	29	11	0	7	16	17	18	4	2	.255/.316/.418	.265	.250	2	SS(49): 2.6	1.4
2012	SLN	MLB	34	531	69	18	3	5	49	44	57	12	4	.264/.325/.346	.247	.289	4.1	SS(120): -1.1	1.6
2013	*SLN*	*MLB*	*35*	*467*	*57*	*20*	*3*	*8*	*41*	*39*	*60*	*13*	*4*	*.267/.329/.385*	*.260*	*.291*	*0.6*	*SS 4*	*2.6*

Furcal's season ended in late August due to an elbow injury, though there's hope the aging shortstop will be ready this spring to play out the second year of his contract. But which Furcal will show up? The All-Star who posted a .333/.391/.460 line through the end of May, or the lineup sinkhole who hit .215/.278/.265 thereafter? The steady veteran gloveman who anchored the infield defense all summer, or the oft-injured clubhouse spectator? The Cardinals have 7 million reasons to hope for the former, but with Furcal now one year older, slower, and more fragile, the odds aren't favorable.

Matt Holliday **LF**
Born: **1/15/1980** Age: **33**
Bats: **R** Throws: **R** Height: **6' 5"**
Weight: **235** Breakout: **2%**
Improve: **32%** Collapse: **5%**
Attrition: **10%** MLB: **95%**
Comparables:
Stan Musial,Josh Willingham,Milton Bradley

YEAR	TEAM	LVL	AGE	PA	R	2B	3B	HR	RBI	BB	SO	SB	CS	AVG_OBP_SLG	TAv	BABIP	BRR	FRAA	WARP
2010	SLN	MLB	30	675	95	45	1	28	103	69	93	9	5	.312/.390/.532	.323	.331	-0.7	LF(155): -2.5	5.5
2011	SLN	MLB	31	516	83	36	0	22	75	60	93	2	1	.296/.388/.525	.315	.330	0	LF(115): -8.1	2.4
2012	SLN	MLB	32	688	95	36	2	27	102	75	132	4	4	.295/.379/.497	.310	.337	0.9	LF(152): -12.5	3.1
2013	*SLN*	*MLB*	*33*	*612*	*81*	*34*	*1*	*24*	*87*	*63*	*109*	*7*	*3*	*.292/.373/.492*	*.307*	*.327*	*-0.9*	*LF -6*	*3.7*

Holliday is perhaps baseball's most overlooked superstar. His production and durability have long been nearly as wonderful and uncelebrated as fresh air and indoor plumbing. Each year since 2006, Big Daddy has stayed healthy enough to reach 500 plate appearances, and productive enough to post a superlative TAv of .299 or greater. The only other players who can match that record are Pujols and Miguel Cabrera; only Joe Mauer and David Wright have managed even five such seasons during that span. Nearly halfway through what was once considered a massive seven-year contract, Holliday's $17 million salary now seems almost a bargain. At 33, Holliday's injury reports annually contain the words "stiffness," "tightness," and "soreness" with greater frequency, but the big left fielder rarely misses more than a game or two at a stretch. His defense slumped somewhat last year, which could presage some age-related range diminishment, but his bat remains as loud and fresh as a spring thunderstorm. PECOTA lets out a figurate yawn while predicting more .300 TAv seasons in his future, and Holliday is as good a bet as any to deliver.

Ryan Jackson **SS**
Born: **5/10/1988** Age: **25**
Bats: **R** Throws: **R** Height: **6' 4"**
Weight: **180** Breakout: **7%**
Improve: **42%** Collapse: **10%**
Attrition: **27%** MLB: **92%**
Comparables:
Rich Aurilia,Ernest Riles,Chico Carrasquel

YEAR	TEAM	LVL	AGE	PA	R	2B	3B	HR	RBI	BB	SO	SB	CS	AVG_OBP_SLG	TAv	BABIP	BRR	FRAA	WARP
2010	QUD	A	22	355	47	13	2	2	27	48	63	6	7	.272/.371/.348	.267	.338	-1.7	SS(83): 4.4	2.1
2010	PMB	A+	22	167	14	10	1	1	8	11	21	3	2	.291/.331/.392	.259	.318	-0.5	SS(40): 5.8	0.8
2010	PMB	A+	22	167	14	10	1	1	8	11	21	3	2	.291/.331/.392	.259	.318	-0.5	SS(1): -0.1	0.8
2011	SFD	AA	23	599	65	34	3	11	73	44	91	2	0	.278/.334/.415	.261	.314	0	--	0.0
2012	MEM	AAA	24	503	60	23	1	10	47	43	75	2	0	.272/.334/.396	.305	.306	1.6	SS(29): 3.5, 2B(2): -0.0	1.3
2012	SLN	MLB	24	18	2	0	0	0	0	1	3	0	0	.118/.167/.118	.073	.143	0.4	2B(7): 0.3	-0.3
2013	*SLN*	*MLB*	*25*	*250*	*25*	*9*	*1*	*3*	*20*	*17*	*48*	*1*	*0*	*.235/.289/.327*	*.224*	*.278*	*-0.4*	*SS 3, 2B 0*	*0.4*

While fans may have fallen in love with the hit summer replacement show *How I Met Pete Kozma*, there are those who think Jackson is a better long-term bet. Defense has long been his calling card, as Jackson makes up for subpar foot speed with quickness, great instincts, and a strong arm. At the plate he has the size and swing to support double-digit home runs, but he struggles against same-side pitching and doesn't draw enough walks to hit at the top of the order. He's not a star in the making, but Jackson could be a fine stopgap at shortstop or second base, and should at least earn a living as a utility player.

Jon Jay **CF**

Born: **3/15/1985** Age: **28**
Bats: **L** Throws: **L** Height: **6' 0"**
Weight: **200** Breakout: **0%**
Improve: **49%** Collapse: **1%**
Attrition: **2%** MLB: **94%**

Comparables:
Shane Victorino,Angel Pagan,Jacoby Ellsbury

YEAR	TEAM	LVL	AGE	PA	R	2B	3B	HR	RBI	BB	SO	SB	CS	AVG_OBP_SLG	TAv	BABIP	BRR	FRAA	WARP
2010	MEM	AAA	25	191	31	16	0	4	32	17	22	13	0	.321/.392/.491	.296	.345	4.2	LF(30): 3.4, CF(11): 0.1	2.0
2010	SLN	MLB	25	323	47	19	2	4	27	24	50	2	4	.300/.359/.422	.283	.350	1.3	RF(61): -4.3, CF(27): 1.7	1.5
2011	SLN	MLB	26	503	56	24	2	10	37	28	81	6	7	.297/.344/.424	.271	.340	0.3	CF(74): 1.8, RF(55): 2.8	1.5
2012	SLN	MLB	27	502	70	22	4	4	40	34	71	19	7	.305/.373/.400	.286	.355	-0.5	CF(116): 9.4	3.2
2013	*SLN*	*MLB*	*28*	*473*	*59*	*23*	*2*	*8*	*44*	*30*	*75*	*12*	*5*	*.287/.344/.411*	*.269*	*.324*	*-0.1*	*CF 0, RF 0*	*1.9*

Quick: who led the Cardinals in WARP last year? Yeah, okay, it was the indestructible catcher with the groovy neck tattoos, but who would have expected Jay to outpace Holliday, Beltran, Craig, and Freese for second place? Sometimes dismissed as a tweener lacking the range for center field or the bat for a corner, Jay has transformed himself into a dynamic center fielder whose bat could play elsewhere. Jay will never have more than gap power, and his on-base percentage was boosted by an unsustainable 15 plunkings, but even with some regression at the plate, his terrific glove makes him an above-average player. Jay won't be eligible for arbitration until after this season, so St. Louis should get his peak years at a discount.

Carson Kelly **3B**

Born: **7/14/1994** Age: **18**
Bats: **R** Throws: **R** Height: **6' 3"**
Weight: **200** Breakout: **0%**
Improve: **44%** Collapse: **56%**
Attrition: **56%** MLB: **100%**

Comparables:
Robin Yount,Wayne Causey,Wayne Causey

YEAR	TEAM	LVL	AGE	PA	R	2B	3B	HR	RBI	BB	SO	SB	CS	AVG_OBP_SLG	TAv	BABIP	BRR	FRAA	WARP
2012	JCY	Rk	17	225	24	10	0	9	25	10	33	0	0	.225/.263/.399	.228	.228	-0.8	3B(35): -6.3	-0.6
2013	*SLN*	*MLB*	*18*	*250*	*19*	*9*	*1*	*6*	*25*	*6*	*63*	*1*	*0*	*.193/.213/.311*	*.188*	*.230*	*-0.3*	*3B -0*	*-1.4*

The Cardinals signed Kelly away from a college commitment last summer based on their belief in his power potential, and the young third baseman displayed a home-run stroke during his rookie-league debut. A native of the Pacific Northwest, Kelly has less experience than most recent draftees since, as any teenage fiction fan knows, games can only be scheduled there during thunderstorms. He struggled with pitch recognition and had difficulty making contact, but the organization believes that will come with time. He doesn't profile as a plus defender despite a strong arm, but if his hit tool can develop he might have enough thump to be an above-average bat at the hot corner.

Pete Kozma **SS**

Born: **4/11/1988** Age: **25**
Bats: **R** Throws: **R** Height: **6' 1"**
Weight: **170** Breakout: **1%**
Improve: **35%** Collapse: **11%**
Attrition: **22%** MLB: **95%**

Comparables:
Bernie Allen,Larry Brown,Ruben Gotay

YEAR	TEAM	LVL	AGE	PA	R	2B	3B	HR	RBI	BB	SO	SB	CS	AVG_OBP_SLG	TAv	BABIP	BRR	FRAA	WARP
2010	SFD	AA	22	570	69	28	2	13	72	56	111	13	2	.243/.316/.384	.245	.282	-0.1	SS(136): 16.1	3.1
2011	MEM	AAA	23	448	48	17	2	3	47	36	91	2	2	.214/.280/.289	.206	.265	0	--	0.0
2011	SLN	MLB	23	22	2	1	0	0	1	4	4	0	0	.176/.333/.235	.211	.231	-0.4	2B(10): 0.0, SS(3): -0.3	-0.1
2012	MEM	AAA	24	500	61	16	3	11	63	41	74	7	4	.232/.292/.355	.212	.251	4.5	2B(21): -1.1, SS(8): -0.4	0.1
2012	SLN	MLB	24	82	11	5	3	2	14	7	19	2	0	.333/.383/.569	.326	.415	1.1	SS(25): 0.5, 2B(1): -0.0	1.2
2013	*SLN*	*MLB*	*25*	*250*	*24*	*10*	*2*	*5*	*24*	*18*	*52*	*3*	*1*	*.229/.284/.349*	*.229*	*.270*	*0.1*	*SS 1, 2B -0*	*0.4*

Buying lottery tickets is a fool's errand, unless you happen to be the fool who buys the winner. When Furcal's injury left them short at shortstop down the stretch, the desperate Cardinals threw up their hands, ran to the liquor store, and bought a fistful of Kozma scratch-offs. To everyone's surprise, the perennially disappointing former top pick spent the month mashing extra-base hits all over the National League and taking part in a number of memorable postseason scenes. Kozma is a true shortstop and has more pop than your normal middle infielder, but his .223/.286/.324 career Triple-A line speaks far more eloquently about his offensive potential than those six magical weeks last summer.

Jake Lemmerman **SS**

Born: **5/4/1989** Age: **24**
Bats: **R** Throws: **R** Height: **6' 2"**
Weight: **192** Breakout: **3%**
Improve: **42%** Collapse: **11%**
Attrition: **32%** MLB: **95%**

Comparables:
Ricky Gutierrez,Denis Menke,Denis Menke

YEAR	TEAM	LVL	AGE	PA	R	2B	3B	HR	RBI	BB	SO	SB	CS	AVG_OBP_SLG	TAv	BABIP	BRR	FRAA	WARP
2010	OGD	Rk	21	303	69	24	2	12	47	31	56	5	4	.363/.441/.610	.350	.427	-2.1	SS(69): -9.0	3.3
2011	RCU	A+	22	469	71	23	2	8	54	47	90	9	3	.292/.379/.420	.286	.355	0	--	0.0
2011	CHT	AA	22	93	11	6	0	2	11	8	22	1	0	.234/.318/.390	.248	.296	0	--	0.0
2012	CHT	AA	23	449	52	29	2	7	46	53	94	8	0	.233/.347/.378	.213	.292	2.4	SS(26): 3.1, 2B(11): 0.5	0.4
2013	*SLN*	*MLB*	*24*	*250*	*23*	*11*	*1*	*5*	*25*	*19*	*64*	*1*	*0*	*.220/.290/.341*	*.231*	*.278*	*-0.4*	*SS -0, 2B 0*	*0.3*

A star shortstop at Duke who was chosen in the fifth round in 2010, Lemmerman finally hit a snag last year after progressing quickly through the Dodgers system. Already strikeout prone for a player with only gap power, his batting average suffered as his BABIP plummeted, and he showed a drastic home-road split. Lemmerman is a gritty, grindy, max-effort type with outstanding fundamentals. He has a compact swing and a good approach at the plate, but his speed and power are below average, and both his arm and his limited range suggest he'll find a home at second base rather than shortstop. The Cardinals, who traded Skip Schumaker for him, have long-term questions at both positions, and Lemmerman will likely compete with Kozma and Jackson for a future utility role.

Yadier Molina **C**

Born: **7/13/1982** Age: **30**
Bats: **R** Throws: **R** Height: **6' 0"**
Weight: **230** Breakout: **0%**
Improve: **32%** Collapse: **6%**
Attrition: **5%** MLB: **96%**

Comparables:
Carlos Ruiz,Tim McCarver,Paul Lo Duca

YEAR	TEAM	LVL	AGE	PA	R	2B	3B	HR	RBI	BB	SO	SB	CS	AVG_OBP_SLG	TAv	BABIP	BRR	FRAA	WARP
2010	SLN	MLB	27	521	34	19	0	6	62	42	51	8	4	.262/.329/.342	.244	.281	-3.8	C(135): 1.4, 1B(7): -0.0	1.8
2011	SLN	MLB	28	518	55	32	1	14	65	33	44	4	5	.305/.349/.465	.283	.311	-4.8	C(136): -0.0, 1B(2): -0.0	2.4
2012	SLN	MLB	29	563	65	28	0	22	76	45	55	12	3	.315/.373/.501	.315	.316	-4.8	C(136): 2.1, 1B(3): 0.1	5.8
2013	*SLN*	*MLB*	*30*	*520*	*59*	*24*	*1*	*12*	*60*	*38*	*50*	*8*	*3*	*.289/.345/.421*	*.274*	*.298*	*-0.7*	*C 1, 1B 0*	*3.2*

The Cardinals rewarded Molina with a long-term deal before last season, and the durable catcher repaid them with a year that not only earned him his fifth Gold Glove, but placed him firmly in the MVP conversation. Molina has no peers behind the dish—he throws his body in front of 58-foot sliders, makes even the best base-stealers think thrice before challenging his lightning arm, and gives confidence to a Cardinals pitching staff whose production always exceeds its talent—but it's been the development of his power bat that's made him a superstar. Molina built on his 2011 offensive breakout by hitting for more power while still making plenty of contact, and he seems to have brought his game to a new level. Even if some of those fly balls start dying at the track, Molina's durability, leadership, and offensive prowess at a defensive position make him as valuable a commodity as you'll find in baseball.

Stephen Piscotty **3B**

Born: **1/14/1991** Age: **22**
Bats: **R** Throws: **R** Height: **6' 4"**
Weight: **185** Breakout: **5%**
Improve: **57%** Collapse: **3%**
Attrition: **10%** MLB: **98%**

Comparables:
Dan Driessen,Matt Dominguez,Glenn Hoffman

YEAR	TEAM	LVL	AGE	PA	R	2B	3B	HR	RBI	BB	SO	SB	CS	AVG_OBP_SLG	TAv	BABIP	BRR	FRAA	WARP
2012	QUD	A	21	237	29	18	1	4	27	18	25	3	0	.295/.376/.448	.359	.320	0.5	3B(3): 0.3	0.2
2013	*SLN*	*MLB*	*22*	*250*	*22*	*11*	*1*	*5*	*25*	*12*	*49*	*1*	*0*	*.234/.281/.349*	*.228*	*.274*	*-0.3*	*3B 0*	*-0.3*

A former Stanford star, Piscotty spent his first pro summer in the Midwest League, showing off the advanced approach and gap power that made him a supplemental first-round pick. No one doubts he will hit, but there's some question as to whether he'll develop the home-run pop hoped for from a top-flight corner man, and whether he has the athleticism and hands to stick at third base. If he has to move down the defensive spectrum he could wind up in right field, where his strong arm would be an asset but the offensive bar is even higher. If he can stick at third—something the Cardinals will give him every opportunity to do—and starts launching a few over the fence he could become a first-division starter, but those are some big ifs.

James Ramsey **CF**

Born: **12/19/1989** Age: **23**
Bats: **L** Throws: **R** Height: **6' 1"**
Weight: **190** Breakout: **6%**
Improve: **47%** Collapse: **8%**
Attrition: **13%** MLB: **91%**

Comparables:
Sil Campusano,Milt Cuyler,Dave Martinez

YEAR	TEAM	LVL	AGE	PA	R	2B	3B	HR	RBI	BB	SO	SB	CS	AVG_OBP_SLG	TAv	BABIP	BRR	FRAA	WARP
2012	PMB	A+	22	247	36	9	3	1	14	33	59	10	2	.229/.333/.314	.235	.309	2.8	CF(10): 0.3	0.7
2013	*SLN*	*MLB*	*23*	*250*	*22*	*9*	*1*	*3*	*21*	*21*	*70*	*4*	*1*	*.207/.278/.299*	*.215*	*.281*	*0.3*	*CF -0*	*-0.4*

The speedy Ramsey, taken in the first round out of Florida State, has solid all-around skills and excellent makeup, but isn't a breathtaking talent. The Cardinals challenged him with an assignment to High-A and Ramsey struggled at the plate, but showed off the defensive chops that make him a true center fielder. At his best, Ramsey works the count, waits for a pitch he can handle, and lashes it into the gap, making the most of his speed. Much like the offices of LesterCorp, Ramsey has a low ceiling and a high floor, meaning it's likely he'll turn into a fourth outfielder, but unlikely he'll be much more.

Shane Robinson **OF**

Born: **10/30/1984** Age: **28**
Bats: **R** Throws: **R** Height: **5' 10"**
Weight: **160** Breakout: **2%**
Improve: **41%** Collapse: **2%**
Attrition: **7%** MLB: **93%**

Comparables:
Dave Gallagher,Rajai Davis,Ryan Freel

YEAR	TEAM	LVL	AGE	PA	R	2B	3B	HR	RBI	BB	SO	SB	CS	AVG_OBP_SLG	TAv	BABIP	BRR	FRAA	WARP
2010	MEM	AAA	25	97	9	5	0	2	13	7	13	3	3	.279/.323/.407	.242	.297	-0.2	CF(26): 0.1	0.0
2011	MEM	AAA	26	193	35	8	3	4	23	19	16	9	1	.299/.366/.455	.287	.305	0	--	0.0
2011	SLN	MLB	26	8	0	0	0	0	0	1	2	0	0	.000/.125/.000	.027	.000	0	CF(5): -0.2, RF(3): 0.0	-0.2
2012	MEM	AAA	27	80	15	4	2	0	3	8	15	5	0	.300/.387/.414	.367	.382	0.8	CF(2): 0.3, RF(1): -0.1	0.2
2012	SLN	MLB	27	181	20	8	0	3	16	14	32	1	0	.253/.309/.355	.248	.295	1.1	CF(37): -2.1, LF(15): 0.3	0.2
2013	*SLN*	*MLB*	*28*	*250*	*26*	*11*	*1*	*4*	*23*	*17*	*41*	*5*	*1*	*.245/.301/.358*	*.243*	*.278*	*0.4*	*CF -0, RF -0*	*0.3*

Robinson is your standard-issue backup outfielder, the kind of player often described as "fundamentally sound" to hide the fact he's more solid than exceptional in the field, and sub-par at the plate. He draws a few walks and slaps a few singles, but has little power. Given that he has both a lower ceiling and a more yellowed birth certificate than Adron Chambers, Robinson will likely be spending another year in Memphis.

Oscar Taveras OF

Born: **6/19/1992** Age: **21**
Bats: **L** Throws: **L** Height: **6' 3"**
Weight: **180** Breakout: **4%**
Improve: **64%** Collapse: **6%**
Attrition: **17%** MLB: **99%**

Comparables:
Vada Pinson,Adam Jones,Ken Griffey

YEAR	TEAM	LVL	AGE	PA	R	2B	3B	HR	RBI	BB	SO	SB	CS	AVG_OBP_SLG	TAv	BABIP	BRR	FRAA	WARP
2010	JCY	Rk	18	229	39	13	3	8	43	12	41	8	5	.322/.367/.526	.323	.370	0.4	CF(29): 1.0, LF(22): 0.6	2.3
2011	QUD	A	19	347	52	27	5	8	62	32	52	1	4	.386/.444/.584	.354	.440	0	--	0.0
2012	SFD	AA	20	531	83	37	7	23	94	42	56	10	1	.321/.380/.572	.341	.323	-2.7	CF(38): 0.8, RF(7): 0.2	2.2
2013	*SLN*	*MLB*	*21*	*250*	*26*	*12*	*2*	*8*	*31*	*13*	*43*	*1*	*0*	*.264/.305/.433*	*.263*	*.290*	*-0.1*	*CF -2, RF 0*	*0.6*

How do you know when a prospect is special? When said prospect starts his first Double-A season as a teenager and ends it as the circuit's MVP, that's how. Taveras is a unique hitting talent, with an innate ability to square up virtually any pitch he can reach. Texas League hurlers tried to stay away from him, but Taveras quickly caught on to their tricks and refused to get himself out; such in-season adjustments against advanced pitching speaks volumes about the young outfielder's future. Taveras is a little stretched in center field, but swings a big enough stick for right, where he could be a .300 hitter with 30 home runs at his peak. The Cardinals are already well-stocked in the outfield, but Taveras should be ready to step in when Beltran's contract expires at year's end, if not before.

Ty Wigginton 4C

Born: **10/11/1977** Age: **35**
Bats: **R** Throws: **R** Height: **6' 1"**
Weight: **230** Breakout: **0%**
Improve: **26%** Collapse: **4%**
Attrition: **26%** MLB: **90%**

Comparables:
Tino Martinez,Julio Franco,David Segui

YEAR	TEAM	LVL	AGE	PA	R	2B	3B	HR	RBI	BB	SO	SB	CS	AVG_OBP_SLG	TAv	BABIP	BRR	FRAA	WARP
2010	BAL	MLB	32	649	63	29	1	22	76	50	116	0	1	.248/.312/.415	.257	.270	-2	1B(97): 2.4, 2B(40): 0.2	1.1
2011	COL	MLB	33	446	52	21	2	15	47	38	84	8	1	.242/.315/.416	.249	.271	0.9	3B(68): -5.9, 1B(36): -1.2	-1.2
2012	PHI	MLB	34	360	40	11	0	11	43	37	81	1	0	.235/.314/.375	.264	.275	-3.2	1B(71): -2.3, 3B(22): -1.3	-0.3
2013	*SLN*	*MLB*	*35*	*356*	*38*	*14*	*1*	*11*	*42*	*26*	*68*	*2*	*1*	*.242/.304/.388*	*.251*	*.273*	*-0.5*	*1B -0, 3B -1*	*0.2*

Wigginton spent last year in Philadelphia as a platoon corner infielder and bench bat, with uninspiring results. Long known for his versatility in the field and ability to mash left-handed pitchers, Wiggy managed to launch double-digit home runs for the ninth time in the last 10 seasons but that's become the extent of his value. He's a liability in the field anywhere but first base, and his productivity against lefties has slowly declined from valuable to serviceable to sub-ho-hum. The Cardinals signed him to a two-year deal as a veteran bench bat, which seems an odd choice given their enviable depth at the corners, but you never know—a few timely late-season hits might just make those millions money well spent.

Patrick Wisdom 3B

Born: **8/27/1991** Age: **21**
Bats: **R** Throws: **R** Height: **6' 3"**
Weight: **210** Breakout: **3%**
Improve: **51%** Collapse: **9%**
Attrition: **24%** MLB: **96%**

Comparables:
Bob Bailey,Kevin Bell,Aramis Ramirez

YEAR	TEAM	LVL	AGE	PA	R	2B	3B	HR	RBI	BB	SO	SB	CS	AVG_OBP_SLG	TAv	BABIP	BRR	FRAA	WARP
2012	BAT	A-	20	279	40	16	5	6	32	31	58	2	1	.282/.373/.465	.330	.346	-0.1	3B(12): -1.1	0.6
2013	*SLN*	*MLB*	*21*	*250*	*22*	*8*	*1*	*5*	*23*	*12*	*77*	*4*	*1*	*.197/.242/.306*	*.200*	*.265*	*0.2*	*3B -1*	*-1.0*

Yet another interesting prospect in a system positively rank with them, Wisdom spent his first pro season raking in short-season ball. Of course that's what you would expect a college draftee to do, but it sure beats *not* raking in short-season ball. Wisdom is a plus defender at third base, with agility, soft hands, and a strong arm. If he can continue to show a good approach at the plate and add some juice to his bat, he could have a career.

Kolten Wong 2B

Born: **10/10/1990** Age: **22**
Bats: **L** Throws: **R** Height: **5' 10"**
Weight: **190** Breakout: **5%**
Improve: **54%** Collapse: **3%**
Attrition: **6%** MLB: **97%**

Comparables:
Derrel Thomas,Jose Altuve,Roberto Alomar

YEAR	TEAM	LVL	AGE	PA	R	2B	3B	HR	RBI	BB	SO	SB	CS	AVG_OBP_SLG	TAv	BABIP	BRR	FRAA	WARP
2011	QUD	A	20	222	39	15	2	5	25	21	24	9	5	.335/.401/.510	.316	.355	0	--	0.0
2012	SFD	AA	21	579	79	23	6	9	52	44	74	21	11	.287/.348/.405	.271	.318	3.8	2B(52): 6.9	1.7
2013	*SLN*	*MLB*	*22*	*250*	*28*	*11*	*2*	*3*	*20*	*14*	*41*	*6*	*2*	*.255/.302/.360*	*.241*	*.293*	*0.1*	*2B -0*	*0.4*

A terrific pure hitter, Wong spent the year lacing line drives around the Texas League and continuing his inevitable march toward the St. Louis second base job. His compact stroke can generate surprising power, though he's more likely to hit .300 in the big leagues than he is to reach 15 home runs. In the field he's solid if unspectacular, with soft hands and a fringy arm that limits him to second base. He's not an All-Star in the making, but he's a solid bet to help the Cardinals finally end their parade of misfits at the keystone.

PITCHERS

Mitchell Boggs

Born: **2/15/1984** Age: **29**
Bats: **R** Throws: **R** Height: **6' 5"** Weight: **215**
Breakout: **36%** Improve: **70%** Collapse: **7%**
Attrition: **13%** MLB: **75%**
Comparables:
Larry Jackson, Jon Leicester, Alejandro Pena

YEAR	TEAM	LVL	AGE	W	L	SV	G	GS	IP	H	HR	BB	SO	BB9	SO9	GB%	BABIP	WHIP	ERA	FIP	FRA	WARP
2010	SLN	MLB	26	2	3	0	61	0	67^{1}	60	5	27	52	3.6	7.0	55%	.279	1.29	3.61	3.91	4.62	0.0
2011	MEM	AAA	27	0	2	0	4	4	14^{2}	12	1	5	14	3.1	8.6	—	.289	1.16	2.45	4.19	4.56	0.0
2011	SLN	MLB	27	2	3	4	51	0	60^{2}	62	4	21	48	3.1	7.1	53%	.314	1.37	3.56	3.41	3.89	0.3
2012	SLN	MLB	28	4	1	0	78	0	73^{1}	56	5	21	58	2.6	7.1	55%	.245	1.05	2.21	3.46	3.93	0.6
2013	*SLN*	*MLB*	*29*	*3*	*1*	*1*	*59*	*0*	*62*	*59*	*6*	*23*	*47*	*3.3*	*6.8*	*50%*	*.300*	*1.32*	*4.22*	*4.05*	*4.59*	*-0.0*

With a heavy mid-90s fastball and a sharp slider, Boggs has long looked like he should be able to dominate hitters in short stretches—and against righties, he sometimes has. In 2012 he recommitted himself to the changeup he had ditched after moving to the bullpen, and the results were eye-opening. Boggs used his new weapon to be effective against lefties for the first time, while allowing a miniscule .190 TAv against same-side hitters. He was a little hit-lucky last year and won't maintain such a low BABIP, but if he can continue to keep lefties out on their front foot, he'll remain one of the league's better set-up men.

Barret Browning

Born: **12/28/1984** Age: **28**
Bats: **L** Throws: **L** Height: **6' 3"** Weight: **205**
Breakout: **21%** Improve: **34%** Collapse: **33%**
Attrition: **14%** MLB: **77%**
Comparables:
Steve Foucault, Jon Switzer, Xavier Hernandez

YEAR	TEAM	LVL	AGE	W	L	SV	G	GS	IP	H	HR	BB	SO	BB9	SO9	GB%	BABIP	WHIP	ERA	FIP	FRA	WARP
2010	ARK	AA	25	5	4	0	25	1	46	38	3	22	44	4.3	8.6	44%	.285	1.30	3.91	3.74	4.90	-0.1
2010	SLC	AAA	25	2	1	0	26	1	42^{2}	61	4	22	41	4.6	8.6	46%	.425	1.94	6.53	4.64	5.30	0.4
2011	SLC	AAA	26	2	1	0	50	2	66^{1}	67	5	35	47	4.7	6.4	56%	.333	1.54	4.61	5.11	6.36	0.1
2012	MEM	AAA	27	2	3	1	35	0	41^{2}	28	1	18	38	3.9	8.2	59%	.255	1.10	1.73	3.59	4.22	0.4
2012	SLN	MLB	27	1	3	0	22	0	19^{1}	18	2	7	11	3.3	5.1	53%	.250	1.29	5.12	4.43	5.01	-0.1
2013	*SLN*	*MLB*	*28*	*1*	*0*	*0*	*27*	*0*	*36^{1}*	*35*	*4*	*16*	*29*	*4.0*	*7.3*	*53%*	*.305*	*1.40*	*4.53*	*4.36*	*4.93*	*-0.2*

We've been waiting years for Browning to make it to the bigs so we could give him a full write-up, complete with cheesy poetical asides (e.g., "how does he LOOGY? Let me count the ways ..."), but now that we realize his first name is actually Gary, it seems anticlimactic. All that leaves us to discuss is Browning's relatively mundane mid-80s fastball, slider, and changeup, which gave hitters fits in Memphis but isn't likely to play a long-term role in a big-league bullpen. Still, the Cardinals kept him on the 40-man roster after his undistinguished debut, so there's a chance he can carve out a niche as a lefty specialist in the city where that role has come to be defined.

Chris Carpenter

Born: **4/27/1975** Age: **38**
Bats: **R** Throws: **R** Height: **6' 7"** Weight: **230**
Breakout: **12%** Improve: **37%** Collapse: **23%**
Attrition: **12%** MLB: **80%**
Comparables:
Greg Maddux, Derek Lowe, Kevin Brown

YEAR	TEAM	LVL	AGE	W	L	SV	G	GS	IP	H	HR	BB	SO	BB9	SO9	GB%	BABIP	WHIP	ERA	FIP	FRA	WARP
2010	SLN	MLB	35	16	9	0	35	35	235	214	21	63	179	2.4	6.9	52%	.278	1.18	3.22	3.71	4.50	1.5
2011	SLN	MLB	36	11	9	0	34	34	237^{1}	243	16	55	191	2.1	7.2	48%	.312	1.26	3.45	3.03	3.73	2.8
2012	SLN	MLB	37	0	2	0	3	3	17	16	2	3	12	1.6	6.4	44%	.264	1.12	3.71	4.14	4.25	0.2
2013	*SLN*	*MLB*	*38*	*3*	*2*	*0*	*8*	*8*	*50^{2}*	*46*	*4*	*11*	*40*	*1.9*	*7.1*	*51%*	*.298*	*1.12*	*3.29*	*3.30*	*3.58*	*0.6*

The list of things most observers wouldn't question about Carpenter is a long one: toughness, fortitude, leadership, pitching acumen, and, of course, height. All were on display last fall when he worked his way back from surgery that removed a rib and neck muscles to help restore normal nerve function to his shoulder, managing to take the mound down the stretch and in the playoffs. Whether he should have done so, however, is a separate question. Carpenter was clearly not right, wriggling through 5 2/3 scoreless innings on guts alone during an NLDS win before losing two games in the NLCS without working into the fifth inning. A healthy Carpenter has always been a productive Carpenter, and the club hopes a full winter of rest will help its co-ace return to form. At some point in the near future, though, Carpenter's body will betray him for the last time, and no amount of Granite State grit and guile will help him get big leaguers out.

Randy Choate

Born: **9/5/1975** Age: **37**
Bats: **L** Throws: **L** Height: **6' 2"** Weight: **200**
Breakout: **15%** Improve: **71%** Collapse: **19%**
Attrition: **6%** MLB: **87%**
Comparables:
Brian Shouse, Mike Stanton, Ron Mahay

YEAR	TEAM	LVL	AGE	W	L	SV	G	GS	IP	H	HR	BB	SO	BB9	SO9	GB%	BABIP	WHIP	ERA	FIP	FRA	WARP
2010	TBA	MLB	34	4	3	0	85	0	44^{2}	41	3	17	40	3.4	8.1	61%	.306	1.30	4.23	3.47	3.88	0.4
2011	FLO	MLB	35	1	1	0	54	0	24^{2}	13	3	13	31	4.7	11.3	63%	.185	1.05	1.82	3.89	4.36	-0.1
2012	LAN	MLB	36	0	0	0	36	0	13^{1}	13	1	9	11	6.1	7.4	69%	.293	1.65	4.05	4.94	4.96	-0.2
2012	MIA	MLB	36	0	0	1	44	0	25^{1}	16	0	9	27	3.2	9.6	61%	.246	0.99	2.49	2.43	2.73	0.4
2013	*SLN*	*MLB*	*37*	*4*	*2*	*1*	*77*	*0*	*38*	*33*	*4*	*14*	*34*	*3.3*	*8.1*	*58%*	*.292*	*1.23*	*3.63*	*3.88*	*3.94*	*0.3*

After missing six weeks in 2011 with elbow inflammation, Choate bounced back to tie for the NL lead in appearances, the second time in three years he's claimed a share of the lead. To their credit, both Ozzie Guillen and Don Mattingly did better jobs last year of picking Choate's spots than managers usually do when it comes to LOOGYs: Choate faced lefties 69 percent of the time and dominated them (.158/.243/.218), thereby minimizing his struggles against righties (.325/.471/.350). The Cardinals, well known for their lefty love, signed him to a three-year deal, during which Choate may be asked to retire Joey Votto about 40 times.

Maikel Cleto

Born: **5/1/1989** Age: **24**
Bats: **R** Throws: **R** Height: **6' 4"** Weight: **235**
Breakout: **20%** Improve: **55%** Collapse: **29%**
Attrition: **19%** MLB: **95%**

Comparables:
Jeff Russell, Willie Fraser, Kyle Lohse

YEAR	TEAM	LVL	AGE	W	L	SV	G	GS	IP	H	HR	BB	SO	BB9	SO9	GB%	BABIP	WHIP	ERA	FIP	FRA	WARP
2010	HDS	A+	21	4	9	0	23	21	102^{1}	125	10	44	83	3.9	7.3	48%	.357	1.65	6.16	4.88	5.94	1.0
2011	PMB	A+	22	1	1	0	5	5	29	20	2	10	33	3.1	10.2	—	.250	1.03	2.48	3.25	3.53	0.0
2011	SFD	AA	22	2	2	0	7	6	34^{1}	40	2	12	36	3.1	9.4	—	.384	1.51	3.93	3.52	3.83	0.0
2011	MEM	AAA	22	5	3	0	13	13	71^{1}	57	6	43	66	5.4	8.3	—	.264	1.40	4.29	4.96	5.39	0.0
2011	SLN	MLB	22	0	0	0	3	0	4^{1}	7	2	4	6	8.3	12.5	47%	.385	2.54	12.46	8.99	10.46	-0.3
2012	MEM	AAA	23	3	2	2	45	0	53^{2}	51	4	22	66	3.7	11.1	49%	.341	1.36	5.37	3.63	4.05	0.7
2012	SLN	MLB	23	0	0	0	9	0	9	13	4	2	15	2.0	15.0	30%	.474	1.67	7.00	6.58	6.46	-0.2
2013	*SLN*	*MLB*	*24*	*2*	*2*	*0*	*17*	*4*	35^{1}	*39*	*5*	*15*	*24*	*3.8*	*6.2*	*47%*	*.314*	*1.52*	*5.50*	*4.95*	*5.98*	*-0.5*

Longer on stuff than production, Cleto has a fastball that can hit triple digits but he hasn't yet figured out what to do with it. His command has improved from "woeful" to "spotty with a chance of meatballs," as he has cut into his walk rate but still gets taken deep way too frequently. Nevertheless, pitchers with his heat and strikeout rate always have a chance, and if Cleto can polish his game in the upper minors and develop a better feel for his slider, he'll be a useful hand in the St. Louis pen.

Samuel Freeman

Born: **6/24/1987** Age: **26**
Bats: **R** Throws: **L** Height: **6' 0"** Weight: **170**
Breakout: **25%** Improve: **48%** Collapse: **26%**
Attrition: **16%** MLB: **84%**

Comparables:
Ken Ryan, John Riedling, Tom Waddell

YEAR	TEAM	LVL	AGE	W	L	SV	G	GS	IP	H	HR	BB	SO	BB9	SO9	GB%	BABIP	WHIP	ERA	FIP	FRA	WARP
2011	PMB	A+	24	0	0	0	7	0	9	8	0	4	7	4.0	7.0	—	.308	1.33	4.00	3.17	3.44	0.0
2011	SFD	AA	24	2	2	3	52	0	59^{1}	53	5	28	52	4.2	7.9	—	.286	1.37	3.03	4.24	4.61	0.0
2012	SFD	AA	25	1	3	1	15	0	17^{1}	12	1	4	12	2.1	6.2	48%	.216	0.92	1.56	3.51	3.38	0.2
2012	MEM	AAA	25	2	2	0	27	0	30^{1}	25	3	12	27	3.6	8.0	42%	.272	1.22	2.08	4.36	4.57	0.2
2012	SLN	MLB	25	0	2	0	24	0	20	17	2	10	18	4.5	8.1	46%	.273	1.35	5.40	4.29	4.43	0.1
2013	*SLN*	*MLB*	*26*	*2*	*1*	*0*	*36*	*0*	36^{2}	*34*	*4*	*16*	*30*	*4.0*	*7.3*	*46%*	*.294*	*1.37*	*4.44*	*4.29*	*4.83*	*-0.1*

Freeman made his big-league debut in June when the St. Louis bullpen was desperate for answers. He didn't pitch well enough to stick, but was more effective after a September call-up. He abets a fastball that can reach the mid-90s with a slider and a changeup, giving him stuff that can work against hitters of all stripes. Freeman doesn't stack strikeouts at quite the rate you'd expect from a prospect, but he avoids ball four well enough that he might have a future in low-leverage relief. A Tommy John survivor, his Arizona Fall League stint was cut short by biceps tendinitis, but he is expected to be healthy enough to compete for a spot at the back of the St. Louis bullpen this spring.

Jaime Garcia

Born: **7/8/1986** Age: **26**
Bats: **L** Throws: **L** Height: **6' 3"** Weight: **215**
Breakout: **29%** Improve: **58%** Collapse: **15%**
Attrition: **8%** MLB: **92%**

Comparables:
Manny Parra, Andy Pettitte, Dallas Braden

YEAR	TEAM	LVL	AGE	W	L	SV	G	GS	IP	H	HR	BB	SO	BB9	SO9	GB%	BABIP	WHIP	ERA	FIP	FRA	WARP
2010	SLN	MLB	23	13	8	0	28	28	163^{1}	151	9	64	132	3.5	7.3	57%	.292	1.32	2.70	3.44	3.87	2.7
2011	SLN	MLB	24	13	7	0	32	32	194^{2}	207	15	50	156	2.3	7.2	55%	.318	1.32	3.56	3.19	4.37	0.9
2012	CRD	Rk	25	0	0	0	1	1	2^{1}	4	0	0	1	0.0	3.9	78%	.444	1.71	0.00	2.58	-2.18	0.0
2012	SFD	AA	25	1	0	0	2	2	10^{1}	8	2	0	11	0.0	9.6	50%	.231	0.77	5.23	3.67	5.40	0.0
2012	MEM	AAA	25	0	1	0	1	1	5	4	1	3	8	5.4	14.4	70%	.333	1.40	3.60	4.87	4.48	0.0
2012	SLN	MLB	25	7	7	0	20	20	121^{2}	136	7	30	98	2.2	7.2	56%	.339	1.36	3.92	3.01	3.57	2.9
2013	*SLN*	*MLB*	*26*	*8*	*6*	*0*	*21*	*21*	121^{2}	*114*	*11*	*33*	*100*	*2.4*	*7.4*	*55%*	*.306*	*1.20*	*3.60*	*3.55*	*3.91*	*1.2*

Garcia missed two months with a sore shoulder but returned in the late going, helping pitch the Cardinals into the postseason with a 2.50 ERA and four wins in September. During his last start the young lefty again felt pain but kept it a secret, tried to gut out his NLDS start, but could only make it through two innings before being shut down. Critics assailed him for foolishly putting his team at risk, though it's fair to ask how difficult it might have been in October for Garcia to walk past Carpenter and tell the skipper he wasn't sound enough to pitch a big game. If Garcia's arm is healthy for spring training, his sinker and wide array of off-speed puzzlers will make him an excellent third starter. At this point, though, both his health and his headspace are major question marks.

John Gast

Born: **2/16/1989** Age: **24**
Bats: **L** Throws: **L** Height: **6' 2"** Weight: **195**
Breakout: **27%** Improve: **69%** Collapse: **18%**
Attrition: **11%** MLB: **95%**

Comparables:
Eric Surkamp, Wade LeBlanc, Jon Niese

YEAR	TEAM	LVL	AGE	W	L	SV	G	GS	IP	H	HR	BB	SO	BB9	SO9	GB%	BABIP	WHIP	ERA	FIP	FRA	WARP
2010	BAT	A-	21	6	0	0	8	6	35	27	1	8	36	2.1	9.3	56%	.340	1.00	1.54	2.56	4.98	0.3
2011	PMB	A+	22	5	4	0	13	12	82	85	7	28	59	3.1	6.5	—	.307	1.38	3.95	4.38	4.76	0.0
2011	SFD	AA	22	4	4	0	13	13	79^{1}	80	9	33	54	3.7	6.1	—	.290	1.42	4.08	4.89	5.32	0.0
2012	SFD	AA	23	4	2	0	8	8	51^{1}	38	5	13	41	2.3	7.2	47%	.243	0.99	1.93	3.77	4.43	0.4
2012	MEM	AAA	23	9	5	0	20	20	109^{1}	124	10	42	86	3.5	7.1	47%	.333	1.52	5.10	4.49	5.95	-0.5
2013	*SLN*	*MLB*	*24*	*3*	*3*	*0*	*8*	*8*	*42*	*42*	*5*	*14*	*32*	*3.0*	*6.9*	*46%*	*.304*	*1.33*	*4.34*	*4.22*	*4.72*	*0.0*

Gast chugged his way into the high minors last year, and the young lefty continued to impress. He flashes solid command of his low-90s fastball and changeup and has started to miss more bats, though his breaking ball still needs work. Gast doesn't have the stuff or ceiling of the organization's more high-octane arms, but he already looks like he could step into the back of a big-league rotation and munch innings. He'll start the season in Triple-A, and another successful year should get him on the 40-man roster and into the organization's long-range plans.

Tyrell Jenkins

Born: **7/20/1992** Age: **20**
Bats: **R** Throws: **R** Height: **6' 5"** Weight: **180**
Breakout: **49%** Improve: **77%** Collapse: **11%**
Attrition: **4%** MLB: **82%**

Comparables:
Dick Brodowski, Catfish Hunter, Milt Pappas

YEAR	TEAM	LVL	AGE	W	L	SV	G	GS	IP	H	HR	BB	SO	BB9	SO9	GB%	BABIP	WHIP	ERA	FIP	FRA	WARP
2010	JCY	Rk	17	0	0	0	2	2	3	2	0	2	2	6.0	6.0	50%	.250	1.33	0.00	4.20	7.42	0.0
2011	JCY	Rk	18	4	2	0	11	11	56	63	3	13	55	2.1	8.8	59%	.333	1.36	3.86	3.37	4.84	0.5
2012	QUD	A	19	4	4	0	19	19	82^{1}	84	5	36	80	3.9	8.7	56%	.338	1.46	5.14	3.62	4.03	0.0
2013	*SLN*	*MLB*	*20*	*2*	*3*	*0*	*8*	*8*	*35*	*38*	*5*	*18*	*22*	*4.5*	*5.8*	*49%*	*.313*	*1.60*	*5.66*	*5.34*	*6.15*	*-0.5*

In his first taste of full-season ball, Jenkins was unable to pitch the full season. Shoulder soreness carved away nearly a month of precious development time. A projectable righty with a long, lean frame, a smooth delivery, and easy heat that can reach the mid-90s, Jenkins still has a lot of rough edges to sand away. He can flash a solid curveball and is making progress with his changeup, but needs to improve his command or more advanced hitters will eat him alive. The Cardinals love his athleticism and believe he'll be able to translate his tools into better production, something he still has plenty of time to do.

Joe Kelly

Born: **6/9/1988** Age: **25**
Bats: **R** Throws: **R** Height: **6' 2"** Weight: **165**
Breakout: **26%** Improve: **48%** Collapse: **16%**
Attrition: **13%** MLB: **95%**

Comparables:
Ned Garver, Todd Burns, Pedro Astacio

YEAR	TEAM	LVL	AGE	W	L	SV	G	GS	IP	H	HR	BB	SO	BB9	SO9	GB%	BABIP	WHIP	ERA	FIP	FRA	WARP
2010	QUD	A	22	6	8	1	26	18	103^{1}	103	3	45	92	3.9	8.0	66%	.337	1.43	4.62	3.72	5.66	0.1
2011	PMB	A+	23	5	2	0	12	11	72^{2}	56	1	34	62	4.2	7.7	—	.275	1.24	2.60	3.59	3.91	0.0
2011	SFD	AA	23	6	4	0	11	11	59^{1}	70	7	25	51	3.8	7.7	—	.358	1.60	5.01	4.71	5.12	0.0
2012	MEM	AAA	24	2	5	0	12	12	72^{1}	75	2	21	45	2.6	5.6	57%	.323	1.33	2.86	3.82	4.52	0.3
2012	SLN	MLB	24	5	7	0	24	16	107	112	10	36	75	3.0	6.3	53%	.306	1.38	3.53	4.04	4.93	0.3
2013	*SLN*	*MLB*	*25*	*5*	*5*	*0*	*20*	*15*	*91^{1}*	*95*	*10*	*33*	*61*	*3.2*	*6.1*	*54%*	*.310*	*1.40*	*4.65*	*4.37*	*5.05*	*-0.3*

Kelly is not considered a top prospect, but injuries forced him into the Cardinals rotation in June and he held down the fort admirably until Garcia returned. His mid-90s sinker can be a genuine worm-killer, but Kelly doesn't miss a lot of bats, his command can be shakier than a dashboard hula dancer, and his off-speed stuff is unremarkable. Given his height and the fact that lefties lit him up last year—only the dessicated remains of Jason Marquis worked 100 innings and allowed a higher TAv than Kelly's .333—it seems likely Kelly's future is in relief, with an occasional spot start.

Kyle Lohse

Born: **10/4/1978** Age: **34**
Bats: **R** Throws: **R** Height: **6' 3"** Weight: **210**
Breakout: **10%** Improve: **39%** Collapse: **26%**
Attrition: **10%** MLB: **84%**

Comparables:
Matt Morris, John Thomson, Hiroki Kuroda

YEAR	TEAM	LVL	AGE	W	L	SV	G	GS	IP	H	HR	BB	SO	BB9	SO9	GB%	BABIP	WHIP	ERA	FIP	FRA	WARP
2010	SFD	AA	31	0	1	0	1	1	5	12	0	0	4	0.0	7.2	36%	.545	2.40	9.00	1.57	2.85	0.2
2010	MEM	AAA	31	1	0	0	3	3	14	9	3	2	14	1.3	9.0	49%	.167	0.79	3.21	4.80	5.41	0.2
2010	SLN	MLB	31	4	8	0	18	18	92	129	9	35	54	3.4	5.3	44%	.364	1.78	6.55	4.44	4.75	0.5
2011	SLN	MLB	32	14	8	0	30	30	188^{1}	178	16	42	111	2.0	5.3	43%	.269	1.17	3.39	3.64	4.45	1.1
2012	SLN	MLB	33	16	3	0	33	33	211	192	19	38	143	1.6	6.1	43%	.262	1.09	2.86	3.55	3.94	2.2
2013	*SLN*	*MLB*	*34*	*11*	*10*	*0*	*29*	*29*	*171^{1}*	*172*	*19*	*38*	*111*	*2.0*	*5.8*	*43%*	*.295*	*1.22*	*4.09*	*4.01*	*4.45*	*0.5*

Over the last two years Lohse has found great success by embodying those most basic of pitching clichés: get ahead of hitters (third highest first-pitch strike rate in baseball), avoid walks (fifth lowest walk rate), and let your defense do the work (14th in contact rate). He's also managed to post a luminous 30-11 record, put up a 3.11 ERA, and unleash an improved slider that's raised his strikeout rate from woeful to merely subpar. All this has helped Lohse make good on the second half of a four-year deal that began with injury, ineffectiveness, and buyer's remorse—a feeling his next employer may soon become familiar with. Lohse gives up lots of fly balls but few of those reach the bleachers, and that (along with his BABIP) is overdue for a regression.

A few more gappers and gopher balls will turn him into more of an innings-muncher than an ace, and while Lohse isn't about to turn into Jeff Suppan, or Braden Looper, or Joel Pineiro, multi-year deals for pitchers of his vintage rarely turn out well.

Lance Lynn

Born: **5/12/1987** Age: **26**
Bats: **R** Throws: **R** Height: **6' 6"** Weight: **250**
Breakout: **23%** Improve: **49%** Collapse: **26%**
Attrition: **20%** MLB: **100%**

Comparables:
Ervin Santana,Steve Busby,Josh Beckett

YEAR	TEAM	LVL	AGE	W	L	SV	G	GS	IP	H	HR	BB	SO	BB9	SO9	GB%	BABIP	WHIP	ERA	FIP	FRA	WARP
2010	MEM	AAA	23	13	10	0	29	29	164	164	21	62	141	3.4	7.7	44%	.301	1.38	4.77	4.81	4.98	1.8
2011	MEM	AAA	24	7	3	0	12	12	75	79	2	25	64	3.0	7.7	—	.344	1.39	3.84	3.50	3.81	0.0
2011	SLN	MLB	24	1	1	1	18	2	34^2	25	3	11	40	2.9	10.4	58%	.272	1.04	3.12	2.85	3.66	0.3
2012	SLN	MLB	25	18	7	0	35	29	176	168	16	64	180	3.3	9.2	46%	.321	1.32	3.78	3.53	3.73	2.7
2013	*SLN*	*MLB*	*26*	*8*	*7*	*0*	*23*	*23*	*129*	*116*	*14*	*44*	*120*	*3.1*	*8.4*	*45%*	*.304*	*1.24*	*3.85*	*3.77*	*4.18*	*0.8*

Lynn spent much of last season going from the penthouse (a 10-2 record and 2.42 ERA in his first 13 starts, which earned him a trip to the All-Star Game) to the outhouse (a 5.89 ERA in his next 12 starts, which earned him a trip to the bullpen) and back again (four straight wins down the stretch when moved back to the rotation). Even during his midseason slide the big righty continued to rack up strikeouts, and his true talent obviously lies somewhere between those two extremes. Lynn can dominate righties when he commands his low-90s fastball and curve, but his dodgy changeup leaves him vulnerable to lefty bats. He's a fourth starter with upside potential.

Seth Maness

Born: **10/14/1988** Age: **24**
Bats: **R** Throws: **R** Height: **6' 1"** Weight: **180**
Breakout: **20%** Improve: **56%** Collapse: **27%**
Attrition: **24%** MLB: **89%**

Comparables:
Justin Germano,Bryan Augenstein,Tommy Hunter

YEAR	TEAM	LVL	AGE	W	L	SV	G	GS	IP	H	HR	BB	SO	BB9	SO9	GB%	BABIP	WHIP	ERA	FIP	FRA	WARP
2011	QUD	A	22	1	0	0	2	0	5	4	0	0	3	0.0	5.4	—	.267	0.80	1.80	2.16	2.35	0.0
2011	BAT	A-	22	0	1	0	10	7	39^2	27	0	3	31	0.7	7.0	75%	.270	0.76	0.91	2.10	3.22	0.5
2011	PMB	A+	22	1	0	0	3	0	8^1	7	0	2	8	2.2	8.6	—	.292	1.08	4.32	2.55	2.77	0.0
2012	PMB	A+	23	3	1	0	7	7	46	45	5	1	29	0.2	5.7	58%	.282	1.00	2.15	3.61	5.46	-0.2
2012	SFD	AA	23	11	3	0	20	20	123^2	122	13	9	83	0.7	6.0	54%	.278	1.06	3.27	3.67	4.89	0.3
2013	*SLN*	*MLB*	*24*	*3*	*3*	*0*	*8*	*8*	*44^2*	*48*	*6*	*10*	*24*	*1.9*	*4.9*	*52%*	*.299*	*1.30*	*4.64*	*4.54*	*5.05*	*-0.2*

Some pitchers can't find the strike zone, others work hard to fill it, but Maness takes a plunger and stuffs it till it overflows. The organization's 2012 Pitcher of the Year used his pinpoint command and control to walk only 10 batters in nearly 170 innings during his full-season debut. An 11th-round pick out of Eastern Carolina, Maness is a small righty with an upper-80s fastball and underwhelming secondary stuff, but he clearly gets the most he can out of it. He spent most of the year as one of the most effective pitchers in the prospect-rich Texas League. He's gotten the organization's attention, and if he can prove his productivity isn't a fluke, he has a chance.

Victor Marte

Born: **11/8/1980** Age: **32**
Bats: **R** Throws: **R** Height: **6' 3"** Weight: **255**
Breakout: **25%** Improve: **58%** Collapse: **28%**
Attrition: **20%** MLB: **68%**

Comparables:
T.J. Mathews,Jay Ritchie,Esteban Yan

YEAR	TEAM	LVL	AGE	W	L	SV	G	GS	IP	H	HR	BB	SO	BB9	SO9	GB%	BABIP	WHIP	ERA	FIP	FRA	WARP
2010	OMA	AAA	29	4	1	3	25	0	40^2	40	3	15	29	3.3	6.4	43%	.289	1.35	3.32	4.22	4.96	0.3
2010	KCA	MLB	29	3	0	0	22	0	27^2	38	8	15	19	4.9	6.2	44%	.323	1.92	9.76	7.28	8.54	-1.0
2011	MEM	AAA	30	2	4	31	55	0	62^1	47	5	20	52	2.9	7.5	—	.243	1.07	1.44	4.17	4.53	0.0
2012	MEM	AAA	31	0	2	3	12	0	12	9	0	7	10	5.2	7.5	61%	.273	1.33	3.00	3.75	3.26	0.2
2012	SLN	MLB	31	3	2	0	48	0	40^1	51	6	14	36	3.1	8.0	50%	.354	1.61	4.91	4.47	4.87	-0.1
2013	*SLN*	*MLB*	*32*	*2*	*1*	*0*	*33*	*0*	*36^2*	*36*	*5*	*15*	*28*	*3.6*	*6.9*	*46%*	*.303*	*1.39*	*4.67*	*4.67*	*5.08*	*-0.2*

Marte managed to hold onto a spot in the Cardinals bullpen until late July, a fact that says more about the state of the St. Louis relief corps than it does about any enduring competence Marte may have shown. The institutional-sized reliever can dial fastballs into the mid-90s but can't command them, frequently leading to line drives that travel even faster. The Cardinals had best hope they can file Marte away in Memphis as a bullpen coupon they don't have to redeem.

Carlos Martinez

Born: **9/2/1991** Age: **21**
Bats: **R** Throws: **R** Height: **6' 1"** Weight: **165**
Breakout: **29%** Improve: **60%** Collapse: **14%**
Attrition: **3%** MLB: **87%**

Comparables:
Alex Fernandez,Arodys Vizcaino,Hayden Penn

YEAR	TEAM	LVL	AGE	W	L	SV	G	GS	IP	H	HR	BB	SO	BB9	SO9	GB%	BABIP	WHIP	ERA	FIP	FRA	WARP
2011	QUD	A	19	3	2	0	8	8	38^2	27	1	14	50	3.3	11.6	—	.299	1.06	2.33	2.51	2.72	0.0
2011	PMB	A+	19	3	3	0	10	10	46	49	2	30	48	5.9	9.4	—	.351	1.72	5.28	4.21	4.58	0.0
2012	PMB	A+	20	2	2	0	7	7	33	29	0	10	34	2.7	9.3	51%	.319	1.18	3.00	2.79	2.47	0.1
2012	SFD	AA	20	4	3	0	15	14	71^1	62	6	22	58	2.8	7.3	63%	.276	1.18	2.90	3.92	4.16	0.2
2013	*SLN*	*MLB*	*21*	*2*	*2*	*0*	*7*	*7*	*37*	*36*	*4*	*14*	*28*	*3.4*	*6.9*	*51%*	*.301*	*1.35*	*4.54*	*4.23*	*4.94*	*-0.0*

Martinez started the season in High-A, finished it in Double-A, and made significant progress toward harnessing his electric stuff. Most impressively, the slight Dominican significantly improved his control, cutting his walk rate in half despite facing more-advanced hitters. His strikeout rate also dropped, but it was clear Martinez was working on finding the plate—with a moving fastball that reaches the high-90s and a solid curve, the whiffs will come. Next on the agenda is improving his command, developing a third pitch, and proving his size and violent delivery can bear up to a starter's workload. If he can manage that, he has the goods to be a front-line starter; if not, the late innings beckon.

Kyle McClellan

Born: 6/12/1984 **Age:** 29
Bats: R **Throws:** R **Height:** 6' 3" **Weight:** 215
Breakout: 29% **Improve:** 57% **Collapse:** 22%
Attrition: 14% **MLB:** 86%

Comparables:
Jim Johnson,Derek Lowe,Dave Schmidt

YEAR	TEAM	LVL	AGE	W	L	SV	G	GS	IP	H	HR	BB	SO	BB9	SO9	GB%	BABIP	WHIP	ERA	FIP	FRA	WARP
2010	SLN	MLB	26	1	4	2	68	0	75^1	58	9	23	60	2.7	7.2	52%	.231	1.08	2.27	4.10	4.49	0.2
2011	SLN	MLB	27	12	7	0	43	17	141^2	143	21	43	76	2.7	4.8	52%	.265	1.31	4.19	4.89	5.85	-1.9
2012	SLN	MLB	28	0	1	0	16	0	18^2	16	2	9	11	4.3	5.3	46%	.237	1.34	5.30	5.12	5.75	-0.1
2013	*SLN*	*MLB*	*29*	*2*	*1*	*0*	*21*	*3*	*38*	*34*	*4*	*11*	*29*	*2.7*	*6.8*	*50%*	*.281*	*1.20*	*3.78*	*3.91*	*4.11*	*0.2*

McClellan started last season in the Cardinals pen but was shelved with a torn elbow ligament in late May, then suffered a labrum tear while rehabbing in late July, ending his season. With a low-90s sinker and a repertoire wider than a Frank Zappa tour band, McClellan has had success as both spot starter and set-up man. Chased out of St. Louis by a new wave of younger, cheaper, and more compelling arms, he'll make a valuable addition to someone else's staff this year if he's healthy.

Shelby Miller

Born: 10/10/1990 **Age:** 22
Bats: R **Throws:** R **Height:** 6' 4" **Weight:** 195
Breakout: 29% **Improve:** 62% **Collapse:** 12%
Attrition: 7% **MLB:** 95%

Comparables:
Bill Gullickson,Chris Tillman,Mark Prior

YEAR	TEAM	LVL	AGE	W	L	SV	G	GS	IP	H	HR	BB	SO	BB9	SO9	GB%	BABIP	WHIP	ERA	FIP	FRA	WARP
2010	QUD	A	19	7	5	0	24	24	104^1	97	7	33	140	2.8	12.1	46%	.346	1.25	3.62	2.83	3.48	2.8
2011	PMB	A+	20	2	3	0	9	9	53	40	2	20	81	3.4	13.8	—	.330	1.13	2.89	2.01	2.19	0.0
2011	SFD	AA	20	9	3	0	16	16	86^2	72	2	33	89	3.4	9.2	—	.308	1.21	2.70	2.90	3.16	0.0
2012	MEM	AAA	21	11	10	0	27	27	136^2	138	24	50	160	3.3	10.5	35%	.327	1.38	4.74	4.95	5.56	0.5
2012	SLN	MLB	21	1	0	0	6	1	13^2	9	0	4	16	2.6	10.5	42%	.273	0.95	1.32	1.89	2.28	0.5
2013	*SLN*	*MLB*	*22*	*3*	*3*	*0*	*9*	*9*	*45^2*	*41*	*6*	*16*	*46*	*3.1*	*9.2*	*40%*	*.308*	*1.26*	*4.01*	*3.94*	*4.36*	*0.3*

A prototypical power pitcher, Miller both entered and exited last season as the team's top starting prospect, but endured a roller-coaster ride in his first Triple-A season. Miller reported to camp significantly underweight after too much winter conditioning, then posted a shocking 6.17 ERA in the first half of the season. Cardinals fans could step back from the ledge, however, after a few tweaks—some mechanical, some emotional—helped Miller post 70 strikeouts and only seven walks in 59 second-half innings and earn a successful September call-up. Miller has premier stuff, with a fastball that can reach the upper 90s and a power curve he can throw for strikes. Still only 22, he's already shown he can get major leaguers to swing and miss, and it's only a matter of time before he's fronting the Cardinals rotation.

Jason Motte

Born: 6/22/1982 **Age:** 31
Bats: R **Throws:** R **Height:** 6' 1" **Weight:** 200
Breakout: 25% **Improve:** 47% **Collapse:** 20%
Attrition: 6% **MLB:** 94%

Comparables:
J.J. Putz,Rafael Betancourt,Robb Nen

YEAR	TEAM	LVL	AGE	W	L	SV	G	GS	IP	H	HR	BB	SO	BB9	SO9	GB%	BABIP	WHIP	ERA	FIP	FRA	WARP
2010	MEM	AAA	28	0	0	0	2	0	2^2	2	0	1	2	3.3	6.7	25%	.250	1.11	3.33	3.21	3.94	0.0
2010	SLN	MLB	28	4	2	2	56	0	52^1	41	5	18	54	3.1	9.3	40%	.275	1.13	2.24	3.32	3.21	0.4
2011	SLN	MLB	29	5	2	9	78	0	68	49	2	16	63	2.1	8.3	46%	.258	0.96	2.25	2.45	3.13	1.1
2012	SLN	MLB	30	4	5	42	67	0	72	49	9	17	86	2.1	10.8	41%	.242	0.92	2.75	3.16	3.71	0.7
2013	*SLN*	*MLB*	*31*	*4*	*2*	*19*	*65*	*0*	*63*	*50*	*6*	*17*	*70*	*2.4*	*10.1*	*41%*	*.292*	*1.06*	*2.85*	*3.03*	*3.09*	*1.2*

A pitcher with Motte's stuff, build, presence, quirks, myopia, and facial hair was destined to be a closer, and after several years of organizational equivocation, the former catcher finally spent a full season dominating the ninth. His approach is as subtle and effective as a sledgehammer, as Motte bludgeons opposing hitters with his overpowering upper-90s fastball and low-90s cutter, and his strikeout-to-walk ratio lives in the same neighborhood as the most dominating relievers in the game (non-Kimbrel division). A late bloomer, Motte is already 30 and will soon get expensive, so the Cardinals will have to decide how much they're willing to pay for the peace of mind a veteran closer can provide.

Edward Mujica

Born: 5/10/1984 **Age:** 29
Bats: R **Throws:** R **Height:** 6' 3" **Weight:** 215
Breakout: 16% **Improve:** 49% **Collapse:** 29%
Attrition: 14% **MLB:** 84%

Comparables:
Lindy McDaniel,Jeff Gray,Rod Beck

YEAR	TEAM	LVL	AGE	W	L	SV	G	GS	IP	H	HR	BB	SO	BB9	SO9	GB%	BABIP	WHIP	ERA	FIP	FRA	WARP
2010	SDN	MLB	26	2	1	0	59	0	69^2	59	14	6	72	0.8	9.3	45%	.256	0.93	3.62	3.91	4.82	-0.2
2011	FLO	MLB	27	9	6	0	67	0	76	64	7	14	63	1.7	7.5	51%	.270	1.03	2.96	3.17	4.02	0.7
2012	JUP	A+	28	0	0	0	2	2	3	0	0	0	2	0.0	6.0	71%	.000	0.00	0.00	2.06	1.73	0.0
2012	MIA	MLB	28	0	3	2	41	0	39	36	6	9	26	2.1	6.0	53%	.252	1.15	4.38	4.57	5.72	-0.3
2012	SLN	MLB	28	0	0	0	29	0	26^1	20	1	3	21	1.0	7.2	51%	.264	0.87	1.03	2.38	3.66	0.3
2013	*SLN*	*MLB*	*29*	*3*	*1*	*2*	*57*	*0*	*61^1*	*56*	*8*	*9*	*50*	*1.3*	*7.4*	*43%*	*.291*	*1.06*	*3.37*	*3.71*	*3.66*	*0.7*

Mujica came to St. Louis at the deadline in exchange for fading prospect Zach Cox, and the former Indian, Padre, and Marlin did yeoman's work solidifying the Cardinals pen down the stretch. The veteran righty has tremendous command of his low-90s fastball, harbors an admirable aversion to ball four, and has cured his chronic troubles with lefty batters through liberal application of the splitter. What made him especially valuable to the Cardinals last year was his ability to keep the ball in the park, but that won't last—he has averaged more than a home run per nine innings in all but one season, mostly pitching in the sprawling fields of San Diego and Miami. Still, he's a reasonably solid seventh-inning arm until someone better and/or cheaper comes along.

Jorge Rondon

Born: **9/16/1988** Age: **24**
Bats: **R** Throws: **R** Height: **6' 2"** Weight: **175**
Breakout: **31%** Improve: **59%** Collapse: **22%**
Attrition: **29%** MLB: **90%**

Comparables:
Gerald Alexander, Lee Tunnell, Al Santorini

YEAR	TEAM	LVL	AGE	W	L	SV	G	GS	IP	H	HR	BB	SO	BB9	SO9	GB%	BABIP	WHIP	ERA	FIP	FRA	WARP
2010	QUD	A	21	4	8	0	29	19	108^2	121	6	65	76	5.4	6.3	59%	.330	1.71	5.30	5.08	6.62	-0.8
2011	PMB	A+	22	1	5	6	21	0	26^2	29	1	13	27	4.4	9.1	—	.364	1.58	4.05	3.31	3.60	0.0
2011	SFD	AA	22	1	8	7	37	0	37^1	43	4	33	30	8.0	7.2	—	.336	2.04	9.16	6.22	6.76	0.0
2012	SFD	AA	23	2	1	4	33	0	34	29	1	16	30	4.2	7.9	53%	.298	1.32	3.44	3.66	4.05	0.3
2012	MEM	AAA	23	0	1	1	13	0	15	12	1	8	20	4.8	12.0	58%	.314	1.33	3.60	3.47	2.58	0.3
2013	*SLN*	*MLB*	*24*	*1*	*2*	*0*	*16*	*4*	*34*	*39*	*5*	*18*	*19*	*4.8*	*4.9*	*49%*	*.314*	*1.68*	*6.14*	*5.58*	*6.67*	*-0.7*

Rondon is a fairly typical relief prospect, with a big arm and big struggles with his control. His fastball can reach the high-90s and his slider can be effective, but his walk rate can be an eyesore. Rondon was able to catch more of the plate last year and the organization rewarded him with a spot on the 40-man roster. If he continues to cut down on the walks, he may someday find a home as a fifth-inning guy.

Trevor Rosenthal

Born: **5/29/1990** Age: **23**
Bats: **R** Throws: **R** Height: **6' 3"** Weight: **190**
Breakout: **25%** Improve: **53%** Collapse: **25%**
Attrition: **9%** MLB: **92%**

Comparables:
Kelvim Escobar, Erv Palica, Bob Moose

YEAR	TEAM	LVL	AGE	W	L	SV	G	GS	IP	H	HR	BB	SO	BB9	SO9	GB%	BABIP	WHIP	ERA	FIP	FRA	WARP
2011	QUD	A	21	7	7	0	22	22	120^1	111	7	39	133	2.9	9.9	—	.328	1.25	4.11	3.20	3.48	0.0
2012	SFD	AA	22	8	6	0	17	17	94	67	6	37	83	3.5	7.9	47%	.243	1.11	2.78	3.59	4.52	0.7
2012	MEM	AAA	22	0	0	0	3	3	15	11	1	5	21	3.0	12.6	61%	.312	1.07	4.20	3.13	3.20	-0.2
2012	SLN	MLB	22	0	2	0	19	0	22^2	14	2	7	25	2.8	9.9	55%	.222	0.93	2.78	3.14	2.97	0.4
2013	*SLN*	*MLB*	*23*	*2*	*2*	*0*	*13*	*6*	*43*	*38*	*5*	*17*	*38*	*3.6*	*8.0*	*49%*	*.294*	*1.29*	*4.01*	*4.13*	*4.35*	*0.2*

Rosenthal's eye-popping performance in last year's postseason, with 15 strikeouts and only two baserunners in almost nine innings of work, was the perfect coda to the young flamethrower's meteoric rise. A year ago Rosenthal hadn't even pitched in Double-A; now, hypnotized by his triple-digit fastball, hyperventilating Cardinals fans are debating whether he'll be the next Bob Gibson or Mariano Rivera. The answer, of course, is neither, but Rosenthal will be stretched out to compete for a rotation job this spring. His heater can be overpowering, especially in short stints, but his secondary pitches still need plenty of work. Rosenthal has already proven he can be a weapon in the late innings, and if he dominates there again this year it may prove difficult to shift him to the rotation later.

Marc Rzepczynski

Born: **8/29/1985** Age: **27**
Bats: **L** Throws: **L** Height: **6' 2"** Weight: **205**
Breakout: **28%** Improve: **66%** Collapse: **15%**
Attrition: **10%** MLB: **85%**

Comparables:
Erik Bedard, Britt Burns, Fernando Valenzuela

YEAR	TEAM	LVL	AGE	W	L	SV	G	GS	IP	H	HR	BB	SO	BB9	SO9	GB%	BABIP	WHIP	ERA	FIP	FRA	WARP
2010	TOR	MLB	24	4	4	0	14	12	63^2	72	8	30	57	4.2	8.1	53%	.342	1.60	4.95	4.54	5.47	0.1
2011	SLN	MLB	25	0	3	0	28	0	22^2	22	1	11	28	4.4	11.1	64%	.368	1.46	3.97	2.69	3.90	0.2
2011	TOR	MLB	25	2	3	0	43	0	39^1	28	2	15	33	3.4	7.6	65%	.248	1.09	2.97	3.42	4.45	0.3
2012	SLN	MLB	26	1	3	0	70	0	46^2	46	7	17	33	3.3	6.4	59%	.281	1.35	4.24	4.76	5.10	-0.2
2013	*SLN*	*MLB*	*27*	*3*	*2*	*1*	*31*	*5*	*44^2*	*40*	*4*	*18*	*41*	*3.6*	*8.2*	*57%*	*.305*	*1.30*	*4.09*	*3.74*	*4.44*	*0.1*

Rzepczynski's job in St. Louis last year was to be a LOOGY. But you can't be a Lefty One-Out Guy if you don't get that one guy out, as was true of "Scrabble" more often than expected last year. When that occurs, you become more of a LOBBY—a Lefty One-Batter Boy—and your organization feels it necessary to bring in Choate on a multi-year deal to get that one guy out. None of which is necessarily bad for Rzepczynski, as his sinker-slider combination can get righties out too, and by lobbying (intentionally or not) to face more and more varied hitters, he could increase his value.

Fernando Salas

Born: **5/30/1985** Age: **28**
Bats: **R** Throws: **R** Height: **6' 3"** Weight: **200**
Breakout: **29%** Improve: **58%** Collapse: **25%**
Attrition: **11%** MLB: **90%**

Comparables:
Huston Street, Chris Ray, Greg McMichael

YEAR	TEAM	LVL	AGE	W	L	SV	G	GS	IP	H	HR	BB	SO	BB9	SO9	GB%	BABIP	WHIP	ERA	FIP	FRA	WARP
2010	MEM	AAA	25	1	0	19	34	0	35^2	26	2	9	44	2.3	11.1	37%	.296	0.98	3.78	2.69	2.96	0.9
2010	SLN	MLB	25	0	0	0	27	0	30^2	28	4	15	29	4.4	8.5	36%	.282	1.40	3.52	4.38	4.37	0.1
2011	MEM	AAA	26	0	0	2	3	0	3	2	0	0	4	0.0	12.0	—	.333	0.67	0.00	3.12	3.39	0.0
2011	SLN	MLB	26	5	6	24	68	0	75	50	7	21	75	2.5	9.0	36%	.226	0.95	2.28	3.13	3.73	0.8
2012	MEM	AAA	27	1	0	1	4	0	4	6	2	0	5	0.0	11.2	17%	.400	1.50	9.00	7.67	10.01	-0.1
2012	SLN	MLB	27	1	4	0	65	0	58^2	56	5	27	60	4.1	9.2	41%	.313	1.41	4.30	3.63	3.50	0.6
2013	*SLN*	*MLB*	*28*	*3*	*1*	*7*	*58*	*0*	*60*	*49*	*6*	*18*	*62*	*2.7*	*9.3*	*37%*	*.290*	*1.11*	*3.13*	*3.33*	*3.40*	*0.9*

Like most of the St. Louis bullpen, Salas struggled early on last season, only to regain his footing in the second half. His stuff—fastball, curveball, and a changeup he feeds to lefties—is nothing special, and Salas has seemingly fallen to the bottom of the bullpen pecking order. With a flood of young arms on the way, his days on the Cardinals staff may be numbered.

Eduardo Sanchez

Born: **2/16/1989** Age: **24**
Bats: **R** Throws: **R** Height: **6' 0"** Weight: **170**
Breakout: **27%** Improve: **57%** Collapse: **17%**
Attrition: **10%** MLB: **92%**

Comparables:
Ed Vande Berg, Mark Clear, Wesley Wright

YEAR	TEAM	LVL	AGE	W	L	SV	G	GS	IP	H	HR	BB	SO	BB9	SO9	GB%	BABIP	WHIP	ERA	FIP	FRA	WARP
2010	SFD	AA	21	1	1	11	24	0	26	22	2	8	27	2.8	9.3	61%	.299	1.15	3.12	3.25	4.81	0.2
2010	MEM	AAA	21	0	0	3	26	0	27	19	2	12	31	4.0	10.3	47%	.280	1.15	1.67	3.81	3.47	0.7
2011	SFD	AA	22	0	1	0	3	0	4^{1}	3	0	2	3	4.2	6.2	—	.231	1.15	4.15	4.76	5.18	0.0
2011	MEM	AAA	22	1	0	0	2	0	3	0	0	0	3	0.0	9.0	—	.000	0.00	0.00	1.78	1.94	0.0
2011	SLN	MLB	22	3	1	5	26	0	30	14	1	16	35	4.8	10.5	34%	.206	1.00	1.80	2.99	4.02	0.2
2012	MEM	AAA	23	2	3	9	30	0	27^{2}	27	3	21	26	6.8	8.5	51%	.299	1.73	5.86	6.12	8.55	-0.3
2012	SLN	MLB	23	0	1	0	17	0	15	11	2	13	13	7.8	7.8	44%	.220	1.60	6.60	5.94	6.64	-0.3
2013	*SLN*	*MLB*	*24*	*2*	*1*	*3*	*36*	*0*	*37^{2}*	*30*	*4*	*17*	*37*	*4.2*	*8.9*	*47%*	*.285*	*1.27*	*3.81*	*3.97*	*4.14*	*0.2*

Sanchez can sometimes make hitters look silly with his mid-90s fastball and slow curve, but he continues to be plagued by awful control. Last year he walked as many batters as he whiffed in his midsummer big-league stint, and was nearly as wild down in Memphis. Sanchez has stuff that can play in high-leverage innings, but if he doesn't learn to harness it soon, he'll never have a career.

Michael Wacha

Born: **7/1/1991** Age: **21**
Bats: **R** Throws: **R** Height: **6' 7"** Weight: **195**
Breakout: **59%** Improve: **71%** Collapse: **14%**
Attrition: **2%** MLB: **91%**

Comparables:
Victor Cruz, Marcos Carvajal, Billy McCool

YEAR	TEAM	LVL	AGE	W	L	SV	G	GS	IP	H	HR	BB	SO	BB9	SO9	GB%	BABIP	WHIP	ERA	FIP	FRA	WARP
2012	CRD	Rk	20	0	0	0	3	2	5	4	1	0	7	0.0	12.6	58%	.273	0.80	1.80	3.23	1.07	0.2
2012	PMB	A+	20	0	0	0	4	0	8	1	0	1	16	1.1	18.0	56%	.111	0.25	0.00	-0.23	0.34	0.3
2012	SFD	AA	20	0	0	0	4	0	8	3	0	3	17	3.4	19.1	67%	.333	0.75	1.12	0.16	0.78	0.3
2013	*SLN*	*MLB*	*21*	*1*	*1*	*1*	*18*	*1*	*38^{1}*	*31*	*4*	*15*	*46*	*3.6*	*10.7*	*47%*	*.307*	*1.19*	*3.37*	*3.33*	*3.66*	*0.4*

The Cardinals were happy to find Wacha still on the board late in the first round of last year's draft, and the former Texas A&M star could hardly have rewarded his new employers with a more impressive pro debut. The towering righty displayed excellent command of his mid-90s fastball, along with a solid changeup and surprisingly improved curveball, while running roughshod over minor-league hitters. Working his way up to Double-A, Wacha struck out almost two batters per inning and walked almost no one, setting up amazingly high expectations for the coming season. Small-sample-size rules apply, of course, but the Cardinals feel they may have uncovered yet another ace-in-waiting.

Adam Wainwright

Born: **8/30/1981** Age: **31**
Bats: **R** Throws: **R** Height: **6' 8"** Weight: **230**
Breakout: **10%** Improve: **34%** Collapse: **27%**
Attrition: **10%** MLB: **89%**

Comparables:
Jose Rijo, Roy Oswalt, John Lackey

YEAR	TEAM	LVL	AGE	W	L	SV	G	GS	IP	H	HR	BB	SO	BB9	SO9	GB%	BABIP	WHIP	ERA	FIP	FRA	WARP
2010	SLN	MLB	28	20	11	0	33	33	230^{1}	186	15	56	213	2.2	8.3	54%	.275	1.05	2.42	2.88	3.51	4.5
2012	SLN	MLB	30	14	13	0	32	32	198^{2}	196	15	52	184	2.4	8.3	52%	.315	1.25	3.94	3.14	3.94	2.7
2013	*SLN*	*MLB*	*31*	*10*	*7*	*0*	*22*	*22*	*143^{2}*	*126*	*12*	*33*	*128*	*2.1*	*8.0*	*50%*	*.296*	*1.10*	*3.17*	*3.19*	*3.44*	*2.2*

Perhaps the happiest story of the season for Cardinals fans was Wainwright's return, as the ace starter came back from a year lost to Tommy John surgery and didn't miss another beat. Just in time, too, as the injury-depleted St. Louis rotation needed his steady production more than ever. The Wagonmaker proved he can still unleash his sinker, cutter, curveball, and changeup to bring a mountain of groundball outs, and his walk and strikeout rates look so much like his peak 2009-10 numbers that great aunts continually confuse them for each other. With the rest of their rotation stocked with question marks (albeit talented ones), the Cardinals should be able to hang their hat on Wainwright.

Jake Westbrook

Born: **9/29/1977** Age: **35**
Bats: **R** Throws: **R** Height: **6' 4"** Weight: **215**
Breakout: **17%** Improve: **48%** Collapse: **25%**
Attrition: **12%** MLB: **79%**

Comparables:
Derek Lowe, Jason Johnson, Jeff Suppan

YEAR	TEAM	LVL	AGE	W	L	SV	G	GS	IP	H	HR	BB	SO	BB9	SO9	GB%	BABIP	WHIP	ERA	FIP	FRA	WARP
2010	CLE	MLB	32	6	7	0	21	21	127^{2}	133	15	44	73	3.1	5.1	54%	.291	1.39	4.65	4.61	5.96	-0.6
2010	SLN	MLB	32	4	4	0	12	12	75	70	5	24	55	2.9	6.6	66%	.281	1.25	3.48	3.55	3.57	1.7
2011	SLN	MLB	33	12	9	0	33	33	183^{1}	208	16	73	104	3.6	5.1	60%	.313	1.53	4.66	4.22	4.51	1.4
2012	SLN	MLB	34	13	11	0	28	28	174^{2}	191	12	52	106	2.7	5.5	59%	.312	1.39	3.97	3.85	4.93	0.6
2013	*SLN*	*MLB*	*35*	*9*	*9*	*0*	*26*	*26*	*151^{1}*	*156*	*16*	*46*	*95*	*2.7*	*5.6*	*56%*	*.305*	*1.34*	*4.47*	*4.23*	*4.86*	*-0.3*

Westbrook is coming off a nice little bounceback year himself. His sinker continues to produce groundball outs at league-leading rates, but last season his walk and strikeout rates moved a few ticks in the right direction. Westbrook can provide excellent production for a fourth or fifth starter, something the Cardinals recognized when they re-upped him for roughly $10 million and a superfluous 2014 mutual option. Now four years removed from elbow surgery, his arm has remained healthy, but we should all expect a few more ancillary problems—like last season's oblique strain—to crop up as Westbrook continues his inexorable creep toward male pattern baldness, early bird specials, and black socks with sandals.

LINEOUTS

HITTERS

PLAYER	TEAM	LVL	AGE	PA	R	2B	3B	HR	RBI	BB	SO	SB-CS	AVG/OBP/SLG	TAv	BABIP	BRR	FRAA	WARP
OF J. Christian	FRE	AAA	32	338	58	23	3	7	35	28	32	12-5	.343/.409/.508	.343	.367	-0.7	CF(47): -5.2, LF(7): -0.3	2.1
	SFN	MLB	32	61	6	1	0	0	2	5	3	2-1	.125/.197/.143	.142	.132	1.1	LF(10): 0.6, RF(8): 0.4	-0.5
OF A. Garcia	QUD	A	20	444	63	34	3	19	74	34	107	3-6	.280/.354/.525	.352	.338	-3.6	LF(20): -2.7, RF(5): 0.1	0.5
C R. Johnson	BUF	AAA	29	178	20	7	1	4	15	9	26	3-2	.207/.253/.335	.228	.219	1.4	C(39): 2.3	0.2
	NYN	MLB	29	58	3	2	0	0	4	4	10	0-0	.250/.298/.288	.204	.302	0.8	C(17): -0.0, P(1): -0.0	0.0
CF C. McElroy	JCY	Rk	19	268	40	11	2	0	22	15	42	24-5	.271/.314/.332	.238	.325	-0.1	CF(44): 1.9	-0.1
OF M. O'Neill	PMB	A+	24	478	56	19	5	0	35	70	24	12-10	.342/.442/.417	.308	.360	-2.4	LF(16): 0.9, CF(7): 0.7	0.4
INF T. Rahmatulla	QUD	A	22	210	37	16	2	7	42	17	36	2-2	.322/.389/.546	.573	.364	-0.3	3B(6): -0.8	1.1
	PMB	A+	22	168	16	4	2	1	7	19	34	0-1	.146/.247/.222	.135	.180	0.3	3B(3): 0.6, 2B(2): 0.3	-0.2
C C. Stanley	PMB	A+	23	170	11	8	1	3	35	6	32	1-0	.280/.300/.401	.277	.320	-2	C(7): -0.1	-0.2
OF C. Tilson	—	—	—	—	—	—	—	—	—	—	—	—	—	—	—	—	—	—
C J. Towles	ROC	AAA	28	189	24	14	0	1	10	12	36	2-4	.214/.280/.315	.220	.263	-0.2	C(39): 0.5, LF(2): -0.2	-0.2
2B B. Valera	BAT	A-	19	305	39	18	4	1	33	18	27	10-6	.316/.359/.418	.308	.344	2.6	2B(34): 1.3, SS(10): -0.8	2.0

As a 33-year-old who has struggled to stay healthy and keep his major-league batting average above the Mendoza line, **Justin Christian**'s big-league days are likely over. **Anthony Garcia** displayed an impressive power bat and a decent approach in his first full professional season; the offensive bar for corner outfielders is high, but if he can put up the same numbers in the high minors, he'll be one to watch. Since **Rob Johnson** cannot hit, frame pitches, or block balls, he's an odd choice to be brought in to compete with Cruz for the backup catcher job. **C.J. McElroy** has a major-league pedigree (he's Chuck's son), little power, and excellent speed, but the fleet outfielder has yet to get on base enough to take much advantage of it. Diminutive outfielder **Mike O'Neill** has no power but is a veritable on-base machine who waits for his pitch and sprays line drives with his short lefty stroke; if he keeps this up at higher levels, the organization may have to take his future a little more seriously. Infield prospect **Tyler Rahmatulla** hit for average and surprising pop in the Midwest League last year but couldn't solve High-A pitching; he can't play shortstop or bat left-handed, but if he continues to barrel everything up the way he did in Quad Cities he could grow into a utility bat. **Cody Stanley** missed 50 games last season after failing a drug test, but when the former fourth-round pick returned he continued to show the solid receiving skills and occasional power that keep him on the prospect radar. New Trier High School star **Charlie Tilson** tore his labrum diving for a ball and missed all of last year; he hopes to be healthy enough to show off his speed, center field defense and gap power in a full-season league this year. Former Astros catcher of the future **J.R. Towles**, owner of a 583 big-league OPS, had his worst minor-league numbers with the Twins' Triple-A team in Rochester last year. **Breyvic Valera** makes solid contact with gap power from both sides of the plate and flashed a decent glove in short-season ball; he can't quite impersonate a shortstop, yet may still grow into a viable utility player.

PITCHERS

PLAYER	TEAM	LVL	AGE	W	L	SV	IP	H	HR	BB	SO	BB9	SO9	GB%	BABIP	WHIP	ERA	FIP	FRA	WARP
S. Blair	CRD	Rk	23	0	0	0	3	1	0	2	1	6.0	3.0	.833	.167	1.00	0.00	5.77	12.09	0.0
	PMB	A+	23	1	3	0	16^{2}	18	1	14	12	7.6	6.5	.456	.304	1.92	5.4	5.25	14.70	0.0
M. Blazek	SFD	AA	23	5	8	0	80	61	11	34	83	3.8	9.3	44%	.254	1.19	4.16	4.38	5.96	-0.2
K. Butler	SFD	AA	23	5	1	25	58^{2}	53	5	23	59	3.5	9.1	39%	.302	1.30	2.76	3.66	3.94	0.7
B. Dickson	MEM	AAA	27	5	11	0	141^{1}	151	17	27	104	1.7	6.6	53%	.307	1.26	3.63	4.39	5.45	0.1
	SLN	MLB	27	0	0	0	6^{1}	10	2	2	6	2.8	8.5	54%	.364	1.89	7.11	6.29	5.85	0.0
E. Fornataro	SFD	AA	24	3	3	5	67^{2}	55	1	17	41	2.3	5.5	60%	.260	1.06	2.39	3.19	3.60	0.6
K. Hald	QUD	A	23	4	5	0	90	88	4	13	77	1.3	7.7	48%	.308	1.12	3.10	2.72	2.55	0.5
	PMB	A+	23	3	4	0	46^{2}	61	3	11	38	2.1	7.3	40%	.359	1.54	3.86	3.37	3.07	0.1
A. Reifer	MEM	AAA	26	1	4	2	64^{1}	64	11	20	44	2.8	6.2	39%	.269	1.31	4.90	5.59	8.79	-0.6
K. Siegrist	PMB	A+	22	6	0	0	55^{1}	33	3	22	41	3.6	6.7	41%	.200	0.99	2.28	4.13	5.55	0.1
	SFD	AA	22	1	2	0	32^{1}	26	4	9	27	2.5	7.5	54%	.247	1.08	3.62	4.52	6.75	-0.2
R. Stock	QUD	A	22	5	2	0	71	61	9	48	66	6.1	8.4	52%	.269	1.54	4.56	5.63	8.93	-0.7
J. Swagerty	—	—	—	—	—	—	—	—	—	—	—	—	—	—	—	—	—	—	—	—

Seth Blair, a former first-rounder from Arizona State, had trouble finding the plate even before losing much of 2012 to a finger issue; with a fastball that can reach the mid-90s and a solid slider, his stuff may work best in the bullpen. Sin City native **Michael Blazek** saw his stuff play up after an in-season move to the bullpen; with his fastball now reaching the mid-90s, the organization saw fit to stash his arm behind glass on the 40-man in preparation for the big club's annual bullpen emergency. **Keith Butler** continued to rack up the strikeouts with his low-90s fastball and sharp slider and forced his way onto the 40-man; a closer in Double-A, his stuff may well work in a set-up role in St. Louis. Having suffered through three years in Memphis with limited access to fresh sushi, lanky strike-thrower **Brandon Dickson** has decided to tote his surprisingly effective sinker-slider combination to Japan this year. Sinkerball enthusiast **Eric Fornataro** doesn't wow with his strikeout numbers, but found success in the Springfield bullpen by working low in the zone and keeping his infielders busy; the organization hopes he can grow into a relief version of Jake Westbrook. Lefty strike-thrower **Kyle Hald** keeps his walks in check and was productive in his first full pro season, but will have to prove himself against Double-A batters before prospect mavens start taking notice. Lightning-armed reliever **Adam Reifer** returned from a knee injury but struggled mightily in the Memphis bullpen, and with so many other premium arms in the system has likely already been passed over. A long-levered lefty with a deceptive delivery, **Kevin Siegrist** could turn into a solid swingman, but even if he grows up to be a LOOGY, that would be quite a feat for a 41st-round pick. Former catcher **Robert Stock** never did turn into soup behind the plate, so the Cardinals moved him to the mound; he missed a few bats in Low-A, but the odds are against him amounting to much in the long run. Late-inning warrior **Jordan Swagerty** can flash mid-90s heat and a plus breaking pitch, but missed all of 2012 after Tommy John surgery; we'll find out later this year how much command the surgeons may have inadvertently removed.

MANAGER: MIKE MATHENY

YEAR	TEAM	W-L	Pythag +/-	Avg PC	100+ P	120+ P	QS	BQS	REL	REL w Zero R	IBB	PH	PH Avg	PH HR	SB2	CS2	SB3	CS3	SAC Att	SAC %	POS SAC	Squeeze	Swing	In Play
2012	SLN	88-74	1	94.2	49	1	99	4	506	400	28	279	.190	1	18	5	1	5	104	73.1%	40	0	287	100

Tony La Russa's first season in St. Louis was a major success. The future Hall of Fame manager led the Cardinals to 88 regular-season wins and a chance to clinch a World Series berth at home in Game Five of the NLCS before losing three straight in ignominious fashion. Sound familiar? Taking over the defending world champions, or replacing a living legend, or propelling a team forward without their franchise player, or managing one of the league's cornerstones without a single day's experience running a clubhouse would be daunting tasks individually. That Mike Matheny was successful while taking on all these challenges at once is a signal achievement. Despite a rash of injuries, particularly in the rotation, Matheny showed flexibility in sorting through his various options, and more often than not he put his players in a position to succeed. While it occasionally felt as if the new skipper was learning on the job, especially early in the season, it's clear the Cardinals are in good hands. It took La Russa six more playoff runs after that 1996 disappointment to finally win a championship in a St. Louis uniform. Cardinals fans are hoping Matheny won't mimic his predecessor in that way, too.

Tampa Bay Rays

2012: THE ONE THAT GOT AWAY

Five years ago, the Tampa Bay Rays were an expansion mistake. Last year, they won 90 games for the fourth time in five seasons, barely missed the playoffs . . . and? Went home with "the worst feeling I've had since I've been here," a Rays official lamented in October. The paradigm has officially shifted. Close is no longer close enough.

If Evan Longoria hadn't missed half the season with a hamstring injury. If free-agent power-strokers Carlos Pena and Luke Scott hadn't seized up. If the Rays had won a few more one-run games or the Baltimore Orioles had lost a few more—or, for that matter, if the Rays hadn't lost consecutive 3-2 games to those Orioles on September 12-13. If they hadn't inexplicably committed the most errors (and had the highest error rate) in the American League, after committing the fewest errors in the majors in 2011. If they hadn't lost eight players (six regulars) to the disabled list in May and June, when they went 26–31. And so on.

RAYS PROSPECTUS

2012 W-L: 90-72, 3rd in AL East

Pythag	.585	3rd	DER	.723	1st
RS/G	4.30	18th	B-Age	29.7	25th
RA/G	3.56	1st	P-Age	27.3	6th
TAv	.265	10th	Salary	$63.6	26th
BRR	-6.9	24th	M$/MW	$1.21	2nd
TAv-P	.243	1st	DL Days	947	12th
FIP	3.46	1st	DL WARP	5.5	5th

Three-Year Park Factors	
Overall	**94**
HR/RH	**97**
HR/LH	**88**
AVG/RH	**98**
AVG/LH	**94**

Tropicana Field (1990)
Att. % of Capacity: 56.5% (25th)
Dim. 315, 410, 404, 404, 322

The Trop is a key character in the Rays saga, an offensive dead zone where lefties hit .214 last season.

The overall plan was, for the most part, sound, as was much of the execution—some of which actually beat expectations. Tampa Bay allowed the fewest runs in the major leagues, and it was a pair of presumably bad breaks that helped them do so: Kyle Farnsworth's early-season injury enabled Fernando Rodney's record-setting year, and Jeff Niemann's cracked fibula opened up a spot in the starting rotation for Alex Cobb, who made the most of it. Jose Molina set a career high for games played at age 37, reducing the need for replacement-level catchers. And the Rays finally found an in-house solution to their shortstop problem: Ben Zobrist, who filled the hole late and put up his highest positional-split OPS (949) in 44 games there.

Yet they finished third in their division.

2013: SMALL POND

Can the Rays succeed in the division of baseball where competition is the toughest, both in terms of on-field talent and dollars spent? Their draft advantages dwindling and their revenue situation remaining grim, they'll continue to go cheek by guile, relying on Joe Maddon's wits, guts, good young pitching, and Longoria's bat, which they secured for 10 more years with an A-Rodian contract extension.

Leaving aside the rigors of the AL East, the issue may simply be that the *The Extra 2%* Jonah Keri celebrated in his 2011 book on the Rays is not only a byword of positive arbitrage, but also the tiny margin for error that makes the club financially vulnerable to negative skew. Needing, perhaps, one more bat to push them into the playoffs last year, the Rays' only notable move was trading cheaply for Ryan Roberts, a middling player who was an unsatisfactory patch for Longoria. Of course, a healthy Longoria could have the same effect as "adding a bat"this year. In case he doesn't, the Rays acted boldly again shortly after the Longoria extension: They traded workhorse starter James Shields, along with Wade Davis, to Kansas City for blue-chip prospect slugger Wil Myers. And in classic Rays (and, frankly, Royals) fashion, they got Dayton Moore to throw in two potential starting pitchers as well.

The Rays enter the second half of their ascendant decade with probably baseball's best and deepest pitching, but without another up-the-middle mainstay: longtime center-fielder B.J. Upton is gone because Tampa Bay couldn't pay his free-agent price. The Rays will hope that Desmond Jennings can fill Upton's shoes, and that someone can fill Jennings's in left. They traded for Yunel Escobar to stabilize shortstop, which tightens up the roster by allowing Zobrist to maximize his natural utility, keeping replacement-level players on the bench. First base and DH remain chronic weaknesses. That's to be expected, as money and power walk in lockstep. But improvement should be made over the sodden output of Pena and Scott—even by James Loney, signed on the cheap at the Winter Meetings, and whomever Maddon pencils in at DH on any given day.

STATE OF THE ORGANIZATION: JUST KEEP SWIMMING

Does success count if no one is there to see it? Tampa Bay finished dead last in the majors in attendance in 2012. Stuart Sternberg & Co. have been pleading for years, with support from virtually all of baseball, including the commissioner, to be freed from their onerous stadium situation, with little progress. Just after last year's World Series, St. Petersburg Mayor Bill Foster firmly rejected Sternberg's latest proposal to get beyond Thunderdome, rejecting his request to investigate sites farther afield in Hillsborough County. The franchise, whose lease at Tropicana Field runs through 2027, seems doomed to the dome.

With revenue stagnant, or functionally shrinking while competing markets have seen growth, the team has built and exploited a strong farm system. But Myers swings the only impact bat in the upper levels of the minors, as the Rays' abundance of top draft picks of the 2000s—like Upton—have already played up or out of the system.

That means that near-devious innovation and creativity must remain the Rays' *modus operandi.* They exploited the compensatory draft-pick system to its fullest in 2011, their free-agent exodus netting them a bonanza of seven supplemental-round selections (Tampa Bay occupied 10 of the draft's first 60 slots). Then along came the new CBA, which seemed almost deliberately designed to punish the Rays. Compensatory picks were virtually eliminated, and new draft spending limits curbed Tampa Bay's ability to bid high on developable talent. The new Competitive Balance Lottery draft actually penalizes successful teams. Only the cap imposed on international free-agent spending would seem to favor the Rays, and they could very well turn their attention overseas as their stateside advantage shrinks. One scout raved about Tampa Bay's program in Venezuela, which has already produced some exciting young pitchers.

Until they outfox the market again, the Rays are hanging their hopes high on the 2011 bumper crop of draftees (almost all of whom you'll find discussed in this chapter). Look, too, for the front office—which lost senior vice president for baseball operations Gerry Hunsicker to the Dodgers—to keep trawling the free-agent deeps and trade-market swamps for smaller fish, or in some cases simply wartier ones. The Rays have not shied away from character risks like Manny Ramirez, Willy Aybar, Josh Lueke, and Matt Bush, and it took just a few days after last season ended for pundits to link them to eyeblack-homophobe Escobar and PED-user Melky Cabrera. They may have dropped the Devil from their nickname, but the Rays still have to dance with him—and sometimes they are him: In December, they made a deal with Faust—the former Fausto Carmona, that is, who was busted for carrying a false identity and now returns as the namesake of Tampa Bay's former closer, Roberto Hernandez.

The fragile issue of "character" is why the Rays' seven minor-league player suspensions last year, the most in baseball, drew more notice than they might have in some other organizations—partly because the violators included two first-rounders. A franchise so heavily dependent on developing its own talent must keep that talent free of taint in order to succeed. Late in 2012, four Bowling Green Hot Rods (including top prospects Ryan Brett and Josh Sale) were suspended after testing positive for amphetamine and methamphetamine. The Rays investigated and concluded that there was no organizational failure to keep players educated and clean, but it didn't seem coincidental that three of the seven suspended Rays farmhands were released after the season. The extra 2 percent is also that toxic, inorganic element that a franchise like Tampa Bay simply cannot afford to carry.

HITTERS

Leslie Anderson **OF**
Born: **3/30/1982** Age: **31**
Bats: **L** Throws: **L** Height: **6' 2"**
Weight: **205** Breakout: **2%**
Improve: **33%** Collapse: **16%**
Attrition: **14%** MLB: **84%**
Comparables:
Willie Montanez, Ray Knight, Shea Hillenbrand

YEAR	TEAM	LVL	AGE	PA	R	2B	3B	HR	RBI	BB	SO	SB	CS	AVG_OBP_SLG	TAv	BABIP	BRR	FRAA	WARP
2010	PCH	A+	28	89	13	3	0	3	11	4	6	0	1	.262/.303/.405	.263	.253	-0.3	LF(9): -1.4, 1B(9): -0.3	-0.1
2010	MNT	AA	28	204	24	11	1	6	25	18	28	3	1	.304/.382/.475	.274	.333	1.8	1B(24): 0.7, LF(18): -1.9	0.6
2010	DUR	AAA	28	129	14	5	0	2	13	5	20	0	0	.328/.357/.418	.264	.376	1.1	LF(22): -2.8, 1B(10): 0.2	0.1
2011	DUR	AAA	29	494	46	24	0	13	65	21	60	2	3	.277/.314/.413	.250	.292	0	--	0.0
2012	DUR	AAA	30	482	63	21	0	14	56	26	56	0	3	.309/.355/.450	.230	.325	1.1	RF(11): 0.3, 1B(11): -0.5	-0.6
2013	*TBA*	*MLB*	*31*	*250*	*23*	*10*	*1*	*6*	*28*	*12*	*43*	*0*	*0*	*.254/.296/.380*	*.251*	*.285*	*-0.5*	*LF -1, 1B -1*	*0.0*

Cuban defector Anderson was pretty much *ropa vieja* going into 2012, his gawky swing, dreadful walk rate, and poor fielding apparently adding up to a $1.725 million mistake by the usually more savvy Rays. But he spent the offseason studying game film and readying himself to deal with changeups, which he said are rarer in Cuba. The result in a second full go-round at Triple-A was better poise at the plate and a rise in production. Anderson even flirted with the International League batting title despite a dropoff against lefties. His fielding improved, too. He enters the final year of his contract with something to build on, if probably no real shot at a big-league job.

Tim Beckham **MI**

Born: **1/27/1990** Age: **23**
Bats: **R** Throws: **R** Height: **6' 1"**
Weight: **190** Breakout: **7%**
Improve: **37%** Collapse: **9%**
Attrition: **15%** MLB: **91%**

Comparables:
Eddie Leon,Roy Smalley,Dale Berra

YEAR	TEAM	LVL	AGE	PA	R	2B	3B	HR	RBI	BB	SO	SB	CS	AVG_OBP_SLG	TAv	BABIP	BRR	FRAA	WARP
2010	PCH	A+	20	542	68	23	5	5	57	62	119	22	14	.256/.344/.359	.253	.328	2.5	SS(126): -21.0	2.2
2010	PCH	A+	20	542	68	23	5	5	57	62	119	22	14	.256/.344/.359	.253	.328	2.5	SS(2): -0.1	2.2
2011	MNT	AA	21	468	82	25	2	7	57	39	91	15	4	.275/.339/.395	.260	.334	0	--	0.0
2011	DUR	AAA	21	111	12	3	2	5	13	3	29	2	1	.255/.282/.462	.245	.306	0	--	0.0
2012	DUR	AAA	22	323	40	10	1	6	28	29	71	6	0	.256/.325/.361	.168	.316	1.8	SS(12): 1.3, 2B(8): -0.5	-0.5
2013	*TBA*	*MLB*	*23*	*250*	*26*	*9*	*1*	*3*	*19*	*19*	*66*	*4*	*2*	*.215/.279/.309*	*.223*	*.282*	*0*	*SS 1, 2B -0*	*0.2*

The biggest news Beckham made last year was for his 50-game recreational-drug suspension in April. When he was playing, the 2008 overall top pick continued to look like the same hot and cold, promising but maddening prospect he has always been. Yet there are signs of progress and change. Beckham dramatically altered his stance midseason and started hitting the ball to right field with more authority. He also played second base for the first time as a pro, increasing his utility and easing worries about his proficiency at shortstop. Beckham was the first guy at the ballpark most days last season, taking his grounders and swings. He has ambition and drive, and he's still young enough to keep watching despite poor results in the AFL.

Jason Bourgeois **OF**

Born: **1/4/1982** Age: **31**
Bats: **R** Throws: **R** Height: **5' 10"**
Weight: **195** Breakout: **0%**
Improve: **30%** Collapse: **3%**
Attrition: **11%** MLB: **84%**

Comparables:
Darryl Hamilton,Tike Redman,Matty Alou

YEAR	TEAM	LVL	AGE	PA	R	2B	3B	HR	RBI	BB	SO	SB	CS	AVG_OBP_SLG	TAv	BABIP	BRR	FRAA	WARP
2010	ROU	AAA	28	261	37	10	3	5	28	21	28	18	6	.345/.402/.477	.299	.373	0.5	CF(48): -5.4	1.3
2010	HOU	MLB	28	136	16	4	1	0	3	13	16	12	4	.220/.294/.268	.203	.252	-0.3	LF(25): -0.1, CF(24): 0.2	-0.5
2011	HOU	MLB	29	252	30	8	2	1	16	10	24	31	6	.294/.323/.357	.244	.324	2.3	CF(34): -2.0, LF(32): 0.0	0.2
2012	OMA	AAA	30	247	41	7	1	3	8	21	24	7	5	.243/.314/.324	.226	.262	-0.2	RF(13): 0.3, CF(11): 0.1	-0.2
2012	KCA	MLB	30	66	10	2	1	0	5	4	4	5	4	.258/.303/.323	.246	.276	0.8	CF(23): 0.5, LF(2): -0.1	0.1
2013	*TBA*	*MLB*	*31*	*250*	*30*	*9*	*2*	*2*	*16*	*14*	*34*	*14*	*5*	*.251/.297/.329*	*.240*	*.283*	*1.2*	*CF -1, LF -0*	*0.2*

Dayton Moore has never met a speedy, banjo-hitting center fielder he could resist. So when the Royals were filling out their roster at the end of spring training last year, it was only natural that Bourgeois found his way to Kansas City. He's hopeless against right-handed pitching, so credit the Royals for using him in a platoon and limiting exposure to his weakness. He was designated for assignment in November, and the Rays signed him to a minor-league deal. He and Rich Thompson will run wild in the Durham outfield as Triple-A insurance for post-surgery Sam Fuld.

Ryan Brett **2B**

Born: **10/9/1991** Age: **21**
Bats: **B** Throws: **R** Height: **5' 10"**
Weight: **180** Breakout: **2%**
Improve: **47%** Collapse: **7%**
Attrition: **11%** MLB: **96%**

Comparables:
Bill Mazeroski,Tim Foli,Glenn Hubbard

YEAR	TEAM	LVL	AGE	PA	R	2B	3B	HR	RBI	BB	SO	SB	CS	AVG_OBP_SLG	TAv	BABIP	BRR	FRAA	WARP
2010	RAY	Rk	18	99	8	5	2	0	9	8	17	12	3	.303/.367/.404	.293	.375	0.4	2B(28): 1.6, SS(1): -0.0	0.8
2011	PRI	Rk	19	270	42	22	5	3	24	26	24	21	3	.300/.370/.471	.307	.321	0.6	2B(34): -0.4	0.9
2012	BGR	A	20	456	77	20	3	6	35	37	73	48	8	.285/.348/.393	.268	.332	4.8	2B(68): -7.9	0.2
2013	*TBA*	*MLB*	*21*	*250*	*29*	*9*	*1*	*2*	*15*	*13*	*59*	*15*	*3*	*.212/.254/.291*	*.209*	*.270*	*1.9*	*2B -1*	*-0.3*

A promotion to High-A Bowling Green saw a compensatory drop in the scrapalicious spark plug's walk rate. Brett still couldn't hit from the right side (.188/.276/.217 in 77 PA), and his 20 errors helped torpedo his fielding rating, although he more than doubled his stolen bases. But did his extra speed come from, well, extra speed? Brett was one of three Hot Rods to draw 50-game suspensions near the end of the season for amphetamine and methamphetamine. Brett vehemently denied the meth use and attributed the reading to Adderall, which he claimed to have taken a single time, and unknowingly. He'll try to hit the ground running when he returns in May.

Reid Brignac **2B**

Born: **1/16/1986** Age: **27**
Bats: **L** Throws: **R** Height: **6' 4"**
Weight: **195** Breakout: **2%**
Improve: **42%** Collapse: **11%**
Attrition: **20%** MLB: **93%**

Comparables:
J.J. Furmaniak,Gene Alley,Jay Bell

YEAR	TEAM	LVL	AGE	PA	R	2B	3B	HR	RBI	BB	SO	SB	CS	AVG_OBP_SLG	TAv	BABIP	BRR	FRAA	WARP
2010	TBA	MLB	24	326	39	13	1	8	45	20	77	3	3	.256/.307/.385	.252	.317	1.9	2B(68): 3.5, SS(50): -0.0	1.5
2011	TBA	MLB	25	264	18	4	0	1	15	10	63	3	1	.193/.227/.221	.174	.254	0.1	SS(91): 5.6	-0.8
2012	DUR	AAA	26	400	45	14	2	8	46	45	79	3	3	.231/.323/.353	.255	.276	1.4	SS(31): -1.4, 2B(1): 0.0	0.2
2012	TBA	MLB	26	22	1	0	0	0	1	1	5	0	0	.095/.136/.095	.091	.125	0	SS(11): 0.2, 3B(4): 0.1	-0.3
2013	*TBA*	*MLB*	*27*	*250*	*23*	*10*	*1*	*4*	*22*	*15*	*58*	*2*	*1*	*.223/.274/.330*	*.227*	*.277*	*-0.4*	*SS -2, 2B 0*	*0.0*

Less than two years after he was handed the starting shortstop job at age 24, Brignac not only handed it back, he couldn't even keep his roster spot. With minor-league options left, virtually nil production in limited at-bats, and still sporting the flitting uppercut swing that has hampered him for years, Brignac was sent to Triple-A for regular playing time. He struggled to hit there, too; more alarmingly, his fielding declined. Without his long-admired glove, Brignac has no value unless he makes dramatic improvements at the plate that may require a total overhaul of his stance and mechanics. The 27-year-old is nearly out of time to make good on the promise that led the Rays to draft him in the second round nine years ago.

Yunel Escobar **SS**

Born: **11/2/1982** Age: **30**
Bats: **R** Throws: **R** Height: **6' 3"**
Weight: **205** Breakout: **4%**
Improve: **28%** Collapse: **6%**
Attrition: **10%** MLB: **91%**

Comparables:
Rafael Furcal,Oscar Robles,Ryan Theriot

YEAR	TEAM	LVL	AGE	PA	R	2B	3B	HR	RBI	BB	SO	SB	CS	AVG_OBP_SLG	TAv	BABIP	BRR	FRAA	WARP
2010	ATL	MLB	27	301	28	12	0	0	19	37	31	5	1	.238/.334/.284	.231	.270	-0.7	SS(74): 10.4	1.3
2010	TOR	MLB	27	266	32	7	0	4	16	19	26	1	1	.275/.340/.356	.245	.296	0.4	SS(60): -5.1	0.1
2011	TOR	MLB	28	590	77	24	3	11	48	61	70	3	3	.290/.369/.413	.284	.316	0.3	SS(132): -3.9	2.9
2012	TOR	MLB	29	608	58	22	1	9	51	35	70	5	1	.253/.300/.344	.232	.273	2	SS(143): 7.2	1.2
2013	*TBA*	*MLB*	*30*	*568*	*64*	*21*	*2*	*8*	*48*	*50*	*70*	*4*	*2*	*.259/.331/.355*	*.261*	*.282*	*-0.8*	*SS 4*	*3.0*

An altogether frustrating season bottomed out in September when Escobar was given a three-game suspension for writing a homophobic slur on his eye black. After hitting .314 against off-speed pitches in 2011, Escobar slipped to .185 last year, helping sabotage his season at the plate. He also saw fewer pitches, leading to a career-worst 5.8 percent walk rate. The Blue Jays sent him to Miami in November's Jose Reyes mega-deal, and a few weeks later, he went intrastate to the Rays, who needed a shortstop so badly that they were glad to grab Escobar and his modest salary.

Cole Figueroa **INF**

Born: **6/30/1987** Age: **26**
Bats: **L** Throws: **R** Height: **5' 11"**
Weight: **180** Breakout: **2%**
Improve: **46%** Collapse: **4%**
Attrition: **14%** MLB: **94%**

Comparables:
Jerry Kenney,Larry Wolfe,Maicer Izturis

YEAR	TEAM	LVL	AGE	PA	R	2B	3B	HR	RBI	BB	SO	SB	CS	AVG_OBP_SLG	TAv	BABIP	BRR	FRAA	WARP
2010	LEL	A+	23	578	88	25	3	4	66	81	54	26	9	.303/.405/.392	.298	.329	1.7	2B(109): -6.2, SS(19): -1.8	3.8
2011	MNT	AA	24	488	71	20	6	5	51	55	41	9	5	.283/.375/.398	.279	.302	0	--	0.0
2012	MNT	AA	25	105	17	6	1	3	12	17	9	1	2	.314/.419/.512	.326	.316	-0.6	--	0.0
2012	DUR	AAA	25	347	32	17	4	2	42	26	22	3	2	.286/.344/.386	.225	.300	0.3	2B(20): -2.8, 3B(19): -0.9	-0.2
2013	*TBA*	*MLB*	*26*	*250*	*26*	*10*	*1*	*2*	*18*	*23*	*33*	*3*	*1*	*.242/.314/.327*	*.244*	*.272*	*-0.1*	*2B -1, 3B -0*	*0.2*

His father Bien was a player, coach, and manager, so it's no surprise that the kid plays an intelligent, steady game and swings a patient bat; his career BB/K rate speaks to inherited baseball acumen. Last season, he adjusted quickly to Triple-A pitching and took the third base job from incumbent slugger Matt Mangini (who was released in August). However, the smallish Figueroa, acquired in the 2009 Jason Bartlett deal, lacks the power for third base and perhaps the range for second, his regular position (he played just under half his games there last season). He may, like his father, top out at Triple-A, but he could become the Rays' Will Rhymes v. 2.0(13).

Mike Fontenot **MI**

Born: **6/9/1980** Age: **33**
Bats: **L** Throws: **R** Height: **5' 9"**
Weight: **165** Breakout: **2%**
Improve: **34%** Collapse: **6%**
Attrition: **13%** MLB: **93%**

Comparables:
Mark Ellis,Ray Durham,Tadahito Iguchi

YEAR	TEAM	LVL	AGE	PA	R	2B	3B	HR	RBI	BB	SO	SB	CS	AVG_OBP_SLG	TAv	BABIP	BRR	FRAA	WARP
2010	CHN	MLB	30	185	14	11	3	1	20	10	28	1	2	.284/.332/.402	.255	.331	-0.3	2B(33): -0.9, 3B(13): 0.2	0.1
2010	SFN	MLB	30	76	10	2	0	0	5	5	13	0	2	.282/.329/.310	.242	.345	0.5	2B(16): 0.5, 3B(6): -0.0	0.2
2011	SFN	MLB	31	252	22	15	3	4	21	25	48	5	1	.227/.304/.377	.250	.267	2.2	SS(37): -1.5, 2B(23): 0.8	0.4
2012	LEH	AAA	32	58	5	6	0	1	7	5	11	0	0	.308/.368/.481	.247	.375	-0.4	2B(3): 0.3, 3B(3): 0.0	0.1
2012	PHI	MLB	32	105	13	2	0	1	5	7	23	0	1	.289/.343/.340	.247	.370	0.6	2B(17): -0.5, 3B(12): 0.6	0.0
2013	*TBA*	*MLB*	*33*	*250*	*25*	*12*	*1*	*4*	*23*	*21*	*51*	*2*	*1*	*.239/.307/.360*	*.250*	*.288*	*-0.3*	*2B -2, SS -0*	*0.5*

The Rays' signing of Fontenot to a minor-league deal betokens their lack of optimism in Brignac, another lefty-swinging, Louisiana-born middle infielder who hasn't lived up to his draft slot (Brignac was a second-rounder, Fontenot first). Fontenot, who has more pop than the stickless Brignac, spent much of last season on the Phillies bench, scrounging 105 plate appearances before he was outrighted to Triple-A on August 1. He'll join a very crowded Durham Bulls infield and, as its elder statesman, is likely to see big-league time, either with Tampa Bay or another team, by season's end.

Sam Fuld **OF**

Born: **11/20/1981** Age: **31**
Bats: **L** Throws: **L** Height: **5' 11"**
Weight: **180** Breakout: **0%**
Improve: **38%** Collapse: **11%**
Attrition: **22%** MLB: **93%**

Comparables:
Danny Heep,Matt Lawton,Elliott Maddox

YEAR	TEAM	LVL	AGE	PA	R	2B	3B	HR	RBI	BB	SO	SB	CS	AVG_OBP_SLG	TAv	BABIP	BRR	FRAA	WARP
2010	IOW	AAA	28	440	69	15	9	4	27	66	37	21	9	.272/.384/.394	.278	.293	0	CF(106): 12.7	4.1
2010	CHN	MLB	28	31	3	1	0	0	3	3	5	0	0	.143/.226/.179	.136	.174	-0.1	LF(7): -0.0, CF(7): 1.0	-0.2
2011	TBA	MLB	29	346	41	18	5	3	27	32	49	20	8	.240/.313/.360	.260	.276	0.5	LF(75): 7.3, RF(9): 0.5	1.7
2012	TBA	MLB	30	107	14	3	2	0	5	8	14	7	2	.255/.318/.327	.241	.298	-0.6	RF(15): 0.2, LF(14): 0.3	0.0
2013	*TBA*	*MLB*	*31*	*250*	*30*	*10*	*3*	*1*	*17*	*26*	*34*	*11*	*4*	*.238/.321/.332*	*.250*	*.273*	*0.7*	*LF 2, CF 0*	*0.7*

During spring training last year, Fuld aggravated a wrist injury he originally sustained in September 2011. The resulting surgery cost him most of the season. In true Legend of Sam Fuld fashion, he returned sooner than expected, in late July, and played in 44 games, although he missed another fortnight in September with a hamstring strain. The Rays know full well that Fuld, whose Super Sam glove comes with a Clark Kent bat, isn't really an every-day player. They'd prefer him as a fourth outfielder, and in 2013 that would be the role in which he'd provide the most value.

Chris Gimenez C

Born: **12/27/1982** Age: **30**
Bats: **R** Throws: **R** Height: **6' 3"**
Weight: **220** Breakout: **4%**
Improve: **29%** Collapse: **8%**
Attrition: **15%** MLB: **90%**

Comparables:
Landon Powell,Ed Bailey,Johnny Roseboro

YEAR	TEAM	LVL	AGE	PA	R	2B	3B	HR	RBI	BB	SO	SB	CS	AVG_OBP_SLG	TAv	BABIP	BRR	FRAA	WARP
2010	COH	AAA	27	219	32	10	0	9	32	20	38	1	1	.276/.339/.464	.262	.298	-1.4	RF(26): -1.7, C(18): 0.2	0.3
2010	CLE	MLB	27	67	6	5	0	1	8	8	22	0	0	.190/.288/.328	.223	.286	-0.4	C(24): 0.0, LF(1): 0.0	0.0
2011	TAC	AAA	28	56	8	1	0	1	4	7	13	0	1	.265/.357/.347	.213	.343	-0.6	C(8): 0.1, 1B(2): 0.0	-0.2
2011	SEA	MLB	28	70	6	1	0	1	6	10	13	0	1	.203/.314/.271	.235	.239	0.3	C(20): -0.4, LF(3): -0.1	0.0
2012	DUR	AAA	29	301	39	15	0	10	49	33	57	0	3	.310/.389/.483	.245	.359	0.1	C(14): -0.3, RF(3): 0.4	0.1
2012	TBA	MLB	29	109	10	4	0	1	9	8	24	0	0	.260/.315/.330	.229	.333	-1.5	C(38): 0.1, LF(1): 0.0	-0.1
2013	*TBA*	*MLB*	*30*	*250*	*25*	*9*	*0*	*6*	*25*	*25*	*62*	*0*	*0*	*.220/.300/.345*	*.242*	*.274*	*-0.6*	*C -0, RF -0*	*0.4*

In February 2012, the Rays, chronically beset by catcheritis, signed Gimenez—who also plays corner infield and outfield—to a minor-league deal. They needed him in the majors almost immediately when Jose Lobaton hit the DL just after Easter. Gimenez performed at just about replacement level until Lobaton returned in late May. Back in Triple-A, Gimenez's OPS flirted with 900 all summer while he waited for the fragile Lobaton to get hurt again, but Lobaton stayed healthy. In some other world, Gimenez forms a catcher-corner infielder/outfielder platoon with lefty-swinging Stephen Vogt, but unfortunately that world is the International League. Nonetheless, an affable, outgoing teammate with multiple skills is an essential 40-man commodity, and Gimenez is likely to log a few major-league at-bats again this year.

Todd Glaesmann OF

Born: **10/24/1990** Age: **22**
Bats: **R** Throws: **R** Height: **6' 5"**
Weight: **220** Breakout: **4%**
Improve: **60%** Collapse: **2%**
Attrition: **10%** MLB: **95%**

Comparables:
John Hale,Wily Mo Pena,Lloyd Moseby

YEAR	TEAM	LVL	AGE	PA	R	2B	3B	HR	RBI	BB	SO	SB	CS	AVG_OBP_SLG	TAv	BABIP	BRR	FRAA	WARP
2010	PRI	Rk	19	261	41	17	5	4	24	13	70	13	6	.233/.296/.398	.249	.311	2.5	CF(46): -2.9, RF(8): -0.7	0.2
2011	BGR	A	20	228	28	8	2	4	21	14	85	6	0	.229/.286/.343	.258	.364	0.2	RF(11): -1.9, CF(1): -0.0	-0.2
2012	BGR	A	21	392	57	17	5	13	53	22	89	8	3	.281/.338/.469	.290	.336	1.5	CF(49): -3.4, LF(12): 0.2	1.1
2012	PCH	A+	21	148	20	8	2	8	22	8	35	0	0	.295/.333/.554	.268	.344	0.3	RF(12): -2.3	-0.1
2013	*TBA*	*MLB*	*22*	*250*	*23*	*8*	*1*	*7*	*26*	*9*	*80*	*3*	*1*	*.203/.240/.334*	*.214*	*.271*	*0.3*	*CF -2, RF -0*	*-0.7*

Glaesmann, a big, athletic outfielder (and former high school quarterback) earned a midseason promotion to high-A and nearly duplicated his low walk and high strikeout rates. He also had a 14-game hitting streak and a spike in home-run rate, leading the Rays farm system in dingers and earning organizational Minor League Player of the Year honors. A 2009 third-rounder (he was the top pick the Rays managed to sign that year), he's a touch old for A-ball—although to be fair, he lost about half of 2011 to injury. If he builds on his breakout 2012 and improves his plate discipline, Glaesmann's rise could accelerate. His power alone makes him worth following.

Tyler Goeddel 3B

Born: **10/20/1992** Age: **20**
Bats: **R** Throws: **R** Height: **6' 5"**
Weight: **180** Breakout: **28%**
Improve: **62%** Collapse: **4%**
Attrition: **29%** MLB: **86%**

Comparables:
Clete Boyer,Adrian Beltre,Wayne Causey

YEAR	TEAM	LVL	AGE	PA	R	2B	3B	HR	RBI	BB	SO	SB	CS	AVG_OBP_SLG	TAv	BABIP	BRR	FRAA	WARP
2012	BGR	A	19	379	52	19	2	6	46	38	94	30	5	.246/.335/.371	.240	.325	5.3	3B(69): 10.3	1.2
2013	*TBA*	*MLB*	*20*	*250*	*26*	*8*	*1*	*4*	*19*	*17*	*78*	*11*	*2*	*.193/.253/.284*	*.206*	*.269*	*1.3*	*3B 2*	*-0.5*

Goeddel's father helped develop HGH (lose that smirk), and his brother Erik pitches in the Mets farm system: genetic brains and brawn. Scouts suggested that Goeddel might take his promising bat and athleticism to center field. The Rays even think he's agile enough to play shortstop (although he'll stay at third), and weren't worried that he made 29 errors at the hot corner last season, 19 of them in his last 40 games. Goeddel is still lanky and wore down as the season progressed. After an 853 April OPS with three homers, it never reached 700 in any subsequent month, and he hit only three more taters the rest of the way. The Rays will wait for him to fill out into full-season form and the third-base profile.

Brandon Guyer OF

Born: **1/28/1986** Age: **27**
Bats: **R** Throws: **R** Height: **6' 2"**
Weight: **210** Breakout: **1%**
Improve: **56%** Collapse: **6%**
Attrition: **9%** MLB: **96%**

Comparables:
Ruben Sierra,Jeff Francoeur,Nate Schierholtz

YEAR	TEAM	LVL	AGE	PA	R	2B	3B	HR	RBI	BB	SO	SB	CS	AVG_OBP_SLG	TAv	BABIP	BRR	FRAA	WARP
2010	TEN	AA	24	410	76	39	6	13	58	27	51	30	3	.344/.395/.588	.330	.368	-0.7	RF(51): -0.4, LF(50): 12.0	6.1
2011	DUR	AAA	25	443	78	29	5	14	61	35	79	16	6	.312/.384/.521	.310	.360	0	--	0.0
2011	TBA	MLB	25	43	7	1	0	2	3	1	9	0	0	.195/.214/.366	.226	.200	0.4	RF(11): -0.2, LF(3): 0.2	0.0
2012	DUR	AAA	26	97	9	3	1	3	13	7	15	2	0	.294/.365/.459	.352	.324	1	RF(5): -0.0, CF(3): 0.0	0.5
2012	TBA	MLB	26	7	2	0	0	1	1	0	1	0	0	.143/.143/.571	.342	.000	0	LF(3): -0.0	0.1
2013	*TBA*	*MLB*	*27*	*250*	*29*	*13*	*2*	*8*	*30*	*12*	*45*	*8*	*1*	*.254/.296/.419*	*.266*	*.280*	*1.2*	*RF -1, LF 0*	*0.8*

It was a rough year for Guyer. In spring training, he loaned Matt Bush the vehicle Bush subsequently drove into a DUI hit-and-run that seriously injured a motorcyclist. With remorse and a $5 million civil suit hanging over him, Guyer nonetheless hit well and got an early-season call-up from Triple-A—and soon thereafter went down for the season with a torn labrum in his non-throwing shoulder, which he originally injured shortly before he was drafted in 2007.

If healthy in 2013, Guyer, a toolsy but incomplete player—iffy plate discipline, questionable routes in the outfield—could contribute as a fourth outfielder. He'll need to have a major breakthrough to earn a starting role, though.

Jake Hager SS
Born: **3/4/1993** Age: **20**
Bats: **R** Throws: **R** Height: **6' 2"**
Weight: **170** Breakout: **9%**
Improve: **29%** Collapse: **11%**
Attrition: **17%** MLB: **93%**
Comparables:
Ted Kazanski, Edgar Renteria, Robin Yount

YEAR	TEAM	LVL	AGE	PA	R	2B	3B	HR	RBI	BB	SO	SB	CS	AVG_OBP_SLG	TAv	BABIP	BRR	FRAA	WARP
2011	PRI	Rk	18	204	29	11	1	4	17	9	26	5	7	.269/.305/.399	.264	.294	-0.7	SS(25): -7.0	-0.4
2012	BGR	A	19	501	63	22	3	10	72	40	60	17	11	.281/.345/.412	.284	.302	-2.2	SS(75): -10.1	0.7
2013	*TBA*	*MLB*	*20*	*250*	*26*	*9*	*1*	*4*	*20*	*12*	*53*	*4*	*3*	*.220/.261/.321*	*.221*	*.262*	*-0.4*	*SS -1*	*-0.1*

The phrase "baseball rat" has been used so often to describe Hager that it's easy to forget that he was a first-round pick in the 2011 draft and cashed a $963,000 bonus check. From Nevada, where the Rays like to go draft-shopping, Hager is already known for his good character and work ethic (on a team that saw three late-season drug suspensions). He availed himself well at Bowling Green, with decent plate discipline and more than bubblegum pop for a young middle infielder (.131 ISO). The Rays think his glove at shortstop is the best in their system after Hak-Ju Lee's, although some scouts are unconvinced, and he slots in nicely behind Lee and Beckham.

Desmond Jennings OF
Born: **10/30/1986** Age: **26**
Bats: **R** Throws: **R** Height: **6' 3"**
Weight: **200** Breakout: **3%**
Improve: **60%** Collapse: **7%**
Attrition: **17%** MLB: **92%**
Comparables:
Lastings Milledge, Chad Huffman, Don Baylor

YEAR	TEAM	LVL	AGE	PA	R	2B	3B	HR	RBI	BB	SO	SB	CS	AVG_OBP_SLG	TAv	BABIP	BRR	FRAA	WARP
2010	DUR	AAA	23	458	82	25	6	3	36	47	67	37	4	.278/.359/.393	.268	.323	6.3	CF(89): 5.3, LF(8): -0.2	3.0
2010	TBA	MLB	23	24	5	1	1	0	2	2	4	2	2	.190/.292/.333	.227	.235	0	RF(5): -0.2, CF(4): 0.4	0.0
2011	DUR	AAA	24	397	68	19	3	12	39	45	78	17	1	.275/.374/.456	.291	.325	0	--	0.0
2011	TBA	MLB	24	287	44	9	4	10	25	31	59	20	6	.259/.356/.449	.299	.303	1.4	LF(53): -0.8, CF(8): -0.2	1.5
2012	TBA	MLB	25	563	85	19	7	13	47	46	120	31	2	.246/.314/.388	.264	.298	5.7	LF(111): 2.0, CF(21): 0.2	2.2
2013	*TBA*	*MLB*	*26*	*476*	*65*	*18*	*5*	*10*	*42*	*43*	*97*	*28*	*5*	*.246/.322/.384*	*.265*	*.291*	*4*	*LF 2, CF 1*	*2.1*

Patience. Because Jennings's explosive 2009 accelerated his projected big-league arrival, expectations skyrocketed, only to inevitably fall back to Earth. Minor injuries delayed his progress and probably kept him from finding a groove in his first season as a big-league starter. Major-league pitchers expanded his strike zone, perhaps exploiting his desire to pull the ball and hit more home runs. As a result, Jennings posted the worst walk-to-strikeout ratio of his pro career. Nonetheless, he is an intelligent, adaptable hitter, and may simply have needed a year to adjust. With B.J. Upton off to collect his millions elsewhere, Jennings inherits center field and its glaring limelight. He is on the cusp of his prime. Hopes—and perhaps pressure—will be even higher.

Elliot Johnson SS
Born: **3/9/1984** Age: **29**
Bats: **B** Throws: **R** Height: **6' 1"**
Weight: **190** Breakout: **2%**
Improve: **45%** Collapse: **6%**
Attrition: **16%** MLB: **94%**
Comparables:
Ronny Cedeno, Jim Fregosi, Gil McDougald

YEAR	TEAM	LVL	AGE	PA	R	2B	3B	HR	RBI	BB	SO	SB	CS	AVG_OBP_SLG	TAv	BABIP	BRR	FRAA	WARP
2010	DUR	AAA	26	481	72	24	5	11	56	37	92	30	6	.319/.367/.475	.278	.372	4.1	SS(70): -0.5, LF(22): 0.1	3.1
2011	TBA	MLB	27	181	20	7	2	4	17	14	53	6	7	.194/.257/.338	.226	.260	-1.7	SS(52): 0.3, 2B(8): 0.2	-0.4
2012	TBA	MLB	28	331	32	10	2	6	33	24	84	18	6	.242/.304/.350	.254	.316	0	SS(100): -2.6, 2B(13): 0.4	0.4
2013	*TBA*	*MLB*	*29*	*281*	*32*	*11*	*2*	*5*	*25*	*21*	*72*	*12*	*4*	*.234/.293/.350*	*.243*	*.298*	*0.8*	*SS -2, 2B -0*	*0.6*

Last year's player card for Johnson concluded: "It is improbable that the Rays carry two offensively challenged shortstops again in 2012." Guess what? The Rays carried the same two offensively challenged shortstops in 2012—the other was Sean Rodriguez—only this time Johnson wasn't quite so challenged. His .254 TAv was actually 12th in the majors among shortstops with 300 PAs, although his negative FRAA seems to have driven his WARP below Rodriguez's. Johnson's bat kept him and his hard-nosed utility on the roster (Joe Maddon seems quite fond of him) while Rodriguez and Brignac were demoted to Triple-A. Still, it is improbable that the Rays carry two offensively challenged shortstops in—wait a minute . . .

Matt Joyce OF
Born: **8/3/1984** Age: **28**
Bats: **L** Throws: **R** Height: **6' 3"**
Weight: **205** Breakout: **1%**
Improve: **62%** Collapse: **1%**
Attrition: **10%** MLB: **100%**
Comparables:
David Justice, Shin-Soo Choo, Roger Maris

YEAR	TEAM	LVL	AGE	PA	R	2B	3B	HR	RBI	BB	SO	SB	CS	AVG_OBP_SLG	TAv	BABIP	BRR	FRAA	WARP
2010	DUR	AAA	25	115	18	8	0	3	12	22	21	1	3	.293/.435/.478	.315	.353	0.4	RF(8): 0.3, LF(7): -0.0	0.9
2010	TBA	MLB	25	261	30	15	3	10	40	40	55	2	2	.241/.360/.477	.297	.273	-2.2	RF(52): 3.6, LF(13): -0.0	1.9
2011	TBA	MLB	26	522	69	32	2	19	75	49	106	13	1	.277/.347/.478	.309	.317	-0.3	RF(126): -4.1, LF(15): 0.2	2.7
2012	TBA	MLB	27	462	55	18	3	17	59	55	102	4	3	.241/.341/.429	.281	.281	2.1	RF(89): -1.2, LF(33): -0.5	1.3
2013	*TBA*	*MLB*	*28*	*448*	*56*	*22*	*3*	*16*	*59*	*53*	*101*	*6*	*3*	*.247/.341/.443*	*.288*	*.291*	*-0.2*	*RF 1, LF 0*	*2.4*

Joyce came roaring out of the gate in 2012, with a 986 OPS and five homers in April. His productivity declined every month after that, though, until a slight uptick in September. It's tempting to assume that Joyce's fade was the effect of five different minor injuries and illnesses that nagged at him all season. He suffered a similar injury-related dropoff in 2011. If he can stay healthy, Joyce could finally put together a full season of the elite performance that earned him an All-Star bid in 2011. But he'll probably also need to improve his production against lefties—a career-long weakness for him—otherwise he could find himself in a platoon role that would limit his at-bats and, consequently, his flickering star potential.

Hak-Ju Lee SS

Born: **11/4/1990** Age: **22**
Bats: **L** Throws: **R** Height: **6' 3"**
Weight: **170** Breakout: **9%**
Improve: **57%** Collapse: **6%**
Attrition: **11%** MLB: **96%**

Comparables:
Edgar Renteria,Jose Valdivielso,Omar Infante

YEAR	TEAM	LVL	AGE	PA	R	2B	3B	HR	RBI	BB	SO	SB	CS	AVG_OBP_SLG	TAv	BABIP	BRR	FRAA	WARP
2010	PEO	A	19	551	85	22	4	1	40	49	86	32	7	.282/.347/.351	.266	.333	6.5	SS(118): 8.4	4.2
2011	PCH	A+	20	454	82	16	11	4	23	42	72	28	14	.317/.389/.442	.296	.380	0	--	0.0
2011	MNT	AA	20	114	16	1	4	1	7	11	22	5	2	.190/.272/.310	.207	.228	0	--	0.0
2012	MNT	AA	21	534	68	15	10	4	37	51	102	37	9	.261/.336/.360	.271	.324	5.5	SS(32): -1.8	1.2
2013	*TBA*	*MLB*	*22*	*250*	*26*	*8*	*2*	*2*	*16*	*15*	*57*	*9*	*2*	*.222/.270/.295*	*.217*	*.281*	*1.2*	*SS 1*	*0.3*

A mild oblique injury in mid-August ended Lee's season a few weeks early. Maybe that's just as well, given that he was hitting .118 in 38 PAs that month—the second year in a row Lee hit a late wall, although to be fair the 2011 decline followed his promotion to Double-A. Lee's first full season at that level surrounded two good months (June and July) with three rough ones. He set a career high in steals, but made 24 errors at shortstop, and his FRAA has fallen steeply as he has advanced. Nonetheless, the Rays love Lee's prototypical speedy-shortstop profile, and they're so high on his glove that he may permanently displace Beckham to second base in Triple-A this year.

Jose Lobaton C

Born: **10/21/1984** Age: **28**
Bats: **B** Throws: **R** Height: **6' 1"**
Weight: **195** Breakout: **7%**
Improve: **42%** Collapse: **17%**
Attrition: **26%** MLB: **92%**

Comparables:
JD Closser,Bob Stinson,Chris Bando

YEAR	TEAM	LVL	AGE	PA	R	2B	3B	HR	RBI	BB	SO	SB	CS	AVG_OBP_SLG	TAv	BABIP	BRR	FRAA	WARP
2010	DUR	AAA	25	271	26	11	0	7	33	27	52	1	0	.261/.337/.394	.250	.306	-2.1	C(62): -0.4	0.6
2011	DUR	AAA	26	224	24	10	1	8	31	37	50	0	0	.293/.410/.489	.316	.362	0	--	0.0
2011	TBA	MLB	26	39	2	1	0	0	0	4	8	0	0	.118/.231/.147	.136	.154	0	C(14): 0.0	-0.3
2012	TBA	MLB	27	197	16	10	0	2	20	24	46	0	1	.222/.323/.317	.241	.289	-1.5	C(66): 0.5	0.0
2013	*TBA*	*MLB*	*28*	*250*	*23*	*10*	*0*	*4*	*22*	*24*	*59*	*0*	*0*	*.217/.297/.321*	*.235*	*.274*	*-0.4*	*C -0*	*0.4*

With Jose Molina setting an unexpected career high for games played, the Rays didn't need as much out of Lobaton (51 starts) as they might have expected. Thank goodness: The fragile Lobaton went down in April for six weeks with shoulder inflammation, which may have helped account for a crummy 16 percent caught-stealing rate. When he came back, he performed at exactly replacement level, and the switch-hitter was useless against right-handers. Strangely, over the last few years, his platoon splits have virtually reversed. Lobaton is one of five upper-minors catchers (Nevin Ashley, Robinson Chirinos, John Jaso, Michel Hernandez) who haven't broken through for the Rays over the last few years. Because he is out of options, he may stick on the roster again anyway.

James Loney 1B

Born: **5/7/1984** Age: **29**
Bats: **L** Throws: **L** Height: **6' 3"**
Weight: **205** Breakout: **1%**
Improve: **53%** Collapse: **11%**
Attrition: **10%** MLB: **95%**

Comparables:
Pete O'Brien,Casey Kotchman,Wally Joyner

YEAR	TEAM	LVL	AGE	PA	R	2B	3B	HR	RBI	BB	SO	SB	CS	AVG_OBP_SLG	TAv	BABIP	BRR	FRAA	WARP
2010	LAN	MLB	26	648	67	41	2	10	88	52	95	10	5	.267/.329/.395	.260	.302	1.5	1B(160): -4.2	0.4
2011	LAN	MLB	27	582	56	30	1	12	65	42	67	4	0	.288/.339/.416	.272	.309	-1.4	1B(150): 3.3	1.3
2012	BOS	MLB	28	106	5	2	0	2	8	5	12	0	0	.230/.264/.310	.212	.241	-0.3	1B(28): 2.6	-0.3
2012	LAN	MLB	28	359	32	18	0	4	33	23	39	0	3	.254/.302/.344	.222	.277	-2.4	1B(105): 1.2	-1.4
2013	*TBA*	*MLB*	*29*	*460*	*46*	*23*	*2*	*9*	*49*	*36*	*60*	*4*	*2*	*.263/.322/.388*	*.265*	*.287*	*-0.6*	*1B -2*	*0.4*

Only the Loney can play first base for the Rays, who specialize in putting discount players at the premium power position (they got Loney for $2 million). A once-promising prospect who posted good numbers as a 22- and 23-year-old with the Dodgers, Loney's offensive numbers cratered last season. His midseason move to Boston did nothing to liven up his bat—in fact, he was worse. Still, Loney is a gifted defensive first baseman and has shown offensive adequacy as recently as 2011. The post-Casey Kotchman Rays will hope for a #MagicofLoney hashtag miracle.

Evan Longoria 3B

Born: **10/7/1985** Age: **27**
Bats: **R** Throws: **R** Height: **6' 3"**
Weight: **210** Breakout: **2%**
Improve: **40%** Collapse: **3%**
Attrition: **5%** MLB: **98%**

Comparables:
Jim Ray Hart,Bob Horner,David Wright

YEAR	TEAM	LVL	AGE	PA	R	2B	3B	HR	RBI	BB	SO	SB	CS	AVG_OBP_SLG	TAv	BABIP	BRR	FRAA	WARP
2010	TBA	MLB	24	661	96	46	5	22	104	72	124	15	5	.294/.372/.507	.313	.336	3.4	3B(151): 7.3	6.9
2011	TBA	MLB	25	574	78	26	1	31	99	80	93	3	2	.244/.355/.495	.319	.239	-2.1	3B(130): 9.1	6.1
2012	TBA	MLB	26	312	39	14	0	17	55	33	61	2	3	.289/.369/.527	.326	.313	-1.7	3B(50): -1.5	2.3
2013	*TBA*	*MLB*	*27*	*351*	*46*	*19*	*1*	*15*	*51*	*39*	*72*	*4*	*2*	*.262/.350/.481*	*.304*	*.293*	*-0.3*	*3B -1*	*2.3*

Longoria hit three home runs in the last game of the 2012 season, erasing any lingering doubt about the soundness of his previously torn hamstring. The injury cost the Rays' hot-cornerstone half the season (and, arguably, a playoff berth for his team). Longoria's hamstrung immobility dealt a major blow to his fielding rating, but he still managed to accumulate 2.3 WARP—the same number as fellow third baseman Chipper Jones in about a third fewer plate appearances, thanks to the highest TAv of Longoria's career. Perhaps the lost time only helped recalibrate Longoria's ludicrously cheap contract to near normal levels. It didn't stay there, however. The Rays bet $100 million on 10 more years of stardom, extending Longoria, hamstring and all, to age 37.

Mikie Mahtook OF

Born: 11/30/1989 **Age:** 23
Bats: R **Throws:** R **Height:** 6' 2"
Weight: 200 **Breakout:** 5%
Improve: 63% **Collapse:** 6%
Attrition: 14% **MLB:** 97%

Comparables:
Bobby Tolan,Jim King,Tito Francona

YEAR	TEAM	LVL	AGE	PA	R	2B	3B	HR	RBI	BB	SO	SB	CS	AVG_OBP_SLG	TAv	BABIP	BRR	FRAA	WARP
2012	PCH	A+	22	386	44	15	7	5	37	29	71	19	6	.290/.358/.419	.255	.347	2.8	CF(13): -0.9, RF(10): 0.4	0.4
2012	MNT	AA	22	169	17	10	1	4	25	11	31	4	3	.248/.308/.405	.166	.283	-0.3	RF(8): 0.4, CF(1): 0.1	-0.2
2013	*TBA*	*MLB*	*23*	*250*	*24*	*9*	*2*	*5*	*24*	*13*	*61*	*6*	*2*	*.224/.270/.338*	*.229*	*.280*	*0.4*	*RF 1, CF 0*	*-0.1*

The Rays fast-tracked this LSU slugger's career, starting Mahtook's climb in high-A and bumping him up to Double-A in late July. They also pushed him out of center field to right, perhaps envisioning him as Joyce's platoon partner in an ideal world. Mahtook had a good first season as a pro but showed little power. The Rays see him as a well-rounded more than a wow player, a solid collegian rather than a star in the making. If he finds his power stroke in 2013, he could reach Triple-A and change their mind.

Jeff Malm 1B

Born: 10/31/1990 **Age:** 22
Bats: L **Throws:** L **Height:** 6' 4"
Weight: 225 **Breakout:** 6%
Improve: 54% **Collapse:** 6%
Attrition: 14% **MLB:** 92%

Comparables:
Gary Thomasson,John Mayberry,Ken Harrelson

YEAR	TEAM	LVL	AGE	PA	R	2B	3B	HR	RBI	BB	SO	SB	CS	AVG_OBP_SLG	TAv	BABIP	BRR	FRAA	WARP
2010	PRI	Rk	19	223	20	9	0	3	25	17	46	2	1	.220/.297/.310	.246	.272	0.5	1B(59): 0.3	-0.2
2011	HUD	A-	20	301	36	15	0	12	47	38	65	3	2	.257/.382/.462	.296	.301	0	--	0.0
2012	BGR	A	21	540	67	36	3	13	61	62	127	6	3	.263/.356/.438	.277	.330	-2.2	1B(61): 1.3, LF(14): 0.0	0.8
2013	*TBA*	*MLB*	*22*	*250*	*20*	*9*	*1*	*4*	*23*	*19*	*75*	*0*	*0*	*.191/.256/.292*	*.209*	*.260*	*-0.4*	*1B -2, LF -0*	*-1.2*

Kevin Goldstein, July 2011: "He needs to keep mashing because that's all he can do as a big, slow first baseman." To that end, 42 percent of Malm's hits last year went for extra bases (the same rate as 2011 in Low-A), including 36 doubles, tied for second in the league with teammate Cameron Seitzer. The Rays would probably like to see him up that percentage even more—break out for 20 homers, say, while racking up dozens more doubles. If he starts to get close to 20 at Port Charlotte, he'll likely move up to Double-A before he reaches the mark. Strikeouts are a given.

Jose Molina C

Born: 6/3/1975 **Age:** 38
Bats: R **Throws:** R **Height:** 6' 3"
Weight: 250 **Breakout:** 2%
Improve: 9% **Collapse:** 15%
Attrition: 23% **MLB:** 63%

Comparables:
Tom Lampkin,Gary Carter,Bob Scheffing

YEAR	TEAM	LVL	AGE	PA	R	2B	3B	HR	RBI	BB	SO	SB	CS	AVG_OBP_SLG	TAv	BABIP	BRR	FRAA	WARP
2010	TOR	MLB	35	183	13	4	0	6	12	9	36	1	0	.246/.304/.377	.234	.280	-2.2	C(56): -0.4	0.2
2011	TOR	MLB	36	191	19	12	1	3	15	15	44	2	1	.281/.342/.415	.276	.363	-1	C(48): -1.3	0.8
2012	TBA	MLB	37	274	27	9	0	8	32	20	60	3	1	.223/.286/.355	.246	.262	-3	C(101): -1.9	0.2
2013	*TBA*	*MLB*	*38*	*250*	*23*	*10*	*1*	*4*	*21*	*16*	*55*	*2*	*1*	*.219/.277/.316*	*.225*	*.265*	*-0.2*	*C -1*	*0.1*

Molina owes Mike Fast big-time. Fast's 2011 research at Baseball Prospectus showed Molina to be by far the best pitch-framer in the business, turning him (and Fast, in fact) into a revered hero almost overnight. The Rays pounced for $1.5 million, and Molina rewarded them by setting a career high for games played (102) at age 37. He'd have played a few more were it not for a late-season hamstring strain, which also interrupted a Yadier-like, week-long hitting spree that separated the offensively challenged Molina from the Mendoza line for good. The Rays were glad to pick up his $1.8 million option in 2013 and hope for similar production.

Wil Myers OF

Born: 12/10/1990 **Age:** 22
Bats: R **Throws:** R **Height:** 6' 4"
Weight: 205 **Breakout:** 2%
Improve: 64% **Collapse:** 0%
Attrition: 5% **MLB:** 98%

Comparables:
Matt Kemp,Ken Griffey,Adam Jones

YEAR	TEAM	LVL	AGE	PA	R	2B	3B	HR	RBI	BB	SO	SB	CS	AVG_OBP_SLG	TAv	BABIP	BRR	FRAA	WARP
2010	BUR	A	19	294	42	19	1	10	45	48	55	10	3	.289/.411/.500	.314	.339	-2.2	C(46): 0.1	2.5
2010	WIL	A+	19	247	28	18	2	4	38	37	39	2	3	.346/.455/.512	.343	.414	-0.1	C(28): -0.2	2.7
2011	NWA	AA	20	416	50	23	1	8	49	52	87	9	2	.254/.353/.393	.259	.312	1.6	RF(48): 1.8, CF(8): 0.1	0.6
2012	NWA	AA	21	152	32	11	1	13	30	16	42	4	1	.343/.414/.731	.375	.412	-0.4	CF(17): 4.2, RF(10): 0.7	2.2
2012	OMA	AAA	21	439	66	15	5	24	79	45	98	2	2	.304/.378/.554	.329	.349	-1.4	CF(51): -10.1, 3B(9): -1.3	1.6
2013	*TBA*	*MLB*	*22*	*250*	*29*	*10*	*1*	*9*	*32*	*24*	*64*	*2*	*1*	*.246/.324/.426*	*.278*	*.301*	*-0.2*	*CF -0, RF 0*	*1.2*

To paraphrase Goldstein, when Jeff Francoeur is blocking Wil Myers, your organization may have a talent-evaluation problem. The Royals tacitly acknowledged their problem by trading Myers to Tampa Bay in the James Shields deal. He recovered from injury and lackadaisical play in 2011 to rebound as the top minor-league bat in

2012. Drafted as a catcher, he moved to right field to shorten his timetable to the majors. Last summer, the Royals had him play a handful of games at third base. Should he stay in right, he has the range and above-average arm needed to play the position. Offensively, he features an unorthodox swing that generates exceptional bat speed and plenty of power. His pitch recognition and contact ability should translate to high on-base ability in the majors. The way is clear for him to shine in the middle of Maddon's lineup.

Ryan Roberts **UT**

Born: **9/19/1980** Age: **32**
Bats: **R** Throws: **R** Height: **6' 0"**
Weight: **185** Breakout: **4%**
Improve: **50%** Collapse: **5%**
Attrition: **9%** MLB: **92%**

Comparables:
Todd Zeile, Richie Hebner, Rance Mulliniks

YEAR	TEAM	LVL	AGE	PA	R	2B	3B	HR	RBI	BB	SO	SB	CS	AVG_OBP_SLG	TAv	BABIP	BRR	FRAA	WARP
2010	RNO	AAA	29	412	62	25	2	11	55	56	73	16	6	.265/.369/.444	.272	.307	1.3	2B(50): 5.0, LF(18): 0.6	1.8
2010	ARI	MLB	29	71	8	4	0	2	9	3	17	0	0	.197/.229/.348	.205	.229	-0.3	LF(14): -0.2, 3B(1): -0.0	-0.3
2011	ARI	MLB	30	555	86	25	2	19	65	66	98	18	9	.249/.341/.427	.278	.275	2.6	3B(107): 0.6, 2B(28): 1.1	2.6
2012	ARI	MLB	31	280	28	9	0	6	34	22	45	6	3	.250/.306/.357	.230	.278	0.9	3B(60): 3.3, 2B(8): -0.3	0.2
2012	TBA	MLB	31	209	23	10	0	6	18	18	47	4	3	.214/.284/.364	.248	.250	-1.2	2B(46): 2.6, 3B(18): 0.9	0.4
2013	*TBA*	*MLB*	*32*	*473*	*52*	*19*	*2*	*11*	*49*	*48*	*93*	*12*	*5*	*.231/.312/.361*	*.254*	*.270*	*0*	*3B 0, 2B -0*	*1.0*

Roberts holds a dubious distinction: He is the only major-league position player the Rays have acquired at the July 31 trade deadline since they became contenders five years ago. What's dubious is that Roberts was no impact bat, nor did the Rays think he'd be one, though they may have secretly hoped otherwise. Roberts was just another branchlet to throw on the pile of infielder kindling (Brignac, Conrad, Johnson, Rodriguez, Rhymes, Sutton) Tampa Bay burned through last season. Despite his half-season of inconsequential production, Tampa Bay nonetheless tendered him a $3 million contract for 2013. That's a regular's salary on Sternberg's payroll, and a suggestion that the team sees untapped every-day potential in Roberts. He did, after all, put up a 1007 OPS in April 2011, the torrid single month on which nearly all his hitting credentials rest.

Sean Rodriguez **INF**

Born: **4/26/1985** Age: **28**
Bats: **R** Throws: **R** Height: **6' 1"**
Weight: **200** Breakout: **2%**
Improve: **49%** Collapse: **1%**
Attrition: **10%** MLB: **93%**

Comparables:
Bobby Crosby, Rico Petrocelli, Jeff Blauser

YEAR	TEAM	LVL	AGE	PA	R	2B	3B	HR	RBI	BB	SO	SB	CS	AVG_OBP_SLG	TAv	BABIP	BRR	FRAA	WARP
2010	TBA	MLB	25	378	53	19	2	9	40	21	97	13	3	.251/.308/.397	.253	.324	0.1	2B(92): 4.0, CF(9): -0.4	1.0
2011	TBA	MLB	26	436	45	20	3	8	36	38	87	11	7	.223/.323/.357	.255	.268	1.6	SS(60): -2.9, 2B(48): 1.5	0.9
2012	TBA	MLB	27	342	36	14	1	6	32	27	75	5	0	.213/.281/.326	.228	.260	0.8	3B(49): 3.8, SS(47): 4.2	0.6
2013	*TBA*	*MLB*	*28*	*341*	*39*	*15*	*2*	*10*	*37*	*29*	*84*	*7*	*2*	*.225/.307/.381*	*.256*	*.274*	*0.2*	*SS -1, 2B -0*	*1.0*

Is it all about the hands? Rodriguez's might be the quickest in baseball: His 118.4 mph homer was the fastest clocked in 2011. But does an over-reliance on the hands and a consequently whippy swing explain his vulnerability against righties? Last August, after two years of decline, he was demoted to Triple-A; two games later, he broke one of those hands when he punched a locker following a petty altercation with Dane De La Rosa (apparently over clubhouse music). So maybe it's about the head, not the hands. Rodriguez spoke last year of his "mindset in the box" (although he did tweak his stance). If he masters his mind—approach and recognition at the plate and elsewhere—he could reward PECOTA's 2013 optimism and far outperform his $1 million salary. Rodriguez's ceiling is significantly higher than he's reached; that's why he's been the Rays' most tantalizing but frustrating player over the last two seasons.

Joshua Sale **LF**

Born: **7/5/1991** Age: **21**
Bats: **L** Throws: **R** Height: **6' 1"**
Weight: **215** Breakout: **4%**
Improve: **59%** Collapse: **9%**
Attrition: **16%** MLB: **96%**

Comparables:
Fernando Martinez, Terry Puhl, Johnny Callison

YEAR	TEAM	LVL	AGE	PA	R	2B	3B	HR	RBI	BB	SO	SB	CS	AVG_OBP_SLG	TAv	BABIP	BRR	FRAA	WARP
2011	PRI	Rk	20	239	24	11	3	4	15	23	41	4	3	.210/.289/.346	.197	.241	-1.1	LF(32): 6.1	-0.2
2012	BGR	A	20	297	35	10	4	10	44	51	62	7	6	.264/.391/.464	.322	.308	-3.8	LF(48): 1.9, RF(3): -0.0	1.4
2013	*TBA*	*MLB*	*21*	*250*	*24*	*7*	*1*	*5*	*22*	*24*	*69*	*3*	*2*	*.193/.270/.308*	*.220*	*.249*	*-0.2*	*LF -1, RF 0*	*-0.6*

Some controversy surrounded Sale's late-season 50-game suspension for amphetamine and methamphetamine. He stated that he didn't take any banned substances but "was unable to uncover enough evidence of my innocence" to appeal. Before the suspension, Sale's almost-full season had topped his weak 2011 rookie-ball trial by miles, and did much to bear out his first-round pedigree (17th overall in 2010). There was worry when he drew an Opening Day assignment to extended spring training, but after an early-May ticket to A-ball he showed power (.201 ISO) and patience (17.2 percent walk rate). If he ends up the Rays' starting left fielder someday, hindsight will reduce the 50-game suspension from a speeding ticket to mere improper equipment. And the world will know that he pronounces it "Sa-LAY."

Luke Scott DH

Born: **6/25/1978** Age: **35**
Bats: **L** Throws: **R** Height: **6' 1"**
Weight: **205** Breakout: **1%**
Improve: **19%** Collapse: **8%**
Attrition: **15%** MLB: **96%**

Comparables:
David Dellucci,Roy Sievers,Norm Cash

YEAR	TEAM	LVL	AGE	PA	R	2B	3B	HR	RBI	BB	SO	SB	CS	AVG_OBP_SLG	TAv	BABIP	BRR	FRAA	WARP
2010	BAL	MLB	32	517	70	29	1	27	72	59	98	2	0	.284/.368/.535	.312	.304	-6.1	1B(19): 0.3, LF(14): -0.0	2.8
2011	BAL	MLB	33	236	24	11	0	9	22	24	54	1	1	.220/.301/.402	.258	.250	-1.1	LF(45): 1.2, 1B(12): -0.5	0.1
2012	TBA	MLB	34	344	35	22	1	14	55	21	80	5	0	.229/.285/.439	.260	.259	-0.4	1B(6): 0.0	0.0
2013	*TBA*	*MLB*	*35*	*309*	*36*	*14*	*1*	*12*	*41*	*30*	*69*	*2*	*0*	*.235/.313/.426*	*.274*	*.269*	*-0.3*	*LF 0, 1B -0*	*1.1*

Like Carlos Pena, Scott was a good lefty-power-bat idea gone bad for the Rays. He missed 48 games with assorted injuries, went 0-41 in a June-July stretch, posted the highest strikeout and lowest walk rates of his career, was worse than ever against southpaws (.149/.211/.264), and cost the Rays the extravagant (for them) sum of $6 million. A replacement-level performance could be had for much less. And Scott didn't even broadcast any of his controversial birther opinions or jocose racial "insensitivity" in the clubhouse to distract us from his poor on-field performance. If he doesn't rebound this season, the end of his career might not be far off.

Richard Shaffer 3B

Born: **3/15/1991** Age: **22**
Bats: **R** Throws: **R** Height: **6' 5"**
Weight: **195** Breakout: **6%**
Improve: **49%** Collapse: **10%**
Attrition: **19%** MLB: **92%**

Comparables:
Dale Berra,Denny Gonzalez,Ken McMullen

YEAR	TEAM	LVL	AGE	PA	R	2B	3B	HR	RBI	BB	SO	SB	CS	AVG_OBP_SLG	TAv	BABIP	BRR	FRAA	WARP
2012	HUD	A-	21	138	25	5	2	4	26	16	31	0	0	.308/.406/.487	.191	.386	0.2	3B(5): -0.9	-0.4
2013	*TBA*	*MLB*	*22*	*250*	*21*	*7*	*1*	*5*	*24*	*17*	*75*	*1*	*0*	*.196/.256/.309*	*.215*	*.261*	*-0.2*	*3B -0*	*-0.6*

The Rays were pleasantly surprised that Shaffer was still there to draft with the 25th pick last year. They love the Clemson Tiger's long, lean body and his quick-twitch bat—some scouts project 25-30 homers in the majors—which distinguishes him from many college power hitters who can't catch up to professional pitching. They also love Shaffer's makeup, which has been an issue with other top Rays picks. Shaffer got right to work in short-season ball, producing an 893 OPS in 33 games and then heading out to the AFL. If Shaffer makes good on his raw power he could move across the diamond to first base, where some think he's a better fit—especially in the Tampa Bay organization, where Longoria has the hot corner locked down for a decade.

Drew Vettleson RF

Born: **7/19/1991** Age: **21**
Bats: **L** Throws: **R** Height: **6' 2"**
Weight: **185** Breakout: **3%**
Improve: **54%** Collapse: **9%**
Attrition: **17%** MLB: **97%**

Comparables:
Bill Russell,Lloyd Moseby,Ed Kirkpatrick

YEAR	TEAM	LVL	AGE	PA	R	2B	3B	HR	RBI	BB	SO	SB	CS	AVG_OBP_SLG	TAv	BABIP	BRR	FRAA	WARP
2011	PRI	Rk	19	267	33	13	4	7	40	27	53	20	6	.282/.357/.462	.283	.333	-0.7	RF(32): 3.5	0.9
2012	BGR	A	20	562	80	24	5	15	69	51	117	20	11	.275/.340/.432	.289	.328	-1.5	RF(88): -5.7, CF(8): -0.4	2.1
2013	*TBA*	*MLB*	*21*	*250*	*24*	*8*	*1*	*5*	*23*	*15*	*70*	*6*	*3*	*.209/.257/.320*	*.219*	*.272*	*0.2*	*RF -1, CF -0*	*-0.6*

Vettleson has much in common with Sale: born two weeks later, also from the Seattle area, and a lefty-swinging outfielder. Sale had the better year (affirming his higher draft slot), albeit in half as much action, but Vettleson held his own and was actually better than Sale in some areas. Vettleson has a great arm, throwing out a slew of baserunners before teams stopped running on him. His platoon splits improved from 2011, too. It speaks to Vettleson's promise that, before the 2012 season started, most pundits in the Rays blogosphere ranked him fifth or sixth among organizational prospects, generally ahead of Sale. The two outfielders stand to wage the sort of multi-year, head-to-head prospect battle that makes farm systems so much fun to follow.

Stephen Vogt C

Born: **11/1/1984** Age: **28**
Bats: **L** Throws: **R** Height: **6' 1"**
Weight: **215** Breakout: **2%**
Improve: **34%** Collapse: **16%**
Attrition: **24%** MLB: **96%**

Comparables:
Ron Hassey,Geno Petralli,Vinny Rottino

YEAR	TEAM	LVL	AGE	PA	R	2B	3B	HR	RBI	BB	SO	SB	CS	AVG_OBP_SLG	TAv	BABIP	BRR	FRAA	WARP
2010	PCH	A+	25	414	56	31	3	8	47	31	46	3	1	.345/.402/.511	.316	.375	0.8	C(30): 0.1, LF(26): -0.2	3.6
2010	PCH	A+	25	414	56	31	3	8	47	31	46	3	1	.345/.402/.511	.316	.375	0.8	1B(1): 0.0, C(1): -0.0	3.6
2011	MNT	AA	26	427	52	21	6	13	85	30	51	4	2	.301/.344/.487	.282	.310	0	--	0.0
2011	DUR	AAA	26	131	15	14	1	4	20	4	29	0	0	.290/.305/.516	.268	.340	0	--	0.0
2012	DUR	AAA	27	396	48	18	4	9	43	42	61	1	0	.272/.350/.424	.252	.306	-2.3	C(16): -0.3, RF(7): 0.3	-0.1
2012	TBA	MLB	27	27	0	0	0	0	0	2	2	0	0	.000/.074/.000	.039	.000	0	C(7): -0.0, LF(2): 0.0	-0.5
2013	*TBA*	*MLB*	*28*	*250*	*23*	*11*	*2*	*5*	*26*	*18*	*45*	*0*	*0*	*.239/.296/.361*	*.246*	*.273*	*-0.2*	*C -0, LF -1*	*0.2*

In Vogt's last at-bat of the final regular-season game of 2012, a bad call at first base denied his bid for an infield single. That extended his career-opening hitless streak to 27 plate appearances. Vogt carries an OF/C/1B business card, awkward mainly because he plays none of those positions especially well. Factor in his advanced age, and he might never get another shot at that hit. Vogt wants to manage someday, and he'll be good at it: He's personable, intelligent, hard-working, and a candid yet diplomatic teammate with a statesman's poise. If he never gets his big-league knock, he can use his career oh-fer to motivate his young charges. For now, he'll go back to whacking Triple-A pitching around the yard while waiting for another chance at box-score glory.

Ben Zobrist **UT**

Born: **5/26/1981** Age: **32**
Bats: **B** Throws: **R** Height: **6' 4"**
Weight: **200** Breakout: **2%**
Improve: **32%** Collapse: **3%**
Attrition: **4%** MLB: **95%**

Comparables:
Milton Bradley,Kosuke Fukudome,Rocky Colavito

YEAR	TEAM	LVL	AGE	PA	R	2B	3B	HR	RBI	BB	SO	SB	CS	AVG_OBP_SLG	TAv	BABIP	BRR	FRAA	WARP
2010	TBA	MLB	29	655	77	28	2	10	75	92	107	24	3	.238/.346/.353	.267	.273	1	RF(103): 3.4, 2B(55): -1.6	2.9
2011	TBA	MLB	30	674	99	46	6	20	91	77	128	19	6	.269/.353/.469	.307	.310	5	2B(131): -5.7, RF(37): 0.1	3.9
2012	TBA	MLB	31	668	88	39	7	20	74	97	103	14	9	.270/.377/.471	.315	.296	-5.2	RF(71): 2.5, 2B(58): -7.0	4.5
2013	*TBA*	*MLB*	*32*	*629*	*78*	*31*	*4*	*17*	*74*	*83*	*114*	*17*	*6*	*.253/.353/.425*	*.289*	*.288*	*0.7*	*2B -2, RF 1*	*4.0*

The August transition to shortstop was classic Zobrist. Once again, he quietly showed his immensely valuable versatility, shoring up a position that had become a sinkhole for the Rays while producing a 900-plus OPS over the last two months of the year. The position change also appears to have lifted Zobrist's sagging FRAA. Zobrist had the 14th-highest BVORP and TAv in all of baseball in 2012. For his elite production and great utility, the Rays paid $4.5 million—and they have him under team control through 2015 for a potential total of $20 million. Isn't that just like Zobrist: His ridiculously team-friendly contract goes mostly unnoticed while Longoria's gets all the attention. Plus, his wife sings the national anthem at the Trop. Here's betting she doesn't charge the Rays a dime.

PITCHERS

Jeff Ames

Born: **1/31/1991** Age: **22**
Bats: **R** Throws: **R** Height: **6' 5"** Weight: **225**
Breakout: **22%** Improve: **52%** Collapse: **21%**
Attrition: **8%** MLB: **90%**

Comparables:
Randall Delgado,Rich Hand,Pete Broberg

YEAR	TEAM	LVL	AGE	W	L	SV	G	GS	IP	H	HR	BB	SO	BB9	SO9	GB%	BABIP	WHIP	ERA	FIP	FRA	WARP
2011	PRI	Rk	20	4	2	1	11	5	30^{1}	40	4	7	39	2.1	11.6	30%	.432	1.55	7.12	3.62	4.31	0.3
2012	HUD	A-	21	6	1	0	14	13	64^{1}	44	1	20	70	2.8	9.8	34%	.269	0.99	1.96	2.76	2.53	0.2
2013	*TBA*	*MLB*	*22*	*1*	*3*	*0*	*8*	*7*	*33*	*34*	*4*	*19*	*26*	*5.0*	*7.2*	*37%*	*.302*	*1.59*	*5.27*	*4.93*	*5.72*	*-0.2*

A Pacific Northwesterner like Sale and Vettleson, Ames was a sleeper supplemental pick in 2011, taken one spot below Tyler Goeddel. Immediately assigned to rookie ball, he put up a dreadful 7.12 ERA despite a 3.04 FIP and superb strikeout and walk rates (11.6 and 2.1 per nine innings). He was assigned to extended spring training to start 2012, worked on simplifying and refining a crude delivery, and then came correct in Low-A with a 2.10 ERA, excellent strikeout-to-walk rates, and only one home run allowed in 64 innings. Ames throws a mid-90s fastball that touched 100 mph in community college. His secondary-pitch development will determine whether he remains a starter or moves to the bullpen, where some pundits already think he belongs.

Christopher Archer

Born: **9/26/1988** Age: **24**
Bats: **R** Throws: **R** Height: **6' 4"** Weight: **185**
Breakout: **32%** Improve: **61%** Collapse: **15%**
Attrition: **11%** MLB: **97%**

Comparables:
Tim Hudson,Floyd Youmans,Ubaldo Jimenez

YEAR	TEAM	LVL	AGE	W	L	SV	G	GS	IP	H	HR	BB	SO	BB9	SO9	GB%	BABIP	WHIP	ERA	FIP	FRA	WARP
2010	DAY	A+	21	7	1	0	15	14	72^{1}	54	4	26	82	3.2	10.2	49%	.288	1.11	2.86	3.09	3.66	1.1
2010	TEN	AA	21	8	2	0	13	13	70	48	2	39	67	5.0	8.6	56%	.275	1.24	1.80	3.60	4.67	1.0
2011	MNT	AA	22	8	7	0	25	25	134^{1}	136	11	80	118	5.4	7.9	—	.318	1.61	4.42	4.62	5.03	0.0
2011	DUR	AAA	22	1	0	0	2	2	13	11	0	6	12	4.2	8.3	—	.297	1.31	0.69	2.78	3.02	0.0
2012	DUR	AAA	23	7	9	0	25	25	128	99	6	62	139	4.4	9.8	49%	.293	1.26	3.66	3.21	3.87	0.7
2012	TBA	MLB	23	1	3	0	6	4	29^{1}	23	3	13	36	4.0	11.0	44%	.290	1.23	4.60	3.35	4.55	0.1
2013	*TBA*	*MLB*	*24*	*3*	*4*	*0*	*10*	*10*	50^{1}	*44*	*5*	*30*	*48*	*5.4*	*8.5*	*48%*	*.288*	*1.48*	*4.36*	*4.37*	*4.74*	*0.1*

Archer cultivates a high-polish, valedictorian persona (and a Yoda-like Twitter feed) that belies a highly animated, heart-on-sleeve mound presence. This split personality suits his pitching, which can be coolly dazzling one minute, coltish and wild the next. In Triple-A last season, Archer again showed his top-shelf stuff—a fastball that reaches 98, a vicious slider, and a developing changeup—while continuing to produce an unsustainable walk rate, although his control improved as the year went on. Archer's six big-league appearances were promising, and he's likely to be first in line for a call-up from Triple-A this year if a starter goes down—or, perhaps, a reliever. Some think he's better suited to the bullpen, but his changeup improved in 2012, and the Rays will probably give Archer every chance to succeed as a starter.

Alex Cobb

Born: **10/7/1987** Age: **25**
Bats: **R** Throws: **R** Height: **6' 3"** Weight: **195**
Breakout: **18%** Improve: **52%** Collapse: **18%**
Attrition: **19%** MLB: **93%**

Comparables:
Enrique Gonzalez,Luke Hochevar,Wade Davis

YEAR	TEAM	LVL	AGE	W	L	SV	G	GS	IP	H	HR	BB	SO	BB9	SO9	GB%	BABIP	WHIP	ERA	FIP	FRA	WARP
2010	MNT	AA	22	7	5	0	23	22	119^{2}	120	7	35	128	2.6	9.6	55%	.342	1.29	2.71	2.98	3.65	2.4
2011	DUR	AAA	23	5	1	0	12	12	67^{1}	61	4	16	70	2.1	9.4	—	.331	1.14	1.87	2.73	2.97	0.0
2011	TBA	MLB	23	3	2	0	9	9	52^{2}	49	3	21	37	3.6	6.3	55%	.284	1.33	3.42	3.65	3.97	0.4
2012	DUR	AAA	24	1	4	0	8	8	41^{1}	44	1	18	44	3.9	9.6	56%	.339	1.50	4.14	2.79	3.14	0.5
2012	TBA	MLB	24	11	9	0	23	23	136^{1}	130	11	40	106	2.6	7.0	60%	.295	1.25	4.03	3.62	4.30	0.8
2013	*TBA*	*MLB*	*25*	*6*	*7*	*0*	*20*	*20*	112^{2}	*110*	*12*	*41*	*87*	*3.2*	*7.0*	*52%*	*.293*	*1.34*	*4.11*	*4.13*	*4.47*	*0.6*

Cobb not only fully recovered from offseason thoracic outlet surgery, he came into spring training having noticeably bulked up. He was assigned to Triple-A, but within a few weeks Adam Lind's comebacker broke Jeff Niemann's leg and Cobb was up in Tampa Bay. He made sure to stick there, gaining confidence as he out-VORPed not only teammate Jeremy Hellickson, to whom he is often compared, but also Roy Halladay. Cobb is all finesse; his 89-91 mph fastball's traction relies on a variable splitter that he throws with two different grips. An intelligent, savvy young pitcher with a demonstrated ability to develop and adjust, he's likely to occupy the fourth or fifth starter role for at least a few years, provided his command doesn't desert him.

Alexander Colome

Born: 12/31/1988 **Age:** 24
Bats: R **Throws:** R **Height:** 6' 3" **Weight:** 184
Breakout: 39% **Improve:** 67% **Collapse:** 15%
Attrition: 16% **MLB:** 95%
Comparables:
Edwin Jackson,Kyle Davies,Tyler Clippard

YEAR	TEAM	LVL	AGE	W	L	SV	G	GS	IP	H	HR	BB	SO	BB9	SO9	GB%	BABIP	WHIP	ERA	FIP	FRA	WARP
2010	BGR	A	21	6	6	0	22	22	114	98	14	45	118	3.6	9.3	48%	.286	1.25	3.95	4.42	4.93	0.9
2010	PCH	A+	21	0	0	0	1	1	4	5	0	0	8	0.0	18.0	1.%	.000	1.25	2.25	0.19	1.23	0.3
2011	PCH	A+	22	9	5	0	19	19	105^{2}	78	8	44	92	3.7	7.8	—	.253	1.15	3.66	4.05	4.40	0.0
2011	MNT	AA	22	3	4	0	9	9	52	41	5	28	31	4.8	5.4	—	.237	1.33	4.15	5.33	5.79	0.0
2012	MNT	AA	23	8	3	0	14	14	75	69	2	34	75	4.1	9.0	47%	.333	1.37	3.48	2.85	2.78	0.3
2012	DUR	AAA	23	0	1	0	3	3	16^{2}	12	1	9	15	4.9	8.1	44%	.262	1.26	3.24	3.94	5.10	-0.1
2013	*TBA*	*MLB*	*24*	*2*	*3*	*0*	*6*	*6*	*33^{2}*	*33*	*4*	*18*	*28*	*5.0*	*7.5*	*45%*	*.297*	*1.55*	*4.99*	*4.69*	*5.43*	*-0.2*

Sort of the mirror-Alex to his lefty counterpart Torres, Colome racks up lots of strikeouts and walks, although not quite to Torres's extreme. He's an old 24, having started his career in 2007 as a free agent, and has already thrown more than 500 innings in the minors. Last year, he earned a late-season promotion to Triple-A but was shut down after three starts with a shoulder injury. He had also missed most of April and May in Double-A with an abdomen strain. Assuming he's healthy, the Rays are likely to send him back to Durham and hope that he'll harness his lively 92-94 mph fastball and sharp curve—and that last year's injuries don't foretell a physical breakdown.

Dane De La Rosa

Born: 2/1/1983 **Age:** 30
Bats: R **Throws:** R **Height:** 6' 8" **Weight:** 245
Breakout: 23% **Improve:** 55% **Collapse:** 33%
Attrition: 12% **MLB:** 88%
Comparables:
Chris Schroder,Greg Aquino,Paul Shuey

YEAR	TEAM	LVL	AGE	W	L	SV	G	GS	IP	H	HR	BB	SO	BB9	SO9	GB%	BABIP	WHIP	ERA	FIP	FRA	WARP
2010	PCH	A+	27	0	0	0	2	0	3	4	0	0	5	0.0	15.0	50%	.500	1.33	3.00	0.10	-0.09	0.2
2010	MNT	AA	27	9	3	4	47	0	73	66	3	26	75	3.2	9.2	54%	.321	1.26	1.97	2.97	3.61	1.2
2011	DUR	AAA	28	6	5	6	52	0	70^{1}	63	8	26	83	3.3	10.6	—	.314	1.27	3.20	3.63	3.95	0.0
2011	TBA	MLB	28	0	0	0	7	0	7^{1}	10	1	3	8	3.7	9.8	52%	.409	1.77	9.82	3.88	3.71	0.1
2012	DUR	AAA	29	0	4	20	54	0	67^{2}	36	2	42	87	5.6	11.6	41%	.243	1.15	2.79	3.01	3.78	0.7
2012	TBA	MLB	29	0	0	0	5	0	5	7	2	2	5	3.6	9.0	53%	.385	1.80	12.60	7.45	10.20	-0.2
2013	*TBA*	*MLB*	*30*	*1*	*1*	*0*	*26*	*0*	*35^{2}*	*31*	*4*	*16*	*37*	*4.1*	*9.4*	*46%*	*.295*	*1.31*	*3.67*	*3.93*	*3.99*	*0.3*

In a second Triple-A season, De La Rosa allowed far fewer hits and far more walks than were his wont, while his strikeout rate spiked. His poor control got him off to a dreadful start, with a 6.61 ERA after 14 appearances. He also had a one-off big-league shellacking in April at Fenway Park. After that, though, his velocity started to increase, climbing from 90-91 to 94-95 by season's end, and he finished the year with a 2.79 ERA and 20 saves as Durham's closer, and three scoreless one-inning appearances with the Rays after a September call-up. De La Rosa is big and durable, and he should see at least some big-league time again this season, more if he can throw mid-90s strikes and command his breaking ball.

Frank De Los Santos

Born: 11/17/1987 **Age:** 25
Bats: L **Throws:** L **Height:** 6' 1" **Weight:** 165
Breakout: 24% **Improve:** 55% **Collapse:** 24%
Attrition: 14% **MLB:** 86%
Comparables:
Jerry Augustine,Chris George,Sean Burnett

YEAR	TEAM	LVL	AGE	W	L	SV	G	GS	IP	H	HR	BB	SO	BB9	SO9	GB%	BABIP	WHIP	ERA	FIP	FRA	WARP
2011	PCH	A+	23	0	1	0	3	1	8	25	3	2	8	2.2	9.0	—	.629	3.38	19.12	7.39	8.03	0.0
2011	MNT	AA	23	3	6	3	33	5	78^{2}	81	3	23	48	2.6	5.5	—	.312	1.32	3.55	3.50	3.80	0.0
2012	MNT	AA	24	4	1	4	24	2	48	45	1	15	26	2.8	4.9	59%	.290	1.25	2.06	3.39	3.65	0.2
2012	DUR	AAA	24	3	1	1	27	0	33	32	2	10	25	2.7	6.8	54%	.294	1.27	2.18	3.61	4.53	0.2
2013	*TBA*	*MLB*	*25*	*1*	*2*	*0*	*11*	*4*	*33*	*40*	*4*	*15*	*14*	*4.0*	*3.9*	*53%*	*.306*	*1.64*	*5.87*	*5.29*	*6.39*	*-0.5*

Get used to reading "slender, hard-throwing Latino lefty" in this section. De Los Santos started scaling the Rays' A-ball rungs in 2007. Moved to the bullpen and promoted to Double-A in 2011, he needed a year and a half to adjust and pitch his way up to Triple-A, where he pitched quite well. De Los Santos relies on a four-seamer that touches 94 with some life, although he leaves it up in the zone too often, and a better two-seamer that gets tons of groundballs. He's much tougher on lefties and probably projects as a LOOGY. De Los Santos was added to the 40-man after 2012. If he continues to handle Triple-A hitters, he could find himself in Tampa Bay before the season ends.

Kyle Farnsworth

Born: **4/14/1976** Age: **37**
Bats: **R** Throws: **R** Height: **6' 5"** Weight: **230**
Breakout: **22%** Improve: **47%** Collapse: **41%**
Attrition: **14%** MLB: **89%**

Comparables:
Joe Borowski, Bob Wickman, Todd Worrell

YEAR	TEAM	LVL	AGE	W	L	SV	G	GS	IP	H	HR	BB	SO	BB9	SO9	GB%	BABIP	WHIP	ERA	FIP	FRA	WARP
2010	ATL	MLB	34	0	2	0	23	0	20	15	2	7	25	3.2	11.2	42%	.271	1.10	5.40	2.96	3.73	0.3
2010	KCA	MLB	34	3	0	0	37	0	44^{2}	40	2	12	36	2.4	7.3	44%	.290	1.16	2.42	3.09	3.43	0.8
2011	TBA	MLB	35	5	1	25	63	0	57^{2}	45	5	12	51	1.9	8.0	51%	.250	0.99	2.18	3.20	3.44	0.8
2012	PCH	A+	36	0	0	0	4	4	4	3	0	0	2	0.0	4.5	42%	.250	0.75	2.25	2.39	2.40	0.0
2012	DUR	AAA	36	0	0	0	2	1	2	2	0	0	4	0.0	18.0	25%	.500	1.00	0.00	-0.84	-3.24	0.1
2012	TBA	MLB	36	1	6	0	34	0	27	22	1	14	25	4.7	8.3	57%	.266	1.33	4.00	3.34	4.14	0.1
2013	*TBA*	*MLB*	*37*	*2*	*1*	*7*	*38*	*0*	35^{2}	*32*	*4*	*12*	*35*	*3.0*	*8.8*	*43%*	*.292*	*1.24*	*3.56*	*3.70*	*3.87*	*0.4*

Farnsworth was the Rays' 2011 bullpen coup, saving 25 games with a 2.18 ERA while pitching more innings than he had in any season since 2007. But he lost most of 2012 to an ailing elbow, limited to just 27 innings and a fragile 0.8 innings per appearance. His numbers were marred by a high walk rate that harked back to his wilder early days but may have been caused by post-injury mechanical rust. If he's healthy, Farnsworth could give someone's bullpen good production for the money. But with his arm starting to show its age, he could also find retirement near at hand.

Brandon Gomes

Born: **7/15/1984** Age: **28**
Bats: **R** Throws: **R** Height: **6' 0"** Weight: **175**
Breakout: **23%** Improve: **50%** Collapse: **33%**
Attrition: **14%** MLB: **87%**

Comparables:
Chris Ray, Ron Davis, Al Hrabosky

YEAR	TEAM	LVL	AGE	W	L	SV	G	GS	IP	H	HR	BB	SO	BB9	SO9	GB%	BABIP	WHIP	ERA	FIP	FRA	WARP
2010	SAN	AA	25	7	2	1	51	0	72^{1}	52	2	25	93	3.1	11.6	43%	.294	1.07	1.87	2.04	2.43	1.9
2011	DUR	AAA	26	0	1	7	20	0	25^{1}	17	1	7	40	2.5	14.2	—	.308	0.95	1.07	1.54	1.67	0.0
2011	TBA	MLB	26	2	1	0	40	0	37	34	3	16	32	3.9	7.8	33%	.290	1.35	2.92	3.76	3.78	0.4
2012	DUR	AAA	27	5	4	9	40	0	55^{1}	44	5	14	73	2.3	11.9	30%	.310	1.05	3.09	2.62	2.67	1.0
2012	TBA	MLB	27	2	2	0	15	0	17^{2}	16	2	12	15	6.1	7.6	37%	.269	1.58	5.09	5.20	5.12	-0.1
2013	*TBA*	*MLB*	*28*	*1*	*1*	*0*	*28*	*0*	35^{2}	*32*	*4*	*14*	*37*	*3.6*	*9.3*	*40%*	*.296*	*1.29*	*3.69*	*3.76*	*4.01*	*0.3*

Delete his four-run, 1/3-inning appearance at Kansas City in June, and Gomes's ERA was 3.12 instead of 5.09. That may be a generous way of saying that relief stats are volatile and don't always tell the whole story, which in Gomes's case is mostly about other pitchers. Tampa Bay's long-haul starters required less mid-inning relief than others. When they did, there were other guys, like Burke Badenhop, holding those innings down. Most bullpens have a sub-replacement mop-up guy (see Sonnanstine, Andy), but there simply wasn't room on Tampa Bay's formidable firefighting force for Gomes's erratic work. He did, after all, have that four-run inning at Kansas City.

Taylor Guerrieri

Born: **12/1/1992** Age: **20**
Bats: **R** Throws: **R** Height: **6' 4"** Weight: **195**
Breakout: **50%** Improve: **79%** Collapse: **10%**
Attrition: **4%** MLB: **83%**

Comparables:
Catfish Hunter, Dick Brodowski, Milt Pappas

YEAR	TEAM	LVL	AGE	W	L	SV	G	GS	IP	H	HR	BB	SO	BB9	SO9	GB%	BABIP	WHIP	ERA	FIP	FRA	WARP
2012	HUD	A-	19	1	2	0	12	12	52	35	0	5	45	0.9	7.8	66%	.243	0.77	1.04	2.12	1.44	0.5
2013	*TBA*	*MLB*	*20*	*2*	*3*	*0*	*7*	*7*	33^{1}	*36*	*4*	*16*	*21*	*4.5*	*5.7*	*51%*	*.297*	*1.58*	*5.39*	*4.94*	*5.86*	*-0.3*

Guerrieri exceeded the first-round hype, overwhelming the New York-Penn League, where he executed and commanded his pitches as well as any Hudson Valley Renegade since Jeremy Hellickson. Guerrieri's smooth, fluid delivery produces a heavy, low-90s fastball and a power curve some think is already big league. It's too early to know whether to go with a scout's 2011 rave that Guerrieri was the best high-school arm he'd ever seen or to downgrade him a little, as BP's Jason Parks did a year later, projecting Guerrieri as "a solid number three." But as soon as Archer leaves the Rays' farm for good, Guerrieri inherits the mantle as the organization's top pitching prospect—and its accompanying expectations.

Jeremy Hellickson

Born: **4/8/1987** Age: **26**
Bats: **R** Throws: **R** Height: **6' 2"** Weight: **185**
Breakout: **31%** Improve: **59%** Collapse: **20%**
Attrition: **15%** MLB: **97%**

Comparables:
Micah Owings, Phil Hughes, Matt Cain

YEAR	TEAM	LVL	AGE	W	L	SV	G	GS	IP	H	HR	BB	SO	BB9	SO9	GB%	BABIP	WHIP	ERA	FIP	FRA	WARP
2010	TBA	MLB	23	4	0	0	10	4	36^{1}	32	5	8	33	2.0	8.2	38%	.267	1.10	3.47	3.85	4.02	0.4
2011	TBA	MLB	24	13	10	0	29	29	189	146	21	72	117	3.4	5.6	36%	.223	1.15	2.95	4.47	4.93	-0.3
2012	TBA	MLB	25	10	11	0	31	31	177	163	25	59	124	3.0	6.3	43%	.262	1.25	3.10	4.55	4.54	0.6
2013	*TBA*	*MLB*	*26*	*9*	*9*	*0*	*26*	*26*	*157*	*137*	*19*	*48*	*129*	*2.8*	*7.4*	*39%*	*.268*	*1.18*	*3.42*	*4.05*	*3.72*	*2.2*

Hellickson followed up his Rookie of the Year 2011 with a similar 2012. In both seasons he led all pitchers in undershooting his SIERA projection, prompting a *Fangraphs* columnist to throw up his hands and complain that "his underlying metrics offer no hints whatsoever as to how the heck he has done what he has." Hellickson's extreme infield-popup tendencies in 2011 regressed in 2012, the Rays defense was worse, and his slightly higher strikeout rate didn't make up the difference. So how'd he do it? Here's a hint: Hellickson's 82.7 percent strand rate led major-league starters. That may not have been a fluke: His LOB percentage placed second in 2011. Closer scrutiny suggests that Hellickson's mechanics improve when he pitches from the stretch. If his strand rate stays high in 2013, we may have to stop calling him lucky and accept Hellickson as a clutch pitcher and therefore a legitimate statistical outlier.

Roberto Hernandez

Born: **12/7/1983** Age: **29**
Bats: **R** Throws: **R** Height: **6' 5"** Weight: **230**
Breakout: **24%** Improve: **60%** Collapse: **25%**
Attrition: **16%** MLB: **82%**

Comparables:
Dock Ellis,Pat Hentgen,Runelvys Hernandez

YEAR	TEAM	LVL	AGE	W	L	SV	G	GS	IP	H	HR	BB	SO	BB9	SO9	GB%	BABIP	WHIP	ERA	FIP	FRA	WARP
2010	CLE	MLB	26	13	14	0	33	33	210^1	203	17	72	124	3.1	5.3	56%	.283	1.31	3.77	4.07	5.10	0.3
2011	CLE	MLB	27	7	15	0	32	32	188^2	205	22	60	109	2.9	5.2	56%	.291	1.40	5.25	4.60	5.65	-1.1
2012	LKC	A	28	1	1	0	2	2	12^1	12	5	1	13	0.7	9.5	54%	.233	1.05	3.65	6.76	13.48	0.0
2012	COH	AAA	28	1	0	0	2	2	12	13	0	3	7	2.2	5.2	56%	.317	1.33	4.50	2.74	1.25	0.0
2012	CLE	MLB	28	0	3	0	3	3	14^1	17	4	3	2	1.9	1.3	50%	.250	1.40	7.53	7.23	7.19	-0.4
2013	*TBA*	*MLB*	*29*	*2*	*3*	*0*	*8*	*8*	*46^2*	*47*	*5*	*18*	*29*	*3.4*	*5.6*	*58%*	*.286*	*1.38*	*4.45*	*4.51*	*4.84*	*0.0*

A hard-throwing sinker-changeup specialist from Distrito Nacional, D.R., with a checkered past and a recent history of underachievement, who rediscovers his magic with the Rays? No, this isn't a player comment for Fernando Rodney. Fausto Carmona, or rather, Roberto Hernandez, was discovered in January 2012 to be living under a false identity and age. He was sent home to find his real stats and thus missed most of the season. The real stats he then manufactured from the mound—three dreadful starts, a 7.53 ERA, and an ankle injury—made his season a total loss. The Rays threw a (for them) mint at Hernandez, adding heavy innings-pitched incentives that suggest they see him not merely as a bullpen replacement for Wade Davis and/or Badenhop; he was one of baseball's best starters in 2007 and could earn a rotation spot again.

J.P. Howell

Born: **4/25/1983** Age: **30**
Bats: **L** Throws: **L** Height: **6' 1"** Weight: **195**
Breakout: **21%** Improve: **50%** Collapse: **17%**
Attrition: **3%** MLB: **90%**

Comparables:
Rob Murphy,Will Ohman,Damaso Marte

YEAR	TEAM	LVL	AGE	W	L	SV	G	GS	IP	H	HR	BB	SO	BB9	SO9	GB%	BABIP	WHIP	ERA	FIP	FRA	WARP
2011	PCH	A+	28	0	1	0	3	3	3^1	3	0	1	4	2.7	10.8	—	.333	1.20	2.70	1.89	2.05	0.0
2011	DUR	AAA	28	0	0	0	4	0	3^2	5	0	1	5	2.5	12.3	—	.500	1.64	0.00	1.33	1.44	0.0
2011	TBA	MLB	28	2	3	1	46	0	30^2	30	5	18	26	5.3	7.6	54%	.287	1.57	6.16	5.44	5.88	-0.4
2012	TBA	MLB	29	1	0	0	55	0	50^1	39	7	22	42	3.9	7.5	53%	.250	1.21	3.04	4.73	5.04	-0.1
2013	*TBA*	*MLB*	*30*	*3*	*1*	*1*	*50*	*0*	*39^2*	*32*	*4*	*18*	*41*	*4.0*	*9.3*	*51%*	*.274*	*1.24*	*3.39*	*3.81*	*3.68*	*0.5*

After Howell's 2010 shoulder labrum surgery, the Rays loyally stuck with him for 46 appearances through a dreadful 2011. He rewarded them with a bounce-back 2012, halving his ERA, albeit with an FRA not much shinier than the previous year's and in mostly short, low-leverage circumstances. Howell's career-high LOB percentage (87.2, eighth-best in baseball) and high HR/FB rate (17.1 percent, after 19.2 in 2011)—plus a strikeout rate well below his 2008-09 heyday—paint a portrait of an escape artist who is about as good as his ability to keep the ball in the yard. But will his strand rate stay so high in 2013?

Josh Lueke

Born: **12/5/1984** Age: **28**
Bats: **R** Throws: **R** Height: **6' 6"** Weight: **235**
Breakout: **27%** Improve: **46%** Collapse: **32%**
Attrition: **7%** MLB: **89%**

Comparables:
Ron Davis,Dan Wheeler,Heath Bell

YEAR	TEAM	LVL	AGE	W	L	SV	G	GS	IP	H	HR	BB	SO	BB9	SO9	GB%	BABIP	WHIP	ERA	FIP	FRA	WARP
2010	HIC	A	25	2	1	10	17	0	19^2	12	0	5	36	2.3	16.4	65%	.324	0.86	0.46	0.94	0.61	1.1
2010	FRI	AA	25	1	1	2	15	0	18^2	18	2	5	26	2.4	12.5	52%	.364	1.23	3.85	2.58	3.04	0.4
2010	WTN	AA	25	1	0	3	6	0	7^1	4	0	0	14	0.0	17.3	39%	.308	0.55	0.00	-0.45	0.48	0.4
2010	TAC	AAA	25	1	0	2	12	0	17^1	14	0	5	18	2.6	9.4	42%	.288	1.10	2.08	2.37	2.77	0.6
2011	TAC	AAA	26	2	4	11	30	0	42^1	34	1	12	35	2.6	7.4	50%	.237	1.09	2.76	3.64	3.08	0.8
2011	SEA	MLB	26	1	1	0	25	0	32^2	34	2	13	29	3.6	8.0	44%	.327	1.44	6.06	3.28	3.96	0.2
2012	DUR	AAA	27	2	6	2	42	0	67^2	85	6	17	71	2.3	9.4	40%	.389	1.51	5.59	2.97	3.87	0.8
2012	TBA	MLB	27	0	0	0	3	0	3^1	9	0	3	2	8.1	5.4	19%	.562	3.60	18.90	4.55	5.40	0.0
2013	*TBA*	*MLB*	*28*	*1*	*1*	*0*	*26*	*0*	*35^2*	*34*	*3*	*12*	*34*	*3.0*	*8.5*	*44%*	*.306*	*1.29*	*3.81*	*3.40*	*4.15*	*0.3*

Those who worried that the grotesque sex-crime skeleton in Lueke's closet would blight the Rays image needn't have: His dismal Triple-A showing limited him to three big-league appearances. Lueke threw copious strikes on the farm, as he usually does, but too many were hard, flat fastballs that were hammered. His 2012 FIP (3.01) causes more optimism than his ERA (5.59), especially if you pardon his .389 BABIP as a fluke. And he's Justin Verlander's nearest PITCHf/x comp, too. But the ugly ERA *included* a midsummer stretch during which Lueke allowed just two runs in 23 innings. However you look at the numbers, they're much worse in contextual comparison: The guy Lueke was traded for, John Jaso, had a breakout season for the Mariners, while Lueke mostly just looked broken.

Parker Markel

Born: **9/15/1990** Age: **22**
Bats: **R** Throws: **R** Height: **6' 5"** Weight: **220**
Breakout: **22%** Improve: **59%** Collapse: **20%**
Attrition: **9%** MLB: **83%**

Comparables:
Edwin Jackson,Bill Pulsipher,Dave Stieb

YEAR	TEAM	LVL	AGE	W	L	SV	G	GS	IP	H	HR	BB	SO	BB9	SO9	GB%	BABIP	WHIP	ERA	FIP	FRA	WARP
2010	RAY	Rk	19	2	0	0	7	0	10^1	8	0	3	13	2.6	11.4	53%	.367	1.07	1.75	1.86	3.87	0.2
2011	HUD	A-	20	3	4	0	13	13	57^1	42	3	23	44	3.6	6.9	—	.248	1.13	3.14	3.98	4.32	0.0
2012	BGR	A	21	11	5	0	24	24	120	117	6	34	96	2.5	7.2	49%	.305	1.26	3.53	3.40	4.14	1.2
2013	*TBA*	*MLB*	*22*	*2*	*3*	*0*	*7*	*7*	*33^1*	*37*	*4*	*16*	*19*	*4.2*	*5.2*	*45%*	*.301*	*1.60*	*5.54*	*5.06*	*6.03*	*-0.4*

Although he shares an alma mater (Yavapai CC) with Curt Schilling, horses don't get much darker than Parker, a 2010 39th-rounder scoped by Rays Four Corners scout Jayson Durocher, who also tracked Nevadan first-rounder Jake Hager. Markel sparkeled immediately, dominating the GCL in his first pro season. He elicited a 2011 barkel of approval from Keith Law, who saw Markel pitch and remarkeled (okay, enough; it's pronounced "Mar-KELL") that he "stole the show" with his mid-90s heater, 81-82 slider and solid changeup. Law, noting Markel's high-effort, top-heavy mechanics and three-quarter arm slot, recommended a move to the bullpen. Sure enough, Markel struggled early in 2012 and lost a month to shoulder soreness. But he recovered and grew stronger as the season progressed, with a season-best 1.75 ERA in August.

Jake McGee

Born: **8/6/1986** Age: **26**
Bats: **L** Throws: **L** Height: **6' 4"** Weight: **230**
Breakout: **28%** Improve: **69%** Collapse: **15%**
Attrition: **5%** MLB: **97%**

Comparables:
Francisco Liriano,J.P. Howell,Johan Santana

YEAR	TEAM	LVL	AGE	W	L	SV	G	GS	IP	H	HR	BB	SO	BB9	SO9	GB%	BABIP	WHIP	ERA	FIP	FRA	WARP
2010	MNT	AA	23	3	7	0	19	19	88^1	81	3	33	100	3.4	10.2	44%	.328	1.29	3.57	2.72	3.32	2.2
2010	DUR	AAA	23	1	1	1	11	1	17^1	9	0	3	27	1.6	14.0	47%	.237	0.69	0.52	0.69	2.04	0.7
2010	TBA	MLB	23	0	0	0	8	0	5	2	0	3	6	5.4	10.8	55%	.182	1.00	1.80	2.45	4.18	0.0
2011	DUR	AAA	24	4	2	9	24	0	33^1	30	4	8	38	2.2	10.3	—	.295	1.14	2.70	3.33	3.62	0.0
2011	TBA	MLB	24	5	2	0	37	0	28	30	5	12	27	3.9	8.7	33%	.312	1.50	4.50	4.74	4.20	-0.1
2012	TBA	MLB	25	5	2	0	69	0	55^1	33	3	11	73	1.8	11.9	44%	.244	0.80	1.95	1.76	1.44	1.6
2013	*TBA*	*MLB*	*26*	*3*	*2*	*0*	*30*	*4*	*41*	*35*	*4*	*15*	*44*	*3.3*	*9.7*	*42%*	*.291*	*1.21*	*3.27*	*3.42*	*3.55*	*0.7*

McGee's move to the bullpen, which happened midway through 2010, paid huge dividends in 2012, his first full major-league season. His 1.6 WAR was the highest in baseball among relievers not used as closers. McGee's approach hasn't changed much: throw, throw, throw that mid-90s heater nearly 90 percent of the time. Perhaps the dramatic improvement in results last season owed to the completion of a gradual, two-year drop in his release point, which has come down about six inches since 2010 and may be a sign that he's getting better arm extension. McGee will reprise his late-inning role in 2013 and could conceivably be the Rays closer in 2014.

Mike Montgomery

Born: **7/1/1989** Age: **23**
Bats: **L** Throws: **L** Height: **6' 5"** Weight: **185**
Breakout: **25%** Improve: **65%** Collapse: **17%**
Attrition: **15%** MLB: **95%**

Comparables:
Jason Vargas,Jon Lester,Jon Niese

YEAR	TEAM	LVL	AGE	W	L	SV	G	GS	IP	H	HR	BB	SO	BB9	SO9	GB%	BABIP	WHIP	ERA	FIP	FRA	WARP
2011	OMA	AAA	21	5	11	0	28	27	150^2	157	15	69	129	4.1	7.7	48%	.310	1.50	5.32	4.88	4.40	1.0
2012	NWA	AA	22	2	6	0	10	10	58	69	12	21	44	3.3	6.8	49%	.318	1.55	6.67	5.69	7.40	-0.8
2012	OMA	AAA	22	3	6	0	17	17	91^2	110	12	43	67	4.2	6.6	48%	.317	1.67	5.69	5.41	6.70	-0.7
2013	*TBA*	*MLB*	*23*	*2*	*3*	*0*	*8*	*8*	43^1	*43*	*5*	*20*	*32*	*4.1*	*6.7*	*48%*	*.287*	*1.44*	*4.66*	*4.61*	*5.06*	*-0.0*

You think you had a bad year? Montgomery, *Baseball America*'s number one Royals prospect after 2011, and BP's number six, opened 2012 in Triple-A, got routinely rocked, was demoted to Double-A, and got rocked even harder. His control began fading his first time through Double-A in 2010 and has been eroding ever since. In Double-A, he tried to refine his command by easing off the power, but left too many pitches over the plate and got abused by Texas League hitters. His physical skills—including three plus pitches—could still work in his favor, but his confidence is shot. Having come to Florida in the Shields trade, his career now rides on the possibility that he can recapture his command under his new organization's tutelage.

Matt Moore

Born: **6/18/1989** Age: **24**
Bats: **L** Throws: **L** Height: **6' 3"** Weight: **205**
Breakout: **32%** Improve: **71%** Collapse: **12%**
Attrition: **10%** MLB: **94%**

Comparables:
Clay Buchholz,Scott Kazmir,Jake McGee

YEAR	TEAM	LVL	AGE	W	L	SV	G	GS	IP	H	HR	BB	SO	BB9	SO9	GB%	BABIP	WHIP	ERA	FIP	FRA	WARP
2010	PCH	A+	21	6	11	0	26	26	144^2	109	7	61	208	3.8	12.9	45%	.325	1.17	3.36	2.62	3.57	2.7
2011	MNT	AA	22	8	3	0	18	18	102^1	68	8	28	131	2.5	11.5	—	.263	0.94	2.20	2.73	2.97	0.0
2011	DUR	AAA	22	4	0	0	9	9	52^2	33	3	18	79	3.1	13.5	—	.291	0.97	1.37	2.06	2.24	0.0
2011	TBA	MLB	22	1	0	0	3	1	9^1	9	1	3	15	2.9	14.5	46%	.381	1.29	2.89	2.20	3.41	0.3
2012	TBA	MLB	23	11	11	0	31	31	177^1	158	18	81	175	4.1	8.9	39%	.294	1.35	3.81	3.88	3.65	2.6
2013	*TBA*	*MLB*	*24*	*7*	*8*	*0*	*22*	*22*	*126*	*108*	*13*	*63*	*137*	*4.5*	*9.8*	*42%*	*.297*	*1.36*	*3.89*	*3.87*	*4.23*	*1.0*

The Rays Longoria'd Moore after he had pitched in just four major-league baseball games, signing him to a five-year, $14 million arb-devouring extension after the 2011 season. The deal could be worth $40 million if all the team options are exercised through 2019. Moore gave the club everything it could want in a rookie fifth starter who earned only the first of those millions. April and May were rough, but he found a two-month groove in midsummer before stumbling to the finish in the stretch drive, perhaps the result of fatigue as he topped his career high in innings pitched. PECOTA is somewhat bearish on Moore, predicting less than a full season of starts from him, but if he's healthy he's a candidate for a breakout performance.

Jeff Niemann

Born: **2/28/1983** Age: **30**
Bats: **R** Throws: **R** Height: **6' 10"** Weight: **260**
Breakout: **10%** Improve: **35%** Collapse: **32%**
Attrition: **13%** MLB: **90%**

Comparables:
Vicente Padilla,Brad Penny,Nate Robertson

YEAR	TEAM	LVL	AGE	W	L	SV	G	GS	IP	H	HR	BB	SO	BB9	SO9	GB%	BABIP	WHIP	ERA	FIP	FRA	WARP
2010	TBA	MLB	27	12	8	0	30	29	174^{1}	159	25	61	131	3.1	6.8	45%	.263	1.26	4.39	4.58	4.91	-0.1
2011	PCH	A+	28	0	0	0	1	1	4	1	0	0	2	0.0	4.5	—	.100	0.25	0.00	2.39	2.60	0.0
2011	DUR	AAA	28	1	1	0	2	2	9^{1}	10	0	3	8	2.9	7.7	—	.333	1.39	3.86	2.49	2.70	0.0
2011	TBA	MLB	28	11	7	0	23	23	135^{1}	131	18	37	105	2.5	7.0	47%	.278	1.24	4.06	4.17	4.37	1.0
2012	PCH	A+	29	0	0	0	2	2	6	9	0	3	6	4.5	9.0	45%	.450	2.00	6.00	3.39	1.56	0.0
2012	DUR	AAA	29	0	0	0	2	2	8^{1}	17	1	2	4	2.2	4.3	42%	.457	2.28	7.56	4.48	7.99	0.0
2012	TBA	MLB	29	2	3	0	8	8	38	30	2	12	34	2.8	8.1	53%	.264	1.11	3.08	3.05	4.00	0.6
2013	*TBA*	*MLB*	*30*	*3*	*3*	*0*	*9*	*9*	*52^{2}*	*49*	*6*	*17*	*41*	*2.9*	*7.0*	*45%*	*.279*	*1.25*	*3.75*	*4.09*	*4.08*	*0.5*

It had just clicked into place for the Big Nyquil: a seven-inning, six-hit, one-run performance against the Yankees on May 9. But in his very next start, Toronto's Adam Lind hit a ball that broke Niemann's right fibula, essentially ending his season. Niemann returned on September 1, also against Toronto, but left that start in the fourth inning with a shoulder strain that shut him down for the year. He has been a solid back-end starter for Tampa Bay when healthy but has missed 186 games with injuries over the last two years. With a crowd of candidates for the starting rotation, Niemann's spot isn't guaranteed. He may have to pitch his way back in.

Jake Odorizzi

Born: **3/27/1990** Age: **23**
Bats: **R** Throws: **R** Height: **6' 3"** Weight: **175**
Breakout: **26%** Improve: **61%** Collapse: **14%**
Attrition: **10%** MLB: **91%**

Comparables:
Juan Cruz,Chris Tillman,Ervin Santana

YEAR	TEAM	LVL	AGE	W	L	SV	G	GS	IP	H	HR	BB	SO	BB9	SO9	GB%	BABIP	WHIP	ERA	FIP	FRA	WARP
2010	WIS	A	20	7	3	1	23	20	120^{2}	99	7	40	135	3.0	10.1	46%	.293	1.15	3.43	3.34	4.21	2.0
2011	WIL	A+	21	5	4	0	15	15	78^{1}	68	4	22	103	2.5	11.8	44%	.373	1.15	2.87	2.18	2.65	1.3
2011	NWA	AA	21	5	3	0	12	12	68^{2}	66	13	22	54	2.9	7.1	31%	.242	1.28	4.72	5.27	5.83	0.2
2012	NWA	AA	22	4	2	0	7	7	38	27	2	10	47	2.4	11.1	36%	.269	0.97	3.32	2.28	3.23	0.9
2012	OMA	AAA	22	11	3	0	19	18	107^{1}	105	12	40	88	3.4	7.4	30%	.292	1.35	2.93	4.65	4.30	1.2
2012	KCA	MLB	22	0	1	0	2	2	7^{1}	8	1	4	4	4.9	4.9	39%	.280	1.64	4.91	5.36	5.94	0.0
2013	*TBA*	*MLB*	*23*	*3*	*3*	*0*	*9*	*9*	*48^{1}*	*47*	*6*	*20*	*38*	*3.7*	*7.1*	*38%*	*.288*	*1.38*	*4.33*	*4.48*	*4.71*	*0.1*

Odorizzi has now been traded for both Zack Greinke and Shields, so if nothing else he's seen as a guy with strong potential. He made his major-league debut last September after a successful Triple-A campaign. His fastball lives in the low 90s and his put-away pitch is a plus curve. As he showed during a cup of coffee in Kansas City, he can be inconsistent with his delivery, which causes him to leave pitches up. He will probably start the season in Durham, but projects as an eventual mid-rotation starter.

Joel Peralta

Born: **3/23/1976** Age: **37**
Bats: **R** Throws: **R** Height: **6' 0"** Weight: **195**
Breakout: **22%** Improve: **43%** Collapse: **38%**
Attrition: **10%** MLB: **91%**

Comparables:
Trevor Hoffman,Tug McGraw,Todd Worrell

YEAR	TEAM	LVL	AGE	W	L	SV	G	GS	IP	H	HR	BB	SO	BB9	SO9	GB%	BABIP	WHIP	ERA	FIP	FRA	WARP
2010	SYR	AAA	34	2	0	20	28	0	33^{1}	24	1	7	38	1.9	10.3	41%	.277	0.93	1.08	2.12	2.21	1.1
2010	WAS	MLB	34	1	0	0	39	0	49	30	5	9	49	1.7	9.0	29%	.200	0.80	2.02	3.05	3.27	0.9
2011	TBA	MLB	35	3	4	6	71	0	67^{2}	44	7	18	61	2.4	8.1	28%	.218	0.92	2.93	3.40	3.82	0.6
2012	TBA	MLB	36	2	6	2	76	0	67	49	9	17	84	2.3	11.3	32%	.261	0.99	3.63	3.09	3.43	0.9
2013	*TBA*	*MLB*	*37*	*3*	*1*	*2*	*56*	*0*	*56^{1}*	*46*	*7*	*16*	*56*	*2.6*	*9.0*	*35%*	*.269*	*1.11*	*3.08*	*3.68*	*3.35*	*1.0*

When he wasn't sparking the biggest pine-tar controversy since George Brett and earning an eight-game suspension from it, king of the rising fastball Peralta saw his performance rise, too, although his ERA (.70 higher than 2011) belied the underlying evidence. Peralta's strikeout rate leaped to 31.8 percent, ninth-best among MLB relievers, and his walk rate and FIP dropped. The ERA is probably explained by an increased home-run rate and a .261 BABIP, which was in line with Peralta's career mark but followed 2011's unrepeatable .218. He was the workhorse of Maddon's bullpen and shows no signs of decline even as he approaches his sunset years. No dummies, the Rays inked him to a new two-year deal after 2012.

David Price

Born: **8/26/1985** Age: **27**
Bats: **L** Throws: **L** Height: **6' 7"** Weight: **225**
Breakout: **27%** Improve: **71%** Collapse: **17%**
Attrition: **20%** MLB: **94%**

Comparables:
Clay Buchholz,Josh Johnson,Jon Lester

YEAR	TEAM	LVL	AGE	W	L	SV	G	GS	IP	H	HR	BB	SO	BB9	SO9	GB%	BABIP	WHIP	ERA	FIP	FRA	WARP
2010	TBA	MLB	24	19	6	0	32	31	208^{2}	170	15	79	188	3.4	8.1	45%	.270	1.19	2.72	3.39	3.79	3.1
2011	TBA	MLB	25	12	13	0	34	34	224^{1}	192	22	63	218	2.5	8.7	45%	.281	1.14	3.49	3.36	3.70	3.1
2012	TBA	MLB	26	20	5	0	31	31	211	173	16	59	205	2.5	8.7	53%	.285	1.10	2.56	3.00	3.69	3.1
2013	*TBA*	*MLB*	*27*	*11*	*9*	*0*	*27*	*27*	*180^{2}*	*150*	*16*	*57*	*172*	*2.9*	*8.6*	*47%*	*.279*	*1.15*	*2.98*	*3.39*	*3.24*	*3.5*

After he won his 20th game, Price was asked whether he felt he'd had a Cy Young season. His answer: "One hundred percent." And who is to argue, other than Justin Verlander? Price established himself as the ace the Rays foresaw when they took him with the first pick in 2007. What stands out is his consistency, both year-to-year and within the season itself. Price almost duplicated many key stats from 2011: walk and strikeout rates,

BABIP, batting average-against, and others. He pitched into the seventh inning in 26 of his 31 starts. It's only a matter of time, and probably not much of it, before Price prices himself out of the Rays' market and perhaps wins his second Cy Young Award in another uniform.

Cesar Ramos

Born: **6/22/1984** Age: **29**
Bats: **L** Throws: **L** Height: **6' 3"** Weight: **205**
Breakout: **7%** Improve: **39%** Collapse: **37%**
Attrition: **37%** MLB: **84%**

Comparables:
Bill Wight,Omar Daal,Lenny DiNardo

YEAR	TEAM	LVL	AGE	W	L	SV	G	GS	IP	H	HR	BB	SO	BB9	SO9	GB%	BABIP	WHIP	ERA	FIP	FRA	WARP
2010	POR	AAA	26	6	7	0	30	15	96	90	7	43	63	4.0	5.9	47%	.290	1.39	3.28	4.63	5.20	0.5
2010	SDN	MLB	26	0	1	0	14	0	8^1	18	1	4	9	4.3	9.7	41%	.515	2.64	11.88	3.95	4.09	0.0
2011	DUR	AAA	27	2	0	0	4	0	4	5	1	2	1	4.5	2.2	—	.267	1.75	4.50	7.49	8.14	0.0
2011	TBA	MLB	27	0	1	0	59	0	43^2	36	4	25	31	5.2	6.4	50%	.248	1.40	3.92	4.76	5.03	-0.1
2012	DUR	AAA	28	5	5	1	25	7	62	58	10	16	46	2.3	6.7	43%	.271	1.19	3.77	4.54	6.44	0.1
2012	TBA	MLB	28	1	0	0	17	1	30	19	2	10	29	3.0	8.7	53%	.221	0.97	2.10	3.18	3.03	0.6
2013	*TBA*	*MLB*	*29*	*2*	*2*	*0*	*25*	*4*	*40^2*	*43*	*5*	*16*	*27*	*3.6*	*5.9*	*46%*	*.298*	*1.45*	*4.67*	*4.65*	*5.07*	*-0.1*

Ramos was actually better against right-handers than lefties in 2012, but he was good against both. Like Gomes, Ramos might have spent the whole year on a big-league roster with a lesser pitching staff. Instead, he threw twice as many Triple-A innings as he logged in the majors. The difference comes mainly from his late-season insertion into the Bulls starting rotation, where he had poor results: His starting ERA of 4.84 was more than double his relief ERA, inflated by six homers in 35 innings as a starter. Ramos perhaps throws too many modest strikes to survive multiple trips through a lineup. The former first-rounder still offers a useful lefty arm if someone figures out how to use it.

Felipe Rivero

Born: **7/5/1991** Age: **21**
Bats: **L** Throws: **L** Height: **6' 1"** Weight: **151**
Breakout: **23%** Improve: **47%** Collapse: **10%**
Attrition: **8%** MLB: **87%**

Comparables:
Mike McCormick,Joel Davis,Ryan Feierabend

YEAR	TEAM	LVL	AGE	W	L	SV	G	GS	IP	H	HR	BB	SO	BB9	SO9	GB%	BABIP	WHIP	ERA	FIP	FRA	WARP
2011	PRI	Rk	19	3	3	0	14	12	60^1	64	7	13	57	1.9	8.5	39%	.306	1.28	4.62	4.34	4.69	0.6
2012	BGR	A	20	8	8	0	27	21	113^1	115	5	29	98	2.3	7.8	53%	.327	1.27	3.41	3.12	3.71	1.5
2013	*TBA*	*MLB*	*21*	*1*	*3*	*0*	*8*	*6*	*33^1*	*37*	*4*	*15*	*20*	*4.2*	*5.5*	*45%*	*.303*	*1.59*	*5.56*	*4.91*	*6.04*	*-0.3*

A slender, hard-throwing lefty (told you!) who can whip it up into the mid-90s, Rivero is a virtual assembly-line product in the Rays southpaw-heavy system. His mechanics are still inconsistent, but he has maintained very good control through three levels, with last year's 2.3 BB9 his highest so far. Last year he generated a lot of groundballs. With Enny Romero and Alex Torres struggling to throw strikes in the upper minors, the way is clear for Rivero to gain traction as the Rays' left-handed starter of the future.

Fernando Rodney

Born: **3/18/1977** Age: **36**
Bats: **R** Throws: **R** Height: **6' 0"** Weight: **220**
Breakout: **29%** Improve: **50%** Collapse: **27%**
Attrition: **8%** MLB: **82%**

Comparables:
Jim Mecir,Dave Smith,Roberto Hernandez

YEAR	TEAM	LVL	AGE	W	L	SV	G	GS	IP	H	HR	BB	SO	BB9	SO9	GB%	BABIP	WHIP	ERA	FIP	FRA	WARP
2010	ANA	MLB	33	4	3	14	72	0	68	70	4	35	53	4.6	7.0	51%	.314	1.54	4.24	4.02	4.19	0.3
2011	SBR	A+	34	0	0	0	2	1	2	2	0	1	3	4.5	13.5	—	.400	1.50	9.00	2.45	2.66	0.0
2011	ANA	MLB	34	3	5	3	39	0	32	26	1	28	26	7.9	7.3	59%	.272	1.69	4.50	4.75	5.72	-0.4
2012	TBA	MLB	35	2	2	48	76	0	74^2	43	2	15	76	1.8	9.2	59%	.220	0.78	0.60	2.08	2.35	1.8
2013	*TBA*	*MLB*	*36*	*3*	*1*	*19*	*55*	*0*	*51^2*	*45*	*4*	*26*	*49*	*4.5*	*8.5*	*52%*	*.284*	*1.36*	*3.76*	*3.82*	*4.09*	*0.4*

Rodney replaced the injured Farnsworth as closer and merely made history: his 0.60 ERA was the lowest ever in a minimum 50-inning season. How did he remake himself? A move to the first-base side of the rubber radically altered his horizontal release point and appears to have helped him locate his two-seamer, which he threw 47 percent of the time, his most ever, and his changeup, which he threw 37 percent of the time. His leg lift appeared to drop a little, too. Moreover, Rodney was comfortable in Tampa Bay after clashing with Mike Scioscia in Anaheim. His walk rate plunged and his save-arrows soared. Maybe he used some of the extras to hunt deer for the elbowed-out Farnsworth. The Rays' 2013 option on Rodney pays him \$2.5 million. If he's only half as good as he was last year, he'll still be a bargain.

Blake Snell

Born: **12/4/1992** Age: **20**
Bats: **L** Throws: **L** Height: **6' 5"** Weight: **180**
Breakout: **25%** Improve: **42%** Collapse: **22%**
Attrition: **36%** MLB: **94%**

Comparables:
Mike McCormick,Bruce Robbins,David Clyde

YEAR	TEAM	LVL	AGE	W	L	SV	G	GS	IP	H	HR	BB	SO	BB9	SO9	GB%	BABIP	WHIP	ERA	FIP	FRA	WARP
2011	RAY	Rk	18	1	2	0	11	8	26^1	30	0	11	26	3.8	8.9	53%	.390	1.56	3.08	2.70	3.66	0.3
2012	PRI	Rk	19	5	1	0	11	11	47^1	34	4	17	53	3.2	10.1	55%	.270	1.08	2.09	3.89	4.96	0.4
2013	*TBA*	*MLB*	*20*	*1*	*3*	*0*	*8*	*8*	*31^2*	*36*	*4*	*22*	*21*	*6.1*	*5.9*	*47%*	*.308*	*1.81*	*6.25*	*5.60*	*6.80*	*-0.5*

Yet another 2011 supplemental first-rounder (and yet another Washingtonian), Snell originally projected lower in the draft, but after he failed to qualify academically for the University of

Washington, the Rays gambled on his signability, and won. Snell swims quietly in the teeming tank of Rays lefties because he doesn't throw that hard and because he's the youngest of them. But he improved all of his numbers in his sophomore pro season, finishing second in the Appalachian League in ERA, striking out more than a batter per inning and getting a lot of grounders with his down-in-the-zone fastball. A command rather than power arm, he'll need to develop secondary pitches in order to climb the ladder.

Alexander Torres
Born: **12/8/1987** Age: **25**
Bats: **L** Throws: **L** Height: **5' 11"** Weight: **175**
Breakout: **34%** Improve: **59%** Collapse: **23%**
Attrition: **15%** MLB: **87%**
Comparables:
Marc Rzepczynski, Tony Saunders, Donnie Veal

YEAR	TEAM	LVL	AGE	W	L	SV	G	GS	IP	H	HR	BB	SO	BB9	SO9	GB%	BABIP	WHIP	ERA	FIP	FRA	WARP
2010	MNT	AA	22	11	6	0	27	27	142^{2}	136	9	70	150	4.4	9.5	53%	.335	1.44	3.47	3.66	4.35	1.7
2011	DUR	AAA	23	9	7	0	27	27	146^{1}	134	7	83	156	5.1	9.6	—	.331	1.48	3.08	3.55	3.86	0.0
2011	TBA	MLB	23	1	1	0	4	0	8	8	0	7	9	7.9	10.1	59%	.364	1.88	3.38	3.81	5.00	0.0
2012	RAY	Rk	24	0	1	0	4	4	11^{1}	7	0	4	17	3.2	13.5	73%	.273	0.97	3.18	1.49	2.83	0.2
2012	DUR	AAA	24	3	7	0	26	14	69	70	6	63	91	8.2	11.9	47%	.370	1.93	7.30	4.52	5.73	0.4
2013	*TBA*	*MLB*	*25*	*2*	*2*	*0*	*9*	*6*	33^{2}	*31*	*3*	*21*	*32*	*5.7*	*8.6*	*53%*	*.303*	*1.57*	*4.70*	*4.33*	*5.11*	*-0.0*

Torres has always had a love-hate relationship with the strike zone, but after a good 2011 included a taste of big-league success, irreconcilable differences ruined his 2012. Torres allowed nearly a walk per inning and was temporarily demoted to the bullpen, where he foundered. In late July, a phantom injury was invented so he could work with Gulf Coast League pitching mentor Marty DeMerritt, whom Torres had known as a youngster in Venezuela. He returned to Durham on the last day of the Triple-A season and threw the best game of his minor-league career, showing simplified mechanics and a slider in place of his curve. If Torres can rebuild his confidence on that performance, he could eventually deliver on his promise as a mid-rotation starter, or thrive in the bullpen.

LINEOUTS

HITTERS

PLAYER	TEAM	LVL	AGE	PA	R	2B	3B	HR	RBI	BB	SO	SB-CS	AVG/OBP/SLG	TAv	BABIP	BRR	FRAA	WARP
2B V. Belnome	TUC	AAA	24	303	28	11	1	5	33	43	72	5-1	.275/.380/.384	.261	.363	-1.9	2B(20): 0.4, 1B(19): -3.6	-0.3
C R. Chirinos	—	—	—	—	—	—	—	—	—	—	—	—	—	—	—	—	—	—
INF B. Conrad	DUR	AAA	32	102	10	5	0	4	12	18	34	0-3	.265/.392/.470	.192	.391	0.4	3B(3): 0.0, 1B(1): -0.0	-0.2
	NAS	AAA	32	85	17	5	1	10	28	11	15	0-1	.405/.482/.905	.458	.408	0.4	2B(10): -0.8, 1B(3): 0.1	2.0
	MIL	MLB	32	44	2	0	0	2	6	3	16	0-0	.075/.136/.225	.140	.043	-0.1	1B(7): -0.1, 2B(4): 0.2	-0.5
	TBA	MLB	32	61	4	5	0	2	9	3	27	0-0	.172/.213/.362	.181	.276	0.6	3B(14): -0.3, 2B(9): -0.2	-0.4
OF J. Feliciano	DUR	AAA	33	467	46	19	1	1	46	25	43	8-3	.270/.312/.326	.222	.295	0	CF(37): 1.2, RF(7): -0.3	-0.4
OF B. Francisco	HOU	MLB	30	90	5	4	0	2	5	5	23	0-0	.247/.289/.365	.237	.317	1	RF(14): -1.0, LF(12): -0.1	-0.3
	TBA	MLB	30	63	4	5	0	2	8	4	16	0-0	.228/.270/.421	.239	.268	0.1	RF(11): -0.4, LF(7): -0.1	-0.2
	TOR	MLB	30	54	5	5	1	0	2	4	10	0-1	.240/.296/.380	.253	.300	-1.3	LF(5): -0.2, RF(4): -0.1	-0.2
3B P. Leonard	BNC	Rk	19	268	37	9	3	14	46	30	55	6-2	.251/.340/.494	.217	.269	0.2	3B(22): 6.6	0.2
DH H. Matsui	DUR	AAA	38	54	3	2	0	0	4	4	10	0-0	.170/.231/.213	.119	.211	-0.2	LF(1): -0.1	-0.1
	TBA	MLB	38	103	7	1	0	2	7	8	22	0-0	.147/.214/.221	.151	.169	0.1	LF(9): -0.4, RF(6): -0.1	-1.2
OF R. Mondesi	HEL	Rk	19	298	43	12	6	5	32	14	87	8-4	.231/.282/.374	.264	.319	1.4	RF(36): 0.9, CF(19): -3.2	0.0
C J. O'Conner	HUD	A-	20	257	39	18	1	5	29	18	73	2-0	.223/.276/.370	.329	.298	0.6	--	0.9
1B C. Seitzer	BGR	A	22	488	50	36	2	4	54	55	83	1-1	.307/.386/.429	.292	.368	-6	1B(48): -1.1, LF(1): 0.0	0.8
OF R. Thompson	DUR	AAA	33	282	41	13	5	2	19	20	35	22-5	.311/.369/.426	.265	.355	5	CF(8): 1.3, LF(5): 0.1	0.6
	LEH	AAA	33	102	6	4	2	0	11	9	18	7-2	.307/.396/.398	.265	.386	-2.1	CF(12): 1.7, RF(2): -0.1	0.0
	TBA	MLB	33	24	5	0	0	0	1	0	5	6-2	.091/.167/.091	.096	.118	0.1	LF(7): -0.2, CF(5): -0.1	-0.4
1B H. Wrigley	MNT	AA	25	137	17	12	0	7	27	15	25	3-0	.270/.350/.541	.294	.289	-1.4	RF(5): -0.8, 1B(1): -0.0	0.0
	DUR	AAA	25	380	39	25	1	13	52	21	78	0-1	.285/.324/.472	.230	.330	-0.3	1B(17): 0.2, RF(2): -0.2	-0.4

Vince Belnome, acquired from San Diego, could become the Rays' next Jeff Keppinger, except one who walks a lot more—or he could become the Rays' next Brooks Conrad. **Robinson Chirinos** lost his entire 2012 season to the disturbingly persistent aftereffects of a spring-training concussion, and his age puts the converted infielder's career into double jeopardy. **Brooks Conrad** was acquired from the Brewers as one of many infielders the Rays threw at their Longorialessness, but he was outrighted to Durham after a month or so of sub-replacement-level performance and will try to be big in Japan in 2013. **Jesus Feliciano** is precisely the kind of aging but brought-my-glove outfielder who leads his Triple-A club in games played despite a .222 TAv, a breathtakingly low walk rate, and exactly one home run in 467 PAs—but hey, he hit that homer off of Dice-K, so he must be a prospect, right? Last season, **Ben Francisco** bounced from Toronto to Houston to Tampa Bay, which acquired him at the end of August to hit lefties. Instead, he hit .176 vs. southpaws, with a 590 OPS and 10 strikeouts in 38 plate appearances. Next. Drafted as a shortstop and shifted to third in his first professional season, **Patrick Leonard** led the Appy League in home runs, has projectable power, and will be 31 when Longoria's contract expires. **Hideki Matsui** was signed as lefty power-bat insurance, but Godzilla was the liability instead of the insurance, ending his great career with a fireless last gasp and then retiring in December. The Rays got **Raul Mondesi Jr.**, son of the former All-Star and older brother of the Royals' Adalberto, a better prospect, from the Brewers for Burke Badenhop. **Justin O'Conner**, the only first-round catcher the Rays have ever drafted, had to spend 2012 at DH due to hip problems. He has a great arm and good athleticism, and if healthy he'll go back behind the dish. Higher draft picks hogged the prospect attention in Bowling Green, but it was 11th-rounder **Cameron Seitzer** whose 815 OPS, eighth in the league, topped them all. **Rich Thompson** got his first career hit on May 17, eight years after his big-league debut, and until his speedy wheels fall off he'll have a Triple-A job somewhere. His prodigious June and July (.367/.400/.580) after an early-season promotion to Triple-A prompted many "Free **Henry Wrigley**" cries as the Rays fiddled while first base burned, but the one-dimensional Big Wrig limped to the finish (.170/.217/.310 in August-September), quieting his claque.

PITCHERS

PLAYER	TEAM	LVL	AGE	W	L	SV	IP	H	HR	BB	SO	BB9	SO9	GB%	BABIP	WHIP	ERA	FIP	FRA	WARP
M. Bush	—	—	—	—	—	—	—	—	—	—	—	—	—	—	—	—	—	—	—	—
R. Carpenter	BGR	A	21	11	8	0	149^2	153	15	23	113	1.4	6.8	42%	.299	1.18	4.09	3.76	4.30	0.9
M. Fleming	MNT	AA	25	4	5	0	63^1	49	6	34	72	4.8	10.2	45%	.281	1.31	3.55	3.81	3.66	0.8
W. Inman	PAW	AAA	25	1	3	6	48^1	35	3	34	60	6.3	11.2	49%	.286	1.43	2.23	3.78	3.77	0.7
A. Liberatore	MNT	AA	25	3	4	8	52	53	4	20	27	3.5	4.7	64%	.295	1.40	2.94	4.61	7.43	-0.5
	DUR	AAA	25	1	1	1	21	18	0	8	21	3.4	9.0	52%	.300	1.24	1.29	2.30	2.23	0.4
L. Pendleton	DUR	AAA	28	8	7	0	129	139	14	55	104	3.8	7.3	32%	.314	1.50	4.81	4.37	4.97	0.5
W. Rodriguez	PCH	A+	22	0	4	0	34	26	3	15	29	4.0	7.7	36%	.250	1.21	5.56	4.42	5.69	-0.2
E. Romero	PCH	A+	21	5	7	0	126	89	5	76	107	5.4	7.6	47%	.244	1.31	3.93	4.19	6.02	-0.2
M. Torra	DUR	AAA	28	12	7	0	147	148	25	26	78	1.6	4.8	36%	.258	1.18	4.10	4.96	7.97	-0.6

Matt Bush's DUI hit-and-run in spring training cost the former overall number-one pick his season and earned him his October release from the Rays and four years in state prison. **Ryan Carpenter**, a 2010 seventh-rounder out of Gonzaga, led Bowling Green in innings pitched and showed great control, tempting one to squint at the relatively unheralded lefty's overall numbers and see the next Andy Pettitte. **Marquis Fleming** took his Bugs Bunny changeup to Durham, but Triple-A coyotes devoured it along with his mid-80s fastball; he hopped right back down to Double-A Montgomery. **Will Inman**, a former Futures Game pitcher, has battled command and elbow issues, but his finesse act, which now plays out of the bullpen, could end up in Tampa Bay if injuries strike. **Adam Liberatore**, a 2010 21st-rounder out of Tennessee Tech, has moved quietly but steadily up the system and, in a late-season stint at Triple-A, put up his best numbers yet. **Lance Pendleton**, a former teammate of Jeff Niemann's at Rice, was in Houston again in spring training last year as an indy-league Sugarland Skeeter when the Rays scooped him up to eat Triple-A innings. **Wilking Rodriguez** has lost much of the last two years to arm injuries, jeopardizing both his development and his spot on the 40-man roster. You can keep from confusing **Enny Romero** with Felipe Rivero, another slight, hard-throwing Latino lefty born in 1991, by looking at his much higher walk rate, and then you can confuse him with Alex Torres instead. **Matt Torra**, a 2005 supplemental first-rounder, a changeup-tossing eater of Triple-A innings—and, apparently, plenty of food—but his good control comes at the cost of copious home runs.

MANAGER: JOE MADDON

YEAR	TEAM	W-L	Pythag +/-	Avg PC	100+ P	120+ P	QS	BQS	REL	REL w Zero R	IBB	PH	PH Avg	PH HR	SB2	CS2	SB3	CS3	SAC Att	SAC %	POS SAC	Squeeze	Swing	In Play
2010	TBA	96-66	1	197.9	159	159	114	5	491	412	68	308	.242	6	25	7	0	1	134	88.1%	116	12	404	120
2011	TBA	91-71	1	102.1	98	5	99	10	438	355	38	129	.252	1	20	8	1	0	63	77.8%	47	5	441	138
2012	TBA	90-72	1	99.9	91	7	90	2	471	415	35	135	.178	3	11	5	1	1	62	67.7%	40	3	354	105

The Baltimore Orioles' 11-game bettering of their Pythagorean record last year was so astonishing that no one much noticed the Rays undershooting theirs by six games, tied for worst in the majors with St. Louis. The disparity cost Tampa Bay a playoff berth. How much of the shortfall can be blamed on Maddon? Should he, for example, have sent Chris Archer back out for a fourth (and game-losing) relief inning in a crushing 14-inning loss to Baltimore in mid-September, right after Archer had labored to escape a bases-loaded, no-outs jam in the 13th? On the other hand, it was a radical defensive realignment Maddon made in that same 13th inning—an emergency two-man outfield and five-man infield—that kept the Orioles from scoring and prolonged the game, which was lost on a two-out walk, a bleeder, and a bloop.

The tactics were emblematic of Maddon's approach: taking risks, putting players where they're not supposed to be (he's King of the Shift), and disregarding any limiting convention of the game. He is an artifex: a creator, a maker, a builder of both systems and cultures. That includes everything from the clubhouse mood—players praise him for making them feel loose, positive, and at ease under any circumstance—to the way he works with his staff to design the Rays' kaleidoscopically variable game plans. Despite group efforts, Maddon is the face of the Rays Way.

What is that Way? If the A's are Moneyball, the Rays are Moneychangerball. Maddon understands the value of currency conversion. He has always been a leader in lineup manipulation, and last year a wave of early-season injuries helped push Maddon to record-setting shuffle-play: 151 unique batting orders, almost one for every game played. As for the Pythagorean sag, anyone who gambles like Maddon does will sometimes find, as Emerson warned, that "the dice of God are always loaded." But he might point out that, in the Rays' four contending years prior to 2012, their cumulative record *exactly* matched its Pythagorean expectation. As he once put it, more simply than Emerson, with a sort of Buddhist detachment: "It's either gonna happen or it's not gonna happen."

Texas Rangers

2012: THE HARE OVERTAKEN

On the heels of back-to-back World Series appearances, the Rangers collapsed down the stretch in 2012, losing both the AL West and the one-game wild-card playoff during a tumultuous three-day span in October. They topped the West for 178 days last season, setting an MLB divisional-era record for most time in first place without winning a division title. While much of the blame focused on the late-season underperformance of stars Josh Hamilton and Ian Kinsler, the club's disappointment was a total team effort.

Well, maybe not quite a *total* team effort. Despite the Rangers' stumble, Adrian Beltre earned AL Player of the Month honors in September after blasting 11 home runs in 26 games, and Mike Napoli, following his mid-September return from injury, added seven homers in his 15 contests. But aside from those two, Rangers position players posted a cumulative .237/.292/.395 slash line after September 1. Lineup stalwarts Kinsler, Elvis Andrus, and Mitch Moreland were almost completely punchless down the stretch. Although Hamilton hit seven round-trippers during that span, he also struck out at a 35 percent clip—a rate that would make Mark Reynolds blush.

On the mound, the story was much the same. Starting pitchers Yu Darvish and Matt Harrison turned in admirable late-season performances, but the remainder of the rotation scuffled. Prior injuries to Neftali Feliz and Colby Lewis appeared to finally take their toll as the club was forced to rely on 21-year-old rookie Martin Perez and long reliever Scott Feldman to make key starts. The lights-out late-inning trio of Joe Nathan, Alexi Ogando, and Mike Adams all had their share of hiccups, as well.

RANGERS PROSPECTUS

2012 W-L: 93-69, 2nd in AL West

Pythag	.563	7th	DER	.708	17th
RS/G	4.99	1st	B-Age	29.8	26th
RA/G	4.36	18th	P-Age	28.1	18th
TAv	.270	5th	Salary	$127.3	7th
BRR	8.4	4th	M$/MW	$2.56	15th
TAv-P	.251	6th	DL Days	609	27th
FIP	3.85	11th	DL WARP	4.6	10th

Three-Year Park Factors	
Overall	109
HR/RH	97
HR/LH	111
AVG/RH	106
AVG/LH	109

Rangers Ballpark in Arlington (1994)
Att. % of Capacity: 88.6% (6th)
Dim. 332, 390, 400, 407, 325

The Rangers' park may have cost them Greinke, but Hamilton's exit sure wasn't because of park factors.

2013: NO MORE SOUR GRAPES

For the first time in a few years, the focus of the Rangers' offseason was more about the club's departures than additions. Looking to bolster its talented-but-thin starting rotation, Texas pursued top free agent Zack Greinke but ultimately lost out to the free-spending Dodgers. Hamilton, of course, left Texas to sign a five-year deal with the division-rival Angels. The offense that led baseball in runs scored last season will have to replace the production of Hamilton, Napoli, and Michael Young. The Rangers enter 2013 with a few extra question marks, and they certainly won't be the odds-on favorite to capture an AL West or a World Series crown. But the roster is still plenty talented enough for a push at a fourth consecutive postseason berth.

There's little doubt the Rangers will be competitive this season; they're even likely to be pretty good, if not very good. Their margin for error, however, may be the kicker. With the Rangers' past lineup depth, the offense could survive a DL stint or three from Hamilton, Cruz, or Beltre with relative ease. That's not likely to be the case this season. Similarly, the starting rotation and bullpen both look solid at the top, with Darvish, Harrison, Nathan, and newcomer Joakim Soria leading the way. But both departments lack experienced depth.

That's where the youngsters come into play. If the Rangers are to reach their full potential in 2013, they'll likely need some help from the top prospects. With Feliz and Lewis slated to miss a sizable chunk to begin the season, the onus could fall on Perez to fill a rotation spot. Alexi Ogando's move back to the starting rotation, coupled with the departures of setup men Adams and Koji Uehara, puts added pressure on Tanner Scheppers, Wilmer Font, and the like to solidify the bullpen's middle-relief roles. On the position-player front, Texas has been insistent on keeping Jurickson Profar, Baseball Prospectus's top prospect in all of baseball, out of trade talks over the last couple of years. He, along with Mike Olt and Leonys Martin, all have a chance to receive regular at-bats this season.

It's not all about the rookies, though. Ron Washington's bunch will also count on a few talented-but-inconsistent players to provide more steady production. Although Darvish and Harrison have cemented themselves atop the Rangers rotation, they're going to need more consistency from the enigmatic Derek Holland. Texas also hired Dave Magadan as hitting coach over the offseason, looking to help guide the offense toward better at-bats and hoping a more consistent approach will mean avoiding the extreme peaks and valleys that plagued a number of the team's hitters in 2012. The core of a successful team is in place, and the raw talent for a pennant-contending squad is present, but it's going to take some molding and perhaps a little luck avoiding the injury bug.

THE STATE OF THE ORGANIZATION: COUNT YOUR CHICKENS

A bitter end to the 2012 campaign followed by an offseason of whiffs on the hot-stove market may not instill great confidence on the surface, but there's no reason to believe that the Rangers are fading in the grand scheme. Texas remains one of baseball's top organizations due to the leadership of general manager Jon Daniels, the ownership's willingness to spend money, and a strong scouting and player-development department.

The Rangers organization has become a mainstay near the top of our annual farm-system rankings, slotting within the top 10 each of the last six years. That stream of talent has played a key role in the club's recent success. It's provided Daniels with a steady pipeline of players to trade or use at the major-league level. In addition to the aforementioned youngsters ready to make their impact in Arlington in 2013, the Rangers have arguably baseball's most talented system in the lower minors. But that shouldn't be much of a surprise based on their investment. Prior to MLB capping signing bonuses for international amateur free agents, the Rangers signed four players—outfielders Jairo Beras and Nomar Mazara, first baseman Ronald Guzman, and left-handed pitcher Yohander Mendez—for approximately $14.5 million.

Whether it's acquiring amateur prospects or signing high-priced free agents, the Rangers ownership group—headlined by Nolan Ryan but fueled by money men Bob Davis and Ray Simpson—have been more than willing to spend with the big boys since purchasing the club and pulling it out of bankruptcy in August 2010. At the time of the purchase, the Rangers had a payroll of approximately $55 million, fourth lowest in baseball. By the start of last season, it had jumped to more than $120 million, sixth highest in the game. Even if the Rangers aren't at their strongest in 2013, there's no reason to believe their window is closing; the organization is seemingly set up for the long haul.

HITTERS

Elvis Andrus SS
Born: **8/26/1988** Age: **24**
Bats: **R** Throws: **R** Height: **6' 1"**
Weight: **200** Breakout: **1%**
Improve: **46%** Collapse: **4%**
Attrition: **7%** MLB: **95%**
Comparables:
Dave Chalk,Aaron Hill,Toby Harrah

YEAR	TEAM	LVL	AGE	PA	R	2B	3B	HR	RBI	BB	SO	SB	CS	AVG_OBP_SLG	TAv	BABIP	BRR	FRAA	WARP
2010	TEX	MLB	21	674	88	15	3	0	35	64	96	32	15	.265/.342/.301	.243	.317	4.9	SS(148): 2.8	2.7
2011	TEX	MLB	22	665	96	27	3	5	60	56	74	37	12	.279/.347/.361	.258	.312	7.1	SS(147): 2.6	2.9
2012	TEX	MLB	23	711	85	31	9	3	62	57	96	21	10	.286/.349/.378	.255	.332	5.8	SS(153): 1.3	2.6
2013	*TEX*	*MLB*	*24*	*659*	*81*	*26*	*6*	*6*	*50*	*53*	*91*	*28*	*11*	*.276/.341/.369*	*.254*	*.309*	*1.6*	*SS -1*	*2.6*

One of the game's top all-around shortstops, Andrus is coming off another steady season both at the plate and in the field. An elite defender with soft hands, flashy range, and strong arm, he improved at making the routine play in 2012, cutting his error total from 25 to 16. As Andrus matures, he becomes a more well-rounded player, and that includes his game at the plate. The Venezuelan has seen an increase in all three slash statistics each of the last two seasons. Often employing an opposite-field approach early in his career, Andrus showed more gap-to-gap power last year while pulling the ball with authority more often. Andrus should further develop and continue that gradual upward trend this season.

Adrian Beltre 3B
Born: **4/7/1979** Age: **34**
Bats: **R** Throws: **R** Height: **6' 0"**
Weight: **220** Breakout: **0%**
Improve: **35%** Collapse: **5%**
Attrition: **10%** MLB: **94%**
Comparables:
Mike Lowell,Michael Young,Aramis Ramirez

YEAR	TEAM	LVL	AGE	PA	R	2B	3B	HR	RBI	BB	SO	SB	CS	AVG_OBP_SLG	TAv	BABIP	BRR	FRAA	WARP
2010	BOS	MLB	31	641	84	49	2	28	102	40	82	2	1	.321/.365/.553	.310	.331	2	3B(154): 15.3	7.6
2011	TEX	MLB	32	525	82	33	0	32	105	25	53	1	1	.296/.331/.561	.309	.273	1	3B(112): 2.9	4.4
2012	TEX	MLB	33	654	95	33	2	36	102	36	82	1	0	.321/.359/.561	.316	.319	-0.4	3B(129): -7.0	4.6
2013	*TEX*	*MLB*	*34*	*589*	*71*	*32*	*2*	*25*	*85*	*32*	*84*	*3*	*1*	*.286/.328/.486*	*.285*	*.298*	*-0.6*	*3B -0*	*2.8*

Two years into Beltre's five-year, $80-million contract, the Rangers couldn't have imagined a better return on their investment. He backed up a strong 2011 with an even better performance in 2012, earning a second consecutive Gold Glove in the process. At the plate, Beltre appears to get better with age, though that theory will be tested toward the end of his contract. He will eventually lose his fantastic range at the hot corner, but he has shown no signs it'll happen in 2013. Thus far, Beltre has given Texas the full package: He hits for average with 30-home-run pop, he provides an elite glove at third base, and his on-field mannerisms are entertaining as ever. Just don't touch him on the head.

Engel Beltre **CF**
Born: **11/1/1989** Age: **23**
Bats: **L** Throws: **L** Height: **6' 3"**
Weight: **180** Breakout: **6%**
Improve: **47%** Collapse: **4%**
Attrition: **11%** MLB: **88%**

Comparables:
Mickey Rivers,Rocco Baldelli,Jay Johnstone

YEAR	TEAM	LVL	AGE	PA	R	2B	3B	HR	RBI	BB	SO	SB	CS	AVG_OBP_SLG	TAv	BABIP	BRR	FRAA	WARP
2010	BAK	A+	20	290	38	11	4	5	35	11	34	10	7	.331/.376/.460	.299	.361	-1.3	CF(68): 3.7	2.3
2010	FRI	AA	20	198	14	4	4	1	14	10	24	8	2	.254/.301/.337	.237	.285	-1.6	CF(48): 7.5, LF(1): 0.1	0.9
2011	FRI	AA	21	482	64	15	6	1	28	28	103	16	6	.231/.285/.300	.197	.299	2	CF(53): 0.4, RF(7): 0.9	-0.8
2012	FRI	AA	22	614	80	17	17	13	55	26	118	36	10	.261/.307/.420	.272	.307	2.2	CF(86): 7.5, RF(1): 0.2	2.9
2013	*TEX*	*MLB*	*23*	*250*	*28*	*9*	*4*	*3*	*19*	*6*	*53*	*9*	*3*	*.235/.263/.346*	*.217*	*.283*	*1.3*	*CF -2, RF 0*	*-0.5*

One of the system's most-talented players, Beltre should advance to Triple-A in 2013 after spending parts of four seasons in the Double-A Texas League. He remains an extremely aggressive hitter but has added some strength. The best defensive outfield prospect in the Rangers system, he provides the full package of speed, range, and arm strength. Beltre's addiction to swinging will always hold him back, but his defense and speed could make him a useful fourth outfielder with the talent to become more. He will presumably use his last remaining option this season, so time is wearing thin.

Julio Borbon **CF**
Born: **2/20/1986** Age: **27**
Bats: **L** Throws: **L** Height: **6' 1"**
Weight: **195** Breakout: **4%**
Improve: **42%** Collapse: **4%**
Attrition: **9%** MLB: **95%**

Comparables:
Willy Taveras,Del Unser,Mickey Rivers

YEAR	TEAM	LVL	AGE	PA	R	2B	3B	HR	RBI	BB	SO	SB	CS	AVG_OBP_SLG	TAv	BABIP	BRR	FRAA	WARP
2010	TEX	MLB	24	468	60	11	4	3	42	19	59	15	7	.276/.309/.340	.234	.313	2.3	CF(133): 3.5, LF(1): 0.0	0.5
2011	ROU	AAA	25	153	27	10	4	0	14	14	22	16	4	.298/.376/.435	.287	.355	0	--	0.0
2011	TEX	MLB	25	98	10	1	3	0	11	3	9	6	2	.270/.305/.348	.247	.296	0.6	CF(32): 0.4	0.2
2012	ROU	AAA	26	585	78	23	8	10	56	37	69	20	8	.304/.349/.433	.261	.331	4.9	CF(24): 3.0, LF(8): -0.9	0.5
2013	*TEX*	*MLB*	*27*	*250*	*30*	*8*	*3*	*3*	*21*	*13*	*36*	*9*	*3*	*.275/.316/.378*	*.248*	*.305*	*0.7*	*CF 1, LF 0*	*0.6*

After appearing in 215 games for the Rangers between 2009 and 2011, Borbon found himself so deep in Ron Washington's doghouse last year that he spent the entire season barking at Triple-A Round Rock. Borbon lost Washington's favor because he couldn't do the "little things," such as get down bunts and avoid outs on the basepaths. An aggressive hitter who has walked at a measly 5 percent rate in the majors, Borbon is a tweener. He's a natural gap-to-gap hitter with marginal power, which isn't the best for utilizing his blazing speed. When he attempts to hit the ball on the ground, he too often becomes a front-foot hitter who struggles to make solid contact. He still has the raw talent to carve out a big-league career, but his next serious opportunity likely will come with another club.

Nelson Cruz **RF**
Born: **7/1/1980** Age: **32**
Bats: **R** Throws: **R** Height: **6' 3"**
Weight: **240** Breakout: **0%**
Improve: **26%** Collapse: **3%**
Attrition: **7%** MLB: **94%**

Comparables:
Hank Aaron,Larry Walker,Ryan Ludwick

YEAR	TEAM	LVL	AGE	PA	R	2B	3B	HR	RBI	BB	SO	SB	CS	AVG_OBP_SLG	TAv	BABIP	BRR	FRAA	WARP
2010	TEX	MLB	30	445	60	31	3	22	78	38	81	17	4	.318/.374/.576	.320	.348	1.4	RF(94): 12.9, LF(14): 0.7	5.2
2011	TEX	MLB	31	513	64	28	1	29	87	33	116	9	5	.263/.312/.509	.279	.288	-2.4	RF(108): 8.2, LF(18): 0.7	1.9
2012	TEX	MLB	31	642	86	45	0	24	90	48	140	8	4	.260/.319/.460	.274	.301	-0.7	RF(151): 7.7, LF(6): -0.1	2.3
2013	*TEX*	*MLB*	*32*	*577*	*79*	*31*	*2*	*28*	*86*	*47*	*132*	*13*	*5*	*.266/.329/.494*	*.288*	*.303*	*0.4*	*RF 5, LF 0*	*3.6*

Cruz and his gargantuan raw power will play a more integral role in the Rangers' offense this season following Josh Hamilton's departure. Part of that role will be staying on the field; he avoided the disabled list for the first time in his big-league career last season, playing in a career-high 159 games. The downside is that he saw a slight overall dip in offensive production. No longer the 20-steal threat that he was in 2009, Cruz has lost some of his athleticism in recent years, reducing his range in right field (though he still wields a cannon for a right arm). The Rangers need Cruz to help carry their lineup this season. A return to his 2009-11 offensive form would be a big step in the right direction, although at his age and with his recent downward trends, that might be asking too much.

Leury Garcia **INF**
Born: **3/18/1991** Age: **22**
Bats: **B** Throws: **R** Height: **5' 8"**
Weight: **153** Breakout: **9%**
Improve: **50%** Collapse: **5%**
Attrition: **9%** MLB: **95%**

Comparables:
Bobby Richardson,Mark Lewis,Luis Castillo

YEAR	TEAM	LVL	AGE	PA	R	2B	3B	HR	RBI	BB	SO	SB	CS	AVG_OBP_SLG	TAv	BABIP	BRR	FRAA	WARP
2010	HIC	A	19	392	57	5	4	3	22	23	57	47	9	.262/.302/.323	.247	.296	4.6	SS(92): 8.3	1.8
2011	MYR	A+	20	482	65	19	5	3	38	28	100	30	12	.256/.306/.342	.232	.324	6.5	SS(81): 2.2	0.7
2012	FRI	AA	21	416	55	12	11	2	30	22	79	31	7	.292/.337/.398	.285	.361	4.6	2B(43): 8.6, SS(29): -1.0	2.7
2013	*TEX*	*MLB*	*22*	*250*	*28*	*8*	*3*	*2*	*16*	*9*	*58*	*14*	*4*	*.235/.266/.317*	*.210*	*.296*	*1.9*	*SS 1, 2B 0*	*0.1*

A shortstop by trade, but blocked at the position, Garcia is being groomed as a super-utility type. With easy range, a plus-plus arm, and excellent speed, the 5-foot-7 Garcia is short in stature but not on premium tools. He's still refining his defensive game, though he took big strides in 2012. After splitting his time between short and second base last season, Garcia saw extended action at both third base and center field in winter ball. He has the ability to play them all at a high level. While Garcia's bat is low on pop, some scouts believe he could hold his own enough to become an every-day shortstop. Ideally, the 22-year-old has one full year of seasoning left in the minors, and that should come at Triple-A this season.

Craig Gentry OF
Born: **11/29/1983** Age: **29**
Bats: **R** Throws: **R** Height: **6' 3"**
Weight: **190** Breakout: **1%**
Improve: **53%** Collapse: **2%**
Attrition: **12%** MLB: **93%**

Comparables:
Chone Figgins,Manny Mota,Kenny Lofton

YEAR	TEAM	LVL	AGE	PA	R	2B	3B	HR	RBI	BB	SO	SB	CS	AVG_OBP_SLG	TAv	BABIP	BRR	FRAA	WARP
2010	OKL	AAA	26	301	43	7	4	4	35	29	47	12	5	.309/.391/.413	.285	.360	1.5	CF(68): 5.6	2.5
2010	TEX	MLB	26	35	4	0	0	0	3	1	11	1	0	.212/.229/.212	.162	.304	0.5	CF(7): -0.5, LF(6): 0.1	-0.2
2011	ROU	AAA	27	123	21	5	1	1	10	11	17	5	1	.245/.325/.336	.240	.283	0	--	0.0
2011	TEX	MLB	27	153	26	5	1	1	13	10	27	18	0	.271/.347/.346	.241	.330	2.5	CF(55): 4.7, RF(7): -0.3	0.8
2012	TEX	MLB	28	269	31	12	3	1	26	14	41	13	7	.304/.367/.392	.272	.364	-1.1	CF(112): 6.7, RF(3): 0.0	1.7
2013	*TEX*	*MLB*	*29*	*250*	*29*	*10*	*2*	*3*	*21*	*16*	*46*	*13*	*3*	*.260/.326/.361*	*.248*	*.310*	*1.4*	*CF 0, RF -0*	*0.6*

The Rangers' primary reserve outfielder in 2012, Gentry proved perfect for his role by providing speed, defense, and even a little offense. Appearing in 121 games, the former 10th-round pick was often a late-inning replacement in center field. He also saw some platoon action against left-handed pitching, hitting .343/.425/.434 vs. southpaws. A fantastic defender in center, the 29-year-old has the full complement of defensive tools: instincts, wheels, and arm. Gentry's limited offensive upside would likely be exposed in an every-day role, but he has become a rock-solid fourth/fifth outfielder.

Ian Kinsler 2B
Born: **6/22/1982** Age: **31**
Bats: **R** Throws: **R** Height: **6' 1"**
Weight: **200** Breakout: **0%**
Improve: **31%** Collapse: **3%**
Attrition: **6%** MLB: **96%**

Comparables:
Roberto Alomar,Brian Roberts,Jose Vidro

YEAR	TEAM	LVL	AGE	PA	R	2B	3B	HR	RBI	BB	SO	SB	CS	AVG_OBP_SLG	TAv	BABIP	BRR	FRAA	WARP
2010	TEX	MLB	28	460	73	20	1	9	45	56	57	15	5	.286/.382/.412	.289	.313	1.6	2B(103): 5.7	3.3
2011	TEX	MLB	29	723	121	34	4	32	77	89	71	30	4	.255/.355/.477	.285	.243	11.6	2B(144): 8.6	5.6
2012	TEX	MLB	30	731	105	42	5	19	72	60	90	21	9	.256/.326/.423	.255	.270	7.2	2B(144): -4.8, 3B(1): -0.0	0.9
2013	*TEX*	*MLB*	*31*	*685*	*98*	*36*	*4*	*22*	*76*	*65*	*88*	*25*	*6*	*.263/.341/.442*	*.277*	*.273*	*2*	*2B -4*	*3.4*

A position change could be in the cards for the Rangers' highly paid second baseman this season. The good news for the club is that Kinsler didn't respond to the possibility by asking for a trade. The Rangers want room in their lineup for top prospect Jurickson Profar, ideally at second base while Kinsler shifts to first. On the surface the move may not be best for Kinsler's positional value, but it would improve the team. At the plate, Kinsler rarely gets cheated with his swings and sometimes sacrifices contact for power. Aggressive to a fault last season, Kinsler's walk rate plummeted from 12.3 to 8.2 percent while his strikeout rate increased from 9.8 percent to 12.3 percent. Though he's coming off the worst offensive season of his career, Kinsler remains in his prime and should rebound.

Leonys Martin CF
Born: **3/6/1988** Age: **25**
Bats: **L** Throws: **R** Height: **6' 2"**
Weight: **180** Breakout: **8%**
Improve: **66%** Collapse: **2%**
Attrition: **10%** MLB: **96%**

Comparables:
Jeff Fiorentino,Dusty Baker,Johnny Grubb

YEAR	TEAM	LVL	AGE	PA	R	2B	3B	HR	RBI	BB	SO	SB	CS	AVG_OBP_SLG	TAv	BABIP	BRR	FRAA	WARP
2011	FRI	AA	23	135	24	9	2	4	24	15	8	10	8	.348/.435/.571	.392	.347	2.1	CF(13): -0.6, RF(2): -0.1	1.3
2011	ROU	AAA	23	192	27	7	1	0	17	11	24	9	2	.263/.316/.314	.230	.303	0	--	0.0
2011	TEX	MLB	23	8	2	1	0	0	0	0	1	0	0	.375/.375/.500	.349	.429	-0.1	CF(8): 0.2	0.1
2012	ROU	AAA	24	260	48	18	2	12	42	24	39	10	9	.359/.422/.610	.340	.392	2.4	CF(10): 1.9, LF(2): 0.2	1.1
2012	TEX	MLB	24	52	6	5	2	0	6	4	12	3	0	.174/.235/.370	.186	.229	-0.2	CF(14): 0.4, LF(4): 0.3	-0.2
2013	*TEX*	*MLB*	*25*	*250*	*35*	*13*	*2*	*6*	*24*	*18*	*47*	*11*	*7*	*.268/.326/.422*	*.264*	*.310*	*-0.3*	*CF -0, LF 0*	*0.8*

When the Rangers gave Martin a five-year, $15.5-million major-league deal in 2011, they wanted him to become their every-day center fielder. Two years later, he remains a prospect with first-division starter potential, but has appeared in only 32 major-league games. Martin, who abused PCL pitching in 55 games last year, could get his first opportunity at regular playing time in 2013. While Martin doesn't have one particularly flashy tool, he's also not below-average in any area. The Rangers would like to see the Cuban improve his baserunning and other nuances. If he does, he shouldn't be far from becoming a solid regular.

Luis Martinez C
Born: **4/3/1985** Age: **28**
Bats: **R** Throws: **R** Height: **6' 1"**
Weight: **210** Breakout: **7%**
Improve: **46%** Collapse: **13%**
Attrition: **26%** MLB: **95%**

Comparables:
Rob Johnson,Chris Bando,Ramon Hernandez

YEAR	TEAM	LVL	AGE	PA	R	2B	3B	HR	RBI	BB	SO	SB	CS	AVG_OBP_SLG	TAv	BABIP	BRR	FRAA	WARP
2010	SAN	AA	25	410	48	16	1	2	31	49	59	3	2	.282/.370/.349	.287	.333	-1.1	C(99): 0.7	3.3
2011	TUC	AAA	26	219	24	17	1	1	28	17	46	2	0	.323/.379/.434	.251	.412	1.1	C(35): -0.0	0.7
2011	SDN	MLB	26	68	7	1	1	1	10	8	14	1	0	.203/.309/.305	.230	.250	1.2	C(19): -0.0	0.1
2012	ROU	AAA	27	247	27	15	2	2	22	26	45	0	0	.270/.350/.386	.295	.327	-0.5	C(13): 0.1	0.1
2012	TEX	MLB	27	19	1	0	0	0	0	0	4	0	0	.111/.158/.111	.108	.143	0	C(9): -0.1	-0.3
2013	*TEX*	*MLB*	*28*	*250*	*23*	*11*	*1*	*3*	*22*	*21*	*52*	*0*	*0*	*.244/.312/.340*	*.236*	*.301*	*-0.3*	*C -0*	*0.5*

A prototypical third catcher, Martinez waits at the end of a team's 40-man roster as insurance. While he wields plus arm strength from behind the plate, he's a pedestrian receiver and an average overall defender. Martinez also provides little with the bat. With one option remaining, the 27-year-old backstop is an up-and-down player who could see time in Arlington this season if the Rangers' thin catching corps falters.

Mitch Moreland 1B

Born: **9/6/1985** Age: **27**
Bats: **L** Throws: **L** Height: **6' 3"**
Weight: **230** Breakout: **1%**
Improve: **45%** Collapse: **9%**
Attrition: **14%** MLB: **89%**

Comparables:
Kent Hrbek,Matt LaPorta,Jason Kubel

YEAR	TEAM	LVL	AGE	PA	R	2B	3B	HR	RBI	BB	SO	SB	CS	AVG_OBP_SLG	TAv	BABIP	BRR	FRAA	WARP
2010	OKL	AAA	24	412	52	29	2	12	65	47	63	2	1	.289/.375/.484	.288	.321	-0.2	RF(80): 2.2, 1B(12): 0.6	2.3
2010	TEX	MLB	24	173	20	4	0	9	25	25	36	3	1	.255/.364/.469	.298	.275	-0.1	1B(40): -3.0, RF(7): -0.2	0.7
2011	TEX	MLB	25	512	60	22	1	16	51	39	92	2	2	.259/.320/.414	.258	.290	0.2	1B(98): -2.8, RF(34): 0.9	-0.1
2012	TEX	MLB	26	357	41	18	0	15	50	23	71	1	1	.275/.321/.468	.264	.306	-2.1	1B(95): 6.3, RF(3): 0.1	1.0
2013	*TEX*	*MLB*	*27*	*369*	*43*	*18*	*1*	*12*	*45*	*31*	*73*	*2*	*1*	*.260/.325/.431*	*.266*	*.294*	*-0.6*	*1B -3, RF -0*	*0.3*

If Kinsler shifts to first base this season, Moreland may slot into a super-sub role. A natural first baseman, Moreland could see increased time in right field and as a designated hitter. When he reached the major leagues in 2010, his patience and ability to use all fields led to immediate success. Over the last two seasons, however, he has sacrificed that for a more pull-happy approach. This hasn't significantly increased his power but has sapped his on-base ability, as teams began employing a lefty overshift against him. He's squarely a second-division starter, though there is room for improvement if he makes the necessary adjustments.

David Murphy LF

Born: **10/18/1981** Age: **31**
Bats: **L** Throws: **L** Height: **6' 5"**
Weight: **205** Breakout: **0%**
Improve: **33%** Collapse: **6%**
Attrition: **13%** MLB: **87%**

Comparables:
Del Ennis,Moises Alou,Hideki Matsui

YEAR	TEAM	LVL	AGE	PA	R	2B	3B	HR	RBI	BB	SO	SB	CS	AVG_OBP_SLG	TAv	BABIP	BRR	FRAA	WARP
2010	TEX	MLB	28	467	54	26	2	12	65	45	71	14	2	.291/.358/.449	.292	.324	-2.8	LF(74): 0.2, RF(51): -2.1	2.0
2011	TEX	MLB	29	440	46	14	2	11	46	33	61	11	6	.275/.328/.401	.253	.299	-2	LF(77): 2.7, RF(32): -0.2	0.1
2012	TEX	MLB	30	521	65	29	3	15	61	54	74	10	5	.304/.380/.479	.302	.333	3.4	LF(120): -0.6, RF(16): -0.1	3.0
2013	*TEX*	*MLB*	*31*	*472*	*55*	*23*	*2*	*13*	*56*	*41*	*81*	*10*	*4*	*.272/.335/.429*	*.272*	*.307*	*0*	*LF 1, RF 0*	*1.8*

After a disappointing 2011 campaign, Murphy rebounded with his best season in 2012, posting career highs in nearly every offensive category. A notorious slow starter, he remained consistent throughout the year and, as a result, also set a personal best in games played. Although the native Texan had success against southpaws last season, the sample was small and ran counter to his career trend. Still, the Rangers may need Murphy to play against both left- and right-handed pitching this season, as the departure of Hamilton likely makes him the club's every-day left fielder. Entering his first year of free agency after 2013, Murphy will be hoping to land a lucrative multi-year deal. But first, he'll have to prove he can handle the expanded role.

Mike Napoli C

Born: **10/31/1981** Age: **31**
Bats: **R** Throws: **R** Height: **6' 1"**
Weight: **215** Breakout: **3%**
Improve: **47%** Collapse: **7%**
Attrition: **7%** MLB: **97%**

Comparables:
Willie McCovey,Carlos Pena,Fred McGriff

YEAR	TEAM	LVL	AGE	PA	R	2B	3B	HR	RBI	BB	SO	SB	CS	AVG_OBP_SLG	TAv	BABIP	BRR	FRAA	WARP
2010	ANA	MLB	28	510	60	24	1	26	68	42	137	4	2	.238/.316/.468	.285	.279	0.5	1B(70): 4.1, C(66): -0.7	3.4
2011	TEX	MLB	29	432	72	25	0	30	75	58	85	4	2	.320/.414/.631	.360	.344	-1.8	C(61): 0.4, 1B(35): -1.3	5.1
2012	TEX	MLB	30	417	53	9	2	24	56	56	125	1	0	.227/.343/.469	.284	.273	0.6	C(72): 1.1, 1B(27): -0.5	2.0
2013	*TEX*	*MLB*	*31*	*395*	*57*	*17*	*1*	*22*	*61*	*44*	*103*	*3*	*1*	*.258/.349/.505*	*.300*	*.303*	*-0.5*	*C -1, 1B -0*	*2.9*

Napoli followed his magical 2011 campaign with a 2012 more in line with his career numbers. For a lifetime .259 hitter, the .320 average he posted two seasons ago looks more like the exception than the rule. However, the Napoli of 2012 remained one of baseball's better hitting backstops, blasting home runs and walking at a 13.4 percent clip. With the power comes strikeouts, though that's not a revelation with Napoli. For much of the offseason Napoli appeared headed for Boston with a three-year, $39 million deal, but the deal crumbled under concerns over Napoli's hip revealed in the required physical. The Red Sox eventually signed him to a one-year deal and the burly slugger figures to be Boston's primary first baseman in 2013 with the occasional start at catcher.

Mike Olt 3B

Born: **8/27/1988** Age: **24**
Bats: **R** Throws: **R** Height: **6' 3"**
Weight: **210** Breakout: **6%**
Improve: **59%** Collapse: **13%**
Attrition: **15%** MLB: **98%**

Comparables:
Scott Moore,Ian Stewart,Troy Glaus

YEAR	TEAM	LVL	AGE	PA	R	2B	3B	HR	RBI	BB	SO	SB	CS	AVG_OBP_SLG	TAv	BABIP	BRR	FRAA	WARP
2010	SPO	A-	21	310	57	16	1	9	43	40	77	6	0	.293/.394/.464	.313	.384	0.3	3B(69): -3.3	1.9
2011	MYR	A+	22	292	39	15	0	14	42	48	70	0	1	.267/.387/.504	.317	.314	-1.9	3B(49): 8.0	2.3
2012	FRI	AA	23	421	65	17	1	28	82	61	101	4	0	.288/.398/.579	.351	.327	1.6	3B(54): -1.3, 1B(9): -0.4	3.6
2012	TEX	MLB	23	40	2	1	0	0	5	5	13	1	1	.152/.250/.182	.204	.227	-1.3	1B(8): 0.7, 3B(5): 0.3	-0.2
2013	*TEX*	*MLB*	*24*	*250*	*30*	*9*	*1*	*10*	*34*	*28*	*72*	*1*	*0*	*.235/.322/.427*	*.270*	*.294*	*-0.3*	*3B 3, 1B 0*	*1.1*

With Olt, the Rangers have baseball's equivalent of a first-world problem. One of the game's top power-hitting prospects, the slick-fielding third baseman is blocked by two-time defending Gold Glove-winner Beltre. Even at 34, Beltre isn't showing any signs of slowing down defensively, so the Rangers began working Olt at first base and right field last season. At the plate, Olt possesses elite bat speed but will likely always have some whiff in his game. When fully developed, he could hit .270 with 30 home runs and a strong walk rate. While he'll be in the mix for a roster spot in 2013, the Rangers might prefer that he marinate in Triple-A a little longer to ensure his deliciousness upon arrival.

A.J. Pierzynski C

Born: **12/30/1976** Age: **36**
Bats: **L** Throws: **R** Height: **6' 4"**
Weight: **225** Breakout: **1%**
Improve: **24%** Collapse: **8%**
Attrition: **23%** MLB: **70%**

Comparables:
Jamie Burke, Darrin Fletcher, Bengie Molina

YEAR	TEAM	LVL	AGE	PA	R	2B	3B	HR	RBI	BB	SO	SB	CS	AVG_OBP_SLG	TAv	BABIP	BRR	FRAA	WARP
2010	CHA	MLB	33	503	43	29	0	9	56	15	39	3	4	.270/.300/.388	.229	.278	-0.8	C(127): -1.6	0.5
2011	CHA	MLB	34	500	38	29	1	8	48	23	33	0	0	.287/.323/.405	.251	.291	-2.7	C(120): -0.8	0.3
2012	CHA	MLB	35	520	68	18	4	27	77	28	78	0	0	.278/.326/.501	.287	.280	-3.1	C(126): -2.2	2.5
2013	*TEX*	*MLB*	*36*	*485*	*46*	*24*	*2*	*10*	*54*	*17*	*59*	*1*	*1*	*.271/.303/.400*	*.243*	*.288*	*-0.8*	*C -1*	*1.1*

Guess who was a free agent this offseason? Pierzynski last posted a .287 TAv in 2003, after which the Twins were able to trade him for Joe Nathan, Francisco Liriano, and Boof Bonser. It's unlikely that the Rangers will be as disappointed as the Giants were in 2004, but he also may not match last season's career-high of 27 home runs. All of the improvement came against right-handed pitchers. Pierzynksi remains baffled by southpaws. The unbalanced stats allowed him to finish 29th in OPS against right-handed pitching, and while that's likely to revert quite a bit, he'll remain an offensive contributor against them. Pierzynski should be a decent stopgap for Texas on a one-year deal.

Jurickson Profar SS

Born: **2/20/1993** Age: **20**
Bats: **B** Throws: **R** Height: **6' 0"**
Weight: **165** Breakout: **13%**
Improve: **48%** Collapse: **6%**
Attrition: **16%** MLB: **91%**

Comparables:
Robin Yount, Bill Mazeroski, Edgar Renteria

YEAR	TEAM	LVL	AGE	PA	R	2B	3B	HR	RBI	BB	SO	SB	CS	AVG_OBP_SLG	TAv	BABIP	BRR	FRAA	WARP
2010	SPO	A-	17	288	42	19	0	4	23	28	46	8	3	.250/.318/.373	.255	.284	-1.3	SS(68): 13.1	2.6
2011	HIC	A	18	516	86	37	8	12	65	65	63	23	9	.286/.390/.493	.315	.309	3.1	SS(83): -3.8	3.5
2012	FRI	AA	19	562	76	26	7	14	62	66	79	16	4	.281/.368/.452	.309	.306	-1.5	SS(71): -2.0, 2B(19): -1.0	2.8
2012	TEX	MLB	19	17	2	2	0	1	2	0	4	0	0	.176/.176/.471	.206	.167	-0.4	2B(5): -0.2, SS(3): -0.1	-0.2
2013	*TEX*	*MLB*	*20*	*250*	*29*	*12*	*2*	*5*	*23*	*20*	*47*	*5*	*2*	*.240/.303/.379*	*.243*	*.276*	*0.3*	*SS 3, 2B -0*	*1.0*

Baseball Prospectus's top prospect on our list of 101, Profar could become a special player at a valuable position. Following a late-season cup of coffee in 2012, the 20-year-old should begin 2013 on the big-league roster. If that happens, the presence of defensive whiz Andrus will force Profar to second base and Kinsler to first. The Curacao native should easily handle the move; he's smooth with the glove at both middle-infield positions. While few are immune to growing pains, the switch-hitting Profar is mature beyond his years both mentally and on the field. With a disciplined approach, he shows the potential to be a .300, 20-home-run bat. Profar may not reach that type of production as a rookie, but he's got a potent mixture of talent and polish.

Konrad Schmidt C

Born: **8/2/1984** Age: **28**
Bats: **R** Throws: **R** Height: **5' 11"**
Weight: **225** Breakout: **2%**
Improve: **29%** Collapse: **17%**
Attrition: **26%** MLB: **96%**

Comparables:
Joe Azcue, Rich Gedman, Bobby Wilson

YEAR	TEAM	LVL	AGE	PA	R	2B	3B	HR	RBI	BB	SO	SB	CS	AVG_OBP_SLG	TAv	BABIP	BRR	FRAA	WARP
2010	MOB	AA	25	440	48	30	3	11	65	32	63	7	3	.315/.378/.490	.308	.353	-4.5	C(93): -0.1	3.5
2010	ARI	MLB	25	9	0	0	0	0	0	1	0	0	0	.125/.222/.125	.149	.125	0	C(2): -0.0	-0.1
2011	RNO	AAA	26	374	47	24	3	9	45	21	66	1	3	.280/.330/.445	.266	.324	0	--	0.0
2012	RNO	AAA	27	374	43	24	0	7	47	25	69	2	0	.277/.338/.413	.165	.326	-0.9	C(40): -0.4	-1.5
2012	ARI	MLB	27	8	1	0	0	0	2	1	2	0	0	.000/.125/.000	.074	.000	0	C(2): 0.2	-0.1
2013	*TEX*	*MLB*	*28*	*250*	*23*	*12*	*1*	*5*	*27*	*14*	*52*	*1*	*0*	*.243/.293/.374*	*.236*	*.289*	*-0.3*	*C -0*	*0.4*

Schmidt was called up by the Diamondbacks in May when Miguel Montero went down with a groin strain, starting a single game behind the plate before the incumbent's health returned. He was recalled when rosters expanded in September, but manager Kirk Gibson's preference to ride Montero down the stretch limited Schmidt's playing time. Schmidt has made solid contact throughout his minor-league career, but he rarely walks and has middling power. His struggles to control the running game limit his utility. Claimed by the Rangers on waivers, Schmidt will take his White Goodman mustache to the AL West in an attempt to carve out a career as a backup catcher.

Brandon Snyder 4C
Born: 11/23/1986 Age: 26
Bats: R Throws: R Height: 6' 3"
Weight: 215 Breakout: 4%
Improve: 57% Collapse: 2%
Attrition: 11% MLB: 92%
Comparables:
Brandon Wood,Howard Johnson,Mike Lowell

YEAR	TEAM	LVL	AGE	PA	R	2B	3B	HR	RBI	BB	SO	SB	CS	AVG_OBP_SLG	TAv	BABIP	BRR	FRAA	WARP
2010	NOR	AAA	23	376	36	22	1	9	43	28	101	4	1	.257/.326/.407	.256	.341	2.8	1B(76): 0.8, 3B(9): -0.9	0.3
2010	BAL	MLB	23	20	1	2	0	0	3	0	3	0	1	.300/.300/.400	.240	.353	-0.8	1B(10): 0.6	0.0
2011	NOR	AAA	24	494	55	21	1	14	71	32	91	1	2	.261/.312/.406	.246	.293	-1.9	1B(49): 3.1, 3B(13): 0.7	-0.2
2011	BAL	MLB	24	17	2	1	0	0	1	3	4	0	0	.231/.412/.308	.277	.333	0.2	1B(5): -0.5	0.0
2012	ROU	AAA	25	92	12	7	0	2	9	4	30	0	0	.253/.286/.402	.207	.364	-0.7	3B(3): 0.5	-0.2
2012	TEX	MLB	25	69	11	2	0	3	9	3	26	0	0	.277/.309/.446	.256	.417	0.7	1B(11): 0.2, 3B(7): -0.2	0.2
2013	*TEX*	*MLB*	*26*	*250*	*24*	*12*	*1*	*7*	*28*	*15*	*68*	*1*	*0*	*.237/.288/.381*	*.237*	*.303*	*-0.4*	*1B -4, 3B -0*	*-0.7*

A former first-round pick, Snyder came up through the Baltimore system before joining the Rangers and appearing in a career-high 40 games last season. Working as a right-handed bench bat, he posted a .318/.348/.568 slash line in a small sample against lefty pitching, but also struck out in 37 percent of his overall plate appearances. In the field, Snyder saw action at all four corner spots—as well as one inning behind the plate—but is a below-average defender in the outfield. He's serviceable at first and third base. Snyder is returning to the Rangers in 2013 on a minor-league deal with a non-roster invite to camp, but the likely increased role of Olt could relegate him to Triple-A.

Geovany Soto C
Born: 1/20/1983 Age: 30
Bats: R Throws: R Height: 6' 2"
Weight: 220 Breakout: 3%
Improve: 36% Collapse: 3%
Attrition: 9% MLB: 94%
Comparables:
Carlton Fisk,Chris Snyder,Johnny Romano

YEAR	TEAM	LVL	AGE	PA	R	2B	3B	HR	RBI	BB	SO	SB	CS	AVG_OBP_SLG	TAv	BABIP	BRR	FRAA	WARP
2010	CHN	MLB	27	387	47	19	0	17	53	62	83	0	1	.280/.393/.497	.307	.324	-2.9	C(104): -1.6	3.2
2011	CHN	MLB	28	474	46	26	0	17	54	45	124	0	0	.228/.310/.411	.252	.280	-2.3	C(121): 3.2	1.4
2012	CHN	MLB	29	197	26	6	1	6	14	19	35	0	0	.199/.284/.347	.227	.215	1	C(52): -0.7	-0.1
2012	TEX	MLB	29	164	19	6	0	5	25	11	41	1	0	.196/.253/.338	.227	.231	0.3	C(43): -0.1	-0.1
2013	*TEX*	*MLB*	*30*	*364*	*43*	*18*	*1*	*13*	*45*	*39*	*84*	*1*	*0*	*.238/.324/.421*	*.267*	*.281*	*-0.6*	*C 0*	*1.9*

Acquired from the Cubs at last season's trading deadline, Soto was non-tendered by the Rangers in the offseason before re-signing on a one-year deal. Other than 2008—when he won NL Rookie of the Year—and 2010, Soto's offensive prowess has underwhelmed, reaching new lows last year. An average defender, the 30-year-old backstop doesn't have the strongest arm, but earns high marks for his receiving skills. Soto should rebound in 2013, but the Rangers would surely settle for replacement-level production.

PITCHERS

Jeff Beliveau
Born: 1/17/1987 Age: 26
Bats: L Throws: L Height: 6' 2" Weight: 190
Breakout: 39% Improve: 52% Collapse: 30%
Attrition: 15% MLB: 90%
Comparables:
Bill Landis,Dave LaRoche,Danny Frisella

YEAR	TEAM	LVL	AGE	W	L	SV	G	GS	IP	H	HR	BB	SO	BB9	SO9	GB%	BABIP	WHIP	ERA	FIP	FRA	WARP
2010	PEO	A	23	0	0	0	6	0	11^1	6	1	6	23	4.8	18.3	57%	.385	1.06	1.59	2.55	2.19	0.4
2010	DAY	A+	23	4	2	2	40	0	53	41	4	23	74	3.9	12.6	43%	.288	1.21	2.89	3.04	3.58	0.8
2011	DAY	A+	24	0	1	2	12	0	17^1	13	0	6	20	3.1	10.4	—	.317	1.10	0.52	2.47	2.68	0.0
2011	TEN	AA	24	6	1	3	41	0	57	37	7	13	69	2.1	10.9	41%	.239	0.88	1.89	3.22	3.05	0.7
2012	IOW	AAA	25	4	5	0	37	0	44	44	4	18	52	3.7	10.6	34%	.348	1.41	3.89	3.71	3.65	0.9
2012	CHN	MLB	25	1	0	0	22	0	17^2	21	5	12	17	6.1	8.7	41%	.314	1.87	4.58	7.10	7.25	-0.4
2013	*TEX*	*MLB*	*26*	*1*	*0*	*0*	*27*	*0*	33^2	*32*	*5*	*18*	*36*	*4.8*	*9.6*	*41%*	*.306*	*1.49*	*4.74*	*4.60*	*5.15*	*0.2*

Ticketed as a reliever very early in his minor-league career, and honored as the Cubs' Minor League Pitcher of the Year in 2011, Beliveau finally got his shot at the majors last year and did nothing impressive with it. Because he has the gift of being left-arm dominant, he's likely to get a few more chances and may even stick somewhere as a LOOGY, but it's looking unlikely that he finds himself as that rara avis, the lefty reliever who can pitch well against right-handers. The Rangers claimed him off waivers.

Lisalverto Bonilla
Born: 6/6/1990 Age: 23
Bats: R Throws: R Height: 6' 2" Weight: 164
Breakout: 22% Improve: 61% Collapse: 18%
Attrition: 11% MLB: 89%
Comparables:
Mike Fornieles,Mickey Lolich,Marcos Carvajal

YEAR	TEAM	LVL	AGE	W	L	SV	G	GS	IP	H	HR	BB	SO	BB9	SO9	GB%	BABIP	WHIP	ERA	FIP	FRA	WARP
2010	PHL	Rk	20	2	1	0	6	6	32^1	32	3	5	38	1.4	10.6	55%	.328	1.15	1.95	2.92	4.45	0.3
2010	WPT	A-	20	1	3	0	10	3	26^1	33	5	12	18	4.1	6.2	46%	.326	1.71	6.50	6.06	6.94	-0.3
2011	LWD	A	21	4	5	4	26	15	106	91	8	29	95	2.5	8.1	58%	.285	1.13	2.80	3.59	3.95	1.0
2012	CLR	A+	22	1	1	1	10	0	13^1	9	0	4	18	2.7	12.1	48%	.290	0.98	1.35	1.59	1.55	0.5
2012	REA	AA	22	2	1	3	21	0	33	22	1	17	46	4.6	12.5	42%	.309	1.18	1.64	2.44	1.97	1.2
2013	*TEX*	*MLB*	*23*	*1*	*2*	*0*	*11*	*4*	*33*	*36*	*5*	*17*	*26*	*4.5*	*7.0*	*47%*	*.311*	*1.60*	*5.51*	*5.14*	*5.99*	*-0.1*

Acquired from Philadelphia as part of the Michael Young deal, Bonilla is a talented righty with a fastball that reaches 95 mph. He'll also mix in a quality changeup and a work-in-progress slider. Following a full-time transition to the bullpen with the Phillies in 2012, the Dominican is expected to remain in that role with Texas. A thumb injury, which required surgery, sidelined Bonilla for the second half of last season, but he returned for the Phillies' instructional league and pitched in winter ball. The 23-year-old is still on the raw side but has seventh- or eighth-inning relief potential. He should open 2013 in the upper minors with a chance at Arlington if he improves his command and breaking ball.

Jake Brigham

Born: **2/10/1988** Age: **25**
Bats: **R** Throws: **R** Height: **6' 4"** Weight: **210**
Breakout: **32%** Improve: **68%** Collapse: **12%**
Attrition: **16%** MLB: **92%**

Comparables:
Dan Wright, Mike Campbell, Scott Sanders

YEAR	TEAM	LVL	AGE	W	L	SV	G	GS	IP	H	HR	BB	SO	BB9	SO9	GB%	BABIP	WHIP	ERA	FIP	FRA	WARP
2010	HIC	A	22	6	5	0	14	13	83	66	5	24	67	2.6	7.3	63%	.256	1.08	3.36	3.78	5.35	0.0
2010	BAK	A+	22	1	5	0	11	10	49^1	67	5	26	39	4.7	7.1	40%	.380	1.89	6.94	5.30	5.68	0.2
2011	FRI	AA	23	6	6	0	35	14	114^1	107	13	55	114	4.3	9.0	44%	.299	1.42	4.49	4.41	5.21	0.4
2012	FRI	AA	24	5	5	0	21	21	124	122	19	46	116	3.3	8.4	46%	.301	1.35	4.28	4.66	5.18	0.2
2012	TEN	AA	24	0	2	0	2	2	3^2	11	1	4	3	9.8	7.4	32%	.556	4.09	19.64	8.33	9.35	0.0
2013	*TEX*	*MLB*	*25*	*2*	*3*	*0*	*6*	*6*	*34^2*	*40*	*6*	*19*	*24*	*4.9*	*6.3*	*45%*	*.311*	*1.70*	*6.21*	*5.71*	*6.75*	*-0.3*

Traded to the Cubs for Soto last July, Brigham made only two appearances with Chicago's Double-A affiliate before succumbing to a season-ending elbow injury. With the Cubs feeling some buyer's remorse, Texas re-acquired him for pitching prospect Barret Loux over the offseason. The Rangers feel Brigham's elbow injury, which didn't require surgery, won't be an issue in the long run, and he should be ready for the start of spring training. On the mound, Brigham's results have rarely matched his electric stuff, which includes a low-to-mid-90s fastball and plus slider-curveball combination. His stuff and fringy command plays up in bursts out of the bullpen, which should be his ultimate destination.

Cody Buckel

Born: **6/18/1992** Age: **21**
Bats: **R** Throws: **R** Height: **6' 2"** Weight: **170**
Breakout: **32%** Improve: **63%** Collapse: **11%**
Attrition: **3%** MLB: **91%**

Comparables:
Felix Hernandez, Matt Cain, Gary Nolan

YEAR	TEAM	LVL	AGE	W	L	SV	G	GS	IP	H	HR	BB	SO	BB9	SO9	GB%	BABIP	WHIP	ERA	FIP	FRA	WARP
2010	RNG	Rk	18	0	0	0	4	0	5	2	0	1	9	1.8	16.2	60%	.200	0.60	0.00	1.26	1.86	0.2
2011	HIC	A	19	8	3	0	23	17	96^2	83	7	27	120	2.5	11.2	51%	.326	1.14	2.61	2.86	3.39	1.8
2012	MYR	A+	20	5	3	0	13	13	75^2	49	2	25	91	3.0	10.8	56%	.269	0.98	1.31	2.35	2.53	1.9
2012	FRI	AA	20	5	5	0	13	10	69	56	7	23	68	3.0	8.9	41%	.280	1.14	3.78	3.85	5.02	0.6
2013	*TEX*	*MLB*	*21*	*2*	*2*	*0*	*8*	*6*	*38^2*	*38*	*5*	*16*	*36*	*3.8*	*8.3*	*47%*	*.304*	*1.39*	*4.43*	*4.26*	*4.82*	*0.4*

With such a varied repertoire, the question isn't what Buckel throws, it's what *doesn't* he throw. During a start, the righty will mix in four- and two-seam fastballs, a cutter, slider, curveball, changeup, and even the occasional "reverse slider," as he calls it. Impressive arsenal aside, it's more about quantity than quality at this point. His fastball averages 89-92 mph but sniffs the mid-90s and is rarely straight. His secondaries aren't particularly nasty, but they're all usable. With a highly cerebral approach and mature feel for pitching, Buckel is a good bet to become a back-end starter with a mid-rotation ceiling. He should open the 2013 campaign in Double-A, with the possibility for a quick Triple-A promotion.

Cory Burns

Born: **10/9/1987** Age: **25**
Bats: **R** Throws: **R** Height: **6' 2"** Weight: **180**
Breakout: **22%** Improve: **44%** Collapse: **25%**
Attrition: **12%** MLB: **93%**

Comparables:
Al Hrabosky, Sammy Gervacio, Chad Cordero

YEAR	TEAM	LVL	AGE	W	L	SV	G	GS	IP	H	HR	BB	SO	BB9	SO9	GB%	BABIP	WHIP	ERA	FIP	FRA	WARP
2010	LKC	A	22	0	0	12	14	0	15^2	13	0	1	25	0.6	14.3	51%	.371	0.89	2.29	0.62	1.21	0.8
2010	KIN	A+	22	1	2	30	40	0	39^1	30	2	13	56	3.0	12.8	65%	.330	1.09	1.83	2.36	3.34	0.8
2011	AKR	AA	23	2	5	35	54	0	59^2	47	3	15	70	2.3	10.6	46%	.322	1.04	2.11	2.47	1.52	1.7
2012	TUC	AAA	24	1	2	3	54	0	66	49	1	17	78	2.3	10.6	57%	.298	1.00	3.14	2.45	2.88	2.0
2012	SDN	MLB	24	0	1	0	17	0	18	26	1	10	18	5.0	9.0	57%	.403	2.00	5.50	3.69	3.30	0.2
2013	*TEX*	*MLB*	*25*	*2*	*1*	*0*	*32*	*0*	*35^2*	*33*	*4*	*13*	*38*	*3.2*	*9.7*	*52%*	*.308*	*1.27*	*3.72*	*3.62*	*4.04*	*0.6*

Burns's funky delivery made him difficult to hit in the minors. His high-80s sinking fastball was treated less kindly in the big leagues. Taken one pick ahead of Paul Goldschmidt in the eighth round of the 2009 draft, Burns is durable and has experience closing at lower levels. His ceiling is that of a middle reliever, but he'll need to throw more strikes than he did in his debut to get there.

Yu Darvish

Born: **8/16/1986** Age: **26**
Bats: **R** Throws: **R** Height: **6' 6"** Weight: **185**
Breakout: **26%** Improve: **54%** Collapse: **13%**
Attrition: **10%** MLB: **99%**

Comparables:
Pedro Martinez, Roger Clemens, Joba Chamberlain

YEAR	TEAM	LVL	AGE	W	L	SV	G	GS	IP	H	HR	BB	SO	BB9	SO9	GB%	BABIP	WHIP	ERA	FIP	FRA	WARP
2010	NIP	NPB	23	12	8	0	26	25	202	158	5	47	222	2.1	9.9	—	.292	1.01	1.78	2.07	2.25	0.0
2011	NIP	NPB	24	18	6	0	28	28	232	156	5	36	276	1.4	10.7	—	.284	0.83	1.44	0.00	0.00	0.0
2012	TEX	MLB	25	16	9	0	29	29	191^1	156	14	89	221	4.2	10.4	48%	.295	1.28	3.90	3.24	3.83	3.1
2013	*TEX*	*MLB*	*26*	*10*	*7*	*0*	*21*	*21*	*156^2*	*132*	*13*	*49*	*177*	*2.8*	*10.1*	*46%*	*.301*	*1.16*	*3.06*	*2.96*	*3.33*	*4.1*

After coming to the United States with much fanfare and lofty expectations, Darvish mostly lived up to the billing in his rookie campaign. The 26-year-old Japanese import owns a deservedly hyped "eight-pitch repertoire," but he found more success late in the season by simplifying his mechanics and narrowing his pitch selection. Once he began relying almost exclusively on his riding four-seamer, hard cutter, and soft curveball, Darvish's walk rates shrank and he pitched into at least the seventh inning in each of his last 10 starts. Already armed with an ideal frame and elite stuff, Darvish showed an ability to make adjustments on the fly that portends continued improvement in 2013.

Neftali Feliz

Born: **5/2/1988** Age: **25**
Bats: **R** Throws: **R** Height: **6' 4"** Weight: **215**
Breakout: **24%** Improve: **49%** Collapse: **23%**
Attrition: **13%** MLB: **92%**

Comparables:
Andy Messersmith,Joba Chamberlain,Karl Spooner

YEAR	TEAM	LVL	AGE	W	L	SV	G	GS	IP	H	HR	BB	SO	BB9	SO9	GB%	BABIP	WHIP	ERA	FIP	FRA	WARP
2010	TEX	MLB	22	4	3	40	70	0	69^1	43	5	18	71	2.3	9.2	36%	.224	0.88	2.73	2.93	3.60	1.1
2011	FRI	AA	23	0	0	0	1	1	1	1	0	0	3	0.0	27.0	%	.000	1.00	0.00	-2.62	-2.88	0.1
2011	TEX	MLB	23	2	3	32	64	0	62^1	42	4	30	54	4.3	7.8	38%	.232	1.16	2.74	3.61	4.72	0.5
2012	FRI	AA	24	0	1	0	1	1	2	1	0	2	4	9.0	18.0	67%	.333	1.50	0.00	2.28	1.71	0.1
2012	ROU	AAA	24	0	1	0	2	2	4^2	4	0	3	4	5.8	7.7	60%	.267	1.50	1.93	4.52	3.99	0.0
2012	TEX	MLB	24	3	1	0	8	7	42^2	28	5	23	37	4.9	7.8	38%	.213	1.20	3.16	4.59	5.79	0.1
2013	*TEX*	*MLB*	*25*	*2*	*1*	*14*	*33*	*2*	*41^1*	*33*	*4*	*16*	*43*	*3.6*	*9.3*	*42%*	*.277*	*1.20*	*3.18*	*3.54*	*3.46*	*1.0*

The owner of a true 80-grade fastball, Feliz transitioned from closer to starting pitcher in 2012 before injuring his elbow in May and undergoing Tommy John surgery nearly three months later. His seven-start stint prior to the injury was erratic, as his command and secondary stuff ranged from above-average to poor. The fireballing Dominican has the pure talent to excel in a starting role, but he'll need to continue refining his slider and changeup while learning to pace his fastball velocity. Even if the Rangers still view Feliz as a starter long-term, the club may choose to use him out of the bullpen for the short term upon his expected return in mid-2013.

Wilmer Font

Born: **5/24/1990** Age: **23**
Bats: **R** Throws: **R** Height: **6' 5"** Weight: **210**
Breakout: **25%** Improve: **50%** Collapse: **25%**
Attrition: **19%** MLB: **92%**

Comparables:
Vinegar Bend Mizell,Eric Wilkins,Ken Cloude

YEAR	TEAM	LVL	AGE	W	L	SV	G	GS	IP	H	HR	BB	SO	BB9	SO9	GB%	BABIP	WHIP	ERA	FIP	FRA	WARP
2010	HIC	A	20	4	1	0	7	7	29^2	35	3	13	33	3.9	10.0	49%	.372	1.62	5.15	4.03	4.42	0.4
2010	BAK	A+	20	1	2	0	9	9	49	38	5	32	52	5.9	9.6	41%	.273	1.43	3.86	5.02	5.11	0.6
2012	MYR	A+	22	2	5	0	23	19	83^1	58	10	37	109	4.0	11.8	36%	.270	1.14	4.21	3.77	4.92	0.7
2012	FRI	AA	22	2	0	1	10	0	15	9	1	7	29	4.2	17.4	60%	.333	1.07	3.00	1.88	3.46	0.3
2012	TEX	MLB	22	0	0	0	3	0	2	0	0	4	1	18.0	4.5	40%	.000	2.00	9.00	8.05	10.60	-0.1
2013	*TEX*	*MLB*	*23*	*2*	*2*	*0*	*9*	*6*	*32^2*	*33*	*4*	*21*	*31*	*5.8*	*8.4*	*39%*	*.304*	*1.64*	*5.41*	*4.82*	*5.88*	*0.0*

A big right-hander with serious velocity, Font is listed at 6-foot-4, 210 pounds but checks in closer to 6-foot-5, 265. After missing the entire 2011 campaign due to Tommy John surgery, he opened last season at High-A Myrtle Beach and finished it in Arlington. The 22-year-old Venezuelan relies primarily on his heavy fastball, which sits in the mid-90s and touches higher in short bursts out of the bullpen. Font's pedestrian secondary stuff and command should limit him to the bullpen long-term, but his lively plus-plus fastball could make him a powerful force in the late innings.

Justin Grimm

Born: **8/16/1988** Age: **24**
Bats: **R** Throws: **R** Height: **6' 4"** Weight: **175**
Breakout: **33%** Improve: **65%** Collapse: **21%**
Attrition: **22%** MLB: **91%**

Comparables:
Justin Verlander,Vance Worley,Carlos Rosa

YEAR	TEAM	LVL	AGE	W	L	SV	G	GS	IP	H	HR	BB	SO	BB9	SO9	GB%	BABIP	WHIP	ERA	FIP	FRA	WARP
2011	HIC	A	22	2	1	0	9	9	50^1	45	5	18	54	3.2	9.7	45%	.292	1.25	3.40	3.92	4.23	0.7
2011	MYR	A+	22	5	2	0	16	16	90^1	84	2	30	73	3.0	7.3	55%	.306	1.26	3.39	3.10	4.31	0.9
2012	FRI	AA	23	9	3	0	16	14	83^2	70	3	14	73	1.5	7.9	50%	.288	1.00	1.72	2.54	3.25	1.4
2012	ROU	AAA	23	2	3	0	9	8	51	53	2	16	30	2.8	5.3	54%	.307	1.35	4.59	4.18	6.24	-0.1
2012	TEX	MLB	23	1	1	0	5	2	14	22	1	3	13	1.9	8.4	45%	.438	1.79	9.00	2.76	3.80	0.3
2013	*TEX*	*MLB*	*24*	*3*	*4*	*0*	*9*	*9*	*51^1*	*55*	*6*	*18*	*37*	*3.1*	*6.6*	*48%*	*.308*	*1.42*	*4.73*	*4.33*	*5.14*	*0.4*

Nickname possibilities aside, Grimm is one of the system's top pitching prospects. A fifth-round pick in 2010, he made his big-league debut last summer, less than two years after he was drafted. A two-pitch guy in college, Grimm has built upon his plus fastball-curveball combo by adding a promising changeup. Now brandishing a starter's complement of weapons, Grimm has the ceiling of a third starter. His velocity and breaking ball could also play in the late innings if he's unable to stick in a rotation. Since the Rangers enter 2013 lacking experienced depth in their pitching ranks, Grimm could be a real Cinderella story.

Matt Harrison
Born: **8/16/1985** Age: **27**
Bats: **L** Throws: **L** Height: **6' 5"** Weight: **240**
Breakout: **27%** Improve: **58%** Collapse: **23%**
Attrition: **13%** MLB: **85%**
Comparables:
Mark Buehrle,Clayton Richard,Andy Pettitte

YEAR	TEAM	LVL	AGE	W	L	SV	G	GS	IP	H	HR	BB	SO	BB9	SO9	GB%	BABIP	WHIP	ERA	FIP	FRA	WARP
2010	FRI	AA	24	0	0	1	2	0	3	3	0	0	4	0.0	12.0	62%	.375	1.00	3.00	0.51	1.34	0.1
2010	OKL	AAA	24	0	1	0	1	1	4^{1}	9	1	1	4	2.1	8.4	59%	.500	2.33	6.28	5.44	5.66	0.0
2010	TEX	MLB	24	3	2	2	37	6	78^{1}	80	10	39	46	4.5	5.3	48%	.270	1.52	4.71	5.10	5.70	-0.4
2011	TEX	MLB	25	14	9	0	31	30	185^{2}	180	13	57	126	2.8	6.1	50%	.290	1.28	3.39	3.55	4.22	2.8
2012	TEX	MLB	26	18	11	0	32	32	213^{1}	210	22	59	133	2.5	5.6	50%	.284	1.26	3.29	3.98	4.67	1.6
2013	*TEX*	*MLB*	*27*	*10*	*10*	*0*	*38*	*25*	*175^{2}*	*181*	*18*	*54*	*116*	*2.8*	*5.9*	*48%*	*.298*	*1.34*	*4.28*	*4.13*	*4.65*	*2.0*

Another key piece in the famous—or infamous, depending on where your rooting interests lie—Mark Teixeira trade, Harrison has steadily improved with each of his full seasons in the major leagues. This southpaw lacks a great breaking ball and doesn't miss a lot of bats, but he features a plus fastball that he lives on and an above-average changeup that induces weak contact. Harrison may be close to reaching his ceiling, which is that of a rock-solid mid-rotation starter.

Derek Holland
Born: **10/9/1986** Age: **26**
Bats: **B** Throws: **L** Height: **6' 3"** Weight: **195**
Breakout: **26%** Improve: **59%** Collapse: **16%**
Attrition: **20%** MLB: **99%**
Comparables:
Brett Myers,Jeremy Bonderman,Jordan Zimmermann

YEAR	TEAM	LVL	AGE	W	L	SV	G	GS	IP	H	HR	BB	SO	BB9	SO9	GB%	BABIP	WHIP	ERA	FIP	FRA	WARP
2010	RNG	Rk	23	0	0	0	1	1	3	0	0	0	6	0.0	18.0	75%	.000	0.00	0.00	0.26	2.31	0.1
2010	OKL	AAA	23	6	2	0	11	11	62^{2}	50	5	18	51	2.6	7.3	47%	.253	1.08	1.87	3.95	4.38	1.1
2010	TEX	MLB	23	3	4	0	14	10	57^{1}	55	6	24	54	3.8	8.5	42%	.297	1.38	4.08	3.99	4.22	0.8
2011	TEX	MLB	24	16	5	0	32	32	198	201	22	67	162	3.0	7.4	48%	.305	1.35	3.95	3.98	4.65	2.0
2012	ROU	AAA	25	0	2	0	2	2	9	11	4	2	5	2.0	5.0	50%	.269	1.44	6.00	9.00	25.31	0.0
2012	TEX	MLB	25	12	7	0	29	27	175^{1}	162	32	52	145	2.7	7.4	44%	.261	1.22	4.67	4.71	5.55	0.4
2013	*TEX*	*MLB*	*26*	*9*	*10*	*0*	*26*	*26*	*155^{1}*	*153*	*21*	*49*	*134*	*2.9*	*7.7*	*44%*	*.294*	*1.30*	*4.23*	*4.18*	*4.59*	*2.0*

Known almost as much for his impressions and adolescent mustache as his pitching, Holland has the stuff to become a consistent force as a second or third starter, but the Rangers are still waiting for it to click. Coming off a strong second half in 2011—highlighted by his masterful World Series performance against St. Louis—Holland's 2012 campaign was filled with peaks and valleys. His plus-plus fastball sits at 92-94 mph with good life, touching higher when necessary. Though his curveball-slider-change combo is unspectacular, it plays well off his fastball when he's able to locate. The 26-year-old southpaw may be the Rangers' most important rotation piece in 2013, and a consistent season would play a big role in propelling the Rangers toward another postseason run.

Tommy Hottovy
Born: **7/9/1981** Age: **31**
Bats: **L** Throws: **L** Height: **6' 2"** Weight: **195**
Breakout: **37%** Improve: **52%** Collapse: **28%**
Attrition: **8%** MLB: **91%**
Comparables:
Bob Howry,Randy Flores,Aaron Fultz

YEAR	TEAM	LVL	AGE	W	L	SV	G	GS	IP	H	HR	BB	SO	BB9	SO9	GB%	BABIP	WHIP	ERA	FIP	FRA	WARP
2010	PME	AA	28	3	2	0	15	0	39^{2}	49	6	20	34	4.5	7.7	37%	.352	1.74	5.21	5.12	5.57	0.1
2010	PAW	AAA	28	0	1	0	26	0	35^{2}	37	5	23	22	5.8	5.5	39%	.278	1.68	4.54	6.15	6.29	-0.6
2011	PME	AA	29	0	0	1	8	0	18^{2}	12	0	4	18	1.9	8.7	—	.250	0.86	1.93	2.12	2.31	0.0
2011	PAW	AAA	29	2	0	1	24	0	36	23	8	9	29	2.2	7.2	49%	.177	0.89	2.75	5.35	5.81	-0.2
2011	BOS	MLB	29	0	0	0	8	0	4	4	0	3	2	6.8	4.5	46%	.308	1.75	6.75	5.06	5.23	0.0
2012	OMA	AAA	30	2	2	7	41	0	50	42	6	16	61	2.9	11.0	42%	.293	1.16	2.52	3.99	3.82	0.8
2012	KCA	MLB	30	0	0	0	9	0	9^{1}	11	2	5	6	4.8	5.8	40%	.321	1.71	2.89	6.47	6.79	-0.2
2013	*TEX*	*MLB*	*31*	*1*	*0*	*0*	*24*	*0*	*34*	*36*	*5*	*15*	*27*	*3.9*	*7.2*	*40%*	*.298*	*1.48*	*5.19*	*4.85*	*5.65*	*0.0*

Acquired from Kansas City for cash considerations in November, Hottovy is a lefty reliever who attacks hitters from a low arm slot. The 31-year-old has just 13 1/3 career innings in the big leagues, but he could still carve out a niche as a specialist. Triple-A left-handers batted just .147/.190/.227 against him last season. Given the Rangers' current stable of short-inning southpaws, he'll likely begin 2013 at Triple-A as LOOGY depth.

Michael Kirkman
Born: **9/18/1986** Age: **26**
Bats: **L** Throws: **L** Height: **6' 5"** Weight: **195**
Breakout: **17%** Improve: **51%** Collapse: **17%**
Attrition: **7%** MLB: **93%**
Comparables:
Phil Coke,Kason Gabbard,Marc Rzepczynski

YEAR	TEAM	LVL	AGE	W	L	SV	G	GS	IP	H	HR	BB	SO	BB9	SO9	GB%	BABIP	WHIP	ERA	FIP	FRA	WARP
2010	OKL	AAA	23	13	3	0	24	22	131	115	8	68	130	4.7	8.9	41%	.296	1.40	3.09	4.02	4.63	2.1
2010	TEX	MLB	23	0	0	0	14	0	16^{1}	9	0	10	16	5.5	8.8	50%	.214	1.16	1.65	2.92	3.04	0.4
2011	ROU	AAA	24	3	3	1	27	7	73	87	6	37	84	4.6	10.4	—	.388	1.70	5.05	4.19	4.56	0.0
2011	TEX	MLB	24	1	1	0	15	0	27^{1}	26	5	12	21	4.0	6.9	37%	.259	1.39	6.59	5.55	5.98	-0.1
2012	ROU	AAA	25	5	1	0	15	8	48	47	5	31	48	5.8	9.0	44%	.336	1.62	5.25	4.96	5.97	0.0
2012	TEX	MLB	25	1	2	0	28	0	35^{1}	24	5	17	38	4.3	9.7	38%	.211	1.16	3.82	4.26	4.38	0.4
2013	*TEX*	*MLB*	*26*	*2*	*2*	*0*	*15*	*5*	*41*	*40*	*5*	*20*	*35*	*4.5*	*7.6*	*42%*	*.293*	*1.47*	*4.74*	*4.54*	*5.15*	*0.3*

An up-and-down player for the last three seasons, Kirkman may have solidified a full-time spot in the Rangers bullpen with his decent 2012 performance. Good thing, too, since he's out of options. While his control wavers, stuff is never a problem. His fastball sits low-to-mid-90s and reaches 97 mph. He can finish hitters off with a swing-and-miss slider that acts more like a power curve. Though he's a lefty, Kirkman has been tougher on righties, who hit just .160/.253/.264 against him last season. His control may render him less consistent than Lindsay Lohan, but it's difficult to let go of a southpaw with plus-plus velocity and a good breaking ball.

Colby Lewis

Born: **8/2/1979** Age: **33**
Bats: **R** Throws: **R** Height: **6' 5"** Weight: **225**
Breakout: **29%** Improve: **52%** Collapse: **18%**
Attrition: **16%** MLB: **83%**

Comparables:
Kelvim Escobar, John Smoltz, Javier Vazquez

YEAR	TEAM	LVL	AGE	W	L	SV	G	GS	IP	H	HR	BB	SO	BB9	SO9	GB%	BABIP	WHIP	ERA	FIP	FRA	WARP
2010	TEX	MLB	30	12	13	0	32	32	201	174	21	65	196	2.9	8.8	39%	.275	1.19	3.72	3.51	3.56	3.8
2011	TEX	MLB	31	14	10	0	32	32	200^1	187	35	56	169	2.5	7.6	35%	.266	1.21	4.40	4.57	5.21	0.6
2012	TEX	MLB	32	6	6	0	16	16	105	99	16	14	93	1.2	8.0	34%	.279	1.08	3.43	3.83	4.14	1.7
2013	*TEX*	*MLB*	*33*	*6*	*6*	*0*	*17*	*17*	*105*	*97*	*13*	*25*	*100*	*2.2*	*8.6*	*39%*	*.290*	*1.17*	*3.63*	*3.62*	*3.95*	*2.1*

Returning to the Rangers on an incentive-laden one year deal, Lewis underwent right elbow surgery last July and is targeting a mid-season return in 2013. After resurrecting his career in Japan, he returned to the majors in 2010, logging 200 innings in consecutive seasons before last year's injury. With his velocity declining over the last two seasons, Lewis becomes a home-run-surrendering machine when his upper-80s fastball misses over the plate. Despite allowing a league-high 35 homers in 2011, he's had success in Arlington thanks to his wipeout slider, which helped him rack up nearly eight strikeouts per nine innings last season. Lewis's velocity may not bounce back post-surgery they way it does for most pitchers because of a degenerative hip, but his solid four-pitch mix and moxie should grant him a few more seasons.

Josh Lindblom

Born: **6/15/1987** Age: **26**
Bats: **R** Throws: **R** Height: **6' 6"** Weight: **240**
Breakout: **37%** Improve: **66%** Collapse: **9%**
Attrition: **15%** MLB: **90%**

Comparables:
A.J. Murray, Carlos Villanueva, Fernando Nieve

YEAR	TEAM	LVL	AGE	W	L	SV	G	GS	IP	H	HR	BB	SO	BB9	SO9	GB%	BABIP	WHIP	ERA	FIP	FRA	WARP
2010	ABQ	AAA	23	3	2	0	40	10	95	143	12	32	84	3.0	8.0	38%	.401	1.84	6.54	4.69	4.81	2.6
2011	CHT	AA	24	1	3	17	34	0	42^1	30	3	14	54	3.0	11.5	—	.293	1.04	2.13	2.95	3.21	0.0
2011	LAN	MLB	24	1	0	0	27	0	29^2	21	0	10	28	3.0	8.5	33%	.276	1.04	2.73	2.32	2.48	0.5
2012	LAN	MLB	25	2	2	0	48	0	47^2	42	9	18	43	3.4	8.1	40%	.266	1.26	3.02	5.11	4.74	-0.1
2012	PHI	MLB	25	1	3	1	26	0	23^1	19	4	17	27	6.6	10.4	31%	.259	1.54	4.63	5.36	5.61	-0.2
2013	*TEX*	*MLB*	*26*	*3*	*2*	*1*	*38*	*3*	*53^1*	*53*	*7*	*20*	*48*	*3.4*	*8.0*	*41%*	*.300*	*1.36*	*4.47*	*4.23*	*4.85*	*0.5*

A former second-round pick of the Dodgers, Lindblom established himself as a reliever with Los Angeles in 2011 before joining the Phillies in last summer's Shane Victorino trade. He came to Texas (along with minor leaguer Bonilla) in exchange for Michael Young over the offseason. On the heels of an excellent showing out of the Dodgers bullpen, Lindblom struggled late last year with the Phillies, with uncharacteristic control issues hampering the right-hander after the trade. Still, he's regarded as a strike-thrower who attacks hitters with a 90-94 mph fastball and usable slider. With a mixture of good-but-not-elite stuff, command, and control, Lindblom should occupy a middle-relief role for the Rangers in 2013.

Mark Lowe

Born: **6/7/1983** Age: **30**
Bats: **L** Throws: **R** Height: **6' 4"** Weight: **210**
Breakout: **39%** Improve: **70%** Collapse: **13%**
Attrition: **5%** MLB: **88%**

Comparables:
Ricardo Rincon, Jim Poole, Pedro Feliciano

YEAR	TEAM	LVL	AGE	W	L	SV	G	GS	IP	H	HR	BB	SO	BB9	SO9	GB%	BABIP	WHIP	ERA	FIP	FRA	WARP
2010	SEA	MLB	27	1	3	0	11	0	10^1	11	1	5	7	4.4	6.1	27%	.312	1.55	3.48	4.40	3.59	0.1
2010	TEX	MLB	27	0	0	0	3	0	3	7	1	1	5	3.0	15.0	30%	.667	2.67	12.00	5.05	3.39	0.1
2011	ROU	AAA	28	1	0	0	6	0	9^1	7	0	4	13	3.9	12.5	—	.318	1.18	2.89	2.28	2.48	0.0
2011	TEX	MLB	28	2	3	1	52	0	45	46	6	19	42	3.8	8.4	50%	.310	1.44	3.80	4.19	4.60	0.4
2012	FRI	AA	29	0	1	0	3	0	4	4	2	2	6	4.5	13.5	30%	.250	1.50	9.00	8.28	10.27	-0.2
2012	ROU	AAA	29	0	0	0	2	0	2	0	0	0	4	0.0	18.0	50%	.000	0.00	0.00	-0.33	0.76	0.1
2012	TEX	MLB	29	0	2	0	36	0	39^1	35	5	13	28	3.0	6.4	34%	.259	1.22	3.43	4.27	4.90	0.2
2013	*TEX*	*MLB*	*30*	*2*	*1*	*0*	*36*	*0*	*35*	*35*	*4*	*14*	*31*	*3.5*	*7.9*	*41%*	*.303*	*1.40*	*4.48*	*4.11*	*4.87*	*0.3*

Armed with a mid-90s fastball and sharp slider, Lowe tantalizes with his talent and frustrates with his inconsistency. Since coming to Texas as part of 2010's Justin Smoak-Cliff Lee trade, the right-hander has worked in middle relief for the Rangers, posting an acceptable 3.63 ERA in two seasons. However, Lowe became an afterthought in the bullpen last September as his velocity dropped a tick and he was battered down the stretch. Iffy command makes him hittable more often than he should be, given his closer-type stuff. Luckily for the Rangers, they should have enough back-end arms to keep him in a middle-relief role this season.

Roman Mendez

Born: 7/25/1990 **Age:** 22
Bats: R **Throws:** R **Height:** 6' 3" **Weight:** 180
Breakout: 20% **Improve:** 52% **Collapse:** 27%
Attrition: 14% **MLB:** 88%
Comparables:
Catfish Hunter,Rich Hand,Moose Haas

YEAR	TEAM	LVL	AGE	W	L	SV	G	GS	IP	H	HR	BB	SO	BB9	SO9	GB%	BABIP	WHIP	ERA	FIP	FRA	WARP
2010	GRN	A	19	0	2	0	6	6	15	29	5	10	18	6.0	10.8	32%	.471	2.60	11.40	8.26	7.25	-0.1
2010	LOW	A-	19	2	3	0	8	8	33	31	5	19	35	5.2	9.5	46%	.286	1.52	4.36	5.14	5.92	-0.2
2010	SPO	A-	19	1	1	0	3	3	11^{2}	19	2	3	13	2.3	10.0	44%	.459	1.88	2.31	4.25	5.70	0.0
2011	HIC	A	20	9	1	1	26	20	117	117	7	45	130	3.5	10.0	36%	.341	1.38	3.31	3.39	3.72	2.3
2012	RNG	Rk	21	0	1	0	3	3	9	7	1	1	7	1.0	7.0	50%	.333	0.89	3.00	4.93	5.03	0.1
2012	MYR	A+	21	4	6	1	18	12	70	69	7	25	71	3.2	9.1	36%	.320	1.34	5.14	4.03	4.42	1.3
2012	FRI	AA	21	2	0	1	5	0	12^{1}	8	2	4	9	2.9	6.6	32%	.171	0.97	1.46	5.14	4.29	0.1
2013	*TEX*	*MLB*	*22*	*1*	*3*	*0*	*8*	*6*	*32^{1}*	*38*	*5*	*16*	*23*	*4.6*	*6.4*	*37%*	*.313*	*1.68*	*6.12*	*5.27*	*6.65*	*-0.2*

Another power arm rising from the Rangers' minor-league ranks, Mendez joined the organization from Boston in the 2010 Jarrod Saltalamacchia trade. Developed mostly as a starting pitcher, the righty finished last season in the Double-A bullpen. Mendez appears more comfortable in relief, as he can let it fly with his mid-90s fastball, slider, and splitter. His secondary stuff shows promise but needs refinement. Although he made a strong impression with his performance as a reliever in big-league camp last year, he needs seasoning and should spend most of 2013 in the minors, with a possible late-season cup of coffee. A breakout season is possible with his talent.

Joe Nathan

Born: 11/22/1974 **Age:** 38
Bats: R **Throws:** R **Height:** 6' 5" **Weight:** 225
Breakout: 28% **Improve:** 50% **Collapse:** 23%
Attrition: 8% **MLB:** 67%
Comparables:
Trevor Hoffman,Tom Henke,Al Reyes

YEAR	TEAM	LVL	AGE	W	L	SV	G	GS	IP	H	HR	BB	SO	BB9	SO9	GB%	BABIP	WHIP	ERA	FIP	FRA	WARP
2011	ROC	AAA	36	0	0	0	3	1	3	2	0	1	5	3.0	15.0	33%	.333	1.00	0.00	0.90	0.91	0.1
2011	MIN	MLB	36	2	1	14	48	0	44^{2}	38	7	14	43	2.8	8.7	37%	.250	1.16	4.84	4.32	4.58	0.3
2012	TEX	MLB	37	3	5	37	66	0	64^{1}	55	7	13	78	1.8	10.9	46%	.306	1.06	2.80	2.74	3.38	1.4
2013	*TEX*	*MLB*	*38*	*3*	*1*	*20*	*55*	*0*	*52^{2}*	*43*	*6*	*15*	*61*	*2.6*	*10.4*	*44%*	*.285*	*1.10*	*3.00*	*3.22*	*3.26*	*1.4*

By signing Nathan to a two-year, $14.75 million deal last offseason, the Rangers were gambling on a resurgence from the veteran closer in his second year removed from Tommy John surgery. That's exactly what they got as Nathan converted 37 saves in 40 attempts. The rebound wasn't a fluke: Nathan's average fastball velocity of 94 mph was his highest since 2007. His power slider-curveball mix was once again a lethal tandem. Now 38, Nathan will begin 2013 in the Rangers' closer role. Fatigue appeared to be an issue late last year, but the club's signing of Joakim Soria—and the possible bullpen return of Feliz—could lighten Nathan's load and keep him fresh for the stretch drive.

Alexi Ogando

Born: 10/5/1983 **Age:** 29
Bats: R **Throws:** R **Height:** 6' 5" **Weight:** 195
Breakout: 14% **Improve:** 37% **Collapse:** 22%
Attrition: 2% **MLB:** 95%
Comparables:
Adam Wainwright,Jose Rijo,Curt Schilling

YEAR	TEAM	LVL	AGE	W	L	SV	G	GS	IP	H	HR	BB	SO	BB9	SO9	GB%	BABIP	WHIP	ERA	FIP	FRA	WARP
2010	FRI	AA	26	0	0	0	7	3	15^{2}	4	1	5	21	2.9	12.0	47%	.103	0.57	1.15	2.28	3.26	0.3
2010	OKL	AAA	26	0	0	1	11	0	15	10	0	6	21	3.6	12.6	44%	.278	1.07	3.00	1.98	2.94	0.4
2010	TEX	MLB	26	4	1	0	44	0	41^{2}	31	2	16	39	3.5	8.4	45%	.257	1.13	1.30	3.02	3.18	0.8
2011	TEX	MLB	27	13	8	0	31	29	169	149	16	43	126	2.3	6.7	38%	.266	1.14	3.51	3.69	4.28	2.7
2012	ROU	AAA	28	0	0	0	2	1	3	1	0	0	5	0.0	15.0	60%	.200	0.33	0.00	0.33	0.22	0.1
2012	TEX	MLB	28	2	0	3	58	1	66	49	9	17	66	2.3	9.0	39%	.237	1.00	3.27	3.68	4.28	0.8
2013	*TEX*	*MLB*	*29*	*4*	*3*	*1*	*36*	*8*	*73*	*64*	*7*	*20*	*67*	*2.5*	*8.2*	*41%*	*.281*	*1.15*	*3.19*	*3.43*	*3.46*	*1.9*

Injuries to Lewis and Feliz facilitated a return to the rotation for Ogando. It's a role in which the Dominican excelled two seasons ago, when he took a bow on the All-Star stage after a dominant first half. Despite his 6-foot-4 frame, Ogando doesn't have the attributes of a traditional starting pitcher. He's almost strictly a two-pitch hurler, featuring an overpowering fastball-slider combination but rarely using a changeup. Still, his ability to command both pitches, while maintaining his mid-90s velocity into the late innings, compensates for his lack of a third offering. The right-hander faded down the stretch as a starter in 2011 before returning to the bullpen in September. The Rangers may have the pitching depth and flexibility to place Ogando in the rotation initially and then transition him to the bullpen as he tires.

Joseph Ortiz

Born: 8/13/1990 **Age:** 22
Bats: L **Throws:** L **Height:** 5' 8" **Weight:** 175
Breakout: 27% **Improve:** 58% **Collapse:** 20%
Attrition: 8% **MLB:** 81%
Comparables:
Oscar Villarreal,Wally Ritchie,Mark Buehrle

YEAR	TEAM	LVL	AGE	W	L	SV	G	GS	IP	H	HR	BB	SO	BB9	SO9	GB%	BABIP	WHIP	ERA	FIP	FRA	WARP
2010	HIC	A	19	4	1	5	26	0	42	30	2	5	59	1.1	12.6	59%	.293	0.83	1.50	1.69	2.99	1.1
2010	BAK	A+	19	0	0	0	2	0	2^{1}	3	0	1	4	3.9	15.7	67%	.500	1.74	3.91	1.56	2.52	0.1
2011	MYR	A+	20	5	5	5	40	0	67	54	4	14	55	1.9	7.4	60%	.245	1.01	2.15	2.99	4.35	0.4
2012	FRI	AA	21	1	2	4	27	0	30^{2}	26	2	6	29	1.8	8.5	49%	.279	1.04	2.35	2.82	2.86	0.7
2012	ROU	AAA	21	1	1	2	24	0	32	31	6	3	23	0.8	6.5	53%	.272	1.06	1.97	4.95	5.91	0.0
2013	*TEX*	*MLB*	*22*	*1*	*0*	*1*	*24*	*0*	*34^{2}*	*37*	*5*	*12*	*25*	*3.3*	*6.5*	*51%*	*.300*	*1.43*	*4.93*	*4.67*	*5.36*	*0.1*

Appropriately nicknamed "Mini-Me" by his teammates, the bowling ball-like Ortiz stands 5-foot-7 and weighs 175 pounds. The southpaw makes up for lack of stature by attacking hitters with impressive fearlessness, wielding a low-90s fastball with a plus slider. He couples the good stuff with excellent command, walking only nine in 62 2/3 innings across two levels last year. Ortiz was added to the Rangers' 40-man roster in November. After limiting Double- and Triple-A lefties to a .214/.222/.398 slash line with a 26 percent strikeout rate last season, the Venezuela native could force his way into the Rangers' lefty relief discussion.

Roy Oswalt

Born: **8/29/1977** Age: **35**
Bats: **R** Throws: **R** Height: **6' 1"** Weight: **190**
Breakout: **19%** Improve: **37%** Collapse: **28%**
Attrition: **7%** MLB: **88%**

Comparables:
Kevin Millwood,Hiroki Kuroda,Kenshin Kawakami

YEAR	TEAM	LVL	AGE	W	L	SV	G	GS	IP	H	HR	BB	SO	BB9	SO9	GB%	BABIP	WHIP	ERA	FIP	FRA	WARP
2010	HOU	MLB	32	6	12	0	20	20	129	109	13	34	120	2.4	8.4	45%	.273	1.11	3.42	3.39	3.88	2.2
2010	PHI	MLB	32	7	1	0	13	12	82^{2}	53	6	21	73	2.3	7.9	52%	.221	0.90	1.74	3.15	3.52	1.6
2011	CLR	A+	33	0	0	0	1	1	5	7	0	1	5	1.8	9.0	—	.412	1.60	5.40	1.99	2.16	0.0
2011	LEH	AAA	33	0	0	0	2	2	10	8	1	4	8	3.6	7.2	—	.259	1.20	2.70	4.14	4.50	0.0
2011	PHI	MLB	33	9	10	0	23	23	139	153	10	33	93	2.1	6.0	47%	.316	1.34	3.69	3.41	3.71	1.5
2012	FRI	AA	34	0	0	0	1	1	3^{1}	5	0	1	3	2.7	8.1	23%	.385	1.80	8.10	2.38	3.37	0.1
2012	ROU	AAA	34	1	1	0	3	3	12	15	1	3	10	2.2	7.5	49%	.368	1.50	5.25	3.83	6.02	-0.2
2012	TEX	MLB	34	4	3	0	17	9	59	79	11	11	59	1.7	9.0	46%	.378	1.53	5.80	4.18	4.44	0.8
2013	*TEX*	*MLB*	*35*	*4*	*4*	*0*	*12*	*12*	*70*	*72*	*8*	*16*	*53*	*2.1*	*6.9*	*49%*	*.302*	*1.27*	*4.09*	*3.86*	*4.45*	*1.0*

Last season's unhappy marriage between Oswalt and the Rangers began with the veteran hurler signing a $4 million deal in late May. His time as a Ranger was marred by his poor performance as a starter: Oswalt was tagged for 69 hits in 46 2/3 innings, as he often missed over the plate with his fastball while struggling to keep hitters off-balance with his soft secondary stuff. The result was an unwanted stint as a reliever and Oswalt's time as a Ranger likely ended when he emptied out his locker shortly after the final pitch of the AL wild-card game. Despite his unwillingness to pitch out of the bullpen—even refusing to work a third inning during one appearance—he was usable in the role.

Martin Perez

Born: **4/4/1991** Age: **22**
Bats: **L** Throws: **L** Height: **6' 1"** Weight: **178**
Breakout: **31%** Improve: **46%** Collapse: **13%**
Attrition: **14%** MLB: **87%**

Comparables:
Steve Avery,Jon Niese,Jimmy Gobble

YEAR	TEAM	LVL	AGE	W	L	SV	G	GS	IP	H	HR	BB	SO	BB9	SO9	GB%	BABIP	WHIP	ERA	FIP	FRA	WARP
2010	FRI	AA	19	5	8	0	24	23	99^{2}	117	12	50	101	4.5	9.1	51%	.344	1.68	5.96	4.22	4.87	0.6
2011	FRI	AA	20	4	2	0	17	16	88^{1}	80	6	36	83	3.7	8.5	45%	.308	1.31	3.16	3.64	3.94	0.8
2011	ROU	AAA	20	4	4	0	10	10	49	72	4	20	37	3.7	6.8	—	.386	1.88	6.43	4.56	4.96	0.0
2012	ROU	AAA	21	7	6	0	22	21	127	122	10	56	69	4.0	4.9	52%	.277	1.40	4.25	5.02	6.85	0.0
2012	TEX	MLB	21	1	4	0	12	6	38	47	3	15	25	3.6	5.9	50%	.333	1.63	5.45	4.10	4.31	0.5
2013	*TEX*	*MLB*	*22*	*3*	*5*	*0*	*12*	*12*	61^{2}	*70*	*8*	*29*	*42*	*4.2*	*6.1*	*48%*	*.312*	*1.61*	*5.59*	*4.94*	*6.07*	*-0.1*

Perez is no stranger to the national prospect scene, having ranked in our top 101 each of the last four years. Unfortunately, he hasn't taken significant steps forward since reaching Triple-A in 2011. Perez's stuff remains excellent. His fastball tops out in the mid-90s and is complemented by a devastating low-80s changeup. He also features two promising, though inconsistent, breaking balls. Despite that, his strikeout rate dropped off significantly last season, along with his ceiling. Once thought to be a potential front-end rotation arm, he's now considered more of a third starter. He scuffled in limited big-league action but showed enough to keep the Rangers front office optimistic. Although Perez may not break camp with the team, he should see action at some point.

Neil Ramirez

Born: **5/25/1989** Age: **24**
Bats: **R** Throws: **R** Height: **6' 4"** Weight: **185**
Breakout: **33%** Improve: **63%** Collapse: **14%**
Attrition: **19%** MLB: **96%**

Comparables:
Tyler Clippard,Rocky Coppinger,Kyle Davies

YEAR	TEAM	LVL	AGE	W	L	SV	G	GS	IP	H	HR	BB	SO	BB9	SO9	GB%	BABIP	WHIP	ERA	FIP	FRA	WARP
2010	HIC	A	21	10	8	0	28	26	140^{1}	150	14	37	142	2.4	9.1	36%	.345	1.33	4.43	3.96	4.38	2.1
2011	MYR	A+	22	0	0	0	1	1	4^{2}	1	0	1	9	1.9	17.4	—	.143	0.43	0.00	0.02	0.02	0.0
2011	FRI	AA	22	1	0	0	6	6	19	13	1	8	24	3.8	11.4	22%	.412	1.11	1.89	2.96	2.28	0.4
2011	ROU	AAA	22	4	3	0	18	18	74^{1}	63	6	35	86	4.2	10.4	—	.308	1.32	3.63	4.17	4.54	0.0
2012	FRI	AA	23	2	5	0	13	12	49^{1}	47	6	16	45	2.9	8.2	34%	.301	1.28	4.20	4.31	4.34	0.6
2012	ROU	AAA	23	6	8	0	15	15	74	78	12	31	63	3.8	7.7	30%	.304	1.47	7.66	5.57	8.68	-0.2
2013	*TEX*	*MLB*	*24*	*2*	*3*	*0*	*7*	*7*	32^{2}	*36*	*5*	*17*	*26*	*4.7*	*7.0*	*33%*	*.304*	*1.61*	*5.89*	*5.16*	*6.40*	*-0.1*

Coming off an eye-opening 2011 campaign, Ramirez looked like a future second or third starter who could contribute in 2012. But the right-hander had his development slowed by myriad issues last season, including an inability to repeat his delivery, a slight velocity dip, and a loss of depth and bite on his once-plus curveball. After 15 Triple-A starts, the problems culminated in a 7.66 ERA—highest in the Pacific Coast League at that time. Ramirez's future is cloudy as he enters

2013, though he did show signs of improvement late in the season at Double-A Frisco, where his fastball began to touch 97 mph once again.

Robert Ross
Born: 6/24/1989 Age: 24
Bats: L Throws: L Height: 6' 0" Weight: 185
Breakout: 24% Improve: 73% Collapse: 17%
Attrition: 6% MLB: 97%
Comparables:
Steve Avery,Jim Abbott,Dick Ellsworth

YEAR	TEAM	LVL	AGE	W	L	SV	G	GS	IP	H	HR	BB	SO	BB9	SO9	GB%	BABIP	WHIP	ERA	FIP	FRA	WARP
2010	HIC	A	21	8	7	0	16	16	94	89	2	20	62	1.9	5.9	65%	.284	1.16	2.59	3.47	4.58	0.6
2010	BAK	A+	21	4	4	0	11	11	52	67	4	17	49	2.9	8.5	63%	.375	1.62	5.37	4.06	5.29	0.5
2011	MYR	A+	22	9	4	0	21	20	123^1	102	1	28	98	2.0	7.2	59%	.297	1.05	2.26	2.57	4.27	0.6
2011	FRI	AA	22	1	1	0	6	6	38	33	5	5	36	1.2	8.5	47%	.228	1.00	2.61	3.59	3.50	0.7
2012	TEX	MLB	23	6	0	0	58	0	65	55	3	23	47	3.2	6.5	63%	.274	1.20	2.22	3.35	4.19	0.9
2013	*TEX*	*MLB*	*24*	*3*	*3*	*0*	*16*	*7*	50^2	*54*	*6*	*19*	*32*	*3.4*	*5.7*	*56%*	*.299*	*1.45*	*4.93*	*4.60*	*5.36*	*0.2*

As a second-year player, Ross will no longer wear his trademark faux cowboy get-up and pink backpack to the bullpen this season. A non-roster invitee last spring, he pitched his way on to the big club and quickly cemented himself as the Rangers' primary lefty reliever, posting a 0.95 ERA over 34 first-half appearances. The second half was less kind. He limped to the finish line with command troubles and minor injuries. Everything Ross throws—including his little-used changeup—has cutting action that consistently missed barrels in 2012. Although the Rangers may give the 23-year-old a look in the rotation, his thin repertoire is better suited for relief work. Ross's production could take a slight step back in 2013, but he should remain an effective bullpen weapon.

Tanner Scheppers
Born: 1/17/1987 Age: 26
Bats: R Throws: R Height: 6' 5" Weight: 200
Breakout: 33% Improve: 56% Collapse: 17%
Attrition: 13% MLB: 87%
Comparables:
Ted Davidson,Juan Oviedo,Fernando Salas

YEAR	TEAM	LVL	AGE	W	L	SV	G	GS	IP	H	HR	BB	SO	BB9	SO9	GB%	BABIP	WHIP	ERA	FIP	FRA	WARP
2011	FRI	AA	24	2	1	0	17	0	23	18	1	9	24	3.5	9.4	52%	.310	1.17	3.13	3.16	2.92	0.2
2011	ROU	AAA	24	2	0	2	11	1	20^2	23	0	12	20	5.2	8.7	—	.383	1.69	4.35	3.88	4.22	0.0
2012	ROU	AAA	25	1	2	11	27	0	31	30	2	4	31	1.2	9.0	38%	.329	1.10	3.48	3.18	3.58	0.4
2012	TEX	MLB	25	1	1	1	39	0	32^1	47	6	9	30	2.5	8.4	44%	.390	1.73	4.45	4.62	4.74	0.3
2013	*TEX*	*MLB*	*26*	*2*	*1*	*0*	*25*	*1*	35^1	*36*	*4*	*11*	*33*	*2.8*	*8.3*	*42%*	*.312*	*1.32*	*4.29*	*3.74*	*4.66*	*0.4*

Once considered a ticking time bomb due to past shoulder troubles, Scheppers has largely maintained a clean bill of health during his three-year career. Best known for his electric velocity, firing a fastball in the mid-to-upper-90s, he also deploys a quality breaking ball that's somewhere between a curve and a slider. For all his overpowering stuff, inconsistent command has held Scheppers back, and it may keep him from reaching his vaunted ceiling. Although the 26-year-old threw more strikes last season, he remained loose within the zone, making him hittable in limited big-league innings. Scheppers is a wild card in the Rangers bullpen mix. With the talent for a breakout season, he'll be counted on to solidify the club's middle-relief corps.

Joakim Soria
Born: 5/18/1984 Age: 29
Bats: R Throws: R Height: 6' 4" Weight: 200
Breakout: 21% Improve: 43% Collapse: 40%
Attrition: 10% MLB: 94%
Comparables:
Bobby Jenks,Lee Smith,Robb Nen

YEAR	TEAM	LVL	AGE	W	L	SV	G	GS	IP	H	HR	BB	SO	BB9	SO9	GB%	BABIP	WHIP	ERA	FIP	FRA	WARP
2010	KCA	MLB	26	1	2	43	66	0	65^2	53	4	16	71	2.2	9.7	49%	.277	1.05	1.78	2.50	2.79	1.7
2011	KCA	MLB	27	5	5	28	60	0	60^1	60	7	17	60	2.5	9.0	43%	.312	1.28	4.03	3.53	4.12	0.6
2013	*TEX*	*MLB*	*29*	*2*	*1*	*17*	*37*	*0*	*37*	*31*	*4*	*10*	*41*	*2.5*	*10.0*	*44%*	*.288*	*1.11*	*3.07*	*3.20*	*3.34*	*0.9*

Soria battled through the 2011 season, and many observers felt he was harboring an injury. Related or not, he went down last spring with elbow soreness that eventually led to his second Tommy John surgery. Soria began throwing six months after the surgery, right on schedule. After the Royals declined their $8 million option for 2013, Soria became a free agent and Texas snapped him up on a two-year deal. Slated for a return to game action in May, a healthy Soria could serve as an excellent eighth-inning option for the Rangers.

Matthew West
Born: 11/21/1988 Age: 24
Bats: R Throws: R Height: 6' 2" Weight: 215
Breakout: 31% Improve: 55% Collapse: 14%
Attrition: 11% MLB: 85%
Comparables:
Esteban Yan,Carlos Castillo,Ron Davis

YEAR	TEAM	LVL	AGE	W	L	SV	G	GS	IP	H	HR	BB	SO	BB9	SO9	GB%	BABIP	WHIP	ERA	FIP	FRA	WARP
2011	SPO	A-	22	1	2	9	23	0	26	23	3	1	35	0.3	12.1	59%	.353	0.92	3.12	2.88	2.79	0.7
2011	MYR	A+	22	0	0	0	1	0	1	1	0	0	0	0.0	0.0	50%	.000	1.00	0.00	3.23	1.71	0.0
2012	MYR	A+	23	0	3	0	17	0	20^1	18	1	16	14	7.1	6.2	52%	.279	1.67	6.64	5.30	6.59	-0.2
2013	*TEX*	*MLB*	*24*	*1*	*0*	*1*	*28*	*0*	32^2	*37*	*5*	*17*	*23*	*4.7*	*6.3*	*47%*	*.310*	*1.65*	*5.86*	*5.34*	*6.37*	*-0.2*

A second-round pick as an infielder in 2007, West converted to the mound during spring training in 2011 and quickly established himself as a legitimate late-inning relief prospect with mid-to-upper-90s velocity and a plus slider. The native Texan appeared to be on the fast track to the major-league bullpen as spring training approached last March, but he was sidetracked by an elbow injury that ultimately required Tommy John surgery. After struggling through 17 appearances at High-A Myrtle Beach last season, the 24-year-old righty finally underwent surgery in August and is expected to miss the bulk of 2013.

LINEOUTS

HITTERS

PLAYER	TEAM	LVL	AGE	PA	R	2B	3B	HR	RBI	BB	SO	SB-CS	AVG/OBP/SLG	TAv	BABIP	BRR	FRAA	WARP
SS H. Alberto	HIC	A	19	272	37	17	1	4	38	18	22	15-4	.337/.385/.463	.321	.354	0.5	SS(31): 3.7, 3B(15): -0.1	2.0
	MYR	A+	19	290	36	11	2	4	34	2	27	9-3	.265/.273/.362	.231	.277	3.1	SS(52): 14.2	1.7
C J. Alfaro	HIC	A	19	300	40	21	5	5	34	16	84	7-3	.261/.320/.430	.288	.355	1.3	C(26): -0.2, 1B(14): -0.6	1.0
1B B. Allen	PCH	A+	26	61	8	3	0	2	4	9	14	0-0	.255/.361/.431	.260	.306	0.6	LF(1): -0.2, 1B(1): -0.0	0.1
	DUR	AAA	26	129	17	9	1	4	14	4	32	0-0	.262/.295/.451	.250	.322	0.3	RF(3): 0.2, LF(3): 0.1	0.0
	OAK	MLB	26	7	0	0	0	0	0	0	5	0-0	.000/.000/.000	.102	.000	0	1B(3): -0.0	-0.1
	TBA	MLB	26	15	3	0	0	1	3	2	4	0-0	.154/.267/.385	.268	.125	-0.1	LF(3): -0.1	0.0
CF L. Brinson	RNG	RK	18	265	54	22	7	7	42	21	74	14-2	.283/.345/.523	.290	.377	0.7	CF(12): -1.5	0
CF J. Butler	ROU	AAA	26	584	93	28	1	20	78	79	128	6-4	.290/.392/.473	.330	.351	-0.4	RF(31): -4.5	0.6
3B J. Gallo	RNG	Rk	18	193	44	10	1	18	43	37	52	6-0	.293/.435/.733	.597	.313	3.3	3B(36): -5.6	-0.3
	SPO	A-	18	67	9	2	0	4	9	11	26	0-0	.214/.343/.464	.281	.308	-0.9	3B(16): 2.1	0.5
1B R. Guzman	RNG	Rk	17	235	29	15	3	1	33	19	42	7-1	.321/.374/.434	.692	.390	0.8	1B(11): -0.3, LF(1): 0.0	0.2
OF N. Mazara	RNG	Rk	17	243	40	13	3	6	39	37	70	5-2	.264/.383/.448	.223	.370	-0.1	RF(13): -1.0	-0.3
2B R. Odor	HIC	A	18	471	60	23	4	10	47	25	65	19-10	.259/.313/.400	.282	.284	1.5	2B(74): -2.5, SS(14): -0.8	1.4
SS L. Sardinas	HIC	A	19	412	65	14	2	2	30	29	52	32-9	.291/.346/.356	.272	.331	3.7	SS(61): -0.7, 2B(12): -0.4	1.6
C E. Whiteside	FRE	AAA	32	229	27	11	1	1	20	17	43	0-1	.224/.296/.303	.237	.275	1	C(40): -0.3	0.5
	SFN	MLB	32	14	3	1	0	0	2	1	4	0-0	.091/.214/.182	.190	.125	0.2	C(11): 0.0	0.1

A rangy middle infielder with a promising hit tool, 19-year-old **Hanser Alberto** hit .397 in the Arizona Fall League this offseason. The system's top catching prospect, 19-year-old Colombia native **Jorge Alfaro** is a ways from the majors but has a sky-high ceiling thanks to his loud tools, including 80-grade arm strength and 70-grade raw power. Signed to a minor-league deal, **Brandon Allen** consistently posts hulking Triple-A numbers but has little to show for it in the majors. Making big-league cameos in each of the last four seasons, he'll provide depth at first base. The Rangers' top pick in last summer's MLB Draft, outfielder **Lewis Brinson** has proven to be less raw than initially thought. A premium athlete with serious bat speed, power potential, and defensive tools, he could possess the organization's highest ceiling. More organizational player than prospect, 26-year-old outfielder **Joey Butler** has posted two consecutive big seasons in Triple-A, but struggles to make contact. Flexing his 80-grade raw power, 2012 supplemental first-round pick **Joey Gallo** made headlines by blasting a rookie-level Arizona League record 18 home runs in just 43 games last summer. First baseman **Ronald Guzman**, signed out of the Dominican Republic for $3.45 million, is a lanky 6-foot-5 lefty with a swing and approach that are mature beyond his 18 years. Lefty-hitting outfielder **Nomar Mazara** signed at the same time as Guzman in July 2011, garnering a club-record $4.95 million bonus. An overall polished game made 19-year-old second baseman **Rougned Odor** a success in full-season ball last year, and he could begin to fly through the system in 2013. One of the system's toolsier players, shortstop **Luis Sardinas** combines elite defensive skills at a premium position with a feel for hitting and plus-plus speed. Claimed off waivers from the Yankees, **Eli Whiteside** is a career backup catcher who will provide added depth behind the plate.

PITCHERS

PLAYER	TEAM	LVL	AGE	W	L	SV	IP	H	HR	BB	SO	BB9	SO9	GB%	BABIP	WHIP	ERA	FIP	FRA	WARP
C. Balester	TOL	AAA	26	1	1	1	47	38	7	12	45	2.3	8.6	41%	.256	1.06	3.64	4.14	6.20	-0.3
	DET	MLB	26	2	0	0	18	14	5	11	12	5.5	6.0	33%	.173	1.39	6.50	7.66	9.99	-0.8
N. Cotts	ROU	AAA	32	2	1	3	31^2	32	2	15	41	4.3	11.7	41%	.358	1.48	4.55	3.41	-0.36	1.2
C. Edwards	SPO	A-	20	2	3	0	47	26	0	19	60	3.6	11.5	50%	.250	0.96	2.11	2.11	2.85	1.3
L. Jackson	HIC	A	20	5	5	0	64	63	4	33	72	4.6	10.1	48%	.347	1.50	4.92	3.92	4.35	0.9
	MYR	A+	20	5	2	0	65^2	67	2	32	74	4.4	10.1	42%	.378	1.51	4.39	3.17	3.78	0.8
K. Kela	RNG	RK	19	0	1	0	11^1	4	0	4	15	3.2	11.9	63%	0.158	0.71	1.59	3.05	2.98	0.3
E. Meek	IND	AAA	29	3	2	1	46	33	3	26	41	5.1	8.0	62%	.242	1.28	2.74	4.18	5.83	-0.3
	PIT	MLB	29	0	0	0	12	14	1	6	8	4.5	6.0	36%	.317	1.67	6.75	4.64	4.47	0.0
Y. Mendez	DRG	Rk	17	2	1	0	45^1	36	1	13	35	2.6	6.9	—	.276	1.08	1.99	2.96	10.29	-0.1
J. Miller	—	—	—	—	—	—	—	—	—	—	—	—	—	—	—	—	—	—	—	—
Y. Tateyama	ROU	AAA	36	4	0	6	39^2	29	2	7	45	1.6	10.2	29%	.276	0.91	1.13	2.66	2.34	0.9
	TEX	MLB	36	1	0	0	17	18	4	6	18	3.2	9.5	35%	.292	1.41	9.00	5.05	7.03	-0.2
N. Tepesch	MYR	A+	23	5	3	0	71^2	68	3	18	59	2.3	7.4	61%	.307	1.20	2.89	3.33	3.97	0.8
	FRI	AA	23	6	3	0	90^1	97	10	26	68	2.6	6.8	52%	.316	1.36	4.28	4.18	5.45	0.3
R. Wells	IOW	AAA	29	3	3	0	43^1	52	6	18	29	3.7	6.0	43%	.354	1.62	7.89	5.58	6.08	0.1
	CHN	MLB	29	1	2	0	28^2	35	1	24	14	7.5	4.4	43%	.333	2.06	5.34	5.33	4.91	0.2
C. Woods	TUL	AA	24	3	2	16	35^2	26	1	8	34	2.0	8.6	61%	.266	0.95	0.76	2.41	2.55	0.9
	CSP	AAA	24	1	2	11	20^2	34	4	11	13	4.8	5.7	49%	.390	2.18	7.40	6.67	7.27	-0.1
J. Yan	ROU	AAA	23	1	1	1	34	35	3	17	24	4.5	6.4	56%	.290	1.53	5.03	5.25	7.56	-0.2

With 185 career big-league innings, non-roster invitee **Collin Balester** should provide bullpen depth. After nearly making the club last spring, veteran lefty reliever **Neal Cotts** pitched well enough in Triple-A to earn another shot this season. A 48th-round pick in 2011, **C.J. Edwards** was nearly unhittable at the short-season levels last summer, running his lively fastball up to 96 mph while spinning a quality curveball. Right-hander **Luke Jackson** needs refinement but features a fastball that reaches 97 mph and a knee-buckling curve. After beginning his career in the bullpen and flashing a fastball up to 100 mph, righty **Keone Kela** could get a crack at starting in 2013. **Evan Meek** made the All-Star team in 2010, dealt with shoulder soreness in 2011, and showed reduced velocity in 2012. Projectable Venezuelan lefty **Yohander Mendez** should make his stateside debut in 2013 after beginning his pro career in the Dominican Summer League. Standing 6-foot-5, the 18-year-old already shows strike-throwing ability with the makings of a wipeout changeup. After Tommy John surgery caused him to miss the entire 2012 campaign, hard-throwing reliever **Justin Miller** is eyeing an early-2013 return and could factor into the Rangers bullpen mix. Returning on a minor-league deal, 37-year-old righty **Yoshinori Tateyama** adds further depth to the Rangers relief corps, but will have to locate his fringy fastball better than he did in 2012. A big righty who pounds the zone with quality stuff, **Nick Tepesch** was solid between High- and Double-A last season while featuring a low-to-mid-90s fastball, a plus cutter, and a rapidly improving curveball. **Randy Wells** was converted from catching to pitching by the Cubs but has struggled in recent years, possibly because of bone chips in his elbow—now removed. A Rule 5 pick over the offseason, side-arming right-hander **Coty Woods** will have a chance to crack the Rangers bullpen with his 88-92 mph fastball, solid-average changeup, and a serviceable slider. Side-arming right-hander **Johan Yan** struggled to retire Triple-A lefties last season but proved a difficult task for fellow righties, attacking with deception and a heavy upper-80s sinker.

MANAGER: RON WASHINGTON

YEAR	TEAM	W-L	Pythag +/-	Avg PC	100+ P	120+ P	QS	BQS	REL	REL w Zero R	IBB	PH	PH Avg	PH HR	SB2	CS2	SB3	CS3	SAC Att	SAC %	POS SAC	Squeeze	Swing	In Play
2010	TEX	90-72	1	196.1	159	158	105	10	482	397	48	164	.229	2	16	6	2	0	164	81.7%	128	6	325	107
2011	TEX	96-66	1	99.2	103	3	99	5	417	335	21	59	.204	1	18	4	2	2	63	73.0%	45	3	374	117
2012	TEX	93-69	1	98.7	87	4	86	3	428	366	15	86	.187	4	10	3	0	1	57	78.9%	41	2	338	96

Since taking over the reins in 2007, Washington has established himself as the most successful manager in Rangers history. In six seasons at the helm, the New Orleans native has set club records with 520 wins, four consecutive winning seasons, three straight postseason berths, and two World Series trips. Of course, with the success comes heightened expectations. The franchise that had posted one lonely postseason victory in the 46 years prior to Washington's arrival has become a distant memory. As a result, the skipper is largely judged against his own successes, and last year's late-season collapse—capped with a wild card-round exit—was viewed as an extreme disappointment.

Cut from the "old school" managerial cloth, Washington defines his own approach as more instinctive than statistical, often preferring to "go with the gut" rather than the numbers. His unorthodox in-game management style has led to criticism, particularly in the hyper-focused microscope of the postseason. Questions have also been raised regarding Washington's loyalty to veteran players such as Michael Young, who appeared in 156 games last season despite posting a -1.5 WARP. Concerns aside, the 61-year-old has proven to be an excellent man-manager who controls and motivates the clubhouse. Washington's players often rave about both his relaxed style and unabashed enthusiasm. His excitable ticks and in-dugout celebrations have become a trademark in recent years.

Like any manager, Washington comes with his share of strengths and flaws, but the bottom line is that he wins. There's something to be said about the consistency and stability he has brought to Texas. Entering 2013, only the Rangers and Yankees can boast postseason trips in each of the last three years. Whether the club can continue its winning ways without Josh Hamilton, Mike Adams, and others will be Washington's next test.

Toronto Blue Jays

2012: CLIPPED WINGS

Injuries defined Toronto's 2012 season, otherwise the Jays might have taken flight like . . . Orioles.

First, the injury bug wrecked a reasonably promising pitching staff, particularly the starting rotation in which Toronto deployed a dozen different pitchers, second-most in the American League. Staff ace Brandon Morrow missed more than two months with a left abdominal strain, while youngsters Kyle Drabek and Drew Hutchison were shut down within days of each other with elbow injuries that eventually required Tommy John surgery.

Healthier than the pitching staff, the Blue Jays lineup was helped by a career year from Edwin Encarnacion, and the team locked him up to a three-year contract extension in July. However, the loss of Jose Bautista for nearly all of the second half threw an entire box of wrenches into the Jays offense. With Bautista in the lineup, the Blue Jays averaged 4.92 runs per game. Without him, that number fell to 3.77, a figure that would have ranked dead last in the American League over the entire season. Compare the scoring difference to that of the Tampa Bay Rays, who were without star third baseman Evan Longoria for more than three months.

Runs Per Game Difference

Player	Tm	With	W/o	Diff
Jose Bautista	TOR	4.92	3.77	1.15
Evan Longoria	TBA	4.79	3.86	0.93

Toronto was 45-45 when Bautista went down with a left wrist injury on July 17, but went 28-44 the rest of the way, so there was plenty of blame for the offensive ineptitude to go around. Adam Lind once again failed to perform at the level that earned him a four-year, $18 million contract after the 2009 season, and third baseman Brett Lawrie fell short of the lofty expectations created by his second-half debut the previous year. Kelly Johnson and Colby Rasmus, acquired weeks apart prior to the 2011 trade deadline, disappointed in their first full seasons in Toronto, and Johnson was allowed to depart as a free agent.

In August, the Blue Jays promoted some of their most promising Triple-A prospects, including center fielder Anthony Gose and shortstop Adeiny Hechavarria. Neither provided a jolt to Toronto's fledgling offense, but Gose finished second on the team in stolen bases despite collecting just 189 plate appearances.

BLUE JAYS PROSPECTUS

2012 W-L: 73-89, 4th in AL East

Pythag	.457	22nd	DER	.709	15th
RS/G	4.42	13th	B-Age	27.7	8th
RA/G	4.84	25th	P-Age	27.1	3rd
TAv	.255	22nd	Salary	$83.7	21st
BRR	3.5	12th	M$/MW	$2.88	19th
TAv-P	.272	26th	DL Days	1329	5th
FIP	4.61	28th	DL WARP	5.3	7th

Three-Year Park Factors	
Overall	104
HR/RH	117
HR/LH	102
AVG/RH	109
AVG/LH	106

Rogers Centre (1989)
Att. % of Capacity: 52.6% (27th)
Dim. 328, 375, 400, 375, 328

He's just one member of the Blue Jays' revamped rotation, but Mark Buehrle may be a poor fit at Rogers.

2013: PECKING ORDER

If 2012 taught the Toronto Blue Jays anything, it taught them there is no time like the present. The unexpected successes of the A's and Orioles caught the baseball-watching world off guard, but more than that, it showed teams that the American League isn't just a play-toy for the Yankees and Rangers. More pertinently, Baltimore's success poked a hole in the invulnerability of Toronto's native division. With Boston attempting a reload, New York older than ever, and Tampa Bay forced into dealing off stud pitchers because almost nobody cares and the Rays essentially play in a converted doublewide, the Blue Jays know that if they patch their holes with productive players, they could push to the front of the line.

In mid-November, the disappointment of the previous season was washed away when the Jays acquired Jose Reyes, Josh Johnson, Mark Buehrle, Emilio Bonifacio, and John Buck from the Miami Marlins in exchange for Henderson Alvarez, Yunel Escobar, Jeff Mathis, and prospects Hechavarria, Jake Marisnick, Justin Nicolino, and Anthony DeSclafani.

For the first time in the lifetimes of all you toddlers out there, the Blue Jays will have to confront the specter of legitimate expectations in 2013. The trade with Miami and the acquisition of R.A. Dickey from the Mets have brought excitement in Toronto to levels not seen since monkeys, armed only with their own feces, engineered a prison break from the Toronto Zoo back in '97. OK, that didn't happen, but it would have been as exciting, right?

The trades not only added talent, they added it in all the right places. Dickey, Johnson, and Buerhle completely remade Toronto's brittle rotation while Reyes represents a massive upgrade over Escobar, even if Reyes comes out on Opening Day with Confederate flags painted on his eye black. The signing of Melky Cabrera pushed Rajai Davis's below-average bat to the bench, and provided yet another middle-of-the-order bat to a lineup now full of them.

Of course, it's not all puppies and rainbows. Toronto's revamped starting rotation carries promise, but also significant risk. New staff ace Dickey will be 38, entering a new league, and trying not to lose his grip on the horns of the raging bull that is the knuckleball. Johnson, having missed nearly 400 days due to injury in 2007-11 and having made more than 14 starts just twice during that time, has a health history that only Rich Harden would envy. In between stays on the disabled list for shoulder and elbow injuries, Johnson went 36-16 with a 2.93 ERA and 8.5 strikeouts per nine innings. While he was healthy last year, he wasn't nearly as dominant, posting a 3.81 ERA and striking out fewer than eight batters per nine innings.

Questions about Buehrle involve efficacy rather than injuries. The lefty has logged more than 200 innings in each of the last dozen seasons, but has never missed many bats (5.1 SO9 for his career). He's entering a division that featured four of the top six ballparks in the American League for home runs in 2012, including Rogers Centre. That's a daunting task for a fly-ball pitcher.

STATE OF THE ORGANIZATION: OUT OF THE NEST

The Blue Jays jettisoned 11 prospects between July and November, including five ranked among their top 10 heading into the season.

The Jays could do this, in part at least, because they had five picks before the start of the second round. Center fielder D.J. Davis, the 17th pick, played 60 games and flashed pop and game-changing speed. Marcus Stroman, the Blue Jays' compensation pick for failing to sign 2011 first-rounder Tyler Beede, reached Double-A before drawing a 50-game suspension at the end of the regular season. Left-hander Matt Smoral was the recipient of an above-slot $2 million bonus as the 50th pick. Overall, the Blue Jays spent $9.3 million on their 2012 draft class, the fifth most in all of baseball. They were one of 10 clubs to exceed their draft allotment and were forced to pay a $330,900 tax, the largest penalty of any club. With the talent exodus from their system the Jays will need each of those dollars to pan out if they want more than a two- or three-year contention window.

In the end, the Blue Jays have split with their recent past in that they are no longer about promise. They are about expectation, production, and results. The time may be right for the Blue Jays to assert themselves. One thing is for certain: They think so.

HITTERS

J.P. Arencibia **C**
Born: **1/5/1986** Age: **27**
Bats: **R** Throws: **R** Height: **6' 2"**
Weight: **210** Breakout: **2%**
Improve: **45%** Collapse: **11%**
Attrition: **12%** MLB: **94%**
Comparables:
Hector Villanueva,Rick Wilkins,Carlton Fisk

YEAR	TEAM	LVL	AGE	PA	R	2B	3B	HR	RBI	BB	SO	SB	CS	AVG_OBP_SLG	TAv	BABIP	BRR	FRAA	WARP
2010	LVG	AAA	24	459	76	36	1	32	85	38	85	0	0	.301/.364/.626	.313	.312	-3.5	C(94): -2.5	3.9
2010	TOR	MLB	24	37	3	1	0	2	4	2	11	0	0	.143/.189/.343	.183	.136	-1.1	C(8): -0.1	-0.3
2011	TOR	MLB	25	486	47	20	4	23	78	36	133	1	1	.219/.282/.438	.258	.255	-2.3	C(122): 1.3	1.5
2012	TOR	MLB	26	372	45	16	0	18	56	18	108	1	0	.233/.275/.435	.252	.281	-0.1	C(94): 1.0	1.1
2013	*TOR*	*MLB*	*27*	*373*	*44*	*17*	*1*	*19*	*55*	*25*	*100*	*1*	*0*	*.235/.290/.456*	*.260*	*.273*	*-0.5*	*C -0*	*1.6*

Arencibia's shortcomings often mask the value of the one thing he does do well: hit for power. He's one of only five American League catchers to have hit at least 40 home runs over the last two seasons. In fact, at 4.7 percent, he's second to Mike Napoli in home-run rate among backstops with at least 800 plate appearances since 2011. Behind the dish, Arencibia has shown improvement in controlling the running game. Opponents ran less often and were caught more often against Arencibia than the AL average.

Jose Bautista **RF**
Born: **10/19/1980** Age: **32**
Bats: **R** Throws: **R** Height: **6' 1"**
Weight: **195** Breakout: **1%**
Improve: **29%** Collapse: **1%**
Attrition: **3%** MLB: **99%**
Comparables:
Bobby Abreu,J.D. Drew,Frank Robinson

YEAR	TEAM	LVL	AGE	PA	R	2B	3B	HR	RBI	BB	SO	SB	CS	AVG_OBP_SLG	TAv	BABIP	BRR	FRAA	WARP
2010	TOR	MLB	29	683	109	35	3	54	124	100	116	9	2	.260/.378/.617	.337	.233	-1.6	RF(113): -13.1, 3B(48): 1.1	6.3
2011	TOR	MLB	30	655	105	24	2	43	103	132	111	9	5	.302/.447/.608	.365	.309	1.4	RF(116): 6.0, 3B(25): 4.1	9.3
2012	TOR	MLB	31	399	64	14	0	27	65	59	63	5	2	.241/.358/.527	.313	.215	4.3	RF(90): 1.4, 1B(4): 0.1	3.4
2013	*TOR*	*MLB*	*32*	*427*	*64*	*17*	*1*	*24*	*70*	*63*	*82*	*5*	*2*	*.256/.373/.518*	*.310*	*.263*	*-0.3*	*RF -1, 3B 1*	*3.1*

Joey Bats was slowly digging his way out of a dreadful start to the year when a wrist injury put him on the shelf in mid-July. He returned to the Jays lineup at the end of August but was back on the disabled list, this time for good, after only two games. Even before injuries wiped out nearly all of the second half for Bautista, he was enduring a largely disappointing season. His over-the-fence power was still there, but an absurd number of balls in play were converted to outs—his .215 BABIP was the lowest among players with at least 300 plate appearances. Toronto's offense fell apart without Bautista, scoring 1.15 fewer runs per game after he went on the disabled list. Wrist injuries have a tendency to sap power, so don't be surprised if his 6.8 percent home-run rate dips. He'll almost certainly have better luck on balls in play, however, so he should see a rebound in batting average.

Emilio Bonifacio UT

Born: **4/23/1985** Age: **28**
Bats: **B** Throws: **R** Height: **6' 0"**
Weight: **200** Breakout: **1%**
Improve: **45%** Collapse: **3%**
Attrition: **10%** MLB: **88%**

Comparables:
Nook Logan,Michael Bourn,Scott Podsednik

YEAR	TEAM	LVL	AGE	PA	R	2B	3B	HR	RBI	BB	SO	SB	CS	AVG_OBP_SLG	TAv	BABIP	BRR	FRAA	WARP
2010	NWO	AAA	25	182	19	8	3	0	11	16	33	8	4	.274/.335/.360	.261	.338	0.4	CF(18): -3.3, 2B(10): -1.9	-0.1
2010	FLO	MLB	25	201	30	6	3	0	10	17	42	12	0	.261/.320/.328	.238	.333	5.6	CF(17): 0.1, SS(9): -1.1	1.0
2011	FLO	MLB	26	641	78	26	7	5	36	59	129	40	11	.296/.360/.393	.274	.372	7.9	SS(67): -5.9, 3B(36): 0.4	2.7
2012	MIA	MLB	27	274	30	3	4	1	11	25	52	30	3	.258/.330/.316	.239	.325	2	CF(51): -3.6, 2B(15): 0.6	-0.4
2013	*TOR*	*MLB*	*28*	*336*	*42*	*12*	*4*	*3*	*25*	*27*	*67*	*20*	*5*	*.262/.322/.359*	*.241*	*.320*	*2.3*	*CF -0, SS -1*	*0.5*

Bonifacio spent most of the 2012 season on the disabled list, missing a combined 98 games due to thumb surgery and a sprained knee. After roving around six different positions for the Marlins in 2011, he settled in center field last year, but the trade to Toronto is likely to result in a return to super-sub duty. Bonifacio's offensive game revolves around his excellent speed—which has fueled an 80 percent success rate on stolen-base attempts—but his bloated strikeout rate eats into his on-base percentage and robs him of opportunities to use those wheels. His versatility and speed should make him an asset as long as he can stay on the field.

Melky Cabrera OF

Born: **8/11/1984** Age: **28**
Bats: **B** Throws: **L** Height: **6' 1"**
Weight: **200** Breakout: **2%**
Improve: **45%** Collapse: **7%**
Attrition: **22%** MLB: **91%**

Comparables:
Shannon Stewart,Carl Crawford,Martin Prado

YEAR	TEAM	LVL	AGE	PA	R	2B	3B	HR	RBI	BB	SO	SB	CS	AVG_OBP_SLG	TAv	BABIP	BRR	FRAA	WARP
2010	ATL	MLB	25	509	50	27	3	4	42	42	64	7	1	.255/.317/.354	.242	.288	-2.4	LF(82): -1.3, CF(55): -0.5	0.0
2011	KCA	MLB	26	706	102	44	5	18	87	35	94	20	10	.305/.339/.470	.287	.332	4.2	CF(143): -17.6, LF(12): 0.2	2.1
2012	SFN	MLB	27	501	84	25	10	11	60	36	63	13	5	.346/.390/.516	.332	.379	0.6	LF(106): 4.5, RF(11): -0.9	5.1
2013	*TOR*	*MLB*	*28*	*512*	*66*	*27*	*3*	*13*	*53*	*36*	*70*	*11*	*4*	*.282/.334/.434*	*.268*	*.305*	*0.2*	*LF -1, CF -1*	*1.6*

Cabrera enjoyed a breakout with the Royals in 2011 before joining the Giants via trade last offseason. Many knowledgeable people felt his 2011 season was fluky and BABIP driven. Those folks were expecting substantial regression for Cabrera last year. Instead, he kicked his play up a notch. That should've confirmed Cabrera had become an impact player, but it didn't because he was suspended for 50 games in August for violating MLB's drug policy. Cabrera was one plate appearance shy of qualifying for the batting title, and he would have won it under the rule that adds that PA as an out, but MLB and the players union, at Cabrera's request, ruled him ineligible, giving the batting crown to Buster Posey. Cabrera's suspension ended early in the postseason, but the Giants declined to roster him. How much of Cabrera's improvement can be tied to his drug use? The Blue Jays signed him to a two-year contract that amounts to a $16 million bet on "not much."

David Cooper 1B

Born: **2/12/1987** Age: **26**
Bats: **L** Throws: **L** Height: **6' 1"**
Weight: **200** Breakout: **5%**
Improve: **58%** Collapse: **5%**
Attrition: **9%** MLB: **96%**

Comparables:
Rafael Palmeiro,Chad Tracy,Daniel Murphy

YEAR	TEAM	LVL	AGE	PA	R	2B	3B	HR	RBI	BB	SO	SB	CS	AVG_OBP_SLG	TAv	BABIP	BRR	FRAA	WARP
2010	NHP	AA	23	553	59	30	1	20	78	52	74	0	0	.257/.328/.442	.268	.267	-3.3	1B(131): 7.0	1.2
2011	LVG	AAA	24	545	77	51	1	9	96	67	43	1	3	.364/.439/.535	.316	.380	-2.5	1B(74): -6.8	1.4
2011	TOR	MLB	24	81	9	7	0	2	12	7	14	0	0	.211/.284/.394	.248	.228	0	1B(15): -0.2	-0.1
2012	LVG	AAA	25	304	45	27	1	10	52	37	34	0	1	.314/.395/.540	.333	.324	-1.4	1B(40): -3.5	1.1
2012	TOR	MLB	25	145	16	11	0	4	11	4	22	0	1	.300/.324/.464	.292	.333	0.2	1B(29): 1.6	0.7
2013	*TOR*	*MLB*	*26*	*250*	*26*	*16*	*0*	*6*	*30*	*19*	*39*	*0*	*0*	*.267/.325/.424*	*.261*	*.295*	*-0.6*	*1B -3*	*-0.1*

Toronto knew it was getting a non-traditional first baseman when it selected Cooper with the 17th pick of the 2008 draft out of Cal. He'll never have better than average power, but Cooper should hit plenty of doubles while maintaining a high batting average. He's played some left field in the past, but not well, and he isn't going to be able to handle playing out there every day. Scouts don't question his bat, but few believe he should be starting for a championship-caliber club.

Rajai Davis OF

Born: **10/19/1980** Age: **32**
Bats: **R** Throws: **R** Height: **5' 11"**
Weight: **195** Breakout: **3%**
Improve: **32%** Collapse: **10%**
Attrition: **23%** MLB: **90%**

Comparables:
Alex Johnson,Dan Gladden,Ralph Garr

YEAR	TEAM	LVL	AGE	PA	R	2B	3B	HR	RBI	BB	SO	SB	CS	AVG_OBP_SLG	TAv	BABIP	BRR	FRAA	WARP
2010	OAK	MLB	29	561	66	28	3	5	52	26	78	50	11	.284/.320/.377	.259	.322	4.7	CF(83): -0.6, LF(47): -1.8	1.5
2011	TOR	MLB	30	338	44	21	6	1	29	15	63	34	11	.237/.273/.350	.225	.292	5	CF(79): -2.8, RF(8): 0.6	-0.6
2012	TOR	MLB	31	487	64	24	3	8	43	29	102	46	13	.257/.309/.378	.242	.314	1	LF(114): 1.0, RF(24): 0.9	0.1
2013	*TOR*	*MLB*	*32*	*428*	*57*	*22*	*4*	*6*	*35*	*23*	*79*	*40*	*11*	*.262/.307/.380*	*.242*	*.311*	*4.2*	*LF -1, CF 0*	*0.6*

Last year, Davis rebounded from a lackluster 2011 campaign to become one of only four players to steal at least 40 bases and knock 35 extra-base hits. Since 2009, Davis's 171 steals trail only Michael Bourn (216) for the most in all of baseball. Originally scheduled to become a free agent after 2012, Davis signed a one-year contract extension to remain in Toronto through 2013, no doubt buying time for Anthony Gose to develop further at Triple-A Buffalo.

Edwin Encarnacion 1B

Born: **1/7/1983** Age: **30**
Bats: **R** Throws: **R** Height: **6' 3"**
Weight: **235** Breakout: **2%**
Improve: **47%** Collapse: **5%**
Attrition: **6%** MLB: **92%**

Comparables:
Justin Morneau,Kevin Youkilis,Kent Hrbek

YEAR	TEAM	LVL	AGE	PA	R	2B	3B	HR	RBI	BB	SO	SB	CS	AVG_OBP_SLG	TAv	BABIP	BRR	FRAA	WARP
2010	TOR	MLB	27	367	47	16	0	21	51	29	60	1	0	.244/.305/.482	.271	.235	1.7	3B(95): -3.2	1.6
2011	TOR	MLB	28	530	70	36	0	17	55	43	77	8	2	.272/.334/.453	.276	.292	-3.6	3B(36): -2.1, 1B(25): -2.4	0.5
2012	TOR	MLB	29	644	93	24	0	42	110	84	94	13	3	.280/.384/.557	.329	.266	-3.9	1B(68): -5.7, LF(3): -0.0	3.6
2013	*TOR*	*MLB*	*30*	*582*	*78*	*27*	*1*	*27*	*86*	*60*	*98*	*7*	*2*	*.258/.342/.476*	*.286*	*.268*	*-0.2*	*1B -1, 3B -1*	*2.5*

It turns out that the key to unlocking the potential in Encarnacion's bat was to take away his third-baseman's glove. Over the last three seasons, the Artist Formerly Known as E5 has hit .238/.280/.497 while playing third base, and .287/.361/.535 while playing first base or serving as the designated hitter. Encarnacion is penciled in as the regular DH in 2013, but he could find his way back on the field if neither Adam Lind nor Cooper asserts himself as a competent major-league first baseman. Encarnacion agreed to a three-year, $29 million contract extension last summer, a deal that will keep him in Toronto through his age-32 season.

Anthony Gose CF

Born: **8/10/1990** Age: **22**
Bats: **L** Throws: **L** Height: **6' 2"**
Weight: **190** Breakout: **7%**
Improve: **61%** Collapse: **3%**
Attrition: **15%** MLB: **95%**

Comparables:
Curt Flood,Lastings Milledge,Grady Sizemore

YEAR	TEAM	LVL	AGE	PA	R	2B	3B	HR	RBI	BB	SO	SB	CS	AVG_OBP_SLG	TAv	BABIP	BRR	FRAA	WARP
2010	CLR	A+	19	461	67	17	11	4	21	32	103	36	27	.263/.321/.385	.257	.335	0	CF(101): 10.8	1.8
2010	CLR	A+	19	461	67	17	11	4	21	32	103	36	27	.263/.321/.385	.257	.335	0	CF(2): -0.0	1.8
2010	DUN	A+	19	113	21	3	2	3	6	13	29	9	5	.255/.357/.426	.274	.328	1.1	CF(25): 1.2	0.7
2011	NHP	AA	20	587	87	20	7	16	59	62	154	70	15	.253/.349/.415	.269	.332	0	--	0.0
2012	LVG	AAA	21	482	87	21	10	5	43	49	101	34	12	.286/.366/.419	.259	.365	7.5	CF(79): -4.5, LF(3): -0.5	0.8
2012	TOR	MLB	21	189	25	7	3	1	11	17	59	15	3	.223/.303/.319	.226	.340	2.2	RF(24): -0.3, CF(22): 1.5	0.0
2013	*TOR*	*MLB*	*22*	*250*	*32*	*9*	*3*	*3*	*18*	*19*	*69*	*14*	*6*	*.228/.295/.342*	*.229*	*.307*	*1*	*CF -3, RF -0*	*-0.3*

Gose became Toronto's no-question center fielder of the future when Jake Marsinick was shipped to Miami in the trade that netted the Blue Jays Josh Johnson, Jose Reyes, and others. He showed improved plate discipline in September, but is still a little rough around the edges and is expected to spend a fair amount of time at Triple-A in 2013. One of the most athletic players in the organization, Gose possesses true plus speed and sneaky pop. The biggest question is how much he'll hit in the big leagues. After a sluggish April, Gose hit .325 in May and June at Triple-A Las Vegas before earning his first cup of coffee in Toronto. If he learns to handle fastballs on the inner half, he should be at least an average hitter.

Maicer Izturis INF

Born: **9/12/1980** Age: **32**
Bats: **B** Throws: **R** Height: **5' 9"**
Weight: **175** Breakout: **2%**
Improve: **40%** Collapse: **18%**
Attrition: **24%** MLB: **93%**

Comparables:
George Kell,Kevin Seitzer,Edgardo Alfonzo

YEAR	TEAM	LVL	AGE	PA	R	2B	3B	HR	RBI	BB	SO	SB	CS	AVG_OBP_SLG	TAv	BABIP	BRR	FRAA	WARP
2010	ANA	MLB	29	238	27	13	1	3	27	21	27	7	3	.250/.321/.363	.257	.272	-0.4	3B(28): 0.1, 2B(22): -1.2	0.6
2011	ANA	MLB	30	494	51	35	0	5	38	33	65	9	6	.276/.334/.388	.266	.311	1.2	2B(49): -0.3, 3B(37): 0.3	1.9
2012	ANA	MLB	31	319	35	11	0	2	20	25	38	17	2	.256/.320/.315	.230	.289	0.1	3B(30): -1.6, 2B(29): -0.1	-0.7
2013	*TOR*	*MLB*	*32*	*335*	*42*	*18*	*1*	*5*	*29*	*27*	*42*	*11*	*3*	*.268/.333/.390*	*.255*	*.293*	*0.4*	*3B -1, 2B 0*	*0.8*

For the second year in a row, Izturis avoided the DL. He did not, however, come close to matching the playing-time career high he set in 2011, because he was quite healthily very, very bad. It's not that anybody expects power from an undersized middle infielder, but other than two home runs, Izturis hit a lone fly ball that landed within 20 feet of the warning track. Pitchers have long treated him as a non-threat: He saw the sixth-most strikes in 2011, and 11th most in 2012, and now he seems unable to make pitchers pay for that largesse. The contract the Angels gave him was the rare three-year deal for a dedicated reserve that worked out, so perhaps that's why the Blue Jays gave him three years, too.

A.J. Jimenez C

Born: **5/1/1990** Age: **23**
Bats: **R** Throws: **R** Height: **6' 0"**
Weight: **200** Breakout: **6%**
Improve: **55%** Collapse: **9%**
Attrition: **8%** MLB: **88%**

Comparables:
Rich Gedman, Charlie Moore, Rene Rivera

YEAR	TEAM	LVL	AGE	PA	R	2B	3B	HR	RBI	BB	SO	SB	CS	AVG_OBP_SLG	TAv	BABIP	BRR	FRAA	WARP
2010	LNS	A	20	292	35	22	0	4	54	18	56	17	4	.305/.356/.435	.280	.374	0.7	C(59): -0.1	2.4
2011	DUN	A+	21	422	49	29	1	4	52	28	60	11	2	.303/.353/.417	.331	.348	0.1	C(38): 0.4	2.0
2012	NHP	AA	22	113	14	4	1	2	10	5	14	2	3	.257/.295/.371	.330	.278	-0.8	C(7): -0.1	0.3
2013	*TOR*	*MLB*	*23*	*250*	*25*	*13*	*1*	*5*	*24*	*11*	*53*	*7*	*2*	*.241/.277/.361*	*.221*	*.287*	*0.4*	*C -1*	*0.1*

Jimenez's season was cut short by a mid-May elbow injury that required Tommy John surgery to correct. When healthy, he's a contributor behind the plate and in the batter's box, though not a power hitter. He's more likely to hit for average than power and his on-base skills are nothing special, though he does have a knack for putting the ball in play. Defensively, Jimenez shows a strong, accurate arm, soft hands, and solid footwork. He'll begin the year back at Double-A New Hampshire, with a midseason promotion to Triple-A not out of the question.

Kelly Johnson 2B

Born: **2/22/1982** Age: **31**
Bats: **L** Throws: **R** Height: **6' 2"**
Weight: **195** Breakout: **2%**
Improve: **34%** Collapse: **8%**
Attrition: **7%** MLB: **81%**

Comparables:
Bobby Grich, Davey Johnson, Junior Spivey

YEAR	TEAM	LVL	AGE	PA	R	2B	3B	HR	RBI	BB	SO	SB	CS	AVG_OBP_SLG	TAv	BABIP	BRR	FRAA	WARP
2010	ARI	MLB	28	671	93	36	5	26	71	79	148	13	7	.284/.370/.496	.297	.339	-1.5	2B(149): -5.3	4.0
2011	ARI	MLB	29	481	59	23	5	18	49	44	132	13	3	.209/.287/.412	.241	.257	1.1	2B(108): -11.5	-1.4
2011	TOR	MLB	29	132	16	4	2	3	9	16	31	3	3	.270/.364/.417	.290	.346	-0.9	2B(33): -1.4	0.6
2012	TOR	MLB	30	581	61	19	2	16	55	62	159	14	2	.225/.313/.365	.248	.292	1.1	2B(136): -4.6	0.2
2013	*TOR*	*MLB*	*31*	*551*	*74*	*27*	*3*	*17*	*60*	*54*	*129*	*12*	*4*	*.245/.323/.421*	*.259*	*.293*	*0.6*	*2B -3*	*1.7*

It's safe to say Toronto lost the August 2011 trade that sent Aaron Hill and John McDonald to Arizona for Johnson. While Hill experienced a bounce-back season that earned him down-ballot MVP consideration, Johnson continued to rack up strikeouts and exhibit diminishing power. For the second consecutive season, Johnson set a career-worst mark in strikeout percentage, his 27.4 percent mark placing sixth among AL qualifiers. History says that second basemen enter the decline phase sooner than most other position players, and at 31, Johnson may already be approaching the end of his days as a viable starter.

Brett Lawrie 3B

Born: **1/18/1990** Age: **23**
Bats: **R** Throws: **R** Height: **6' 1"**
Weight: **215** Breakout: **6%**
Improve: **63%** Collapse: **1%**
Attrition: **7%** MLB: **97%**

Comparables:
Gordon Beckham, Hank Blalock, Ryan Zimmerman

YEAR	TEAM	LVL	AGE	PA	R	2B	3B	HR	RBI	BB	SO	SB	CS	AVG_OBP_SLG	TAv	BABIP	BRR	FRAA	WARP
2010	HUN	AA	20	609	90	36	16	8	63	47	118	30	13	.285/.345/.451	.274	.349	2.5	2B(131): 5.2	3.2
2011	LVG	AAA	21	329	64	24	6	18	61	26	53	13	2	.353/.415/.661	.349	.383	-1.9	3B(42): 2.7	2.3
2011	TOR	MLB	21	171	26	8	4	9	25	16	31	7	1	.293/.373/.580	.335	.318	0.2	3B(43): 9.3	3.0
2012	TOR	MLB	22	536	73	26	3	11	48	33	86	13	8	.273/.324/.405	.261	.311	2.4	3B(123): 20.5, SS(1): -0.0	3.6
2013	*TOR*	*MLB*	*23*	*456*	*62*	*23*	*5*	*13*	*49*	*28*	*85*	*15*	*6*	*.273/.324/.444*	*.268*	*.311*	*1.1*	*3B 5, 2B -0*	*2.2*

Lawrie wasn't able to match the offensive fireworks of his major-league debut, but he did provide league-average production and stellar defense at the hot corner in his first full season. Despite missing a month down the stretch with an oblique injury, Lawrie led all of baseball in Fielding Runs Above Average with 20.48, edging former Blue Jay Aaron Hill (20.46). His over-the-fence power was mitigated by an inordinate number of groundballs. In the minors, 44.2 percent of balls in play were hit on the ground, but that number spiked to 50.7 percent last year, five percentage points higher than the AL average. If he's able to regain his fly-ball stroke, expect an uptick in power production.

Adam Lind DH

Born: **7/17/1983** Age: **29**
Bats: **L** Throws: **L** Height: **6' 2"**
Weight: **220** Breakout: **5%**
Improve: **41%** Collapse: **9%**
Attrition: **13%** MLB: **86%**

Comparables:
Hank Blalock, Ben Broussard, Micah Hoffpauir

YEAR	TEAM	LVL	AGE	PA	R	2B	3B	HR	RBI	BB	SO	SB	CS	AVG_OBP_SLG	TAv	BABIP	BRR	FRAA	WARP
2010	TOR	MLB	26	613	57	32	3	23	72	38	144	0	0	.237/.287/.425	.245	.277	-2.6	LF(16): -0.6, 1B(11): 0.5	-0.7
2011	TOR	MLB	27	542	56	16	0	26	87	32	107	1	1	.251/.295/.439	.265	.265	2	1B(109): -4.6	-0.1
2012	LVG	AAA	28	143	24	10	0	8	29	15	26	1	0	.392/.448/.664	.348	.436	-3.5	1B(25): -1.6	0.8
2012	TOR	MLB	28	353	28	14	2	11	45	29	61	0	0	.255/.314/.414	.260	.282	-0.1	1B(61): -3.6	-0.4
2013	*TOR*	*MLB*	*29*	*393*	*46*	*20*	*1*	*16*	*55*	*28*	*77*	*1*	*0*	*.267/.322/.462*	*.272*	*.297*	*-0.6*	*1B 0, LF -0*	*1.0*

Lind's 2008, when he hit 35 homers with an OPS over 900, set the world afire and heralded the coming of a new star in Toronto. In the 1,508 plate appearances since, he has hit .246/.296/.428. As you can see, Lind's problems are beautiful multifaceted gemstones, highly prized by the aristocracy for their richness and complexity. Put bluntly, dude can't hit lefties, play defense, or get on base. Other than that, Mrs. Lincoln . . . ? His four-year, $18 million deal expires after this season. Here's hoping he invested wisely.

Mike McCoy UT

Born: **4/2/1981** Age: **32**
Bats: **R** Throws: **R** Height: **5' 10"**
Weight: **180** Breakout: **1%**
Improve: **31%** Collapse: **8%**
Attrition: **10%** MLB: **85%**

Comparables:
Jose Offerman, Jamey Carroll, Glenn Hubbard

YEAR	TEAM	LVL	AGE	PA	R	2B	3B	HR	RBI	BB	SO	SB	CS	AVG_OBP_SLG	TAv	BABIP	BRR	FRAA	WARP
2010	LVG	AAA	29	259	48	14	1	6	26	37	31	17	2	.310/.405/.469	.287	.330	3.7	SS(47): 8.9, CF(5): 0.4	3.0
2010	TOR	MLB	29	90	9	4	0	0	3	8	20	5	1	.195/.267/.244	.198	.258	1.7	2B(14): 1.4, LF(8): 0.6	-0.1
2011	LVG	AAA	30	186	33	6	0	2	20	33	23	14	5	.311/.440/.392	.322	.358	-0.5	SS(12): -0.1, CF(6): -0.0	0.7
2011	TOR	MLB	30	228	26	8	0	2	10	25	41	12	2	.198/.291/.269	.225	.240	2	SS(26): 1.4, CF(16): 0.6	0.1
2012	LVG	AAA	31	349	46	13	1	3	31	58	51	21	10	.263/.386/.349	.250	.306	-0.8	2B(20): 0.1, 3B(18): 0.3	0.3
2012	TOR	MLB	31	56	10	1	0	1	7	4	6	2	1	.173/.232/.250	.183	.178	0.2	2B(8): 0.2, 3B(6): 0.3	-0.4
2013	*TOR*	*MLB*	*32*	*250*	*32*	*9*	*1*	*3*	*17*	*30*	*46*	*13*	*4*	*.230/.324/.319*	*.233*	*.272*	*0.9*	*SS 1, 2B -0*	*0.3*

A prototypical up-and-down Triple-A insurance piece, McCoy has played parts of the last four seasons in the major leagues, collecting more than 90 plate appearances only once. His value lies in his ability to play all over the diamond. In a mere 32 games last year, he saw time at six different positions. McCoy owns a career .273 on-base percentage, but he's an efficient base stealer (84 percent success rate) when he is able to get on.

Mike Nickeas C

Born: **2/13/1983** Age: **30**
Bats: **R** Throws: **R** Height: **6' 1"**
Weight: **215** Breakout: **1%**
Improve: **33%** Collapse: **11%**
Attrition: **14%** MLB: **90%**

Comparables:
Gary Bennett, Jerry Grote, Tom Lampkin

YEAR	TEAM	LVL	AGE	PA	R	2B	3B	HR	RBI	BB	SO	SB	CS	AVG_OBP_SLG	TAv	BABIP	BRR	FRAA	WARP
2010	BIN	AA	27	318	27	15	0	5	33	49	43	1	1	.283/.403/.396	.287	.323	-2	C(77): 0.4, 1B(3): -0.2	2.1
2010	NYN	MLB	27	10	0	0	0	0	0	0	5	0	0	.200/.200/.200	.121	.400	0	C(4): -0.0	-0.1
2011	BUF	AAA	28	192	15	9	0	2	15	16	27	0	0	.214/.286/.304	.192	.239	-1	C(40): 0.5, 1B(1): 0.0	-0.7
2011	NYN	MLB	28	59	4	1	0	1	6	4	11	0	1	.189/.246/.264	.200	.220	0.6	C(20): -0.1	0.0
2012	BUF	AAA	29	75	10	6	0	1	6	6	9	0	0	.364/.405/.500	.314	.397	-0.9	C(20): 0.7	0.5
2012	NYN	MLB	29	122	8	3	0	1	13	8	27	0	0	.174/.242/.229	.189	.220	-0.4	C(45): 0.5	-0.5
2013	*TOR*	*MLB*	*30*	*250*	*23*	*10*	*1*	*4*	*23*	*22*	*50*	*0*	*0*	*.227/.300/.331*	*.226*	*.269*	*-0.4*	*C 0, 1B -0*	*0.2*

Not all major leaguers are the best player to emerge from their high school, but poor Nickeas is only the third-best *catcher* to come from Westlake High School in Southern California. Hell, he's not even the best catcher named Mike from the school, given that Mike Lieberthal also went there. (Gerald Laird is the third, if you were wondering.) At least Nickeas made the honor roll, which probably helped him get into Georgia Tech. Which is the alma mater of Jason Varitek and Matt Wieters. Nickeas can't hit the broad side of a baseball, but he fully lives up to Nichols's Law: He carries a good defensive reputation.

Colby Rasmus CF

Born: **8/11/1986** Age: **26**
Bats: **L** Throws: **L** Height: **6' 3"**
Weight: **200** Breakout: **2%**
Improve: **57%** Collapse: **3%**
Attrition: **7%** MLB: **99%**

Comparables:
Chris Young, Richard Hidalgo, Fred Lynn

YEAR	TEAM	LVL	AGE	PA	R	2B	3B	HR	RBI	BB	SO	SB	CS	AVG_OBP_SLG	TAv	BABIP	BRR	FRAA	WARP
2010	SLN	MLB	23	534	85	28	3	23	66	63	148	12	8	.276/.361/.498	.304	.354	2.4	CF(133): -18.6	2.5
2011	SLN	MLB	24	386	61	14	6	11	40	45	77	5	2	.246/.332/.420	.265	.286	0.4	CF(92): -3.0	0.7
2011	TOR	MLB	24	140	14	10	0	3	13	5	39	0	0	.173/.201/.316	.189	.217	-0.3	CF(35): -0.6	-0.9
2012	TOR	MLB	25	625	75	21	5	23	75	47	149	4	3	.223/.289/.400	.241	.259	0.8	CF(145): -8.4	-0.4
2013	*TOR*	*MLB*	*26*	*567*	*75*	*25*	*4*	*22*	*68*	*50*	*134*	*6*	*3*	*.244/.314/.437*	*.260*	*.286*	*-0.3*	*CF -7*	*1.1*

Look past the hype, the controversy surrounding his exit from St. Louis, and his excellent 2010 season, and you'll see that for the past two seasons Colby Rasmus has been a below-replacement-level player. That's not what was expected of an outfielder many saw as a perennial All-Star. Still, Rasmus is only 26, plays an acceptable center field, walks a little bit, and has some pop in his bat. Also, he posted an 859 OPS in center field as a 23-year-old, so maybe that's still in there somewhere. See? It's a hard thing to look past. Another year of lousy production, however, will make it easier.

Jose Reyes SS

Born: **6/11/1983** Age: **30**
Bats: **B** Throws: **R** Height: **6' 2"**
Weight: **200** Breakout: **5%**
Improve: **36%** Collapse: **3%**
Attrition: **7%** MLB: **94%**

Comparables:
Barry Larkin, Jimmy Rollins, Nomar Garciaparra

YEAR	TEAM	LVL	AGE	PA	R	2B	3B	HR	RBI	BB	SO	SB	CS	AVG_OBP_SLG	TAv	BABIP	BRR	FRAA	WARP
2010	NYN	MLB	27	603	83	29	10	11	54	31	63	30	10	.282/.321/.428	.269	.301	3.9	SS(133): -5.6	3.0
2011	NYN	MLB	28	586	101	31	16	7	44	43	41	39	7	.337/.384/.493	.312	.353	4.6	SS(124): -1.3	5.4
2012	MIA	MLB	29	716	86	37	12	11	57	63	56	40	11	.287/.347/.433	.286	.298	4.4	SS(160): -17.0	2.7
2013	*TOR*	*MLB*	*30*	*648*	*93*	*34*	*11*	*15*	*67*	*50*	*66*	*36*	*9*	*.293/.348/.464*	*.281*	*.306*	*4.2*	*SS -7*	*4.1*

A year after signing a six-year, $106 million deal, Reyes was sent to Toronto in the November blockbuster. Despite a rough year defensively, he hushed critics who claimed that he couldn't stay healthy by appearing in 160 games, his highest total since 2007. Reyes maintained his stolen-base rate as well. Now he'll face a new batch of injury question marks surrounding his ability to avoid leg ailments on the Rogers Centre turf. Assuming he can stay off the disabled list, and that the -17 FRAA that marred his 2012 WARP is an outlier, Reyes should provide significant surplus value in 2013, with his paycheck holding steady at $10 million for one more year before spiking to $16 million in 2014 and $22 million thereafter.

Moises Sierra OF

Born: **9/24/1988** Age: **24**
Bats: **R** Throws: **R** Height: **6' 1"**
Weight: **225** Breakout: **2%**
Improve: **54%** Collapse: **3%**
Attrition: **8%** MLB: **95%**

Comparables:
Ron Swoboda,Leon Durham,Dwight Evans

YEAR	TEAM	LVL	AGE	PA	R	2B	3B	HR	RBI	BB	SO	SB	CS	AVG_OBP_SLG	TAv	BABIP	BRR	FRAA	WARP
2011	NHP	AA	22	551	81	19	3	18	67	39	93	16	14	.277/.342/.436	.270	.307	0	--	0.0
2012	LVG	AAA	23	422	62	16	1	17	63	39	86	7	6	.289/.360/.472	.278	.333	-1.7	RF(72): 0.6, CF(6): -0.2	1.2
2012	TOR	MLB	23	157	14	4	0	6	15	8	44	1	0	.224/.274/.374	.222	.278	-0.7	RF(39): -0.0	-0.5
2013	*TOR*	*MLB*	*24*	*250*	*27*	*9*	*1*	*9*	*31*	*17*	*66*	*2*	*1*	*.235/.292/.397*	*.243*	*.288*	*-0.4*	*RF -3, LF 0*	*-0.2*

Sierra has clubbed 41 home runs over the last two years, a testament to increased trust in his hands that has finally allowed him to tap into his above-average power. He has a chance to hit in the bottom third of a major-league lineup while providing solid defense and a plus arm in right field. Sierra has below-average speed and instincts on the bases, leading to a 62 percent stolen-base success rate in 105 tries. He's aggressive and isn't likely to post impressive batting averages or on-base percentages, but he could carve out a long career as a bench player capable of playing all three outfield positions.

Josh Thole C

Born: **10/28/1986** Age: **26**
Bats: **L** Throws: **R** Height: **6' 2"**
Weight: **215** Breakout: **4%**
Improve: **48%** Collapse: **3%**
Attrition: **15%** MLB: **94%**

Comparables:
Tim McCarver,Clay Dalrymple,Yadier Molina

YEAR	TEAM	LVL	AGE	PA	R	2B	3B	HR	RBI	BB	SO	SB	CS	AVG_OBP_SLG	TAv	BABIP	BRR	FRAA	WARP
2010	BUF	AAA	23	191	20	19	1	2	17	22	25	0	0	.267/.354/.430	.267	.302	-1.3	C(48): -1.2	0.6
2010	NYN	MLB	23	227	17	7	1	3	17	24	25	1	0	.277/.357/.366	.254	.305	1.1	C(61): 1.4	1.2
2011	NYN	MLB	24	386	22	17	0	3	40	38	47	0	2	.268/.345/.344	.253	.300	-3	C(102): 1.8	0.7
2012	NYN	MLB	25	354	24	15	0	1	21	27	50	0	0	.234/.294/.290	.206	.273	0.9	C(99): 0.6	-0.6
2013	*TOR*	*MLB*	*26*	*340*	*34*	*17*	*1*	*5*	*32*	*30*	*44*	*1*	*1*	*.264/.334/.375*	*.249*	*.292*	*-0.6*	*C 1*	*1.2*

Theories abound regarding Thole's drop from useful hitter to miserable one. A September report had him claiming that he'd sold out for more pull power and was returning to a shorter swing, though (small sample alert!) he didn't hit any better after that announcement than he had before. Alternatively, Ty Wigginton concussed him in a collision in May, and Thole had been hitting .284/.356/.370 before the injury. Or maybe it was a fluke. Or maybe the league found his weak point. There are a lot of moving parts and post-hoc rationales, but a lefty catcher who can put up a .350 OBP is worth trying to figure out. Thole also caught Johan Santana's no-hitter, so that's something.

Bobby Wilson C

Born: **4/8/1983** Age: **30**
Bats: **R** Throws: **R** Height: **6' 1"**
Weight: **210** Breakout: **1%**
Improve: **28%** Collapse: **14%**
Attrition: **16%** MLB: **94%**

Comparables:
Mark Salas,Dave Valle,Bill Fahey

YEAR	TEAM	LVL	AGE	PA	R	2B	3B	HR	RBI	BB	SO	SB	CS	AVG_OBP_SLG	TAv	BABIP	BRR	FRAA	WARP
2010	ANA	MLB	27	106	12	6	0	4	15	8	23	0	0	.229/.288/.417	.250	.261	0.7	C(38): -0.4, 1B(1): -0.0	0.4
2011	ANA	MLB	28	127	5	8	0	1	8	10	16	0	2	.189/.252/.288	.196	.208	-0.4	C(47): 0.6, 1B(6): -0.0	-0.3
2012	ANA	MLB	29	201	19	5	0	3	13	15	33	0	0	.211/.277/.292	.218	.243	0.4	C(72): -0.2, 1B(4): 0.1	-0.3
2013	*TOR*	*MLB*	*30*	*250*	*25*	*12*	*0*	*5*	*25*	*19*	*46*	*1*	*0*	*.237/.298/.365*	*.231*	*.268*	*-0.5*	*C -0, 1B -0*	*0.3*

"I'm done with Twitter," Wilson tweeted in July. "Try to be fan friendly and all I get is criticism. I wasn't blessed with 5 tools. I worked hard to get here." It's true: Wilson is a 48th-round pick who racked up more than 100 days of service time in the majors before he ever got to start a game. He carved out a comfortable living as the glove Mike Scioscia could love, and if his batting isn't enough for fans, it's enough to keep a career going for five or 10 years as a backup. His OPS+ in 2012 was 67; 13 teams gave at least 20 games to a backup catcher who was worse, while the Mets, Royals and Orioles gave at least 20 games to *two* backup catchers who were worse. In the end, the Angels waived Wilson and the Jays snagged him. Wilson's Twitter handle, meanwhile, was snatched up by Ms. Betsy Webb, who is "loving life and all it has to offer."

PITCHERS

Mark Buehrle

Born: **3/23/1979** Age: **34**
Bats: **L** Throws: **L** Height: **6' 3"** Weight: **230**
Breakout: **21%** Improve: **50%** Collapse: **18%**
Attrition: **11%** MLB: **92%**

Comparables:
Jarrod Washburn,Mark Hendrickson,Dick Donovan

YEAR	TEAM	LVL	AGE	W	L	SV	G	GS	IP	H	HR	BB	SO	BB9	SO9	GB%	BABIP	WHIP	ERA	FIP	FRA	WARP
2010	CHA	MLB	31	13	13	0	33	33	210^{1}	246	17	49	99	2.1	4.2	47%	.313	1.40	4.28	3.87	4.32	2.8
2011	CHA	MLB	32	13	9	0	31	31	205^{1}	221	21	45	109	2.0	4.8	47%	.294	1.30	3.59	4.02	4.46	2.1
2012	MIA	MLB	33	13	13	0	31	31	202^{1}	197	26	40	125	1.8	5.6	43%	.270	1.17	3.74	4.22	4.83	0.9
2013	*TOR*	*MLB*	*34*	*11*	*8*	*0*	*25*	*25*	*161^{2}*	*178*	*21*	*36*	*94*	*2.0*	*5.2*	*46%*	*.300*	*1.32*	*4.43*	*4.39*	*4.82*	*1.0*

Signed to a four-year, $58 million deal during the Marlins' December 2011 splurge, Buehrle was billed as a top-of-the-rotation complement to injury-prone ace Johnson. But Buehrle is a quality innings-eater, not a dominant force. The lefty's FIP has bloated over the past three years, and that decline in skill figures to continue as he enters his mid-30s. The Marlins sent him north with Reyes in the megadeal, and moving to the American League East isn't likely to do Buehrle any favors. Alex Anthopoulos and the Jays could be in for some buyer's remorse if his soft-tossing ways fail to translate.

Brett Cecil

Born: **7/2/1986** Age: **26**
Bats: **R** Throws: **L** Height: **6' 2"** Weight: **235**
Breakout: **28%** Improve: **66%** Collapse: **18%**
Attrition: **21%** MLB: **95%**

Comparables:
Alex Fernandez,Luke Hochevar,Johnny Cueto

YEAR	TEAM	LVL	AGE	W	L	SV	G	GS	IP	H	HR	BB	SO	BB9	SO9	GB%	BABIP	WHIP	ERA	FIP	FRA	WARP
2010	LVG	AAA	23	2	0	0	2	2	11	13	0	2	11	1.6	9.0	46%	.394	1.36	2.45	2.13	3.37	0.4
2010	TOR	MLB	23	15	7	0	28	28	172^2	175	18	54	117	2.8	6.1	44%	.293	1.33	4.22	4.00	4.59	1.6
2011	LVG	AAA	24	8	2	0	12	12	78^2	89	15	24	63	2.7	7.2	44%	.300	1.44	5.26	5.58	7.48	-0.1
2011	TOR	MLB	24	4	11	0	20	20	123^2	122	22	42	87	3.1	6.3	40%	.267	1.33	4.73	5.13	5.65	-0.2
2012	NHP	AA	25	3	2	0	9	9	42^2	44	2	14	34	3.0	7.2	46%	.294	1.36	3.38	3.34	3.05	0.3
2012	LVG	AAA	25	1	2	0	6	6	39^2	36	1	7	33	1.6	7.5	49%	.311	1.08	2.50	2.93	3.29	1.1
2012	TOR	MLB	25	2	4	0	21	9	61^1	70	11	23	51	3.4	7.5	40%	.324	1.52	5.72	4.99	5.02	0.1
2013	*TOR*	*MLB*	*26*	*6*	*4*	*0*	*14*	*14*	*86^1*	*89*	*12*	*29*	*66*	*3.0*	*6.8*	*47%*	*.297*	*1.37*	*4.55*	*4.49*	*4.95*	*0.5*

Formerly one of the Blue Jays' top pitching prospects, Cecil has spent the last two seasons bouncing between Toronto and Triple-A. He was moved to the major-league bullpen in September and was arguably less effective in that role. In nine starts, he posted a 5.72 ERA and a .286 opponents' batting average. Out of the bullpen, his ERA stayed roughly the same (5.73), but batters hit .326 off of him. He did a much better job of keeping the ball in the yard as a reliever, however, allowing no home runs in 11 innings of work after averaging nearly two long balls per nine innings as a starter. With the Jays' suddenly stacked starting rotation, Cecil may not receive another chance as a starter in Toronto, and his most likely role is that of a multi-inning reliever in the middle innings.

Steve Delabar

Born: **7/17/1983** Age: **29**
Bats: **R** Throws: **R** Height: **6' 6"** Weight: **220**
Breakout: **26%** Improve: **52%** Collapse: **37%**
Attrition: **23%** MLB: **94%**

Comparables:
Jason Motte,Ugueth Urbina,Edwar Ramirez

YEAR	TEAM	LVL	AGE	W	L	SV	G	GS	IP	H	HR	BB	SO	BB9	SO9	GB%	BABIP	WHIP	ERA	FIP	FRA	WARP
2011	HDS	A+	27	1	1	3	7	0	12^1	12	0	8	20	5.8	14.6	—	.414	1.62	4.38	3.14	3.41	0.0
2011	WTN	AA	27	1	3	12	23	0	30^2	23	0	26	30	7.6	8.8	—	.280	1.60	2.05	3.99	4.34	0.0
2011	TAC	AAA	27	1	1	0	10	0	13	11	0	6	18	4.2	12.5	50%	.500	1.31	0.69	2.86	0.21	0.6
2011	SEA	MLB	27	1	1	0	6	0	7	5	1	4	7	5.1	9.0	31%	.267	1.29	2.57	5.06	5.54	-0.1
2012	TAC	AAA	28	0	1	1	9	0	12	11	0	12	12	9.0	9.0	46%	.314	1.92	3.75	4.92	5.02	0.1
2012	SEA	MLB	28	2	1	0	34	0	36^2	23	9	11	46	2.7	11.3	48%	.182	0.93	4.17	5.04	6.27	-0.4
2012	TOR	MLB	28	2	2	0	27	0	29^1	23	3	15	46	4.6	14.1	41%	.323	1.30	3.38	2.77	2.64	0.7
2013	*TOR*	*MLB*	*29*	*2*	*1*	*1*	*45*	*0*	*51^1*	*42*	*6*	*21*	*64*	*3.8*	*11.2*	*42%*	*.296*	*1.24*	*3.68*	*3.45*	*4.00*	*0.8*

Delabar flamed out of pro ball after a little more than four seasons in the Padres organization, never advancing past High-A. After being released in 2008, he went on to pitch in the independent Frontier and Can-Am leagues before taking all of 2010 off to work as a substitute teacher. After a year away from the game, he signed a minor-league deal with Seattle, and he reached the major leagues for six games at the end of 2011. Delabar was traded to Toronto for outfielder Eric Thames last July, and he used his upper-90s fastball to rack up 14.1 strikeouts per nine innings out of the Blue Jays bullpen. He doesn't have the profile of a future closer, with iffy secondary offerings and shaky command, but he should occupy a high-leverage role in the back of the bullpen this year.

R.A. Dickey

Born: **10/29/1974** Age: **38**
Bats: **R** Throws: **R** Height: **6' 3"** Weight: **220**
Breakout: **10%** Improve: **29%** Collapse: **26%**
Attrition: **10%** MLB: **77%**

Comparables:
Dennis Martinez,Derek Lowe,Early Wynn

YEAR	TEAM	LVL	AGE	W	L	SV	G	GS	IP	H	HR	BB	SO	BB9	SO9	GB%	BABIP	WHIP	ERA	FIP	FRA	WARP
2010	BUF	AAA	35	4	2	0	8	8	60^2	55	3	8	37	1.2	5.5	56%	.272	1.04	2.22	3.26	4.04	1.0
2010	NYN	MLB	35	11	9	0	27	26	174^1	165	13	42	104	2.2	5.4	56%	.276	1.19	2.84	3.67	4.39	2.8
2011	NYN	MLB	36	8	13	0	33	32	208^2	202	18	54	134	2.3	5.8	52%	.278	1.23	3.28	3.74	4.38	1.9
2012	NYN	MLB	37	20	6	0	34	33	233^2	192	24	54	230	2.1	8.9	48%	.275	1.05	2.73	3.31	3.74	4.1
2013	*TOR*	*MLB*	*38*	*12*	*8*	*0*	*26*	*26*	*175^1*	*176*	*22*	*54*	*126*	*2.7*	*6.5*	*50%*	*.291*	*1.31*	*4.22*	*4.32*	*4.59*	*1.5*

Dickey released a memoir last season, but he also wrote an instruction manual for how to be a better pitcher: Keep your BABIP and your walks steady while striking out way more guys. He won the NL Cy Young with that approach and will now see if he can keep up the performance in the AL East. The 38-year-old knuckleballer with a sense of humor and a love of English literature climbed Kilimanjaro in the offseason, so fans should love him even if his ERA were 4.73 instead of 2.73. But the two-year, $25 million extension the Jays signed him to means they are banking on more than a lovefest. The acquisition of a reigning Cy Young winner means Toronto wants to play hardball in baseball's toughest division.

Kyle Drabek

Born: 12/8/1987 Age: 25
Bats: R Throws: R Height: 6' 2" Weight: 220
Breakout: 29% Improve: 59% Collapse: 10%
Attrition: 14% MLB: 93%

Comparables:
Jason Hirsh,John Smoltz,Anibal Sanchez

YEAR	TEAM	LVL	AGE	W	L	SV	G	GS	IP	H	HR	BB	SO	BB9	SO9	GB%	BABIP	WHIP	ERA	FIP	FRA	WARP
2010	NHP	AA	22	14	9	0	27	27	162	126	12	68	132	3.8	7.3	50%	.253	1.20	2.94	4.03	4.77	1.2
2010	TOR	MLB	22	0	3	0	3	3	17	18	2	5	12	2.6	6.4	61%	.320	1.35	4.76	4.05	5.23	0.1
2011	LVG	AAA	23	5	4	0	15	15	75	111	12	41	45	4.9	5.4	50%	.340	2.03	7.44	6.38	5.24	0.8
2011	TOR	MLB	23	4	5	0	18	14	78^{2}	87	10	55	51	6.3	5.8	45%	.310	1.81	6.06	5.55	6.60	-0.9
2012	TOR	MLB	24	4	7	0	13	13	71^{1}	67	10	47	47	5.9	5.9	55%	.274	1.60	4.67	5.57	6.49	-0.6
2013	*TOR*	*MLB*	*25*	*4*	*4*	*0*	*12*	*12*	*66^{2}*	*69*	*9*	*34*	*47*	*4.6*	*6.3*	*47%*	*.292*	*1.53*	*5.11*	*5.07*	*5.56*	*-0.0*

The second Tommy John surgery of his career cost Drabek the final four months of the 2012 season and put his status for the first half of 2013 in jeopardy. Before the injury, Drabek showed little progress in controlling his pitches, posting a 9:19 strikeout-to-walk ratio over his final five starts. His pedigree and talent will afford him more opportunities to establish himself in the majors, but the odds are now longer than ever.

Jason Frasor

Born: 8/9/1977 Age: 35
Bats: R Throws: R Height: 5' 10" Weight: 180
Breakout: 18% Improve: 55% Collapse: 30%
Attrition: 21% MLB: 75%

Comparables:
Kiko Calero,Scot Shields,Trever Miller

YEAR	TEAM	LVL	AGE	W	L	SV	G	GS	IP	H	HR	BB	SO	BB9	SO9	GB%	BABIP	WHIP	ERA	FIP	FRA	WARP
2010	TOR	MLB	32	3	4	4	69	0	63^{2}	61	4	27	65	3.8	9.2	47%	.318	1.38	3.68	3.28	3.32	1.3
2011	CHA	MLB	33	1	2	0	20	0	17^{2}	20	3	11	20	5.6	10.2	35%	.354	1.75	5.09	5.04	4.15	0.1
2011	TOR	MLB	33	2	1	0	44	0	42^{1}	38	4	15	37	3.2	7.9	41%	.283	1.25	2.98	3.75	4.36	0.4
2012	DUN	A+	34	0	0	0	2	0	2	0	0	0	4	0.0	18.0	1.%	.000	0.00	0.00	-0.61	1.21	0.1
2012	TOR	MLB	34	1	1	0	50	0	43^{2}	42	6	22	53	4.5	10.9	42%	.333	1.47	4.12	4.05	5.23	0.1
2013	*TOR*	*MLB*	*35*	*2*	*1*	*1*	*45*	*0*	*41^{2}*	*38*	*5*	*18*	*42*	*3.9*	*9.1*	*43%*	*.298*	*1.35*	*4.07*	*4.04*	*4.42*	*0.4*

Frasor missed nearly two months of the second half with a right forearm strain, and was used exclusively in low-leverage situations upon his return in September. Effectiveness against right-handed hitters has allowed him to carve out a solid-if-unspectacular nine-year career, but his lack of an effective out pitch against lefties limits him to a middle-relief role.

Justin Germano

Born: 8/6/1982 Age: 30
Bats: R Throws: R Height: 6' 3" Weight: 210
Breakout: 14% Improve: 39% Collapse: 20%
Attrition: 19% MLB: 88%

Comparables:
Moose Haas,Jim Archer,Bob Friend

YEAR	TEAM	LVL	AGE	W	L	SV	G	GS	IP	H	HR	BB	SO	BB9	SO9	GB%	BABIP	WHIP	ERA	FIP	FRA	WARP
2010	AKR	AA	27	2	1	0	7	1	19^{1}	17	0	4	16	1.9	7.5	61%	.298	1.09	2.80	2.32	3.50	0.4
2010	COH	AAA	27	3	2	1	17	6	53^{1}	49	8	10	37	1.7	6.2	52%	.255	1.11	3.38	4.47	5.20	0.2
2010	CLE	MLB	27	0	3	0	23	1	35^{1}	27	6	8	29	2.0	7.4	42%	.216	0.99	3.31	4.80	5.24	0.0
2011	COH	AAA	28	1	2	3	16	6	49	50	5	4	39	0.7	7.2	—	.315	1.10	4.22	3.40	3.70	0.0
2011	CLE	MLB	28	0	1	0	9	0	12^{2}	15	1	5	5	3.6	3.6	38%	.298	1.58	5.68	4.96	4.92	0.0
2012	PAW	AAA	29	9	4	0	17	16	105	82	15	13	72	1.1	6.2	48%	.220	0.90	2.40	4.16	5.32	-0.4
2012	BOS	MLB	29	0	0	0	1	0	5^{2}	5	0	2	7	3.2	11.1	33%	.333	1.24	0.00	1.63	1.14	0.3
2012	CHN	MLB	29	2	10	0	13	12	64	81	7	19	45	2.7	6.3	48%	.339	1.56	6.75	4.37	5.01	0.3
2013	*TOR*	*MLB*	*30*	*4*	*3*	*0*	*21*	*10*	*75^{1}*	*84*	*12*	*19*	*46*	*2.3*	*5.5*	*49%*	*.296*	*1.37*	*4.94*	*4.81*	*5.37*	*0.1*

The name Germano sounds well traveled, with the illusion to Germany and the rather Italian tinge at the end. Germano himself is well-travelled, with stops in San Diego, Cincinnati, San Diego again, Japan, Cleveland, Boston, and Chicago. As with many pitchers similarly well-travelled, he has not traveled very well, unless you consider him a wandering earned-run salesman of sorts. Germano has traveled once again to Toronto, where he has exciting possibilities as a bad reliever or an awful starter.

J.A. Happ

Born: 10/19/1982 Age: 30
Bats: L Throws: L Height: 6' 7" Weight: 200
Breakout: 25% Improve: 64% Collapse: 12%
Attrition: 15% MLB: 89%

Comparables:
Jason Jennings,Ted Lilly,Randy Wolf

YEAR	TEAM	LVL	AGE	W	L	SV	G	GS	IP	H	HR	BB	SO	BB9	SO9	GB%	BABIP	WHIP	ERA	FIP	FRA	WARP
2010	CLR	A+	27	0	1	0	1	1	3	3	0	0	2	0.0	6.0	64%	.273	1.00	6.00	2.10	4.42	0.0
2010	REA	AA	27	1	0	0	3	3	12^{1}	18	3	4	10	2.9	7.3	51%	.303	1.79	8.05	6.12	7.19	-0.1
2010	LEH	AAA	27	0	1	0	5	4	22^{1}	26	3	15	22	6.1	8.9	51%	.348	1.84	4.84	5.09	5.19	0.0
2010	HOU	MLB	27	5	4	0	13	13	72	60	7	35	61	4.4	7.6	41%	.265	1.32	3.75	4.18	4.82	0.3
2010	PHI	MLB	27	1	0	0	3	3	15^{1}	13	1	12	9	7.0	5.3	37%	.250	1.63	1.76	5.13	5.03	0.0
2011	OKL	AAA	28	1	0	0	3	3	18	11	0	9	16	4.5	8.0	—	.239	1.11	1.50	3.51	3.81	0.0
2011	HOU	MLB	28	6	15	0	28	28	156^{1}	157	21	83	134	4.8	7.7	35%	.298	1.54	5.35	4.66	4.85	0.7
2012	HOU	MLB	29	7	9	0	18	18	104^{1}	112	17	39	98	3.4	8.5	48%	.315	1.45	4.83	4.53	4.81	0.7
2012	TOR	MLB	29	3	2	0	10	6	40^{1}	35	2	17	46	3.8	10.3	38%	.317	1.29	4.69	2.75	2.62	1.3
2013	*TOR*	*MLB*	*30*	*8*	*7*	*0*	*22*	*22*	*119*	*120*	*17*	*52*	*98*	*4.0*	*7.4*	*40%*	*.296*	*1.45*	*4.82*	*4.72*	*5.24*	*0.4*

Last October, Happ became the eighth Toronto pitcher to end his season early when a break was discovered in his right foot. This season you'd expect him to step back into his slot in the back of the rotation, and on a team that hadn't just acquired three good starting pitchers, that would happen. Happ should be a perfectly cromulent fourth or fifth starter. He gets his strikeouts (a career high 9.0 SO9 last season), but walks and hard-hit balls have been a problem. He's always been a starter, but on this team he's a long man out of the pen. Considering his four-seam fastball has jumped 1.6 mph to 91.2 mph since arriving in the majors, maybe that's a blessing in disguise.

Casey Janssen
Born: **9/17/1981** Age: **31**
Bats: **R** Throws: **R** Height: **6' 4"** Weight: **225**
Breakout: **27%** Improve: **54%** Collapse: **27%**
Attrition: **6%** MLB: **92%**
Comparables:
Bruce Sutter,Gene Garber,Chad Qualls

YEAR	TEAM	LVL	AGE	W	L	SV	G	GS	IP	H	HR	BB	SO	BB9	SO9	GB%	BABIP	WHIP	ERA	FIP	FRA	WARP
2010	TOR	MLB	28	5	2	0	56	0	68^2	74	8	21	63	2.8	8.3	47%	.327	1.38	3.67	3.82	4.37	0.6
2011	NHP	AA	29	0	0	0	5	0	5	1	0	1	7	1.8	12.6	—	.111	0.40	0.00	1.21	1.32	0.0
2011	LVG	AAA	29	0	0	0	1	0	2	1	0	0	3	0.0	13.5	—	.250	0.50	0.00	0.78	0.85	0.0
2011	TOR	MLB	29	6	0	2	55	0	55^2	47	2	14	53	2.3	8.6	49%	.296	1.10	2.26	2.49	3.31	1.1
2012	TOR	MLB	30	1	1	22	62	0	63^2	44	7	11	67	1.6	9.5	44%	.240	0.86	2.54	3.03	3.50	1.2
2013	*TOR*	*MLB*	*31*	*2*	*1*	*5*	*46*	*0*	49^2	*48*	*6*	*14*	*44*	*2.5*	*8.1*	*48%*	*.301*	*1.25*	*3.80*	*3.84*	*4.13*	*0.7*

After two years of serving as a solid middle reliever, Janssen received an opportunity to close after Sergio Santos was lost for the year with a right shoulder injury. Janssen converted 22 of 25 save chances while setting career bests in strikeouts, hits, and walks per nine innings. Not too shabby. Janssen is a versatile pitcher capable of working in any of the late innings, but not the overwhelming power arm of your typical major-league closer, relying more on deception and an above-average fastball/slider combination to retire hitters on either side. No one said typical was better.

Jeremy Jeffress
Born: **9/21/1987** Age: **25**
Bats: **R** Throws: **R** Height: **6' 1"** Weight: **210**
Breakout: **31%** Improve: **53%** Collapse: **14%**
Attrition: **5%** MLB: **90%**
Comparables:
Chan Ho Park,Jon Meloan,Dustin McGowan

YEAR	TEAM	LVL	AGE	W	L	SV	G	GS	IP	H	HR	BB	SO	BB9	SO9	GB%	BABIP	WHIP	ERA	FIP	FRA	WARP
2010	WIS	A	22	0	0	0	5	0	8	0	0	3	14	3.4	15.8	60%	.000	0.38	0.00	1.61	2.07	0.3
2010	BRV	A+	22	0	0	1	8	0	10	10	0	7	14	6.3	12.6	44%	.370	1.70	5.40	2.74	3.77	0.1
2010	HUN	AA	22	1	1	3	11	0	14^1	8	0	2	15	1.3	9.4	63%	.229	0.70	1.26	1.92	2.93	0.3
2010	MIL	MLB	22	1	0	0	10	0	10	8	0	6	8	5.4	7.2	57%	.286	1.40	2.70	3.31	3.69	0.2
2011	NWA	AA	23	1	3	0	9	8	31^2	32	2	22	20	6.3	5.7	63%	.274	1.71	4.26	5.21	6.61	-0.1
2011	OMA	AAA	23	2	3	3	16	3	24	27	5	18	24	6.8	9.0	53%	.419	1.88	7.12	6.87	7.29	0.0
2011	KCA	MLB	23	1	1	1	14	0	15^1	12	1	11	13	6.5	7.6	58%	.262	1.50	4.70	4.37	5.90	-0.1
2012	NWA	AA	24	0	0	1	1	0	1^1	0	0	1	3	6.8	20.2	%	.000	0.75	0.00	1.03	0.19	0.1
2012	OMA	AAA	24	5	4	2	37	0	58	52	4	25	61	3.9	9.5	51%	.313	1.33	4.97	3.75	4.44	0.4
2012	KCA	MLB	24	0	0	0	13	0	13^1	19	0	13	13	8.8	8.8	49%	.404	2.40	6.75	4.02	4.91	0.0
2013	*TOR*	*MLB*	*25*	*1*	*1*	*0*	*23*	*1*	33^1	*32*	*4*	*21*	*32*	*5.5*	*8.7*	*49%*	*.303*	*1.57*	*5.02*	*4.73*	*5.45*	*-0.0*

Jeffress is Nuke LaLoosh incarnate, complete with fabled million-dollar arm and 10-cent head. With the raw power to light up the radar gun with triple digits, he can't find the strike zone to save his life. As one might expect, those control issues have been his downfall. He seemed to piece together a decent performance in Triple-A last summer and was a bit unlucky in the ERA department with a 60 percent strand rate. But the Royals ran out of patience and sold him to Toronto for cash considerations.

Chad Jenkins
Born: **12/22/1987** Age: **25**
Bats: **R** Throws: **R** Height: **6' 5"** Weight: **235**
Breakout: **31%** Improve: **58%** Collapse: **19%**
Attrition: **27%** MLB: **76%**
Comparables:
Greg Reynolds,Brad Rigby,Mike Esposito

YEAR	TEAM	LVL	AGE	W	L	SV	G	GS	IP	H	HR	BB	SO	BB9	SO9	GB%	BABIP	WHIP	ERA	FIP	FRA	WARP
2010	LNS	A	22	5	4	0	13	13	79^1	87	5	13	64	1.5	7.3	56%	.327	1.26	3.63	3.34	4.92	0.5
2010	DUN	A+	22	2	6	0	13	13	62^1	73	6	18	42	2.6	6.1	54%	.307	1.46	4.33	4.21	5.56	-0.3
2011	DUN	A+	23	4	5	0	11	11	67^1	71	3	14	44	1.9	5.9	58%	.305	1.26	3.07	3.28	5.28	0.1
2011	NHP	AA	23	5	7	0	16	16	100^1	93	8	27	74	2.4	6.6	—	.284	1.20	4.13	3.84	4.17	0.0
2012	NHP	AA	24	5	9	0	20	20	114^1	145	17	31	57	2.4	4.5	49%	.327	1.54	4.96	5.08	8.23	0.0
2012	TOR	MLB	24	1	3	0	13	3	32	32	5	11	16	3.1	4.5	43%	.262	1.34	4.50	5.20	5.30	0.0
2013	*TOR*	*MLB*	*25*	*3*	*4*	*0*	*10*	*10*	52^1	*65*	*9*	*19*	*24*	*3.3*	*4.1*	*48%*	*.306*	*1.61*	*6.08*	*5.61*	*6.61*	*-0.5*

Only injuries in Toronto got Jenkins the promotion to make his major-league debut last year. His performance did little to warrant it. The 20th pick of the 2009 draft, he nearly doubled his home-run rate while striking out fewer than five batters per nine innings in his second year at Double-A New Hampshire. He was used mostly in low-leverage situations out of the bullpen before wrapping up the year with a trio of unspectacular starts. His fly-ball tendencies and inability to miss bats make him a risky option for a team that fancies itself a contender, but he does have two quality pitches, a low-90s fastball and an above-average slider, which could make him a useful bullpen piece down the road.

Josh Johnson
Born: 1/31/1984 Age: 29
Bats: L Throws: R Height: 6' 8" Weight: 250
Breakout: 16% Improve: 46% Collapse: 24%
Attrition: 7% MLB: 94%
Comparables:
Barry Zito,Erik Bedard,CC Sabathia

YEAR	TEAM	LVL	AGE	W	L	SV	G	GS	IP	H	HR	BB	SO	BB9	SO9	GB%	BABIP	WHIP	ERA	FIP	FRA	WARP
2010	FLO	MLB	26	11	6	0	28	28	183^{2}	155	7	48	186	2.4	9.1	48%	.298	1.11	2.30	2.44	2.82	4.8
2011	FLO	MLB	27	3	1	0	9	9	60^{1}	39	2	20	56	3.0	8.4	52%	.239	0.98	1.64	2.61	3.38	1.1
2012	MIA	MLB	28	8	14	0	31	31	191^{1}	180	14	65	165	3.1	7.8	47%	.302	1.28	3.81	3.44	3.80	2.8
2013	*TOR*	*MLB*	*29*	*10*	*5*	*0*	*21*	*21*	*134^{2}*	*127*	*13*	*39*	*121*	*2.6*	*8.1*	*48%*	*.300*	*1.23*	*3.52*	*3.53*	*3.83*	*2.4*

A spate of arm injuries—ranging from a torn elbow ligament in 2007 to shoulder inflammation in 2011—finally began to take its toll on Johnson, who made 31 starts for the first time since 2009, but did so as a number-two caliber starter, not as one of the most dominant pitchers in the National League. The 29-year-old is still plenty useful, even with his fastball down to 93 mph (from 95), because he pairs it with an outstanding slider and above-average command. If his health holds up for a second consecutive year, Johnson has the weapons to succeed despite moving to a more hitter-friendly ballpark in a tougher league. Johnson is the most talented starter the Blue Jays have had at their disposal since they sent Roy Halladay to the Phillies in December 2009.

Aaron Laffey
Born: 4/15/1985 Age: 28
Bats: L Throws: L Height: 6' 1" Weight: 200
Breakout: 15% Improve: 42% Collapse: 21%
Attrition: 14% MLB: 81%
Comparables:
Curt Simmons,Tom Glavine,Eric DuBose

YEAR	TEAM	LVL	AGE	W	L	SV	G	GS	IP	H	HR	BB	SO	BB9	SO9	GB%	BABIP	WHIP	ERA	FIP	FRA	WARP
2010	LKC	A	25	0	0	0	2	1	2	2	1	0	3	0.0	13.5	80%	.250	1.00	4.50	7.11	5.88	0.0
2010	AKR	AA	25	0	0	0	1	0	1	1	0	0	0	0.0	0.0	1.%	.333	1.00	0.00	3.36	4.27	0.0
2010	COH	AAA	25	0	1	0	10	4	27	29	1	16	12	5.3	4.0	46%	.306	1.67	3.67	4.66	6.95	-0.4
2010	CLE	MLB	25	2	3	0	29	5	55^{2}	62	1	28	28	4.5	4.5	52%	.316	1.62	4.53	3.89	4.78	0.2
2011	SWB	AAA	26	0	1	0	2	1	3^{2}	5	0	2	1	4.9	2.5	46%	.455	1.91	7.36	5.15	5.92	0.0
2011	NYA	MLB	26	2	1	0	11	0	10^{2}	13	0	5	6	4.2	5.1	38%	.351	1.69	3.38	3.91	3.65	0.2
2011	SEA	MLB	26	1	1	0	36	0	42^{2}	54	7	16	24	3.4	5.1	54%	.315	1.64	4.01	5.26	5.52	-0.4
2012	LVG	AAA	27	3	5	0	11	11	63^{2}	77	6	20	38	2.8	5.4	56%	.327	1.52	4.52	4.78	6.41	0.1
2012	TOR	MLB	27	4	6	0	22	16	100^{2}	100	17	37	48	3.3	4.3	50%	.258	1.36	4.56	5.54	6.44	-0.6
2013	*TOR*	*MLB*	*28*	*5*	*4*	*0*	*39*	*12*	*94^{2}*	*106*	*12*	*38*	*51*	*3.6*	*4.9*	*53%*	*.302*	*1.52*	*5.22*	*4.97*	*5.67*	*-0.2*

Cleveland gave up on Laffey as a starting pitcher in 2010, but injuries challenged the Blue Jays' depth and put them in a position to offer him 16 big-league starts last year. His inability to miss bats makes it unlikely that he'll be able to sustain the sliver of success he had in 2012, but he's the kind of depth piece organizations like to have around, preferably at Triple-A.

Brad Lincoln
Born: 5/25/1985 Age: 28
Bats: L Throws: R Height: 6' 1" Weight: 210
Breakout: 16% Improve: 47% Collapse: 24%
Attrition: 13% MLB: 91%
Comparables:
Johnny Podres,John Smiley,Eric Milton

YEAR	TEAM	LVL	AGE	W	L	SV	G	GS	IP	H	HR	BB	SO	BB9	SO9	GB%	BABIP	WHIP	ERA	FIP	FRA	WARP
2010	IND	AAA	25	7	5	0	17	17	94	83	9	24	84	2.3	8.0	42%	.280	1.14	4.12	3.74	5.09	0.9
2010	PIT	MLB	25	1	4	0	11	9	52^{2}	66	9	15	25	2.6	4.3	39%	.306	1.54	6.66	5.52	6.26	-0.3
2011	IND	AAA	26	7	8	0	19	19	111^{2}	115	6	21	94	1.7	7.6	43%	.314	1.22	4.19	3.06	4.39	0.9
2011	PIT	MLB	26	2	3	0	12	8	47^{2}	54	4	16	29	3.0	5.5	53%	.312	1.47	4.72	4.00	4.39	0.2
2012	IND	AAA	27	1	0	0	2	2	12	10	0	0	9	0.0	6.8	57%	.286	0.83	2.25	2.16	2.94	0.3
2012	PIT	MLB	27	4	2	1	28	5	59^{1}	51	8	14	60	2.1	9.1	39%	.276	1.10	2.73	3.62	3.07	1.2
2012	TOR	MLB	27	1	0	0	24	0	28^{2}	29	6	10	28	3.1	8.8	47%	.291	1.36	5.65	4.86	6.23	-0.2
2013	*TOR*	*MLB*	*28*	*5*	*3*	*0*	*21*	*11*	*73*	*79*	*11*	*21*	*54*	*2.6*	*6.7*	*43%*	*.300*	*1.37*	*4.79*	*4.54*	*5.20*	*0.2*

Despite making all 88 of his minor-league appearances as a starting pitcher, most of Lincoln's major-league work has come out of the bullpen. Toronto acquired him from Pittsburgh for Travis Snider at last summer's trade deadline in an exchange of disappointing ex-first-round picks. While he was effective in Pittsburgh, Lincoln wasn't the same pitcher in the American League, putting more runners on base while surrendering more home runs and striking fewer hitters out. By September, Lincoln was mostly relegated to middle-inning work, entering in high-leverage situations in only two of his dozen September appearances. He fares much better against left-handed batters, so he could have a future as a lefty specialist.

Aaron Loup
Born: 12/19/1987 Age: 25
Bats: L Throws: L Height: 6' 0" Weight: 180
Breakout: 18% Improve: 49% Collapse: 28%
Attrition: 7% MLB: 93%
Comparables:
Oscar Villarreal,Julian Tavarez,Donnie Moore

YEAR	TEAM	LVL	AGE	W	L	SV	G	GS	IP	H	HR	BB	SO	BB9	SO9	GB%	BABIP	WHIP	ERA	FIP	FRA	WARP
2010	LNS	A	22	3	2	2	35	5	73^{1}	79	4	22	73	2.7	9.0	45%	.366	1.38	4.54	3.43	4.94	0.7
2011	DUN	A+	23	4	3	5	48	0	65^{2}	67	6	27	56	3.7	7.7	51%	.342	1.43	4.66	4.38	4.97	0.1
2012	NHP	AA	24	0	3	3	37	0	45^{1}	46	4	14	43	2.8	8.5	51%	.326	1.32	2.78	3.71	3.34	0.6
2012	TOR	MLB	24	0	2	0	33	0	30^{2}	26	0	2	21	0.6	6.2	57%	.277	0.91	2.64	1.87	2.69	0.7
2013	*TOR*	*MLB*	*25*	*1*	*1*	*0*	*24*	*1*	*34*	*37*	*4*	*12*	*25*	*3.3*	*6.5*	*47%*	*.308*	*1.46*	*4.97*	*4.32*	*5.40*	*-0.0*

One of the most pleasant surprises in the organization last year, Loup reached Toronto in the second half and proved to be valuable in left-on-left matchups in the later innings. A ninth-round pick out of Tulane in 2009, Loup offers a straight low-90s fastball, a slurvy slider, and a deceptive, jerky delivery that is particularly difficult for left-handed hitters to track. He doesn't have the stuff to profile in the later innings, but he could have a few years of solid sixth- and seventh-inning work in his future.

Brandon Lyon

Born: 8/10/1979 Age: **33**
Bats: **R** Throws: **R** Height: **6' 2"** Weight: **200**
Breakout: **20%** Improve: **36%** Collapse: **33%**
Attrition: **20%** MLB: **89%**

Comparables:
Mike Timlin, Lee Gardner, LaTroy Hawkins

YEAR	TEAM	LVL	AGE	W	L	SV	G	GS	IP	H	HR	BB	SO	BB9	SO9	GB%	BABIP	WHIP	ERA	FIP	FRA	WARP
2010	HOU	MLB	30	6	6	20	79	0	78	68	2	31	54	3.6	6.2	42%	.272	1.27	3.12	3.36	3.26	1.3
2011	OKL	AAA	31	0	0	0	2	0	2	2	0	0	0	0.0	0.0	—	.286	1.00	0.00	3.78	4.11	0.0
2011	HOU	MLB	31	3	3	4	15	0	13^{1}	27	4	5	6	3.4	4.1	47%	.411	2.40	11.48	7.12	7.69	-0.3
2012	HOU	MLB	32	0	2	0	37	0	36	37	3	11	35	2.8	8.8	37%	.330	1.33	3.25	3.36	3.12	0.6
2012	TOR	MLB	32	4	0	1	30	0	25	19	2	9	28	3.2	10.1	42%	.266	1.12	2.88	3.05	3.35	0.5
2013	*TOR*	*MLB*	*33*	*2*	*1*	*2*	*48*	*0*	*45^{1}*	*45*	*5*	*15*	*36*	*3.0*	*7.1*	*43%*	*.293*	*1.33*	*4.07*	*4.04*	*4.42*	*0.5*

A good if not great reliever, Lyon gets a bit of a bum rap because he was on the receiving end of Ed Wade's silly three-year contract offer. Even if it was a bad contract the moment crayon met paper, it's hard to blame Lyon for that. To his credit, he pitched well as an Astro when he was healthy, a four-word disclaimer that conveniently leaves out the 2011 season, when a tear in his labrum and a detached biceps tendon made pitching difficult and pitching *well* impossible. He bounced back last season, although the surgery took a couple of ticks off his fastball. A free agent, he'll find a one-year landing spot for his 50 perfectly adequate innings somewhere.

Deck McGuire

Born: 6/23/1989 Age: **24**
Bats: **R** Throws: **R** Height: **6' 7"** Weight: **220**
Breakout: **18%** Improve: **53%** Collapse: **28%**
Attrition: **33%** MLB: **86%**

Comparables:
Kyle Lohse, Collin Balester, Jose Acevedo

YEAR	TEAM	LVL	AGE	W	L	SV	G	GS	IP	H	HR	BB	SO	BB9	SO9	GB%	BABIP	WHIP	ERA	FIP	FRA	WARP
2011	DUN	A+	22	7	4	0	19	18	104^{2}	89	9	38	102	3.3	8.8	41%	.260	1.21	2.75	3.82	4.19	0.6
2011	NHP	AA	22	2	1	0	4	3	20^{2}	20	4	7	22	3.0	9.6	—	.296	1.31	4.35	4.96	5.39	0.0
2012	NHP	AA	23	5	15	0	28	28	144	162	22	62	97	3.9	6.1	41%	.310	1.56	5.88	5.26	7.36	-0.6
2013	*TOR*	*MLB*	*24*	*2*	*3*	*0*	*7*	*7*	*39^{2}*	*45*	*7*	*19*	*25*	*4.4*	*5.7*	*40%*	*.301*	*1.63*	*6.01*	*5.67*	*6.53*	*-0.4*

Toronto's top pick in the 2010 draft, McGuire was expected to move quickly but he hit a wall at Double-A New Hampshire last year. He led the Eastern League with 1.38 home runs allowed per nine innings and placed third with a 1.56 WHIP. McGuire was never expected to develop into an ace, but he was viewed as a polished arm who would assert himself as a solid back-of-the-rotation innings-eater in short order. The Jays could have used a guy like that when injuries devastated their starting rotation last year, but McGuire never inspired enough confidence to warrant a promotion. The good news is that, if he can ever solve Double-A hitters, he no longer has the pinball machine environment of Las Vegas to look forward to at the next level.

Brandon Morrow

Born: 7/26/1984 Age: **28**
Bats: **R** Throws: **R** Height: **6' 4"** Weight: **195**
Breakout: **22%** Improve: **53%** Collapse: **29%**
Attrition: **15%** MLB: **94%**

Comparables:
Edinson Volquez, Hideo Nomo, Daisuke Matsuzaka

YEAR	TEAM	LVL	AGE	W	L	SV	G	GS	IP	H	HR	BB	SO	BB9	SO9	GB%	BABIP	WHIP	ERA	FIP	FRA	WARP
2010	TOR	MLB	25	10	7	0	26	26	146^{1}	136	11	66	178	4.1	10.9	40%	.342	1.38	4.49	3.13	3.95	2.9
2011	DUN	A+	26	0	2	0	3	3	9^{1}	13	0	6	11	5.8	10.6	47%	.294	2.04	7.71	2.96	2.64	0.2
2011	TOR	MLB	26	11	11	0	30	30	179^{1}	162	21	69	203	3.5	10.2	37%	.299	1.29	4.72	3.67	4.03	2.9
2012	DUN	A+	27	0	0	0	2	2	6	8	0	3	6	4.5	9.0	47%	.471	1.83	1.50	2.89	3.00	0.2
2012	NHP	AA	27	1	0	0	3	3	14^{1}	10	2	3	12	1.9	7.5	39%	.216	0.91	2.51	3.97	4.73	0.0
2012	TOR	MLB	27	10	7	0	21	21	124^{2}	98	12	41	108	3.0	7.8	42%	.252	1.11	2.96	3.60	4.14	1.9
2013	*TOR*	*MLB*	*28*	*9*	*5*	*0*	*21*	*21*	*118^{1}*	*103*	*13*	*50*	*126*	*3.8*	*9.6*	*39%*	*.292*	*1.29*	*3.81*	*3.77*	*4.14*	*1.8*

Perpetually everyone's favorite breakout candidate, Morrow finally broke out last season. Then he just broke. Morrow's strained oblique muscle was severe enough to cause him to miss 64 games. On a per-inning basis Morrow was more valuable than ever, but while his ERA looked good, his strikeouts didn't keep up. On the plus side, his walks declined for a third straight season, but his strikeouts, always his calling card and the reason he's perpetually everyone's favorite breakout candidate, dropped off significantly from over 10 to under 8 per nine innings. Without the Ks, Morrow is just another guy, but if he's fully recovered from his oblique he stands a good chance to put in that excellent season everyone knows is in there somewhere.

Sean Nolin

Born: 12/26/1989 **Age:** 23
Bats: L **Throws:** L **Height:** 6' 6" **Weight:** 235
Breakout: 26% **Improve:** 59% **Collapse:** 21%
Attrition: 24% **MLB:** 96%
Comparables:
Scott Olsen, Danny Duffy, Andrew Oliver

YEAR	TEAM	LVL	AGE	W	L	SV	G	GS	IP	H	HR	BB	SO	BB9	SO9	GB%	BABIP	WHIP	ERA	FIP	FRA	WARP
2010	BLJ	Rk	20	0	0	0	1	1	2	1	0	1	4	4.5	18.0	%	.500	1.00	0.00	1.01	1.94	0.1
2010	AUB	A-	20	0	2	0	6	6	19^{1}	25	0	9	22	4.2	10.3	46%	.424	1.76	6.06	2.90	3.39	0.5
2011	LNS	A	21	4	4	1	25	21	108^{1}	102	9	31	113	2.6	9.4	—	.321	1.23	3.49	3.32	3.61	0.0
2012	DUN	A+	22	9	0	0	17	15	86^{1}	72	7	21	90	2.2	9.4	45%	.293	1.08	2.19	3.23	3.76	1.0
2012	NHP	AA	22	1	0	0	3	3	15	9	0	6	18	3.6	10.8	42%	.273	1.00	1.20	2.20	2.33	0.2
2013	*TOR*	*MLB*	*23*	*2*	*2*	*0*	*7*	*7*	*34*	*35*	*5*	*15*	*30*	*4.0*	*7.8*	*43%*	*.306*	*1.47*	*4.95*	*4.67*	*5.38*	*0.1*

Thanks to the trades with the Mets and Marlins, Nolin will begin the season as one of the best prospects in Toronto's system. But thanks to those same deals, there isn't much room for him on the big-league roster. Fortunately, neither qualifies as a huge problem. Nolin has more development left anyway, with just 15 innings thrown above A-ball, although his overall refinement hints that he may be ready sometime this season.

Darren Oliver

Born: 10/6/1970 **Age:** 42
Bats: R **Throws:** L **Height:** 6' 3" **Weight:** 200
Breakout: 35% **Improve:** 49% **Collapse:** 40%
Attrition: 12% **MLB:** 72%
Comparables:
Larry Andersen, Trevor Hoffman, Hoyt Wilhelm

YEAR	TEAM	LVL	AGE	W	L	SV	G	GS	IP	H	HR	BB	SO	BB9	SO9	GB%	BABIP	WHIP	ERA	FIP	FRA	WARP
2010	TEX	MLB	39	1	2	1	64	0	61^{2}	53	4	15	65	2.2	9.5	49%	.310	1.10	2.48	2.61	3.11	1.1
2011	TEX	MLB	40	5	5	2	61	0	51	47	3	11	44	1.9	7.8	43%	.282	1.14	2.29	2.81	2.89	1.3
2012	TOR	MLB	41	3	4	2	62	0	56^{2}	43	3	15	52	2.4	8.3	46%	.272	1.02	2.06	2.90	3.56	0.9
2013	*TOR*	*MLB*	*42*	*3*	*1*	*1*	*51*	*0*	*46*	*42*	*5*	*13*	*41*	*2.6*	*8.1*	*46%*	*.293*	*1.21*	*3.43*	*3.68*	*3.72*	*0.8*

People see Oliver as a LOOGY. He isn't. He's just a good relief pitcher. However, baseball is a grind and Oliver will be 43 years young next season. At press time he didn't know if he wanted to do it anymore. It's understandable, after 19 years with nine teams, that he might want to call it a career. Over the past two seasons, Oliver has held a reverse platoon split, which is something for someone who holds lefties to just over a 600 OPS. If he decides he's got one more in him, expect more of the same.

Roberto Osuna

Born: 7/2/1995 **Age:** 17
Bats: R **Throws:** R **Height:** 6' 3" **Weight:** 230
Breakout: --% **Improve:** --% **Collapse:** --%
Attrition: --% **MLB:** --%
Comparables:
--

YEAR	TEAM	LVL	AGE	W	L	SV	G	GS	IP	H	HR	BB	SO	BB9	SO9	GB%	BABIP	WHIP	ERA	FIP	FRA	WARP
2012	BLU	Rk	16	1	0	0	7	4	24	18	1	6	24	2.2	9.0	49%	.274	1.00	1.50	3.24	4.25	0.2
2012	VAN	A-	16	1	0	0	5	5	19^{2}	14	1	9	25	4.1	11.4	44%	.265	1.17	3.20	2.97	3.98	0.3
2013	*TOR*	*A-*	—	—	—	—	—	—	—	—	—	—	—	—	—	—	—	—	—	—	—	—

It isn't very often that a 17-year-old pitching prospect can be described as "polished" or "physically mature," but that's what the Blue Jays have in Osuna. A nephew of former major-league reliever Antonio Osuna, Roberto had his rights purchased from the Mexico City Red Devils in 2011 for $1.5 million. He lacks the projection of Luis Heredia, another high-profile signing out of Mexico, but he profiles as a solid mid-rotation starter if he's able to keep his conditioning under control. Toronto is typically conservative with its pitching prospects, but Osuna's polish and poise could earn him an Opening Day assignment to the Midwest League just two months after his 18th birthday.

Luis Perez

Born: 1/20/1985 **Age:** 28
Bats: L **Throws:** L **Height:** 6' 1" **Weight:** 160
Breakout: 26% **Improve:** 57% **Collapse:** 19%
Attrition: 15% **MLB:** 83%
Comparables:
Brian Burres, Willard Nixon, Bob Ojeda

YEAR	TEAM	LVL	AGE	W	L	SV	G	GS	IP	H	HR	BB	SO	BB9	SO9	GB%	BABIP	WHIP	ERA	FIP	FRA	WARP
2010	NHP	AA	25	5	6	0	13	12	73^{1}	67	6	37	49	4.5	6.0	59%	.280	1.42	4.54	4.77	6.32	-0.4
2010	LVG	AAA	25	5	5	0	15	15	86^{2}	107	5	47	56	4.9	5.8	58%	.345	1.78	6.12	5.08	6.84	-0.4
2011	LVG	AAA	26	2	2	0	8	8	45	37	5	23	43	4.6	8.6	63%	.276	1.33	4.60	5.05	5.08	0.3
2011	TOR	MLB	26	3	3	0	37	4	65	74	9	27	54	3.7	7.5	61%	.327	1.55	5.12	4.68	5.63	-0.2
2012	TOR	MLB	27	2	2	0	35	0	42	38	3	16	39	3.4	8.4	50%	.307	1.29	3.43	3.47	4.43	0.3
2013	*TOR*	*MLB*	*28*	*2*	*2*	*0*	*14*	*5*	*39*	*41*	*5*	*19*	*28*	*4.4*	*6.4*	*55%*	*.302*	*1.55*	*5.35*	*4.89*	*5.81*	*-0.1*

Perez has some meat on his fastball, or at least he did before tearing the ulnar collateral ligament in his pitching elbow. He underwent Tommy John surgery in late July. He may be able to return before the 2013 season is out, but considering his mediocre performance to date, the Blue Jays won't hold their breath waiting for him.

Esmil Rogers

Born: **8/14/1985** Age: **27**
Bats: **R** Throws: **R** Height: **6' 2"** Weight: **190**
Breakout: **32%** Improve: **58%** Collapse: **13%**
Attrition: **22%** MLB: **88%**

Comparables:
Kirk McCaskill,Garrett Olson,Jack McDowell

YEAR	TEAM	LVL	AGE	W	L	SV	G	GS	IP	H	HR	BB	SO	BB9	SO9	GB%	BABIP	WHIP	ERA	FIP	FRA	WARP
2010	CSP	AAA	24	3	3	0	12	11	61	62	6	19	53	2.8	7.8	52%	.308	1.33	5.75	4.26	5.10	1.2
2010	COL	MLB	24	2	3	0	28	8	72	94	5	26	66	3.2	8.2	52%	.385	1.67	6.12	3.47	4.02	1.5
2011	TUL	AA	25	0	1	0	1	1	4	5	1	1	2	2.2	4.5	50%	.267	1.50	2.25	6.38	7.50	-0.1
2011	CSP	AAA	25	1	2	0	5	5	23	36	3	5	15	2.0	5.9	46%	.400	1.78	6.26	5.09	6.33	0.3
2011	COL	MLB	25	6	6	0	18	13	83	110	14	47	63	5.1	6.8	43%	.352	1.89	7.05	5.58	5.80	0.2
2012	CLE	MLB	26	3	1	0	44	0	53	47	5	12	54	2.0	9.2	48%	.294	1.11	3.06	3.08	3.58	0.8
2012	COL	MLB	26	0	2	0	23	0	25^2	36	2	18	29	6.3	10.2	48%	.425	2.10	8.06	4.23	3.86	0.5
2013	*TOR*	*MLB*	*27*	*4*	*3*	*0*	*29*	*8*	*69*	*76*	*9*	*28*	*56*	*3.6*	*7.3*	*45%*	*.319*	*1.51*	*5.17*	*4.49*	*5.62*	*-0.1*

Rogers was once a highly regarded prospect in Colorado's system, but he never managed to find the kind of success expected of him in the rotation. He finally moved to the bullpen full time last year, and after his midseason trade to Cleveland he began to thrive. Rogers has always been more of a control than a command guy, and in the pen, where he can work in short bursts, he doesn't have to worry about being as fine with his pitches or about giving hitters different looks. He was pitching in favorable low-leverage situations, sure, and he may not have the command to be a seventh- or eighth-inning guy, but he definitely has the stuff to be a solid reliever if he can just keep the walks at a reasonable rate.

Ricky Romero

Born: **11/6/1984** Age: **28**
Bats: **R** Throws: **L** Height: **6' 1"** Weight: **215**
Breakout: **13%** Improve: **59%** Collapse: **22%**
Attrition: **11%** MLB: **92%**

Comparables:
John Smoltz,Anibal Sanchez,Noah Lowry

YEAR	TEAM	LVL	AGE	W	L	SV	G	GS	IP	H	HR	BB	SO	BB9	SO9	GB%	BABIP	WHIP	ERA	FIP	FRA	WARP
2010	TOR	MLB	25	14	9	0	32	32	210	189	15	82	174	3.5	7.5	56%	.289	1.29	3.73	3.60	4.86	1.8
2011	TOR	MLB	26	15	11	0	32	32	225	176	26	80	178	3.2	7.1	56%	.242	1.14	2.92	4.23	5.12	0.9
2012	TOR	MLB	27	9	14	0	32	32	181	198	21	105	124	5.2	6.2	55%	.311	1.67	5.77	5.09	6.07	-1.1
2013	*TOR*	*MLB*	*28*	*12*	*8*	*0*	*27*	*27*	*169^2*	*166*	*18*	*73*	*133*	*3.9*	*7.1*	*53%*	*.297*	*1.41*	*4.47*	*4.30*	*4.86*	*1.0*

Look up broken in the dictionary and you'll see this joke. But also a picture of Ricky Romero. Famously taken over Troy Tulowitzki in the 2005 draft, Romero managed to turn himself from trivia answer/punch line into a bona fide top-of-the-rotation starter, or at least the closest approximation the Blue Jays had. Romero was the Opening Day starter for Toronto and on June 5 was 7-1 with a respectable 4.02 ERA. After that he was 6-14 with a 7.10 ERA. In 102 innings he struck out 64 and walked 66. Rumors of an injury abounded and he finally underwent surgery to remove bone chips from his elbow at the end of October. If that was the problem, then, thanks to the big trades, Toronto has itself a pretty good fifth starter. If not . . . well, you can probably guess what happens next.

Aaron Sanchez

Born: **7/1/1992** Age: **20**
Bats: **R** Throws: **R** Height: **6' 5"** Weight: **190**
Breakout: **42%** Improve: **61%** Collapse: **10%**
Attrition: **3%** MLB: **85%**

Comparables:
Milt Pappas,Dick Brodowski,Sandy Koufax

YEAR	TEAM	LVL	AGE	W	L	SV	G	GS	IP	H	HR	BB	SO	BB9	SO9	GB%	BABIP	WHIP	ERA	FIP	FRA	WARP
2010	BLJ	Rk	17	0	2	0	8	8	19	19	1	12	28	5.7	13.3	52%	.419	1.63	1.42	3.77	3.91	0.4
2010	AUB	A-	17	0	1	0	2	2	6	4	0	5	9	7.5	13.5	60%	.267	1.50	4.50	2.97	4.75	0.1
2011	BLU	Rk	18	3	2	1	11	6	42^2	45	4	18	43	3.8	9.1	46%	.352	1.48	5.48	4.32	6.89	-0.1
2011	VAN	A-	18	0	1	0	3	3	11^2	8	0	8	13	6.2	10.0	48%	.172	1.37	4.63	3.70	3.35	0.3
2012	LNS	A	19	8	5	0	25	18	90^1	64	3	51	97	5.1	9.7	63%	.280	1.27	2.49	3.56	3.82	0.4
2013	*TOR*	*MLB*	*20*	*2*	*2*	*0*	*9*	*7*	*32^1*	*34*	*5*	*22*	*27*	*6.2*	*7.4*	*50%*	*.308*	*1.74*	*5.94*	*5.58*	*6.45*	*-0.2*

Sanchez entered the year as arguably the Blue Jays' top pitching prospect, and his surface numbers suggest a successful full-season debut at Class-A Lansing. He finished among the league leaders in earned run average and hits per nine innings, but he also walked 51 batters in just over 90 innings of work. He's just 19, so there's still plenty of time to hone his command, but he's had three years of professional instruction and shown very little progress harnessing his plus stuff. Sanchez will head to the Florida State League in 2013, but could be challenged if hitters learn to sit back and wait for him to throw a strike.

Sergio Santos

Born: **7/4/1983** Age: **29**
Bats: **R** Throws: **R** Height: **6' 3"** Weight: **230**
Breakout: **19%** Improve: **40%** Collapse: **48%**
Attrition: **18%** MLB: **95%**

Comparables:
Bryan Harvey,Chris Schroder,Michael Wuertz

YEAR	TEAM	LVL	AGE	W	L	SV	G	GS	IP	H	HR	BB	SO	BB9	SO9	GB%	BABIP	WHIP	ERA	FIP	FRA	WARP
2010	CHA	MLB	26	2	2	1	56	0	51^2	53	2	26	56	4.5	9.8	45%	.345	1.53	2.96	3.07	3.77	0.8
2011	CHA	MLB	27	4	5	30	63	0	63^1	41	6	29	92	4.1	13.1	43%	.269	1.11	3.55	2.90	3.05	1.4
2012	TOR	MLB	28	0	1	2	6	0	5	6	1	4	4	7.2	7.2	50%	.333	2.00	9.00	6.45	4.89	0.0
2013	*TOR*	*MLB*	*29*	*2*	*1*	*16*	*37*	*0*	*35^1*	*30*	*4*	*16*	*43*	*4.2*	*10.8*	*42%*	*.306*	*1.31*	*3.67*	*3.60*	*3.99*	*0.5*

Surgery to repair a fraying labrum in his right shoulder ended Santos's season after just six appearances, but he's expected to be ready for the start of 2013. When healthy, Santos operates in the mid-90s with his fastball and shows off a loose mid-80s slider that he sometimes struggles to command. A former first-round pick as a shortstop, Santos shows the aggressiveness and confidence of a productive closer, but will likely begin the year in a set-up role to Janssen.

Mickey Storey
Born: **3/16/1986** Age: **27**
Bats: **R** Throws: **R** Height: **6' 3"** Weight: **185**
Breakout: **22%** Improve: **45%** Collapse: **40%**
Attrition: **24%** MLB: **87%**
Comparables:
Tom Niedenfuer,Shawn Kelley,Fernando Salas

YEAR	TEAM	LVL	AGE	W	L	SV	G	GS	IP	H	HR	BB	SO	BB9	SO9	GB%	BABIP	WHIP	ERA	FIP	FRA	WARP
2010	MID	AA	24	5	4	8	43	1	71	58	5	22	63	2.8	8.0	45%	.269	1.13	3.30	3.37	4.23	0.8
2010	SAC	AAA	24	1	1	1	11	0	13	15	3	5	14	3.5	9.7	44%	.316	1.54	5.54	5.58	5.21	0.1
2011	MID	AA	25	3	3	4	27	0	38	41	3	13	31	3.1	7.3	—	.330	1.42	4.03	4.04	4.39	0.0
2011	OKL	AAA	25	1	0	2	23	0	29^{1}	35	3	12	28	3.7	8.6	—	.368	1.60	3.99	4.43	4.82	0.0
2012	OKL	AAA	26	7	4	2	38	2	65	62	8	14	72	1.9	10.0	42%	.313	1.17	3.05	3.83	2.78	0.8
2012	HOU	MLB	26	0	1	0	26	0	30^{1}	27	2	10	34	3.0	10.1	39%	.312	1.22	3.86	2.84	3.15	0.5
2013	*TOR*	*MLB*	*27*	*1*	*0*	*0*	*25*	*0*	36^{2}	*35*	*5*	*12*	*35*	*3.0*	*8.7*	*43%*	*.295*	*1.28*	*4.10*	*4.05*	*4.45*	*0.3*

The Neverending Storey: Claimed by Toronto—after being claimed by Houston—after being claimed by the Yankees . . . from Houston. The reliever's strikeout rate doesn't look like it belongs to a righty whose fastball barely topped 90 and was crushed to the tune of a .343 TAv, but it's the off-speed stuff that makes him interesting: 28 of his 34 Ks came on his slider and slow curve, which he commands well. As a free-talent pickup, he's promising, but if hitters learn to let the slow stuff go by and feast on his fastball, Storey's next chapter might make his team want to turn the page.

Marcus Stroman
Born: **5/1/1991** Age: **22**
Bats: **R** Throws: **R** Height: **5' 10"** Weight: **185**
Breakout: **17%** Improve: **45%** Collapse: **33%**
Attrition: **19%** MLB: **79%**
Comparables:
Phil Paine,Ryan Wagner,Reggie Harris

YEAR	TEAM	LVL	AGE	W	L	SV	G	GS	IP	H	HR	BB	SO	BB9	SO9	GB%	BABIP	WHIP	ERA	FIP	FRA	WARP
2012	VAN	A-	21	1	0	0	7	0	11^{1}	8	0	3	15	2.4	11.9	48%	.296	0.97	3.18	1.47	2.97	0.3
2012	NHP	AA	21	2	0	0	8	0	8	8	1	6	8	6.8	9.0	62%	.304	1.75	3.38	5.08	5.94	0.0
2013	*TOR*	*MLB*	*22*	*1*	*0*	*1*	*26*	*0*	33^{1}	*36*	*5*	*17*	*26*	*4.6*	*7.2*	*46%*	*.306*	*1.58*	*5.44*	*5.12*	*5.91*	*-0.2*

Toronto's second first-round pick in last summer's draft, Stroman elicits a lot of Tom Gordon comparisons because he delivers plus velocity from a slight frame. He pitched in the rotation at Duke, but some believe his future is in the back of the bullpen as a shutdown reliever. As a starter, he shows command of four pitches, including a mid-90s fastball and a two-plane, mid-80s slider, as well as feel for a solid changeup. He worked as a reliever after signing, reaching Double-A New Hampshire by August, before a positive drug test earned him a 50-game suspension. He'll miss the first month of 2013 serving the balance of that suspension, but could be on the fast track once he returns.

Carlos Villanueva
Born: **11/28/1983** Age: **29**
Bats: **R** Throws: **R** Height: **6' 3"** Weight: **230**
Breakout: **25%** Improve: **53%** Collapse: **20%**
Attrition: **10%** MLB: **87%**
Comparables:
Chris Smith,Gaylord Perry,Yunesky Maya

YEAR	TEAM	LVL	AGE	W	L	SV	G	GS	IP	H	HR	BB	SO	BB9	SO9	GB%	BABIP	WHIP	ERA	FIP	FRA	WARP
2010	MIL	MLB	26	2	0	1	50	0	52^{2}	48	7	22	67	3.8	11.4	36%	.313	1.33	4.61	3.77	3.97	0.6
2011	DUN	A+	27	0	0	0	1	1	1	1	0	0	0	0.0	0.0	—	.200	1.00	0.00	3.39	3.68	0.0
2011	TOR	MLB	27	6	4	0	33	13	107	103	11	32	68	2.7	5.7	37%	.271	1.26	4.04	4.14	4.93	0.6
2012	TOR	MLB	28	7	7	0	38	16	125^{1}	113	23	46	122	3.3	8.8	38%	.275	1.27	4.16	4.66	4.78	1.0
2013	*TOR*	*MLB*	*29*	*6*	*4*	*1*	*46*	*10*	104^{1}	*101*	*15*	*33*	*92*	*2.9*	*8.0*	*40%*	*.292*	*1.29*	*4.18*	*4.25*	*4.54*	*1.0*

Villanueva began the year in the bullpen, but moved into the rotation shortly before the All-Star break. He performed admirably before falling apart in September, going 1-4 with an 8.10 ERA in five starts. Before that collapse, he struck out nearly a batter per inning while posting a 2.83 ERA in 10 July-August outings. He'd never been more than a spot starter before Toronto's pitching woes forced him into rotation duty last summer, but he performed well enough that most believe he could hold up as a solid fourth starter.

LINEOUTS

HITTERS

PLAYER	TEAM	LVL	AGE	PA	R	2B	3B	HR	RBI	BB	SO	SB-CS	AVG/OBP/SLG	TAv	BABIP	BRR	FRAA	WARP
3B K. Ahrens	DUN	A+	23	477	59	17	1	8	53	60	87	1-1	.240/.338/.345	.259	.282	-4.7	3B(69): 0.3, 1B(14): -1.5	0.0
CF D. Davis	BLJ	Rk	17	190	30	7	2	4	12	18	54	18-7	.233/.339/.374	.481	.324	0.4	CF(1): -0.1	0.2
	BLU	Rk	17	53	9	3	1	1	6	4	10	6-2	.340/.415/.511	.339	.417	0.5	CF(7): 0.2	0.3
MI R. Goins	NHP	AA	24	618	66	33	4	7	61	47	78	15-9	.289/.342/.403	.270	.323	-0.6	SS(39): -1.4, 2B(6): 0.7	1.2
1B L. Jimenez	TAC	AAA	30	536	64	32	2	20	81	64	97	3-0	.310/.394/.514	.304	.356	-5.5	1B(38): -3.8	1.5
	SEA	MLB	30	18	0	0	0	0	0	1	4	0-0	.059/.111/.059	.071	.077	0	--	-0.3
OF R. Langerhans	SLC	AAA	32	401	59	21	6	11	54	63	113	6-6	.250/.369/.446	.268	.343	-3	RF(30): -0.3, LF(27): 2.1	0.0
2B C. Lopes	BLU	Rk	19	205	33	16	5	4	29	15	34	6-1	.280/.343/.484	.302	.324	1.6	2B(26): 1.7, SS(7): 1.2	1.4
C S. Nessy	BLU	Rk	19	178	26	8	0	8	23	13	47	0-0	.256/.320/.456	.275	.308	-0.7	C(33): 0.2	0.8
C S. Ochinko	DUN	A+	24	119	21	12	0	1	13	10	16	0-0	.306/.370/.444	.290	.352	0.2	C(18): 0.3	0.7
	NHP	AA	24	231	26	11	1	8	29	8	40	0-0	.264/.304/.435	.256	.290	-4.1	C(15): -0.1, 1B(1): -0.0	-0.6
OF K. Pillar	LNS	A	23	375	49	20	4	5	57	35	53	35-6	.322/.390/.451	.253	.371	0.6	LF(10): 0.4, RF(5): 0.3	0.4
	DUN	A+	23	178	16	8	2	1	34	5	17	16-3	.323/.339/.415	.305	.342	1.8	RF(15): -0.7, CF(12): -0.9	1.0
2B R. Schimpf	DUN	A+	24	419	59	29	3	14	61	48	89	4-2	.266/.353/.479	.301	.311	-1.5	2B(48): -1.1, 3B(12): 0.3	1.6
	NHP	AA	24	137	21	8	0	8	15	23	32	3-1	.279/.412/.568	.215	.324	1	3B(6): 0.3, LF(3): -0.4	0.0
INF O. Vizquel	TOR	MLB	45	163	13	5	1	0	7	7	17	3-2	.235/.265/.281	.195	.261	-2.3	2B(24): -0.8, 3B(18): 1.2	-0.7

After spending parts of four seasons at High-A Dunedin, former first-round pick **Kevin Ahrens** has officially earned the "bust" tag. The 17th-overall pick in last June's draft, **D.J. Davis** may be even faster than Cincinnati's Billy Hamilton, and he showed better-than-expected on-base skills in his debut. **Ryan Goins** gets lost in the shuffle of Toronto middle-infield prospects, perhaps rightfully so given his age, but he has shown a knack for making contact and getting on base over the last two seasons. In his eighth organization (including a detour to Japan), 280-lb. **Luis Jimenez** finally made his major-league debut and, probably, swan song. **Ryan Langerhans** was the veteran hired to give the Angels' hot prospect "more time to develop," meaning when Mike Trout tore up the bigs, Langerhans languished at Salt Lake: Now he can languish in Buffalo. **Christian Lopes** signed for supplemental-first-round money in the eighth round of the 2011 draft and flashed surprising pop in his short-season debut. Toronto's depth behind the plate has allowed it to move big-bodied bonus baby **Santiago Nessy** slowly through the organization. **Sean Ochinko** was promoted to Double-A New Hampshire when elbow surgery shelved A.J. Jimenez in mid-May. Like many of Toronto's hitting prospects, Ochinko has been old for his leagues, but the former LSU Tiger has interesting pop and could grind his way to a backup job at some point. **Kevin Pillar** has done nothing but hit since signing with the Blue Jays out of the 32nd round of the 2011 draft, compiling a .331/.375/.469 over a season and a half. Actually, he's been hitting since his days at Cal State Dominguez Hills, where he once strung together a 54-game hitting streak. **Ryan Schimpf**'s profile is one that should be familiar if you've read these comments in order: on-base skills, old for his league, future bench player. One of the modern era's finest defensive shortstops, **Omar Vizquel** finally reached the end of the line in 2012, hanging up his spikes after a dazzling 24-year career that spanned four decades and put him in the Hall of Fame conversation.

PITCHERS

PLAYER	TEAM	LVL	AGE	W	L	SV	IP	H	HR	BB	SO	BB9	SO9	GB%	BABIP	WHIP	ERA	FIP	FRA	WARP
D. Barnes	DUN	A+	22	1	2	34	51^1	37	3	16	63	2.8	11.0	39%	.276	1.03	1.40	2.63	2.76	1.2
R. Coello	LVG	AAA	27	4	1	0	42	31	4	18	43	3.9	9.2	44%	.260	1.17	3.00	4.14	5.20	0.5
	TOR	MLB	27	0	1	0	6^1	10	2	4	11	5.7	15.6	12%	.533	2.21	12.79	6.05	5.34	0.0
E. Crawford	LVG	AAA	25	1	4	0	27^2	38	2	12	20	3.9	6.5	61%	.379	1.81	6.83	4.68	6.20	0.0
	TOR	MLB	25	0	0	0	8	10	3	4	5	4.5	5.6	42%	.304	1.75	6.75	8.55	8.04	-0.3
S. Dyson	DUN	A+	24	2	0	0	28^2	35	1	5	16	1.6	5.0	68%	.337	1.40	4.08	3.36	5.84	0.0
	NHP	AA	24	2	2	9	45^1	38	2	15	22	3.0	4.4	67%	.248	1.17	2.38	4.06	7.38	-0.4
	TOR	MLB	24	0	0	0	0^2	4	0	2	1	27.0	13.5	80%	.800	9.00	40.50	9.05	6.60	0.0
C. Everts	LVG	AAA	27	3	2	2	61	53	2	32	53	4.7	7.8	51%	.295	1.39	3.10	3.93	4.38	0.9
S. Gracey	DUN	A+	25	2	3	1	28^1	27	3	11	42	3.5	13.3	55%	.364	1.34	3.81	2.97	3.71	0.5
	NHP	AA	25	0	0	0	26	26	1	14	18	4.8	6.2	51%	.309	1.54	3.81	4.05	4.99	0.0
D. Hutchison	TOR	MLB	21	5	3	0	58^2	59	8	20	49	3.1	7.5	46%	.291	1.35	4.60	4.43	5.38	-0.1
D. McGowan	—	—	—	—	—	—	—	—	—	—	—	—	—	—	—	—	—	—	—	—
D. Norris	BLU	Rk	19	2	3	0	35	44	4	13	38	3.3	9.8	46%	.370	1.63	7.97	4.30	6.31	-0.1
J. Perez	NAS	AAA	33	4	2	0	40	32	3	20	54	4.5	12.1	60%	.322	1.30	3.60	3.52	3.94	0.4
	MIL	MLB	33	0	1	0	7	6	2	8	10	10.3	12.9	44%	.286	2.00	5.14	7.85	8.56	-0.2
J. Stilson	DUN	A+	21	3	0	0	54^1	56	2	19	47	3.1	7.8	52%	.331	1.38	2.82	3.25	4.13	0.7
	NHP	AA	21	2	4	1	50	54	6	23	44	4.1	7.9	41%	.326	1.54	5.04	4.56	5.51	0.0
R. Thompson	SAC	AAA	27	4	2	3	62	46	7	23	58	3.3	8.4	41%	.230	1.11	3.34	4.38	5.76	0.1
	ANA	MLB	27	0	1	0	2^1	5	1	1	3	3.9	11.6	44%	.500	2.57	15.43	7.33	6.74	-0.1
	OAK	MLB	27	0	0	0	0^2	1	0	0	0	0.0	0.0	33%	.333	1.50	0.00	3.05	3.95	0.0

Danny Barnes converted 34 of 36 save opportunities for Dunedin, the most saves in the Florida State League, and has a 12.5 SO9 in 156 2/3 professional innings. **Robert Coello** could be a useful middle relief piece, as his heavy low-90s fastball is effective when he doesn't leave it over the middle of the plate. **Evan Crawford** offers two plus pitches from the left side, including a heavy low-90s fastball, but unreliable control is likely to keep him out of the highest of high-leverage spots. Lefties have a difficult time tracking him, so he could have a nice career as a LOOGY. **Sam Dyson** raced through the organization and made his major-league debut barely a year after being taken in the fourth round of the 2011 draft, but he'll have to find a way to increase his 4.6 SO9 in order to realize his middle-relief potential. Former fifth-overall pick **Clint Everts** had his climb to the big leagues stalled by arm injuries, including 2004 Tommy John surgery, but has reinvented himself as a reliever and finds himself on the cusp. Inconsistent control is the only thing standing between **Scott Gracey**'s plus fastball and a job in the Blue Jays bullpen. **Drew Hutchison** struggled through his first four starts, but was mostly effective until right elbow soreness shut him down in mid-June, followed by Tommy John surgery in August and rehab that should last all of 2013. **Dustin McGowan** has missed most of the last two seasons with various shoulder injuries, and it's anyone's guess what he'll be able to contribute going forward as the Blue Jays have him under contract through 2014. **Daniel Norris** was the recipient of an above-slot $2 million signing bonus in 2011, but mechanical inconsistencies contributed to disastrous results in his debut. Vagabond reliever **Juan Perez** dazzled the kiddies in Nashville but face-planted in Milwaukee, earning his release. Lefties who can throw 95 are hard to come by, so he'll add an eighth organization to his dance card this year with Toronto. **John Stilson** was a potential first-round pick in 2011 before shoulder trouble knocked him down draft boards. Toronto signed him out of the third round and he reached Double-A in his debut. **Rich Thompson** made a single appearance for the Athletics in April and spent the rest of his season in Sacramento, despite the lure of a three-headed hydra of Australian relievers in the bullpen, and now he's off to the Blue Jays.

MANAGER: JOHN GIBBONS

Here's an easy way to remember new Blue Jays manager John Gibbons: He has the same name as the guy who managed the team five seasons and three managers ago. This just in: The new Gibbons is, in fact, the same Gibbons as the old Gibbons.

Gibbons (Gibbons!) replaces John Farrell, whose two-year tenure with Toronto ended unceremoniously after his love of his former employer, the Boston Red Sox, was requited. Boston needed a new manager not named Valentine and Farrell wanted to be that guy, so not wanting a guy who didn't want to be their guy, the Jays shipped Farrell east for shortstop Mike Aviles, who was quickly flipped to Cleveland for Esmil Rogers.

Re-enter Gibbons, whose first tenure with the team lasted for parts of five seasons and resulted in a 305-305 record. Not too bad in retrospect, but Gibbons's performance was pockmarked by physical confrontations with his own players, first Shea Hillenbrand, then Ted Lilly. Yet there are reasons to feel confidence in Gibbons's return. Despite the fighting, Gibbons is almost universally liked among those in the game. Even former pugilistic foe Hillenbrand endorsed his hiring, saying of Gibbons, "He's a great guy!" When even the guy you came to blows with calls you a great guy, you're officially a great guy.

Gibbons brings more to the table than great-guyness, as his in-game strategy eschews sacrifice bunts and stolen bases. Last season several Jays were thrown out with Jose Bautista hitting, a peculiar type of self-defeat unlikely to repeat itself on Gibbons's watch.

While his handling of the pitching staff came under fire during his first run—he occasionally worked his starting pitchers' pitch counts into the 120s—it's easy to see that misunderstanding of pitcher safety corrected with Toronto's forward-thinking front office.

A surprising choice, Gibbons has the skills, the players, and the experience to prove himself the right choice. All he must do now is win.

Washington Nationals

2012: CHEERS

The Nationals featured a top-three pitching staff and a top-five lineup, an accomplishment no other National League club could boast. Highlighted by Bryce Harper's sensational rise to Rookie of the Year, but led by a stellar starting rotation and a strong bullpen, the Nationals won a franchise-record 98 games and held sole possession of first place in the NL East from early June to the finish. That meant the end of a 31-year playoff drought that dated back to Montreal and the prime of Andre Dawson.

Nationals pitchers posted the lowest earned-run average in the league and were third in strikeouts. Offseason acquisitions Gio Gonzalez and Edwin Jackson combined with the returning Stephen Strasburg, the unleashed Jordan Zimmermann, and Ross Detwiler to start 93 percent of Washington's games. That figure that would have been higher had Strasburg not been shut down with an innings limit similar to the one that had shortened Zimmermann's season in 2011, though Strasburg's shutdown was far more controversial because the games he missed meant something.

The offense was carried by an explosive infield whose regulars—Adam LaRoche, Danny Espinosa, Ian Desmond, and Ryan Zimmerman—combined for 100 home runs and a .273/.332/.473 slash line. But unlike the rotation, the lineup battled its share of injuries. Michael Morse began the year on the disabled list with a right shoulder strain, and fellow outfielder Jayson Werth missed 75 games after fracturing his left forearm in early May. Wilson Ramos was lost for the year with a torn ACL a week after Werth's injury, and All-Star shortstop Desmond missed nearly a month in July and August with an oblique strain. Though he missed only two weeks' worth of games, third baseman Zimmerman battled right shoulder soreness and inflammation throughout the year and had postseason surgery to correct the injury.

Though he wasn't the team's best position player, 19-year-old outfielder Harper garnered more attention than any other hitter on the Nationals roster. After a hot start, Harper posted pedestrian numbers through the summer before taking off in September, hitting .330/.400/.643 with seven home runs and five stolen bases. He edged out Arizona pitcher Wade Miley for the National League Rookie of the Year award, collecting more than half of the first-place votes.

NATIONALS PROSPECTUS

2012 W-L: 98-64, 1st in NL East

Pythag	.594	1st	DER	.718	4th
RS/G	4.51	10th	B-Age	27.1	4th
RA/G	3.67	3rd	P-Age	26.9	2nd
TAv	.267	7th	Salary	$94.6	15th
BRR	-21.3	30th	M$/MW	$1.64	7th
TAv-P	.245	3rd	DL Days	1171	10th
FIP	3.58	2nd	DL WARP	3.6	15th

Three-Year Park Factors	
Overall	99
HR/RH	109
HR/LH	106
AVG/RH	102
AVG/LH	105

Nationals Park (2008)
Att. % of Capacity: 70.9% (14th)
Dim. 328, 379, 404, 370, 325

The Nationals are built to win at any park, finishing with +37 in homers at home, and +28 on the road.

2013: HAPPY DAYS

Four-fifths of the Nationals starting rotation is slated to return. The club signed Dan Haren to replace Jackson, who departed via free agency. The team also bolstered its outfield defense by trading former first-rounder Alex Meyer to Minnesota for center fielder Denard Span. Washington enters the season as a favorite to repeat as division leaders, with the stiffest competition figuring to come from Atlanta.

The acquisition of Span gives the Nationals one of the league's best up-the-middle defenses, assuming Ramos returns to his duties behind the plate. Span also provides the lineup with a more traditional leadoff hitter, allowing manager Davey Johnson to move Werth further down in the order to take advantage of his run-producing abilities. With Span and Harper atop the lineup, Zimmerman, Morse, and Werth will have plenty of opportunities to drive in runs.

The starting rotation will once again be a strength, but depth took a hit when the club elected to non-tender John Lannan. Haren will slide into Jackson's vacated turn. Haren was only available because the Angels declined his option after back issues contributed to the worst full season of his career. If any one of their starters goes down, the Nationals will be forced to turn to Tom Gorzelanny, Yunesky Maya, Tanner Roark, or Paul Demny to fill in. Reliever Ryan Perry, the Tigers' top pick in the 2008 draft, began the transition to starting last summer, and he could be an emergency option if the need arises.

Washington boasted one of the National League's best bullpens in 2012, and the majority of those relievers are returning this year, the exceptions being free-agent lefty specialists Sean Burnett and Mike Gonzalez. Closer Drew Storen missed the first half with a right elbow injury, but after experiments with Henry Rodriguez and Brad Lidge came to an end in May, Tyler Clippard solidified the ninth inning, converting 32 of 37 save chances. Storen will resume closing duties this year, but Clippard gives the Nationals quality, proven insurance in the eighth inning.

The Nationals lineup has significant depth, led by fourth outfielder Roger Bernadina and utility infielder Steve Lombardozzi. Both players performed admirably when injuries to regulars forced them into playing every day at various points last year. Moore gives Johnson a power bat off the bench who is capable of playing first base and the outfield corners. The biggest area of concern is catcher—the team went through six of them last year, and none were capable of delivering Ramos's combination of offense and defense. Kurt Suzuki, acquired in a midseason deal from Oakland, returns. Johnson has said Suzuki will get a lot of playing time while Ramos eases back into the swing of things. Suzuki is a capable backup, but Ramos is the catcher of the future.

STATE OF THE ORGANIZATION: FULL HOUSE

There are two ways an organization can use its farm system. The first, and most common, is as a pipeline for cost-controlled major-league talent. The second method is to keep only the bluest of the blue-chippers and use the rest in trades that strengthen the major-league roster.

The Nationals have successfully deployed the second of those strategies since the end of the 2011 season, using minor-league depth to acquire big-league contributors such as Gonzalez, Span, and Suzuki. It's difficult to find flaws in that approach, as it has landed them a Cy Young contender, one of the league's finest all-around center fielders, and a backup catcher capable of starting for a number of clubs. The downside is that those transactions have depleted much of Washington's upper-level prospect ranks, but most organizations would gladly accept that if the tradeoff was consistent playoff contention.

Third baseman Anthony Rendon and center fielder Brian Goodwin, two of the Nationals' top three picks in 2011, reached Double-A last year and rank among the club's best hopes. Rendon, in particular, qualifies as one of baseball's top prospects, though ankle injuries have hounded him since his college days and limited him to a paltry 43 games across three levels last year.

The young core of the Nationals' roster, including Harper, Strasburg, Zimmerman, Zimmermann, Espinosa, and Desmond, is under control for several seasons, all but ensuring a competitive squad in the nation's capitol for years to come.

HITTERS

Roger Bernadina LF
Born: **6/12/1984** Age: **29**
Bats: **L** Throws: **L** Height: **6' 3"**
Weight: **200** Breakout: **1%**
Improve: **46%** Collapse: **3%**
Attrition: **15%** MLB: **95%**
Comparables:
Aaron Rowand, Tony Gonzalez, Jackie Brandt

YEAR	TEAM	LVL	AGE	PA	R	2B	3B	HR	RBI	BB	SO	SB	CS	AVG_OBP_SLG	TAv	BABIP	BRR	FRAA	WARP
2010	SYR	AAA	26	69	8	2	1	2	8	6	5	7	2	.377/.426/.541	.318	.382	-1.4	CF(11): -0.5, RF(1): -0.0	0.5
2010	WAS	MLB	26	461	52	18	3	11	47	35	93	16	2	.246/.307/.384	.248	.288	3.1	RF(77): -3.6, LF(43): -2.3	0.1
2011	SYR	AAA	27	188	26	9	0	6	14	18	47	14	5	.250/.339/.415	.288	.315	1.5	CF(21): -4.2, LF(7): 0.3	0.5
2011	WAS	MLB	27	337	40	12	2	7	27	22	63	17	3	.243/.301/.362	.243	.285	1.4	CF(56): -6.0, LF(36): 1.2	-0.4
2012	WAS	MLB	28	261	25	11	0	5	25	28	53	15	3	.291/.372/.405	.284	.359	-1.3	LF(54): 0.0, CF(37): 0.1	1.3
2013	*WAS*	*MLB*	*29*	*276*	*37*	*11*	*2*	*6*	*25*	*22*	*56*	*15*	*3*	*.260/.323/.389*	*.255*	*.308*	*1.5*	*CF -1, LF 0*	*0.7*

After back-to-back years of the same underwhelming results, Bernadina made a fundamental change in his approach for the first time as a major leaguer. He became more patient at the plate, and results were felt throughout his stat line. The 4 percent spike in walk rate sent him into double digits, making his 20 percent strikeout rate quite a bit more palatable. Meanwhile, he found better pitches to hit and did more damage with them. At Bernadina's age, it's a real question whether the improvement can stick. But it's not out of line with his minor-league work, so it isn't outlandish to assume he has matured as a hitter.

Corey Brown OF

Born: **11/26/1985** Age: **27**
Bats: **L** Throws: **L** Height: **6' 2"**
Weight: **205** Breakout: **0%**
Improve: **58%** Collapse: **3%**
Attrition: **6%** MLB: **93%**

Comparables:
Jimmie Hall,Jim Edmonds,Curtis Granderson

YEAR	TEAM	LVL	AGE	PA	R	2B	3B	HR	RBI	BB	SO	SB	CS	AVG_OBP_SLG	TAv	BABIP	BRR	FRAA	WARP
2010	MID	AA	24	386	63	14	8	10	49	52	93	19	1	.320/.416/.502	.319	.421	2.9	CF(78): -1.9, LF(1): -0.1	3.4
2010	SAC	AAA	24	148	21	4	3	5	20	11	36	3	1	.193/.250/.378	.212	.219	2	CF(30): 2.2, RF(12): 0.8	0.0
2011	SYR	AAA	25	462	50	18	3	14	39	47	134	4	7	.235/.326/.402	.242	.317	-0.9	CF(69): 2.6, LF(11): 1.2	0.1
2011	WAS	MLB	25	3	0	0	0	0	0	0	2	0	0	.000/.000/.000	.002	.000	0	--	-0.1
2012	SYR	AAA	26	554	83	22	9	25	71	59	139	18	7	.285/.365/.523	.290	.349	-2.5	CF(71): -2.7, LF(22): -0.4	1.9
2012	WAS	MLB	26	27	4	2	0	1	3	1	9	0	0	.200/.231/.400	.243	.267	0.3	LF(7): 0.3, CF(2): 0.1	0.1
2013	*WAS*	*MLB*	*27*	*250*	*33*	*9*	*2*	*9*	*28*	*21*	*71*	*5*	*2*	*.242/.310/.418*	*.257*	*.309*	*0.4*	*CF -2, LF -0*	*0.5*

In his third go-round at Triple-A, Brown finally got the hang of it, putting together a huge season in Syracuse and displaying the best of his skills. He has always been a power-speed guy whose ceiling was tamped down by his inability to make consistent contact. His 2012 breakthrough was no different: He still struck out 25 percent of the time, but he managed to pack a lot of damage into the other 75 percent of his plate appearances. He looks like a 26th, even 27th type of guy for the Nationals, shuttling between Syracuse and Washington a couple of times a year.

Mark DeRosa LF

Born: **2/26/1975** Age: **38**
Bats: **R** Throws: **R** Height: **6' 1"**
Weight: **220** Breakout: **0%**
Improve: **12%** Collapse: **11%**
Attrition: **20%** MLB: **56%**

Comparables:
Dusty Baker,Minnie Minoso,Monte Irvin

YEAR	TEAM	LVL	AGE	PA	R	2B	3B	HR	RBI	BB	SO	SB	CS	AVG_OBP_SLG	TAv	BABIP	BRR	FRAA	WARP
2010	SFN	MLB	35	104	9	3	0	1	10	9	16	0	2	.194/.279/.258	.194	.224	-1.4	LF(21): 0.5, 2B(7): -0.0	-0.6
2011	SFN	MLB	36	97	9	2	0	0	12	8	18	1	1	.279/.351/.302	.263	.348	1.6	3B(16): -1.0, 1B(10): -0.1	0.3
2012	WAS	MLB	37	101	13	5	0	0	6	14	18	1	0	.188/.300/.247	.207	.235	-1.1	3B(11): 0.0, LF(9): -0.5	-0.5
2013	*WAS*	*MLB*	*38*	*250*	*27*	*10*	*1*	*7*	*29*	*22*	*50*	*2*	*1*	*.245/.319/.390*	*.257*	*.284*	*-0.4*	*3B -0, LF -0*	*0.5*

Remember when DeRosa was a strong everyday player? Hard to blame you if you don't, considering that it was all the way back in his early 30s. Now 38, DeRosa is struggling for 100 plate appearances a season, let alone 100 games played. He can still ostensibly be maneuvered around the field, playing six positions in his limited time last year, but that remains something done at the peril of the team in charge of him at this age.

Ian Desmond SS

Born: **9/20/1985** Age: **27**
Bats: **R** Throws: **R** Height: **6' 3"**
Weight: **210** Breakout: **1%**
Improve: **44%** Collapse: **8%**
Attrition: **14%** MLB: **94%**

Comparables:
Tyler Greene,Jim Fregosi,Elliot Johnson

YEAR	TEAM	LVL	AGE	PA	R	2B	3B	HR	RBI	BB	SO	SB	CS	AVG_OBP_SLG	TAv	BABIP	BRR	FRAA	WARP
2010	WAS	MLB	24	574	59	27	4	10	65	28	109	17	5	.269/.308/.392	.252	.317	1.6	SS(148): -8.6, RF(1): -0.0	1.1
2011	WAS	MLB	25	639	65	27	5	8	49	35	139	25	10	.253/.298/.358	.245	.317	4.8	SS(152): -3.6	1.1
2012	WAS	MLB	26	547	72	33	2	25	73	30	113	21	6	.292/.335/.511	.290	.332	1.1	SS(128): -14.6	1.5
2013	*WAS*	*MLB*	*27*	*532*	*71*	*27*	*3*	*14*	*55*	*29*	*109*	*19*	*6*	*.270/.314/.425*	*.262*	*.315*	*1.3*	*SS -3*	*2.3*

While the advanced metrics can't seem to agree on Desmond's defensive value, there is no doubting his offensive impact. The power he showed in flashes throughout his career prior to 2012 finally came together, resulting in 25 home runs, enough to lead the league among shortstops. Desmond made an All-Star appearance and won the Silver Slugger Award. Desmond's power emergence and the growth of the team as a whole have allowed the Nationals to slot him lower in the lineup, where he is a much better fit given his strikeout and walk rates.

Danny Espinosa SS

Born: **4/25/1987** Age: **26**
Bats: **B** Throws: **R** Height: **6' 1"**
Weight: **190** Breakout: **4%**
Improve: **52%** Collapse: **4%**
Attrition: **12%** MLB: **99%**

Comparables:
Kelly Johnson,Geronimo Pena,Sean Rodriguez

YEAR	TEAM	LVL	AGE	PA	R	2B	3B	HR	RBI	BB	SO	SB	CS	AVG_OBP_SLG	TAv	BABIP	BRR	FRAA	WARP
2010	HAR	AA	23	434	66	16	4	18	54	33	94	20	8	.262/.333/.464	.284	.300	-0.8	SS(98): -0.8	3.1
2010	SYR	AAA	23	108	14	2	1	4	15	8	22	5	3	.295/.349/.463	.272	.338	0.5	SS(17): -1.6, 2B(7): 0.5	0.5
2010	WAS	MLB	23	112	16	4	1	6	15	9	30	0	2	.214/.277/.447	.251	.239	1.6	2B(25): -0.0, SS(2): 0.3	0.4
2011	WAS	MLB	24	658	72	29	5	21	66	57	166	17	6	.236/.323/.414	.265	.292	2.7	2B(158): 11.6	2.8
2012	WAS	MLB	25	658	82	37	2	17	56	46	189	20	6	.247/.315/.402	.255	.333	-0.3	2B(126): 2.9, SS(36): 3.1	1.4
2013	*WAS*	*MLB*	*26*	*618*	*83*	*27*	*3*	*20*	*67*	*45*	*164*	*17*	*6*	*.239/.308/.410*	*.254*	*.297*	*0.8*	*2B -2, SS 0*	*1.9*

The defensive metrics are united in their opinion that Espinosa, unlike his double-play partner, carries major value in the field. He cuts into that value with his bat thanks to a ton of swings-and-misses. His 29 percent strikeout rate was seventh-worst in baseball and his 189 total strikeouts led the National League. With just 24 games at Triple-A before reaching the majors, he's still learning on the job, and at 26, it's more than reasonable to assume he has yet to tap into his full offensive potential. The switch-hitter has shown he can handle lefties much better than righties, so while the depth of the lineup allows the Nationals to take the burden off of Espinosa as a top-third guy, he can probably hang in there when facing southpaws.

Jesus Flores **C**

Born: **10/26/1984** Age: **28**
Bats: **R** Throws: **R** Height: **6' 2"**
Weight: **230** Breakout: **4%**
Improve: **31%** Collapse: **19%**
Attrition: **27%** MLB: **95%**

Comparables:
Rich Gedman,John Bateman,Eddie Taubensee

YEAR	TEAM	LVL	AGE	PA	R	2B	3B	HR	RBI	BB	SO	SB	CS	AVG_OBP_SLG	TAv	BABIP	BRR	FRAA	WARP
2011	SYR	AAA	26	218	17	15	0	5	30	5	54	0	0	.234/.252/.378	.214	.288	-1.7	C(38): -0.2	-0.4
2011	WAS	MLB	26	91	5	6	0	1	2	5	27	0	0	.209/.253/.314	.204	.293	-1.5	C(22): -0.5	-0.4
2012	WAS	MLB	27	296	22	12	1	6	26	13	59	1	2	.213/.248/.329	.202	.247	-1.8	C(79): -0.7	-1.4
2013	*WAS*	*MLB*	*28*	*259*	*25*	*12*	*1*	*7*	*27*	*13*	*61*	*1*	*1*	*.236/.279/.376*	*.232*	*.287*	*-0.4*	*C -0*	*0.4*

The former Rule 5 pickup from the Mets hasn't been the same since his 29-game breakout in 2009, and injuries, underperformance, and the acquisition of Kurt Suzuki led to his non-tendering by the Nationals. Capable backstops don't usually linger on the wire too long, so Flores will latch on somewhere either as a backup or as a Triple-A starter on hand for depth.

Brian Goodwin **CF**

Born: **11/2/1990** Age: **22**
Bats: **L** Throws: **L** Height: **6' 2"**
Weight: **195** Breakout: **3%**
Improve: **67%** Collapse: **2%**
Attrition: **11%** MLB: **94%**

Comparables:
Willie Mays,Grady Sizemore,Lastings Milledge

YEAR	TEAM	LVL	AGE	PA	R	2B	3B	HR	RBI	BB	SO	SB	CS	AVG_OBP_SLG	TAv	BABIP	BRR	FRAA	WARP
2012	HAG	A	21	266	47	18	1	9	38	43	39	15	4	.324/.438/.542	.366	.357	0.4	CF(48): 2.0	3.3
2012	HAR	AA	21	186	17	8	1	5	14	18	50	3	3	.223/.306/.373	.254	.288	0.3	CF(35): -3.3	0.2
2013	*WAS*	*MLB*	*22*	*250*	*31*	*10*	*1*	*7*	*24*	*22*	*63*	*5*	*2*	*.230/.301/.371*	*.242*	*.284*	*0*	*CF -2*	*0.1*

The 2011 first-round pick tore up Hagerstown until mid-July, when the Nationals challenged him with a level-skipping promotion to Double-A. The stats fell back to earth, but scouts were impressed with how Goodwin handled the failure. Undeterred by stumbling to the finish line of the regular season, Goodwin went down to Arizona and mashed the ball in the Fall League, with 11 of his 19 hits going for extra bases. He then shined brightest in the AFL All-Star Game, clubbing a home run and double with all eyes on him. This five-tool stud gives the Nationals yet another future outfielder, though he's still a few years off.

Bryce Harper **OF**

Born: **10/16/1992** Age: **20**
Bats: **L** Throws: **R** Height: **6' 4"**
Weight: **225** Breakout: **17%**
Improve: **79%** Collapse: **2%**
Attrition: **8%** MLB: **94%**

Comparables:
Mike Trout,Ken Griffey,Justin Upton

YEAR	TEAM	LVL	AGE	PA	R	2B	3B	HR	RBI	BB	SO	SB	CS	AVG_OBP_SLG	TAv	BABIP	BRR	FRAA	WARP
2011	HAG	A	18	305	49	17	1	14	46	44	61	19	5	.318/.423/.554	.324	.372	0.8	RF(40): 3.0, CF(15): -1.1	2.6
2011	HAR	AA	18	147	14	7	1	3	12	15	26	7	2	.256/.329/.395	.238	.294	1.9	LF(27): -1.2	0.0
2012	SYR	AAA	19	84	8	4	1	1	3	9	14	1	1	.243/.325/.365	.259	.288	-0.4	CF(10): -0.7, RF(5): -0.3	0.0
2012	WAS	MLB	19	597	98	26	9	22	59	56	120	18	6	.270/.340/.477	.291	.310	5.4	CF(92): 1.5, RF(63): 2.7	4.5
2013	*WAS*	*MLB*	*20*	*495*	*71*	*22*	*4*	*18*	*57*	*44*	*104*	*17*	*5*	*.261/.327/.448*	*.275*	*.300*	*1.3*	*CF -0, RF 1*	*2.3*

Thanks to the explosion of Mike Trout, Harper's brilliant rookie campaign has been somewhat undersold, but he exceeded even the wildest expectations. Though he had been struggling early in Triple-A, he got a surprise call-up in late April because the Nats needed an impact bat, since they seemed to be losing one a day. He lived up to the hype immediately, doubling and making a dynamite throw in his debut, then stealing home off of Cole Hamels in his eighth game. He hit the proverbial rookie wall in July, at one point posting a 501 OPS in 34 games, but he rebounded brilliantly, hitting 12 home runs with a 1045 OPS in his final 44 contests. What will he do for an encore? Improvement isn't out of the question. Harper has been graded with easy 80 power by throngs of scouts and analysts. The sky's the limit.

Destin Hood **OF**

Born: **4/3/1990** Age: **23**
Bats: **R** Throws: **R** Height: **6' 2"**
Weight: **225** Breakout: **6%**
Improve: **64%** Collapse: **10%**
Attrition: **20%** MLB: **95%**

Comparables:
Jim McAnany,Ollie Brown,Jim King

YEAR	TEAM	LVL	AGE	PA	R	2B	3B	HR	RBI	BB	SO	SB	CS	AVG_OBP_SLG	TAv	BABIP	BRR	FRAA	WARP
2010	HAG	A	20	537	56	30	3	5	65	33	119	5	7	.285/.337/.388	.267	.367	0.8	RF(69): -1.1, LF(60): -5.3	0.7
2011	POT	A+	21	536	61	29	5	13	83	58	96	21	6	.276/.364/.445	.274	.319	-0.7	RF(81): 5.1, LF(10): 0.7	1.2
2012	HAR	AA	22	389	45	20	3	3	45	24	89	6	1	.245/.301/.344	.233	.315	-0.3	RF(73): -6.0, LF(4): -0.3	-1.2
2013	*WAS*	*MLB*	*23*	*250*	*21*	*11*	*1*	*3*	*22*	*13*	*64*	*2*	*1*	*.227/.272/.324*	*.215*	*.295*	*-0.1*	*RF -0, LF -1*	*-0.7*

A wrist injury stunted Hood's development in 2012. He remains an ultra-talented prospect the team loves and holds in high esteem. His bat should play well in either left or right field, though he will need to deliver some value through speed and defense to make up for his power not matching that of a prototypical corner outfielder. There's still plenty of development to be done here. It remains to be seen whether the rough 2012 will derail his ETA of 2014.

Adam LaRoche **1B**
Born: **11/6/1979** Age: **33**
Bats: **L** Throws: **L** Height: **6' 4"**
Weight: **205** Breakout: **2%**
Improve: **33%** Collapse: **1%**
Attrition: **11%** MLB: **88%**
Comparables:
Brad Hawpe,Roy Sievers,Fred McGriff

YEAR	TEAM	LVL	AGE	PA	R	2B	3B	HR	RBI	BB	SO	SB	CS	AVG_OBP_SLG	TAv	BABIP	BRR	FRAA	WARP
2010	ARI	MLB	30	615	75	37	2	25	100	48	172	0	1	.261/.320/.468	.271	.330	-2.4	1B(146): 9.7	2.0
2011	WAS	MLB	31	177	15	4	0	3	15	25	37	1	0	.172/.288/.258	.208	.205	1.7	1B(43): 3.0	-0.7
2012	WAS	MLB	32	647	76	35	1	33	100	67	138	1	1	.271/.343/.510	.303	.298	-3.3	1B(153): 10.8	3.6
2013	*WAS*	*MLB*	*33*	*514*	*61*	*26*	*1*	*21*	*72*	*48*	*124*	*1*	*1*	*.252/.321/.451*	*.271*	*.298*	*-1*	*1B -0*	*0.9*

Pitching and LaRoche sustained the Nationals in April as they scored a paltry 3.4 runs per game while managing to hold the opposite to just 2.7 runs of their own. LaRoche and Jayson Werth were the only regulars with an OPS north of 713 that month, and LaRoche's 964 was leaps and bounds ahead of even Werth at 806. He didn't slow down from there. June was his worst month by OPS at just 718, but seven of his 16 hits were home runs. He picked the perfect time for arguably the best year of his career, and he cashed in by re-signing with the Nationals for two years and $24 million. An underrated aspect of the venerable LaRoche is that he also plays sharp defense at first base.

Sandy Leon **C**
Born: **3/13/1989** Age: **24**
Bats: **B** Throws: **R** Height: **6' 0"**
Weight: **175** Breakout: **3%**
Improve: **23%** Collapse: **7%**
Attrition: **10%** MLB: **90%**
Comparables:
Yorvit Torrealba,Javier Valentin,Charlie Moore

YEAR	TEAM	LVL	AGE	PA	R	2B	3B	HR	RBI	BB	SO	SB	CS	AVG_OBP_SLG	TAv	BABIP	BRR	FRAA	WARP
2010	HAG	A	21	385	48	10	6	2	36	50	79	3	5	.249/.345/.335	.268	.317	-2.7	C(91): 0.4	2.4
2011	POT	A+	22	416	36	21	1	6	43	33	69	1	3	.251/.312/.362	.220	.292	-3.5	C(77): 0.7	0.2
2012	HAR	AA	23	149	15	12	0	1	19	9	16	1	0	.311/.358/.422	.276	.342	0.5	C(31): -0.1	0.7
2012	SYR	AAA	23	64	8	5	0	2	4	12	12	0	0	.346/.469/.558	.328	.421	-2.1	C(14): 0.2	0.4
2012	WAS	MLB	23	36	2	2	0	0	2	4	11	0	0	.267/.389/.333	.294	.421	-1.3	C(12): -0.2	0.1
2013	*WAS*	*MLB*	*24*	*250*	*22*	*10*	*1*	*3*	*21*	*19*	*56*	*0*	*0*	*.233/.297/.325*	*.226*	*.292*	*-0.4*	*C -0*	*0.2*

The emergence of Leon, who went from High-A to the majors last year, allowed the team the freedom to non-tender Flores. Leon will almost certainly start the season in Triple-A with Suzuki and Wilson Ramos handling the big-league duties, but he gives Washington great defensive depth behind the dish. With Suzuki a free agent after this year, Leon is eyeing the backup job for 2014.

Steve Lombardozzi **UT**
Born: **9/20/1988** Age: **24**
Bats: **B** Throws: **R** Height: **6' 1"**
Weight: **170** Breakout: **1%**
Improve: **33%** Collapse: **7%**
Attrition: **11%** MLB: **97%**
Comparables:
Johnny Giavotella,Felix Millan,Ken Boswell

YEAR	TEAM	LVL	AGE	PA	R	2B	3B	HR	RBI	BB	SO	SB	CS	AVG_OBP_SLG	TAv	BABIP	BRR	FRAA	WARP
2010	POT	A+	21	507	71	30	9	1	38	49	60	20	10	.293/.364/.409	.281	.329	2.2	2B(107): -11.8	1.4
2010	HAR	AA	21	118	19	5	2	5	11	12	15	4	2	.295/.373/.524	.316	.306	0.2	2B(31): -2.7	1.0
2011	HAR	AA	22	291	40	12	7	4	23	18	38	16	3	.309/.366/.454	.307	.348	2.1	2B(46): -4.8, SS(3): -0.4	1.0
2011	SYR	AAA	22	325	46	13	2	4	29	21	40	14	5	.310/.354/.408	.232	.344	0.6	2B(39): 0.6, SS(5): -0.1	-0.3
2011	WAS	MLB	22	32	3	1	0	0	1	1	4	0	0	.194/.219/.226	.167	.222	-0.7	2B(3): -0.0, 3B(3): 0.3	-0.3
2012	WAS	MLB	23	416	40	16	3	3	27	19	46	5	3	.273/.317/.354	.249	.304	-2.7	2B(51): 5.3, LF(41): -0.6	0.4
2013	*WAS*	*MLB*	*24*	*366*	*42*	*16*	*3*	*4*	*29*	*20*	*50*	*10*	*4*	*.267/.314/.370*	*.245*	*.296*	*0.5*	*2B -1, LF 0*	*0.5*

Lombardozzi sports a legitimate hit tool that elevates him from a defensive replacement to a super-utility infielder who's a perfect fit on a National League ballclub. If he could add some patience to his game as well, he could even be stretched into a second-division starter. There is no power present and none coming, but teams could do a lot worse than having Lombardozzi plug holes around their infield while racking up 350-400 plate appearances.

Chris Marrero **1B**
Born: **7/2/1988** Age: **24**
Bats: **R** Throws: **R** Height: **6' 4"**
Weight: **210** Breakout: **8%**
Improve: **64%** Collapse: **2%**
Attrition: **13%** MLB: **95%**
Comparables:
Chris Parmelee,Darin Erstad,Paul Konerko

YEAR	TEAM	LVL	AGE	PA	R	2B	3B	HR	RBI	BB	SO	SB	CS	AVG_OBP_SLG	TAv	BABIP	BRR	FRAA	WARP
2010	HAR	AA	22	577	73	28	0	18	82	43	102	1	3	.294/.353/.450	.281	.337	-3.7	1B(133): 0.3	1.3
2011	SYR	AAA	23	546	59	30	0	14	69	58	97	3	2	.300/.375/.449	.287	.349	3.7	1B(90): 5.5	2.1
2011	WAS	MLB	23	117	6	5	0	0	10	4	27	0	0	.248/.274/.294	.217	.318	-0.7	1B(31): -0.1	-0.8
2012	SYR	AAA	23	144	13	6	1	0	12	16	28	0	0	.244/.333/.307	.226	.313	0.2	1B(24): -1.4	-0.7
2013	*WAS*	*MLB*	*24*	*250*	*24*	*11*	*0*	*5*	*27*	*16*	*50*	*0*	*0*	*.260/.311/.384*	*.251*	*.309*	*-0.5*	*1B -5*	*-0.6*

It feels like the former first-round pick has been around forever, especially when you consider that he ranked 28th on Baseball Prospectus's Top 100 list all the way back in 2008. Marrero's 2012 was cut short by multiple injuries, and he played just 53 games. Yet he's only 24, meaning there's still a glimmer of hope that he can deliver on his prospect potential. The problem is that his bat has regressed to the point that it won't play at first base, the only position he's manned since he last stood in an outfield in 2007. See why it's just a glimmer of hope? Despite seven seasons of minor-league ball, he only has 690 plate appearances in Triple-A, so he'll head there for more seasoning in 2013.

Tyler Moore OF

Born: 1/30/1987 Age: 26
Bats: R Throws: R Height: 6' 3''
Weight: 185 Breakout: 2%
Improve: 45% Collapse: 3%
Attrition: 14% MLB: 97%

Comparables:
Orlando Cepeda,Nate Colbert,Will Clark

YEAR	TEAM	LVL	AGE	PA	R	2B	3B	HR	RBI	BB	SO	SB	CS	AVG_OBP_SLG	TAv	BABIP	BRR	FRAA	WARP
2010	POT	A+	23	553	78	43	3	31	111	40	125	0	0	.269/.324/.552	.308	.299	-1.9	1B(124): 12.6	4.7
2011	HAR	AA	24	561	70	35	4	31	90	30	139	2	0	.270/.314/.532	.307	.307	-0.3	1B(94): 3.2	2.5
2012	SYR	AAA	25	115	15	6	1	9	26	12	26	1	0	.307/.374/.653	.311	.324	-1.9	1B(20): 2.4, LF(3): -0.3	0.6
2012	WAS	MLB	25	171	20	9	0	10	29	14	46	3	0	.263/.327/.513	.278	.310	-2.2	LF(39): -4.0, 1B(14): -0.3	-0.2
2013	*WAS*	*MLB*	*26*	*250*	*31*	*12*	*1*	*13*	*39*	*15*	*66*	*1*	*0*	*.249/.296/.482*	*.271*	*.287*	*-0.3*	*1B -4, LF -0*	*0.2*

Moore needed just 29 games in Triple-A before the Nats deemed him worthy of the call, though as with Harper, their options were limited by mounting injuries. The power-heavy college product rewarded the team's trust with a quality debut that included a team-high .513 slugging percentage, though in only 171 plate appearances. The trade for Denard Span and re-signing of LaRoche will make it a challenge for Moore to find playing time.

Michael Morse OF

Born: 3/22/1982 Age: 31
Bats: R Throws: R Height: 6' 6''
Weight: 230 Breakout: 1%
Improve: 51% Collapse: 4%
Attrition: 9% MLB: 96%

Comparables:
Marcus Thames,Jim Rice,Josh Hamilton

YEAR	TEAM	LVL	AGE	PA	R	2B	3B	HR	RBI	BB	SO	SB	CS	AVG_OBP_SLG	TAv	BABIP	BRR	FRAA	WARP
2010	SYR	AAA	28	60	12	2	0	3	8	8	11	0	0	.255/.367/.471	.256	.270	-0.1	1B(6): 0.1, RF(5): -0.1	0.1
2010	WAS	MLB	28	293	36	12	2	15	41	22	64	0	1	.289/.352/.519	.300	.330	-3.7	RF(72): 1.2, 1B(19): 0.3	1.5
2011	WAS	MLB	29	575	73	36	0	31	95	36	126	2	3	.303/.360/.550	.319	.344	1.3	1B(85): -0.0, LF(55): -1.9	3.4
2012	WAS	MLB	30	430	53	17	1	18	62	16	97	0	1	.291/.321/.470	.276	.339	-4.9	LF(67): -3.9, RF(36): 1.5	0.1
2013	*WAS*	*MLB*	*31*	*436*	*54*	*21*	*1*	*20*	*64*	*26*	*98*	*1*	*1*	*.279/.330/.484*	*.287*	*.323*	*-0.9*	*LF -0, 1B -1*	*1.8*

If told to guess whether Morse's batting average or slugging percentage would stick from his breakout season, you better believe 10-of-10 would have gone with power. Alas, they would have been wrong. It was an odd season for Morse, though, as a lat injury pushed his 2012 debut to June and then he endured a host of nagging injuries. Perhaps those injuries contributed to his peculiar batted-ball profile: His groundball rate soared by 11 percent while his fly-ball rate plummeted just as much. Power remained a part of his game, just less so than in 2011. Meanwhile, he now has three straight years of BABIPs fit for a speedy leadoff hitter, so it just might be a skill connected to the hard contact he generates.

Eury Perez CF

Born: 5/30/1990 Age: 23
Bats: R Throws: R Height: 6' 1''
Weight: 180 Breakout: 3%
Improve: 49% Collapse: 7%
Attrition: 13% MLB: 90%

Comparables:
Rocco Baldelli,Morris Nettles,Gary Woods

YEAR	TEAM	LVL	AGE	PA	R	2B	3B	HR	RBI	BB	SO	SB	CS	AVG_OBP_SLG	TAv	BABIP	BRR	FRAA	WARP
2010	HAG	A	20	491	88	17	5	3	42	23	74	64	13	.299/.331/.381	.285	.335	14.1	CF(113): 7.1, RF(16): -0.7	5.2
2011	POT	A+	21	465	54	9	2	1	41	22	63	45	15	.283/.319/.321	.261	.326	2.6	CF(87): 3.2, LF(6): 0.5	1.3
2012	HAR	AA	22	373	34	11	2	0	30	7	53	26	10	.299/.325/.342	.273	.351	1.6	CF(71): 8.3, RF(2): -0.1	2.7
2012	SYR	AAA	22	173	21	7	1	0	10	8	26	20	5	.333/.373/.390	.255	.398	1.9	CF(22): 2.4, LF(10): -0.1	0.7
2012	WAS	MLB	22	5	3	0	0	0	0	0	0	3	0	.200/.200/.200	.164	.200	-0.6	CF(4): -0.1, LF(3): -0.0	-0.1
2013	*WAS*	*MLB*	*23*	*250*	*30*	*9*	*1*	*1*	*15*	*5*	*46*	*18*	*5*	*.264/.284/.327*	*.221*	*.312*	*1.8*	*CF -2, LF -0*	*-0.3*

Perez is a speed-only outfielder capable of posting an identical batting average, on-base percentage, and slugging percentage in a season if it weren't for a handful of speed doubles. Perhaps that is overstating things, but his 4 percent walk rate since arriving in stateside rookie ball in 2009 leaves a lot to be desired. He has maintained solid batting averages, but he'll need more of a refined approach in the majors to become anything more than a fifth outfielder/defensive replacement/pinch-runner. At 23, there's still time to improve, and game-changing speed like his will get a long leash to see if he can put it together.

Wilson Ramos C

Born: 8/10/1987 Age: 25
Bats: R Throws: R Height: 6' 1''
Weight: 220 Breakout: 3%
Improve: 52% Collapse: 3%
Attrition: 8% MLB: 92%

Comparables:
Ted Simmons,Miguel Montero,Johnny Pramesa

YEAR	TEAM	LVL	AGE	PA	R	2B	3B	HR	RBI	BB	SO	SB	CS	AVG_OBP_SLG	TAv	BABIP	BRR	FRAA	WARP
2010	ROC	AAA	22	295	25	14	0	5	30	12	49	1	2	.241/.278/.345	.217	.274	-0.5	C(53): -0.9	0.0
2010	SYR	AAA	22	82	14	3	1	3	8	3	12	0	0	.316/.341/.494	.282	.344	0.7	C(18): 0.3	0.9
2010	MIN	MLB	22	28	2	3	0	0	1	0	3	0	0	.296/.321/.407	.258	.333	0	C(7): -0.1	0.1
2010	WAS	MLB	22	54	3	4	0	1	4	2	9	0	0	.269/.296/.404	.239	.310	-1.2	C(15): 0.1	0.1
2011	WAS	MLB	23	435	48	22	1	15	52	38	76	0	2	.267/.334/.445	.269	.297	0.7	C(108): -1.4	2.0
2012	WAS	MLB	24	96	11	2	0	3	10	12	19	0	0	.265/.354/.398	.284	.306	0.4	C(24): 0.3	0.5
2013	*WAS*	*MLB*	*25*	*250*	*27*	*12*	*1*	*7*	*29*	*17*	*44*	*0*	*0*	*.264/.317/.421*	*.261*	*.294*	*-0.5*	*C 0*	*1.1*

A torn ACL cut Ramos's season short and left the Nationals with a season-long struggle to find adequate offense behind the dish. Ramos had a breakout 2011 season as a rookie, with a balanced approach that landed him in the top 10 among catchers by virtually any measure of composite value. Davey Johnson has indicated that Ramos will be worked back into the starting role slowly as he recovers, especially with a veteran like Suzuki on hand. Ramos is still the future for the Nationals, a potential star-caliber player.

Tony Renda 2B
Born: **1/24/1991** Age: **22**
Bats: **R** Throws: **R** Height: **5' 11"**
Weight: **170** Breakout: **6%**
Improve: **50%** Collapse: **5%**
Attrition: **9%** MLB: **94%**
Comparables:
Mark Lewis,Glenn Hubbard,Luis Rivas

YEAR	TEAM	LVL	AGE	PA	R	2B	3B	HR	RBI	BB	SO	SB	CS	AVG_OBP_SLG	TAv	BABIP	BRR	FRAA	WARP
2012	AUB	A-	21	334	47	9	0	0	32	31	33	15	3	.264/.341/.295	.257	.294	3.1	2B(54): 3.9	0.8
2013	*WAS*	*MLB*	*22*	*250*	*23*	*8*	*1*	*2*	*16*	*13*	*52*	*4*	*1*	*.212/.254/.279*	*.197*	*.259*	*0.1*	*2B 1*	*-0.6*

The undersized 2012 second-rounder from Cal has been tabbed as "scrappy," "a sparkplug," and "gritty" because he often plays above his pure talent. The easy (read: lazy) comparison to Dustin Pedroia is dangerous because it places an unfair burden on Renda simply because of his size and ethnicity. He is a pure hitter with good foot and bat speed. If he hits in the pros like he did at Cal, he will quickly force his way onto prospect lists even though the tools report will be underwhelming.

Anthony Rendon 3B
Born: **6/6/1990** Age: **23**
Bats: **R** Throws: **R** Height: **6' 1"**
Weight: **190** Breakout: **3%**
Improve: **66%** Collapse: **4%**
Attrition: **13%** MLB: **94%**
Comparables:
Matt Tuiasosopo,Eric Chavez,Ron Santo

YEAR	TEAM	LVL	AGE	PA	R	2B	3B	HR	RBI	BB	SO	SB	CS	AVG_OBP_SLG	TAv	BABIP	BRR	FRAA	WARP
2012	HAR	AA	22	82	14	3	1	3	3	11	16	0	0	.162/.305/.368	.281	.163	2	3B(15): 1.2	0.6
2013	*WAS*	*MLB*	*23*	*250*	*25*	*9*	*2*	*7*	*29*	*22*	*57*	*1*	*0*	*.227/.301/.377*	*.246*	*.271*	*-0.1*	*3B 1*	*0.3*

Rendon touched four levels in his pro debut, though he only managed 43 games in all as injuries once again cut down the promising prospect. They have been a problem throughout his career, dating back to his time at Rice. A future with health on his side would be an extremely bright one. He put on a show in the hitter-friendly Arizona Fall League, hitting .338, smacking 11 extra-base hits, and walking 15 times compared to just 14 strikeouts. Rendon has everything you want in a batter's profile as well as the ability to capably field his position, leaving his upside on a plane with current Nationals third baseman Ryan Zimmerman and NL East foe David Wright.

Will Rhymes INF
Born: **4/1/1983** Age: **30**
Bats: **L** Throws: **R** Height: **5' 10"**
Weight: **155** Breakout: **2%**
Improve: **31%** Collapse: **1%**
Attrition: **13%** MLB: **94%**
Comparables:
Billy Goodman,Dave Cash,Fernando Vina

YEAR	TEAM	LVL	AGE	PA	R	2B	3B	HR	RBI	BB	SO	SB	CS	AVG_OBP_SLG	TAv	BABIP	BRR	FRAA	WARP
2010	TOL	AAA	27	421	59	20	7	2	35	36	35	22	5	.305/.362/.415	.272	.321	3.1	2B(65): 0.2, 3B(13): -1.1	1.8
2010	DET	MLB	27	213	30	12	3	1	19	14	16	0	3	.304/.350/.414	.277	.326	-1.3	2B(53): 2.1	1.0
2011	TOL	AAA	28	464	57	17	4	3	24	46	46	13	8	.306/.377/.390	.260	.337	-2.6	2B(61): -3.3, LF(5): -0.5	-0.1
2011	DET	MLB	28	99	13	3	0	0	2	11	12	1	0	.235/.323/.271	.228	.274	-0.3	2B(24): -1.1	-0.3
2012	DUR	AAA	29	194	19	5	3	4	21	18	19	2	3	.256/.326/.390	.264	.265	-0.6	2B(12): -0.2, 3B(3): 0.1	0.1
2012	TBA	MLB	29	137	11	2	1	1	8	10	17	1	2	.228/.299/.285	.228	.255	0.6	2B(31): 1.8, 3B(15): 0.7	0.3
2013	*WAS*	*MLB*	*30*	*250*	*28*	*10*	*2*	*2*	*19*	*19*	*27*	*5*	*3*	*.266/.326/.359*	*.245*	*.288*	*-0.1*	*2B -2, 3B -0*	*0.3*

Just two years removed from being the Opening Day second baseman for the Tigers, Rhymes now finds himself on the outside of prospecthood looking in, although he does offer good plate discipline, decent infield utility, and a perspicacious Twitter feed as a bench player or Triple-A call-up candidate. The Nationals signed him to a minor-league deal after the Rays let him go.

Carlos Rivero INF
Born: **5/20/1988** Age: **25**
Bats: **R** Throws: **R** Height: **6' 4"**
Weight: **200** Breakout: **15%**
Improve: **55%** Collapse: **6%**
Attrition: **17%** MLB: **96%**
Comparables:
Andy Carey,Aramis Ramirez,Carlos Guillen

YEAR	TEAM	LVL	AGE	PA	R	2B	3B	HR	RBI	BB	SO	SB	CS	AVG_OBP_SLG	TAv	BABIP	BRR	FRAA	WARP
2010	AKR	AA	22	444	39	16	2	6	43	28	81	0	3	.232/.281/.325	.223	.274	-3.3	SS(107): 10.4	0.6
2011	REA	AA	23	538	70	36	0	15	66	38	106	5	3	.275/.331/.440	.263	.321	0.4	3B(64): -6.3	0.0
2012	SYR	AAA	24	498	57	28	1	10	64	33	87	6	5	.303/.347/.435	.266	.352	0.1	3B(82): 12.1, 1B(16): -0.7	2.5
2013	*WAS*	*MLB*	*25*	*250*	*22*	*12*	*1*	*5*	*26*	*11*	*51*	*1*	*1*	*.247/.282/.366*	*.232*	*.292*	*-0.5*	*3B 0, SS 0*	*-0.1*

A former top prospect in the Indians organization, Rivero stalled out at Double-A and bounced around before the Nationals plucked him from the Phillies. Last season he enjoyed a career year in Triple-A after shifting to a more contact-oriented approach at the expense of some power. The result is a post-hype prospect who is starting to pay dividends. He came up as a shortstop, though his future may be at third base: He played the hot corner for most of 2012, in addition to 17 games at short. The Nationals could have a solid utility man on their hands with the potential for a bit more. All essentially for free, too.

Matthew Skole **3B**

Born: **7/30/1989** Age: **23**
Bats: **L** Throws: **R** Height: **6' 5"**
Weight: **230** Breakout: **6%**
Improve: **59%** Collapse: **5%**
Attrition: **8%** MLB: **95%**

Comparables:
Troy Glaus,Brandon Wood,Andy Van Slyke

YEAR	TEAM	LVL	AGE	PA	R	2B	3B	HR	RBI	BB	SO	SB	CS	AVG_OBP_SLG	TAv	BABIP	BRR	FRAA	WARP
2011	AUB	A-	21	319	43	23	1	5	48	42	52	2	1	.290/.382/.438	.285	.338	-1.9	3B(45): -8.2	-0.2
2012	HAG	A	22	448	73	18	0	27	92	94	116	10	0	.286/.438/.574	.341	.345	-2.8	3B(90): -6.3	4.0
2012	POT	A+	22	76	11	10	1	0	12	5	17	1	0	.314/.355/.486	.330	.407	0.6	3B(8): 0.5	0.5
2013	*WAS*	*MLB*	*23*	*250*	*28*	*9*	*1*	*9*	*32*	*30*	*72*	*0*	*0*	*.220/.314/.394*	*.253*	*.276*	*-0.3*	*3B -0*	*0.3*

Skole mashed his way through Hagerstown in his full-season debut, hitting 27 home runs before earning a late-season promotion to High-A. Additionally, he walked 94 times in Hagerstown and another five in Potomac, which gave him the highest walk total of anyone below Double-A and the second highest in all of the minor leagues. The power profile is no fluke. It's exactly what he was expected to deliver after pounding the ACC with 47 home runs in his three years at Georgia Tech. His peak value is obviously at third base, a position he can handle defensively, but given the logjam there he could be forced across the diamond, which would eat into, but not totally destroy, his value.

Denard Span **CF**

Born: **2/27/1984** Age: **29**
Bats: **L** Throws: **L** Height: **6' 1"**
Weight: **210** Breakout: **0%**
Improve: **44%** Collapse: **3%**
Attrition: **8%** MLB: **96%**

Comparables:
Lenny Green,Shane Victorino,Johnny Damon

YEAR	TEAM	LVL	AGE	PA	R	2B	3B	HR	RBI	BB	SO	SB	CS	AVG_OBP_SLG	TAv	BABIP	BRR	FRAA	WARP
2010	MIN	MLB	26	705	85	24	10	3	58	60	74	26	4	.264/.331/.348	.248	.294	2.3	CF(153): 7.5	2.1
2011	MIN	MLB	27	311	37	11	5	2	16	27	36	6	1	.264/.328/.359	.257	.297	2.2	CF(67): 7.6	1.4
2012	MIN	MLB	28	568	71	38	4	4	41	47	62	17	6	.283/.342/.395	.270	.315	-1.1	CF(125): 6.8	2.3
2013	*WAS*	*MLB*	*29*	*486*	*60*	*20*	*5*	*6*	*41*	*44*	*61*	*16*	*5*	*.281/.351/.391*	*.266*	*.310*	*1.3*	*CF 2*	*2.2*

His new trainers in Washington would do well to stop listening to Span when he claims to feel fine. After suffering from a nasty concussion in 2011, Span pushed to come back too quickly and went 2-for-35 before being shut down for another month. Last year, instead of going on the DL for a sprained shoulder, Span refused an MRI due to his claustrophobia and assured Twins manager Ron Gardenhire he could come back in a couple of days. He took 10 days off, returned for four games, reinjured the shoulder, and was out another two weeks. Undeniably, Span plays the game hard and, when healthy, is a good leadoff hitter and a strong defender in center.

Kurt Suzuki **C**

Born: **10/4/1983** Age: **29**
Bats: **R** Throws: **R** Height: **6' 0"**
Weight: **195** Breakout: **0%**
Improve: **40%** Collapse: **8%**
Attrition: **16%** MLB: **95%**

Comparables:
Ken Retzer,Carlos Ruiz,Brayan Pena

YEAR	TEAM	LVL	AGE	PA	R	2B	3B	HR	RBI	BB	SO	SB	CS	AVG_OBP_SLG	TAv	BABIP	BRR	FRAA	WARP
2010	OAK	MLB	26	544	55	18	2	13	71	33	49	3	2	.242/.303/.366	.244	.245	-3.5	C(123): -2.7	0.7
2011	OAK	MLB	27	515	54	26	0	14	44	38	64	2	2	.237/.301/.385	.258	.244	-1.6	C(129): -1.7	1.2
2012	OAK	MLB	28	278	19	15	0	1	18	9	53	1	0	.218/.250/.286	.200	.267	-1.7	C(75): -1.1	-0.6
2012	WAS	MLB	28	164	17	5	0	5	25	11	20	1	0	.267/.321/.404	.269	.274	-0.3	C(42): 0.5	0.6
2013	*WAS*	*MLB*	*29*	*430*	*43*	*21*	*1*	*10*	*48*	*24*	*50*	*3*	*1*	*.261/.312/.395*	*.254*	*.274*	*-0.7*	*C -1*	*1.5*

Suzuki has long derived the bulk of his value from his work behind the plate, but he put a huge burden on himself to remain a positive value player with Oakland last year by carrying a .200 True Average at the dish. Not even Jose Molina's pitch framing and defense could counteract that kind of bat. Suzuki was dealt on August 3, to loud lamenting by A's pitchers. It turned out to be a boon for Suzuki, though. He surged, posting a .269 TAv with the Nats, his second-best total ever. Now he finds himself with the starting job as Ramos heals from a torn ACL. Suzuki is making nearly $6.5 million in 2013, which is the final guaranteed year of his contract. It is unlikely he could do enough to earn his $8.5 million team option for 2014.

Michael Taylor **CF**

Born: **3/26/1991** Age: **22**
Bats: **R** Throws: **R** Height: **6' 3"**
Weight: **190** Breakout: **9%**
Improve: **54%** Collapse: **5%**
Attrition: **18%** MLB: **93%**

Comparables:
Nelson Mathews,Gary Geiger,David Green

YEAR	TEAM	LVL	AGE	PA	R	2B	3B	HR	RBI	BB	SO	SB	CS	AVG_OBP_SLG	TAv	BABIP	BRR	FRAA	WARP
2010	NAT	Rk	19	149	14	4	3	1	12	14	31	1	2	.195/.278/.297	.232	.247	-0.1	SS(19): 0.9, 2B(9): 0.2	0.4
2011	HAG	A	20	488	64	26	7	13	68	32	120	23	12	.253/.310/.432	.243	.316	1.5	CF(78): -3.8, RF(16): 0.3	-0.3
2012	POT	A+	21	431	51	33	2	3	37	40	113	19	9	.242/.318/.362	.242	.335	1.2	CF(86): 9.8, RF(1): -0.2	2.0
2013	*WAS*	*MLB*	*22*	*250*	*22*	*10*	*1*	*3*	*20*	*13*	*74*	*7*	*3*	*.197/.241/.296*	*.194*	*.266*	*0.2*	*CF -1, RF -0*	*-1.1*

Perhaps this Michael Taylor will enjoy a better fate than the former uber-prospect of the same name in the Oakland organization. Like the Oakland version, this Taylor has tools for days, though they come in a compact 6-foot-2 frame compared to Oakland's behemoth. In a perfect world, this version could become a power-speed center fielder headlining a lineup, but he is a long way from that potential. He needs to focus on making better contact and starting to shave that massive strikeout rate. Taylor has struck out in over a quarter of his plate appearances as a professional.

Chad Tracy **3B**

Born: **5/22/1980** Age: **33**
Bats: **L** Throws: **R** Height: **6' 3"**
Weight: **215** Breakout: **1%**
Improve: **34%** Collapse: **13%**
Attrition: **22%** MLB: **86%**

Comparables:
Jim Spencer,Javier Valentin,David Segui

YEAR	TEAM	LVL	AGE	PA	R	2B	3B	HR	RBI	BB	SO	SB	CS	AVG_OBP_SLG	TAv	BABIP	BRR	FRAA	WARP
2010	IOW	AAA	30	96	21	8	0	5	18	5	9	0	1	.396/.427/.648	.371	.403	1.1	3B(19): 1.4	1.6
2010	SWB	AAA	30	73	14	5	0	6	18	4	6	0	0	.324/.361/.662	.336	.286	0.1	3B(14): -0.1, 1B(2): -0.1	0.9
2010	CHN	MLB	30	49	6	2	0	0	5	5	15	0	0	.250/.327/.295	.229	.379	0.3	3B(10): -0.7, 1B(2): -0.0	0.0
2010	FLO	MLB	30	111	5	6	0	1	10	6	21	0	0	.245/.297/.333	.221	.296	0.3	3B(24): 0.9, 1B(5): 0.0	0.0
2012	WAS	MLB	32	105	7	7	0	3	14	10	15	0	0	.269/.343/.441	.282	.289	-1.4	1B(14): 0.4, 3B(10): 0.2	0.4
2013	*WAS*	*MLB*	*33*	*250*	*24*	*13*	*0*	*6*	*28*	*16*	*42*	*0*	*0*	*.255/.304/.388*	*.246*	*.285*	*-0.5*	*3B -0, 1B -0*	*0.2*

Yes, this is *that* Chad Tracy, the one who hit 27 home runs for Arizona in 2005. After a heavy fade in his late-20s, he spent 2011 in Japan before returning and latching on with the Nationals. He broke camp with the team and was off to a great start when a strained groin cut him down for two months. He was adequate upon returning from injury, and overall, his season has to be considered a success, all 105 plate appearances of it. Signed to a one-year extension in August, Tracy had arthroscopic surgery on his left knee in October, but he should be ready to vie for a bench spot in spring training.

Jayson Werth **RF**

Born: **5/20/1979** Age: **34**
Bats: **R** Throws: **R** Height: **6' 6"**
Weight: **220** Breakout: **1%**
Improve: **29%** Collapse: **2%**
Attrition: **9%** MLB: **93%**

Comparables:
Larry Walker,Ken Singleton,Dwight Evans

YEAR	TEAM	LVL	AGE	PA	R	2B	3B	HR	RBI	BB	SO	SB	CS	AVG_OBP_SLG	TAv	BABIP	BRR	FRAA	WARP
2010	PHI	MLB	31	652	106	46	2	27	85	82	147	13	3	.296/.388/.532	.324	.352	-0.3	RF(135): -1.6, CF(21): -0.4	5.8
2011	WAS	MLB	32	649	69	26	1	20	58	74	160	19	3	.232/.330/.389	.262	.286	2.1	RF(134): 3.0, CF(19): 2.0	1.9
2012	WAS	MLB	33	344	42	21	3	5	31	42	57	8	2	.300/.387/.440	.303	.356	-1	RF(76): 5.3, CF(11): -1.0	2.0
2013	*WAS*	*MLB*	*34*	*389*	*51*	*18*	*1*	*15*	*51*	*45*	*91*	*10*	*2*	*.259/.351/.447*	*.285*	*.312*	*0.6*	*RF 2, CF -0*	*2.3*

Werth suffered through an abysmal season on the heels of signing his $126 million contract, but he was in the midst of wiping away that memory when he fractured his left wrist and missed 75 games. He was great again once he returned, seemingly changing his approach to adapt to his new role in the leadoff spot. He has always drawn walks, but he drastically cut his strikeout rate from 25 percent to 17. His new-found groundball approach seems to have drained his power, but some of that should return: He suffered through a criminally low 5 percent home-run-per-fly-ball rate in 2012.

Ryan Zimmerman **3B**

Born: **9/28/1984** Age: **28**
Bats: **R** Throws: **R** Height: **6' 4"**
Weight: **230** Breakout: **1%**
Improve: **46%** Collapse: **1%**
Attrition: **7%** MLB: **97%**

Comparables:
Bobby Thomson,Edwin Encarnacion,Chipper Jones

YEAR	TEAM	LVL	AGE	PA	R	2B	3B	HR	RBI	BB	SO	SB	CS	AVG_OBP_SLG	TAv	BABIP	BRR	FRAA	WARP
2010	WAS	MLB	25	603	85	32	0	25	85	69	98	4	1	.307/.388/.510	.308	.334	-0.7	3B(137): -10.4	3.4
2011	WAS	MLB	26	440	52	21	2	12	49	41	73	3	1	.289/.355/.443	.282	.326	-0.7	3B(97): -1.7	2.2
2012	WAS	MLB	27	641	93	36	1	25	95	57	116	5	2	.282/.346/.478	.287	.313	-0.3	3B(145): 5.7	4.0
2013	*WAS*	*MLB*	*28*	*565*	*71*	*29*	*1*	*22*	*80*	*51*	*97*	*3*	*1*	*.285/.351/.478*	*.293*	*.312*	*-0.8*	*3B 2*	*3.4*

A June series in Colorado is credited as the turning point of Zimmerman's season, which ended up being excellent despite a slump of nearly three months. He entered Coors Field with a 597 season OPS, but went 7-for-19 with two homers in the four-game set and his season took off. In the 89 games starting with that series, Zimmerman hit .319, posted a 967 OPS, and popped 22 of his 25 home runs. He had nursed a shoulder injury through the bulk of his slump, and may have benefited from a well-timed cortisone shot. The franchise cornerstone is in the thick of his prime and should remain a star-level talent for several more years.

PITCHERS

Fernando Abad

Born: **12/17/1985** Age: **27**
Bats: **L** Throws: **L** Height: **6' 3"** Weight: **215**
Breakout: **21%** Improve: **46%** Collapse: **32%**
Attrition: **14%** MLB: **89%**

Comparables:
Terry Mathews,Gabe White,Tom Gorman

YEAR	TEAM	LVL	AGE	W	L	SV	G	GS	IP	H	HR	BB	SO	BB9	SO9	GB%	BABIP	WHIP	ERA	FIP	FRA	WARP
2010	CCH	AA	24	4	3	0	14	4	39^{2}	48	3	6	33	1.4	7.5	43%	.360	1.36	2.49	2.95	4.01	0.4
2010	ROU	AAA	24	0	0	0	5	0	6^{1}	5	1	2	9	2.9	12.9	33%	.286	1.11	1.43	3.74	3.80	0.1
2010	HOU	MLB	24	0	1	0	22	0	19	14	3	5	12	2.4	5.7	32%	.196	1.00	2.84	4.69	5.15	0.0
2011	AST	Rk	25	0	0	0	2	0	2	1	0	0	2	0.0	9.0	60%	.200	0.50	0.00	1.42	1.94	0.1
2011	OKL	AAA	25	2	3	0	29	0	30	32	4	6	31	1.8	9.3	–	.326	1.27	4.80	4.05	4.40	0.0
2011	HOU	MLB	25	1	4	0	29	0	19^{2}	28	5	9	15	4.1	6.9	39%	.333	1.88	7.32	6.30	6.69	-0.4
2012	OKL	AAA	26	2	0	2	13	3	27^{2}	33	3	7	28	2.3	9.1	34%	.366	1.45	3.90	3.92	3.77	0.4
2012	HOU	MLB	26	0	6	0	37	6	46	57	6	19	38	3.7	7.4	43%	.359	1.65	5.09	4.61	3.82	0.6
2013	*WAS*	*MLB*	*27*	*3*	*2*	*0*	*34*	*4*	45^{2}	*47*	*6*	*13*	*35*	*2.6*	*7.0*	*39%*	*.312*	*1.32*	*4.59*	*4.23*	*4.99*	*-0.1*

Abad's 88 games with the Astros are likely to be remembered by few, fondly by fewer still. He knows how to throw four pitches, so he was tried as a starting pitcher last year when Houston was in dire straits. It didn't go well. He has a compact short-arm delivery that leaves him in good fielding position and shuts down the running game. But as far as retiring batters goes, his only success to date has been against the left-handed variety, against whom he still sports a sub-.300 career on-base percentage allowed.

Bill Bray
Born: **6/5/1983** Age: **30**
Bats: **L** Throws: **L** Height: **6' 4"** Weight: **225**
Breakout: **43%** Improve: **65%** Collapse: **15%**
Attrition: **4%** MLB: **91%**
Comparables:
Jack Taschner,Rob Murphy,George Sherrill

YEAR	TEAM	LVL	AGE	W	L	SV	G	GS	IP	H	HR	BB	SO	BB9	SO9	GB%	BABIP	WHIP	ERA	FIP	FRA	WARP
2010	LYN	A+	27	0	0	0	4	0	4^2	1	0	2	9	3.8	17.2	43%	.143	0.64	0.00	0.85	2.21	0.2
2010	LOU	AAA	27	0	0	1	6	0	5^2	2	0	1	7	1.6	11.1	25%	.167	0.53	0.00	1.36	-0.49	0.3
2010	CIN	MLB	27	0	2	0	35	0	28^1	21	4	10	30	3.2	9.5	39%	.233	1.09	4.13	3.88	4.20	0.3
2011	CIN	MLB	28	5	3	0	79	0	48^1	35	3	17	44	3.2	8.2	34%	.246	1.08	2.98	3.16	3.92	0.4
2012	DYT	A	29	1	0	0	2	0	2^2	0	0	1	4	3.4	13.5	80%	.000	0.38	0.00	1.48	-2.27	0.1
2012	LOU	AAA	29	1	0	0	14	0	12	17	1	12	10	9.0	7.5	43%	.390	2.42	9.00	5.57	6.63	-0.2
2012	CIN	MLB	29	0	0	0	14	0	8^2	6	2	14	7	14.5	7.3	27%	.200	2.31	5.19	9.37	10.88	-0.5
2013	*WAS*	*MLB*	*30*	*3*	*1*	*1*	*53*	*0*	37^2	*31*	*4*	*15*	*38*	*3.7*	*9.1*	*40%*	*.292*	*1.24*	*3.61*	*3.76*	*3.92*	*0.4*

Left-groin and low-back injuries ruined Bray's 2012, just as injuries have marred many seasons in his career. He made five appearances in April, then missed two months, then got into nine more games before calling it a season at the beginning of September. Even when he was healthy, he couldn't throw strikes. He returns to his original organization on a minor-league deal and will hope for more health and strikes this year.

Tyler Clippard
Born: **2/14/1985** Age: **28**
Bats: **R** Throws: **R** Height: **6' 4"** Weight: **200**
Breakout: **32%** Improve: **63%** Collapse: **25%**
Attrition: **13%** MLB: **84%**
Comparables:
Billy Sadler,Rich Gossage,Eric Hull

YEAR	TEAM	LVL	AGE	W	L	SV	G	GS	IP	H	HR	BB	SO	BB9	SO9	GB%	BABIP	WHIP	ERA	FIP	FRA	WARP
2010	WAS	MLB	25	11	8	1	78	0	91	69	8	41	112	4.1	11.1	29%	.284	1.21	3.07	3.21	4.18	0.8
2011	WAS	MLB	26	3	0	0	72	0	88^1	48	11	26	104	2.6	10.6	24%	.197	0.84	1.83	3.14	3.12	1.4
2012	WAS	MLB	27	2	6	32	74	0	72^2	55	7	29	84	3.6	10.4	32%	.259	1.16	3.72	3.36	3.47	1.0
2013	*WAS*	*MLB*	*28*	*3*	*1*	*10*	*62*	*0*	*70*	*52*	*8*	*26*	*77*	*3.4*	*9.9*	*33%*	*.274*	*1.12*	*3.04*	*3.60*	*3.30*	*1.2*

Pitching up in the zone is frowned upon, but try telling that to Clippard, who has ranked in the bottom five in the majors in groundball rate in each of the past three seasons. Primarily a fastball-changeup pitcher, with cutters sprinkled in to give like-handed hitters a different look, Clippard relied more on his off-speed offerings in 2012 while ably filling Drew Storen's shoes in the ninth inning. The bespectacled righty's free-falling changeup is a weapon against left-handed batters, and its remarkable contrast with his 93-mph heater has helped the former Yankees farmhand to develop into one of the senior circuit's most feared relievers. Clippard figures to return to eighth-inning work to begin the season, but if Storen endures another injury or a slump, he'll be first in line for save opportunities.

Ross Detwiler
Born: **3/6/1986** Age: **27**
Bats: **R** Throws: **L** Height: **6' 6"** Weight: **185**
Breakout: **24%** Improve: **54%** Collapse: **14%**
Attrition: **12%** MLB: **88%**
Comparables:
Sergio Mitre,Doug Mathis,Mitch Talbot

YEAR	TEAM	LVL	AGE	W	L	SV	G	GS	IP	H	HR	BB	SO	BB9	SO9	GB%	BABIP	WHIP	ERA	FIP	FRA	WARP
2010	POT	A+	24	0	0	0	2	2	6	6	1	1	6	1.5	9.0	67%	.294	1.17	1.50	4.07	4.44	0.1
2010	HAR	AA	24	2	2	0	7	7	32^2	38	1	7	31	1.9	8.5	49%	.345	1.38	2.48	2.69	3.15	1.2
2010	SYR	AAA	24	1	0	0	1	1	5	5	0	1	2	1.8	3.6	80%	.333	1.20	1.80	3.09	4.71	0.0
2010	WAS	MLB	24	1	3	0	8	5	29^2	34	5	14	17	4.2	5.2	44%	.296	1.62	4.25	5.67	5.99	-0.1
2011	SYR	AAA	25	6	6	0	16	16	87^1	98	4	32	63	3.3	6.5	52%	.351	1.49	4.53	3.52	4.37	0.7
2011	WAS	MLB	25	4	5	0	15	10	66	63	7	20	41	2.7	5.6	46%	.272	1.26	3.00	4.18	4.51	0.2
2012	WAS	MLB	26	10	8	0	33	27	164^1	149	15	52	105	2.8	5.8	53%	.263	1.22	3.40	4.09	4.78	0.4
2013	*WAS*	*MLB*	*27*	*8*	*7*	*0*	*24*	*24*	124^2	*129*	*13*	*42*	*81*	*3.1*	*5.9*	*49%*	*.306*	*1.37*	*4.56*	*4.27*	*4.96*	*-0.1*

Three years removed from surgery to repair a torn labrum in his right hip, Detwiler does not have the overpowering stuff typically associated with top-10 draft picks, but he logged the 13th-best ERA among NL starters thanks to the Nationals' elite defense. As long as Detwiler continues to throw his fastball, curveball, and changeup for strikes, he will be an adequate fifth starter in a star-studded rotation. Sadly, though, his performance on the mound may never live up to his Twitter handle, @nationaldet.

Zach Duke

Born: **4/19/1983** Age: **30**
Bats: **L** Throws: **L** Height: **6' 2"** Weight: **205**
Breakout: **18%** Improve: **56%** Collapse: **17%**
Attrition: **19%** MLB: **79%**

Comparables:
Mike Maroth, Jack Kralick, Claude Osteen

YEAR	TEAM	LVL	AGE	W	L	SV	G	GS	IP	H	HR	BB	SO	BB9	SO9	GB%	BABIP	WHIP	ERA	FIP	FRA	WARP
2010	ALT	AA	27	0	0	0	2	2	7	5	1	1	1	1.3	1.3	44%	.333	0.86	2.57	5.36	6.98	-0.2
2010	PIT	MLB	27	8	15	0	29	29	159	212	25	51	96	2.9	5.4	49%	.338	1.65	5.72	4.98	5.31	0.1
2011	VIS	A+	28	1	0	0	1	1	5	5	0	0	4	0.0	7.2	—	.333	1.00	1.80	2.35	2.56	0.0
2011	RNO	AAA	28	1	0	0	1	1	5^{1}	7	2	1	2	1.7	3.4	—	.263	1.50	8.44	8.47	9.21	0.0
2011	ARI	MLB	28	3	4	1	21	9	76^{2}	101	6	19	32	2.2	3.8	50%	.339	1.57	4.93	3.96	4.76	0.5
2012	SYR	AAA	29	15	5	0	26	26	164^{1}	178	16	39	91	2.1	5.0	53%	.298	1.32	3.51	4.05	6.07	-1.3
2012	WAS	MLB	29	1	0	0	8	0	13^{2}	11	0	4	10	2.6	6.6	41%	.262	1.10	1.32	2.55	2.40	0.4
2013	*WAS*	*MLB*	*30*	*4*	*4*	*0*	*11*	*11*	*65*	*73*	*8*	*15*	*35*	*2.0*	*4.8*	*50%*	*.312*	*1.35*	*4.80*	*4.42*	*5.21*	*-0.3*

As sixth starters go, you could do a lot worse than Duke. The lefty doesn't miss many bats, but he also seldom misses the strike zone, a skill that—with the Nationals' quality defense—makes him a serviceable rotation option if injuries strike. Duke's multimillion-dollar-paycheck days are in the rearview mirror, and after returning to Washington on a one-year deal, he'll strive to become the new John Lannan. The Nationals survived 2012 without needing a rotation replacement to make more than six starts, but given the question marks surrounding Dan Haren's back and the elbow troubles in Stephen Strasburg and Jordan Zimmermann's not-too-distant pasts, Duke may back into a double-digit assignment this year.

Christian Garcia

Born: **8/24/1985** Age: **27**
Bats: **R** Throws: **R** Height: **6' 6"** Weight: **215**
Breakout: **24%** Improve: **55%** Collapse: **21%**
Attrition: **11%** MLB: **90%**

Comparables:
Francisco Cruceta, Danny Darwin, Andrew Bailey

YEAR	TEAM	LVL	AGE	W	L	SV	G	GS	IP	H	HR	BB	SO	BB9	SO9	GB%	BABIP	WHIP	ERA	FIP	FRA	WARP
2010	TRN	AA	24	1	0	0	1	1	5^{2}	2	0	1	3	1.6	4.7	53%	.133	0.53	0.00	3.36	3.83	0.0
2011	AUB	A-	25	3	1	1	10	0	18^{1}	17	1	2	28	1.0	13.7	64%	.333	1.04	2.95	1.84	2.83	0.3
2011	SYR	AAA	25	0	0	0	1	0	2	0	0	1	2	4.5	9.0	—	.000	0.50	0.00	2.74	2.97	0.0
2012	HAR	AA	26	1	0	7	18	0	20	13	0	6	28	2.7	12.6	59%	.283	0.95	1.35	1.30	1.75	0.8
2012	SYR	AAA	26	1	1	14	27	0	32^{1}	18	0	11	38	3.1	10.6	70%	.231	0.90	0.56	1.83	3.13	0.6
2012	WAS	MLB	26	0	0	0	13	0	12^{2}	8	2	2	15	1.4	10.7	31%	.222	0.79	2.13	3.77	4.90	0.0
2013	*WAS*	*MLB*	*27*	*2*	*1*	*0*	*32*	*0*	*38*	*32*	*4*	*14*	*38*	*3.4*	*9.1*	*51%*	*.299*	*1.23*	*3.73*	*3.67*	*4.06*	*0.3*

A third-round pick by the Yankees in 2004, Garcia took the road less traveled through the minor leagues, waiting eight years for his major-league debut, changing organizations in 2011, and requiring three elbow surgeries along the way. The righty has never lacked for stuff—as demonstrated by his minor-league strikeout rates and his numbers in a cup of coffee last September—and his four-pitch arsenal led Johnson to ponder converting him to a starter for 2013. Washington's rotation is full, so Garcia will be ticketed for Triple-A if he doesn't secure a bullpen gig out of spring training. As long as his ligaments stay hinged, he should have a bright future in the nation's capital.

Lucas Giolito

Born: **7/14/1994** Age: **18**
Bats: **R** Throws: **R** Height: **6' 7"** Weight: **225**
Breakout: **--%** Improve: **--%** Collapse: **--%**
Attrition: **--%** MLB: **--%**

Comparables:
--

YEAR	TEAM	LVL	AGE	W	L	SV	G	GS	IP	H	HR	BB	SO	BB9	SO9	GB%	BABIP	WHIP	ERA	FIP	FRA	WARP
2012	NAT	Rk	17	0	0	0	1	1	2	2	0	0	1	0.0	4.5	—	.333	1.00	4.50	2.20	2.65	0.0

Once considered the top high-school pitching prospect in the 2012 draft, Giolito slipped 15 spots before the Nationals happily scooped him up for an above-slot bonus of $2.925 million. Giolito required Tommy John surgery in August, postponing his ascent up the minor-league ladder for most of the 2013 season, but assuming he regains his mid-90s fastball and knee-buckling curve, he has the talent to jump back onto the fast track to Nationals Park. Developing a trustworthy changeup to go with the power breaker would go a long way toward enabling Giolito to reach his ace ceiling.

Michael Gonzalez

Born: **5/23/1978** Age: **35**
Bats: **R** Throws: **L** Height: **6' 3"** Weight: **215**
Breakout: **23%** Improve: **46%** Collapse: **36%**
Attrition: **21%** MLB: **86%**

Comparables:
John Hiller, Lee Smith, Kerry Wood

YEAR	TEAM	LVL	AGE	W	L	SV	G	GS	IP	H	HR	BB	SO	BB9	SO9	GB%	BABIP	WHIP	ERA	FIP	FRA	WARP
2010	ORI	Rk	32	0	0	0	2	2	2	1	0	0	3	0.0	13.5	%	.250	0.50	0.00	0.51	2.60	0.1
2010	ABE	A-	32	0	1	0	4	1	5	7	2	0	5	0.0	9.0	56%	.357	1.40	5.40	6.67	7.65	-0.1
2010	BOW	AA	32	1	0	0	4	0	4	2	1	1	4	2.2	9.0	20%	.111	0.75	2.25	5.36	5.74	0.0
2010	NOR	AAA	32	0	0	0	2	1	1^{2}	3	0	2	4	10.6	21.2	50%	.750	2.94	10.59	2.11	-0.33	0.2
2010	BAL	MLB	32	1	3	1	29	0	24^{2}	18	1	14	31	5.1	11.3	36%	.283	1.30	4.01	2.76	3.04	0.5
2011	BAL	MLB	33	2	2	1	49	0	46^{1}	46	7	18	46	3.5	8.9	41%	.302	1.38	4.27	4.33	4.34	0.3
2011	TEX	MLB	33	0	0	0	7	0	7	5	0	3	5	3.9	6.4	50%	.250	1.14	5.14	2.92	3.64	0.1
2012	SYR	AAA	34	0	0	0	1	0	1^{1}	0	0	0	2	0.0	13.5	1.%	.000	0.00	0.00	0.16	1.97	0.0
2012	WAS	MLB	34	0	0	0	47	0	35^{2}	31	2	16	39	4.0	9.8	43%	.309	1.32	3.03	3.02	2.59	0.8
2013	*WAS*	*MLB*	*35*	*2*	*1*	*1*	*44*	*0*	*38^{1}*	*31*	*4*	*14*	*42*	*3.3*	*10.0*	*41%*	*.296*	*1.17*	*3.39*	*3.46*	*3.68*	*0.5*

For a setup man with a long track record of trampling opposing lefties, Gonzalez sure has bounced around a lot, chiefly because his medical history is just as long. Gonzalez underwent Tommy John surgery in 2007, watched most of the 2010 season while rehabbing rotator cuff and labrum woes, and needed knee surgery last offseason to repair a torn meniscus in his left knee. As long as he stays healthy, Gonzalez will be a valuable contributor to any bullpen, though his manager should understand the folly of letting him face righties in high-leverage spots.

Gio Gonzalez

Born: **9/19/1985** Age: **27**
Bats: **R** Throws: **L** Height: **6' 1"** Weight: **205**
Breakout: **21%** Improve: **54%** Collapse: **26%**
Attrition: **5%** MLB: **93%**

Comparables:
Dustin McGowan, Chad Billingsley, Edinson Volquez

YEAR	TEAM	LVL	AGE	W	L	SV	G	GS	IP	H	HR	BB	SO	BB9	SO9	GB%	BABIP	WHIP	ERA	FIP	FRA	WARP
2010	OAK	MLB	24	15	9	0	33	33	200^{2}	171	15	92	171	4.1	7.7	51%	.274	1.31	3.23	3.75	4.33	1.7
2011	OAK	MLB	25	16	12	0	32	32	202	175	17	91	197	4.1	8.8	48%	.287	1.32	3.12	3.68	3.94	2.3
2012	WAS	MLB	26	21	8	0	32	32	199^{1}	149	9	76	207	3.4	9.3	50%	.267	1.13	2.89	2.87	3.36	3.7
2013	*WAS*	*MLB*	*27*	*12*	*8*	*0*	*28*	*28*	171^{2}	*144*	*16*	*68*	*165*	*3.6*	*8.7*	*48%*	*.291*	*1.24*	*3.60*	*3.68*	*3.91*	*1.7*

Gonzalez delivered his best campaign to date after coming over from the A's. He earned his second consecutive All-Star Game trip and placed third in the NL Cy Young vote. The southpaw has improved his walk and strikeout rates in each of his first three major-league seasons, and, paired with Strasburg, he gives the Nationals a formidable one-two punch atop the rotation. If the strides Gonzalez has taken to date are real, the five-year, $42 million extension he signed last January—at the time the largest contract ever for a pitcher in his first year of arbitration eligibility—will prove to be one of the league's great bargains.

Dan Haren

Born: **9/17/1980** Age: **32**
Bats: **R** Throws: **R** Height: **6' 6"** Weight: **215**
Breakout: **12%** Improve: **30%** Collapse: **38%**
Attrition: **14%** MLB: **86%**

Comparables:
Josh Beckett, Aaron Harang, Ben Sheets

YEAR	TEAM	LVL	AGE	W	L	SV	G	GS	IP	H	HR	BB	SO	BB9	SO9	GB%	BABIP	WHIP	ERA	FIP	FRA	WARP
2010	ANA	MLB	29	5	4	0	14	14	94	84	8	25	75	2.4	7.2	41%	.274	1.16	2.87	3.42	4.01	0.7
2010	ARI	MLB	29	7	8	0	21	21	141	161	23	29	141	1.9	9.0	42%	.336	1.35	4.60	3.91	4.27	3.0
2011	ANA	MLB	30	16	10	0	35	34	238^{1}	211	20	33	192	1.2	7.3	45%	.272	1.02	3.17	3.02	3.75	3.0
2012	SBR	A+	31	0	0	0	1	1	5	7	0	0	2	0.0	3.6	39%	.389	1.40	3.60	3.01	-1.54	0.0
2012	ANA	MLB	31	12	13	0	30	30	176^{2}	190	28	38	142	1.9	7.2	41%	.302	1.29	4.33	4.20	4.48	0.7
2013	*WAS*	*MLB*	*32*	*13*	*8*	*0*	*27*	*27*	178^{1}	*165*	*21*	*29*	*154*	*1.5*	*7.8*	*43%*	*.295*	*1.09*	*3.33*	*3.49*	*3.62*	*2.4*

Angels GM Jerry DiPoto knew he had some tough decisions to make after the 2012 season, but picking up Haren's $15.5 million option didn't figure to be one of them. Then Haren turned in the worst year of his career. The Angels once bought low on a slumping Haren, but this slumping Haren is much more troubling than the 2010 version shopped by the Diamondbacks. His velocity dropped another mile per hour, continuing a steady five-year decline. Lost fastball velocity forces him to his lesser pitches: Haren threw far more splitters and cutters (66 percent combined) than he did in 2010 (41 percent), when he had more heat. Haren's inability to set up his secondary pitches with a strong fastball allows hitters to sit on them. In 2010, Haren got whiffs on nearly 18 percent of his secondary pitches—in 2012, 12 percent. The Nationals signed Haren for one year, $13 million. There's buying low, and there's buying late.

Cole Kimball

Born: **8/1/1985** Age: **27**
Bats: **R** Throws: **R** Height: **6' 4"** Weight: **225**
Breakout: **31%** Improve: **56%** Collapse: **13%**
Attrition: **9%** MLB: **92%**

Comparables:
Esmerling Vasquez, Bob Trowbridge, John Axford

YEAR	TEAM	LVL	AGE	W	L	SV	G	GS	IP	H	HR	BB	SO	BB9	SO9	GB%	BABIP	WHIP	ERA	FIP	FRA	WARP
2010	POT	A+	24	3	0	6	19	0	24^{2}	17	0	8	27	2.9	9.8	43%	.283	1.01	1.82	2.43	2.97	0.6
2010	HAR	AA	24	5	1	12	38	0	54	33	4	31	74	5.2	12.3	44%	.248	1.19	2.33	3.58	3.50	1.3
2011	SYR	AAA	25	1	0	5	12	0	13^{2}	8	0	8	14	5.3	9.2	45%	.250	1.17	0.00	2.94	3.18	0.2
2011	WAS	MLB	25	1	0	0	12	0	14	8	0	11	11	7.1	7.1	31%	.222	1.36	1.93	3.99	3.63	0.2
2012	NAT	Rk	26	0	0	0	1	1	1	1	0	0	1	0.0	9.0	33%	.333	1.00	0.00	1.43	1.17	0.1
2012	HAG	A	26	0	0	0	1	1	1	1	0	0	2	0.0	18.0	%	.500	1.00	0.00	-0.42	0.86	0.1
2012	POT	A+	26	0	1	0	3	2	3^{1}	6	3	0	2	0.0	5.4	31%	.231	1.80	10.80	14.79	19.98	0.0
2012	HAR	AA	26	0	0	0	1	0	0^{1}	1	0	1	0	27.0	0.0	50%	.500	6.00	0.00	12.20	13.94	-0.1
2013	*WAS*	*MLB*	*27*	*1*	*0*	*1*	*28*	*0*	35^{1}	*32*	*4*	*21*	*31*	*5.4*	*7.8*	*39%*	*.298*	*1.51*	*4.96*	*4.70*	*5.39*	*-0.3*

Kimball made his major-league debut in 2011, and he immediately etched his name in the history books—sort of. The flamethrower became one of only five Liveball Era pitchers to log at least 14 innings, walk at least seven batters per nine, and post an ERA below 2.00 in a season. All of that is to say that when Kimball finally returns from July 2011 rotator-cuff surgery—hopefully in spring training—he'll need to rein in the walks. The hefty Brooklyn native has the gas to succeed in a seventh-inning role, provided he can keep his shoulder intact and harness his aim.

Ryan Mattheus

Born: **11/10/1983** Age: **29**
Bats: **R** Throws: **R** Height: **6' 4"** Weight: **215**
Breakout: **31%** Improve: **51%** Collapse: **21%**
Attrition: **24%** MLB: **86%**

Comparables:
Todd Frohwirth, Chad Bradford, Ramon Troncoso

YEAR	TEAM	LVL	AGE	W	L	SV	G	GS	IP	H	HR	BB	SO	BB9	SO9	GB%	BABIP	WHIP	ERA	FIP	FRA	WARP
2010	NAT	Rk	26	0	1	0	6	3	6	5	0	1	6	1.5	9.0	65%	.294	1.00	1.50	2.01	4.26	0.1
2010	VER	A-	26	1	0	0	4	1	5^{1}	3	0	2	5	3.4	8.5	67%	.200	0.94	0.00	2.72	2.57	0.2
2011	HAR	AA	27	2	1	4	13	0	14^{2}	9	1	5	18	3.1	11.0	57%	.250	0.95	2.45	3.07	4.06	0.2
2011	SYR	AAA	27	0	0	2	9	0	10	3	0	3	10	2.7	9.0	59%	.136	0.60	0.00	2.14	3.05	0.2
2011	WAS	MLB	27	2	2	0	35	0	32	26	1	15	12	4.2	3.4	53%	.236	1.28	2.81	4.24	4.79	-0.1
2012	POT	A+	28	0	1	0	1	0	1	2	2	0	0	0.0	0.0	20%	.000	2.00	18.00	29.39	30.49	-0.2
2012	HAR	AA	28	0	0	0	2	0	2	0	0	1	3	4.5	13.5	25%	.000	0.50	4.50	1.70	2.30	0.1
2012	WAS	MLB	28	5	3	0	66	0	66^{1}	57	8	19	41	2.6	5.6	49%	.253	1.15	2.85	4.46	5.06	-0.3
2013	*WAS*	*MLB*	*29*	*3*	*1*	*0*	*54*	*0*	*54*	*50*	*6*	*19*	*40*	*3.2*	*6.6*	*51%*	*.287*	*1.28*	*4.03*	*4.22*	*4.39*	*0.2*

Mattheus, like Clippard, is a converted starter whose deep arsenal makes him serviceable against both left- and right-handed batters. Unlike Clippard, though, Mattheus relies on a sinker-slider combination to generate groundball contact, a *modus operandi* tailored for success in front of the Nationals' rangy infielders. Mattheus hung a few too many of those sliders during the second half, serving up seven of the eight homers he allowed after the All-Star break, but he compensated for that damage by inducing 12 double-play balls, good for second among all relievers. The Sacramento-area native will be back in his familiar middle-inning role this season, and for deep-league fantasy owners, he is a reasonable bet to improve on his 2012 total of 18 holds.

Yunesky Maya

Born: **8/28/1981** Age: **31**
Bats: **R** Throws: **R** Height: **6' 0"** Weight: **170**
Breakout: **8%** Improve: **46%** Collapse: **29%**
Attrition: **15%** MLB: **92%**

Comparables:
Billy O'Dell, Dave Goltz, Frank Lary

YEAR	TEAM	LVL	AGE	W	L	SV	G	GS	IP	H	HR	BB	SO	BB9	SO9	GB%	BABIP	WHIP	ERA	FIP	FRA	WARP
2010	NAT	Rk	28	0	0	0	2	2	7	3	0	2	5	2.6	6.4	74%	.158	0.71	1.29	3.36	4.81	0.0
2010	POT	A+	28	0	1	0	1	1	4	7	1	3	4	6.8	9.0	47%	.429	2.50	13.50	7.66	6.69	-0.1
2010	SYR	AAA	28	1	1	0	2	2	10^{1}	8	0	5	9	4.4	7.9	60%	.267	1.26	0.87	3.00	4.00	0.1
2010	WAS	MLB	28	0	3	0	5	5	26	30	3	11	12	3.8	4.2	34%	.300	1.58	5.88	5.18	5.78	-0.1
2011	SYR	AAA	29	4	9	0	22	22	129^{2}	133	14	28	98	1.9	6.8	48%	.292	1.24	5.00	3.89	4.90	0.3
2011	WAS	MLB	29	1	1	0	10	5	32^{2}	40	3	10	15	2.8	4.1	45%	.330	1.53	5.23	4.37	4.91	-0.2
2012	SYR	AAA	30	11	10	0	28	28	167	158	20	40	89	2.2	4.8	50%	.257	1.19	3.88	4.48	6.21	-1.1
2013	*WAS*	*MLB*	*31*	*3*	*3*	*0*	*12*	*9*	56^{1}	*56*	*7*	*16*	*38*	*2.5*	*6.0*	*47%*	*.296*	*1.27*	*4.17*	*4.32*	*4.53*	*0.2*

Remember when Maya, a Cuban import who made a name for himself in the World Baseball Classic, was starting September games for the Nationals after taking the mound only five times in the minors? Then-manager Jim Riggleman trotted out 14 different starting pitchers that year, with Maya netting five assignments down the stretch. If you'd told Nationals fans then that in just two years their team would be winning the franchise's first division title since 1981 with a dominant rotation, they'd have laughed you all the way to Montreal. Maya throws strikes, but lacks swing-and-miss stuff, and while the four-year major-league deal he signed in 2010 will keep him employed this year, it may be his last guaranteed paycheck in the States.

Ryan Perry

Born: **2/13/1987** Age: **26**
Bats: **R** Throws: **R** Height: **6' 5"** Weight: **200**
Breakout: **32%** Improve: **65%** Collapse: **16%**
Attrition: **15%** MLB: **86%**

Comparables:
Jose Capellan, Fernando Hernandez, Ray Narleski

YEAR	TEAM	LVL	AGE	W	L	SV	G	GS	IP	H	HR	BB	SO	BB9	SO9	GB%	BABIP	WHIP	ERA	FIP	FRA	WARP
2010	TOL	AAA	23	0	0	0	3	0	3^{2}	1	0	4	4	9.7	9.7	67%	.111	1.35	0.00	4.37	4.80	0.0
2010	DET	MLB	23	3	5	2	60	0	62^{2}	55	6	23	45	3.3	6.5	46%	.269	1.24	3.59	4.20	4.85	0.2
2011	TOL	AAA	24	3	0	7	20	0	32^{2}	24	1	9	30	2.5	8.3	41%	.226	1.01	3.03	2.72	4.00	0.2
2011	DET	MLB	24	2	0	0	36	0	37	39	1	21	24	5.1	5.8	38%	.317	1.62	5.35	3.98	4.41	0.3
2012	HAR	AA	25	2	4	0	13	13	73	59	3	22	46	2.7	5.7	56%	.263	1.11	2.84	3.54	4.43	0.4
2012	SYR	AAA	25	1	1	2	11	0	12	16	0	7	14	5.2	10.5	48%	.516	1.92	4.50	2.82	3.31	0.2
2012	WAS	MLB	25	1	0	0	7	0	8	12	2	2	3	2.2	3.4	37%	.357	1.75	10.12	6.39	6.95	-0.2
2013	*WAS*	*MLB*	*26*	*2*	*1*	*0*	*24*	*2*	37^{1}	*34*	*4*	*15*	*30*	*3.6*	*7.3*	*46%*	*.297*	*1.32*	*4.12*	*4.19*	*4.48*	*0.1*

When the Tigers grabbed Perry with the 21st pick of the 2008 draft, he was supposed to be on the fast track to ninth-inning work. But even dating back to his days as a collegian at the University of Arizona, Perry's strikeout numbers have never matched his raw stuff. He throws a high-90s fastball and a slider that flashes wipeout movement, but neither pitch is dependable because of erratic command and wayward mechanics. Acquired by the Nationals for Collin Balester in December 2011, Perry is out of options, so he will need to show substantial progress this spring to stay in the organization. Failing that, another team might gamble on his long-lost upside, stashing Perry in Triple-A and hoping for the best.

Matt Purke

Born: **7/17/1990** Age: **22**
Bats: **L** Throws: **L** Height: **6' 5"** Weight: **180**
Breakout: **22%** Improve: **37%** Collapse: **33%**
Attrition: **30%** MLB: **88%**

Comparables:
Jerry Reuss,Buddy Carlyle,Brad Hand

YEAR	TEAM	LVL	AGE	W	L	SV	G	GS	IP	H	HR	BB	SO	BB9	SO9	GB%	BABIP	WHIP	ERA	FIP	FRA	WARP
2012	HAG	A	21	0	2	0	3	3	15^{1}	15	1	12	14	7.0	8.2	49%	.318	1.76	5.87	5.14	6.11	0.3
2013	*WAS*	*MLB*	*22*	*2*	*3*	*0*	*7*	*7*	*35*	*38*	*5*	*18*	*23*	*4.5*	*5.8*	*45%*	*.309*	*1.58*	*5.62*	*5.29*	*6.11*	*-0.5*

Another example, along with Giolito, of general manager Mike Rizzo's willingness to gamble on elite arms, Purke had top-10 talent but dropped to the third round in 2011 because of injury concerns. Signed to a major-league deal out of Texas Christian University, he endured a rocky professional debut in the Sally League before visiting Dr. Lewis Yocum and succumbing to surgery to relieve bursitis in his troublesome left shoulder. Purke was given a clean bill of health after that procedure, and he expects to be at full strength come spring training, so there is ample hope that he may yet reward the Nationals' $4 million investment.

Henry Rodriguez

Born: **2/25/1987** Age: **26**
Bats: **R** Throws: **R** Height: **6' 1"** Weight: **220**
Breakout: **34%** Improve: **65%** Collapse: **16%**
Attrition: **15%** MLB: **86%**

Comparables:
Al Alburquerque,Juan Morillo,Daniel Bard

YEAR	TEAM	LVL	AGE	W	L	SV	G	GS	IP	H	HR	BB	SO	BB9	SO9	GB%	BABIP	WHIP	ERA	FIP	FRA	WARP
2010	OAK	MLB	23	1	0	0	29	0	27^{2}	25	2	13	33	4.2	10.7	41%	.319	1.37	4.55	3.12	4.06	0.3
2011	HAR	AA	24	0	0	0	3	1	4	3	0	0	7	0.0	15.8	20%	.600	0.75	0.00	-0.09	-3.21	0.2
2011	SYR	AAA	24	0	0	0	6	0	8^{1}	5	0	6	9	6.5	9.7	50%	.188	1.32	1.08	3.24	4.77	0.0
2011	WAS	MLB	24	3	3	2	59	0	65^{2}	54	1	45	70	6.2	9.6	47%	.299	1.51	3.56	3.21	3.81	0.6
2012	HAR	AA	25	0	0	0	3	0	3	0	0	1	4	3.0	12.0	60%	.000	0.33	0.00	1.53	1.50	0.1
2012	SYR	AAA	25	0	0	2	4	0	4	0	0	4	3	9.0	6.8	78%	.000	1.00	0.00	4.66	4.58	0.0
2012	WAS	MLB	25	1	3	9	35	0	29^{1}	19	4	22	31	6.8	9.5	39%	.205	1.40	5.83	5.15	6.49	-0.4
2013	*WAS*	*MLB*	*26*	*2*	*1*	*3*	*36*	*0*	36^{2}	*29*	*3*	*21*	*41*	*5.2*	*10.1*	*46%*	*.300*	*1.38*	*3.92*	*3.75*	*4.26*	*0.2*

Rodriguez and Gio Gonzalez uncorked the same number of wild pitches (10) last year, but while the lefty starter amassed that total over nearly 200 innings, the righty reliever, who also came over from Oakland, did so in fewer than 30. From a pure stuff standpoint, Rodriguez is unparalleled: If you measure effectiveness by whiff percentage, then his fastball, which touches triple digits, is his third-best pitch. But, as the Nationals discovered when they wanted Rodriguez to supplant Storen as their closer, the gas is useless if it doesn't find the tank. Rodriguez had an eventful 2012 on top of the wildness, missing a month after slamming his index finger in a bathroom door, then straining his back, and eventually requiring surgery to remove bone fragments from his elbow. He'll report to spring training looking for a fresh start and a chance to win back Johnson's trust.

Craig Stammen

Born: **3/9/1984** Age: **29**
Bats: **R** Throws: **R** Height: **6' 4"** Weight: **200**
Breakout: **24%** Improve: **47%** Collapse: **21%**
Attrition: **10%** MLB: **96%**

Comparables:
Jason Hammel,Pat Misch,Chris Bosio

YEAR	TEAM	LVL	AGE	W	L	SV	G	GS	IP	H	HR	BB	SO	BB9	SO9	GB%	BABIP	WHIP	ERA	FIP	FRA	WARP
2010	SYR	AAA	26	2	0	0	3	3	20	18	2	3	10	1.4	4.5	54%	.246	1.05	2.25	4.19	5.50	-0.1
2010	WAS	MLB	26	4	4	0	35	19	128	151	13	41	85	2.9	6.0	52%	.327	1.50	5.13	4.08	4.44	1.6
2011	SYR	AAA	27	10	7	0	25	24	142	163	18	40	127	2.5	8.0	55%	.330	1.43	4.75	3.96	5.27	-0.1
2011	WAS	MLB	27	1	1	0	7	0	10^{1}	3	0	4	12	3.5	10.5	50%	.136	0.68	0.87	1.83	1.40	0.4
2012	WAS	MLB	28	6	1	1	59	0	88^{1}	70	7	36	87	3.7	8.9	47%	.265	1.20	2.34	3.49	3.70	1.1
2013	*WAS*	*MLB*	*29*	*4*	*3*	*0*	*26*	*8*	*72*	*71*	*8*	*20*	*49*	*2.5*	*6.1*	*51%*	*.294*	*1.26*	*4.17*	*4.12*	*4.53*	*0.2*

Another member of the Nationals' stable of starters-turned-relievers, Stammen added a few ticks to his fastball in his first full major-league season working out of the bullpen, performing well in a middle-inning gig. The righty contributed two-plus innings in 28 of his 59 trips to the bump, and—like Clippard and Mattheus—he enjoyed positive results against both left- and right-handed hitters. With his sinker bumping up from fringy to average, and enhancing his already above-average slider as a result, Stammen should continue to hold down the bridge job that he earned out of spring training last year.

Drew Storen

Born: **8/11/1987** Age: **25**
Bats: **B** Throws: **R** Height: **6' 3"** Weight: **180**
Breakout: **25%** Improve: **46%** Collapse: **24%**
Attrition: **10%** MLB: **94%**

Comparables:
Chad Cordero,Adam Wainwright,Huston Street

YEAR	TEAM	LVL	AGE	W	L	SV	G	GS	IP	H	HR	BB	SO	BB9	SO9	GB%	BABIP	WHIP	ERA	FIP	FRA	WARP
2010	HAR	AA	22	0	0	4	7	0	9^{1}	5	1	1	11	1.0	10.6	50%	.211	0.65	0.97	2.72	3.23	0.2
2010	SYR	AAA	22	0	0	0	6	0	7^{1}	7	0	2	4	2.5	4.9	48%	.304	1.23	1.23	3.02	3.48	0.1
2010	WAS	MLB	22	4	4	5	54	0	55^{1}	48	3	22	52	3.6	8.5	41%	.296	1.27	3.58	3.29	3.54	0.9
2011	WAS	MLB	23	6	3	43	73	0	75^{1}	57	8	20	74	2.4	8.8	48%	.246	1.02	2.75	3.29	3.73	0.8
2012	POT	A+	24	1	0	0	5	1	6	4	1	1	8	1.5	12.0	60%	.214	0.83	3.00	3.39	3.92	0.1
2012	HAR	AA	24	0	0	0	1	0	0^{2}	3	1	1	0	13.5	0.0	20%	.500	6.00	54.00	27.20	17.46	-0.1
2012	WAS	MLB	24	3	1	4	37	0	30^{1}	22	0	8	24	2.4	7.1	52%	.265	0.99	2.37	2.44	2.52	0.7
2013	*WAS*	*MLB*	*25*	*2*	*1*	*13*	*39*	*0*	39^{2}	*32*	*4*	*11*	*38*	*2.4*	*8.8*	*44%*	*.287*	*1.08*	*2.93*	*3.43*	*3.19*	*0.7*

Surgery to remove bone chips from Storen's elbow kept the closer sidelined until late July, but upon returning to the mound, he was as effective as ever. Storen almost immediately regained his velocity, using his mid-90s sinker to keep the ball in the yard, and in 21 regular-season appearances from August 21 onward, he recorded 16 strikeouts without walking a batter. The Stanford product's season ended miserably, with a four-run meltdown in Game Five of the NLDS, but he'll come to spring training with a clear head and a reasonable chance to lead the majors in saves. Don't forget, he placed sixth in that category on an 80-win Nationals team two years ago.

Stephen Strasburg
Born: **7/20/1988** Age: **24**
Bats: **R** Throws: **R** Height: **6' 5"** Weight: **220**
Breakout: **22%** Improve: **54%** Collapse: **9%**
Attrition: **5%** MLB: **98%**
Comparables:
Jered Weaver, Max Scherzer, Joba Chamberlain

YEAR	TEAM	LVL	AGE	W	L	SV	G	GS	IP	H	HR	BB	SO	BB9	SO9	GB%	BABIP	WHIP	ERA	FIP	FRA	WARP
2010	WAS	MLB	21	5	3	0	12	12	68	56	5	17	92	2.2	12.2	47%	.319	1.07	2.91	2.11	3.01	1.6
2011	HAG	A	22	0	1	0	3	3	6^{1}	9	1	3	13	4.3	18.5	50%	.500	1.89	9.95	3.37	1.98	0.3
2011	POT	A+	22	0	0	0	1	1	3	2	0	0	5	0.0	15.0	86%	.286	0.67	0.00	-0.10	1.41	0.2
2011	HAR	AA	22	1	0	0	1	1	6	1	0	0	4	0.0	6.0	—	.071	0.17	0.00	2.58	2.80	0.0
2011	SYR	AAA	22	0	0	0	1	1	5	2	0	0	7	0.0	12.6	80%	.200	0.40	1.80	0.44	2.64	0.1
2011	WAS	MLB	22	1	1	0	5	5	24	15	0	2	24	0.8	9.0	42%	.242	0.71	1.50	1.24	2.55	0.7
2012	WAS	MLB	23	15	6	0	28	28	159^{1}	136	15	48	197	2.7	11.1	44%	.311	1.15	3.16	2.87	3.17	4.4
2013	*WAS*	*MLB*	*24*	*9*	*5*	*0*	*22*	*22*	119^{1}	*92*	*10*	*29*	*140*	*2.2*	*10.6*	*48%*	*.300*	*1.01*	*2.60*	*2.67*	*2.82*	*3.1*

Twenty-five starts into Strasburg's 2012 season, his ERA stood at 2.85, and it was fair to wonder if the flamethrower might pass the Nationals' eye test and avoid a looming shutdown. But Strasburg coughed up five earned runs in two of his ensuing three starts, and Rizzo—adamant about preserving his prized asset's arm, in the face of said asset's own wishes and rebukes from fans—pulled the plug. Whether Strasburg would have thrown a perfect game his next time out or shredded his elbow trying is now irrelevant; what matters is that, 18 months after elbow surgery, he is back to full strength and in hot pursuit of a Cy Young Award. From a stuff standpoint, a healthy Strasburg can go toe-to-toe with Justin Verlander—the only pitcher who topped him in WARP last year—and now that the kid gloves are coming off, he'll have a fair chance to jockey with the Tigers ace for the top spot on the leaderboard.

Chien-Ming Wang
Born: **3/31/1980** Age: **33**
Bats: **R** Throws: **R** Height: **6' 4"** Weight: **230**
Breakout: **13%** Improve: **43%** Collapse: **23%**
Attrition: **14%** MLB: **72%**
Comparables:
Jeff Suppan, Sidney Ponson, Tomo Ohka

YEAR	TEAM	LVL	AGE	W	L	SV	G	GS	IP	H	HR	BB	SO	BB9	SO9	GB%	BABIP	WHIP	ERA	FIP	FRA	WARP
2011	HAG	A	31	0	0	0	1	1	3	4	0	0	3	0.0	9.0	82%	.364	1.33	6.00	2.53	1.65	0.2
2011	POT	A+	31	0	0	0	1	1	4	1	0	2	2	4.5	4.5	67%	.111	0.75	0.00	3.73	4.12	0.1
2011	HAR	AA	31	2	0	0	2	2	11	8	0	0	3	0.0	2.5	41%	.273	0.73	0.00	2.86	4.13	0.1
2011	SYR	AAA	31	0	1	0	2	2	10^{2}	15	2	2	9	1.7	7.6	55%	.361	1.59	6.75	4.83	6.54	-0.3
2011	WAS	MLB	31	4	3	0	11	11	62^{1}	67	8	13	25	1.9	3.6	53%	.272	1.28	4.04	4.53	5.57	-0.5
2012	HAG	A	32	1	0	0	1	1	6	3	1	1	7	1.5	10.5	33%	.143	0.67	1.50	3.91	4.76	0.1
2012	POT	A+	32	0	1	0	2	2	8	7	0	2	4	2.2	4.5	59%	.259	1.12	4.50	3.14	4.32	0.2
2012	HAR	AA	32	1	5	0	9	9	45^{1}	59	7	9	33	1.8	6.6	59%	.342	1.50	6.75	4.35	6.05	0.0
2012	SYR	AAA	32	2	0	0	3	3	20^{2}	26	1	5	8	2.2	3.5	61%	.338	1.50	4.35	4.03	5.96	-0.2
2012	WAS	MLB	32	2	3	0	10	5	32^{1}	50	5	15	15	4.2	4.2	54%	.375	2.01	6.68	5.89	6.85	-0.5
2013	*WAS*	*MLB*	*33*	*4*	*4*	*0*	*11*	*11*	57^{1}	*63*	*7*	*17*	*32*	*2.7*	*5.0*	*54%*	*.308*	*1.40*	*4.93*	*4.56*	*5.36*	*-0.3*

Re-signed by the Nationals to a $4 million deal after bouncing back from shoulder surgery in 2011, Wang was bitten by the injury bug again last spring, spending two months on the shelf with a hamstring strain, and then two more months off the field in the summer with a hip ailment. In between those disabled-list stints, he showed signs of wear from the mélange of maladies that have derailed his career, beginning with the Lisfranc sprain he incurred while running the bases in 2008. Wang still features a bowling-ball sinker, but the pitch's velocity is down to 91 from its 93-mph peak, and his once-solid control betrayed him in 2012. There's still enough here for a healthy Wang to serve as a fifth starter or swingman, but agent Alan Nero will struggle to do better than a minor-league hitch this time around.

Jordan Zimmermann
Born: **5/23/1986** Age: **27**
Bats: **R** Throws: **R** Height: **6' 3"** Weight: **220**
Breakout: **19%** Improve: **61%** Collapse: **16%**
Attrition: **5%** MLB: **96%**
Comparables:
Jeremy Bonderman, Scott Baker, Alex Fernandez

YEAR	TEAM	LVL	AGE	W	L	SV	G	GS	IP	H	HR	BB	SO	BB9	SO9	GB%	BABIP	WHIP	ERA	FIP	FRA	WARP
2010	WAS	MLB	24	1	2	0	7	7	31	31	8	10	27	2.9	7.8	50%	.261	1.32	4.94	5.88	6.38	-0.3
2011	WAS	MLB	25	8	11	0	26	26	161^{1}	154	12	31	124	1.7	6.9	41%	.292	1.15	3.18	3.13	3.81	2.2
2012	WAS	MLB	26	12	8	0	32	32	195^{2}	186	18	43	153	2.0	7.0	44%	.288	1.17	2.94	3.55	3.76	3.8
2013	*WAS*	*MLB*	*27*	*11*	*8*	*0*	*28*	*28*	161^{1}	*150*	*18*	*36*	*133*	*2.0*	*7.4*	*44%*	*.297*	*1.15*	*3.62*	*3.67*	*3.94*	*1.7*

Two-and-a-half years removed from Tommy John surgery, Zimmermann is slowly shedding the "league's best-kept secret" tag, though he is now overshadowed by Strasburg and Gonzalez.

He's a human Don't Walk sign, one of only six qualifying starters to rank among the top 15 in BB/PA in each of the past two seasons. Zimmermann's fastball, which averages 94 mph, was the third hardest among NL starters in 2012, trailing only Strasburg and Jeff Samardzija, and he complements it with a quality slider and curveball. If Zimmermann can stay healthy and find a way to notch a modest uptick in strikeouts, he has the control and savvy to contend for Cy Young honors in tvhe coming years.

LINEOUTS

HITTERS

PLAYER	TEAM	LVL	AGE	PA	R	2B	3B	HR	RBI	BB	SO	SB-CS	AVG/OBP/SLG	TAv	BABIP	BRR	FRAA	WARP
OF B. Carroll	SYR	AAA	29	417	55	23	2	10	50	44	97	7-5	.250/.333/.407	.269	.310	1.5	RF(76): 2.4, CF(9): 1.8	1.4
OF E. Komatsu	SYR	AAA	24	123	16	4	0	3	14	13	13	2-5	.269/.355/.394	.270	.278	-2	LF(14): -0.0, CF(9): -0.9	-0.2
	MIN	MLB	24	37	2	0	0	0	1	4	3	0-0	.219/.297/.219	.207	.233	0.4	RF(6): 0.1, CF(2): -0.1	-0.2
	SLN	MLB	24	21	3	0	0	0	0	2	2	0-0	.211/.286/.211	.188	.235	0.3	RF(4): -0.0, CF(3): 0.1	-0.1
C C. Maldonado	SYR	AAA	33	187	20	7	0	6	11	27	42	0-0	.210/.326/.369	.236	.248	-3.2	C(40): -0.0, 1B(1): -0.0	-0.2
	WAS	MLB	33	12	0	0	0	0	1	2	4	0-0	.000/.182/.000	.112	.000	0	C(4): -0.0	-0.2
SS J. Martinson	HAG	A	23	321	68	11	3	10	63	47	88	23-3	.272/.391/.449	.304	.367	5.9	SS(59): 7.2	3.5
	POT	A+	23	265	36	2	4	12	43	21	79	7-2	.215/.279/.409	.226	.258	2.1	SS(34): 0.9, 3B(9): -0.5	-0.2
RF B. Miller	AUB	A-	22	127	20	11	3	4	21	10	36	0-0	.292/.354/.549	.316	.387	0.5	RF(12): 0.4, LF(1): -0.2	0.5
C J. Solano	SYR	AAA	26	57	8	2	0	0	2	3	6	0-0	.250/.298/.288	.204	.277	0.1	C(9): 0.3	-0.2
	WAS	MLB	26	37	6	3	0	2	6	2	5	1-0	.314/.351/.571	.322	.321	0.7	C(11): -0.2	0.5
SS Z. Walters	POT	A+	22	207	24	8	1	5	24	10	43	6-3	.269/.304/.399	.271	.318	0.9	SS(25): -0.7, 3B(7): -0.7	0.5
	HAR	AA	22	172	23	11	4	6	19	8	38	1-0	.293/.326/.518	.314	.350	0	SS(29): -0.6	1.0
	SYR	AAA	22	105	9	4	0	1	6	6	28	0-0	.214/.260/.286	.193	.290	-0.5	SS(22): 2.7	-0.2

Given the Nationals' outfield depth at all levels, **Brett Carroll** couldn't have chosen a worse place to try to land a job. The same goes for **Erik Komatsu**, though at least he's five years younger than Carroll. Any team with an injured catcher will have the Nats on speed dial, as **Carlos Maldonado** is yet another viable veteran backstop knocking around in the organization. The impressive power-speed profile of **Jason Martinson** would be more appealing if he could a) make regular contact or b) realistically stick at shortstop. **Brandon Miller** was drafted by the Nationals twice, improving his stock 44 rounds from 2010 to 2012, and he possesses an intriguing skill set built on massive power and tremendous athleticism. Adding to the Nationals' throng of catchers, **Jhonatan Solano** will squeeze in somewhere in the organization to get some playing time. The Nationals aggressively pushed **Zach Walters** through three levels; they like the potential his bat can offer around the diamond, though the hope is he can stay at shortstop.

PITCHERS

PLAYER	TEAM	LVL	AGE	W	L	SV	IP	H	HR	BB	SO	BB9	SO9	GB%	BABIP	WHIP	ERA	FIP	FRA	WARP
D. Cortes	—	—	—	—	—	—	—	—	—	—	—	—	—	—	—	—	—	—	—	—
E. Davis	HAR	AA	25	7	3	5	64^1	61	5	18	69	2.5	9.7	52%	.327	1.23	2.52	2.95	3.34	0.9
P. Demny	HAR	AA	22	6	8	0	123^2	138	13	61	97	4.4	7.1	45%	.326	1.61	5.46	4.75	6.02	-0.5
N. Karns	HAG	A	24	3	0	2	44^1	23	1	21	61	4.3	12.4	50%	.237	0.99	2.03	2.74	3.55	1.0
	POT	A+	24	8	4	0	71^2	47	1	26	87	3.3	10.9	53%	.287	1.02	2.26	2.39	2.96	1.8
M. MacDougal	LAN	MLB	35	0	0	0	5^2	9	0	6	4	9.5	6.4	32%	.409	2.65	7.94	4.90	5.80	-0.1
B. Mooneyham	AUB	A-	22	2	2	0	42^1	36	2	16	29	3.4	6.2	49%	.262	1.23	2.55	3.78	5.38	-0.1
T. Roark	SYR	AAA	25	6	17	0	147^2	161	14	47	130	2.9	7.9	45%	.332	1.41	4.39	3.81	5.16	0.2
J. Smoker	NAT	Rk	23	1	0	0	5	3	0	1	3	1.8	5.4	69%	.231	0.80	1.8	3.43	4.84	0
	POT	A+	23	0	0	0	1^2	2	0	1	2	5.4	10.8	20%	.400	1.80	10.8	6.39	6.38	0
	HAG	A	23	0	1	1	3	3	1	4	1	12.0	3.0	60%	.222	2.33	15.0	11.25	18.11	-0.3
S. Solis	—	—	—	—	—	—	—	—	—	—	—	—	—	—	—	—	—	—	—	—

Once a top 100 prospect, **Dan Cortes** missed most of last season after failing his physical. He's only 26, so better health and control could eventually lead to a middle-relief future. ⚾ Impressed with **Erik Davis**'s 0.56 ERA showing in the Dominican Winter League, the Nationals added the righty to their 40-man roster. With a strong showing in spring training and at Triple-A Syracuse, he could make a bullpen cameo before September. ⚾ A sixth-round pick in 2008, **Paul Demny** has seen his strike-out rates erode on his way up the ladder, and he may need to shift to the bullpen to earn a look. ⚾ Though **Nathan Karns** was used as a starter in High-A last year, his above-average fastball and plus curveball could project better in a bullpen role; if Karns is to remain in the rotation, where he has a mid-rotation ceiling, he'll need to refine his changeup and avoid injury despite a jerky delivery. ⚾ **Mike MacDougal** returned to the Nationals organization after flaming out in Chavez Ravine, and while he still throws gas, his control was erratic even in Triple-A ⚾ A sturdy left-hander from Stanford, **Brett Mooneyham** has a big-league arm, but he needs to develop a swing-and-miss pitch. ⚾ **Tanner Roark** held his own for Triple-A Syracuse in 2012, after needing two years to solve Double-A, and he'll be among the top candidates for a promotion to the big club if the injury bug bites Washington's pitching staff this year. ⚾ Injuries and the resulting ineffectiveness have mired **Josh Smoker** in the lower levels, and the 2007 first-rounder, who once had an impressive array of pitches, is now a long shot to ever reach the majors. ⚾ **Sammy Solis** has fourth-starter potential if his elbow heals from surgery and his secondary pitches come along.

MANAGER: DAVEY JOHNSON

YEAR	TEAM	W-L	Pythag +/-	Avg PC	100+ P	120+ P	QS	BQS	REL	REL w Zero R	IBB	PH	PH Avg	PH HR	SB2	CS2	SB3	CS3	SAC Att	SAC %	POS SAC	Squeeze	Swing	In Play
2011	WAS	40-43	0	84.0	12	0	33	3	271	218	19	137	.179	1	11	3	0	0	58	74.1%	19	1	170	51
2012	WAS	98-64	1	93.6	48	1	97	2	482	378	32	244	.288	4	18	4	1	1	80	72.5%	27	1	303	78

The reigning National League Manager of the Year, Johnson returns for a second season at the helm, after which he will move back upstairs in a consulting role. Johnson earned the award by steering the Nationals to 98 wins, and his most salient contribution was emphasizing on-base percentage over speed and contact skills at the top of the batting order. Few skippers would have considered Jayson Werth—who stole only eight bases in 81 games—a leadoff man, and many would have succumbed to the middle-infielder-must-bat-second rule; Johnson bucked both trends, using Werth and Bryce Harper to catalyze his offense, and his team was better for it.

The decision to use Henry Rodriguez over Tyler Clippard to supplant Drew Storen in the ninth inning proved less prescient, and Johnson may have allowed Sean Burnett to face too many righties, but his bullpen management on the whole was palatable. With nearly two decades of managing experience, Johnson has a keen understanding of the rules, which he demonstrated in the pine-tar incident surrounding Rays reliever Joel Peralta in June, though his choice of insults in the aftermath of the ejection—calling Joe Maddon a "weird wuss" because he "has a Tweeter"— left much to be desired. Blending old-school style with some new-school methods, Johnson issues his share of free passes and occasionally calls for a bewildering sacrifice bunt, but his philosophy on lineup construction ensures that he won't impede his team's success.

Sabermetrician Wanted, Must Have MFA

Russell A. Carleton

Wanted: Highly qualified analyst for Major League front office. Must have experience in analyzing large baseball-related dataset and MFA or equivalent. Please send examples of projects completed using major statistical package (SPSS, STATA, R, Minitab) and draft of Great American novel/poetry compilation/video of recent art installation. Dancers welcome.

I was once talking to my boss at my day job about "that baseball thing" I do on the side. She doesn't follow baseball, but when I told her that I apply advanced statistical modeling to figuring out what strategies worked and which players had hidden value, she got the basic idea. Then, she asked me how many people do . . . y'know . . . whatever it is that I do.

I wasn't quite sure how to answer that. After all, what exactly is it that I do? There are thousands of people who write on the Internet about baseball. There are fewer, but still a substantial number, who analyze the game through the lens of advanced stats. A subset of those conduct their own research. I confess that I picked a number out of the air and mumbled that I thought it to be somewhere around a hundred. She replied that I must be part of an elite group. I chided her about the difference between "elite" and "small." She chuckled. But it was the sort of conversation that gives one an existential tummy ache. What exactly am I doing with my free time?

I often find myself in an odd place in my practice of the magical arts of sabermetrics. In theory, I am a scientist searching for objective information about the game of baseball. In practice, I am a writer who produces content for a website. Sometimes that works together beautifully. I'll set out to look at some issue that's relevant to the game at the moment, or just some timeless question that people argue over. And sometimes, an elegant, statistically significant finding that's slightly counterintuitive in a quirky and interesting way will fall into my lap. And I'll write an article about it that will be widely discussed and retweeted. And that's nice . . . until the next Monday, when I'll be scheduled to deliver another piece, preferably with another finding that's elegant and statistically significant and slightly counterintuitive in a quirky and interesting way. Despite the fact that I'm well aware of the inherent conflict in this arrangement—I've taught research methods at the undergraduate level—for some reason, it never really bothered me until recently.

I think there's a structural problem in sabermetrics as it is currently practiced that's actually damaging the field. No, I'm not here to cry a eulogy for sabermetrics. No "It was a joyful endeavor, but there's no more to be found, and perhaps we should move along to solving world hunger or analyzing elections or something useful like that." In fact, I believe that sabermetrics as a discipline has barely scratched the surface of what's out there. So long as baseball is played by humans, or perhaps even if life should imitate art and the Nintendo prophecy of robots with guns playing baseball comes true, there will always be more to figure out. My worry is that sabermetrics could achieve a lot more than it already has but we're holding ourselves back.

The problem is that we're not behaving enough like artists. Or 3-year-olds. Either will do.

People who have worked in real research labs know that science doesn't really operate on a predictable schedule with fascinating things to write about weekly. It's a slow process that builds over years, and most of the time it isn't that interesting. I went to graduate school. I know of what I speak. I spent a lot of time in my car going to interviews where the person might not show up, and even if s/he did, I would spend most of the rest of the day typing in answers into a spreadsheet for later analysis. At the end, there were some cool things to be found. But only after about three years of hearing my then-girlfriend, now-wife wondering why I couldn't hang out on Saturday afternoons. (Sorry, sweetie. I had to drive 25 miles to get that interview.)

Yet somehow, I've resolved (or learned to ignore) the cognitive dissonance that comes with the thought that sabermetrics has married what should be a scientific endeavor to the culture of the blogosphere. We adopted the model of writing on a regular basis whether we had something worth reporting or not. I once taught a class in research methods. I think I'd have given myself a C- if I had proposed such a model.

There's a serious consequence to trying to be a scientist and an entertainer at the same time. In order to be able to write *something*, there has to be an angle. The readers want it to be "interesting," and writing an "I had this great theory, but it didn't pan out" piece . . . isn't. Trust me, I've written a few of them. That p-value had better be less than .05, or else. Statistical non-significance doesn't get page views and links. I wonder how often statistically non-significant things are simply scrapped in favor of another article that will have more impressive results. I know at least one researcher (that would be me) who has done it. In science more broadly, this is called the "file-drawer problem," and it has many of the same effects: There may have been five studies that showed no link between the two variables I studied, and those were done in a more rigorous way, but mine is the only one available on the Internet.

If the incentives in a system point toward producing statistically significant findings, the best way to make sure that I have a significant finding to report is to tread on familiar ground. It's easy enough to tweak an existing theory, and on the very practical end of things, to use code that I've already written for another article. I just need to modify it a little. It's also best to use simple models with only a couple of variables. Not only do I save all that time by not having to set up a complex database or write crazy amounts of new code, but using simpler statistical models makes it easier for me to find significance. It's a lot easier to write up a bivariate correlation than a mixed linear model. Of course, there's the tiny problem that simple models assume a simple reality, and reality is never that simple. There can be all sorts of complexities hiding beneath that seemingly innocuous p-value.

The problem with treading familiar ground is that you never wander afield and take a risk. If the risk doesn't work, you're left with nothing to write about. Nothing, that is, except your failure to, on a week's notice, intuit some greater truth about the game of baseball that no one has thought of before and then back it up with impeccable numerical gymnastics. After having done the same thing the previous week. And the week before.

For what it's worth, sometimes, there are breakthroughs that come from making small adjustments to established models. But realistically, what often results is not an iPod, a game-changer, but a slightly better CD player. It takes "outside the box thinking" (or your favorite business-cliché equivalent)—not to mention a lot of work—to invent an iPod. A flash of creativity. When the ecosystem doesn't encourage people to be creative, the ecosystem won't produce a lot of those flashes. Sure, they happen, but I wonder what could have been if I had felt more free at the canvas.

My daughter is in an experimental phase of her artistic life. She's 3. She occasionally breaks out the toy xylophone for a thrash-metal version of "Old McDonald" (and yes, it sounds exactly like you think it does). I guess she's trying to write her own concept album. Lately, she's been working on a series of monotone portraits of her Little People toys. In other words, she grabbed a marker and scribbled out a 3-year-old's approximation of a human form and said it was the Fireman Guy (Miguel, I think). Before that, she and most of the kitchen table were into finger paint. Before that, it had been abstract watercolor paintings and mixing colors just to see what would come out, usually various shades of brown. She didn't care. Before *that*, she would apply paint to ink stamps and sometimes the business end of the stamp would land on the paper in front of her. Most of the time, even. It doesn't really matter how it turns out anyway. It's all in fun. Toddlers have a way of not caring who's watching.

Maybe there was a time when sabermetrics was like that. I don't go back to the days of the Usenet group rec.sports.baseball, where many of the sabermetric Hall of Fame first balloters got their start. Back then, there were teams that were tinkering with the idea of quantitative analysis in the front office. Baseball has always been a numerical game, after all, but the folks with the calculators were generally baseball lifers, most of them already on the inside, who had a fondness for numbers. And Bill James.

At some point along the way, someone started to notice the outsiders, who had migrated from Usenet to the blogosphere and the mainstream media, and some of them got hired by teams, which was (and still is) really cool. It's a sign that teams in Major League Baseball believe that the sabermetric movement has value that's worth paying actual money for. Now there is a well-marked trail to get from a blog to the front office, and you don't even get dysentery along the way. I suppose that given that I have consulted for teams, I can't really complain too loudly, but I wonder if this didn't do some harm to the sabermetric movement as a whole. Sabermetricians all grew up fans of the game, and surely had fantasies of one day making it to the major leagues. Mine realistically ended when I was 10 (and I'm being generous to myself), but fantasies die hard. The thought of making it into the game *somehow* is a siren that sings "Take Me Out to the Ball Game." It's hard for any baseball geek to ignore. That allure is a bit of an 800-pound gorilla in the room that's never openly discussed. Nor are the effects it might have.

I worry that we who profess to be objective scientists of baseball are breaking one of the cardinal rules of science: *Let the facts lead.* I know I have felt a certain need for self-censorship over what topics I address in my research. Should I write about the folly of signing middling middle relievers to multi-year, multmillion-dollar contracts? Will this be brought up in the interview I'm hoping to score?

There must be a fearlessness in science. Even if someone is watching, facts are facts and everyone else will just have to deal with it. Sure, in a perfect world, the people I'm trying to critique and impress at the same time will have an open mind about my thesis that they are fools. But all the same, just in case they aren't so forgiving, maybe I should shelve that article for now.

Maybe I've sold out.

*

I'm married to a knitter. She's the kind that has moved on from dishcloths and scarves and designs her own knitwear. She once taught me how to knit. I've taken her to a few baseball games. That's what married couples do. Sometimes, she'll be working on something and she'll "frog" or "tink" some sock or sweater or stuffed animal that she's been working on. There's apparently a knitting slang for unraveling the thing that you just spent a bunch of time creating. It makes me glad my hobby doesn't have little pseudo-words for important concepts that sound silly when said out loud.

I don't know if there are any sabermetric knitters. Or dancers. Or sculptors. And that bothers me. It seems that most of the people with whom I interact are economists and physicists and computer scientists and other quantitatively savvy people. There's nothing wrong with those disciplines or being skilled in the dark arts of the spreadsheet. For too long, baseball mostly ignored or even ridiculed the idea that these disciplines might have something to offer to the game. That's been remedied: Now even teams that fans assume are downright Luddite have analytics departments, many of them featuring former Baseball Prospectus writers. It would, however, be an equal act of arrogance to assume that quantitative modeling is the only way to discover new and exciting things about baseball. We sabermetricians are good, but we're not omnipotent.

The natural (and social) sciences, as fields, come with their own biases. Chief among them is an assumption that the world around us operates according to well-defined and orderly laws and that these laws can be discovered experimentally. What appears to be complex can be understood. It's just a matter of engineering the right data-collection widget to measure it. The way to discover new things is to do more experiments with more power!

For the most part, that works out great, but it has a nasty side effect in practice. Perhaps we, as a species, really can understand the complexities of the universe with more experimentation and better data. What happens when this honest scientific method is combined with the all-too-common hubris of thinking that, by virtue of my general awesomeness, it will be *me* who cracks the code? The p-value on a simple bivariate correlation is less than .05, *ergo* I am a genius. Maybe I just glanced at (and over-simplified) something that I don't fully understand. I wouldn't be the first. Or the last.

Complex systems are, by definition, hard to understand, and there is a certain anxiety that springs from the unknown. If we can't explain then we can't predict, and that sort of uncertainty is hard to live with. It's a lot more reassuring to say, "I figured it out!" rather than "I need to study it more!" Try as we might, even within the confines of the scientific method, we are still dealing with human emotion, no matter how hard we try to avoid it. Chaos is scary. A couple of neat equations that fit nicely on a napkin are much nicer to look at. Any variance can be dismissed as statistical noise. It's easy to run a regression, get a significant finding, write an article about it, and state confidently that the matter is closed. If enough people leave the matter alone and neglect to question the original study, it becomes a matter of settled fact. Questioning settled facts is a revolutionary act, and revolutionaries aren't generally welcome in any era, even the sabermetric one.

And this is why we need sabermetric artists. It is the novelist who has the freedom to explore what the world would look like to a person given a different set of assumptions about reality. It is the dancer who may experiment with new ideas of having a team of people move together to achieve some goal. It is the photographer who spends the time looking at a common object from a different angle to create a work of beauty. It is the knitter who sees how thousands of individual stitches form a coherent whole. Artists have the luxury of inhabiting a space where boundaries can (and should) be pushed and assumptions questioned.

They have that luxury because there's a societally understood safe distance between art and reality . Artists have societal permission to say uncomfortable things because "it's just art." The good artists push those boundaries all the time without care for who's watching, and they deliver messages that people would never accept coming from the pen of a scientist. I envy them for that.

It's not that sabermetricians are incapable of thinking outside the box, or generating creative new ideas. In fact, didn't that used to be our thing?

If there ever was a "stats vs. scouts" standoff to speak of, it was supposed to be about the idea that outsiders with spreadsheets would never be able to understand the nuances that could only be spotted with 20 years of experience of watching bad high-school baseball. Here were a bunch of nerds pushing the boundaries of what counted as useful baseball information and creating new assumptions about the game. Now I worry that we have instead created an island within the baseball world where anything that isn't backed up with hard evidence and a regression equation is simply ignored. Like the pigs in George Orwell's *Animal Farm*, have we become the very thing that we sought to depose?

I would never argue that any jolly old chap who comes up with a half-baked theory as to how the game of baseball works is correct. In fact, the next step is to test whether that theory fits with actual data. But in agreeing to hear someone out and test out the idea, there's an implicit acknowledgment: You might be right. You might very well be wrong, but it's an open question, and for a moment, I will allow my mind to live with the unknowing. When old baseball chestnuts are trotted out (and, yes, largely debunked), that's an example of the system working the way it's supposed to. But if we're to live up to the Jamesian definition of sabermetrics being the search for objective knowledge about baseball, then we do not have the luxury of picking what it is we focus our microscopes on .

*

I wish I could bring together a group of artists who were at least passingly familiar with baseball in general. I'd feed them lunch, encourage them to talk on the subject of baseball, and start a tape recorder. I'd ask for a group of 3-year-olds, but after trying to explain the concept of the Leverage Index to my daughter, I decided that this would be impractical. Lunch would probably end up on the floor, and the tape recorder would be filled with off-key renditions of "Old Ben McDonald." Perhaps there would be a BABIP here and a BABIP there.

I don't know what the results would be. Perhaps the novelist would critique the manner in which managers construct a narrative for the game. Maybe the painter would question whether the use of color in the stadium is somehow influencing the team, or the dancer would try to figure out the best between-pitch movements for fielders to ensure they're ready for the ball. The poet might muse about the soul-crushing experience of the minor leagues. The 3-year-old would probably wonder if she could have dessert.

Some of the ideas would be useless. But even just taking a moment to look at life from a different angle might provide a tiny smidgen of insight. That's the point. There's plenty of technical skill in the sabermetric movement. We've bled a lot of the creativity and insight that used to be our calling card out of the system. We need to have a frank conversation about how that happened and how we can get that creativity and insight back.

In a counterintuitive and slightly quirky in an interesting way, we would be better scientists if we acted more like artists.

The Baseball Prospectus Top 101 Prospects

Jason Parks with Nick Faleris, Mark Anderson, Chris Mellen, Hudson Belinsky, Joe Hamrahi, and Jason Cole

1. Jurickson Profar, SS, Rangers

It's funny how fast scouting opinion can change. Back in the summer of 2009, Profar was viewed by many (if not most) scouting departments as a pitching prospect, and not the position player he envisioned. With a collection of solid-average to plus tools and instincts that grade off the chart, Profar has developed into the top position prospect in the game, painting all of the doubters as fools with the same stroke that paints the Rangers as prophets.

2. Oscar Taveras, OF, Cardinals

With a swing that is equal parts beauty and violence, Taveras took another step forward in 2012 to emerge as the most feared offensive prospect in the game. His attack is rooted in elite bat speed, the kind that alters a pitcher's approach, and executed with tremendous bat control, a command over his weapon that rarely accompanies such brutal force. The 20-year-old Dominican projects to be a .300 hitter with 30-plus home-run potential, which could make him a perennial All-Star and middle-of-the-order monster at the highest level.

3. Gerrit Cole, RHP, Pirates

If it's possible for an overall top pick to be underrated, Gerrit Cole is somehow underrated. With prototypical size and strength, combined with a well-above-average arsenal, Cole fits the profile of a future number-one starter. So far in his professional career, the results have only been solid, not spectacular, which has caused some to question whether he has the ability to make full use of his skill set. However, the 22-year-old is only one season into his professional journey, and he has all the characteristics of a major-league giant, the kind you don't want to get caught underestimating based on a debut sample.

4. Dylan Bundy, RHP, Orioles

Bundy started his professional baseball career with 30 innings in the Sally League, where the then-19-year-old allowed a meager five hits while striking out 40 full-season hitters. Yeah, that's normal. He continued his assault on the minors upon subsequent promotions up the chain before arriving at the major-league level in late September. Bundy can do it all on a mound, using a plus-plus fastball, a hammer curve, an advanced changeup, and pitchability beyond his years to dominate much older and more experienced competition. When it comes to pitching prospects, they don't often come with as much promise and polish as Bundy, who could develop into a top starter in short order.

5. Zack Wheeler, RHP, Mets

When you trade a prospect for a veteran rental, as the Giants did to get Carlos Beltran in 2011, you cross your fingers and hope the prospect doesn't become Zack Wheeler. The once-projectable dream has developed into the projectable reality, a prototypical top-of–the-rotation starter in the making. Armed with a potent four-pitch mix that continues to gain an edge, Wheeler is on the doorstep of the majors, where his impact potential and six years of team control could make him one of the more valuable young players in the game.

6. Jose Fernandez, RHP, Marlins

Call it an "it factor." Refer to the player as "a dude." Say the player has special qualities that make him stand out among his peers. Fernandez is one of those guys. With size, strength, an electric arsenal, and an "it factor" that would scare Stephen King, Fernandez exploded in his first full season of work, reaching the Florida State League and improving with each start. He's a dude.

7. Wil Myers, CF, Rays

As a 21-year-old, Myers destroyed the upper minors, hitting a combined .314/.387/.600 over two stops and becoming the poster boy of the minor leagues in the process. Despite the warranted accolades, Myers was made available by the Royals and was moved in a package for two major-league arms in the offseason. With a balanced approach at the plate to go along with contact ability and above-average pop, Myers could come back to haunt Kansas City: His floor is a major-league regular and his ceiling could make him an All-Star.

8. Byron Buxton, CF, Twins

You can make a case that Buxton has the most impressive collection of raw tools in the minors, with elite speed, an above-average arm, and plus projections on the bat. A potential disruptive force in all phases of the game, Buxton has the talent to eventually sit atop this list, but the 19-year-old is far from a finished product. He'll face big challenges at the full-season level in 2013.

9. Taijuan Walker, RHP, Mariners

A gifted athlete with long levers and a high-octane arsenal, Walker jumped a level to Double-A in 2012, where the teenager's raw stuff didn't disappoint. With a fastball that can work in the plus-plus range, two above-average secondary offerings, and an improving changeup, Walker has the raw gifts to develop into something special.

10. Francisco Lindor, SS, Indians

A classic shortstop with tools and instincts, Lindor is a top-10 prospect despite a limited professional résumé and a statistical output that is unlikely to impress upon first glance. But with proper context and eyewitness scouting reports, the monster that is Lindor comes into focus: a gifted defender who wasn't overwhelmed at the plate as an 18-year-old in a pitcher-friendly full-season league. That's a pretty picture.

11. Jameson Taillon, RHP, Pirates

The second selection in the 2011 draft, Taillon has everything you want in a classic Texas power pitcher: big size, big stuff, big competitor, and finally, he's a Texan. The 21-year-old continues on his developmental journey, having reached the Double-A level at the end of the 2012 season, when the total package started to come together and the high-impact profile started offering-high impact production. Allow for another season in the minors, but then pencil Taillon into the Pirates rotation for the next decade.

12. Xander Bogaerts, SS, Red Sox

You know you have special offensive skills when the biggest debate is focused on your defensive profile rather than your bat. Nobody seems to question Bogaerts' ability to crush baseballs, which is something that he does better than most young hitters in the game. With an easy and loose swing and near-elite bat speed, Bogaerts can send ropes all over the field, and projects to hit for both average and power at the highest level. He might be able to stick around at shortstop for a while, which will only increase his value, but his long-term position is most likely at the hot corner, where his bat will define his profile and could carry him to All-Star heights.

13. Kevin Gausman, RHP, Orioles

Viewed by many as the top pitching prospect available in the 2012 draft, Gausman might not take long proving those evaluators correct, as the LSU product fits the profile of a fast-moving, high-end major-league arm. Armed with an explosive plus-plus fastball, a slider that misses bats, and a changeup that should end up as his third above-average offering, Gausman has the arsenal, the size, and the pitchability to develop into a number-two starter on a contending team.

14. Billy Hamilton, CF, Reds

In the time it'll take you to read this paragraph, Billy Hamilton will steal three bases and be back in the dugout calming the smoke coming off his feet. With speed that somehow grades above elite, Hamilton is a true catalytic weapon, a player who influences the way others play the game based on his involvement. If the bat can offer minor utility, the legs will cement his value, both on base and in the field, where a move to center will take full advantage of his physical gifts and give him range that few players can match.

15. Travis d'Arnaud, C, Mets

One of the rarest commodities in the game is a catcher with skills on both sides of the ball, the kind who can control the running game and a pitching staff while swinging a stick that isn't an easy out. The recently traded d'Arnaud fits this rare profile, bringing a balanced skill set to the table and a first-division future to the Mets, a team in need of a young, cornerstone player at a premium position.

16. Shelby Miller, RHP, Cardinals

After a shaky first half of the season, when his fastball velocity was inconsistent, Miller found his form and once again emerged as one of the most promising young arms in baseball. Another Texas-born power arm, Miller can pump his fastball in the mid-90s, touching higher when he wants to reach back and get it. Both his curveball and his changeup will flash plus potential and should settle into that grade through repetition. If the command sharpens without losing the edge on the raw stuff, Miller could be a major-league force to reckon with.

17. Tyler Skaggs, LHP, Diamondbacks

Skaggs keeps getting better, year after year, outing after outing. The stuff continues to find polish without losing its punch. A 6'3" lefty with a sneaky-plus fastball that plays up despite sitting in the low-90s, a deceptive changeup that fades away from righties, and a monster curveball that he can throw for strikes or use as a chase pitch, Skaggs profiles as a number-three starter. The 21-year-old could be even more than that if he keeps taking steps forward.

18. Albert Almora, CF, Cubs

The sixth pick in the 2012 draft, Almora has a solid-average to plus tool collection and the baseball instincts to drive those raw physical gifts beyond their on-paper capacity. In a 33-game professional sample, the 18-year-old showed off his potential at the plate and his preternatural instincts in the field, a potent combination that could make him one of the more valuable players in the game if he reaches his ceiling.

19. Austin Hedges, C, Padres

Multiple sources have referred to Hedges as the best defensive catcher to come out of high school in the last decade, an advanced receiver with a top-flight arm and all the intangibles necessary for the demanding mental position. The almost universal praise for the defensive skill set puts enormous pressure on his average-at-best bat, where merely adequate offensive utility could make him an All-Star. Yes, the defensive profile is that good.

20. Javier Baez, SS, Cubs

Not many players in the minors have the high-end tools necessary to develop into the top prospect in the game. Baez is one of them. With bat speed that draws comparisons to Gary Sheffield, Baez has elite potential at the plate, with a hit tool that projects to be a plus weapon and raw power that grades out near the top of the chart. His ultra-aggressive approach could be his undoing, but with a better plan of attack, the execution could push his prospect status to the next level. This could be a very special player.

21. Miguel Sano, 3B, Twins

If you like tape-measure home runs and raw power that grades as an 80 on the 20-80 scale, you are going to love Miguel Sano. The Dominican teenager made his full-season debut in 2012, ripping 60 extra-base hits against much older competition in a league that is notoriously difficult on hitters. Sano has a long, leveraged swing and a propensity to strike out, but the raw power is game-changing, and in the ever-evolving landscape of baseball, where one-dimensional power bats are dinosaurs, he could provide middle-of-the-order value by hitting 35-plus bombs a season.

22. Addison Russell, SS, Athletics

When he was selected in the first round of the 2012 draft, Russell was viewed by many as a bat-first shortstop who was likely to move off the position on his way up the chain. But with an improved body and professional instruction, the 18-year-old looks like a candidate to stick around up the middle, making his plus offensive skill set shine even brighter. Russell can straight-up rip the ball, showing an advanced ability to make hard contact to all fields, with power that already shows up in game action. If the bat continues to play at a high level, and the defensive chops prove to be sustainable as he advances, Russell could emerge as a top-tier prospect.

23. Christian Yelich, CF, Marlins

As a 20-year-old, Yelich hit .330 in the Florida State League and showed why the Marlins made him the 23rd pick in the 2010 draft. With impressive bat speed and even more impressive bat control, Yelich projects to hit for a high average, and with his gap-to-gap power approach, he has the potential to produce a lot of extra-base hits. As he continues to mature as a hitter, some of those doubles will no doubt turn into home runs, making Yelich a dual threat at the plate and a prototypical number-three hitter.

24. Trevor Bauer, RHP, Indians

Bauer experienced an unexpected prospect dip during his first full season in the minors, a season filled with dominating performances and frustrating setbacks. His eccentric routines and self-serving approach to pitching get the ink, but inconsistent results and shaky command are key components in his status slump, which ultimately led the Diamondbacks to trade him to the Indians in the offseason. Bauer's upside hasn't changed, and if he can refine his command and keep the eccentricities of his approach in a better line with organizational philosophies, his future as a high-end starter will be preserved.

25. Jonathan Singleton, 1B, Astros

With the prospect spotlight shining on him heading into the 2012 season, Singleton didn't disappoint at Double-A, showing improved in-game power to go along with a mature, discerning approach at the plate. The 21-year-old lacks defensive versatility, and he isn't going to wow onlookers with his athletic displays on base, but he can rake, and that's what he will be paid to do in the major leagues. It might take a few seasons for the power numbers to find value at the position, but he will eventually settle in as a middle-of-the-order force for a team in desperate need of a middle-of-the-order-force.

26. Carlos Correa, SS, Astros

One of the toolsiest players available in the 2012 draft, Correa went number one overall and signed a slot-friendly deal with the Astros for around $5 million. You can frame the signing however you want, but the Astros didn't go cheap on talent in order to go cheap on price. Correa is a legit five-tool prospect with instincts for the game, the kind of talent who can change the fortunes of an organization by developing into a cost-controlled superstar.

27. Jackie Bradley, CF, Red Sox

His bat is solid, but isn't going to hang in the middle of the order; his speed is solid, but isn't going to dazzle the eye with Hamiltonian maneuvers in the running game. So why is Jackie Bradley the 27th best prospect in the minors? Because his defensive profile in center field is well above average, with tremendous instincts for the position that allow his average speed to play far beyond his paper grade, giving him plus range, a very good glove, and an accurate arm. The total package is a plus-plus defender at a premium position, with enough bat to keep pitchers honest and the type of natural baseball feel that makes everything in the tool chest play beyond expectations.

28. Noah Syndergaard, RHP, Mets

A big-bodied Texan with a big-bodied fastball and good pitchability, Syndergaard fits the profile of a future number-two starter. While he's far from a finished product, the intimidating righty can already pump a mid-90s fastball low in the zone, where the late action makes it difficult to square up. Beyond the heater, the secondary arsenal is already showing its quality, with a very promising changeup that he can turn over very well and a hard, biting curveball that has plus potential. He'll move up to High-A in 2013, and if the stuff continues to refine, could find himself among the top arms in the minors by the end of the season.

29. Chris Archer, RHP, Rays

Armed with one of the best sliders in baseball, Archer could be a high-leverage bullpen monster on the back of his easy plus-fastball and a destructive slider. But with improved command and a step forward with the changeup, Archer could develop into a high-end rotation piece, with an electric arsenal and a late-innings mentality. Either way, he has impact potential, and will be a heavy contributor for the Rays in 2013.

30. Mike Olt, 3B, Rangers

With a well-above-average defensive profile at the hot corner and plus power in his bat, Olt projects as a first-division talent. But with Adrian Beltre firmly entrenched at third for the Rangers, Olt looks like a trade chip or a positional journeyman on the roster, with the athleticism and versatility to play both outfield corners and first base. Regardless of where he plays on the diamond, Olt's bat will contribute, with an average hit tool and enough raw power to hit 25-plus home runs at his peak.

31. Archie Bradley, RHP, Diamondbacks

Bradley's overall package shows the key ingredients to develop into a front-of-the-rotation type down the line, with a potentially elite arsenal at his disposal. His stuff overmatched hitters in the Midwest League last season as he racked up 152 strikeouts in 136 innings and limited batters to 87 hits. Bradley's fastball is explosive, sitting 93–95 mph with strong angle and life, while the curveball is a tight knee-bender that misses bats and is continuing to improve. The key needs going forward are the progression of his changeup and control. Both are below-average, with progress a must to reach his full potential. There's fair risk he won't reach his ceiling, but the reward and major-league profile could be huge with development strides over the next few seasons.

32. Aaron Sanchez, RHP, Blue Jays

Making his full-season debut in 2012, Sanchez proved to be ahead of the competition, fanning 97 batters while only allowing 64 hits in 90 1/3 innings. The 20-year-old possesses the raw stuff to develop three above-average or better pitches, including an easy mid-90s fastball that explodes on batters and a classic 12-to-6 curveball with plenty of bite to generate swings and misses. While Sanchez's command is below average, his athleticism gives him the promise to iron out some of the roughness with his delivery. That could enhance his command as he continues to mature, potentially giving him a second-starter ceiling.

33. Mike Zunino, C, Mariners

The third pick in the 2012 draft, this catcher out of the University of Florida quickly hit the ground running as a professional, finishing up the year with a cameo in Double-A. Zunino's bat speed allows him to get the fat part of the bat on pitches to create consistent backspin and profile for average-to-better power. He also shows strong catch-and-throw mechanics behind the dish. There's some work to do with both his receiving skills and learning the finer points of the defensive game, but he's a polished product capable of reaching the majors in 2013 and beginning to put his foothold on a regular catching role.

34. Trevor Story, SS, Rockies

The 20-year-old proved he could hold his own with both the bat and glove during his debut in full-season ball, posting a .277/.367/.505 line with Asheville while drawing strong marks for being able to stick at shortstop. Story's easy swing and plus bat speed enable him to make hard contact, with a 15-20 home-run ceiling within his reach. The swing can get long, and Story needs to focus more on using the whole field to produce consistent contact. Given his power and defensive profile at a premium position, he's a prospect who can develop into a valuable big leaguer if the tools progress to full utility.

35. Anthony Rendon, 3B, Nationals

The sixth pick in the 2011 draft continued to be hindered with ankle injuries, suffering another fracture last season, which limited him to just 43 games. On the positive side, Rendon spent the bulk of those games in Double-A, and when he does take the field, his skills are advanced. He has a strong approach at the plate and the eye to quickly differentiate offerings. These traits combine with his natural bat speed and smooth, easy swing to produce a lot of hard contact. Hitting comes naturally to Rendon. The big questions are whether he can stay healthy and if there will be any lingering defensive effects from his injuries. Rendon previously moved well at third base, with the profile of an above-average defender. With the developmental progress he's made, if Rendon can get a healthy season under his belt, he could make a quick rise through the upper minors and get a taste of the big leagues this year.

36. Jorge Soler, RF, Cubs

Soler signed a nine-year deal with the Cubs as an international free agent in June after defecting from Cuba, then appeared in 34 games between rookie ball and Low-A. Soler possesses plus-plus raw power thanks to natural strength, easy bat speed, and loft in his swing, though hitches in that swing and his approach could limit the in-game results. Still, he has the potential to approach 30 home runs. The rest of his offensive game is in the early stages of developing and will likely take some time to come up to speed. Soler's plus arm gives him the defensive profile of a right fielder, one who can play as average or better. There's work to do ironing out his swing mechanics and risk that the power won't fully show, but it's a package that can develop into a middle-of-the-order bat and peak as a first-division regular for a number of seasons.

37. Nick Castellanos, 3B, Tigers

Castellanos quickly proved he was ahead of the curve in High-A last year, hitting .405 in 55 games before getting the bump to Double-A. Although he cooled off after the promotion and had some of his deficiencies exposed by the more advanced pitching, the 20-year-old is one of the rising hitting prospects in the game. Castellanos flashes quick, powerful hands and the type of barrel control to be a .300 hitter in the majors with continued refinement of his approach. While the power has yet to show in game action, he creates lift and strong backspin with his swing, and that can translate into solid-average to plus power down the line. The questions surround Castellanos's ultimate position: He showed improvement at the hot corner last year, but he's blocked there by Miguel Cabrera, and the Tigers gave him a long look last year in right field, where he might end up.

38. Matt Barnes, RHP, Red Sox

Boston's first-round pick in 2011, Barnes quickly established himself in 2012 as a pitching prospect on the rise. After tearing up Low-A over the course of five starts, he continued to miss bats in High-A, piling up 91 strikeouts in 93 innings. Barnes' 93-95 mph fastball is his best pitch, and he's shown the ability to work both sides of the plate and generate easy, exploding velocity. The 22-year-old can stand to tighten up the curve and needs continued progress with feeling the changeup. Both will be tested in the upper minors, but are viable secondary offerings, giving Barnes the package to profile as a solid third starter for the Red Sox in coming seasons.

39. Rymer Liriano, RF, Padres

The development path has been slow and steady for Liriano since he signed as an international free agent in 2007: He reached Double-A in 2012. Liriano has put solid work into building a professional approach, and he's shown improvement with his pitch-recognition skills. These will continue to be tested, as he was on the susceptible side against soft stuff during his 53 games with San Antonio. Liriano's quick wrists, strong forearms, and natural strength give him plus power potential, but he's yet to really figure out how to begin tapping into it. At 21, the outfielder is still learning the game and polishing his tools. There's a lot of risk in Liriano's game coming to fruition, especially his hit tool, but the payout can be an above-average regular in right field if things click to their fullest.

40. David Dahl, CF, Rockies

Although just 18, Dahl is on the polished side for a player just entering the professional ranks, posting an impressive .379/.423/.625 line in 65 games of short-season ball. Possessing strong tools across the board, Dahl's package is highlighted by his plus hit tool and defensive ability in center field. He's a pure hitter with an idea about how to execute his craft at a young age. While the power may not translate into big home-run totals, the stroke can play in the form of doubles and a lot of hard line drives into both gaps. Dahl has a ways to go, but his ceiling is high and he could prove to be a strong pick for the Rockies at 10th overall in 2012.

41. Kyle Zimmer, RHP, Royals

The Royals' top pick last June, Zimmer represents everything the organization needs in a prospect. A high-ceiling pitcher with the upside of a second starter, Zimmer can move quickly through the minor leagues. With a young lineup in need of high-end pitching to take them to the next level, the Royals may have their guy with Zimmer and his mid- to low-90s fastball, plus curve, and strong overall profile. He could arrive in the big leagues in 2014 and could end up fronting the Kansas City rotation by the time James Shields departs.

42. Kaleb Cowart, 3B, Angels

Overall, the Angels system lacks punch and it could be a while before additional youth arrives to help Mike Trout carry the torch into the future. Cowart may lead the next minor wave of talent, representing a classic third-base profile with good hitting ability, newfound patience, and the potential for plus power at his peak. He also has a strong defensive profile and could help solidify the left side of the infield for a team that will have several aging stars when he arrives in late 2014.

43. Carlos Martinez, RHP, Cardinals

The Cardinals have an enviable stable of young power arms all approaching big-league readiness. Martinez has some of the most impressive arm strength in the Cards system, touching triple digits on several occasions and generally sitting at 95-97 mph. His curveball could be an excellent pitch as well, giving him a late-inning profile at a minimum. If his mechanics and changeup gain consistency, he still has a chance to be an overpowering starter.

44. Gregory Polanco, CF, Pirates

While the top of the Pirates prospect list features multiple front-line starting pitchers, Polanco represents arguably the best position prospect in the organization. He has legitimately loud tools across the board, headlined by excellent athleticism, natural hitting ability, and an up-the-middle defensive profile. His game also features projectable power, a strong arm, and plus running ability. It's an impressive pile of tools for a 21-year-old prospect who has time to marinate in the minor leagues while Andrew McCutchen holds down center field in Pittsburgh.

45. Trevor Rosenthal, RHP, Cardinals

Rosenthal made a name for himself with some big-time velocity in the 2012 postseason and he has the potential to offer much more than that to the Cardinals down the line. He can reach 100 mph with his fastball in short bursts and rests comfortably in the 92–96 range as a starter. His arsenal is rounded out by a potential plus curveball, a useable changeup, and an improving cutter. For as much as he could provide in the bullpen, the Cardinals may be better served to have him sit in the middle of their rotation over the next few years.

46. Aaron Hicks, CF, Twins

Scouts have been waiting for Hicks to break out for years now and he finally put his tools to use on the field in 2012. By hitting .286/.384/.460 in his first exposure to Double-A, Hicks has vaulted himself into the Twins' immediate outfield plans. He is a complete tool shed with an elite arm, strong center-field defense, an excellent understanding of the strike zone, solid hitting ability, and good pop. Hicks could be an impact big-league center fielder for a very long time, giving the Twins the dynamic player they crave as they await the arrival of Sano and Buxton.

47. Gary Sanchez, C, Yankees

Yankees fans should be used to discussions of catching prospects who can hit a ton but can't really catch. That story previously played out during Jesus Montero's development, and the narrative applies to Sanchez as well. A potential offensive monster, Sanchez uses an aggressive approach at the plate to hit for both a good average and plenty of power. Few scouts believe he can stick at catcher, but that won't matter if his bat lives up to its billing. Offensively, Sanchez could be knocking on the door to New York in 2014.

48. Taylor Guerrieri, RHP, Rays

While Guerrieri didn't look like the overpowering right-hander the Rays took in the 2011 draft, he still looked like a top-flight pitching prospect in his debut season. Guerrieri currently uses a well-commanded low-90s sinking fastball to set up both a curveball and changeup that have at least above-average projection. The Rays have had little trouble developing pitchers over the years, and Guerrieri could be the next front-line type in that pipeline.

49. Bubba Starling, CF, Royals

One of the most impressive raw athletes in all the minor leagues, Starling is a baseball lottery ticket. He has ridiculous tools, the complete set necessary to become a superstar if given the time to develop and mature, but they're all quite raw because he was a multi-sport star in high school. If he becomes just an average hitter, the rest of his offensive abilities project as plus to go along with his center-field defensive profile.

50. Danny Hultzen, LHP, Mariners

The Mariners shocked many in the industry by taking Hultzen with the second pick in the 2011 draft. The club scouted him heavily throughout the spring and pulled the trigger based on its belief in both his ceiling and his high floor. Hultzen has a bundle of at-least-average pitches, and while he struggled to throw strikes at times last year, he should have a quality command/control profile down the line. Some scouts see Hultzen as a future third starter while others see an inning-eating number four.

51. Mason Williams, CF, Yankees

Williams has the tools and potential impact ability to be the next young stud in New York. With plus-plus speed, he can patrol center field with the best of them. Offensively, he is a gifted hitter with the potential to hit .300 at the highest levels. Scouts are split on his power projection, but most see average home-run power and plenty of doubles and triples. The Yankees have dealt many of their high-end prospects over the years, but Williams may be the type of impact athlete they'll want to keep and allow to burst onto the scene in the Big Apple.

52. Julio Teheran, RHP, Braves

While his prospect stock may seem in free fall, Teheran is still very highly regarded across the game. His fastball works in the low- to mid-90s and he commands it well to all parts of the strike zone. He has a plus changeup that can be a lethal weapon in any count. Questions linger about the ultimate fate of his breaking ball, but even without significant progress, Teheran could still be a mid-rotation starter, possibly more if he finally discovers a feel for his breaker.

53. Luis Heredia, RHP, Pirates

The Pirates made a huge splash on the international market with the $2.6 million signing bonus handed to the then-16-year-old Mexican. A massive 6-foot-6 and 200-plus pounds, Heredia has a mature frame, but needs to add strength to reach his ceiling. He shows plus velocity and some feel for a downer curveball and fading changeup that could give him a quality three-pitch mix. Projections for Heredia's future range from the front of a big-league rotation to the back, and everything in between.

54. Arodys Vizcaino, RHP, Cubs

Vizcaino was the highlight in the package of prospects the Cubs received for left-hander Paul Maholm and outfielder Reed Johnson in July, even though he missed the entire 2012 season due to injury. When healthy—which has not been often enough throughout his career—Vizcaino has an electric arsenal that plays up out of the bullpen. His mid-90s fastball can reach 98 mph in short stints and his plus curveball seemingly gets better in relief. In exchange for two modest veterans, the Cubs may have received their closer of the future.

55. George Springer, CF, Astros

Northeast-area scouts were treated to a rare display of high-end tools at the college level when Springer took the field for Connecticut in 2011. He was an easy first-round pick for the Astros that summer and he reached Double-A in just his second professional season in 2012. Springer has the speed and athleticism to handle center field and the arm to support a move to right. His speed plays on the bases and he also has excellent raw power. His hitting ability could be a developmental hurdle, but even without full development, he has enough other tools and the all-out style of play to have a lengthy big-league career.

56. Michael Wacha, RHP, Cardinals

Wacha raced up pre-draft boards with an outstanding spring season at Texas A&M but tumbled in the draft and fell into the Cardinals' lap with the 19th pick. After signing for $1.9 million, Wacha dominated across three levels, including four appearances at Double-A, posting a 0.86 ERA with 40 strikeouts in 21 innings. While he lacks the front-of-the-rotation ceiling his raw numbers suggest because his stuff is more solid than spectacular, Wacha can still fit nicely as a third starter, and he could reach that ceiling very quickly.

57. Nolan Arenado, 3B, Rockies

Some players have a knack for hitting that cannot be taught. Arenado is one of them. His excellent bat speed and uncanny control of the barrel allow him to hit for a high average, something he should be able to do against MLB pitching. Defensively, he fits nicely at third base and the only thing keeping him from owning the prototypical third-base profile is his power projection. Arenado should be ready soon and when he arrives in the majors he could hit .290 with 15 home runs and 30 doubles.

58. Adalberto Mondesi, SS, Royals

The Royals have been lauded for having a loaded system in recent years, and that trend is not going to stop any time soon. Mondesi could be the next elite prospect the club develops, and he could ascend to that throne by the end of the 2013 season. His defense at shortstop is already very good and there's little doubt he'll stick at that position. He's a natural hitter with unexpected power projection, giving him the potential to develop into an all-around stud. Alcides Escobar may be holding down shortstop for now, but Mondesi is the future in Kansas City.

59. Martin Perez, LHP, Rangers

Perez has long been viewed as a future rotation anchor for the Rangers, and despite being on the prospect radar for five years, he will enter the 2013 season at just 22 years old. His fastball and changeup are both plus offerings and he mixes in a curveball, slider, and new two-seam fastball that also keep hitters off balance. He still needs to improve his command, but with a deep arsenal and youth on his side, Perez's odds of becoming a solid number-three starter are very good.

60. Oswaldo Arcia, RF, Twins

As the Twins begin an all-out rebuild of their big-league roster, Arcia could be a factor in the composition of the next contending team in Minnesota. Arcia is a natural hitter with quick hands and plus bat speed that could allow him to hit .290 in the big leagues. He swings the bat hard and generates easy pop to all fields with 15-20 home-run potential. His arm is an asset in the outfield. The Twins needs offensive firepower and Arcia could help provide that as soon as the end of the 2013 campaign.

61. Max Fried, LHP, Padres

Selected seventh in the 2012 draft, Fried is an exciting blend of projectability, "now" stuff, and mound presence, all rolled into a workhorse frame and lefty profile. The former UCLA commit reaches as high as the mid-90s with his fastball and pairs it with two effective secondary offerings in a 12-to-6 curve and a changeup. He projects as a possible front-end arm with three potential plus-or-better weapons at his disposal, and is advanced enough to tackle full-season ball in 2013.

62. Yordano Ventura, RHP, Royals

Generally, diminutive right-handed pitchers tend not to make appearances on top-prospect lists, but Ventura is an easy exception to the trend. With an explosive fastball and hard breaking ball that each rate as plus-plus offerings, he profiles as a potential second or third starter with a nice fallback as a late-inning power arm. Ventura's lively heater and hard spinner are each products of an incredibly fast arm and mechanics that allow that arm unfettered ability to do its work. The late action on the fastball and two-plane break on the curve help to quell the typical "short pitcher" plane concerns, though the young flamethrower will need a more consistent off-speed pitch to turn over upper-level line-ups consistently. He should start 2013 back in Double-A at Northwest Arkansas.

63. J.R. Graham, RHP, Braves

As with Ventura, Graham's stuff outdistances his physicality, giving him a shot to start in spite of an atypical starter's body. The former Santa Clara University standout boasts three legit swing-and-miss offerings in a low-90s sinker, a four-seamer that bumps 95–97 mph, and a tight low- to mid-80s slider. Graham chewed through 148 innings last summer with little trouble and has a chance to project to an MLB rotation if he can continue to refine his developing changeup. He could reach Atlanta by mid-2013 if the Braves wish to utilize his power in the 'pen.

64. Kyle Gibson, RHP, Twins

Gibson left the University of Missouri as a high-floor, moderate-ceiling arm and now, with a Tommy John surgery under his belt, remains essentially the same type of arm as he nears the start of his major-league career. The former first-rounder's bread and butter is a plus changeup that plays well due to good arm-speed deception, command, and abrupt late drop. The fastball is a solid-average offering that follows a similar plate trajectory as his change, increasing the effectiveness of each and allowing Gibson some wiggle room when he misses his spots. The breaker is an angled slider with good levels and some bite, though he is still looking to regain feel for the offering post-surgery. Gibson started the Arizona Fall League off with a bang, and despite seeing some diminution in stuff over the course of the fall, he remains poised to break through with the big club this year. Long term, he looks like a good number three or soft number two starter.

65. Kyle Crick, RHP, Giants

Crick is blessed with a workhorse build and a big arm, flaunting mid-90s velocity and a second gear that makes squaring the pitch difficult for hitters. Questions remain as to where the final velo spread of Crick's pitches will fall once he masters command of his fastball, but few question the pitch grading out as at least plus. Crick has multiple secondary pitches, including a slider, change, and curve, and he shows some comfort with each. Currently his most advanced breaker, the slider, comes with low- to mid-80s velocity and good depth, while the curve is loopier, with less defined shape. With around two years of focused pitching experience under his belt (he was not a full-time pitcher until his senior year of high school), Crick has made large strides quickly. Though significant development remains ahead, the early returns have all been positive, and with continued growth he could reach a lofty ceiling as a legit front-end arm.

66. Alen Hanson, SS, Pirates

The young Dominican middle-infielder enjoyed a breakout season in the Midwest League last summer, showcasing a plus hit tool from both sides of the plate. Hanson's calling card is loud contact produced by his above-average bat speed and ability to find the ball with the barrel of the bat. As with many young hitters, he's still learning to recognize pitches and work the count in his favor; as he refines this skill he should see a decrease in strikeouts and "giveaway" at-bats. The 20-year-old will jump to High-A Bradenton this year, where evaluators will look for improved footwork and feel at shortstop. Hanson profiles well at second base should a move down the defensive spectrum be required.

67. Jesse Biddle, LHP, Phillies

Out of high school Biddle drew comparisons to Andy Pettitte due to similar frames, deliveries, and arsenals (though Biddle's fastball variation is a two-seamer, rather than a cutter). That comparison largely holds true three years later, as the 27th selection in the 2010 draft has sharpened his consistency across the board and darkened the line delineating his breaking balls. Biddle projects as a mid-rotation arm capable of eating innings and missing bats. Though his fastball velocity is average, the big depth in his curve and his ability to mix four pitches helps to keep hitters off balance while slowing their bats. He should be tested at Double-A Reading to start 2013, and could force his way to Philly next summer.

68. Wily Peralta, RHP, Brewers

Peralta logged 29 innings with the Brew Crew in 2012 over six appearances, five starts, more than holding his own. A big body with an even bigger fastball, Peralta routinely tops 95 mph with his heaters—both the two- and four-seam variety. While the bore on his two-seamer helps to miss barrels, the tight velo spread between his fastballs and his slider and changeup can allow hitters to key into two speeds, which may limit his effectiveness as he turns over major-league lineups. He profiles as a mid-rotation arm, but he has a little more upside remaining if he can find more success disrupting hitters' timing at the plate.

69. Allen Webster, RHP, Red Sox

Drafted in the 18th round of the 2009 draft by the Dodgers and signed for a mere $20,000, Webster may have been obtained at a bargain for the second time last summer when the Red Sox were able to wrestle him away from Los Angeles as part of the giant salary dump that shipped Carl Crawford, Josh Beckett, and Adrian Gonzalez out of town. Webster's fastball-changeup combo can be devastating, each pitch coming with late action, making them difficult to elevate. The fastball can reach the mid-90s without losing life, and Webster's off-speed pitch flashes plus-plus when he turns it over properly, making it disappear late in its trajectory. Webster should open 2013 in Triple-A Pawtucket and could peak as a second or third starter depending on his ability to smooth out command issues and refine his mid-80s slider.

70. Lucas Giolito, RHP, Nationals

High school teammates with Fried at Harvard Westlake in Southern California in 2012, Giolito likewise bypassed the opportunity to play college ball at UCLA in order to start his pro career. Selected 16th by the Nationals, Giolito already flashes two plus-plus offerings in his fastball and hard downer curve, with his changeup still developing. The shadow of one elbow surgery already hangs over the imposing former prep star, but his upside as a true number one starter separates him from many of those who share the back third of this list with him.

71. Jake Marisnick, CF, Marlins

A third-round pick of the Blue Jays in 2009, Marisnick was a key piece in the monster 12-player Florida-Toronto trade in November, which netted the Jays Jose Reyes, Josh Johnson, and Mark Buehrle, among others. Marisnick is a toolsy asset who draws future plus grades across the board from some evaluators. His enticing profile, however, comes with a high degree of risk, mostly due to the non-zero chance he outgrows center field, as well as concerns with mechanical shortcomings in his swing. He stands at a crossroads, likely heading back to Double-A to begin the 2013 season and the next stage of his development, with perhaps equal odds he will shoot up this list or drop off completely a year from now.

72. Nick Franklin, MI, Mariners

A short stroke and solid bat-to ball skills from the left side have helped Franklin post solid offensive numbers through each level of the minors prior to some struggles (particularly from the right side) during his first taste of Triple-A ball in 2012. The young middle-infielder, and former first rounder (27th overall in 2009), profiles as a second-division starter, with solid-average grades in the hit, power, run, and glove departments. His fringe-average arm strength and merely adequate range will likely limit him to second base as an every-day player, though he could fill in at short. Franklin should start 2013 back in Triple-A, where his strong feel for the game should help him with his next set of developmental adjustments. He should get his first taste of major-league action this summer.

73. Justin Nicolino, LHP, Marlins

Along with Marisnick, Nicolino was part of the seven-player package sent from Toronto to Miami in November in the Reyes trade. Nicolino profiles as a potential mid-rotation arm, with advanced pitchability and a feel for sequencing and pitch placement that belies his age and experience. A fringe-average fastball plays up a grade due to command and heavy action, with his changeup mirroring everything about the heater, save for velocity. His curve lacks flash, but is serviceable as a third offering and can change a batter's eye level. There is still projection left in Nicolino's frame and, potentially, in his arsenal, making him an interesting follow, and potential riser, for 2013.

74. Brian Goodwin, CF, Nationals

After being drafted in the 17th round of the 2009 draft by the White Sox, Goodwin passed on the opportunity to play pro ball, instead attending and performing well at UNC for a year before a suspension led the North Carolina native to transfer to Miami-Dade Junior College. Goodwin responded well, periodically putting five tools on display in the lead-up to the 2011 draft, ultimately going in the supplemental first round. Goodwin has a chance to grow into a legit five-tool center fielder but while he continues to refine his approach at the plate and his reads and routes in the field, he is at least a year away. His speed allows him to cover the gaps and his arm is plenty strong, though lacking in accuracy at times due to inconsistent setting of his lower half. Goodwin could profile as a top-of-the-order threat on the strength of his compact swing and overall solid feel for the craft, and if all breaks right he will provide the Nationals with positive value in the field, at the plate, and on the bases.

75. Hak-Ju Lee, SS, Rays

Lee's star has dimmed a bit over his past two stints at Double-A Montgomery, but he remains a potential long-term fix for the Rays at shortstop. A smooth defender, Lee has all the makings of an every-day shortstop, including clean lines, soft hands, a lower half that works, and a quick and accurate left-side arm. Offensively, Lee will need to continue to add strength to grow into the gap-to-gap threat he will need to be in order to keep big-league pitchers honest.

At his best, Lee can work the ball the other the way and is an above-average baserunner, adding value both with stolen bases and with good reads and execution on balls in play. He profiles best as a bottom-third bat that can provide value in the field and on the base paths. The Rays will likely afford him a full developmental year at Triple-A Durham before giving him a shot to take over the six spot in St. Pete come 2014.

76. Jorge Alfaro, C, Rangers

The Legend is the rare backstop who's average or better in all five tools, including an 80 arm and solid defensive profile. Alfaro is young, which is good because his game needs a lot of refinement. Defensively, he needs to improve his lateral movement and footwork on the catch-and-throw side, which can too often push his rifle shots off target. At the plate, he carries some thunder in his bat but needs to quiet his approach and keep his swing on a cleaner path to contact, in addition to working more advantageous hitter's counts. The Rangers can afford to give Alfaro the time and coaching necessary to reach his impressive ceiling. If he gets there he could be one of the top catchers in the game. Alfaro will play his age-20 season in High-A Myrtle Beach.

77. Casey Kelly, RHP, Padres

Kelly was knocked around some in his first taste of major-league ball last year, giving up 16 hits and five home runs over his second two starts (eight total innings pitched). Still, the stuff is there for Kelly to develop into a solid mid-rotation arm that can log 200-plus innings. Through the minors, he relied on a heavy fastball and plus curve to hold hitters at bay, with a solid-if-unspectacular changeup mixed in. In order to thrive in the majors, he'll need to show better command of all three offerings, and he may need to tease a better differential between the low-90s fastball and the mid-80s change. Kelly could open the 2013 season in the Padres rotation, and with minimal improvement he could become a fixture there.

78. Robert Stephenson, RHP, Reds

Stephenson was the 27th selection in a loaded 2011 draft class, and in just 65 pro innings he's already rewarded Cincinnati for its $2 million investment. The former NorCal prep standout has dazzled in limited action, reaching the upper-90s with his fastball and consistently clocking in the 93–96 mph range from start to start. Listed at 6-foot-2, 190 pounds, Stephenson still carries some room to add strength, which should help him to maintain velocity as he hangs more innings on his arm over shorter rest. Stephenson has work to do on both his change and his breaking ball, though the former showed solid growth with attention over the past year. He has front-end upside but many reps to go before realizing that potential. He'll likely tackle a full season in the Midwest League in 2013.

79. Yasiel Puig, OF, Dodgers

Puig signed a seven-year, $42 million deal with the Dodgers before the international cap took effect, leaving many in the industry scratching their heads over the price tag and the player. With limited exposure, Puig's skill set was a mystery to many, with impressive raw power the premium tool in the package. The professional sample remains small, and the questions about his profile remain, but the 22-year-old Cuban did show off his offensive promise in a 23-game tease in rookie ball and High-A. Puig could emerge as a prototypical corner bat in the coming years, justifying his hefty price tag and making the Dodgers look smart for taking the risk.

80. Jonathan Schoop, 2B, Orioles

Schoop's most ardent supporters point to top-shelf bat speed, emerging power, soft hands, and a quick transfer and release in projecting him as an above-average offensive-minded second baseman. Evaluators less sold on the 20-year-old Curacao native point to an inconsistent—and at times lengthy—bat path and thickening lower half as evidence of a limited offensive upside and a likely shift to third base or right field. Schoop should start 2013 back in Double-A Bowie, with Baltimore hoping to add him to a 2014 up-the-middle contingent consisting of former and potential All-Stars Adam Jones in center field, Matt Wieters behind the plate, and Manny Machado at shortstop.

81. Chris Owings, SS, Diamondbacks

After struggling to hit in the California League in 2011, Owings repeated the level and began 2012 with High-A Visalia, this time as a 20-year-old. The results were positive; in 59 games, the 2009 first-round pick posted a solid .324/.362/.544 line, prompting a promotion to Mobile. He struggled in his first exposure to Double-A, but 2012 was an overall successful year, and Owings is one step closer to actualizing the tools that could make him an every-day player at an up-the-middle position.

82. Michael Choice, CF, Athletics

A fractured hand cost Choice the final months of the 2012 season, but the overall body of work wasn't too shabby; in just a tick over 400 PAs he posted a .287/.356/.423 line. He continued to strike out at an unhealthy rate, but he's entering his age-23 season and the tools that made him a very high draft pick are still present.

83. Jake Odorizzi, RHP, Rays

The Rays dealt from an area of depth when they shipped James Shields and Wade Davis to Kansas City for Wil Myers and "prospects." Odorizzi's inclusion was a bit puzzling, as the Rays rotation was already jam-packed. Odorizzi is ready to be a middle- to back-end starter in the big leagues right now, and the Rays acquired six years of team control on him. It's not clear he'll have a starting role to begin 2013, but he should have a chance to crack the rotation at some point in the season.

84. Jedd Gyorko, 3B, Padres

Gyorko belted 30 home runs and reached Triple-A in 2012, but Chase Headley broke out for the Padres, and management appears to be set on keeping Headley, who can reach free agency after the 2014 season. Gyorko has enough bat to profile smoothly at third base, but he was tested at second base last year, where his offense would be more than enough to make him an above-average regular. It may be too soon to tell if he can handle the position, but if he can, the Padres could have a very juicy piece of fruit on the farm. If he can't, he might be a solid trade candidate.

85. Dan Straily, RHP, Athletics

A 24th-round pick in 2009, Straily exploded onto the prospect scene in 2012. The stuff was underwhelming when he tackled the Midwest and California leagues in 2010 and 2011, but it took big steps forward in 2012. Straily reached the majors and made an impact, and the departure of Brandon McCarthy could allow him to sneak into Oakland's rotation to start 2013.

86. Luis Sardinas, SS, Rangers

He's been overshadowed from day one by fellow international-free-agent shortstop Jurickson Profar, so it's often forgotten that Sardinas has even louder defensive tools than the top prospect in the game. Because of assorted shoulder injuries, Sardinas hasn't been able to gain traction on the field, but a healthy 2012 campaign put him back on the prospect map, where his plus defensive skill set, 70-grade speed, and plus-potential hit tool once again reminded the industry of his high ceiling.

87. Zach Lee, RHP, Dodgers

Once viewed as an unsignable arm with first-round upside, Lee signed in 2010 when the Dodgers went way over slot on the 28th pick, and it looks like the club made a strong choice. Lee reached Double-A in 2012. He possesses a solid arsenal that should make him at least a solid-average rotation cog, and there's a bit more projection in the body. Los Angeles kept him out of midseason trades, then bolstered its rotation with Zack Greinke and Hyun-Jin Ryu, so the Dodgers can take their time with Lee.

88. Alex Meyer, RHP, Twins

The 6-foot-9 former Kentucky Wildcat struck out 139 batters in 129 innings in his pro debut. Meyer is a power arm with a strong fastball-slider combination, and he adds some punch to Minnesota's minor-league system. His ceiling is high, and he could be good enough to justify trading Denard Span to get him.

89. Matt Davidson, 3B, Diamondbacks

After a modest 2011 campaign with High-A Visalia, Davidson was, statistically, a little bit better with Double-A Mobile in 2012, trimming his strikeout rate and bumping his walk rate. He also made strides at third base, and now he figures to be a solid-average player there. Arizona's midseason acquisition of Chris Johnson clogs the position for now, but Davidson could be good enough to create a competition down the line.

90. Kolten Wong, 2B, Cardinals

Wong's instincts and makeup allowed St. Louis some comfort when it challenged him with a Double-A assignment, and Wong didn't disappoint. In his first full pro season, Wong had a strong year at Double-A, posting a .287/.348/.405 line over 579 PAs. The 22-year-old's hit tool impressed again in the Arizona Fall League, and he could challenge for Daniel Descalso's spot at some point in 2013.

91. Tony Cingrani, LHP, Reds

With a fastball that routinely works in the plus-velocity range and touches higher, and a changeup that some sources have put a plus-plus grade on, Cingrani was able to chew up minor-league hitters, forcing weak contact or missing bats altogether. Some question his ability to stick in a big-league rotation, mostly because of a fringy breaking ball and only adequate command, but with impressive size and two plus pitches, Cingrani's role in the bullpen isn't cemented quite yet.

92. James Paxton, LHP, Mariners

Paxton has taken an odd path, but it looks like it's going to lead him to Seattle's rotation soon. After losing his NCAA eligibility for improper contact with agent Scott Boras, the southpaw played a year of independent-league baseball, and the M's took a stab at him in the fourth round of the 2010 draft. Paxton lives on a mid-90s fastball and a plus curveball. Command issues slowed him down in 2012, but overall it was a solid effort at Double-A, and Paxton could compete for a rotation spot in 2013.

93. Christian Bethancourt, C, Braves

On the surface, 2012 was a down year for Bethancourt, but if we take a step back we can see modest production at Double-A from a 20-year-old. A .243/.275/.291 line over 288 PAs might remind you of Jeff Mathis, but Bethancourt's story hasn't been written yet. It's unlikely he'll make a name for himself with the stick, but he has a chance to be one of the better defensive players at an up-the-middle position. If he hits just a little, he's going to have a career.

94. Tyrell Jenkins, RHP, Cardinals

A 2010 first-round pick, Jenkins is still adding stamina to his athletic frame. He racked up 82 1/3 innings in his first exposure to a full-season league, and he struck out nearly a batter per inning. He's sitting in the low 90s and getting by with his secondary stuff, so a promotion to High-A, where he should add another 25–30 innings to his workload, seems like the next logical step.

95. Clayton Blackburn, RHP, Giants

Statistically, it was a special year for Blackburn, who mastered Low-A in his first full season as a pro. A 16th-round pick out of Edmond, Oklahoma, Blackburn burst onto the prospect scene in 2012 with a plus sinker, ridiculous control of the strike zone, and a 7.94 strikeout-to-walk ratio. He turned 20 in January and he's ready to take a plunge into the hitter's paradise that is the California League, where a high ground-ball rate might keep him out of trouble.

96. Dorssys Paulino, SS, Indians

Paulino entered 2012 having not yet recorded a single plate appearance as a pro, and now he will enter 2013 as one of the most exciting young prospects in baseball. As a 17-year-old he destroyed the Arizona Rookie League and moved on to short-season Mahoning Valley, where he didn't dominate, but did show off his tools. Paulino is the dream: an up-the-middle prospect with plus-hit-tool projection. There's a long way to go, but he could make the jump to full-season ball in 2013, where his prospect status could explode.

97. Sean Nolin, LHP, Blue Jays

A strong year at High-A Dunedin was rewarded with a late-season jump to Double-A, where Nolin continued to dominate. On the whole, the big left-hander put together a 2.04 ERA across 101 1/3 innings, striking out 108 and walking just 27. A midseason lat injury slowed Nolin down, but his four-pitch repertoire and advanced pitchability should give him a boost toward the highest level in 2013. There's no clear rotation spot for Nolin in Toronto right now, so the Jays can take their time with him.

98. Michael Fulmer, RHP, Mets

Fulmer is the final Oklahoma right-hander in our rankings who will play his 2013 season as a 20-year-old. He has heat, running his fastball up to 95, and an excellent slider that receives plus grades. In 2012, he successfully tackled Low-A, posting a 2.74 ERA over 108 1/3 innings and striking out 101 while walking just 38. He'll need to work on his third offering (a changeup), but the tools are in place for Fulmer to pitch in the middle of a rotation. He should start 2013 in High-A.

99. Lewis Brinson, CF, Rangers

When Texas nabbed Brinson with the 29th pick in the 2012 draft, many saw it as a reach for a toolsy outfielder who would take plenty of time to develop. As it turns out, Brinson isn't as raw as you might have thought. While there are some weaknesses in his swing, he made a lot of hard contact and displayed all five tools in his first sips of professional baseball in the Arizona Rookie League and at instructs. The ceiling is sky-high, and the 18-year-old could be part of another loaded Rangers affiliate in Low-A Hickory in 2013.

100. Tyler Thornburg, RHP, Brewers

Thornburg started 2012 with Double-A Hunstville and ended it with the Brewers. The 24-year-old was very good in the upper minors, and had a few brief stops in Milwaukee throughout the year. He's got a solid three-pitch mix, but concerns about the maximum effort in his delivery cause some scouts to question his shelf-life as a starter. Thornburg is ready to go, and he should have a chance to win himself a job in spring training.

101. Delino DeShields Jr., 2B, Astros

After a rough first try, DeShields was back at Low-A Lexington for a second time to start 2012. This time, he hit the ground running, swiping 83 bags in 97 attempts while hitting .298/.401/.439 before a promotion to High-A. The 20-year-old finished the season with 101 stolen bases, second in the minor leagues to Billy Hamilton. DeShields has the makings of a plus hit tool and has good on-base skills, too. He isn't without weaknesses, but he's a fantastic prospect who could be headed for a full season of the hitter-friendly California League in 2013.

Team Name Codes

CODE	TEAM	LEAGUE	AFFILIATION	NAME
ABE	Aberdeen	NYP	Orioles	IronBirds
ABQ	Albuquerque	PCL	Dodgers	Isotopes
AKR	Akron	EAS	Indians	Aeros
ALT	Altoona	EAS	Pirates	Curve
ANA	Los Angeles	AL	-	Angels
ANG	AZL Angels	AZL	Angels	-
ARI	Arizona	NL	-	Diamondbacks
ARK	Arkansas	TEX	Angels	Travelers
ASH	Asheville	SAL	Rockies	Tourists
AST	GCL Astros	GCL	Astros	-
ATH	AZL Athletics	AZL	Athletics	-
ATL	Atlanta	NL	-	Braves
AUB	Auburn	NYP	Nationals	Doubledays
AUG	Augusta	SAL	Giants	GreenJackets
BAK	Bakersfield	CAL	Reds	Blaze
BAL	Baltimore	AL	-	Orioles
BAT	Batavia	NYP	Cardinals	Muckdogs
BGR	Bowling Green	MID	Rays	Hot Rods
BIL	Billings	PIO	Reds	Mustangs
BIN	Binghamton	EAS	Mets	Mets
BIR	Birmingham	SOU	White Sox	Barons
BLJ	GCL Blue Jays	GCL	Blue Jays	-
BLT	Beloit	MID	Twins	Snappers
BLU	Bluefield	APP	Blue Jays	Blue Jays
BNC	Burlington	APP	Royals	Royals
BOI	Boise	NOR	Cubs	Hawks
BOS	Boston	AL	-	Red Sox
BOW	Bowie	EAS	Orioles	Baysox
BRA	GCL Braves	GCL	Braves	-
BRD	Bradenton	FSL	Pirates	Marauders
BRI	Bristol	APP	White Sox	White Sox
BRO	Brooklyn	NYP	Mets	Cyclones
BRR	AZL Brewers	AZL	Brewers	-
BRV	Brevard County	FSL	Brewers	Manatees
BUF	Buffalo	INT	Mets	Bisons
BUR	Burlington	MID	Athletics	Bees
CAR	Carolina	CAR	Indians	Mudcats
CCH	Corpus Christi	TEX	Astros	Hooks
CDR	Cedar Rapids	MID	Angels	Kernels
CHA	Chicago	AL	-	White Sox
CHB	Chiba Lotte	NPB	-	Marines
CHN	Chicago	NL	-	Cubs
CHR	Charlotte	INT	White Sox	Knights
CHT	Chattanooga	SOU	Dodgers	Lookouts
CHU	Chunichi	NPB	-	Dragons
CIN	AZL Reds	AZL	Reds	-
CIN	Cincinnati	NL	-	Reds
CLE	AZL Indians	AZL	Indians	-
CLE	Cleveland	AL	-	Indians
CLN	Clinton	MID	Mariners	LumberKings
CLR	Clearwater	FSL	Phillies	Threshers
COH	Columbus	INT	Indians	Clippers
COL	Colorado	NL	-	Rockies
CRD	GCL Cardinals	GCL	Cardinals	-
CSC	Charleston	SAL	Yankees	RiverDogs
CSP	Colorado Springs	PCL	Rockies	Sky Sox
CUB	AZL Cubs	AZL	Cubs	-
DAC	DSL D-backs/Reds	DSL	-	-
DAN	DSL Angels	DSL	Angels	-
DAS	DSL Astros	DSL	Astros	-
DAT	DSL Athletics	DSL	Athletics	-
DAY	Daytona	FSL	Cubs	Cubs
DBL	DSL Blue Jays	DSL	Blue Jays	-
DBR	DSL Braves	DSL	Braves	-
DBW	DSL Brewers	DSL	Brewers	-
DCA	DSL Cardinals	DSL	Cardinals	-
DCH	DSL Cubs2	DSL	Cubs	-
DCU	DSL Cubs1	DSL	Cubs	-
DDI	DSL D-backs	DSL	Diamondbacks	-
DDO	DSL Dodgers	DSL	Dodgers	-
DDR	DSL Rays	DSL	Rays	-
DEL	Delmarva	SAL	Orioles	Shorebirds
DET	Detroit	AL	-	Tigers
DGI	DSL Giants	DSL	Giants	-
DIA	AZL D-backs	AZL	Diamondbacks	-
DIN	DSL Indians	DSL	Indians	-
DME	DSL Mets1	DSL	Mets	-
DML	DSL Marlins	DSL	Marlins	-
DMR	DSL Mariners	DSL	Mariners	-
DNV	Danville	APP	Braves	Braves
DOD	AZL Dodgers	AZL	Dodgers	-
DOR	DSL Orioles	DSL	Orioles	-
DPA	DSL Padres	DSL	Padres	-
DPH	DSL Phillies	DSL	Phillies	-
DPI	DSL Pirates1	DSL	Pirates	-
DPT	DSL Pirates2	DSL	Pirates	-
DRD	DSL Reds	DSL	Reds	-
DRG	DSL Rangers	DSL	Rangers	-
DRO	DSL Rockies	DSL	Rockies	-
DRS	DSL Red Sox	DSL	Red Sox	-
DRY	DSL Royals	DSL	Royals	-
DTI	DSL Tigers	DSL	Tigers	-
DTW	DSL Twins	DSL	Twins	-
DUN	Dunedin	FSL	Blue Jays	Blue Jays
DUR	Durham	INT	Rays	Bulls
DWA	DSL Nationals	DSL	Nationals	-

CODE	TEAM	LEAGUE	AFFILIATION	NAME
DWS	DSL White Sox	DSL	White Sox	-
DYA	DSL Yankees1	DSL	Yankees	-
DYN	DSL Yankees2	DSL	Yankees	-
DYT	Dayton	MID	Reds	Dragons
ELZ	Elizabethton	APP	Twins	Twins
ERI	Erie	EAS	Tigers	SeaWolves
EUG	Eugene	NOR	Padres	Emeralds
EVE	Everett	NOR	Mariners	AquaSox
FKU	Fukuoka	NPB	-	Hawks
FRD	Frederick	CAR	Orioles	Keys
FRE	Fresno	PCL	Giants	Grizzlies
FRI	Frisco	TEX	Rangers	RoughRiders
FTM	Fort Myers	FSL	Twins	Miracle
FTW	Fort Wayne	MID	Padres	TinCaps
GIA	AZL Giants	AZL	Giants	-
GJR	Grand Junction	PIO	Rockies	Rockies
GRB	Greensboro	SAL	Marlins	Grasshoppers
GRF	Great Falls	PIO	White Sox	Voyagers
GRL	Great Lakes	MID	Dodgers	Loons
GRN	Greenville	SAL	Red Sox	Drive
GRV	Greeneville	APP	Astros	Astros
GWN	Gwinnett	INT	Braves	Braves
HAG	Hagerstown	SAL	Nationals	Suns
HAR	Harrisburg	EAS	Nationals	Senators
HDS	High Desert	CAL	Mariners	Mavericks
HEL	Helena	PIO	Brewers	Brewers
HIC	Hickory	SAL	Rangers	Crawdads
HNS	Hanshin	NPB	-	Tigers
HOU	Houston	NL	-	Astros
HRO	Hiroshima Toyo	NPB	-	Carp
HUD	Hudson Valley	NYP	Rays	Renegades
HUN	Huntsville	SOU	Brewers	Stars
IDA	Idaho Falls	PIO	Royals	Chukars
IND	Indianapolis	INT	Pirates	Indians
IOW	Iowa	PCL	Cubs	Cubs
JAM	Jamestown	NYP	Marlins	Jammers
JAX	Jacksonville	SOU	Marlins	Suns
JCY	Johnson City	APP	Cardinals	Cardinals
JUP	Jupiter	FSL	Marlins	Hammerheads
KAN	Kannapolis	SAL	White Sox	Intimidators
KCA	Kansas City	AL	-	Royals
KNC	Kane County	MID	Royals	Cougars
KNG	Kingsport	APP	Mets	Mets
LAK	Lakeland	FSL	Tigers	Flying Tigers
LAN	Los Angeles	NL	-	Dodgers
LEH	Lehigh Valley	INT	Phillies	IronPigs
LEL	Lake Elsinore	CAL	Padres	Storm
LEX	Lexington	SAL	Astros	Legends
LKC	Lake County	MID	Indians	Captains
LNC	Lancaster	CAL	Astros	JetHawks
LNS	Lansing	MID	Blue Jays	Lugnuts
LOU	Louisville	INT	Reds	Bats
LOW	Lowell	NYP	Red Sox	Spinners
LVG	Las Vegas	PCL	Blue Jays	51s
LWD	Lakewood	SAL	Phillies	BlueClaws
LYN	Lynchburg	CAR	Braves	Hillcats
MEM	Memphis	PCL	Cardinals	Redbirds
MET	DSL Mets2	DSL	Mets	-
MHV	Mahoning Valley	NYP	Indians	Scrappers
MIA	Miami	NL	-	Marlins
MID	Midland	TEX	Athletics	RockHounds
MIL	Milwaukee	NL	-	Brewers
MIN	Minnesota	AL	-	Twins
MIS	Mississippi	SOU	Braves	Braves
MNT	Montgomery	SOU	Rays	Biscuits
MOB	Mobile	SOU	Diamondbacks	BayBears
MOD	Modesto	CAL	Rockies	Nuts
MRL	GCL Marlins	GCL	Marlins	-
MRN	AZL Mariners	AZL	Mariners	-
MSO	Missoula	PIO	Diamondbacks	Osprey
MYR	Myrtle Beach	CAR	Rangers	Pelicans
NAS	Nashville	PCL	Brewers	Sounds
NAT	GCL Nationals	GCL	Nationals	-
NBR	New Britain	EAS	Twins	Rock Cats
NHP	New Hampshire	EAS	Blue Jays	Fisher Cats
NIP	Nippon Ham	NPB	-	Fighters
NOR	Norfolk	INT	Orioles	Tides
NWA	NW Arkansas	TEX	Royals	Naturals
NWO	New Orleans	PCL	Marlins	Zephyrs
NYA	New York	AL	-	Yankees
NYN	New York	NL	-	Mets
OAK	Oakland	AL	-	Athletics
OGD	Ogden	PIO	Dodgers	Raptors
OKL	Oklahoma City	PCL	Astros	RedHawks
OMA	Omaha	PCL	Royals	Storm Chasers
ONE	Connecticut	NYP	Tigers	Tigers
ORI	GCL Orioles	GCL	Orioles	-
ORM	Orem	PIO	Angels	Owlz
ORX	Orix	NPB	-	Buffaloes
PAW	Pawtucket	INT	Red Sox	Red Sox
PCH	Charlotte	FSL	Rays	Stone Crabs
PDR	AZL Padres	AZL	Padres	-
PEN	Pensacola	SOU	Reds	Blue Wahoos
PEO	Peoria	MID	Cubs	Chiefs
PHI	Philadelphia	NL	-	Phillies
PHL	GCL Phillies	GCL	Phillies	-
PIR	GCL Pirates	GCL	Pirates	-
PIT	Pittsburgh	NL	-	Pirates
PMB	Palm Beach	FSL	Cardinals	Cardinals
PME	Portland	EAS	Red Sox	Sea Dogs
POT	Potomac	CAR	Nationals	Nationals
PRI	Princeton	APP	Rays	Rays
PUL	Pulaski	APP	Mariners	Mariners
QUD	Quad Cities	MID	Cardinals	River Bandits
RAK	Rakuten	NPB	-	Golden Eagles
RAY	GCL Rays	GCL	Rays	-
RCU	Rnch. Cucam.	CAL	Dodgers	Quakes
REA	Reading	EAS	Phillies	Phillies
RIC	Richmond	EAS	Giants	Flying Squirrels
RNG	AZL Rangers	AZL	Rangers	-
RNO	Reno	PCL	Diamondbacks	Aces
ROC	Rochester	INT	Twins	Red Wings

CODE	TEAM	LEAGUE	AFFILIATION	NAME
ROM	Rome	SAL	Braves	Braves
ROU	Round Rock	PCL	Rangers	Express
ROY	AZL Royals	AZL	Royals	-
RSX	GCL Red Sox	GCL	Red Sox	-
SAC	Sacramento	PCL	Athletics	River Cats
SAN	San Antonio	TEX	Padres	Missions
SAV	Savannah	SAL	Mets	Sand Gnats
SBN	South Bend	MID	Diamondbacks	Silver Hawks
SBR	Inland Empire	CAL	Angels	66ers
SCO	State College	NYP	Pirates	Spikes
SDN	San Diego	NL	-	Padres
SEA	Seattle	AL	-	Mariners
SEI	Seibu	NPB	-	Lions
SFD	Springfield	TEX	Cardinals	Cardinals
SFN	San Francisco	NL	-	Giants
SJO	San Jose	CAL	Giants	Giants
SLC	Salt Lake	PCL	Angels	Bees
SLM	Salem	CAR	Red Sox	Red Sox
SLN	St. Louis	NL	-	Cardinals
SLO	Salem-Keizer	NOR	Giants	Volcanoes
SLU	St. Lucie	FSL	Mets	Mets
SPO	Spokane	NOR	Rangers	Indians
STA	Staten Island	NYP	Yankees	Yankees
STO	Stockton	CAL	Athletics	Ports
SWB	Scranton/WB	INT	Yankees	Yankees
SYR	Syracuse	INT	Nationals	Chiefs
TAC	Tacoma	PCL	Mariners	Rainiers
TAM	Tampa	FSL	Yankees	Yankees
TBA	Tampa Bay	AL	-	Rays
TCV	Tri-City	NYP	Astros	ValleyCats
TEN	Tennessee	SOU	Cubs	Smokies
TEX	Texas	AL	-	Rangers
TGR	GCL Tigers	GCL	Tigers	-
TOL	Toledo	INT	Tigers	Mud Hens
TOR	Toronto	AL	-	Blue Jays
TRI	Tri-City	NOR	Rockies	Dust Devils
TRN	Trenton	EAS	Yankees	Thunder
TUC	Tucson	PCL	Padres	Padres
TUL	Tulsa	TEX	Rockies	Drillers
TWI	GCL Twins	GCL	Twins	-
VAN	Vancouver	NOR	Blue Jays	Canadians
VER	Vermont	NYP	Athletics	Lake Monsters
VIS	Visalia	CAL	Diamondbacks	Rawhide
VPH	VSL PHI	VSL	Phillies	VSL Phillies
VSE	VSL SEA	VSL	Mariners	VSL Mariners
VTB	VSL TB	VSL	Rays	VSL Rays
VTI	VSL DET	VSL	Tigers	VSL Tigers
WAS	Washington	NL	-	Nationals
WIL	Wilmington	CAR	Royals	Blue Rocks
WIS	Wisconsin	MID	Brewers	Timber Rattlers
WMI	West Michigan	MID	Tigers	Whitecaps
WNS	Winston-Salem	CAR	White Sox	Dash
WPT	Williamsport	NYP	Phillies	Crosscutters
WTN	Jackson	SOU	Mariners	Generals
WVA	West Virginia	SAL	Pirates	Power
YAK	Yakima	NOR	Diamondbacks	Bears
YAN	GCL Yankees	GCL	Yankees	-
YKL	Yakult	NPB	-	Swallows
YKO	Yokohama DeNa	NPB	-	BayStars
YOM	Yomiuri	NPB	-	Giants

PECOTA Leaderboards

HITTERS

Home Runs

RANK	NAME	TEAM	HR
1	Albert Pujols	ANA	34
1	Miguel Cabrera	DET	34
3	Ryan Braun	MIL	33
4	Prince Fielder	DET	32
5	Giancarlo Stanton	MIA	31
5	Curtis Granderson	NYA	31
7	Adam Dunn	CHA	30
7	Jay Bruce	CIN	30
9	Mark Trumbo	ANA	28
9	Nelson Cruz	TEX	28
11	Dan Uggla	ATL	27
11	Mark Reynolds	CLE	27
11	Adrian Gonzalez	LAN	27
11	Edwin Encarnacion	TOR	27
15	Paul Konerko	CHA	26
15	Alfonso Soriano	CHN	26
15	Carlos Pena	HOU	26
15	Aramis Ramirez	MIL	26
19	Josh Hamilton	ANA	25
19	Josh Willingham	MIN	25
19	Mark Teixeira	NYA	25
19	Adrian Beltre	TEX	25

Runs Batted In

RANK	NAME	TEAM	RBI
1	Miguel Cabrera	DET	109
2	Albert Pujols	ANA	104
3	Prince Fielder	DET	103
4	Ryan Braun	MIL	101
5	Adrian Gonzalez	LAN	94
6	Robinson Cano	NYA	92
7	Jay Bruce	CIN	91
8	Adam Dunn	CHA	88
9	Aramis Ramirez	MIL	87
9	Matt Holliday	SLN	87
11	Nelson Cruz	TEX	86
11	Edwin Encarnacion	TOR	86
13	Dan Uggla	ATL	85
13	Paul Konerko	CHA	85
13	Giancarlo Stanton	MIA	85
13	Curtis Granderson	NYA	85
13	Adrian Beltre	TEX	85
18	Josh Hamilton	ANA	84
18	Adam Jones	BAL	84
18	Billy Butler	KCA	84

Runs Scored

RANK	NAME	TEAM	R
1	Ian Kinsler	TEX	98
2	Curtis Granderson	NYA	97
3	Miguel Cabrera	DET	95
3	Ryan Braun	MIL	95
5	Albert Pujols	ANA	94
6	Prince Fielder	DET	93
6	Jose Reyes	TOR	93
8	Michael Bourn	ATL	87
9	Jimmy Rollins	PHI	86
10	Mike Trout	ANA	85
10	Rickie Weeks	MIL	85
10	Andrew McCutchen	PIT	85
13	Dustin Pedroia	BOS	84
13	Adrian Gonzalez	LAN	84
15	Shane Victorino	BOS	83
15	Danny Espinosa	WAS	83
17	Starlin Castro	CHN	82
18	Alex Gordon	KCA	81
18	Matt Holliday	SLN	81
18	Elvis Andrus	TEX	81

Stolen Bases

RANK	NAME	TEAM	SB
1	Michael Bourn	ATL	48
2	Rajai Davis	TOR	40
3	Billy Hamilton	CIN	38
3	Coco Crisp	OAK	38
5	B.J. Upton	ATL	37
6	Jose Reyes	TOR	36
7	Mike Trout	ANA	35
8	Ben Revere	PHI	33
9	Drew Stubbs	CLE	31
9	Juan Pierre	MIA	31
9	Ichiro Suzuki	NYA	31
12	Everth Cabrera	SDN	30
13	Shane Victorino	BOS	29
13	Jarrod Dyson	KCA	29
13	Angel Pagan	SFN	29
16	Jimmy Rollins	PHI	28
16	Desmond Jennings	TBA	28
16	Elvis Andrus	TEX	28
19	Alcides Escobar	KCA	26
19	Norichika Aoki	MIL	26

Batting Average

RANK	NAME	TEAM	AVG
1	Joe Mauer	MIN	0.316
2	Miguel Cabrera	DET	0.314
3	Ryan Braun	MIL	0.303
4	Joey Votto	CIN	0.300
5	Albert Pujols	ANA	0.299
5	Troy Tulowitzki	COL	0.299
7	Carlos Gonzalez	COL	0.298
7	Norichika Aoki	MIL	0.298
9	Billy Butler	KCA	0.297
10	Buster Posey	SFN	0.295
10	Pablo Sandoval	SFN	0.295
12	Dustin Pedroia	BOS	0.294
12	Victor Martinez	DET	0.294
14	Robinson Cano	NYA	0.293
14	Jose Reyes	TOR	0.293
16	Matt Holliday	SLN	0.292
17	Ichiro Suzuki	NYA	0.291
18	DJ LeMahieu	COL	0.290
19	Mike Trout	ANA	0.289
19	Starlin Castro	CHN	0.289
19	Salvador Perez	KCA	0.289
19	Yadier Molina	SLN	0.289

On Base Percentage

RANK	NAME	TEAM	OBP
1	Joe Mauer	MIN	0.402
2	Joey Votto	CIN	0.401
3	Prince Fielder	DET	0.394
4	Miguel Cabrera	DET	0.392
5	Nick Johnson	BAL	0.387
6	Albert Pujols	ANA	0.384
7	Lance Berkman	SLN	0.379
8	Matt Holliday	SLN	0.373
8	Jose Bautista	TOR	0.373
10	Troy Tulowitzki	COL	0.370
11	Shin-Soo Choo	CIN	0.368
12	Buster Posey	SFN	0.367
13	Dan Johnson	CHA	0.366
13	Adrian Gonzalez	LAN	0.366
13	Ryan Braun	MIL	0.366
16	Carlos Santana	CLE	0.364
16	Dexter Fowler	COL	0.364
18	Dustin Pedroia	BOS	0.362
18	Norichika Aoki	MIL	0.362
18	Kevin Youkilis	NYA	0.362

SLG

RANK	NAME	TEAM	SLG
1	Miguel Cabrera	DET	0.564
2	Albert Pujols	ANA	0.554
3	Ryan Braun	MIL	0.551
4	Giancarlo Stanton	MIA	0.543
5	Joey Votto	CIN	0.534
6	Troy Tulowitzki	COL	0.528
7	Prince Fielder	DET	0.525
8	Jose Bautista	TOR	0.518
9	Carlos Gonzalez	COL	0.517
10	Wilin Rosario	COL	0.512
11	Mike Napoli	TEX	0.505
12	Nelson Cruz	TEX	0.494
13	Matt Holliday	SLN	0.492
14	Robinson Cano	NYA	0.491
15	Josh Hamilton	ANA	0.490
15	Aramis Ramirez	MIL	0.490
15	Allen Craig	SLN	0.490
18	Ryan Howard	PHI	0.489
19	Matt Kemp	LAN	0.488
20	Adrian Gonzalez	LAN	0.487

ISO

RANK	NAME	TEAM	ISO
1	Giancarlo Stanton	MIA	0.276
2	Jose Bautista	TOR	0.262
3	Albert Pujols	ANA	0.255
4	Miguel Cabrera	DET	0.250
5	Ryan Braun	MIL	0.248
6	Mike Napoli	TEX	0.247
7	Wilin Rosario	COL	0.246
8	Ryan Howard	PHI	0.241
9	Prince Fielder	DET	0.239
10	Adam Dunn	CHA	0.235
11	Dan Johnson	CHA	0.235
12	Joey Votto	CIN	0.234
13	Tyler Moore	WAS	0.233
14	Jay Bruce	CIN	0.229
14	Troy Tulowitzki	COL	0.229
16	Nelson Cruz	TEX	0.228
17	Mark Teixeira	NYA	0.226
18	Mark Reynolds	CLE	0.225
18	Curtis Granderson	NYA	0.225
20	Donnie Murphy	MIL	0.223

True Average

RANK	NAME	TEAM	TAV
1	Albert Pujols	ANA	0.330
2	Miguel Cabrera	DET	0.327
3	Joey Votto	CIN	0.326
4	Prince Fielder	DET	0.317
5	Ryan Braun	MIL	0.315
6	Giancarlo Stanton	MIA	0.312
7	Jose Bautista	TOR	0.310
8	Adrian Gonzalez	LAN	0.307
8	Buster Posey	SFN	0.307
8	Matt Holliday	SLN	0.307
11	Joe Mauer	MIN	0.305
12	Evan Longoria	TBA	0.304
13	Mike Trout	ANA	0.302
13	Matt Kemp	LAN	0.302
15	Pablo Sandoval	SFN	0.301
15	Lance Berkman	SLN	0.301

17	Mike Napoli	TEX	0.300
18	Andrew McCutchen	PIT	0.299
19	Hanley Ramirez	LAN	0.298
19	Carlos Quentin	SDN	0.298

Wins Above Replacement Player, American League

RANK	NAME	TEAM	WARP
1	Albert Pujols	ANA	6.3
2	Miguel Cabrera	DET	5.3
3	Robinson Cano	NYA	4.4
4	Joe Mauer	MIN	4.2
5	Mike Trout	ANA	4.1
5	Carlos Santana	CLE	4.1
5	Jose Reyes	TOR	4.1
8	Prince Fielder	DET	4.0
8	Ben Zobrist	TBA	4.0
10	Josh Hamilton	ANA	3.9

Wins Above Replacement Player, National League

RANK	NAME	TEAM	WARP
1	Ryan Braun	MIL	5.5
2	Andrew McCutchen	PIT	4.6
3	Adrian Gonzalez	LAN	4.3
4	Joey Votto	CIN	4.2
4	Buster Posey	SFN	4.2
6	Giancarlo Stanton	MIA	4.0
7	Justin Upton	ARI	3.8
8	Matt Holliday	SLN	3.7
9	Miguel Montero	ARI	3.6
9	Starlin Castro	CHN	3.6

Wins Above Replacement Player, Catcher

RANK	NAME	TEAM	WARP
1	Joe Mauer	MIN	4.2
1	Buster Posey	SFN	4.2
3	Carlos Santana	CLE	4.1
4	Miguel Montero	ARI	3.6
5	Brian McCann	ATL	3.5
6	Yadier Molina	SLN	3.2
7	Mike Napoli	TEX	2.9
8	Matt Wieters	BAL	2.7
9	Carlos Ruiz	PHI	2.5
10	Alex Avila	DET	2.4

Wins Above Replacement Player, First Base

RANK	NAME	TEAM	WARP
1	Albert Pujols	ANA	6.3
2	Adrian Gonzalez	LAN	4.3
3	Joey Votto	CIN	4.2
4	Prince Fielder	DET	4.0
5	Billy Butler	KCA	3.2
6	Mark Teixeira	NYA	2.7
7	Edwin Encarnacion	TOR	2.5
8	David Ortiz	BOS	2.2
8	Paul Konerko	CHA	2.2
10	Adam Dunn	CHA	1.9
10	Kendrys Morales	SEA	1.9

Wins Above Replacement Player, Second Base

RANK	NAME	TEAM	WARP
1	Robinson Cano	NYA	4.4
2	Ben Zobrist	TBA	4.0
3	Dustin Pedroia	BOS	3.7
4	Ian Kinsler	TEX	3.4
5	Dan Uggla	ATL	3.0
5	Jason Kipnis	CLE	3.0
7	Omar Infante	DET	2.7
8	Howard Kendrick	ANA	2.6
9	Aaron Hill	ARI	2.4
10	Chase Utley	PHI	2.3

Wins Above Replacement Player, Third Base

RANK	NAME	TEAM	WARP
1	Miguel Cabrera	DET	5.3
2	David Wright	NYN	3.5
3	Ryan Zimmerman	WAS	3.4
4	Pablo Sandoval	SFN	3.0
5	Chase Headley	SDN	2.9
6	Adrian Beltre	TEX	2.8
7	Kevin Youkilis	NYA	2.6
8	David Freese	SLN	2.5
9	Alex Rodriguez	NYA	2.4
10	Aramis Ramirez	MIL	2.3
10	Evan Longoria	TBA	2.3

Wins Above Replacement Player, Shortstop

RANK	NAME	TEAM	WARP
1	Jose Reyes	TOR	4.1
2	Starlin Castro	CHN	3.6
3	Hanley Ramirez	LAN	3.5
4	Yunel Escobar	TBA	3.0
5	Jimmy Rollins	PHI	2.9
6	J.J. Hardy	BAL	2.7
7	Asdrubal Cabrera	CLE	2.6
7	Rafael Furcal	SLN	2.6
7	Elvis Andrus	TEX	2.6
10	Troy Tulowitzki	COL	2.4

Wins Above Replacement Player, Left Field

RANK	NAME	TEAM	WARP
1	Ryan Braun	MIL	5.5
2	Josh Hamilton	ANA	3.9
3	Alex Gordon	KCA	3.7
3	Matt Holliday	SLN	3.7
5	Josh Willingham	MIN	2.9
5	Yoenis Cespedes	OAK	2.9
7	Martin Prado	ATL	2.7
8	Carlos Gonzalez	COL	2.4
9	Desmond Jennings	TBA	2.1
10	Jason Kubel	ARI	1.9

Wins Above Replacement Player, Center Field

RANK	NAME	TEAM	WARP
1	Andrew McCutchen	PIT	4.6
2	Mike Trout	ANA	4.1
3	Curtis Granderson	NYA	3.6
4	Adam Jones	BAL	3.5
5	Matt Kemp	LAN	3.3
6	B.J. Upton	ATL	3.2
7	Angel Pagan	SFN	2.8
8	Shane Victorino	BOS	2.5
8	Austin Jackson	DET	2.5
10	Alejandro De Aza	CHA	2.3
10	Bryce Harper	WAS	2.3

Wins Above Replacement Player, Right Field

RANK	NAME	TEAM	WARP
1	Giancarlo Stanton	MIA	4.0
2	Justin Upton	ARI	3.8
3	Nelson Cruz	TEX	3.6
4	Shin-Soo Choo	CIN	3.4
5	Jason Heyward	ATL	3.3
5	Jay Bruce	CIN	3.3
7	Jose Bautista	TOR	3.1
8	Andre Ethier	LAN	3.0
8	Hunter Pence	SFN	3.0
8	Carlos Beltran	SLN	3.0

Wins Above Replacement Player, Rookies

RANK	NAME	TEAM	WARP
1	Wil Myers	TBA	1.2
2	Billy Hamilton	CIN	1.1
2	Mike Olt	TEX	1.1
4	Adam Eaton	ARI	1.0
4	Mike Zunino	SEA	1.0
4	Jurickson Profar	TEX	1.0
7	Xander Bogaerts	BOS	0.9
7	Jacob Elmore	HOU	0.9
9	Nick Ahmed	ATL	0.8
9	Evan Gattis	ATL	0.8
9	Brock Holt	BOS	0.8
9	Travis d'Arnaud	NYN	0.8
9	Jedd Gyorko	SDN	0.8
9	Brandon Guyer	TBA	0.8
9	Leonys Martin	TEX	0.8

Wins Above Replacement Player, Improvement

RANK	NAME	TEAM	WARP 2012	WARP 2013	WARP DIFF
1	Jeff Francoeur	KCA	-3.0	0.6	3.6
2	Drew Stubbs	CLE	-1.6	1.4	3.0
2	Jesus Montero	SEA	-0.7	2.3	3.0
4	Lucas Duda	NYN	-1.5	1.4	2.9
5	Brian McCann	ATL	0.8	3.5	2.7
6	Albert Pujols	ANA	3.7	6.3	2.6
6	Ryan Raburn	DET	-2.0	0.6	2.6
6	Michael Young	PHI	-1.5	1.1	2.6
6	Hunter Pence	SFN	0.4	3.0	2.6
10	J.D. Martinez	HOU	-2.4	0.1	2.5

Wins Above Replacement Player, Greatest Declines

RANK	NAME	TEAM	WARP 2012	WARP 2013	WARP DIFF
1	Mike Trout	ANA	9.1	4.1	5.0
2	Aaron Hill	ARI	5.9	2.4	3.5
2	Melky Cabrera	TOR	5.1	1.6	3.5
4	Austin Jackson	DET	5.4	2.5	2.9
5	Buster Posey	SFN	7.0	4.2	2.8
6	Alex Rios	CHA	4.6	1.9	2.7
6	Adam LaRoche	WAS	3.6	0.9	2.7
8	Yadier Molina	SLN	5.8	3.2	2.6
9	Carlos Ruiz	PHI	4.9	2.5	2.4
9	Chase Headley	SDN	5.3	2.9	2.4

PITCHERS

Wins

RANK	NAME	TEAM	W
1	Justin Verlander	DET	16
2	Felix Hernandez	SEA	14
3	Ian Kennedy	ARI	13
3	Clayton Kershaw	LAN	13
3	Zack Greinke	LAN	13
3	Dan Haren	WAS	13
7	Trevor Cahill	ARI	12
7	Mat Latos	CIN	12
7	Justin Masterson	CLE	12
7	Max Scherzer	DET	12
7	Anibal Sanchez	DET	12
7	James Shields	KCA	12
7	CC Sabathia	NYA	12
7	Matt Cain	SFN	12
7	R.A. Dickey	TOR	12
7	Ricky Romero	TOR	12
7	Gio Gonzalez	WAS	12

Strikeouts

RANK	NAME	TEAM	SO
1	Justin Verlander	DET	205
2	Clayton Kershaw	LAN	196
3	Felix Hernandez	SEA	193
4	Tim Lincecum	SFN	187
5	Zack Greinke	LAN	186
6	Yovani Gallardo	MIL	185
7	Yu Darvish	TEX	177
8	Max Scherzer	DET	174
9	CC Sabathia	NYA	172
9	David Price	TBA	172
11	Jon Lester	BOS	171
12	Cole Hamels	PHI	169
13	Ian Kennedy	ARI	168

14	C.J. Wilson	ANA	167
15	James Shields	KCA	165
15	Gio Gonzalez	WAS	165
17	Cliff Lee	PHI	164
18	Chris Sale	CHA	163
18	Mat Latos	CIN	163
20	A.J. Burnett	PIT	161

Earned Run Average (min. 125 IP)

RANK	NAME	TEAM	ERA
1	Clayton Kershaw	LAN	2.62
2	Felix Hernandez	SEA	2.80
3	Zack Greinke	LAN	2.84
4	Roy Halladay	PHI	2.86
5	Cliff Lee	PHI	2.90
6	Tim Lincecum	SFN	2.95
7	Matt Cain	SFN	2.96
8	Jered Weaver	ANA	2.98
8	Justin Verlander	DET	2.98
8	David Price	TBA	2.98
11	Chris Sale	CHA	3.05
11	Josh Beckett	LAN	3.05
13	Yu Darvish	TEX	3.06
14	CC Sabathia	NYA	3.10
15	Cole Hamels	PHI	3.11
16	Adam Wainwright	SLN	3.17
17	Mat Latos	CIN	3.19
17	Madison Bumgarner	SFN	3.19
19	Dan Haren	WAS	3.33
20	C.J. Wilson	ANA	3.38

Walks plus Hits per Innings Pitched (min. 125 IP)

RANK	NAME	TEAM	WHIP
1	Roy Halladay	PHI	1.03
1	Cliff Lee	PHI	1.03
3	Zack Greinke	LAN	1.05
4	Cole Hamels	PHI	1.06
5	Clayton Kershaw	LAN	1.07
6	Josh Beckett	LAN	1.08
7	Matt Cain	SFN	1.09
7	Dan Haren	WAS	1.09
9	Mat Latos	CIN	1.10
9	Adam Wainwright	SLN	1.10
11	Jered Weaver	ANA	1.11
12	Madison Bumgarner	SFN	1.12
13	Justin Verlander	DET	1.13
13	Felix Hernandez	SEA	1.13
15	Chris Sale	CHA	1.14
15	CC Sabathia	NYA	1.14
17	Ian Kennedy	ARI	1.15
17	Johnny Cueto	CIN	1.15
17	Tim Lincecum	SFN	1.15
17	David Price	TBA	1.15
17	Jordan Zimmermann	WAS	1.15

Saves

RANK	NAME	TEAM	SV
1	Craig Kimbrel	ATL	38
2	J.J. Putz	ARI	37
3	John Axford	MIL	35
4	Chris Perez	CLE	31
4	Jose Valverde	DET	31
6	Joel Hanrahan	BOS	30
6	Jonathan Papelbon	PHI	30
8	Mariano Rivera	NYA	29
9	Heath Bell	ARI	28
10	Brian Wilson	SFN	24
11	Carlos Marmol	CHN	22
12	Jonathan Broxton	CIN	20
12	Brandon League	LAN	20
12	Juan Oviedo	MIA	20
12	Joe Nathan	TEX	20
16	Jason Motte	SLN	19
16	Fernando Rodney	TBA	19
18	Jim Johnson	BAL	18
18	Rafael Soriano	NYA	18
18	Huston Street	SDN	18

Strikeouts per Nine Innings (min. 125 IP)

RANK	NAME	TEAM	SO9
1	Yu Darvish	TEX	10.1
2	Chris Sale	CHA	10.0
3	Matt Moore	TBA	9.8
4	Tim Lincecum	SFN	9.7
5	Max Scherzer	DET	9.6
6	Yovani Gallardo	MIL	9.4
7	Clayton Kershaw	LAN	9.2
8	Justin Verlander	DET	9.1
9	Zack Greinke	LAN	9.0
9	Edinson Volquez	SDN	9.0
11	Francisco Liriano	CHA	8.9
12	Bud Norris	HOU	8.7
12	Gio Gonzalez	WAS	8.7
14	Tommy Hanson	ANA	8.6
14	Felix Hernandez	SEA	8.6
14	David Price	TBA	8.6
17	Jon Lester	BOS	8.5
18	Ubaldo Jimenez	CLE	8.4
18	CC Sabathia	NYA	8.4
18	Lance Lynn	SLN	8.4

Wins Above Replacement Player

RANK	NAME	TEAM	WARP
1	Justin Verlander	DET	4.8
2	CC Sabathia	NYA	4.2
2	Felix Hernandez	SEA	4.2
4	Clayton Kershaw	LAN	4.1
4	Yu Darvish	TEX	4.1
6	Jon Lester	BOS	3.5

6	Mat Latos	CIN	3.5
6	Zack Greinke	LAN	3.5
6	David Price	TBA	3.5
10	Jered Weaver	ANA	3.3
10	Chris Sale	CHA	3.3
12	Cliff Lee	PHI	3.1
12	Stephen Strasburg	WAS	3.1
14	Matt Cain	SFN	2.8
15	C.J. Wilson	ANA	2.7
15	Roy Halladay	PHI	2.7
15	Tim Lincecum	SFN	2.7
18	Josh Beckett	LAN	2.6
18	Cole Hamels	PHI	2.6
20	Jake Peavy	CHA	2.5

Wins Above Replacement Player, Rookies

RANK	NAME	TEAM	WARP
1	Kyuji Fujikawa	CHN	1.0
2	Carter Capps	SEA	0.7
3	Trevor Bauer	CLE	0.6
3	Steven Rodriguez	LAN	0.6
3	Mark Montgomery	NYA	0.6
3	Cory Burns	TEX	0.6
7	Tony Cingrani	CIN	0.5
7	Cody Allen	CLE	0.5
7	Alejandro Ramos	MIA	0.5
7	Jose Fernandez	MIA	0.5
7	Anthony Slama	MIN	0.5
7	Evan Scribner	OAK	0.5

Wins Above Replacement Player, Improvement

RANK	NAME	TEAM	WARP 2012	WARP 2013	WARP DIFF
1	Tim Lincecum	SFN	-0.6	2.7	3.3
2	Ervin Santana	KCA	-2.0	1.1	3.2
3	Tommy Hanson	ANA	-0.5	1.9	2.4
4	Jered Weaver	ANA	1.0	3.3	2.3
4	Jon Lester	BOS	1.2	3.5	2.3
6	Tim Hudson	ATL	-0.2	1.9	2.1
6	Clay Buchholz	BOS	-0.3	1.8	2.1
6	Ricky Romero	TOR	-1.0	1.0	2.1
9	Josh Beckett	LAN	0.7	2.6	1.9
9	Clayton Richard	SDN	-2.2	-0.3	1.9

Wins Above Replacement Player, Decline

RANK	NAME	TEAM	WARP 2012	WARP 2013	WARP DIFF
1	Wade Miley	ARI	2.9	0.1	2.8
2	R.A. Dickey	TOR	3.7	1.5	2.2
3	Jason Hammel	BAL	2.7	0.8	1.9
4	J. Zimmermann	WAS	3.5	1.7	1.8
5	Mike Fiers	MIL	2.9	1.2	1.7
5	A.J. Burnett	PIT	2.8	1.0	1.7
5	Gio Gonzalez	WAS	3.4	1.7	1.7
8	Jeff Samardzija	CHN	2.3	0.6	1.6
8	Lance Lynn	SLN	2.4	0.8	1.6
8	Matt Moore	TBA	2.7	1.0	1.6

Contributors

The BP Team

R.J. Anderson lives in Florida and joined Prospectus in 2011. In the past, Anderson's work has appeared on ESPN, SLAM, and Wired, as well as in the *Wall Street Journal* and *USA Today*. His nightmares include an endless loop of Hank Blalock playing third base.

Bradley Ankrom is a Baseball Analyst with Bloomberg Sports. His writing has appeared in various places in print and on the web, including Baseball Prospectus, The Score, and the (Lewiston, Maine) *Sun Journal*. He currently resides in New York City with his dog Rufus and the spirit of their departed feline friend, El Gato.

Theorizing that one could write everywhere within his own lifetime, **Michael Bates** stepped into his Internet accelerator, The Platoon Advantage, and vanished... He woke to find himself on several sites, including Baseball Prospectus, SBNation, Getting Blanked, NotGraphs, and ESPN's SweetSpot, driven by an unknown force to change the Hall of Fame for the better by getting Jeff Bagwell elected. His only guide on this journey is Bill Parker, his heterosexual life-mate, who appears as a voice of relative reason only Mike can see and hear. And so Bates finds himself leaping from blog to blog, striving to put right what once went wrong, and hoping each time that his next leap will be the leap home. Oh boy.

Craig Brown is a co-founder of Royals Authority and now writes at Royals Review. He has contributed to ESPN.com and The Hardball Times and has published two annuals dedicated to the exploits of the Royals. A Kansas City native, he inherited his passion for the game from his grandfather, who took him to countless games and taught him to keep score and signed him up for SABR as an eight-year-old. He still lives in the area with his wife and two daughters, who kindly tolerate his obsession with the game. He booed Robinson Cano at the 2012 Home Run Derby.

Russell A. Carleton grew up in Cleveland, Ohio, cheering for the Indians, moved to Chicago, where he developed an unrequited crush on the Cubs, and now lives in Atlanta with his wife and kids working as a research consultant. Somewhere in the middle he got a Ph.D. in clinical psychology, wrote for the websites Statistically Speaking and Baseball Prospectus, and served as a consultant to two teams in Major League Baseball. When he was young, his babysitter also babysat the kids of John Farrell and Tom Candiotti.

Derek Carty is the Fantasy Manager for Baseball Prospectus. In the past, he has had his work published by The Hardball Times, ESPN Insider, SportsIllustrated.com, NBC's Rotoworld, FOXSports.com, and *USA Today*. In expert league competition, he has three championships with nine top-three finishes and is the youngest champion in the history of LABR—the longest-running expert league in existence. He is the only active fantasy writer to have graduated from the MLB Scouting Bureau's Scout Development Program (aka Scout School) and is the COO of Fantasy Squared, a market-style game in which users "buy" and "sell" shares of events that transpire in an underlying fantasy league (either private or expert).

Jason Cole covers the entire Texas Rangers organization at LoneStarDugout.com and is a contributor to the prospect and draft coverage at Baseball Prospectus. During the baseball season, he wears a tie and plays broadcaster by working color commentary on Frisco RoughRiders telecasts in the Dallas-Fort Worth Metroplex. Jason resides in Austin, Texas, and is a product of St. Edward's University. This is his first year contributing to the Baseball Prospectus annual.

Jason Collette is someone in constant motion, whether it be at a computer, on a people mover, or on an airplane. By day, he helps make our public schools a better place for technology. By night, he consumes baseball like a fraternity brother consumes cheap beer, and thanks his wife daily for tolerating his crazy schedule.

Ken Funck contributes the occasional "Changing Speeds" column to BaseballProspectus.com, focusing on issues both absurd and sublime, and has written for the Baseball Prospectus annual each year since winning the inaugural Prospectus Idol competition in 2009. Ken spends his days managing Business Intelligence systems and lives outside Madison, Wisconsin (America's greatest small city), with his ever-supportive wife, Stephanie, their children, Max and Abby, one cat, two dogs, two kayaks, one canoe, and an almost frighteningly large mounted walleye.

Jay Jaffe is the founder of the 12-year-old Futility Infielder website *(www.futilityinfielder.com)*, one of the oldest baseball blogs. He's been a part of Baseball Prospectus since 2004, writing the Prospectus Hit and Run column, covering the annual Hall of Fame balloting, contributing to eight BP annuals as well as *It Ain't Over 'Til It's Over, Mind Game, Extra Innings,* and the two-volume *Best of Baseball Prospectus 1996–2011*. In 2012, he joined SportsIllustrated.com to write the daily Hit and Run blog at *mlb.si.com*. Over the past two years, he has been a recurring guest "Clubhouse Consultant" on MLB Network's *Clubhouse Confidential* show. He has placed third in the famous Milwaukee Brewers sausage race, dropped an F-bomb in the *Wall Street Journal*, and been voted into the Baseball Writers Association of America.

King Kaufman is the manager of the Writer Program at Bleacher Report. For most of the '00s, he wrote a daily sports column for Salon.com. Before that he covered boxing for the *San Francisco Examiner*. He has written chapters in anthologies about Neifi Perez, Ron Cey, and Mike Tyson, and hopes to get them all together for dinner someday. He lives in the Excelsior District of San Francisco.

Matthew Kory is an author of Baseball Prospectus, a writer at SB Nation's Over the Monster Red Sox blog, a stay-at-home dad, and author of the Walnut Street Journal best sellers, *400,000,000 Things You Absolutely Should Have Done Ten Seconds Ago* and *The Best Things In Life Are Stolen Which Is Why You Just Paid For This Book*. He lives, drinks, and doesn't sleep in Portland, Oregon, with or near his beautiful wife, Stephanie, and his twin boys, Wyatt and Sacha. He personally put a banana in the tailpipe of the Noodle and Doodle Bus.

Ben Lindbergh is the Editor-in-Chief of Baseball Prospectus. He co-hosts the daily BP podcast, Effectively Wild, contributes regularly to ESPN Insider, and is a member of the Baseball Writers' Association of America (BBWAA). This is his fourth year contributing to the BP annual. A recent graduate of Georgetown University, Ben makes his home on the western shore of his native Manhattan, where he can keep a close eye on New Jersey.

Ian Miller is one-half of Productive Outs and one-fourth of the band Kowloon Walled City. He lives with a wonderful woman and a terrible cat in Oakland, California, and often wonders what he did to deserve such an awesome life.

Sam Miller is an author at Baseball Prospectus, co-host of the Effectively Wild podcast, and a contributor to *ESPN the Magazine*. He previously covered a variety of news beats for the Orange County Register before moving into sports in 2009. He lives in Long Beach, California, with his wife and daughter.

SABR member **Rob McQuown** is a lifelong Cubs fan who was inspired by a *Bill James Abstract* to join STATS, Inc., where he was first published in the *The Scouting Report*, 1993. Since then, neither starting up multiple dot-coms or years in big corporate life could pull him convincingly away from his first love, baseball. Getting restarted in the industry in 2006 with *Baseball Daily Digest*, he was welcomed to the Baseball Prospectus team as a programmer and writer when BDD became a subsidiary of BP. He has contributed extensive web content with both words and programs for numerous sites, as well as writing sections of *Graphical Player*, 2010 and 2011 editions.

Bill Parker is a practicing attorney with a wonderful wife and two amazing and active young sons. So naturally, he has nothing *but* time to write about baseball on the Internet. As such, he co-founded The Platoon Advantage, and has appeared as a Designated Columnist at SB Nation, Baseball Prospectus, ESPN.com and The Score's Getting Blanked blog. He was born and now lives once again in St. Paul, Minnesota, following stops essentially everywhere else. He's a long-time reader, first-time author of the Baseball Prospectus annual, and after family and baseball, devotes himself to spreading awareness and love for the short-lived television show *Sports Night* and the works of Stephen Sondheim.

Jason Parks officially joined the Baseball Prospectus roster in 2011, having spent the three previous three years covering the Texas Rangers minor-league system for Baseball Time in Arlington (BBTiA) and masquerading as a scout in Mexico. A native Texan, Jason now calls Brooklyn his home, living in the Bushwick neighborhood with his three cats, his three personalities, and his quality haircut.

Daniel Rathman is an author of Baseball Prospectus who joined as an intern in the fall of 2011. He graduated from Tufts University with a degree in economics last May, and participated in the Diamond Dollars Case Competition at the SABR Analytics Conference last March. Daniel previously interned for New England Sports Network. This is his first year contributing to the annual.

Josh Shepardson is a graduate from SUNY Cortland's Sport Management undergraduate program and a resident of Central New York. He has been writing about fantasy sports since late 2009 and joined Baseball Prospectus in June of 2012. He aspires to eventually turn his current passion of writing about fantasy sports into his full-time profession.

Adam Sobsey's weekly Baseball Prospectus column debuted in January 2012. He has been a beat writer covering the Triple-A Durham Bulls since 2009 and is currently working on a documentary project about the team and its milieu. He is also an award-winning playwright, with work produced in New York, Texas, California, and North Carolina, and an MFA in Writing from the Michener Center for Writers at the University of Texas-Austin. He lives in Durham with his wife, and disagrees with Crash Davis that Susan Sontag is overrated.

Paul Sporer began writing for Baseball Prospectus in 2012. Before that his work could be found at various outlets on the Internet including PaulSporer.com, which has been around since 2006 and still houses his work, including the well-known Starting Pitcher Guide, released annually in the winter. He and his beloved beagle Curtis (named after former Detroit Tiger Granderson) spend their summers enjoying the blistering Texas heat glued to the MLB At Bat app watching as many games as possible, including every Tigers one.

Cecilia Tan has been writing about baseball since that book report on *The Reggie Jackson Story* when she was in fifth grade. She is currently Publications Director for SABR and editor of the *Baseball Research Journal,* as well as longtime editor of the *Yankees Annual.* She still writes occasionally for the oldest baseball blog on the Internet, Why I Like Baseball.

Doug Thorburn is a product of the Baseball Prospectus farm system. He was scouted by Joe Hamrahi, developed his writing skills at Baseball Daily Digest, and made his BP debut in 2012 with his "Raising Aces" column focused on the science of pitching. Prior to joining BP, he was the director of the motion-analysis program at the National Pitching Association, where he co-authored a book with NPA founder Tom House titled *Arm Action, Arm Path, & the Perfect Pitch.* A baseball lifer, Thorburn got his start as an intern in the front office of the Sacramento River Cats, and later earned an M.B.A. in sports business management. Doug resides in Morgan Hill, California, with his lovely new bride, Caitlin, and their two Siberian Huskies, Echo and Briar.

Jason Wojciechowski is a union lawyer in Los Angeles with a fondness for TV, labor history, and yelling. He lives with Austen Rachlis, the human to whom he is wed, and Joey from the Bronx, Tami Taylor, and Louise Archer, the cats by whom he is enslaved.

Colin Wyers, by day, is a mild-mannered writer and database administrator for Baseball Prospectus. By night, he is *also* a mild-mannered writer and database administrator for Baseball Prospectus.

Geoff Young has been a regular contributor to Baseball Prospectus since 2009, most recently as author of the "Western Front" column, which focuses on the AL and NL West divisions. This is his second appearance in the BP annual. Geoff's work also was featured in *Best of Baseball Prospectus: 1996–2011.* In the past, he has written for The Hardball Times, ESPN.com, and other outlets. He founded Ducksnorts, which covered the Padres from 1997 to 2011, publishing online content and three books under that title. Geoff lives in San Diego with his patient wife, Sandra.

Acknowledgments

Bradley Ankrom: Steve and Cheryl Ankrom, Mark Anderson, R.J. Anderson, James Bailey, Bill Baer, Tommy Bennett, Riley Breckenridge, Grant Brisbee, Derek Carty, Brad Ciolek, Jason Cole, Kimball Crossley, Jeff Euston, Drew Fairservice, Mike Ferrin, Peter Gammons, Craig Glaser, Conor Glassey, Kevin Goldstein, Jay Jaffe, Zachary Levine, Ben Lindbergh, Chris Mellen, Ian Miller, Sam Miller, Marc Normandin, Dustin Parkes, Jason Parks, Jeff Passan, David Pease, Mike Petriello, Tommy Rancel, Travis Reitsma, Daniel Rathman, Juan Rodriguez, Emma Span, Andrew Stoeten, Jason Wojciechowski, Geoff Young, Alec Zumwalt.

Michael Bates: Mike: Melissa, Charlie, Marcia Rose, mom and dad, Charles Bassett, Deacon David and Diane Lapinski, Bill Parker, and Marvin Miller.

Craig Brown: Joe Hamrahi, Marc Normandin, Cecilia Tan, Clark Fosler, Nick Scott, Jeff Zimmerman, Josh Duggan, Connor Moylan, Max Rieper, Will McDonald, Greg Schaum Evan Brunell, Rob Blackstein, Rob Neyer, and Rex Hudler.

Derek Carty: Joe Hamrahi, Ryan Lind, Jason Parks, Cecilia Tan, and multiple anonymous baseball insiders.

Jason Cole: Jason Parks, Joe Hamrahi, Cecilia Tan, Joey Matschulat, and a slew of anonymous scouts.

Jason Collette: My wife, Sarah, my children, Jacob & Emma, my mother's love for baseball, and my deceased mother-in-law for her encouragement throughout the years.

Ken Funck: Doug Ross, Zach Eveland, Christina Kahrl, Rany Jazayerli, Joe Sheehan, Clay Davenport, Gary Huckabay, Steven Goldman, John Perrotto, Ben Lindbergh, King Kaufman, Cecilia Tan, Stephani Bee, Joe Hamrahi, Kevin Goldstein, Will Carroll, Rob Neyer, Chris Anderson, Gary Atkins, Frank Berta, Jon Bourdon, Randy Cross, Don Egan, Larry Hirt, John Kostyo, Mike Martin, Kraig Rowe, Bill Severn, Ale Asylum, The Asylum Rats, Bump In The Night, and The Whole Fam Damily.

Jay Jaffe: Emma Span, Bryan Jaffe, Nick Stone, Issa Clubb, Brian Kenny, Duke Castiglione, Norm Wamer, Steve Kaplowitz, Thyrl Nelson, Alex Belth, Steven Goldman, Marc Carig, Peter Abraham, Keith Law, Jonah Keri, Mike Ferrin.

King Kaufman: Jane Paris and Buster and Daisy for tolerating a too-busy husband and dad at holiday time, Cecilia Tan for being a great editing partner, and the BP team for being amazingly talented.

Ian Miller: would like to thank Josh Shepardson and Grant Brisbee for pointing out potentially life-threatening errors in his work.

Sam Miller: Ryan Ghan, Scott Servais, Jeff Sullivan, Jay Yencich.

Bill Parker: Kristine, Jamie, Danny Parker, mom and dad, Edella Erickson, Mike Bates, and Kirby Puckett.

Daniel Rathman: Joe Capozzi, Juan C. Rodriguez, Hudson Belinsky, Bradley Ankrom, Jason Parks, Ben Lindbergh, Mark Anderson, Evan Brunell, Joe Hamrahi, Steven Goldman, R.J. Anderson, and several anonymous scouts.

Adam Sobsey: Heather Mallory, Chaim Bloom, R. J. Anderson, Jason Collette, Ben Lindbergh, Charlie Montoyo.

Paul Sporer: Curtis the Beagle, Mark Anderson, Jason Collette, Sean Forman, Gino Barrica, Joe Hamrahi, Scarlett Johansson, Chandler Parks, Melissa Parks, Cody Sporer, Dorothy Sporer, Paul Sporer Sr., Cecilia Tan, King Kaufman, and Antonio Vivaldi, whose music underscores all of my writing sessions.

Cecilia Tan: Joe Hamrahi, David Pease, Ben Lindbergh, and everyone who keeps Baseball Prospectus at the top of its game, Keith R.A. DeCandido, James Murray, King Kaufman.

Doug Thorburn: Tom House, Ryan Sienko, Eric Andrews, Joe Donohue, Joe Hamrahi, Ben Lindbergh, Gary Huckabay, Baseball Prospectus writers past and present.

Jason Wojciechowski: Shaun Boyle, Jason Churchill, Dan Evans, Chris Migliaccio, Marc Normandin, Evan Seckular.

Colin Wyers: Thanks to my parents, my daughter Tessa, the lovely Liz Roscher—and to all of you, for all your support for everything we do.

Geoff Young: Steph Bee, Corey Brock, Bruce Campbell, John Conniff, Jeff Creps, Dan Evans, Joe Hamrahi, Dan Hayes, A.J. Hinch, King Kaufman, Tom Krasovic, Jason Parks, Bernie Pleskoff, Troy Renck, SABR, Patrick Saunders, Randy Smith, Sandra Tokashiki, and anyone else inadvertently missed.

Index

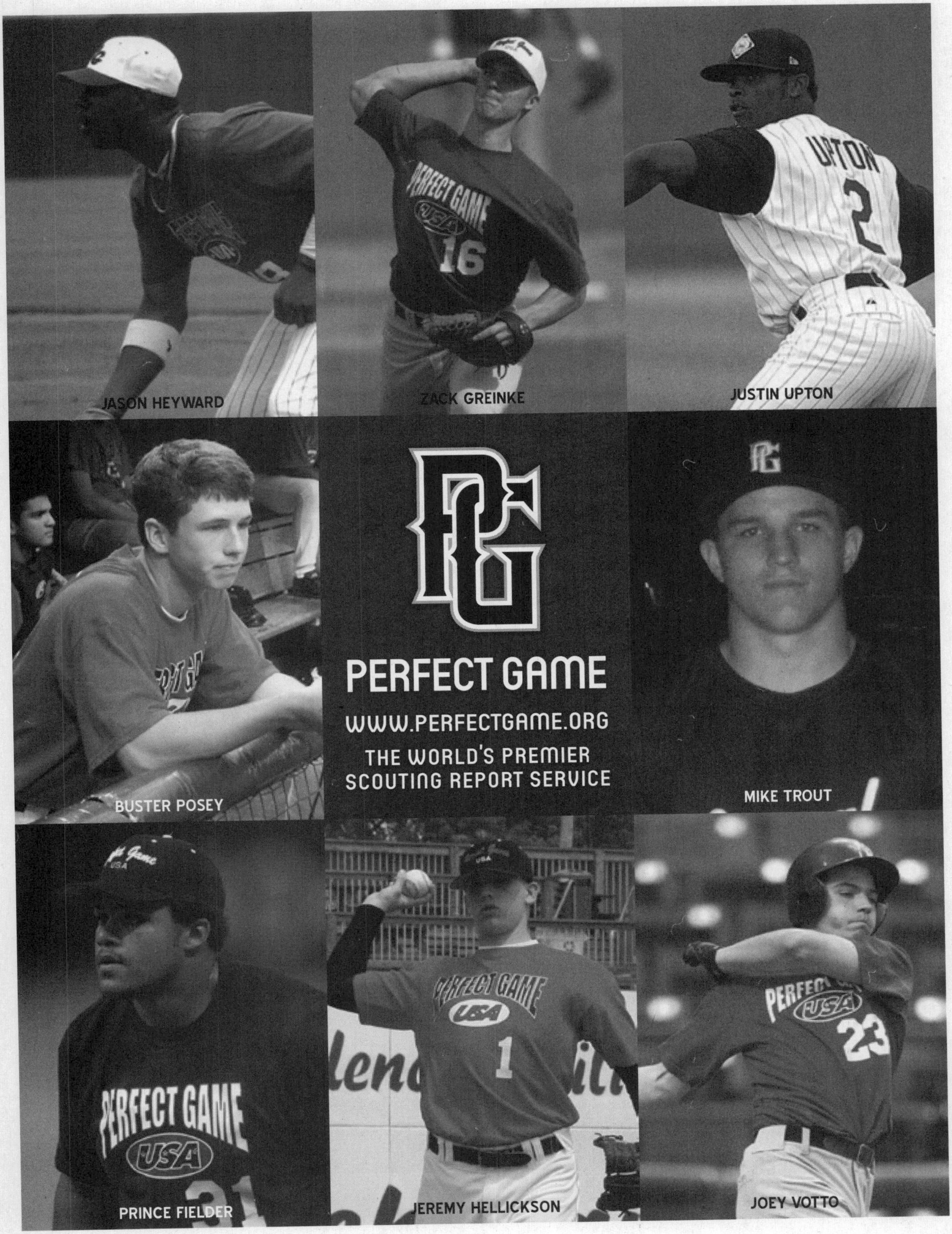
JASON HEYWARD
ZACK GREINKE
JUSTIN UPTON
PERFECT GAME
WWW.PERFECTGAME.ORG
THE WORLD'S PREMIER
SCOUTING REPORT SERVICE
BUSTER POSEY
MIKE TROUT
PRINCE FIELDER
JEREMY HELLICKSON
JOEY VOTTO

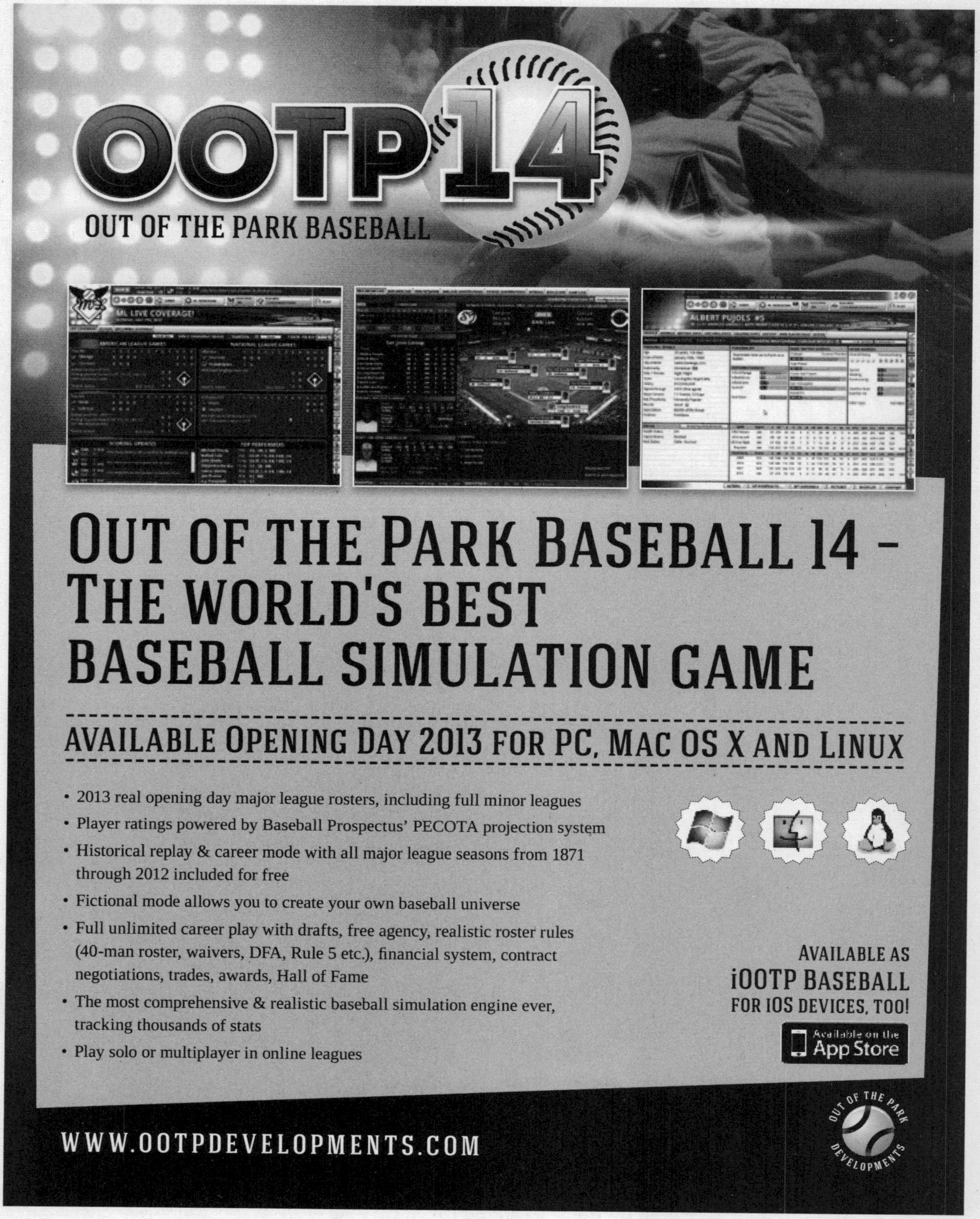
OOTP 14
OUT OF THE PARK BASEBALL
OUT OF THE PARK BASEBALL 14 - THE WORLD'S BEST BASEBALL SIMULATION GAME
AVAILABLE OPENING DAY 2013 FOR PC, MAC OS X AND LINUX
• 2013 real opening day major league rosters, including full minor leagues
• Player ratings powered by Baseball Prospectus' PECOTA projection system
• Historical replay & career mode with all major league seasons from 1871 through 2012 included for free
• Fictional mode allows you to create your own baseball universe
• Full unlimited career play with drafts, free agency, realistic roster rules (40-man roster, waivers, DFA, Rule 5 etc.), financial system, contract negotiations, trades, awards, Hall of Fame
• The most comprehensive & realistic baseball simulation engine ever, tracking thousands of stats
• Play solo or multiplayer in online leagues
AVAILABLE AS iOOTP BASEBALL FOR IOS DEVICES, TOO!
Available on the App Store
WWW.OOTPDEVELOPMENTS.COM
OUT OF THE PARK DEVELOPMENTS